Classics of American Political and Constitutional Thought

Volume 1

Origins through the Civil War

Classics of American Political and Constitutional Thought

Volume 1

Origins through the Civil War

Edited, with Introductions, by
Scott J. Hammond
Kevin R. Hardwick
Howard L. Lubert

Hackett Publishing Company, Inc.
Indianapolis/Cambridge

Printed in the United States of America

12 11 10 09 08 07 1 2 3 4 5 6 7

For further information, please address:

Hackett Publishing Company, Inc.
P.O. Box 44937
Indianapolis, IN 46244-0937

www.hackettpublishing.com

Text design by Meera Dash
Composition by Scribe
Printed at Edwards Brothers, Inc.

Library of Congress Cataloging-in-Publication Data

Classics of American political and constitutional thought / edited, with introductions, by Scott J. Hammond, Kevin R. Hardwick, and Howard L. Lubert.
p. cm.
ISBN-13: 978-0-87220-786-8 (pbk. set) ISBN-13:978-0-87220-787-5 (cloth set)

1. Constitutional history—United States—Sources. 2. United States—Politics and government—Sources. I. Hammond, Scott J. II. Hardwick, Kevin R., 1961– III. Lubert, Howard L. (Howard Leslie), 1966–
JK31.C54 2007
320.473—dc22

2006046824

ISBN-13 (Vol. 1): 978-0-87220-883-4 (pbk.) ISBN-13 (Vol. 1): 978-0-87220-884-1 (cloth)

The paper used in this publication meets the minimum requirements of American National Standard for Information Sciences—Permanence of Paper for Printed Library Materials, ANSI Z39.48–1984.

Acknowledgments

Many friends and colleagues have contributed in various ways to this project. In recognition of their kind support, advice, and guidance, we thank the following individuals. For providing informed opinions and needed input regarding either the content of our selections or the style of our presentation, we thank John "Chris" Arndt, Herman Belz, William Hawk, Raymond "Skip" Hyser, Iain MacLean, Charles Miller, Henry Myers, Steve Reich, Margaret Williams, Jacqueline Walker, and our anonymous reviewers. For material support as well as the occasional boost to morale, we thank all of our good colleagues in both the department of Political Science and the department of History here at James Madison University. We also thank Rob Gardner, one of our graduate assistants, for his help in transcribing text.

We are especially grateful to James Madison University for generous assistance in funding this venture. In particular, we thank Phil Bigler and the James Madison Center for a generous financial contribution that helped to underwrite a substantial portion of this project. Additionally, we thank the Provost Office, as well as Linda Halpern and the JMU summer grants program. Without all of this additional funding from our home university the final shape and substance of this project would have been decidedly different, and not for the better.

Finally, we thank the expert staff at Hackett Publishing for their good counsel, enthusiastic devotion, and inexhaustible patience. Specifically, we thank Rick Todhunter, our editor at Hackett; Fred Courtwright, our permissions guru; and Meera Dash, Hackett's managing editor, and her amazing staff of skilled and tireless copyeditors. In particular we are grateful to Carrie Wagner and her important contribution toward the completion of this project. Without them, this book would not be in your hands. Even so, we, the editors who are fortunate enough to have our name on the cover, assume full responsibility for the content of this text.

Finally, we dedicate this book to our families, without whom there would be nothing at all.

To our wives, Chereé, Jan, and Caroline, and our children,
Adriana, Neil, Carolyn, Eleanor, and Sarah

Contents

4 Toward a More Perfect Union 329

5 The Ratification Debate 454

6 Liberty, Authority, and the Implementation of Government 597

7 Liberty, Morality, and Nationalism 691

8 Liberty, Order, and the Market 821

The Declaration of Independence

When in the course of human events, it becomes necessary for one people to dissolve the political bands which have connected them with another, and to assume among the powers of the earth, the separate and equal station to which the laws of nature and of nature's God entitle them, a decent respect to the opinions of mankind requires that they should declare the causes which impel them to the separation.

We hold these truths to be self-evident,

That all men are created equal; that they are endowed by their Creator with certain unalienable rights; that among these are life, liberty, and the pursuit of happiness; that, to secure these rights, governments are instituted among men, deriving their just powers from the consent of the governed; that whenever any form of government becomes destructive of these ends, it is the right of the people to alter or to abolish it, and to institute new government, laying its foundation on such principles, and organizing its powers in such form, as to them shall seem most likely to effect their safety and happiness. Prudence, indeed, will dictate that governments long established should not be changed for light and transient causes; and accordingly all experience hath shown that mankind are more disposed to suffer, while evils are sufferable than to right themselves by abolishing the forms to which they are accustomed. But when a long train of abuses and usurpations, pursuing invariably the same object, evinces a design to reduce them under absolute despotism, it is their right, it is their duty, to throw off such government, and to provide new guards for their future security. Such has been the patient sufferance of these colonies; and such is now the necessity which constrains them to alter their former systems of government. The history of the present King of Great Britain is a history of repeated injuries and usurpations, all having in direct object the establishment of an absolute tyranny over these states. To prove this, let facts be submitted to a candid world.

He has refused his assent to laws, the most wholesome and necessary for the public good.

He has forbidden his governors to pass laws of immediate and pressing importance, unless suspended in their operation till his assent should be obtained; and, when so suspended, he has utterly neglected to attend to them.

He has refused to pass other laws for the accommodation of large districts of people, unless those people would relinquish the right of representation in the legislature, a right inestimable to them, and formidable to tyrants only.

He has called together legislative bodies at places unusual, uncomfortable, and distant from the depository of their public records, for the sole purpose of fatiguing them into compliance with his measures.

He has dissolved representative houses repeatedly, for opposing, with manly firmness, his invasions on the rights of the people.

He has refused for a long time, after such dissolutions, to cause others to be elected; whereby the legislative powers, incapable of annihilation, have returned to the people at large for their exercise; the state remaining, in the mean time, exposed to all the dangers of invasions from without and convulsions within.

He has endeavored to prevent the population of these states; for that purpose obstructing the laws for naturalization of foreigners; refusing to pass others to encourage their migration hither, and raising the conditions of new appropriations of lands.

He has obstructed the administration of justice, by refusing his assent to laws for establishing judiciary powers.

He has made judges dependent on his will alone, for the tenure of their offices, and the amount and payment of their salaries.

He has erected a multitude of new offices, and sent hither swarms of officers to harass our people and eat out their substance.

He has kept among us, in times of peace, standing armies, without the consent of our legislatures.

He has affected to render the military independent of, and superior to, the civil power.

He has combined with others to subject us to a jurisdiction foreign to our Constitution and unacknowledged by our laws, giving his assent to their acts of pretended legislation:

For quartering large bodies of armed troops among us;

For protecting them, by a mock trial, from punishment for any murders which they should commit on the inhabitants of these states;

For cutting off our trade with all parts of the world;

For imposing taxes on us without our consent;

For depriving us, in many cases, of the benefits of trial by jury;

For transporting us beyond seas, to be tried for pretended offenses;

For abolishing the free system of English laws in a neighboring province, establishing therein an arbitrary government, and enlarging its boundaries, so as to render it at once an example and fit instrument for introducing the same absolute rule into these colonies;

For taking away our charters, abolishing our most valuable laws, and altering fundamentally the forms of our governments;

For suspending our own legislatures, and declaring themselves invested with power to legislate for us in all cases whatsoever.

He has abdicated government here, by declaring us out of his protection and waging war against us.

He has plundered our seas, ravaged our coasts, burned our towns, and destroyed the lives of our people.

He is at this time transporting large armies of foreign mercenaries to complete the works of death, desolation, and tyranny already begun with circumstances of cruelty and perfidy scarcely paralleled in the most barbarous ages, and totally unworthy the head of a civilized nation.

He has constrained our fellow-citizens, taken captive on the high seas, to bear arms against their country, to become the executioners of their friends and brethren, or to fall themselves by their hands.

He has excited domestic insurrection among us, and has endeavored to bring on the inhabitants of our frontiers the merciless Indian savages, whose known rule of warfare is an undistinguished destruction of all ages, sexes, and conditions.

In every stage of these oppressions we have petitioned for redress in the most humble terms; our repeated petitions have been answered only by repeated injury. A prince, whose character is thus marked by every act which may define a tyrant, is unfit to be the ruler of a free people.

Nor have we been wanting in our attentions to our British brethren. We have warned them, from time to time, of attempts by their legislature to extend an unwarrantable jurisdiction over us. We have reminded them of the circumstances of our emigration and settlement here. We have appealed to their native justice and magnanimity; and we have conjured them, by the ties of our common kindred, to disavow these usurpations which would inevitably interrupt our connections and correspondence. They too, have been deaf to the voice of justice and of consanguinity. We must, therefore, acquiesce in the necessity which denounces our separation, and hold them as we hold the rest of mankind, enemies in war, in peace friends.

We, therefore, the representatives of the United States of America, in General Congress assembled, appealing to the Supreme Judge of the world for the rectitude of our intentions, do, in the name and by the authority of the good people of these colonies, solemnly publish and declare, That these United Colonies are, and of right ought to be, free and independent states; that they are absolved from all allegiance to the British crown and that all political connection between them and the state of Great Britain is, and ought to be, totally dissolved; and that, as free and independent states, they have full power to levy war, conclude peace, contract alliances, establish commerce, and do all other acts and things which independent states may of right do. And for the support of this declaration, with a firm reliance on the protection of Divine Providence, we mutually pledge to each other our lives, our fortunes, and our sacred honor.

[Signed by] John Hancock [President]

New Hampshire
Josiah Bartlett,
Wm. Whipple,
Matthew Thornton.

Massachusetts Bay
Saml. Adams,
John Adams,
Robt. Treat Paine,
Elbridge Gerry

Rhode Island
STEP. HOPKINS,
WILLIAM ELLERY.

Connecticut
ROGER SHERMAN,
SAM'EL HUNTINGTON,
WM. WILLIAMS,
OLIVER WOLCOTT.

New York
WM. FLOYD,
PHIL. LIVINGSTON,
FRANS. LEWIS,
LEWIS MORRIS.

New Jersey
RICHD. STOCKTON,
JNO. WITHERSPOON,
FRAS. HOPKINSON,
JOHN HART,
ABRA. CLARK.

Pennsylvania
ROBT. MORRIS
BENJAMIN RUSH,
BENJA. FRANKLIN,
JOHN MORTON,
GEO. CLYMER,
JAS. SMITH,
GEO. TAYLOR,
JAMES WILSON,
GEO. ROSS.

Delaware
CAESAR RODNEY,
GEO. READ,
THO. M'KEAN.

Maryland
SAMUEL CHASE,
WM. PACA,
THOS. STONE,
CHARLES CARROLL of Carrollton.

Virginia
GEORGE WYTHE,
RICHARD HENRY LEE,
TH. JEFFERSON,
BENJA. HARRISON,
THS. NELSON, JR.,
FRANCIS LIGHTFOOT LEE,
CARTER BRAXTON.

North Carolina
WM. HOOPER,
JOSEPH HEWES,
JOHN PENN.

South Carolina
EDWARD RUTLEDGE,
THOS. HAYWARD, JUNR.,
THOMAS LYNCH, JUNR.,
ARTHUR MIDDLETON.

Georgia
BUTTON GWINNETT,
LYMAN HALL,
GEO. WALTON.

The Constitution of the United States

We the People of the United States, in Order to form a more perfect Union, establish Justice, insure domestic Tranquility, provide for the common defense, promote the general Welfare, and secure the Blessings of Liberty to ourselves and our Posterity, do ordain and establish this Constitution for the United States of America.

Article I

Section 1. All legislative Powers herein granted shall be vested in a Congress of the United States, which shall consist of a Senate and House of Representatives.

Section 2. The House of Representatives shall be composed of Members chosen every second Year by the People of the several States, and the Electors in each State shall have the Qualifications requisite for Electors of the most numerous Branch of the State Legislature.

No Person shall be a Representative who shall not have attained to the Age of twenty five Years, and been seven Years a Citizen of the United States, and who shall not, when elected, be an Inhabitant of that State in which he shall be chosen.

Representatives and direct Taxes shall be apportioned among the several States which may be included within this Union, according to their respective Numbers, which shall be determined by adding to the whole Number of free Persons, including those bound to Service for a Term of Years, and excluding Indians not taxed, three fifths of all other Persons. The actual Enumeration shall be made within three Years after the first Meeting of the Congress of the United States, and within every subsequent Term of ten Years, in such Manner as they shall by Law direct. The Number of Representatives shall not exceed one for every thirty Thousand, but each State shall have at Least one Representative; and until such enumeration shall be made, the State of New Hampshire shall be entitled to chuse three, Massachusetts eight, Rhode-Island and Providence Plantations one, Connecticut five, New-York six, New Jersey four, Pennsylvania eight, Delaware one, Maryland six, Virginia ten, North Carolina five, South Carolina five, and Georgia three.

When vacancies happen in the Representation from any State, the Executive Authority thereof shall issue Writs of Election to fill such Vacancies.

The House of Representatives shall chuse their Speaker and other Officers; and shall have the sole Power of Impeachment.

Section 3. The Senate of the United States shall be composed of two Senators from each State, chosen by the Legislature thereof, for six Years; and each Senator shall have one Vote.

Immediately after they shall be assembled in Consequence of the first Election, they shall be divided as equally as may be into three Classes. The Seats of the Senators of the first Class shall be vacated at the Expiration of the second Year, of the second Class at the Expiration of the fourth Year, and of the third Class at the Expiration of the sixth Year, so that one third may be chosen every second Year; and if Vacancies happen by Resignation, or otherwise, during the Recess of the Legislature of any State, the Executive thereof may make temporary Appointments until the next Meeting of the Legislature, which shall then fill such Vacancies.

No Person shall be a Senator who shall not have attained to the Age of thirty Years, and been nine Years a Citizen of the United States, and who shall not, when elected, be an Inhabitant of that State for which he shall be chosen.

The Vice President of the United States shall be President of the Senate, but shall have no Vote, unless they be equally divided.

The Senate shall chuse their other Officers, and also a President pro tempore, in the Absence of the Vice President, or when he shall exercise the Office of President of the United States.

The Senate shall have the sole Power to try all Impeachments. When sitting for that Purpose, they shall be on Oath or Affirmation. When the President of the United States is tried, the Chief Justice shall preside: And no Person shall be convicted without the Concurrence of two thirds of the Members present.

Judgment in Cases of Impeachment shall not extend further than to removal from Office, and disqualification to hold and enjoy any Office of honor, Trust or Profit under the United States: but the Party convicted shall nevertheless be liable and subject to Indictment, Trial, Judgment and Punishment, according to Law.

Section 4. The Times, Places and Manner of holding Elections for Senators and Representatives, shall be prescribed in each State by the Legislature thereof; but the Congress may at any time by Law make or alter such Regulations, except as to the Places of choosing Senators.

The Congress shall assemble at least once in every Year, and such Meeting shall be on the first Monday in December, unless they shall by Law appoint a different Day.

Section 5. Each House shall be the Judge of the Elections, Returns and Qualifications of its own Members, and a Majority of each shall constitute a Quorum to do Business; but a smaller Number may adjourn from day to day, and may be authorized to compel the Attendance of absent Members, in such Manner, and under such Penalties as each House may provide.

Each House may determine the Rules of its Proceedings, punish its Members for disorderly Behaviour, and, with the Concurrence of two thirds, expel a Member.

Each House shall keep a Journal of its Proceedings, and from time to time publish the same, excepting such Parts as may in their Judgment require Secrecy; and the Yeas and Nays of the Members of either House on any question shall, at the Desire of one fifth of those Present, be entered on the Journal.

Neither House, during the Session of Congress, shall, without the Consent of the other, adjourn for more than three days, nor to any other Place than that in which the two Houses shall be sitting.

Section 6. The Senators and Representatives shall receive a Compensation for their Services, to be ascertained by Law, and paid out of the Treasury of the United States. They shall in all Cases, except Treason, Felony and Breach of the Peace, be privileged from Arrest during their Attendance at the Session of their respective Houses, and in going to and returning from the same; and for any Speech or Debate in either House, they shall not be questioned in any other Place.

No Senator or Representative shall, during the Time for which he was elected, be appointed to any civil Office under the Authority of the United States, which shall have been created, or the Emoluments whereof shall have been increased during such time; and no Person holding any Office under the United States, shall be a Member of either House during his Continuance in Office.

Section 7. All Bills for raising Revenue shall originate in the House of Representatives; but the Senate may propose or concur with Amendments as on other Bills.

Every Bill which shall have passed the House of Representatives and the Senate, shall, before it become a Law, be presented to the President of the United States; If he approve he shall sign it, but if not he shall return it, with his Objections to that House in which it shall have originated, who shall enter the Objections at large on their Journal, and proceed to reconsider it. If after such Reconsideration two thirds of that House shall agree to pass the Bill, it shall be sent, together with the Objections, to the other House, by which it shall likewise be reconsidered, and if approved by two thirds of that House, it shall become a Law. But in all such Cases the Votes of both Houses shall be determined by yeas and Nays, and the Names of the Persons voting for and against the Bill shall be entered on the Journal of each House respectively. If any Bill shall not be returned by the President within ten Days (Sundays excepted) after it shall have been presented to him, the Same shall be a Law, in like Manner as if he had signed it, unless the Congress by their Adjournment prevent its Return, in which Case it shall not be a Law.

Every Order, Resolution, or Vote to which the Concurrence of the Senate and House of Representatives may be necessary (except on a question of Adjournment) shall be presented to the President of the United States; and before the Same shall take Effect, shall be approved by him, or being disapproved by him, shall be repassed by two thirds of the Senate and House of Representatives, according to the Rules and Limitations prescribed in the Case of a Bill.

Section 8. The Congress shall have Power To lay and collect Taxes, Duties, Imposts and Excises, to pay the Debts and provide for the common Defence and general Welfare of the United States; but all Duties, Imposts and Excises shall be uniform throughout the United States;

To borrow Money on the credit of the United States;

To regulate Commerce with foreign Nations, and among the several States, and with the Indian Tribes;

To establish an uniform Rule of Naturalization, and uniform Laws on the subject of Bankruptcies throughout the United States;

To coin Money, regulate the Value thereof, and of foreign Coin, and fix the Standard of Weights and Measures;

To provide for the Punishment of counterfeiting the Securities and current Coin of the United States;

To establish Post Offices and post Roads;

To promote the Progress of Science and useful Arts, by securing for limited Times to Authors and Inventors the exclusive Right to their respective Writings and Discoveries;

To constitute Tribunals inferior to the supreme Court;

To define and punish Piracies and Felonies committed on the high Seas, and Offences against the Law of Nations;

To declare War, grant Letters of Marque and Reprisal, and make Rules concerning Captures on Land and Water;

To raise and support Armies, but no Appropriation of Money to that Use shall be for a longer Term than two Years;

To provide and maintain a Navy;

To make Rules for the Government and Regulation of the land and naval Forces;

To provide for calling forth the Militia to execute the Laws of the Union, suppress Insurrections and repel Invasions;

To provide for organizing, arming, and disciplining, the Militia, and for governing such Part of them as may be employed in the Service of the United States, reserving to the States respectively, the Appointment of the Officers, and the Authority of training the Militia according to the discipline prescribed by Congress;

To exercise exclusive Legislation in all Cases whatsoever, over such District (not exceeding ten Miles square) as may, by Cession of particular States, and the Acceptance of Congress, become the Seat of the Government of the United States, and to exercise like Authority over all Places purchased by the Consent of the Legislature of the State in which the Same shall be, for the Erection of Forts, Magazines, Arsenals, dock-Yards, and other needful Buildings;—And

To make all Laws which shall be necessary and proper for carrying into Execution the foregoing Powers, and all other Powers vested by this Constitution in the Government of the United States, or in any Department or Officer thereof.

Section 9. The Migration or Importation of such Persons as any of the States now existing shall think proper to admit, shall not be prohibited by the Congress prior to the Year one thousand eight hundred and eight, but a Tax or duty may be imposed on such Importation, not exceeding ten dollars for each Person.

The Privilege of the Writ of Habeas Corpus shall not be suspended, unless when in Cases of Rebellion or Invasion the public Safety may require it.

No Bill of Attainder or ex post facto Law shall be passed.

No Capitation, or other direct, Tax shall be laid, unless in Proportion to the Census or Enumeration herein before directed to be taken.

No Tax or Duty shall be laid on Articles exported from any State.

No Preference shall be given by any Regulation of Commerce or Revenue to the Ports of one State over those of another: nor shall Vessels bound to, or from, one State, be obliged to enter, clear, or pay Duties in another.

No Money shall be drawn from the Treasury, but in Consequence of Appropriations made by Law; and a regular Statement and Account of the Receipts and Expenditures of all public Money shall be published from time to time.

No Title of Nobility shall be granted by the United States: And no Person holding any Office of Profit or Trust under them, shall, without the Consent of the Congress, accept of any present, Emolument, Office, or Title, of any kind whatever, from any King, Prince, or foreign State.

Section 10. No State shall enter into any Treaty, Alliance, or Confederation; grant Letters of Marque and Reprisal; coin Money; emit Bills of Credit; make any Thing but gold and silver Coin a Tender in Payment of Debts; pass any Bill of Attainder, ex post facto Law, or Law impairing the Obligation of Contracts, or grant any Title of Nobility.

No State shall, without the Consent of the Congress, lay any Imposts or Duties on Imports or Exports, except what may be absolutely necessary for executing its inspection Laws: and the net Produce of all Duties and Imposts, laid by any State on Imports or Exports, shall be for the Use of the Treasury of the United States; and all such Laws shall be subject to the Revision and Controul of the Congress.

No State shall, without the Consent of Congress, lay any Duty of Tonnage, keep Troops, or Ships of War in time of Peace, enter into any Agreement or Compact with another State, or with a foreign Power, or engage in War, unless actually invaded, or in such imminent Danger as will not admit of delay.

Article II

Section 1. The executive Power shall be vested in a President of the United States of America. He shall hold his Office during the Term of four Years, and, together with the Vice President, chosen for the same Term, be elected, as follows:

Each State shall appoint, in such Manner as the Legislature thereof may direct, a Number of Electors, equal to the whole Number of Senators and Representatives to which the State may be entitled in the Congress: but no Senator or Representative, or Person holding an Office of Trust or Profit under the United States, shall be appointed an Elector.

The Electors shall meet in their respective States, and vote by Ballot for two Persons, of whom one at least shall not be an Inhabitant of the same State with themselves. And they shall make a List of all the Persons voted for, and of the Number of Votes for each; which List they shall sign and certify, and transmit sealed to the Seat of the Government of the United States, directed to the President of the Senate. The President of the Senate shall, in the Presence of the Senate and House of Representatives, open all the Certificates, and the Votes shall then be counted. The Person having the greatest Number of Votes shall be the President, if such Number be a Majority of the whole Number of Electors appointed; and if there be more than one who have such Majority, and have an equal Number of Votes, then the House of Representatives shall immediately chuse by Ballot one of them for President; and if no Person have a Majority, then from the five highest on the List the said House shall in like Manner chuse the President. But in choosing the President, the Votes shall be taken by States, the Representation from each State having one Vote; A quorum for this Purpose shall consist of a Member or Members from two thirds of the States, and a Majority of all the States shall be necessary to a Choice. In every Case, after the Choice of the President, the Person having the greatest Number of Votes of the Electors shall be the Vice President. But if there should remain two or more who have equal Votes, the Senate shall chuse from them by Ballot the Vice President.

The Congress may determine the Time of choosing the Electors, and the Day on which they shall give their Votes; which Day shall be the same throughout the United States.

No Person except a natural born Citizen, or a Citizen of the United States, at the time of the Adoption of this Constitution, shall be eligible to the Office of President; neither shall any Person be eligible to that Office who shall not have attained to the Age of thirty five Years, and been fourteen Years a Resident within the United States.

In Case of the Removal of the President from Office, or of his Death, Resignation, or Inability to discharge the Powers and Duties of the said Office, the Same shall devolve on the Vice President, and the Congress may by Law provide for the Case of Removal, Death, Resignation or Inability, both of the President and Vice President, declaring what Officer shall then act as President, and such Officer shall act accordingly, until the Disability be removed, or a President shall be elected.

The President shall, at stated Times, receive for his Services, a Compensation, which shall neither be increased nor diminished during the Period for which he shall have been elected, and he shall not receive within that Period any other Emolument from the United States, or any of them.

Before he enter on the Execution of his Office, he shall take the following Oath or Affirmation:—"I do solemnly swear (or affirm) that I will faithfully execute the Office of President of the United States, and will to the best of my Ability, preserve, protect and defend the Constitution of the United States."

Section 2. The President shall be Commander in Chief of the Army and Navy of the United States, and of the Militia of the several States, when called into the actual Service of the United States; he may require the Opinion, in writing, of the principal Officer in each of the executive Departments, upon any Subject relating to the Duties of their respective Offices, and he shall have Power to grant Reprieves and Pardons for Offences against the United States, except in Cases of Impeachment.

He shall have Power, by and with the Advice and Consent of the Senate, to make Treaties, provided two thirds of the Senators present concur; and he shall nominate, and by and with the Advice and Consent of the Senate, shall appoint Ambassadors, other public Ministers and Consuls, Judges of the supreme Court, and all other Officers of the United States, whose Appointments are not herein otherwise provided for, and which shall be established by Law: but the Congress may by Law vest the Appointment of such inferior Officers, as they think proper, in the President alone, in the Courts of Law, or in the Heads of Departments.

The President shall have Power to fill up all Vacancies that may happen during the Recess of the Senate, by granting Commissions which shall expire at the End of their next Session.

Section 3. He shall from time to time give to the Congress Information of the State of the Union, and recommend to their Consideration such Measures as he shall judge necessary and expedient; he may, on extraordinary Occasions, convene both Houses, or either of them, and in Case of Disagreement between them, with Respect to the Time of Adjournment, he may adjourn them to such Time as he shall think proper; he shall receive Ambassadors and other public Ministers; he shall take Care that the Laws be faithfully executed, and shall Commission all the Officers of the United States.

Section 4. The President, Vice President and all civil Officers of the United States, shall be removed from Office on Impeachment for, and Conviction of, Treason, Bribery, or other high Crimes and Misdemeanors.

Article III

Section 1. The judicial Power of the United States shall be vested in one supreme Court, and in such inferior Courts as the Congress may from time to time ordain and establish. The Judges, both of the supreme and inferior Courts, shall hold their Offices during good Behaviour, and shall, at stated Times, receive for their Services, a Compensation, which shall not be diminished during their Continuance in Office.

Section 2. The judicial Power shall extend to all Cases, in Law and Equity, arising under this Constitution, the Laws of the United States, and Treaties made, or which shall be made, under their Authority;—to all Cases affecting Ambassadors, other public Ministers and Consuls;—to all Cases of admiralty and maritime Jurisdiction;—to Controversies to which the United States shall be a Party;—to Controversies between two or more States;—between a State and Citizens of another State;—between Citizens of different States,—between Citizens of the same State claiming Lands under Grants of different States, and between a State, or the Citizens thereof, and foreign States, Citizens or Subjects.

In all Cases affecting Ambassadors, other public Ministers and Consuls, and those in which a State shall be Party, the supreme Court shall have original Jurisdiction. In all the other Cases before mentioned, the supreme Court shall have appellate Jurisdiction, both as to Law and Fact, with such Exceptions, and under such Regulations as the Congress shall make.

The Trial of all Crimes, except in Cases of Impeachment, shall be by Jury; and such Trial shall be held in the State where the said Crimes shall have been committed; but when not committed within any State, the Trial shall be at such Place or Places as the Congress may by Law have directed.

Section 3. Treason against the United States shall consist only in levying War against them, or in adhering to their Enemies, giving them Aid and Comfort. No Person shall be convicted of Treason unless on the Testimony of two Witnesses to the same overt Act, or on Confession in open Court.

The Congress shall have Power to declare the Punishment of Treason, but no Attainder of Treason shall work Corruption of Blood, or Forfeiture except during the Life of the Person attainted.

Article IV

Section 1. Full Faith and Credit shall be given in each State to the public Acts, Records, and judicial Proceedings of every other State. And the Congress may by general Laws prescribe the Manner in which such Acts, Records and Proceedings shall be proved, and the Effect thereof.

Section 2. The Citizens of each State shall be entitled to all Privileges and Immunities of Citizens in the several States.

A Person charged in any State with Treason, Felony, or other Crime, who shall flee from Justice, and be found in another State, shall on Demand of the executive Authority of the State from which he fled, be delivered up, to be removed to the State having Jurisdiction of the Crime.

No Person held to Service or Labour in one State, under the Laws thereof, escaping into another, shall, in Consequence of any Law or Regulation therein, be discharged from such Service or Labour, but shall be delivered up on Claim of the Party to whom such Service or Labour may be due.

Section 3. New States may be admitted by the Congress into this Union; but no new State shall be formed or erected within the Jurisdiction of any other State; nor any State be formed by the Junction of two or more States, or Parts of States, without the Consent of the Legislatures of the States concerned as well as of the Congress.

The Congress shall have Power to dispose of and make all needful Rules and Regulations respecting the Territory or other Property belonging to the United States; and nothing in this Constitution shall be so construed as to Prejudice any Claims of the United States, or of any particular State.

Section 4. The United States shall guarantee to every State in this Union a Republican Form of Government, and shall protect each of them against Invasion; and on Application of the Legislature, or of the Executive (when the Legislature cannot be convened) against domestic Violence.

Article V

The Congress, whenever two thirds of both Houses shall deem it necessary, shall propose Amendments to this Constitution, or, on the Application of the Legislatures of two thirds of the several States, shall call a Convention for proposing Amendments, which, in either Case, shall be valid to all Intents and Purposes, as Part of this Constitution, when ratified by the Legislatures of three fourths of the several States, or by Conventions in three fourths thereof, as the one or the other Mode of Ratification may be proposed by the Congress; Provided that no Amendment which may be made prior to the Year One thousand eight hundred and eight shall in any Manner affect the first and fourth Clauses in the Ninth Section of the first Article; and that no State, without its Consent, shall be deprived of its equal Suffrage in the Senate.

Article VI

All Debts contracted and Engagements entered into, before the Adoption of this Constitution, shall be as valid against the United States under this Constitution, as under the Confederation.

This Constitution, and the Laws of the United States which shall be made in Pursuance thereof; and all Treaties made, or which shall be made, under the Authority of the United States, shall be the supreme Law of the Land; and the Judges in every State shall be bound thereby, any Thing in the Constitution or Laws of any State to the Contrary notwithstanding.

The Senators and Representatives before mentioned, and the Members of the several State Legislatures, and all executive and judicial Officers, both of the United States and of the several States, shall be bound by Oath or Affirmation, to support this Constitution; but no religious Test shall ever be required as a Qualification to any Office or public Trust under the United States.

Article VII

The Ratification of the Conventions of nine States, shall be sufficient for the Establishment of this Constitution between the States so ratifying the Same. Done in Convention by the Unanimous Consent of the States present the Seventeenth Day of September in the Year of our Lord one thousand seven hundred and Eighty seven and of the Independence of the United States of America the Twelfth In witness whereof We have hereunto subscribed our Names,

GO. WASHINGTON—
Pres. and deputy from Virginia

[Signed also by the deputies of twelve States.]

Delaware
Geo: Read
Gunning Bedford jun
John Dickinson
Richard Bassett
Jaco: Broom

Maryland
James MCHenry
Dan of ST ThoS. Jenifer
DanL Carroll.

Virginia
John Blair—
James Madison Jr.

North Carolina
WM Blount
RichD. Dobbs Spaight.
Hu Williamson

South Carolina
J. Rutledge
Charles Cotesworth Pinckney
Charles Pinckney
Pierce Butler.

Georgia
William Few
Abr Baldwin

New Hampshire
John Langdon
Nicholas Gilman

Massachusetts
Nathaniel Gorham
Rufus King

Connecticut
WM. SamL. Johnson
Roger Sherman

New York
Alexander Hamilton

New Jersey
Wil: Livingston
David Brearley.
WM. Paterson.
Jona: Dayton

Pennsylvania
B Franklin
Thomas Mifflin
RobT Morris
Geo. Clymer
ThoS. FitzSimons
Jared Ingersoll
James Wilson.
Gouv Morris

Attest William Jackson
Secretary

Amendments to the Constitution

Amendment I

Congress shall make no law respecting an establishment of religion, or prohibiting the free exercise thereof; or abridging the freedom of speech, or of the press; or the right of the people peaceably to assemble, and to petition the Government for a redress of grievances.

Amendment II

A well regulated Militia, being necessary to the security of a free State, the right of the people to keep and bear Arms, shall not be infringed.

Amendment III

No Soldier shall, in time of peace be quartered in any house, without the consent of the Owner, nor in time of war, but in a manner to be prescribed by law.

Amendment IV

The right of the people to be secure in their persons, houses, papers, and effects, against unreasonable searches and seizures, shall not be violated, and no Warrants shall issue, but upon probable cause, supported by Oath or affirmation, and particularly describing the place to be searched, and the persons or things to be seized.

Amendment V

No person shall be held to answer for a capital, or otherwise infamous crime, unless on a presentment or indictment of a Grand Jury, except in cases arising in the land or naval forces, or in the Militia, when in actual service in time of War or public danger; nor shall any person be subject for the same offence to be twice put in jeopardy of life or limb; nor shall be compelled in any criminal case to be a witness against himself, nor be deprived of life, liberty, or property, without due process of law; nor shall private property be taken for public use, without just compensation.

Amendment VI

In all criminal prosecutions, the accused shall enjoy the right to a speedy and public trial, by an impartial jury of the State and district wherein the crime shall have been committed, which district shall have been previously ascertained by law, and to be informed of the nature and cause of the accusation; to be confronted with the witnesses against him; to have compulsory process for obtaining witnesses in his favor, and to have the Assistance of Counsel for his defence.

Amendment VII

In Suits at common law, where the value in controversy shall exceed twenty dollars, the right of trial by jury shall be preserved, and no fact tried by a jury, shall be otherwise re-examined in any Court of the United States, than according to the rules of the common law.

Amendment VIII

Excessive bail shall not be required, nor excessive fines imposed, nor cruel and unusual punishments inflicted.

Amendment IX

The enumeration in the Constitution of certain rights, shall not be construed to deny or disparage others retained by the people.

Amendment X

The powers not delegated to the United States by the Constitution, nor prohibited by it to the States, are reserved to the States respectively, or to the people.

Amendment XI

The Judicial power of the United States shall not be construed to extend to any suit in law or equity, commenced or prosecuted against one of the United States by Citizens of another State, or by Citizens or Subjects of any Foreign State.

Amendment XII

The Electors shall meet in their respective states, and vote by ballot for President and Vice-President, one of whom, at least, shall not be an inhabitant of the same state with themselves; they shall name in their ballots the person voted for as President, and in distinct ballots the person voted for as Vice-President, and they shall make distinct lists of all persons voted for as President, and of all persons voted for as Vice-President, and of the number of votes for each, which lists they shall sign and certify, and transmit sealed to the seat of the government of the United States, directed to the President of the Senate;—The President of the Senate shall, in the presence of the Senate and House of Representatives, open all the certificates and the votes shall then be counted;—The person having the greatest number of votes for President, shall be the President, if such number be a majority of the whole number of Electors appointed; and if no person have such majority, then from the persons having the highest numbers not exceeding three on the list of those voted for as President, the House of Representatives shall choose immediately, by ballot, the President. But in choosing the President, the votes shall be taken by states, the representation from each state having one vote; a quorum for this purpose shall consist of a member or members from two-thirds of the states, and a majority of all the states shall be necessary to a choice. And if the House of Representatives shall not choose a President whenever the right of choice shall devolve upon them, before the fourth day of March next following, then the Vice-President shall act as President, as in the case of the death or other constitutional disability of the President—The person having the greatest number of votes as Vice-President, shall be the Vice-President, if such number be a majority of the whole number of Electors appointed, and if no person have a majority, then from the two highest numbers on the list, the Senate shall choose the Vice-President; a quorum for the purpose shall consist of two-thirds of the whole number of Senators, and a majority of the whole number shall be necessary to a choice. But no person constitutionally ineligible to the office of President shall be eligible to that of Vice-President of the United States.

Amendment XIII

Section 1. Neither slavery nor involuntary servitude, except as a punishment for crime whereof the party shall have been duly convicted, shall exist within the United States, or any place subject to their jurisdiction.

Section 2. Congress shall have power to enforce this article by appropriate legislation.

Amendment XIV

Section 1. All persons born or naturalized in the United States, and subject to the jurisdiction thereof, are citizens of the United States and of the State wherein they reside. No State shall make or enforce any law which shall abridge the privileges or immunities of citizens of the United States; nor shall any State deprive any person of life, liberty, or property, without due process of law; nor deny to any person within its jurisdiction the equal protection of the laws.

Section 2. Representatives shall be apportioned among the several States according to their respective numbers, counting the whole number of persons in each State, excluding Indians not taxed. But when the right to vote at any election for the choice of electors for President and Vice President of the United States, Representatives in Congress, the Executive and Judicial officers of a State, or the members of the Legislature thereof, is denied to any of the male inhabitants of such State, being twenty-one years of age, and citizens of the United States, or in any way abridged, except for participation in rebellion, or other crime, the basis of representation therein shall be reduced in the proportion which the number of such male citizens shall bear to the whole number of male citizens twenty-one years of age in such State.

Section 3. No person shall be a Senator or Representative in Congress, or elector of President and Vice President, or hold any office, civil or military, under the United States, or under any State, who, having previously taken an oath, as a member of Congress, or as an officer of the United States, or as a member of any State legislature, or as an executive or judicial officer of any State, to support the Constitution of the United States, shall have engaged in insurrection or rebellion against the same, or given aid or comfort to the enemies thereof. But Congress may by a vote of two-thirds of each House, remove such disability.

Section 4. The validity of the public debt of the United States, authorized by law, including debts incurred for payment of pensions and bounties for services in suppressing insurrection or rebellion, shall not be questioned. But neither the United States nor any State shall assume or pay any debt or obligation incurred in aid of insurrection or rebellion against the United States, or any claim for the loss or emancipation of any slave; but all such debts, obligations and claims shall be held illegal and void.

Section 5. The Congress shall have power to enforce, by appropriate legislation, the provisions of this article.

Amendment XV

Section 1. The right of citizens of the United States to vote shall not be denied or abridged by the United States or by any State on account of race, color, or previous condition of servitude.

Section 2. The Congress shall have power to enforce this article by appropriate legislation.

Amendment XVI

The Congress shall have power to lay and collect taxes on incomes, from whatever source derived, without apportionment among the several States, and without regard to any census or enumeration.

Amendment XVII

The Senate of the United States shall be composed of two Senators from each State, elected by the people thereof, for six years; and each Senator shall have one vote. The electors in each State shall have the qualifications requisite for electors of the most numerous branch of the State legislatures.

When vacancies happen in the representation of any State in the Senate, the executive authority of such State shall issue writs of election to fill such vacancies: Provided, that the legislature of any State may empower the executive thereof to make temporary appointments until the people fill the vacancies by election as the legislature may direct.

This amendment shall not be so construed as to affect the election or term of any Senator chosen before it becomes valid as part of the Constitution.

Amendment XVIII

Section 1. After one year from the ratification of this article the manufacture, sale, or transportation of intoxicating liquors within, the importation thereof into, or the exportation thereof from the United States and all territory subject to the jurisdiction thereof for beverage purposes is hereby prohibited.

Section 2. The Congress and the several States shall have concurrent power to enforce this article by appropriate legislation.

Section 3. This article shall be inoperative unless it shall have been ratified as an amendment to the Constitution by the legislatures of the several States, as provided in the Constitution, within seven years from the date of the submission hereof to the States by the Congress.

Amendment XIX

The right of citizens of the United States to vote shall not be denied or abridged by the United States or by any State on account of sex.

Congress shall have power to enforce this article by appropriate legislation.

Amendment XX

Section 1. The terms of the President and Vice President shall end at noon on the 20th day of January, and the terms of Senators and Representatives at noon on the 3d day of January, of the years in which such terms would have ended if this article had not been ratified; and the terms of their successors shall then begin.

Section 2. The Congress shall assemble at least once in every year, and such meeting shall begin at noon on the 3d day of January, unless they shall by law appoint a different day.

Section 3. If, at the time fixed for the beginning of the term of the President, the President elect shall have died, the Vice President elect shall become President. If a President shall not have been chosen before the time fixed for the beginning of his term, or if the President elect shall have failed to qualify, then the Vice President elect shall act as President until a President shall have qualified; and the Congress may by law provide for the case wherein neither a President elect nor a Vice President elect shall have qualified, declaring who shall then act as President, or the manner in which one who is to act shall be selected, and such person shall act accordingly until a President or Vice President shall have qualified.

Section 4. The Congress may by law provide for the case of the death of any of the persons from whom the House of Representatives may choose a President whenever the right of choice shall have devolved upon them, and for the case of the death of any of the persons from whom the Senate may choose a Vice President whenever the right of choice shall have devolved upon them.

Section 5. Sections 1 and 2 shall take effect on the 15th day of October following the ratification of this article.

Section 6. This article shall be inoperative unless it shall have been ratified as an amendment to the Constitution by the legislatures of three-fourths of the several States within seven years from the date of its submission.

Amendment XXI

Section 1. The eighteenth article of amendment to the Constitution of the United States is hereby repealed.

Section 2. The transportation or importation into any State, Territory, or possession of the United States for delivery or use therein of intoxicating liquors, in violation of the laws thereof, is hereby prohibited.

Section 3. This article shall be inoperative unless it shall have been ratified as an amendment to the Constitution by conventions in the several States, as provided in the Constitution, within seven years from the date of the submission hereof to the States by the Congress.

Amendment XXII

Section 1. No person shall be elected to the office of the President more than twice, and no person who has held the office of President, or acted as President, for more than two years of a term to which some other person was elected President shall be elected to the office of the President more than once. But this article shall not apply to any person holding the office of President when this article was proposed by the Congress, and shall not prevent any person who may be holding the office of President, or acting as President, during the term within which this article becomes operative from holding the office of President or acting as President during the remainder of such term.

Section 2. This article shall be inoperative unless it shall have been ratified as an amendment to the Constitution by the legislatures of three-fourths of the several states within seven years from the date of its submission to the states by the Congress.

Amendment XXIII

Section 1. The District constituting the seat of government of the United States shall appoint in such manner as the Congress may direct:

A number of electors of President and Vice President equal to the whole number of Senators and Representatives in Congress to which the District would be entitled if it were a state, but in no event more than the least populous state; they shall be in addition to those appointed by the states, but they shall be considered, for the purposes of the election of President and Vice President, to be electors appointed by a state; and they shall meet in the District and perform such duties as provided by the twelfth article of amendment.

Section 2. The Congress shall have power to enforce this article by appropriate legislation.

Amendment XXIV

Section 1. The right of citizens of the United States to vote in any primary or other election for President or Vice President, for electors for President or Vice President, or for Senator or Representative in Congress, shall not be denied or abridged by the United States or any state by reason of failure to pay any poll tax or other tax.

Section 2. The Congress shall have power to enforce this article by appropriate legislation.

Amendment XXV

Section 1. In case of the removal of the President from office or of his death or resignation, the Vice President shall become President.

Section 2. Whenever there is a vacancy in the office of the Vice President, the President shall nominate a Vice President who shall take office upon confirmation by a majority vote of both Houses of Congress.

Section 3. Whenever the President transmits to the President pro tempore of the Senate and the Speaker of the House of Representatives his written declaration that he is unable to discharge the powers and duties of his office, and until he transmits to them a written declaration to the contrary, such powers and duties shall be discharged by the Vice President as Acting President.

Section 4. Whenever the Vice President and a majority of either the principal officers of the executive departments or of such other body as Congress may by law provide, transmit to the President pro tempore of the Senate and the Speaker of the House of Representatives their written declaration that the President is unable to discharge the powers and duties of his office, the Vice President shall immediately assume the powers and duties of the office as Acting President.

Thereafter, when the President transmits to the President pro tempore of the Senate and the Speaker of the House of Representatives his written declaration that no inability exists, he shall resume the powers and duties of his office unless the Vice President and a majority of either the principal officers of the executive department or of such other body as Congress may by law provide, transmit within four days to the President pro tempore of the Senate and the Speaker of the House of Representatives their written declaration that the President is unable to discharge the powers and duties of his office. Thereupon Congress shall decide the issue, assembling within forty-eight hours for that purpose if not in session. If the Congress, within twenty-one days after receipt of the latter written declaration, or, if Congress is not in session, within twenty-one days after Congress is required to assemble, determines by two-thirds vote of both Houses that the President is unable to discharge the powers and duties of his office, the Vice President shall continue to discharge the same as Acting President; otherwise, the President shall resume the powers and duties of his office.

Amendment XXVI

Section 1. The right of citizens of the United States, who are 18 years of age or older, to vote, shall not be denied or abridged by the United States or any state on account of age.

Section 2. The Congress shall have the power to enforce this article by appropriate legislation.

Amendment XXVII

No law varying the compensation for the services of the Senators and Representatives shall take effect until an election of Representatives shall have intervened.

1

Absolutism and the Ancient Constitution

This chapter examines the process of constituting new political societies that began when English colonists arrived in North America.[1] Though far from home, they insisted they possessed the same traditional "rights of Englishmen" that they had enjoyed in England. The third charter of the colony of Virginia, for example, empowered the Virginia Company and its officers "to ordain and make such Laws and Ordinances, for the Good and Welfare of the said Plantation, as to them from Time to Time, shall be thought requisite and meet: So always, as the same be not contrary to the Laws and Statutes of this our Realm of England." Whatever else settlers believed they were doing when they emigrated from England, they did not envision themselves becoming less English, legally or culturally, than their compatriots who remained at home. Quite the contrary, as they set about establishing working political and social institutions in the colonies, they modeled themselves self-consciously on England. "Whatsoever we did, or ought to have, done, when we lived in England," said the Puritan John Winthrop in his famous 1630 lay sermon, "A Model of Christian Charity," "the same must we do, and more also, where we go."

But just what were those English rights? The seventeenth century was a period of political, religious, and constitutional settlement. Even as English monarchs authorized settlements in the New World, they and their subjects struggled to resolve intense controversies over the nature of English state religion and the extent and character of English state authority. Early in the century, English monarchs claimed absolute, divine authority, which implied that the rights of subjects existed at the will of the sovereign. When English kings attempted to rule without the advice and consent of Parliament, common-law lawyers asserted the primacy of the "ancient constitution," the source of English rights under which all English people—royal, noble, or common—were obliged to live. In the view of those who celebrated Parliament as a check on the authority of the monarch, traditional English rights—the right to be secure from arbitrary arrest and imprisonment, trial by jury, security of private property from arbitrary taking or taxation, and so on—were grounded in the tried-and-true practices of the English people from time immemorial.

Seventeenth-century English monarchs, like their European peers, grounded their claims to authority in religion. In this sense, the seventeenth-century English constitution was profoundly religious. But while almost everyone in England agreed that the state religion was Protestant, the exact nature of the English church remained unsettled. Prior to the English civil wars, the Church of England was highly conservative, from the point of view of many reformers. The church as established under

1. From the accession of James I to the English throne in 1603 until the Act of Union with Scotland in 1707, the three kingdoms of England, Scotland, and Ireland were joined only by their allegiance to a common king. With the significant exception of New Amsterdam, conquered by the English in 1664, all of the mainland colonies that would later become the United States were English. There were no colonies settled under Irish authority in North America, and only one abortive attempt to establish a colony by Scotland. While all of the colonies contained settlers from all three realms, the legal, constitutional, and political character of every mainland colony was substantively English.

Queen Elizabeth I and her Stuart successors retained numerous Catholic elements, including a liturgy; a hierarchy of priests, deans, bishops, and archbishops; altar rails and other elements of sacred architecture; and clerical vestments. King James I resisted efforts to "purify" the church of its remaining Catholic influences, recognizing astutely the potential for theological conflict to expand from learned discourse to actual violence. James' less gifted son Charles I lacked his father's political competence. Charles appointed bishops and archbishops who challenged key Protestant doctrines like justification by faith, in the process mobilizing Englishmen committed to the reformed tradition to political action.

One legacy of this struggle over the character of the English Church was the settlement of a series of religiously inspired colonies in New England. Some reformers separated themselves from the state church and emigrated from England to more thoroughly Protestant countries; one such congregation, known to us today as the "Pilgrims," took advantage of the opportunity to relocate to the English New World, and established the Plymouth colony in 1620. A much larger and more vigorous migration, lasting from 1630 until roughly 1642 and including more than 20,000 men, women, and children, founded and settled in the Massachusetts Bay colony. These men and women remained engaged with the ongoing contest in England, and hoped by the example of their "errand into the wilderness" that they would inspire religious reform in England. In the 1630s they set up additional colonies in Hartford, New Haven, and Rhode Island.

In Rhode Island, the minister Roger Williams and his followers created a government that radically separated church and state and formally protected religious liberty. But Rhode Island was an exception. All of the other New England colonies strove to institute biblical commonwealths in which a uniform religious practice was regulated by law. Massachusetts, for example, reserved the death penalty for those who worshiped "any god, but the lord god," practiced witchcraft, or committed blasphemy. Nathaniel Ward, minister of the town of Ipswich in Massachusetts, declared in his 1647 "Simple Cobbler of Aggawam" that "God doth no where in his word tolerate Christian States, to give Tolerations to such adversaries of his Truth, if they have power in their hands to suppresse them." In the 1650s, when Quakers first appeared in Massachusetts and disrupted religious services there, authorities prosecuted them under the colony's law. Convicted with scrupulous care, Massachusetts authorities fined, whipped, and ultimately expelled them from the colony. When several Quakers persisted and returned to the colony, Massachusetts sentenced and hanged four of them.

Between 1639 and 1660, the English endured a period of deep civil and religious strife. By 1642, civil wars erupted, organized around the person of the king, on the one hand, and the institution of Parliament, on the other, and ending only with the trial and execution of King Charles I. Abolition of lords and monarchy followed, and then a period of profound instability. English theorists and statesmen struggled with little success to define a legitimate nonmonarchical government. As the condemned king had poignantly noted, "if power without law may make laws, may alter the fundamental laws of the kingdom, I do not know what subject he is in England that can be sure of his life or anything that he calls his own." Parliament's legitimacy and authority were intimately tied to the monarchy, and with the death of the king, ultimately could not be sustained. A coup in 1653 replaced Parliament with military rule, which, when efforts to find a legitimate basis for that authority ultimately failed, by 1655 devolved into the military dictatorship of Oliver Cromwell.

Upon Cromwell's death, English statesmen restored the monarchy in 1660. The new king, Charles II, son of the man whom Parliament had executed in 1649, returned England to its traditional form of government. He restored the House of Lords and revived his father's and grandfather's pretensions to rule by divine right. He likewise restored the Church of England to its privileged established position. Within the church, numerous prominent theologians emphasized the capacity of "right reason" to deduce from human experience principles of correct behavior. Scientists like Robert Boyle and Isaac Newton, as well as philosophers like John Locke, celebrated the capacity of the human mind to apprehend the laws of nature as God had created them. As rational religion, with its emphasis on human liberty, became the orthodox position of the Church of England, even those most committed to reformed Christianity, whether in England or in the colonies, felt the need to adapt their thinking.

The restored monarchy, however, continued to confront religious suspicion. In 1688, when a son was born to King James II and his Catholic wife, powerful Protestants orchestrated a nearly bloodless revolution. Like their grandfather James I, the later Stuart kings, Charles II and James II, had proclaimed the divine nature of their authority. But when, unable to tolerate a Catholic monarch, the English replaced James II with the reliably Protestant William of Orange, they justified their action by employing theories of social contract. As early as 1683, the Whig politician Algernon Sydney, accused of plotting to kill the king, had forcefully declared "that the right and power of magistrates in every country is that which the laws of that country made it to be," and "that those laws were to be observed, and the oaths taken by them, having the force of a contract between magistrate and people, could not be violated without danger of dissolving the whole fabric." This was a line of thinking developed with considerable sophistication by the great social contract philosopher John Locke. In his *First Treatise of Government*, Locke demolished the patriarchal metaphor that had proved so instrumental in articulating divine right. In his *Second Treatise*, Locke grounded just and legitimate government in the reasoned consent of the governed. The authority of legitimate government originated from a contract with the people, in which the people gave up some of their natural rights in exchange for just, contractually limited government. When a king overstepped his authority, as it was claimed that James II had done, it was appropriate that the people replace him. In the aftermath of the Glorious Revolution, then, England possessed a limited, constitutional monarchy and a Protestant religious establishment.

The political struggles that culminated in the Glorious Revolution of 1688 also ended an effort to define the constitution of the rapidly growing empire, leaving the various English colonies in an ambiguous relationship with their mother country. The languages of social compact and natural law, which proved so valuable in redefining monarchical authority, could also be employed by the colonists to resist English claims of absolute dominion. Thus, the multiple English settlements of the seventeenth century exercised a profound influence over subsequent political and constitutional developments in what would become the United States of America. When eighteenth-century efforts to define the imperial constitution insisted upon the primacy of the King-in-Parliament, they encountered a long and well-developed strain of colonial argument that defined the colonial legislatures, governed by a representative of the king to be sure, as the guarantor of the colonists' English rights. That confrontation, which will be illuminated by documents in subsequent chapters of this volume, proved both explosive and revolutionary.

James I

Address before Parliament (1610)

[. . .] The state of monarchy is the supremest thing upon earth, for kings are not only God's lieutenants upon earth and sit upon God's throne, but even by God himself they are called gods. There be three principal similitudes that illustrate the state of monarchy: one taken out of the word of God, and the two other out of the grounds of policy and philosophy. In the Scriptures kings are called gods, and so their power after a certain relation compared to the Divine power. Kings are also compared to fathers of families; for a king is truly parens patriae, the politic father of his people. And lastly, kings are compared to the head of this microcosm of the body of man.

Kings are justly called gods for that they exercise a manner or resemblance of the divine power upon earth. For if you will consider the attributes of God, you shall see how they agree in the person of a king. God has the power to create, or destroy, or make, or unmake at his pleasure, to give life, or send death, to judge all, and to be judged nor accountable to none; to raise low things, and to make high things low at his pleasure, and to God are both soul and body due. And the like power have kings: they make and unmake their subjects; they have the power of raising and casting down, of life and of death; judges over all their subjects, and in all cases, and yet accountable to none but God only. They have the power to exalt low things and abase high things, and make of their subjects like men at chess: a pawn to take a bishop or a knight, and to cry up and down any of their subjects, as they do their money. And to the king is due both the affection of the soul and the service of the body of his subjects. [. . .]

As for the father of a family, they had of old under the law of nature patriam potestatem, which was potestatem vitae et necis, over their children or family. . . . Now a father may dispose of his inheritance to his children at his pleasure: yea, even disinherit the eldest upon just occasions, and prefer the youngest, according to his liking; make them beggars or rich at his pleasure; restrain, or banish out of his presence, as he finds them give cause of offence, or restore them again with the penitent sinner. So may the king deal with his subjects.

And lastly, as the head of the natural body, the head has the power of directing all the members of the body to that use which the judgment of the head thinks most convenient. It may apply sharp cures, or cut off corrupt members, let blood in what proportion it thinks fit, and as the body may spare, but yet is all this power ordained by God ad aedificationem, non ad destructionem. For though God have power of destruction as well as of creation or maintenance, yet will it not agree with the wisdom of God to exercise his power in the destruction of nature and overturning of the whole frame of things, since his creatures were made that his glory might thereby be the better expressed. So were he a foolish father that would disinherit or destroy his children without a cause, or leave off the careful education of them. And it were an idle head that would in place of physic so poison or phlebotomize the body as might breed a dangerous distemper or destruction thereof. [. . .]

Early Colonial Documents

The Third Charter of Virginia (March 12, 1611)

JAMES, by the Grace of God, King of England; Scotland, France, and Ireland; Defender of the Faith; To all to whom these Presents shall come, Greeting. WHEREAS at the humble Suit of divers and sundry our loving Subjects, as well Adventurers as Planters of the first Colony in Virginia, and for the Propagation of Christian Religion, and Reclaiming of People barbarous, to Civility and Humanity, We have, by our Letters-Patents, bearing Date at Westminster, the three-and-twentieth Day of May, in the seventh Year of our Reign of England, France, and Ireland, and the two-and-fortieth of Scotland, GIVEN and GRANTED unto them that they and all such and so many of our loving Subjects as should from time to time, for ever after, be joined with them as Planters or Adventurers in the said Plantation, and their Successors, for ever, should be one Body politick, incorporated by the Name of The Treasurer and Company of Adventurers and; Planters of the city of London for the first Colony in Virginia;

And whereas also for the greater Good and Benefit of the said Company, and for the better Furtherance, Strengthening, and Establishing of the said Plantation, we did further GIVE, GRANT and CONFIRM, by our Letters-Patents unto the said Company and their Successors, for ever, all those Lands, Countries or Territories, situate, lying and being in that Part of America called Virginia, [. . .].

We therefore tendering the good and happy Success of the said Plantation, both in Regard of the General Weal of human Society, as in Respect of the Good of our own Estate and Kingdoms, and being willing to give Furtherance unto all good Means that may advance the Benefit of the said Company, and which may secure the Safety of our loving Subjects planted in our said Colony, under the Favour and Protection of God Almighty, and of our Royal Power and Authority, have therefore of our especial Grace, certain Knowledge, and mere Motion, given, granted, and confirmed, and for Us, our Heirs and Successors, we do by these Presents give, grant, and confirm to the said Treasurer and Company of Adventurers and Planters of the city of London for the first Colony in Virginia, and to their Heirs and Successors for ever, [. . .] all and singular Soils, Lands, Grounds, Havens, Ports, Rivers, Waters, Fishings, Mines and Minerals, as well Royal Mines of Gold and Silver, as other Mines and Minerals, Pearls, precious Stones, Quarries, and all and singular other Commodities, Jurisdictions, Royalties, Privileges, Franchises, and Preheminences, [. . .] within the said Tract of Land upon the Main, [. . .]. Provided always, that the said [. . .] Premises herein mentioned, or by these Presents intended or meant to be granted, be not actually possessed or inhabited by any other Christian Prince or Estate, nor be within the Bounds, Limits, or Territories of the Northern Colony heretofore by Us granted to be planted by divers of our loving Subjects in the North Parts of Virginia. To HAVE AND TO HOLD, possess and enjoy, [. . .] with all and singular the said Soils, Lands, Grounds, and all and singular other the Premises heretofore by these Presents granted or mentioned to be granted to them, the said Treasurer and Company of Adventurers and Planters of the City of London for the first Colony in Virginia, and to their Heirs; Successors, and Assigns, for ever, to the sole and proper Use and Behoof of them the said Treasurer and Company, and their Heirs and Successors and Assigns, for ever; TO BE HOLDEN OF US, our Heirs and Successors, as of our Manor of East-Greenwich, in Free and common Soccage, and not in Capite; YIELDING AND PAYING therefore to Us, our Heirs and Successors, the fifth Part of the Ore of all Gold and Silver which shall be there gotten, had, or obtained for all Manner of Services whatsoever. [. . .]

And we do hereby ordain and grant by these Presents, that the said Treasurer and Company of Adventurers and Planters aforesaid, shall and may, once every week, or oftener, at their Pleasure, hold, and keep a Court and Assembly for the better Order and Government of the said Plantation, and such Things as shall concern the same; And that any five Persons of our Council for the said first Colony in Virginia, for the Time being, of which Company the Treasure, or his Deputy, to be always one, and the Number of fifteen others, at the least, of the Generality of the said Company, assembled together in such Manner, as is and hath been heretofore used and accustomed, shalt be said, taken, held, and reputed to be, and shall be a sufficient Court of the said Company, for the handling and ordering, and dispatching of all such casual and particular Occurrences, and accidental Matters, of less Consequence and Weight, as shall from Time to Time happen, touching and concerning the said Plantation.

And that nevertheless, for the handling, ordering, and disposing of Matters and Affairs of greater Weight and Importance, and such as shall or may, in any Sort, concern the Weal Publick and general Good of the said Company and Plantation, as namely, the Manner of Government from Time to Time to be used, the ordering and Disposing of the Lands and Possessions, and the settling and establishing of a Trade there, or such like, there shall be held and kept every Year, upon the last Wednesday, save one, of Hillary Term, Easter, Trinity, and Michaelmas Terms, for ever, one great, general, and solemn Assembly, which four Assemblies shall be stiled and called, The four Great and General Courts of the Council and Company of Adventurers for Virginia; In all and every of which said Great and General Courts, so assembled, our Will and Pleasure is, and we do, for Us, our Heirs and Successors, for ever, Give and Grant to the said Treasurer and Company, and their Successors for ever, by these Presents, that they, the said Treasurer and Company, or the greater Number of them, so assembled, shall and may have full Power and Authority, from Time to Time, and at all Times hereafter, to elect and chuse discreet Persons, to be of our said Council for the said first Colony in Virginia, and to nominate and appoint such Officers as they shall think fit and requisite, for the Government, managing, ordering, and dispatching of the Affairs of the said Company; And shall likewise have full Power and Authority, to ordain and make such Laws and Ordinances, for the Good and Welfare of the said Plantation, as to them from Time to Time, shall be thought requisite and meet: So always, as the same be not contrary to the Laws and Statutes of this our Realm of England; And shall, in like Manner, have Power and Authority, to expulse, disfranchise, and put out of and from their said Company and Society for ever, all and every such Person and Persons, as having either promised or subscribed their Names to become Adventurers to the said Plantation, of the said first Colony in Virginia, or having been nominated for Adventurers in these or any other our Letters-Patents, or having been otherwise admitted and nominated to be of the said Company, have nevertheless either not put in any adventure at all for and towards the said Plantation, or else have refused or neglected, or shall refuse and neglect to bring in his or their Adventure, by Word or Writing, promised within six Months after the same shall be so payable and due. [. . .] And We do, for Us, our Heirs and Successors, further give and grant to the said Treasurer and Company, or their Successors forever, that the said Treasurer and Company, or the greater Part of them for the Time being, so in a full and general Court assembled as aforesaid, shall and may from Time to Time, and at all times forever hereafter, elect choose and admit into their Company, and Society, any Person or Persons, as well Strangers and Aliens born in any Part beyond the Seas wheresoever, being in Amity with us, as our natural Liege Subjects born in any our Realms and Dominions: And that all such Persons so elected, chosen, and admitted to be of the said Company as aforesaid, shall thereupon be taken, reputed, and held, and shall be free Members of the said Company, and shall have, hold, and enjoy all and singular Freedoms, Liberties, Franchises, Privileges, Immunities, Benefits, Profits, and Commodities whatsoever, to the said Company in any Sort belonging or appertaining, as fully, freely and amply as any other Adventurers now being, or which hereafter at any Time shall be of the said Company, hash, have, shall, may, might, or ought to have and enjoy the same to all Intents and Purposes whatsoever. And We do further of our especial Grace, certain Knowledge, and mere Motion, for Us, our Heirs and Successors, give and grant unto the said Treasurer and Company, and their Sucessors for ever, by these Presents, that it shall be lawful and free for them and their

Assigns, at all and every Time and Times hereafter, out of any our Realms and Dominions whatsoever, to take, lead, carry, and transport in and into the said Voyage, and for and towards the said Plantation of our said first Colony in Virginia, all such and so many of our loving Subjects, or any other Strangers that will become our loving Subjects, and live under our Allegiance, as shall willingly accompany them in the said Voyages and Plantation, with Shipping, Armour, Weapons, Ordnance, Munition, Powder, Shot, Victuals, and all Manner of Merchandises and Wares, and all Manner of Clothing, Implements, Furniture, Beasts, Cattle, Horses, Mares, and all other Things necessary for the said Plantation, and for their Use and Defence, and for Trade with the People there, and in passing and returning to and from, without paying or yielding any Subsidy, Custom, or Imposition, either inward or outward, or any other Duty to Us, our Heirs and Successors, for the same, for the Space of Seven Years from the Date of these Presents.

And We do further, for Us, our Heirs and Successors, give and grant to the said Treasurer and Company, and their Successors forever, by these Presents, that the said Treasurer of that Company, or his Deputy for the Time being, or any two other of the said Council, for the said first Colony in Virginia, for the Time being, or any two other at all Times hereafter, and from Time to Time, have full Power and authority to minister and give the Oath and Oaths of Supremacy and Allegiance, or either of them, to all and every Person and Persons, which shall at any Time or Times hereafter, go or pass to the said Colony in Virginia:

And further, that it shall be lawful likewise for the said Treasurer, or his Deputy for the Time being, or any two or others of our said Council, for the said first Colony in Virginia, for the Time being, from Time to Time, and at all Times hereafter to minister such a formal Oath, as by their discretion shall be reasonably devised, as well unto any Person or Persons employed in, for, or touching the said Plantation, for their honest, faithful and just Discharge of their Service in all such Matters as shall be committed unto them, for the Good and Benefit of the said Company, Colony and Plantation; As also unto such other Person or Persons as the said Treasurer, or his Deputy, with two others of the said Council shall think meet, for the Examination or clearing of the Truth, in any Cause whatsoever, concerning the said Plantation, or any Business from thence proceeding, or thereunto belonging. [. . .]

In witness whereof we have caused these our Letters to be made Patents. Witness Ourself, at Westminster, the twelfth Day of March, in the ninth Year of our Reign of England, France, and Ireland, and of Scotland the five and fortieth.

The Mayflower Compact (1620)

Agreement between the Settlers at New Plymouth: 1620

In the name of God, amen. We, whose names are underwritten, the Loyal Subjects of our dread Sovereign Lord King *James*, by the Grace of God, of *Great Britain, France*, and *Ireland*, King, *Defender of the Faith*, &c. Having undertaken for the Glory of God, and Advancement of the Christian Faith, and the Honour of our King and Country, a Voyage to plant the first Colony in the northern Parts of *Virginia*; Do by these Presents, solemnly and mutually, in the Presence of God and one another, covenant and combine ourselves together into a civil Body Politick, for our better Ordering and Preservation, and Furtherance of the Ends aforesaid: And by Virtue hereof do enact, constitute, and frame, such just and equal Laws, Ordinances, Acts, Constitutions, and Officers, from time to time, as shall be thought most meet and convenient for the general Good of the Colony; unto which we promise all due Submission and Obedience. In witness whereof we have hereunto subscribed our names at *Cape-Cod* the eleventh of November, in the Reign of our Sovereign Lord King *James,* of *England, France,* and *Ireland,* the eighteenth, and of *Scotland* the fifty-fourth, *Anno Domini*; 1620.

Mr. John Carver, Mr. William Bradford, Mr. Edward Winslow, Mr. William Brewster, Isaac Allerton, Myles Standish, John Alden, John Turner, Francis Eaton, James Chilton, John Craxton, John Billington, Joses Fletcher, John Goodman, Mr. Samuel Fuller, Mr. Christopher Martin, Mr. William Mullins, Mr. William White, Mr. Richard Warren, John Howland, Mr. Steven Hopkins, Digery Priest, Thomas Williams, Gilbert Winslow, Edmund Margesson, Peter Brown, Richard Britteridge, George Soule, Edward Tilly, John Tilly, Francis Cooke, Thomas Rogers, Thomas Tinker, John Ridgdale, Edward Fuller, Richard Clark, Richard Gardiner, Mr. John Allerton, Thomas English, Edward Doten, Edward Liester.

Fundamental Orders of Connecticut (1639)

For as much as it hath pleased Almighty God by the wise disposition of his divine providence so to order and dispose of things that we the Inhabitants and Residents of Windsor, Hartford and Wethersfield are now cohabiting and dwelling in and upon the River of Connectecotte and the lands thereunto adjoining; and well knowing where a people are gathered together the word of God requires that to maintain the peace and union of such a people there should be an orderly and decent Government established according to God, to order and dispose of the affairs of the people at all seasons as occasion shall require; do therefore associate and conjoin ourselves to be as one Public State or Commonwealth; and do for ourselves and our successors and such as shall be adjoined to us at any time hereafter, enter into Combination and Confederation together, to maintain and preserve the liberty and purity of the Gospel of our Lord Jesus which we now profess, as also, the discipline of the Churches, which according to the truth of the said Gospel is now practiced amongst us; as also in our civil affairs to be guided and governed according to such Laws, Rules, Orders and Decrees as shall be made, ordered, and decreed as followeth:

1. It is Ordered, sentenced, and decreed, that there shall be yearly two General Assemblies or Courts, the one the second Thursday in April, the other the second Thursday in September following; the first shall be called the Court of Election, wherein shall be yearly chosen from time to time, so many Magistrates and other public Officers as shall be found requisite: Whereof one to be chosen Governor for the year ensuing and until another be chosen, and no other Magistrate to be chosen for more than one year: provided always there be six chosen besides the Governor, which being chosen and sworn according to an Oath recorded for that purpose, shall have the power to administer justice according to the Laws here established, and for want thereof, according to the Rule of the Word of God; which choice shall be made by all that are admitted freemen and have taken the Oath of Fidelity, and do cohabit within this Jurisdiction having been admitted Inhabitants by the major part of the Town wherein they live or the major part of such as shall be then present.

2. It is Ordered, sentenced, and decreed, that the election of the aforesaid Magistrates shall be in this manner: every person present and qualified for choice shall bring in (to the person deputed to receive them) one single paper with the name of him written in it whom he desires to have Governor, and that he that hath the greatest number of papers shall be Governor for that year. And the rest

of the Magistrates or public officers to be chosen in this manner: the Secretary for the time being shall first read the names of all that are to be put to choice and then shall severally nominate them distinctly, and every one that would have the person nominated to be chosen shall bring in one single paper written upon, and he that would not have him chosen shall bring in a blank; and every one that hath more written papers than blanks shall be a Magistrate for that year; which papers shall be received and told by one or more that shall be then chosen by the court and sworn to be faithful therein; but in case there should not be six chosen as aforesaid, besides the Governor, out of those which are nominated, than he or they which have the most written papers shall be a Magistrate or Magistrates for the ensuing year, to make up the aforesaid number.

3. It is Ordered, sentenced, and decreed, that the Secretary shall not nominate any person, nor shall any person be chosen newly into the Magistracy which was not propounded in some General Court before, to be nominated the next election; and to that end it shall be lawful for each of the Towns aforesaid by their deputies to nominate any two whom they conceive fit to be put to election; and the Court may add so many more as they judge requisite.

4. It is Ordered, sentenced, and decreed, that no person be chosen Governor above once in two years, and that the Governor be always a member of some approved Congregation, and formerly of the Magistracy within this Jurisdiction; and that all the Magistrates, Freemen of this Commonwealth; and that no Magistrate or other public officer shall execute any part of his or their office before they are severally sworn, which shall be done in the face of the court if they be present, and in case of absence by some deputed for that purpose.

5. It is Ordered, sentenced, and decreed, that to the aforesaid Court of Election the several Towns shall send their deputies, and when the Elections are ended they may proceed in any public service as at other Courts. Also the other General Court in September shall be for making of laws, and any other public occasion, which concerns the good of the Commonwealth.

6. It is Ordered, sentenced, and decreed, that the Governor shall, either by himself or by the Secretary, send out summons to the Constables of every Town for the calling of these two standing Courts one month at least before their several times: And also if the Governor and the greatest part of the Magistrates see cause upon any special occasion to call a General Court, they may give order to the Secretary so to do within fourteen days' warning: And if urgent necessity so required, upon a shorter notice, giving sufficient grounds for it to the deputies when they meet, or else be questioned for the same; And if the Governor and major part of Magistrates shall either neglect or refuse to call the two General standing Courts or either of them, as also at other times when the occasions of the Commonwealth require, the Freemen thereof, or the major part of them, shall petition to them so to do; if then it be either denied or neglected, the said Freemen, or the major part of them, shall have the power to give order to the Constables of the several Towns to do the same, and so may meet together, and choose to themselves a Moderator, and may proceed to do any act of power which any other General Courts may.

7. It is Ordered, sentenced, and decreed, that after there are warrants given out for any of the said General Courts, the Constable or Constables of each Town, shall forthwith give notice distinctly to the inhabitants of the same, in some public assembly or by going or sending from house to house, that at a place and time by him or them limited and set, they meet and assemble themselves together to elect and choose certain deputies to be at the General Court then following to agitate the affairs of the Commonwealth; which said deputies shall be chosen by all that are admitted Inhabitants in the several Towns and have taken the oath of fidelity; provided that none be chosen a Deputy for any General Court which is not a Freeman of this Commonwealth.

The aforesaid deputies shall be chosen in manner following: every person that is present and qualified as before expressed, shall bring the names of such, written in several papers, as they desire to have chosen for that employment, and these three or four, more or less, being the number agreed on to be chosen for that time, that have the greatest number of papers written for them shall be deputies for that Court; whose names shall be endorsed on the back side of the warrant and returned into the

Court, with the Constable or Constables' hand unto the same.

8. It is Ordered, sentenced, and decreed, that Windsor, Hartford, and Wethersfield shall have power, each Town, to send four of their Freemen as their deputies to every General Court; and Whatsoever other Town shall be hereafter added to this Jurisdiction, they shall send so many deputies as the Court shall judge meet, a reasonable proportion to the number of Freemen that are in the said Towns being to be attended therein; which deputies shall have the power of the whole Town to give their votes and allowance to all such laws and orders as may be for the public good, and unto which the said Towns are to be bound.

9. It is Ordered, sentenced, and decreed, that the deputies thus chosen shall have power and liberty to appoint a time and a place of meeting together before any General Court, to advise and consult of all such things as may concern the good of the public, as also to examine their own Elections, whether according to the order, and if they or the greatest part of them find any election to be illegal they may seclude such for present from their meeting, and return the same and their reasons to the Court; and if it be proved true, the Court may fine the party or parties so intruding, and the Town, if they see cause, and give out a warrant to go to a new election in a legal way, either in part or in whole. Also the said deputies shall have power to fine any that shall be disorderly at their meetings, or for not coming in due time or place according to appointment; and they may return the said fines into the Court if it be refused to be paid, and the Treasurer to take notice of it, and to escheat or levy the same as he does other fines.

10. It is Ordered, sentenced, and decreed, that every General Court, except such as through neglect of the Governor and the greatest part of the Magistrates the Freemen themselves do call, shall consist of the Governor, or some one chosen to moderate the Court, and four other Magistrates at least, with the major part of the deputies of the several Towns legally chosen; and in case the Freemen, or major part of them, through neglect or refusal of the Governor and major part of the Magistrates, shall call a Court, it shall consist of the major part of Freemen that are present or their deputies, with a Moderator chosen by them: In which said General Courts shall consist the supreme power of the Commonwealth, and they only shall have power to make laws or repeal them, to grant levies, to admit of Freemen, dispose of lands undisposed of, to several Towns or persons, and also shall have power to call either Court or Magistrate or any other person whatsoever into question for any misdemeanor, and may for just causes displace or deal otherwise according to the nature of the offense; and also may deal in any other matter that concerns the good of this Commonwealth, except election of Magistrates, which shall be done by the whole body of Freemen.

In which Court the Governor or Moderator shall have power to order the Court, to give liberty of speech, and silence unseasonable and disorderly speakings, to put all things to vote, and in case the vote be equal to have the casting voice. But none of these Courts shall be adjourned or dissolved without the consent of the major part of the Court.

11. It is Ordered, sentenced, and decreed, that when any General Court upon the occasions of the Commonwealth have agreed upon any sum, or sums of money to be levied upon the several Towns within this Jurisdiction, that a committee be chosen to set out and appoint what shall be the proportion of every Town to pay of the said levy, provided the committee be made up of an equal number out of each Town.

14th January 1639 the 11 Orders above said are voted.

The Maryland Toleration Act (1649)

An Act Concerning Religion

Forasmuch as in a well governed and Christian Common Weath matters concerning Religion and the honor of God ought in the first place to bee taken, into serious consideracion and endeavoured to bee settled, Be it therefore ordered and enacted by the Right Honourable Cecilius Lord Baron of Baltemore absolute Lord and Proprietary of this Province with the advise and consent of this Generall Assembly:

That whatsoever person or persons within this Province and the Islands thereunto belonging shall from henceforth blaspheme God, that is Curse him, or deny our Saviour Jesus Christ to bee the sonne of God, or shall deny the holy Trinity the father sonne and holy Ghost, or the Godhead of any of the said Three persons of the Trinity or the Unity of the Godhead, or shall use or utter any reproachfull Speeches, words or language concerning the said Holy Trinity, or any of the said three persons thereof, shalbe punished with death and confiscation or forfeiture of all his or her lands and goods to the Lord Proprietary and his heires.

And bee it also Enacted by the Authority and with the advise and assent aforesaid, That whatsoever person or persons shall from henceforth use or utter any reproachfull words or Speeches concerning the blessed Virgin Mary the Mother of our Saviour or the holy Apostles or Evangelists or any of them shall in such case for the first offence forfeit to the said Lord Proprietary and his heirs Lords and Proprietaries of this Province the summe of five pound Sterling or the value thereof to be Levyed on the goods and chattells of every such person soe offending, but in case such Offender or Offenders, shall not then have goods and chattells sufficient for the satisfyeing of such forfeiture, or that the same bee not otherwise speedily satisfyed that then such Offender or Offenders shalbe publiquely whipt and bee imprisoned during the pleasure of the Lord Proprietary or the Lieutenant or cheife Governor of this Province for the time being. And that every such Offender or Offenders for every second offence shall forfeit tenne pound sterling or the value thereof to bee levyed as aforesaid, or in case such offender or Offenders shall not then have goods and chattells within this Province sufficient for that purpose then to bee publiquely and severely whipt and imprisoned as before is expressed. And that every person or persons before mentioned offending herein the third time, shall for such third Offence forfeit all his lands and Goods and bee for ever banished and expelled out of this Province.

And be it also further Enacted by the same authority advise and assent that whatsoever person or persons shall from henceforth uppon any occasion of Offence or otherwise in a reproachful manner or Way declare call or denominate any person or persons whatsoever inhabiting, residing, traffiqueing, trading or comerceing within this Province or within any the Ports, Harbors, Creeks or Havens to the same belonging an heritick, Scismatick, Idolator, puritan, Independant, Prespiterian popish prest, Jesuite, Jesuited papist, Lutheran, Calvenist, Anabaptist, Brownist, Antinomian, Barrowist, Roundhead, Separatist, or any other name or terme in a reproachfull manner relating to matter of Religion shall for every such Offence forfeit and loose the somme of tenne shillings sterling or the value thereof to bee levyed on the goods and chattells of every such Offender and Offenders, the one half thereof to be forfeited and paid unto the person and persons of whom such reproachfull words are or shalbe spoken or uttered, and the other half thereof to the Lord Proprietary and his heires Lords and Proprietaries of this Province. But if such person or persons who shall at any time utter or speake any such reproachfull words or Language shall not have Goods or Chattells sufficient and overt within this Province to bee taken to satisfie the penalty aforesaid or that the same bee not otherwise speedily satisfyed, that then the person or persons soe offending shalbe publickly whipt, and shall suffer imprisonment without baile or maineprise untill hee, shee or they respectively shall satisfy the party soe offended or greived by such reproachfull Language by asking him or her respectively forgivenes publiquely for such his Offence before the Magistrate of cheife Officer or Officers of the Towne or place where such Offence shalbe given.

And be it further likewise Enacted by the Authority and consent aforesaid That every person and persons within this Province that shall at any time hereafter prophane the Sabbath or Lords day called Sunday by frequent swearing, drunkennes or by any uncivill or disorderly recreacion, or by working on that day when absolute necessity doth not require it shall for every such first offence forfeit 2*s* 6*d* sterling or the value thereof, and for the second offence 5*s* sterling or the value thereof, and for the third offence and soe for every time he shall offend in like manner afterwards 10*s* sterling or the value thereof. And in case such offender and offenders shall not have sufficient goods or chattells within this Province to satisfy any of the said Penalties respectively hereby imposed for prophaning the Sabbath or Lords day called Sunday as aforesaid, That in Every such case the partie soe offending shall for the first and second offence in that kinde be imprisoned till hee or shee shall publickly in open Court before the cheife Commander Judge or Magistrate, of that County Towne or precinct where such offence shalbe committed acknowledg the Scandall and offence he hath in that respect given against God and the good and civill Governement of this Province, And for the third offence and for every time after shall also bee publickly whipt.

And whereas the inforceing of the conscience in matters of Religion hath frequently fallen out to be of dangerous Consequence in those commonwealthes where it hath been practised, And for the more quiett and peaceable governement of this Province, and the better to preserve mutuall Love and amity amongst the Inhabitants thereof, Be it Therefore also by the Lord Proprietary with the advise and consent of this Assembly Ordeyned and enacted (except as in this present Act is before Declared and sett forth) that noe person or persons whatsoever within this Province, or the Islands, Ports, Harbors, Creekes, or havens thereunto belonging professing to beleive in Jesus Christ, shall from henceforth bee any waies troubled, Molested or discountenanced for or in respect of his or her religion nor in the free exercise thereof within this Province or the Islands thereunto belonging nor any way compelled to the beleife or exercise of any other Religion against his or her consent, soe as they be not unfaithfull to the Lord Proprietary, or molest or conspire against the civill Governement established or to bee established in this Province under him or his heires. And that all and every person and persons that shall presume Contrary to this Act and the true intent and meaning thereof directly or indirectly either in person or estate willfully to wrong disturbe trouble or molest any person whatsoever within this Province professing to beleive in Jesus Christ for or in respect of his or her religion or the free exercise thereof within this Province other than is provided for in this Act that such person or persons soe offending, shalbe compelled to pay trebble damages to the party soe wronged or molested, and for every such offence shall also forfeit 20*s* sterling in money or the value thereof, half thereof for the use of the Lord Proprietary, and his heires Lords and Proprietaries of this Province, and the other half for the use of the party soe wronged or molested as aforesaid, Or if the partie soe offending as aforesaid shall refuse or bee unable to recompense the party soe wronged, or to satisfy such fyne or forfeiture, then such Offender shalbe severely punished by publick whipping and imprisonment during the pleasure of the Lord Proprietary, or his Lieutenant or cheife Governor of this Province for the tyme being without baile or maineprise.

And bee it further alsoe Enacted by the authority and consent aforesaid That the Sheriff or other Officer or Officers from time to time to bee appointed and authorized for that purpose, of the County Towne or precinct where every particular offence in this present Act conteyned shall happen at any time to bee committed and whereupon there is hereby a forfeiture fyne or penalty imposed shall from time to time distraine and seise the goods and estate of every such person soe offending as aforesaid against this present Act or any part thereof, and sell the same or any part thereof for the full satisfaccion of such forfeiture, fine, or penalty as aforesaid, Restoring unto the partie soe offending the Remainder or overplus of the said goods or estate after such satisfaccion soe made as aforesaid.

The freemen have assented.

John Winthrop

Model of Christian Charity (1630)

God Almighty in His most holy and wise providence, hath so disposed of the condition of mankind, as in all times some must be rich, some poor, some high and eminent in power and dignity; others mean and in submission.

The Reason hereof:

1st Reason. First to hold conformity with the rest of His world, being delighted to show forth the glory of his wisdom in the variety and difference of the creatures, and the glory of His power in ordering all these differences for the preservation and good of the whole, and the glory of His greatness, that as it is the glory of princes to have many officers, so this great king will have many stewards, counting himself more honored in dispensing his gifts to man by man, than if he did it by his own immediate hands.

2nd Reason. Secondly, that He might have the more occasion to manifest the work of his Spirit: first upon the wicked in moderating and restraining them, so that the rich and mighty should not eat up the poor, nor the poor and despised rise up against and shake off their yoke. Secondly, in the regenerate, in exercising His graces in them, as in the great ones, their love, mercy, gentleness, temperance etc., and in the poor and inferior sort, their faith, patience, obedience etc.

3rd Reason. Thirdly, that every man might have need of others, and from hence they might be all knit more nearly together in the bonds of brotherly affection. From hence it appears plainly that no man is made more honorable than another or more wealthy etc., out of any particular and singular respect to himself, but for the glory of his Creator and the common good of the creature, man. Therefore God still reserves the property of these gifts to Himself as Ezek. 16:17, He there calls wealth, His gold and His silver, and Prov. 3:9, He claims their service as His due, "Honor the Lord with thy riches," etc.—All men being thus (by divine providence) ranked into two sorts, rich and poor; under the first are comprehended all such as are able to live comfortably by their own means duly improved; and all others are poor according to the former distribution.

There are two rules whereby we are to walk one towards another: Justice and Mercy. These are always distinguished in their act and in their object, yet may they both concur in the same subject in each respect; as sometimes there may be an occasion of showing mercy to a rich man in some sudden danger or distress, and also doing of mere justice to a poor man in regard of some particular contract, etc.

There is likewise a double Law by which we are regulated in our conversation towards another. In both the former respects, the Law of Nature and the Law of Grace (that is, the moral law or the law of the gospel) to omit the rule of justice as not properly belonging to this purpose otherwise than it may fall into consideration in some particular cases. By the first of these laws, man as he was enabled so withal is commanded to love his neighbor as himself. Upon this ground stands all the precepts of the moral law, which concerns our dealings with men. To apply this to the works of mercy, this law requires two things. First, that every man afford his help to another in every want or distress. Secondly, that he perform this out of the same affection which makes him careful of his own goods, according to the words of our Savior (from Matthew 7:12), whatsoever ye would that men should do to you. This was practiced by Abraham and Lot in entertaining the angels and the old man of Gibea.

The law of Grace or of the Gospel hath some difference from the former (the law of nature), as in these respects: First, the law of nature was given to man in the estate of innocence. This of the Gospel in the estate of regeneracy. Secondly, the former propounds one man to another, as the same flesh and image of God. This as a brother in Christ also, and in the communion of the same Spirit, and so teacheth to put a difference between Christians and others. Do good to all, especially to the household of faith. Upon this ground the Israelites were to put a difference between the brethren of such as were strangers, though not of the Canaanites. Thirdly, the Law of Nature would give no rules for dealing with enemies, for all are to be considered as friends in the state of innocence, but the Gospel commands love to an enemy. Proof: If thine enemy hunger, feed him; "Love your enemies. . . . Do good to them that hate you" (Matt. 5:44).

This law of the Gospel propounds likewise a difference of seasons and occasions. There is a time when a Christian must sell all and give to the poor, as they did in the Apostles' times. There is a time also when Christians (though they give not all yet) must give beyond their ability, as they of Macedonia (2 Cor. 8). Likewise, community of perils calls for extraordinary liberality, and so doth community in some special service for the church. Lastly, when there is no other means whereby our Christian brother may be relieved in his distress, we must help him beyond our ability rather than tempt God in putting him upon help by miraculous or extraordinary means. This duty of mercy is exercised in the kinds: giving, lending and forgiving (of a debt). [. . .]

Having already set forth the practice of mercy according to the rule of God's law, it will be useful to lay open the grounds of it also, being the other part of the Commandment and that is the affection from which this exercise of mercy must arise, the Apostle tells us that this love is the fulfilling of the law, not that it is enough to love our brother and so no further; but in regard of the excellency of his parts giving any motion to the other as the soul to the body and the power it hath to set all the faculties at work in the outward exercise of this duty; as when we bid one make the clock strike, he doth not lay hand on the hammer, which is the immediate instrument of the sound, but sets on work the first mover or main wheel; knowing that will certainly produce the sound which he intends. So the way to draw men to the works of mercy, is not by force of Argument from the goodness or necessity of the work; for though this cause may enforce, a rational mind to some present act of mercy, as is frequent in experience, yet it cannot work such a habit in a soul, as shall make it prompt upon all occasions to produce the same effect, but by framing these affections of love in the heart which will as naturally bring forth the other, as any cause doth produce the effect.

The definition which the Scripture gives us of love is this: Love is the bond of perfection. First it is a bond or ligament. Secondly, it makes the work perfect. There is no body but consists of parts and that which knits these parts together, gives the body its perfection, because it makes each part so contiguous to others as thereby they do mutually participate with each other, both in strength and infirmity, in pleasure and pain. To instance in the most perfect of all bodies: Christ and his Church make one body. The several parts of this body considered a part before they were united, were as disproportionate and as much disordering as so many contrary qualities or elements, but when Christ comes, and by his spirit and love knits all these parts to himself and each to other, it is become the most perfect and best proportioned body in the world (Eph. 4:15–16). Christ, by whom all the body being knit together by every joint for the furniture thereof, according to the effectual power which is in the measure of every perfection of parts, a glorious body without spot or wrinkle; the ligaments hereof being Christ, or his love, for Christ is love (1 John 4:8). So this definition is right. Love is the bond of perfection.

From hence we may frame these conclusions:

First of all, true Christians are of one body in Christ (1 Cor. 12). Ye are the body of Christ and members of their part. All the parts of this body being thus united are made so contiguous in a special relation as they must needs partake of each other's strength and infirmity; joy and sorrow, weal and woe. If one member suffers, all suffer with it, if one be in honor, all rejoice with it.

Secondly, the ligaments of this body which knit together are love.

Thirdly, no body can be perfect which wants its proper ligament.

Fourthly, All the parts of this body being thus united are made so contiguous in a special relation as they must needs partake of each other's strength and infirmity, joy and sorrow, weal and woe (1 Cor. 12:26). If one member suffers, all suffer with it; if one be in honor, all rejoice with it.

Fifthly, this sensitivity and sympathy of each other's conditions will necessarily infuse into each part a native desire and endeavor, to strengthen, defend, preserve and comfort the other. To insist a little on this conclusion being the product of all the former, the truth hereof will appear both by precept and pattern. 1 John 3:16, "We ought to lay down our lives for the brethren." Gal. 6:2, "Bear ye one another's burden's and so fulfill the law of Christ."

For patterns we have that first of our Savior who, out of his good will in obedience to his father, becoming a part of this body and being knit with it in the bond of love, found such a native sensitivity of our infirmities and sorrows as he willingly yielded himself to death to ease the infirmities of the rest of his body, and so healed their sorrows. From the like sympathy of parts did the Apostles and many thousands of the Saints lay down their lives for Christ. Again the like we may see in the members of this body among themselves. Rom. 9—Paul could have been contented to have been separated from Christ, that the Jews might not be cut off from the body. It is very observable what he professeth of his affectionate partaking with every member; "Who is weak (saith he) and I am not weak? Who is offended and I burn not?" And again (2 Cor. 7:13), "Therefore we are comforted because ye were comforted." Of Epaphroditus he speaketh (Phil. 2:25–30) that he regarded not his own life to do him service. So Phoebe and others are called the servants of the church. Now it is apparent that they served not for wages, or by constraint, but out of love. The like we shall find in the histories of the church, in all ages; the sweet sympathy of affections which was in the members of this body one towards another; their cheerfulness in serving and suffering together; how liberal they were without repining, harborers without grudging, and helpful without reproaching; and all from hence, because they had fervent love amongst them; which only makes the practice of mercy constant and easy.

The next consideration is how this love comes to be wrought. Adam in his first estate was a perfect model of mankind in all their generations, and in him this love was perfected in regard of the habit. But Adam, himself rent from his Creator, rent all his posterity also one from another; whence it comes that every man is born with this principle in him to love and seek himself only, and thus a man continueth till Christ comes and takes possession of the soul and infuseth another principle, love to God and our brother, and this latter having continual supply from Christ, as the head and root by which he is united, gets predominant in the soul, so by little and little expels the former. 1 John 4:7—Love cometh of God and every one that loveth is born of God, so that this love is the fruit of the new birth, and none can have it but the new creature. Now when this quality is thus formed in the souls of men, it works like the Spirit upon the dry bones. Ezek. 37:7—"Bone came to bone." It gathers together the scattered bones, or perfect old man Adam, and knits them into one body again in Christ, whereby a man is become again a living soul.

The third consideration is concerning the exercise of this love, which is twofold, inward or outward. The outward hath been handled in the former preface of this discourse. From unfolding the other we must take in our way that maxim of philosophy, "simile simili gaudet," or like will to like; for as of things which are turned with disaffection to each other, the ground of it is from a dissimilitude or arising from the contrary or different nature of the things themselves; for the ground of love is an apprehension of some resemblance in the things loved to that which affects it. This is the cause why the Lord loves the creature, so far as it hath any of his Image in it; He loves his elect because they are like Himself, He beholds them in His beloved son.

So a mother loves her child, because she thoroughly conceives a resemblance of herself in it. Thus it is between the members of Christ; each discerns, by the work of the Spirit, his own Image and resemblance in another, and therefore cannot but love him as he loves himself. Now when the soul, which is of a sociable nature, finds anything like to itself, it is like Adam when Eve was brought to him. She must be one with himself. This is flesh of my flesh (saith he) and bone of my bone. So the soul conceives a great delight in it; therefore she desires nearness and familiarity with it. She hath a great propensity to do it good and receives such content in it, as fearing the miscarriage of her beloved, she bestows it in the inmost closet of her heart. She will not endure that it shall want any good which she can give it. If by occasion she be withdrawn from the company of it, she is still looking towards the place where she left her beloved. If she heard it groan, she is with it presently. If she find it sad and disconsolate, she sighs and moans with it. She hath no such joy as to see her beloved merry and thriving. If she see it wronged, she cannot hear it without passion. She sets no bounds to her affections, nor hath any thought of reward. She finds recompense enough in the exercise of her love towards it.

We may see this acted to life in Jonathan and David. Jonathan a valiant man endued with the spirit of love, so soon as he discovered the same spirit in David had presently his heart knit to him by this ligament of love; so that it is said he loved him as his own soul, he takes so great pleasure in him, that he strips himself to adorn his beloved. His father's kingdom was not so precious to him as his beloved David, David shall have it with all his heart. Himself desires no more but that he may be near to him to rejoice in his good. He chooseth to converse with him in the wilderness even to the hazard of his own life, rather than with the great Courtiers in his father's Palace. When he sees danger towards him, he spares neither rare pains nor peril to direct it. When injury was offered his beloved David, he would not bear it, though from his own father. And when they must part for a season only, they thought their hearts would have broke for sorrow, had not their affections found vent by abundance of tears. Other instances might be brought to show the nature of this affection; as of Ruth and Naomi, and many others; but this truth is cleared enough. If any shall object that it is not possible that love shall be bred or upheld without hope of requital, it is granted; but that is not our cause; for this love is always under reward. It never gives, but it always receives with advantage:

First in regard that among the members of the same body, love and affection are reciprocal in a most equal and sweet kind of commerce.

Secondly, in regard of the pleasure and content that the exercise of love carries with it, as we may see in the natural body. The mouth is at all the pains to receive and mince the food which serves for the nourishment of all the other parts of the body; yet it hath no cause to complain; for first the other parts send back, by several passages, a due proportion of the same nourishment, in a better form for the strengthening and comforting the mouth. Secondly, the labor of the mouth is accompanied with such pleasure and content as far exceeds the pains it takes. So is it in all the labor of love among Christians. The party loving, reaps love again, as was showed before, which the soul covets more then all the wealth in the world.

Thirdly, nothing yields more pleasure and content to the soul then when it finds that which it may love fervently; for to love and live beloved is the soul's paradise both here and in heaven. In the State of wedlock there be many comforts to learn out of the troubles of that condition; but let such as have tried the most, say if there be any sweetness in that condition comparable to the exercise of mutual love.

From the former considerations arise these conclusions:

First, this love among Christians is a real thing, not imaginary.

Secondly, this love is as absolutely necessary to the being of the body of Christ, as the sinews and other ligaments of a natural body are to the being of that body.

Thirdly, this love is a divine, spiritual, nature; free, active, strong, courageous, permanent; undervaluing all things beneath its proper object and of all the graces, this makes us nearer to resemble the virtues of our heavenly father.

Fourthly, it rests in the love and welfare of its beloved. For the full certain knowledge of those truths concerning the nature, use, and excellency of this grace, that which the holy ghost hath left recorded, 1 Cor. 13, may give full satisfaction, which is needful for every true member of this lovely body of the Lord Jesus, to work upon their hearts by prayer, meditation continual exercise at least of the special influence of this grace, till Christ be formed in them and they in him, all in each other, knit together by this bond of love.

It rests now to make some application of this discourse, by the present design, which gave the occasion of writing of it. Herein are four things to be propounded; first the persons, secondly, the work, thirdly the end, fourthly the means.

First, for the persons. We are a company professing ourselves fellow members of Christ, in which respect only, though we were absent from each other many miles, and had our employments as far distant, yet we ought to account ourselves knit together by this bond of love and live in the exercise of it, if we would have comfort of our being in Christ. This was notorious in the practice of the Christians in former times; as is testified of the Waldenses, from the mouth of one of the adversaries Aeneas Sylvius "mutuo ament pene antequam norunt"—they use to love any of their own religion even before they were acquainted with them.

Secondly for the work we have in hand. It is by a mutual consent, through a special overvaluing providence and a more than an ordinary approbation of the churches of Christ, to seek out a place of cohabitation and consortship under a due form of government both civil and ecclesiastical. In such cases as this, the care of the public must oversway all private respects, by which, not only conscience, but mere civil policy, doth bind us. For it is a true rule that particular estates cannot subsist in the ruin of the public.

Thirdly, the end is to improve our lives to do more service to the Lord; the comfort and increase of the body of Christ, whereof we are members, that ourselves and posterity may be the better preserved from the common corruptions of this evil world, to serve the Lord and work out our salvation under the power and purity of his holy ordinances.

Fourthly, for the means whereby this must be effected. They are twofold, a conformity with the work and end we aim at. These we see are extraordinary, therefore we must not content ourselves with usual ordinary means. Whatsoever we did, or ought to have done, when we lived in England, the same must we do, and more also, where we go. That which the most in their churches maintain as truth in profession only, we must bring into familiar and constant practice; as in this duty of love, we must love brotherly without dissimulation, we must love one another with a pure heart fervently. We must bear one another's burdens. We must not look only on our own things, but also on the things of our brethren.

Neither must we think that the Lord will bear with such failings at our hands as he doth from those among whom we have lived; and that for these three reasons:

First, in regard of the more near bond of marriage between Him and us, wherein He hath taken us to be His, after a most strict and peculiar manner, which will make Him the more jealous of our love and obedience. So He tells the people of Israel, you only have I known of all the families of the earth, therefore will I punish you for your transgressions.

Secondly, because the Lord will be sanctified in them that come near Him. We know that there were many that corrupted the service of the Lord; some setting up altars before his own; others offering both strange fire and strange sacrifices also; yet there came no fire from heaven, or other sudden judgment upon them, as did upon Nadab and Abihu, whom yet we may think did not sin presumptuously.

Thirdly, when God gives a special commission He looks to have it strictly observed in every article; When He gave Saul a commission to destroy Amaleck, He indented with him upon certain articles, and because he failed in one of the least, and that upon a fair pretense, it lost him the kingdom, which should have been his reward, if he had observed his commission.

Thus stands the cause between God and us. We are entered into covenant with Him for this work. We have taken out a commission. The Lord hath given us leave to draw our own articles. We have professed to enterprise these and those accounts, upon these and those ends. We have hereupon besought Him of favor and blessing. Now if the Lord shall please to hear us, and bring us in peace to the place we desire, then hath He ratified this covenant and sealed our commission, and will expect a strict performance of the articles contained in it; but if we shall neglect the observation of these articles which are the ends we have propounded, and, dissembling with our God, shall fall to embrace this present world and prosecute our carnal intentions, seeking great things for ourselves and our posterity, the Lord will surely break out in wrath against us, and be revenged of such a people, and make us know the price of the breach of such a covenant.

Now the only way to avoid this shipwreck, and to provide for our posterity, is to follow the counsel of Micah, to do justly, to love mercy, to walk humbly with our God. For this end, we must be knit together, in this work, as one man. We must entertain each other in brotherly affection. We must be willing to abridge ourselves of our superfluities, for the supply of others' necessities. We must uphold a familiar commerce together in all meekness, gentleness, patience and liberality. We must delight in each other; make others' conditions our own; rejoice together, mourn together, labor and suffer together, always having before our eyes our commission and community in the work, as members of the same body. So shall we keep the unity of the spirit in the bond of peace. The Lord will be our God, and delight to dwell among us, as His own people, and will command a blessing upon us in all our ways, so that we shall see much more of His wisdom, power, goodness and truth, than formerly we have been acquainted with. We shall find that the God of Israel is among us, when ten of us shall be able to resist a thousand of our enemies; when He shall make us a praise and glory that men shall say of succeeding plantations, "may the Lord make it like that of New England." For we must consider that we shall be as a city upon a hill. The eyes of all people are upon us. So that if we shall deal falsely with our God in this work we have undertaken, and so cause Him to withdraw His present help from us, we shall be made a story and a by-word through the world. We shall open the mouths of enemies to speak evil of the ways of God, and all professors for God's sake. We shall shame the faces of many of God's worthy servants, and cause their prayers to be turned into curses upon us till we be consumed out of the good land whither we are going. And to shut this discourse with that exhortation of Moses, that faithful servant of the Lord, in his last farewell to Israel, Deut. 30. "Beloved, there is now set before us life and death, good and evil," in that we are commanded this day to love the Lord our God, and to love one another, to walk in his ways and to keep his Commandments and his ordinance and his laws, and the articles of our Covenant with Him, that we may live and be multiplied, and that the Lord our God may bless us in the land whither we go to possess it. But if our hearts shall turn away, so that we will not obey, but shall be seduced, and worship other Gods, our pleasure and profits, and serve them; it is propounded unto us this day, we shall surely perish out of the good land whither we pass over this vast sea to possess it.

Therefore let us choose life,
that we, and our Seed,
may live; by obeying His
voice, and cleaving to Him,
for He is our life, and
our prosperity.

Little Speech on Liberty (1645)

I suppose something may be expected from me, upon this charge that is befallen me which moves me to speak now to you; yet I intend not to intermeddle in the proceedings of the court or with any of the persons concerned therein. Only I bless God that I see an issue of this troublesome business. I also acknowledge the justice of the court, and, for mine own part, I am well satisfied, I was publicly charged, and I am publicly and legally acquitted, which is all I did expect or desire. And though this be sufficient for my justification before men, yet not so before the God, who hath seen so much amiss in my dispensations (and even in this affair) as calls me to be humble. For to be publicly and criminally charged in this court is matter of humiliation (and I desire to make a right use of it), notwithstanding I be thus acquitted. If her father had spit in her face (saith the Lord concerning Miriam), should she not have been ashamed seven days? Shame had lien upon her, whatever the occasion had been. I am unwilling to stay you from your urgent affairs, yet give me leave (upon this special occasion) to speak a little more to this assembly. It may be of some good use, to inform and rectify the judgments of some of the people, and may prevent such distempers as have arisen amongst us. The great questions that have troubled the country are about the authority of the magistrates and the liberty of the people. It is yourselves who have called us to this office, and, being called by you, we have our authority from God, in way of an ordinance, such as hath the image of God eminently stamped upon it, the contempt and violation whereof hath been vindicated with examples of divine vengeance. I entreat you to consider that, when you choose magistrates, you take them from among yourselves, men subject to like passions as you are. Therefore, when you see infirmities in us, you should reflect upon your own, and that would make you bear the more with us, and not be severe censurers of the failings of your magistrates, when you have continual experience of the like infirmities in yourselves and others. We account him a good servant who breaks not his covenant. The covenant between you and us is the oath you have taken of us, which is to this purpose: that we shall govern you and judge your causes by the rules of God's laws and our own, according to our best skill. When you agree with a workman to build you a ship or house, etc., he undertakes as well for his skill as for his faithfulness, for it is his profession, and you pay him for both. But when you call one to be a magistrate, he doth not profess nor undertake to have sufficient skill for that office, nor can you furnish him with gifts, etc., therefore you must run the hazard of his skill and ability. But if he fail in faithfulness, which by his oath he is bound unto, that he must answer for. If it fall out that the case be clear to common apprehension, and the rule clear also, if he transgress here, the error is not in the skill, but in the evil of the will: it must be required of him. But if the case be doubtful, or the rule doubtful, to men of such understanding and parts as your magistrates are, if your magistrates should err here, yourselves must bear it.

For the other point concerning liberty, I observe a great mistake in the country about that. There is a twofold liberty, natural (I mean as our nature is now corrupt) and civil or federal. The first is common to man with beasts and other creatures. By this, man, as he stands in relation to man simply, hath liberty to do what he lists; it is a liberty to evil as well as to good. This liberty is incompatible and inconsistent with authority and cannot endure the least restraint of the most just authority. The exercise and maintaining of this liberty makes men grow more evil and in time to be worse than brute beasts: *omnes sumus licentia deteriores.* This is that great enemy of truth and peace, that wild beast, which all of the ordinances of God are bent against, to restrain and subdue it. The other kind of liberty I call civil or federal; it may also be termed moral, in reference to the covenant between God and man, in the moral law, and the politic covenants and constitutions amongst men themselves. This liberty is the proper end and object of authority and cannot subsist without it; and it is a liberty to that only which is good, just, and honest. This liberty you are to stand for, with the hazard (not only of your goods, but) of your lives, if need be. Whatsoever crosseth this is not authority but a distemper thereof. This liberty is maintained and exercised in a way of subjection to authority; it is of the same kind of liberty wherewith Christ hath made us free. The women's own choice makes such a man her husband; yet, being so chosen, he is her lord, and she is to be subject to him, yet in a way of liberty, not of bondage; and a true wife accounts her subjection her honor and freedom and would not think her condition safe and free but in her subjection to her husband's authority. Such is the liberty of the church under the authority of Christ, her king and husband; his yoke is so easy and sweet to her as a bride's ornaments; and if through forwardness or wantonness, etc., she shake it off, at any time, she is at no rest in her spirit, until she take it up again; and whether her lord smiles upon her and embraceth her in his arms, or whether he frowns, or rebukes, or smites her, she apprehends the sweetness of his love in all, and is refreshed, supported, and instructed by every such dispensation of his authority over her. On the other side, ye know who they are that complain of this yoke and say, Let us break their bands, etc.; we will not have this man to rule over us. Even so, brethren, it will be between you and your magistrates. If you want to stand for your natural corrupt liberties, and will do what is good in your own eyes, you will not endure the least weight of authority, but will murmur, and oppose, and be always striving to shake off that yoke; but if you will be satisfied to enjoy such civil and lawful liberties, such as Christ allows you, then will you quietly and cheerfully submit unto that authority which is set over you, in all the administrations of it, for your good. Wherein, if we fail at any time, we hope we shall be willing (by God's assistance) to hearken to good advice from any of you, or in any other way of God; so shall your liberties be preserved in upholding the honor and power of authority amongst you.

Nathaniel Ward

The Simple Cobbler of Aggawam (1647)

Sathan is now in his passions, hee feeles his passion approaching; he loves to fish in royled waters. Though that Dragon cannot sting the vitals of the Elect mortally, yet that Beelzebub can fly-blow their Intellectuals miserably: The finer Religion grows, the finer he spins his Cobwebs, he will hold pace with Christ so long as his wits will serve him. He sees himself beaten out of grosse Idolatries, Heresies, Ceremonies, where the Light breakes forth with power; he will therefore bestirre him to prevaricate Evangelicall Truths, and Ordinances, that if they will needs be walking, yet they shall *laborare varicibus,* and not keep their path: he will put them out of time and place; Assascinating for his Engineers, men of Paracelsian parts, well complexioned for honesty; for, such are fittest to Mountebanke his Chimistry into sicke Churches and weake Judgements.

Nor shall he need to stretch his strength overmuch in this worke: Too many men having not laid their foundation sure, nor ballasted their Spirits deep with humility and feare, are prest enough of themselves to evaporate their owne apprehensions. Those that are acquainted with Story know, it hath ever been so in new Editions of Churches: Such as are least able, are most busy to pudder in the rubbish, and to raise dust in the eyes of more steady Repayrers. Civill Commotions make room for uncivill practises: Religious mutations, for irreligious opinions: Change of aire, discovers corrupt bodies: Reformation of Religion, unsound mindes. He that hath any well-faced phancy in his Crowne, and doth not vent it now, feares, the pride of his own heart will dub him duns for ever. Such a one will trouble the whole *Israel* of God with his most untimely births, though he makes the bones of his vanity stick up, to the view and griefe of all that are godly wise. The devill desires no better sport then to see light heads handle their heelcs, and fetch their carreers in a time, when the Roofe of Liberty stands open.

The next perplexed Question, with pious and ponderous men, will be: What should be done for the healing of these comfortlesse exulcerations. I am the unablest adviser of a thousand, the unworthiest of ten thousand; yet I hope I may presume to assert what follows without just offence.

First, such as have given or taken any unfriendly reports of us *New-English,* should doe well to recollect themselves. We have been reputed a Colluvies of wild Opinionists, swarmed into a remote wildernes to find elbow-roome for our phanatick Doctrines and practises: I trust our diligence past, and constant sedulity against such persons and courses, will plead better things for us. I dare take upon me, to be the Herauld of *New-England* so farre, as to proclaime to the world, in the name of our Colony, that all Familists, Antinomians, Anabaptists, and other Enthusiasts, shall have free Liberty to keep away from us, and such as will come to be gone as fast as they can, the sooner the better.

Secondly, I dare averre, that God doth no where in his word tolerate Christian States, to give Tolerations to such adversaries of his Truth, if they have power in their hands to suppresse them.

Here is lately brought us an Extract of a *Magna Charta,* so called, compiled between the Sub-planters of a *West-Indian* Island; whereof the first article of constipulation, firmely provides free stable-roome and litter for all kinde of consciences, be they never so dirty or jadish; making it actionable, yea, treasonable, to disturb any man in his Religion, or to discommend it, whatever it be. We are very sorry to see such professed profanenesse in *English* Professors, as industriously to lay their Religious foundations on the ruine of true Religion; which strictly bindes every conscience to contend earnestly for the Truth: to preserve unity of spirit, faith and Ordinances, to be all like-minded, of one accord; every man to take his brother into his Christian care: to stand fast with one spirit, with one minde, striving together for the faith of the Gospel: and by no meanes to permit Heresies or erroneous opinions: But God abhorring such loathsome beverages, hath in his righteous judgement blasted that enterprize, which might otherwise have prospered well, for ought *I* know: I presume their case is generally known ere this.

If the devill might have his free option, I beleeve he would ask nothing else, but liberty to enfranchize all other Religions, and to embondage the true; nor should he need: It is much to be feared, that laxe Tolerations upon State-pretences and planting necessities, will be the next subtle Stratagem he will spread, to distate the Truth of God and supplant the peace of the Churches. Tolerations in things tolerable, exquisitely drawn out by the lines of the Scripture, and pensill of the Spirit, are the sacred favours of Truth, the due latitudes of Love, the faire Compartiments of Christian fraternity: but irregular dispensations, dealt forth by the facilities of men, are the frontiers of errour, the redoubts of Schisme, the perillous irritaments of carnall enmity.

My heart hath naturally detested foure things: The standing of the Apocrypha in the Bible; Forrainers dwelling in my Countrey, to crowd out native Subjects into the corners of the Earth; Alchymized coines; Tolerations of divers Religions, or of one Religion in segregant shapes: He that willingly assents to the last, if he examines his heart by daylight, his conscience will tell him, he is either an Atheist, or an Heretique, or an Hypocrite, or at best a captive to some lust: polchpiety is the greatest impiety in the world. True Religion is *Ignis probationis*, which doth *congregare homogenea & segregare heterogenia*.

Not to tolerate tilings meerly indifferent to weak consciences, argues a conscience too strong: pressed uniformity in these, causes much disunity. To tolerate more than indifferents, is not to deale indifferently with God; He that doth it, takes his Scepter out of His hand, and bids Him stand by. The power of all Religion and Ordinances, lies in their purity: their purity in their simplicity: then are mixtures pernicious. I lived in a City, where a Papist Preached in one Church, a Lutheran in another, a Calvinist in a third; a Lutheran one part of the day, a Calvinist the other, in the same Pulpit: the Religion of that place was but motly and meagre, their affections Leopard-like.

If the whole Creature should conspire to doe the Creator a mischiefe, or offer him an insolency, it would be in nothing more, then in erecting untruths against his Truth, or by sophisticating his Truths with humane medley's: the removing of some one iota in Scripture, may draw out all the life, and traverse all the Truth of the whole Bible: but to authorise an untruth, by a Toleration of State, is to build a Sconce against the walls of Heaven, to batter God out of his Chaire: To tell a practicall lye, is a great sinne, but yet transient; but to set up a Theoricall untruth, is to warrant every lye that lyes from its root to the top of every branch it hath.

I would willingly hope that no Member of the Parliament hath skilfully ingratiated himselfe into the hearts of the House, that he might watch a time to midwife out some ungracious Toleration for his own turne, and for the sake of that, some others. I would also hope that a word of generall caution should not bee particularly misapplied. Yet good Gentlemen, looke well about you, and remember how *Tiberius* plaid the Fox with the Senate *of Rome*, and how *Fabius Maximus* cropt his eares for his cunning.

That State is wise, that will improve all paines and patience rather to compose, then tolerate differences in Religion. There is no divine Truth, but hath much Celestiall fire in it from the Spirit of Truth: nor no irreligious untruth, without its proportion of Antifire from the Spirit of Error to contradict it: the zeale of the one, the virulency of the other, must necessarily kindle Combustions. Fiery diseases seated in the spirit, embroile the whole frame of the body; others more externall and coole, are lesse dangerous. They which divide in Religion, divide in God; they who divide in him, divide beyond *Genus Generalissimum*, where there is no reconciliation, without atonement; that is, without uniting in him, who is One, and in his Truth, which is also one.

Wise are those men who will be perswaded rather to live within the pale of Truth where they may bee quiet, than in the purliev's, where they are sure to bee hunted ever and anon, doe Authority what it can. Every singular Opinion, hath a singular opinion of it self; and he that holds it, a singular opinion of himself, and a simple opinion of all contra-sentients: he that confutes them, must confute all three at once, or else he does nothing; which will not be done without more stirre then the peace of the State or Church can indure.

And prudent are those Christians, that will rather give what may be given, then hazard all by yeelding nothing. To sell all peace of Country, to buy some peace of Conscience unseasonably, is more avarice than thrift, imprudence than patience: they deale not equally, that set any Truth of God at such a rate; but they deale wisely that will stay till the Market is fallen.

My prognosticks deceive me not a little, if once within three seven yeares, peace prove not such a penny worth at most Marts in Christendome, that he that would not lay downe his money, his lust, his opinion, his will, I had almost said the best flower of his Crowne, for it, while he might have had it; will tell his owne heart, he plaid the very ill husband.

Concerning Tolerations I may further assert.

That Persecution of true Religion, and Toleration of false, are the *Jannes* and *Jambres* to the Kingdome of Christ, whereof the last is farre the worst. Augustines tongue had not owed his mouth one penny-rent though it had never spake word more in it, but this, *Nullum malum pejus libertate errandi*.

He that is willing to tolerate any Religion, or discrepant way of Religion, besides his owne, unlesse it be in matters meerly indifferent, either doubts of his owne, or is not sincere in it.

He that is willing to tolerate any unsound Opinion, that his owne may also be tolerated, though never so sound, will for a need hang Gods Bible at the Devills girdle.

Every Toleration of false Religions, or Opinions hath as many Errors and sinnes in it, as all the false Religions and Opinions it tolerates, and one sound one more.

That State that will give Liberty of Conscience in matters of Religion, must give Liberty of Conscience and Conversation in their Morall Lawes, or else the Fiddle will be out of tune, and some of the strings cracke.

He that will rather make an irreligious quarrell with other Religions, then try the Truth of his own by valuable Arguments, and peaceable Sufferings; either his Religion, or himself is irreligious.

Experience will teach Churches and Christians, that it is farre better to live in a State united, though somewhat Corrupt, then in a State, whereof some Part is Incorrupt, and all the rest divided.

I am not altogether ignorant of the eight Rules given by Orthodox Divines, about giving Tolerations, yet with their favour I dare affirme, That there is no Rule given by God for any State to give an Affirmative Toleration to any false Religion, or Opinion whatsoever; they must connive in some Cases, but may not concede in any.

That the State of *England* (so farre as my Intelligence serves) might in time have prevented with ease, and may yet without any great difficulty deny both Toleration, and Connivances *salva Republica*.

That if the State of *England* shall either willingly Tolerate, or weakly connive at such Courses, the Church of that Kingdome will sooner become the Devills Dancing-Schoole, then Gods-Temple: The Civill State a Beare-garden, then an Exchange: The whole Realme a Pais base, then an *England*. And what pity it is, that that Country which hath been the Staple of Truth to all Christendome, should now become the Aviary of Errors to the whole World, let every fearing heart judge. [. . .]

Concerning Novelties of opinions; I shall expresse my thoughts in these briefe passages. First, that Truth is the best boone God ever gave the world: there is nothing in the world, any further then Truth makes it so; it is better than any creat' *Ens* or *Bonum*, which are but Truths twins. Secondly, the least Truth of Gods Kingdome, doth in its place, uphold the whole kingdome of his Truths; Take away the least *vericulum* out of the world, and it unworlds all, potentially, and may unravell the whole texture actually, if it be not conserved by an Arme of extraordinary power. Thirdly, the least Evangelicall Truth, is more worth than all the Civill Truths in the world, that are meerly so. Fourthly, that Truth is the Parent of all Liberty whether politicall or personall; so much untruth, so much thraldome, *John* 8. 32.

Hence it is, that God is so jealous of his Truths, that he hath taken order in his due Justice: First, that no practicall sin is so sinfull as some errour in judgement; no men so accursed with indelible infamy and dedolent impenitency, as Authours of Heresie. Secondly, that the least Error, if grown sturdy and pressed, shall set open the Spittle-doore of all the squint-ey'd, wry-necked, and brasen-faced Errors that are or ever were of that litter; if they be not enough to serve its turne, it will beget more, though it hath not one crust of reason to maintain them. Thirdly, that, that State which will permit Errors in Religion, shall admit Errors in Policy unavoydably.

Fourthly, that that Policy which will suffer irreligious errors, shall suffer the losse of so much Liberty in one kinde or other, I will not exempt *Venice, Rhaguse,* the *Nether-lands,* or any.

An easie head may soon demonstrate, that the prementioned Planters, by Tolerating all Religions, had immazed themselves in the most intolerable confusions and inextricable thraldomes the world ever heard of. I am perswaded the Devill himselfe was never willing with their proceedings, for feare it would break his winde and wits to attend such a Province. I speak it seriously according to my meaning. How all Religions should enjoy their liberty, Justice its due regularity, Civill cohabitation morall honesty, in one and the same Jurisdiction, is beyond the Artique of my comprehension. If the whole conclave of Hell can so compromise, exadverse, and diametriall contradictions, as to compolitize such a multimonstrous maufrey of heteroclytes and quicquidlibets quietly; I trust I may say with all humble reverence, they can doe more then the Senate of Heaven. My *modus loquendi* pardoned; I entirely wish much welfare and more wisdome to that Plantation. [. . .]

James Harrington

Oceana (1656)

Janotti, the most excellent describer of the Commonwealth of Venice, divides the whole series of government into two times or periods: the one ending with the liberty of Rome, which was the course or empire, as I may call it, of ancient prudence, first discovered to mankind by God himself in the fabric of the commonwealth of Israel, and afterward picked out of his footsteps in nature, and unanimously followed by the Greeks and Romans; the other beginning with the arms of Caesar, which, extinguishing liberty, were the transition of ancient into modern prudence, introduced by those inundations of Huns, Goths, Vandals, Lombards, Saxons, which, breaking the Roman Empire, deformed the whole face of the world with those ill-features of government, which at this time are become far worse in these western parts, except Venice, which, escaping the hands of the barbarians by virtue of its impregnable situation, has had its eye fixed upon ancient prudence, and is attained to a perfection even beyond the copy.

Relation being had to these two times, government (to define it de jure, or according to ancient prudence) is an art whereby a civil society of men is instituted and preserved upon the foundation of common right or interest; or, to follow Aristotle and Livy, it is the empire of laws, and not of men.

And government (to define it de facto, or according to modern prudence) is an art whereby some man, or some few men, subject a city or a nation, and rule it according to his or their private interest; which, because the laws in such cases are made according to the interest of a man, or of some few families, may be said to be the empire of men, and not of laws.

The former kind is that which Machiavel (whose books are neglected) is the only politician that has gone about to retrieve; and that Leviathan (who would have his book imposed upon the universities) goes about to destroy. For "it is," says he, "another error of Aristotle's politics that in a well-ordered commonwealth, not men should govern, but the laws. What man that has his natural senses, though he can neither write nor read, does not find himself governed by them he fears, and believes can kill or hurt him when he obeys not? or, who believes that the law can hurt him, which is but words and paper, without the hands and swords of men?" I confess that the magistrate upon his bench is that to the law which a gunner upon his platform is to his cannon. Nevertheless, I should not dare to argue with a man of any ingenuity after this manner. A whole army, though they can neither write nor read, are not afraid of a platform, which they know is but earth or stone; nor of a cannon, which, without a hand to give fire to it, is but cold iron; therefore a whole army is afraid of one man. But of this kind is the ratiocination of Leviathan, as I shall show in divers places that come in my way, throughout his whole politics, or worse; as where he says, "of Aristotle and of Cicero, of the Greeks, and of the Romans, who lived under popular States, that they derived those rights, not from the principles of nature, but transcribed them into their books out of the practice of their own commonwealths, as grammarians describe the rules of language out of poets." Which is as if a man should tell famous Harvey that he transcribed his circulation of the blood, not out of the principles of nature, but out of the anatomy of this or that body.

To go on therefore with his preliminary discourse, I shall divide it, according to the two definitions of government relating to Janotti's two times, in two parts: the first, treating of the principles of government in general, and according to the ancients; the second, treating of the late governments of Oceana in particular, and in that of modern prudence.

Government, according to the ancients, and their learned disciple Machiavel, the only politician of later ages, is of three kinds: the government of one man, or of the better sort, or of the whole people; which, by their more learned names, are called monarchy, aristocracy, and democracy. These they hold, through their proneness to degenerate, to be all evil. For whereas they that govern should govern according to reason, if they govern according to passion they do that which they should not do. Wherefore, as reason and passion are two things, so government by reason is one thing, and the corruption of government by passion is another thing, but not always another government: as a body that is alive is one thing, and a body that is dead is another thing, but not always another creature, though the corruption of one comes at length to be the generation of another. The corruption then of monarchy is called tyranny; that of aristocracy, oligarchy and that of democracy, anarchy. But legislators, having found these three governments at the best to be naught, have invented another, consisting of a mixture of them all, which only is good. This is the doctrine of the ancients.

But Leviathan is positive that they are all deceived, and that there is no other government in nature than one of the three; as also that the flesh of them cannot stink, the names of their corruptions being but the names of men's fancies, which will be understood when we are shown which of them was Senatus Populusque Romanus.

To go my own way, and yet to follow the ancients, the principles of government are twofold: internal, or the goods of the mind; and external, or the goods of fortune. The goods of the mind are natural or acquired virtues, as wisdom, prudence, and courage, etc. The goods of fortune are riches. There be goods also of the body, as health, beauty, strength; but these are not to be brought into account upon this score, because if a man or an army acquires victory or empire, it is more from their discipline, arms, and courage than from their natural health, beauty, or strength, in regard that a people conquered may have more of natural strength, beauty, and health, and yet find little remedy. The principles of government then are in the goods of the mind, or in the goods of fortune. To the goods of the mind answers authority; to the goods of fortune, power or empire. Wherefore Leviathan, though he be right where he says that "riches are power," is mistaken where he says that "prudence, or the reputation of prudence, is power"; for the learning or prudence of a man is no more power than the learning or prudence of a book or author, which is properly authority. A learned writer may have authority though he has no power; and a foolish magistrate may have power, though he has otherwise no esteem or authority. The difference of these two is observed by Livy in Evander, of whom he says that he governed rather by the authority of others than by his own power.

To begin with riches, in regard that men are hung upon these, not of choice as upon the other, but of necessity and by the teeth; forasmuch as he who wants bread is his servant that will feed him, if a man thus feeds a whole people, they are under his empire.

Empire is of two kinds, domestic and national, or foreign and provincial.

Domestic empire is founded upon dominion. Dominion is property, real or personal; that is to say, in lands, or in money and goods.

Lands, or the parts and parcels of a territory, are held by the proprietor or proprietors, lord or lords of it, in some proportion; and such (except it be in a city that has little or no land, and whose revenue is in trade) as is the proportion or balance of dominion or property in land, such is the nature of the empire.

If one man be sole landlord of a territory, or overbalance the people, for example, three parts in four, he is grand seignior; for so the Turk is called from his property, and his empire is absolute monarchy.

If the few or a nobility, or a nobility with the clergy, be landlords, or overbalance the people to the like proportion, it makes the Gothic balance (to be shown at large in the second part of this discourse), and the empire is mixed monarchy, as that of Spain, Poland, and late of Oceana.

And if the whole people be landlords, or hold the lands so divided among them that no one man, or number of men, within the compass of the few or aristocracy, overbalance them, the empire (without the interposition of force) is a commonwealth.

If force be interposed in any of these three cases, it must either frame the government to the foundation, or the foundation to the government; or holding the government not according to the balance, it is not natural, but violent; and therefore if it be at the devotion of a prince, it is tyranny; if at the devotion of the few, oligarchy; or if in the power of the people, anarchy: Each of which confusions, the balance standing otherwise, is but of short continuance, because against the nature of the balance, which, not destroyed, destroys that which opposes it.

But there be certain other confusions, which, being rooted in the balance, are of longer continuance, and of worse consequence; as, first, where a nobility holds half the property, or about that proportion, and the people the other half; in which case, without altering the balance there is no remedy but the one must eat out the other, as the people did the nobility in Athens, and the nobility the people in Rome. Secondly, when a prince holds about half the dominion, and the people the other half (which was the case of the Roman emperors, planted partly upon their military colonies and partly upon the Senate and the people), the government becomes a very shambles, both of the princes and the people. Somewhat of this nature are certain governments at this day, which are said to subsist by confusion. In this case, to fix the balance is to entail misery; but in the three former, not to fix it is to lose the government. [. . .]

But Leviathan, though he seems to skew at antiquity, following his furious master Carneades, has caught hold of the public sword, to which he reduces all manner and matter of government; as, where he affirms this opinion (that any monarch receives his power by covenant; that is to say, upon conditions) "to proceed from the not understanding this easy truth, that covenants being but words and breath, have no power to oblige, contain, constrain, or protect any man, but what they have from the public sword." But as he said of the law, that without this sword it is but paper, so he might have thought of this sword, that without a hand it is but cold iron. The hand which holds this sword is the militia of a nation; and the militia of a nation is either an army in the field, or ready for the field upon occasion. But an army is a beast that has a great belly, and must be fed: wherefore this will come to what pastures you have, and what pastures you have will come to the balance of property, without which the public sword is but a name or mere spitfrog. Wherefore, to set that which Leviathan says of arms and of contracts a little straighter, he that can graze this beast with the great belly, as the Turk does his Timariots, may well deride him that imagines he received his power by covenant, or is obliged to any such toy. It being in this case only that covenants are but words and breath. But if the property of the nobility, stocked with their tenants and retainers, be the pasture of that beast, the ox knows his master's crib; and it is impossible for a king in such a constitution to reign otherwise than by covenant; or if he break it, it is words that come to blows.

"But," says he, "when an assembly of men is made sovereign, then no man imagines any such covenant to have part in the institution." But what was that by Publicola of appeal to the people, or that whereby the people had their tribunes? "Fie," says he, "nobody is so dull as to say that the people of Rome made a covenant with the Romans, to hold the sovereignty on such or such conditions, which, not performed, the Romans might depose the Roman people." In which there be several remarkable things; for he holds the Commonwealth of Rome to have consisted of one assembly, whereas it consisted of the Senate and the people; that they were not upon covenant, whereas every law enacted by them was a covenant between them; that the one assembly was made sovereign, whereas the people, who only were sovereign, were such from the beginning, as appears by the ancient style of their covenants or laws—"The Senate has resolved, the people have decreed," that a council being made sovereign, cannot be made such upon conditions, whereas the Decemvirs being a council that was made sovereign, was made such upon conditions; that all conditions or covenants making a sovereign being made, are void; whence it must follow that, the Decemviri being made, were ever after the lawful government of Rome, and that it was unlawful for the Commonwealth of Rome to depose the Decemvirs; as also that Cicero, if he wrote otherwise out of his commonwealth, did not write out of nature. But to come to others that see more of this balance.

You have Aristotle full of it in divers places, especially where he says, that "immoderate wealth, as where one man or the few have greater possessions than the equality or the frame of the commonwealth will bear, is an occasion of sedition, which ends for the greater part in monarchy and that for this cause the ostracism has been received in divers places, as in Argos and Athens. But that it were better to prevent the growth in the beginning, than, when it has got head, to seek the remedy of such an evil."

Machiavel has missed it very narrowly and more dangerously for not fully perceiving that if a commonwealth be galled by the gentry it is by their overbalance, he speaks of the gentry as hostile to popular governments, and of popular governments as hostile to the gentry; and makes us believe that the people in such are so enraged against them, that where they meet a gentleman they kill him: which can never be proved by any one example, unless in civil war, seeing that even in Switzerland the gentry are not only safe, but in honor. But the balance, as I have laid it down, though unseen by Machiavel, is that which interprets him, and that which he confirms by his judgment in many others as well as in this place, where he concludes, "That he who will go about to make a commonwealth where there be many gentlemen, unless he first destroys them, undertakes an impossibility. And that he who goes about to introduce monarchy where the condition of the people is equal, shall never bring it to pass, unless he cull out such of them as are the most turbulent and ambitious, and make them gentlemen or noblemen, not in name but in effect; that is, by enriching them with lands, castles, and treasures, that may gain them power among the rest, and bring in the rest to dependence upon themselves, to the end that, they maintaining their ambition by the prince, the prince may maintain his power by them."

Wherefore, as in this place I agree with Machiavel, that a nobility or gentry, overbalancing a popular government, is the utter bane and destruction of it; so I shall show in another, that a nobility or gentry, in a popular government, not overbalancing it, is the very life and soul of it. [. . .]

I come to the principles of authority, which are internal, and founded upon the goods of the mind. These the legislator that can unite in his government with those of fortune, comes nearest to the work of God, whose government consists of heaven and earth; which was said by Plato, though in different words, as, when princes should be philosophers, or philosophers princes, the world would be happy. And says Solomon: "There is an evil which I have seen under the sun, which proceeds from the ruler (enimvero neque nobilem, neque ingenuum, nec libertinum quidem armis praeponere, regia utilitas est). Folly is set in great dignity, and the rich (either in virtue and wisdom, in the goods of the mind, or those of fortune upon that balance which gives them a sense of the national interest) sit in low places. I have seen servants upon horses, and princes walking as servants upon the earth." Sad complaints, that the principles of power and of authority, the goods of the mind and of fortune, do not meet and twine in the wreath or crown of empire! Wherefore, if we have anything of piety or of prudence, let us raise ourselves out of the mire of private interest to the contemplation of virtue, and put a hand to the removal of "this evil from under the sun"; this evil against which no government that is not secured can be good; this evil from which the government that is secure must be perfect. Solomon tells us that the cause of it is from the ruler, from those principles of power, which, balanced upon earthly trash, exclude the heavenly treasures of virtue, and that influence of it upon government which is authority. We have wandered the earth to find out the balance of power; but to find out that of authority we must ascend, as I said, nearer heaven, or to the image of God, which is the soul of man.

The soul of man (whose life or motion is perpetual contemplation or thought) is the mistress of two potent rivals, the one reason, the other passion, that are in continual suit; and, according as she gives up her will to these or either of them, is the felicity or misery which man partakes in this mortal life.

For, as whatever was passion in the contemplation of a man, being brought forth by his will into action, is vice and the bondage of sin; so whatever was reason in the contemplation of a man, being brought forth by his will into action, is virtue and the freedom of soul.

Again, as those actions of a man that were sin acquire to himself repentance or shame, and affect others with scorn or pity, so those actions of a man that are virtue acquire to himself honor, and upon others authority.

Now government is no other than the soul of a nation or city: wherefore that which was reason in the debate of a commonwealth being brought forth by the result, must be virtue; and forasmuch as the soul of a city or nation is the sovereign power, her virtue must be law. But the government whose law is virtue, and whose virtue is law, is the same whose empire is authority, and whose authority is empire. [. . .]

Again, if the liberty of a man consists in the empire of his reason, the absence whereof would betray him to the bondage of his passions, then the liberty of a commonwealth consists in the empire of her laws, the absence whereof would betray her to the lust of tyrants. And these I conceive to be the principles upon which Aristotle and Livy (injuriously accused by Leviathan for not writing out of nature) have grounded their assertion, "that a commonwealth is an empire of laws and not of men." But they must not carry it so. "For," says he, "the liberty whereof there is so frequent and honorable mention in the histories and philosophy of the ancient Greeks and Romans, and the writings and discourses of those that from them have received all their learning in the politics, is not the liberty of particular men, but the liberty of the commonwealth." He might as well have said that the estates of particular men in a commonwealth are not the riches of particular men, but the riches of the commonwealth; for equality of estates causes equality of power, and equality of power is the liberty, not only of the commonwealth, but of every man. [. . .]

But seeing they that make the laws in commonwealths are but men, the main question seems to be, how a commonwealth comes to be an empire of laws, and not of men? or how the debate or result of a commonwealth is so sure to be according to reason; seeing they who debate, and they who resolve, be but men? "And as often as reason is against a man, so often will a man be against reason."

This is thought to be a shrewd saying, but will do no harm; for be it so that reason is nothing but interest, there be divers interests, and so divers reasons.

As first, there is private reason, which is the interest of a private man.

Secondly, there is reason of state, which is the interest (or error, as was said by Solomon) of the ruler or rulers, that is to say, of the prince, of the nobility, or of the people.

Thirdly there is that reason, which is the interest of mankind, or of the whole. "Now if we see even in those natural agents that want sense, that as in themselves they have a law which directs them in the means whereby they tend to their own perfection, so likewise that another law there is, which touches them as they are sociable parts united into one body, a law which binds them each to serve to others' good, and all to prefer the good of the whole, before whatsoever their own particular; as when stones, or heavy things, forsake their ordinary wont or centre, and fly upward, as if they heard themselves commanded to let go the good they privately wish, and to relieve the present distress of nature in common." There is a common right, law of nature, or interest of the whole, which is more excellent, and so acknowledged to be by the agents themselves, than the right or interest of the parts only. "Wherefore, though it may be truly said that the creatures are naturally carried forth to their proper utility or profit, that ought not to be taken in too general a sense; seeing divers of them abstain from their own profit, either in regard of those of the same kind, or at least of their young."

Mankind then must either be less just than the creature, or acknowledge also his common interest to be common right. And if reason be nothing else but interest, and the interest of mankind be the right interest, then the reason of mankind must be right reason. Now compute well; for if the interest of popular government come the nearest to the interest of mankind, then the reason of popular government must come the nearest to right reason.

But it may be said that the difficulty remains yet; for be the interest of popular government right reason, a man does not look upon reason as it is right or wrong in itself, but as it makes for him or against him. Wherefore, unless you can show such orders of a government as, like those of God in nature, shall be able to constrain this or that creature to shake off that inclination which is more peculiar to it, and take up that which regards the common good or interest, all this is to no more end than to persuade every man in a popular government not to carve himself of that which he desires most, but to be mannerly at the public table, and give the best from himself to decency and the common interest. But that such orders may be established as may, nay must, give the upper hand in all cases to common right or interest, notwithstanding the nearness of that which sticks to every man in private, and this in a way of equal certainty and facility, is known even to girls, being no other than those that are of common practice with them in divers cases. For example, two of them have a cake yet undivided, which was given between them: that each of them therefore might have that which is due, "Divide," says one to the other, "and I will choose; or let me divide, and you shall choose." If this be but once agreed upon, it is enough; for the divident, dividing unequally, loses, in regard that the other takes the better half. Wherefore she divides equally, and so both have right. "Oh, the depth of the wisdom of God." And yet "by the mouths of babes and sucklings has He set forth His strength"; that which great philosophers are disputing upon in vain is brought to light by two harmless girls, even the whole mystery of a commonwealth, which lies only in dividing and choosing. Nor has God (if his works in nature be understood) left so much to mankind to dispute upon as who shall divide and who choose, but distributed them forever into two orders, whereof the one has the natural right of dividing, and the other of choosing. [. . .]

By what has been shown in reason and experience, it may appear, that though commonwealths in general be governments of the senate proposing, the people resolving, and the magistracy executing, yet some are not so good at these orders as others, through some impediment or defect in the frame, balance, or capacity of them, according to which they are of divers kinds. [. . .]

An equal commonwealth is such a one as is equal both in the balance or foundation, and in the superstructure; that is to say, in her agrarian law and in her rotation.

An equal agrarian is a perpetual law, establishing and preserving the balance of dominion by such a distribution, that no one man or number of men, within the compass of the few or aristocracy, can come to overpower the whole people by their possessions in lands.

As the agrarian answers to the foundation, so does rotation to the superstructures.

Equal rotation is equal vicissitude in government, or succession to magistracy conferred for such convenient terms, enjoying equal vacations, as take in the whole body by parts, succeeding others, through the free election or suffrage of the people.

The contrary, whereunto is prolongation of magistracy, which, trashing the wheel of rotation, destroys the life or natural motion of a commonwealth.

The election or suffrage of the people is most free, where it is made or given in such a manner that it can neither oblige nor disoblige another, nor through fear of an enemy, or bashfulness toward a friend, impair a man's liberty.

Wherefore, says Cicero, the tablet or ballot of the people of Rome (who gave their votes by throwing tablets or little pieces of wood secretly into urns marked for the negative or affirmative) was a welcome constitution to the people, as that which, not impairing the assurance of their brows, increased the freedom of their judgment. I have not stood upon a more particular description of this ballot, because that of Venice exemplified in the model is of all others the most perfect.

An equal commonwealth (by that which has been said) is a government established upon an equal agrarian, arising into the superstructures or three orders, the Senate debating and proposing, the people resolving, and the magistracy executing, by an equal rotation through the suffrage of the people given by the ballot. For though rotation may be without the ballot, and the ballot without rotation, yet the ballot not only as to the ensuing model includes both, but is by far the most equal way; for which cause under the name of the ballot I shall hereafter understand both that and rotation too. [. . .]

But there be who say (and think it a strong objection) that, let a commonwealth be as equal as you can imagine, two or three men when all is done will govern it; and there is that in it which, notwithstanding the pretended sufficiency of a popular State, amounts to a plain confession of the imbecility of that policy, and of the prerogative of monarchy; forasmuch as popular governments in difficult cases have had recourse to dictatorian power, as in Rome.

To which I answer, that as truth is a spark to which objections are like bellows, so in this respect our commonwealth shines; for the eminence acquired by suffrage of the people in a commonwealth, especially if it be popular and equal, can be ascended by no other steps than the universal acknowledgment of virtue: and where men excel in virtue, the commonwealth is stupid and unjust, if accordingly they do not excel in authority. Wherefore this is both the advantage of virtue, which has her due encouragement, and of the commonwealth, which has her due services. These are the philosophers which Plato would have to be princes, the princes which Solomon would have to be mounted, and their steeds are those of authority, not empire; or, if they be buckled to the chariot of empire, as that of the dictatorian power, like the chariot of the sun, it is glorious for terms and vacations or intervals. And as a commonwealth is a government of laws and not of men, so is this the principality of virtue, and not of man; if that fail or set in one, it rises in another who is created his immediate successor. And this takes away that vanity from under the sun, which is an error proceeding more or less from all other rulers under heaven but an equal commonwealth. [. . .]

But let a commonwealth be equal or unequal, it must consist, as has been shown by reason and all experience, of the three general orders; that is to say, of the Senate debating and proposing, of the people resolving, and of the magistracy executing. Wherefore I can never wonder enough at Leviathan, who, without any reason or example, will have it that a commonwealth consists of a single person, or of a single assembly; nor can I sufficiently pity those "thousand gentlemen, whose minds, which otherwise would have wavered, he has framed (as is affirmed by himself) in to a conscientious obedience (for so he is pleased to call it) of such a government."

But to finish this part of the discourse, which I intend for as complete an epitome of ancient prudence, and in that of the whole art of politics, as I am able to frame in so short a time:

The two first orders, that is to say, the Senate and the people, are legislative, whereunto answers that part of this science which by politicians is entitled "of laws"; and the third order is executive, to which answers that part of the same science which is styled "of the frame and course of courts or judicatories." A word to each of these will be necessary.

And first for laws: they are either ecclesiastical or civil, such as concern religion or government.

Laws, ecclesiastical, or such as concern religion, according to the universal course of ancient prudence, are in the power of the magistrate; but, according to the common practice of modern prudence, since the papacy, torn out of his hands.

But, as a government pretending to liberty, and yet suppressing liberty of conscience (which, because religion not according to a man's conscience can to him be none at all, is the main) must be a contradiction, so a man that, pleading for the liberty of private conscience, refuses liberty to the national conscience, must be absurd.

A commonwealth is nothing else but the national conscience. And if the conviction of a man's private conscience produces his private religion, the conviction of the national conscience must produce a national religion. Whether this be well reasoned, as also whether these two may stand together, will best be shown by the examples of the ancient commonwealths taken in their order. . . .

[. . .] A people, says Machiavel, that is corrupt, is not capable of a commonwealth. But in showing what a corrupt people is, he has either involved himself, or me; nor can I otherwise come out of the labyrinth, than by saying, the balance altering a people, as to the foregoing government, must of necessity be corrupt; but corruption in this sense signifies no more than that the corruption of one government, as in natural bodies, is the generation of another. Wherefore if the balance alters from monarchy, the corruption of the people in this case is that which makes them capable of a commonwealth. But whereas I am not ignorant that the corruption which he means is in manners, this also is from the balance. For the balance leading from monarchical into popular abates the luxury of the nobility, and, enriching the people, brings the government from a more private to a more public interest which coming nearer, as has been shown, to justice and right reason, the people upon a like alteration is so far from such a corruption of manners as should render them incapable of a commonwealth, that of necessity they must thereby contract such a reformation of manners as will bear no other kind of government. On the other side, where the balance changes from popular to oligarchical or monarchical, the public interest, with the reason and justice included in the sane, becomes more private; luxury is introduced in the room of temperance, and servitude in that of freedom, which causes such a corruption of manners both in the nobility and people, as, by the example of Rome in the time of the Triumvirs, is more at large discovered by the author to have been altogether incapable of a commonwealth. [. . .]

To conclude, Oceana, or any other nation of no greater extent, must have a competent nobility, or is altogether incapable of monarchy; for where there is equality of estates, there must be equality of power, and where there is equality of power, there can be no monarchy. [. . .]

SAMUEL PUFENDORF

On the Law of Nature and Nations (1672)

Book Two, Chapter 3
On the Law of Nature in General

1. Seeing that man's condition did not allow him to live without law and to act by a vague impulse, as it were, without regard to any norm, it follows that we should inquire about the most common rule of human actions to which all men as rational animals must conform themselves. This rule, which has customarily been designated the right (*ius*) or law (*lex*) of nature, may also be called the universal and everlasting law because it binds the entire race of mortals and, unlike positive laws, is not subject to change. What sort of law it is, how it comes to be known, the proofs on which it rests, and what ought to be referred to it and what to positive law, must all be more carefully investigated, because if this foundation is not correctly laid everything built thereon will necessarily collapse of itself. [. . .]

4. Some lay down as the object of the natural law those acts which are morally necessary or base of themselves, and which are therefore in their own nature either owed or illicit, and for this reason understood as necessarily prescribed or forbidden by God. This feature, they maintain, distances natural law not only from human law but also from divine voluntary or positive law, which does not prescribe or forbid things that are of themselves and by their own nature owed or illicit, but makes things illicit or owed by forbidding or prescribing them. For the things forbidden by the natural law are not base because God has forbidden them, they say, but God forbade them because they were base in themselves. Similarly, those which are prescribed by that same law are not made honorable or necessary because they are prescribed by God, but they are prescribed because they are honorable in themselves. [. . .]

Now besides the fact that it would remain obscure, if this opinion were admitted, just what those acts are which are in themselves illicit, and by what sign they may be clearly known apart from other acts, and likewise what the most obvious reason is that they are such, it has also been shown above [. . .] that no acts are owed or illicit in themselves before being made so through law. Nor can anyone be moved to wonder: If all morality of human actions depends on law, could God not have formed the law of nature in such a way that it would prescribe the opposites of the things now prescribed; so that, for example, killing, stealing, adultery, and false accusation would be among the mutual duties of man, while exhibiting gratitude, keeping pacts, repaying loans, and the like would be among those that are forbidden?

It may seem vain and impudent here to ask what God could have done, since it is well known what He has done. Nonetheless, if anyone takes pleasure in the uprooting even of vanities, one can easily reply that such wondering plainly involves a contradiction. For even if no necessity compelled God to create man at all, . . . still, once He had determined to create him as a rational and social animal the natural law could not but accord with him, not from an absolute necessity but a hypothetical one. For if man had been bound to the opposite duties, no social animal would have been produced, but another, wild and rude kind of living thing.

Despite this fact, it nonetheless remains firm that all acts whatsoever are indifferent previous to any law. For God, in the very act of deciding to create man, that is an animal for whom not all acts should be indifferent, also established a law for him at the same time. But it does not follow either, from our assertion that all acts are in themselves indifferent previous to law, that God could if He had wished have ordained that He be worshipped by blasphemies or disregard. [. . .] For a rational creature, that is one into whom God has placed the faculty to apprehend things as they are, cannot conceive God in any other way than as endowed not only with a certain infinite superiority, but also with supreme sovereignty over himself. For otherwise he would conceive a lifeless idol, or anything whatever, rather than God. [. . .]

13. Most men agree that the natural law is to be derived from man's reason itself, and therefore that it flows from the injunctions of this faculty when it is functioning correctly. [. . .] Thus, even the Sacred Scriptures declare that the law has been inscribed on men's hearts. It is evident here, in our judgment, that even though the Divine Scriptures shed additional light to make the natural law more clearly known, it can nonetheless be investigated and firmly demonstrated even without that assistance, through the rational powers which the Creator has granted to and still preserves in us. But we hardly think it necessary, in this respect, to insist that the general precepts of the natural law, at least, have been produced or, so to speak, impressed upon men's minds at birth itself, in the form of distinct and actual propositions which a man can articulate upon acquiring the use of speech without any further education or reflection. For anyone so curious as to observe with any care the gradual emergence of children from their infantile ignorance will easily recognize this as a baseless fiction. Nor should we overlook the fact that the Sacred Scriptures commonly describe infancy as a time of ignorance about the upright and the base, and our riper age as one of knowledge thereof. [. . .]

Therefore, the sense in which we maintain that the natural law is a dictate of right reason is this: The human understanding has a faculty that enables it to see clearly from a contemplation of the human condition that it ought necessarily to live according to the norm of this law, and that enables it at the same time to discover the principle from which the law's precepts can be firmly and plainly demonstrated. [. . .] The fact that most men have no knowledge or grasp of how the natural law's precepts may be formally demonstrated, and that most of them usually learn and observe the natural law from custom or the course of ordinary life, poses no obstacle to this. For we also see artisans doing many things by imitation every day, or with the aid of instruments which they themselves do not know how to explain; yet the things they thus devise can nonetheless be called scientific and rationally grounded.

These things also clarify how we are to gauge whether reason's derivation of the natural law is correct, or how it is determined whether a certain dictate proceeds from right or depraved reason. As everyone knows, the dictates of right reason are true principles in agreement with the properly observed and examined nature of things, and derived from true first principles by valid deduction. A dictate of depraved reason, on the other hand, occurs when someone either posits false principles or, through syllogistic error [*asullogistian*], formulates false conclusions. For in saying that the natural law is impressed on us by the nature of things, we imply that it is true.

This is because nature indicates only what exists and is never the cause of anything containing falsehood—something that arises, as we know, from the error of men. [. . .]

14. It seems to us that there is no more direct and appropriate way of discovering the natural law than to contemplate carefully man's nature, condition, and inclinations, though this consideration must necessarily include as well a reflection on other things external to man, especially those capable of benefitting or harming him in some way. For whether the law has been imposed on man to promote his happiness or to check his wickedness (which would lead to his own destruction), there is no more fruitful way to learn the law than by examining the kinds of assistance and restraint he needs.

The first thing, therefore, that man has in common with all living things which are aware of themselves is that he loves himself to the highest degree, is eager to preserve himself in every way, and strives to acquire those things that seem good to him and to repel those that seem evil. [. . .]

Besides this love of and eagerness to preserve himself by all means, we also find in man an extreme weakness and a natural neediness. Hence, if we were to conceive him as abandoned to himself in this world without any assistance from other men, his life could seem to have been given him as a punishment. It is evident as well that, after the Divinity, no greater help and relief can come to a man than from other men. For even though we find the strength of individuals to preserve themselves so slight that they need the help of many things and men in order to live well and comfortably (since individuals would lack both the strength and the time to produce most of the things that are most useful and supremely necessary for men, if many men had not joined their efforts together), they can, on the other hand, still provide many things for the uses of others which they themselves do not need, and which would therefore be of no use to themselves if they were not dispensed to other men. [. . .]

It must also be noted here, however, that in setting forth man's condition we have given priority to self-love not because one should always prefer oneself to everyone else or assess everything in terms of one's own interest, proposing this to oneself (insofar as it has been separated from others' advantage) as one's highest goal; but because man, being naturally aware of his own existence before that of others, naturally loves himself before he cares for them. Besides, the task of caring for myself belongs more properly to me than to anyone else. For even if we set our sights upon the common good, since I too am a part of humankind whose preservation should be of some concern, the distinct and special care of myself can surely rest on no one else as much as it does on me.

15. Once these things have been established, it is easy to discover the foundation of the natural law. Man, it is clearly apparent, is an animal most eager to preserve himself, essentially in need, ill-equipped to maintain himself without the aid of those who are like him, and very well suited for the mutual promotion of advantages. All the same, he is often malicious, insolent, easily annoyed, and both ready and able to inflict harm. For this kind of animal to be safe and enjoy the goods that befall his worldly condition, it is necessary that he be sociable. That is, he must will to be united with those who are similar to himself and conduct himself toward them in such a way that they are provided with no cause to hurt him, but instead have reason to maintain or promote his advantage. [. . .]

And so the fundamental law of nature will be this: "Any man must, inasmuch as he can, cultivate and maintain toward others a peaceable sociality that is consistent with the native character and end of humankind in general." For sociality, as we understand it here, is not merely a tendency to form particular societies, whose purpose and manner of formation can also be evil, like an association of thieves—as if just any intention for joining oneself to another would do. Rather, we mean by it a kind of disposition whereby a man is understood to be joined to every other man by ties of benevolence, peace, and charity, and therefore by a mutual obligation. And so it is utterly false to claim that the sociality we are introducing is indifferent as to whether a society is good or evil. [. . .]

As for Hobbes's rather clever deduction of natural laws solely from the care for one's own welfare, it must be noted at the start, concerning that demonstration, that it does indeed clearly establish that it is conducive to men's welfare that they lead their lives according to those dictates of reason. Yet it cannot be immediately concluded that man has a right to apply them as a means toward his own preservation, and that he is therefore bound to observe them as by some law. Hence those dictates of reason must, in order to receive the force of law, be deduced from an altogether different principle.

Next we must also take great precautions lest anyone conclude from this that when a person appears to himself to have secured his own welfare, there is no reason to consider that of others, or that I can as I please insult someone who contributes nothing to my welfare, or does not have enough strength to harm it. For the reason we said that man is a sociable animal is also that men are more suited to promote their mutual advantages than any other living being, just as on the contrary, no animal can experience more harm from man than man himself. Indeed, the excellence and perfection of any man is the more resplendent insofar as he contributes more to the advantage of the rest; and these very deeds are considered the noblest and to demand the highest wisdom, since on the contrary, even a man of little worth and a fool can bother and hurt others. [. . .]

Indeed, reason is also quite insistent that one who has his own welfare and preservation at heart cannot renounce the care of others. For since our safety and happiness depend for a large part on the benevolence and help of others, and indeed men's nature is such that they wish to be repaid in kind for their good deeds, and when this does not happen they put aside the spirit of beneficence, surely no sane person can set his own preservation as a goal for himself in such a way as to divest himself of all regard for others. But rather, the more rationally a person loves himself the more he will see to it, by means of his services, that others love him. For no one can with any reason expect that men will be ready and willing to devote their efforts to making happy those whom they have found to be malevolent, untrustworthy, ungrateful, and inhumane toward themselves; but it must rather be believed that other men will lie in wait in order to restrain and eradicate such individuals.

17. Next, though individual men unite with certain men into a particular society or group in order to reap some special advantage for themselves, it does not follow that human nature in general is not meant for sociality, or I myself not bound to be social toward one from whom I anticipate receiving no particular benefit. For it is surely obvious that the uniting together of certain men into a certain kind of society comes either from a special harmony of minds or other qualities, or from the fact that they think it more possible for themselves to obtain a particular end among these than among those. Still, besides the fact that as a rule it does not befit any man not to live in any particular society, those connected by no other bond than their humanity must also willingly cultivate among themselves that common sociality and peace. This consists almost entirely in refraining from unjust harms and, to the extent that one's stricter obligations allow, in the mutual promotion and sharing of advantages and goods.

18. It readily appears from this what response should be made to the following objection: "If men loved one another naturally, that is, as men, no reason could be given why everyone does not love everyone equally, as they are equally men, or why they frequent the society of those who honor or profit them more than the rest." This objection confuses that common sociality with special, narrower kinds of societies, and common love with that which stems from special causes. For that common love really does require no other reason than the fact of being a man, since nature has, indeed, for the reasons mentioned above, established a general sort of friendship among men, from which no one is to be excluded unless he has made himself unworthy of it through monstrous crimes. [. . .]

[N]ature did not order us to be sociable so that we might neglect the care of ourselves. Rather, men cultivate sociability so that we can, through a mutual sharing of assistance and goods, more adequately provide for our own goods. And although someone primarily has his own advantage before his eyes when he joins himself to some particular society, and only secondarily that of his fellows (insofar as the former cannot be obtained without these), this does not prevent him from being bound to strive after his own advantage in such a way that the advantage of society is not hurt or injury inflicted on its individual members, or, now and then, to care for the good of society by considering his own advantage as less important.

19. Furthermore, this principle for deducing the natural law is not only true and evident, in our opinion, but also so sufficient and adequate that there is no precept of the natural law regarding other men whose reason is not ultimately derived from it. Yet, as

we shall soon show, for such dictates of reason to have the force of law it must be presupposed that God exists and that His providence governs all things, especially humankind. For we cannot support Grotius's claim, in the *Prolegomena*, that natural laws "would have a certain validity even if we should grant what cannot be granted without the greatest impiety: that there is no God, or that He does not care about human affairs." For if anyone went so far as to assume that impious and absurd hypothesis and conceived the human race to have sprung from itself, then those dictates of reason could in no way have the force of law, as this necessarily supposes a superior. [. . .]

And so it must absolutely be maintained that the obligation of the natural law is from God Himself, the Creator and supreme governor of the human race, Who by virtue of His sovereignty over men, His creatures, has bound them to its observance. And this can be demonstrated by the light of reason. We are supposing now that God is the maker and ruler of the universe, since wise men have for a long time clearly shown this to be so and no pious person will dispute it. Since He formed the nature of things and of man in such a way that the latter cannot be preserved without a sociable life (and for this reason placed into him a mind capable of grasping ideas conducive to that end, instilling these into men's minds through the motion of natural things, which derives from Himself as prime mover, and clearly manifesting their necessary connection and truth), it is no doubt understood that He also wished man to adjust his actions to that native character, as it were, which He is seen to have specially assigned to the life of men over that of brutes. But since this may be obtained in no other way than by observing the natural law, the Creator has understandably obligated men to observe it, not as a means they have chosen to invent and can change as they desire, but as one expressly ordained by Himself for procuring this end. [. . .]

Book Three, Chapter 2
That All Men Be Considered Naturally Equal

1. In addition to that love which man has for his own life, body, and things, and because of which he cannot avoid repelling or fleeing everything tending to their destruction, we also find embedded in his mind a very delicate self-esteem. And if anyone detracts from this in any way, he is usually no less, but in fact often more upset than if some harm is done to his body or things. Although this esteem is heightened by various causes, its primary basis seems to be human nature itself. Indeed, the very word 'man' is thought to contain a certain dignity, and the ultimate as well as the most effective argument for deflecting others' rude insults is taken to be: "Surely I am not a dog or a beast, but as much a man as you." [. . .]

Now since human nature belongs equally to all men, and since one cannot lead a social life with someone by whom one is not esteemed at least as a man, it follows as a precept of the natural law that "Everyone must esteem and treat other men as his natural equals, or as men in the same sense as he." [. . .]

Because of their equal freedom, however, a more prudent person cannot claim for himself a right to rule a more imprudent one without the latter's consent, especially if the latter professes himself content with whatever skill he has. For, indeed, though equality of strength can also prevent a man from brashly insulting another (since it is risky to contend with an equal, and foolish to wish upon another an evil that is equally destructive to oneself), the equality we are dealing with here, and which is of the highest importance for humankind to keep intact, is nonetheless of a different kind. Indeed, nature has revealed here the cleverness that she also exhibits in other matters, by measuring out her physical and mental goods to mortals in different porportions, amid whose variety the equality of which we are treating maintains a proper harmony. Thus, just as in well-founded commonwealths citizens exceed one another in dignity or wealth, while freedom belongs equally to all, so also, no matter how greatly someone excels others in mental or physical endowments, he is no less bound to exercise toward them the same duties of the natural law that he expects of them, and his endowments do not give him more of a license to afflict them with injuries. Nor does stingy nature or slender fortune as such condemn anyone to a worse position than others in regard to the enjoyment of a common right (*ius*). Rather, that which one person can demand or expect of another can—other things being equal—be demanded or expected of him by others as well; and whatever law (*ius*) someone has set up for another is quite appropriately followed by himself. [. . .]

4. From this equality which we have posited flow certain precepts whose observance has the greatest impact on the preservation of peace and friendship among mortals. Here it is evident, right at the beginning, that he who wishes to avail himself of the labors of others for his own advantage should also make himself useful to them in turn. As the proverb says, "Hand washes hand." For one who demands that others be of service to him but desires always to be exempt surely deems them inferior to himself. And one who exhibits such an attitude cannot avoid seriously offending others and giving them a pretext to break the peace. [. . .]

And surely, just as opposite judgments about things that agree with one another imply a contradiction, so also does the laying down of different rules for two entirely similar cases, namely mine and someone else's. Indeed, since everyone knows his own nature perfectly well, and that of other men (at least their general inclinations) no less than that, it follows that someone who decides differently about another's right than about his own, despite their similarity, contradicts himself in a most familiar matter and gives proof of a seriously ill mind. For no good reason can be given why something I consider right for myself should, if all other things are equal, be considered wrong for another. [. . .]

Algernon Sidney

Apology (1683)

Men, Brethren, and Fathers; Friends, Countrymen, and Strangers:—It may be expected that I should now say some great matters unto you; but the rigor of the season and the infirmities of my age, increased by a close imprisonment of above five months, do not permit me. Moreover, we live in an age that maketh truth pass for treason; I dare not say anything contrary unto it, and the ears of those that are about me will probably be found too tender to hear it. My trial and condemnation sufficiently evidence this.

West, Rumsey, and Keyling, who were brought to prove the plot[1] said no more of me than that they knew me not; and some others equally unknown to me had used my name, and that of some others, to give a little reputation unto their designs. The Lord Howard is too infamous by his life, and the many perjuries not to be denied, or rather sworn by himself, to deserve mention; and being a single witness he would be of no value, tho he had been of unblemished credit, or had not seen and confessed that the crimes committed by him would be pardoned only for committing more; and even the pardon promised could not be obtained till the drudgery of swearing was over.

This being laid aside, the whole matter is reduced to the papers said to be found in my closet by the king's officers, without any other proof of their being written by me, than what is taken from suppositions upon the similitude of a hand that is easily counterfeited, and which hath been lately declared in the Lady Carr's case to be no lawful evidence in criminal causes. But if I had been seen to write them, the matter would not be much altered. They plainly appear to relate unto a large treatise written long since in answer to Filmer's book, which, by all intelligent men, is thought to be grounded upon wicked principles, equally pernicious unto magistrates and people. If he might publish unto the world his opinion: that all men are born under a necessity derived from the

1. [The Rye House Plot, an attempt to assassinate Charles II.]

laws of God and nature, to submit unto an absolute kingly government, which could be restrained by no law or oath; and that he that hath the power, whether he came unto it by creation, election, inheritance, usurpation, or any other way, had the right; and none must oppose his will, but the persons and estates of his subjects must be indispensably subject unto it; I know not why I might not have published my opinion to the contrary, without the breach of any law I have yet known. I might as freely as he have declared publicly my thoughts, and the reasons upon which they were grounded; and I am persuaded to believe that God has left nations unto the liberty of setting up such governments as best please themselves.

The magistrates are set up for the good of nations, not nations for the honor and glory of magistrates; that the right and power of magistrates in every country is that which the laws of that country made it to be; that those laws were to be observed, and the oaths taken by them, having the force of a contract between magistrate and people, could not be violated without danger of dissolving the whole fabric; that usurpation could give no right, and the most dangerous of all enemies unto kings were they, who, raising their power to an exorbitant height, allowed unto usurpers all the rights belonging unto it; that such usurpations being seldom compassed without the slaughter of the reigning person, or family, the worst of all villains was thereby rewarded with the most glorious privileges; that if such doctrines were received, they would stir up men to the destruction of princes with more violence than all the passions that have hitherto raged in the hearts of the most unruly; that none could be safe, if such a reward were proposed unto any that could destroy them; that few would be so gentle as to spare even the best, if by their destruction a vile usurper could become God's anointed and by the most execrable wickedness invest himself with that divine character.

By these means I am brought to this place. The Lord forgive these practises, and avert the evils that threaten the nation from them. The Lord sanctify these my sufferings unto me, and tho I fall as a sacrifice unto idols, suffer not idolatry to be established in the land. Bless Thy people and save them. Defend Thy own cause, and defend those who defend it. Stir up such as are faint, direct those that are willing, confirm those that waver, give wisdom and integrity unto all. Order all things so as may most redound unto Thine own glory. Grant that I may die glorifying Thee for all Thy mercies, and that at the last Thou hast permitted me to be singled out as a witness of Thy truth; and even by the confession of my opposers, for that old cause in which I was from my youth engaged and for which Thou hast often and wonderfully declared Thyself.

Discourses Concerning Government (1689)

Introduction.

Having lately seen a book entitled *Patriarcha*, written by Sir Robert Filmer, concerning the universal and undistinguished right of all kings, I thought a time of leisure might be well employed in examining his doctrine, and the questions arising from it; which seem so far to concern all mankind, that, besides the influence upon our future life, they may be said to comprehend all that in this world deserves to be cared for. If he say true, there is but one government in the world that can have anything of justice in it: and those who have hitherto been esteemed the best and wisest of men, for having constituted commonwealths or kingdoms; and taken much pains so to proportion the powers of several magistracies, that they might all concur in procuring the publick good; or so to divide the powers between the magistrates and people, that a well-regulated harmony might be preserved in the whole, were the most unjust and foolish of all men. [. . .]

[. . .] I have been sometimes apt to wonder, how things of this nature could enter into the head of any man: Or, if no wickedness or folly be so great, but some may fall into it, I could not well conceive why they should publish it to the world. But these thoughts ceased, when I considered that a people from all ages in love with liberty, and desirous to maintain their own privileges, could never be brought to resign them, unless they were made to believe that in conscience they ought to do it; which could not be, unless they were also persuaded to believe, that there was a law set to all mankind which none might transgress, and which put the examination of all those matters out of their power. [. . .]

[. . .] This, as he thinks, is farther sweetened, by asserting, that he doth not inquire what the rights of a people are, but from whence; not considering, that whilst he denies they can proceed from the laws of natural liberty, or any other root than the grace and bounty of the prince, he declares they can have none at all. For as liberty solely consists in an independency upon the will of another, and by the name of slave we understand a man, who can neither dispose of his person nor goods, but enjoys all at the will of his master; there is no such thing in nature as a slave, if those men or nations are not slaves, who have no other title to what they enjoy, than the grace of the prince, which he may revoke whensoever he pleaseth. But there is more than ordinary extravagance in his assertion, that *the greatest liberty in the world is for a people to live under a monarch*, when his whole book is to prove, that this monarch hath his right from God and nature, is endowed with an unlimited power of doing what he pleaseth, and can be restrained by no law. If it be liberty to live under such a government, I desire to know what is slavery. [. . .]

Such as enter into Society, must in some degree diminish their Liberty.

Reason leads them to this: No one man or family is able to provide that which is requisite for their convenience or security, whilst everyone has an equal right to everything, and none acknowledges a superior to determine the controversies, that upon such occasions must continually arise, and will probably be so many and great, that mankind cannot bear them. [. . .] All the regular kingdoms in the world are commonwealths; yet there is nothing of absurdity in saying, that man cannot continue in the perpetual and entire fruition of the liberty that God hath given him. The liberty of one is thwarted by that of another; and whilst they are all equal, none will yield to any, otherwise than by a general consent. This is the ground of all just governments; for violence or fraud can create no right; and the same consent gives the form to them all, how much soever they differ from each other. Some small numbers of men, living within the precincts of one city, have, as it were, cast into a common stock, the right which they had of governing themselves and children, and by common consent joining in one body, exercised such power over every single person as seemed beneficial to the whole; and this men call perfect *democracy*. Others chose rather to be governed by a select number of such as most excelled in wisdom and virtue; and this, according to the signification of the word, was called *aristocracy*: Or when one man excelled all others, the government was put into his hands under the name of *monarchy*. But the wisest, best, and far the greatest part of mankind, rejecting these simple species, did form governments mixed or composed of the three, as shall be proved hereafter, which commonly received their respective denomination from the part that prevailed, and did deserve praise or blame, as they were well or ill proportioned.

It were a folly hereupon to say, that the liberty for which we contend, is of no use to us, since we cannot endure the solitude, barbarity, weakness, want, misery and dangers that accompany it whilst we live alone, nor can enter into a society without resigning it; for the choice of that society, and the liberty of framing it according to our own wills, for our own good, is all we seek. This remains to us whilst we form governments, that we ourselves are judges how far 'tis good for us to recede from our natural liberty; which is of so great importance, that from thence only we can know whether we are freemen or slaves; and the difference between the best government and the worst, doth wholly depend upon a right or wrong exercise of that power. If men are naturally free, such as have wisdom and understanding will always frame good governments: But if they are born under the necessity of perpetetual slavery, no wisdom can be of use to them; but all must forever depend on the will of their lords, how cruel, mad, proud or wicked soever they be.

Goverment is not instituted for the good of the Governor, but of the Governed; and Power is not an Advantage, but a Burden.

The follies with which our author endeavours to corrupt and trouble the world, seem to proceed from his fundamental mistakes of the ends for which governments are constituted; and from an opinion, that an excessive power is good for the governor, or the diminution of it a prejudice: whereas common sense teaches, and all good men acknowledge, that governments are not set up for the advantage, profit, pleasure or glory of one or a few men, but for the good of the society. For this reason Plato and Aristotle find no more certain way of distinguishing between a lawful king and a tyrant, than that the first seeks to procure the common good, and the other his own pleasure or profit; and doubt not to declare, that he who according to his institution was the first, destroys his own being , and degenerates into the latter, if he deflect from that rule: He that was the best of men, becomes the worst; and the father or shepherd of the people makes himself their enemy. And we may from hence collect, that in all controversies concerning the power of magistrates, we are not to examine what conduces to their profit or glory, but what is good for the publick.

His second error is no less gross and mischievous than the first; and that absolute power to which he would exalt the chief magistrate, would be burdensome, and desperately dangerous if he had it. The highest places are always slippery: Men's eyes dazzle when they are carried up to them; and all falls from them are mortal. Few kings or tyrants, say Juvenal, go down to the grave in peace; and he did not imprudently couple them together, because in his time few or no kings were known who were not tyrants. Dionysius thought no man left a tyranny, till he was drawn out by the heels. [. . .] The moral sense of Jotham's wise parable is eternal: The bramble coveted the power, which the vine, olive and fig tree refused. The worst and basest of men are ambitious of the highest places, which the best and wisest reject; [. . .]

Liberty produceth Virtue, Order and Stability: Slavery is accompanied with Vice, Weakness and Misery.

Our author's judgment, as well as inclinations to virtue, are manifested in the preference he gives to the manners of the Assyrians and other Eastern nations, before the Grecians and Romans: Whereas the first were never remarkable for anything, but pride, lewdness, treachery, cruelty, cowardice, madness, and hatred to all that is good; whilst the others excelled in wisdom, valour, and all the virtues that deserve imitation. This was so well observed by St. Augustine, that he brings no stronger argument to prove, that God leaves nothing that is good in man unrewarded, than that he gave the dominion of the best part of the world to the Romans, who in moral virtues excelled all other nations. And I think no example can be alleged of a free people that has ever been conquer'd by an absolute monarch, unless he did incomparably surpass them in riches and strength; whereas many great kings have been overthrown by small republicks: and the success being constantly the same, it cannot be attributed to fortune, but must necessarily be the production of virtue and good order. Machiavelli discoursing of these matters, finds virtue to be so essentially necessary to the establishment and preservation of liberty, that he thinks it impossible for a corrupted people to set up a good government, or for a tyranny to be introduced if they be virtuous; and makes this conclusion, *That where the matter* (that is, the body of the people) *is not corrupted, tumults and disorders do no hurt; and where it is corrupted, good laws do no good:* Which being confirmed by reason and experience, I think no wise man has ever contradicted him.

But I do not more wonder that Filmer should look upon absolute monarchy to be the nurse of virtue, tho we see they did never subsist together, than that he should attribute order and stability to it; whereas order doth principally consist in appointing to everyone his right place, office, or work; and this lays the whole weight of the government upon one person, who very often does neither deserve, nor is able to bear the least part of it. Plato, Aristotle, Hooker, and (I may say in short) all wise men have held, that order required that the wisest, best, and most valiant men, should be placed in the offices where wisdom, virtue and valour are requisite. [. . .]

Aristotle proves, that no man is to be entrusted with an absolute Power, by shewing that no one knows how to execute it, but such a man as is not to be found.

Our author having falsely cited and perverted the sense of Aristotle, now brings him in saying, *That a perfect kingdom is that wherein the king rules all according to his own will.* But tho I have read his books of government with some attention, I can find no such thing in them, unless the word which signifies *mere* or *absolute* may be justly translated into *perfect;* which is so far from Aristotle's meaning, that he distinguishes the absolute or despotical kingdoms from the legitimate; and commending the latter, gives no better name than that of *barbarous* to the first, which he says can agree only with the nature of such nations as are base and stupid, little differing from beasts; and having no skill to govern, or courage to defend themselves, must resign all to the will of one that will take care of them. Yet even this cannot be done, unless he that should take that care be wholly exempted from the vices which oblige the others to stand in need of it; for otherwise 'tis no better than if a sheep should undertake to govern sheep, or a hog to command swine; Aristotle plainly saying, *That as men are by nature equal, if it were possible all should be magistrates.* But that being repugnant to the nature of government, he finds no other way of solving the difficulty, than by *obeying and commanding alternately;* that they may do by turns that which they cannot do all together, and to which no one man has more right than another, because they are all by nature equal. This might be composed by a more compendious way, if, according to our author's doctrine, possession could give a right. But Aristotle speaking like a philosopher, and not like a publick enemy of mankind, examines what is just, reasonable, and beneficial to men, that is, what ought to be done, and which being done, is to be accounted just, and therefore to be supported by good men. But as *that which is unjust in the beginning, can never have the effect of justice;* and it being manifestly unjust for one or a few men to assume a power over those who by nature are equal to them, no such power can be just or beneficial to mankind; nor fit to be upheld by good men, if it be unjust and prejudicial. In the opinion of Aristotle, this natural equality continues till virtue makes the distinction, which must be either simply compleat and perfect in itself, so that he who is endued with it, is a god among men, or relatively, as far as concerns civil society, and the ends for which it is constituted, that is, defence, and the obtaining of justice. This requires a mind unbiased by passion, full of goodness and wisdom, firm against all the temptations to ill, that may arise from desire or fear; tending to all manner of good, through a perfect knowledge and affection to it; and this to such a degree, that he or they have more of these virtues and excellencies than all the rest of the society, tho computed together: Where such a man is found, he is by nature a king, and 'tis best for the nation where he is that he govern. If a few men, tho equal and alike among themselves, have the same advantages above the rest of the people, nature for the same reason seems to establish an aristocracy in that place; and the power is more safely committed to them, than left in the hands of the multitude. But if this excellency of virtue do not appear in one, nor in a few men, the right and power is by nature equally lodged in all; and to assume or appropriate that power to one, or a few men, is unnatural and tyrannical, which in Aristotle's language comprehends all that is detestable and abominable.

If any man should think Aristotle a trifler, for speaking of such a man as can never be found, I answer, that he went as far as his way could be warranted by reason or nature, and was obliged to stop there by the defect of his subject. He could not say that the government of one was simply good, when he knew so many qualifications were required in the person to make it so; nor that it is good for a nation to be under the power of a fool, a coward, or a villain, because 'tis good to be under a man of admirable wisdom, valour, industry and goodness; or that the government of one should be continued in such as by chance succeed in a family, because it was given to the first who had all the virtues required, tho all the reasons for which the power was given fail in the successor; much less could he say that any government was good, which was not good for those whose good only it was constituted to promote.

Moreover, by shewing who only is fit to be a monarch, or may be made such, without violating the laws of nature and justice, he shews who cannot be one: and he who says that no such man is to be found, as according to the opinion of Aristotle can be a monarch, does most ridiculously allege his authority in favour of monarchs, or the power which some amongst us would attribute to them. If anything therefore may be concluded from his words, 'tis this, that since no power ought to be admitted which is not just; that none can be just which is not good, profitable to the people, and conducing to the ends for which it is constituted; that no man can know how to direct the power to those ends, can deserve, or administer it, unless he do so far excel all those that are under him in wisdom, justice, valour and goodness, as to possess more of those virtues than all of them: I say, if no such man or succession of men be found, no such power is to be granted to any man, or succession of men. But if such power be granted, the laws of nature and reason are overthrown, and the ends for which societies are constituted, utterly perverted, which necessarily implies an annihilation of the grant. And if a grant so made by those who have a right of setting up a government among themselves, do perish through its own natural iniquity and perversity, I leave it to any man, whose understanding and manners are not so entirely corrupted as those of our author, to determine what name ought to be given to that person, who not excelling all others in civil and moral virtues, in the proportion requir'd by Aristotle, does usurp a power over a nation, and what obedience the people owe to such a one. But if his opinion deserve our regard, the king by having those virtues is *omnium optimus*, and the best guide to the people, *to lead them to happiness by the ways of virtue*. And he who assumes the same power, without the qualifications requir'd, is *tyrannus omnium pessimus*, leading the people to all manner of ill, and in consequence to destruction.

The Liberty of a People is the gift of God and Nature.

If any man ask how nations come to have the power of doing these things, I answer, that liberty being only an exemption from the dominion of another, the question ought not to be, how a nation can come to be free, but how a man comes to have a dominion over it; for till the right of dominion be proved and justified, liberty subsists as arising from the nature and being of a man. Tertullian speaking of the emperors says, *ab eo imperium a quo spiritus*; and we taking man in his first condition may justly say, *ab eo libertas a quo spiritus*; for no man can owe more than he has received. The creature having nothing, and being nothing but what the creator makes him, must owe all to him, and nothing to anyone from whom he has received nothing. Man therefore must be naturally free, unless he be created by another power than we have yet heard of. The obedience due to parents arises from hence, in that they are the instruments of our generation; and we are instructed by the light of reason, that we ought to make great returns to those from whom under God we have received all. When they die we are their heirs, we enjoy the same rights, and devolve the same to our posterity. God only who confers this right upon us, can deprive us of it: and we can no way understand that he does so, unless he had so declared by express revelation, or had set some distinguishing marks of dominion and subjection upon men; and, as an ingenious person not long since said, caused some to be born with crowns upon their heads, and all others with saddles upon their backs. This liberty therefore must continue, till it be either forfeited or willingly resigned. The forfeiture is hardly comprehensible in a multitude that is not entered into any society; for as they are all equal, and *equals can have no right over each other*, no man can forfeit anything to one who can justly demand nothing, unless it may be by a personal injury, which is nothing to this case; because where there is no society, one man is not bound by the actions of another. All cannot join in the same act, because they are joined in none; or if they should, no man could recover, much less transmit the forfeiture; and not being transmitted, it perishes as if it had never been, and no man can claim anything from it.

'Twill be no less difficult to bring resignation to be subservient to our author's purpose; for men could not resign their liberty, unless they naturally had it in themselves. Resignation is a publick declaration of their assent to be governed by the person to whom they resign; that is, they do by that act constitute him to be their governor. This necessarily puts us upon the inquiry, why they do resign, how they will be governed, and proves the governor to be their creature; and the right of disposing the government must be in them, or they who receive it can have none. This is so evident to common sense, that it were impertinent to ask who made Carthage, Athens, Rome or Venice to be free cities. Their charters were not from men, but from God and nature. When a number of Phoenicians had found a port on the coast of Africa, they might perhaps agree with the inhabitants for a parcel of ground, but they brought their liberty with them. When a company of

Latins, Sabines and Tuscans met together upon the banks of the Tiber, and chose rather to build a city for themselves, than to live in such as were adjacent, they carried their liberty in their own breasts, and had hands and swords to defend it. This was their charter; and Romulus could confer no more upon them, than Dido upon the Carthaginians. [. . .] 'Tis agreed by mankind, that subjection and protection are relative; and that he who cannot protect those that are under him, in vain pretends to a dominion over them. The only ends for which governments are constituted, and obedience render'd to them, are the obtaining of justice and protection; and they who cannot provide for both, give the people a right of taking such ways as best please themselves, in order to their own safety. [. . .]

[. . .] When the fierce barbarity of the Saxons came to be softened by a more gentle climate, the arts and religion they learnt, taught them to reform their manners, and better enabled them to frame laws for the preservation of their liberty, but no way diminished their love to it: and tho the Normans might desire to get the lands of those who had joined with Harold, and of others into their hands; yet when they were settled in the country, and by marriages united to the ancient inhabitants, they became true Englishmen, and no less lovers of liberty and resolute defenders of it than the Saxons had been. There was then neither conquering Norman nor conquered Saxon, but a great and brave people composed of both, united in blood and interest in the defence of their common rights, which they so well maintained, that no prince since that time has too violently encroached upon them, who, as the reward of his folly, has not lived miserably and died shamefully.

Such actions of our ancestors do not, as I suppose, savour much of the submission which patrimonial slaves do usually render to the will of their lord. On the contrary, whatsoever they did was by a power inherent in themselves to defend that liberty in which they were born. All their kings were created upon the same condition, and for the same ends. Alfred acknowledged he found and left them perfectly free; and the confession of Offa, that they had not made him king for his own merits, but for the defence of their liberty, comprehends all that were before and after him. They well knew how great the honour was, to be made head of a great people, and rigorously exacted the performance of the ends for which such a one was elevated, severely punishing those who basely and wickedly betray'd the trust reposed in them, and violated all that is most sacred among men; which could not have been unless they were naturally free, for the liberty that has no being cannot be defended. [. . .]

William Penn

Frame of Government of Pennsylvania (February 2, 1683)

The Frame of the Government of the Province of Pennsylvania and, Territories thereunto annexed, in America.

To all persons, to whom these presents may come. Whereas king *Charles* the Second, by his letters patents, under the great seal of England, bearing date the fourth day of March in the thirty and third year of the lying, for divers considerations therein mentioned, hath been graciously pleased to give and grant unto me *William Penn* (by the name of *William Penn,* Esquire, son and heir of Sir *William Penn,* deceased) and to my heirs and assigns for ever, all that tract of land or province called Pennsylvania, in America, with divers great powers, preheminencies, royalties, jurisdictions and authorities, necessary for the well-being and government thereof. And whereas, the king's dearest brother *James,* duke of

York and Albany, &c., by his deeds of feoffment, under his hand and seal, duly perfected, bearing date the four and twentieth day of August, one thousand six hundred eighty and two, did grant Unto me, my heirs and assigns, all that tract of land, lying and being from twelve miles northward of *Newcastle,* upon Delaware river, in *America,* to Cape Hinlopen, upon the said river and bay of *Delaware* southward, together with all royalties, franchises, duties, jurisdictions, liberties and privileges hereunto belonging.

Now know ye, That for the well-being and good government of the said province and territories hereunto annexed, and for the encouragement of all the freemen and planters, that may be therein concerned, in pursuance of the rights and powers aforementioned, I, the said *William Penn,* have declared, granted, and confirmed, and by these presents, for me, my heirs and assigns, do declare, grant and confirm unto all the freemen, planters and adventurers of, in and to the said province and territories thereof, these liberties, franchises and properties, so far as in me lieth, to be held, enjoyed and kept by the freemen, planters and adventurers of and in the said province of *Pennsylvania,* and territories thereunto annexed, for ever.

Imprimis, That the government of this province and territories thereof, shall, from time to time, according to the powers of the patent and deeds of feoffment aforesaid, consist of the Proprietary and Governor, and freemen of the said province and territories thereof, in form of provincial Council and General Assembly; which provincial Council shall consist of eighteen persons, being three out of each county, and which Assembly shall consist of thirty-six persons, being six out of each county, men of most note for their virtue, wisdom and ability; by whom all laws shall be made, officers chosen, and public affairs transacted, as is hereafter limited and declared.

II. There being three persons already chosen for every respective county of this province and territories thereof, to serve in the provincial Council, one of them for three years; one for two years, and one for one year; and one of them to go off yearly, in every county; that on the tenth day of the first month yearly, for ever after, the freemen of the said province and territories thereof, shall meet together, in the most convenient place, in every county of this province and territories thereof, then and there to chuse one person, qualified as aforesaid, in every county, being one-third of the number to serve in provincial Council, for three years; it being intended, that one-third of the whole provincial Council, consisting and to consist of eighteen persons, falling off yearly, it shall be yearly supplied with such yearly elections, as aforesaid; and that one person shall not continue in longer than three years; and in case any member shall decease before the last election, during his time, that then, at the next election ensuing his decease, another shall be chosen to supply his place for the remaining time he was to have served, and no longer.

III. That, after the first seven years, every one of the said third parts, that goeth yearly off, shall be incapable of being chosen again for one whole year following, that so all that are capable and qualified, as aforesaid, may be fitted for government, and have a share of the care and burden of it.

IV. That the provincial Council in all cases and matters of moment, as their arguing upon bills to be passed into laws, or proceedings about erecting of courts of justice, sitting in judgment upon criminals impeached, and choice of officers, in such manner as is herein after expressed, not less than two-thirds of the whole shall make a *quorum;* and that the consent and approbation of two-thirds of that *quorum* shall be had in all such cases, or matters, of moment: and that, in all cases and matters of lesser moment, one-third of the whole shall make a *quorum,* the majority of which shall and may always determine in such cases and causes of lesser moment.

V. That the Governor and provincial Council shall have the power of preparing and proposing to the Assembly, hereafter mentioned, all bills, which they shall see needful, and that shall, at any time, be past into laws, within the said province and territories thereof, which bills shall be published and affixed to the most noted places, in every county of this province and territories thereof, twenty days before the meeting of the Assembly, in order to passing them into laws.

VI. That the Governor and provincial Council shall take care that all laws, statutes and ordinances, which shall, at any time, be made within the said province and territories, be duly and diligently executed.

VII. That the Governor and provincial Council shall, at all times, have the care of the peace and safety of this province and territories thereof; and that nothing be, by any person, attempted, to the subversion of this frame of government.

VIII. That the Governor and provincial Council shall, at all times, settle and order the situation of all cities, and market towns, in every county, modelling therein all public buildings, streets and market places; and shall appoint all necessary roads and highways, in this province and territories thereof.

IX. That the Governor and provincial Council shall, at all times, have power to inspect the management of the public treasury, and punish those who shall convert any part thereof to any other use, than what hath been agreed upon by the Governor, provincial Council and Assembly.

X. That the Governor and provincial Council shall erect and order all public schools, and encourage and reward the authors of useful sciences and laudable inventions in the said province and territories thereof.

XI. That one-third part of the provincial Council, residing with the Governor, from time to time, shall with the Governor have the care of the management of public affairs, relating to the peace, justice, treasury and improvement of the province and territories, and to the good education of youth, and sobriety of the manners of the inhabitants therein, as aforesaid.

XII. That the Governor, or his Deputy, shall always preside in the provincial Council, and that he shall, at no time, therein perform any public act of state whatsoever, that shall, or may, relate unto the justice, trade, treasury, or safety of the province and territories as aforesaid, but by and with the advice and consent of the provincial Council thereof.

XIII. And to the end that all bills prepared and agreed by the Governor and provincial Council, as aforesaid may yet have the more full concurrence of the freemen of the province and territories thereof, it is declared, granted and confirmed, that, at the time and place in every county for the choice of one person to serve in provincial Council, as aforesaid, the respective Members thereof, at their said meeting, shall yearly chuse out of themselves six persons of most note, for virtue, wisdom and ability, to serve in Assembly, as their representatives, who shall yearly meet on the tenth day of the third month, in the capital town or city of the said province, unless the Governor and provincial Council shall think fit to appoint another place to meet in, where, during eight days, the several Members may confer freely with one another; and if any of them see meet, with a committee of the provincial Council, which shall be, at that time, purposely appointed, to receive from any of them proposals for the alterations, or amendments, of any of the said proposed and promulgated bills; and on the ninth day from their so meeting, the said Assembly, after their reading over the proposed bills, by the Clerk of the provincial Council, and the occasions and motives for them being opened by the Governor or his Deputy, shall, upon the question by him put, give their affirmative or negative, which to them seemeth best, in such manner as is hereafter expressed: but not less than two-thirds shall make a quorum in the passing of all bills into laws, and choice of such officers as are by them to be chosen.

XIV. That the laws so prepared and proposed, as aforesaid, that are assented to by the Assembly, shall be enrolled as laws of this province and territories thereof, with this stile: *By the Governor, with the assent and approbation of the freemen in provincial Council and Assembly met,* and from henceforth the meetings, sessions, acts, and proceedings of the Governor, provincial Council and Assembly, shall be stiled and called, *The meeting, sessions and proceedings of the General Assembly of the province of Pennsylvania, and the territories thereunto belonging.*

XV. And that the representatives of the people in provincial Council and Assembly, may, in after ages, bear some proportion with the increase and multiplying of the people, the number of such representatives of the people may be, from time to time, increased and enlarged, so as at no time, the number exceeds seventy-two for the provincial Council, and two hundred for the Assembly; the appointment and proportion of which number, as also the laying and methodizing of the choice of such representatives in future time, most equally to the division of the country, or number of the inhabitants, is left to the Governor and provincial Council to propose, and the Assembly to resolve, so that the order of proportion be strictly observed, both in the choice of the Council and the respective committees thereof, viz.: one third to go off, and come in yearly.

XVI. That from and after the death of this present Governor, the provincial Council shall, together with the succeeding Governor, erect, from time to time, standing courts of justice, in such places and number as they shall judge convenient for the good government of the said province and territories thereof; and that the provincial Council shall, on the thirteenth day of the second month then next ensuing, elect and present to the Governor, or his Deputy, a double number of persons, to serve for Judges, Treasurers, and Masters of the Rolls, within the said province and territories, to continue so long as they shall well behave themselves, in those capacities respectively; and the freemen of the said province, in an Assembly met on the thirteenth day of the third month, yearly, shall elect and then present to the Governor, or his Deputy, a double number of persons to serve for Sheriffs, Justices of the Peace, and Coroners, for the year next ensuing; out of which respective elections and presentments, the Governor, or his Deputy, shall nominate and commissionate the proper number for each office, the third day after the said respective presentments; or else the first named in such presentment, for each office, as aforesaid, shall stand and serve in that office, the time before respectively limited; and in case of death or default, such vacancy shall be supplied by the Governor and provincial Council in manner aforesaid.

XVII. That the Assembly shall continue so long as may be needful to impeach criminals, fit to be there impeached, to pass such bills into laws as are proposed to them, which they shall think fit to pass into laws, and till such time as the Governor and provincial Council shall declare, that they have nothing further to propose unto them, for their assent and approbation, and that declaration shall be a dismiss to the assembly, for that time; which Assembly shall be, notwithstanding, capable of assembling together, upon the summons of the Governor and provincial Council, at any time, during that year, if the Governor and provincial Council shall see occasion for their so assembling.

XVIII. That all the elections of members, of representatives of the people to serve in provincial Council and Assembly, and all questions to be determined by both or either of them, that relate to choice of officers, and all, or any other personal matters, shall be resolved or determined by the *ballot*, and all things relating to the preparing and passing of bills into laws, shall be openly declared and resolved by the vote.

XIX. That, at all times, when the Proprietary and Governor shall happen to be an infant, and under the age of one and twenty years, and no guardians or commissioners are appointed in writing, by the father of the said infant, or that such guardian shall be deceased, that during such minority, the provincial Council shall, from time to time, as they shall see meet, constitute and appoint guardians and commissioners, not exceeding three, one of which shall preside as deputy, and chief guardian, during such minority, and shall have and execute, with the consent of one of the other two, all the power of a Governor, in all public affairs and concerns of the said province and territories thereof, according to charter; which said guardian so appointed, shall also have the care and oversight of the estate of the said minor, and be yearly accountable and responsible for the same to the provincial Council, and the provincial Council to the minor, when of age, or to the next heir, in case of the minor's death, for the trust before expressed.

XX. That as often as any days of the month mentioned in any article of this charter, shall fall upon the first day of the week, commonly called the *Lord's* day, the business appointed for that day, shall be deferred until the next day, unless in cases of emergency.

XXI. And, for the satisfaction and encouragement of all aliens, I do give and grant, that, if any alien, who is, or shall be a purchaser, or who doth, or shall, inhabit in this province or territories thereof, shall decease at any time before he can well be naturalized, his right and interest therein shall notwithstanding descend to his wife and children, or other his relations, be he testate, or intestate, according to the laws of this province or territories thereof, in such cases provided, in as free and ample manner, to all intents and purposes, as if the said alien had been naturalized.

XXII. And that the inhabitants of this province and territories thereof may be accommodated with such food and sustenance, as God, in His providence, hath freely afforded, I do also further grant to the inhabitants of this province and territories thereof, liberty to fowl arid hunt upon the lands they hold, and all other lands therein not inclosed; and to fish, in all waters in the said lands, and in all rivers and rivulets in, and belonging to, this province and territories thereof, with liberty to draw his or their fish on shore on any man's lands, so as it be not to the detriment, or annoyance of the owner thereof, except such lands as do lie upon inland rivulets that are not bootable, or which are, or may be hereafter erected into manors.

XXIII. And that all the inhabitants of this province and territories thereof, whether purchasers or others, may have the last worldly pledge of my good and kind intentions to them and theirs, I do give, grant and confirm to all and every one of them, full and quiet possession of their respective lands, to which they have any lawful or equitable claim, saving only such rents and services for the same, as are, or customarily ought to be, reserved to me, my heirs or assigns.

XXIV. That no act, law, or ordinance whatsoever, shall, at any time hereafter, be made or done by the Proprietary and Governor of this province, and territories hereunto belonging, his heirs or assigns, or by the freemen in provincial Council or Assembly, to alter, change or diminish the form or effect of this charter, or any part or clause thereof, contrary to the true intent and meaning thereof, without the consent of the Proprietary and Governor, his heirs or assigns, and six parts of seven of the said freemen in provincial Council and Assembly met.

XXV. And lastly, I, the said *William Penn*, Proprietary and Governor of the province of *Pennsylvania*, and territories thereunto belonging, for me, my heirs and assigns, have solemnly declared, granted and confirmed, and do hereby solemnly declare, grant and confirm, that neither I, my heirs nor assigns, shall procure, or do, any thing or things, whereby the liberties, in this charter contained and expressed, shall be infringed or broken: and if any thing be procured, by any person or persons, contrary to these premises, it shall be held of no force or effect. In witness whereof, I, the said *William Penn*, at Philadelphia, in *Pennsylvania*, have unto this present charter of liberties set my hand and broad seal, this second day of the second month, in the year of our Lord one thousand six hundred and eighty and three, being the five and thirtieth year of the king, and the third year of my government.

William Penn.

This within *charter*, which we have distinctly heard read and thankfully received, shall be by us inviolably kept, at Philadelphia, the second day of the second month, one thousand six hundred eighty and three.

The members of the provincial Council present.

William Markham, John Moll,
William Haige, Christopher Taylor,
John Simcock, William Clayton,
Francis Whittwel, Thomas Holme

William Clark, William Biles, James
Harrison, John Richardson, Philip
Thomas Lenman, Secr. Gov.
Richard Ingelo, Cl. Coun.

The Members of the Assembly present:

Casparus Harman, John Darby,
Benjamin Williams, William Guest,
Valentine Hollingsworth, James
Boyden, Bennony Bishop, John
Beazor, John Harding, Andrews
Bringston, Simon Irons, John Wood,
John Curtis, Daniel Brown, William
Futcher, John Kipshaven, Alexander
Molestine, Robert Bracy, senior,
Thomas Bracy, William Yardly, John
Hastings, Robert Wade, Thomas
Hassald, John Hart, Robert Hall,
Robert Bedwell, William Simsmore,
Samuel Darke, Robert Lucas, James
Williams, John Blunston, John
Songhurst, John Hill, Nicholas Waln,
Thomas Fitzwater, John Clows, Luke
Watson, Joseph Phipps, Dennis
Rotchford, John Brinklair, Henry
Bowman, Cornelius Verhoofe, John
Southworth, Cl. Synod.

Some of the inhabitants of Philadelphia present:

William Howell, Edmund Warner,
Henry Lewis, Samuel Miles.

Charter of Privileges Granted by William Penn, Esq. to the Inhabitants of Pennsylvania and Territories (October 28, 1701)

WILLIAM PENN, Proprietary and Governor of the Province of *Pensilvania* and Territories thereunto belonging, To all to whom these Presents shall come, sendeth Greeting. WHEREAS King CHARLES *the Second*, by His Letters Patents, under the Great Seal of *England*, bearing Date the *Fourth* Day of *March* in the Year *One Thousand Six Hundred and Eighty-one*, was graciously pleased to give and grant unto me, and my Heirs and Assigns for ever, this Province of Pennsilvania, with divers great Powers and Jurisdictions for the well Government thereof.

AND WHEREAS the King's dearest Brother, JAMES *Duke of* YORK *and* ALBANY, &c. by his Deeds of Feoffment, under his Hand and Seal duly perfected, bearing Date the *Twenty-Fourth* Day of August, *One Thousand Six Hundred Eighty and Two*, did grant unto me, my Heirs and Assigns, all that Tract of Land, now called the Territories of *Pensilvania*, together with Powers and Jurisdictions for the good Government thereof.

AND WHEREAS for the Encouragement of all the Freemen and Planters, that might be concerned in the said Province and Territories, and for the good Government thereof, I the said WILLIAM PENN, in the Year *One Thousand Six Hundred Eighty and Three*, for me, my Heirs and Assigns, did grant and confirm unto all the Freemen Planters and Adventurers therein, divers Liberties, Franchises and Properties, as by the said Grant, entituled, *The* FRAME *of the Government of the Province of* Pensilvania, *and Territories thereunto belonging, in* America, may appear; which Charter or Frame being found in some Parts of it, not so suitable to the present Circumstances of the Inhabitants, was in the *Third* Month, in the Year One Thousand Seven Hundred, delivered up to me, by *Six* Parts of Seven of the Freemen of this Province and Territories, in General Assembly met, Provision being made in the said Charter, for that End and Purpose.

AND WHEREAS I was then pleased to promise, That I would restore the said Charter to them again, with necessary Alterations, or in lieu thereof, give them another, better adapted to answer the present Circumstances and Conditions of the said Inhabitants; which they have now, by their Representatives in General Assembly met at *Philadelphia*, requested me to grant.

KNOW YE THEREFORE, That for the further Well-being and good Government of the said Province, and Territories; and in Pursuance of the Rights and Powers before-mentioned, I the said William Penn do declare, grant and confirm, unto all the Freemen, Planters and Adventurers, and other Inhabitants of this Province and Territories, these following Liberties, Franchises and Privileges, so far as in me lieth, to be held, enjoyed and kept, by the Freemen, Planters and Adventurers, and other Inhabitants of and in the said Province and Territories hereunto annexed, for ever.

First

BECAUSE no People can be truly happy, though under the greatest Enjoyment of Civil Liberties, if abridged of the Freedom of their Consciences, as to their Religious Profession and Worship: And Almighty God being the only Lord of Conscience, Father of Lights and Spirits; and the Author as well as Object of all divine Knowledge, Faith and Worship, who only doth enlighten the Minds, and persuade and convince the Understandings of People, I do hereby grant and declare, That no Person or Persons, inhabiting in this Province or Territories, who shall confess and acknowledge One almighty God, the Creator, Upholder and Ruler of the World; and profess him or themselves obliged to live quietly under the Civil Government, shall be in any Case molested or prejudiced, in his or their Person or Estate, because of his or their conscientious Persuasion or Practice, nor be compelled to frequent or maintain any religious Worship, Place or Ministry, contrary to his or their Mind, or to do or super any other Act or Thing, contrary to their religious Persuasion.

AND that all Persons who also profess to believe in *Jesus Christ*, the Saviour of the World, shall be capable (notwithstanding their other Persuasions and Practices in Point of Conscience and Religion) to serve this Government in any Capacity, both legislatively and executively, he or they solemnly promising, when lawfully required, Allegiance to the King as Sovereign, and Fidelity to the Proprietary and Governor, and taking the Attests as now established by the Law made at *New-Castle*, in the Year *One Thousand and Seven Hundred*, entitled, *An Act directing the Attests of several Officers and Ministers*, as now amended and confirmed this present Assembly.

II

FOR the well governing of this Province and Territories, there shall be an Assembly yearly chosen, by the Freemen thereof, to consist of *Four* Persons out of each County, of most Note for Virtue, Wisdom and Ability, (or of a greater number at any Time, as the Governor and Assembly shall agree) upon the *First* Day of *October* for ever; and shall sit on the *Fourteenth* Day of the same Month, at *Philadelphia*, unless the Governor and Council for the Time being, shall see Clause to appoint another Place within the said Province or Territories: Which Assembly shall have Power to chuse a Speaker and other their Officers; and shall be Judges of the Qualifications and Elections of their own Members; sit upon their own Adjournments; appoint (committees; prepare Bills in order to pass into Laws; impeach Criminals, and redress Grievances; and shall have all other Powers and Privileges of an Assembly, according to the Rights of the free-born Subjects of *England*, and as is usual in any of the King's Plantations in *America*.

AND if any County or Counties, shall refuse or neglect to chuse their respective Representatives as aforesaid, or if chosen, do not meet to serve in Assembly, those who are so chosen and met, shall have the full Power of an Assembly, in as ample Manner as if all the Representatives had been chosen and met, provided they are not less than *Two Thirds* of the whole Number that ought to meet.

AND that the Qualifications of Electors and Elected, and all other Matters and Things relating to Elections of Representatives to serve in Assemblies, though not herein particularly expressed, shall be and remain as by a Law of this Government, made at *New-Castle* in the Year *One Thousand Seven Hundred*, entitled, *An Act to ascertain the Number of Members of Assembly, and to regulate the Elections*.

III

THAT the Freemen in each respective County at the Time and Place of Meeting for Electing their Representatives to serve in Assembly, may as often as there shall be Occasion, chuse a double Number of Persons to present to the Governor for Sheriffs and Coroners to serve for *Three* Years, if so long they behave themselves well; out of which respective Elections and Presentments, the Governor shall nominate and commissionate one for each of the said Offices, the *Third* Day after such Presentment, or else the First named in such Presentment, for each Office as aforesaid, shall stand and serve in that Office for the Time before respectively limited; and in Case of Death or Default, such Vacancies shall be supplied by the Governor, to serve to the End of the said Term.

PROVIDED ALWAYS, That if the said Freemen shall at any Time neglect or decline to chuse a Person or Persons for either or both the aforesaid Offices then and in such Case, the Persons that are or shall be in the respective Offices of Sheriffs or Coroners, at the Time of Election, shall remain therein, until they shall be removed by another Election as aforesaid.

AND that the Justices of the respective Counties shall or may nominate and present to the Governor *Three* Persons, to serve for Clerk of the Peace for the said County, when there is a Vacancy, one of which the Governor shall commissionate within Ten Days after such Presentment, or else the *First* nominated shall serve in the said Office during good Behavior.

IV

THAT the Laws of this Government shall be in this Stile, viz. *By the Governor, with the Consent and Approbations of the Freemen in General Assembly Met*; and shall be, after Confirmation by the Governor, forthwith recorded in the Rolls Office, and kept at *Philadelphia*, unless the Governor and Assembly shall agree to appoint another Place.

V

THAT all Criminals shall have the same Privileges of Witnesses and Council as their Prosecutors.

VI

THAT no Person or Persons shall or may, at any Time hereafter, be obliged to answer any Complaint, Matter or Thing whatsoever, relating to Property, before the Governor and Council, or in any other Place, but in ordinary Course of Justice, unless Appeals thereunto shall be hereafter by Law appointed.

VII

THAT no Person within this Government, shall be licensed by the Governor to keep an Ordinary, Tavern or House of Publick Entertainment, but such who are first recommended to him, under the Hands of the Justices of the respective Counties, signed in open Court; which Justices are and shall be hereby impowered, to suppress and forbid any Person, keeping such Publick-House as aforesaid, upon their Misbehaviour, on such Penalties as the Law doth or shall direct; and to recommend others from time to time, as they shall see Occasion.

VIII

IF any person, through Temptation or Melancholy, shall destroy himself; his Estate, real and personal, shall notwithstanding descend to his Wife and Children, or Relations, as if he had died a natural Death; and if any Person shall be destroyed or killed by Casualty or Accident, there shall be no Forfeiture to the Governor by reason thereof.

AND no Act, Law or Ordinance whatsoever, shall at any Time hereafter, be made or done, to alter, change or diminish the Form or Effect of this Charter, or of any Part or Clause therein, contrary to the true Intent and Meaning thereof, without the Consent of the Governor for the Time being, and *Six* Parts of *Seven* of the Assembly met.

BUT because the Happiness of Mankind depends so much upon the Enjoying of Liberty of their Consciences as aforesaid, I do hereby solemnly declare, promise and grant, for me, my Heirs and Assigns, That the *First* Article of this Charter relating to Liberty of Conscience, and every Part and Clause therein, according to the true Intent and Meaning thereof, shall be kept and remain, without any Alteration, inviolably for ever.

AND LASTLY, I the said *William Penn*, Proprietary and Governor of the Province of *Pensilvania*, and Territories thereunto belonging, for myself, my Heirs and Assigns, have solemnly declared, granted and confirmed, and do hereby solemnly declare, grant and confirm, That neither I, my Heirs or Assigns, shall procure or do any Thing or Things whereby the Liberties In this Charter contained and expressed, nor any Part thereof, shall be infringed or broken: And if any thing shall be procured or done, by any Person or Persons, contrary to these Presents, it shall be held of no Force or Effect.

IN WITNESS whereof, I the said *William Penn*, at *Philadelphia* in *Pensilvania*, have unto this present Charter of Liberties, set my Hand and broad Seal, this *Twenty-Eighth* Day of *October*, in the Year of Our Lord *One Thousand Seven Hundred and One*, being the *Thirteenth* Year of the Reign of King William the *Third*, over *England, Scotland, France* and *Ireland*, &c. and the *Twenty-First* Year of my Government.

AND NOTWITHSTANDING the Closure and Test of this present Charter as aforesaid, I think fit to add this following Proviso thereunto, as Part of the same, *That is to say*, That notwithstanding any Clause or Clauses in the above-mentioned Charter, obliging the Province and Territories to join together in Legislation, I am content, and do hereby declare, that if the Representatives of the Province and Territories shall not hereafter agree to join together in Legislation, and that the same shall be signified unto me, or my Deputy, in open Assembly, or otherwise from under the Hands and Seals of the Representatives, for the Time being, of the Province and Territories, or the major Part of either of them, at any Time within *Three* Years from the Date hereof, that in such Case, the Inhabitants of each of the *Three* Counties of this

Province, shall not have less than Eight Persons to represent them in Assembly, for the Province; and the Inhabitants of the Town of *Philadelphia* (when the said Town is incorporated) Two Persons to represent them in Assembly; and the Inhabitants of each County in the Territories, shall have as many Persons to represent them in a distinct Assembly for the Territories, as shall be by them requested as aforesaid.

NOTWITHSTANDING which Separation of the Province and Territories, in Respect of Legislation, I do hereby promise, grant and declare, That the Inhabitants of both Province and Territories, shall separately enjoy all other Liberties, Privileges and Benefits, granted jointly to them in this Charter, any Law, Usage or Custom of this Government heretofore made and practiced, or any Law made and passed by this General Assembly, to the Contrary hereof, notwithstanding.

WILLIAM PENN.

THIS CHARTER of PRIVILEGES *being distinctly read in Assembly; and the whole and every Part thereof, being approved of and agreed to, by Us, we do thankfully receive the same from, our Proprietary and Governor, at* Philadelphia, *this* Twenty-Eighth *Day of* October, One Thousand Seven Hundred and One. *Signed on Behalf, and by Order of the Assembly,*

per JOSEPH GROWDON, *Speaker.*

EDWARD SHIPPEN,
PHINEAS PEMBERTON,
SAMUEL CARPENTER,
GRIFFITH OWEN,
CALEB PUSEY,
THOMAS STORY,
Proprietary and Governor's Council.

RESOLUTIONS OF THE GERMANTOWN MENNONITES (February 18,1688)

This is to the monthly meeting held at Richard Worrell's:

These are the reasons why we are against the traffic of men-body, as followeth: Is there any that would be done or handled at this manner? viz., to be sold or made a slave for all the time of his life? How fearful and faint-hearted are many at sea, when they see a strange vessel, being afraid it should be a Turk, and they should be taken, and sold for slaves into Turkey. Now, what is this better done, than Turks do? Yea, rather it is worse for them, which say they are Christians; for we hear that the most part of such negers are brought hither against their will and consent, and that many of them are stolen. Now, though they are black, we cannot conceive there is more liberty to have them slaves, as it is to have other white ones. There is a saying, that we should do to all men like as we will be done ourselves; making no difference of what generation, descent, or colour they are. And those who steal or rob men, and those who buy or purchase them, are they not all alike? Here is liberty of conscience, which is right and reasonable; here ought to be likewise liberty of the body, except of evil-doers, which is another case. But to bring men hither, or to rob and sell them against their will, we stand against. In Europe there are many oppressed for conscience sake; and here there are those oppressed which are of a black colour. And we who know that men must not commit adultery some do commit adultery in others, separating wives from their husbands, and giving them to others: and some sell the children of these poor creatures to other men. Ah! do consider well this thing, you who do it, if you would be done at this manner and if it is done according to Christianity! You surpass Holland and Germany in this thing. This makes an ill report in all those countries of Europe, where they hear of [it], that the Quakers do here handel men as they handel there the cattle. And for that reason some have no mind or inclination to come hither. And who shall maintain this your cause, or plead for it? Truly, we cannot do so, except you shall inform us better hereof, viz.: that Christians have liberty to practice these things. Pray, what thing in the world can be done worse towards us, than if men should rob or steal us away, and sell us for slaves to strange countries; separating husbands from their wives and children. Being now this is not done in the manner we would be done at; therefore, we contradict, and are against this traffic of men-body. And we who profess that it is not lawful to steal, must, likewise, avoid to purchase such things as are stolen, but rather help to stop this robbing and stealing, if possible. And such men ought to be delivered out of the hands of the robbers, and set free as in Europe. Then is Pennsylvania to have a good report, instead, it hath now a bad one, for this sake, in other countries; Especially whereas the Europeans are desirous to know in what manner the Quakers do rule in their province; and most of them do look upon us with an envious eye. But if this is done well, what shall we say is done evil?

If once these slaves (which they say are so wicked and stubborn men,) should join themselves [to] fight for their freedom, and handel their masters and mistresses, as they did handel them before; will these masters and mistresses take the sword at hand and war against these poor slaves, like, as we are able to believe, some will not refuse to do? Or, have these poor negers not as much right to fight for their freedom, as you have to keep them slaves?

Now consider well this thing, if it is good or bad. And in case you find it to be good to handel these blacks in that manner, we desire and require you hereby lovingly, that you may inform us herein, which at this time never was done, viz., that Christians have such a liberty to do so. To the end we shall be satisfied on this point, and satisfy likewise our good friends and acquaintances in our native country, to whom it is a terror, or fearful thing, that men should be handelled so in Pennsylvania.

This is from our meeting at Germantown, held ye 18th of the 2d month, 1688, to be delivered to the monthly meeting at Richard Worrell's.

Garret Henderich,
Derick op de Graeff,
Francis Daniel Pastorius,
Abram op de Graeff.

JOHN LOCKE

Second Treatise of Government (1689)

Chapter 1
Of Civil Government

1. It having been shewn in the foregoing discourse,[1]

1. That Adam had not, either by natural right of fatherhood, or by positive donation from God, any such authority over his children, or dominion over the world, as is pretended:
2. That if he had, his heirs, yet, had no right to it:
3. That if his heirs had, there being no law of

1. [Locke here refers to his *First Treatise of Government*, written earlier but published simultaneously with the *Second Treatise* in 1689. In the former, Locke devotes the entire treatise to the demolition of Sir Robert Filmer's *Patriarcha*, which argued for the divine right of kings as ordained by God through Adam, the first king, from whom all subsequent kingship descends.]

nature, nor positive law of God, that determines, which is the right heir in all cases that may arise, the right of succession, and consequently of bearing rule, could not have been certainly determined:

4. That if even that had been determined, yet the knowledge of which is the eldest line of Adam's posterity, being so long since utterly lost, that in the races of mankind and families of the world, there remains not to one above another the least pretence to be the eldest house, and to have the right of inheritance:

All these premises having, as I think, been clearly made out, it is impossible that the rulers now on earth, should make any benefit, or derive any the least shadow of authority from that, which is held to be the fountain of all power, *Adam's private dominion and paternal jurisdiction;* so that he that will not give just occasion to think that all government in the world is the product only of force and violence, and that men live together by no other rules but that of beasts, where the strongest carries it, and so lay a foundation for perpetual disorder and mischief, tumult, sedition, and rebellion (things that the followers of that hypothesis so loudly cry out against) must of necessity find out another rise of government, another original of political power, and another way of designing and knowing the persons that have it, than what Sir Robert Filmer hath taught us.

2. To this purpose, I think it may not be amiss, to set down what I take to be political power; that the power of a *magistrate* over a subject may be distinguished from that of a *father* over his children, a *master* over his servant, a *husband* over his *wife*, and a *lord* over his slave. All which distinct powers happening sometimes together in the same man, if he be considered under these different relations, it may help us to distinguish these powers one from another, and shew the difference betwixt a ruler of a commonwealth, a father of a family, and a captain of a galley.

3. *Political power*, then, I take to be a *right* of making laws and penalties of death, and consequently all less penalties for the regulating and preserving of property, and of employing the force of the community, in the execution of such laws, and in the defence of the commonwealth from foreign injury; and all this only for the public good.

Chapter 2
Of the State of Nature

4. To understand political power, right, and derive it from its original, we must consider what state all men are naturally in, and that is, a *state of perfect freedom* to order their actions, and dispose of their possessions and persons, as they think fit, within the bounds of the law of nature; without asking leave, or depending upon the will of any other man.

A *state* also of *equality*, wherein all the power and jurisdiction is reciprocal, no one having more than another; there being nothing more evident, than that creatures of the same species and rank, promiscuously born to all the same advantages of nature, and the use of the same faculties, should also be equal one amongst another without subordination or subjection; unless the lord and master of them all should, by any manifest declaration of his will, set one above another, and confer on him, by an evident and clear appointment, an undoubted right to dominion and sovereignty.

5. This *equality* of men by nature, the judicious Hooker looks upon as so evident in itself, and beyond all question, that he makes it the foundation of that obligation to mutual love amongst men, on which he builds the duties we owe one another, and from whence he derives the great maxims of *justice* and *charity*. His words are, "The like natural inducement hath brought men to know, that it is no less their duty to love others than themselves; for seeing those things which are equal, must needs all have one measure; if I cannot but wish to receive good, even as much at every man's hands, as any man can wish unto his own soul, how should I look to have any part of my desire herein satisfied, unless myself be careful to satisfy the like desire, which is undoubtedly in other men, being of one and the same nature? To have any thing offered them repugnant to this desire, must needs in all respects grieve them as much as me; so that if I do harm, I must look to suffer, there being no reason that others should shew greater measure of love to me, than they have by me shewed unto them: my desire therefore to be loved of my equals in nature, as

much as possibly may be, imposeth upon me a natural duty of bearing to themward fully the like affection: From which relation of equality between ourselves and them that are as ourselves, what several rules and canons natural reason hath drawn, for direction of life, no man is ignorant." Eccl. Pol. L. I.

6. But though this be *a state of liberty*, yet *it is not a state of licence:* though man in that state have an uncontrolable liberty to dispose of his person or possessions, yet he has not liberty to destroy himself, or so much as any creature in his possession, but where some nobler use than its bare preservation calls for it. The *state of nature* has a law of nature to govern it, which obliges every one: And reason, which is that law, teaches all mankind, who will but consult it, that being all *equal and independent*, no one ought to harm another in his life, health, liberty, or possessions. For men being all the workmanship of one omnipotent and infinitely wise Maker; all the servants of one sovereign master, sent into the world by his order, and about his business; they are his property, whose workmanship they are, made to last during his, not another's pleasure. And being furnished with like faculties, sharing all in one community of nature, there cannot be supposed any such subordination among us, that may authorize us to destroy another, as if we were made for one another's uses, as the inferior ranks of creatures are for ours. Every one, as he is *bound to preserve himself*, and not to quit his station wilfully, so by the like reason, when his own preservation comes not in competition, ought he, as much as he can, *to preserve the rest of mankind*, and may not, unless it be to do justice to an offender, take away or impair the life, or what tends to the preservation of life, the liberty, health, limb, or goods of another.

7. And that all men may be restrained from invading others rights, and from doing hurt to one another, and the law of nature be observed, which willeth the peace and *preservation of all mankind*, the *execution* of the law of nature is, in that state, put into every man's hands, whereby every one has a right to punish the transgressors of that law to such a degree as may hinder its violation. For the *law of nature* would, as all other laws that concern men in this world, be in vain, if there were no body that in the state of nature had a *power to execute* that law, and thereby preserve the innocent and restrain offenders. And if any one in the state of nature may punish another for any evil he has done, every one may do so. For in that *state of perfect equality*, where naturally there is no superiority or jurisdiction of one over another, what any may do in prosecution of that law, every one must needs have a right to do.

8. And thus, in the state of nature, *one man comes by a power over another;* but yet no absolute or arbitrary power, to use a criminal, when he has got him in his hands, according to the passionate heats, or boundless extravagancy of his own will; but only to retribute to him, so far as calm reason and conscience dictate, what is proportionate to his *transgression;* which is so much as may serve for *reparation* and *restraint.* For these two are the only reasons, why one man may lawfully do harm to another, which is that we call *punishment.* In transgressing the law of nature, the offender declares himself to live by another rule than that of reason and common equity, which is that measure God has set to the actions of men, for their mutual security; and so he becomes dangerous to mankind, the tye, which is to secure them from injury and violence, being slighted and broken by him. Which being a trespass against the whole species, and the peace and safety of it, provided for by the law of nature; every man upon this score, by the right he hath to preserve mankind in general, may restrain, or, where it is necessary, destroy things noxious to them, and so may bring such evil on any one, who hath transgressed that law, as may make him repent the doing of it, and thereby deter him, and by his example others, from doing the like mischief. And in this case, and upon this ground, *every man hath a right to punish the offender, and be executioner of the law of nature.* [. . .]

13. To this strange doctrine, viz. That *in the state of nature every one has the executive power* of the law of nature, I doubt not but it will be objected, that it is unreasonable for men to be judges in their own cases, that self-love will make men partial to themselves and their friends: And on the other side, that ill nature, passion and revenge will carry them too far in punishing others; and hence nothing but confusion and disorder will follow, and that therefore God hath certainly appointed government to restrain the partiality and violence of men. I easily grant, that civil government is the proper remedy for the inconveniencies of the state of nature, which must certainly be great, where men may be judges in their own case, since it

is easy to be imagined, that he who was so unjust as to do his brother an injury, will scarce be so just as to condemn himself for it: But I shall desire those who make this objection, to remember, that *absolute monarchs* are but men, and if government is to be the remedy of those evils, which necessarily follow from men's being judges in their own cases, and the state of nature is therefore not to be endured, I desire to know what kind of government that is, and how much better it is than the state of nature, where one man commanding a multitude, has the liberty to be judge in his own case, and may do to all his subjects whatever he pleases, without the least liberty to any one to question or control those who execute his pleasure? and in whatsoever he doth, whether led by reason, mistake or passion, must be submitted to? Much better it is in the state of nature, wherein men are not bound to submit to the unjust will of another: And if he that judges, judges amiss in his own, or any other case, he is answerable for it to the rest of mankind. [. . .]

Chapter 3
Of the State of War

16. The *state of war* is a state of *enmity* and *destruction*: And therefore declaring by word or action, not a passionate and hasty, but a sedate settled design upon another man's life, *puts him in a state of war* with him against whom he has declared such an intention, and so has exposed his life to the other's power to be taken away by him, or any one that joins with him in his defence, and espouses his quarrel: it being reasonable and just I should have a right to destroy that which threatens me with destruction. For *by the fundamental law of nature, man being to be preserved* as much as possible, when all cannot be preserved, the safety of the innocent is to be preferred: And one may destroy a man who makes war upon him, or has discovered an enmity to his being, for the same reason that he may kill a *wolf* or a *lion;* because such men are not under the ties of the common law of reason, have no other rule, but that of force and violence, and so may be treated as beasts of prey, those dangerous and noxious creatures, that will be sure to destroy him whenever he falls into their power.

17. And hence it is, that he who attempts to get another man into his absolute power, does thereby *put himself into a state of war* with him; it being to be understood as a declaration of a design upon his life. For I have reason to conclude, that he who would get me into his power without my consent, would use me as he pleased when he got me there, and destroy me too when he had a fancy to it; for no body can desire to *have me in his absolute power* unless it be to compel me by force to that which is against the right of my freedom, i.e. make me a slave. To be free from such force is the only security of my preservation; and reason bids me look on him, as an enemy to my preservation, who would take away that freedom which is the fence to it; so that he who makes an *attempt to enslave* me, thereby puts himself into a state of war with me. He that, in the state of nature, *would take away the freedom* that belongs to any one in that state, must necessarily be supposed to have a design to take away every thing else, that *freedom* being the foundation of all the rest: As he that, in the state of society, would take away the freedom belonging to those of that society or commonwealth, must be supposed to design to take away from them every thing else, and so be looked on as *in a state of war.*

18. This makes it lawful for a man to *kill a thief,* who has not in the least hurt him, nor declared any design upon his life, any farther, than by the use of force, so to get him in his power, as to take away his money, or what he pleases, from him; because using force, where he has no right, to get me into his power, let his pretence be what it will, I have no reason to suppose, that he, who would *take away my liberty,* would not, when he had me in his power, take away every thing else. And therefore it is lawful for me to treat him as one who has put *himself into a state of war* with me, i.e. kill him if I can; for to that hazard does he justly expose himself, whoever introduces a state of war, and is aggressor in it.

19. And here we have the plain *difference between the state of nature and the state of war;* which however some men have confounded, are as far distant, as a state of peace, good will, mutual assistance and preservation, and a state of enmity, malice, violence and mutual destruction, are one from another. Men living together according to reason, without a common superior on earth, with authority to judge between them, is *properly the state of nature.* But force, or a declared design of force, upon the person

of another, where there is no common superior on earth to appeal to for relief, *is the state of war:* And it is the want of such an appeal gives a man the right of war even against an aggressor, though he be in society and a fellow subject. [. . .]

21. To avoid this *state of war* (wherein there is no appeal but to heaven, and wherein every the least difference is apt to end, where there is no authority to decide between the contenders) is one great *reason of men's putting themselves into society,* and quitting the state of nature. For where there is an authority, a power on earth, from which relief can be had by *appeal,* there the continuance of the *state of war* is excluded, and the controversy is decided by that power. [. . .]

Chapter 4
Of Slavery

22. The *natural liberty* of man is to be free from any superior power on earth, and not to be under the will or legislative authority of man, but to have only the law of nature for his rule. The *liberty of man,* in society, is to be under no other legislative power, but that established, by consent, in the commonwealth; nor under the dominion of any will, or restraint of any law, but what that legislative shall enact, according to the trust put in it. Freedom then is not what Sir Robert Filmer tells us, O, A. 55. "a liberty for every one to do what he lists, to live as he pleases, and not to be tied by any laws:" But *freedom of men under government,* is, to have a standing rule to live by, common to every one of that society, and made by the legislative power erected in it; a liberty to follow my own will in all things, where the rule prescribes not; and not to be subject to the inconstant, uncertain, unknown, arbitrary will of another man: As *freedom of nature* is, to be under no other restraint but the law of nature.

23. This freedom from absolute, arbitrary power, is so necessary to, and closely joined with a man's preservation, that he cannot part with it, but by what forfeits his preservation and life together. For a man, not having the power of his own life, cannot, by compact, or his own consent, enslave himself to any one, nor put himself under the absolute, arbitrary power of another, to take away his life, when he pleases. No body can give more power than he has himself; and he that cannot take away his own life, cannot give another power over it. Indeed, having by his fault forfeited his own life, by some act that deserves death; he, to whom he has forfeited it, may (when he has him in his power) delay to take it, and make use of him to his own service, and he does him no injury by it. For, whenever he finds the hardship of his slavery outweigh the value of his life, it is in his power, by resisting the will of his master, to draw on himself the death he desires.

24. This is the perfect condition of *slavery,* which is nothing else, but *the state of war continued, between a lawful conqueror and a captive.* For, if once compact enter between them, and make an agreement for a limited power on the one side, and obedience on the other, the state of war and slavery ceases, as long as the compact endures. For, as has been said, no man can, by agreement, pass over to another that which he hath not in himself, a power over his own life. [. . .]

Chapter 5
Of Property

25. Whether we consider natural *reason,* which tells us, that men, being once born, have a right to their preservation, and consequently to meat and drink, and such other things as nature affords for their subsistence: or *revelation,* which gives us an account of those grants God made of the world to Adam, and to Noah, and his sons, it is very clear, that God, as King David says, *Psal.* cxv. 16, "has given the earth to the children of men," given it to mankind in common. But this being supposed, it seems to some a very great difficulty how any one should ever come to have a *property* in any thing: I will not content myself to answer, that if it be difficult to make out *property,* upon a supposition, that God gave the world to Adam, and his posterity in common; it is impossible that any man, but one universal monarch, should have any property upon a supposition, that God gave the world to Adam, and his heirs in succession, exclusive of all the rest of his posterity. But I shall endeavour to shew, how men might come to have a *property* in several parts of that which God gave to mankind in common, and that without any express compact of all the commoners.

26. God, who hath given the world to men in common, hath also given them reason to make use of it to the best advantage of life, and convenience. The earth, and all that is therein, is given to men for the support and comfort of their being. And though all the fruits it naturally produces, and beasts it feeds, belong to mankind in common, as they are produced by the spontaneous hand of nature; and no body has originally a private dominion, exclusive of the rest of mankind, in any of them, as they are thus in their natural state: yet being given for the use of men, there must of necessity be *a means to appropriate* them some way or other, before they can be of any use, or at all beneficial to any particular man. The fruit, or venison, which nourishes the wild Indian, who knows no enclosure, and is still a tenant in common, must be his, and so his, i.e. a part of him, that another can no longer have any right to it, before it can do him any good for the support of his life.

27. Though the earth, and all inferior creatures, be common to all men, yet every man has a property in his own person: this no body has any right to but himself. The labour of his body, and the work of his hands, we may say, are properly his. Whatsoever then he removes out of the state that nature hath provided, and left it in, he hath mixed his labour with, and joined to it something that is his own, and thereby makes it his property. It being by him removed from the common state nature hath placed it in, it hath by this labour something annexed to it, that excludes the common right of other men. For this labour being the unquestionable property of the labourer, no man but he can have a right to what that is once joined to, at least where there is enough, and as good, left in common for others.

28. He that is nourished by the acorns he picked up under an oak, or the apples he gathered from the trees in the wood, has certainly appropriated them to himself. No body can deny but the nourishment is his. I ask then, when did they begin to be his? When he digested? Or when he eat? Or when he boiled? Or when he brought them home? Or when he picked them up? And it is plain, if the first gathering made them not his, nothing else could. That *labour* put a distinction between them and common: that added something to them more than nature, the common mother of all, had done; and so they became his private right. And will any one say he had no right to those acorns or apples he thus appropriated, because he had not the consent of all mankind to make them his? Was it a robbery thus to assume to himself what belonged to all in common? If such a consent as that was necessary, man had starved, notwithstanding the plenty God had given him. We see in *commons*, which remain so by compact, that it is the taking any part of what is common, and removing it out of the state nature leaves it in, which *begins the property*; without which the common is of no use. And the taking of this or that part does not depend on the express consent of all the commoners. Thus the grass my horse has bit; the turfs my servant has cut; and the ore I have digged in any place, where I have a right to them in common with others, become my *property*, without the assignation or consent of any body. The *labour* that was mine, removing them out of that common state they were in, hath *fixed* my *property* in them. [...]

31. It will perhaps be objected to this, that *if gathering the acorns, or other fruits of the earth, &c.* makes a right to them, then any one may engross as much as he will. To which I answer, Not so. The same law of nature, that does by this means give us property, does also *bound* that *property* too. "God has given us all things richly," 1 *Tim.* vi. 17, is the voice of reason confirmed by inspiration. But how far has he given it us? *To enjoy.* As much as any one can make use of to any advantage of life before it spoils, so much he may by his labour fix a property in: whatever is beyond this, is more than his share, and belongs to others. Nothing was made by God for man to spoil or destroy. And thus, considering the plenty of natural provisions there was a long time in the world, and the few spenders; and to how small a part of that provision the industry of one man could extend itself, and engross it to the prejudice of others; especially keeping within the *bounds*, set by reason, *of* what might serve for his *use*; there could be then little room for quarrels or contentions about property so established.

32. But the *chief matter of property* being now not the fruits of the earth, and the beasts that subsist on it, but the *earth itself*; as that which takes in, and carries with it all the rest: I think it is plain, that *property* in that too is acquired as the former. *As much land* as a man tills, plants, improves, cultivates, and can use the product of, so much is his *property*. He by his labour does, as it were, enclose it from the common.

Nor will it invalidate his right, to say every body else has an equal title to it; and therefore he cannot appropriate, he cannot enclose, without the consent of all his fellow commoners, all mankind. God, when he gave the world in common to all mankind, commanded man also to labour, and the penury of his condition required it of him. God and his reason commanded him to subdue the earth, i.e. improve it for the benefit of life, and therein lay out something upon it that was his own, his labour. He that, in obedience to this command of God, subdued, tilled, and sowed any part of it, thereby annexed to it something that was his *property*, which another had no title to, nor could without injury take from him. [. . .]

35. It is true, in *land* that is *common* in England, or any other country, where there is plenty of people under government, who have money and commerce, no one can enclose or appropriate any part, without the consent of all his fellow-commoners: Because this is left common by compact, i.e. by the law of the land, which is not to be violated. And though it be common, in respect of some men, it is not so to all mankind, but is the joint property of this country, or this parish. Besides, the remainder, after such enclosure, would not be as good to the rest of the commoners, as the whole was when they could all make use of the whole: whereas in the beginning and first peopling of the great common of the world, it was quite otherwise. The law man was under, was rather for appropriating. God commanded, and his wants forced him to *labour*. That was his *property* which could not be taken from him wherever he had fixed it. And hence subduing or cultivating the earth, and having dominion, we see are joined together. The one gave title to the other. So that God, by commanding to subdue, gave authority so far to *appropriate*: And the condition of human life, which requires labour and materials to work on, necessarily introduces private possessions.

36. The *measure of property* nature has well set by the extent of men's *labour, and the conveniences of life*: No man's labour could subdue or appropriate all; nor could his enjoyment consume more than a small part; so that it was impossible for any man, this way, to intrench upon the right of another, or acquire to himself a property, to the prejudice of his neighbour, who would still have room for as good, and as large a possession (after the other had taken out his) as before it was appropriated. This *measure* did confine every man's *possession* to a very moderate proportion, and such as he might appropriate to himself, without injury to any body, in the first ages of the world, when men were more in danger to be lost, by wandering from their company, in the then vast wilderness of the earth, than to be straitened for want of room to plant in. And the same measure may be allowed still without prejudice to any body, as full as the world seems. For supposing a man, or family, in the state they were at first peopling of the world by the children of Adam, or Noah; let him plant in some inland, vacant places of America, we shall find that the *possessions* he could make himself, upon the *measures* we have given, would not be very large, nor, even to this day, prejudice the rest of mankind, or give them reason to complain, or think themselves injured by this man's encroachment, though the race of men have now spread themselves to all the corners of the world, and do infinitely exceed the small number was at the beginning. Nay, the extent of *ground* is of so little value, *without labour*, that I have heard it affirmed, that in Spain itself a man may be permitted to plough, sow, and reap, without being disturbed, upon land he has no other title to, but only his making use of it. But, on the contrary, the inhabitants think themselves beholden to him, who by his industry on neglected and consequently waste land, has increased the stock of corn, which they wanted. But be this as it will, which I lay no stress on; this I dare boldly affirm, that the same *rule of propriety*, (*viz.*) that every man should have as much as he could make use of, would hold still in the world, without straitening any body, since there is land enough in the world to suffice double the inhabitants, had not the *invention of money*, and the tacit agreement of men to put a value on it, introduced (by consent) larger possessions, and a right to them; which, how it has done, I shall by and by shew more at large.

37. This is certain, that in the beginning, before the desire of having more than man needed had altered the intrinsic value of things, which depends only on their usefulness to the life of man; or had *agreed, that a little piece of yellow metal*, which would keep without wasting or decay, should be worth a great piece of flesh, or a whole heap of corn; though men had a right to appropriate, by their

labour, each one to himself as much of the things of nature as he could use: yet this could not be much, nor to the prejudice of others, where the same plenty was still left to those who would use the same industry. To which let me add, that he who appropriates land to himself by his labour, does not lessen, but increase the common stock of mankind. For the provisions serving to the support of human life, produced by one acre of enclosed and cultivated land, are (to speak much within compass) ten times more than those which are yielded by an acre of land of an equal richness lying waste in common. And therefore he that encloses land, and has a greater plenty of the conveniencies of life from ten acres, than he could have from an hundred left to nature, may truly be said to give ninety acres to mankind. For his labour now supplies him with provisions out of ten acres, which were by the product of an hundred lying in common. I have here rated the improved land very low, in making its product but as ten to one, when it is much nearer an hundred to one. For I ask, whether in the wild woods and uncultivated waste of America, left to nature, without any improvement, tillage, or husbandry, a thousand acres yield the needy and wretched inhabitants as many conveniencies of life, as ten acres equally fertile land do in Devonshire, where they are well cultivated? [. . .]

40. Nor is it so strange, as perhaps before consideration it may appear, that the *property of labour* should be able to over-balance the community of land. For it is *labour* indeed that *puts the difference of value* on every thing; and let any one consider what the difference is between an acre of land planted with tobacco or sugar, sown with wheat or barley, and an acre of the same land lying in common, without any husbandry upon it, and he will find, that the improvement of *labour makes* the far greater part of the value. I think it will be but a very modest computation to say, that of the *products* of the earth useful to the life of man, nine tenths are the *effects of labour*: nay, if we will rightly estimate things as they come to our use, and cast up the several expences about them, what in them is purely owing to *nature*, and what to *labour*, we shall find, that in most of them ninety-nine hundredths are wholly to be put on the account of *labour*. [. . .]

45. Thus *labour*, in the beginning, *gave a right of property*, wherever any one was pleased to employ it upon what was common, which remained a long while the far greater part, and is yet more than mankind makes use of. Men, at first, for the most part, contented themselves with what unassisted nature offered to their necessities: and though afterwards, in some parts of the world, (where the increase of people and stock, with the *use of money*, had made land scarce, and so of some value) the several *communities* settled the bounds of their distinct territories, and by laws within themselves regulated the properties of the private men of their society, and so, by *compact* and agreement, *settled the property* which labour and industry began; and the leagues that have been made between several states and kingdoms, either expressly or tacitly disowning all claim and right to the land in the others possession, have, by common consent, given up their pretences to their natural common right, which originally they had to those countries, and so have, by *positive agreement, settled a property* amongst themselves, in distinct parts and parcels of the earth; yet there are still *great tracts of ground* to be found, which (the inhabitants thereof not having joined with the rest of mankind, in the consent of the use of their common money) *lie waste*, and are more than the people who dwell on it do, or can make use of, and so still lie in common. Though this can scarce happen amongst that part of mankind that have consented to the use of money.

46. The greatest part of *things really useful* to the life of man, and such as the necessity of subsisting made the first commoners of the world look after, as it doth the Americans now, *are* generally things of *short duration*; such as, if they are not consumed by use, will decay and perish of themselves: gold, silver, and diamonds, are things that fancy or agreement hath put the value on, more than real use, and the necessary support of life. Now of those good things which nature hath provided in common, every one had a right, (as hath been said) to as much as he could use, and property in all that he could affect with his labour; all that his *industry* could extend to, to alter from the state nature had put it in, was his. He that *gathered* a hundred bushels of acorns or apples, had thereby a *property* in them, they were his goods as soon as gathered. He was only to look, that he used them before they spoiled, else he took more than his share, and robbed others. And indeed it was

a foolish thing, as well as dishonest, to hoard up more than he could make use of. If he gave away a part to any body else, so that it perished not uselessly in his possession, these he also made use of. And if he also bartered away plums, that would have rotted in a week, for nuts that would last good for his eating a whole year, he did no injury; he wasted not the common stock; destroyed no part of the portion of goods that belonged to others, so long as nothing perished uselessly in his hands. Again, if he would give his nuts for a piece of metal, pleased with its colour; or exchange his sheep for shells, or wool for a sparkling pebble or a diamond, and keep those by him all his life, he invaded not the right of others, he might heap up as much of these durable things as he pleased; the *exceeding of the bounds of* his *just property* not lying in the largeness of his possession, but the perishing of any thing uselessly in it.

47. And thus *came in the use of money*, some lasting thing that men might keep without spoiling, and that by mutual consent men would take in exchange for the truly useful, but perishable supports of life. [. . .]

49. [. . .] [I]n the beginning all the world was America, and more so than that is now; for no such thing as *money* was any where known. Find out something that hath the *use and value of money* amongst his neighbours, you shall see the same man will begin presently to *enlarge* his possessions.

50. But since gold and silver, being little useful to the life of man in proportion to food, raiment, and carriage, has its *value* only from the consent of men, whereof *labour* yet *makes*, in great part, the *measure*, it is plain, that men have agreed to a disproportionate and unequal *possession of the earth*, they having, by a tacit and voluntary consent, found out a way how a man may fairly possess more land than he himself can use the product of, by receiving in exchange for the overplus, gold and silver, which may be hoarded up without injury to any one; these metals not spoiling or decaying in the hands of the possessor. This partage of things in an inequality of private possessions, men have made practicable out of the bounds of society, and without compact, only by putting a value on gold and silver, and tacitly agreeing in the use of money. For in governments, the laws regulate the right of property, and the possession of land is determined by positive constitutions. [. . .]

Chapter 6
Of Paternal Power

[. . .] 57. The law, that was to govern Adam, was the same that was to govern all his posterity, *the law of reason*. But his offspring having another way of entrance into the world, different from him, by a natural birth, that produced them ignorant and without the use of *reason*, they were not presently *under that law*; for no body can be under a law, which is not promulgated to him: and this law being promulgated or made known by *reason* only, he that is not come to the use of his *reason*, cannot be said to be *under this law*; and Adam's children, being not presently as soon as born, *under this law of reason*, were not presently free. For law, in its true notion, is not so much the limitation, as the direction of a *free and intelligent* agent to his proper interest, and prescribes no farther than is for the general good of those under that law. Could they be happier without it, the law, as an useless thing, would of it self vanish: and that ill deserves the name of confinement which hedges us in only from bogs and precipices. So that, however it may be mistaken, *the end of law* is not to abolish or restrain, but *to preserve and enlarge freedom*. For in all the states of created beings capable of laws, *where there is no law, there is no freedom*. For liberty is to be free from restraint and violence from others which cannot be where there is no law: but freedom is not, as we are told, "a liberty for every man to do what he lists:" (for who could be free, when every other man's humour might domineer over him?) but a liberty to dispose, and order as he lists, his person, actions, possessions, and his whole property, within the allowance of those laws under which he is, and therein not to be subject to the arbitrary will of another, but freely follow his own. [. . .]

61. Thus we are *born free*, as we are born rational; not that we have actually the exercise of either: age, that brings one, brings with it the other too. And thus we see how *natural freedom and subjection to parents* may consist together, and are both founded on the same principle. [. . .]

63. The *freedom* then of man, and liberty of acting according to his own will, is *grounded* on his having *reason*, which is able to instruct him in that law he is to govern himself by, and make him know how far he is left to the freedom of his own will. To turn him

loose to an unrestrained liberty, before he has reason to guide him, is not the allowing him the privilege of his nature to be free; but to thrust him out amongst brutes, and abandon him to a state as wretched, and as much beneath that of a man, as theirs. This is that which puts the *authority* into the *parents* hands to govern the *minority* of their children. God hath made it their business to employ this care on their offspring, and hath placed in them suitable inclinations of tenderness and concern to temper this power, to apply it, as his wisdom designed it, to the children's good as long as they should need to be under it.

64. But what reason can hence advance this care of the *parents* due to their offspring into an *absolute arbitrary dominion* of the father, whose power reaches no farther than, by such a discipline as he finds most effectual, to give such strength and health to their bodies, such vigour and rectitude to their minds, as may best fit his children to be most useful to themselves and others; and, if it be necessary to his condition, to make them work, when they are able, for their own subsistence. But in this power the *mother* too has her share with the *father*.

65. Nay, *this* power so little belongs to the father by any peculiar right of nature, but only as he is guardian of his children, that when he quits his care of them, he loses his power over them, which goes along with their nourishment and education, to which it is inseparably annexed; and it belongs as much to the foster-father of an exposed child, as to the natural father of another. So little power does the bare *act of begetting* give a man over his issue; if all his care ends there, and this be all the title he hath to the name and authority of a father. [. . .] His command over his children is but temporary, and reaches not their life or property: it is but a help to the weakness and imperfection of their nonage, a discipline necessary to their education: and though a father may dispose of his own possessions as he pleases, when his children are out of danger of perishing for want, yet his power extends not to the lives or goods, which either their own industry, or another's bounty has made theirs; nor to their liberty neither, when they are once arrived to the infranchisement of the years of discretion. The *father's empire* then ceases, and can from thence forwards no more dispose of the liberty of his son, than that of any other man: and it must be far from an absolute or perpetual jurisdiction, from which a man may withdraw himself, having licence from divine authority to *leave father and mother, and cleave to his wife*. [. . .]

Chapter 7
Of Political or Civil Society

[. . .] 87. Man being born, as has been proved, with a title to perfect freedom, and an uncontrolled enjoyment of all the rights and privileges of the law of nature, equally with any other man, or number of men in the world, hath by nature a power, not only to preserve his property, that is, his life, liberty, and estate, against the injuries and attempts of other men; but to judge of and punish the breaches of that law in others, as he is persuaded the offence deserves, even with death itself, in crimes where the heinousness of the fact, in his opinion, requires it. But because no *political* society can be, nor subsist, without having in itself the power to preserve the property, and, in order thereunto, punish the offences of all those of that society; there and there only is *political society*, where every one of the members hath quitted his natural power, resigned it up into the hands of the community in all cases that excludes him not from appealing for protection to the law established by it. And thus all private judgment of every particular member being excluded, the community comes to be umpire by settled standing rules, indifferent, and the same to all parties; and by men having authority from the community, for the execution of those rules, decides all the differences that may happen between any members of that society concerning any matter of right; and punishes those offences which any member hath committed against the society, with such penalties as the law has established, whereby it is easy to discern, who are, and who are not, in *political society* together. Those who are united into one body, and have a common established law and judicature to appeal to, with authority to decide controversies between them, and punish offenders, *are in civil society* one with another: but those who have no such common appeal, I mean on earth, are still in the state of nature, each being, where there is no other, judge for himself, and executioner: which is, as I have before shewed, the perfect *state of nature*.

88. And thus the commonwealth comes by a power to set down what punishment shall belong to

the several transgressions which they think worthy of it, committed amongst the members of that society, (which is the *power of making laws*) as well as it has the power to punish any injury done unto any of its members, by any one that is not of it, (which is the power of war and peace,) and all this for the preservation of the property of all the members of that society, as far as is possible. But though every man who has entered into civil society, and is become a member of any commonwealth, has thereby quitted his power to punish offences against the law of nature, in prosecution of his own private judgment; yet with the judgment of offences, which he has given up to the legislative in all cases, where he can appeal to the magistrate, he has given a right to the commonwealth to employ his force, for the execution of the judgments of the commonwealth whenever he shall be called to it; which indeed are his own judgments, they being made by himself, or his representative. And herein we have the original of the legislative and executive power of civil society, which is to judge by standing laws, how far offences are to be punished, when committed within the commonwealth; and also to determine, by occasional judgments founded on the present circumstances of the fact, how far injuries from without are to be vindicated; and in both these to employ all the force of all the members, when there shall be need.

89. Whenever therefore any number of men are so united into one society, as to quit every one his executive power of the law of nature, and to resign it to the public, there and there only is a political, or civil society. And this is done, wherever any number of men, in the state of nature, enter into society to make one people, one body politic, under one supreme government; or else when any one joins himself to, and incorporates with any government already made. For hereby he authorizes the society, or, which is all one, the legislative thereof, to make laws for him, as the public good of the society shall require; to the execution whereof, his own assistance (as to his own degrees) is due. And this puts men out of a state of nature into that of a commonwealth, by setting up a judge on earth, with authority to determine all the controversies, and redress the injuries that may happen to any member of the commonwealth: which judge is the legislative, or magistrate appointed by it. And wherever there are any number of men, however associated, that have no such decisive power to appeal to, there they are still in the state of nature. [. . .]

Chapter 8
Of the Beginning of Political Societies

95. Men being, as has been said, by nature, all free, equal, and independent, no one can be put out of this estate, and subjected to the political power of another, without his own consent. The only way, whereby any one divests himself of his natural liberty, and puts on the *bonds of civil society*, is by agreeing with other men to join and unite into a community, for their comfortable, safe, and peaceable living one amongst another, in a secure enjoyment of their properties, and a greater security against any, that are not of it. This any number of men may do, because it injures not the freedom of the rest; they are left as they were in the liberty of the state of nature. When any number of men have so *consented to make one community or government*, they are thereby presently incorporated, and make *one body politic*, wherein the *majority* have a right to act and conclude the rest.

96. For when any number of men have, by the consent of every individual, made a *community*, they have thereby made that *community* one body, with a power to act as one body, which is only by the will and determination of the majority. For that which acts any community, being only the *consent* of the individuals of it, and it being necessary to that which is one body to move one way; it is necessary the body should move that way whither the greater force carries it, which is the *consent of the majority*: or else it is impossible it should act or continue one body, one community, which the consent of every individual that united into it, agreed that it should; and so every one is bound by that consent to be concluded by the majority. And therefore we see, that in assemblies, impowered to act by positive laws, where no number is set by that positive law which impowers them, the *act of the majority* passes for the act of the whole, and of course determines, as having, by the law of nature and reason, the power of the whole.

97. And thus every man, by consenting with others to make one body politic under one government, puts himself under an obligation, to every one of that

society, to submit to the determination of the majority, and to be concluded by it; or else this *original compact*, whereby he with others incorporate into one society, would signify nothing, and be no compact, if he be left free, and under no other ties than he was in before in the state of nature. For what appearance would there be of any compact? What new engagement if he were no farther tied by any decrees of the society, than he himself thought fit, and did actually consent to? This would be still as great a liberty, as he himself had before his compact, or any one else in the state of nature hath, who may submit himself, and consent to any acts of it if he thinks fit.

98. For if *the consent of the majority* shall not, in reason, be received as *the act of the whole*, and conclude every individual; nothing but the consent of every individual can make any thing to be the act of the whole: But such a consent is next to impossible ever to be had, if we consider the infirmities of health, and avocations of business, which in a number, though much less than that of a commonwealth, will necessarily keep many away from the public assembly. To which if we add the variety of opinions, and contrariety of interests, which unavoidably happen in all collections of men, the coming into society upon such terms would be only like Cato's coming into the theatre, only to go out again. Such a constitution as this would make the mighty *leviathan* of a shorter duration, than the feeblest creatures, and not let it outlast the day it was born in: which cannot be supposed, till we can think, that rational creatures should desire and constitute societies only to be dissolved. For where the majority cannot conclude the rest, there they cannot act as one body, and consequently will be immediately dissolved again.

99. Whosoever therefore out of a state of nature unite into a community, must be understood to give up all the power, necessary to the ends for which they unite into society, to the majority of the community, unless they expressly agreed in any number greater than the majority. And this is done by barely agreeing to *unite into one political society*, which is *all the compact* that is, or needs be, between the individuals, that enter into, or make up a commonwealth. And thus that, which begins and actually *constitutes any political society*, is nothing, but the consent of any number of freemen capable of a majority, to unite and incorporate into such a society. And this is that, and that only, which did, or could give beginning to any lawful government in the world. [. . .]

Chapter 9
Of the Ends of Political Society and Government

123. If man in the state of nature be so free, as has been said; if he be absolute lord of his own person and possessions, equal to the greatest, and subject to no body, why will he part with his freedom? why will he give up this empire, and subject himself to the dominion and control of any other power? To which it is obvious to answer, that though in the state of nature he hath such a right, yet the enjoyment of it is very uncertain, and constantly exposed to the invasion of others. For all being kings as much as he, every man his equal, and the greater part no strict observers of equity and justice, the enjoyment of the property he has in this state is very unsafe, very unsecure. This makes him willing to quit this condition, which, however free, is full of fears and continual dangers: and it is not without reason, that he seeks out, and is willing to join in society with others, who are already united, or have a mind to unite, for the mutual preservation of their lives, liberties, and estates, which I call by the general name, property.

124. The great and *chief end*, therefore, of men's uniting into commonwealths, and putting themselves under government, *is the preservation of their property*. To which in the state of nature there are many things wanting.

First, There wants an established, settled, known law, received and allowed by common consent to be the standard of right and wrong, and the common measure to decide all controversies between them. For though the law of nature be plain and intelligible to all rational creatures; yet men being biassed by their interest, as well as ignorant for want of studying it, are not apt to allow of it as a law binding to them in the application of it to their particular cases.

125. Secondly, In the state of nature there wants *a known and indifferent judge*, with authority to determine all differences according to the established law. For every one in that state being both judge and executioner of the law of nature, men being partial to themselves, passion and revenge is very apt to carry

them too far, and with too much heat, in their own cases; as well as negligence, and unconcernedness, to make them too remiss in other men's.

126. Thirdly, In the state of nature, there often wants power to back and support the sentence when right, and to give it due execution. They who by any injustice offended, will seldom fail, where they are able, by force to make good their injustice; such resistance many times makes the punishment dangerous, and frequently destructive, to those who attempt it.

127. Thus mankind, notwithstanding all the privileges of the state of nature, being but in an ill condition, while they remain in it, are quickly driven into society. Hence it comes to pass that we seldom find any number of men live any time together in this state. The inconveniencies that they are therein exposed to, by the irregular and uncertain exercise of the power every man has of punishing the transgressions of others, make them take sanctuary under the established laws of government, and therein seek *the preservation of their property*. It is this makes them so willingly give up every one his single power of punishing, to be exercised by such alone, as shall be appointed to it amongst them; and by such rules as the community, or those authorized by them to that purpose, shall agree on. And in this we have the original *right and rise of both the legislative and executive power*, as well as of the governments and societies themselves. [. . .]

131. But though men, when they enter into society, give up the equality, liberty, and executive power they had in the state of nature, into the hands of the society, to be so far disposed of by the legislative, as the good of the society shall require; yet it being only with an intention in every one the better to preserve himself, his liberty and property; (for no rational creature can be supposed to change his condition with an intention to be worse) the power of the society, or legislative constituted by them, *can never be supposed to extend farther, than the common good;* but is obliged to secure every one's property, by providing against those three defects above mentioned, that made the state of nature so unsafe and uneasy. And so whoever has the legislative or supreme power of any commonwealth, is bound to govern by established standing laws, promulgated and known to the people, and not by extemporary decrees; by indifferent and upright judges, who are to decide controversies by those laws; and to employ the force of the community at home, *only in the execution of such laws;* or abroad to prevent or redress foreign injuries, and secure the community from inroads and invasion. And all this to be directed to no other *end,* but the *peace, safety,* and *public good* of the people. [. . .]

Chapter 11
Of the Extent of the Legislative Power

134. The great end of men's entering into society being the enjoyment of their properties in peace and safety, and the great instrument and means of that being the laws established in that society; the *first and fundamental positive law* of all commonwealths *is the establishing of the legislative* power; as the *first and fundamental natural law,* which is to govern even the legislative itself, *is the preservation of the society,* and (as far as will consist with the public good) of every person in it. This *legislative* is not only *the supreme power* of the commonwealth, but sacred and unalterable in the hands where the community have once placed it; nor can any edict of any body else, in what form soever conceived, or by what power soever backed, have the force and obligation of a law, which has not its *sanction* from that *legislative* which the public has chosen and appointed; for without this the law could not have that, which is absolutely necessary to its being a *law,*[2] *the consent of the society;* over

2. "The lawful power of making laws to command whole politic societies of men, belonging so properly unto the same entire societies, that for any prince or potentate of what kind soever upon earth, to exercise the same of himself, and not by express commission immediately and personally received from God, or else by authority derived at the first from their consent, upon whose persons they impose laws, it is no better than mere tyranny. Laws they are not therefore which public approbation hath not made so." Hooker's Eccl. Pol. L. I. Sect. 10. "Of this point therefore we are to note, that sith men naturally have no full and perfect power to command whole politic multitudes of men, therefore utterly without our consent, we could in such sort be at no man's commandment living. And to be commanded we do consent when that society, whereof we be a part, hath at any time before consented, without revoking the same after by the like universal agreement.

Laws therefore human, of what kind so ever, are available by consent." Ibid.

whom no body can have a power to make laws, but by their own consent, and by authority received from them; and therefore all the obedience, which by the most solemn ties any one can be obliged to pay, ultimately terminates in this supreme power, and is directed by those laws which it enacts; nor can any oaths to any foreign power whatsoever, or any domestic subordinate power, discharge any member of the society from his *obedience to the legislative*, acting pursuant to their trust; nor oblige him to any obedience contrary to the laws so enacted, or farther than they do allow; it being ridiculous to imagine one can be tied ultimately to obey any power in the society, which is not the supreme.

135. Though the legislative, whether placed in one or more, whether it be always in being, or only by intervals, though it be the supreme power in every commonwealth; yet,

First, It is *not*, nor can possibly be absolutely *arbitrary* over the lives and fortunes of the people. For it being but the joint power of every member of the society given up to that person, or assembly, which is legislator, it can be no more than those persons had in a state of nature before they entered into society, and gave up to the community. For no body can transfer to another more power than he has in himself; and no body has an absolute arbitrary power over himself, or over any other, to destroy his own life, or take away the life or property of another. A man, as has been proved, cannot subject himself to the arbitrary power of another; and having in the state of nature no arbitrary power over the life, liberty, or possession of another, but only so much as the law of nature gave him for the preservation of himself and the rest of mankind; this is all he doth, or can give up to the commonwealth, and by it to the legislative power, so that the legislative can have no more than this. Their power, in the utmost bounds of it, is *limited to the public good* of the society. It is a power, that hath no other end but preservation, and therefore can never[3] have a right to destroy, enslave, or designedly to impoverish the subjects. The obligations of the law of nature cease not in society, but only in many cases are drawn closer, and have by human laws known penalties annexed to them, to enforce their observation. Thus the law of nature stands as an eternal rule to all men, legislators as well as others. The rules that they make for other men's actions, must, as well as their own and other men's actions, be conformable to the law of nature, i.e. to the will of God, of which that is a declaration; and the *fundamental law of nature being the preservation of mankind*, no human sanction can be good or valid against it.

136. Secondly,[4] The legislative or supreme authority cannot assume to itself a power to rule, by extemporary, arbitrary decrees, but *is bound to dispense justice*, and decide the rights of the subject, *by promulgated, standing laws, and known authorised judges*. For the law of nature being unwritten, and so nowhere to be found, but in the minds of men; they who through passion, or interest, shall miscite, or misapply it, cannot so easily be convinced of their mistake, where there is no established judge: and so it serves not, as it ought, to determine the rights, and fence the properties of those that live under it; especially where every one is judge, interpreter, and executioner of it too, and that in his own case: and he that has right on

3. "Two foundations there are which bear up public societies, the one a natural inclination, whereby all men desire sociable life and fellowship; the other an order, expressly or secretly agreed upon, touching the manner of their union in living together: the latter is that which we call the law of a commonweal, the very soul of a politic body, the parts whereof are by law animated, held together, and set on work in such actions as the common good requireth. Laws politic, ordained for external order and regiment amongst men, are never framed as they should be, unless presuming the will of man to be inwardly obstinate, rebellious, and averse from all obedience to the sacred laws of his nature; in a word, unless presuming man to be, in regard of his depraved mind, little better than a wild beast, they do accordingly provide notwithstanding, so to frame his outward actions, that they be no hindrance unto the common good, for which societies are instituted. Unless they do this, they are not perfect." Hooker's Eccl. Pol. L. I. Sect. 10.

4. "Human laws are measures in respect of men whose actions they must direct, howbeit such measures they are as have also their higher rules to be measured by, which rules are two, the law of God, and the law of nature; so that laws human must be made according to the general laws of nature, and without contradiction to any positive law of scripture, otherwise they are ill made." Hooker's Eccl. Pol. L. 3. Sect. 9.

"To constrain men to any thing inconvenient doth seem unreasonable." Ibid. L. I. Sect. 10.

his side, having ordinarily but his own single strength, hath not force enough to defend himself from injuries, or to punish delinquents. To avoid these inconveniencies, which disorder men's properties in the state of nature, men unite into societies, that they may have the united strength of the whole society to secure and defend their properties, and may have standing rules to bound it, by which every one may know what is his. To this end it is that men give up all their natural power to the society which they enter into, and the community put the legislative power into such hands as they think fit: with this trust, that they shall be governed by *declared laws,* or else their peace, quiet, and property will still be at the same uncertainty, as it was in the state of nature.

137. Absolute arbitrary power, or governing without *settled standing laws,* can neither of them consist with the ends of society and government, which men would not quit the freedom of the state of nature for, and tie themselves up under, were it not to preserve their lives, liberties, and fortunes, and by *stated rules* of right and property to secure their peace and quiet. It cannot be supposed that they should intend, had they a power so to do, to give to any one, or more, an *absolute arbitrary power* over their persons and estates, and put a force into the magistrate's hand to execute his unlimited will arbitrarily upon them. This were to put themselves into a worse condition than the state of nature, wherein they had a liberty to defend their right against the injuries of others, and were upon equal terms of force to maintain it, whether invaded by a single man, or many in combination. [. . .]

138. *Thirdly,* The *supreme power cannot take* from any man part of his property without his own consent. For the preservation of property being the end of government, and that for which men enter into society, it necessarily supposes and requires, that the people should *have property,* without which they must be supposed to lose that, by entering into society, which was the end for which they entered into it; too gross an absurdity for any man to own. *Men* therefore *in society having property,* they have such right to the goods, which by the law of the community are theirs, that no body hath a right to take their substance or any part of it from them, without their own consent; without this they have no property at all. For I have truly no property in that, which another can by right take from me, when he pleases, against my consent. Hence it is a mistake to think, that the *supreme or legislative power* of any commonwealth can do what it will, and dispose of the estates of the subject arbitrarily, or take any part of them at pleasure. This is not much to be feared in governments where the legislative consists, wholly or in part, in assemblies which are variable, whose members, upon the dissolution of the assembly, are subjects under the common laws of their country, equally with the rest. But in governments, where the legislative is in one lasting assembly always in being, or in one man, as in absolute monarchies, there is danger still, that they will think themselves to have a distinct interest from the rest of the community; and so will be apt to increase their own riches and power by taking what they think fit from the people. For a man's property is not at all secure, though there be good and equitable laws to set the bounds of it between him and his fellow subjects, if he who commands those subjects, have power to take from any private man, what part he pleases of his property, and use and dispose of it as he thinks good.

139. But government, into whatsoever hands it is put, being, as I have before shewed, intrusted with this condition, and *for this end,* that men might have and secure their properties; the prince, or senate, however it may have power to make laws, for the regulating of property between the subjects one amongst another, yet can never have a power to take to themselves the whole, or any part of the subject's property, without their own consent. For this would be in effect to leave them no property at all. [. . .]

140. It is true, governments cannot be supported without great charge, and it is fit every one who enjoys his share of the protection, should pay out of his estate his proportion for the maintenance of it. But still it must be with his own consent, i.e. the consent of the majority, giving it either by themselves, or their representatives chosen by them. For if any one shall claim a *power to lay* and levy *taxes* on the people, by his own authority, and without such consent of the people, he thereby invades the *fundamental law of property,* and subverts the end of government. For what property have I in that, which another may by right take when he pleases, to himself?

141. *Fourthly,* The *legislative cannot transfer the power of making laws* to any other hands. For it being

but a delegated power from the people, they who have it cannot pass it over to others. The people alone can appoint the form of the commonwealth, which is by constituting the legislative, and appointing in whose hands that shall be. And when the people have said, we will submit to rules, and be governed by laws made by such men, and in such forms, no body else can say other men shall make laws for them; nor can the people be bound by any laws, but such as are enacted by those whom they have chosen, and authorized to make laws for them. The power of the legislative being derived from the people by a positive voluntary grant and institution, can be no other than what that positive grant conveyed, which being only to make laws, and not to make legislators, the legislative can have no power to transfer their authority of making laws and place it in other hands.

142. These are the bounds which the trust, that is put in them by the society and the law of God and nature, have *set to the legislative* power of every commonwealth, in all forms of government. [. . .]

Chapter 12
Of the Legislative, Executive, and Federative Power of the Commonwealth

143. The legislative power is that, which has a right *to direct how the force of the commonwealth* shall be employed for preserving the community and the members of it. But because those laws which are constantly to be executed, and whose force is always to continue, may be made in a little time; therefore there is no need, that the legislative should be always in being, not having always business to do. And because it may be too great a temptation to human frailty, apt to grasp at power, for the same persons, who have the power of making laws, to have also in their hands the power to execute them, whereby they may exempt themselves from obedience to the laws they make, and suit the law, both in its making and execution, to their own private advantage, and thereby come to have a distinct interest from the rest of the community, contrary to the end of society and government: therefore in well ordered commonwealths, where the good of the whole is so considered, as it ought, the legislative power is put into the hands of divers persons, who, duly assembled, have by themselves, or jointly with others, a power to make laws; which when they have done, being separated again, they are themselves subject to the laws they have made; which is a new and near tie upon them, to take care that they make them for the public good.

144. But because the laws, that are at once, and in a short time made, have a constant and lasting force, and need a *perpetual execution,* or an attendance thereunto: therefore it is necessary there should be a *power always in being,* which should see to the execution of the laws that are made, and remain in force. And thus the legislative and executive power come often to be separated.

145. There is another power in every commonwealth, which one may call *natural,* because it is that which answers to the power every man naturally had before he entered into society. For though in a commonwealth, the members of it are distinct persons still in reference to one another, and as such are governed by the laws of the society; yet in reference to the rest of mankind, they make one body, which is, as every member of it before was, still in the state of nature with the rest of mankind. Hence it is, that the controversies that happen between any man of the society with those that are out of it, are managed by the public; and an injury done to a member of their body engages the whole in the reparation of it. So that, under this consideration, the whole community is one body in the state of nature, in respect of all other states or persons out of its community.

146. This therefore contains the power of war and peace, leagues and alliances, and all the transactions, with all persons and communities without the commonwealth; and may be called federative, if any one pleases. So the thing be understood, I am indifferent as to the name.

147. These two powers, executive and federative, though they be really distinct in themselves, yet one comprehending the execution of the municipal laws of the society within itself, upon all that are parts of it; the other the management of the *security and interest of the public without,* with all those that it may receive benefit or damage from; yet they are always almost united. And though this *federative power* in the well or ill management of it be of great moment to the commonwealth, yet it is much less capable to be directed by antecedent, standing, positive laws, than

the executive; and so must necessarily be left to the prudence and wisdom of those whose hands it is in, to be managed for the public good. For the laws that concern subjects one amongst another, being to direct their actions, may well enough precede them. But what is to be done in reference to foreigners, depending much upon their actions, and the variation of designs, and interests, must be left in great part to the prudence of those who have this power committed to them, to be managed by the best of their skill, for the advantage of the commonwealth.

148. Though, as I said, the executive and federative power of every community be really distinct in themselves, yet they are hardly to be separated, and placed at the same time in the hands of distinct persons. For both of them requiring the force of the society for their exercise, it is almost impracticable to place the force of the commonwealth in distinct, and not subordinate hands; or that the executive and federative power should be placed in persons that might act separately, whereby the force of the public would be under different commands: which would be apt some time or other to cause disorder and ruin.

Chapter 13
Of the Subordination of the Powers of the Commonwealth

149. Though in a constituted commonwealth, standing upon its own basis, and acting according to its own nature, that is, acting for the preservation of the community, there can be but *one supreme power*, which is the *legislative*, to which all the rest are and must be subordinate; yet the legislative being only a fiduciary power to act for certain ends, there remains still *in the people a supreme power to remove or alter the legislative*, when they find the legislative act contrary to the trust reposed in them. For all *power given with trust* for the attaining an end, being limited by that end; whenever that end is manifestly neglected or opposed, the trust must necessarily be forfeited, and the power devolve into the hands of those that gave it, who may place it anew where they shall think best for their safety and security. And thus the *community* perpetually *retains a supreme power* of saving themselves from the attempts and designs of any body, even of their legislators, whenever they shall be so foolish, or so wicked, as to lay and carry on designs against the liberties and properties of the subject. For no man, or society of men, having a power to deliver up their preservation, or consequently the means of it, to the absolute will and arbitrary dominion of another; whenever any one shall go about to bring them into such a slavish condition, they will always have a right to preserve what they have not a power to part with; and to rid themselves of those who invade this fundamental, sacred, and unalterable law of self-preservation, for which they entered into society. And thus the community may be said in this respect to be *always the supreme power*, but not as considered under any form of government, because this power of the people can never take place till the government be dissolved. [. . .]

Chapter 14
Of Prerogative

159. Where the legislative and executive power are in distinct hands, (as they are in all moderated monarchies and well-framed governments) there the good of the society requires, that several things should be left to the discretion of him that has the executive power. For the legislators not being able to foresee, and provide by laws, for all that may be useful to the community, the executor of the laws having the power in his hands, has by the common law of nature a right to make use of it for the good of the society, in many cases, where the municipal law has given no direction, till the legislative can conveniently be assembled to provide for it. Many things there are, which the law can by no means provide for; and those must necessarily be left to the discretion of him that has the executive power in his hands, to be ordered by him as the public good and advantage shall require: nay, it is fit that the laws themselves should in some cases give way to the executive power, or rather to this fundamental law of nature and government, viz. That, as much as may be, all the members of the society are to be preserved. For since many accidents may happen, wherein a strict and rigid observation of the laws may do harm; (as not to pull down an innocent man's house to stop the fire, when the next to it is burning) and a man may come sometimes within the reach of the law, which

makes no distinction of persons, by an action that may deserve reward and pardon; it is fit the ruler should have a power, in many cases, to mitigate the severity of the law, and pardon some offenders. For the *end of government* being the *preservation of all*, as much as may be, even the guilty are to be spared, where it can prove no prejudice to the innocent.

160. This power to act according to discretion, for the public good, without the prescription of the law, and sometimes even against it, is that which is called *prerogative*. For since in some governments the law-making power is not always in being, and is usually too numerous, and so too slow for the dispatch requisite to execution; and because also it is impossible to foresee, and so by laws to provide for all accidents and necessities that may concern the public, or to make such laws as will do no harm, if they are executed with an inflexible rigour on all occasions, and upon all persons that may come in their way; therefore there is a latitude left to the executive power, to do many things of choice which the laws do not prescribe.

161. This power, whilst employed for the benefit of the community, and suitably to the trust and ends of the government, *is undoubted prerogative*, and never is questioned. For the people are very seldom or never scrupulous or nice in the point; they are far from examining prerogative, whilst it is in any tolerable degree employed for the use it was meant; that is, for the good of the people, and not manifestly against it. But if there comes to be a *question* between the executive power and the people, about a thing claimed as a *prerogative*, the tendency of the exercise of such prerogative to the good or hurt of the people will easily decide that question. [. . .]

163. And therefore they have a very wrong notion of government, who say, that the people have *encroached upon the prerogative*, when they have got any part of it to be defined by positive laws. For in so doing they have not pulled from the prince any thing that of right belonged to him, but only declared, that that power which they indefinitely left in his or his ancestors hands, to be exercised for their good, was not a thing which they intended him when he used it otherwise. For the end of government being the good of the community, whatsoever alterations are made in it, tending to that end, cannot be an encroachment upon any body, since no body in government can have a right tending to any other end: and those only are encroachments which prejudice or hinder the public good. Those who say otherwise, speak as if the prince had a distinct and separate interest from the good of the community, and was not made for it; the root and source from which spring almost all those evils and disorders which happen in kingly governments. And indeed, if that be so, the people under his government are not a society of rational creatures, entered into a community for their mutual good; they are not such as have set rulers over themselves, to guard and promote that good; but are to be looked on as an herd of inferior creatures under the dominion of a master, who keeps them and works them for his own pleasure or profit. If men were so void of reason, and brutish, as to enter into society upon such terms, prerogative might indeed be, what some men would have it, an arbitrary power to do things hurtful to the people.

164. But since a rational creature cannot be supposed, when free, to put himself into subjection to another, for his own harm; (though, where he finds a good and wise ruler, he may not perhaps think it either necessary or useful to set precise bounds to his power in all things) prerogative can be nothing but the people's permitting their rulers to do several things, of their own free choice, where the law was silent, and sometimes too against the direct letter of the law, for the public good; and their acquiescing in it when so done. For as a good prince, who is mindful of the trust put into his hands, and careful of the good of his people, cannot have too much prerogative, that is, power to do good; so a weak and ill prince, who would claim that power which his predecessors exercised without the direction of the law, as a prerogative belonging to him by right of his office, which he may exercise at his pleasure, to make or promote an interest distinct from that of the public, gives the people an occasion to claim their right, and limit that power, which, whilst it was exercised for their good, they were content should be tacitly allowed. [. . .]

168. The old question will be asked in this matter of prerogative, "But who shall be judge when this power is made a right use of?" I answer: between an executive power in being, with such a prerogative, and a legislative that depends upon his will for their convening, there can be no *judge on earth*; as there can be none between the legislative and the people, should either the executive or the legislative, when

they have got the power in their hands, design, or go about to enslave or destroy them. The people have no other remedy in this, as in all other cases where they have no judge on earth, but to *appeal to heaven.* For the rulers, in such attempts, exercising a power the people never put into their hands, (who can never be supposed to consent that any body should rule over them for their harm) do that which they have not a right to do. And where the body of the people, or any single man, is deprived of their right, or is under the exercise of a power without right, and have no appeal on earth, then they have a liberty to appeal to heaven, whenever they judge the cause of sufficient moment. And therefore, *though the people cannot* be *judge,* so as to have, by the constitution of that society, any superior power to determine and give effective sentence in the case; yet they have, by a law antecedent and paramount to all positive laws of men, reserved that ultimate determination to themselves which belongs to all mankind, where there lies no appeal on earth, viz. to judge, whether they have just cause to make their appeal to heaven. And this judgment they cannot part with, it being out of a man's power so to submit himself to another, as to give him a liberty to destroy him; God and nature never allowing a man so to abandon himself, as to neglect his own preservation: and since he cannot take away his own life, neither can he give another power to take it. Nor let any one think, this lays a perpetual foundation for disorder; for this operates not, till the inconveniency is so great, that the majority feel it, and are weary of it, and find a necessity to have it amended. But this the executive power, or wise princes, never need come in the danger of: and it is the thing, of all others, they have most need to avoid, as of all others the most perilous. [. . .]

Chapter 18
Of Tyranny

199. As usurpation is the exercise of power, which another hath a right to, so *tyranny is the exercise of power beyond right,* which no body can have a right to. And this is making use of the power any one has in his hands, not for the good of those who are under it, but for his own private separate advantage.—When the governor, however intitled, makes not the law, but his will, the rule; and his commands and actions are not directed to the preservation of the properties of his people, but the satisfaction of his own ambition, revenge, covetousness, or any other irregular passion.

200. If one can doubt this to be truth, or reason, because it comes from the obscure hand of a subject, I hope the authority of a king will make it pass with him. King James the first, in his speech to the parliament, 1603, tells them thus: "I will ever prefer the weal of the public, and of the whole commonwealth, in making of good laws and constitutions, to any particular and private ends of mine. Thinking ever the wealth and weal of the commonwealth to be my greatest weal and worldly felicity; a point wherein a lawful king doth directly differ from a tyrant. For I do acknowledge, that the special and greatest point of difference that is between a rightful king and an usurping tyrant, is this, that whereas the proud and ambitious tyrant doth think his kingdom and people are only ordained for satisfaction of his desires and unreasonable appetites, the righteous and just king doth by the contrary acknowledge himself to be ordained for the procuring of the wealth and property of his people." [. . .]

202. *Wherever law ends, tyranny begins,* if the law be transgressed to another's harm; and whosoever in authority exceeds the power given him by the law, and makes use of the force he has under his command, to compass that upon the subject, which the law allows not, ceases in that to be a magistrate; and, acting without authority, may be opposed as any other man, who by force invades the right of another. [. . .]

Chapter 19
Of the Dissolution of Government

[. . .] 212. Besides this overturning from without, *governments are dissolved from within.*

First, When the *legislative* is *altered.* Civil society being a state of peace, amongst those who are of it, from whom the state of war is excluded by the umpirage, which they have provided in their legislative, for the ending all differences that may arise amongst any of them; it is in their legislative, that the members of a commonwealth are united, and combined together into one coherent living body. This *is the soul that gives form, life, and unity* to the commonwealth: from hence the several members have their mutual influence, sympathy, and connexion; and therefore, when the legislative is broken, or dissolved, dissolution and death follows. For, *the essence and union of the society* consisting in having one will, the legislative, when once established by the majority, has the declaring, and as it were keeping of that will. The *constitution of the legislative* is the first and fundamental act of society, whereby provision is made for the *continuation of their union,* under the direction of persons, and bonds of laws, made by persons authorized thereunto, by the consent and appointment of the people; without which no one man, or number of men, amongst them, can have authority of making laws that shall be binding to the rest. When any one, or more, shall take upon them to make laws, whom the people have not appointed so to do, they make laws without authority, which the people are not therefore bound to obey; by which means they come again to be out of subjection, and may constitute to themselves a new legislative, as they think best, being in full liberty to resist the force of those, who without authority would impose any thing upon them. Every one is at the disposure of his own will, when those who had, by the delegation of the society, the declaring of the public will, are excluded from it, and others usurp the place, who have no such authority or delegation. [. . .]

219. There is one way more whereby such a government may be dissolved, and that is, when he who has the supreme executive power neglects and abandons that charge, so that the laws already made can no longer be put in execution. This is demonstratively to reduce all to anarchy, and so effectually to *dissolve the government.* For laws not being made for themselves, but to be, by their execution, the bonds of the society, to keep every part of the body politic in its due place and function; when that totally ceases, the *government* visibly *ceases,* and the people become a confused multitude, without order or connexion. Where there is no longer the administration of justice, for the securing of men's rights, nor any remaining power within the community to direct the force, or provide for the necessities of the public; there certainly is *no government left.* Where the laws cannot be executed, it is all one as if there were no laws; and a government without laws is, I suppose, a mystery in politics, inconceivable to human capacity, and inconsistent with human society.

220. In these and the like cases, *when the government is dissolved,* the people are at liberty to provide for themselves, by erecting a new legislative, differing from the other, by the change of persons, or form, or both, as they shall find it most for their safety and good. For the *society* can never, by the fault of another, lose the native and original right it has to preserve itself; which can only be done by a settled legislative, and a fair and impartial execution of the laws made by it. But the state of mankind is not so miserable that they are not capable of using this remedy, till it be too late to look for any. To tell *people* they *may provide for themselves,* by erecting a new legislative, when by oppression, artifice, or being delivered over to a foreign power, their old one is gone, is only to tell them, they may expect relief when it is too late, and the evil is past cure. This is in effect no more, than to bid them first be slaves, and then to take care of their liberty; and when their chains are on, tell them, they may act like freemen. This, if barely so, is rather mockery than relief; and men can never be secure from tyranny, if there be no means to escape it, till they are perfectly under it: And therefore it is, that they have not only a right to get out of it, but to prevent it.

221. There is, therefore, secondly, another way whereby *governments are dissolved,* and that is, when the legislative, or the prince either of them, act contrary to their trust.

First, The *legislative acts against the trust* reposed in them, when they endeavour to invade the property of the subject, and to make themselves, or any part of the community, masters, or arbitrary disposers of the lives, liberties, or fortunes of the people.

222. The reason why men enter into society, is the preservation of their property; and the end why they choose and authorize a legislative, is, that there may be laws made, and rules set, as guards and fences to the properties of all the members of the society: to limit the power, and moderate the dominion, of every part and member of the society. For since it can never be supposed to be the will of the society, that the legislative should have a power to destroy that, which every one designs to secure, by entering into society, and for which the people submitted themselves to legislators of their own making, whenever

the *legislators endeavour to take away and destroy the property of the people,* or to reduce them to slavery under arbitrary power, they put themselves into a state of war with the people, who are thereupon absolved from any farther obedience, and are left to the common refuge, which God hath provided for all men, against force and violence. Whensoever therefore the *legislative* shall transgress this fundamental rule of society; and either by ambition, fear, folly or corruption, *endeavour to grasp* themselves, *or put into the hands of any other an absolute power* over the lives, liberties, and estates of the people; by this breach of trust they *forfeit the power,* the people had put into their hands, for quite contrary ends, and it devolves to the people, who have a right to resume their original liberty, and, by the establishment of a new legislative, (such as they shall think fit) provide for their own safety and security, which is the end for which they are in society. What I have said here, concerning the legislative in general, holds true also concerning the supreme executor, who having a double trust put in him, both to have a part in the legislative, and the supreme execution of the law, acts against both, when he goes about to set up his own arbitrary will, as the law of the society. He *acts* also *contrary to his trust,* when he either employs the force, treasure, and offices of the society to corrupt the *representatives,* and gain them to his purposes; or openly pre-engages the *electors,* and prescribes to their choice, such, whom he has by solicitations, threats, promises, or otherwise, won to his designs: and employs them to bring in such, who have promised before-hand, what to vote, and what to enact. Thus to regulate candidates and electors, and new model the ways of election, what is it but to cut up the government by the roots, and poison the very fountain of public security? for the people having reserved to themselves the choice of their *representatives,* as the fence to their properties, could do it for no other end, but that they might always be freely chosen, and so chosen, freely act, and advise, as the necessity of the commonwealth, and the public good should, upon examination and mature debate, be judged to require. This, those who give their votes before they hear the debate, and have weighed the reasons on all sides, are not capable of doing. To prepare such an assembly as this, and endeavour to set up the declared abettors of his own will, for the true representatives of the people, and the law-makers of the society, is certainly as great a *breach of trust,* and as perfect a declaration of a design to subvert the government, as is possible to be met with. To which if one shall add rewards and punishments visibly employed to the same end, and all the arts of perverted law made use of, to take off and destroy all that stand in the way of such a design, and will not comply and consent to betray the liberties of their country, it will be past doubt what is doing. What power they ought to have in the society, who thus employ it contrary to the trust that went along with it in its first institution, is easy to determine; and one cannot but see, that he, who has once attempted any such thing as this, cannot any longer be trusted.

223. To this perhaps it will be said, that the people being ignorant, and always discontented, to lay the foundation of government in the unsteady opinion and uncertain humour of the people, is to expose it to certain ruin; and *no government will be able long to subsist,* if the people may set up a new legislative, whenever they take offence at the old one. To this I answer, quite the contrary. People are not so easily got out of their old forms as some are apt to suggest. They are hardly to be prevailed with to amend the acknowledged faults in the frame they have been accustomed to. And if there be any original defects, or adventitious ones introduced by time, or corruption: it is not an easy thing to get them changed, even when all the world sees there is an opportunity for it. This slowness and aversion in the people to quit their old constitutions, has in the many revolutions which have been seen in this kingdom, in this and former ages, still kept us to, or, after some interval of fruitless attempts, still brought us back again to, our old legislative of king, lords, and commons: and whatever provocations have made the crown be taken from some of our princes heads, they never carried the people so far as to place it in another line.

224. But it will be said, this *hypothesis* lays a *ferment for* frequent *rebellion.* To which I *answer,*

First, no more than any other *hypothesis:* for when the people are made miserable, and find themselves *exposed to the ill usage of arbitrary power,* cry up their governors as much as you will, for *sons of Jupiter;* let them be sacred or divine, descended, or authorized from heaven; give them out for whom or what you please, the same will happen. *The people generally ill treated*, and contrary to right, will be ready upon any occasion to ease themselves of a burden that sits heavy upon them. They will wish, and seek for the opportunity, which in the change, weakness, and accidents of human affairs, seldom delays long to offer itself. He must have lived but a little while in the world, who has not seen examples of this in his time; and he must have read very little, who cannot produce examples of it in all sorts of governments in the world.

225. *Secondly*, I answer, such *revolutions happen* not upon every little mismanagement in public affairs. *Great mistakes* in the ruling part, many wrong and inconvenient laws, and all the slips of human frailty, will be *borne by the people* without mutiny or murmur. But if a long train of abuses, prevarications and artifices, all tending the same way, make the design visible to the people, and they cannot but feel what they lie under, and see whither they are going; it is not to be wondered, that they should then rouse themselves, and endeavour to put the rule into such hands which may secure to them the ends for which government was at first erected; and without which, ancient names, and specious forms, are so far from being better, that they are much worse, than the state of nature, or pure anarchy; the inconveniencies being all as great and as near, but the remedy farther off and more difficult.

226. *Thirdly*, I answer, that *this doctrine* of a power in the people of providing for their safety anew, by a new legislative, when their legislators have acted contrary to their trust, by invading their property, is the *best fence against rebellion*, and the probablest means to hinder it. For *rebellion* being an opposition, not to persons, but authority, which is founded only in the constitutions and laws of the government; those, whoever they be, who by force break through, and by force justify their violation of them, are truly and properly *rebels*. For when men, by entering into society and civil government, have excluded force, and introduced laws for the preservation of property, peace, and unity amongst themselves; those who set up force again in opposition to the laws, do *rebellare*, that is, bring back again the state of war, and are properly rebels: Which they who are in power, (by the pretence they have to authority, the temptation of force they have in their hands, and the flattery of those about them) being likeliest to do; the properest way to prevent the evil, is to shew them the danger and injustice of it, who are under the greatest temptation to run into it.

227. In both the forementioned cases, when either the legislative is changed, or the legislators act contrary to the end for which they were constituted, those who are guilty are *guilty of rebellion*; for if any one by force takes away the established legislative of any society, and the laws by them made pursuant to their trust, he thereby takes away the umpirage, which every one had consented to, for a peaceable decision of all their controversies, and a bar to the state of war amongst them. They who remove, or change the legislative, take away this decisive power, which no body can have but by the appointment and consent of the people; and so destroying the authority which the people did, and no body else can set up, and introducing a power which the people hath not authorized, they actually *introduce a state of war*, which is that of force without authority; and thus by removing the legislative established by the society, (in whose decisions the people acquiesced and united, as to that of their own will) they untie the knot, and *expose the people anew to the state of war*. And if those, who by force take away the legislative, are *rebels*, the *legislators* themselves, as has been shewn, can be no less esteemed so; when they, who were set up for the protection and preservation of the people, their liberties and properties, shall by force invade and endeavour to take them away; and so they putting themselves into a state of war with those who made them the protectors and guardians of their peace, are properly, and with the greatest aggravation, *rebellantes*, rebels. [. . .]

240. Here, it is like, the common question will be made, *Who shall be judge*, whether the prince or legislative act contrary to their trust? This, perhaps, ill-affected and factious men may spread amongst the people, when the prince only makes use of his due prerogative. To this I reply, "The people shall be judge;" for who shall be *judge* whether his trustee or deputy acts well, and according to the trust reposed in him, but he who deputes him, and must by having deputed him, have still a power to discard him, when he fails in his trust? If this be reasonable in particular cases of private men, why should it be otherwise in that of the greatest moment, where the welfare of millions is concerned, and also where the evil, if not

prevented, is greater, and the redress very difficult, dear, and dangerous?

241. But farther, this question, ("Who shall be judge?") cannot mean that there is no judge at all. For where there is no judicature on earth, to decide controversies amongst men, God in heaven is judge. He alone, it is true, is judge of the right. But *every man* is *judge* for himself, as in all other cases, so in this, whether another hath put himself into a state of war with him, and whether he should appeal to the supreme judge, as Jephthah did.

242. If a controversy arise betwixt a prince and some of the people, in a matter where the law is silent, or doubtful, and the thing be of great consequence, I should think the proper *umpire*, in such a case, should be the body of the *people*: for in cases where the prince hath a trust reposed in him, and is dispensed from the common ordinary rules of the law; there, if any men find themselves aggrieved, and think the prince acts contrary to, or beyond that trust, who so proper to *judge* as the body of the *people*, (who, at first, lodged that trust in him) how far they meant it should extend? But if the prince, or whoever they be in the administration, decline that way of determination, the appeal then lies no where but to heaven; force between either persons, who have no known superior on earth, or which permits no appeal to a judge on earth, being properly a state of war, wherein the appeal lies only to heaven; and in that state the *injured party must judge* for himself, when he will think fit to make use of that appeal, and put himself upon it.

243. To conclude, The *power that every individual gave the society*, when he entered into it, can never revert to the individuals gain, as long as the society lasts, but will always remain in the community; because without this there can be no community, no commonwealth, which is contrary to the original agreement: so also when the society hath placed the legislative in any assembly of men, to continue in them and their successors, with direction and authority for providing such successors, the *legislative can never revert to the people* whilst that government lasts: Because, having provided a legislative with power to continue for ever, they have given up their political power to the legislative, and cannot resume it. But if they have set limits to the duration of their legislative, and made this supreme power in any person, or assembly, only temporary; or else, when by the miscarriages of those in authority, it is forfeited; upon the forfeiture, or at the determination of the time set, *it reverts to the society*, and the people have a right to act as supreme, and continue the legislative in themselves; or erect a new form, or under the old form place it in new hands, as they think good.

English Bill of Rights (1689)

An Act Declaring the Rights and Liberties of the Subject and Settling the Succession of the Crown

Whereas the Lords Spiritual and Temporal and Commons assembled at Westminster, lawfully, fully and freely representing all the estates of the people of this realm, did upon the thirteenth day of February in the year of our Lord one thousand six hundred eighty-eight [old style date] present unto their Majesties, then called and known by the names and style of William and Mary, prince and princess of Orange, being present in their proper persons, a certain declaration in writing made by the said Lords and Commons in the words following, viz.:

- Whereas the late King James the Second, by the assistance of divers evil counsellors, judges and ministers employed by him, did endeavour to subvert and extirpate the

Protestant religion and the laws and liberties of this kingdom;

- By assuming and exercising a power of dispensing with and suspending of laws and the execution of laws without consent of Parliament; By committing and prosecuting divers worthy prelates for humbly petitioning to be excused from concurring to the said assumed power;
- By issuing and causing to be executed a commission under the great seal for erecting a court called the Court of Commissioners for Ecclesiastical Causes;
- By levying money for and to the use of the Crown by pretence of prerogative for other time and in other manner than the same was granted by Parliament;
- By raising and keeping a standing army within this kingdom in time of peace without consent of Parliament, and quartering soldiers contrary to law;
- By causing several good subjects being Protestants to be disarmed at the same time when papists were both armed and employed contrary to law;
- By violating the freedom of election of members to serve in Parliament;
- By prosecutions in the Court of King's Bench for matters and causes cognizable only in Parliament, and by divers other arbitrary and illegal courses;
- And whereas of late years partial corrupt and unqualified persons have been returned and served on juries in trials, and particularly divers jurors in trials for high treason which were not freeholders;
- And excessive bail hath been required of persons committed in criminal cases to elude the benefit of the laws made for the liberty of the subjects;
- And excessive fines have been imposed;
- And illegal and cruel punishments inflicted;
- And several grants and promises made of fines and forfeitures before any conviction or judgment against the persons upon whom the same were to be levied;
- All which are utterly and directly contrary to the known laws and statutes and freedom of this realm;

And whereas the said late King James the Second having abdicated the government and the throne being thereby vacant, his Highness the prince of Orange (whom it hath pleased Almighty God to make the glorious instrument of delivering this kingdom from popery and arbitrary power) did (by the advice of the Lords Spiritual and Temporal and divers principal persons of the Commons) cause letters to be written to the Lords Spiritual and Temporal being Protestants, and other letters to the several counties, cities, universities, boroughs and cinque ports, for the choosing of such persons to represent them as were of right to be sent to Parliament, to meet and sit at Westminster upon the two and twentieth day of January in this year one thousand six hundred eighty and eight, in order to such an establishment as that their religion, laws and liberties might not again be in danger of being subverted, upon which letters elections having been accordingly made;

And thereupon the said Lords Spiritual and Temporal and Commons, pursuant to their respective letters and elections, being now assembled in a full and free representative of this nation, taking into their most serious consideration the best means for attaining the ends aforesaid, do in the first place (as their ancestors in like case have usually done) for the vindicating and asserting their ancient rights and liberties declare:

- That the pretended power of suspending the laws or the execution of laws by regal authority without consent of Parliament is illegal;
- That the pretended power of dispensing with laws or the execution of laws by regal authority, as it hath been assumed and exercised of late, is illegal;
- That the commission for erecting the late Court of Commissioners for Ecclesiastical Causes, and all other commissions and courts of like nature, are illegal and pernicious;
- That levying money for or to the use of the Crown by pretence of prerogative, without grant of Parliament, for longer time, or in

other manner than the same is or shall be granted, is illegal;

- That it is the right of the subjects to petition the king, and all commitments and prosecutions for such petitioning are illegal;
- That the raising or keeping a standing army within the kingdom in time of peace, unless it be with consent of Parliament, is against law;
- That the subjects which are Protestants may have arms for their defence suitable to their conditions and as allowed by law;
- That election of members of Parliament ought to be free;
- That the freedom of speech and debates or proceedings in Parliament ought not to be impeached or questioned in any court or place out of Parliament;
- That excessive bail ought not to be required, nor excessive fines imposed, nor cruel and unusual punishments inflicted;
- That jurors ought to be duly impaneled and returned, and jurors which pass upon men in trials for high treason ought to be freeholders;
- That all grants and promises of fines and forfeitures of particular persons before conviction are illegal and void;
- And that for redress of all grievances, and for the amending, strengthening and preserving of the laws, Parliaments ought to be held frequently.

And they do claim, demand and insist upon all and singular the premises as their undoubted rights and liberties, and that no declarations, judgments, doings or proceedings to the prejudice of the people in any of the said premises ought in any wise to be drawn hereafter into consequence or example; to which demand of their rights they are particularly encouraged by the declaration of his Highness the prince of Orange as being the only means for obtaining a full redress and remedy therein. [. . .]

2

Liberty and Monarchy under the "Balanced" Constitution

The eighteenth-century English essayist Joseph Addison, in his "Letter against Parties," shared secondhand an account from his "worthy friend, Sir Roger," describing an event from his days as a young schoolboy. A simple question regarding the name and location of a street, Addison recounted, sparked sectarian vitriol from all quarters. One respondent accused the author of being a "Popish Cur" simply for using the street's traditional name, while another deemed him a "Prickeared Cur"—*prick-ear* serving to disparage Puritans for their short hair—if he acceded to modify the name of the street more in line with Puritan sensibilities. Addison told this story to illustrate the level of divisiveness in British society in the late sixteenth and early seventeenth centuries, and to demonstrate the ubiquity, even over the smallest things, of the dangers of party and the "Spirit of Division as rends a Government in to two distinct People." Addison's concern over the problems of political and religious division reflected the lingering memory of sectarian strife in the English imagination. In the still nascent liberal societies of England and its colonies, worry about the debilitating, corrosive effects of "party" or "faction" pervaded the public discourses that informed the thinking of eighteenth-century statesmen and scholars throughout the British Atlantic.

This chapter explores the writing of scholars as well as statesmen who sought ways to understand factionalism even as the seeds of democracy were sown on both sides of the Atlantic. Often they came to similar conclusions. Twenty-five years after Addison published his essay, in a speech on the occasion of his election as Speaker of the Virginia House of Burgesses, Sir John Randolph celebrated the spirit of disinterest at the highest level of Virginia's government. Randolph praised Colonial Governor William Gooch for rising above party interest, noting that the "abstruse" art of governing is frustrated by the "pride and interest of the person that governs." Scottish philosopher David Hume analyzed the same set of issues. Hume affirmed without equivocation that "factions subvert government, render laws impotent, and beget the fiercest animosities among men of the same nation," particularly those factions that are driven by principles—ideas—and not simply personal allegiance or affiliation. By finding ways to disperse power, the abuse of power by both king and lord protector, by oligarchs and demagogues, could be mitigated, and perhaps prevented. Even before democracy emerged to dominate the world stage, the problems of faction—omnipresent in a healthy republic—were a matter of focus.

The French philosopher Charles Louis Secondat, Baron de la Brède et de Montesquieu, developed his theory of power checking power in response to these concerns. For Montesquieu, liberty was only possible in "moderate" governments, those governments wherein there is no abuse of power. This could only be ensured through the dispersal of power, and the setting of separated mechanisms of power in counterpoise against one another. Equilibrium was the key to sound government, framed by the rule of law and sustained by the careful checking of the forces of power. Hume and Montesquieu both recognized the realities of the contest between authority and liberty, and found the solution not in the choice of one over the other, but in the balance between them.

These ideas proved especially resonant in the American colonies. In the decades after the Glorious Revolution, British government ended its efforts to formally subordinate the colonies to imperial authority. A long period of "salutary neglect" followed, leaving colonial legislatures to manage most of their affairs by their own lights. A large, self-reliant and literate population emerged, eager to absorb the ideas of Hume and Montesquieu, as well as James Harrington, John Locke, and Algernon Sydney, and a particularly powerful set of essays by two popular English social critics, Thomas Gordon and John Trenchard. Initially in response to the South Sea Bubble scandal of 1721, their essays, penned under the pseudonyms "Independent Whig" and, more famously, "Cato," developed into an expansive advocacy of liberty against traditional abuses of power. Influenced by Locke and Sydney, Gordon and Trenchard championed free press and religious toleration. Their writings soon became associated, especially in the colonies, with defiance of tyranny and the promotion of greater freedom. Some historians view the Cato letters as the most influential set of documents shaping the growing liberal spirit within the colonies, arming the colonists with intellectual weapons that would prove especially powerful during the crises of the 1760s and 1770s.

The ambiguous relationship of colonies to the larger empire could on occasion evoke real anxiety in the colonies, and led some colonial thinkers to inspired, if intermittent, consideration of the nature of liberty. Even before the clarion protests of Gordon and Trenchard, colonist John Wise of Ipswich held to the essential reality of a "Natural Right [by which] all Men are born free." For Wise, we are both sociable and free individuals, and we cannot be the one without the other, a sentiment echoing the previous conclusions of John Locke and, before him, Richard Hooker. Wise's political theory represents a turn in the colonial mind toward a modern conception of liberty and democracy, one that would await full development in the politically charged atmosphere of the 1760s and early 1770s leading up to the American Revolution.

Few colonists soldiered so steadfastly in the cause of liberty than Jonathan Mayhew. Fifteen years before the Stamp Act crisis—partly noted for the slogan "no taxation without representation," a phrase attributed by some to Mayhew—the Boston cleric thundered against the restoration of the reputation of King Charles I in his sermon titled "A Discourse Concerning Unlimited Submission and Non-Resistance to the Higher Power." Delving into the long tradition of English liberties and limited monarchy, Mayhew's argument concluded that the regicide of Charles, or any monarch, is within the rights of all people faced with violations of their ancient liberties. Mayhew's sermon is notable because it returns to the text of St. Paul's Epistle to the Romans to argue that submission to civil authority was never intended as acquiescence to the tyrant. Long after Mayhew's bold declamation, John Adams noted the widespread influence of Mayhew's ideas. Mayhew, like Gordon and Trenchard before him and Adams after, vigorously advanced the growing cause of liberty as the essential principle of a just society.

William Livingston of New Jersey, who would eventually become an important actor in the American Revolution, considered liberty to be a vital requisite to both the enjoyment of life's gifts and the fostering of character. "The Subjects of a free State," Livingston averred, "have something open and generous in their Carriage; something of Grandeur and Sublimity in their Appearance, resulting from their Freedom and Independence," not to be found under the yoke of absolute monarchy. Mild and limited government, for Livingston, meant a lawful, free, and happy citizenry capable of a more developed sense of the responsibilities of freedom.

Questions regarding freedom penetrate still more deeply when framed within the theology of Calvinism. In response to the Arminian doctrine of conditioned election, which allows for free will, the Calvinist theologian Jonathan Edwards called for a revival of the older Calvinist belief in unconditional election and irresistible grace. That is, according to Genevan theologian John Calvin and his followers, one is predestined for salvation and cannot work toward redemption. There are no conditions attached to one's election, for election is predetermined even before time. Arminianism—first developed by Dutch Calvinist Johannes Arminius—allows for conditional grace, the belief that human free will can resist God's call. However, Arminians still held to a notion that God could foresee who would answer the call; the key difference was found in the role of the will of the elect to choose the right answer. Additionally, the Arminian doctrine held that it is still possible to "fall from grace," an idea in opposition to the Calvinist notion that the elect are eternally saved. Edwards demanded a return to the spirit of Calvin's original doctrine of total depravity, unconditional grace, limited atonement, irresistible grace, and perseverance of the saints. God's grace is given arbitrarily, for Edwards, and any question concerning liberty must first confront this essential principle.

The implications of such theological debates, rarefied and abstract as they may seem, are immense. If Edwards is correct, the good society should be ordered along the lines of the earlier biblical commonwealths of New England (Rhode Island excepted). Human nature, depraved and weak, requires the guidance of law if an orderly, stable society is to be achieved. The concerns of the state and the concerns of religion are thoroughly implicated, each with the other. The liberal religious rationalism of Edwards' opponents, on the other hand, is considerably more compatible with the privatization of religion and the separation of church and state. In an Arminian conception, what matters is the inculcation of the right dispositions in the human will, the development of correct human faculties that will lead the individual to salvation. Freedom of conscience, then, is the more pressing concern, not the restraint of depravity. Such questions would reappear throughout the development of the concept of liberty within the American tradition.

Finally, confronting the embrace of liberty in the colonies, the problem of slavery continued to fix the attention of many colonial writers. William Byrd, Peter Fontaine, and the writings of the Georgia Trustees foreshadowed the festering problems of racial misapprehension and the aggravations of slavery as they persist in infecting American life and culture. The presence of an enslaved labor, while not yet a volatile issue, nonetheless would eventually prove to be the most divisive aspect within the young American nation, a division that would have been understood by Addison as a danger equal to the religious strife of the previous century.

Joseph Addison

Letter against Parties (1711)

Ne pueri, ne tanta animis assuescite bella:
Neu patriæ validas in viscera vertite vires.
Vir.

My worthy Friend Sir Roger, when we are talking of the Malice of Parties, very frequently tells us an Accident that happened to him when he was a School-Boy, which was at the Time. when the Feuds ran high between the Round-heads and Cavaliers. This worthy Knight being then but a Strippling, had Occasion to enquire which was the Way to St. *Anne*'s Lane, upon which the Person whom he spoke to, instead of answering his Question, called him a young Popish Cur, and asked him who had made *Anne* a Saint? The Boy being in some Confusion, enquired of the next he met, which was the Way to *Anne*'s Lane; but was called a Prick-eared Cur for his Pains, and instead of being shewn the Way, was told, that she had been a Saint before he was born, and would be one after he was hanged. Upon this, says Sir Roger, I did not think fit to repeat the former Question, but going into every Lane of the Neighbourhood, asked what they called the Name of that Lane. By which ingenious Artifice he found out the Place he enquired after, without giving Offence to any Party. Sir Roger, generally closes this Narrative with Reflections on the Mischief that Parties do in the Country; how they spoil good Neighbourhood, and make honest Gentlemen hate one another; besides that they manifestly tend to the Prejudice of the Land-Tax, and the Destruction of the Game.

There cannot a greater Judgment befall a Country than such a dreadful Spirit of Division as rends a Government into two distinct People, and makes them greater Strangers and more averse to one another, than if they were actually two different Nations. The Effects of such a Division are pernicious to the last degree; not only with Regard to those Advantages which they give the Common Enemy, but to those private Evils which they produce in the Heart of almost every particular Person. This Influence is very fatal both to Mens Morals and their Understandings; It sinks the Virtue of a Nation, and not only so, but destroys even Common Sense.

A furious Party-Spirit, when it rages in its full Violence, exerts it self in Civil War and Bloodshed; and when it is under its greatest Restraints naturally breaks out in Falsehood, Detraction, Calumny, and a partial Administration of Justice. In a Word, It fills a Nation with Spleen and Rancour, and extinguishes all the Seeds of Good-Nature, Compassion and Humanity.

Plutarch says very finely, That a Man should not allow himself to hate even his Enemies, because, says he, if you indulge this Passion in some Occasions, it will rise of it self in others; if you hate your Enemies, you will contract such a vicious Habit of Mind, as by Degrees will break out upon those who are your Friends, or those who are indifferent to you. I might here observe how admirably this Precept of Morality (which derives the Malignity of Hatred from the Passion it self, and not from its Object) answers to that great Rule which was dictated to the World about an Hundred Years before this Philosopher wrote; but instead of that, I shall only take notice, with a real Grief of Heart, that the Minds of many good Men among us appear sowered with Party-Principles, and alienated from one another in such a manner, as seems to me altogether inconsistent with the Dictates either of Reason or Religion. Zeal for a Publick Cause is apt to breed Passions in the Hearts of virtuous Persons, to which the Regard of their own private Interest would never have betrayed them.

If this Party-Spirit has so ill an Effect on our Morals, it has likewise a very great one upon our Judgments. We often hear a poor insipid Paper or Pamphlet cryed up, and sometimes a noble Piece depreciated, by those who are of a different Principle from the Author. One who is actuated by this Spirit is almost under an

Incapacity of discerning either real Blemishes or Beauties. A Man of Merit in a different Principle, is like an Object seen in two different Mediums, that appears crooked or broken, however straight and entire it may be in it self. For this Reason there is scarce a Person of any Figure in *England* who does not go by two contrary Characters, as opposite to one another as Light and Darkness. Knowledge and Learning suffer in a particular manner from this strange Prejudice, which at present prevails amongst all Ranks and Degrees in the *British* Nation. As Men formerly became eminent in learned Societies by their Parts and Acquisitions, they now distinguish themselves by the Warmth and Violence with which they espouse their respective Parties. Books are valued upon the like Considerations: An Abusive Scurrilous Style passes for Satyr, and a dull Scheme of Party-Notions is called fine Writing.

There is one Piece of Sophistry practised by both Sides, and that is the taking any scandalous Story that has been ever whispered or invented of a private Man, for a known undoubted Truth, and raising suitable Speculations upon it. Calumnies that have been never proved, or have been often refuted, are the ordinary Postulatums of these infamous Scribblers, upon which they proceed as upon first Principles granted by all Men, though in their Hearts they know they are false, or at best very doubtful. When they have laid these Foundations of Scurrility, it is no wonder that their Superstructure is every way answerable to them. If this shameless Practice of the present Age endures much longer, Praise and Reproach will cease to be Motives of Action in good Men.

There are certain Periods of Time in all Governments when this inhuman Spirit prevails. *Italy* was long torn in pieces by the *Guelfes* and *Gibellines,* and *France* by those who were for and against the League: But it is very unhappy for a Man to be born in such a stormy and tempestuous Season. It is the restless Ambition of Artful Men that thus breaks a People into Factions, and draws several well-meaning Persons to their Interest by a Specious Concern for their Country. How many honest Minds are filled with uncharitable and barbarous Notions, out of their Zeal for the Publick Good? What Cruelties and Outrages would they not commit against Men of an adverse Party, whom they would honour and esteem, if instead of considering them as they are represented, they knew them as they are? Thus are Persons of the greatest Probity seduced into shameful Errors and Prejudices, and made bad Men even by that noblest of Principles, the Love of their Country. I cannot here forbear mentioning the Famous *Spanish* Proverb, *If there were neither Fools, nor Knaves in the World, all People would be of one Mind.*

For my own part, I could heartily wish that all Honest Men would enter into an Association, for the Support of one another against the Endeavours of those whom they ought to look upon as their Common Enemies, whatsoever side they may belong to. Were there such an honest Body of Neutral Forces, we should never see the worst of Men in great Figures of Life, because they are useful to a Party; nor the best unregarded, because they are above practising those Methods which would be grateful to their Faction. We should then single every Criminal out of the Herd, and hunt him down, however formidable and overgrown he might appear: On the contrary, we should shelter distressed Innocence, and defend Virtue, however beset with Contempt or Ridicule, Envy or Defamation. In short, we should not any longer regard our Fellow-Subjects as Whigs or Tories, but should make the Man of Merit our Friend, and the Villain our Enemy.

John Wise

A Vindication of New England Churches (1717)

[. . .] 1. I Shall disclose several Principles of Natural Knowledge; plainly discovering the Law of Nature; or the true sentiments of Natural Reason, with Respect to Mans Being and Government. And in this Essay I shall peculiarly confine the discourse to two heads, *viz.*

1. Of the Natural [in distinction to the Civil] and then,
2. Of the Civil Being of Man. And I shall Principally take Baron *Puffendorff* for my Chief Guide and Spokesman.

1. I shall consider Man in a state of Natural Being, as a Free-Born Subject under the Crown of Heaven, and owing Homage to none but God himself. It is certain Civil Government in General, is a very Admirable Result of Providence, and an Incomparable Benefit to Man-kind, yet must needs be acknowledged to be the Effect of Humane Free-Compacts and not of Divine Institution; it is the Produce of Mans Reason, of Humane and Rational Combinations, and not from any direct Orders of Infinite Wisdom, in any positive Law wherein is drawn up this or that Scheme of Civil Government. Government [says the Lord *Warrington*] is necessary—in that no Society of Men can subsist without it; and that Particular Form of Government is necessary which best suits the Temper and Inclination of a People. Nothing can be Gods Ordinance, but what he has particularly Declared to be such; there is no particular Form of Civil Government described in Gods Word, neither does Nature prompt it. [. . .]

But to proceed under the head of a State of Natural Being, I shall more distinctly Explain the State of Humane Nature in its Original Capacity, as Man is placed on Earth by his Maker, and Cloathed with many Investitures, and Immunities which properly belong to Man separately considered. As,

1. The Prime Immunity in Mans State, is that he is most properly the Subject of the Law of Nature. He is the Favourite Animal on Earth; in that this Part of Gods Image, *viz.* Reason is Congenate with his Nature, wherein by a Law Immutable, Instampt upon his Frame, God has provided a Rule for Men in all their Actions; obliging each one to the performance of that which is Right, not only as to Justice, but likewise as to all other Moral Vertues, the which is nothing but the Dictate of Right Reason founded in the Soul of Man. [. . .] That which is to be drawn from Mans Reason, flowing from the true Current of that Faculty, when unperverted, may be said to be the Law of Nature; on which account, the Holy Scriptures declare it written on Mens hearts. For being indowed with a Soul, you may know from your self, how, and what you ought to act, Rom. 2. 14. *These having not a Law, are a Law to themselves*. So that the meaning is, when we acknowledge the Law of Nature to be the dictate of Right Reason, we must mean that the Understanding of Man is Endowed with such a power, as to be able, from the Contemplation of humane Condition to discover a necessity of Living agreeably with this Law: And likewise to find out some Principle, by which the Precepts of it, may be clearly and solidly Demonstrated. The way to discover the Law of Nature in our own State, is by a narrow Watch, and accurate Contemplation of our Natural Condition, and propensions. Others say this is the way to find out the Law of Nature. *scil.* If a Man any ways doubts, whether What he is going to do to another Man be agreeable to the Law of Nature, then let him suppose himself to be in that other Mans Room; And by this Rule effectually Executed. A Man must be a very dull Scholar to Nature not to make Proficiency in the Knowledge of her Laws. But more Particularly in pursuing our Condition for the discovery of the Law of Nature, this is very obvious to view, *viz.*

1. A Principle of Self-Love, and Self-Preservation, is very predominant in every Mans Being.
2. A Sociable Disposition.
3. An Affection or Love to Man-kind in General. And to give such Sentiments the force of a Law, we must suppose a God who takes care of all Mankind, and has thus obliged each one, as a Subject of higher Principles of Being, then meer Instincts. For that all Law properly considered, supposes a capable Subject, and a Superiour Power; And the Law of God which is Binding, is published by the Dictates of Right Reason as other ways: Therefore says *Plutarch, To follow God and obey Reason is the same thing.* But moreover that God has Established the Law of Nature, as the General Rule of Government, is further Illustrable from the many Sanctions in Providence, and from the Peace and Guilt of Conscience in them that either obey, or violate the Law of Nature. But moreover, the foundation of the Law of Nature with relation to Government, may be thus Discovered. *Scil.* Man is a Creature extreamly desirous of his own Preservation; of himself he is plainly Exposed to many Wants, unable to secure his own safety, and Maintenance without the Assistance of his fellows; and he is also able of returning Kindness by the furtherance of mutual Good; But yet Man is often found to be Malicious, Insolent and easily Provoked, and as powerful in Effecting mischief, as he is ready in designing it. Now that such a Creature may be Preserved, it is necessary that he be Sociable; that is, that he be capable and disposed to unite himself to those of his own species, and to Regulate himself towards them, that they may have no fair Reason to do him harm; but rather incline to promote his Interests, and secure his Rights and Concerns. This then is a Fundamental Law of Nature, that every Man as far as in him lies, do maintain a Sociableness with others, agreeable with the main end and disposition of humane Nature in general. For this is very apparent, that Reason and Society render Man the most potent of all Creatures. And Finally, from the Principles of Sociableness it follows as a fundamental Law of Nature, that Man is not so Wedded to his own Interest, but that he can make the Common good the mark of his Aim: And hence he becomes Capacitated to enter into a Civil State by the Law of Nature; for without this property in Nature, *viz.* Sociableness, which is for Cementing of parts, every Government would soon molder and dissolve.

2. The Second Great Immunity of Man is an Orginal Liberty Instampt upon his Rational Nature. He that intrudes upon this Liberty, Violates the Law of Nature. In this Discourse I shall wave the Consideration of Mans Moral Turpitude, but shall view him Physically as a Creature which God has made and furnished essentially with many Ennobling Immunities, which render him the most August Animal in the World, and still, whatever has happened since his Creation, he remains at the upper-end of Nature, and as such is a Creature of a very Noble Character. For as to his Dominion, the whole frame of the Lower Part of the Universe is devoted to his use, and at his Command; and his Liberty under the Conduct of Right Reason, is equal with his trust. Which Liberty may be briefly Considered, Internally as to his Mind, and Externally as to his Person.

1. The Internal Native Liberty of Mans Nature in general implies, a faculty of Doing or Omitting things according to the Direction of his Judgment. But in a more special meaning, this Liberty does not consist in a loose and ungovernable Freedom, or in an unbounded Licence of Acting. Such Licence is disagreeing with the condition and dignity of Man, and would make Man of a lower and meaner Constitution than Bruit Creatures; who in all their Liberties are kept under a better and more Rational Government, by their Instincts. Therefore as *Plutarch* says, *Those Persons only who live in Obedience to Reason, are worthy to be accounted free: They alone live as they Will, who have Learnt what they ought to Will.* So that the true Natural Liberty of Man, such as really and truely agrees to him, must be understood, as he is

Guided and Restrained by the Tyes of Reason, and Laws of Nature; all the rest is Brutal, if not worse.

2. Mans External Personal, Natural Liberty, Antecedent to all Humane parts, or Alliances must also be considered. And so every Man must be conceived to be perfectly in his own Power and disposal, and not to be controuled by the Authority of any other. And thus every Man, must be acknowledged equal to every Man, since all Subjection and all Command are equally banished on both sides; and considering all Men thus at Liberty, every Man has a Prerogative to Judge for himself, *viz.* What shall be most for his Behoof, Happiness and Well-being.

3. The Third Capital Immunity belonging to Mans Nature, is an equality amongst Men; Which is not to be denyed by the Law of Nature, till Man has Resigned himself with all his Rights for the sake of a Civil State; and then his Personal Liberty and Equality is to be cherished, and preserved to the highest degree, as will consist with all just distinctions amongst Men of Honour, and shall be agreeable with the publick Good. For Man has a high valuation of himself, and the passion seems to lay its first foundation [not in Pride, but] really in the high and admirable Frame and Constitution of Humane Nature. The Word Man, says my Author, is thought to carry somewhat of Dignity in its sound; and we commonly make use of this as the most proper and prevailing Argument against a rude Insulter, *viz. I am not a Beast or a Dog, but am a Man as well as your self.* Since then Humane Nature agrees equally with all persons; and since no one can live a Sociable Life with another that does not own or Respect him as a Man; It follows as a Command of the Law of Nature, that every Man Esteem and treat another as one who is naturally his Equal, or who is a Man as well as he. There be many popular, or plausible Reasons that greatly Illustrate this Equality, *viz.* that we all Derive our Being from one stock, the same Common Father of humane Race. On this Consideration *Boethius* checks the pride of the Insulting Nobility.

Quid Genus et Proavos Strepitis?
Si Primordia Vestra,
Auteremque Deum Spectas,
Nullus Degener Extat
Nisi vitiis Pejora Fovens,
Proprium Deserat Orturn.

Fondly our first Descent we Boast;
If whence at first our Breath we Drew,
The common springs of Life we view,
The Airy Notion soon is Lost.

The Almighty made us equal all;
But he that slavishly complyes
To do the Drudgery of Vice,
Denyes his high Original.

And also that our Bodies are Composed of matter, frail, brittle, and lyable to be destroyed by thousand Accidents; we all owe our Existence to the same Method of propagation. The Noblest Mortal in his Entrance on to the Stage of Life, is not distinguished by any pomp or of passage from the lowest of Mankind; and our Life hastens to the same General Mark: Death observes no Ceremony, but Knocks as loud at the Barriers of the Court, as at the Door of the Cottage. This Equality being admitted, bears a very great force in maintaining Peace and Friendship amongst Men. For that he who would use the Assistance of others, in promoting his own Advantage, ought as freely to be at their service, when they want his help on the like Occasions. *One Good turn Requires another,* is the Common Proverb; for otherwise he must need esteem others unequal to himself, who constantly demands their Aid, and as constantly denies his own. And whoever is of this Insolent Temper, cannot but highly displease those about him, and soon give Occasion of the Breach of the Common Peace. It was a Manly Reproof which *Charactacus* gave the *Romans. Nun Si vos Omnibus etc.* What! because you desire to be Masters of all Men, does it follow therefore that all Men should desire to be your Slaves, for that it is a Command of Natures Law, that no Man that has not obtained a particular and special Right, shall arrogate to himself a Larger share than his fellows, but shall admit others to equal Priviledges with himself. So that the Principle of Equality in a Natural State, is peculiarly transgressed by Pride, which is when a Man without sufficient reason prefers himself to others. And though as *Hensius,* Paraphrases upon *Aristotle's* Politicks to this Purpose. *viz. Nothing is more suitable to Nature, then that those who Excel in Understanding and Prudence, should Rule and Controul those who are less happy in those Advantages,* etc. Yet we must note, that there is room for an Answer, *scil.* That it would be the greatest absurdity to believe, that Nature actually Invests the Wise with a Sovereignity over the weak; or with a Right of forcing them against their Wills; for that no Sovereignty can be Established, unless some Humane Deed, or Covenant Precede: Nor does Natural fitness for Government make a Man presently Governour over another; for that as *Ulpian* says, *by a Natural Right all Men are born free;* and Nature having set all Men upon a Level and made them Equals, no Servitude or Subjection can be conceived without Inequality; and this cannot be made without Usurpation or Force in others, or Voluntary Compliance in those who Resign their freedom, and give away their degree of Natural Being. And thus we come,

2. To consider Man in a Civil State of Being; wherein we shall observe the great difference between a Natural, and Political State; for in the Latter State many Great disproportions appear, or at least many obvious distinctions are soon made amongst Men; which Doctrine is to be laid open under a few heads.

1. Every Man considered in a Natural State, must be allowed to be Free, and at his own dispose; yet to suit Mans Inclinations to Society; And in a peculiar manner to gratify the necessity he is in of publick Rule and Order, he is Impelled to enter into a Civil Community; and Divests himself of his Natural Freedom, and puts himself under Government; which amongst other things Comprehends the Power of Life and Death over Him; together with Authority to Injoyn him some things to which he has an utter Aversation, and to prohibit him other things, for which he may have as strong an Inclination; so that he may be often under this Authority, obliged to Sacrifice his Private, for the Publick Good. So that though Man is inclined to Society, yet he is driven to a Combination by great necessity. For that the true and leading Cause of forming Governments, and yielding up Natural Liberty, and throwing Mans Equality into a Common Pile to be new Cast by the Rules of fellowship; was really and truly to guard themselves against the Injuries Men were lyable to Interchangeably; for none so Good to Man, as Man, and yet none a greater Enemy. So that,

2. The first Humane Subject and Original of Civil Power is the People. For as they have a Power every Man over himself in a Natural State, so upon a Combination they can and do bequeath this Power unto others; and settle it according as their united discretion shall Determine. For that this is very plain, that when the Subject of Sovereign Power is quite Extinct, that Power returns to the People again. And when they are free, they may set up what species of Government they please; or if they rather incline to it, they may subside into a State of Natural Being, if it be plainly for the best. In the *Eastern* Country of the *Mogul,* we have some resemblance of the Case; for upon the Death of an absolute Monarch, they live so many days without a Civil Head; but in that *Interregnum,* those who survive the Vacancy, are glad to get into a Civil State again; and usually they are in a very Bloody Condition when they return under the Covert of a new Monarch; this project is to endear the People to a Tyranny, from the Experience they have so lately had of an Anarchy.

3. The formal Reason of Government is the Will of a Community, yielded up and surrendered to some other Subject, either of one particular Person, or more, Conveyed in the following manner.

Let us conceive in our Mind a multitude of Men, all Naturally Free and Equal; going about voluntarily, to Erect themselves into a new Common-Wealth. Now their Condition being such, to bring themselves into a Politick Body, they must needs Enter into divers Covenants.

1. They must Interchangeably each Man Covenant to joyn in one lasting Society, that they may be capable to concert the measures of their safety, by a Publick Vote.

2. A Vote or Decree must then nextly pass to set up some Particular speecies of Government over them. And if they are joyn in their first Compact upon absolute Terms, to stand to the Decision of the first Vote concerning the Species of Government: Then all are bound by the Majority to acquiesce in that particular Form thereby settled, though their own private Opinion, incline them to some other Model,

3. After a Decree has specified the Particular form of Government, then there will be need of a New Covenant, whereby those on whom Sovereignty is conferred, engage to take care of the Common Peace, and Welfare. And the Subjects on the other hand, to yield them faithful Obedience. In which Covenant is Included that Submission and Union of Wills, by which a State may be conceived to be but

one Person. So that the most proper Definition of a Civil State, is this, *viz.* A Civil State is a Compound Moral Person whose Will (United by those Covenants before passed) is the Will of all; to the end it may Use, and Apply the strength and riches of Private Persons towards maintaining the Common Peace, Security, and Well-being of all. Which may be conceived as tho' the whole State was now become but one Man; in which the aforesaid Covenants may be supposed under Gods Providence, to be the Divine *Fiat*, Pronounced by God, let us make Man. And by way of resemblance the aforesaid Being may be thus Anatomized.

1. The Sovereign Power is the Soul infused, giving Life and Motion to the whole Body.
2. Subordinate Officers are the Joynts by which the Body moves.
3. Wealth and Riches are the Strength.
4. Equity and Laws are the Reason.
5. Councellors the Memory.
6. *Salus Populi*, or the Happiness of the People, is the End of its Being; or main Business to be attended and done.
7. Concord amongst the Members, and all Estates, is the Health.
8. Sedition is Sickness, and Civil War Death.

4. The Parts of Sovereignty may be considered: So,

1. As it Prescribes the Rule of Action: It is rightly termed *Legislative Power.*
2. As it determines the Controversies of Subjects by the Standard of those Rules. So is it justly Termed Judiciary Power.
3. As it Arms the Subjects against Foreigners, or forbids Hostility, so its called the Power of Peace and War.
4. As it takes in Ministers for the discharge of Business, so it is called the Right of Appointing Magistrates. So that all great Officers and Publick Servants, must needs owe their Original to the Creating Power of Sovereignty. So that those whose Right it is to Create, may Dissolve the being of those who are Created, unless they cast them into an Immortal Frame. And yet must needs be dissoluble if they justly forfeit their being to their Creators.
5. The Chief End of Civil Communities, is, that Men thus conjoyned, may be secured against the Injuries, they are lyable to from their own Kind. For if every Man could secure himself singly; It would be great folly for him, to Renounce his Natural Liberty, in which every Man is his own King and Protector.
6. The Sovereign Authority besides that it inheres in every State as in a Common and General Subject. So farther according as it resides in some One Person, or in a Council (consisting of some Select Persons, or of all the Members of a Community) as in a proper and particular Subject, so it produced different Forms of Commonwealths, *viz.* Such as are either simple and regular, or mixt. [. . .]

Mixt Governments, which are various and of divers kinds [not now to be Enumerated] yet possibly the fairest in the World is that which has a Regular Monarchy; [in Distinction to what is Dispotick] settled upon a Noble Democracy as its Basis. And each part of the Government is so adjusted by Pacts and Laws that renders the whole Constitution an *Elisium.* It is said of the *British* Empire, *That it is such a Monarchy, as that by the necessary subordinate Concurrence of the Lords and Commons, in the Making and Repealing all Statutes or Acts of Parliament; it hath the main Advantages of an Aristocracy, and of a Democracy, and yet free from the Disadvantages and Evils of either. It is such a Monarchy, as by most Admirable Temperament affords very much to the Industry, Liberty, and Happiness of the Subject, and reserves enough for the Majesty and Prerogative of any King, who will own his People as Subjects, not as Slaves. It is a Kingdom, that of all the Kingdoms of the World, is most like to the Kingdom of Jesus Christ, whose Yoke is easy, and Burden light.* Present State of *England 1st.*

John Trenchard and Thomas Gordon

Cato's Letters (1719–1723)

Letter 33

Sir,

Considering what sort of a creature man is it is scarce possible to put him under too many restraints, when he is possessed of great power: He may possibly use it well; but they act most prudently, who, supposing that he would use it ill, inclose him within certain bounds, and make it terrible to him to exceed them.

Men that are above all fear, soon grow above all shame. [. . .] Even Nero had lived a great while inoffensively, and reigned virtuously: But finding at last that he might do what he would, he let loose his appetite for blood, and committed such mighty, such monstrous, such unnatural slaughters and outrages, as none but a heart bent on the study of cruelty could have devised. [. . .] [D]iscovering, by degrees, that [the people] would bear any thing, and his soldiers would execute every thing, he grew into an open defiance with mankind, and daily and wantonly wallowed in their blood. Having no other rival, he seemed to rival himself, and every day's wickedness was blacker than another.

Yet Nero was not the worst of all men: There have been thousands as bad as he, and only wanted the same opportunity to shew it. And there actually have been many princes in the world who have shed more blood, and done more mischief to mankind, than Nero did. I could instance in a late one, who destroyed more lives than ever Nero destroyed, perhaps an hundred to one. It makes no difference, that Nero committed butcheries out of cruelty, and the other only for his glory: However the world may be deceived by the change of names into an abhorrence of the one, and an admiration of the other; it is all one to a nation, when they are to be slaughtered, whether they be slaughtered by the hangman or by dragoons, in prison or in the field; nor is ambition better than cruelty, when it begets mischief as great.

It is nothing strange, that men, who think themselves unaccountable, should act unaccountably, and that all men would be unaccountable if they could: Even those who have done nothing to displease, do not know but some time or other they may; and no man cares to be at the entire mercy of another. Hence it is, that if every man had his will, all men would exercise dominion, and no man would suffer it. It is therefore owing more to the necessities of men, than to their inclinations, that they have put themselves under the restraint of laws, and appointed certain persons, called magistrates, to execute them; otherwise they would never be executed, scarce any man having such a degree of virtue as willingly to execute the laws upon himself; but, on the contrary, most men thinking them a grievance, when they come to meddle with themselves and their property. [Pompey] made laws when they suited his occasions, and broke them when they thwarted his will. And it is the character of almost every man possessed of Pompey's power: They intend them for a security to themselves, and for a terror to others. This shews the distrust that men have of men; and this made a great philosopher call the state of nature, a state of war; which definition is true in a restrained sense, since human societies and human laws are the effect of necessity and experience: Whereas were all men left to the boundless liberty which they claim from nature, every man would be interfering and quarrelling with another; every man would be plundering the acquisitions of another; the labour of one man would be the property of another; weakness would be the prey of force; and one man's industry would be the cause of another man's idleness.

Hence grew the necessity of government; which was the mutual contract of a number of men, agreeing upon certain terms of union and society, and putting themselves under penalties, if they violated these terms, which were called laws, and put into the hands of one or more men to execute. And thus men quitted part of their natural liberty to acquire civil security. But frequently the remedy proved worse than the disease; and human society had often no enemies so great as their own magistrates; who, where-ever they were trusted with too much power, always abused it, and grew mischievous to those who made them what they were. Rome, while she was free (that is, while she kept her magistrates within due bounds) could defend herself against all the world, and conquer it: But being enslaved (that is, her magistrates having broke their bounds) she could not defend herself against her own single tyrants, nor could they defend her against her foreign foes and invaders; for by their madness and cruelties they had destroyed her virtue and spirit, and exhausted her strength. This shews that those magistrates that are at absolute defiance with a nation, either cannot subsist long, or will not suffer the nation to subsist long; and that mighty traitors, rather than fall themselves, will pull down their country. [. . .]

The world is governed by men, and men by their passions; which, being boundless and insatiable, are always terrible when they are not controuled. Who was ever satiated with riches, or surfeited with power, or tired with honours? There is a tradition concerning Alexander, that having penetrated to the Eastern Ocean, and ravaged as much of this world as he knew, he wept that there was never another world for him to conquer. This, whether true or no, shews the spirit of the man, and indeed of human nature, whose appetites are infinite.

People are ruined by their ignorance of human nature; which ignorance leads them to credulity, and too great a confidence in particular men. They fondly imagine that he, who, possessing a great deal by their favour, owes them great gratitude, and all good offices, will therefore return their kindness: But, alas! How often are they mistaken in their favourites and trustees; who, the more they have given them, are often the more incited to take all, and to return destruction for generous usage. The common people generally think that great men have great minds, and scorn base actions; which judgment is so false, that the basest and worst of all actions have been done by great men: Perhaps they have not picked private pockets, but they have done worse; they have often disturbed, deceived, and pillaged the world: And he who is capable of the highest mischief, is capable of the meanest: He who plunders a country of a million of money, would in suitable circumstances steal a silver spoon; and a conqueror, who steals and pillages a kingdom, would, in an humbler fortune, rifle a portmanteau, or rob an orchard.

Political jealousy, therefore, in the people, is a necessary and laudable passion. But in a chief magistrate, a jealousy of his people is not so justifiable, their ambition being only to preserve themselves; whereas it is natural for power to be striving to enlarge itself, and to be encroaching upon those that have none. The most laudable jealousy of a magistrate is to be jealous for his people; which will shew that he loves them, and has used them well: But to be jealous *of* them, would denote that he has evil designs against them, and has used them ill. The people's jealousy tends to preserve liberty; and the prince's to destroy it. Venice is a glorious instance of the former, and so is England; and all nations who have lost their liberty, are melancholy proofs of the latter.

Power is naturally active, vigilant, and distrustful; which qualities in it push it upon all means and expedients to fortify itself, and upon destroying all opposition, and even all seeds of opposition, and make it restless as long as any thing stands in its way. It would do what it pleases, and have no check. Now, because liberty chastises and shortens power, therefore power would extinguish liberty; and consequently liberty has too much cause to be exceeding jealous, and always upon her defense. Power has many advantages over her; it has generally numerous guards, many creatures, and much treasure; besides, it has more craft and experience, less honesty and innocence: And whereas power can, and for the most part does, subsist where liberty is not, liberty cannot subsist without power; so that she has, as it were, the enemy always at her gates.

Some have said that magistrates being accountable to none but God ought to know no other restraint. But this reasoning is as frivolous as it is wicked; for no good man cares how many punishments and penalties lie in his way to an offence which he does not intend to commit: A man who does not mean to commit murder, is not sorry that murder is punished with death. And as to wicked men, their being accountable to God, whom they do not fear, is no security to use against their folly and malice; and to say that we ought to have no security against them, is to insult common sense, and give the lie to the first law of nature, that of self-preservation. Human reason says, that there is no obedience, no regard due to those rulers, who govern by no rule but their lust. Such men are no rulers; they are outlaws; who, being at defiance with God and man, are protected by no law of God, or of reason. By what precept, moral or divine, are we forbid to kill a wolf, or burn an infected ship? Is it unlawful to prevent wickedness and misery, and to resist the authors of them? Are crimes sanctified by their greatness? And is he who robs a country, and murders ten thousand, less a criminal, then he who steals single guineas, and takes away single lives? Is there any sin in preventing, and restraining, or resisting the greatest sin that can be committed, that of oppressing and destroying mankind by wholesale? Sure there never were such open, such shameless, such selfish impostors, as the advocates for lawless power! It is a damnable sin to oppress them; yet it is a damnable sin to oppose them when they oppress, or gain by oppression of others! When they are hurt themselves ever so little, or but think themselves hurt, they are the loudest of all men in their complaints, and the most outrageous in their behaviour: But when others are plundered, oppressed, and butchered, complaints are sedition; and to seek redress, is damnation. Is not this to be the authors of all wickedness and falsehood?

To conclude: Power, without control, appertains to God alone; and no man ought to be trusted with what no man is equal to. In truth there are so many passions, and inconsistencies, and so much selfishness, belonging to human nature, that we can scarce be too much upon our guard against each other. The only security which we can have that men will be honest, is to make it their interest to be honest; and the best defense which we can have against their being knaves, is to make it terrible to them to be knaves. As there are many men wicked in some stations, who would be innocent in others; the best way is to make wickedness unsafe in any station.

Letter 38

Sir,

[. . .] In most parts of the earth there is neither light nor liberty; and even in the best parts of it they are but little encouraged, and coldly maintained; there being, in all places, many engaged, through interest, in a perpetual conspiracy against them. They are the two greatest civil blessings, inseparable in their interests, and the mutual support of each other; and whoever would destroy one of them, must destroy both. Hence it is, that we every where find tyranny and imposture, ignorance and slavery, joined together; and oppressors and deceivers mutually aiding and paying constant court to each other. Where-ever truth is dangerous, liberty is precarious.

Of all the sciences that I know in the world, that of government concerns us most, and is the easiest to be known, and yet is the least understood. Most of those who manage it would make the lower world believe that there is I know not what difficulty and mystery in it, far above vulgar understandings; which proceeding of theirs is direct craft and imposture: Every ploughman knows a good government from a bad one, from the effects of it: he knows whether the fruits of his labour be his own, and whether he enjoy them in peace and security: And if he do not know the principles of government, it is for want of thinking and enquiry, for they lie open to common sense; but people are generally taught not to think of them at all, or to think wrong of them.

What is government, but a trust committed by all, or the most, to one, or a few, who are to attend upon the affairs of all, that every one may, with the more security, attend upon his own? A great and honourable trust; but too seldom honourably executed; those who possess it having it often more at heart to increase their power, than to make it useful; and to be terrible, rather than beneficent. It is therefore a trust, which ought to be bounded with many and strong restraints, because power renders men wanton, insolent to others, and fond of themselves. Every violation therefore of this trust, where such violation is considerable, ought to meet with proportionable punishment; and the smallest violation of it ought to meet with some, because indulgence to the least faults of magistrates may be cruelty to a whole people.

Honesty, diligence, and plain sense, are the only talents necessary for the executing of this trust; and the public good is its only end: As to refinements and finesses, they are often only the false appearances of wisdom and parts, and oftener tricks to hide guilt and emptiness; and they are generally mean and dishonest: they are the arts of jobbers in politicks, who, playing their own game under the publick cover, subsist upon poor shifts and expedients; starved politicians, who live from hand to mouth, from day to day, and following the little views of ambition, avarice, revenge, and the like personal passions, are ashamed to avow them, yet want souls great enough to forsake them; small wicked statesmen, who make a private market of the publick, and deceive it, in order to sell it.

These are the poor parts which great and good governors scorn to play, and cannot play; their designs, like their stations, being purely publick, are open and undisguised. They do not consider their people as their prey, nor lie in ambush for their subjects; nor dread, and treat and surprize them like enemies, as all ill magistrates do; who are not governors, but jailers and sponges, who chain them and squeeze them, and yet take it very ill if they do but murmur; which is yet much less than a people so abused ought to do. There have been times and countries, when publick ministers and publick enemies have been the same individual men. What a melancholy reflection is this, that the most terrible and mischievous foes to a nation should be its own magistrates! And yet in every enslaved country, which is almost every country, this is their woeful case.

Honesty and plainness go always together, and the makers and multipliers of mysteries, in the political way, are shrewdly to be suspected of dark designs. Cincinnatus was taken from the plough to save and defend the Roman state; an office which he executed honestly and successfully, without the grimace and gains of a statesman. Nor did he afterwards continue obstinately at the head of affairs, to form a party, raise a fortune, and settle himself in power: As he came into it with universal consent, he resigned it with universal applause.

It seems that government was not in those days become a trade, at least a gainful trade. Honest Cincinnatus was but a farmer: And happy had it been for the Romans, if, when they were enslaved, they could have taken the administration out of the hands of the emperors, and their refined politicians, and committed it to such farmers, or any farmers. It is certain, that many of their imperial governors acted more ridiculously than a board of ploughmen would have done, and more barbarously than a club of butchers could have done.

But some have said, It is not the business of private man to meddle with government. A bold, false, and dishonest saying; and whoever says it, either knows not what he says, or cares not, or slavishly speaks the sense of others. It is a cant now almost forgot in England, and which never prevailed but when liberty and the constitution were attacked, and never can prevail but upon the like occasion.

It is a vexation to be obliged to answer nonsense, and confute absurdities: But since it is and has been the great design of this paper to maintain and explain the glorious principles of liberty, and to expose the arts of those who would darken or destroy them; I shall here particularly shew the wickedness and stupidity of the above saying; which is fit to come from no mouth but that of a tyrant or a slave, and can never be heard by any man of an honest and free soul, without horror and indignation: It is, in short, a saying, which ought to render the man who utters it for ever incapable of place or credit in a free country, as it shews the malignity of his heart, and the baseness of his nature, and as it is the pronouncing of a doom upon our constitution. A crime, or rather a complication of crimes, for which a lasting infamy ought to be but part of the punishment.

But to the falsehood of the thing: Publick truths ought never to be kept secrets; and they who do it, are guilty of a solecism, and a contradiction: Every man ought to know what it concerns all to know. Now, nothing upon earth is of a more universal nature than government; and every private man upon earth has a concern in it, because in it is concerned, and nearly and immediately concerned, his virtue, his property, and the security of his person: And where all these are best preserved and advanced, the government is best administered; and where they are not, the government is impotent, wicked, or unfortunate; and where the government is so, the people will be so, there being always and every where a certain sympathy and analogy between the nature of the government and the nature of the people. This holds true in every instance. Public men are the patterns of private;

and the virtues and vices of the governors become quickly the virtues and vices of the governed. [. . .]

Good government does, on the contrary, produce great virtue, much happiness, and many people. Greece and Italy, while they continued free, were each of them, for the number of inhabitants, like one continued city; for virtue, knowledge, and great men, they were the standards of the world; and that age and country that could come nearest to them, has ever since been reckoned the happiest. Their government, their free government, was the root of all these advantages, and of all this felicity and renown; and in these great and fortunate states the people were the principals in the government; laws were made by their judgment and authority, and by their voice and commands were magistrates created and condemned. The city of Rome could conquer the world; nor could the great Persian monarch, the greatest then upon earth, stand before the face of one Greek city. [. . .]

What is the publick, but the collective body of private men, as every private man is a member of the publick? And as the whole ought to be concerned for the preservation of every private individual, it is the duty of every individual to be concerned for the whole, in which himself is included.

One man, or a few men, have often pretended the publick, and meant themselves, and consulted their own personal interest, in instances essential to its well-being; but the whole people, by consulting their own interest, consult the publick, and act for the publick by acting for themselves: This is particularly the spirit of our constitution, in which the whole nation is represented; and our records afford instances, where the House of Commons have declined entering upon a question of importance, till they had gone into the country, and consulted their principals, the people: So far were they from thinking that private men had no right to meddle with government. In truth, our whole worldly happiness and misery (abating for accidents and diseases) are owing to the order or mismanagement of government; and he who says that private men have no concern with government, does wisely and modestly tell us, that men have no concern in that which concerns them most; it is saying that people ought not to concern themselves whether they be naked or clothed, fed or starved, deceived or instructed, and whether they be protected or destroyed: What nonsense and servitude in a free and wise nation! [. . .]

Letter 60

Sir,

There is no government now upon earth, which owes its formation or beginning to the immediate revelation of God, or can derive its existence from such revelation: It is certain, on the contrary, that the rise and institution or variation of government, from time to time, is within the memory of men or of histories; and that every government, which we know at this day in the world, was established by the wisdom and force of mere men, and by the concurrence of means and causes evidently human. Government therefore can have no power, but such as men can give, and such as they actually did give, or permit for their own sakes: Nor can any government be in fact framed but by consent, if not of every subject, yet of as many as can compel the rest; since no man, or council of men, can have personal strength enough to govern multitudes by force, or can claim to themselves and their families any superiority, or natural sovereignty over their fellow-creatures naturally as good as them. Such strength, therefore, where-ever it is, is civil and accumulative strength, derived from the laws and constitutions of the society, of which the governors themselves are but members.

So that to know the jurisdiction of governors, and its limits, we must have recourse to the institution of government, and ascertain those limits by the measure of power, which men in the state of nature have over themselves and one another: And as no man can take from many, who are stronger than him, what they have no mind to give him; and he who has not consent must have force, which is itself the consent of the stronger; so no man can give to another either what is none of his own, or what in its own nature is inseparable from himself; as his religion particularly is.

Every man's religion is his own; nor can the religion of any man, of what nature or figure soever, be the religion of another man, unless he also chooses it; which action utterly excludes all force, power, or government. Religion can never come without conviction, nor can conviction come from civil authority; religion, which is the fear of God, cannot be subject to power, which is the fear of man. It is a relation between God and our own souls only, and consists in a disposition of mind to obey the will of our great Creator, in the manner which we think most acceptable to him. It is independent upon all human directions, and superior to them; and consequently uncontrollable by external force, which cannot reach the free faculties of the mind, or inform the understanding, much less convince it. Religion therefore, which can never be subject to the jurisdiction of another, can never be alienated to another, or put in his power.

Nor has any man in the state of nature power over his own life, or to take away the life of another, unless to defend his own, or what is as much his own, namely, his property. This power therefore, which no man has, no man can transfer to another.

Nor could any man in the state of nature, have a right to violate the property of another; that is, what another had acquired by his art or labour; or to interrupt him in his industry and enjoyments, as long as he himself was not injured by that industry and those enjoyments. No man therefore could transfer to the magistrate that right which he had not himself.

No man in his senses was ever so wild as to give an unlimited power to another to take away his life, or the means of living, according to the caprice, passion, and unreasonable pleasure of that other: But if any man restrained himself from any part of his pleasures, or parted with any portion of his acquisitions, he did it with the honest purpose of enjoying the rest with the greater security, and always in subserviency to his own happiness, which no man will or can willingly and intentionally give away to any other whatsoever.

And if any one, through his own inadvertence, or by the fraud or violence of another, can be drawn into so foolish a contract, he is relievable by the eternal laws of God and reason. No engagement that is wicked and unjust can be executed without injustice and wickedness: This is so true, that I question whether there be a constitution in the world which does not afford, or pretend to afford, a remedy for relieving ignorant, distressed, and unwary men, trepanned into such engagements by artful knaves, or frightened into them by imperious ones. So that here the laws of nature and general reason supersede the municipal and positive laws of nations; and no where oftener than in England. What else was the design, and ought to be the business, of our courts of equity? And I hope whole countries and societies are no more exempted from the privileges and protection of reason and equity, than are private particulars.

Here then is the natural limitation of the magistrate's authority: He ought not to take what no man ought to give; nor exact what no man ought to perform: All he has is given him, and those that gave it must judge of the application. In government there is no such relation as lord and slave, lawless will and blind submission; nor ought to be amongst men. [. . .]

So that the nature of government does not alter the natural right of men to liberty, which in all political societies is alike their due: But some governments provide better than others for the security and impartial distribution of that right. There has been always such a constant and certain fund of corruption and malignity in human nature, that it has been rare to find that man, whose views and happiness did not center in the gratification of his appetites, and worst appetites, his luxury, his pride, his avarice, and lust of power; and who considered any publick trust reposed in him, with any other view, than as the means to satiate such unruly and dangerous desires! And this has been most eminently true of great men, and those who aspired to dominion. They were first made great for the sake of the publick, and afterwards at its expense. And if they had been content to have been moderate traitors, mankind would have been still moderately happy; but their ambition and treason observing no degrees, there was no degree of vileness and misery which the poor people did not often feel.

The appetites therefore of men, especially of great men, are carefully to be observed and stayed, or else they will never stay themselves. The experience of every age convinces us, that we must not judge of men by what they ought to do, but by what they will do; and all history affords but few instances of men trusted with great power without abusing it, when with security they could. The servants-of society, that is to say, its magistrates, did almost universally serve it by seizing it, selling it, or plundering it; especially when they were left by the society unlimited as to their duty and wages. In that case these faithful stewards generally took all; and, being servants, made slaves of their masters.

For these reasons, and convinced by woeful and eternal experience, societies found it necessary to lay restraints upon their magistrates or publick servants, and to put checks upon those who would otherwise put chains upon them; and therefore these societies set themselves to model and form national constitutions with such wisdom and art, that the publick interest should be consulted and carried at the same time, when those entrusted with the administration of it were consulting and pursuing their own.

Hence grew the distinction between arbitrary and free governments: Not that more or less power was vested in the one than in the other; nor that either of them lay under less or more obligations, in justice, to protect their subjects, and study their ease, prosperity, and security, and to watch for the same. But the power and sovereignty of magistrates in free countries was so qualified, and so divided into different channels, and committed to the direction of so many different men, with different interests and views, that the majority of them could seldom or never find their account in betraying their trust in fundamental instances. Their emulation, envy, fear, or interest, always made them spies and checks upon one another. By all which means the people have often come at the heads of those who forfeited their heads, by betraying the people.

In despotick governments things went far otherwise, those governments having been framed otherwise; if the same could be called governments, where the rules of publick power were dictated by private and lawless lust; where folly and madness often swayed the scepter, and blind rage wielded the sword. The whole wealth of the state, with its civil or military power, being in the prince, the people could have no remedy but death and patience, while he oppressed them by the lump, and butchered them by thousands: Unless perhaps the ambition or personal resentments of some of the instruments of his tyranny procured a revolt, which rarely mended their condition.

The only secret therefore in forming a free government, is to make the interests of the governors and of the governed the same, as far as human policy can contrive. Liberty cannot be preserved any other way. [. . .] And where the persons interested are too numerous, or live too distant to meet together on all emergencies, they must moderate necessity by prudence, and act by deputies, whose interest is the same with their own, and whose property is so intermingled with theirs, and so engaged upon the same bottom, that principals and deputies must stand and fall together. When the deputies thus act for their own interest, by acting for the interest of their principals; when they can make no law but what they themselves, and their posterity, must be subject to; when they can give no money, but what they must pay their share of; when they can do no mischief, but what must fall upon their own heads in common with their countrymen; their principals may then expect good laws, little mischief, and much frugality. [. . .]

Letter 62

Sir,

[. . .] By liberty, I understand the power which every man has over his own actions, and his right to enjoy the fruit of his labour, art, and industry, as far as by it he hurts not the society, or any members of it, by taking from any member, or by hindering him from enjoying what he himself enjoys. The fruits of a man's honest industry are the just rewards of it, ascertained to him by natural and eternal equity, as is his title to use them in the manner which he thinks fit: And thus, with the above limitations, every man is sole lord and arbiter of his own private actions and property. A character of which no man living can divest him but by usurpation, or his own consent.

The entering into political society, is so far from a departure from his natural right, that to preserve it was the sole reason why men did so; and mutual protection and assistance is the only reasonable purpose of all reasonable societies. To make such protection practicable, magistracy was formed, with power to defend the innocent from violence, and to punish those that offered it; nor can there be any other pretence for magistracy in the world. In order to this good end, the magistrate is entrusted with conducting and applying the united force of the community; and with exacting such a share of every man's property, as is necessary to preserve the whole, and to defend every man and his property from foreign and domestick injuries. These are the boundaries of the power of the magistrate, who deserts his function whenever he breaks them. By the laws of society, he is more limited and restrained than any man amongst them; since, while they are absolutely free in all their actions, which purely concern themselves; all his actions, as a publick person, being for the sake of society, must refer to it, and answer the ends of it.

It is a mistaken notion in government, that the interest of the majority is only to be consulted, since in society every man has a right to every man's assistance in the enjoyment and defense of his private property; otherwise the greater number may sell the lesser, and divide their estates amongst themselves; and so, instead of a society, where all peaceable men are protected, become a conspiracy of the many against the minority. With as much equity may one man wantonly dispose of all, and violence may be sanctified by mere power.

And it is as foolish to say, that government is concerned to meddle with the private thoughts and actions of men, while they injure neither the society, nor any of its members. Every man is, in nature and reason, the judge and disposer of his own domestick affairs; and, according to the rules of religion and equity, every man must carry his own conscience. So that neither has the magistrate a right to direct the private behaviour of men; nor has the magistrate, or any body else, any manner of power to model people's speculations, no more than their dreams. Government being intended to protect men from the injuries of one another, and not to direct them in their own affairs, in which no one is interested but themselves; it is plain, that their thoughts and domestick concerns are exempted entirely from its jurisdiction: In truth, men's thoughts are not subject to their own jurisdiction.

Idiots and lunaticks indeed, who cannot take care of themselves, must be taken care of by others: But whilst men have their five senses, I cannot see what the magistrate has to do with actions by which the society cannot be affected; and where he meddles with such, he meddles impertinently or tyrannically. Must the magistrate tie up every man's legs, because some men fall into ditches? Or, must he put out their eyes, because with them they see lying vanities? Or, would it become the wisdom and care of governors to establish a travelling society, to prevent people, by a proper confinement, from throwing themselves into wells, or over precipices; or to endow a fraternity of physicians and surgeons all over the nation, to take care of their subjects' health, without being consulted; and to vomit, bleed, purge, and scarify them at pleasure, whether they would or no, just as these established judges of health should think fit? If this were the case, what a stir and hubbub should we soon see kept about the established potions and lancets? Every man, woman, or child, though ever so healthy, must be a patient, or woe be to them! The best diet and medicines would soon grow pernicious from any other hand; and their pills alone, however ridiculous, insufficient, or distasteful, would be attended with a blessing.

Let people alone, and they will take care of themselves, and do it best; and if they do not, a sufficient punishment will follow their neglect, without the magistrate's interposition and penalties. It is plain, that such busy care and vicious intrusion into the personal affairs, or private actions, thoughts, and imaginations of men, has in it more craft than kindness; and is only a device to mislead people, and pick their pockets, under the false presence of the publick and their private good. To quarrel with any man for his opinions, humours, or the fashion of his clothes, is an offence taken without being given. What is it to a magistrate how I wash my hands, or cut my corns; what fashion or colours I wear, or what notions I entertain, or what gestures I use, or what words I pronounce, when they please me, and do him and my neighbour no hurt? As well may he determine the colour of my hair, and control my shape and features.

True and impartial liberty is therefore the right of every man to pursue the natural, reasonable, and religious dictates of his own mind; to think what he will, and act as he thinks, provided he acts not to the prejudice of another; to spend his own money himself, and lay out the produce of his labour his own way; and to labour for his own pleasure and profit, and not for others who are idle, and would live and riot by pillaging and oppressing him, and those that are like him.

So that civil government is only a partial restraint put by the laws of agreement and society upon natural and absolute liberty, which might otherwise grow licentious: And tyranny is an unlimited restraint put upon natural liberty, by the will of one or a few. Magistracy, amongst a free people, is the exercise of power for the sake of the people; and tyrants abuse the people, for the sake of power. Free government is the protecting the people in their liberties by stated rules: Tyranny is a brutish struggle for unlimited liberty to one or a few, who would rob all others of their liberty, and act by no rule but lawless lust.

So much for an idea of civil liberty. I will now add a word or two, to shew how much it is the delight and passion of mankind; and then shew its advantages. The love of liberty is an appetite so strongly implanted in the nature of all living creatures, that even the appetite of self-preservation, which is allowed to be the strongest, seems to be contained in it; since by the means of liberty they enjoy the means of preserving themselves, and of satisfying their desires in the manner which they themselves choose and like best. Many animals can never be tamed, but feel the bitterness of restraint in the midst of the kindest usage; and rather than bear it, grieve and starve themselves to death; and some beat out their brains against their prisons.

Where liberty is lost, life grows precarious, always miserable, often intolerable. Liberty is, to live upon one's own terms; slavery is, to live at the mere mercy of another; and a life of slavery is, to those who can bear it, a continual state of uncertainty and wretchedness, often an apprehension of violence, often the lingering dread of a violent death: But by others, when no other remedy is to be had, death is reckoned a good one. And thus, to many men, and to many other creatures, as well as men, the love of liberty is beyond the love of life. [. . .]

Men eternally cowed and oppressed by haughty and insolent governors, made base themselves by the baseness of that sort of government, and become slaves by ruling over slaves, want spirit and souls to meet in the field freemen, who scorn oppressors, and are their own governors, or at least measure and direct the power of their governors.

Education alters nature, and becomes stronger. Slavery, while it continues, being a perpetual awe upon the spirits, depresses them, and sinks natural courage; and want and fear, the concomitants of bondage, always produce despondency and baseness; nor will men in bonds ever fight bravely, but to be free. Indeed, what else should they fight for; since every victory that they gain for a tyrant, makes them poorer and fewer; and, increasing his pride, increases his cruelty, with their own misery and chains?

Those, who, from terror and delusion, the frequent causes and certain effects of servitude, come to think their governors greater than men, as they find them worse, will be as apt to think themselves less: And when the head and the heart are thus both gone, the hands will signify little. They who are used like beasts, will be apt to degenerate into beasts. But those, on the contrary, who, by the freedom of their government and education, are taught and accustomed to think freely of men and things, find, by comparing one man with another, that all men are naturally alike; and that their governors, as they have the same face, constitution, and shape with themselves, and are subject to the same sickness, accidents, and death, with the meanest of their people; so they possess the same passions and faculties of the mind which their subjects possess, and not better. They therefore scorn to degrade and prostrate themselves, to adore those of their own species, however covered with titles, and disguised by power: They consider them as their own creatures; and, as far as they surmount themselves, the work of their own hands, and only the chief servants of the state, who have no more power to do evil than one of themselves, and are void of every privilege and superiority, but to serve them and the state. They know it to be a contradiction in religion and reason, for any man to have a right to do evil; that not to resist any man's wickedness, is to encourage it; and that they have the least reason to bear evil and oppression from their governors, who of all men are the most obliged to do them good. They therefore detest slavery, and despise or pity slaves; and, adoring liberty alone, as they who see its beauty and feel its advantages always will, it is no wonder that they are brave for it.

Indeed liberty is the divine source of all human happiness. To possess, in security, the effects of our industry, is the most powerful and reasonable incitement to be industrious: And to be able to provide for our children, and to leave them all that we have, is the best motive to beget them. But where property is precarious, labour will languish. The privileges of thinking, saying, and doing what we please, and of growing as rich as we can, without any other restriction, than that by all this we hurt not the publick, nor one another, are the glorious privileges of liberty; and its effects, to live in freedom, plenty, and safety.

These are privileges that increase mankind, and the happiness of mankind. And therefore countries are generally peopled in proportion as they are free, and are certainly happy in that proportion: And upon the same tract of land that would maintain a hundred thousand freemen in plenty, five thousand slaves would starve. In Italy, fertile Italy, men die sometimes of hunger amongst the sheaves, and in a plentiful harvest; for what they sow and reap is none of their own; and their cruel and greedy governors, who live by the labour of their wretched vassals, do not suffer them to eat the bread of their own earning, nor to sustain their lives with their own hands.

Liberty naturally draws new people to it, as well as increases the old stock; and men as naturally run when they dare from slavery and wretchedness, whithersoever they can help themselves. Hence great cities losing their liberty become deserts, and little towns by liberty grow great cities [. . .]

[. . .] [A]ll civil happiness and prosperity is inseparable from liberty; and [. . .] tyranny cannot make men, or societies of men, happy, without departing from its nature, and giving them privileges inconsistent with tyranny. And here is an unanswerable argument, amongst a thousand others, against absolute power in a single man. Nor is there one way in the world to give happiness to communities, but by sheltering them under certain and express laws, irrevocable at any man's pleasure. [. . .]

Even where absolute princes are not tyrants, there ministers will be tyrants. But it is indeed impossible for an arbitrary prince to be otherwise, since oppression is absolutely necessary to his being so. Without giving his people liberty, he cannot make them happy; and by giving them liberty, he gives up his own power. So that to be and continue arbitrary, he is doomed to be a tyrant in his own defense. The oppression of the people, corruption, wicked counsellors, and pernicious maxims in the court, and every where baseness, ignorance, and chains, must support tyranny, or it cannot be supported. So that in such governments there are inevitable grievances, without possible redress; misery, without mitigation or remedy; whatever is good for the people, is bad for their governors; and what is good for the governors, is pernicious to the people.

William Byrd

Letter to John Perceval, Earl of Egmont (July 12, 1736)

Virginia

My Lord

I had the honour of your Lordships commands of the 9th of September, and since that have the pleasure of conversing a great deal with your picture. It is incomparably well done & the painter has not only hit your ayr, but some of the vertues too which usd to soften and enliven your features. So that every connoisseur that sees it, can see t'was drawn for a generous, benevolent, & worthy person. It is no wonder perhaps that I could discern so many good things in the portrait, when I knew them so well in the original, just like those who pick out the meaning of the Bible, altho' in a strange language, because they were acquainted with the subject before. But I own I was pleasd to find some strangers able to read your Lordships character on the canvas, as plain as if they had been physiognomists by profession.

Your Lordships opinion concerning rum & Negros is certainly very just, and your excluding both of them from your colony of Georgia will be very happy; tho' with respect to rum, the saints of New England I fear will find out some trick to evade your Act of Parliament. They have a great dexterity at palliating a perjury so well as to leave no taste of it in the mouth, nor can any people like them slip through a penal statute. They will give some other name to their rum, which they may safely do, because it goes by that of kill-devil in this country from its banefull qualitys. A watchfull eye must be kept on these foul traders or all the precautions of the trustees will be vain.

I wish my Lord we could be blesst with the same prohibitions. They import so many Negros hither, that I fear this colony will some time or other be confirmd by the name of New Guinea. I am sensible of many bad consequences of multiplying these Ethiopians amongst us. They blow up the pride, & ruin the industry of our white people, who seing a rank of poor creatures below them, detest work for fear it shoud make them look like slaves. Then that poverty which will ever attend upon idleness, disposes them as much to pilfer, as it dos the Portuguese, who account it much more like a gentleman to steal, than to dirty their hands with labour of any kind.

Another unhappy effect of many Negros, is, the necessity of being severe. Numbers make them insolent, & then foul means must do, what fair will not. We have however nothing like the inhumanity here, that is practiced in the islands, & God forbid we ever shoud. But these base tempers require to be rid with a tort rein, or they will be apt to throw their rider. Yet even this is terrible to a good naturd man, who must submit to be either a fool or a fury. And this will be more our unhappy case, the more Negros are increased amongst us.

But these private mischiefs are nothing if compared to the publick danger. We have already at least 10,000 men of these descendants of Ham fit to bear arms, & their numbers increase every day as well by birth as importation. And in case there should arise a man of desperate courage amongst us, exasperated by a desperate fortune, he might with more advantage than Cataline, kindle a sevile war. Such a man might be dreadfully mischievous before any opposition could be formed against him, and tinge our rivers as wide as they are with blood. Besides the calamitys which woud be brought upon us by such an attempt, it woud cost our mother country many a fair million to make us as profitable as we are at present.

It were therefore worth the consideration of a British Parliament, my Lord, to put an end to this unchristian traffick of makeing merchandize of our fellow creatures. At least the farther importation of them into our colonys should be prohibited lest they prove as troublesome & dangerous every where, as they have been lately in Jamaica, where besides a vast expense of mony, they have cost the lives of many of His Majestys subjects. We have mountains in Virginia too, to which they may retire as safely, and do as much mischief as they do in Jamaica. All these matters duly considerd, I wonder the legislature will indulge a few ravenous traders to the danger of the publick safety, and such traders as woud freely sell their fathers, their elder brothers, & even the wives of their bosomes, if they could black their faces & get any thing by them.

I intirely agree with your Lordship in the detestation you seem to have for that diabolical liquor rum, which dos more mischief to peoples industry & morals than any thing except gin and the pope. And if it were not a little too poetical, I should fancy, as the Gods of old were said to quaff nectar, so the devils are fobbd off with rumm. Tho' my dear country men would think this unsavory spirit much too good for devils, because they are fonder of it than they are of their wives & children, for they often sell the bread out of their mouths, to buy rumm to put in their own. Thrice happy Georgia, if it be in the power of any law to keep out so great an enimy to health industry & vertue! The new setlers there had much better plant vinyards like Noah, & get drunk with their own wine.

I wish Mr. Oglethorp after he has put his generous scheme in execution in that favorite colony, would make the tour of the continent, & then I shoud hope for the pleasure of seeing him in some of his planetary motions. I was acquainted with him formerly, when I coud see he had the seeds of vertue in him, which have since grown up into fruit. Heaven give both your Lordship & him success in your disinterested endeavours for makeing Georgia a very flourishing & happy place. And methinks if he were Governour of Carolina, with a power of appointing a lieutenant Governour of Georgia, he might do more service by far, than by visiting it only sometimes. Because things are apt to run into strange abuses in this part of the world, without an uninterrupted vigilance.

I have met with disappointment in the little colony I expected from Switzerland. Some body deluded them to Carolina, where most of them I understand are dead. They woud probably have had better luck at the place I intended for them, which is as healthy as any in America, the soil very good, & full of cool & delightfull streams.

Not a syllable have I heard this long time of any of the Southwell family. They are so unkind as to drop me, distance being in their reckoning the same as death; but I must be dead indeed not to remember them and wish them all the health & prosperity in the world. If your Lordship will be so good as to give them a place in the much coveted account of your own family, it will be entertaining in a high degree to your Lordship's &c.

Lord Egmont

SIR JOHN RANDOLPH

Re-Election Speech (1736)

Mr. Speaker elect, with the House, went to attend the governor in the Council Chamber and speak as followeth:

The House of Burgesses have, in obedience to your commands, proceeded to the choice of a speaker; and having elected me, do now present me for your approbation. And as I have never yet tried my strength in perverting the use of speech, which was given us for the true discovering, and not to disguise our minds, I dare not make my first essay in this place, and before this assembly; but without arraigning the small abilities I have, I humbly submit myself to your judgment.

Then the governor spake thus:

Gentlemen, the choice you have made of a speaker is greatly to my satisfaction.

After the governor's speech, Mr. Speaker replied:

I humbly thank you for this your favourable opinion, which I don't pretend to deserve, but will use it as a proper admonition, whereby I ought to regulate my conduct in the exercise of the office you are now pleased to confirm me in, which I do not intend to magnify to the degree some have done, feeling we are no more than the representative body of a colony, naturally and justly dependent upon the mother kingdom, whose power is circumscribed by very narrow bounds, and whose influence is of small extent. All we pretend to is to be of some importance to those who send us hither, and to have some share in their protection and the security of their lives, liberties, and properties.

The planters who sustained the heat and burden of the first settlement of this plantation were miserably harassed by the government in the form it was then established, which had an unnatural power of ruling by martial law, and constitutions passed by a Council in England, without the consent of the people, which were no better. This made the name of Virginia so infamous that we see the impressions of those times hardly yet worn out in other countries, especially among the vulgar. And such have been in all ages and for ever must continue to be the effects of an arbitrary despotic power, of which the Company in London, in whom all dominion and property was then lodged, were so sensible that they resolved to establish another form of government more agreeable and suitable to the temper and genius of the English nation. And accordingly, in July, 1621, passed a charter under their Common Seal, which was founded upon powers before granted by charters under the Great Seal of England, whereby they ordered and declared that for preventing injustice and oppression for the future and for advancing the strength and prosperity of the colony there should be two supreme councils; one to be called the Council of State, consisting of the governor and certain councillors, particularly named, to serve as a council of advice to the governor; the other to be called by the governor yearly, consisting of the Council of State and two burgesses, to be chosen by the inhabitants of every town, hundred, or other plantation, to be called the General Assembly. And to have free power to treat, consult, and conclude of all things concerning the public weal; and to enact such laws for the behoof of the colony and the good government thereof as from time to time should appear necessary or requisite, commanding them to imitate and follow the policy, form of government, laws, customs, manner of trial, and other administration of justice used in England; and providing that no orders of their General Court should bind the colony unless ratified in the General Assemblies. This is the original of our constitution, confirmed by King James the first, by King Charles the first, upon his accession to the throne, and by all the crowned heads of England and Great Britain, successively, upon the appointment of every new governor, with very little alteration. Under it we are grown to whatever we now have to boast of. And from hence, the House of Burgesses do derive diverse privileges which they have long enjoyed, and claim as their undoubted right. Freedom of speech is the very essence of their being because without it nothing could be thoroughly debated, nor could they be looked upon as a council; an exemption from arrests, confirmed by a positive law; otherwise their counsels and debates might be frequently interrupted and their body diminished by the loss of its members; a protection for their estates to prevent all occasions to withdraw them from the necessary duty of their attendance; a power over their own members, that they may be answerable to no other jurisdiction for anything done in the House; and a sole right of determining all questions concerning their own elections lest contrary judgments in the courts of law might thwart or destroy theirs.

All these I say, besides others which spring out of them, are incident to the nature and constitution of our body; and I am commanded by the House to offer a petition in their behalf that you will be pleased to discountenance all attempts that may be offered against them and assist us with your authority in supporting and maintaining them against all insults whatsoever. And lastly, I must beg your favour to myself, that you will not construe my actions with too much severity, nor impute my particular errors and failings to the House.

To which the governor answered:

The House of Burgesses may always depend upon my care to support them in their ancient rights and privileges.

And then Mr. Speaker went on:

We have long experienced your love and good will to the people of this country, and observe with what readiness you exert it upon all occasions.

The art of governing well is thought to be the most abstruse, as well as the usefullest science in the world, and when it is learnt to some degree of perfection it is very difficult to put it in practice, being often opposed by the pride and interest of the person that governs. But you have showed how easy it is to give universal satisfaction to the people under your government. You have met them and heard their grievances in frequent assemblies and have had the pleasure of seeing none of them proceed from your administration. You have not been intoxicated with the power committed to you by his Majesty but have used it like a faithful trustee for the public good and with proper cautions; raised no debates about what it might be able to do of itself, but on all important occasions have suffered it to unite with that of the other parts of the legislature. You never propose matters without supposing your opinion subject to the examination of others, nor strove to make other men's reason blindly and implicitly obedient to yours, but have always calmly acquiesced in the contrary opinion. And lastly, you have extirpated all factions from among us by discountenancing public animosities, and plainly proved that none can arise, or be lasting, but from the countenance and encouragement of a governor. *Hinc illae Artes.*

I do not mention these things for the sake of enlarging my periods nor for flattery, nor for conciliating favour, for if I know myself at all I have none of the arts of the first nor the address that is necessary for the other. And I hope I shall never be one of those who bestow their commendations upon all men alike; upon those who deserve it as well as those who do not.

Permit me then, sir, to beseech you to go on in the same steady course. Finish the character you have been almost nine years establishing. Let it remain unblemished and a pattern to those who shall come after you. Make us the envy of the king's other plantations and put those governors out of countenance who make tyranny their glory, and though they know their master's will, fancy it a dishonor to perform it.

Jonathan Edwards

Northampton Covenant (1742)

Copy of a Covenant

Entered into and subscribed, by the people of God at Northampton, and owned before God in his house as their vow to the Lord, and made a solemn act of public worship, by the congregation in general that were above fourteen years of age, on a day of fasting and prayer for the continuance and increase of the gracious presence of God in that place.

March 16th, 1742. Acknowledging God's great goodness to us, a sinful, unworthy people, in the blessed manifestations and fruits of his gracious presence in this town, both formerly and lately, and particularly in the very late spiritual revival; [. . .] we do this day present ourselves before the Lord, to renounce our evil ways; we put away our abominations from before God's eyes, and with one accord, to renew our engagements to seek and serve God: and particularly do now solemnly promise and vow to the Lord as follows:

In all our conversations, concerns, and dealings with our neighbor, we will have a strict regard to rules of honesty, justice, and uprightness, that we don't overreach or defraud our neighbor in any matter, and either willfully, or through want of care, injure him in any of his honest possessions or rights, and in all our communication will have a tender respect, not only to our own interest, but also to the interest of our neighbor; and will carefully endeavor, in everything, to do to others as we should expect, or think reasonable, that they should do to us, if we were in their case, and they in ours.

And particularly we will endeavor to render everyone his due, and will take heed to ourselves, that we don't injure our neighbor, and give him just cause of offense, by willfully or negligently forbearing to pay our honest debts.

And wherein any of us, upon strict examination of our past behavior, may be conscious to ourselves, that we have by any means wronged any of our neighbors in their outward estate, we will not rest, till we have made that restitution, or given that satisfaction, which the rules of moral equity require; or if we are, on a strict and impartial search, conscious to ourselves that we have in any other respect considerably injured our neighbor, we will truly endeavor to do that which we in our consciences suppose Christian rules require, in order to a reparation of the injury, and removing the offense given thereby. [. . .]

And we promise that we will be very careful to avoid doing anything to our neighbor from a spirit of revenge. And that we will take great care that we do not, for private interest or our own honor, or to maintain ourselves against those of a contrary party, or to get our wills, or to promote any design in opposition to others, do those things which we, on the most impartial consideration are capable of, can think in our consciences will tend to wound religion, and the interests of Christ's kingdom.

And particularly, that so far as any of us, by Divine Providence, have any special influence upon others, to lead them in the management of public affairs, we will not make our own worldly gain, or honor, or interest in the affections of others, or getting the better of any of a contrary party, that are in any respect our competitors, or the bringing or keeping them down, our governing aim, to the prejudice of the interest of religion, and the honour of Christ.

And in the management of any public affair, wherever there is a difference of opinions, concerning any outward possessions, privileges, rights, or properties, we will not willingly violate justice for private interest: and with the greatest strictness and watchfulness, will avoid all unchristian bitterness, vehemence, and heat of spirit; yea, though we should think ourselves injured by a contrary party; and in the time of the management of such affairs, will especially watch over ourselves, our spirits, and our tongues, to avoid all unchristian inveighings, reproachings, bitter reflectings, judging and ridiculing others, either in public meetings or in private conversation, either to men's faces, or behind their backs; but will greatly endeavor, so far as we are concerned, that all should be managed with Christian humility, gentleness, quietness, and love.

And those of us that are in youth do promise never to allow ourselves in any diversions or pastimes, in meetings, or companies of young people, that we, in our consciences, upon sober consideration, judge not well to consist with, or would sinfully tend to hinder, the devoutest and most engaged spirit in religion, or indispose the mind for that devout and profitable attendance on the duties of the closet, which is most agreeable to God's will, or that we, in our most impartial judgment, can think tends to rob God of that honor which he expects, by our orderly serious attendance on family worship.

And furthermore we promise that we will strictly avoid all freedoms and familiarities in company, so tending either to stir up or gratify a lust of lasciviousness that we cannot in our consciences think will be approved by the infinitely pure and holy eye of God, or that we can think, on serious and impartial consideration, we should be afraid to practice, if we expected in a few hours to appear before that holy God, to give an account of ourselves to him, as fearing they would be condemned by him as unlawful and impure.

We also promise with great watchfulness to perform relative duties required by Christian rules, in the families we belong to, as we stand related respectively, towards parents and children, husbands and wives, brothers and sisters, masters or mistresses, and servants.

And we now appear before God, depending on Divine grace and assistance, solemnly to devote our whole lives, to be laboriously spent in the business of religion; ever making it our greatest business, without backsliding from such a way of living, not hearkening to the solicitations of our sloth, and other corrupt inclinations, or the temptations of the world, that tend to draw us off from it. [. . .]

And being sensible of our weakness and the deceitfulness of our own hearts, and our proneness to forget our most solemn vows and lose our resolutions, we promise to be often strictly examining ourselves by these promises, especially before the sacrament of the Lord's supper; and beg of God that he would, for Christ's sake, keep us from wickedly dissembling in these our solemn vows; and that he who searches our hearts, and ponders the path of our feet, would, from time to time, help us in trying ourselves by this covenant, and help us to keep covenant with him, and not leave us to our own foolish, wicked, and treacherous hearts.

DAVID HUME

Essays Moral, Political and Literary (1742, revised 1777)

Essay III
That Politics May Be Reduced to a Science

It is a question with several, whether there be any essential difference between one form of government and another, and whether every form may not become good or bad, according as it is well or ill administered.[1] Were it once admitted that all governments are alike, and that the only difference consists in the character and conduct of the governors, most political disputes would be at an end, and all *zeal* for one constitution above another must be esteemed mere bigotry and folly. But, though a friend to moderation, I cannot forbear condemning this sentiment, and should be sorry to think that human affairs admit

1. For forms of government let fools contest,
Whate'er is best administer'd is best.
Essay on Man, Book III

of no greater stability than what they receive from the casual humours and characters of particular men.

It is true, those who maintain that the goodness of all government consists in the goodness of the administration, may cite many particular instances in history where the very same government, in different hands, has varied suddenly into the two opposite extremes of good and bad. Compare the French government under Henry III and under Henry IV. Oppression, levity, artifice on the part of the rulers; faction, sedition, treachery, rebellion, disloyalty on the part of the subjects: these compose the character of the former miserable era. But when the patriot and heroic prince who succeeded was once firmly seated on the throne, the government, the people, everything seemed to be totally changed; and all from the difference of the temper and conduct of these two sovereigns. Instances of this kind may be multiplied, almost without number, from ancient as well as modern history, foreign as well as domestic.

But here it may be proper to make a distinction. All absolute governments must very much depend on the administration; and this is one of the great inconveniences attending that form of government. But a republican and free government would be an obvious absurdity, if the particular checks and controls provided by the constitution had really no influence, and made it not the interest, even of bad men, to act for the public good. Such is the intention of these forms of government, and such is their real effect, where they are wisely constituted; as on the other hand, they are the source of all disorder, and of the blackest crimes, where either skill or honesty has been wanting in their original frame and institution.

So great is the force of laws, and of particular forms of government, and so little dependence have they on the humours and tempers of men, that consequences almost as general and certain may sometimes be deduced from them, as any which the mathematical sciences afford us.

The constitution of the Roman republic gave the whole legislative power to the people, without allowing a negative voice either to the nobility or consuls. This unbounded power they possessed in a collective, not in a representative body. The consequences were: when the people, by success and conquest, had become very numerous, and had spread themselves to a great distance from the capital, the city-tribes, though the most contemptible, carried almost every vote; they were, therefore, most cajoled by every one that affected popularity; they were supported in idleness by the general distribution of corn, and by particular bribes, which they received from almost every candidate; by this means, they became every day more licentious, and the Campus Martius was a perpetual scene of tumult and sedition; armed slaves were introduced among these rascally citizens, so that the whole government fell into anarchy, and the greatest happiness which the Romans could look for was the despotic power of the Cæsars. Such are the effects of democracy without a representative.

A nobility may possess the whole or any part of the legislative power of a state in two different ways. Either every nobleman shares the power as part of the whole body, or the whole body enjoys the power as composed of parts, which have each a distinct power and authority. The Venetian aristocracy is an instance of the first kind of government; the Polish of the second. In the Venetian government the whole body of nobility possesses the whole power, and no nobleman has any authority which he receives not from the whole. In the Polish government every nobleman, by means of his fiefs, has a distinct hereditary authority over his vassals, and the whole body has no authority but what it receives from the concurrence of its parts. The different operations and tendencies of these two species of government might be made apparent even *a priori*. A Venetian nobility is preferable to a Polish, let the humours and education of men be ever so much varied. A nobility who possess their power in common will preserve peace and order, both among themselves and their subjects; and no member can have authority enough to control the laws for a moment. The nobles will preserve their authority over the people, but without any grievous tyranny, or any breach of private property; because such a tyrannical government promotes not the interests of the whole body, however it may that of some individuals. There will be a distinction of rank between the nobility and people, but this will be the only distinction in the state. The whole nobility will form one body, and the whole people another, without any of those private feuds and animosities which spread ruin and desolation everywhere. It is easy to see the disadvantages of a Polish nobility in every one of these particulars.

It is possible so to constitute a free government, as that a single person, call him doge, prince, or king, shall possess a large share of power, and shall form a proper balance or counterpoise to the other parts of the legislature. This chief magistrate may be either *elective* or *hereditary*; and though the former institution may, to a superficial view, appear the most advantageous, yet more accurate inspection will discover in it greater inconveniences than in the latter, and such as are founded on causes and principles eternal and immutable. The filling of the throne, in such a government, is a point of too great and too general interest not to divide the whole people into factions; whence a civil war, the greatest of ills, may be apprehended, almost with certainty, upon every vacancy. The prince elected must be either a *foreigner* or a *native*. The former will be ignorant of the people whom he is to govern; suspicious of his new subjects, and suspected by them; giving his confidence entirely to strangers, who will have no other care but of enriching themselves in the quickest manner, while their master's favour and authority are able to support them. A native will carry into the throne all his private animosities and friendships, and will never be viewed in his elevation without exciting the sentiment of envy in those who formerly considered him as their equal. Not to mention that a crown is too high a reward ever to be given to merit alone, and will always induce the candidates to employ force, or money, or intrigue, to procure the votes of the electors; so that such an election will give no better chance for superior merit in the prince, than if the state had trusted to birth alone for determining their sovereign.

It may therefore be pronounced as an universal axiom in politics, *That an hereditary prince, a nobility without vassals, and a people voting by their representatives, form the best monarchy, aristocracy and democracy*. [. . .]

Legislators, therefore, ought not to trust the future government of a state entirely to chance, but ought to provide a system of laws to regulate the administration of public affairs to the latest posterity. Effects will always correspond to causes; and wise regulations in any commonwealth are the most valuable legacy that can be left to future ages. In the smallest court or office, the stated forms and methods by which business must be conducted are found to be a considerable check on the natural depravity of mankind. Why should not the case be the same in public affairs? Can we ascribe the stability and wisdom of the Venetian government, through so many ages, to anything but the form of government? And is it not easy to point out those defects in the original constitution which produced the tumultuous governments of Athens and Rome, and ended at last in the ruin of these two famous republics? And so little dependence has this affair on the humours and education of particular men, that one part of the same republic may be wisely conducted, and another weakly, by the very same men, merely on account of the difference of the forms and institutions by which these parts are regulated. [. . .]

The ages of greatest public spirit are not always most eminent for private virtue. Good laws may beget order and moderation in the government, where the manners and customs have instilled little humanity or justice into the tempers of men. The most illustrious period of the Roman history, considered in a political view, is that between the beginning of the first and end of the last Punic war, the due balance between the nobility and people being then fixed by the contests of the tribunes, and not being yet lost by the extent of conquests. Yet at this very time, the horrid practice of poisoning was so common that, during part of a season, a *Prætor* punished capitally for this crime above three thousand persons in a part of Italy, and found informations of this nature still multiplying upon him. [. . .]

Here, then, is a sufficient inducement to maintain with the utmost *zeal*, in every free state, those forms and institutions by which liberty is secured, the public good consulted, and the avarice or ambition of particular men restrained and punished. Nothing does more honour to human nature, than to see it susceptible of so noble a passion; as nothing can be a greater indication of meanness of heart in any man, than to see him destitute of it. A man who loves only himself, without regard to friendship and desert, merits the severest blame; and a man who is only susceptible of friendship, without public spirit, or a regard to the community, is deficient in the most material part of virtue. [. . .]

Essay V
Of the Origin of Government

Man, born in a family, is compelled to maintain society from necessity, from natural inclination, and from habit. The same creature, in his farther progress, is engaged to establish political society in order to administer justice; without which there can be no peace among them, nor safety, nor mutual intercourse. We are, therefore, to look upon all the vast apparatus of our government as having ultimately no other object or purpose but the distribution of justice. [. . .]

All men are sensible of the necessity of justice to maintain peace and order; and all men are sensible of the necessity of peace and order for the maintenance of society. Yet, notwithstanding this strong and obvious necessity, such is the frailty or perverseness of our nature, it is impossible to keep men, faithfully and unerringly, in the paths of justice. Some extraordinary circumstances may happen, in which a man finds his interests to be more promoted by fraud or rapine, than hurt by the breach which his injustice makes in the social union. But much more frequently, he is seduced from his great and important, but distant interests, by the allurement of present, though often very frivolous temptations. This great weakness is incurable in human nature.

Men must, therefore, endeavour to palliate what they cannot cure. They must institute some persons, under the appellation of magistrates, whose peculiar office it is to point out the decrees of equity, to punish transgressors, to correct fraud and violence, and to oblige men, however reluctant, to consult their own real and permanent interests. In a word, *obedience* is a new duty which must be invented to support that of *justice*; and the ties of equity must be corroborated by those of allegiance.

But still, viewing matters in an abstract light, it may be thought that nothing is gained by this alliance, and that the factitious duty of obedience, from its very nature, lays as feeble a hold of the human mind, as the primitive and natural duty of justice. Peculiar interests and present temptations may overcome the one as well as the other. They are equally exposed to the same inconvenience. And the man who is inclined to be a bad neighbour must be led by the same motives, well or ill understood, to be a bad citizen and subject. Not to mention that the magistrate himself may often be negligent, or partial, or unjust in his administration.

Experience, however, proves that there is a great difference between the cases. Order in society, we find, is much better maintained by means of government; and our duty to the magistrate is more strictly guarded by the principles of human nature, than our duty to our fellow-citizens. The love of dominion is so strong in the breast of man, that many not only submit to, but court all the dangers, and fatigues, and cares of government; and men, once raised to that station, though often led astray by private passions, find, in ordinary cases, a visible interest in the impartial administration of justice. The persons who first attain this distinction by the consent, tacit or express, of the people, must be endowed with superior personal qualities of valour, force, integrity, or prudence, which command respect and confidence; and after government is established, a regard to birth, rank, and station has a mighty influence over men, and enforces the decrees of the magistrate. The prince or leader exclaims against every disorder which disturbs his society. He summons all his partisans and all men of probity to aid him in correcting and redressing it; and he is readily followed by all indifferent persons in the execution of his office. He soon acquires the power of rewarding these services; and in the progress of society, he establishes subordinate ministers and often a military force, who find an immediate and a visible interest in supporting his authority. Habit soon consolidates what other principles of human nature had imperfectly founded; and men, once accustomed to obedience, never think of departing from that path in which they and their ancestors have constantly trod, and to which they are confined by so many urgent and visible motives.

But though this progress of human affairs may appear certain and inevitable, and though the support which allegiance brings to justice be founded on obvious principles of human nature, it cannot be expected that men should beforehand be able to discover them, or foresee their operation. Government commences more casually and more imperfectly. It is probable that the first ascendant of one man over multitudes began during a state of war, where the superiority of courage and of genius discovers itself most visibly, where unanimity and concert are most requisite, and where the pernicious effects of disorder are most sensibly felt. The long continuance of that state, an incident common among savage tribes, ensured the people to submission; and if the chieftain possessed as much equity as prudence and valour, he became, even during peace, the arbiter of all differences, and could gradually, by a mixture of force and consent, establish his authority. The benefit sensibly felt from his influence made it be cherished by the people, at least by the peaceable and well disposed among them; and if his son enjoyed the same good qualities, government advanced the sooner to maturity and perfection; but was still in a feeble state, till the farther progress of improvement procured the magistrate a revenue, and enabled him to bestow rewards on the several instruments of his administration, and to inflict punishments on the refractory and disobedient. Before that period, each exertion of his influence must have been particular, and founded on the peculiar circumstances of the case. After it, submission was no longer a matter of choice in the bulk of the community, but was rigorously exacted by the authority of the supreme magistrate.

In all governments, there is a perpetual intestine struggle, open or secret, between *authority* and *liberty*; and neither of them can ever absolutely prevail in the contest. A great sacrifice of liberty must necessarily be made in every government; yet even the authority which confines liberty can never, and perhaps ought never, in any constitution, to become quite entire and uncontrollable. The sultan is master of the life and fortune of any individual, but will not be permitted to impose new taxes on his subjects; a French monarch can impose taxes at pleasure, but would find it dangerous to attempt the lives and fortunes of individuals. Religion also, in most countries, is commonly found to be a very intractable principle; and other principles or prejudices frequently resist all the authority of the civil magistrate, whose power, being founded on opinion, can never subvert other opinions, equally rooted with that of his title to dominion. The government which, in common appellation, receives the appellation of free, is that which admits of a partition of power among several members, whose united authority is no less, or is commonly greater than that of any monarch, but who, in the usual course of administration, must act by general and equal laws that are previously known to all the members and to all their subjects. In this sense, it must be owned that liberty is the perfection of civil society; but still authority must be acknowledged essential to its very existence; and in those contests which so often take place between the one and the other, the latter may, on that account, challenge the preference. Unless perhaps one may say (and it may be said with some reason) that a circumstance which is essential to the existence of civil society must always support itself, and needs be guarded with less jealousy, than one that contributes only to its perfection, which the indolence of men is so apt to neglect, or their ignorance to overlook.

Essay VI
On the Independence of Parliament

Political writers have established it as a maxim that, in contriving any system of government, and fixing the several checks and controls of the constitution, every man ought to be supposed a *knave*, and to have no other end, in all his actions, than private interest. By this interest we must govern him, and by means of it make him, notwithstanding his insatiable avarice and ambition, co-operate to public good. Without this, say they, we shall in vain boast of the advantages of any constitution, and shall find, in the end, that we have no security for our liberties or possessions, except the good-will of our rulers; that is, we shall have no security at all.

It is, therefore, a just *political* maxim, that *every man must be supposed a knave*; though, at the same time, it appears somewhat strange that a maxim should be true in *politics*, which is false in *fact*. But to satisfy us on this head, we may consider that men are generally more honest in their private than in their public capacity, and will go greater lengths to serve a party, than when their own private interest is alone concerned. Honour is a great check upon mankind; but where a considerable body of men act together, this check is in a great measure removed, since a man is sure to be approved of by his own party for what promotes the common interest, and he soon learns to despise the clamors of adversaries.

To which we may add that every court or senate is determined by the greater number of voices; so that, if self-interest influences only the majority (as it will always do) the whole senate follows the allurements of this separate interest, and acts as if it contained not one member who had any regard to public interest and liberty.

When there offers, therefore, to our censure and examination any plan of government, real or imaginary, where the power is distributed among several courts and several orders of men, we should always consider the separate interest of each court, and each order; and if we find that, by the skilful division of power, this interest must necessarily, in its operation, concur with public, we may pronounce that government to be wise and happy. If, on the contrary, separate interest be not checked, and be not directed to the public, we ought to look for nothing but faction, disorder, and tyranny from such a government. In this opinion I am justified by experience, as well as by the authority of all philosophers and politicians, both ancient and modern. [. . .]

Essay VIII
Of Parties in General

[. . .] As much as legislators and founders of states ought to be honoured and respected among men, as much ought the founders of sects and factions to be detested and hated, because the influence of faction is directly contrary to that of laws. Factions subvert government, render laws impotent, and beget the fiercest animosities among men of the same nation, who ought to give mutual assistance and protection to each other. And what should render the founders of parties more odious is the difficulty of extirpating these weeds, when once they have taken root in any state. They naturally propagate themselves for many centuries, and seldom end but by the total dissolution of that government in which they are sown. They are, besides, plants which grow most plentifully in the richest soil; and though absolute governments be not wholly free from them, it must be confessed that they rise more easily, and propagate themselves faster in free governments, where they always infect the legislature itself, which alone could be able, by the steady application of rewards and punishments, to eradicate them.

Factions may be divided into *personal* and *real*, that is, into factions founded on personal friendship or animosity among such as compose the contending parties, and into those founded on some real difference of sentiment or interest. The reason of this distinction is obvious, though I must acknowledge that parties are seldom found pure and unmixed, either of the one kind or the other. It is not often seen that a government divides into factions where there is no difference in the views of the constituent members, either real or apparent, trivial or material; and in those factions which are founded on the most real and most material difference, there is always observed a great deal of personal animosity or affection. But notwithstanding this mixture, a party may be denominated either personal or real, according to that principle which is predominant, and is found to have the greatest influence.

Personal factions arise most easily in small republics. Every domestic quarrel, there, becomes an affair of state. Love, vanity, emulation, any passion, as well as ambition and resentment, begets public division. The *Neri* and *Bianchi* of Florence, the *Fregosi* and *Adorni* of Genoa, the *Colonesi* and *Orsini* of modern Rome, were parties of this kind.

Men have such a propensity to divide into personal factions that the smallest appearance of real difference will produce them. What can be imagined more trivial than the difference between one colour of livery and another in horse races? Yet this difference begat two most inveterate factions in the Greek empire, the *Prasini* and *Veneti*, who never suspended their animosities till they ruined that unhappy government. [. . .]

Real factions may be divided into those from *interest*, from *principle*, and from *affection*. Of all factions, the first are the most reasonable, and the most excusable. Where two orders of men, such as the nobles and the people, have a distinct authority in a government not very accurately balanced and modelled, they naturally follow a distinct interest; nor can we reasonably expect a different conduct, considering that degree of selfishness implanted in human nature. It requires great skill in a legislator to prevent such parties; and many philosophers are of opinion that this secret, like the *grand elixir*, or *perpetual motion*, may amuse men in theory but can never possibly be reduced to practice. In despotic governments, indeed, factions often do not appear; but they are not the less real, or rather they are more real and more pernicious upon that very account. The distinct orders of men, nobles and people, soldiers and merchants, have all a distinct interest; but the more powerful oppresses the weaker with impunity, and without resistance, which begets a seeming tranquillity in such governments. [. . .]

Parties from *principle*, especially abstract speculative principle, are known only to modern times, and are, perhaps, the most extraordinary and unaccountable phenomenon that has yet appeared in human affairs. Where different principles beget a contrariety of conduct, which is the case with all different political principles, the matter may be more easily explained. A man who esteems the true right of government to lie in one man or one family cannot easily agree with his fellow-citizen who thinks that another man or family is possessed of this right. Each naturally wishes that right may take place, according to his own notions of it. But where the difference of principle is attended with no contrariety of action, but every one may follow his own way without interfering with his neighbour, as happens in all religious controversies, what madness, what fury can beget such unhappy and such fatal divisions?

Two men travelling on the highway, the one east, the other west, can easily pass each other, if the way be broad enough; but two men, reasoning upon opposite principles of religion, cannot so easily pass without shocking, though one should think that the way were also, in that case, sufficiently broad, and that each might proceed without interruption in his own course. But such is the nature of the human mind that it always lays hold on every mind that approaches it; and as it is wonderfully fortified by an unanimity of sentiments, so is it shocked and disturbed by any contrariety. Hence the eagerness which most people discover in a dispute; and hence their impatience of opposition, even in the most speculative and indifferent opinions.

This principle, however frivolous it may appear, seems to have been the origin of all religious wars and divisions. But as this principle is universal in human nature, its effects would not have been confined to one age, and to one sect of religion, did it not there concur with other more accidental causes, which raise it to such a height as to produce the greatest misery and devastation. Most religions of the ancient world arose in the unknown ages of government, when men were as yet barbarous and uninstructed, and the prince, as well as the peasant, was disposed to receive, with implicit faith, every pious tale of fiction which was offered to him. The magistrate embraced the religion of the people and, entering cordially into the care of sacred matters, naturally acquired an authority in them, and united the ecclesiastical with the civil power. But the Christian religion, arising while principles directly opposite to it were firmly established in the polite part of the world, who despised the nation that first broached this novelty, no wonder that, in such circumstances, it was but little countenanced by the civil magistrate, and that the priesthood was allowed to engross all the authority in the new sect. So bad a use did they make of this power, even in those early times, that the primitive persecutions may perhaps *in part* be ascribed to the violence instilled by them into their followers. And the same principles of priestly government continuing after Christianity became the established religion, they have engendered a spirit of persecution which has ever since been the poison of human society, and the source of the most inveterate factions in every government. Such divisions, therefore, on the part of the people, may justly be esteemed factions of *principle*; but, on the part of the priests, who are the prime movers, they are really factions of *interest*.

There is another cause (beside the authority of the priests, and the separation of the ecclesiastical and civil powers) which has contributed to render Christendom the scene of religious wars and divisions. Religions that arise in ages totally ignorant and barbarous consist mostly of traditional tales and fictions, which may be different in every sect, without being contrary to each other; and even when they are contrary, every one adheres to the tradition of his own sect, without much reasoning or disputation. But as philosophy was widely spread over the world at the time when Christianity arose, the teachers of the new sect were obliged to form a system of speculative opinions, to divide, with some accuracy, their articles of faith, and to explain, comment, confute, and defend with all the subtlety of argument and science. Hence naturally arose keenness in dispute, when the Christian religion came to be split into new divisions and heresies; and this keenness assisted the priests in their policy of begetting a mutual hatred and antipathy among their deluded followers. Sects of philosophy, in the ancient world, were more zealous than parties of religion; but in modern times, parties of religion are more furious and enraged than the most cruel factions that ever arose from interest and ambition.

I have mentioned parties from *affection* as a kind of *real* parties, beside those from *interest* and *principle*. By parties from affection, I understand those which are founded on the different attachments of men towards particular families and persons whom they desire to rule over them. These factions are often very violent, though, I must own, it may seem unaccountable that men should attach themselves so strongly to persons with whom they are no wise acquainted, whom perhaps they never saw, and from whom they never received, nor can ever hope for any favour. Yet this we often find to be the case, and even with men who, on other occasions, discover no great generosity of spirit, nor are found to be easily transported by friendship beyond their own interest. We are apt to think the relation between us and our sovereign very close and intimate. The splendor of majesty and power bestows an importance on the fortunes even of a single person. And when a man's good-nature does not give him this imaginary interest, his ill-nature will, from spite and opposition to persons whose sentiments are different from his own.

Idea of a Perfect Commonwealth (1754)

It is not with forms of government, as with other artificial contrivances; where an old engine may be rejected, if we can discover another more accurate and commodious, or where trials may safely be made, even though the success be doubtful. An established government has an infinite advantage, by that very circumstance of its being established; the bulk of mankind being governed by authority, not reason, and never attributing authority to any thing that has not the recommendation of antiquity. To tamper, therefore, in this affair, or try experiments merely upon the credit of supposed argument and philosophy, can never be the part of a wise magistrate, who will bear a reverence to what carries the marks of age; and though he may attempt some improvements for the public good, yet will he adjust his innovations, as much as possible, to the ancient fabric, and preserve entire the chief pillars and supports of the constitution.

The mathematicians of Europe have been much divided concerning that figure of a ship, which is the most commodious for sailing; and Huygens, who at last determined the controversy, is justly thought to have obliged the learned, as well as commercial world; though Columbus had sailed to America, and Sir Francis Drake made the tour of the world, without any such discovery. As one form of government must be allowed more perfect than another, independent of the manners and humours of particular men; why may we not enquire what is the most perfect of all, though the common botched and inaccurate governments seem to serve the purposes of society, and though it be not so easy to establish a new system of government, as to build a vessel upon a new construction? The subject is surely the most worth curiosity of any the wit of man can possibly devise. And who knows, if this controversy were fixed by the universal consent of the wise and learned, but, in some future age, an opportunity might be afforded by reducing the theory to practice, either by a dissolution of some old government, or by the combination of men to form a new one, in some distant part of the world? In all cases, it must be advantageous to know what is most perfect in the kind, that we may be able to bring any real constitution or form of government as near it as possible, by such gentle alterations and innovations as may not give too great disturbance to society. [. . .]

All plans of government, which suppose great reformation in the manners of mankind, are plainly imaginary. Of this nature, are the Republic of Plato, and the Utopia of Sir Thomas More. The Oceana is the only valuable model of a commonwealth, that has yet been offered to the public. [. . .]

The chief defects of the Oceana seem to be these. First, Its rotation is inconvenient, by throwing men, of whatever abilities, by intervals, out of public employments. Secondly, Its Agrarian is impracticable. Men will soon the art, which was practiced in ancient Rome, of concealing their possessions under other people's name; till at last, the abuse will become so common, that they will throw off even the appearance of restraint. Thirdly, The Oceana provides not a sufficient security for liberty, or the redress of grievances. The senate must propose, and the people consent; by which means, the senate have not only a negative upon the people, but, what is of much greater consequence, their negative goes before the votes of the people. Were the King's negative of the same nature in the English constitution, and could he prevent any bill from coming into parliament, he would be an absolute monarch. As his negative follows the votes of the houses, it is of little consequence: Such a difference is there in the manner of placing the same thing. When a popular bill has been debated in parliament, is brought to maturity, all its conveniencies and inconveniencies, weighed and balanced; if afterwards it be presented for the royal assent, few princes will venture to reject the unanimous desire of the people. But could the King crush a disagreeable bill in embryo (as was the case, for some time, in the Scottish parliament, by means of the lords of the articles), the British government would have no balance, nor would grievances ever be redressed: And it is certain, that exorbitant power proceeds not, in any government, from new laws, so much as from neglecting to remedy the abuses, which frequently rise from the old ones. A government, says Machiavel, must often be brought back to its original principles. It appears then, that, in the Oceana, the whole legislature may be said to rest in the senate; which Harrington would own to be an inconvenient form of government, especially after the Agrarian is abolished.

Here is a form of government, to which I cannot, in theory, discover any considerable objection. [. . .] We will conclude this subject, with observing the falsehood of the common opinion, that no large state, such as France or Great Britain, could ever be modelled into a commonwealth, but that such a form of government can only take place in a city or small territory. The contrary seems probable. Though it is more difficult to form a republican government in an extensive country than in a city; there is more facility, once when it is formed, of preserving it steady and uniform, without tumult and faction. It is not easy, for the distant parts of a large state to combine in any plan of free government; but they easily conspire in the esteem and reverence for a single person, who, by means of this popular favour, may seize the power, and forcing the more obstinate to submit, may establish a monarchical government. On the other hand, a city readily concurs in the same notions of government, the natural equality of property favors liberty, and the nearness of habitation enables the citizens mutually to assist each other. Even under absolute princes, the subordinate government of cities is commonly republican; while that of counties and provinces is monarchical. But these same circumstances, which facilitate the erection of commonwealths in cities, render their constitution more frail and uncertain. Democracies are turbulent. For however the people may be separated or divided into small parties, either in their votes or elections; their near habitation in a city will always make the force of popular tides and currents very sensible. Aristocracies are better adapted for peace and order, and accordingly were most admired by ancient writers; but they are jealous and oppressive. In a large government, which is modelled with masterly skill, there is compass and room enough to refine the democracy, from the lower people, who may be admitted into the first elections or first concoction of the commonwealth, to the higher magistrates, who direct all the movements. At the same time, the parts are so distant and remote, that it is very difficult, either by intrigue, prejudice, or passion, to hurry them into any measures against the public interest.

It is needless to enquire, whether such a government would be immortal. I allow the justness of the poet's exclamation on the endless projects of human race, Man and for ever! The world itself probably is not immortal. Such consuming plagues may arise as would leave even a perfect government a weak prey to its neighbors. We know not to what length enthusiasm, or other extraordinary movements of the human mind, may transport men, to the neglect of all order and public good. Where difference of interest is removed, whimsical and unaccountable factions often arise, from personal favour or enmity. Perhaps, rust may grow to the springs of the most accurate political machine, and disorder its motions. Lastly, extensive conquests, when pursued, must be the ruin of every free government; and of the more perfect governments sooner than the imperfect; because of the very advantages which the former possess above the latter. And though such a state ought to establish a fundamental law against conquests; yet republics have ambition as well as individuals, and present interest makes men forgetful of their posterity. It is a sufficient incitement to human endeavours, that such a government would flourish for many ages; without pretending to bestow, on any work of man, that immortality, which the Almighty seems to have refused to his own productions.

GEORGIA TRUSTEES

A Brief Account of the Causes That Have Retarded the Progress of the Colony of Georgia (1743)

[. . .] But as if the difficulties arising from indifferent lands, and discouraging tenures, were not sufficient to humble and prepare them for the other severities they have met with, they were totally prohibited the importation, use, or even sight of Negroes. In spite of all endeavours to disguise this point, it is as clear as light itself, that Negroes are as essentially necessary to the cultivation of Georgia, as axes, hoes, or any other utensil of agriculture. So that if a colony was designed able but to subsist itself, their prohibition was inconsistent; if a garrison only was intended, the very inhabitants were needless. But all circumstances considered, it looked as if the assistance of human creatures, who have been called slaves, as well as subject to the treatment of such, were incongruous with a system that proceeded to confer the thing, but to spare the odium of the appellation. Experience would too soon have taught them the parity of their conditions, in spite of a mere nominal difference. The only English clergymen, who were ever countenanced there, declared they never desired to see Georgia a rich, but a godly colony; and the blind subjection the poor Salzburgers are under to the Rev. Mr. Boltzius, who has furnished such extraordinary extracts in some accounts of Georgia, published here, will be too evident from some of the annexed depositions to call for any descant.

The pretended content and satisfaction of the people of Ebenezer, without Negroes, will plainly appear to be the dictates of spiritual tyranny, and only the wretched acquiescence of people, who were in truth unacquainted with the privilege of choosing for themselves.

It is acknowledged indeed that the present war, and late invasion, may furnish the enemies of the colony with the most plausible objections that could occur, against the allowance of black slaves; but these reasons have not always existed, nor have the trustees ever declared any resolution to admit them, at any other juncture. But if it plainly appears that Georgia, as a colony, cannot barely exist without them, surely an admission of them under limitations, suitable to the present situation of affairs, is absolutely necessary to its support; since want and famine must be more dreadful and insuperable invaders, than any living enemy. Besides, the honorable trustees were informed by a letter from Mr. Stirling and others, of the falsehood of the contented and comfortable situation the people of Darien were affirmed to be in; and that they were bought with a number of cattle, and extensive promises of future rewards when they signed their petition against Negroes.

Montesquieu

Spirit of the Laws (1748)

Part One, Book One
On Laws in General

Chapter 1
On laws in their relation with the various beings

Laws, taken in the broadest meaning, are the necessary relations deriving from the nature of things; and in this sense, all beings have their laws: the divinity has its laws, the material world has its laws, the intelligence superior to man have their laws, the beasts have their laws, man has his laws.

Those who have said that *a blind fate has produced all the effects that we see in the world* have said a great absurdity; for what greater absurdity is there than a blind fate that could have produced intelligent beings?

There is, then, a primitive reason; and laws are both the relations that exist between it and the different beings, and the relations of these various beings to each other.

God is related to the universe, as creator and preserver; the laws according to which he created are those according to which he preserves; he acts according to these rules because he knows them; he knows them because he made them; he made them because they are related to his wisdom and his power.

As we see that the world, formed by the motion of matter and devoid of intelligence, still continues to exist, its motions must have invariable laws; and, if one could imagine another world than this, it would have consistent rules or it would be destroyed.

Thus creation, which appears to be an arbitrary act, presupposes rules as invariable as the fate claimed by atheists. It would be absurd to say that the creator, without these rules, could govern the world, since the world would not continue to exist without them.

These rules are a consistently established relation. Between one moving body and another moving body, it is in accord with relations of mass and velocity that all motions are received, increased, diminished, or lost; every diversity is *uniformity*, every change is *consistency*.

Particular intelligent beings can have laws that they have made, but they also have some that they have not made. Before there were intelligent beings, they were possible; therefore, they had possible relations and consequently possible laws. Before laws were made, there were possible relations of justice. To say that there is nothing just or unjust but what positive laws ordain or prohibit is to say that before a circle was drawn, all its radii were not equal.

Therefore, one must admit that there are relations of fairness prior to the positive law that establishes them, so that, for example, assuming that there were societies of men, it would be just to conform to their laws; so that, if there were intelligent beings that had received some kindness from another being, they ought to be grateful for it; so that, if one intelligent being had created another intelligent being, the created one ought to remain in its original dependency; so that one intelligent being who has done harm to another intelligent being deserves the same harm in return, and so forth.

But the intelligent world is far from being as well governed as the physical world. For, though the intelligent world also has laws that are invariable by their nature, unlike the physical world, it does not follow its laws consistently. The reason for this is that particular intelligent beings are limited by their nature and are consequently subject to error; futhermore, it is in their nature to act by themselves. Therefore, they do not consistently follow their primitive laws or even always follow the laws they give themselves. [. . .]

Man, as a physical being, is governed by invariable laws like other bodies. As an intelligent being, he constantly violates the laws god has established and changes those he himself establishes; he must guide himself, and yet he is a limited being; he is subject to ignorance and error, as are all finite intelligences; he loses even the imperfect knowledge he has. As a feeling creature, he falls subject to a thousand passions. Such a being could at any moment forget his creator; god has called him back to him by the laws of religion. Such a being could at any moment forget himself; philosophers have reminded him of himself by the laws of morality. Made for living in society, he could forget his fellows; legislators have returned him to his duties by political and civil laws.

Chapter 2
On the laws of nature

Prior to all these laws are the laws of nature, so named because they derive uniquely from the constitution of our being. To know them well, one must consider a man before the establishment of societies. The laws he would receive in such a state will be the laws of nature.

The law that impresses on us the idea of a creator and thereby leads us toward him is the first of the *natural laws* in importance, though not first in the order of these laws. A man in the state of nature would have the faculty of knowing rather than knowledge. It is clear that his first ideas would not be speculative ones; he would think of the preservation of his being before seeking the origin of his being. Such a man would at first feel only his weakness; his timidity would be extreme: and as for evidence, if it is needed on this point, savages have been found in forests,[1] everything makes them tremble, everything makes them flee.

In this state, each feels himself inferior; he scarcely feels himself an equal. Such men would not seek to attack one another, and peace would be the first natural law.

Hobbes gives men first the desire to subjugate one another, but this is not reasonable. The idea of empire and domination is so complex and depends on so many other ideas, that it would not be the one they would first have.

Hobbes asks, *If men are not naturally in a state of war, why do they always carry arms and why do they have keys to lock their doors?* But one feels that what can happen to men only after the establishment of societies, which induced them to find motives for attacking others and for defending themselves, is attributed to them before that establishment.

Man would add the feeling of his needs to the feeling of his weakness. Thus another natural law would be the one inspiring him to seek nourishment.

I have said that fear would lead men to flee one another, but the marks of mutual fear would soon persuade them to approach one another. They would also be so inclined by the pleasure one animal feels at the approach of an animal of its own kind. In addition, the charm that the two sexes inspire in each other by their difference would increase this pleasure, and the natural entreaty they always make to one another would be a third law.

Besides feelings, which belong to men from the outset, they also succeed in gaining knowledge; thus they have a second bond, which other animals do not have. Therefore, they have another motive for uniting, and the desire to live in society is a fourth natural law.

Chapter 3
On positive laws

As soon as men are in society, they lose their feeling of weakness; the equality that was among them ceases, and the state of war begins.

Each particular society comes to feel its strength, producing a state of war among nations. The individuals within each society begin to feel their strength; they seek to turn their favor the principal advantages of this society, which brings about a state of war among them.

These two sorts of states of war bring about the establishment of laws among men. Considered as inhabitants of a planet so large that different peoples are necessary, they have laws bearing on the relation that these peoples have with one another, and this is the RIGHT OF NATIONS. Considered as living in a society that must be maintained, they have laws concerning the relation between those who govern and those who are governed, and this is the POLITICAL RIGHT. Further, they have laws concerning the relation that all citizens have with one another, and this is the CIVIL RIGHT.

The *right of nations* is by nature founded on the principle that the various nations should do to one another in times of peace the most good possible,

---

1. Witness the savage who was found in the forests of Hanover and who lived in England in the reign of George I.

and in times of war the least ill possible, without harming their true interests.

The object of war is victory; of victory, conquest; of conquest, preservation. All the laws that form the *right of nations* should derive from this principle and the preceding one.

All nations have a right of nations; and even the Iroquois, who eat their prisoners, have one. They send and receive embassies; they know rights of war and peace: the trouble is that their right of nations is not founded on true principles.

In addition to the right of nations, which concerns all societies, there is a *political right* for each one. A society could not continue to exist without a government. *"The union of all individual strengths,"* as Gravina aptly says, "forms what is called the POLITICAL STATE."

The strength of the whole society may be put in the hands of *one alone* or in the hands of *many*. Since nature has established paternal power, some have thought that government by one alone is most in conformity with nature. But the example of paternal power proves nothing. For, if the power of the father is related to government by one alone, then after the death of the father, the power of the brothers, or after the death of the brothers, the power of the first cousins, is related to government by many. Political power necessarily includes the union of many families.

It is better to say that the government most in conformity with nature is the one whose particular arrangement best relates to the disposition of the people for whom it is established.

Individual strengths cannot be united unless all wills are united. *The union of these wills*, as Gravina again aptly says, *is what is called the* CIVIL STATE.

Law in general is human reason insofar as it governs all the peoples of the earth; and the political and civil laws of each nation should be only the particular cases to which human reason is applied.

Laws should be so appropriate to the people for whom they are made that it is very unlikely that the laws of one nation can suit another.

Laws must relate to the nature and the principle of the government that is established or that one wants to establish, whether those laws form it as do political laws, or maintain it, as do civil laws.

They should be related to the *physical aspect* of the country; to the climate, be it freezing, torrid, or temperate; to the properties of the terrain, its location and extent; to the way of life of the peoples, be they plowmen, hunters, or herdsmen; they should relate to the degree of liberty that the constitution can sustain, to the religion of the inhabitants, their inclinations, their wealth, their number, their commerce, their mores and their manners; finally, the laws are related to one another, to their origin, to the purpose of the legislator, and to the order of things on which they are established. They must be considered from all these points of view.

This is what I undertake to do in this work. I shall examine all these relations; together they form what is called THE SPIRIT OF THE LAWS.

I have made no attempt to separate *political* from *civil* laws, for, as I do not treat laws but the spirit of the laws, and as this spirit consists in the various relations that laws may have with various things, I have had to follow the natural order of laws less than that of these relations and of these things.

I shall first examine the relations that laws have with the nature and the principle of each government, and, as this principle has a supreme influence on the laws, I shall apply myself to understanding it well; and if I can once establish it, the laws will be seen to flow from it as from their source. I shall then proceed to other relations that seem to be more particular.

Chapter 5
On laws relative to the nature of the despotic state

A result of the nature of despotic power is that the one man who exercises it has it likewise exercised by another. A man whose five senses constantly tell him that he is everything and that others are nothing is naturally lazy, ignorant, and voluptuous. Therefore, he abandons the public business. But, if he entrusted this business to many people, there would be disputes among them; there would be intrigues to be the first slave; the prince would be obliged to return to administration. Therefore it is simpler for him to abandon them to a vizir[2] who will instantly have the

2. Eastern kings always have vizirs, says [John] Chardin [*Voyages*, "Description du gouvernement"; chap. 5, "Des charges"; 5, 339–340; 1811 edn.].

same power as he. In this state, the establishment of a vizir is a fundamental law.

It is said that a certain pope, upon his election, overcome with his inadequacy, at first made infinite difficulties. Finally, he agreed to turn all matters of business over to his nephew. He was awestruck and said, "I would never have believed that it could be so easy." It is the same for the princes of the East. When, from that prison where eunuchs have weakened their hearts and spirits and have often left them ignorant even of their estate, these princes are withdrawn to be put on the throne, they are stunned at first; but when they have appointed a vizir, when in their seraglio they have given themselves up to the most brutal passions, when in the midst of a downtrodden court they have followed their most foolish caprices, they would never have believed that it could be so easy.

The more extensive the empire, the larger the seraglio, and the more, consequently, the prince is drunk with pleasures. Thus, in these states, the more peoples the prince has to govern, the less he thinks about government; the greater the matters of business, the less deliberation they are given.

Part One, Book Three On the Principles of the Three Governments

Chapter 1 The difference between the nature of the government and its principle

After having examined the laws relative to the nature of each government, one must look at those that are relative to its principle.

There is this difference[3] between the nature of the government and its principle: its nature is that which makes it what it is, and its principle, that which makes it act. The one is its particular structure, and the others the human passions that set it in motion.

Now, the laws should be no less relative to the principle of each government than to its nature. Therefore, this principle must be sought. I shall do so in this book.

Chapter 2 On the principle of the various governments

I have said that the nature of republican government is that the people as a body, or certain families, have the sovereign power; the nature of monarchical government is that the prince has the sovereign power, but that he exercises it according to established laws; the nature of despotic government is that one alone governs according to his wills and caprices. Nothing more is needed for me to find their three principles; they derive naturally from this. I shall begin with republican government, and I shall first speak of the democratic government.

Chapter 3 On the principle of democracy

There need not be much integrity for a monarchical or despotic government to maintain or sustain itself. The force of the laws in the one and the prince's ever-raised arm in the other can rule or contain the whole. But in a popular state there must be an additional spring, which is VIRTUE.

What I say is confirmed by the entire body of history and is quite in conformity with the nature of things. For it is clear that less virtue is needed in a monarchy, where the one who sees to the execution of the laws judges himself above the laws, than in a popular government, where the one who sees to the execution of the laws feels that he is subject to them himself and that he will bear their weight.

It is also clear that the monarch who ceases to see to the execution of the laws, through bad counsel or negligence, may easily repair the damage; he has only to change his counsel or correct his own negligence. But in a popular government when the laws have ceased to be executed, as this can come only from the corruption of the republic, the state is already lost.

It was a fine spectacle in the last century to see the impotent attempts of the English to establish democracy among themselves. As those who took part in public affairs had no virtue at all, as their

---

3. This difference is very important, and I shall draw many consequences from it; it is the key to an infinity of laws.

ambition was excited by the success of the most audacious one[4] and the spirit of one faction was repressed only by the spirit of another, the government was constantly changing; the people, stunned, sought democracy and found it nowhere. Finally, after much motion and many shocks and jolts, they had to come to rest on the very government that had been proscribed.

When Sulla wanted to return liberty to Rome, it could no longer be accepted; Rome had but a weak remnant of virtue, and as it had ever less, instead of reawakening after Caeser, Tiberius, Caius, Claudius, Nero, and Domitian, it became ever more enslaved; all the blows were struck against tyrants, none against tyranny.

The political men of Greece who lived under popular government recognized no other force to sustain it than virtue. Those of today speak to us only of manufacturing, commerce, finance, wealth, and even luxury.

When that virtue ceases, ambition enters those hearts that can admit it, and avarice enters them all. Desires change their objects: that which one used to love, one loves no longer. One was free under the laws, one wants to be free against them. Each citizen is like a slave who has escaped from his master's house. What was a *maxim* is now called *severity*; what was a *rule* is now called *constraint*; what was *vigilance* is now called *fear*. There, frugality, not the desire to possess, is avarice. Formerly the goods of individuals made up the public treasury; the public treasury has now become the patrimony of individuals. The republic is a cast-off husk, and its strength is no more than the power of a few citizens and the license of all.

Chapter 4
On the principle of aristocracy

Just as there must be virtue in popular government, there must also be virtue in the aristocratic one. It is true that it is not as absolutely required.

The people, who are with respect to the nobles what the subjects are with respect to the monarch, are contained by the nobles laws. Therefore, they need virtue less than the people of a democracy. But how will the nobles be contained? Those who should see to the execution of the laws against their fellows will instantly feel that they act against themselves. Virtue must, therefore, be in this body by the nature of the constitution.

Aristocratic government has a certain strength in itself that democracy does not have. In aristocratic government, the nobles form a body, which, by its prerogative and for its particular interest, represses the people; having laws is enough to insure that they will be executed.

But it is as easy for this body to repress the others as it is difficult for it to repress itself.[5] Such is the nature of this constitution that it seems to put under the power of the laws the same people it exempts from them.

Now such a body may repress itself in only two ways: either by a great virtue that makes the nobles in some way equal to their people, which may form a great republic; or by a lesser virtue, a certain moderation that renders the nobles at least equal among themselves, which brings about their preservation.

Therefore, *moderation* is the soul of these governments. I mean the moderation founded on virtue, not the one that comes from faintheartedness and from laziness of soul.

Chapter 5
That virtue is not the principle of monarchical government

In monarchies, politics accomplishes great things with as little virtue as it can, just as in the finest machines art employs as few motions, forces, and wheels as possible.

The state continues to exist independently of love of the homeland, desire for true glory, self-renunciation, sacrifice of one's dearest interests, and all those heroic virtues we find in the ancients and know only by hearsay.

The laws replace all these virtues, for which there is no need; the state excuses you from them: here an action done noiselessly is in a way inconsequential.

Though all crimes are by their nature public, truly public crimes are nevertheless distinguished

4. Cromwell.

5. Public crimes can be punished there because they are the business of all; private crimes will not be punished there, because it is not the business of all to punish them.

from private crimes, so called because they offend an individual more than the whole society.

Now, in republics private crimes are more public, that is, they run counter to the constitution of the state more than against individuals; and, in monarchies, public crimes are more private, that is, they run counter to individual fortunes more than against the constitution of the state itself.

I beg that no one be offended by what I have said; I have followed all the histories. I know very well that virtuous princes are not rare, but I say that in a monarchy it is very difficult for the people to be virtuous.[6]

Read what the historians of all times have said about the courts of monarchs; recall the conversations of men from every country about the wretched character of courtiers: these are not matters of speculation but of sad experience.

Ambition in idleness, meanness in arrogance, the desire to enrich oneself without work, aversion to truth, flattery, treachery, perfidy, the abandonment of all one's engagements, the scorn of the duties of citizens, the fear of the prince's virtue, the expectation of his weaknesses, and more than all that, the perpetual ridicule cast upon virtue, these form, I believe, the character of the greater number of courtiers, as observed in all places and at all times. Now, it is very awkward for most of the principal men of a state to be dishonest people and for the inferiors to be good people, for the former to be deceivers and the latter to consent to be no more than dupes.

If there is some unfortunate honest man among the people,[7] hints Cardinal Richelieu in his *Political Testament*, a monarch should be careful not to employ him.[8] So true is it that virtue is not the spring of this government! Certainly, it is not excluded, but it is not its spring.

Chapter 6
How virtue is replaced in monarchical government

I hasten and I lengthen my steps, so that none will believe I satirize monarchical government. No; if one spring is missing, monarchy has another. HONOR, that is, the prejudice of each person and each condition, takes the place of the political virtue of which I have spoken and represents it everywhere. It can inspire the finest actions; joined with the force of the laws, it can lead to the goal of government as does virtue itself.

Thus, in well-regulated monarchies everyone will be almost a good citizen, and one will rarely find someone who is a good man; for, in order to be a good man,[9] one must have the intention of being one[10] and love the state less for oneself than for itself.

Chapter 7
On the principle of monarchy

Monarchical government assumes, as we have said, preeminences, ranks, and even a hereditary nobility. The nature of *honor* is to demand preferences and distinctions; therefore, honor has, in and of itself, a place in this government.

Ambition is pernicious in a republic. It has good effects in monarchy; it gives life to that government; and it has this advantage, that it is not dangerous because it can constantly be repressed.

You could say that it is like the system of the universe, where there is a force constantly repelling all bodies from the center and a force of gravitation attracting them to it. Honor makes all the parts of the body politic move; its very action binds them, and each person works for the common good, believing he works for his individual interests.

---

6. I speak here about political virtue, which is moral virtue in the sense that it points toward the general good, very little about individual moral virtues, and not at all about that virtue which relates to revealed truths. This will be seen in book 5, chap. 2 [below].

7. To be understood in the sense of the preceding note.

8. There it is said, "One must not employ people of low degree; they are too austere and too difficult" [Cardinal Richelieu, *Testament politique*, pt. I, chap. 4, sec. I; pp. 237–238; 1947 edn.].

9. These words, *good man*, are to be taken here only in a political sense.

10. See note 6.

Speaking philosophically, it is true that the honor that guides all the parts of the state is a false honor, but this false honor is as useful to the public as the true one would be to the individuals who could have it.

And is it not impressive that one can oblige men to do all the difficult actions and which require force, with no reward other than the renown of these actions?

Part One, Book Four That the Laws of Education Should Be Relative to the Principles of the Government

Chapter 5 On education in republican government

It is in republican government that the full power of education is needed. Fear in despotic governments arises of itself from threats and chastisements; honor in monarchies is favored by the passions and favors them in turn; but political virtue is a renunciation of oneself, which is always a very painful thing.

One can define this virtue as love of the laws and the homeland. This love, requiring a continuous preference of the public interest over one's own, produces all the individual virtues; they are only that preference.

This love is singularly connected with democracies. In them alone, government is entrusted to each citizen. Now government is like all things in the world; in order to preserve it, one must love it.

One never hears it said that kings do not love monarchy or that despots hate despotism.

Therefore, in a republic, everything depends on establishing this love, and education should attend to inspiring it. But there is a sure way for children to have it; it is for the fathers themselves to have it.

One is ordinarily in charge of giving one's knowledge to one's children and even more in charge of giving them one's own passions.

If this does not happen, it is because what was done in the father's house is destroyed by impressions from the outside.

It is not young people who degenerate; they are ruined only when grown men have already been corrupted.

Part One, Book Eight On the Corruption of the Principles of the Three Governments

Chapter 1 The general idea of this book

The corruption of each government almost always begins with that of its principles.

Chapter 2 On the corruption of the principle of democracy

The principle of democracy is corrupted not only when the spirit of equality is lost but also when the spirit of extreme equality is taken up and each one wants to be the equal of those chosen to command. So the people, finding intolerable even the power they entrust to the others, want to do everything themselves: to deliberate for the senate, to execute for the magistrates, and to cast aside all the judges.

Then there can no longer be virtue in the republic, the people want to perform the magistrates' functions; therefore, the magistrates are no longer respected. The senate's deliberations no longer carry weight; therefore, there is no longer consideration for senators or, consequently, for elders. And if there is no respect for elders, neither will there be any for fathers; husbands no longer merit deference nor masters, submission. Everyone will come to love this license; the restraint of commanding will be as tiresome as that of obeying had been. Women, children, and slaves will submit to no one. There will no longer be mores or love of order, and finally, there will no longer be virtue.

One sees in Xenophon's *Symposium* an artless depiction of a republic whose people have abused equality. Each guest in turn gives his reason for being pleased with himself. "I am pleased with myself," says Charmides, "because of my poverty. When I was rich I was obliged to pay court to slanderers, well aware that I was more likely to receive ill from them than to cause them any; the republic constantly asked for a new payment; I could not travel. Since becoming poor, I have acquired authority; no one threatens me, I threaten the others; I can go or stay. The rich now rise from their seats and make way for me. Now I am a king, I was a slave; I used to pay a tax to the republic, today the republic feeds me; I no longer fear loss, I expect to acquire."

The people fall into this misfortune when those to whom they entrust themselves, wanting to hide their own corruption, seek to corrupt the people. To keep the people from seeing their own ambition, they speak only of the people's greatness; to keep the people from perceiving their avarice, they constantly encourage that of the people.

Corruption will increase among those who corrupt, and it will increase among those who are already corrupted. The people will distribute among themselves all the public funds; and, just as they will join the management of business to their laziness, they will want to join the amusements of luxury to their poverty. But given their laziness and their luxury, only the public treasure can be their object.

One must not be astonished to see votes given for silver. One cannot give the people much without taking even more from them; but, in order to take from them, the state must be overthrown. The more the people appear to take advantage of their liberty, the nearer they approach the moment they are to lose it. Petty tyrants are formed, having all the vices of a single one. What remains of liberty soon becomes intolerable. A single tyrant rises up, and the people lose everything, even the advantages of their corruption.

Therefore, democracy has to avoid two excesses: the spirit of inequality, which leads it to aristocracy or to the government of one alone, and the spirit of extreme equality, which leads it to the despotism or one alone, as the despotism of one alone ends by conquest. [. . .]

Chapter 3
On the spirit of extreme equality

As far as the sky is from the earth, so far is the true spirit of equality from the spirit of extreme equality. The former consists neither in making everyone command nor in making no one command, but in obeying and commanding one's equals. It seeks not to have no master but to have only one's equals for masters.

In the state of nature, men are born in equality, but they cannot remain so. Society makes them lose their equality, and they become equal again only through the laws.

The difference between the democracy that is regulated and the one that is not is that, in the former, one is equal only as a citizen, and, in the latter, one is also equal as a magistrate, senator, judge, father, husband, or master.

The natural place of virtue is with liberty, but virtue can no more be found with extreme liberty than with servitude.

Chapter 16
Distinctive properties of the republic

It is in the nature of a republic to have only a small territory; otherwise, it can scarcely continue to exist. In a large republic, there are large fortunes, and consequently little moderation in spirits: the depositories are too large to put in the hands of a citizen; interests become particularized; at first a man feels he can be happy, great, and glorious without his homeland; and soon, that he can be great only on the ruins of his homeland.

In a large republic, the common good is sacrificed to a thousand considerations; it is subordinated to exceptions; it depends upon accidents. In a small one, the public good is better felt, better known, lies nearer to each citizen; abuses are less extensive there and consequently less protected.

What made Lacedaemonia last so long is that, after all its wars, it always remained within its territory. Lacedaemonia's only goal was liberty; the only advantage of its liberty was glory.

It was in the spirit of the Greek republics for them to be as satisfied with their lands as they were with their laws. Athens was seized with ambition and transmitted it to Lacedaemonia; but this was in order to command free peoples rather than to govern slaves; to be at the head of the union rather than to shatter it. All was lost when a monarchy rose up, a government whose spirit tends more toward expansion.

It is difficult for any government other than the republican to continue to exist in a single town unless there are particular circumstances.[11] A prince of such a small state would naturally be inclined to

11. As when a small sovereign maintains himself between two great states by their mutual jealousy; but he exists only precariously.

oppression because he would have a great power and few ways to enjoy it or to make it respected; therefore he would trample his people greatly. Then again, such a prince would be easily oppressed by a foreign force or even by a domestic force; the people could come together and unite against him at any moment. Now, when the prince of a single town is driven from his town, the proceeding is finished; if he has several towns, it has just begun.

Chapter 20
Consequence of the preceding chapters

If the natural property of small states is to be governed as republics, that of medium-sized ones, to be subject to a monarch, and that of large empires to be dominated by a despot, it follows that, in order to preserve the principles of the established government, the state must be maintained at the size it already has and that it will change its spirit to the degree to which its boundaries are narrowed or extended.

Part Two, Book Nine
On the Laws in Their Relation with Defensive Force

Chapter 1
How republics provide for their security

If a republic is small, it is destroyed by a foreign force; if it is large, it is destroyed by an internal vice.

This dual drawback taints democracies and aristocracies equally, whether they are good or whether they are bad. The ill is in the thing itself; there is no form that can remedy it.

Thus, it is very likely that ultimately men would have been obliged to live forever under the government of one alone if they had not devised a kind of constitution that has all the internal advantages of republican government and the external force of monarchy. I speak of the federal republic.

This form of government is an agreement by which many political bodies consent to become citizens of the larger state that they want to form. It is a society of societies that make a new one, which can be enlarged by new associates that unite with it.

Such associations made Greece flourish for so long. By using them, the Romans attacked the universe, and with their use alone, the universe defended itself from the Romans; and when Rome had reached its greatest height, the barbarians were able to resist it by associations made beyond the Danube and the Rhine, associations made from fright.

Because of them, Holland,[12] Germany, and the Swiss leagues are regarded in Europe as eternal republics.

Associations of towns were more necessary formerly than they are today. A city without power risked greater perils. Conquest made it lose not only executive and legislative power, as today, but also all property among men.[13]

This sort of republic. able to resist external force, can be maintained at its size without internal corruption: the form of this society curbs every drawback.

One who might want to usurp could scarcely have equal credit in all the confederated states. If he became too strong in one state, he would alarm all the others; if he subjugated a part, the part still free could resist him with forces independent of those he had usurped and overwhelm him before he had completely established himself.

If a sedition occurs in one of the members of the confederation, the others can pacify it. If some abuses are introduced somewhere, they are corrected by the healthy parts. This state can perish in one place without perishing in another; the confederation can be dissolved and the confederates remain sovereign.

Composed of small republics, it enjoys the goodness of the internal government of each one; and, with regard to the exterior, it has, by the force of the association, all the advantages of large monarchies.

---

12. It is formed of about fifty republics, all of them different from one another. [François Michel] Janiçon, *Etat présent de la République des Provinces-Unies* [I, 76; 1729 edn].

13. Civil liberty, goods, women, children, temples, and even sepulchers.

Chapter 2
That the federal constitution should be composed of states of the same nature, above all of republican states

The Canaanites were destroyed because they were small monarchies that had not confederated and did not have a common defense. This is because it is not in the nature of small monarchies to confederate.

The federal republic of Germany is composed of free towns and small states subject to princes. Experience shows that it is more imperfect than the federal republics of Holland and Switzerland.

The spirit of monarchy is war and expansion; the spirit of republics is peace and moderation. The only way these two sorts of governments can continue to exist together in one federal republic is by force. [. . .]

The federal republic of Germany, composed of princes and free towns, continues to exist because it has a leader who is, in a way, the magistrate of the union and, in a way, the monarch.

Chapter 3
Other things required in the federal republic

In the republic of Holland, one province cannot make an alliance without the consent of the others. This law is good and even necessary in the federal republic. It is missing from the German constitution, where it would curb the misfortunes that can come to all the members from the imprudence, ambition, or avarice of one alone. A republic united in a political confederation has given itself entirely and has nothing more to give.

It is unlikely that the states that associate will be of the same size and have equal power. The republic of the Lycians[14] was an association of twenty-three towns; the large ones had three votes in the common council; the medium-sized ones, two; the small ones, one. The republic of Holland is composed of seven provinces, large and small, each having one vote.

The towns of Lycia[15] paid the costs in proportion to their votes. The provinces of Holland cannot follow this proportion; they must follow that of their power.

In Lycia,[16] the judges and magistrates of the towns were elected by the common council in the proportion that we have said. In the republic of Holland, they are not elected by the common council, and each town names its magistrates. If one had to propose a model of a fine federal republic, I would choose the republic of Lycia.

Part Two, Book Eleven
On the Laws that Form Political Liberty in Its Relation with the Constitution

Chapter 1
General idea

I distinguish the laws that form political liberty in its relation with the constitution from those that form it in its relation with the citizen. The first are the subject of the present book; I shall discuss the second in the next book.

Chapter 2
The various significations given to the word liberty

No word has received more different significations and has struck minds in so many ways as has *liberty*. Some have taken it for the ease of removing the one to whom they had given tyrannical power; some, for the faculty of electing the one whom they were to obey; others, for the right to be armed and to be able to use violence; yet others, for the privilege of being governed only by a man of their own nation, or by their own laws.[17] For a certain people liberty has long been the usage of wearing a long beard.[18] Men have

14. Strabo [*Geographica*], bk. 14 [14.3.3].

15. Ibid. [Strabo, *Geographica*, 14.3.3].

16. Strabo [*Geographica*], bk. 14 [14.3.3].

17. Cicero [*Epistolae ad Atticum* 6.1.15] says, "I have copied Scaevola's edict, which permits the Greeks to end their differences among themselves according to their laws; this makes them regard themselves as free peoples."

18. The Muscovites could not bear Czar Peter's order to cut them off.

given this name to one form of government and have excluded the others. Those who had tasted republican government put it in this government; those who had enjoyed monarchical government placed it in monarchy.[19] In short, each has given the name of *liberty* to the government that was consistent with his customs or his inclinations; and as, in a republic, one does not always have visible and so present the instruments of the ills of which one complains and as the very laws seem to speak more and the executors of the law to speak less, one ordinarily places liberty in republics and excludes it from monarchies. Finally, as in democracies the people seem very nearly to do what they want, liberty has been placed in this sort of government and the power of the people has been confused with the liberty of the people.

Chapter 3
What liberty is

It is true that in democracies the people seem to do what they want, but political liberty in no way consists in doing what one wants. In a state, that is, in a society where there are laws, liberty can consist only in having the power to do what one should want to do and in no way being constrained to do what one should not want to do.

One must put oneself in mind of what independence is and what liberty is. Liberty is the right to do everything the laws permit; and if one citizen could do what they forbid, he would no longer have liberty because the others would likewise have this same power.

Chapter 4
Continuation of the same subject

Democracy and aristocracy are not free states by their nature. Political liberty is found only in moderate governments. But it is not always in moderate states. It is present only when power is not abused, but it has eternally been observed that any man who has power is led to abuse it; he continues until he finds limits. Who would think it! Even virtue has need of limits.

So that one cannot abuse power, power must check power by the arrangement of things. A constitution can be such that no one will be constrained to do the things the law does not oblige him to do or be kept from doing the things the law permits him to do.

Chapter 5
On the purpose of various states

Although all states have the same purpose in general, which is to maintain themselves, yet each state has a purpose that is peculiar to it. Expansion was the purpose of Rome; war, that of Lacedaemonia; religion, that of the Jewish laws; commerce, that of Marseilles; public tranquillity, that of the laws of China;[20] navigation, that of the laws of the Rhodians; natural liberty was the purpose of the police of the savages; in general, the delights of the prince are the purpose of the despotic states; his glory and that of his state, that of monarchies; the independence of each individual is the purpose of the laws of Poland, and what results from this is the oppression of all.[21]

There is also one nation in the world whose constitution has political liberty for its direct purpose. We are going to examine the principles on which this nation founds political liberty. If these principles are good, liberty will appear there as in a mirror.

Not much trouble need be taken to discover political liberty in the constitution. If it can be seen where it is, if it has been found, why seek it?

Chapter 6
On the constitution of England

In each state there are three sorts of powers: legislative power, executive power over the things depending on the right of nations, and executive power over the things depending on civil right.

By the first, the prince or the magistrate makes laws for a time or for always and corrects or abrogates those that have been made. By the second, he makes peace or war, sends or receives embassies, establishes security, and prevents invasions. By the third, he punishes crimes or judges disputes between

19. The Cappadocians refused the republican state the Romans offered them.

20. The natural purpose of a state having no enemies on the outside or believing them checked by barriers.

21. Drawback of the *liberum veto*.

individuals. The last will be called the power of judging, and the former simply the executive power of the state.

Political liberty in a citizen is that tranquillity of spirit which comes from the opinion each one has of his security, and in order for him to have this liberty the government must be such that one citizen cannot fear another citizen.

When legislative power is united with executive power in a single person or in a single body of the magistracy, there is no liberty, because one can fear that the same monarch or senate that makes tyrannical laws will excute them tyrannically.

Nor is there liberty if the power of judging is not separate from legislative power and from executive power. If it were joined to legislative power, the power over the life and liberty of the citizens would be arbitary, for the judge would be the legislator. If it were joined to executive power, the judge could have the force of an oppressor.

All would be lost if the same man or the same body of principal men, either of nobles, or of the people, exercised these three powers: that of making the laws, that of executing public resolutions, and that of judging the crimes or the disputes of individuals.

In most kingdoms in Europe, the goverment is moderate because the prince, who has the first two powers, leaves the exercise of the third to his subjects. Among the Turks, where the three powers are united in the person of the sultan, an atrocious despotism reigns.

In the Italian republics, where the three powers are united, there is less liberty than in our monarchies. Thus, in order to maintain itself, the government needs means as violent as in the government of the Turks; witness the state inquisitors[22] and the lion's maw into which an informer can, at any moment, throw his note of accusation.

Observe the possible situation of a citizen in these republics. The body of the magistracy, as executor of the laws, retains all the power it has given itself as legislator. It can plunder the state by using its general wills; and, as it also has the power of judging, it can destroy each citizen by using its particular wills.

There, all power is one; and although there is none of the external pomp that reveals a despotic prince, it is felt at every moment.

Thus princes who have wanted to make themselves despotic have always begun by uniting in their person all the magistracies, and many kings of Europe have begun by uniting all the great posts of their state.

I do believe that the pure hereditary aristocracy of the Italian republics is not precisely like the despotism of Asia. The multitude of magistrates sometimes softens the magistracy; not all the nobles always concur in the same designs; there various tribunals are formed that temper one another. Thus, in Venice, the *Great Council* has legislation; the *Pregadi*, execution; *Quarantia*, the power of judging. But the ill is that these different tribunals are formed of magistrates taken from the same body; this makes them nearly a single power.

The power of judging should not be given to a permanent senate but should be exercised by persons drawn from the body of the people[23] at certain times of the year in the manner prescribed by law to form a tribunal which lasts only as long as necessity requires.

In this fashion the power of judging, so terrible among men, being attached neither to a certain state nor to a certain profession, becomes, so to speak, invisible and null. Judges are not continually in view; one fears the magistracy, not the magistrates.

In important accusations, the criminal in cooperation with the law must choose the judges, or at least he must be able to challenge so many of them that those who remain are considered to be of his choice.

The two other powers may be given instead to magistrates or to permanent bodies because they are exercised upon no individual, the one being only the general will of the state, and the other, the execution of that general will.

But though tribunals should not be fixed, judgments should be fixed to such a degree that they are never anything but a precise text of the law. If judgments were the individual opinion of a judge, one would live in this society without knowing precisely what engagements one has contracted.

---

22. In Venice.

23. As in Athens.

Further, the judges must be of the same condition as the accused, or his peers, so that he does not suppose that he has fallen into the hands of people inclined to do him violence.

If the legislative power leaves to the executive power the right to imprison citizens who can post bail for their conduct, there is no longer any liberty, unless the citizens are arrested in order to respond without delay to an accusation of a crime the law has rendered capital; in this case they are really free because they are subject only to the power of the law.

But if the legislative power believed itself endangered by some secret conspiracy against the state or by some correspondence with its enemies on the outside, it could, for a brief and limited time, permit the executive power to arrest suspected citizens who would lose their liberty for a time only so that it would be preserved forever.

And this is the only means consistent with reason of replacing the tyrannical magistracy of the *ephors* and the *state inquisitors* of Venice, who are also despotic.

As, in a free state, every man, considered to have a free soul, should be governed by himself, the people as a body should have legislative power; but, as this is impossible in large states and is subject to many drawbacks in small ones, the people must have their representatives do all that they themselves cannot do.

One knows the needs of one's own town better than those of other towns, and one judges the ability of one's neighbors better than that of one's other compatriots. Therefore, members of the legislative body must not be drawn from the body of the nation at large; it is proper for the inhabitants of each principal town to choose a representative from it.

The great advantage of representatives is that they are able to discuss public business. The people are not at all appropriate for such discussions; this forms one of the great drawbacks of democracy.

It is not necessary that the representatives, who have been generally instructed by those who have chosen them, be instructed about each matter of business in particular, as is the practice in the Diets of Germany. It is true that, in their way, the word of the deputies would better express the voice of the nation; but it would produce infinite delays and make each deputy the master of all the others, and on the most pressing occasions the whole force of the nation could be checked by a caprice.

Mr. Sidney says properly that when the deputies represent a body of people, as in Holland, they should be accountable to those who have commissioned them; it is another thing when they are deputed by boroughs, as in England.

In choosing a representative, all citizens in the various districts should have the right to vote except those whose estate is so humble that they are deemed to have no will of their own.

A great vice in most ancient republics was that the people had the right to make resolutions for action, resolutions which required some execution, which altogether exceeds the people's capacity. The people should not enter the government except to choose their representatives; this is quite within their reach. For if there are few people who know the precise degree of a man's ability, yet every one is able to know, in general, if the one he chooses sees more clearly than most of the others.

Nor should the representative body be chosen in order to make some resolution for action, a thing it would not do well, but in order to make laws or in order to see if those they have made have been well executed; these are things it can do very well and that only it can do well.

In a state there are always some people who are distinguished by birth, wealth, or honors; but if they were mixed among the people and if they had only one voice like the others, the common liberty would be their enslavement and they would have no interest in defending it, because most of the resolutions would be against them. Therefore, the part they have in legislation should be in proportion to the other advantages they have in the state, which will happen if they form a body that has the right to check the enterprises of the people, as the people have the right to check theirs.

Thus, legislative power will be entrusted both to the body of the nobles and to the body that will be chosen to represent the people, each of which will have assemblies and deliberations apart and have separate views and interests.

Among the three powers of which we have spoken, that of judging is in some fashion, null. There remain only two; and, as they need a power whose regulations temper them, that part of the legislative body composed of the nobles is quite appropriate for producing this effect.

The nobility should be hereditary. In the first place, it is so by its nature; and, besides, it must have a great interest in preserving its prerogatives, odious in themselves, and which, in a free state, must always be endangered.

But, as a hereditary power could be induced to follow its particular interests and forget those of the people, in the things about which one has a sovereign interest in corrupting, for instance, in the laws about levying silver coin, it must take part in legislation only through its faculty of vetoing and not through its faculty of enacting.

I call the right to order by oneself, or to correct what has been ordered by another, the *faculty of enacting*. I call the right to render null a resolution taken by another the *faculty of vetoing*, which was the power of the tribunes of Rome. And, although the one who has the faculty of vetoing can also have the right to approve, this approval is no more than a declaration that one does not make use of one's faculty of vetoing, and it derives from that faculty.

The executive power should be in the hands of a monarch, because the part of the government that almost always needs immediate action is better administered by one than by many, whereas what depends on legislative power is often better ordered by many than by one.

If there were no monarch and the executive power were entrusted to a certain number of persons drawn from the legislative body, there would no longer be liberty, because the two powers would be united, the same persons sometimes belonging and always able to belong to both.

If the legislative body were not convened for a considerable time, there would no longer be liberty. For one of two things would happen: either there would no longer be any legislative resolution and the state would fall into anarchy; or these resolutions would be made by the executive power, and it would become absolute.

It would be useless for the legislative body to be convened without interruption. That would inconvenience the representatives and besides would overburden the executive power, which would not think of executing, but of defending its prerogatives and its right to execute. [. . .]

The legislative body should not convene itself. For a body is considered to have a will only when it is convened; and if it were not convened unanimously, one could not identify which part was truly the legislative body, the part that was convened or the one that was not. For if it had the right to prorogue itself, it could happen that it would never prorogue itself; this would be dangerous in the event that it wanted to threaten executive power. Besides, there are some times more suitable than others for convening the legislative body; therefore, it must be the executive power that regulates, in relation to the circumstances it knows, the time of the holding and duration of these assemblies.

If the executive power does not have the right to check the enterprises of the legislative body, the latter will be despotic, for it will wipe out all the other powers, since it will be able to give to itself all the power it can imagine.

But the legislative power must not have the reciprocal faculty of checking the executive power. For, as execution has the limits of its own nature, it is useless to restrict it; besides, executive power is always exercised on immediate things. And the power of the tribunes in Rome was faulty in that it checked not only legislation but even execution; this caused great ills.

But if, in a free state, legislative power should not have the right to check executive power, it has the right and should have the faculty to examine the manner in which the laws it has made have been executed: [. . .]

But, whether or not this examination is made, the legislative body should not have the power to judge the person, and consequently the conduct, of the one who executes. His person should be sacred because, as he is necessary to the state so that the legislative body does not become tyrannical, if he were accused or judged there would no longer be liberty.

In this case, the state would not be a monarchy but an unfree republic. But, as he who executes cannot execute badly without having as ministers wicked counselors who hate the law although the laws favor them as men, these counselors can be sought out and punished. [. . .]

Although in general the power of judging should not be joined to any part of the legislative power, this is subject to three exceptions founded on the particular interests of the one who is to be judged.

Important men are always exposed to envy; and if they were judged by the people, they could be endangered and would not enjoy the privilege of the last citizen of a free state, of being judged by his peers. Therefore, nobles must not be called before the ordinary tribunals of the nation but before that part of the legislative body composed of nobles.

It could happen that the law, which is simultaneously clairvoyant and blind, might be too rigorous in certain cases. But the judges of the nation are, as we have said, only the mouth that pronounces the words of the law, inanimate beings who can moderate neither its force nor its rigor. Therefore, the part of the legislative body, which we have just said is a necessary tribunal on another occasion, is also one on this occasion; it is for its supreme authority to moderate the law in favor of the law itself by pronouncing less rigorously than the law.

It could also happen that a citizen, in matters of public business, might violate the rights of the people and commit crimes that the established magistrates could not or would not want to punish. But, in general, the legislative power cannot judge, and even less so in this particular case, where it represents the interested party, the people. Therefore, it can be only the accuser. But, before whom will it make its accusation? Will it bow before the tribunals of law, which are lower than it and are, moreover, composed of those who, being also of the people, would be swept along by the authority of such a great accuser? No: in order to preserve the dignity of the people and the security of the individual, that part of the legislature drawn from the people must make its accusation before the part of the legislature drawn from the nobles, which has neither the same interests nor the same passions.

This last is the advantage of this government over most of the ancient republics, where there was the abuse that the people were judge and accuser at the same time.

Executive power, as we have said, should take part in legislation by its faculty of vetoing; otherwise it will soon be stripped of its prerogatives. But if legislative power takes part in execution, executive power will equally be lost.

If the monarch took part in legislation by the faculty of enacting, there would no longer be liberty. But as in spite of this, he must take part in legislation in order to defend himself, he must take part in it by the faculty of vetoing. [. . .]

Here, therefore, is the fundamental constitution of the government of which we are speaking. As its legislative body is composed of two parts, the one will be chained to the other by their reciprocal faculty of vetoing. The two will be bound by the executive power, which will itself be bound by the legislative power.

The form of these three powers should be rest or inaction. But as they are constrained to move by the necessary motion of things, they will be forced to move in concert.

As executive power belongs to the legislative only through its faculty of vetoing, it cannot enter into the discussion of public business. It is not even necessary for it to propose, because, as it can always disapprove of resolutions, it can reject decisions on propositions it would have wanted left unmade. [. . .]

If the executive power enacts on the raising of public funds without the consent of the legislature, there will no longer be liberty, because the executive power will become the legislator on the most important point of legislation.

If the legislative power enacts, not from year to year, but forever, on the raising of public funds, it runs the risk of losing its liberty, because the executive power will no longer depend upon it; and when one holds such a right forever, it is unimportant whether that right comes from oneself or from another. The same is true if the legislative power enacts, not from year to year, but forever, about the land and sea forces, which it should entrust to the executive power. [. . .]

Since all human things have an end, the state of which we are speaking will lose its liberty; it will perish. Rome, Lacedaemonia, and Carthage have surely perished. This state will perish when legislative power is more corrupt than executive power.

It is not for me to examine whether at present the English enjoy this liberty or not. It suffices for me to say that it is established by their laws, and I seek no further.

I do not claim hereby to disparage other governments, or to say that this extreme political liberty should humble those who have only a moderate one. How could I say that, I who believe that the excess even of reason is not always desirable and that men almost always accommodate themselves better to middles than to extremities?

Harrington, in his *Oceana*, has also examined the furthest point of liberty to which the constitution of a state can be carried. But of him it can be said that he sought this liberty only after misunderstanding it, and that he built Chalcedon with the coast of Byzantium before his eyes.

Part Two, Book Twelve On the Laws that Form Political Liberty in Relation to the Citizen

Chapter 1 The idea of this book

It is not enough to treat political liberty in its relation to the constitution; it must be shown in its relation to the citizen.

I have said that, in the former instance, liberty is formed by a certain distribution of the three powers, but in the latter it must be considered with a different idea in view. It consists in security or in one's opinion of one's security.

It can happen that the constitution is free and that the citizen is not. The citizen can be free and the constitution not. In these instances, the constitution will be free by right and not in fact; the citizen will be free in fact and not by right.

Only the disposition of the laws, and especially of the fundamental laws, forms liberty in its relation to the constitution. But, in the relation to the citizen, mores, manners, and received examples can give rise to it and certain civil laws can favor it, as we shall see in the present book.

Further, as in most states liberty is more hampered, countered, or beaten down than is required by their constitutions, it is well to speak of the particular laws that, in each constitution, can aid or run counter to the principle of the liberty of which each government can admit.

Chapter 2 On the liberty of the citizen

Philosophical liberty consists in the exercise of one's will or, at least (if all systems must be mentioned), in one's opinion that one exerts one's will. Political liberty consists in security or, at least, in the opinion one has of one's security.

This *security* is never more attacked than by public or private accusations. Therefore, the citizen's liberty depends principally on the goodness of the criminal laws. [. . .]

Chapter 3 Continuation of the same subject

The laws that send a man to his death on the deposition of a single witness are fatal to liberty. Reason requires two, because a witness who affirms and an accused who denies produce a division, and there must be a third for a decision. [. . .]

Chapter 4 That liberty is favored by the nature of penalties, and by their proportion

It is the triumph of liberty when criminal laws draw each penalty from the particular nature of the crime. All arbitrariness ends; the penalty does not ensue from the legislator's capriciousness but from the nature of the thing, and man does not do violence to man.

There are four sorts of crimes. Those of the first kind run counter to religion; those of the second, to mores; those of the third, to tranquility; those of the fourth, to the security of the citizens. The penalties inflicted should derive from the nature of each of these kinds.

I include in the class of crimes concerning religion only those that attack it directly, such as all cases of simple sacrilege. For crimes of disturbing the exercise of religion are of the nature of those that run counter to the tranquility or the security of the citizens and should be shifted to these classes.

In order for the penalty against simple sacrilege to be drawn from the nature[24] of the thing, it should consist in the deprivation of all the advantages given

24. St. Louis made such exaggerated laws against those who swore that the Pope felt obliged to caution him about it. This prince moderated his zeal and softened his laws. See his *Ordinances*. [*Recueil général des anciennes lois françaises. Capétiens*, 216.2; see also 218.1; 1, 341–342, 346].

by religion: expulsion from the temples; deprivation of the society of the faithful for a time or forever; shunning the presence of the sacrilegious; execration, detestation, and exorcism.

In the things that disturb the tranquility or security of the state, hidden actions are a concern of human justice. But in those that wound the divinity, where there is no public action, there is no criminal matter; it is all between the man and god who knows the measure and the time of his vengeance. For if the magistrate, confusing things, even searches out hidden sacrilege, he brings an inquisition to a kind of action where it is not necessary; he destroys the liberty of citizens by aiming against them the zeal of both timid and brash consciences.

The ill came from the idea that the divinity must be avenged. But one must make divinity honored, and one must never avenge it. Indeed, if one were guided by the latter idea, where would punishments end? If men's laws are to avenge an infinite being, they will be ruled by his infinity and not by the weakness, ignorance, and caprice of human nature.

An historian of Provence[25] reports a fact that paints very clearly for us what this idea of avenging the divinity can produce in weak spirits. A Jew, accused of having blasphemed the Holy Virgin, was condemned to be flayed. Masked knights with knives in their hands mounted the scaffold and drove away the executioner in order to avenge the honor of the Holy Virgin themselves . . . I certainly do not want to anticipate the reader's reflections.

The second class is of crimes against the mores: these are the violation of public or individual continence, that is, of the police concerning how one should enjoy the pleasures associated with the use of one's senses and with corporal union. The penalties for these crimes should also be drawn from the nature of the thing. Deprivation of the advantages that society has attached to the purity of mores, fines, shame, the constraint to hide oneself, public infamy, and expulsion from the town and from society; finally, all the penalties within the correctional jurisdiction suffice to repress the temerity of the two sexes. Indeed, these things are founded less on wickedness than on forgetting or despising oneself.

Here it is a question only of crimes that involve mores alone, not of those that also run counter to public security, such as kidnapping and rape, which are of the fourth kind.

The crimes of the third class are those that run counter to the citizens' tranquility, and the penalties for them should be drawn from the nature of the thing and relate to that tranquility, such as deprivation, exile, corrections, and other penalties that restore men's troubled spirits and return them to the established order.

I restrict crimes against tranquility to the things that are a simple breach of police; the ones that, while disturbing tranquility, attack security at the same time, should be put in the fourth class.

The penalties for these last crimes are what are called punishments. They are a kind of retaliation, which causes the society to refuse to give security to a citizen who has deprived or has wanted to deprive another of it. This penalty is derived from the nature of the thing and is drawn from reason and from the sources of good and evil. A citizen deserves death when he has violated security so far as to take or to attempt to take a life. The death penalty is the remedy, as it were, for a sick society. When one violates security with respect to goods there can be reasons for the penalty to be capital; but it would perhaps be preferable, and it would be more natural, if the penalty for crimes committed against the security of goods were punished by the loss of goods. And that ought to be so, if fortunes were common or equal; but as those who have no goods more readily attack the goods of others, the corporal penalty has had to replace the pecuniary penalty.

All that I say is drawn from nature and is quite favorable to the citizen's liberty.

Chapter 6
On the crime against nature

Please god that I may not diminish the horror that one has for a crime that religion, morality, and policy condemn in turn. It would have to be proscribed if it did no more than give to one sex the weaknesses of the other and prepare for an infamous old age by a shameful youth. What I shall say will leave it all of its stigma and will bear only on the tyranny that can take an unfair advantage of even the horror in which it should be held.

25. Father Bougerel.

As it is in the nature of this crime to be hidden, legislators have often punished it on the deposition of a child. This opened wide the door to calumny. "Justinian," says Procopius,[26] "published a law against this crime; he made inquiries about those who were guilty of it, not only after the law was made but before. The deposition of a witness, sometimes a child, sometimes a slave, sufficed, especially against the rich and those who were of the faction of the *Greens*."

It is singular that among ourselves three crimes, magic, heresy, and the crime against nature, of which it can be proved that the first does not exist, that the second is susceptible to infinite distinctions, interpretations and limitations, and that the third is often hidden, were all three punished by the penalty of burning.

I shall assert that the crime against nature will not make much progress in a society unless the people are also inclined to it by some custom, as among the Greeks, where the young people performed all their exercises naked, as among ourselves where education at home is no longer the usage, as among the Asians where some individuals have a large number of wives whom they scorn while others can have none. Do not clear the way for this crime, let it be proscribed by an exact police, as are all the violations of mores, and one will immediately see nature either defend her rights or take them back. Gentle, pleasing, charming, nature has scattered pleasures with a liberal hand; and by overwhelming us with delights, she prepares us with our children through whom we are born again, as it were, for satisfactions greater even than those delights.

Chapter 11
On thoughts

A certain Marsyas dreamed he cut the throat of Dionysius.[27] Dionysius had him put to death, saying that Marsyas would not have dreamed it at night if he had not thought it during the day. This was a great tyranny; for, even if he had thought it, he had not attempted it.[28] Laws are charged with punishing only external actions.

26. [Procopius] *Anecdota sive Historia arcana* [19. 11].

27. Plutarch [*Vit.*], *Dion* [9.5].

28. Thought must be joined to some sort of action.

Chapter 12
On indiscreet speech

Nothing makes the crime of high treason more arbitrary than when indiscreet speech becomes its material. Discourse is so subject to interpretation, there is so much difference between indiscretion and malice and so little in the expressions they use, that the law can scarcely subject speech to a capital penalty, unless it declares explicitly which speech is subject to it.[29]

Speech does not form a *corpus delicti:* it remains only an idea. Most frequently it has no meaning in itself but rather in the tone in which it is spoken. Often when repeating the same words, one does not express the same meaning; the meaning depends on the link the words have with other things. Silence sometimes expresses more than any speech. Nothing is so equivocal. How, then, can one make speech a crime of high treason? Wherever this law is established, not only is there no longer liberty, there is not even its shadow. [. . .]

I do not intend to diminish the indignation one should have against those who want to stigmatize the glory of their prince, but I do say that if one wants to moderate despotism, punishing with a simple correction will suit these occasions better than an accusation of high treason, which is always terrible, even to the innocent.[30]

Actionable acts are not an everyday occurrence; they may be observed by many people: a false accusation over facts can easily be clarified. The words that are joined to an act take on the nature of that action. Thus a man who goes into the public square to exhort the subjects to revolt becomes guilty of high treason, because the speech is joined to the act and participates in it. It is not speech that is punished but an act committed in which speech is used. [. . .]

29. "It should not be punished as a crime unless it be set down in the letter of the law or established by examples in the law" [L.], says Modestinus in Law 7, para. 3 of the *Digest* [*Corpus Juris Civilis, Digest* 48.4.7.3]; *ad legem Juliam maiestatis.*

30. "It is in no way easy to interpret the deceits of language" [L.], Modestinus, in Law 7, para. 3 of the *Digest* [*Corpus Juris Civilis, Digest* 48.4.7.3]; *ad legem Juliam maiestatis.*

Chapter 13
On writings

Writings contain something more permanent than speech, but when they do not prepare the way for high treason, they are not material to the crime of high treason. [. . .]

Satirical writings are scarcely known in despotic states, where dejection on the one hand and ignorance on the other produce neither the talent nor the will to write them. In democracy, they are not prevented, for the very reason that they are prohibited in the government of one alone. As they are usually composed against powerful people, they flatter the spitefulness of the people who govern in a democracy. In a monarchy, they are prohibited, but they have been made an object of police rather than of crime. They can amuse the general spitefulness, console malcontents, reduce envy of those in high positions, give the people the patience to suffer, and make them laugh about their sufferings.

Aristocracy is the government that most proscribes satirical works. Magistrates there are little sovereigns who are not big enough to scorn insults. If in monarchy some barb is thrown against the monarch, he is so high that the barb does not reach him. An aristocratic lord is pierced through and through. Thus, the decemvirs, who formed an aristocracy, punished satirical writings with death.[31]

Chapter 19
How the usage of liberty is suspended in a republic

There are, in the states where one sets the most store by liberty, laws that violate it for a single person in order to keep it for all. Such are what are called *bills of attainder*[32] in England. They are related to those laws of Athens that were enacted against an individual[33] provided they were made by the vote of six thousand citizens. They are related to those laws made in Rome against individual citizens, which were called *privileges*.[34] They were made only in the great estates of the people. But, however the people made them, Cicero wanted them abolished, because the force of the law consists only in its being enacted for everyone.[35] I admit, however, that the usage of the freest peoples that ever lived on earth makes me believe that there are cases where a veil has to be drawn, for a moment, over liberty, as one hides the statues of the gods.

Part Four, Book 20
On the Laws in Their Relation to Commerce. Considered in its Nature and Distinctions

Chapter 1
On commerce

The following material would require more extensive treatment, but the nature of this work does not permit it. I should like to glide on a tranquil river; I am dragged along by a torrent.

Commerce cures destructive prejudices, and it is an almost general rule that everywhere there are gentle mores, there is commerce and that everywhere there is commerce, there are gentle mores.

Therefore, one should not be surprised if our mores are less fierce than they were formerly. Commerce has spread knowledge of the mores of all

31. The Law of Twelve Tables.

32. It is not enough, in the tribunals of the kingdom, for there to be a piece of evidence that convinces the judges; this piece of evidence must also be formal, that is, legal; and the law requires there to be two witnesses against the accused; an additional piece of evidence would not suffice. Now if a man, presumed guilty of what is called a high crime, had found a way to keep the witnesses from appearing so that it was impossible to condemn him under the law, one could bring a special bill of attainder against him, that is, make a singular law concerning his person. One proceeds as with any other bill: it must pass the two Houses and the king must give his consent, otherwise there is no *bill*, that is, no judgment. The accused can have his advocates speak against the *bill*, and one can speak for the *bill* in the House.

33. "A law concerning a single individual ought not to be proposed unless six thousand have considered it" [L.] Andocides, *Orationes, De mysteriis* [87]. This is ostracism.

34. "Proposed concerning private individuals" [L.]. Cicero, *De legibus*, bk. 3 [3.19.44–45].

35. "A decree and law over all" [L.]. Cicero, ibid. [*De legibus* 3.19.44].

nations everywhere; they have been compared to each other, and good things have resulted from this.

One can say that the laws of commerce perfect mores for the same reason that these same laws ruin mores. Commerce corrupts pure mores,[36] and this was the subject of Plato's complaints; it polishes and softens barbarous mores, as we see every day.

Chapter 2
On the spirit of commerce

The natural effect of commerce is to lead to peace. Two nations that trade with each other become reciprocally dependent; if one has an interest in buying, the other has an interest in selling, and all unions are founded on mutual needs.

But, if the spirit of commerce unites nations, it does not unite individuals in the same way. We see that in countries[37] where one is affected only by the spirit of commerce, there is traffic in all human activities. [. . .]

Chapter 4
On commerce in the various governments

Commerce is related to the constitution. In government by one alone, it is ordinarily founded on luxury, and though it is also founded on real needs, its principal object is to procure for the nation engaging in it all that serves its arrogance, its delights, and its fancies. In government by many, it is more often founded on economy. Traders, eyeing all the nations of the earth, take to one what they bring from another. This is how the republics of Tyre, Carthage, Marseilles, Florence, Venice, and Holland engaged in commerce.

This kind of traffic concerns the government of many by its nature and monarchical government on occasion. For, as it is founded only on the practice of gaining little and even of gaining less than any other nation and of being compensated only by gaining continually, it is scarcely possible for it to be done by a people among whom luxury is established who spend much and who see only great objects.

In keeping with these ideas, Cicero said so well:[38] "I do not like a people to be both the rulers and the clerks of the universe." Indeed, one would have to assume that each individual in this state and even the whole state always had a head full of both great projects and small ones, which is contradictory.

Yet the greatest enterprises are also undertaken in those states which subsist by economic commerce, and they show a daring not to be found in monarchies: here is the reason for it.

One commerce leads to another, the small to the middling, the middling to the great, and he who earlier desired to gain little arrives at a position where he has no less of a desire to gain a great deal.

Moreover, the great enterprises of the traders are always necessarily mixed with public business. But, public business is for the most part as suspect to the merchants in monarchies as it appears safe to them in republican states. Therefore, great commercial enterprises are not for monarchies, but for the government by many.

In short, one's belief that one's prosperity is more certain in these states makes one undertake everything, and because one believes that what one has acquired is secure, one dares to expose it in order to acquire more; only the means for acquisition are at risk; now, men expect much of their fortune.

I do not mean that any monarchies are totally excluded from economic commerce, but they are less inclined to it by its nature; I do not mean that the republics we know are entirely without the commerce of luxury, but it is less related to their constitution.

As for the despotic state, it is useless to talk about it. General rule: in a nation that is in servitude, one works more to preserve than to acquire; in a free nation, one works more to acquire than to preserve.

---

36. Caesar says of the Gauls that the proximity and commerce of Marseilles had spoiled them so that they, who had formerly always vanquished the Germans, had become inferior to them. [Gaius Julius Caesar] *De bello Gallico*, bk. 6 [6.24].

37. Holland.

38. "I do not wish the same people to be both the ruler and customs officer for the world" [L.] [Cicero, *De republica* 4.7].

Chapter 7
The spirit of England concerning commerce

Almost none of England's tariffs with other nations are regular; tariffs change, so to speak, with each parliament, as it lifts or imposes particular duties. England has also wanted to preserve its independence in this matter. Sovereignly jealous of the commerce that is done there, it binds itself with few treaties and depends only on its laws.

Other nations have made commercial interests give way to political interests: England has always made its political interests give way to the interests of its commerce.

This is the people in the world who have best known how to take advantage of each of these three great things at the same time: religion, commerce, and liberty.

Chapter 12
On the liberty of commerce

Liberty of commerce is not a faculty granted to traders to do what they want; this would instead be the servitude of commerce. That which hampers those who engage in commerce does not, for all that, hamper commerce. It is in countries of liberty that the trader finds innumerable obstacles; the laws never thwart him less than in countries of servitude.

England prohibits the export of its wool; it wants coal brought to the capital by sea; it does not permit the export of horses unless they are gelded; the ships[39] from its colonies that trade in Europe are to anchor in England. It hampers the trader, but it does so in favor of commerce.

39. Navigation Act of 1660 [*The Statutes of the Realm*, 12 Car., vol. 2, chap. 18; 5, 246–250; 1963 edn; consider the Act of Interregnum, October 9, 1651]. It was only in wartime that those [merchants] of Boston and Philadelphia sent the vessels carrying their goods directly to the Mediterranean.

Part Four, Book 21
On Laws in Their Relation to Commerce, Considered in the Revolutions It Has Had in the World

Chapter 20
How commerce in Europe penetrated barbarism

When the philosophy of Aristotle was brought to the West, the shrewd minds, who are the great minds in times of ignorance, found it very agreeable. The schoolmen were infatuated with it and took from this philosopher[40] many explanations on lending at interest, whereas its very natural source was the gospel; they condemned it without distinction and in every case. Thus, commerce, which was the profession only of mean people, also became that of dishonest people; for, whenever one prohibits a thing that is naturally permitted or necessary, one only makes dishonest the people who do it.

Commerce passed to a nation then covered with infamy, and soon it was no longer distinguished from the most horrible usuries, from monopolies, from the levy of subsidies, and from all the dishonest means of acquiring silver.

The Jews,[41] who were made wealthy by their exactions, were pillaged with the same tyranny by the princes, a thing that consoled the people and did not relieve them.

What happened in England will give an idea of what was done in other countries. When King John[42]

40. See Aristotle, *Pol.*, bk. 1, chaps. 9, 10 [1256b40–1258b8].

41. See in [Pierre de Marca] *Marca Hispanica*, the constitutions of Aragon of the years 1228 [chap. 507, pp. 1415–1416; see also pp. 522–528; 1688 edn] and 1231 [chap. 511, 1233, p. 1427; 1688 edn]; in [Nicolas] Brussel [*Nouvel examen de l'usage général des fiefs en France pendant le XIe, le XIIe, le XIIIe et le XIVe siècle*], the agreement of 1206 reached between the king, the countess of Champagne, and Guy de Dampierre. [Actually 1200, vol. 2, *Chartres, lettres-patentes, traités*; xxii–xxiii; 1727 edn.]

42. [John] Stow, in his *Survey of London*, bk. 3, p. 54 ["Coleman Street Ward"; I, 279–280; 1908 edn; pp. 250–251; 1929 edn].

imprisoned the Jews in order to have their goods, there were few who did not have at least an eye put out; thus did this king conduct his chamber of justice. A Jew who had had seven teeth pulled out, one each day, gave ten thousand silver marks on the eighth. From Aaron, a Jew of York, Henry III got fourteen thousand silver marks and ten thousand for the queen. In those times, one did violently what is done in Poland today with some measure. As the kings were not able to search into the pockets of their subjects because of their privileges, they tortured the Jews, who were not regarded as citizens.

Finally, the custom was introduced of confiscating the goods of the Jews who embraced Christianity. We know of this outlandish custom from the law abrogating it.[43] The reasons given for it have been very empty; it has been said that one wanted to test them and make nothing remain of their enslavement to the devil. But, it is clear that this confiscation was a kind of right of amortization[44] of the taxes which the prince or the lords levied on the Jews and which they were denied when the latter embraced Christianity. In those times, men were regarded as lands. And, I shall note in passing how much one has toyed with that nation from one century to another. Their goods were confiscated when they wanted to be Christians, and soon afterwards they were burned when they did not want to be Christians.

Nevertheless, one saw commerce leave this seat of harassment and despair. The Jews, proscribed by each country in turn, found the means for saving their effects. In that way, they managed to fix their refuges forever; a prince who wanted very much to be rid of them would not, for all that, be in a humor to rid himself of their silver.

They invented letters of exchange,[45] and in this way commerce was able to avoid violence and maintain itself everywhere, for the richest trader had only invisible goods, which could be sent everywhere and leave no trace anywhere.

Theologians were obliged to curb their principles, and commerce, which had been violently linked to bad faith, returned, so to speak, to the bosom of integrity.

Thus, to the speculations of the schoolmen we owe all the misfortunes[46] that accompanied the destruction of commerce; and to the avarice of princes we owe the establishment of a device that puts it, in a way, out of their power.

Since that time princes have had to govern themselves more wisely than they themselves would have thought, for it turned out that great facts of authority were so clumsy that experience itself has made known that only goodness of government brings prosperity.

One has begun to be cured of Machiavellianism, and one will continue to be cured of it. There must be more moderation in councils. What were formerly called *coups d'état* would at present, apart from their horror, be only imprudences.

And, happily, men are in a situation such that, though their passions inspire in them the thought of being wicked, they nevertheless have an interest in not being so.

---

43. Edict given at Baville, April 4, 1392. [Actually Abbeville, April 25, 1393. *Recueil général des anciennes lois françaises*, 181; 6, 728–729.]

44. In France, the Jews were serfs subject to mortmain and the lords inherited from them. [Nicolas] Brussel reports an agreement of 1206 between the king and Thibaut, Count of Champagne, by which it was agreed that the Jews of the one would not lend in the land of the other. [Nicolas Brussel, *Nouvel examen de l'usage général des fiefs en France pendant le XIe, le XIIe, le XIIIe et le XIVe siècles.* Actually 1200, vol. 2, *Chartes, lettres-patentes, traités;* xxii–xxiii; 1727 edn.]

45. It is known that under Philip Augustus and Philip the Tall, the Jews, driven out of France took refuge in Lombardy and that there they gave the foreign traders and travelers secret letters for those to whom they had entrusted their effects in France, with which their debts were paid.

46. See, in the Corpus of the Law, *Novellae Leonis* 83, which revokes the law of Basil, his father. The law of Basil is in [Konstantin] Hermenopoulus [*Manuale legum sive Hexabiblos*] under "Leon," bk. 3, tit. 7, para. 27 [3.7.24].

Part Four, Book 22
On the Laws in Their Relation to the Use of Money

Chapter 1
The reason for the use of money

Peoples who have little in the way of commodities for commerce, such as savages, and peoples with a police who have only two or three kinds, trade by exchange. Thus the Moorish caravans that go to Timbuktu in the heart of Africa to barter salt for gold need no money. The Moor puts his salt in a pile; the Negro, his gold dust in another; if there is not enough gold, the Moor takes back some of his salt or the Negro adds to his gold, until the parties agree.

But when a people deals in a large number of commodities, there must necessarily be money, because a metal that is easy to transport saves much of the cost one would be obliged to incur if one always proceeded by exchange. [. . .]

Chapter 2
On the nature of money

Money is a sign representing the value of all commodities. Some metal is chosen, so that the sign will be durable,[47] will be little worn by use, and can be divided many times without being destroyed. A precious metal is chosen so that the sign can be carried easily. A metal is an altogether appropriate common measure because it can easily be reduced to the same grade. Each state stamps it, so that the form reflects the grade and the weight and so that both may be known simply by looking at it.

Before using metals, the Athenians used oxen,[48] and the Romans sheep, but one ox is not the same as another in the way one piece of metal can be the same as another.

As silver is the sign of the values of commodities, paper is a sign of the value of silver, and when the paper is good, it represents silver so well that there is no difference in its effect.

Just as silver is the sign of a thing and represents it, each thing is a sign of silver and represents it; and a state is prosperous insofar as, on the one hand, the silver indeed represents all things, and on the other, all things indeed represent silver, and they are signs of one another; that is, their relative value is such that one can have the first as soon as one has the other. This happens only in a moderate government, but it does not always happen in a moderate government; for example, if the laws favor an unjust debtor, the things belonging to him do not represent silver and are not a sign of it. With regard to despotic government, it would be a marvel if things there represented their sign; tyranny and distrust make everyone bury his silver;[49] therefore, things there do not represent silver at all.

Legislators have sometimes used such art that things have not only represented silver by their nature but they have become money like silver itself. Caesar[50] as dictator permitted debtors to give lands in payment to their creditors at the price they fetched before the civil war. Tiberius[51] ordered that those who wanted silver could have it from the public treasury by pledging lands worth double the amount. Under Caesar, lands were the money that paid all debts; under Tiberius, ten thousand sesterces of land became the money in common use, like five thousand sesterces of silver.

Chapter 11
On the operations the Romans performed on monies

Whatever acts of authority have been performed on monies in our time in France in two consecutive

47. Salt, used in Abyssinia, has the shortcoming of constantly wasting away.

48. Herodotus [*The Persian Wars*] in Clio [1.94], tells us that the Lydians discovered the art of minting money; the Greeks took it from them; the ancient ox was stamped on the money of Athens. I have seen one of these coins in the Earl of Pembroke's collection.

49. It is an old usage in Algiers for each father of a family to have a buried treasure. Laugier de Tassy, *Histoire du royaume d'Alger* [chap. 8, "Des Mœurs et des Coutumes des Algériens"; p. 117; 1720 edn].

50. See Julius Caesar, *De bello Civili*, bk. 3 [3.1].

51. Tacitus [*Annales*], bk. 6 [6.17].

ministries, the Romans performed even greater ones, not at the time of the corrupt republic or at that of the republic which was only anarchy, but when, having the full force of the institution, as much by its wisdom as by its courage, after vanquishing the towns of Italy, it disputed empire with the Carthaginians. [. . .]

In the First Punic War[52] the as, which was supposed to be of twelve ounces of copper, weighed only two, and in the Second Punic War, it weighed only one. This retrenching corresponds to what we today call expansion of the currency; to remove half the silver from an ecu of six livres in order to make two ecus, or to make it worth twelve livres, is precisely the same thing.

There remains no record of the way the Romans performed their operation in the First Punic War, but what they did in the Second points to a remarkable wisdom. The republic was not in a position to pay its debts; the as weighed two ounces of copper; and the denarius, valued at ten ases, weighed twenty ounces of copper. The republic made the as of one ounce of copper;[53] it gained half on its creditors; it paid a denarius with these ten ounces of copper. This operation gave the state a great jolt: it should have been as small as possible; the operation contained an injustice: it should have been as small as possible; its object was the liberation of the republic from its citizens: it could not, therefore, have been the liberation of the citizens from themselves: this brought about a second operation, and one ordered that the denarius, which had until then been only ten ases, would contain sixteen. It resulted from this double operation that, while the creditors of the republic lost half,[54] those of the individuals lost only a fifth;[55] commodities increased only a fifth; the real change in the money was only a fifth; the other consequences can be seen.

52. Pliny the Elder, *Naturalis historiae*, bk. 33, art. 13 [33.13.44–35].

53. Ibid. [Pliny the Elder, *Naturalis historiae* 33.13.44].

54. They received ten ounces of copper for twenty.

55. They received sixteen ounces of copper for twenty.

Chapter 12
The circumstances in which the Romans performed their operations on money

Long ago there was very little silver or gold in Italy; this country has few if any gold or silver mines: when Rome was taken by the Gauls there were only a thousand pounds of gold there.[56] Still, the Romans sacked several powerful towns and carried their wealth home. For a long time they used only copper money; it was only after the peace of Pyrrhus that they had enough silver to make money of it:[57] they made denarii with this metal, which were valued at ten ases[58] or ten pounds of copper. Therefore, the proportion of silver to copper was as 1 to 960, for, as the Roman denarius was valued at ten ases or ten pounds of copper, it was valued at 120 ounces of copper and, as the same denarius was valued at an eighth of an ounce of silver,[59] this gives the proportion we have just mentioned.

When Rome became the master of this part of Italy, with Greece and Sicily as her closest neighbours, little by little it found itself between two rich peoples, the Greeks and the Carthaginians; its silver increased at home; and, as the proportion of 1 to 960 between silver and copper could no longer be sustained, Rome performed various operations on the monies, of which we know nothing. We know only that at the beginning of the Second Punic War, the Roman denarius was valued at only twenty ounces of copper[60] and that thus the proportion between silver and copper was only 1 to 160. The reduction was quite considerable, for the republic gained five-sixths

56. Pliny the Elder, [*Naturalis historiae*] bk. 33, art. 5 [33.5.14].

57. [Johann] Freinsheim [*Supplementorum Livianorum*], decade 2, bk. 5 [15.6].

58. Ibid. [Freinsheim, *Supplementorum Livianorum*, 15.6]. They also struck halves called "quinaires" and quarters called "sesterces."

59. [Guillaume Budé, *De Asse et partibus eius*, bk. 1; 2, 3; 1969 edn.] According to Budé, an eighth; according to others, a seventh.

60. Pliny the Elder, *Naturalis historiae*, bk. 33, art. 13 [33.13.45].

on all the copper money, but one had done only what the nature of thing required and had reestablished the proportion between the metals that served as money.

The peace that ended the First Punic War had left the Romans masters of Sicily. They soon entered Sardinia; they began to know Spain: the stock of silver continued to increase in Spain; an operation was performed reducing the silver denarius from twenty ounces to sixteen,[61] and it had the effect of putting silver and copper back in proportion; this proportion was 1 to 160; it had been 1 to 128.

Study the Romans: their superiority will never be more evident than in the choice of the circumstances in which they did good and evil things.

Chapter 13
Operations on the monies at the time of the emperors

In the operations performed on the monies during the republic, one proceeded by way of retrenchment; the state disclosed its needs to the people and did not try to seduce them. Under the emperors, one proceeded by alloying metals: these princes, reduced to despair by their very liberalities, were obliged to tamper with the monies, an indirect path which decreased the ill but appeared not to touch it; one took back part of the gift and hid one's hand, and, without speaking of decrease in pay or largess, these were diminished.

One can still see in some collections[62] what are called plated metals, which have only a sheath of silver covering the copper. [. . .]

Didius Julianus began the weakening. One finds that the money of Caracalla was more than half alloy;[63] that of Alexander Severus two-thirds;[64] the weakening continued; and under Galienus, one saw only silvered copper.[65]

One can feel that these violent operations could not occur in our time; a prince would deceive himself and would deceive no one else. The exchange has taught the banker to compare all the monies of the world and set them at their just value; the grade of monies can no longer be kept secret. If a prince begins to alloy precious metal with copper, everyone continues to do so and does it for him; strong specie leave first and return to him weakened. If, like the Roman emperors, he weakened silver without weakening gold, he would see the gold suddenly disappear and he would be reduced to his bad silver. The exchange, [. . .] has curtailed the great acts of authority, or at least the success of the great acts of authority.

61. Ibid. [Pliny the Elder, *Naturalis historiae*, 33.13.45.]

62. See Father [Louis] Jobert, *The Knowledge of Medals* (Paris, 1739), p. 59 [chaps. 2, 8, pp. 13–14, 93–94; 1715 edn].

63. See [Louis] Savot [*Discours sur les medailles antiques*], pt. 2, chap. 12 [p. 95, 1627 edn], and the *Journal des Sçavans*, July 28, 1681 [340–342] concerning a discovery of 50,000 medals.

64. Ibid. [Louis Savot, *Discours sur les medailles antiques*, pp. 95–96; 1627 edn.]

65. Ibid. [Louis Savot, *Discours sur les medailles antiques*, p. 97; 1627 edn.]

Jonathan Mayhew

A Discourse Concerning Unlimited Submission and Non-Resistance to the Higher Powers (1750)

Let us now trace the apostle's reasoning in favor of submission to the *higher powers*, a little more particularly and exactly.[1] For by this it will appear, on one hand, how good and conclusive it is, for submission to those rulers who exercise their power in a proper manner: And, on the other, how weak and trifling and in connected it is, if it be supposed to be meant by the apostle to show the obligation and duty of obedience to tyrannical, oppressive rulers in common with others of a different character.

The apostle enters upon his subject thus—*Let every soul be subject unto the higher powers; for there is no power but of God: the powers that be, are ordained of God.* Here he urges the duty of obedience from this topic of argument, that civil rulers, as they are supposed to fulfill the pleasure of God, are the ordinance of God. But how is this an argument for obedience to such rulers as do not perform the pleasure of God, by doing good; but the pleasure of the devil, by doing evil; and such as are not, therefore, *God's ministers*, but the devil's! *Whosoever, therefore, resisteth the power, resisteth the ordinance of God; and they that resist, shall receive to themselves damnation.* Here the apostle argues, that those who resist a reasonable and just authority, which is agreeable to the will of God, do really resist the will of God himself; and will, therefore, be punished by him. But how does this prove, that those who resist a lawless, unreasonable power, which is contrary to the will of God, do therein resist the will and ordinance of God? Is resisting those who resist God's will, the same thing with resisting God? Or shall those who do so, *receive to themselves damnation! For rulers are not a terror to good works, but to the evil. Wilt thou then not be afraid of the power? Do that which is good; and thou shalt have praise of the same. For he is the minister of God to thee for good.* Here the apostle argues more explicitly than he had before done, for revering, and submitting to, magistracy, from this consideration, that such as really performed the duty of magistrates, would be enemies only to the evil actions of men, and would befriend and encourage the good; and so be a common blessing to society. But how is this an argument, that we must honor, and submit to, such magistrates as are not enemies to the evil actions of men; but to the good; and such as are not a common blessing, but a common curse, to society! *But if thou do that which is evil, be afraid: For he is the minister of God, a revenger, to execute wrath upon him that doth evil.* Here the apostle argues from the nature and end of magistracy, that such as did evil, (and such only) had reason to be afraid of the *higher powers*; it being part of their office to punish evil doers, no less than to defend and encourage such as do well. But if magistrates are unrighteous; if they are *respecters of persons*; if they are partial in their administration of justice; then those who do well have as much reason to *be afraid*, as those that do evil: there can be no safety for the good, nor any peculiar ground of terror to the unruly and injurious. So that, in this case, the main end of civil government will be frustrated, And what reason is there for submitting to that government, which does by no means answer the design of government? *Wherefore ye must needs be subject not only for wrath, but also for conscience sake.* Here the apostle argues the duty of a chearful and conscientious submission to civil government, from the nature and end of magistracy as he had before laid it down, i.e. as the design of it was to punish evil doers, and to support and encourage such as do well; and as it must, if so exercised, be agreeable to the will of God. But how does what he here says, prove the duty of a cheerful and conscientious subjection to those who forfeit the character of rulers? to those who encourage the bad,

1. [Mayhew's sermon is based on his interpretation of St. Paul's Epistle to the Romans, Chapter 13.]

and discourage the good? The argument here used no more proves it to be a sin to resist such rulers, than it does, to *resist the devil*, that he may *flee from us*. For one is as truly the *minister of God* as the other. *For, for this cause pay you tribute also; for they are God's ministers, attending continually upon this very thing.* Here the apostle argues the duty of paying taxes, from this consideration, that those who perform the duty of rulers, are continually attending upon the public welfare. But how does this argument conclude for paying taxes to such princes as are continually endeavouring to ruin the public? And especially when such payment would facilitate and promote this wicked design! *Render therefore to all their dues; tribute, to whom tribute is due; custom, to whom custom; fear, to whom fear; honor, to whom honor.* Here the apostle sums up what he had been saying concerning the duty of subjects to rulers. And his argument stands thus—"Since magistrates who execute their office well, are common benefactors to society; and may, in that respect, be properly stiled the *ministers and ordinance of God*; and since they are constantly employed in the service of the public; it becomes you to pay them tribute and custom; and to reverence, honor, and submit to, them in the execution of their respective offices." This is apparently good reasoning. But does this argument conclude for the duty of paying tribute, custom, reverence, honor, and obedience, to such persons as (although they bear the title of rulers) use all their power to hurt and injure the public? such as are not *God's ministers*, but *satan's?* such as do not take care of, and attend upon, the public interest, but their own, to the ruin of the public? that is, in short, to such as have no natural and just claim at all to tribute, custom, reverence, honor and obedience? It is to be hoped that those who have any regard to the apostle's character as an inspired writer, or even as a man of common understanding, will not represent him as reasoning in such a loose incoherent manner; and drawing conclusions which have not the least relation to his premises. For what can be more absurd than an argument thus framed? "Rulers are, by their office, bound to consult the public welfare and the good of society: therefore you are bound to pay them tribute, to honor, and to submit to them, even when they destroy the public welfare, and are a common pest to society, by acting in direct contradiction to the nature and end of their office."

Thus, upon a careful review of the apostle's reasoning in this passage, it appears that his arguments to enforce submission, are of such a nature, as to conclude only in favour of submission *to such rulers as he himself describes;* i.e. such as rule for the good of society, which is the only end of their institution. Common tyrants, and public oppressors, are not intitled to obedience from their subjects, by virtue of any thing here laid down by the inspired apostle.

I now add, farther, that the apostle's argument is so far from proving it to be the duty of people to obey, and submit to, such rulers as act in contradiction to the public good,[2] and so to the design of their office, that it proves *the direct contrary.* For, please to observe, that if the end of all civil government, be the good of society; if this be the thing that is aimed at in constituting civil rulers; and if the motive and argument for submission to government, be taken from the apparent usefulness of civil authority; it follows, that when no such good end can be answered by submission, there remains no argument or motive to enforce it; if instead of this good end's being brought about by submission, a *contrary end* is brought about, and the ruin and misery of society effected by it, here is a plain and positive reason against submission in all such cases, should they ever happen. And therefore, in such cases, a regard to the public welfare, ought to make us with-hold from our rulers, that obedience and subjection which it would, otherwise, be our duty to render to them. If it be our duty, for example, to obey our king, merely for this reason, that he rules for the public welfare, (which is the only argument the apostle makes use of) it follows, by a parity of reason, that when he turns tyrant, and makes his subjects his prey to devour and to destroy, instead of his charge to defend and cherish, we are bound to throw off our allegiance to him, and to resist; and that according to the tenor of the apostle's argument in this passage. Not to discontinue our allegiance, in this case, would be to join with the sovereign in promoting the slavery and misery of that

---

2. This does not intend, their acting so in *a few particular instances*, which the best of rulers may do through mistake, &c. but their acting so *habitually*; and in a manner which plainly shows, that they aim at making themselves great, by the ruin of their subjects.

society, the welfare of which, we ourselves, as well as our sovereign, are indispensably obliged to secure and promote, as far as in us lies. It is true the apostle puts no case of such a tyrannical prince; but by his grounding his argument for submission wholly upon the good of civil society; it is plain he implicitly authorises, and even requires us to make resistance, whenever this shall be necessary to the public safety and happiness. Let me make use of this easy and familiar *similitude* to illustrate the point in hand—Suppose God requires a family of children, to obey their father and not to resist him; and inforces his command with this argument; that the superintendence and care and authority of a just and kind parent, will contribute to the happiness of the whole family; so that they ought to obey him for their own sakes more than for his: Suppose this parent at length runs distracted, and attempts, in his mad fit, to cut all his children's throats: Now, in this case, is not the reason before assigned, why these children should obey their parent while he continued of a sound mind, namely, *their common good*, a reason equally conclusive for disobeying and resisting him, since he is become delirious, and attempts their ruin? It makes no alteration in the argument, whether this parent, properly speaking, loses his reason; or does, while he retains his understanding, that which is as fatal in its consequences, as any thing he could do, were he really deprived of it. This similitude needs no formal application—

But it ought to be remembred, that if the duty of universal obedience and non-resistance to our king or prince, can be argued from this passage, the same unlimited submission under a republican, or any other form of government; and even to all the subordinate powers in any particular state, can be proved by it as well: which is more than those who alledge it for the mentioned purpose, would be willing should be inferred from it. So that this passage does not answer their purpose; but really overthrows and confutes it. This matter deserves to be more particularly considered.—The advocates for unlimited submission and passive obedience, do, if I mistake not, always speak with reference to kingly or monarchical government, as distinguished from all other forms; and, with reference to submitting to the will of the king, in distinction from all subordinate officers, acting beyond their commission, and the authority which they have received from the crown. It is not pretended that any person besides kings, have a divine right to do what they please, so that no one may resist them, without incurring the guilt of factiousness and rebellion. If any other supreme powers oppress the people, it is generally allowed, that the people may get redress, by resistance, if other methods prove ineffectual. And if any officers in a kingly government, go beyond the limits of that power which they have derived from the crown, (the supposed original source of all power and authority in the state) and attempt, illegally, to take away the properties and lives of their fellow subjects, they may be *forcibly* resisted, at least till application can be made to the crown. But as to the sovereign himself, he may not be resisted in any case; nor any of his officers, while they confine themselves within the bounds which he has prescribed to them. This is, I think, a true sketch of the principles of those who defend the doctrine of passive obedience and non-resistance. Now there is nothing in scripture which supports this scheme of political principles. As to the passage under consideration, the apostle here speaks of civil rulers in *general*; of all persons in *common*, vested with authority for the good of society, without any particular reference to one form of government, more than to another; or to the supreme power in any particular state, more than to subordinate powers. The apostle does not concern himself with the different forms of government.[3] This he supposes left intirely to human prudence and discretion. Now the consequence of this is, that unlimited and passive obedience, is no more enjoined in this passage, under monarchical government; or to the supreme power in any state, than

---

3. The essence of government (I mean *good* government; and this is the *only* government which the apostle treats of in this passage) consists in the *making* and *executing of good laws*—laws attempered to the common felicity of the *governed*. And if this be, *in fact*, done, it is evidently, in it self, a thing of no consequence at all, what the *particular* form of government is;—whether the legislative and executive power be lodged in *one and the same* person, or in *different* persons;—whether in *one* person, whom we call an *absolute monarch*;—whether in a *few*, so as to constitute an *aristocrasy*—whether in *many*, so as to constitute a *republic*; or whether in three *co-ordinate branches*, in such manner

under all other species of government, which answer the end of government; or, to all the subordinate degrees of civil authority, from the highest to the lowest. Those, therefore, who would from this passage infer the guilt of resisting kings, in all cases whatever, though acting ever so contrary to the design of their office, must, if they will be consistent, go much farther, and infer from it the guilt of resistance under all other forms of government; and of resisting *any petty officer* in the state, tho' acting beyond his commission, in the most arbitrary, illegal manner possible. The argument holds equally strong in both cases. All civil rulers, as such, are the *ordinance* and *ministers of God;* and they are all, by the nature of their office, and in their respective spheres and stations, bound to consult the public welfare. With the same reason therefore, that any deny unlimited and passive obedience to be here injoined under a republic or aristocrasy, or any other established form of civil government; or to subordinate powers, acting in an illegal and oppressive manner; (with the same reason) others may deny, that such obedience is enjoined to a king or monarch, or any civil power whatever. For the apostle says nothing that is *peculiar to kings;* what he says, extends equally to *all* other persons whatever, vested with any civil office. They are all, in exactly the same sense, the *ordinance of God;* and the *ministers of God;* and obedience is equally enjoined to be paid to them all. For, as the apostle expresses it, *there is* NO POWER *but of God:* And we are required to *render to* ALL *their* DUES; and not MORE than their DUES. And what these *dues* are, and to *whom* they are to be *rendered,* the apostle *sayeth not;* but leaves to the reason and consciences of men to determine.

Thus it appears, that the common argument, grounded upon this passage, in favor of universal, and passive obedience, really overthrows itself, by proving too much, if it proves any thing at all; namely, that no civil officer is, in any case whatever, to be resisted, though acting in express contradiction to the design of his office; which no man, in his senses, ever did, or can assert. [. . .]

[. . .] To conclude: Let us all learn to be *free,* and to be *loyal.* Let us not profess ourselves vassals to the lawless pleasure of any man on earth. But let us remember, at the same time, government is *sacred,* and not to be *trifled* with. It is our happiness to live under the government of a PRINCE who is satisfied with ruling according to law; as every other *good prince* will—We enjoy under his administration all the liberty that is proper and expedient for us. It becomes us, therefore, to be contented, and dutiful subjects. Let us prize our freedom; but not *use our liberty for a cloke of maliciousness.* There are men who strike at *liberty* under the term *licentiousness.* There are others who aim at *popularity* under the disguise of *patriotism.* Be aware of both. *Extremes* are dangerous. There is at present amongst *us,* perhaps, more danger of the *latter,* than of the *former.* For which reason I would exhort you to pay all due Regard to the government over us; to the KING and all in authority; and to *lead a quiet and peaceable life.*—And while I am speaking of loyalty to our *earthly Prince,* suffer me just to put you in mind to be loyal also to the supreme RULER of the universe, *by whom kings reign, and princes decree justice.* To which king eternal immortal, invisible, even to the ONLY WISE GOD, be all honor and praise, DOMINION and thanksgiving, through JESUS CHRIST our LORD. AMEN.

---

as to make the government *partake* something of *each* of these forms; and to be, at the same time, *essentially different* from them *all.* If the *end* be attained, it is enough. But no form of government seems to be so unlikely to accomplish this *end,* as *absolute monarchy*—Nor is there any one that has so little pretence to a *divine original,* unless it be in this sense, that God *first* introduced it into, and thereby overturned, the common wealth of *Israel,* as a *curse* upon that people for their *folly* and *wickedness,* particularly in *desiring* such a government. (See I *Sam.* viii. chap.) Just so God, before, sent *Quails* amongst them, as a *plague,* and a *curse,* and not as a *blessing. Numb.* chap. xi.

William Livingston

Essays from the *Independent Reflector* (1752–1753)

December 21, 1752—The Different Effects of an Absolute and a Limited Monarch: The Glory of a Prince Ruling According to Law, Superior to that of an Arbitrary Sovereign; with the peculiar Happiness of the British Nation

When one considers the Difference between an absolute, and a limited Monarchy, it seems unaccountable, that any Person in his Senses, should prefer the former to the latter. For, notwithstanding the pretended Advantages under an unlimited Prince, Despotism is a Task above the Capacity of human Nature. Power of all Kinds is intoxicating; but boundless Power, is insupportable by the giddy and arrogant Mind of MAN. So exalted an Elevation, hath seldom fail'd to turn the Head of its Possessor. The frail and delicate Structure of the human Eye, is not more incapable of enduring the dazzling Lustre of the Sun, than the Heart of Man, the bewitching Charms of despotic Sovereignty. Hence most absolute Monarchs have acted more like imperial Wolves, or rather Beasts in human Shape, than rational and intelligent Beings. 'Tis true, that a Prince, who would never abuse his uncontroulable Authority, might, in some Instances, promote the public Welfare, beyond a Ruler whose Hands are tied by the Law: But such a Prince is rather a Creature of the Imagination, than a real Existence; and so unequal are the Chances against it, that it is the Height of Phrensy, to make the Experiment.

In *limited* Monarchies, the Pride and Ambition of Princes, and their natural Lust for Dominion, are check'd and restrained. If they violate their Oath, and sap the fundamental Constitution of the State, the People have a Right to resist them; because by that Means they put themselves in the Condition of private Persons, and act with unauthoritative Power: For such is all the Power they can have, inconsistent with, or in Opposition to the Laws. Hence they are to be considered, as in a State of Nature, to have broke the original Compact, abdicated their Thrones, and introduced a Necessity of repelling Force by Force.

But where the People have voluntarily resigned their natural Liberty, without any Restriction, as in *absolute* Monarchies; they must be content to fall a Prey to the brutal Passions of their Sovereign, whenever he thinks fit to resemble Satan, under the Character of the Lord's Anointed. Thanks be to GOD, this is not our Case. Our sage and provident Ancestors, were inspired with too great a Love for *Liberty*, and too tender a Concern for the Happiness of their Posterity, to make such an unconditional Submission, and entail upon them so fatal a Calamity: For, such is the Nature of our excellent Constitution, that amidst all the Prerogatives of the Crown, which are great and splendid, the *Liberty of the Subject*, is secure and inviolable. How must it swell the Breast of every BRITON, with Transport! while he surveys the despicable Slaves of *unlimited* Princes, to reflect, that his Person and Property are guarded by Laws, which the Sovereign himself cannot infringe: Nay, that in a Trial between his King and himself, his Majesty is obliged to put himself upon the Country, and submit the Controversy to the Decision of the Peers of his Subject. [. . .]

Liberty gives an inexpressible Charm to all our Enjoyments. It imparts a Relish to the most indifferent Pleasure, and renders the highest Gratification the more consummately delightful. It is the Refinement of Life; it sooths and alleviates our Toils; smooths the rugged Brow of Adversity, and endears and enhances every Acquisition. The Subjects of a free State, have something open and generous in their Carriage; something of Grandeur and Sublimity in their Appearance, resulting from their Freedom and Independence, that is never to be met with in those dreary Abodes, where the embittering Circumstance of a precarious Property, mars the Relish of every Gratification, and damps the most magnanimous

Spirits. They can think for themselves; publish their Sentiments, and animadvert on Religion and Government, secure and unmolested.

> *O happy Men, born under good Stars,*
> *Where, what is honest, you may freely think;*
> *Speak what you think, and write what you do speak;*
> *Not bound to servile Soothings!*
>
> MARSTON'S *Fawn*.

But in *absolute* Monarchies, the whole Country is overspread with a dismal Gloom. *Slavery* is stamp'd on the Looks of the Inhabitants; and Penury engraved on their Visages, in strong and legible Characters. To prevent Complaints, the Press is prohibited; and a Vindication of the natural Rights of Mankind, is Treason. Every generous Spirit is broke and depressed: Human Nature is degraded, insulted, spurn'd, and outrag'd: The lovely Image of GOD, is defaced and disfigur'd, and the Lord of the Creation treated like the bestial Herd. The liberal Sciences languish: The politer Arts droop their Heads: Merit is banished to Cells and Deserts; and Virtue frowned into Dungeons, or dispatched to the Gallies: Iniquity is exalted: Goodness trod under Foot: Truth perverted; and the barbarous Outrages of Tyranny, sanctified and adored. The Fields lie waste and uncultivate: Commerce is incumbered with supernumerary Duties: The Tyrant riots in the Spoils of his People; and drains their Purses, to replenish his insatiate Treasury. He wages War against his own Subjects: Rapine and Plunder are his royal Amusements: His Sword is Reason and Law. *Stet pro Ratione voluntas.* For the Extent of Territory, and to flatter his boundless Ambition, the Blood of the Subject is inhumanly squander'd; and a whole Nation devoted to Indigence and Ruin. Or if he spares the Wretches a miserable Morsel; ecclesiastic Tyranny snatches it up like a rapacious Vulture. Persecuting Zeal slashes the devouring Torch, and bathes the Sword in unbelieving Blood. [. . .]

But far otherwise, is the Condition of a free People. Under the mild and gentle Administration of a *limited* Prince, every Thing looks chearful and happy, smiling and serene. Agriculture is encouraged, and proves the annual Source of immense Riches to the Kingdom: The Earth opens her fertile Bosom to the Ploughshare, and luxuriant Harvests diffuse Wealth and Plenty thro' the Land: The Fields stand thick with Corn: The Pastures smile with Herbage: The Hills and Vallies are cover'd with Flocks and Herds: Manufacturies flourish; and unprecarious Plenty recompenses the Artificer's Toil: In a Word, Nothing is seen but universal Joy and Festivity. Such is the Happiness of the People, under the blissful Reign of a good King. But do they get a Prince, whose Heart is poison'd with Regard to regal Authority, and who vainly imagines; that the Grandeur of Princes consists in making themselves feared; and accordingly plays the Devil in the Name of the Lord: They boldly assert their Rights, and call aloud for Justice; They cannot, they will not be enslaved. Sooner shall the royal Sinner have the Honour of Martyrdom, and the *Lord's Anointed* perish for his Iniquity, than the whole Frame of the Government be unhinged and dissolved.

At the same Time, that the Happiness of a *limited* Monarchy, exceeds that of a *despotic* Government, the Person of their King is much safer, as well as his Glory far superior, to the specious Glare, the tinsel Lustre, of an arbitrary Prince: He is beloved by a nation of Freemen and Heroes; while the other is fear'd and flattered by a Crowd of fawning Slaves and abject Dependents: He reigns in the Breasts of his People; and while he preserves their Affection, his Throne is founded on a Rock: Their Lives and Fortunes are at his Service. Where Inclination prompts, there needs no Force to compel, and where that is wanting, all Force is ineffectual. It may overpower, but it cannot conquer. The first Opportunity that offers, their Vengeance will break out; and break out like a smothered Flame, with redoubled Fury: But the King, who has the Love of his People, is safe and happy: They revere him as their Father, their Benefactor; and consider their Prosperity inseparably connected with his. How miserably deluded, therefore, are such Princes, who place their Felicity in arbitrary Power? For without the Love of their Subjects, vain is Force, or rather the Exertion of it, their Ruin. Force will be resisted with Force; and a War once commenced, the Relation of King and Subject is forgotten, and both consider each other as Enemies, and the Worst of Enemies.

It is not standing Armies, numerous Guards, or a rich Exchequer, that constitute the Safety and Glory of a Monarch. These can only inspire Terror; and that no longer than the People are in a Capacity to defy them. The Prince, who hath Nothing else to maintain himself in the Possession of his Throne, holds it by a precarious Tenure: The Impotence of his People is his only Strength; and when they acquire sufficient Power, he is undone: But a King, who pursues true Glory and real Greatness, will never aim at absolute Dominion. Lawless Power, is a Power over Slaves, and void of every Thing sublime and generous. Obedience by Compulsion, is the Obedience of Vassals, who without Compulsion would disobey. The Affection of the People is the only Source of a chearful and rational Obedience; and such Obedience is the brightest Jewel in the Royal Diadem. [. . .]

January 25, 1753—Public Virtue to Be Distinguished by Public Honors: The Selling of Offices, which Require Skill and Confidence, a Dismal Omen of the Declension of a State

Omnia venalia Romæ. SAL.

O cives, cives, querenda Pecunia primum est,
Virtus post nummos,— HOR.

No State or Government can long continue in a flourishing Condition, without observing a proper Discrimination between the Blameable and Praiseworthy of its Subjects. Nor is the Punishment of the Flagitious, a sufficient Encouragement to Virtue, without, moreover, rewarding the eminently deserving. As the licentious Criminal ought to be crush'd by the violated Laws of the Common-Wealth, so also should her dutious Children, who devote their Studies, and consecrate their Talents to her Service, be crowned with her distinguishing Honours. A meer Exemption from Punishment, is too feeble a Spur to great and arduous Undertakings: It only supposes a Man innocent, or negatively virtuous, but is no Recompense to superior Desert, and conspicuous Merit. It is but a small Satisfaction, that we are exempted from the Gallows or Pillory, because we are not Rogues and Villains, while we reap no Benefit by being signally good and meritorious. 'Tis true, every Man ought to promote the Prosperity of his Country, from a sublimer Motive than his private Advantage: But it is extremely difficult, for the best of Men, to divest themselves of Self-Interest: Nor is it rational, to expect great Geniuses, accomplished Heroes, or any other illustrious Characters, in a Government that overlooks Merit; and, like the Grave, buries the Best and the Worst in one promiscuous and undistinguished Oblivion. Such is the Degeneracy of human Nature, that Punishments to deter, without Rewards to allure, are not sufficient to fix the roving Mind of Man, in the uninterrupted Practice of public Virtue. Hence the Government which inflicts the One, without any Provision for the Other, is partial and fundamentally defective; but that, on the Contrary, which makes the Service of the Public, the most efficacious Means of promoting the true Interest of every Individual, affords the strongest Proofs of its political Wisdom. GOD himself, hath annexed *Rewards and Punishments*, as the Conditions of the Obedience or Disloyalty of his free and intelligent Creatures. He, whose Omniscience pervades the Heart of Man, hath not denounced his Vengeance, to deter him from Evil, without super-adding his Promises, as Inducements to Virtue. [. . .] The Ambition natural to the Mind of Man, wants, at least, the Prospect of Fame and Honour, to keep him in the Pursuit of Glory. [. . .] But the pleasing and animating View of being distinguished by his Country, from the common Run of his Species, in proportion to his Merit, is a perpetual Stimulation to Virtue: It is kind of intellectual Gale, that fans the Fire of Ambition, and preserves him from Lassitude in his Pursuit of Glory. Not that he will really obtain the Satisfaction he has in View: All our Hopes of Happiness, from any Thing beneath the Sun, must, by Necessity of Nature, be delusive. No sooner do we arrive to the Point proposed, but the Object on which we had placed our Felicity, eludes our Embrace like a Fantom: Instead of a JUNO, we are deceived with a Cloud. [. . .]

The *Athenians* and *Lacedæmonians* conferred the Honours of the State, according to the real Worth of the Candidates. In those celebrated Common-Wealths, Men rose to the first Rank, by the Strength of their Genius, and their personal Valour. This naturally gave Rise to a numerous Race of Heroes, and produced a Multitude of Philosophers, Statesmen, Poets and Orators: And yet so great was the public Frugality, as to enable them to leave no Merit unrewarded. A Twig of Laurel was as illustrious a Distinction as a splendid Pension. All the Honour conferred on MILTIADES, who delivered *Athens*, from the Invasion of *Persia*, was the placing his Picture at the Head of the Commanders in the *Piazza*, where the Battle of *Marathon* was painted. This Parsimony in the Distribution of Rewards, made them the more glorious: But when the State became corrupted by the Extravagance of their Magistrates, and decreed Three Hundred Statues to DEMETRIUS PHALEREUS, their Favours became multiplied and threadbare, and consequently useless and contemptible.

Justly celebrated for this essential Article of sound Politicks, is a neighboring Nation, equally famous for their good Cookery, and political Subtlety; The *French* are not more remarkable for the Slaughter of Frogs, the cutting of Capers, or the Consumption of Fricassees, than for their Wisdom, in preferring Persons in proportion to their Deserts. Hence it is, that their Officers, both civil and military, are, perhaps, inferior to none in *Europe*.

With Pleasure I write it, and with Pleasure will it be read, that we rather surpass than rival them in this important Point of political Wisdom. How happy the Nation among whom public Venality and the Sale of Offices, is prohibited by Law! It is impossible for a Man devoid of Merit, to be elevated to an eminent Post; or, for superior Worth to languish in Obscurity and Indigence. SALLUST mentions the Sale of Offices, as a deadly Symptom of the approaching Dissolution of *Rome*. And indeed, I cannot conceive, how a State can long escape its final Period, after the Introduction of an universal Venality: But our Laws have wisely provided against this ruinous Mischief. By our excellent Constitution, an Office, either of the Grant of the King or the Subject, which concerns the Administration or the Proceeding of Justice, the King's Revenue, the Common-Wealth, the Interest and Safety of the Subject, or the like, granted to a Man unexpert, and of insufficient Skill for the Exercise or Execution of it, is meerly void; and the Party disabled by Law to take it, *pro commodo regis & populi:* And no Man, tho' never so skillful and expert, is capable of a judicial Office, in Reversion. Again, where any *bargaining*, or *giving of Money*, or any *Matter of Reward*, etc. for Offices, is mentioned, it shall render the Purchaser incapable. Such being the Law, it affects me with singular Pleasure, to reflect, by Way of Illation, that all our Officers are Men of Skill and Capacity; and that none of them have been guilty of this political Simony, of purchasing their Posts; because that would be supposing our Superior to have acted contrary to Law; which would be the Height of Absurdity, and a most ill-mannerly Reflection. It would indeed infer little less than Perjury, and be an injurious Calumny on their Reputations. It must, therefore, be taken for granted; that they were preferred for their personal Merit, and that no sinister Consideration entered into the Thoughts of the Grantor.

May 10, 1753—A Discant on the Origin, Nature, Use and Abuse of Civil Government

[. . .] In the Field of Nature, almost every Phenomenon that presents itself to the Philosopher, passes equally under the Observation of any Man that has the Use of his Senses. But with this Difference, the former by the Exercise of his Reason, investigates the Causes, discovers the Natures, and traces the Design and Tendency of those natural Appearances; while the latter contents himself with a bare Sensibility of their having occurred. The Physician, thro' his Acquaintance with the Constitution of the animal Nature of Man, sees every Disorder to which his Patient is subject: His Knowledge of the various and different Properties of the several Parts of the vegetable Creation, furnishes him with proper Remedies for those Disorders, while the Patient, by his own unhappy Feeling, is barely convinced that he is subject to Sickness and Mortality, without being able to dissipate the former, or prolong the Event of the latter. Thus it is in civil Polity. Examples alone can never teach the Magistrate the Rules of true Government, nor lay open to him the Basis upon which a well-regulated Community should be founded. Does he turn his Attention to the Monuments of ancient History, he beholds a thousand exemplary Facts crowding in upon his Mind, attended with Circumstances sufficient to enamour him with their Beauty, or terrify him with their Deformity. He sees that a NERO, a CALIGULA, were Monsters equally formidable to themselves and to their Subjects; while TRAJAN could taste the Sweets of real Felicity, in being the Father of his Country, and a Lover of Mankind. But if we consider those different Springs from which good or bad Actions flow; the different Principles, Prejudices, Passions and Interests, that variously influence every civil Event, it will appear undeniably evident, that the Force of Example can never teach a Ruler the Methods of just Administration. He must carry his Inquiries much higher, view Government in its first Rise, trace Communities back to their Original, and acquaint himself with the formal Reasons of Society. Such Investigations as these, will convince him, that Communities were formed not for the Advantage of one Man, but for the Good of the whole Body: That Government was instituted, not to give the Ruler a Power of reigning despotically over the Subject, but to preserve and promote the true Interest and Happiness of both: Thus he will learn, that while he acts agreable to the true End of his Institution, he justly merits the Love and Obedience of his Subjects, and that he cannot deviate from it, without involving both in Misery; and must consequently, forfeit his Right of Government. Would he grow wise by Example, he must view Facts not only as having happened; he must investigate the Causes whence they sprung, discover the Motives upon which former Rulers have acted, the Passions and Vices to which they were subject, and the Principles of Virtue whereby they were influenced. Furnished with this important Stock of Knowledge, he will be enabled to determine what Qualifications are expedient to form the true Character of a just and wise Ruler, and what Acts are necessary to promote the real Happiness of a People.

[. . .] Men of true Principles would rather return to a State of primitive Freedom, in which every Man has a Right to be his own Carver, than be the Slaves of the greatest Monarch, or even suffer under the most unlimited Democracy in the Universe. It is true, that Society is the most eligible State in which Man can exist; nor can it also be denied, that Government is absolutely necessary for the Happiness of Society. But still, it will appear to every one who is not bigoted to the slavish Doctrines of *passive Obedience* and *Non-Resistance*, to be the height of Madness, to purchase the Advantages of Society, by giving up all our Title to Liberty. Government, at best, is a Burden, tho' a necessary one. Had Man been wise from his Creation, he would always have been free. We might have enjoyed the Gifts of liberal Nature, unmolested, unrestrained. It is the Depravity of Mankind, that has necessarily introduced Government; and so great is this Depravity, that without it, we could scarcely subsist: Yet who does not see, that our Nature would teach us to live void of that Restraint, could we receive all the Advantages arising from a Subjection of this Kind, or greater, in a State of absolute Liberty and Independence? Who can deny, that we have ceded a Part of our original Freedom, to secure to us the rest, together with the other Blessings of Life? Without this Prospect, it is plain, no Man would ever subject himself to the Dominion and Rule of another. And therefore, tho' Government is necessary to our Well-being, it must be such as is consistent with it. [. . .]

The very Notion of Government, supposes in some Person or other, a Right to decree and execute Justice; and therefore this Power may be well or ill applied, as such Person may be inclined to act, either upon public Motives, or Views of Self-interest. Deprive the Ruler of this discretionary Power, you destroy the Government; grant it to him, and your Liberties are at best precarious. The only Conclusion that can be drawn from hence is, that a People should be careful of yielding too much of their original Power, even to the most just Ruler, and always retain the Privilege of degrading him whenever he acts in Contradiction to the Design of his Institution. [. . .]

It would, indeed, be unreasonable to expect, that by elevating the Magistrate above the common Level of his fellow Creatures, he should be deprived of those Passions which constitute a Part of his Nature. Far from desiring this, as they are necessary in private Life to stimulate Man to Action, they are much more so in public Stations, where the Ruler's Duty requires the utmost Efforts of human Nature. He should neither be dispassionate, nor disinterested, but should make his Passions and Interest center in the Happiness of his People: Let him soar upon the Wings of Ambition, but let the State mount with him the Summit of real Grandeur: Is his Courage matchless and undaunted, it should be exercised with Wisdom in the Defence of his Country: Is he armed with Power, let it be exerted in executing Vengeance against the Enemies of the State: Is his Nature generous and benevolent; it should deluge down Favours and Blessings upon his Subjects: In short, as he is the Vicegerent of Heaven, let his Administration bear all possible Resemblance to the Government of the supreme Ruler of the Universe.

From what has hitherto been advanced, I am evidently far from encouraging a Spirit of unbounded Licentiousness in the People: It is, I hope, a Charge that never will be laid against me. I have already enforced the Necessity of civil Government, and preferred the English Constitution as the most eligible in Nature. Nor do I want Reason to convince me, that a due Obedience of the Subject, is absolutely requisite under a Government like ours, or that Libertinism unrestrained, has a natural Tendency to destroy it. Let us be content with that Portion of our natural Liberty, which we thought proper to retain at the original Formation of the Community, neither encroaching on the Prerogative of the civil Magistrate, nor suffering our indisputable Rights to be invaded. Let us watchfully observe the Actions of the most just and temperate Ruler, and vigilantly guard against the Attacks of lawless and arbitrary Sway: But let us still remember, that as the Magistrate is cloathed with Power for the Security of the Subject, the People cannot strip him of his Authority, without reducing themselves to their original Independency, the most joyless uncomfortable State in which human Nature can possibly exist.

August 2 and 9, 1753—The Absurdity of the Civil Magistrate's Interfering in Matters of Religion (in two parts)

(Part One, Aug. 2) Mankind being naturally free, and with respect to a Right of Dominion, upon a perfect Equality; it is absurd to suppose, that any Man, or Body of Men, would ever have consented to resign that Freedom, and Equality, by submitting to the Government and Controul of another, but for some Advantages they expected from such Submission. Nor would they have acted rationally in thus subjecting themselves from the Prospect of any Advantages unequivalent to their natural Liberty, voluntarily surrendered; because that would have been parting with a greater for a lesser Good, or an Alienation of an inestimable Jewel, without a valuable Consideration. It is therefore unreasonable to imagine they had less in View, than a Remedy for the Inconveniences that sprang from a State of Nature, in which, for want of a Judge, armed with proper Authority, to decide Controversies, the Weak were a perpetual Prey to the Powerful, who were under no other Restraint from violating the Possessions of their Neighbors, than the Dictates of Reason, which were seldom sufficiently regarded. [. . .] Nothing, therefore, but what is injurious to the Society, or some particular Member of it, can be the proper Object of civil Punishment; because, nothing else falls within the Design of forming the Society. For this, and this only, was the Magistrate invested with his Power, over the Persons who submitted themselves to him. But the religious Opinions and Speculations of the Subject, cannot be prejudicial to the Society, as a Society; nor to any particular Member of it; because such Opinions and Speculations are not injurious either to the Person or Possession of another: And all that is necessary to the Welfare of the Society, is, that no such Injury be committed. Matters of Religion relate to another World, and have nothing to do with the Interest of the State. The first resides in the Minds and Consciences of Men; the latter in the outward Peace and Prosperity of the Public. It is the Business of the civil Power, to see that the Common-Wealth suffer no Injury, whether it be attempted on a religious, or any other Pretence. But provided he hurt no Man, every Subject has a Right to be protected in the Exercise of the Liberty of thinking about Religion, as he judges proper, as well as of acting in Conformity thereto. Religious Opinions and Speculations come not therefore within the Design of cloathing the Magistrate with a Superiority over the Subject; nor are they proper Objects for the Exercise of his Authority. Neither did there arise any Inconveniences from such Opinions in a State of Nature, nor consequently could their Regulation or Restraint, be any Part of the Origin or Intention of entering into civil Society. And every Exertion of Power contrary to, or which was no Part of, the Design of creating the Magistrate, must of Necessity be Usurpation and Tyranny. It must be injurious and oppressive, and all his Decisions concerning Matters of Religion, are to be regarded as unauthoritative Adjudications. For surely it could never enter into the Heart of Man to submit his Judgment in Matters of Religion to his Ruler, not only because it is impossible for all his Subjects to concur with him in Opinion, but also because no Man, of any Religion at all, would reduce himself to the Necessity of worshipping God in a Manner he thought disagreable to him; which must often be the Case, if he is obliged to be of the Magistrate's Religion. From all which it clearly follows, that the civil Power hath no Jurisdiction over the Sentiments or Opinions of the Subject, till such Opinions break out into Actions prejudicial to the Community, and then it is not the Opinion, but the Action that is the Object of the Punishment. For tho' a Man entertained such Opinions as would, if reduced to Practice, be dangerous to the Society, yet while they lie dormant in his Breast, they injure no Man: and if no Person is injured, no Crime is committed; and without a Crime, there can be no Room for Punishment. [. . .]

(Part Two, Aug. 9) Having in my last Paper shewn, that Government was a Means calculated to secure Mankind in the free and unmolested Enjoyment of their political Rights, every Perversion of such Means must evidently be an Abuse of Government, and an Infringement of that native Power in Man from which all civil Authority by Delegation originally sprang. Power unduly exercised becomes Oppression; and that Liberty, for the Preservation of which civil Power was instituted, degenerates into Slavery. It was wisely observed by one of the greatest Patrons of English Liberty and Learning, that *wheresoever Law ends Tyranny begins*; and it might justly be added, that *whenever the Legislature pervert the true Intention of that Power with which they are invested, by instituting such Laws, as tend to abridge the Liberty of human Nature, it is the Height of Tyranny and Oppression*. Nay, it is so much worse than open Violence, as they screen their Conduct under the specious Appearance of Law and Equity.

But among the many Instances of the Abuse of Government, there is none more immediately destructive of the natural Rights of Mankind, than the Interposition of the secular Arm in Matters purely religious. The Efficacy of human Laws is limited to the exterior Acts of Man, as they affect Society, and consequently can enforce nothing as a Duty, but what springs from the Circumstances of Man, considered as a Member of Society. [. . .]

[H]ow great is the Absurdity to suppose, that Government was ever designed to *enslave* the *Consciences of Men!* Is it possible for Man to divest himself of Thought, which is essential to our Existence? Equally preposterous is it to suppose, that the inward Exertions of the Soul, should be regulated by any external Laws. The Understanding, upon surveying a Set of Ideas that form a Proposition, must either determine, that it be true or false; or the Judgment must be suspended for want of clearer Light and Information. But in either Case can the Force of civil Authority have any Efficacy? The Mind must, if at all, be determined by the highest apparent Reason, and of that the *Mind itself* is the only *competent Judge*. [. . .]

The Restraint of civil Authority, in different Countries and Ages, upon the free Exercise of human Reason, has ever been attended with a Decay of all valuable Knowledge and Literature. It is as impossible for the Sciences to grow and flourish under the Frowns and Terrors of Oppression, as for a People to breath Liberty under the savage Administration of a Tyrant. The Advancement of Learning depends upon the free Exercise of Thought; it is therefore absurd to suppose, that it should thrive under a Government that makes it Treason even for a Man to think. How injurious this is to the Cause of Religion, requires no great Sagacity to conceive. The Enlargement of our reasoning Powers depends entirely upon the Exercise of them, to which nothing can be more conducive than the Encouragement of Learning. Our Duties increase with our Knowledge, and no Man has so much Reason to be religious as he whose Knowledge is most extensive. It has therefore always been the Care of the wisest Administrations, to encourage a Liberty of Thought; and as he who thinks freely is most likely to think aright, that Religion which proceeds from a Man's own free Thoughts, must certainly be the most agreeable to the Deity. [. . .]

Peter Fontaine

Letters (1756–1757)

March 2, 1756

Dear Brothers:—Yours of the 30th October, 1754, came to hand the February following, when I was very ill of the gout, which confined me to the middle of April, and took me again in September, but did not confine me so long. Thus much with regard to my troublesome companion.

My sister came to reside with us in the beginning of last October, but we had no long enjoyment of her company, for she departed this life the last day of December, after a five days' illness, which though very sharp, she bore with a truly Christian patience and resignation to the Divine will, spending her last breath in prayers for all her relations and acquaintances, and in blessing me and my little family, one by one, as we stood in tears around her. The first thing she said to me when she came to my house was: "Brother I am come to die with you." Her countenance was cheerful, and I was in hopes that her words would not be so soon accomplished. During the little time she was with us, she did me and my family much good by her pious exhortations, and she instructed my little ones in commendable works they were unacquainted with before, which she was very capable to teach them. She had, after her duty to God, taken the excellent daughter, Proverbs 31st chapter, the 18th verse to the end, for her pattern; and she kept all about her employed, and would often wish she had strength to do more herself, and not be the only lazy person in the family; and yet in that short time, besides her daily task in the Bible, four chapters and the Psalms for the day, she had read the best part of "The Persecutions of the Vaudois of Piedmont," a pretty large folio by John Liger, a minister of that country. She concluded her labors here in the sixty-sixth year of her age, and by the truly Christian manner of her death gave us great comfort, who were eye-witnesses of it. This being the last scene she acted on this troublesome stage of life, I have transmitted it to you faithfully, and I hope we may all imitate her faith and constancy.

As to news, you have a better account in the public papers than I can give you.

Hitherto we have been shamefully defeated by the enemy, not for want of men to carry on the war, but of money and proper military discipline.

The French as you observe are bad neighbors, and the Indians not one jot better, neither of which any treaties can bind, so that though a peace should be concluded at home, and you should reap the benefit of it, till the floating walls are unmanned and laid up, the enemy will make use of that cessation of hostilities to distress us. It would be no peace for us here, for, until the English colonies can, by exerting themselves, force the enemy to retreat from their borders, the people will be cut off piecemeal under pretence of an Indian war. The French will furnish the Indians with arms, ammunition, scalping-knives and leaders, to harass us continually; and may it not be of evil consequence to tie up our hands by a peace just now? Is not this delivering us over to the tyranny of fear, an imperious master more dreadful than a thousand deaths? No doubt peace is a jewel more to be desired than any thing else this world affords, could it be expected to be a real peace; but to put off the evil day, because you or I, who are old, may by that time be out of harm's way, and leave the conflict to our children, is not acting a generous, but a dastardly part.

The other evil you mention, our intestine enemies, our slaves, increase daily. The females are far more prolific than the white women, for, living upon a simple diet, upon bread, water, pulse, roots and herbs, seldom tasting meat of any sort, and drinking no strong drink, and being used to labor in the ground, they seldom miscarry, have strong healthy children, liable to no distempers. When our mother country shall vouchsafe to consider us a part of herself, she may perhaps not suffer such multitudes to be brought from Africa to pleasure a company, and overrun a dutiful colony.

May God preserve you, is the hearty prayer of your affectionate brother and humble servant,

PETER FONTAINE

March 30, 1757

DEAR BROTHER MOSES:—As I was obliged to take my consignments out of the hands of Hanbury and Farrell, it has occasioned some miscarriages and delays of our letters. Thomas Knox, Esq., in Bristol, and Robert Cary, Esq., in London, manage for me now. I am favored with yours, and brother and sister Torin's letters, dated December, 1756, and January, 1757, received the 11th March. Yours and our kind relations' prayers for me and mine, give me great comfort, as I am persuaded they have a favorable audience at the Throne of Grace. Dear brother, the best thing we can do for one another at this distance, is to send up our petitions continually to the centre of our hope, love, filial affection and fear, where they meet in an instant, join us to our Heavenly Father, to our blessed Redeemer, and one to another. Thus we shall be disposed to turn our faces now towards our heavenly rest, where we shall ere long meet, see one another, and by God's grace and mercy live for ever. When our thoughts take this direction the darkest scenes of life disappear, or are only noticed as small rubs on our journey thither. Oh! let us not be concerned at the measure or duration of afflictions sent to bring us back from our strayings. Let us not open our lips in complaints, but, with holy David, be dumb, and be content that all our affairs should be managed by Him whom our soul loveth, and who we are persuaded loveth us, and who saith to the sword and to the pestilence, what he formerly said to the sea, Thus far shalt thou rage, and no farther, and there shall thy proud waves be stayed.

Now, to answer your first query—whether by our breach of treaties we have not justly exasperated the bordering nations of Indians against us, and drawn upon ourselves the barbarous usage we meet with from them and the French? To answer this fully would take up much time. I shall only hint at some things which we ought to have done, and which we did not do at our first settlement amongst them, and which we might have learnt long since from the practice of our enemies the French. I am persuaded we were not deficient in the observation of treaties, but as we got the land by concession, and not by conquest, we ought to have intermarried with them, which would have incorporated us with them effectually, and made of them stanch friends, and, which is of still more consequence, made many of them good Christians; but this our wise politicians at home put an effectual stop to at the beginning of our settlement here, for when they heard that Rolfe had married Pocahontas, it was deliberated in Council, whether he had not committed high treason by so doing, that is, marrying an Indian Princess; and had not some troubles intervened which put a stop to the inquiry, the poor man might have been hanged up for doing the most just, the most natural, the most generous and politic action that ever was done this side of the water. This put an effectual stop to all intermarriages afterwards. Our Indian traders have indeed their squaws, alias whores, at the Indian towns where they trade, but leave their offspring like bulls or boars to be provided for at random by their mothers. As might be expected, some of these bastards have been the leading men or war captains that have done us so much mischief. This ill-treatment was sufficient to create jealousy in the natural man's breast, and made the Indians look upon us as false and deceitful friends, and cause all our endeavors to convert them to be ineffectual. But here methinks I can hear you observe, What! Englishmen intermarry with Indians? But I can convince you that they are guilty of much more heinous practices, more unjustifiable in the sight of God and man (if that, indeed, may be called a bad practice), for many base wretches amongst us take up with Negro women, by which means the country swarms with mulatto bastards, and these mulattoes, if but three generations removed from the black father or mother, may, by the indulgence of the laws of the country, intermarry with the white people, and actually do every day so marry. Now, if, instead of this abominable practice which hath polluted the blood of many amongst us, we had taken Indian wives in the first place, it would have made them some compensation for their lands. They are a free people, and the offspring would not be born in a state of slavery. We should become rightful heirs to their lands, and should not have smutted our blood, for the Indian children when born are as white as Spaniards or Portuguese, and were it not for the practice of going naked in the summer and besmearing themselves with bears' grease, &c., they would continue white; and had we thought fit to make them our wives, they would readily have complied with our fashion of wearing clothes all the year round; and by doing justice to these poor benighted heathen, we should have introduced Christianity amongst them. Your own reflections upon these hints will be a sufficient answer to your first query. I shall only add that General Johnson's success was owing, under God, to his fidelity to the Indians, and his generous conduct to his Indian wife, by whom he hath several hopeful sons, who are all war-captains, the bulwarks with him of the five nations, and loyal subjects to their mother country.

As to your second query, if enslaving our fellow creatures be a practice agreeable to Christianity, it is answered in a great measure in many treatises at home, to which I refer you. I shall only mention something of our present state here.

Like Adam we are all apt to shift off the blame from ourselves and lay it upon others, how justly in our case you may judge. The negroes are enslaved by the negroes themselves before they are purchased by the masters of the ships who bring them here. It is to be sure at our choice whether we buy them or not, so this then is our crime, folly, or whatever you will please to call it. But, our Assembly, foreseeing the ill consequences of importing such numbers amongst us, hath often attempted to lay a duty upon them which would amount to a prohibition, such as ten or twenty pounds a head, but no Governor dare pass such a law, having instructions to the contrary from the Board of Trade at home. By this means they are forced upon us, whether we will or will not. This plainly shows the African Company hath the advantage of the colonies, and may do as it pleases with the Ministry.

Indeed, since we have been exhausted of our little stock of cash by the war, the importation has stopped; our poverty then is our best security. There is no more picking for their ravenous jaws upon bare bones, but should we begin to thrive they will be at the same again. All our taxes are now laid upon slaves and on shippers of tobacco, which they wink at while we are in danger of being torn from them, but we durst not do it in time of peace, it being looked upon as the highest presumption to lay any burden upon trade. This is our part of the grievance, but to live in Virginia without slaves is morally impossible. Before our troubles, you could not hire a servant or slave for love or money, so that unless robust enough to cut wood, to go to mill, to work at the hoe, &c., you must starve, or board in some family where they both fleece and half starve you. There is no set price upon corn, wheat and provisions, so they take advantage of the necessities of strangers, who are thus obliged to purchase some slaves and land. This of course draws us all into the original sin and curse of the country of purchasing slaves, and this is the reason we have no merchants, traders or artificers of any sort but what become planters in a short time.

A common laborer, white or black, if you can be so much favored as to hire one, is a shilling sterling or fifteen pence currency per day; a bungling carpenter two shillings or two shillings and sixpence per day; besides diet and lodging. That is, for a lazy fellow to get wood and water, £19. 16. 3, current per annum; add to this seven or eight pounds more and you have a slave for life.

My last to you was in March, 1756. The 9th of April following I had a son born whose name is Abraham, a fine child, praised be God, the biggest I ever had; he has eight teeth.

I have had a severe fit of the gout this winter, and am just able to write.

We hear the Brest fleet is out, and Louis the 15th dead. If they come to Virginia we must take to the woods and fight behind the trees. We have no other fortification but the Lord of Hosts, if he be on our side we shall give them a great deal of trouble. May he be your protection and ours, is the daily and sincere prayer of, dear brother,

Your affectionate, humble servant,

Peter Fontaine

3

THE AMERICAN REVOLUTION

In the Treaty of Paris of 1763, Great Britain triumphantly concluded the Seven Years War. British armies and navies had thoroughly defeated France, not just in North America but throughout the world. Great Britain took possession of French colonial interests worldwide, which in North America included Canada and the eastern Mississippi River valley. North American colonists, like Britons everywhere, celebrated the decisive end to twenty years of intermittent imperial struggle. People in every colony expressed profound satisfaction in their identities as British subjects. And yet, over the next dozen or so years, British initiatives and colonial responses revealed deep and principled political divisions between the home government and the colonies. By 1776, the chasm seemed unbridgeable. But even before the Declaration of Independence, thoughtful observers on both sides of the Atlantic recognized that real constitutional issues were at stake. This chapter focuses on documents that illuminate both the evolution of the political arguments and the core political and constitutional ideas and values at their center.

The Seven Years War had placed an unprecedented strain on the imperial treasury. Britain's national debt nearly doubled in size over the course of the war, reaching £132 million in 1763. Moreover, victory placed fresh demands on British finances. The acquisition of France's vast North American territories required an ongoing British military presence. Government planners determined that it would require 10,000 men to adequately garrison and defend the newly conquered lands, at an annual cost of £225,000. When treasury officials audited the North American customs service, they discovered that the cost for collecting imperial taxes there each year was more than the revenue the taxes produced. The administration of George Grenville responded by putting into place policies aimed at eliminating corruption in tax collection and increasing the revenue generated in the American colonies. The Sugar Act (1764) and the Stamp Act (1765) were central to these purposes. The Stamp Act, Grenville hoped, would bring in a modest £60,000 in revenue to contribute to the costs of defending the North American colonies. Given the evident prosperity there, what could be more reasonable than requiring the colonists to pay a small portion of the costs of their own defense?

Members of Parliament conducted a robust debate over whether these new policies—in particular, the Stamp Act—were prudent or even legal. In the end, persuaded of its power to tax the colonies, and brushing aside warnings that parliamentary taxes "would go down with [the] people like Chopt hay," Parliament enacted the legislation by overwhelming margins. In response, the colonial legislatures, separately and collectively, drafted formal protests. Meanwhile, individual colonists wrote pamphlets decrying the policies. They instituted an economic boycott against British merchants. And, they rioted. What had been for decades a stable, if somewhat ambiguous, political and constitutional relationship between Britain and the American colonies was suddenly thrown into doubt. "Every thing went prosperously for both Countries," Benjamin Franklin wrote in 1768, "'till the Idea of Taxing us by the Power of Parliament unfortunately enter'd the Heads of your Ministers, which has occasion'd a publick Discussion of Questions that had better never been started, and thrown all into Confusion."

As Franklin's remark suggests, the true revolution began with the passage of these two acts, for their passage precipitated the first systematic, theoretical inquiry into the constitutional relationship between the American colonies and Britain. Indeed, one might argue, as John Adams later would, that the revolution began even earlier in 1761, when Boston attorney James Otis impassionedly argued that Parliament could not legally authorize the issuance of writs of assistance. "Otis was a flame of fire," Adams recalled. "[W]ith a promptitude of classical allusions, a depth of research, a rapid summary of historical events and dates, a profusion of legal authorities, a prophetic glance of his eyes into futurity, and a rapid torrent of impetuous eloquence, he hurried away all before him. American Independence was then and there born. . . . In fifteen years, that is in 1776, he grew up to manhood, and declared himself free." Thus, years before the colonists famously dumped tea into Boston Harbor, years before declaring independence, British Americans questioned the political and constitutional bonds that united them with Great Britain.

The colonists had to respond to two different arguments invoked by British authorities as justification for the new taxes. First, British leaders claimed that the colonists were represented in Parliament, despite the fact that the colonists were legally disenfranchised from parliamentary elections. Many in Parliament adopted the theory of virtual representation, arguing that every member of Parliament in fact represented the interests of all who lived under the British Crown, there being no distinct constituencies but rather one common interest shared by all British subjects. Any given member of Parliament represented equally the interests of York and New York, regardless of residence or local attachments. In the American press, most colonists rejected virtual representation, affirming that representatives were delegates of particular constituencies and thus bound to act on behalf of their local interests. Some, like Daniel Dulany, suggested that even if virtual representation were theoretically viable, the colonists were not virtually represented in Parliament. Others simply rejected the idea of virtual representation altogether. Furthermore, most colonists rejected suggestions that the colonies be permitted to send representatives to Parliament.

The second argument the American colonists confronted was the claim that sovereignty in Great Britain was indivisible and located in Parliament. British leaders routinely defined parliamentary sovereignty as unlimited. For example, English jurist William Blackstone wrote that "sovereignty and legislature are indeed convertible terms" and explained that Parliament was thus omnipotent, its power being "absolute and without control." Accordingly, there was in Parliament's view no legal justification for colonial resistance to the Sugar and Stamp Acts. The colonies were legally subordinate to Parliament and hence obligated to comply with its statutes. With a few notable exceptions, the colonists initially responded to the claim of parliamentary sovereignty by arguing that Parliament had the legal authority to legislate for the colonies in external matters—principally commercial affairs. Jurisdiction over the colonies' internal matters—including the power to tax—resided with the colonial legislatures. Many scholars see in this articulation the early signs of the modern federalism that would become a core principle in American constitutionalism.

This argument, however, proved to be of little practical value. The colonists soon found themselves responding to a series of commercial laws whose real intent was to raise tax revenue in the colonies. Over the next few years tensions in the colonies worsened. The arrival of British troops in Boston, followed by the Boston Massacre in 1770, seemed to confirm colonial suspicions of an impending British tyranny. The Boston Tea Party in 1773 suggested to the British that the colonists were riotous people intent on resisting lawful British rule. By 1774, when Parliament enacted the Coercive Acts and the First Continental Congress convened, most colonists had concluded that Parliament had no legal authority over them whatsoever. Each colony was an independent political entity, connected to the other colonies (and to England) as a result of their allegiance to a common king. American colonists, Thomas Jefferson explained, freely choose upon emigrating from the "mother country . . . to continue their union with her by submitting themselves to the same common sovereign, who was thereby made the central link connecting the several parts of the empire thus newly multiplied." Remarkably, this position was staked out by a few colonists in the early years of the crisis, but it would take nearly a decade for the rest of the colonists to catch up.

Ultimately, in their responses to various parliamentary measures and arguments, American colonists revisited transcendent political questions—questions they would continue to debate vigorously as they struggled to construct an American government in the wake of independence. This political discourse would radically transform how they understood core political concepts. For example, whereas in 1766 John Adams could not distinguish between a constitution and government, comparing the former to the "nerves, fibres, and muscles" of the human body and to the inner workings of a clock, the colonists a decade later clearly differentiated the concepts. As Thomas Paine wrote, a constitution is "a thing *antecedent* to a government." It is "the act [not] of its government, but of the people constituting a government." That is, government is "only the creature of a constitution." Bound to this new understanding of a constitution was a new conception of popular sovereignty, one that made the will of the people "not a thing in name only, but in fact." A constitution, as an expression of the popular will, was now a legally prior and binding body of laws. Given that according to British constitutional theory, Parliament was sovereign and could, in Blackstone's words, "change and create afresh even the constitution of the kingdom," it was no surprise that the colonists concluded that "the English have no fixed Constitution." Many colonists turned to an older, alternative approach, anticipated by the seventeenth-century English jurist Sir Edward Coke, who held that those statutes of Parliament repugnant to the common law were to be considered void. James Otis, for example, argued in the 1760s that legislation must be accountable to common-law principles. As the constitutional crisis with England intensified, such ideas gained currency among the colonists, who were already thinking in terms of a constitution as a fixed framework and higher rule under which legislators were to operate.

Finally, the revolutionary focus on rights, along with the emerging notion of a constitution as a binding body of law, are manifest in the constitutions the colonists began to write in the wake of independence. Indeed, the priority of rights, the idea that "governments are instituted" to "secure" unalienable rights, is suggested by the very placement of bills of rights in constitutions like Virginia's and Pennsylvania's. And while many of the rights found in these documents are drawn from the British constitutional tradition, Americans also began to claim new rights, in particular the right to the "free exercise of religion." Not all states initially recognized an uncompromised right to religious liberty; still, the Revolution, and the arguments made to legitimate it, invited oppressed religious sects to demand more than mere religious toleration. The claim to religious freedom, expressed famously in Isaac Backus' argument against ecclesiastical taxes, would finally, with the assistance of James Madison and Thomas Jefferson in 1785, establish itself as a core American constitutional principle.

James Otis

Against Writs of Assistance (recorded, with notes, by John Adams)[1] (1761)

May it please your Honors: I was desired by one of the court to look, into the books, and consider the question now before them concerning Writs of Assistance. I have accordingly considered it, and now appear not only in obedience to your order, but likewise in behalf of the inhabitants of this town, who have presented another petition, and out of regard to the liberties of the subject. And I take this opportunity to declare that whether under a fee or not (for in such a cause as this I despise a fee) I will to my dying day oppose, with all the powers and faculties God has given me, all such instruments of slavery on the one hand and villainy on the other as this Writ of Assistance is.

It appears to me the worst instrument of arbitrary power, the most destructive of English liberty and the fundamental principles of law, that ever was found in an English law-book. I must therefore beg your Honors' patience and attention to the whole range of an argument that may perhaps appear uncommon in many things, as well as to points of learning that are more remote and unusual, that the whole tendency of my design may the more easily be perceived, the conclusions better descend, and the force of them be better felt. I shall not think much of my pains in this cause, as I engaged in it from principle.

I was solicited to argue this cause as Advocate-General; and, because I would not, I have been charged with desertion from my office. To this charge I can give a very sufficient answer. I renounced that office and I argue this cause from the same principle; and I argue it with the greater pleasure, as it is in favor of British liberty, at a time when we hear the greatest monarch upon earth declaring from his throne that he glories in the name of Briton and that the privileges of his people are dearer to him than the most valuable prerogatives of his crown; and as it is in opposition to a kind of power, the exercise of which in former periods of history cost one king of England his head and another his throne. I have taken more pains in this cause than I ever will take again, although my engaging in this and another popular cause has raised much resentment. But I think I can sincerely declare that I cheerfully submit myself to every odious name for conscience' sake; and from my soul I despise all those whose guilt, malice, or folly has made them my foes. Let the consequences be what they will, I am determined to proceed. The only principles of public conduct that are worthy of a gentleman or a man are to sacrifice estate, ease, health, and applause, and even life, to the sacred calls of his country.

These manly sentiments, in private life, make good citizens; in public life, the patriot and the hero. I do not say that, when brought to the test, I shall be invincible. I pray God I may never be brought to the melancholy trial; but, if ever I should, it will then be known how far I can reduce to practice principles which I know to be founded in truth. In the meantime I will proceed to the subject of this writ.

Your Honors will find in the old books concerning the office of a justice of the peace precedents of general warrants to search suspected houses. But in more modern books you will find only special warrants to search such and such houses, specially named, in which the complainant has before sworn that he suspects his goods are concealed; and will find it adjudged that special warrants only are legal. In the same manner I rely on it, that the writ prayed for in this petition, being general, is illegal. It is a power

1. [According to historical record, this speech ran for approximately five hours, but we possess only a small fragment from the opening. The first six paragraphs are attributed to Otis; the remainder of this document is a summary of Adams' notes presenting Otis' argument.]

that places the liberty of every man in the hands of every petty officer. I say I admit that special Writs of Assistance, to search special places, may be granted to certain persons on oath; but I deny that the writ now prayed for can be granted, for I beg leave to make some observations on the writ itself, before I proceed to other Acts of Parliament.

In the first place, the writ is universal, being directed "to all and singular justices, sheriffs, constables, and all other officers and subjects"; so that, in short, it is directed to every subject in the King's dominions. Every one with this writ may be a tyrant; if this commission be legal, a tyrant in a legal manner, also, may control, imprison, or murder any one within the realm. In the next place, it is perpetual; there is no return. A man is accountable to no person for his doings. Every man may reign secure in his petty tyranny, and spread terror and desolation around him, until the trump of the Archangel shall excite different emotions in his soul. In the third place, a person with this writ, in the daytime, may enter all houses, shops, etc., at will, and command all to assist him. Fourthly, by this writ not only deputies, etc., but even their menial servants, are allowed to lord it over us. What is this but to have the curse of Canaan with a witness on us: to be the servants of servants, the most despicable of God's creation?

[John Adams' Summary of the Remainder]

Now, one of the most essential branches of English liberty is the freedom of one's house. A man's house is his castle; and whilst he is quiet, he is as well guarded as a prince in his castle. This writ, if it should be declared legal, would totally annihilate this privilege. Custom-house officers may enter our houses when they please; we are commanded to permit their entry. Their menial servants may enter, may break locks, bars, and everything in their way; and whether they break through malice or revenge, no man, no court can inquire. Bare suspicion without oath is sufficient.

This wanton exercise of this power is not a chimerical suggestion of a heated brain. I will mention some facts. Mr. Pew had one of these writs, and, when Mr. Ware succeeded him, he endorsed this writ over to Mr. Ware; so that these writs are negotiable from one officer to another; and so your Honors have no opportunity of judging the persons to whom this vast power is delegated. Another instance is this: Mr. Justice Walley had called this same Mr. Ware before him, by a constable, to answer for a breach of the Sabbath-day Acts, or that of profane swearing. As soon as he had finished, Mr. Ware asked him if he had done. He replied, "Yes." "Well then," said Mr. Ware, "I will show you a little of my power. I command you to permit me to search your house for uncustomed goods"—and went on to search the house from the garret to the cellar; and then served the constable in the same manner!

But to show another absurdity in this writ: if it should be established, I insist upon it every person, by the 14th Charles Second, has this power as well as the custom-house officers. The words are: "It shall be lawful for any person or persons authorized," etc. What a scene does this open! Every man prompted by revenge, ill-humor, or wantonness to inspect the inside of his neighbor's house, may get a Writ of Assistance. Others will ask it from self-defence; one arbitrary exertion will provoke another, until society be involved in tumult and in blood.

A dissertation on the rights of man in a state of nature. He asserted that every man, merely natural, was an independent sovereign, subject to no law but the law written on his heart and revealed to him by his Maker, in the constitution of his nature and the inspiration of his understanding and his conscience. His right to his life, his liberty, no created being could rightfully contest. Nor was his right to his property less incontestable. The club that he had snapped from a tree, for a staff or for defense, was his own. His bow and arrow were his own; if by a pebble he had killed a partridge or a squirrel, it was his own. No creature, man or beast, had a right to take it from him. If he had taken an eel or a smelt or a sculpin, it was his property. In short, he sported upon this topic with so much wit and humor, and at the same time with so much indisputable truth and reason, that he was not less entertaining than instructive.

He asserted that these rights were inherent and inalienable. That they never could be surrendered or alienated but by idiots or madmen and all the acts of idiots and lunatics were void and not obligatory, by all the laws of God and man. Nor were the poor Negroes forgotten. Not a Quaker in Philadelphia or Mr. Jefferson in Virginia ever asserted the rights of Negroes in stronger terms. Young as I was and ignorant as I was, I shuddered at the doctrine he taught; and I have all my life shuddered, and still shudder, at the consequences that may be drawn from such premises. Shall we say that the rights of masters and servants clash and can be decided only by force? I adore the idea of gradual abolitions! but who shall decide how fast or how slowly these abolitions shall be made? From individual independence he proceeded to association. If it was inconsistent with the dignity of human nature to say that men were gregarious animals, like wild geese, it surely could offend no delicacy to say they were social animals by nature, that there were natural sympathies, and, above all, the sweet attraction of the sexes, which must soon draw them together in little groups, and by degrees in larger congregations, for mutual assistance and defense. And this must have happened before any formal covenant, by express words or signs, was concluded. When general councils and deliberations commenced, the objects could be no other than the mutual defense and security of every individual for his life, his liberty, and his property. To suppose them to have surrendered these in any other way than by equal rules and general consent was to suppose them idiots or madmen whose acts were never binding. To suppose them surprised by fraud or compelled by force into any other compact, such fraud and such force could confer no obligation. Every man had a right to trample it underfoot whenever he pleased. In short, he asserted these rights to be derived only from nature and the Author of nature; that they were inherent, inalienable, and indefeasible by any laws, pacts, contracts, covenants, or stipulations which man could devise. These principles and these rights were wrought into the English constitution as fundamental laws. And under this head he went back to the old Saxon laws and to Magna Carta and the fifty confirmations of it in Parliament and the executions ordained against the violators of it and the national vengeance which had been taken on them from time to time, down to the Jameses and Charleses, and to the position of rights and the Bill of Rights and the revolution.

He asserted that the security of these rights to life, liberty, and property had been the object of all those struggles against arbitrary power, temporal and spiritual, civil and political, military and ecclesiastical, in every age. He asserted that our ancestors, as British subjects, and we their descendants, as British subjects, were entitled to all those rights by the British constitution as well as by the law of nature and our provincial character as much as any inhabitant of London or Bristol or any part of England, and were not to be cheated out of them by any phantom of "virtual representation" or any other fiction of law or politics or any monkish trick of deceit and hypocrisy.

He then examined the Acts of Trade, one by one, and demonstrated that, if they were considered as revenue laws, they destroyed all our security of property, liberty, and life, every right of nature and the English constitution and the charter of the province. Here he considered the distinction between "external and internal taxes," at that time a popular and commonplace distinction. But he asserted that there was no such distinction in theory or upon any principle but "necessity." The necessity that the commerce of the Empire should be under one direction was obvious. The Americans had been so sensible of this necessity that they had connived at the distinction between external and internal taxes, and had submitted to the Acts of Trade as regulations of commerce but never as taxations or revenue laws. Nor had the British government till now ever dared to attempt to enforce them as taxations or revenue laws.

The Navigation Act he allowed to be binding upon us because we had consented to it by our own legislature. Here he gave a history of the Navigation Act of the first of Charles II, a plagiarism from Oliver Cromwell. In 1675, after repeated letters and orders from the King, Governor Leverett very candidly informs His Majesty that the law had not been executed because it was thought unconstitutional, Parliament not having authority over us.

Rights of the British Colonies Asserted and Proved (1764)

Here indeed opens to view a large field; but I must study brevity—Few people have extended their enquiries after the foundation of any of their rights, beyond a charter from the crown. There are others who think when they have got back to old *Magna Charta,* that they are at the beginning of all things. They imagine themselves on the borders of Chaos (and so indeed in some respects they are) and see creation rising out of the unformed mass, or from nothing. Hence, say they, spring all the rights of men and of citizens.—But liberty was better understood, and more fully enjoyed by our ancestors, before the coming in of the first Norman Tyrants than ever after, 'till it was found necessary, for the salvation of the kingdom, to combat the arbitrary and wicked proceedings of the Stuarts. [. . .]

The deliverance under God wrought by the prince of Orange, afterwards deservedly made King Wm. 3d. was as joyful an event to the colonies as to Great-Britain: In some of them, steps were taken in his favour as soon as in England.

They all immediately acknowledged King William and Queen Mary as their lawful Sovereign. And such has been the zeal and loyalty of the colonies ever since for that establishment, and for the protestant succession in his present Majesty's illustrious family, that I believe there is not one man in an hundred (except in Canada) who does not think himself under the best national civil constitution in the world.

Their loyalty has been abundantly proved, especially in the late war. Their affection and reverence for their mother country is unquestionable. They yield the most chearful and ready obedience to her laws, particularly to the power of that august body the parliament of Great-Britain, the supreme legislative of the kingdom and in dominions. These I declare are my own sentiments of duty and loyalty. I also hold it clear that the act of Queen Anne, which makes it high treason to deny "that the King, with and by the authority of parliament, is able to make laws and statutes of sufficient force and validity to *limit and bind* the crown, and the descent, limitation, inheritance and *government* thereof" is founded on the principles of liberty and the British constitution: And he that would palm the doctrine of unlimited passive obedience and non-resistance upon mankind, and thereby or by any other means serve the cause of the Pretender, is not only a fool and a knave, but a rebel against common sense, as well as the laws of God, of Nature, and his Country.

I also lay it down as one of the first principles from whence I intend to deduce the civil rights of the British colonies, that all of them are subject to, and dependent on Great-Britain; and that therefore as over subordinate governments, the parliament of Great-Britain has an undoubted power and lawful authority to make acts for the general good, that by naming them, shall and ought to be equally binding, as upon the subjects of Great-Britain within the realm. This principle, I presume will be readily granted on the other side of the Atlantic. It has been practiced upon for twenty years to my knowledge, in the province of the *Massachusetts-Bay;* and I have ever received it, that it has been so from the beginning, in this and the sister provinces, thro' the continent.[1]

I am aware, some will think it is time for me to retreat, after having expressed the power of the British parliament in quite so strong terms. But 'tis from and under this very power and its acts, and from the common law, that the political and civil rights of the Colonists are derived: And upon those grand pillars of liberty shall my defence be rested. At present therefore, the reader may suppose, that there is not one provincial charter on the continent; he may, if he pleases, imagine all taken away, without fault, without forfeiture, without tryal or notice. All this really happened to some of them in the last century. I would have the reader carry his imagination still further, and suppose a time may come, when instead

---

1. This however was formally declared as to Ireland, but so lately as the reign of G. 1. Upon the old principles of conquest the Irish could not have so much to say for an exemption, as the unconquered Colonists.

of a process at common law, the parliament shall give a decisive blow to every charter in America, and declare them all void. Nay it shall also be granted, that 'tis barely possible, the time may come, when the real interest of the whole may require an act of parliament to annihilate all those charters. What could follow from all this, that would shake one of the essential, natural, civil or religious rights of the Colonists? Nothing. They would be men, citizens and british subjects after all. No act of parliament can deprive them of the liberties of such, unless any will contend that an act of parliament can make slaves not only of one, but of two millions of the commonwealth. And if so, why not of the whole? I freely own, that I can find nothing in the laws of my country, that would justify the parliament in making one slave, nor did they ever professedly undertake to make one.

Two or three innocent colony charters have been threatened with destruction an hundred and forty years past. I wish the present enemies of those harmless charters would reflect a moment, and be convinced that an act of parliament that should demolish those bugbears to the foes of liberty, would not reduce the Colonists to a state of absolute slavery. The worst enemies of the charter governments are by no means to be found in England. 'Tis a piece of justice due to Great-Britain to own, they are and have ever been natives of or residents in the colonies. A set of men in America, without honour or love to their country, have been long grasping at powers, which they think unattainable while these charters stand in the way. But they will meet with insurmountable obstacles to their project for enslaving the British colonies, should those, arising from provincial charters be removed. It would indeed seem very hard and severe, for those of the colonists, who have charters, with peculiar priviledges, to loose them. They were given to their ancestors, in consideration of their sufferings and merit, in discovering and settling America. Our fore-fathers were soon worn away in the toils of hard labour on their little plantations, and in war with the Savages. They thought they were earning a sure inheritance for their posterity. Could they imagine it would ever be tho't just to deprive them or theirs of their charter priviledges! Should this ever be the case, there are, thank God, natural, inherent and inseperable rights as men, and as citizens, that would remain after the so much wished for catastrophe, and which, whatever became of charters, can never be abolished *de jure*, if *de facto*, till the general conflagration.[2] Our rights as men and free born British subjects, give all the Colonists enough to make them very happy in comparison with the subjects of any other prince in the world.

Every British subject born on the continent of America, or in any other of the British dominions, is by the law of God and nature, by the common law, and by act of parliament, (exclusive of all charters from the Crown) entitled to all the natural, essential; inherent and inseparable rights of our fellow subjects in Great-Britain. Among those rights are the following, which it is humbly conceived no man or body of men, not excepting the parliament, justly, equitably and consistently with their own rights and the constitution, can take away.

1st. *That the supreme and subordinate powers of legislation should be free and sacred in the hands where the community have once rightfully placed them.*

2dly. *The supreme national legislative cannot be altered justly 'till the commonwealth is dissolved, nor a subordinate legislative taken away without forfeiture or other good cause.* Nor then can the subjects in the subordinate government be reduced to a state of slavery, and subject to the despotic rule of others. A state has no right to make slaves of the conquered. Even when the subordinate right of legislature is forfeited, and so declared, this cannot affect the natural persons either of those who were invested with it, or the inhabitants,[3] so far as to deprive them of the rights of subjects and of men—The colonists will have an equitable right notwithstanding any such forfeiture of charter, to be represented in Parliament, or to have some new subordinate legislature among themselves. It would be best if they had both. Deprived however

---

2. The fine defence of the provincial charters by *Jeremy Dummer*, Esq.; the late very able and learned agent for the province of the *Massachusetts Bay*, makes it needless to go into a particular consideration of charter priviledges. That piece is unanswerable, but by power and might, and other arguments of that kind.

3. See Magna Charta, the Bill of Rights. 3 Mod. 152 2. Salkeld 411. Vaughan 300.

of their common rights as subjects, they cannot lawfully be, while they remain such. A representation in Parliament from the several Colonies, since they are become so large and numerous, as to be called on not to maintain provincial government, civil and military among themselves, for this they have chearfully done, but to contribute towards the support of a national standing army, by reason of the heavy national debt, when they themselves owe a large one, contracted in the common cause, can't be tho't an unreasonable thing, nor if asked, could it be called an immodest request. *Qui sentit commodum sentire debet et onus*, has been tho't a maxim of equity. But that a man should bear a burthen for other people, as well as himself, without a return, never long found a place in any law-book or decrees, but those of the most despotic princes. Besides the equity of an American representation in parliament, a thousand advantages would result from it. It would be the most effectual means of giving those of both countries a thorough knowledge of each others interests; as well as that of the whole, which are inseparable. [. . .]

No representation of the Colonies in parliament alone, would however be equivalent to a subordinate legislative among themselves; nor so well answer the ends of increasing their prosperity and the commerce of Great-Britain. It would be impossible for the parliament to judge so well, of their abilities to bear taxes, impositions on trade, and other duties and burthens, or of the local laws that might be really needful, as a legislative here.

3dly. *No legislative, supreme or subordinate, has a right to make itself arbitrary.*

It would be a most manifest contradiction, for a free legislative, like that of Great-Britain, to make itself arbitrary.

4thly. *The supreme legislative cannot justly assume a power of ruling by extempore arbitrary decrees, but is bound to dispense justice by known settled rules*, and by duly *authorized independant judges.*

5thly. *The supreme power cannot take from any man any part of his property*, without his consent in *person, or by representation.*

6thly. *The legislature cannot transfer the power of making laws to any other hands.*

These are their bounds, which by God and nature are fixed, hitherto have they a right to come, and no further.

1. *To govern by stated laws.*

2. *Those laws should have no other end ultimately, but the good of the people.*

3. *Taxes are not to be laid on the people, but by their consent in person, or by deputation.*

4. *Their whole power is not transferable.*[4]

These are the first principles of law and justice, and the great barriers of a free state, and of the British constitution in particular. I ask, I want no more—Now let it be shown how 'tis reconcileable with these principles, or to many other fundamental maxims of the British constitution, as well as the natural and civil rights, which by the laws of their country, all British subjects are intitled to, as their best inheritance and birth-right, that all the northern colonies, who are without one representative in the house of Commons, should be taxed by the British parliament.

That the colonists, black and white, born here, are free born British subjects, and entitled to all the essential civil rights of such, is a truth not only manifest from the provincial charters, from the principles of the common law, and acts of parliament; but from the British constitution, which was reestablished at the revolution, with a professed design to secure the liberties of all the subjects to all generations.[5]

In the 12 and 13 of Wm. cited above, the liberties of the subject are spoken of as their best birthrights—No one ever dreamt, surely, that these liberties were confined to the realm. At that rate, no British subjects in the dominions could, without a manifest contradiction, be declared entitled to all the privileges of subjects born within the realm, to all intents and purposes, which are rightly given foreigners, by parliament, after residing seven years. These expressions of parliament, as well as of the charters, must be vain and empty sounds, unless we are allowed the essential rights of our fellow-subjects in Great-Britain.

Now can there be any liberty, where property is taken away without consent? Can it with any colour of truth, justice or equity, be affirmed, that the

4. See Locke on Government. B. II. C. xi.

5. See the convention, and acts confirming it.

northern colonies are represented in parliament? Has this whole continent of near three thousand miles in length, and in which and his other American dominions, his Majesty has, or very soon will have, some millions of as good, loyal and useful subjects, white and black, as any in the three kingdoms, the election of one member of the house of commons?

Is there the least difference, as to the consent of the Colonists, whether taxes and impositions are laid on their trade, and other property, by the crown alone, or by the parliament. As it is agreed on all hands, the Crown alone cannot impose them, we should be justifiable in refusing to pay them, but must and ought to yield obedience to an act of parliament, tho' erroneous, 'till repealed.

I can see no reason to doubt, but that the imposition of taxes, whether on trade, or on land, or houses, or ships, on real or personal, fixed or floating property, in the colonies, is absolutely irreconcileable with the rights of the Colonists, as British subjects, and as men. I say men, for in a state of nature, no man can take my property from me, without my consent: If he does, he deprives me of my liberty, and makes me a slave. If such a proceeding is a breach of the law of nature, no law of society can make it just— The very act of taxing, exercised over those who are not represented, appears to me to be depriving them of one of their most essential rights, as freemen; and if continued, seems to be in effect an entire disfranchisement of every civil right. For what one civil right is worth a rush, after a man's property is subject to be taken from him at pleasure, without his consent. If a man is not his *own assessor* in person, or by deputy, his liberty is gone, or lays intirely at the mercy of others.

I think I have heard it said, that when the Dutch are asked why they enslave their colonies, their answer is, that the liberty of Dutchmen is confined to Holland; and that it was never intended for Provincials in America, or anywhere else. A sentiment this, very worthy of modern Dutchmen; but if their brave and worthy ancestors had entertained such narrow ideas of liberty, seven poor and distressed provinces would never have asserted their rights against the whole Spanish monarchy, of which the present is but a shadow. It is to be hoped, none of our fellow subjects of Britain, great or small, have borrowed this Dutch maxim of plantation politics; if they have, they had better return it from whence it came; indeed they had. Modern Dutch or French maxims of state, never will suit with a British constitution. It is a maxim, that the King can do no wrong; and every good subject is bound to believe his King is not inclined to do any. We are blessed with a prince who has given abundant demonstrations, that in all his actions, he studies the good of his people, and the true glory of his crown, which are inseparable. It would therefore, be the highest degree of impudence and disloyalty to imagine that the King, at the head of his parliament, could have any, but the most pure and perfect intentions of justice, goodness and truth, that human nature is capable of. All this I say and believe of the King and parliament, in all their acts; even in that which so nearly affects the interest of the colonists; and that a most perfect and ready obedience is to be yielded to it, while it remains in force. I will go further, and readily admit, that the intention of the ministry was not only to promote the public good, by this act; but that Mr. Chancellor of the Exchequer had therein a particular view to the "ease, the quiet, and the good will of the Colonies," he having made this declaration more than once. Yet I hold that 'tis possible he may have erred in his kind intentions towards the Colonies, and taken away our fish, and given us a stone. With regard to the parliament, as infallability belongs not to mortals, 'tis possible *they* may have been misinformed and deceived. The power of parliament is uncontroulable, but by themselves, and we must obey. They only can repeal their own acts. There would be an end of all government, if one or a number of subjects or subordinate provinces should take upon them so far to judge of the justice of an act of parliament, as to refuse obedience to it. If there was nothing else to restrain such a step, prudence ought to do it, for forceably resisting the parliament and the King's laws, is high treason. Therefore let the parliament lay what burthens they please on us, we must, it is our duty to submit and patiently bear them, till they will be pleased to relieve us. And tis to be presumed, the wisdom and justice of that august assembly, always will afford us relief by repealing such acts, as through mistake, or other human infirmities, have been suffered to pass, if they can be convinced that their proceedings are not constitutional, or not for the common good. . . .

To say the parliament is absolute and arbitrary, is a contradiction. The parliament cannot make 2 and 2, 5: Omnipotency cannot do it. The supreme power in a state, is *jus dicere* only:—*jus dare*, strictly speaking, belongs alone to God. Parliaments are in all cases to *declare* what is for the good of the whole; but it is not the *declaration* of parliament that makes it so: There must be in every instance, a higher authority, viz. GOD. Should an act of parliament be against any of *his* natural laws, which are *immutably* true, *their* declaration would be contrary to eternal truth, equity and justice, and consequently void: and so it would be adjudged by the parliament itself, when convinced of their mistake. Upon this great principle, parliaments repeal such acts, as soon as they find they have been mistaken, in having declared them to be for the public good, when in fact they were not so. When such mistake is evident and palpable, as in the instances in the appendix, the judges of the executive courts have declared the act "of a whole parliament void." See here the grandeur of the British constitution! See the wisdom of our ancestors! The supreme *legislative*, and the supreme *executive*, are a perpetual check and balance to each other. If the supreme executive errs, it is informed by the supreme legislative in parliament: If the supreme legislative errs, it is informed by the supreme executive in the King's courts of law.—Here, the King appears, as represented by his judges, in the highest lustre and majesty, as supreme executor of the commonwealth; and he never shines brighter, but on his Throne, at the head of the supreme legislative. This is government! This, is a constitution! to preserve which, either from foreign or domestic foes, has cost oceans of blood and treasure in every age; and the blood and the treasure have upon the whole been well spent. [. . .]

The Colonies have been so remarkable for loyalty, that there never has been any instance of rebellion or treason in them. This loyalty is in very handsome terms acknowledged by the author of the administration of the colonies. "It has been often suggested that care should be taken in the administration of the plantations, lest, in some future time, these colonies should become independent of the mother country. But perhaps it may be proper on this occasion, nay, it is justice to say it, that if, by becoming independent, is meant a revolt, nothing is further from their nature, their interest, their thoughts. If a defection from the *alliance* of the mother country be suggested, it ought to be, and can be truly said, that their spirit abhors the sense of such; their attachment to the protestant succession in the house of Hanover, will ever stand unshaken; and nothing can eradicate from their hearts their natural and almost mechanical, affection to Great Britain, which they conceive under no other sense, nor call by any other name than that of *home*. Any such suggestion, therefore, is a false and unjust aspersion on their principles and affections; and can arise from nothing but an intire ignorance of their circumstances."[6] After all this loyalty, it is a little hard to be charged with claiming, and represented as aspiring after, independency. The inconsistency of this I leave. We have said that the loyalty of the colonies has never been suspected; this must be restricted to a just suspicion. For it seems there have long been groundless suspicions of us in the minds of individuals. And there have always been those who have endeavoured to magnify these chimerical fears. [. . .]

We all think ourselves happy under Great-Britain. We love, esteem and reverence our mother country, and adore our King. And could the choice of independency be offered the colonies, or subjection to Great-Britain upon any terms above absolute slavery, I am convinced they would accept the latter. The ministry, in all future generations may rely on it, that British America will never prove undutiful, till driven to it, as the last fatal resort against ministerial oppression, which will make the wisest mad, and the weakest strong.

These colonies are and always have been, "entirely subject to the crown," in the legal sense of the terms. But if any politician of "tampering activity, of wrongheaded inexperience, misled to be meddling,"[7] means, by "curbing the colonies in time," and by "being made entirely subject to the crown;" that this subjection should be absolute, and confined to the crown, he had better have suppressed his wishes. This never will nor can be done, without making the colonists vassals of the crown. Subjects they are; their lands they hold of the crown, by common soccage, the freest feudal tennure, by which any

---

6. [From Thomas Pownall's 1764 treatise, *The Administration of the Colonies.*]

7. [From Pownall's *Administration.*]

hold their lands in England, or any where else. Would these gentlemen carry us back to the state of the Goths and Vandals, and revive all the military tenures and bondage which our fore-fathers could not bear? It may be worth noting here, that few if any instances can be given, where colonies have been disposed to forsake or disobey a tender mother: But history is full of examples, that armies stationed as guards over provinces, have seized the prey for their general, and given him a crown at the expence of his master. Are all ambitious generals dead? Will no more rise up hereafter? The danger of a standing army in remote provinces is much greater to the metropolis, than at home. Rome found the truth of this assertion, in her Sylla's, her Pompey's and Caesars; but she found it too late: Eighteen hundred years have roll'd away since her ruin. A continuation of the same liberties that have been enjoyed by the colonists since the revolution, and the same moderation of government exercised towards them, will bind them in perpetual lawful and willing subjection, obedience and love to Great-Britain: She and her colonies will both prosper and flourish: The monarchy will remain in sound health and full vigor at that blessed period, when the proud arbitrary tyrants of the continent shall either unite in the deliverance of the human race, or resign their crowns. Rescued, human nature must and will be, from the general slavery that has so long triumphed over the species. Great-Britain has done much towards it: What a Glory will it be for her to complete the work throughout the world! . . .

The sum of my argument is, That civil government is of God: That the administrators of it were originally the whole people: That they might have devolved it on whom they pleased: That this devolution is fiduciary, for the good of the whole; That by the British constitution, this devolution is on the King, lords and commons, the supreme, sacred and uncontroulable legislative power, not only in the realm, but thro' the dominions: That by the abdication, the original compact was broken to pieces: That by the revolution, it was renewed, and more firmly established, and the rights and liberties of the subject in all parts of the dominions, more fully explained and confirmed: That in consequence of this establishment, and the acts of succession and union, his Majesty George III. is rightful king and sovereign, and with his parliament, the supreme legislative of Great Britain; France and Ireland, and the dominions thereto belonging: That this constitution is the most free one, and by far the best, now existing on earth: That by this constitution, every man in the dominion is a free man: That no parts of his Majesty's dominions can be taxed without their consent: That every part has a right to be represented in the supreme or some subordinate legislature: That the refusal of this, would seem to be a contradiction in practice to the theory of the constitution: That the colonies are subordinate dominions, and are now in such a state, as to make it best for the good of the whole, that they should not only be continued in the enjoyment of subordinate legislation, but be also represented in some proportion to their number and estates, in the grand legislature of the nation: That this would firmly unite all parts of the British empire, in the greatest peace and prosperity; and render it invulnerable and perpetual.

Stephen Hopkins

The Rights of the Colonies Examined (1764)

Providence, Rhode Island

Mid the low murmurs of submissive fear
And mingled rage, my Hampden *rasi'd his voice,*
And to the laws appeal'd. . . .

THOMPSON'S *Liberty*

Liberty is the greatest blessing that men enjoy, and slavery the heaviest curse that human nature is capable of. This being so makes it a matter of the utmost importance to men which of the two shall be their portion. Absolute liberty is, perhaps, incompatible with any kind of government. The safety resulting from society, and the advantage of just and equal laws, hath caused men to forego some part of their natural liberty, and submit to government. This appears to be the most rational account of its beginning, although, it must be confessed, mankind have by no means been agreed about it. Some have found its origin in the divine appointment; others have thought it took its rise from power; enthusiasts have dreamed that dominion was founded in grace. Leaving these points to be settled by the descendants of Filmer, Cromwell, and Venner, we will consider the British constitution as it at present stands, on Revolution principles, and from thence endeavor to find the measure of the magistrate's power and the people's obedience.

This glorious constitution, the best that ever existed among men, will be confessed by all to be founded by compact and established by consent of the people. By this most beneficent compact British subjects are to be governed only agreeable to laws to which themselves have some way consented, and are not to be compelled to part with their property but as it is called for by the authority of such laws. The former is truly liberty; the latter is really to be possessed of property and to have something that may be called one's own.

On the contrary, those who are governed at the will of another, or of others, and whose property may be taken from them by taxes or otherwise without their own consent and against their will, are in the miserable condition of slaves. "For liberty solely consists in an independency upon the will of another; and by the name of slave we understand a man who can neither dispose of his person or goods, but enjoys all at the will of his master," says Sidney on government. These things premised, whether the British American colonies on the continent are justly entitled to like privileges and freedom as their fellow subjects in Great Britain are, shall be the chief point examined. In discussing this question we shall make the colonies in New England, with whose rights we are best acquainted, the rule of our reasoning, not in the least doubting but all the others are justly entitled to like rights with them.

New England was first planted by adventurers who left England, their native country, by permission of King CHARLES I, and at their own expense transported themselves to America, with great risk and difficulty settled among savages, and in a very surprising manner formed new colonies in the wilderness. Before their departure the terms of their freedom and the relation they should stand in to the mother country in their emigrant state were fully settled: they were to remain subject to the King and dependent on the kingdom of Great Britain. In return they were to receive protection and enjoy all the rights and privileges of freeborn Englishmen.

This is abundantly proved by the charter given to the Massachusetts colony while they were still in England, and which they received and brought over with them as the authentic evidence of the conditions they removed upon. The colonies of Connecticut and Rhode Island also afterwards obtained charters from the crown, granting them the like ample privileges. By all these charters, it is in the most express and solemn manner granted that these adventurers, and their children after them forever, should have and enjoy all the freedom and liberty that the subjects in England enjoy; that they might make laws for their own government suitable to their circumstances, not repugnant to but as near as might be agreeable to the laws of England; that they might purchase lands, acquire goods, and use trade for their advantage, and have an absolute property in whatever they justly acquired. These, with many other gracious privileges, were granted them by several kings; and they were to pay as an acknowledgment to the crown only one-fifth part of the ore of gold and silver that should at any time be found in the said colonies, in lieu of, and full satisfaction for, all dues and demands of the crown and kingdom of England upon them.

There is not anything new or extraordinary in these rights granted to the British colonies. The colonies from all countries, at all times, have enjoyed equal freedom with the mother state. Indeed, there would be found very few people in the world willing to leave their native country and go through the fatigue and hardship of planting in a new uncultivated one for the sake of losing their freedom. They who settle new countries must be poor and, in course, ought to be free. Advantages, pecuniary or agreeable, are not on the side of emigrants, and surely they must have something in their stead. [. . .] [The colonies] have always enjoyed as much freedom as the mother state from which they went out. And will anyone suppose the British colonies in America are an exception to this general rule? Colonies that came out from a kingdom renowned for liberty, from a constitution founded on compact, from a people of all the sons of men the most tenacious of freedom; who left the delights of their native country, parted from their homes and all their conveniences, searched out and subdued a foreign country with the most amazing travail and fortitude, to the infinite advantage and emolument of the mother state; that removed on a firm reliance of a solemn compact and royal promise and grant that they and their successors forever should be free, should be partakers and sharers in all the privileges and advantages of the then English, now British constitution.

If it were possible a doubt could yet remain, in the most unbelieving mind, that these British colonies are not every way justly and fully entitled to equal liberty and freedom with their fellow subjects in Europe, we might show that the Parliament of Great Britain have always understood their rights in the same light.

By an act passed in the thirteenth year of the reign of his late Majesty, King George II, entitled An Act For Naturalizing Foreign Protestants, etc., and by another act, passed in the twentieth year of the same reign, for nearly the same purposes, by both which it is enacted and ordained "that all foreign Protestants who had inhabited and resided for the space of seven years or more in any of His Majesty's colonies in America" might, on the conditions therein mentioned, be naturalized, and thereupon should "be deemed, adjudged, and taken to be His Majesty's natural-born subjects of the kingdom of Great Britain to all intents, constructions, and purposes, as if they, and every one of them, had been or were born within the same." No reasonable man will here suppose the Parliament intended by these acts to put foreigners who had been in the colonies only seven years in a better condition than those who had been born in them or had removed from Britain thither, but only to put these foreigners on an equality with them; and to do this, they are obliged to give them all the rights of natural-born subjects of Great Britain.

From what hath been shown, it will appear beyond a doubt that the British subjects in America have equal rights with those in Britain; that they do not hold those rights as a privilege granted them, nor enjoy them as a grace and favor bestowed, but possess them as an inherent, indefeasible right, as they and their ancestors were freeborn subjects, justly and naturally entitled to all the rights and advantages of the British constitution.

And the British legislative and executive powers have considered the colonies as possessed of these rights, and have always heretofore, in the most tender and parental manner, treated them as their dependent, though free, condition required. The protection promised on the part of the crown, with cheerfulness and great gratitude we acknowledge, hath at all times been given to the colonies. The dependence of the colonies to Great Britain hath been fully testified by a constant and ready obedience to all the commands of his present Majesty and his royal predecessors, both men and money having been raised in them at all times when called for with as much alacrity and in as large proportions as hath been done in Great Britain, the ability of each considered. It must also be confessed with thankfulness that the first adventurers and their successors, for one hundred and thirty years, have fully enjoyed all the freedoms and immunities promised on their first removal from England. But here the scene seems to be unhappily changing: the British ministry, whether induced by a jealousy of the colonies by false informations, or by some alteration in the system of political government, we have no information; whatever hath been the motive, this we are sure of: the Parliament in their last session passed an act limiting, restricting, and burdening the trade of these colonies much more than had ever been done before, as also for greatly enlarging the power and jurisdiction of the courts of admiralty in the colonies; and also came to a resolution that it might be necessary to establish stamp duties and other internal taxes to be collected within them. This act and this resolution have caused great uneasiness and consternation among the British subjects on the continent of America: how much reason there is for it we will endeavor, in the most modest and plain manner we can, to lay before our readers.

In the first place, let it be considered that although each of the colonies hath a legislature within itself to take care of its interests and provide for its peace and internal government, yet there are many things of a more general nature, quite out of the reach of these particular legislatures, which it is necessary should be regulated, ordered, and governed. One of this kind is the commerce of the whole British empire, taken collectively, and that of each kingdom and colony in it as it makes a part of that whole. Indeed, everything that concerns the proper interest and fit government of the whole commonwealth, of keeping the peace, and subordination of all the parts towards the whole and one among another, must be considered in this light. Amongst these general concerns, perhaps, money and paper credit, those grand instruments of all commerce, will be found also to have a place. These, with all other matters of a general nature, it is absolutely necessary should have a general power to direct them, some supreme and overruling authority with power to make laws and form regulations for the good of all, and to compel their execution and observation. It being necessary some such general power should exist somewhere, every man of the least knowledge of the British constitution will be naturally led to look for and find it in the Parliament of Great Britain. That grand and august legislative body must from the nature of their authority and the necessity of the thing be justly vested with this power. Hence it becomes the indispensable duty of every good and loyal subject cheerfully to obey and patiently submit to all the acts, laws, orders, and regulations that may be made and passed by Parliament for directing and governing all these general matters.

Here it may be urged by many, and indeed with great appearance of reason, that the equity, justice, and beneficence of the British constitution will require that the separate kingdoms and distant colonies who are to obey and be governed by these general laws and regulations ought to be represented, some way or other, in Parliament, at least whilst these general matters are under consideration. Whether the colonies will ever be admitted to have representatives in Parliament, whether it be consistent with their distant and dependent state, and whether if it were admitted it would be to their advantage, are questions we will pass by, and observe that these colonies ought in justice and for the very evident good of the whole commonwealth to have notice of every new measure about to be pursued and new act that is about to be passed, by which their rights, liberties, or interests will be affected. They ought to have such notice, that they may appear and be heard by their agents, by counsel, or written representation, or by some other equitable and effectual way.

The colonies are at so great a distance from England that the members of Parliament can generally have but little knowledge of their business, connections, and interest but what is gained from people who have been there; the most of these have so slight a knowledge themselves that the informations they can give are very little to be depended on, though they may pretend to determine with confidence on matters far above their reach. All such kind of informations are too uncertain to be depended on in the transacting business of so much consequence and in which the interests of two millions of free people are so deeply concerned. There is no kind of inconveniency or mischief can arise from the colonies having such notice and being heard in the manner above mentioned; but, on the contrary, very great mischiefs have already happened to the colonies, and always must be expected, if they are not heard before things of such importance are determined concerning them.

Had the colonies been fully heard before the late act had been passed, no reasonable man can suppose it ever would have passed at all in the manner it now stands; for what good reason can possibly be given for making a law to cramp the trade and ruin the interests of many of the colonies, and at the same time lessen in a prodigious manner the consumption of the British manufactures in them? These are certainly the effects this act must produce; a duty of three pence per gallon on foreign molasses is well known to every man in the least acquainted with it to be much higher than that article can possibly bear, and therefore must operate as an absolute prohibition. This will put a total stop to our exportation of lumber, horses, flour, and fish to the French and Dutch sugar colonies; and if anyone supposes we may find a sufficient vent for these articles in the English islands in the West Indies, he only verifies what was just now observed, that he wants truer information. Putting an end to the importation of foreign molasses at the same time puts an end to all the costly distilleries in these colonies, and to the rum trade to the coast of Africa, and throws it into the hands of the French. With the loss of the foreign molasses trade, the cod fishery of the English in America must also be lost and thrown also into the hands of the French. That this is the real state of the whole business is not fancy; this, nor any part of it, is not exaggeration but a sober and most melancholy truth. [. . .]

Enlarging the power and jurisdiction of the courts of vice-admiralty in the colonies is another part of the same act, greatly and justly complained of. Courts of admiralty have long been established in most of the colonies, whose authority were circumscribed within moderate territorial jurisdictions; and these courts have always done the business necessary to be brought before such courts for trial in the manner it ought to be done and in a way only moderately expensive to the subjects; and if seizures were made or informations exhibited without reason or contrary to law, the informer or seizor was left to the justice of the common law, there to pay for his folly or suffer for his temerity. But now this course is quite altered, and a customhouse officer may make a seizure in Georgia of goods ever so legally imported, and carry the trial to Halifax at fifteen hundred miles distance; and thither the owner must follow him to defend his property; and when he comes there, quite beyond the circle of his friends, acquaintance, and correspondents, among total strangers, he must there give bond and must find sureties to be bound with him in a large sum before he shall be admitted to claim his own goods; when this is complied with, he hath a trial and his goods acquitted. If the judge can be prevailed on (which it is very well known may too easily be done) to certify there was only probable cause for making the seizure, the unhappy owner shall not maintain any action against the illegal seizor for damages or obtain any other satisfaction, but he may return to Georgia quite ruined and undone in conformity to an act of Parliament. Such unbounded encouragement and protection given to informers must call to everyone's remembrance Tacitus' account of the miserable condition of the Romans in the reign of Tiberius their emperor, who let loose and encouraged the informers of that age. Surely if the colonies had been fully heard before this has been done, the liberties and properties of the Americans would not have been so much disregarded.

The resolution of the House of Commons, come into during the same session of Parliament, asserting their rights to establish stamp duties and internal taxes to be collected in the colonies without their own consent, hath much more, and for much more reason, alarmed the British subjects in America than anything that had ever been done before. These resolutions, carried into execution, the colonies cannot help but consider as a manifest violation of their just and long-enjoyed rights. For it must be confessed by all men that they who are taxed at pleasure by others cannot possibly have any property, can have nothing to be called their own. They who have no property can have no freedom, but are indeed reduced to the most abject slavery, are in a condition far worse than countries conquered and made tributary, for these have only a fixed sum to pay, which they are left to raise among themselves in the way that they may think most equal and easy, and having paid the stipulated sum the debt is discharged, and what is left is their own. This is much more tolerable than to be taxed at the mere will of others, without any bounds, without any stipulation and agreement, contrary to their consent and against their will. If we are told that those who lay these taxes upon the colonies are men of the highest character for their wisdom, justice, and integrity, and therefore cannot be supposed to deal hardly, unjustly, or unequally by any; admitting and really believing that all this is true, it will make no alteration in the nature of the case. For one who is bound to obey the will of another is as really a slave though he may have a good master as if he had a bad one; and this is stronger in politic bodies than in natural ones, as the former have perpetual succession and remain the same; and although they may have a very good master at one time, they may have a very bad one at another. And indeed, if the people in, America are to be taxed by the representatives of the people in Britain, their malady is an increasing evil that must always grow greater by time. Whatever burdens are laid upon the Americans will be so much taken off the Britons; and the doing this will soon be extremely popular, and those who put up to be members of the House of Commons must obtain the votes of the people by promising to take more and more of the taxes off them by putting it on the Americans. This must most assuredly be the case, and it will not be in the power even of the Parliament to prevent it; the people's private interest will be concerned and will govern them; they will have such, and only such, representatives as will act agreeable to this their interest; and these taxes laid on Americans will be always a part of the supply bill, in which the other branches of the legislature can make no alteration. And in truth, the subjects in the colonies will be taxed at the will and pleasure of their fellow subjects in Britain. How equitable and how just this may be must be left to every impartial man to determine. [. . .]

We are not insensible that when liberty is in danger, the liberty of complaining is dangerous; yet a man on a wreck was never denied the liberty of roaring as loud as he could, says Dean Swift. And we believe no good reason can be given why the colonies should not modestly and soberly inquire what right the Parliament of Great Britain have to tax them. We know such inquiries by a late letter writer have been branded with the little epithet of *mushroom policy;* and he insinuates that for the colonies to pretend to claim any privileges will draw down the resentment of the Parliament on them. Is the defense of liberty become so contemptible, and pleading for just rights so dangerous? Can the guardians of liberty be thus ludicrous? Can the patrons of freedom be so jealous and so severe? If the British House of Commons are rightfully possessed of a power to tax the colonies in America, this power must be vested in them by the British constitution, as they are one branch of the great legislative body of the nation. As they are the representatives of all the people in Britain, they have beyond doubt all the power such a representation can possibly give; yet great as this power is, surely it cannot exceed that of their constituents. And can it possibly be shown that the people in Britain have a sovereign authority over their fellow subjects in America? Yet such is the authority that must be exercised in taking people's estates from them by taxes, or otherwise without their consent. In all aids granted to the crown by the Parliament, it is said with the greatest propriety, "We freely give unto Your Majesty"; for they give their own money and the money of those who have entrusted them with a proper power for that purpose. But can they with the same propriety give away the money of the Americans, who have never given any such power? Before a thing can be justly given away, the giver must certainly have acquired a property in it; and have the people in Britain justly acquired such a property in the goods and estates of the people in these colonies that they may give them away at pleasure?

In an imperial state, which consists of many separate governments each of which hath peculiar privileges and of which kind it is evident the empire of Great Britain is, no single part, though greater than another part, is by that superiority entitled to make laws for or to tax such lesser part; but all laws and all taxations which bind the whole must be made by the whole. This may be fully verified by the empire of Germany, which consists of many states, some powerful and others weak, yet the powerful never make laws to govern or to tax the little and weak ones, neither is it done by the emperor, but only by the diet, consisting of the representatives of the whole body. Indeed, it must be absurd to suppose that the common people of Great Britain have a sovereign and absolute authority over their fellow subjects in America, or even any sort of power whatsoever over them; but it will be still more absurd to suppose they can give a power to their representatives which they have not themselves. If the House of Commons do not receive this authority from their constituents it will be difficult to tell by what means they obtained it, except it be vested in them by mere superiority and power.

Should it be urged that the money expended by the mother country for the defense and protection of America, and especially during the late war, must justly entitle her to some retaliation from the colonies, and that the stamp duties and taxes intended to be raised in them are only designed for that equitable purpose; if we are permitted to examine how far this may rightfully vest the Parliament with the power of taxing the colonies we shall find this claim to have no sort of equitable foundation. In many of the colonies, especially those in New England, who were planted, as before observed, not at the charge of the crown or kingdom of England, but at the expense of the planters themselves, and were not only planted but also defended against the savages and other enemies in long and cruel wars which continued for an hundred years almost without intermission, solely at their own charge; and in the year 1746, when the Duke D'Anville came out from France with the most formidable French fleet that ever was in the American seas, enraged at these colonies for the loss of Louisbourg the year before and with orders to make an attack on them; even in this greatest exigence, these colonies were left to the protection of Heaven and their own efforts. These colonies having thus planted and defended themselves and removed all enemies from their borders, were in hopes to enjoy peace and recruit their state, much exhausted by these long struggles; but they were soon called upon to raise men and send out to the defense of other colonies, and to make conquests for the crown. They dutifully obeyed the requisition, and with ardor entered into those services and continued in them until all encroachments were removed, and all Canada, and even the Havana, conquered. They most cheerfully complied with every call of the crown; they rejoiced, yea even exulted, in the prosperity and exaltation of the British empire. But these colonies, whose bounds were fixed and whose borders were before cleared from enemies by their own fortitude and at their own expense, reaped no sort of advantage by these conquests: they are not enlarged, have not gained a single acre of land, have no part in the Indian or interior trade. The immense tracts of land subdued and no less immense and profitable commerce acquired all belong to Great Britain, and not the least share or portion to these colonies, though thousands of their men have lost their lives and millions of their money have been expended in the purchase of them, for great part of which we are yet in debt, and from which we shall not in many years be able to extricate ourselves. Hard will be the fate, yea cruel the destiny, of these unhappy colonies if the reward they are to receive for all this is the loss of their freedom; better for them Canada still remained French, yea far more eligible that it ever should remain so than that the price of its reduction should be their slavery.

If the colonies are not taxed by Parliament, are they therefore exempted from bearing their proper share in the necessary burdens of government? This by no means follows. Do they not support a regular internal government in each colony as expensive to the people here as the internal government of Britain is to the people there? Have not the colonies here, at all times when called upon by the crown, raised money for the public service, done it as cheerfully as the Parliament have done on like occasions? Is not this the most easy, the most natural, and most constitutional way of raising money in the colonies? What occasion then to distrust the colonies—what necessity to fall on an invidious and unconstitutional method to compel them to do what they have ever done freely? Are not the people in the colonies as loyal and dutiful subjects as any age or nation ever produced; and are they not as useful to the kingdom, in this remote quarter of the world, as their fellow subjects are who dwell in Britain? The Parliament, it is confessed, have power to regulate the trade of the whole empire; and hath it not full power, by this means, to draw all the money and all the wealth of the colonies into the mother country at pleasure? What motive, after all this, can remain to induce the Parliament to abridge the privileges and lessen the rights of the most loyal and dutiful subjects, subjects justly entitled to ample freedom, who have long enjoyed and not abused or forfeited their liberties, who have used them to their own advantage in dutiful subserviency to the orders and interests of Great Britain? Why should the gentle current of tranquillity that has so long run with peace through all the British states, and flowed with joy and happiness in all her countries, be at last obstructed, be turned out of its true course into unusual and winding channels by which many of those states must be ruined, but none of them can possibly be made more rich or more happy? [. . .]

We finally beg leave to assert that the first planters of these colonies were pious Christians, were faithful subjects who, with a fortitude and perseverance little known and less considered, settled these wild countries, by God's goodness and their own amazing labors, thereby added a most valuable dependence to the crown of Great Britain; were ever dutifully subservient to her interests; so taught their children that not one has been disaffected to this day, but all have honestly obeyed every royal command and cheerfully submitted to every constitutional law; have as little inclination as they have ability to throw off their dependency; have carefully avoided every offensive measure and every interdicted manufacture; have risked their lives as they have been ordered, and furnished their money when it has been called for; have never been troublesome or expensive to the mother country; have kept due order and supported a regular government; have maintained peace and practiced Christianity; and in all conditions, and in every relation, have demeaned themselves as loyal, as dutiful, and as faithful subjects ought; and that no kingdom or state hath, or ever had, colonies more quiet, more obedient, or more profitable than these have ever been.

May the same divine goodness that guided the first planters, protected the settlements, inspired Kings to be gracious, Parliaments to be tender, ever preserve, ever support our present gracious King; give great wisdom to his ministers and much understanding to his Parliaments; perpetuate the sovereignty of the British constitution, and the filial dependency and happiness of all the colonies.

THOMAS WHATELY

The Regulations Lately Made (1765)

The Revenue that may be raised by the Duties which have been already, or by these [stamp dates] if they should be hereafter imposed, are all equally applied by Parliament, *towards defraying the necessary Expences of defending, protecting, and securing, the British Colonies and Plantations in America:* Not that on the one hand an *American* Revenue might not have been applied to different Purposes; or on the other, that *Great Britain* is to contribute nothing to these: The very Words of the Act of Parliament and of the Resolution of the House of Commons imply, that the whole of the Expence is not to be charged upon the Colonies: They are under no Obligation to provide for this or any other particular national Expence; neither can they claim any Exemption from general Burthens; but being a part of the *British* Dominions, are to share all necessary Services with the rest. This in *America* does indeed first claim their Attention: They are immediately, they are principally concerned in it; and the Inhabitants of their Mother-Country would justly and loudly complain, if after all their Efforts for the Benefit of the Colonies, when every Point is gained, and every wish accomplished, they, and they alone should be called upon still to answer every additional Demand, that the Preservation of these Advantages, and the Protection of the Colonies from future Dangers, may occasion: *Great Britain* has a Right at all Times, she is under a Necessity, upon this Occasion, to demand their Assistance; but still she requires it in the Manner most suitable to their Circumstances; for by appropriating this Revenue towards the Defence and Security of the Provinces where it is raised, the Produce of it is kept in the Country, the People are not deprived of the Circulation of what Cash they have amongst themselves, and thereby the severest Oppression of an

American Tax, that of draining the Plantations of Money which they can so ill spare, is avoided. What Part they ought to bear of the national Expence, that is necessary for their Protection, must depend upon their Ability, which is not yet sufficiently known: to the whole they are certainly unequal, that would include all the military and all the naval Establishment, all Fortifications which it may be thought proper to erect, the Ordnance and Stores that must be furnished, and the Provisions which it is necessary to supply; but surely a Part of this great Disbursement, a large Proportion at least of some particular Branches of it, cannot be an intolerable Burthen upon such a Number of Subjects, upon a Territory so extensive, and upon the Wealth which they collectively possess. As to the Quota which each Individual must pay, it will be difficult to persuade the Inhabitants of this Country, where the neediest Cottager pays out of his Pittance, however scanty, and how hardly so ever earned, our high Duties and Customs and Excise in the Price of all his Consumption; it will be difficult I say, to persuade those who see, who suffer, or who relieve such Oppression; that the *West Indian* out of his Opulence, and the *North American* out of his Competency, can contribute no more than it is now pretended they can afford towards the Expence of Services, the Benefit of which, as a Part of this Nation they share, and as Colonists they peculiarly enjoy. They have indeed their own civil Governments besides to support; but *Great Britain* has her civil Government too; she has also a large Peace Establishment to maintain; and the national Debt, tho' so great a Part, and that the heaviest Part of it has been incurred by a War undertaken for the Protection of the Colonies, lies solely still upon her.

The Reasonableness, and even the Necessity of requiring an *American* Revenue being admitted, the Right of the Mother Country to impose such a Duty upon her Colonies, if duly considered, cannot be questioned: they claim it is true the Privilege, which is common to all *British* Subjects, of being taxed only with their own Consent, given by their Representatives; and may they ever enjoy the Privilege in all its Extent: May this sacred Pledge of Liberty be preserved inviolate, to the utmost Verge of our Dominions, and to the latest Page of our History! but let us not limit the legislative Rights of the *British* People to Subjects of Taxation only: No new Law whatever can bind us that is made without the Concurrence of our Representatives. The Acts of Trade and Navigation, and all other Acts that relate either to ourselves or to the Colonies, are founded upon no other Authority; they are not obligatory if a Stamp Act is not, and every Argument in support of an Exemption from the Superintendance of the *British* Parliament in the one Case, is equally applicable to the others. The Constitution knows no Distinction; the Colonies have never attempted to make one; but have acquiesced under several parliamentary Taxes. The 6 *Geo.* II. c. 13. which has been already referred to, lays heavy Duties on all foreign Rum, Sugar, and Melasses, imported into the *British* Plantations: the Amount of the Impositions has been complained of; the Policy of the Laws has been objected to; but the Right of making such a Law, has never been questioned. These however, it may be said, are Duties upon Imports only, and there some imaginary Line has been supposed to be drawn; but had it ever existed, it was passed long before, for by 25 *Charles* II. c. 7. enforced by 7 and 8 *Wil* and *Mary*, c. 22. and by 1 *Geo.* I. c. 12. the Exports of the *West Indian* Islands, not the Merchandize purchased by the Inhabitants, nor the Profits they might make by their Trade, but the Property they had at the Time, the Produce of their Lands, was taxed, by the Duties then imposed upon Sugar, Tobacco, Cotton, Indigo, Ginger, Logwood, Fustick, and Cocoa, exported from one *British* Plantation to another.

It is in vain to call these only Regulations of Trade; the Trade of *British* Subjects may not be regulated by such Means, without the Concurrence of their Representatives. Duties laid for these Purposes, as well as for the Purposes of Revenue, are still Levies of Money upon the People. The Constitution again knows no Distinction between Impost Duties and internal Taxation; and if some speculative Difference should be attempted to be made, it certainly is contradicted by Fact; for an internal Tax also was laid on the Colonies by the Establishment of a Post Office there; which, however it may be represented, will, upon a Perusal of 9 *Anne* c. 10. appear to be essentially a Tax, and that of the most authoritative Kind; for it is enforced by Provisions, more peculiarly prohibitory and compulsive, than others are usually attended with: The Conveyance of Letters thro' any other Channel is forbidden, by which

Restrictions, the Advantage which might be made by public Carriers and others of this Branch of their Business is taken away; and the Passage of Ferries is declared to be free for the Post, the Ferrymen being compellable immediately on Demand to give their Labour without pay, and the Proprietors being obliged to furnish the Means of Passage to the Post without Recompence. These Provisions are indeed very proper, and even necessary; but certainly Money levied by such Methods, the Effect of which is intended to be a Monopoly of the Carriage of Letters to the Officers of this Revenue, and by Means of which the People are forced to pay the Rates imposed upon all their Correspondence, is a public Tax to which they must submit, and not meerly a Price required of them for a private Accommodation. The Act treats this and the *British* Postage upon exactly the same Footing, and expressly calls them both *a Revenue.* The Preamble of it declares, that the new Rates are fixed in the Manner therein specified with a View *to enable her Majesty in some Measure to carry on and finish the War.* The Sum of 700*l. per* Week out of all *the Duties arising from time to time by virtue of this Act is* appropriated for that Purpose, and for other necessary Occasions; the Surplus after other Deductions, was made part of the civil List Revenues; it continued to be thus applied during the Reigns of *George* I: and *George* II. and on his present Majesty's Accession to the Throne, when the Civil List was put upon a different Establishment, the Post Office Revenues were carried with the others *to the aggregate Fund, to be applied to the Uses, to which the said Fund is or shall be applicable.* If all these Circumstances do not constitute a Tax, I do not know what do: the Stamp Duties are not marked with stronger Characters, to entitle them to that Denomination; and with respect to the Application of the Revenue, the Power of the Parliament of *Great Britain* over the Colonies was then held up much higher than it has been upon the present Occasion. The Revenue arising from the Postage in *America* is blended with that of *England,* is applied in Part to the carrying on of a continental War, and other public Purposes; the Remainder of it to the Support of the Civil List; and now the whole of it to the Discharge of the National Debt by Means of the aggregate Fund; all these are Services that are either national or particular to *Great Britain;* but the Stamp Duties and the others that were laid last Year, are appropriated to such Services only as more particularly relate to the Colonies; and surely if the Right of the *British* Parliament to impose the one be acknowledged; that of laying on the other cannot be disputed. The Post-Office has indeed been called a meer Convenience; which therefore the People always chearfully pay for. After what has been said, this Observation requires very little Notice; I will not call the Protection and Security of the Colonies, to which the Duties in question are applied , by so low a Name as Convenience.

The Instances that have been mentioned prove, that the Right of the Parliament of *Great Britain* to impose Taxes of every Kind on the Colonies, has been always admitted; but were there no Precedents to support the Claim, it would still be incontestable, being founded on the Principles of our Constitution; for the Fact is, that the Inhabitants of the Colonies are represented in Parliament: they do not indeed chuse the Members of that Assembly; neither are Nine Tenths of the People of *Britain* Electors; for the Right of Election is annexed to certain Species of Property, to peculiar Franchises, and to Inhabitancy in some particular Places; but these Descriptions comprehend only a very small Part of the Land, the Property, and the People of this Island: all Copyhold, all Leasehold Estates, under the Crown, under the Church, or under private Persons, tho' for Terms ever so long; all landed Property in short, that is not Freehold, and all monied Property whatsoever are excluded: the Possessors of these have no Votes in the Election of Members of Parliament; Women and Persons under Age be their Property ever so large, and all of it Freehold, have none. The Merchants of *London,* a numerous and respectable Body of Men, whose Opulence exceeds all that *America* could collect; the Proprietors of that vast Accumulation of Wealth, the public Funds; the Inhabitants of *Leeds,* of *Halifax,* of *Birmingham,* and of *Manchester,* Towns that are each of them larger than the Largest in the Plantations; many of less Note that are yet incorporated; and that great Corporation the *East India* Company, whose Rights over the Countries they possess, fall little short of Sovereignty, and whose Trade and whose Fleets are sufficient to constitute them a maritime Power, are all in the same Circumstances; none of them chuse their Representatives; and yet are they not represented in Parliament? Is their vast Property subject to Taxes without their Consent? Are they all arbitrarily bound by Laws to which they have not agreed? The Colonies are in exactly the same Situation: All *British* Subjects are really in the same; none are actually, all are virtually represented in Parliament; for every Member of Parliament sits in the House, not as Representative of his own Constituents, but as one of that august Assembly by which all the Commons of *Great Britain* are represented. Their Rights and their Interests, however his own Borough may be affected by general Dispositions, ought to be the great Objects of his Attention, and the only Rules for his Conduct; and to sacrifice these to a partial Advantage in favour of the Place where he was chosen, would be a Departure from his Duty: if it were otherwise, *Old Sarum* would enjoy Privileges essential to Liberty, which are denied to *Birmingham* and to *Manchester;* but as it is, they and the Colonies and all *British* Subjects whatever, have an equal Share in the general Representation of the Commons of *Great Britain,* and are bound by the Consent of the Majority of that House, whether their own particular Representatives consented to or opposed the Measures there taken, or whether they had or had not particular Representatives there.

The Inhabitants of the Colonies however have by some been supposed to be excepted, because they are represented in their respective Assemblies. So are the Citizens of *London* in their Common Council; and yet so far from excluding them from the national Representation, it does not impeach their Right to chuse Members of Parliament: it is true, that the Powers vested in the Common Council of *London,* are not equal to those which the Assemblies in the Plantations enjoy; but still they are legislative Powers, to be exercised within their District, and over their Citizens; yet not exclusively of the general Superintendance of the great Council of the Nation: The Subjects of a By-law and of an Act of Parliament may possibly be the same; yet it never was imagined that the Privileges of *London* were incompatible with the Authority of Parliament; and indeed what Contradiction, what Absurdity, does a double Representation imply? What difficulty is there in allowing both, tho' both should even be vested with equal legislative Powers, if the one is to be exercised for local, and the other for general Purposes? and where is the Necessity that the Subordinate Power must derogate from the superior Authority? It would be a singular Objection to a Man's Vote for a Member of Parliament, that being represented in a provincial, he cannot be represented in a national Assembly; and if this is not sufficient Ground for an Objection, neither is it for an Exemption, or for any Pretence of an Exclusion.

The Charter and the proprietary Governments in *America,* are in this Respect, on the same Footing with the Rest. The comprehending them also, both in a provincial and national Representation, is not necessarily attended with any Inconsistency, and nothing contained in their Grants can establish one; for all who took those Grants were *British* Subjects, inhabiting *British* Dominions, and who at the Time of taking, were indisputably under the Authority of Parliament; no other Power can abridge that Authority, or dispense with the Obedience that is due to it: those therefore, to whom the Charters were originally given, could have no Exemption granted to them: and what the Fathers never received, the Children cannot claim as an Inheritance; nor was it ever in Idea that they should; even the Charters themselves, so far from allowing guard against the Supposition.

And after all, does any Friend to the Colonies desire the Exemption? he cannot, if he will reflect but a Moment on the Consequences. We value the Right of being represented in the national Legislature as the dearest Privilege we enjoy; how justly would the Colonies complain, if they alone were deprived of it? They acknowledge Dependence upon their Mother Country; but that Dependence would be Slavery not Connection, if they bore no Part in the Government of the whole: they would then indeed be in a worse Situation than the Inhabitants of *Britain,* for these are all of them virtually, tho' few of them are actually represented in the *House of Commons;* if the Colonies were not, they could not expect that their Interests and their Privileges would be any otherwise considered there, than as subservient to those of *Great Britain;* for to deny the Authority of a Legislature, is to surrender all Claims to a Share in its Councils; and if this were the Tenor of their Charters, a Grant more insidious and more replete with Mischief, could not have been invented: a permanent Title to a Share in national Councils, would be exchanged for a precarious Representation in a provincial Assembly; and a Forfeiture of their Rights would be couched under the Appearance of Privileges; they would be reduced from Equality to Subordination, and be at the same Time deprived of the Benefits, and liable to the Inconveniences, both of Independency and of Connection. Happily for them, this is not their Condition. They are on the contrary a Part, and an important Part of the Commons of *Great Britain:* they are represented in Parliament, in the same Manner as those Inhabitants of *Britain* are, who have not Voices in Elections; and they enjoy, with the Rest of their Fellow-subjects the inestimable Privilege of not being bound by any Laws, or subject to any Taxes, to which the Majority of the Representatives of the Commons have not consented.

If there really were any Inconsistency between a national and a provincial Legislature, the Consequence would be the Abolition of the latter; for the Advantages that attend it are purely local: the District it is confined to might be governed without it, by means of the national Representatives; and it is unequal to great general Operations; whereas the other is absolutely necessary for the Benefit and Preservation of the whole: But so far are they from being incompatible, that they will be seldom found to interfere with one another: The Parliament will not often have occasion to exercise its Power over the Colonies, except for those Purposes, which the Assemblies cannot provide for. A general Tax is of this Kind; the Necessity for it, the Extent, the Application of it, are Matters which Councils limited in their Views and in their Operations cannot properly judge of; and when therefore the national Council determine these Particulars, it does not encroach on the other, it only exercises a Power which that other does not pretend to, never claimed, or wished, nor can ever be vested with: The latter remains in exactly the same State as it was before, providing for the same Services, by the same Means, and on the same Subjects; but conscious of its own Inability to answer greater Purposes than those for which it was instituted, it leaves the care of more general Concerns to that higher Legislature, in whose Province alone the Direction of them always was, is, and will be. The Exertion of that Authority which belongs to its universal Superintendance, neither lowers the Dignity, nor deprecates the Usefulness of more limited Powers: They retain all that they ever had, and are really incapable of more.

The Concurrence therefore of the provincial Representatives cannot be necessary in great public Measures to which none but the national Representatives are equal: The Parliament of *Great Britain* not only may but must tax the Colonies, when the public Occasions require a Revenue there: The present Circumstances of the Nation require one now; and a Stamp Act, of which we have had so long an Experience in this, and which is not unknown in that Country, seems an eligible Mode of Taxation. From all these Considerations, and from many others which will occur upon Reflexion and need not be suggested, it must appear *proper to charge certain Stamp Duties in the Plantations to be applied towards defraying the necessary Expences of defending, protecting, and securing the British Colonies and Plantations in America.* This Vote of the House of Commons closed the Measures taken last Year on the Subject of the Colonies: They appear to have been founded upon true Principles of Policy, of Commerce, and of Finance; to be wise with respect to the Mother-Country: just and even beneficial to the Plantations; and therefore it may reasonably be expected that either in their immediate Operations, or in their distant Effects, they will improve the Advantages we possess, confirm the Blessings we enjoy, and promote the public Welfare.

Jared Ingersoll

Letter to Thomas Fitch (February 11, 1765)

London

Sr

Since my last to you, I have been honoured with yours of the 7th of December, in which you inform me that the Genl Assembly have been pleased to desire my Assistance while here in any Matters that may concern the Colony. Be so good, Sr, in return as to Assure the Assembly that I have not only a Due Sense of the honour they have done me by placing this Confidence in me, but that I have ever since my arrival here, from Motives of Inclination, as well as Duty, done every thing in my Power to promote the Colony's Interests.

The principal Attention has been to the Stamp bill that has been preparing to Lay before Parliament for taxing America. The Point of the Authority of Parliament to impose such Tax I found on my Arrival here was so fully and Universally yielded, that there was not the least hopes of making any impressions that way. Indeed it has appeared since that the House would not suffer to be brought in, nor would any one Member Undertake to Offer to the House, any Petition from the Colonies that held forth ye Contrary of that Doctrine. I own I advised the Agents if possible to get that point Canvassed that so the Americans might at least have the Satisfaction of having the point Decided upon a full Debate, but I found it could not be done, and here before I proceed to acquaint you with the Steps that have been taken, in this Matter, I beg leave to give you a Summary of the Arguments which are made Use of in favour of such Authority.

The House of Commons, say they, is a branch of the supreme legislature of the Nation, & which in its Nature is supposed to represent, or rather to stand in the place of, the Commons, that is, of the great body of the people, who are below the dignity of peers; that this house of Commons Consists of a certain number of Men Chosen by certain people of certain places, which Electors, by the Way, they Insist, are not a tenth part of the people, and that the Laws, rules and Methods by which their number is ascertained have arose by degrees & from various Causes & Occasions, and that this house of Commons, therefore, is now fixt and ascertained & is a part of the Supreme unlimited power of the Nation, as in every State there must be some unlimited Power and Authority; and that when it is said they represent the Commons of England, it cannot mean that they do so because those Commons choose them, for in fact by far the greater part do not, but because by their Constitution they must themselves be Commoners, and not Peers, and so the Equals, or of the same Class of Subjects, with the Commons of the Kingdom. They further urge, that the only reason why America has not been heretofore taxed in the fullest Manner, has been merely on Account of their Infancy and Inability; that there have been, however, not wanting Instances of the Exercise of this Power, in the various regulations of the American trade, the Establishment of the post Office &c, and they deny any Distinction between what is called an internal & external Tax as to the point of the Authority imposing such taxes. And as to the Charters in the few provinces where there are any, they say, in the first place, the King cannot grant any that shall exempt them from the Authority of one of the branches of the great body of Legislation, and in the second place say the King has not done, or attempted to do it. In that of Pensilvania the Authority of Parliament to impose taxes is expressly mentioned & reserved; in ours tis said, our powers are generally such as are *According to the Course of other Corporations in England* (both which Instances by way of Sample were mentioned & referred to by Mr Grenville in the House); in short they say a Power to tax is a necessary Part of every Supreme Legislative Authority, and that if they have not that Power over America, they have none, & then America is at once a Kingdom of itself.

On the other hand those who oppose the bill say, it is true the Parliament have a supreme unlimited Authority over every Part & Branch of the Kings dominions and as well over Ireland as any other place, yet we believe a British parliament will never think it prudent to tax Ireland. Tis true they say, that the Commons of England & of the british Empire are all represented in and by the house of Commons, but this representation is confessedly on all hands by Construction & Virtually only as to those who have no hand in choosing the representatives, and that the Effects of this implied Representation here & in America must be infinitely different in the Article of Taxation. Here in England the Member of Parliament is equally known to the Neighbour who elects & to him who does not; the Friendships, the Connections, the Influences are spread through the whole. If by any Mistake an Act of Parliament is made that prove injurious and hard the Member of Parliament here sees with his own Eyes and is moreover very accessible to the people, not only so, but the taxes are laid equally by one Rule and fall as well on the Member himself as on the people. But as to America, from the great distance in point of Situation, from the almost total unacquaintedness, Especially in the more northern Colonies, with the Members of Parliament, and they with them, or with the particular Ability & Circumstances of one another, from the Nature of this very tax laid upon others not Equally & in Common with ourselves, but with express purpose to Ease ourselves, we think, say they, that it will be only to lay a foundation of great Jealousy and Continual Uneasiness, and that to no purpose, as we already by the Regulations upon their trade draw from the Americans all that they can spare, at least they say this Step should not take place untill or unless the Americans are allowed to send Members to Parliament; for *who of you,* said Coll Barre Nobly in his Speech in the house upon this Occasion, *who of you reasoning upon this Subject feels warmly from the Heart* (putting his hand to his own breast) for *the Americans as they would for themselves or as you would for the people of your own native Country?* and to this point M[r] Jackson produced Copies of two Acts of Parliament granting the priviledge of having Members to the County Palitine of Chester & the Bishoprick of Durham upon Petitions preferred for that purpose in the Reign of King Henry the Eighth and Charles the first, the preamble of which Statutes counts upon the Petitions from those places as setting forth that being in their general Civil Jurisdiction Exempted from the Common Law Courts &c, yet being Subject to the general Authority of Parliament, were taxed in Common with the rest of ye Kingdom, which taxes by reason of their having no Members in Parliament to represent their Affairs, often proved hard and injurious &c and upon that ground they had the priviledge of sending Members granted them—& if this, say they, could be a reason in the case of Chester and Durham, how much more so in the case of America.

Thus I have given you, I think, the Substance of the Arguments on both sides of that great and important Question of the right & also of the Expediency of taxing America by Authority of Parliament. I cannot, however, Content myself without giving you a Sketch of what the aforementioned M[r] Barre said in Answer to some remarks made by M[r] Ch. Townsend in a Speech of his upon this Subject. I ought here to tell you that the Debate upon the American Stamp bill came on before the house for the first time last Wednesday, when the same was open'd by M[r] Grenville the Chanceller of the Exchequer, in a pretty lengthy Speech, & in a very able and I think in a very candid manner he opened the Nature of the Tax, Urged the Necessity of it, Endeavoured to obviate all Objections to it—and took Occasion to desire the House to give y[e] bill a most Serious and Cool Consideration & not suffer themselves to be influenced by any resentments which might have been kindled from any thing they might have heard out of doors—alluding I suppose to the N. York and Boston Assemblys' Speeches & Votes—that this was a matter of revenue which was of all things the most interesting to y[e] Subject &c. The Argument was taken up by several who opposed the bill (viz) by Alderman Beckford, who, and who only, seemed to deny y[e] Authority of Parliament, by Col. Barre, M[r] Jackson, S[r] William Meredith and some others. M[r] Barre, who by the way I think, & I find I am not alone in my Opinion, is one of the finest Speakers that the House can boast of, having been some time in America as an Officer in the Army, & having while there, as I had known before, contracted many Friendships with American Gentlemen, & I believe Entertained much more favourable Opinions of them than some of his profession have done, Delivered a very handsome & moving Speech upon the bill & against the same, Concluding by saying that he was very sure that Most who Should hold up their hands to the Bill must be under a Necessity of acting very much in the dark, but added, perhaps as well in the Dark as any way.

After him Mr Charles Towsend spoke in favour of the Bill—took Notice of several things Mr Barre had said, and concluded with the following or like Words: —And now will these Americans, Children planted by our Care, nourished up by our Indulgence until they are grown to a Degree of Strength & Opulence, and protected by our Arms, will they grudge to contribute their mite to releive us from the heavy weight of the that burden which we lie under? When he had done, Mr Barre rose and having explained something which he had before said & which Mr Townsend had been remarking upon, he then took up the beforementioned Concluding words of Mr Townsend, and in a most spirited & I thought an almost inimitable manner, said—

"They planted by your Care? No! your Oppressions planted em in America. They fled from your Tyranny to a then uncultivated and unhospitable Country—where they exposed themselves to almost all the hardships to which human Nature is liable, and among others to the Cruelties of a Savage foe, the most subtle and I take upon me to say the most formidable of any People upon the face of Gods Earth. And yet, actuated by Principles of true english Lyberty, they met all these hardships with pleasure, from the hands of those who should have been their Friends.

"They nourished by *your* indulgence? they grew by your neglect of Em:—as soon as you began to care about them, that Care was Excercised in sending persons to rule over them, in one Department and another, who were perhaps the Deputies of Deputies to some Member of this house—sent to Spy out their Lyberty, to misrepresent their actions & to prey upon Em; men whose behaviour on many Occasions has caused the Blood of those Sons of Liberty to recoil within them; men promoted to the highest Seats of Justice, some, who to my knowledge were glad by going to a foreign Country to Escape being brought to the Bar of a Court of Justice in their own.

"They protected by *your* Arms? they have nobly taken up Arms in your defence, have Exerted a Valour amidst their constant & Laborious industry for the defence of a Country, whose frontier, while drench'd in blood, its interior Parts have yielded all its little Savings to your Emolument. And beleive me, remember I this Day told you so, that same Spirit of freedom which actuated that people at first, will accompany them still.—But prudence forbids me to explain myself further. God knows I do not at this Time speak from motives of party Heat, what I deliver are the genuine Sentiments of my heart; however superiour to me in general knowledge and Experience the reputable body of this house may be, yet I claim to know more of America than most of you, having seen and been conversant in that Country. The People I beleive are as truly Loyal as any Subjects the King has, but a people Jealous of their Lyberties and who will vindicate them, if ever they should be violated—but the Subject is too delicate & I will say no more."

These sentiments were thrown out so intirely without premeditation, so forceably and so firmly, and the breaking off so beautifully abrupt, that the whole house sat awhile as Amazed, intently Looking and without answering a Word.

I own I felt Emotions that I never felt before & went the next Morning & thank'd Coll Barre in behalf of my Country for his noble and spirited Speech.

However, Sr after all that was said, upon a Division of the house upon the Question, there was about 250 to about 50 in favour of the Bill. [. . .]

The Virginia Resolutions as Printed by the *Newport Mercury* (June 24, 1765)

Whereas the Hon. House of Commons, in England, have of late drawn into Question, how far the General Assembly of this Colony hath Power to enact Laws for laying of Taxes and imposing Duties, payable by the People of this his Majesty's most antient Colony: For settling and ascertaining the same to all future Times, the House of Burgesses of this present General Assembly have come to the following Resolves:—

Resolved, That the first Adventurers, Settlers of this his Majesty's Colony and Dominion of Virginia, brought with them and transmitted to their Posterity, and all other his Majesty's Subjects since inhabiting in this his Majesty's Colony, all the Privileges and Immunities that have at any Time been held, enjoyed and possessed by the People of Great-Britain.

Resolved, That by two Royal Charters, granted by King *James* the First, the Colony aforesaid are declared and entitled to all Privileges and Immunities of natural born Subjects, to all Intents and Purposes, as if they had been abiding and born within the Realm of England.

Resolved, That his Majesty's liege People of this his antient Colony have enjoy'd the Right of being thus govern'd, by their own Assembly, in the Article of Taxes and internal Police; and that the same have never been forfeited, or any other Way yielded up, but have been constantly recogniz'd by the King and People of Britain.

Resolved, therefore, That the General Assembly of this Colony, together with his Majesty or his Substitutes, have, in their Representative Capacity, the only exclusive Right and Power to lay Taxes and Imposts upon the Inhabitants of this Colony: And that every Attempt to vest such Power in any other Person or Persons whatever, than the General Assembly aforesaid, is illegal, unconstitutional and unjust, and have a manifest Tendency to destroy British as well as American Liberty.

Resolved, That his Majesty's liege People, the Inhabitants of this Colony, are not bound to yield Obedience to any Law or Ordinance whatever, designed to impose any Taxation whatsoever upon them, other than the Laws or Ordinances of the General Assembly aforesaid.

Resolved, That any Person, who shall, by speaking or writing, assert or maintain, that any Person or Persons, other than the General Assembly of this Colony, have any Right or Power to impose or lay any Taxation on the People here, shall be deemed an Enemy to this his Majesty's Colony.

RESOLUTIONS OF THE STAMP ACT CONGRESS (October 19, 1765)

The members of this Congress, sincerely devoted, with the warmest sentiments of affection and duty to His Majesty's Person and Government, inviolably attached to the present happy establishment of the Protestant succession, and with minds deeply impressed by a sense of the present and impending misfortunes of the British colonies on this continent; having considered as maturely as time will permit the circumstances of the said colonies, esteem it our indispensable duty to make the following declarations of our humble opinion, respecting the most essential rights and liberties Of the colonists, and of the grievances under which they labour, by reason of several late Acts of Parliament.

I. That His Majesty's subjects in these colonies, owe the same allegiance to the Crown of *Great-Britain,* that is owing from his subjects born within the realm, and all due subordination to that august body the Parliament of *Great Britain.*

II. That His Majesty's liege subjects in these colonies, are entitled to all the inherent rights and liberties of his natural born subjects within the kingdom *of Great-Britain.*

III. That it is inseparably essential to the freedom of a people, and the undoubted right *of Englishmen,* that no taxes be imposed on them, but with their own consent, given personally, or by their representatives.

IV. That the people of these colonies are not, and from their local circumstances cannot be, represented in the House of Commons in *Great-Britain.*

V. That the only representatives of the people of these colonies, are persons chosen therein by themselves, and that no taxes ever have been, or can be constitutionally imposed on them, but by their respective legislatures.

VI. That all supplies to the Crown, being free gifts of the people, it is unreasonable and inconsistent with the principles and spirit of the *British* Constitution, for the people of *Great-Britain* to grant to His Majesty the property of the colonists.

VII. That trial by jury is the inherent and invaluable right of every *British* subject in these colonies.

VIII. That the late Act of Parliament, entitled, *An Act for granting and applying certain Stamp Duties, and other Duties, in the British colonies and plantations in America, etc.*, by imposing taxes on the inhabitants of these colonies, and the said Act, and several other Acts, by extending the jurisdiction of the courts of Admiralty beyond its ancient limits, have a manifest tendency to subvert the rights and liberties of the colonists.

IX. That the duties imposed by several late Acts of Parliament, from the peculiar circumstances of these colonies, will be extremely burthensome and grievous; and from the scarcity of specie, the payment of them absolutely impracticable.

X. That as the profits of the trade of these colonies ultimately center in *Great-Britain,* to pay for the manufactures which they are obliged to take from thence, they eventually contribute very largely to all supplies granted there to the Crown.

XI. That the restrictions imposed by several late Acts of Parliament, on the trade of these colonies, will render them unable to purchase the manufactures of *Great-Britain.*

XII. That the increase, prosperity, and happiness of these colonies, depend on the full and free enjoyment of their rights and liberties, and an intercourse with *Great-Britain* mutually affectionate and advantageous.

XIII. That it is the right of the *British* subjects in these colonies, to petition the King, Or either House of Parliament.

Lastly, That it is the indispensable duty of these colonies, to the best of sovereigns, to the mother country, and to themselves, to endeavour by a loyal and dutiful address to his Majesty, and humble applications to both Houses of Parliament, to procure the repeal of the Act for granting and applying certain stamp duties, of all clauses of any other Acts of Parliament, whereby the jurisdiction of the Admiralty is extended as aforesaid, and of the other late Acts for the restriction *of American* commerce.

William Pym

Letter to the *London General Evening Post* and the *Newport Mercury* (1765)

The people in our American colonies lay a very great stress upon the importance of their charters, and imagine that the privileges granted to their ancestors, at the time of their original establishment, must infallibly exempt them from participating in the least inconvenience of the Mother country, though the Mother country must share in every inconvenience of theirs. This mode of reasoning is however no less new than it is extraordinary: and one would almost be tempted to imagine that the persons, who argue in this manner, were alike unacquainted with the nature of the colonies and the constitution of this kingdom.

I shall very readily grant, that the colonies at the time of their first settling might receive particular indulgences from the Crown, to encourage adventurers to go over; and I will also grant, that these charters should be as inviolably adhered to as the nature of public contingencies will admit. But at the same time let me inform my fellow subjects of America, that a resolution of the British parliament can at any time set aside all the charters that have ever been granted by our monarchs; and that consequently nothing can be more idle than this pompous exclamation about their charter exemptions, whenever such a resolution has actually passed.

The great business of the British Legislative power is, to consult upon what new laws may be necessary for the general good of the British dominions, and to remove any casual inconveniencies which may arise from the existence of their former acts. In the prosecution of this important end, they cannot expect but what the most salutary laws will prove oppressive to some part of the people. However no injury, which may be sustained by individuals, is to prevent them from promoting the welfare of the community; for if they debated till they framed an ordinance agreeable to the wishes of every body, 'twould be utterly impossible for them ever to frame any ordinance at all.

If then the Legislative power of this country have a right to alter or annul those public acts which were solemnly passed by former princes and former parliaments; it must be a necessary consequence that they have an equal right to annul the private charters of former princes also; and that these charters, which are by no means to be set in the same degree of importance with our laws, are at least every whit as subject to their jurisdiction and authority. This is a circumstance which the assembly of Virginia in particular should have attended to before their late unaccountable resolutions; and 'tis what I hope the assemblies of our other settlements will judiciously attend to, if they find the least propensity to follow the extraordinary example of their Sister-colony. [. . .]

I am very well aware that the present impatience, which the whole kingdom feels at the least increase of taxes, will naturally create a number of friends for the colonies: but at the same time let us consider that the propriety of the tax, which has excited such a ferment among our American fellow-subjects, is not now the foundation of dispute. The question now is, Whether those American subjects are, or are not, bound by the resolutions of a British parliament? If they are *not*, they are entirely a separate people from us, and the mere reception of officers appointed in this kingdom, is nothing but an idle farce of government, which it is by no means our interest to keep up, if it is to produce us no benefit but the honour of protecting them whenever they are attacked by their enemies. On the other hand, if the people of America *are* bound by the proceedings of the English legislature, what excuse can the Virginians possibly make for the late indecent vote (to give it no harsher appellation) of their assembly. The present crisis, Sir, is really an alarming one; and after all the blood and treasure which we have expended in defence of the colonies, it is now questioned, whether we have any interest in those colonies at all.

If the people of Virginia were offended either with the tax itself, or with the mode of taxation, the proper method of proceeding would have been to petition the parliament, to point out the grievances arising from it, and to solicit the necessary redress. This is the invariable manner in which all the rest of their fellow-subjects (at least the European part of their fellow subjects) have acted in cases of a like nature. But to think of bullying their King, and the august Council of the Mother country, into an acquiescence with their sentiments, by a rash and hot headed vote; not only must expose them to the ridicule, but to the resentment of every considerate man who wishes well either to their interest or to the prosperity of this kingdom.

The people of the colonies know very well that the taxes of the Mother country are every day increasing; and can they expect that no addition whatsoever will be made to theirs? They know very well that a great part of our national debt was contracted in establishing them on a firm foundation, and protecting them from the arbitrary attempts of their implacable enemies.—Can anything then be so unreasonable, as a refusal of their assistance to wipe a little of it off? For my own part I am as much astonished at their want of justice, as I am surprized at their want of gratitude; and cannot help declaring it as my opinion, that we ought to shew but a very small share of sensibility for the circumstances of those people who are so utterly regardless of ours. To be sure, Sir, in assisting the colonies we had an eye to our own interest. It would be ridiculous otherwise to squander away our blood and our treasure in their defence. But certainly the benefit was mutual; and consequently the disadvantage should be mutual too. If we reap emoluments from the existence of the colonies, the colonies owe every thing to our encouragement and protection. As therefore we share in the same prosperity, we ought to participate of the same distress; and nothing can be more inequitable, than the least disinclination to bear a regular portion of those disbursements, which were applied to support the general interest both of the mother-country and themselves.

William Pym

Daniel Dulany

Considerations on the Propriety of Imposing Taxes in the British Colonies (1765)

In the constitution of *England*, the three principal forms of government, monarchy, aristocracy, and democracy, are blended together in certain proportions; but each of these orders, in the exercise of the legislative authority, hath its peculiar department, from which the others are excluded. In this division, the *granting of supplies*, or *laying taxes*, is deemed to be the province of the house of commons, as the representative of the people. . . . All supplies are supposed to flow from their gift; and the other orders are permitted only to assent, or reject generally, not to propose any modification, amendment, or partial alteration of it.

This observation being considered, it will undeniably appear, that, in framing the late *Stamp Act*, the commons acted in the character of representative of the colonies. They assumed it as the principle of that measure, and the *propriety* of it must therefore stand, or fall, as the principle is true, or false: For the preamble sets forth, that the commons of *Great-Britain* had resolved to *give and grant* the several rates and duties imposed by the act; but what right had the commons of *Great-Britain* to be thus munificent at the expence of the commons of *America?* . . . To give property not belonging to the giver, and without the consent of the owner, is such evident and flagrant injustice, in *ordinary cases,* that few are hardy enough to avow it; and therefore, when it really happens, the fact is disguised and varnished over by the most plausible pretences the ingenuity of the giver can suggest. . . . But it is alledged that there is a *virtual,* or *implied representation* of the colonies springing out of the constitution of the *British* government: And it must be confessed on all hands, that, as the representation is not actual, it is virtual, or it doth not exist at all; for no third kind of representation can be imagined. The colonies claim the privilege, which is common to all *British subjects,* of being taxed *only* with their own consent given by their representatives, and all the advocates for the *Stamp Act* admit this claim. Whether, therefore, upon the whole matter, the imposition of the *Stamp Duties* is a *proper* exercise of constitutional authority, or not, depends upon the single question, Whether the commons of *Great Britain* are *virtually* the representatives of the commons of *America,* or not.

The advocates for the Stamp Act admit, in express terms, that "the colonies do not choose members of parliament," "but they assert that the colonies are *virtually* represented in the same manner with the non-electors resident in *Great Britain.*"

How have they proved this position? Where have they defined, or precisely explained what they mean by the expression, *virtual representation?* As it is the very hinge upon which the rectitude of the taxation turns, something more satisfactory than mere assertion, more solid than a form of expression, is necessary: for how can it be seriously expected, that men, who think themselves injuriously affected in their properties and privileges, will be convinced and reconciled by a fanciful phrase, the meaning of which can't be precisely ascertained by those who use it, or properly applied to the purpose for which it hath been advanced?

They argue, that "the right of election being annexed to certain species of property, to franchises, and inhabitancy in some particular places, a very small part of the land, the property, and the people of *England* are comprehended in those descriptions. All landed property, not freehold, and all monied property, are *excluded.* The merchants of *London,* the proprietors of the public funds, the inhabitants of *Leeds, Halifax, Birmingham,* and *Manchester,* and that great corporation of the *East-India* company, *none of them* choose their representatives, and yet are they all represented in parliament, and the colonies being *exactly* in *their* situation, are represented in the *same manner.*"

Now, this argument, which is all that their invention hath been able to supply, is totally defective; for, it consists of facts not true, and of conclusions inadmissible.

It is so far from being true, that all the persons enumerated under the character of *non-electors,* are in that predicament, that it is indubitably certain there is *no* species of property, landed, or monied, which is not possessed by *very many* of the *British electors.*

I shall undertake to disprove the supposed similarity of situation, whence the same kind of representation is deduced, of the inhabitants of the colonies, and of the *British* non-electors; and, if I succeed, the notion of a *virtual representation* of the colonies must fail, which, in truth, is a mere cob web, spread to catch the unwary, and intangle the weak. I would be understood: I am upon a question of *propriety,* not of power; and, though some may be inclined to think it is to little purpose to discuss the one, when the other is irresistible, yet are they different considerations; and, at the same time that I invalidate the claim upon which it is founded, I may very consistently recommend a submission to the law, whilst it endures. I shall say nothing of the use I intend by the discussion; for if it should not be perceived by the sequel, there is no use in it, and, if it should appear then, it need not be premised.

Lessees for years, copyholders, proprietors of the public funds, inhabitants of *Birmingham, Leeds, Halifax,* and *Manchester,* merchants of the city of *London,* or members of the corporation of the *East-India* company, are, *as such,* under no personal incapacity to be electors; for they may acquire the right of election, and there are *actually* not only a considerable number of electors in each of the classes of lessees for years, etc. but in many of them, if not all, even members of parliament. The interests therefore of the non-electors, the electors, and the representatives, are individually the same; to say nothing of the connection among neighbours, friends, and relations. The security of the non-electors against oppression, is, that their oppression will fall also upon the electors and the representatives. The one can't be injured, and the other indemnified.

Further, if the non-electors should not be taxed by the *British* parliament, they would not be taxed *at all*; and it would be iniquitous as well as a solecism, in the political system, that they should partake of all the benefits resulting from the imposition, and application of taxes, and derive an immunity from the circumstance of not being qualified to vote. Under this constitution then, a double or virtual representation may be reasonably supposed. The electors, who are inseparably connected in their interests with the non-electors, may be justly deemed to be the representatives of the non-electors, at the same time they exercise their personal privilege in the right of election; and the members chosen, therefore, the representatives of both. This is the only rational explanation of the expression, *virtual representation*. None has been advanced by the assertors of it, and their meaning can only be inferred from the instances, by which they endeavour to elucidate it, and no other meaning can be stated, to which the instances apply.

It is an essential principle of the *English* constitution, that the subject shall not be taxed without his consent, which hath not been introduced by any particular law, but necessarily results from the nature of that mixed government; for, without it, the order of democracy could not exist. [. . .]

The situation of the non-electors in *England*—their capacity to become electors—their inseparable connection with those who are electors, and their representatives—their security against oppression resulting from this connection, and the necessity of imagining a double or virtual representation, to avoid iniquity and absurdity, have been explained—the inhabitants of the colonies are, *as such*, incapable of being electors, the privilege of election being exerciseable only in person, and therefore if *every* inhabitant of *America* had the requisite freehold, not *one* could vote, but upon the supposition of his ceasing to be an inhabitant of *America*, and becoming a resident of *Great-Britain*, a supposition which would be impertinent, because it shifts the question—should the colonies not be taxed by *Parliamentary impositions*, their respective legislatures have a regular, adequate, and constitutional authority to tax them, and therefore there would not necessarily be an iniquitous and absurd exemption, from their not being represented by *the house of commons*.

There is not that intimate and inseparable relation between the *electors of* Great-Britain, and the *Inhabitants of the colonies*, which must inevitably involve both in the same taxation; on the contrary, not a single *actual* elector in *England*, might be immediately affected by a taxation in *America*, imposed by a statute which would have a general operation and effect, upon the properties of the inhabitants of the colonies. The latter might be oppressed in a thousand shapes, without any Sympathy, or exciting any alarm in the former. Moreover, even acts, oppressive and injurious to the colonies in an extreme degree, might become popular in *England*, from the promise or expectation, that the very measures which depressed the colonies, would give ease to the Inhabitants of *Great-Britain*. It is indeed true, that the interests of *England* and the colonies are allied, and an injury to the colonies produced into all [its] consequences, will eventually affect the mother country; yet these consequences being generally remote, are not at once foreseen; they do not immediately alarm the fears, and engage the passions of the *English* electors; the connection between a freeholder of *Great-Britain*, and a *British American* being deductible only thro' a train of reasoning, which few will take the trouble, or can have opportunity, if they have capacity, to investigate; wherefore the relation between the *British Americans*, and the *English electors*, is a knot too infirm to be relied on as a competent security, especially against the force of a present, counteracting expectation of relief.

If it would have been a just conclusion, that the *colonies* being exactly in the *same* situation with the *non-electors* of *England*, are *therefore* represented in the same manner; it ought to be allowed, that the reasoning is solid, which, after having evinced a total *dissimilarity* of situation, infers, that their representation is *different*.

If the commons of *Great-Britain* have no right by the constitution, to GIVE AND GRANT property *not* belonging to themselves or others, without their consent actually or virtually given; If the claim of the colonies not to be taxed *without their consent*, signified by their representatives, is well founded; if it appears that the colonies are not actually represented by the commons of *Great-Britain*, and that the notion of a double or virtual representation, doth not with any propriety apply to the people of *America;* then the principle of the *Stamp act*, must be given up as indefensible on the point of representation, and the validity of it rested upon the *power* which they who framed it, have to carry it into execution. . . .

The colonies have a complete and adequate legislative authority, and are not only represented in their assemblies, but in *no other manner.* The power of making bye-laws vested in the common council is inadequate and incomplete, being bounded by a few particular subjects; and the common council are actually represented too, by having a choice of members to serve in parliament. How then can the reason of the exemption from internal parliamentary taxations, claimed by the colonies, apply to the citizens of *London?*

The power described in the provincial charters, is to make laws, and in the exercise of that power, the colonies are bounded by no other limitations than what result from their subordination to, and dependence upon *Great Britain.* The term *bye-laws* is as novel, and improper, when applied to the *parliament* of Great Britain; and it is as absurd and insensible, to call a colony a common corporation, because not an independent kingdom, and the powers of each to make laws and bye-laws, are limited, tho' not comparable in their extent, and the variety of their objects, as it would be to call lake *Erie*, a *Duck-puddle*, because not the atlantic ocean.

Should the analogy between the *colonies* and *corporations* be even admitted for a moment, in order to see what would be the consequence of the *postulatum*, it would only amount to this, The *colonies* are vested with as complete authority to all intents and purposes to tax themselves, as any *English corporation* is to make a bye-law, in any imaginable instance for any local purpose whatever, and the *parliament* doth not make laws for *corporations* upon subjects, in every respect proper for *bye-laws.*

But I don't rest the matter upon this, or any other circumstance, however considerable, to prove the impropriety of a taxation by the *British* parliament. I rely upon the fact, that not one inhabitant in any colony is, or can be *actually* or *virtually* represented by the *British house of commons*, and therefore, that the Stamp duties are severely imposed.

But it has been alledged, that if the right to *give and grant* the property of the colonies by an internal taxation is denied by the house of commons, the subordination and dependence of the colonies, and the superintendence of the *British* parliament can't be consistently establish'd. . . . That any supposed line of distinction between the two cases, is but "a whimsical imagination, a chimerical speculation against fact and experience." . . . Now, under favour, I conceive there is more confidence, than solidity in this assertion; and it may be satisfactorily and easily proved, that the subordination and dependence of the colonies may be preserved, and the *supreme authority* of the mother country be firmly supported, and yet the principle of representation, and the right of the *British* house of commons flowing from *it*, to *give and grant* the property of the commons of *America*, be denied.

The colonies are dependent upon *Great Britain*, and the supreme authority vested in the king, lords, and commons, may justly be exercised to secure, or preserve their dependence, whenever necessary for that purpose. This authority results from, and is implied in the idea of the relation subsisting between *England* and her colonies; for, considering the nature of human affections, the inferior is not to be trusted with providing regulations to prevent his rising to an equality with his superior. But, though the right of the superior to use the proper means for preserving the subordination of his inferior is admitted, yet it does not necessarily follow, that he has a right to seize the property of his inferior when he pleases, or to command him in every thing; since, in the degrees of it, there may very well exist a *dependence* and *inferiority*, without absolute *vassalage* and *slavery.* In what the superior may *rightfully* controul, or compel, and in what the inferior ought to be at liberty to act without controul or compulsion, depends upon the nature of the dependence, and the degree of the subordination; and, these being ascertained, the measure of obedience, and submission, and the extent of the authority and superintendence will be settled. When powers, compatible with the relation between the superior and inferior, have, by express compact, been granted to, and accepted by, the latter, and have been, after that compact, repeatedly recognized by the former—When they may be exercised effectually upon every occasion without any injury to that relation, the authority of the superior can't properly interpose; for, by the powers vested in the inferior, is the superior limited.

By their constitutions of government, the colonies are empowered to impose internal taxes. This power is compatible with their dependence, and hath been expressly recognized by *British* ministers and the *British* parliament, upon many occasions; and it may be exercised effectually without striking at, or impeaching, in any respect, the superintendence of the *British* parliament. May not then the line be distinctly and justly drawn between such acts as are necessary, or proper, for preserving or securing the dependence of the colonies, and such as are not necessary or proper for that very important purpose?

When the powers were conferred upon the colonies, they were conferred too as privileges and immunities, and accepted as such; or, to speak more properly, the privileges belonging necessarily to them as *British* subjects, were solemnly declared and confirmed by their charters, and they who settled in *America* under the encouragement and faith of these charters, understood, not only that They *might*, but that it was their *right* to exercise those powers without controul, or prevention. In some of the charters the distinction is expressed, and the strongest declarations made, and the most solemn assurances given, that the settlers should not have their property taxed without their own consent by their representatives; though their legislative authority is limited at the same time, by the subordination implied in their relation, and They are therefore restrained for making acts of assembly repugnant to the laws of *England;* and, had the distinction not been expressed, the powers given would have implied it, for, if the parliament may in any case interpose, when the authority of the colonies is adequate to the occasion, and not limited by their subordination to the mother country, it may in every *case,* which would make *another* appellation more proper to describe their condition, than the name by which their inhabitants have been usually called, and have gloried in.

Because the parliament may, when the relation between *Great Britain* and her colonies calls for an exertion of her superintendence, bind the colonies by statute, therefore a parliamentary interposition in every other instance, is justifiable, is an inference that may be denied. . . .

It appears to me that there is a clear and necessary Distinction between an Act imposing a tax for *the single purpose of revenue,* and those Acts which have been made for the *regulation of trade,* and have produced some revenue in consequence of their effect and operation as regulations of trade. The colonies claim the privileges of British subjects. It has been proved to be inconsistent with those privileges to tax them without their own consent, and it hath been demonstrated that a tax imposed by Parliament is a tax without their consent.

The subordination of the colonies, and the authority of the Parliament to preserve it, have been fully acknowledged. Not only the welfare, but perhaps the existence of the mother country as an independent kingdom, may rest upon her trade and navigation, and these so far upon her intercourse with the colonies, that if this should be neglected, there would soon be an end to that commerce whence her greatest wealth is derived, and upon which her maritime power is principally founded. From these considerations, the right of the British Parliament to regulate the trade of the colonies, may be justly deduced; a denial of it would contradict the admission of the subordination, and of the authority to preserve it, resulting from the nature of the relation between the mother country and her colonies. It is a common and frequently the most proper method to regulate trade by duties on imports and exports. The authority of the mother country to regulate the trade of the colonies being unquestionable, what regulations are the most proper, are to be of course submitted to the determination of the Parliament; and if an incidental revenue should be produced by such regulations, these are not therefore unwarrantable.

A right to impose an internal tax on the colonies, without their consent *for the single purpose of revenue,* is denied, a right to regulate their trade without their consent is admitted. The imposition of a duty, may, in some instances, be the proper regulation. If the claims of the mother country and the colonies should seem on such an occasion to interfere, and the point of right to be doubtful, (which I take to be otherwise) it is easy to guess that the determination will be on the side of power, and that the inferior will be constrained to submit. . . .

Any oppression of the colonies, would intimate an opinion of them I am persuaded they do not deserve, and their security as well as honour ought to engage them to confute. When contempt is mixed with injustice, and insult with violence, which is the case when an injury is done to him who hath the means of redress in his power; if the injured hath one inflammable grain of honour in his breast, his resentment will invigorate his pursuit of reparation, and animate his efforts to obtain an effectual security against a repetition of the outrage.

If the case supposed should really happen, the resentment I should recommend would be a legal, orderly, and prudent resentment, to be expressed in a zealous and vigorous industry, in an immediate use and unabating application of the advantages we derive from our situation . . . a resentment which could not fail to produce effects as beneficial to the mother country as to the colonies, and which a regard to her welfare as well as our own, ought to inspire us with on such an occasion.

The general assemblies would not, I suppose, have it in their power to encourage by laws, the prosecution of this beneficial, this necessary measure: but they might promote it almost as effectually by their example. I have in my younger days seen fine sights, and been captivated by their dazzling pomp and glittering splendor; but the sight of our representatives, all adorned in compleat dresses of their own leather, and flax, and wool, manufactured by the art and industry of the inhabitants of *Virginia*, would excite, not the gaze of admiration, the flutter of an agitated imagination, or the momentary amusement of a transient scene, but a calm, solid, heart-felt delight. Such a sight would give me more pleasure than the most splendid and magnificent spectacle the most exquisite taste ever painted, the richest fancy ever imagined, realized to the view . . . as much more pleasure as a good mind would receive from the contemplation of virtue, than of elegance; of the spirit of patriotism, than the ostentation of opulence.

Not only, "as a friend to the colonies," but as an inhabitant having my all at stake upon their welfare I desire an "exemption from taxes imposed *without my consent*, and" I have reflected longer than "a moment upon the consequences:" I value it as one of the dearest privileges I enjoy: I acknowledge dependance on *Great Britain*, but I can perceive a degree of it without slavery, and I disown all other. I do not expect that the interests of the colonies will be considered by some men, but in subserviency to other regards. The effects of luxury, and venality, and oppression, posterity may perhaps experience, and SUFFICIENT FOR THE DAY WILL BE THE EVIL THEREOF.

JOHN ADAMS

Clarendon, No. 3 (January 27, 1766)

You are pleased to charge the Colonists with ignorance of the British constitution—But let me tell you there is not even a *Son of Liberty* among them who has not manifested a deeper knowledge of it, and a warmer attachment to it, than appears in any of your late writings. They know the true constitution and all the resources of liberty in it, as well as in the law of nature which is one principal foundation of it, and in the temper and character of the people, much better than you, if we judge by your late most impudent pieces, or than your patron and master, if we judge by his late conduct.

The people in America have discovered the most accurate judgment about the real constitution, I say, by their whole behaviour, excepting the excesses of a few, who took advantage of the general enthusiasm, to perpetrate their ill designs: tho' there has been great enquiry, and some apparent puzzle among them about a formal, logical, technical definition of it. Some have defined it to [be] the practice of parliament; others, the judgments and precedents of the King's courts; but either of these definitions would make it a constitution of wind and weather, because, the parliaments have sometimes voted the King absolute and the judges have sometimes adjudg'd him to be so. Some have call'd it custom, but this is as fluctuating and variable as the other. Some have call'd it the most perfect combination of human powers in society, which finite wisdom has yet contrived and reduced to practice, for the preservation of liberty and the production of happiness. This is rather a character of the constitution, and a just observation concerning it, than a regular definition of it; and leaves us still to dispute what it is. Some have said that the whole body of the laws; others that King, Lords, and Commons, make the constitution. There has also been much inquiry and dispute about the essentials and fundamentals of the constitution, and many definitions and descriptions have been attempted: But there seems to be nothing satisfactory to a rational mind, in any of these definitions: Yet I cannot say, that I am at any loss about any man's meaning when he speaks of the British constitution, or of the essentials and fundamentals of it.

What do we mean when we talk of the constitution of the human body? What by a strong and robust, or a weak and feeble constitution? Do we not mean certain contextures of the nerves, fibres, and muscles, or certain qualities of the blood and juices, as fizy, or watery, phlegmatic or fiery, acid or alkaline? We can never judge of any constitution without considering the *end* of it; and no judgment can be formed of the human constitution, without considering it as productive of *life* or *health* or *strength*. The physician shall tell one man that certain kinds of exercise, or diet, or medicine, are not adapted to his constitution, that is, not compatible with his *health*, which he would readily agree are the most productive of *health* in another. The patient's habit abounds with acid, and acrimonious juices: Will the doctor order vinegar, lemmon juice, barberries and cramberries, to work a cure? These would be unconstitutional remedies; calculated to increase the evil, which arose from the want of a balance, between the acid and alkaline ingredients, in his composition. If the patient's nerves are overbraced, will the doctor advise to jesuits bark? There is a certain quantity of exercise, diet, and medicine, best adapted to every man's constitution, will keep him in the best health and spirits, and contribute the most to the prolongation of his life. These determinate quantities are not perhaps known to him, or any other person: but here lies the proper province of the physician to study his constitution and give him the best advice what and how much he may eat and drink; when and how long he shall sleep; how far he may walk or ride in a day; what air and weather he may improve for this purpose; when he shall take physick, and of what sort it shall be; in order to preserve and perfect his *health*, and prolong his *life*. But there are certain other parts of the body, which the *physician* can in no case have any *authority* to *destroy* or *deprave*; which may properly be called *stamina vitae*, or *essentials* and *fundamentals of the constitution*. Parts, without which life itself cannot be preserved a moment. Annihilate the heart, lungs, brain, animal spirits, blood; any one of these, and life will depart at once. These may be strictly called fundamentals, of the human constitution: Tho' the limbs may be all amputated, the eyes put out, and many other mutilations practiced to impair the strength, activity and other attributes of the man; and yet the essentials to life may remain, unimpaired many years.

Similar observations may be made with equal propriety concerning every kind of machinery. A clock has also a constitution, that is a certain combination of weights, wheels and levers, calculated for a certain use and end, the mensuration of time. Now the constitution of a clock, does not imply such a perfect constructure of movement as shall never go too fast or too slow, as shall never gain nor lose a second of time, in a year or century. This is the proper business of Quare, Tomlinson, and Graham, to execute the workmanship like artists, and come as near to perfection, i.e. as near to a perfect mensuration of time, as the human eye and finger will allow. But yet there are certain parts of a clock, without which, it will not go at all, and you can have from it no better account of the time of day, than from the ore of gold, silver brass and iron, out of which it was wrought. These parts therefore are the essentials and fundamentals of a clock.

Let us now enquire whether the same reasoning is not applicable in all its parts to government. For government is a frame, a scheme, a system, a combination of powers, for a certain end, viz. the good of the whole community. The public good, the salus populi is the professed end of all government, the most despotic, as well as the most free. I shall enter into no examination which kind of government, whether either of the forms of the schools, or any mixture of them is the best calculated for this end. This is the proper inquiry of the founders of Empires. I shall take for granted, what I am sure no Briton will controvert, viz. that Liberty is essential to the public good, the salus populi. And here lies the difference between the British constitution, and other forms of government, viz. that Liberty is its end, its use, its designation, drift and scope, as much as grinding corn is the use of a mill, the transportation of burdens the end of a ship, the mensuration of time the scope of a watch, or life and health the designation of the human body.

Were I to define the British constitution, therefore, I should say, it is a limited monarchy, or a mixture of the three forms of government commonly known in the schools, reserving as much of the monarchial splendor, the aristocratical independency, and the democratical freedom, as are necessary, that each of these powers may have a controul both in legislation and execution, over the other two, for the preservation of the subjects liberty.

According to this definition, the first grand division of constitutional powers is, into those of legislation and those of execution. In the power of legislation, the King, Lords, Commons, and People, are to be considered as essential and fundamental parts of the constitution. I distinguish between the house of commons, and the people who depute them, because there is in nature and fact a real difference; and these last have as important a department in the constitution as the former, I mean the power of election. The constitution is not grounded on "the enormous faith of millions made for one." It stands not on the supposition that kings are the favourites of heaven; that their power is more divine than the power of the people, and unlimited but by their own will and discretion. It is not built on the doctrine that a few nobles or rich commons have a right to inherit the earth, and all the blessings and pleasures of it: and that the multitude, the million, the populace, the vulgar, the mob, the herd and the rabble, as the great always delight to call them, have no rights at all, and were made only for their use, to be robbed and butchered at their pleasure. No, it stands upon this principle, that the meanest and lowest of the people, are, by the unalterable indefeasible laws of God and nature, as well intitled to the benefit of the air to breathe, light to see, food to eat, and clothes to wear, as the nobles or the king. All men are born equal: and the drift of the British constitution is to preserve as much of this equality, as is compatible with the people's security against foreign invasions and domestic usurpation. It is upon these fundamental principles, that popular power was placed as essential in the constitution of the legislature; and the constitution would be as compleat without a kingly as without a popular power. This popular power however, when the numbers grew large, became impracticable to be exercised by the universal and immediate suffrage of the people: and this impracticability has introduced from the feudal system, an expedient which we call a representation. This expedient is only an equivalent for the suffrage of the whole people, in the common management of public concerns. It is in reality nothing more than this, the people chuse attornies to vote for them in the great council of the nation, reserving always the fundamentals of the government, reserving also a right to give their attornies instructions how to vote, and a right, at certain stated intervals of choosing a new, discarding an old attorney, and choosing a wiser and a better. And it is this reservation, of fundamentals, of the right of giving instructions, and of new elections, which creates a popular check, upon the whole government which alone secures the constitution from becoming an aristocracy, or a mixture of monarchy and aristocracy only.

The other grand division of power, is that of execution. And here the King is by the constitution, supreme executor of the laws, and is always present in person or by his judges, in his courts, distributing justice among the people. But the executive branch of the constitution, as far as respects the administration of justice, has in it a mixture of popular power too. The judges answer to questions of law: but no further. Were they to answer to questions of fact as well as law, being few they might be easily corrupted; being commonly rich and great, they might learn to despise the common people, and forget the feelings of humanity: and then the subject's liberty and security would be lost. But by the British constitution, *ad questionem facti respondent juratores*, the jurors answer to the question of fact. In this manner the subject is guarded, in the execution of the laws. The people choose a grand jury to make enquiry and presentment of crimes. Twelve of these must agree in finding the Bill. And the petit jury must try the same fact over again, and find the person guilty before he can be punished. Innocence therefore, is so well protected in this wise constitution, that no man can be punished till twenty four of his Neighbours have said upon oath, that he is guilty. So it is also in the tryal of causes between party and party: No man's property or liberty can be taken from him, till twelve men in his Neighbourhood, have said upon oath, that by laws of his own making it ought to be taken away, i.e. that the facts are such as to fall within such laws.

Thus it seems to appear that two branches of popular power, voting for members of the house of commons, and tryals by juries, the one in the legislative and the other in the executive part of the constitution are as essential and fundamental, to the great end of it, the preservation of the subject's liberty, to preserve the balance and mixture of the government, and to prevent its running into an oligarchy or aristocracy; as the lords and commons are to prevent its becoming an absolute monarchy. These two popular powers therefore are the heart and lungs, the main spring, and the center wheel, and without them, the body must die; the watch must run down; the government must become arbitrary, and this our law books have settled to be the death of the laws and constitution. In these two powers consist wholly, the liberty and security of the people: They have no other fortification against wanton, cruel power: no other indemnification against being ridden like horses, fleeced like sheep, worked like cattle, and fed and cloathed like swine and hounds: No other defence against fines, imprisonments, whipping posts, gibbets, bastenadoes and racks. This is that constitution which has prevailed in Britain from an immense antiquity: It prevailed, and the House of Commons and tryals by juries made a part of it, in Saxon times, as may be abundantly proved by many monuments still remaining in the Saxon language: That constitution which had been for so long a time the envy and admiration of surrounding nations: which has been, no less than five and fifty times, since the Norman conquest, attacked in parliament, and attempted to be altered, but without success; which has been so often defended by the people of England, at the expence of oceans of their blood, and which, cooperating with the invincible spirit of liberty, inspired by it into the people, has never yet failed to work the ruin of the authors of all settled attempts to destroy it.

What a fine reflection and consolation is it for a man to reflect that he can be subjected to no laws, which he does not make himself, or constitute some of his friends to make for him: his father, brother, neighbour, friend, a man of his own rank, nearly of his own education, fortune, habits, passions, prejudices, one whose life and fortune and liberty are to be affected like those of his constituents, by the laws he shall consent to for himself and them. What a satisfaction is it to reflect, that he can lie under the imputation of no guilt, be subjected to no punishment, lose none of his property, or the necessaries, conveniencies or ornaments of life, which indulgent providence has showered around him: but by the judgment of his peers, his equals, his neighbours, men who know him, and to whom he is known; who have no end to serve by punishing him; who wish to find him innocent, if charged with a crime; and are indifferent, on which side the truth lies, if he disputes with his neighbour.

Your writings, Mr. Pym, have lately furnished abundant Proofs, that the infernal regions, have taken from you, all your shame, sense, conscience and humanity: otherwise I would appeal to them who has discovered the most ignorance of the British constitution; you who are for exploding the whole system of popular power, with regard to the Americans, or they who are determined to stand by it, in both its branches, with their lives and fortunes?

Richard Bland

An Inquiry into the Rights of the British Colonies (1766)

Sir,

I take the Liberty to address you, as the Author of "The Regulations lately made concerning the Colonies, and the Taxes imposed upon them considered." It is not to the Man, whoever you are, that I address myself; but it is to the Author of a Pamphlet which, according to the Light I view it in, endeavours to fix Shackles upon the American Colonies: Shackles which, however nicely polished, can by no Means sit easy upon Men who have just Sentiments of their own Rights and Liberties. [. . .]

The Question is whether the Colonies are represented in the British Parliament or not? You affirm it to be an indubitable Fact that they are represented, and from thence you infer a Right in the Parliament to impose Taxes of every Kind upon them. You do not insist upon the Power, but upon the Right of Parliament to impose Taxes upon the Colonies. This is certainly a very proper Distinction, as Right and Power have very different Meanings, and convey very different Ideas; For had you told us that the Parliament of Great Britain have Power, by the Fleets and Armies of the Kingdom, to impose Taxes and to raise Contributions upon the Colonies, I should not have presumed to dispute the Point with you; but as you insist upon the Right only, I must beg Leave to differ from you in Opinion, and shall give my Reasons for it.

But I must first recapitulate your Arguments in Support of this Right in the Parliament. You say the Inhabitants of the Colonies do not indeed choose Members of Parliament, neither are nine Tenths of the People of Britain Electors; for the Right of Election is annexed to certain Species of Property, to peculiar Franchises, and to Inhabitancy in some particular Places. But these Descriptions comprehend only a very small Part of the Lands, the Property and People of Britain; all Copy-Hold, all Leave-Hold Estates under the Crown, under the Church, or under private Persons, though for Terms ever so long; all landed Property in short that is not Freehold, and all monied Property whatsoever, are excluded. The Possessors of these have no Votes in the Election of Members of Parliament; Women and Persons under Age, be their Property ever so large, and all of it Freehold, have none: The Merchants of London, a numerous and respectable Body of Men, whose Opulence exceeds all that America can collect; the Proprietors of that vast Accumulation of Wealth, the Publick Funds; the Inhabitants of Leeds, of Halifax, of Birmingham, and of Manchester, Towns that are each of them larger than the largest in the Plantations; many of lesser Note, that are incorporated; and that great Corporation the East India Company, whose Rights over the Countries they possess fall very little short of Sovereignty, and whose Trade and whose Fleets are sufficient to constitute them a maritime Power, are all in the same Circumstances: And yet are they not represented in Parliament? Is their vast Property subject to Taxation without their Consent? Are they all arbitrarily bound by Laws to which they have not agreed? The Colonies are exactly in the same Situation; all British Subjects are really in the same; none are actually, all are virtually, represented in Parliament: For every Member of Parliament sits in the House not as a Representative of his own Constituents, but as one of that august Assembly by which all the Commons of Great Britain are represented.

This is the Sum of what you advance, in all the Pomp at Parliamentary Declamation, to prove that the Colonies are represented in Parliament, and therefore subject to their Taxation; but notwithstanding this Way of reasoning, I cannot comprehend how Men who are excluded from voting at the Election of Members of Parlament can be represented in that Assembly, or how those who are elected do not sit in the House as Representatives of their Constituents. These Assertions appear to me not only paradoxical, but contrary to the fundamental Principles of the English Constitution.

To illustrate this important Disquisition, I conceive we must recur to the civil Constitution of England, and from thence deduce and ascertain the Rights and Privileges of the People at the first Establishment of the government, and discover the Alterations that have been made in them from Time to Time; and it is from the Laws of the Kingdom, founded upon the Principles of the Law of Nature, that we are to show the Obligation every Member of the State is under to pay Obedience to its Institutions. From these Principles I shall endeavour to prove that the Inhabitants of Britain, who have no Vote in the Election of Members of Parliament, are not represented in that Assembly, and yet that they owe Obedience to the Laws of Parliament; which, as to them, are constitutional, and not arbitrary. As to the Colonies, I shall consider them afterwards. [. . .]

Men in a State of Nature are absolutely free and independent of one another as to sovereign Jurisdiction,[1] but when they enter into a Society, and by their own Consent become Members of it, they must submit to the Laws of the Society according to which they agree to be governed; for it is evident, by the very Act of Association, that each Member subjects himself to the Authority of that Body in whom, by common Consent, the legislative Power of the State is placed: But though they must submit to the Laws, so long as they remain Members of the Society, yet they retain so much of their natural Freedom as to have a Right to retire from the Society, to renounce the Benefits of it, to enter into another Society, and to settle in another Country; for their Engagements to the Society, and their Submission to the publick Authority of the State, do not oblige them to continue in it longer than they find it will conduce to their Happiness, which they have a natural Right to promote. This natural Right remains with every Man, and he cannot justly be deprived of it by any civil Authority. Every Person therefore who is denied his Share in the Legislature of the State to which he had an original Right, and every Person who from his particular Circumstances is excluded from this great Privilege, and refuses to exercise his natural Right of quitting the Country, but remains in it, and continues to exercise the Rights of a Citizen in all other Respects, must be subject to the Laws which by these Acts he *implicitly*, or to use your own Phrase, *virtually* consents to: For Men may subject themselves to Laws, by consenting to them *implicitly;* that is, by conforming to them, by adhering to the Society, and accepting the Benefits of its Constitution, as well, as *explicitly* and directly, in their own Persons, or by their Representatives, substituted in their Room.[2] Thus, if a Man whose Property does not entitle him to be an Elector of Members of Parliament, and therefore cannot be represented, or have any Share in the Legislature,

> inherits or takes any Thing by the Laws of the Country to which he has no indubitable Right in Nature, or which, if he has a Right to it, he cannot tell how to get or keep without the Aid of the Laws and the Advantage of Society, then, when he takes this Inheritance, or whatever it is, *with* it he takes and owns the Laws that gave it him. And since the Security he has from the Laws of the Country, in Respect of his Person and Rights, is the *Equivalent* for his Submission to them, he cannot accept *that* Security without being obliged, in Equity, to pay *this* Submission: Nay his very continuing in the Country shows that he either likes the Constitution, or likes it better, notwithstanding the Alteration made in it to his Disadvantage, than any other; or at least thinks it better, in his Circumstances, to conform to it, than to seek any other; that is, he is content to be comprehended in it.

From hence it is evident that the Obligation of the Laws of Parliament upon the People of Britain who have no Right to be Electors does not arise from their being *virtually* represented, but from a quite different Principle; a Principle of the Law of Nature, true, certain, and universal, applicable to every Sort of Government, and not contrary to the common Understandings of Mankind.

If what you say is a real Fact, that nine Tenths of the People of Britain are deprived of the high Privilege of being Electors, it shows a great Defect in the present Constitution, which has departed so much from its original Purity; but never can prove that

1. Vattel's Law of Nature. Lock on Civil Govern. Wollaston's Rel. of Nat.

2. Wollaston's Rel. of Nat.

those People are even *virtually* represented in Parliament. And here give me Leave to observe that it would be a Work worthy of the best patriotick Spirits in the Nation to effectuate an Alteration in this putrid Part of the Constitution; and, by restoring it to its pristine Perfection, prevent any "Order or Rank of the Subjects from imposing upon or binding the rest without their Consent." But, I fear, the Gangrene has taken too deep Hold to be eradicated in these Days of Venality.

But if those People of Britain who are excluded from being Electors are not represented in Parliament, the Conclusion is much stronger against the People of the Colonies being represented; who are considered by the British Government itself, in every Instance of Parliamentary Legislation, as a distinct People. It has been determined by the Lords of the Privy Council that "Acts of Parliament made in England without naming the foreign Plantations will not bind them." Now, what can be the Reason of this Determination, but that the Lords of the Privy Council are of Opinion the Colonies are a distinct People from the Inhabitants of Britain, and are not represented in Parliament. If, as you contend, the Colonies are *exactly in the same Situation* with the Subjects in Britain, the Laws will in every Instance be equally binding upon them, as upon those Subjects, unless you can discover two Species of *virtual* Representation; the one to respect the Subjects in Britain, and always existing in Time of Parliament; the other to respect the Colonies, a mere Non-Entity, if I may be allowed the Term, and never existing but when the Parliament thinks proper to produce it into Being by any particular Act in which the Colonies happen to be named. But I must examine the Case of the Colonies more distinctly.

It is in vain to search into the civil Constitution of England for Directions in fixing the proper Connexion between the Colonies and the Mother Kingdom; I mean what their reciprocal Duties to each other are, and what Obedience is due from Children to the general Parent. The planting Colonies from Britain is but of recent Date, and nothing relative to such Plantation can be collected from the ancient Laws of the Kingdom; neither can we receive any better Information by extending our Inquiry into the History of the Colonies established by the several Nations in the more early Ages of the World. All the Colonies (except those of Georgia and Nova Scotia) formed from the English Nation, in North America, were planted in a Manner, and under a Dependence, of which there is not an Instance in all the Colonies of the Ancients; and therefore, I conceive, it must afford a good Degree of Surprise to find an English Civilian[3] giving it as his Sentiment that the English Colonies ought to be governed by the Roman Laws, and for no better Reason than because the Spanish Colonies, as he says, are governed by those Laws. The Romans established their Colonies in the Midst of vanquished Nations, upon Principles which best secured their Conquests; the Privileges granted to them were not always the same; their Policy in the Government of their Colonies and the conquered Nations being always directed by arbitrary Principles to the End they aimed at, the subjecting the whole Earth to their Empire. But the Colonies in North America, except those planted within the present Century, were founded by Englishmen; who, becoming private Adventurers, established themselves, without any Expense to the Nation, in this uncultivated and almost uninhabited Country; so that their Case is plainly distinguishable from that of the Roman, or any other Colonies of the ancient World.

As then we can receive no Light from the Laws of the Kingdom, or from ancient History, to direct us in our Inquiry, we must have Recourse to the Law of Nature, and those Rights of Mankind which flow from it.

I have observed before that when Subjects are deprived of their civil Rights, or are dissatisfied with the Place they hold in the Community, they have a natural Right to quit the Society of which they are Members, and to retire into another Country. Now when Men exercise this Right, and withdraw themselves from their Country, they recover their natural Freedom and Independence: The Jurisdiction and Sovereignty of the State they have quitted ceases; and if they unite, and by common Consent take Possession of a new Country, and form themselves into a Political Society, they become a sovereign State, independent of the State from which they separated.

3. Strahan in his Preface to Domat.

If then the Subjects of England have a natural Right to relinquish their Country, and by retiring from it, and associating together, to form a new political Society and independent State, they must have a Right, by Compact with the Sovereign of the Nation, to remove into a new Country, and to form a civil Establishment upon the Terms of the Compact. In such a Case, the Terms of the Compact must be obligatory and binding upon the Parties; they must be the Magna Charta, the fundamental Principles of Government, to this new Society; and every Infringement of them must be wrong, and may be opposed. It will be necessary then to examine whether any such Compact was entered into between the Sovereign and those English Subjects who established themselves in America.

You have told us that "before the first and great Act of Navigation the Inhabitants of North America were but a few unhappy Fugitives, who had wandered thither to enjoy their civil and religious Liberties, which they were deprived of at Home." If this was true, it is evident, from what has been said upon the Law of Nature, that they have a Right to a civil independent Establishment of their own, and that Great Britain has no *Right* to interfere in it. But you have been guilty of a gross Anachronism in your Chronology, and a great Errour in your Account of the first Settlement of the Colonies in North America; for it is a notorious Fact that they were not settled by Fugitives from their native Country, but by Men who came over voluntarily, at their own Expense, and under Charters from the Crown, obtained for that Purpose, long before the first and great Act of Navigation. [. . .]

From this Detail of the Charters, and other Acts of the Crown, under which the first Colony in North America was established, it is evident that "the Colonists were not a few unhappy Fugitives who had wandered into a distant Part of the World to enjoy their civil and religious Liberties, which they were deprived of at home," but had a regular Government long before the first Act of Navigation, and were respected as a distinct State, independent, as to their *internal* Government, of the original Kingdom, but united with her, as to their *external* Polity, in the closest and most intimate League and Amity, under the same Allegiance, and enjoying the Benefits of a reciprocal Intercourse.

But allow me to make a Reflection or two upon the preceding Account of the first Settlement of an English Colony in North America.

America was no Part of the Kingdom of England; it was possessed by a savage People, scattered through the Country, who were not subject to the English Dominion, nor owed Obedience to its Laws. This independent Country was settled by Englishmen at their own Expense, under particular Stipulations with the Crown: These Stipulations then must be the sacred Band of Union between England and her Colonies, and cannot be infringed without Injustice. But you Object that "no Power can abridge the Authority of Parliament, which has never exempted any from the Submission they owe to it; and no other Power can grant such an Exemption."

I will not dispute the Authority of the Parliament, which is without Doubt supreme within the Body of the Kingdom, and cannot be abridged by any other Power; but may not the King have Prerogatives which he has a Right to exercise without the Consent of Parliament? If he has, perhaps that of granting License to his Subjects to remove into a *new* Country, and to settle therein upon particular Conditions, may be one. If he has no such Prerogative, I cannot discover how the Royal Engagements can be made good, that "the Freedom and other Benefits of the British Constitution" shall be secured to those People who shall settle in a new Country under such Engagements; the Freedom, and other Benefits of the British Constitution, cannot be secured to a People without they are exempted from being taxed by any Authority but that of their Representatives, chosen by themselves. This is an essential Part of British Freedom; but if the King cannot grant such an Exemption, in Right of his Prerogative, the Royal Promises cannot be fulfilled; and all Charters which have been granted by our former Kings, for this Purpose, must be Deceptions upon the Subjects who accepted them, which to say would be a high Reflection upon the Honour of the Crown. But there was a Time when some Parts of England itself were exempt from the Laws of Parliament: The Inhabitants of the County Palatine of Chester were not subject to such Laws[4] *ab antiquo*,

4. Petyt's Rights of the Commons. King's Vale Royal of England.

because they did not send Representatives to Parliament, but had their own *Commune Concilium;* by whose Authority, with the Consent of their Earl, their Laws were made. If this Exemption was not derived originally from the Crown, it must have arisen from that great Principle in the British Constitution by which the Freemen in the Nation are not subject to any Laws but such as are made by Representatives elected by themselves to Parlament; so that, in either Case, it is an Instance extremely applicable to Colonies, who contend for no other Right but that of directing their *internal* Government by Laws made with their own Consent, which has been preserved to them by repeated Acts and Declarations of the Crown.

The Constitution of the Colonies, being established upon the Principles of British Liberty, has never been infringed by the immediate Act of the Crown; but the Powers of Government, agreeably to this Constitution, have been constantly declared in the King's Commissions to their Governours, which, as often as they pass the Great Seal, are *new* Declarations and Confirmations of the Rights of the Colonies. Even in the Reign of Charles the Second, a Time by no Means favourable to Liberty, these Rights of the Colonies were maintained inviolate; for when it was thought necessary to establish a permanent Revenue for the Support of Government in Virginia, the King did not apply to the English Parliament, but to the General Assembly, and sent over an Act, under the Great Seal of England, by which it was enacted "by the King's Most Excellent Majesty, by and with the Consent of the General Assembly," that two Shillings per Hogshead upon all Tobacco exported, one Shilling and Threepence per Tun upon Shipping, and Sixpence per Poll for every Person imported, not being actually a Mariner in Pay, were to be paid for ever as a Revenue for the Support of the Government in the Colony.

I have taken Notice of this Act, not only because it shows the proper Fountain from whence all Supplies to be raised in the Colonies ought to flow, but also as it affords an Instance that Royalty itself did not disdain formerly to be named as a Part of the Legislature of the Colony; though now, to serve a Purpose destructive of their Rights, and to introduce Principles of Despotism unknown to a free Constitution, the Legislature of the Colonies are degraded even below the Corporation of a petty Borough in England.

It must be admitted that after the Restoration the Colonies lost that Liberty of Commerce with foreign Nations they had enjoyed before that Time.

As it became a fundamental Law of the other States of Europe to prohibit all foreign Trade with the Colonies, England demanded such an exclusive Trade with her Colonies. This was effected by the Act of 25th Charles 2d, and some other subsequent Acts; which not only circumscribed the Trade of the Colonies with foreign Nations within very narrow Limits, but imposed Duties upon several Articles of their own Manufactory exported from one Colony to another. These Acts, which imposed severer Restrictions upon the Trade of the Colonies than were imposed upon the Trade of England, deprived the Colonies, so far as these Restrictions extended, of the Privileges of English Subjects, and constituted an unnatural Difference between Men under the same Allegiance, born equally free, and entitled to the same civil Rights. In this Light did the People of Virginia view the Act of 25th Charles 2d, when they sent Agents to the English Court to represent against "Taxes and Impositions being laid on the Colony by any Authority but that of their General Assembly." The Right of imposing *internal* Duties upon their Trade by Authority of Parliament was then disputed, though you say it was never called into Question; and the Agents sent from Virginia upon this Occasion obtained a Declaration from Charles 2d the 19th of April 1676, under his Privy Seal, that Impositions or "Taxes ought not be laid upon the Inhabitants and Proprietors of the Colony but by the common Consent of the General Assembly, except such Impositions as the Parliament should lay on the Commodities imported into England from the Colony:" And he ordered a Charter to be made out, and to pass the Great Seal, for securing this Right, among others, to the Colony.

But whether the Act of 25th Charles 2d, or any of the other Acts, have been complained of as Infringements of the Rights of the Colonies or not, is immaterial; for if a Man of superior Strength takes my Coat from me, that cannot give him a Right to my Cloak, nor am I obliged to submit to be deprived of all my Estate because I may have given up some Part of it without Complaint. Besides, I have proved irrefragably that the Colonies are not represented in Parliament, and consequently, upon your own Position, that no new Law can bind them that is made without the Concurrence of their Representatives; and if so, then every Act of Parliament that imposes *internal* Taxes upon the Colonics is an Act of *Power*, and not of *Right*. I must speak freely, I am considering a Question which affects the *Rights* of above two Millions of as loyal Subjects as belong to the British Crown, and must use Terms adequate to the Importance of it; I say that *Power* abstracted from *Right* cannot give a just Title to Dominion. If a Man invades my Property, he becomes an Aggressor, and puts himself into a State of War with me: I have a Right to oppose this Invader; If I have not Strength to repel him, I must submit, but he acquires no Right to my Estate which he has usurped. Whenever I recover Strength I may renew my Claim, and attempt to regain my Possession; if I am never strong enough, my Son, or his Son, may, when able, recover the natural Right of his Ancestor which has been unjustly taken from him.

I hope I shall not be charged with Insolence, in delivering the Sentiments of an honest Mind with Freedom: I am speaking of the *Rights* of a People; *Rights* imply *Equality* in the Instances to which they belong, and must be treated without Respect to the Dignity of the Persons concerned in them. If "the British Empire in Europe and in America is the same *Power*," if the "Subjects in both are the same People, and all equally participate in the Adversity and Prosperity of the Whole," what Distinctions can the Difference of their Situations make, and why is this Distinction made between them? Why is the Trade of the Colonies more circumscribed than the Trade of Britain? And why are Impositions laid upon the one which are not laid upon the other? If the Parliament "have a *Right* to impose Taxes of *every Kind* upon the Colonies," they ought in Justice, as the same People, to have the same Sources to raise them from: Their Commerce ought to be equally free with the Commerce of Britain, otherwise it will be loading them with Burthens at the same Time that they are deprived of Strength to sustain them; it will be forcing them to make Bricks without Straw. I acknowledge the Parliament is the sovereign legislative Power of the British Nation, and that by a full Exertion of their Power they can deprive the Colonists of the Freedom and other Benefits of the British Constitution which have been secured to them by our Kings; they can abrogate all their civil Rights and Liberties; but by what *Right* is it that the Parliament can exercise such a Power over the Colonists, who have as natural a Right to the Liberties and Privileges of Englishmen as if they were actually resident within the Kingdom? The Colonies are subordinate to the Authority of Parliament; subordinate I mean in Degree, but not absolutely so: For if by a Vote of the British Senate the Colonists were to be delivered up to the Rule of a French or Turkish Tyranny, they may refuse Obedience to such a Vote, and may oppose the Execution of it by Force. Great is the Power of Parliament, but, great as it is, it cannot, constitutionally, deprive the People of their *natural* Rights; nor, in Virtue of the same Principle, can it deprive them of their *civil* Rights, which are founded in Compact, without their own Consent. There is, I confess, a considerable Difference between these two Cases as to the Right of Resistance: In the first, if the Colonists should be dismembered from the Nation by Act of Parliament, and abandoned to another Power, they have a natural Right to defend their Liberties by open Force, and may lawfully resist; and, if they are able, repel the Power to whose Authority they are abandoned. But in the other, if they are deprived of their civil Rights, if great and manifest Oppressions are imposed upon them by the State on which they are dependent, their Remedy is to lay their Complaints at the Foot of the Throne, and to suffer patiently rather than disturb the publick Peace, which nothing but a Denial of Justice can excuse them in breaking. But if this Justice should be denied, if the most humble and dutiful Representations should be rejected, nay not even deigned to be received, what is to be done? To such a Question Thucydides would make the Corinthians reply, that if "a decent and condescending Behaviour is shown on the Part of the Colonies, it would be base in the Mother State to press too far on such Moderation:" And he would make the Corcyreans answer, that "every Colony, whilst used in a proper Manner, ought to pay Honour and Regard to its Mother State; but, when treated with Injury and Violence, is become an Alien. They were not sent out to be the Slaves, but to be the Equals of those that remain behind."

But, according to your Scheme, the Colonies are to be prohibited from uniting in a Representation of their general Grievances to the common Sovereign. This Moment "the British Empire in Europe and in America is the same Power; its Subjects in both are the same People; each is equally important to the other, and mutual Benefits, mutual Necessities, cement their Connection." The next Moment "the Colonies are unconnected with each other, different in their Manners, opposite in their Principles, and clash in their Interests and in their Views, from Rivalry in Trade, and the Jealousy of Neighbourhood. This happy Division, which was effected by Accident, is to be continued throughout by Design; and all Bond of Union between them" is excluded from your vast System. *Divide et impera* is your Maxim in Colony Administration, lest "an Alliance should be formed dangerous to the Mother Country." Ungenerous Insinuation! detestable Thought! abhorrent to every Native of the Colonies! who, by an Uniformity of Conduct, have ever demonstrated the deepest Loyalty to their King, as the Father of his People, and an unshaken Attachment to the Interest of Great Britain. But you must entertain a most despicable Opinion of the Understandings of the Colonists to imagine that they will allow Divisions to be fomented between them about inconsiderable Things, when the closest Union becomes necessary to maintain in a constitutional Way their dearest Interests. [. . .]

The Colonies upon the Continent of North America lie united to each other in one Tract of Country, and are equally concerned to maintain their common Liberty. If he will attend then to the Laws of Attraction in natural as well as political Philosophy, he will find that Bodies in Contact, and cemented by mutual Interests, cohere more strongly than those which are at a Distance, and have no common Interests to preserve. But this natural Law is to be destroyed; and the Colonies, whose real Interests are the same, and therefore ought to be united in the closest Communication, are to be disjoined, and all intercommunication between them prevented. But how is this System of Administration to be established? Is it to be done by a military Force, quartered upon private Families? Is it to be done by extending the Jurisdiction of Courts of Admiralty, and thereby depriving the Colonists of legal Trials in the Courts of common Law? Or is it to be done by harassing the Colonists, and giving overbearing Taxgatherers an Opportunity of ruining Men, perhaps better Subjects than themselves by dragging them from one Colony to another, before Prerogative Judges, exercising a despotick Sway in Inquisitorial Courts? Oppression has produced very great and unexpected Events: The Helvetick Confederacy, the States of the United Netherlands, are Instances in the Annals of Europe of the glorious Actions a petty People, in Comparison, can perform when united in the Cause of Liberty. May the Colonies ever remain under a constitutional Subordination to Great Britain! It is their Interest to live under such a Subordination; and it is their Duty, by an Exertion of all their Strength and Abilities, when called upon by their common Sovereign, to advance the Grandeur and the Glory of the Nation. May the Interests of Great Britain and her Colonies be ever united, so as that whilst they are retained in a legal and just Dependence no unnatural or unlimited Rule may be exercised over them; but that they may enjoy the Freedom, and other Benefits of the British Constitution, to the latest Page in History!

Britannus Americanus

Untitled (Boston, 1766)

When the first settlers of this country had transplanted themselves here, they were to be considerered, either as in the state of nature, or else as subjects of that kingdom from whence they had migrated: If they were in the state of nature, they were then entitled to all the rights of nature; no power on earth having any *just* authority, to molest them in the enjoyment of the least of these rights, unless they either had or should forfeit them by an invasion of the rights of other: If the Crown and people of England had at that time, no right, property or claim to that part of the earth, which they had fix'd upon to settle and inhabit, it follows, that in the suppos'd state of nature, neither the crown nor people of England had any *lawful* and *equitable* authority or controul over them more than the inhabitants of the moon: they had a right to connect themselves, for the sake of their own advantage and security, either with the natives, or any other people upon the globe, who were willing to be connected with them: It is a fact, that they chose to erect a government of their own, much under the same form, as that was, which they had formerly been under in Europe; and chose the King of England for *their* King, whose subjects they had been in their state of society before their emigration.—Thus upon the foregoing supposition, the King of *Old* England became connected with the settlers of *New* England, and *their* King: But the people of England could have no more political connection with them or power of jurisdiction over them, than they now have with or over the people of Hanover, who are also subjects of the same King: And if they have since obtain'd no power of jurisdiction, by virtue of any treaty, compact agreement or consent, in which *alone,* all *legal* jurisdiction has its establishment, the people here still remain under the most sacred tie, the subject of the *King* of Great-Britain; but utterly unaccountable to, and uncontrollable by the *people* of Great-Britain, or any body of them whatever; their compact being with the King only, to him alone they submitted, to be govern'd by him, agreable to the terms of that compact, contain'd in their charter.

But on the other supposition, if after their arrival here they remained, as undoubtedly they did, the subjects of the Kingdom of England, they then remain'd without the necessity of charter declarations to confirm it justly entitled to all and every the rights, liberties, privileges and immunities of such; for to talk of English subjects who are free, and of other English subjects, not *so* free, provided they have not legally forfeited *any part* of their freedom, appears to be absurd.—Of all the rights of Englishmen, those of consenting to their own laws, and being tried by juries, are the most material and important: Upon the present supposition, the parliament of England has no more lawful power to make an act which shall deprive the people of *New* England of those rights, than they have to make an act to deprive the people of *Old* England of the same rights: If these are the indefeasible rights of the one, so they must be of the other; they being *fellow subjects,* and standing upon *equal* footing: The people of *Old* England would think it very unjust, to have an act of parliament made, which should deprive them of the unalienable rights of the constitution; just so would the people of *New* England think, and for the same reason; and human nature being the same and both being animated with the same love of freedom and equally attached to the same happy constitution, such a law in either case would probably produce the same effects: it is hoped the people of England will never think it necessary for them to make such laws for the Colonies, for it might prove a *fatal* necessity: It might at least be *detrimental* to Great Britain in *proportion* as the Colonies are *important* to her: Would not such laws, in a *moral* view, cut the thread of political connection and obligation? Does not allegiance infer protection? Has not the latter the strongest claim? Would men ever have had the idea of allegiance to an earthly Prince, had they not first found it necessary to form a government on earth, under God, to protect their natural rights? Is not therefore the Subject's allegiance first due to the constitution of government. which secures the natural rights of the governed; and as a necessary means thereof circumscribes and limits the power of those, whom they have or shall constitute to be their legislators and governors, whether Kings, or Parliaments, or both?

To ascertain the rights of the New-England subjects, the King early gave them a Charter, in which it was declared, what those rights were; and to show his royal mind, that by their attempting at their own cost and pains, to settle a new world, they could by no means be thought to have forfeited their rights as Englishmen: He expressly declares them and their posterity entitled to all those rights, as fully as if they had remained in England. Indeed, if they could possibly have been suppos'd to have lost their rights, by means of their emigration, being yet *innocent* people, and subject to *no other* power on earth, they must have been reduced to a state of nature and independence; for to talk of English subjects without any of the rights of the constitution, is a solicism.

It was not possible for them to enjoy these Rights without erecting a legislative and other powers of government among themselves: For it was not possible for them at such a distance, to have that *weight* and *importance* in the legislative power in England, which every *individual* there has a right to by the constitution, and by act of parliament is declared actually to have: The granting them show the power of government was not mere *favor*, but that which was *right, fit, equitable*; for without it they must have been depriv'd of that right, which others enjoy'd who were no more than their *equals*; and which were some of them the essential rights of nature, as well as the constitution, and therefore inseparable from them either as men or subjects.—By virtue of these powers of government they now stand (as in all respects they ought in justice) upon a footing with their *fellow subjects* in England. Their laws are now made, with the consent of representatives of *their* own free election; which laws like those made by the two houses of the British parliament, are laid before the Sovereign, who has the same power of rejection, *upon both:* Would it not then be just as equitable, and just as consistent with the British constitution, which extends to all his Majesty's *British* subjects throughout his dominions, for the representatives of the people of New-England, or any other colony, to make a law to tax their *fellow subjects* in England, as for their representatives to make a law to tax *their* fellow subjects in the colonies?

LETTER TO THE *PENNSYLVANIA JOURNAL* (March 13, 1766)

To the Printer.

We have had lately several hints among the articles of intelligence from Great-Britain, that a proposal was likely to be made, to allow the colonies *Representatives* in *Parliament*; with a view to quiet our uneasiness, and remove our principal objection against the Stamp Act. Some of their political writers have warmly recommended it, as the only way to set us on equal footing with themselves, and secure to the parliament the right they claim to tax us; others have espoused it as the means to annihilate effectually the power of our assemblies, which it seems they will gladly do if they can. A proposal so insidious as this, ought to be maturely considered, and its baneful tendency exposed to public view, that if they attempt to insnare us this way, we may be sufficiently guarded against it. [. . .]

It is easy to see that this proposal, if adopted by the colonies, will involve them in a very burdensome expence—can do them no service—will expose them to great and irreparable evils, and therefore that it would be the height of infatuation to comply with it if offered. It will involve them in a very burdensome expence—We have few gentlemen in the colonies, who have fortunes sufficient to enable them, and fewer still I fear who have public spirit enough to be willing to reside at the court of Great Britain at their own expence. To send them there without handsome appointments for their support, would be throwing them into the very jaws of temptation; it would be to make it in some sort necessary for many of them at least to betray their trust. They must then be reputably supported by their respective colonies. But it is well known that a gentleman cannot live at court reputably, or even decently in a public character, for less than £500 *per annum;* and if the damage arising from their absence from their private affairs be estimated (which in common justice ought to be done) in most cases the above-mentioned sum must be doubled. If then, upon an average, each of the colonies be admitted to send four members to parliament (which number will give them no great weight in the house of commons, which consists of 558 members) the charge of supporting them will amount of £4000 sterling *per annum* to each colony; which vastly exceeds the current expences of government in most of them, and would be an extremely grievous addition to the other burdens they at present labour under.

Again, this scheme, if adopted, would not only be grievously expensive to the colonies, but can do them no service. For we may take it for granted that Great Britain will never offer us such a number of representatives in the house, as would give us any considerable weight or influence there. To allow the colonies such a number of members in the house of commons, as would enable them to carry points against the mother country, when a competition of interests arises, would be in effect to resign her own independency, which we may be assured she never will do. It would be unsafe to allow even such a number, as to be able to turn the scale for, or against the ministry; which a few might often do if they took care to be united. For if they have weight enough to render a ministry secure against the attacks of their enemies, or overthrow them by joining in the opposition, that very circumstance will render them considerable; and they will seldom want opportunities to encrease their strength, if they are watchful to improve them. For the colonies are growing fast in population and wealth, and consequently in influence; as these increase it will be natural to suppose their number of representatives ought to increase. Vast tracts of land remain to be settled, which will afford ample room for at least as many new colonies, as we now possess on the coast: these when settled, will have as good a claim to a representation in the house, as we now have. Our members already there will have it easily in their power, if they are only united, to introduce any reasonable number of new ones, by seizing such favourable conjunctures as often will occur; as for instance, when the ministry cannot stand their ground without their assistance. Thus the strength of the Americans in the house will be continually increasing, and that of the Britons as distinguished from it, will be at a stand: and it is easy to see that the former must in time overtop the latter.

Whenever the American interest obtains the ascendency in the house, it will be in the power of our representatives to remove the seat of government to their native country, (which is to be supposed they will be forward enough to do, as their own interest would be eminently promoted by it) and then Great-Britain, from being the head of a vast empire, will dwindle away to an American province. Nor is this event to be regarded as a remote contingency; in one century such a revolution might easily be effected. [. . .] It requires no large share of penetration to foresee it: Great-Britain will certainly foresee and prevent it, as her own dignity and importance are ruined if it be not prevented. Therefore if a representation in parliament is offered us, it will be limited to so small a number of members, as will effectually prevent our having any weight or influence there. But what imaginable service can such a representation do us? It is only when a supposed collision of interest between Great Britain and the Colonies arises, that having members in parliament can be of any importance. But in an assembly, where for [far?] the greater part of the members have their residence and whole interest in Britain, and where every thing is decided by a majority of votes, to expect the interest of America, when supposed to be opposite to theirs, would be generally considered, is as absurd as to expect a steady and inviolable distribution of justice from men when admitted to be judges in their own cause. It would be to suppose men are not generally to be swayed by their own interests, contrary to the universal experience of all ages. [. . .]

But if this scheme on the one hand, promises no advantage, it affords a prospect of infinite damage on the other. When venality and corruption reign with such unlimited sway, as it is known they have done in Britain for many years past, excepting one or two short intervals, it requires no ordinary stock of virtue to resist the torrent. Though I have the most honourable sentiments of my countrymen, yet I may suppose they have the same passions with other men. They will be liable to the artful attacks of bribery in some form or other, and we never can have any assurance they will not fall before them. Their living at such a distance from their native country, without any private emolument from their faithful discharge of their trust, may in many instances increase the temptation; especially when the prevalency of universal example is known to be sufficient to make almost any practice appear reputable, or at least to take off the shame and disgrace, that would otherwise attend it, and which is one of our strongest guards against all base actions. It may be viewed then as a probable event, that American Representations would be more or less infected with the common contagion. If in some unfortunate period they should be induced to betray their trust, by concurring in some iniquitous scheme to ruin us, either by passing injurious and oppressive laws, or levying burthensome and oppressive taxes, such as we should not be able to bear, what regular method should we have to rid ourselves of them? We could not pretend to say they were unconstitutional, for they are supposed to be enacted by an assembly, where we are duly represented: and what could hinder our having all our liberties sold one after another, if our representatives were villanous enough to sell, and the ministry disposed to buy them; it is plain they will be in a state of great insecurity, if they depend on the fidelity of a few individuals at such a distance from us. [. . .]

But the disadvantages attending this scheme, if ever adopted, are not barely such as may happen, if our members of Parliament should be corrupted; a subversion of our fundamental liberties, will be implied in the very nature of it. We have now a right to claim full and compleat legislation in every province; but if the scheme I am considering takes place, this claim must be at an end. Though it would be necessary for various purposes, that our provincial assemblies should continue, yet their powers of Legislation must be subordinate to the general legislature of the whole empire. For a colony to be represented in two distinct legislative bodies, equal and independent of each other, and the laws of each to be equally binding at the same time, would be a perfect solecism in any system of government; for it is plain such equal and independent powers would frequently clash, which can issue in nothing but anarchy and confusion. Supreme and independent legislation must subsist somewhere in every state; but on the supposition before us, it can subsist no where but in the parliament of Great-Britain, which would be considered as the general legislature of the whole empire. Britain, though but a part would have the whole influence, and govern every thing as her own interests directed. In a confederacy of states, independent of each other, yet united under one head, such as I conceive the British empire at present to be, all the powers of legislation may subsist full and compleat in each part, and their respective legislatures be absolutely independent of each other; at least so far that the acts of one may not be liable to be repealed by another. In this case there is no proper subordination of one part to another, though the power and influence of one of these confederate states may be vastly superior to any of the rest, or indeed to all of them united. If then the lesser states surrender their powers of free and independent legislation to a general diet, or parliament made up of representatives from every part, but where the proportion of members deligated by each are so adjusted, that the larger and more important state secures to herself the whole influence; and will always be able to direct every determination as she pleases, it is plain that the powers of legislation are lodged in her alone, and the lesser states are no longer confederates belonging to the same body, but are as really subjected to the larger, as if they had been conquered by her arms. Thus in the case before us, if we accept of a representation in parliament, we do from the very nature of the thing, by our own act and deed surrender our powers of legislation to the parliament, and no such thing as any compleat legislative authority can subsist any longer in America. Our provincial assemblies would be little more than petty corporations, having power to make a few bylaws for present conveniency.

If a general legislature was erected for the whole British empire in America, composed of delegates from each colony, (which indeed would be a very desirable event) the several provincial legislatures would be necessarily subordinated to it; and though their powers of legislation would be still independent of each other, yet the exercise of them would be subject to such limitations as arise from the nature of their subordination. But this would be subjecting each part regularly to the whole; not subjecting the whole to *one part*. There is a very wide difference between subordinating the provincial legislatures to a general legislature, where each province has its due share of influence, and where no collision of interests between the members of such general and provincial legislatures is supposable; and subordinating them all to an assembly, where none of them will have any influence, and where a collision of interest between the members of said assembly, and the several parts subjected to them, is frequently supposable. It is indeed hard to conceive of a worse system of government than that to which we shall subject ourselves, if we accept of a representation in parliament. It will be in vain to clamour about oppressive taxes, injurious restrictions on trade, manufactures, &c we must submit to whatever impositions they see fit to lay upon us; for all will be perfectly agreeable to the genius and spirit of the constitution we shall have expressly adopted. Our dependence on Britain, instead of being lessened, will be vastly increased. We shall have indeed the shadow of liberty, but be destitute of the substance. Our influence in the British legislature will in reality be no more than it is now, but instead of being free from its jurisdiction, we shall be regularly and properly subject to it. They will have a right by the very constitution, to command our purses and persons at pleasure. Our liberties, our lives, and every thing that is dear, will be at their mercy. They may indeed for a while be *gentle masters*, but they will be our *masters* still, though they permit us the enjoyment of our privileges during pleasure. [. . .]

This is I think a fair, but imperfect delineation of the horrid consequences of our accepting a representation in parliament. Surely nothing but compleat infatuation can ever induce the colonies to embrace a scheme so fraught with ruin. It will be virtually to surrender our liberty and property to be held by the meer will and pleasure of a body of men in Britain; it will be to put it in their power to enslave us whenever they please. If such a proposal is made, let it be treated as it deserves; let it be considered as a base crafty device to ensnare us; let it be rejected universally with scorn and indignation. Let those that urge its acceptance, if any such villains be found, be considered as enemies to their country. Let us steadily persist in maintaining our freedom, and though the struggle may be hard, let us not doubt of coming off victorious at last.

F. L.

Samuel Adams

Circular Letter from the Massachusetts House of Representatives to the Speakers of Other Houses of Representatives (February 11, 1768)

Sir,

The House of Representatives of this Province have taken into their serious Consideration, the great difficultys that must accrue to themselves & their Constituents, by the operation of several acts of Parliament imposing Duties & Taxes on the American Colonys.

As it is a Subject in which every Colony is deeply interested they have no reason to doubt but your

Assembly is deeply impressd with its Importance & that such constitutional measures will be come into as are proper. It seems to be necessary, that all possible Care should be taken, that the Representations of the several Assembly upon so delicate a point, should harmonize with each other: The House therefore hope that this letter will be candidly considerd in no other Light, than as expressing a Disposition freely to communicate their mind to a Sister Colony, upon a common Concern in the same manner as they would be glad to receive the Sentiments of your or any other House of Assembly on the Continent.

The House have humbly represented to the ministry, their own Sentiments that His Majestys high Court of Parliament is the supreme legislative Power over the whole Empire: That in all free States the Constitution is fixd; & as the supreme Legislative derives its Power & Authority from the Constitution, it cannot overleap the Bounds of it without destroying its own foundation: That the Constitution ascertains & limits both Sovereignty & allegiance, & therefore, his Majestys American Subjects who acknowlege themselves bound by the Ties of Allegiance, have an equitable Claim to the full enjoyment of the fundamental Rules of the British Constitution. That it is an essential unalterable Right in nature, ingrafted into the British Constitution, as a fundamental Law & ever held sacred & irrevocable by the Subjects within the Realm, that what a man has honestly acquird is absolutely his own, which he may freely give, but cannot be taken from him without his consent: That the American Subjects may therefore exclusive of any Consideration of Charter Rights, with a decent firmness adapted to the Character of free men & Subjects assert this natural and constitutional Right.

It is moreover their humble opinion, which they express with the greatest Deferrence to the Wisdom of the Parliament that the Acts made there imposing Duties on the People of this province with the sole & express purpose of raising a Revenue, are Infringements of their natural & constitutional Rights because as they are not represented in the British Parliament His Majestys Commons in Britain by those Acts grant their Property without their consent.

This House further are of Opinion that their Constituents considering their local Circumstances cannot by any possibility be represented in the Parliament, & that it will forever be impracticable that they should be equally represented there & consequently not at all; being seperated by an Ocean of a thousand leagues: and that his Majestys Royal Predecessors for this reason were graciously pleased to form a subordinate legislature here that their subjects might enjoy the unalienable Right of a Representation. Also that considering the utter Impracticability of their ever being fully & equally represented in parliament, & the great Expence that must unavoidably attend even a partial representation there, this House think that a taxation of their Constituents, even without their Consent, grievous as it is, would be preferable to any Representation that could be admitted for them there.

Upon these principles, & also considering that were the right in Parliament ever so clear, yet, for obvious reasons it would be beyond the rules of Equity that their Constituents should be taxed on the manufactures of Great Britain here, in Addition to the dutys they pay for them in England, & other Advantages arising to Great Britain from the Acts of trade, this House have preferrd a humble dutifull & loyal Petition to our most gracious Sovereign, & made such Representations to his Majestys Ministers, as they apprehended would tend to obtain redress.

They have also submitted to Consideration whether any People can be said to enjoy any degree of Freedom if the Crown in addition to its undoubted Authority of constituting a Governor, should also appoint him such a Stipend as it may judge proper without the Consent of the people & at their Expence; and whether while the Judges of the Land & other Civil officers hold not their Commission during good Behavior, their having salarys appointed for them by the Crown independent of the people hath not a tendency to subvert the principles of Equity & endanger the Happiness & Security of the Subject.

In addition to these measures the House have wrote a Letter to their Agent, Mr De Berdt, the Sentiments of which he is directed to lay before the ministry: wherein they take Notice of the hardships of the Act for preventing Mutiny & Desertion, which requires the Governor & Council to provide enumerated Articles for the Kings marching troops & the People to pay the Expences; & also of the Commission of the Gentlemen appointed Commissioners of the Customs to reside in America, which authorizes them to make as many Appointments as they think fit & to pay the Appointees what sum they please, for whose Mal Conduct they are not accountable—from whence it may happen that officers of the Crown may be multiplyd to such a degree as to become dangerous to the Liberty of the people by Virtue of a Commission which doth not appear to this House to derive any such Advantages to Trade as many have been led to expect.

These are the Sentiments & proceedings of this House; & as they have too much reason to believe that the Enemys of the Colonys have represented them to his Majestys Ministers & the parliament as factious disloyal & having a disposition to make themselves independent of the Mother Country, they have taken occasion in the most humble terms to assure his Majesty & his ministers that with regard to the People of this province & as they doubt not of all the colonies the charge is unjust.

The house is fully satisfyd that your Assembly is too generous and enlargd in sentiment, to believe, that this Letter proceeds from an Ambition of taking the Lead or dictating to the other Assemblys: They freely submit their opinions to the Judgment of others, & shall take it kind in your house to point out to them any thing further which may be thought necessary.

This House cannot conclude without expressing their firm Confidence in the King our common head & Father, that the united & dutifull Supplications of his distressed American Subjects will meet with his royal & favorable Acceptance.

Benjamin Rush

Letter to Ebenezer Hazard (October 22, 1768)

London

My dear Sir,

Was I condemned to the galleys of France and allowed but one hour's liberty in the whole year, I think I would employ part of it in writing to you. Your very friendly letter dated in July came safe to hand. I rejoice to hear you are again so comfortably settled in Mr. Noel's family. Mr. DeBerdt has been at his country seat ever since I came to London, so that I have had no opportunity of speaking to him about the Ohio lands. As soon as he comes to town you may depend upon my doing everything in my power to serve you in conjunction with him.

My whole time is now employed in attending lectures and hospitals and in visiting those places in London which are most worthy the notice of a stranger. I went a few days ago in company with a Danish physician to visit the House of Lords and the House of Commons. When I went into the first, I felt as if I walked on sacred ground. I gazed for some time at the Throne with emotions that I cannot describe. I asked our guide if it was common for strangers to set down upon it. He told me no, but upon my importuning him a good deal I prevailed upon him to allow me the liberty. I accordingly advanced towards it and sat in it for a considerable time. When I first got into it, I was seized with a kind of horror which for some time interrupted my ordinary train of thinking. "This," said I (in the words of Dr. Young), "is the golden period of the worldly man's wishes. His passions conceive, his hopes aspire after nothing beyond *this Throne*." I endeavored to arrange my thoughts into some order, but such a crowd of ideas poured in upon my mind that I can scarcely recollect one of them. From this I went into the House of Commons. I cannot say I felt as if I walked on "sacred ground" here. This, thought I, is the place where the infernal scheme for enslaving America was first broached. Here the usurping Commons first endeavored to rob the King of his supremacy over the colonies and to divide it among themselves. O! cursed haunt of venality, bribery, and corruption! In the midst of these reflections I asked where Mr. Pitt (alas! now Lord Chatham) stood when he spoke in favor of repealing the Stamp Act. "Here," said our guide, "on this very spot." I then went up to it, sat down upon it for some time, and fancying myself surrounded with a crowded House, rose up from my seat and began to repeat part of his speech: "When the scheme for taxing America," said I, "was first proposed, I was unhappily confined to my bed. But had some kind hand brought me and laid me down upon *this* floor, I would have bore a public testimony against it. Americans are the sons, not the bastards of Englishmen. I rejoice that America has resisted." O sir! How grand must have been the entertainment to have heard this once illustrious patriot declaiming with more than Roman eloquence in favor of his distant oppressed countrymen! I was ready to kiss the very walls that had re-echoed to his voice upon that glorious occasion, and to ask them to repeat again the enchanting sounds. You see my paper obliges me to conclude myself, as usual, yours most affectionately,

B: RUSH

JOHN DICKINSON

Letters from a Farmer in Pennsylvania (1768)

Letter II

My dear Countrymen,

There is another late act of parliament, which appears to me to be unconstitutional, and as destructive to the liberty of these colonies, as that mentioned in my last letter; that is, the act for granting the duties on paper, glass, etc.

The parliament unquestionably possesses a legal authority to *regulate* the trade of *Great Britain*, and all her colonies. Such an authority is essential to the relation between a mother country and her colonies; and necessary for the common good of all. He who considers these provinces as states distinct from the *British Empire*, has very slender notions of *justice*, or of their *interests*. We are but parts of a *whole*; and therefore there must exist a power somewhere, to preside, and preserve the connection in due order. This power is lodged in the parliament; and we are as much dependent on *Great Britain*, as a perfectly free people can be on another.

I have looked over *every statute* relating to these colonies, from their first settlement to this time; and I find every one of them founded on this principle, till the *Stamp Act* administration. *All before*, are calculated to regulate trade, and preserve or promote a mutually beneficial intercourse between the several constituent parts of the empire; and though many of them imposed duties on trade, yet those duties were always imposed *with design* to restrain the commerce of one part, that was injurious to another, and thus to promote the general welfare. The raising of a revenue thereby was never intended. Thus the King, by his judges in his courts of justice, imposes fines, which all together amount to a very considerable sum, and contribute to the support of government: But this is merely a consequence arising from restrictions that only meant to keep peace and prevent confusion; and surely a man would argue very loosely, who should conclude from hence, that the King has a right to levy money in general upon his subjects. Never did the *British* parliament, till the period above mentioned, think of imposing duties in *America* FOR THE PURPOSE OF RAISING A REVENUE. Mr. *Greenville* first introduced this language, in the preamble to the 4th of GEO. III Chap. 15, which has these words—"And whereas it is just and necessary that A REVENUE BE RAISED IN YOUR

MAJESTY'S SAID DOMINIONS IN AMERICA, *for defraying the expenses of defending, protecting, and securing the same:* We your Majesty's most dutiful and loyal subjects, THE COMMONS OF GREAT BRITAIN, in parliament assembled, being desirous to make some provision in this present session of parliament, TOWARD RAISING THE SAID REVENUE IN AMERICA, have resolved to GIVE and GRANT unto your Majesty the several rates and duties herein after mentioned." etc.

A few months after came the *Stamp Act,* which reciting this, proceeds in the same strange mode of expression, thus—"And whereas it is just and necessary, that provision be made FOR RAISING A FURTHER REVENUE WITHIN YOUR MAJESTY'S DOMINIONS IN AMERICA, *towards defraying the said expences,* we your Majesty's most dutiful and loyal subjects, the COMMONS OF GREAT BRITAIN, etc. GIVE and GRANT," etc. as before.

The last act, granting duties upon paper, etc. carefully pursues these modern precedents. The preamble is, "Whereas it is expedient THAT A REVENUE SHOULD BE RAISED IN YOUR MAJESTY'S DOMINIONS IN AMERICA, *for making a more certain and adequate provision for defraying the charge of the administration of justice, and the support of civil government in such provinces, where it shall be found necessary; and towards further defraying the expences of defending, protecting and securing the said dominions, we your Majesty's most dutiful and loyal subjects,* the COMMONS OF GREAT BRITAIN, etc. GIVE and GRANT," etc. as before.

Here we may observe an authority *expressly* claimed and exerted to impose duties on these colonies; not for the regulation of trade; not for the preservation or promotion of a mutually beneficial intercourse between the several constituent parts of the empire, heretofore the *sole objects* of parliamentary institutions; *but for the single purpose of levying money upon us.*

This I call an innovation; and a most dangerous innovation.[1] It may perhaps be objected, that *Great Britain* has a right to lay what duties she pleases upon her exports,[2] and it makes no difference to us, whether they are paid here or there.

To this I answer. These colonies require many things for their use, which the laws of *Great Britain* prohibit them from getting any where but from her. Such are paper and glass.

That we may legally be bound to pay any *general* duties on these commodities, relative to the regulation of trade, is granted; but we being *obliged by her laws* to take them from *Great Britain,* any *special* duties imposed on their exportation *to us only, with intention to raise a revenue from us only,* are as much *taxes* upon us, as those imposed by the *Stamp Act.* [. . .]

Why was the *Stamp Act* then so pernicious to freedom? It did not enact, that every man in the colonies *should* buy a certain quantity of paper—No: It only directed, that no instrument of writing should be valid in law, if not made on stamped paper, etc.

The makers of that act knew full well, that the confusions that would arise from the disuse of writings, would COMPEL the colonies to use the stamped paper, and therefore to pay the taxes imposed. For this reason the *Stamp Act* was said to be a law THAT WOULD EXECUTE ITSELF. For the very same reason, the last act of parliament, if it is granted to have any force here, WILL EXECUTE ITSELF, and will be attended with the very same consequences to *American* liberty.

Some persons perhaps may say that this act lays us under no necessity to pay the duties imposed because we may ourselves manufacture the articles on which they are laid; whereas by the *Stamp Act* no instrument of writing could be good unless made on *British* paper, and that too stamped. [. . .]

---

1. "It is worthy observation how quietly subsidies, granted in forms *usual* and *accustomable* (though heavy) are borne; such a power hath use and custom. On the other side, what discontentments and disturbances subsidies *framed in a new mold* do raise (SUCH AN INBRED HATRED NOVELTY DOTH HATCH) is evident by examples of former times." Lord *Coke's* 2nd Institute, p. 33.

2. Some people think that *Great Britain* has the same right to impose duties on the exports to these colonies, as on the exports to *Spain* and *Portugal,* etc. Such persons attend so much to the idea of exportation, that they entirely drop *that of the connection between the mother country and her colonies.* If *Great Britain* had always claimed, and exercised an authority to compel *Spain* and *Portugal* to import manufactures from her only, the cases would be parallel: But as she never pretended to such a right, they are at liberty to get them where they please; and if they chuse to take them from her, rather than from other nations, they voluntarily consent to pay the duties imposed on them.

But can any man, acquainted with *America*, believe this possible? I am told there are but two or three *Glass-Houses* on this continent, and but very few *Paper-Mills;* and suppose more should be erected, a long course of years must elapse, before they can be brought to perfection. This continent is a country of planters, farmers, and fishermen; not of manufactures. The difficulty of establishing particular manufactures in such a country, is almost insufferable. For one manufacture is connected with others in such a manner, that it may be said to be impossible to establish one or two without establishing several others. The experience of many nations may convince us of this truth.

Inexpressible therefore must be our distresses in evading the late acts, by the disuse of *British* paper and glass. Nor will this be the extent of our misfortune, if we admit the legality of that act.

Great Britain has prohibited the manufacturing *iron* and *steel* in these colonies, without any objection being made to her *right* of doing it. The *like* right she must have to prohibit any other manufacture among us. Thus she is possessed of an undisputed *precedent* on that point. This authority, she will say, is founded on the *original intention* of settling these colonies; that is, that she should manufacture for them, and that they should supply her with materials. The *equity* of this policy, she will also say, has been universally acknowledged by the colonies, who never have made the least objection to statutes for that purpose; and will further appear by the *mutual benefits* flowing from this usage, ever since the settlement of these colonies.

Our great advocate, Mr. *Pitt*, in his speeches on the debate concerning the repeal of the *Stamp Act*, acknowledged, that *Great Britain* could restrain our manufactures. His words are these—"This kingdom, as the supreme governing and legislative power, has always bound the colonies by her regulations and restrictions in trade, in navigation, in MANUFACTURES—in everything, *except that of taking their money out of their pockets* WITHOUT THEIR CONSENT." Again he says, "We may bind their trade, CONFINE THEIR MANUFACTURES, and exercise every power whatever, *except that of taking their money out of their pockets* WITHOUT THEIR CONSENT."

Here then, my dear countrymen, ROUSE yourselves, and behold the ruin hanging over your heads. If you ONCE admit, that *Great Britain* may lay duties upon her exportations to us, *for the purpose of levying money on us only*, she then will have nothing to do, but to lay those duties on the articles which she prohibits us to manufacture—and the tragedy of *American* liberty is finished. We have been prohibited from procuring manufactures, in all cases, any where but from *Great Britain* (excepting linens, which we are permitted to import directly from *Ireland*). We have been prohibited, in some cases, from manufacturing for ourselves; and may be prohibited in others. We are therefore exactly in the situation of a city besieged, which is surrounded by the works of the besiegers in every part *but one*. If *that* is closed up, no step can be taken, *but to surrender at discretion*. If *Great Britain* can order us to come to her for necessaries we want, and can order us to pay what taxes she pleases before we take them away, or when we land them here, we are as abject slaves as *France* and *Poland* can show in wooden shoes and with uncombed hair.[3] [. . .]

Upon the whole, the single question is, whether the parliament can legally impose duties to be paid *by the people of these colonies only*, FOR THE SOLE PURPOSE OF RAISING A REVENUS, *on commodities which she obliges us to take from her alone*, or, in other words, whether the parliament can legally take money out of our pockets, without our consent. If they can, our boasted liberty is but

Vox et praeterea nihil.

A sound and nothing else.

A Farmer

Letter IV

My dear Countrymen,

An objection, I hear, has been made against my second letter, which I would willingly clear up before I proceed. "There is," say these objectors, "a material difference between the *Stamp Act* and the *late act* for

3. The peasants of *France* wear wooden shoes; and the vassals of *Poland* are remarkable for matted hair which never can be combed.

laying a duty on paper, etc. that justifies the conduct of those who opposed the former, and yet are willing to submit to the latter. The duties imposed by the *Stamp Act* were *internal* taxes; but the present are *external*, and therefore the parliament may have a right to impose them."

To this I answer, with a total denial of the power of parliament to lay upon these colonies any *"tax"* whatever. [. . .]

To the word *"tax,"* I annex that meaning which the constitution and history of *England* require to be annexed to it; that is—that it is *an imposition on the subject, for the sole purpose of levying money.*

In the early ages of our monarchy, certain services were rendered to the crown *for the general good.* These were personal.[4] But in process of time, such institutions being found inconvenient, gifts and grants of their own property were made by the people. [. . .] All these sums were levied upon the people by virtue of their voluntary gift.[5] Their intention was to support the *national honor and interest.* Some of those grants comprehended duties arising from trade; being imports on merchandizes. These Lord Chief Justice *Coke* classes under "subsidies," and "parliamentary aids." They are also called "customs." But whatever the name was, they were always considered as *gifts of the people to the crown, to be employed for public uses.*

Commerce was at a low ebb, and surprising instances might be produced how little it was attended to for a succession of ages. The terms that have been mentioned, and, among the rest, that of "tax," had obtained a national, parliamentary meaning, drawn from the principles of the constitution, long before any *Englishman* thought of *imposition of duties, for the regulation of trade.* [. . .]

In the national, parliamentary sense insisted on, the word "tax"[6] was certainly understood by the congress at New York, whose resolves may be said to form the *American* "bill of rights."

The third, fourth, fifth, and sixth resolves, are thus expressed.

III. "That it is *inseparably essential to the freedom of a people, and the undoubted right of Englishmen,* that NO TAX be imposed on them, *except with their own consent,* given personally, or by their representatives."

IV. "That the people of the colonies are not, and from their local circumstances, cannot be represented in the house of commons in *Great Britain.*"

V. "That the only representatives of the people of the colonies, are the persons chosen therein by themselves; and that NO TAXES ever have been, or can be constitutionally imposed on them, but by their respective legislatures."

VI. "That ALL *supplies to the crown,* being free gifts of the people, it is *unreasonable, and inconsistent with the principles and spirit of the* British *constitution,* for the people of *Great Britain* to grant to his Majesty *the property of the colonies.*"

Here is no distinction made between *internal* and *external* taxes. It is evident from the short reasoning thrown into these resolves, that every imposition "to

---

4. It is very worthy of remark, how watchful our wise ancestors were, lest their *services* should be increased beyond what the law allowed. No man was bound to go out of the realm to serve the King. Therefore, even in the conquering reign of *Henry the Fifth,* when the martial spirit of the nation was highly inflamed by the heroic courage of their Prince, and by his great success, they still carefully guarded against the establishment of illegal services. "When this point (says Lord Chief Justice *Coke*) concerning maintenance of wars out of *England,* came in question, the COMMONS did make their *continual claim* of their *ancient freedom* and *birthright,* as in the first of *Henry the Fifth,* and in the seventh of *Henry the Fifth,* etc. the COMMONS made a PROTEST, that they were not bound to the maintenance of war in *Scotland, Ireland, Calice, France, Normandy,* or other *foreign* parts, and caused their PROTESTS to be entered into the parliament rolls, where they yet remain; which, in effect, agrees with that which, upon like occasion, was made in the parliament of the 15th *Edward* I." (2d Inst. p. 528)

5. These gifts entirely depending on the pleasure of the donors, were proportioned to the abilities of the several ranks of people who gave, and were regulated by *their* opinion of the public necessities. Thus *Edward* I had in his 11th year a *thirtieth* from the *laity,* a *twentieth* from the *clergy;* in his 22nd year a TENTH from the *laity,* a *sixth* from *London,* and other corporate towns, *half of their benefices* from the *clergy;* in his 23d year an *eleventh* from the *barons* and others, a *tenth* from the *clergy;* a *seventh* from the *burgesses,* etc. (*Hume's Hist. of England*)

6. In this sense *Montesquieu* uses the word "tax," in his 13th book of *Spirit of Laws.*

grant to his Majesty *the property of the colonies,"* was thought a "tax"; and that every such imposition, if laid any other way, than "with their consent, given personally, or by their representatives," was not only "unreasonable, and inconsistent with the principles and spirit of the *British* constitution," but destructive "to the freedom of a people."

This language is clear and important. A "TAX" means an imposition to raise money. Such persons therefore as speak of *internal* and *external* "TAXES," I pray may pardon me, if I object to that expression, as applied to the privileges and interests of these colonies. There may be *internal* and *external* IMPOSITIONS, founded on *different principles*, and having *different tendencies*; every "tax" being an imposition, though every imposition is not a "tax." But *all taxes* are founded on the *same principle*; and have the *same tendency*.

External impositions, for the regulation of our trade, do not "grant to his Majesty *the property of the colonies."* They only *prevent the colonies acquiring property*, in things not necessary, in a manner judged to be injurious to the welfare of the whole empire. But the last statute respecting us, "grants to his Majesty *the property of the colonies,"* by laying duties on the manufactures of *Great Britain* which they MUST take, and which she settled them, on purpose that they SHOULD take.

WHAT *tax* can be more *internal* than this?[7] Here is money drawn, *without their consent*, from a society, who have constantly enjoyed a constitutional mode of raising all money among themselves. The payment of this *tax* they have no possible method of avoiding; as they cannot do without the commodities on which it is laid, and they cannot manufacture these commodities themselves. Besides, if this unhappy country should be so lucky as to elude this act, by getting parchment enough, in the place of paper, or by reviving the ancient method of writing on wax and bark, and by inventing something to serve instead of glass, her ingenuity would stand her in little stead; for then the parliament would have nothing to do but to prohibit such manufactures, or to lay a tax on *hats* and WOOLEN CLOTHS, which they have already prohibited the colonies *from supplying each other with*; or on instruments and tools of *steel* and *iron*, which they have prohibited the provincials *from manufacturing at all*:[8] And then, what little gold and silver they have, must be torn from their hands, or they will not be able, in a short time, to get an ax[9] for cutting their firewood, nor a plough for raising their food. In what respect, therefore, I beg leave to ask, is the late act preferable to the *Stamp Act*, or more consistent with the liberties of the colonies? For my own part, I regard them both with equal apprehension; and think they ought to be in the same manner opposed.

Habemus quidem senatus consultum, tanquam gladium in vagina repositum.

We have a statute, laid up for future use, like a sword in the scabbard.

A Farmer

---

7. It seems to be evident, that Mr. *Pitt*, in his defense of *America*, during the debate concerning the repeal of the *Stamp Act*, by "*internal* taxes," meant any duties "for the purpose of raising a revenue"; and by "*external* taxes," meant duties imposed "for the regulation of trade." His expressions are these—"If the gentleman does not understand the differences between *internal* and *external* taxes, I cannot help it; but there is a plain distinction between taxes levied FOR THE PURPOSES OF RAISING A REVENUE, and duties imposed FOR THE REGULATION OF TRADE, for the accommodation of the subject; although, in the consequences, some revenue might incidentally arise from the latter."

These words were in Mr. *Pitt's* reply to Mr. *Greenville*, who said he could not understand the difference between external and internal taxes.

8. "And that pig and bar iron, made in his Majesty's colonies in America, may be further manufactured in this kingdom, be it further enacted by the authority aforesaid, that from and after the twenty-fourth day of June, 1750, no mill, or other engine, for slitting or rolling of iron, or any plating forge, to work with a tilt hammer, or any furnace for making steel, shall be erected; or, after such erection, continued in any of his Majesty's colonies in America." 23d *Geo.* II. Chap. 29, Sect. 9.

9. Though these particulars are mentioned as being absolutely necessary, yet perhaps they are not more so than glass in our severe winters, to keep out the cold from our houses; or than paper, without which such inexpressible confusions must ensue.

Letter VI

My dear Countrymen,

It may perhaps be objected against the arguments that have been offered to the public, concerning the legal power of the parliament, "that it has always exercised the power of improving duties, for the purposes of raising a revenue on the productions of these colonies carried to Great Britain, which may be called a tax on them." To this objection I answer, that this is no violation of the rights of the colonies, it being implied in the relation between them and *Great Britain*, that they should not carry such commodities to other nations, as should enable them to interfere with the mother country. The imposition of duties on these commodities, when brought to her, is only a consequence of her parental right; and if the point is thoroughly examined, the duties will be found to be laid on the people of the mother country. Whatever they are, they must proportionably raise the price of the goods, and consequently must be paid by the consumers. In this light they were considered by the parliament in the 25th Charles II. Chap. 7, Sect. 2, which says, that the productions of the plantations were carried from one to another free from all customs, "while the subjects of this your kingdom of *England* have paid *great customs and impositions for what of them have been* SPENT HERE," etc.

Besides, if *Great Britain* exports these commodities again, the duties will injure her own trade, so that she cannot hurt us, without plainly and immediately hurting herself; and this is our check against her acting arbitrarily in this respect.

It may be perhaps further objected, "that it being granted that statutes made for regulating trade, are binding upon us, it will be difficult for any persons, but the makers of the laws, to determine, which of them are made for the regulating of trade, and which for raising a revenue; and that from hence may arise confusion."

To this I answer, that the objection is of no force in the present case, or such as resemble it; because the act now in question, is formed expressly FOR THE SOLE PURPOSE OF RAISING A REVENUE.

However, supposing the design of parliament had not been expressed, the objection seems to me of no weight, with regard to the influence which those who may make it, might expect it ought to have on the conduct of these colonies.

It is true that *impositions for raising a revenue*, may be hereafter called *regulations of trade*: But names will not change the nature of things. Indeed we ought firmly to believe, what is an undoubted truth, confirmed by the unhappy experience of many states heretofore free, that UNLESS THE MOST WATCHFUL ATTENTION BE EXERTED, A NEW SERVITUDE MAY BE SLIPPED UPON US, UNDER THE SANCTION OF USUAL AND RESPECTABLE TERMS. [. . .]

All artful rulers, who strive to extend their power beyond its just limits, endeavor to give to their attempts as much semblance of legality as possible. Those who succeed them may venture to go a little further; for each new encroachment will be strengthened by a former. "That which is now supported by examples, growing old, will become an example itself,"[*] and thus support fresh usurpations.

A FREE people therefore can never be too quick in observing, nor too firm in opposing the beginnings of *alteration* either in *form* or *reality*, respecting institutions formed for their security. The first kind of alteration leads to the last: Yet, on the other hand, nothing is more certain, than that the *forms* of liberty may be retained, when the *substance* is gone. In government, as well as in religion, "The *letter* killeth, but the *spirit* giveth life."[10] [. . .]

Ought not the people therefore to watch? to observe facts? to search into causes? to investigate designs? And have they not a right of JUDGING from the evidence before them, on no slighter points than their *liberty* and *happiness?* It would be less than trifling, whenever a *British* government is established, to make use of any arguments to prove such a right. It is sufficient to remind the reader of the day, on the anniversary of which the first of these letters is dated.

I will now apply what has been said to the present question.

The *nature* of any impositions laid by parliament on these colonies, must determine the *design* in laying them. It may not be easy in every instance to discover that design. Whenever it is doubtful, I think submission cannot be dangerous; nay, it must be right, for, in my opinion, there is no privilege these

10. II Corinthians 3:6.

colonies claim, which they ought in *duty* and *prudence* more earnestly to maintain and defend, than the authority of the *British* parliament to regulate the trade of all her dominions. Without this authority, the benefits she enjoys from our commerce, must be lost to her: The blessings we enjoy from our dependence upon her, must be lost to us. Her strength must decay; her glory vanish; and she cannot suffer without our partaking in her misfortune. *Let us therefore cherish her interests as our own, and give her everything, that it becomes* FREEMEN *to give or to receive.*

The *nature* of any impositions she may lay upon us may, in general, be known, by considering how far they relate to the preserving, in due order, at the connection between the several parts of the *British* empire. One thing we may be assured of, which is this—Whenever she imposes duties on commodities, to be paid only upon their exportation from *Great Britain* to these colonies, it is not a regulation of trade, but a design to raise a revenue upon us. Other instances may happen, which it may not be necessary at present to dwell on. I hope these colonies will never, to their latest existence, want understanding sufficient to discover the intentions of those who rule over them, nor the resolution necessary for asserting their interests. They will always have the same rights, that all free states have, of judging when their privileges are invaded, and of using all prudent measures for preserving them.

Quocirca vivite fortes
Fortiaque adversis opponite pectora rebus.

Wherefore keep up your spirits, and gallantly oppose this adverse course of affairs.

A Farmer

Letter VII

My dear Countrymen,

Some of you, perhaps, filled, as I know your breasts are, with loyalty to our most excellent Prince, and with love to our dear mother country, may feel yourselves inclined, by the affections of your hearts, to approve every action of those whom you so much venerate and esteem. A prejudice thus flowing from goodness of disposition, is amiable indeed. I wish it could be indulged without danger. Did I think this possible, the error should have been adopted, and not opposed by me. But in truth, all men are subject to the frailties of nature; and therefore whatever regard we entertain for the persons of those who govern us, we should always remember that their conduct, as *rulers,* may be influenced by human infirmities.

When any laws, injurious to these colonies, are passed, we cannot suppose, that any injury was intended us by his Majesty, or the Lords. For the assent of the crown and peers to laws, seems, as far as I am able to judge, to have been vested in them, more for their own security, than for any other purpose. On the other hand, it is the particular business of the people, to inquire and discover what regulations are useful for themselves, and to digest and present them in the form of bills, to the other orders, to have them enacted into laws. Where these laws are to bind *themselves,* it may be expected, that the house of commons will very carefully consider them: But when they are making laws that are not designed to bind *themselves,* we cannot imagine that their deliberations will be as cautious and scrupulous, as in their own case. [. . .]

There are two ways of laying taxes. One is, by imposing a certain sum on particular kinds of property, to be paid by the *user* or *consumer,* or by rating the *person* at a certain sum. The other is, by imposing a certain sum on particular kinds of property, to be paid by the seller.

When a man pays the first sort of tax, he *knows with certainty,* that he pays so much money for a tax. The *consideration* for which he pays it, is remote, and, it may be, does not occur to him. He is sensible too, that he is *commanded and obliged* to pay it *as a tax;* and therefore people are apt to be displeased with this sort of tax.

The other sort of tax is submitted to in a very different manner. [. . .]

The merchant or importer, who pays the duty at first, will not consent to be so much money out of pocket. He therefore proportionally raises the price of his goods. It may then be said to be a contest between him and the person offering to buy, who shall lose the duty. This must be decided by the nature of the commodities, and the purchaser's demand for them. If they are mere luxuries, he is at liberty to do as he pleases, and if he buys, he does it voluntarily: But if they are absolute *necessaries,* or *conveniences*, which use and custom have made requisite for the comfort of life, and which he is not permitted, by the power imposing the duty, to get *elsewhere*, there the seller has a plain advantage, and the buyer *must* pay the duty. In fact, the seller is nothing less than a collector of the tax for the power that imposed it. If these duties then are extended to the necessaries and conveniences of life in general, and enormously increased, the people must at length become indeed "most exquisitely sensible of their slavish situation." Their happiness therefore entirely depends on the moderation of those who have authority to impose the duties.

I shall now apply these observations to the late act of parliament. Certain duties are thereby imposed on paper and glass, imported into these colonies. By the laws of *Great Britain* we are prohibited to get these articles from any other part of the world. We cannot at present, nor for many years to come, tho' we should apply ourselves to these manufacturers with the utmost industry, make enough ourselves for our own use. That paper and glass are not only convenient, but absolutely necessary for us, I imagine very few will contend. Some perhaps, who think mankind grew wicked and luxurious, as soon as they found out another way of communicating their sentiments than by speech, and another way of dwelling than in caves, may advance so whimsical an opinion. But I presume no body will take the unnecessary trouble of refuting them.

From these remarks I think it evident, that we *must* use paper and glass; that what we use, *must* be *British;* and that we must pay the duties imposed, unless those who sell these articles, are so generous as to make us presents of the duties they pay.

Some persons may think this act of no consequence, because the duties are so *small.* A fatal error. *That* is the very circumstance most alarming to me. For I am convinced, that the authors of this law would never have obtained an act to raise so trifling a sum as it must do, had they not intended by *it* to establish a *precedent* for future use. To console ourselves with the smallness of the duties, is to walk deliberately into the snare that is set for us, praising the *neatness* of the workmanship. Suppose the duties imposed by the late act could be paid by these distressed colonies with the utmost ease, and that the purposes to which they are to be applied, were the most reasonable and equitable that can be conceived, the contrary of which I hope to demonstrate before these letters are concluded; yet even in such a supposed case, these colonies ought to regard the act with abhorrence. For WHO ARE A FREE PEOPLE? Not *those*, over whom government is reasonable and equitably exercised, but *those*, who live under a government so *constitutionally checked and controlled,* that proper provision is made against its being otherwise exercised.

The late act is founded on the destruction of this constitutional security. If the parliament have a right to lay a duty of Four Shillings and Eight-pence on a hundred weight of glass, or a ream of paper, they have a right to lay a duty of any other sum on either. They may raise the duty, as the author before quoted says has been done in some countries, till it "exceeds seventeen or eighteen times the value of the commodity." In short, it they have a right *to* levy a tax of *one penny* upon us, they have a right to levy a *million* upon us: For where does their right stop? At any given number of Pence, Shillings or Pounds? To attempt to limit their right, after granting it to exist at all, is as contrary to reason—as granting it to exist at all, is contrary to justice. If *they* have any right to tax *us*—then, whether *our own money* shall continue in *our own pockets* or not, depends no longer on *us,* but on *them.* "There is nothing which" we "can call our own; or, to use the words of Mr. Locke—WHAT PROPERTY HAVE" WE "IN THAT, WHICH ANOTHER MAY, BY RIGHT, TAKE WHEN HE PLEASES, TO HIMSELF?"[11]

These duties, which will inevitably be levied upon us—which are now levying upon us—are *expressly* laid FOR THE SOLE PURPOSE OF TAKING MONEY. This is the true definition of "*taxes.*" They are therefore *taxes.* This money is to be taken from *us. We* are therefore taxed. *Those* who are *taxed* without their own consent, expressed by themselves or their representatives, are *slaves. We are taxed* without our own consent, expressed by ourselves or our representatives. *We* are therefore—SLAVES.[12]

Miserabile vulgus.

A miserable tribe.

A Farmer

---

11. Lord *Cambden's* speech.

12. "It is my opinion, that this kingdom has no right to lay A TAX upon the colonies"—"The *Americans* are the SONS,

Letter XI

My dear Countrymen,

I have several times, in the course of these letters, mentioned the late act of parliament, as being the *foundation* of future measures injurious to these colonies; and the belief of this truth I wish to prevail, because I think it necessary to our safety.

A perpetual *jealousy*, respecting liberty, is absolutely requisite in all free states. The very texture of their constitution, in *mixed* governments, demands it. For the *cautions* with which power is distributed among the several orders, *imply*, that *each* has that share which is proper for the general welfare, and therefore that any further acquisition must be pernicious. *Machiavel* employs a whole chapter in his discourses,[13] to prove that a state, to be long lived, must be frequently corrected, and reduced to its first principles. But of all states that have existed, there never was any, in which this jealousy could be more proper than in these colonies. For the government here is not only *mixed*, but *dependent*, which circumstance occasions *a peculiarity in its form*, of a very delicate nature.

Two reasons induce me to desire, that this spirit of apprehension may be always kept up among us, in its utmost vigilance. The first is this—that as the happiness of these provinces indubitably consists in their connection with *Great Britain*, any separation between them is less likely to be occasioned by civil discords, if every disgusting measure is opposed singly, and *while it is new:* For in this manner of proceeding, every such measure is most likely to be

---

not the BASTARDS of *England*"—"The distinction between LEGISLATION and TAXATION is essentially necessary to liberty"—"The COMMONS of *America*, represented in their several assemblies, have ever been in possession of this their constitutional right, of GIVING AND GRANTING THEIR OWN MONEY. They would have been SLAVES, if they had not enjoyed it." "The idea of a *virtual representation of America* in this house, is the most contemptible idea that ever entered into the head of man—It does not deserve a serious refutation." (Mr. Pitt's *Speech on the Stamp-Act*)

That great and excellent man Lord *Cambden*, maintains the same opinion. His speech in the house of peers, on the declaratory bill of the sovereignty of *Great Britain* over the colonies, has lately appeared in our papers. The following extracts so perfectly agree with, and confirm the sentiments avowed in these letters, that it is hoped the inserting them in this note will be excused.

"As the affair is of the *utmost importance*, and in its consequences may involve the *fate of kingdoms*, I took the strictest review of my arguments; I re-examined all my authorities; fully determined, if I found myself mistaken, publicly to own my mistake, and give up my opinion: But my searches have more and more convinced me, that the *British* parliament have NO RIGHT TO TAX the *Americans*"—"Nor is the doctrine new; it is as old as the constitution; it grew up with it; indeed it is its support"—"TAXATION and REPRESENTATION are inseparably united. GOD hath joined them: No *British* parliament can separate them: To endeavor to do it, is to stab our vitals."

"My position is this—I repeat it—I will maintain it to my last hour—TAXATION and REPRESENTATION are inseparable—this position is founded on the laws of nature; it is more, it is itself AN ETERNAL LAW OF NATURE; for whatever is a man's own, is absolutely his own; NO MAN HATH A RIGHT TO TAKE IT FROM HIM WITHOUT HIS CONSENT, either expressed by himself or representative; *whoever attempts to do it, attempts an injury;* WHOEVER DOES IT, COMMITS A ROBBERY; HE THROWS DOWN THE DISTINCTION BETWEEN LIBERTY AND SLAVERY." "There is not a *blade of grass*, which, when taxed, *was not taxed by the consent of the proprietor.*" "The forefathers of the *Americans* did not leave their native country, and subject themselves to every danger and distress, TO BE REDUCED TO A STATE OF SLAVERY. They did not give up their rights: They looked for protection, and *not for* CHAINS, from their mother country. By her they expected to be defended in the possession of their property, and not to be deprived of it: For should the present power continue, THERE IS NOTHING WHICH THEY CAN CALL THEIR OWN; or, to use the words of Mr. Locke, "WHAT PROPERTY HAVE THEY IN THAT, WHICH ANOTHER MAN, BY RIGHT, TAKE, WHEN HE PLEASES, TO HIMSELF?""

It is impossible to read this speech, and Mr. *Pitt's*, and not be charmed with the generous zeal for the rights of mankind that glows in every sentence. These great and good men, animated by the subject they speak upon, seem to rise above all the former glorious exertions of their abilities. A foreigner might be tempted to think they are *Americans*, asserting, with all the ardor of patriotism, and all the anxiety of apprehension, the cause of their native land—and not *Britons*, striving to stop their mistaken countrymen from oppressing others. Their reasoning is not only just—it is, as Mr. *Hume* says of the eloquence of Demosthenes, "vehement." It is disdain, anger, boldness, freedom, involved in a continual stream of argument.

13. *Machiavel's Discourses—Book* 3. *Chap.* I.

rectified. On the other hand, oppressions and dissatisfactions being permitted to accumulate—*if ever* the governed throw off the load, *they will do more.* A people does not reform with moderation. The rights of the subject therefore cannot be *too often* considered, explained or asserted: And whoever attempts to do this, shows himself, whatever may be the rash and peevish reflections of pretended wisdom, and pretended duty, a friend to *those* who injudiciously exercise their power, as well as to *them,* over whom it is so exercised. [. . .]

[T]here is no other people mentioned in history, that I recollect, who have been so constantly watchful of their liberty, and so successful in their struggles for it, as the *English.* This consideration leads me to the second reason, why I "desire that the spirit of apprehension may be always kept among us in its utmost vigilance."

The first principles of government are to be looked for in human nature. Some of the best writers have asserted, and it seems with good reason, that "government is founded on *opinion.*"[14]

Custom undoubtedly has a mighty force in producing *opinion,* and reigns in nothing more arbitrarily than in public affairs. It gradually reconciles us to objects even of dread and detestation; and I cannot but think these lines of Mr. *Pope* as applicable to vice in *politics,* as to vice in *ethics*—

Vice is a monster of so horrid mien,
As to be hated, needs but to be seen;
Yet *seen too oft,* familiar with her face,
We first *endure,* then *pity,* then *embrace.*

When an act injurious to freedom has been *once* done, and the people *bear* it, the *repetition* of it is most likely to meet with submission. For as the *mischief* of the one was found to be tolerable, they will hope that of the second will prove so too; and they will not regard the *infamy* of the last, because they are stained with that of the first.

Indeed nations, in general, are not apt to *think* until they *feel;* and therefore nations in general have lost their liberty: For as violations of the rights of the *governed,* are commonly not only *specious,* but *small* at the beginning, they spread over the multitude in such a manner, as to touch individuals but slightly.[15] Thus they are disregarded. The power or profit that arises from these violations, *centering in few persons,* is to them considerable. For this reason the *governors* having in view their particular purposes, successfully preserve a uniformity of conduct for attaining them. They regularly increase the first injuries, till at length the inattentive people are compelled to perceive the heaviness of their burdens—They begin to complain and inquire—but too late. They find their oppressors so strengthened by success, and themselves so entangled in examples of express authority on the part of their rulers, and of tacit recognition on their own part, that they are quite confounded: For millions entertain no other idea of the *legality* of power, than that it is founded on the exercise of power. They voluntarily fasten their chains, by adopting a pusillanimous *opinion,* "that there will be too much *danger* in attempting a remedy"—or another *opinion* no less fatal—"that the government has a *right* to treat them as it does." They then seek a wretched relief for their minds, by persuading themselves, that to yield their *obedience,* is to discharge their *duty.* The deplorable *poverty of spirit,* that prostrates all the dignity

14. "Opinion is of two kinds, *viz., opinion* of INTEREST, and *opinion* of RIGHT. By *opinion* of *interest,* I chiefly understand, *the sense of the public advantage which is reaped from government;* together with the persuasion, that the particular government which is established, *is equally advantageous* with any other, *that could be easily settled.*"

"*Right* is of two kinds, *right* to *power,* and *right* to *property.* What prevalence *opinion* of the first kind has over mankind, may easily be understood, by observing the attachment which all nations have to their ancient government, and even to those names which have had the sanction of antiquity. *Antiquity always begets the opinion of right*"—"It is sufficiently understood, that the *opinion of right to property,* is of the greatest moment in all matters of government." (*Hume's Essays*)

15. "The *republic* is always *attacked* with greater vigor, than it is *defended:* For the *audacious* and *profligate,* prompted by their natural enmity to it, are *easily impelled* to act by the *least nod* of their *leaders:* Whereas the HONEST, I know not why, are generally *slow* and *unwilling* to stir, and *neglecting always* the BEGINNINGS *of things,* are *never roused* to exert themselves, but by the *last necessity:* So that through IRRESOLUTION and DELAY, when they would be glad to compound at last for the QUIET, at the expense even of their HONOR, they *commonly lose them* BOTH." (CICERO'S *Orat. for* SEXTIUS)

bestowed by divine providence on our nature—*of course succeeds.*

From these reflections I conclude, that every free state should incessantly watch, and instantly take alarm on any addition being made to the power exercised over them. Innumerable instances might be produced to show, from what slight beginnings the most extensive consequences have flowed: But I shall select two only from the history of England. [. . .]

These facts are sufficient to support what I have said. It is true, that all the mischiefs apprehended by our ancestors from a *standing army* and *excise*, have not *yet happened*: But it does not follow from this, that they *will not happen*. The inside of a house may catch fire, and the most valuable apartments be ruined, before the flames burst out. The question in these cases is not, what evil *has actually attended* particular measures—but, what evil, in the nature of things, *is likely to attend* them. Certain circumstances may for some time delay effects, that *were reasonably expected*, and that *must ensue*. There was a long period, after the *Romans* had prorogued his command to *Q. Publilius Philo*, before *that example* destroyed their liberty. All our kings, from the revolution to the present reign, have been *foreigners*. Their *ministers* generally continued but a short time in authority and they themselves were *mild* and *virtuous* princes.

A bold, *ambitious* prince, possessed of *great abilities*, firmly *fixed* in his throne *by descent*, served by *ministers like* himself, and rendered either *venerable* or *terrible* by the *glory of his successes*, may execute what his predecessors did not dare to attempt. *Henry* the Fourth tottered in his seat during his whole reign. *Henry* the Fifth drew the strength of that kingdom into *France*, to carry on his wars there, and left the *commons* at home, *protesting*, "that the people were not bound to serve out of the realm."

It is true, that a strong spirit of liberty subsists at present in *Great Britain*, but what reliance is to be placed in the *temper* of a people, when the prince is possessed of an unconstitutional power, our own history can sufficiently inform us. When *Charles* the Second had strengthened himself by the return of the garrison of *Tangier*, "*England* (says *Rapin*) saw on a sudden an *amazing revolution;* saw herself *stripped of all her rights and privileges*, excepting such as the king should vouchsafe to grant her: And what is *more astonishing*, the *English* themselves *delivered up* these very rights and privileges to *Charles* the Second, which they had so *passionately*, and, if I may say it, *furiously* defended against the designs of *Charles* the First." This happened only *thirty-six* years after this last prince had been beheaded.

Some persons are of opinion, that liberty is not violated, but by such *open* acts of force; but they seem to be greatly mistaken. I could mention a period within these forty years, when almost as great a change of disposition was produced by the SECRET measures of a *long* administration, as by *Charles's* violence. Liberty, perhaps, is never exposed to so much danger, as when the people believe there is the least; for it may be subverted, and yet they not think so.

Public disgusting acts are seldom practised by the ambitious, at the beginning of their designs. Such conduct *silences* and *discourages* the weak, and the wicked, who would otherwise have been their *advocates* or *accomplices*. It is of great consequence, to allow those who, upon any account, are inclined to favor them, something specious to say in their defense. Their power may be fully established, tho' it would not be safe for them to do *whatever they please*. For there are things, which, at some times, even *slaves* will not bear. *Julius Caesar*, and *Oliver Cromwell*, did not dare to assume the title *of king*. The *Grand Seignor* dares not lay a *new tax*. The king of *France* dares not be a *protestant*. Certain popular points may be left untouched, and yet freedom be extinguished. The commonalty of Venice imagine themselves free, because they are permitted to do what they ought not. But I quit a subject, that would lead me too far from my purpose.

By the late act of parliament, taxes are to be levied upon us, for "defraying the charge of the *administration of justice*—the support of *civil government*—and the expenses of defending his Majesty's dominions in *America*."

If any man doubts what ought to be the conduct of these colonies on this occasion, I would ask him these questions.

Has not the parliament *expressly* AVOWED their INTENTION of raising money from US FOR CERTAIIN PURPOSES? Is not this scheme *popular* in *Great Britain?* Will the taxes, imposed by the late act, *answer those purposes?* If it will, must it not take an immense sum from us? If it will not, *is it to be expected*, that the parliament will not *fully execute* their INTENTION when it is *pleasing at home*, and *not opposed here?* Must not this be done by imposing NEW *taxes?* Will not every addition, thus made to our taxes, be an addition to the power of the *British* legislature, by *increasing the number of officers* employed in the collection? Will not every additional tax therefore render it *more difficult* to abrogate any of them? When a branch of revenue is once established, does it not appear to many people *invidious* and *undutiful*, to attempt to abolish it? If taxes, sufficient to *accomplish the* INTENTION of the parliament, are imposed by the parliament, *what taxes will remain* to be imposed by our assemblies? If *no material taxes remain* to be imposed by them, what must become of *them*, and the *people* they represent?

"If any person considers these things, and yet thinks our liberties are in no danger, I wonder at that person's security."[16]

One other argument is to be added, which, by itself, I hope, will be sufficient to convince the most incredulous man on this continent, that the late act of parliament is *only* designed to be a PRECEDENT, whereon the future vassalage of these colonies may be established.

Every duty thereby laid on articles of *British* manufacture, is laid on some commodity, upon the exportation of which from *Great Britain*, a *drawback* is payable. Those *drawbacks*, in most of the articles, are *exactly double* to the *duties* given by the late act. The parliament therefore might, in *half a dozen lines*, have raised MUCH MORE MONEY, only by *stopping the drawbacks* in the hands of the officers at home, on exportation to these colonies, than by this solemn imposition of taxes upon us, to be collected here. Probably, the artful contrivers of this act formed it in this manner, in order to reserve to themselves, in case of any objections being made to it, this specious pretence—"that the drawbacks are gifts to the colonies, and that the late act only lessens those gifts." But the truth is, that the drawbacks are intended for the encouragement and promotion of *British* manufactures and commerce, and are allowed on exportation to *any foreign parts*, as well as on exportation to these provinces. Besides, care has been taken to slide into the act, some articles on which there are no drawbacks. However, the *whole duties* laid by the late act on *all* the articles therein specified are *so small*, that they will not amount to *as much as* the *drawbacks* which are allowed on *part* of them only. If therefore, *the sum to be obtained by the late act*, had been the *sole object* in forming it, there would not have been any occasion for "the COMMONS of *Great Britain*, to GIVE and GRANT to his Majesty RATES and DUTIES for *raising a revenue* IN *his Majesty's dominions* in America, for making a more certain and adequate provision for defraying the charges of the administration of justice, the support of civil government, and the expense of defending the said dominions"; nor would there have been any occasion for an expensive board of commissioners,[17] and all the other new charges to which we are made liable.

Upon the whole, for my part, I regard the late act as an *experiment made of our disposition*. It is a bird sent out over the waters, to discover, whether the waves, that lately agitated this part of the world with such violence, have yet *subsided*. If *this adventurer* gets footing here, we shall quickly find it to be of the kind described by the poet.[18]

Infelix vates.

A direful foreteller of future calamities.

A Farmer

16. *Demosthenes's* 2d Philippic.

17. The expense of this board, I am informed, is between Four and Five thousand Pounds Sterling a year. The establishment of officers, for collecting the revenue in *America*, amounted before to Seven Thousand Six Hundred Pounds *per annum;* and yet, says the author of "The regulation of the colonies," "the whole remittance from *all* the taxes in the colonies, at an average of *thirty years*, has not amounted to One Thousand Nine Hundred Pounds a year, and in that sum Seven or Eight Hundred Pounds *per annum* only, have been remitted from *North America*."

The smallness of the revenue arising from the duties in *America*, demonstrates that they were intended only as REGULATIONS OF TRADE: And can any person be so blind to truth, so dull of apprehension in a matter of unspeakable importance to his country, as to imagine, that the board of commissioners lately established at such a charge, is instituted to assist in collecting One Thousand Nine Hundred Pounds a year, or the trifling duties imposed by the late act? Surely every man on this continent must perceive, that they are established for the care of a NEW SYSTEM OF REVENUE, which is but now begun.

18. "Dira caelaeno," etc. *Virgil, Aeneid* 3.

Letter XII

My dear Countrymen,

Some states have lost their liberty by *particular accidents:* But this calamity is generally owing to the *decay of virtue.* A *people* is travelling fast to destruction, when *individuals* consider *their* interests as distinct from *those of the public.* Such notions are fatal to their country, and to themselves. Yet how many are there, so *weak* and *sordid* as to *think* they perform *all the offices of life,* if they earnestly endeavor to increase their own *wealth, power,* and *credit,* without the least regard for the society, under the protection of which they live. [. . .]

Though I always reflect, with a high pleasure, on the integrity and understanding of my countrymen, which, joined with a pure and humble devotion to the great and gracious author of every blessing they enjoy, will, I hope, ensure to them, and their posterity, all temporal and eternal happiness; yet when I consider, that in every age and country there have been bad men, my heart, at this threatening period, is so full of apprehension, as not to permit me to believe, but that there may be some on this continent, *against whom you ought to be upon your guard—*

Our *vigilance* and our *union* are *success* and *safety.* Our *negligence* and our *division* are *distress* and *death.* They are *worse*—They are *shame* and *slavery.* Let us equally shun the benumbing stillness of *overweening sloth,* and the feverish activity of that *ill informed zeal,* which busies itself in maintaining *little, mean* and *narrow* opinions. Let us, with a truly wise *generosity* and *charity*, banish and discourage all *illiberal distinctions,* which may arise from differences in *situation,* forms of *government,* or modes of *religion.* Let us consider ourselves as MEN—FREEMEN—CHRISTIAN FREEMEN—*separated from the rest of the world, and firmly bound together* by the *same rights, interests* and *dangers.* Let *these* keep our attention inflexibly fixed on the GREAT OBJECTS, which we must CONTINUALLY REGARD, in order to *preserve those rights, to promote those interests,* and to *avert those dangers.*

Let these *truths* be indelibly impressed on our minds—*that* we *cannot be* HAPPY, *without being* FREE—that we cannot be free, *without being secure in our property*—that *we* cannot be secure in our property, *if, without our consent, others may, as by right, take it away*—that *taxes imposed on us by parliament,* do thus take it away—that *duties laid for the sole purpose of raising money,* are taxes—that *attempts* to lay such duties *should be instantly and firmly opposed*—that this opposition can never be effectual, *unless it is the united effort of these provinces*—that therefore BENEVOLENCE *of temper towards each other,* and UNANIMITY *of counsels,* are essential to the welfare of the whole—and lastly, that for this reason, every man among us, who in any manner would encourage either *dissension, dissidence,* or *indifference,* between these colonies, is an enemy to *himself,* and *to his country.*

The belief of these truths, I verily think, my countrymen, is indispensably necessary to your happiness. I beseech you, therefore, "teach them diligently unto your children, and talk of them when you sit in your houses, and when you walk by the way, and when you lie down, and when you rise up."[19]

What have these colonies to *ask,* while they continue free? Or what have they to *dread,* but insidious attempts to subvert their freedom? *Their prosperity* does not depend on *ministerial favors doled out* to *particular* provinces. *They* form *one* political body, of which *each colony is a member. Their happiness* is founded on *their constitution;* and is to be promoted, by preserving that constitution in unabated vigor, *throughout every part.* A spot, a speck of decay, however small the limb on which it appears, and however remote it may seem from the vitals, should be alarming. We have *all the rights* requisite for our prosperity. The legal authority of *Great Britain* may indeed lay hard restrictions upon us; but, like the spear of *Telephus,* it will cure as well as wound. Her unkindness will instruct and compel us, after some time, to discover, in our *industry* and *frugality,* surprising remedies—*if our rights continue unviolated:* For as long as the *products* of our *labor,* and the *rewards* of our *care, can properly* be called *our own,* so long it will be worth our while to be *industrious* and *frugal.* But if when we plow—sow—reap—gather—and thresh—we find, that we plow—sow—reap—gather—and thresh *for others,* whose PLEASURE is to

---

19. Deuteronomy 6:7.

be the SOLE LIMITATION *how much* they shall *take,* and *how much* they shall *leave,* WHY should we repeat the unprofitable toil? *Horses* and *oxen* are content with *that portion of the fruits of their work,* which their *owners* assign them, in order to keep them strong enough to raise successive crops; but even *these beasts* will not submit to draw for their *masters,* until they are *subdued* by *whips* and *goads.*

Let us take care of our *rights,* and we *therein* take care of *our prosperity.* "SLAVERY IS EVER PRECEDED BY SLEEP."[20]

[W]hatever kind of *minister* he is, that attempts to innovate a *single* iota in the privileges of these colonies, him I hope you will *undauntedly oppose;* and that you will never suffer yourselves to be either *cheated or frightened* into any *unworthy obsequiousness.* On such emergencies you may surely, without presumption, believe, that ALMIGHTY GOD himself will look down upon your righteous contest with gracious approbation. You will be a *"band of brothers,"* cemented by the dearest ties—and strengthened with inconceivable supplies of force and constancy, by that sympathetic ardor, which animates good men, confederated in a good cause. Your *honor* and *welfare* will be, as they now are, most intimately concerned; and besides—*you are assigned by divine providence,* in the appointed order of things, the *protectors of unborn ages,* whose *fate* depends upon your *virtue.* Whether *they* shall arise the *generous* and *indisputable heirs* of the noblest patrimonies, or the *dastardly and hereditary drudges* of imperious task-masters, YOU MUST DETERMINE.

To discharge this double duty to *yourselves,* and to your *posterity,* you have nothing to do, but to call forth into use the *good sense* and *spirit* of which you are possessed. You have nothing to do, but to conduct your affairs *peaceably—prudently—firmly—jointly.* By *these means* you will support the character of *freemen,* without losing that of *faithful subjects*—a good character in any government—one of the best under a *British* government. You will *prove,* that *Americans* have that true *magnanimity* of soul, that can resent injuries, without falling into rage; and that tho' your devotion to *Great Britain* is the most affectionate, yet you can make PROPER DISTINCTIONS, and know what you owe *to yourselves,* as well as *to her*—You will, at the same time that you advance your *interests,* advance your *reputation*—You will convince the world of the *justice of your demands,* and the *purity of your intentions.* While all mankind must, with unceasing applauses, confess, that YOU indeed DESERVE liberty, who so *well understand* it, so *passionately love* it, so *temperately enjoy* it, and so *wisely, bravely,* and *virtuously assert, maintain,* and *defend* it.

Certe ego libertatem, quae mihi a parente meo tradita est, experiar:
Verum id frustra an ob rem faciam, in vestra manu situm est, quirites.

For my part, I am resolved to contend for the liberty delivered down to me by my ancestors, but whether I shall do it effectually or not, depends on you, my countrymen. "How littlesoever one is able to write, yet when the liberties of one's country are threatened, it is still more difficult to be silent."

A *Farmer*

Is there not the strongest probability, that if the universal sense of these colonies is immediately expressed by RESOLVES of the assemblies, in support of their rights, by INSTRUCTIONS to their agents on the subject, and by PETITIONS to the crown and parliament for redress, these measures will have the same success now, that they had in the time of the *STAMP ACT.*

20. *Montesquieu's* Spirit of Laws, Book 14, Chap. 13.

Thomas Hutchinson

A Dialogue between an American and a European Englishman (1768)

European: America is in a very different state from what it was when I saw you last in England.

American: I am sensible of it, and the worst circumstance is that there seems to be no prospect of recovering our former state.

European: Whose fault is that?

American: You will say it is our fault, we think it is yours. You assumed and exercised an authority over us which we thought you had no right to do. We asserted our rights and sent our humble remonstrances, but you would not receive them. We refused to submit to your act, obliged the officers you had appointed to carry it into execution to resign their trusts; we threatened to break off all commerce with you and to live upon our own produce and manufactures; you were alarmed and thought it prudent to repeal the act which was so grievous to us. It seems some of our patriots unwarily complained of the grievance as being an internal tax and therefore the more unconstitutional. You took the advantage of this distinction and passed another act imposing what you call external taxes. We are now convinced that our rights are equally affected by the one and the other. We are Englishmen, and the property of Englishmen is not to be taken from them without their consent. We never gave our consent to these acts neither in person nor by our representatives. In short, if the Parliament [have][1] this authority over us, we are no better than slaves.

European: Hold, my friend, be calm. This dispute, like all other party disputes in affairs of government <as well as religion>, has been carried on with great zeal and warmth of temper. This temper must subside before there can be any room to hope for an accommodation.

You complained first of internal taxes, now of external. Give me leave to ask you whether you think that the Parliament may exercise any authority whatsoever over the colonies without an abridgment of their natural rights.

American: The colonists have always allowed that it is no violation of their rights to have such regulations made in their trade as shall prevent foreign nations receiving benefit from them to the prejudice of Great Britain.[2]

European: Consider a little before you make this concession. Do not you rather mean that you are willing to submit to regulations in your trade, provided you may be exempt from all obligation to submit to other acts of Parliament? Is not every law a restraint upon your natural liberty, and is it not as much a part of the English constitution to be governed by laws in general made by ourselves or our representatives as to be taxed by ourselves or our representatives?

American: Admit that all legislation in which we have not a share is an abridgment of our rights, yet taxation is more peculiarly so. There is an absurdity in the very form of it. We the Commons of Great Britain give [. . .] the money of the people of America, which does not belong to us.

European: Let this exemption from taxes be your right in a more eminent degree. Still, the other, viz., a general exemption from all [laws] <in which you

---

1. [Throughout this selection, some words appear in square brackets (as shown here) or angled brackets (in the next paragraph). All text enclosed in angled brackets represents material added or deleted by Hutchinson in his revisions of this text: words that appear in italic type were deleted, and those in regular type were added. Words enclosed in square brackets were added by a twentieth-century editor when the selection was first published.]

2. Dulany.

have no voice you will challenge> as your right also in a less degree. Now what security have we that as soon as you are relieved from external taxes you will not alter your mind and not incline any longer to submit to regulations of your trade? If you deal ingenuously you must acknowledge that you intend a perfect independence upon the Parliament of Great Britain.

AMERICAN: We admit "the authority of Parliament in all cases which can consist with the fundamental rights of nature and the constitution.."[3] [. . .]

EUROPEAN: We must come closer to the point. What sort of connection do you imagine there is between Great Britain and her colonies? Are you and we parts of one and the same empire or are we not?

AMERICAN: We are certainly under one and the same sovereign.

EUROPEAN: So are Great Britain and Hanover. But how happens it that we are under the same sovereign?

AMERICAN: Before our ancestors left England they acknowledged the King of England for their sovereign; they came away with his permission and under his protection, and to him they <promised and we still> owe allegiance.

EUROPEAN: Your ancestors <while they were in England> acknowledged the Parliament to be the supreme legislative power of the realm as well as the King to be the supreme executive power. How came the executive power to continue and not the legislative?

AMERICAN: The King might retain the executive power and also his share in the legislative <in each colony> without any abridgment of our <ancestors'> rights as Englishmen; the Parliament could not retain their legislative power without depriving <them> of those rights, for after their removal they could no longer be represented, and their sovereign, sensible of this, by charter or commissions made provision in every colony for legislatures within themselves.

EUROPEAN: Your ancestors, you allow, until their embarkation were subject to Parliamentary authority, and I am willing further to allow that by removing from one part of the empire where they always had been represented in Parliament to another part where they could not be represented, they must be abridged of some of the rights of Englishmen if Parliament still exercised its authority, but you are to remember that this was the voluntary act of your ancestors for their own benefit. They were at full liberty either to stay and enjoy this privilege or to go and be deprived of it, but the Parliament did nothing which your ancestors could urge as a relinquishing of any part of their right, and if the King intended to grant an independent legislative authority in each colony, which I shall convince you by and by he did not, such grant would have been absolutely void. Which, under these circumstances, is more reasonable: that you should lose some part of the rights which you might have enjoyed if you would have remained, or that Parliament should lose all the authority it had over you?

AMERICAN: We do not rest altogether upon our rights as Englishmen. We go farther and challenge the rights of nature, for which we have a charter from the great author of our beings and which the mere accident of being born under a government of one form or another cannot deprive us of, not that I <*think*> that we cannot support our claim upon the mere rights of Englishmen and the principles of the English constitution. Therefore I will first consider our rights as Englishmen. [. . .] <In all the monarchical governments in Europe the disposal of new discovered countries hath been left to the prince. This seems to have been an universal law of which it may no more be necessary to show the rise than of many other laws which are acquiesced in. By virtue thereof the Kings of England and Scotland have disposed of the plantations as having been discovered for their use by their subjects, and this law for two centuries has been tacitly acknowledged, and I have no doubt that> both James and Charles the First supposed they had a right to the part of America which had been discovered under commissions from preceding princes without any control from Parliament. James we know made a grant of Arcady to his Scotch subjects and Sir William Alexander began a settlement there about the year 1620. If the settlement had gone on, must the colony have been bound by acts of the Parliament of England? No, the Parliament would have given themselves no more concern about them than about the French in Canada. We see that Charles the First soon after gave this country of

3. Massch [*torn*] to the King.

Arcady to the French. He might as well have given Massachusetts Bay which joins to it, the French having the same claim to both, and if he had done it there is no doubt the English Parliament would have been as silent in the last case as they were in the first. It is not, therefore, the country or territory where we are settled which give the Parliament authority over us, it must be because <our ancestors, whilst in England, were> subjects to this authority; and we their posterity, let us be born in any part of the globe whatsoever, <you will pretend> must always remain so. Subjects we are and ever shall be to the King of England. This was the contract our ancestors made for themselves and their posterity, from him they expected protection, to him they owed allegiance, but no such contract was made expressly or by implication with the Parliament. And the conduct of Parliament for many years after the colonies were planted shows that they had no apprehensions of such an authority. New Plymouth began in 1620, Barbados and the Leeward Islands in 1625, Massachusetts in 1628, and several other colonies soon after; but the first act of Parliament that is in force respecting the trade of the colonies was made in 1660. As soon as the nation began to taste the sweets of commerce with the colonies, the Parliament was for engrossing the whole. The colonies were great sufferers by this restraint. The regulations, however, were submitted [to] and by length of time they are so established as [to b]ecome part of our constitution, but [we] have never been required to submit to acts imposing taxes or duties for the purposes of revenue until within these few years, and to such acts I think neither we nor our posterity ever shall submit, and if they are carried into execution it must be by means of the superiority of the strength of the nation to that of the colonies.

EUROPEAN: I am glad to find you will allow acts for regulating your trade by force of long usage are become part of your constitution. This is gaining something, <if we can but fix you there.> But I am not content with this. I must examine the principles you rely upon and the historical facts urged in your favour. There is no inferring from the acts of such princes as James or Charles what was the constitution of England. There was no <new> constitution settled at the [*Glorious*] Revolution. The Bill of Rights was declaratory. In former reigns there had been a deviation. Whatever King James might imagine, I cannot be convinced that a grant of Nova Scotia made by him under the Great Seal of Scotland was worth one farthing, but a grant from the King of Spain would have been every whit as good, nor am I sure that the cession of Acadia to the French, if it had not been a contested country of which the French had very early possession, would have been acquiesced in. [. . .] At present we are arguing from the principles of the English constitution. Now allegiance (in an English subject) is not local but perpetual. The contract you pretend your ancestors made with their prince can do you neither good nor harm. You would have been just as much held to your allegiance without it as with it, and as far as you owe allegiance to the King so far you owe it to the King in Parliament, your posterity within the English dominions will always owe the same allegiance <and I know not how the King could discharge them from it>. [. . .]

EUROPEAN: It seems enough for my purpose to show that your ancestors <*acknowledged the right of England to*> the territory of which they took possession <as a part of the dominions of the crown of England>. Why else did they seek for grants from the crown before they left England? Why did they not upon their arrival become subjects to the Indian princes? Instead of that, they took a formal possession for and in behalf of the government of England by virtue of charters and commissions from the crown, and this possession has been continued to this day, and the whole territory so possessed has been <de facto> for more than a century the dominions of England, and I know of no one circumstance that can give a claim to an inhabitant of those dominions to an exemption from the supreme authority any more than if their ancestors had remained in England and you their posterity had been born there. Has not there been a continual passing and repassing ever since just the same as from London to Wales and Wales to London? Have not many of you, born in America, been Members of Parliament in England, and were not many of your present members of the legislatures in the colonies born in England? You and we have always been considered as parts of the same government. <If you refuse your subjection to the authority of England, what right have you to protection from England? If you consider America only

under the same sovereign with England, all who are born in America are aliens. By what right then from time to time have you taken estates in England by descent when by the laws of England you are aliens and incapable of inheriting?>

AMERICAN: The Parliament, it is certain, have not exercised their legislative authority over us in the same manner as they have done over England, and except in a few instances you will not pretend yourself that their acts have any respect to us.

EUROPEAN: I will consider that presently, but I must first show you that you are erroneous in your facts relative to the first settlement of the colonies and the attention of Parliament upon that occasion. [. . .] In 1642 we find the House of Commons passed a memorable vote in favour of the then most flourishing colony, the Massachusetts Bay, exempting the inhabitants from taxes and duties as well in the colony as in England. Now I think a power of exemption must imply a power of imposition, and besides, this very colony thanked the House of Commons for this favour granted them—a strong instance of the early sense the <Parliament and> colonies had of the connection which continued between them. You will find in Scobell's Statutes the Parliament in the years 1650 and 1656 exercising its authority over the trade of the colonies. [. . .] As soon as the nation was restored to its constitutional form of government, acts of Parliament were passed in the 12–14–15–22 and 23rd and 25th of King Charles the 2d asserting the Parliamentary right over the colonies. If any of the colonies disobeyed these acts they never denied the authority which made them. [. . .] Upon the Revolution even in the Convention a bill passed the House of Commons for restoring plantation charters which had been surrendered, which bill was earnestly solicited by the agents of one of the colonies. And has not the Parliament ever since been frequently exercising its authority by general regulations or by acts respecting particular colonies—nay, private acts, which respect individuals or particular companies? In short, when you can make the authority of Parliament serve for your protection or benefit in any respect, you have been ready to own and even seek it; when any burden is to be laid upon you, however equitable, you shun it and refuse submission to it. It is true indeed that the Parliament in scarce any instance has thought fit to lay any taxes upon the colonies. Perhaps their infant state and inability to do anything more than support themselves might be the reason; but this reason now ceases. Indulgence showed in delaying to exercise the right ought not to be urged against the right itself.

Having thus shown that the Parliament cannot be said to have <given up> their authority over the colonies by neglecting the exercise of it, I will endeavour to show why they have not been in the constant use and exercise of it in the same manner they have over subjects in England. The settlement of the colonies was not made in consequence of any preconcerted plan. It seems to be owing to mere chance or accident rather than design. After many attempts for more than 50 years by particular undertakers to make a settlement in Virginia there seems to have been no prospect of success when all at once the world was surprised with the great and populous colonies of New England which in 8 or 10 years from their beginning were become so considerable as to leave no room to doubt of their permanence. Their charter from the crown being, as I before observed, intended only for a corporation in England like other corporations, they had the power granted of making bylaws which were not to be repugnant to the laws of the realm. The laws of the realm were the laws for this corporation as much as for any other corporation in England, but where any special rules or laws were necessary for the carrying on their particular affairs, such rules to bind their own members, they had power to establish. When the principal settlers removed, they carried their charter with them, set up that corporation in America which was designed to remain in England, made a body of laws for their government, certainly very different from the laws of England. The <*full*> force of the expression *not repugnant to the laws of England* <in a charter for a corporation without the realm must be as much as this, viz.,> that no laws of the corporation can be of any validity which are contrary to the laws of England made immediately to respect such corporation. This mode of expression was observed in the charters and commissions to the colonies which sprang from or were settled after this first colony in New England. [. . .] Now if the colonies had been settled upon a projected plan I think the laws of England would have continued the general rule of law for all the colonies, and all acts of

Parliament subsequent to the settlement would have been understood to extend to the whole dominions unless from the nature or subject matter of them or an express exception in them they could not be understood to have this general extent. The several colonies by their legislatures might have been empowered to make local laws or orders not inconsistent with the general rule of law and always subject to the supreme legislative authority. The administration of justice could not have been the same as in England but perhaps there might have been no more material difference than between the courts for Wales and those for the rest of England. I fancy if you had been settled upon this plan, besides avoiding the great uncertainty which most colonies are now under, sometimes adopting the law of England and sometimes not in similar cases we should have had no dispute at this day whether the authority of Parliament <extended to> America or not. [. . .]

AMERICAN: I cannot think that the people under any government can be obliged to submit to what is in its nature unjust. <Let us re-assume the argument from which we digressed.> All government is or ought to have been instituted for the <*good*> <sake> of the people. There are certain natural rights which as men we are entitled to and which we can never be supposed to give up to any authority whatsoever. There are certain fundamental principles of the English constitution, and to any act contrary to those fundamentals the people are not obliged to submit. I think every man has a natural right to dispose of his own property. It is a fundamental of the English constitution, a part of Magna Charta, that all supplies be made by the Commons, in other words by the people. The very term ["]give and grant["] must intend that it comes from the owner. These fundamentals set bounds to Parliamentary power, and the great oracle of the English law, Lord Coke, says in his Reports that acts made against the fundamental principles of the constitution are void. If void, certainly there is no obligation to submit to them. Nay, by the constitution it may well be questioned whether the Parliament of England can be considered as the Parliament for the colonies. We know the sense the Parliament *itself* has had of itself. In a statute of 1 of King James the First a Parliament is said to be when all the whole body of the realm and every particular member thereof either in person or by representation upon their own free election are by the laws of the realm deemed to be personally present in Parliament. You have not given me a sufficient answer upon these points, but if you had been able to do it I have a farther argument. Admitting the power, which I never shall do, yet it has not been thought equitable to exercise it for more than a century past, and there is no more pretence from equity now than there has been in any former time.

EUROPEAN: I am willing to consider every point as fully as you please and we will now take them in the order you have advanced them. I agree with you that government is to be considered as instituted for the sake of the people, but that every individual has a right to judge when the acts of government are just and unjust and to submit or not submit accordingly I can't so readily concede. Only think a little and you must be convinced that this is a doctrine repugnant to <*the very idea of*> government. I have no idea but this of the difference between a state of nature and a state of government. In a state of I nature am in no case subject to the controul of any other person except to redress or repel a wrong done or intended to be done him. <By entering into> [a] state of government I subject myself to a power constituted over a society of which I become a member. It is immaterial in whom this power is lodged. Such power must be lodged somewhere or there is no government. You say, such submission must be intended only in matters that are just. I say, this is no submission at all, for if every man is at liberty to judge what is just and what is unjust and submit or not submit accordingly, he is free, as far as he pleases, from that power to which he professes himself to be a subject, which is a contradiction in terms. Just the same may be said of those natural rights which you say every man retains notwithstanding his being in a state of government. If I am at liberty to judge what is my natural right, which I have thus reserved, and what not, I may exempt myself from every act of government, for every act lays me under some restraint which I have a natural right to be free from. But pray tell me <which of our> natural rights in a state of government must be supposed to be reserved?

AMERICAN: <To instance in one of many, because most to our purpose,> I retain my natural right of disposing of my property either by my own consent or by my representative.

European: You are not the first American who has confounded the general principles of government with the principles of the particular constitution of the English government, which we shall consider presently. But what is there which makes it more reasonable in the nature of the thing for you to retain a right of disposing of your property than of your liberty? Certainly the latter <*is*> <may be> more valuable to you than the former. To answer the ends of government it may be more necessary that the former should be at the disposal of the supreme authority than the latter, and in many cases which may happen, it is equally necessary that both should be so.

American: A line must be drawn somewhere <both as to liberty and property.> It may be difficult perhaps to determine by any general rules where the line shall be. It may depend upon particular cases, but it can never be supposed that a man who enters into a state of government merely for his own benefit may have all his property taken from him and he himself be bought and sold at the will and pleasure of the supreme authority. He certainly had better have remained in his natural state. This doctrine of Passive Obedience and Non-resistance never had any advocates among us <Americans>.

European: The question now is not which is best, a state of nature or a state of government and civil society. Indeed nothing can make me doubt which is best. Such disorders and confusions as of late have prevailed not in the colonies only but in the <kingdom> from whence they sprang <perhaps are necessary to convince men of the deplorable state they would be in without government and to reconcile them to the restraint of their natural liberties>. We are considering what degree of submission is due from persons who have brought themselves into a state of government. Now if individuals or any particular parts of a government may resist whensoever they shall apprehend themselves aggrieved, instead of order, <peace,> and a state of general security—the great ends of government—we may well expect tumults, wars, and a state of general danger. You have been taught by some of your writers to use the terms Passive Obedience and Non-resistance, which are deservedly odious as they were applied by the sycophants of the court in the last century when kings were said to be *jure divino,* and let their government be ever so arbitrary and tyrannical and the whole body of the people be ever so much dissatisfied, no redress was to be had, their commands were to be obeyed or the penalty of the breach of them patiently submitted to.

American: I am willing to carry my principles of submission as far as the great Mr. Locke did his <and no farther. He says,> "the supreme power cannot take from any man part of his property without his own consent; for the preservation of property being the end of government and that for which men enter into society, it necessarily supposes and requires that the people should have property without which they must be supposed to lose that by entering into society which was the end for which they entered into it, too gross an absurdity for any man to own."[4] He afterwards goes on, "It is true, governments cannot be supported without great charge and it is fit everyone who enjoys his share of the protection should pay out of his estate his proportion for the maintainance of it. But still, it must be with his own consent, i.e., the consent of the majority, giving it either by themselves or their representatives chosen by them. For if anyone shall claim a power to lay and levy taxes upon the people by his own authority and without such consent of the people, he thereby invades the fundamental law of property and subverts the end of government. For what property have I in that which another may by right take when he pleases to himself?"[5]

European: I reverence Mr. Locke as much as you can. I think I have advanced nothing which is not supported by his authority. You will find him saying in another place that "every man, by consenting with others to make one body politic under one government, puts himself under an obligation to every one of that society to submit to the determination of the majority and to be concluded by it, or else the original compact whereby he with others incorporated into one society would signify nothing and be no compact if he be left free and under no other ties than he was [in] before in the state of nature. For what appearance would there be of any compact? What new engagement if he were no further tied by any decrees of the society than he himself thought fit

4. B 2d, Sect. 138.
5. B 2, Sect. 140.

and did actually consent to? This would be still as great a liberty as he himself had before his compact, or any one else in the state of nature hath who may submit himself and consent to any acts of it if he thinks fit."[6] He adds, "Whosoever out of a state of nature unites into a community must be understood to give up all the power necessary to the ends for which they unite into society to the majority of the community, unless they expressly agreed in any number greater than the majority."[7] These ends he tells us are the preservation of their lives, liberties, and estates which he calls by the general name property[8] <"No man *in civil society* can be exempted from the laws of it, for if any man may do what he thinks fit and there be no appeal on earth for redress or security against any harm he shall do, I ask whether he be not perfectly still in the state of nature and so can be no part or member of *that civil society*, unless anyone will say the state of nature and civil society are one and the same thing."[9]>

When I consider these other parts of Mr. Locke's treatise I never can believe that in those which you refer to he <could intend> that it <is> a principle in government that any individual or any number of individuals short of the majority may refuse submission to every act of government which he or they determine in their own minds abridge them of more of their natural rights than the ends for which such government was instituted make necessary. If individuals have good right to refuse submission I think upon the same reason the executive and judiciary powers of such government ought to refuse to cause any laws to be executed against a subject who thinks them unnecessary to such ends, the absurdity of which doctrine I fancy you readily conceive of.

AMERICAN: <I will not allow> that courts and judges in any government are to observe laws that are contrary to the <*fundamentals of the constitution*> ends for which such government was instituted.

EUROPEAN: If I was a judge I should not think myself at liberty to determine whether an act of Parliament is or is not expedient for the community; it's enough for me that the act is part of the law which I have sworn I will make the rule of my judgment, and although I may be of opinion that such act <will> affect the property of particular subjects unequally, yet I consider that the property of these subjects from the very nature of government is at the disposal of the supreme authority for the good of the whole not in such easy and just proportions only as those subjects themselves shall judge necessary to promote his good but as the supreme authority shall judge it so. <Besides, if I should agree with you, what will you get by it? If you once allow courts and juries to observe the laws or not according to their discretion, instead of being governed by known, established laws you are subjected to an arbitrary government by making the legislative and executive powers one and the same.> If you will suppose an act of Parliament may require a judge to do anything in its nature immoral or contrary to his duty to the supreme legislator of the world, in this case I would quit my post and subject myself to penalty rather than obey it. But if you had not interrupted me, I should have further observed to you that if you take the whole of Mr. Locke's work together you will find he intends no more by the passage you think so favorable to your cause than this, viz., that when the <*legislative and executive*> powers <of government> shall cease to make the ends for which government is instituted the rule of government, the people are under no moral obligation to continue subject to them but may revolt and remove their governors or mold themselves into any other form of government they think proper.

AMERICAN: If the body of the people are under no moral obligation to continue subject, I do not see why individuals or any lesser part of the people should be obliged from a moral consideration.

EUROPEAN: Admitting what you say, yet it's enough for my purpose that the judiciary and executive powers of any government are obliged to carry the laws of it <which are not in their nature immoral> into execution as long as it continues to exist.

AMERICAN: As a judge, you say yourself you would do nothing immoral but would sooner quit your post or subject yourself to any penalty. To carry acts of Parliament into execution which are contrary to natural justice is doing a thing immoral.

EUROPEAN: <You may suppose such a law that a judge ought to quit his post rather than carry it into

6. B 2, Ch, 8. Sect. 97.
7. Sect. 99.
8. Sect. 123.
9. B 2, C 7, Sect. 94.

execution, but> a thing may be immoral or unjust under some circumstances, as particularly in a state of nature, and under other circumstances, as in a state of government, may be moral and just. By your submission to government, as I have already observed, you have given up your property to the disposal of the supreme authority which otherwise would have remained to your disposal, and a judge or court only holds you to your own agreement. You are not the only British subjects who <are obliged to submit> to acts of Parliament which they conceive not agreeable to natural justice. Do not you imagine that the Roman Catholics think it unequal for them to pay taxes double to what Protestants of the same estates pay?

American: I hope you do not compare us to Roman Catholics. They have no reason to complain. The principles of their religion are repugnant to government. They hold that no faith is to be kept with heretics. They are such dangerous subjects that anything short of banishment is a favour shown them.

European: But few Roman Catholics at this day will own what you affirm to be a principle of their religion. Protestants will force that and many other tenets as absurd upon them let them disclaim them as much as they will. However, for argument sake, I will admit they hold this principle. <If they do they will say it is a matter of conscience and it is contrary to justice to mulct a man for following the dictates of conscience. A Roman Catholic cannot sit in Parliament nor can he vote for anyone to represent him. Upon your principles he ought not to be taxed at all, but he is taxed double to other subjects of the same estates. The supreme authority acknowledge that it is a principle in the constitution that no man's property shall be taken from him without his consent in person or by his representative, but they say there is a higher principle than this—*Salus Populi*, the great end of all government—that it is incompatible with this principle that Roman Catholics should share in the government of a Protestant nation, but that it is very agreeable to it and necessary to the ends of government that they should be taxed and double taxed to the support of the nation. But consider to what length this principle will carry you. Why may you not urge> that a war in which the state is engaged is contrary to natural justice and refuse to pay any taxes to support it as that you are taxed by a power where you are not represented and refused to pay it on that account? The Quakers say that all war is unlawful and scruple paying to the support of it, but your legislatures in the colonies find a way to compel them by distressing, imprisoning, etc. Now I cannot see how you can justify exercising your authority to compel them to an act which they think contrary to natural justice and at the same time urge an exemption from acts of a power you acknowledge to be the supreme authority over you because such acts are contrary to natural justice. You justify yourselves by saying the Quakers are people under your authority and your legislatures have a right to judge when to apply their property to answer the great end of government and when not. [. . .]

American: Notwithstanding all you have said, I can easily conceive that there may be certain fundamental principles of government and that the people of which such government is constituted are freed from all obligation to subjection when the supreme authority departs from these fundamentals, and as we know of no government which has constituted an umpire or judge to determine when these principles are departed from, every man's own conscience must be the judge and he must follow the evidence of truth in his own mind and submit or not submit accordingly. He would not have been obliged to submit if such a constitution had not been formed. When the condition upon which he submitted is not performed he returns to the rights of his original state of nature and all obligation to submit ceases.

European: Such a compact as you suppose would be a mere rope of sand. I challenge you to give me an instance of any one government from the creation of the world established upon such fundamentals which have continued for a long series of time without alteration. On the other hand, look into the history of any government you please and take it for granted that it was first formed by the mutual compact of every individual, you will find that in a course of years frequent material alterations have been made in fundamental points not by subsequent new agreements made by each individual but by acts of the supreme authority of such governments, and such alterations become to all intents and purposes parts of the constitution. After all you have said in defence of your tenet, it appears to me absurd to the greatest degree to suppose a government consisting of individuals each of whom may plead an exemption from all the laws of such government which appears [*sic*] to him to be contrary to his natural rights or to natural justice, and that such plea ought to prevail with the judiciary and executive powers.

AMERICAN: All that you have said is far from convincing me that to take my property from me without my consent in person or by my representative is not contrary to natural justice, and although you seem to suppose all that is said of original contracts is merely ideal, yet it will amount to the same thing if it be contrary to the ends for which governments must have been instituted <if we could trace them back to their original formation> and if instead of having property secured it must be rendered more precarious than in a state of nature. Upon this natural principle the English constitution was first formed or, I care not which, from time immemorial has been established; from thence Englishmen derive a darling maxim that no charges shall be levied of the people but by authority of Parliament, not because the Parliament is the supreme authority of the English government but because in the supreme authority so constituted every man is or ought to be, not virtually, as you express yourselves without any meaning, but actually represented.

EUROPEAN: If you Americans have not preserved all the rights of Englishmen you certainly retain one of their distinguishing qualities. You are obstinately tenacious of what you have once, though upon mistaken grounds, conceived to be your rights. However, since we have begun I am willing to go through, and will now proceed to examine your claim upon the principles of the English constitution. You say there are certain fundamentals in the English constitution and to an act contrary to them the subject is not held to submit. I readily admit it to be the happiness of the English constitution that there are certain fundamental principles, plain and intelligible, which in all judicatories are to be considered as the rule for construing law in all cases where there is room for doubt or uncertainty, but I should think it a great misfortune if when, in a long course of time and a total change of circumstances, the reason for establishing these principles ceased there should be no power subsisting to alter or repeal even these fundamentals. I will put you in mind of the very first in the list of fundamentals: *Ecclesia Anglicana libera sit et habeat omnia jura sua integra*, or in English, all ecclesiastical persons shall enjoy all their lawful jurisdictions inviolate. You are alarmed with a proposal of appointing a single bishop for America. What a deplorable condition would you be in if the Church should be restored to the same state it was in when Magna Charta was enacted or established or at any time between that and the reformation? How many other <fundamental> parts of Magna Charta are repealed by acts of Parliament or by changes in the state of the nation rendered null and altogether impossible to be executed. Indeed, I know of no principle in the English constitution more fundamental and which is more certain always to remain than this, viz., that no act can be made or passed in any Parliament which it shall not be in the power of a subsequent Parliament to alter and repeal. You will find this in the same author, Lord Coke, whom you cite to show that acts contrary to fundamentals are void. I am sensible that <*this*> doctrine is received in all parts of the colonies, and in some of your writers we find such positions as these: no act of Parliament can deprive us of the liberties of men, citizens, and British subjects; the supreme power cannot take from any man any part of his property without his consent in person or by representation. <*The Parliament is to govern by stated laws.*> It seems to have been the grand point which some of these writers have had in view to captivate their readers with big sounding words. Examine these positions. Does not every change from a state of nature into government more or less deprive us of the rights we enjoyed as men? In Europe, governments in general breathe more of the spirit of liberty. In Asia the climate or some other cause inclines to despotism. No prince in Asia has a right to deprive me of my natural liberty by compelling me to become his subject, but if for the sake of his protection I become or continue his subject, I have as much submitted my <natural> rights to his government there although I have parted with more of them as I should have done in Europe in what we call free governments. What this writer means by the rights of citizens is very uncertain seeing you will scarce find any two cities where they are just the same, and the rights of British subjects vary in every age and perhaps every session of Parliament. And as to the second position, why should my property be exempt from the supreme power more than any other of my natural rights?

AMERICAN: Before you proceed any farther I desire you to recollect that you are now to show that these are not the principles of the English constitution but you are going back to show that they have not their foundation in nature.

EUROPEAN: Your writers have so often blended them together or in their arguments run from one to the other that I hope it will be some excuse to continue myself as you would have me. I have no idea of any government's being unalterable. The power which established it may dissolve it. The King, nobles, and people of Britain we will suppose to have settled certain fundamental principles of government. You may suppose that the King has acquired by such settlement a prerogative which the other two branches may not deprive him of, and the nobles and people may acquire respective rights as unalterable, but if King, nobles, and people agree to make an alteration in what were before fundamentals, who is there to complain?

AMERICAN: Not the King nor the nobles because it is their own act, but the people may justly complain that their representatives have given up what they had no right to do, nay though such a departure from fundamental principles should not be disapproved by the major part of the people, yet the minor part who did disapprove it ought not to be held by it. No act contrary to these fundamentals should be binding because the representative has assumed a power which was never delegated to it.

EUROPEAN: You should consider how these fundamentals were settled at first. We will suppose that in the days of King John, the first Henrys, or Edwards the fundamental principles of government were settled; or go back if you will to any time since Julius Caesar landed and we have any knowledge of Britain: have the people ever assembled together in one body so as that we may suppose these fundamentals to have been settled by the majority of individuals? If not, as no doubt you will allow, it must have been done by a less number either elected to represent the whole or assuming such representation without any election. Why has not the representative as good right at this day to alter fundamentals as it had at that day to establish them? The same power may just as well alter them and in fact from time to time have been making continual alterations ever since we have any knowledge of the history of the constitution.

AMERICAN: I never supposed when I gave my voice for my representative in our provincial assembly that I gave him an unlimited power. We have a known constitution, and if the representative of the people gives up the rights they are entitled to by that constitution he has assumed a power never delegated to him, and the act is void.

<Or if> we return to Great Britain. I have often read and heard that when the Septennial Act was under consideration the opposers of the bill argued that it was unconstitutional that the people when they chose their representatives chose them for three years only, that continuing themselves four years longer was assuming a power which was not delegated, and such a bill if it should pass into an act would be void.

EUROPEAN: The great caution you use in expressing your reasons to support your principles is of itself a sufficient answer to them. You choose to give the sentiments of those who were against the act while it was a bill but do not think proper to declare it to be your own sentiment that it is a void act now it is passed. You know it would be criminal in you to do it, and why? Because if individuals were at liberty to declare acts of the supreme authority to be void and refuse submission to them, the government would soon be dissolved. You disallow the Septennial Act, and may as well disallow all the acts passed by the first septennial Parliament if not by all the Parliaments since; another deems some other acts unconstitutional, and so on until perhaps few or none would be left approved by all. However, therefore, you may satisfy yourself that merely in a moral sense you are not bound to <conform to such> a law, you will never find a court of judicature which will think your sense of your obligations sufficient *<excuse>* <reason> to exempt you from the *<penal consequences of not conforming to>* <operation of> the law. Their judgments must be determined by acts of Parliament. If later acts militate with former, how early so ever—even those you call fundamental—the later must be the rule.

AMERICAN: Surely we may suppose a government to have known established fundamentals settled by agreement of the individuals at their first formation into a government. Several of the colonies in America were first formed in that manner. Admit, for argument sake, that they had continued to this day in the same form without any commissions or charters from the crown or any authority in England, would the supreme authority of such government have a right at this day to pass acts contrary to these fundamentals? Would not such acts be utterly void?

EUROPEAN: We may suppose such a government as you mention not to be so numerous as to prevent its being an absolute democracy and the whole people may at stated times or occasions all be assembled for acts of government, or we may suppose it to be so increased as to render it impracticable for the people so to assemble and their voices to be collected, and they may call themselves a commonwealth and the people be represented in a senate, which in this case be the supreme authority; in the other case the supreme authority would remain in the body of the people. In either case the acts of this supreme authority would be binding though they altered the fundamentals. In the latter case, if the individuals remained the same as when they first combined, would not it be in their power to rescind their own act? If the first formers were extinct, their posterity surely would say, what right had our ancestors to bind us by any irrevocable act of theirs? If the supreme authority be in the senate, they are in the place of the body of the people. You will say, perhaps the people never delegated the power of departing from fundamentals: admit it and see what will be the consequence. Not that every man or every part of the community may refuse obedience to such acts, for this, as I observed before, would be directly contrary to the fundamental principle in all government, but the body of the people may rise and change the rulers or change the very form of the government, and this they may do at all times and on all occasions, just when they please. But every individual must take the consequence of a mistake if he attempts to stir up the body of a people to a revolt and should be disappointed. In a moral view he may perhaps be innocent <whether his attempt succeeds or not>, but consider him as a member of the political body and he must be pronounced guilty by the judiciary powers of that society if he fails of success. This is a principle essential to the nature of government and to the English constitution as well as all others.

AMERICAN: Admit all you say to be true, and yet it does not touch our case. Suppose it reasonable and necessary that the lesser part of the whole should submit to the greater part of the whole, it does not follow that one-third part of the whole must submit to the major part of the other two-thirds, but this is the unfortunate case of us Americans.

EUROPEAN: How can it be otherwise? You say yourselves that your remote situation makes it impossible for you to be represented in Parliament to your advantage. What else would you propose?

AMERICAN: We propose that no taxes should be laid upon us but by our own legislatures, that we should be governed <in general> by laws of our making, but in matters of commerce we are willing to be restrained by acts of the British Parliament, for as we depend upon you for protection against the other powers of Europe we do not think it reasonable that we should carry on trade beneficial to them and detrimental to you.

EUROPEAN: If we could be certain even of this it would be something. But what assurance have we that you will not very soon complain of this restraint upon your trade, which deprives you of the means of increasing your property, as much as you now do of the revenue acts, which take from you a part of your property? By your present conduct you give us all imaginable reason to expect it. What is the cause of that enmity against the commissioners and other officers of the customs? No one instance has ever been shown of oppression or rigour in the execution of their office. You say it is laying unnecessary burdens upon your trade. We know that you are much less burdened than your fellow subjects in England. We know that notwithstanding all care and endeavours to prevent it, there is much more smuggling in the colonies in proportion to their trade than there is in England. In short, there is no need of proving that the principles I have advanced are just by any other instance than what has occurred among yourselves. Admit that you are not subject to all the laws and you will presently be subject to none. As we concede, so you advance. I would not give up the least iota of our right, but I would exercise this right with discretion, with equity, and even with a degree of partiality, but when I had once determined how far I would exercise it, at all events such determination should never be departed from.

AMERICAN: You may find it more difficult than you imagine.

EUROPEAN: I would provide for the worst, though I am really of opinion when once you are convinced that we are in earnest that we shall have but little trouble with you. You have a few desperate men among you, some of them can never be in worse circumstances than they are at present, and if they could reduce all to a chaos upon a new creation they might have a chance of better, but the generality of your people who are in easy circumstances will not care to part with their estates and see their families miserable; they will willingly sacrifice those desperadoes to provide for their own future security. There are an hundred ways of restraining you in your trade and manufactures. One ship of war in each of your principal ports, with such powers as in your case would be no more than reasonable, would reduce every colony in a very few months. The rage of the people would break out not against us but against the heads of the faction in each colony who have been stirring up sedition and substituting a phantom, a mere imaginary good, in the room of the greatest blessing, Liberty in as great a degree as will consist with a state of government.

AMERICAN: I am ready to acknowledge that the most considerate part of the people in America have no great opinion of the virtue of their present leaders. There are very few of them who will ever be left executors to any will or entrusted with the guardianship of any children or have the care of any private affairs, but let them act from what principles they may, they have certainly been the instruments of saving us from slavery; the tumults and riots which they stirred up after the Stamp Act were the cause of the repeal of it. The opposition they are now making to the importation of goods from Great Britain will distress your tradesmen so that you will not be able to avoid repealing the other revenue acts also. These measures, it cannot be denied, are distressing to ourselves and we are in a state of such disorder that if it was to be perpetual any rational man would choose to live in France or Spain or any other of the governments in Europe which are called absolute, but we are submitting to a very great temporary evil in order to obtain a lasting good.

EUROPEAN: I should not have forgot your confederacies for stopping importation from Great Britain. Pray, do you think such combinations are to be tolerated?

AMERICAN: They are our dernier resort, and we are of opinion they are legal and constitutional.

[EUROPEAN]: For the ley gens I could wish their ignorance might be their excuse, but for professed lawyers, for members of your Councils and Houses of Burgesses or Representatives, for the judges and officers of your courts, their ignorance shall not excuse them. I wish the laws may be carried into execution against them and, that none may plead ignorance, for the future I wish an act of Parliament may pass immediately subjecting all who shall thus combine or any ways abet or encourage such combinations to express and severe penalties, and that this act may be constantly read at the opening of every court where the offence shall be made cognizable in each of the colonies or plantations.

AMERICAN: You know that in England there is no carrying an act of Parliament into execution against the opinion of the body of the people.

EUROPEAN: I know that when an act is made which is found by experience to be inexpedient, that it will be repealed, but you can show me no instance of an act repealed because one or more of the counties in England denied the authority of Parliament to pass the act, and if you can give no better reason than your opposing this authority, I think your revenue acts never ought to be repealed, but as I really think them inexpedient I wish all which are made for the purpose of a revenue may be repealed, but I would have effectual provision made in the same act for strengthening the authority of Parliament in all cases wherein it has been or may be judged proper to exercise it, that the colonists may see their opposition to the authority of Parliament had not the least tendency to bring about the repeal.

AMERICAN: In despotic governments laws which are contrary to the general bent of the people may, for a long time, be executed, but in free governments, such as all parts of the English governments are or ought to be, this can never be the case. What judicial, what ministerial, officers will ever carry such laws into execution?

EUROPEAN: Laws against the general bent of the people, I agree with you, cannot long continue in the English constitution, but laws against the bent of particular parts of the people are and must oftentimes <in every constitution> be enforced by the authority of the whole. [. . .]

[The manuscript breaks off at this point. [. . .]]

Samuel Adams

Letter to the *Boston Gazette* (February 27, 1769)

In the days of the Stuarts, it was look'd upon by some men as a high degree of prophaness, for any subject to enquire into what was called the *mysteries* of government: *James* the first thundered his anathema against Dr. *Cowel*, for his daring presumption in treating of—those *mysteries*; and forbad his subjects to read his books, or even to keep them in their houses. In those days *passive obedience, non-resistance*, the *divine hereditary right* of kings, and their being accountable to God alone, were doctrines generally taught, believ'd and practiced: But behold the sudden transition of human affairs! In the very next reign the people assum'd the right of *free enquiry*, into the nature and end of government, and the conduct of those who were entrusted with it: *Laud* and *Strafford* were bro't to the block; and after the horrors of a civil war, in which some of the best blood of the nation was spilt as water upon the ground, they finally called to account, arraign'd, adjudg'd, condemn'd and even executed the monarch himself! and for a time held his son and heir in exile. The two sons of *Charles* the first, after the death of *Oliver Cromwell*, reigned in their turns; but by copying after their father, their administration of government was *grievous* to their subjects, and *infamous* abroad. *Charles* the second indeed reign'd till he died; but his brother *James* was oblig'd to abdicate the throne, which made room for *William* the third, and his royal consort *Mary*, the daughter of the unfortunate *James*—This was the fate of a race of Kings, bigotted to the greatest degree to the doctrines of *slavery* and regardless of the *natural, inherent, divinely hereditary* and *indefeasible* rights of their subjects.—At the revolution, the British constitution was again restor'd to its original principles, declared in the bill of rights; which was afterwards pass'd into a law, and stands as a bulwark to the natural rights of subjects. "To vindicate these rights, says Mr. *Blackstone*, when actually violated or attack'd, the subjects of England are entitled first to the regular administration and *free course of justice* in the courts of law—next to the right of *petitioning the King* and parliament for redress of grievances—and lastly, to the right of *having and using arms for self-preservation and defence*." These he calls "auxiliary subordinate rights, which serve principally as *barriers* to protect and maintain inviolate the three great and primary rights of *personal security, personal liberty* and *private property*": And that of *having arms for their defence* he tells us is "a public allowance, under due restrictions, of the *natural right of resistance and self preservation*, when the sanctions of society and laws are found *insufficient* to restrain the *violence of oppression*."—How little do those persons attend to the rights of the constitution, if they know anything about them, who find fault with a late vote of this town, calling upon the inhabitants to *provide themselves with arms for their defence* at any time; but more especially, when they had reason to fear, there would be a necessity of the means of self preservation against the *violence of oppression*.—Every one knows that the exercise of the military power is forever *dangerous* to civil rights; and we have had recent instances of *violences* that have been offer'd to *private subjects*, and the last week, even *to a magistrate in the execution of his office!*—Such violences are no more than might have been expected from *military troops*: A power, which is apt enough at all times to take a wanton lead, even when in the midst of civil society; but more especially so, when they are led to believe that they are become *necessary*, to awe a spirit of *rebellion*, and *preserve peace and good order*. But there are some persons, who would, if possibly they could, perswade the people *never to make use* of their *constitutional* rights or terrify them from doing it. No wonder that a resolution of this town to *keep arms* for its own defence, should be represented as having at bottom a *secret intention* to oppose the landing of the King's troops: when those very persons, who gave it this colouring, had before represented the peoples petitioning their

Sovereign, as proceeding from a *factious* and *rebellious* spirit; and would now insinuate that there is an *impropriety* in their addressing even a *plantation Governor* upon public business—Such are the times we are fallen into!

The Rights of the Colonists (November 20, 1772)

The Report of the Committee of Correspondence to the Boston Town Meeting.

I. Natural Rights of the Colonists as Men

Among the natural rights of the Colonists are these: First, a right to life; Secondly, to liberty; Thirdly, to property; together with the right to support and defend them in the best manner they can. These are evident branches of, rather than deductions from, the duty of self-preservation, commonly called the first law of nature.

All men have a right to remain in a state of nature as long as they please; and in case of intolerable oppression, civil or religious, to leave the society they belong to, and enter into another.

When men enter into society, it is by voluntary consent; and they have a right to demand and insist upon the performance of such conditions and previous limitations as form an equitable original compact.

Every natural right not expressly given up, or, from the nature of a social compact, necessarily ceded, remains.

All positive and civil laws should conform, as far as possible, to the law of natural reason and equity.

As neither reason requires nor religion permits the contrary, every man living in or out of a state of civil society has a right peaceably and quietly to worship God according to the dictates of his conscience.

"Just and true liberty, equal and impartial liberty," in matters spiritual and temporal, is a thing that all men are clearly entitled to by the eternal and immutable laws of God and nature, as well as by the law of nations and all well-grounded municipal laws, which must have their foundation in the former.

In regard to religion, mutual toleration in the different professions thereof is what all good and candid minds in all ages have ever practised, and, both by precept and example, inculcated on mankind. And it is now generally agreed among Christians that this spirit of toleration, in the fullest extent consistent with the being of civil society, is the chief characteristical mark of the Church. Insomuch that Mr. Locke has asserted and proved, beyond the possibility of contradiction on any solid ground, that such toleration ought to be extended to all whose doctrines are not subversive of society. The only sects which he thinks ought to be, and which by all wise laws are excluded from such toleration, are those who teach doctrines subversive of the civil government under which they live. The Roman Catholics or Papists are excluded by reason of such doctrines as these, that princes excommunicated may be deposed, and those that they call heretics may be destroyed without mercy; besides their recognizing the Pope in so absolute a manner, in subversion of government, by introducing, as far as possible into the states under whose protection they enjoy life, liberty, and property, that solecism in politics, imperium in imperio, leading directly to the worst anarchy and confusion, civil discord, war, and bloodshed.

The natural liberty of man, by entering into society, is abridged or restrained, so far only as is necessary for the great end of society, the best good of the whole.

In the state of nature every man is, under God, judge and sole judge of his own rights and of the injuries done him. By entering into society he agrees to an arbiter or indifferent judge between him and his neighbors; but he no more renounces his original right than by taking a cause out of the ordinary course of law, and leaving the decision to referees or indifferent arbitrators.

In the last case, he must pay the referees for time and trouble. He should also be willing to pay his just quota for the support of government, the law, and the constitution; the end of which is to furnish indifferent and impartial judges in all cases that may happen, whether civil, ecclesiastical, marine, or military.

The natural liberty of man is to be free from any superior power on earth, and not to be under the will or legislative authority of man, but only to have the law of nature for his rule.

In the state of nature men may, as the patriarchs did, employ hired servants for the defence of their lives, liberties, and property; and they should pay them reasonable wages. Government was instituted for the purposes of common defence, and those who hold the reins of government have an equitable, natural right to an honorable support from the same principle that "the laborer is worthy of his hire." But then the same community which they serve ought to be the assessors of their pay. Governors have no right to seek and take what they please; by this, instead of being content with the station assigned them, that of honorable servants of the society, they would soon become absolute masters, despots, and tyrants. Hence, as a private man has a right to say what wages he will give in his private affairs, so has a community to determine what they will give and grant of their substance for the administration of public affairs. And, in both cases, more are ready to offer their service at the proposed and stipulated price than are able and willing to perform their duty.

In short, it is the greatest absurdity to suppose it in the power of one, or any number of men, at the entering into society, to renounce their essential natural rights, or the means of preserving those rights; when the grand end of civil government, from the very nature of its institution, is for the support, protection, and defence of those very rights; the principal of which, as is before observed, are Life, Liberty, and Property. If men, through fear, fraud, or mistake, should in terms renounce or give up any essential natural right, the eternal law of reason and the grand end of society would absolutely vacate such renunciation. The right to freedom being the gift of God Almighty, it is not in the power of man to alienate this gift and voluntarily become a slave.

II. The Rights of the Colonists as Christians

These may be best understood by reading and carefully studying the institutes of the great Law Giver and Head of the Christian Church, which are to be found clearly written and promulgated in the New Testament.

By the act of the British Parliament, commonly called the Toleration Act, every subject in England, except Papists, &c., was restored to, and re-established in, his natural right to worship God according to the dictates of his own conscience. And, by the charter of this Province, it is granted, ordained, and established (that is, declared as an original right) that there shall be liberty of conscience allowed in the worship of God to all Christians, except Papists, inhabiting, or which shall inhabit or be resident within, such Province or Territory. Magna Charta itself is in substance but a constrained declaration or proclamation and promulgation in the name of the King, Lords, and Commons, of the sense the latter had of their original, inherent, indefeasible natural rights, as also those of free citizens equally perdurable with the other. That great author, that great jurist, and even that court writer, Mr. Justice Blackstone, holds that this recognition was justly obtained of King John, sword in hand. And per adventure it must be one day, sword in hand, again rescued and preserved from total destruction and oblivion.

III. The Rights of the Colonists as Subjects

A commonwealth or state is a body politic, or civil society of men, united together to promote their mutual safety and prosperity by means of their union.

The absolute rights of Englishmen and all freemen, in or out of civil society, are principally personal security, personal liberty, and private property.

All persons born in the British American Colonies are, by the laws of God and nature and by the common law of England, exclusive of all charters from the Crown, well entitled, and by acts of the British Parliament are declared to be entitled, to all the natural, essential, inherent, and inseparable rights, liberties, and privileges of subjects born in Great Britain or within the realm. Among those rights are the following, which no man, or body of men, consistently with their own rights as men and citizens, or members of society, can for themselves give up or take away from others.

First, "The first fundamental, positive law of all common wealths or states is the establishing the legislative power. As the first fundamental natural law, also, which is to govern even the legislative power itself, is the preservation of the society."

Secondly, The Legislative has no right to absolute, arbitrary power over the lives and fortunes of the people; nor can mortals assume a prerogative not only too high for men, but for angels, and therefore reserved for the exercise of the Deity alone.

"The Legislative cannot justly assume to itself a power to rule by extempore arbitrary decrees; but it is bound to see that justice is dispensed, and that the rights of the subjects be decided by promulgated, standing, and known laws, and authorized independent judges"; that is, independent, as far as possible, of Prince and people. "There should be one rule of justice for rich and poor, for the favorite at court, and the countryman at the plough."

Thirdly, The supreme power cannot justly take from any man any part of his property, without his consent in person or by his representative.

These are some of the first principles of natural law and justice, and the great barriers of all free states and of the British Constitution in particular. It is utterly irreconcilable to these principles and to many other fundamental maxims of the common law, common sense, and reason that a British House of Commons should have a right at pleasure to give and grant the property of the Colonists. (That the Colonists are well entitled to all the essential rights, liberties, and privileges of men and freemen born in Britain is manifest not only from the Colony charters in general, but acts of the British Parliament.) The statute of the 13th of Geo. 2, C. 7, naturalizes even foreigners after seven years' residence. The words of the Massachusetts charter are these: "And further, our will and pleasure is, and we do hereby for us, our heirs, and successors, grant, establish, and ordain, that all and every of the subjects of us, our heirs, and successors, which shall go to, and inhabit within our said Province or Territory, and every of their children, which shall happen to be born there or on the seas in going thither or returning from thence, shall have and enjoy all liberties and immunities of free and natural subjects within any of the dominions of us, our heirs, and successors, to all intents, constructions, and purposes whatsoever as if they and every one of them were born within this our realm of England."

Now what liberty can there be where property is taken away without consent? Can it be said with any color of truth and justice, that this continent of three thousand miles in length, and of a breadth as yet unexplored, in which, however, it is supposed there are five millions of people, has the least voice, vote, or influence in the British Parliament? Have they all together any more weight or power to return a single member to that House of Commons who have not inadvertently, but deliberately, assumed a power to dispose of their lives, liberties, and properties, than to choose an Emperor of China? Had the Colonists a right to return members to the British Parliament, it would only be hurtful; as, from their local situation and circumstances, it is impossible they should ever be truly and properly represented there. The inhabitants of this country, in all probability, in a few years, will be more numerous than those of Great Britain and Ireland together; yet it is absurdly expected by the promoters of the present measures that these, with their posterity to all generations, should be easy, while their property shall be disposed of by a House of Commons at three thousand miles' distance from them, and who cannot be supposed to have the least care or concern for their real interest; who have not only no natural care for their interest, but must be in effect bribed against it, as every burden they lay on the Colonists is so much saved or gained to themselves. Hitherto, many of the Colonists have been free from quit rents; but if the breath of a British House of Commons can originate an act for taking away all our money, our lands will go next, or be subject to rack rents from haughty and relentless landlords, who will ride at ease, while we are trodden in the dirt. The Colonists have been branded with the odious names of traitors and rebels only for complaining of their grievances. How long such treatment will or ought to be borne, is submitted.

Thomas Hutchinson

Speech of the Governor to the Two Houses (January 6, 1773)

Gentlemen of the Council, and
Gentlemen of the House of Representatives,

I have nothing in special command from his Majesty to lay before you at this time; I have general instructions to recommend to you, at all times, such measures as may tend to promote that peace and order, upon which your own happiness and prosperity, as well as his Majesty's service, very much depend. That the government is at present in a disturbed and disordered state, is a truth too evident to be denied. The cause of this disorder, appears to me equally evident. I wish I may be able to make it appear so to you, for then, I may not doubt that you will agree with me in the proper measures for the removal of it. I have pleased myself, for several years past, with hopes, that the cause would cease of itself, and the effect with it, but I am disappointed; and I may not any longer, consistent with my duty to the King, and my regard to the interest of the province, delay communicating my sentiments to you upon a matter of so great importance. [. . .]

When our predecessors first took possession of this plantation, or colony, under a grant and charter from the Crown of England, it was their sense, and it was the sense of the kingdom, that they were to remain subject to the supreme authority of Parliament. This appears from the charter itself, and from other irresistible evidence. This supreme authority has, from time to time, been exercised by Parliament, and submitted to by the colony, and hath been, in the most express terms, acknowledged by the Legislature, and, except about the time of the anarchy and confusion in England, which preceded the restoration of King Charles the Second, I have not discovered that it has been called in question, even by private or particular persons, until within seven or eight years last past. Our provincial or local laws have, in numerous instances, had relation to acts of Parliament, made to respect the plantations in general, and this colony in particular, and in our Executive Courts, both Juries and Judges have, to all intents and purposes, considered such acts as part of our rule of law. Such a constitution, in a plantation, is not peculiar to England, but agrees with the principles of the most celebrated writers upon the law of nations, that "when a nation takes possession of a distant country, and settles there, that country, though separated from the principal establishment, or mother country, naturally becomes a part of the state, equally with its ancient possessions."

So much, however, of the spirit of liberty breathes through all parts of the English constitution, that, although from the nature of government, there must be one supreme authority over the whole, yet this constitution will admit of subordinate powers with Legislative and Executive authority, greater or less, according to local and other circumstances. Thus we see a variety of corporations formed within the kingdom, with powers to make and execute such by-laws as are for their immediate use and benefit, the members of such corporations still remaining subject to the general laws of the kingdom. We see also governments established in the plantations, which, from their separate and remote situation, require more general and extensive powers of legislation within themselves, than those formed within the kingdom, but subject, nevertheless, to all such laws of the kingdom as immediately respect them, or are designed to extend to them; and, accordingly, we, in this province have, from the first settlement of it, been left to the exercise of our Legislative and Executive powers, Parliament occasionally, though rarely, interposing, as in its wisdom has been judged necessary.

Under this constitution, for more than one hundred years, the laws both of the supreme and subordinate authority were in general, duly executed; offenders against them have been brought to condign punishment, peace and order have been maintained, and the people of this province have experienced as largely the advantages of government, as, perhaps, any people upon, the globe; and they have, from time to time, in the most public manner expressed their sense of it, and, once in every year, have offered up their united thanksgivings to God for the enjoyment of these privileges, and, as often, their united prayers for the continuance of them.

At length the constitution has been called in question, and the authority of the Parliament of Great Britain to make and establish laws for the inhabitants of this province has been, by many, denied. What was at first whispered with caution, was soon after openly asserted in print; and, of late, a number of inhabitants, in several of the principal towns in the province, having assembled together in their respective towns, and have assumed the name of legal town meetings, have passed resolves, which they have ordered to be placed upon their town records, and caused to be printed and published in pamphlets and newspapers. I am sorry that it is thus become impossible to conceal, what I could wish had never been made public. I will not particularize these resolves or votes, and shall only observe to you in general, that some of them deny the supreme authority of Parliament, and so are repugnant to the principles of the constitution, and that others speak of this supreme authority, of which the King is a constituent part, and to every act of which his assent is necessary, in such terms as have a direct tendency to alienate the affections of the people from their Sovereign, who has ever been most tender of their rights, and whose person, crown, and dignity, we are under every possible obligation to defend and support. In consequence of these resolves, committees of correspondence are formed in several of those towns, to maintain the principles upon which they are founded.

I know of no arguments, founded in reason, which will be sufficient to support these principles, or to justify the measures taken in consequence of them. It has been urged, that the sole power of making laws is granted, by charter, to a Legislature established in the province, consisting of the King, by his Representative the Governor, the Council, and the House of Representatives; that, by this charter, there are likewise granted, or assured to the inhabitants of the province, all the liberties and immunities of free and natural subjects, to all intents, constructions and purposes whatsoever, as if they had been born within the realms or England; that it is part of the liberties of English subjects, which has its foundation in nature, to be governed by laws made by their consent in person, or by their representative; that the subjects in this province are not, and cannot be represented in the Parliament of Great Britain, and, consequently, the acts of that Parliament cannot be binding upon them.

I do not find, gentlemen, in the charter, such an expression as sole power, or any words which import it. The General Court has, by charter, full power to make such laws, as are not repugnant to the laws of England. A favorable construction has been put upon this clause, when it has been allowed to intend such laws of England only, as are expressly declared to respect us. Surely then this is, by charter, a reserve of power and authority to Parliament to bind us by such laws, at least, as are made expressly to refer to us, and consequently, is a limitation of the power given to the General Court. Nor can it be contended, that, by the limits of free and natural subjects, is to be understood an exemption from acts of Parliament, because not represented there, seeing it is provided by the same charter, that such acts shall be in force; and if they that make the objection to such acts, will read the charter with attention, they must be convinced that this grant of liberties and immunities is nothing more than a declaration and assurance on the part of the Crown, that the place, to which their predecessors were about to remove, was, and would be considered as part of the dominions of the Crown of England, and, therefore, that the subjects of the Crown so removing, and those born there, or in their passage thither, or in their passage from thence, would not become aliens, but would, throughout all parts of the English dominions, wherever they might happen to be, as well as within the colony, retain the liberties and immunities of free and natural subjects, their removal from, or not being born within the realm notwithstanding. If the plantations be part of the dominions of the Crown, this clause in the charter does not confer or reserve any liberties, but what would have been enjoyed without it, and what the inhabitants of every other colony do enjoy where they are without a charter. If the plantations are not the dominions of the Crown, will not all that are born here, be considered as born out of the liegeance of the King of England, and, whenever they go into any parts of the dominions, will they not be deemed aliens to all intents and purposes, this grant in the charter notwithstanding?

They who claim exemption from acts of Parliament by virtue of their rights as Englishmen, should consider that it is impossible the rights of English subjects should be the Same, in every respect, in all parts of the dominions. It is one of their rights as English subjects, to be governed by laws made by persons, in whose election they have, front time to time, a voice; they remove from the kingdom, where, perhaps, they were in the full exercise of this right, to the plantations, where it cannot be exercised, or where the exercise of it would be of no benefit to them. Does it follow that the government, by their removal from one part of the dominions to another, loses its authority over that part to which they remove, and that they are freed from the subjection they were under before; or do they expect that government should relinquish its authority because they cannot enjoy this particular right? Will it not rather be said, that by this, their voluntary removal, they have relinquished for a time at least, one of the rights of an English subject, which they might, if they pleased, have continued to enjoy, and may again enjoy, whensoever they will return to the place where it can be exercised?

They who claim exemption, as part of their rights by nature, should consider that every restraint which men are laid under by a state of government, is a privation of part of their natural rights; and of all the different forms of government which exist, there can be no two of them in which the departure from natural rights is exactly the same. Even in case of representation by election, do they not give up part of their natural rights when they consent to be represented by such person as shall be chosen by the majority of the electors, although their own voices may be for some other person? And is it not contrary to their natural rights to be obliged to submit to a representative for seven years, or even one year, after they are dissatisfied with his conduct, although they gave their voices for him when he was elected? This must, therefore, be considered as an objection against a state of government, rather than against any particular form.

If what I have said shall not be sufficient to satisfy such as object to the supreme authority of Parliament over the plantations, there may something further be added to induce them to an acknowledgment of it, which, I think, will well deserve their consideration. I know of no line that can be drawn between the supreme authority of Parliament and the total independence of the colonies: it is impossible there should be two independent Legislatures in one and the same state; for, although there may be but one head, the King, yet the two Legislative bodies will make two governments as distinct as the kingdoms of England and Scotland before the union. If we might be suffered to be altogether independent of Great Britain, could we have any claim to the protection of that government, of which we are no longer a part? Without this protection, should we not become the prey of one or the other powers of Europe, such as should first seize upon us? Is there any thing which we have more reason to dread than independence? I hope it never will be our misfortune to know, by experience, the difference between the liberties of an English colonist, and those of the Spanish, French, or Dutch.

If then, the supremacy of Parliament over the whole British dominions shall no longer be denied, it will follow that the mere exercise of its authority can be no matter of grievance. If it has been, or shall be exercised in such way and manner as shall appear to be grievous, still this cannot be sufficient ground for immediately denying or renouncing the authority, or refusing to submit to it. The acts and doings of authority, in the most perfect form of government, will not always be thought just and equitable by all the parts of which it consists; but it is the greatest absurdity, to admit the several parts to be at liberty to obey, or disobey, according as the acts of such authority may be approved, or disapproved of by them, for this necessarily works a dissolution of the government. The manner, then, of obtaining redress, must be by representations and endeavors, in such ways and forms, as the established rules of the constitution prescribe or allow, in order to make any matters, alleged to be grievances, appear to be really such; but, I conceive it is rather the mere exercise of this authority, which is complained of as a grievance, than any heavy burdens which have been brought upon the people by means of it. [. . .]

I have disclosed my sentiments to you without reserve. Let me entreat you to consider them calmly, and not be too sudden in your determination. If my principles of government are right, let us adhere to them. With the same principles, our ancestors were easy and happy for a long course of years together, and I know of no reason to doubt of your being equally easy and happy. The people, influenced by you, will desist from their unconstitutional principles, and desist from their irregularities, which are the consequence of them; they will be convinced that every thing which is valuable to them, depend upon their connexion with their parent state; that this connexion cannot be carried in any other way, than such as will also continue their dependence upon the supreme authority of the British dominions; and that, notwithstanding this dependence, they will enjoy as great a proportion of those, to which they have a claim by nature, or as Englishmen, as can be enjoyed by a plantation or colony.

If I am wrong in my principles of government, or in the inferences which I have drawn from them, I wish to be convinced of my error. Independence, I may not allow myself to think that you can possibly have in contemplation. If you can conceive of any other constitutional dependence than what I have mentioned, if you are of opinion, that upon any other principles our connexion with the state from which we sprang, can be continued, communicate your sentiments to me with the same freedom and unreservedness, as I have communicated mine to you.

I have no desire, gentlemen, by any thing I have said, to preclude you from seeking relief, in a constitutional way, in any cases in which you have heretofore, or may hereafter suppose that you are aggrieved; and, although I should not concur with you in sentiment, I will, notwithstanding, do nothing to lessen the weight which your representations may deserve. I have laid before you what I think are the principles of your constitution; if you do not agree with me, I wish to know your objections; they may be convincing to me, or I may be able to satisfy you of the insufficiency of them. In either case, I hope we shall put an end to those irregularities, which ever will be the portion of a government where the supreme authority is controverted, and introduce that tranquillity, which seems to have taken place in most of the colonies upon the continent.

T. Hutchinson

Bowdoin, Gray, Otis, Hall, et al.

Answer of the Council to the Speech of Governor Hutchinson (January 25, 1773)

May it please your Excellency,

The Board have considered your Excellency's speech to both Houses, with the attention due to the object of it; and, we hope, with the candor you were pleased to recommend to them. We thank you for the promise, that, "if we shall not agree with you in sentiment, you will, with candor, likewise receive and consider what we may offer in answer."

Your speech informs the two Houses, that this government is at present in a disturbed and disordered state; that the cause of this disorder is the unconstitutional principles adopted by the people, in questioning the supreme authority of Parliament; and that the proper measure for removing the disorder, must be the substituting of contrary principles. [. . .]

With regard to the present disordered state of the government, it can have no reference to tumults or riots; from which this government is as free as any other, whatever. If your Excellency meant, only, that the province is discontented, and in a state of uneasiness, we should entirely agree with you; but you will permit us to say, that we are not so well agreed in the cause of it. The uneasiness, which was a general one, throughout the colonies, began when you inform, the authority of Parliament was first called in question, viz. about seven or eight years ago. Your mentioning that particular time, might have suggested to your Excellency the true cause of the origin and continuance of that uneasiness.

At that time, the stamp act, then lately made, began to operate; which, with some preceding and succeeding acts of Parliament, subjecting the colonies to taxes, without their consent, was the original cause of all the uneasiness which has happened since; and has also occasioned an inquiry into the nature and extent of the authority, by which they were made. The late town meetings in several towns, are instanced of both. These are mentioned by your Excellency, in proof of a disordered state. But, though we do not approve of some of their resolves, we think they had a clear right to instruct their Representatives in any subject they apprehended to be of sufficient importance to require it; which necessarily implies a previous consideration and expression of their minds on that subject, however mistaken they may be concerning it.

When a community, great or small, think their rights and privileges infringed, they will express their uneasiness in a variety of ways; some of which, may be highly improper and criminal. So far as any of an atrocious nature have taken place, we would express our abhorrence of them; and, as we have always done, hitherto, we shall continue to do everything in our power, to discourage and suppress them. But it is in vain to hope that this can be done effectually, so long as the cause of the uneasiness exists. Your Excellency will perceive that the *cause* you assign, is, by us, supposed to be an *effect*, derived from the original cause, above mentioned; the removal of which, will remove its effects.

To obtain this removal, we agree with you in the method pointed out in your speech, where you say, "the manner of obtaining redress must be by representation, and endeavors, in such ways and forms as the constitution allows, in order to make any matters alleged to be grievances, appear to be really such."

This method has been pursued repeatedly. Petitions to Parliament have gone from the colonies, and from this colony in particular; but without success. Some of them, in a former Ministry, were previously shewn to the Minister, who, as we have been informed, advised the Agents to postpone presenting them to the House of Commons, till the first reading of the bill they referred to; when, being presented, a rule of the House against receiving petitions on money bills, was urged for rejecting them, and they were rejected, accordingly; and other petitions, for want of formality, or whatever was the reason, have had the same fate. This we mention, not by way of censure on that honorable House, but in some measure to account for the conduct of those persons, who, despairing of redress, in a constitutional way, have denied the just authority of Parliament; concerning which, we shall now give our own sentiments, intermixed with observations on those of your Excellency.

You are pleased to observe, that when our predecessors first took possession of this colony, under a grant and charter from the Crown of England, it was their sense, and the sense of the whole kingdom, that they were to remain subject to the supreme authority of Parliament; and to prove that subjection, the greater part of your speech is employed.

In order to a right conception of this matter, it is necessary to guard against any improper idea of the term *supreme* authority. In your idea of it, your Excellency seems to include *unlimited* authority; for, you are pleased to say, that you know of no line which can be drawn between the supreme authority of Parliament, and the real independence of the colonies. But if no such line can be drawn, a denial of that authority, in any instance whatever, implies and amounts to a declaration of total independence. But if supreme authority, includes unlimited authority, the subjects of it are emphatically slaves; and equally so, whether residing in the colonies, or Great Britain. And, indeed, in this respect, all the nations on earth, among whom government exists in any of its forms, would be alike conditioned, excepting so far as the mere grace and favor of their Governors might make a difference, for from, the nature of government there must be, as your Excellency has observed, one supreme authority over the whole.

We cannot think, that when our predecessors took possession of this colony, it was their sense, or the sense of the kingdom, that they were to remain subject to the supreme authority of Parliament in this idea of it. Nor can we find, that this appears from the charter; or, that such authority has ever been exercised by Parliament, submitted to by the colony, or acknowledged by the Legislature.

Supreme, or unlimited authority, can with fitness, belong only to the Sovereign of the universe; and that fitness is derived from the perfection of his nature. To such authority, directed by infinite wisdom and infinite goodness, is due both active and passive obedience; which, as it constitutes the happiness of rational creatures, should, with cheerfulness, and from choice, be unlimitedly paid by them. But, this can be said with truth, of no other authority whatever. If, then, from the nature and end of government, the supreme authority of every government is limited, the supreme authority of Parliament must be limited; and the inquiry will be, what are the limits of that authority, with regard to this colony? To fix them with precision, to determine the exact lines of right and wrong in this case, as in some others, is difficult; and we have not the presumption to attempt it. But we humbly hope, that, as we are personally and relatively, in our public and private capacities, for ourselves, for the whole province, and posterity, so deeply interested in this important subject, it will not be deemed arrogance to give some general sentiments upon it, especially as your Excellency's speech has made it absolutely necessary. [. . .]

Magna Charta declares, that no aid shall be imposed in the kingdom, unless by the Common Council of the kingdom, except to redeem the King's person, &c. And that all cities, boroughs, towns, and ports, shall have their liberties and free customs; and shall have the Common Council of the kingdom, concerning the assessment of their aids, except in the cases aforesaid.

The statute of the 34th of Edward I. *de tallio non concedendo*, declares, that no tallage or aid should be laid or levied by the King or his heirs, in the realm, without the good will and assent of the Archbishops, Bishops, Earls, Barons, Knights, Burgesses, and others, the freemen of the commonalty of this realm. A statute of the 25th Edward III. enacts, that from thenceforth, no person shall be compelled to make any loans to the King, against his will, because such loans were against reason and the franchise of the land.

The petition of rights in the 3d of Charles I. in which are cited the two foregoing statutes, declares, that, by those statutes, and other good laws and statutes of the realm, his Majesty's subjects inherited this freedom, that they should not be compelled to contribute to any tax, tallage, aid, or other like charge, not set by common consent of Parliament.

And the statute of the 1st of William III. for declaring the rights and liberties of the subject, and settling the succession of the Crown, declares, that the levying of money for, or to the use of the Crown, by pretence of prerogative, without grant of Parliament for longer time, or in any other manner than the same is, or shall be granted, is illegal.

From these authorities, it appears an essential part of the English constitution, that no tallage, or aid, or tax, shall be laid or levied without the good will and assent of the freedom of the commonalty of the realm. If this could be done without their assent, their property would be in the highest degree precarious; or rather they could not, with fitness, be said to have any property at all. At best, they would be only the holders of it for the use of the Crown, and the Crown be the real proprietor. This would be vassalage in the extreme, from which the generous nature of Englishmen have been so abhorrent, that they have bled with freedom in defence of this part of their constitution, which has preserved them from it; and influenced by the same generosity, they can never view with disapprobation, any lawful measures taken by us for the defence of our own constitution, which entitles us to the same rights and privileges with themselves. These were derived to us from common law, which is the inheritance of all his Majesty's subjects; have been recognized by acts of Parliament, and confirmed by the province charter, which established its constitution; and which charter, has been recognized by acts of Parliament also. [. . .] From all which it appears, that the inhabitants of this colony are clearly entitled to all the rights and privileges of free and natural subjects; which certainty must include that most essential one, that no aid or taxes be levied on them, without their own consent, signified by their Representatives.

But, from the clause in the charter, relative to the power granted to the General Court, to make laws not repugnant to the laws of England, your Excellency draws this inference, that surely this is, by charter, a reserve of power and authority to Parliament, to bind us by such laws, at least, as are made to refer to us, and consequently is a limitation of the power given to the General Court. If it be allowed, that, by that clause there was a reserve of power to Parliament, to bind the province, it was only by such laws as were in being at the time the charter was granted; for, by the charter, there is nothing appears to make it refer to any parliamentary laws, that should be afterwards made; and therefore, it will not support your Excellency's inference.

The grant of power to the General Court to make laws, runs thus—"full power and authority, from time to time, to make and ordain, and establish, all manner of wholesome and reasonable laws, orders, statutes and ordinances, directions and instructions, either with penalties or without, so as the same be not repugnant or contrary to the laws of this our realm of England, as they shall judge to be for the good and welfare of our said province." We humbly conceive an inference very different from your Excellency's, and a very just one too, maybe drawn from this clause, if attention be given to the description of the orders and laws that were to be made. They were to be wholesome, reasonable, and for the good and welfare of the province; and in order that they might be so, it is provided, that they be not repugnant or contrary to the laws of the realm, which were then in being; by which proviso, all the liberties and immunities of free and natural subjects within the realm, were more effectually secured to the inhabitants of the province, agreeable to another clause in the charter, whereby those liberties and immunities are expressly granted to them; and accordingly, the power of the General Court is so far limited, that they shall not make orders and laws to take away or diminish those liberties and immunities.

This construction appears to us a just one, and perhaps may appear so to your Excellency, if you will please to consider, that, by another part of the charter, effectual care was taken for preventing the General Assembly passing of orders and laws repugnant to, or that in any way might militate with acts of Parliament then or since made, or that might be exceptionable in any other respect whatever; for the charter reserves to his Majesty the appointment of the Governor, whose assent is necessary in the passing of all orders and laws; after which, they are to be sent to England, for the royal approbation or disallowance; by which double control, effectual care is taken to prevent the establishment of any improper orders or laws, whatever. Besides, your Excellency is sensible that letters patent must be construed one part with another, and all the parts of them together, so as to make the whole harmonize and agree. But your Excellency's construction of the paragraph empowering the General Court to make orders and laws, does by no means harmonize and agree with the paragraph granting liberties and immunities; [. . .]

If the former paragraph (in this supposed case) be binding on this people, the latter must be binding on the Crown, which thereby became guarantee of those rights and privileges, or it must be supposed that one party is held by a compact and the other not; which supposition is against reason and against law; and therefore, destroys the foundation of the inference. Supposing it well founded, however, it would not from thence follow, that the charter intended such laws as should subject the inhabitants of this province to taxes, without their consent; for, (as it appears above) it grants to them all the rights and liberties of free and natural subjects; of which, one of the most essential is, a freedom from all taxes not consented to by themselves. Nor could the parties, either grantor or grantees, intend such laws. The royal grantor could not, because his grant contradicts such intention, and because it is inconsistent with every idea of royalty and royal wisdom, to grant what it does not intend to grant. And it will be readily allowed, that the grantees could not intend such laws; not only on account of their inconsistency with the grant, but because their acceptance of a charter, subjecting them to such laws, would be voluntary slavery.

Your Excellency next observes, "that it cannot be contended, that, by the liberties of free and natural subjects, is to be understood an exemption from acts of Parliament, because not represented there, seeing it is provided by the charter, that such acts shall be in force." If the observations we have made above, and our reasoning on them be just, it will appear, that no such provision is made in the charter; and, therefore, that the deductions and inferences derived from the supposition of such provision, are not well founded. And with respect to representation in Parliament, as it is one of the essential liberties of free and natural subjects, and properly makes those who enjoy it, liable to parliamentary acts, so in reference to the inhabitants of this province, who are entitled to all the liberties of such subjects, the impossibility of their being duly represented in Parliament, does clearly exempt them from all such acts, at least, as have been or shall be made by Parliament, to tax them; representation and taxation being, in our opinion, constitutionally inseparable. [. . .]

"If the plantations be part of the dominions of the Crown, this clause in the charter, granting liberties and immunities, does not," your Excellency observes, "confer or reserve any liberties, but what would have been enjoyed without it; and what the inhabitants of every other colony do enjoy, where they are without a charter." Although the colonies, considered as part of the dominions of the Crown, are entitled to equal liberties, the inhabitants of this colony, think it a happiness, that those liberties are confirmed and secured to them by a charter; whereby the honor and faith of the Crown are pledged, that those liberties shall not be violated. And for protection in them, we humbly look up to his present Majesty, our rightful and lawful Sovereign, as children to a father, able and disposed to assist and relieve them; humbly imploring his Majesty, that his subjects of this province, ever faithful and loyal, and ever accounted such, till the stamp act existed, and who, in the late war, and upon all other occasions, have demonstrated that faithfulness and loyalty, by their vigorous and unexampled exertions in his service, may have their grievances redressed, and be restored to their just rights.

Your Excellency next observes, "that it is impossible the rights of English subjects should be the same in every respect, in all parts of the dominions," and instances in the right of "being governed by laws made by persons, in whose election they have a voice." When "they remove from the kingdom to the plantations, where it cannot be enjoyed," you ask, "will it not be said, by this voluntary removal, they have relinquished, for a time at least, one of the rights of an English subject, which they might, if they pleased, have continued to enjoy, and may again enjoy, whenever they will return to the place where it can be exercised?"

When English subjects remove from the kingdom to the plantations, with their property, they not only relinquish that right *de facto*, but it ought to cease in the kingdom *de jure*. But it does not from thence follow, that they relinquish that right in reference to the plantation or colony, to which they remove. On the contrary, having become inhabitants of that colony, and qualified according to the laws of it, they can exercise that right, equally with the other inhabitants of it. And their right, on like conditions, will travel with them through all the colonies, wherein a Legislature, similar to that of the kingdom, is established. And therefore, in this respect, and, we suppose, in all other essential respects, it is not impossible the rights of English subjects should be the same in all parts of the dominions, under a like form of Legislature.

This right of representation, is so essential and indisputable, in regard of all laws for levying taxes, that a people under any form of government, destitute of it, is destitute of freedom: of that degree of freedom, for the preservation of which, government was instituted; and without which, government degenerates into despotism. It cannot, therefore, be given up, or taken away, without making a breach in the essential rights of nature.

But your Excellency is pleased to say, "that they who claim exemption as part of their rights by nature, should consider that every restraint which men are laid under by a state of government, is a privation of part of their natural rights. Even in case of representation by election, do they not give up part of their natural rights, when they consent to be represented by such persons as shall be chosen by the majority of the electors, although their own voices may be for some other person. And is it not contrary to their natural rights, to be obliged to submit to a representation for seven years, or even one year, after they are dissatisfied with his conduct, although they gave their voices for him, when he was elected? This must, therefore, be considered as an objection against a state of government, rather than against any particular form."

Your Excellency's premises are true, but we do not think your conclusion follows from them. It is true, that every restraint of government is a privation of natural right; and the two cases you have been pleased to mention, may be instances of that privation. But, as they arise from the nature of society and government; and as government is necessary to secure other natural rights, infinitely more valuable, they cannot, therefore, be considered as an objection, either against a state government, or against any particular form of it.

Life, liberty, property, and the disposal of that property, with our own consent, are natural rights.

Will any one put the other in competition with these; or infer, that, because those others must be given up in a state of government, these must be given up also? The preservation of these rights, is the great end of government. But is it probable, they will be effectually secured by a government, which the proprietors of them, have no part in the direction of, and over which, they have no power or influence, whatever? Hence, is deductible representation, which being necessary to preserve these invaluable rights of nature, is itself, for that reason, a natural right, coinciding with, and running into that great law of nature, self preservation.

Thus have we considered the most material parts of your Excellency's speech, and, agreeable to your desire, disclosed to you our sentiments on the subject of it. "Independence," as you have rightly judged, "we have not in contemplation." We cannot, however, adopt your principles of government, or acquiesce in all the inferences you have drawn from them.

We have the highest respect for that august body, the Parliament, and do not presume to prescribe the exact limits of its authority; yet, with the deference which is due to it, we are humbly of opinion, that, as all human authority is, in the nature of it, and ought to be, limited, it cannot, constitutionally, extend, for the reasons we have suggested, to the levying of taxes, in any form, on his Majesty's subjects in this province.

[Hon. J. Bowdoin, H. Gray, J. Otis, and S. Hall, were the committee of Council, who prepared the above.]

MASSACHUSETTS HOUSE OF REPRESENTATIVES (S. ADAMS, J. HANCOCK, ET AL.)

Answer of the House of Representatives to the Speech of the Governor (January 26, 1773)

May it please your Excellency,

Your Excellency's speech to the General Assembly, at the opening of this session, has been read with great attention in this House.

We fully agree with your Excellency, that our own happiness, as well as his Majesty's service, very much depends upon peace and order; and we shall at all times take such measures as are consistent with our constitution, and the rights of the people, to promote and maintain them. That the government at present is in a very disturbed state, is apparent. But we cannot ascribe it to the people's having adopted unconstitutional principles, which seems to be the cause assigned for it by your Excellency. It appears to us, to have been occasioned rather by the British House of Commons assuming and exercising a power inconsistent with the freedom of the constitution, to give and grant the property of the colonists, and appropriate the same without their consent.

It is needless for us to inquire what were the principles that induced the councils of the nation to so new and unprecedented a measure. But, when the Parliament, by an act of their own, expressly declared, that the King, Lords, and Commons, of the nation "have, and of right ought to have full power and authority to make laws and statutes of sufficient force and validity, to bind the colonies and people of America, subjects of the Crown of Great Britain, in all cases whatever," and in consequence hereof, another revenue act was made, the minds of the people were filled with anxiety, and they were justly alarmed with apprehensions of the total extinction of their liberties. [. . .]

You are pleased to say, that, "when our predecessors first took possession of this plantation, or colony, under a grant and charter from the Crown of England, it was their sense, and it was the sense of the kingdom, that they were to remain subject to the supreme authority of Parliament;" whereby we understand your Excellency to mean, in the sense of the declaratory act of Parliament afore mentioned, in all cases whatever. And, indeed, it is difficult, if possible, to draw a line of distinction between the universal authority of Parliament over the colonies, and no authority at all. It is, therefore, necessary for us to inquire how it appears, for your Excellency has not shown it to us, that when, or at the time that our predecessors took possession of this plantation, or colony, under a grant and charter from the Crown of England, it was their sense, and the sense of the kingdom, that they were to remain subject to the authority of Parliament. [. . .]

Previous to a direct consideration of the charter granted to the province or colony, and the better to elucidate the true sense and meaning of it, we would take a view of the state of the English North American continent at the time, when, and after possession was first taken of any part of it, by the Europeans. It was then possessed by heathen and barbarous people, who had, nevertheless, all that right to the soil, and sovereignty in and over the lands they possessed, which God had originally given to man. Whether their being heathen, inferred any right or authority to christian princes, a right which had long been assumed by the Pope, to dispose of their lands to others, we will leave to your Excellency, or any one of understanding and impartial judgment, to consider. It is certain, they had in no other sense, forfeited them to any power in Europe. Should the doctrine be admitted, that the discovery of lands owned and possessed by pagan people, gives to any christian prince a right and title to the dominion and property, still it is vested in the Crown alone. It was an acquisition of foreign territory, not annexed to the realm of England, and, therefore, at the absolute disposal of the Crown. For we take it to be a settled point, that the King has a constitutional prerogative, to dispose of and alienate, any part of his territories not annexed to the realm. In the exercise of this prerogative, Queen Elizabeth granted the first American charter and, claiming a right by virtue of discovery, then supposed to be valid, to the lands which are now possessed by the colony of Virginia, she conveyed to Sir Walter Rawleigh, the property, dominion, and sovereignty thereof, to be held of the Crown, by homage, and a certain render, without any reservation to herself, of any share in the Legislative and Executive authority. After the attainder of Sir Walter, King James the I. created two Virginian companies, to be governed each by laws, transmitted to them by his Majesty, and not by the Parliament, with power to establish, and cause to be made, a coin to pass current among them; and vested with all liberties, franchises and immunities, within any of his other dominions, to all intents and purposes, as if they had been abiding and born within the realm. A declaration similar to this, is contained in the first charter of this colony, and in those of other American colonies, which shows that the colonies were not intended, or considered to be within the realm of England, though within the allegiance of the English Crown. After this, another charter was granted by the same King James, to the Treasurer and Company of Virginia, vesting them with full power and authority, to make, ordain, and establish, all manner of orders, laws, directions, instructions, forms and ceremonies of governments, and magistracy, fit and necessary, and the same to abrogate, &c. without any reservation for securing their subjection to the Parliament, and future laws of England. A third charter was afterwards granted by the same King, to the Treasurer and Company of Virginia, vesting them with power and authority to make laws, with an addition of this clause, "so, always, that the same be not contrary to the laws and statutes of this our realm of England." The same clause was afterwards copied into the charter of this and other colonies, with certain variations, such as, that these laws should be "consonant to reason," not repugnant to the laws of England, "as nearly as conveniently may be to the laws, statutes and rights of England," &c. These modes of expression, convey the same meaning, and serve to show an intention, that the laws of the colonies should be as much as possible, conformable in the spirit of them, to the principles and fundamental laws of the English constitution, its rights and statutes then in being, and by no means to bind the colonies to a subjection to the supreme authority of the English Parliament. And that this is the true intention, we think it further evident from this consideration, that no acts of any colony Legislative, are ever brought into Parliament for inspection there, though the laws made in some of them, like the acts of the British Parliament, are laid before the King for his dissent or allowance. [. . .]

These charters, as well as that afterwards granted to Lord Baltimore, and other charters, are repugnant to the idea of Parliamentary authority; and, to suppose a Parliamentary authority over the colonies, under such charters, would necessarily induce that solecism in politics, *imperium in imperio*. And the King's repeatedly exercising the prerogative of disposing of the American territory by such charters, together with the silence of the nation thereupon, is an evidence that it was an acknowledged prerogative. [. . .]

Having taken a view of the several charters of the first colony in America, if we look into the old charter of this colony, we shall find it to be grounded on the same principle; that the right of disposing the territory granted therein, was vested in the Crown, as being that Christian Sovereign who first discovered it, when in the possession of heathens; and that it was considered as being not within the realm, but being only within the Fee and Seignory of the King. As, therefore, it was without the realm of England, must not the King, if he had designed that the Parliament should have had any authority over it, have made a special reservation for that purpose, which was not done? [. . .]

The King, in the first charter to this colony, expressly grants, that it "shall be construed, reputed and adjudged in all cases, most favorably on the behalf and for the benefit and behoof of the said Governor and Company, and their successors—any matter, cause or thing, whatsoever, to the contrary notwithstanding." It is one of the liberties of free and natural subjects, born and abiding within the realm, to be governed, as your Excellency observes, "by laws made by persons, in whose elections they, from time to time, have a voice." This is an essential right. For nothing is more evident, than, that any people, who are subject to the unlimited power of another, must be in a state of abject slavery. It was easily and plainly foreseen, that the right of representation in the English Parliament, could not be exercised by the people of this colony. It would be impracticable, if consistent with the English constitution. And for this reason, that this colony might have and enjoy all the liberties and immunities of free and natural subjects within the realm, as stipulated in the charter, it was necessary, and a Legislative was accordingly constituted within the colony; one branch of which, consists of Representatives chosen by the people, to make all laws, statutes, ordinances, &c. for the well ordering and governing the same, not repugnant to the laws of England, or, as nearly as conveniently might be, agreeable to the fundamental laws of the English constitution. We are, therefore, still at a loss to conceive, where your Excellency finds it "provided in the same charter, that such acts," viz. acts of Parliament, made expressly to refer to us, "shall be in force" in this province. There is nothing to this purpose, expressed in the charter, or in our opinion, even implied in it. And surely it would be very absurd, that a charter, which is evidently formed upon a supposition and intention, that a colony is and should be considered as not within the realm; and declared by the very Prince who granted it, to be not within the jurisdiction of Parliament, should yet provide, that the laws which the same Parliament should make, expressly to refer to that colony, should be in force therein. Your Excellency is pleased to ask, "does it follow, that the government, by their (our ancestors) removal from one part of the dominions to another, loses its authority over that part to which they remove; and that they are freed from the subjection they were under before?" We answer, if that part of the King's dominions, to which they removed, was not then a part of the realm, and was never annexed to it, the Parliament lost no authority over it, having never had such authority; and the emigrations were consequently freed from the subjection they were under before their removal. The power and authority of Parliament, being constitutionally confined within the limits of the realm, and the nation collectively, of which alone it is the representing and Legislative Assembly. Your Excellency further asks, "will it not rather be said, that by this, their voluntary removal, they have relinquished, for a time, at least, one of the rights of an English subject, which they might, if they pleased, have continued to enjoy, and may again enjoy, whenever they return to the place where it can be exercised?" To which we answer; they never did relinquish the right to be governed by laws, made by persons in whose election they had a voice. The King stipulated with them, that they should have and enjoy all the liberties of free and natural subjects, born within the realm, to all intents, purposes and constructions, whatsoever; that is, that they should be as free as those, who were to abide within the realm: consequently, he stipulated with them, that they should enjoy and exercise this most essential right, which discriminates freemen from vassals, uninterruptedly, in its full sense and meaning; and they did, and ought still to exercise it, without the necessity of returning, for the sake of exercising it, to the nation or state of England. [. . .]

Your Excellency is disposed to compare this government to the variety of corporations, formed within the kingdom, with power to make and execute by-laws, &c.; and, because they remain subject to the supreme authority of Parliament, to infer, that this colony is also subject to the same authority: this reasoning appears to us not just. The members of those corporations are resident within the kingdom; and residence subjects them to the authority of Parliament, in which they are also represented; whereas the people of this colony are not resident within the realm. The charter was granted, with the express purpose to induce them to reside without the realm; consequently, they are not represented in Parliament there. But, we would ask your Excellency, are any of the corporations, formed within the kingdom, vested with the power of erecting other subordinate corporations? of enacting and determining what crimes shall be capital? and constituting courts of common law, with all their officers, for the hearing, trying and punishing capital offenders with death? These and many other powers vested in this government, plainly show, that it is to be considered as a corporation, in no other light, than as every state is a corporation. Besides, appeals from the courts of law here, are not brought before the House of Lords; which shows, that the peers of the realm, are not the peers of America: but all such appeals are brought before the King in council, which is a further evidence, that we are not within the realm.

We conceive enough has been said, to convince your Excellency, that, when our predecessors first took possession of this plantation, or colony, by a grant and charter from the Crown of England, it *was not*, and never had been the sense of the kingdom, that they were to remain subject to the supreme authority of Parliament. We will now, with your Excellency's leave, inquire what *was* the sense of our ancestors, of this very important matter.

And, as your Excellency has been pleased to tell us, you have not discovered, that the supreme authority of Parliament has been called in question, even by private and particular persons, until within seven or eight years past; except about the time of the anarchy and confusion in England, which preceded the restoration of King Charles the II. we beg leave to remind your Excellency of some parts of your own history of Massachusetts Bay. [. . .] By the history, it appears to have been the opinion of those persons of influence, "that the subjects of any prince or state, had a natural right to remove to any other state, or to another quarter of the world, unless the state was weakened or exposed by such remove; and, even in that case, if they were deprived of the right of all mankind, liberty of conscience, it would justify a separation, and upon their removal, their subjection determined and ceased." That "the country to which they had removed, was claimed and possessed by independent princes, whose right to the lordship and sovereignty thereof had been acknowledged by the Kings of England," an instance of which is quoted in the margin. "That they themselves had actually purchased, for valuable consideration, not only the soil, but the dominion, the lordship and sovereignty of those princes;" without which purchase, "in the sight of God and men, they had no right or title to what they possessed." They had received a charter of incorporation from the King, from whence arose a new kind of subjection, namely, "a voluntary, civil subjection;" and by this compact, "they were to be governed by laws made by themselves." Thus it appears to have been the sentiments of private persons, though persons by whose sentiments the public conduct was influenced, that their removal was a justifiable separation from the mother state, upon which, their subjection to that state, determined and ceased. [. . .]

The first act of Parliament, made expressly to refer to the colonies, was after the restoration. In the reign of King Charles the II. several such acts passed. And the same history informs us, there was a difficulty in conforming to them; and the reason of this difficulty is explained in a letter of the General Assembly to their Agent, quoted in the following words; "they apprehended them to be an invasion of the rights, liberties and properties of the subjects of his Majesty, in the colony, they not being represented in Parliament, and according to the usual sayings of the learned in the law, the laws of England were bounded within the four seas, and did not reach America: However, as his Majesty had signified his pleasure, that those acts should be observed in the Massachusetts, they had made provision, by a law of the colony, that they should be strictly attended." Which provision, by a law of their own, would have been superfluous, if they had admitted the supreme authority of Parliament. [. . .]

But, still further to show the sense of our ancestors, respecting this matter, we beg leave to recite some parts of a narrative, presented to the Lords of Privy Council, by Edward Randolph, in the year 1676, which we find in your Excellency's collection of papers lately published. Therein it is declared to be the sense of the colony, "that no law is in force or esteem there, but such as are made by the General Court; and, therefore, it is accounted a breach of their privileges, and a betraying of the liberties of their commonwealth, to urge the observation of the laws of England." [. . .] And, further, "there is no notice taken, of the act of navigation, plantation or any other laws, made in England for the regulation of trade." [. . .] And further, "he (the Governor) freely declared to me, that the laws made by your Majesty and, your Parliament, obliged them in nothing, but what consists with the interests of that colony; that the Legislative power and authority is, and abides in them solely." And in the same Mr. Randolph's letter to the Bishop of London, July 14, 1682, he says, "this independence in government is claimed and daily practiced." And your Excellency being then sensible, that this was the sense of our ancestors, in a marginal note, in the same collection of papers, observes, that, "this, viz. the provision made for observing the acts of trade, is very extraordinary, for this provision was an act of the colony, declaring the acts of trade shall be in force there." [. . .]

Thus we see, from your Excellency's history and publications, the sense our ancestors had of the jurisdiction of Parliament, under the first charter. Very different from that, which your Excellency in your speech, apprehends it to have been. [. . .]

Soon after the arrival of the charter, viz. in 1692, your Excellency's history informs us, "the first act" of this Legislative, was a sort of Magna Charta, asserting and setting forth their general privileges, and this clause was among the rest; "no aid, tax, tallage, assessment, custom, loan, benevolence, or imposition whatever, shall be laid, assessed, imposed, or levied on any of their Majesty's subjects, or their estates, on any pretence whatever, but by the act and consent of the Governor, Council, and Representatives of the people assembled in General Court." And though this act was disallowed, it serves to show the sense which the General Assembly, contemporary with the granting the charter, had of their sole and exclusive right to legislate for the colony. The history says, "the other parts of the act were copied from Magna Charta;" by which, we may conclude that the Assembly then construed the words, "not repugnant to the laws," to mean, conformable to the fundamental principles of the English constitution. And it is observable, that the Lords of Privy Council, so lately as in the reign of Queen Anne, when several laws enacted by the General Assembly were laid before her Majesty for her allowance, interpreted the words in this charter, "not repugnant to the laws of England," by the words, "as nearly as conveniently may be agreeable to the laws and statutes of England." And her Majesty was pleased to disallow those acts, not because they were repugnant to any law or statute of England, made expressly to refer to the colony, but because divers persons, by virtue thereof, were punished, without being tried by their peers in the ordinary "courts of law," and "by the ordinary rules and known methods of justice," contrary to the express terms of Magna Charta, which was a statute in force at the time of granting the charter, and declaratory of the rights and liberties of the subjects within the realm.

You are pleased to say, that "our provincial or local laws have, in numerous instances, had relation to acts of Parliament, made to respect the plantations, and this colony in particular." The authority of the Legislature, says the same author who is quoted by your Excellency, "does not extend so far as the fundamentals of the constitution. They ought to consider the fundamental laws as sacred, if the nation has not in very express terms, given them the power to change them. For the constitution of the state ought to be fixed; and since that was first established by the nation, which afterwards trusted certain persons with the Legislative power, the fundamental laws are excepted from their commission." Now the fundamentals of the constitution of this province, are stipulated in the charter; the reasoning, therefore, in this case, holds equally good. Much less, then, ought any acts or doings of the General Assembly, however numerous, to neither of which your Excellency has pointed us, which barely relate to acts of Parliament made to respect the plantations in general, or this colony in particular, to be taken as an acknowledgment of this people, or even of the Assembly, which inadvertently passed those acts, that we are subject to the supreme authority of Parliament; and with still less reason are the decisions in the executive courts to determine this point. If they have adopted that "as part of the rule of law," which, in fact, is not, it must be imputed to inattention or error in judgment, and cannot justly be urged as an alteration or restriction of the Legislative authority of the province.

Before we leave this part of your Excellency's speech, we would observe, that the great design of our ancestors, in leaving the kingdom of England, was to be freed from a subjection to its spiritual laws and courts, and to worship God according to the dictates of their consciences. Your Excellency, in your history observes, that their design was "to obtain for themselves and their posterity, the liberty of worshipping God in such manner as appeared to them most agreeable to the sacred scriptures." And the General Court themselves declared in 1651, that "seeing just cause to fear the persecution of the then Bishop, and high commission for not conforming to the ceremonies of those under their power, they thought it their safest course, to get to this outside of the world, but of their view, and beyond their reach." But, if it had been their sense, that they were still to be subject to the supreme authority of Parliament, they must have known that their design might, and probably would be frustrated; that the Parliament, especially considering the temper of those times, might make what ecclesiastical laws they pleased, expressly to refer to them, and place them in the same circumstances with respect to religious matters, to be relieved from which, was the design of their removal; and we would add, that if your Excellency's construction of the clause in our present charter is just, another clause therein, which provides for liberty of conscience for all christians, except papists, may be rendered void by an act of Parliament made to refer to us, requiring a conformity to the rites and mode of worship in the church of England, or any other.

Thus we have endeavored to show the sense of the people of this colony under both charters; and, if there have been in any late instances a submission *to* acts of Parliament, it has been, in our opinion, rather from inconsideration, or a reluctance at the idea of contending with the parent state, than from a conviction or acknowledgment of the Supreme Legislative authority of Parliament.

Your Excellency tells us, "you know of no line that can be drawn between the supreme authority of Parliament and the total independence of the colonies." If there be no such line, the consequence is, either that the colonies are the vassals of the Parliament, or that they are totally independent. As it cannot be supposed to have been the intention of the parties in the compact, that we should be reduced to a state of vassalage, the conclusion is, that it was their sense, that we were thus independent. "It is impossible," your Excellency says, "that there should be two independent Legislatures in one and the same state." May we not then further conclude, that it was their sense, that the colonies were, by their charters, made distinct states from the mother country? Your Excellency adds, "for although there may be but one head, the King, yet the two Legislative bodies will make two governments as distinct as the kingdoms of England and Scotland, before the union." Very true, may it please your Excellency; and if they interfere not with each other, what hinders, but that being united in one head and common Sovereign, they may live happily in that connection, and mutually support and protect each other? Notwithstanding all the terrors which your Excellency has pictured to us as the effects of a total independence, there is more reason to dread the consequences of absolute uncontrolled power, whether of a nation or a monarch, than those of a total independence. It would be a misfortune to know by experience, the difference between the liberties of an English colonist and those of the Spanish, French, and Dutch: and since the British Parliament has passed an act, which is executed even with rigor, though not voluntarily submitted to, for raising a revenue, and appropriating the same, without the consent of the people who pay it, and have claimed a power of making such laws as they please, to order and govern us, your Excellency will excuse us in asking, whether you do not think we already experience too much of such a difference, and have not reason to fear we shall soon be reduced to a worse situation than that of the colonies of France, Spain, or Holland?

If your Excellency expects to have the line of distinction between the supreme authority of Parliament, and the total independence of the colonies drawn by us, we would say it would be an arduous undertaking, and of very great importance to all the other colonies; and therefore, could we conceive of such a line, we should be unwilling to propose it, without their consent in Congress.

To conclude, these are great and profound questions. It is the grief of this House, that, by the ill policy of a late injudicious administration, America has been driven into the contemplation of them. And we cannot but express our concern, that your Excellency, by your speech, has reduced us to the unhappy alternative, either of appearing by our silence to acquiesce in your Excellency's sentiments, or of thus freely discussing this point.

After all that we have said, we would be far from being understood to have in the least abated that just sense of allegiance which we owe to the King of Great Britain, our rightful Sovereign; and should the people of this province be left to the free and full exercise of all the liberties and immunities granted to them by charter, there would be no danger of an independence on the Crown. Our charters reserve great power to the Crown in its Representative, fully sufficient to balance, analogous to the English constitution, all the liberties and privileges granted to the people. All this your Excellency knows full well; and whoever considers the power and influence, in all their branches, reserved by our charter, to the Crown, will be far from thinking that the Commons of this province are too independent.

[This answer was reported by Mr. S. Adams, Mr. Hancock, Maj. Hawley, Col. Bowers, Mr. Hobson, Maj. Foster, Mr. Phillips, and Col. Thayer.]

PHILLIS WHEATLEY

Letter to Reverend Samson Occum (March 11, 1774)

The Connecticut Gazette

Rev'd and honor'd Sir,

I have this Day received your obliging kind Epistle, and am greatly satisfied with your Reasons respecting the Negroes, and think highly reasonable what you offer in Vindication of their natural Rights: Those that invade them cannot be insensible that the divine Light is chasing away the thick Darkness which broods over the Land of Africa; and the Chaos which has reign'd so long, is converting into beautiful Order, and reveals more and more clearly, the glorious Dispensation of civil and religious Liberty, which are so inseparably united, that there is little or no Enjoyment of one without the other: Otherwise, perhaps, the Israelites had been less solicitous for their Freedom from Egyptian Slavery; I don't say they would have been contented without it, by no Means, for in every human Breast, God has implanted a Principle, which we call Love of Freedom; it is impatient of Oppression, and pants for Deliverance; and by the Leave of our modern Egyptians I will assert, that the same Principle lives in us. God grant Deliverance in his own Way and Time, and get him honour upon all those whose Avarice impels them to countenance and help forward the Calamities of their fellow Creatures. This I desire not for their Hurt, but to convince them of the strange Absurdity of their Conduct whose Words and Actions are so diametrically opposite. How well the cry for Liberty, and the reverse Disposition for the exercise of oppressive Power over others agree,—I humbly think it does not require the Penetration of a Philosopher to determine.—

Phillis Wheatley

Declaration and Resolves of the First Continental Congress (October 14, 1774)

Whereas, since the close of the last war, the British parliament, claiming a power, of right, to bind the people of America by statutes in all cases whatsoever, hath, in some acts, expressly imposed taxes on them, and in others, under various presences, but in fact for the purpose of raising a revenue, hath imposed rates and duties payable in these colonies, established a board of commissioners, with unconstitutional powers, and extended the jurisdiction of courts of admiralty, not only for collecting the said duties, but for the trial of causes merely arising within the body of a county:

And whereas, in consequence of other statutes, judges, who before held only estates at will in their offices, have been made dependant on the crown alone for their salaries, and standing armies kept in times of peace: And whereas it has lately been resolved in parliament, that by force of a statute, made in the thirty-fifth year of the reign of King Henry the Eighth, colonists may be transported to England, and tried there upon accusations for treasons and misprisions, or concealments of treasons committed in the colonies, and by a late statute, such trials have been directed in cases therein mentioned:

And whereas, in the last session of parliament, three statutes were made; one entitled, "An act to discontinue, in such manner and for such time as are therein mentioned, the landing and discharging, lading, or shipping of goods, wares and merchandise, at the town, and within the harbour of Boston, in the province of Massachusetts-Bay in New England;" another entitled, "An act for the better regulating the government of the province of Massachusetts-Bay in New England;" and another entitled, "An act for the impartial administration of justice, in the cases of persons questioned for any act done by them in the execution of the law, or for the suppression of riots and tumults, in the province of the Massachusetts-Bay in New England;" and another statute was then made, "for making more effectual provision for the government of the province of Quebec, etc." All which statutes are impolitic, unjust, and cruel, as well as unconstitutional, and most dangerous and destructive of American rights:

And whereas, assemblies have been frequently dissolved, contrary to the rights of the people, when they attempted to deliberate on grievances; and their dutiful, humble, loyal, and reasonable petitions to the crown for redress, have been repeatedly treated with contempt, by his Majesty's ministers of state:

The good people of the several colonies of New-Hampshire, Massachusetts-Bay, Rhode Island and Providence Plantations, Connecticut, New-York, New-Jersey, Pennsylvania, Newcastle, Kent, and Sussex on Delaware, Maryland, Virginia, North-Carolina and South-Carolina, justly alarmed at these arbitrary proceedings of parliament and administration, have severally elected, constituted, and appointed deputies to meet, and sit in general Congress, in the city of Philadelphia, in order to obtain such establishment, as that their religion, laws, and liberties, may not be subverted: Whereupon the deputies so appointed being now assembled, in a full and free representation of these colonies, taking into their most serious consideration, the best means of attaining the ends aforesaid, do, in the first place, as Englishmen, their ancestors in like cases have usually done, for asserting and vindicating their rights and liberties, DECLARE,

That the inhabitants of the English colonies in North-America, by the immutable laws of nature, the principles of the English constitution, and the several charters or compacts, have the following RIGHTS:

Resolved, N.C.D. 1. That they are entitled to life, liberty and property: and they have never ceded to any foreign power whatever, a right to dispose of either without their consent.

Resolved, N.C.D. 2. That our ancestors, who first settled these colonies, were at the time of their emigration from the mother country, entitled to all the rights, liberties, and immunities of free and natural-born subjects, within the realm of England.

Resolved, N.C.D. 3. That by such emigration they by no means forfeited, surrendered, or lost any of those rights, but that they were, and their descendants now are, entitled to the exercise and enjoyment of all such of them, as their local and other circumstances enable them to exercise and enjoy.

Resolved, 4. That the foundation of English liberty, and of all free government, is a right in the people to participate in their legislative council: and as the English colonists are not represented, and from their local and other circumstances, cannot properly be represented in the British parliament, they are entitled to a free and exclusive power of legislation in their several provincial legislatures, where their right of representation can alone be preserved, in all cases of taxation and internal polity, subject only to the negative of their sovereign, in such manner as has been heretofore used and accustomed: But, from the necessity of the case, and a regard to the mutual interest of both countries, we cheerfully consent to the operation of such acts of the British parliament, as are bona fide, restrained to the regulation of our external commerce, for the purpose of securing the commercial advantages of the whole empire to the mother country, and the commercial benefits of its respective members; excluding every idea of taxation internal or external, for raising a revenue on the subjects, in America, without their consent.

Resolved, N.C.D. 5. That the respective colonies are entitled to the common law of England, and more especially to the great and inestimable privilege of being tried by their peers of the vicinage, according to the course of that law.

Resolved, N.C.D. 6. That they are entitled to the benefit of such of the English statutes, as existed at the time of their colonization; and which they have, by experience, respectively found to be applicable to their several local and other circumstances.

Resolved, N.C.D. 7. That these, his Majesty's colonies, are likewise entitled to all the immunities and privileges granted and confirmed to them by royal charters, or secured by their several codes of provincial laws.

Resolved, N.C.D. 8. That they have a right peaceably to assemble, consider of their grievances, and petition the king; and that all prosecutions, prohibitory proclamations, and commitments for the same, are illegal.

Resolved, N.C.D. 9. That the keeping a standing army in these colonies, in times of peace, without the consent of the legislature of that colony, in which such army is kept, is against law.

Resolved, N.C.D. 10. It is indispensably necessary to good government, and rendered essential by the English constitution, that the constituent branches of the legislature be independent of each other; that, therefore, the exercise of legislative power in several colonies, by a council appointed, during pleasure, by the crown, is unconstitutional, dangerous and destructive to the freedom of American legislation.

All and each of which the aforesaid deputies, in behalf of themselves, and their constituents, do claim, demand, and insist on, as their indubitable rights and liberties, which cannot be legally taken from them, altered or abridged by any power whatever, without their own consent, by their representatives in their several provincial legislature.

In the course of our inquiry, we find many infringements and violations of the foregoing rights, which, from an ardent desire, that harmony and mutual intercourse of affection and interest may be restored, we pass over for the present, and proceed to state such acts and measures as have been adopted since the last war, which demonstrate a system formed to enslave America.

Resolved, N.C.D. That the following acts of parliament are infringements and violations of the rights of the colonists; and that the repeal of them is essentially necessary, in order to restore harmony between Great Britain and the American colonies, viz.

The several acts of Geo. III. ch. 15, and ch. 34.-5 Geo. III. ch. 25.-6 Geo. ch. 52.-7 Geo. III. ch. 41 and ch. 46.-8 Geo. III. ch. 22. which impose duties for the purpose of raising a revenue in America, extend the power of the admiralty courts beyond their ancient limits, deprive the American subject of trial by jury, authorize the judges certificate to indemnify the prosecutor from damages, that he might otherwise be liable to, requiring oppressive security from a claimant of ships and goods seized, before he shall be allowed to defend his property, and are subversive of American rights.

Also 12 Geo. III. ch. 24, intituled, "An act for the better securing his majesty's dockyards, magazines, ships, ammunition, and stores," which declares a new offence in America, and deprives the American subject of a constitutional trial by jury of the vicinage, by authorizing the trial of any person, charged with the committing any offence described in the said act, out of the realm, to be indicted and tried for the same in any shire or county within the realm.

Also the three acts passed in the last session of parliament, for stopping the port and blocking up the harbour of Boston, for altering the charter and government of Massachusetts-Bay, and that which is entitled, "An act for the better administration of justice, etc."

Also the act passed in the same session for establishing the Roman Catholic religion, in the province of Quebec, abolishing the equitable system of English laws, and erecting a tyranny there, to the great danger (from so total a dissimilarity of religion, law and government) of the neighboring British colonies, by the assistance of whose blood and treasure the said country was conquered from France.

Also the act passed in the same session, for the better providing suitable quarters for officers and soldiers in his majesty's service, in North-America.

Also, that the keeping a standing army in several of these colonies, in time of peace, without the consent of the legislature of that colony, in which such army is kept, is against law.

To these grievous acts and measures, Americans cannot submit, but in hopes their fellow subjects in Great Britain will, on a revision of them, restore us to that state, in which both countries found happiness and prosperity, we have for the present, only resolved to pursue the following peaceable measures: 1. To enter into a non-importation, non-consumption, and non-exportation agreement or association. 2. To prepare an address to the people of Great-Britain, and a memorial to the inhabitants of British America: and 3. To prepare a loyal address to his majesty, agreeable to resolutions already entered into.

Isaac Backus

A History of New England with Particular Reference to the Baptists, Volume 2 (1774)

September 7, [1774] [. . .] They [. . .] were in earnest for me to go to the Association and also to the Congress at Philadelphia, and represented that now was the most likely time to obtain our religious liberty that we had ever known. [. . .]

September 14. The Association were all unanimous that I should go to Philadelphia. [. . .]

The Association gave to Mr. Backus the following certificate:

To the Honorable Delegates of the several colonies in North America, met in a general Congress in Philadelphia:

Honorable Gentlemen: As the Antipaedobaptist churches in New England are most heartily concerned for the preservation and defense of the rights and privileges of this country, and are deeply affected by the encroachments upon the same, which have lately been made by the British parliament, and are willing to unite with our dear countrymen, vigorously to pursue every prudent measure for relief, so we would beg leave to say that, as a distinct denomination of Protestants, we conceive that we have an equal claim to charter-rights with the rest of our fellow-subjects; and yet have long been denied the free and full enjoyment of those rights, as to the support of religious worship. Therefore we, the elders and brethren of twenty Baptist churches met in Association at Medfield, twenty miles from Boston, September 14, 1774, have unanimously chosen and sent unto you the reverend and beloved Mr. Isaac Backus as our agent, to lay our case, in these respects, before you, or otherwise to use all the prudent means he can for our relief. [. . .]

These resolves were carried by said agent to that city; where he met with an Association of Baptist Churches, from several adjacent colonies who elected a large Committee to assist in the affair, and by their request a conference was procured in the evening of October 14, with the Honorable Delegates from our Province to Congress, in the presence of several more of their members, and other gentleman. It was opened by reading a brief memorial of our chief grievances in Massachusetts, on religious accounts. [. . .]

It claimed liberty of conscience for the Baptists in Massachusetts Bay, both as a natural and as a charter right, and showed how this right had been violated by various enactments of the General Assembly. [. . .] It closed as follows:

"It may now be asked, *What is the liberty desired?* The answer is: As the kingdom of Christ is not of this world, and religion is a concern between God and the soul, with which no human authority can intermeddle, consistently with the principles of Christianity, and according to the dictates of Protestantism, we claim and expect the liberty of worshipping God according to our consciences, not being obliged to support a ministry we cannot attend, whilst we demean ourselves as faithful subjects. These we have an undoubted right to, as men, as Christians, and by charter as inhabitants of Massachusetts Bay. [. . .]"

John Adams made a long speech and Samuel Adams another; both of whom said, "There is, indeed, an ecclesiastical establishment in our province; but a very slender one, hardly to be called an establishment." When they would permit, we brought up facts, which they tried to explain away, but could not. Then they shifted their plea, and asserted that our General Court was clear of blame, and had always been ready to hear our complaints, and to grant all reasonable help, whatever might have been done by executive officers; and S. Adams and R. T. Paine spent near an hour more on this plea. When they stopped, I told them I was very sorry to have any accusations to bring against the government which I belonged to, and which I would gladly serve to the utmost of my power, but I must say that facts proved the contrary to their plea; and gave a short account of our Legislature's treatment of Ashfield, which was very puzzling to them. In their plea, S. Adams tried to represent that *regular* Baptists were quite easy among us; and more than once insinuated that these complaints came from enthusiasts who made it a merit to suffer persecution; and also that enemies had a hand therein. Paine said, there was nothing of conscience in the matter; it was only a contending about paying a little money; and also that we would not be neighborly and let them know who we were, which was all they wanted, and they would readily exempt us.

In answer, I told them they might call it enthusiasm or what they pleased; but I freely own, before all these gentlemen, that it is absolutely a point of conscience with me; for I cannot give in the certificates they require without implicitly acknowledging that power in man which I believe belongs only to God. This shocked them; and Cushing said: "*It quite altered the case*; for if it were a point of conscience, he had nothing to say to that." And the conference of about four hours continuance, closed with their promising to do what they could for our relief; though to deter us from thinking of their coming upon equal footing with us as to religion, John Adams at one time said, we might as well expect a change in the solar system, as to expect they would give up their establishment.

1775 Memorial to the Massachusetts Assembly

Our real grievances are, that we, as well as our fathers, have, from time to time, been taxed on religious accounts where we were not represented; and when we have sued for our rights, our causes have been tried by interested judges. That the Representatives in former Assemblies, as well as the present, were elected by virtue only of civil and worldly qualifications, is a truth so evident, that we presume it need not be proved to this Assembly; and for a civil Legislature to impose religious taxes, is, we conceive, a power which their constituents never had to give; and is therefore going entirely out of their jurisdiction. . . . Under the legal dispensation, where God himself prescribed the exact proportion of what the people were to give, yet none but persons of the worst characters ever attempted to *take it by force*. I Sam. ii. 12, 16; Mic. iii. 5–9. How daring then, must it be for any to do it for Christ's ministers, who says, *My kingdom is not of this world!* . . . We beseech this honorable Assembly to take these matters into their wise and serious consideration, before him who has said, With what measure ye mete it shall be measured to you again. Is not all America now appealing to heaven against the injustice of being taxed where we are not represented, and against being judged by men who are interested in getting away our money? And will heaven approve of your *doing the same thing* to your fellow servants? No, surely. . . . We have no desire of representing this government as the worst of any who have imposed religious taxes; we fully believe the contrary. Yet, as we are persuaded that an entire freedom from being taxed by civil rulers to religious worship, is not a mere favor, from any man or men in the world, but a right and property granted us by God, who commands us to stand fast in it, we have not only the same reason to refuse an acknowledgement of such a taxing power here, as America has the above-said power, but also, according to our present light, we should wrong our consciences in allowing that power to men, which we believe belongs only to God.

Thomas Jefferson

A Summary View of the Rights of British America (July 1774)

Resolved that it be an instruction to the said deputies when assembled in General Congress with the deputies from the other states of British America to propose to the said Congress that an humble and dutiful address be presented to his majesty begging leave to lay before him as chief magistrate of the British empire the united complaints of his majesty's subjects in America; complaints which are excited by many unwarrantable incroachments and usurpations, attempted to be made by the legislature of one part of the empire, upon those rights which god and the laws have given equally and independently to all. To represent to his majesty that these his states have often individually made humble application to his imperial throne, to obtain thro' [its] intervention some redress of their injured rights; to none of which was ever even an answer condescended. Humbly to hope that this their joint address, penned in the language of truth, and divested of those expressions of servility which would persuade his majesty that we are asking favors and not rights, shall obtain from his majesty a more respectful acceptance. And this his majesty will think we have reason to expect when he reflects that he is no more than the chief officer of the people, appointed by the laws, and circumscribed with definite powers, to assist in working the great machine of government erected for their use, and consequently subject to their superintendance. And in order that these our rights, as well as the invasions of them, may be laid more fully before his majesty, to take a view of them from the origin and first settlement of these countries.

To remind him that our ancestors, before their emigration to America, were the free inhabitants of the British dominions in Europe, and possessed a right, which nature has given to all men, of departing from the country in which chance, not choice has placed them, of going in quest of new habitations, and of there establishing new societies, under such laws and regulations as to them shall seem most likely to promote public happiness. That their Saxon ancestors had under this universal law, in like manner, left their native wilds and woods in the North of Europe, had possessed themselves of the island of Britain then less charged with inhabitants, and had established there that system of laws which has so long been the glory and protection of that country. Nor was ever any claim of superiority or dependance asserted over them by that mother country from which they had migrated: and were such a claim made it is beleived his majesty's subjects in Great Britain have too firm a feeling of the rights derived to them from their ancestors to bow down the sovereignty of their state before such visionary pretensions. And it is thought that no circumstance has occurred to distinguish materially the British from the Saxon emigration. America was conquered, and her settlements made and firmly established, at the expence of individuals, and not of the British public. Their own blood was spilt in acquiring lands for their settlement, their own fortunes expended in making that settlement effectual. For themselves they fought, for themselves they conquered, and for themselves alone they have right to hold. No shilling was ever issued from the public treasures of his majesty or his ancestors for their assistance, till of very late times, after the colonies had become established on a firm and permanent footing. That then indeed, having become valuable to Great Britain for her commercial purposes, his parliament was pleased to lend them assistance against an enemy who would fain have drawn to herself the benefits of their commerce to the great aggrandisement of herself and danger of Great Britain. Such assistance, and in such circumstances, they had often before given to Portugal and other allied states, with whom they carry on a commercial intercourse. Yet these states never supposed that, by calling in her aid, they thereby submitted themselves to her sovereignty. Had such terms been proposed, they would have rejected them with disdain, and trusted for better to the moderation of their enemies, or to a vigorous exertion of their own force. We do not however mean to underrate those aids, which to us were doubtless valuable, on whatever principles granted: but we would shew that they cannot give a title to that authority which the British parliament would arrogate over us; and that they may amply be repaid, by our giving to the inhabitants of Great Britain such exclusive privileges in trade as may be advantageous to them, and at the same time not too restrictive to ourselves. That settlements having been thus effected in the wilds of America, the emigrants thought proper to adopt that system of laws under which they had hitherto lived in the mother country, and to continue their union with her by submitting themselves to the same common sovereign, who was thereby made the central link connecting the several parts of the empire thus newly multiplied.

But that not long were they permitted, however far they thought themselves removed from the hand of oppression, to hold undisturbed the rights thus acquired at the hazard of their lives and loss of their fortunes. A family of princes was then on the British throne, whose treasonable crimes against their people brought on them afterwards the exertion of those sacred and sovereign rights of punishment, reserved in the hands of the people for cases of extreme necessity, and judged by the constitution unsafe to be delegated to any other judicature. While every day brought forth some new and unjustifiable exertion of power over their subjects on that side the water, it was not to be expected that those here, much less able at that time to oppose the designs of despotism, should be exempted from injury. Accordingly that country which had been acquired by the lives, the labors and the fortunes of individual adventurers, was by these princes at several times parted out and distributed among the favorites and followers of their fortunes; and by an assumed right of the crown alone were erected into distinct and independent governments; a measure which it is beleived his majesty's prudence and understanding would prevent him from imitating at this day; as no exercise of such a power of dividing and dismembering a country has ever occurred in his majesty's realm of England, tho' now of very antient standing; nor could it be justified or acquiesced under there or in any other part of his majesty's empire.

That the exercise of a free trade with all parts of the world, possessed by the American colonists as of natural right, and which no law of their own had taken away or abridged, was next the object of unjust incroachment. Some of the colonies having thought proper to continue the administration of their government in the name and under the authority of his majesty king Charles the first, whom notwithstanding his late deposition by the Common-wealth of England, they continued in the sovereignty of their state, the Parliament for the Common-wealth took the same in high offence, and assumed upon themselves the power of prohibiting their trade with all other parts of the world except the island of Great

Britain. This arbitrary act however they soon recalled, and by solemn treaty entered into on the 12th. day of March 1651, between the said Commonwealth by their Commissioners and the colony of Virginia by their house of Burgesses, it was expressly stipulated by the 8th. article of the said treaty that they should have "free trade as the people of England do enjoy to all places and with all nations according to the laws of that Commonwealth." But that, upon the restoration of his majesty King Charles the second, their rights of free commerce fell once more a victim to arbitrary power: and by several acts of his reign as well as of some of his successors the trade of the colonies was laid under such restrictions as shew what hopes they might form from the justice of a British parliament were its uncontrouled power admitted over these states. History has informed us that bodies of men as well as individuals are susceptible of the spirit of tyranny. A view of these acts of parliament for regulation, as it has been affectedly called, of the American trade, if all other evidence were removed out of the case, would undeniably evince the truth of this observation. Besides the duties they impose on our articles of export and import, they prohibit our going to any Markets Northward of cape Finesterra in the kingdom of Spain for the sale of commodities which Great Britain will not take from us, and for the purchase of others with which she cannot supply us; and that for no other than the arbitrary purpose of purchasing for themselves by a sacrifice of our rights and interests, certain privileges in their commerce with an allied state, who, in confidence that their exclusive trade with America will be continued while the principles and power of the British parliament be the same, have induldged themselves in every exorbitance which their avarice could dictate, or our necessities extort: have raised their commodities called for in America to the double and treble of what they sold for before such exclusive privileges were given them, and of what better commodities of the same kind would cost us elsewhere; and at the same time give us much less for what we carry thither, than might be had at more convenient ports. That these acts prohibit us from carrying in quest of other purchasers the surplus of our tobaccoes remaining after the consumption of Great Britain is supplied: so that we must leave them with the British merchant for whatever he will please to allow us, to be by him reshipped to foreign markets, where he will reap the benefits of making sale of them for full value. That to heighten still the idea of parliamentary justice, and to shew with what moderation they are like to exercise power, where themselves are to feel no part of [its] weight, we take leave to mention to his majesty certain other acts of British parliament, by which they would prohibit us from manufacturing for our own use the articles we raise on our own lands with our own labor. By an act passed in the 5th. year of the reign of his late majesty king George the second an American subject is forbidden to make a hat for himself of the fur which he has taken perhaps on his own soil. An instance of despotism to which no parrallel can be produced in the most arbitrary ages of British history. By one other act passed in the 23d. year of the same reign, the iron which we make we are forbidden to manufacture; and, heavy as that article is, and necessary in every branch of husbandry, besides commission and insurance, we are to pay freight for it to Great Britain, and freight for it back again, for the purpose of supporting, not men, but machines, in the island of Great Britain. In the same spirit of equal and impartial legislation is to be viewed the act of parliament passed in the 5th. year of the same reign, by which American lands are made subject to the demands of British creditors, while their own lands were still continued unanswerable for their debts; from which one of these conclusions must necessarily follow, either that justice is not the same thing in America as in Britain, or else that the British parliament pay less regard to it here than there. But that we do not point out to his majesty the injustice of these acts with intent to rest on that principle the cause of their nullity, but to shew that experience confirms the propriety of those political principles which exempt us from the jurisdiction of the British parliament. The true ground on which we declare these acts void is that the British parliament has no right to exercise authority over us.

That these exercises of usurped power have not been confined to instances alone in which themselves were interested; but they have also intermeddled with the regulation of the internal affairs of the colonies. The act of the 9th. of Anne for establishing a post office in America seems to have had little connection with British convenience, except that of accomodating his majesty's ministers and favorites with the sale of a lucrative and easy office.

That thus have we hastened thro' the reigns which preceded his majesty's, during which the violation of our rights were less alarming, because repeated at more distant intervals, than that rapid and bold succession of injuries which is likely to distinguish the present from all other periods of American story. Scarcely have our minds been able to emerge from the astonishment into which one stroke of parliamentary thunder has involved us, before another more heavy and more alarming is fallen on us. Single acts of tyranny may be ascribed to the accidental opinion of a day; but a series of oppressions, begun at a distinguished period, and pursued unalterably thro' every change of ministers, too plainly prove a deliberate, systematical plan of reducing us to slavery.

That the act passed in the 4th. year of his majesty's reign intitled "an act [for granting certain duties"], one other act passed in the 5th. year of his reign intitled "an act [for granting and applying certain stamp duties"], one other act passed in the 6th. year of his reign intitled "an act [for the better securing the dependency of his majesty's dominions in America"], and one other act passed in the 7th. year of his reign intitled "an act [for granting duties on paper, tea, etc."] form that connected chain of parliamentary usurpation which has already been the subject of frequent applications to his majesty and the houses of Lords and Commons of Great Britain; and, no answers having yet been condescended to any of these, we shall not trouble his majesty with a repetition of the matters they contained.

But that one other act passed in the same 7th. year of his reign, having been a peculiar attempt, must ever require peculiar mention. It is intitled "an act [for suspending the legislature of New York."] One free and independent legislature hereby takes upon itself to suspend the powers of another, free and independent as itself, thus exhibiting a phaenomenon, unknown in nature, the creator and creature of [its] own power. Not only the principles of common sense, but the common feelings of human nature must be surrendered up, before his majesty's subjects here can be persuaded to beleive that they hold their political existence at the will of a British parliament. Shall these governments be dissolved, their property annihilated, and their people reduced to a state of nature, at the imperious breath of a body of men whom they never saw, in whom they never confided, and over whom they have no powers of punishment or removal, let their crimes against the American public be ever so great? Can any one reason be assigned why 160,000 electors in the island of Great Britain should give law to four millions in the states of America, every individual of whom is equal to every individual of them in virtue, in understanding, and in bodily strength? Were this to be admitted, instead of being a free people, as we have hitherto supposed, and mean to continue, ourselves, we should suddenly be found the slaves, not of one, but of 160,000 tyrants, distinguished too from all others by this singular circumstance that they are removed from the reach of fear, the only restraining motive which may hold the hand of a tyrant.

That by "an act to discontinue in such manner and for such time as are therein mentioned the landing and discharging lading or shipping of goods wares and merchandize at the town and within the harbor of Boston in the province of Massachusett's bay in North America" which was passed at the last session of British parliament, a large and populous town, whose trade was their sole subsistence, was deprived of that trade, and involved in utter ruin. Let us for a while suppose the question of right suspended, in order to examine this act on principles of justice. An act of parliament had been passed imposing duties on teas to be paid in America, against which act the Americans had protested as inauthoritative. The East India company, who till that time had never sent a pound of tea to America on their own account, step forth on that occasion the asserters of parliamentary right, and send hither many ship loads of that obnoxious commodity. The masters of their several vessels however, on their arrival in America, wisely attended to admonition, and returned with their cargoes. In the province of New England alone the remonstrances of the people were disregarded, and a compliance, after being many days waited for, was flatly refused. Whether in this the master of the vessel was governed by his obstinacy or his instructions, let those who know, say. There are extraordinary situations which require extraordinary interposition. An exasperated people, who feel that they possess power, are not easily restrained within limits strictly regular. A number of them assembled in the town of Boston, threw the tea into the ocean and dispersed without doing any other act of violence. If in this they did wrong, they were known, and were amenable to the laws of the land, against which it could not be objected that they had ever in any instance been obstructed or diverted from their regular course in favor of popular offenders. They should therefore not have been distrusted on this occasion. But that ill-fated colony had formerly been bold in their enmities against the house of Stuart, and were now devoted to ruin by that unseen hand which governs the momentous affairs of this great empire. On the partial representations of a few worthless ministerial dependants, whose constant office it has been to keep that government embroiled, and who by their treacheries hope to obtain the dignity of the British knighthood, without calling for a party accused, without asking a proof, without attempting a distinction between the guilty and the innocent, the whole of that antient and wealthy town is in a moment reduced from opulence to beggary. Men who had spent their lives in extending the British commerce, who had invested in that place the wealth their honest endeavors had merited, found themselves and their families thrown at once on the world for subsistence by [its] charities. Not the hundredth part of the inhabitants of that town had been concerned in the act complained of; many of them were in Great Britain and in other parts beyond sea; yet all were involved in one indiscriminate ruin, by a new executive power unheard of till then, that of a British parliament. A property of the value of many millions of money was sacrifised to revenge, not repay, the loss of a few thousands. This is administering justice with a heavy hand indeed! And when is this tempest to be arrested in [its] course? Two wharfs are to be opened again when his majesty shall think proper: the residue which lined the extensive shores of the bay of Boston are forever interdicted the exercise of commerce. This little exception seems to have been thrown in for no other purpose than that of setting a precedent for investing his majesty with legislative powers. If the pulse of his people shall beat calmly under this experiment, another and another will be tried till the measure of despotism be filled up. It would be an insult on common sense to pretend that this exception was made in order to restore [its] commerce to that great town. The trade which cannot be received at two wharfs alone, must of necessity be transferred to some other place; to which it will soon be followed by that of the two wharfs. Considered in this light it would be an insolent and cruel mockery at the annihilation of the town of Boston.

By the act for the suppression of riots and tumults in the town of Boston, passed also in the last session of parliament, a murder committed there is, if the governor pleases, to be tried in the court of King's bench in the island of Great Britain, by a jury of Middlesex. The witnesses too, on receipt of such a sum as the Governor shall think it reasonable for them to expend, are to enter into recognisance to appear at the trial. This is in other words taxing them to the amount of their recognisance; and that amount may be whatever a Governor pleases. For who does his majesty think can be prevailed on to cross the Atlantick for the sole purpose of bearing evidence to a fact? His expences are to be borne indeed as they shall be estimated by a Governor; but who are to feed the wife and children whom he leaves behind, and who have had no other subsistence but his daily labor? Those epidemical disorders too, so terrible in a foreign climate, is the cure of them to be estimated among the articles of expence, and their danger to be warded off by the almighty power of a parliament? And the wretched criminal, if he happen to have offended on the American side, stripped of his privilege of trial by peers, of his vicinage, removed from the place where alone full evidence could be obtained, without money, without counsel, without friends, without exculpatory proof, is tried before judges predetermined to condemn. The cowards who would suffer a countryman to be torn from the bowels of their society in order to be thus offered a sacrifice to parliamentary tyranny, would merit that everlasting infamy now fixed on the authors of the act! A clause for a similar purpose had been introduced into an act passed in the 12th. year of his majesty's reign entitled "an act for the better securing and preserving his majesty's dock-yards, magazines, ships, ammunition and stores," against which as meriting the same censures the several colonies have already protested.

That these are the acts of power assumed by a body of men foreign to our constitutions, and unacknowledged by our laws; against which we do, on behalf of the inhabitants of British America, enter this our solemn and determined protest. And we do earnestly intreat his majesty, as yet the only mediatory power between the several states of the British empire, to recommend to his parliament of Great Britain the total revocation of these acts, which however nugatory they be, may yet prove the cause of further discontents and jealousies among us.

That we next proceed to consider the conduct of his majesty, as holding the executive powers of the laws of these states, and mark out his deviations from the line of duty. By the constitution of Great Britain as well as of the several American states, his majesty possesses the power of refusing to pass into a law any bill which has already passed the other two branches of legislature. His majesty however and his ancestors, conscious of the impropriety of opposing their single opinion to the united wisdom of two houses of parliament, while their proceedings were unbiassed by interested principles, for several ages past have modestly declined the exercise of this power in that part of his empire called Great Britain. But by change of circumstances, other principles than those of justice simply have obtained an influence on their determinations. The addition of new states to the British empire has produced an addition of new, and sometimes opposite interests. It is now therefore the great office of his majesty to resume the exercise of his negative power, and to prevent the passage of laws by any one legislature of the empire which might bear injuriously on the rights and interests of another. Yet this will not excuse the wanton exercise of this power which we have seen his majesty practice on the laws of the American legislatures. For the most trifling reasons, and sometimes for no conceivable reason at all, his majesty has rejected laws of the most salutary tendency. The abolition of domestic slavery is the great object of desire in those colonies where it was unhappily introduced in their infant state. But previous to the infranchisement of the slaves we have, it is necessary to exclude all further importations from Africa. Yet our repeated attempts to effect this by prohibitions, and by imposing duties which might amount to a prohibition, have been hitherto defeated by his majesty's negative: thus preferring the immediate advantages of a few British corsairs to the lasting interests of the American states, and to the rights of human nature deeply wounded by this infamous practice. Nay the single interposition of an interested individual against a law was scarcely ever known to fail of success, tho' in the opposite scale were placed the interests of a whole country. That this is so shameful an abuse of a power trusted with his majesty for other purposes, as if not reformed would call for some legal restrictions.

With equal inattention to the necessities of his people here, has his majesty permitted our laws to lie neglected in England for years, neither confirming them by his assent, nor annulling them by his negative: so that such of them as have no suspending clause, we hold on the most precarious of all tenures, his majesty's will, and such of them as suspend themselves till his majesty's assent be obtained we have feared might be called into existence at some future and distant period, when time and change of circumstances shall have rendered them destructive to his people here. And to render this grievance still more oppressive, his majesty by his instructions has laid his governors under such restrictions that they can pass no law of any moment unless it have such suspending clause: so that, however immediate may be the call for legislative interposition, the law cannot be executed till it has twice crossed the Atlantic, by which time the evil may have spent its whole force.

But in what terms reconcileable to majesty and at the same time to truth, shall we speak of a late instruction to his majesty's governor of the colony of Virginia, by which he is forbidden to assent to any law for the division of a county, unless the new county will consent to have no representative in assembly? That colony has as yet affixed no boundary to the Westward. Their Western counties therefore are of indefinite extent. Some of them are actually seated many hundred miles from their Eastern limits. Is it possible then that his majesty can have bestowed a single thought on the situation of those people, who, in order to obtain justice for injuries however great or small, must, by the laws of that colony, attend their county court at such a distance, with all their witnesses, monthly, till their litigation be determined? Or does his majesty seriously wish, and publish it to the world, that his subjects should give up the glorious right of representation, with all the benefits derived from that, and submit themselves the absolute slaves of his sovereign will? Or is it rather meant to confine the legislative body to their present numbers, that they may be the cheaper bargain whenever they shall become worth a purchase?

One of the articles of impeachment against Tresilian and the other judges of Westminster Hall in the reign of Richard the second, for which they suffered death as traitors to their country, was that they had advised the king that he might dissolve his parliament at any time: and succeeding kings have adopted the opinion of these unjust judges. Since the establishment however of the British constitution at the glorious Revolution on [its] free and antient principles, neither his majesty nor his ancestors have exercised such a power of dissolution in the island of Great Britain; and when his majesty was petitioned by the united voice of his people there to dissolve the present parliament, who had become obnoxious to them, his ministers were heard to declare in open parliament that his majesty possessed no such power by the constitution. But how different their language and his practice here! To declare as their duty required the known rights of their country, to oppose the usurpation of every foreign judicature, to disregard the imperious mandates of a minister or governor, have been the avowed causes of dissolving houses of representatives in America. But if such powers be really vested in his majesty, can he suppose they are there placed to awe the members from such purposes as these? When the representative body have lost the confidence of their constituents, when they have notoriously made sale of their most valuable rights, when they have assumed to themselves powers which the people never put into their hands, then indeed their continuing in office becomes dangerous to the state, and calls for an exercise of the power of dissolution. Such being the causes for which the representative body should and should not be dissolved, will it not appear strange to an unbiassed observer that that of Great Britain was not dissolved, while those of the colonies have repeatedly incurred that sentence?

But your majesty or your Governors have carried this power beyond every limit known or provided for by the laws. After dissolving one house of representatives, they have refused to call another, so that for a great length of time the legislature provided by the laws has been out of existence. From the nature of things, every society must at all times possess within itself the sovereign powers of legislation. The feelings of human nature revolt against the supposition of a state so situated as that it may not in any emergency provide against dangers which perhaps threaten immediate ruin. While those bodies are in existence to whom the people have delegated the powers of legislation, they alone possess and may exercise those powers. But when they are dissolved by the lopping off one or more of their branches, the power reverts to the people, who may use it to unlimited extent, either assembling together in person, sending deputies, or in any other way they may think proper. We forbear to trace consequences further; the dangers are conspicuous with which this practice is replete.

That we shall at this time also take notice of an error in the nature of our landholdings, which crept in at a very early period of our settlement. The introduction of the Feudal tenures into the kingdom of England, though antient, is well enough understood to set this matter in a proper light. In the earlier ages of the Saxon settlement feudal holdings were certainly altogether unknown, and very few, if any, had been introduced at the time of the Norman conquest. Our Saxon ancestors held their lands, as they did their personal property, in absolute dominion, disencumbered with any superior, answering nearly to the nature of those possessions which the Feudalists term Allodial: William the Norman first introduced that system generally. The lands which had belonged to those who fell in the battle of Hastings, and in the subsequent insurrections of his reign, formed a considerable proportion of the lands of the whole kingdom. These he granted out, subject to feudal duties, as did he also those of a great number of his new subjects, who by persuasions or threats were induced to surrender them for that purpose. But still much was left in the hands of his Saxon subjects, held of no superior, and not subject to feudal conditions. These therefore by express laws, enacted to render uniform the system of military defence, were made liable to the same military duties as if they had been feuds: and the Norman lawyers soon found means to saddle them also with all the other feudal burthens. But still they had not been surrendered to the king, they were not derived from his grant, and therefore they were not holden of him. A general principle indeed was introduced that "all lands in England were held either mediately or immediately of the crown": but this was borrowed from those holdings which were truly feudal, and only applied to others for the purposes of illustration. Feudal holdings were therefore but exceptions out of the Saxon laws of possession, under which all lands were held in absolute right. These therefore still form the basis or groundwork of the Common law, to prevail wheresoever the exceptions have not taken place. America was not conquered by William the Norman, nor [its] lands surrendered to him or any of his successors. Possessions there are undoubtedly of the Allodial nature. Our ancestors however, who migrated hither, were laborers, not lawyers. The fictitious principle that all lands belong originally to the king, they were early persuaded to beleive real, and accordingly took grants of their own lands from the crown. And while the crown continued to grant for small sums and on reasonable rents, there was no inducement to arrest the error and lay it open to public view. But his majesty has lately taken on him to advance the terms of purchase and of holding to the double of what they were, by which means the acquisition of lands being rendered difficult, the population of our country is likely to be checked. It is time therefore for us to lay this matter before his majesty, and to declare that he has no right to grant lands of himself. From the nature and purpose of civil institutions, all the lands within the limits which any particular society has circumscribed around itself, are assumed by that society, and subject to their allotment only. This may be done by themselves assembled collectively, or by their legislature to whom they may have delegated sovereign authority: and, if they are allotted in neither of these ways, each individual of the society may appropriate to himself such lands as he finds vacant, and occupancy will give him title.

That, in order to inforce the arbitrary measures before complained of, his majesty has from time to time sent among us large bodies of armed forces, not made up of the people here, nor raised by the authority of our laws. Did his majesty possess such a right as this, it might swallow up all our other rights whenever he should think proper. But his majesty has no right to land a single armed man on our shores; and those whom he sends here are liable to our laws for the suppression and punishment of Riots, Routs, and unlawful assemblies, or are hostile bodies invading us in defiance of law. When in the course of the late war it became expedient that a body of Hanoverian troops should be brought over for the defence of Great Britain, his majesty's grandfather, our late sovereign, did not pretend to introduce them under any authority he possessed. Such a measure would have given just alarm to his subjects in Great Britain, whose liberties would not be safe if armed men of another country, and of another spirit, might be brought into the realm at any time without the consent of their legislature. He therefore applied to parliament who passed an act for that purpose, limiting the number to be brought in and the time they were to continue. In like manner is his majesty restrained in every part of the empire. He possesses indeed the executive power of the laws in every state; but they are the laws of the particular state which he is to administer within that state, and not those of any one within the limits of another. Every state must judge for itself the number of armed men which they may safely trust among them, of whom they are to consist, and under what restrictions they are to be laid. To render these proceedings still more criminal against our laws, instead of subjecting the military to the civil power, his majesty has expressly made the civil subordinate to the military. But can his majesty thus put down all law under his feet? Can he erect a power superior to that which erected himself? He has done it indeed by force; but let him remember that force cannot give right.

That these are our grievances which we have thus laid before his majesty with that freedom of language and sentiment which becomes a free people, claiming their rights as derived from the laws of nature, and not as the gift of their chief magistrate. Let those flatter, who fear: it is not an American art. To give praise where it is not due, might be well from the venal, but would ill beseem those who are asserting the rights of human nature. They know, and will therefore say, that kings are the servants, not the proprietors of the people. Open your breast Sire, to liberal and expanded thought. Let not the name of George the third be a blot in the page of history. You are surrounded by British counsellors, but remember that they are parties. You have no ministers for American affairs, because you have none taken from among us, nor amenable to the laws on which they are to give you advice. It behoves you therefore to think and to act for yourself and your people. The great principles of right and wrong are legible to every reader: to pursue them requires not the aid of many counsellors. The whole art of government consists in the art of being honest. Only aim to do your duty, and mankind will give you credit where you fail. No longer persevere in sacrificing the rights of one part of the empire to the inordinate desires of another: but deal out to all equal and impartial right. Let no act be passed by any one legislature which may infringe on the rights and liberties of another. This is the important post in which fortune has placed you, holding the balance of a great, if a well poised empire. This, Sire, is the advice of your great American council, on the observance of which may perhaps depend your felicity and future fame, and the preservation of that harmony which alone can continue both to Great Britain and America the reciprocal advantages of their connection. It is neither our wish nor our interest to separate from her. We are willing on our part to sacrifice every thing which reason can ask to the restoration of that tranquility for which all must wish. On their part let them be ready to establish union on a generous plan. Let them name their terms, but let them be just. Accept of every commercial preference it is in our power to give for such things as we can raise for their use, or they make for ours. But let them not think to exclude us from going to other markets, to dispose of those commodities which they cannot use, nor to supply those wants which they cannot supply. Still less let it be proposed that our properties within our own territories shall be taxed or regulated by any power on earth but our own. The god who gave us life, gave us liberty at the same time: the hand of force may destroy, but cannot disjoin them. This, Sire, is our last, our determined resolution: and that you will be pleased to interpose with that efficacy which your earnest endeavors may insure to procure redress of these our great grievances, to quiet the minds of your subjects in British America against any apprehensions of future incroachment, to establish fraternal love and harmony thro' the whole empire, and that that may continue to the latest ages of time, is the fervent prayer of all British America.

Alexander Hamilton

The Farmer Refuted (1775)

Sir,[1]

I resume my pen, in reply to the curious epistle, you have been pleased to favour me with; and can assure you, that, notwithstanding, I am naturally of a grave and phlegmatic disposition, it has been the source of abundant merriment to me. The spirit that breathes throughout is so rancorous, illiberal and imperious: The argumentative part of it so puerile and fallacious: The misrepresentations of facts so palpable and flagrant: The criticisms so illiterate, trifling and absurd. [. . .]

Having thus, briefly, delivered my sentiments of your performance in general, I shall proceed to a particular examination of it, so far, as may be requisite, towards placing it in that just point of light in which it ought to stand. I flatter myself, I shall find no difficulty in obviating the objections you have produced, against the Full Vindication; and in shewing, that your View of the Controversy between Great-Britain and the Colonies, is not only partial and unjust, but diametrically opposite to the first principles of civil society. [. . .]

1. [Hamilton wrote *The Farmer Refuted* as part of a particularly exercised debate with the loyalist Samuel Seabury.]

Here, I expect, you will exclaim with your usual vehemence and indecency; you are now espousing the cause of a party! It is the most daring impudence and falsehood to assert the contrary! I can, by no means, conceive, that an opposition to a small herd of mal-contents, among whom, you have thought proper to rank, and a zealous attachment to the general measures of America can be denominated the effect of a party spirit. You, Sir, and your adherents may be justly deemed a faction, because you compose a small number inimical to the common voice of your country. To determine the truth of this affirmation, it is necessary to take a comprehensive view of all the colonies. [. . .]

Your envenomed pen has endeavored to sully the characters of our continental representatives, with the presumptuous charges of ignorance, knavery, sedition, rebellion, treason and tyranny; a tremendous catalogue indeed! Nor have you treated their friends and adherents, with any greater degree of complaisance. You have also delineated the mercantile body, as entirely devoid of principle; and the several committees as bands of robbers and petty tyrants. In short, except the few who are of your own complexion and stamp, "the *virtuous* friends of order and good government," you have not hesitated to exercise your obloquy and malevolence against the whole continent.

These things being considered, it is manifest, that, in my answer to your Free Thoughts, I treated you with more lenity than you had a right to expect; and did, by no means, observe the strict law of retaliation. None, but yourself, will think, you can, with the least propriety, complain of abuse. [. . .]

I shall, for the present, pass over to that part of your pamphlet, in which you endeavour to establish the supremacy of the British Parliament over America. After a proper eclaircissement of this point, I shall draw such inferences, as will sap the foundation of every thing you have offered.

The first thing that presents itself is a wish, that "I had, explicitly, declared to the public my ideas of the *natural rights* of mankind. Man, in a state of nature (you say) may be considered, as perfectly free from all restraints of *law* and *government*, and, then, the weak must submit to the strong."

I shall, henceforth, begin to make some allowance for that enmity, you have discovered to the *natural rights* of mankind. For, though ignorance of them in this enlightened age cannot be admitted, as a sufficient excuse for you; yet, it ought, in some measure, to extenuate your guilt. If you will follow my advice, there still may be hopes of your reformation. Apply yourself, without delay, to the study of the law of nature. I would recommend to your perusal, Grotius, Puffendorf, Locke, Montesquieu, and Burlemaqui. I might mention other excellent writers on this subject; but if you attend, diligently, to these, you will not require any others.

There is so strong a similitude between your political principles and those maintained by Mr. Hobbs,[2] that, in judging from them, a person might very easily *mistake* you for a disciple of his. His opinion was, exactly, coincident with yours, relative to man in a state of nature. He held, as you do, that he was, then, perfectly free from all restraint of *law* and *government*. Moral obligation, according to him, is derived from the introduction of civil society; and there is no virtue, but what is purely artificial, the mere contrivance of politicians, for the maintenance of social intercourse. But the reason he run into this absurd and impious doctrine, was, that he disbelieved the existence of an intelligent superintending principle, who is the governor, and will be the final judge of the universe.

As you, sometimes, swear *by him that made you*, I conclude, your sentiment does not correspond with his, in that which is the basis of the doctrine, you both agree in; and this makes it impossible to imagine whence this congruity between you arises. To grant, that there is a supreme intelligence, who rules the world, and has established laws to regulate the actions of his creatures; and, still, to assert, that man, in a state of nature, may be considered as perfectly free from all restraints of *law* and *government*, appear to a common understanding, altogether irreconcilable.

Good and wise men, in all ages, have embraced a very dissimilar theory. They have supposed, that the deity, from the relations, we stand in, to himself and to each other, has constituted an eternal and immutable law, which is, indispensably, obligatory upon all mankind, prior to any human institution whatever.

2. [I.e., Thomas Hobbes.]

This is what is called the law of nature, "which, being coeval with mankind, and dictated by God himself, is, of course, superior in obligation to any other. It is binding over all the globe, in all countries, and at all times. No human laws are of any validity, if contrary to this; and such of them as are valid, derive all their authority, mediately, or immediately, from this original." BLACKSTONE.

Upon this law, depend the natural rights of mankind, the supreme being gave existence to man, together with the means of preserving and beatifying that existence. He endowed him with rational faculties, by the help of which, to discern and pursue such things, as were consistent with his duty and interest, and invested him with an inviolable right to personal liberty, and personal safety.

Hence, in a state of nature, no man had any *moral* power to deprive another of his life, limbs, property or liberty; nor the least authority to command, or exact obedience from him; except that which arose from the ties of consanguinity.

Hence also, the origin of all civil government, justly established, must be a voluntary compact, between the rulers and the ruled; and must be liable to such limitations, as are necessary for the security of the *absolute rights* of the latter; for what original title can any man or set of men have, to govern others, except their own consent? To usurp dominion over a people, in their own despite, or to grasp at a more extensive power than they are willing to entrust, is to violate that law of nature, which gives every man a right to his personal liberty; and can, therefore, confer no obligation to obedience.

"The principal aim of society is to protect individuals, in the enjoyment of those absolute rights, which were vested in them by the immutable laws of nature; but which could not be preserved, in peace, without that mutual assistance, and intercourse, which is gained by the institution of friendly and social communities. Hence it follows, that the first and primary end of human laws, is to maintain and regulate these *absolute rights* of individuals." BLACKSTONE.

If we examine the pretensions of parliament, by this criterion, which is evidently, a good one, we shall, presently detect their injustice. First, they are subversive of our natural liberty, because an authority is assumed over us, which we by no means assent to. And secondly, they divest us of that moral security, for our lives and properties, which we are intitled to, and which it is the primary end of society to bestow. For such security can never exist, while we have no part in making the laws, that are to bind us; and while it may be the interest of our uncontrolled legislators to oppress us as much as possible.

To deny these principles will be not less absurd, than to deny the plainest axioms: I shall not, therefore, attempt any further illustration of them.

You say, "when I assert, that since Americans have not, by any act of theirs, empowered the British parliament to make laws for them, it follows they can have no just authority to do it, I advance a position subversive of that dependence, which all colonies must, from their very nature, have on the mother country." The premises from which I drew this conclusion, are indisputable. You have not detected any fallacy in them; but endeavor to overthrow them by deducing a false and imaginary consequence. My principles admit the only dependence which can subsist, consistent with any idea of civil liberty, or with the future welfare of the British empire, as will appear hereafter.

"The dependence of the colonies, on the mother country," (you assert) "has ever been acknowledged. It is an impropriety of speech, to talk of an independent colony: The words independent and colony, convey contradictory ideas, much like *killing* and *sparing*. As soon as a colony becomes independent on the parent state, it ceases to be any longer a colony, just as when you *kill* a sheep, you cease to *spare* him."

In what sense, the dependance of the colonies on the mother country, has been acknowledged, will appear from those circumstances of their political history, which I shall, by and by, recite. The term colony signifies nothing more, than a body of people drawn from the mother country, to inhabit some distant place, or the country it self so inhabited. As to the degrees and modifications of that subordination, which is due to the parent state, these must depend upon other things, besides the mere act of emigration, to inhabit or settle a distant country. These must be ascertained, by the spirit of the constitution of the mother country, by the compacts for the purpose of colonizing, and, more especially, by the law of nature, and that *supreme law* of every society—*its own happiness*.

The idea of colony does not involve the idea of slavery. There is a wide difference, between the dependence of a free people, and the submission of slaves. The former I allow, the latter I reject with disdain. Nor does the notion of a colony imply any subordination to our fellow subjects, in the parent state, while there is one common sovereign established. The dependence of the colonies, on Great-Britain, is an ambiguous and equivocal phrase. It may, either mean dependence on the people of Great-Britain, or on the King. In the former sense, it is absurd and unaccountable: In the latter it is just and rational. No person will affirm, that a French colony is independent, on the parent state, though it acknowledge the King of France as rightful sovereign. Nor can it, with any greater propriety, be said, that an English colony is independent, while it bears allegiance to the King of Great-Britain. The difference, between their dependence, is only that which distinguishes civil liberty from slavery; and results from the different genius of the French and English constitution.

But you deny, that "we can be liege subjects to the King of Great-Britain, while we disavow the authority of parliament." You endeavour to prove it thus, "The King of Great Britain was placed on the throne, by virtue of an act of parliament; and he is King of America, by virtue of being King of Great-Britain. He is therefore King of America by act of parliament: And, if we disclaim that authority of Parliament, which made him our King, we, in fact, reject him from being our King; for we disclaim that authority, by which he is King at all."

Admitting, that the King of Great Britain was enthroned by virtue of an act of parliament, and that he is King of America, because he is King of Great-Britain, yet the act of parliament is not the *efficient cause* of his being the King of America: It is only the *occasion* of it. He is King of America, by virtue of a compact between us and the Kings of Great-Britain. These colonies were planted and settled by the Grants, and under the Protection of English Kings, who entered into covenants with us for themselves, their heirs and successors; and it is from these covenants, that the duty of protection on their part, and the duty of allegiance on ours arise.

So that, to disclaim, the authority of a British Parliament over us, does by no means imply the dereliction of our allegiance to British Monarchs. Our compact takes no cognizance of the manner of their accession to the throne. It is sufficient for us, that they are Kings of England.

The most valid reasons can be assigned for our allegiance to the King of Great-Britain; but not one of the least force or plausibility for our subjection to parliamentary decrees.

We hold our lands in America by virtue of charters from British Monarchs; and are under no obligations to the lords or commons for them: Our title is similar and equal to that, by which they possess their lands; and the King is the legal fountain of both: this is one grand source of our obligation to allegiance. [. . .]

The right of parliament to legislate for us cannot be accounted for upon any reasonable grounds. The constitution of Great Britain is very properly called a limited monarchy, the people having reserved to themselves a share in the legislature, as a check upon the regal authority, to prevent its degenerating into despotism and tyranny. The very aim and intention of the democratical part, or the house of commons, is to secure the rights of the people. Its very being depends upon those rights. Its whole power is derived from them, and must be terminated by them.

It is the unalienable birth-right of every Englishman, who can be considered as *a free agent* to participate in framing the laws which are to bind him, either as to his life or property. But, as many inconveniences would result from the exercise of this right, in person, it is appointed by the constitution, that he shall delegate it to another. Hence he is to give his vote in the election of some person he chuses to confide in as his representative. This right no power on earth can divest him of. It was enjoyed by his ancestors time immemorial; recognized and established by Magna Charta, and is essential to the existence of the constitution. Abolish this privilege, and the house of commons is annihilated.

But what was the use and design of this privilege? To secure his life and property from the attacks of exorbitant power. And in what manner is this done? By giving him the election of those, who are to have the disposal and regulation of them, and whose interest is in every respect connected with his.

The representative in this case is bound by every possible tie to consult the advantage of his constituent. Gratitude for the high and honorable trust reposed in him demands a return of attention and regard to the advancement of his happiness. Self-interest, that most powerful incentive of human actions, points and attracts towards the same object.

The duration of his trust is not perpetual; but must expire in a few years, and if he is desirous of the future favour of his constituents, he must not abuse the present instance of it; but must pursue the end, for which he enjoys it; otherwise he forfeits it, and defeats his own purpose. Besides, if he consent to any laws hurtful to his constituent, he is bound by the same, and must partake in the disadvantage of them. His friends, relations, children, all whose ease and comfort are dear to him, will be in a like predicament. And should he concur in any flagrant acts of injustice or oppression, he will be within the reach of popular vengeance, and this will restrain him within due bounds.

To crown the whole, at the expiration of a few years, if their representatives have abused their trust, the people have it in their power to change them, and to elect others, who may be more faithful and more attached to their interest.

These securities, the most powerful that human affairs will admit of, have the people of Britain, for the good deportment of their representatives towards them. They may have proved, at some times, and on some occasions, defective; but, upon the whole, they have been found sufficient. [. . .]

The fundamental source of all your errors, sophisms and false reasonings is a total ignorance of the natural rights of mankind. Were you once to become acquainted with these, you could never entertain a thought, that all men are not, by nature, entitled to a parity of privileges. You would be convinced, that natural liberty is a gift of the beneficent Creator to the whole human race, and that civil liberty is founded in that; and cannot be wrested from any people, without the most manifest violation of justice. *Civil liberty, is only natural liberty, modified and secured by the sanctions of civil society.* It is not a thing, in its own nature, precarious and dependent on human will and caprice; but is conformable to the constitution of man, as well as necessary to the *well-being* of society.

Upon this principle, colonists as well as other men, have a right to civil liberty: For, if it be conducive to the happiness of society (and reason and experience testify that it is) it is evident, that every society, of whatsoever kind, has an absolute and perfect right to it, which can never be with-held without cruelty and injustice. [. . .][3]

Sir, I have taken a pretty general survey of the American Charters; and proved to the satisfaction of every unbiassed person, that they are intirely, discordant with that sovereignty of parliament, for which you are an advocate. The disingenuity of your extracts (to give it no harsher name) merits the severest censure; and will no doubt serve to discredit all your former, as well as future labours, in your favourite cause of despotism.

It is true, that New-York has no Charter. But, if it could support its claim to liberty in no other way, it might, with justice, plead the common principles of colonization: for, it would be unreasonable, to seclude one colony, from the enjoyment of the most important privileges of the rest. There is no need, however, of this plea: The sacred rights of mankind are not to be rummaged for, among old parchments, or musty records. They are written, as with a sun beam, in the whole *volume* of human nature, by the hand of the divinity itself; and can never be erased or obscured by mortal power.

The nations of Turkey, Russia, France, Spain, and all other despotic kingdoms, in the world, have an inherent right, when ever they please, to shake off the yoke of servitude, (though sanctified by the immemorial usage of their ancestors;) and to model their government, upon the principles of civil liberty. [. . .]

[. . .] If we look forward to a period not far distant, we shall perceive, that the productions of our country will infinitely exceed the demands, which Great-Britain and her connections can possibly have for them; and, as we shall then be greatly advanced in population, our wants will be proportionably increased. These circumstances will open an ample field, for extortion and oppression.

The legislative authority of Parliament would always be ready to silence our murmurs, by tyrannical edicts: These would be enforced, by a formidable

---

3. [Here Hamilton launches into a "survey of the political history of the colonies," an exhaustive study of charters and statutes supportive of his claim that Parliament holds no sovereign authority over the colonies.]

army, kept up among us, for the purpose. The slightest struggles, to recover our lost liberty, would become dangerous and even capital. Those hated things Continental Conventions, by which there might be a communion of councils and measures, would be interdicted. Non-importation and non-exportation agreements would, in effect, be made *seditious, illegal,* and *treasonable:* No remedy would be left, but in the clemency of our oppressors; a wretched one indeed, and such as no prudent man would confide in! In whatever light, we consider the matter, we shall find, that we must effectually seal our bondage by adopting the mode you recommend.

Agreeable to your own concession, Great-Britain is abundantly recompensed for the naval protection she affords, by the *principal profits* of our trade: It can, therefore, with no colour of justice, be urged upon us, to permit her to raise a revenue through that channel.

But, after all, let us suppose, that the emolument which arises, from the simple and abstracted regulation of our trade, is inadequate to the protection, we derive, from the parent state; does it follow, that her just demands cannot be satisfied, unless we put it in her power to ruin us? When did the colonies refuse to contribute their proportion, towards defraying the expenses of government? During the war, our contributions were so liberal and generous, that we were thought to have done more, than our part, and restitution was accordingly made. Massachusetts, that injured, insulted and calumniated country was foremost in displaying its loyalty; and was neither parsimonious of its men nor money. But, notwithstanding this, no confidence, it seems is due to our virtue, or fidelity; but every thing is to be trusted to the wisdom and disinterestedness of a British Parliament.

We do not expect, or require, that all should depend upon our integrity or generosity; but only a part: And this every rule of equity intitles us to. We have assented to the exercise of a power, which gives a certainty to Great-Britain of a vast annual income: Any further aids, that may be necessary, ought to be intrusted to our fidelity: When the circumstances of two parties will not admit of precise boundaries to the duty of each, it is not a dictate of justice to put one entirely into the power of the other. If the mother country would desist from grasping at too much, and permit us to enjoy the privileges of freemen, interest would concur with duty, and lead us to the performance of it. We should be sensible of the advantages of a mutual intercourse and connection; and should esteem the welfare of Britain, as the best security for our own. She may, by kind treatment secure our attachment in the powerful bands of self-interest. This is the conduct that prudence and sound policy point out; but alas! to her own misfortune, as well as ours, she is blind and infatuated.

If we take futurity into the account, as we no doubt ought to do, we shall find, that, in fifty or sixty years, America will be in no need of protection from Great-Britain. She will then be able to protect herself, both at home and abroad. She will have a plenty of men and a plenty of materials to provide and equip a formidable navy. She will indeed owe a debt of gratitude to the parent state, for past services; but the scale will then begin to turn in her favour, and the obligation, for future services, will be on the side of Great-Britain. It will be the interest of the latter to keep us without a fleet, and, by this means to continue to regulate our trade, as before. But, in thus withholding the means of protection, which we have, within our own reach, she will chiefly consult her own advantage, and oblige herself much more, than us. At that æra, to enjoy the privilege of enriching herself, by the direction of our commerce, and at the same time, to derive supports from our youthful vigor and strength, against all her enemies, and, thereby to extend her conquests over them, will give her reason to bless the times that gave birth to these colonies.[. . .]

I imagine, Sir, I have, by this time, pretty fully and satisfactorily answered every thing, contained in your letter, of any consequence: The parts, I have left unattended to, are such as cannot operate, materially, to the prejudice of the cause I espouse; but I should not have neglected them, had it not been, that I have already taken a very ample range; and it would, perhaps, be imprudent to delay a conclusion.

Whatever opinion may be entertained of my sentiments and intentions, I attest that being, whose all-seeing eye penetrates the inmost recesses of the heart, that I am not influenced (in the part I take) by any unworthy motive—that, if I am in an error, it is my judgment, not my heart, that errs. That I earnestly lament the unnatural quarrel, between the parent state and the colonies; and most ardently wish for a speedy reconciliation, a perpetual and *mutually* beneficial union, that I am a warm advocate for limited monarchy, and an unfeigned well-wisher to the present Royal Family.

But on the other hand, I am inviolably attached to the essential rights of mankind, and the true interests of society. I consider civil liberty, in a genuine unadulterated sense, as the greatest of terrestrial blessings. I am convinced, that the whole human race is intitled to it; and, that it can be wrested from no part of them, without the blackest and most aggravated guilt.

I verily believe also, that the best way to secure a permanent and happy union, between Great-Britain and the colonies, is to permit the latter to be as free, as they desire. To abridge their liberties, or to exercise any power over them, which they are unwilling to submit to, would be a perpetual source of discontent and animosity. A continual jealousy would exist on both sides. This would lead to tyranny, on the one hand, and to sedition and rebellion, on the other. Impositions, not really grievous in themselves, would be thought so; and the murmurs arising from thence, would be considered as the effect of a turbulent ungovernable spirit. These jarring principles would, at length, throw all things into disorder; and be productive of an irreparable breach, and a total disunion.

That harmony and mutual confidence may speedily be restored, between all the parts of the British empire, is the favourite wish of one, who feels the warmest sentiments of good will to mankind, who bears no enmity to you, and who is,

A sincere Friend to America.

John Wesley

A Calm Address to Our American Colonies (1775)

London

Brethren and Countrymen,

1. The grand question which is now debated (and with warmth enough on both sides), is this, Has the English Parliament power to tax the American colonies?

In order to determine this, let us consider the nature of our colonies. An English colony is, a number of persons to whom the king grants a charter, permitting them to settle in some far country as a corporation, enjoying such powers as the charter grants, to be administered in such a manner as the charter prescribes. As a corporation they make laws for themselves: but as a corporation subsisting by a grant from higher authority, to the control of that authority, they still continue subject.

Considering this, nothing can be more plain, than that the supreme power in England has a legal right of laying any tax upon them for any end beneficial to the whole empire.

2. But you object, "It is the privilege of a freeman and an Englishman to be taxed only by his own consent. And this consent is given for every man by his representative in Parliament. But we have no representation in Parliament. Therefore we ought not to be taxed thereby."

I answer, This argument proves too much. If the Parliament cannot tax you, because you have no representation therein, for the same reason it can make no laws to bind you. If a freeman cannot be taxed without his own consent, neither can he be punished without it: for whatever holds with regard to taxation, holds with regard to all other laws. Therefore he who denies the English Parliament the power of taxation, denies it the right of making any laws at all. But this power over the colonies you have never disputed: you have always admitted statutes, for the punishment of offences, and for the preventing or redressing of inconveniences. And the reception of any law draws after it by a chain which cannot be broken, the necessity of admitting taxation.

3. But I object to the very foundation of your plea. That "every freeman is governed by laws to which he has consented, " as confidently as it has been asserted, it is absolutely false. In wide-extended dominions, a very small part of the people are concerned in making laws. This, as all public business, must be done by delegation, the delegates are chosen by a select number. And those that are not electors, who are far the greater part, stand by, idle and helpless spectators.

The case of electors is little better. When they are near equally divided, almost half of them must be governed, not only without, but even against their own consent.

And how has any man consented to those laws, which were made before he was born? Our consent to these, nay and to the laws now made even in England, is purely passive. And in every place, as all men are born the subjects of some state or other, so they are born, passively, as it were consenting to the laws of that state. Any other than this kind of consent, the condition of civil life does not allow.

4. But you say, *You are intitled to life, liberty and property by nature: and that you have never ceded to any sovereign power, the right to dispose of those without your consent.*

While you speak as the naked sons of nature, this is certainly true. But you presently declare, *Our ancestors at the time they settled these colonies, were intitled to all the rights of natural-born subjects, within the realm of England.* This likewise is true: but when this is granted, the boast of original rights is at an end. You are no longer in a state of nature, but sink down to colonists, governed by a charter. If your ancestors were subjects, they acknowledged a sovereign: if they had a right to English privileges, they were accountable to English laws, and had ceded to the king and Parliament, *the power of disposing without their consent, of both their lives, liberties and properties.* And did the Parliament cede to them, a dispensation from the obedience, which they owe as natural subjects? Or any degree of independence, not enjoyed by other Englishmen?

5. *They did not indeed,* as you observe, *by emigration forfeit any of those privileges: but they were, and their descendents now are intitled to all such as their circumstances enable them to enjoy.*

That they who form a colony by a lawful charter, forfeit no privilege thereby, is certain. But what they do not forfeit by any judicial sentence, they may lose by natural effects. When a man voluntarily comes into America, he may lose what he had when in Europe. Perhaps he had a right to vote for a knight or burgess: by crossing the sea he did not forfeit this right. But it is plain, he has made the exercise of it no longer possible. He has reduced himself from a voter to one of the innumerable multitude that have no votes.

6. But you say, *As the colonies are not represented in the British Parliament, they are entitled to a free power of legislation. For they inherit all the right which their ancestors had of enjoying all the privileges of Englishmen.*

They do inherit all the privileges which their ancestors had: but they can inherit no more. Their ancestors left a country where the representatives of the people were elected by men particularly qualified, and where those who wanted that qualification were bound by the decisions of men whom they had not deputed. You are the descendants of men who either had no votes, or resigned them by emigration. You have therefore exactly what your ancestors left you: not a vote in making laws, nor in chusing legislators, but the happiness of being protected by laws, and the duty of obeying them.

What your ancestors did not bring with them, neither they nor their descendants have acquired. They have not, by abandoning their right in one legislature, acquired a right to constitute another: any more than the multitudes in England who have no vote, have a right to erect a Parliament for themselves.

7. *However the colonies have a right to all the privileges granted them by royal charters, or secured to them by provincial laws.*

The first clause is allowed: they have certainly a right to all the privileges granted them by the royal charters. But as to the second there is a doubt: provincial laws may grant privileges to individuals of the province. But surely no province can confer provincial privileges on itself! They have a right to all which the king has given them; but not to all which they have given themselves.

A corporation can no more assume to itself, privileges which it had not before, than a man can, by his own act and deed, assume titles or dignities. The legislature of a colony may be compared to the vestry of a large parish: which may lay a cess on its inhabitants, but still regulated by the law: and which (whatever be its internal expenses) is still liable to taxes laid by superior authority.

The charter of Pennsylvania has a clause admitting, in express terms, taxation by Parliament. If such a clause be not inferred in other charters, it must be omitted as not necessary; because it is manifestly implied in the very nature of subordinate government: all countries which are subject to laws, being liable to taxes.

It is true, *The first settlers in Massachusetts-Bay were promised an exemption from taxes for seven years.* But does not this very exemption imply, that they were to pay them afterwards?

If there is in the charter of any colony a clause exempting them from taxes for ever, then undoubtedly they have a right to be so exempted. But if there is no such clause, then the English Parliament has the same right to tax them as to tax any other English subjects.

8. All that impartially consider what has been observed, must readily allow, that the English Parliament has undoubted right to tax all the English colonies.

But whence then is all this hurry and tumult? Why is America all in an uproar? If you can yet give yourselves time to think, you will see, the plain case is this.

A few years ago, you were assaulted by enemies, whom you were not well able to resist. You represented this to your mother-country, and desired her assistance. You was largely assisted, and by that means wholly delivered from all your enemies.

After a time, your mother-country desiring to be reimbursed for some part of the large expence she had been at, laid a small tax (which she had always a right to do) on one of her colonies.

But how is it possible, that the taking of this reasonable and legal step, should have set all America in a flame?

I will tell you my opinion freely; and perhaps you will not think it improbable. I speak the more freely, because I am unbiased: I have nothing to hope or fear from either side. I gain nothing either by the government or by the Americans, and probably never shall. And I have no prejudice to any man in America: I love you as my brethren and countrymen.

9. My opinion is this. We have a few men in England, who are determined enemies to monarchy. Whether they hate his present majesty on any other ground, than because he is a king, I know not. But they cordially hate his office, and have for some years been undermining it with all diligence, in hopes of erecting their grand idol, their dear commonwealth upon its ruins. I believe they have let very few into their design (although many forward it, without knowing any thing of the matter): but they are steadily pursuing it, as by various other means, so in particular by inflammatory papers, which are industriously and continually dispersed, throughout the town and country: by this method they have already wrought thousands of the people, even to the pitch of madness. By the same, only varied according to your circumstances, they have likewise inflamed America. I make no doubt, but these very men are the original cause of the present breach between England and her colonies. And they are still pouring oil into the flame, studiously incensing each against the other, and opposing under a variety of pretences, all measures of accommodation. So that although the Americans, in general, love the English, and the English in general, love the Americans (all, I mean that are not yet cheated and exasperated by these artful men), yet the rupture is growing wider every day, and none can tell where it will end.

These good men hope it will end, in the total defection of North America from England. If this were effected, they trust the English in general would be so irreconcilably disgusted, that they should be able, with or without foreign assistance, entirely to overturn the government: especially while the main of both the English and Irish forces, are at so convenient a distance.

10. But, my brethren, would this be any advantage to you? Can you hope for a more desirable form of government, either in England or America, than that which you now enjoy? After all the vehement

cry for liberty, what more liberty can you have? What more religious liberty can you desire, than that which you enjoy already? May not every one among you worship God according to his own conscience? What civil liberty can you desire, which you are not already possessed of? Do not you sit without restraint, *every man under his own vine?* Do you not, every one, high or low, enjoy the fruit of your labour? This is real, rational liberty, such as is enjoyed by Englishmen alone; and not by any other people in the habitable world. Would the being independent of England make you more free? Far, very far from it. It would hardly be possible for you to steer clear, between anarchy and tyranny. But suppose, after numberless dangers and mischiefs, you should settle into one or more republics: would a republican government give you more liberty, either religious or civil? By no means. No governments under heaven are so despotic as the republican: no subjects are governed in so arbitrary a manner, as those of a commonwealth. If any one doubt of this, let him look at the subjects of Venice, of Genoa, or even of Holland. Should any man talk or write of the Dutch government as every cobler does of the English, he would be laid in irons, before he knew where he was. And then wo be to him! Republics shew no mercy.

11. "But if we submit to one tax, more will follow." Perhaps so, and perhaps not. But if they did; if you were taxed (which is quite improbable) equal with Ireland or Scotland, still were you to prevent this by renouncing connection with England, the remedy would be worse than the disease. For O! what convulsions must poor America feel, before any other government was settled? Innumerable mischiefs must ensue, before any general form could be established. And the grand mischief would ensue, when it was established; when you had received a yoke, which you could not shake off.

12. Brethren, open your eyes! Come to yourselves! Be no longer the dupes of designing men. I do not mean any of your countrymen in America: I doubt whether any of these are in the secret. The designing men, the Ahithophels, are in England; those who have laid their scheme so deep and covered it so well, that thousands who are ripening it, suspect nothing at all of the matter. These well-meaning men, sincerely believing, that they are serving their country, exclaim against grievances, which either never existed, or are aggravated above measure, and thereby inflame the people more and more, to the wish of those who are behind the scene. But be not you duped any longer: do not ruin yourselves for them that owe you no good will, that now employ you only for their own purposes, and in the end will give you no thanks. They love neither England nor America, but play one against the other, in subserviency to their grand design, of overturning the English government. Be warned in time. Stand and consider before it is too late; before you have entailed confusion and misery on your latest posterity. Have pity upon your mother country! Have pity upon your own! Have pity upon yourselves, upon your children, and upon all that are near and dear to you! Let us not bite and devour one another, lest we be consumed one of another! O let us follow after peace! Let us put away our sins; the real ground of all our calamities! Which never will or can be thoroughly removed, till we fear God and honour the king. [. . .]

Thomas Paine

Common Sense (1776)

Introduction

Perhaps the sentiments contained in the following pages, are not yet sufficiently fashionable to procure them general favour; a long habit of not thinking a thing *wrong*, gives it a superficial appearance of being *right*, and raises at first a formidable outcry in defence of custom. But the tumult soon subsides. Time makes more converts than reason.

As a long and violent abuse of power, is generally the Means of calling the right of it in question (and in matters too which might never have been thought of, had not the Sufferers been aggravated into the inquiry) and as the K—— of England had undertaken in his *own Right*, to support the Parliament in what he calls *Theirs*, and as the good people of this country are grievously oppressed by the combination, they have an undoubted privilege to inquire into the pretensions of both, and equally to reject the usurpation of either.

In the following sheets, the author hath studiously avoided every thing which is personal among ourselves. Compliments as well as censure to individuals make no part thereof. The wise, and the worthy, need not the triumph of a pamphlet; and those whose sentiments are injudicious, or unfriendly, will cease of themselves unless too much pains are bestowed upon their conversion.

The cause of America is in a great measure the cause of all mankind. Many circumstances hath, and will arise, which are not local, but universal, and through which the principles of all Lovers of Mankind are affected, and in the Event of which, their Affections are interested. The laying a Country desolate with Fire and Sword, declaring War against the natural rights of all Mankind, and extirpating the Defenders thereof from the Face of the Earth, is the concern of every Man to whom Nature hath given the Power of feeling; of which Class, regardless of Party Censure, is the

Author.

PS. The Publication of this new Edition hath been delayed, with a View of taking notice (had it been necessary) of any Attempt to refute the Doctrine of Independence: As no Answer hath yet appeared, it is now presumed that none will, the Time needful for getting such a Performance ready for the Public being considerably past.

Who the Author of this Production is, is wholly unnecessary to the Public, as the Object for Attention is the *Doctrine itself*, not the *Man*. Yet it may not be unnecessary to say, That he is unconnected with any Party, and under no sort of Influence public or private, but the influence of reason and principle.

Of the Origin and Design of Government in General. With Concise Remarks on the English Constitution

Some writers have so confounded society with government, as to leave little or no distinction between them; whereas they are not only different, but have different origins. Society is produced by our wants, and government by our wickedness; the former promotes our happiness *positively* by uniting our affections, the latter *negatively* by restraining our vices. The one encourages intercourse, the other creates distinctions. The first is a patron, the last a punisher.

Society in every state is a blessing, but government even in its best state is but a necessary evil; in its worst state an intolerable one; for when we suffer, or are exposed to the same miseries *by a government*, which we might expect in a country *without government*, our calamities are heightened by reflecting that we furnish the means by which we suffer. Government, like dress, is the badge of lost innocence; the palaces of kings are built on the ruins of the bowers of paradise. For were the impulses of conscience clear, uniform, and irresistibly obeyed, man would need no other lawgiver; but that not being the case, he finds it necessary to surrender up a part of his property to furnish means for the protection of the rest; and this he is induced to do by the same prudence which in every other case advises him out of two evils to choose the least. *Wherefore*, security being the true design and end of government, it unanswerably follows that whatever *form* thereof appears most likely to ensure it to us, with the least expense and greatest benefit, is preferable to all others.

In order to gain a clear and just idea of the design and end of government, let us suppose a small number of persons settled in some sequestered part of the earth, unconnected with the rest, they will then represent the first peopling of any country, or of the world. In this state of natural liberty, society will be their first thought. A thousand motives will excite them thereto, the strength of one man is so unequal to his wants, and his mind so unfitted for perpetual solitude, that he is soon obliged to seek assistance and relief of another, who in his turn requires the same. Four or five united would be able to raise a tolerable dwelling in the most of a wilderness, but *one* man might labour out the common period of life without accomplishing any thing; when he had felled his timber he could not remove it, nor erect it after it was removed; hunger in the mean time would urge him from his work, and every different want call him a different way. Disease, nay even misfortune would be death, for though neither might be mortal, yet either would disable him from living, and reduce him to a state in which he might rather be said to perish than to die.

Thus necessity, like a gravitating power, would soon form our newly arrived emigrants into society, the reciprocal blessings of which, would supersede, and render the obligations of law and government unnecessary while they remained perfectly just to each other; but as nothing but heaven is impregnable to vice, it will unavoidably happen, that in proportion as they surmount the first difficulties of emigration, which bound them together in a common cause, they will begin to relax in their duty and attachment to each other; and this remissness, will point out the necessity, of establishing some form of government to supply the defect of moral virtue.

Some convenient tree will afford them a State-House, under the branches of which, the whole colony may assemble to deliberate on public matters. It is more than probable that their first laws will have the title only of REGULATIONS, and be enforced by no other penalty than public disesteem. In this first parliament every man, by natural right will have a seat.

But as the colony increases, the public concerns will increase likewise, and the distance at which the members may be separated, will render it too inconvenient for all of them to meet on every occasion as at first, when their number was small, their habitations near, and the public concerns few and trifling. This will point out the convenience of their consenting to leave the legislative part to be managed by a select number chosen from the whole body, who are supposed to have the same concerns at stake which those have who appointed them, and who will act in the same manner as the whole body would act were they present. If the colony continue increasing, it will become necessary to augment the number of the representatives, and that the interest of every part of the colony may be attended to, it will be found best to divide the whole into convenient parts, each part sending its proper number; and that the *elected* might never form to themselves an interest separate from the *electors*, prudence will point out the propriety of having elections often; because as the *elected* might by that means return and mix again with the general body of the *electors* in a few months, their fidelity to the public will be secured by the prudent reflection of not making a rod for themselves. And as this frequent interchange will establish a common interest with every part of the community, they will mutually and naturally support each other, and on this (not on the unmeaning name of king) depends the *strength of government, and the happiness of the governed.*

Here then is the origin and rise of government; namely, a mode rendered necessary by the inability of moral virtue to govern the world; here too is the design and end of government, viz. freedom and security. And however our eyes may be dazzled with snow, or our ears deceived by sound; however prejudice may warp our wills, or interest darken our understanding, the simple voice of nature and of reason will say, it is right.

I draw my idea of the form of government from a principle in nature, which no art can overturn, viz. that the more simple any thing is, the less liable it is to be disordered, and the easier repaired when disordered; and with this maxim in view, I offer a few remarks on the so much boasted constitution of England. That it was noble for the dark and slavish times in which it was erected is granted. When the world was overrun with tyranny the least remove therefrom was a glorious rescue. But that it is imperfect, subject to convulsions, and incapable of producing what it seems to promise, is easily demonstrated.

Absolute governments (tho' the disgrace of human nature) have this advantage with them, that they are simple; if the people suffer, they know the head from which their suffering springs, know likewise the remedy, and are not bewildered by a variety of causes and cures. But the constitution of England is so exceedingly complex, that the nation may suffer for years together without being able to discover in which part the fault lies, some will say in one and some in another, and every political physician will advise a different medicine.

I know it is difficult to get over local or long standing prejudices, yet if we will suffer ourselves to examine the component parts of the English constitution, we shall find them to be the base remains of two ancient tyrannies, compounded with some new republican materials.

First.—The remains of monarchical tyranny in the person of the king.

Secondly.—The remains of aristocratical tyranny in the persons of the peers.

Thirdly.—The new republican materials, in the persons of the commons, on whose virtue depends the freedom of England.

The two first, by being hereditary, are independent of the people; wherefore in a *constitutional sense* they contribute nothing towards the freedom of the state.

To say that the constitution of England is a *union* of three powers reciprocally *checking* each other, is farcical, either the words have no meaning, or they are flat contradictions.

To say that the commons is a check upon the king, presupposes two things.

First.—That the king is not to be trusted without being looked after, or in other words, that a thirst for absolute power is the natural disease of monarchy.

Secondly.—That the commons, by being appointed for that purpose, are either wiser or more worthy of confidence than the crown.

But as the same constitution which gives the commons a power to check the king by withholding the supplies, gives afterwards the king a power to check the commons, by empowering him to reject their other bills; it again supposes that the king is wiser than those whom it has already supposed to be wiser than him. A mere absurdity!

There is something exceedingly ridiculous in the composition of monarchy; it first excludes a man from the means of information, yet empowers him to act in cases where the highest judgement is required. The state of a king shuts him from the world, yet the business of a king requires him to know it thoroughly; wherefore the different parts, unnaturally opposing and destroying each other, prove the whole character to be absurd and useless.

Some writers have explained the English constitution thus; the king, say they, is one, the people another; the peers are an house in behalf of the king; the commons in behalf of the people; but this hath all the distinctions of an house divided against itself; and though the expressions be pleasantly arranged, yet when examined they appear idle and ambiguous; and it will always happen, that the nicest construction that words are capable of, when applied to the description of some thing which either cannot exist, or is too incomprehensible to be within the compass of description, will be words of sound only, and though they may amuse the ear, they cannot inform the mind, for this explanation includes a previous question, viz. *How came the king by a power which the people are afraid to trust, and always obliged to check?* Such a power could not be the gift of a wise people, neither can any power, *which needs checking*, be from God; yet the provision, which the constitution makes, supposes such a power to exist.

But the provision is unequal to the task; the means either cannot or will not accomplish the end, and the whole affair is a *felo de se*; for as the greater weight will always carry up the less, and as all the wheels of a machine are put in motion by one, it only remains to know which power in the constitution has the most weight, for that will govern; and though the others, or a part of them, may clog, or, as the phrase is, check the rapidity of its motion, yet so long as they cannot stop it, their endeavors will be ineffectual; the first moving power will at last have its way, and what it wants in speed is supplied by time.

That the crown is this overbearing part in the English constitution needs not be mentioned, and that it derives its whole consequence merely from being the giver of places and pensions is self-evident, wherefore, though we have been wise enough to shut and lock a door against absolute monarchy, we at the same time have been foolish enough to put the crown in possession of the key.

The prejudice of Englishmen, in favour of their own government by king, lords, and commons, arises as much or more from national pride than reason. Individuals are undoubtedly safer in England than in some other countries, but the *will* of the king is as much the *law* of the land in Britain as in France, with this difference, that instead of proceeding directly from his mouth, it is handed to the people under the most formidable shape of an act of parliament. For the fate of Charles the First, hath only made kings more subtle—not more just.

Wherefore, laying aside all national pride and prejudice in favour of modes and forms, the plain truth is, that *it is wholly owing to the constitution of the people, and not to the constitution of the government* that the crown is not as oppressive in England as in Turkey.

An inquiry into the *constitutional errors* in the English form of government is at this time highly necessary; for as we are never in a proper condition of doing justice to others, while we continue under the influence of some leading partiality, so neither are we capable of doing it to ourselves while we remain fettered by any obstinate prejudice. And as a man, who is attached to a prostitute, is unfitted to choose or judge of a wife, so any prepossession in favour of a rotten constitution of government will disable us from discerning a good one.

Of Monarchy and Hereditary Succession

Mankind being originally equals in the order of creation, the equality could only be destroyed by some subsequent circumstance; the distinctions of rich, and poor, may in a great measure be accounted for, and that without having recourse to the harsh, ill-sounding names of oppression and avarice. Oppression is often the *consequence*, but seldom or never the *means* of riches; and though avarice will preserve a man from being necessitously poor, it generally makes him too timorous to be wealthy.

But there is another and greater distinction for which no truly natural or religious reason can be assigned, and that is, the distinction of men into KINGS and SUBJECTS. Male and female are the distinctions of nature, good and bad are the distinctions of heaven; but how a race of men came into the world so exalted above the rest, and distinguished like some new species, is worth inquiring into, and whether they are the means of happiness or of misery to mankind.

In the early ages of the world, according to the scripture chronology, there were no kings; the consequence of which was there were no wars; it is the pride of kings which throw mankind into confusion. Holland without a king hath enjoyed more peace for this last century than any of the monarchial govenments in Europe. Antiquity favours the same remark; for the quiet and rural lives of the first patriarchs hath a happy something in them, which vanishes away when we come to the history of Jewish royalty.

Government by kings was first introduced into the world by the heathens, from whom the children of Israel copied the custom. It was the most prosperous invention the Devil ever set on foot for the promotion of idolatry. The Heathens paid divine honours to their deceased kings, and the Christian world hath impoved on the plan by doing the same to their living ones. How impious is the title of *sacred majesty* applied to a worm, who in the midst of his splendour is crumbling into dust.

As the exalting one man so greatly above the rest cannot be justified on the equal rights of nature, so neither can it be defended on the authority of scripture; for the will of the Almighty, as declared by

Gideon and the prophet Samuel, expressly disapproves of government by kings. All anti-monarchial parts of scripture have been very smoothly glossed over in monarchial governments, but they undoubtedly merit the attention of countries which have their governments yet to form. *'Render unto Caesar the things which are Caesar's'* is the scriptural doctrine of the courts, yet it is no support of monarchial government, for the Jews at that time were without a king, and in a state of vassalage to the Romans.

Near three thousand years passed away from the Mosaic account of the creation, till the Jews under a national delusion requested a king. Till then their form of government (except in extraordinary cases, where the Almighty interposed) was a kind of republic administered by a judge and the elders of the tribes. Kings they had none, and it was held sinful to acknowledge any being under that title but the Lord of Hosts. And when a man seriously reflects on the idolatrous homage which is paid to the persons of kings, he need not wonder, that the Almighty, ever jealous of his honour, should disapprove of a form of government which so impiously invades the prerogative of heaven.

Monarchy is ranked in scripture as one of the sins of the Jews, for which a curse in reserve is denounced against them. The history of that transaction is worth attending to.

The children of Israel being oppressed by the Midianites, Gideon marched against them with a small army, and victory, through the divine interposition, decided in his favour. The Jews, elate with success, and attributing it to the generalship of Gideon, proposed making him a king, saying, *Rule thou over us, thou and thy son and thy son's son.* Here was temptation in its fullest extent; not a kingdom only, but a hereditary one, but Gideon in the piety of his soul replied, *I will not rule over you, neither shall my son rule over you,* THE LORD SHALL RULE OVER YOU. Words need not be more explicit; Gideon doth not decline the honour but denieth their right to give it; neither doth he compliment them with invented declarations of his thanks, but in the positive style of a prophet charges them with disaffection to their proper sovereign, the King of Heaven.

About one hundred and thirty years after this, they fell again into the same error. The hankering which the Jews had for the idolatrous customs of the Heathens, is something exceedingly unaccountable; but so it was, that laying hold of the misconduct of Samuel's two sons, who were entrusted with some secular concerns, they came in an abrupt and clamorous manner to Samuel, saying, *Behold thou art old, and thy sons walk not in thy ways, now make us a king to judge us like all the other nations.* And here we cannot but observe that their motives were bad, viz. that they might be *like* unto other nations, i.e. the Heathens, whereas their true glory laid in being as much *unlike* them as possible. *But the thing displeased Samuel when they said, give us a king to judge us; and Samuel prayed unto the Lord, and the Lord said unto Samuel, Hearken unto the voice of the people in all that they say unto thee, for they have not rejected thee, but they have rejected me,* THAT I SHOULD NOT REIGN OVER THEM. *According to all the works which they have done since the day that I brought them up out of Egypt, even unto this day; wherewith they have forsaken me and served other Gods; so do they also unto thee. Now therefore hearken unto their voice, howbeit, protest solemnly unto them and shew them the manner of the king that shall reign over them,* i.e. not of any particular king, but the general manner of the kings of the earth, whom Israel was so eagerly copying after. And notwithstanding the great distance of time and difference of manners, the character is still in fashion. *And Samuel told all the words of the Lord unto the people, that asked of him a king. And he said, This shall be the manner of the king that shall reign over you; he will take your sons and appoint them for himself for his chariots, and to be his horsemen, and some shall run before his chariots* (this description agrees with the present mode of impressing men) *and he will appoint him captains over thousands and captains over fifties, and will set them to ear his ground and to reap his harvest, and to make his instruments of war, and instruments of his chariots; and he will take your daughters to be confectionaries and to be cooks and to be bakers* (this describes the expense and luxury as well as the oppression of kings) *and he will take your fields and your olive yards, even the best of them, and give them to his servants; and he will take the tenth of your seed, and of your vineyards, and give them to his officers and to his servants* (by which we see that bribery, corruption, and favouritism are the standing vices of kings) *and he will take the tenth of your men servants, and your maid servants, and your goodliest young men and your asses, and put them to his work; and he will take the tenth of your sheep, and ye shall be his servants, and ye shall cry out in that day because of your king which ye shall have chosen,* AND THE LORD WILL NOT HEAR YOU IN THAT DAY. This accounts for the continuation of monarchy; neither do the characters of the few good kings which have lived since, either sanctify the title, or blot out the sinfulness of the origin; the high encomuim given of David takes no notice of him *officially as a king,* but only as a man after God's own heart. *Nevertheless the People refused to obey the voice of Samuel, and they said, Nay, but we will have a king over us, that we may be like all the nations, and that our king may judge us, and go out before us and fight our battles.* Samuel continued to reason with them, but to no purpose; he set before them their ingratitude, but all would not avail; and seeing them fully bent on their folly, he cried out *I will call unto the Lord, and he shall send thunder and rain* (which then was a punishment, being a time of wheat harvest) *that ye may perceive and see that your wickedness is great which ye have done in the sight of the Lord,* IN ASKING YOU A KING. *So Samuel called unto the Lord, and the Lord sent thunder and rain that day, and all the people greatly feared the Lord and Samuel. And all the people said unto Samuel, Pray for thy servants unto the Lord thy God that we die not, for* WE HAVE ADDED UNTO OUR SINS THIS EVIL, TO ASK A KING. These portions of scripture are direct and positive. They admit of no equivocal construction. That the Almighty hath here entered his protest against monarchial government is true, or the scripture is false. And a man hath good reason to believe that there is as much of king-craft, as priest-craft in witholding the scripture from the public in Popish countries. For monarchy in every instance is the Popery of government.

To the evil of monarchy we have added that of hereditary succession; and as the first is a degradation and lessening of ourselves, so the second, claimed as a matter of right, is an insult and and imposition on posterity. For all men being originally equals, no *one* by *birth* could have a right to set up his own family in perpetual preference to all others for ever, and though himself might deserve *some* decent degree of honours of his contemporaries, yet his descendants might be far too unworthy to inherit them. One of the strongest *natural* proofs of the folly of hereditary right in kings, is, that nature disapproves of it, otherwise she would not so frequently turn it into ridicule by giving mankind an *ass for a lion.*

Secondly, as no man at first could possess any other public honours than were bestowed upon him, to the givers of those honours could have no power to give away the right of posterity, and though they might say 'We choose you for *our* head,' they could not without manifest injustice to their children say 'that your children and your children's children shall reign over *ours* for ever.' Because such an unwise, unjust, unnatural compact might (perhaps) in the next succession put them under the government of a rogue or a fool. Most wise men, in their private sentiments, have ever treated hereditary right with contempt; yet it is one of those evils, which when once established is not easily removed; many submit from fear, others from superstition, and the more powerful part shares with the king the plunder of the rest.

This is supposing the present race of the kings in the world to have had an honourable origin; whereas it is more than probable, that could we take off the dark covering of antiquity, and trace them to their first rise, that we should find the first of them nothing better than the principal ruffian of some restless gang, whose savage manners or pre-eminence in subtlety obtained him the title of chief among plunderers; and who by increasing in power, and extending his depredations, over-awed the quiet and defenceless to purchase their safety by frequent contributions. Yet his electors could have no idea of giving hereditary right to his descendants, because such a perpetual exclusion of themselves was incompatible with the free and unrestrained principles they professed to live by. Wherefore, hereditary succession in the early ages of monarchy could not take place as a matter of claim, but as something casual or complimental; but as few or no records were extant in those days, and traditionary history stuffed with fables, it was very easy, after the lapse of a few generations, to trump up some superstitious tale, conveniently timed, Mahomet like, to cram hereditary right down the throats of the vulgar. Perhaps the disorders which threatened, or seemed to threaten on the decease of a leader and the choice of a new one (for elections among ruffians could not be very orderly) induced many at first to favour hereditary pretensions; by which means it happened, as it hath happened since, that what at first was submitted to as a convenience, was afterwards claimed as a right.

England, since the conquest, hath known some few good monarchs, but groaned beneath a much larger number of bad ones, yet no man in his senses can say that their claim under William the Conqueror is a very honourable one. A French bastard landing with an armed banditti, and establishing himself king of England against the consent of the natives, is in plain terms a very paltry rascally original.—It certainly hath no divinity in it. However, it is needless to spend much time in exposing the folly of hereditary right, if there are any so weak as to believe it, let them promiscuously worship the ass and lion, and welcome. I shall neither copy their humility, nor disturb their devotion.

Yet I should be glad to ask how they suppose kings came at first? The question admits but of three answers, viz. either by lot, by election, or by usurpation. If the first king was taken by lot, it establishes a precedent for the next, which excludes hereditary succession. Saul was by lot yet the succession was not hereditary, neither does it appear from that transaction there was any intention it ever should. If the first king of any country was by election, that likewise establishes a precedent for the next; for to say, that the *right* of all future generations is taken away, by the act of the first electors, in their choice not only of a king, but of a family of kings for ever, hath no parallel in or out of scripture but the doctrine of original sin, which supposes the free will of all men lost in Adam; and from such comparison, and it will admit of no other, hereditary succession can derive no glory. For as in Adam all sinned, and as in the first electors all men obeyed; as in the one all mankind were subjected to Satan, and in the other to Sovereignty; as our innocence was lost in the first, and our authority in the last; and as both disable us from re-assuming some former state and privilege, it unanswerably follows that original sin and hereditary succession are parallels. Dishonourable rank! Inglorious connection! Yet the most subtle sophist cannot produce a juster simile.

As to usurpation, no man will be so hardy as to defend it; and that William the Conqueror was an usurper is a fact not to be contradicted. The plain truth is, that the antiquity of English monarchy will not bear looking into.

But it is not so much the absurdity as the evil of hereditary succession which concerns mankind. Did it ensure a race of good and wise men it would have the seal of divine authority, but as it opens a door to the *foolish*, the *wicked*, and the *improper*, it hath in it the nature of oppression. Men who look upon themselves born to reign, and other to obey, soon grow insolent; selected from the rest of mankind their minds are early poisoned by importance; and the world they act in differs so materially from the world at large, that they have but little opportunity of knowing its true interests, and when they succeed to the government are frequently the most ignorant and unfit of any throughout the dominions.

Another evil which attends hereditary succession it, that the throne is subject to be possessed by a minor at any age; all which time the regency, acting under the cover of a king, have every opportunity and inducement to betray their trust. The same national misfortune happens, when a king worn out with age and infirmity, enters the last stange of human weakness. In both these cases the public becomes a prey to every miscreant, who can tamper successfully with the follies either of age or infancy.

The most plausible plea, which hath ever been offered in favour of hereditary succession, is, that it preserves a nation from civil wars; and were this true, it would be weighty; whereas, it is the most barefaced falsity ever imposed upon mankind. The whole history of England disowns the fact. Thirty kings and two minors have reigned in that distracted kingdom since the conquest, in which time there have been (including the Revolution) no less than eight civil wars and nineteen rebellions. Wherefore instead of making for peace, it makes against it, and destroys the very foundation it seems to stand on.

The contest for monarchy and succession, between the houses of York and Lancaster, laid England in a scene of blood for many years. Twelve pitched battles, besides skirmishes and sieges, were fought between Henry and Edward. Twice was Henry prisoner to Edward, who in his turn was prisoner to Henry. And so uncertain is the fate of war and the temper of a nation, when nothing but personal matters are the ground of a quarrel, that Henry was taken in triumph from a prison to a palace, and Edward obliged to fly from a palace to a foreign land; yet, as sudden transitions of temper are seldom lasting, Henry in his turn was driven from the throne, and Edward recalled to succeed him. The parliament always following the strongest side.

This contest began in the reign of Henry the Sixth, and was not entirely extinguished till Henry the Seventh, in whom the families were united. Including a period of 67 years, viz. from 1422 to 1489.

In short, monarchy and succession have laid (not this or that kingdom only) but the world in blood and ashes. 'Tis a form of government which the word of God bears testimony against, and blood will attend it.

If we inquire into the business of a king, we shall find that in some countries they have none; and after sauntering away their lives without pleasure to themselves or advantage to the nation, withdraw from the scene, and leave their successors to tread the same idle round. In absolute monarchies the whole weight of business civil and military, lies on the king; the children of Israel in their request for a king, urged this plea 'that he may judge us, and go out before us and fight our battles.' But in countries where he is neither a judge nor a general, as in E——d, a man would be puzzled to know what *is* his business.

The nearer any government approaches to a republic the less business there is for a king. It is somewhat difficult to find a proper name for the government of E——. Sir William Meredith calls it a republic; but in its present state it is unworthy of the name, because the corrupt influence of the crown, by having all the places in its disposal, hath so effectually swallowed up the power, and eaten out the virtue of the house of commons (the republican part in the constitution) that the government of England is nearly as monarchical as that of France or Spain. Men fall out with names without understanding them. For it is the republican and not the monarchical part of the constitution of England which Englishmen glory in, viz. the liberty of choosing an house of commons from out of their own body—and it is easy to see that when the republican virtue fails, slavery ensues. Why is the constitution of E——d sickly, but because monarchy hath poisoned the republic, the crown hath engrossed the commons?

In England a k—— hath little more to do than to make war and give away places; which in plain terms, is to impoverish the nation and set it together by the ears. A pretty business indeed for a man to be allowed eight hundred thousand sterling a year for, and worshipped into the bargain! Of more worth is one honest man to society, and in the sight of God, than all the crowned ruffians that ever lived.

Thoughts on the Present State of American Affairs

In the following pages I offer nothing more than simple facts, plain arguments, and common sense; and have no other preliminaries to settle with the reader, than that he will divest himself of prejudice and prepossession, and suffer his reason and his feelings to determine for themselves; that he will put *on*, or rather that he will not put *off*, the true character of a man, and generously enlarge his views beyond the present day.

Volumes have been written on the subject of the struggle between England and America. Men of all ranks have embarked in the controversy, from different motives, and with various designs; but all have been ineffectual, and the period of debate is closed. Arms, as the last resource, decide the contest; the appeal was the choice of the king, and the continent hath accepted the challenge. [. . .]

The sun never shined on a cause of greater worth. 'Tis not the affair of a city, a country, a province, or a kingdom, but of a continent—of at least one eighth part of the habitable globe. 'Tis not the concern of a day, a year, or an age; posterity are virtually involved in the contest, and will be more or less affected, even to the end of time, by the proceedings now. Now is the seed time of continental union, faith and honour. The least fracture now will be like a name engraved with the point of a pin on the tender rind of a young oak; the wound will enlarge with the tree, and posterity read it in full grown characters. [. . .]

I have heard it asserted by some, that as America hath flourished under her former connection with Great Britain, that the same connection is necessary towards her future happiness, and will always have the same effect. Nothing can be more fallacious than this kind of argument. We may as well assert, that because a child has thrived upon milk, that it is never to have meat; or that the first twenty years of our lives is to become a precedent for the next twenty. But even this is admitting more than is true, for I answer roundly, that America would have flourished as much, and probably much more, had no European power had any thing to do with her. The commerce by which she hath enriched herself are the necessaries of life, and will always have a market while eating is the custom of Europe.

But she has protected us, say some. That she hath engrossed us is true, and defended the continent at our expense as well as her own is admitted, and she would have defended Turkey from the same motive, viz. the sake of trade and dominion.

Alas, we have been long led away by ancient prejudices, and made large sacrifices to superstition. We have boasted the protection of Great Britain, without considering, that her motive was *interest* not *attachment;* that she did not protect us from *our enemies* on *our account,* but from *her enemies* on *her own account,* from those who had no quarrel with us on any *other account,* and who will always be our enemies on the *same account.* Let Britain wave her pretensions to the continent, or the continent throw off the dependence, and we should be at peace with France and Spain were they at war with Britain. The miseries of Hanover last war ought to warn us against connections. [. . .]

But Britain is the parent country, say some. Then the more shame upon her conduct. Even brutes do not devour their young, nor savages make war upon their families; wherefore the assertion, if true, turns to her reproach; but it happens not to be true, or only partly so, and the phrase *parent* or *mother country* hath been Jesuitically adopted by the —— and his parasites, with a low papistical design of gaining an unfair bias on the credulous weakness of our minds. Europe, and not England, is the parent country of America. This new world hath been the asylum for the persecuted lovers of civil and religious liberty from *every part* of Europe. Hither have they fled, not from the tender embraces of the mother, but from the cruelty of the monster; and it is so far true of England, that the same tyranny which drove the first emigrants from home, pursues their descendants still.

In this extensive quarter of the globe, we forget the narrow limits of three hundred and sixty miles (the extent of England) and carry our friendship on a larger scale; we claim brotherhood with every European Christian, and triumph in the generosity of the sentiment. [. . .]

Much hath been said of the united strength of Britain and the colonies, that in conjunction they might bid defiance to the world. But this is mere presumption; the fate of war is uncertain, neither do the expressions mean any thing; for this continent would never suffer itself to be drained of inhabitants to support the British arms in either Asia, Africa, or Europe.

Besides, what have we to do with setting the world at defiance? Our plan is commerce, and that, well attended to, will secure us the peace and friendship of all Europe; because it is the interest of all Europe to have America a *free port.* Her trade will always be a protection, and her barrenness of gold and silver secure her from invaders.

I challenge the warmest advocate for reconciliation, to shew, a single advantage that this continent can reap, by being connected with Great Britain. I repeat the challenge, not a single advantage is derived. Our corn will fetch its price in any market in Europe, and our imported goods must be paid for buy them where we will.

But the injuries and disadvantages we sustain by that connection, are without number; and our duty to mankind at large, as well as to ourselves, instruct us to renounce the alliance: Because, any submission to, or dependence on Great Britain, tends directly to involve this continent in European wars and quarrels; and sets us at variance with nations, who would otherwise seek our friendship, and against whom, we have neither anger nor complaint. As Europe is our market for trade, we ought to form no partial connection with any part of it. It is the true interest of America to steer clear of European contentions, which she never can do, while by her dependence on Britain, she is made the make-weight in the scale of British politics. [. . .]

The authority of Great Britain over this continent, is a form of government, which sooner or later must have an end: And a serious mind can draw no true pleasure by looking forward, under the painful and positive conviction, that what he calls 'the present constitution' is merely temporary. As parents, we can have no joy, knowing that *this government* is not sufficiently lasting to ensure any thing which we may bequeath to posterity: And by a plain method of argument, as we are running the next generation into debt, we ought to do the work of it, otherwise we use them meanly and pitifully. In order to discover the line of our duty rightly, we should take our children in our hand, and fix our station a few years farther into life; that eminence will present a prospect, which a few present fears and prejudices conceal from our sight. [. . .]

Men of passive tempers look somewhat lightly over the offences of Britain, and, still hoping for the best, are apt to call out, '*Come we shall be friends again for all this.*' But examine the passions and feelings of mankind. Bring the doctrine of reconciliation to the touchstone of nature, and then tell me, whether you can hereafter love, honour, and faithfully serve the power that hath carried fire and sword into your land? If you cannot do all these, then are you only deceiving yourselves, and by your delay bringing ruin upon posterity. Your future connection with Britain, whom you can neither love nor honour, will be forced and unnatural, and being formed only on the plan of present convenience, will in a little time fall into a relapse more wretched than the first. But if you say, you can still pass the violations over, then I ask, Hath your house been burnt? Hath your property been destroyed before your face? Are your wife and children destitute of a bed to lie on, or bread to live on? Have you lost a parent or a child by their hands, and yourself the ruined and wretched survivor? If you have not, then are you not a judge of those who have. But if you have, and can still shake hands with the murderers, then are you unworthy the name of husband, father, friend, or lover, and whatever may be your rank or title in life, you have the heart of a coward, and the spirit of a sycophant.

This is not inflaming or exaggerating matters, but trying them by those feelings and affections which nature justifies, and without which, we should be incapable of discharging the social duties of life, or enjoying the felicities of it. I mean not to exhibit horror for the purpose of provoking revenge, but to awaken us from fatal and unmanly slumbers, that we may pursue determinately some fixed object. It is not in the power of Britain or of Europe to conquer America, if she did not conquer herself by *delay* and *timidity*. The present winter is worth an age if rightly employed, but if lost or neglected, the whole continent will partake of the misfortune; and there is no punishment which that man will not deserve, be he who, or what, or where he will, that may be the means of sacrificing a season so precious and useful.

It is repugnant to reason, to the universal order of things, to all examples from the former ages, to suppose, that this continent can longer remain subject to any external power. The most sanguine in Britain does not think so. The utmost stretch of human wisdom cannot, at this time compass a plan short of separation, which can promise the continent even a year's security. Reconciliation is and was a fallacious dream. Nature hath deserted the connection, and Art cannot supply her place. For, as Milton wisely expressed, 'Never can true reconcilement grow where wounds of deadly hate have pierced so deep.'

Every quiet method for peace hath been ineffectual. Our prayers have been rejected with disdain; and only tended to convince us, that nothing flatters vanity, or confirms obstinacy in kings more than repeated petitioning—and nothing hath contributed more than that very measure to make the kings of Europe absolute: Witness Denmark and Sweden. Wherefore since nothing but blows will do, for God's sake, let us come to a final separation, and not leave the next generation to be cutting throats, under the violated unmeaning names of parent and child.

But the most powerful of all arguments, is, that nothing but independence, i.e. a continental form of government, can keep the peace of the continent and preserve it inviolate from civil wars. [. . .]

The colonies have manifested such a spirit of good order and obedience to continental government, as is sufficient to make every reasonable person easy and happy on that head. No man can assign the least pretence for his fears, on any other grounds, that such as are truly childish and ridiculous, that one colony will be striving for superiority over another.

Where there are no distinctions there can be no superiority, perfect equality affords no temptation. The republics of Europe are all (and we may say always) in peace. Holland and Switzerland are without wars, foreign or domestic: Monarchical governments, it is true, are never long at rest; the crown itself is a temptation to enterprising ruffians at *home*; and that degree of pride and insolence ever attendant on regal authority, swells into a rupture with foreign powers, in instances, where a republican government, by being formed on more natural principles, would negotiate the mistake.

If there is any true cause of fear respecting independence, it is because no plan is yet laid down. Men do not see their way out—Wherefore, as an opening into that business, I offer the following hints; at the same time modestly affirming, that I have no other opinion of them myself, than that they may be the means of giving rise to something better. Could the straggling thoughts of individuals be collected, they would frequently form materials for wise and able men to improve to useful matter.

Let the assemblies be annual, with a President only. The representation more equal. Their business wholly domestic, and subject to the authority of a Continental Congress.

Let each colony be divided into six, eight, or ten, convenient districts, each district to send a proper number of delegates to Congress, so that each colony send at least thirty. The whole number in Congress will be at least 390. Each Congress to sit and to choose a president by the following method. When the delegates are met, let a colony be taken from the whole thirteen colonies by lot, after which let the whole Congress choose (by ballot) a president from out of the delegates of *that* province. In the next Congress, let a colony be taken by lot from twelve only, omitting that colony from which the president was taken in the former Congress, and so proceeding on till the whole thirteen shall have had their proper rotation. And in order that nothing may pass into a law but what is satisfactorily just, not less than three fifths of the Congress to be called a majority.—He that will promote discord, under a government so equally formed as this, would join Lucifer in his revolt.

But as there is a peculiar delicacy, from whom, or in what manner, this business must first arise, and as it seems most agreeable and consistent, that it should come from some intermediate body between the governed and the governors, that is between the Congress and the people, let a Continental Conference be held, in the following manner, and for the following purpose.

A committee of twenty-six members of Congress, viz. two for each colony. Two members for each house of assembly, or Provincial convention, and five representatives of the people at large, to be chosen in the capital city or town of each province, for, and in behalf of the whole province, by as many qualified voters as shall think proper to attend from all parts of the province for that purpose; or, if more convenient, the representatives may be chosen in two or three of the most populous parts thereof. In this conference, thus assembled, will be united, the two grand principles of business, *knowledge* and *power*. The members of Congress, Assemblies, or Conventions, by having had experience in national concerns, will be able and useful counsellors, and the whole, being empowered by the people will have a truly legal authority.

The conferring members being met, let their business be to frame a Continental Charter, or Charter of the United Colonies; (answering to what is called the Magna Charta of England) fixing the number and manner of choosing members of Congress, members of Assembly, with their date of sitting, and drawing the line of business and jurisdiction between them: (Always remembering, that our strength is continental, not provincial:) Securing freedom and property to all men, and above all things the free exercise of religion, according to the dictates of conscience; which such other matter as is necessary for a charter to contain. Immediately after which, the said conference to dissolve, and the bodies which shall be chosen conformable to the said charter, to be the legislators and governors of this continent and for the time being: Whose peace and happiness, may God preserve, Amen.

Should any body of men be hereafter delegated for this or some similar purpose, I offer them the following extracts from that wise observer on governments *Dragonetti*. 'The science,' says he, 'of the politician consists in fixing the true point of happiness and freedom. Those men would deserve the gratitude of ages, who should discover a mode of government that contained the greatest sum of individual happiness, with the least national expense.' —*Dragonetti on Virtue and Rewards*.

But where says some is the King of America? I'll tell you Friend, he reigns above, and doth not make havoc of mankind like the Royal —— of Britain. Yet that we may not appear to be defective even in earthly honours, let a day be solemnly set apart for proclaiming the charter; let it be brought forth placed on the divine law, the word of God; let a crown be placed thereon, by which the world may know, that so far as we approve of monarchy, that in

America THE LAW IS KING. For as in absolute governments the King is law, so in free countries the law *ought* to be King; and there ought to be no other. But lest any ill use should afterwards arise, let the crown at the conclusion of the ceremony be demolished, and scattered among the people whose right it is.

A government of our own is our natural right: And when a man seriously reflects on the precariousness of human affairs, he will become convinced, that it is infinitely wiser and safer, to form a constitution of our own in a cool deliberate manner, while we have it in our power, than to trust such an interesting event to time and chance. [. . .]

Ye that tell us of harmony and reconciliation, can ye restore to us the time that is past? Can ye give to prostitution its former innocence? Neither can ye reconcile Britain and America. The last cord now is broken, the people of England are presenting addresses against us. There are injuries which nature cannot forgive; she would cease to be nature if she did. As well can the lover forgive the ravisher of his mistress, as the continent forgive the murders of Britain. The Almighty hath implanted in us these unextinguishable feelings for good and wise purposes. They are the guardians of his image in our hearts. They distinguish us from the herd of common animals. The social compact would dissolve, and justice be extirpated from the earth, or have only a casual existence were we callous to the touches of affection. The robber and the murderer, would often escape unpunished, did not the injuries which our tempers sustain, provoke us into justice.

O ye that love mankind! Ye that dare oppose, not only the tyranny, but the tyrant, stand forth! Every spot of the old world is over-run with oppression. Freedom hath been hunted round the globe. Asia, and Africa, have long expelled her.—Europe regards her like a stranger, and England hath given her warning to depart. O! receive the fugitive, and prepare in time an asylum for mankind.

On the Present Ability of America, with Some Miscellaneous Reflections

I have never met with a man, either in England or America, who hath not confessed his opinion, that a separation between the countries, would take place one time or other. And there is no instance in which we have shewn less judgement, than in endeavoring to describe, what we call, the ripeness or fitness of the Continent for independence.

As all men allow the measure, and vary only in their opinion of the time, let us, in order to remove mistakes, take a general survey of things and endeavour if possible, to find out the *very* time. But we need not go far, the inquiry ceases at once, for the *time hath found us.* The general concurrence, the glorious union of all things prove the fact.

It is not in numbers but in unity, that our great strength lies; yet our present numbers are sufficient to repel the force of all the world. The Continent hath, at this time, the largest body of armed and disciplined men of any power under Heaven; and is just arrived at that pitch of strength, in which no single colony is able to support itself, and the whole, when united can accomplish the matter, and either more, or, less than this, might be fatal in its effects. Our land force is already sufficient, and as to naval affairs, we cannot be insensible, that Britain would never suffer an American man of war to be built while the continent remained in her hands. Wherefore we should be no forwarder an hundred years hence in that branch, than we are now; but the truth is, we should be less so, because the timber of the country is every day diminishing, and that which will remain at last, will be far off and difficult to procure. [. . .]

Debts we have none; and whatever we may contract on this account will serve as a glorious memento of our virtue. Can we but leave posterity with a settled form of government, an independent constitution of its own, the purchase at any price will be cheap. But to expend millions for the sake of getting a few vile acts repealed, and routing the present ministry only, is unworthy the charge, and is using posterity with the utmost cruelty; because it is leaving them the great work to do, and a debt upon their backs, from which they derive no advantage. Such a thought is unworthy a man of honour, and is the true characteristic of a narrow heart and a pedling politician. [. . .]

No country on the globe is so happily situated, so internally capable of raising a fleet as America. Tar, timber, iron, and cordage are her natural produce. We need go abroad for nothing. Whereas the Dutch, who make large profits by hiring out their ships of war to the Spaniards and Portuguese, are obliged to import most of the materials they use. We ought to view the building of a fleet as an article of commerce, it being the natural manufactory of this country. It is the best money we can lay out. A navy when finished is worth more than it cost. And is that nice point in national policy, in which commerce and protection are united. Let us build; if we want them not, we can sell; and by that means replace our paper currency with ready gold and silver.

In point of manning a fleet, people in general run into great errors; it is not necessary that one-fourth part should be sailors. The Terrible privateer, Captain Death, stood the hottest engagement of any ship last war, yet had not twenty sailors on board, though her complement of men was upwards of two hundred. A few able and social sailors will soon instruct a sufficient number of active land-men in the common work of a ship. Wherefore, we never can be more capable to begin on maritime matters than now, while our timber is standing, our fisheries blocked up, and our sailors and shipwrights out of employ. [. . .]

In almost every article of defense we abound. Hemp flourishes even to rankness, so that we need not want cordage. Our iron is superior to that of other countries. Our small arms equal to any in the world. Cannon we can cast at pleasure. Saltpetre and gunpowder we are every day producing. Our knowledge is hourly improving. Resolution is our inherent character, and courage hath never yet forsaken us. Wherefore, what is it that we want? Why is it that we hesitate? From Britain we can expect nothing but ruin. If she is once admitted to the government of America again, this Continent will not be worth living in. Jealousies will be always arising; insurrections will be constantly happening; and who will go forth to quell them? Who will venture his life to reduce his own countrymen to a foreign obedience? The difference between Pennsylvania and Connecticut, respecting some unlocated lands, shews the insignificance of a B——sh government, and fully proves, that nothing but Continental authority can regulate Continental matters.

Another reason why the present time is preferable to all others, is, that the fewer our numbers are, the more land there is yet unoccupied, which instead of being lavished by the k—— on his worthless dependants, may be hereafter applied, not only to the discharge of the present debt, but to the constant support of government. No nation under heaven hath such an advantage as this.

The infant state of the Colonies, as it is called, so far from being against, is an argument in favour of independence. We are sufficiently numerous, and were we more so, we might be less united. It is a matter worthy of observation, that the more a country is peopled, the smaller their armies are. In military numbers, the ancients far exceeded the moderns: and the reason is evident, for trade being the consequence of population, men become too much absorbed thereby to attend to any thing else. Commerce diminishes the spirit, both of patriotism and military defence. And history sufficiently informs us, that the bravest achievements were always accomplished in the nonage of a nation. With the increase of commerce, England hath lost its spirit. The city of London, notwithstanding its numbers, submits to continued insults with the patience of a coward. The more men have to lose, the less willing are they to venture. The rich are in general slaves to fear, and submit to courtly power with the trembling duplicity of a spaniel.

Youth is the seed time of good habits, as well in nations as in individuals. It might be difficult, if not impossible, to form the Continent into one government half a century hence. The vast variety of interests, occasioned by an increase of trade and population, would create confusion. Colony would be against colony. Each being able might scorn each other's assistance: and while the proud and foolish gloried in their little distinctions, the wise would lament that the union had not been formed before. Wherefore, the *present time* is the *true time* for establishing it. The intimacy which is contracted in infancy, and the friendship which is formed in misfortune, are, of all others, the most lasting and unalterable. Our present union is marked with both these characters: we are young, and we have been distressed; but our concord hath withstood our troubles, and fixes a memorable era for posterity to glory in. [. . .]

As to religion, I hold it to be the indispensable duty of all government, to protect all conscientious professors thereof, and I know of no other business which government hath to do therewith. Let a man throw aside that narrowness of soul, that selfishness of principle, which the niggards of all professions are so unwilling to part with, and he will be at once delivered of his fears on that head. Suspicion is the companion of mean souls, and the bane of all good society. For myself I fully and conscientiously believe, that it is the will of the Almighty, that there should be diversity of religious opinions among us: It affords a larger field of our christian kindness. Were we all of one way of thinking, our religious dispositions would want matter for probation; and on this liberal principle, I look on the various denominations among us, to be like children of the same family, differing only, in what is called their Christian names. [. . .]

To CONCLUDE, however strange it may appear to some, or however unwilling they may be to think so, matters not, but many strong and striking reasons may be given, to shew, that nothing can settle our affairs so expeditiously as an open and determined declaration for independence. Some of which are,

First.—It is the custom of nations, when any two are at war, for some other powers, not engaged in the quarrel, to step in as mediators, and bring about the preliminaries of a peace: but while America calls herself the subject of Great Britain, no power, however well disposed she may be, can offer her mediation. Wherefore, in our present state we may quarrel on for ever.

Secondly.—It is unreasonable to suppose, that France or Spain will give us any kind of assistance, if we mean only to make use of that assistance for the purpose of repairing the breach, and strengthening the connection between Britain and America; because, those powers would be sufferers by the consequences.

Thirdly.—While we profess ourselves the subjects of Britain, we must, in the eye of foreign nations, be considered as rebels. The precedent is somewhat dangerous to *their peace,* for men to be in arms under the name of subjects; we on the spot, can solve the paradox: but to unite resistance and subjection, requires an idea much too refined for common understanding.

Fourthly.—Were a manifesto to be published, and dispatched to foreign courts, setting forth the miseries we have endured, and the peaceable methods we have ineffectually used for redress; declaring, at the same time, that not being able, any longer to live happily or safely under the cruel disposition of the B——sh court, we had been driven to the necessity of breaking off all connection with her; at the same time assuring all such courts of our peaceable disposition towards them, and of our desire of entering into trade with them: Such a memorial would produce more good effects to this Continent, than if a ship were freighted with petition to Britain.

Under our present denomination of British subjects we can neither be received nor heard abroad: The custom of all courts is against us, and will be so, until, by an independence, we take rank with other nations.

These proceedings may at first appear strange and difficult; but, like all other steps which we have already passed over, will in a little time become familiar and agreeable; and, until an independence is declared, the Continent will feel itself like a man who continues putting off some unpleasant business from day to day, yet knows it must be done, hates to set about it, wishes it over, and is continually haunted with the thoughts of its necessity.

Candidus [James Chalmers]

Plain Truth; Addressed to the Inhabitants of America, Containing Remarks on a Late Pamphlet, Entitled, Common Sense (1776)

I have now before me the Pamphlet, entitled COMMON SENSE; on which I shall remark with freedom and candour. It may not be improper to remind my readers, that the investigation of my subject, demands the utmost freedom of enquiry. I therefore entreat his indulgence; and that he will carefully remember, that intemperate zeal, is as injurious to liberty, as a manly discussion of facts is friendly to it. "Liberty, says the great MONTESQUIEU, is a right of doing whatever the laws permit; and if a citizen could do what they forbid, he would no longer be possessed of liberty, because all his fellow citizens would have the same power." In the beginning of his pamphlet, the Author asserts, that society in every state is a blessing. This in the sincerity of my heart I deny; for it is supreme misery to be associated with those, who to promote their ambitious purposes, flagitiously pervert the ends of political society. I do not say that our Author is indebted to BURGH'S POLITICAL DISQUISITIONS, or to ROUSSEAU'S Social Compact for his definition of Government, and his large Tree; although I wish he had favoured his readers with the following extract from that sublime reasoner. "To investigate those conditions of society which may best answer the purpose of nations, would require the abilities of some superior intelligence, who should be witness to all the passions of men, but be subject itself to none, who should have no connections with human nature, but should have a perfect knowledge of it: A Being, in short, whose happiness should be independent of us, and who would nevertheless employ itself about us. It is the province of Gods to make the laws for Men." With the utmost deference to the celebrated ROUSSEAU, I cannot indeed imagine, that laws even so constructed, would materially benefit our imperfect race; unless omniscience deigned previously to exalt our nature. The judicious reader will therefore perceive, that malevolence only, is requisite to declaim against, and arraign the most perfect governments. Our *Political Quack*, avails himself of this trite expedient, to cajole the people into the most abject slavery, under the delusive name of independence. His first indecent attack is against the English constitution; which with all its imperfections, is, and ever will be the pride and envy of mankind. To this panegyric involuntarily our author subscribes, by granting individuals to be safer in England, than in any other part of Europe. He indeed insidiously attributes this pre-eminent excellency, to the constitution of the people, rather than to our excellent constitution. To such contemptible subterfuge is our Author reduced, I would ask him, why did not the constitution of the people afford them superior safety, in the reign of Richard the Third, Henry the Eighth, and other tyrannic princes? Many pages might indeed be filled with encomiums bestowed on our excellent constitution, by illustrious authors of different nations.

This beautiful system (according to MONTESQUIEU) our constitution is a compound of Monarchy, Aristocracy, and Democracy. But it is often said, that the Sovereign, by honours and appointments, influences the Commons. The profound and elegant HUME agitating this question, thinks, to this circumstance, we are in part indebted for our supreme felicity; since without such controul in the Crown, our Constitution would immediately degenerate into Democracy; a government, which in the sequel, I hope to prove ineligible. Were I asked marks of the best government, and the purpose of political society, I would reply, the encrease, preservation, and prosperity of its members, in no quarter of the Globe, are those marks so certainly to be found, as in Great Britain, and her dependencies. After our Author has employed several pages, to break the bounds of society by debasing Monarchs: He says, "The plain truth is, that the antiquity of English Monarchy will not bear looking into."

HUME treating of the original contract, has the following melancholy, but sensible observation, "Yet reason tells us, that there is no property in durable objects, such as lands, and houses, when carefully examined, in passing from hand to hand, but must in some period, have been founded in fraud and injustice. The necessities of human society, neither in private or public life, will allow of such an accurate enquiry; and there is no virtue or moral duty, but what may, with facility, be refined away, if we indulge a false philosophy, in sifting and scrutinizing, by every captious rule of logic, in every light or position in which it may be placed."

Say ye votaries of honour and truth, can we adduce a stronger proof of our Author's turpitude, than his quoting the anti-philosophical story of the Jews, to debase Monarchy, and the best of Monarchs. Briefly examining the story of this contemptible race, more barbarous than our savages: "We find their history a continued succession of miracles, astonishing our imaginations, and exercising our faith. After wandering forty years in horrid desarts, they are chiefly condemned to perish for their perverseness, although under the immediate dominion of the KING OF HEAVEN. At length, they arrive in the sterile country of Palestine; which they conquer, by exterminating the inhabitants, and warring like Demons. The inhabitants of the adjoining regions, justly therefore held them in detestation, and the Jews finding themselves constantly abhorred, have ever since hated all mankind. This people, as destitute of arts and industry, and humanity, had not even in their language a word expressive of education. We might indeed remind our Author, who so readily drags in the Old Testament to support his sinister measures; that we could draw from that source, many texts, favourable to Monarchy, were we not conscious, that the Mosaic Law, gives way to the Gospel Dispensation. The reader no doubt will be gratified by the following extract from a most primitive Christian. "Christianity is a spiritual religion, relative only to celestial objects. The Christian's inheritance is not of this world. He performs his duty it is true, but this he does with a profound indifference for the good or ill success of his endeavors: Provided he hath nothing to reproach himself, it is of little consequence to him whether matters go well or ill here below. If the state be in a flourishing condition, he can hardly venture to rejoice in the public felicity, least he should be puffed up, with the inordinate price of his country's glory. If the state decline, he blesses the hand of GOD, that humbles his people to the dust."

Having defined the best government, I will humbly attempt to describe good Kings by the following unerring rule. The best Princes are constantly calumniated by the envenomed tongues and pens of the most worthless of their subjects. For this melancholy truth, do I appeal to the testimony of impartial historians; and long experience. The noble impartial historian Sully, speaking of the almost divine Henry the Fourth of France says, "Thus was the godlike prince represented (by the discontented of these days) almost throughout his whole kingdom, as a furious, and implacable tyrant: They were never without one set of arguments to engage his catholic nobility in a rebellion against him; and another to sow sedition among his protestant officers and gentry." HUME says, that the cruel unrelenting tyrant, Philip the Second of Spain, with his infernal Inquisition, was not more detested by the people of the Netherlands; than was the humane Charles, with his inoffensive Liturgy; by his mutinous subjects. The many unmerited insults offered to our gracious Sovereign; by the unprincipled Wilkes, and others down to this late Author; will forever disgrace humanity. For he says, "that monarchy was the most prosperous invention the Devil ever set on foot for the promotion of idolatry. It is the pride of Kings which throws mankind into confusion: In short, continues this Author, monarchy and succession, have laid not this or that kingdom only, but the World in blood and ashes." How deplorably wretched the condition of mankind, could they believe such execrable flagitious jargon. Unhappily indeed, mankind in every age are susceptible of delusion; but surely our Author's poison carries its antidote with it. Attentive to the spirit of his publication, we fancy ourselves in the barbarous fifteenth century: in which period our Author would have figured with his "Common Sense——and blood will attend it."

After his terrible anathema against our venerable constitution, and monarchy; let us briefly examine a democratical state; and see whether or not it is a government less sanguinary. This government is extremely plausible, and indeed flattering to the pride of mankind. The demagogues therefore, to seduce the people into their criminal designs ever hold up democracy to them: although conscious it never did, nor ever will answer in practice. If we believe a great Author, "There never existed, nor ever will exist a real democracy in the World." If we examine the republics of Greece and Rome, we ever find them in a state of war domestic or foreign. Our Author therefore makes no mention of these ancient States. "When Alexander ordered all the exiles, to be restored throughout the cities, it was found that the whole amounted to twenty thousand, the remains probably of still greater slaughters and massacres. What an astonishing number in so narrow a country as ancient Greece? and what domestic confusion, jealousy, partiality, revenge, heart-burnings must tear those cities, where factions were wrought up to such a degree of fury and despair." Apian's history of the civil wars of Rome, contains the most frightening picture of massacres, proscriptions, and forfeitures that ever were presented to the world.

The excellent Montesquieu declares, "That a democracy supposes the concurrence of a number of circumstances rarely united, in the first place, it is requisite that the state itself should be of small extent; so that the people might be easily assembled and personally known to each other. Secondly, the simplicity of their manners, should be such as to prevent a multiplicity of affairs, and perplexity in discussing them: And thirdly, there should subsist a great degree of equality between them, in point of right and authority: Lastly, there should be little or no luxury, for luxury must either be the effect of wealth, or it must make it necessary. It corrupts at once, both rich and poor: The one, by the possession, and the other, by the want of it." To this may be added continues the same Author, "that no government is so subject to CIVIL WARS, and INTESTINE COMMOTIONS, as that of the democratical or popular form; because, no other tends so strongly and so constantly to alter, nor requires so much vigilance, and fortitude to preserve it from alteration. It is indeed, in such a constitution, particularly, that a Citizen should always be armed with fortitude, constancy; and should every day, in the sincerity of his heart, guard against corruption, arising either from selfishness in himself, or in his compatriots; for if it once enters into public transactions, to root it out afterwards would be miraculous." [. . .]

I shall humbly endeavour to shew, that our author shamefully misrepresents facts, is ignorant of the true state of Great Britain and her Colonies, utterly unqualified for the arduous task, he has presumptuously assumed; and ardently intent on seducing us to that precipice on which himself stands trembling. To elucidate my strictures, I must with fidelity expose the circumstances of Great Britain and her colonies. If therefore, in the energy of description, I unfold certain bold and honest truths with simplicity, the judicious reader will remember, that true knowledge of our situation, is as essential to our safety, as ignorance thereof may endanger it. In the English provinces, exclusive of negroe and other slaves, we have one hundred and sixty thousand; or one hundred and seventy thousand men capable of bearing arms. If we deduct the people called Quakers, Anabaptists, and other religionists averse to arms; a considerable part of the emigrants, and those having a grateful predilection for the ancient constitution and parent state, we shall certainly reduce the first number to sixty or seventy thousand men. Now admitting those equal to the Roman legions, can we suppose them capable of defending against the power of Britain, a country nearly twelve hundred miles extending on the ocean. Suppose, our troops assembled in New-England, if the Britons see not fit to assail them, they haste to and desolate our other provinces, which eventually would reduce New England. If by dividing our forces, we pretend to defend our provinces, we also are infallibly undone. Our most fertile provinces, filled with unnumbered domestic enemies, slaves; intersected by navigable rivers, every where accessible to the fleets and armies of Britain, can make no defense. If without the medium of passion and prejudice, we view our other provinces, half armed, destitute of money and a navy: We must confess, that no power ever engaged such POTENT ANTAGONISTS, under such peculiar circumstances of infelicity. In the better days of Rome, she permitted no regular troops to defend her. Men destitute of property she admitted not into her militia, (her only army). I have been extremely concerned at the separation of the Connecticut men from our army. It augur'd not an ardent enthusiasm for liberty and glory. We still have an army before Boston, and I should be extremely happy to hear substantial proofs of their glory. I am still hopeful of great things from our army before Boston, when joined by the regiments now forming, which WANT OF BREAD will probably soon fill. Notwithstanding the predilection I have for my countrymen, I remark with grief, that hitherto our troops have displayed but few marks of Spartan or Roman enthusiasm. In the sincerity of my heart, I adjure the reader to believe, that no person is more sensibly afflicted by hearing the enemies of America remark, that no General ever fell singly and so ingloriously unrevenged before the inauspicious affair of Quebec. I am under no doubt, however, that we shall become as famed for martial courage, as any nation ever the sun beheld. Sanguine as I am, respecting the virtue and courage of my countrymen, depending on the history of mankind, since the Christian Æra, I cannot however imagine, the zeal for liberty will to such glorious efforts of heroism, as religious enthusiasm hath often impelled its votaries to perform. [. . .]

With the utmost deference to the honorable Congress; I do not view the most distant gleam of aid from foreign powers. The princes alone, capable of succouring us, are the Sovereigns of France and Spain. If according to our Author, we possess an eighth part of the habitable globe, and actually have a check on the West India commerce of England. The French indigo, and other valuable West India commodities, and the Spanish galeons, are in great jeopardy from our power. The French and Spaniards are therefore wretched politicians, if they do not assist England, in reducing her colonies to obedience.——Pleasantry apart! Can we be so deluded, to expect aid from those princes, which inspiring their subjects with a relish for liberty, might eventually shake their arbitrary thrones.——Natural avowed enemies to our sacred cause: Will they cherish, will they support the flame of liberty in America? Ardently intent, on extinguishing its latent dying sparks in their respective dominions. Can we believe, that those princes will offer an example so dangerous to their subjects and colonies, by aiding those provinces to independence? If independent, aggrandized by infinite numbers from every part of Europe, this Continent would rapidly attain power astonishing to imagination. Soon, very soon would we be conditioned to conquer Mexico, and all their West India settlements, which to annoy, or possess, we indeed are most happily situated. Simple and obvious as these truths are, can they be unknown to the people and princes of Europe? Be it however admitted, that those princes unmindful of the fatal policy of RICHLIEU'S arming Charles's subjects against him, and the more fatal policy of LEWIS the fourteenth permitting our glorious deliverer to effect the Revolution. I say, be it admitted, that those princes regardless of future consequences, and the ineptitude of the times, are really disposed to succour us. Say, ye friends of liberty and mankind, would no danger accrue from an army of French and Spaniards in the bosom of America? would ye not dread their junction with the Canadians and Savages, and with the numerous Roman Catholics, dispersed throughout the Colonies?

Let us now briefly view the pre-eminently envied state of Great Britain. If we regard the power of Britain, unembarrassed with Continental connections, and the political balance, we may justly pronounce her what our author does, America;—"A match for all Europe." Amazing were the efforts of England, in the war of Queen Ann, when little benefited by colony commerce, and e'er she had availed herself of the courage, good sense, and numbers of the people of Scotland and Ireland.

That England then prescribed laws to Europe, will be long remembered. Last war, her glory was, if possible, more eminently exalted, in every quarter of the globe did victory hover round her armies and navies, and her fame re-echoed from pole to pole. At present Great Britain is the umpire of Europe. [. . .]

But continues our author, "What have we to do with setting the world at defiance? our plan is commerce, and that well attended to, will secure us the peace and friendship of all Europe. Because it is the interest of all Europe, to have America a free-port, her trade will always be her protection, and her barrenness of gold and silver, will secure her from invaders."

I am perfectly satisfied, that we are in no condition to set the world at defiance, that commerce and the protection of Great Britain will secure us peace, and the friendship of all Europe. But I deny, that it is the interest of all Europe, to have American a free port, unless they are desirous of depopulating their dominions. His assertions, that barrenness of gold and silver will secure us from invaders, is indeed highly pleasant, have we not a much better security from invasions, viz. the most numerous and best disciplined army under heaven; or has our author already disbanded it. Pray how much gold and silver do the mines of Flanders produce? and what country so often as seen its unhappy fields drenched with blood, and fertilised with human gore. The princes of Europe have long dreaded the migration of their subjects to America; and we are sensible, that the king of Prussia is said more than once to have hanged Newlanders, or those who seduced his subjects to emigrate. I also humbly apprehend, that Britain is part of Europe. Now *old gentleman*, as you have clearly shewn, that we have a check upon her West India trade? Is it her interest to give us a greater check upon it, by permitting America (as you express it) to become a free port [?] Can we suppose it to be her interest to lose her valuable commerce to the Colonies, which effectually she would do, by giving up America to become your free port [?] If therefore it is the interest of all Europe, to have American as a free port: The people of Britain are extremely simple to expend so many millions sterling to prevent it. [. . .]

"Every quiet method of peace has been ineffectual; our prayers have been rejected with disdain." I do not indeed agree with the people of England in saying, that those, who so successfully laboured to widen the breach——desired nothing less than peace. That they who shortly were to command the most numerous and best disciplined army under Heaven; and a navy fit to contend with the fleets of England; imagining, *the time had found us*, disdained to be just. I highly venerate a majority of the Delegates. I have not indeed the honour of knowing all the worthy members; however, I wish the Gentlemen of the Congress, 'ere they entered on their important charge, had been better acquainted, with the strength of our friends in parliament. I sincerely lament, that the King did not receive the last excellent petition from the Congress; and I as sincerely wish, the Gentlemen of the Congress had not addressed themselves at that juncture, to the people of Ireland. "As to government matters," (continues our Author), "it is not in the power of Britain to do this Continent justice: The business of it will soon be too weighty and intricate to be managed with any tolerable degree of convenience, by a power so very distant from us, and so very ignorant of us; for if they cannot conquer us, they cannot govern us. The difference between Pennsylvania, and Connecticut, respecting some unlocated lands, shews the insignificance of a British government, and fully proves, that nothing but Continental authority can regulate Continental matters."

Until the present unhappy period, Great Britain has afforded to all mankind, the most perfect proof of her wise, lenient, and magnanimous government of the Colonies——The proofs to which we already have alluded, viz. our supreme felicity, and amazing increase. Than the affair of the Connecticut invaders; Omnipotence only could grant us stronger reasons for praying a continuance of our former beneficent government. Most certainly, every dispassionate person, as well as the plundered Pennsylvanians, must confess; that the Arm of Great Britain alone detained those Free-booters aforesaid, from seising the city of Philadelphia, to which without all doubt, they have as just a claim, as to those fertile regions in Pennsylvania, which they surreptitiously have possessed themselves of. In wrath to mankind, should Heaven permit our Author's new fangled government to exist; I, as a friend to Pennsylvanians, advise them to explore new settlements, and avoid the cruel mortification of being expelled by the *Saints* from their delicious abodes and pleasing fields.——"But (says the Author) the most powerful argument is, that nothing but independence, (that is a Continental form of government) can keep the peace of the Continent, and preserve it inviolate from civil wars. I dread the event of a reconciliation now with Britain, as it is more than probable, that it will be followed by revolt somewhere; the consequences of which may be far more fatal than all the malice of Britain. Thousands are already ruined by British barbarity, thousands more will probably share the same fate. These men have other feelings, than those who have nothing suffered: All they now possess is liberty, what they before enjoyed is sacrificed to its service, and having nothing more to lose, they disdain all submission."

Here we cannot mistake our author's meaning, that if one or more of the middle or southern Colonies reconcile with Great Britain, they will have war to sustain with New England; "the consequences of which may be more detrimental, than all the malice of Britain." This terrible denunciation, fortunately for such Colonies; is as futile as its author. Should Great Britain re-establish her authority in the said Colonies by negociation; surely it is not temerity to add, that the weight of Britain, in the scale of those provinces, would preponderate against the power of New England. If Britain should reduce the Colonies by arms, (which may Heaven avert!) The New England provinces will have as little inclination, as ability, to disturb the peace of their neighbours. I do indeed most sincerely compassionate those unhappy men, who are ruined by our unfortunate distractions. I do fervently pray, that Britain, and the Colonies may most effectually consider their peculiar infelicity. Such attention will do infinite honour to the parent state; who cannot view them as enemies, but as men unhappily irritated by the impolitic measures of Great Britain. [. . .]

Here I humbly apprehend our author's meaning is truly conspicuous. This Continent fifty years hence, infallibly will be richer, and much better peopled than at present; consequently abler to effect a revolution. But alas e're that period, our author will forever be forgotten; impelled therefore by his villainous ambition, he would rather precipitate his country into every species of horror, misery, and desolation, rather than forego his fancied protectorship. "But if you have, (says our author) and still can shake hands with the murderers, then are ye unworthy the name of husband, father, friend, or lover, and whatever may be your rank or title in life, you have the heart of a coward, and the spirit of a sycophant, &c. To talk of friendship with those in whom our reason forbids us to have faith, and our affections wounded through a thousand pores, instructs us to detest is madness and folly."

Ye that are not drunk with fanaticism answer me? Are these words dictated by peace, or base foul revenge, the constant attendant on COWARDS and sycophants; Does our author so perfectly veried in scripture, mean to conduct us to peace or desolation; or is he fit to legislate for men or Devils? Nations after desolating each other, (happily for mankind,) forgive, forget, and reconcile; like individuals who quarrel, reconcile, and become friends. Following the laudable example of the CONGRESS; we lately have most readily shaken hands with our inveterate enemies the Canadians, who have scalped nearly as many of our people as the British troops have done: Why therefore may we not forgive and reconcile ——by no means, it blasts our author's ambitious purposes. The English and Scotch, since the first Edward's time, have alternately slaughtered each other . . . to the amount of several hundred thousand: And now view each other as subjects, despising the efforts of certain turbulent spirits, tending to rekindle the ancient animosity. Many of the unhappy men criminally engaged with the Pretender: reconciled by humane treatment to that family against whom they rebelled, served in their armies a few years after. Indeed the conduct of the Canadians to our troops, as effectually illustrates our doctrine, as it reprobates the Anti-christian, diabolical tenets of our author. [. . .]

The author of Common Sense confidently affirms, "that our trade will always be its protection. . . ." Hitherto we have treated of reconciliation on the principles of our being as potent as Great Britain. Let us now consider our army, nearly as I have stated it, and our navy as an object by no means sublunary. It now behooves us well to consider, whether it were better to enter the harbour of peace with Great Britain, or plunge the ship into all the horrors of war.—Of civil war. As peace and a happy extension of commerce, are objects infinitely better for Great Britain; than war and diminution of her commerce. It therefore is her interest to grant us every species of indulgence, consistent with our constitutional dependence, should war continue, there can be no doubt of the annihilation of our ships, ports and commerce, by Great Britain. The King's ships now in New England, unhappily are more than sufficient to ruin the ports and commerce of these provinces. [. . .] I would remind our author of the constant language, and apparent purport of all ranks in opposition to Great Britain: "We have (say they) been the happiest people on earth, and would continue to be so, should Great Britain renounce her claim of taxation. We have no sinister views, we claim not independence; No! Perish the thought." Such I believe also was the tenor of the petitions from the Congress to his Majesty. Now I would ask every man of sentiment, what opinion our friends in Great Britain, nay the whole world will entertain of us, if in gratefully, and madly adopting our author's frantic schemes, we reject reasonable terms of reconciliation? Will they not most assuredly believe, that our popular leaders, have by infinite art, deluded the unwary people into their pre-concerted schemes; on supposition, *that the time had found us?* Those acquainted with Britain must confess, that the minority in parliament, hitherto have been our main prop. Now independency for ever annihilates this our best resource. Let us admit a part of the minority, republicans, or what is more probable, bent on removing the present ministry from their power. Our author's schemes annihilates all their consequence, all their opposition. In case of our independence, should a BARRE, or BURKE, patronize our government; such patrons, would infallibly participate the fate of the great and good DEWITS; be torn in pieces by the furious People.——If my remarks are founded on truth, it results, *that the time hath not found us;* that independency is inexpedient, ruinous, and impracticable, and that reconciliation with Great Britain on good terms, is our sole resource. 'Tis this alone, will render us respectable; it is this alone, will render us numerous; it is this only, will make us happy.

I shall no longer detain my reader, but conclude with a few remarks on our Author's scheme. The people of those Colonies would do well to consider the character, fortune, and designs of our Author, and his independents; and compare them with those of the most amiable and venerable personages in, and out of the Congress, who abominate such nefarious measures. I would humbly observe, that the specious science of politics, is of all others, the most delusive. Soon after the Revolution; the ablest states-men in England, and other parts of Europe; confidently predicted National ruin, infallible ruin, soon as the public debt exceeded fifty millions sterling. The nation now indebted nearly thrice that sum; is not arrived at the zenith of her credit and power. It is perhaps possible to form a specious system of government on paper which may seem practicable, and to have the consent of the people; yet it will not answer in practice nor retain their approbation upon trial. "All plans of government (says HUME) which suppose great reformation in the manners of mankind, are merely imaginary."

The fabricators of Independency have too much influence; to be entrusted in such arduous and important concerns. This reason alone, were sufficient at present, to deter us from altering the Constitution. It would be as inconsistent in our leaders in this hour of danger to form a government; as it were for a Colonel forming his battalion in the face of an enemy, to stop to write an essay on war.

This author's Quixotic system, is really an insult to our understanding; it is infinitely inferior to HUME'S idea of a perfect Common Wealth, which notwithstanding his acknowledged greatness of genius, is still reprehensible. It is not our business to examine, in what manner this author's associates, acquired their knowledge in national affairs; but we may predict, that his scheme of independency would soon, very soon give way to a govenment imposed on us, by some Cromwell of our armies. Nor is this sentiment unnatural, if we are attentive to constant experience, and human nature. The sublime MONTESQUIEU, so aptly quoted by the Congress, unhappily corroborates our doctrine, "from (says he) a manner of thinking that prevails amongst mankind. They set a higher value upon courage than timorousness, on activity than prudence, on strength than counsel. Hence, the army will ever despise a senate, and respect their own officers. They will naturally slight the order sent them by a body of men whom they look upon as cowards, and therefore unworthy to command them, so that as soon as the army depends on the legislative body, it becomes a military one;" and if the contrary has ever happened, it has been owing to some extraordinary circumstances, such as Holland being able to drown her garrisons, and the Venetians having it in their power to compel their troops to obedience by the vicinity of the European armies. Resources to which we forever must be strangers. If independence takes place, the New England men by their consequence therein; will assume a superiority, impatiently to be born by the other Colonies.

Notwithstanding our Author's fine words about toleration: Ye sons of peace and true christianity; believe me, it were folly supreme, madness, to expect angelic toleration from New-England, where she has constantly been detested, persecuted and execrated. Even in vain would our Author: or our CROMWELL cherish toleration; for the people of New-England, not yet arrived in the seventeenth or eighteenth century, would reprobate her.——It is more than probable to suppose, that the New-England governments would have no objection to an Agrarian law; nor is it unreasonable to suppose, that such division of property would be very agreeable to the soldiers. Indeed their General could not perhaps with safety to his existence as a General, refuse them so reasonable a gratification, particularly, as he will have more than one occasion for their services. Let us however admit that our General and troops, contradicting the experience of ages; do not assume the sovereignty. Released from foreign war; we would probably be plunged into all the misery of anarchy and intestine war. Can we suppose that the people of the south, would submit to have the seat of Empire at Philadelphia, or in New England; or that the people oppressed by a change of government, contrasting their misery with their former happy state, would not invite Britain to reassume the sovereignty. [. . .]

Ye respectable descendants of the planters from Holland and [Switzerland]; who acknowledge, that your fathers have instructed you to felicitate yourselves in existing under the benign British government. And have taught you to execrate the Government of Holland and other popular states, where the unhappy people unacquainted with trial by jury and other peculiar felicities of British subjects are [. . .] under the harrow of oppressive Demagogues. Do ye possess the wisdom to continue your happiness by a well regulated connection with Britain?

Volumes were insufficient to describe the horror, misery and desolation, awaiting the people at large in the syren form of American independence. In short, I affirm that it would be most excellent policy in those who wish for TRUE LIBERTY to submit by an advantageous reconciliation to the authority of Great Britain; "to accomplish in the long run, what they cannot do by hypocrisy, fraud and force in the short one."

INDEPENDENCE AND SLAVERY ARE SYNONYMOUS TERMS.

FINIS.

Carter Braxton

Letter to Landon Carter (April 14, 1776)

Dear Sir,

In this much elevated Station to which I fear I was improperly called by my Country, it has been my desire to seek the Advice and opinions of my friends that I might with better Judgment determine on the important matters that daily occur. In this number Nature gave me a right to rank you, & my knowledge taught me to expect your Wisdom & Experience would be a luminary in the present maze of Politicks, the intricacies and windings of which I own often puzzles my Understanding. To assist in finding a Clue by which my Country may be safely & honourably directed thro this labyrinth shall be my peculiar Study & Attention. If in this pursuit I differ in Sentiment with some of my Countrymen I flatter myself their Charity will prevent any injurious imputations on the motives that influence my Actions.

Independency & total Seperation from Great Britain are the interesting Subjects of all ranks of Men & often agitate our Body. It is in truth a delusive Bait which Men inconsiderately catch at without knowing the hook to which it is affixed. It is an Object to be wished for by every American; when it can be obtained with Safety & Honor. That this is not the moment I will prove by Arguments that to me are decisive & which exist with certainty. Your refined notion of our publick Honor being engaged to await the terms to be offered by Commissioners operates strongly with me & many others & makes the first reason I would offer. My next is that America is in too defenseless a State for the declaration having no Alliance with a naval Power nor as yet any Fleet of Consequence of her own to protect that trade which is so essential to the prosecution of the War & without which I know we cannot go on much longer. It is said by the Advocates for Seperation that France will undoubtedly assist us after we have asserted the State, and therefore they urge us to make the experiment.

Would such a blind, precipitate measure as this be justified by Prudence, first to throw off our Connection with G. Britain and then give ourselves up to the Arms of France [?] Would not this Court so famous for Intrigues & Deception avail herself of our Situation & from it exact much severer terms than if we were to treat with her before hand & settle the terms of any future alliance [?] Surely she would, but the truth of the matter is, there are some who are afraid to await the Arrival of Commissioners, lest the dispute should be accommodated much ag[ains]t their Will even upon the Admission of our own terms. For however strange it may appear I am satisfied that the eastern Colonies do not mean to have a Reconciliation and in this I am justified by publick & private Reasons.

To illustrate my Opinion I will beg leave to mention them. Two of the new England Colonies enjoy a Government purely democratical the Nature & Principle of which both civil & religious are so totally incompatible with Monarchy that they have ever lived in a restless State under it. The other two tho not so popular in their frame bordered so near upon it that Monarchical Influence hung very heavy on them. The best opportunity in the World being now offered them to throw off all Subjection & embrace their darling Democracy, they are determined to accept it.

These are aided by those of a private Nature but not less cogent. The Colonies of Massachusetts & Connecticut who rule the other two have Claims on the Province of Pensylvania in the whole for near one third of the Land within their Provincial Bounds & indeed the Claim extended to its full extent comes within four Miles of this City. This dispute was carried to the King & Council & with them it now lies. The eastern Colonies unwilling they should now be the Arbiters have exerted their Claim by force & have at this time eight hundred Men in Arms upon the upper part of this Land called Wyoming, where they are peaceble at present only thro the Influence of the Congress. There naturally then arises a heart burning & Jealousy between these People & they must have two very different Objects in View.

The Province of New York is not without her Fears & apprehensions from the Temper of her Neighbours, their great Swarms & small Territory.

Even Virginia is not free from Claims on Pennsylvania nor Maryland from those on Virginia. Some of the delegates from our Colony carry their Ideas of right to Lands so far to the eastward that the middle Colonies dread their being swallowed up between the Claims of them & those from the East. And yet without any Adjustment of their disputes & a variety of other matters, some are for lugging us into Independence. But so long as these remain unsettled & Men act upon the Principles they ever have done, you may rely no such thing will be generally agreed on. Upon viewing the secret movements of Men & things I am convinced the Assertion of Independence is far off. If it was to be now asserted, the Continent would be torn in pieces by intestine Wars & Convulsions.

Previous to Independence all disputes must be healed & Harmony prevail. A grand Continental League must be formed & a superintending Power also. When these necessary Steps are taken & I see a Coalition formed sufficient to withstand the Power of Britain or any other, then am I for an independent State & all its Consequences, as then I think they will produce Happiness to America. It is a true saying of a Wit—We must hang together or seperately. I will not beg yr pardon for intruding this long Letter upon yr old age which I judged necessary in my Situation & to conclude by assuring you I am with great regard, your affect Nephew,

Carter Braxton

John Adams

Letter to Mercy Warren (April 16, 1776)

Madam Not untill Yesterdays Post, did your agreable Favour of March the Tenth, come to my Hands. It gave me great Pleasure and altho in the distracted Kind of Life, I am obliged to lead, I cannot promise to deserve a Continuance of so excellent a Correspondence yet I am determined by Scribbling Something or other, be it what it may, to provoke it.

The Ladies I think are the greatest Politicians, that I have the Honour to be acquainted with, not only because they act upon the Sublimest of all the Principles of Policy, viz. [that] Honesty is the best Policy, but because they consider Questions more coolly, than those who are heated with Party Zeal, and inflamed with the bitter Contentions of active public Life.

I know of no Researches in any of the sciences more ingenious than those which have been made after the best Forms of Government nor can there be a more agreable Employment to a benevolent Heart. The Time is now approaching, when the Colonies will find themselves under a Necessity of engaging in Earnest in this great and indispensible Work. I have ever Thought it the most difficult and dangerous Part of the Business Americans have to do, in this mighty Contest, to continue some Method for the Colonies to glide insensibly, from under the old Government, into a peaceable and contented Submission to new ones. It is a long Time since this opinion was conceivd, and it has never been out of my Mind, my constant Endeavour has been to convince Gentlemen of the Necessity of turning their Thoughts to these Subjects. At present the sense of this Necessity seems to be general, and Measures are taking which must terminate in a compleat Revolution. There is Danger of Convulsions. But I hope, not great ones.

The Form of Government, which you admire, when its Principles are pure is admirable indeed. It is productive of every Thing, which is great and excellent among Men. But its Principles are as easily destroyed, as human Nature is corrupted. Such a Government is only to be supported by pure Religion, or Austere Morals. Public Virtue cannot exist in a Nation without private, and public Virtue is the only Foundation of Republics. There must be a positive Passion for the public good, the public Interest, Honour, Power, and Glory, established in the Minds of the People, or there can be no Republican Government, nor any real Liberty. And this public Passion must be superiour to all private Passions. Men must be ready, they must pride themselves, and be happy to sacrifice their private Pleasures, Passions, and Interests, nay their private Friendships and dearest Connections, when they Stand in Competition with the Right of Society.

Is there in the World a Nation, which deserves this Character [?] There have been several, but they are no more. Our dear Americans perhaps have as much of it as any Nation now existing, and New England perhaps has more than the rest of America. But I have seen all along my Life, Such Selfishness, and Littleness even in New England, that I sometimes tremble to think that, altho We are engaged in the best Cause that ever employed the Human Heart, yet the Prospect of success is doubtfull not for Want of Power or of Wisdom, but of Virtue.

The Spirit of Commerce, Madam, which even insinuates itself into Families, and influences holy Matrimony, and thereby corrupts the Morals of Families as well as destroys their Happiness, it is much to be feared is incompatible with that purity of Heart, and Greatness of soul which is necessary for an happy Republic. This Same Spirit of Commerce is as rampant in New England as in any Part of the World. Trade is as well understood and as passionately loved there as any where. Even the Farmers, and Tradesmen are addicted to Commerce. And it is too true, that Property is generally the standard of Respect there as much as any where. While this is the Case there is great Danger that a Republican Government would be very factious and turbulent there. Divisions in Elections are much to be dreaded. Every Man must sincerely set himself to root out his Passions, Prejudices and Attachments, and to get the better of his private Interest. The only reputable Principle and Doctrine must be that all Things must give Way to the public.

This is very grave and Solemn Discourse to a Lady. True, and I thank God, that his Providence has made me Acquainted with two Ladies at least, who can bear it.

I think Madam, that the Union of the Colonies, will continue and be more firmly cemented. But We must move slowly. Patience, Patience, Patience! I am obliged to invoke this every Morning of my Life, every Noon, and every Evening.

It is Surprising to me that any among you should flatter themselves with an Accommodation. Every Appearance is against it, to an Attentive observer. The Story of Commissioners is a Bubble. Their real Errant is an Insult. But popular Passions and Fancies will have their Course, you may as well reason down a Gale of Wind. You expect, if a certain Bargain Should be complied with, to be made acquainted with noble and Royal Characters. But in this you will be disappointed. Your Correspondent has neither Principles, nor Address, nor Abilities, for such Scenes. And others are as sensible of it, I assure you as he is. They must be Persons of more Complaisance and Ductility of Temper as well as better Accomplishments for such great Things.

He wishes for nothing less. He wishes for nothing more than to retire from all public Stages, and public Characters, great and Small, to his Farm and his Attorneys office. And to both these he must return.

Thoughts on Government (April 1776)

If I was equal to the task of forming a plan for the government of a colony, I should be flattered with your request, and very happy to comply with it; because as the divine science of politicks is the science of social happiness, and the blessings of society depend entirely on the constitutions of government, which are generally institutions that last for many generations, there can be no employment more agreeable to a benevolent mind, than a research after the best.

Pope flattered tyrants too much when he said,

For forms of government let fools contest,
That which is best administered is best.

Nothing can be more fallacious than this: But poets read history to collect flowers not fruits—they attend to fanciful images, not the effects of social institutions. Nothing is more certain from the history of nations, and the nature of man, than that some forms of government are better fitted for being well administered than others.

We ought to consider, what is the end of government, before we determine which is the best form. Upon this point all speculative politicians will agree, that the happiness of society is the end of government, as all Divines and moral Philosophers will agree that the happiness of the individual is the end of man. From this principle it will follow, that the form of government, which communicates ease, comfort, security, or in one word happiness to the greatest number of persons, and in the greatest degree, is the best.

All sober enquiries after truth, ancient and modern, Pagan and Christian, have declared that the happiness of man, as well as his dignity consists in virtue. Confucius, Zoroaster, Socrates, Mahomet, not to mention authorities really sacred, have agreed in this.

If there is a form of government then, whose principle and foundation is virtue, will not every sober man acknowledge it better calculated to promote the general happiness than any other form?

Fear is the foundation of most governments; but is so sordid and brutal a passion, and renders men, in whose breasts it predominates, so stupid, and miserable, that Americans will not be likely to approve of any political institution which is founded on it.

Honor is truly sacred, but holds a lower rank in the scale of moral excellence than virtue. Indeed the former is but a part of the latter, and consequently has not equal pretensions to support a frame of government productive of human happiness.

The foundation of every government is some principle or passion in the minds of the people. The noblest principles and most generous affections in our nature then, have the fairest chance to support the noblest and most generous models of government.

A man must be indifferent to the sneers of modern Englishmen to mention in their company the names of Sidney, Harrington, Locke, Milton, Nedham, Neville, Burnet, and Hoadley. No small fortitude is necessary to confess that one has read them. The wretched condition of this country, however, for ten or fifteen years past, has frequently reminded me of their principles and reasonings. They will convince any candid mind, that there is no good government but what is Republican. That the only valuable part of the British constitution is so; because the very definition of a Republic, is "an Empire of Laws, and not of men." That, as a Republic is the best of governments, so that particular arrangement of the powers of society, or in other words that form of government, which is best contrived to secure an impartial and exact execution of the laws, is the best of Republics.

Of Republics, there is an inexhaustable variety, because the possible combinations of the powers of society, are capable of innumerable variations.

As good government, is an empire of laws, how shall your laws be made? In a large society, inhabiting an extensive country, it is impossible that the whole should assemble, to make laws: The first necessary step then, is, to depute power from the many, to a few of the most wise and good. But by what rules shall you chuse your Representatives? Agree upon the number and qualifications of persons, who shall have the benefit of choosing, or annex this priviledge to the inhabitants of a certain extent of ground.

The principal difficulty lies, and the greatest care should be employed in constituting this Representative Assembly. It should be in miniature, an exact portrait of the people at large. It should think, feel, reason, and act like them. That it may be the interest of this Assembly to do strict justice at all times, it should be an equal representation, or in other words equal interest among the people should have equal interest in it. Great care should be taken to effect this, and to prevent unfair, partial, and corrupt elections. Such regulations, however, may be better made in times of greater tranquility than the present, and they will spring up of themselves naturally, when all the powers of government come to be in the hands of the people's friends. At present it will be safest to proceed in all established modes to which the people have been familiarised by habit.

A representation of the people in one assembly being obtained, a question arises whether all the powers of government, legislative, executive, and judicial, shall be left in this body? I think a people cannot be long free, nor ever happy, whose government is in one Assembly. My reasons for this opinion are as follow.

1. A single Assembly is liable to all the vices, follies and frailties of an individual. Subject to fits of humour, starts of passion, flights of enthusiasm, partialities of prejudice, and consequently productive of hasty results and absurd judgments: And all these errors ought to be corrected and defects supplied by some controuling power.

2. A single Assembly is apt to be avaricious, and in time will not scruple to exempt itself from burthens which it will lay, without compunction, on its constituents.

3. A single Assembly is apt to grow ambitious, and after a time will not hesitate to vote itself perpetual. This was one fault of the long parliament, but more remarkably of Holland, whose Assembly first voted themselves from annual to septennial, then for life, and after a course of years, that all vacancies happening by death, or otherwise, should be filled by themselves, without any application to constituents at all.

4. A Representative Assembly, altho' extremely well qualified, and absolutely necessary as a branch of the legislature, is unfit to exercise the executive power, for want of two essential properties, secrecy and dispatch.

5. A Representative Assembly is still less qualified for the judicial power; because it is too numerous, too slow, and too little skilled in the laws.

6. Because a single Assembly, possessed of all the powers of government, would make arbitrary laws for their own interest, execute all laws arbitrarily for their own interest, and adjudge all controversies in their own favour.

But shall the whole power of legislation rest in one Assembly? Most of the foregoing reasons apply equally to prove that the legislative power ought to be more complex—to which we may add, that if the legislative power is wholly in one Assembly, and the executive in another, or in a single person, these two powers will oppose and enervate upon each other, until the contest shall end in war, and the whole power, legislative and executive, be usurped by the strongest.

The judicial power, in such case, could not mediate, or hold the balance between the two contending powers, because the legislative would undermine it. And this shews the necessity too, of giving the executive power a negative upon the legislative, otherwise this will be continually encroaching upon that.

To avoid these dangers let a [distinct] Assembly be constituted, as a mediator between the two extreme branches of the legislature, that which represents the people and that which is vested with the executive power.

Let the Representative Assembly then elect by ballot, from among themselves or their constituents, or both, a distinct Assembly, which for the sake of perspicuity we will call a Council. It may consist of any number you please, say twenty or thirty, and should have a free and independent exercise of its judgment, and consequently a negative voice in the legislature.

These two bodies thus constituted, and made integral parts of the legislature, let them unite, and by joint ballot choose a Governor, who, after being stripped of most of those badges of domination called prerogatives, should have a free and independent exercise of his judgment, and be made also an integral part of the legislature. This I know is liable to objections, and if you please you may make him only President of the Council, as in Connecticut: But as the Governor is to be invested with the executive power, with consent of Council, I think he ought to have a negative upon the legislative. If he is annually elective, as he ought to be, he will always have so much reverence and affection for the People, their Representatives and Councillors, that although you give him an independent exercise of his judgment, he will seldom use it in opposition to the two Houses, except in cases the public utility of which would be conspicuous, and some such cases would happen.

In the present exigency of American affairs, when by an act of Parliament we are put out of the royal protection, and consequently discharged from our allegiance; and it has become necessary to assume government for our immediate security, the Governor, Lieutenant-Governor, Secretary, Treasurer, Commissary, Attorney-General, should be chosen by joint Ballot, of both Houses. And these and all other elections, especially of Representatives, and Councillors, should be annual, there not being in the whole circle of the sciences, a maxim more infallible than this, "Where annual elections end, there slavery begins."

These great men, in this respect, should be, once a year

> Like bubbles on the sea of matter borne,
> They rise, they break, and to that sea return.

This will teach them the great political virtues of humility, patience, and moderation, without which every man in power becomes a ravenous beast of prey.

This mode of constituting the great offices of state will answer very well for the present, but if, by experiment, it should be found inconvenient, the legislature may at its leisure devise other methods of creating them, by elections of the people at large, as in Connecticut, or it may enlarge the term for which they shall be chosen to seven years, or three years, or for life, or make any other alterations which the society shall find productive of its ease, its safety, its freedom, or in one word, its happiness.

A rotation of all offices, as well as of Representatives and Councillors, has many advocates, and is contended for with many plausible arguments. It would be attended no doubt with many advantages, and if the society has a sufficient number of suitable characters to supply the great number of vacancies which would be made by such a rotation, I can see no objection to it. These persons may be allowed to serve for three years, and then excluded three years, or for any longer or shorter term.

Any seven or nine of the legislative Council may be made a Quorum, for doing business as a Privy Council, to advise the Governor in the exercise of the executive branch of power, and in all acts of state.

The Governor should have the command of the militia, and of all your armies. The power of pardons should be with the Governor and Council.

Judges, Justices and all other officers, civil and military, should be nominated and appointed by the

Governor, with the advice and consent of Council, unless you choose to have a government more popular; if you do, all officers, civil and military, may be chosen by joint ballot of both Houses, or in order to preserve the independence and importance of each House, by ballot of one House, concurred by the other. Sheriffs should be chosen by the freeholders of counties—so should Registers of Deeds and Clerks of Counties.

All officers should have commissions, under the hand of the Governor and seal of the Colony.

The dignity and stability of government in all its branches, the morals of the people and every blessing of society, depends so much upon an upright and skillful administration of justice, that the judicial power ought to be distinct from both the legislative and executive, and independent upon both, that so it may be a check upon both, as both should be checks upon that. The Judges therefore should always be men of learning and experience in the laws, of exemplary morals, great patience, calmness, coolness and attention. Their minds should not be distracted with jarring interests; they should not be dependant upon any man or body of men. To these ends they should hold estates for life in their offices, or in other words their commissions should be during good behaviour, and their salaries ascertained and established by law. For misbehaviour the grand inquest of the Colony, the House of Representatives, should impeach them before the Governor and Council, where they should have time and opportunity to make their defence, but if convicted should be removed from their offices, and subjected to such other punishment as shall be thought proper.

A Militia Law requiring all men, or with very few exceptions, besides cases of conscience, to be provided with arms and ammunition, to be trained at certain seasons, and requiring counties, towns, or other small districts to be provided with public stocks of ammunition and entrenching utensils, and with some settled plans for transporting provisions after the militia, when marched to defend their country against sudden invasions, and requiring certain districts to be provided with field-pieces, companies of matrosses and perhaps some regiments of light horse, is always a wise institution, and in the present circumstances of our country indispensible.

Laws for the liberal education of youth, especially of the lower class of people, are so extremely wise and useful, that to a humane and generous mind, no expence for this purpose would be thought extravagant.

The very mention of sumptuary laws will excite a smile. Whether our countrymen have wisdom and virtue enough to submit to them I know not. But the happiness of the people might be greatly promoted by them, and a revenue saved sufficient to carry on this war forever. Frugality is a great revenue, besides curing us of vanities, levities and fopperies which are real antidotes to all great, manly and warlike virtues.

But must not all commissions run in the name of a king? No. Why may they not as well run thus, "The Colony of —— to A. B. greeting," and be tested by the Governor?

Why may not writs, instead of running in the name of a King, run thus, "The Colony of —— to the Sheriff, &c." and be tested by the Chief Justice.

Why may not indictments conclude, "against the peace of the Colony of —— and the dignity of the same?"

A Constitution, founded on these principles, introduces knowledge among the People, and inspires them with a conscious dignity, becoming Freemen. A general emulation takes place, which causes good humour, sociability, good manners, and good morals to be general. That elevation of sentiment, inspired by such a government, makes the common people brave and enterprizing. That ambition which is inspired by it makes them sober, industrious and frugal. You will find among them some elegance, perhaps, but more solidity; a little pleasure, but a great deal of business—some politeness, but more civility. If you compare such a country with the regions of domination, whether Monarchial or Aristocratical, you will fancy yourself in Arcadia or Elisium.

If the Colonies should assume governments separately, they should be left entirely to their own choice of the forms, and if a Continental Constitution should be formed, it should be a Congress, containing a fair and adequate Representation of the Colonies, and its authority should sacredly be confined to these cases, viz. war, trade, disputes between Colony and Colony, the Post-Office, and the unappropriated lands of the Crown, as they used to be called.

These Colonies, under such forms of government, and in such a union, would be unconquerable by all the Monarchies of Europe.

You and I, my dear Friend, have been sent into life, at a time when the greatest law-givers of antiquity would have wished to have lived. How few of the human race have ever enjoyed an opportunity of making an election of government more than of air, soil, or climate, for themselves or their children. When! Before the present epocha, had three millions of people full power and a fair opportunity to form and establish the wisest and happiest government that human wisdom can contrive? I hope you will avail yourself and your country of that extensive learning and indefatigable industry which you possess, to assist her in the formations of the happiest governments, and the best character of a great People. For myself, I must beg you to keep my name out of sight, for this feeble attempt, if it should be known to be mine, would oblige me to apply to myself those lines of the immortal John Milton, in one of his sonnets,

> I did but teach the age to quit their cloggs
> By the plain rules of ancient Liberty,
> When lo! a barbarous noise surrounded me,
> Of owls and cuckoos, asses, apes and dogs.

The Virginia Declaration of Rights (June 12, 1776)

A declaration of rights made by the representatives of the good people of Virginia, assembled in full and free convention; which rights do pertain to them and their posterity, as the basis and foundation of government.

Section 1. That all men are by nature equally free and independent and have certain inherent rights, of which, when they enter into a state of society, they cannot, by any compact, deprive or divest their posterity; namely, the enjoyment of life and liberty, with the means of acquiring and possessing property, and pursuing and obtaining happiness and safety.

Sec. 2. That all power is vested in, and consequently derived from, the people; that magistrates are their trustees and servants and at all times amenable to them.

Sec. 3. That government is, or ought to be, instituted for the common benefit, protection, and security of the people, nation, or community; of all the various modes and forms of government, that is best which is capable of producing the greatest degree of happiness and safety and is most effectually secured against the danger of maladministration; and that, when any government shall be found inadequate or contrary to these purposes, a majority of the community hath an indubitable, inalienable, and indefeasible right to reform, alter, or abolish it, in such manner as shall be judged most conducive to the public weal.

Sec. 4. That no man, or set of men, are entitled to exclusive or separate emoluments or privileges from the community, but in consideration of public services; which, not being descendible, neither ought the offices of magistrate, legislator, or judge to be hereditary.

Sec. 5. That the legislative and executive powers of the state should be separate and distinct from the judiciary; and that the members of the two first may be restrained from oppression, by feeling and participating the burdens of the people, they should, at fixed periods, be reduced to a private station, return into that body from which they were originally taken, and the vacancies be supplied by frequent, certain, and regular elections, in which all, or any part, of the former members, to be again eligible, or ineligible, as the laws shall direct.

Sec. 6. That elections of members to serve as representatives of the people, in assembly, ought to be free; and that all men, having sufficient evidence of permanent common interest with, and attachment to, the community, have the right of suffrage and cannot be taxed or deprived of their property for public uses without their own consent, or that of their representatives so elected, nor bound by any law to which they have not, in like manner, assented for the public good.

SEC. 7. That all power of suspending laws, or the execution of laws, by any authority, without consent of the representatives of the people, is injurious to their rights and ought not to be exercised.

SEC. 8. That in all capital or criminal prosecutions a man hath a right to demand the cause and nature of his accusation, to be confronted with the accusers and witnesses, to call for evidence in his favor, and to a speedy trial by an impartial jury of twelve men of his vicinage, without whose unanimous consent he cannot be found guilty; nor can he be compelled to give evidence against himself; that no man be deprived of his liberty, except by the law of the land or the judgment of his peers.

SEC. 9. That excessive bail ought not to be required, nor excessive fines imposed, nor cruel and unusual punishments inflicted.

SEC. 10. That general warrants, whereby an officer or messenger may be commanded to search suspected places without evidence of a fact committed, or to seize any person or persons not named, or whose offense is not particularly described and supported by evidence, are grievous and oppressive and ought not to be granted.

SEC. 11. That in controversies respecting property, and in suits between man and man, the ancient trial by jury is preferable to any other and ought to be held sacred.

SEC. 12. That the freedom of the press is one of the great bulwarks of liberty and can never be restrained but by despotic governments.

SEC. 13. That a well-regulated militia, or composed of the body of the people, trained to arms, is the proper, natural, and safe defense of a free state; that standing armies, in time of peace, should be avoided as dangerous to liberty; and that in all cases the military should be under strict subordination to, and governed by, the civil power.

SEC. 14. That the people have a right to uniform government; and, therefore, that no government separate from or independent of the government of Virginia ought to be erected or established within the limits thereof.

SEC. 15. That no free government, or the blessings of liberty, can be preserved to any people, but by a firm adherence to justice, moderation, temperance, frugality, and virtue, and by frequent recurrence to fundamental principles.

SEC. 16. That religion, or the duty which we owe to our Creator, and the manner of discharging it, can be directed only by reason and conviction, not by force or violence; and therefore all men are equally entitled to the free exercise of religion, according to the dictates of conscience; and that it is the mutual duty of all to practice Christian forbearance, love, and charity toward each other.

FOUR LETTERS ON INTERESTING SUBJECTS (1776)

Letter IV

Among the many publications which have appeared on the subject of political Constitutions, none, that I have seen, have properly defined what is meant by *a Constitution*, that word having been bandied about without any determinate sense being affixed thereto. A Constitution, and a form of government, are frequently confounded together, and spoken of as synonimous things; whereas they are not only different, but are established for different purposes: All countries have some form of government, but few, or perhaps none, have truly a Constitution. The form of government in England is by a king, lords and commons; but if you ask an Englishman what he means when he speaks of the English Constitution, he is unable to give you any answer. The truth is, the English have no fixed Constitution. The prerogative of the crown, it is true, is under several restrictions; but the legislative power, which includes king, lords and commons, is under none; and whatever acts *they* pass, are laws, be they ever so oppressive or arbitrary. England is likewise defective in Constitution in three other material points, viz. The crown, by virtue of a patent from itself, can increase the number of the lords (one of the legislative branches) at his pleasure. Queen Ann created six in one day, for the purpose of making a majority for carrying a bill then passing, who were afterwards distinguished by the name of the six occasional lords. Lord Bathurst, the father of the present chancellor, is the only surviving one. The crown can likewise, by a patent, incorporate any town or village, small or great, and empower it to send members to the house of commons, and fix what the precise number of the electors shall be. And an act of the legislative power, that is, an act of king, lords, and commons, can again diminish the house of commons to what number they please, by disfranchising any county, city or town.

It is easy to perceive that individuals by agreeing to erect forms of government, (for the better security of themselves) must give up some part of their liberty for that purpose; and it is the particular business of a Constitution to mark out *how much* they shall give up. In this sense it is easy to see that the English have no Constitution, because they have given up every thing; their legislative power being unlimited without either condition or controul, except in the single instance of trial by Juries. No country can be called *free* which is governed by an absolute power; and it matters not whether it be an absolute royal power or an absolute legislative power, as the consequences will be the same to the people. That England is governed by the latter, no man can deny, there being, as is said before, no Constitution in that country which says to the legislative powers, "Thus far shalt thou go, and no farther." There is nothing to prevent them passing a law which shall exempt themselves from the payment of taxes, or which shall give the house of commons power to sit for life, or to fill up the vacancies by appointing others, like the Corporation of Philadelphia. In short, an act of parliament, to use a court phrase, can do any thing but make a man a woman.

A Constitution, when completed, resolves the two following questions: First, What shall the form of government be? And secondly, What shall be its power? And the last of these two is far more material than the first. The Constitution ought likewise to make provision in those cases where it does not empower the legislature to act.

The forms of government are numerous, and perhaps the simplest is the best. The notion of checking by having different houses, has but little weight in it, when inquired into, and in all cases it tends to embarrass and prolong business; besides, what kind of checking is it that one house is to receive from another? or which is the house that is most to be trusted to? They may fall out about forms and precedence, and check one another's honour and tempers, and thereby produce petulances and ill-will, which a more simple form of government would have prevented. That some kind of convenience might now and then arise from having two houses, is granted, and the same may be said of twenty houses; but the question is, whether such a mode would not produce more hurt than good. The more houses the more parties; and perhaps the ill consequence to this country would be, that the landed interest would get into one house, and the commercial interest into the other; and by that means a perpetual and dangerous opposition would be kept up, and no business be got through: Whereas, were there a large, equal and annual representation in one house *only*, the different parties, by being thus blended together, would hear each other's arguments, which advantage they cannot have if they sit in different houses. To say, there ought to be two houses, because there are two sorts of interest, is the very reason why there ought to be but one, and *that one* to consist of every sort. The lords and commons in England formerly made but one house; and it is evident, that by separating men you lessen the quantity of knowledge, and increase the difficulties of business. However, let the form of government be what it may, in this, or other provinces, so long as it answers the purpose of the people, and they approve it, they will be happy under it. That which suits one part of the Continent may not in every thing suit another; and when each is pleased, however variously, the matter is ended. No man is a true republican, or worthy of the name, that will not give up his single voice to that of the public:

his private opinion he may retain; it is obedience only that is his duty.

The chief convenience arising from two houses is, that the second may sometimes amend small imperfections which would otherwise pass; yet, there is nearly as much chance of their making alterations for the worse as the better; and the supposition that a single house may become arbitrary, can with more reason be said of two; because their strength is greater. Besides, when all the supposed advantages arising from two houses are put together, they do not appear to balance the disadvantage. A division in one house will not retard business, but serves rather to illustrate; but a difference between two houses may produce serious consequences. In queen Ann's reign a quarrel arose between the upper and lower house, which was carried to such a pitch that the nation was under very terrifying apprehensions, and the house of commons was dissolved to prevent worse mischief. A like instance was nearly happening about six years ago, when the members of each house very affronting turned one another by force out of doors: The two best bills in the last sessions in England were entirely lost by having two houses: the bill for encreasing liberty of conscience, by taking off the necessity of subscription to the thirty-nine articles, Athanasian creed, &c. after passing the lower house by a very great majority, was thrown out by the upper one; and at the time that the nation was starving with the high price of corn, the bill for regulating the importation and exportation of grain, after passing the lower house, was lost by a *difference* between the two, and when returned from the upper one was thrown on the floor by the commons, and indignantly trampled under foot.—Perhaps most of the Colonies will have two houses, and it will probably be of benefit to have some little difference in the forms of government, as those which do not like one, may r[es]ide in another, and by trying different experiments, the best form will the sooner be found out, as the preference at present rests on conjecture.

Government is generally distinguished into three parts, Executive, Legislative and Judicial; but this is more a distinction of words than things. Every king or governor in giving his assent to laws acts legislatively, and not executively: The house of lords in England is both a legislative and judicial body. In short, the distinction is perplexing, and however we may refine and define, there is no more than two powers in any government, viz. the power to make laws, and the power to execute them; for the judical power is only a branch of the executive, the Chief of every country being the first magistrate.

A Constitution should lay down some permanent ratio, by which the representation should afterwards encrease or decrease with the number of inhabitants; for the right of representation, which is a natural one, ought not to depend upon the will and pleasure of future legislatures. And for the same reason perfect liberty of conscience; security of person against unjust imprisonments, similar to what is called the Habeas Corpus act; the mode of trial in all law and criminal cases; in short, all the great rights which man never mean, nor ever ought, to lose, should be *guaranteed*, not *granted*, by the Constitution; for at the forming a Constitution we ought to have in mind, that whatever is left to be secured by law only, may be altered by another law. That Juries ought to be judges of law, as well as fact, should be clearly described; for though in some instances Juries may err, it is generally from tenderness, and on the right side. A man cannot be *guilty* of a *good* action, yet if the fact only is to be proved (which is Lord Mansfield's doctrine) and the Jury not empowered to determine in their own minds, whether the fact proved to be done is a crime or not, a man may hereafter be found guilty of going to church or meeting. [. . .]

It is the part of a Constitution to fix the manner in which the officers of government shall be chosen, and determine the principal outlines of their power, their time of duration, manner of commissioning them, &c. The line, so far as respects their election, seems easy, which is, by the representatives of the people; provincial officers can be chosen no other way, because the whole province cannot be convened, any more than the whole of the Associators could be convened for choosing generals. Civil officers for towns and countries may easily be chosen by election. The mode of choosing delegates for Congress deserves consideration, as they are not officers but legislators. Positive provincial instructions have a tendency to disunion, and, if admitted, will one day or other rend the Continent of America. A continental Constitution, when fixed, will be the best boundaries of Congressional power, and in matters for the general good, they ought to be as free as assemblies.

The notion, which some have, of excluding the military from the legislature is unwise, because it has a tendency to make them form a distinct party of their own. Annual elections, strengthened by some kind of periodical exclusion, seem the best guard against the encroachments of power; suppose the exclusion was triennial, that is, that no person should be returned a member of assembly for more than three succeeding years, nor be capable of being returned again till he had been absent three years. Such a mode would greatly encrease the circle of knowledge, make men cautious how they acted, and prevent the disagreeableness of giving offence, by removing some, to make room for others of equal, or perhaps superior, merit. Something of the same kind may be practiced respecting Presidents or Governors, not to be eligible after a certain number of returns; and as no person, after filling that rank, can, consistent with character, descend to any other office or employment; and as it may not always happen that the most wealthy are the most capable, some decent provision therefore should be made for them in their retirement from the world. Whoever reflects on this, will see many good advantages arising from it.

Modest and decent honorary titles, so as they be neither hereditary, nor convey legislative authority, are of use in a state; they are, when properly conferred, the badges of merit. The love of the public is the chief reward which a generous man seeks; and, surely! if *that* be an honour, the mode of conferring it must be so likewise.

Next to the forming a good Constitution, is the means of p[re]serving it. If once the legislative power breaks in upon it, the effect will be the same as if a kingly power did it. The Constitution, in either case, will receive its death wound, and "the outward and visible sign," or mere form of government only will remain. "I wish," says Lord Camden, "that the maxim of Machiavel was followed, that of examining a Constitution, at certain periods, according to its first principles; this would correct abuses, and supply defects." The means here pointed out for preserving a Constitution are easy, and some article in the Constitution may provide, that at the expiration of every seven or any other number of years a *Provincial Jury* shall be elected, to enquire if any inroads have been made in the Constitution, and to have power to remove them; but not to make alterations, unless a clear majority of all the inhabitants shall so direct.

Farther observations were intended to have been offered in these letters, but the sudden turn of military affairs hath prevented them; I shall therefore conclude with remarking, that perfection in government, like perfection in all other earthly things, is not to be hoped for. A single house, or a duplication of them, will alike have their evils; and the defect is incurable, being founded in the nature of man, and the instability of things.

John Adams

Letters to Abigail Adams (July 3, 1776)

[1]

Yesterday the greatest Question was decided, which ever was debated in America, and a greater perhaps, never was or will be decided among Men. A Resolution was passed without one dissenting Colony "that these united Colonies, are, and of right ought to be free and independent States, and as such, they have, and of Right ought to have full Power to make War, conclude Peace, establish Commerce, and to do all the other Acts and Things, which other States may rightfully do." You will see in a few days a Declaration setting forth the Causes, which have impell'd Us to this mighty Revolution, and the Reasons which will justify it, in the Sight of God and Man. A Plan of Confederation will be taken up in a few days.

When I look back to the Year 1761, and recollect the Argument concerning Writs of Assistance, in the Superiour Court, which I have hitherto considered as the Commencement of the Controversy, between Great Britain and America, and run through the whole Period from that Time to this, and recollect the series of political Events, the Chain of Causes and Effects, I am surprised at the Suddenness, as well as Greatness of this Revolution. Britain has been fill'd with Folly, and America with Wisdom, at least this is my Judgment. Time must determine. It is the Will of Heaven, that the two Countries should be sundered forever. It may be the Will of Heaven that America shall suffer Calamities still more wasting and Distresses yet more dreadful. If this is to be the Case, it will have this good Effect, at least: it will inspire Us with many Virtues, which We have not, and correct many Errors, Follies, and Vices, which threaten to disturb, dishonour, and destroy Us. The Furnace of Affliction produces Refinement, in States as well as Individuals. And the new Governments we are assuming, in every Part, will require a Purification from our Vices, and an Augmentation of our Virtues or they will be no Blessings. The People will have unbounded Power. And the People are extreamly addicted to Corruption and Venality, as well as the Great. I am not without Apprehensions from this Quarter. But I must submit all my Hopes and Fears, to an overruling Providence, in which, unfashionable as the Faith may be, I firmly believe.

[2]

Had a Declaration of Independency been made seven Months ago, it would have been attended with many great and glorious Effects. We might before this Hour, have formed Alliances with foreign States. We should have mastered Quebec and been in Possession of Canada. [. . .]

But on the other Hand, the Delay of this Declaration to this Time, has many great Advantages attending it. The Hopes of Reconciliation, which were fondly entertained by Multitudes of honest and well meaning tho weak and mistaken People, have been gradually and at last totally extinguished. Time has been given for the whole People, maturely to consider the great Question of Independence and to ripen their Judgments, dissipate their Fears, and allure their Hopes, by discussing it in News Papers and Pamphletts, by debating it, in Assemblies, Conventions, Committees of Safety and Inspection, in Town and County Meetings, as well as in private Conversations, so that the whole People in every Colony of the 13, have now adopted it, as their own Act. This will cement the Union, and avoid those Heats and perhaps Convulsions which might have been occasioned, by such a Declaration Six Months ago.

But the Day is past. The Second Day of July 1776, will be the most memorable Epocha, in the History of America. I am apt to believe that it will be celebrated, by succeeding Generations, as the great anniversary Festival. It ought to be commemorated, as the Day of Deliverance by solemn Acts of Devotion to God Almighty. It ought to be solemnized with Pomp and Parade, with Shews, Games, Sports, Guns, Bells, Bonfires and Illuminations from one End of this Continent to the other from this Time forward forever more. You will think me transported with Enthusiasm but I am not. I am well aware of the Toil and Blood and Treasure, that it will cost Us to maintain this Declaration, and support and defend these States. Yet through all the Gloom I can see the Rays of ravishing Light and Glory. I can see that the End is more than worth all the Means. And that Posterity will tryumph in that Days Transaction, even altho We should rue it, which I trust in God We shall not.

Benjamin Rush

Letter to Patrick Henry (July 16, 1776)

My dear friend,

I congratulate you less upon the acct. of your late honourable Appointment than upon the declaration of the freedom & independance of the American colonies. Such inestimable blessings can not be too joyfully received, nor purchased at too high a price. They would be cheaply bought at the loss of all the towns & of every fourth, or even third man in America. I tremble to think of the mischiefs that would have spread thro' this country had we continued our dependance upon G Britain twenty years longer. The contest two years ago found us contaminated with British customs, manners & ideas of government. We begin to be purified from some of them. In particular we dare to speak freely & justly of royal & hereditary power. In a few years we shall vie I hope for wisdom with the Citizens of Athens. But our Virtue will I hope know no bounds. The Conduct of our Militia upon a late Alarm from New York gives me reason to think we may make any thing we please of Americans. Were our officers equal to our men, I believe we might drive a whole Army of Howes & Burgoynes into the Ocean in a few days. They implore their generals every hour for the liberty of attacking our enemies. War, liberty & independance is the common language of them all.

Providence has frowned upon our Arms in Canada. I sometimes think that country has been earned by the March of Col. Arnold, & the heroic Achievements & death of the gallant Montgomery, and that the banner of liberty will be planted on some future day by the States of America upon the walls of Quebec. Perhaps this opinion is nothing but the effect of a Veneration bordering upon idolatry for the Services & merit of those illustrious heroes.

The States of America cannot be a Nation without War. They will have Wars in Europe. Canada may be reserved to the Crown of Britain as a nursery of enemies to the States on purpose to keep alive their martial virtue. If this be the case, it becomes us to reconcile ourselves to the Loss of Canada, and to resolve it into the goodness of that being with whom "all partial evil is universal good."

Have you not violated a fundamental principle of liberty in excluding the clergy from your Legislatures? I know their danger in a free government but I would rather see them excluded from civil power by custom than by law. They have property, wives & children, & of course are citizens of a community. Why therefore Should they be Abridged of any one priviledge which Other citizens enjoy? Is it not a fact that by investing any men with more, or confining them to fewer priviledges than members of a community enjoy in general we render those men the enemies of that community? Perhaps all the Mischief which the clergy have done in all countries has arisen from the first of the above causes. Will not the clause in your Charter which excludes Clergymen from your Legislature hand down to posterity as well as hold up to the World an idea that you looked upon the Christian religion as well as its Ministers as unfriendly to good government? I wish our governments would treat religion of all kinds, & ministers of all denominations as if no such things or beings existed in the world. They mutually destroy each Other when any Attempts are made by either to support each other.

Benjamin Franklin

Letter to Lord Howe (July 20, 1776)

My Lord,

I received safe the Letters your Lordship so kindly forwarded to me, and beg you to accept my Thanks.

The Official Dispatches to which you refer me, contain nothing more than what we had seen in the Act of Parliament, viz. Offers of Pardon upon Submission; which I was sorry to find, as it must give your Lordship Pain to be sent so far on so hopeless a Business.

Directing Pardons to be offered the Colonies, who are the very Parties injured, expresses indeed that Opinion of our Ignorance, Baseness, & Insensibility which your uninform'd and proud Nation has long been pleased to entertain of us; but it can have no other Effect than that of increasing our Resentment. It is impossible we should think of Submission to a Government, that has with the most wanton Barbarity and Cruelty, burnt our defenceless Towns in the midst of Winter, excited the Savages to massacre our Farmers, and our Slaves to murder their Masters, and is even now bringing foreign Mercenaries to deluge our Settlements with Blood. These atrocious Injuries have extinguished every remaining Spark of Affection for that Parent Country we once held so dear. But were it possible for us to forget and forgive them, it is not possible for *you* (I mean the British Nation) to forgive the People you have so heavily injured; you can never confide again in those as Fellow Subjects, & permit them to enjoy equal Freedom, to whom you know you have given such just Cause of lasting Enmity. And this must impel you, were we again under your Government, to endeavour the breaking our Spirit by the severest Tyranny, & obstructing by every means in your Power our growing Strength and Prosperity.

But your Lordship mentions "the Kings paternal Solicitude for promoting the Establishment of lasting *Peace* and Union with the Colonies." If by *Peace* is here meant, a Peace to be entered into between Britain and America as distinct States now at War, and his Majesty has given your Lordship Powers to treat with us of such a Peace, I may venture to say, tho' without Authority, that I think a Treaty for that purpose not yet quite impracticable, before we enter into Foreign Alliances. But I am persuaded you have no such Powers. Your Nation, tho' by punishing those American Governors who have created & fomented the Discord, rebuilding our burnt Towns, & repairing as far as possible the Mischiefs done us, She might yet recover a great Share of our Regard & the greatest part of our growing Commerce, with all the Advantage of that additional Strength to be derived from a Friendship with us; I know too well her abounding Pride and deficient Wisdom, to believe she will ever take such Salutary Measures. Her Fondness for Conquest as a Warlike Nation, her Lust of Dominion as an Ambitious one, and her Thirst for a gainful Monopoly as a Commercial one (none of them legitimate Causes of War) will all join to hide from her Eyes every View of her true Interests; and continually goad her on in these ruinous distant Expeditions, so destructive both of Lives and Treasure, that must prove as pernicious to her in the End as the Croisades formerly were to most of the Nations of Europe.

I have not the Vanity, my Lord, to think of intimidating by thus predicting the Effects of this War; for I know it will in England have the Fate of all my former Predictions, not to be believed till the Event shall verify it.

Long did I endeavour with unfeigned and unwearied Zeal, to preserve from breaking, that fine & noble China Vase the British Empire: for I knew that being once broken, the separate Parts could not retain even their Share of the Strength or Value that existed in the Whole, and that a perfect Re-Union of those Parts could scarce even be hoped for. Your Lordship may possibly remember the Tears of Joy that wet my Cheek, when, at your good Sister's in London, you once gave me Expectations that a Reconciliation might soon take place. I had the Misfortune to find those Expectations disappointed, & to be treated as the Cause of the Mischief I was labouring to prevent. My Consolation under that groundless and malevolent Treatment was, that I retained the Friendship of many Wise & Good Men in that Country, and among the rest some I have in the Regard of Lord Howe.

The well founded Esteem, and permit me to say Affection, which I shall always have for your Lordship; makes it painful to me to see you engag'd in conducting a War, the great Ground of which, as expressed in your Letter, is, "the Necessity of preventing the American Trade from passing into foreign Channels." To me it seems that neither the obtaining or retaining of any Trade, how valuable soever, is an Object for which Men may justly Spill each others Blood, that the true and sure means of extending and securing Commerce is the goodness and cheapness of Commodities, & that the profits of no Trade can ever be equal to the Expence of compelling it, and of holding it, by Fleets and Armies. I consider this War against us therefore, as both unjust, and unwise; and I am persuaded cool dispassionate Posterity will condemn to Infamy those who advised it; and that even Success will not save from some degree of Dishonour, those who voluntarily engag'd to conduct it. I know your great Motive in coming hither was the Hope of being instrumental in a Reconciliation; and I believe when you find that impossible on any Terms given you to propose, you will relinquish so odious a Command, and return to a more honourable private Station. With the greatest and most sincere Respect, I have the honour to be; My Lord, Your Lordships most obedient humble Servant.

Notes of Debates in Congress (1776)

July 30, 1776

[Article 17 of the Articles, giving each state one vote in Congress, debated]

Dr. Franklin: Let the smaller Colonies give equal Money and Men, and then have an equal Vote. But if they have an equal Vote, without bearing equal Burthens, a Confederation upon such iniquitous Principles, will never last long.

Dr. Witherspoon: We all agree that there must and shall be a Confederation, for this War. It will diminish the Glory of our Object, and depreciate our Hope. It will damp the Ardor of the People. The greatest danger We have is of Disunion among ourselves. Is it not plausible, that the small States will be oppressed by the great ones. The Spartans and Helotes—the Romans and their Dependents.

Every Colony is a distinct Person. States of Holland.

Clark: We must apply for Pardons, if We dont confederate.[. . .]

Wilson: [. . .] We should settle upon some Plan of Representation.

[Article 11 now debated, addressing proportional contributions to the federal government]

Chase: Moves that the Word, White, should be inserted in the 11. Article. The Negroes are wealth. Numbers are not a certain Rule of wealth. It is the best Rule We can lay down. Negroes a Species of Property-personal Estate. If Negroes are taken into the Computation of Numbers, to ascertain Wealth, they ought to be in settling the Representation. The Massachusetts Fisheries, and Navigation ought to be taken into Consideration. The young and old Negroes are a Burthen to their owners. The Eastern Colonies have a great Advantage, in Trade. This will give them a Superiority. We shall be governed by our Interests, and ought to be. If I am satisfied, in the Rule of levying and appropriating Money, I am willing the small Colonies may have a Vote.

WILSON: If the War continues 2 Years, each Soul will have 40 dollars to pay of the public debt. It will be the greatest Encouragement to continue Slave keeping, and to increase them, that can be to exempt them from the Numbers which are to vote and pay. . . . Slaves are Taxables in the Southern Colonies. It will be partial and unequal. Some Colonies have as many black as white. . . . These will not pay more than half what they ought. Slaves prevent freemen cultivating a Country. It is attended with many Inconveniences.

LYNCH: If it is debated, whether their Slaves are their Property, there is an End of the Confederation. Our Slaves being our Property, why should they be taxed more than the Land, Sheep, Cattle, Horses, &c. Freemen cannot be got, to work in our Colonies. It is not in the Ability, or Inclination of freemen to do the Work that the Negroes do. Carolina has taxed their Negroes. So have other Colonies, their Lands.

DR. FRANKLIN: Slaves rather weaken than strengthen the State, and there is therefore some difference between them and Sheep. Sheep will never make any Insurrections.

RUTLEDGE: . . . I shall be happy to get rid of the idea of Slavery. The Slaves do not signify Property. The old and young cannot work. The Property of some Colonies are to be taxed, in others not. The Eastern Colonies will become the Carriers for the Southern. They will obtain Wealth for which they will not be taxed.

Aug. 1, 1776

[Continuation of the debate of 30 July on Article 11]

HOOPER: N.C. is a striking Exception to the general Rule that was laid down Yesterday, that the Riches of a Country are in Proportion to the Numbers of Inhabitants. A Gentleman of 3 or 400 Negroes, dont raise more corn than feeds them. A Labourer cant be hired for less than £24 a Year in Mass. Bay. The neat profit of a Negro is not more than 5 or 6£ per Annum. I wish to see the day that Slaves are not necessary. Whites and Negroes cannot work together. Negroes are Goods and Chattells, are Property. A Negro works under the Impulse of fear—has no Care of his Masters Interest. [One-half of a blank page follows in the manuscript.]

17. Art. [now discussed]

Dr. Franklin moves that Votes should be in Proportion to Numbers.

Mr. Middleton moves that the Vote should be according to what they pay.

Sherman thinks We ought not to vote according to Numbers. We are rep[resentative]s of States not Individuals. States of Holland. The Consent of every one is necessary. 3 Colonies would govern the whole but would not have a Majority of Strength to carry those Votes into Execution.

The Vote should be taken two Ways. Call the Colonies and call the Individuals, and have a Majority of both.

DR. RUSH: Abbe Reynauld has attributed the Ruin of the united Provinces to 3 Causes. The principal one is that the Consent of every State is necessary. The other that the Members are obliged to consult their Constituents upon all Occasions.

We lose an equal Representation. We represent the People. It will tend to keep up colonial Distinctions. We are now a new Nation. Our Trade, Language, Customs, Manners dont differ more than they do in G. Britain.

The more a Man aims at serving America the more he serves his Colony.

It will promote Factions in Congress and in the States.

It will prevent the Growth of Freedom in America. We shall be lo[a]th to admit new Colonies into the Confederation. If We vote by Numbers Liberty will be always safe. Mass. is contiguous to 2 small Colonies, R. [I.] and N. H. Pen. is near N. J. and D. Virginia is between Maryland and N. Carolina.

We have been to[o] free with the Word Independence. We are dependent on each other—not totally independent States.

Montesquieu pronounced the Confederation of Licea the best that ever was made. The Cities had different Weights in the Scale.

China is not larger than one of our Colonies. How populous.

It is said that the small Colonies deposit their All. This is deceiving Us with a Word.

I would not have it understood, that I am pleading the Cause of Pensilvania. When I entered that door, I considered myself a Citizen of America.

DR. WITHERSPOON: Representation in England is unequal. Must I have 3 Votes in a County because I have 3 times as much Money as my Neighbour. Congress are to determine the Limits of Colonies.

G[OVERNOR] HOPKINS: A momentous Question. Many difficulties on each Side. 4 larger, 5 lesser, 4 stand indifferent. V.M.P.M. make more than half the People. 4 may alw [A blank occurs here in the manuscript.]

C., N.Y., 2 Carolinas, not concerned at all. The dissinterested Coolness of these Colonies ought to determine. I can easily feel the Reasoning of the larger Colonies. Pleasing Theories always gave Way to the Prejudices, Passions, and Interests of Mankind.

The Germanic Confederation. The K. of Prussia has an equal Vote. The Helvetic Confederacy. It cant be expected that 9 Colonies will give Way to be governed by 4. The Safety of the whole depends upon the distinctions of Colonies.

DR. FRANKLIN: I hear many ingenious Arguments to perswade Us that an unequal Representation is a very good Thing. If We had been born and bred under an unequal Representation We might bear it. But to sett out with an unequal Representation is unreasonable.

It is said the great Colonies will swallow up the less. Scotland said the same Thing at the Union.

DR. WITHERSPOON: Rises to explain a few Circumstances relating to Scotland. That was an incorporating Union, not a federal. The Nobility and Gentry resort to England.

In determining all Questions, each State shall have a Weight in Proportion to what it contributes to the public Expences of the united States.

Aug. 2d, [1776]

Limiting the Bounds of States which by Charter &c. extend to the South Sea.

Sherman thinks the Bounds ought to be settled. A Majority of States have no Claim to the South Sea. Moves this Amendment, to be subs[t]ituted in Place of this Clause and also instead of the 15th Article.

No Lands to be seperated from any State, which are already settled, or become private Property.

Chase denys that any Colony has a Right, to go to the South Sea.

HARRISON: How came Maryland by its Land? but by its Charter: By its Charter Virginia owns to the South Sea. Gentlemen shall not pare away the Colony of Virginia. R. Island has more Generosity, than to wish the Massachusetts pared away. Delaware does not wish to pare away Pensilvania.

HUNTINGTON: Admit there is danger, from Virginia, does it follow that Congress has a Right to limit her Bounds? The Consequence is not to enter into Confederation. But as to the Question of Right, We all unite against mutilating Charters. I cant agree to the Principle. We are a Spectacle to all Europe. I am not so much alarmed at the Danger, from Virginia, as some are. My fears are not alarmed. They have acted as noble a Part as any. I doubt not the Wisdom of Virginia will limit themselves. A Mans Right does not cease to be a Right because it is large. The Question of Right must be determined by the Principles of the common Law.

STONE: This Argument is taken up upon very wrong Ground. It is considered as if We were voting away the Territory of particular Colonies, and Gentlemen work themselves up into Warmth, upon that Supposition. Suppose Virginia should. The small Colonies have a Right to Happiness and Security. They would have no Safety if the great Colonies were not limited. We shall grant Lands in small Quantities, without Rent, or Tribute, or purchase Money. It is said that Virginia is attacked on every Side. Is it meant that Virginia shall sell the Lands for their own Emolument?

All the Colonies have defended these Lands vs. the K. of G.B., and at the Expence of all. Does Virginia intend to establish Quitrents?

I dont mean that the united States shall sell them to get Money by them.

JEFFERSON: I protest vs. the Right of Congress to decide, upon the Right of Virginia. Virginia has released all Claims to the Lands settled by Maryland &c.

John Witherspoon

Speech in Congress (July 30, 1776)

The absolute necessity of union to the vigour and success of those measures on which we are already entered, is felt and confessed by every one of us, without exception; so far, indeed, that those who have expressed their fears or suspicions of the existing confederacy proving abortive, have yet agreed in saying that there must and shall be a confederacy for the purposes of, and till the finishing of this war. So far it is well; and so far it is pleasing to hear them express their sentiments. But I intreat gentlemen calmly to consider how far the giving up all hopes of a lasting confederacy among these states, for their future security and improvement, will have an effect upon the stability and efficacy of even the temporary confederacy, which all acknowledge to be necessary? I am fully persuaded, that when it ceases to be generally known, that the delegates of the provinces consider a lasting union as impracticable, it will greatly derange the minds of the people, and weaken their hands in defence of their country, which they have now undertaken with so much alacrity and spirit. I confess it would to me greatly diminish the glory and importance of the struggle, whether considered as for the rights of mankind in general, or for the prosperity and happiness of this continent in future times.

It would quite depreciate the object of hope, as well as place it at a greater distance. For what would it signify to risk our possessions and shed our blood to set ourselves free from the encroachments and oppression of Great Britain—with a certainty, as soon as peace was settled with them of a more lasting war, a more unnatural, more bloody, and much more hopeless war, among the colonies themselves? Some of us consider ourselves as acting for posterity at present, having little expectation of living to see all things fully settled, and the good consequences of liberty taking effect. But how much more uncertain the hope of seeing the internal contests of the colonies settled upon a lasting and equitable footing?

One of the greatest dangers I have always considered the colonies as exposed to at present, is treachery among themselves, augmented by bribery and corruption from our enemies. But what force would be added to the arguments of seducers, if they could say with truth, that it was of no consequence whether we succeeded against Great Britain or not; for we must, in the end, be subjected, the greatest part of us, to the power of one or more of the strongest or largest of the American states? And here I would apply the argument which we have so often used against Great Britain—that in all history we see that the slaves of freemen, and the subject states of republics, have been of all others the most grievously oppressed. I do not think the records of time can produce an instance of slaves treated with so much barbarity as the Helotes by the Lacedemonians, who were the most illustrious champions for liberty in all Greece; or of provinces more plundered and spoiled than the states conquered by the Romans, for one hundred years before Caesar's dictatorship. The reason is plain; there are many great men in free states. There were many consular gentlemen in that great republic, who all considered themselves as greater than kings, and must have kingly fortunes, which they had no other way of acquiring but by governments of provinces, which lasted generally but one year, and seldom more than two.

In what I have already said, or may say, or any cases I may state, I hope every gentleman will do me the justice to believe, that I have not the most distant view to particular persons or societies, and mean only to reason from the usual course of things, and the prejudices inseparable from men as such. And can we help saying, that there will be a much greater degree, not only of the corruption of particular persons, but the defection of particular provinces from the present confederacy, if they consider our success itself as only a prelude to a contest of a more dreadful nature, and indeed much more properly a civil war than that which now often obtains the name? Must not small colonies in particular be in danger of saying, we must secure ourselves? If the colonies are independent states, separate and disunited, after this war, we may be sure of coming off by the worse. We are in no condition to contend with several of them. Our trade in general, and our trade with them, must be upon such terms as they shall be pleased to prescribe. What will be the consequence of this? Will they not be ready to prefer putting themselves under the protection of Great Britain, France or Holland, rather than submit to the tyranny of their neighbours, who were lately their equals? Nor would it be at all impossible, that they should enter into such rash engagements as would prove their own destruction, from a mixture of apprehended necessity and real resentment.

Perhaps it may be thought that breaking off this confederacy, and leaving it unfinished after we have entered upon it, will be only postponing the duty to some future period? Alas, nothing can exceed the absurdity of that supposition. Does not all history cry out, that a common danger is the great and only effectual means of settling difficulties, and composing differences. Have we not experienced its efficacy in producing such a degree of union through these colonies, as nobody would have prophesied, and hardly any would have expected?

If therefore, at present, when the danger is yet imminent, when it is so far from being over, that it is but coming to its height, we shall find it impossible to agree upon the terms of this confederacy, what madness is it to suppose that there ever will be a time, or that circumstances will so change, as to make it even probable, that it will be done at an after season? Will not the very same difficulties that are in our way, be in the way of those who shall come after us? Is it possible that they should be ignorant of them, or inattentive to them? Will they not have the same jealousies of each other, the same attachment to local prejudices, and particular interest? So certain is this, that I look upon it as on the repentance of a sinner— Every day's delay, though it adds to the necessity, yet augments the difficulty, and takes from the inclination.

There is one thing that has been thrown out, by which some seem to persuade themselves of, and others to be more indifferent about the success of a confederacy—that from the nature of men, it is to be expected, that a time must come when it will be dissolved and broken in pieces. I am none of those who either deny or conceal the depravity of human nature, till it is purified by the light of truth, and renewed by the Spirit of the living God. Yet I apprehend there is no force in that reasoning at all. Shall we establish nothing good, because we know it cannot be eternal? Shall we live without government, because every constitution has its old age, and its period? Because we know that we shall die, shall we take no pains to preserve or lengthen out life? Far from it, Sir: it only requires the more watchful attention, to settle government upon the best principles and in the wisest manner, that it may last as long as the nature of things will admit.

But I beg leave to say something more, though with some risk that it will be thought visionary and romantic. I do expect, Mr. President a progress, as in every other human art, so in the order and perfection of human society, greater than we have yet seen; and why should we be wanting to ourselves in urging it forward? It is certain, I think that human science and religion have kept company together, and greatly assisted each other's progress in the world. I do not say that intellectual and moral qualities are in the same proportion in particular persons; but they have a great and friendly influence upon one another, in societies and larger bodies.

There have been great improvements, not only in human knowledge, but in human nature; the progress of which can be easily traced in history. Every body is able to look back to the time in Europe, when the liberal sentiments that now prevail upon the rights of conscience, would have been looked upon as absurd. It is but little above two hundred years since that enlarged system called the balance of power, took place; and I maintain, that it is a greater step from the former disunited and hostile situation of kingdoms and states, to their present condition, than it would be from their present condition to a state of more perfect and lasting union. It is not impossible, that in future times all the states on one quarter of the globe, may see it proper by some plan of union, to perpetuate security and peace; and sure I am, a well planned confederacy among the states of America, may hand down the blessings of peace and public order to many generations. The union of the seven provinces of the Low Countries, has never yet been broken; and they are of very different degrees of strength and wealth. Neither have the Cantons of Switzerland ever broken among themselves, though there are some of them protestants, and some of them papists, by public establishment. Not only so, but these confederates are seldom engaged in a war with other nations. Wars are generally between monarchs, or single states that are large. A confederation of itself keeps war at a distance from the bodies of which it is composed.

For all these reasons, Sir, I humbly apprehend, that every argument from honour, interest, safety and necessity, conspire in pressing us to a confederacy; and if it be seriously attempted, I hope, by the blessing of God upon our endeavours, it will be happily accomplished.

The Dominion of Providence over the Passions of Men (1776)

Surely the Wrath of Man shall praise thee;
the remainder of Wrath shalt thou restrain.
Psalm LXXVI.10

There is not a greater evidence either of the reality or the power of religion, than a firm belief of God's universal presence, and a constant attention to the influence and operation of his providence. It is by this means that the Christian may be said, in the emphatical scripture language, "to walk with God, and to endure as seeing him who is invisible."

[. . .] There is the greater need to take notice of this, that men are not generally sufficiently aware of the distinction between the law of God and his purpose; they are apt to suppose, that as the temper of the sinner is contrary to the one, so the outrages of the sinner are able to defeat the other; than which nothing can be more false. The truth is plainly asserted, and nobly expressed by the psalmist in the text, "Surely the wrath of man shall praise thee; the remainder of wrath shalt thou restrain."

This psalm was evidently composed as a song of praise for some signal victory obtained, which was at the same time a remarkable deliverance from threatening danger. [. . .]

The truth, then, asserted in this text, which I propose to illustrate and improve, is, That all the disorderly passions of men, whether exposing the innocent to private injury, or whether they are the arrows of divine judgment in public calamity, shall, in the end, be to the praise of God: Or, to apply it more particularly to the present state of the American colonies, and the plague of war, The ambition of mistaken princes, the cunning and cruelty of oppressive and corrupt ministers, and even the inhumanity of brutal soldiers, however dreadful, shall finally promote the glory of God, and in the mean time, while the storm continues, his mercy and kindness shall appear in prescribing bounds to their rage and fury.

In discoursing on this subject, it is my intention, through the assistance of divine grace,

I. To point out to you in some particulars, how the wrath of man praises God.

II. To apply these principles to our present situation, by inferences of truth for your instruction and comfort, and by suitable exhortations to duty in the important crisis.

In the first place, I am to point out to you in some particulars, how the wrath of man praises God. [. . .]

In the first place, the wrath of man praises God, as it is an example and illustration of divine truth, and clearly points out the corruption of our nature, which is the foundation stone of the doctrine of redemption. Nothing can be more absolutely necessary to true religion, than a clear and full conviction of the sinfulness of our nature and state. Without this there can be neither repentance in the sinner, nor humility in the believer. [. . .]

But where can we have a more affecting view of the corruption of our nature, than in the wrath of man, when exerting itself in oppression, cruelty and blood? [. . .] All the disorders in human society, and the greatest part even of the unhappiness we are exposed to, arises from the envy, malice, covetousness, and other lusts of man. If we and all about us were just what we ought to be in all respects, we should not need to go any further for heaven, for it would be upon earth. But war and violence present a spectacle still more awful. How affecting is it to think, that the lust of domination should be so violent and universal? [. . .] It is shocking to think, since the first murder of Abel by his brother Cain, what havock has been made of man by man in every age. What is it that fills the pages of history, but the wars and contentions of princes and empires? What vast numbers has lawless ambition brought into the field, and delivered as a prey to the destructive sword?

If we dwell a little upon the circumstances, they become deeply affecting. [. . .]

But if this may be justly said of all wars between man and man, what shall we be able to say that is suitable to the abhorred scene of civil war between citizen and citizen? How deeply affecting is it, that those who are the same in complexion, the same in blood, in language, and in religion, should, notwithstanding, butcher one another with unrelenting rage, and glory in the deed? That men should lay waste the fields of their fellow subjects, with whose provision they themselves had been often fed, and consume with devouring fire those houses in which they had often found a hospitable shelter. [. . .]

But what I mean at this time to prove by the preceding reflections, and wish to impress on your minds, is the depravity of our nature. James iv. i. "From whence come wars and fighting among you? come they not hence even from your lusts that war in your members?" Men of lax and corrupt principles, take great delight in speaking to the praise of human nature, and extolling its dignity, without distinguishing what it was, at its first creation, from what it is in its present fallen state. These fine speculations are very grateful to a worldly mind. They are also much more pernicious to uncautious and unthinking youth, than even the temptations to a dissolute and sensual life, against which they are fortified by the dictates of natural conscience, and a sense of public shame. But I appeal from these visionary reasonings to the history of all ages, and the inflexible testimony of daily experience. These will tell us what men have been in their practice, and from thence you may judge what they are by nature, while unrenewed. If I am not mistaken, a cool and candid attention, either to the past history, or present state of the world, but above all, to the ravages of lawless power, ought to humble us in the dust. It should at once lead us to acknowlege the just view given us in scripture of our lost state; to desire the happy influence of renewing grace each for ourselves; and to long for the dominion of righteousness and peace, when "men shall beat their swords into plow-shares, and their spears into pruning hooks; when nation shall not lift up sword against nation, neither shall they learn war any more." Mic iv. 3. [. . .]

II. Proceed now to the second general head, which was to apply the principles illustrated above to our present situation, by inferences of truth for your instruction and comfort, and by suitable exhortations to duty in this important crisis. And,

In the first place, I would take the opportunity on this occasion, and from this subject, to press every hearer to a sincere concern for his own soul's salvation. [. . .]

2. From what has been said upon this subject, you may see what ground there is to give praise to God for his favors already bestowed on us, respecting the public cause. It would be a criminal inattention not to observe the singular interposition of Providence hitherto, in behalf of the American colonies. It is however impossible for me, in a single discourse, as well as improper at this time, to go through every step of our past transactions, I must therefore content myself with a few remarks. How many discoveries have been made of the designs of enemies in Britain and among ourselves, in a manner as unexpected to us as to them, and in such season as to prevent their effect? What surprising success has attended our encounters in almost every instance? Has not the boasted discipline of regular and veteran soldiers been turned into confusion and dismay, before the new and maiden courage of freemen, in defence of their property and right? In what great mercy has blood been spared on the side of this injured country? Some important victories in the south have been gained with so little loss, that enemies will probably think it has been dissembled; as many, even of ourselves thought, till time rendered it undeniable. But these were comparatively of small moment. The signal advantage we have gained by the evacuation of Boston, and the shameful flight of the army and navy of Britain, was brought about without the loss of a man. To all this

we may add, that the counsels of our enemies have been visibly confounded, so that I believe that I may say with truth, that there is hardly any step which they have taken, but it has operated strongly against themselves, and been more in our favor, than if they had followed a contrary course. [. . .]

3. From what has been said you may learn what encouragement you have to put your trust in God, and hope for his assistance in the present important conflict. He is the Lord of hosts, great in might, and strong in battle. Whoever hath his countenance and approbation, shall have the best at last. I do not mean to speak prophetically, but agreeably to the analogy of faith, and the principles of God's moral government. Some have observed that true religion, and in her train, dominion, riches, literature, and arts, have taken their course in a slow and gradual manner, from east to west, since the earth was settled after the flood, and from thence forebode the future glory of America. I leave this as a matter rather of conjecture than certainty, but observe, that if your cause is just, if your principles are pure, and if your conduct is prudent, you need not fear the multitude of opposing hosts.

If your cause is just—you may look with confidence to the Lord and intreat him to plead it as his own. You are all my witnesses, that this is the first time of my introducing any political subject into the pulpit. At this season however, it is not only lawful but necessary, and I willingly embrace the opportunity of declaring my opinion without any hesitation, that the cause in which America is now in arms, is the cause of justice, of liberty, and of human nature. So far as we have hitherto proceeded, I am satisfied that the confederacy of the colonies, has not been the effect of pride, resentment, or sedition, but of a deep and general conviction, that our civil and religious liberties, and consequently in a great measure the temporal and eternal happiness of us and our posterity, depended on the issue. The knowledge of God and his truths have from the beginning of the world been chiefly, if not entirely, confined to those parts of the earth, where some degree of liberty and political justice were to be seen, and great were the difficulties with which they had to struggle from the imperfection of human society, and the unjust decisions of usurped authority. There is not a single instance in history in which civil liberty was lost, and religious liberty preserved entire. If therefore we yield up our temporal property, we at the same time deliver the conscience into bondage.

You shall not, my brethren, hear from me in the pulpit, what you have never heard from me in conversation, I mean railing at the king personally, or even his ministers and the parliament, and people of Britain, as so many barbarous savages. Many of their actions have probably been worse than their intentions. That they should desire unlimited dominion, if they can obtain or preserve it, is neither new nor wonderful. I do not refuse submission to their unjust claims, because they are corrupt or profligate, although probably many of them are so, but because they are men, and therefore liable to all the selfish bias inseparable from human nature. I call this claim unjust, of making laws to bind us in all cases whatsoever, because they are separated from us, independent of us, and have an interest in opposing us. Would any man who could prevent it, give up his estate, person, and family, to the disposal of his neighbour, although he had liberty to chuse the wisest and the best master? Surely not. This is the true and proper hinge of the controversy between Great-Britain and America. It is however to be added, that such is their distance from us, that a wise and prudent administration of our affairs is as impossible as the claim of authority is unjust. Such is and must be their ignorance of the state of things here, so much time must elapse before an error can be seen and remedied, and so much injustice and partiality must be expected from the arts and misrepresentation of interested persons, that for these colonies to depend wholly upon the legislature of Great-Britain, would be like many other oppressive connexions, injury to the master, and ruin to the slave.

The management of the war itself on their part, would furnish new proof of this, if any were needful. Is it not manifest with what absurdity and impropriety they have conducted their own designs? We had nothing so much to fear as dissension, and they have by wanton and unnecessary cruelty forced us into union. At the same time to let us see what we have to expect, and what would be the fatal consequence of unlimited submission, they have uniformly called those acts *lenity*, which filled this whole continent with resentment and horror. The ineffable disdain expressed by our fellow subject, in saying, "That he would not harken to America, till she was at his feet," has armed more men, and inspired more deadly rage, than could have been done by laying waste a whole province with fire and sword. Again we wanted not numbers, but time, and they sent over handful after handful till we were ready to oppose a multitude greater than they have to send. In fine, if there was one place stronger than the rest, and more able and willing to resist, there they made the attack, and left the others till they were duly informed, completely incensed, and fully furnished with every instrument of war.

I mention these things, my brethren, not only as grounds of confidence in God, who can easily overthrow the wisdom of the wise, but as decisive proofs of the impossibility of these great and growing states, being safe and happy when every part of their internal polity is dependant on Great Britain. If, on account of their distance, and ignorance of our situation, they could not conduct their own quarrel with propriety for one year, how can they give direction and vigor to every department of our civil constitutions from age to age? There are fixed bounds to every human thing. When the branches of a tree grow very large and weighty, they fall off from the trunk. The sharpest sword will not pierce when it cannot reach. And there is a certain distance from the seat of government, where an attempt to rule will either produce tyranny and helpless subjection, or provoke resistance and effect a separation.

I have said, if your principles are pure—the meaning of this is, if your present opposition to the claims of the British ministry does not arise from a seditious and turbulent spirit, or a wanton contempt of legal authority; from a blind and factious attachment to particular persons or parties; or from a selfish rapacious disposition, and a desire to turn public confusion to private profit—but from a concern for the interest of your country, and the safety of yourselves and your posterity. On this subject I cannot help observing, that though it would be a miracle if there were not many selfish persons among us, and discoveries now and then made of mean and interested transactions, yet they have been comparatively inconsiderable both in number and effect. In general, there has been so great a degree of public spirit, that we have much more reason to be thankful for its vigor and prevalence, than to wonder at the few appearances of dishonesty or disaffection. It would be very uncandid to ascribe the universal ardor that has prevailed among all ranks of men, and the spirited exertions in the most distant colonies, to any thing else than public spirit. Nor was there ever perhaps in history so general a commotion from which religious differences have been so entirely excluded. Nothing of this kind has as yet been heard, except of late in the absurd, but malicious and detestable attempts of our few remaining enemies to introduce them. At the same time I must also, for the honor of this country observe, that though government in the ancient forms has been so long unhinged, and in some colonies not sufficient care taken to substitute another in its place; yet has there been, by common consent, a much greater degree of order and public peace, than men of reflection and experience foretold or expected. From all these circumstances I conclude favorably of the principles of the friends of liberty, and do earnestly exhort you to adopt and act upon those which have been described, and resist the influence of every other.

Once more, if to the justice of your cause, and the purity of your principles, you add prudence in your conduct, there will be the greatest reason to hope, by the blessing of God, for prosperity and success. By prudence in conducting this important struggle, I have chiefly in view union, firmness, and patience. Every body must perceive the absolute necessity of union. It is indeed in every body's mouth, and therefore instead of attempting to convince you of its importance, I will only caution you against the usual causes of division. If persons of every rank, instead of implicitly complying with the orders of those whom they themselves have chosen to direct, will needs judge every measure over again, when it comes to be put in execution; if different classes of men intermix their little private views, or clashing interest with public affairs, and marshal into parties, the merchant against the landholder, and the landholder against the merchant; if local provincial pride and jealousy arise, and you allow yourselves to speak with contempt of the courage, character, manners, or even language of particular places, you are doing a greater injury to the common cause, than you are aware of. If such practices are admitted among us, I shall look upon it as one of the most dangerous symptoms, and if they become general, a presage of approaching ruin.

By firmness and patience, I mean a resolute adherence to your duty, and laying your account with many difficulties, as well as occasional disappointments. In a former part of this discourse, I have cautioned you against ostentation and vain glory. Be pleased farther to observe that extremes often beget one another, the same persons who exult extravagantly on success, are generally most liable to despondent timidity on every little inconsiderable defeat. Men of this character are the bane and corruption of every society or party to which they belong, but they are especially the ruin of an army, if suffered to continue in it. Remember the vicissitude of human things, and the usual course of providence. How often has a just cause been reduced to the lowest ebb, and yet when firmly adhered to, has become finally triumphant. I speak this now while the affairs of the colonies are in so prosperous a state, lest this propriety itself should render you less able to bear unexpected misfortunes—the sum of the whole is, that the blessing of God is only to be looked for by those who are not wanting in the discharge of their own duty. I would neither have you to trust in an arm of flesh, nor sit with folded hands and expect that miracles should be wrought in your defence—this is a sin which is in scripture stiled tempting God. In opposition to it, I would exhort you as Joab did the host of Israel, who, though he does not appear to have had a spotless character throughout, certainly in this instance spoke like a prudent general and a pious man. 2 Sam. x. 12. "Be of good courage, and let us behave ourselves valiantly for our people and for the cities of our God, and let the Lord do that which is good in his sight."

I shall now conclude this discourse by some exhortations to duty, founded upon the truths which have been illustrated above, and suited to the interesting state of this country at the present time; and,

1. Suffer me to recommend to you an attention to the public interest of religion, or in other words, zeal for the glory of God and the good of others. I have already endeavored to exhort sinners to repentance; what I have here in view is to point out to you the concern which every good man ought to take in the national character and manners, and the means which he ought to use for promoting public virtue, and bearing down impiety and vice. This is a matter of the utmost moment, and which ought to be well understood, both in its nature and principles. Nothing is more certain than that a general profligacy and corruption of manners make a people ripe for destruction. A good form of government may hold the rotten materials together for some time, but beyond a certain pitch, even the best constitution will be ineffectual, and slavery must ensue. On the other hand, when the manners of a nation are pure, when true religion and internal principles maintain their vigour, the attempts of the most powerful enemies to oppress them are commonly baffled and disappointed. This will be found equally certain, whether we consider the great principles of God's moral government, or the operation and influence of natural causes.

What follows from this? That he is the best friend to American liberty, who is most sincere and active in promoting true and undefiled religion, and who sets himself with the greatest firmness to bear down profanity and immorality of every kind. Whoever is an avowed enemy to God, I scruple not to call him an enemy to his country. Do not suppose, my brethren, that I mean to recommend a furious and angry zeal for the circumstantials of religion, or the contentions of one sect with another about their peculiar distinctions. I do not wish you to oppose any body's religion, but every body's wickedness. Perhaps there are few surer marks of the reality of religion, than when a man feels himself more joined in spirit to a true holy person of a different denomination, than to an irregular liver of his own. It is therefore your duty in this important and critical season to exert yourselves, every one in his proper sphere, to stem the tide of prevailing vice, to promote the knowledge of God, the reverence of his name and worship, and obedience to his laws.

Perhaps you will ask, what it is that you are called to do for this purpose farther than your own personal duty? I answer this itself when taken in its proper extent is not a little. The nature and obligation of visible religion is, I am afraid, little understood and less attended to.

Many from a real or pretended fear of the imputation of hypocrisy, banish from their conversation and carriage every appearance of respect and submission to the living God. What a weakness and meanness of spirit does it discover, for a man to be ashamed in the presence of his fellow sinners, to profess that reverence to almighty God which he inwardly feels: The truth is, he makes himself truly liable to the accusation which he means to avoid. It is as genuine and perhaps a more culpable hypocrisy to appear to have less religion than you really have, than to appear to have more. This false shame is a more extensive evil than is commonly apprehended. We contribute constantly, though insensibly, to form each other's character and manners; and therefore, the usefulness of a strictly holy and conscientious deportment is not confined to the possessor, but spreads its happy influence to all that are within its reach. I need scarcely add, that in proportion as men are distinguished by understanding, literature, age, rank, office, wealth, or any other circumstance, their example will be useful on the one hand, or pernicious on the other.

But I cannot content myself with barely recommending a silent example. There is a dignity in virtue which is entitled to authority, and ought to claim it. In many cases it is the duty of a good man, by open reproof and opposition, to wage war with profaneness. There is a scripture precept delivered in very singular terms, to which I beg your attention; "Thou shalt not hate thy brother in thy heart, but shalt in any wise rebuke him, and not suffer sin upon him." How prone are many to represent reproof as flowing from ill nature and surliness of temper? The spirit of God, on the contrary, considers it as the effect of inward hatred, or want of genuine love, to forbear reproof, when it is necessary or may be useful. I am sensible there may in some cases be a restraint from prudence, agreeably to that caution of our Saviour, "Cast not your pearls before swine, lest they trample them under their feet, and turn again and rent you." Of this every man must judge as well as he can for himself; but certainly, either by open reproof, or expressive silence, or speedy departure from such society, we ought to guard against being partakers of other men's sins.

To this let me add, that if all men are bound in some degree, certain classes of men are under peculiar obligations, to the discharge of this duty. Magistrates, ministers, parents, heads of families, and those whom age has rendered venerable, are called to use their authority and influence for the glory of God and the good of others. Bad men themselves discover an inward conviction of this, for they are often liberal in their reproaches of persons of grave characters or religious profession, if they bear with patience the profanity of others. Instead of enlarging on the duty of men in authority in general, I must particularly recommend this matter to those who have the command of soldiers inlisted for the defence of their country. The cause is sacred, and the champions for it ought to be holy. Nothing is more grieving to the heart of a good man, than to hear from those who are going to the field, the horrid sound of cursing and blasphemy; it cools the ardor of his prayers, as well as abates his confidence and hope in God. Many more circumstances affect me in such a case, than I can enlarge upon, or indeed easily enumerate at present; the glory of God, the interest of the deluded sinner, going like a devoted victim, and imprecating vengeance on his own head, as well as the cause itself committed to his care. We have sometimes taken the liberty to forebode the downfall of the British empire, from the corruption and degeneracy of the people. Unhappily the British soldiers have been distinguished among all the nations in Europe, for the most shocking profanity. Shall we then pretend to emulate them in this internal distinction, or rob them of the horrid privilege? God forbid. Let the officers of the army in every degree remember, that as military subjection, while it lasts, is the most complete of any, it is in their power greatly to restrain, if not wholly to banish, this flagrant enormity.

2. I exhort all who are not called to go into the field, to apply themselves with the utmost diligence to works of industry. It is in your power by this mean not only to supply the necessities, but to add to the strength of your country. Habits of industry prevailing in a society, not only increase its wealth, as their immediate effect, but they prevent the introduction of many vices, and are intimately connected with sobriety and good morals. Idleness is the mother or nurse of almost every vice; and want, which is its inseparable companion, urges men on to the most abandoned and destructive courses. Industry, therefore is a moral duty of the greatest moment, absolutely necessary to national prosperity, and the sure way of obtaining the blessing of God. I would also observe, that in this, as in every other part of God's government, obedience to his will is as much a natural mean, as a meritorious cause, of the advantage we wish to reap from it. Industry brings up a firm and hardy race. He who is inured to the labor of the field, is prepared for the fatigues of a campaign.

The active farmer who rises with the dawn and follows his team or plow, must in the end be an overmatch for those effeminate and delicate soldiers, who are nursed in the lap of self-indulgence, and whose greatest exertion is in the important preparation for, and tedious attendance on, a masquerade, or midnight ball.

3. In the last place, suffer me to recommend to you frugality in your families, and every other article of expence. This the state of things among us renders absolutely necessary, and it stands in the most immediate connexion both with virtuous industry, and active public spirit. Temperance in meals, moderation and decency in dress, furniture and equipage, have, I think, generally been characteristics of a distinguished patriot. And when the same spirit pervades a people in general, they are fit for every duty, and able to encounter the most formidable enemy. The general subject of the preceding discourse has been the wrath of man praising God. If the unjust oppression of your enemies, which withholds from you many of the usual articles of luxury and magnificence, shall contribute to make you clothe yourselves and your children with the works of your own hands, and cover your tables with the salutary productions of your own soil, it will be a new illustration of the same truth, and a real happiness to yourselves and your country.

I could wish to have every good thing done from the purest principles and the noblest views. Consider, therefore, that the Christian character, particularly the self-denial of the gospel, should extend to your whole deportment. In the early times of Christianity, when adult converts were admitted to baptism, they were asked among other questions, Do you renounce the world, its shews, its pomp, and its vanities? I do. The form of this is still preserved in the administration of baptism, where we renounce the devil, the world, and the flesh. This certainly implies not only abstaining from acts of gross intemperance and excess, but a humility of carriage, a restraint and moderation in all your desires. The same thing, as it is suitable to your Christian profession, is also necessary to make you truly independent in yourselves, and to feed the source of liberality and charity to others, or to the public. The riotous and wasteful liver, whose craving appetites make him constantly needy, is and must be subject to many masters, according to the saying of Solomon, "The borrower is servant to the lender." But the frugal and moderate person, who guides his affairs with discretion, is able to assist in public counsels by a free and unbiassed judgment, to supply the wants of his poor brethren, and sometimes, by his estate and substance to give important aid to a sinking country.

Upon the whole, I beseech you to make a wise improvement of the present threatening aspect of public affairs, and to remember that your duty to God, to your country, to your families, and to yourselves, is the same. True religion is nothing else but an inward temper and outward conduct suited to your state and circumstances in providence at any time. And as peace with God and conformity to him, adds to the sweetness of created comforts while we possess them, so in times of difficulty and trial, it is in the man of piety and inward principle, that we may expect to find the uncorrupted patriot, the useful citizen, and the invincible soldier. God grant that in America true religion and civil liberty may be inseparable, and that the unjust attempts to destroy the one, may in the issue tend to the support and establishment of both.

Benjamin Rush

Notes for a Speech in Congress (August 1, 1776)

Question of great importance

The Abbe Reynall, an author who predicted so exactly all the circumstances of the present contr[overs]y 7 years ago, informs us that the liberties of the 7 United Provinces were lost from the foll[owin]g causes.

1. Perfect unan[imit]y being required in their counsels.

2. Each province & city being unable to assent to anything 'till it had cons[ulte]d its Constituents.

3. Each province having an equal Vote.

From the experience we have had of the effects of the second of these causes—much weight in the last. We have lived to see several colonies well nigh ruind—nay more—the union of the whole well nigh dissolved—by the fatal operation of instructions, & I apprehend many of us will live to see greater evils to indiv[idua]l states, & to the whole if each state is all [owe]d a seperate Vote.

I am not able to point out all the mischiefs &c. In every case of doubtful issue it becomes us to imitate the mariner who has lost sight of the sun—keep eye steadily fixed upon his compass—thus we should keep our eyes steadily fixed on the principles of reason & rules of justice.

Shall attempt to point out the misch[ief] of this mode of vot[ing].

1. [dist?]. Equal repress[entation] the found[ation] of liberty. To face the effects of unequal representa-tion] would be to point out the principal cause of the downfall of liberty in most of the free States of the world.

The members of the congress it is true are app[ointe]d by States, but repress[ent] the people—& no State hath a right to alienate the privilege of equal representation: it belongs solely [*to*] the people. The Objects before us are the people's rights, not the rights of States. Every man in America stands related to two legislative bodies—he deposits his property, liberty & life with his own State, but his trade [*and*] Arms, the means of enriching & defending himself & his honor, he deposits with the congress.

If entitled to equal rep[resentation] in the first case, why not in the second?

I add further—that the people of America have been accustomed to view the Congress without the intervent[ion] of the states to which they belonged. And no wonder—the constitution & leaders of their states betrayed them—they looked up [to] the congress & it saved them. [. . .]

2. Evil—keeps up colony distinctions—we are now One people—a new nation—our Interests, language & trade not more divided than they are among the people in Britain who with a Better form of gov-ernment] might have been happy & free under one complete System of Laws forever. Strange if we cannot, who are bound only by a few, & those chiefly in the time of war.

But I go further—our variety of interests is an Advantage to us—had our produce or manufactures between the same in our colony, more reason for jealousy—but the variety of both in every State points out that heaven intended us for one people.

Colony distinctions should be lost here. The more any man forgets the State which gave his birth, or which he represents, the better member of congress, & as in private life the more a man promotes the happiness of his neighb[ors], the more *finally* his own. So the more a man aims to promote the honor & happiness of the whole continent, the more certainly his own state. Every Act of the Conf[ederatio]n is general—all tend to the advancement of the whole.

3. Promote faction—a majority of the people, not states, will determine questions out of doors, and wherever we go contrary to their sentiments they will resent it—perhaps with arms. Already the States & people have divided upon the subject of independence. Bad consequences from it perc[eive]d—perhaps not fully known. Perhaps they will be known & felt in the course of the present war.

4. By this mode of representation we check the progress of freedom in this country. We shall soon experience such inconv[eniencie]s from voting by colonies that we will not readily admit small colonies into the confederation. But if they vote by numbers congress may judge when to admit colonies just as legislatures judge when to admit counties. If we do, whole system of confed[eratio]n be altered.

Sir I am alarmed at the consequences of the mode of voting proposed in this article. If we vote by numbers I maintain that we cannot deposit too much of our liberty & safety in the hands of the congress. They cannot be put out to better interest any where. Here colony factions may be destroyed—here the Aristocratic will cease to pant for a title—or to complain of the inequality of mankind. But if we vote by colonies I maintain that we cannot deposit too little in the hands of the congress. The Scheme is big with ruin, not only to one but to all the colonies.

But Sir, providence has held up a testim[on]y against this manner of voting. If ever colonies should think of having seperate interests, it must be those that are contiguous to each other. Now Sir let us examine the rel[ationshi]p which the several colonies have to each other. M. Bay lies contiguous to Rh. Island & New Hamshire—Pens[ylvania] to New Jersey & the *lower Counties*—N. Carolina to South Carolina & Georgia. If they vote by Colonies, think of the weight any one of these three large martial colonies will derive from their neighbours—but if by numbers they can derive no advantage from them that will not be ballanced by the members who will Vote in the other large colonies that are remote from it.

Sir, some of the colonies have lost sight of their true situation by being too familiar with the word *independance*. When confed[erate]d Sir, they are independant states, but in their seperate capacity, as they are *defendant* states, They cannot exist without each other. Our weakness, & strength of enemies, &c require it. Their dependance differs from former dependance on the crown of &c, in their still retaining their freedom. The congress interferes with no internal legislature, & each colony has a voice in proportion to the services it renders the states.

I have heard it said, that if we vote by Colonies 3 can bind the whole. If this the case, these three colonies are so seperated [*they*] can have no interest but within the interest of the whole. But if by Colonies don't the minority of people bind majority?

By one article, 7 Colonies are to assess proport[ion] of taxes [for] each colony. Is there no danger from this to the large colonies? Is [*it*] not Subjecting them to the very evil We fled from G.B. to avoid—taxation without representation?

They say small colonies will plunge them into a war &c—no—here let 3/4 or 4/5 Determine.

Appeal once more to history to determine the question. Montesquieu pronounces the Confed[eratio]n of *Lycia* the best in the world. 25 cities, large ones 3 votes, second size 2, small ones one. Strabo says the happiest & freest people in the world.

But suppose 9 now include a majority—will this always be the case? May not some one from excell[enc]y of laws, soil, climate, become more popul[ous] than Whole? But, again suppose only 8 concur—shall we have no peace, alliances, money, &c? Or shall we [bribe?], persuade &c the 9th colony, or dissolve without doing any thing?

They say small Colonies deposit their *all*. Suppose we admit 8 or 10 Colonies with 5000 or 10000 inhabitants each. They deposit all too, but would the smallest colony among us be *now* willing to give each of them a Vote equal with itself? I believe not. But Sir—We are deceived here with a word. To suppose that a colony deposits *all* its liberty in the Congress is to give it one life—to make it as one man. This Idea is a most dangerous one. It is to contract millions to a span [. . .], & whether it is, intended or no, it is to invest the Congress with the power of a Caligula.

I might mention the advantages of voting by numbers. If any exclusive advantages from it will induce Colonies to cultivate the arts of population—to reform, & perfect their gov[ernmen]ts, to destroy religious establish[men]ts & to keep down arb[itrar]y power of every kind.

I am not plead[in]g the Cause of Pensylvania. In half a century she may be and probably will be as near the smallest as she now is the greatest states. New Hamshire & Georgia will probably receive most benefit from it if any exclusive Advantages from repres[entatio]n by numbers. No Sir—I am pleading the cause of the Continent—of mankind—of posterity.

I shall not say I will not sign the confed[erac]y if we vote by numbers—but I will say that every man who does, signs the death warrant of the liberties of America.

Propose a plan—every 5000 a member; when the congress amounts to above 100, encrease the proportion of people who are to send a member.

This is not the most perfect that can be wished; is certainly much better than the worst that can be contrived.

Henry Laurens

Letter to John Laurens (August 14, 1776)

Charles Town

My Negroes there all to a Man are strongly attached to me, so are all of mine in this Country, hitherto not one of them has attempted to desert on the contrary those who are more exposed hold themselves always ready to fly from the Enemy in case of a sudden descent—many hundreds of that Colour have been stolen and decoyed by the Servants of King George the third—Captains of British Ships of War & Noble Lords have busied themselves in such inglorious pilferage to the disgrace of their Master & disgrace of their Cause—these Negroes were first enslaved by the English—Acts of Parliament have established the Slave Trade in favour of the home residing English and almost totally prohibited the Americans from reaping any share of it—Men of War Forts Castles Governors Companies & Committees are employed & authorized by the English Parliament to protect regulate & extend the Slave Trade—Negroes are brought by English Men and sold as Slaves to Americans—Bristol Liverpoole Manchester Birmingham [etc.] live upon the Slave Trade the British Parliament now employ their Men of War to steal those Negroes from the Americans to whom they had sold them, pretending to set the poor wretches free but basely trepan & sell them into ten fold worse Slavery in the West Indies, where probably they will become the property of Englishmen again and of some who sit in Parliament; what meanness! what complicated wickedness appears in this scene! O England, how changed! how fallen!

You know my Dear Sir. I abhor Slavery, I was born in a Country where Slavery had been established by British Kings & Parliaments as well as by the Laws of that Country Ages before my existence, I found the Christian Religion and Slavery growing under the same authority and cultivation—I nevertheless disliked it—in former days there was no combating the prejudices of Men supported by Interest, the day I hope is approaching when from principles of gratitude as well as justice every Man will strive to be foremost in shewing his readiness to comply with the Golden Rule; not less than £20000 [sterling] would all my Negroes produce if sold at public Auction tomorrow, I am not the Man who enslaved them, they are indebted to English Men for that favour, nevertheless I am devising means for manumitting many of them and for cutting off the entail of Slavery —great powers oppose me, the Laws and Customs of my Country, my own & the avarice of my Country Men—What will my Children say if I deprive them of so much Estate? These are difficulties but not insuperable I will do as much as I can in my time and leave the rest to a better hand. I am not one of those who arrogate the peculiar care of Providence in each fortunate event, nor one of those who dare trust in Providence for defence and security of their own Liberty while they enslave and wish to continue in Slavery, thousands who are as well intitled to freedom as themselves—I perceive the work before me is great. I shall appear to many as a promoter not only of strange but of dangerous doctrines, it will therefore be necessary to proceed with caution, you are apparently deeply Interested in this affair but as I have no doubts concerning your concurrence and approbation I most sincerely wish for your advice & assistance & hope to receive both in good time. [. . .]

Concord Town Meeting Resolution (October 21, 1776)

At a meeting of the Inhabitants of the Town of Concord being free and twenty one years of age and upward, met by adjournment on the twenty first Day of October 1776 to take into Consideration a Resolve of the Honorable House of Representatives of this State on the 17th of September Last, the Town Resolved as follows—

Resolve 1st. That this State being at Present destitute of a Properly established form of Government, it is absolutely necessary that one should be immediately formed and established—

Resolve 2d. That the Supreme Legislative, either in their Proper Capacity, or in Joint Committee, are by no means a Body proper to form and Establish a Constitution, or form of Government; for Reasons following. first Because we Conceive that a Constitution in its Proper Idea intends a System of Principles Established to Secure the Subject in the Possession and enjoyment of their Rights and Privileges, against any Encroachments of the Governing Part—

2d. Because the Same Body that forms a Constitution have of Consequence a power to alter it.

3d. Because a Constitution alterable by the Supreme Legislative is no Security at all to the Subject against any Encroachment of the Governing part on any, or on all of their Rights and privileges.

Resolve 3d. That it appears to this Town highly necessary and Expedient that a Convention, or Congress be immediately Chosen, to form and establish a Constitution, by the Inhabitants of the Respective Towns in this State, being free and of twenty one years of age, and upwards, in Proportion as the Representatives of this State formerly ware Chosen; the Convention or Congress not to Consist of a greater number then the House of assembly of this State heretofore might Consist of, Except that each Town and District shall have Liberty to Send one Representative or otherwise as Shall appear meet to the Inhabitants of this State in General.

Resolve 4th. That when the Convention, or Congress have formed a Constitution they adjourn for a Short time, and Publish their Proposed Constitution for the Inspection and Remarks of the Inhabitants of this State.

Resolve 5th. That the Honorable House of assembly of this State be Desired to Recommend it to the Inhabitants of the State to Proceed to Chuse a Convention or Congress for the Purpose above said as soon as Possable.

Thomas Paine

The *Crisis*, No. 1 (1776)

THESE are the times that try men's souls. The summer soldier and the sunshine patriot will, in this crisis, shrink from the service of their country; but he that stands it now, deserves the love and thanks of man and woman. Tyranny, like hell, is not easily conquered; yet we have this consolation with us, that the harder the conflict, the more glorious the triumph. What we obtain too cheap, we esteem too lightly: it is dearness only that gives every thing its value. Heaven knows how to put a proper price upon its goods; and it would be strange indeed if so celestial an article as FREEDOM should not be highly rated. Britain, with an army to enforce her tyranny, has declared that she has a right (not only to TAX) but "to BIND US in ALL CASES WHATSOEVER," and if being bound in that manner, is not slavery, then is there not such a thing as slavery upon earth. Even the expression is impious; for so unlimited a power can belong only to God.

Whether the independence of the continent was declared too soon, or delayed too long, I will not now enter into as an argument; my own simple opinion is, that had it been eight months earlier, it would have been much better. We did not make a proper use of last winter, neither could we, while we were in a dependent state. However, the fault, if it were one, was all our own; we have none to blame but ourselves. But no great deal is lost yet. All that Howe has been doing for this month past, is rather a ravage than a conquest, which the spirit of the Jerseys, a year ago, would have quickly repulsed, and which time and a little resolution will soon recover. [. . .]

I have as little superstition in me as any man living, but my secret opinion has ever been, and still is, that God Almighty will not give up a people to military destruction, or leave them unsupportedly to perish, who have so earnestly and so repeatedly sought to avoid the calamities of war, by every decent method which wisdom could invent. Neither have I so much of the infidel in me, as to suppose that He has relinquished the government of the world, and given us up to the care of devils; and as I do not, I cannot see on what grounds the king of Britain can look up to heaven for help against us: a common murderer, a highwayman, or a house-breaker, has as good a pretence as he.

'Tis surprising to see how rapidly a panic will sometimes run through a country. All nations and ages have been subject to them. Britain has trembled like an ague at the report of a French fleet of flat-bottomed boats; and in the fourteenth [fifteenth] century the whole English army, after ravaging the kingdom of France, was driven back like men petrified with fear; and this brave exploit was performed by a few broken forces collected and headed by a woman, Joan of Arc. Would that heaven might inspire some Jersey maid to spirit up her countrymen, and save her fair fellow sufferers from ravage and ravishment! Yet panics, in some cases, have their uses; they produce as much good as hurt. Their duration is always short; the mind soon grows through them, and acquires a firmer habit than before. But their peculiar advantage is, that they are the touchstones of sincerity and hypocrisy, and bring things and men to light, which might otherwise have lain forever undiscovered. In fact, they have the same effect on secret traitors, which an imaginary apparition would have upon a private murderer. They sift out the hidden thoughts of man, and hold them up in public to the world. Many a disguised Tory has lately shown his head, that shall penitentially solemnize with curses the day on which Howe arrived upon the Delaware.

As I was with the troops at Fort Lee, and marched with them to the edge of Pennsylvania, I am well acquainted with many circumstances, which those who live at a distance know but little or nothing of. Our situation there was exceedingly cramped, the place being a narrow neck of land between the North River and the Hackensack. Our force was inconsiderable, being not one-fourth so great as Howe could bring against us. We had no army at hand to have relieved the garrison, had we shut ourselves up and stood on our defence. Our ammunition, light artillery, and the best part of our stores, had been removed, on the apprehension that Howe would endeavor to penetrate the Jerseys, in which case Fort Lee could be of no use to us; for it must occur to every thinking man, whether in the army or not, that these kind of field forts are only for temporary purposes, and last in use no longer than the enemy directs his force against the particular object which such forts are raised to defend. Such was our situation and condition at Fort Lee on the morning of the 20th of November, when an officer arrived with information that the enemy with 200 boats had landed about seven miles above; Major General Green, who commanded the garrison, immediately ordered them under arms, and sent express to General Washington at the town of Hackensack, distant by the way of the ferry = six miles. Our first object was to secure the bridge over the Hackensack, which laid up the river between the enemy and us, about six miles from us, and three from them. General Washington arrived in about three-quarters of an hour, and marched at the head of the troops towards the bridge, which place I expected we should have a brush for; however, they did not choose to dispute it with us, and the greatest part of our troops went over the bridge, the rest over the ferry, except some which passed at a mill on a small creek, between the bridge and the ferry, and made their way through some marshy grounds up to the town of Hackensack, and there passed the river. We brought off as much baggage as the wagons could contain, the rest was lost. The simple object was to bring off the garrison, and march them on till they could be strengthened by the Jersey or Pennsylvania militia, so as to be enabled to make a stand. We staid four days at Newark, collected our out-posts with some of the Jersey militia, and marched out twice to meet the enemy, on being informed that they were advancing, though our numbers were greatly inferior to theirs. Howe, in my little opinion, committed a great error in generalship in not throwing a body of forces off from Staten Island through Amboy, by which means he might have seized all our stores at Brunswick, and intercepted our march into Pennsylvania; but if we believe the power of hell to be limited, we must likewise believe that their agents are under some providential control.

I shall not now attempt to give all the particulars of our retreat to the Delaware; suffice it for the present to say, that both officers and men, though greatly harassed and fatigued, frequently without rest, covering, or provision, the inevitable consequences of a long retreat, bore it with a manly and martial spirit. All their wishes centred in one, which was, that the country would turn out and help them to drive the enemy back. Voltaire has remarked that King William never appeared to full advantage but in difficulties and in action; the same remark may be made on General Washington, for the character fits him. There is a natural firmness in some minds which cannot be unlocked by trifles, but which, when unlocked, discovers a cabinet of fortitude; and I reckon it among those kind of public blessings, which we do not immediately see, that God hath blessed him with uninterrupted health, and given him a mind that can even flourish upon care.

I shall conclude this paper with some miscellaneous remarks on the state of our affairs; and shall begin with asking the following question, Why is it that the enemy have left the New England provinces, and made these middle ones the seat of war? The answer is easy: New England is not infested with Tories, and we are. I have been tender in raising the cry against these men, and used numberless arguments to show them their danger, but it will not do to sacrifice a world either to their folly or their baseness. The period is now arrived, in which either they or we must change our sentiments, or one or both must fall. And what is a Tory? Good God! what is he? I should not be afraid to go with a hundred Whigs against a thousand Tories, were they to attempt to get into arms. Every Tory is a coward; for servile, slavish, self-interested fear is the foundation of Toryism; and a man under such influence, though he may be cruel, never can be brave.

But, before the line of irrecoverable separation be drawn between us, let us reason the matter together: Your conduct is an invitation to the enemy, yet not one in a thousand of you has heart enough to join him. Howe is as much deceived by you as the American cause is injured by you. He expects you will all take up arms, and flock to his standard, with muskets on your shoulders. Your opinions are of no use to him, unless you support him personally, for 'tis soldiers, and not Tories, that he wants.

I once felt all that kind of anger, which a man ought to feel, against the mean principles that are held by the Tories: a noted one, who kept a tavern at Amboy, was standing at his door, with as pretty a child in his hand, about eight or nine years old, as I ever saw, and after speaking his mind as freely as he thought was prudent, finished with this unfatherly expression, "Well! give me peace in my day." Not a man lives on the continent but fully believes that a separation must some time or other finally take place, and a generous parent should have said, "If there must be trouble, let it be in my day, that my child may have peace;" and this single reflection, well applied, is sufficient to awaken every man to duty. Not a place upon earth might be so happy as America. Her situation is remote from all the wrangling world, and she has nothing to do but to trade with them. A man can distinguish himself between temper and principle, and I am as confident, as I am that God governs the world, that America will never be happy till she gets clear of foreign dominion. Wars, without ceasing, will break out till that period arrives, and the continent must in the end be conqueror; for though the flame of liberty may sometimes cease to shine, the coal can never expire.

America did not, nor does not want force; but she wanted a proper application of that force. Wisdom is not the purchase of a day, and it is no wonder that we should err at the first setting off. From an excess of tenderness, we were unwilling to raise an army, and trusted our cause to the temporary defence of a well-meaning militia. A summer's experience has now taught us better; yet with those troops, while they were collected, we were able to set bounds to the progress of the enemy, and, thank God! they are again assembling. I always considered militia as the best troops in the world for a sudden exertion, but they will not do for a long campaign. Howe, it is probable, will make an attempt on this city [Philadelphia]; should he fail on this side the Delaware, he is ruined. If he succeeds, our cause is not ruined. He stakes all on his side against a part on ours; admitting he succeeds, the consequence will be, that armies from both ends of the continent will march to assist their suffering friends in the middle states; for he cannot go everywhere, it is impossible. I consider Howe as the greatest enemy the Tories have; he is bringing a war into their country, which, had it not been for him and partly for themselves, they had been clear of. Should he now be expelled, I wish with all the devotion of a Christian, that the names of Whig and Tory may never more be mentioned; but should the Tories give him encouragement to come, or assistance if he come, I as sincerely wish that our next year's arms may expel them from the continent, and the Congress appropriate their possessions to the relief of those who have suffered in well-doing. A single successful battle next year will settle the whole. America could carry on a two years' war by the confiscation of the property of disaffected persons, and be made happy by their expulsion. Say not that this is revenge, call it rather the soft resentment of a suffering people, who, having no object in view but the good of all, have staked their own all upon a seemingly doubtful event. Yet it is folly to argue against determined hardness; eloquence may strike the ear, and the language of sorrow draw forth the tear of compassion, but nothing can reach the heart that is steeled with prejudice.

Quitting this class of men, I turn with the warm ardor of a friend to those who have nobly stood, and are yet determined to stand the matter out: I call not upon a few, but upon all: not on this state or that state, but on every state: up and help us; lay your shoulders to the wheel; better have too much force than too little, when so great an object is at stake. Let it be told to the future world, that in the depth of winter, when nothing but hope and virtue could survive, that the city and the country, alarmed at one common danger, came forth to meet and to repulse it. Say not that thousands are gone, turn out your tens of thousands; throw not the burden of the day upon Providence, but "show your faith by your works," that God may bless you. It matters not where you live, or what rank of life you hold, the evil or the blessing will reach you all. The far and the near, the home counties and the back, the rich and the poor, will suffer or rejoice alike. The heart that feels not now is dead; the blood of his children will curse his cowardice, who shrinks back at a time when a little might have saved the whole, and made them happy. I love the man that can smile in trouble, that can gather strength from distress, and grow brave by reflection. 'Tis the business of little minds to shrink; but he whose heart is firm, and whose conscience approves his conduct, will pursue his principles unto death. My own line of reasoning is to myself as straight and clear as a ray of light. Not all the treasures of the world, so far as I believe, could have induced me to support an offensive war, for I think it murder; but if a thief breaks into my house, burns and destroys my property, and kills or threatens to kill me, or those that are in it, and to "bind me in all cases whatsoever" to his absolute will, am I to suffer it? What signifies it to me, whether he who does it is a king or a common man; my countryman or not my countryman; whether it be done by an individual villain, or an army of them? If we reason to the root of things we shall find no difference; neither can any just cause be assigned why we should punish in the one case and pardon in the other. Let them call me rebel and welcome, I feel no concern from it; but I should suffer the misery of devils, were I to make a whore of my soul by swearing allegiance to one whose character is that of a sottish, stupid, stubborn, worthless, brutish man. I conceive likewise a horrid idea in receiving mercy from a being, who at the last day shall be shrieking to the rocks and mountains to cover him, and fleeing with terror from the orphan, the widow, and the slain of America.

There are cases which cannot be overdone by language, and this is one. There are persons, too, who see not the full extent of the evil which threatens them; they solace themselves with hopes that the enemy, if he succeed, will be merciful. It is the madness of folly, to expect mercy from those who have refused to do justice; and even mercy, where conquest is the object, is only a trick of war; the cunning of the fox is as murderous as the violence of the wolf, and we ought to guard equally against both. Howe's first object is, partly by threats and partly by promises, to terrify or seduce the people to deliver up their arms and receive mercy. The ministry recommended the same plan to Gage, and this is what the tories call making their peace, "a peace which passeth all understanding" indeed! A peace which would be the immediate forerunner of a worse ruin than any we have yet thought of. Ye men of Pennsylvania, do reason upon these things! Were the back counties to give up their arms, they would fall an easy prey to the Indians, who are all armed: this perhaps is what some Tories would not be sorry for. Were the home counties to deliver up their arms, they would be exposed to the resentment of the back counties who would then have it in their power to chastise their defection at pleasure. And were any one state to give up its arms, that state must be garrisoned by all Howe's army of Britons and Hessians to preserve it from the anger of the rest. Mutual fear is the principal link in the chain of mutual love, and woe be to that state that breaks the compact. Howe is mercifully inviting you to barbarous destruction, and men must be either rogues or fools that will not see it. I dwell not upon the vapors of imagination; I bring reason to your ears, and, in language as plain as A, B, C, hold up truth to your eyes.

I thank God, that I fear not. I see no real cause for fear. I know our situation well, and can see the way out of it. While our army was collected, Howe dared not risk a battle; and it is no credit to him that he decamped from the White Plains, and waited a mean opportunity to ravage the defenceless Jerseys; but it is great credit to us, that, with a handful of men, we sustained an orderly retreat for near an hundred miles, brought off our ammunition, all our field pieces, the greatest part of our stores, and had four rivers to pass. None can say that our retreat was precipitate, for we were near three weeks in performing it, that the country might have time to come in. Twice we marched back to meet the enemy, and remained out till dark. The sign of fear was not seen in our camp, and had not some of the cowardly and disaffected inhabitants spread false alarms through the country, the Jerseys had never been ravaged. Once more we are again collected and collecting; our new army at both ends of the continent is recruiting fast, and we shall be able to open the next campaign with sixty thousand men, well armed and clothed. This is our situation, and who will may know it. By perseverance and fortitude we have the prospect of a glorious issue; by cowardice and submission, the sad choice of a variety of evils—a ravaged country—a depopulated city—habitations without safety, and slavery without hope—our homes turned into barracks and bawdy-houses for Hessians, and a future race to provide for, whose fathers we shall doubt of. Look on this picture and weep over it! and if there yet remains one thoughtless wretch who believes it not, let him suffer it unlamented.

Common Sense
December 23, 1776

Carter Braxton

A Native of This Colony (1776)

An Address to the Convention of the Colony and Ancient Dominion of Virginia on the Subject of Government in General, and Recommending a Particular Form to Their Attention

Virginia

Gentlemen,

When despotism had displayed her banners, and with unremitting ardour and fury scattered her engines of oppression through this wide extended continent, the virtuous opposition of the people to its progress relaxed the tone of government in almost every colony, and occasioned in many instances a total suspension of law. These inconveniences, however, were natural, and the mode readily submitted to, as there was then reason to hope that justice would be done to our injured country; the same laws, executed under the same authority, soon regain their former use and lustre; and peace, raised on a permanent foundation, bless this our native land.

But since these hopes have hitherto proved delusive, and time, instead of bringing us relief, daily brings forth new proofs of British tyranny, and thereby separates us further from that reconciliation we so ardently wished; does it not become the duty of your, and every other Convention, to assume the reins of government, and no longer suffer the people to live without the benefit of law, and order the protection it affords? Anarchy and riot will follow a continuance of its suspension, and render the enjoyment of our liberties and future quiet at least very precarious.

Presuming that this object will, ere long, engage your attention, and fully persuaded that when it does it will be considered with all the candour and deliberation due to its importance, I have ventured to collect my sentiments on the subject, and in a friendly manner offer them to your consideration. Should they suggest any hints that may tend to improve or embellish the fabric you are about to erect, I shall deem myself happy in having contributed my might to the benefit of a people I esteem, and a country to which I owe every obligation.

Taking for granted, therefore, the necessity of instituting a government capable of affording all the blessings of which the most cruel attempts have been made to deprive us, the first inquiry will be, which of the various forms is best adapted to our situation, and will in every respect most probably answer our purpose.

Various are the opinions of men on this subject, and different are the plans proposed for your adoption. Prudence will direct you to examine them with a jealous eye, and weigh the pretensions of each with care, as well as impartiality. Your, and your children's welfare depends upon the choice. Let it therefore neither be marked by a blind attachment to ancient prejudices on the one hand, or a restless spirit of innovation on the other.

Although all writers agree in the object of government, and admit that it was designed to promote and secure the happiness of every member of society, yet their opinions, as to the systems most productive of this general benefit, have been extremely contradictory. As all these systems are said to move on separate and distinct principles, it may not be improper to analyse them, and by that means shew the manner of their operations.

Government is generally divided into two parts, its *mode or form of constitution,* and the *principle* intended to direct it.

The simple forms of government are despotism, monarchy, aristocracy, and democracy. Out of these an infinite variety of combinations may be deduced. The absolute unlimited controul of one man describes *despotism,* whereas *monarchy* compels the Sovereign to rule agreeable to certain fundamental laws. *Aristocracy* vests the sovereignty of a state in a few nobles, and *democracy* allows it to reside in the body of the people, and is thence called a popular government.

Each of these forms are actuated by different *principles*. The subjects of an unlimited despotic Prince, whose will is their only rule of conduct, are influenced by the principle of *fear*. In a monarchy limited by laws the people are insensibly led to the pursuit of *honour*, they feel an interest in the greatness of their Princes, and, inspired by a desire of glory, rank, and promotion, unite in giving strength and energy to the whole machine. Aristocracy and democracy claim for their principle *public virtue*, or a regard for the public good independent of private interest.

Let us inquire from which of these several [ ] we should take a cion to ingraft on our wild one, see which is most congenial to our soil, and by the extent and strength of its branches best calculated to shelter the people from the rage of those tempests which often darken the political hemisphere. I will not deny, whatever others may do, that individuals have enjoyed a certain degree of happiness under all these forms. Content, and consequently happiness, depend more on the state of our minds than external circumstances, and some men are satisfied with fewer enjoyments than others. Upon these occasions the inclinations of men, which are often regulated by what they have seen and experienced, ought to be consulted. It cannot be wise to draw them further from their former institutions than obvious reasons and necessity will justify. Should a form of government directly opposite to the ancient one, under which they have been happy, be introduced and established, will they not, on the least disgust, repine at the change, and be disposed even to acts of violence in order to regain their former condition. Many examples in the history of almost every country prove the truth of this remark.

What has been the government of Virginia, and in a revolution how is its spirit to be preserved, are important questions. The better to discuss these points, we should take a view of the constitution of England, because by that model ours was constructed, and under it we have enjoyed tranquillity and security. Our ancestors, the English, after contemplating the various forms of government, and experiencing, as well as perceiving, the defects of each, wisely refused to resign their liberties either to the single man, the few, or the many. They determine to make a compound of each the foundation of their government, and of the most valuable parts of them all to build a superstructure that should surpass all others, and bid defiance to time to injure, or any thing, except national degeneracy and corruption, to demolish.

In rearing this fabric, and connecting its parts, much time, blood, and treasure were expended. By the vigilance, perseverance, and activity of innumerable martyrs, the happy edifice was at length completed under the auspices of the renowned King William in the year 1688. They wisely united the hereditary succession of the Crown with the good behaviour of the Prince; they gave respect and stability to the legislature, by the independence of the Lords, and security, as well as importance to the people, by being parties with their Sovereign in every act of legislation. Here then our ancestors rested from their long and laborious pursuit, and saw many good days in the peaceable enjoyment of the fruit of their labours. Content with having provided against the ills which had befallen them, they seemed to have forgot, that although the seeds of destruction might be excluded from their constitution, they were, nevertheless, to be found in those by whom their affairs were administered.

Time, the improver, as well as destroyer, of all things, discovered to them, that the very man who had wrought their deliverance was capable of pursuing measures leading to their destruction. Much is it to be lamented, that this magnanimous Prince, ascending a throne beset with uncertainty and war, was induced, by the force of both, to invent and practise the art of *funding* to supply his wants, and create an interest that might support him in possession of his Crown. He succeeded to his wish, and thereby established a monied interest, which was followed by levying of taxes, by a host of tax-gatherers, and a long train of dependents on the Crown. The practice grew into system, till at length the Crown found means to break down those barriers which the constitution had assigned to each branch of the legislature, and effectively destroyed the independence of both Lords and Commons. These breaches, instead of being repaired as soon as discovered, were, by the supineness of the nation permitted to widen by daily practice, till, finally, the influence of the Crown pervaded and overwhelmed the whole people, and gave birth to the many calamities which we now bewail, and for the removal of which the united efforts of America are at this time exerted.

Men are prone to condemn the whole, because a part is objectionable; but certainly it would, in the present case, be more wise to consider, whether, if the constitution was brought back to its original state, and its present imperfections remedied, it would not afford more happiness than any other. If the independence of the Commons could be secured, and the dignity of the Lords preserved, how can a government be better formed for the preservation of freedom? And is there any thing more easy than this? If placemen and pensioners were excluded a seat in either House, and elections made triennial, what danger could be apprehended for prerogative? I have the best authority for asserting, that with these improvements, added to the suppression of boroughs, and giving the people an equal and adequate representation, England would have remained a land of liberty to the latest ages.

Judge of the *principle* of this constitution by the great effects it has produced. Their code of laws, the boast of Englishmen and of freedom; the rapid progress they have made in trade, in arts and sciences; the respect they commanded from their neighbours, then gaining the empire of the sea; are all powerful arguments of the wisdom of that constitution and government, which raised the people of that island to their late degree of greatness. But though I admire their perfections, I must mourn their faults; and though I would guard against, and cast off their oppression, yet would I retain all their wise maxims, and derive advantage from their mistakes and misfortunes. The testimony of the learned Montesquieu in favour of the English constitution is very respectable. "There is (says he) one nation in the world that has for the direct end of its constitution political liberty." Again he says, "It is not my business to examine whether the English actually enjoy this liberty or not; sufficient it is for my purpose to observe, that it is established by their laws, and I inquire no further."

This constitution, and these laws, have also been those of Virginia, and let it be remembered, that under them she flourished and was happy. The same principles which led the English to greatness animates us. To that principle our laws, our customs, and our manners, are adapted, and it would be perverting all order to oblige us, by a novel government, to give up our laws, our customs, and our manners.

However necessary it may be to shake off the authority of arbitrary British dictators, we ought, nevertheless, to adopt and perfect that system, which England has suffered to be grossly abused, and the experience of ages has taught us to venerate. This, like almost every thing else, is perhaps liable to objections, and probably the difficulty of adopting a limited monarchy will be largely insisted on. Admit this objection to have weight, and that we cannot in every instance assimulate a government to that, yet no good reason can be assigned why the same *principle*, or spirit, may not in a great measure be preserved. But, honourable as this spirit is, we daily see it calumniated by advocates for popular governments, and rendered obnoxious to all whom their artifices can influence or delude. The systems recommended to the colonies seem to accord with the temper of the times, and are fraught with all the tumult and riot incident to simple democracy; systems which many think it their interest to support, and without doubt will be industriously propagated among you. The best of these systems exist only in theory, and were never confirmed by the experience, even of those who recommend them. I flatter myself, therefore, that you will not quit a substance actually enjoyed, for a shadow or phantom, by which, instead of being benefited, many have been misled and perplexed.

Let us examine the principles they assign to their government, and try its merits by the unerring standard of truth. In a late pamphlet it is thus stated: The happiness of man, as well as his dignity, consists in virtue; *if there be a form of government, then, whose principle is virtue, will not every sober man acknowledge it better calculated to promote the general happiness of society than any other form.* Virtue is the principle of a republic, therefore a republic is the best form of government.

The author, with what design I know not, seems to have cautiously blended *private* with *public* virtue, as if for the purpose of confounding the two, and thereby recommending his plan under the amiable appearance of courting *virtue*. It is well known that *private* and *public* virtue are materially different. The happiness and dignity of man I admit consists in the practice of *private* virtues, and to this he is stimulated by the rewards promised to such conduct. In this he acts for himself, and with a view of promoting his own particular welfare. *Public* virtue, on the other hand, means a disinterested attachment to the public good, exclusive and independent of all private and selfish interest, and which, though sometimes possessed by a few individuals, never characterised the mass of the people in any state. And this is said to be the principle of democratical governments, and to influence every subject of it to pursue such measures as conduce to the prosperity of the whole. A man, therefore, to qualify himself for a member of such a community, must divest himself of all interested motives, and engage in no pursuits which do not ultimately redound to the benefit of society. He must not, through ambition, desire to be great, because it would destroy that equality on which the security of the government depends; nor ought he to be rich, lest he be tempted to indulge himself in those luxuries, which, though lawful, are not expedient, and might occasion envy and emulation. Should a person deserve the esteem of his fellow citizens, and become popular, he must be neglected, if not banished, lest his growing influence disturb the equilibrium. It is remarkable, that neither the justice of Aristides, or the bravery of Themistocles, could shield them from the darts of envy and jealousy; nor are modern times without examples of the same kind.

To this species of government every thing that looks like elegance and refinement is inimical, however necessary to the introduction of manufactures, and the cultivation of arts and sciences. Hence, in some ancient republics, flowed those numberless sumptuary laws, which restrained men to plainness and similarity in dress and diet, and all the mischiefs which attend Agrarian laws, and unjust attempts to maintain their idol equality by an equal division of property.

Schemes like these may be practicable in countries so steril by nature as to afford a scanty supply of the necessaries, and none of the conveniences, of life; but they can never meet with a favourable reception from people who inhabit a country to which Providence has been more bountiful. They will always claim a right of using and enjoying the fruits of their honest industry, unrestrained by any ideal principles of government, and will gather estates for themselves and children without regarding the whimsical impropriety of being richer than their neighbours. These are rights which freemen will never consent to relinquish, and after fighting for deliverance from one species of tyranny, it would be unreasonable to expect they should tamely acquiesce under another.

The truth is, that men will not be poor from choice or compulsion, and these governments can exist only in countries where the people are so from necessity. In all others they have ceased almost as soon as erected, and in many instances been succeeded by despotism, and the arbitrary sway of some usurper, who had before perhaps gained the confidence of the people by eulogiums on liberty, and possessing no property of his own, by most disinterestedly opposing depredations on that of his neighbours.

The most considerable state in which the shadow of democracy exists (for it is far from being purely so) is that of the united provinces of Holland, &c. Their territories are confined within narrow limits, and the exports of their own produce very inconsiderable. Trade is the support of that people, and, however said to be considerable, will not admit of luxury. With the greatest parsimony and industry, they, as a people, can but barely support themselves, although individuals among them may amass estates. I own they have exhibited to mankind an example of perseverance and magnanimity that appeared like a prodigy. By the profits of their trade they maintained large armies, and supported a navy equal to the first in their day of warfare; but their military strength, as well as the form of their government, have long since given way. Their navy has dwindled into a few ships of war, and their government into an aristocracy, as unhappy and despotic as the one of which we complain.

The state of Venice, once a republic, is now governed by one of the worst of despotisms. In short, I do not recollect a single instance of a nation who supported this form of government for any length of time, or with any degree of greatness; which convinces me, as it has many others, that the principle contended for is ideal and a mere creature of a warm imagination. [. . .]

That I may not tire your patience, I will now proceed to delineate the method in which I would distribute the powers of government, so as to devise the best code of laws, engage their due execution, and secure the liberties of the people. It is agreed by most writers on this subject, that this power should be divided into three parts, each independent of, but having connection with each other. Let the people, in the first place, choose their usual number of Representatives, and let this right return to them every third year.

Let these Representatives when convened, elect a Governor, to continue in authority during his good behavior, of which the two houses of Council of State and Assembly should jointly be the Judges, and by majority of voices supply any vacancy in that office, which may happen by dismission, death, or resignation.

Let the Representatives also choose out of the Colony at large, twenty-four proper persons to constitute, a Council of State, who should form a distinct or intermediate branch of the legislature, and hold their places for life, in order that they might possess all the weight, stability and dignity due to the importance of their office. Upon the death or resignation of any of the members let the Assembly appoint another to succeed him.

Let no member of either house, except the Treasurer, hold a post of profit in the government.

Let the Governor have a Privy Council of seven to advise with, tho' they should not be members of either house.

Let the Judges of the Courts of Common Law and Chancery be appointed by the Governor, with the advice of his Privy Council, to hold their offices during their good behaviour, but should be excluded a seat in either house.

Let the Treasurer, Secretary, and other great officers of state be chosen by the lower house, and proper salaries assigned to them as well as to the Judges, &c. &c.

Let all military officers be appointed by the Governor, and all other inferior civil ones.

Let the different Courts appoint their own clerks. The Justices in each county should be paid for their services, and required to meet for the dispatch of business every three months. Let five of them be authorized to form a Court to hear and determine causes, and the others impowered to keep the peace, & c. & c.

These are the out lines of a government which should, I think, preserve the principle of our constitution, and secure the freedom and happiness of the people better than any other.

The Governor will have dignity to command necessary respect and authority, to enable him to execute the laws, without being deterred by the fear of giving offence, and yet be amenable to the other branches of the legislature for every violation of the rights of the people. If this great officer was exposed to the uncertain issue of frequent elections, he would be induced to relax and abate the vigorous execution of the laws whenever such conduct would increase his popularity. Should he, by discharging his duty with impartiality give offence to men of weight and influence, he would be liable to all the opposition, threats, and insults which resentment could suggest; and which few men in such a dependent state would have sufficient resolution to neglect and dispise. Hence it would follow, that the apprehensions of losing his election would frequently induce him to court the favour of the great, at the expense of the duties of his station and the public good. For these, and a variety of other reasons, this office should be held during good behaviour.

The Council of State who are to constitute the second branch of the legislature should be for life. They ought to be well informed of the policy and laws of other states, and therefore should be induced by the permanence of their appointment to devote their time to such studies as may best qualify them for that station. They will acquire firmness from their independency, and wisdom from their reflection and experience, and appropriate both to the good of the state. Upon any disagreement between the Governor and lower house, this body will mediate and adjust such difference, will investigate the propriety of laws, and often propose such as may be of public utility for the adoption of the legislature. Being secluded from offices of profit, they will not be seduced from their duty by pecuniary considerations.

The Representatives of the people will be under no temptation to swerve from the design of their institution by bribery or corruption; all lucrative posts being denied them. And should they on any occasion be influenced by improper motives, the short period of their duration will give their constituents an opportunity of depriving them of power to do injury. The Governor and the members of the Council of State, should be restrained from intermeddling farther in the elections of Representatives, than merely by giving their votes.

The internal government and police of the Colony being thus provided for, the next object of inquiry that presents itself is, how a superintending power over the whole Continent shall be raised, and with what powers invested. Such a power is confessed on all hands to be necessary, as well for the purpose of connecting the Colonies, as for the establishment of many general regulations to which the provincial legislatures will not be competent.

Let a Congress therefore be appointed, composed of members from each Colony in proportion to their number of souls; to convene at any place that may be agreed upon, as often as occasion may require. Let them have power to adjust disputes between Colonies, regulate the affairs of trade, war, peace, alliances, &c. but they should by no means have authority to interfere with the internal police or domestic concerns of any Colony, but confined strictly to such general regulations, as tho' necessary for the good of the whole, cannot be established by any other power.

But whether you settle the affairs of government in this, or any other manner, let me recommend to your serious attention the speedy adjustment of all disputes about the boundaries of your Colony, before they rise to such a height as to threaten great uneasiness and inquietude.

The claim of the Proprietors of Indiana on one side, and that of Kantuckee, on the other, should be fairly and impartially heard and determined, and notice given to the claimants to attend, that ample justice may be done. In the mean time, would it not be proper to give notice, that none of those lands should be sold or settled, until it was known to whom they appertain. The claims of the Indiana Company are stated in a pamphlet, (sent for your perusal) and patronized by the opinions of some eminent lawyers. But this should not prevent a strict and thorough investigation of the matter. Both claims, it is certain, cannot be good. If the treaty of Stanwix should be adjudged valid and the right given up to the country of Indiana, that same treaty will confirm to the Colony on the lands on this side the Ohio from its mouth, along the river, up to the Pennsylvania lands in the direction of the place called Kittaniny in that province. In which bounds are included the lands claimed and settled by Mr. Henderson.

Our colonial right to those lands being settled, would it not be proper to sell all such as may be unappropriated for the use of the Colony, and apply the monies to the payment of the vast burden of taxes we shall have to incur by this war? The sooner you determine this, the more effectually you will frustrate the design avowed by the author of a late pamphlet, of seizing all unappropriated lands for the use of the Continent; a design, in which, I own, I see as few traces of justice, as in many other of his schemes.

Having compleated the remarks I intended to make, I hope, whatever reception they may meet with, you will impute them to my zeal for our country's welfare; the only motive that ever shall induce me to offer my opinion or advice.

I am,
Gentlemen,
With the greatest regard,
Your devoted Friend,

A NATIVE

4

Toward a More Perfect Union

When on June 7, 1776, Richard Henry Lee arose before Congress and offered a resolution in favor of independence, he proposed a second one calling for the creation of a permanent confederation among the colonies. Congress adopted both proposals and formed two committees—one to draft a declaration of independence, the other, to draft articles of union. The former, famously staffed by Thomas Jefferson, John Adams, Benjamin Franklin, Roger Sherman, and Robert R. Livingston, produced a document ever since lauded as an inspired expression of humankind's right to and desire for political liberty. The other committee, headed by John Dickinson of Pennsylvania, helped create a document that soon elicited a steady stream of criticism and scorn, and which today is typically described as a failure in political vision. The selections in this chapter illustrate the efforts of American statesmen to produce a workable national constitution in the years immediately following the Declaration of Independence.

It is not surprising that the call for independence was attended by a call for the creation of an American union. To successfully wage war against Great Britain required foreign assistance; foreign nations, particularly France, which had a vested interest in driving Britain from America, would not provide aid unless the colonies could demonstrate the political will to unite. "[N]o foreign Court will attend to our applications for Assistance," Samuel Chase, a signer of the Declaration and a future Supreme Court justice, wrote, "before We are confederated. What Contract will a foreign State make with Us, when We cannot agree among Ourselves?" As one congressional delegate warned bluntly, "We must apply for Pardons, if We dont [*sic*] confederate."

In many ways, Congress' task in forming articles of union was far more demanding than drafting a declaration of independence. The theoretical framework for independence, articulated by the "great Mr. *Locke*," already existed. A decade of parliamentary statutes and royal edicts gave the colonists a lengthy list of grievances that they believed justified political independence from Britain. All that was required was the remarkably able pen of Jefferson to state the colonists' case in eloquent, moving language.

The case with articles of union was far different. It is worth remembering that a mere ten years earlier Dickinson himself had written that independence would produce in America a "Multitude of Commonwealths, Crimes and Calamities, of mutual Jealousies, Hatreds, Wars and Devastations; till at last the exhausted Provinces shall sink into Slavery under the yoke of some fortunate Conqueror." "History," he worried, "seems to prove that this must be the deplorable Fate of these Colonies whenever they become independent." Dickinson's remarks were not unusual. As colonial leaders knew full well, substantial differences—economic, religious, ethnic, and social—divided the colonies. In 1775 John Adams concluded that "the Characters of Gentlemen in the four New England colonies, differ as much from those in the others, as that of the Common People differs, that is as much as several distinct Nations almost." The "Consequences of this Disimilitude of Character," he worried, might well be "fatal."

Thus, Dickinson and his fellow delegates had a tall order to fill when they began to write a constitution for this new union they titled the "United States of America." Disagreement over how the new government would be structured, what powers it would possess—indeed, over the very nature of the union itself—plagued debates over the Articles of Confederation. Further, work on the Articles proceeded intermittently, as Congress was preoccupied with the very real matter of conducting war. Disputes over the

Articles continued even after Congress adopted them. An argument over Western land claims delayed formal adoption of the Articles until 1781, and by then, weaknesses in the Articles were growing increasingly evident to many of the country's leaders.

Congress could claim some successes under the aegis of the Articles. The American Confederation managed to obtain significant and invaluable foreign aid during the Revolutionary War, conducted that war against and concluded a favorable peace with Britain, and enacted the Northwest Ordinance, which contained provisions that have often been referred to as America's first *national* bill of rights. More often than not, however, flaws in the Articles delayed or denied critical governmental action. The Articles' "deficiencies" quickly became apparent to statesmen like James Madison and Alexander Hamilton, who spent the better part of a decade criticizing the Articles and calling for reform. Many of these deficiencies reflected a lack of congressional power: its inability to regulate interstate commerce, to raise armies, and to tax. Other deficiencies were structural: the lack of an independent executive and of a judiciary with final determination over federal questions. Some deficiencies went to the core of constitutional theory itself; for example, the fact that the Articles were not popularly ratified.

Even in the face of seemingly obvious deficiencies, respected voices like those of Richard Henry Lee resisted fundamental changes to the Articles. Lee asserted in 1783 that, "he had rather see Congress a rope of sand than a rod of Iron," perhaps expressing a fear of strong, distant centralized government that grew acute during the decade prior to independence. He certainly objected to increasing Congress' powers under the existing constitutional plan. Still, the deficiencies delineated by critics like Madison and Hamilton indisputably weakened the vitality of the central government. The union created by the Articles of Confederation was one of the strongest ever to have existed, but it was not at all clear that it could long endure. People like Lee acknowledged the need for change but emphasized that any proposed remedies must be considered with extraordinary care. "[T]he first maxim of a man who loves liberty should be," he wrote in a 1785 letter to Samuel Adams, "never to grant to Rulers an atom of power that is not most clearly & indispensably necessary for the safety and well being of Society." Incremental revisions within the existing framework of the Articles would suffice to address the most pressing problems. "Happily for us," he continued, "our political disease admits of simple remedies for its cure, if rightly judged of, and wisely practised upon."

Some American statesmen suggested continuity between the principles that structure the United States Constitution and those inherent to the Articles of Confederation. Madison, for example, asserted that "the truth is that the great principles of the Constitution proposed by the [1787] Convention may be considered less as absolutely new than as the expansion of principles which are found in the Articles of Confederation. The misfortune under the latter system has been that these principles are so feeble and confined as to . . . require a degree of enlargement which gives to the new system the aspect of an entire transformation of the old." Madison wrote these words during the struggle to ratify the work of the Constitutional Convention in Philadelphia, and it is possible they merely reflect his desire to portray the proposed 1787 Constitution as less controversial.

Indeed, to critics of the new Constitution like Richard Henry Lee, it was not at all apparent that the Articles and the Constitution shared the same intellectual tradition. Consider, for example, the structure and powers of government under the Articles. The government they established consisted of a unicameral legislature, with executive and judicial functions handled by committees. Lee suggested that such a framework failed to meet the structural requirement for the separation of powers and, more broadly, republican government. He argued that under the Articles Congress was an executive power and thus should not wield independent taxing power. Did the Articles embody the modern principle of federalism that would be bedrock for the 1787 Constitution? Congress possessed some powers exclusively, but it lacked enforcement power. Moreover, while Article II restricted states' powers (by delegating to them only those powers not expressly granted to Congress), the states possessed powers often attributed to sovereign nations, such as the power to coin money and the power to naturalize citizens.

Some in Congress argued that the states should have the power to judge for themselves whether to comply with particular congressional requisitions—requisitions that textually speaking were binding on them. And some states pursued diplomatic relations with foreign countries, despite the Articles' ban on such acts.

Many of the men who framed the Articles of Confederation perceived that America consisted of a multiplicity of regional identities, defined by vastly different climates, economic institutions, social mores, religious practices, and even languages. As we will see in the next chapter, when they analyzed the factors, beyond the structure of political institutions and powers, necessary to establish and maintain a republic, they drew the conclusion that state identities of necessity had to be maintained. Many Anti-Federalists argued that the multiplicity of regional identities necessarily mitigated against a successful, unified national government on a continental scale. Federalists like Hamilton and Madison devoted considerable energy to countering this conclusion. Nonetheless, the question of national character was already being discussed and debated in the 1780s. One might argue that for Hector St. John de Crèvecoeur, equality was an important characteristic of life in America that helped to create a national identity and sustain a republican way of life. Likewise, Jefferson seemed to associate husbandry with republican government, locating in the breasts of yeoman farmers the virtues necessary to sustain liberty.[1] At the same time, Washington worried that a republic could not be sustained where "thirteen sovereign, independent, disunited States are in the habit of discussing & refusing compliance with" congressional requisitions. Indeed, he worried that the deficiencies of the Articles and the political exigencies they were producing might ultimately induce the people to once again embrace monarchical government.

---

1. Our use of the terms "republic" and "republicanism," along with related phrases such as "republican principles," warrants explanation. There is among scholars robust debate about the philosophical traditions that shaped the American political tradition. Scholars variously point to different traditions—including Old Whig constitutionalism, the Scottish Enlightenment, Protestant Christianity, as well as republicanism and Lockean liberalism—as the dominant influence in the American Founding. The chief scholarly argument, however, pits the classical republican tradition against a liberal tradition grounded in the writings of Thomas Hobbes and John Locke. While scholars generally argue that some or all of these sources influenced the Founding, most scholars argue in favor of republicanism or liberalism as the predominant philosophic influence. Scholars emphasizing republican influences claim that the political language of the Founding emphasized civic virtue and the common good, while articulating a strong fear about the dangers of political corruption. Scholars who stress the liberal tradition argue that the language of natural rights, which prioritized the individual, dominated eighteenth-century American discourse. Our use of the term "republicanism" in chapter introductions is not intended to signal our view of the debate. Rather, we employ the term more broadly, using it as shorthand to refer to the Founders' commitment to the rule of law, individual rights, and those civil dispositions they saw as essential to maintaining free government.

Articles of Confederation (1777, 1781)

To all to whom these Presents shall come, we the undersigned Delegates of the States affixed to our Names send greeting.

Articles of Confederation and perpetual Union between the states of New Hampshire, Massachusetts-bay Rhode Island and Providence Plantations, Connecticut, New York, New Jersey, Pennsylvania, Delaware, Maryland, Virginia, North Carolina, South Carolina and Georgia.

I

The Stile of this Confederacy shall be
"The United States of America."

II

Each state retains its sovereignty, freedom, and independence, and every power, jurisdiction, and right, which is not by this Confederation expressly delegated to the United States, in Congress assembled.

III

The said States hereby severally enter into a firm league of friendship with each other, for their common defense, the security of their liberties, and their mutual and general welfare, binding themselves to assist each other, against all force offered to, or attacks made upon them, or any of them, on account of religion, sovereignty, trade, or any other pretense whatever.

IV

The better to secure and perpetuate mutual friendship and intercourse among the people of the different States in this Union, the free inhabitants of each of these States, paupers, vagabonds, and fugitives from justice excepted, shall be entitled to all privileges and immunities of free citizens in the several States; and the people of each State shall free ingress and regress to and from any other State, and shall enjoy therein all the privileges of trade and commerce, subject to the same duties, impositions, and restrictions as the inhabitants thereof respectively, provided that such restrictions shall not extend so far as to prevent the removal of property imported into any State, to any other State, of which the owner is an inhabitant; provided also that no imposition, duties or restriction shall be laid by any State, on the property of the United States, or either of them.

If any person guilty of, or charged with, treason, felony, or other high misdemeanor in any State, shall flee from justice, and be found in any of the United States, he shall, upon demand of the Governor or executive power of the State from which he fled, be delivered up and removed to the State having jurisdiction of his offense.

Full faith and credit shall be given in each of these States to the records, acts, and judicial proceedings of the courts and magistrates of every other State.

V

For the most convenient management of the general interests of the United States, delegates shall be annually appointed in such manner as the legislatures of each State shall direct, to meet in Congress on the first Monday in November, in every year, with a power reserved to each State to recall its delegates, or any of them, at any time within the year, and to send others in their stead for the remainder of the year.

No State shall be represented in Congress by less than two, nor more than seven members; and no person shall be capable of being a delegate for more than three years in any term of six years; nor shall any person, being a delegate, be capable of holding any office under the United States, for which he, or another for his benefit, receives any salary, fees or emolument of any kind.

Each State shall maintain its own delegates in a meeting of the States, and while they act as members of the committee of the States.

In determining questions in the United States in Congress assembled, each State shall have one vote.

Freedom of speech and debate in Congress shall not be impeached or questioned in any court or place out of Congress, and the members of Congress shall be protected in their persons from arrests or imprisonments, during the time of their going to and from, and attendence on Congress, except for treason, felony, or breach of the peace.

VI

No State, without the consent of the United States in Congress assembled, shall send any embassy to, or receive any embassy from, or enter into any conference, agreement, alliance or treaty with any King, Prince or State; nor shall any person holding any office of profit or trust under the United States, or any of them, accept any present, emolument, office or title of any kind whatever from any King, Prince or foreign State; nor shall the United States in Congress assembled, or any of them, grant any title of nobility.

No two or more States shall enter into any treaty, confederation or alliance whatever between them, without the consent of the United States in Congress assembled, specifying accurately the purposes for which the same is to be entered into, and how long it shall continue.

No State shall lay any imposts or duties, which may interfere with any stipulations in treaties, entered into by the United States in Congress assembled, with any King, Prince or State, in pursuance of any treaties already proposed by Congress, to the courts of France and Spain.

No vessel of war shall be kept up in time of peace by any State, except such number only, as shall be deemed necessary by the United States in Congress assembled, for the defense of such State, or its trade; nor shall any body of forces be kept up by any State in time of peace, except such number only, as in the judgement of the United States in Congress assembled, shall be deemed requisite to garrison the forts necessary for the defense of such State; but every State shall always keep up a well-regulated and disciplined militia, sufficiently armed and accoutered, and shall provide and constantly have ready for use, in public stores, a due number of field pieces and tents, and a proper quantity of arms, ammunition and camp equipage.

No State shall engage in any war without the consent of the United States in Congress assembled, unless such State be actually invaded by enemies, or shall have received certain advice of a resolution being formed by some nation of Indians to invade such State, and the danger is so imminent as not to admit of a delay till the United States in Congress assembled can be consulted; nor shall any State grant commissions to any ships or vessels of war, nor letters of marque or reprisal, except it be after a declaration of war by the United States in Congress assembled, and then only against the Kingdom or State and the subjects thereof, against which war has been so declared, and under such regulations as shall be established by the United States in Congress assembled, unless such State be infested by pirates, in which case vessels of war may be fitted out for that occasion, and kept so long as the danger shall continue, or until the United States in Congress assembled shall determine otherwise.

VII

When land forces are raised by any State for the common defense, all officers of or under the rank of colonel, shall be appointed by the legislature of each State respectively, by whom such forces shall be raised, or in such manner as such State shall direct, and all vacancies shall be filled up by the State which first made the appointment.

VIII

All charges of war, and all other expenses that shall be incurred for the common defense or general welfare, and allowed by the United States in Congress assembled, shall be defrayed out of a common treasury, which shall be supplied by the several States in proportion to the value of all land within each State, granted or surveyed for any person, as such land and the buildings and improvements thereon shall be estimated according to such mode as the United States in Congress assembled, shall from time to time direct and appoint.

The taxes for paying that proportion shall be laid and levied by the authority and direction of the legislatures of the several States within the time agreed upon by the United States in Congress assembled.

IX

The United States in Congress assembled, shall have the sole and exclusive right and power of determining on peace and war, except in the cases mentioned in the sixth article—of sending and receiving ambassadors—entering into treaties and alliances, provided that no treaty of commerce shall be made whereby the legislative power of the respective States shall be restrained from imposing such imposts and duties on foreigners, as their own people are subjected to, or from prohibiting the exportation or importation of any species of goods or commodities whatsoever—of establishing rules for deciding in all cases, what captures on land or water shall be legal, and in what manner prizes taken by land or naval forces in the service of the United States shall be divided or appropriated—of granting letters of marque and reprisal in times of peace—appointing courts for the trial of piracies and felonies committed on the high seas and establishing courts for receiving and determining final appeals in all cases of captures, provided that no member of Congress shall be appointed a judge of any of the said courts.

The United States in Congress assembled shall also be the last resort on appeal in all disputes and differences now subsisting or that hereafter may arise between two or more States concerning boundary, jurisdiction or any other causes whatever; which authority shall always be exercised in the manner following. Whenever the legislative or executive authority or lawful agent of any State in controversy with another shall present a petition to Congress stating the matter in question and praying for a hearing, notice thereof shall be given by order of Congress to the legislative or executive authority of the other State in controversy, and a day assigned for the appearance of the parties by their lawful agents, who shall then be directed to appoint by joint consent, commissioners or judges to constitute a court for hearing and determining the matter in question: but if they cannot agree, Congress shall name three persons out of each of the United States, and from the list of such persons each party shall alternately strike out one, the petitioners beginning, until the number shall be reduced to thirteen; and from that number not less than seven, nor more than nine names as Congress shall direct, shall in the presence of Congress be drawn out by lot, and the persons whose names shall be so drawn or any five of them, shall be commissioners or judges, to hear and finally determine the controversy, so always as a major part of the judges who shall hear the cause shall agree in the determination: and if either party shall neglect to attend at the day appointed, without showing reasons, which Congress shall judge sufficient, or being present shall refuse to strike, the Congress shall proceed to nominate three persons out of each State, and the secretary of Congress shall strike in behalf of such party absent or refusing; and the judgement and sentence of the court to be appointed, in the manner before prescribed, shall be final and conclusive; and if any of the parties shall refuse to submit to the authority of such court, or to appear or defend their claim or cause, the court shall nevertheless proceed to pronounce sentence, or judgement, which shall in like manner be final and decisive, the judgement or sentence and other proceedings being in either case transmitted to Congress, and lodged among the acts of Congress for the security of the parties concerned: provided that every commissioner, before he sits in judgement, shall take an oath to be administered by one of the judges of the supreme or superior court of the State, where the cause shall be tried, "well and truly to hear and determine the matter in question, according to the best of his judgement, without favor, affection or hope of reward": provided also, that no State shall be deprived of territory for the benefit of the United States.

All controversies concerning the private right of soil claimed under different grants of two or more States, whose jurisdictions as they may respect such lands, and the States which passed such grants are adjusted, the said grants or either of them being at the same time claimed to have originated antecedent to such settlement of jurisdiction, shall on the petition of either party to the Congress of the United States, be finally determined as near as may be in the same manner as is before prescribed for deciding disputes respecting territorial jurisdiction between different States.

The United States in Congress assembled shall also have the sole and exclusive right and power of regulating the alloy and value of coin struck by their own authority, or by that of the respective States—fixing the standards of weights and measures throughout the United States—regulating the trade and managing all affairs with the Indians, not members of any of the States, provided that the legislative right of any State within its own limits be not infringed or violated—establishing or regulating post offices from one State to another, throughout all the United States, and exacting such postage on the papers passing through the same as may be requisite to defray the expenses of the said office—appointing all officers of the land forces, in the service of the United States, excepting regimental officers—appointing all the officers of the naval forces, and commissioning all officers whatever in the service of the United States—making rules for the government and regulation of the said land and naval forces, and directing their operations.

The United States in Congress assembled shall have authority to appoint a committee, to sit in the recess of Congress, to be denominated "A Committee of the States," and to consist of one delegate from each State; and to appoint such other committees and civil officers as may be necessary for managing the general affairs of the United States under their direction—to appoint one of their members to preside, provided that no person be allowed to serve in the office of president more than one year in any term of three years; to ascertain the necessary sums of money to be raised for the service of the United States, and to appropriate and apply the same for defraying the public expenses—to borrow money, or emit bills on the credit of the United States, transmitting every half-year to the respective States an account of the sums of money so borrowed or emitted—to build and equip a navy—to agree upon the number of land forces, and to make requisitions from each State for its quota, in proportion to the number of white inhabitants in such State; which requisition shall be binding, and thereupon the legislature of each State shall appoint the regimental officers, raise the men and cloath, arm and equip them in a solid-like manner, at the expense of the United States; and the officers and men so cloathed, armed and equipped shall march to the place appointed, and within the time agreed on by the United States in Congress assembled. But if the United States in Congress assembled shall, on consideration of circumstances judge proper that any State should not raise men, or should raise a smaller number of men than the quota thereof, such extra number shall be raised, officered, cloathed, armed and equipped in the same manner as the quota of each State, unless the legislature of such State shall judge that such extra number cannot be safely spread out in the same, in which case they shall raise, officer, cloath, arm and equip as many of such extra number as they judge can be safely spared. And the officers and men so cloathed, armed, and equipped, shall march to the place appointed, and within the time agreed on by the United States in Congress assembled.

The United States in Congress assembled shall never engage in a war, nor grant letters of marque or reprisal in time of peace, nor enter into any treaties or alliances, nor coin money, nor regulate the value thereof, nor ascertain the sums and expenses necessary for the defense and welfare of the United States, or any of them, nor emit bills, nor borrow money on the credit of the United States, nor appropriate money, nor agree upon the number of vessels of war, to be built or purchased, or the number of land or sea forces to be raised, nor appoint a commander in chief of the army or navy, unless nine States assent to the same: nor shall a question on any other point, except for adjourning from day to day be determined, unless by the votes of the majority of the United States in Congress assembled.

The Congress of the United States shall have power to adjourn to any time within the year, and to any place within the United States, so that no period of adjournment be for a longer duration than the space of six months, and shall publish the journal of their proceedings monthly, except such parts thereof relating to treaties, alliances or military operations, as in their judgement require secrecy; and the yeas and nays of the delegates of each State on any question shall be entered on the journal, when it is desired by any delegates of a State, or any of them, at his or their request shall be furnished with a transcript of the said journal, except such parts as are above excepted, to lay before the legislatures of the several States.

X

The Committee of the States, or any nine of them, shall be authorized to execute, in the recess of Congress, such of the powers of Congress as the United States in Congress assembled, by the consent of the nine States, shall from time to time think expedient to vest them with; provided that no power be delegated to the said Committee, for the exercise of which, by the Articles of Confederation, the voice of nine States in the Congress of the United States assembled be requisite.

XI

Canada acceding to this confederation, and adjoining in the measures of the United States, shall be admitted into, and entitled to all the advantages of this Union; but no other colony shall be admitted into the same, unless such admission be agreed to by nine States.

XII

All bills of credit emitted, monies borrowed, and debts contracted by, or under the authority of Congress, before the assembling of the United States, in pursuance of the present confederation, shall be deemed and considered as a charge against the United States, for payment and satisfaction whereof the said United States, and the public faith are hereby solemnly pledged.

XIII

Every State shall abide by the determination of the United States in Congress assembled, on all questions which by this confederation are submitted to them. And the Articles of this Confederation shall be inviolably observed by every State, and the Union shall be perpetual; nor shall any alteration at any time hereafter be made in any of them; unless such alteration be agreed to in a Congress of the United States, and be afterwards confirmed by the legislatures of every State.

And Whereas it hath pleased the Great Governor of the World to incline the hearts of the legislatures we respectively represent in Congress, to approve of, and to authorize us to ratify the said Articles of Confederation and perpetual Union. Know Ye that we the undersigned delegates, by virtue of the power and authority to us given for that purpose, do by these presents, in the name and in behalf of our respective constituents, fully and entirely ratify and confirm each and every of the said Articles of Confederation and perpetual Union, and all and singular the matters and things therein contained: And we do further solemnly plight and engage the faith of our respective constituents, that they shall abide by the determinations of the United States in Congress assembled, on all questions, which by the said Confederation are submitted to them. And that the Articles thereof shall be inviolably observed by the States we respectively represent, and that the Union shall be perpetual.

In Witness whereof we have hereunto set our hands in Congress. Done at Philadelphia in the State of Pennsylvania the ninth day of July in the Year of our Lord One Thousand Seven Hundred and Seventy-Eight, and in the Third Year of the independence of America.

[Agreed to by Congress 15 November 1777 In force after ratification by Maryland, 1 March 1781]

Alexander Hamilton

Letter to James Duane (September 3, 1780)

Dr. Sir

Agreeably to your request and my promise I sit down to give you my ideas of the defects of our present system, and the changes necessary to save us from ruin. They may perhaps be the reveries of a projector rather than the sober views of a politician. You will judge of them, and make what use you please of them.

The fundamental defect is a want of power in Congress. It is hardly worth while to show in what this consists, as it seems to be universally acknowledged, or to point out how it has happened, as the only question is how to remedy it. It may however be said that it has originated from three causes—an excess of the spirit of liberty which has made the particular states show a jealousy of all power not in their own hands; and this jealousy has led them to exercise a right of judging in the last resort of the measures recommended by Congress, and of acting according to their own opinions of their propriety or necessity, a diffidence in Congress of their own powers, by which they have been timid and indecisive in their resolutions, constantly making concessions to the states, till they have scarcely left themselves the shadow of power; a want of sufficient means at their disposal to answer the public exigencies and of vigor to draw forth those means; which have occasioned them to depend on the states individually to fulfil their engagements with the army, and the consequence of which has been to ruin their influence and credit with the army, to establish its dependence on each state separately rather than *on them,* that is rather than on the whole collectively. [. . .]

But the confederation itself is defective and requires to be altered; it is neither fit for war, nor peace. The idea of an uncontrollable sovereignty in each state, over its internal police, will defeat the other powers given to Congress, and make our union feeble and precarious. There are instances without number, where acts necessary for the general good, and which rise out of the powers given to Congress must interfere with the internal police of the states, and there are as many instances in which the particular states by arrangements of internal police can effectually though indirectly counteract the arrangements of Congress. You have already had examples of this for which I refer you to your own memory.

The confederation gives the states individually too much influence in the affairs of the army; they should have nothing to do with it. The entire formation and disposal of our military forces ought to belong to Congress. It is an essential cement of the union; and it ought to be the policy of Congress to destroy all ideas of state attachments in the army and make it look up wholly to them. For this purpose all appointments promotions and provisions whatsoever ought to be made by them. It may be apprehended that this may be dangerous to liberty. But nothing appears more evident to me, than that we run much greater risk of having a weak and disunited federal government, than one which will be able to usurp upon the rights of the people. Already some of the lines of the army would obey their states in opposition to Congress notwithstanding the pains we have taken to preserve the unity of the army—if any thing would hinder this it would be the personal influence of the General, a melancholy and mortifying consideration.

The forms of our state constitutions must always give them great weight in our affairs and will make it too difficult to bend them to the persuit of a common interest, too easy to oppose whatever they do not like and to form partial combinations subversive of the general one. There is a wide difference between our situation and that of an empire under one simple form of government, distributed into counties provinces or districts, which have no legislatures but merely magistratical bodies to execute the laws of a common sovereign. Here the danger is that the sovereign will have too much power to oppress the parts of which it is composed. In our case, that of an empire composed of confederated states each with a government completely organised within itself, having all the means to draw its subjects to a close dependence on itself—the danger is directly the reverse. It is that the common sovereign will not have power sufficient to unite the different members together, and direct the common forces to the interest and happiness of the whole. [. . .]

Our own experience should satisfy us. We have felt the difficulty of drawing out the resources of the country and inducing the states to combine in equal exertions for the common cause. The ill success of our last attempt is striking. Some have done a great deal, others little or scarcely any thing. The disputes about boundaries &c. testify how flattering a prospect we have of future tranquillity, if we do not frame in time a confederacy capable of deciding the differences and compelling the obedience of the respective members.

The confederation too gives the power of the purse too intirely to the state legislatures. It should provide perpetual funds in the disposal of Congress—by a land tax, poll tax, or the like. All imposts upon commerce ought to be laid by Congress and appropriated to their use, for without certain revenues, a government can have no power; that power, which holds the purse strings absolutely, must rule. This seems to be a medium, which without making Congress altogether independent will tend to give reality to its authority.

Another defect in our system is want of method and energy in the administration. This has partly resulted from the other defect, but in a great degree from prejudice and the want of a proper executive. Congress have kept the power too much into their own hands and have meddled too much with details of every sort. Congress is properly a deliberative corps and it forgets itself when it attempts to play the executive. It is impossible such a body, numerous as it is, constantly fluctuating, can ever act with sufficient decision, or with system. Two thirds of the members, one half the time, cannot know what has gone before them or what connection the subject in hand has to what has been transacted on former occasions. The members, who have been more permanent, will only give information, that promotes the side they espouse, in the present case, and will as often mislead as enlighten. The variety of business must distract, and the proneness of every assembly to debate must at all times delay.

Lately Congress, convinced of these inconveniences, have gone into the measure of appointing boards. But this is in my opinion a bad plan. A single man, in each department of the administration, would be greatly preferable. It would give us a chance of more knowledge, more activity, more responsibility and of course more zeal and attention. Boards partake of a part of the inconveniences of larger assemblies. Their decisions are slower their energy less their responsibility more diffused. They will not have the same abilities and knowledge as an administration by single men. Men of the first pretensions will not so readily engage in them, because they will be less conspicuous, of less importance, have less opportunity of distinguishing themselves. The members of boards will take less pains to inform themselves and arrive to eminence, because they have fewer motives to do it. All these reasons conspire to give a preference to the plan of vesting the great executive departments of the state in the hands of individuals. As these men will be of course at all times under the direction of Congress, we shall blend the advantages of a monarchy and republic in our constitution. [. . .]

A third defect is the fluctuating constitution of our army. This has been a pregnant source of evil; all our military misfortunes, three fourths of our civil embarrassments are to be ascribed to it. The General has so fully enumerated the mischief of it in a late letter [. . .] to Congress that I could only repeat what he has said, and will therefore refer you to that letter.

The imperfect and unequal provision made for the army is a fourth defect which you will find delineated in the same letter. Without a speedy change the army must dissolve; it is now a mob, rather than an army, without cloathing, without pay, without provision, without morals, without discipline. We begin to hate the country for its neglect of us; the country begins to hate us for our oppressions of them. Congress have long been jealous of us; we have now lost all confidence in them, and give the worst construction to all they do. Held together by the slenderest ties we are ripening for a dissolution.

The present mode of supplying the army—by state purchases—is not one of the least considerable defects of our system. It is too precarious a dependence, because the states will never be sufficiently impressed with our necessities. Each will make its own ease a primary object, the supply of the army a secondary one. The variety of channels through which the business is transacted will multiply the number of persons employed and the opportunities of embezzling public money. From the popular spirit on which most of the governments turn, the state agents, will be men of less character and ability, nor will there be so rigid a responsibility among them as there might easily be among those in the employ of the continent, of course not so much diligence care or economy. Very little of the money raised in the several states will go into the Continental treasury, on pretence, that it is all exhausted in providing the quotas of supplies, and the public will be without funds for the other demands of governments. The expence will be ultimately much greater and the advantages much smaller. We actually feel the insufficiency of this plan and have reason to dread under it a ruinous extremity of want. [. . .]

I shall now propose the remedies, which appear to me applicable to our circumstances, and necessary to extricate our affairs from their present deplorable situation.

The first step must be to give Congress powers competent to the public exigencies. This may happen in two ways, one by resuming and exercising the discretionary powers I suppose to have been originally vested in them for the safety of the states and resting their conduct on the candor of their country men and the necessity of the conjuncture: the other by calling immediately a convention of all the states with full authority to conclude finally upon a general confederation, stating to them beforehand explicity the evils arising from a want of power in Congress, and the impossibility of supporting the contest on its present footing, that the delegates may come possessed of proper sentiments as well as proper authority to give to the meeting. Their commission should include a right of vesting Congress with the whole or a proportion of the unoccupied lands, to be employed for the purpose of raising a revenue, reserving the jurisdiction to the states by whom they are granted.

The first plan, I expect will be thought too bold an expedient by the generality of Congress; and indeed their practice hitherto has so rivetted the opinion of their want of power, that the success of this experiment may very well be doubted.

I see no objection to the other mode, that has any weight in competition with the reasons for it. The Convention should assemble the 1st of November next, the sooner, the better; our disorders are too violent to admit of a common or lingering remedy. The reasons for which I require them to be vested with plenipotentiary authority are that the business may suffer no delay in the execution, and may in reality come to effect. A convention may agree upon a confederation; the states individually hardly ever will. We must have one at all events, and a vigorous one if we mean to succeed in the contest and be happy hereafter. As I said before, to engage the states to comply with this mode, Congress ought to confess to them plainly and unanimously the impracticability of supporting our affairs on the present footing and without a solid coercive union. I ask that the Convention should have a power of vesting the whole or a part of the unoccupied land in Congress, because it is necessary that body should have some property as a fund for the arrangements of finance; and I know of no other land that can be given them.

The confederation in my opinion should give Congress complete sovereignty; except as to that part of internal police, which relates to the rights of property and life among individuals and to raising money by internal taxes. It is necessary, that every thing, belonging to this, should be regulated by the state legislatures. Congress should have complete sovereignty in all that relates to war, peace, trade, finance, and to the management of foreign affairs, the right of declaring war of raising armies, officering, paying them, directing their motions in every respect, of equipping fleets and doing the same with them, of building fortifications arsenals magazines &c. &c., of malting peace on such conditions as they think proper, of regulating trade, determining with what countries it shall be carried on, granting indulgences laying prohibitions on all the articles of export or import, imposing duties granting bounties & premiums for raising exporting importing and applying to their own use the product of these duties, only giving credit to the states on whom they are raised in the general account of revenues and expences, instituting Admiralty courts &c., of coining money, establishing banks on such terms, and with such privileges as they think proper, appropriating funds and doing whatever else relates to the operations of finance transacting every thing with foreign nations making alliances offensive and defensive, treaties of commerce, &c. &c.

The confederation should provide certain perpetual revenues, productive and easy of collection, a land tax, poll tax or the like, which together with the duties on trade and the unlocated lands would give Congress a substantial existence, and a stable foundation for their schemes of finance. What more supplies were necessary should be occasionally demanded of the states, in the present mode of quotas.

The second step I would recommend is that Congress should instantly appoint the following great officers of state—A secretary for foreign affairs—A President of war—A President of Marine—A Financier—A President of trade; instead of this last a board of Trade may be preferable as the regulations of trade are slow and gradual and require prudence and experience (more than other qualities), for which boards are very well adapted.

Congress should choose for these offices, men of the first abilities, property and character in the continent—and such as have had the best opportunities of being acquainted with the several branches. [. . .]

These offices should have nearly the same powers and functions as those in France analogous to them, and each should be chief in his department, with subordinate boards composed of assistant clerks &c. to execute his orders.

In my opinion a plan of this land would be of inconceivable utility to our affairs; its benefits would be very speedily felt. It would give new life and energy to the operations of government. Business would be conducted with dispatch method and system. A million of abuses now existing would be corrected, and judicious plans would be formed and executed for the public good. [. . .]

And, in future, My Dear Sir, two things let me recommend, as fundamental rules for the conduct of Congress—to attach the army to them by every motive, to maintain an air of authority (not domineering) in all their measures with the states. The manner in which a thing is done has more influence than is commonly imagined. Men are governed by opinion; this opinion is as much influenced by appearances as by realities; if a Government appears to be confident of its own powers, it is the surest way to inspire the same confidence in others; if it is diffident, it may be certain, there will be a still greater diffidence in others, and that its authority will not only be distrusted, controverted, but contemned.

I wish too Congress would always consider that a kindness consists as much in the manner as in the thing: the best things done hesitatingly and with an ill grace lose their effect, and produce disgust rather than satisfaction or gratitude. In what Congress have at any time done for the army, they have commonly been too late: They have seemed to yield to importunity rather than to sentiments of justice or to a regard to the accommodation of their troops. An attention to this idea is of more importance than it may be thought. I who have seen all the workings and progress of the present discontents, am convinced, that a want of this has not been among the most inconsiderable causes.

You will perceive My Dear Sir this letter is hastily written and with a confidential freedom, not as to a member of Congress, whose feelings may be sore at the prevailing clamours; but as to a friend who is in a situation to remedy public disorders, who wishes for nothing so much as truth, and who is desirous of information, even from those less capable of judging than himself. I have not even time to correct and copy and only enough to add that I am very truly and affectionately D Sir

Your most Obed ser

A. Hamilton

Liberty Pole

James Madison

Letter to Thomas Jefferson (1781)

The necessity of arming Congress with coercive powers arises from the shameful deficiency of some of the States which are most capable of yielding their apportioned supplies, and the military exactions to which others already exhausted by the enemy and our own troops are in consequence exposed. Without such powers too in the general government, the whole confederacy may be insulted and the most salutary measures frustrated by the most inconsiderable State in the Union. At a time when all the other States were submitting to the loss and inconveniency of an embargo on their exports, Delaware absolutely declined coming into the measure, and not only defeated the general object of it, but enriched herself at the expence of those who did their duty.

The expediency however of making the proposed application to the States will depend on the probability of their complying with it. If they should refuse, Congress will be in a worse situation than at present: for as the confederation now stands, and according to the nature even of alliances much less intimate, there is an implied right of coer[c]io[n] against the delinquent party, and the exercise of it by Congress whenever a palpable necessity occurs will probably be acquiesced in.

It may be asked perhaps by what means Congress could exercise such a power if the States were to invest them with it? As long as there is a regular army on foot a small detachment from it, acting under Civil authority, would at any time render a voluntary contribution of supplies due from a State, an eligible alternative. But there is a still more easy and efficacious mode. The situation of most of the States is such, that two or three vessels of force employed against their trade will make it their interest to yield prompt obidience to all just requisitions on them. With respect to those States that have little or no foreign trade of their own it is provided that all inland trade with such states as supply them with foreign merchandize may be interdicted and the concurrence of the latter may be enforced in case of refusal by operations on their foreign trade.

There is a collateral reason which interests the States who are feeble in maritime resources, in such a plan. If a naval armament was considered as the proper instrument of general Government, it would be both preserved in a respectable State in time of peace, and it would be an object to mann it with Citizens taken in due proportions from every State. A Navy so formed and under the orders of the general Council of the States, would not only be a guard against aggression & insults from abroad; but without it what is to protect the Southern States for many years to come against the insults & aggressions of their N. Brethren.

I am Dear [Sir] Yr. sincere friend & obt. servt.

J. Madison Junr.

Hector St. Jean de Crèvecoeur

Letters from an American Farmer (1782)

Letter III: What Is an American?

I wish I could be acquainted with the feelings and thoughts which must agitate the heart and present themselves to the mind of an enlightened Englishman, when he first lands on this continent. He must greatly rejoice that he lived at a time to see this fair country discovered and settled; he must necessarily feel a share of national pride, when he views the chain of settlements which embellishes these extended shores. When he says to himself, this is the work of my countrymen, who, when convulsed by factions, afflicted by a variety of miseries and wants, restless and impatient, took refuge here. They brought along with them their national genius, to which they principally owe what liberty they enjoy, and what substance they possess. Here he sees the industry of his native country displayed in a new manner, and traces in their works the embrios of all the arts, sciences, and ingenuity which flourish in Europe. Here he beholds fair cities, substantial villages, extensive fields, an immense country filled with decent houses, good roads, orchards, meadows, and bridges, where an hundred years ago all was wild, woody and uncultivated! What a train of pleasing ideas this fair spectacle must suggest; it is a prospect which must inspire a good citizen with the most heartfelt pleasure. The difficulty consists in the manner of viewing so extensive a scene. He is arrived on a new continent; a modern society offers itself to his contemplation, different from what he had hitherto seen. It is not composed, as in Europe, of great lords who possess every thing and of a herd of people who have nothing. Here are no aristocratical families, no courts, no kings, no bishops, no ecclesiastical dominion, no invisible power giving to a few a very visible one; no great manufacturers employing thousands, no great refinements of luxury. The rich and the poor are not so far removed from each other as they are in Europe. Some few towns excepted, we are all tillers of the earth, from Nova Scotia to West Florida. We are a people of cultivators, scattered over an immense territory communicating with each other by means of good roads and navigable rivers, united by the silken bands of mild government, all respecting the laws, without dreading their power, because they are equitable. We are all animated with the spirit of an industry which is unfettered and unrestrained, because each person works for himself. If he travels through our rural districts he views not the hostile castle, and the haughty mansion, contrasted with the clay-built hut and miserable cabin, where cattle and men help to keep each other warm, and dwell in meanness, smoke, and indigence. A pleasing uniformity of decent competence appears throughout our habitations. The meanest of our log-houses is a dry and comfortable habitation. Lawyer or merchant are the fairest titles our towns afford; that of a farmer is the only appellation of the rural inhabitants of our country. It must take some time ere he can reconcile himself to our dictionary, which is but short in words of dignity, and names of honour. There, on a Sunday, he sees a congregation of respectable farmers and their wives, all clad in neat homespun, well mounted, or riding in their own humble waggons. There is not among them an esquire, saving the unlettered magistrate. There he sees a parson as simple as his flock, a farmer who does not riot on the labour of others. We have no princes, for whom we toil, starve, and bleed: we are the most perfect society now existing in the world. Here man is free; as he ought to be; nor is this pleasing equality so transitory as many others are. Many ages will not see the shores of our great lakes replenished with inland nations, nor the unknown bounds of North America entirely peopled. Who can tell how far it extends? Who can tell the millions of men whom it will feed and contain? for no European foot has as yet travelled half the extent of this mighty continent!

The next wish of this traveller will be to know whence came all these people? they are mixture of English, Scotch, Irish, French, Dutch, Germans, and Swedes. From this promiscuous breed, that race now called Americans have arisen. The eastern provinces must indeed be excepted, as being the unmixed descendants of Englishmen. I have heard many wish that they had been more intermixed also: for my part, I am no wisher, and think it much better as it has happened. They exhibit a most conspicuous figure in this great and variegated picture; they too enter for a great share in the pleasing perspective displayed in these thirteen provinces. I know it is fashionable to reflect on them, but I respect them for what they have done; for the accuracy and wisdom with which they have settled their territory; for the decency of their manners; for their early love of letters; their ancient college, the first in this hemisphere; for their industry; which to me who am but a farmer, is the criterion of everything. There never was a people, situated as they are, who with so ungrateful a soil have done more in so short a time. Do you think that the monarchical ingredients which are more prevalent in other governments, have purged them from all foul stains? Their histories assert the contrary.

In this great American asylum, the poor of Europe have by some means met together, and in consequence of various causes; to what purpose should they ask one another what countrymen they are? Alas, two thirds of them had no country. Can a wretch who wanders about, who works and starves, whose life is a continual scene of sore affliction or pinching penury; can that man call England or any other kingdom his country? A country that had no bread for him, whose fields procured him no harvest, who met with nothing but the frowns of the rich, the severity of the laws, with jails and punishments; who owned not a single foot of the extensive surface of this planet? No! urged by a variety of motives, here they came. Every thing has tended to regenerate them; new laws, a new mode of living, a new social system; here they are become men: in Europe they were as so many useless plants, wanting vegetative mould, and refreshing showers; they withered, and were mowed down by want, hunger, and war; but now by the power of transplantation, like all other plants they have taken root and flourished! Formerly they were not numbered in any civil lists of their country, except in those of the poor; here they rank as citizens. By what invisible power has this surprising metamorphosis been performed? By that of the laws and that of their industry. The laws, the indulgent laws, protect them as they arrive, stamping on them the symbol of adoption; they receive ample rewards for their labours; these accumulated rewards procure them lands; those lands confer on them the title of freemen, and to that title every benefit is affixed which men can possibly require. This is the great operation daily performed by our laws. From whence proceed these laws? From our government. Whence the government? It is derived from the original genius and strong desire of the people ratified and confirmed by the crown. This is the great chain which links us all, this is the picture which every province exhibits. [. . .]

What attachment can a poor European emigrant have for a country where he had nothing? The knowledge of the language, the love of a few kindred as poor as himself, were the only cords that tied him: his country is now that which gives him land, bread, protection, and consequence: Ubi panis ibi patria ["Where bread is, there is one's country"], is the motto of all emigrants. What then is the American, this new man? He is either an European, or the descendant of an European, hence that strange mixture of blood, which you will find in no other country. I could point out to you a family whose grandfather was an Englishman, whose wife was Dutch, whose son married a French woman, and whose present four sons have now four wives of different nations. He is an American, who leaving behind him all his ancient prejudices and manners, receives new ones from the new mode of life he has embraced, the new government he obeys, and the new rank he holds. He becomes an American by being received in the broad lap of our great Alma Mater. Here individuals of all nations are melted into a new race of men, whose labours and posterity will one day cause great changes in the world. Americans are the western pilgrims, who are carrying along with them that great mass of arts, sciences, vigour, and industry which began long since in the east; they will finish the great circle. The Americans were once scattered all over Europe; here they are incorporated into one of the finest systems of population which has ever appeared, and which will hereafter become distinct by the power of the different climates they inhabit. The American ought therefore to love this country much better than that wherein either he or his forefathers were born. Here the rewards of his industry follow with equal steps the progress of his labour; his labour is founded on the basis of nature, self-interest; can it want a stronger allurement? Wives and children, who before in vain demanded of him a morsel of bread, now, fat and frolicsome, gladly help their father to clear those fields whence exuberant crops are to arise to feed and to clothe them all; without any part being claimed, either by a despotic prince, a rich abbot, or a mighty lord. Here religion demands but little of him; a small voluntary salary to the minister, and gratitude to God; can he refuse these? The American is a new man, who acts upon new principles; he must therefore entertain new ideas, and form new opinions. From involuntary idleness, servile dependence, penury, and useless labour, he has passed to toils of a very different nature, rewarded by ample subsistence.——This is an American. [. . .]

As I have endeavored to shew you how Europeans become Americans; it may not be disagreeable to shew you likewise how the various Christian sects introduced, wear out, and how religious indifference becomes prevalent. When any considerable number of a particular sect happen to dwell contiguous to each other, they immediately erect a temple, and there worship the Divinity agreeably to their own peculiar ideas. Nobody disturbs them. If any new sect springs up in Europe, it may happen that many of its professors will come and settle in America. As they bring their zeal with them, they are at liberty to make proselytes if they can, and to build a meeting and to follow the dictates of their consciences; for neither the government nor any other power interferes. If they are peaceable subjects, and are industrious, what is it to their neighbours how and in what manner they think fit to address their prayers to the Supreme Being? But if the sectaries are not settled close together, if they are mixed with other denominations, their zeal will cool for want of fuel, and will be extinguished in a little time. Then the Americans become as to religion, what they are as to country, allied to all. In them the name of Englishman, Frenchman, and European is lost, and in like manner, the strict modes of Christianity as practised in Europe are lost also. This effect will extend itself still farther hereafter, and though this may appear to you as a strange idea, yet it is a very true one. I shall be able perhaps hereafter to explain myself better, in the meanwhile, let the following example serve as my first justification.

Let us suppose you and I to be travelling; we observe that in this house, to the right, lives a Catholic, who prays to God as he has been taught, and believes in transubstantiation; he works and raises wheat, he has a large family of children, all hale and robust; his belief, his prayers offend nobody. About one mile farther on the same road, his next neighbour may be a good honest plodding German Lutheran, who addresses himself to the same God, the God of all, agreeably to the modes he has been educated in, and believes in consubstantiation; by so doing he scandalizes nobody; he also works in his fields, embellishes the earth, clears swamps, &c. What has the world to do with his Lutheran principles? He persecutes nobody, and nobody persecutes him, he visits his neighbours, and his neighbours visit him. Next to him lives a seceder, the most enthusiastic of all sectaries; his zeal is hot and fiery, but separated as he is from others of the same complexion, he has no congregation of his own to resort to, where he might cabal and mingle religious pride with worldly obstinacy. He likewise raises good crops, his house is handsomely painted, his orchard is one of the fairest in the neighbourhood. How does it concern the welfare of the country, or of the province at large, what this man's religious sentiments are, or really whether he has any at all? He is a good farmer, he is a sober, peaceable, good citizen: William Penn himself would not wish for more. This is the visible character, the invisible one is only guessed at, and is nobody's business. Next again lives a Low Dutchman, who implicitly believes the rules laid down by the synod of Dort. He conceives no other idea of a clergyman than that of an hired man; if he does his work well he will pay him the stipulated sum; if not he will dismiss him, and do without his sermons, and let his church be shut up for years. But notwithstanding this coarse idea, you will find his house and farm to be the neatest in all the country; and you will judge by his waggon and fat horses, that he thinks more of the affairs of this world than of those of the next. He is sober and laborious, therefore he is all he ought to be as to the affairs of this life; as for those of the next, he must trust to the great Creator. Each of these people instruct their children as well as they can, but these instructions are feeble compared to those which are given to the youth of the poorest class in Europe. Their children will therefore grow up less zealous and more indifferent in matters of religion than their parents. The foolish vanity, or rather the fury of making Proselytes, is unknown here; they have no time. The seasons call for all their attention, and thus in a few years, this mixed neighbourhood will exhibit a strange religious medley, that will be neither pure Catholicism nor pure Calvinism. A very perceptible indifference even in the first generation, will become apparent; and it may happen that the daughter of the Catholic will marry the son of the seceder, and settle by themselves at a distance from their parents. What religious education will they give their children? A very imperfect one. If there happens to be in the neighbourhood any place of worship, we will suppose a Quaker's meeting; rather than not shew their fine clothes, they will go to it, and some of them may perhaps attach themselves to that society. Others will remain in a perfect state of indifference; the children of these zealous parents will not be able to tell what their religious principles are, and their grandchildren still less. The neighborhood of a place of worship generally leads them to it, and the action of going thither, is the strongest evidence they can give of their attachment to any sect. The Quakers are the only people who retain a fondness for their own mode of worship; for be they ever so far separated from each other, they hold a sort of communion with the society, and seldom depart from its rules, at least in this country. Thus all sects are mixed as well as all nations; thus religious indifference is imperceptibly disseminated from one end of the continent to the other; which is at present one of the strongest characteristics of the Americans. Where this will reach no one can tell, perhaps it may leave a vacuum fit to receive other systems. Persecution, religious pride, the love of contradiction, are the food of what the world commonly calls religion. These motives have ceased here: zeal in Europe is confined; here it evaporates in the great distance it has to travel; there it is a grain of powder inclosed, here it burns away in the open air, and consumes without effect. [. . .]

Europe contains hardly any other distinctions but lords and tenants; this fair country alone is settled by freeholders, the possessors of the soil they cultivate, members of the government they obey, and the framers of their own laws, by means of their representatives. This is a thought which you have taught me to cherish; our difference from Europe, far from diminishing, rather adds to our usefulness and consequence as men and subjects. Had our forefathers remained there, they would only have crowded it, and perhaps prolonged those convulsions which had shook it so long. Every industrious European who transports himself here may be compared to a sprout growing at the foot of a great tree; it enjoys and draws but a little portion of sap; wrench it from the parent roots, transplant it, and it will become a tree bearing fruit also. Colonists are therefore entitled to the consideration due to the most useful subjects; a hundred families barely existing in some parts of Scotland, will here in six years, cause an annual exportation of 10,000 bushels of wheat: 100 bushels being but a common quantity for an industrious family to sell, if they cultivate good land. It is here then that the idle may be employed, the useless become useful, and the poor become rich; but by riches I do not mean gold and silver, we have but little of those metals; I mean a better sort of wealth, cleared lands, cattle, good houses, good cloaths, and an increase of people to enjoy them.

There is no wonder that this country has so many charms, and presents to Europeans so many temptations to remain in it. A traveller in Europe becomes a stranger as soon as he quits his own kingdom; but it is otherwise here. We know, properly speaking, no strangers; this is every person's country; the variety of our soils, situations, climates, governments, and produce, hath something which must please every body. No sooner does an European arrive, no matter of what condition, than his eyes are opened upon the fair prospect; he hears his language spoke, he retraces many of his own country manners, he perpetually hears the names of families and towns with which he is acquainted; he sees happiness and prosperity in all places disseminated; he meets with hospitality, kindness, and plenty every where; he beholds hardly any poor, he seldom hears of punishments and executions; and he wonders at the elegance of our towns, those miracles of industry and freedom. He cannot admire enough our rural districts, our convenient roads, good taverns, and our many accommodations; he involuntarily loves a country where every thing is so lovely. When in England, he was a mere Englishman; here he stands on a larger portion of the globe, not less than its fourth part, and may see the productions of the north, in iron and naval stores; the provisions of Ireland, the grain of Egypt, the indigo, the rice of China. He does not find, as in Europe, a crouded society, where every place is over-stocked; he does not feel that perpetual collision of parties, that difficulty of beginning, that contention which oversets so many. There is room for every body in America; has he any particular talent, or industry? he exerts it in order to procure a livelihood, and it succeeds. Is he a merchant? the avenues of trade are infinite; is he eminent in any respect? he will be employed and respected. Does he love a country life? pleasant farms present themselves; he may purchase what he wants, and thereby become an American farmer. Is he a labourer, sober and industrious? he need not go many miles, nor receive many informations before he will be hired, well fed at the table of his employer, and paid four or five times more than he can get in Europe. Does he want uncultivated lands? Thousands of acres present themselves, which he may purchase cheap. Whatever be his talents or inclinations, if they are moderate, he may satisfy them. I do not mean that every one who comes will grow rich in a little time; no, but he may procure an easy, decent maintenance, by his industry. Instead of starving he will be fed, instead of being idle he will have employment; and these are riches enough for such men as come over here. The rich stay in Europe, it is only the middling and the poor that emigrate. Would you wish to travel in independent idleness, from north to south, you will find easy access, and the most chearful reception at every house; society without ostentation, good cheer without pride, and every decent diversion which the country affords, with little expence. It is no wonder that the European who has lived here a few years, is desirous to remain; Europe with all its pomp, is not to be compared to this continent, for men of middle stations, or labourers.

An European, when he first arrives, seems limited in his intentions, as well as in his views, but he very suddenly alters his scale; two hundred miles formerly appeared a very great distance, it is now but a trifle; he no sooner breathes our air than he forms schemes, and embarks in designs he never would have thought of in his own country. There the plenitude of society confines many useful ideas, and often extinguishes the most laudable schemes which here ripen into maturity. Thus Europeans become Americans.

But how is this accomplished in that croud of low, indigent people, who flock here every year from all parts of Europe? I will tell you; they no sooner arrive than they immediately feel the good effects of that plenty of provisions we possess: they fare on our best food and they are kindly entertained; their talents, character, and peculiar industry are immediately inquired into; they find countrymen everywhere disseminated, let them come from whatever part of Europe. Let me select one as an epitome of the rest; he is hired, he goes to work, and works moderately; instead of being employed by a haughty person, he finds himself with his equal, placed at the substantial table of the farmer, or else at an inferior one as good; his wages are high, his bed is not like that bed of sorrow on which he used to lie: if he behaves with propriety, and is faithful, he is caressed, and becomes as it were a member of the family. He begins to feel the effects of a sort of resurrection; hitherto he had not lived, but simply vegetated; he now feels himself a man, because he is treated as such; the laws of his own country had overlooked him in his insignificancy; the laws of this cover him with their mantle. Judge what an alteration there must arise in the mind and thoughts of this man; he begins to forget his former servitude and dependence, his heart involuntarily swells and glows; this first swell inspires him with those new thoughts which constitute an American. What love can he entertain for a country where his existence was a burthen to him; if he's a generous good man, the love of this new adoptive parent will sink deep into his heart. He looks around, and sees many a prosperous person, who but a few years before was as poor as himself. This encourages him much, he begins to form some little scheme, the first, alas, he ever formed in his life. If he is wise he thus spends two or three years, in which time he acquires knowledge, the use of tools, the modes of working the lands, felling trees, &c. This prepares the foundation of a good name, the most useful acquisition he can make. He is encouraged, he has gained friends; he is advised and directed, he feels bold, he purchases some land; he gives all the money he has brought over, as well as what he has earned, and trusts to the God of harvests for the discharge of the rest. His good name procures him credit. He is now possessed of the deed, conveying to him and his posterity the fee simple and absolute property of two hundred acres of land, situated on such a river. What an epocha in this man's life! He is become a freeholder, from perhaps a German boor—he is now an American, a Pennsylvanian, an English subject. He is naturalized, his name is enrolled with those of the other citizens of the province. Instead of being a vagrant, he has a place of residence; he is called the inhabitant of such a county, or of such a district, and for the first time in his life counts for something; for hitherto he has been a cypher. I only repeat what I have heard man say, and no wonder their hearts should glow, and be agitated with a multitude of feelings, not easy to describe. From nothing to start into being; from a servant to the rank of a master; from being the slave of some despotic prince, to become a free man, invested with lands, to which every municipal blessing is annexed! What a change indeed! It is in consequence of that change that he becomes an American. This great metamorphosis has a double effect, it extinguishes all his European prejudices, he forgets that mechanism of subordination, that servility of disposition which poverty had taught him. [. . .]

After a foreigner from any part of Europe is arrived, and become a citizen; let him devoutly listen to the voice of our great parent, which says to him, "Welcome to my shores, distressed European; bless the hour in which thou didst see my verdant fields, my fair navigable rivers, and my green mountains! If thou wilt work, I have bread for thee; if thou wilt be honest, sober, and industrious, I have greater rewards to confer on thee—ease and independence. I will give thee fields to feed and cloath thee; a comfortable fireside to sit by, and tell thy children by what means thou hast prospered; and a decent bed to repose on. I shall endow thee beside with the immunities of a freeman. If thou wilt carefully educate thy children, teach them gratitude to God, and reverence to that government, that philanthropic government, which has collected here so many men and made them happy. I will also provide for thy progeny; and to every good man this ought to be the most holy, the most Powerful, the most earnest wish he can possibly form, as well as the most consolatory prospect when he dies. Go thou and work and till; thou shalt prosper, provided thou be just, grateful and industrious. [. . .]"

Thomas Jefferson

Notes on the State of Virginia (1782)

Query 14

[. . .] Many of the laws which were in force during the monarchy being relative merely to that form of government, or inculcating principles inconsistent with republicanism, the first assembly which met after the establishment of the commonwealth appointed a committee to revise the whole code, to reduce it into proper form and volume, and report it to the assembly. This work has been executed by three gentlemen, and reported; but probably will not be taken up till a restoration of peace shall leave to the legislature leisure to go through such a work.

The plan of the revisal was this. The common law of England, by which is meant, that part of the English law which was anterior to the date of the oldest statutes extant, is made the basis of the work. It was thought dangerous to attempt to reduce it to a text: it was therefore left to be collected from the usual monuments of it. Necessary alterations in that, and so much of the whole body of the British statutes, and of acts of assembly, as were thought proper to be retained, were digested into 126 new acts, in which simplicity of stile was aimed at, as far as was safe. The following are the most remarkable alterations proposed:

To change the rules of descent, so as that the lands of any person dying intestate shall be divisible equally among all his children, or other representatives, in equal degree.

To make slaves distributable among the next of kin, as other moveables.

To have all public expences, whether of the general treasury, or of a parish or county, (as for the maintenance of the poor, building bridges, courthouses, &c.) supplied by assessments on the citizens, in proportion to their property.

To hire undertakers for keeping the public roads in repair, and indemnify individuals through whose lands new roads shall be opened.

To define with precision the rules whereby aliens should become citizens, and citizens make themselves aliens.

To establish religious freedom on the broadest bottom.

To emancipate all slaves born after passing the act. The bill reported by the revisors does not itself contain this proposition; but an amendment containing it was prepared, to be offered to the legislature whenever the bill should be taken up, and further directing, that they should continue with their parents to a certain age, then be brought up, at the public expence, to tillage, arts or sciences, according to their geniusses, till the females should be eighteen, and the males twenty-one years of age, when they should be colonized to such place as the circumstances of the time should render most proper, sending them out with arms, implements of household and of the handicraft arts, feeds, pairs of the useful domestic animals, &c. to declare them a free and independent people, and extend to them our alliance and protection, till they shall have acquired strength; and to send vessels at the same time to other parts of the world for an equal number of white inhabitants; to induce whom to migrate hither, proper encouragements were to be proposed. It will probably be asked, Why not retain and incorporate the blacks into the state, and thus save the expence of supplying, by importation of white settlers, the vacancies they will leave? Deep rooted prejudices entertained by the whites; ten thousand recollections, by the blacks, of the injuries they have sustained; new provocations; the real distinctions which nature has made; and many other circumstances, will divide us into parties, and produce convulsions which will probably never end but in the extermination of the one or the other race.—To these objections, which are political, may be added others, which are physical and moral. The first difference which strikes us is that of colour. Whether the black of the negro resides in the reticular membrane between the skin and scarf-skin, or in the scarf-skin itself; whether it proceeds from the colour of the blood, the colour of the bile, or from that of some other secretion, the difference is fixed in nature, and is as real as if its seat and cause were better known to us. And is this difference of no importance? Is it not the foundation of a greater or less share of beauty in the two races? Are not the fine mixtures of red and white, the expressions of every passion by greater or less suffusions of colour in the one, preferable to that eternal monotony, which reigns in the countenances, that immoveable veil of black which covers all the emotions of the other race? Add to these, flowing hair, a more elegant symmetry of form, their own judgment in favour of the whites, declared by their preference of them, as uniformly as is the preference of the Oranootan for the black women over those of his own species. The circumstance of superior beauty, is thought worthy attention in the propagation of our horses, dogs, and other domestic animals; why not in that of man? Besides those of colour, figure, and hair, there are other physical distinctions proving a difference of race. They have less hair on the face and body. They secrete less by the kidnies, and more by the glands of the skin, which gives them a very strong and disagreeable odour. This greater degree of transpiration renders them more tolerant of heat, and less so of cold, than the whites. Perhaps too a difference of structure in the pulmonary apparatus, which a late ingenious[1] experimentalist has discovered to be the principal regulator of animal heat, may have disabled them from extricating, in the act of inspiration, so much of that fluid from the outer air, or obliged them in expiration, to part with more of it. They seem to require less sleep. A black, after hard labour through the day,

1. Crawford.

will be induced by the slightest amusements to sit up till midnight, or later, though knowing he must be out with the first dawn of the morning. They are at least as brave, and more adventuresome. But this may perhaps proceed from a want of forethought, which prevents their seeing a danger till it be present. When present, they do not go through it with more coolness or steadiness than the whites. They are more ardent after their female: but love seems with them to be more an eager desire, than a tender delicate mixture of sentiment and sensation. Their griefs are transient. Those numberless afflictions, which render it doubtful whether heaven has given life to us in mercy or in wrath, are less felt, and sooner forgotten with them. In general, their existence appears to participate more of sensation than reflection. To this must be ascribed their disposition to sleep when abstracted from their diversions, and unemployed in labour. An animal whose body is at rest, and who does not reflect, must be disposed to sleep of course. Comparing them by their faculties of memory, reason, and imagination, it appears to me, that in memory they are equal to the whites; in reason much inferior, as I think one could scarcely be found capable of tracing and comprehending the investigations of Euclid; and that in imagination they are dull, tasteless, and anomalous. It would be unfair to follow them to Africa for this investigation. We will consider them here, on the same stage with the whites, and where the facts are not apocryphal on which a judgment is to be formed. It will be right to make great allowances for the difference of condition, of education, of conversation, of the sphere in which they move. Many millions of them have been brought to, and born in America. Most of them indeed have been confined to tillage, to their own homes, and their own society: yet many have been so situated, that they might have availed themselves of the conversation of their masters; many have been brought up to the handicraft arts, and from that circumstance have always been associated with the whites. Some have been liberally educated, and all have lived in countries where the arts and sciences are cultivated to a considerable degree, and have had before their eyes samples of the best works from abroad. The Indians, with no advantages of this kind, will often carve figures on their pipes not destitute of design and merit. They will crayon out an animal, a plant, or a country, so as to prove the existence of a germ in their minds which only wants cultivation. They astonish you with strokes of the most sublime oratory; such as prove their reason and sentiment strong, their imagination glowing and elevated. But never yet could I find that a black had uttered a thought above the level of plain narration; never see even an elementary trait of painting or sculpture. In music they are more generally gifted than the whites with accurate ears for tune and time, and they have been found capable of imagining a small catch.[2] Whether they will be equal to the composition of a more extensive run of melody, or of complicated harmony, is yet to be proved. Misery is often the parent of the most affecting touches in poetry.—Among the blacks is misery enough, God knows, but no poetry. Love is the peculiar; oestrum of the poet. Their love is ardent, but it kindles the senses only, not the imagination. Religion indeed has produced a Phyllis Whately; but it could not produce a poet. The compositions published under her name are below the dignity of criticism. The heroes of the Dunciad are to her, as Hercules to the author of that poem. Ignatius Sancho has approached nearer to merit in composition; yet his letters do more honour to the heart than the head. They breathe the purest effusions of friendship and general philanthropy, and shew how great a degree of the latter may be compounded with strong religious zeal. He is often happy in the turn of his compliments, and his stile is easy and familiar, except when he affects a Shandean fabrication of words. But his imagination is wild and extravagant, escapes incessantly from every restraint of reason and taste, and, in the course of its vagaries, leaves a tract of thought as incoherent and eccentric, as is the course of a meteor through the sky. His subjects should often have led him to a process of sober reasoning: yet we find him always substituting sentiment for demonstration. Upon the whole, though we admit him to the first place among those of his own colour who have presented themselves to the public judgment, yet when we compare him with the

---

2. The instrument proper to them is the Banjar, which they brought hither from Africa, and which is the original of the guitar, its chords being precisely the four lower chords of the guitar.

writers of the race among whom he lived, and particularly with the epistolary class, in which he has taken his own stand, we are compelled to enroll him at the bottom of the column. This criticism supposes the letters published under his name to be genuine, and to have received amendment from no other hand; points which would not be of easy investigation. The improvement of the blacks in body and mind, in the first instance of their mixture with the whites, has been observed by every one, and proves that their inferiority is not the effect merely of their condition of life. We know that among the Romans, about the Augustan age especially, the condition of their slaves was much more deplorable than that of the blacks on the continent of America. The two sexes were confined in separate apartments, because to raise a child cost the master more than to buy one. Cato, for a very restricted indulgence to his slaves in this particular,[3] took from them a certain price. But in this country the slaves multiply as fast as the free inhabitants. Their situation and manners place the commerce between the two sexes almost without restraint.—The same Cato, on a principle of; oeconomy, always sold his sick and superannuated slaves. He gives it as a standing precept to a master visiting his farm, to sell his old oxen, old waggons, old tools, old and diseased servants, and every thing else become useless. 'Vendat boves vetulos, plaustrum vetus, ferramenta vetera, servum senem, servum morbosum, & si quid aliud supersit vendat.' Cato de re rustica. c. 2. The American slaves cannot enumerate this among the injuries and insults they receive. It was the common practice to expose in the island (Suet. Claud. 25) of Aesculapius, in the Tyber, diseased slaves, whose cure was like to become tedious. The Emperor Claudius, by an edict, gave freedom to such of them as should recover, and first declared, that if any person chose to kill rather than to expose them, it should be deemed homicide. The exposing them is a crime of which no instance has existed with us; and were it to be followed by death, it would be punished capitally. We are told of a certain Vedius Pollio, who, in the presence of Augustus, would have given a slave as food to his fish, for having broken a glass. With the Romans, the regular method of taking the evidence of their slaves was under torture. Here it has been thought better never to resort to their evidence. When a master was murdered, all his slaves, in the same house, or within hearing, were condemned to death. Here punishment falls on the guilty only, and as precise proof is required against him as against a freeman. Yet notwithstanding these and other discouraging circumstances among the Romans, their slaves were often their rarest artists. They excelled too in science, insomuch as to be usually employed as tutors to their master's children. Epictetus, Terence, and Phaedrus, were slaves. But they were of the race of whites. It is not their condition then, but nature, which has produced the distinction.—Whether further observation will or will not verify the conjecture, that nature has been less bountiful to them in the endowments of the head, I believe that in those of the heart she will be found to have done them justice. That disposition to theft with which they have been branded, must be ascribed to their situation, and not to any depravity of the moral sense.

The man, in whose favour no laws of property exist, probably feels himself less bound to respect those made in favour of others. When arguing for ourselves, we lay it down as a fundamental, that laws, to be just, must give a reciprocation of right: that, without this, they are mere arbitrary rules of conduct, founded in force, and not in conscience: and it is a problem which I give to the master to solve, whether the religious precepts against the violation of property were not framed for him as well as his slave? And whether the slave may not as justifiably take a little from one, who has taken all from him, as he may slay one who would slay him? That a change in the relations in which a man is placed should change his ideas of moral right and wrong, is neither new, nor peculiar to the colour of the blacks. Homer tells us it was so 2600 years ago. [. . .]

> Jove fix'd it certain, that whatever day
> Makes man a slave, takes half his worth away.
>
> *Od.*17.323

But the slaves of which Homer speaks were whites. Notwithstanding these considerations which must weaken their respect for the laws of property, we find among them numerous instances of the most rigid

3. *Tos dolos etaxen orismeno nomismatos omilein tais therapainisin.*—Plutarch. Cato.

integrity, and as many as among their better instructed masters, of benevolence, gratitude, and unshaken fidelity.—The opinion, that they are inferior in the faculties of reason and imagination, must be hazarded with great diffidence. To justify a general conclusion, requires many observations, even where the subject may be submitted to the Anatomical knife, to Optical glasses, to analysis by fire, or by solvents. How much more then where it is a faculty, not a substance, we are examining; where it eludes the research of all the senses; where the conditions of its existence are various and variously combined; where the effects of those which are present or absent bid defiance to calculation; let me add too, as a circumstance of great tenderness, where our conclusion would degrade a whole race of men from the rank in the scale of beings which their Creator may perhaps have given them. To our reproach it must be said, that though for a century and a half we have had under our eyes the races of black and of red men, they have never yet been viewed by us as subjects of natural history. I advance it therefore as a suspicion only, that the blacks, whether originally a distinct race, or made distinct by time and circumstances, are inferior to the whites in the endowments both of body and mind. It is not against experience to suppose, that different species of the same genus, or varieties of the same species, may possess different qualifications. Will not a lover of natural history then, one who views the gradations in all the races of animals with the eye of philosophy, excuse an effort to keep those in the department of man as distinct as nature has formed them? This unfortunate difference of colour, and perhaps of faculty, is a powerful obstacle to the emancipation of these people. Many of their advocates, while they wish to vindicate the liberty of human nature, are anxious also to preserve its dignity and beauty. Some of these, embarrassed by the question 'What further is to be done with them?' join themselves in opposition with those who are actuated by sordid avarice only. Among the Romans emancipation required but one effort. The slave, when made free, might mix with, without staining the blood of his master. But with us a second is necessary, unknown to history. When freed, he is to be removed beyond the reach of mixture.

The revised code further proposes to proportion crimes and punishments. This is attempted on the following scale.

I. Crimes whose punishment extends to *Life*.

1. High treason.	Death by hanging. Forfeiture of lands and goods to the commonwealth.	
2. Petty treason.	Death by hanging. Dissection. Forfeiture of half the lands and goods to the representatives of the party slain.	
3. Murder.	1. by poison.	Death by poison. Forfeiture of one-half as before.
	2. in Duel.	Death by hanging. Gibbeting, if the challenger. Forfeiture of one-half as before, unless it be the party challenged, then the forfeiture is to the commonwealth.
	3. in any other way.	Death by hanging. Forfeiture of one-half as before.
4. Manslaughter.	The second offence is murder.	

II. Crimes whose punishment goes to *Limb*.

1. Rape, 2. Sodomy,	Dismemberment.
3. Maiming, 4. Disfiguring	Retaliation, and the forfeiture of half the lands and goods to the sufferer.

III. Crimes punishable by *Labour*.

1. Manslaughter, 1st offence.	Labour VII. years for the public.	Forfeiture of half as in murder.
2. Counterfeiting money.	Labour VI. years.	Forfeiture of lands and goods to the commonwealth.

Crime	Punishment	
3. Arson. 4. Asportation of vessels.	Labour V. years.	Reparation three-fold.
5. Robbery. 6. Burglary.	Labour IV. years.	Reparation double.
7. House-breaking. 8. Horse-stealing.	Labour III. years.	Reparation.
9. Grand Larceny.	Labour II. years.	Reparation. Pillory.
10. Petty Larceny.	Labour I. year.	Reparation. Pillory.
11. Pretensions to witch-craft, &c.	Ducking.	Stripes.
12. Excusable homicide. 13. Suicide. 14. Apostacy. Heresy.	to be pitied, not punished.	

Pardon and privilege of clergy are proposed to be abolished; but if the verdict be against the defendant, the court in their discretion, may allow a new trial. No attainder to cause a corruption of blood, or forfeiture of dower. Slaves guilty of offences punishable in others by labour, to be transported to Africa, or elsewhere, as the circumstances of the time admit, there to be continued in slavery. A rigorous regimen proposed for those condemned to labour.

Another object of the revisal is, to diffuse knowledge more generally through the mass of the people. This bill proposes to lay off every county into small districts of five or six miles square, called hundreds, and in each of them to establish a school for teaching reading, writing, and arithmetic. The tutor to be supported by the hundred, and every person in it entitled to send their children three years gratis, and as much longer as they please, paying for it. These schools to be under a visitor, who is annually to chuse the boy, of best genius in the school, of those whose parents are too poor to give them further education, and to send him forward to one of the grammar schools, of which twenty are proposed to be erected in different parts of the country, for teaching Greek, Latin, geography, and the higher branches of numerical arithmetic. Of the boys thus sent in any one year, trial is to be made at the grammar schools one or two years, and the best genius of the whole selected, and continued six years, and the residue dismissed. By this means twenty of the best geniusses will be raked from the rubbish annually, and be instructed, at the public expence, so far as the grammer schools go. At the end of six years instruction, one half are to be discontinued (from among whom the grammar schools will probably be supplied with future masters); and the other half, who are to be chosen for the superiority of their parts and disposition, are to be sent and continued three years in the study of such sciences as they shall chuse, at William and Mary college, the plan of which is proposed to be enlarged, as will be hereafter explained, and extended to all the useful sciences. The ultimate result of the whole scheme of education would be the teaching all the children of the state reading, writing, and common arithmetic: turning out ten annually of superior genius, well taught in Greek, Latin, geography, and the higher branches of arithmetic: turning out ten others annually, of still superior parts, who, to those branches of learning, shall have added such of the sciences as their genius shall have led them to: the furnishing to the wealthier part of the people convenient schools, at which their children may be educated, at their own expence.—The general objects of this law are to provide an education adapted to the years, to the capacity, and the condition of every one, and directed to their freedom and happiness. Specific details were not proper for the law. These must be the business of the visitors entrusted with its execution. The first stage of this education being the schools of the hundreds, wherein the great mass of the people will receive their instruction, the principal foundations of future order will be laid here. Instead therefore of putting the Bible and Testament into the hands of the children, at an age when their judgments are not sufficiently matured for religious enquiries, their memories may here be stored with the most useful facts from Grecian, Roman, European and American history such as, when further developed as their judgments advance in strength, may teach them how to work out their own greatest happiness, by shewing them that it does not depend on the condition of life in which chance has placed them, but is always the result of a good conscience, good health, occupation, and freedom in all just pursuits.—Those whom either the wealth of their parents or the adoption of the state shall destine to higher degrees of learning, will go on to the grammar schools, which constitute the next stage, there to be instructed in the languages. The learning Greek and Latin, I am told, is going into disuse in Europe. I know not what their manners and occupations may call for: but it would be very ill-judged in us to follow their example in this instance. There is a certain period of life, say from eight to fifteen or sixteen years of age, when the mind, like the body, is not yet firm enough for laborious and close operations. If applied to such, it falls an early victim to premature exertion; exhibiting indeed at first, in these young and tender subjects, the flattering appearance of their being men while they are yet children, but ending in reducing them to be children when they should be men. The memory is then most susceptible and tenacious of impressions; and the learning of languages being chiefly a work of memory, it seems precisely fitted to the powers of this period, which is long enough too for acquiring the most useful languages antient and modern. I do not pretend that language is science. It is only an instrument for the attainment of science. But that time is not lost which is employed in providing tools for future operation: more especially as in this case the books put into the hands of the youth for this purpose may be such as will at the same time impress their minds with useful facts and good principles. If this period be suffered to pass in idleness, the mind becomes lethargic and impotent, as would the body it inhabits if unexercised during the same time. The sympathy between body and mind during their rise, progress and decline, is too strict and obvious to endanger our being misled while we reason from the one to the other.—As soon as they are of sufficient age, it is supposed they will be sent on from the grammar schools to the university, which constitutes our third and last stage, there to study those sciences which may be adapted to their views.—By that part of our plan which prescribes the selection of the youths of genius from among the classes of the poor, we hope to avail the state of those talents which nature has sown as liberally among the poor as the rich, but which perish without use, if not sought for and cultivated.—But of all the views of this law none is more important, none more legitimate, than that of rendering the people the safe, as they are the ultimate, guardians of their own liberty. For this purpose the reading in the first stage, where *they* will receive their whole education, is proposed, as has been said, to be chiefly historical. History by apprising them of the past will enable them to judge of the future; it will avail them of the experience of other times and other nations; it will qualify them as judges of the actions and designs of men; it will enable them to know ambition under every disguise it may assume; and knowing it, to defeat its views. In every government on earth is some trace of human weakness, some germ of corruption and degeneracy, which cunning will discover, and wickedness insensibly open, cultivate, and improve. Every government degenerates when trusted to the rulers of the people alone. The people themselves therefore are its only safe depositories. And to render even them safe their minds must be improved to a certain degree. This indeed is not all that is necessary, though it be essentially necessary. An amendment of our constitution must here come in aid of the public education. The influence over government must be shared among all the people. If every individual which composes their mass participates of the ultimate authority, the government will be safe; because the corrupting the whole mass will exceed any private resources of wealth: and public ones cannot be provided but by levies on the people. In this case every man would have to pay his own price. The government of Great-Britain has been corrupted, because but one man in ten has a right to vote for members of parliament. The sellers of the government therefore get nine-tenths of their price clear. It has been thought that corruption is restrained by confining the right of suffrage to a few of the wealthier of the people: but it would be more effectually restrained by an extension of that right to such numbers as would bid defiance to the means of corruption.

Lastly, it is proposed, by a bill in this revisal, to begin a public library and gallery, by laying out a certain sum annually in books, paintings, and statues.

Query 18

Manners—The particular customs and manners that may happen to be received in that state?

It is difficult to determine on the standard by which the manners of a nation may be tried, whether *catholic*, or *particular*. It is more difficult for a native to bring to that standard the manners of his own nation, familiarized to him by habit. There must doubtless be an unhappy influence on the manners of our people produced by the existence of slavery among us. The whole commerce between master and slave is a perpetual exercise of the most boisterous passions, the most unremitting despotism on the one part, and degrading submissions on the other. Our children see this, and learn to imitate it; for man is an imitative animal. This quality is the germ of all education in him. From his cradle to his grave he is learning to do what he sees others do. If a parent could find no motive either in his philanthropy or his self-love, for restraining the intemperance of passion towards his slave, it should always be a sufficient one that his child is present. But generally it is not sufficient. The parent storms, the child looks on, catches the lineaments of wrath, puts on the same airs in the circle of smaller slaves, gives a loose to his worst of passions, and thus nursed, educated, and daily exercised in tyranny, cannot but be stamped by it with odious peculiarities. The man must be a prodigy who can retain his manners and morals undepraved by such circumstances. And with what execration should the statesman be loaded, who permitting one half the citizens thus to trample on the rights of the other, transforms those into despots, and these into enemies, destroys the morals of the one part, and the amor patriae of the other. For if a slave can have a country in this world, it must be any other in preference to that in which he is born to live and labour for another: in which he must lock up the faculties of his nature, contribute as far as depends on his individual endeavours to the vanishment of the human race, or entail his own miserable condition on the endless generations proceeding from him. With the morals of the people, their industry also is destroyed. For in a warm climate, no man will labour for himself who can make another labour for him. This is so true, that of the proprietors of slaves a very small proportion indeed are ever seen to labour. And can the liberties of a nation be thought secure when we have removed their only firm basis, a conviction in the minds of the people that these liberties are of the gift of God? That they are not to be violated but with his wrath? Indeed I tremble for my country when I reflect that God is just: that his justice cannot sleep for ever: that considering numbers, nature and natural means only, a revolution of the wheel of fortune, an exchange of situation, is among possible events: that it may become probable by supernatural interference! The Almighty has no attribute which can take side with us in such a contest.—But it is impossible to be temperate and to pursue this subject through the various considerations of policy, of morals, of history natural and civil. We must be contented to hope they will force their way into every one's mind. I think a change already perceptible, since the origin of the present revolution. The spirit of the master is abating, that of the slave rising from the dust, his condition mollifying, the way I hope preparing, under the auspices of heaven, for a total emancipation, and that this is disposed, in the order of events, to be with the consent of the masters, rather than by their extirpation.

Query 19

Manufactures—The present state of manufactures, commerce, interior and exterior trade?

We never had an interior trade of any importance. Our exterior commerce has suffered very much from the beginning of the present contest. During this time we have manufactured within our families the most necessary articles of cloathing. Those of cotton will bear some comparison with the same kinds of manufacture in Europe; but those of wool, flax and hemp are very coarse, unsightly, and unpleasant: and such is our attachment to agriculture, and such our preference for foreign manufactures, that be it wise or unwise, our people will certainly return as soon as they can, to the raising raw materials, and exchanging them for finer manufactures than they are able to execute themselves.

The political oeconomists of Europe have established it as a principle that every state should endeavour to manufacture for itself: and this principle, like many others, we transfer to America, without calculating the difference of circumstance which should often produce a difference of result. In Europe the lands are either cultivated, or locked up against the cultivator. Manufacture must therefore be resorted to of necessity not of choice, to support the surplus of their people. But we have an immensity of land courting the industry of the husbandman. Is it best then that all our citizens should be employed in its improvement, or that one half should be called off from that to exercise manufactures and handicraft arts for the other? Those who labour in the earth are the chosen people of God, if ever he had a chosen people, whose breasts he has made his peculiar deposit for substantial and genuine virtue. It is the focus in which he keeps alive that sacred fire, which otherwise might escape from the face of the earth. Corruption of morals in the mass of cultivators is a phaenomenon of which no age nor nation has furnished an example. It is the mark set on those, who not looking up to heaven, to their own soil and industry, as does the husbandman, for their subsistance, depend for it on the casualties and caprice of customers. Dependance begets subservience and venality, suffocates the germ of virtue, and prepares fit tools for the designs of ambition. This, the natural progress and consequence of the arts, has sometimes perhaps been retarded by accidental circumstances: but, generally speaking, the proportion which the aggregate of the other classes of citizens bears in any state to that of its husbandmen, is the proportion of its unsound to its healthy parts, and is a good-enough barometer whereby to measure its degree of corruption. While we have land to labour then, let us never wish to see our citizens occupied at a work-bench, or twirling a distaff. Carpenters, masons, smiths, are wanting in husbandry: but, for the general operations of manufacture, let our work-shops remain in Europe. It is better to carry provisions and materials to workmen there, than bring them to the provisions and materials, and with them their manners and principles. The loss by the transportation of commodities across the Atlantic will be made up in happiness and permanence of government. The mobs of great cities add just so much to the support of pure government, as sores do to the strength of the human body. It is the manners and spirit of a people which preserve a republic in vigour. A degeneracy in these is a canker which soon eats to the heart of its laws and constitution.

Benjamin Banneker

Letter to Thomas Jefferson (August 19, 1791)

I am fully sensible of the greatness of that freedom, which I take with you on the present occasion; a liberty which seemed to me scarcely allowable, when I reflected on that distinguished and dignified station in which you stand, and the almost general prejudice and prepossession, which is so prevalent in the world against those of my complexion.

I suppose it is a truth too well attested to you, to need a proof here, that we are a race of beings, who have long labored under the abuse and censure of the world; that we have long been looked upon with an eye of contempt; and that we have long been considered rather as brutish than human, and scarcely capable of mental endowments.

Sir, I hope I may safely admit, in consequence of that report which hath reached me, that you are a man far less inflexible in sentiments of this nature, than many others; that you are measurably friendly, and well disposed towards us; and that you are willing and ready to lend your aid and assistance to our relief, from those many distresses, and numerous calamities, to which we are reduced. Now Sir, if this is founded in truth, I apprehend you will embrace every opportunity, to eradicate that train of absurd and false ideas and opinions, which so generally prevails with respect to us; and that your sentiments are concurrent with mine, which are, that one universal Father hath given being to us all; and that he hath not only made us all of one flesh, but that he hath also, without partiality, afforded us all the same sensations and endowed us all with the same faculties; and that however variable we may be in society or religion, however diversified in situation or color, we are all of the same family, and stand in the same relation to him.

Sir, if these are sentiments of which you are fully persuaded, I hope you cannot but acknowledge, that it is the indispensable duty of those, who maintain for themselves the rights of human nature, and who possess the obligations of Christianity, to extend their power and influence to the relief of every part of the human race, from whatever burden or oppression they may unjustly labor under; and this, I apprehend, a full conviction of the truth and obligation of these principles should lead all to. Sir, I have long been convinced, that if your love for yourselves, and for those inestimable laws, which preserved to you the rights of human nature, was founded on sincerity, you could not but be solicitous, that every individual, of whatever rank or distinction, might with you equally enjoy the blessings thereof; neither could you rest satisfied short of the most active effusion of your exertions, in order to their promotion from any state of degradation, to which the unjustifiable cruelty and barbarism of men may have reduced them.

Sir, I freely and cheerfully acknowledge, that I am of the African race, and in that color which is natural to them of the deepest dye; and it is under a sense of the most profound gratitude to the Supreme Ruler of the Universe, that I now confess to you, that I am not under that state of tyrannical thraldom, and inhuman captivity, to which too many of my brethren are doomed, but that I have abundantly tasted of the fruition of those blessings, which proceed from that free and unequalled liberty with which you are favored; and which, I hope, you will willingly allow you have mercifully received, from the immediate hand of that Being, from whom proceedeth every good and perfect Gift.

Sir, suffer me to recall to your mind that time, in which the arms and tyranny of the British crown were exerted, with every powerful effort, in order to reduce you to a state of servitude: look back, I entreat you, on the variety of dangers to which you were exposed; reflect on that time, in which every human aid appeared unavailable, and in which even hope and fortitude wore the aspect of inability to the conflict, and you cannot but be led to a serious and grateful sense of your miraculous and providential preservation; you cannot but acknowledge, that the present freedom and tranquility which you enjoy you have mercifully received, and that it is the peculiar blessing of Heaven.

This, Sir, was a time when you clearly saw into the injustice of a state of slavery, and in which you had just apprehensions of the horrors of its condition. It was now that your abhorrence thereof was so excited, that you publicly held forth this true and invaluable doctrine, which is worthy to be recorded and remembered in all succeeding ages: "We hold these truths to be self-evident, that all men are created equal; that they are endowed by their Creator with certain unalienable rights, and that among these are, life, liberty, and the pursuit of happiness." Here was a time, in which your tender feelings for yourselves had engaged you thus to declare, you were then impressed with proper ideas of the great violation of liberty, and the free possession of those blessings, to which you were entitled by nature; but, Sir, how pitiable is it to reflect, that although you were so fully convinced of the benevolence of the Father of Mankind, and of his equal and impartial distribution of these rights and privileges, which he hath conferred upon them, that you should at the same time counteract his mercies, in detaining by fraud and violence so numerous a part of my brethren, under groaning captivity and cruel oppression, that you should at the same time be found guilty of that most criminal act, which you professedly detested in others, with respect to yourselves.

I suppose that your knowledge of the situation of my brethren, is too extensive to need a recital here; neither shall I presume to prescribe methods by which they may be relieved, otherwise than by recommending to you and all others, to wean yourselves from those narrow prejudices which you have imbibed with respect to them, and as Job proposed to his friends, "put your soul in their souls' stead;" thus shall your hearts be enlarged with kindness and benevolence towards them; and thus shall you need neither the direction of myself or others, in what manner to proceed herein. And now, Sir, although my sympathy and affection for my brethren hath caused my enlargement thus far, I ardently hope, that your candor and generosity will plead with you in my behalf, when I make known to you, that it was not originally my design; but having taken up my pen in order to direct to you, as a present, a copy of an Almanac, which I have calculated for the succeeding year, I was unexpectedly and unavoidably led thereto.

Thomas Jefferson

Letter to Benjamin Banneker (August 30, 1791)

Philadelphia

Sir,—I thank you sincerely for your letter of the 19th instant and for the Almanac it contained. No body wishes more than I do to see such proofs as you exhibit, that nature has given to our black brethren, talents equal to those of the other colors of men, and that the appearance of a want of them is owing merely to the degraded condition of their existence both in Africa & America. I can add with truth, that no body wishes more ardently to see a good system commenced for raising the condition both of their body & mind to what it ought to be, as fast as the imbecility of their present existence, and other circumstances which cannot be neglected, will admit. I have taken the liberty of sending your Almanac to Monsieur de Condorcet, Secretary of the Academy of Sciences at Paris, and member of the Philanthropic society because I considered it as a document to which your whole colour had a right for their justification against the doubts which have been entertained of them. I am with great esteem, Sir Your most obedt humble servt.

James Madison

Notes on Debates in Congress (February 21, 1783)

Mr. Mercer made some remarks tending to a reconsideration of the act declaring general funds to be necessary, which revived the discussion of that subject.

Mr. Madison said that he had observed throughout the proceedings of Congress relative to the establishment of such funds that the power delegated to Congress by the confederation had been very differently construed by different members & that this difference of construction had materially affected their reasonings & opinions on the several propositions which had been made; that in particular it had been represented by sundry members that Congress was merely an Executive body; and therefore that it was inconsistent with the principles of liberty & the spirit of the Constitution, to submit to them a permanent revenue which wd. be placing the purse & the sword in the same hands; that he wished the true doctrine of the confederation to be ascertained as it might perhaps remove some embarrassments; and towards that end would offer his ideas on the subject.

He said that he did not conceive in the first place that the opinion was sound that the power of Congress in cases of revenue was in no respect Legislative, but merely Executive: and in the second place that admitting the power to be Executive a permanent revenue collected & dispensed by them in the discharge of the debts to wch. it sd. be appropriated, would be inconsistent with the nature of an Executive body, or dangerous to the liberties of the republic.

As to the first opinion he observed that by the articles of Confederation Congs. had clearly & expressly the right to fix the quantum of revenue necessary for the public exigences, &c to require the same from the States respectively in proportion to the value of their land; that the requisitions thus made were a law to the States, as much as the acts of the latter for complying with them were a law to their individual members: that the foederal constitution was as sacred & obligatory as the internal constitutions of the several States; and that nothing could justify the States in disobeying acts warranted by it, but some previous abuse or infraction on the part of Congs.; that as a proof that the power of fixing the quantum & making requisitions of money, was considered as a legislative power over the purse, he would appeal to the proposition made by the British Minister of giving this power to the B. Parliamt. & leaving to the American assemblies the privilege of complying in their own modes; & to the reasonings of Congress & the several States on that proposition. He observed further that by the articles of Confederation was delegated to Congs. a right to borrow money indefinitely, and emit bills of Credit which was a species of borrowing, for repayment & redemption of which the faith of the States was pledged & their legislatures constitutionally bound. He asked whether these powers were reconcileable with the idea that Congress was a body merely Executive? He asked what would be thought in G. B. from whose constitution our Political reasonings were so much drawn, of an attempt to prove that a power of making requisitions of money on the Parliament, & of borrowing money for discharge of which the Parlt sd. be bound, might be annexed to the Crown without changing its quality of an Executive branch; and that the leaving to the Parliamt. the mode only of complying with the requisitions of the Crown, would be leaving to it its supreme & exclusive power of Legislation?

As to the second point he referred again to the British Constitution & the mode in which provision was made for the public debts; observing that although the Executive had no authority to contract a debt; yet that when a debt had been authorized or admitted by the parliament a permanent & irrevocable revenue was granted by the Legislature, to be collected & dispensed by the Executive; and that this practice had never been deemed a subversion of the Constitution or a dangerous association of a power over the purse with the power of the Sword.

If these observations were just as he conceived them to be, the establishment of a permanent revenue not by any assumed authority of Congress, but by the authority of the States at the recommendation of Congs: to be collected & applied by the latter to the discharge of the public debts, could not be deemed inconsistent with the spirit of the foederal constitution, or subversive of the principles of liberty; and that all objections drawn from such a supposition ought [to] be withdrawn. Whether other objections of sufficient weight might not lie agst. such an establishmt. was another question. For his part altho' for various reasons he had wished for such a plan as most eligible, he had never been sanguine that it was practicable & the discussions which had taken place had finally satisfied him that it would be necessary to limit the call for a general revenue to duties on commerce & to call for the deficiency in the most permanent way that could be reconciled with a revenue established within each State separately & appropriated to the Common Treasury. He said the rule which he had laid down to himself in this business was to concur in every arrangemt. that sd. appear necessary for an honorable & just fulfillment of the public engagements; & in no measure tending to augment the power of Congress which sd appear to be unnecessary; and particularly disclaimed the idea of perpetuating a public debt.

Mr. Lee in answer to Mr. Madison said the doctrine maintained by him was pregnant with dangerous consequences to the liberties of the confederated States; that notwithstanding the specious arguments that had been employed it was an established truth that the purse ought not to be put into the same hands with the Sword; that like arguments had been used in favor of Ship money in the reign of Charles I it being then represented as essential to the support of the Govt., that the Executive should be assured of the means of fulfilling its engagements for the public service: He said it had been urged by several in behalf of such an establishment for public credit that without it Congress was nothing more than a rope of sand. On this head he would be explicit; he had rather see Congress a rope of sand than a rod of Iron. He urged finally as a reason why some States would not & ought not to concur in granting to Congress a permanent revenue, that some States as Virga, would receive back a small part by paymt. from the U. S. to its Citizens; whilst others as Pena. wd. receive a vast surplus; & consequently be enriched by draining the former of its wealth.

Mr. Mercer said if he conceived the foederal compact to be such as it had been represented he would immediately withdraw from Congress & do every thing in his power to destroy its existence: that if Congs. had a right to borrow money as they pleased and to make requisitions on the States that wd. be binding on them, the liberties of the States were ideal; that requisitions ought to be consonant to the Spirit of liberty; that they should go frequently & accompanied with full information, that the States must be left to judge of the nature of them, of their abilities to comply with them & to regulate their compliance accordingly; he laid great stress on the omission of Congs. to transmit half yearly to the States an acct. of the monies borrowed by them &c. and even insinuated that this omission had absolved the States in some degree from the engagements.

Memorial and Remonstrance against Religious Assessments (June 20, 1785)

To the Honorable the General Assembly
of the Commonwealth of Virginia
A Memorial and Remonstrance

We the subscribers, citizens of the said Commonwealth, having taken into serious consideration, a Bill printed by order of the last Session of General Assembly, entitled "A Bill establishing a provision for Teachers of the Christian Religion," and conceiving that the same if finally armed with the sanctions of a law, will be a dangerous abuse of power, are bound as faithful members of a free State to remonstrate against it, and to declare the reasons by which we are determined. We remonstrate against the said Bill,

1. Because we hold it for a fundamental and undeniable truth, "that Religion or the duty which we owe to our Creator and the manner of discharging it, can be directed only by reason and conviction, not by force or violence." [Virginia Declaration of Rights, art. 16] The Religion then of every man must be left to the conviction and conscience of every man; and it is the right of every man to exercise it as these may dictate. This right is in its nature an unalienable right. It is unalienable, because the opinions of men, depending only on the evidence contemplated by their own minds cannot follow the dictates of other men: It is unalienable also, because what is here a right towards men, is a duty towards the Creator. It is the duty of every man to render to the Creator such homage and such only as he believes to be acceptable to him. This duty is precedent, both in order of time and in degree of obligation, to the claims of Civil Society. Before any man can be considered as a member of Civil Society, he must be considered as a subject of the Governour of the Universe: And if a member of Civil Society, who enters into any subordinate Association, must always do it with a reservation of his duty to the General Authority; much more must every man who becomes a member of any particular Civil Society, do it with a saving of his allegiance to the Universal Sovereign.

We maintain therefore that in matters of Religion, no mans right is abridged by the institution of Civil Society and that Religion is wholly exempt from its cognizance. True it is, that no other rule exists, by which any question which may divide a Society, can be ultimately determined, but the will of the majority; but it is also true that the majority may trespass on the rights of the minority.

2. Because if Religion be exempt from the authority of the Society at large, still less can it be subject to that of the Legislative Body. The latter are but the creatures and vicegerents of the former. Their jurisdiction is both derivative and limited: it is limited with regard to the co-ordinate departments, more necessarily is it limited with regard to the constituents. The preservation of a free Government requires not merely, that the metes and bounds which separate each department of power be invariably maintained; but more especially that neither of them be suffered to overleap the great Barrier which defends the rights of the people. The Rulers who are guilty of such an encroachment, exceed the commission from which they derive their authority, and are Tyrants. The People who submit to it are governed by laws made neither by themselves nor by an authority derived from them, and are slaves.

3. Because it is proper to take alarm at the first experiment on our liberties. We hold this prudent jealousy to be the first duty of Citizens, and one of the noblest characteristics of the late Revolution. The free men of America did not wait till usurped power had strengthened itself by exercise, and entangled the question in precedents. They saw all the consequences in the principle, and they avoided the consequences by denying the principle. We revere this lesson too much soon to forget it. Who does not see that the same authority which can establish Christianity, in exclusion of all other Religions, may establish with the same ease any particular sect of Christians, in exclusion of all other Sects? that the same authority which can force a citizen to contribute three pence only of his property for the support of any one establishment, may force him to conform to any other establishment in all cases whatsoever?

4. Because the Bill violates that equality which ought to be the basis of every law, and which is more indispensible, in proportion as the validity or expediency of any law is more liable to be impeached. If "all men are by nature equally free and independent," [Virginia Declaration of Rights, art. 1] all men are to be considered as entering into Society on equal conditions; as relinquishing no more, and therefore retaining no less, one than another, of their natural rights. Above all are they to be considered as retaining an "*equal* title to the free exercise of Religion according to the dictates of Conscience." [Virginia Declaration of Rights, art. 16] Whilst we assert for ourselves a freedom to embrace, to profess and to observe the Religion which we believe to be of divine origin, we cannot deny an equal freedom to those whose minds have not yet yielded to the evidence which has convinced us. If this freedom be abused, it is an offence against God, not against man: To God, therefore, not to man, must an account of it be rendered. As the Bill violates equality by subjecting some to peculiar burdens, so it violates the same principle, by granting to others peculiar exemptions. Are the Quakers and Menonists the only sects who think a compulsive support of their Religions unnecessary and unwarrantable? Can their piety alone be entrusted with the care of public worship? Ought their Religions to be endowed above all others with extraordinary privileges by which proselytes may be enticed from all others? We think too favorably of the justice and good sense of these denominations to believe that they either covet pre-eminences over their fellow citizens or that they will be seduced by them from the common opposition to the measure.

5. Because the Bill implies either that the Civil Magistrate is a competent Judge of Religious Truth; or that he may employ Religion as an engine of Civil policy. The first is an arrogant pretension falsified by the contradictory opinions of Rulers in all ages, and throughout the world: the second an unhallowed perversion of the means of salvation.

6. Because the establishment proposed by the Bill is not requisite for the support of the Christian Religion. To say that it is, is a contradiction to the Christian Religion itself, for every page of it disavows a dependence on the powers of this world: it is a contradiction to fact; for it is known that this Religion both existed and flourished, not only without the support of human laws, but in spite of every opposition from them, and not only during the period of miraculous aid, but long after it had been left to its own

evidence and the ordinary care of Providence. Nay, it is a contradiction in terms; for a Religion not invented by human policy, must have pre-existed and been supported, before it was established by human policy. It is moreover to weaken in those who profess this Religion a pious confidence in its innate excellence and the patronage of its Author; and to foster in those who still reject it, a suspicion that its friends are too conscious of its fallacies to trust it to its own merits.

7. Because experience witnesseth that ecclesiastical establishments, instead of maintaining the purity and efficacy of Religion, have had a contrary operation. During almost fifteen centuries has the legal establishment of Christianity been on trial. What have been its fruits? More or less in all places, pride and indolence in the Clergy, ignorance and servility in the laity, in both, superstition, bigotry and persecution. Enquire of the Teachers of Christianity for the ages in which it appeared in its greatest lustre; those of every sect, point to the ages prior to its incorporation with Civil policy. Propose a restoration of this primitive State in which its Teachers depended on the voluntary rewards of their flocks, many of them predict its downfall. On which Side ought their testimony to have greatest weight, when for or when against their interest?

8. Because the establishment in question is not necessary for the support of Civil Government. If it be urged as necessary for the support of Civil Government only as it is a means of supporting Religion, and it be not necessary for the latter purpose, it cannot be necessary for the former. If Religion be not within the cognizance of Civil Government how can its legal establishment be necessary to Civil Government? What influence in fact have ecclesiastical establishments had on Civil Society? In some instances they have been seen to erect a spiritual tyranny on the ruins of the Civil authority; in many instances they have been seen upholding the thrones of political tyranny: in no instance have they been seen the guardians of the liberties of the people. Rulers who wished to subvert the public liberty, may have found an established Clergy convenient auxiliaries. A just Government instituted to secure & perpetuate it needs them not. Such a Government will be best supported by protecting every Citizen in the enjoyment of his Religion with the same equal hand which protects his person and his property; by neither invading the equal rights of any Sect, nor suffering any Sect to invade those of another.

9. Because the proposed establishment is a departure from that generous policy, which, offering an Asylum to the persecuted and oppressed of every Nation and Religion, promised a lustre to our country, and an accession to the number of its citizens. What a melancholy mark is the Bill of sudden degeneracy? Instead of holding forth an Asylum to the persecuted, it is itself a signal of persecution. It degrades from the equal rank of Citizens all those whose opinions in Religion do not bend to those of the Legislative authority. Distant as it may be in its present form from the Inquisition, it differs from it only in degree. The one is the first step, the other the last in the career of intolerance. The magnanimous sufferer under this cruel scourge in foreign Regions, must view the Bill as a Beacon on our Coast, warning him to seek some other haven, where liberty and philanthrophy in their due extent, may offer a more certain repose from his Troubles.

10. Because it will have a like tendency to banish our Citizens. The allurements presented by other situations are every day thinning their number. To superadd a fresh motive to emigration by revoking the liberty which they now enjoy, would be the same species of folly which has dishonoured and depopulated flourishing kingdoms.

11. Because it will destroy that moderation and harmony which the forbearance of our laws to intermeddle with Religion has produced among its several sects. Torrents of blood have been spilt in the old world, by vain attempts of the secular arm, to extinguish Religious discord, by proscribing all difference in Religious opinion. Time has at length revealed the true remedy. Every relaxation of narrow and rigorous policy, wherever it has been tried, has been found to assuage the disease. The American Theatre has exhibited proofs that equal and compleat liberty, if it does not wholly eradicate it, sufficiently destroys its malignant influence on the health and prosperity of the State. If with the salutary effects of this system under our own eyes, we begin to contract the bounds of Religious freedom, we know no name that will too severely reproach our folly. At least let warning be taken at the first fruits of the threatened innovation. The very appearance of the Bill has transformed "that Christian forbearance,

love and charity," [Virginia Declaration of Rights, art. 16] which of late mutually prevailed, into animosities and jealousies, which may not soon be appeased. What mischiefs may not be dreaded, should this enemy to the public quiet be armed with the force of a law?

12. Because the policy of the Bill is adverse to the diffusion of the light of Christianity. The first wish of those who enjoy this precious gift ought to be that it may be imparted to the whole race of mankind. Compare the number of those who have as yet received it with the number still remaining under the dominion of false Religions; and how small is the former! Does the policy of the Bill tend to lessen the disproportion? No; it at once discourages those who are strangers to the light of revelation from coming into the Region of it; and countenances by example the nations who continue in darkness, in shutting out those who might convey it to them. Instead of Levelling as far as possible, every obstacle to the victorious progress of Truth, the Bill with an ignoble and unchristian timidity would circumscribe it with a wall of defence against the encroachments of error.

13. Because attempts to enforce by legal sanctions, acts obnoxious to so great a proportion of Citizens, tend to enervate the laws in general, and to slacken the bands of Society. If it be difficult to execute any law which is not generally deemed necessary or salutary, what must be the case, where it is deemed invalid and dangerous? And what may be the effect of so striking an example of impotency in the Government, on its general authority?

14. Because a measure of such singular magnitude and delicacy ought not to be imposed, without the clearest evidence that it is called for by a majority of citizens, and no satisfactory method is yet proposed by which the voice of the majority in this case may be determined, or its influence secured. "The people of the respective counties are indeed requested to signify their opinion respecting the adoption of the Bill to the next Session of Assembly." But the representation must be made equal, before the voice either of the Representatives or of the Counties will be that of the people. Our hope is that neither of the former will, after due consideration, espouse the dangerous principle of the Bill. Should the event disappoint us, it will still leave us in full confidence, that a fair appeal to the latter will reverse the sentence against our liberties.

15. Because finally, "the equal right of every citizen to the free exercise of his Religion according to the dictates of conscience" is held by the same tenure with all our other rights. If we recur to its origin, it is equally the gift of nature; if we weigh its importance, it cannot be less dear to us; if we consult the "Declaration of those rights which pertain to the good people of Virginia, as the basis and foundation of Government," it is enumerated with equal solemnity, or rather studied emphasis. Either then, we must say, that the Will of the Legislature is the only measure of their authority; and that in the plenitude of this authority, they may sweep away all our fundamental rights; or, that they are bound to leave this particular right untouched and sacred: Either we must say, that they may controul the freedom of the press, may abolish the Trial by Jury, may swallow up the Executive and Judiciary Powers of the State; nay that they may despoil us of our very right of suffrage, and erect themselves into an independent and hereditary Assembly or, we must say, that they have no authority to enact into law the Bill under consideration. We the Subscribers say, that the General Assembly of this Commonwealth have no such authority: And that no effort may be omitted on our part against so dangerous an usurpation, we oppose to it, this remonstrance; earnestly praying, as we are in duty bound, that the Supreme Lawgiver of the Universe, by illuminating those to whom it is addressed, may on the one hand, turn their Councils from every act which would affront his holy prerogative, or violate the trust committed to them: and on the other, guide them into every measure which may be worthy of his blessing, may redound to their own praise, and may establish more firmly the liberties, the prosperity and the happiness of the Commonwealth.

Richard Henry Lee

Letter to Samuel Adams (March 14, 1785)

The selfishness and corruption of Europe I have no doubt about, and therefore wish most sincerely that our free Republics may not suffer themselves to be changed and wrongly wrought upon by the corrupt maxims of policy that pervade European Councils—where artful and refined plausibility is forever called in to aid the most pernicious designs. It would seem as if there were a general jealosy beyond the water, of the powerful effects to be derived from Republican virtue here, and so we hear a constant cry from thence, echoed & reechoed here by all Expectants from the Treasury of the United States—That Congress must have more power—That we cannot be secure & happy until Congress command implicitly both purse & sword. So that our confederation must be perpetually changing to answer sinister views in the greater part, until every fence is thrown down that was designed to protect & cover the rights of Mankind. It is a melancholy consideration that many wise & good men have, some how or other, fallen in with these ruinous opinions. I think Sir that the first maxim of a man who loves liberty should be, never to grant to Rulers an atom of power that is not most clearly & indispensably necessary for the safety and well being of Society. To say that these Rulers are revocable, and holding their places during pleasure may not be supposed to design evil for self-aggrandizement, is affirming what I cannot easily admit. Look to history and see how often the liberties of mankind have been oppressed & ruined by the same delusive hopes & falacious reasoning. The fact is, that power poisons the mind of its possessor and aids him to remove the shackles that restrain itself. To be sure, all things human must partake of human infirmity, and therefore the Confederation should not be presumptuously called an infallible system for all times and all situations—but tho' this is true, yet as it is a great and fundamental system of Union & Security, no change should be admitted until proved to be necessary by the fairest fullest & most mature experience. Upon these principles I have ever been opposed to the 5 P Cent imposts, My idea is still that of the Confederation, Fix the sum, apportion it & let every State by its own means, and in its own way faithfully & honestly make its payment. That the now federal mode of apportionment is productive of delay, of great expence, and still liable to frequent change, is certain. And therefore I see no inconvenience in so far altering the Confederation as to make the Rule of Apportionment lie upon the numbers as stated in the recommendation of Congress upon that Subject. But I can never agree that this Body shall dictate the mode of Taxation, or that the collection shall in any manner be subject to Congressional controul. It is said that this will more effectually secure the Revenue—But how so? if a spirit prevails to neglect a duty imposed by the Confederation, may not the same spirit render abortive at any time Acts passed for granting the Impost? Besides that we are depending for the payment of our debts upon uncertainty, when the most certain revenues of the State ought to be appropriated for that purpose. Whilst every good man wishes great punctuality to prevail in the payment of debts, he must at the same time condemn and discourage large importations which impoverish by increasing the balance of trade against us. So that from this system we are to expect our greatest good from our greatest evil. A good physician will tell you that contrary indications of cure threaten danger to human life, and by a just parity of reason, contrary indications threaten danger to the Political body. But happily for us, our political disease admits of simple remedies for its cure, if rightly judged of, and wisely practised upon. Let it be therefore the effort of every Patriot to encourage a punctual payment of each State's quota of the foederal demand, and let the money be found in ways most agreable to the circumstances of every State. This is the plan of the Confederation, and this I own will be mine, until more satisfactory experience has proved its inefficacy.

Letter to George Mason (May 15, 1787)

It has given me much pleasure to be informed that General Washington and yourself have gone to the Convention. We may hope, from such efforts, that alterations beneficial will take place in our Federal Constitution, if it shall be found, on deliberate inquiry, that the evils now felt do flow from errors in that constitution; but, alas! sir, I fear it is more in vicious manners, than mistakes in form, that we must seek for the causes of the present discontent. The present causes of complaint seem to be, that Congress cannot command the money necessary for the just purposes of paying debts, or for supporting the federal government; and that they cannot make treaties of commerce, unless power unlimited, of regulating trade be given. The Confederation now gives right to name the sums necessary, and to apportion the quotas by a rule established. This rule is, unfortunately, very difficult of execution, and, therefore the recommendations of Congress on this subject have not been made in federal mode; so that States have thought themselves justified in non-compliance. If the rule were plain and easy, and refusal were then to follow demand, I see clearly, that no form of government whatever, short of force, will answer; for the same want of principle that produces neglect now, will do so under any change not supported by power compulsory; the difficulty certainly is, how to give this power in such manner as that it may only be used to good, and not abused to bad, purposes. Whoever shall solve this difficulty will receive the thanks of this and future generations. With respect to the want of power to make treaties of trade, for want of legislation, to regulate the general commerce, it appears to me, that the right of making treaties, and the legislative power contended for are essentially different things; the former may be given and executed without the danger attending upon the States parting with their legislative authority, in the instance contended for. If the third paragraph of the sixth article were altered, by striking out the words, in pursuance of any treaties already proposed by Congress, to the courts of France and Spain; and the proviso stricken out of the first section in the ninth article, Congress would then have a complete and unlimited right of making treaties of all kinds, and, so far, I really think it both right and necessary; but this is very different from, and in danger far short of, giving an exclusive power of regulating trade. A minister of Congress may go to a foreign court with full power to make a commercial treaty; but if he were to propose to such court that the eight northern States in this Union, should have the exclusive right of carrying the products of the five southern States, or of supplying these States with foreign articles, such a proposition of monopoly would be rejected; and, therefore, no danger here from the power of making treaty; but a legislative right to regulate trade through the States may, in a thousand artful modes, be so abused as to produce the monopoly aforesaid, to the extreme oppression of the staple States, as they are called. I do not say that this would be done, but I contend that it might be done; and, where interest powerfully prompts, it is greatly to be feared that it would be done. Whoever has served long in Congress, knows that the restraint of making the consent of nine States necessary, is feeble and incompetent. Some will sometimes sleep, and some will be negligent, but it is certain that improper power not given cannot be improperly used.

The human mind is too apt to rush from one extreme to another; it appears, by the objections that came from the different States, when the Confederation was submitted for consideration, that the universal apprehension was, of the too great, not the defective powers of Congress. Whence this immense change of sentiment, in a few years? For now the cry is power, give Congress power. Without reflecting that every free nation, that hath ever existed, has lost its liberty by the same rash impatience, and want of necessary caution. I am glad, however, to find, on this occasion, that so many gentlemen, of competent years, are sent to the Convention, for, certainly, "youth is the season of credulity, and confidence a plant of slow growth in an aged bosom." The States have been so unpardonably remiss, in furnishing their federal quotas, as to make impost necessary, for a term of time, with a provisional security, that the money arising shall be unchangeably applied to the payment of their public debts; that accounts of the application, shall be annually sent to each State; and the collecting officers appointed by, and be amenable to the States: or, if not so, very strong preventives and correctives of official abuse and misconduct, interpose, to shield the people from oppression.

Give me leave, sir, to detain you a moment longer, with a proposition that I have not heard mentioned. It is that the right of making paper money shall be exclusively vested in Congress; such a right will be clearly within the spirit of the fourth section of the ninth article of the present confederation. This appears to me, to be a restraint of the last importance to the peace and happiness of the Union, and of every part of it. Knaves assure, and fools believe, that calling paper money, and making it tender, is the way to be rich and happy; thus the national mind is kept in constant ferment; and the public councils in continual disturbance by the intrigues of wicked men, for fraudulent purposes, for speculating designs. This would be a great step towards correcting morals, and suppressing legislative frauds, which, of all frauds, is the most hateful to society. Do you not think, sir, that it ought to be declared, by the new system, that any State act of legislation that shall contravene, or oppose, the authorized acts of Congress, or interfere with the expressed rights of that body, shall be *ipso facto* void, and of no force whatsoever?

My respects, if you please, to your brethren of the Convention, from this State, and pardon me for the liberty I have taken of troubling you with my sentiments on the interesting business that calls you to Philadelphia.

Northwest Ordinance (1787)

An Ordinance for the government of the Territory of the United States northwest of the River Ohio

Section 1. *Be it ordained by the United States in Congress assembled,* That the said territory, for the purposes of temporary government, be one district, subject, however, to be divided into two districts, as future circumstances may, in the opinion of Congress, make it expedient. [. . .]

Sec. 13. And, for extending the fundamental principles of civil and religious liberty, which form the basis whereon these republics, their laws and constitutions are erected; to fix and establish those principles as the basis of all laws, constitutions, and governments, which forever hereafter shall be formed in the said territory: to provide also for the establishment of States, and permanent government therein, and for their admission to a share in the federal councils on an equal footing with the original States, at as early periods as may be consistent with the general interest:

Sec. 14. It is hereby ordained and declared by the authority aforesaid, That the following articles shall be considered as articles of compact between the original States and the people and States in the said territory and forever remain unalterable, unless by common consent, to wit:

Art. 1. No person, demeaning himself in a peaceable and orderly manner, shall ever be molested on account of his mode of worship or religious sentiments, in the said territory.

Art. 2. The inhabitants of the said territory shall always be entitled to the benefits of the writ of *habeas corpus,* and of the trial by jury; of a proportionate representation of the people in the legislature; and of judicial proceedings according to the course of the common law. All persons shall be bailable, unless for capital offenses, where the proof shall be evident or the presumption great. All fines shall be moderate;

and no cruel or unusual punishments shall be inflicted. No man shall be deprived of his liberty or property, but by the judgment of his peers or the law of the land; and, should the public exigencies make it necessary, for the common preservation, to take any person's property, or to demand his particular services, full compensation shall be made for the same. And, in the just preservation of rights and property, it is understood and declared, that no law ought ever to be made, or have force in the said territory, that shall, in any manner whatever, interfere with or affect private contracts or engagements, *bona fide*, and without fraud, previously formed.

Art. 3. Religion, morality, and knowledge, being necessary to good government and the happiness of mankind, schools and the means of education shall forever be encouraged. The utmost good faith shall always be observed towards the Indians; their lands and property shall never be taken from them without their consent; and, in their property, rights, and liberty, they shall never be invaded or disturbed, unless in just and lawful wars authorized by Congress; but laws founded in justice and humanity, shall from time to time be made for preventing wrongs being done to them, and for preserving peace and friendship with them.

Art. 4. The said territory, and the States which may be formed therein, shall forever remain a part of this Confederacy of the United States of America, subject to the Articles of Confederation, and to such alterations therein as shall be constitutionally made; and to all the acts and ordinances of the United States in Congress assembled, conformable thereto. The inhabitants and settlers in the said territory shall be subject to pay a part of the federal debts contracted or to be contracted, and a proportional part of the expenses of government, to be apportioned on them by Congress according to the same common rule and measure by which apportionments thereof shall be made on the other States; and the taxes for paying their proportion shall be laid and levied by the authority and direction of the legislatures of the district or districts, or new States, as in the original States, within the time agreed upon by the United States in Congress assembled. The legislatures of those districts or new States, shall never interfere with the primary disposal of the soil by the United States in Congress assembled, nor with any regulations Congress may find necessary for securing the title in such soil to the bona fide purchasers. No tax shall be imposed on lands the property of the United States; and, in no case, shall nonresident proprietors be taxed higher than residents. The navigable waters leading into the Mississippi and St. Lawrence, and the carrying places between the same, shall be common highways and forever free, as well to the inhabitants of the said territory as to the citizens of the United States, and those of any other States that may be admitted into the confederacy, without any tax, impost, or duty therefor.

Art. 5. There shall be formed in the said territory, not less than three nor more than five States; and the boundaries of the States, as soon as Virginia shall alter her act of cession, and consent to the same, shall become fixed and established as follows, to wit: The western State in the said territory, shall be bounded by the Mississippi, the Ohio, and Wabash Rivers; a direct line drawn from the Wabash and Post Vincents, due North, to the territorial line between the United States and Canada; and, by the said territorial line, to the Lake of the Woods and Mississippi. The middle State shall be bounded by the said direct line, the Wabash from Post Vincents to the Ohio, by the Ohio, by a direct line, drawn due north from the mouth of the Great Miami, to the said territorial line, and by the said territorial line. The eastern State shall be bounded by the last mentioned direct line, the Ohio, Pennsylvania, and the said territorial line: *Provided, however,* and it is further understood and declared, that the boundaries of these three States shall be subject so far to be altered, that, if Congress shall hereafter find it expedient, they shall have authority to form one or two States in that part of the said territory which lies north of an east and west line drawn through the southerly bend or extreme of Lake Michigan. And, whenever any of the said States shall have sixty thousand free inhabitants therein, such State shall be admitted, by its delegates, into the Congress of the United States, on an equal footing with the original States in all respects whatever, and shall be at liberty to form a permanent constitution and State government: *Provided,* the constitution and government so to be formed, shall be republican, and in conformity to the principles contained in these articles; and, so far as it can be consistent with the general interest of the confederacy, such admission shall be allowed at an earlier period, and when there may be a less number of free inhabitants in the State than sixty thousand.

Art. 6. There shall be neither slavery nor involuntary servitude in the said territory, otherwise than in the punishment of crimes whereof the party shall have been duly convicted: *Provided, always,* That any person escaping into the same, from whom labor or service is lawfully claimed in any one of the original States, such fugitive may be lawfully reclaimed and conveyed to the person claiming his or her labor or service as aforesaid.

Be it ordained by the authority aforesaid, That the resolutions of the 23rd of April, 1784, relative to the subject of this ordinance, be, and the same are hereby repealed and declared null and void.

Done by the United States, in Congress assembled, the 13th day of July, in the year of our Lord 1787, and of their sovereignty and independence the twelfth.

George Washington

Letter to John Jay (August 15, 1786)

[. . .] Your sentiments, that our affairs are drawing rapidly to a crisis, accord with my own. What the event will be, is also beyond the reach of my foresight. We have errors to correct; we have probably had too good an opinion of human nature in forming our confederation. Experience has taught us, that men will not adopt and carry into execution measures the best calculated for good, without the intervention of a coercive power. I do not conceive we can exist long as a nation without having lodged some where a power, which will pervade the whole Union in as energetic a manner, as the authority of the State Governments extends over the several States.

To be fearful of investing Congress, constituted as that body is, with ample authorities for national purposes, appears to me the very climax of popular absurdity and madness. Could Congress exert them for the detriment of the public, without injuring themselves in an equal or greater proportion? Are not their interests inseparably connected with those of their constituents? By the rotation of appointment, must they not mingle frequently with the mass of Citizens? Is it not rather to be apprehended, if they were possessed of the powers before described, that the individual members would be induced to use them, on many occasions, very timidly and inefficaciously for fear of losing their popularity and future election? We must take human nature as we find it: perfection falls not to the share of mortals. Many are of opinion that Congress have too frequently made use of the suppliant humble tone of requisition, in applications to the States, when they had a right to assert their imperial dignity and command obedience. Be that as it may, requisitions are a perfect nihility where thirteen sovereign independent disunited States are in the habit of discussing and refusing compliance with them at their option. Requisitions are actually little better than a jest and a bye word throughout the land. If you tell the Legislatures they have violated the Treaty of Peace, and invaded the prerogatives of the confederacy, they will laugh in your face. What then is to be done? Things cannot go on in the same train forever. It is much to be feared, as you observe, that the better kind of people, being disgusted with the circumstances, will have their minds prepared for any revolution whatever. We are apt to run from one extreme into another. To anticipate and prevent disastrous contingencies, would be the part of wisdom and patriotism.

What astonishing changes a few years are capable of producing. I am told that even respectable characters speak of a monarchical form of Government without horror. From thinking proceeds speaking, thence to acting is often but a single step. But how irrevocable and tremendous! what a triumph for our enemies to verify their predictions! what a triumph for the advocates of despotism to find that we are incapable of governing ourselves, and that systems founded on the basis of equal liberty are merely ideal and fallacious! Would to God that wise measures may be taken in time to avert the consequences we have but too much reason to apprehend.

JOHN JAY

Letter to George Washington (January 7, 1787)

New York

Dear Sir:

They who regard the public good with more attention and attachment than they do mere personal concerns must feel and confess the force of such sentiments as are expressed in your letter to me by Colonel Humphrey last fall. The situation of our affairs calls not only for reflection and prudence, but for exertion. What is to be done? is a common question not easy to answer.

Would the giving *any* further degree of power to Congress do the business? I am much inclined to think it would not, for among other reasons there will always be members who will find it convenient to make their seats subservient to partial and personal purposes; and they who may be able and willing to concert and promote useful and national measures will seldom be unembarrassed by the ignorance, prejudices, fears, or interested views of others.

In so large a body secrecy and despatch will be too uncommon; and foreign as well as local influence will frequently oppose and sometimes prostrate the worst measures. Large assemblies often misunderstand or neglect the obligations of character, honour, and dignity, and will collectively do or omit things which individual gentlemen in private capacities would not approve. As the many divide blame and also divide credit, too little a portion of either falls to each man there to affect him strongly, even in cases where the whole blame or the whole credit must be national. It is not easy for those to think and feel as sovereigns who have been always accustomed to think and feel as subjects.

The executive business of sovereignty depending on so many wills, and those wills moved by such a variety of contradictory motives and inducements, will in general be but feebly done. Such a sovereignty, however theoretically responsible, cannot be effectually so in its departments and officers without adequate judicatories. I therefore promise myself nothing very desirable from any change which does not divide the sovereignty into its proper departments. Let Congress legislate—let others execute—let others judge.

Shall we have a king? Not in my opinion while other experiments remain untried. Might we not have a governor-general limited in his prerogatives and duration? Might not Congress be divided into an upper and lower house—the former appointed for life, the latter annually,—and let the governor-general (to preserve the balance), with the advice of a council, formed for that only purpose, of the great judicial officers, have a negative on their acts? Our government should in some degree be suited to our manners and circumstances, and they, you know, are not strictly democratical. What powers should be granted to the government so constituted is a question which deserves much thought. I think the more the better, the States retaining only so much as may be necessary for domestic purposes, and all their principal officers, civil and military, being commissioned and removable by the national government. These are short hints. Details would exceed the limits of a letter, and to you be superfluous.

A convention is in contemplation, and I am glad to find your name among those of its intended members. To me the policy of *such* a convention appears questionable; their authority is to be derived from acts of the State legislatures. Are the State legislatures authorized, either by themselves or others, to alter constitutions? I think not; they who hold commissions can by virtue of them neither retrench nor extend the powers conveyed to them. Perhaps it is intended that this convention shall not ordain, but only recommend; if so, there is danger that their recommendations will produce endless discussion, perhaps jealousies and party heats.

Would it not be better for Congress plainly and in strong terms to declare that the present Federal Government is inadequate to the purposes for which it was instituted; that they forbear to point out its particular defects or to ask for an extension of any particular powers, lest improper jealousies should thence arise; but that in their opinion it would be expedient for the people of the States without delay to appoint State conventions (in the way they choose their general assemblies), with the sole and express power of appointing deputies to a general convention who, or the majority of whom, should take into consideration the Articles of Confederation, and make such alterations, amendments, and additions thereto as to them should appear necessary and proper, and which being by them ordained and published should have the same force and obligation which all or any of the present articles now have? No alterations in the government should, I think, be made, nor if attempted will easily take place, unless deducible from the only source of just authority—*the People.*

Accept, my dear sir, my warmest and most cordial wishes for your health and happiness, and believe me to be with the greatest respect and esteem,

Your most obedient servant,

John Jay

George Washington

Letter to John Jay (March 10, 1787)

Mount Vernon

Dear Sir:

I am indebted to you for two letters. The first, introductory of Mr. Anstey, needed no apology; nor will any be necessary on future similar occasions. The other, of the 7th of January, is on a very interesting subject, deserving very particular attention.

How far the revision of the federal system, and giving more adequate powers to Congress, may be productive of an efficient government, I will not, under my present view of the matter, pretend to decide. That many inconveniences result from the present form, none can deny; those enumerated in your letter are so obvious and sensibly felt, that no logic can controvert, nor is it probable that any change of conduct will remove them; and that all attempts to alter or amend it will be like the propping of a house which is ready to fall, and which no shores can support (as many seem to think), may also be true.

But is the public mind matured for such an important change as the one you have suggested? What would be the consequence of a premature attempt?

My opinion is, that this country has yet to *feel* and *see* a little more before it can be accomplished. A thirst for power, and the bantling—I had like to have said MONSTER—sovereignty, which have taken such fast hold of the States individually, will, when joined by the many whose personal consequence in the line of State politics will in a manner be annihilated, form a strong phalanx against it; and when to these, the few who can hold posts of honour or profit in the national government are compared with the many who will see but little prospect of being noticed, and the discontents of others who may look for appointments, the opposition would be altogether irresistible, till the mass as well as the more discerning part of the community shall see the necessity.

Among men of reflection, few will be found, I believe, who are not *beginning* to think that our system is better in theory than practice; and that, notwithstanding the boasted virtue of America, it is more than probable we shall exhibit the last melancholy proof that mankind are not competent to their own government, without the means of coercion, in the sovereign. Yet I would try what the wisdom of the proposed Convention will suggest, and what can be effected by their counsels. It may be the last peaceable mode of essaying the practicability of the present form, without a greater lapse of time than the exigency of our affairs will admit. In strict propriety, a Convention so holden may not be legal; Congress, however, may give it a colouring by recommendation which would fit it more to the taste, without proceeding to a definition of powers: this, however constitutionally it might be done, would not in my opinion be expedient; for delicacy on the one hand, and jealousy on the other, would produce a mere nihil. [. . .]

James Madison

Vices of the Political System of the United States (1787)

1. Failure of the States to comply with the Constitutional requisitions. This evil has been so fully experienced both during the war and since the peace, results so naturally from the number and independent authority of the States and has been so uniformly examplified in every similar Confederacy, that it may be considered as not less radically and permanently inherent in, than it is fatal to the object of, the present System.

2. Encroachments by the States on the federal authority. Examples of this are numerous and repetitions may be foreseen in almost every case where any favorite object of a State shall present a temptation. Among these examples are the wars and Treaties of Georgia with the Indians—The unlicensed compacts between Virginia and Maryland, and between Pena. & N. Jersey—the troops raised and to be kept up by Massts.

3. Violations of the law of nations and of treaties. From the number of Legislatures, the sphere of life from which most of their members are taken, and the circumstances under which their legislative business is carried on, irregularities of this kind must frequently happen. Accordingly not a year has passed without instances of them in some one or other of the States. The Treaty of peace—the treaty with France—the treaty with Holland have each been violated. The causes of these irregularities must necessarily produce frequent violations of the law of nations in other respects.

As yet foreign powers have not been rigorous in animadverting on us. This moderation however cannot be mistaken for a permanent partiality to our faults, or a permanent security agst. those disputes with other nations, which being among the greatest of public calamities, it ought to be least in the power of any part of the Community to bring on the whole.

4. Trespasses of the States on the rights of each other. These are alarming symptoms, and may be daily apprehended as we are admonished by daily experience. See the law of Virginia restricting foreign vessels to certain ports—of Maryland in favor of vessels belonging to her own citizens—of N. York in favor of the same.

Paper money, instalments of debts, occlusion of Courts, making property a legal tender, may likewise be deemed aggressions on the rights of other States. As the Citizens of every State aggregately taken stand more or less in the relation of Creditors or debtors, to the Citizens of every other States, Acts of the debtor State in favor of debtors, affect the Creditor State, in the same manner, as they do its own citizens who are relatively creditors towards other citizens. This remark may be extended to foreign nations. If the exclusive regulation of the value and alloy of coin was properly delegated to the federal authority, the policy of it equally requires a controul on the States in the cases above mentioned. It must have been meant 1. to preserve uniformity in the circulating medium throughout the nation. 2. to prevent those frauds on the citizens of other States, and the subjects of foreign powers, which might disturb the tranquility at home, or involve the Union in foreign contests.

The practice of many States in restricting the commercial intercourse with other States, and putting their productions and manufactures on the same footing with those of foreign nations, though not contrary to the federal articles, is certainly adverse to the spirit of the Union, and tends to beget retaliating regulations, not less expensive & vexatious in themselves, than they are destructive of the general harmony.

5. Want of concert in matters where common interest requires it. This defect is strongly illustrated in the state of our commercial affairs. How much has the national dignity, interest, and revenue suffered from this cause? Instances of inferior moment are the want of uniformity in the laws concerning naturalization & literary property; of provision for national seminaries, for grants of incorporation for national purposes, for canals and other works of general utility, wch. may at present be defeated by the perverseness of particular States whose concurrence is necessary.

6. Want of guaranty to the States of their Constitutions & laws against internal violence. The confederation is silent on this point and therefore by the second article the hands of the federal authority are tied. According to Republican Theory, Right and power being both vested in the majority, are held to be synonimous. According to fact and experience a minority may in an appeal to force, be an overmatch for the majority. 1. If the minority happen to include all such as possess the skill and habits of military life, & such as possess the great pecuniary resources, one third only may conquer the remaining two thirds. 2. One third of those who participate in the choice of the rulers, may be rendered a majority by the accession of those whose poverty excludes them from a right of suffrage, and who for obvious reasons will be more likely to join the standard of sedition than that of the established Government. 3. Where slavery exists the republican Theory becomes still more fallacious.

7. Want of sanction to the laws, and of coercion in the Government of the Confederacy. A sanction is essential to the idea of law, as coercion is to that of Government. The federal system being destitute of both, wants the great vital principles of a Political Cons[ti]tution. Under the form of such a Constitution, it is in fact nothing more than a treaty of amity of commerce and of alliance, between so many independent and Sovereign States. From what cause could so fatal an omission have happened in the articles of Confederation? from a mistaken confidence that the justice, the good faith, the honor, the sound policy, of the several legislative assemblies would render superfluous any appeal to the ordinary motives by which the laws secure the obedience of individuals: a confidence which does honor to the enthusiastic virtue of the compilers, as much as the inexperience of the crisis apologizes for their errors. The time which has since elapsed has had the double effect, of increasing the light, and tempering the warmth, with which the arduous work may be revised. It is no longer doubted that a unanimous and punctual obedience of 13 independent bodies, to the acts of the federal Government, ought not be calculated on. Even during the war, when external danger supplied in some degree the defect of legal & coercive sanctions, how imperfectly did the States fulfil their obligations to the Union? In time of peace, we see already what is to be expected. How indeed could it be otherwise? In the first place, Every general act of the Union must necessarily bear unequally hard on some particular member or members of it. Secondly the partiality of the members to their own interests and rights, a partiality which will be fostered by the Courtiers of popularity, will naturally exaggerate the inequality where it exists, and even suspect it where it has no existence. Thirdly a distrust of the voluntary compliance of each other may prevent the compliance of any, although it should be the latent disposition of all.

Here are causes & pretexts which will never fail to render federal measures abortive. If the laws of the States, were merely recommendatory to their citizens, or if they were to be rejudged by County authorities, what security, what probability would exist, that they would be carried into execution? Is the security or probability greater in favor of the acts of Congs. which depending for their execution on the will of the state legislatures, wch. are tho' nominally authoritative, in fact recommendatory only.

8. **Want of ratification by the people of the articles of Confederation.** In some of the States the Confederation is recognized by, and forms a part of the constitution. In others however it has received no other sanction than that of the Legislative authority. From this defect two evils result: 1. Whenever a law of a State happens to be repugnant to an act of Congress, particularly when the latter is of posterior date to the former, it will be at least questionable whether the latter must not prevail; and as the question must be decided by the Tribunals of the State, they will be most likely to lean on the side of the State. 2. As far as the Union of the States is to be regarded as a league of sovereign powers, and not as a political Constitution by virtue of which they are become one sovereign power, so far it seems to follow from the doctrine of compacts, that a breach of any of the articles of the confederation by any of the parties to it, absolves the other parties from their respective obligations, and gives them a right if they chuse to exert it, of dissolving the Union altogether.

9. **Multiplicity of laws in the several States.** In developing the evils which viciate the political system of the U.S. it is proper to include those which are found within the States individually, as well as those which directly affect the States collectively, since the former class have an indirect influence on the general malady and must not be overlooked in forming a compleat remedy. Among the evils then of our situation may well be ranked the multiplicity of laws from which no State is exempt. As far as laws are necessary, to mark with precision the duties of those who are to obey them, and to take from those who are to administer them a discretion, which might be abused, their number is the price of liberty. As far as the laws exceed this limit, they are a nusance: a nusance of the most pestilent kind. Try the Codes of the several States by this test, and what a luxuriancy of legislation do they present. The short period of independency has filled as many pages as the century which preceded it. Every year, almost every session, adds a new volume. This may be the effect in part, but it can only be in part, of the situation in which the revolution has placed us. A review of the several codes will shew that every necessary and useful part of the least voluminous of them might be compressed into one tenth of the compass, and at the same time be rendered tenfold as perspicuous.

10. **Mutability of the laws of the States.** This evil is intimately connected with the former yet deserves a distinct notice as it emphatically denotes a vicious legislation. We daily see laws repealed or superseded, before any trial can have been made of their merits: and even before a knowledge of them can have reached the remoter districts within which they were to operate. In the regulations of trade this instability becomes a snare not only to our citizens but to foreigners also.

11. **Injustice of the laws of States.** If the multiplicity and mutability of laws prove a want of wisdom, their injustice betrays a defect still more alarming: more alarming not merely because it is a greater evil in itself, but because it brings more into question the fundamental principle of republican Government, that the majority who rule in such Governments, are the safest Guardians both of public Good and of private rights. To what causes is this evil to be ascribed?

These causes lie 1. in the Representative bodies. 2. in the people themselves.

1. Representative appointments are sought from 3 motives. 1. ambition 2. personal interest. 3. public good. Unhappily the two first are proved by experience to be most prevalent. Hence the candidates who feel them, particularly, the second, are most industrious, and most successful in pursuing their object: and forming often a majority in the legislative Councils, with interested views, contrary to the interest, and views, of their Constituents, join in a perfidious sacrifice of the latter to the former. A succeeding election it might be supposed, would displace the offenders, and repair the mischief. But how easily are base and selfish measures, masked by pretexts of public good and apparent expediency? How frequently

will a repetition of the same arts and industry which succeeded in the first instance, again prevail on the unwary to misplace their confidence?

How frequently too will the honest but unenlightened representative be the dupe of a favorite leader, veiling his selfish views under the professions of public good, and varnishing his sophistical arguments with the glowing colours of popular eloquence?

2. A still more fatal if not more frequent cause lies among the people themselves. All civilized societies are divided into different interests and factions, as they happen to be creditors or debtors—Rich or poor—husbandmen, merchants or manufacturers—members of different religious sects—followers of different political leaders—inhabitants of different districts—owners of different kinds of property &c &c. In republican Government the majority however composed, ultimately give the law. Whenever therefore an apparent interest or common passion unites a majority what is to restrain them from unjust violations of the rights and interests of the minority, or of individuals? Three motives only 1. a prudent regard to their own good as involved in the general and permanent good of the Community. This consideration although of decisive weight in itself, is found by experience to be too often unheeded. It is too often forgotten, by nations as well as by individuals that honesty is the best policy. 2dly. respect for character. However strong this motive may be in individuals, it is considered as very insufficient to restrain them from injustice. In a multitude its efficacy is diminished in proportion to the number which is to share the praise or the blame. Besides, as it has reference to public opinion, which within a particular Society, is the opinion of the majority, the standard is fixed by those whose conduct is to be measured by it. The public opinion without the Society, will be little respected by the people at large of any Country. Individuals of extended views, and of national pride, may bring the public proceedings to this standard, but the example will never be followed by the multitude. Is it to be imagined that an ordinary citizen or even an assemblyman of R. Island in estimating the policy of paper money, ever considered or cared in what light the measure would be viewed in France or Holland; or even in Massts or Connect.? It was a sufficient temptation to both that it was for their interest: it was a sufficient sanction to the latter that it was popular in the State; to the former that it was so in the neighbourhood. 3dly. will Religion the only remaining motive be a sufficient restraint? It is not pretended to be such on men individually considered. Will its effect be greater on them considered in an aggregate view? quite the reverse. The conduct of every popular assembly acting on oath, the strongest of religious ties, proves that individuals join without remorse in acts, against which their consciences would revolt if proposed to them under the like sanction, separately in their closets. When indeed Religion is kindled into enthusiasm, its force like that of other passions, is increased by the sympathy of a multitude. But enthusiasm is only a temporary state of religion, and while it lasts will hardly be seen with pleasure at the helm of Government. Besides as religion in its coolest state, is not infallible, it may become a motive to oppression as well as a restraint from injustice. Place three individuals in a situation wherein the interest of each depends on the voice of the others, and give to two of them an interest opposed to the rights of the third? Will the latter be secure? The prudence of every man would shun the danger. The rules & forms of justice suppose & guard against it. Will two thousand in a like situation be less likely to encroach on the rights of one thousand? The contrary is witnessed by the notorious factions & oppressions which take place in corporate towns limited as the opportunities are, and in little republics when uncontrouled by apprehensions of external danger. If an enlargement of the sphere is found to lessen the insecurity of private rights, it is not because the impulse of a common interest or passion is less predominant in this case with the majority; but because a common interest or passion is less apt to be felt and the requisite combinations less easy to be formed by a great than by a small number. The Society becomes broken into a greater variety of interests, of pursuits, of passions, which check each other, whilst those who may feel a common sentiment have less opportunity of communication and concert. It may be inferred that the inconveniences of popular States contrary to the prevailing Theory, are in proportion not to the extent, but to the narrowness of their limits.

The great desideratum in Government is such a modification of the Sovereignty as will render it sufficiently neutral between the different interests and factions, to controul one part of the Society from invading the rights of another, and at the same time sufficiently controuled itself, from setting up an interest adverse to that of the whole Society. In absolute Monarchies, the prince is sufficiently, neutral towards his subjects, but frequently sacrifices their happiness to his ambition or his avarice. In small Republics, the sovereign will is sufficiently controuled from such a Sacrifice of the entire Society, but is not sufficiently neutral towards the parts composing it. As a limited Monarchy tempers the evils of an absolute one; so an extensive Republic meliorates the administration of a small Republic.

An auxiliary desideratum for the melioration of the Republican form is such a process of elections as will most certainly extract from the mass of the Society the purest and noblest characters which it contains; such as will at once feel most strongly the proper motives to pursue the end of their appointment, and be most capable to devise the proper means of attaining it.

Letter to George Washington (April 16, 1787)

Dear Sir,—I have been honoured with your letter of the 31 March, and find with much pleasure, that your views of the reform which ought to be pursued by the Convention give a sanction to those which I have entertained. Temporising applications will dishonor the Councils which propose them, and may foment the internal malignity of the disease, at the same time that they produce an ostensible palliation of it. Radical attempts although unsuccessful will at least justify the authors of them.

Having been lately led to revolve the subject which is to undergo the discussion of the Convention, and formed in my mind *some* outlines of a new system, I take the liberty of submitting them without apology to your eye.

Conceiving that an individual independence of the States is utterly irreconcileable with their aggregate sovereignty, and that a consolidation of the whole into one simple republic would be as inexpedient as it is unattainable, I have sought for some middle ground, which may at once support a due supremacy of the national authority, and not exclude the local authorities wherever they can be subordinately useful.

I would propose as the groundwork that a change be made in the principle of representation. According to the present form of the Union, in which the intervention of the States is in all great cases necessary to effectuate the measures of Congress, an equality of suffrage, does not destroy the inequality of importance in the several members. No one deny that Virginia and Massachusetts, have more weight and influence, both within and without Congress than Delaware or Rhode Island. Under a system which would operate in many essential points without the intervention of the State legislatures, the case would be materially altered. A vote in the national Councils from Delaware, would then have the same effect and value as one from the largest State in the Union. I am ready to believe that such a change would not be attended with much difficulty. A majority of the States, and those of greatest influence, will regard it as favorable to them. To the northern States it will be recommended by their present populousness; to the southern, by their expected advantage in this respect. The lesser States must in every event yield to the predominant will. But the consideration which particularly urges a change in the representation is that it will obviate the principal objections of the larger States to the necessary concessions of power.

I would propose next that in addition to the present federal powers, the national Government should be armed with positive and compleat authority in all cases which require uniformity; such as the regulation of trade, including the right of taxing both exports and imports, the fixing the terms and forms of naturalization, &c, &c.

Over and above this positive power, a negative *in all cases whatsoever* on the legislative acts of the States, as heretofore exercised by the Kingly prerogative, appears to me to be absolutely necessary, and to be the least possible encroachment on the State jurisdictions. Without this defensive power, every positive power that can be given on paper will be evaded and defeated. The States will continue to invade the National jurisdiction, to violate treaties and the law of nations and to harass each other with rival and spiteful measures dictated by mistaken views of interest. Another happy effect of this prerogative would be its controul on the internal vicissitudes of State policy, and the aggressions of interested majorities on the rights of minorities and of individuals. The great desideratum, which has not yet been found for Republican Governments seems to be some disinterested and dispassionate umpire in disputes between different passions and interests in the State. The majority who alone have the right of decision, have frequently an interest, real or supposed in abusing it. In Monarchies the Sovereign is more neutral to the interests and views of different parties; but unfortunately he too often forms interests of his own repugnant to those of the whole. Might not the national prerogative here suggested be found sufficietly disinterested for the decision of local questions of policy, whilst it would itself be sufficiently restrained from the pursuit of interests adverse to those of the whole Society? There has not been any moment since the peace at which the representatives of the Union would have given an assent to paper money or any other measure of a kindred nature.

The national supremacy ought also to be extended, as I conceive, to the Judiciary departments. If those who are to expound and apply the laws are connected by their interests and their oaths with the particular States wholly, and not with the Union, the participation of the Union in the making of the laws may be possibly rendered unavailing. It seems at least necessary that the oaths of the Judges should include a fidelity to the general as well as local constitution, and that an appeal should lie to some National tribunal in all cases to which foreigners or inhabitants of other States may be parties. The admiralty jurisdiction seems to fall entirely within the purview of the national Government.

The National supremacy in the Executive departments is liable to some difficulty, unless the officers administering them could be made appointable by the supreme Government. The Militia ought certainly to be placed in some form or other under the authority which is entrusted with the general protection and defence.

A Government composed of such extensive powers should be well organized and balanced. The legislative department might be divided into two branches; one of them chosen every years [sic] by the people at large, or by the Legislatures; the other to consist of fewer members, to hold their places for a longer term, and to go out in such a rotation as always to leave in office a large majority of old members. Perhaps the negative on the laws might be most conveniently exercised by this branch. As a further check, a Council of revision including the great ministerial officers might be superadded.

A National Executive must also be provided. I have scarcely ventured as yet to form my own opinion either of the manner in which it ought to be constituted or of the authorities with which it ought to be cloathed.

An article should be inserted expressly guarantying the tranquillity of the States against internal as well as external dangers.

In like manner the right of coercion should be expressly declared. With the resources of Commerce in hand, the National administration might always find means of exerting it either by sea or land. But the difficulty and awkwardness of operating by force on the collective will of a State render it particularly desirable that the necessity of it might be precluded. Perhaps the negative on the laws might create such a mutuality of dependence between the central and particular authorities, as to answer this purpose or, perhaps, some defined objects of taxation might be submitted along with commerce, to the general authority.

To give a new System its proper validity and energy, a ratification must be obtained from the people, and not merely from the ordinary authority of the Legislatures. This will be the more essential as inroads on the *existing Constitutions* of the States will be unavoidable. [. . .]

Notes on the Debates in the Federal Convention (1787)

Tuesday, May 29

Mr. Randolph then opened the main business.

He expressed his regret that it should fall to him, rather than those, who were of longer standing in life and political experience, to open the great subject of their mission. But, as the convention had originated from Virginia, and his colleagues supposed that some proposition was expected from them, they had imposed this task on him. He then commented on the difficulty of the crisis, and necessity of preventing the fulfilment of the prophecies of the American downfall. He observed that in revising the federal system we ought to inquire 1. into the properties, which such a government ought to possess, 2. the defects of the confederation, 3. the danger of our situation & 4. the remedy.

1. The Character of such a government ought to secure 1. against foreign invasion: 2. against dissentions between members of the Union, or seditions in particular states: 3. to procure to the several States, various blessings, of which an isolated situation was incapable: 4. to be able to defend itself against incroachment: & 5. to be paramount to the state constitutions.

2. In speaking of the defects of the confederation he professed a high respect for its authors, and considered them, as having done all that patriots could do, in the then infancy of science, of constitutions, & of confederacies,—when the inefficiency of requisitions was unknown—no commercial discord had arisen among any states—no rebellion had appeared as in Massts.—foreign debts had not become urgent—the havoc of paper money had not been foreseen—treaties had not been violated—and perhaps nothing better could be obtained from the jealousy of the states with regard to their sovereignty.

He then proceeded to enumerate the defects:

1. that the confederation produced no security against foreign invasion; congress not being permitted to prevent a war nor to support it by their own authority—Of this he cited many examples; most of which tended to shew, that they could not cause infractions of treaties or of the law of nations, to be punished: that particular states might by their conduct provoke war without controul; and that neither militia nor draughts being fit for defence on such occasions, inlistments only could be successful, and these could not be executed without money.
2. that the federal government could not check the quarrels between states, nor a rebellion in any, not having constitutional power nor means to interpose according to the exigency:
3. that there were many advantages, which the U.S. might acquire, which were not attainable under the confederation—such as a productive impost—counteraction of the commercial regulations of other nations—pushing of commerce ad libitum—&c &c.
4. that the federal government could not defend itself against the incroachments from the states.
5. that it was not even paramount to the state constitutions, ratified, as it was in many of the states.

3. He next reviewed the danger of our situation, appealed to the sense of the best friends of the U.S.—the prospect of anarchy from the laxity of government every where; and to other considerations.

4. He the proceeded to the remedy; the basis of which he said must be the republican principle.

He proposed as conformable to his ideas the following resolutions, which he explained one by one [Here insert ye Resolutions annexed.]

Resolutions proposed by Mr. Randolph in Convention May 29, 1787

1. Resolved that the Articles of Confederation ought to be so corrected & enlarged as to accomplish the objects proposed by their institution; namely, "common defence, security of liberty and general welfare."

2. Resd. therefore that the rights of suffrage in the National Legislature ought to be proportioned to the Quotas of contribution, or to the number of free inhabitants, as the one or the other rule may seem best in different cases.

3. Resd. that the National Legislature ought to consist of two branches.

4. Resd. that the members of the first branch of the National Legislature ought to be elected by the people of the several States every _____ for the term of _____; to be of the age of _____ years at least, to receive liberal stipends by [which] they may be compensated for the devotion of their time to public service; to be ineligible to any office established by a particular State, or under the authority of the United States, except those peculiarly belonging to the functions of the first branch, during the term of service, and for the space of _____ after its expiration; to be incapable of reelection for the space of _____ after the expiration of their term of service, and to be subject to recall.

5. Resold. that the members of the second branch of the National Legislature ought to be elected by those of the first, out of a proper number of persons nominated by the individual Legislatures, to be of the age of _____ years at least; to hold their offices for a term sufficient to ensure their independency; to receive liberal stipends, by which they may be compensated for the devotion of their time to public service; and to be ineligible to any office established by a particular State, or under the authority of the United States, except those peculiarly belonging to the functions of the second branch, during the term of service, and for the space of _____ after the expiration thereof.

6. Resolved that each branch ought to possess the right of originating Acts; that the National Legislature ought to be impowered to enjoy the Legislative Rights vested in Congress by the Confederation & moreover to legislate in all cases to which the separate States are incompetent, or in which the harmony of the United States may be interrupted by the exercise of individual Legislation; to negative all laws passed by the several States, contravening in the opinion of the National Legislature the articles of Union; and to call forth the force of the Union agst. any member of the Union failing to fulfill its duty under the articles thereof.

7. Resd, that a National Executive be instituted; to be chosen by the National Legislature for the term of _____ years, to receive punctually at stated times, a fixed compensation for the services rendered, in which no increase or diminution shall be made so as to affect the Magistracy, existing at the time of increase or diminution, and to be ineligible a second time; and that besides a general authority to execute the National laws, it ought to enjoy the Executive rights vested in Congress by the Confederation.

8. Resd. that the Executive and a convenient number of the National Judiciary, ought to compose a Council of revision with authority to examine every act of the National Legislature before it shall operate, & every act of a particular Legislature before a Negative thereon shall be final; and that the dissent of the said Council shall amount to a rejection, unless the Act of the National Legislature be again passed, or that of a particular Legislature be again negatived by _____ of the members of each branch.

9. Resd. that a National Judiciary be established to consist of one or more supreme tribunals, and of inferior tribunals to be chosen by the National Legislature, to hold their offices during good behaviour; and to receive punctually at stated times fixed compensation for their services, in which no increase or diminution shall be made so as to affect the persons actually in office at the time of such increase or diminution. That the jurisdiction of the inferior tribunals shall be to hear & determine in the first instance, and of the supreme tribunal to hear and determine in the dernier resort, all piracies & felonies on the high seas, captures from an enemy; cases in which foreigners or citizens of other States applying to such jurisdictions may be interested, or which respect the collection of the National revenue; impeachments of any National officers, and questions which may involve the national peace and harmony.

10. Resolvd. that provision ought to be made for the admission of States lawfully arising within the limits of the United States, whether from a voluntary junction of Government & Territory or otherwise, with the consent of a number of voices in the National legislature less than the whole.

11. Resd. that a Republican Government & the territory of each State, except in the instance of a voluntary junction of Government & territory, ought to be guarantied by the United States to each State.

12. Resd. that provision ought to be made for the continuance of Congress and their authorities and privileges, until a given day after the reform of the articles of Union shall be adopted, and for the completion of all their engagements.

13. Resd. that provision ought to be made for the amendment of the Articles of Union whensoever it shall seem necessary, and that the assent of the National Legislature ought not to be required thereto.

14. Resd. that the Legislative Executive & Judiciary powers within the several States ought to be bound by oath to support the articles of Union.

15. Resd. that the amendments which shall be offered to the Confederation, by the Convention ought at a proper time, or times, after the approbation of Congress to be submitted to an assembly or assemblies of Representatives, recommended by the several Legislatures to be expressly chosen by the people, to consider & decide thereon.

He concluded with an exhortation, not to suffer the present opportunity of establishing general peace, harmony, happiness and liberty in the U. S. to pass away unimproved.

It was then Resolved—That the House will tomorrow resolve itself into a Committee of the Whole House to consider of the state of the American Union.—and that the propositions moved by Mr. Randolph be referred to the said Committee.

Wednesday, May 30

1st resolution from Mr. Randol[ph]

Mr. R. wishes to have that resol. dissented to. The resol. postponed to take up the following:

1st. That a union of the States merely foederal will not accomplish the object proposed by the articles of confederation, namely, "common defence, security of liberty, and general welfare."

Mr. C. Pinkney wishes to know whether the establishment of this Resolution is intended as a ground for a consolidation of the several States into one.

Mr. Randol[ph] has nothing further in contemplation than what the propositions, he has submitted yesterday has [sic] expressed.

2. Resolved that no treaty or treaties between the whole or a less number of the States in their sovereign capacities will accomplish their common defence, liberty or welfare.

3. Resolved therefore that a national governmen[t] ought to be established consisting of a supreme legislature, judiciary and executive.

Mr Whythe [sic] presumes from the silence of the house that the gentn. are prepared to pass on the resolution and proposes its being put.

Mr. Butler does not think the house prepared, that he is not. Wishes Mr. Randolph to shew that the existence of the States cannot be preserved by any other mode than a national government.

Gen. Pinkney thinks agreeing to the resolve is declaring that the convention does not act under the authority of the recommendation of Congress.

The first resolution postponed to take up the 3d. viz.—Resolved that a national government ought to be established consisting of a supreme legislature, judiciary and executive.

1787, 21 Febry. Resolution of Congress

Resolved that in the opinion of Congress it is expedient that on the 2d Monday of May next a convention of delegates who shall have been appointed by the several States to be held at Philada. for the sole and expres[s] purpose of revising the articles of confederation, and reporting to Congress and the several legislatures, such alterations and provisions therein as shall when agreeed [sic] to in Congress, and confirmed by the States, render the federal constitution, adequate to the exigencies of government and the preservation of the union.

Mr. Randolph explains the intention of the 3d Resolution. Repeats the substance of his yesterdays observations. It is only meant to give the national government a power to defend and protect itself. To take therefore from the respective legislatures or States, no more sover[e]ignty than is competent to this end.

Mr. Dickinson. Under obligations to the gentlemen who brought forward the systems laid before the house yesterday. Yet differs from the mode of proceeding to which the resolutions or propositions before the Committee lead. Would propose a more simple mode. All agree that the confederation is defective all agree that it ought to be amended. We are a nation altho' consisting of parts or States—we are also confederated, and he hopes we shall always remain confederated. The enquiry should be—

1. What are the legislative powers which we should vest in Congress.
2. What judiciary powers.
3. What executive powers.

We may resolve therefore, in order to let us into the business. That the confederation is defective; and then proceed to the definition of such powers as may be thought adequate to the objects for which it was instituted.

Mr. E. Gerry. Does not rise to speak to the merits of the question before the Committee but to the mode.

A distinction has been made between a federal and national government. We ought not to determine that there is this distinction for if we do, it is questionable not only whether this convention can propose an government totally different or whether Congress itself would have a right to pass such a resolution as that before the house. The commission from Massachusets empowers the deputies to proceed agreeably to the recommendation of Congress. This the foundation of the convention. If we have a right to pass this resolution we have a right to annihilate the confederation.

Proposes—In the opinion of this convention, provision should be made for the establishment of a federal legislative, judiciary, and executive.

Governeur Morris. Not yet ripe for a decision, because men seem to have affixed different explanations to the terms before the house. 1. We are not now under a federal gover[n]ment. 2. There is no such thing. A federal government is that which has a right to compel every part to do its duty. The federal gov. has no such compelling capacities, whether considered in their legislative, judicial or Executive qualities.

The States in their appointments Congress in their recommendations point directly to the establishment of a supreme government capable of "the common defence, security of liberty and general welfare."

Cannot conceive of a government in which there can exist two supremes. A federal agreement which each party may violate at pleasure cannot answer the purpose. One government better calculated to prevent wars or render them less expensive or bloody than many.

We had better take a supreme government now, than a despot twenty years hence—for come he must.

Mr. Reed, Genl. [Pinckney] 2dng proposes—In order to carry into execution the design of the States in——this meeting and to accomplish the objects proposed by the confederation resolved that A more effective government consisting of a legislative judiciary and executive ought to be established.

In order to carry into execution.

Mr. R. King—The object of the motion from Virginia, an establishment of a government that is to act upon the whole people of the U.S.

The object of the motion from Delaware seems to have application merely to the strengthening the confederation by some additional powers.

Mr. Madison—The motion does go to bring out the sense of the house—whether the States shall be governed by one power. If agreed to it will decide nothing. The meaning of the States that the confed. is defect. and ought to be amended. [. . .]

Monday, June 4

In Committee of the Whole

The Question was resumed on motion of Mr. Pinkney 2ded by Wilson, "shall the blank for the number of the Executive be filled with a single person?"

Mr. Wilson was in favor of the motion. It had been opposed by the gentleman from Virga. [Mr.

Randolph] but the arguments used had not convinced him. He observed that the objections of Mr. R. were levelled not so much agst. the measure itself, as agst. its unpopularity, If he could suppose that it would occasion a rejection of the plan of which it should form a part, though the part was an important one, yet he would give it up rather than lose the whole. On examination he could see no evidence of the alledged antipathy of the people. On the contrary he was persuaded that it does not exist. All know that a single magistrate is not a King. One fact has great weight with him. All the 13 States tho agreeing in scarce any other instance, agree in placing a single magistrate at the head of the Governt. The idea of three heads has taken place in none. The degree of power is indeed different; but there are no co-ordinate heads. In addition to his former reasons for preferring a unity, he would mention another. The *tranquility* not less than the vigor of the Govt. he thought would be favored by it. Among three equal members, he foresaw nothing but uncontrouled, continued, & violent animosities; which would not only interrupt the public administration; but diffuse their poison thro' the other branches of Govt., thro' the States, and at length thro' the people at large. If the members were to be unequal in power the principle of the opposition to the unity was given up. If equal, the making them an odd number would not be a remedy. In Courts of Justice there are two sides only to a question. In the Legislative & Executive departmts. questions have commonly many sides. Each member therefore might espouse a separate one & no two agree.

Mr. Sherman. This matter is of great importance and ought to be well considered before it is determined. Mr. Wilson he said had observed that in each State a single magistrate was placed at the head of the Govt. It was so he admitted, and properly so, and he wished the same policy to prevail in the federal Govt. But then it should be also remarked that in all the States there was a Council of advice, without which the first magistrate could not act. A council he thought necessary to make the establishment acceptable to the people. Even in G.B. the King has a Council; and though he appoints it himself, its advice has its weight with him, and attracts the Confidence of the people.

Mr. Williamson asks Mr. Wilson whether he means to annex a Council.

Mr. Wilson means to have no Council, which oftener serves to cover, than prevent malpractices.

Mr . Gerry was at a loss to discover the policy of three members for the Executive. It Wd. be extremely inconvenient in many instances, particularly in military matters, whether relating to the militia, an army, or a navy. It would be a general with three heads.

On the question for a single Executive it was agreed to Massts. ay. Cont. ay. N.Y. no. Pena. ay. Del. no. Maryd. no. Virg. ay. [Mr. R. & Mr. Blair no—Docr. McCg. Mr. M. & Gen W. ay. Col. Mason being no, but not in house, Mr. Wythe ay but gone home]. N.C. ay. S.C. ay. Georga ay.

First Clause of Proposition 8th relating to a *Council of Revision* taken into consideration.

Mr. Gerry doubts whether the Judiciary ought to form a part of it, as they will have a sufficient check agst. encroachments on their own department by their exposition of the laws, which involved a power of deciding on their Constitutionality. In some States the Judges had actually set aside laws as being agst. the Constitution. This was done too with general approbation. It was quite foreign from the nature of ye. office to make them judges of the policy of public measures. He moves to postpone the clause in order to propose "that the National Executive shall have a right to negative any Legislative act which shall not be afterwards passed by _____ parts of each branch of the national Legislature."

Mr. King seconds the motion, observing that the Judges ought to be able to expound the law as it should come before them, free from the bias of having participated in its formation.

Mr. Wilson thinks neither the original proposition nor the amendment go far enough. If the Legislative Exetv & Judiciary ought to be distinct & independent. The Executive ought to have an absolute negative. Without such a self-defense the Legislature can at any moment sink it into non-existence. He was for varying the proposition in such a manner as to give the Executive & Judiciary jointly an absolute negative.

On the question to postpone in order to take Mr. Gerry's proposition into consideration it was agreed to, Masss. ay. Cont. no. N.Y. ay. Pa. ay. Del. no. Maryd. no. Virga. no. N.C. ay. S.C. ay. Ga. ay.

Mr. Gerry's proposition being now before Committee, Mr. Wilson & Mr. Hamilton move that the last part of it [viz. Wch. Sl. not be afterwds. passed unless by parts of each branch of the National legislature] be struck out, so as to give the Executive an absolute negative on the laws. There was no danger they thought of such a power being too much exercised. It was mentioned by Col. Hamilton that the King of G.B. had not exerted his negative since the Revolution.

Mr. Gerry sees no necessity for so great a controul over the legislature as the best men in the Community would be comprised in the two branches of it.

Doc. Franklin, said he was sorry to differ from his colleague for whom he had a very great respect, on any occasion, but he could not help it on this. He had had some experience of this check in the Executive on the Legislature, under the proprietary Government of Pena. The negative of the Governor was constantly made use of to extort money. No good law whatever could be passed without a private bargain with him. An increase of his salary, or some donation, was always made a condition; till at last it became the regular practice, to have orders in his favor on the Treasury, presented along with the bills to be signed, so that he might actually receive the former before he should sign the latter. When the Indians were scalping the western people, and notice of it arrived, the concurrence of the Governor in the means of self-defence could not be got, till it was agreed that his Estate should be exempted from taxation: so that the people were to fight for the security of his property, whilst he was to bear no share of the burden. This was a mischievous sort of check. If the Executive was to have a Council, such a power would be less objectionable. It was true the King of G.B. had not, as was said, exerted his negative since the Revolution; but that matter was easily explained. The bribes and emoluments now given to the members of parliament rendered it unnecessary, every thing being done according to the will of the Ministers. He was afraid, if a negative should be given as proposed, that more power and money would be demanded, till at last eno' would be gotten to influence & bribe the Legislature into a compleat subjection to the will of the Executive.

Mr. Sherman was agst. enabling any one man to stop the will of the whole. No one man could be found so far above all the rest in wisdom. He thought we ought to avail ourselves of his wisdom in revising the laws, but not permit him to overule the decided and cool opinions of the Legislature.

Mr. Madison supposed that if a proper proportion of each branch should be required to overrule the objections of the Executive, it would answer the same purpose as an absolute negative. It would rarely if ever happen that the Executive constituted as ours is proposed to be would, have firmness eno' to resist the legislature, unless backed by a certain part of the body itself. The King of G.B. with all his splendid attributes would not be able to withstand ye. unanimous and eager wishes of both houses of Parliament. To give such a prerogative would certainly be obnoxious to the temper of this Country; its present temper at least.

Mr. Wilson believed as others did that this power would seldom be used. The Legislature would know that such a power existed, and would refrain from such laws, as it would be sure to defeat. Its silent operation would therefore preserve harmony and prevent mischief. The case of Pena formerly was very different from its present case. The Executive was not then as now to be appointed by the people. It will not in this case as in the one cited be supported by the head of a Great Empire, actuated by a different & sometimes opposite interest. The salary too is now proposed to be fixed by the Constitution, or if Dr. F.'s idea should be adopted all salary whatever interdicted. The requiring a large proportion of each House to overrule the Executive check might do in peaceable times; but there might be tempestuous moments in which animosities may run high between the Executive and Legislative branches, and in which the former ought to be able to defend itself.

Mr. Butler had been in favor of a single Executive Magistrate; but could he have entertained an idea that a compleat negative on the laws was to be given him he certainly should have acted very differently. It had been observed that in all countries the Executive power is in a constant course of increase. This was certainly the case in G.B. Gentlemen seemed to think that we had nothing to apprehend from an abuse of the Executive power. But why might not a Cataline or a Cromwell arise in this Country as well as in others.

Mr. Bedford was opposed to every check on the Legislative, even the Council of Revision first proposed. He thought it would be sufficient to mark out in the Constitution the boundaries to the Legislative Authority, which would give all the requisite security to the rights of the other departments. The Representatives of the people were the best Judges of what was for their interest, and ought to be under no external controul whatever. The two branches would produce a sufficient controul within the Legislature itself.

Col. Mason observed that a vote had already passed he found [he was out at the time] for vesting the executive powers in a single person. Among these powers was that of appointing to offices in certain cases. The probable abuses of a negative had been well explained by Dr. F. as proved by experience, the best of all tests. Will not the same door be opened here. The Executive may refuse its assent to necessary measures till new appointments shall be referred to him; and having by degrees engrossed all these into his own hands, the American Executive, like the British, will by bribery & influence, save himself the trouble & odium of exerting his negative afterwards. We are Mr. Chairman going very far in this business. We are not indeed constituting a British Government, but a more dangerous monarchy, an elective one. We are introducing a new principle into our system, and not necessary as in the British Govt. where the Executive has greater rights to defend. Do gentlemen mean to pave the way to hereditary Monarchy? Do they flatter themselves that the people will ever consent to such an innovation? If they do I venture to tell them, they are mistaken. The people never will consent. And do gentlemen consider the danger of delay, and the still greater danger of a rejection, not for a moment but forever, of the plan which shall be proposed to them. Notwithstanding the oppressions & injustice experienced among us from democracy; the genius of the people is in favor of it, and the genius of the people must be consulted. He could not but consider the federal system as in effect dissolved by the appointment of this Convention to devise a better one. And do gentlemen look forward to the dangerous interval between the extinction of an old, and the establishment of a new Governmt. and to the scenes of confusion which may ensue. He hoped that nothing like a Monarchy would ever be attempted in this Country. A hatred to its oppressions had carried the people through the late Revolution. Will it not be eno' to enable the Executive to suspend offensive laws, till they shall be coolly revised, and the objections to them overruled by a greater majority than was required in the first instance. He never could agree to give up all the rights of the people to a single Magistrate. If more than one had been fixed on, greater powers might have been entrusted to the Executive. He hoped this attempt to give such powers would have its weight hereafter as an argument for increasing the number of the Executive. Col. Mason had mentioned the circumstance of appointing officers. He knew how that point would be managed. No new appointment would be suffered as heretofore in Pensa. unless it be referred to the Executive; so that all profitable offices will be at his disposal. The first man put at the helm will be a good one. No body knows what sort may come afterwards. The Executive will be always increasing here, as elsewhere, till it ends in a Monarchy.

On the question for striking out so as to give Executive an absolute negative—Massts. no. Cont. no. N.Y. no. Pa. no. Dl. no. Md. no. Va. no. N.C. no. S.C. no. Georga. no.

Mr. Butler moved that the Resoln. be altered so as to read—"Resolved that the National Executive have a power to suspend any Legislative act for the term of _____."

Doc. Franklin seconds the motion.

Mr. Gerry observed that a power of suspending might do all the mischief dreaded from the negative of useful laws; without answering the salutary purpose of checking unjust or unwise ones.

On question for giving this suspending power all the States, to wit Massts. Cont. N.Y. Pa. Del. Maryd. Virga. N.C. S.C. Georgia were No.

On a question for enabling *two thirds* of each branch of the Legislature to overrule the revisionary check: it passed in the affirmative sub silentio; and was inserted in the blank of Mr. Gerry's motion.

On the question on Mr. Gerry's motion which gave the Executive alone without the Judiciary the revisionary controul on the laws unless overruled by two-thirds of each branch; Massts. ay. Cont. no. N.Y. ay. Pa. ay. Del. ay. Maryd. no. Va. ay. N.C. ay. S.C. ay. Geo. ay.

Tuesday, June 5

In Committee of the Whole

Governor Livingston from New Jersey, took his seat.

The words, "one or more" were struck out before "inferior tribunals" as an amendment to the last clause of Resoln. 9th The Clause—"that the National Judiciary be chose by the National Legislature," being under consideration.

Mr. Wilson opposed the appointmt. of Judges by the National Legisl: Experience shewed the impropriety of such appointments by numerous bodies. Intrigue, partiality, and concealment were the necessary consequences. A principal reason for unity in the executive was that officers might be appointed by a single, responsible person.

Mr. Rutlidge was by no means disposed to grant so great a power to any single person. The people will think we are leaning too much towards Monarchy. He was against establishing any national tribunal except a single supreme one. The State tribunals are most proper to decide in all cases in the first instance.

Docr. Franklin observed that two modes of chusing the Judges had been mentioned, to wit, by the Legislature and by the Executive. He wished such other modes to be suggested as might occur to other gentlemen; it being a point of great moment. He would mention one which he had understood was practiced in Scotland. He then in a brief and entertaining manner related a Scotch mode, in which the nomination proceeded from the Lawyers, who always selected the ablest of the profession in order to get rid of him, and share his practice among themselves. It was here he said the interest of the electors to make the best choice, which should always be made the case if possible.

Mr. Madison disliked the election of the Judges by the Legislature or any numerous body. Besides, the danger of intrigue and partiality, many of the members were not judges of the requisite qualifications. The Legislative talents which were very different from those of a Judge, commonly recommended men to the favor of Legislative Assemblies. It was known too that the accidental circumstances of presence and absence, of being a member or not a member, had a very undue influence on the appointment. On the other hand he was not satisfied with referring the appointment to the Executive. He rather inclined to give it to the Senatorial branch, as numerous eno' to be confided in—as not so numerous as to be governed by the motives of the other branch; and as being sufficiently stable and independent to follow their deliberate judgments. He hinted this only and moved that the *appointment by the Legislature* might be struck out, & a blank left to be hereafter filled on maturer reflection.

Mr. Wilson seconds it.

On the question for striking out. Massts. ay. Cont. no. N.Y. ay. N.J. ay. Pena.ay. Del. Ay. Md. ay. N.C. ay. S.C.no. Geo.ay.

Propos.15 for "*recommending Conventions under appointment of the people to ratify the new Constitution*" &c. being taken up.

Mr. Sharman thought such a popular ratification unnecessary: the articles of Confederation providing for changes and alterations with the assent of Congs. and ratification of State Legislatures.

Mr. Madison thought this provision essential. The articles of Confedn. themselves were defective in this respect, resting in many of the States on the Legislative sanction only. Hence in conflicts between acts of the States, and of Congs. especially where the former are of posterior date, and the decision is to be made by State tribunals, an uncertainty must necessarily prevail, or rather perhaps a certain decision in favor of the State authority. He suggested also that as far as the articles of Union were to be considered as a Treaty only of a particular sort, among the Governments of Independent States, the doctrine might be set up that a breach of any one article, by any of the parties, absolved the other parties from the whole obligation. For these reasons as well as others he thought it indispensable that the new Constitution should be ratified in the most unexceptionable form, and by the supreme authority of the people themselves.

Mr. Gerry observed that in the Eastern States the Confedn. had been sanctioned by the people themselves. He seemed afraid of referring the new system to them. The people in that quarter have at this time the wildest ideas of Government in the world. They were for abolishing the Senate in Massts. and giving all the other powers of Govt. to the other branch of the Legislature.

Mr. King supposed that the last article of ye Confedn. rendered the legislature competent to the ratification. The people of the Southern States where the federal articles had been ratified by the Legislatures only, had since *impliedly* given their sanction to it. He thought notwithstanding that there might be policy in varying the mode. A Convention being a single house, the adoption may more easily be carried thro' it, than thro' the Legislatures where there are several branches. The Legislatures also being to lose power, will be most likely to raise objections. The people having already parted with the necessary powers it is immaterial to them, by which Government they are possessed, provided they be well employed.

Mr. Wilson took this occasion to lead the Committee by a train of observations to the idea of not suffering a disposition in the plurality of States to confederate anew on better principles, to be defeated by the inconsiderate or selfish opposition of a few States. He hoped the provision for ratifying would be put on such a footing as to admit of such a partial union, with a door open for the accession of the rest.

Mr. Pinkney hoped that in case the experiment should not unanimously take place nine States might be authorized to unite under the same Governt.

Mr. Rutlidge havg. obtained a rule for reconsideration of the clause for establishing inferior tribunals under the national authority, now moved that that part of the clause in propos. 9. should be expunged: arguing that the State Tribunals might and ought to be left in all cases to decide in the first instance the right of appeal to the supreme national tribunal being sufficient to secure the national rights & uniformity of Judgmts.: that it was making an unnecessary encroachment oil the jurisdiction of the States and creating unnecessary obstacles to their adoption of the new system.

Mr. Sherman 2ded the motion.

Mr. Madison observed that unless inferior tribunals were dispersed throughout the Republic with *final* jurisdiction in *many* cases, appeals would be multiplied to a most oppressive degree; that besides, an appeal would not in many cases be a remedy. What was to be done after improper Verdicts in State tribunals obtained under the biassed directions of a dependent Judge, or the local prejudices of an undirected jury? To remand the cause for a new trial would answer no purpose. To order a new trial at the Supreme bar would oblige the parties to bring up their witnesses, tho' ever so distant from the seat of the Court. An effective Judiciary establishment commensurate to the legislative authority, was essential. A Government without a proper Executive & Judiciary would be the mere trunk of a body, without arms or legs to act or move.

Mr. Wilson opposed the motion on like grounds. He said the admiralty jurisdiction ought to be given wholly to the national Government, as it related to cases not within the jurisdiction of particular states, & to a scene in which controversies with foreigners would be most likely to happen.

Mr. Sherman was in favor of the motion. He dwelt chiefly on the supposed expensiveness of having a new set of Courts, when the existing State Courts would answer the same purpose. Mr. Dickinson contended strongly that if there was to be a National Legislature, there ought to be a national Judiciary, and that the former ought to have authority to institute the latter. On the question for Mr. Rutlidge's motion to strike out "inferior tribunals."

Massts. divided. Cont. ay. N.Y. divd. N.J. ay. Pa. no. Del. no. Md. no. Va. no. N.C. ay. S.C. ay. Geo. ay.

Mr. Wilson & Mr. Madison then moved, in pursuance of the idea expressed above by Mr. Dickinson, to add to Resol: 9. the words following "that the National Legislature be empowered to institute inferior tribunals." They observed that there was a distinction between establishing such tribunals absolutely, and giving a discretion to the Legislature to establish or not establish them. They repeated the necessity of some such provision.

Mr. Butler. The people will not bear such innovations. The States will revolt at such encroachments. Supposing such an establishment to be useful, we must not venture on it. We must follow the example of Solon who gave the Athenians not the best Govt. he could devise; but the best they wd. receive.

Mr. King remarked as to the comparative expence that the establishment of inferior tribunals wd. cost infinitely less than the appeals that would be prevented by them.

On this question as moved by Mr. W. & Mr. M. Mass. ay. Ct. no. N.Y. divd. N.J. ay. Pa. ay. Del. ay. Md. ay. Va. ay. N.C. ay. S.C. no. Geo. ay.

Wednesday, June 6

In Committee of the Whole

Mr. Pinkney according to previous notice & rule obtained, moved "that the first branch of the national Legislature be elected by the State Legislatures, and not by the people." contending that the people were less fit Judges in such a case, and that the Legislatures would be less likely to promote the adoption of the new Government, if they were to be excluded from all share in it.

Mr. Rutlidge 2ded the motion.

Mr. Gerry. Much depends on the mode of election. In England, the people will probably lose their liberty from the smallness of the proportion having a right of suffrage. Our danger arises from the opposite extreme: hence in Massts. the worst men get into the Legislature. Several members of that Body had lately been convicted of infamous crimes. Men of indigence, ignorance & baseness, spare no pains, however dirty to carry their point agst. men who are superior to the artifices practised. He was not disposed to run into extremes. He was as much principled as ever agst. aristocracy and monarchy. It was necessary on the one hand that the people should appoint one branch of the Govt. in order to inspire them with the necessary confidence. But he wished the election on the other to be so modified as to secure more effectually a just preference of merit. His idea was that the people should nominate certain persons in certain districts, out of whom the State Legislatures shd. make the appointment.

Mr. Wilson. He wished for vigor in the Govt., but he wished that vigorous authority to flow immediately from the legitimate source of all authority. The Govt. ought to possess not only 1st. the *force*, but 2dly. the *mind* or *sense* of the people at large. The Legislature ought to be the most exact transcript of the whole Society. Representation is made necessary only because it is impossible for the people to act collectively. The opposition was to be expected he said from the *Governments*, not from the Citizens of the States. The latter had parted as was observed [by Mr. King] with all the necessary powers; and it was immaterial to them, by whom they were exercised, if well exercised. The State officers were to be the losers of power. The people he supposed would be rather more attached to the national Govt. than to the State Govts. as being more important in itself, and more flattering to their pride. There is no danger of improper elections if made by large districts. Bad elections proceed from the smallness of the districts which give an opportunity to bad men to intrigue themselves into office.

Mr. Sherman. If it were in view to abolish the State Govts. the elections ought to be by the people. If the State Govts. are to be continued, it is necessary in order to preserve harmony between the National & State Govts. that the elections to the former shd. be made by the latter. The right of participating in the National Govt. would be sufficiently secured to the people by their election of the State Legislatures. The objects of the Union, he thought were few. 1. defence agst. foreign danger. 2. agst. internal disputes & a resort to force. 3. Treaties with foreign nations. 4. regulating foreign commerce, & drawing revenue from it. These & perhaps a few lesser objects alone rendered a Confederation of the States necessary. All other matters civil & criminal would be much better in the hands of the States. The people are more happy in small than large States. States may indeed be too small as Rhode Island, & thereby be too subject to faction. Some others were perhaps too large, the powers of Govt. not being able to pervade them. He was for giving the General Govt. power to legislate and execute within a defined province.

Col. Mason. Under the existing Confederacy, Congs. represent the *States* not the *people* of the States: their acts operate on the *States*, not on the individuals. The case will be changed in the new plan of Govt. The people will be represented; they ought therefore to choose the Representatives. The requisites in actual representation are that the Reps. should sympathize with their constituents; shd. think as they think, & feel as they feel; and that for these purposes shd. even be residents among them. Much he sd. had been alledged agst. democratic elections. He admitted that much might be said; but it was to be considered that no Govt. was free from imperfections & evils; and that improper elections in many instances, were inseparable from Republican Govts. But compare these with the advantage of this Form in favor of the rights of the people, in favor of human nature. He was persuaded there was a better chance for proper elections by the people, if divided into large districts, than by the State Legislatures. Paper money had been issued by the latter when the former were against it. Was it to be supposed that the State Legislatures then wd. not send to the Natl. legislature patrons of such projects, if the choice depended on them.

Mr. Madison considered an election of one branch at least of the Legislature by the people immediately, as a clear principle of free Govt. and that this mode under proper regulations had the additional advantage of securing better representatives, as well as of avoiding too great an agency of the State Governments in the General one.—He differed from the member from Connecticut [Mr. Sharman] in thinking the objects mentioned to be all the principal ones that required a National Govt. Those were certainly important and necessary objects; but he combined with them the necessity of providing more effectually for the security of private rights, and the steady dispensation of Justice. Interferences with these were evils which had more perhaps than any thing else, produced this convention. Was it to be supposed that republican liberty could long exist under the abuses of it practised in some of the States. The gentleman [Mr. Sharman] had admitted that in a very small State, faction & oppression wd. prevail. It was to be inferred then that wherever these prevailed the State was too small. Had they not prevailed in the largest as well as the smallest tho' less than in the smallest; and were we not thence admonished to enlarge the sphere as far as the nature of the Govt. would admit. This was the only defence agst. the inconveniencies of democracy consistent with the democratic form of Govt. All civilized Societies would be divided into different Sects, Factions, & interests, as they happened to consist of rich & poor, debtors & creditors, the landed, the manufacturing, the commercial interests, the inhabitants of this district or that district, the followers of this political leader or that political leader, the disciples of this religious Sect or that religious Sect. In all cases where a majority are united by a common interest or passion, the rights of the minority are in danger. What motives are to restrain them? A prudent regard to the maxim that honesty is the best policy is found by experience to be as little regarded by bodies of men as by individuals. Respect for character is always diminished in proportion to the number among whom the blame or praise is to be divided. Conscience, the only remaining tie, is known to be inadequate in individuals: In large numbers, little is to be expected from it. Besides, Religion itself may become a motive to persecution & oppression.—These observations are verified by the Histories of every Country antient & modern. In Greece & Rome the rich & poor, the creditors & debtors, as well as the patricians & plebians alternately oppressed each other with equal unmercifulness. What a source of oppression was the relation between the parent cities of Rome, Athens & Carthage, & their respective provinces: the former possessing the power, & the latter being sufficiently distinguished to be separate objects of it? Why was America so justly apprehensive of Parliamentary injustice? Because G. Britain had a separate interest real or supposed, & if her authority had been admitted, could have pursued that interest at our expence. We have seen the mere distinction of colour made in the most enlightened period of time, a ground of the most oppressive dominion ever exercised by man over man. What has been the source of those unjust laws complained of among ourselves? Has it not been the real or supposed interest of the major number? Debtors have defrauded their creditors. The landed interest has borne hard on the mercantile interest. The Holders of one species of property have thrown a disproportion of taxes on the holders of another species. The lesson we are to draw from the whole is that where a majority are united by a common sentiment, and have an opportunity, the rights of the minor party become insecure. In a Republican Govt. the Majority if united have always an opportunity. The only remedy is to enlarge the Sphere, & thereby divide the community into so great a number of interests & parties, that in the 1st place a majority will not be likely at the same moment to have a common interest separate from that of the whole or of the minority; and in the 2d place, that in case they shd. have such an interest, they may not be apt to unite in the pursuit of it. It was incumbent on us then to try this remedy, and with that view to frame a republican system on such a scale & in such a form as will controul all the evils wch. have been experienced.

Mr. Dickenson considered it as essential that one branch of the Legislature shd. be drawn immediately from the people; and as expedient that the other shd. be chosen by the Legislatures of the States. This combination of the State Govts. with the national Govt. was as politic as it was unavoidable. In the formation of the Senate we ought to carry it through such a refining process as will assimilate it as near as may be to the House of Lords in England. He repeated his warm eulogiums on the British Constitution. He was for a strong National Govt. but for leaving the States a considerable agency in the System. The objection agst. making the former dependent on the latter might be obviated by giving to the Senate an authority permanent & irrevocable for three, five or seven years. Being thus independent they will speak & decide with becoming freedom.

Mr. Read. Too much attachment is betrayed to the State Governts. We must look beyond their continuance. A national Govt. must soon of necessity swallow all of them up. They will soon be reduced to the mere office of electing the National Senate. He was agst. patching up the old federal System: he hoped the idea wd. be dismissed. It would be like putting new cloth on an old garment. The confederation was founded on temporary principles. It cannot last: it cannot be amended. If we do not establish a good Govt. on new principles, we must either go to ruin, or have the work to do over again. The people at large are wrongly suspected of being averse to a Genl. Govt. The aversion lies among interested men. Mr. Pierce was for an election by the people as to the 1st branch & by the States as to the 2d branch; by which means the Citizens of the States wd. be represented both *individually & collectively*.

General Pinkney wished to have a good National Govt. & at the same time to leave a considerable share of power in the States. An election of either branch by the people scattered as they are in many States, particularly in S. Carolina was totally impracticable. He differed from gentlemen who thought that a choice by the people wd. be a better guard agst. bad measures, than by the Legislatures. A majority of the people in S. Carolina were notoriously for paper money as a legal tender; the Legislature had refused to make it a legal tender. The reason was that the latter had some sense of character and were restrained by that consideration. The State Legislatures also he said would be more jealous, & more ready to thwart the National Govt., if excluded from a participation in it. The Idea of abolishing these Legislatures wd. never go down.

Mr. Wilson, would not have spoken again, but for what had fallen from Mr. Read; namely, that the idea of preserving the State Govts. ought to be abandoned. He saw no incompatibility between the National & State Govts. provided the latter were restrained to certain local purposes; nor any probability of their being devoured by the former. In all confederated Systems antient & modern the reverse had happened; the Generality being destroyed gradually by the usurpations of the parts composing it.

On the question for electing the 1st branch by the State Legislatures as moved by Mr. Pinkney: it was negatived: Mass. no. Ct. ay. N.Y. no. N.J. ay. Pa. no. Del. no. Md. no. Va. no. N.C. no. S.C. ay. Geo. no.

Mr. Wilson moved to reconsider the vote excluding the Judiciary from a share in the revision of the laws, and to add after "National Executive" the words "with a convenient number of the national Judiciary"; remarking the expediency of reinforcing the Executive with the influence of that Department.

Mr. Madison 2ded the motion. He observed that the great difficulty in rendering the Executive competent to its own defence arose from the nature of Republican Govt. which could not give to an individual citizen that settled pre-eminence in the eyes of the rest, that weight of property, that personal interest agst. betraying the [. . .] national interest, which appertain to an hereditary magistrate. In a Republic personal merit alone could be the ground of political exaltation, but it would rarely happen that this merit would be so pre-eminent as to produce universal acquiescence. The Executive Magistrate would be envied & assailed by disappointed competitors: His firmness therefore wd. need support. He would not possess those great emoluments from his station, nor that permanent stake in the public interest which wd. place him out of the reach of foreign corruption: He would stand in need therefore of being controuled as well as supported. An association of the Judges in his revisionary function wd. both double the advantage and diminish the danger. It wd. also enable the Judiciary Department the better to defend itself agst. Legislative encroachments. Two objections had been made 1st that the Judges ought not to be subject to the bias which a participation in the making of laws might give in the exposition of them. 2dly that the Judiciary Departmt. ought to be separate & distinct from the other great Departments.

The 1st objection had some weight; but it was much diminished by reflecting that a small proportion of the laws coming in question before a Judge wd. be such wherein he had been consulted; that a small part of this proportion wd. be so ambiguous as to leave room for his prepossessions; and that but a few cases wd. probably arise in the life of a Judge under such ambiguous passages. How much good on the other hand wd. proceed from the perspicuity, the conciseness, and the systematic character wch. the Code of laws wd. receive from the Judiciary talents. As to the 2d objection, it either had no weight, or it applied with equal weight to the Executive & to the Judiciary revision of the laws. The maxim on which the objection was founded required a separation of the Executive as well as of the Judiciary from the Legislature & from each other. There wd. in truth however be no improper mixture of these distinct powers in the present case. In England, whence the maxim itself had been drawn, the Executive had an absolute negative on the laws; and the supreme tribunal of Justice [the House of Lords] formed one of the other branches of the Legislature. In short whether the object of the revisionary power was to restrain the Legislature from encroaching on the other coordinate Departments, or on the rights of the people at large; or from passing laws unwise in their principle, or incorrect in their form, the utility of annexing the wisdom and weight of the Judiciary to the Executive seemed incontestable.

Mr. Gerry thought the Executive, whilst standing alone wd. be more impartial than when he cd. be covered by the sanction & seduced by the sophistry of the Judges.

Mr. King. If the Unity of the Executive was preferred for the sake of responsibility, the policy of it is as applicable to the revisionary as to the Executive power.

Mr. Pinkney had been at first in favor of joining the heads of the principal departmts. the Secretary of War, of foreign affairs &—in the council of revision. He had however relinquished the idea from a consideration that these could be called in by the Executive Magistrate whenever he pleased to consult them. He was opposed to an introduction of the Judges into the business.

Col. Mason was for giving all possible weight to the revisionary institution. The Executive power ought to be well secured agst. Legislative usurpations on it. The purse & the sword ought never to get into the same hands whether Legislative or Executive.

Mr. Dickenson. Secrecy, vigor & despatch are not the principal properties reqd. in the Executive. Important as these are, that of responsibility is more so, which can only be preserved; by leaving it singly to discharge its functions. He thought too a junction of the Judiciary to it, involved an improper mixture of powers.

Mr. Wilson remarked, that the responsibility required belonged to his Executive duties. The revisionary duty was an extraneous one, calculated for collateral purposes.

Mr. Williamson, was for substituting a clause requiring 2/3 for every effective act of the Legislature, in place of the revisionary provision.

On the question forjoining the Judges to the Executive in the revisionary business, Mass. no. Cont. ay. N.Y. ay. N.J. no. Pa. no. Del. no. Md. no. Va. ay. N.C. no. S.C. No. Geo. no.

Mr. Pinkney gave notice that tomorrow he should move for the reconsideration of that clause in the sixth Resolution adopted by the Comme. which vests a negative in the National Legislature on the laws of the several States.

The Come. rose & the House adjd. to 11 OC.

Thursday, June 7

In Committee of the Whole

The Clause providing for ye. appointment of the 2d branch of the national Legislature, having lain blank since the last vote on the mode of electing it, to wit, by the 1st branch, Mr. Dickenson now moved "that the members of the 2d branch ought to be chosen by the individual Legislatures."

Mr. Sharman seconded the motion; observing that the particular States would thus become interested in supporting the national Govermt. and that a due harmony between the two Governments would be maintained. He admitted that the two ought to have separate and distinct jurisdictions, but that they ought to have a mutual interest in supporting each other.

Mr. Pinkney. If the small States should be allowed one Senator only, the number will be too great, there will be 80 at least.

Mr. Dickenson had two reasons for his motion. 1. because the sense of the States would be better collected through their Governments; than immediately from the people at large; 2. because he wished the Senate to consist of the most distinguished characters, distinguished for their rank in life and their weight of property, and bearing as strong a likeness to the British House of Lords as possible; and he thought such characters more likely to be selected by the State Legislatures, than in any other mode. The greatness of the number was no objection with him. He hoped there would be 80 and twice 80 of them. If their number should be small, the popular branch could not be balanced by them. The legislature of a numerous people ought to be a numerous body.

Mr. Butler was anxious to know the ratio of representation before he gave any opinion.

Mr. Wilson. If we are to establish a national Government, that Government ought to flow from the people at large. If one branch of it should be chosen by the Legislatures, and the other by the people, the two branches will rest on different foundations, and dissensions will naturally arise between them. He wished the Senate to be elected by the people as well as the other branch, and the people might be divided into proper districts for the purpose & moved to postpone the motion of Mr. Dickenson, in order to take up one of that import.

Mr. Morris 2ded him.

Mr. Read proposed "that the Senate should be appointed by the Executive Magistrate out of a proper number of persons to be nominated by the individual legislatures." He said he thought it his duty, to speak his mind frankly. Gentlemen he hoped would not be alarmed at the idea. Nothing short of this approach towards a proper model of Government would answer the purpose, and he thought it best to come directly to the point at once.—His proposition was not seconded nor supported.

Mr. Madison, if the motion [of Mr. Dickenson] should be agreed to, we must either depart from the doctrine of proportional representation; or admit into the Senate a very large number of members. The first is inadmissible, being evidently unjust. The second is inexpedient. The use of the Senate is to consist in its proceeding with more coolness, with more system, & with more wisdom, than the popular branch. Enlarge their number and you communicate to them the vices which they are meant to correct. He differed from Mr. D. who thought that the additional number would give additional weight to the body. On the contrary it appeared to him that their weight would be in an inverse ratio to their number. The example of the Roman Tribunes was applicable. They lost their influence and power, in proportion as their number was augmented. The reason seemed to be obvious: They were appointed to take care of the popular interests & pretensions at Rome, because the people by reason of their numbers could not act in concert; were liable to fall into factions among themselves, and to become a prey to their aristocratic adversaries. The more the representatives of the people therefore were multiplied, the more they partook of the infirmities of their constituents, the more liable they became to be divided among themselves either from their own indiscretions or the artifices of the opposite faction, and of course the less capable of fulfilling their trust. When the weight of a set of men depends merely on their personal characters; the greater the number the greater the weight. When it depends on the degree of political authority lodged in them the smaller the number the greater the weight. These considerations might perhaps be combined in the intended Senate; but the latter was the material one.

Mr. Gerry. 4 modes of appointing the Senate have been mentioned. 1. by the 1st branch of the National Legislature. This would create a dependence contrary to the end proposed. 2. by the National Executive. This is a stride towards monarchy that few will think of. 3. by the people. The people have two great interests, the landed interest, and the commercial including the stockholders. To draw both branches from the people will leave no security to the latter interest; the people being chiefly composed of the landed interest, and erroneously supposing, that the other interests are adverse to it. 4. by the Individual Legislatures. The elections being carried thro' this refinement, will be most likely to provide some check in favor of the commercial interest agst. the landed; without which oppression will take place, and no free Govt. can last long where that is the case. He was therefore in favor of this last.

Mr. Dickenson. The preservation of the States in a certain degree of agency is indispensable. It will produce that collision between the different authorities which should be wished for in order to check each other. To attempt to abolish the States altogether, would degrade the Councils of our Country, would be impracticable, would be ruinous. He compared the proposed National System to the Solar System, in which the States were the planets, and ought to be left to move freely in their proper orbits. The Gentleman from Pa. [Mr. Wilson] wished he said to extinguish these planets. If the State Governments were excluded from all agency in the national one, and all power drawn from the people at large, the consequence would be that the national Govt. would move in the same direction as the State Govts. now do, and would run into all the same mischiefs. The reform would only unite the 13 small streams into one great current pursuing the same course without any opposition whatever. He adhered to the opinion that the Senate ought to be composed of a large number, and that their influence from family weight & other causes would be increased thereby. He did not admit that the Tribunes lost their weight in proportion as their no. was augmented and gave a historical sketch of this institution. If the reasoning of [Mr. Madison] was good it would prove that the number of the Senate ought to be reduced below ten, the highest no. of the Tribunitial corps.

Mr. Wilson. The subject it must be owned is surrounded with doubts and difficulties. But we must surmount them. The British Governmt. cannot be our model. We have no materials for a similar one. Our manners, our laws, the abolition of entails and of primogeniture, the whole genius of the people, are opposed to it. He did not see the danger of the States being devoured by the Nationl. Govt. On the contrary, he wished to keep them from devouring the national Govt. He was not however for extinguishing these planets as was supposed by Mr. D.—neither did he on the other hand, believe that they would warm or enlighten the Sun. Within their proper orbits they must still be suffered to act for subordinate purposes for which their existence is made essential by the great extent of our Country. He could not comprehend in what manner the landed interest wd. be rendered less predominant in the Senate, by an election through the medium of the Legislatures then by the people themselves. If the Legislatures, as was now complained, sacrificed the commercial to the landed interest, what reason was there to expect such a choice from them as would defeat their own views. He was for an election by the people in large districts which wd. be most likely to obtain men of intelligence & uprightness; subdividing the districts only for the accomodation of voters.

Mr. Madison could as little comprehend in what manner family weight, as desired by Mr. D. would be more certainly conveyed into the Senate through elections by the State Legislatures, than in some other modes. The true question was in what mode the best choice wd. be made? If an election by the people, or thro' any other channel than the State Legislatures promised as uncorrupt & impartial a preference of merit, there could surely be no necessity for an appointment by those Legislatures. Nor was it apparent that a more useful check would be derived thro' that channel than from the people thro' some other. The great evils complained of were that the State Legislatures run into schemes of paper money &c. whenever solicited by the people, & sometimes without even the sanction of the people. Their influence then, instead of checking a like propensity in the National Legislature, may be expected to promote it. Nothing can be more contradictory than to say that the Natl. Legislature witht. a proper check, will follow the example of the State Legislatures, & in the same breath, that the State Legislatures are the only proper check.

Mr. Sharman opposed elections by the people in districts, as not likely to produce such fit men as elections by the State Legislatures.

Mr. Gerry insisted that the commercial & monied interest wd. be more secure in the hands of the State Legislatures, than of the people at large. The former have more sense of character, and will be restrained by that from injustice. The people are for paper money when the Legislatures are agst. it. In Massts. the County Conventions had declared a wish for a *depreciating* paper that wd. sink itself. Besides, in some States there are two Branches in the Legislature, one of which is somewhat aristocratic. There wd. therefore be so far a better chance of refinement in the choice. There seemed, he thought to be three powerful objections agst. elections by districts. 1. it is impracticable; the people cannot be brought to one place for the purpose; and whether brought to the same place or not, numberless frauds wd. be unavoidable. 2. small States forming part of the same district with a large one, or large part of a large one, wd. have no chance of gaining an appointment for its citizens of merit. 3. a new source of discord wd. be opened between different parts of the same district.

Mr. Pinkney thought the 2d branch ought to be permanent & independent, & that the members of it wd. be rendered more so by receiving their appointment from the State Legislatures. This mode wd. avoid the rivalships & discontents incident to the election by districts. He was for dividing the States into three classes according to their respective sizes, & for allowing to the 1st. class three members—to the 2d. two, & to the 3d. one. On the question for postponing Mr. Dickinson's motion referring the appointment of the Senate to the State Legislatures, in order to consider Mr. Wilson's for referring it to the people.

Mass. no. Cont no. N.Y. no. N.J. no. Pa. ay. Del. no. Md. no. Va. no. N.C. no. S.C. no. Geo. no.

Col. Mason. whatever power may be necessary for the Natl. Govt. a certain portion must necessarily be left in the States. It is impossible for one power to pervade the extreme parts of the U.S. so as to carry equal justice to them. The State Legislatures also ought to have some means of defending themselves agst. encroachments of the Natl. Govt. In every other department we have studiously endeavored to provide for its self-defence. Shall we leave the States alone unprovided with the means for this purpose? And what better means can we provide than the giving them some share in, or rather to make them a constituent part of, the Natl. Establishment. There is danger on both sides no doubt; but we have only seen the evils arising on the side of the State Govts. Those on the other side remain to be displayed. The example of Congs. does not apply. Congs. had no power to carry their acts into execution as the Natl. Govt. will have.

On Mr. Dickinson's motion for an appointment of the Senate by the State—Legislatures.

Mass, ay. Ct. ay. N.Y. ay. Pa. ay. Del. ay. Md. ay. Va. ay N.C. ay. S.C. ay. Geo. ay.

Saturday, June 9

In Committee of the Whole

Mr. Patterson moves that the Committee resume the clause relating to the rule of suffrage in the Natl. Legislature.

Mr. Brearly seconds him. He was sorry he said that any question on this point was brought into view. It had been much agitated in Congs. at the time of forming the Confederation, and was then rightly settled by allowing to each sovereign State an equal vote. Otherwise the smaller States must have been destroyed instead of being saved. The substitution of a ratio, he admitted carried fairness on the face of it; but on a deeper examination was unfair and unjust. Judging of the disparity of the States by the quota of Congs. Virga. would have 16 votes, and Georgia but one. A like proportion to the others will make the whole number ninity. There will be 3 large states, and 10 small ones. The large States by which he meant Massts. Pena. & Virga. will carry every thing before them. It had been admitted, and was known to him from facts within N. Jersey that where large & small counties were united into a district for electing representatives for the district, the large counties always carried their point, and Consequently that the large States would do so. Virga. with her sixteen votes will be a solid column indeed, a formidable phalanx. While Georgie with her Solitary vote, and the other little States will be obliged to throw themselves constantly into the scale of some large one, in order to have any weight at all. He had come to the convention with a view of being as useful as he could in giving energy and stability to the federal Government. When the proposition for destroying the equality of votes came forward, he was astonished, he was alarmed. Is it fair then it will be asked that Georgia should have an equal vote with Virga.? He would not say it was. What remedy then? One only, that a map of the U.S. be spread out, that all the existing boundaries be erased, and that a new partition of the whole be made into 13 equal parts.

Mr. Patterson considered the proposition for a proportional representation as striking at the existence of the lesser States. He wd. premise however to an investigation of this question some remarks on the nature structure and powers of the Convention. The Convention he said was formed in pursuance of an Act of Congs. that this act was recited in several of the Commissions, particularly that of Massts. which he required to be read: that the amendment of the confederacy was the object of all the laws and commissions on the subject; that the articles of the Confederation were therefore the proper basis of all the proceedings of the Convention. We ought to keep within its limits, or we should be charged by our Constituents with usurpation, that the people of America were sharpsighted and not to be deceived. But the Commissions under which we acted were not only the measure of our power, they denoted also the sentiments of the States on the subject of our deliberation. The idea of a national Govt. as contradistinguished from a federal one, never entered into the mind of any of them, and to the public mind we must accomodate ourselves. We have no power to go beyond the federal scheme, and if we had the people are not ripe for any other. We must follow the people; the people will not follow us.—The *proposition* could not be maintained whether considered in reference to us as a nation, or as a confederacy. A confederacy supposes sovereignty in the members composing it & sovereignty supposes equality. If we are to be considered as a nation, all State distinctions must be abolished, the whole must be thrown into hotchpot, and when an equal division is made, then there may be fairly an equality of representation. He held up Virga. Massts. & Pa. as the three large States, and the other ten as small ones; repeating the calculations of Mr. Brearly as to the disparity of votes which wd. take place, and affirming that the small States would never agree to it. He said there was no more reason that a great individual State contributing much, should have more votes than a small one contributing little, than that a rich individual citizen should have more votes than an indigent one. If the rateable property of A was to that of B as 40 to 1, ought A for that reason to have 40 times as many votes as B. Such a principle would never be admitted, and if it were admitted would put B entirely at the mercy of A. As A has more to be protected than B so he ought to contribute more for the common protection. The same may be said of a large State wch. has more to be protected than a small one. Give the large States an influence in proportion to their magnitude, and what will be the consequence? Their ambition will be proportionally increased, and the small States will have every thing to fear. It was once proposed by Galloway & some others that America should be represented in the British Parlt. and then be bound by its laws. America could not have been entitled to more than 1/3 of the no. of Representatives which would fall to the share of G.B. Would American rights & interests have been safe under an authority thus constituted? It has been said that if a Natl. Govt. is to be formed so as to operate on the people and not on the States, the representatives ought to be drawn from the people. But why so? May not a Legislature filled by the State Legislatures operate on the people who chuse the State Legislatures? or may not a practicable coercion be found. He admitted that there was none such in the existing System.—He was attached strongly to the plan of the existing confederacy, in which the people chuse their Legislative representatives; and the Legislatures their federal representatives. No other amendments were wanting than to mark the orbits of the States with due precision, and provide for the use of coercion, which was the great point. He alluded to the hint thrown out heretofore by Mr. Wilson of the necessity to which the large States might be reduced of confederating among themselves, by a refusal of the others to concur. Let them unite if they please, but let them remember that they have no authority to compel the others to unite. N. Jersey will never confederate on the plan before the Committee. She would be swallowed up. He had rather submit to a monarch, to a despot, than to such a fate. He would not only oppose the plan here but on his return home do every thing in his power to defeat it there.

Mr. Wilson hoped if the Confederacy should be dissolved, that a *majority*, that a *minority* of the States would unite for their safety. He entered elaborately into the defence of a proportional representation, stating for his first position that as all authority was derived from the people, equal numbers of people ought to have an equal no. of representatives, and different numbers of people different numbers of representatives. This principle had been improperly violated in the Confederation, owing to the urgent circumstances of the time. As to the case of A & B, stated by Mr. Patterson, he observed that in districts as large as the States, the number of people was the best measure of their comparative wealth. Whether therefore wealth or numbers were to form the ratio it would be the same. Mr. P. admitted persons, not property to be the measure of suffrage. Are not the Citizens of Pena. equal to those of N. Jersey? does it require 150 of the former to balance 50 of the latter? Representatives of different districts ought clearly to hold the same proportion to each other, as their respective Constituents hold to each other. If the small States will not confederate on this plan, Pena. & he presumed some other States, would not confederate on any other. We have been told that each State being sovereign, all are equal. So each man is naturally a sovereign over himself, and all men are therefore naturally equal. Can he retain this equality when he becomes a member of Civil Government? He can not. As little can a Sovereign State, when it becomes a member of a federal Governt. If N.J. will not part with her Sovereignty it is in vain to talk of Govt. A new partition of the States is desireable, but evidently & totally impracticable.

Friday, June 15

Mr. Patterson, laid before the Convention the plan which he said several of the deputations wished to be substituted in place of that proposed by Mr. Randolph. After some little discussion of the most proper mode of giving it a fair deliberation it was agreed that it should be referred to a Committee of the whole, and that in order to place the two plans in due comparison, the other should be recommitted. At the earnest desire of Mr. Lansing & some other gentlemen, it was also agreed that the Convention should not go into Committee of the whole on the subject till tomorrow, by which delay the friends of the plan proposed by Mr. Patterson wd. be better prepared to explain & support it, and all would have an opportuy. of taking copies.

The propositions from N. Jersey moved by Mr. Patterson were in the words following.

1. Resd. that the articles of Confederation ought to be so revised, corrected & enlarged, as to render the federal Constitution adequate to the exigencies of Government, & the preservation of the Union.

2. Resd. that in addition to the powers vested in the U. States in Congress, by the present existing articles of Confederation, they be authorized to pass acts for raising a revenue, by levying a duty or duties on all goods or merchandizes of foreign growth or manufacture, imported into any part of the U. States, by Stamps on paper, vellum or parchment, and by a postage on all letters or packages passing through the general post-office, to be applied to such federal purposes as they shall deem proper & expedient; to make rules & regulations for the collection thereof; and the same from time to time, to alter & amend in such manner as they shall think proper: to pass Acts for the regulation of trade & commerce as well with foreign nations as with each other: provided that all punishments, fines, forfeitures & penalties to be incurred for contravening such acts rules and regulations shall be adjudged by the Common law Judiciaries of the State in which any offence contrary to the true intent & meaning of such Acts rules & regulations shall have been committed or perpetrated, with liberty of commencing in the first instance all suits & prosecutions for that purpose in the superior common law Judiciary in such State, subject nevertheless, for the correction of all errors, both in law & fact in rendering Judgment, to an appeal to the Judiciary of the U. States.

3. Resd. that whenever requisitions shall be necessary, instead of the rule for making requisitions mentioned in the articles of Confederation, the United States in Congs. be authorized to make such requisitions in proportion to the whole number of white & other free citizens & inhabitants of every age sex and condition including those bound to servitude for a term of years & three fifths of all other persons not comprehended in the foregoing description, except Indians not paying taxes; that if such requisitions be not complied with, in the time specified therein, to direct the collection thereof in the non complying States & for that purpose to devise and pass acts directing & authorizing the same; provided that none of the powers hereby vested in the U. States in Congs. shall be exercised without the consent of at least _____ States, and in that proportion if the number of Confederated States should hereafter be increased or diminished.

4. Resd. that the U. States in Congs. be authorized to elect a federal Executive to consist of _____

persons, to continue in office for the term of _____ years, to receive punctually at stated times a fixed compensation for their services, in which no increase or diminution shall be made so as to affect the persons composing the Executive at the time of such increase or diminution, to be paid out of the federal treasury; to be incapable of holding any other office or appointment during their time of service and for _____ years thereafter; to be ineligible a second time, & removeable by Congs. on application by a majority of the Executives of the several States; that the Executives besides their general authority to execute the federal acts ought to appoint all federal officers not otherwise provided for, & to direct all military operations; provided that none of the persons composing the federal Executive shall on any occasion take command of any troops, so as personally to conduct any enterprise as General or in other capacity.

5. Resd. that a federal Judiciary be established to consist of a supreme Tribunal the Judges of which to be appointed by the Executive, & to hold their offices during good behaviour, to receive punctually at stated times a fixed compensation for their services in which no increase or diminution shall be made, so as to affect the persons actually in office at the time of such increase or diminution; that the Judiciary so established shall have authority to hear & determine in the first instance on all impeachments of federal officers, & by way of appeal in the dernier resort in all cases touching the rights of Ambassadors, in all cases of captures from an enemy, in all cases of piracies & felonies on the high Seas, in all cases in which foreigners may be interested, in the construction of any treaty or treaties, or which may arise on any of the Acts for regulation of trade, or the collection of the federal Revenue: that none of the Judiciary shall during the time they remain in office be capable of receiving or holding any other office or appointment during their time of service, or for _____ thereafter.

6. Resd. that all Acts of the U. States in Congs. made by virtue & in pursuance of the powers hereby & by the articles of Confederation vested in them, and all Treaties made & ratified under the authority of the U. States shall be the supreme law of the respective States so far forth as those Acts or Treaties shall relate to the said States or their Citizens, and that the Judiciary of the several States shall be bound thereby in their decisions, any thing in the respective laws of the Individual States to the contrary notwithstanding; and that if any State, or any body of men in any State shall oppose or prevent yd. carrying into execution such acts or treaties, the federal Executive shall be authorized to call forth ye. power of the Confederated States, or so much thereof as may be necessary to enforce and compel an obedience to such Acts, or an observance of such Treaties.

7. Resd. that provision be made for the admission of new States into the Union.

8. Resd. the rule for naturalization ought to be the same in every State.

9. Resd. that a Citizen of one State committing an offense in another State of the Union, shall be deemed guilty of the same offense as if it had been committed by a Citizen of the State in which the offense was committed.

Adjourned.

Saturday, June 16

In Committee of the Whole on Resolutions Proposed by Mr. P & Mr. R

Mr. Lansing called for the reading of the 1st resolution of each plan, which he considered as involving principles directly in contrast; that of Mr. Patterson says he sustains the sovereignty of the respective States, that of Mr. Randolph distroys it: the latter requires a negative on all the laws of the particular States; the former, only certain general powers for the general good. The plan of Mr. R. in short absorbs all power except what may be exercised in the little local matters of the States which are not objects worthy of the supreme cognizance. He grounded his preference of Mr. P.'s plan, chiefly on two objections agst. that of Mr. R. 1. want of power in the Convention to discuss & propose it. 2. the improbability of its being adopted.

1. He was decidedly of opinion that the power of the Convention was restrained to amendments of a federal nature, and having for their basis the Confederacy in being. The Act of Congress The tenor of the Acts of the States, the Commissions produced by the several deputations all proved this. And this

limitation of the power to an amendment of the Confederacy, marked the opinion of the States, that it was unnecessary & improper to go farther. He was sure that this was the case with his State. N. York would never have concurred in sending deputies to the convention, if she had supposed the deliberations were to turn on a consolidation of the States, and a National Government.

2. was it probable that the States would adopt & ratify a scheme, which they had never authorized us to propose? and which so far exceeded what they regarded as sufficient? We see by their several Acts particularly in relation to the plan of revenue proposed by Cong. in 1783, not authorized by the Articles of Confederation, what were the ideas they then entertained. Can so great a change be supposed to have already taken place. To rely on any change which is hereafter to take place in the sentiments of the people would be trusting to too great an uncertainty. We know only what their present sentiments are. And it is in vain to propose what will not accord with these. The States will never feel a sufficient confidence in a general Government to give it a negative on their laws. The Scheme is itself totally novel. There is no parallel to it to be found. The authority of Congress is familiar to the people, and an augmentation of the powers of Congress will be readily approved by them.

Mr. Patterson, said as he had on a former occasion given his sentiments on the plan proposed by Mr. R. he would now avoiding repetition as much as possible give his reasons in favor of that proposed by himself. He preferred it because it accorded 1. with the powers of the Convention, 2. with the sentiments of the people. If the confederacy was radically wrong, let us return to our States, and obtain larger powers, not assume them of ourselves. I came here not to speak my own sentiments, but the sentiments of those who sent me. Our object is not such a Governmt as may be best in itself, but such a one as our Constituents have authorized us to prepare, and as they will approve. If we argue the matter on the supposition that no Confederacy at present exists, it can not be denied that all the States stand on the footing of equal sovereignty. All therefore must concur before any can be bound. If a proportional representation be right, why do we not vote so here? If we argue on the fact that a federal compact actually exists, and consult the articles of it we still find an equal Sovereignty to be the basis of it. He reads the 5th art: of Confederation giving each State a vote—& the 13th declaring that no alteration shall be made without unanimous consent. This is the nature of all treaties. What is unanimously done, must be unanimously undone. It was observed [by Mr. Wilson] that the larger States gave up the point, not because it was right but because the circumstances of the moment urged the concession. Be it so. Are they for that reason at liberty to take it back. Can the donor resume his gift without the consent of the donee. This doctrine may be convenient, but it is a doctrine that will sacrifice the lesser States. The large States acceded readily to the confederacy. It was the small ones that came in reluctantly and slowly. N. Jersey & Maryland were the two last, the former objecting to the want of power in Congress over trade: both of them to the want of power to appropriate the vacant territory to the benefit of the whole.—If the sovereignty of the States is to be maintained, the Representatives must be drawn immediately from the States, not from the people: and we have no power to vary the idea of equal sovereignty. The only expedient that will cure the difficulty, is that of throwing the States into Hotchpot. To say that this is impracticable, will not make it so. Let it be tried, and we shall see whether the Citizens of Massts. Pena. & Va. accede to it. It will be objected that Coercion will be impracticable. But will it be more so in one plan than the other? Its efficacy will depend on the quantum of power collected, not on its being drawn from the States, or from the individuals; and according to his plan it may be exerted on individuals as well as according that of Mr. R. A distinct executive & Judiciary also were equally provided by his plan. It is urged that two branches in the Legislature are necessary. Why? for the purpose of a check. But the reason of the precaution is not applicable to this case. Within a particular State, where party heats prevail, such a check may be necessary. In such a body as Congress it is less necessary, and besides, the delegations of the different States are checks on each other. Do the people at large complain of Congs.? No, what they wish is that Congs. may have more power. If the power now proposed be not eno', the people hereafter will make additions to it. With proper powers Congs. will act with more energy & wisdom than the proposed Natl. Legislature; being fewer in number, and more secreted & refined by the mode of election. The plan of Mr. R. will also be enormously expensive. Allowing Georgia & Del. two representatives each in the popular branch the aggregate number of that branch will be 180. Add to it half as many for the other branch and you have 270 members coming once at least a year from the most distant as well as the most central pails of the republic. In the present deranged state of our finances can so expensive a system be seriously though of? By enlarging the powers of Congs. the greatest part of this expence will be saved, and all purposes will be answered. At least a trial ought to be made.

Mr. Wilson entered into a contrast of the principal points of the two plans so far he said as there had been time to examine the one last proposed. These points were 1. in the Virga. plan there are 2 & in some degree 3 branches in the Legislature: in the plan from N.J. there is to be a *single* legislature—only 2. Representation of the people at large is the basis of the one:—the State Legislatures, the pillars of the other—3. proportional representation prevails in one:—equality of suffrage in the other—4. A single Executive Magistrate is at the head of the one:—a plurality is held out in the other.—5. in the one the majority of the people of the U.S. must prevail:—in the other a minority may prevail. 6. the Natl. Legislature is to make laws in all cases to which the separate States are incompetent &—:—in place of this Congs. are to have additional power in a few cases only—7. A negative on the laws of the States:—in place of this coertion to be substituted—8. The Executive to be removeable on impeachment & conviction;—in one plan: in the other to be removeable at the instance of majority of the Executives of the States—9. Revision of the laws provided for in one:—no such check in the other—10. inferior national tribunals in one:—none such in the other. 11. In ye. one jurisdiction of Natl. tribunals to extend &c—; an appellate jurisdiction only allowed in the other. 12. Here the jurisdiction is to extend to all cases affecting the Nationl. peace & harmony: there, a few cases only are marked out. 13. finally ye. ratification is in this to be by the people themselves:—in that by the legislative authorities according to the 13 art: of Confederation.

With regard to the *power of the Convention*, he conceived himself authorized to *conclude nothing*, but to be at liberty to *propose any thing*. In this particular he felt himself perfectly indifferent to the two plans.

With *regard to the sentiments of the people*, he conceived it difficult to know precisely what they are. Those of the particular circle in which one moved, were commonly mistaken for the general voice. He could not persuade himself that the State Govts. & Sovereignties were so much the idols of the people, nor a Natl. Govt. so obnoxious to them, as some supposed. Why sd. a Natl. Govt. be unpopular? Has it less dignity? will each Citizen enjoy under it less liberty or protection? Will a Citizen of *Delaware* be degraded by becoming a Citizen of the *United States?* Where do the people look at present for relief from the evils of which they complain? Is it from an internal reform of their Govts.? no, Sir. It is from the Natl. Councils that relief is expected. For these reasons he did not fear, that the people would not follow us into a national Govt. and it will be a further recommendation of Mr. R.'s plan that it is to be submitted to *them*, and not to the *Legislatures*, for ratification.

Proceeding now to the 1st point on which he had contrasted the two plans, he observed that anxious as he was for some augmentation of the federal powers, it would be with extreme reluctance indeed that he could ever consent to give powers to Congs. he had two reasons either of wch. was sufficient. 1. Congs. as a Legislative body does not stand on the people. 2. it is a *single* body. He would not repeat the remarks he had formerly made on the principles of Representation. He would only say that an inequality in it, has ever been a poison contaminating every branch of Govt. In G. Britain where this poison has had a full operation, the security of private rights is owing entirely to the purity of Her tribunals of Justice, the Judges of which are neither appointed nor paid, by a venal Parliament. The political liberty of that Nation, owing to the inequality of representation is at the mercy of its rulers. He means not to insinuate that there is any parallel between the situation of that Country & ours at present. But it is a lesson we ought not to disregard, that the smallest bodies in G.B. are notoriously the most corrupt. Every other source of influence must also be stronger in small than large bodies of men. When Lord Chesterfield had told us that one of the Dutch provinces had been seduced into the views of France, he need not have added, that it was not Holland, but one of the *smallest* of them. There are facts among ourselves which are known to all. Passing over others, he will only remark that the *Impost*, so anxiously wished for by the public was defeated not by any of the *larger* States in the Union. 2. *Congress is a single Legislature.* Despotism comes on Mankind in different Shapes, sometimes in an Executive, sometimes in a Military, one. Is there no danger of a Legislative despotism? Theory & practice both proclaim it. If the Legislative authority be not restrained, there can be neither liberty nor stability; and it can only be restrained by dividing it within itself, into distinct and independent branches. In a single House there is no check, but the inadequate one, of the virtue & good sense of those who compose it.

On another great point, the contrast was equally favorable to the plan reported by the Committee of the whole. It vested the Executive powers in a single Magistrate. The plan of N. Jersey, vested them in a plurality. In order to controul the Legislative authority, you must divide it. In order to controul the Executive you must unite it. One man will be more responsible than three. Three will contend among themselves till one becomes the master of his colleagues. In the triumvirates of Rome first Caesar, then Augustus, are witnesses of this truth. The Kings of Sparta, & the Consuls of Rome prove also the factious consequences of dividing the Executive Magistracy. Having already taken up so much time he wd. not he sd. proceed to any of the other points. Those on which he had dwelt, are sufficient of themselves: and on a decision of them, the fate of the others will depend.

Mr. Pinkney, the whole comes to this, as he conceived. Give N. Jersey an equal vote, and she will dismiss her scruples, and concur in the Natil. system. He thought the Convention authorized to go any length in recommending, which they found necessary to remedy the evils which produced this Convention.

Mr. Elseworth proposed as a more distinctive form of collecting the mind of the Committee on the subject, "that the Legislative power of the U.S. should remain in Congs." This was not seconded though it seemed better calculated for the purpose than the 1st proposition of Mr. Patterson in place of which Mr. E. wished to substitute it.

Mr. Randolph, was not scrupulous on the point of power. When the salvation of the Republic was at stake, it would be treason to our trust, not to propose what we found necessary. He painted in strong colours, the imbecility of the existing Confederacy, & the danger of delaying a substantial reform. In answer to the objection drawn from the sense of our Constituents as denoted by their acts relating to the Convention and the objects of their deliberation, he observed that as each State acted separately in the case, it would have been indecent for it to have charged the existing Constitution with all the vices which it might have perceived in it. The first State that set on foot this experiment would not have been justified in going so far, ignorant as it was of the opinion of others, and sensible as it must have been of the uncertainty of a successful issue to the experiment. There are certainly seasons of a peculiar nature where the ordinary cautions must be dispensed with; and this is certainly one of them. He wd. not as far as depended on him leave any thing that seemed necessary, undone. The present moment is favorable, and is probably the last that will offer.

The true question is whether we shall adhere to the federal plan, or introduce the national plan. The insufficiency of the former has been fully displayed by the trial already made. There are but two modes, by which the end of a Genl. Govt. can be attained: the 1st is by coercion as proposed by Mr. P.s plan 2. by real legislation as propd. by the other plan. Coercion he pronounced to be *impracticable, expensive, cruel to individuals.* It tended also to habituate the instruments of it to shed the blood & riot in the spoils of their fellow Citizens, and consequently trained them up for the service of ambition. We must resort therefor' to a National *Legislation over individuals,* for which Congs. are unfit. To vest such power in them, would be blending the Legislative with the Executive, contrary to the recd. maxim on this subject: If the Union of these powers heretofore in Congs. has been safe, it has been owing to the general impotency of that body. Congs. are moreover not elected by the people, but by the Legislatures who retain even a power of recall. They have therefore no will of their own, they are a mere diplomatic body, and are always obsequious to the views of the States, who are always encroaching on the authority of the U. States. A provision for harmony among the States, as in trade, naturalization &c.—for crushing rebellion.

Whenever it may rear its crest—and for certain other general benefits, must be made. The powers for these purposes, can never be given to a body, inadequate as Congress are in point of representation, elected in the mode in which they are, and possessing no more confidence than they do: for notwithstanding what has been said to the contrary, his own experience satisfied him that a rooted distrust of Congress pretty generally prevailed. A Natl. Govt. alone, property constituted, will answer the purpose; and he begged it to be considered that the present is the last moment for establishing one. After this select experiment, the people will yield to despair.

The Committee rose & the House adjourned.

Monday, June 18

In Committee of the Whole on the Propositions of Mr. Patterson & Mr. Randolph

Mr. Hamilton, had been hitherto silent on the business before the Convention, partly from respect to others whose superior abilities age & experience rendered him unwilling to bring forward ideas dissimilar to theirs, and partly from his delicate situation with respect to his own State, to whose sentiments as expressed by his Colleagues, he could by no means accede. The crisis however which now marked our affairs, was too serious to permit any scruples whatever to prevail over the duty imposed on every man to contribute his efforts for the public safety & happiness. He was obliged therefore to declare himself unfriendly to both plans. He was particularly opposed to that from N. Jersey, being fully convinced, that no amendment of the Confederation, leaving the States in possession of their Sovereignty could possibly answer the purpose. On the other hand he confessed he was much discouraged by the amazing extent of Country in expecting the desired blessings from any general sovereignty that could be substituted.—As to the powers of the Convention, he thought the doubts started on that subject had arisen from distinctions & reasonings too subtle. A *federal* Govt. he conceived to mean an association of independent Communities into one. Different Confederacies have different powers, and exercise them in different ways. In some instances the powers are exercised over collective bodies; in others over individuals, as in the German Diet—& among ourselves in cases of piracy. Great latitude therefore must be given to the signification of the term. The plan last proposed departs itself from the *federal* idea, as understood by some, since it is to operate eventually on individuals. He agreed moreover with the Honble gentleman from Va. [Mr. R.] that we owed it to our Country, to do on this emergency whatever we should deem essential to its happiness. The States sent us here to provide for the exigences of the Union. To rely on & propose any plan not adequate to these exigences, merely because it was not clearly within our powers, would be to sacrifice the means to the end. It may be said that the *States* can not *ratify* a plan not within the purview of the article of Confederation providing for alterations & amendments. But may not the States themselves in which no constitutional authority equal to this purpose exists in the Legislatures, have had in view a reference to the people at large. In the Senate of N. York, a proviso was moved, that no act of the Convention should be binding untill it should be referred to the people & ratified; and the motion was lost by a single voice only, the reason assigned agst. it being, that it might possibly be found an inconvenient shackle.

The great question is what provision shall we make for the happiness of our Country? He would first make a comparative examination of the two plans—prove that there were essential defects in both—and point out such changes as might render a *national one,* efficacious.—The great & essential principles necessary for the support of Government are 1. an active & constant interest in supporting it. This principle does not exist in the States in favor of the federal Govt. They have evidently in a high degree, the esprit de corps. They constantly pursue internal interests adverse to those of the whole. They have their particular debts—their particular plans of finance &c. All these when opposed to, invariably prevail over the requisitions & plans of Congress. 2. The love of power. Men love power. The same remarks are applicable to this principle.

The States have constantly shewn a disposition rather to regain the powers delegated by them than to part with more, or to give effect to what they had parted with. The ambition of their demagogues is known to hate the controul of the Genl. Government. It may be remarked too that the Citizens have not that anxiety to prevent a dissolution of the Genl. Govt. as of the particular Govts. A dissolution of the latter would be fatal; of the former would still leave the purposes of Govt. attainable to a considerable degree. Consider what such a State as Virga. will be in a few years, a few compared with the life of nations. How strongly will it feet its importance & self-sufficiency? 3. An habitual attachment of the people. The whole force of this tie is on the side of the State Govt. Its sovereignty is immediately before the eyes of the people: its protection is immediately enjoyed by them. From its hand distributive justice, and all those acts which familiarize & endear Govt. to a people, are dispensed to them. 4. *Force* by which may be understood a *coertion of laws or coertion of arms.* Congs. have not the former except in few cases. In particular States, this coercion is nearly sufficient; tho' he held it in most cases, not entirely so. A certain portion of military force is absolutely necessary in large communities. Mass. is now feeling this necessity & making provision for it. But how can this force be exerted on the States collectively. It is impossible. It amounts to a war between the parties. Foreign powers also will not be idle spectators. They will interpose, the confusion will increase, and a dissolution of the Union ensue. 5. *influence.* he did not mean corruption, but a dispensation of those regular honors & emoluments, which produce an attachment to the Govt. Almost all the weight of these is on the side of the States; and must continue so as long as the States continue to exist. All the passions then we see, of avarice, ambition, interest, which govern most individuals, and all public bodies, fall into the current of the States, and do not flow in the stream of the Genl. Govt. The former therefore will generally be an overmatch for the Genl. Govt. and render any confederacy, in its very natuve precarious. Theory is in this case fully confirmed by experience, The Amphyctionic Council had it would seem ample powers for general purposes. It had in particular the power of fining and using force agst. delinquent members. What was the consequence. Their decrees were mere signals of war. The Phocian war is a striking example of it. Philip at length taking advantage of their disunion, and insinuating himself into their Councils, made himself master of their fortunes. The German Confederacy affords another lesson. The authority of Charlemagne seemed to be as great as could be necessary. The great feudal chiefs however, exercising their local sovereignties, soon felt the spirit & found the means of, encroachments, which reduced the imperial authority to a nominal sovereignty. The Diet has succeeded, which tho' aided by a Prince at its head, of great authority independently of his imperial attributes, is a striking illustration of the weakness of Confederated Governments. Other examples instruct us in the same truth. The Swiss cantons have scarce any Union at all, and have been more than once at war with one another—How then are all these evils to be avoided? only by such a compleat sovereignty in the general Governmt. as will turn all the strong principles & passions above mentioned on its side. Does the scheme of N. Jersey produce this effect? does it afford any substantial remedy whatever? On the contrary it labors under great defects, and the defect of some of its provisions will destroy the efficacy of others. It gives a direct revenue to Congs. but this will not be sufficient. The balance can only be supplied by requisitions: which experience proves can not be relied on. If States are to deliberate on the mode, they will also deliberate on the object of the supplies, and will grant or not grant as they approve or disapprove of it. The delinquency of one will invite and countenance it in others. Quotas too must in the nature of things be so unequal as to produce the same evil. To what standard will you resort? Land is a fallacious one. Compare Holland with Russia: France or Engd. with other countries of Europe. Pena. with N. Carola. will the relative pecuniary abilities in those instances, correspond with the relative value of land. Take numbers of inhabitants for the rule and make like comparison of different countries, and you will find it to be equally unjust. The different degrees of industry and improvement in different Countries render the first object a precarious measure of wealth. Much depends too on *situation.* Cont. N. Jersey & N. Carolina, not being commercial States & contributing to the wealth of the commercial ones, can never bear quotas assessed by the ordinary rules of proportion.

They will & must fail in their duty, their example will be followed, and the Union itself be dissolved. Whence then is the national revenue to be drawn? from Commerce? even from exports which notwithstanding the common opinion are fit objects of moderate taxation, from excise, &c &c, These tho' not equal, are less unequal than quotas. Another destructive ingredient in the plan, is that equality of suffrage which is so much desired by the small States. It is not in human nature that Va. & the large States should consent to it, or if they did that they shd. long abide by it. It shocks too much the ideas of Justice, and every human feeling. Bad principles in a Govt. tho slow are sure in their operation and will gradually destroy it. A doubt has been raised whether Congs. at present have a right to keep Ships or troops in time of peace. He leans to the negative. Mr. Ps. plan provides no remedy.—If the powers proposed were adequate, the organization of Congs. is such that they could never be properly & effectually exercised. The members of Congs. being chosen by the States & subject to recall, represent all the local prejudices. Should the powers be found effectual, they will from time to time be heaped on them, till a tyrannic sway shall be established. The general power whatever be its form if it preserves itself, must swallow up the State powers. Otherwise it will be swallowed up by them. It is agst. all the principles of a good Government to vest the requisite powers in such a body as Congs. Two Sovereignties can not coexist within the same limits. Giving powers to Congs. must eventuate in a bad Govt. or in no Govt. The plan of N. Jersey therefore will not do. What then is to be done? Here he was embarrassed. The extent of the Country to be governed, discouraged him. The expence of a general Govt was also formidable; unless there were such a diminution of expence on the side of the State Govts. as the case would admit. If they were extinguished, he was persuaded that great oeconomy might be obtained by substituting a general Govt. He did not mean however to shock the public opinion by proposing such a measure. On the other hand he saw no *other* necessity for declining it. They are not necessary for any of the great purposes of commerce, revenue, or agriculture. Subordinate authorities he was aware would be necessary. There must be district tribunals: corporations for local purposes. But cui bono, the vast & expensive apparatus now appertaining to the States. The only difficulty of a serious nature which occurred to him, was that of drawing representatives from the extremes to the center of the Community. What inducements can be offered that will suffice? The moderate wages for the 1st branch would only be a bait to little demagogues. Three dollars or thereabouts he supposed would be the utmost. The Senate he feared from a similar cause, would be filled by certain undertakers who wish for particular offices under the Govt. This view of the subject almost led to him despair that a Republican Govt. could be established over so great an extent. He was sensible at the same time that it would be unwise to propose one of any other form. In his private opinion he had no scruple in declaring, supported as he was by the opinions of so many of the wise & good, that the British Govt. was the best in the world: and that he doubted much whether any thing short of it would do in America. He hoped Gentlemen of different opinions would bear with him in this, and begged them to recollect the change of opinion on this subject which had taken place and was still going on. It was once thought that the power of Congs. was amply sufficient to secure the end of their institution. The error was now seen by every one. The members most tenacious of republicanism, he observed, were as loud as any in declaiming agst. the vices of democracy. This progress of the public mind led him to anticipate the time, when others as well as himself would join in the praise bestowed by Mr. Neckar on the British Constitution, namely, that it is the only Govt. in the world "which unites public strength with individual security."—In every community where industry is encouraged, there will be a division of it into the few & the many. Hence separate interests will arise. There will be debtors & creditors &c. Give all power to the many, they will oppress the few. Give all power to the few, they will oppress the many. Both therefore ought to have power, that each may defend itself agst. the other. To the want of this check we owe our paper money, instalment laws &c. To the proper adjustment of it the British owe the excellence of their Constitution. Their house of Lords is a most noble institution. Having nothing to hope for by a change, and a sufficient interest by means of their property, in being faithful to the national interests they form a permanent barrier agst. every pernicious innovation, whether attempted on the part of the Crown or of the Commons. No temporary Senate will have firmness eno' to answer the purpose. The Senate [of Maryland] which seems to be so much appealed to, has not yet been sufficiently tried. Had the people been unanimous & eager, in the late appeal to them on the subject of a paper emission they would have yielded to the torrent. Their acquiescing in such an appeal is a proof of it.—Gentlemen differ in their opinions concerning the necessary checks, from the different estimates they form of the human passions. They suppose seven years a sufficient period to give the senate an adequate firmness, from not duly considering the amazing violence & turbulence of the democratic spirit. When a great object of Govt. is pursued, which seizes the popular passions, they spread like wild fire, and become irresistable. He appealed to the gentlemen from the N. England States whether experience had not there verified the remark.—As to the Executive, it seemed to be admitted that no good one could be established on Republican principles. Was not this giving up the merits of the question: for can there be a good Govt. without a good Executive. The English model was the only good one on this subject. The Hereditary interest of the King was so interwoven with that of the Nation, and his personal emoluments so great, that he was placed above the danger of being corrupted from abroad—and at the same time was both sufficiently independent and sufficiently controuled, to answer the purpose of the institution at home, one of the weak sides of Republics was their being liable to foreign influence & corruption. Men of little character, acquiring great power become easily the tools of intermedling Neighbours. Sweeden was a striking instance, The French & English had each their parties during the late Revolution which was effected by the predominant influence of the former.—What is the inference from all these observations? That we ought to go as far in order to attain stability and permanency, as republican principles will admit. Let one branch of the Legislature hold their places for life or at least during good behaviour. Let the Executive also be for life. He appealed to the feelings of the members present whether a term of seven years, would induce the sacrifices of private affairs which an acceptance of public trust would require, so so as to ensure the services of the best Citizens. On this plan we should have in the Senate a permanent will, a weighty interest, which would answer essential purposes. But is this a Republican Govt., it will be asked? Yes if all the Magistrates are appointed, and vacancies are filled, by the people, or a process of election originating with the people. He was sensible that an Executive constituted as he proposed would have in fact but little of the power and independence that might be necessary. On the other plan of appointing him for 7 years, he thought the Executive ought to have but little power. He would be ambitious, with the means of making creatures; and as the object of his ambition wd. be to *prolong* his power, it is probable that in case of a war, he would avail himself of the emergence, to evade or refuse a degradation from his place. An Executive for life has not this motive for forgetting his fidelity, and will therefore be a safer depository of power. It will be objected probably, that such an Executive will be an *elective Monarch*, and will give birth to the tumults which characterize that form of Govt. He wd. reply that *Monarch* is an indefinite term. It marks not either the degree or duration of power. If this Executive Magistrate wd. be a monarch for life—the other propd. by the Report from the Comtte of the whole, wd. be a monarch for seven years. The circumstance of being elective was also applicable to both. It had been observed by judicious writers that elective monarchies wd. be the best if they could be guarded agst. the *tumults* excited by the ambition and intrigues of competitors. He was not sure that tumults were an inseparable evil. He rather thought this character of Elective Monarchies had been taken rather from particular cases than from general principles. The election of Roman Emperors was made by the *Army*. In *Poland* the election is made by great rival *princes* with independent power, and ample means, of raising commotions. In the German Empire, the appointment is made by the Electors & Princes, who have equal motives & means, for exciting cabals & parties. Might not such a mode of election be devised among ourselves as will defend the community agst. these effects in any dangerous degree? Having made these observations he would read to the Committee a sketch of a plan which he shd. prefer to either of those under consideration. He was aware that it went beyond the ideas of most members. But will such a plan be adopted out of doors? In return he would ask will the people adopt the other plan? At present they will adopt neither. But he sees the Union dissolving or already dissolved—he sees evils operating in the States which must soon cure the people of their fondness for democracies—he sees that a great progress has been already made & is still going on in the public mind. He thinks therefore that the people will in time be unshackled from their prejudices; and whenever that happens, they will themselves not be satisfied at stopping where the plan of Mr. R. wd. place them, but be ready to go as far at least as he proposes. He did not mean to offer the paper he had sketched as a proposition to the Committee. It was meant only to give a more correct view of his ideas, and to suggest the amendments which he should probably propose to the plan of Mr. R. in the proper stages of its future discussion. He read his sketch in the words following: to wit

I. The Supreme Legislative power of the United States of America to be vested in two different bodies of men; the one to be called the Assembly, the other the Senate who together shall form the Legislature of the United States with power to pass all laws whatsoever subject to the Negative hereafter mentioned.

II. The Assembly to consist of persons elected by the people to serve for three years.

III. The Senate to consist of persons elected to serve during good behaviour; their election to be made by electors chosen for that purpose by the people: in order to this the States to be divided into election districts. On the death, removal or resignation of any Senator his place to be filled out of the district from which he came.

IV. The supreme Executive authority of the United States to be vested in a Governour to be elected to serve during good behaviour—the election to be made by Electors chosen by the people in the Election Districts aforesaid—The authorities & functions of the Executive to be as follows: to have a negative on all laws about to be passed, and the execution of all laws passed, to have the direction of war when authorized or begun; to have with the advice and approbation of the Senate the power of making all treaties; to have the sole appointment of the heads or chief officers of the departments of Finance, War and Foreign Affairs; to have the nomination of all other officers (Ambassadors to foreign Nations included) subject to the approbation or rejection of the Senate; to have the power of pardoning all offences except Treason; which he shall not pardon without the approbation of the Senate.

V. On the death, resignation or removal of the Governour his authorities to be exercised by the President of the Senate till a Successor be appointed.

VI. The Senate to have the sole power of declaring war, the power of advising and approving all Treaties, the power of approving or rejecting all appointments of officers except the heads or chiefs of the departments of Finance War and foreign affairs.

VII. The supreme Judicial authority to be vested in Judges to hold their offices during good behaviour with adequate and permanent salaries. This Court to have original jurisdiction in all causes of capture, and an appellative jurisdiction in all causes in which the revenues of the general Government or the Citizens of foreign Nations are concerned.

VIII. The Legislature of the United States to have power to institute Courts in each State for the determination of all matters of general concern.

IX. The Governour Senators and all officers of the United States to be liable to impeachment for mal- and corrupt conduct; and upon conviction to be removed from office, & disqualified for holding any-place of trust or profit—All impeachments to be tried by a Court to consist of the Chief or Judge of the superior Court of Law of each State, provided such Judge shall hold his place during good behavior, and have a permanent salary.

X. All laws of the particular States contrary to the Constitution or laws of the United States to be utterly void; and the better to prevent such laws being passed, the Governour or president of each State shall be appointed by the General Government and shall have a negative upon the laws about to be passed in the State of which he is Governour or President.

XI. No State to have any forces land or Naval; and the Militia of all the States to be under the sole and exclusive direction of the United States, the officers of which to be appointed and commissioned by them.

On these several articles he entered into explanatory observations corresponding with the principles of his introductory reasoning.

Committee rose & the House Adjourned.

Tuesday, June 19

In Committee of Whole of the Propositions of Mr. Patterson

Mr. Patterson's plan was again at large before the Committee.

Mr. Madison. Much stress had been laid by some gentlemen on the want of power in the Convention to propose any other than a *federal* plan. To what had been answered by others, he would only add, that neither of the characteristics attached to a *federal* plan would support this objection. One characteristic, was that in a *federal* Government, the power was exercised not on the people individually; but on the people *collectively*, on the *States*. Yet in some instances as in piracies, captures &c. the existing Confederacy, and in many instances, the amendments to it proposed by Mr. Patterson, must operate immediately on individuals. The other characteristic was that a *federal* Govt. derived its appointments not immediately from the people, but from the States which they respectively composed. Here too were facts on the other side. In two of the States, Connect. and Rh. Island, the delegates to Congs. were chosen, not by the Legislatures, but by the people at large; and the plan of Mr. P. intended no change in this particular.

It had been alledged [by Mr. Patterson], that the Confederation having been formed by unanimous consent, could be dissolved by unanimous Consent only. Does this doctrine result from the nature of compacts? does it arise from any particular stipulation in the articles of Confederation? If we consider the federal union as analogous to the fundamental compact by which individuals compose one Society, and which must in its theoretic origin at least, have been the unanimous act of the component members, it can not be said that no dissolution of the compact can be effected without unanimous consent. A breach of the fundamental principles of the compact by a pail of the Society would certainly absolve the other part from their obligations to it. If the breach of *any* article by *any* of the parties, does not set the others at liberty, it is because, the contrary is *implied* in the compact itself, and particularly by that law of it, which gives an indefinite authority to the majority to bind the whole in all cases. This latter circumstance shews that we are not to consider the federal Union as analogous to the social compact of individuals: for if it were so, a Majority would have a fight to bind the rest, and even to form a new Constitution for the whole, which the Gentn. from N. Jersey would be among the last to admit. If we consider the federal Union as analogous not to the social compacts among individual men: but to the conventions among individual States. What is the doctrine resulting from these conventions? Clearly, according to the Expositors of the law of Nations, that a breach of any one article, by any one party, leaves all the other parties at liberty, to consider the whole convention as dissolved, unless they choose rather to compel the delinquent party to repair the breach. In some treaties indeed it is expressly stipulated that a violation of particular articles shall not have this consequence, and even that particular articles shall remain in force during war, which in general is understood to dissolve all subsisting Treaties. But are there any exceptions of this sort to the Articles of confederation? So far from it that there is not even an express stipulation that force shall be used to compell an offending member of the Union to discharge its duty. He observed that the violations of the federal articles had been numerous & notorious. Among the most notorious was an act of N. Jersey herself, by which she *expressly refused* to comply with a constitutional requisition of Congs. and yielded no farther to the expostulations of their deputies, than barely to rescind her vote of refusal without passing any positive act of compliance. He did not wish to draw any rigid inferences frorn these observations. He thought it proper however that the true nature of the existing confederacy should be investigated, and he was not anxious to strengthen the foundations on which it now stands. Proceeding to the consideration of Mr. Patterson's plan, he stated the object of a proper plan to be twofold. 1. to preserve the Union. 2. to provide a Governmt. that will remedy the evils felt by the States both in their united and individual capacities. Examine Mr. P.s plan, & say whether it promises satisfaction in these respects.

1. Will it prevent those violations of the law of nations & of Treaties which if not prevented must involve us in the calamities of foreign wars? The tendency of the States to these violations has been

manifested in sundry instances. The files of Congs. contain complaints already, from almost every nation with which treaties have been formed. Hitherto indulgence has been shewn to us. This can not be the permanent disposition of foreign nations. A rupture with other powers is among the greatest of national calamities. It ought therefore to be effectually provided that no part of a nation shall have it in its power to bring them on the whole. The existing Confederacy does not sufficiently provide against this evil. The proposed amendment to it does not supply the omission. It leaves the will of the States as uncontrouled as ever.

2. Will it prevent encroachments on the federal authority? A tendency to such encroachments has been sufficiently exemplified, among ourselves, as well in every other confederated republic antient and Modern. By the federal articles, transactions with the Indians appertain to Congs. Yet in several instances, the States have entered into treaties & wars with them. In like manner no two or more States can form among themselves any treaties &c. without the consent of Congs. Yet Virga. & Maryd. in one instance—Pena. & N. Jersey in another, have entered into compacts, without previous application or subsequent apology. No State again can of right raise troops in time of peace without the like consent. Of all cases of the league, this seems to require the most scrupulous observance. Has not Massts, notwithstanding, the most powerful member of the Union, already raised a body of troops? Is she not now augmenting them, without having even deigned to apprise Congs. of Her intention? In fine—Have we not seen the public land dealt out to Cont. to bribe her acquiescence in the decree constitutionally awarded agst. her claim on the territory of Pena.? for no other possible motive can account for the policy of Congs. in that measure?—If we recur to the examples of other confederacies, we shall find in all of them the same tendency of the parts to encroach on the authority of the whole. He then reviewed the Amphyctionic & Achaean confederacies among the antients, and the Helvetic, Germanic & Belgic among the moderns, tracing their analogy to the U. States—in the constitution and extent of their federal authorities—in the tendency of the particular members to usurp on these authorities; and to bring confusion & ruin on the whole.—He observed that the plan of Mr. Patterson besides omitting a controul over the States as a general defence of the federal prerogatives was particularly defective in two of its provisions. 1. Its ratification was not to be by the people at large, but by the *legislatures*. It could not therefore render the Acts of Congs. in pursuance of their powers, even legally *paramount* to the Acts of the States. 2. It gave to the federal Tribunal an appellate jurisdiction only—even in the criminal cases enumerated, The necessity of any such provision supposed a danger of undue acquittals in the State tribunals. Of what avail cd. an appellate tribunal be, after an acquittal? Besides in most if not all of the States, the Executives have by their respective *Constitutions* the right of pardg. How could this be taken from them by a *legislative* ratification only?

3. Will it prevent trespasses of the States on each other? Of these enough has been already seen. He instanced Acts of Virga. & Maryland which give a preference to their own Citizens in cases where the Citizens of other States are entitled to equality of privileges by the Aticles of Confederation. He considered the emissions of paper money & other kindred measures as also aggressions. The States relatively to one an other being each of them either Debtor or Creditor; The creditor States must suffer unjustly from every emission by the debtor States. We have seen retaliating acts on this subject which threatened danger not to the harmony only, but the tranquility of the Union. The plan of Mr. Patterson, not giving even a negative on the acts of the States, left them as much at liberty as ever to execute their unrighteous projects agst. each other.

4. Will it secure the internal tranquility of the States themselves? The insurrections in Massts. admonished all the States of the danger to which they were exposed. Yet the plan of Mr. P. contained no provisions for supplying the defect of the Confederation on this point. According to the Republican theory indeed, Right & power being both vested in the majority, are held to be synonimous. According to fact & experience, a minority may in an appeal to force be an overmatch for the majority. 1. If the minority happen to include all such as possess the skill & habits of military life, with such as possess the great pecuniary resources, one third may conquer the remaining two thirds. 2. one third of those who participate in the choice of rulers may be rendered a

majority by the accession of those whose poverty disqualifies them from a suffrage, & who for obvious reasons may be more ready to join the standard of sedition than that of the established Government. 3. where slavery exists, the Republican Theory becomes still more fallacious.

5. Will it secure a good internal legislation & administration to the particular States? In developing the evils which vitiate the political system of the U.S. it is proper to take into view those which prevail within the States individually as well as those which affect them collectively: Since the former indirectly affect the whole; and there is great reason to believe that the pressure of them had a full share in the motives which produced the present Convention. Under this head he enumerated and animadverted on 1. the multiplicity of the laws passed by the several States. 2. the mutability of their laws. 3.the injustice of them. 4. the impotence of them: observing that Mr. Patterson's plan contained no remedy for this dreadful class of evils, and could not therefore be received as an adequate provision for the exigences of the Community.

6. Will it secure the Union agst. the influence of foreign powers over its members. He pretended not to say that any such influence had yet been tried: but it was naturally to be expected that occasions would produce it. As lessons which claimed particular attention, he cited the intrigues practised among the Amphyctionic Confederates first by the Kings of Persia, and afterwards fatally by Philip of Macedon: among the Achaeans, first by Macedon & afterwards no less fatally by Rome: among the Swiss by Austria, France & the lesser neighbouring powers: among the members of the Germanic Body by France, England, Spain & Russia—: and in the Belgic Republic, by all the great neighbouring powers. The plan of Mr. Patterson, not giving to the general Councils any negative on the will of the particular States, left the door open for the like pernicious machinations among ourselves.

7. He begged the smaller States which were most attached to Mr. Patterson's plan to consider the situation in which it would leave them. In the first place they would continue to bear the whole expence of maintaining their Delegates in Congress. It ought not to be said that if they were willing to bear this burden, no others had a right to complain. As far as it led the small States to forbear keeping up a representation, by which the public business was delayed, it was evidently a matter of common concern. An examination of the minutes of Congress would satisfy every one that the public business had been frequently delayed by this cause; and that the States most frequently unrepresented in Congs. were not the larger States. He reminded the convention of another consequence of leaving on a small State the burden of maintaining a Representation in Congs. During a considerable period of the War, one of the Representatives of Delaware, in whom alone before the signing of the Confederation the entire vote of that State and after that event one half of its vote, frequently resided, was a Citizen & Resident of Penna. and held an office in his own State incompatible with an appointment from it to Congs. During another period, the same State was represented by three delegates two of whom were citizens of Penna. and the third a Citizen of New Jersey. These expedients must have been intended to avoid the burden of supporting delegates from their own State. But whatever might have been ye. cause, was not in effect the vote of one State doubled, and the influence of another increased by it? In the 2d place The coercion, on which the efficacy of the plan depends, can never be exerted but on themselves. The larger States will be impregnable, the smaller only can feel the vengeance of it. He illustrated the position by the history of the Amphyctionic Confederates: and the ban of the German Empire. It was the cobweb wch. could entangle the weak, but would be the sport of the strong.

8. He begged them to consider the situation in which they would remain in case their pertinacious adherence to an inadmissible plan, should prevent the adoption of any plan. The contemplation of such an event was painful; but it would be prudent to submit to the task of examining it at a distance, that the means of escaping it might be the more readily embraced. Let the Union of the States be dissolved, and one of two consequences must happen. Either the States must remain individually independent & sovereign; or two or more Confederacies must be formed among them. In the first event would the small States be more secure agst. the ambition & power of their larger neighbours, than they would be under a general Government pervading with equal

energy every part of the Empire, and having an equal interest in protecting every part agst. every other part? In the second, can the smaller expect that their larger neighbours would confederate with them on the principle of the present confederacy, which gives to each member, an equal suffrage; or that they would exact less severe concessions from the smaller States, than are proposed in the scheme of Mr. Randolph?

The great difficulty lies in the affair of Representation; and if this could be adjusted, all others would be surmountable. It was admitted by both the gentlemen from N. Jersey [Mr. Brearly and Mr. Patterson] that it would not be *just to allow Virga.* which was 16 times as large as Delaware an equal vote only. Their language was that it would not be *safe for Delaware* to allow Virga. 16 times as many votes. The expedient proposed by them was that all the States should be thrown into one mass and a new partition be made into 13 equal parts. Would such a scheme be practicable? The dissimilarities existing in the rules of property, as well as in the manners, habits and prejudices of the different States, amounted to a prohibition of the attempt. It had been found impossible for the power of one of the most absolute princes in Europe [K. of France] directed by the wisdom of one of the most enlightened and patriotic Ministers [Mr. Neckar] that any age has produced to equalize in some points only the different usages & regulations of the different provinces. But admitting a general amalgamation and repartition of the States to be practicable, and the danger apprehended by the smaller States from a proportional representation to be real; would not a particular and voluntary coalition of these with their neighbours, be less inconvenient to the whole community, and equally effectual for their own safety. If N. Jersey or Delaware conceived that an advantage would accrue to them from an equalization of the States, in which case they would necessaryly form a junction with their neighbours, why might not this end be attained by leaving them at liberty by the Constitution to form such a junction whenever they pleased? And why should they wish to obtrude a like arrangement on all the States, when it was, to say the least, extremely difficult, would be obnoxious to many of the States, and when neither the inconveniency, nor the benefit of the expedient to themselves, would be lessened, by confining it to themselves.—The prospect of many new States to the Westward was another consideration of importance. If they should come into the Union at all, they would come when they contained but few inhabitants. If they shd. be entitled to vote according to their proportions of inhabitants, all would be right & safe. Let them have an equal vote, and a more objectionable minority than ever might give law to the whole.

On a question for postponing generally the 1st proposition of Mr. Patterson's plan, it was agreed to: N.Y. & N.J. only being no—

On the question moved by Mr. King whether the Committee should rise & Mr. Randolphs propositions be re-reported without alteration, which was in fact a question whether Mr. R's should be adhered to as preferable to those of Mr. Patterson:

(Of Mr. Randolph's plan as reported from the Committee) the 1. propos: "that a Natl. Govt. ought to be established consisting &c." being taken up in the House. Mr. Wilson observed that by a Natl. Govt. he did not mean one that would swallow up the State Govts. as seemed to be wished by some gentlemen. He was tenacious of the idea of preserving the latter. He thought, contrary to the opinion of [Col. Hamilton] that they might not only subsist but subsist on friendly terms with the former. They were absolutely necessary for certain purposes which the former could not reach. All large Governments must be subdivided into lesser jurisdictions. As Examples he mentioned Persia, Rome, and particularly the divisions & subdivisions of England by Alfred.

Col. Hamilton coincided with the proposition as it stood in the Report. He had not been understood yesterday. By an abolition of the States, he meant that no boundary could be drawn between the National & State Legislatures; that the former must therefore have indefinite authority. If it were limited at all, the rivalship of the States would gradually subvert it. Even as Corporations the extent of some of them as Va. Massts. &c. would be formidable. As *States,* he thought they ought to be abolished. But he admitted the necessity of leaving in them, subordinate jurisdictions. The examples of Persia & the Roman Empire, cited by [Mr. Wilson] were he thought in favor of his doctrine: the great powers delegated to the Satraps & proconsuls, having frequently produced revolts, and schemes of independence.

Mr. King, wished as every thing depended on this proposition, that no objections might be improperly indulged agst. the phraseology of it. He conceived that the import of the terms "States" "Sovereignty" "*national*" "federal," had been often used & applied in the discussions inaccurately & delusively. The States were not "Sovereigns" in the sense contended for by some. They did not possess the peculiar features of sovereignty, they could not make war, nor peace, nor alliances nor treaties. Considering them as political Beings, they were dumb, for they could not speak to any foreign Sovereign whatever. They were deaf, for they could not hear any propositions from such Sovereign. They had not even the organs or faculties of defence or offence, for they could not of themselves raise troops, or equip vessels, for war. On the other side, if the Union of the States comprizes the idea of a confederation, it comprizes that also of consolidation. A Union of the States is a Union of the men composing them, from whence a *national* character results to the whole. Congs. can act alone without the States—they can act & their acts will be binding agst. the Instructions of the States. If they declare war: war is de jure declared—captures made in pursuance of it are lawful—No acts of the States can vary the situation, or prevent the judicial consequences. If the States therefore retained some portion of their sovereignty, they had certainly divested themselves of essential portions of it. If they formed a confederacy in some respects—they formed a Nation in others—The Convention could clearly deliberate on & propose any alterations that Congs. could have done under ye. federal articles, and could not Congs. propose by virtue of the last article, a change in any article whatever: and as well that relating to the equality of suffrage, as any other. He made these remarks to obviate some scruples which had been expressed. He doubted much the practicability of annihilating the States; but thought that much of their power ought to be taken from them.

Mr. Martin, said he considered that the separation from G.B. placed the 13 States in a state of Nature towards each other; that they would have remained in that state till this time, but for the confederation; that they entered into the confederation on the footing of equality; that they met now to to amend it on the same footing, and that he could never accede to a plan that would introduce an inequality and lay 10 States at the mercy of Va. Massts. and Penna.

Mr. Wilson, could not admit the doctrine that when the Colonies became independent of G. Britain, they became independent also of each other. He read the declaration of Independence, observing thereon that the *United Colonies* were declared to be free & independent States; and inferring that they were independent, not *individually* but *Unitedly* and that they were confederated as they were independent, States.

Col. Hamilton, assented to the doctrine of Mr. Wilson. He denied the doctrine that the States were thrown into a State of Nature. He was not yet prepared to admit the doctrine that the Confederacy, could be dissolved by partial infractions of it. He admitted that the States met now on an equal footing but could see no inference from that against concerting a change of the system in this particular. He took this occasion of observing for the purpose of appeasing the fears of the small States, that two circumstances would render them secure under a National Govt. in which they might lose the equality of rank they now held: one was the local situation of the 3 largest States Virga. Masts. & Pa. They were separated from each other by distance of place, and equally so, by all the peculiarities which distinguish the interests of one State from those of another. No combination therefore could be dreaded. In the second place, as there was a gradation in the States from Va. the largest down to Delaware the smallest, it would always happen that ambitious combinations among a few States might & wd. be counteracted by defensive combinations of greater extent among the rest. No combination has been seen among large Counties merely as such, agst. lesser Counties. The more close the Union of the States, and the more compleat the authority of the whole: the less opportunity will be allowed the stronger States to injure the weaker.

Adjd.

Tuesday, June 26

In Convention

The duration of the 2d branch under consideration.

Mr. Ghorum moved to fill the blank with "six years," one third of the members to go out every second year.

Mr. Wilson 2ded the motion.

Mr. Read movd. that the term be nine years. This wd. admit of a very convenient rotation, one third going out triennially. He wd. still prefer "during good behaviour," but being little supported in that idea, he was willing to take the longest term that could be obtained.

Mr. Broome 2ded the motion.

Mr. Madison. In order to judge of the form to be given to this institution, it will be proper to take a view of the ends to be served by it. These were first to protect the people agst. their rulers: secondly to protect the people agst. the transient impressions into which they themselves might be led. A people deliberating in a temperate moment, and with the experience of other nations before them, on the plan of Govt. most likely to secure their happiness, would first be aware, that those chargd. with the public happiness, might betray their trust. An obvious precaution agst. this danger wd. be to divide the trust between different bodies of men, who might watch & check each other. In this they wd. be governed by the same prudence which has prevailed in organizing the subordinate departments of Govt., where all business liable to abuses is made to pass thro' separate hands, the one being a check on the other. It wd. next occur to such a people, that they themselves were liable to temporary errors, thro' want of information as to their true interest, and that men chosen for a short term, & employed but a small portion of that in public affairs, might err from the same cause. This reflection wd. naturally suggest that the Govt. be so constituted, as that one of its branches might have an oppy. of acquiring a competent knowledge of the public interests. Another reflection equally becoming a people on such an occasion, wd. be that they themselves, as well as a numerous body of Representatives, were liable to err also, from fickleness and passion. A necessary fence agst. this danger would be to select a portion of enlightened citizens, whose limited number, and firmness might seasonably interpose agst. impetuous councils. It ought finally to occur to a people deliberating on a Govt. for themselves, that as different interests necessarily result from the liberty meant to be secured, the major interest might under sudden impulses be tempted to commit injustice on the minority. In all civilized Countries the people fall into different classes havg a real or supposed difference of interests. There will be creditors & debtors, farmers, merchts. & manufacturers. There will be particularly the distinction of rich & poor. It was true as had been observd. [by Mr. Pinkney] we had not among us those hereditary distinctions, of rank which were a great source of the contests in the ancient Govts. as well as the modern States of Europe, nor those extremes of wealth or poverty which characterize the latter. We cannot however be regarded even at this time, as one homogeneous mass, in which every thing that affects a part will affect in the same manner the whole. In framing a system which we wish to last for ages, we shd. not lose sight of the changes which ages will produce. An increase of population will of necessity increase the proportion of those who will labour under all the hardships of life, & secretly sigh for a more equal distribution of its blessings. These may in time outnumber those who are placed above the feelings of indigence. According to the equal laws of suffrage, the power will slide into the hands of the former. No agrarian attempts have yet been made in this Country, but symtoms, of a leveling spirit, as we have understood, have sufficiently appeared in a certain quarters to give notice of the future danger. How is this danger to be guarded agst. on republican principles? How is the danger in all cases of interested coalitions to oppress the minority to be guarded agst.? Among other means by the establishment of a body in the Govt. sufficiently respectable for its wisdom & virtue, to aid on such emergences, the preponderance of justice by throwing its weight into that scale. Such being the objects of the second branch in the proposed Govt. he thought a considerable duration ought to be given to it. He did not conceive that the term of nine years could threaten any real danger; but in pursuing his particular ideas on the subject, he should require that the long term allowed to the 2d branch should not commence till such a period of life, as would render a perpetual disqualification to be re-elected little inconvenient either in a public or private view. He observed that as it was more than probable we were now digesting a plan which in its operation wd. decide for ever the fate of Republican Govt. we ought not only to provide every guard to liberty that its preservation cd. require, but be equally careful to supply the defects which our own experience had particularly pointed out.

Mr. Gerry wished we could be united in our ideas concerning a permanent Govt. All aim at the same end, but there are great differences as to the means. One circumstance He thought should be carefully attended to. There were not 1/1000 part of our fellow citizens who were not agst. every approach towards Monarchy. Will they ever agree to a plan which seems to make such an approach. The Convention ought to be extremely cautious in what they hold out to the people. Whatever plan may be proposed will be espoused with warmth by many out of respect to the quarter it proceeds from as well as from an approbation of the plan itself. And if the plan should be of such a nature as to rouse a violent opposition, it is easy to foresee that discord & confusion will ensue, and it is even possible that we may become a prey to foreign powers. He did not deny the position of Mr. Madison, that the majority will generally violate justice when they have an interest in so doing; But did not think there was any such temptation in this Country. Our situation was different from that of G. Britain: and the great body of lands yet to be parcelled out & settled would very much prolong the difference. Notwithstanding the symtoms of injustice which had marked many of our public Councils, they had not proceeded so far as not to leave hopes, that there would be a sufficient sense of justice & virtue for the purpose of Govt. He admitted the evils arising from a frequency of elections: and would agree to give the Senate a duration of four or five years. A longer term would defeat itself. It never would be adopted by the people.

Mr. Wilson did not mean to repeat what had fallen from others, but wd. add an observation or two which he believed had not yet been suggested. Every nation may be regarded in two relations 1. to its own citizens. 2. to foreign nations. It is therefore not only liable to anarchy & tyranny within, but has wars to avoid & treaties to obtain from abroad. The Senate will probably be the depositary of the powers concerning the latter objects. It ought therefore to be made respectable in the eyes of foreign Nations. The true reason why G. Britain has not yet listened to a commercial treaty with us has been, because she had no confidence in the stability or efficacy of our Government 9 years with a rotation, will provide these desirable qualities; and give our Govt. an advantage in this respect over Monarchy itself. In a monarchy much must always depend on the temper of the man. In such a body, the personal character will be lost in the political. He wd add another observation. The popular objection agst. appointing any public body for a long term was that it might by gradual encroachments prolong itself first into a body for life, and finally become a hereditary one. It would be a satisfactory answer to this objection that as 1/3 would go out triennially, there would be always three divisions holding their places for unequal terms, and consequently acting under the influence of different views, and different impulses.—On the question for 9 years, 1/3 to go out triennially Massts. no. Cont. no. N.Y. no. N.J. no. Pa. ay. Del. ay. Md. no. Va. ay. N.C. no. S.C. no. Gen. no.

On the question for 6 years 1/3 to go out biennially Massts. ay. Cont. ay. N.Y. no. N.J. no. Pa. ay. Del. ay. Md. ay. Va. ay. N.C. ay. S.C. no. Geo. no.

"To receive fixt stipends by which they may be compensated for their services." considered.

General Pinkney proposed "that no Salary should be allowed." As this [the Senatorial] branch was meant to represent the wealth of the Country, it ought to be composed of persons of wealth; and if no allowance was to be made the wealthy alone would undertake the service. He moved to strike out the clause.

Doc. Franklin seconded the motion. He wished the Convention to stand fair with the people. There were in it a number of young men who would probably be of the Senate. If lucrative appointments should be recommended we might be chargeable with having carved out places for ourselves. On the question, Masts. Connecticut Pa. Md. S. Carolina ay. N.Y. N.J. Del. Virga. N.C. Gen. no.

Mr. Elseworth moved to strike out "to be paid out of the natil. Treasury" and insert "to be paid by their respective States." If the Senate was meant to strengthen the Govt. it ought to have the confidence of the States. The States will have an interest in keeping up a representation, and will make such provision for supporting the members as will ensure their attendance.

Mr. Madison considered this a departure from a fundamental principle, and subverting the end intended by allowing the Senate a duration of 6 years. They would if this motion should be agreed to, hold their places during pleasure; during the pleasure of the State Legislatures. One great end of the institution was, that being a firm, wise and impartial body, it might not only give stability to the Genl. Govt. in its operations on individuals, but hold an even balance among different States. The motion would make the Senate like Congress, the mere Agents & Advocates of State interests & views, instead of being the impartial umpires & Guardians of justice and general Good. Congs. had lately by the establishment of a board with full powers to decide on the mutual claims be—between the U. States & the individual States, fairly acknowledged themselves to be unfit for discharging this part of the business referred to them by the Confederation.

Mr. Dayton considered the payment of the Senate by the States as fatal to their independence. He was decided for paying them out of the Natl. Treasury.

On the question of payment of the Senate to be left to the States as moved by Mr. Elseworth. Massts. no. Cont. ay. N.Y. ay. N.J. ay. Pa. no. Del. no. Md. no. Va. no. N.C. no. S.C. ay. Geo. ay.

Col. Mason. He did not rise to make any motion, but to hint an idea which seemed to be proper for consideration. One important object in constituting the Senate was to secure the rights of property. To give them weight & firmness for this purpose, a considerable duration in office was thought necessary. But a longer term than 6 years, would be of no avail in this respect, if needy persons should be appointed. He suggested therefore the propriety of annexing to the office a qualification of property. He thought this would be very practicable; as the rules of taxation would supply a scale for measuring the degree of wealth possessed by every man.

Thursday, June 28

Mr. L. Martin resumed his discourse, contending that the Genl. Govt. ought to be formed for the States, not for individuals: that if the States were to have votes in proportion to their numbers of people, it would be the same thing whether their representatives were chosen by the Legislatures or the people; the smaller States would be equally enslaved; that if the large States have the same interest with the smaller as was urged, there could be no danger in giving them an equal vote; they would not injure themselves, and they could not injure the large ones on that supposition without injuring themselves and if the interests were not the same the inequality of suffrage wd—be dangerous to the smaller States: that it will be in vain to propose any plan offensive to the rulers of the States, whose influence over the people will certainly prevent their adopting it: that the large States were weak at present in proportion to their extent: & could only be made formidable to the small ones, by the weight of their votes; that in case a dissolution of the Union should take place, the small States would have nothing to fear from their power; that if in such a case the three great States should league themselves together, the other ten could do so too: & that he had rather see partial Confederacies take place, than the plan on the table. This was the substance of the residue of his discourse which was delivered with much diffuseness & considerable vehemence.

Mr. Lansing & Mr. Dayton moved to strike out "not" so that the 7 art: might read that the rights of suffrage in the 1st branch ought to be according to the rule established by the Confederation.

Mr. Dayton expressed great anxiety that the question might not be put till tomorrow; Governr. Livingston being kept away by indisposition, and the representation of N. Jersey thereby suspended.

Mr. Williamson thought that if any political truth could be grounded on mathematical demonstration, it was that if the states were equally sovereign now, and parted with equal proportions of sovereignty, that they would remain equally sovereign. He could not comprehend how the smaller States would be injured in the case, and wished some gentleman would vouchsafe a solution of it. He observed that the small States, if they had a plurality of votes would have an interest in throwing the burdens off their own shoulders on those of the large ones. He begged that the expected addition of new States from the Westward might be kept in view. They would be small States, they would be poor States, they would be unable to pay in proportion to their numbers; their distance from market rendering the produce of their labour less valuable; they would consequently be tempted to combine for the purpose of laying burdens on commerce & consumption which would fall with greatest weight on the old States.

Mr. Madison sd. he was much disposed to concur in any expedient not inconsistent with fundamental principles, that could remove the difficulty concerning the rule of representation. But he could neither be convinced that the rule contended for was just, nor necessary for the safety of the small States agst. the large States. That it was not just, had been conceded by Mr. Brearly & Mr. Patterson themselves. The expedient proposed by them was a new partition of the territory of the U. States. The fallacy of the reasoning drawn from the equality of Sovereign States in the formation of compacts, lay in confounding mere Treaties, in which were specified certain duties to which the parties were to be bound, and certain rules by which their subjects were to be reciprocally governed in their intercourse, with a compact by which an authority was created paramount to the parties, & making laws for the government of them. If France, England & Spain were to enter into a Treaty for the regulation of commerce &c. with the Prince of Monacho & 4 or 5 other of the smallest sovereigns of Europe, they would not hesitate to treat as equals, and to make the regulations perfectly reciprocal. Wd. the case be the same if a Council were to be formed of deputies from each with authority and discretion, to raise money, levy troops, determine the value of coin &c? Would 30 or 40 million of people submit their fortunes into the hands, of a few thousands? If they did it would only prove that they expected more from the terror of their superior force, than they feared from the selfishness of their feeble associates. Why are Counties of the same States represented in proportion to their numbers? Is it because the representatives are chosen by the people themselves? so will be the representatives in the National Legislature. Is it because, the larger have more at stake than the smaller? The case will be the same with the larger & smaller States. Is it because the laws are to operate immediately on their persons & properties? The same is the case in some degree as the articles of confederation stand; the same will be the case in a far greater degree under the plan proposed to be substituted. In the cases of captures, of piracies, and of offenses in a federal army, the property & persons of individuals depend on the laws of Congs. By the plan proposed a compleat power of taxation, the highest prerogative of supremacy is proposed to be vested in the National Govt. Many other powers are added which assimilate it to the Govt. of individual States. The negative on the State laws proposed, will make it an essential branch of the State Legislatures & of course will require that it should be exercised by a body established on like principles with the other branch of those Legislatures.—That it is not necessary to secure the small States agst. the large ones he conceived to be equally obvious: Was a combination of the large ones dreaded? this must arise either from some interest common to Va. Massts. & Pa. & distinguishing them from the other States or from the mere circumstance of similarity of size. Did any such common interest exist? In point of situation they could not have been more effectually separated from each other by the most jealous citizen of the most jealous State. In point of manners, Religion and the other circumstances, which sometimes beget affection between different communities, they were not more assimilated than the other States.—In point of the staple productions they were as dissimilar as any three other States in the Union.

The Staple of Masts. was *fish*, of Pa. *flower*, of Va. *Tobo*. Was a Combination to be apprehended from the mere circumstance of equality of size? Experience suggested no such danger. The journals of Congs. did not present any peculiar association of these States in the votes recorded. It had never been seen that different Counties in the same State, conformable in extent, but disagreeing in other circumstances, betrayed a propensity to such combinations. Experience rather taught a contrary lesson. Among individuals of superior eminence & weight in society, rivalships were much more frequent than coalitions. Among independent nations preeminent over their neighbours, the same remark was verified. Carthage & Rome tore one another to pieces instead of uniting their forces to devour the weaker nations of the Earth. The Houses of Austria & France were hostile as long as they remained the greatest powers of Europe. England & France have succeeded to the pre-eminence & to the enmity. To this principle we owe perhaps our liberty. A coalition between those powers would have been fatal to us. Among the principal members of antient & modern confederacies, we find the same effect from the same cause. The contentions, not the coalitions of Sparta, Athens & Thebes, proved fatal to the smaller members of the Amphyctionic Confederacy. The contentions, not the combinations of Prussia & Austria, have distracted & oppressed the Germanic empire. Were the large States formidable *singly* to their smaller neighbours? On this supposition the latter ought to wish for such a general Govt. as will operate with equal energy on the former as on themselves. The more lax the band, the more liberty the larger will have to avail themselves of their superior force. Here again Experience was an instructive monitor. What is ye situation of the weak compared with the strong in those stages of civilization in which the violence of individuals is least controuled by an efficient Government? The Heroic period of Antient Greece the feudal licentiousness of the middle ages of Europe, the existing condition of the American Savages, answer this question. What is the situation of the minor sovereigns in the great society of independent nations, in which the more powerful are under no controul but the nominal authority of the law of Nations? Is not the danger to the former exactly in proportion to their weakness. But there are cases still more in point. What was the condition of the weaker members of the Amphyctionic Confederacy. Plutarch (life of Themistocles) will inform us that it happened but too often that the strongest cities corrupted & awed the weaker, and that judgment went in favor of the more powerful party. What is the condition of the lesser States in the German Confederacy? We all know that they are exceedingly trampled upon and that they owe their safety as far as they enjoy it, partly to their enlisting themselves, under the rival banners of the preeminent members, partly to alliances with neighbouring Princes which the Constitution of the Empire does not prohibit. What is the state of things in the lax system of the Dutch Confederacy? Holland contains about 1/2 the people, supplies about 1/2 of the money, and by her influence, silently & indirectly governs the whole Republic. In a word; the two extremes before us are a perfect separation & a perfect incorporation, of the 13 States. In the first case they would be independent nations subject to no law, but the law of nations. In the last, they would be mere counties of one entire republic, subject to one common law. In the first case the smaller states would have every thing to fear from the larger. In the last they would have nothing to fear. The true policy of the small States therefore lies in promoting those principles & that form of Govt. which will most approximate the States to the condition of Counties. Another consideration may be added. If the Genl. Govt. be feeble, the large States distrusting its continuance, and foreseeing that their importance & security may depend on their own size & strength, will never submit to a partition. Give to the Genl. Govt. sufficient energy & permanency, & you remove the objection. Gradual partitions of the large, & junctions of the small States will be facilitated, and time may effect that equalization, which is wished for by the small States, now, but can never be accomplished at once.

Mr. Wilson. The leading argument of those who contend for equality of votes among the States is that the States as such being equal, and being represented not as districts of individuals, but in their political & corporate capacities, are entitled to an equality of suffrage. According to this mode of reasoning the representation of the burroughs in Engld which has been allowed on all hands to be the rotten part of the Constitution, is perfectly right & proper. They are like the States represented in their corporate capacity like the States therefore they are entitled to equal voices, old Sarum to as many as London. And instead of the injury supposed hitherto to be done to London, the true ground of complaint lies with old Sarum; for London instead of two which is her proper share, sends four representatives to Parliament.

Mr. Sherman. The question is not what rights naturally belong to men; but how they may be most equally & effectually guarded in Society. And if some give up more than others in order to attain this end, there can be no room for complaint. To do otherwise, to require an equal concession from all, if it would create danger to the rights of some, would be sacrificing the end to the means. The rich man who enters into Society along with the poor man, gives up more than the poor man. Yet with an equal vote he is equally safe. Were he to have more votes than the poor man in proportion to his superior stake, the rights of the poor man would immediately cease to be secure. This consideration prevailed when the articles of confederation were formed.

The determination of the question from striking out the word "not" was put off till tomorrow at the request of the Deputies of N. York.

Dr. Franklin. Mr. President: The small progress we have made after 4 or five weeks close attendance & continual reasonings with each other—our different sentiments on almost every question, several of the last producing as many noes as ays, is methinks a melancholy proof of the imperfection of the Human Understanding. We indeed seem to feel our own want of political wisdom, since we have been running about in search of it. We have gone back to ancient history for models of Government, and examined the different forms of those Republics which having been formed with the seeds of their own dissolution now no longer exist. And we have viewed Modern States all round Europe, but find none of their Constitutions suitable to our circumstances.

In this situation of this Assembly, groping as it were in the dark to find political truth, and scarce able to distinguish it when presented to us, how has it happened, Sir, that we have not hitherto once thought of humbly applying to the Father of lights to illuminate our understandings? In the beginning of the Contest with G. Britain, when we were sensible of danger we had daily prayer in this room for the divine protection.—Our prayers, Sir, were heard, and they were graciously answered. All of us who were engaged in the struggle must have observed frequent instances of a Superintending providence in our favor. To that kind providence we owe this happy opportunity of consulting in peace on the means of establishing our future national felicity. And have we now forgotten that powerful friend? or do we imagine that we no longer need his assistance? I have lived, Sir, a long time, and the longer I live, the more convincing proofs I see of this truth—*that God governs in the affairs of men.* And if a sparrow cannot fall to the ground without his notice, is it probable that an empire can rise without his aid? We have been assured, Sir, in the sacred writings, that "except the Lord build the House they labour in vain that build it." I firmly believe this; and I also believe that without his concurring aid we shall succeed in this political building no better than the Builders of Babel: We shall be divided by our little partial local interests; our projects will be confounded, and we ourselves shall become a reproach and bye word down to future ages. And what is worse, mankind may hereafter from this unfortunate instance, despair of establishing Governments by Human Wisdom and leave it to chance, war and conquest.

I therefore beg leave to move—that henceforth prayers imploring the assistance of Heaven, and its blessings on our deliberations, be held in this Assembly every morning before we proceed to business, and that one or more of the Clergy of this City be requested to officiate in that service———

Mr. Sharman seconded the motion.

Mr. Hamilton & several others expressed their apprehensions that however proper such a resolution might have been at the beginning of the convention, it might at this late day, 1. bring on it some disagreeable animadversions & 2. lead the public to believe that the embarrassments and dissentions within the convention, had suggested this measure. It was answered by Doc. F. Mr. Sherman & others, that the past omission of a duty could not justify a further omission—that the rejection of such a proposition would expose the Comvention to more unpleasant animadversions than the adoption of it: and that the alarm out of doors that might be excited for the state of thing, within would at least be as likely to do good as ill.

Mr. Williamson, observed that the true cause of the omission could not be mistaken. The Convention had no funds.

Mr. Randolph proposed in order to give a favorable aspect to ye. measure, that a sermon be preached at the request of the convention on 4th of July, the anniversary of Independence,—& thenceforward prayers be used in ye Convention every morning. Dr. Frankn. 2ded this motion. After several unsuccessful attempts for silently postponing the matter by adjourng. the adjournment was at length carried, without any vote on the motion.

Friday, June 29

In Convention

Doctr. Johnson. The controversy must be endless whilst Gentlemen differ in the grounds of their arguments; Those on one side considering the States as districts of people composing one political Society; those on the other considering them as so many political societies. The fact is that the States do exist as political Societies, and a Govt. is to be formed for them in their political capacity, as well as for the individuals composing them. Does it not seem to follow, that if the States as such are to exist they must be armed with some power of self-defence. This is the idea of [Col. Mason] who appears to have looked to the bottom of this matter. Besides the Aristocratic and other interests, which ought to have the means of defending themselves, the States have their interests as such, and are equally entitled to likes means. On the whole he thought that as in some respects the States are to be considered in their political capacity, and in others as districts of individual citizens, the two ideas embraced on different sides, instead of being opposed to each other, ought to be combined; that in *one* branch the *people,* ought to be represented; in the *other* the *States.*

Mr. Ghorum. The States as now confederated have no doubt a right to refuse to be consolidated, or to be formed into any new system. But he wished the small States which seemed most ready to object, to consider which are to give up most, they or the larger ones. He conceived that a rupture of the Union wd. be an event unhappy for all, but surely the large States would be least unable to take care of themselves, and to make connections with one another. The weak therefore were most interested in establishing some general system for maintaining order. If among individuals, composed partly of weak, and partly of strong, the former most need the protection of law & Government, the case is exactly the same with weak & powerful States. What would be the situation of Delaware (for these things he found must be spoken out, & it might as well be done first as last) what wd. be the situation of Delaware in case of a separation of the States? Would she not lie at the mercy of Pennsylvania? would not her true interest lie in being consolidated with her, and ought she not now to wish for such a union with Pa. under one Govt. as will put it out of the power of Pena. to oppress her? Nothing can be more ideal than the danger apprehended by the States, from their being formed into one nation. Massts. was originally three colonies, viz. old Massts. Plymouth—& the province of Mayne. These apprehensions existed then. An incorporation took place; all parties were safe & satisfied; and every distinction is now forgotten. The case was similar with Connecticut & Newhaven. The dread of union was reciprocal; the consequence of it equally salutary and satisfactory. In like manner N. Jersey has been made one society out of two parts. Should a separation of the States take place, the fate of N. Jersey wd, be worst of all. She has no foreign commerce & can have but little. Pa. & N. York will continue to levy taxes on her consumption. If she consults her interest she wd. beg of all things to be annihilated. The apprehensions of the small States ought to be appeased by another reflection. Massts. will be divided. The province of Maine is already considered as approaching the term of its annexation to it; and Pa. will probably not increase, considering the present state of her population, & other events that may happen. On the whole he considered a Union of the States as necessary to their happiness, & a firm Genl. Govt. as necessary to their Union. He shd. consider it as his duty if his colleagues viewed the matter in the same light he did to stay here as long as any other State would remain with them, in order to agree on some plan that could with propriety be recommended to the people.

Mr. Read. He shd. have no objection to the system if it were truly national, but it has too much of a federal mixture in it. The little States he thought had not much to fear. He suspected that the large States felt their want of energy, & wished for a Genl. Govt. to supply the defect. Massts. was evidently labouring under her weakness and he believed Delaware wd. not be in much danger if in her neighbourhood. Delaware had enjoyed tranquility & he flattered himself wd. continue to do so. He was not however so selfish as not to wish for a good Genl. Govt. In order to obtain one the whole States must be incorporated. If the States remain, the representatives of the large ones will stick together, and carry every thing before them. The Executive also will be chosen under the influence of this partiality, and will betray it in his administration. These jealousies are inseparable from the scheme of leaving the States in existence. They must be done away. The ungranted lands also which have been assumed by particular States must also be given up. He repeated his approbation of the plan of Mr. Hamilton, & wished it to be substituted in place of that on the table.

Mr. Madison agreed with Doc. Johnson, that the mixed nature of the Govt. ought to be kept in view; but thought too much stress was laid on the rank of the States as political societies. There was a gradation, he observed from the smallest corporation, with the most limited powers, to the largest empire with the most perfect sovereignty. He pointed out the limitations on the sovereignty of the States, as now confederated their laws in relation to the paramount law of the Confederacy were analogous to that of bye laws to the supreme law within a State. Under the proposed Govt. the powers of the States will be much farther reduced. According to the views of every member, the Genl. Govt. will have powers far beyond those exercised by the British Parliament, when the States were part of the British Empire. It will in particular have the power, without the consent of the State Legislatures, to levy money directly on the people themselves; and therefore not to divest such *unequal* portions of the people as composed the several States, of an *equal* voice, would subject the system to the reproaches & evils which have resulted from the vicious representation in G.B.

He entreated the gentlemen representing the small States to renounce a principle wch. was confessedly unjust, which cd. never be admitted, & if admitted must infuse mortality into a Constitution which we wished to last forever. He prayed them to ponder well the consequences of suffering the Confederacy to go to pieces. It had been sd. that the want of energy in the large states wd. be a security to the small. It was forgotten that this want of energy proceeded from the supposed security of the States agst. all external danger. Let each state depend on itself for its security, & let apprehensions arise of danger, from distant powers or from neighbouring States, & the languishing condition of all the States, large as well as small, wd. soon be transformed into vigorous & high toned Govts. His great fear was that their Govts. wd. then have too much energy, that these might not only be formidable in the large to the small States, but fatal to the internal liberty of all. The same causes which have rendered the old world the Theatre of incessant wars, & have banished liberty from the face of it, wd. soon produce the same effects here. The weakness & jealousy of the small States wd. quickly introduce some regular military force agst. sudden danger from their powerful neighbours. The example wd. be followed by others, and wd. soon become universal. In time of actual war, great discretionary powers are constantly given to the Executive Magistrate. Constant apprehension of war, has the same tendency to render the head too large for the body. A standing military force, with an overgrown Executive will not long be safe companions to liberty. The means of defence agst. foreign danger, have been always the instruments of tyranny at home. Among the Romans it was a standing maxim to excite a war, whenever a revolt was apprehended. Throughout all Europe, the armies kept up under the pretext of defending, have enslaved the people. It is perhaps questionable, whether the best concerted system of absolute power in Europe cd. maintain itself in a situation, where no alarms of external danger cd. tame the people to the domestic yoke. The insular situation of G. Britain was the principal cause of her being an exception to the general fate of Europe. It has rendered less defence necessary, and admitted a kind of defence wch. cd. not be used for the purpose of oppression.—These consequences he conceived ought to be apprehended whether the States should run into a total separation from each other, or shd. enter into partial confederacies. Either event wd. be truly deplorable; & those who might be accessary to either, could never be forgiven by their Country, nor by themselves.

Mr. Hamilton observed that individuals forming political Societies modify their rights differently, with regard to suffrage. Examples of it are found in all the States. In all of them some individuals are deprived of the right altogether, not having the requisite qualification of property. In some of the States the right of suffrage is allowed in some cases and refused in others. To vote for a member in one branch, a certain quantum of property, to vote for a member in another branch of the Legislature, a higher quantum of property is required. In like manner States may modify their right of suffrage differently, the larger exercising a larger, the smaller a smaller share of it. But as States are a collection of individual men which ought we to respect most, the rights of the people composing them, or of the artificial beings resulting from the composition. Nothing could be more preposterous or absurd than to sacrifice the former to the latter. It has been sd. that if the smaller States renounce their *equality*, they renounce at the same time their *liberty*. The truth is it is a contest for power, not for liberty. Will the men composing the small States be less free than those composing the larger. The State of Delaware having 40,000 souls will *lose power*, if she has 1/10 only of the votes allowed to Pa. having 400,000: but will the people of Del: *be less free*, if each citizen has an equal vote with each citizen of Pa. He admitted that common residence within the same State would produce a certain degree of attachment; and that this principle might have a certain influence in public affairs. He thought however that this might by some precautions be in a great measure excluded: and that no material inconvenience could result from it, as there could not be any ground for combination among the States whose influence was most dreaded. The only considerable distinction of interests, lay between the carrying & non-carrying States, which divide instead of uniting the largest States. No considerable inconvenience had been found from the division of the State of N. York into different districts of different sizes.

Some of the consequences of a dissolution of the Union, and the establishment of partial confederacies, had been pointed out. He would add another of a most serious nature. Alliances will immediately be formed with different rival & hostile nations of Europe, who will foment disturbances among ourselves, and make us parties to all their own quarrels. Foreign Nations having American dominions are & must be jealous of us. Their representatives betray the utmost anxiety for our fate, & for the result of this meeting, which must have an essential influence on it.—It had been said that respectability in the eyes of foreign Nations was not the object at which we aimed; that the proper object of republican Government was domestic tranquility & happiness. This was an ideal distinction. No Governmt. could give us tranquility & happiness at home, which did not possess sufficient stability and strength to make us respectable abroad. This was the critical moment for forming such a Government. We should run every risk in trusting to future amendments. As yet we retain the habits of union. We are weak & sensible of our weakness. Henceforward the motives will become feebler, and the difficulties greater. It is a miracle that we were now here exercising our tranquil & free deliberations on the subject. It would be madness to trust to future miracles. A thousand causes must obstruct a reproduction of them.

Mr. Gerry urged that we never were independent States, were not such now, & never could be even on the principles of the Confederation. The States & the advocates for them were intoxicated with the idea of their *sovereignty*. He was a member of Congress at the time the federal articles were formed. The injustice of allowing each State an equal vote was long insisted on. He voted for it, but it was agst. his Judgment, and under the pressure of public danger, and the obstinacy of the lesser States. The present confederation he considered as dissolving. The fate Of the Union will be decided by the Convention. If they do not agree on something, few delegates will probably be appointed to Congs. If they do Congs. will probably be kept up till the new System should be adopted. He lamented that instead of coming here like a band of brothers, belonging to the same family, we seemed to have brought with us the spirit of political negociators. *Independent*, was once familiar & understood; though it seemed now so strange & obscure. He read those passages in the articles of Confederation, which describe them in that language.

On the question as moved by Mr. Lansing. Shall the word "not" be struck out.

Massts. no. Cont. ay. N.Y. ay. N.J. sly. Pa. no. Del. ay. Md. divd. Va. no. N.C. no. S.C. no. Geo. no.

On the motion to agree to the clause as reported, that the rule of suffrage in the 1st branch ought not to be according to that established by the articles of Confederation.

Mass. ay. Cont. no. N.Y. no. N.J. no. Pa. ay. Del. no. Md. divd. Va. ay. N.C. ay. S.C. ay. Geo. ay.

Mr. Elseworth moved that the rule of suffrage in the 2d branch be the same with that established by the articles of confederation. He was not sorry on the whole he said that the vote just passed, had determined against this rule in the first branch. He hoped it would become a ground of compromise with regard to the 2d branch. We were partly national; partly federal. The proportional representation in the first branch was conformable to the national principle & would secure the large States agst. the small. An equality of voices was conformable to the federal principle and was necessary to secure the Small States agst. the large. He trusted that on this middle ground a compromise would take place. He did not see that it could on any other. And if no compromise should take place, our meeting would not only be in vain but worse than in vain. To the Eastward he was sure Massts. was the only State that would listen to a proposition for excluding the States as equal political Societies, from an equal voice in both branches. The others would risk every consequence rather than part with so dear a right. An attempt to deprive them of it, was at once cutting the body of America in two, and as he supposed would be the case, somewhere about this part of it. The large States he conceived would notwithstanding the equality of votes, have an influence that would maintain their superiority. Holland, as had been admitted [by Mr. Madison] had, notwithstanding a like equality in the Dutch Confederacy, a prevailing influence in the public measures. The power of self-defence was essential to the small States. Nature had given it to the smallest insect of the creation. He could never admit that there was no danger of combinations among the large States. They will like individuals find out and avail themselves of the advantage to be gained by it. It was true the danger would be greater, if they were contiguous and had a more immediate common interest. A defensive combination of the small States was rendered more difficult by their greater number. He would mention another consideration of great weight. The existing confederation was founded on the equality of the States in the article of suffrage: was it meant to pay no regard to this antecedent plighted faith. Let a Strong Executive, a Judiciary & Legislative power be created; but Let not too much be attempted; by which all may be lost. He was not in general a half-way man, yet he preferred doing half the good we could, rather than do nothing at all. The other half may be added, when the necessity shall be more fully experienced.

Mr. Baldwin could have wished that the powers of the General Legislature had been defined, before the mode of constituting it had been agitated. He should vote against the motion of Mr. Elseworth, tho' he did not like the Resolution as it stood in the Report of the Committee of the whole. He thought the second branch ought to be the representation of property, and that in forming it therefore some reference ought to be had to the relative wealth of their Constituents, and to the principles on which the Senate of Massts. was constituted. He concurred with those who thought it wd. be impossible for the Genl. Legislature to extend its cares to the local matters of the States.

Adjd.

Thursday, July 5

In Convention

Mr. Gerry delivered in from the Committee appointed on Monday last the following Report.

"The Committee to whom was referred the 8th Resol. of the Report from the Committee of the whole House, and so much of the 7th as has not been decided on, submit the following Report: That the subsequent propositions be recommended to the Convention on condition that both shall be generally adopted. 1. That in the 1st branch of the Legislature each of the States now in the Union shall be allowed 1 member for every 40,000 inhabitants of the description reported in the 7th Resolution of the Come. of the whole House: that each State not containing that number shall be allowed 1 member: that all bills for raising or appropriating money, and for fixing the Salaries of the officers of the Governt. of the U. States shall originate in the 1st branch of the Legislature, and shall not be altered or amended by the 2d branch: and that no money shall be drawn from the public Treasury but in pursuance of appropriations to be orginated in the 1st branch II. That in the 2d branch each State shall have an equal vote."

Mr. Ghorum observed that as the report consisted of propositions mutually conditional he wished to hear some explanations touching the grounds on which the conditions were estimated.

Mr. Gerry. The Committee were of different opinions as well as the Deputations from which the Come. were taken, and agreed to the Report merely in order that some ground of accomodation might be proposed. Those opposed to the equality of votes have only assented conditionally; and if the other side do not generally agree will not be under any obligation to support the Report.

Mr. Madison. could not regard the exclusive privilege of originating money bills as any concession on the side of the small States. Experience proved that it had no effect. If seven States in the upper branch wished a bill to be originated, they might surely find some member from some of the same States in the lower branch who would originate it. The restriction as to amendments was of as little consequence. Amendments could be handed privately by the Senate to members in the other house. Bills could be negatived that they might be sent up in the desired shape. If the Senate should yield to the obstinacy of the 1st branch the use of that body as a check would be lost. If the 1st branch should yield to that of the Senate, the privilege would be nugatory. Experience had also shewn both in G.B. and the States having a similar regulation that it was a source of frequent & obstinate altercations. These considerations had produced a rejection of a like motion on a former occasion when judged by its own merits. It could not therefore be deemed any concession on the present, and left in force all the objections which had prevailed agst. allowing each State an equal voice. He conceived that the Convention was reduced to the alternative of either departing from justice in order to conciliate the smaller States, and the minority of the people of the U.S. or of displeasing these by justly gratifying the larger States and the majority of the people. He could not himself hesitate as to the option he ought to make. The Convention with justice & the majority of the people on their side, had nothing to fear. With injustice and the minority on their side they had every thing to fear. It was in vain to purchase concord in the Convention on terms which would perpetuate discord among their Constituents. The Convention ought to pursue a plan which would bear the test of examination, which would be espoused & supported by the enlightened and impartial part of America, & which they could themselves vindicate and urge. It should be considered that altho' at first many may judge of the system recommended, by their opinion of the Convention, yet finally all will judge of the Convention by the System. The merits of the System alone can finally & effectually obtain the public suffrage. He was not apprehensive that the people of the small States would obstinately refuse to accede to a Govt. founded on just principles, and promising them substantial protection. He could not suspect that Delaware would brave the consequences of seeking her fortunes apart from the other States, rather than submit to such a Govt. much less could he suspect that she would pursue the rash policy of courting foreign support, which the warmth of one of her representatives [Mr. Bedford] had suggested, or if she shd. that any foreign nation wd. be so rash as to hearken to the overture. As little could he suspect that the people of N. Jersey notwithstanding the decided tone of the gentlemen from that State, would choose rather to stand on their own legs, and bid defiance to events, than to acquiesce under an establishment founded on principles the justice of which they could not dispute, and absolutely necessary to redeem them from the exactions levied on them by the commerce of the neighbouring States. A review of other States would prove that there was as little reason to apprehend an inflexible opposition elsewhere. Harmony in the Convention was no doubt much to be desired. Satisfaction to all the States, in the first instance still more so. But if the principal States comprehending a majority of the people of the U.S. should concur in a just & judicious plan, he had the firmest hopes, that all the other States would by degrees accede to it.

Mr. Govr. Morris thought the form as well as the matter of the Report objectionable. It seemed in the first place to render amendments impracticable. In the next place, it seemed to involve a pledge to agree to the 2d part if the 1st shd. be agreed to. He conceived the whole aspect of it to be wrong. He came here as a Representative of America; he flattered himself he came here in some degree as a Representative of the whole human race; for the whole human race will be affected by the proceedings of this Convention. He wished gentlemen to extend their views beyond the present moment of time; beyond the narrow limits of place from which they derive their political origin. If he were to believe some things which he had heard, he should suppose that we were assembled to truck and bargain for our particular States. He cannot descend to think that any gentlemen are really actuated by these views. We must look forward to the effects of what we do. These alone ought to guide us. Much has been said of the sentiments of the people. They were unknown. They could not be known. All that we can infer is that if the plan we recommend be reasonable & right; all who have reasonable minds and sound intentions will embrace it, notwithstanding what had been said by some gentlemen. Let us suppose that the larger States shall agree; and that the smaller refuse: and let us trace the consequences. The opponents of the system in the smaller States will no doubt make a party, and a noise for a time, but the ties of interest, of kindred & of common habits which connect them with the other States will be too strong to be easily broken. In N. Jersey particularly he was sure a great many would follow the sentiments of Pena. & N. York. This Country must be united. If persuasion does not unite it, the sword will. He begged that this consideration might have its due weight. The scenes of horror attending civil commotion can not be described, and the conclusion of them will be worse than the term of their continuance. The stronger party will then make traytors of the weaker; and the Gallows & Halter will finish the work of the sword. How far foreign powers would be ready to take part in the confusions he would not say. Threats that they will be invited have it seems been thrown out. He drew the melancholy picture of foreign intrusions as exhibited in the History of Germany, & urged it as a standing lesson to other nations. He trusted that the Gentlemen who may have hazarded Such expressions, did not entertain them till they reached their own lips. But returning to the Report he could not think it in any respect calculated for the public good. As the 2d branch is now constituted, there will be constant disputes & appeals to the States which will undermine the Genl. Government & controul & annihilate the 1st branch. Suppose that the delegates from Massts. & Rho I. in the Upper House disagree, and that the former are outvoted. What Results? they will immediately declare that their State will not abide by the decision, and make such representations as will produce the same effect. The same may happen to Virga. & other States. Of what avail then will be what is on paper. State attachments, and State importance have been the bane of this Country. We can not annihilate; but we may perhaps take out the teeth of the serpents. He wished our ideas to be enlarged to the true interest of man, instead of being circumscribed within the narrow compass of a particular Spot. And after all how little can be the motive yielded by selfishness for such a policy. Who can say whether he himself, much less whether his children, will the next year be an inhabitant of this or that State.

Mr. Bedford. He found that what he had said as to the small States being taken by the hand, had been misunderstood; and he rose to explain. He did not mean that the small States would court the aid & interposition of foreign powers. He meant that they would not consider the federal compact as dissolved until it should be so by the Acts of the large States. In this case The consequence of the breach of faith on their part, and the readiness of the small States to fulfill their engagements, would be that foreign Nations having demands on this Country would find it their interest to take the small States by the hand, in order to do themselves justice. This was what he meant. But no man can foresee to what extremities the small States may be driven by oppression. He observed also in apology that some allowance ought to be made for the habits of his profession in which warmth was natural & sometimes necessary. But is there not an apology in what was said by [Mr. Govt. Morris] that the sword is to unite: by Mr. Ghorum that Delaware must be annexed to Penna. and N. Jersey divided between Pena. and N. York. To hear such language without emotion, would be to renounce the feelings of a man and the duty of a Citizen—As to the propositions of the Committee, the lesser States have thought it necessary to have a security somewhere. This has been thought necessary for the Executive Magistrate of the proposed Govt. who has a sort of negative on the laws; and is it not of more importance that the States should be protected, than that the Executive branch of the Govt. shd. be protected. In order to obtain this, the smaller States have conceded as to the constitution of the first branch, and as to money bills. If they be not gratified by correspondent concessions as to the 2d branch is it to be supposed they will ever accede to the plan; and what will be the consequence if nothing should be done! The condition of the U. States requires, that something should be immediately done. It will be better that a defective plan should be adopted, than that none should be recommended, He saw no reason why defects might not be supplied by meetings 10, 15, or 20 years hence.

Mr. Gerry. Tho' he had assented to the Report in the Committee, be had very material objections to it. We were however in a peculiar situation. We were neither the same Nation nor different Nations. We ought not therefore to pursue the one or the other of these ideas too closely. If no compromise should take place what will be the consequence. A secession he foresaw would take place; for some gentlemen seem decided on it; two different plans will be proposed; and the result no man could foresee. If we do not come to some agreement among ourselves some foreign sword will probably do the work for us.

Mr. Mason. The Report was meant not as specific propositions to be adopted, but merely as a general ground of accomodation. There must be some accomodation on this point, or we shall make little further progress in the work. Accomodation was the object of the House in the appointment of the Committee; and of the Committee in the Report they had made. And however liable the Report might be to objections, he thought it preferable to an appeal to the world by the different sides, as had been talked of by some Gentlemen. It could not be more inconvenient to any gentleman to remain absent from his private affairs, than it was for him: but he would bury his bones in this City rather than expose his Country to the Consequences of a dissolution of the Convention without any thing being done. The 1st proposition in the report for fixing the representation in the 1st branch, one member for every 40,000 inhabitants, being taken up.

Mr. Govr. Morris objected to that scale of apportioment. He thought property ought to be taken into the estimate as well as the number of inhabitants. Life & liberty were generally said to be of more value, than property. An accurate view of the matter would nevertheless prove that property was the main object of Society. The savage State was more favorable to liberty than the Civilized; and sufficiently so to life. It was preferred by all men who had not acquired a taste for property; it was only renounced for the sake of property which could only be secured by the restraints of regular Government. These ideas might appear to some new, but they were nevertheless just. If property then was the main object of Govt. certainly it ought to be one measure of the influence due to those who were to be affected by the Governmt. He looked forward also to that range of New States which wd. soon be formed in the West. He thought the rule of representation ought to be so fixed as to secure to the Atlantic States a prevalence in the National Councils. The new States will know less of the public interest than these, will have an interest in many respects different, in particular will be little scrupulous of involving the Community in wars the burdens & operations of which would fall chiefly on the maritime States. Provision ought therefore to be made to prevent the maritime States from being hereafter outvoted by them. He thought this might be easily done by irrevocably fixing the number of representatives which the Atlantic States should respectively have, and the number which each new State will have. This wd. not be unjust, as the Western settlers wd. previously know the conditions on which they were to possess their lands. It would be politic as it would recommend the plan to the present as well as future interest of the States which must decide the fate of it.

Col, Mason said the case of new States was not unnoticed in the Committee; but it was thought and he was himself decidedly of opinion that if they made a part of the Union, they ought to be subject to no unfavorable discriminations. Obvious considerations required it.

Friday, July 13

In Convention

On the motion of Mr. Randolph, the vote of Saturday last authorising the Legislre. to adjust from time to time, the representation upon the principles of *wealth* & numbers of inhabitants was reconsidered by common consent in order to strike out "Wealth" and adjust the resolution to that requiring periodical revisions according to the number of whites & three fifths of the blacks:

Mr. Govr. Morris opposed the alteration as leaving still an incoherence. If Negroes were to be viewed as inhabitants, and the revision was to proceed on the principle of numbers of inhabts. they ought to be added in their entire number, and not in the proportion of 3/5. If as property, the word wealth was right, and striking it out, would produce the very inconsistency which it was meant to get rid of.—The train of business & the late turn which it had taken, had led him he said, into deep meditation on it, and He wd. candidly state the result. A distinction had been set up & urged, between the Nn. & Southn. States. He had hitherto considered this doctrine as heretical. He still thought the distinction groundless. He sees however that it is persisted in, and that the Southn. Gentlemen will not be satisfied unless they see the way open to their gaining a majority in the public Councils. The consequence of such a transfer of power from the maritime to the interior & landed interest will he foresees be such an oppression of commerce, that he shall be obliged to vote for ye. vicious principle of equality in the 2d branch in order to provide some defence for the N. States agst. it. But to come more to the point; either this distinction is fictitious or real; if fictitious let it be dismissed & let us proceed with due confidence. If it be real, instead of attempting to blend incompatible things, let us at once take a friendly leave of each other. There can be no end of demands for security if every particular interest is to be entitled to it. The Eastern States may claim it for their fishery, and for other objects, as the Southn. States claim it for their peculiar objects. In this struggle between the two ends of the Union, what part ought the middle States in point of policy to take: to join their Eastern brethren according to his ideas. If Southn. States get the power into their hands, and be joined as they will be with the interior Country, they will inevitably bring on a war with Spain for the Mississippi. This language is already held the interior Country having no property nor interest exposed on the sea, will be little affected by such a war. He wished to know what security the Northn. & middle States will have agst. this danger. It has been said that N.C., S.C., and Georgia only will in a little time have a majority of the people of America. They must in that case include the great interior Country, and every thing was to be apprehended from their getting the power into their hands.

Mr. Butler. The security the Southn. States want is that their negroes may not be taken from them, which some gentlemen within or without doors, have a very good mind to do. It was not supposed that N.C., S.C. & Geo. would have more people than all the other States, but many more relatively to the other States than they now have. The people & strength of America are evidently bearing Southwardly & S. westwdly.

Mr. Wilson. If a general declaration would satisfy any gentleman he had no indisposition to declare his sentiments. Conceiving that all men wherever placed have equal rights and are equally entitled to confidence, he viewed without apprehension the period when a few States should contain the superior number of people. The majority of people wherever found ought in all questions to govern the minority. If the interior Country should acquire this majority, it will not only have the right, but will avail themselves of it whether we will or no. This jealousy misled the policy of G. Britain with regard to America. The fatal maxims espoused by her were that the Colonies were growing too fast, and that their growth must be stinted in time. What were the consequences? first. enmity on our part, then actual separation. Like consequences will result on the part of the interior settlements, if like jealousy & policy be pursued on ours. Further, if numbers be not a proper rule, why is not some better rule pointed out. No one has yet ventured to attempt it. Congs. have never been able to discover a better. No State as far as he had heard, has suggested any other. In 1783, after elaborate discussion of a measure of wealth all were satisfied then as they are now that the rule of numbers, does not differ much from the combined rule of numbers & wealth. Again he could not agree that property was the sole or the primary object of Governt. & society. The cultivation & improvement of the human mind was the most noble object. With respect to this object, as well as to other personal rights, numbers were surely the natural & precise measure of Representation. And with respect to property, they could not vary much from the precise measure. In no point of view however could the establishmt. of numbers as the rule of representation in the 1st branch vary his opinion as to the impropriety of letting a vicious principle into the 2d branch.—On the Question to strike out *wealth*, & to make the change as moved by Mr. Randolph, it passed in the affirmative—

Mas. ay. Cont. ay. N.J. ay. Pa. ay. Del. divd. Md. ay. Va. ay. N.C. ay. S.C. ay. Geo. ay.

Saturday, July 14

In Convention

Mr. Rutlidge proposed to reconsider the two propositions touching the originating of money bills in the first & the equality of votes in the second branch.

Mr. Sherman was for the question on the whole at once. It was he said a conciliatory plan, it had been considered in all its parts, a great deal of time had been spent on it, and if any part should now be altered, it would be necessary to go over the whole ground again.

Mr. L. Martin urged the question on the whole. He did not like many parts of it. He did not like having two branches, nor the inequality of votes in the 1st branch. He was willing however to make trial of the plan, rather than do nothing.

Mr. Wilson traced the progress of the report through its several stages, remarking yt. when on the question concerning an equality of votes, the House was divided, our Constituents had they voted as their representatives did, would have stood as 2/3 agst. the equality, and 1/3 only in favor of it. This fact would ere long be known, and it will appear that this fundamental point has been carried by 1/3 agst. 2/3. What hopes will our Constituents entertain when they find that the essential principles of justice have been violated in the outset of the Govermnt. As to the privilege of originating money bills, it was not considered by any as of much moment, and by many as improper in itself. He hoped both clauses wd. be reconsidered. The equality of votes was a point of such critical importance, that every opportunity ought to be allowed, for discussing and collecting the mind of the Convention on it.

Mr. L. Martin denies that there were 2/3 agst. the equality of votes. The States that please to call themselves large, are the weakest in the Union. Look at Masts. Look at Virga. Are they efficient States? He was for letting a separation take place if they desired it. He had rather there should be two Confederacies, than one founded on any other principle than an equality of votes in the 2d branch at least.

Mr. Wilson was not surprised that those who say that a minority is more than the majority should say that the minority is stronger than the majority. He supposed the next assertion will be that they are richer also; though he hardly expected it would be persisted in when the States shall be called on for taxes & troops—

The reconsideration being tacitly agreed to.

Mr. Pinkney moved that instead of an equality of votes, the States should be represented in the 2d branch as follows: N.H. by. 2. members. Mas. 4. R.I. 1 Cont. 3. N.Y. 3. N.J. 2. Pa. 4. Del 1. Md. 3. Virga. 5. N.C. 3. S.C. 3. Geo. 2. making in the whole 36.

Mr. Wilson seconds the motion.

Mr. Dayton. The smaller States can never give up their equality. For himself he would in no event yield that security for their rights.

Mr. Madison expressed his apprehensions that if the proper foundation of Govenmt—was destroyed, by substituting an equality in place of a proportional Representation, no proper superstructure would be raised. If the small States really wish for a Government armed with the powers necessary to secure their liberties, and to enforce obedience on the larger members as well as on themselves he could not help thinking them extremely mistaken in their means. He reminded them of the consequences of laying the existing confederation on improper principles. All the principal parties to its compilation, joined immediately in mutilating & fettering the Govermnt. in such a manner that it has disappointed every hope placed on it. He appealed to the doctrine & arguments used by themselves on a former occasion. It had been very properly observed by [Mr. Patterson] that Representation was an expedient by which the meeting of the people themselves was rendered unnecessary; and that the representatives ought therefore to bear a proportion to the votes which their constituents if convened, would respectively have. Was not this remark as applicable to one branch of the Representation as to the other? But it had been said that the Governt. would in its operation be partly federal, partly national; that altho' in the latter respect the Representatives of the people ought to be in proportion to the people: yet in the former it ought to be according to the number of States. If there was any solidity in this distinction he was ready to abide by it, if there was none it ought to be abandoned. In all cases where the Genl. Government is to act on the people, let the people be represented and the votes be proportional. In all cases where the Governt. is to act on the States as such, in like manner as Congs. now act on them, let the States be represented & the votes be equal. This was the true ground of compromise if there was any ground at all. But he denied that there was any ground. He called for a single instance in which the Genl. Govt. was not to operate on the people individually. The practicability of making laws, with coercive sanctions, for the States as Political bodies, had been exploded on all hands. He observed that the people of the large States would in some way or other secure to themselves a weight proportioned to the importance accruing from their superior numbers. If they could not effect it by a proportional representation in the Govt. they would probably accede to no Govt. which did not in great measure depend for its efficacy on their voluntary cooperation; in which case they would indirectly secure their object. The existing confederacy proved that where the Acts of the Genl. Govt. were to be executed by the particular Govts. the latter had a weight in proportion to their importance. No one would say that either in Congs. or out of Congs. Delaware had equal weight with Pensylva. If the latter was to supply ten times as much money as the former, and no compulsion could be used, it was of ten times more importance, that she should voluntarily furnish the supply. In the Dutch confederacy the votes of the Provinces were equal. But Holland which supplies about half the money, governs the whole republic. He enumerated the objections agst. an equality of votes in 2d branch, notwithstanding the proportional representation in the first. 1. the minority could negative the will of the majority of the people. 2. they could extort measures by making them a condition of their assent to other necessary measures. 3. they could obtrude measures on the majority by virtue of the peculiar powers which would be vested in the Senate. 4. the evil instead of being cured by time, would increase with every new State that should be admitted, as they must all be admitted on the principle of equality. 5. the perpetuity it would give to the preponderance of the Northn. agst. the Southn. Scale was a serious consideration. It seemed now to be pretty well understood that the real difference of interests lay, not between the large & small but between the N. & Southn. States. The institution of slavery & its consequences formed the line of discrimination. There were 5 States on the South, 8 on the Northn. side of this line. Should a proportl. representation take place it was true, the N. side would still outnumber the other; but not in the same degree, at this time; and every day would tend towards an equilibrium.

Mr. Wilson would add a few words only. If equality in the 2d branch was an error that time would correct, he should be less anxious to exclude it being sensible that perfection was unattainable in any plan; but being a fundamental and a perpetual error, it ought by all means to be avoided. A vice in the Representation, like an error in the first concoction, must be followed by disease, convulsions, and finally death itself. The justice of the general principle of proportional representation has not in argument at least been yet contradicted. But it is said that a departure from it so far as to give the States an equal vote in one branch of the Legislature is essential to their preservation. He had considered this position maturely, but could not see its application. That the States ought to be preserved he admitted. But does it follow that an equality of votes is necessary for the purpose? Is there any reason to suppose that if their preservation should depend more on the large than on the small States the security of the States agst. the Genl. Government would be diminished? Are the large States less attached to their existence, more likely to commit suicide, than the small? An equal vote then is not necessary as far as he can conceive: and is liable among other objections to this insuperable one: The great fault of the existing confederacy is its inactivity. It has never been a complaint agst. Congs. that they governed overmuch. The complaint has been that they have governed too little. To remedy this defect we were sent here. Shall we effect the cure by establishing an equality of votes as is proposed? no: this very equality carries us directly to Congress: to the system which it is our duty to rectify. The small States cannot indeed act, by virtue of this equality, but they may controul the Govt. as they have done in Congs. This very measure is here prosecuted by a minority of the people of America. Is then the object of the Convention likely to be accomplished in this way? Will not our Constituents say? we sent you to form an efficient Govt. and you have given us one more complex indeed, but having all the weakness of the former Governt. He was anxious for uniting all the States under one Governt. He knew there were some respectable men who preferred three confederacies, united by offensive & defensive alliances. Many things may be plausibly said, some things may be justly said, in favor of such a project. He could not however concur in it himself, but he thought nothing so pernicious as bad first principles.

Mr. Elseworth asked two questions one of Mr. Wilson, whether he had ever seen a good measure fail in Congs. for want of a majority of States in its favor? He had himself never known such an instance: the other of Mr. Madison whether a negative lodged with the majority of the States even the smallest, could be more dangerous than the qualified negative proposed to be lodged in a single Executive Magistrate, who must be taken from some one State?

Mr. Sherman, signified that his expectation was that the Genl. Legislature would in some cases act on the *federal principle*, of requiring quotas. But he thought it ought to be empowered to carry their own plans into execution, if the States should fail to supply their respective quotas.

On the question for agreeing to Mr. Pinkney's motion for allowing N.H. 2. Mas. 4. &c—it passed in the negative Mas. no. Mr. King ay. Mr. Ghorum absent. Cont. no. N.J. no. Pa. ay. Del. no. Md. ay. Va. ay. N.C. no. S.C. ay. Geo. no.

Adjourned.

Tuesday, July 17

In Convention

"To be chosen by the National Legisl:"

Mr. Governr. Morris was pointedly agst. his being so chosen. He will be the mere creature of the Legisl: if appointed & impeachable by that body. He ought to be elected by the people at large, by the freeholders of the Country. That difficulties attend this mode, he admits. But they have been found superable in N.Y. & in Cont. and would he believed be found so, in the case of an Executive for the U. States. If the people should elect, they will never fail to prefer some man of distinguished character, or services: some man, if he might so speak, of continental reputation.—If the Legislature elect, it will be the work of intrigue, of cabal, and of faction; it will be like the election of a pope by a conclave of cardinals; real merit will rarely be the title to the appointment. He moved to strike out "National Legislature" & insert "citizens of U.S."

Mr. Sherman thought that the sense of the Nation would be better expressed by the Legislature, than by the people at large. The latter will never be sufficiently informed of characters, and besides will never give a majority of votes to any one man. They will generally vote for some man in their own State, and the largest State will have the best chance for the appointment. If the choice be made by the Legislre. A majority of voices may be made necessary to constitute an election.

Mr. Wilson. Two arguments have been urged agnt. an election of the Executive Magistrate by the people. 1 the example of Poland where an Election of the supreme Magistrate is attended with the most dangerous commotions. The cases he observed were totally dissimilar. The Polish nobles have resources & dependents which enable them to appear in force, and to threaten the Republic as well as each other. In the next place the electors all assemble in one place: which would not be the case with us. The 2d argt. is that a *majority* of the people would never concur. It might be answered that the concurrence of a majority of people is not a necessary principle of election, nor required as such in any of the States. But allowing the objection all its force, it may be obviated by the expedient used in Massts. where the Legislature by majority of voices, decide in case a majority of people do not concur in favor of one of the candidates. This would restrain the choice to a good nomination at least, and prevent in a great degree intrigue & cabal. A particular objection with him agst. an absolute election by the Legislre. was that the Exec: in that case would be too dependent to stand the mediator between the intrigues & sinister views of the Representatives and the general liberties & interests of the people.

Mr. Pinkney did not expect this question would again have been brought forward; an Election by the people being liable to the most obvious & striking objections. They will be led by a few active & designing men. The most populous States by combining in favor of the same individual will be able to carry their points. The Natl. Legislature being most immediately interested in the laws made by themselves, will be most attentive to the choice of a fit man to carry them properly into execution.

Mr. Govr. Morris. It is said that in case of an election by the people the populous States will combine & elect whom they please. Just the reverse. The people of such States cannot combine. If their be any combination it must be among their representatives in the Legislature. It is said the people will be led by a few designing men. This might happen in a small district. It can never happen throughout the continent. In the election of a Govr. of N. York, it sometimes is the case in particular spots, that the activity & intrigues of little partizans are successful, but the general voice of the State is never influenced by such artifices. It is said the multitude will be uninformed. It is true they would be uninformed of what passed in the Legislative Conclave, if the election were to be made there; but they will not be uninformed of those great & illustrious characters which have merited their esteem & confidence. If the Executive be chosen by the Natl. Legislature, he will not be independent on it; and if not independent, usurpation

& tyranny on the part of the Legislature will be the consequence. This was the case in England in the last Century. It has been the case in Holland, where their Senates have engrossed all power. It has been the case every where. He was surprised that an election by the people at large should ever have been likened to the polish election of the first Magistrate. An election by the Legislature will bear a real likeness to the election by the Diet of Poland. The great must be the electors in both cases, and the corruption & cabal wch. are known to characterise the one would soon find their way into the other. Appointments made by numerous bodies, are always worse than those made by single responsible individuals, or by the people at large.

Col. Mason. It is curious to remark the different language held at different times. At one moment we are told that the Legislature is entitled to thorough confidence, and to indifinite power. At another, that it will be governed by intrigue & corruption, and cannot be trusted at all. But not to dwell on this inconsistency he would observe that a Government which is to last ought at least to be practicable. Would this be the case if the proposed election should be left to the people at large. He conceived it would be as unnatural to refer the choice of a proper character for chief Magistrate to the people, as it would, to refer a trial of colours to a blind man. The extent of the Country renders it impossible that the people can have the requisite capacity to judge of the respective pretensions of the Candidates.

Mr. Wilson could not see the contrariety stated [by Col. Mason]. The Legislre. might deserve confidence in some respects, and distrust in others. In acts which were to affect them & yr. Constituents precisely alike confidence was due. In others jealousy was warranted. The appointment to great offices, where the Legislre. might feel many motives, not common to the public confidence was surely misplaced. This branch of business it was notorious was most corruptly managed of any that had been committed to legislative bodies.

Mr. Williamson conceived that there was the same difference between an election in this case, by the people and by the legislature, as between an appt. by lot, and by choice. There are at present distinguished characters, who are known perhaps to almost every man. This will not always be the case. The people will be sure to vote for some man in their own State, and the largest State will be sure to succeed. This will not be Virga. however. Her slaves will have no suffrage. As the Salary of the Executive will be fixed, and he will not be eligible a 2d time, there will not be such a dependence on the Legislature as has been imagined.

Question on an election by the people instead of the Legislature; which 30 passed in the negative.

Mas. no. Cont. no. N.J. no. Pa. ay. Del. no. Md. no. Va. no. N.C. no. S.C. no. Geo. no.

Mr. L. Martin moved that the Executive be chosen by Electors appointed by the several Legislatures of the individual States.

Mr. Broome 2ds. On the Question, it passed in the negative.

Mas. no. Cont. no. N.J. no. Pa. no. Del. ay. Md. ay. Va. no. N.C. no. S.C. no. Gen. no.

On the question on the words "to be chosen by the Nationl. Legislature" it passed unanimously in the affirmative.

Wednesday, July 18

In Convention

Resol. 11 "that a Natl. Judiciary be estabd. to consist of one supreme tribunal." agd. to nem. con. "The Judges of which to be appointd. by the 2d branch of the Natl. Legislature."

Mr. Ghorum Wd. prefer an appointment by the 2d branch to an appointmt. by the whole Legislature; but he thought even that branch too numerous, and too little personally responsible, to ensure a good choice. He suggested that the Judges be appointed by the Execuve. with the advice & consent of the 2d branch, in the mode prescribed by the constitution of Massts. This mode had been long practised in that country, & was found to answer perfectly well.

Mr. Wilson still wd. prefer an appointmt. by the Executive; but if that could not be attained, wd. prefer in the next place, the mode suggested by Mr. Ghorum. He thought it his duty however to move in the first instance "that the Judges be appointed by the Executive." Mr. Govr. Morris 2ded the motion.

Mr. L. Martin was strenuous for an appt. by the 2d branch. Being taken from all the States it wd. be best informed of characters & most capable of making a fit choice.

Mr. Mason. The mode of appointing the Judges may depend in some degree on the mode of trying impeachments of the Executive. If the Judges were to for a tribunal for that purpose, they surely ought not to be appointed by the Executive. There were insuperable objections besides agst. referring the appointment to the Executive. He mentioned as one, that as the Seat of Govt. must be in some one State, and the Executive would remain in office for a considerable time, for 4, 5, or 6 years at least, he would insensibly form local & personal attachments within the particular State that would deprive equal merit elsewhere, of an equal chance of promotion.

Mr. Ghorum. As the Executive will be responsible in point of character at least, for a judicious and faithful discharge of his trust, he will be careful to took through all the States for proper characters. The Senators will be as likely to form their attachments at the seat of Govt. where they reside, as the Executive. If they can not get the man of the particular State to which they may respectively belong, they will be indifferent to the rest. Public bodies feel no personal responsibility, and give full play to intrigue & cabal. Rh. Island is a full illustration of the insensibility to character, produced by a participation of numbers, in dishonorable measures, and of the length to which a public body may carry wickedness & cabal.

Mr. Govr. Morris supposed it would be improper for an impeachmt. of the Executive to be tried before the Judges. The latter would in such case be drawn into intrigues with the Legislature and an impartial trial would be frustrated. As they wd. be much about the Seat of Govt. they might even be previously consulted & arrangements might be made for a prosecution of the Executive. He thought therefore that no argument could be drawn from the probability of such a plan of impeachments agst. the motion before the House.

Mr. Madison, suggested that the Judges might be appointed by the Executive with the concurrence of 1/3 at least, of the 2d branch. This would unite the advantage of responsibility in the Executive with the security afforded in the 2d branch agst. any incautious or corrupt nomination by the Executive.

Mr. Sherman was clearly for an election by the Senate. It would be composed of men nearly equal to the Executive, and would of course have on the whole more wisdom. They would bring into their deliberations a more diffusive knowledge of characters. It would be less easy for candidates to intrigue with them, than with the Executive Magistrate. For these reasons he thought there would be a better security for a proper choice in the Senate than in the Executive.

Mr. Randolph. It is true that when the appt. of the Judges was vested in the 2d branch an equality of votes had not been given to it. Yet he had rather leave the appointmt. there than give it to the Executive. He thought the advantage of personal responsibility might be gained in the Senate by requiring the respective votes of the members to be entered on the Journal. He thought too that the hope of receiving appts. would be more diffusive if they depended on the Senate, the members of which wd. be diffusively known, than if they depended on a single man who could not be personally known to a very great extent; and consequently that opposition to the System, would be so far weakened.

Mr. Bedford thought there were solid reasons agst. leaving the appointment to the Executive. He must trust more to information than the Senate. It would put it in his power to gain over the larger States, by gratifying them with a preference of their Citizens. The responsibility of the Executive so much talked of was chimerical. He could not be punished for mistakes.

Mr. Ghorum remarked that the Senate could have no better information than the Executive. They must like him, trust to information from the members belonging to the particular State where the Candidates resided. The Executive would certainly be more answerable for a good appointment, as the whole blame of a bad one would fall on him alone. He did not mean that he would be answerable under any other penalty than that of public censure, which with honorable minds was a sufficient one.

On the question for referring the appointment of the Judges to the Executive, instead of the 2d branch, Mas. ay. Cont. no. Pa. ay. Del. no. Md. no. Va. no. N.C. no. S.C. no.—Geo. absent.

12. Resol: "that Natl. Legislature be empowered to appoint inferior tribunals."

Mr. Butler could see no necessity for such tribunals. The State Tribunals might do the business.

Mr. L. Martin concurred. They will create jealousies & oppositions in the State tribunals, with the jurisdiction of which they will interfere.

Mr. Ghorum. There are in the States already federal Courts with jurisdiction for trial of piracies &c. committed on the Seas. No complaints have been made by the States or the Courts of the States. Inferior tribunals are essential to render the authority of the Natl. Legislature effectual.

Mr. Randolph observed that the Courts of the States can not be trusted with the administration of the National laws. The objects of jurisdiction are such as will often place the General & local policy at variance.

Mr. Govr. Morris urged also the necessity of such a provision.

Mr. Sherman was willing to give the power to the Legislature but wished them to make use of the State Tribunals whenever it could be done, with safety to the general interest.

Col. Mason thought many circumstances might arise not now to be foreseen, which might render such a power absolutely necessary.

On question for agreeing to 12. Resol: empowering the National Legislature to appoint "inferior tribunals." Agd. to nem. con.

Resol. 16. "That a Republican Constitution & its. existing laws ought to be guarantied to each State by the U. States."

Mr. Govr. Morris thought the Resol: very objectionable. He should be very unwilling that such laws as exist in R. Island should be guaranteid.

Mr. Wilson. The object is merely to secure the States agst. dangerous commotions, insurrections and rebellions.

Col. Mason. If the Genl. Govt. should have no right to suppress rebellions agst. particular States, it will be in a bad situation indeed. As Rebellions agst. itself originate in & agst. individual States, it must remain a passive Spectator of its own subversion.

Mr. Randolph. The Resoln. has 2. objects. 1. to secure Republican Government. 2. to suppress domestic commotions. He urged the necessity of both these provisions.

Mr. Madison moved to substitute "that the Constitutional authority of the States shall be guarantied to them respectively agst. domestic as well as foreign violence."

Docr. McClurg seconded the motion.

Mr. Houston was afraid of perpetuating the existing Constitutions of the States. That of Georgia was a very bad one, and he hoped would be revised & amended. It may also be difficult for the Genl. Govt. to decide between contending parties each of which claim the sanction of the Constitution.

Mr . L. Martin was for leaving the States to suppress Rebellions themselves.

Mr. Ghorum thought it strange that a Rebellion should be known to exist in the Empire, and the Genl. Govt. shd. be restrained from interposing to subdue it. At this rate an enterprising Citizen might erect the standard of Monarchy in a particular State, might gather together partizans from all quarters, might extend his views from State to State, and threaten to establish a tyranny over the whole & the Genl. Govt. be compelled to remain an inactive witness of its own destruction. With regard to different parties in a State; as long as they confine their disputes to words, they will be harmless to the Genl. Govt. & to each other. If they appeal to the sword, it will then be necessary for the Genl. Govt., however difficult it may be to decide on the merits of their contest, to interpose & put an end to it.

Mr. Carrol. Some such provision is essential. Every State ought to wish for it. It has been doubted whether it is a casus federis at present. And no room ought to be left for such a doubt hereafter.

Mr. Randolph moved to add as amendt. to the motion; "and that no State be at liberty to form any other than a Republican Govt."

Mr. Madison seconded the motion.

Mr. Rutlidge thought it unnecessary to insert any guarantee. No doubt could be entertained but that Congs. had the authority if they had the means to co-operate with any State in subduing a rebellion. It was & would be involved in the nature of the thing.

Mr. Wilson moved as a better expression of the idea that a Republican form of Governmt. shall be guarantied to each State & that each State shall be protected agst. foreign & domestic violence.

This seeming to be well received, Mr. Madison & Mr. Randolph withdrew their propositions & on the Question for agreeing to Mr. Wilson's motion, it passed nem. con.

Thursday, July 19

In Convention

On reconsideration of the vote rendering the Executive re-eligible a 2d time, Mr. Martin moved to reinstate the words, "to be ineligible a 2d time."

Mr. Governeur Morris. It is necessary to take into one view all that relates to the establishment of the Executive; on the due formation of which must depend the efficacy & utility of the Union among the present and future States. It has been a maxim in Political Science that Republican Government is not adapted to a large extent of Country, because the energy of the Executive Magistracy can not reach the extreme parts of it. Our Country is an extensive one. We must either then renounce the blessings of the Union, or provide an Executive with sufficient vigor to pervade every part of it. This subject was of so much importance that he hoped to be indulged in an extensive view of it. One great object of the Executive is to controul the Legislature. The Legislature will continually seek to aggrandize & perpetuate themselves; and will seize those critical moments produced by war, invasion or convulsion for that purpose. It is necessary then that the Executive Magistrate should be the guardian of the people, even of the lower classes, agst. Legislative tyranny, against the Great & the wealthy who in the course of things will necessarily compose the Legislative body. Wealth tends to corrupt the mind & to nourish its love of power, and to stimulate it to oppression. History proves this to be the spirit of the opulent. The check provided in the 2d branch was not meant as a check on Legislative usurpations of power, but on the abuse of lawful powers, on the propensity in the 1st branch to legislate too much to run into projects of paper money & similar expedients. It is no check on Legislative tyranny. On the contrary it may favor it, and if the 1st branch can be seduced may find the means of success. The Executive therefore ought to be so constituted as to be the great protector of the Mass of the people.—It is the duty of the Executive to appoint the officers & to command the forces of the Republic: to appoint 1. ministerial officers for the administration of public affairs. 2. officers for the dispensation of Justice. Who will be the best Judges whether these appointments be well made? The people at large, who will know, will see, will feel the effects of them. Again who can judge so well of the discharge of military duties for the protection & security of the people, as the people themselves who are to be protected & secured?—He finds too that the Executive is not to be re-eligible. What effect will this have?

1. It will destroy the great incitement to merit public esteem by taking away the hope of being rewarded with a reappointment. It may give a dangerous turn to one of the strongest passions in the human breast. The love of fame is the great spring to noble & illustrious actions. Shut the Civil road to Glory & he may be compelled to seek it by the sword.

2. It will tempt him to make the most of the short space of time allotted him, to accumulate wealth and provide for his friends.

3. It will produce violations of the very constitution it is meant to secure. In moments of pressing danger the tried abilities and established character of a favorite Magistrate will prevail over respect for the forms of the Constitution. The Executive is also to be impeachable. This is a dangerous part of the plan. It will hold him in such dependence that he will be no check on the Legislature, will not be a firm guardian of the people and of the public interest. He will be the tool of a faction, of some leading demagogue in the Legislature. These then are the faults of the Executive establishment as now proposed. Can no better establishmt. be devised? If he is to be the Guardian of the people let him be appointed by the people? If he is to be a check on the Legislature let him not be impeachable. Let him be of short duration, that he may with propriety be re-eligible. It has been said that the candidates for this office will not be known to the people. If they be known to the Legislature, they must have such a notoriety and eminence of Character, that they can not possibly be unknown to the people at large. It cannot be possible that a man shall have sufficiently distinguished himself to merit this high trust without having his character proclaimed by fame throughout the Empire. As to the danger from an unimpeachable magistrate he could not regard it as formidable. There must be certain great officers of State; a minister of finance, of war, of foreign affairs &c. These he presumes will exercise their functions in subordination to the Executive, and will be amenable by impeachment to the

public Justice. Without these ministers the Executive can do nothing of consequence. He suggested a biennial election of the Executive at the time of electing the 1st branch, and the Executive to hold over, so as to prevent any interregnum in the administration. An election by the people at large throughout so great an extent of country could not be influenced, by those little combinations and those momentary lies which often decide popular elections within a narrow sphere. It will probably, be objected that the election will be influenced by the members of the Legislature; particularly of the 1st branch, and that it will be nearly the same thing with an election by the Legislature itself. It could not be denied that such an influence would exist. But it might be answered that as the Legislature or the candidates for it would be divided, the enmity of one part would counteract the friendship of another: that if the administration of the Executive were good, it would be unpopular to oppose his reelection, if bad it ought to be opposed & a reappointmt. prevented; and lastly that in every view this indirect dependence on the favor of the Legislature could not be so mischievous as a direct dependence for his appointment. He saw no alternative for making the Executive independent of the Legislature but either to give him his office for life, or make him eligible by the people—Again, it might be objected that two years would be too short a duration. But he believes that as long as he should behave himself well, he would be continued in his place. The extent of the Country would secure his re-election agst. the factions & discontents of particular States. It deserved consideration also that such an ingredient in the plan would render it extremely palatable to the people. These were the general ideas which occurred to him on the subject, and which led him to wish & move that the whole constitution of the Executive might undergo reconsideration.

Mr. Randolph urged the motion of Mr. L. Martin for restoring the words making the Executive ineligible a 2d time. If he ought to be independent, he should not be left under a temptation to court a re-appointment. If he should be re-appointable by the Legislature, he will be no check on it. His revisionary power will be of no avail. He had always thought & contended as he still did that the danger apprehended by the little States was chimerical; but those who thought otherwise ought to be peculiarly anxious for the motion. If the Executive be appointed, as has been determined, by the Legislature, he will probably be appointed either by joint ballot of both houses, or be nominated by the 1st and appointed by the 2d branch. In either case the large States will preponderate. If he is to court the same influence for his re-appointment, will he not make his revisionary power, and all the other functions of his administration subservient to the views of the large States. Besides, is there not great reason to apprehend that in case he should be re-eligible, a false complaisance in the Legislature might lead them to continue an unfit man in office in preference to a fit one. It has been said that a constitutional bar to reappointment will inspire unconstitutional endeavours to perpetuate himself. It may be answered that his endeavours can have no effect unless the people be corrupt to such a degree as to render all precautions hopeless: to which may be added that this argument supposes him to be more powerful & dangerous, than other arguments which have been used, admit, and consequently calls for stronger fetters on his authority. He thought an election by the Legislature with an incapacity to be elected a second time would be more acceptable to the people that the plan suggested by Mr. Govr. Morris.

Mr. King did not like the ineligibility. He thought there was great force in the remark of Mr. Sherman, that he who has proved himself to be most fit for an Office, ought not to be excluded by the constitution fron, holding it. He would therefore prefer any other reasonable plan that could be substituted. He was much disposed to think that in such cases the people at large would chuse wisely. There was indeed some difficulty arising from the improbability of a general concurrence of the people in favor of any one man. On the whole he was of opinion that an appointment by electors chosen by the people for the purpose, would be liable to fewest objections.

Mr. Patterson's ideas nearly coincided he said with those of Mr. King. He proposed that the Executive should be appointed by Electors to be chosen by the States in a ratio that would allow one elector to the smallest and three to the largest States. Mr. Wilson. It seems to be the unanimous sense that the Executive should not be appointed by the Legislature, unless he be rendered in-eligible a 2d time: he perceived with pleasure that the idea was gaining ground, of an election mediately or immediately by the people.

Mr. Madison. If it be a fundamental principle of free Govt. that the Legislative, Executive & Judiciary powers should be *separately* exercised, it is equally so that they be *independently* exercised. There is the same & perhaps greater reason why the Executive shd. be independent of the Legislature, than why the Judiciary should: A coalition of the two former powers would be more immediately & certainly dangerous to public liberty. It is essential then that the appointment of the Executive should either be drawn from some source, or held by some tenure, that will give him a free agency with regard to the Legislature. This could not be if he was to be appointable from time to time by the Legislature. It was not clear that an appointment in the 1st instance even with an eligibility afterwards would not establish an improper connection between the two departments. Certain it was that the appointment would be attended with intrigues and contentions that ought not to be unnecessarily admitted. He was disposed for these reasons to refer the appointment to some other source. The people at large was in his opinion the fittest in itself. It would be as likely as any that could be devised to produce an Executive Magistrate of distinguished Character. The people generally could only know & vote for some Citizen whose merits had rendered him an object of general attention & esteem. There was one difficulty however of a serious nature attending an immediate choice by the people. The right of Suffrage was much more diffusive in the Northern than the Southern States; and the latter could have no influence in the election on the score of the Negroes. The substitution of electors obviated this difficulty and seemed on the whole to be liable to fewest objections.

Mr. Gerry. If the Executive is to be elected by the Legislature he certainly ought not to be re-eligible. This would make him absolutely dependent. He was agst. a popular election. The people are uninformed, and would be misled by a few designing men. He urged the expediency of an appointment of the Executive by Electors to be chosen by the State Executives. The people of the States will then choose the 1st branch: The legislatures of the States the 2d branch of the National Legislature, and the Executives of the States, the National Executive. This he thought would form a strong attachnt. in the States to the National System. The popular mode of electing the chief Magistrate would certainly be the worst of all. If he should be so elected & should do his duty, he will be turned out for it like Govr. Bowdoin in Massts. & President Sullivan in N. Hamshire.

On the question on Mr. Govr. Morris motion to reconsider generally the constitution of the Executive. Mas. ay. Ct. ay. N.J. ay. & all the others ay.

Mr. Elseworth moved to strike out the appointmt. by the Natl. Legislature, and insert to be chosen by electors appointed, by the Legislatures of the States in the following ratio; to wit—one for each State not exceeding 200,000 inhabits., two for each above yt. number & not exceeding 300,000, and three for each State exceeding 300,000.

Mr. Broome 2ded the motion.

Mr. Rutlidge was opposed to all the modes except the appointmt. by the Natl. Legislature. He will be sufficiently independent, if he be not re-eligible.

Mr. Gerry preferred the motion of Mr. Elseworth to an appointmt. by the Natl. Legislature, or by the people; tho' not to an appt. by the State Executives. He moved that the electors proposed by Mr. E. should be 25 in number, and allotted in the following proportion. to N.H. 1. to Mas. 3. to R.I. 1. to Cont. 2. to N.Y. 2.

The question as moved by Mr. Elseworth being divided, on the 1st part shall ye. Natl. Executive be appointed by Electors? Mas. divd. Cont. ay. N.J. ay. Pa. ay. Del. ay. Md. ay. Va. ay. N.C. no. S.C. no. Geo. no.

On 2d part shall the Electors be chosen by 14 State Legislatures? Mas. ay. Cont. ay. N.J. ay. Pa. ay. Del. ay. Md. ay. Va. no. N.C. ay. S.C. no. Geo. ay.

The part relating to the ratio in which the States sd. chuse electors was postponed nem. con.

Saturday, July 21

In Convention

Mr. Wilson moved as an amendment to Resoln. 10 that the supreme Natl. Judiciary should be associated with the Executive in the Revisionary power. This proposition had been before made and failed: but he was so confirmed by reflection in the opinion of its utility, that he thought it incumbent on him to make another effort. The Judiciary ought to have an opportunity of remonstrating agst. projected encroachments on the people as well as on themselves. It had been said that the Judges, as expositors of the Laws would have an opportunity of defending their constitutional rights. There was weight in this observation; but this power of the Judges did not go far enough. Laws may be unjust, may be unwise, may be dangerous, may be destructive; and yet may not be so unconstitutional as to justify the Judges in refusing to give them effect. Let them have a share in the Revisionary power, and they will have an opportunity of taking notice of these characters of a law, and of counteracting, by the weight of their opinions the improper views of the Legislature.—

Mr. Madison 2ded the motion.

Mr. Ghorum did not see the advantage of employing the Judges in this way. As Judges they are not to be presumed to possess any peculiar knowledge of the mere policy of public measures. Nor can it be necessary as a security for their constitutional rights. The Judges in England have no such additional provision for their defence, yet their jurisdiction is not invaded. He thought it would be best to let the Executive alone be responsible, and at most to authorize him to call on Judges for their opinions.

Mr. Elseworth approved heartily of the motion. The aid of the Judges will give more wisdom & firmness to the Executive. They will possess a systematic and accurate knowledge of the Laws, which the Executive can not be expected always to possess. The law of Nations also will frequently come into question. Of this the Judges alone will have competent information.

Mr. Madison considered the object of the motion as of great importance to the meditated Constitution. It would be useful to the Judiciary deparmt. by giving it an additional opportunity of defending itself agst. Legislative encroachments; It would be useful to the Executive, by inspiring additional confidence & firmness in exerting the revisionary power: It would be useful to the Legislature by the valuable assistance it would give in preserving a consistency, conciseness, perspicuity & technical propriety in the laws, qualities peculiarly necessary; & yet shamefully wanting in our republican Codes. It would moreover be useful to the Community at large as an additional check agst. a pursuit of those unwise & unjust measures which constituted so great a portion of our calamities. If any solid objection could be urged agst. the motion, it must be on the supposition that it tended to give too much strength either to the Executive or Judiciary. He did not think there was the least ground for this apprehension. It was much more to be apprehended that notwithstanding this co-operation of the two departments, the Legislature would still be an overmatch for them. Experience in all the States had evinced a powerful tendency in the Legislature to absorb all power into its vortex. This was the real source of danger to the American Constitutions; & suggested the necessity of giving every defensive authority to the other departments that was consistent with republican principles.

Mr. Mason said he had always been a friend to this provision. It would give a confidence to the Executive, which he would not otherwise have, and without which the Revisionary power would be of little avail.

Mr. Gerry did not expect to see this point which had undergone full discussion, again revived. The object he conceived of the Revisionary power was merely to secure the Executive department agst. legislative encroachment. The Executive therefore who will best know and be ready to defend his rights ought alone to have the defence of them. The motion was liable to strong objections. It was combining & mixing together the Legislative & the other departments. It was establishing an improper coalition between the Executive & Judiciary departments. It was making Statesmen of the Judges; and setting them up as the guardians of the Rights of the people. He relied for his part on the Representatives of the people as the guardians of their Rights & interests. It was making the Expositors of the Laws, the Legislators which ought never to be done. A better expedient for correcting the laws, would be to appoint as had been done in Pena. a person or persons of proper skill, to draw bills for the Legislature.

Mr. Govr. Morris. Some check being necessary on the Legislature, the question is in what hands it should be lodged. On one side it was contended that the Executive alone ought to exercise it. He did not think that an Executive appointed for 6 years, and impeachable whilst in office wd. be a very effectual check. On the other side it was urged that he ought to be reinforced by the Judiciary department. Agst. this it was objected that Expositors of laws ought to have no hand in making them, and arguments in favor of this had been drawn from England. What weight was due to them might be easily determined by an attention to facts. The truth was that the Judges in England had a great share in ye. Legislation. They are consulted in difficult & doubtful cases. They may be & some of them are members of the Legislature. They are or may be members of the privy Council, and can there advise the Executive as they will do with us if the motion succeeds. The influence the English Judges may have in the latter capacity in strengthening the Executive check can not be ascertained, as the King by his influence in a manner dictates the laws. There is one difference in the two Cases however which disconcerts all reasoning from the British to our proposed Constitution. The British Executive has so great an interest in his prerogatives and such powerful means of defending them that he will never yield any part of them. The interest of our Executive is so inconsiderable & so transitory, and his means of defending it so feeble, that there is the justest ground to fear his want of firmness in resisting encroachments. He was extremely apprehensive that the auxiliary firmness & weight of the Judiciary would not supply the deficiency. He concurred in thinking the public liberty in greater danger from Legislative usurpations than from any other source. It had been said that the Legislature ought to be relied on as the proper Guardians of liberty. The answer was short and conclusive. Either bad laws will be pushed or not. On the latter supposition no check will be wanted. On the former a strong check will be necessary: And this is the proper supposition. Emissions of paper money, largesses to the people—a remission of debts and similar measures, will at some times be popular, and will be pushed for that reason. At other times such measures will coincide with the interests of the Legislature themselves, & that will be a reason not less cogent for pushing them. It may be thought that the people will not be deluded and misled in the latter case. But experience teaches another lesson. The press is indeed a great means of diminishing the evil, yet it is found to be unable to prevent it altogether.

Mr. L. Martin. Considered the association of the Judges with the Executive as a dangerous innovation; as well as one which could not produce the particular advantage expected from it. A knowledge of Mankind, and of Legislative affairs cannot be presumed to belong in a higher degree to the Judges than to the Legislature. And as to the Constitutionality of laws, that point will come before the Judges in their proper official character. In this character they have a negative on the laws. Join them with the Executive in the Revision and they will have a double negative. It is necessary that the Supreme Judiciary should have the confidence of the people. This will soon be lost, if they are employed in the task of remonstrating agst. popular measures of the Legislature. Besides in what mode & proportion are they to vote in the Council of Revision?

Mr. Madison could not discover in the proposed association of the Judges with the Executive in the Revisionary check on the Legislature any violation of the maxim which requires the great departments of power to be kept separate & distinct. On the contrary he thought it an auxiliary precaution in favor of the maxim. If a Constitutional discrimination of the departments on paper were a sufficient security to each agst. encroachments of the others, all further provisions would indeed be superfluous. But experience had taught us a distrust of that security; and that it is necessary to introduce such a balance of powers and interests, as will guarantee the provisions on paper. Instead therefore of contenting ourselves with laying down the Theory in the Constitution that each department ought to be separate & distinct, it was proposed to add a defensive power to each which should maintain the Theory in practice. In so doing we did not blend the departments together. We erected effectual barriers for keeping them separate. The most regular example of this theory was in the British Constitution. Yet it was not only the practice there to admit the Judges to a seat in the legislature, and in the Executive Councils, and to submit to their previous examination all laws of a certain description, but it was a part of *their* Constitution that the Executive might negative any law whatever; a part of their Constitution which had been universally regarded as calculated for the preservation of the whole. The objection agst. a union of the Judiciary & Executive branches in the revision of the laws, had either no foundation or was not carried far enough. If such a Union was an improper mixture of powers, or such a Judiciary check on the laws, was inconsistent with the Theory of a free Constitution, it was equally so to admit the Executive to any participation in the making of laws; and the revisionary plan ought to be discarded altogether.

Col. Mason Observed that the defence of the Executive was not the sole object of the Revisionary power. He expected even greater advantages from it. Notwithstanding the precautions taken in the Constitution of the Legislature, it would still so much resemble that of the individual States, that it must be expected frequently to pass unjust and pernicious laws. This restraining power was therefore essentially necessary. It would have the effect not only of hindering the final passage of such laws; but would discourage demagogues from attempting to get them passed. It had been said [by Mr. L. Martin] that if the Judges were joined in this check on the laws, they would have a double negative, since in their expository capacity of Judges they would have one negative. He would reply that in this capacity they could impede in one case only, the operation of laws. They could declare an unconstitutional law void. But with regard to every law however unjust oppressive or pernicious, which did not come plainly under this description, they would be under the necessity as Judges to give it a free course. He wished the further use to be made of the Judges, of giving aid in preventing every improper law. Their aid will be the more valuable as they are in the habit and practice of considering laws in their true principles, and in all their consequences.

Mr. Wilson. The separation of the departments does not require that they should have separate objects but that they should act separately tho' on the same objects. It is necessary that the two branches of the Legislature should be separate and distinct, yet they are both to act precisely on the same object.

Mr. Gerry had rather give the Executive an absolute negative for its own defence than thus to blend together the Judiciary & Executive departments. It will bind them together in an offensive and defensive alliance agst. the Legislature, and render the latter unwilling to enter into a contest with them.

Mr. Govr. Morris was surprised that any defensive provision for securing the effectual separation of the departments should be considered as an improper mixture of them. Suppose that the three powers, were to be vested in three persons, by compact among themselves; that one was to have the power of making, another of executing, and a third of judging, the laws. Would it not be very natural for the two latter after having settled the partition on paper, to observe, and would not candor oblige the former to admit, that as a security agst. legislative acts of the former which might easily be so trained as to undermine the powers of the two others, the two others ought to be armed with a veto for their own defence, or at least to have an opportunity of stating their objections agst. acts of encroachment? And would any one pretend that such a right tended to blend & confound powers that ought to be separately exercised? As well might it be said that If three neighbours had three distinct farms, a right in each to defend his farm agst. his neighbours, tended to blend the farms together.

Mr. Ghorum. All agree that a check on the Legislature is necessary. But there are two objections agst. admitting the Judges to share in it which no observations on the other side seem to obviate. The 1st is that the Judges ought to carry into the exposition of the laws no prepossessions with regard to them. 2d that as the Judges will outnumber the Executive, the revisionary check would be thrown entirely out of the Executive hands, and instead of enabling him to defend himself, would enable the Judges to sacrifice him.

Mr. Wilson. The proposition is certainly not liable to all the objections which have been urged agst. it. According [to Mr. Gerry] it will unite the Executive & Judiciary in an offensive & defensive alliance agst. the Legislature. According to Mr. Ghorum it will lead to a subversion of the Executive by the Judiciary irifluence. To the first gentleman the answer was obvious; that the joint weight of the two departments was necessary to balance the single weight of the Legislature. To the 1st objection stated by the other Gentleman it might be answered that supposing the prepossion to mix itself with the exposition, the evil would be overbalanced by the advantages promised by the expedient. To the 2d objection, that such a rule of voting might be provided in the detail as would guard agst. it.

Mr. Rutlidge thought the Judges of all men the most unfit to be concerned in the revisionary Council. The Judges ought never to give their opinion on a law till it comes before them. He thought it equally unnecessary. The Executive could advise with the officers of State, as of war, finance &c. and avail himself of their information & opinions.

On Question on Mr. Wilson's motion for joining the Judiciary in the Revision of laws it passed in the negative—Mas. no. Cont. ay. N.J. not present. Pa. divd. Del. no. Md. ay. Va. ay. N.C. no. S.C. no. Geo. divd. 9 Resol. 10, giving the Ex. a qualified veto, without the amendt, was then agd. to nem. con.

The motion made by Mr. Madison July 18. & then postponed, "that the Judges shd. be nominated by the Executive & such nominations become appointments unless disagreed to by 213 of the 2d branch of the Legislature," was now resumed.

Mr. Madison stated as his reasons for the motion. 1. that it secured the responsibility of the Executive who would in general be more capable & likely to select fit characters than the Legislature, or even the 2d b. of it, who might hide their selfish motives under the number concerned in the appointment.—2. that in case of any flagrant partiality or error, in the nomination it might be fairly presumed that 2/3 of the 2d brancli would join in putting a negative on it. 3. that as the 2d b. was very differently constituted when the appointment of the Judges was formerly referred to it, and was now to be composed of equal votes from all the States, the principle of compromise which had prevailed in other instances required in this that their shd. be a concurrence of two authorities, in one of which the people, in the other the States, should be represented. The Executive Magistrate wd. be considered as a national officer, acting for and equally sympathising with every part of the U. States. If the 2d branch alone should have this power, the Judges might be appointed by a minority of the people, tho' by a majority, of the States, which could not be justified on any principle as their proceedings were to relate to the people, rather than to the States: and as it would moreover throw the appointments entirely into the hands of ye. Northern States, a perpetual ground of jealousy & discontent would be furnished to the Southern States.

Mr. Pinkney was for placing the appointmt. in the 2d b. exclusively. The Executive will possess neither the requisite knowledge of characters, nor confidence of the people for so high a trust.

Mr. Randolph wd. have preferred the mode of appointmt. proposed formerly by Mr. Ghorum, as adopted in the Constitution of Massts. but thought the motion depending so great an improvement of the clause as it stands, that he anxiously wished it success. He laid great stress on the responsibility of the Executive as a security for fit appointments. Appointments by the Legislatures have generally resulted from cabal, from personal regard, or some other consideration than a title derived from the proper qualifications. The same inconveniencies will proportionally prevail, if the appointments be be referred to either branch of the Legislature or to any other authority administered by a number of individuals.

Mr. Elseworth would prefer a negative in the Executive on a nomination by the 2d branch, the negative to be overruled by a concurrence of 2/3 of the 2d b. to the mode proposed by the motion; but preferred an absolute appointment by the 2d branch to either. The Executive will be regarded by the people with a jealous eye. Every power for augmenting unnecessarily his influence will be disliked. As he will be stationary it was not to be supposed he could have a better knowledge of characters. He will be more open to caresses & intrigues than the Senate. The right to supersede his nomination will be ideal only. A nomination under such circumstances will be equivalent to an appointment.

Mr. Govr. Morris supported the motion. 1. The States in their corporate capacity will frequently have an interest staked on the determination of the Judges. As in the Senate the States are to vote the Judges ought not to be appointed by the Senate. Next to the impropriety of being Judge in one's own cause, is the appointment of the Judge, 2. It had been said the Executive would be uninformed of characters. The reverse was ye. truth. The Senate will be so. They must take the character of candidates from the flattering pictures drawn by their friends. The Executive in the necessary intercourse with every part of the U.S. required by the nature of his administration, will or may have the best possible information. 3. It had been said that a jealousy would be entertained of the Executive. If the Executive can be safely trusted with the command of the army, there cannot surely be any reasonable ground of Jealousy in the present case. He added that if the objections agst. an appointment of the Executive by the Legislature, had the weight that had been allowed there must be some weight in the objection to an appointment of the Judges by the Legislature or by any part of it.

Mr. Gerry. The appointment of the Judges like every other part of the Constitution shd. be so modelled as to give satisfaction both to the people and to the States. The mode under consideration will give satisfaction to neither. He could not conceive that the Executive could be as well informed of characters throughout the Union, as the Senate. It appeared to him also a strong objection that 2/3 of the Senate were required to reject a nomination of the Executive. The Senate would be constituted in the same manner as Congress. And the appointments of Congress have been generally good.

Mr. Madison observed that he was not anxious that 2/3 should be necessary to disagree to a nomination. He had given this form to his motion chiefly to vary it the more clearly from one which had just been rejected. He was content to obviate the objection last made, and accordingly so varied the motion as to let a majority reject.

Col. Mason found it his duty to differ from his colleagues in their opinions & reasonings on this subject. Notwithstanding the form of the proposition by which the appointment seemed to be divided between the Executive & Senate, the appointment was substantially vested in the former alone. The false complaisance which usually prevails in such cases will prevent a disagreement to the first nominations. He considered the appointment by the Executive as a dangerous prerogative. It might even give him an influence over the Judiciary department itself. He did not think the difference of interest between the Northern and Southern States could be properly brought into this argument. It would operate & require some precautions in the case of regulating navigation, commerce & imposts; but he could not see that it had any connection with the Judiciary department.

On the question, the motion now being that the executive should nominate, & such nominations should become appointments unless disagreed to by the Senate Mas. ay. Ct. no. Pa. ay. Del. no. Md. no. Va. ay. N.C. no. S.C. no. Geo. no.

On question for agreeing to the clause as it stands by which the Judges are to be appointed by 2d branch Mas. no. Ct. ay. Pa. no. Del. ay. Md. ay. Va. no. N.C. ay. S.C. ay. Geo. ay.

Adjourned.

Tuesday, July 24

In Convention

The appointment of the Executive by Electors reconsidered.

Mr. Houston moved that he be appointed by the "Natl. Legislature," instead of "Electors appointed by the State Legislatures" according to the last decision of the mode. He dwelt chiefly on the improbability, that capable men would undertake the service of Electors from the more distant States.

Mr. Gerry opposed it. He thought there was no ground to apprehend the danger urged by Mr. Houston. The election of the Executive Magistrate will be considered as of vast importance and will excite great earnestness. The best men, the Governours of the States will not hold it derogatory from their character to be the electors. If the motion should be agreed to, it will be necessary to make the Executive ineligible a 2d time, in order to render him independent of the Legislature; which was an idea extremely repugnant to his way of thinking.

Mr. Strong supposed that there would be no necessity, if the Executive should be appointed by the Legislature, to make him ineligible a 2d time; as new elections of the Legislature will have intervened; and he will not depend for his 2d appointment on the same sett of men as his first was recd. from. It had been suggested that gratitude for his past appointment wd. produce the same effect as dependence for his future appointment. He thought very differently. Besides this objection would lie agst. the Electors who would be objects of *gratitude* as well as the Legislature. It was of great importance not to make the Govt. too complex which would be the case if a new seft of men like the Electors should be introduced into it. He thought also that the first characters in the States would not feel sufficient motives to undertake the office of Electors.

Mr. Williamson was for going back to the original ground; to elect the Executive for years and render hint ineligible a 2d time. The proposed Electors would certainly not be men of the 1st nor even of the 2d grade in the States. These would all prefer a seat either in the Senate or the other branch of the Legislature. He did not like the Unity in the Executive. He had wished the Executive power to be lodged in three men taken from three districts into which the States should be divided. As the Executive is to have a kind of veto on the laws, and there is an essential difference of interests between the N. & S. States, particularly in the carrying trade, the power will be dangerous, if the Executive is to be taken from part of the Union, to the part from which he is not taken. The case is different here from what it is in England; where there is a sameness of interests throughout the Kingdom. Another objection agst. a single Magistrate is that he will be an elective King, and will feel the spirit of one. He will spare no pains to keep himself in for life, and will then lay a train for the succession of his children. It was pretty certain he thought that we should at some time or other have a King; but he wished no precaution to be omitted that might postpone the event as long as possible.—Ineligibility a 2d time appeared to him to be the best precaution. With this precaution he had no objection to a longer term than 7 years. He would go as far as 10 or 12 years.

Mr. Gerry moved that the Legislatures of the States should vote by ballot for the Executive in the same proportions as it had been proposed they should chuse electors; and that in case a majority of the votes should not center on the same person, the 1st branch of the Natl. Legislature should chuse two out of the 4 candidates having most votes, and out of these two, the 2d branch should chose the Executive.

Question on Mr. Houston's motion that the Executive be appd. by Nal. Legislature

N.H. ay. Mas. ay. Ct. no. N.J. ay. Pa. no. Del. ay. Md. no. Va. no. N.C. ay. S.C. ay. Geo. ay.

Mr. L. Martin & Mr. Gerry moved to re-instate the ineligibility of the Executive a 2d time.

Mr. Elseworth. With many this appears a natural consequence of his being elected by the Legislature. It was not the case with him. The Executive he thought should be reelected if his conduct proved him worthy of it. And he will be more likely to render himself worthy of it if he be rewardable with it. The most eminent characters also will be more willing to accept the trust under this condition, than if they foresee a necessary degradation at a fixd. period.

Mr. Gerry. That the Executive shd. be independent of the Legislature is a clear point. The longer the duration of his appointment the more will his dependence be diminished. It will be better then for him to continue 10, 15, or even 20, years and be ineligible afterwards.

Mr. L. Martin, suspending his motion as to the ineligibility, moved that the appointmt. of the Executive shall continue for Eleven years.

Mr. Gerry suggested fifteen years.

Mr. King twenty years. This is the medium life of princes.

Mr. Davie Eight years.

Mr. Wilson. The difficulties & perplexities into which the House is thrown proceed from the election by the Legislature which he was sorry had been reinstated. The inconveniency of this mode was such that he would agree to almost any length of time in order to get rid of the dependence which must result from it. He was persuaded that the longest term would not be equivalent to a proper mode of election; unless indeed it should be during good behaviour. It seemed to be supposed that at a certain advance in life, a continuance in office would cease to be agreeable to the officer, as well as desirable to the public. Experience had shewn in a variety of instances that both a capacity & inclination for public service existed—in very advanced stages. He mentioned the instance of a Doge of Venice who was elected after he was 80 years of age. The popes have generally been elected at very advanced periods, and yet in no case had a more steady or a better concerted policy been pursued than in the Court of Rome. If the Executive should come into office at 35 years of age, which he presumes may happen & his continuance should be fixt at 15 years. at the age of 50 in the very prime of life, and with all the aid of experience, he must be cast aside like a useless hulk. What an irreparable loss would the British Jurisprudence have sustained, had the age of 50 been fixt there as the ultimate limit of capacity or readiness to serve the public. The great luminary [Ld. Mansfield] held his seat for thirty years after his arrival at that age. Notwithstanding what had been done he could not but hope that a better mode of election would yet be adopted; and one that would be more agreeable to the general sense of the House. That time might be given for further deliberation he wd. move that the present question be postponed till tomorrow.

Mr. Broom seconded the motion to postpone.

Mr. Gerry. We seem to be entirely at a loss on this head. He would suggest whether it would not be adviseable to refer the clause relating to the Executive to the Committee of detail to be appointed. Perhaps they will be able to hit on something that may unite the various opinions which have been thrown out.

Mr. Govr. Morris. Of all possible modes of appointment that by the Legislature is the worst. If the Legislature is to appoint and to impeach or to influence the impeachment, the Executive will be the mere creature of it. He had been opposed to the impeachment but was now convinced that impeachments must be provided for, if the appt. was to be of any duration. No man wd. say, that an Executive known to be in the pay of an Enemy, should not be removeable in some way or other. He had been charged heretofore [by Col. Mason] with inconsistency in pleading for confidence in the Legislature on some occasions, & urging a distrust on others. The charge was not well founded. The Legislature is worthy of unbounded confidence in some respects, and liable to equal distrust in others. When their interest coincides precisely with that of their Constituents, as happens in many of their Acts, no abuse of trust is to be apprehended. When a strong personal interest happens to be opposed to the general interest, the Legislature can not be too much distrusted. In all public bodies there are two parties. The Executive will necessarily be more connected with one than with the other. There will be a personal interest therefore in one of the parties to oppose as well as in the other to support him. Much had been said of the intrigues that will be practised by the Executive to get into office. Nothing had been said on the other side of the intrigues to get him out of office. Some leader of the party will always covet his seat, will perplex his administration, will cabal with the Legislature, till he succeeds in supplanting him. This was the way in which the King of England was got out, he meant the real King, the Minister. This was the way in which Pitt [Ld. Chatham] forced himself into place. Fox was for pushing the matter still farther. if he carried his India bill, which he was very near doing, he would have made the Minister, the King in form almost as well as in substance. Our President will be the British Minister, yet we are about to make him appointable by the Legislature, Something had been said of the danger of Monarchy. If a good government should not now be formed, if a good organization of the Executive should not be provided, he doubted whether we should not have something worse than a limited Monarchy. In order to get rid of the dependence of the Executive on the Legislature, the expedient of making him ineligible a 2d time had been devised. This was as much as to say we shd. give him the benefit of experience, and then deprive ourselves of the use of it. But make him ineligible a 2d time—and prolong his duration even to 15—years, will he by any wonderful interposition of providence at that period cease to be a man? No he will be unwilling to quit his exaltation, the road to his object thro' the Constitution will be shut; he will be in possession of the sword, a civil war will ensue, and the Commander of the victorious army on which ever side, will be the despot of America. This consideration renders him particularly anxious that the Executive should be properly constituted. The vice here would not, as in some other parts of the system be curable. It is the most difficult of all rightly to balance the Executive. Make him too weak: The Legislature will usurp his powers: Make him too strong, He will usurp on the Legislature. He preferred a short period, a re-eligibility, but a different mode of election. A long period would prevent an adoption of the plan: it ought to do so. He shd. himself be afraid to trust it. He was not prepared to decide on Mr. Wilson's mode of election just hinted by him. He thought it deserved consideration It would be better that chance sd. decide than intrigue.

On a question to postpone the consideration of the Resolution on the subject of the Executive

N.H. no. Mas. no. Ct. ay. N.J. no. Pa. ay. Del. divd. Md. ay. Va. ay. N.C. no. S.C. no. Geo. no.

Mr. Wilson then moved that the Executive be chosen every _____ years by _____ Electors to be taken by lot from the Natl Legislature who shall proceed immediately to the choice of the Executive and not separate until it be made. [. . .]

Mr. Gerry. This is committing too much to chance. If the lot should fall on a sett of unworthy men, an unworthy Executive must be saddled on the Country. He thought it had been demonstrated that no possible mode of electing by the Legislature could be a good one.

Mr. King. The lot might fall on a majority from the same State which wd. ensure the election of a man from that State. We ought to be governed by reason, not by chance. As nobody seemed to be satisfied, he wished the matter to be postponed.

Mr. Wilson did not move this as the best mode. His opinion remained unshaken that we ought to resort to the people for the election. He seconded the postponement.

On a question whether the last motion was in order, it was determined in the affirmative; 7. ays. 4 noes.

On the question of postponent. it was agreed to nem. con.

Wednesday, July 25

In Convention

Clause relating to the Executive again under consideration.

Mr. Madison. There are objections agst. every mode that has been, or perhaps can be proposed. The election must be made either by some existing authority under the Natil. or State Constitutions—or by some special authority derived from the people—or by the people themselves.—The two Existing authorities under the Natl. Constitution wd. be the Legislative & Judiciary. The latter he presumed was out of the question. The former was in his Judgment liable to insuperable objections. Besides the general influence of that mode on the independence of the Executive, 1. the election of the Chief Magistrate would agitate & divide the legislature so much that the public interest would materially suffer by it. Public bodies are always apt to be thrown into contentions, but into more violent ones by such occasions than by any others. 2. the candidate would intrigue with the Legislature, would derive his appointment from the predominant faction, and be apt to render his administration subservient to its views. 3. The Ministers of foreign powers would have and make use of, the opportunity to mix their intrigues & influence with the Election. Limited as the powers of the Executive are, it will be an object of great moment with the great rival powers of Europe who have American possessions, to have at the head of our Governmt. a man attached to their respective politics & interests. No pains, nor perhaps expense, will be spared, to gain from the Legislature an appointmt. favorable to their wishes. Germany & Poland are witnesses of this danger. In the former, the election of the Head of the Empire, till it became in a manner hereditary, interested all Europe, and was much influenced by foreign interference. In the latter, altho' the elective Magistrate has very little real power, his election has at all times produced the most eager interference of foreign princes, and has in fact at length slid entirely into foreign hands. The existing authorities in the States are the Legislative, Executive & Judiciary. The appointment of the Natl. Executive by the first, was objectionable in many points of view, some of which had been already mentioned. He would mention one which of itself would decide his opinion. The Legislatures of the States had betrayed a strong propensity to a variety of pernicious measures. One object of the Natl. Legislre. was to controul this propensity. One object of the Natl. Executive, so far as it would have a negative on the laws, was to controul the Natl. Legislature, so far as it might be infected with a similar propensity. Refer the appointmt. of the Natl. Executive to the State Legislatures, and this controuling purpose may be defeated. The Legislatures can & will act with some kind of regular plan, and will promote the appointmt. of a man who will not oppose himself to a favorite object. Should a majority of the Legislatures at the time of election have the same object, or different objects of the same kind, the Natl. Executive would be rendered subservient to them.—An appointment by the State Executives, was liable among other objections to this insuperable one, that being standing bodies, they could & would be courted, and intrigued with by the Candidates, by their partizans, and by the Ministers of foreign powers. The State judiciarys had not & he presumed wd. not be proposed as a proper source of appointment. The option before us then lay between an appointment by Electors chosen by the people and an immediate appointment by the people. He thought the former mode free from many of the objections which had been urged agst. it, and greatly preferable to an appointment by the Natl. Legislature. As the electors would be chosen for the occasion, would meet at once, & proceed immediately to an appointment, there would be very little opportunity for cabal, or corruption. As a farther precaution, it might be required that they should meet at some place, distinct from the seat of Govt. and even that no person within a certain distance of the place at the time shd. be eligible. This Mode however had been rejected so recently & by so great a majority that it probably would not be proposed anew. The remaining mode was an election by the people or rather by the qualified part of them, at large: With all its imperfections he liked this best. He would not repeat either the general argumts. for or the objections agst. this mode. He would only take notice of two difficulties which he admitted to have weight. The first arose from the disposition in the people to prefer a Citizen of their own State, and the disadvantage this wd. throw on the smaller States. Great as this objection might be he did not think it equal to such as lay agst. every other mode which had been proposed. He thought too that some expedient might be hit upon that would obviate it. The second difficulty arose from the disproportion of qualified voters in the N. & S. States, and the disadvantages which this mode would throw on the latter. The answer to this objection was 1. that this disproportion would be continually decreasing under the influence of the Republican laws introduced in the S. States, and the more rapid increase of their population. 2. That local considerations must give way to the general interest. As an individual from the S. States he was willing to make the sacrifice.

Mr. Elseworth. The objection drawn from the different sizes of the States, is unanswerable. The Citizens of the largest States would invariably prefer the Candidate within the State; and the largest States wd. invariably have the man.

Mr. Pinkney moved that the election by the Legislature be qualified with a proviso that no person be eligible for more than 6 years in any twelve years. He thought this would have all the advantage & at the same time avoid in some degree the inconveniency, of an absolute ineligibility a 2d time.

Col. Mason approved the idea. It had the sanction of experience in the instance of Congs. and some of the Executives of the States. It rendered the Executive as effectually independent, as an ineligibility after his first election, and opened the way at the same time for the advantage of his future services. He preferred on the whole the election by the Natl. Legislature: Tho' Candor obliged him to admit, that there was great danger of foreign influence, as had been suggested. This was the most serious objection with him that had been urged.

Mr. Butler. The two great evils to be avoided are cabal at home, & influence from abroad. It will be difficult to avoid either if the Election be made by the Natl. Legislature. On the other hand: The Govt. should not be made so complex & unwieldy as to disgust the States. This would be the case, if the election shd. be referred to the people. He liked best an election by Electors chosen by the Legislatures of the States. He was agst. are—eligibility at all events. He was also agst. a ratio of votes in the States. An equality should prevail in this case. The reasons for departing from it do not hold in the case of the Executive as in that of the Legislature.

Mr. Govr. Morris was agst. a rotation in every case. It formed a political School, in wch we were always governed by the scholars, and not by the Masters. The evils to be guarded agst. in this case are 1. the undue influence of the Legislature. 2. instability of Councils. 3. misconduct in office. To guard agst. the first, we run into the second evil. We adopt a rotation which produces instability of Councils. To avoid Sylla we fall into Charibdis. A change of men is ever followed by a change of measures. We see this fully exemplified in the vicissitudes among ourselves, particularly in the State of Pena. The self-sufficiency of a victorious party scorns to tread in the paths of their predecessors. Rehoboam will not imitate Soloman. 2. the Rotation in office will not prevent intrigue and dependence on the Legislature. The man in office will look forward to the period at which he will become re-eligible. The distance of the period, the improbability of such a protraction of his life will be no obstacle. Such is the nature of man, formed by his benevolent author no doubt for wise ends, that altho' he knows his existence to be limited to a span, he takes his measures as if he were to live forever. But taking another supposition, the inefficacy of the expedient will be manifest. If the magistrate does not look forward to his re-election to the Executive, he will be pretty sure to keep in view the opportunity of his going into the Legislature itself. He will have little objection then to an extension of power on a theatre where he expects to act a distinguished part; and will be very unwilling to take any step that may endanger his popularity with the Legislature, on his influence over which the figure he is to make will depend. 3. To avoid the third evil, impeachments will be essential, and hence an additional reason agst.

an election by the Legislature. He considered an election by the people as the best, by the Legislature as the worst, mode. Putting both these aside, he could not but favor the idea of Mr. Wilson, of introducing a mixture of lot. It will diminish, if not destroy both cabal & dependence.

Mr. Williamson was sensible that strong objections lay agst. an election of the Executive by the Legislature, and that it opened a door for foreign influence. The principal objection agst. an election by the people seemed to be, the disadvantage under which it would place the smaller States. He suggested as a cure for this difficulty, that each man should vote for 3 candidates, One of those he observed would be probably of his own State, the other 2. of some other States, and as probably of a small as a large one.

Mr. Govr. Morris liked the idea, suggesting as an amendment that each man should vote for two persons one of whom at least should not be of his own State.

Mr. Madison also thought something valuable might be made of the suggestion with the proposed amendment of it. The second best man in this case would probably be the first, in fact. The only objection which occurred was that each Citizen after havg. given his vote for his favorite fellow Citizen, wd. throw away his second on some obscure Citizen of another State, in order to ensure the object of his first choice. But it could hardly be supposed that the Citizens of many States would be so sanguine of having their favorite elected, as not to give their second vote with sincerity to the next object of their choice. It might moreover be provided in favor of the smaller States that the Executive should not be eligible more than times in years from the same State.

Mr. Gerry. A popular election in this case is radically vicious. The ignorance of the people would put it in the power of some one set of men dispersed through the Union & acting in Concert to delude them into any appointment. He observed that such a Society of men existed in the Order of the Cincinnati. They are respectable, United, and influencial. They will in fact elect the chief Magistrate in every instance, if the election be referred to the people. His respect for the characters composing this Society could not blind him to the danger & impropriety of throwing such a power into their hands.

Mr. Dickenson. As far as he could judge from the discussions which had taken place during his attendance, insuperable objections lay agst. an election of the Executive by the Natl. Legislature; as also by the Legislatures or Executives of the States. He had long leaned towards an election by the people which he regarded as the best & purest source. Objections he was aware lay agst. this mode, but not so great he thought as agst. the other modes. The greatest difficulty in the opinion of the House seemed to arise from the partiality of the States to their respective Citizens. But, might not this very partiality be turned to a useful purpose. Let the people of each State chuse its best Citizen. The people will know the most eminent characters of their own States, and the people of different States will feel an emulation in selecting those of which they will have the greatest reason to be proud. Out of the thirteen names thus selected, an Executive Magistrate may be chosen either by the Natl. Legislature, or by Electors appointed by it.

On a question which was moved for postponing Mr. Pinkney's motion; in order to make way for some such proposition as had been hinted by Mr. Williamson & others: it passed in the negative. N.H. no. Mas. no. Ct. ay. N.J. ay. Pa. ay. Del. no. Md. ay. Va. ay. N.C. no. S.C. no. Geo. no.

On Mr. Pinkney's motion that no person shall serve in the Executive more than 6 years in 12 years, it passed in the negative.

Wednesday, August 22

In Convention

Art VII sect 4. resumed. Mr. Sherman was for leaving the clause as it stands. He disapproved of the slave trade; yet as the States were now possessed of the right to import slaves, as the public good did not require it to be taken from them, & as it was expedient to have as few objections as possible to the proposed scheme of Government, he thought it best to leave the matter as we find it. He observed that the abolition of Slavery seemed to be going on in the U.S. & that the good sense of the several States would probably by degrees compleat it. He urged on the Convention the necessity of despatching its business.

Col Mason. This infernal trafic originated in the avarice of British Merchants. The British Govt. constantly checked the attempts of Virginia to put a stop to it. The present question concerns not the importing States alone but the whole Union. The evil of having slaves was experienced during the late war. Had slaves been treated as they might have been by the Enemy, they would have proved dangerous instruments in their hands. But their folly dealt by the slaves, as it did by the Tories. He mentioned the dangerous insurrections of the slaves in Greece and Sicily; and the instructions given by Cromwell to the Commissioners sent to Virginia, to arm the servants & slaves, in case other means of obtaining its submission should fail. Maryland & Virginia he said had already prohibited the importation of slaves expressly. N. Carolina had done the same in substance. All this would be in vain if S. Carolina & Georgia be at liberty to import. The Western People are already calling out for slaves for their new lands, and will fill that Country with slaves if they can be got thro' S. Carolina & Georgia. Slavery discourages arts & manufactures. The poor despise labor when performed by slaves. They prevent the immigration of Whites, who really enrich & strengthen a Country. They produce the most pernicious effect on manners. Every master of slaves is born a petty tyrant. They bring the judgment of heaven on a Country. As nations can not be rewarded or punished in the next world they must be in this. By an inevitable chain of causes & effects providence punishes national sins, by national calamities. He lamented that some of our Eastern brethren had from a lust of gain embarked in this nefarious traffic. As to the States being in possession of the Right to import, this was the case with many other rights, now to be property given up. He held it essential in every point of view that the Genl. Govt. should have power to prevent the increase of slavery.

Mr. Elsworth. As he had never owned a slave could not judge of the effects of slavery on character: He said however that if it was to be considered in a moral light we ought to go farther and free those already in the Country.—As slaves also multiply so fast in Virginia & Maryland that it is cheaper to raise than import them, whilst in the sickly rice swamps foreign supplies are necessary, if we go no farther than is urged, we shall be unjust towards S. Carolina & Georgia. Let us not intermeddle. As population increases poor laborers will be so plenty as to render slaves useless. Slavery in time will not be a speck in our Country. Provision is already made in Connecticut for abolishing it. And the abolition has already taken place in Massachusetts. As to the danger of insurrections from foreign influence, that will become a motive to kind treatment of the slaves.

Mr. Pinkney. If slavery be wrong, it is justified by the example of all the world. He cited the case of Greece Rome & other antient States; the sanction given by France England, Holland & other modern States, In all ages one half of mankind have been slaves. If the S. States were let alone they will probably of themselves stop importations. He wd. himself as a Citizen of S. Carolina vote for it. An attempt to take away the right as proposed will produce serious objections to the Constitution which he wished to see adopted.

General Pinkney declared it to be his firm opinion that if himself & all his colleagues were to sign the Constitution & use their personal influence, it would be of no avail towards obtaining the assent of their Constituents. S. Carolina & Georgia cannot do without slaves. As to Virginia she will gain by stopping the importations. Her slaves will rise in value, & she has more than she wants. It would be unequal to require S.C. & Georgia to confederate on such unequal terms. He said the Royal assent before the Revolution had never been refused to S. Carolina as to Virginia. He contended that the importation of slaves would be for the interest of the whole Union. The more slaves, the more produce to employ the carrying trade; The more consumption also, and the more of this, the more of revenue for the common treasury. He admitted it to be reasonable that slaves should be dutied like other imports, but should consider a rejection of the clause as an exclusion of S. Carola. from the Union.

Mr. Baldwin had conceived national objects atone to be before the Convention, not such as like the present were of a local nature. Georgia was decided on this point. That State has always hitherto supposed a Genl. Governmt. to be the pursuit of the central States who wished to have a vortex for every thing—that her distance would preclude her from equal advantage—& that she could not prudently purchase it by yielding national powers. From this it might be understood in what light she would view an attempt to abridge one of her favorite prerogatives. If left to herself, she may probably put a stop to the evil. As one ground for this conjecture, he took notice of the sect of _____ which he said was a respectable class of people, who carried their ethics beyond the mere *equality of men*, extending their humanity to the claims of the whole animal creation.

Mr. Wilson observed that if S.C. & Georgia were themselves disposed to get rid of the importation of slaves in a short time as had been suggested, they would never refuse to Unite because the importation might be prohibited. As the Section now stands all articles imported are to be taxed. Slaves alone are exempt. This is in fact a bounty on that article.

Mr. Gerry thought we had nothing to do with the conduct of the States as to Slaves, but ought to be careful not to give any sanction to it.

Mr. Dickenson considered it as inadmissible on every principle of honor & safety that the importation of slaves should be authorised to the States by the Constitution. The true question was whether the national happiness would be promoted or impeded by the importation, and this question ought to be left to the National Govt. not to the States particularly interested. If Engd. & France permit slavery, slaves are at the same time excluded from both those Kingdoms. Grecce and Rome were made unhappy by their slaves. He could not believe that the Southn. States would refuse to confederate on the account apprehended; especially as the power was not likely to be immediately exercised by the Genl. Government.

Mr. Williamson stated the law of N. Carolina on the subject, to wit that it did not directly prohibit the importation of slaves. It imposed a duty of £5 on each slave imported from Africa. £10 on each from elsewhere, & £50 on each from a State licensing manumission. He thought the S. States could not be members of the Union if the clause shd. be rejected, and that it was wrong to force any thing down, not absolutely necessary, and which any State must disagree to.

Mr. King thought the subject should be considered in a political light only. If two States will not agree to the Constitution as stated on one side, he could affirm with equal belief on the other, that great & equal opposition would be experienced from the other States. He remarked on the exemption of slaves from duty whilst every other import was subjected to it, as an inequality that could not fail to strike the commercial sagacity of the Northn. & middle States.

Mr. Langdon was strenuous for giving the power to the Genl. Govt. He cd. not with a good conscience leave it with the States who could then go on with the traffic, without being restrained by the opinions here given that they will themselves cease to import slaves.

Genl. Pinkney thought himself bound to declare candidly that he did not think S. Carolina would stop her importations of slaves in any short time, but only stop them occasionally as she now does. He moved to commit the clause that slaves might be made liable to an equal tax with other imports which he thought right & wch. wd. remove one difficulty that had been started.

Mr. Rutlidge. If the Convention thinks that N.C. S.C. & Georgia will ever agree to the plan, unless their right to import slaves be untouched, the expectation is vain. The people of those States will never be such fools as to give up so important an interest. He was strenuous agst. striking out the Section, and seconded the motion of Genl. Pinkney for a commitment.

Mr. Govr. Morris wished the whole subject to be committed including the clauses relating to taxes on exports & to a navigation act. These things may form a bargain among the Northern & Southern States.

Mr. Butler declared that he never would agree to the power of taxing exports.

Mr. Sherman said it was better to let the S. States import slaves than to part with them, if they made that a sine qua non. He was opposed to a tax on slaves imported as making the matter worse, because it implied they were property. He acknowledged that if the power of prohibiting the importation should be given to the Genl. Government that it would be exercised. He thought it would be its duty to exercise the power.

Mr. Read was for the commitment provided the clause concerning taxes on exports should also be committed.

Mr. Randolph was for committing in order that some middle ground might, if possible, be found. He could never agree to the clause as it stands. He wd. sooner risk the constitution. He dwelt on the dilemma to which the Convention was exposed. By agreeing to the clause, it would revolt the Quakers, the Methodists, and many others in the States having no slaves. On the other hand, two States might be lost to the Union. Let us then, he said, try the chance of a commitment.

On the question for committing the remaining part of Sect. 4 & 5. of art: 7. N.H. no. Mas. abst. Cont. ay N.J. ay. Pa. no. Del. no. Maryd. ay. Va. ay. N.C. ay S.C. ay. Geo. ay.

Mr. Pinkney & Mr. Langdon moved to commit Sect. 6. as to navigation act by two thirds of each House.

Mr. Gorham did not see the propriety of it. Is it meant to require a greater proportion of votes? He desired it to be remembered that the Eastern States had no motive to Union but a commercial one. They were able to protect themselves. They were not afraid of external danger, and did not need the aid of the Southn. States.

Mr. Wilson wished for a commitment in order to reduce the proportion of votes required.

Mr. Elsworth was for taking the plan as it is. This widening of opinions has a threatening aspect. If we do not agree on this middle & moderate ground he was afraid we should lose two States, with such others as may be disposed to stand aloof, should fly into a variety of shapes & directions, and most probably into several confederations and not without bloodshed.

On Question for committing 6 Sect. as to navigation act to a member from each State—N.H. ay. Mas. ay. Ct. no. N.J. no. Pa. ay. Del. ay. Md. ay. Va. ay. N.C. ay. S.C. ay. Geo. ay.

Tuesday, September 4

In Convention

Mr Brearly from the Committee of eleven made a further partial Report as follows:

The Committee of Eleven to whom sundry resolutions &c were referred on the 31st of August, report that in their opinion the following additions and alterations should be made to the Report before the Convention, viz.

(4) After the word 'Excellency' in sect. 1. art. 10. to be inserted. 'He shall hold his office during the term of four years, and together with the vice-President, chosen for the same term, be elected in the following manner, viz. Each State shall appoint in such manner as its Legislature may direct, a number of electors equal to the whole number of Senators and members of the House of Representatives to which the State may be entitled in the Legislature. The Electors shalt meet in their respective States, and vote by ballot for two persons, of whom one at least shall not be an inhabitant of the same State with themselves; and they shall make a list of all the persons voted for, and of the number of votes for each, which list they shall sign and certify and transmit sealed to the Seat of the Genl. Government, directed to the President of the Senate—The President of the Senate shall in that House open all the certificates; and the votes shall be then & there counted. The Person having the greatest number of votes shall be the President, if such number be a majority of that of the electors; and if there be more than one who have such majority, and have an equal number of votes, then the Senate shall immediately choose by ballot one of them for President: but if no person have a majority, then from the five highest on the list, the Senate shall choose by ballot the President. And in every case after the choice of the President, the person having the greatest number of votes shall be vice-president: but if there should remain two or more who have equal votes, the Senate shall choose from them the vice-President. The Legislature may determine the time of choosing and assembling the Electors, and the manner of certifying and transmitting their votes. [. . .]

Wednesday, September 5

In Convention

The Report made Yesterday as to the appointment of the Executive being taken up.

Mr. Pinkney renewed his opposition to the mode, arguing 1. that the electors will not have sufficient knowledge of the fittest men, & will be swayed by an attachment to the eminent men of their respective States. Hence 2dly the dispersion of the votes would leave the appointment with the Senate, and as the Presidents reappointment will thus depend on the Senate he will be the mere creature of that body. 3. He will combine with the Senate agst. the House of

Representatives. 4. This change in the mode of election was meant to get rid of the ineligibility of the President a second time, whereby he will become fixed for life under the auspices of the Senate.

Col. Mason admitted that there were objections to an appointment by the Legislature as originally planned. He had not yet made up his mind, but would state his objections to the mode proposed by the Committee. 1. It puts the appointment in fact into the hands of the Senate, as it will rarely happen that a majority of the whole votes will fall on any one candidate: and as the Existing President will always be one of the 5 highest, his reappointment will of course depend on the Senate. 2. Considering the powers of the President & those of the Senate, if a coalition should be established between these two branches, they will be able to subvert the Constitution. The great objection with him would be removed by depriving the Senate of the eventual election. He accordingly moved to strike out the words "if such number be a majority of that of the electors."

Mr. Williamson 2ded the motion. He could not agree to the clause without some such modification. He preferred making the highest tho' not having a majority of the votes, President, to a reference of the matter to the Senate. Referring the appointment to the Senate lays a certain foundation for corruption & aristocracy. On the motion of Col: Mason, N.H. no. Mas. no. Ct. no. N.J. no. Pa. no. Del. no. Md. ay. Va. no. N.C. ay. S.C. no. Geo. no.

Mr. Wilson moved to strike out "Senate" and insert the word "Legislature."

Mr. Madison considered it as a primary object to render an eventual resort to any part of the Legislature improbable. He was apprehensive that the proposed alteration would turn the attention of the large States too much to the appointment of candidates, instead of aiming at an effectual appointment of the officer, as the large States would predominate in the Legislature which would have the final choice out of the Candidates. Whereas if the Senate in which the small States predominate should have this final choice, the concerted effort of the large States would be to make the appointment in the first instance conclusive.

Mr. Randolph. We have in some revolutions of this plan made a bold stroke for Monarchy. We are now doing the same for an aristocracy. He dwelt on the tendency of such an influence in the Senate over the election of the President in addition to its other powers, to convert that body into a real & dangerous Aristocracy.

Mr. Dickinson was in favor of giving the eventual election to the Legislature, instead of the Senate. It was too much influence to be superadded to that body.

On the question moved by Mr. Wilson, N.H. divd. Mas. no. Ct. no. N.J. no. Pa. ay. Del. no. Md. no. Va. ay. N.C. no. S.C. ay. Geo. no.

Thursday, September 6

In Convention

Mr. Gerry proposed, as the President was to be elected by the Senate out of the five highest candidates, that if he should not at the end of his term be re-elected by a majority of the Electors, and no other candidate should have a Majority, the eventual election should be made by the Legislature. This he said would relieve the President from his particular dependence on the Senate for his continuance in office.

Mr. Govr. Morris thought favorably of Mr. Gerry's proposition. It would free the President from being tempted in naming to Offices, to Conform to the will of the Senate, & thereby virtually give the appointments to office, to the Senate.

Mr. Wilson said that he had weighed carefully the report of the Committee for remodelling the constitution of the Executive; and on combining it with other parts of the plan, he was obliged to consider the whole as having a dangerous tendency to aristocracy; as throwing a dangerous power into the hands of the Senate. They will have in fact, the appointment of the President, and through his dependence on them, the virtual appointment to offices; among others the offices of the Judiciary Department. They are to make Treaties; and they are to try all impeachments. In allowing them thus to make the Executive & Judiciary appointments, to be the Court of impeachments, and to make Treaties which are to be laws of the land, the Legislative, Executive & Judiciary powers are all blended in one branch of the Government.

The power of making Treaties involves the case of subsidies, and here as an additional evil, foreign influence is to be dreaded. According to the plan as it now stands, the President will not be the man of the people as he ought to be, but the Minion of the Senate. He cannot even appoint a tide-waiter without the Senate. He had always thought the Senate too numerous a body for making appointments to office. The Senate, will moreover in all probability be in constant Session. They will have high salaries. And with all those powers, and the President in their interest, they will depress the other branch of the Legislature, and aggrandize themselves in proportion. Add to all this, that the Senate sitting in conclave, can by holding up to their respective States various and improbable candidates, contrive so to scatter their votes, as to bring the appointment of the President ultimately before themselves. Upon the whole, he thought the new mode of appointing the President, with some amendments, a valuable improvement; but he could never agree to purchase it at the price of the ensuing parts of the Report, nor befriend a system of which they make a part.

Mr. Govr. Morris expressed his wonder at the observations of Mr. Wilson so far as they preferred the plan in the printed Report to the new modification of it before the House, and entered into a comparative view of the two, with an eye to the nature of Mr. Wilson's objections to the last. By the first the Senate he observed had a voice in appointing the President out of all the Citizens of the U.S: by this they were limited to five candidates previously nominated to them, with a probability of being barred altogether by the successful ballot of the Electors. Here surely was no increase of power. They are now to appoint Judges nominated to them by the President. Before they had the appointment without any agency whatever of the President. Here again surely no additional power. If they are to make Treaties as the plan now stands, the power was the same in the printed plan. If they are to try impeachments, the Judges must have been triable by them before. Wherein then lay the dangerous tendency of the innovations to establish an aristocracy in the Senate? As to the appointment of officers, the weight of sentiment in the House, was opposed to the exercise of it by the President alone; though it was not the case with himself. If the Senate would act as was suspected, in misleading the States into a fallacious disposition of their votes for a President, they would, if the appointment were withdrawn wholly from them, make such representations in their several States where they have influence, as would favor the object of their partiality.

Mr. Hamilton said that he had been restrained from entering into the discussions by his dislike of the Scheme of Govt. in General; but as he meant to support the plan to be recommended, as better than nothing, he wished in this place to offer a few remarks. He liked the new modification, on the whole, better than that in the printed Report. In this the President was a Monster elected for seven years, and ineligible afterwards; having great powers, in appointments to office, & continually tempted by this constitutional disqualification to abuse them in order to subvert the Government. Although he should be made re-eligible, still if appointed by the Legislature, he would be tempted to make use of corrupt influence to be continued in office. It seemed peculiarly desireable therefore that some other mode of election should be devised. Considering the different views of different States, & the different districts Northern Middle & Southern, he concurred with those who thought that the votes would not be concentered, and that the appointment would consequently in the present mode devolve on the Senate. The nomination to offices will give great weight to the President. Here then is a mutual connection & influence, that will perpetuate the President, and aggrandize both him & the Senate. What is to be the remedy? He saw none better than to let the highest number of ballots, whether a majority or not, appoint the President. What was the objection to this? Merely that too small a number might appoint. But as the plan stands, the Senate may take the candidate having the smallest number of votes, and make him President.

On a question on the clause referring the eventual appointment of the President to the Senate, N.H. ay. Mas. ay. Ct. ay. N.J. ay. Pa. ay. Del. ay. Va. ay. N.C. no. Here the call ceased.

Mr. Madison made a motion requiring 2/3 at least of the Senate to be present at the choice of a President. Mr. Pinkney 2ded the motion.

Mr. Gorham thought it a wrong principle to require more than a majority in any case. In the present case it might prevent for a long time any choice of a President.

On the question moved by Mr. M. & Mr. P., N.H. ay: Mas. abst. Ct. no. N.J. no. Pa. no. Del. no. Md. ay. Va. ay. N.C. ay. S.C. ay. Geo. ay.

Mr. Willamson suggested as better than an eventual choice by the Senate, that this choice should be made by the Legislature, voting *by States* and not *per capita.*

Mr. Sherman suggested the House of Reps as preferable to the Legislature, and moved, accordingly, to strike out the words "The Senate shall immediately choose &c." and insert "The House of Representatives shall immediately choose by ballot one of them for President, the members from each State having one vote."

Col. Mason liked the latter mode best as lessening the aristocratic influence of the Senate.

On the Motion of Mr. Sherman, N.H. ay. Mas. ay. Ct. ay. N.J. ay. Pa. ay. Del. no. Md. ay. Va. ay. N.C. ay. S.C. ay. Gen. ay.

Friday, September 7

In Convention

Mr. Gerry moved "that in the election of President by the House of Representatives, no State shall vote by less than three members, and where that number may not be allotted to a State, it shall be made up by its Senators; and a concurrence of a majority of all the States shall be necessary to make such choice." Without some such provision five individuals might possibly be competent to an election; these being a majority of two thirds of the existing number of States; and two thirds being a quorum for this business.

Mr. Madison 2ded the motion.

Mr. Read observed that the States having but one member only in the House of Reps. would be in danger of having no vote at all in the election: the sickness or absence either of the Representative or one of the Senators would have that effect.

Mr. Madison replied that, if one member of the House of Representatives should be left capable of voting for the State, the states having one Representative only would still be subject to that danger. He thought it an evil that so small a number at any rate should be authorized, to elect. Corruption would be greatly facilitated by it. The mode itself was liable to this further weighty objection that the representatives of a *Minority* of the people, might reverse the choice of a *majority* of the *States* and of the *people,* He wished some cure for this inconveniency might yet be provided.

Mr. Gerry withdrew the first part of his motion; and on the—Question on the 2d part viz. "and a concurrence of a majority of all the States shall be necessary to make such choice" to follow the words "a member or members from two thirds of the States"—

It was agreed to nem: con:

Section 3. (see Sept. 4). "The vice President shall be ex-officio President of the Senate."

Mr. Gerry opposed this regulation. We might as well put the President himself at the head of the Legislature. The close intimacy that must subsist between the President & vice-president makes it absolutely improper. He was agst. having any vice President.

Mr. Govr. Morris. The vice president then will be the first heir apparent that ever loved his father. If there should be no vice president, the President of the Senate would be temporary successor which would amount to the same thing.

Mr. Sherman saw no danger in the case. If the vice-President were not to be President of the Senate, he would be without employment, and some member by being made President must be deprived of his vote, unless when an equal division of votes might happen in the Senate, which would be but seldom.

Mr. Randolph concurred in the opposition to the clause.

Mr. Willamson, observed that such an officer as vice-President was not wanted. He was introduced only for the sake of a valuable mode of election which required two to be chosen at the same time.

Col. Mason thought the office of vice-President an encroachment on the rights of the Senate; and that it mixed too much the Legislative & Executive, which as well as the Judiciary departments, ought to be kept as separate as possible. He took occasion to express his dislike of any reference whatever of the power to make appointments to either branch of the Legislature. On the other hand he was averse to vest so dangerous a power in the President alone. As a method for avoiding both, he suggested that a privy

Council of six members to the president should be established; to be chosen for six years by the Senate, two out of the Eastern two out of the middle, and two out of the Southern quarters of the Union, & to go out in rotation two every second year; the concurrence of the Senate to be required only in the appointment of Ambassadors, and in making treaties, which are more of a legislative nature. This would prevent the constant sitting of the Senate which he thought dangerous, as well as keep the departments separate & distinct. It would also save the expence of constant sessions of the Senate. He had he said always considered the Senate as too unwieldy & expensive for appointing officers, especially the smallest, such as tide waiters &c. He had not reduced his idea to writing, but it could be easily done if it should be found acceptable.

On the question shall the vice President be ex officio President of the Senate? N.H. ay. Mas. ay. Ct. ay. N.J. no. Pa. ay. Del ay. Mas no. Va. ay. N.C. abst. S.C. ay. Geo. ay.

The other parts of the same Section (3) were then agreed to.

The Section 4.—to wit, "The President by & with the advice and consent of the Senate shall have power to make Treaties &c."

Mr. Wilson moved to add, after the word "Senate" the words, "and House of Representatives." As treaties he said are to have the operation of laws, they ought to have the sanction of laws also. The circumstance of secrecy in the business of treaties formed the only objection; but this he thought, so far as it was inconsistent with obtaining the Legislative sanction, was outweighed by the necessity of the latter.

Mr. Sherman thought the only question that could be made was whether the power could be safely trusted to the Senate. He thought it could; and that the necessity of secresy in the case of treaties forbade a reference of them to the whole Legislature.

Mr. Fitzimmon 2ded the motion of Mr. Wilson, & on the question N.H. no. Mas. no. Ct. no. N.J. no. Pa. ay. Del. no. Md. no. Va. no. N.C. no. S.C. no. Geo. no.

The first sentence as to making treaties was then Agreed to: nem: con:

"He shall nominate &c Appoint Ambassadors &c."

Mr. Wilson objected to the mode of appointing, as blending a branch of the Legislature with the Executive. Good laws are of no effect without a good Executive; and there can be no good Executive without a responsible appointment of officers to execute. Responsibility is in a manner destroyed by such an agency of the Senate. He would prefer the council proposed by Col. Mason, provided its advice should not be made obligatory on the President.

Mr. Pinkney was against joining the Senate in these appointments, except in the instance of Ambassadors whom he thought ought not to be appointed by the President.

Mr. Govr. Morris said that as the President was to nominate, there would be responsibility, and as the Senate was to concur, there would be security. As Congress now make appointments there is no responsibility.

Mr. Gerry. The idea of responsibility in the nomination to offices is chimerical. The President can not know all characters, and can therefore always plead ignorance.

Mr. King. As the idea of a Council proposed by Col. Mason has been supported by Mr. Wilson, he would remark that most of the inconveniencies charged on the Senate are incident to a Council of Advice. He differed from those who thought the Senate would sit constantly. He did not suppose it was meant that all the minute officers were to be appointed by the Senate, or any other original source, but by the higher officers of the departments to which they belong. He was of opinion also that the people wold be alarmed at an unnecessary creation of new Corps which must increase the expence as well as influence of the Government.

On the question on these words in the clause viz.—"He shall nominate & by & with the advice and consent of the Senate, shall appoint ambassadors, and other public ministers (and Consuls) Judges of the Supreme Court." Agreed to nem. con. the insertion of "and consuls" having first taken place.

Section 4. "The President by and with the advice and consent of the Senate shall have power to make Treaties"—"*But no treaty shall be made without the consent of two thirds of the members present*"—this last being before the House.

Mr. Wilson thought it objectionable to require the concurrence of 2/3 which puts it in the power of a minority to controul the will of a majority.

Mr. King concurred in the objection; remarking that as the Executive was here joined in the business, there was a check which did not exist in Congress where The concurrence of 2/3 was required.

Mr. Madison moved to insert after the word "treaty" the words "except treaties of peace" allowing these to be made with less difficulty than other treaties.—It was agreed to nem: con:

Mr. Madison then moved to authorise a concurrence of two thirds of the Senate to make treaties of peace, without the concurrence of the President.—The President he said would necessarily derive so much power and importance from a state of war that he might be tempted, if authorised, to impede a treaty of peace.

Mr. Butler 2ded the motion.

Mr. Gorham thought the precaution unnecessary as the means of carrying on the war would not be in the hands of the President, but of the Legislature.

Mr. Govr. Morris thought the power of the President in this case harmless; and that no peace ought to be made without the concurrence of the President, who was the general Guardian of the National interests.

Mr. Butler was strenuous for the motion, as a necessary security against ambitious & corrupt Presidents. He mentioned the late perfidious policy of the Statholder in Holland; and the artifices of the Duke of Marlbro' to prolong the war of which he had the management.

Mr. Gerry was of opinion that in treaties of peace a greater rather than less proportion of votes was necessary, than in other treaties. In Treaties of peace the dearest interests will be at stake, as the fisheries, territory &c. In treaties of peace also there is more danger to the extremities of the Continent, of being sacrificed, than on any other occasions.

Mr. Williamson thought that Treaties of peace should be guarded at least by requiring the same concurrence as in other Treaties.

On the motion of Mr. Madison & Mr. Butler, N.H. no. Mas. no. Ct. no. N.J. no. Pa. no. Del. no. Md. ay. Va. no. N.C. no. S.C. ay. Geo. ay.

On the part of the clause concerning treaties amended by the exception as to Treaties of peace, N.H. ay. Mas. ay. Ct. ay. N.J. no. Pa. no. Del. ay. Md. ay. Va. ay. N.C. ay. S.C. ay. Geo. no.

"And may require the opinion in writing of the principal officer in each of the Executive Departments, upon any subject relating to the duties of their respective offices," being before the House.

Col. Mason said that in rejecting a Council to the President we were about to try an experiment on which the most despotic Governments had never ventured. The Grand Signor himself had his Divan. He moved to postpone the consideration of the clause in order to take up the following:

"That it be an instruction to the Committee of the States to prepare a clause or clauses for establishing an Executive Council, as a Council of State, for the President of the U. States, to consist of six members, two of which from the Eastern, two from the middle, and two from the Southern States, with a Rotation and duration of office similar to those of the Senate; such Council to be appointed by the Legislature or by the Senate."

Doctor Franklin 2ded the motion. We seemed he said too much to fear cabals in appointments by a number, and to have too much confidence in those of single persons. Experience shewed that caprice, the intrigues of favorites & mistresses, &c were nevertheless the means most prevalent in monarchies. Among instances of abuse in such modes of appointment, he mentioned the many bad Governors appointed in G.B. for the Colonies. He thought a Council would not only be a check on a bad President but be a relief to a good one.

Mr. Govr. Morris. The question of a Council was considered in the Committee, where it was judged that the Presidt. by persuading his Council, to concur in his wrong measures, would acquire their protection for them.

Mr. Wilson approved of a Council in preference to making the Senate a party to appointmts.

Mr. Dickenson was for a Council. It wd. be a singular thing if the measures of the Executive were not to undergo some previous discussion before the President.

Mr. Madison was in favor of the instruction to the Committee proposed by Col. Mason.

The motion of Mr. Mason was negatived. Maryd. ay. S.C. ay. Geo. ay—N.H. no. Mas. no. Ct. no. N.J. no Pa. no. Del. no. Va. no. N.C. no.

Saturday, September 15

In Convention

[. . .] Art 1. Sect. 10. (paragraph 2). "No State shall, without the consent of Congress lay imposts or duties on imports or exports; nor with such consent, but to the use of the Treasury of the U. States."

In consequence of the proviso moved by Col. Mason: and agreed to on the 13 Sept., this part of the section was laid aside in favor of the following substitute viz. "No State shall, without the consent of Congress, lay any imposts or duties on imports or exports, except what may be absolutely necessary for executing its Inspection laws; and the nett produce of all duties and imposts, laid by any State on imports or exports, shall be for the use of the Treasury of the U.S.; and all such laws shall be subject to the revision and controul of the Congress."

On a motion to strike out the last part "and all such laws shall be subject to the revision and controul of the Congress" it passed in the negative. N.H. no. Mas. no. Ct. no. N.J. no. Pa. divd. Del. no. Md. no. Va. ay. N.C. ay. S.C. no. Geo. ay.

The substitute was then agreed to: Virga. alone being in the negative.

The remainder of the paragraph being under consideration—viz.—"nor keep troops nor ships of war in time of peace, nor enter into any agreement or compact with another State, nor with any foreign power. Nor engage in any way, unless it shall be actually invaded by enemies, or the danger of invasion be so imminent as not to admit of delay, until Congress can be consulted."

Mr. McHenry & Mr. Carrol moved that "no State shall be restrained from laying duties of tonnage for the purpose of clearing harbours and erecting lighthouses."

Col. Mason in support of this explained and urged the situation of the Chesapeak which peculiarly required expences of this sort.

Mr. Govr. Morris. The States are not restrained from laying tonnage as the Constitution now Stands. The exception proposed will imply the contrary, and will put the States in a worse condition than the gentleman [Col Mason] wishes.

Mr. Madison. Whether the States are now restrained from laying tonnage duties depends on the extent of the power "to regulate commerce." These terms are vague, but seem to exclude this power of the States. They may certainly be restrained by Treaty. He observed that there were other objects for tonnage Duties as the support of Seamen &c. He was more & more convinced that the regulation of Commerce was in its nature indivisible and ought to be wholly under one authority.

Mr. Sherman. The power of the U. States to regulate trade being supreme can controul interferences of the State regulations when such interferences happen; so that there is no danger to be apprehended from a concurrent jurisdiction.

Mr . Langdon insisted that the regulation of tonnage was an essential part of the regulation of trade, and that the States ought to have nothing to do with it. On motion "that no State shall lay any duty on tonnage without the Consent of Congress," N.H. ay. Mas. ay. Ct. divd. N.J. ay. Pa. no. Del. ay. Md. ay. Va. no. N.C. no. S.C. ay. Geo. no.

The remainder of the paragraph was then remoulded and passed as follows viz.—"No State shall without the consent of Congress, lay any duty of tonnage, keep troops or ships of war in time of peace, enter into any agreement or compact with another State, or with a foreign power, or engage in war, unless actually invaded, or in such imminent danger as will not admit of delay."

Art: II. Sect. 2. "he shall have power to grant reprieves and pardons for offences against the U.S. &c"

Mr. Randolph moved to "except cases of treason." The prerogative of pardon in these cases was too great a trust. The President may himself be guilty. The Traytors may be his own instruments.

Col. Mason supported the motion.

Mr. Govr. Morris had rather there should be no pardon for treason, than let the power devolve on the Legislature.

Mr. Wilson. Pardon is necessary for cases of treason, and is best placed in the hands of the Executive. If he be himself a party to the guilt he can be impeached and prosecuted.

Mr. King thought it would be inconsistent with the Constitutional separation of the Executive &

Legislative powers to let the prerogative be exercised by the latter. A Legislative body is utterly unfit for the purpose. They are governed too much by the passions of the moment. In Massachussets, one assembly would have hung all the insurgents in that State: the next was equally disposed to pardon them all. He suggested the expedient of requiring the concurrence of the Senate in Acts of Pardon.

Mr. Madison admitted the force of objections to the Legislature, but the pardon of treasons was so peculiarly improper for the President that he should acquiesce in the transfer of it to the former, rather than leave it altogether in the hands of the latter. He would prefer to either an association of the Senate as a Council of advice, with the President.

Mr. Randolph could not admit the Senate into a share of the Power. the great danger to liberty lay in a combination between the President & that body.

Col. Mason. The Senate has already too much power. There can be no danger of too much lenity in legislative pardons, as the Senate must concur, & the President moreover can require 2/3 of both Houses.

On the motion of Mr. Randolph, N.H. no. Mas. no. Ct. divd. N.J. no. Pa. no. Del. no. Md. no. Va. ay. N.C. no. S.C. no. Geo. ay.

[. . .] Art. V. "The Congress, whenever two thirds of both Houses shall deem necessary, or on the application of two thirds of the Legislatures of the several States shall propose amendments to this Constitution, which shall be valid to all intents and purposes as part thereof, when the same shall have been ratified by three fourths at least of the Legislatures of the several States, or by Conventions in three fourths thereof, as the one or the other mode of ratification may be proposed by the Congress: Provided that no amendment which may be made prior to the year 1808 shall in any manner affect the I & 4 clauses in the 9. section of article 1."

Mr. Sherman expressed his fears that three fourths of the States might be brought to do things fatal to particular States, as abolishing them altogether or depriving them of their equality in the Senate. He thought it reasonable that the proviso in favor of the States importing slaves should be extended so as to provide that no State should be affected in its internal police, or deprived of its equality in the Senate.

Col. Mason thought the plan of amending the Constitution exceptionable & dangerous. As the proposing of amendments is in both the modes to depend, in the first immediately, in the second, ultimately, on Congress, no amendments of the proper kind would ever be obtained by the people, if the Government should become oppressive, as he verily believed would be the case.

Mr. Govr. Morris & Mr. Gerry moved to amend the article so as to require a Convention on application of 2/3 of the Sts.

Mr. Madison did not see why Congress would not be as much bound to propose amendments applied for by two thirds of the States as to call a Convention on the like application. He saw no objection however against providing for a Convention for the purpose of amendments, except only that difficulties might arise as to the form, the quorum &c. which in Constitutional regulations ought to be as much as possible avoided.

The motion Of Mr. Gov. Morris & Mr. Gerry was agreed to nem: con: [see the first part of the article as finally past]

Mr. Sherman moved to strike out of art. V. after "legislatures" the words "of three fourths" and so after the word "Conventions" leaving future Conventions to act in this matter, like the present Conventions according to circumstances.

On this motion, N.H. divd. Mas. ay. Ct. ay. N.J. ay. Pa. no. Del. no. Md. no. Va. no. N.C. no. S.C. no. Geo. no. [. . .]

Mr. Sherman moved according to his idea above expressed to annex to the end of the article a further proviso "that no State shall without its consent be affected in its internal police, or deprived of its equal suffrage in the Senate."

Mr. Madison. Begin with these special provisos, and every State will insist on them, for their boundaries, exports &c.

On the motion of Mr. Sherman, N.H. no. Mas. no. Ct. ay. N.J. ay. Pa. no. Del. ay. Md. no. Va. no. N.C. no. S.C. no. Geo. no.

Mr. Sherman then moved to strike out art V altogether.

Mr. Brearley 2ded the motion, on which N.H. no. Mas. no. Ct. ay. N.J. ay. Pa. no. Del. divd. Md. no S.C. no. N.C. no. Geo. no.

Mr. Govr. Morris moved to annex a further proviso—"that no State, without its consent shall be deprived of its equal suffrage in the Senate."

This motion being dictated by the circulating murmurs of the small States was agreed to without debate, no one opposing it, or on the question, saying no.

Col. Mason expressing his discontent at the power given to Congress by a bare majority to pass navigation acts, which he said would not only enhance the freight, a consequence he did not so much regard—but would enable a few rich merchants in Philada N. York & Boston, to monopolize the Staples of the Southern States & reduce their value perhaps 50 Per Ct.—moved a further proviso "that no law in nature of a navigation act be passed before the year 1808, without the consent of 2/3 of each branch of the Legislature."

On this motion N.H. no. Mas. no. Ct. no. N.J. no. Pa. no. Del. no. Md. ay. Va. ay. N.C. abst. S.C. no. Geo. ay.

Mr. Randolph animadverting on the indefinite and dangerous power given by the Constitution to Congress, expressing the pain he felt at differing from the body of the Convention, on the close of the great & awful subject of their labours, and anxiously wishing for some accomodating expedient which would relieve him from his embarrassments, made a motion importing "that amendments to the plan might be offered by the State Conventions, which should be submitted to and finally decided on by another general Convention." Should this proposition be disregarded, it would he said be impossible for him to put his name to the instrument. Whether he should oppose it afterwards he would not then decide but he would not deprive himself of the freedom to do so in his own State, if that course should be prescribed by his final judgment.

Col: Mason 2ded & followed Mr. Randolph in animadversions on the dangerous power and structure of the Government, concluding that it would end either in monarchy, or a tyrannical aristocracy; which, he was in doubt, but one or other, he was sure. This Constitution had been formed without the knowledge or idea of the people. A second Convention will know more of the sense of the people, and be able to provide a system more consonant to it. It was improper to say to the people, take this or nothing. As the Constitution now stands, he could neither give it his support or vote in Virginia; and he could not sign here what he could not support there. With the expedient of another Convention as proposed, he could sign.

Mr. Pinkney. These declarations from members so respectable at the close of this important scene, give a peculiar solemnity to the present moment. He descanted on the consequences of calling forth the deliberations & amendments of the different States on the subject of Government at large. Nothing but confusion & contrariety could spring from the experiment. The States will never agree in their plans, and the Deputies to a second Convention coming together under the discordant impressions of their Constituents, will never agree. Conventions are serious things, and ought not to be repeated. He was not without objections as well as others to the plan. He objected to the contemptible weakness & dependence of the Executive. He objected to the power of a majority only of Congs. over Commerce. But apprehending the danger of a general confusion, and an ultimate decision by the sword, he should give the plan his support.

Mr. Gerry, stated the objections which determined him to withhold his name from the Constitution. 1. the duration and reeligibility of the Senate. 2. the power of the House of Representatives to conceal their journals. 3. the power of Congress over the places of election. 4. the unlimited power of Congress over their own compensation. 5. Massachusetts has not a due share of Representatives allotted to her. 6. 3/5 of the Blacks are to be represented as if they were freemen. 7. Under the power over commerce, monopolies may be established. 8. The vice president being made head of the Senate. He could however he said get over all these, if the rights of the Citizens were not rendered insecure 1. by the general power of the Legislature to make what laws they may please to call necessary and proper. 2. raise armies and money without limit. 3. to establish a tribunal without juries, which will be a Star-chamber as to Civil cases. Under such a view of the Constitution, the best that could be done he conceived was to provide for a second general Convention.

On the question on the proposition of Mr. Randolph. All the States answered—no.

On the question to agree to the Constitution, as amended. All the States ay.

The Constitution was then ordered to be engrossed.

And the House adjourned.

Monday, September 17

In Convention

The engrossed Constitution being read,

Doc. Franklin rose with a speech in his hand, which he had reduced to writing for his own conveniency, and which Mr. Wilson read in the words following.

Mr. President,

I confess that there are several parts of this constitution which I do not at present approve, but I am not sure I shall never approve them: For having lived long, I have experienced many instances of being obliged by better information, or fuller consideration, to change opinions even on important subjects, which I once thought right, but found to be otherwise. It is therefore that the older I grow, the more apt I am to doubt my own judgment, and to pay more respect to the judgment of others. Most men indeed as well as most sects in Religion, think themselves in possession of all truth, and that wherever others differ from them it is so far error. Steele a Protestant in a Dedication tells the Pope, that the only difference between our Churches in their opinions of the certainty of their doctrines is, the Church of Rome is infallible and the Church of England is never in the wrong. But though many private persons think almost as highly of their own infallibility as of that of their sect, few express it so naturally as a certain french lady, who in a dispute with her sister, said "I don't know how it happens, Sister but I meet with no body but myself, that's always in the right—*Il n'y a que moi qui a toujours raison.*"

In these sentiments, Sir, I agree to this Constitution with all its faults, if they are such; because I think a general Government necessary for us, and there is no form of Government but what may be a blessing to the people if well administered, and believe farther that this is likely to be well administered for a course of years, and can only end in Despotism, as other forms have done before it, when the people shall become so corrupted as to need despotic Government, being incapable of any other. I doubt too whether any other Convention we can obtain, may be able to make a better Constitution. For when you assemble a number of men to have the advantage of their joint wisdom, you inevitably assemble with those men, all their prejudices, their passions, their errors of opinion, their local interests, and their selfish views. From such an assembly can a perfect production be expected? It therefore astonishes me, Sir, to find this system approaching so near to perfection as it does, and I think it will astonish our enemies, who are waiting with confidence to hear that our councils are confounded like those of the Builders of Babel, and that our States are on the point of separation, only to meet hereafter for the purpose of cutting one another's throats. Thus I consent, Sir, to this Constitution because I expect no better, and because I am not sure, that it is not the best. The opinions I have had of its errors, I sacrifice to the public good. I have never whispered a syllable of them abroad. Within these walls they were born, and here they shall die. If every one of us in returning to our Constituents were to report the objections he has had to it, and endeavor to gain partizans in support of them, we might prevent its being generally received, and thereby lose all the salutary effects & great advantages resulting naturally in our favor among foreign Nations as well as among ourselves, from our real or apparent unanimity. Much of the strength & efficiency of any Government in procuring and securing happiness to the people, depends, on opinion, on the general opinion of the goodness of the Government, as well as of the wisdom and integrity of its Governors. I hope therefore that for our own sakes as a part of the people, and for the sake of posterity, we shall act heartily and unanimously in recommending this Constitution (if approved by Congress & confirmed by the Conventions) wherever our influence may extend, and turn our future thoughts & endeavors to the means of having it well administred.

On the whole, Sir, I can not help expressing a wish that every member of the Convention who may still have objections to it, would with me, on this occasion doubt a little of his own infallibility, and to make manifest our unanimity, put his name to this instrument.—

He then moved that the Constitution be signed by the members and offered the following as a convenient form viz. "Done in Convention by the unanimous consent of *the States* present the 17th. of Sept.

&c—In Witness whereof we have hereunto subscribed our names." [. . .]

Mr. Randolph then rose and with an allusion to the observations of Doc. Franklin apologized for his refusing to sign the Constitution notwithstanding the vast majority & venerable names that would give sanction to its wisdom and its worth. He said however that he did not mean by this refusal to decide that he should oppose the Constitution without doors. He meant only to keep himself free to be governed by his duty as it should be prescribed by his future judgment. He refused to sign, because he thought the object of the Convention would be frustrated by the alternative which it presented to the people. Nine States will fail to ratify the plan and confusion must ensue. With such a view of the subject he ought not, he could not, by pledging himself to support the plan, restrain himself from taking such steps as might appear to him most consistent with the public good.

Doc. Franklin expressed his fears from what Mr. Randolph had said, that he thought himself alluded to in the remarks offered this morning to the House. He declared that when drawing up that paper he did not know that any particular member would refuse to sign his name to the instrument, and hoped to be so understood. He professed a high sense of obligation to Mr. Randolph for having brought forward the plan in the first instance, and for the assistance he had given in its progress, and hoped that he would yet lay aside his objections, and by concurring with his brethren, prevent the great mischief which the refusal of his name might produce. [. . .]

Mr. Gerry described the painful feelings of his situation, and the embarrassment under which he rose to offer any further observations on the subject wch. had been finally decided. Whilst the plan was depending, he had treated it with all the freedom he thought it deserved. He now felt himself bound as he was disposed to treat it with the respect due to the Act of the Convention. He hoped he should not violate that respect in declaring on this occasion his fears that a Civil war may result from the present crisis of the U.S. In Massachussetts, particularly he saw the danger of this calamitous event—In that State there are two parties, one devoted to Democracy, the worst he thought of all political evils, the other as violent in the opposite extreme. From the collision of these in opposing and resisting the Constitution, confusion was greatly to be feared. He had thought it necessary, for this & other reasons that the plan should have been proposed in a more mediating shape, in order to abate the heat and opposition of parties. As it has been passed by the Convention, he was persuaded it would have a contrary effect. He could not therefore by signing the Constitution pledge himself to abide by it at all events. The proposed form made no difference with him. But if it were not otherwise apparent, the refusals to sign should never be known from him. Alluding to the remarks of Doc. Franklin, he could not he said but view them as levelled at himself and the other gentlemen who meant not to sign; [. . .]

On the motion of Doc. Franklin, N.H. ay. Mas. ay. Ct. ay. N.J. ay. Pa. ay. Del. ay. Md. ay. Va. ay. N.C. ay. S.C. divd. Geo. ay.

The members then proceeded to sign the instrument.

Whilst the last members were signing it Doc. Franklin looking towards The President's Chair, at the back of which a rising sun happened to be painted, observed to a few members near him, that Painters had found it difficult to distinguish in their art a rising from a setting sun. I have said he, often and often in the course of the Session, and the vicisitudes of my hopes and fears as to its issue, looked at that behind the President without being able to tell whether it was rising or setting: But now at length I have the happiness to know that it is a rising and not a setting Sun.

The Constitution being signed by all the members except Mr. Randolph, Mr. Mason, and Mr. Gerry who declined giving it the sanction of their names, the Convention dissolved itself by an Adjournment sine die— [. . .]

James Madison

5

The Ratification Debate

This chapter focuses on the debates surrounding ratification of the Constitution. The dedication of an entire chapter to this debate is justified. Rarely in human history have a people been empowered, as Americans were in 1787–1788, to freely debate and vote on the form of government they will live under. "[I]t seems to have been reserved to the people of this country," Alexander Hamilton wrote in the first *Federalist* essay, "by their conduct and example, to decide the important question, whether societies of men are really capable or not of establishing good government from reflection and choice, or whether they are forever destined to depend for their political constitutions on accident and force." Moreover, most of the commentaries produced during these debates are cogent works of political theory, worthy of study in their own right. And as Thomas Jefferson wrote, *The Federalist* "may fairly enough be regarded as the most authentic exposition of the text of the federal Constitution, as understood by the Body which prepared and the Authority which accepted it." Even today, justices of the Supreme Court routinely refer to *The Federalist* in their opinions.

The Constitution called for special conventions in each state to vote on ratification, with approval of nine conventions "sufficient for the Establishment of this Constitution between the States so ratifying the Same." The men who drafted the proposed United States Constitution considered this process essential to its adoption. Using the amendment process laid out in the Articles of Confederation—unanimous approval by the state legislatures—would have doomed the Constitution. As Edmund Randolph explained, "Whose opposition will be most likely to be excited [against] the System? That of the local demagogues who will be degraded by it from the importance they now hold." Further, relying on state legislatures for ratification raised constitutional problems. "[I]t would be wrong to refer the plan to [the state legislatures]," George Mason argued, "because succeeding Legislatures having equal authority could undo the acts of their predecessors; and the National Govt. would stand in each State on the weak and tottering foundation of an Act of Assembly."

Thus, constitutional and political reasons led the Framers to bypass the ratification process found in the Articles. This move was controversial. Congress had called the Philadelphia convention "for the sole and express purpose of revising the Articles of Confederation." Ignoring the process outlined in the Articles—and more generally, replacing the Articles with a new Constitution—hardly seemed to the Constitution's critics to be consistent with *revising* the Articles. Also controversial was the Framers' insistence that the state ratifying conventions be limited to a simple up-or-down vote. The Framers worried that if the conventions were allowed to attach amendments to the proposed Constitution, ratification would be delayed and likely denied, as states would adopt different versions of the Constitution. Calls for a second convention to take up potential amendments were likewise rejected, though some ratifying conventions still called for one. Conventions are rarely exempt from "the pestilential influence of party animosities," James Madison explained. The Philadelphia convention was an aberration; additional conventions would lack the give-and-take that allowed the Philadelphia delegates to produce a Constitution most could agree on.

Six of the delegates opposed the convention's final work. Three of those delegates left Philadelphia before the convention had concluded its business, but Edmund Randolph, Elbridge Gerry, and George

Mason were present on the last day of the convention—and despite an eloquent appeal by Benjamin Franklin for unanimity, they refused to sign. The Framers had hoped that unanimity among the delegates, along with the weight that Franklin's and Washington's support carried, would sway public opinion decisively in favor of adoption. Instead, they found themselves immersed in a real political battle. The Anti-Federalists (the name used to designate the Constitution's opponents) were strong in many states and dominant in at least three. Moreover, when in December 1787 Luther Martin began to publish his history of the Convention (later published as *The Genuine Information . . .*), the Framers found their motives questioned. Now, in addition to having to fend off criticism of various constitutional provisions, the Framers faced charges that they had arrived in Philadelphia intent on undermining popular rule.

The Framers, then, had to argue for the Constitution by answering charges that the Constitution failed—and perhaps was designed to fail—to uphold republican principles. (The Framers, it should be noted, were equally capable of vilifying their opponents.) Their first test was in Pennsylvania, where the Anti-Federalists leveled various charges against the proposed Constitution, including the powerful one that it lacked a bill of rights. James Wilson answered this charge in his statehouse speech. His answer was less than persuasive, a rare case when the Framers' arguments were weaker than those offered by the Anti-Federalists.

The Anti-Federalists also objected vigorously that under the Constitution there would be too few elected representatives to represent the nation's increasingly large and diverse populace. In turn, it would be impossible for people to hold their representatives accountable. The result would be a population suspicious of their leaders and an elected but aristocratic ruling class who were out of touch and thus inclined to abuse power. Indeed, such a legislature would be more likely to exercise the excessive powers granted to the central government. Herein lay another core Anti-Federalist fear—that the Constitution anticipated the future consolidation of all power in a central government. The Anti-Federalists raised other objections as well, including (but not limited to) the lack of term limits; Congress' unrestricted taxing power; the violation of the political maxim regarding the importance for republican government of annual elections; the delegation of executive powers to the Senate; the constitutional assumption of a large, heterogeneous population; and the power of judicial review.

The Federalist, Hamilton's brainchild, remains the greatest political and theoretical response to the Anti-Federalists. While by January 1788, five state conventions had approved the Constitution, ratification was still uncertain. The Anti-Federalists had shown fight in Pennsylvania, and their numbers were strong in the still-to-vote key states of New York, Massachusetts, and Virginia. Eager to present a comprehensive argument for ratification to the public, Hamilton solicited the help of Madison and John Jay, and on October 27, 1787, published the first of eighty-five essays under the pseudonym of "Publius." Completed with remarkable haste, the essays present: (1) an argument for the need to retain the Union (essays #1–14); (2) the argument that no revised version of the Articles was sufficient to preserve the Union (essays #15–22); (3) the necessity of an energetic government at least as powerful as that proposed to preserve the Union (essays #23–36); (4) a consideration of the "general form of the proposed government," with an emphasis on federal-state relations (essays #37–46); and (5) an overview of the "particular structure" of the government (essays #47–84). These essays, later combined into one volume, have entered the canon of the great classics of political philosophy, and remain one of the more authoritative sources consulted by those who seek a deeper understanding of the origins and nature of the Constitution.

Alexander Hamilton, James Madison, John Jay ("Publius")

The Federalist Papers (1787–1788)

7

Alexander Hamilton

November 17, 1787

To the People of the State of New York.

It is sometimes asked, with an air of seeming triumph, what inducements, could the states have, if disunited, to make war upon each other? It would be a full answer to this question to say—precisely the same inducements, which have, at different times, deluged in blood all the nations in the world. But unfortunately for us, the question admits of a more particular answer. There are causes of difference within our immediate contemplation, of the tendency of which, even under the restraints of a federal constitution, we have had sufficient experience to enable us to form a judgment of what might be expected, if those restraints were removed.

Territorial disputes have at all times been found one of the most fertile sources of hostility among nations. Perhaps the greatest proportion of the wars that have desolated the earth have sprung from this origin. This cause would exist, among us, in full force. We have a vast tract of unsettled territory within the boundaries of the United States. There still are discordant and undecided claims between several of them; and the dissolution of the union would lay a foundation for similar claims between them all. It is well known, that they have heretofore had serious and animated discussions concerning the right to the lands which were ungranted at the time of the revolution, and which usually went under the name of crown-lands. The states within the limits of whose colonial governments they were comprised have claimed them as their property; the others have contended that the rights of the crown in this article devolved upon the union; especially as to all that part of the Western territory which, either by actual possession, or through the submission of the Indian proprietors, was subjected to the jurisdiction of the king of Great-Britain, till it was relinquished in the treaty of peace. This, it has been said, was at all events an acquisition to the confederacy by compact with a foreign power. It has been the prudent policy of congress to appease this controversy, by prevailing upon the states to make cessions to the United States for the benefit of the whole. This has been so far accomplished, as under a continuation of the union, to afford a decided prospect of an amicable termination of the dispute. A dismemberment of the confederacy however would revive this dispute, and would create others on the same subject. At present, a large part of the vacant Western territory is by cession at least, if not by any anterior right, the common property of the union. If that were at an end, the states which have made cessions, on a principle of federal compromise, would be apt, when the motive of the grant had ceased, to reclaim the lands as a reversion. The other states would no doubt insist on a proportion, by right of representation. Their argument would be that a grant, once made, could not be revoked; and that the justice of their participating in territory acquired, or secured by the joint efforts of the confederacy remained undiminished. If contrary to probability it should be admitted by all the states, that each had a right to a share of this common stock, there would still be a difficulty to be surmounted, as to a proper rule of apportionment. Different principles would be set up by different states for this purpose; and as they would affect the opposite interests of the parties, they might not easily be susceptible of a pacific adjustment.

In the wide field of Western territory, therefore, we perceive an ample theatre for hostile pretensions, without any umpire or common judge to interpose between the contending parties. To reason from the past to the future we shall have good ground to apprehend, that the sword would sometimes be appealed to as the arbiter of their differences. The circumstances of the dispute between Connecticut and Pennsylvania, respecting the lands at Wyoming, admonish us, not to be sanguine in expecting an easy accommodation of such differences. The articles of confederation obliged the parties to submit the matter to the decision of a federal court. The submission was made, and the court decided in favour of Pennsylvania. But Connecticut gave strong indications of dissatisfaction with that determination; nor did she appear to be entirely resigned to it, till by negotiation and management something like an equivalent was found for the loss she supposed herself to have sustained. Nothing here said is intended to convey the slightest censure on the conduct of that state. She no doubt sincerely believed herself to have been injured by the decision; and states like individuals, acquiesce with great reluctance in determinations to their disadvantage. [. . .]

The competitions of commerce would be another fruitful source of contention. The states less favourably circumstanced would be desirous of escaping from the disadvantages of local situation, and of sharing in the advantages of their more fortunate neighbours. Each state, or separate confederacy, would pursue a system of commercial polity peculiar to itself. This would occasion distinctions, preferences and exclusions, which would beget discontent. The habits of intercourse, on the basis of equal privileges, to which we have been accustomed from the earliest settlement of the country, would give a keener edge to those causes of discontent, than they would naturally have, independent of this circumstance. *We should be ready to denominate injuries those things which were in reality the justifiable acts of independent sovereignties consulting a distinct interest.* The spirit of enterprise, which characterises the commercial part of America, has left no occasion of displaying itself unimproved. It is not at all probable that this unbridled spirit would pay much respect to those regulations of trade, by which particular states might endeavour to secure exclusive benefits to their own citizens. The infractions of these regulations on one side, the efforts to prevent and repel them on the other, would naturally lead to outrages, and these to reprisals and wars.

The opportunities, which some states would have of rendering others tributary to them, by commercial regulations, would be impatiently submitted to by the tributary states. The relative situation of New-York, Connecticut and New-Jersey, would afford an example of this kind. New-York, from the necessities of revenue, must lay duties on her importations. A great part of these duties must be paid by the inhabitants of the two other states in the capacity of consumers of what we import. New-York would neither be willing nor able to forego this advantage. Her citizens would not consent that a duty paid by them should be remitted in favour of the citizens of her neighbours; nor would it be practicable, if there were not this impediment in the way, to distinguish the customers in our own markets. Would Connecticut and New-Jersey long submit to be taxed by New-York for her exclusive benefit? Should we be long permitted to remain in the quiet and undisturbed enjoyment of a metropolis, from the possession of which we derived an advantage so odious to our neighbours, and, in their opinion, so oppressive? Should we be able to preserve it against the incumbent weight of Connecticut on the one side, and the co-operating pressure of New-Jersey on the other? These are questions that temerity alone will answer in the affirmative.

The public debt of the union would be a further cause of collision between the separate states or confederacies. The apportionment, in the first instance, and the progressive extinguishment, afterwards, would be alike productive of ill humour and animosity. How would it be possible to agree upon a rule of apportionment satisfactory to all? There is scarcely any, that can be proposed, which is entirely free from real objections. These, as usual, would be exaggerated by the adverse interests of the parties. There are even dissimilar views among the states, as to the general principle of discharging the public debt. Some of them, either less impressed with the importance of national credit, or because their citizens have little, if any, immediate interest in the question, feel an indifference, if not a repugnance to the payment of the domestic debt, at any rate. These would be inclined to magnify the difficulties of a distribution. Others of them, a numerous body of whose citizens are creditors to the public, beyond the proportion of the state in the total amount of the national debt, would be strenuous for some equitable and effectual provision. The procrastinations of the former would excite the resentments of the latter. The settlement of a rule would in the mean time be postponed, by real differences of opinion and affected delays. The citizens of the states interested, would clamour, foreign powers would urge, for the satisfaction of their just demands; and the peace of the states would be hazarded to the double contingency of external invasion and internal contention.

Suppose the difficulties of agreeing upon a rule surmounted, and the apportionment made. Still there is great room to suppose, that the rule agreed upon would, upon experiment, be found to bear harder upon some states than upon others. Those which were sufferers by it would naturally seek for a mitigation of the burthen. The others would as naturally be disinclined to a revision, which was likely to end in an increase of their own incumbrances. Their refusal would be too plausible a pretext to the complaining states to withhold their contributions, not to be embraced with avidity; and the non compliance of these states with their engagements would be a ground of bitter dissention and altercation. If even the rule adopted should in practice justify the equality of its principle, still delinquencies in payment, on the part of some of the states, would result from a diversity of other causes—the real deficiency of resources—the mismanagement of their finances, accidental disorders in the administration of the government—and in addition to the rest the reluctance with which men commonly part with money for purposes, that have outlived the exigencies which produced them, and interfere with the supply of immediate wants. Delinquencies from whatever causes would be productive of complaints, recriminations and quarrels. There is perhaps nothing more likely to disturb the tranquillity of nations, than their being bound to mutual contributions for any common object, which does not yield an equal and coincident benefit. For it is an observation as true, as it is trite, that there is nothing men differ so readily about as the payment of money. [. . .]

8

Alexander Hamilton

November 20, 1787

To the People of the State of New York.

Assuming it therefore as an established truth that the several states, in case of disunion, or such combinations of them as might happen to be formed out of the wreck of the general confederacy, would be subject to those vicissitudes of peace and war, of friendship and enmity with each other, which have fallen to the lot of all neighbouring nations not united under one government, let us enter into a concise detail of some of the consequences that would attend such a situation.

War between the states, in the first periods of their separate existence, would be accompanied with much greater distresses than it commonly is in those countries, where regular military establishments have long obtained. The disciplined armies always kept on foot on the continent of Europe, though they bear a malignant aspect to liberty and economy, have notwithstanding been productive of the signal advantage, of rendering sudden conquests impracticable, and of preventing that rapid desolation, which used to mark the progress of war, prior to their introduction. The art of fortification has contributed to the same ends. The nations of Europe are encircled with chains of fortified places, which mutually obstruct invasion. Campaigns are wasted in reducing two or three frontier garrisons, to gain admittance into an enemy's country. Similar impediments occur at every step, to exhaust the strength and delay the progress of an invader. Formerly an invading army would penetrate into the heart of a neighbouring country, almost as soon as intelligence of its approach could be received; but now a comparatively small force of disciplined troops, acting on the defensive with the aid of posts, is able to impede and finally to frustrate the enterprises of one much more considerable. The history of war, in that quarter of the globe, is no longer a history of nations subdued and empires overturned, but of towns taken and retaken, of battles that decide nothing, of retreats more beneficial than victories, of much effort and little acquisition.

In this country the scene would be altogether reversed. The jealousy of military establishments, would postpone them as long as possible. The want of fortifications leaving the frontiers of one state open to another, would facilitate inroads. The populous states would with little difficulty over-run their less populous neighbours. Conquests would be as easy to be made as difficult to be retained. War therefore would be desultory and predatory. Plunder and devastation ever march in the train of irregulars. The calamities of individuals would make the principal figure in the events, which would characterise our military exploits.

This picture is not too highly wrought, though I confess, it would not long remain a just one. Safety from external danger is the most powerful director of national conduct. Even the ardent love of liberty will, after a time, give way to its dictates. The violent destruction of life and property incident to war—the continual effort and alarm attendant on a state of continual danger, will compel nations the most attached to liberty, to resort for repose and security, to institutions, which have a tendency to destroy their civil and political rights. To be more safe they, at length, become willing to run the risk of being less free.

The institutions chiefly alluded to are STANDING ARMIES, and the correspondent appendages of military establishments. Standing armies, it is said, are not provided against in the new constitution, and it is thence inferred, that they would exist under it.[1] This inference, from the very form of the proposition, is, at best problematical and uncertain. But STANDING ARMIES it may be replied, must inevitably result from a dissolution of the confederacy. Frequent war, and constant apprehension, which require a state of as constant preparation, will infallibly produce them. The weaker states or confederacies, would first have recourse to them, to put themselves upon an equality with their more potent neighbours. They would endeavour to supply the inferiority of population and resources, by a more regular and effective system of defence, by disciplined troops and by fortifications. They would, at the same time, be necessitated to strengthen the executive arm of government; in doing which, their constitutions would acquire a progressive direction towards monarchy. It is of the nature of war to increase the executive at the expence of the legislative authority.

The expedients which have been mentioned would soon give the states, or confederacies that made use of them, a superiority over their neighbours. Small states, or states of less natural strength, under vigorous governments, and with the assistance of disciplined armies, have often triumphed over large states, or states of greater natural strength, which have been destitute of these advantages. Neither the pride, nor the safety of the more important states, or confederacies, would permit them long to submit to this mortifying and adventitious inferiority. They would quickly resort to means similar to those by which it had been effected, to reinstate themselves in their lost pre-eminence. Thus we should in a little time see established in every part of this country, the same engines of despotism which have been the scourge of the old world. This at least would be the natural course of things, and our reasonings will be the more likely to be just, in proportion as they are accommodated to this standard.

These are not vague inferences drawn from supposed or speculative defects in a constitution, the whole power of which is lodged in the hands of the people, or their representatives and delegates, but they are solid conclusions drawn from the natural and necessary progress of human affairs.

It may perhaps be asked, by way of objection to this, why did not standing armies spring up out of the contentions which so often distracted the ancient republics of Greece? Different answers equally satisfactory, may be given to this question. The industrious habits of the people of the present day, absorbed in the pursuits of gain, and devoted to the improvements of agriculture and commerce are incompatible with the condition of a nation of soldiers, which was the true condition of the people of those republics. The means of revenue, which have been so greatly multiplied by the encrease of gold and silver, and of the arts of industry, and the science of finance, which is the offspring of modern times,

---

1. This objection will be fully examined in its proper place, and it will be shown that the only rational precaution which could have been taken on this subject has been taken; and a much better one than is to be found in any constitution that has been heretofore framed in America, most of which contain no guard at all on this subject.

concurring with the habits of nations, have produced an intire revolution in the system of war, and have rendered disciplined armies, distinct from the body of the citizens, the inseparable companion of frequent hostility.

There is a wide difference also, between military establishments in a country, seldom exposed by its situation to internal invasions, and in one which is often subject to them, and always apprehensive of them. The rulers of the former can have no good pretext, if they are even so inclined, to keep on foot armies so numerous as must of necessity be maintained in the latter. These armies being, in the first case, rarely, if at all, called into activity for interior defence, the people are in no danger of being broken to military subordination. The laws are not accustomed to relaxations, in favor of military exigencies—the civil state remains in full vigor, neither corrupted nor confounded with the principles or propensities of the other state. The smallness of the army renders the natural strength of the community an overmatch for it; and the citizens, not habituated to look up to the military power for protection, or to submit to its oppressions, neither love nor fear the soldiery: They view them with a spirit of jealous acquiescence in a necessary evil, and stand ready to resist a power which they suppose may be exerted to the prejudice of their rights.

The army under such circumstances, may usefully aid the magistrate to suppress a small faction, or an occasional mob, or insurrection; but it will be unable to enforce encroachments against the united efforts of the great body of the people.

In a country, in the predicament last described, the contrary of all this happens. The perpetual menacings of danger oblige the government to be always prepared to repel it—its armies must be numerous enough for instant defence. The continual necessity for their services enhances the importance of the soldier, and proportionably degrades the condition of the citizen. The military state becomes elevated above the civil. The inhabitants of territories, often the theatre of war, are unavoidably subjected to frequent infringements on their rights, which serve to weaken their sense of those rights; and by degrees, the people are brought to consider the soldiery not only as their protectors, but as their superiors. The transition from this disposition to that of considering them as masters, is neither remote, nor difficult: But it is very difficult to prevail upon a people under such impressions, to make a bold, or effectual resistance, to usurpations, supported by the military power. [. . .]

If we are wise enough to preserve the union, we may for ages enjoy an advantage similar to that of an insulated situation. Europe is at a great distance from us. Her colonies in our vicinity, will be likely to continue too much disproportioned in strength, to be able to give us any dangerous annoyance. Extensive military establishments cannot, in this position, be necessary to our security. But if we should be disunited, and the integral parts should either remain separated, or which is most probable, should be thrown together into two or three confederacies, we should be in a short course of time, in the predicament of the continental powers of Europe—our liberties would be a prey to the means of defending ourselves against the ambition and jealousy of each other. [. . .]

9

Alexander Hamilton

November 21, 1787

To the People of the State of New York.

A firm union will be of the utmost moment to the peace and liberty of the states as a barrier against domestic faction and insurrection. It is impossible to read the history of the petty republics of Greece and Italy, without feeling sensations of horror and disgust at the distractions with which they were continually agitated, and at the rapid succession of revolutions, by which they were kept in a state of perpetual vibration, between the extremes of tyranny and anarchy. [. . .]

From the disorders that disfigure the annals of those republics, the advocates of despotism have drawn arguments, not only against the forms of republican government, but against the very principles of civil liberty. They have decried all free government, as inconsistent with the order of society, and have indulged themselves in malicious exultation over its friends and partizans. Happily for mankind, stupendous fabrics reared on the basis of liberty, which have flourished for ages, have in a few glorious instances refuted their gloomy sophisms. And, I trust, America will be the broad and solid foundation of other edifices not less magnificent, which will be equally permanent monuments of their errors.

But it is not to be denied that the portraits, they have sketched of republican government, were too just copies of the originals from which they were taken. If it had been found impracticable, to have devised models of a more perfect structure, the enlightened friends to liberty would have been obliged to abandon the cause of that species of government as indefensible. The science of politics, however, like most other sciences has received great improvement. The efficacy of various principles is now well understood, which were either not known at all, or imperfectly known to the ancients. The regular distribution of power into distinct departments—the introduction of legislative ballances and checks—the institution of courts composed of judges, holding their offices during good behaviour—the representation of the people in the legislature by deputies of their own election—these are either wholly new discoveries or have made their principal progress towards perfection in modern times. They are means, and powerful means, by which the excellencies of republican government may be retained and its imperfections lessened or avoided. To this catalogue of circumstances, that tend to the amelioration of popular systems of civil government, I shall venture, however novel it may appear to some, to add one more on a principle, which has been made the foundation of an objection to the new constitution, I mean the ENLARGEMENT of the ORBIT within which such systems are to revolve either in respect to the dimensions of a single state, or to the consolidation of several smaller states into one great confederacy. [. . .]

The utility of a confederacy, as well to suppress faction and to guard the internal tranquillity of states, as to increase their external force and security, is in reality not a new idea. It has been practiced upon in different countries and ages, and has received the sanction of the most applauded writers, on the subjects of politics. The opponents of the PLAN proposed have with great assiduity cited and circulated the observations of Montesquieu on the necessity of a contracted territory for a republican government. But they seem not to have been apprised of the sentiments of that great man expressed in another part of his work, nor to have adverted to the consequences of the principle to which they subscribe, with such ready acquiescence.

When Montesquieu recommends a small extent for republics, the standards he had in view were of dimensions, far short of the limits of almost every one of these states. Neither Virginia, Massachusetts, Pennsylvania, New-York, North-Carolina, nor Georgia, can by any means be compared with the models, from which he reasoned and to which the terms of his description apply. If we therefore take his ideas on this point, as the criterion of truth, we shall be driven to the alternative, either of taking refuge at once in the arms of monarchy, or of splitting ourselves into an infinity of little jealous, clashing, tumultuous commonwealths, the wretched nurseries of unceasing discord and the miserable objects of universal pity or contempt. [. . .]

Referring the examination of the principle itself to another place, as has been already mentioned, it will be sufficient to remark here, that in the sense of the author who has been most emphatically quoted upon the occasion, it would only dictate a reduction of the SIZE of the more considerable MEMBERS of the union; but would not militate against their being all comprehended in one confederate government. And this is the true question, in the discussion of which we are at present interested.

So far are the suggestions of Montesquieu from standing in opposition to a general union of the states, that he explicitly treats of a CONFEDERATE REPUBLIC as the expedient for extending the sphere of popular government and reconciling the advantages of monarchy with those of republicanism.

"It is very probable (says he[2]) that mankind would have been obliged, at length, to live constantly under the government of a SINGLE PERSON, had they not contrived a kind of constitution, that has all the internal advantages of a republican, together with the external force of a monarchial government. I mean a CONFEDERATE REPUBLIC.

2. *Spirit of Laws*, Vol. 1. Book IX. Chap. I.

"This form of government is a convention, by which several smaller *states* agree to become members of a larger *one*, which they intend to form. It is a kind of assemblage of societies, that constitute a new one, capable of encreasing by means of new associations, till they arrive to such a degree of power as to be able to provide for the security of the united body.

"A republic of this kind, able to withstand an external force, may support itself without any internal corruption. The form of this society prevents all manner of inconveniences.

"If a single member should attempt to usurp the supreme authority, he could not be supposed to have an equal authority and credit, in all the confederate states. Were he to have too great influence over one, this would alarm the rest. Were he to subdue a part, that which would still remain free might oppose him with forces, independent of those which he had usurped, and overpower him before he could be settled in his usurpation.

"Should a popular insurrection happen, in one of the confederate states, the others are able to quell it. Should abuses creep into one part, they are reformed by those that remain sound. The state may be destroyed on one side, and not on the other; the confederacy may be dissolved, and the confederates preserve their sovereignty.

"As this government is composed of small republics it enjoys the internal happiness of each, and with respect to its external situation it is possessed, by means of the association of all the advantages of large monarchies."

I have thought it proper to quote at length these interesting passages, because they contain a luminous abrigement of the principal arguments in favour of the union, and must effectually remove the false impressions, which a misapplication of other parts of the work was calculated to produce. They have at the same time an intimate connection with the more immediate design of this paper; which is to illustrate the tendency of the union to repress domestic faction and insurrection.

A distinction, more subtle than accurate has been raised between a *confederacy* and a *consolidation* of the states. The essential characteristic of the first is said to be, the restriction of its authority to the members in their collective capacities, without reaching to the individuals of whom they are composed. It is contended that the national council ought to have no concern with any object of internal administration. An exact equality of suffrage between the members has also been insisted upon as a leading feature of a confederate government. These positions are in the main arbitrary; they are supported neither by principle nor precedent. It has indeed happened that governments of this kind have generally operated in the manner, which the distinction, taken notice of, supposes to be inherent in their nature—but there have been in most of them extensive exceptions to the practice, which serve to prove as far as example will go, that there is no absolute rule on the subject. And it will be clearly shewn, in the course of this investigation, that as far as the principle contended for has prevailed, it has been the cause of incurable disorder and imbecility in the government.

The definition of a *confederate republic* seems simply to be, an "assemblage of societies" or an association of two or more states into one state. The extent, modifications and objects of the federal authority are mere matters of discretion. So long as the separate organization of the members be not abolished, so long as it exists by a constitutional necessity for local purposes, though it should be in perfect subordination to the general authority of the union, it would still be, in fact and in theory, an association of states, or a confederacy. The proposed constitution, so far from implying an abolition of the state governments, makes them constituent parts of the national sovereignty by allowing them a direct representation in the senate, and leaves in their possession certain exclusive and very important portions of sovereign power. This fully corresponds, in every rational import of the terms, with the idea of a federal government.

In the Lycian confederacy, which consisted of twenty-three CITIES or republics, the largest were intitled to *three* votes in the COMMON COUNCIL, those of the middle class to *two* and the smallest to *one*. The COMMON COUNCIL had the appointment of all the judges and magistrates of the respective CITIES. This was certainly the most delicate species of interference in their internal administration; for if there be any thing, that seems exclusively appropriated to the local jurisdictions, it is the appointment of their own officers. Yet Montesquieu, speaking of this association, says "Were I to give a model of an excellent confederate republic, it would be that of Lycia." Thus we perceive that the distinctions insisted upon were not within the contemplation of this enlightened civilian, and we shall be led to conclude that they are the novel refinements of an erroneous theory.

10

James Madison

November 22, 1787

To the People of the State of New York.

Among the numerous advantages promised by a well constructed union, none deserves to be more accurately developed than its tendency to break and control the violence of faction. The friend of popular governments, never finds himself so much alarmed for their character and fate, as when he contemplates their propensity to this dangerous vice. He will not fail therefore to set a due value on any plan which, without violating the principles to which he is attached, provides a proper cure for it. The instability, injustice and confusion introduced into the public councils, have in truth been the mortal diseases under which popular governments have every where perished; as they continue to be the favorite and fruitful topics from which the adversaries to liberty derive their most specious declamations. The valuable improvements made by the American constitutions on the popular models, both ancient and modern, cannot certainly be too much admired; but it would be an unwarrantable partiality, to contend that they have as effectually obviated the danger on this side as was wished and expected. Complaints are every where heard from our most considerate and virtuous citizens, equally the friends of public and private faith, and of public and personal liberty; that our governments are too unstable; that the public good is disregarded in the conflicts of rival parties; and that measures are too often decided, not according to the rules of justice, and the rights of the minor party; but by the superior force of an interested and over-bearing majority. However anxiously we may wish that these complaints had no foundation, the evidence of known facts will not permit us to deny that they are in some degree true. It will be found indeed, on a candid review of our situation, that some of the distresses under which we labor, have been erroneously charged on the operation of our governments; but it will be found, at the same time, that other causes will not alone account for many of our heaviest misfortunes; and particularly, for that prevailing and increasing distrust of public engagements, and alarm for private rights, which are echoed from one end of the continent to the other. These must be chiefly, if not wholly, effects of the unsteadiness and injustice, with which a factious spirit has tainted our public administration.

By a faction I understand a number of citizens, whether amounting to a majority or minority of the whole, who are united and actuated by some common impulse of passion, or of interest, adverse to the rights of other citizens or to the permanent and aggregate interests of the community.

There are two methods of curing the mischiefs of faction: the one, by removing its causes; the other, by controling its effects.

There are again two methods of removing the causes of faction: the one by destroying the liberty which is essential to its existence, the other, by giving to every citizen the same opinions, the same passions, and the same interests.

It could never be more truly said than of the first remedy, that it is worse than the disease. Liberty is to faction, what air is to fire, an aliment without which it instantly expires. But it could not be a less folly to abolish liberty, which is essential to political life, because it nourishes faction, than it would be to wish the annihilation of air, which is essential to animal life, because it imparts to fire its destructive agency.

The second expedient is as impracticable, as the first would be unwise. As long as the reason of man continues fallible, and he is at liberty to exercise it, different opinions will be formed. As long as the connection subsists between his reason and his self-love, his opinions and his passions will have a reciprocal influence on each other; and the former will be objects to which the latter will attach themselves. The diversity in the faculties of men from which the rights of property originate, is not less an insuperable obstacle to an uniformity of interests. The protection of these faculties is the first object of government. From the protection of different and unequal faculties of acquiring property, the possession of different degrees and kinds of property immediately results: and from the influence of these on the sentiments and views of the respective proprietors, ensues a division of the society into different interests and parties.

The latent causes of faction are thus sown in the nature of man; and we see them every where brought into different degrees of activity, according to the different circumstances of civil society. A zeal for different opinions concerning religion, concerning government and many other points, as well of speculation as of practice; an attachment to different leaders ambitiously contending for pre-eminence and power; or to persons of other descriptions whose fortunes have been interesting to the human passions, have in turn divided mankind into parties, inflamed them with mutual animosity, and rendered them much more disposed to vex and oppress each other, than to co-operate for their common good. So strong is this propensity of mankind to fall into mutual animosities, that where no substantial occasion presents itself, the most frivolous and fanciful distinctions have been sufficient to kindle their unfriendly passions, and excite their most violent conflicts. But the most common and durable source of factions, has been the various and unequal distribution of property. Those who hold, and those who are without property, have ever formed distinct interests in society. Those who are creditors, and those who are debtors, fall under a like discrimination. A landed interest, a manufacturing interest, a mercantile interest, a monied interest, with many lesser interests, grow up of necessity in civilized nations, and divide them into different classes, actuated by different sentiments and views. The regulation of these various and interfering interests forms the principal task of modern legislation, and involves the spirit of party and faction in the necessary and ordinary operations of government.

No man is allowed to be a judge in his own cause; because his interest would certainly bias his judgment, and, not improbably, corrupt his integrity. With equal, nay with greater reason, a body of men, are unfit to be both judges and parties, at the same time; yet, what are many of the most important acts of legislation, but so many judicial determinations, not indeed concerning the rights of single persons, but concerning the rights of large bodies of citizens; and what are the different classes of legislators, but advocates and parties to the causes which they determine? Is a law proposed concerning private debts? It is a question to which the creditors are parties on one side, and the debtors on the other. Justice ought to hold the balance between them. Yet the parties are and must be themselves the judges; and the most numerous party, or, in other words, the most powerful faction must be expected to prevail. Shall domestic manufactures be encouraged, and in what degree, by restrictions on foreign manufactures? are questions which would be differently decided by the landed and the manufacturing classes; and probably by neither, with a sole regard to justice and the public good. The apportionment of taxes on the various descriptions of property, is an act which seems to require the most exact impartiality; yet, there is perhaps no legislative act in which greater opportunity and temptation are given to a predominant party, to trample on the rules of justice. Every shilling with which they over-burden the inferior number, is a shilling saved to their own pockets.

It is in vain to say, that enlightened statesmen will be able to adjust these clashing interests, and render them all subservient to the public good. Enlightened statesmen will not always be at the helm: Nor, in many cases, can such an adjustment be made at all, without taking into view indirect and remote considerations, which will rarely prevail over the immediate interest which one party may find in disregarding the rights of another, or the good of the whole.

The inference to which we are brought, is, that the *causes* of faction cannot be removed; and that relief is only to be sought in the means of controling its *effects*.

If a faction consists of less than a majority, relief is supplied by the republican principle, which enables the majority to defeat its sinister views by regular vote: It may clog the administration, it may convulse the society; but it will be unable to execute and mask its violence under the forms of the constitution. When a majority is included in a faction, the form of popular government on the other hand enables it to sacrifice to its ruling passion or interest, both the public good and the rights of other citizens. To secure the public good, and private rights against the danger of such a faction, and at the same time to preserve the spirit and the form of popular government, is then the great object to which our enquiries are directed. Let me add that it is the great desideratum, by which alone this form of government can be rescued from the opprobrium under which it has so long labored, and be recommended to the esteem and adoption of mankind.

By what means is this object attainable? Evidently by one of two only. Either the existence of the same passion or interest in a majority at the same time must be prevented; or the majority, having such co-existent passion or interest, must be rendered, by their number and local situation, unable to concert and carry into effect schemes of oppression. If the impulse and the opportunity be suffered to coincide, we well know that neither moral nor religious motives can be relied on as an adequate control. They are not found to be such on the injustice and violence of individuals, and lose their efficacy in proportion to the number combined together; that is, in proportion as their efficacy becomes needful.

From this view of the subject, it may be concluded, that a pure democracy, by which I mean a society consisting of a small number of citizens, who assemble and administer the government in person, can admit of no cure for the mischiefs of faction. A common passion or interest will, in almost every case, be felt by a majority of the whole; a communication and concert results from the form of government itself; and there is nothing to check the inducements to sacrifice the weaker party, or an obnoxious individual. Hence it is, that such democracies have ever been spectacles of turbulence and contention; have ever been found incompatible with personal security or the rights of property; and have in general been as short in their lives, as they have been violent in their deaths. Theoretic politicians, who have patronized this species of government, have erroneously supposed, that by reducing mankind to a perfect equality in their political rights, they would, at the same time, be perfectly equalized and assimilated in their possessions, their opinions, and their passions.

A republic, by which I mean a government in which the scheme of representation takes place, opens a different prospect, and promises the cure for which we are seeking. Let us examine the points in which it varies from pure democracy, and we shall comprehend both the nature of the cure, and the efficacy which it must derive from the union.

The two great points of difference between a democracy and a republic are, first, the delegation of the government, in the latter, to a small number of citizens elected by the rest: secondly, the greater number of citizens and greater sphere of country, over which the latter may be extended.

The effect of the first difference is, on the one hand to refine and enlarge the public views, by passing them through the medium of a chosen body of citizens, whose wisdom may best discern the true interest of their country, and whose patriotism and love of justice, will be least likely to sacrifice it to temporary or partial considerations. Under such a regulation, it may well happen that the public voice pronounced by the representatives of the people, will be more consonant to the public good, than if pronounced by the people themselves convened for the purpose. On the other hand, the effect may be inverted. Men of factious tempers, of local prejudices, or of sinister designs, may by intrigue, by corruption or by other means, first obtain the suffrages, and then betray the interests of the people. The question resulting is, whether small or extensive republics are most favorable to the election of proper guardians of the public weal: and it is clearly decided in favor of the latter by two obvious considerations.

In the first place it is to be remarked that however small the republic may be, the representatives must be raised to a certain number, in order to guard against the cabals of a few; and that however large it may be, they must be limited to a certain number, in order to guard against the confusion of a multitude. Hence the number of representatives in the two cases, not being in proportion to that of the constituents, and being proportionally greatest in the small republic, it follows, that if the proportion of fit characters, be not less, in the large than in the small republic, the former will present a greater option, and consequently a greater probability of a fit choice.

In the next place, as each representative will be chosen by a greater number of citizens in the large than in the small republic, it will be more difficult for unworthy candidates to practise with success the vicious arts, by which elections are too often carried; and the suffrages of the people being more free, will be more likely to centre on men who possess the most attractive merit, and the most diffusive and established characters.

It must be confessed, that in this, as in most other cases, there is a mean, on both sides of which inconveniencies will be found to lie. By enlarging too much the number of electors, you render the representative too little acquainted with all their local circumstances and lesser interests; as by reducing it too much, you render him unduly attached to these, and too little fit to comprehend and pursue great and national objects. The federal constitution forms a happy combination in this respect; the great and aggregate interests being referred to the national, the local and particular, to the state legislatures.

The other point of difference is, the greater number of citizens and extent of territory which may be brought within the compass of republican, than of democratic government; and it is this circumstance principally which renders factious combinations less to be dreaded in the former, than in the latter. The smaller the society, the fewer probably will be the distinct parties and interests composing it, the fewer the distinct parties and interests, the more frequently will a majority be found of the same party; and the smaller the number of individuals composing a majority, and the smaller the compass within which they are placed, the more easily will they concert and execute their plans of oppression. Extend the sphere, and you take in a greater variety of parties and interests; you make it less probable that a majority of the whole will have a common motive to invade the rights of other citizens; or if such a common motive exists, it will be more difficult for all who feel it to discover their own strength, and to act in unison with each other. Besides other impediments, it may be remarked, that where there is a consciousness of unjust or dishonorable purposes, communication is always checked by distrust, in proportion to the number whose concurrence is necessary.

Hence it clearly appears, that the same advantage, which a republic has over a democracy, in controling the effects of faction, is enjoyed by a large over a small republic—is enjoyed by the union over the states composing it. Does this advantage consist in the substitution of representatives, whose enlightened views and virtuous sentiments render them superior to local prejudices, and to schemes of injustice? It will not be denied, that the representation of the union will be most likely to possess these requisite endowments. Does it consist in the greater security afforded by a greater variety of parties, against the event of any one party being able to outnumber and oppress the rest? In an equal degree does the encreased variety of parties, comprised within the union, encrease this security. Does it, in fine, consist in the greater obstacles opposed to the concert and accomplishment of the secret wishes of an unjust and interested majority? Here, again, the extent of the union gives it the most palpable advantage.

The influence of factious leaders may kindle a flame within their particular states, but will be unable to spread a general conflagration through the other states: A religious sect, may degenerate into a political faction in a part of the confederacy; but the variety of sects dispersed over the entire face of it, must secure the national councils against any danger from that source: A rage for paper money, for an abolition of debts, for an equal division of property, or for any other improper or wicked project, will be less apt to pervade the whole body of the union, than a particular member of it; in the same proportion as such a malady is more likely to taint a particular county or district, than an entire state.

In the extent and proper structure of the union, therefore, we behold a republican remedy for the diseases most incident to republican government. And according to the degree of pleasure and pride, we feel in being republicans, ought to be our zeal in cherishing the spirit, and supporting the character of federalists.

11

Alexander Hamilton

November 24, 1787

To the People of the State of New York.

The importance of the union, in a commercial light, is one of those points, about which there is least room to entertain a difference of opinion, and which has in fact commanded the most general assent of men, who have any acquaintance with the subject. This applies as well to our intercourse with foreign countries, as with each other.

There are appearances to authorise a supposition, that the adventurous spirit, which distinguishes the commercial character of America, has already excited uneasy sensations in several of the maritime powers of Europe. They seem to be apprehensive of our too great interference in that carrying trade, which is the support of their navigation and the foundation of their naval strength. Those of them, which have colonies in America, look forward, to what this country is capable of becoming, with painful solicitude. They foresee the dangers, that may threaten their American dominions from the neighbourhood of states, which have all the dispositions, and would possess all the means, requisite to the creation of a powerful marine. Impressions of this kind will naturally indicate the policy of fostering divisions among us, and of depriving us as far as possible of an ACTIVE COMMERCE in our own bottoms. This would answer the threefold purpose of preventing our interference in their navigation, of monopolising the profits of our trade, and of clipping the wings, by which we might soar to a dangerous greatness. Did not prudence forbid the detail, it would not be difficult to trace by facts the workings of this policy to the cabinets of ministers.

If we continue united, we may counteract a policy so unfriendly to our prosperity in a variety of ways. By prohibitory regulations, extending at the same time throughout the states, we may oblige foreign countries to bid against each other, for the privileges of our markets. This assertion will not appear chimerical to those who are able to appreciate the importance to any manufacturing nation of the markets of three millions of people—increasing in rapid progression, for the most part exclusively addicted to agriculture, and likely from local circumstances to remain in this disposition and the immense difference there would be to the trade and navigation of such a nation, between a direct communication in its own ships, and an indirect conveyance of its products and returns, to and from America, in the ships of another country. Suppose, for instance, we had a government in America, capable of excluding Great-Britain (with whom we have at present no treaty of commerce) from all our ports, what would be the probable operation of this step upon her politics? Would it not enable us to negotiate with the fairest prospect of success for commercial privileges of the most valuable and extensive kind in the dominions of that kingdom? When these questions have been asked, upon other occasions, they have received a plausible but not a solid or satisfactory answer. It has been said, that prohibitions on our part would produce no change in the system of Britain; because she could prosecute her trade with us, through the medium of the Dutch, who would be her immediate customers and paymasters for those articles which were wanted for the supply of our markets. But would not her navigation be materially injured, by the loss of the important advantage of being her own carrier in that trade? Would not the principal part of its profits be intercepted by the Dutch, as a compensation for their agency and risk? Would not the mere circumstance of freight occasion a considerable deduction? Would not so circuitous an intercourse facilitate the competitions of other nations, by enhancing the price of British commodities in our markets, and by transferring to other hands the management of this interesting branch of the British commerce?

A mature consideration of the objects, suggested by these questions, will justify a belief, that the real disadvantages to Great-Britain from such a state of things, conspiring with the prepossessions of a great part of the nation in favour of the American trade, and with the importunities of the West-India islands, would produce a relaxation in her present system, and would let us into the enjoyment of privileges in the markets of those islands and elsewhere, from which our trade would derive the most substantial benefits. Such a point gained from the British government, and which could not be expected without an equivalent in exemptions and immunities in our markets, would be likely to have a correspondent effect on the conduct of other nations, who would not be inclined to see themselves, altogether supplanted in our trade.

A further resource for influencing the conduct of European nations towards us, in this respect would arise from the establishment of a federal navy. There can be no doubt, that the continuance of the union, under an efficient government, would put it in our power, at a period not very distant, to create a navy, which, if it could not vie with those of the great maritime powers, would at least be of respectable weight, if thrown into the scale of either of two contending parties. This would be more particularly the case in relation to operations in the West-Indies. A few ships of the line sent opportunely to the reinforcement of either side, would often be sufficient to decide the fate of a campaign, on the event of which interests of the greatest magnitude were suspended. Our position is in this respect a very commanding one. And if to this consideration we add that of the usefulness of supplies from this country, in the prosecution of military operations in the West-Indies, it will readily be perceived, that a situation so favourable would enable us to bargain with great advantage for commercial privileges. A price would be set not only upon our friendship, but upon our neutrality. By a steady adherance to the union we may hope ere long to become the arbiter of Europe in America; and to be able to incline the balance of European competitions in this part of the world as our interest may dictate.

But in the reverse of this eligible situation we shall discover, that the rivalships of the parts would make them checks upon each other, and would frustrate all the tempting advantages, which nature has kindly placed within our reach. In a state so insignificant, our commerce would be a prey to the wanton intermeddlings of all nations at war with each other; who, having nothing to fear from us, would with little scruple or remorse supply their wants by depredations on our property, as often as it fell in their way. The rights of neutrality will only be respected, when they are defended by an adequate power. A nation, despicable by its weakness, forfeits even the privilege of being neutral.

Under a vigorous national government, the natural strength and resources of the country, directed to a common interest, would baffle all the combinations of European jealousy to restrain our growth. [. . .]

But in a state of disunion these combinations might exist, and might operate with success. It would be in the power of the maritime nations, availing themselves of our universal impotence, to prescribe the conditions of our political existence; and as they have a common interest in being our carriers, and still more in preventing our being theirs, they would in all probability combine to embarrass our navigation in such a manner, as would in effect destroy it, and confine us to a PASSIVE COMMERCE. We should thus be compelled to content ourselves with the first price of our commodities, and to see the profits of our trade snatched from us to enrich our enemies and persecutors. That unequalled spirit of enterprise, which signalises the genius of the American Merchants and Navigators, and which is in itself an inexhaustible mine of national wealth, would be stifled and lost; and poverty and disgrace would overspread a country, which with wisdom might make herself the admiration and envy of the world. [. . .]

An unrestrained intercourse between the states themselves will advance the trade of each, by an interchange of their respective productions, not only for the supply of reciprocal wants at home, but for exportation to foreign markets. The veins of commerce in every part will be replenished, and will acquire additional motion and vigour from a free circulation of the commodities of every part. Commercial enterprise will have much greater scope, from the diversity in the productions of different states. When the staple of one fails, from a bad harvest or unproductive crop, it can call to its aid the staple of another. The variety not less than the value of products for exportation, contributes to the activity of foreign commerce. It can be conducted upon much better terms, with a large number of materials of a given value, than with a small number of materials of the same value; arising from the competitions of trade and from the fluctuations of markets. Particular articles may be in great demand, at certain periods, and unsaleable at others; but if there be a variety of articles it can scarcely happen that they should all be at one time in the latter predicament; and on this account the operations of the merchant would be less liable to any considerable obstruction, or stagnation. The speculative trader will at once perceive the force of these observations; and will acknowledge that the aggregate ballance of the commerce of the United States would bid fair to be much more favorable, than that of the thirteen states, without union, or with partial unions.

It may perhaps be replied to this, that whether the states are united, or disunited, there would still be an intimate intercourse between them which would answer the same ends: But this intercourse would be fettered, interrupted and narrowed by a multiplicity of causes; which in the course of these papers have been amply detailed. An unity of commercial, as well as political interests, can only result from an unity of government. [. . .]

14

James Madison

November 30, 1787

To the People of the State of New York.

We have seen the necessity of the union as our bulwark against foreign danger, as the conservator of peace among ourselves, as the guardian of our commerce and other common interests, as the only substitute for those military establishments which have subverted the liberties of the old world; and as the proper antidote for the diseases of faction, which have proved fatal to other popular governments, and of which alarming symptoms have been betrayed by our own. All that remains, within this branch of our enquiries, is to take notice of an objection, that may be drawn from the great extent of country which the union embraces. A few observations on this subject will be the more proper, as it is perceived that the adversaries of the new constitution are availing themselves of a prevailing prejudice, with regard to the practicable sphere of republican administration, in order to supply by imaginary difficulties, the want of those solid objections, which they endeavor in vain to find.

The error which limits republican government to a narrow district, has been unfolded and refuted in preceding papers. I remark here only, that it seems to owe its rise and prevalence, chiefly to the confounding of a republic with a democracy: And applying to the former reasonings drawn from the nature of the latter. The true distinction between these forms was also adverted to on a former occasion. It is, that in a democracy, the people meet and exercise the government in person; in a republic they assemble and administer it by their representatives and agents. A democracy consequently must be confined to a small spot. A republic may be extended over a large region. [. . .]

As the natural limit of a democracy is that distance from the central point, which will just permit the most remote citizens to assemble as often as their public functions demand; and will include no greater number than can join in those functions; so the natural limit of a republic is that distance from the center, which will barely allow the representatives of the people to meet as often as may be necessary for the administration of public affairs. Can it be said, that the limits of the United States exceed this distance? It will not be said by those who recollect that the Atlantic coast is the longest side of the union; that during the term of thirteen years, the representatives of the states have been almost continually assembled; and that the members from the most distant states are not chargeable with greater intermissions of attendance, than those from the states in the neighbourhood of congress. [. . .]

Favorable as this view of the subject may be, some observations remain which will place it in a light still more satisfactory.

In the first place it is to be remembered, that the general government is not to be charged with the whole power of making and administering laws. Its jurisdiction is limited to certain enumerated objects, which concern all the members of the republic, but which are not to be attained by the separate provisions of any. The subordinate governments which can extend their care to all those other objects, which can be separately provided for, will retain their due authority and activity. Were it proposed by the plan of the convention to abolish the governments of the particular states, its adversaries would have some ground for their objection, though it would not be difficult to shew that if they were abolished, the general government would be compelled by the principle of self-preservation, to reinstate them in their proper jurisdiction.

A second observation to be made is, that the immediate object of the federal constitution is to secure the union of the Thirteen Primitive states, which we know to be practicable; and to add to them such other states, as may arise in their own bosoms or in their neighbourhoods, which we cannot doubt to be equally practicable. The arrangements that may be necessary for those angles and fractions of our territory, which lie on our north western frontier, must be left to those whom further discoveries and experience will render more equal to the task.

Let it be remarked in the third place, that the intercourse throughout the union will be daily facilitated by new improvements. Roads will every where be shortened, and kept in better order; accommodations for travellers will be multiplied and meliorated;

an interior navigation on our eastern side will be opened throughout, or nearly throughout the whole extent of the Thirteen states. The communication between the western and Atlantic districts, and between different parts of each, will be rendered more and more easy by those numerous canals with which the beneficence of nature has intersected our country, and which art finds it so little difficult to connect and complete.

A fourth and still more important consideration is, that as almost every state will on one side or other, be a frontier, and will thus find in a regard to its safety, an inducement to make some sacrifices for the sake of the general protection; so the states which lie at the greatest distance from the heart of the union, and which of course may partake least of the ordinary circulation of its benefits, will be at the same time immediately contiguous to foreign nations, and will consequently stand on particular occasions, in greatest need of its strength and resources. It may be inconvenient for Georgia or the states forming our western or North Eastern borders to send their representatives to the seat of government, but they would find it more so to struggle alone against an invading enemy, or even to support alone the whole expence of those precautions, which may be dictated by the neighbourhood of continual danger. If they should derive less benefit therefore from the union in some respects, than the less distant states, they will derive greater benefit from it in other respects, and thus the proper equilibrium will be maintained throughout.

I submit to you my fellow citizens, these considerations, in full confidence that the good sense which has so often marked your decisions, will allow them their due weight and effect; and that you will never suffer difficulties, however formidable in appearance or however fashionable the error on which they may be founded, to drive you into the gloomy and perilous scene into which the advocates for disunion would conduct you. Hearken not to the unnatural voice which tells you that the people of America, knit together as they are by so many chords of affection, can no longer live together as members of the same family; can no longer continue the mutual guardians of their mutual happiness; can no longer be fellow citizens of one great respectable and flourishing empire. Hearken not to the voice which petulantly tells you that the form of government recommended for your adoption is a novelty in the political world; that it has never yet had a place in the theories of the wildest projectors; that it rashly attempts what it is impossible to accomplish. No my countrymen, shut your ears against this unhallowed language. Shut your hearts against the poison which it conveys; the kindred blood which flows in the veins of American citizens, the mingled blood which they have shed in defence of their sacred rights, consecrate their union, and excite horror at the idea of their becoming aliens, rivals, enemies. And if novelties are to be shunned, believe me the most alarming of all novelties, the most wild of all projects, the most rash of all attempts, is that of rending us in pieces, in order to preserve our liberties and promote our happiness. But why is the experiment of an extended republic to be rejected merely because it may comprise what is new? Is it not the glory of the people of America, that whilst they have paid a decent regard to the opinions of former times and other nations, they have not suffered a blind veneration for antiquity, for custom, or for names, to overrule the suggestions of their own good sense, the knowledge of their own situation, and the lessons of their own experience? To this manly spirit, posterity will be indebted for the possession, and the world for the example of the numerous innovations displayed on the American theatre, in favor of private rights and public happiness. Had no important step been taken by the leaders of the revolution for which a precedent could not be discovered, no government established of which an exact model did not present itself, the people of the United States might, at this moment, have been numbered among the melancholy victims of misguided councils, must at best have been labouring under the weight of some of those forms which have crushed the liberties of the rest of mankind. Happily for America, happily we trust for the whole human race, they pursued a new and more noble course. They accomplished a revolution which has no parallel in the annals of human society: They reared the fabrics of governments which have no model on the face of the globe. They formed the design of a great confederacy, which it is incumbent on their successors to improve and perpetuate. If their works betray imperfections, we wonder at the fewness of them. If they erred most in the structure of the union; this was the work most difficult to be executed; this is the work which has been new modelled by the act of your convention, and it is that act on which you are now to deliberate and to decide.

15

Alexander Hamilton

December 1, 1787

To the People of the State of New York.

In the course of the preceding papers, I have endeavoured, my fellow citizens, to place before you in a clear and convincing light, the importance of union to your political safety and happiness. I have unfolded to you a complication of dangers to which you would be exposed should you permit that sacred knot which binds the people of America together to be severed or dissolved by ambition or by avarice, by jealousy or by misrepresentation. [. . .]

In pursuance of the plan, which I have laid down, for the discussion of the subject, the point next in order to be examined is the "insufficiency of the present confederation to the preservation of the union." It may perhaps be asked, what need is there of reasoning or proof to illustrate a position, which is not either controverted or doubted; to which the understandings and feelings of all classes of men assent; and which in substance is admitted by the opponents as well as by the friends of the new constitution?—It must in truth be acknowledged that however these may differ in other respects, they in general appear to harmonise in this sentiment at least, that there are material imperfections in our national system, and that something is necessary to be done to rescue us from impending anarchy. The facts that support this opinion are no longer objects of speculation. They have forced themselves upon the sensibility of the people at large, and have at length extorted from those, whose mistaken policy has had the principal share in precipitating the extremity, at which we are arrived, a reluctant confession of the reality of those defects in the scheme of our federal government, which have been long pointed out and regretted by the intelligent friends of the union.

We may indeed with propriety be said to have reached almost the last stage of national humiliation. There is scarcely any thing that can wound the pride, or degrade the character of an independent nation, which we do not experience. Are there engagements to the performance of which we are held by every tie respectable among men? These are the subjects of constant and unblushing violation. Do we owe debts to foreigners and to our own citizens contracted in a time of imminent peril, for the preservation of our political existence? These remain without any proper or satisfactory provision for their discharge. Have we valuable territories and important posts in the possession of a foreign power, which by express stipulations ought long since to have been surrendered? These are still retained, to the prejudice of our interests not less than of our rights. Are we in a condition to resent, or to repel the aggression? We have neither troops nor treasury nor government.[3] Are we even in a condition to remonstrate with dignity? The just imputations on our own faith, in respect to the same treaty, ought first to be removed. Are we entitled by nature and compact to a free participation in the navigation of the Mississippi? Spain excludes us from it. Is public credit an indispensable resource in time of public danger? We seem to have abandoned its cause as desperate and irretrievable. Is commerce of importance to national wealth? Ours is at the lowest point of declension. Is respectability in the eyes of foreign powers a safeguard against foreign encroachments? The imbecility of our government even forbids them to treat with us: Our ambassadors abroad are the mere pageants of mimic sovereignty. Is a violent and unnatural decrease in the value of land a symptom of national distress? The price of improved land in most parts of the country is much lower than can be accounted for by the quantity of waste land at market, and can only be fully explained by that want of private and public confidence, which are so alarmingly prevalent among all ranks and which have a direct

3. I mean for the union.

tendency to depreciate property of every kind. Is private credit the friend and patron of industry? That most useful kind which relates to borrowing and lending is reduced within the narrowest limits, and this still more from an opinion of insecurity than from a scarcity of money. To shorten an enumeration of particulars which can afford neither pleasure nor instruction it may in general be demanded, what indication is there of national disorder, poverty and insignificance that could befal a community so peculiarly blessed with natural advantages as we are, which does not form a part of the dark catalogue of our public misfortunes?

This is the melancholy situation, to which we have been brought by those very maxims and councils, which would now deter us from adopting the proposed constitution; and which not content with having conducted us to the brink of a precipice, seem resolved to plunge us into the abyss, that awaits us below. Here, my countrymen, impelled by every motive that ought to influence an enlightened people, let us make a firm stand for our safety, our tranquillity, our dignity, our reputation. Let us at last break the fatal charm which has too long seduced us from the paths of felicity and prosperity.

It is true, as has been before observed, that facts too stubborn to be resisted have produced a species of general assent to the abstract proposition that there exist material defects in our national system; but the usefulness of the concession, on the part of the old adversaries of federal measures, is destroyed by a strenuous opposition to a remedy, upon the only principles, that can give it a chance of success. While they admit that the government of the United States is destitute of energy; they contend against conferring upon it those powers which are requisite to supply that energy: They seem still to aim at things repugnant and irreconcilable—at an augmentation of federal authority without a diminution of state authority—at sovereignty in the union and complete independence in the members. They still in fine seem to cherish with blind devotion the political monster of an *imperium in imperio*. This renders a full display of the principal defects of the confederation necessary, in order to shew, that the evils we experience do not proceed from minute or partial imperfections, but from fundamental errors in the structure of the building which cannot be amended otherwise than by an alteration in the first principles and main pillars of the fabric.

The great and radical vice in the construction of the existing confederation is in the principle of LEGALISATION for STATES or GOVERNMENTS, in their CORPORATE or COLLECTIVE CAPACITIES and as contradistinguished from the INDIVIDUALS of whom they consist. Though this principle does not run through all the powers delegated to the union; yet it pervades and governs those, on which the efficacy of the rest depends. Except as to the rule of apportionment, the United States have an indefinite discretion to make requisitions for men and money; but they have no authority to raise either by regulations extending to the individual citizens of America. The consequence of this is, that though in theory their resolutions concerning those objects are laws, constitutionally binding on the members of the union, yet in practice they are mere recommendations, which the states observe or disregard at their option. [. . .]

There is nothing absurd or impracticable in the idea of a league or alliance between independent nations, for certain defined purposes precisely stated in a treaty; regulating all the details of time, place, circumstance and quantity; leaving nothing to future discretion; and depending for its execution on the good faith of the parties. Compacts of this kind exist among all civilized nations subject to the usual vicissitudes of peace and war, of observance and non observance, as the interests or passions of the contracting powers dictate. In the early part of the present century, there was an epidemical rage in Europe for this species of compacts; from which the politicians of the times fondly hoped for benefits which were never realized. With a view to establishing the equilibrium of power and the peace of that part of the world, all the resources of negotiation were exhausted, and triple and quadruple alliances were formed; but they were scarcely formed before they were broken, giving an instructive but afflicting lesson to mankind how little dependence is to be placed on treaties which have no other sanction than the obligations of good faith; and which oppose general considerations of peace and justice to the impulse of any immediate interest or passion.

If the particular states in this country are disposed to stand in a similar relation to each other, and to drop the project of a general DISCRETIONARY SUPERINTENDENCE, the scheme would indeed be pernicious, and would entail upon us all the mischiefs that have been enumerated under the first head; but it would have the merit of being at least consistent and practicable. Abandoning all views towards a confederate government, this would bring us to a simple alliance offensive and defensive; and would place us in a situation to be alternately friends and enemies of each other as our mutual jealousies and rivalships nourished by the intrigues of foreign nations should prescribe to us.

But if we are unwilling to be placed in this perilous situation; if we will still adhere to the design of a national government, or which is the same thing of a superintending power under the direction of a common council, we must resolve to incorporate into our plan those ingredients which may be considered as forming the characteristic difference between a league and a government; we must extend the authority of the union to the persons of the citizens,—the only proper objects of government.

Government implies the power of making laws. It is essential to the idea of a law, that it be attended with a sanction; or, in other words, a penalty or punishment for disobedience. If there be no penalty annexed to disobedience, the resolutions or commands which pretend to be laws will in fact amount to nothing more than advice or recommendation. This penalty, whatever it may be, can only be inflicted in two ways; by the agency of the courts and ministers of Justice, or by military force; by the COERTION of the magistracy, or by the COERTION of arms. The first kind can evidently apply only to men—the last kind must of necessity be employed against bodies politic, or communities or states. It is evident, that there is no process of a court by which their observance of the laws can in the last resort be enforced. Sentences may be denounced against them for violations of their duty; but these sentences can only be carried into execution by the sword. In an association where the general authority is confined to the collective bodies of the communities that compose it, every breach of the laws must involve a state of war, and military execution must become the only instrument of civil obedience. Such a state of things can certainly not deserve the name of government, nor would any prudent man choose to commit his happiness to it.

There was a time when we were told that breaches, by the states, of the regulations of the federal authority were not to be expected—that a sense of common interest would preside over the conduct of the respective members, and would beget a full compliance with all the constitutional requisitions of the union. This language at the present day would appear as wild as a great part of what we now hear from the same quarter will be thought, when we shall have received further lessons from that best oracle of wisdom, experience. It at all times betrayed an ignorance of the true springs by which human conduct is actuated, and belied the original inducements to the establishment of civil power. Why has government been instituted at all? Because the passions of men will not conform to the dictates of reason and justice, without constraint. Has it been found that bodies of men act with more rectitude or greater disinterestedness than individuals? The contrary of this has been inferred by all accurate observers of the conduct of mankind; and the inference is founded upon obvious reasons. Regard to reputation has a less active influence, when the infamy of a bad action is to be divided among a number, than when it is to fall singly upon one. A spirit of faction which is apt to mingle its poison in the deliberations of all bodies of men, will often hurry the persons of whom they are composed into improprieties and excesses, for which they would blush in a private capacity.

In addition to all this, there is in the nature of sovereign power an impatience of controul, that disposes those who are invested with the exercise of it, to look with an evil eye upon all external attempts to restrain or direct its operations. From this spirit it happens that in every political association which is formed upon the principle of uniting in a common interest a number of lesser sovereignties, there will be found a kind of excentric tendency in the subordinate or inferior orbs, by the operation of which there will be a perpetual effort in each to fly off from the common center. This tendency is not difficult to be accounted for. It has its origin in the love of power. Power controuled or abridged is almost always the rival and enemy of that power by which it is controuled or abriged. This simple proposition will teach us how little reason there is to expect, that the persons, entrusted with the administration of the affairs of the particular members of a confederacy, will at all times be ready, with perfect good humour, and an unbiassed regard to the public weal, to execute the resolutions or decrees of the general authority. The reverse of this results from the constitution of man.

If therefore the measures of the confederacy cannot be executed, without the intervention of the particular administrations, there will be little prospect of their being executed at all. The rulers of the respective members, whether they have a constitutional right to do it or not, will undertake to judge of the propriety of the measures themselves. They will consider the conformity of the thing proposed or required to their immediate interests or aims, the momentary conveniences or inconveniences that would attend its adoption. All this will be done, and in a spirit of interested and suspicious scrutiny, without that knowledge of national circumstances and reasons of state, which is essential to a right judgment, and with that strong predilection in favour of local objects, which can hardly fail to mislead the decision. The same process must be repeated in every member of which the body is constituted; and the execution of the plans, framed by the councils of the whole, will always fluctuate on the discretion of the ill-informed and prejudiced opinion of every part. [. . .]

In our case, the concurrence of thirteen distinct sovereign wills is requisite under the confederation to the complete execution of every important measure, that proceeds from the union. It has happened as was to have been foreseen. The measures of the union have not been executed; and the delinquencies of the states have step by step matured themselves to an extreme; which has at length arrested all the wheels of the national government, and brought them to an awful stand. Congress at this time scarcely possess the means of keeping up the forms of administration; till the states can have time to agree upon a more substantial substitute for the present shadow of a federal government. Things did not come to this desperate extremity at once. The causes which have been specified produced at first only unequal and disproportionate degrees of compliance with the requisitions of the union. The greater deficiencies of some states furnished the pretext of example and the temptation of interest to the complying, or to the least delinquent states. Why should we do more in proportion than those who are embarked with us in the same political voyage? Why should we consent to bear more than our proper share of the common burthen? These were suggestions which human selfishness could not withstand, and which even speculative men, who looked forward to remote consequences, could not, without hesitation, combat. Each state yielding to the persuasive voice of immediate interest or convenience has successively withdrawn its support, till the frail and tottering edifice seems ready to fall upon our heads and to crush us beneath its ruins.

22

Alexander Hamilton

December 14, 1787

To the People of the State of New York.

In addition to the defects already enumerated in the existing federal system, there are others of not less importance, which concur in rendering it altogether unfit for the administration of the affairs of the union.

The want of a power to regulate commerce is by all parties allowed to be of the number. The utility of such a power has been anticipated under the first head of our inquiries; and for this reason as well as from the universal conviction entertained upon the subject, little need be added in this place. It is indeed evident, on the most superficial view, that there is no object, either as it respects the interests of trade or finance that more strongly demands a federal superintendence. The want of it has already operated as a bar to the formation of beneficial treaties with foreign powers; and has given occasions of dissatisfaction between the states. No nation acquainted with the nature of our political association would be unwise enough to enter into stipulations with the United States, conceding on their part privileges of importance, while they were apprised that the engagements on the part of the union, might at any moment be violated by its members; and while they found from experience that they might enjoy every advantage they desired in our markets, without granting us any return, but such as their momentary convenience might suggest. [. . .]

The interfering and unneighbourly regulations of some states contrary to the true spirit of the union, have in different instances given just cause of umbrage and complaint to others; and it is to be feared that examples of this nature, if not restrained by a national controul, would be multiplied and extended till they became not less serious sources of animosity and discord, than injurious impediments to the intercourse between the different parts of the confederacy. "The commerce of the German empire,[4] is in continual trammels from the multiplicity of the duties which the several princes and states exact upon the merchandizes passing through their territories; by means of which the fine streams and navigable rivers with which Germany is so happily watered, are rendered almost useless." Though the genius of the people of this country might never permit this description to be strictly applicable to us, yet we may reasonably expect, from the gradual conflicts of state regulations, that the citizens of each, would at length come to be considered and treated by the others in no better light than that of foreigners and aliens.

The power of raising armies, by the most obvious construction of the articles of the confederation, is merely a power of making requisitions upon the states for quotas of men. This practice, in the course of the late war, was found replete with obstructions to a vigorous and to an economical system of defence. It gave birth to a competition between the states, which created a kind of auction for men. In order to furnish the quotas required of them, they outbid each other, till bounties grew to an enormous and insupportable size. The hope of a still further increase afforded an inducement to those who were disposed to serve to procrastinate their inlistment; and disinclined them to engaging for any considerable periods. Hence slow and scanty levies of men in the most critical emergencies of our affairs—short inlistments at an unparalleled expence—continual fluctuations in the troops, ruinous to their discipline, and subjecting the public safety frequently to the perilous crisis of a disbanded army. Hence also those oppressive expedients for raising men which were upon several occasions practised, and which nothing but the enthusiasm of liberty would have induced the people to endure. [. . .]

The right of equal suffrage among the states is another exceptionable part of the confederation. Every idea of proportion, and every rule of fair representation conspire to condemn a principle, which gives to Rhode-Island an equal weight in the scale of power with Massachusetts, or Connecticut, or New-York; and to Delaware, an equal voice in the national deliberations with Pennsylvania or Virginia, or North-Carolina. Its operation contradicts that fundamental maxim of republican government, which requires that the sense of the majority should prevail. Sophistry may reply, that sovereigns are equal, and that a majority of the votes of the states will be a majority of confederated America. But this kind of logical legerdemain will never counteract the plain suggestions of justice and common sense. It may happen that this majority of states is a small minority of the people of America;[5] and two thirds of the people of America, could not long be persuaded, upon the credit of artificial distinctions and syllogistic subtleties, to submit their interests to the management and disposal of one third. The larger states would after a while revolt from the idea of receiving the law from the smaller. To acquiesce in such a privation of their due importance in the political scale, would be not merely to be insensible to the love of power, but even to sacrifice the desire of equality. It is neither rational to expect the first, nor just to require the last—the smaller states considering how peculiarly their safety and welfare depend on union, ought readily to renounce a pretension; which, if not relinquished would prove fatal to its duration.

It may be objected to this, that not seven but nine states, or two thirds of the whole number must consent to the most important resolutions; and it may be thence inferred, that nine states would always comprehend a majority of the inhabitants of the union.

4. *Encyclopedia,* article *Empire.*

5. New-Hampshire, Rhode-Island, New-Jersey, Delaware, Georgia, South-Carolina and Maryland, are a majority of the whole number of the states, but they do not contain one third of the people.

But this does not obviate the impropriety of an equal vote between states of the most unequal dimensions and populousness; nor is the inference accurate in point of fact; for we can enumerate nine states which contain less than a majority of the people;[6] and it is constitutionally possible, that these nine may give the vote. Besides there are matters of considerable moment determinable by a bare majority; [. . .]

But this is not all; what at first sight may seem a remedy, is in reality a poison. To give a minority a negative upon the majority (which is always the case where more than a majority is requisite to a decision) is in its tendency to subject the sense of the greater number to that of the lesser number. Congress from the non-attendance of a few states have been frequently in the situation of a Polish diet, where a single veto has been sufficient to put a stop to all their movements. A sixtieth part of the union, which is about the proportion of Delaware and Rhode-Island, has several times been able to oppose an intire bar to its operations. This is one of those refinements which in practice has an effect, the reverse of what is expected from it in theory. The necessity of unanimity in public bodies, or of something approaching towards it, has been founded upon a supposition that it would contribute to security. But its real operation is to embarrass the administration, to destroy the energy of government, and to substitute the pleasure, caprice or artifices of an insignificant, turbulent or corrupt junto, to the regular deliberations and decisions of a respectable majority. In those emergencies of a nation, in which the goodness or badness, the weakness or strength of its government, is of the greatest importance, there is commonly a necessity for action. The public business must in some way or other go forward. If a pertinacious minority can controul the opinion of a majority respecting the best mode of conducting it; the majority in order that something may be done, must conform to the views of the minority; and thus the sense of the smaller number will over-rule that of the greater, and give a tone to the national proceedings. Hence tedious delays—continual negotiation and intrigue—contemptible compromises of the public good. And yet in such a system, it is even happy when such compromises can take place: For upon some occasions, things will not admit of accommodation; and then the measures of government must be injuriously suspended or fatally defeated. It is often, by the impracticability of obtaining the concurrence of the necessary number of votes, kept in a state of inaction. Its situation must always savour of weakness—sometimes border upon anarchy.

It is not difficult to discover that a principle of this kind gives greater scope to foreign corruption as well as to domestic faction, than that which permits the sense of the majority to decide; though the contrary of this has been presumed. The mistake has proceeded from not attending with due care to the mischiefs that may be occasioned by obstructing the progress of government at certain critical seasons. When the concurrence of a large number is required by the constitution to the doing of any national act, we are apt to rest satisfied that all is safe, because nothing improper will be likely *to be done;* but we forget how much good may be prevented, and how much ill may be produced, by the power of hindering that which is necessary from being done, and of keeping affairs in the same unfavorable posture in which they may happen to stand at particular periods.

Suppose for instance we were engaged in a war, in conjunction with one foreign nation against another. Suppose the necessity of our situation demanded peace, and the interest or ambition of our ally led him to seek the prosecution of the war, with views that might justify us in making separate terms. In such a state of things, this ally of ours would evidently find it much easier by his bribes and intrigues to tie up the hands of government from making peace, where two thirds of all the votes were requisite to that object, than where a simple majority would suffice. In the first case he would have to corrupt a smaller number; in the last a greater number. Upon the same principle it would be much easier for a foreign power with which we were at war, to perplex our councils and embarrass our exertions. And in a commercial view we may be subjected to similar inconveniences. A nation, with which we might have a treaty of commerce, could with much greater facility prevent our forming a connection with her competitor in trade; though such a connection should be ever so beneficial to ourselves.

6. Add New-York and Connecticut, to the foregoing seven, and they will still be less than a majority.

Evils of this description ought not to be regarded as imaginary. One of the weak sides of republics, among their numerous advantages, is that they afford too easy an inlet to foreign corruption. An hereditary monarch, though often disposed to sacrifice his subjects to his ambition, has so great a personal interest in the government, and in the external glory of the nation, that it is not easy for a foreign power to give him an equivalent for what he would sacrifice by treachery to the state. The world has accordingly been witness to few examples of this species of royal prostitution, though there have been abundant specimens of every other kind.

In republics, persons elevated from the mass of the community, by the suffrages of their fellow-citizens, to stations of great pre-eminence and power, may find compensations for betraying their trust, which to any but minds actuated by superior virtue, may appear to exceed the proportion of interest they have in the common stock, and to over-balance the obligations of duty. Hence it is that history furnishes us with so many mortifying examples of the prevalency of foreign corruption in republican governments. [. . .]

A circumstance, which crowns the defects of the confederation, remains yet to be mentioned—the want of a judiciary power. Laws are a dead letter without courts to expound and define their true meaning and operation. The treaties of the United States to have any force at all, must be considered as part of the law of the land. Their true import as far as respects individuals, must, like all other laws, be ascertained by judicial determinations. To produce uniformity in these determinations, they ought to be submitted in the last resort, to one SUPREME TRIBUNAL. And this tribunal ought to be instituted under the same authority which forms the treaties themselves. These ingredients are both indispensable. If there is in each state, a court of final jurisdiction, there may be as many different final determinations on the same point, as there are courts. There are endless diversities in the opinions of men. We often see not only different courts, but the judges of the same court differing from each other. To avoid the confusion which would unavoidably result from the contradictory decisions of a number of independent judicatories, all nations have found it necessary to establish one court paramount to the rest—possessing a general superintendance, and authorised to settle and declare in the last resort an uniform rule of civil justice.

This is the more necessary where the frame of the government is so compounded, that the laws of the whole are in danger of being contravened by the laws of the parts. In this case if the particular tribunals are invested with a right of ultimate jurisdiction, besides the contradictions to be expected from difference of opinion, there will be much to fear from the bias of local views and prejudices, and from the interference of local regulations. As often as such an interference was to happen, there would be reason to apprehend, that the provisions of the particular laws might be preferred to those of the general laws; from the deference with which men in office naturally look up to that authority to which they owe their official existence.

The treaties of the United States, under the present constitution, are liable to the infractions of thirteen different legislatures, and as many different courts of final jurisdiction, acting under the authority of those legislatures. The faith, the reputation, the peace of the whole union, are thus continually at the mercy of the prejudices, the passions, and the interests of every member of which it is composed. Is it possible that foreign nations can either respect or confide in such a government? Is it possible that the people of America will longer consent to trust their honor, their happiness, their safety, on so precarious a foundation?

In this review of the confederation, I have confined myself to the exhibition of its most material defects; [. . .] It must be by this time evident to all men of reflection, who are either free from erroneous prepossessions, or can divest themselves of them, that it is a system so radically vicious and unsound, as to admit not of amendment but by an entire change in its leading features and characters.

The organization of congress, is itself utterly improper for the exercise of those powers which are necessary to be deposited in the union. A single assembly may be a proper receptacle of those slender, or rather fettered authorities, which have been heretofore delegated to the federal head; but it would be inconsistent with all the principles of good government, to intrust it with those additional powers which even the moderate and more rational adversaries of the proposed constitution admit ought to reside in the United States. If that plan should not be adopted; and if the necessity of union should be able to withstand the ambitious aims of those men, who may indulge magnificent schemes of personal aggrandizement from its dissolution; the probability would be, that we should run into the project of conferring supplementary powers upon congress as they are now constituted; and either the machine, from the intrinsic feebleness of its structure, will moulder into pieces in spite of our ill-judged efforts to prop it; or by successive augmentations of its force and energy, as necessity might prompt, we shall finally accumulate in a single body, all the most important prerogatives of sovereignty; and thus entail upon our posterity, one of the most execrable forms of government that human infatuation ever contrived. Thus we should create in reality that very tyranny, which the adversaries of the new constitution either are, or affect to be solicitous to avert.

It has not a little contributed to the infirmities of the existing federal system, that it never had a ratification by the PEOPLE. Resting on no better foundation than the consent of the several legislatures; it has been exposed to frequent and intricate questions concerning the validity of its powers; and has in some instances given birth to the enormous doctrine of a right of legislative repeal. Owing its ratification to the law of a state, it has been contended, that the same authority might repeal the law by which it was ratified. However gross a heresy it may be, to maintain that *a party* to *a compact* has a right to revoke that *compact*, the doctrine itself has had respectable advocates. The possibility of a question of this nature, proves the necessity of laying the foundations of our national government deeper than in the mere sanction of delegated authority. The fabric of American Empire ought to rest on the solid basis of THE CONSENT OF THE PEOPLE. The streams of national power ought to flow immediately from that pure original fountain of all legitimate authority.

23

Alexander Hamilton

December 18, 1787

To the People of the State of New York.

The necessity of a constitution, at least equally energetic with the one proposed, to the preservation of the union, is the point, at the examination of which we are now arrived.

This enquiry will naturally divide itself into three branches—the objects to be provided for by a federal government—the quantity of power necessary to the accomplishment of those objects—the persons upon whom that power ought to operate. Its distribution and organization will more properly claim our attention under the succeeding head.

The principal purposes to be answered by union are these—The common defence of the members—the preservation of the public peace as well against internal convulsions as external attacks—the regulation of commerce with other nations and between the states—the superintendence of our intercourse, political and commercial, with foreign countries.

The authorities essential to the care of the common defence are these—to raise armies—to build and equip fleets—to prescribe rules for the government of both—to direct their operations—to provide for their support. These powers ought to exist without limitation: *Because it is impossible to foresee or to define the extent and variety of national exigencies, and the correspondent extent and variety of the means which may be necessary to satisfy them.* The circumstances that endanger the safety of nations are infinite; and for this reason no constitutional shackles can wisely be imposed on the power to which the care of it is committed. This power ought to be coextensive with all the possible combinations of such circumstances; and ought to be under the direction of the same councils, which are appointed to preside over the common defence.

This is one of those truths, which to a correct and unprejudiced mind, carries its own evidence along with it; and may be obscured, but cannot be made plainer by argument or reasoning. It rests upon axioms as simple as they are universal. The *means* ought to be proportioned to the *end;* the persons, from whose agency the attainment of any *end* is expected, ought to possess the *means* by which it is to be attained.

Whether there ought to be a federal government intrusted with the care of the common defence, is a question in the first instance open to discussion; but the moment it is decided in the affirmative, it will follow, that that government ought to be cloathed with all the powers requisite to the complete execution of its trust. And unless it can be shewn, that the circumstances which may affect the public safety are reducible within certain determinate limits; unless the contrary of this position can be fairly and rationally disputed, it must be admitted, as a necessary consequence, that there can be no limitation of that authority, which is to provide for the defence and protection of the community, in any matter essential to its efficacy; that is, in any matter essential to the *formation, direction* or *support* of the NATIONAL FORCES.

Defective as the present confederation has been proved to be, this principle appears to have been fully recognized by the framers of it; though they have not made proper or adequate provision for its exercise. Congress have an unlimited discretion to make requisitions of men and money—to govern the army and navy—to direct their operations. As their requisitions are made constitutionally binding upon the states, who are in fact under the most solemn obligations to furnish the supplies required of them, the intention evidently was, that the United States should command whatever resources were by them judged requisite to the "common defence and general welfare." It was presumed that a sense of their true interests, and a regard to the dictates of good faith, would be found sufficient pledges for the punctual performance of the duty of the members to the federal head.

The experiment has, however demonstrated, that this expectation was ill founded and illusory; and the observations made under the last head, will, I imagine, have sufficed to convince the impartial and discerning, that there is an absolute necessity for an entire change in the first principles of the system: That if we are in earnest about giving the union energy and duration, we must abandon the vain project of legislating upon the states in their collective capacities: We must extend the laws of the federal government to the individual citizens of America: We must discard the fallacious scheme of quotas and requisitions, as equally impracticable and unjust. The result from all this is, that the union ought to be invested with full power to levy troops; to build and equip fleets, and to raise the revenues, which will be required for the formation and support of an army and navy, in the customary and ordinary modes practiced in other governments.

If the circumstances of our country are such, as to demand a compound instead of a simple, a confederate instead of a sole government, the essential point which will remain to be adjusted, will be to discriminate the OBJECTS, as far as it can be done, which shall appertain to the different provinces or departments of power; allowing to each the most ample authority for fulfilling the objects committed to its charge. Shall the union be constituted the guardian of the common safety? Are fleets and armies and revenues necessary to this purpose? The government of the union must be empowered to pass all laws, and to make all regulations which have relation to them. The same must be the case, in respect to commerce, and to every other matter to which its jurisdiction is permitted to extend. Is the administration of justice between the citizens of the same state, the proper department of the local governments? These must possess all the authorities which are connected with this object, and with every other that may be allotted to their particular cognizance and direction. Not to confer in each case a degree of power, commensurate to the end, would be to violate the most obvious rules of prudence and propriety, and improvidently to trust the great interests of the nation to hands, which are disabled from managing them with vigour and success.

Who so likely to make suitable provisions for the public defence, as that body to which the guardianship of the public safety is confided—which, as the center of information, will best understand the extent and urgency of the dangers that threaten—as the representative of the WHOLE will feel itself most deeply interested in the preservation of every part—which, from the responsibility implied in the duty assigned to it, will be most sensibly impressed with the necessity of proper exertions—and which, by the extension of its authority throughout the states, can alone establish uniformity and concert in the plans and measures, by which the common safety is to be secured? Is there not a manifest inconsistency in devolving upon the federal government the care of the general defence, and leaving in the state governments the *effective* powers, by which it is to be provided for? Is not a want of co-operation the infallible consequence of such a system? And will not weakness, disorder, an undue distribution of the burthens and calamities of war, an unnecessary and intolerable increase of expence, be its natural and inevitable concomitants?

Have we not had unequivocal experience of its effects in the course of the revolution, which we have just achieved?

Every view we may take of the subject, as candid enquirers after truth, will serve to convince us, that it is both unwise and dangerous to deny the federal government an unconfined authority in respect to all those objects which are intrusted to its management. It will indeed deserve the most vigilant and careful attention of the people, to see that it be modelled in such a manner, as to admit of its being safely vested with the requisite powers. [. . .] A government, the constitution of which renders it unfit to be trusted with all the powers, which a free people *ought to delegate to any government*, would be an unsafe and improper depository of the NATIONAL INTERESTS, wherever THESE can with propriety be confided, the co-incident powers may safely accompany them. [. . .] And the adversaries of the plan, promulgated by the convention would have given a better impression of their candor if they had confined themselves to showing that the internal structure of the proposed government, was such as to render it unworthy of the confidence of the people. [. . .] The POWERS are not too extensive for the OBJECTS of federal administration, or in other words, for the management of our NATIONAL INTERESTS; nor can any satisfactory argument be framed to shew that they are chargeable with such an excess. If it be true, as has been insinuated by some of the writers on the other side, that the difficulty arises from the nature of the thing, and that the extent of the country will not permit us to form a government, in which such ample powers can safely be reposed, it would prove that we ought to contract our views, and resort to the expedient of separate confederacies, which will move within more practicable spheres. [. . .]

I trust, however, that the impracticability of one general system cannot be shewn. [. . .] I flatter myself, that the observations which have been made in the course of these papers, have served to place the reverse of that position in as clear a light as any matter still in the womb of time and experience can be susceptible of. This at all events must be evident, that the very difficulty itself drawn from the extent of the country, is the strongest argument in favor of an energetic government; for any other can certainly never preserve the union of so large an empire. [. . .]

25

Alexander Hamilton

December 21, 1787

To the People of the State of New York.

[. . .] Reasons have been already given to induce a supposition, that the state governments will too naturally be prone to a rivalship with that of the union, the foundation of which will be the love of power; and that in any contest between the federal head and one of its members, the people will be most apt to unite with their local government: If in addition to this immense advantage, the ambition of the members should be stimulated by the separate and independent possession of military forces, it would afford too strong a temptation, and too great facility to them to make enterprises upon, and finally to subvert the constitutional authority of the union. On the other hand, the liberty of the people would be less safe in this state of things, than in that which left the national forces in the hands of the national government. As far as an army may be considered as a dangerous weapon of power, it had better be in those hands, of which the people are most likely to be jealous, than in those of which they are least likely to be jealous. For it is a truth which the experience of all ages has attested, that the people are commonly most in danger, when the means of injuring their rights are in the possession of those of whom they entertain the least suspicion.

The framers of the existing confederation, fully aware of the danger to the union from the separate possession of military forces by the states, have in express terms, prohibited them from having either ships or troops, unless with the consent of congress. The truth is, that the existence of a federal government and military establishments, under state authority, are not less at variance with each other, than a due supply of the federal treasury and the system of quotas and requisitions.

There are other lights besides those already taken notice of, in which the impropriety of restraints on the discretion of the national legislature will be equally manifest. The design of the objection, which has been mentioned, is to preclude standing armies in time of peace; though we have never been informed how far it is desired the prohibition should extend; whether to raising armies as well as to *keeping them up* in a season of tranquility or not. If it be confined to the latter, it will have no precise signification, and it will be ineffectual for the purpose intended. When armies are once raised, what shall be denominated "keeping them up," contrary to the sense of the constitution? What time shall be requisite to ascertain the violation? Shall it be a week, a month, or a year? Or shall we say, they may be continued as long as the danger which occasioned their being raised continues? This would be to admit that they might be kept up *in time of peace* against threatening, or impending danger; which would be at once to deviate from the literal meaning of the prohibition, and to introduce an extensive latitude of construction. Who shall judge of the continuance of the danger? This must undoubtedly be submitted to the national government—and the matter would then be brought to this issue, that the national government, to provide against apprehended danger, might, in the first instance, raise troops, and might afterwards keep them on foot, as long as they supposed the peace or safety of the community was in any degree of jeopardy. It is easy to perceive, that a discretion so latitudinary as this, would afford ample room for eluding the force of the provision. [. . .]

If to obviate this consequence, it should be resolved to extend the prohibition to the *raising* of armies in time of peace, the United States would then exhibit the most extraordinary spectacle, which the world has yet seen—that of a nation incapacitated by its constitution to prepare for defence, before it was actually invaded. [. . .] We must receive the blow before we could even prepare to return it. All that kind of policy by which nations anticipate distant danger, and meet the gathering storm, must be abstained from, as contrary to the genuine maxims of a free government. We must expose our property and liberty to the mercy of foreign invaders, and invite them, by our weakness, to seize the naked and defenceless prey, because we are afraid that rulers, created by our choice—dependent on our will—might endanger that liberty, by an abuse of the means necessary to its preservation.

Here I expect we shall be told, that the Militia of the country is its natural bulwark, and would be at all times equal to the national defence. This doctrine in substance had like to have lost us our independence. It cost millions to the United States, that might have been saved. The facts, which from our own experience forbid a reliance of this kind, are too recent to permit us to be the dupes of such a suggestion. The steady operations of war against a regular and disciplined army, can only be successfully conducted by a force of the same kind. Considerations of economy, not less than of stability and vigor, confirm this position. The American Militia, in the course of the late war, have by their valour on numerous occasions, erected eternal monuments to their fame; but the bravest of them feel and know, that the liberty of their country could not have been established by their efforts alone, however great and valuable they were. War, like most other things, is a science to be acquired and perfected by diligence, by perseverance, by time, and by practice.

All violent policy, contrary to the natural and experienced course of human affairs, defeats itself. Pennsylvania at this instant affords an example of the truth of this remark. The bill of rights of that state declares, that standing armies are dangerous to liberty, and ought not to be kept up in time of peace. Pennsylvania, nevertheless, in a time of profound peace, from the existence of partial disorders in one or two of her counties, has resolved to raise a body of troops; and in all probability, will keep them up as long as there is an appearance of danger to the public peace. The conduct of Massachusetts affords a lesson on the same subject, though on different ground. That state (without waiting for the sanction of congress as the articles of the confederation require) was compelled to raise troops to quell a domestic insurrection, and still keeps a corps in pay to prevent a revival of the spirit of revolt. [. . .] Cases are likely to occur under our governments, as well as under those of other nations, which will sometimes render a military force in time of peace essential to the security of the society; and [. . .] it is therefore improper, in this respect, to controul the legislative discretion. [. . .]

Nations pay little regard to rules and maxims calculated in their very nature to run counter to the necessities of society. Wise politicians will be cautious about fettering the government with restrictions, that cannot be observed; because they know that every breach of the fundamental laws, though dictated by necessity, impairs that sacred reverence, which ought to be maintained in the breast of rulers towards the constitution of a country, and forms a precedent for other breaches, where the same plea of necessity does not exist at all, or is less urgent and palpable.

27

Alexander Hamilton

December 25, 1787

To the People of the State of New York.

It has been urged in different shapes that a constitution of the kind proposed by the convention, cannot operate without the aid of a military force to execute its laws. [. . .] As far as I have been able to divine the latent meaning of the objectors, it seems to originate in a pre-supposition that the people will be disinclined to the exercise of federal authority in any matter of an internal nature. [. . .] Let us enquire what ground there is to presuppose that disinclination in the people. Unless we presume, at the same time, that the powers of the general government will be worse administered than those of the state governments, there seems to be no room for the presumption of ill-will, disaffection or opposition in the people. I believe it may be laid down as a general rule, that their confidence in and obedience to a government, will commonly be proportioned to the goodness or badness of its administration. [. . .]

Various reasons have been suggested in the course of these papers, to induce a probability that the general government will be better administered than the particular governments: The principal of which are that the extension of the spheres of election will present a greater option, or latitude of choice to the people, that through the medium of the state legislatures,—who are select bodies of men, and who are to appoint the members of the national senate,—there is reason to expect that this branch will generally be composed with peculiar care and judgment: That these circumstances promise greater knowledge and more comprehensive information in the national councils: And that on account of the extent of the country from which those, to whose direction they will be committed, will be drawn, they will be less apt to be tainted by the spirit of faction, and more out of the reach of those occasional ill humors or temporary prejudices and propensities, which in smaller societies frequently contaminate the public deliberations, beget injustice and oppression of a part of the community, and engender schemes, which though they gratify a momentary inclination or desire, terminate in general distress, dissatisfaction and disgust. [. . .] Until satisfactory reasons can be assigned to justify an opinion, that the federal government is likely to be administered in such a manner as to render it odious or contemptible to the people, there can be no reasonable foundation for the supposition, that the laws of the union will meet with any greater obstruction from them, or will stand in need of any other methods to enforce their execution, than the laws of the particular members. [. . .]

I will in this place hazard an observation which will not be the less just, because to some it may appear new; which is, that the more the operations of the national authority are intermingled in the ordinary exercise of government; the more the citizens are accustomed to meet with it in the common occurrences of their political life; the more it is familiarised to their sight and to their feelings; the further it enters into those objects which touch the most sensible cords, and put in motion the most active springs of the human heart; the greater will be the probability that it will conciliate the respect and attachment of the community. Man is very much a creature of habit. A thing that rarely strikes his senses will generally have but transient influence upon his mind. A government continually at a distance and out of sight, can hardly be expected to interest the sensations of the people. The inference is, that the authority of the union, and the affections of the citizens towards it, will be strengthened rather than weakened by its extension to what are called matters of internal concern; and that it will have less occasion to recur to force in proportion to the familiarity and comprehensiveness of its agency. The more it circulates through those channels and currents, in which the passions of mankind naturally flow, the less will it require the aid of the violent and perilous expedients of compulsion. [. . .]

The plan reported by the convention, by extending the authority of the federal head to the individual citizens of the several states, will enable the government to employ the ordinary magistracy of each in the execution of its laws. It is easy to perceive that this will tend to destroy, in the common apprehension, all distinction between the sources from which they might proceed; and will give the federal government the same advantage for securing a due obedience to its authority, which is enjoyed by the government of each state; in addition to the influence on public opinion, which will result from the important consideration of its having power to call to its assistance and support the resources of the whole union. It merits particular attention in this place, that the laws of the confederacy, as to the *enumerated* and *legitimate* objects of its jurisdiction, will become the SUPREME LAW of the land; to the observance of which, all officers legislative, executive and judicial in each state, will be bound by the sanctity of an oath. Thus the legislatures, courts and magistrates of the respective members will be incorporated into the operations of the national government, *as far as its just and constitutional authority extends*; and will be rendered auxiliary to the enforcement of its laws.[7] Any man, who will pursue by his own reflections the consequences of this situation, will perceive that there is good ground to calculate upon a regular and peaceable execution of the laws of the union; if its powers are administered with a common share of prudence. [. . .]

30 [29]

Alexander Hamilton

December 28, 1787

To the People of the State of New York.

It has been already observed, that the federal government ought to possess the power of providing for the support of the national forces; in which proposition was intended to be included the expence of raising troops, of building and equipping fleets, and all other expences in any wise connected with military arrangements and operations. But these are not the only objects to which the jurisdiction of the union, in respect to revenue, must necessarily be empowered to extend—It must embrace a provision for the support of the national civil list—for the payment of the national debts contracted, or that may be contracted—and in general for all those matters which will call for disbursements out of the national treasury. The conclusion is, that there must be interwoven in the frame of the government, a general power of taxation in one shape or another.

Money is with propriety considered as the vital principle of the body politic; as that which sustains its life and motion, and enables it to perform its most essential functions. A complete power therefore to procure a regular and adequate supply of revenue, as far as the resources of the community will permit, may be regarded as an indispensable ingredient in every constitution. From a deficiency in this particular, one of two evils must ensue; either the people must be subjected to continual plunder as a substitute for a more eligible mode of supplying the public wants, or the government must sink into a fatal atrophy, and in a short course of time perish. [. . .]

The present confederation, feeble as it is, intended to repose in the United States, an unlimited power of providing for the pecuniary wants of the union. But proceeding upon an erroneous principle, it has been done in such a manner as entirely to have frustrated the intention. Congress by the articles which compose that compact (as has already been stated) are authorised to ascertain and call for any sums of money necessary, in their judgment, to the service of the United States; and their requisitions, if conformable to the rule of apportionment, are in every constitutional sense obligatory upon the states. These have no right to question the propriety of the demand—no discretion beyond that of devising the ways and means of furnishing the sums demanded. But though this be strictly and truly the case; though the assumption of such a right would be an infringement of the articles of union; though it may seldom or never have been avowedly claimed; yet in practice it has been constantly exercised; and would continue to be so, as long as the revenues of the confederacy should remain dependent on the intermediate agency of its members. [. . .]

7. The sophistry which has been employed to show that this will tend to the destruction of the state governments will, in its proper place, be fully detected.

What remedy can there be for this situation but, in a change of the system, which has produced it? In a change of the fallacious and delusive system of quotas and requisitions? What substitute can there be imagined for this *ignis fatuus* in finance, but that of permitting the national government to raise its own revenues by the ordinary methods of taxation, authorised in every well ordered constitution of civil government? Ingenious men may declaim with plausibility on any subject; but no human ingenuity can point out any other expedient to rescue us from the inconveniences and embarrassments, naturally resulting from defective supplies of the public treasury.

The more intelligent adversaries of the new constitution admit the force of this reasoning; but they qualify their admission by a distinction between what they call *internal* and *external* taxation. The former they would reserve to the state governments; the latter, which they explain into commercial imposts, or rather duties on imported articles, they declare themselves willing to concede to the federal head. This distinction, however, would violate that fundamental maxim of good sense and sound policy, which dictates that every POWER ought to be proportionate to its OBJECT; and would still leave the general government in a kind of tutelage to the state governments, inconsistent with every idea of vigor or efficiency. Who can pretend that commercial imposts are or would be alone equal to the present and future exigencies of the union? Taking into the account the existing debt, foreign and domestic, upon any plan of extinguishment, which a man moderately impressed with the importance of public justice and public credit could approve, in addition to the establishments, which all parties will acknowledge to be necessary, we could not reasonably flatter ourselves, that this resource alone, upon the most improved scale, would even suffice for its present necessities. Its future necessities admit not of calculation or limitation; and upon the principle, more than once adverted to, the power of making provision for them as they arise, ought to be equally unconfined. I believe it may be regarded as a position, warranted by the history of mankind, that *in the usual progress of things, the necessities of a nation in every stage of its existence will be found at least equal to its resources.* [. . .]

If the opinions of those who contend for the distinction which has been mentioned, were to be received as evidence of truth, one would be led to conclude that there was some known point in the economy of national affairs, at which it would be safe to stop, and to say, thus far the ends of public happiness will be promoted by supplying the wants of government, and all beyond this is unworthy of our care or anxiety. How is it possible that a government half supplied and always necessitous, can fulfil the purposes of its institution—can provide for the security,—advance the prosperity—or support the reputation of the commonwealth? How can it ever possess either energy or stability, dignity or credit, confidence at home or respectability abroad? How can its administration be any thing else than a succession of expedients temporising, impotent, disgraceful? How will it be able to avoid a frequent sacrifice of its engagements to immediate necessity? How can it undertake or execute any liberal or enlarged plans of public good?

Let us attend to what would be the effects of this situation in the very first war in which we should happen to be engaged. We will presume for argument sake, that the revenue arising from the import duties answers the purposes of a provision for the public debt, and of a peace establishment for the union. Thus circumstanced, a war breaks out. What would be the probable conduct of the government in such an emergency? Taught by experience that proper dependence could not be placed on the success of requisitions: unable by its own authority to lay hold of fresh resources, and urged by considerations of national danger, would it not be driven to the expedient of diverting the funds already appropriated from their proper objects to the defence of the state? It is not easy to see how a step of this kind could be avoided; and if it should be taken, it is evident that it would prove the destruction of public credit at the very moment that it was become essential to the public safety. To imagine that at such a crisis credit might be dispensed with, would be the extreme of infatuation. In the modern system of war, nations the most wealthy are obliged to have recourse to large loans. A country so little opulent as ours, must feel this necessity in a much stronger degree. But who would lend to a government that prefaced its overtures for borrowing, by an act which demonstrated that no reliance could be placed on the steadiness of its measures for paying? The loans it might be able to procure, would be as limited in their extent as burthensome in their conditions. They would be made upon the same principles that usurers commonly lend to bankrupt and fraudulent debtors; with a sparing hand, and at enormous premiums. [. . .]

The power of creating new funds upon new objects of taxation by its own authority, would enable the national government to borrow, as far as its necessities might require. Foreigners as well as the citizens of America, could then reasonably repose confidence in its engagements; but to depend upon a government, that must itself depend upon thirteen other governments for the means of fulfilling its contracts, when once its situation is clearly understood, would require a degree of credulity, not often to be met with in the pecuniary transactions of mankind, and little reconcileable with the usual sharp-sightedness of avarice.

Reflections of this kind, may have trifling weight with men, who hope to see realized in America, the halcyon scenes of the poetic or fabulous age; but to those who believe we are likely to experience a common portion of the vicissitudes and calamities, which have fallen to the lot of other nations, they must appear entitled to serious attention. Such men must behold the actual situation of their country with painful solicitude, and deprecate the evils which ambition or revenge might, with too much facility, inflict upon it.

33 [31]

Alexander Hamilton

January 2, 1788

To the People of the State of New York.

The residue of the argument against the provisions in the constitution, in respect to taxation, is ingrafted upon the following clauses; the last clause of the eighth section of the first article, authorises the national legislature "to make all laws which shall be *necessary* and *proper*, for carrying into execution *the powers* by that constitution vested in the government of the United States, or in any department or officer thereof"; and the second clause of the sixth article declares, that "the constitution and the Laws of the United States made *in pursuance thereof*, and the treaties made by their authority shall be the *supreme law* of the land; any thing in the constitution or laws of any state to the contrary notwithstanding."

These two clauses have been the sources of much virulent invective and petulant declamation against the proposed constitution, they have been held up to the people, in all the exaggerated colours of misrepresentation, as the pernicious engines by which their local governments were to be destroyed and their liberties exterminated—as the hideous monster whose devouring jaws would spare neither sex nor age, nor high nor low, nor sacred nor profane; and yet strange as it may appear, after all this clamour, to those who may not have happened to contemplate them in the same light, it may be affirmed with perfect confidence, that the constitutional operation of the intended government would be precisely the same, if these clauses were entirely obliterated, as if they were repeated in every article. They are only declaratory of a truth, which would have resulted by necessary and unavoidable implication from the very act of constituting a federal government, and vesting it with certain specified powers. [. . .]

What is a power, but the ability or faculty of doing a thing? What is the ability to do a thing but the power of employing the *means* necessary to its execution? What is a LEGISLATIVE power but a power of making LAWS? What are the *means* to execute a LEGISLATIVE power but LAWS? What is the power of laying and collecting taxes but a *legislative power*, or a power of *making laws*, to lay and collect taxes? What are the proper means of executing such a power but *necessary* and *proper* laws?

This simple train of enquiry furnishes us at once with a test of the true nature of the clause complained of. It conducts us to this palpable truth, that a power to lay and collect taxes must be a power to pass all laws *necessary* and *proper* for the execution of that power; and what does the unfortunate and calumniated provision in question do more than declare the same truth; to wit, that the national legislature to whom the power of laying and collecting taxes had been previously given, might in the execution of that power pass all laws *necessary* and *proper* to carry it into effect? I have applied these observations thus particularly to the power of taxation, because it is the immediate subject under consideration, and because it is the most important of the authorities proposed to be conferred upon the union. But the same process will lead to the same result in relation to all other powers declared in the constitution. And it is *expressly* to execute these powers, that the sweeping clause, as it has been affectedly called, authorises the national legislature to pass all *necessary* and *proper* laws. If there be anything exceptionable, it must be sought for in the specific powers, upon which this general declaration is predicated. The declaration itself, though it may be chargeable with tautology or redundancy, is at least perfectly harmless.

But SUSPICION may ask why then was it introduced? The answer is, that it could only have been done for greater caution, and to guard against all cavilling refinements in those who might hereafter feel a disposition to curtail and evade the legitimate authorities of the union. The convention probably foresaw what it has been a principal aim of these papers to inculcate that the danger which most threatens our political welfare, is, that the state governments will finally sap the foundations of the union; and might therefore think it necessary, in so cardinal a point, to leave nothing to construction. [. . .]

But it may be again asked, who is to judge of the *necessity* and *propriety* of the laws to be passed for executing the powers of the union? I answer first that this question arises as well and as fully upon the simple grant of those powers, as upon the declaratory clause: And I answer in the second place, that the national government, like every other, must judge in the first instance of the proper exercise of its powers; and its constituents in the last. If the federal government should overpass the just bounds of its authority, and make a tyrannical use of its powers; the people whose creature it is must appeal to the standard they have formed, and take such measures to redress the injury done to the constitution, as the exigency may suggest and prudence justify. The propriety of a law in a constitutional light, must always be determined by the nature of the powers upon which it is founded. Suppose by some forced constructions of its authority (which indeed cannot easily be imagined) the federal legislature should attempt to vary the law of descent in any state; would it not be evident that in making such an attempt it had exceeded its jurisdiction and infringed upon that of the state? Suppose again that upon the pretence of an interference with its revenues, it should undertake to abrogate a land tax imposed by the authority of a state, would it not be equally evident that this was an invasion of that concurrent jurisdiction in respect to this species of tax which its constitution plainly supposes to exist in the state governments? [. . .]

But it is said, that the laws of the union are to be the *supreme law* of the land. What inference can be drawn from this or what would they amount to, if they were not to be supreme? It is evident they would amount to nothing. A LAW by the very meaning of the term includes supremacy. It is a rule which those to whom it is prescribed are bound to observe. This results from every political association. If individuals enter into a state of society the laws of that society must be the supreme regulator of their conduct. If a number of political societies enter into a larger political society, the laws which the latter may enact, pursuant to the powers entrusted to it by its constitution, must necessarily be supreme over those societies, and the individuals of whom they are composed. It would otherwise be a mere treaty, dependent on the good faith of the parties, and not a government; which is only another word for POLITICAL POWER AND SUPREMACY. But it will not follow from this doctrine that acts of the larger society which are *not pursuant* to its constitutional powers but which are invasions of the residuary authorities of the smaller societies will become the supreme law of the land. These will be merely acts of usurpation and will deserve to be treated as such. Hence we perceive that the clause which declares the supremacy of the laws of the union, like the one we have just before considered, only declares a truth, which flows immediately and necessarily from the institution of a federal government. It will not, I presume, have escaped observation that it *expressly* confines this supremacy to laws made *pursuant to the constitution*; which I mention merely as an instance of caution in the convention; since that limitation would have been to be understood though it had not been expressed.

Though a law therefore for laying a tax for the use of the United States would be supreme in its nature, and could not legally be opposed or controuled, yet a law for abrogating or preventing the collection of a tax laid by the authority of a state (unless upon imports and exports) would not be the supreme law of the land, but an usurpation of power not granted by the constitution. [. . .] The inference from the whole is—that the individual states would, under the proposed constitution, retain an independent and uncontroulable authority to raise revenue to any extent of which they may stand in need by every kind of taxation except duties on imports and exports. [. . .]

39 [38]

James Madison

January 16, 1788

To the People of the State of New York.

[. . .] The first question that offers itself is, whether the general form and aspect of the government be strictly-republican? It is evident that no other form would be reconcileable with the genius of the people of America; with the fundamental principles of the revolution; or with that honorable determination, which animates every votary of freedom, to rest all our political experiments on the capacity of mankind for self-government. If the plan of the convention therefore be found to depart from the republican character, its advocates must abandon it as no longer defensible. [. . .]

We may define a republic to be, or at least may bestow that name on, a government which derives all its powers directly or indirectly from the great body of the people; and is administered by persons holding their offices during pleasure, for a limited period, or during good behaviour. It is *essential* to such a government, that it be derived from the great body of the society, not from an inconsiderable proportion, or a favored class of it; otherwise a handful of tyrannical nobles, exercising their oppressions by a delegation of their powers, might aspire to the rank of republicans, and claim for their government the honorable title of republic. It is *sufficient* for such a government, that the persons administering it be appointed, either directly or indirectly, by the people; and that they hold their appointments by either of the tenures just specified; otherwise every government in the United States, as well as every other popular government that has been or can be well organized or well executed, would be degraded from the republican character. According to the constitution of every state in the union, some or other of the officers of government are appointed indirectly only by the people. According to most of them the chief magistrate himself is so appointed. And according to one, this mode of appointment is extended to one of the co-ordinate branches of the legislature. According to all the constitutions also, the tenure of the highest offices is extended to a definite period, and in many instances, both within the legislative and executive departments, to a period of years. According to the provisions of most of the constitutions, again, as well as according to the most respectable and received opinions on the subject, the members of the judiciary department are to retain their offices by the firm tenure of good behaviour.

On comparing the constitution planned by the convention, with the standard here fixed, we perceive at once that it is in the most rigid sense conformable to it. The house of representatives, like that of one branch at least of all the state legislatures, is elected immediately by the great body of the people. The senate, like the present congress, and the senate of Maryland, derives its appointment indirectly from the people. The president is indirectly derived from the choice of the people, according to the example in most of the states. Even the judges, with all other officers of the union, will, as in the several states, be the choice, though a remote choice, of the people themselves. The duration of the appointments is equally conformable to the republican standard, and to the model of the state constitutions. The house of representatives is periodically elective as in all the states: and for the period of two years as in the state of South-Carolina. The senate is elective for the period of six years; which is but one year more than the period of the senate of Maryland; and but two more than that of the senates of New-York and Virginia. The president is to continue in office for the period of four years; as in New-York and Delaware, the chief magistrate is elected for three years, and in South-Carolina for two years. In the other states the election is annual. In several of the states however, no explicit provision is made for the impeachment of the chief magistrate. And in Delaware and Virginia, he is not impeachable till out of office. The president of the United States is impeachable at any time during his continuance in office. The tenure by which the judges are to hold their places, is, as it unquestionably ought to be, that of good behaviour. The tenure of the ministerial offices generally will be a subject of legal regulation, conformably to the reason of the case, and the example of the state constitutions.

Could any further proof be required of the republican complexion of this system, the most decisive one might be found in its absolute prohibition of titles of nobility, both under the federal and the state governments; and in its express guarantee of the republican form to each of the latter.

But it was not sufficient, say the adversaries of the proposed constitution, for the convention to adhere to the republican form. They ought, with equal care, to have preserved the *federal* form, which regards the union as a *confederacy* of sovereign states; instead of which, they have framed a *national* government, which regards the union as a *consolidation* of the states. And it is asked by what authority this bold and radical innovation was undertaken. The handle which has been made of this objection requires, that it should be examined with some precision.

Without enquiring into the accuracy of the distinction on which the objection is founded, it will be necessary to a just estimate of its force, first to ascertain the real character of the government in question; secondly, to enquire how far the convention were authorised to propose such a government; and thirdly, how far the duty they owed to their country, could supply any defect of regular authority.

First. In order to ascertain the real character of the government it may be considered in relation to the foundation on which it is to be established; to the sources from which its ordinary powers are to be drawn; to the operation of those powers; to the extent of them; and to the authority by which future changes in the government are to be introduced.

On examining the first relation, it appears on one hand that the constitution is to be founded on the assent and ratification of the people of America, given by deputies elected for the special purpose; but on the other, that this assent and ratification is to be given by the people, not as individuals composing one entire nation; but as composing the distinct and independent states to which they respectively belong. It is to be the assent and ratification of the several states, derived from the supreme authority in each state, the authority of the people themselves. The act therefore establishing the constitution, will not be a *national* but a *federal* act.

That it will be a federal and not a national act, as these terms are understood by the objectors, the act of the people as forming so many independent states, not as forming one aggregate nation, is obvious from this single consideration that it is to result neither from the decision of a *majority* of the people of the union, nor from that of a *majority* of the states. It must result from the *unanimous* assent of the several states that are parties to it, differing no other wise from their ordinary assent than in its being expressed, not by the legislative authority, but by that of the people themselves. Were the people regarded in this transaction as forming one nation, the will of the majority of the whole people of the United States, would bind the minority; in the same manner as the majority in each state must bind the minority; and the will of the majority must be determined either by a comparison of the individual votes; or by considering the will of the majority of the states, as evidence of the will of a majority of the people of the United States. Neither of these rules has been adopted. Each state in ratifying the constitution, is considered as a sovereign body independent of all others, and only to be bound by its own voluntary act. In this relation then the new constitution will, if established, be a *federal* and not a *national* constitution.

The next relation is to the sources from which the ordinary powers of government are to be derived. The house of representatives will derive its powers from the people of America, and the people will be represented in the same proportion, and on the same principle, as they are in the legislature of a particular state. So far the government is *national* not *federal.* The senate on the other hand will derive its powers from the states, as political and co-equal societies; and these will be represented on the principle of equality in the senate, as they now are in the existing congress. So far the government is *federal,* not *national.* The executive power will be derived from a very compound source. The immediate election of the president is to be made by the states in their political characters. The votes allotted to them, are in a compound ratio, which considers them partly as distinct and co-equal societies; partly as unequal members of the same society. The eventual election, again is to be made by that branch of the legislature which consists of the national representatives; but in this particular act, they are to be thrown into the form of individual delegations from so many distinct and co-equal bodies politic. From this aspect of the government, it appears to be of a mixed character presenting at least as many *federal* as *national* features.

The difference between a federal and national government as it relates to the *operation of the government*, is, by the adversaries of the plan of the convention, to consist in this, that in the former, the powers operate on the political bodies composing the confederacy, in their political capacities: In the latter, on the individual citizens, composing the nation, in their individual capacities. On trying the constitution by this criterion, it falls under the *national*, not the *federal* character; though perhaps not so compleatly, as has been understood. In several cases and particularly in the trial of controversies to which states may be parties, they must be viewed and proceeded against in their collective and political capacities only. But the operation of the government on the people in their individual capacities, in its ordinary and most essential proceedings, will on the whole, in the sense of its opponents, designate it in this relation, a *national* government.

But if the government be national with regard to the *operation* of its powers, it changes its aspect again when we contemplate it in relation to the *extent* of its powers. The idea of a national government involves in it, not only an authority over the individual citizens; but an indefinite supremacy over all persons and things, so far as they are objects of lawful government. Among a people consolidated into one nation, this supremacy is compleatly vested in the national legislature. Among communities united for particular purposes, it is vested partly in the general, and partly in the municipal legislatures. In the former case, all local authorities are subordinate to the supreme; and may be controuled, directed or abolished by it at pleasure. In the latter the local or municipal authorities form distinct and independent portions of the supremacy, no more subject within their respective spheres to the general authority, than the general authority is subject to them, within its own sphere. In this relation then the proposed government cannot be deemed a *national* one; since its jurisdiction extends to certain enumerated objects only, and leaves to the several states a residuary and inviolable sovereignty over all other objects. It is true that in controversies relating to the boundary between the two jurisdictions, the tribunal which is ultimately to decide, is to be established under the general government. But this does not change the principle of the case. The decision is to be impartially made, according to the rules of the constitution; and all the usual and most effectual precautions are taken to secure this impartiality. Some such tribunal is clearly essential to prevent an appeal to the sword, and a dissolution of the compact; and that it ought to be established under the general, rather than under the local governments; or to speak more properly, that it could be safely established under the first alone, is a position not likely to be combated.

If we try the constitution by its last relation, to the authority by which amendments are to be made, we find it neither wholly *national*, nor wholly *federal*. Were it wholly national, the supreme and ultimate authority would reside in the *majority* of the people of the union; and this authority would be competent at all times, like that of a majority of every national society, to alter or abolish its established government. Were it wholly federal on the other hand, the concurrence of each state in the union would be essential to every alteration that would be binding on all. The mode provided by the plan of the convention is not founded on either of these principles. In requiring more than a majority, and particularly, in computing the proportion by *states*, not by *citizens*, it departs from the *national*, and advances towards the *federal* character: In rendering the concurrence of less than the whole number of states sufficient, it loses again the *federal*, and partakes of the *national* character.

The proposed constitution therefore, even when tested by the rules laid down by its antagonists, is in strictness neither a national nor a federal constitution; but a composition of both. In its foundation, it is federal, not national; in the sources from which the ordinary powers of the government are drawn, it is partly federal, and partly national: in the operation of these powers, it is national, not federal: In the extent of them again, it is federal, not national: And finally, in the authoritative mode of introducing amendments, it is neither wholly federal, nor wholly national.

47 [46]

James Madison

January 30, 1788

To the People of the State of New York.

[. . .] One of the principal objections inculcated by the more respectable adversaries to the constitution, is its supposed violation of the political maxim, that the legislative, executive and judiciary departments ought to be separate and distinct. In the structure of the federal government, no regard, it is said, seems to have been paid to this essential precaution in favor of liberty. The several departments of power are distributed and blended in such a manner, as at once to destroy all symmetry and beauty of form; and to expose some of the essential parts of the edifice to the danger of being crushed by the disproportionate weight of other parts.

No political truth is certainly of greater intrinsic value or is stamped with the authority of more enlightened patrons of liberty than that on which the objection is founded. The accumulation of all powers legislative, executive and judiciary in the same hands, whether of one, a few or many, and whether hereditary, self appointed, or elective, may justly be pronounced the very definition of tyranny. Were the federal constitution therefore really chargeable with this accumulation of power or with a mixture of powers having a dangerous tendency to such an accumulation, no further arguments would be necessary to inspire a universal reprobation of the system. I persuade myself however, that it will be made apparent to every one, that the charge cannot be supported, and that the maxim on which it relies, has been totally misconceived and misapplied. [. . .]

The oracle who is always consulted and cited on this subject, is the celebrated Montesquieu. If he be not the author of this invaluable precept in the science of politics, he has the merit at least of displaying, and recommending it most effectually to the attention of mankind. Let us endeavour in the first place to ascertain his meaning on this point.

The British constitution was to Montesquieu, what Homer has been to the didactic writers on epic poetry. As the latter have considered the work of the immortal bard, as the perfect model from which the principles and rules of the epic art were to be drawn, and by which all similar works were to be judged; so this great political critic appears to have viewed the constitution of England, as the standard, or to use his own expression, as the mirror of political liberty; and to have delivered in the form of elementary truths, the several characteristic principles of that particular system. That we may be sure then not to mistake his meaning in this case, let us recur to the source from which the maxim was drawn.

On the slightest view of the British constitution we must perceive, that the legislative, executive and judiciary departments are by no means totally separate and distinct from each other. The executive magistrate forms an integral part of the legislative authority. He alone has the prerogative of making treaties with foreign sovereigns, which when made have, under certain limitations, the force of legislative acts. All the members of the judiciary department are appointed by him; can be removed by him on the address of the two houses of Parliament, and form, when he pleases to consult them, one of his constitutional councils. One branch of the legislative department forms also, a great constitutional council to the executive chief; as on another hand, it is the sole depositary of judicial power in cases of impeachment, and is invested with the supreme appellate jurisdiction, in all other cases. The judges again are so far connected with the legislative department, as often to attend and participate in its deliberations, though not admitted to a legislative vote.

From these facts by which Montesquieu was guided it may clearly be inferred, that in saying "there can be no liberty where the legislative and executive powers are united in the same person, or body of magistrates," or "if the power of judging be not separated from the legislative and executive powers," he did not mean that these departments ought to have no *partial agency* in, or no *controul* over the acts of each other. His meaning, as his own words import, and still more conclusively as illustrated by the example in his eye, can amount to no more than this, that where the *whole* power of one department is exercised by the same hands which possess the *whole* power of another department, the fundamental principles of a free constitution, are subverted. This would not have been the case in the constitution examined by him, if the king who is the sole executive magistrate, had possessed also the compleat legislative power, or the supreme administration of justice; or if the entire legislative body, had possessed the supreme judiciary, or the supreme executive authority. This however is not among the vices of that constitution. The magistrate in whom the whole executive power resides cannot of himself make a law, though he can put a negative on every law, nor administer justice in person, though he has the appointment of those who do administer it. The judges can exercise no executive prerogative, though they are shoots from the executive stock, nor any legislative function, though they may be advised with by the legislative councils. The entire legislature, can perform no judiciary act, though by the joint act of two of its branches, the judges may be removed from their offices; and though one of its branches is possessed of the judicial power in the last resort. The entire legislature again can exercise no executive prerogative, though one of its branches constitutes the supreme executive magistracy; and another, on the impeachment of a third, can try and condemn all the subordinate officers in the executive department.

The reasons on which Montesquieu grounds his maxim are a further demonstration of his meaning. "When the legislative and executive powers are united in the same person or body" says he, "there can be no liberty, because apprehensions may arise lest *the same* monarch or senate should *enact* tyrannical laws, to *execute* them in a tyrannical manner." Again "Were the power of judging joined with the legislative, the life and liberty of the subject would be exposed to arbitrary controul, for *the judge* would then be *the legislator.* Were it joined to the executive power, *the judge* might behave with all the violence of *an oppressor.*" [. . .]

If we look into the constitutions of the several states we find that notwithstanding the emphatical, and in some instances, the unqualified terms in which this axiom has been laid down, there is not a single instance in which the several departments of power have been kept absolutely separate and distinct. New-Hampshire, whose constitution was the last formed, seems to have been fully aware of the impossibility and inexpediency of avoiding any mixture whatever of these departments; and has qualified the doctrine by declaring "that the legislative, executive and judiciary powers ought to be kept as separate from, and independent of each other *as the nature of a free government will admit; or as is consistent with that chain of connection, that binds the whole fabric of the constitution in one indissoluble bond of unity and amity.*" Her constitution accordingly mixes these departments in several respects. The senate which is a branch of the legislative department is also a judicial tribunal for the trial of impeachments. The president who is the head of the executive department, is the presiding member also of the senate; and besides an equal vote in all cases, has a casting vote in case of a tie. The executive head is himself eventually elective every year by the legislative department; and his council is every year chosen by and from the members of the same department. Several of the officers of state are also appointed by the legislature. And the members of the judiciary department are appointed by the executive department.

The constitution of Massachusetts has observed a sufficient though less pointed caution in expressing this fundamental article of liberty. It declares "that the legislative department shall never exercise the executive and judicial powers, or either of them: The executive shall never exercise the legislative and judicial powers, or either of them: The judicial shall never exercise the legislative and executive powers, or either of them." This declaration corresponds precisely with the doctrine of Montesquieu as it has been explained, and is not in a single point violated by the plan of the convention. It goes no farther than to prohibit any one of the entire departments from exercising the powers of another department. In the very constitution to which it is prefixed, a partial mixture of powers has been admitted. The executive magistrate has a qualified negative on the legislative body; and the senate, which is a part of the legislature, is a court of impeachment for members both of the executive and judiciary departments. The members of the judiciary department again are appointable by the executive department, and removeable by the same authority, on the address of the two legislative branches. Lastly, a number of the officers of government are annually appointed by the legislative department. As the appointment to offices, particularly executive offices, is in its nature an executive function, the compilers of the constitution have in this last point at least, violated the rule established by themselves. [. . .]

The constitution of New-York contains no declaration on this subject; but appears very clearly to have been framed with an eye to the danger of improperly blending the different departments. It gives nevertheless to the executive magistrate a partial controul over the legislative department; and what is more, gives a like controul to the judiciary department, and even blends the executive and judiciary departments in the exercise of this controul. In its council of appointment, members of the legislative are associated with the executive authority in the appointment of officers both executive and judiciary. And its court for the trial of impeachments and correction of errors, is to consist of one branch of the legislature and the principal members of the judiciary department. [. . .]

The language of Virginia is still more pointed on this subject. Her constitution declares, "that the legislative, executive and judiciary departments, shall be separate and distinct; so that neither exercise the powers properly belonging to the other; nor shall any person exercise the powers of more than one of them at the same time; except that the justices of the county courts shall be eligible to either house of assembly." Yet we find not only this express exception, with respect to the members of the inferior courts; but that the chief magistrate with his executive council are appointable by the legislature; that two members of the latter are triennially displaced at the pleasure of the legislature; and that all the principal offices, both executive and judiciary, are filled by the same department. The executive prerogative of pardon, also is in one case vested in the legislative department. [. . .]

In citing these cases in which the legislative, executive and judiciary departments, have not been kept totally separate and distinct, I wish not to be regarded as an advocate for the particular organizations of the several state governments. I am fully aware that among the many excellent principles which they exemplify, they carry strong marks of the haste, and still stronger of the inexperience, under which they were framed. It is but too obvious that in some instances, the fundamental principle under consideration has been violated by too great a mixture, and even an actual consolidation of the different powers; and that in no instance has a competent provision been made for maintaining in practice the separation delineated on paper. What I have wished to evince is, that the charge brought against the proposed constitution, of violating a sacred maxim of free government, is warranted neither by the real meaning annexed to that maxim by its author; nor by the sense in which it has hitherto been understood in America. [. . .]

48 [47]

James Madison

February 1, 1788

To the People of the State of New York.

It was shewn in the last paper, that the political apothegm there examined, does not require that the legislative, executive and judiciary departments should be wholly unconnected with each other. I shall undertake in the next place, to shew that unless these departments be so far connected and blended, as to give to each a constitutional controul over the others, the degree of separation which the maxim requires as essential to a free government, can never in practice, be duly maintained.

It is agreed on all sides, that the powers properly belonging to one of the departments, ought not to be directly and compleatly administered by either of the other departments. It is equally evident, that neither of them ought to possess directly or indirectly, an overruling influence over the others in the administration of their respective powers. It will not be denied, that power is of an encroaching nature, and that it ought to be effectually restrained from passing the limits assigned to it. After discriminating therefore in theory, the several classes of power, as they may in their nature be legislative, executive, or judiciary; the next and most difficult task, is to provide some practical security for each against the invasion of the others. What this security ought to be, is the great problem to be solved.

Will it be sufficient to mark with precision the boundaries of these departments in the constitution of the government, and to trust to these parchment barriers against the encroaching spirit of power? This is the security which appears to have been principally relied on by the compilers of most of the American constitutions. But experience assures us, that the efficacy of the provision has been greatly over-rated; and that some more adequate defence is indispensibly necessary for the more feeble, against the more powerful members of the government. The legislative department is every where extending the sphere of its activity, and drawing all power into its impetuous vortex.

The founders of our republics have so much merit for the wisdom which they have displayed, that no task can be less pleasing than that of pointing out the errors into which they have fallen. A respect for truth however obliges us to remark, that they seem never for a moment to have turned their eyes from the danger to liberty from the overgrown and all-grasping prerogative of an hereditary magistrate, supported and fortified by an hereditary branch of the legislative authority. They seem never to have recollected the danger from legislative usurpations; which by assembling all power in the same hands, must lead to the same tyranny as is threatened by executive usurpations.

In a government, where numerous and extensive prerogatives are placed in the hands of a hereditary monarch, the executive department is very justly regarded as the source of danger, and watched with all the jealousy which a zeal for liberty ought to inspire. In a democracy, where a multitude of people exercise in person the legislative functions, and are continually exposed by their incapacity for regular deliberation and concerted measures, to the ambitious intrigues of their executive magistrates, tyranny may well be apprehended on some favorable emergency, to start up in the same quarter. But in a representative republic, where the executive magistracy is carefully limited both in the extent and the duration of its power; and where the legislative power is exercised by an assembly, which is inspired by a supposed influence over the people with an intrepid confidence in its own strength; which is sufficiently numerous to feel all the passions which actuate a multitude; yet not so numerous as to be incapable of pursuing the objects of its passions, by means which reason prescribes; it is against the enterprising ambition of this department, that the people ought to indulge all their jealousy and exhaust all their precautions.

The legislative department derives a superiority in our governments from other circumstances. Its constitutional powers being at once more extensive and less susceptible of precise limits, it can with the greater facility, mask under complicated and indirect measures, the encroachments which it makes on the co-ordinate departments. It is not unfrequently a question of real nicety in legislative bodies, whether the operation of a particular measure, will, or will not extend beyond the legislative sphere. On the other side, the executive power being restrained within a narrower compass, and being more simple in its nature; and the judiciary being described by land marks, still less uncertain, projects of usurpation by either of these departments, would immediately betray and defeat themselves. Nor is this all: As the legislative department alone has access to the pockets of the people, and has in some constitutions full discretion, and in all, a prevailing influence over the pecuniary rewards of those who fill the other departments, a dependence is thus created in the latter, which gives still greater facility to encroachments of the former.

I have appealed to our own experience for the truth of what I advance on this subject. [. . .]

The first example is that of Virginia, a state which, as we have seen, has expressly declared in its constitution, that the three great departments ought not to be intermixed. The authority in support of it is Mr. Jefferson, who, besides his other advantages for remarking the operation of the government, was himself the chief magistrate of it. In order to convey fully the ideas with which his experience had impressed him on this subject, it will be necessary to quote a passage of some length from his very interesting "Notes on the state of Virginia." (p. 195). "All the powers of government, legislative, executive and judiciary, result to the legislative body. The concentrating these in the same hands is precisely the definition of despotic government. It will be no alleviation that these powers will be exercised by a plurality of hands, and not by a single one. One hundred and seventy-three despots would surely be as oppressive as one. Let those who doubt it turn their eyes on the republic of Venice. As little will it avail us that they are chosen by ourselves. An *elective despotism*, was not the government we fought for; but one which should not only be founded on free principles, but in which the powers of government should be so divided and balanced among several bodies of magistracy, as that no one could transcend their legal limits, without being effectually checked and restrained by the others. For this reason that convention which passed the ordinance of government, laid its foundation on this basis, that the legislative, executive and judiciary departments should be separate and distinct, so that no person should exercise the powers of more than one of them at the same time. *But no barrier was provided between these several powers.* The judiciary and executive members were left dependent on the legislative for their subsistence in office, and some of them for their continuance in it. If therefore the legislature assumes executive and judiciary powers, no opposition is likely to be made; nor if made can be effectual; because in that case, they may put their proceeding into the form of an act of assembly, which will render them obligatory on the other branches. They have accordingly *in many* instances *decided rights* which should have been left to *judiciary controversy*; and *the direction of the executive during the whole time of their session, is becoming habitual and familiar.*"

The other state which I shall have for an example, is Pennsylvania; and the other authority the council of censors which assembled in the years 1783 and 1784. A part of the duty of this body, as marked out by the constitution was, "to enquire whether the constitution had been preserved inviolate in every part; and whether the legislative and executive branches of government had performed their duty as guardians of the people, or assumed to themselves, or exercised other or greater powers than they are entitled to by the constitution." In the execution of this trust, the council were necessarily led to a comparison, of both the legislative and executive proceedings, with the constitutional powers of these departments; and from the facts enumerated, and to the truth of most of which, both sides in the council subscribed, it appears that the constitution had been flagrantly violated by the legislature in a variety of important instances.

A great number of laws had been passed violating without any apparent necessity, the rule requiring that all bills of a public nature, shall be previously printed for the consideration of the people; although this is one of the precautions chiefly relied on by the constitution, against improper acts of the legislature.

The constitutional trial by jury had been violated; and powers assumed, which had not been delegated by the constitution.

Executive powers had been usurped.

The salaries of the judges, which the constitution expressly requires to be fixed, had been occasionally varied; and cases belonging to the judiciary department, frequently drawn within legislative cognizance and determination.

Those who wish to see the several particulars falling under each of these heads, may consult the journals of the council which are in print. Some of them, it will be found may be imputable to peculiar circumstances connected with the war: But the greater part of them may be considered as the spontaneous shoots of an ill-constituted government. [. . .]

The conclusion which I am warranted in drawing from these observations is, that a mere demarkation on parchment of the constitutional limits of the several departments, is not a sufficient guard against those encroachments which lead to a tyrannical concentration of all the powers of government in the same hands.

49 [48]

James Madison

February 2, 1788

To the People of the State of New York.

The author of the "Notes on the state of Virginia," quoted in the last paper, has subjoined to that valuable work, the draught of a constitution which had been prepared in order to be laid before a convention expected to be called in 1783 by the legislature, for the establishment of a constitution for that commonwealth. The plan, like every thing from the same pen, marks a turn of thinking original, comprehensive and accurate; and is the more worthy of attention, as it equally displays a fervent attachment to republican government, and an enlightened view of the dangerous propensities against which it ought to be guarded. One of the precautions which he proposes, and on which he appears ultimately to rely as a palladium to the weaker departments of power, against the invasions of the stronger, is perhaps altogether his own, and as it immediately relates to the subject of our present enquiry, ought not to be overlooked.

His proposition is, "that whenever any two of the three branches of government shall concur in opinion, each by the voices of two thirds of their whole number, that a convention is necessary for altering the constitution or *correcting breaches of it*, a convention shall be called for the purpose."

As the people are the only legitimate fountain of power, and it is from them that the constitutional charter, under which the several branches of government hold their power, is derived; it seems strictly consonant to the republican theory, to recur to the same original authority, not only whenever it may be necessary to enlarge, diminish, or new-model the powers of government; but also whenever any one of the departments may commit encroachments on the chartered authorities of the others. The several departments being perfectly co-ordinate by the terms of their common commission, neither of them, it is evident, can pretend to an exclusive or superior right of settling the boundaries between their respective powers; and how are the encroachments of the stronger to be prevented, or the wrongs of the weaker to be redressed, without an appeal to the people themselves; who, as the grantors of the commission, can alone declare its true meaning and enforce its observance?

There is certainly great force in this reasoning, and it must be allowed to prove, that a constitutional road to the decision of the people, ought to be marked out, and kept open, for certain great and extraordinary occasions. But there appear to be insuperable objections against the proposed recurrence to the people, as a provision in all cases for keeping the several departments of power within their constitutional limits.

In the first place, the provision does not reach the case of a combination of two of the departments against a third. If the legislative authority, which possesses so many means of operating on the motives of the other departments, should be able to gain to its interest either of the others, or even one-third of its members, the remaining department could derive no advantage from this remedial provision. I do not dwell however on this objection, because it may be thought to lie rather against the modification of the principle, than against the principle itself.

In the next place, it may be considered as an objection inherent in the principle, that as every appeal to the people would carry an implication of some defect in the government, frequent appeals would in great measure deprive the government of that veneration, which time bestows on every thing, and without which perhaps the wisest and freest governments would not possess the requisite stability. If it be true that all governments rest on opinion, it is no less true that the strength of opinion in each individual, and its practical influence on his conduct, depend much on the number which he supposes to have entertained the same opinion. The reason of man, like man himself is timid and cautious, when left alone; and acquires firmness and confidence, in proportion to the number with which it is associated. When the examples, which fortify opinion, are *antient* as well as *numerous*, they are known to have a double effect. In a nation of philosophers, this consideration ought to be disregarded. A reverence for the laws, would be sufficiently inculcated by the voice of an enlightened reason. But a nation of philosophers is as little to be expected as the philosophical race of kings wished for by Plato. And in every other nation, the most rational government will not find it a superfluous advantage, to have the prejudices of the community on its side.

The danger of disturbing the public tranquility by interesting too strongly the public passions, is a still more serious objection against a frequent reference of constitutional questions, to the decision of the whole society. Notwithstanding the success which has attended the revisions of our established forms of government, and which does so much honour to the virtue and intelligence of the people of America, it must be confessed, that the experiments are of too ticklish a nature to be unnecessarily multiplied. We are to recollect that all the existing constitutions were formed in the midst of a danger which repressed the passions most unfriendly to order and concord; of an enthusiastic confidence of the people in their patriotic leaders, which stifled the ordinary diversity of opinions on great national questions; of a universal ardor for new and opposite forms, produced by a universal resentment and indignation against the antient government; and whilst no spirit of party, connected with the changes to be made, or the abuses to be reformed, could mingle its leaven in the operation. The future situations in which we must expect to be usually placed, do not present any equivalent security against the danger which is apprehended.

But the greatest objection of all is, that the decisions which would probably result from such appeals, would not answer the purpose of maintaining the constitutional equilibrium of the government. We have seen that the tendency of republican governments is to an aggrandizement of the legislative, at the expence of the other departments. The appeals to the people therefore would usually be made by the executive and judiciary departments. But whether made by one side or the other, would each side enjoy equal advantages on the trial? Let us view their different situations. The members of the executive and judiciary departments, are few in number, and can be personally known to a small part only of the people. The latter by the mode of their appointment, as well as, by the nature and permanency of it, are too far removed from the people to share much in their prepossessions. The former are generally the objects of jealousy: And their administration is always liable to be discoloured and rendered unpopular. The members of the legislative department, on the other hand, are numerous. They are distributed and dwell among the people at large. Their connections of blood, of friendship and of acquaintance, embrace a great proportion of the most influencial part of the society. The nature of their public trust implies a personal influence among the people, and that they are more immediately the confidential guardians of the rights and liberties of the people. With these advantages, it can hardly be supposed that the adverse party would have an equal chance for a favorable issue.

But the legislative party would not only be able to plead their cause most successfully with the people. They would probably be constituted themselves the judges. The same influence which had gained them an election into the legislature, would gain them a seat in the convention. If this should not be the case with all, it would probably be the case with many, and pretty certainly with those leading characters, on whom every thing depends in such bodies. The convention in short would be composed chiefly of men, who had been, who actually were, or who expected to be, members of the department whose conduct was arraigned. They would consequently be parties to the very question to be decided by them.

It might however sometimes happen, that appeals would be made under circumstances less adverse to the executive and judiciary departments. The usurpations of the legislature might be so flagrant and so sudden, as to admit of no specious colouring. A strong party among themselves might take side with the other branches. The executive power might be in the hands of a peculiar favorite of the people. In such a posture of things, the public decision might be less swayed by prepossessions in favor of the legislative party. But still it could never be expected to turn on the true merits of the question. It would inevitably be connected with the spirit of pre-existing parties, or of parties springing out of the question itself. It would be connected with persons of distinguished character and extensive influence in the community. It would be pronounced by the very men who had been agents in, or opponents of the measures, to which the decision would relate. The *passions* therefore not *the reason*, of the public, would sit in judgment. But it is the reason of the public alone that ought to controul and regulate the government. The passions ought to be controuled and regulated by the government.

We found in the last paper that mere declarations in the written constitution, are not sufficient to restrain the several departments within their legal limits. It appears in this, that occasional appeals to the people would be neither a proper nor an effectual provision, for that purpose. How far the provisions of a different nature contained in the plan above quoted, might be adequate, I do not examine. Some of them are unquestionably founded on sound political principles, and all of them are framed with singular ingenuity and precision.

51 [50]

James Madison

February 6, 1788

To the People of the State of New York.

To what expedient then shall we finally resort for maintaining in practice the necessary partition of power among the several departments, as laid down in the constitution? The only answer that can be given is, that as all these exterior provisions are found to be inadequate, the defect must be supplied, by so contriving the interior structure of the government, as that its several constituent parts may, by their mutual relations, be the means of keeping each other in their proper places. [. . .]

In order to lay a due foundation for that separate and distinct exercise of the different powers of government, which to a certain extent, is admitted on all hands to be essential to the preservation of liberty, it is evident that each department should have a will of its own; and consequently should be so constituted, that the members of each should have as little agency as possible in the appointment of the members of the others. Were this principle rigorously adhered to, it would require that all the appointments for the supreme executive, legislative, and judiciary magistracies, should be drawn from the same fountain of authority, the people, through channels, having no communication whatever with one another. Perhaps such a plan of constructing the several departments would be less difficult in practice than it may in contemplation appear. Some difficulties however, and some additional expence, would attend the execution of it. Some deviations therefore from the principle must be admitted. In the constitution of the judiciary department in particular, it might be inexpedient to insist rigorously on the principle; first, because peculiar qualifications being essential in the members, the primary consideration ought to be to select that mode of choice, which best secures these qualifications; secondly, because the permanent tenure by which the appointments are held in that department, must soon destroy all sense of dependence on the authority conferring them.

It is equally evident that the members of each department should be as little dependent as possible on those of the others, for the emoluments annexed to their offices. Were the executive magistrate, or the judges, not independent of the legislature in this particular, their independence in every other would be merely nominal.

But the great security against a gradual concentration of the several powers in the same department, consists in giving to those who administer each department, the necessary constitutional means, and personal motives, to resist encroachments of the others. The provision for defence must in this, as in all other cases, be made commensurate to the danger of attack. Ambition must be made to counteract ambition. The interest of the man must be connected with the constitutional rights of the place. It may be a reflection on human nature, that such devices should be necessary to controul the abuses of government. But what is government itself but the greatest of all reflections on human nature? If men were angels, no government would be necessary. If angels were to govern men, neither external nor internal controuls on government would be necessary. In framing a government which is to be administered by men over men, the great difficulty lies in this: You must first enable the government to controul the governed; and in the next place, oblige it to controul itself. A dependence on the people is no doubt the primary controul on the government; but experience has taught mankind the necessity of auxiliary precautions.

This policy of supplying by opposite and rival interests, the defect of better motives, might be traced through the whole system of human affairs, private as well as public. We see it particularly displayed in all the subordinate distributions of power; where the constant aim is to divide and arrange the several offices in such a manner as that each may be a check on the other; that the private interest of every individual, may be a centinel over the public rights. These inventions of prudence cannot be less requisite in the distribution of the supreme powers of the state.

But it is not possible to give to each department an equal power of self defence. In republican government the legislative authority necessarily predominates. The remedy for this inconveniency is, to divide the legislature into different branches; and to render them by different modes of election, and different principles of action, as little concerned with each other, as the nature of their common functions, and their common dependence on the society, will admit. It may even be necessary to guard against dangerous encroachments by still further precautions. As the weight of the legislative authority requires that it should be thus divided, the weakness of the executive may require, on the other hand, that it should be fortified. An absolute negative, on the legislature, appears at first view to be the natural defence with which the executive magistrate should be armed. But perhaps it would be neither altogether safe, nor alone sufficient. On ordinary occasions, it might not be exerted with the requisite firmness; and on extraordinary occasions, it might be perfidiously abused. May not this defect of an absolute negative be supplied, by some qualified connection between this weaker department, and the weaker branch of the stronger department, by which the latter may be led to support the constitutional rights of the former, without being too much detached from the rights of its own department? [. . .]

There are moreover two considerations particularly applicable to the federal system of America, which place that system in a very interesting point of view.

First. In a single republic, all the power surrendered by the people is submitted to the administration of a single government; and the usurpations are guarded against by a division of the government into distinct and separate departments. In the compound republic of America, the power surrendered by the people, is first divided between two distinct governments, and then the portion allotted to each, subdivided among distinct and separate departments. Hence a double security arises to the rights of the people. The different governments will controul each other; at the same time that each will be controuled by itself.

Second. It is of great importance in a republic, not only to guard the society against the oppression of its rulers; but to guard one part of the society against the injustice of the other part. Different interests necessarily exist in different classes of citizens. If a majority be united by a common interest, the rights of the minority will be insecure. There are but two methods of providing against this evil: The one by creating a will in the community independent of the majority, that is, of the society itself; the other by comprehending in the society so many separate descriptions of citizens, as will render an unjust combination of a majority of the whole, very improbable, if not impracticable. The first method prevails in all governments possessing an hereditary or self-appointed authority. This at best is but a precarious security; because a power independent of the society may as well espouse the unjust views of the major, as the rightful interests, of the minor party, and may possibly be turned against both parties. The second method will be exemplified in the federal republic of the United States. Whilst all authority in it will be derived from and dependent on the society, the society itself will be broken into so many parts, interests and classes of citizens, that the rights of individuals or of the minority, will be in little danger from interested combinations of the majority. In a free government, the security for civil rights must be the same as that for religious rights. It consists in the one case in the multiplicity of interests, and in the other, in the multiplicity of sects. The degree of security in both cases will depend on the number of interests and sects; and this may be presumed to depend on the extent of country and number of people comprehended under the same government. This view of the subject must particularly recommend a proper federal system to all the sincere and considerate friends of republican government: Since it shews that in exact proportion as the territory of the union may be formed into more circumscribed confederacies or states, oppressive combinations of a majority will be facilitated, the best security under the republican form, for the rights of every class of citizens, will be diminished; and consequently, the stability and independence of some member of the government, the only other security, must be proportionally increased. Justice is the end of government. It is the end of civil society. It ever has been, and ever will be pursued, until it be obtained, or until liberty be lost in the pursuit. In a society under the forms of which the stronger faction can readily unite and oppress the weaker, anarchy may as truly be said to reign, as in a state of nature where the weaker individual is not secured against the violence of the stronger: And as in the latter state even the stronger individuals are prompted by the uncertainty of their condition, to submit to a government which may protect the weak as well as themselves: So in the former state, will the more powerful factions or parties be gradually induced by a like motive, to wish for a government which will protect all parties, the weaker as well as the more powerful. It can be little doubted, that if the state of Rhode Island was separated from the confederacy, and left to itself, the insecurity of rights under the popular form of government within such narrow limits, would be displayed by such reiterated oppressions of factious majorities, that some power altogether independent of the people would soon be called for by the voice of the very factions whose misrule had proved the necessity of it. In the extended republic of the United States, and among the great variety of interests, parties and sects which it embraces, a coalition of a majority of the whole society could seldom take place on any other principles than those of justice and the general good: Whilst there being thus less danger to a minor from the will of the major party, there must be less pretext also, to provide for the security of the former, by introducing into the government a will not dependent on the latter; or in other words, a will independent of the society itself. It is no less certain than it is important, notwithstanding the contrary opinions which have been entertained, that the larger the society, provided it lie within a practicable sphere, the more duly capable it will be of self government. And happily for the *republican cause*, the practicable sphere may be carried to a very great extent, by a judicious modification and mixture of the *federal principle*.

53 [52]

James Madison

February 9, 1788

To the People of the State of New York.

I shall here perhaps be reminded of a current observation, "that where annual elections end, tyranny begins." If it be true as has often been remarked, that sayings which become proverbial, are generally founded in reason, it is not less true that when once established, they are often applied to cases to which the reason of them does not extend. I need not look for a proof beyond the case before us. What is the reason on which this proverbial observation is founded? No man will subject himself to the ridicule of pretending that any natural connection subsists between the sun or the seasons, and the period within which human virtue can bear the temptations of power. Happily for mankind, liberty is not in this respect confined to any single point of time; but lies within extremes, which afford sufficient latitude for all the variations which may be required by the various situations and circumstances of civil society. [. . .] Turning our attention to the periods established among ourselves, for the election of the most numerous branches of the state legislatures, we find them by no means coinciding any more in this instance, than in the elections of other civil magistrates. In Connecticut and Rhode-Island, the periods are half-yearly. In the other states, South-Carolina excepted, they are annual. In South-Carolina, they are biennial; as is proposed in the federal government. [. . .] Yet it would be not easy to shew that Connecticut or Rhode-Island is better governed, or enjoys a greater share of rational liberty than South-Carolina. [. . .]

In searching for the grounds of this doctrine, I can discover but one, and that is wholly inapplicable to our case. The important distinction so well understood in America between a constitution established by the people, and unalterable by the government; and a law established by the government, and alterable by the government, seems to have been little understood and less observed in any other country. Wherever the supreme power of legislation has resided, has been supposed to reside also, a full power to change the form of the government. Even in Great-Britain, where the principles of political and civil liberty have been most discussed; and where we hear most of the rights of the constitution, it is maintained that the authority of the parliament is transcendent and uncontroulable, as well with regard to the constitution, as the ordinary objects of legislative provision. They have accordingly, in several instances, actually changed, by legislative acts, some of the most fundamental articles of the government. They have in particular, on several occasions, changed the period of election; and on the last occasion, not only introduced septennial, in place of triennial elections; but by the same act continued themselves in place four years beyond the term for which they were elected by the people. An attention to these dangerous practices has produced a very natural alarm in the votaries of free government, of which frequency of elections is the corner stone; and has led them to seek for some security to liberty against the danger to which it is exposed. Where no constitution paramount to the government, either existed or could be obtained, no constitutional security similar to that established in the United States, was to be attempted. Some other security therefore was to be sought for; and what better security would the case admit, than that of selecting and appealing to some simple and familiar portion of time, as a standard for measuring the danger of innovations, for fixing the national sentiment, and for uniting the patriotic exertions. The most simple and familiar portion of time, applicable to the subject, was that of a year; and hence the doctrine has been inculcated by a laudable zeal to erect some barrier against the gradual innovations of an unlimited government, that the advance towards tyranny was to be calculated by the distance of departure from the fixed point of annual elections. But what necessity can there be of applying this expedient to a government, limited as the federal government will be, by the authority of a paramount constitution? Or who will pretend that the liberties of the people of America will not be more secure under biennial elections, unalterably fixed by such a constitution, than those of any other nation would be, where elections were annual or even more frequent, but subject to alterations by the ordinary power of the government?

The second question stated is, whether biennial elections be necessary or useful? The propriety of answering this question in the affirmative will appear from several very obvious considerations.

No man can be a competent legislator who does not add to an upright intention and a sound judgment, a certain degree of knowledge of the subjects on which he is to legislate. A part of this knowledge may be acquired by means of information which lie within the compass of men in private as well as public stations. Another part can only be attained, or at least thoroughly attained, by actual experience in the station which requires the use of it. The period of service ought therefore in all such cases to bear some proportion to the extent of practical knowledge, requisite to the due performance of the service. The period of legislative service established in most of the states for the more numerous branch is, as we have seen, one year. The question then may be put into this simple form; does the period of two years bear no greater proportion to the knowledge requisite for federal legislation, than one year does to the knowledge requisite for state legislation? [. . .]

In a single state the requisite knowledge, relates to the existing laws which are uniform throughout the state, and with which all the citizens are more or less conversant; and to the general affairs of the state, which lie within a small compass, are not very diversified, and occupy much of the attention and conversation of every class of people. The great theatre of the United States presents a very different scene. The laws are so far from being uniform, that they vary in every state; whilst the public affairs of the union are spread throughout a very extensive region, and are extremely diversified by the local affairs connected with them, and can with difficulty be correctly learnt in any other place, than in the central councils, to which a knowledge of them will be brought by the representatives of every part of the empire. Yet some knowledge of the affairs, and even of the laws of all the states, ought to be possessed by the members from each of the states. How can foreign trade be properly regulated by uniform laws, without some acquaintance with the commerce, the ports, the usages, and the regulations, of the different states? How can the trade between the different states be duly regulated without some knowledge of their relative situations in these and other points? How can taxes be judiciously imposed, and effectually collected, if they be not accommodated to the different laws and local circumstances relating to these objects in the different states? How can uniform regulations for the militia be duly provided without a similar knowledge of some internal circumstances by which the states are distinguished from each other? These are the principal objects of federal legislation, and suggest most forceably, the extensive information which the representatives ought to acquire. The other inferior objects will require a proportional degree of information with regard to them.

It is true that all these difficulties will by degrees be very much diminished. The most laborious task will be the proper inauguration of the government, and the primeval formation of a federal code. Improvements on the first draught will every year become both easier and fewer. Past transactions of the government will be a ready and accurate source of information to new members. The affairs of the union will become more and more objects of curiosity and conversation among the citizens at large. And the increased intercourse among those of different states will contribute not a little to diffuse a mutual knowledge of their affairs, as this again will contribute to a general assimilation of their manners and laws. But with all these abatements the business of federal legislation must continue so far to exceed both in novelty and difficulty, the legislative business of a single state as to justify the longer period of service assigned to those who are to transact it.

A branch of knowledge which belongs to the acquirements of a federal representative, and which has not been mentioned, is that of foreign affairs. In regulating our own commerce he ought to be not only acquainted with the treaties between the United States and other nations, but also with the commercial policy and laws of other nations. He ought not to be altogether ignorant of the law of nations, for that as far as it is a proper object of municipal legislation is submitted to the federal government. And although the house of representatives is not immediately to participate in foreign negotiations and arrangements, yet from the necessary connection between the several branches of public affairs, those particular branches will frequently deserve attention in the ordinary course of legislation, and will sometimes demand particular legislative sanction and co-operation. Some portion of this knowledge may no doubt be acquired in a man's closet; but some of it also can only be derived from the public sources of information; and all of it will be acquired to best effect by a practical attention to the subject during the period of actual service in the legislature.

There are other considerations of less importance perhaps, but which are not unworthy of notice. The distance which many of the representatives will be obliged to travel, and the arrangements rendered necessary by that circumstance, might be much more serious objections with fit men to this service if limited to a single year than if extended to two years. No argument can be drawn on this subject from the case of the delegates to the existing congress. They are elected annually it is true; but their re-election is considered by the legislative assemblies almost as a matter of course. The election of the representatives by the people would not be governed by the same principle.

A few of the members, as happens in all such assemblies, will possess superior talents, will by frequent re-elections, become members of long standing; will be thoroughly masters of the public business, and perhaps not unwilling to avail themselves of those advantages. The greater the proportion of new members, and the less the information of the bulk of the members, the more apt will they be to fall into the snares that may be laid for them. This remark is no less applicable to the relation which will subsist between the house of representatives and the senate.

It is an inconvenience mingled with the advantages of our frequent elections, even in single states where they are large and hold but one legislative session in the year, that spurious elections cannot be investigated and annulled in time for the decision to have its due effect. If a return can be obtained, no matter by what unlawful means, the irregular member, who takes his seat of course, is sure of holding it a sufficient time, to answer his purposes. Hence a very pernicious encouragement is given to the use of unlawful means for obtaining irregular returns. Were elections for the federal legislature to be annual, this practice might become a very serious abuse, particularly in the more distant states. Each house is, as it necessarily must be, the judge of the elections, qualifications and returns of its members, and whatever improvements may be suggested by experience for simplifying and accelerating the process in disputed cases. So great a portion of a year would unavoidably elapse, before an illegitimate member could be dispossessed of his seat, that the prospect of such an event, would be little check to unfair and illicit means of obtaining a seat.

All these considerations taken together warrant us in affirming that biennial elections will be as useful to the affairs of the public, as we have seen that they will be safe to the liberties of the people.

54 [53]

James Madison

February 12, 1788

To the People of the State of New York.

The next view which I shall take of the house of representatives, relates to the apportionment of its members to the several states, which is to be determined by the same rule with that of direct taxes.

It is not contended that the number of people in each state ought not to be the standard for regulating the proportion of those who are to represent the people of each state. The establishment of the same rule for the apportionment of taxes, will probably be as little contested. [. . .]

But does it follow from an admission of numbers for the measure of representation, or of slaves combined with free citizens, as a ratio of taxation, that slaves ought to be included in the numerical rule of representation? Slaves are considered as property, not as persons. They ought therefore to be comprehended in estimates of taxation which are founded on property, and to be excluded from representation which is regulated by a census of persons. This is the objection, as I understand it, stated in its full force. I shall be equally candid in stating the reasoning which may be offered on the opposite side.

We subscribe to the doctrine, might one of our southern brethren observe, that representation relates more immediately to persons, and taxation more immediately to property, and we join in the application of this distinction to the case of our slaves. But we must deny the fact that slaves are considered merely as property, and in no respect whatever as persons. The true state of the case is, that they partake of both these qualities; being considered by our laws, in some respects, as persons, and in other respects, as property. In being compelled to labor not for himself, but for a master; in being vendible by one master to another master; and in being subject at all times to be restrained in his liberty, and chastised in his body, by the capricious will of another, the slave may appear to be degraded from the human rank, and classed with those irrational animals, which fall under the legal denomination of property. In being protected on the other hand in his life and in his limbs, against the violence of all others, even the master of his labor and his liberty; and in being punishable himself for all violence committed against others; the slave is no less evidently regarded by the law as a member of the society; not as a part of the irrational creation; as a moral person, not as a mere article of property. The federal constitution therefore, decides with great propriety on the case of our slaves, when it views them in the mixt character of persons and of property. This is in fact their true character. It is the character bestowed on them by the laws under which they live; and it will not be denied that these are the proper criterion; because it is only under the pretext that the laws have transformed the negroes into subjects of property, that a place is disputed them in the computation of numbers; and it is admitted that if the laws were to restore the rights which have been taken away, the negroes could no longer be refused an equal share of representation with the other inhabitants.

This question may be placed in another light. It is agreed on all sides, that numbers are the best scale of wealth and taxation, as they are the only proper scale of representation. Would the convention have been impartial or consistent, if they had rejected the slaves from the list of inhabitants when the shares of representation were to be calculated; and inserted them on the lists when the tariff of contributions was to be adjusted? Could it be reasonably expected that the southern states would concur in a system which considered their slaves in some degree as men, when burdens were to be imposed, but refused to consider them in the same light when advantages were to be conferred? [. . .]

It may be replied perhaps that slaves are not included in the estimate of representatives in any of the states possessing them. They neither vote themselves, nor increase the votes of their masters. Upon what principle then ought they to be taken into the federal estimate of representation? In rejecting them altogether, the constitution would in this respect have followed the very laws which have been appealed to, as the proper guide.

This objection is repelled by a single observation. It is a fundamental principle of the proposed constitution, that as the aggregate number of representatives allotted to the several states, is to be determined by a federal rule founded on the aggregate number of inhabitants, so the right of choosing this allotted number in each state is to be exercised by such part of the inhabitants, as the state itself may designate. The qualifications on which the right of suffrage depend, are not perhaps the same in any two states. In some of the states the difference is very material. In every state, a certain proportion of inhabitants are deprived of this right by the constitution of the state, who will be included in the census by which the federal constitution apportions the representatives. In this point of view, the southern states might retort the complaint, by insisting, that the principle laid down by the convention required that no regard should be had to the policy of particular states towards their own inhabitants; and consequently, that the slaves as inhabitants should have been admitted into the census according to their full number, in like manner with other inhabitants, who by the policy of other states, are not admitted to all the rights of citizens. A rigorous adherence however to this principle is waved by those who would be gainers by it. All that they ask is, that equal moderation be shewn on the other side. Let the case of the slaves be considered as it is in truth a peculiar one. Let the compromising expedient of the constitution be mutually adopted, which regards them as inhabitants, but as debased by servitude below the equal level of free inhabitants, which regards the *slave* as divested of two fifth of the *man*.

After all may not another ground be taken on which this article of the constitution, will admit of a still more ready defence? We have hitherto proceeded on the idea that representation related to persons only, and not at all to property. But is it a just idea? Government is instituted no less for protection of the property, than of the persons of individuals. The one as well as the other, therefore may be considered as represented by those who are charged with the government. Upon this principle it is, that in several of the states, and particularly in the state of New-York, one branch of the government is intended more especially to be the guardian of property, and is accordingly elected by that part of the society which is most interested in this object of government. In the federal constitution, this policy does not prevail. The rights of property are committed into the same hands with the personal rights. Some attention ought therefore to be paid to property in the choice of those hands.

For another reason the votes allowed in the federal legislature to the people of each state, ought to bear some proportion to the comparative wealth of the states. States have not like individuals, an influence over each other arising from superior advantages of fortune. [. . .] A state possesses no such influence over other states. It is not probable that the richest state in the confederacy will ever influence the choice of a single representative in any other state. Nor will the representatives of the larger and richer states possess any other advantage in the federal legislature over the representatives of other states, than what may result from their superior number alone; as far therefore as their superior wealth and weight may justly entitle them to any advantage, it ought to be secured to them by a superior share of representation. [. . .]

Such is the reasoning which an advocate for the southern interests might employ on this subject: And although it may appear to be a little strained in some points, yet on the whole, I must confess, that it fully reconciles me to the scale of representation, which the convention have established. [. . .]

55 [54]

James Madison

February 13, 1788

To the People of the State of New York.

The number of which the house of representatives is to consist, forms another, and a very interesting point of view under which this branch of the federal legislature may be contemplated. Scarce any article indeed in the whole constitution seems to be rendered more worthy of attention, by the weight of character and the apparent force of argument, with which it has been assailed. The charges exhibited against it are, first, that so small a number of representatives will be an unsafe depositary of the public interests; secondly, that they will not possess a proper knowledge of the local circumstances of their numerous constituents; thirdly, that they will be taken from that class of citizens which will sympathize least with the feelings of the mass of the people, and be most likely to aim at a permanent elevation of the few on the depression of the many. [. . .]

In general it may be remarked on this subject, that no political problem is less susceptible of a precise solution, than that which relates to the number most convenient for a representative legislature: Nor is there any point on which the policy of the several states is more at variance; whether we compare their legislative assemblies directly with each other, or consider the proportions which they respectively bear to the number of their constituents. [. . .] A very considerable difference is observable among states nearly equal in population. The number of representatives in Pennsylvania is not more than one-fifth of that in [Massachusetts]. New-York, whose population is to that of South-Carolina as six to five, has little more than one third of the number of representatives. As great a disparity prevails between the states of Georgia and Delaware, or Rhode-Island. In Pennsylvania the representatives do not bear a greater proportion to their constituents than of one for every four or five thousand. In Rhode-Island, they bear a proportion of at least one for every thousand. And according to the constitution of Georgia, the proportion may be carried to one for every ten electors; and must unavoidably far exceed the proportion in any of the other states.

Another general remark to be made is, that the ratio between the representatives and the people, ought not to be the same where the latter are very numerous, as where they are very few. Were the representatives in Virginia to be regulated by the standard in Rhode-Island, they would at this time amount to between four and five hundred; and twenty or thirty years hence, to a thousand. On the other hand, the ratio of Pennsylvania, if applied to the state of Delaware, would reduce the representative assembly of the latter to seven or eight members. Nothing can be more fallacious than to found our political calculations on arithmetical principles. Sixty or seventy men, may be more properly trusted with a given degree of power than six or seven. But it does not follow, that six or seven hundred would be proportionally a better depositary. And if we carry on the supposition to six or seven thousand, the whole reasoning ought to be reversed. The truth is, that in all cases a certain number at least seems to be necessary to secure the benefits of free consultation and discussion, and to guard against too easy a combination for improper purposes: As on the other hand, the number ought at most to be kept within a certain limit, in order to avoid the confusion and intemperance of a multitude. In all very numerous assemblies, of whatever characters composed, passion never fails to wrest the sceptre from reason. Had every Athenian citizen been a Socrates; every Athenian assembly would still have been a mob.

It is necessary also to recollect here the observations which were applied to the case of biennial elections. For the same reason that the limited powers of the congress and the controul of the state legislatures, justify less frequent elections than the public safety might otherwise require; the members of the congress need be less numerous than if they possessed the whole power of legislation, and were under no other than the ordinary restraints of other legislative bodies.

With these general ideas in our minds, let us weigh the objections which have been stated against the number of members proposed for the house of representatives. It is said in the first place, that so small a number cannot be safely trusted with so much power.

The number of which this branch of the legislature is to consist at the outset of the government, will be sixty five. Within three years a census is to be taken, when the number may be augmented to one for every thirty thousand inhabitants; and within every successive period of ten years, the census is to be renewed, and augmentations may continue to be made under the above limitation. [. . .]

The true question to be decided then is whether the smallness of the number, as a temporary regulation, be dangerous to the public liberty: Whether sixty five members for a few years, and a hundred or two hundred for a few more, be a safe depositary for a limited and well guarded power of legislating for the United States? I must own that I could not give a negative answer to this question, without first obliterating every impression which I have received with regard to the present genius of the people of America, the spirit, which actuates the state legislatures, and the principles which are incorporated with the political character of every class of citizens. I am unable to conceive that the people of America in their present temper, or under any circumstances which can speedily happen, will chuse, and every second year repeat the choice of sixty-five or an hundred men, who would be disposed to form and pursue a scheme of tyranny or treachery. I am unable to conceive that the state legislatures which must feel so many motives to watch, and which possess so many means of counteracting the federal legislature, would fail either to detect or to defeat a conspiracy of the latter against the liberties of their common constituents. I am equally unable to conceive that there are at this time, or can be in any short time, in the United States any sixty-five or an hundred men capable of recommending themselves to the choice of the people at large, who would either desire or dare within the short space of two years, to betray the solemn trust committed to them. [. . .]

From what quarter can the danger proceed? Are we afraid of foreign gold? If foreign gold could so easily corrupt our federal rulers, and enable them to ensnare and betray their constituents, how has it happened that we are at this time a free and independent nation? The congress which conducted us through the revolution were a less numerous body than their successors will be; they were not chosen by nor responsible to their fellow citizens at large; though appointed from year to year, and recallable at pleasure, they were generally continued for three years; and prior to the ratification of the federal articles, for a still longer term; they held their consultations always under the veil of secrecy; they had the sole transaction of our affairs with foreign nations; through the whole course of the war, they had the fate of their country more in their hands, than it is to be hoped will ever be the case with our future representatives; and from the greatness of the prize at stake and the eagerness of the party which lost it, it may well be supposed, that the use of other means than force would not have been scrupled; yet we know by happy experience that the public trust was not betrayed; nor has the purity of our public councils in this particular ever suffered even from the whispers of calumny.

Is the danger apprehended from the other branches of the federal government? But where are the means to be found by the president or the senate, or both? Their emoluments of office it is to be presumed will not, and without a previous corruption of the house of representatives cannot, more than suffice for very different purposes: Their private fortunes, as they must all be American citizens, cannot possibly be sources of danger. The only means then which they can possess, will be in the dispensation of appointments. Is it here that suspicion rests her charge? Sometimes we are told that this fund of corruption is to be exhausted by the president in subduing the virtue of the senate. Now the fidelity of the other house is to be the victim. The improbability of such a mercenary and perfidious combination of the several members of government standing on as different foundations as republican principles will well admit, and at the same time accountable to the society over which they are placed, ought alone to quiet this apprehension. But fortunately the constitution has provided a still further safeguard. The members of the congress are rendered ineligible to any civil offices that may be created or of which the emoluments may be increased, during the term of their election. No offices therefore can be dealt out to the existing members, but such as may become vacant by ordinary casualties; and to suppose that these would be sufficient to purchase the guardians of the people, selected by the people themselves, is to renounce every rule by which events ought to be calculated, and to substitute an indiscriminate and unbounded jealousy, with which all reasoning must be vain. The sincere friends of liberty who give themselves up to the extravagancies of this passion are not aware of the injury they do their own cause. As there is a degree of depravity in mankind which requires a certain degree of circumspection and distrust: So there are other qualities in human nature, which justify a certain portion of esteem and confidence. Republican government presupposes the existence of these qualities in a higher degree than any other form. Were the pictures which have been drawn by the political jealousy of some among us, faithful likenesses of the human character, the inference would be that there is not sufficient virtue among men for self-government; and that nothing less than the chains of despotism can restrain them from destroying and devouring one another.

57 [56]

James Madison

February 19, 1788

To the People of the State of New York.

The third charge against the house of representatives is, that it will be taken from that class of citizens which will have least sympathy with the mass of the people, and be most likely to aim at an ambitious sacrifice of the many to the aggrandizement of the few.

Of all the objections which have been framed against the federal constitution, this is perhaps the most extraordinary. Whilst the objection itself is levelled against a pretended oligarchy, the principle of it strikes at the very root of republican government.

The aim of every political constitution is or ought to be first to obtain for rulers, men who possess most wisdom to discern, and most virtue to pursue the common good of the society; and in the next place, to take the most effectual precautions for keeping them virtuous, whilst they continue to hold their public trust. The elective mode of obtaining rulers is the characteristic policy of republican government. The means relied on in this form of government for preventing their degeneracy are numerous and various. The most effectual one is such a limitation of the term of appointments, as will maintain a proper responsibility to the people.

Let me now ask what circumstance there is in the constitution of the house of representatives, that violates the principles of republican government; or favors the elevation of the few on the ruins of the many? Let me ask whether every circumstance is not, on the contrary, strictly conformable to these principles; and scrupulously impartial to the rights and pretensions of every class and description of citizens?

Who are to be the electors of the federal representatives? Not the rich more than the poor; not the learned more than the ignorant; not the haughty heirs of distinguished names, more than the humble sons of obscure and unpropitious fortune. The electors are to be the great body of the people of the United States. They are to be the same who exercise the right in every state of electing the correspondent branch of the legislature of the state.

Who are to be the objects of popular choice? Every citizen whose merit may recommend him to the esteem and confidence of his country. No qualification of wealth, of birth, of religious faith, or of civil profession, is permitted to fetter the judgment or disappoint the inclination of the people.

If we consider the situation of the men on whom the free suffrages of their fellow citizens may confer the representative trust, we shall find it involving every security which can be devised or desired for their fidelity to their constituents.

In the first place, as they will have been distinguished by the preference of their fellow citizens, we are to presume, that in general, they will be somewhat distinguished also, by those qualities which entitle them to it, and which promise a sincere and scrupulous regard to the nature of their engagements.

In the second place, they will enter into the public service under circumstances which cannot fail to produce a temporary affection at least to their constituents. There is in every breast a sensibility to marks of honor, of favor, of esteem, and of confidence, which, apart from all considerations of interest, is some pledge for grateful and benevolent returns. Ingratitude is a common topic of declamation against human nature; and it must be confessed, that instances of it are but too frequent and flagrant both in public and in private life. But the universal and extreme indignation which it inspires, is itself a proof of the energy and prevalence of the contrary sentiment.

In the third place, those ties which bind the representative to his constituents are strengthened by motives of a more selfish nature. His pride and vanity attach him to a form of government which favors his pretensions, and gives him a share in its honors and distinctions. Whatever hopes or projects might be entertained by a few aspiring characters, it must generally happen that a great proportion of the men deriving their advancement from their influence with the people, would have more to hope from a preservation of the favor, than from innovations in the government subversive of the authority of the people.

All these securities however would be found very insufficient without the restraint of frequent elections. Hence, in the fourth place, the house of representatives is so constituted as to support in the members an habitual recollection of their dependence on the people. Before the sentiments impressed on their minds by the mode of their elevation, can be effaced by the exercise of power, they will be compelled to anticipate the moment when their power is to cease, when their exercise of it is to be reviewed, and when they must descend to the level from which they were raised; there for ever to remain, unless a faithful discharge of their trust shall have established their title to a renewal of it.

I will add as a fifth circumstance in the situation of the house of representatives, restraining them from oppressive measures, that they can make no law which will not have its full operation on themselves and their friends, as well as on the great mass of the society. This has always been deemed one of the strongest bonds by which human policy can connect the rulers and the people together. It creates between them that communion of interests and sympathy of sentiments of which few governments have furnished examples; but without which every government degenerates into tyranny. If it be asked what is to restrain the house of representatives from making legal discriminations in favor of themselves and a particular class of the society? I answer, the genius of the whole system, the nature of just and constitutional laws, and above all the vigilant and manly spirit which actuates the people of America, a spirit which nourishes freedom, and in return is nourished by it.

If this spirit shall ever be so far debased as to tolerate a law not obligatory on the legislature as well as on the people, the people will be prepared to tolerate anything but liberty.

Such will be the relation between the house of representatives and their constituents. Duty, gratitude, interest, ambition itself, are the cords by which they will be bound to fidelity and sympathy with the great mass of the people. It is possible that these may all be insufficient to controul the caprice and wickedness of man. But are they not all that government will admit, and that human prudence can devise? Are they not the genuine and the characteristic means by which republican government provides for the liberty and happiness of the people? Are they not the identical means on which every state government in the union, relies for the attainment of these important ends? What then are we to understand by the objection which this paper has combated? What are we to say to the men who profess the most flaming zeal for republican government, yet boldly impeach the fundamental principle of it; who pretend to be champions for the right and the capacity of the people to chuse their own rulers, yet maintain that they will prefer those only who will immediately and infallibly betray the trust committed to them? [. . .]

62 [61]

James Madison

February 27, 1788

To the People of the State of New York.

Having examined the constitution of the house of representatives, and answered such of the objections against it as seemed to merit notice, I enter next on the examination of the senate. The heads into which this member of the government may be considered, are—I. the qualifications of senators—II. the appointment of them by the state legislatures—III. the equality of representation in the senate—IV. the number of senators, and the term for which they are to be elected—V. the powers vested in the senate.

I. The qualifications proposed for senators, as distinguished from those of representatives, consist in a more advanced age, and a longer period of citizenship. A senator must be thirty years of age at least; as a representative, must be twenty-five. And the former must have been a citizen nine years; as seven years are required for the latter. The propriety of these distinctions is explained by the nature of the senatorial trust; which requiring greater extent of information and stability of character, requires at the same time that the senator should have reached a period of life most likely to supply these advantages; and which participating immediately in transactions with foreign nations, ought to be exercised by none who are not thoroughly weaned from the prepossessions and habits incident to foreign birth and education. The term of nine years appears to be a prudent mediocrity between a total exclusion of adopted citizens, whose merit and talents may claim a share in the public confidence; and an indiscriminate and hasty admission of them, which might create a channel for foreign influence on the national councils. [. . .]

III. The equality of representation in the senate is another point, which, being evidently the result of compromise between the opposite pretensions of the large and the small states, does not call for much discussion. If indeed it be right that among a people thoroughly incorporated into one nation, every district ought to have a *proportional* share in the government; and that among independent and sovereign states bound together by a simple league, the parties however unequal in size, ought to have an *equal* share in the common councils, it does not appear to be without some reason, that in a compound republic partaking both of the national and federal character, the government ought to be founded on a mixture of the principles of proportional and equal representation. But it is superfluous to try by the standard of theory, a part of the constitution which is allowed on all hands to be the result not of theory, but "of a spirit of amity, and that mutual deference and concession which the peculiarity of our political situation rendered indispensable." A common government with powers equal to its objects, is called for by the voice, and still more loudly by the political situation of America. A government founded on principles more consonant to the wishes of the larger states, is not likely to be obtained from the smaller states. The only option then for the former lies between the proposed government and a government still more objectionable. Under this alternative the advice of prudence must be, to embrace the lesser evil; and instead of indulging a fruitless anticipation of the possible mischiefs which may ensue, to contemplate rather the advantageous consequences which may qualify the sacrifice.

In this spirit it may be remarked, that the equal vote allowed to each state, is at once a constitutional recognition of the portion of sovereignty remaining in the individual states, and an instrument for preserving that residuary sovereignty. So far the equality ought to be no less acceptable to the large than to the small states; since they are not less solicitous to guard by every possible expedient against an improper consolidation of the states into one simple republic.

Another advantage accruing from this ingredient in the constitution of the senate, is the additional impediment it must prove against improper acts of legislation. No law or resolution can now be passed without the concurrence first of a majority of the people, and then of a majority of the states. It must be acknowledged that this complicated check on legislation may in some instances be injurious as well as beneficial; and that the peculiar defence which it involves in favour of the smaller states would be more rational, if any interests common to them, and distinct from those of the other states, would otherwise be exposed to peculiar danger. But as the larger states will always be able by their power over the supplies to defeat unreasonable exertions of this prerogative of the lesser states; and as the facility and excess of law-making seem to be the diseases to which our governments are most liable, it is not impossible that this part of the constitution may be more convenient in practice than it appears to many in contemplation.

IV. The number of senators and the duration of their appointment come next to be considered. In order to form an accurate judgment on both these points, it will be proper to enquire into the purposes which are to be answered by a senate; and in order to ascertain these it will be necessary to review the inconveniencies which a republic must suffer from the want of such an institution.

First. It is a misfortune incident to republican government, though in a less degree than to other governments, that those who administer it, may forget their obligations to their constituents, and prove unfaithful to their important trust. In this point of view, a senate, as a second branch of the legislative assembly, distinct from, and dividing the power with, a first, must be in all cases a salutary check on the government. It doubles the security to the people, by requiring the concurrence of two distinct bodies in schemes of usurpation or perfidy, where the ambition or corruption of one, would otherwise be sufficient. This is a precaution founded on such clear principles, and now so well understood in the United States, that it would be more than superfluous to enlarge on it. I will barely remark that as the improbability of sinister combinations will be in proportion to the dissimilarity in the genius of the two bodies; it must be politic to distinguish them from each other by every circumstance which will consist with a due harmony in all proper measures, and with the genuine principles of republican government.

Second. The necessity of a senate is not less indicated by the propensity of all single and numerous assemblies, to yield to the impulse of sudden and violent passions, and to be seduced by factious leaders, into intemperate and pernicious resolutions. Examples on this subject might be cited without number; and from proceedings within the United States, as well as from the history of other nations. But a position that will not be contradicted need not be proved. All that need be remarked is that a body which is to correct this infirmity ought itself be free from it, and consequently ought to be less numerous. It ought moreover to possess great firmness, and consequently ought to hold its authority by a tenure of considerable duration.

Third. Another defect to be supplied by a senate lies in a want of due acquaintance with the objects and principles of legislation. It is not possible that an assembly of men called for the most part from pursuits of a private nature, continued in appointment for a short time, and led by no permanent motive to devote the intervals of public occupation to a study of the laws, the affairs and the comprehensive interests of their country, should, if left wholly to themselves, escape a variety of important errors in the exercise of their legislative trust. It may be affirmed, on the best grounds, that no small share of the present embarrassments of America is to be charged on the blunders of our governments; and that these have proceeded from the heads rather than the hearts of most of the authors of them. What indeed are all the repealing, explaining and amending laws, which fill and disgrace our voluminous codes, but so many monuments of deficient wisdom. [. . .]

A good government implies two things; first, fidelity to the object of government, which is the happiness of the people; secondly, a knowledge of the means by which that object can be best attained. Some governments are deficient in both these qualities: Most governments are deficient in the first. I scruple not to assert that in the American governments, too little attention has been paid to the last. The federal constitution avoids this error; and what merits particular notice, it provides for the last in a mode which increases the security for the first.

Fourth. The mutability in the public councils, arising from a rapid succession of new members, however qualified they may be, points out in the strongest manner, the necessity of some stable institution in the government. Every new election in the states, is found to change one half of the representatives. From this change of men must proceed a change of opinions; and from a change of opinions, a change of measures. But a continual change even of good measures is inconsistent with every rule of prudence, and every prospect of success. [. . .]

In the first place it forfeits the respect and confidence of other nations, and all the advantages connected with national character. An individual who is observed to be inconstant to his plans, or perhaps to carry on his affairs without any plan at all, is marked at once by all prudent people as a speedy victim to his own unsteadiness and folly. His more friendly neighbours may pity him; but all will decline to connect their fortunes with his; and not a few will seize the opportunity of making their fortunes out of his. One nation is to another what one individual is to another; with this melancholy distinction perhaps, that the former with fewer of the benevolent emotions than the latter, are under fewer restraints also from taking undue advantage of the indiscretions of each other. Every nation consequently whose affairs betray a want of wisdom and stability, may calculate on every loss which can be sustained from the more systematic policy of its wiser neighbours. But the best instruction on this subject is unhappily conveyed to America by the example of her own situation. She finds that she is held in no respect by her friends; that she is the derision of her enemies; and that she is a prey to every nation which has an interest in speculating on her fluctuating councils and embarrassed affairs.

The internal effects of a mutable policy are still more calamitous. It poisons the blessings of liberty itself. It will be of little avail to the people that the laws are made by men of their own choice, if the laws be so voluminous that they cannot be read, or so incoherent that they cannot be understood; if they be repealed or revised before they are promulged, or undergo such incessant changes that no man who knows what the law is to-day can guess what it will be to-morrow. Law is defined to be a rule of action; but how can that be a rule, which is little known and less fixed?

Another effect of public instability is the unreasonable advantage it gives to the sagacious, the enterprising and the moneyed few, over the industrious and uninformed mass of the people. Every new regulation concerning commerce or revenue, or in any manner affecting the value of the different species of property, presents a new harvest to those who watch the change, and can trace its consequences; a harvest reared not by themselves but by the toils and cares of the great body of their fellow citizens. This is a state of things in which it may be said with some truth that laws are made for the *few* not for the *many*.

In another point of view great injury results from an unstable government. The want of confidence in the public councils damps every useful undertaking; the success and profit of which may depend on a continuance of existing arrangements. What prudent merchant will hazard his fortunes in any new branch of commerce, when he knows not but that his plans may be rendered unlawful before they can be executed? What farmer or manufacturer will lay himself out for the encouragement given to any particular cultivation or establishment, when he can have no assurance that his preparatory labors and advances will not render him a victim to an inconstant government? In a word no great improvement or laudable enterprise, can go forward, which requires the auspices of a steady system of national policy.

But the most deplorable effect of all is that diminution of attachment and reverence which steals into the hearts of the people, towards a political system which betrays so many marks of infirmity, and disappoints so many of their flattering hopes. No government any more than an individual will long be respected, without being truly respectable, nor be truly respectable without possessing a certain portion of order and stability.

63 [62]

James Madison

March 1, 1788

To the People of the State of New York.

A fifth desideratum illustrating the utility of a senate, is the want of a due sense of national character. Without a select and stable member of the government, the esteem of foreign powers will not only be forfeited by an unenlightened and variable policy, proceeding from the causes already mentioned; but the national councils will not possess that sensibility to the opinion of the world, which is perhaps not less necessary in order to merit, than it is to obtain, its respect and confidence.

An attention to the judgment of other nations is important to every government for two reasons: The one is, that independently of the merits of any particular plan or measure, it is desireable on various accounts, that it should appear to other nations as the offspring of a wise and honorable policy: The second is, that in doubtful cases, particularly where the national councils may be warped by some strong passion, or momentary interest, the presumed or known opinion of the impartial world, may be the best guide that can be followed. What has not America lost by her want of character with foreign nations? And how many errors and follies would she not have avoided, if the justice and propriety of her measures had in every instance been previously tried by the light in which they would probably appear to the unbiassed part of mankind?

Yet however requisite a sense of national character may be, it is evident that it can never be sufficiently possessed by a numerous and changeable body. It can only be found in a number so small, that a sensible degree of the praise and blame of public measures may be the portion of each individual; or in an assembly so durably invested with public trust, that the pride and consequence of its members may be sensibly incorporated with the reputation and prosperity of the community. [. . .]

I add as a *sixth* defect, the want in some important cases of a due responsibility in the government to the people, arising from that frequency of elections, which in other cases produces this responsibility. The remark will perhaps appear not only new but paradoxical. It must nevertheless be acknowledged, when explained, to be as undeniable as it is important.

Responsibility in order to be reasonable must be limited to objects within the power of the responsible party; and in order to be effectual, must relate to operations of that power, of which a ready and proper judgment can be formed by the constituents. The objects of government may be divided into two general classes; the one depending on measures which have singly an immediate and sensible operation; the other depending on a succession of well chosen and well connected measures, which have a gradual and perhaps unobserved operation. The importance of the latter description to the collective and permanent welfare of every country needs no explanation. And yet it is evident, that an assembly elected for so short a term as to be unable to provide more than one or two links in a chain of measures, on which the general welfare may essentially depend, ought not to be answerable for the final result, any more than a steward or tenant, engaged for one year, could be justly made to answer for places or improvements, which could not be accomplished in less than half a dozen years. Nor is it possible for the people to estimate the *share* of influence which their annual assemblies may respectively have on events resulting from the mixed transactions of several years. It is sufficiently difficult at any rate to preserve a personal responsibility in the members of a *numerous* body, for such acts of the body as have an immediate, detached and palpable operation on its constituents.

The proper remedy for this defect must be an additional body in the legislative department, which, having sufficient permanency to provide for such objects as require a continued attention, and a train of measures, may be justly and effectually answerable for the attainment of those objects.

Thus far I have considered the circumstances which point out the necessity of a well constructed senate, only as they relate to the representatives of the people. To a people as little blinded by prejudice, or corrupted by flattery, as those whom I address, I shall not scruple to add, that such an institution may be sometimes necessary, as a defence to the people against their own temporary errors and delusions. As the cool and deliberate sense of the community ought in all governments, and actually will in all free governments ultimately prevail over the views of its rulers; so there are particular moments in public affairs, when the people stimulated by some irregular passion, or some illicit advantage, or misled by the artful misrepresentations of interested men, may call for measures which they themselves will afterwards be the most ready to lament and condemn. In these critical moments, how salutary will be the interference of some temperate and respectable body of citizens, in order to check the misguided career, and to suspend the blow meditated by the people against themselves, until reason, justice and truth, can regain their authority over the public mind? What bitter anguish would not the people of Athens have often escaped, if their government had contained so provident a safeguard against the tyranny of their own passions? Popular liberty might then have escaped the indelible reproach of decreeing to the same citizens, the hemlock on one day, and statues on the next.

It may be suggested that a people spread over an extensive region, cannot like the crowded inhabitants of a small district, be subject to the infection of violent passions; or to the danger of combining in the pursuit of unjust measures. I am far from denying that this is a distinction of peculiar importance. I have on the contrary endeavoured in a former paper, to shew that it is one of the principal recommendations of a confederated republic. At the same time this advantage ought not to be considered as superseding the use of auxiliary precautions. It may even be remarked that the same extended situation which will exempt the people of America from some of the dangers incident to lesser republics, will expose them to the inconveniency of remaining for a longer time, under the influence of those misrepresentations which the combined industry of interested men may succeed in distributing among them. [. . .]

70 [69]

Alexander Hamilton

March 15, 1788

To the People of the State of New York.

There is an idea, which is not without its advocates, that a vigorous executive is inconsistent with the genius of republican government. The enlightened well wishers to this species of government must at least hope that the supposition is destitute of foundation; since they can never admit its truth, without at the same time admitting the condemnation of their own principles. Energy in the executive is a leading character in the definition of good government. It is essential to the protection of the community against foreign attacks: It is not less essential to the steady administration of the laws, to the protection of property against those irregular and high handed combinations, which sometimes interrupt the ordinary course of justice, to the security of liberty against the enterprises and assaults of ambition, of faction and of anarchy. Every man the least conversant in Roman story knows how often that republic was obliged to take refuge in the absolute power of a single man, under the formidable title of dictator, as well against the intrigues of ambitious individuals, who aspired to the tyranny, and the seditions of whole classes of the community, whose conduct threatened the existence of all government, as against the invasions of external enemies, who menaced the conquest and destruction of Rome.

There can be no need however to multiply arguments or examples on this head. A feeble executive implies a feeble execution of the government. A feeble execution is but another phrase for a bad execution: And a government ill executed, whatever it may be in theory, must be in practice a bad government.

Taking it for granted, therefore, that all men of sense will agree in the necessity of an energetic executive; it will only remain to inquire, what are the ingredients which constitute this energy—how far can they be combined with those other ingredients which constitute safety in the republican sense? And how far does this combination characterise the plan, which has been reported by the convention?

The ingredients which constitute energy in the executive are, unity—duration—an adequate provision for its support—competent powers.

The ingredients which constitute safety in the republican sense are, a due dependence on the people—a due responsibility.

Those politicians and statesmen, who have been the most celebrated for the soundness of their principles, and for the justness of their views, have declared in favor of a single executive and a numerous legislature. They have with great propriety considered energy as the most necessary qualification of the former, and have regarded this as most applicable to power in a single hand; while they have with equal propriety considered the latter as best adapted to deliberation and wisdom, and best calculated to conciliate the confidence of the people and to secure their privileges and interests.

That unity is conducive to energy will not be disputed. Decision, activity, secrecy, and dispatch will generally characterise the proceedings of one man, in a much more eminent degree, than the proceedings of any greater number; and in proportion as the number is increased, these qualities will be diminished.

This unity may be destroyed in two ways; either by vesting the power in two or more magistrates of equal dignity and authority; or by vesting it ostensibly in one man, subject in whole or in part to the controul and co-operation of others, in the capacity of counsellors to him. Of the first the two consuls of Rome may serve as an example; of the last we shall find examples in the constitutions of several of the states. New-York and New-Jersey, if I recollect right, are the only states, which have entrusted the executive authority wholly to single men.[8] Both these methods of destroying the unity of the executive have their partisans; but the votaries of an executive council are the most numerous. They are both liable, if not to equal, to similar objections; and may in most lights be examined in conjunction.

The experience of other nations will afford little instruction on this head. As far however as it teaches any thing, it teaches us not to be inamoured of plurality in the executive. [. . .]

But quitting the dim light of historical research, and attaching ourselves purely to the dictates of reason and good sense, we shall discover much greater cause to reject than to approve the idea of plurality in the executive, under any modification whatever.

Wherever two or more persons are engaged in any common enterprize or pursuit, there is always danger of difference of opinion. If it be a public trust or office in which they are cloathed with equal dignity and authority, there is peculiar danger of personal emulation and even animosity. From either and especially from all these causes, the most bitter dissentions are apt to spring. Whenever these happen, they lessen the respectability, weaken the authority, and distract the plans and operations of those whom they divide. If they should unfortunately assail the supreme executive magistracy of a country, consisting of a plurality of persons, they might impede or frustrate the most important measures of the government, in the most critical emergencies of the state. And what is still worse, they might split the community into the violent and irreconcilable factions, adhering differently to the different individuals who composed the magistracy.

Men often oppose a thing merely because they have had no agency in planning it, or because it may have been planned by those whom they dislike. But if they have been consulted and have happened to disapprove, opposition then becomes in their estimation an indispensable duty of self love. They seem to think themselves bound in honor, and by all the motives of personal infallibility to defeat the success of what has been resolved upon, contrary to their sentiments. Men of upright, benevolent tempers have too many opportunities of remarking with horror, to what desperate lengths this disposition is sometimes carried, and how often the great interests of society are sacrificed to the vanity, to the conceit and to the obstinacy of individuals, who have credit enough to make their passions and their caprices interesting to mankind. Perhaps the question now before the public may in its consequences afford melancholy proofs

---

8. New-York has no council except for the single purpose of appointing to offices; New-Jersey has a council, whom the governor may consult. But I think from the terms of the constitution their resolutions do not bind him.

of the effects of this despicable frailty, or rather detestable vice in the human character.

Upon the principles of a free government, inconveniencies from the source just mentioned must necessarily be submitted to in the formation of the legislature; but it is unnecessary and therefore unwise to introduce them into the constitution of the executive. It is here too that they may be most pernicious. In the legislature, promptitude of decision is oftener an evil than a benefit. The differences of opinion, and the jarrings of parties in that department of the government, though they may sometimes obstruct salutary plans, yet often promote deliberation and circumspection; and serve to check excesses in the majority. When a resolution too is once taken, the opposition must be at an end. That resolution is a law, and resistance to it punishable. But no favourable circumstances palliate or atone for the disadvantages of dissention in the executive department. Here they are pure and unmixed. There is no point at which they cease to operate. They serve to embarrass and weaken the execution of the plan or measure, to which they relate, from the first step to the final conclusion of it. They constantly counteract those qualities in the executive, which are the most necessary ingredients in its composition, vigour and expedition, and this without any counterballancing good. In the conduct of war, in which the energy of the executive is the bulwark of the national security, every thing would be to be apprehended from its plurality.

It must be confessed that these observations apply with principal weight to the first case supposed, that is to a plurality of magistrates of equal dignity and authority; a scheme the advocates for which are not likely to form a numerous sect: But they apply, though not with equal, yet with considerable weight, to the project of a council, whose concurrence is made constitutionally necessary to the operations of the ostensible executive. An artful cabal in that council would be able to distract and to enervate the whole system of administration. If no such cabal should exist, the mere diversity of views and opinions would alone be sufficient to tincture the exercise of the executive authority with a spirit of habitual feebleness and dilatoriness.

But one of the weightiest objections to a plurality in the executive, and which lies as much against the last as the first plan, is that it tends to conceal faults, and destroy responsibility. Responsibility is of two kinds, to censure and to punishment. The first is the most important of the two; especially in an elective office. Men, in public trust, will much oftener act in such a manner as to render them unworthy of being any longer trusted, than in such a manner as to make them obnoxious to legal punishment. But the multiplication of the executive adds to the difficulty of detection in either case. It often becomes impossible, amidst mutual accusations, to determine on whom the blame or the punishment of a pernicious measure, or series of pernicious measures ought really to fall. It is shifted from one to another with so much dexterity, and under such plausible appearances, that the public opinion is left in suspense about the real author. The circumstances which may have led to any national miscarriage or misfortune are sometimes so complicated, that where there are a number of actors who may have had different degrees and kinds of agency, though we may clearly see upon the whole that there has been mismanagement, yet it may be impracticable to pronounce to whose account the evil which may have been incurred is truly chargeable.

"I was overruled by my council. The council were so divided in their opinions, that it was impossible to obtain any better resolution on the point." These and similar pretexts are constantly at hand, whether true or false. And who is there that will either take the trouble or incur the odium of a strict scrutiny into the secret springs of the transaction? Should there be found a citizen zealous enough to undertake the unpromising task, if there happen to be a collusion between the parties concerned, how easy is it to cloath the circumstances with so much ambiguity, as to render it uncertain what was the precise conduct of any of those parties?

In the single instance in which the governor of this state is coupled with a council, that is in the appointment to offices, we have seen the mischiefs of it in the view now under consideration. Scandalous appointments to important offices have been made. Some cases indeed have been so flagrant, that ALL PARTIES have agreed in the impropriety of the thing. When enquiry has been made, the blame has been laid by the governor on the members of the council; who on their part have charged it upon his nomination: While the people remain altogether at a loss to determine by whose influence their interests have been committed to hands so unqualified, and so manifestly improper. In tenderness to individuals, I forbear to descend to particulars.

It is evident from these considerations, that the plurality of the executive tends to deprive the people of the two greatest securities they can have for the faithful exercise of any delegated power; first, the restraints of public opinion, which lose their efficacy as well on account of the division of the censure attendant on bad measures among a number, as on account of the uncertainty on whom it ought to fall; and secondly, the opportunity of discovering with facility and clearness the misconduct of the persons they trust, in order either to their removal from office, or to their actual punishment, in cases which admit of it. [. . .]

The idea of a council to the executive, which has so generally obtained in the state constitutions, has been derived from that maxim of republican jealousy, which considers power as safer in the hands of a number of men than of a single man. If the maxim should be admitted to be applicable to the case, I should contend that the advantage on that side would not counterballance the numerous disadvantages on the opposite side. But I do not think the rule at all applicable to the executive power. I clearly concur in opinion in this particular with a writer whom the celebrated Junius pronounces to be "deep, solid and ingenious," that, "the executive power is more easily confined when it is one":[9] That it is far more safe there should be a single object for the jealousy and watchfulness of the people; and in a word that all multiplication of the executive is rather dangerous than friendly to liberty. [. . .]

71 [70]

Alexander Hamilton

March 18, 1788

To the People of the State of New York.

Duration in office has been mentioned as the second requisite to the energy of the executive authority. This has relation to two objects: To the personal firmness of the executive magistrate in the employment of his constitutional powers; and to the stability of the system of administration which may have been adopted under his auspices. With regard to the first, it must be evident, that the longer the duration in office, the greater will be the probability of obtaining so important an advantage. It is a general principle of human nature, that a man will be interested in whatever he possesses, in proportion to the firmness or precariousness of the tenure, by which he holds it; will be less attached to what he holds by a momentary or uncertain title, than to what he enjoys by a durable or certain title; and of course will be willing to risk more for the sake of the one, than for the sake of the other. This remark is not less applicable to a political privilege, or honor, or trust, than to any article of ordinary property. The inference from it is, that a man acting in the capacity of chief magistrate, under a consciousness, that in a very short time he *must* lay down his office, will be apt to feel himself too little interested in it, to hazard any material censure or perplexity, from the independent exertion of his powers, or from encountering the ill-humors, however transient, which may happen to prevail either in a considerable part of the society itself, or even in a predominant faction in the legislative body. If the case should only be, that he *might* lay it down, unless continued by a new choice; and if he should be desirous of being continued, his wishes conspiring with his fears would tend still more powerfully to corrupt his integrity, or debase his fortitude. In either case feebleness and irresolution must be the characteristics of the station.

There are some, who would be inclined to regard the servile pliancy of the executive to a prevailing current, either in the community, or in the legislature, as its best recommendation. But such men entertain very crude notions, as well of the purposes for which government was instituted, as of the true means by which the public happiness may be promoted. The republican principle demands, that the deliberate sense of the community should govern the conduct of those to whom they entrust the management of their affairs; but it does not require an unqualified complaisance to every sudden breese of passion, or to every transient impulse which the people may receive from the arts of men, who flatter

9. De Lolme.

their prejudices to betray their interests. It is a just observation, that the people commonly *intend* the PUBLIC GOOD. This often applies to their very errors. But their good sense would despise the adulator, who should pretend that they always *reason right* about the *means* of promoting it. They know from experience, that they sometimes err; and the wonder is, that they so seldom err as they do; beset as they continually are by the wiles of parasites and sycophants, by the snares of the ambitious, the avaricious, the desperate; by the artifices of men, who possess their confidence more than they deserve it, and of those who seek to possess, rather than to deserve it. When occasions present themselves in which the interests of the people are at variance with their inclinations, it is the duty of the persons whom they have appointed to be the guardians of those interests, to withstand the temporary delusion, in order to give them time and opportunity for more cool and sedate reflection. Instances might be cited, in which a conduct of this kind has saved the people from very fatal consequences of their own mistakes, and has procured lasting monuments of their gratitude to the men, who had courage and magnanimity enough to serve them at the peril of their displeasure.

But however inclined we might be to insist upon an unbounded complaisance in the executive to the inclinations of the people, we can with no propriety contend for a like complaisance to the humors of the legislature. The latter may sometimes stand in opposition to the former; and at other times the people may be entirely neutral. In either supposition, it is certainly desirable that the executive should be in a situation to dare to act his own opinion with vigor and decision.

The same rule, which teaches the propriety of a partition between the various branches of power, teaches likewise that this partition ought to be so contrived as to render the one independent of the other. To what purpose separate the executive, or the judiciary, from the legislative, if both the executive and the judiciary are so constituted as to be at the absolute devotion of the legislative? Such a separation must be merely nominal and incapable of producing the ends for which it was established. It is one thing to be subordinate to the laws, and another to be dependent on the legislative body. The first comports with, the last violates, the fundamental principles of good government; and whatever may be the forms of the constitution, unites all power in the same hands. The tendency of the legislative authority to absorb every other, has been fully displayed and illustrated by examples, in some preceding numbers. In governments purely republican, this tendency is almost irresistable. The representatives of the people, in a popular assembly, seem sometimes to fancy that they are the people themselves; and betray strong symptoms of impatience and disgust at the least sign of opposition from any other quarter; as if the exercise of its rights by either the executive or judiciary, were a breach of their privilege and an outrage to their dignity. They often appear disposed to exert an imperious controul over the other departments; and as they commonly have the people on their side, they always act with such momentum as to make it very difficult for the other members of the government to maintain the balance of the constitution.

It may perhaps be asked how the shortness of the duration in office can affect the independence of the executive on the legislature, unless the one were possessed of the power of appointing or displacing the other? One answer to this enquiry may be drawn from the principle already remarked, that is from the slender interest a man is apt to take in a short lived advantage, and the little inducement it affords him to expose himself on account of it to any considerable inconvenience or hazard. Another answer [. . .] will result from the consideration of the influence of the legislative body over the people, which might be employed to prevent the re-election of a man, who by an upright resistance to any sinister project of that body, should have made himself obnoxious to its resentment. [. . .]

It cannot be affirmed, that a duration of four years or any other limited duration would completely answer the end proposed; but it would contribute towards it in a degree which would have a material influence upon the spirit and character of the government. Between the commencement and termination of such a period there would always be a considerable interval, in which the prospect of annihilation would be sufficiently remote not to have an improper effect upon the conduct of a man endued with a tolerable portion of fortitude; and in which he might reasonably promise himself, that there would be time enough, before it arrived, to make the community sensible of the propriety of the measures he might incline to pursue. Though it be probable, that as he approached the moment when the public were by a new election to signify their sense of his conduct, his confidence and with it, his firmness would decline; yet both the one and the other would derive support from the opportunities, which his previous continuance in the station had afforded him of establishing himself in the esteem and good will of his constituents. He might then hazard with safety, in proportion to the proofs he had given of his wisdom and integrity, and to the title he had acquired to the respect and attachment of his fellow citizens. [. . .]

73 [72]

Alexander Hamilton

March 21, 1788

To the People of the State of New York.

[. . .] The last of the requisites to energy which have been enumerated are competent powers. Let us proceed to consider those which are proposed to be vested in the president of the United States.

The first thing that offers itself to our observation, is the qualified negative of the president upon the acts or resolutions of the two houses of the legislature; or in other words his power of returning all bills with objections; to have the effect of preventing their becoming laws, unless they should afterwards be ratified by two thirds of each of the component members of the legislative body.

The propensity of the legislative department to intrude upon the rights and to absorb the powers of the other departments, has been already more than once suggested; the insufficiency of a mere parchment delineation of the boundaries of each, has also been remarked upon; and the necessity of furnishing each with constitutional arms for its own defence, has been inferred and proved. From these clear and indubitable principles results the propriety of a negative, either absolute or qualified, in the executive, upon the acts of the legislative branches. Without the one or the other the former would be absolutely unable to defend himself against the depredations of the latter. He might gradually be stripped of his authorities by successive resolutions, or annihilated by a single vote. And in the one mode or the other, the legislative and executive powers might speedily come to be blended in the same hands. If even no propensity had ever discovered itself in the legislative body, to invade the rights of the executive, the rules of just reasoning and theoretic propriety would of themselves teach us, that the one ought not to be left at the mercy of the other, but ought to possess a constitutional and effectual power of self defence.

But the power in question has a further use. It not only serves as a shield to the executive, but it furnishes an additional security against the enaction of improper laws. It establishes a salutary check upon the legislative body calculated to guard the community against the effects of faction, precipitancy, or of any impulse unfriendly to the public good, which may happen to influence a majority of that body.

The propriety of a negative, has upon some occasions been combated by an observation, that it was not to be presumed a single man would possess more virtue or wisdom, than a number of men; and that unless this presumption should be entertained, it would be improper to give the executive magistrate any species of controul over the legislative body.

But this observation when examined will appear rather specious than solid. The propriety of the thing does not turn upon the supposition of superior wisdom or virtue in the executive: But upon the supposition that the legislative will not be infallible: That the love of power may sometimes betray it into a disposition to encroach upon the rights of the other members of the government; that a spirit of faction may sometimes pervert its deliberations; that impressions of the moment may sometimes hurry it into measures which itself on maturer reflection would condemn. The primary inducement to conferring the power in question upon the executive, is to enable him to defend himself; the secondary one is to encrease the chances in favor of the community, against the passing of bad laws, through haste, inadvertence, or design. The oftener a measure is brought under examination, the greater the diversity in the situations of those who are to examine it, the less must be the danger of those errors which flow from want of due deliberation, or of those missteps which proceed from the contagion of some common passion or interest. It is far less probable, that culpable views of any kind should infect all the parts of the government, at the same moment and in relation to the same object, than that they should by turns govern and mislead every one of them.

It may perhaps be said, that the power of preventing bad laws includes that of preventing good ones; and may be used to the one purpose as well as to the other. But this objection will have little weight with those who can properly estimate the mischiefs of that inconstancy and mutability in the laws, which form the greatest blemish in the character and genius of our governments. They will consider every institution calculated to restrain the excess of law-making, and to keep things in the same state in which they may happen to be at any given period, as much more likely to do good than harm; because it is favorable to greater stability in the system of legislation. The injury which may possibly be done by defeating a few good laws will be amply compensated by the advantage of preventing a number of bad ones.

Nor is this all. The superior weight and influence of the legislative body in a free government, and the hazard to the executive in a trial of strength with that body, afford a satisfactory security, that the negative would generally be employed with great caution, and that there would oftener be room for a charge of timidity than of rashness, in the exercise of it. [. . .]

It is evident that there would be greater danger of his not using his power when necessary, than of his using it too often, or too much. An argument indeed against its expediency has been drawn from this very source. It has been represented on this account as a power odious in appearance; useless in practice. But it will not follow, that because it might be rarely exercised, it would never be exercised. In the case for which it is chiefly designed, that of an immediate attack upon the constitutional rights of the executive, or in a case in which the public good was evidently and palpably sacrificed, a man of tolerable firmness would avail himself of his constitutional means of defence, and would listen to the admonitions of duty and responsibility. In the former supposition, his fortitude would be stimulated by his immediate interest in the power of his office; in the latter by the probability of the sanction of his constituents; who though they would naturally incline to the legislative body in a doubtful case, would hardly suffer their partiality to delude them in a very plain case. I speak now with an eye to a magistrate possessing only a common share of firmness. There are men, who under any circumstances will have the courage to do their duty at every hazard.

But the convention have pursued a mean in this business; which will both facilitate the exercise of the power vested in this respect in the executive magistrate, and make its efficacy to depend on the sense of a considerable part of the legislative body. Instead of an absolute negative, it is proposed to give the executive the qualified negative already described. This is a power, which would be much more readily exercised than the other. A man who might be afraid to defeat a law by his single VETO, might not scruple to return it for re-consideration; subject to being finally rejected only in the event of more than one third of each house concurring in the sufficiency of his objections. He would be encouraged by the reflection, that if his opposition should prevail, it would embark in it a very respectable proportion of the legislative body, whose influence would be united with his in supporting the propriety of his conduct, in the public opinion. A direct and categorical negative has something in the appearance of it more harsh, and more apt to irritate, than the mere suggestion of argumentative objections to be approved or disapproved, by those to whom they are addressed. In proportion as it would be less apt to offend, it would be more apt to be exercised; and for this very reason it may in practice be found more effectual. It is to be hoped that it will not often happen, that improper views will govern so large a proportion as two-thirds of both branches of the legislature at the same time; and this too in defiance of the counterpoising weight of the executive. It is at any rate far less probable, that this should be the case, than that such views should taint the resolutions and conduct of a bare majority. A power of this nature, in the executive, will often have a silent and unperceived though forcible operation. When men engaged in unjustifiable pursuits are aware, that obstructions may come from a quarter which they cannot controul, they will often be restrained, by the bare apprehension of opposition, from doing what they would with eagerness rush into, if no such external impediments were to be feared. [. . .]

78

Alexander Hamilton

May 28, 1788

To the People of the State of New York.

We proceed now to an examination of the judiciary department of the proposed government.

In unfolding the defects of the existing confederation, the utility and necessity of a federal judicature have been clearly pointed out. It is the less necessary to recapitulate the considerations there urged; as the propriety of the institution in the abstract is not disputed: The only questions which have been raised being relative to the manner of constituting it, and to its extent. To these points therefore our observations shall be confined.

The manner of constituting it seems to embrace these several objects—1st. The mode of appointing the judges.—2d. The tenure by which they are to hold their places. [. . .]

As to the tenure by which the judges are to hold their places: This chiefly concerns their duration in office; the provisions for their support; and the precautions for their responsibility.

According to the plan of the convention, all the judges who may be appointed by the United States are to hold their offices *during good behaviour,* which is conformable to the most approved of the state constitutions; and among the rest, to that of this state. Its propriety having been drawn into question by the adversaries of that plan, is no light symptom of the rage for objection which disorders their imaginations and judgments. The standard of good behaviour for the continuance in office of the judicial magistracy is certainly one of the most valuable of the modern improvements in the practice of government. In a monarchy it is an excellent barrier to the despotism of the prince: In a republic it is a no less excellent barrier to the encroachments and oppressions of the representative body. And it is the best expedient which can be devised in any government, to secure a steady, upright and impartial administration of the laws.

Whoever attentively considers the different departments of power must perceive, that in a government in which they are separated from each other, the judiciary, from the nature of its functions, will always be the least dangerous to the political rights of the constitution; because it will be least in a capacity to annoy or injure them. The executive not only dispenses the honors, but holds the sword of the community. The legislature not only commands the purse, but prescribes the rules by which the duties and rights of every citizen are to be regulated. The judiciary on the contrary has no influence over either the sword or the purse, no direction either of the strength or of the wealth of the society, and can take no active resolution whatever. It may truly be said to have neither FORCE nor WILL, but merely judgment; and must ultimately depend upon the aid of the executive arm even for the efficacy of its judgments.

This simple view of the matter suggests several important consequences. It proves incontestibly that the judiciary is beyond comparison the weakest of the three departments of power;[10] that it can never attack with success either of the other two; and that all possible care is requisite to enable it to defend itself against their attacks. It equally proves, that though individual oppression may now and then proceed from the courts of justice, the general liberty of the people can never be endangered from that quarter: I mean, so long as the judiciary remains truly distinct from both the legislative and executive. For I agree that "there is no liberty, if the power of judging be not separated from the legislative and executive powers."[11] And it proves, in the last place, that as liberty can have nothing to fear from the judiciary alone, but would have every thing to fear from its union with either of the other departments; that as all the effects of such an union must ensue from a dependence of the former on the latter, notwithstanding a nominal and apparent separation; that as from the natural feebleness of the judiciary, it is in continual jeopardy of being overpowered, awed or influenced by its coordinate branches; and that as nothing can contribute so much to its firmness and independence, as permanency in office, this quality may therefore be justly regarded as an indispensable ingredient in its

---

10. The celebrated Montesquieu speaking of them says, "of the three powers above mentioned, the JUDICIARY is next to nothing." *Spirit of Laws,* Vol. 1, page 186.

11. Idem. page 181.

constitution; and in a great measure as the citadel of the public justice and the public security.

The complete independence of the courts of justice is peculiarly essential in a limited constitution. By a limited constitution I understand one which contains certain specified exceptions to the legislative authority; such for instance as that it shall pass no bills of attainder, no *ex post facto* laws, and the like. Limitations of this kind can be preserved in practice no other way than through the medium of the courts of justice; whose duty it must be to declare all acts contrary to the manifest tenor of the constitution void. Without this, all the reservations of particular rights or privileges would amount to nothing.

Some perplexity respecting the right of the courts to pronounce legislative acts void, because contrary to the constitution, has arisen from an imagination that the doctrine would imply a superiority of the judiciary to the legislative power. It is urged that the authority which can declare the acts of another void, must necessarily be superior to the one whose acts may be declared void. As this doctrine is of great importance in all the American constitutions, a brief discussion of the grounds on which it rests cannot be unacceptable.

There is no position which depends on clearer principles, than that every act of a delegated authority, contrary to the tenor of the commission under which it is exercised, is void. No legislative act therefore contrary to the constitution can be valid. To deny this would be to affirm that the deputy is greater than his principal; that the servant is above his master; that the representatives of the people are superior to the people themselves; that men acting by virtue of powers may do not only what their powers do not authorise, but what they forbid.

If it be said that the legislative body are themselves the constitutional judges of their own powers, and that the construction they put upon them is conclusive upon the other departments, it may be answered, that this cannot be the natural presumption, where it is not to be collected from any particular provisions in the constitution. It is not otherwise to be supposed that the constitution could intend to enable the representatives of the people to substitute their *will* to that of their constituents. It is far more rational to suppose that the courts were designed to be an intermediate body between the people and the legislature, in order, among other things, to keep the latter within the limits assigned to their authority. The interpretation of the laws is the proper and peculiar province of the courts. A constitution is in fact, and must be, regarded by the judges as a fundamental law. It therefore belongs to them to ascertain its meaning as well as the meaning of any particular act proceeding from the legislative body. If there should happen to be an irreconcileable variance between the two, that which has the superior obligation and validity ought of course to be preferred; or in other words, the constitution ought to be preferred to the statute, the intention of the people to the intention of their agents.

Nor does this conclusion by any means suppose a superiority of the judicial to the legislative power. It only supposes that the power of the people is superior to both; and that where the will of the legislature declared in its statutes, stands in opposition to that of the people declared in the constitution, the judges ought to be governed by the latter, rather than the former. They ought to regulate their decisions by the fundamental laws, rather than by those which are not fundamental.

This exercise of judicial discretion in determining between two contradictory laws, is exemplified in a familiar instance. It not uncommonly happens, that there are two statutes existing at one time, clashing in whole or in part with each other, and neither of them containing any repealing clause or expression. In such a case, it is the province of the courts to liquidate and fix their meaning and operation: So far as they can by any fair construction be reconciled to each other; reason and law conspire to dictate that this should be done. Where this is impracticable, it becomes a matter of necessity to give effect to one, in exclusion of the other. The rule which has obtained in the courts for determining their relative validity is that the last in order of time shall be preferred to the first. But this is mere rule of construction, not derived from any positive law, but from the nature and reason of the thing. It is a rule not enjoined upon the courts by legislative provision, but adopted by themselves, as consonant to truth and propriety, for the direction of their conduct as interpreters of the law. They thought it reasonable, that between the interfering acts of an *equal* authority, that which was the last indication of its will, should have the preference.

But in regard to the interfering acts of a superior and subordinate authority, of an original and derivative power, the nature and reason of the thing indicate the converse of that rule as proper to be followed. They teach us that the prior act of a superior ought to be preferred to the subsequent act of an inferior and subordinate authority; and that, accordingly, whenever a particular statute contravenes the constitution, it will be the duty of the judicial tribunals to adhere to the latter, and disregard the former.

It can be of no weight to say, that the courts on the pretence of a repugnancy, may substitute their own pleasure to the constitutional intentions of the legislature. This might as well happen in the case of two contradictory statutes; or it might as well happen in every adjudication upon any single statute. The courts must declare the sense of the law; and if they should be disposed to exercise WILL instead of JUDGMENT, the consequence would equally be the substitution of their pleasure to that of the legislative body. The observation, if it proved any thing, would prove that there ought to be no judges distinct from that body.

If then the courts of justice are to be considered as the bulwarks of a limited constitution against legislative encroachments, this consideration will afford a strong argument for the permanent tenure of judicial offices, since nothing will contribute so much as this to that independent spirit in the judges, which must be essential to the faithful performance of so arduous a duty.

This independence of the judges is equally requisite to guard the constitution and the rights of individuals from the effects of those ill humours which the arts of designing men, or the influence of particular conjunctures, sometimes disseminate among the people themselves, and which, though they speedily give place to better information and more deliberate reflection, have a tendency in the mean time to occasion dangerous innovations in the government, and serious oppressions of the minor party in the community. Though I trust the friends of the proposed constitution will never concur with its enemies[12] in questioning that fundamental principle of republican government, which admits the right of the people to alter or abolish the established constitution whenever they find it inconsistent with their happiness; yet it is not to be inferred from this principle, that the representatives of the people, whenever a momentary inclination happens to lay hold of a majority of their constituents incompatible with the provisions in the existing constitution, would on that account be justifiable in a violation of those provisions; or that the courts would be under a greater obligation to connive at infractions in this shape, than when they had proceeded wholly from the cabals of the representative body. Until the people have by some solemn and authoritative act annulled or changed the established form, it is binding upon themselves collectively, as well as individually; and no presumption, or even knowledge of their sentiments, can warrant their representatives in a departure from it, prior to such an act. But it is easy to see that it would require an uncommon portion of fortitude in the judges to do their duty as faithful guardians of the constitution, where legislative invasions of it had been instigated by the major voice of the community.

But it is not with a view to infractions of the constitution only that the independence of the judges may be an essential safeguard against the effects of occasional ill humours in the society. These sometimes extend no farther than to the injury of the private rights of particular classes of citizens, by unjust and partial laws. Here also the firmness of the judicial magistracy is of vast importance in mitigating the severity, and confining the operation of such laws. It not only serves to moderate the immediate mischiefs of those which may have been passed, but it operates as a check upon the legislative body in passing them; who, perceiving that obstacles to the success of an iniquitous intention are to be expected from the scruples of the courts, are in a manner compelled by the very motives of the injustice they meditate, to qualify their attempts. [. . .]

That inflexible and uniform adherence to the rights of the constitution and of individuals, which we perceive to be indispensable in the courts of justice, can certainly not be expected from judges who hold their offices by a temporary commission. Periodical appointments, however regulated, or by whomsoever made, would in some way or other be fatal to their necessary independence. If the power of making them was committed either to the executive or legislature, there would be danger of an improper complaisance to the branch which possessed it; if to both, there would be

12 Vide Protest of the minority of the convention of Pennsylvania, Martin's speech, &c.

an unwillingness to hazard the displeasure of either; if to the people, or to persons chosen by them for the special purpose, there would be too great a disposition to consult popularity, to justify a reliance that nothing would be consulted but the constitution and the laws.

There is yet a further and a weighty reason for the permanency of the judicial offices; which is deducible from the nature of the qualifications they require. It has been frequently remarked with great propriety, that a voluminous code of laws is one of the inconveniences necessarily connected with the advantages of a free government. To avoid an arbitrary discretion in the courts, it is indispensable that they should be bound down by strict rules and precedents, which serve to define and point out their duty in every particular case that comes before them; and it will readily be conceived from the variety of controversies which grow out of the folly and wickedness of mankind, that the records of those precedents must unavoidably swell to a very considerable bulk, and must demand long and laborious study to acquire a competent knowledge of them. Hence it is that there can be but few men in the society, who will have sufficient skill in the laws to qualify them for the stations of judges. And making the proper deductions for the ordinary depravity of human nature, the number must be still smaller of those who unite the requisite integrity with the requisite knowledge. These considerations apprise us, that the government can have no great option between fit characters; and that a temporary duration in office, which would naturally discourage such characters from quitting a lucrative line of practice to accept a seat on the bench, would have a tendency to throw the administration of justice into hands less able, and less well qualified to conduct it with utility and dignity. In the present circumstances of this country, and in those in which it is likely to be for a long time to come, the disadvantages on this score would be greater than they may at first sight appear; but it must be confessed that they are far inferior to those which present themselves under the other aspects of the subject. [. . .]

James Wilson

Speech on Ratification (1787)

State House, 6 October 1787,
Pennsylvania Packet, 10 October 1787

Mr. Chairman and Fellow Citizens, Having received the honour of an appointment to represent you in the late convention, it is, perhaps, my duty to comply with the request of many gentlemen, whose characters and judgments I sincerely respect, and who have urged that this would be a proper occasion to lay before you any information, which will serve to elucidate and explain the principles and arrangements of the constitution that has been submitted to the consideration of the United States. I confess that I am unprepared for so extensive and so important a disquisition: but the insidious attempts, which are clandestinely and industriously made to pervert and destroy the new plan, induce me the more readily to engage in its defence: and the impressions of four months constant attendance to the subject, have not been so easily effaced, as to leave me without an answer to the objections which have been raised.

It will be proper, however, before I enter into the refutation of the charges that are alleged, to mark the leading discrimination between the state constitutions, and the constitution of the United States. When the people established the powers of legislation under their separate governments, they invested their representatives with every right and authority which they did not in explicit terms reserve: and therefore upon every question, respecting the jurisdiction of the house of assembly, if the frame of government is silent, the jurisdiction is efficient and complete. But in delegating fœderal powers, another criterion was necessarily introduced: and the congressional authority is to be collected, not from tacit implication, but from the positive grant, expressed in the instrument of union. Hence, it is evident, that in the former case, everything which is not reserved, is given: but in the latter, the reverse of the proposition prevails, and every thing which is not given, is reserved. This distinction being recognized, will furnish an answer to those who think the omission of a bill of rights, a defect in the proposed constitution: for it would have been superfluous and absurd, to have stipulated with a fœderal body of our own creation, that we should enjoy those privileges, of which we are not divested either by the intention or the act that has brought that body into existence. For instance, the liberty of the press, which has been a copious subject of declamation and opposition: what controul can proceed from the fœderal government, to shackle or destroy that sacred palladium of national freedom? If, indeed, a power similar to that which has been granted for the regulation of commerce, had been granted to regulate literary publications, it would have been as necessary to stipulate that the liberty of the press should be preserved inviolate, as that the impost should be general in its operation. [. . .]

In truth, then, the proposed system possesses no influence whatever upon the press; and it would have been merely nugatory, to have introduced a formal declaration upon the subject; nay, that very declaration might have been construed to imply that some degree of power was given, since we undertook to define its extent.

Another objection that has been fabricated against the new constitution, is expressed in this disingenuous form—"the trial by jury is abolished in civil cases." I must be excused, my fellow citizens, if, upon this point, I take advantage of my professional experience, to detect the futility of the assertion. Let it be remembered, then, that the business of the fœderal constitution was not local, but general—not limited to the views and establishments of a single state, but co-extensive with the continent, and comprehending the views and establishments of thirteen independent sovereignties. When, therefore, this subject was in discussion, we were involved in difficulties, which pressed on all sides, and no precedent could be discovered to direct our course. The cases open to a jury, differed in the different states; it was therefore impracticable, on that ground, to have made a general rule. The want of uniformity would have rendered any reference to the practice of the states idle and useless: and it could not, with any propriety, be said, that "the trial by jury shall be as heretofore:" since there has never existed any fœderal system of jurisprudence, to which the declaration could relate. Besides, it is not in all cases that the trial by jury is adopted in civil questions: for causes depending in courts of admiralty, such as relate to maritime captures, and such as are agitated in the courts of equity, do not require the intervention of that tribunal. How, then, was the line of discrimination to be drawn? The convention found the task too difficult for them: and they left the business as it stands—in the fullest confidence, that no danger could possibly ensue, since the proceedings of the supreme court are to be regulated by the congress, which is a faithful representation of the people: and the oppression of government is effectually barred, by declaring that in all criminal cases, the trial by jury shall be preserved.

This constitution, it has been further urged, is of a pernicious tendency, because it tolerates a standing army in the time of peace. This has always been a popular topic of declamation: and yet I do not know a nation in the world, which has not found it necessary and useful to maintain the appearance of strength in a season of the most profound tranquility. Nor is it a novelty with us; for under the present articles of confederation, congress certainly possesses this reprobated power: and the exercise of it is proved at this moment by the cantonments along the banks of the Ohio. But what would be our national situation, were it otherwise? Every principle of policy must be subverted, and the government must declare war before they are prepared to carry it on. Whatever may be the provocation, however important the object in view, and however necessary dispatch and secrecy may be, still the declaration must precede the preparation, and the enemy will be informed of your intention, not only before you are equipped for an attack, but even before you are fortified for a defence. The consequence is too obvious to require any further delineation; and no man, who regards the dignity and safety of his country, can deny the necessity of a military force, under the controul, and with the restrictions which the new constitution provides.

James Madison

Letter to Thomas Jefferson (October 24, 1787)

You will herewith receive the result of the Convention, which continued its Session till the 17th of September. I take the liberty of making some observations on the subject which will help to make up a letter, if they should answer no other purpose.

It appeared to be the sincere and unanimous wish of the Convention to cherish and preserve the Union of the States. No proposition was made, no suggestion was thrown out, in favor of a partition of the Empire into two or more Confederacies.

It was generally agreed that the objects of the Union could not be secured by any system founded on the principle of a confederation of sovereign States. A *voluntary* observance of the federal law by all the members, could never be hoped for. A *compulsive* one could evidently never be reduced to practice, and if it could, involved equal calamities to the innocent & the guilty, the necessity of a military force both obnoxious & dangerous, and in general, a scene resembling much more a civil war, than the administration of a regular Government.

Hence was embraced the alternative of a Government which instead of operating, on the States, should operate without their intervention on the individuals composing them; and hence the change in the principle and proportion of representation.

This ground-work being laid, the great objects which presented themselves were 1. to unite a proper energy in the Executive and a proper stability in the Legislative departments, with the essential characters of Republican Government. 2. to draw a line of demarkation which would give to the General Government every power requisite for general purposes, and leave to the States every power which might be most beneficially administered by them. 3. to provide for the different interests of different parts of the Union. 4. to adjust the clashing pretensions of the large and small States. Each of these objects was pregnant with difficulties. The whole of them together formed a task more difficult than can be well conceived by those who were not concerned in the execution of it. Adding to these considerations the natural diversity of human opinions on all new and complicated subjects, it is impossible to consider the degree of concord which ultimately prevailed as less than a miracle.

The first of these objects as it respects the Executive, was peculiarly embarrassing. On the question whether it should consist of a single person, or a plurality of coordinate members, on the mode of appointment, on the duration in office, on the degree of power, on the re-eligibility, tedious and reiterated discussions took place. The plurality of co-ordinate members had finally but few advocates. Governour Randolph was at the head of them. The modes of appointment proposed were various, as by the people at large—by electors chosen by the people—by the Executives of the States—by the Congress, some preferring a joint ballot of the two Houses—some a separate concurrent ballot allowing to each a negative on the other house—some a nomination of several canditates by one House, out of whom a choice should be made by the other. Several other modifications were started. The expedient at length adopted seemed to give pretty general satisfaction to the members. As to the duration in office, a few would have preferred a tenure during good behaviour—a considerable number would have done so, in case an easy & effectual removal by impeachment could be settled. It was much agitated whether a long term, seven years for example, with a subsequent & perpetual ineligibility, or a short term with a capacity to be re-elected, should be fixed. In favor of the first opinion were urged the danger of a gradual degeneracy of re-elections from time to time, into first a life and then a hereditary tenure, and the favorable effect of an incapacity to be reappointed, on the independent exercise of the Executive authority. On the other side it was contended that the prospect of necessary degradation, would discourage the most dignified characters from aspiring to the office, would take away the principal motive to the faithful discharge of its duties—the hope of being rewarded with a reappointment, would stimulate ambition to violent efforts for holding over the constitutional term—and instead of producing an independent administration, and a firmer defence of the constitutional rights of the department, would render the officer more indifferent to the importance of a place which he would soon be obliged to quit for ever, and more ready to yield to the incroachmts. of the Legislature of which he might again be a member. The questions concerning the degree of power turned chiefly on the appointment to offices, and the controul on the Legislature. An *absolute* appointment to all offices—to some offices—to no offices, formed the scale of opinions on the first point. On the second, some contended for an absolute negative, as the only possible mean of reducing to practice, the theory of a free Government which forbids a mixture of the Legislative & Executive powers. Others would be content with a revisionary power to be overruled by three fourths of both Houses. It was warmly urged that the judiciary department should be associated in the revision. The idea of some was that a separate revision should be given to the two departments—that if either objected two thirds; if both three fourths, should be necessary to overrule.

In forming the Senate, the great anchor of the Government, the questions as they came within the first object turned mostly on the mode of appointment, and the duration of it. The different modes proposed were, 1. by the House of Representatives 2. by the Executive, 3. by electors chosen by the people for the purpose. 4. by the State Legislatures. On the point of duration, the propositions descended from good-behavior to four years, through the intermediate terms of nine, seven, six, & five years. The election of the other branch was first determined to be triennial, and afterwards reduced to biennial.

The second object, the due partition of power, between the General & local Governments, was perhaps of all, the most nice and difficult. A few contended for an entire abolition of the States; some for indefinite power of Legislation in the Congress, with a negative on the laws of the States: some for such a power without a negative: some for a limited power of legislation, with such a negative: the majority finally for a limited power without the negative. The question with regard to the Negative underwent repeated discussions, and was finally rejected by a bare majority. As I formerly intimated to you my opinion in favor of this ingredient, I will take this occasion of explaining myself on the subject. Such a check on the States appears to me necessary 1. to prevent encroachments on the General authority. 2. to prevent instability and injustice in the legislation of the States.

1. Without such a check in the whole over the parts, our system involves the evil of imperia in imperio. If a compleat supremacy some where is not necessary in every Society, a controuling power at least is so, by which the general authority may be defended against encroachments of the subordinate authorities, and by which the latter may be restrained from encroachments on each other. If the supremacy of the British Parliament is not necessary as has been contended, for the harmony of that Empire; it is evident I think that without the royal negative or some equivalent controul, the unity of the system would be destroyed. The want of some such provision seems to have been mortal to the antient Confederacies, and to be the disease of the modern. Of the Lycian Confederacy little is known. That of the Amphyctions is well known to have been rendered of little use whilst it lasted, and in the end to have been destroyed by the predominance of the local over the federal authority. The same observation may be made, on the authority of Polybius, with regard to the Achaean League. The Helvetic System scarcely amounts to a Confederacy, and is distinguished by too many peculiarities, to be a ground of comparison. The case of the United Netherlands is in point. The authority of a Statholder, the influence of a Standing army, the common interest in the conquered possessions, the pressure of surrounding danger, the guarantee of foreign powers, are not sufficient to secure the authority and interests of the generality, agst. the antifederal tendency of the provincial sovereignties. The German Empire is another example. A Hereditary chief with vast independent resources of wealth and power, a federal Diet, with ample parchment authority, a regular Judiciary establishment, the influence of the neighbourhood of great & formidable Nations, have been found unable either to maintain the subordination of the members, or to prevent their mutual contests & encroachments. Still more to the purpose is our own experience both during the war and since the peace. Encroachments of the States on the general authority, sacrifices of national to local interests, interferences

of the measures of different States, form a great part of the history of our political system. It may be said that the new Constitution is founded on different principles, and will have a different operation. I admit the difference to be material. It presents the aspect rather of a feudal system of republics, if such a phrase may be used, than of a Confederacy of independent States. And what has been the progress and event of the feudal Constitutions? In all of them a continual struggle between the head and the inferior members, until a final victory has been gained in some instances by one, in others, by the other of them. In one respect indeed there is a remarkable variance between the two cases. In the feudal system the sovereign, though limited, was independent; and having no particular sympathy of interests with the great Barons, his ambition had as full play as theirs in the mutual projects of usurpation. In the American Constitution the general authority will be derived entirely from the subordinate authorities. The Senate will represent the States in their political capacity; the other House will represent the people of the States in their individual capacity. The former will be accountable to their constituents at moderate, the latter at short periods. The President also derives his appointment from the States, and is periodically accountable to them. This dependence of the General, on the local authorities, seems effectually to guard the latter against any dangerous encroachments of the former: Whilst the latter, within their respective limits, will be continually sensible of the abridgment of their power, and be stimulated by ambition to resume the surrendered portion of it. We find the representatives of Counties and corporations in the Legislatures of the States, much more disposed to sacrifice the aggregate interest, and even authority, to the local views of their Constituents: than the latter to the former. I mean not by these remarks to insinuate that an esprit de corps will not exist in the national Government or that opportunities may not occur, of extending its jurisdiction in some points. I mean only that the danger of encroachments is much greater from the other side, and that the impossibility of dividing powers of legislation, in such a manner, as to be free from different constructions by different interests, or even from ambiguity in the judgment of the impartial, requires some such expedient as I contend for. Many illustrations might be given of this impossibility. How long has it taken to fix, and how imperfectly is yet fixed the legislative power of corporations, though that power is subordinate in the most compleat manner? The line of distinction between the power of regulating trade and that of drawing revenue from it, which was found on fair discussion, to be absolutely undefinable. No distinction seems to be more obvious than that between spirtual and temporal matters. Yet whever they have been made objects of legislation, they have clashed and contended with each other, till one or the other has gained the supremacy. Even the Boundaries between the Executive, Legislative & Judiciary powers, though in general so strongly marked in themselves, consist in many instances of mere shades of difference. It may be said that the Judicial authority under our new system will keep the States within their proper limits, and supply the place of a negative on their laws. The answer is, that it is more convenient to prevent the passage of a law, than to declare it void after it is passed; that this will be particularly the case, where the law aggrieves individuals, who may be unable to support an appeal agst. a State to the supreme Judicary; that a State which would violate the Legislative rights of the Union, would not be very ready to obey a Judicial decree in support of them, and that a recurrence to force, which in the event of disobedience would be necessary, is an evil which the new Constitution meant to exclude as far as possible.

2. A constitutional negative on the laws of the States seems equally necessary to secure individuals agst. encroachments on their rights. The mutability of the laws of the States is found to be a serious evil. The injustice of them has been so frequent and so flagrant as to alarm the most stedfast friends of Republicanism. I am persuaded I do not err in saying that the evils issuing from these sources contributed more to that uneasiness which produced the Convention, and prepared the public mind for general reform, than those which accrued to our national character and interest from the inadequacy of the Confederation to its immediate objects. A reform therefore which does not make provision for private rights, must be materially defective. The restraints agst. paper emissions, and violations of contracts are not sufficient. Supposing them to be effectual as far as they go, they are short of the mark. Injustice may be effected by such an infinitude of legislative expedients, that where the disposition exists it can only be controuled by some

provision which reaches all cases whatsoever. The partial provision made, supposes the disposition which will evade it. It may be asked how private rights will be more secure under the Guardianship of the General Government than under the State Governments, since they are both founded on the republican principle which refers the ultimate decision to the will of the majority, and are distinguished rather by the extent within which they will operate, than by any material difference in their structure. A full discussion of this question would, if I mistake not, unfold the true principles of Republican Government, and prove in contradiction to the concurrent opinions of theoretical writers, that this form of Goverment, in order to effect its purposes, must operate not within a small but an extensive sphere. I will state some of the ideas which have occurred to me on this subject. Those who contend for a simple Democracy, or a pure republic, actuated by the sense of the majority, and operating within narrow limits, assume or suppose a case which is altogether fictitious. They found their reasoning on the idea, that the people composing the Society, enjoy not only an equality of political rights; but that they have all precisely the same interests, and the same feelings in every respect. Were this in reality the case, their reasoning would be conclusive. The interest of the majority would be that of the minority also; the decisions could only turn on mere opinion concerning the good of the whole, of which the major voice would be the safest criterion; and within a small sphere, this voice could be most easily collected, and the public affairs most accurately managed. We know however that no Society ever did or can consist of so homogeneous a mass of Citizens. In the savage State indeed, an approach is made towards it; but in that State little or no Government is necessary. In all civilized Societies, distinctions are various and unavoidable. A distinction of property results from that very protection which a free Government gives to unequal faculties of acquiring it. There will be rich and poor; creditors and debtors; a landed interest, a monied interest, a mercantile interest, a manufacturing interest. These classes may again be subdivided according to the different productions of different situations & soils, & according to different branches of commerce, and of manufactures. In addition to these natural distinctions, artificial ones will be founded, on accidental differences in political, religious or other opinions, or an attachment to the persons of leading individuals. However erroneous or ridiculous these grounds of dissention and faction may appear to the enlightened Statesman, or the benevolent philosopher, the bulk of mankind who are neither Statesmen nor Philosophers, will continue to view them in a different light. It remains then to be enquired whether a majority having any common interest, or feeling any common passion, will find sufficient motives to restrain them from oppressing the minority. An individual is never allowed to be a judge or even a witness in his own cause. If two individuals are under the biass of interest or enmity agst. a third, the rights of the latter could never be safely referred to the majority of the three. Will two thousand individuals be less apt to oppress one thousand, or two hundred thousand, one hundred thousand? Three motives only can restrain in such cases. 1. a prudent regard to private or partial good, as essentially involved in the general and permanent good of the whole. This ought no doubt to be sufficient of itself. Experience however shews that it has little effect on individuals, and perhaps still less on a collection of individuals, and least of all on a majority with the public authority in their hands. If the former are ready to forget that honest is the best policy; the last do more. They often proceed on the converse of the maxim: that whatever is politic is honest. 2. respect for character. This motive is not found sufficient to restrain individuals from injustice, and loses its efficacy in proportion to the number which is to divide the praise or the blame. Besides as it has reference to public opinion, which is that of the majority, the Standard is fixed by those whose conduct is to be measured by it. 3. Religion. The inefficacy of this restraint on individuals is well known. The conduct of every popular Assembly, acting on oath, the strongest of religious ties, shews that individuals join without remorse in acts agst. which their consciences would revolt, if proposed to them seperately in their closets. When Indeed Religion is kindled into enthusiasm, its force like that of other passions is increased by the sympathy of a multitude. But enthusiasm is only a temporary state of Religion, and whilst it lasts will hardly be seen with pleasure at the helm. Even in its coolest state, it has been much oftener a motive to oppression than a restraint from it. If then there must be different interests and parties in Society; and a majority when united by a common interest or passion can not be restrained from oppressing the minority, what remedy can be found in a republican Government, where the majority must ultimately decide, but that of giving such an extent to its sphere, that no common interest or passion will be likely to unite a majority of the whole number in an unjust pursuit. In a large Society, the people are broken into so many interests and parties, that a common sentiment is less likely to be felt, and the requisite concert less likely to be formed, by a majority of the whole. The same security seems requisite from the civil as for the religious rights of individuals. If the same sect form a majority and have the power, other sects will be sure to be depressed. Divide et impera, the reprobated axiom of tyranny, is under certain qualifications, the only policy, by which a republic can be administered on just principles. It must be observed however that this doctrine can only hold within a sphere of a mean extent. As in too small a sphere oppressive combinations may be too easily formed agst. the weaker party; so in too extensive a one, a defensive concert may be rendered too difficult against the oppression of those entrusted with the administration. The great desideratum in Government is, so to modify the sovereignty as that it may be sufficiently neutral between different parts of the Society to controul one part from invading the rights of another, and at the same time sufficiently controuled itself, from setting up an interest adverse to that of the entire Society. In absolute monarchies, the Prince may be tolerably neutral towards different classes of his subjects, but may sacrifice the happiness of all to his personal ambition or avarice. In small republics, the sovereign will is controuled from such a sacrifice of the entire Society, but is not sufficiently neutral towards the parts composing it. In the extended Republic of the United States, The General Government would hold a pretty even balance between the parties of particular States, and be at the same time sufficiently restrained by its dependence on the community, from betraying its general interests.

Begging pardon for this immoderate digression I return to the third object abovementioned, the adjustment of the different interests of different parts of the Continent. Some contended for an unlimited power over trade including exports as well as imports, and over slaves as well as other imports; some for such a power, provided the concurrence of two thirds of both House were required; Some for such a qualification of the power, with an exemption of exports and slaves, others for an exemption of exports only. The result is seen in the Constitution. S. Carolina & Georgia were inflexible on the point of the slaves.

The remaining object created more embarrassment, and a greater alarm for the issue of the Convention than all the rest put together. The little States insisted on retaining their equality in both branches, unless a compleat abolition of the State Governments should take place; and made an equality in the Senate a sine qua non. The large States on the other hand urged that as the new Government was to be drawn principally from the people immediately and was to operate directly on them, not on the States; and consequently as the States wd. lose that importance which is now proportioned to the importance of their voluntary compliances with the requisitions of Congress, it was necessary that the representation in both Houses should be in proportion to their size. It ended in the compromise which you will see, but very much to the dissatisfaction of several members from the large States.

Letter to Thomas Jefferson (October 17, 1788)

The little pamphlet herewith inclosed will give you a collective view of the alterations which have been proposed for the new Constitution. Various and numerous as they appear they certainly omit many of the true grounds of opposition. The articles relating to Treaties—to paper money, and to contracts, created more enemies than all the errors in the System positive & negative put together.

It is true, nevertheless, that not a few, particularly in Virginia, have contended for the proposed alterations from the most honorable and patriotic motives; and that among the advocates for the Constitution there are some who wish for further guards to public liberty and individual rights. As far as these may consist of a constitutional declaration of the most essential rights, it is probable they will be added; though there are many who think such addition unnecessary, and not a few who think it misplaced in such a Constitution. There is scarce any point on which the party in opposition is so much divided as to its importance and its propriety. My own opinion has always been in favor of a bill of rights, provided it be so framed as not to imply powers not meant to be included in the enumeration. At the same time, I have never thought the omission a material defect, nor been anxious to supply it even by *subsequent* amendment, for any other reason than that it is anxiously desired by others. I have favored it because I supposed it might be of use, and, if properly executed, could not be of disservice.

I have not viewed it in an important light—1. Because I conceive that in a certain degree, though not in the extent argued by Mr. Wilson, the rights in question are reserved by the manner in which the federal powers are granted. 2. Because there is great reason to fear that a positive declaration of some of the most essential rights could not be obtained in the requisite latitude. I am sure that the rights of conscience in particular, if submitted to public definition, would be narrowed much more than they are likely ever to be by an assumed power. One of the objections in New England was, that the Constitution, by prohibiting religious tests, opened a door for Jews, Turks, and infidels. 3. Because the limited powers of the federal Government, and the jealousy of the subordinate Governments, afford a security which has not existed in the case of the State Governments, and exists in no other. 4. Because experience proves the inefficacy of a bill of rights on those occasions when its controul is most needed. Repeated violations of these parchment barriers have been committed by overbearing majorities in every State.

In Virginia, I have seen the bill of rights violated in every instance where it has been opposed to a popular current. Notwithstanding the explicit provision contained in that instrument for the rights of conscience, it is well known that a religious establishment would have taken place in that State, if the Legislative majority had found, as they expected, a majority of the people in favor of the measure; and I am persuaded that if a majority of the people were now of one sect, the measure would still take place, and on narrower ground than was then proposed, notwithstanding the additional obstacle which the law has since created.

Wherever the real power in a Government lies, there is the danger of oppression. In our Governments the real power lies in the majority of the community, and the invasion of private rights is *chiefly* to be apprehended, not from acts of Government contrary to the sense of its constituents, but from acts in which the Government is the mere instrument of the major number of the Constituents. This is a truth of great importance, but not yet sufficiently attended to; and is probably more strongly impressed on my mind by facts and reflections suggested by them than on yours, which has contemplated abuses of power issuing from a very different quarter. Wherever there is an interest and power to do wrong, wrong will generally be done, and not less readily by a powerful and interested party than by a powerful and interested prince. The difference, so far as it relates to the superiority of republics over monarchies, lies in the less degree of probability that interest may prompt abuses of power in the former than in the latter; and in the security in the former against an oppression of more than the smaller part of the Society, whereas, in the latter, it may be extended in a manner to the whole.

The difference, so far as it relates to the point in question—the efficacy of a bill of rights in controuling abuses of power—lies in this: that in a monarchy the latent force of the nation is superior to that of the Sovereign, and a solemn charter of popular rights must have a great effect as a standard for trying the validity of public acts, and a signal for rousing and uniting the superior force of the community; whereas, in a popular Government, the political and physical power may be considered as vested in the same hands, that is, in a majority of the people, and, consequently the tyrannical will of the Sovereign is not to be controuled by the dread of an appeal to any other force within the community.

What use, then, it may be asked, can a bill of rights serve in popular Governments? I answer, the two following, which, though less essential than in other Governments, sufficiently recommend the precaution: 1. The political truths declared in that solemn manner acquire by degrees the character of fundamental maxims of free Government, and as they become incorporated with the national sentiment, counteract the impulses of interest and passion. 2. Although it be generally true, as above stated, that the danger of oppression lies in the interested majorities of the people rather than in usurped acts of the Government, yet there may be occasions on which the evil may spring from the latter source; and on such, a bill of rights will be a good ground for an appeal to the sense of the community. Perhaps, too, there may be a certain degree of danger that a succession of artful and ambitious rulers may, by gradual and well-timed advances, finally erect an independent Government on the subversion of liberty. Should this danger exist at all, it is prudent to guard against it, especially when the precaution can do no injury.

At the same time I must own that I see no tendency in our Governments to danger on that side. It has been remarked that there is a tendency in *all* Governments to an augmentation of power at the expence of liberty. But the remark, as usually understood, does not appear to me well founded. Power, when it has attained a certain degree of energy and independence, goes on generally to further degrees. But when below that degree, the direct tendency is to further degrees of relaxation, until the abuses of liberty beget a sudden transition to an undue degree of power. With this explanation the remark may be true; and in the latter sense only is it, in my opinion, applicable to the existing Governments in America. It is a melancholy reflection that liberty should be equally exposed to danger whether the Government have too much or too little power, and that the line which divides these extremes should be so inaccurately defined by experience.

Supposing a bill of rights to be proper, the articles which ought to compose it admit of much discussion. I am inclined to think that *absolute* restrictions in cases that are doubtful, or where emergencies may overrule them, ought to be avoided. The restrictions, however strongly marked on paper, will never be regarded when opposed to the decided sense of the public; and after repeated violations, in extraordinary cases will lose even their ordinary efficacy. Should a Rebellion or insurrection alarm the people as well as the Government, and a suspension of the Habeas Corpus be dictated by the alarm, no written prohibitions on earth would prevent the measure. Should an army in time of peace be gradually established in our neighbourhood by Britain or Spain, declarations on paper would have as little effect in preventing a standing force for the public safety. The best security against these evils is to remove the pretext for them.

With regard to Monopolies, they are justly classed among the greatest nuisances in Government. But is it clear that, as encouragements to literary works and ingenious discoveries, they are not too valuable to be wholly renounced? Would it not suffice to reserve in all cases a right to the public to abolish the privilege, at a price to be specified in the grant of it? Is there not, also, infinitely less danger of this abuse in our Governments than in most others? Monopolies are sacrifices of the many to the few. Where the power is in the few, it is natural for them to sacrifice the many to their own partialities and corruptions. Where the power, as with us, is in the many, not in the few, the danger cannot be very great that the few will be thus favored. It is much more to be dreaded that the few will be unnecessarily sacrificed to the many.

Thomas Jefferson

Letter to James Madison (March 15, 1789)

Paris

[. . .] Your thoughts on the subject of the Declaration of rights in the letter of Oct 17. I have weighed with great satisfaction. Some of them had not occurred to me before, but were acknoleged just in the moment they were presented to my mind. In the arguments in favor of a declaration of rights, you omit one which has great weight with me, the legal check which it puts into the hands of the judiciary. This is a body, which if rendered independent & kept strictly to their own department merits great confidence for their learning & integrity. In fact what degree of confidence would be too much for a body composed of such men as Wythe, Blair & Pendleton? On characters like these the "*civium ardor prava jubentium*" would make no impression. I am happy to find that on the whole you are a friend to this amendment. The Declaration of rights is like all other human blessings alloyed with some inconveniences, and not accomplishing fully it's object. But the good in this instance vastly overweighs the evil. I cannot refrain from making short answers to the objections which your letter states to have been raised. 1. That the rights in question are reserved by the manner in which the federal powers are granted. Answer. A constitutive act may certainly be so formed as to need no declaration of rights. The act itself has the force of a declaration as far as it goes; and if it goes to all material points nothing more is wanting. In the draught of a constitution which I had once a thought of proposing in Virginia, & printed afterwards, I endeavored to reach all the great objects of public liberty, and did not mean to add a declaration of rights. Probably the object was imperfectly executed; but the deficiencies would have been supplied by others, in the course of discussion. But in a constitutive act which leaves some precious articles unnoticed, and raises implications against others, a declaration of rights becomes necessary by way of supplement. This is the case of our new federal constitution. This instrument forms us into one state as to certain objects, and gives us a legislative & executive body for these objects. It should therefore guard us against their abuses of power within the field submitted to them. 2. A positive declaration of some essential rights could not be obtained in the requisite latitude. Answer. Half a loaf is better than no bread. If we cannot secure all our rights, let us secure what we can. 3. The limited powers of the federal government & jealousy of the subordinate governments afford a security which exists in no other instance. Answer. The first member of this seems resolvable into the first objection before stated. The jealousy of the subordinate governments is a precious reliance. But observe that those governments are only agents. They must have principles furnished them whereon to found their opposition. The declaration of rights will be the text whereby they will try all the acts of the federal government. In this view it is necessary to the federal government also; as by the same text they may try the opposition of the subordinate governments. 4. Experience proves the inefficacy of a bill of rights. True. But tho' it is not absolutely efficacious under all circumstances, it is of great potency always, and rarely inefficacious. A brace the more will often keep up the building which would have fallen with that brace the less. There is a remarkable difference between the characters of the Inconveniences which attend a Declaration of rights, & those which attend the want of it. The inconveniences of the Declaration are that it may cramp government in it's useful exertions. But the evil of this is short-lived, trivial & reparable. The inconveniences of the want of a Declaration are permanent, afflicting & irreparable. They are in constant progression from bad to worse. The executive in our governments is not the sole, it is scarcely the principal object of my jealousy. The tyranny of the legislatures is the most formidable dread at present, and will be for long years. That of the executive will come in it's turn, but it will be at a remote period. I know there are some among us who would now establish a monarchy. But they are inconsiderable in number and weight of character. The rising race are all republicans. We were educated in royalism; no wonder if some of us retain that idolatry still. Our young people are educated in republicanism, an apostasy from that to royalism is unprecedented & impossible. I am much pleased with the prospect that a declaration of rights will be added; and hope it will be done in that way which will not endanger the whole frame of the government, or any essential part of it.

George Clinton

Cato, No. 4 (1787)

It is remarked by Montesquieu, in treating of republics, that *in all magistracies, the greatness of the power must be compensated by the brevity of the duration; and that a longer time than a year, would be dangerous.* It is therefore obvious to the least intelligent mind, to account why, great power in the hands of a magistrate, and that power connected, with a considerable duration, may be dangerous to the liberties of a republic—the deposit of vast trusts in the hands of a single magistrate, enables him in their exercise, to create a numerous train of dependants—this tempts his *ambition,* which in a republican magistrate is also remarked, *to be pernicious* and the duration of his office for any considerable time favours his views, gives him the means and time to perfect and execute his designs—*he therefore fancies that he may be great and glorious by oppressing his fellow citizens, and raising himself to permanent grandeur on the ruins of his country.*—And here it may be necessary to compare the vast and important powers of the president, together with his continuance in office with the foregoing doctrine—his eminent magisterial situation will attach many adherents to him, and he will be surrounded by expectants and courtiers—his power of nomination and influence on all appointments—the strong posts in each state comprised within his superintendance, and garrisoned by troops under his direction—his controul over the army, militia, and navy—the unrestrained power of granting pardons for treason, which may be used to screen from punishment, those whom he had secretly instigated to commit the crime, and thereby prevent a discovery of his own guilt—his duration in office for four years: these, and various other principles evidently prove the truth of the position—that if the president is possessed of ambition, he has power and time sufficient to ruin his country.

Though the president, during the sitting of the legislature, is assisted by the senate, yet he is without a constitutional council in their recess—he will therefore be unsupported by proper information and advice, and will generally be directed by minions and favorites, or a council of state will grow out of the principal officers of the great departments, the most dangerous council in a free country.

The ten miles square, which is to become the seat of government, will of course be the place of residence for the president and the great officers of state—the same observations of a great man will apply to the court of a president possessing the powers of a monarch, that is observed of that of a monarch—*ambition with idleness—baseness with pride—the thirst of riches without labour—aversion to truth—flattery—treason—perfidy—violation of engagements—contempt of civil duties—hope from the magistrate's weakness; but above all, the perpetual ridicule of virtue*—these, he remarks, are the characteristics by which the courts in all ages have been distinguished.

The language and the manners of this court will be what distinguishes them from the rest of the community, not what assimilates them to it, and in being remarked for a behaviour that shews they are not *meanly born,* and in adulation to people of fortune and power.

The establishment of a vice-president is as unnecessary as it is dangerous. This officer, for want of other employment, is made president of the senate, thereby blending the executive and legislative powers, besides always giving to some one state, from which he is to come, an unjust preeminence.

It is a maxim in republics, that the representative of the people should be of their immediate choice; but by the manner in which the president is chosen he arrives to this office at the fourth or fifth hand, nor does the highest vote, in the way he is elected, determine the choice—for it is only necessary that he should be taken from the highest of five, who may have a plurality of votes.

Compare your past opinions and sentiments with the present proposed establishment, and you will find, that if you adopt it, that it will lead you into a system which you heretofore reprobated as odious. Every American whig, not long since, bore his emphatic testimony against a monarchical government, though limited, because of the dangerous inequality that it created among citizens as relative to their rights and property; and wherein does this president, invested with his powers and prerogatives, essentially differ from the king of Great-Britain (save as to name, the creation of nobility and some immaterial incidents, the offspring of absurdity and locality). [T]he direct prerogatives of the president, as springing from his political character, are among the following:—It is necessary, in order to distinguish him from the rest of the community, and enable him to keep, and maintain his court, that the compensation for his services; or in other words, his revenue should be such as to enable him to appear with the splendor of a prince; he has the power of receiving embassadors from, and a great influence on their appointments to foreign courts; as also to make treaties, leagues, and alliances with foreign states, assisted by the senate, which when made, become the supreme law of the land: he is a constituent part of the legislative power; for every bill which shall pass the house of representatives and senate, is to be presented to him for approbation; if he approves of it, he is to sign it, if he disapproves, he is to return it with objections, which in many cases will amount to a complete negative; and in this view he will have a great share in the power of making peace, coining money, etc. and all the various objects of legislation, expressed or implied in this Constitution: for though it may be asserted that the king of Great-Britain has the express power of making peace or war, yet he never thinks it prudent so to do without the advice of his parliament from whom he is to derive his support, and therefore these powers, in both president and king, are substantially the same: he is the generalissimo of the nation, and of course, has the command and controul of the army, navy and militia; he is the general conservator of the peace of the union—he may pardon all offences, except in cases of impeachment, and the principal fountain of all offices and employments. Will not the exercise of these powers therefore tend either to the establishment of a vile and arbitrary aristocracy, or monarchy? The safety of the people in a republic depends on the share or proportion they have in the government; but experience ought to teach you, that when a man is at the head of an elective government invested with great powers, and interested in his reelection, in what circle appointments will be made; by which means *an imperfect aristocracy* bordering on monarchy may be established.

An Old Whig, No. 5 (1787)

In order that people may be sufficiently impressed, with the necessity of establishing a Bill of Rights in the forming of a new constitution, it is very proper to take a short view of some of those liberties, which it is of the greatest importance for Freemen to retain to themselves, when they surrender up a part of their natural rights for the good of society.

The first of these, which it is of the utmost importance for the people to retain to themselves, which indeed they have not even the right to surrender, and which at the same time it is of no kind of advantage to government to strip them of, is the Liberty of Conscience. I know that a ready answer is at hand, to any objections upon this head. We shall be told that in this enlightened age, the rights of conscience are perfectly secure: There is no necessity of guarding them; for no man has the remotest thoughts of invading them. If this be the case, I beg leave to reply that now is the very time to secure them.—Wise and prudent men always take care to guard against danger beforehand, and to make themselves safe whilst it is yet in their power to do it without inconvenience or risk.—[W]ho shall answer for the ebbings and flowings of opinion, or be able to say what will be the fashionable frenzy of the next generation? It would have been treated as a very ridiculous supposition, a year ago, that the charge of witchcraft would cost a person her life in the city of Philadelphia; yet the fate of the unhappy old woman called *Corbmaker*, who was beaten—repeatedly wounded with knives—mangled and at last killed in our streets, in obedience to the commandment which requires "that we shall not suffer a witch to live," without a possibility of punishing or even of detecting the authors of this inhuman folly, should be an example to warn us how little we ought to trust to the unrestrained discretion of human nature.

Uniformity of opinion in science, morality, politics or religion, is undoubtedly a very great happiness to mankind; and there have not been wanting zealous champions in every age, to promote the means of securing so invaluable a blessing. If in America we have not lighted up fires to consume Heretics in religion, if we have not persecuted unbelievers to promote the unity of the faith, in matters which pertain to our final salvation in a future world, I think we have all of us been witness to something very like the same spirit, in matters which are supposed to regard our political salvation in this world. In Boston it seems at this very moment, that no man is permitted to publish a doubt of the infalibility of the late convention, without giving up his name to the people, that he may be delivered over to speedy destruction; and it is but a short time since the case was little better in this city. Now this is a portion of the very same spirit, which has so often kindled the fires of the inquisition: and the same Zealot who would hunt a man down for a difference of opinion upon a political question which is the subject of public enquiry, if he should happen to be fired with zeal for a particular species of religion, would be equally intolerant. The fact is, that human nature is still the same that ever it was: the fashion indeed changes; but the seeds of superstition, bigotry and enthusiasm, are too deeply implanted in our minds, ever to be eradicated; and fifty years hence, the French may renew the persecution of the Huguenots, whilst the Spaniards in their turn may become indifferent to their forms of religion. They are idiots who trust their future security to the whim of the present hour. One extreme is always apt to produce the contrary, and those countries, which are now the most lax in their religious notions, may in a few years become the most rigid, just as the people of this country from not being able to bear any continental government at all, are now flying into the opposite extreme of surrendering up all the powers of the different states, to one continental government.

The more I reflect upon the history of mankind, the more I am disposed to think that it is our duty to secure the essential rights of the people, by every precaution; for not an avenue has been left unguarded, through which oppression could possibly enter in any government[,] without some enemy of the public peace and happiness improving the opportunity to break in upon the liberties of the people; and none have been more frequently successful in the attempt, than those who have covered their ambitious designs under the garb of a fiery zeal for religious orthodoxy. What has happened in other countries and in other ages, may very possibly happen again in our own country, and for aught we know, before the present generation quits the stage of life. We ought therefore in a *bill of rights* to secure, in the first place, by the most express stipulations, the sacred rights of conscience. Has this been done in the constitution, which is now proposed for the consideration of the people of this country?—Not a word on this subject has been mentioned in any part of it; but we are left in this important article, as well as many others, entirely to the mercy of our future rulers.

But supposing our future rulers to be wicked enough to attempt to invade the rights of conscience; I may be asked how will they be able to effect so horrible a design? I will tell you my friends—*The unlimited power of taxation* will give them the command of all the treasures of the continent; *a standing army* will be wholly at their devotion, and the authority which is given them over the *militia*, by virtue of which they may, if they please, change all the officers of the militia on the continent in one day, and put in new officers whom they can better trust; by which they can subject all the militia to strict military laws, and punish the disobedient with death, or otherwise, as they shall think right: by which they can march the militia back and forward from one end of the continent to the other, at their discretion; these powers, if they should ever fall into bad hands, may be abused to the worst of purposes. Let us instance one thing arising from this right of organizing and governing the militia. Suppose a man alledges that he is conscientiously scrupulous of bearing Arms.—By the bill of rights of Pennsylvania he is bound only to pay an equivalent for his personal service.—What is there in the new proposed constitution to prevent his being dragged like a Prussian soldier to the camp and there compelled to bear arms?—This will depend wholly upon the wisdom and discretion of the future legislature of the continent in the framing their militia laws; and I have lived long enough to hear the practice *of commuting personal service for a paltry fine* in time of war and foreign invasion most severely reprobated by some persons who ought to have judged more rightly on the subject—Such flagrant oppressions as these I dare say will not happen at the beginning of the new government; probably not till the powers of government shall be firmly fixed; but it is a duty we owe to ourselves and our posterity if possible to prevent their ever happening. I hope and trust that there are few persons at present hardy enough to entertain thoughts of creating any religious establishment for this country; although I have lately read a piece in the newspaper, which speaks of *religious* as well as civil and military *offices*, as being hereafter to be disposed of by the new government; but if a majority of the continental legislature should at any time think fit to establish a form of religion, for the good people of this continent, with all the pains and penalties which in other countries are annexed to the establishment of a national church, what is there in the proposed constitution to hinder their doing so? Nothing; for we have no bill of rights, and every thing therefore is in their power and at their discretion. And at whose discretion? We know not any more than we know the fates of those generations which are yet unborn.

ROBERT YATES

Brutus Essays (1787–1788)

I

October 18, 1787

To the Citizens of the State of New-York.

When the public is called to investigate and decide upon a question in which not only the present members of the community are deeply interested, but upon which the happiness and misery of generations yet unborn is in great measure suspended, the benevolent mind cannot help feeling itself peculiarly interested in the result.

In this situation, I trust the feeble efforts of an individual, to lead the minds of the people to a wise and prudent determination, cannot fail of being acceptable to the candid and dispassionate part of the community. Encouraged by this consideration, I have been induced to offer my thoughts upon the present important crisis of our public affairs.

Perhaps this country never saw so critical a period in their political concerns. We have felt the feebleness of the ties by which these United-States are held together, and the want of sufficient energy in our present confederation, to manage, in some instances, our general concerns. Various expedients have been proposed to remedy these evils, but none have succeeded. At length a Convention of the states has been assembled, they have formed a constitution which will now, probably, be submitted to the people to ratify or reject, who are the fountain of all power, to whom alone it of right belongs to make or unmake constitutions, or forms of government, at their pleasure. The most important question that was ever proposed to your decision, or to the decision of any people under heaven, is before you, and you are to decide upon it by men of your own election, chosen specially for this purpose. If the constitution, offered to your acceptance, be a wise one, calculated to preserve the invaluable blessings of liberty, to secure the inestimable rights of mankind, and promote human happiness, then, if you accept it, you will lay a lasting foundation of happiness for millions yet unborn; generations to come will rise up and call you blessed. You may rejoice in the prospects of this vast extended continent becoming filled with freemen, who will assert the dignity of human nature. You may solace yourselves with the idea, that society, in this favoured land, will fast advance to the highest point of perfection; the human mind will expand in knowledge and virtue, and the golden age be, in some measure, realised. But if, on the other hand, this form of government contains principles that will lead to the subversion of liberty—if it tends to establish a despotism, or, what is worse, a tyrannic aristocracy; then, if you adopt it, this only remaining asylum for liberty will be shut up, and posterity will execrate your memory.

Momentous then is the question you have to determine, and you are called upon by every motive which should influence a noble and virtuous mind, to examine it well, and to make up a wise judgment. It is insisted, indeed, that this constitution must be received, be it ever so imperfect. If it has its defects, it is said, they can be best amended when they are experienced. But remember, when the people once part with power, they can seldom or never resume it again but by force. Many instances can be produced in which the people have voluntarily increased the powers of their rulers; but few, if any, in which rulers have willingly abridged their authority. This is a sufficient reason to induce you to be careful, in the first instance, how you deposit the powers of government.

With these few introductory remarks, I shall proceed to a consideration of this constitution:

The first question that presents itself on the subject is, whether a confederated government be the best for the United States or not? Or in other words, whether the thirteen United States should be reduced to one great republic, governed by one legislature, and under the direction of one executive and judicial; or whether they should continue thirteen confederated republics, under the direction and control of a supreme federal head for certain defined national purposes only?

This enquiry is important, because, although the government reported by the convention does not go to a perfect and entire consolidation, yet it approaches so near to it, that it must, if executed, certainly and infallibly terminate in it.

This government is to possess absolute and uncontroulable power, legislative, executive and judicial, with respect to every object to which it extends, for by the last clause of section 8th, article 1st, it is declared "that the Congress shall have power to make all laws which shall be necessary and proper for carrying into execution the foregoing powers, and all other powers vested by this constitution, in the government of the United States; or in any department or office thereof." And by the 6th article, it is declared "that this constitution, and the laws of the United States, which shall be made in pursuance thereof, and the treaties made, or which shall be made, under the authority of the United States, shall be the supreme law of the land; and the judges in every state shall be bound thereby, any thing in the constitution, or law of any state to the contrary notwithstanding." It appears from these articles that there is no need of any intervention of the state governments, between the Congress and the people, to execute any one power vested in the general government, and that the constitution and laws of every state are nullified and declared void, so far as they are or shall be inconsistent with this constitution, or the laws made in pursuance of it, or with treaties made under the authority of the United States.—The government then, so far as it extends, is a complete one, and not a confederation. It is as much one complete government as that of New-York or Massachusetts, has as absolute and perfect powers to make and execute all laws, to appoint officers, institute courts, declare offences, and annex penalties, with respect to every object to which it extends, as any other in the world. So far therefore as its powers reach, all ideas of confederation are given up and lost. It is true this government is limited to certain objects, or to speak more properly, some small degree of power is still left to the states, but a little attention to the powers vested in the general government, will convince every candid man, that if it is capable of being executed, all that is reserved for the individual states must very soon be annihilated, except so far as they are barely necessary to the organization of the general government. The powers of the general legislature extend to every case that is of the least importance—there is nothing valuable to human nature, nothing dear to freemen, but what is within its power. It has authority to make laws which will affect the lives, the liberty, and property of every man in the United States; nor can the constitution or laws of any state, in any way prevent or impede the full and complete execution of every power given. The legislative power is competent to lay taxes, duties, imposts, and excises;—there is no limitation to this power, unless it be said that the clause which directs the use to which those taxes, and duties shall be applied, may be said to be a limitation: but this is no restriction of the power at all, for by this clause they are to be applied to pay the debts and provide for the common defence and general welfare of the United States; but the legislature have authority to contract debts at their discretion; they are the sole judges of what is necessary to provide for the common defence, and they only are to determine what is for the general welfare; this power therefore is neither more nor less, than a power to lay and collect taxes, imposts, and excises, at their pleasure; not only [is] the power to lay taxes unlimited, as to the amount they may require, but it is perfect and absolute to raise them in any mode they please. No state legislature, or any power in the state governments, have any more to do in carrying this into effect, than the authority of one state has to do with that of another. In the business therefore of laying and collecting taxes, the idea of confederation is totally lost, and that of one entire republic is embraced. It is proper here to remark, that the authority to lay and collect taxes is the most important of any power that can be granted; it connects with it almost all other powers, or at least will in process of time draw all other after it; it is the great mean of protection, security, and defence, in a good government, and the great engine of oppression and tyranny in a bad one. This cannot fail of being the case, if we consider the contracted limits which are set by this constitution, to the late [state?] governments, on this article of raising money. No state can emit paper money—lay any duties, or imposts, on imports, or exports, but by consent of the Congress; and then the net produce shall be for the benefit of the United States: the only mean therefore left, for any state to support its government and discharge its debts, is by direct taxation; and the United States have also power to lay and collect taxes, in any way they please. Every one who has thought on the subject, must be convinced that but small sums of money can be collected in any country, by direct taxe[s], when the foederal government begins to exercise the right of taxation in all its parts, the legislatures of the several states will find it impossible to raise monies to support their governments. Without money they cannot be supported, and they must dwindle away, and, as before observed, their powers absorbed in that of the general government. [. . .]

How far the clause in the 8th section of the 1st article may operate to do away all idea of confederated states, and to effect an entire consolidation of the whole into one general government, it is impossible to say. The powers given by this article are very general and comprehensive, and it may receive a construction to justify the passing almost any law. A power to make all laws, which shall be *necessary and proper*, for carrying into execution, all powers vested by the constitution in the government of the United States, or any department or officer thereof, is a power very comprehensive and definite [indefinite?], and may, for ought I know, be exercised in a such manner as entirely to abolish the state legislatures. Suppose the legislature of a state should pass a law to raise money to support their government and pay the state debt, may the Congress repeal this law, because it may prevent the collection of a tax which they may think proper and necessary to lay, to provide for the general welfare of the United States? For all laws made, in pursuance of this constitution, are the supreme lay of the land, and the judges in every state shall be bound thereby, any thing in the constitution or laws of the different states to the contrary notwithstanding.—By such a law, the government of a particular state might be overturned at one stroke, and thereby be deprived of every means of its support.

It is not meant, by stating this case, to insinuate that the constitution would warrant a law of this kind; or unnecessarily to alarm the fears of the people, by suggesting, that the federal legislature would be more likely to pass the limits assigned them by the constitution, than that of an individual state, further than they are less responsible to the people. But what is meant is, that the legislature of the United States are vested with the great and uncontroulable powers, of laying and collecting taxes, duties, imposts, and excises; of regulating trade, raising and supporting armies, organizing, arming, and disciplining the militia, instituting courts, and other general powers. And are by this clause invested with the power of making all laws, *proper and necessary*, for carrying all these into execution; and they may so exercise this power as entirely to annihilate all the state governments, and reduce this country to one single government. And if they may do it, it is pretty certain they will; for it will be found that the power retained by individual states, small as it is, will be a clog upon the wheels of the government of the United States; the latter therefore will be naturally inclined to remove it out of the way. Besides, it is a truth confirmed by the unerring experience of ages, that every man, and every body of men, invested with power, are ever disposed to increase it, and to acquire a superiority over every thing that stands in their way. This disposition, which is implanted in human nature, will operate in the federal legislature to lessen and ultimately to subvert the state authority, and having such advantages, will most certainly succeed, if the federal government succeeds at all. It must be very evident then, that what this constitution wants of being a complete consolidation of the several parts of the union into one complete government, possessed of perfect legislative, judicial, and executive powers, to all intents and purposes, it will necessarily acquire in its exercise and operation.

Let us now proceed to enquire, as I at first proposed, whether it be best the thirteen United States should be reduced to one great republic, or not? It is here taken for granted, that all agree in this, that whatever government we adopt, it ought to be a free one; that it should be so framed as to secure the liberty of the citizens of America, and such an one as to admit of a full, fair, and equal representation of the people. The question then will be, whether a government thus constituted, and founded on such principles, is practicable, and can be exercised over the whole United States, reduced into one state?

If respect is to be paid to the opinion of the greatest and wisest men who have ever thought or wrote on the science of government, we shall be constrained to conclude, that a free republic cannot succeed over a country of such immense extent, containing such a number of inhabitants, and these encreasing in such rapid progression as that of the whole United States. Among the many illustrious authorities which might be produced to this point, I shall content myself with quoting only two. The one is the baron de Montesquieu, spirit of laws, chap. xvi. vol. I [book VIII]. "It is natural to a republic to have only a small territory, otherwise it cannot long subsist. In a large republic there are men of large fortunes, and consequently of less moderation; there are trusts too great to be placed in any single subject; he has interest of his own; he soon begins to think that he may be happy, great and glorious, by oppressing his fellow citizens; and that he may raise himself to grandeur on the ruins of his country. In a large republic, the public good is sacrificed to a thousand views; it is subordinate to exceptions, and depends on accidents. In a small one, the interest of the public is easier perceived, better understood, and more within the reach of every citizen; abuses are of less extent, and of course are less protected." Of the same opinion is the marquis Beccarari.

History furnishes no example of a free republic, any thing like the extent of the United States. The Grecian republics were of small extent; so also was that of the Romans. Both of these, it is true, in process of time, extended their conquests over large territories of country; and the consequence was, that their governments were changed from that of free governments to those of the most tyrannical that ever existed in the world.

Not only the opinion of the greatest men, and the experience of mankind, are against the idea of an extensive republic, but a variety of reasons may be drawn from the reason and nature of things, against it. In every government, the will of the sovereign is the law. In despotic governments, the supreme authority being lodged in one, his will is law, and can be as easily expressed to a large extensive territory as to a small one. In a pure democracy the people are the sovereign, and their will is declared by themselves; for this purpose they must all come together to deliberate, and decide. This kind of government cannot be exercised, therefore, over a country of any considerable extent; it must be confined to a single city, or at least limited to such bounds as that the people can conveniently assemble, be able to debate, understand the subject submitted to them, and declare their opinion concerning it.

In a free republic, although all laws are derived from the consent of the people, yet the people do not declare their consent by themselves in person, but by representatives, chosen by them, who are supposed to know the minds of their constituents, and to be possessed of integrity to declare this mind.

In every free government, the people must give their assent to the laws by which they are governed. This is the true criterion between a free government and an arbitrary one. The former are ruled by the will of the whole, expressed in any manner they may agree upon; the latter by the will of one, or a few. If the people are to give their assent to the laws, by persons chosen and appointed by them, the manner of the choice and the number chosen, must be such, as to possess, be disposed, and consequently qualified to declare the sentiments of the people; for if they do not know, or are not disposed to speak the sentiments of the people, the people do not govern, but the sovereignty is in a few. Now, in a large extended country, it is impossible to have a representation, possessing the sentiments, and of integrity, to declare the minds of the people, without having it so numerous and unwieldly, as to be subject in great measure to the inconveniency of a democratic government.

The territory of the United States is of vast extent; it now contains near three millions of souls, and is capable of containing much more than ten times that number. Is it practicable for a country, so large and so numerous as they will soon become, to elect a representation, that will speak their sentiments, without their becoming so numerous as to be incapable of transacting public business? It certainly is not.

In a republic, the manners, sentiments, and interests of the people should be similar. If this be not the case, there will be a constant clashing of opinions; and the representatives of one part will be continually striving against those of the other. This will retard the operations of government, and prevent such conclusions as will promote the public good. If we apply this remark to the condition of the United States, we shall be convinced that it forbids that we should be one government. The United States includes a variety of climates. The productions of the different parts of the union are very variant, and their interests, of consequence, diverse. Their manners and habits differ as much as their climates and productions; and their sentiments are by no means coincident. The laws and customs of the several states are, in many respects, very diverse, and in some opposite; each would be in favor of its own interests and customs, and, of consequence, a legislature, formed of representatives from the respective parts, would not only be too numerous to act with any care or decision, but would be composed of such heterogenous and discordant principles, as would constantly be contending with each other.

The laws cannot be executed in a republic, of an extent equal to that of the United States, with promptitude.

The magistrates in every government must be supported in the execution of the laws, either by an armed force, maintained at the public expence for that purpose; or by the people turning out to aid the magistrate upon his command, in case of resistance. [. . .]

A free republic will never keep a standing army to execute its laws. It must depend upon the support of its citizens. But when a government is to receive its support from the aid of the citizens, it must be so constructed as to have the confidence, respect, and affection of the people. Men who, upon the call of the magistrate, offer themselves to execute the laws, are influenced to do it either by affection to the government, or from fear; where a standing army is at hand to punish offenders, every man is actuated by the latter principle, and therefore, when the magistrate calls, will obey: but, where this is not the case, the government must rest for its support upon the confidence and respect which the people have for their government and laws. The body of the people being attached, the government will always be sufficient to support and execute its laws, and to operate upon the fears of any faction which may be opposed to it, not only to prevent an opposition to the execution of the laws themselves, but also to compel the most of them to aid the magistrate; but the people will not be likely to have such confidence in their rulers, in a republic so extensive as the United States, as necessary for these purposes. The confidence which the people have in their rulers, in a free republic, arises from their knowing them, from their being responsible to them for their conduct, and from the power they have of displacing them when they misbehave: but in a republic of the extent of this continent, the people in general would be acquainted with very few of their rulers: the people at large would know little of their proceedings, and it would be extremely difficult to change them. The people in

Georgia and New-Hampshire would not know one another's mind, and therefore could not act in concert to enable them to effect a general change of representatives. The different parts of so extensive a country could not possibly be made acquainted with the conduct of their representatives, nor be informed of the reasons upon which measures were founded. The consequence will be, they will have no confidence in their legislature, suspect them of ambitious views, be jealous of every measure they adopt, and will not support the laws they pass. Hence the government will be nerveless and inefficient, and no way will be left to render it otherwise, but by establishing an armed force to execute the laws at the point of the bayonet—a government of all others the most to be dreaded.

In a republic of such vast extent as the United-States, the legislature cannot attend to the various concerns and wants of its different parts. It cannot be sufficiently numerous to be acquainted with the local condition and wants of the different districts, and if it could, it is impossible it should have sufficient time to attend to and provide for all the variety of cases of this nature, that would be continually arising.

In so extensive a republic, the great officers of government would soon become above the control of the people, and abuse their power to the purpose of aggrandizing themselves, and oppressing them. The trust committed to the executive offices, in a country of the extent of the United-States, must be various and of magnitude. The command of all the troops and navy of the republic, the appointment of officers, the power of pardoning offences, the collecting of all the public revenues, and the power of expending them, with a number of other powers, must be lodged and exercised in every state, in the hands of a few. When these are attended with great honor and emolument, as they always will be in large states, so as greatly to interest men to pursue them, and to be proper objects for ambitious and designing men, such men will be ever restless in their pursuit after them. They will use the power, when they have acquired it, to the purposes of gratifying their own interest and ambition, and it is scarcely possible, in a very large republic, to call them to account for their misconduct, or to prevent their abuse of power.

These are some of the reasons by which it appears, that a free republic cannot long subsist over a country of the great extent of these states. If then this new constitution is calculated to consolidate the thirteen states into one, as it evidently is, it ought not to be adopted.

II

November 1, 1787

I flatter myself that my last address established this position, that to reduce the Thirteen States into one government, would prove the destruction of your liberties.

But lest this truth should be doubted by some, I will now proceed to consider its merits.

Though it should be admitted, that the argument[s] against reducing all the states into one consolidated government, are not sufficient fully to establish this point; yet they will, at least, justify this conclusion, that in forming a constitution for such a country, great care should be taken to limit and definite its powers, adjust its parts, and guard against an abuse of authority. How far attention has been paid to these objects, shall be the subject of future enquiry. When a building is to be erected which is intended to stand for ages, the foundation should be firmly laid. The constitution proposed to your acceptance, is designed not for yourselves alone, but for generations yet unborn. The principles, therefore, upon which the social compact is founded, ought to have been clearly and precisely stated, and the most express and full declaration of rights to have been made—But on this subject there is almost an entire silence.

If we may collect the sentiments of the people of America, from their own most solemn declarations, they hold this truth as self evident, that all men are by nature free. No one man, therefore, or any class of men, have a right, by the law of nature, or of God, to assume or exercise authority over their fellows. The origin of society then is to be sought, not in any natural right which one man has to exercise authority over another, but in the united consent of those who associate. The mutual wants of men, at first dictated the propriety of forming societies; and when they were established, protection and defence pointed out the necessity of instituting government. In a state of nature every individual pursues his own interest; in this pursuit it frequently happened, that the possessions or enjoyments of one were sacrificed to the views and designs of another; thus the weak were a prey to the strong, the simple and unwary were subject to impositions from those who were more crafty and designing. In this state of things, every individual was insecure; common interest therefore directed, that government should be established, in which the force of the whole community should be collected, and under such directions, as to protect and defend every one who composed it. The common good, therefore, is the end of civil government, and common consent, the foundation on which it is established. To effect this end, it was necessary that a certain portion of natural liberty should be surrendered, in order, that what remained should be preserved: how great a proportion of natural freedom is necessary to be yielded by individuals, when they submit to government, I shall not now enquire. So much, however, must be given up, as will be sufficient to enable those, to whom the administration of the government is committed, to establish laws for the promoting the happiness of the community, and to carry those laws into effect. But it is not necessary, for this purpose, that individuals should relinquish all their natural rights. Some are of such a nature that they cannot be surrendered. Of this kind are the rights of conscience, the right of enjoying and defending life, etc. Others are not necessary to be resigned, in order to attain the end for which government is instituted, these therefore ought not to be given up. To surrender them, would counteract the very end of government, to wit, the common good. From these observations it appears, that in forming a government on its true principles, the foundation should be laid in the manner I before stated, by expressly reserving to the people such of their essential natural rights, as are not necessary to be parted with. The same reasons which at first induced mankind to associate and institute government, will operate to influence them to observe this precaution. If they had been disposed to conform themselves to the rule of immutable righteousness, government would not have been requisite. It was because one part exercised fraud, oppression, and violence on the other, that men came together, and agreed that certain rules should be formed, to regulate the conduct of all, and the power of the whole community lodged in the hands of rulers to enforce an obedience to them. But rulers have the same propensities as other men; they are as likely to use the power with which they are vested for private purposes, and to the injury and oppression of those over whom they are placed, as individuals in a state of nature are to injure and oppress one another. It is therefore as proper that bounds should be set to their authority, as that government should have at first been instituted to restrain private injuries.

This principle, which seems so evidently founded in the reason and nature of things, is confirmed by universal experience. Those who have governed, have been found in all ages ever active to enlarge their powers and abridge the public liberty. This has induced the people in all countries, where any sense of freedom remained, to fix barriers against the encroachments of their rulers. The country from which we have derived our origin, is an eminent example of this. Their magna charta and bill of rights have long been the boast, as well as the security, of that nation. I need say no more, I presume, to an American, than, that this principle is a fundamental one, in all the constitutions of our own states; there is not one of them but what is either founded on a declaration or bill of rights, or has certain express reservation of rights interwoven in the body of them. From this it appears, that at a time when the pulse of liberty beat high and when an appeal was made to the people to form constitutions for the government of themselves, it was their universal sense, that such declarations should make a part of their frames of government. It is therefore the more astonishing, that this grand security, to the rights of the people, is not to be found in this constitution.

It has been said, in answer to this objection, that such declaration[s] of rights, however requisite they might be in the constitutions of the states, are not necessary in the general constitution, because, "in the former case, every thing which is not reserved is given, but in the latter the reverse of the proposition prevails, and every thing which is not given is reserved." It requires but little attention to discover, that this mode of reasoning is rather specious than solid. The powers, rights, and authority, granted to the general government by this constitution, are as complete, with respect to every object to which they extend, as that of any state government—It reaches to every thing which concerns human happiness—Life, liberty, and property, are under its controul. There is the same reason, therefore, that the exercise of power, in this case, should be restrained within proper limits, as in that of the state governments. To set this matter in a clear light, permit me to instance some of the articles of the bills of rights of the individual states, and apply them to the case in question.

For the security of life, in criminal prosecutions, the bills of rights of most of the states have declared, that no man shall be held to answer for a crime until he is made fully acquainted with the charge brought against him; he shall not be compelled to accuse, or furnish evidence against himself—The witnesses against him shall be brought face to face, and he shall be fully heard by himself or counsel. That it is essential to the security of life and liberty, that trial of facts be in the vicinity where they happen. Are not provisions of this kind as necessary in the general government, as in that of a particular state? The powers vested in the new Congress extend in many cases to life; they are authorised to provide for the punishment of a variety of capital crimes, and no restraint is laid upon them in its exercise, save only, that "the trial of all crimes, except in cases of impeachment, shall be by jury; and such trial shall be in the state where the said crimes shall have been committed." No man is secure of a trial in the county where he is charged to have committed a crime; he may be brought from Niagara to New-York, or carried from Kentucky to Richmond for trial for an offence, supposed to be committed. What security is there, that a man shall be furnished with a full and plain description of the charges against him? That he shall be allowed to produce all proof he can in his favor? That he shall see the witnesses against him face to face, or that he shall be fully heard in his own defence by himself or counsel?

For the security of liberty it has been declared, "that excessive bail should not be required, nor excessive fines imposed, nor cruel or unusual punishments inflicted—That all warrants, without oath or affirmation, to search suspected places, or seize any person, his papers or property, are grievous and oppressive."

These provisions are as necessary under the general government as under that of the individual states; for the power of the former is as complete to the purpose of requiring bail, imposing fines, inflicting punishments, granting search warrants, and seizing persons, papers, or property, in certain cases, as the other.

Does not the same necessity exist of reserving this right, under this national compact, as in that of these states? Yet nothing is said respecting it. In the bills of rights of the states it is declared, that a well regulated militia is the proper and natural defence of a free government—That as standing armies in time of peace are dangerous, they are not to be kept up, and that the military should be kept under strict subordination to, and controuled by the civil power.

The same security is as necessary in this constitution, and much more so; for the general government will have the sole power to raise and to pay armies, and are under no controul in the exercise of it; yet nothing of this is to be found in this new system.

I might proceed to instance a number of other rights, which were as necessary to be reserved, such as, that elections should be free, that the liberty of the press should be held sacred; but the instances adduced, are sufficient to prove, that this argument is without foundation.—Besides, it is evident, that the reason here assigned was not the true one, why the framers of this constitution omitted a bill of rights; if it had been, they would not have made certain reservations, while they totally omitted others of more importance. We find they have, in the 9th section of the 1st article, declared, that the writ of habeas corpus shall not be suspended, unless in cases of rebellion—that no bill of attainder, or expost facto law, shall be passed—that no title of nobility shall be granted by the United States, &c. If every thing which is not given is reserved, what propriety is there in these exceptions? Does this constitution any where grant the power of suspending the habeas corpus, to make expost facto laws, pass bills of attainder, or grant titles of nobility? It certainly does not in express terms. The only answer that can be given is, that these are implied in the general powers granted. With equal truth it may be said, that all the powers, which the bills of right, guard against the abuse of, are contained or implied in the general ones granted by this constitution.

So far it is from being true, that a bill of rights is less necessary in the general constitution than in those of the states, the contrary is evidently the fact.—This system, if it is possible for the people of America to accede to it, will be an original compact: and being the last, will, in the nature of things, vacate every former agreement inconsistent with it. For it being a plan of government received and ratified by the whole people, all other forms, which are in existence at the time of its adoption, must yield to it. [. . .]

It is therefore not only necessarily implied thereby, but positively expressed that the different state constitutions are repealed and entirely done away so far as they are inconsistent with this, with the laws which shall be made in pursuance thereof, or with treaties made or which shall be made, under the authority of the United States; of what avail will the constitutions of the respective states be to preserve the rights of its citizens? should they be plead, the answer would be the constitution of the United States, and the laws made in pursuance thereof, is the supreme law, and all legislatures and judicial officers, whether of the general or state governments, are bound by oath to support it. No priviledge, reserved by the bills of rights, or secured by the state government, can limit the power granted by this, or restrain any laws made in pursuance of it. It stands therefore on its own bottom, and must receive a construction by itself without any reference to any other—And hence it was of the highest importance, that the most precise and express declarations and reservations of rights should have been made.

VI

December 27, 1787

[. . .] I have, in my former papers, offered a variety of arguments to prove, that a simple free government could not be exercised over this whole continent and that therefore we must either give up our liberties and submit to an arbitrary one, or frame a constitution on the plan of confederation. Further reasons might be urged to prove this point—but it seems unnecessary, because the principal advocates of the new constitution admit of the position. The question therefore between us, this being admitted, is, whether or not this system is so formed as either directly to annihilate the state governments, or that in its operation it will certainly effect it. [. . .]

The general government is to be vested with authority to levy and collect taxes, duties, and excises; the separate states have also power to impose taxes, duties, and excises, except that they cannot lay duties on exports and imports without the consent of Congress. Here then the two governments have concurrent jurisdiction; both may lay impositions of this kind. But then the general government have superadded to this power, authority to make all laws which shall be necessary and proper for carrying the foregoing power into execution. Suppose then that both governments should lay taxes, duties, and excises, and it should fall so heavy on the people that they would be unable, or be so burdensome that they would refuse to pay them both—would it not be necessary that the general legislature should suspend the collection of the state tax? It certainly would. For, if the people could not, or would not pay both, they must be discharged from the tax to the state, or the tax to the general government could not be collected.—The conclusion therefore is inevitable, that the respective state governments will not have the power to raise one shilling in any way, but by the permission of the Congress. I presume no one will pretend, that the states can exercise legislative authority, or administer justice among their citizens for any length of time, without being able to raise a sufficiency to pay those who administer their governments.

If this be true, and if the states can raise money only by permission of the general government, it follows that the state governments will be dependent on the will of the general government for their existence. [. . .]

It was observed in my last number,[1] that the power to lay and collect duties and excises, would invest the Congress with authority to impose a duty and excise on every necessary and convenience of life. As the principal object of the government, in laying a duty or excise, will be, to raise money, it is obvious, that they will fix on such articles as are of the most general use and consumption; because, unless great quantities of the article, on which the duty is laid, is used, the revenue cannot be considerable. We may therefore presume, that the articles which will be the

1. [Essay 5, not included in this volume.]

object of this species of taxes will be either the real necessaries of life; or if not these, such as from custom and habit are esteemed so. I will single out a few of the productions of our own country, which may, and probably will, be of the number.

Cider is an article that most probably will be one of those on which an excise will be laid, because it is one, which this country produces in great abundance, which is in very general use, is consumed in great quantities, and which may be said too not to be a real necessary of life. An excise on this would raise a large sum of money in the United States. How would the power, to lay and collect an excise on cider, and to pass all laws proper and necessary to carry it into execution, operate in its exercise? It might be necessary, in order to collect the excise on cider, to grant to one man, in each county, an exclusive right of building and keeping cider mills, and oblige him to give bonds and security for payment of the excise; or, if this was not done, it might be necessary to license the mills, which are to make this liquor, and to take from them security, to account for the excise; or, if otherwise, a great number of officers must be employed, to take account of the cider made, and to collect the duties on it.

Porter, ale, and all kinds of malt liquors, are articles that would probably be subject also to an excise. It would be necessary, in order to collect such an excise, to regulate the manufactory of these, that the quantity made might be ascertained, or otherwise security could not be had for the payment of the excise. Every brewery must then be licensed, and officers appointed, to take account of its product, and to secure the payment of the duty, or excise, before it is sold. Many other articles might be named, which would be objects of this species of taxation, but I refrain from enumerating them. It will probably be said, by those who advocate this system, that the observations already made on this head, are calculated only to inflame the minds of the people, with the apprehension of dangers merely imaginary. That there is not the least reason to apprehend, the general legislature will exercise their power in this manner. To this I would only say, that these kinds of taxes exist in Great Britain, and are severely felt. The excise on cider and perry, was imposed in that nation a few years ago, and it is in the memory of everyone, who read the history of the transaction, what great tumults it occasioned.

This power, exercised without limitation, will introduce itself into every corner of the city, and country—It will wait upon the ladies at their toilette, and will not leave them in any of their domestic concerns; it will accompany them to the ball, the play, and the assembly; it will go with them when they visit, and will, on all occasions, sit beside them in their carriages, nor will it defect them even at church; it will enter the house of every gentleman, watch over his cellar, wait upon his cook in the kitchen, follow the servants into the parlor, preside over the table, and note down all he eats or drinks; it will attend him to his bedchamber, and watch him while he sleeps; it will take cognizance of the professional mail in his office, or his study; it will watch the merchant in the counting house, or in his store; it will follow the mechanic to his shop, and in his work, and will haunt him in his family, and in his bed; it will be a constant companion of the industrious farmer in all his labor, it will be with him in the house, and in the field, observe the toil of his hands, and the sweat of his brow; it will penetrate into the most obscure cottage; and finally, it will light upon the head of every person in the United States. To all these different classes of people, and in all these circumstances, in which it will attend them, the language in which it will address them, will be GIVE! GIVE!

A power that has such latitude, which reaches every person in the community to every conceivable circumstance, and lays hold of every species of property they possess and which has no bounds set to it but the discretion of those who exercise it. I say, such a power must necessarily, from its very nature, swallow up all the power of the state governments.

I shall add but one other observation on this head, which is this—It appears to me a solecism, for two men, or bodies of men, to have unlimited power respecting the same object. It contradicts the scripture maxim, which saith, "no man can serve two masters," the one power or the other must prevail, or else they will destroy each other, and neither of them effect their purpose. It may be compared to two mechanic powers, acting upon the same body in opposite directions, the consequence would be, if the powers were equal, the body would remain in a state of rest, or if the force of the one was superior to that of the other, the stronger would prevail, and overcome the resistance of the weaker.

But it is said, by some of the advocates of this system, "That the idea that Congress can levy taxes at pleasure, is false, and the suggestion wholly unsupported: that the preamble to the constitution is declaratory of the purposes of the union, and the assumption of any power not necessary to establish justice, etc. to provide for the common defense, etc. will be unconstitutional. Besides, in the very clause which gives the power of levying duties and taxes, the purposes to which the money shall be appropriated, are specified, viz. to pay the debts, and provide for the common defense and general welfare."[2] I would ask those, who reason thus, to define what ideas are included under the terms, to provide for the common defense and general welfare? Are these terms definite, and will they be understood in the same manner, and to apply to the same cases by everyone? No one will pretend they will. It will then be matter of opinion, what tends to the general welfare; and the Congress will be the only judges in the matter. To provide for the general welfare, is an abstract proposition, which mankind differ in the explanation of, as much as they do on any political or moral proposition that can be proposed; the most opposite measures may be pursued by different parties, and both may profess, that they have in view the general welfare; and both sides may be honest in their professions, or both may have sinister views. Those who advocate this new constitution declare, they are influenced by a regard to the general welfare; those who oppose it, declare they are moved by the same principle; and I have no doubt but a number on both sides are honest in their professions; and yet nothing is more certain than this, that to adopt this constitution, and not to adopt it, cannot both of them be promotive of the general welfare.

It is as absurd to say, that the power of Congress is limited by these general expressions, "to provide for the common safety, and general welfare," as it would be to say, that it would be limited, had the constitution said they should have power to lay taxes, etc. at will and pleasure. Were this authority given, it might be said, that under it the legislature could not do injustice, or pursue any measures, but such as were calculated to promote the public good, and happiness. For every man, rulers as well as others, are bound by the immutable laws of God and reason, always to will what is right. It is certainly right and fit, that the governors of every people should provide for the common defense and general welfare; every government, therefore, in the world, even the greatest despot, is limited in the exercise of his power. But however just this reasoning may be, it would be found, in practice, a most pitiful restriction. The government would always say, their measures were designed and calculated to promote the public good; and there being no judge between them and the people, the rulers themselves must, and would always, judge for themselves.

There are others of the favorers of this system, who admit, that the power of the Congress under it, with respect to revenue, will exist without limitation, and contend, that so is ought to be.

It is said, "The power to raise armies, to build and equip fleets, and to provide for their support ought to exist without limitation, because it is impossible to foresee, or to define, the extent and variety of national exigencies, or the correspondent extent and variety of the means which may be necessary to satisfy them."

This, it is said, "is one of those truths which, to correct and unprejudiced minds, carries its own evidence along with it. It rests upon axioms as simple as they are universal: the means ought to be proportioned to the end; the person, from whose agency the attainment of any end is expected, ought to possess the means by which it is to be attained."[3] [. . .]

But with submission to this author's better judgment, I humbly conceive his reasoning will appear, upon examination, more specious than solid. The means, says the gentleman, ought to be proportioned to the end; admit the proposition to be true it is then necessary to inquire, what is the end of the government of the United States, in order to draw any just conclusions from it. Is this end simply to preserve the general government, and to provide for the common defense and general welfare of the union only? certainly not[;] for beside this, the state governments are to be supported, and provision made for the managing such of their internal concerns as are allotted to

2. Vide an examination into the leading principles of the federal constitution, printed in Philadelphia, Page 34.

3. Vide the Federalist, No. 23.

them. It is admitted, "that the circumstances of our country are such, as to demand a compound, instead of a simple, a confederate, instead of a sole government," that the objects of each ought to be pointed out, and that each ought to possess ample authority to execute the powers committed to them. The government then, being complex in its nature, the end it has in view is so also; and it is as necessary, that the state governments should possess the means to attain the ends expected from them, as for the general government. Neither the general government, nor the state governments, ought to be vested with all the powers proper to be exercised for promoting the ends of government. The powers are divided between them—certain ends are to be attained by the one, and other certain ends by the other; and these, taken together, include all the ends of good government. This being the case, the conclusion follows, that each should be furnished with the means, to attain the ends, to which they are designed.

To apply this reasoning to the case of revenue; the general government is charged with the case of providing for the payment of the debts of the United States; supporting the general government, and providing for the defense of the union. To obtain these ends, they should be furnished with means. But does it hence follow, that they should command all the revenues of the United States! Most certainly it does not. For if so, it will follow, that no means will be left to attain other ends, as necessary to the happiness of the country, as those committed to their care. The individual states have debts to discharge; their legislatures and executives are to be supported, and provision is to be made for the administration of justice in the respective states. For those objects the general government has no authority to provide; nor is it proper it should. It is clear then, that the states should have the command of such revenues, as to answer the ends they have to obtain. To say, "that the circumstances that endanger the safety of nations are infinite," and from hence to infer, that all the sources of revenue in the states should be yielded to the general government, is not conclusive reasoning: for the Congress are authorized only to control in general concerns, and not regulate local and internal ones; and these are as essentially requisite to be provided for as those. The peace and happiness of a community is as intimately connected with the prudent direction of their domestic affairs, and the due administration of justice among themselves, as with a competent provision for their defense against foreign invaders, and indeed more so.

Upon the whole, I conceive, that there cannot be a clearer position than this, that the state governments ought to have an uncontrollable power to raise a revenue, adequate to the exigencies of their governments; and, I presume, no such power is left them by this constitution.

XI

January 31, 1788

The nature and extent of the judicial power of the United States, proposed to be granted by this constitution, claims our particular attention.

Much has been said and written upon the subject of this new system on both sides, but I have not met with any writer, who has discussed the judicial powers with any degree of accuracy. And yet it is obvious, that we can form but very imperfect ideas of the manner in which this government will work, or the effect it will have in changing the internal police and mode of distributing justice at present subsisting in the respective states, without a thorough investigation of the powers of the judiciary and of the manner in which they will operate. This government is a complete system, not only for making, but for executing laws. And the courts of law, which will be constituted by it, are not only to decide upon the constitution and the laws made in pursuance of it, but by officers subordinate to them to execute all their decisions. The real effect of this system of government, will therefore be brought home to the feelings of the people, through the medium of the judicial power. It is, moreover, of great importance, to examine with care the nature and extent of the judicial power; because those who are to be vested with it, are to be placed in a situation altogether unprecedented in a free country. They are to be rendered totally independent, both of the people and the legislature, both with respect to their offices and salaries. No errors they may commit can be corrected by any power above them, if any such power there be, nor can they be removed from office for making ever so many erroneous adjudications.

The only cause for which they can be displaced, is conviction of treason, bribery, and high crimes and misdemeanors.

This part of the plan is so modeled, as to authorize the courts, not only to carry into execution the powers expressly given, but where these are wanting or ambiguously expressed, to supply what is wanting by their own decisions.

That we may be enabled to form a just opinion on this subject, I shall, in considering it,

First. Examine the nature and extent of the judicial powers—and

Second. Inquire, whether the courts who are to exercise them, are so constituted as to afford reasonable ground of confidence, that they will exercise them for the general good. [. . .]

In article third, section 2nd, it is said, "The judicial power shall extend to all cases in law and equity arising under this constitution, the laws of the United States, and treaties made, or which shall be made, under their authority, etc."

The first article to which this power extends, is, all cases in law and equity arising under this constitution.

What latitude of construction this clause should receive, it is not easy to say. At first view, one would suppose, that it meant no more than this, that the courts under the general government should exercise, not only the powers of courts of law, but also that of courts of equity, in the manner in which those powers are usually exercised in the different states. But this cannot be the meaning, because the next clause authorizes the courts to take cognizance of all cases in law and equity arising under the laws of the United States; this last article, I conceive, conveys as much power to the general judicial as any of the state courts possess.

The cases arising under the constitution must be different from those arising under the laws, or else the two clauses mean exactly the same thing.

The cases arising under the constitution must include such, as bring into question its meaning, and will require an explanation of the nature and extent of the powers of the different departments under it.

This article, therefore, vests the judicial with a power to resolve all questions that may arise on any case on the construction of the constitution, either in law or in equity.

First. They are authorized to determine all questions that may arise upon the meaning of the constitution in law. This article vests the courts with authority to give the constitution a legal construction, or to explain it according to the rules laid down for construing a law.—These rules give a certain degree of latitude of explanation. According to this mode of construction, the courts are to give such meaning to the constitution as comports best with the common, and generally received acceptation of the words in which it is expressed, regarding their ordinary and popular use, rather than their grammatical propriety. Where words are dubious, they will be explained by the context. The end of the clause will be attended to, and the words will be understood, as having a view to it; and the words will not be so understood as to bear no meaning or a very absurd one.

Second. The judicial are not only to decide questions arising upon the meaning of the constitution in law, but also in equity.

By this they are empowered, to explain the constitution according to the reasoning spirit of it, without being confined to the words or letter.

"From this method of interpreting laws (says Blackstone) by the reason of them, arises what we call equity"; which is thus defined by Grotius, "the correction of that, wherein the law, by reason of its universality, is deficient; for since in laws all cases cannot be foreseen, or expressed, it is necessary, that when the decrees of the law cannot be applied to particular cases, there should somewhere be a power vested of [adapting the law to] those circumstances, which had they been foreseen the legislator would have expressed; and these are the cases, which according to Grotius, lex non exacte definit, sed arbitrio boni viri permittet."

The same learned author observes, "That equity, thus depending essentially upon each individual case, there can be no established rules and fixed principles of equity laid down, without destroying its very essence, and reducing it to a positive law."

From these remarks, the authority and business of the courts of law, under this clause, may be understood.

They will give the sense of every article of the constitution, that may from time to time come before them. And in their decisions they will not confine themselves to any fixed or established rules, but will determine, according to what appears to them, the reason and spirit of the constitution. The opinions of the supreme court, whatever they may be, will have the force of law; because there is no power provided in the constitution, that can correct their errors, or control their adjudications. From this court there is no appeal. And I conceive the legislature themselves, cannot set aside a judgment of this court, because they are authorized by the constitution to decide in the last resort. The legislature must be controlled by the constitution, and not the constitution by them. They have therefore no more right to set aside any judgment pronounced upon the construction of the constitution, than they have to take from the president, the chief command of the army and navy, and commit it to some other person. The reason is plain; the judicial and executive derive their authority from the same source, that the legislature do theirs; and therefore in all cases, where the constitution does not make the one responsible to, or controllable by the other, they are altogether independent of each other.

The judicial power will operate to effect, in the most certain, but yet silent and imperceptible manner, what is evidently the tendency of the constitution:—I mean, an entire subversion of the legislative, executive, and judicial powers of the individual states. Every adjudication of the supreme court, on any question that may arise upon the nature and extent of the general government, will affect the limits of the state jurisdiction. In proportion as the former enlarge the exercise of their powers, will that of the latter be restricted.

That the judicial power of the United States, will lean strongly in favor of the general government, and will give such an explanation to the constitution, as will favor an extension of its jurisdiction, is very evident from a variety of considerations.

First. The constitution itself strongly countenances such a mode of construction. Most of the articles in this system, which convey powers of any considerable importance, are conceived in general and indefinite terms, which are either equivocal, ambiguous, or which require long definitions to unfold the extent of their meaning. The two most important powers committed to any government, those of raising money, and of raising and keeping up troops, have already been considered, and shown to be [unlimited] by anything but the discretion of the legislature. The clause which vests the power to pass all laws which are proper and necessary, to carry the powers given into execution, it has been shown, leaves the legislature at liberty, to do everything, which in their judgment is best. It is said, I know, that this clause confers no power on the legislature, which they would not have had without it—though I believe this is not the fact, yet, admitting it to be, it implies that the constitution is not to receive an explanation strictly, according to its letter; but more power is implied than is expressed. And this clause, if it is to be considered, as explanatory of the extent of the powers given, rather than giving a new power, is to be understood as declaring, that in construing any of the articles conveying power, the spirit, intent, and design of the clause, should be attended to, as well as the words in their common acceptation. [. . .]

Second. Not only will the constitution justify the courts in inclining to this mode of explaining it, but they will be interested in using this latitude of interpretation. Every body of men invested with office are tenacious of power; they feel interested, and hence it has become a kind of maxim, to hand down their offices, with all its rights and privileges, unimpaired to their successors; the same principle will influence them to extend their power, and increase their rights; this of itself will operate strongly upon the courts to give such a meaning to the constitution in all cases where it can possibly be done, as will enlarge the sphere of their own authority. Every extension of the power of the general legislature, as well as of the judicial powers, will increase the powers of the courts; and the dignity and importance of the judges, will be in proportion to the extent and magnitude of the powers they exercise. I add, it is highly probable the emolument of the judges will be increased, with the increase of the business they will have to transact and its importance. From these considerations the judges will be interested to extend the powers of the courts, and to construe the constitution as much as possible, in such a way as to favor it; and that they will do it, appears probable. [. . .]

XII

February 7, 1788

In my last, I showed, that the judicial power of the United States under the first clause of the second section of article eight, would be authorized to explain the constitution, not only according to its letter, but according to its spirit and intention; and having this power, they would strongly incline to give it such a construction as to extend the powers of the general government, as much as possible, to the diminution, and finally to the destruction, of that of the respective states.

I shall now proceed to show how this power will operate in its exercise to effect these purposes. [. . .]

First. How it will tend to extend the legislative authority. [. . .]

It is to be observed, that the supreme court has the power, in the last resort, to determine all questions that may arise in the course of legal discussion, on the meaning and construction of the constitution. This power they will hold under the constitution, and independent of [the] legislature. The latter can no more deprive the former of this right, than either of them, or both of them together, can take from the president, with the advice of the senate, the power of making treaties, or appointing ambassadors.

In determining these questions, the court must and will assume certain principles, from which they will reason, in forming their decisions. These principles, whatever they may be, when they become fixed, by a course of decisions, will be adopted by the legislature, and will be the rule by which they will explain their own powers. This appears evident from this consideration, that if the legislature pass laws, which, in the judgment of the court, they are not authorized to do by the constitution, the court will not take notice of them; for it will not be denied, that the constitution is the highest or supreme law. And the courts are vested with the supreme and uncontrollable power, to determine, in all cases that come before them, what the constitution means; they cannot, therefore, execute a law, which, in their judgment, opposes the constitution, unless we can suppose they can make a superior law give way to an inferior. The legislature, therefore, will not go over the limits by which the courts may adjudge they are confined. And there is little room to doubt but that they will come up to those bounds, as often as occasion and opportunity may offer, and they may judge it proper to do it. For as on the one hand, they will not readily pass laws which they know the courts will not execute, so on the other, we may be sure they will not scruple to pass such as they know they will give effect, as often as they may judge it proper.

From these observations it appears, that the judgment of the judicial, on the constitution, will become the rule to guide the legislature in their construction of their powers.

What the principles are, which the courts will adopt, it is impossible for us to say; but taking up the powers as I have explained them in my last number, which they will possess under this clause, it is not difficult to see, that they may, and probably will, be very liberal ones.

We have seen, that they will be authorized to give the constitution a construction according to its spirit and reason, and not to confine themselves to its letter.

To discover the spirit of the constitution, it is of the first importance to attend to the principal ends and designs it has in view. These are expressed in the preamble, in the following words, viz. "We, the people of the United States, in order to form a more perfect union, establish justice, insure domestic tranquillity, provide for the common defense, promote the general welfare, and secure the blessings of liberty to ourselves and our posterity, do ordain and establish this constitution," etc. If the end of the government is to be learned from these words, which are clearly designed to declare it, it is obvious it has in view every object which is embraced by any government. The preservation of internal peace—the due administration of justice—and to provide for the defense of the community, seems to include all the objects of government; but if they do not, they are certainly comprehended in the words, "to provide for the general welfare." If it be further considered, that this constitution, if it is ratified, will not be a compact entered into by states, in their corporate capacities, but an agreement of the people of the United States, as one great body politic, no doubt can remain, but that the great end of the constitution, if it is to be collected from the preamble, in which its end is declared, is to constitute a government which is to extend to every case for which any government is instituted, whether external or internal. The courts, therefore, will establish this as a principle in expounding the constitution, and will give every part of it such an explanation, as will give latitude to every department under it, to take cognizance of every matter, not only that affects the general and national concerns of the union, but also of such as relate to the administration of private justice, and to regulating the internal and local affairs of the different parts.

Such a rule of exposition is not only consistent with the general spirit of the preamble, but it will stand confirmed by considering more minutely the different clauses of it.

The first object declared to be in view is, "To form a perfect union." It is to be observed, it is not an union of states or bodies corporate; had this been the case the existence of the state governments, might have been secured. But it is a union of the people of the United States considered as one body, who are to ratify this constitution, if it is adopted. Now to make a union of this kind perfect, it is necessary to abolish all inferior governments, and to give the general one complete legislative, executive, and judicial powers to every purpose. The courts therefore will establish it as a rule in explaining the constitution: To give it such a construction as will best tend to perfect the union or take from the state government every power of either making or executing laws. The second object is "to establish justice." This must include not only the idea of instituting the rule of justice, or of making laws which shall be the measure or rule of right, but also of providing for the application of this rule or of administering justice under it. And under this the courts will in their decisions extend the power of the government to all cases they possibly can, or otherwise they will be restricted in doing what appears to be the intent of the constitution they should do, to wit, pass laws and provide for the execution of them, for the general distribution of justice between man and man. Another end declared is "to insure domestic tranquillity." This comprehends a provision against all private breaches of the peace, as well as against all public commotions or general insurrections; and to attain the object of this clause fully, the government must exercise the power of passing laws on these subjects, as well as of appointing magistrates with authority to execute them. And the courts will adopt these ideas in their expositions. I might proceed to the other clauses, in the preamble, and it would appear by a consideration of all of them separately, as it does by taking them together, that if the spirit of this system is to be known from its declared end and design in the preamble, its spirit is to subvert and abolish all the powers of the state government, and to embrace every object to which any government extends.

As it sets out in the preamble with this declared intention, so it proceeds in the different parts with the same idea. Any person, who will peruse the eighth section with attention, in which most of the powers are enumerated, will perceive that they either expressly or by implication extend to almost everything about which any legislative power can be employed. But if this equitable mode of construction is applied to this part of the constitution; nothing can stand before it.

This will certainly give the first clause in that article a construction which I confess I think the most natural and grammatical one, to authorize the Congress to do anything which in their judgment will tend to provide for the general welfare, and this amounts to the same thing as general and unlimited powers of legislation in all cases.

February 14, 1788

This same manner of explaining the constitution, will fix a meaning, and a very important one too, to the twelfth clause of the same section, which authorizes the Congress to make all laws which shall be proper and necessary for carrying into effect the foregoing powers, etc. A voluminous writer in favor of this system, has taken great pains to convince the public, that this clause means nothing: for that the same powers expressed in this, are implied in other parts of the constitution. Perhaps it is so, but still this will undoubtedly be an excellent auxiliary to assist the courts to discover the spirit and reason of the constitution, and when applied to any and every of the other clauses granting power, will operate powerfully in extracting the spirit from them. [. . .]

It is obvious that these courts will have authority to decide upon the validity of the laws of any of the states, in all cases where they come in question before them. Where the constitution gives the general government exclusive jurisdiction, they will adjudge all laws made by the state, in such cases, *void ab* [*initio*]. Where the constitution gives them concurrent jurisdiction, the laws of the United States must prevail, because they are the supreme law. In such cases, therefore, the laws of the state legislatures must be repealed, restricted, or so construed, as to give full effect to the laws of the union on the same subject. From these remarks it is easy to see, that in proportion as the general government acquires power and jurisdiction, by the liberal construction which the judges may give the constitution, will those of the states lose their rights, until they become so trifling and unimportant, as not to be worth having. [. . .]

XIII

February 21, 1788

Having in the two preceding numbers, examined the nature and tendency of the judicial power, as it respects the explanation of the constitution, I now proceed to the consideration of the other matters, of which it has cognizance.—[. . .]

The next paragraph which gives a power to decide in law and equity, on all cases arising under treaties, is unintelligible to me. I can readily comprehend what is meant by deciding a case under a treaty. For as treaties will be the law of the land, every person who have rights or privileges secured by treaty, will have aid of the courts of law, in recovering them. But I do not understand, what is meant by equity arising under a treaty. I presume every right which can be claimed under a treaty, must be claimed by virtue of some article or clause contained in it, which gives the right in plain and obvious words; or at least, I conceive, that the rules for explaining treaties, are so well ascertained, that there is no need of having recourse to an equitable construction. If under this power, the courts are to explain treaties, according to what they conceive are their spirit, which is nothing less than a power to give them whatever extension they may judge proper, it is a dangerous and improper power. The cases affecting ambassadors, public ministers, and consuls—of admiralty and maritime jurisdiction; controversies to which the United States are a party, and controversies between states, it is proper should be under the cognizance of the courts of the union, because none but the general government, can, or ought to pass laws on their subjects. But, I conceive the clause which extends the power of the judicial to controversies arising between a state and citizens of another state, improper in itself, and will, in its exercise, prove most pernicious and destructive.

It is improper, because it subjects a state to answer in a court of law, to the suit of an individual. This is humiliating and degrading to a government, and, what I believe, the supreme authority of no state ever submitted to.

The states are now subject to no such actions. All contracts entered into by individuals with states, were made upon the faith and credit of the states; and the individuals never had in contemplation any compulsory mode of obliging the government to fulfil its engagements.

The evil consequences that will flow from the exercise of this power, will best appear by tracing it in its operation. The constitution does not direct the mode in which an individual shall commence a suit against a state or the manner in which the judgement of the court shall be carried into execution, but it gives the legislature full power to pass all laws which shall be proper and necessary for the purpose. And they certainly must make provision for these purposes, or otherwise the power of the judicial will be nugatory. For, to what purpose will the power of a judicial be, if they have no mode, in which they can call the parties before them? Or of what use will it be, to call the parties to answer, if after they have given judgement, there is no authority to execute the judgment? We must, therefore, conclude, that the legislature will pass laws which will be effectual in this head. An individual of one state will then have a legal remedy against a state for any demand he may have against a state to which he does not belong. Every state in the union is largely indebted to individuals. For the payment of these debts they have given notes payable to the bearer. At least this is the case in this state. Whenever a citizen of another state becomes possessed of one of these notes, he may commence an action in the supreme court of the general government; and I cannot see any way in which he can be prevented from recovering. It is easy to see, that when this once happens, the notes of the state will pass rapidly from the hands of citizens of the state to those of other states.

And when the citizens of other states possess them, they may bring suits against the state for them, and by this means, judgments and executions may be obtained against the state for the whole amount of the state debt. It is certain the state, with the utmost exertions it can make, will not be able to discharge the debt she owes, under a considerable number of years, perhaps with the best management, it will require twenty or thirty years to discharge it. This new system will protract the time in which the ability of the state will enable them to pay off their debt, because all the funds of the state will be transferred to the general government, except those which arise from internal taxes.

The situation of the states will be deplorable. By this system, they will surrender to the general government, all the means of raising money, and at the same time, will subject themselves to suits at law, for the recovery of the debts they have contracted in effecting the revolution.

The debts of the individual states will amount to a sum, exceeding the domestic debt of the United States; these will be left upon them, with power in the judicial of the general government, to enforce their payment, while the general government will possess an exclusive command of the most productive funds, from which the states can derive money, and a command of every other source of revenue paramount to the authority of any state.

It may be said that the apprehension that the judicial power will operate in this manner is merely visionary, for that the legislature will never pass laws that will work these effects. Or if they were disposed to do it, they cannot provide for levying an execution on a state, for where will the officer find property whereon to levy?

To this I would reply, if this is a power which will not or cannot be executed, it was useless and unwise to grant it to the judicial. For what purpose is a power given which it is imprudent or impossible to exercise? If it be improper for a government to exercise a power, it is improper they should be vested with it. And it is unwise to authorise a government to do what they cannot effect.

As to the idea that the legislature cannot provide for levying an execution on a state, I believe it is not well founded. I presume the last paragraph of the 8th section of article 1, gives the Congress express power to pass any laws they may judge proper and necessary for carrying into execution the power vested in the judicial department. [. . .] The only difficulty is, on whom shall process be served, when a state is a party, and how shall execution be levied. With regard to the first, the way is easy, either the executive or legislative of the state may be notified, and upon proof being made of the service of the notice, the court may proceed to a hearing of the cause. Execution may be levied on any property of the state, either real or personal. The treasury may be seized by the officers of the general government, or any lands the property of the state, may be made subject to seizure and sale to satisfy any judgment against it. [. . .]

If the power of the judicial under this clause will extend to the cases above stated, it will, if executed, produce the utmost confusion, and in its progress, will crush the states beneath its weight.

XIV

March 6, 1788

It may still be insisted that this clause does not take away the trial by jury on appeals, but that this may be provided for by the legislature, under that paragraph which authorises them to form regulations and restrictions for the court in the exercise of this power.

The natural meaning of this paragraph seems to be no more than this, that Congress may declare, that certain cases shall not be subject to the appellate jurisdiction, and they may point out the mode in which the court shall proceed in bringing up the causes before them, the manner of their taking evidence to establish the facts, and the method of the courts proceeding. But I presume they cannot take from the court the right of deciding on the fact, any more than they can deprive them of the right of determining on the law, when a cause is once before them; for they have the same jurisdiction as to fact, as they have as to the law. But supposing the Congress may under this clause establish the trial by jury on appeals, it does not seem to me that it will render this article much less exceptionable. An appeal from one court and jury, to another court and jury, is a thing altogether unknown in the laws of our state, and in most of the states in the union. A practice of this kind prevails in the eastern states; actions are there commenced in the inferior courts, and an appeal lies from them on the whole merits to the superior courts: the consequence is well known, very few actions are determined in the lower courts; it is rare that a case of any importance is not carried by appeal to the supreme court, and the jurisdiction of the inferior courts is merely nominal; this has proved so burthensome to the people in Massachusetts, that it was one of the principal causes which excited the insurrection in that state, in the year past; very few sensible and moderate men in that state but what will admit, that the inferior courts are almost entirely useless, and answer very little purpose, save only to accumulate costs against the poor debtors who are already unable to pay their just debts.

But the operation of the appellate power in the supreme judicial of the United States, would work infinitely more mischief than any such power can do in a single state.

The trouble and expence to the parties would be endless and intolerable. No man can say where the supreme court are to hold their sessions, the presumption is, however, that it must be at the seat of the general government: in this case parties must travel many hundred miles, with their witnesses and lawyers, to prosecute or defend a suit; no man of midling fortune, can sustain the expence of such a law suit, and therefore the poorer and midling class of citizens will be under the necessity of submitting to the demands of the rich and the lordly, in cases that will come under the cognizance of this court. If it be said, that to prevent this oppression, the supreme court will set in different parts of the union, it may be replied, that this would only make the oppression somewhat more tolerable, but by no means so much as to give a chance of justice to the poor and midling class. It is utterly impossible that the supreme court can move into so many different parts of the Union, as to make it convenient or even tolerable to attend before them with witnesses to try causes from every part of the United states; if to avoid the expence and inconvenience of calling witnesses from a great distance, to give evidence before the supreme court, the expedient of taking the deposition of witnesses in writing should be adopted, it would not help the matter. It is of great importance in the distribution of justice that witnesses should be examined face to face, that the parties should have the fairest opportunity of cross examining them in order to bring out the whole truth; there is something in the manner in which a witness delivers his testimony which cannot be committed to paper, and which yet very frequently gives a complexion to his evidence, very different from what it would bear if committed to writing, besides the expence of taking written testimony would be enormous; those who are acquainted with the costs that arise in the courts, where all the evidence is taken in writing, well know that they exceed beyond all comparison those of the common law courts, where witnesses are examined viva voce.

The costs accruing in courts generally advance with the grade of the court. [. . .] We have just reason to suppose, that the costs in the supreme general court will exceed either of our courts; the officers of the general court will be more dignified than those of the states, the lawyers of the most ability will practice in them, and the trouble and expence of attending them will be greater. From all these considerations, it appears, that the expence attending suits in the supreme court will be so great, as to put it out of the power of the poor and midling class of citizens to contest a suit in it.

From these remarks it appears, that the administration of justice under the powers of the judicial will be dilatory; that it will be attended with such an heavy expence as to amount to little short of a denial of justice to the poor and middling class of people who in every government stand most in need of the protection of the law; and that the trial by jury, which has so justly been the boast of our fore fathers as well as ourselves is taken away under them.

These extraordinary powers in this court are the more objectionable, because there does not appear the least necessity for them, in order to secure a due and impartial distribution of justice.

The want of ability or integrity, or a disposition to render justice to every suitor, has not been objected against the courts of the respective states: so far as I have been informed, the courts of justice in all the states, have ever been found ready, to administer justice with promptitude and impartiality according to the laws of the land; It is true in some of the states, paper money has been made, and the debtor authorised to discharge his debts with it, at a depreciated value, in orders, tender laws have been passed, obliging the creditor to receive on execution other property than money in discharge of his demand, and in several of the states laws have been made unfavorable to the creditor and tending to render property insecure.

But these evils have not have not happened from any defect in the judicial departments of the states [. . .] All the acts of our legislature, which have been charged with being of this complexion, have uniformly received the strictest construction by the judges, and have been extended to no cases but to such as came within the strict letter of the law. In this way, have our courts, I will not say evaded the law, but so limited it in its operation as to work the least possible injustice. [. . .]

No pretext therefore, can be formed, from the conduct of the judicial courts which will justify giving such poweres to the supreme general court, for their decisions have been such as to give just ground of confidence in them, that they will firmly adhere to the principles of rectitude, and there is no necessity of lodging these powers in the courts, in order to guard against the evils justly complained of, on the subject of security of property under this constitution. For it has provided, "that no state shall emit bills of credit, or make any thing butgold and silver coin a tender in payment of debts." It has also declared, that "no state shall pass any law impairing the obligation of contracts."—These prohibitions give the most perfect security against those attacks upon property which I am sorry to say some of the states have but too wantonly made, by passing laws sanctioning fraud in the debtor against his creditor. For "this constitution will be the supreme law of the land, and the judges in every state will be bound thereby; any thing in the constitution and laws of any state to the contrary notwithstanding."

The courts of the respective states might therefore have been securely trusted, with deciding all cases between man and man, whether citizens of the same state or of different states, or between foreigners and citizens, and indeed for ought I see every case that can arise under the constitution or laws of the United States, ought in the first instance to be tried in the court of the state, except those which might arise between states, such as respect ambassadors, or other public ministers, and perhaps such as call in question the claim of lands under grants from different states. The state courts would be under sufficient control, if writs of error were allowed from the state courts to the supreme court of the union, according to the practice of the courts in England and of this state, on all cases in which the laws of the union are concerned, and perhaps to all cases in which a foreigner is a party.

This method would preserve the good old way of administering justice, would bring justice to every man's door, and preserve the inestimable right of trial by jury. It would be following, as near as our circumstances will admit, the practice of the courts in England, which is almost the only thing I would wish to copy in their government.

XV

March 20, 1788

I said in my last number, that the supreme court under this constitution would be exalted above all other power in the government, and subject to no controul. The business of this paper will be to illustrate this, and to show the danger that will result from it. I question whether the world ever saw, in any period of it, a court of justice invested with such immense powers, and yet placed in a situation so little responsible. Certain it is, that in England, and in the several states, where we have been taught to believe, the courts of law are put upon the most prudent establishment, they are on a very different footing.

The judges in England, it is true, hold their offices during their good behaviour, but then their determinations are subject to correction by the house of lords; and their power is by no means so extensive as that of the proposed supreme court of the union.—I believe they in no instance assume the authority to set aside an act of parliament under the idea that it is inconsistent with their constitution. They consider themselves bound to decide according to the existing laws of the land, and never undertake to controul them by adjudging that they are inconsistent with the constitution—much less are they vested with the power of giving an *equitable* construction to the constitution.

The judges in England are under the controul of the legislature, for they are bound to determine according to the laws passed by them. But the judges under this constitution will controul the legislature, for the supreme court are authorised in the last resort, to determine what is the extent of the powers of the Congress; they are to give the constitution an explanation, and there is no power above them to set aside their judgment. The framers of this constitution appear to have followed that of the British, in rendering the judges independent, by granting them their offices during good behaviour, without following the constitution of England, in instituting a tribunal in which their errors may be corrected; and without adverting to this, that the judicial under this system have a power which is above the legislative, and which indeed transcends any power before given to a judicial by any free government under heaven.

I do not object to the judges holding their commissions during good behaviour. I suppose it a proper provision provided they were made properly responsible. But I say, this system has followed the English government in this, while it has departed from almost every other principle of their jurisprudence, under the idea, of rendering the judges independent; which, in the British constitution, means no more than that they hold their places during good behaviour, and have fixed salaries, they have made the judges *independent,* in the fullest sense of the word. There is no power above them, to controul any of their decisions. There is no authority that can remove them, and they cannot be controuled by the laws of the legislature. In short, they are independent of the people, of the legislature, and of every power under heaven. Men placed in this situation will generally soon feel themselves independent of heaven itself. [. . .]

I have said that the judges under this system will be *independent* in the strict sense of the word: To prove this I will show—That there is no power above them that can controul their decisions, or correct their errors. There is no authority that can remove them from office for any errors or want of capacity, or lower their salaries, and in many cases their power is superior to that of the legislature.

First. There is no power above them that can correct their errors or controul their decisions—The adjudications of this court are final and irreversible, for there is no court above them to which appeals can lie, either in error or on the merits. In this respect it differs from the courts in England, for there the house of lords is the highest court, to whom appeals, in error, are carried from the highest of the courts of law.—

Second. They cannot be removed from office or suffer a dimunition of their salaries, for any error in judgement or want of capacity.

It is expressly declared by the constitution,—"That they shall at stated times receive a compensation for their services which shall not be diminished during their continuance in office."

The only clause in the constitution which provides for the removal of the judges from office, is that which declares, that "the president, vice-president, and all civil officers of the United States, shall be removed from office, on impeachment for, and conviction of treason, bribery, or other high crimes and misdemeanors." By this paragraph, civil officers, in which the judges are included, are removable only for crimes. Treason and bribery are named, and the rest are included under the general terms of high crimes and misdemeanors.—Errors in judgement, or want of capacity to discharge the duties of the office, can never be supposed to be included in these words, *high crimes and misdemeanors.* A man may mistake a case in giving judgment, or manifest that he is incompetent to the discharge of the duties of a judge, and yet give no evidence of corruption or want of integrity. To support the charge, it will be necessary to give in evidence some facts that will show, that the judges commited the error from wicked and corrupt motives.

Third. The power of this court is in many cases superior to that of the legislature. I have showed, in a former paper,[4] that this court will be authorised to decide upon the meaning of the constitution, and that, not only according to the natural and obvious meaning of the words, but also according to the spirit and intention of it. In the exercise of this power they will not be subordinate to, but above the legislature. For all the departments of this government will receive their powers, so far as they are expressed in the constitution, from the people immediately, who

4. [I.e., Essay 11, above.]

are the source of power. The legislature can only exercise such powers as are given them by the constitution, they cannot assume any of the rights annexed to the judicial, for this plain reason, that the same authority which vested the legislature with their powers, vested the judicial with theirs—both are derived from the same source, both therefore are equally valid, and the judicial hold their powers independently of the legislature, as the legislature do of the judicial.—The supreme court then have a right, independent of the legislature, to give a construction to the constitution and every part of it, and there is no power provided in this system to correct their construction or do it away. If, therefore, the legislature pass any laws, inconsistent with the sense the judges put upon the constitution, they will declare it void; and therefore in this respect their power is superior to that of the legislature. In England the judges are not only subject to have their decisions set aside by the house of lords, for error, but in cases where they give an explanation to the laws or constitution of the country, contrary to the sense of the parliament, though the parliament will not set aside the judgement of the court, yet, they have authority, by a new law, to explain a former one, and by this means to prevent a reception of such decisions. But no such power is in the legislature. The judges are supreme—and no law, explanatory of the constitution, will be binding on them.

From the preceding remarks, which have been made on the judicial powers proposed in this system, the policy of it may be fully developed.

I have, in the course of my observation on this constitution, affirmed and endeavored to show, that it was calculated to abolish entirely the state governments, and to melt down the states into one entire government, for every purpose as well internal and local, as external and national. In this opinion the opposers of the system have generally agreed—and this has been uniformly denied by its advocates in public. Some individuals, indeed, among them, will confess, that it has this tendency, and scruple not to say, it is what they wish; and I will venture to predict, without the spirit of prophecy, that if it is adopted without amendments, or some such precautions as will ensure amendments immediately after its adoption, that the same gentlemen who have employed their talents and abilities with such success to influence the public mind to adopt this plan, will employ the same to persuade the people, that it will be for their good to abolish the state governments as useless and burdensome.

Perhaps nothing could have been better conceived to facilitate the abolition of the state governments than the constitution of the judicial. They will be able to extend the limits of the general government gradually, and by insensible degrees, and to accomodate themselves to the temper of the people. Their decisions on the meaning of the constitution will commonly take place in cases which arise between individuals, with which the public will not be generally acquainted; one adjudication will form a precedent to the next, and this to a following one. [. . .] In this situation, the general legislature, might pass one law after another, extending the general and abridging the state jurisdictions, and to sanction their proceedings would have a course of decisions of the judicial to whom the constitution has committed the power of explaining the constitution. [. . .]

Had the construction of the constitution been left with the legislature, they would have explained it at their peril; if they exceed their powers, or sought to find, in the spirit of the constitution, more than was expressed in the letter, the people from whom they derived their power could remove them, and do themselves right; and indeed I can see no other remedy that the people can have against their rulers for encroachments of this nature. A constitution is a compact of a people with their rulers; if the rulers break the compact, the people have a right and ought to remove them and do themselves justice; but in order to enable them to do this with the greater facility, those whom the people chuse at stated periods, should have the power in the last resort to determine the sense of the compact; if they determine contrary to the understanding of the people, an appeal will lie to the people at the period when the rulers are to be elected, and they will have it in their power to remedy the evil; but when this power is lodged in the hands of men independent of the people, and of their representatives, and who are not, constitutionally, accountable for their opinions, no way is left to controul them but *with a high hand and an outstretched arm.*

XVI

April 10, 1788

When great and extraordinary powers are vested in any man, or body of men, which in their exercise, may operate to the oppression of the people, it is of high importance that powerful checks should be formed to prevent the abuse of it.

Perhaps no restraints are more forcible, than such as arise from responsibility to some superior power.—Hence it is that the true policy of a republican government is, to frame it in such manner, that all persons who are concerned in the government, are made accountable to some superior for their conduct in office.—This responsibility should ultimately rest with the People. To have a government well administered in all its parts, it is requisite the different departments of it should be separated and lodged as much as may be in different hands. The legislative power should be in one body, the executive in another, and the judicial in one different from either—But still each of these bodies should be accountable for their conduct. Hence it is impracticable, perhaps, to maintain a perfect distinction between these several departments—For it is difficult, if not impossible, to call to account the several officers in government, without in some degree mixing the legislative and judicial. The legislature in a free republic are chosen by the people at stated periods, and their responsibility consists, in their being amenable to the people. When the term, for which they are chosen, shall expire, who will then have opportunity to displace them if they disapprove of their conduct—but it would be improper that the judicial should be elective, because their business requires that they should possess a degree of law knowledge, which is acquired only by a regular education, and besides it is fit that they should be placed, in a certain degree in an independent situation, that they may maintain firmness and steadiness in their decisions. As the people therefore ought not to elect the judges, they cannot be amenable to them immediately, some other mode of amenability must therefore be devised for these, as well as for all other officers which do not spring from the immediate choice of the people: this is to be effected by making one court subordinate to another, and by giving them cognizance of the behaviour of all officers; but on this plan we at last arrive at some supreme, over whom there is no power to controul but the people themselves. This supreme controling power should be in the choice of the people, or else you establish an authority independent, and not amenable at all, which is repugnant to the principles of a free government. Agreeable to these principles I suppose the supreme judicial ought to be liable to be called to account, for any misconduct, by some body of men, who depend upon the people for their places; and so also should all other great officers in the State, who are not made amenable to some superior officers. This policy seems in some measure to have been in view of the framers of the new system, and to have given rise to the institution of a court of impeachments—How far this Court will be properly qualified to execute the trust which will be reposed in them, will be the business of a future paper to investigate. To prepare the way to do this, it shall be the business of this, to make some remarks upon the constitution and powers of the Senate, with whom the power of trying impeachments is lodged.

The following things may be observed with respect to the constitution of the Senate.

First. They are to be elected by the legislatures of the States and not by the people, and each State is to be represented by an equal number.

Second. They are to serve for six years, except that one third of those first chosen are to go out of office at the expiration of two years, one third at the expiration of four years, and one third at the expiration of six years, after which this rotation is to be preserved, but still every member will serve for the term of six years.

Third. If vacancies happen by resignation or otherwise, during the recess of the legislature of any State, the executive is authorised to make temporary appointments until the next meeting of the legislature.

Fourth. No person can be a senator who has not arrived to the age of thirty years, been nine years a citizen of the United States, and who is not at the time he is elected an inhabitant of the State for which he is elected.

The apportionment of members of Senate among the States is not according to numbers, or the importance of the States; but is equal. This, on the plan of a consolidated government, is unequal and improper; but is proper on the system of confederation—on this principle I approve of it. It is indeed the only feature of any importance in the constitution of a confederated government. It was obtained after a vigorous struggle of that part of the Convention who were in favor of preserving the state governments. It is to be regretted, that they were not able to have infused other principles into the plan, to have secured the government of the respective states, and to have marked with sufficient precision the line between them and the general government.

The term for which the senate are to be chosen, is in my judgment too long, and no provision being made for a rotation will, I conceive, be of dangerous consequence.

It is difficult to fix the precise period for which the senate should be chosen. It is a matter of opinion, and our sentiments on the matter must be formed, by attending to certain principles. Some of the duties which are to be performed by the senate, seem evidently to point out the propriety of their term of service being extended beyond the period of that of the assembly. Besides as they are designed to represent the aristocracy of the country, it seems fit they should possess more stability, and so continue a longer period than that branch who represent the democracy. The business of making treaties and some other which it will be proper to commit to the senate, requires that they should have experience, and therefore that they should remain some time in office to acquire it.—But still it is of equal importance that they should not be so long in office as to be likely to forget the hand that formed them, or be insensible of their interests. Men long in office are very apt to feel themselves independent [and] to form and pursue interests separate from those who appointed them. And this is more likely to be the case with the senate, as they will for the most part of the time be absent from the state they represent, and associate with such company as will possess very little of the feelings of the middling class of people. For it is to be remembered that there is to be *a federal city*, and the inhabitants of it will be the great and the mighty of the earth. For these reasons I would shorten the term of their service to four years. Six years is a long period for a man to be absent from his home, it would have a tendency to wean him from his constituents.

A rotation in the senate, would also in my opinion be of great use. It is probable that senators once chosen for a state will, as the system now stands, continue in office for life. The office will be honorable if not lucrative. The persons who occupy it will probably wish to continue in it, and therefore use all their influence and that of their friends to continue in office.—Their friends will be numerous and powerful, for they will have it in their power to confer great favors; besides it will before long be considered as disgraceful not to be re re-elected. It will therefore be considered as a matter of delicacy to the character of the senator not to return him again.—Every body acquainted with public affairs knows how difficult it is to remove from office a person who is [has?] long been in it. It is seldom done except in cases of gross misconduct. It is rare that want of competent ability procures it. To prevent this inconvenience I conceive it would be wise to determine, that a senator should not be eligible after he had served for the period assigned by the constitution for a certain number of years; perhaps three would be sufficient. A farther benefit would be derived from such an arrangement; it would give opportunity to bring forward a greater number of men to serve their country, and would return those, who had served, to their state, and afford them the advantage of becoming better acquainted with the condition and politics of their constituents. It farther appears to me proper, that the legislatures should retain the right which they now hold under the confederation, of recalling their members. It seems an evident dictate of reason, that when a person authorises another to do a piece of business for him, he should retain the power to displace him, when he does not conduct according to his pleasure. This power in the state legislatures, under confederation, has not been exercised to the injury of the government, nor do I see any danger of its being so exercised under the new system. It may operate much to the public benefit.

These brief remarks are all I shall make on the organization of the senate. The powers with which they are invested will require a more minute investigation.

This body will possess a strange mixture of legislative, executive and judicial powers, which in my opinion will in some cases clash with each other.

1. They are one branch of the legislature, and in this respect will possess equal powers in all cases with the house of representatives; for I consider the clause which gives the house of representatives the right of originating bills for raising a revenue as

merely nominal, seeing the senate be authorised to propose or concur with amendments.

2. They are a branch of the executive in the appointment of ambassadors and public ministers, and in the appointment of all other officers, not otherwise provided for; whether the forming of treaties, in which they are joined with the president, appertains to the legislative or the executive part of the government, or to neither, is not material.

3. They are part of the judicial, for they form the court of impeachments. It has been a long established maxim, that the legislative, executive and judicial departments in government should be kept distinct. It is said, I know, that this cannot be done. And therefore that this maxim is not just, or at least that it should only extend to certain leading features in a government. I admit that this distinction cannot be perfectly preserved. In a due ballanced government, it is perhaps absolutely necessary to give the executive qualified legislative powers, and the legislative or a branch of them judicial powers in the last resort. It may possibly also, in some special cases, be adviseable to associate the legislature, or a branch of it, with the executive, in the exercise of acts of great national importance. But still the maxim is a good one, and a separation of these powers should be sought as far as is practicable. I can scarcely imagine that any of the advocates of the system will pretend, that it was necessary to accumulate all these powers in the senate.

There is a propriety in the senate's possessing legislative powers; this is the principal end which should be held in view in their appointment. I need not here repeat what has so often and ably been advanced on the subject of a division of the legislative power into two branches—The arguments in favor of it I think conclusive. But I think it equally evident, that a branch of the legislature should not be invested with the power of appointing officers. This power in the senate is very improperly lodged for a number of reasons—These shall be detailed in a future number.

FEDERAL FARMER (1787–1788)

Letter VII

December 31, 1787

Dear sir,

In viewing the various governments instituted by mankind, we see their whole force reducible to two principles—the important springs which alone move the machines, and give them their intended influence and control, are force and persuasion: by the former men are compelled, by the latter they are drawn. We denominate a government despotic or free, as the one or other principle prevails in it. Perhaps it is not possible for a government to be so despotic, as not to operate persuasively on some of its subjects; nor is it, in the nature of things, I conceive, for a government to be so free, or so supported by voluntary consent, as never to want force to compel obedience to the laws. In despotic governments one man, or a few men, independent of the people, generally make the laws, command obedience, and inforce it by the sword: one-fourth part of the people are armed, and obliged to endure the fatigues of soldiers, to oppress the others and keep them subject to the laws. In free governments the people, or their representatives, make the laws; their execution is principally the effect of voluntary consent and aid; the people respect the magistrate, follow their private pursuits, and enjoy the fruits of their labour with very small deductions for the public use. The body of the people must evidently prefer the latter species of government; and it can be only those few, who may be well paid for the part they take in enforcing despotism, that can, for a moment, prefer the former. Our true object is to give full efficacy to one principle, to arm persuasion on every side, and to render force as little necessary as possible. Persuasion is never dangerous not even in despotic governments; but military force, if often applied internally, can never fail to destroy the love and confidence, and break the spirits, of the people; and to render it totally impracticable and unnatural for him or them who govern, and yield to this force against the people, to hold their places by the peoples' elections. [. . .]

Government must exist—If the persuasive principle be feeble, force is infallibly the next resort—The moment the laws of congress shall be disregarded they must languish, and the whole system be convulsed—that moment we must have recourse to this next resort, and all freedom vanish.

It being impracticable for the people to assemble to make laws, they must elect legislators, and assign men to the different departments of the government. In the representative branch we must expect chiefly to collect the confidence of the people, and in it to find almost entirely the force of persuasion. In forming this branch, therefore, several important considerations must be attended to. It must possess abilities to discern the situation of the people and of public affairs, a disposition to sympathize with the people, and a capacity and inclination to make laws congenial to their circumstances and condition: it must afford security against interested combinations, corruption and influence; it must possess the confidence, and have the voluntary support of the people.

I think these positions will not be controverted, nor the one I formerly advanced, that a fair and equal representation is that in which the interests, feelings, opinions and views of the people are collected, in such manner as they would be were the people all assembled. Having made these general observations, I shall proceed to consider further my principal position, viz. that there is no substantial representation of the people provided for in a government, in which the most essential powers, even as to the internal police of the country, are proposed to be lodged; and to propose certain amendments as to the representative branch: 1st, That there ought to be *an increase of the numbers of representatives*: And, 2dly, That the elections of them ought to be better secured. [. . .]

In fixing this branch, the situation of the people must be surveyed, and the number of representatives and forms of election apportioned to that situation. When we find a numerous people settled in a fertile and extensive country, possessing equality, and few or none of them oppressed with riches or wants, it ought to be the anxious care of the constitution and laws, to arrest them from national depravity, and to preserve them in their happy condition. A virtuous people make just laws, and good laws tend to preserve unchanged a virtuous people. A virtuous and happy people by laws uncongenial to their characters, may easily be gradually changed into servile and depraved creatures. Where the people, or their representatives, make the laws, it is probable they will generally be fitted to the national character and circumstances, unless the representation be partial, and the imperfect substitute of the people. However, the people may be electors, if the representation be so formed as to give one or more of the natural classes of men in the society an undue ascendency over the others, it is imperfect; the former will gradually become masters, and the latter slaves. It is the first of all among the political balances, to preserve in its proper station each of these classes. We talk of balances in the legislature, and among the departments of government; we ought to carry them to the body of the people. Since I advanced the idea of balancing the several orders of men in a community, in forming a genuine representation, and seen that idea considered as chimerical, I have been sensibly struck with a sentence in the marquis Beccaria's treatise: this sentence was quoted by congress in 1774, and is as follows:—"In every society there is an effort continually tending to confer on one part the height of power and happiness, and to reduce the others to the extreme of weakness and misery; the intent of good laws is to oppose this effort, and to diffuse their influence universally and equally." Add to this Montesquieu's opinion, that "in a free state every man, who is supposed to be a free agent, ought to be concerned in his own government: therefore, the legislative should reside in the whole body of the people, or their representatives." It is extremely clear that these writers had in view the several orders of men in society, which we call aristocratical, democratical, mercantile, mechanic, &c. and perceived the efforts they are constantly, from interested and ambitious views, disposed to make to elevate themselves and oppress others. Each order must have a share in the business of legislation actually and efficiently. It is deceiving a people to tell them they are electors, and can chuse their legislators, if they cannot, in the nature of things, chuse men from among themselves, and genuinely like themselves. I wish you to take another idea along with you; we are not only to balance these natural efforts, but we are also to guard against accidental combinations; combinations founded in the connections of offices and private interests, both evils which are increased in proportion as the number of men, among which the elected must be, are decreased. To set this matter in a proper point of view, we must form some general ideas and descriptions of the different classes of men, as they may be divided by occupations and politically: the first class is the aristocratical. There are three kinds of aristocracy spoken of in this country—the first is a constitutional one, which does not exist in the United States in our common acceptation of the word. Montesquieu, it is true, observes, that where a part of the persons in a society, for want of property, age, or moral character, are excluded any share in the government, the others, who alone are the constitutional electors and elected, form this aristocracy; this according to him, exists in each of the United States, where a considerable number of persons, as all convicted of crimes, under age, or not possessed of certain property, are excluded any share in the government; the second is an aristocratic faction, a junto of unprincipled men, often distinguished for their wealth or abilities, who combine together and make their object their private interests and aggrandizement; the existence of this description is merely accidental, but particularly to be guarded against. The third is the natural aristocracy; this term we use to designate a respectable order of men, the line between whom and the natural democracy is in some degree arbitrary; we may place men on one side of this line, which others may place on the other, and in all disputes between the few and the many, a considerable number are wavering and uncertain themselves on which side they are, or ought to be. In my idea of our natural aristocracy in the United States, I include about four or five thousand men; and among these I reckon those who have been placed in the offices of governors, of members of Congress, and state senators generally, in the principal officers of Congress, of the army and militia, the superior judges, the most eminent professional men, &c. and men of large property—the other persons and orders in the community form the natural democracy; this includes in general the yeomanry, the subordinate officers, civil and military, the fishermen, mechanics and traders, many of the merchants and professional men. It is easy to perceive that men of these two classes, the aristocratical, and democratical, with views equally honest, have sentiments widely different, especially respecting public and private expenses, salaries, taxes, &c. Men of the first class associate more extensively, have a high sense of honor, possess abilities, ambition, and general knowledge: men of the second class are not so much used to combining great objects; they possess less ambition, and a larger share of honesty: their dependence is principally on middling and small estates, industrious pursuits, and hard labour, while that of the former is principally on the emoluments of large estates, and of the chief offices of government. Not only the efforts of these two great parties are to be balanced, but other interests and parties also, which do not always oppress each other merely for want of power, and for fear of the consequences; though they, in fact, mutually depend on each other; yet such are their general views, that the merchants alone would never fail to make laws favourable to themselves and oppressive to the farmers, &c. the farmers alone would act on like principles; the former would tax the land, the latter the trade. The manufacturers are often disposed to contend for monopolies, buyers make every exertion to lower prices, and sellers to raise them; men who live by fees and salaries endeavour to raise them, and the part of the people who pay them, endeavour to lower them; the public creditors to augment the taxes, and the people at large to lessen them. Thus, in every period of society, and in all the transactions of men, we see parties verifying the observation made by the Marquis; and those classes which have not their sentinels in the government, in proportion to what they have to gain or lose, must infallibly be ruined. Efforts among parties are not merely confined to property; they contend for rank and distinctions; all their passions in turn are enlisted in political controversies—Men, elevated in society, are often disgusted with the changeableness of the democracy, and the latter are often agitated with the passions of jealousy and envy: the yeomanry possess a large share of property and strength, are nervous and firm in their opinions and habits—the mechanics of towns are ardent and changeable, honest and credulous, they are inconsiderable for numbers, weight and strength, not always sufficiently stable for the supporting free governments; the fishing interest partakes partly of the strength and stability of the landed, and partly of the changeableness of the mechanic interest. As to merchants and traders, they are our agents in almost all money transactions; give activity to government, and possess a considerable share of influence in it. It has been observed by an able writer, that frugal industrious merchants are generally advocates for liberty. It is an observation, I believe, well founded, that the schools produce but few advocates for republican forms of government; gentlemen of the law, divinity, physic, &c. probably form about a fourth part of the people; yet their political influence, perhaps, is equal to that of all the other descriptions of men; if we may judge from the appointments to Congress, the legal characters will often, in a small representation, be the majority; but the more the representatives are increased, the more of the farmers, merchants, &c. will be found to be brought into the government.

These general observations will enable you to discern what I intend by different classes, and the general scope of my ideas, when I contend for uniting and balancing their interests, feelings, opinions, and views in the legislature; we may not only so unite and balance these as to prevent a change in the government by the gradual exaltation of one part to the depression of others, but we may derive many other advantages from the combination and full representation; a small representation can never be well informed as to the circumstances of the people, the members of it must be too far removed from the people, in general, to sympathize with them, and too few to communicate with them: a representation must be extremely imperfect where the representatives are not circumstanced to make the proper communications to their constituents, and where the constituents in turn cannot, with tolerable convenience, make known their wants, circumstances, and opinions, to their representatives; where there is but one representative to 30,000, or 40,000 inhabitants, it appears to me, he can only mix, and be acquainted with a few respectable characters among his constituents, even double the federal representation, and then there must be a very great distance between the representatives and the people in general represented. [. . .]

Could we get over all our difficulties respecting a balance of interests and party efforts, to raise some and oppress others, the want of sympathy, information and intercourse between the representatives and the people, an insuperable difficulty will still remain, I mean the constant liability of a small number of representatives to private combinations; the tyranny of the one, or the licentiousness of the multitude, are, in my mind, but small evils, compared with the factions of the few. It is a consideration well worth pursuing, how far this house of representatives will be liable to be formed into private juntos, how far influenced by expectations of appointments and offices, how far liable to be managed by the president and senate, and how far the people will have confidence in them.

Letter XIV

January 17, 1788

Dear sir,

It is a good general rule, that the legislative, executive, and judicial powers, ought to be kept distinct; but this, like other general rules, has its exceptions; and without these exceptions we cannot form a good government, and properly balance its parts: and we can determine only from reason, experience, and a critical inspection of the parts of the government, how far it is proper to intermix those powers. Appointments, I believe, in all mixed governments, have been assigned to different hands—some are made by the executive, some by the legislature, some by the judges, and some by the people. It has been thought advisable by the wisest nations, that the legislature should so far exercise executive and judicial powers as to appoint some officers, judge of the elections of its members, and impeach and try officers for misconduct—that the executive should have a partial share in legislation—that judges should appoint some subordinate officers, and regulate so far as to establish rules for their own proceedings. Where the members of the government, as the house, the senate, the executive, and judiciary, are strong and complete, each in itself, the balance is naturally produced, each party may take the powers congenial to it, and we have less need to be anxious about checks, and the subdivision of powers.

If after making the deductions, already alluded to, from the general power to appoint federal officers the residuum shall be thought to be too large and unsafe, and to place an undue influence in the hands of the president and council, a further deduction may be made, with many advantages, and, perhaps, with but a few inconveniencies; and that is, by giving the appointment of a few great officers to the legislature—as of the commissioners of the treasury—of the comptroller, treasurer, master coiner, and some of the principal officers in the money department—of the sheriffs or marshals of the United States—of states attorneys, secretary of the home department, and secretary at war, perhaps, of the judges of the supreme court—of major-generals and admirals. The appointments of these officers, who may be at the heads of the great departments of business, in carrying into execution the national system, involve in them a variety of considerations; they will not often occur and the power to make them ought to remain in safe hands. Officers of the above description are appointed by the legislatures in some of the states, and in some not. We may, I believe, presume that the federal legislature will possess sufficient knowledge and discernment to make judicious appointments: however, as these appointments by the legislature tend to increase a mixture of power, to lessen the advantages of impeachment and responsibility, I would by no means contend for them any further than it may be necessary for reducing the power of the executive within the bounds of safety. To determine, with propriety, how extensive power the executive ought to possess relative to appointments, we must also examine the forms of it, and its other powers; and these forms and other powers I shall now proceed briefly to examine. [. . .]

Viewing the principles and checks established in the election of the president, and especially considering the several states may guard the appointment of the electors as they shall judge best, I confess there appears to be a judicious combination of principles and precautions. Were the electors more numerous than they will be, in case the representation be not increased, I think, the system would be improved; not that I consider the democratic character so important in the choice of the electors as in the choice of representatives: be the electors more or less democratic, the president will be one of the very few of the most elevated characters. But there is danger, that a majority of a small number of electors may be corrupted and influenced, after appointed electors, and before they give their votes, especially if a considerable space of time elapse between the appointment and voting. I have already considered the advisory council in the executive branch: there are two things further in the organization of the executive, to which I would particularly draw your attention; the first, which, is a single executive. I confess, I approve; the second, by which any person from period to period may be re-elected president, I think very exceptionable.

Each state in the union has uniformly shown its preference for a single executive, and generally directed the first executive magistrate to act in certain cases by the advice of an executive council. Reason, and the experience of enlightened nations, seem justly to assign the business of making laws to numerous assemblies; and the execution of them, principally, to the direction and care of one man. Independent of practice a single man seems to be peculiarly well circumstanced to superintend the execution of laws with discernment and decision, with promptitude and uniformity: the people usually point out a first man—he is to be seen in civilized as well as uncivilized nations—in republics as well as in other governments. In every large collection of people there must be a visible point serving as a common centre in the government, towards which to draw their eyes and attachments. The constitution must fix a man, or a congress of men, superior in the opinion of the people, to the most popular men in the different parts of the community, else the people will be apt to divide and follow their respective leaders. Aspiring men, armies and navies, have not often been kept in tolerable order by the decrees of a senate or an executive council. The advocates for lodging the executive power in the hands of a number of equals, as an executive council, say, that much wisdom may be collected in such a council, and that it will be safe; but they agree, that it cannot be so prompt and responsible as a single man—they admit that such a council will generally consist of the aristocracy, and not stand so indifferent between it and the people as a first magistrate. But the principal objection made to a single man is, that when possessed of power he will be constantly struggling for more, disturbing the government, and encroaching on the rights of others. It must be admitted, that men, from the monarch down to the porter, are constantly aiming at power and importance and this propensity must be as constantly guarded against in the forms of the government. Adequate powers must be delegated to those who govern, and our security must be in limiting, defining, and guarding the exercise of them, so that those given shall not be abused, or made use of for openly or secretly seizing more. Why do we believe this abuse of power peculiar to a first magistrate? Is it because in the wars and contests of men, one man has often established his power over the rest? Or are men naturally fond of accumulating powers in the hands of one man? I do not see any similitude between the cases of those tyrants, who have sprung up in the midst of wars and tumults, and the cases of limited executives in established governments; nor shall we, on a careful examination, discover much likeness between the executives in Sweden, Denmark, Holland, &c. which have, from time to time, increased their powers, and become more absolute, and the executives, whose powers are well ascertained and defined, and which remain, by the constitution, only for a short and limited period in the hands of any one man or family. A single man, or family, can long and effectually direct its exertions to one point. There may be many favourable opportunities in the course of a man's life to seize on additional powers, and many more where powers are hereditary; and there are many circumstances favourable to usurpation, where the powers of the man or family are undefined, and such as often may be unduly extended before the people discover it. If we examine history attentively, we shall find that such exertions, such opportunities, and such circumstances as these have attended all the executives which have usurped upon the rights of the people, and which appear originally to have been, in some degree, limited. Admitting that moderate and even well defined powers, long in the hands of the same man or family, will, probably, be unreasonably increased, it will not follow that even extensive powers placed in the hands of a man only for a few years will be abused. The Roman consuls and Carthaginian sufferers possessed extensive powers while in office; but being annually appointed, they but seldom, if ever, abused them. The Roman dictators often possessed absolute power while in office; but usually being elected for short periods of time, no one of them for ages usurped upon the rights of the people. The kings of France, Spain, Sweden, Denmark, &c. have become absolute merely from the encroachments and abuse of power made by the nobles. As to kings, and limited monarchs, generally, history furnishes many more instances in which their powers have been abridged or annihilated by the nobles or people, or both, than in which they have been increased or made absolute; and in almost all the latter cases, we find the people were inattentive and fickle, and evidently were not born to be free. I am the more particular respecting this subject, because I have heard many mistaken observations relative to it. Men of property, and even men who hold powers for themselves and posterity, have too much to lose, wantonly to hazard a shock of the political system; the game must be large, and the chance of winning great, to induce them to risque what they have, for the uncertain prospect of gaining more. Our executive may be altogether elective, and possess no power, but as the substitute of the people, and that well limited, and only for a limited time. The great object is, in a republican government, to guard effectually against perpetuating any portion of power, great or small, in the same man or family; this perpetuation of power is totally uncongenial to the true spirit of republican governments: on the one hand the first executive magistrate ought to remain in office so long as to avoid instability in the execution of the laws; on the other, not so long as to enable him to take any measures to establish himself. The convention, it seems, first agreed that the president should be chosen for seven years, and never after to be eligible. Whether seven years is a period too long or not, is rather matter of opinion; but clear it is, that this mode is infinitely preferable to the one finally adopted. When a man shall get the chair, who may be re-elected, from time to time, for life, his greatest object will be to keep it; to gain friends and votes, at any rate; to associate some favourite son with himself, to take the office after him: whenever he shall have any prospect of continuing the office in himself and family, he will spare no artifice, no address, and no exertions, to increase the powers and importance of it; the servile supporters of his wishes will be placed in all offices, and tools constantly employed to aid his views and sound his praise. A man so situated will have no permanent interest in the government to lose, by contests and convulsions in the state, but always much to gain, and frequently the seducing and flattering hope of succeeding. If we reason at all on the subject, we must irresistibly conclude, that this will be the case with nine tenths of the presidents; we may have, for the first president, and, perhaps, one in a century or two afterwards (if the government should withstand the attacks of others) a great and good man, governed by superior motives; but these are not events to be calculated upon in the present state of human nature.

A man chosen to this important office for a limited period, and always afterwards rendered, by the constitution, ineligible, will be governed by very different considerations: he can have no rational hopes or expectations of retaining his office after the expiration of a known limited time, or of continuing the office in his family, as by the constitution there must be a constant transfer of it from one man to another, and consequently from one family to another. No man will wish to be a mere cypher at the head of the government: the great object of each president then will be, to render his government a glorious period in the annals of his country. When a man constitutionally retires from office, he retires without pain; he is sensible he retires because the laws direct it, and not from the success of his rivals, nor with that public disapprobation which being left out, when eligible, implies. It is said, that a man knowing that at a given perïod he must quit his office, will unjustly attempt to take from the public, and lay in store the means of support and splendor in his retirement; there can, I think, be but very little in this observation. The same constitution that makes a man eligible for a given period only, ought to make no man eligible till he arrive to the age of forty or forty-five years: if he be a man of fortune, he will retire with dignity to his estate; if not, he may, like the Roman consuls, and other eminent characters in republics, find an honorable support and employment in some respectable office. A man who must, at all events, thus leave his office, will have but few or no temptations to fill its dependant offices with his tools, or any particular set of men; whereas the man constantly looking forward to his future elections, and, perhaps, to the aggrandizement of his family, will have every inducement before him to fill all places with his own props and dependants. [. . .]

On the whole, it would be, in my opinion, almost as well to create a limited monarchy at once, and give some family permanent power and interest in the community, and let it have something valuable to itself to lose in convulsions in the state, and in attempts of usurpation, as to make a first magistrate eligible for life, and to create hopes and expectations in him and his family, of obtaining what they have not. In the latter case, we actually tempt them to disturb the state, to foment struggles and contests, by laying before them the flattering prospect of gaining much in them without risking any thing. [. . .]

I shall conclude my observations on the organization of the legislature and executive, with making some remarks, rather as a matter of amusement, on the branch, or partial negative, in the legislation:—The third branch in the legislature may answer three valuable purposes, to impede in their passage hasty and intemperate laws, occasionally to assist the senate or people, and to prevent the legislature from encroaching upon the executive or judiciary. In Great Britain the king has a complete negative upon all laws, but he very seldom exercises it. This may be well lodged in him, who possesses strength to support it, and whose family has independent and hereditary interests and powers, rights and prerogatives, in the government, to defend: but in a country where the first executive officer is elective, and has no rights, but in common with the people, a partial negative in legislation, as in Massachusetts and New-York, is, in my opinion, clearly best: in the former state, as before observed, it is lodged in the governor alone; in the latter, in the governor, chancellor, and judges of the supreme court—the new constitution lodges it in the president. This is simply a branch of legislative power, and has in itself no relation to executive or judicial powers. The question is, in what hands ought it to be lodged, to answer the three purposes mentioned the most advantageously? The prevailing opinion seems to be in favour of vesting it in the hands of the first executive magistrate. I will not say this opinion is ill founded. The negative, in one case, is intended to prevent hasty laws, not supported and revised by two-thirds of each of the two branches; in the second, it is to aid the weaker branch; and in the third, to defend the executive and judiciary. To answer these ends, there ought, therefore, to be collected in the hands which hold this negative, firmness, wisdom, and strength; the very object of the negative is occasional opposition to the two branches. By lodging it in the executive magistrate, we give him a share in making the laws, which he must execute; by associating the judges with him, as in New-York, we give them a share in making the laws, upon which they must decide as judicial magistrates; this may be a reason for excluding the judges: however, the negative in New-York is certainly well calculated to answer its great purposes: the governor and judges united must possess more firmness and strength, more wisdom and information, than either alone, and also more of the confidence of the people; and as to the balance among the departments, why should the executive alone hold the scales, and the judicial be left defenceless? I think the negative in New-York is found best in practice; we see it there frequently and wisely put upon the measures of the two branches; whereas in Massachusetts it is hardly ever exercised, and the governor, I believe, has often permitted laws to pass to which he had substantial objections, but did not make them; he, however, it is to be observed, is annually elected.

Letter XV

January 18, 1788

Dear sir,

It is an observation of an approved writer, that judicial power is of such a nature, that when we have ascertained and fixed its limits, with all the caution and precision we can, it will yet be formidable, somewhat arbitrary and despotic—that is, after all our cares, we must leave a vast deal to the discretion and interpretation—to the wisdom, integrity, and politics of the judges—These men, such is the state even of the best laws, may do wrong, perhaps, in a thousand cases, sometimes with, and sometimes without design, yet it may be impracticable to convict them of misconduct. These considerations show, how cautious a free people ought to be in forming this, as well as the other branches of their government, especially when connected with other considerations equally deserving of notice and attention. When the legislature makes a bad law, or the first executive magistrate usurps upon the rights of the people, they discover the evil much sooner, than the abuses of power in the judicial department; the proceedings of which are far more intricate, complex, and out of their immediate view. A bad law immediately excites a general alarm; a bad judicial determination, though not less pernicious in its consequences, is immediately felt, probably, by a single individual only, and noticed only by his neighbours, and a few spectators in the court. In this country, we have been always jealous of the legislature, and especially the executive; but not always of the judiciary: but very few men attentively consider the essential parts of it, and its proceedings, as they tend to support or to destroy free government: only a few professional men are in a situation properly to do this; and it is often all edged, that instances have not frequently occurred, in which they have been found very alert watchmen in the cause of liberty, or in the cause of democratic republics. Add to these considerations, that particular circumstances exist at this time to increase our inattention to limiting properly the judicial powers, we may fairly conclude, we are more in danger of sowing the seeds of arbitrary government in this department than in any other. In the unsettled state of things in this country, for several years past, it has been thought, that our popular legislatures have, sometimes, departed from the line of strict justice, while the law courts have shown a disposition more punctually to keep to it. We are not sufficiently attentive to the circumstances, that the measures of popular legislatures naturally settle down in time, and gradually approach a mild and just medium; while the rigid systems of the law courts naturally become more severe and arbitrary, if not carefully tempered and guarded by the constitution, and by laws, from time to time. [. . .]

As the trial by jury is provided for in criminal causes, I shall confine my observations to civil causes—and in these, I hold it is the established right of the jury by the common law, and the fundamental laws of this country, to give a general verdict in all cases when they chuse to do it, to decide both as to law and fact, whenever blended together in the issue put to them. Their right to determine as to facts will not be disputed, and their right to give a general verdict has never been disputed, except by a few judges and lawyers, governed by despotic principles. Coke, Hale, Holt, Blackstone, De Lo[l]me, and almost every other legal or political writer, who has written on the subject, has uniformly asserted this essential and important right of the jury. Juries in Great-Britain and America have universally practiced accordingly. Even Mansfield, with all his wishes about him, dare not directly avow the contrary. What fully confirms this point is, that there is no instance to be found, where a jury was ever punished for finding a general verdict, when a special one might, with propriety, have been found. The jury trial, especially politically considered, is by far the most important feature in the judicial department in a free country, and the right in question is far the most valuable part, and the last that ought to be yielded, of this trial. Juries are constantly and frequently drawn from the body of the people, and freemen of the country; and by holding the jury's right to return a general verdict in all cases sacred, we secure to the people at large, their just and rightful control in the judicial department. If the conduct of judges shall be severe and arbitrary, and tend to subvert the laws, and change the forms of government, the jury may check them, by deciding against their opinions and determinations, in similar cases. It is true, the freemen of a country are not always minutely skilled in the laws, but they have common sense in its purity, which seldom or never errs in making and applying laws to the condition of the people, or in determining judicial causes, when stated to them by the parties. The body of the people, principally, bear the burdens of the community; they of right ought to have a control in its important concerns, both in making and executing the laws, otherwise they may, in a short time, be ruined. Nor is it merely this control alone we are to attend to; the jury trial brings with it an open and public discussion of all causes, and excludes secret and arbitrary proceedings. This, and the democratic branch in the legislature, as was formerly observed, are the means by which the people are let into the knowledge of public affairs—are enabled to stand as the guardians of each others rights, and to restrain, by regular and legal measures, those who otherwise might infringe upon them. I am not unsupported in my opinion of the value of the trial by jury; not only British and American writers, but De Lo[l]me, and the most approved foreign writers, hold it to be the most valuable part of the British constitution, and indisputably the best mode of trial ever invented. [. . .]

In the civil law process the trial by jury is unknown; the consequence is, that a few judges and dependant officers, possess all the power in the judicial department. Instead of the open fair proceedings of the common law, where witnesses are examined in open court, and may be cross examined by the parties concerned—where council is allowed, &c. we see in the civil law process judges alone, who always, long previous to the trial, are known and often corrupted by ministerial influence, or by parties. Judges once influenced, soon become inclined to yield to temptations, and to decree for him who will pay the most for their partiality. It is, therefore, we find in the Roman, and almost all governments, where judges alone possess the judicial powers and try all cases, that bribery has prevailed. This, as well as the forms of the courts, naturally lead to secret and arbitrary proceedings—to taking evidence secretly—exparte, &c. to perplexing the cause—and to hasty decisions:—but, as to jurors, it is quite impracticable to bribe or influence them by any corrupt means; not only because they are untaught in such affairs, and possess the honest characters of the common freemen of a country; but because it is not, generally, known till the hour the cause comes on for trial, what persons are to form the jury.

But it is said, that no words could be found by which the states could agree to establish the jury-trial in civil causes. I can hardly believe men to be serious, who make observations to this effect. The states have all derived judicial proceedings principally from one source, the British system; from the same common source the American lawyers have almost universally drawn their legal information. All the states have agreed to establish the trial by jury, in civil as well as in criminal causes. The several states, in congress, found no difficulty in establishing it in the Western Territory, in the ordinance passed in July 1787. We find, that the several states of congress, in establishing government in that territory, agreed, that the in inhabitants of it, should always be entitled to the benefit of the trial by jury. Thus in few words, the jury trial is established in its full extent; and the convention with as much ease, have established the jury trial in criminal cases. In making a constitution, we are substantially to fix principles. [. . .]

By the common law, in Great Britain and America, there is no appeal from the verdict of the jury, as to facts, to any judges whatever—the jurisdiction of the jury is complete and final in this; and only errors in law are carried up to the house of lords, the special supreme court in Great Britain; or to the special supreme courts in Connecticut, New-York, New-Jersey, &c. Thus the juries are left masters as to facts: but, by the proposed constitution, directly the opposite principles is established. An appeal will lay in all appellate causes from the verdict of the jury, even as to mere facts, to the judges of the supreme court. Thus, in effect, we establish the civil law in this point; for if the jurisdiction of the jury be not final, as to facts, it is of little or no importance.

By art. 3. sect. 2. "the judicial power shall extend to all cases in law and equity, arising under this constitution, the laws of the United States," &c. What is here meant by equity? what is equity in a case arising under the constitution? possibly the clause might have the same meaning, were the words "in law and equity," omitted. Cases in law must differ widely from cases in law and equity. At first view, by thus joining the word equity with the word law, if we mean any thing, we seem to mean to give the judge a discretionary power. The word equity, in Great Britain, has in time acquired a precise meaning—chancery proceedings there are now reduced to system—but this is not the case in the United States. In New-England, the judicial courts have no powers in cases in equity, except those dealt out to them by the legislature, in certain limited portions, by legislative acts. In New-York, Maryland, Virginia, and South Carolina, powers to decide, in cases of equity, are vested in judges distinct from those who decide in matters of law: and the states generally seem to have carefully avoided giving unlimitedly, to the same judges, powers to decide in cases in law and equity. Perhaps, the clause would have the same meaning were the words, "this constitution," omitted: there is in it either a careless complex misuse of words, in themselves of extensive signification, or there is some meaning not easy to be comprehended. Suppose a case arising under the constitution—suppose the question judicially moved, whether, by the constitution, congress can suppress a state tax laid on polls, lands, or as an excise duty, which may be supposed to interfere with a federal tax. By the letter of the constitution, congress will appear to have no power to do it: but then the judges may decide the question on principles of equity as well as law. Now, omitting the words, "in law and equity," they may decide according to the spirit and true meaning of the constitution, as collected from what must appear to have been the intentions of the people when they made it. Therefore, it would seem, that if these words mean any thing, they must have a further meaning: yet I will not suppose it intended to lodge an arbitrary power or discretion in the judges, to decide as their conscience, their opinions, their caprice, or their politics might dictate. Without dwelling on this obscure clause, I will leave it to the examination of others.

Letter XVI

January 20, 1788

Dear sir,

Having gone through with the organization of the government, I shall now proceed to examine more particularly those clauses which respect its powers. I shall begin with those articles and stipulations which are necessary for accurately ascertaining the extent of powers, and what is given, and for guarding, limiting, and restraining them in their exercise. We often find, these articles and stipulations placed in bills of rights; but they may as well be incorporated in the body of the constitution, as selected and placed by themselves. The constitution, or whole social compact, is but one instrument, no more or less, than a certain number of articles or stipulations agreed to by the people, whether it consists of articles, sections, chapters, bills of rights, or parts of any other denomination, cannot be material. Many needless observations, and idle distinctions, in my opinion, have been made respecting a bill of rights. On the one hand, it seems to be considered as a necessary distinct limb of the constitution, and as containing a certain number of very valuable articles, which are applicable to all societies; and, on the other, as useless, especially in a federal government, possessing only enumerated power—nay, dangerous, as individual rights are numerous, and not easy to be enumerated in a bill of rights, and from articles, or stipulations, securing some of them, it may be inferred, that others not mentioned are surrendered. There appears to me to be general indefinite propositions without much meaning—and the man who first advanced those of the latter description, in the present case, signed the federal constitution, which directly contradicts him. The supreme power is undoubtedly in the people, and it is a principle well established in my mind, that they reserve all powers not expressly delegated by them to those who govern; this is as true in forming a state as in forming a federal government. There is no possible distinction but this founded merely in the different modes of proceeding which take place in some cases. In forming a state constitution, under which to manage not only the great but the little concerns of a community: the powers to be possessed by the government are often too numerous to be enumerated; the people to adopt the shortest way often give general powers, indeed all powers, to the government, in some general words, and then, by a particular enumeration, take back, or rather say they however reserve certain rights as sacred, and which no laws shall be made to violate: hence the idea that all powers are given which are not reserved; but in forming a federal constitution, which *ex vi termine*, supposes state governments existing, and which is only to manage a few great national concerns, we often find it easier to enumerate particularly the powers to be delegated to the federal head, than to enumerate particularly the individual rights to be reserved; and the principle will operate in its full force, when we carefully adhere to it. When we particularly enumerate the powers given, we ought either carefully to enumerate the rights reserved, or be totally silent about them; we must either particularly enumerate both, or else suppose the particular enumeration of the powers given adequately draws the line between them and the rights reserved, particularly to enumerate the former and not the latter, I think most advisable: however, as men appear generally to have their doubts about these silent reservations, we might advantageously enumerate the powers given, and then in general words, according to the mode adopted in the 2d art. of the confederation, declare all powers, rights and privileges, are reserved, which are not explicitly and expressly given up. People, and very wisely too, like to be express and explicit about their essential rights, and not to be forced to claim them on the precarious and unascertained tenure of inferences and general principles, knowing that in any controversy between them and their rulers, concerning those rights, disputes may be endless, and nothing certain:—But admitting, on the general principle, that all rights are reserved of course, which are not expressly surrendered, the people could with sufficient certainty assert their rights on all occasions, and establish them with ease, still there are infinite advantages in particularly enumerating many of the most essential rights reserved in all cases; and as to the less important ones, we may declare in general terms, that all not expressly surrendered are reserved. We do not by declarations change the nature of things, or create new truths, but we give existence, or at least establish in the minds of the people truths and principles which they might never otherwise have thought of, or soon forgot. If a nation means its systems, religious or political, shall have duration, it ought to recognize the leading principles of them in the front page of every family book. What is the usefulness of a truth in theory, unless it exists constantly in the minds of the people, and has their assent:—we discern certain rights, as the freedom of the press, and the trial by jury, &c. which the people of England and of America of course believe to be sacred, and essential to their political happiness, and this belief in them is the result of ideas at first suggested to them by a few able men, and of subsequent experience; while the people of some other countries hear these rights mentioned with the utmost indifference; they think the privilege of existing at the will of a despot much preferable to them. Why this difference amongst beings every way formed alike. The reason of the difference is obvious—it is the effect of education, a series of notions impressed upon the minds of the people by examples, precepts and declarations. When the people of England got together, at the time they formed Magna Charta, they did not consider it sufficient, that they were indisputably entitled to certain natural and unalienable rights, not depending on silent titles, they, by a declaratory act, expressly recognized them, and explicitly declared to all the world, that they were entitled to enjoy those rights; they made an instrument in writing, and enumerated those they then thought essential, or in danger, and this wise men saw was not sufficient; and therefore, that the people might not forget these rights, and gradually become prepared for arbitrary government, their discerning and honest leaders caused this instrument to be confirmed near forty times, and to be read twice a year in public places, not that it would lose its validity without such confirmations, but to fix the contents of it in the minds of the people, as they successively come upon the stage.—Men, in some countries do not remain free, merely because they are entitled to natural and unalienable rights; men in all countries are entitled to them, not because their ancestors once got together and enumerated them on paper, but because, by repeated negotiations and declarations, all parties are brought to realize them, and of course to believe them to be sacred. Were it necessary, I might shew the wisdom of our past conduct, as a people in not merely comforting ourselves that we were entitled to freedom, but in constantly keeping in view, in addresses, bills of rights, in news-papers, &c. the particular principles on which our freedom must always depend.

It is not merely in this point of view, that I urge the engrafting in the constitution additional declaratory articles. The distinction, in itself just, that all powers not given are reserved, is in effect destroyed by this very constitution, as I shall particularly demonstrate—and even independent of this, the people, by adopting the constitution, give many general undefined powers to congress, in the constitutional exercise of which, the rights in question may be effected. Gentlemen who oppose a federal bill of rights, or further declaratory articles, seem to view the subject in a very narrow imperfect manner. These have for their objects, not only the enumeration of the rights reserved, but principally to explain the general powers delegated in certain material points, and to restrain those who exercise them by fixed known boundaries. [. . .]

To make declaratory articles unnecessary in an instrument of government, two circumstances must exist; the rights reserved must be indisputably so, and in their nature defined; the powers delegated to the government, must be precisely defined by the words that convey them, and clearly be of such extent and nature as that, by no reasonable construction, they can be made to invade the rights and prerogatives intended to be left in the people.

The first point urged, is, that all power is reserved not expressly given, that particular enumerated powers only are given, that all others are not given, but reserved, and that it is needless to attempt to restrain congress in the exercise of powers they possess not. This reasoning is logical, but of very little importance in the common affairs of men; but the constitution does not appear to respect it even in any view. To prove this, I might cite several clauses in it. I shall only remark on two or three. By article 1, section 9, "No title of nobility shall be granted by congress." Was this clause omitted, what power would congress have to make titles of nobility? in what part of the constitution would they find it? The answer must be, that congress would have no such power—that the people, by adopting the constitution, will not part with it. Why then by a negative clause, restrain congress from doing what it would have no power to do? This clause, then, must have no meaning, or imply, that were it omitted, congress would have the power in question, either upon the principle that some general words in the constitution may be so construed as to give it, or on the principle that congress possess the powers not expressly reserved. But this clause was in the confederation, and is said to be introduced into the constitution from very great caution. Even a cautionary provision implies a doubt, at least, that it is necessary; and if so in this case, clearly it is also alike necessary in all similar ones. The fact appears to be, that the people in forming the confederation, and the convention, in this instance, acted, naturally, they did not leave the point to be settled by general principles and logical inferences; but they settle the point in a few words, and all who read them at once understand them.

The trial by jury in criminal as well as in civil causes, has long been considered as one of our fundamental rights, and has been repeatedly recognized and confirmed by most of the state conventions. But the constitution expressly establishes this trial in criminal, and wholly omits it in civil causes. The jury trial in criminal causes, and the benefit of the writ of habeas corpus, are already as effectually established as any of the fundamental or essential rights of the people in the United States. This being the case, why in adopting a federal constitution do we now establish these, and omit all others, or all others, at least, with a few exceptions, such as again agreeing there shall be no ex post facto laws, no titles of nobility, &c. We must consider this constitution when adopted as the supreme act of the people, and in construing it hereafter, we and our posterity must strictly adhere to the letter and spirit of it, and in no instance depart from them: in construing the federal constitution, it will be not only impracticable, but improper to refer to the state constitutions. They are entrirely distinct instruments and inferior acts: besides, by the people's now establishing certain fundamental rights, it is strongly implied, that they are of opinion, that they would not otherwise be secured as a part of the federal system, or be regarded in the federal administration as fundamental. Further, these same rights, being established by the state constitutions, and secured to the people, our recognizing them now, implies, that the people thought them insecure by the state establishments, and extinguished or put afloat by the new arrangement of the social system, unless re-established.—Further, the people, thus establishing some few rights, and remaining totally silent about others similarly circumstanced, the implication indubitably is, that they mean to relinquish the latter, or at least feel indifferent about them. Rights, therefore, inferred from general principles of reason, being precarious and hardly ascertainable in the common affairs of society, and the people, in forming the federal constitution, explicitly shewing they conceive these rights to be thus circumstanced, and accordingly proceed to enumerate and establish some of them, the conclusion will be, that they have established all which they esteem valuable and sacred. On every principle, then, the people especially having began, ought to go through enumerating, and establish particularly all the rights of individuals, which can by any possibility come in question in making and executing federal laws. I have already observed upon the excellency and importance of the jury trial in civil as well as in criminal causes, instrad of establishing it in criminal causes only; we ought to establish it generally;—instead of the clause of forty or fifty words relative to this subject, why not use the language that has always been used in this country, and say, "the people of the United States shall always be entitled to the trial by jury." This would shew the people still hold the right sacred, and enjoin it upon congress substantially to preserve the jury trial in all cases, according to the usage and custom of the country. [. . .]

Security against ex post facto laws, the trial by jury, and the benefits of the writ of habeas corpus, are but a part of those inestimable rights the people of the United States are entitled to, even in judicial proceedings, by the course of the common law. These may be secured in general words, as in New York, the Western Territory, &c. by declaring the people of the United States shall always be entitled to judicial proceedings according to the course of the common law, as used and established in the said states. Perhaps it would be better to enumerate the particular essential rights the people are entitled to in these proceedings, as has been done in many of the states, and as has been done in England. In this case, the people may proceed to declare, that no man shall be held to answer at any offence, till the same be fully described to him; nor to furnish evidence against himself: that, except in the government of the army or navy, no person shall be tried for any offence, whereby he may incur loss of life, or an infamous punishment, until he be first indicted by a grand jury: that every person shall have a right to produce all proofs that may be favourable to him, and to meet the witnesses against him face to face: that every person shall be entitled to obtain right and justice freely and without delay: that all persons shall have a right to be secure from all unreasonable searches and seizures of their persons, houses, papers, or possessions,; and that all warrants shall be deemed contrary to this right, if the foundation of them be not previously supported by oath, and there be not in them a special designation of persons or objects of search, arrest, or seizure: and that no person shall be exiled or molested in his person or effects, otherwise than by the judgment of his peers, or according to the law of the land. A celebrated writer observes upon this last article, that in itself it may be said to comprehend the whole end of political society. These rights are not necessarily reserved, they are established, or enjoyed but in few countries: they are stipulated rights, almost peculiar to British and American laws. In the execution of those laws, individuals, by long custom, by magna charta, bills of rights &c. have become entitled to them. A man, at first, by act of parliament, became entitled to the benefits of the writ of habeas corpus—men are entitled to these rights and benefits in the judicial proceedings of our state courts generally: but it will by no means follow, that they will be entitled to them in the federal courts, and have a right to assert them, unless secured and established by the constitution or federal laws. We certainly, in federal processes, might as well claim the benefits of the writ of habeas corpus, as to claim trial by a jury—the right to have council—to have witnesses face to face—to be secure against unreasonable search warrants, &c. was the constitution silent as to the whole of them:—but the establishment of the former, will evince that we could not claim them without it; and the omission of the latter, implies they are relinquished, or deemed of no importance. These are rights and benefits individuals acquire by compact; they must claim them under compacts, or immemorial usage—it is doubtful, at least, whether they can be claimed under immemorial usage in this country; and it is, therefore, we generally claim them under compacts, as charters and constitutions.

The people by adopting the federal constitution, give congress general powers to institute a distinct and new judiciary, new courts, and to regulate all proceedings in them, under the eight limitations mentioned in a former letter; and the further one, that the benefits of the habeas corpus act shall be enjoyed by individuals. Thus general powers being given to institute courts, and regulate their proceedings, with no provision for securing the rights principally in question, may not congress so exercise those powers, and constitutionally too, as to destroy those rights? clearly, in my opinion, they are not in any degree secured. But, admitting the case is only doubtful, would it not be prudent and wise to secure them and remove all doubts, since all agree the people ought to enjoy these valuable rights, a very few men excepted, who seem to be rather of opinion that there is little or nothing in them? Were it necessary I might add many observations to show their value and political importance.

The constitution will give congress general powers to raise and support armies. General powers carry with them incidental ones, and the means necessary to the end. In the exercise of these powers, is there any provision in the constitution to prevent the quartering of soldiers on the inhabitants? you will answer, there is not. This may sometimes be deemed a necessary measure in the support of armies; on what principle can the people claim the right to be exempt from this burden? they will urge, perhaps, the practice of the country, and the provisions made in some of the state constitutions—they will be answered, that their claim thus to be exempt, is not founded in nature, but only in custom and opinion, or at best, in stipulations in some of the state constitutions, which are local, and inferior in their operation, and can have no control over the general government—that they had adopted a federal constitution—had noticed several rights, but had been totally silent about this exemption—that they had given general powers relative to the subject, which, in their operation, regularly destroyed the claim. Though it is not to be presumed, that we are in any immediate danger from this quarter, yet it is fit and proper to establish, beyond dispute, those rights which are particularly valuable to individuals, and essential to the permanency and duration of free government. An excellent writer observes, that the English, always in possession of their freedom, are frequently unmindful of the value of it: we, at this period, do not seem to be so well off, having, in some instances abused ours; many of us are quite disposed to barter it away for what we call energy, coercion, and some other terms we use as vaguely as that of liberty—There is often as great a rage for change and novelty in politics, as in amusements and fashions.

All parties apparently agree, that the freedom of the press is a fundamental right, and ought not to be restrained by any taxes, duties, or in any manner whatever. Why should not the people, in adopting a federal constitution, declare this, even if there are only doubts about it. But, say the advocates, all powers not given are reserved.—true; but the great question is, are not powers given, in the exercise of which this right may be destroyed? The people's or the printers claim to a free press, is founded on the fundamental laws, that is, compacts, and state constitutions, made by the people. The people, who can annihilate or alter those constitutions, can annihilate or limit this right. This may be done by giving general powers, as well as by using particular words. [. . .] By art. 1. sect. 8. congress will have power to lay and collect taxes, duties, imposts and excise. By this congress will clearly have power to lay and collect all kind of taxes whatever—taxes on houses, lands, polls, industry, merchandise, &c.—taxes on deeds, bonds, and all written instruments—on writs, pleas, and all judicial proceedings, on licences, naval officers papers, &c. on newspapers, advertisements, &c. and to require bonds of the naval officers, clerks, printers, &c. to account for the taxes that may become due on papers that go through their hands. Printing, like all other business, must cease when taxed beyond its profits; and it appears to me, that a power to tax the press at discretion, is a power to destroy or restrain the freedom of it. There may be other powers given, in the exercise of which this freedom may be effected; and certainly it is of too much importance to be left thus liable to be taxed, and constantly to constructions and inferences. A free press is the channel of communication as to mercantile and public affairs; by means of it the people in large countries ascertain each other's sentiments; are enabled to unite, and become formidable to those rulers who adopt improper measures. Newspapers may sometimes be the vehicles of abuse, and of many things not true; but these are but small inconveniencies, in my mind, among many advantages. A celebrated writer, I have several times quoted, speaking in high terms of the English liberties, says, "lastly the key stone was put to the arch, by the final establishment of the freedom of the press."

Letter XVII

January 23, 1788

Dear sir,

I believe the people of the United States are full in the opinion, that a free and mild government can be preserved in their extensive territories, only under the substantial forms of a federal republic. As several of the ablest advocates for the system proposed, have acknowledged this (and I hope the confessions they have published will be preserved and remembered) I shall not take up time to establish this point. A question then arises, how far that system partakes of a federal republic.—I observed in a former letter, that it appears to be the first important step to a consolidation of the states; that its strong tendency is to that point.

But what do we mean by a federal republic? and what by a consolidated government? To erect a federal republic, we must first make a number of states on republican principles; each state with a government organized for the internal management of its affairs: The states, as such, must unite under a federal head, and delegate to it powers to make and execute laws in certain enumerated cases, under certain restrictions; this head may be a single assembly, like the present congress, or the Amphictionic council; or it may consist of a legislature, with one or more branches; of an executive, and of a judiciary. To form a consolidated, or one entire government, there must be no state, or local governments, but all things, persons and property, must be subject to the laws of one legislature alone; to one executive, and one judiciary. Each state government, as the government of New Jersey, &c. is a consolidated, or one entire government, as it respects the counties, towns, citizens and property within the limits of the state.—The state governments are the basis, the pillar on which the federal head is placed, and the whole together, when formed on elective principles, constitute a federal republic. A federal republic in itself supposes state or local governments to exist, as the body or props, on which the federal head rests, and that it cannot remine a moment after they cease. In erecting the federal government, and always in its councils, each state must be known as a sovereign body; but in erecting this government, I conceive, the legislature of the state, by the expressed or implied assent of the people, or the people of the state, under the direction of the government of it, may accede to the federal compact: Nor do I conceive it to be necessarily a part of a confederacy of states, that each have an equal voice in the general councils. A confederated republic being organized, each state must retain powers for managing its internal police, and all delegate to the union power to manage general concerns: The quantity of power the union must possess is one thing, the mode of exercising the powers given, is quite a different consideration; and it is the mode of exercising them, that makes one of the essential distinctions between one entire or consolidated government, and a federal republic; that is, however the government may be organized, if the laws of the union, in most important concerns, as in levying and collecting taxes, raising troops, &c. operate immediately upon the persons and property of individuals, and not on states, extend to organizing the militia, &c.

the government, as to its administration, as to making and executing laws, is not federal, but consolidated. To illustrate my idea—the union makes a requisition, and assigns to each state its quota of men or monies wanted; each state, by its own laws and officers, in its own way, furnishes its quota: here the state governments stand between the union and individuals; the laws of the union operate only on states, as such, and federally: Here nothing can be done without the meetings of the state legislatures—but in the other case the union, though the state legislatures should not meet for years together, proceeds immediately, by its own laws and officers, to levy and collect monies of individuals, to inlist men, form armies, &c. here the laws of the union operate immediately on the body of the people, on persons and property; in the same manner the laws of one entire consolidated government operate.—These two modes are very distinct, and in their operation and consequences have directly opposite tendencies: The first makes the existence of the state governments indispensable, and throws all the detail business of levying and collecting the taxes, &c. into the hands of those governments, and into the hands, of course, of many thousand officers solely created by, and dependent on the state. The last entirely excludes the agency of the respective states, and throws the whole business of levying and collecting the taxes, &c. into the hands of many thousand officers solely created by, and dependent upon the union, and makes the existence of the state government of no consequence in the case. It is true, congress in raising any given sum in direct taxes, must by the constitution, raise so much of it in one state, and so much in another, by a fixed rule, which most of the states some time since agreed to: But this does not effect the principle in question, it only secures each state against any arbitrary proportions. The federal mode is perfectly safe and eligible, founded in the true spirit of a confederated republic there could be no possible exception to it, did we not find by experience, that the states will sometimes neglect to comply with the reasonable requisitions of the union. It being according to the fundamental principles of federal republics, to raise men and monies by requisitions, and for the states individually to organize and train the militia, I conceive, there can be no reason whatever for departing from them, except this, that the states sometimes neglect to comply with reasonable requisitions, and that it is dangerous to attempt to compel a delinquent state by force, as it may often produce a war. We ought, therefore, to enquire attentively, how extensive the evils to be guarded against are, and cautiously limit the remedies to the extent of the evils. I am not about to defend the confederation, or to charge the proposed constitution with imperfections not in it; but we ought to examine facts, and strip them of the false colorings often given them by incautious observations, by unthinking or designing men. We ought to premise, that laws for raising men and monies, even in consolidated governments, are not often punctually complied with. [. . .] I agree there have been instances in the republics of Greece, Holland, &c. in the course of several centuries, of states neglecting to pay their quotas of requisitions; but it is a circumstance certainly deserving of attention, whether these nations which have depended on requisitions principally for their defence, have not raised men and monies nearly as punctually as entire governments, which have taxed directly; whether we have not found the latter as often distressed for the want of troops and monies, as the former. [. . .]

As to the United States, the separate states lay taxes directly, and the union calls for taxes by way of requisitions; and is it a fact, that more monies are due in proportion on requisitions in the United States, than on the state taxes directly laid?—It is but about ten years since congress begun to make requisitions, and in that time, the monies, &c. required, and the bounties given for men required of the states, have amounted, specie value, to about 36 millions dollars, about 24 millions of dollars of which have been actually paid; and a very considerable part of the 12 millions not paid, remains so not so much from the neglect of the states, as from the sudden changes in paper money, &c. which in a great measure rendered payments of no service, and which often induced the union indirectly to relinquish one demand, by making another in a different form. Before we totally condemn requisitions, we ought to consider what immense bounties the states gave, and what prodigious exertions they made in the war, in order to comply with the requisitions of congress; and if since the peace they have been delinquent, ought we not carefully to enquire, whether that delinquency is to be imputed solely to the nature of requisitions? ought it not in part to be imputed to two other causes? I mean first, an opinion, that has extensively prevailed, that the requisitions for domestic interest have not been founded on just principles; and secondly, the circumstance, that the government itself, by proposing imposts, &c. has departed virtually from the constitutional system; which proposed changes, like all changes proposed in government, produce an inattention and negligence in the execution of the government in being.

I am not for depending wholly on requisitions; but I mention these few facts to show they are not so totally futile as many pretend. For the truth of many of these facts I appeal to the public records; and for the truth of the others, I appeal to many republican characters, who are best informed in the affairs of the United States. Since the peace, and till the convention reported, the wisest men in the United States generally supposed, that certain limited funds would answer the purposes of the union: and though the states are by no means in so good a condition as I wish they were, yet, I think, I may very safely affirm, they are in a better condition than they would be had congress always possessed the powers of taxation now contended for. The fact is admitted, that our federal government does not possess sufficient powers to give life and vigor to the political system; and that we experience disappointments, and several inconveniencies; but we ought carefully to distinguish those which are merely the consequences of a severe and tedious war, from those which arise from defects in the federal system. There has been an entire revolution in the United States within thirteen years, and the least we can compute the waste of labour and property at, during that period, by the war, is three hundred million of dollars. Our people are like a man just recovering from a severe fit of sickness. It was the war that disturbed the course of commerce, introduced floods of paper money, the stagnation of credit, and threw many valuable men out of steady business. From these sources our greatest evils arise; men of knowledge and reflection must perceive it;—but then, have we not done more in three or four years past, in repairing the injuries of the war, by repairing houses and estates, restoring industry, frugality, the fisheries, manufactures, &c. and thereby laying the foundation of good government, and of individual and political happiness, than any people ever did in a like time; we must judge from a view of the country and facts, and not from foreign newspapers, or our own, which are printed chiefly in the commercial towns, where imprudent living, imprudent importations, and many unexpected disappointments, have produced a despondency, and a disposition to view every thing on the dark side. Some of the evils we feel, all will agree, ought to be imputed to the defective administration of the governments. From these and various considerations, I am very clearly of opinion, that the evils we sustain, merely on account of the defects of the confederation, are but as a feather in the balance against a mountain, compared with those which would, infallibly, be the result of the loss of general liberty, and that happiness men enjoy under a frugal, free, and mild government.

Heretofore we do not seem to have seen danger any where, but in giving power to congress, and now no where but in congress wanting powers; and, without examining the extent of the evils to be remedied, by one step, we are for giving up to congress almost all powers of any importance without limitation. The defects of the confederation are extravagantly magnified, and every species of pain we feel imputed to them: and hence it is inferred, there must be a total change of the principles, as well as forms of government: and in the main point, touching the federal powers, we rest all on a logical inference, totally inconsistent with experience and sound political reasoning.

It is said, that as the federal head must make peace and war, and provide for the common defence, it ought to possess all powers necessary to that end: that powers unlimited, as to the purse and sword, to raise men and monies, and form the militia, are necessary to that end; and, therefore, the federal head ought to possess them. This reasoning is far more specious than solid: it is necessary that these powers so exist in the body politic, as to be called into exercise whenever necessary for the public safety; but it is by no means true, that the man, or congress of men, whose duty it more immediately is to provide for the common defence, ought to possess them without limitation. But clear it is, that if such men, or congress, be not in a situation to hold them without danger to liberty, he or they ought not to possess them. It has long been thought to be a well founded position, that the purse and sword ought not to be placed in the same hands in a free government. Our wise ancestors have carefully separated them—placed the sword in the hands of their king, even under considerable limitations, and the purse in the hands of the commons alone: yet the king makes peace and war, and it is his duty to provide for the common defence of the nation. This authority at least goes thus far—that a nation, well versed in the science of government, does not conceive it to be necessary or expedient for the man entrusted with the common defence and general tranquility, to possess unlimitedly the powers in question, or even in any considerable degree. Could he, whose duty it is to defend the public, possess in himself independently, all the means of doing it consistent with the public good, it might be convenient: but the people of England know that their liberties and happiness would be in infinitely greater danger from the king's unlimited possession of these powers, than from all external enemies and internal commotions to which they might be exposed: therefore, though they have made it his duty to guard the empire, yet they have wisely placed in other hands, the hands of their representatives, the power to deal out and control the means. In Holland their high mightinesses must provide for the common defence, but for the means they depend, in a considerable degree, upon requisitions made on the state or local assemblies. Reason and facts evince, that however convenient it might be for an executive magistrate, or federal head, more immediately charged with the national defence and safety, solely, directly, and independently to possess all the means; yet such magistrate, or head, never ought to possess them, if thereby the public liberties shall be endangered. The powers in question never have been, by nations wise and free, deposited, nor can they ever be, with safety any where but in the principal members of the national system:—where these form one entire government, as in Great-Britain, they are separated and lodged in the principal members of it. But in a federal republic, there is quite a different organization; the people form this kind of government, generally, because their territories are too extensive to admit of their assembling in one legislature, or of executing the laws on free principles under one entire government. They convene in their local assemblies, for local purposes, and for managing their internal concerns, and unite their states under a federal head for general purposes. It is the essential characteristic of a confederated republic, that this head be dependant on, and kept within limited bounds by, the local governments; and it is because, in these alone, in fact, the people can be substantially assembled or represented. It is, therefore, we very universally see, in this kind of government, the congressional powers placed in a few hands, and accordingly limited, and specifically enumerated: and the local assemblies strong and well guarded, and composed of numerous members. Wise men will always place the controlling power where the people are substantially collected by their representatives. By the proposed system, the federal head will possess, without limitation, almost every species of power that can, in its exercise, tend to change the government, or to endanger liberty; while in it, I think it has been fully shown, the people will have but the shadow of representation, and but the shadow of security for their rights and liberties. In a confederated republic, the division of representation, &c. in its nature, requires a correspondent division and deposit of powers, relative to taxes and military concerns: and I think the plan offered stands quite alone, in confounding the principles of governments in themselves totally distinct. I wish not to exculpate the states for their improper neglects in not paying their quotas of requisitions; but, in applying the remedy, we must be governed by reason and facts. It will not be denied, that the people have a right to change the government when the majority chuse it, if not restrained by some existing compact—that they have a right to displace their rulers, and consequently to determine when their measures are reasonable or not—and that they have a right, at any time, to put a stop to those measures they may deem prejudicial to them, by such forms and negatives as they may see fit to provide. From all these, and many other well founded considerations, I need not mention, a question arises, what powers shall there be delegated to the federal head, to insure safety, as well as energy, in the government? I think there is a safe and proper medium pointed out by experience, by reason, and facts. When we have organized the government, we ought to give power to the union, so far only as experience and present circumstances shall direct, with a reasonable regard to time to come. Should future circumstances, contrary to our expectations, require that further powers be transferred to the union, we can do it far more easily, than get back those we may now imprudently give. The system proposed is untried: candid advocates and opposers admit, that it is, in a degree, a mere experiment, and that its organization is weak and imperfect; surely then, the safe ground is cautiously to vest power in it, and when we are sure we have given enough for ordinary exigencies, to be extremely careful how we delegate powers, which, in common cases, must necessarily be useless or abused, and of very uncertain effect in uncommon ones.

By giving the union power to regulate commerce, and to levy and collect taxes by imposts, we give it an extensive authority, and permanent productive funds, I believe quite as adequate to the present demands of the union, as excises and direct taxes can be made to the present demands of the separate states. The state governments are now about four times as expensive as that of the union; and their several state debts added together, are nearly as large as that of the union—Our impost duties since the peace have been almost as productive as the other sources of taxation, and when under one general system of regulations, the probability is, that those duties will be very considerably increased: Indeed the representation proposed will hardly justify giving to congress unlimited powers to raise taxes by imposts, in addition to the other powers the union must necessarily have. It is said, that if congress possess only authority to raise taxes by imposts, trade probably will be overburdened with taxes, and the taxes of the union be found inadequate to any uncommon exigencies: To this we may observe, that trade generally finds its own level, and will naturally and necessarily heave off any undue burdens laid upon it: further, if congress alone possess the impost, and also unlimited power to raise monies by excises and direct taxes, there must be much more danger that two taxing powers, the union and states, will carry excises and direct taxes to an unreasonable extent, especially as these have not the natural boundaries taxes on trade have. However, it is not my object to propose to exclude congress from raising monies by internal taxes, as by duties, excises, and direct taxes; but my opinion is, that congress, especially in its proposed organization, ought not to raise monies by internal taxes, except in strict conformity to the federal plan; that is, by the agency of the state governments in all cases, except where a state shall neglect, for an unreasonable time, to pay its quota of a requisition; and never where so many of the state legislatures as represent a majority of the people, shall formally determine an excise law or requisition is improper, in their next session after the same be laid before them. We ought always to recollect that the evil to be guarded against is found by our own experience, and the experience of others, to be mere neglect in the states to pay their quotas; and power in the union to levy and collect the neglecting states quotas with interest, is fully adequate to the evil. By this federal plan, with this exception mentioned, we secure the means of collecting the taxes by the usual process of law, and avoid the evil of attempting to compel or coerce a state; and we avoid also a circumstance, which never yet could be, and I am fully confident never can be, admitted in a free federal republic; I mean a permanent and continued system of tax laws of the union, executed in the bowels of the states by many thousand officers, dependent as to the assessing and collecting federal taxes, solely upon the union. On every principle then, we ought to provide, that the union render an exact account of all monies raised by imposts and other taxes; and that whenever monies shall be wanted for the purposes of the union, beyond the proceeds of the impost duties, requisitions shall be made on the states for the monies so wanted; and that the power of laying and collecting shall never be exercised, except in cases where a state shall neglect, a given time, to pay its quota. This mode seems to be strongly pointed out by the reason of the case, and spirit of the government; and I believe, there is no instance to be found in a federal republic, where the congressional powers ever extended generally to collecting monies by direct taxes or excises. Creating all these restrictions, still the powers of the union in matters of taxation, will be too unlimited; further checks, in my mind, are indispensably necessary. Nor do I conceive, that as full a representation as is practicable in the federal government, will afford sufficient security: the strength of the government, and the confidence of the people, must be collected principally in the local assemblies; every part or branch of the federal head must be feeble, and unsafely trusted with large powers. A government possessed of more power than its constituent parts will justify, will not only probably abuse it, but be unequal to bear its own burden; it may as soon be destroyed by the pressure of power, as languish and perish for want of it.

There are two ways further of raising checks, and guarding against undue combinations and influence in a federal system. The first is, in levying taxes, raising and keeping up armies, in building navies, in forming plans for the militia, and in appropriating monies for the support of the military, to require the attendance of a large proportion of the federal representatives, as two-thirds or three-fourths of them; and in passing laws, in these important cases, to require the consent of two-thirds or three-fourths of the members present. The second is, by requiring that certain important laws of the federal head, as a requisition or a law for raising monies by excise shall be laid before the state legislatures, and if disapproved of by a given number of them, say by as many of them as represent a majority of the people, the law shall have no effect. Whether it would be advisable to adopt both, or either of these checks, I will not undertake to determine. We have seen them both exist in confederated republics. The first exists substantially in the confederation, and will exist in some measure in the plan proposed, as in choosing a president by the house, in expelling members; in the senate, in making treaties, and in deciding on impeachments, and in the whole in altering the constitution. The last exists in the United Netherlands, but in a much greater extent. The first is founded on this principle, that these important measures may, sometimes, be adopted by a bare quorum of members, perhaps, from a few states, and that a bare majority of the federal representatives may frequently be of the aristocracy, or some particular interests, connections, or parties in the community, and governed by motives, views, and inclinations not compatible with the general interest.—The last is founded on this principle, that the people will be substantially represented, only in their state or local assemblies; that their principal security must be found in them; and that, therefore, they ought to have ultimately a constitutional control over such interesting measures.

I have often heard it observed, that our people are well informed, and will not submit to oppressive governments; that the state governments will be their ready advocates, and possess their confidence, mix with them, and enter into all their wants and feelings. This is all true; but of what avail will these circumstances be, if the state governments, thus allowed to be the guardians of the people, possess no kind of power by the forms of the social compact, to stop, in their passage, the laws of congress injurious to the people. State governments must stand and see the law take place; they may complain and petition—so may individuals; the members of them, in extreme cases, may resist, on the principles of self-defence—so may the people and individuals.

It has been observed, that the people, in extensive territories, have more power, compared with that of their rulers, than in small states. Is not directly the opposite true? The people in a small state can unite and act in concert, and with vigour; but in large territories, the men who govern find it more easy to unite, while people cannot; while they cannot collect the opinions of each part, while they move to different points, and one part is often played off against the other.

It has been asserted, that the confederate head of a republic at best, is in general weak and dependent;—that the people will attach themselves to, and support their local governments, in all disputes with the union. Admit the fact: is it any way to remove the inconvenience by accumulating powers upon a weak organization? The fact is, that the detail administration of affairs, in this mixed republic, depends principally on the local governments; and the people would be wretched without them: and a great proportion of social happiness depends on the internal administration of justice, and on internal police. The splendor of the monarch, and the power of the government are one thing. The happiness of the subject depends on very different causes: but it is to the latter, that the best men, the greatest ornaments of human nature, have most carefully attended: it is to the former tyrants and oppressors have always aimed.

Melancton Smith

Speeches (1788)

June 20, 1788

Mr. Smith again rose—He most heartily concurred in sentiment with the honorable gentleman who opened the debate yesterday, that the discussion of the important question now before them ought to be entered on with a spirit of patriotism; with minds open to conviction; with a determination to form opinions only on the merits of the question, from those evidences which should appear in the course of the investigation. [. . .]

He was as strongly impressed with the necessity of a Union, as any one could be: He would seek it with as much ardor. In the discussion of this subject, he was disposed to make every reasonable concession, and indeed to sacrifice everything for a Union, except the liberties of his country, than which he could contemplate no greater misfortune. But he hoped we were not reduced to the necessity of sacrificing or even endangering our liberties to preserve the Union. If that was the case, the alternative was dreadful. But he would not now say that the adoption of the Constitution would endanger our liberties; because that was the point to be debated, and the premises should be laid down previously to the drawing of any conclusion. He wished that all observations might be confined to this point; and that declamation and appeals to the passions might be omitted.

Why, said he, are we told of our weaknesses? Of the defenseless condition of the southern parts of our state? Of the exposed situation of our capital? Of Long Island surrounded by water, and exposed to the incursions of our neighbors in Connecticut? Of Vermont having separated from us and assumed the powers of a distinct government; And of the Northwest part of our state being in the hands of a foreign enemy? [. . .] The defects of the Old Confederation needed as little proof as the necessity of an Union: But there was no proof in all this, that the proposed Constitution was a good one. Defective as the Old Confederation is, he said, no one could deny but it was possible we might have a worse government. But the question was not whether the present Confederation be a bad one; but whether the proposed Constitution be a good one. [. . .]

He was pleased that thus early in the debate, the honorable gentleman had himself shown, that the intent of the Constitution was not a Confederacy, but a reduction of all the states into a consolidated government. He hoped the gentleman would be complaisant enough to exchange names with those who disliked the Constitution, as it appeared from his own concession that they were Federalists, and those who advocated it Anti-Federalists. He begged leave, however, to remind the gentleman, that Montesquieu, with all the examples of modern and ancient Republics in view, gives it as his opinion, that a confederated Republic has all the internal advantages of a Republic, with the external force of a Monarchical Government. He was happy to find an officer of such high rank recommending to the other officers of Government, and to those who are members of the Legislature, to be unbiased by any motives of interest or state importance. Fortunately for himself, he was out of the verge of temptations of this kind, not having the honor to hold any office under the state. But then he was exposed, in common with other gentlemen of the Convention, to another temptation, against which he thought it necessary that we should be equally guarded:—If, said he, this constitution is adopted, there will be a number of honorable and lucrative offices to be filled, and we ought to be cautious lest an expectancy of some of them should influence us to adopt without due consideration.

We may wander, said he, in the fields of fancy without end, and gather flowers as we go: It may be entertaining—but it is of little service to the discovery of truth:—We may on one side compare the scheme advocated by our opponents to golden images, with feet part of iron and part of clay; and on the other, to a beast dreadful and terrible, and strong exceedingly, having great iron teeth, which devours, breaks in pieces, and stamps the residue with his feet: And after all, said he, we shall find that both these allusions are taken from the same vision; and their true meaning must be discovered by sober reasoning.

He would agree with the honorable gentleman, that perfection in any system of government was not to be looked for. If that was the object, the debates on the one before them might soon be closed.—But he would observe that this observation applied with equal force against changing any systems—especially against material and radical changes.—Fickleness and inconstancy, he said, was characteristic of a free people; and in framing a Constitution for them, it was, perhaps the most difficult thing to correct this spirit, and guard against the evil effects of it—he was persuaded it could not be altogether prevented without destroying their freedom—it would be like attempting to correct a small indisposition in the habit of the body, by fixing the patient in a confirmed consumption.—This fickle and inconstant spirit was the more dangerous in bringing about changes in the government. The instance that had been adduced by the gentleman from sacred history, was an example in point to prove this: The nation of Israel having received a form of civil government from Heaven, enjoyed it for a considerable period; but at length laboring under pressures, which were brought upon them by their own misconduct and imprudence, instead of imputing their misfortunes to their true causes, and making a proper improvement of their calamities, by a correction of their errors, they imputed them to a defect in their constitution; they rejected their Divine Ruler, and asked Samuel to make them a King to judge them, like other nations. Samuel was grieved at their folly; but still, by the command of God, he hearkened to their voice; though not until he had solemnly declared unto them the manner in which the King should reign over them. "This, (says Samuel) shall be the manner of the King that shall reign over you. He will take your sons and appoint them for himself, for his chariots, and for his horsemen, and some shall run before his chariots; and he will appoint him captains over thousands, and captains over fifties, and will set them to ear his ground, and to reap his harvest, and to make his instruments of war, and instruments of his chariots. And he will take your daughters to be confectioneries, and to be cooks, and to be bakers. And he will take your fields, and your vineyards, and your olive yards, even the best of them, and give them to his servants. And he will take the tenth of your seed, and of your vineyards, and give to his officers and to his servants. And he will take your men servants and your maid servants, and your goodliest young men, and your asses, and put them to his work. He will take the tenth of your sheep: And ye shall be his servants. And ye shall cry out in that day, because of your King which ye have chosen you; and the Lord will not hear you in that day."—How far this was applicable to the subject he would not now say; it could be better judged of when they had gone through it.—On the whole he wished to take up this matter with candor and deliberation.

He would now proceed to state his objections to the clause just read (section 2 of article I, clause 3). His objections were comprised under three heads: First. the rule of apportionment is unjust; second. there is no precise number fixed on below which the house shall not be reduced; third. it is inadequate. In the first place the rule of apportionment of the representatives is to be according to the whole number of the white inhabitants, with three-fifths of all others; that is in plain English, each state is to send Representatives in proportion to the number of freemen, and three-fifths of the slaves it contains. He could not see any rule by which slaves are to be included in the ratio of representation: The principle of a representation, being that every free agent should be concerned in governing himself, it was absurd to give that power to a man who could not exercise it—slaves have no will of their own: The very operation of it was to give certain privileges to those people who were so wicked as to keep slaves. He knew it would be admitted that this rule of apportionment was founded on unjust principles, but that it was the result of accommodation; which he supposed we should be under the necessity of admitting, if we meant to be in union with the Southern States, though utterly repugnant to his feelings. In the second place, the number was not fixed by the Constitution, but left at the discretion of the Legislature; perhaps he was mistaken; it was his wish to be informed. He understood from the Constitution, that sixty-five Members were to compose the House of

Representatives for three years; that after that time a census was to be taken, and the numbers to be ascertained by the Legislature on the following principles: First, they shall be apportioned to the respective States according to numbers; second, each State shall have one at least; third, they shall never exceed one to every thirty thousand. If this was the case, the first Congress that met might reduce the number below what it now is; a power inconsistent with every principle of a free government, to leave it to the discretion of the rulers to determine the number of the representatives of the people. There was no kind of security except in the integrity of the men who were entrusted; and if you have no other security, it is idle to contend about Constitutions. In the third place, supposing Congress should declare that there should be one representative for every thirty thousand of the people, in his opinion it would be incompetent to the great purposes of representation. It was, he said, the fundamental principle of a free government, that the people should make the laws by which they were to be governed: He who is controlled by another is a slave; and that government which is directed by the will of any one or a few, or any number less than is the will of the community, is a government for slaves.

The next point was, how was the will of the community to be expressed? It was not possible for them to come together; the multitude would be too great: In order, therefore to provide against this inconvenience, the scheme of representation had been adopted, by which the people deputed others to represent them. Individuals entering into society became one body, and that body ought to be animated by one mind; and he conceived that every form of government should have that complexion. It was true that notwithstanding all the experience we had from others, it had not appeared that the experiment of representation had been fairly tried: there was something like it in the ancient republics, in which, being of small extent, the people could easily meet together, though instead of deliberating, they only considered of those things which were submitted to them by their magistrates. In Great Britain representation had been carried much further than in any government we knew of, except our own; but in that country it now had only a name. America was the only country, in which the first fair opportunity had been offered. When we were Colonies, our representation was better than any that was then known: Since the revolution we had advanced still nearer to perfection. He considered it as an object, of all others the most important, to have it fixed on its true principle; yet he was convinced that it was impracticable to have such a representation in a consolidated government. However, said he, we may approach a great way toward perfection by increasing the representation and limiting the powers of Congress. He considered that the great interests and liberties of the people could only be secured by the State Governments. He admitted, that if the new government was only confined to great national objects, it would be less exceptionable; but it extended to every thing dear to human nature. That this was the case could be proved without any long chain of reasoning:—for that power which had both the purse and the sword, had the government of the whole country, and might extend its powers to any and to every object. He had already observed, that by the true doctrine of representation, this principle was established—that the representative must be chosen by the free will of the majority of his constituents: It therefore followed that the representative should be chosen from small districts. This being admitted, he would ask, could sixty-five men, for three million, or one for thirty thousand, be chosen in this manner? Would they be possessed of the requisite information to make happy the great number of souls that were spread over this extensive country?—There was another objection to the clause: If great affairs of government were trusted to a few men, they would be more liable to corruption. Corruption, he knew, was unfashionable among us, but he supposed that Americans were like other men; and though they had hitherto displayed great virtues, still they were men; and therefore such steps should be taken as to prevent the possibility of corruption. We were now in that stage of society, in which we could deliberate with freedom;—how long it might continue, God only knew! Twenty years hence, perhaps, these maxims might become unfashionable; we already hear, said he, in all parts of the country, gentlemen ridiculing that spirit of patriotism and love of liberty, which carried us through all our difficulties in times of danger.—When patriotism was already nearly hooted out of society, ought we not to take some precautions against the progress of corruption?

He had one more observation to make, to show that the representation was insufficient—Government, he said, must rest for its execution, on the good opinion of the people, for if it was made in heaven, and had not the confidence of the people, it could not be executed: that this was proved, by the example given by the gentleman, of the Jewish theocracy. It must have a good setting out, or the instant it takes place there is an end of liberty. He believed that the inefficacy of the old Confederation, had arisen from that want of confidence; and this caused in a great degree by the continual declamation of gentlemen of importance against it from one end of the continent to the other, who had frequently compared it to a rope of sand. It had pervaded every class of citizens, and their misfortunes, the consequences of idleness and extravagance, were attributed to the defects of that system. At the close of the war, our country had been left in distress; and it was impossible that any government on earth could immediately retrieve it; it must be time and industry alone that could effect it. He said he would pursue these observations no further at present,—And concluded with making the following motion:

"Resolved, That it is proper that the number of representatives be fixed at the rate of one for every twenty thousand inhabitants, to be ascertained on the principles mentioned in the second section of the first article of the Constitution, until they amount to three hundred; after which they shall be apportioned among the States, in proportion to the number of inhabitants of the States respectively: And that before the first enumeration shall be made, the several States shall be entitled to choose double the number of representatives for that purpose, mentioned in the Constitution."

June 21, 1788

Mr. M. Smith. [. . .] To determine whether the number of representatives proposed by this Constitution is sufficient, it is proper to examine the qualifications which this house ought to possess, in order to exercise their powers discreetly for the happiness of the people. The idea that naturally suggests itself to our minds, when we speak of representatives is, that they resemble those they represent; they should be a true picture of the people; possess the knowledge of their circumstances and their wants; sympathize in all their distresses, and be disposed to seek their true interests. The knowledge necessary for the representatives of a free people, not only comprehends extensive political and commercial information, such as is acquired by men of refined education, who have leisure to attain to high degrees of improvement, but it should also comprehend that kind of acquaintance with the common concerns and occupations of the people, which men of the middling class of life are in general much better competent to, than those of a superior class. To understand the true commercial interests of a country, not only requires just ideas of the general commerce of the world, but also, and principally, a knowledge of the productions of your own country and their value, what your soil is capable of producing, the nature of your manufactures, and the capacity of the country to increase both. To exercise the power of laying taxes, duties, and excises with discretion, requires something more than an acquaintance with the abstruse parts of the system of finance. It calls for a knowledge of the circumstances and ability of the people in general, a discernment how the burdens imposed will bear upon the different classes.

From these observations results this conclusion that the number of representatives should be so large, as that while it embraces men of the first class, it should admit those of the middling class of life. I am convinced that this Government is so constituted, that the representatives will generally be composed of the first class in the community, which I shall distinguish by the name of the natural aristocracy of the country. I do not mean to give offense by using this term. I am sensible this idea is treated by many gentlemen as chimerical. I shall be asked what is meant by the natural aristocracy—and told that no such distinction of classes of men exists among us. It is true it is our singular felicity that we have no legal or hereditary distinctions of this kind; but still there are real differences: Every society naturally divides itself into classes. The author of nature has bestowed on some greater capacities than on others—birth, education, talents, and wealth, create distinctions among men as visible and of as much influence as titles, stars, and garters. In every society, men of this class will command a superior degree of respect—and if the government is so constituted as to admit but few to exercise the powers of it, it will, according to the natural course of things, be in their hands. Men in the middling class, who are qualified as representatives, will not be so anxious to be chosen as those of the first. When the number is so small the office will be highly elevated and distinguished—the style in which the members live will probably be high—circumstances of this kind, will render the place of a representative not a desirable one to sensible, substantial men, who have been used to walk in the plain and frugal paths of life.

Besides, the influence of the great will generally enable them to succeed in elections—it will be difficult to combine a district of country containing thirty or forty thousand inhabitants, frame your election laws as you please, in any one character; unless it be in one of conspicuous, military, popular, civil, or legal talents. The great easily form associations; the poor and middling class form them with difficulty. If the elections be by plurality, as probably will be the case in this state, it is almost certain, none but the great will be chosen—for they easily unite their interest—The common people will divide, and their divisions will be promoted by the others. There will be scarcely a chance of their uniting, in any other but some great man, unless in some popular demagogue, who will probably be destitute of principle. A substantial yeoman of sense and discernment, will hardly ever be chosen. From these remarks it appears that the government will fall into the hands of the few and the great. This will be a government of oppression. I do not mean to declaim against the great, and charge them indiscriminately with want of principle and honesty.—The same passions and prejudices govern all men. The circumstances in which men are placed in a great measure give a cast to the human character. Those in middling circumstances, have less temptation—they are inclined by habit and the company with whom they associate, to set bounds to their passions and appetites—if this is not sufficient, the want of means to gratify them will be a restraint—they are obliged to employ their time in their respective callings—hence the substantial yeomanry of the country are more temperate, of better morals, and less ambition than the great. The latter do not feel for the poor and middling class; the reasons are obvious—they are not obliged to use the pains and labor to procure property as the other.—They feel not the inconveniences arising from the payment of small sums. The great consider themselves above the common people—entitled to more respect—do not associate with them—they fancy themselves to have a right of preeminence in everything. In short, they possess the same feelings, and are under the influence of the same motives, as a hereditary nobility. I know the idea that such a distinction exists in this country is ridiculed by some—But I am not the less apprehensive of danger from their influence on this account—Such distinctions exist all the world over—have been taken notice of by all writers on free government—and are founded in the nature of things. It has been the principal care of free governments to guard against the encroachments of the great. Common observation and experience prove the existence of such distinctions. Will anyone say, that there does not exist in this country the pride of family, of wealth, of talents; and that they do not command influence and respect among the common people? Congress, in their address to the inhabitants of the province of Quebec, in 1775, state this distinction in the following forcible words quoted from the Marquis Beccaria. "In every human society, there is an essay continually tending to confer on one part the height of power and happiness, and to reduce the other to the extreme of weakness and misery. The intent of good laws is to oppose this effort, and to diffuse their influence universally and equally." We ought to guard against the government being placed in hands of this class—They cannot have that sympathy with their constituents which is necessary to connect them closely to their interest: Being in the habit of profuse living, they will be profuse in the public expenses. They find no difficulty in paying their taxes, and therefore do not feel the public burdens: Besides if they govern, they will enjoy the emoluments of the government. The middling class, from their frugal habits, and feeling themselves the public burdens, will be careful how they increase them.

But I may be asked, would you exclude the first class in the community, from any share in legislation? I answer by no means—they would be more dangerous out of power than in it—they would be factious—discontented and constantly disturbing the government—it would also be unjust—they have their liberties to protect as well as others—and the largest share of property. But my idea is, that the Constitution should be so framed as to admit this class, together with a sufficient number of the middling class to control them. You will then combine the abilities and honesty of the community—a proper degree of information, and a disposition to pursue the public good. A representative body, composed principally of respectable yeomanry is the best possible security to liberty.—When therefore this class in society pursue their own interest, they promote that of the public, for it is involved in it.

In so small a number of representatives, there is great danger from corruption and combination. A great politician has said that every man has his price. I hope this is not true in all its extent—But I ask the gentlemen to inform, what government there is, in which it has not been practiced. Notwithstanding all that has been said of the defects in the Constitution of the ancient Confederacies of the Grecian Republics, their destruction is to be imputed more to this cause than to any imperfection in their forms of government. This was the deadly poison that effected their dissolution. This is an extensive country, increasing in population and growing in consequence. Very many lucrative offices will be in the grant of the government, which will be the object of avarice and ambition. How easy will it be to gain over a sufficient number, in the bestowment of these offices, to promote the views and purposes of those who grant them! Foreign corruption is also to be guarded against. A system of corruption is known to be the system of government in Europe. It is practiced without blushing. And we may lay it to our account it will be attempted among us. The most effectual as well as natural security against this, is a strong democratic branch in the legislature frequently chosen, including in it a number of the substantial, sensible yeomanry of the country. Does the house of representatives answer this description? I confess, to me they hardly wear the complexion of a democratic branch—they appear the mere shadow of representation. The whole number in both houses amounts to ninety-one—Of these forty-six make a quorum; and twenty-four of those being secured, may carry any point. Can the liberties of three million people be securely trusted in the hands of twenty-four men? Is it prudent to commit to so small a number the decision of the great questions which come before them? Reason revolts at the idea.

The honorable gentleman from New York has said that sixty-five members in the house of representatives are sufficient for the present situation of the country, and taking it for granted that they will increase as one for thirty thousand, in twenty-five years they will amount to two hundred. It is admitted by this observation that the number fixed in the Constitution, is not sufficient without it is augmented. It is not declared that an increase shall be made, but is left at the discretion of the legislature, by the gentleman's own concession; therefore the Constitution is imperfect. We certainly ought to fix in the Constitution those things which are essential to liberty. If anything falls under this description, it is the number of the legislature. To say, as this gentleman does, that our security is to depend upon the spirit of the people, who will be watchful of their liberties, and not suffer them to be infringed, is absurd. It would equally prove that we might adopt any form of government. I believe were we to create a despot, he would not immediately dare to act the tyrant; but it would not be long before he would destroy the spirit of the people, or the people would destroy him. If our people have a high sense of liberty, the government should be congenial to this spirit—calculated to cherish the love of liberty, while yet it had sufficient force to restrain licentiousness. Government operates upon the spirit of the people, as well as the spirit of the people operates upon it—and if they are not conformable to each other, the one or the other will prevail. In a less time than twenty-five years, the government will receive its tone. What the spirit of the country may be at the end of that period, it is impossible to foretell: Our duty is to frame a government friendly to liberty and the rights of mankind, which will tend to cherish and cultivate a love of liberty among our citizens. If this government becomes oppressive it will be by degrees: It will aim at its end by disseminating sentiments of government opposite to republicanism; and proceed from step to step in depriving the people of a share in the government. A recollection of the change that has taken place in the minds of many in this country in the course of a few years, ought to put us upon our guard. Many who are ardent advocates for the new system, reprobate republican principles as chimerical and such as ought to be expelled from society. Who would have thought ten years ago, that the very men who risked their lives and fortunes in support of republican principles, would now treat them as the fictions of fancy?—A few years ago we fought for liberty—We framed a general government on free principles—We placed the state legislatures, in whom the people have a full and fair representation, between Congress and the people. We were then, it is true, too cautious; and too much restricted the powers of the general government. But now it is proposed to go into the contrary, and a more dangerous extreme; to remove all barriers; to give the New Government free access to our pockets, and ample command of our persons; and that without providing for a genuine and fair representation of the people. No one can say what the progress of the change of sentiment may be in twenty-five years. The same men who now cry up the necessity of an energetic government, to induce a compliance with this system, may in much less time reprobate this in as severe terms as they now do the confederation, and may as strongly urge the necessity of going as far beyond this, as this is beyond the Confederation.—Men of this class are increasing—they have influence, talents, and industry—It is time to form a barrier against them. And while we are willing to establish a government adequate to the purposes of the union, let us be careful to establish it on the broad basis of equal liberty.

JOHN ADAMS

Letter to Roger Sherman (July 18, 1789)

Dear Sir: In my letter of yesterday I think it was demonstrated that the English government is a republic, and that the regal negative upon the laws is essential to that republic. Because without it that government would not be what it is, a monarchical republic, and, consequently, could not preserve the balance of power between the executive and legislative powers, nor that other balance which is in the legislature—between the one, the few, and the many in which two balances the excellence of that form of government must consist.

Let us now inquire whether the new constitution of the United States is or is not a monarchical republic like that of Great Britain. The monarchical and the aristocratical power in our constitution, it is true, are not hereditary; but this makes no difference in the nature of the power, in the nature of the balance, or in the name of the species of government. It would make no difference in the power of a judge or justice, or general or admiral, whether his commission were for life or years. His authority during the time it lasted would be the same whether it were for one year or twenty, or for life, or descendible to his eldest son. The people, the nation, in whom all power resides originally, may delegate their power for one year or for ten years, for years or for life; or may delegate it in fee simple or fee tail, if I may so express myself; or during good behavior, or at will, or till further orders.

A nation might unanimously create a dictator or a despot for one year or more, or for life, or for perpetuity with hereditary descent. In such a case, the dictator for one year would as really be a dictator for the time his power lasted as the other would be whose power was perpetual and descendible. A nation in the same manner might create a simple monarchy for years, life, or perpetuity, and in either case the creature would be equally a simple monarch during the continuance of his power. So the people of England might create king, lords, and commons for a year, or for several years, or for life, and in any of these cases their government would be a monarchical republic, or, if you will, a limited monarchy during its continuance, as much as it is now when the king and nobles are hereditary. They might make their house of commons hereditary too. What the consequence of this would be it is easy to foresee; but it would not in the first moment make any change in the legal power, nor in the name of the government.

Let us now consider what our constitution is and see whether any other name can with propriety be given it, than that of a monarchical republic or, if you will, a limited monarchy. The duration of our president is neither perpetual nor for life; it is only for four years; but his power during those four years is much greater than that of an avoyer, a consul, a podestà, a doge, a stadtholder; nay, than a king of Poland; nay, than a king of Sparta. I know of no first magistrate in any republican government, excepting England and Neuchâtel, who possesses a constitutional dignity, authority, and power comparable to his. The power of sending and receiving ambassadors, of raising and commissioning all officers, of managing the treasures, the internal and external affairs of the nation; nay, the whole executive power, coextensive with the legislative power, is vested in him, and he has the right, and his is the duty, to take care that the laws be faithfully executed. These rights and duties, these prerogatives and dignities are so transcendent that they must naturally and necessarily excite in the nation all the jealousy, envy, fears, apprehensions, and opposition that are so constantly observed in England against the crown.

That these powers are necessary I readily admit. That the laws cannot be executed without them; that the lives, liberties, properties and characters of the citizens cannot be secure without their protection, is most clear. But it is equally certain, I think, that they ought to have been still greater, or much less. The limitations upon them in the cases of war, treaties, and appointments to office, and especially the limitation on the president's independence as a branch of the legislative, will be the destruction of this constitution and involve us in anarchy, if not amended. I shall pass over all particulars for the present, except the last, because that is now the point in dispute between you and me. Longitude and the philosopher's stone have not been sought with more earnestness by philosophers than a guardian of the laws has been studied by legislators from Plato to Montesquieu; but every project has been found to be no better than committing the lamb to the custody of the wolf, except that one which is called a *balance of power*. A simple sovereignty in one, a few, or many has no balance and therefore no laws. A divided sovereignty without a balance, or, in other words, where the division is unequal, is always at war and consequently has no laws. In our constitution the sovereignty—that is, the legislative power—is divided into three branches. The house and senate are equal, but the third branch, though essential, is not equal. The president must pass judgment upon every law, but in some cases his judgment may be overruled. These cases will be such as attack his constitutional power; it is, therefore, certain he has not equal power to defend himself, or the constitution, or the judicial power, as the senate and house have.

Power naturally grows. Why? Because human passions are insatiable. But that power alone can grow which already is too great, that which is unchecked, that which has no equal power to control it. The legislative power in our constitution is greater than the executive; it will, therefore, encroach because both aristocratical and democratical passions are insatiable. The legislative power will increase, the executive will diminish. In the legislature the monarchical power is not equal either to the aristocratical or democratical; it will, therefore, decrease while the other will increase. Indeed, I think the aristocratical power is greater than either the monarchical or democratical. That will, therefore, swallow up the other two.

In my letter of yesterday, I think it was proved that a republic might make the supreme executive an integral part of the legislature. In this, it is equally demonstrated, as I think, that our constitution ought to be amended by a decisive adoption of that expedient. If you do not forbid me, I shall write to you again.

Letter to Samuel Adams (October 18, 1790)

Dear Sir,—I am thankful to our common friend, as well as to you, for your favor of the fourth, which I received last night. My fears are in unison with yours, that hay, wood, and stubble, will be the materials of the new political buildings in Europe, till men shall be more enlightened and friendly to each other.

You agree, that there are undoubtedly principles of political architecture. But, instead of particularizing any of them, you seem to place all your hopes in the universal, or at least more general, prevalence of knowledge and benevolence. I think with you, that knowledge and benevolence ought to be promoted as much as possible; but, despairing of ever seeing them, sufficiently general for the security of society, I am for seeking institutions which may supply in some degree the defect. If there were no ignorance, error, or vice, there would be neither principles nor systems of civil or political government.

I am not often satisfied with the opinions of Hume; but in this he seems well founded, that all projects of government, founded in the supposition or expectation of extraordinary degrees of virtue, are evidently chimerical. Nor do I believe it possible, humanly speaking, that men should ever be greatly improved in knowledge or benevolence, without assistance from the principles and system of government.

I am very willing to agree with you in fancying, that in the greatest improvements of society, government will be in the republican form. It is a fixed principle with me, that all good government is and must be republican. But, at the same time, your candor will agree with me, that there is not in lexicography a more fraudulent word. Whenever I use the word *republic* with approbation, I mean a government in which the people have collectively, or by representation, an essential share in the sovereignty. The republican forms of Poland and Venice are much worse, and those of Holland and Bern very little better, than the monarchical form in France before the late revolution. By the republican form, I know you do not mean the plan of Milton, Nedham, or Turgot. For, after a fair trial of its miseries, the simple monarchical form will ever be, as it has ever been, preferred to it by mankind. Are we not, my friend, in danger of rendering the word *republican* unpopular in this country by an indiscreet, indeterminate, and equivocal use of it? The people of England have been obliged to wean themselves from the use of it, by making it unpopular and unfashionable, because they found it was artfully used by some, and simply understood by others, to mean the government of their interregnum parliament. They found they could not wean themselves from that destructive form of government so entirely, as that a mischievous party would not still remain in favor of it, by any other means than by making the words *republic* and *republican* unpopular. They have succeeded to such a degree, that, with a vast majority of that nation, a republican is as unamiable as a witch, a blasphemer, a rebel, or a tyrant. If, in this country, the word *republic* should be generally understood, as it is by some, to mean a form of government inconsistent with a mixture of three powers, forming a mutual balance, we may depend upon it that such mischievous effects will be produced by the use of it as will compel the people of America to renounce, detest, and execrate it as the English do. With these explanations, restrictions, and limitations, I agree with you in your love of republican governments, but in no other sense.

With you, I have also the honor most perfectly to harmonize in your sentiments of the humanity and wisdom of promoting education in knowledge, virtue, and benevolence. But I think that these will confirm mankind in the opinion of the necessity of preserving and strengthening the dikes against the ocean, its tides and storms. Human appetites, passions, prejudices, and self-love will never be conquered by benevolence and knowledge alone, introduced by human means. The millennium itself neither supposes nor implies it. All civil government is then to cease, and the Messiah is to reign. That happy and holy state is therefore wholly out of this question. You and I agree in the utility of universal education; but will nations agree in it as fully and extensively as we do, and be at the expense of it? We know, with as much certainty as attends any human knowledge, that they will not. We cannot, therefore, advise the people to depend for their safety, liberty, and security, upon hopes and blessings which we know will not fall to their lot. If we do our duty then to the people, we shall not deceive them, but advise them to depend upon what is in their power and will relieve them.

Philosophers, ancient and modern, do not appear to me to have studied nature, the whole of nature, and nothing but nature. Lycurgus's principle was war and family pride; Solon's was what the people would bear, &c. The best writings of antiquity upon government, those, I mean, of Aristotle, Zeno, and Cicero, are lost. We have human nature, society, and universal history to observe and study, and from these we may draw all the real principles which ought to be regarded. Disciples will follow their masters, and interested partisans their chieftains; let us like it or not, we cannot help it. But if the true principles can be discovered, and fairly, fully, and impartially laid before the people, the more light increases, the more the reason of them will be seen, and the more disciples they will have. Prejudice, passion, and private interest, which will always mingle in human inquiries, one would think might be enlisted on the side of truth, at least in the greatest number; for certainly the majority are interested in the truth, if they could see to the end of all its consequences. "Kings have been deposed by aspiring nobles." True, and never by any other. "These" (the nobles, I suppose,) "have waged everlasting war against the common rights of men." True, when they have been possessed of the *summa imperii* in one body, without a check. So have the plebeians; so have the people; so have kings; so has human nature, in every shape and combination, and so it ever will. But, on the other hand, the nobles have been essential parties in the preservation of liberty, whenever and wherever it has existed. In Europe, they alone have preserved it against kings and people, wherever it has been preserved; or, at least, with very little assistance from the people. One hideous despotism, as horrid as that of Turkey, would have been the lot of every nation of Europe, if the nobles had not made stands. By nobles, I mean not peculiarly an hereditary nobility, or any particular modification, but the natural and actual aristocracy among mankind. The existence of this you will not deny. You and I have seen four noble families rise up in Boston,—the CRAFTS, GORES, DAWES, and AUSTINS. These are as really a nobility in our town, as the Howards, Somersets, Berties, &c., in England. Blind, undistinguishing reproaches against the aristocratical part of mankind, a division which nature has made, and we cannot abolish, are neither pious nor benevolent. They are as pernicious as they are false. They serve only to foment prejudice, jealousy, envy, animosity, and malevolence. They serve no ends but those of sophistry, fraud, and the spirit of party. It would not be true, but it would not be more egregiously false, to say that the people have waged everlasting war against the rights of men.

"The love of liberty," you say, "is interwoven in the soul of man." So it is, according to La Fontaine, in that of a wolf; and I doubt whether it be much more rational, generous, or, social, in one than in the other, until in man it is enlightened by experience, reflection, education, and civil and political institutions, which are at first produced, and constantly supported and improved by a few; that is, by the nobility. The wolf, in the fable, who preferred running in the forest, lean and hungry, to the sleek, plump, and round sides of the dog, because he found the latter was sometimes restrained, had more love of liberty than most men. The numbers of men in all ages have preferred ease, slumber, and good cheer to liberty, when they have been in competition. We must not then depend alone upon the love of liberty in the soul of man for its preservation. Some political institutions must be prepared, to assist this love against its enemies. Without these, the struggle will ever end only in a change of impostors. When the people, who have no property, feel the power in their own hands to determine all questions by a majority, they ever attack those who have property, till the injured men of property lose all patience, and recur to finesse, trick, and stratagem, to outwit those who have too much strength, because they have too many hands to be resisted any other way. Let us be impartial, then, and speak the whole truth. Till we do, we shall never discover all the true principles that are necessary. The multitude, therefore, as well as the nobles, must have a check. This is one principle.

"Were the people of England free, after they had obliged King John to concede to them their ancient rights?" The people never did this. There was no people who pretended to any thing. It was the nobles alone. The people pretended to nothing but to be villains, vassals, and retainers to the king or the nobles.

The nobles, I agree, were not free, because all was determined by a majority of their votes, or by arms, not by law. Their feuds deposed their "Henrys, Edwards, and Richards," to gratify lordly ambition, patrician rivalry, and "family pride." But, if they had not been deposed, those kings would have become despots, because the people would not and could not join the nobles in any regular and constitutional opposition to them. They would have become despots, I repeat it, and that by means of the villains, vassals, and retainers aforesaid. It is not family pride, my friend, but family popularity, that does the great mischief, as well as the great good. Pride, in the heart of man, is an evil fruit and concomitant of every advantage; of riches, of knowledge, of genius, of talents, of beauty, of strength, of virtue, and even of piety. It is sometimes ridiculous, and often pernicious. But it is even sometimes, and in some degree, useful. But the pride of families would be always and only ridiculous, if it had not family popularity to work with. The attachment and devotion of the people to some families inspires them with pride. As long as gratitude or interest, ambition or avarice, love, hope, or fear, shall be human motives of action, so long will numbers attach themselves to particular families. When the people will, in spite of all that can be said or done, cry a man or a family up to the skies, exaggerate all his talents and virtues, not hear a word of his weakness or faults, follow implicitly his advice, detest every man he hates, adore every man he loves, and knock down all who will not swim down the stream with them, where is your remedy? When a man or family are thus popular, how can you prevent them from being proud? You and I know of instances in which popularity has been a wind, a tide, a whirlwind. The history of all ages and nations is full of such examples.

Popularity, that has great fortune to dazzle; splendid largesses, to excite warm gratitude; sublime, beautiful, and uncommon genius or talents, to produce deep admiration; or any thing to support high hopes and strong fears, will be proud; and its power will be employed to mortify enemies, gratify friends, procure votes, emoluments, and power. Such family popularity ever did, and ever will govern in every nation, in every climate, hot and cold, wet and dry, among civilized and savage people, Christians and Mahometans, Jews and Heathens. Declamation against family pride is a pretty, juvenile exercise, but unworthy of statesmen. They know the evil and danger is too serious to be sported with. The only way, God knows, is to put these families into a hole by themselves, and set two watches upon them; a superior to them all on one side, and the people on the other.

There are a few popular men in the Massachusetts, my friend, who have, I fear, less honor, sincerity, and virtue, than they ought to have. These, if they are not guarded against, may do another mischief. They may excite a party spirit and a mobbish spirit, instead of the spirit of liberty, and produce another Wat Tyler's rebellion. They can do no more. But I really think their party language ought not to be countenanced, nor their shibboleths pronounced. The miserable stuff that they utter about the *well-born* is as despicable as themselves. The *ἐυγενεῖς* of the Greeks, the *bien nées* of the French, the *welgebohren* of the Germans and Dutch, the *beloved families* of the Creeks, are but a few samples of national expressions of the same thing, for which every nation on earth has a similar expression. One would think that our scribblers were all the sons of redemptioners or transported convicts. They think with Tarquin, "*In novo populo, ubi omnis repentina atque ex virtute nobilitas fit, futurum locum forti ac strenuo viro.*"

Let us be impartial. There is not more of family pride on one side, than of vulgar malignity and popular envy on the other. Popularity in one family raises envy in others. But the popularity of the least deserving will triumph over envy and malignity; while that which is acquired by real merit, will very often be overborne and oppressed by it.

Let us do justice to the people and to the nobles; for nobles there are, as I have before proved, in Boston as well as in Madrid. But to do justice to both, you must establish an arbitrator between them. This is another principle.

It is time, that you and I should have some sweet communion together. I do not believe, that we, who have preserved for more than thirty years an uninterrupted friendship, and have so long thought and acted harmoniously together in the worst of times, are now so far asunder in sentiment as some people pretend; in full confidence of which, I have used this freedom, being ever your warm friend.

John Adams

Discourses on Davila (1789)

Second Discourse

Men, in their primitive conditions, however savage, were undoubtedly gregarious; and they continue to be social, not only in every stage of civilization, but in every possible situation in which they can be placed. As nature intended them for society, she has furnished them with passions, appetites, and propensities, as well as a variety of faculties, calculated both for their individual enjoyment, and to render them useful to each other in their social connections. There is none among them more essential or remarkable, than the *passion for distinction.* A desire to be observed, considered, esteemed, praised, beloved, and admired by his fellows, is one of the earliest, as well as keenest dispositions discovered in the heart of man. If any one should doubt the existence of this propensity, let him go and attentively observe the journeymen and apprentices in the first workshop, or the oarsmen in a cockboat, a family or a neighborhood, the inhabitants of a house or the crew of a ship, a school or a college, a city or a village, a savage or civilized people, a hospital or a church, the bar or the exchange, a camp or a court. Wherever men, women, or children, are to be found, whether they be old or young, rich or poor, high or low, wise or foolish, ignorant or learned, every individual is seen to be strongly actuated by a desire to be seen, heard, talked of, approved and respected, by the people about him, and within his knowledge.

Moral writers have, by immemorial usage, a right to make a free use of the poets.

> The love of praise, howe'er conceal'd by art,
> Reigns, more or less, and glows, in every heart;
> The proud, to gain it, toils on toils endure,
> The modest shun it, but to make it sure.
> O'er globes and sceptres, now on thrones it swells,
> Now, trims the midnight lamp in college cells.
> 'Tis tory, whig—it plots, prays, preaches, pleads,
> Harangues in Senates, squeaks in masquerades.
> It aids the dancer's heel, the writer's head,
> And heaps the plain with mountains of the dead;
> Nor ends with life; but nods in sable plumes,
> Adorns our hearse, and flatters on our tombs.

A regard to the sentiments of mankind concerning him, and to their dispositions towards him, every man feels within himself; and if he has reflected, and tried experiments, he has found, that no exertion of his reason, no effort of his will, can wholly divest him of it. In proportion to our affection for the notice of others is our aversion to their neglect; the stronger the desire of the esteem of the public, the more powerful the aversion to their disapprobation; the more exalted the wish for admiration, the more invincible the abhorrence of contempt. Every man not only desires the consideration of others, but he frequently compares himself with others, his friends or his enemies; and in proportion as he exults when he perceives that he has more of it than they, he feels a keener affliction when he sees that one or more of them, are more respected than himself.

This passion, while it is simply a desire to excel another, by fair industry in the search of truth, and the practice of virtue, is properly called *Emulation.* When it aims at power, as a means of distinction, it is *Ambition.* When it is in a situation to suggest the sentiments of fear and apprehension, that another, who is now inferior, will become superior, it is denominated *Jealousy.* When it is in a state of mortification, at the superiority of another, and desires to bring him down to our level, or to depress him below us, it is properly called *Envy.* When it deceives a man into a belief of false professions of esteem or admiration, or into a false opinion of his importance in the judgment of the world, it is *Vanity.* These observations alone would be sufficient to show, that this propensity, in all its branches, is a principal source of the virtues and vices, the happiness and misery of human life; and that the history of mankind is little more than a simple narration of its operation and effects.

There is in human nature, it is true, simple *Benevolence,* or an affection for the good of others; but alone it is not a balance for the selfish affections. Nature then has kindly added to benevolence, the desire of reputation, in order to make us good members of society. *Spectemur agendo* expresses the great principle of activity for the good of others. Nature has sanctioned the law of self-preservation by rewards and punishments. The rewards of selfish activity are life and health; the punishments of negligence and indolence are want, disease, and death. Each individual, it is true, should consider, that nature has enjoined the same law on his neighbor, and therefore a respect for the authority of nature would oblige him to respect the rights of others as much as his own. But reasoning as abstruse, though as simple as this, would not occur to all men. The same nature therefore has imposed another law, that of promoting the good, as well as respecting the rights of mankind, and has sanctioned it by other rewards and punishments. The rewards in this case, in this life, are *esteem* and *admiration* of others; the punishments are *neglect* and *contempt;* nor may any one imagine that these are not as real as the others. The desire of the esteem of others is as real a want of nature as hunger; and the neglect and contempt of the world as severe a pain as the gout or stone. It sooner and oftener produces despair, and a detestation of existence; of equal importance to individuals, to families, and to nations. It is a principal end of government to regulate this passion, which in its turn becomes a principal means of government. It is the only adequate instrument of order and subordination in society, and alone commands effectual obedience to laws, since without it neither human reason, nor standing armies, would ever produce that great effect. Every personal quality, and every blessing of fortune, is cherished in proportion to its capacity of gratifying this universal affection for the esteem, the sympathy, admiration and congratulations of the public. Beauty in the face, elegance of figure, grace of attitude and motion, riches, honors, every thing is weighed in the scale, and desired, not so much for the pleasure they afford, as the attention they command. As this is a point of great importance, it may be pardonable to expatiate a little upon these particulars.

Why are the personal accomplishments of beauty, elegance, and grace, held in such high estimation by mankind? Is it merely for the pleasure which is received from the sight of these attributes? By no means. The taste for such delicacies is not universal; in those who feel the most lively sense of them, it is but a slight sensation, and of shortest continuance; but those attractions command the notice and attention of the public; they draw the eyes of spectators. This is the charm that makes them irresistible. Is it for such fading perfections that a husband or a wife is chosen? Alas, it is well known, that a very short familiarity totally destroys all sense and attention to such properties; and on the contrary, a very little time and habit destroy all the aversion to ugliness and deformity, when unattended with disease or ill temper. Yet beauty and address are courted and admired, very often, more than discretion, wit, sense, and many other accomplishments and virtues, of infinitely more importance to the happiness of private life, as well as to the utility and ornament of society. Is it for the momentous purpose of dancing and drawing, painting and music, riding or fencing, that men or women are destined in this life or any other? Yet those who have the best means of education, bestow more attention and expense on those, than on more solid acquisitions. Why? Because they attract more forcibly the attention of the world, and procure a better advancement in life. Notwithstanding all this, as soon as an establishment in life is made, they are found to have answered their end, are neglected and laid aside.

Is there any thing in birth, however illustrious or splendid, which should make a difference between one man and another? If, from a common ancestor, the whole human race is descended, they are all of the same family. How then can they distinguish families into the more or the less ancient? What advantage is there in an illustration of an hundred or a thousand years? Of what avail are all these histories, pedigrees, traditions? What foundation has the whole science of genealogy and heraldry? Are there differences in the breeds of men, as there are in those of horses? If there are not, these sciences have no foundation in reason; in prejudice they have a very solid one. All that philosophy can say is, that there is a general presumption, that a man has had some advantages of education, if he is of a family of note. But this advantage must be derived from his father and mother chiefly, if not wholly; of what importance is it then, in this view, whether the family is twenty generations upon record, or only two?

The mighty secret lies in this:—An illustrious descent attracts the notice of mankind. A single drop of royal blood, however illegitimately scattered, will make any man or woman proud or vain. Why? Because, although it excites the indignation of many, and the envy of more, it still attracts the *attention* of the world. Noble blood, whether the nobility be hereditary or elective, and indeed, more in republican governments than in monarchies, least of all in despotisms, is held in estimation for the same reason. It is a name and a race that a nation has been interested in, and is in the habit of respecting. Benevolence, sympathy, congratulation, have been so long associated to those names in the minds of the people, that they are become national habits. National gratitude descends from the father to the son, and is often stronger to the latter than the former. It is often excited by remorse, upon reflection on the ingratitude and injustice with which the former has been treated. When the names of a certain family are read in all the gazettes, chronicles, records, and histories of a country for five hundred years, they become known, respected, and delighted in by every body. A youth, a child of this extraction, and bearing this name, attracts the eyes and ears of all companies long before it is known or inquired whether he be a wise man or a fool. His name is often a greater distinction than a title, a star, or a garter. This it is which makes so many men proud, and so many others envious of illustrious descent. The pride is as irrational and contemptible as the pride of riches, and no more. A wise man will lament that any other distinction than that of merit should be made. A good man will neither be proud nor vain of his birth, but will earnestly improve every advantage he has for the public good. A conning man will carefully conceal his pride; but will indulge it in secret the more effectually, and improve his advantage to greater profit. But was any man ever known so wise, or so good, as really to despise birth or wealth? Did you ever read of a man rising to public notice, from obscure beginnings, who was not reflected on? Although, with every liberal mind, it is an honor and a proof of merit, yet it is a disgrace with mankind in general. What a load of sordid obloquy and envy has every such man to carry! The contempt that is thrown upon obscurity of ancestry, augments the eagerness for the stupid adoration that is paid to its illustration.

This desire of the consideration of our fellowmen, and their congratulations in our joys, is not less invincible than the desire of their sympathy in our sorrows. It is a determination of our nature, that lies at the foundation of our whole moral system in this world, and may be connected essentially with our destination in a future state.

Third Discourse

Why do men pursue riches? What is the end of avarice?

The labor and anxiety, the enterprises and adventures, that are voluntarily undertaken in pursuit of gain, are out of all proportion to the utility, convenience, or pleasure of riches. A competence to satisfy the wants of nature, food and clothes, a shelter from the seasons, and the comforts of a family, may be had for very little. The daily toil of the million, and of millions of millions, is adequate to a complete supply of these necessities and conveniences. With such accommodations, thus obtained, the appetite is keener, the digestion more easy and perfect, and repose is more refreshing, than among the most abundant superfluities and the rarest luxuries. For what reason, then, are any mortals averse to the situation of the farmer, mechanic, or laborer? Why do we tempt the seas and encompass the globe? Why do any men affront heaven and earth to accumulate wealth, which will forever be useless to them? Why do we make an ostentatious display of riches? Why should any man be proud of his purse, houses, lands, or gardens? or, in better words, why should the rich man glory in his riches? What connection can there be between wealth and pride?

The answer to all these questions is, *because riches attract the attention, consideration, and congratulations of mankind*; it is not because the rich have really more of ease or pleasure than the poor. Riches force the opinion on a man that he is the object of the congratulations of others, and he feels that they attract the complaisance of the public. His senses all inform him, that his neighbors have a natural disposition to harmonize with all those pleasing emotions and agreeable sensations, which the elegant accommodations around him are supposed to excite.

His imagination expands, and his heart dilates at these charming illusions. His attachment to his possessions increases as fast as his desire to accumulate more; not for the purposes of beneficence or utility, but from the desire of illustration.

Why, on the other hand, should any man be ashamed to make known his poverty? Why should those who have been rich, or educated in the houses of the rich, entertain such an aversion, or be agitated with such terror, at the prospect of losing their property? or of being reduced to live at a humbler table? in a meaner house? to walk, instead of riding? or to ride without their accustomed equipage or retinue? Why do we hear of madness, melancholy, and suicides, upon bankruptcy, loss of ships, or any other sudden fall from opulence to indigence, or mediocrity? Ask your reason, what disgrace there can be in poverty? What moral sentiment of approbation, praise, or honor can there be in a palace? What dishonor in a cottage? What glory in a coach? What shame in a wagon? Is not the sense of propriety and sense of merit as much connected with an empty purse as a full one? May not a man be as estimable, amiable, and respectable, attended by his faithful dog, as if preceded and followed by a train of horses and servants? All these questions may be very wise, and the stoical philosophy has her answers ready. But if you ask the same questions of nature, experience, and mankind, the answers will be directly opposite to those of *Epictetus*, namely,—that there is more respectability, in the eyes of the greater part of mankind, in the gaudy trappings of wealth, than there is in genius or learning, wisdom or virtue.

The poor man's conscience is clear; yet he is ashamed. His character is irreproachable; yet he is neglected and despised. He feels himself out of the sight of others, groping in the dark. Mankind take no notice of him. He rambles and wanders unheeded. In the midst of a crowd, at church, in the market, at a play, at an execution, or coronation, he is in as much obscurity as he would be in a garret or a cellar. He is not disapproved, censured, or reproached; *he is only not seen.* This total inattention is to him mortifying, painful, and cruel. He suffers a misery from this consideration, which is sharpened by the consciousness that others have no fellow-feeling with him in this distress. If you follow these persons, however, into their scenes of life, you will find that there is a kind of figure which the meanest of them all endeavors to make; a kind of little grandeur and respect, which the most insignificant study and labor to procure in the small circle of their acquaintances. Not only the poorest mechanic, but the man who lives upon common charity, nay, the common beggars in the streets; and not only those who may be all innocent, but even those who have abandoned themselves to common infamy, as pirates, highwaymen, and common thieves, court a set of admirers, and plume themselves upon that superiority which they have, or fancy they have, over some others. There must be one, indeed, who is the last and lowest of the human species. But there is no risk in asserting, that there is no one who believes and will acknowledge himself to be the man. To be wholly overlooked, and to know it, are intolerable. Instances of this are not uncommon. When a wretch could no longer attract the notice of a man, woman, or child, he must be respectable in the eyes of his dog. "Who will love me then?" was the pathetic reply of one, who starved himself to feed his mastiff, to a charitable passenger, who advised him to kill or sell the animal. In this "*who will love me then?*" there is a key to the human heart; to the history of human life and manners; and to the rise and fall of empires. To feel ourselves unheeded, chills the most pleasing hope, damps the most fond desire, checks the most agreeable wish, disappoints the most ardent expectations of human nature.

Is there in science and letters a reward for the labor they require? Scholars learn the dead languages of antiquity, as well as the living tongues of modern nations; those of the east, as well as the west. They puzzle themselves and others with metaphysics and mathematics. They renounce their pleasures, neglect their exercises, and destroy their health, for what? Is curiosity so strong? Is the pleasure that accompanies the pursuit and acquisition of knowledge so exquisite? If *Crusoe*, on his island, had the library of *Alexandria*, and a certainty that he should never again see the face of man, would he ever open a volume? Perhaps he might; but it is very probable he would read but little. A sense of duty; a love of truth; a desire to alleviate the anxieties of ignorance, may, no doubt, have an influence on some minds. But the universal object and idol of men of letters is *reputation*. It is the *notoriety*, the *celebration*, which constitutes the charm that is to compensate the loss of appetite and sleep, and sometimes of riches and honors.

The same ardent desire of the *congratulations* of others in our joys, is the great incentive to the pursuit of honors. This might be exemplified in the career of civil and political life. That we may not be too tedious, let us instance in military glory.

Is it to be supposed that the regular standing armies of Europe engage in the service from pure motives of patriotism? Are their officers men of contemplation and devotion, who expect their reward in a future life? Is it from a sense of moral or religious duty that they risk their lives and reconcile themselves to wounds? Instances of all these kinds may be found. But if any one supposes that all or the greater part of these heroes are actuated by such principles, he will only prove that he is unacquainted with them. Can their pay be considered as an adequate encouragement? This, which is no more than a very simple and moderate subsistence, would never be a temptation to renounce the chances of fortune in other pursuits, together with the pleasures of domestic life, and submit to this most difficult and dangerous employment. No, it is the consideration and the chances of laurels which they acquire by the service.

The soldier compares himself with his fellows, and contends for promotion to be a corporal. The corporals vie with each other to be sergeants. The sergeants will mount breaches to be ensigns. And thus every man in an army is constantly aspiring to be something higher, as every citizen in the commonwealth is constantly struggling for a better rank, that he may draw the observation of more eyes.

Fifth Discourse

> The senate's thanks, the Gazette's pompous tale,
> With force resistless o'er the brave prevail.
> This power has praise, that virtue scarce can warm,
> Till fame supplies the universal charm.
>
> JOHNSON

The result of the preceding discourses is, that avarice and ambition, vanity and pride, jealousy and envy, hatred and revenge, as well as the love of knowledge and desire of fame, are very often nothing more than various modifications of that desire of the attention, consideration, and congratulations of our fellow men, which is the great spring of social activity; that all men compare themselves with others, especially those with whom they most frequently converse, those who, by their employments or amusements, professions or offices, present themselves most frequently at the same time to the view and thoughts of that public, little or great, to which every man is known; that emulations and rivalries naturally and necessarily are excited by such comparisons; that the most heroic actions in war, the sublimest virtues in peace, and the most useful industry in agriculture, arts, manufactures, and commerce, proceed from such emulations on the one hand, and jealousies, envy, enmity, hatred, revenge, quarrels, factions, seditions, and wars on the other. The final cause of this constitution of things is easy to discover. Nature has ordained it, as a constant incentive to activity and industry, that, to acquire the attention and complacency, the approbation and admiration of their fellows, men might be urged to constant exertions of beneficence. By this destination of their natures, men of all sorts, even those who have the least of reason, virtue or benevolence, are chained down to an incessant servitude to their fellow creatures; laboring without intermission to produce something which shall contribute to the comfort, convenience, pleasure, profit, or utility of some or other of the species, they are really thus constituted by their own vanity, slaves to mankind. Slaves, I say again. For what a folly is it! On a selfish system, what are the thoughts, passions, and sentiments, of mankind to us?

> "What's fame? A fancied life in others' breath." [. . .]

Eighth Discourse

> First follow nature; and your judgment frame
> By her just standard, which is still the same.
>
> POPE

The world grows more enlightened. Knowledge is more equally diffused. Newspapers, magazines, and circulating libraries have made mankind wiser. Titles and distinctions, ranks and orders, parade and ceremony, are all going out of fashion. This is roundly and frequently asserted in the streets, and sometimes on theatres of higher *rank:* Some truth there is in it; and if the opportunity were temperately improved, to the reformation of abuses, the rectification of errors, and the dissipation of pernicious prejudices, a great advantage it might be. But, on the other hand, false inferences may be drawn from it, which may make mankind wish for the age of dragons, giants, and fairies. If all decorum, discipline, and subordination are to be destroyed, and universal Pyrrhonism, anarchy, and insecurity of property are to be introduced, nations will soon wish their books in ashes, seek for darkness and ignorance, superstition and fanaticism, as blessings, and follow the standard of the first mad despot, who, with the enthusiasm of another Mahomet, will endeavor to obtain them.

Are riches, honors, and beauty going out of fashion? Is not the rage for them, on the contrary, increased faster than improvement in knowledge? As long as either of these are in vogue, will there not be emulations and rivalries? Does not the increase of knowledge in any man increase his emulation; and the diffusion of knowledge among men multiply rivalries? Has the progress of science, arts, and letters yet discovered that there are no passions in human nature? no ambition, avarice, or desire of fame? Are these passions cooled, diminished, or extinguished? Is the rage for admiration less ardent in men or women? Have these propensities less a tendency to divisions, controversies, seditions, mutinies, and civil wars than formerly? On the contrary, the more knowledge is diffused, the more the passions are extended, and the more furious they grow. Had Cicero less vanity, or Cæsar less ambition, for their vast erudition? Had the King of Prussia less of one than the other? There is no connection in the mind between science and passion, by which the former can extinguish or diminish the latter. It on the contrary sometimes increases them by giving them exercise. [. . .]

The increase and dissemination of knowledge, instead of rendering unnecessary the checks of emulation and the balances of rivalry in the orders of society and constitution of government, augment the necessity of both. It becomes the more indispensable that every man should know his place, and be made to keep it. Bad men increase in knowledge as fast as good men; and science, arts, taste, sense, and letters, are employed for the purposes of injustice and tyranny, as well as those of law and liberty; for corruption, as well as for virtue.

FRENCHMEN! Act and think like yourselves! confessing human nature, be magnanimous and wise. Acknowledging and boasting yourselves to be men, avow the feelings of men. The affectation of being exempted from passions is inhuman. The grave pretension to such singularity is solemn hypocrisy. Both are unworthy of your frank and generous natures. Consider that government is intended to set bounds to passions which nature has not limited; and to assist reason, conscience, justice, and truth, in controlling interests, which, without it, would be as unjust as uncontrollable.[1]

AMERICANS! Rejoice, that from experience you have learned wisdom; and instead of whimsical and fantastical projects, you have adopted a promising essay towards a well-ordered government. Instead of following any foreign example, to return to *the legislation of confusion*, contemplate the means of restoring decency, honesty, and order in society, by preserving and completing, if any thing should be found necessary to complete the balance of your government. In a well-balanced government, reason, conscience, truth, and virtue, must be respected by all parties, and exerted for the public good. Advert to the principles on which you commenced that glorious self-defence, which, if you behave with steadiness and consistency, may ultimately loosen the chains of all mankind. If you will take the trouble to read over the memorable proceedings of the town of Boston, on the twenty-eighth day of October, 1772, when the Committee of Correspondence of twenty-one persons was appointed to state the rights of the colonists as men, as Christians, and as subjects, and to publish them to the world, with the infringements and violations of them, you will find the great principles of civil and religious liberty for which you have contended so successfully, and which the world is contending for after your example. I could transcribe with pleasure the whole of this immortal pamphlet, which is a real picture of the sun of liberty rising on the human race; but shall select only a few words more directly to the present purpose.

"The first fundamental, positive law of all commonwealths or states is the establishment of the legislative power." Page 9.

"It is absolutely necessary in a mixed government like that of this province, that a *due proportion* or *balance* of power should be established among the

1. Americans paid no attention or regard to this. And a blind, mad rivalry between the north and the south is destroying all morality and sound policy. God grant that division, civil war, murders, assassination, and massacres may not soon grow out of these rivalries of states, families, and individuals.

several branches of the legislative. Our ancestors received from King William and Queen Mary a charter, by which it was understood by both parties in the contract, that such a proportion or balance was fixed; and, therefore, every thing which renders any one branch of the legislative more independent of the other two than it was originally designed, is an alteration of the constitution."

AMERICANS! in your Congress at Philadelphia, on Friday, the fourteenth day of October, 1774, you laid down the fundamental principles for which you were about to contend, and from which it is to be hoped you will never depart. For asserting and vindicating your rights and liberties, you declared, "That, by the immutable laws of nature, the principles of the English constitution and your several charters or compacts, you were entitled to life, liberty, and property; that your ancestors were entitled to all the rights, liberties, and immunities of free and natural born subjects in England; that you, their descendants, were entitled to the exercise and enjoyment of all such of them as your local and other circumstances enabled you to exercise and enjoy. That the foundation of English liberty and of all free governments, is a right in the people to participate in their legislative council. That you were entitled to the common law of England, and more especially to the great and inestimable privilege of being tried by your peers of the vicinage, according to the course of that law. *That it is indispensably necessary to good government, and rendered essential by the English constitution, that the constituent branches of the legislature be independent of each other*." These among others you then claimed, demanded, and insisted on, as your indubitable rights and liberties. These are the principles on which you first united and associated, and if you steadily and consistently maintain them, they will not only secure freedom and happiness to yourselves and your posterity, but your example will be imitated by all Europe, and in time, perhaps, by all mankind. The nations are in travail, and great events must have birth.

"The minds of men are in movement from the Boristhenes to the Atlantic. Agitated with new and strong emotions, they swell and heave beneath oppression, as the seas within the polar circle, at the approach of spring. The genius of philosophy, with the touch of Ithuriel's spear, is trying the establishments of the earth. The various forms of prejudice, superstition, and servility, start up in their true shapes, which had long imposed upon the world, under the revered semblances of honor, faith, and loyalty. Whatever is loose must be shaken; whatever is corrupted must be lopped away; whatever is not built on the broad basis of public utility must be thrown to the ground. Obscure murmurs gather and swell into a tempest; the spirit of inquiry, like a severe and searching wind, penetrates every part of the great body politic; and whatever is unsound, whatever is infirm, shrinks at the visitation. Liberty, led by philosophy, diffuses her blessings to every class of men; and even extends a smile of hope and promise to the poor African, the victim of hard, impenetrable avarice. Man, as man, becomes an object of respect. Tenets are transferred from theory to practice. The glowing sentiment, the lofty speculation, no longer serve 'but to adorn the pages of a book.' They are brought home to men's business and bosoms; and what, some centuries ago, it was daring but to think, and dangerous to express, is now realized and carried into effect. Systems are analyzed into their first principles, and principles are fairly pursued to their legitimate consequences."

This is all enchanting. But amidst our enthusiasm, there is great reason to pause and preserve our sobriety. It is true that the first empire of the world is breaking the fetters of human reason and exerting the energies of redeemed liberty. In the glowing ardor of her zeal, she condescends, Americans, to pay the most scrupulous attention to your maxims, principles, and example. There is reason to fear she has copied from you errors which have cost you very dear. Assist her, by your example, to rectify them before they involve her in calamities as much greater than yours, as her population is more unwieldy, and her situation more exposed to the baleful influence of rival neighbors. Amidst all their exultations, Americans and Frenchmen should remember that the perfectibility of man is only human and terrestrial perfectibility. Cold will still freeze, and fire will never cease to burn; disease and vice will continue to disorder, and death to terrify mankind. Emulation next to self-preservation will forever be the great spring of human actions, and the balance of a well-ordered government will alone be able to prevent that emulation from degenerating into dangerous ambition, irregular rivalries, destructive factions, wasting seditions, and bloody, civil wars.

The great question will forever remain, *who shall work?* Our species cannot all be idle. Leisure for study must ever be the portion of a few. The number employed in government must forever be very small. Food, raiment, and habitations, the indispensable wants of all, are not to be obtained without the continual toil of ninety-nine in a hundred of mankind. As rest is rapture to the weary man, those who labor little will always be envied by those who labor much, though the latter in reality be probably the most enviable. With all the encouragements, public and private, which can ever be given to general education, and it is scarcely possible they should be too many or too great, the laboring part of the people can never be learned. The controversy between the rich and the poor, the laborious and the idle, the learned and the ignorant, distinctions as old as the creation, and as extensive as the globe, distinctions which no art or policy, no degree of virtue or philosophy can ever wholly destroy, will continue, and rivalries will spring out of them. These parties will be represented in the legislature, and must be balanced, or one will oppress the other. There will never probably be found any other mode of establishing such an equilibrium, than by constituting the representation of each an independent branch of the legislature, and an independent executive authority, such as that in our government, to be a third branch and a mediator or an arbitrator between them. Property must be secured, or liberty cannot exist. But if unlimited or unbalanced power of disposing property, be put into the hands of those who have no property, France will find, as we have found, the lamb committed to the custody of the wolf. In such a case, all the pathetic exhortations and addresses of the national assembly to the people, to respect property, will be regarded no more than the warbles of the songsters of the forest. The great art of lawgiving consists in balancing the poor against the rich in the legislature, and in constituting the legislative a perfect balance against the executive power, at the same time that no individual or party can become its rival. The essence of a free government consists in an effectual control of rivalries. The executive and the legislative powers are natural rivals; and if each has not an effectual control over the other, the weaker will ever be the lamb in the paws of the wolf. The nation which will not adopt an equilibrium of power must adopt a despotism. [. . .]

6

Liberty, Authority, and the Implementation of Government

In October 1788, following the ratification of the new federal Constitution, the Continental Congress conducted its last business and adjourned for good. In the process, Americans closed a period of extended and anxious constitutional debate. The Federalist victory seemed to presage political tranquillity, as Anti-Federalists, who shared the Federalist fear of anarchy, fell into line in support of the new national government. But within just a few years, American statesmen and politicians again divided into bitter and partisan argument. The stakes for which they contended seemed every bit as high as those that had characterized the ratification debates. As evidenced by the selections in this chapter, the task of implementing the new government, and the practical policies that it would pursue, rapidly produced fundamental contention over just what kind of place the new nation would be.

Presidential electors meeting in the various state capitols on February 4, 1789, unanimously chose George Washington to serve as the nation's first president. Washington, who enjoyed the admiration, indeed reverence, of most Americans, brought immediate legitimacy to the new government. Washington further enhanced the government's authority by his cabinet choices: Thomas Jefferson, as secretary of state; the brilliant Alexander Hamilton as secretary of the treasury; and Edmund Randolph, as attorney general. Henry Knox, a massive man and well respected, had served as secretary of war since 1785 and remained at that post under Washington, establishing continuity with the earlier regime. All of them were nationalists. All of them, save Jefferson, had been strong proponents of the Constitution during the ratification debates.

Hamilton's efforts to restore financial stability to the national government led to the first fractures. Throughout 1790 and early 1791, Hamilton produced a series of reports that aimed to provide the United States with the financial infrastructure to become a major commercial and military power, while at the same time solidifying the country's most powerful financial interests in support of the national government. Hamilton took as his model the government of Great Britain, which—however reviled by many American republicans—possessed the robust fiscal institutions necessary to sustain and wield enormous power throughout the world. He proposed to create a national debt; assume federal responsibility for the Revolutionary War debts of the states (in the process rewarding financial speculators); charter a national bank to serve as the nation's financial agent; establish excise taxes, including a tax on whiskey, in order to provide a steady stream of revenue for the national government; and implement proactive government support for manufacturing enterprise.

Hamilton's vision for America as a great power, capable of projecting force and power in the world on an equal standing with the great European states, and the means he proposed to achieve it, alarmed Americans committed to a more republican vision of American greatness. Jefferson and James Madison assumed leadership of the "republican interest" that the Hamiltonian program elicited. Hamilton's proposals, they feared, siphoned monies from agriculture to support manufacturing, commercial, and financial interests. In the judgment of Hamilton's critics, a republican state required vigilant and committed citizens in order to sustain freedom and to stave off corruption. Independent, landowning farmers, in this view, were the most inclined to develop the kind of civic character necessary to sustain republican government. Thus, proposals that weakened agriculture threatened the entire project of crafting a stable polity on the basis of popular sovereignty. For Jefferson, Madison, and those who agreed with them, the various features of Hamilton's fiscal plan loomed darkly as a menace to the legacy of the American Revolution.

By mid-1793, Jefferson had broken with Washington's administration, resigning his position as secretary of state. In the same year, the French Revolution turned radical and bloody. Revolutionaries in France executed the king, numerous members of the aristocracy, and priests. When war broke out between Great Britain and France, partisans in the United States aligned with either France or Britain. Federalists tended to see in the French Revolution the specter of anarchy; Jefferson and Madison emphasized French republicanism and the invaluable support France had provided during the American Revolution. Dispute over the merits of Hamilton's fiscal plan, and the deeper and competing visions for America's future that that dispute clarified, increasingly employed symbols and rhetoric derived from the French Revolution. Federalists understood themselves to be the legitimate defenders of law, order, stability, and religion, and as argument grew steadily more heated, they characterized their opponents as wild-eyed radical enemies of those values. The politicians and statesmen who opposed them, meanwhile, feared the resurrection of something akin to monarchical tyranny, reading into Federalist celebration of Great Britain an underlying hostility to popular government.

Federalist suspicion that many Americans lacked the capacity for prudent self-government received fresh confirmation in 1794. In that year backcountry farmers in several states organized to prevent collection of the national excise tax on distilled spirits, an element of Hamilton's financial program. Living in regions cut off from commercial markets by bad roads and primitive waterways, these farmers realized that the only profitable way to transport and sell their grain was to distill it. Just as earlier "rebels" had evoked the spirit of liberty before the Revolution, and again during Shays' Rebellion, supporters of the Whiskey Rebellion viewed the new tax as an exercise in tyranny. Federalists, however, emphasized the importance of the rule of law and the maintenance of public order. Washington sent an army of some 13,000 militiamen to disperse the "rebellion."

By the mid-1790s, the political comity that ratification of the Constitution had seemed to promise dissolved into discord and distrust. The opposition had coalesced into a recognizable political party. Whereas Federalists tended to emphasize ordered liberty, and distrusted the capacity of average citizens to govern themselves prudentially, the Republican Party of Jefferson and Madison aligned itself with popular democracy and expressed greater faith in the capacity of most citizens to make wise public decisions. The new party rapidly acquired an infrastructure to disseminate its critique of Federalist governance to the public. A fiercely partisan Republican press disparaged both Federalist policies and the character of Federalist politicians.

In a society in which gentlemen still valued their personal honor, and in which legitimate claims to govern were intimately tied to personal character, the emergence of an opposition party seemed to portend not a healthy and vigorous democratic public sphere but rather demagoguery and anarchy. Federalists, who identified themselves as *the* legitimate government, perceived the new party as a fundamental threat to the newly installed national constitution. In 1798, they overreacted, passing national legislation designed to silence their critics. In order to limit the perceived threat from radical French émigrés, they extended the residency requirement for citizenship from five to fourteen years and passed the Alien Act to permit the government to deport noncitizens whom they deemed a threat to public order. Most dangerous of all, from the perspective of the Republican Party, they passed the Sedition Act, which made it a crime for any person to write, print, or publish "any false, scandalous and malicious writing . . . against the government of the United States, or either house of Congress . . . , or the President . . . with intent to defame . . . or to bring them, or either of them, into contempt or disrepute; or to excite against them, or either or any of them, the hatred of the good people of the United States." Jefferson and Madison responded by drafting the Virginia and Kentucky Resolutions, the latter raising the constitutional specter of nullification, and both challenging the Sedition Act on First Amendment grounds. The Federalist overreaction in 1798 powerfully energized supporters of the Republican Party and contributed to Jefferson's victory in the election of 1800.

Henry Knox

Report on White Outrages (1788)

[The secretary of war reports] That it appears . . . that the white inhabitants on the frontiers of North Carolina in the vicinity of Chota on the Tenessee river, have frequently committed the most unprovoked and direct outrages against the Cherokee Indians.

That this unworthy conduct is an open violation of the treaty of peace made by the United States with the said Indians at Hopewell on the Keowee the 30th of November 1785.

That the said enormities have arisen at length to such an height as to amount to an actual although informal war of the said white inhabitants against the said Cherokees.

That the unjustifiable conduct of the said inhabitants has most probably been dictated by the avaricious desire of obtaining the fertile lands possessed by the said Indians of which and particularly of their ancient town of Chota they are exceedingly tenacious. . . .

That . . . by an upright and honorable construction of the treaty of Hopewell the United States have pledged themselves for the protection of the said Indians within the boundaries described by the said treaty and that the principles of good Faith sound policy and every respect which a nation, owes to its own reputation and dignity require if the union possess sufficient power that it be exerted to enforce a due observance of the said treaty.

That in order to vindicate the sovereignty of the Union from reproach, your secretary is of opinion, that, the sentiments, and decision, of Congress should be fully expressed to the said white inhabitants, who have so flagitiously stained the American name.

That the agent of Indian affairs should disperse among the said people a proclamation to be issued by Congress on the subject. That the said proclamation should recite such parts of said treaty as are obligatory on the Union and a declaration of the firm determination of Congress to enforce the same. That all persons who have settled on any of the said lands unless the same shall have been fairly purchased of the said Indians shall be warned at their peril to depart previously to a day to be affixed.

That in order to carry efficiently into effect the determinations of Congress the commanding officer of the troops on the Ohio should be directed to make himself acquainted of the best routes by which a body of three hundred men could be transported most easily and expeditiously to Chota on the Tenessee river, and report the same to the secretary at war.

That in case the Proclamation of Congress should be attended with no effect that the said commanding officer should be directed to move as early in the spring of the next year as the season should admit with a body of three hundred troops to Chota and there to act according to the special instructions he shall receive from the Secretary at War. [. . .]

Your Secretary begs leave to observe that he is utterly at a loss to devise any other mode of correcting effectually the evils specified than the one herein proposed. That he conceives it of the highest importance to the peace of the frontiers that all the Indian tribes should rely with security on the treaties they have made or shall make with the United States. That unless this shall be the case the powerful tribes of the Creeks Choctaws and Chickesaws will be able to keep the frontiers of the southern states constantly embroiled with hostilities, and that all the other tribes will have good grounds not only according to their own opinions but according to the impartial judgements of the civilized part of the human race for waging perpetual war against the citizens of the United States. [. . .]

Tribal Council of the Delaware and Twelve Additional Tribes (1793)

Money to us is of no value, and to most of us unknown; and as no consideration whatever can induce us to sell the lands on which we get sustenance for our women and children, we hope we may be allowed to point out a mode by which your settlers may be easily removed, and peace thereby obtained.

We know that these settlers are poor, or they would never have ventured to live in a country which has been in continual trouble ever since they crossed the Ohio. Divide, therefore, this large sum of money which you have offered us among these people; give to each, also, a proportion of what you say you would give to us annually, over and above this very large sum of money, and we are persuaded they would most readily accept of it in lieu of the lands you sold them. If you add, also, the great sums you must expend in raising and paying armies with a view to force us to yield you our country, you will certainly have more than sufficient for the purpose of repaying these settlers for all their labor and their improvements.

You have talked to us about concessions. It appears strange that you should expect any from us, who have only been defending our just rights against your invasions. We want peace. Restore to us our country, and we shall be enemies no longer.

We desire you to consider, brothers, that our only demand is the peaceable possession of a small part of our once great country. Look back and review the lands from whence we have been driven to this spot. We can retreat no farther, because the country behind hardly affords food for its present inhabitants, and we have therefore resolved to leave our bones in this small space to which we are now confined.

Red Jacket (Segoyewatha)

Speech in Response to White Missionaries (1805)

Friend and Brother: It was the will of the Great Spirit that we should meet together this day. He orders all things, and has given us a fine day for our council. He has taken his garment from before the sun and caused it to shine with brightness upon us. For all these things we thank the Great Ruler, and Him *only!*

Brother, this council-fire was kindled by you. It was at your request that we came together at this time. We have listened with joy to what you have said. You requested us to speak our minds freely. This gives us great joy, for we now consider that we stand upright before you and can speak what we think. All have heard your voice and can speak to you as one man. Our minds are agreed.

Brother, listen to what we say. There was a time when our forefathers owned this great island. Their seats extended from the rising to the setting sun. The Great Spirit had made it for the use of Indians. He had created the buffalo, the deer and other animals for food. He had made the bear and the beaver. Their skins served us for clothing. He had scattered them over the country and taught us how to take them. He had caused the earth to produce corn for bread. All this he had done for his red children because he loved them. If we had some disputes about our hunting-ground, they were generally settled without the shedding of much blood. But an evil day came upon us. Your forefathers crossed the great water and landed upon this island. Their numbers were small. They found us friends and not enemies. They told us they had fled from their own country on account of wicked men, and had come here to enjoy their religion. They asked for a small seat. We took pity on them and granted their request, and they sat down amongst us. We gave them corn and meat; they gave us poison [liquor] in return.

The white people, brother, had now found our country. Tidings were carried back, and more came amongst us. Yet we did not fear them. We took them to be friends. They called us brothers; we believed them, and gave them a larger seat. At length their numbers had greatly increased. They wanted more land; they wanted our country. Our eyes were opened, and our minds became uneasy. Wars took place. Indians were hired to fight against Indians, and many of our people were destroyed. They also brought strong liquor amongst us. It was strong and powerful and has slain thousands.

Brother, our seats were once large, and yours were small. You have now become a great people, and we have scarcely a place left to spread our blankets. You have got our country, but are not satisfied; you want to force your religion upon us.

Brother, continue to listen. You say that you are sent to instruct us how to worship the Great Spirit agreeable to his mind; and if we do not take hold of the religion which you white people teach, we shall be unhappy hereafter. You say that you are right, and we are lost. How do we know this to be true? We understand that your religion is written in a book. If it was intended for us as well as you, why has not the Great Spirit given to us—and not only to us, but to our forefathers—the knowledge of that book, with the means of understanding it rightly? We only know what you tell us about it. How shall we know when to believe, being so often deceived by the white people?

Brother, you say there is but one way to worship and serve the Great Spirit. If there is but one religion, why do you white people differ so much about it? Why not all agree, as you can all read the book?

Brother, we do not understand these things. We are told that your religion was given to your forefathers, and has been handed down from father to son. We, also, have a religion which was given to our forefathers, and has been handed down to us, their children. We worship in that way. It teaches us to be thankful for all the favors we receive; to love each other, and be united. We never quarrel about religion, because it is a matter which concerns each man and the Great Spirit.

Brother, we do not wish to destroy your religion or take it from you; we only want to enjoy our own.

Brother, we have been told that you have been preaching to the white people in this place. These people are our neighbors. We are acquainted with them. We will wait a little while and see what effect your preaching has upon them. If we find it does them good, makes them honest and less disposed to cheat Indians, we will consider again of what you have said.

Brother, you have now heard our talk, and this is all we have to say at present. As we are going to part, we will come and take you by the hand, and hope the Great Spirit will protect you on your journey, and return you safely to your friends.

Speech in Response to Land Speculators (1811)

Brother!—We opened our ears to the talk you lately delivered to us, at our council-fire. In doing important business it is best not to tell long stories, but come to it in a few words. We therefore shall not repeat your talk, which is fresh in our minds. We have well considered it, and the advantage and disadvantages of your offers. We request your attention to our answer, which is not from the speaker alone, but from all the Sachems and Chiefs now around our council-fire.

Brother!—We know that great men, as well as great nations, have different interests and different minds, and do not see the same light—but we hope our answer will be agreeable to you and your employers.

Brother!—Your application for the purchase of our lands is to our minds very extraordinary. It has been made in a crooked manner. You have not walked in the straight path pointed out by the great Council of your nation. You have no writings from your great Father, the President. In making up our minds we have looked back, and remembered how the Yorkers purchased our lands in former times. They bought them, piece after piece—for a little money paid to a few men in our nation, and not to all our brethren—until our planting and hunting-grounds have become very small, and if we sell *them*, we know not where to spread our blankets.

Brother!—You tell us your employers have purchased of the Council of Yorkers a right to buy our lands. We do not understand how this can be. The lands do not belong to the Yorkers; they are ours, and were given to us by the Great Spirit.

Brother!—We think it strange that you should jump over the lands of our brethren in the East to come to our council-fire so far off, to get our lands. When we sold our lands in the East to the white people, we determined never to sell those we kept, which are as small as we can comfortably live on.

Brother!—You want us to travel with you and look for new lands. If we should sell our lands and move off into a distant country towards the setting sun, we should be looked upon in the country to which we go as foreigners and strangers. We should be despised by the red as well as the white men, and we should soon be surrounded by the white people, who will there also kill our game, and come upon our lands and try to get them from us.

Brother!—We are determined not to sell our lands, but to continue on them. We like them. They are fruitful, and produce us corn in abundance for the support of our women and children, and grass and herbs for our cattle.

Brother!—At the treaties held for the purchase of our lands, the white men, with sweet voices and smiling faces, told us they loved us, and that they would not cheat us, but that the king's children on the other side of the lake would cheat us. When we go on the other side of the lake, the king's children tell us *your* people will cheat us. These things puzzle our heads, and we believe that the Indians must take care of themselves, and not trust either in your people, or in the king's children.

Brother!—At a late council we requested our agents to tell you that we would not sell our lands, and we think you have not spoken to our agents, or they would have told you so, and we should not have met you at our council-fire at this time.

Brother!—The white people buy and sell false rights to our lands, and your employers have, you say, paid a great price for their rights. They must have a plenty of money to spend it in buying false rights to lands belonging to Indians. The loss of it will not hurt them, but our lands are of great value to us, and we wish you to go back with our talk to your employers, and tell them and the Yorkers that they have no right to buy and sell false rights to our lands.

Brother!—We hope you clearly understand the ideas we have offered. This is all we have to say.

GEORGE WASHINGTON

Inaugural Address (April 30, 1789)

Fellow Citizens of the Senate
and the House of Representatives.

Among the vicissitudes incident to life, no event could have filled me with greater anxieties than that of which the notification was transmitted by your order, and received on the fourteenth day of the present month. On the one hand, I was summoned by my Country, whose voice I can never hear but with veneration and love, from a retreat which I had chosen with the fondest predilection, and, in my flattering hopes, with an immutable decision, as the asylum of my declining years: a retreat which was rendered every day more necessary as well as more dear to me, by the addition of habit to inclination, and of frequent interruptions in my health to the gradual waste committed on it by time. On the other hand, the magnitude and difficulty of the trust to which the voice of my Country called me, being sufficient to awaken in the wisest and most experienced of her citizens, a distrustful scrutiny into his qualifications, could not but overwhelm with dispondence, one, who, inheriting inferior endowments from nature and unpractised in the duties of civil administration, ought to be peculiarly conscious of his own deficiencies. In this conflict of emotions, all I dare aver, is, that it has been my faithful study to collect my duty from a just appreciation of every circumstance, by which it might be affected. All I dare hope, is, that, if in executing this task I have been too much swayed by a grateful remembrance of former instances, or by an affectionate sensibility to this transcendent proof, of the confidence of my fellow-citizens; and have thence too little consulted my incapacity as well as disinclination for the weighty and untried cares before me; my error will be palliated by the motives which misled me, and its consequences be judged by my Country, with some share of the partiality in which they originated.

Such being the impressions under which I have, in obedience to the public summons, repaired to the present station; it would be peculiarly improper to omit in this first official Act, my fervent supplications to that Almighty Being who rules over the Universe, who presides in the Councils of Nations, and whose providential aids can supply every human defect, that his benediction may consecrate to the liberties and happiness of the People of the United States, a Government instituted by themselves for these essential purposes: and may enable every instrument employed in its administration to execute with success, the functions allotted to his charge. In tendering this homage to the Great Author of every public and private good I assure myself that it expresses your sentiments not less than my own; nor those of my fellow-citizens at large, less than either. No People can be bound to acknowledge and adore the invisible hand, which conducts the Affairs of men more than the People of the United States. Every step, by which they have advanced to the character of an independent nation, seems to have been distinguished by some token of providential agency. And in the important revolution just accomplished in the system of their United Government, the tranquil deliberations and voluntary consent of so many distinct communities, from which the event has resulted, cannot be compared with the means by which most Governments have been established, without some return of pious gratitude along with an humble anticipation of the future blessings which the past seem to presage. These reflections, arising out of the present crisis, have forced themselves too strongly on my mind to be suppressed. You will join with me I trust in thinking, that there are none under the influence of which, the proceedings of a new and free Government can more auspiciously commence.

By the article establishing the Executive Department, it is made the duty of the President "to recommend to your consideration, such measures as he shall judge necessary and expedient." The circumstances under which I now meet you, will acquit me from entering into that subject, farther than to refer to the Great Constitutional Charter under which you are assembled; and which, in defining your powers, designates the objects to which your attention is to be given. It will be more consistent with those circumstances, and far more congenial with the feelings which actuate me, to substitute, in place of a recommendation of particular measures, the tribute that is due to the talents, the rectitude, and the patriotism which adorn the characters selected to devise and adopt them. In these honorable qualifications, I behold the surest pledges, that as on one side, no local prejudices, or attachments; no seperate views, nor party animosities, will misdirect the comprehensive and equal eye which ought to watch over this great assemblage of communities and interests: so, on another, that the foundations of our National policy will be laid in the pure and immutable principles of private morality; and the pre-eminence of a free Government, be exemplified by all the attributes which can win the affections of its Citizens, and command the respect of the world.

I dwell on this prospect with every satisfaction which an ardent love for my Country can inspire:

since there is no truth more thoroughly established, than that there exists in the oeconomy and course of nature, an indissoluble union between virtue and happiness, between duty and advantage, between the genuine maxims of an honest and magnanimous policy, and the solid rewards of public prosperity and felicity: Since we ought to be no less persuaded that the propitious smiles of Heaven, can never be expected on a nation that disregards the eternal rules of order and right, which Heaven itself has ordained: And since the preservation of the sacred fire of liberty, and the destiny of the Republican model of Government, are justly considered as deeply, perhaps as finally staked, on the experiment entrusted to the hands of the American people.

Besides the ordinary objects submitted to your care, it will remain with your judgment to decide, how far an exercise of the occasional power delegated by the Fifth article of the Constitution is rendered expedient at the present juncture by the nature of objections which have been urged against the System, or by the degree of inquietude which has given birth to them. Instead of undertaking particular recommendations on this subject, in which I could be guided by no lights derived from official opportunities, I shall again give way to my entire confidence in your discernment and pursuit of the public good: For I assure myself that whilst you carefully avoid every alteration which might endanger the benefits of an United and effective Government, or which ought to await the future lessons of experience; a reverence for the characteristic rights of freemen, and a regard for the public harmony, will sufficiently influence your deliberations on the question how far the former can be more impregnably fortified, or the latter be safely and advantageously promoted.

To the preceeding observations I have one to add, which will be most properly addressed to the House of Representatives. It concerns myself, and will therefore be as brief as possible. When I was first honoured with a call into the Service of my Country, then on the eve of an arduous struggle for its liberties, the light in which I contemplated my duty required that I should renounce every pecuniary compensation. From this resolution I have in no instance departed. And being still under the impressions which produced it, I must decline as inapplicable to myself, any share in the personal emoluments, which may be indispensably included in a permanent provision for the Executive Department; and must accordingly pray that the pecuniary estimates for the Station in which I am placed, may, during my continuance in it, be limited to such actual expenditures as the public good may be thought to require.

Having thus imported to you my sentiments, as they have been awakened by the occasion which brings us together, I shall take my present leave; but not without resorting once more to the benign parent of the human race, in humble supplication that since he has been pleased to favour the American people, with opportunities for deliberating in perfect tranquility, and dispositions for deciding with unparellelled unanimity on a form of Government, for the security of their Union, and the advancement of their happiness; so his divine blessing may be equally *conspicuous* in the enlarged views, the temperate consultations, and the wise measures on which the success of this Government must depend.

Letter to the United Baptist Churches of Virginia (May 1789)

Gentlemen,

I request that you will accept my best acknowledgments for your congratulation on my appointment to the first office in the nation. The kind manner in which you mention my past conduct equally claims the expression of my gratitude.

After we had, by the smiles of Heaven on our exertions, obtained the object for which we contended, I retired at the conclusion of the war, with an idea that my country could have no farther occasion for my services, and with the intention of never entering again into public life: But when the exigence of my country seemed to require me once more to engage in public affairs, an honest conviction of duty superseded my former resolution, and became my apology for deviating from the happy plan which I had adopted.

If I could have entertained the slightest apprehension that the Constitution framed in the Convention, where I had the honor to preside, might possibly endanger the religious rights of any ecclesiastical Society, certainly I would never have placed my signature to it; and if I could now conceive that the general Government might ever be so administered as to render the liberty of conscience insecure, I beg you will be persuaded that no one would be more zealous than myself to establish effectual barriers against the horrors of spiritual tyranny, and every species of religious persecution—For you, doubtless, remember that I have often expressed my sentiment, that every man, conducting himself as a good citizen, and being accountable to God alone for his religious opinions, ought to be protected in worshipping the Deity according to the dictates of his own conscience.

While I recollect with satisfaction that the religious Society of which you are Members, have been, throughout America, uniformly, and almost unanimously, the firm friends to civil liberty, and the persevering Promoters of our glorious revolution; I cannot hesitate to believe that they will be the faithful Supporters of a free, yet efficient, general Government. Under this pleasing expectation I rejoice to assure them that they may rely on my best wishes and endeavors to advance their prosperity.

In the meantime be assured, Gentlemen, that I entertain a proper sense of your fervent supplications to God for my temporal and eternal happiness.

James Madison and Alexander White

Debates in the First Congress (June 16–18, 1789)

Mr. Madison. [. . .] I am clearly of opinion with the gentleman from South-Carolina (Mr. Smith,) that we ought in this and every other case to adhere to the constitution, so far as it will serve as a guide to us, and that we ought not to be swayed in our decisions by the splendor of the character of the present chief magistrate, but to consider it with respect to the merit of men who, in the ordinary course of things, may be supposed to fill the chair. I believe the power here declared is a high one, and in some respects a dangerous one; but in order to come to a right decision on this point, we must consider both sides of the question. The possible abuses which may spring from the single will of the first magistrate, and the abuse which may spring from the combined will of the executive and the senatorial qualification.

When we consider that the first magistrate is to be appointed at present by the suffrages of three millions of people, and in all human probability in a few years time by double that number, it is not to be presumed that a vicious or bad character will be selected. If the government of any country on the face of the earth was ever effectually guarded against the election of ambitious or designing characters to the first office of the state, I think it may with truth be said to be the case under the constitution of the United States. With all the infirmities incident to a popular election, corrected by the particular mode of conducting it, as directed under the present system, I think we may fairly calculate, that the instances will be very rare in which an unworthy man will receive that mark of the public confidence which is required to designate the president of the United States. Where the people are disposed to give so great an elevation to one of their fellow citizens, I own that I am not afraid to place my confidence in him; especially when I know he is impeachable for any crime or misdemeanor, before the senate, at all times; and that at all events he is impeachable before the community at large every four years, and liable to be displaced if his conduct shall have given umbrage during the time he has been in office. Under these circumstances, although the trust is a high one, and in some degree perhaps a dangerous one, I am not sure but it will be safer here than placed where some gentlemen suppose it ought to be.

It is evidently the intention of the constitution that the first magistrate should be responsible for the executive department; so far therefore as we do not make the officers who are to aid him in the duties of that department responsible to him, he is not responsible to his country. Again, is there no danger that an officer when he is appointed by the concurrence of the senate, and has friends in that body, may chuse rather to risk his establishment on the favor of that branch, than rest it upon the discharge of his duties to the satisfaction to the executive branch, which is constitutionally authorised to inspect and controul his conduct? And if it should happen that the officers connect themselves with the senate, they may mutually support each other, and for want of efficacy reduce the power of the president to a mere vapor, in which case his responsibility would be annihilated, and the expectation of it unjust. The high executive officers, joined in cabal with the senate, would lay the foundation of discord, and end in an assumption of the executive power, only to be removed by a revolution in the government. I believe no principle is more clearly laid down in the constitution than that of responsibility. After premising this, I will proceed to an investigation of the merits of the question upon constitutional ground. [. . .]

By a strict examination of the constitution on what appears to be its true principles, and considering the great departments of the government in the relation they have to each other, I have my doubts whether we are not absolutely tied down to the construction declared in the bill. In the first section of the 1st article, it is said, that all legislative powers herein granted shall be vested in a congress of the United States. In the second article it is affirmed, that the executive power shall be vested in a president of the United States of America. In the third article it is declared, that the judicial power of the United States shall be vested in one supreme court, and in such inferior courts as congress may from time to time ordain and establish. I suppose it will be readily admitted, that so far as the constitution has separated the powers of these great departments, it would be improper to combine them together, and so far as it has left any particular department in the entire possession of the powers incident to that department, I conceive we ought not to qualify them farther than they are qualified by the constitution. The legislative powers are vested in congress, and are to be exercised by them uncontrolled by any other department, except the constitution has qualified it otherwise. The constitution has qualified the legislative power by authorising the president to object to any act it may pass, requiring, in this case two-thirds of both houses to concur in making a law; but still the absolute legislative power is vested in the congress with this qualification alone.

The constitution affirms, that the executive power shall be vested in the president: Are there exceptions to this proposition? Yes there are. The constitution says that, in appointing to office, the senate shall be associated with the president, unless in the case of inferior officers, when the law shall otherwise direct. Have we a right to extend this exception? I believe not. If the constitution has invested all executive power in the president, I venture to assert, that the legislature has no right to diminish or modify his executive authority.

The question now resolves itself into this, Is the power of displacing an executive power? I conceive that if any power whatsoever is in its nature executive it is the power of appointing, overseeing, and controlling those who execute the laws. If the constitution had not qualified the power of the president in appointing to office, by associating the senate with him in that business, would it not be clear that he would have the right by virtue of his executive power to make such appointment? Should we be authorised, in defiance of that clause in the constitution—"The executive power shall be vested in a president," to unite the senate with the president in the appointment to office? I conceive not. If it is admitted we should not be authorised to do this, I think it may be disputed whether we have a right to associate them in removing persons from office, the one power being as much of an executive nature as the other, and the first only is authorised by being excepted out of the general rule established by the constitution, in these words, "the executive power shall be vested in the president." [. . .]

Several constructions have been put upon the constitution relative to the point in question. The gentleman from Connecticut (Mr. Sherman) has advanced a doctrine which was not touched upon before. He seems to think (if I understood him right), that the power of displacing from office is subject to legislative discretion; because it having a right to create, it may limit or modify as is thought proper. I shall not say but at first view this doctrine may seem to have some plausibility: But when I consider, that the constitution clearly intended to maintain a marked distinction between the legislative, executive, and judicial powers of government; and when I consider, that if the legislature has a power, such as contended for, they may subject, and transfer at discretion, powers from one department of government to another; they may, on that principle, exclude the president altogether from exercising any authority in the removal of officers; they may give it to the senate alone, or the president and senate combined; they may vest it in the whole congress, or they may reserve it to be exercised by this house. When I consider the consequences of this doctrine, and compare them with the true principles of the constitution, I own that I cannot subscribe to it.

Another doctrine which has found very respectable friends, has been particularly advocated by the gentleman from South-Carolina (Mr. Smith). It is this; when an officer is appointed by the president and senate, he can only be displaced from malfeasance in his office by impeachment: I think this would give a stability to the executive department so far as it may be described by the heads of departments, which is more incompatible with the genius of republican government in general, and this constitution in particular, than any doctrine which has yet been proposed. The danger to liberty, the danger of mal-administration has not yet been found to lay so much in the facility of introducing improper persons into office, as in the difficulty of displacing those who are unworthy of the public trust. If it is said that an officer once appointed shall not be displaced without the formality required by impeachment, I shall be glad to know what security we have for the faithful administration of the government. Every individual in the long chain which extends from the highest to the lowest link of the executive magistracy, would find a security in his situation which would relax his fidelity and promptitude in the discharge of his duty.

The doctrine, however, which seems to stand most in opposition to the principles I contend for, is that the power to annul an appointment is in the nature of things incidental to the power which makes the appointment. I agree that if nothing more was said in the constitution than that the president, by and with the advice and consent of the senate, should appoint to office, there would be great force in saying that the power of removal resulted by a natural implication from the power of appointing. But there is another part of the constitution no less explicit than the one on which the gentleman's doctrine is founded, it is that part which declares, that the executive power shall be vested in a president of the United States. The association of the senate with the president in exercising that particular function, is an exception to this general rule; and exceptions to general rules, I conceive, are ever to be taken strictly. But there is another part of the constitution which inclines in my judgment, to favor the construction I put upon it; the president is required to take care that the laws be faithfully executed. If the duty to see the laws faithfully executed be required at the hands of the executive magistrate, it would seem that it was generally intended he should have that species of power which is necessary to accomplish that end. Now if the officer when once appointed, is not to depend upon the president for his official existence, but upon a distinct body (for where there are two negatives required either can prevent the removal), I confess I do not see how the president can take care that the laws be faithfully executed. It is true by a circuitous operation, he may obtain an impeachment, and even without this it is possible he may obtain the concurrence of the senate for the purpose of displacing an officer; but would this give that species of control to the executive magistrate which seems to be required by the constitution? I own if my opinion was not contrary to that entertained by what I suppose to be the minority on this question, I should be doubtful of being mistaken, when I discovered how inconsistent that construction would make the constitution with itself. I can hardly bring myself to imagine the wisdom of the convention who framed the constitution, contemplated such incongruity.

There is another maxim which ought to direct us in expounding the constitution, and is of great importance. It is laid down in most of the constitutions or bills of rights in the republics of America, it is to be found in the political writings of the most celebrated civilians, and is every where held as essential to the preservation of liberty, That the three great departments of government be kept separate and distinct; and if in any case they are blended, it is in order to admit a partial qualification in order more effectually to guard against an entire consolidation. I think, therefore, when we review the several parts of this constitution, when it says that the legislative powers shall be vested in a congress of the United States under certain exceptions, and the executive power vested in the president with certain exceptions, we must suppose they were intended to be kept separate in all cases in which they are not blended, and ought consequently to expound the constitution so as to blend them as little as possible.

Every thing relative to the merits of the question as distinguished from a constitutional question, seems to turn on the danger of such a power vested in the president alone. But when I consider the checks under which he lies in the exercise of this power, I own to you I feel no apprehensions but what arise from the dangers incidental to the power itself; for dangers will be incidental to it, vest it where you please. I will not reiterate what was said before with respect to the mode of election, and the extreme improbability that any citizen will be selected from the mass of citizens who is not highly distinguished by his abilities and worth; in this alone we have no small security for the faithful exercise of this power. But, throwing that out of the question, let us consider the restraints he will feel after he is placed in that elevated station. It is to be remarked that the power in this case will not consist so much in continuing a bad man in office, as in the danger of displacing a good one. Perhaps the great danger, as has been observed, of abuse in the executive power, lies in the improper continuance of bad men in office. But the power we contend for will not enable him to do this; for if an unworthy man be continued in office by an unworthy president, the house of representatives can at any time impeach him, and the senate can remove him, whether the president chuses or not. The danger then consists merely in this: the president can displace from office a man whose merits require that he should be continued in it. What will be the motives which the president can feel for such abuse of his power, and the restraints that operate to prevent it? In the first place, he will be impeachable by this house, before the senate, for such an act of mal-administration; for I contend that the wanton removal of meritorious officers would subject him to impeachment and removal from his own high trust. But what can be his motives for displacing a worthy man? It must be that he may fill the place with an unworthy creature of his own. Can he accomplish this end? No; he can place no man in the vacancy whom the senate shall not approve; and if he could fill the vacancy with the man he might chuse, I am sure he would have little inducement to make an improper removal. Let us consider the consequences. The injured man will be supported by the popular opinion; the community will take side with him against the president; it will facilitate those combinations, and give success to those exertions which will be pursued to prevent his re-election. To displace a man of high merit, and who from his station may be supposed a man of extensive influence, are considerations which will excite serious reflections beforehand in the mind of any man who may fill the presidential chair; the friends of those individuals, and the public sympathy will be against him. If this should not produce his impeachment before the senate, it will amount to an impeachment before the community, who will have the power of punishment by refusing to re-elect him. But suppose this persecuted individual, cannot obtain revenge in this mode; there are other modes in which he could make the situation of the president very inconvenient, if you suppose him resolutely bent on executing the dictates of resentment. If he had not influence enough to direct the vengeance of the whole community, he may probably be able to obtain an appointment in one or other branch of the legislature; and being a man of weight, talents and influence in either case, he may prove to the president troublesome indeed. We have seen examples in the history of other nations, which justifies the remark I now have made. Though the prerogatives of the British king are great as his rank, and it is unquestionably known that he has a positive influence over both branches of the legislative body, yet there have been examples in which the appointment and removal of ministers has been found to be dictated by one or other of those branches. Now if this is the case with an hereditary monarch, possessed of those high prerogatives and furnished with so many means of influence; can we suppose a president elected for four years only dependent upon the popular voice impeachable by the legislature? Little if at all distinguished for wealth, personal talents, or influence from the head of the department himself; I say, will he bid defiance to all these considerations, and wantonly dismiss a meritorious and virtuous officer? Such abuse of power exceeds my conception: If any thing takes place in the ordinary course of business of this kind, my imagination cannot extend to it on any rational principle. But let us not consider the question on one side only; there are dangers to be contemplated on the other. Vest this power in the senate jointly with the president, and you abolish at once that great principle of unity and responsibility in the executive department, which was intended for the security of liberty and the public good. If the president should possess alone the power of removal from office, those who are employed in the execution of the law will be in their proper situation, and the chain of dependence be preserved; the lowest officers, the middle grade, and the highest, will depend, as they ought, on the president, and the president on the community. The chain of dependence therefore terminates in the supreme body, namely, in the people; who will possess besides, in aid of their original power, the decisive engine of impeachment. Take the other supposition, that the power should be vested in the senate, on the principle that the power to displace is necessarily connected with the power to appoint. It is declared by the constitution, that we may by law vest the appointment of inferior officers, in the heads of departments, the power of removal being incidental, as stated by some gentlemen. Where does this terminate? If you begin with the subordinate officers, they are dependent on their superior, he on the next superior, and he on whom?—on the senate, a permanent body; a body, by its particular mode of election, in reality existing for ever; a body possessing that proportion of aristocratic power which the constitution no doubt thought wise to be established in the system, but which some have strongly excepted against: And let me ask gentlemen, is there equal security in this case as in the other? Shall we trust the senate, responsible to individual legislatures, rather than the person who is responsible to the whole community? It is true the senate do not hold their offices for life, like aristocracies recorded in the historic page; yet the fact is they will not possess that responsibility for the exercise of executive powers which would render it safe for us to vest such powers in them. But what an aspect will this give to the executive? Instead of keeping the departments of government distinct, you make an executive out of one branch of the legislature; you make the executive a two-headed monster, to use the expression of the gentleman from New-Hampshire (Mr. Livermore); you destroy the great principle of responsibility, and perhaps have the creature divided in its will, defeating the very purposes for which an unity in the executive was instituted. These objections do not lie against such an arrangement as the bill establishes. I conceive that the president is sufficiently accountable to the community; and if this power is vested in him, it will be vested where its nature requires it should be vested; if any thing in its nature is executive it must be that power which is employed in superintending and seeing that the laws are faithfully executed; the laws cannot be executed but by officers appointed for that purpose; therefore those who are over such officers naturally possess the executive power. If any other doctrine be admitted, what is the consequence? You may set the senate at the head of the executive department, or you may require that the officers hold their places during the pleasure of this branch of the legislature, if you cannot go so far as to say we shall appoint them; and by this means you link together two branches of the government which the preservation of liberty requires to be constantly separated.

Another species of argument has been urged against this clause. It is said, that it is improper, or at least unnecessary to come to any decision on this subject. It has been said by one gentleman, that it would be officious in this branch of the legislature to expound the constitution, so far as it relates to the division of power between the president and senate; it is incontrovertably of as much importance to this branch of the government as to any other, that the constitution should be preserved entire. It is our duty, so far as it depends upon us, to take care that the powers of the constitution be preserved entire to every department of government; the breach of the constitution in one point, will facilitate the breach in another; a breach in this point may destroy that equilibrium by which the house retains its consequence and share of power; therefore we are not chargeable with an officious interference; besides, the bill, before it can have effect, must be submitted to both those branches who are particularly interested in it; the senate may negative, or the president may object if he thinks it unconstitutional.

But the great objection drawn from the source to which the last arguments would lead us is, that the legislature itself has no right to expound the constitution; that wherever its meaning is doubtful, you must leave it to take its course, until the judiciary is called upon to declare its meaning. I acknowledge, in the ordinary course of government, that the exposition of the laws and constitution devolves upon the judicial. But, I beg to know, upon what principle it can be contended, that any one department draws from the constitution greater powers than another, in marking out the limits of the powers of the several departments. The constitution is the charter of the people to the government; it specifies certain great powers as absolutely granted, and marks out the departments to exercise them. If the constitutional boundary of either be brought into question, I do not see that any one of these independent departments has more right than another to declare their sentiments on that point. [. . .]

Mr. White—It is not contended, that the power which this bill proposes to vest is given to the president in express terms by the constitution; or that it can be inferred from any particular clause in that instrument. It is sought for from another source, the general nature of executive power. It is on this principle the clause is advocated, or I mistake the arguments urged by my colleague.[1] It was said by that gentleman, that the constitution having invested the president with a general executive power, thereby all those powers were vested which were not expressly excepted; and therefore he possessed the power of removal. This is a doctrine not to be learned in American governments; is no part of the constitution of the union. Each state has an executive magistrate; but look at his powers, and I believe it will not be found that he has in any one, of necessity, the right of appointing or removing officers. In Virginia, I know, all the great officers are appointed by the general assembly. Few, if any, of a subordinate nature are appointed by the governor, without some modification. The case is generally the same in the other states. If the doctrine of the gentleman is to be supported by examples, it must be by those brought from beyond the Atlantic; we must also look there for rules to circumscribe the latitude of this principle, if indeed it can be limited. Upon the principle by which the executive powers are expounded, must the legislative be determined. Hence we are to infer, that congress have all legislative powers not expressly excepted in the constitution. If this is the case, and the president is invested with all executive powers not excepted, I do not know that there can be a more arbitrary government. The president will have the powers of the most absolute monarch, and the legislature all the powers of the most sovereign legislature, except in those particular instances in which the constitution has defined their limits. This I take to be a clear and necessary deduction from the principle on which the clause in the bill is founded. [. . .]

1. [I.e., Madison.]

Thomas Jefferson

Letter to Nehemiah Dodge and Others, a Committee of the Danbury Baptist Association, in the State of Connecticut (January 1, 1802)

Gentlemen,

The affectionate sentiments of esteem and approbation which you are so good as to express towards me, on behalf of the Danbury Baptist Association, give me the highest satisfaction. My duties dictate a faithful and zealous pursuit of the interests of my constituents, and in proportion as they are persuaded of my fidelity to those duties, the discharge of them becomes more and more pleasing.

Believing with you that religion is a matter which lies solely between man and his God, that he owes account to none other for his faith or his worship, that the legislative powers of government reach actions only, and not opinions, I contemplate with sovereign reverence that act of the whole American people which declared that their legislature should "make no law respecting an establishment of religion, or prohibiting the free exercise thereof," thus building a wall of separation between church and State. Adhering to this expression of the supreme will of the nation in behalf of the rights of conscience, I shall see with sincere satisfaction the progress of those sentiments which tend to restore to man all his natural rights, convinced he has no natural right in opposition to his social duties.

I reciprocate your kind prayers for the protection and blessing of the common Father and Creator of man, and tender you for yourselves and your religious association, assurances of my high respect and esteem.

Letter to Benjamin Hawkins (February 18, 1803)

Washington

Dear Sir, [. . .] Altho' you will receive, thro' the official channel of the War Office, every communication necessary to develop to you our views respecting the Indians, and to direct your conduct, yet, supposing it will be satisfactory to you, and to those with whom you are placed, to understand my personal dispositions and opinions in this particular, I shall avail myself of this private letter to state them generally. I consider the business of hunting as already become insufficient to furnish clothing and subsistence to the Indians. The promotion of agriculture, therefore, and household manufacture, are essential in their preservation, and I am disposed to aid and encourage it liberally. This will enable them to live on much smaller portions of land, and indeed will render their vast forests useless but for the range of cattle; for which purpose, also, as they become better farmers, they will be found useless, and even disadvantageous. While they are learning to do better on less land, our increasing numbers will be calling for more land, and thus a coincidence of interests will be produced between those who have lands to spare, and want other necessaries, and those who have such necessaries to spare, and want lands. This commerce, then, will be for the good of both, and those who are friends to both ought to encourage it. You are in the station peculiarly charged with this interchange, and who have it peculiarly in your power to promote among the Indians a sense of the superior value of a little land, well cultivated, over a great deal, unimproved, and to encourage them to make this estimate truly. The wisdom of the animal which amputates & abandons to the hunter the parts for which he is pursued should be theirs, with this difference, that the former sacrifices what is useful, the latter what is not. In truth, the ultimate point of rest & happiness for them is to let our settlements and theirs meet and blend together, to intermix, and become one people. Incorporating themselves with us as citizens of the U.S., this is what the natural progress of things will of course bring on, and it will be better to promote than to retard it. Surely it will be better for them to be identified with us, and preserved in the occupation of their lands, than be exposed to the many casualties which may endanger them while a separate people. I have little doubt but that your reflections must have led you to view the various ways in which their history may terminate, and to see that this is the one most for their happiness. And we have already had an application from a settlement of Indians to become citizens of the U.S. It is possible, perhaps probable, that this idea may be so novel as that it might shock the Indians, were it even hinted to them. Of course, you will keep it for your own reflection; but, convinced of its soundness, feel it consistent with pure morality to lead them towards it, to familiarize them to the idea that it is for their interest to cede lands at times to the U.S. and for us thus to procure gratifications to our citizens, from time to time, by new acquisitions of land. From no quarter is there at present so strong a pressure on this subject as from Georgia for the residue of the fork of Oconee & Ockmulgee; and indeed I believe it will be difficult to resist it. As it has been mentioned that the Creeks had at one time made up their minds to sell this, and were only checked in it by some indiscretions of an individual, I am in hopes you will be able to bring them to it again. I beseech you to use your most earnest endeavors; for it will relieve us here from a great pressure, and yourself from the unreasonable suspicions of the Georgians which you notice, that you are more attached to the interests of the Indians than of the U.S. and throw cold water on their willingness to part with lands. It is so easy to excite suspicion, that none are to be wondered at; but I am in hopes it will be in your power to quash them by effecting the object. [. . .]

ALEXANDER HAMILTON

Report on Public Credit (January 9, 1790)

Treasury Department

The Secretary of the Treasury, in obedience to the resolution of the House of Representatives, of the twenty-first day of September last, has, during the recess of Congress, applied himself to the consideration of a proper plan for the support of the Public Credit, with all the attention which was due to the authority of the House, and to the magnitude of the object.

In the discharge of this duty, he has felt, in no small degree, the anxieties which naturally flow from a just estimate of the difficulty of the task, from a well-founded diffidence of his own qualifications for executing it with success, and from a deep and solemn conviction of the momentous nature of the truth contained in the resolution under which his investigations have been conducted, "That an *adequate* provision for the support of the Public Credit, is a matter of high importance to the honor and prosperity of the United States."

With an ardent desire that his well-meant endeavors may be conducive to the real advantage of the nation, and with the utmost deference to the superior judgment of the House, he now respectfully submits the result of his enquiries and reflections, to their indulgent construction.

In the opinion of the Secretary, the wisdom of the House, in giving their explicit sanction to the proposition which has been Stated, cannot but be applauded by all, who will seriously consider, and trace through their obvious consequences, these plain and undeniable truths.

That exigencies are to be expected to occur, in the affairs of nations, in which there will be a necessity for borrowing.

That loans in times of public danger, especially from foreign war, are found an indispensable resource, even to the wealthiest of them.

And that in a country, which, like this, is possessed of little active wealth, or in other words, little monied capital, the necessity for that resource, must, in such emergencies, be proportionably urgent.

And as on the one hand, the necessity for borrowing in particular emergencies cannot be doubted, so on the other, it is equally evident, that to be able to borrow upon *good terms,* it is essential that the credit of a nation should be well established.

For when the credit of a country is in any degree questionable, it never fails to give an extravagant premium, in one shape or another, upon all the loans it has occasion to make. Nor does the evil end here; the same disadvantage must be sustained upon whatever is to be bought on terms of future payment.

From this constant necessity of *borrowing* and *buying dear,* it is easy to conceive how immensely the expenses of a nation, in a course of time, will be augmented by an unsound state of the public credit.

To attempt to enumerate the complicated variety of mischief in the whole system of the social economy, which proceed from a neglect of the maxims that uphold public credit, and justify the solicitude manifested by the House on this point, would be an improper intrusion on their time and patience.

In so strong a light nevertheless do they appear to the Secretary, that on their due observance at the present critical juncture, materially depends, in his judgment, the individual and aggregate prosperity of the citizens of the United States; their relief from the embarrassments they now experience; their character as a People; the cause of good government.

If the maintenance of public credit, then, be truly so important, the next enquiry which suggests itself is, by what means it is to be effected? The ready answer to which question is, by good faith, by a punctual performance of contracts. States, like individuals, who observe their engagements, are respected and trusted: while the reverse is the fate of those, who pursue an opposite conduct.

Every breach of the public engagements, whether from choice or necessity, is in different degrees hurtful to public credit. When such a necessity does truly exist, the evils of it are only to be palliated by a scrupulous attention, on the part of the government, to carry the violation no farther than the necessity absolutely requires, and to manifest, if the nature of the case admits of it, a sincere disposition to make reparation, whenever circumstances shall permit. But with every possible mitigation, credit must suffer, and numerous mischief ensue. It is therefore highly important, when an appearance of necessity seems to press upon the public councils, that they should examine well its reality, and be perfectly assured, that there is no method of escaping from it, before they yield to its suggestions. For though it cannot safely be affirmed, that occasions have never existed, or may not exist, in which violations of the public faith, in this respect, are inevitable; yet there is great reason to believe, that they exist far less frequently than precedents indicate; and are oftenest either pretended through levity, or want of firmness, or supposed through want of knowledge. Expedients might often have been devised to effect, consistently with good faith, what has been done in contravention of it. Those who are most commonly creditors of a nation, are, generally speaking, enlightened men; and there are signal examples to warrant a conclusion, that when a candid and fair appeal is made to them, they will understand their true interest too well to refuse their concurrence in such modifications of their claims, as any real necessity may demand.

While the observance of that good faith, which is the basis of public credit, is recommended by the strongest inducements of political expediency, it is enforced by considerations of still greater authority. There are arguments for it, which rest on the immutable principles of moral obligation. And in proportion as the mind is disposed to contemplate, in the order of Providence, an intimate connection between public virtue and public happiness, will be its repugnancy to a violation of those principles.

This reflection derives additional strength from the nature of the debt of the United States. It was the price of liberty. The faith of America has been repeatedly pledged for it, and with solemnities, that give peculiar force to the obligation. There is indeed reason to regret that it has not hitherto been kept; that the necessities of the war, conspiring with inexperience in the subjects of finance, produced direct infractions; and that the subsequent period has been a continued scene of negative violation, or non-compliance. But a diminution of this regret arises from the reflection, that the last seven years have exhibited an earnest and uniform effort, on the part of the government of the union, to retrieve the national credit, by doing justice to the creditors of the nation; and that the embarrassments of a defective constitution, which defeated this laudable effort, have ceased.

From this evidence of a favorable disposition, given by the former government, the institution of a new one, coated with powers competent to calling forth the resources of the community, has excited correspondent expectations. A general belief, accordingly, prevails, that the credit of the United States will quickly be established on the firm foundation of an effectual provision for the existing debt. The influence, which this has had at home, is witnessed by the rapid increase, that has taken place in the market value of the public securities. From January to November, they rose thirty-three and a third per cent, and from that period to this time, they have risen fifty per cent more. And the intelligence from abroad announces effects proportionably favorable to our national credit and consequence.

It cannot but merit particular attention, that among ourselves the most enlightened friends of good government are those, whose expectations are the highest.

To justify and preserve their confidence; to promote the encreasing respectability of the American name; to answer the calls of justice; to restore landed property to its due value; to furnish new resources both to agriculture and commerce; to cement more closely the union of the states; to add to their security against foreign attack; to establish public order on the basis of an upright and liberal policy. These are the great and invaluable ends to be secured, by a proper and adequate provision, at the present period, for the support of public credit. [. . .]

The Secretary has now completed the objects, which he proposed to himself, to comprise in the present report. He has, for the most part, omitted details, as well to avoid fatiguing the attention of the House, as because more time would have been desirable even to digest the general principles of the plan. If these should be found right, the particular modifications will readily suggest themselves in the progress of the work.

The Secretary, in the views which have directed his pursuit of the subject, has been influenced, in the first place, by the consideration, that his duty from the very terms of the resolution of the House, obliged him to propose what appeared to him an adequate provision for the support of the public credit, adapted at the same time to the real circumstances of the United States; and in the next, by the reflection, that measures which will not bear the test of future unbiased examination, can neither be productive of individual reputation, nor (which is of much greater consequence) public honor, or advantage.

Deeply impressed, as the Secretary is, with a full and deliberate conviction, that the establishment of public credit, upon the basis of a satisfactory provision, for the public debt, is, under the present circumstances of this country, the true desideratum towards relief from individual and national embarrassments; that without it, these embarrassments will be likely to press still more severely upon the community—He cannot but indulge an anxious wish, that an effectual plan for that purpose may, during the present session, be the result of the united wisdom of the legislature.

He is fully convinced, that it is of the greatest importance, that no further delay should attend the making of the requisite provision; not only, because it will give a better impression of the good faith of the country, and will bring earlier relief to the creditors; both which circumstances are of great moment to public credit: but, because the advantages to the community, from raising stock, as speedily as possible, to its natural value, will be incomparably greater, than any that can result from its continuance below that standard. No profit, which could be derived from purchases in the market, on account of the government, to any practicable extent, would be an equivalent for the loss, which would be sustained by the purchases of foreigners, at a low value. [. . .]

Report on a National Bank (December 13, 1790)

Treasury Department

In obedience to the order of the House of Representatives of the ninth day of August last, requiring the Secretary of the Treasury to prepare and report on this day such further provision as may, in his opinion, be necessary for establishing the public Credit

The said Secretary further respectfully reports

That from a conviction (as suggested in his report No. 1 herewith presented) That a National Bank is an Institution of primary importance to the prosperous administration of the Finances, and would be of the greatest utility in the operations connected with the support of the Public Credit, his attention has been drawn to devising the plan of such an institution, upon a scale, which will intitle it to the confidence, and be likely to render it equal to the exigencies of the Public.

Previously to entering upon the detail of this plan, he entreats the indulgence of the House, towards some preliminary reflections naturally arising out of the subject, which he hopes will be deemed, neither useless, nor out of place. Public opinion being the ultimate arbiter of every measure of Government, it can scarcely appear improper, in deference to that, to accompany the origination of any new proposition with explanations, which the superior information of those, to whom it is immediately addressed, would render superfluous.

It is a fact well understood, that public Banks have found admission and patronage among the principal and most enlightened commercial nations. They have successively obtained in Italy, Germany, Holland, England and France, as well as in the United States. And it is a circumstance, which cannot but have considerable weight, in a candid estimate of their tendency, that after an experience of centuries, there exists not a question about their utility in the countries in which they have been so long established. Theorists and men of business unite in the acknowledgment of it.

Thomas Jefferson

On the Constitutionality of a National Bank (February 15, 1791)

The bill for establishing a National Bank undertakes, among other things

1. To form the subscribers into a Corporation.
2. To enable them, in their corporate capacities to receive grants of land; and so far is against the laws of *Mortmain*.[1]
3. To make alien subscribers capable of holding lands, and so far is against the laws of *Alienage*.
4. To transmit these lands, on the death of a proprietor, to a certain line of successors: and so far changes the course of *Descents*.

1. Though the constitution controuls the laws of Mortmain so far as to permit Congress itself to hold lands for certain purposes, yet not so far as to permit them to communicate a similar right to other corporate bodies.

5. To put the lands out of the reach of forfeiture or escheat and so far is against the laws of *Forfeiture and Escheat.*
6. To transmit personal chattels to successors in a certain line: and so far is against the laws of *Distribution.*
7. To give them the sole and exclusive right of banking under the national authority: and so far is against the laws of Monopoly.
8. To communicate to them a power to make laws paramount to the laws of the states: for so they must be construed, to protect the institution from the controul of the state legislatures; and so, probably they will be construed.

I consider the foundation of the Constitution as laid on this ground that "all powers not delegated to the U.S. by the Constitution, not prohibited by it to the states, are reserved to the states or to the people" [XIIth Amendmt.]. To take a single step beyond the boundaries thus specially drawn around the powers of Congress, is to take possession of a boundless field of power, no longer susceptible of any definition.

The incorporation of a bank, and other powers assumed by this bill have not, in my opinion, been delegated to the U.S. by the Constitution.

I. They are not among the powers specially enumerated, for these are

1. A power to *lay taxes* for the purpose of paying the debts of the U.S. But no debt is paid by this bill, nor any tax laid. Were it a bill to raise money, its origination in the Senate would condemn it by the constitution.
2. "to borrow money." But this bill neither borrows money, nor ensures the borrowing it. The proprietors of the bank will be just as free as any other money holders, to lend or not to lend their money to the public. The operation proposed in the bill, first to lend them two millions, and then borrow them back again, cannot change the nature of the latter act, which will still be a payment, and not a loan, call it by what name you please.
3. "to regulate commerce with foreign nations, and among the states, and with the Indian tribes." To erect a bank, and to regulate commerce, are very different acts. He who erects a bank creates a subject of commerce in its bills: so does he who makes a bushel of wheat, or digs a dollar out of the mines. Yet neither of these persons regulates commerce thereby. To erect a thing which may be bought and sold, is not to prescribe regulations for buying and selling. Besides; if this was an exercise of the power of regulating commerce, it would be void, as extending as much to the internal commerce of every state, as to its external. For the power given to Congress by the Constitution, does not extend to the internal regulation of the commerce of a state (that is to say of the commerce between citizen and citizen) which remains exclusively with its own legislature; but to its external commerce only, that is to say, its commerce with another state, or with foreign nations or with the Indian tribes. Accordingly the bill does not propose the measure as a "regulation of trade," but as "productive of considerable advantage to trade."

Still less are these powers covered by any other of the special enumerations.

II. Nor are they within either of the general phrases, which are the two following.

1. To lay taxes to provide for the general welfare of the U.S., that is to say, "to lay taxes for *the purpose* of providing for the general welfare." For the laying of taxes is the *power* and the general welfare the *purpose* for which the power is to be exercised. They are not to lay taxes *ad libitum for any purpose they please;* but only *to pay the debts or provide for the welfare of the Union.* In like manner they are not *to do anything they please* to provide for the general welfare, but only *to lay taxes* for that purpose. To consider the latter phrase, not as describing the purpose of the first, but as giving a distinct and independent power to do any act they please,

which might be for the good of the Union, would render all the preceding and subsequent enumerations of power completely useless. It would reduce the whole instrument to a single phrase, that of instituting a Congress with power to do whatever would be for the good of the U.S. and as they would be the sole judges of the good or evil, it would be also a power to do whatever evil they pleased. It is an established rule of construction, where a phrase will bear either of two meanings, to give it that which will allow some meaning to the other parts of the instrument, and not that which would render all the others useless. Certainly no such universal power was meant to be given them. It was intended to lace them up straitly within the enumerated powers, and those without which, as means, these powers could not be be carried into effect. It is known that the very power now proposed *as a means,* was rejected *as an end,* by the Convention which formed the constitution. A proposition was made to them to authorize Congress to open canals, and an amendatory one to empower them to incorporate. But the whole was rejected, and one of the reasons of rejection urged in debate was that then they would have a power to erect a bank, which would render the great cities, where there were prejudices and jealousies on that subject adverse to the reception of the constitution.

2. The second general phrase is "to make all laws *necessary* and proper for carrying into execution the enumerated powers." But they can all be carried into execution without a bank. A bank therefore is not *necessary,* and consequently not authorised by this phrase.

It has been much urged that a bank will give great facility, or convenience in the collection of taxes. Suppose this were true: yet the constitution allows only the means which are "necessary," not those which are merely "convenient" for effecting the enumerated powers. If such a latitude of construction be allowed to this phrase as to give any non-enumerated power, it will go to every one, for there is no one which ingenuity may not torture into a *convenience, in some way or other,* to *some one* of so long a list of enumerated powers. It would swallow up all the delegated powers, and reduce the whole to one phrase as before observed. Therefore it was that the constitution restrained them to the *necessary* means, that is to say, to those means without which the grant of the power would be nugatory.

But let us examine this *convenience,* and see what it is. The report on this subject, page 3. states the only *general* convenience to be the preventing the transportation and re-transportation of money between the states and the treasury. (For I pass over the increase of circulating medium ascribed to it as a merit, and which, according to my ideas of paper money is clearly a demerit.) Every state will have to pay a sum of tax-money into the treasury: and the treasury will have to pay, in every state, a part of the interest on the public debt, and salaries to the officers of government resident in that state. In most of the states there will still be a surplus of tax-money to come up to the seat of government for the officers residing there. The payments of interest and salary in each state may be made by treasury-orders on the state collector. This will take up the greater part of the money he has collected in his state, and consequently prevent the great mass of it from being drawn out of the state. If there be a balance of commerce in favour of that state against the one in which the government resides, the surplus of taxes will be remitted by the bills of exchange drawn for that commercial balance. And so it must be if there was a bank. But if there be no balance of commerce, either direct or circuitous, all the banks in the world could not bring up the surplus of taxes but in the form of money. Treasury orders then and bills of exchange may prevent the displacement of the main mass of the money collected, without the aid of any bank: and where these fail, it cannot be prevented even with that aid.

Perhaps indeed bank bills may be a more *convenient* vehicle than treasury orders. But a little *difference* in the degree of *convenience,* cannot constitute the necessity which the constitution makes the ground for assuming any non-enumerated power.

Besides; the existing banks will without a doubt, enter into arrangements for lending their agency: and the more favourable, as there will be a competition among them for it: whereas the bill delivers us up bound to the national bank, who are free to refuse all arrangement, but on their own terms, and the public not free, on such refusal, to employ any other bank. That of Philadelphia, I believe, now does this business, by their post-notes, which by an arrangement with the treasury, are paid by any state collector to whom they are presented. This expedient alone suffices to prevent the existence of that *necessity* which may justify the assumption of a non-enumerated power as a means for carrying into effect an enumerated one. The thing may be done, and has been done, and well done without this assumption; therefore it does not stand on that degree of *necessity* which can honestly justify it.

It may be said that a bank, whose bills would have a currency all over the states, would be more convenient than one whose currency is limited to a single state. So it would be still more convenient that there should be a bank whose bills should have a currency all over the world. But it does not follow from this superior conveniency that there exists anywhere a power to establish such a bank; or that the world may not go on very well without it.

Can it be thought that the Constitution intended that for a shade or two of *convenience*, more or less, Congress should be authorised to break down the most antient and fundamental laws of the several states, such as those against Mortmain, the laws of alienage, the rules of descent, the acts of distribution, the laws of escheat and forfeiture, the laws of monopoly? Nothing but a necessity invincible by any other means, can justify such a prostration of laws which constitute the pillars of our whole system of jurisprudence. Will Congress be too strait-laced to carry the constitution into honest effect, unless they may pass over the foundation-laws of the state-governments for the slightest convenience to theirs?

The Negative of the President is the shield provided by the constitution to protect against the invasions of the legislature: 1. The right of the Executive. 2. Of the Judiciary. 3. Of the states and state legislatures. The present is the case of a right remaining exclusively with the states and is consequently one of those intended by the constitution to be placed under his protection.

It must be added however, that unless the President's mind on a view of every thing which is urged for and against this bill, is tolerably clear that it is unauthorised by the constitution, if the pro and the con hang so even as to balance his judgment, a just respect for the wisdom of the legislature would naturally decide the balance in favour of their opinion. It is chiefly for cases where they are clearly misled by error, ambition, or interest, that the constitution has placed a check in the negative of the President.

ALEXANDER HAMILTON

Opinion on the Constitutionality of a National Bank (February 23, 1791)

The Secretary of the Treasury having perused with attention the papers containing the opinions of the Secretary of State and the Attorney-General, concerning the constitutionality of the bill for establishing a national bank, proceeds, according to the order of the President, to submit the reasons which have induced him to entertain a different opinion. [. . .]

In entering upon the argument, it ought to be premised that the objections of the Secretary of State and the Attorney-General are founded on a general denial of the authority of the United States to erect corporations. The latter, indeed, expressly admits, that if there be anything in the bill which is not warranted by the Constitution, it is the clause of incorporation.

Now it appears to the Secretary of the Treasury that this *general principle* is *inherent* in the very *definition* of government, and *essential* to every step of the progress to be made by that of the United States, namely: That every power vested in a government is in its nature *sovereign*, and includes, by *force* of the *term*, a right to employ all the *means* requisite and fairly applicable to the attainment of the ends of such *power*, and which are not precluded by restrictions and exceptions specified in the Constitution, or not immoral, or not contrary to the *essential ends* of political society. [. . .]

The circumstance that the powers of sovereignty are in this country divided between the National and State governments, does not afford the distinction required. It does not follow from this, that each of the portion of powers delegated to the one or to the other, is not sovereign with *regard to its proper objects*. It will only follow from it, that each has sovereign power as to certain *things*, and not as to other things. To deny that the Government of the United States has sovereign power, as to its declared purposes and trusts, because its power does not extend to all cases, would be equally to deny that the State governments have sovereign power in any case, because their power does not extend to every case. The tenth section of the first article of the Constitution exhibits a long list of very important things which they may not do. And thus the United States would furnish the singular spectacle of a *political society* without *sovereignty*, or of a people governed, without *government*.

If it would be necessary to bring proof to a proposition so clear, as that which affirms that the powers of the Federal Government, as to *its objects*, were sovereign, there is a clause of its Constitution which would be decisive. It is that which declares that the Constitution, and the laws of the United States made in pursuance of it, and all treaties made, or which shall be made, under their authority, shall be the *supreme law of the land*. The power which can create the *supreme law of the land* in any case, is doubtless *sovereign* as to such case.

This general and indisputable principle puts at once an end to the *abstract* question, whether the United States have power to erect a *corporation*; that is to say, to give a *legal* or *artificial capacity* to one or more persons, distinct from the *natural*. For it is unquestionably incident to *sovereign* power to erect corporations, and consequently to that of the United States, in *relation* to the *objects* intrusted to the management of the government. The difference is this: where the authority of the government is general, it can create corporations in all *cases*; where it is confined to certain branches of legislation, it can create corporations only in those cases.

Here, then, as far as concerns the reasonings of the Secretary of State and the Attorney-General, the affirmative of the constitutionality of the bill might be permitted to rest. It will occur to the President, that the principle here advanced has been untouched by either of them.

For a more complete elucidation of the point, nevertheless, the arguments which they had used against the power of the government to erect corporations, however foreign they are to the great and fundamental rule which has been stated, shall be particularly examined. And after showing that they do not tend to impair its force, it shall also be shown that the power of incorporation, incident to the government in certain cases, does fairly extend to the particular case which is the object of the bill.

The first of these arguments is, that the foundation of the Constitution is laid on this ground: 'That all powers not delegated to the United States by the Constitution, nor prohibited by it to the States, are reserved to the States, or to the people.' Whence it is meant to be inferred, that Congress can in no case exercise any power not included in those enumerated in the Constitution. And it is affirmed, that the power of erecting a corporation is not included in any of the enumerated powers.

The main proposition here laid down, in its true signification, is not to be questioned. It is nothing more than a consequence of this republican maxim, that all government is a delegation of power. But how much is delegated in each case is a question of fact, to be made out by fair reasoning and construction, upon the particular provisions of the Constitution, taking as guides the general principles and general ends of governments.

It is not denied that there are *implied*, as well as *express powers*, and that the *former* are as effectually delegated as the *latter*. And for the sake of accuracy it shall be mentioned that there is another class of powers, which may be properly denominated *resulting powers*. It will not be doubted that if the United

States should make a conquest of any of the territories of its neighbors, they would possess sovereign jurisdiction over the conquered territory. This would be rather a result from the whole mass of the powers of the government, and from the nature of political society, than a consequence of either of the powers specially enumerated.

But be this as it may, it furnishes a striking illustration of the general doctrine contended for; it shows an extensive case, in which a power of erecting corporations is either implied in, or would result from, some or all of the powers vested in the National Government. The jurisdiction acquired over such conquered country would certainly be competent to any species of legislation.

To return:—It *is* conceded that *implied powers* are to be considered as delegated equally with *express ones.* Then it follows, that as a power of erecting a corporation may as well be *implied* as any other thing, it may as well be employed as an *instrument* or *means* of carrying into execution any of the specified powers, as any other *instrument* or *means* whatever. The only question must be in this, as in every other, case, whether the means to be employed, or, in this instance, the corporation to be erected, has a natural relation to any of the acknowledged objects or lawful ends of the government. Thus a corporation may not be erected by Congress for superintending the police of the city of Philadelphia, because they are not authorized to *regulate* the police of that city. But one may be erected in relation to the collection of taxes, or to the trade with foreign countries, or to the trade between the States, or with the Indian tribes; because it is the province of the Federal Government to *regulate* those objects, and because it is incident to a general *sovereign* or *legislative* power to regulate a thing, to employ all the means which relate to its regulation to the best and greatest advantage. [. . .]

Through this mode of reasoning respecting the right of employing all the means requisite to the execution of the specified powers of the government, it is to be objected, that none but necessary and proper means are to be employed; and the Secretary of State maintains, that no means are to be considered necessary but those without which the grant of the power would be nugatory. Nay, so far does he go in his restrictive interpretation of the word, as even to make the case of necessity which shall warrant the constitutional exercise of the power to depend on casual and temporary circumstances; an idea which alone refutes the construction. [. . .]

It is essential to the being of the national government, that so erroneous a conception of the meaning of the word *necessary* should be exploded.

It is certain, that neither the grammatical nor popular sense of the term requires that construction. According to both, *necessary* often means no more than *needful, requisite, incidental, useful,* or *conducive to.* It is a common mode of expression to say, that it is necessary for a government or a person to do this or that thing, when nothing more is intended or understood, than that the interests of the government or person require, or will be promoted by, the doing of this or that thing. The imagination can be at no loss for exemplifications of the use of the word in this sense. And it is the true one in which it is to be understood as used in the Constitution. The whole turn of the clause containing it indicates, that it was the intent of the Convention, by that clause, to give a liberal latitude to the exercise of the specified powers. The expressions have peculiar comprehensiveness. They are, 'to make all laws necessary and proper for carrying into execution the *foregoing powers,* and all other powers vested by the Constitution in the Government of the United States, or in any department or officer thereof.'

To understand the word as the Secretary of States does, would be to depart from its obvious and popular sense, and to give it a restrictive operation, an idea never before entertained. It would be to give it the same force as if the word *absolutely* or *indispensably* had been prefixed to it. [. . .]

It may be truly said of every government, as well as of that of the United States, that it has only a right to pass such laws as are necessary and proper to accomplish the objects intrusted to it. For no government has a right to do *merely what it pleases.* Hence, by a process of reasoning similar to that of the Secretary of State, it might be proved that neither of the State governments has the right to incorporate a bank. It might be shown that all the public business of the State could be performed without a bank, and inferring thence that it was unnecessary, it might be argued that it could not be done, because it is against the rule which has been just mentioned. A like mode of reasoning would prove that there was no power to incorporate the inhabitants of a town, with a view to a more perfect police. For it is certain that an incorporation may be dispensed with, though it is better to have one. It is to be remembered that there is no *express* power in any State constitutions to erect corporations.

The degree in which a measure is necessary can never be a test of the legal right to adopt it; that must be a matter of opinion, and can only be a test of expediency. The relation between the measure and the *end*; between the nature of the *means* employed towards the execution of a power, and the object of that power, must be the criterion of constitutionality, not the more or less of *necessity* or *utility*.

The practice of the government is against the rule of construction advocated by the Secretary of State. Of this, the act concerning lighthouses, beacons, buoys, and public piers is a decisive example. This, doubtless, must be referred to the powers of regulating trade, and is fairly relative to it. But it cannot be affirmed that the exercise of that power in this instance was strictly *necessary*, or that the power itself would be *nugatory*, without that of regulating establishments of this nature.

This restrictive interpretation of the word *necessary* is also contrary to this sound maxim of construction; namely, that the powers contained in a constitution of government, especially those which concern the general administration of the affairs of a country, its finances, trade, defence, etc., ought to be construed liberally in advancement of the public good. This rule does not depend on the particular form of a government, or on the particular demarcation of the boundaries of its powers, but on the nature and objects of government itself. The means by which national exigencies are to be provided for, national inconveniences obviated, national prosperity promoted, are of such infinite variety, extent, and complexity, that there must of necessity be great latitude of discretion in the selection and application of those means. Hence, consequently, the necessity and propriety of exercising the authorities intrusted to a government on principles of liberal construction. [. . .]

But while on the one hand the construction of the Secretary of State is deemed inadmissible, it will not be contended, on the other, that the clause in question gives any *new* or *independent* power. But it gives an explicit sanction to the doctrine of *implied powers*, and is equivalent to an admission of the proposition that the government, as to its *specified powers* and *objects*, has plenary and sovereign authority, in some cases paramount to the States; in others, co-ordinate with it. For such is the plain import of the declaration, that it may pass all laws necessary and proper to carry into execution those powers.

It is no valid objection to the doctrine to say, that it is calculated to extend the power of the General Government throughout the entire sphere of State legislation. The same thing has been said [. . .] with regard to every exercise of power *by implication* or *construction*. [. . .]

The truth is, that difficulties on this point are inherent in the nature of the Federal Constitution; they result inevitably from a division of the legislative power. The consequence of this division is, that there will be cases clearly within the power of the National Government; others, clearly without its powers; and a third class, which will leave room for controversy and difference of opinion, and concerning which a reasonable latitude of judgment must be allowed.

But the doctrine which is contended for is not chargeable with the consequences imputed to it. It does not affirm that the National Government is sovereign in all respects, but that it is sovereign to a certain extent—that is, to the extent of the objects of its specified powers.

It leaves, therefore, a criterion of what is constitutional, and of what is not so. This criterion is the end, to which the measure relates as a means. If the end be clearly comprehended within any of the specified powers, and if the measure have an obvious relation to that end, and is not forbidden by any particular provision of the Constitution, it may safely be deemed to come within the compass of the national authority. [. . .]

Report on the Subject of Manufacturers (December 5, 1791)

The Secretary of the Treasury in obedience to the order of ye House of Representatives, of the 15th day of January 1790, has applied his attention, at as early a period as his other duties would permit, to the subject of Manufactures; and particularly to the means of promoting such as will tend to render the United States, independent on foreign nations, for military and other essential supplies. And he there upon respectfully submits the following Report.

The expediency of encouraging manufactures in the United States, which was not long since deemed very questionable, appears at this time to be pretty generally admitted. The embarrassments, which have obstructed the progress of our external trade, have led to serious reflections on the necessity of enlarging the sphere of our domestic commerce: the restrictive regulations, which in foreign markets abrige the vent of the increasing surplus of our Agricultural produce, serve to beget an earnest desire, that a more extensive demand for that surplus may be created at home: And the complete success, which has rewarded manufacturing enterprise, in some valuable branches, conspiring with the promising symptoms, which attend some less mature essays, in others, justify a hope, that the obstacles to the growth of this species of industry are less formidable than they were apprehended to be; and that it is not difficult to find, in its further extension; a full indemnification for any external disadvantages, which are or may be experienced, as well as an accession of resources, favourable to national independence and safety. [. . .]

It is now proper to proceed a step further, and to enumerate the principal circumstances, from which it may be inferred—That manufacturing establishments not only occasion a possitive augmentation of the Produce and Revenue of the Society, but that they contribute essentially to rendering them greater than they could possibly be, without such establishmeats. These circumstances are—

1. The division of Labour.
2. An extension of the use of Machinery.
3. Additional employment to classes of the community not ordinarily engaged in the business.
4. The promoting of emigration from foreign Countries.
5. The furnishing greater scope for the diversity of talents and dispositions which discriminate men from each other.
6. The affording a more ample and various field for enterprize.
7. The creating in some instances a new, and securing in all, a more certain and steady demand for the surplus produce of the soil.

Each of these circumstances has a considerable influence upon the total mass of industrious effort in a community. Together, they add to it a degree of energy and effect, which are not easily conceived. Some comments upon each of them, in the order in which they have been stated, may serve to explain their importance.

I. As to the Division of Labour.

It has justly been observed, that there is scarcely any thing of greater moment in the œconomy of a nation, than the proper division of labour. The seperation of occupations causes each to be carried to a much greater perfection, than it could possible acquire, if they were blended. This arises principally from three circumstances.

1st—The greater skill and dexterity naturally resulting from a constant and undivided application to a single object. It is evident, that these properties must increase, in proportion to the separation and simplification of objects and the steadiness of the attention devoted to each; and must be less, in proportion to the complication of objects, and the number among which the attention is distracted.

2nd. The œconomy of time—by avoiding the loss of it, incident to a frequent transition from one operation to another of a different nature. This depends on various circumstances—the transition itself—the orderly disposition of the impliments, machines and materials employed in the operation to be relinquished—the preparatory steps to the commencement of a new one—the interruption of the impulse, which the mind of the workman acquires, from being engaged in a particular operation—the distractions hesitations and reluctances, which attend the passage from one kind of business to another.

3rd. An extension of the use of Machinery. A man occupied on a single object will have it more in his power, and will be more naturally led to exert his imagination in devising methods to facilitate and abrige labour, than if he were perplexed by a variety of independent and dissimilar operations. Besides this, the fabrication of Machines, in numerous instances, becoming itself a distinct trade, the Artist who follows it, has all the advantages which have been enumerated, for improvement in his particular art; and in both ways the invention and application of machinery are extended.

And from these causes united, the mere separation of the occupation of the cultivator, from that of the Artificer, has the effect of augmenting the *productive powers* of labour, and with them, the total mass of the produce or revenue of a Country. In this single view of the subject, therefore, the utility of Artificers or Manufacturers, towards promoting an increase of productive industry, is apparent.

II. As to an extension of the use of Machinery a point which though partly anticipated requires to be placed in one or two additional lights.

The employment of Machinery forms an item of great importance in the general mass of national industry. 'Tis an artificial force brought in aid of the natural force of man; and, to all the purposes of labour, is an increase of hands; an accession of strength, *unencumbered too by the expence of maintaining the laborer.* May it not therefore be fairly inferred, that those occupations, which give greatest scope to the use of this auxiliary, contribute most to the general Stock of industrious effort, and, in consequence, to the general product of industry?

It shall be taken for granted, and the truth of the position referred to observation, that manufacturing pursuits are susceptible in a greater degree of the application of machinery, than those of Agriculture. If so all the difference is lost to a community, which, instead of manufacturing for itself, procures the fabrics requisite to its supply from other Countries. The substitution of foreign for domestic manufactures is a transfer to foreign nations of the advantages accruing from the employment of Machinery, in the modes in which it is capable of being employed, with most utility and to the greatest extent.

The Cotton Mill invented in England, within the last twenty years, is a signal illustration of the general proposition, which has been just advanced. In consequence of it, all the different processes for spining Cotton are performed by means of Machines, which are put in motion by water, and attended chiefly by women and Children; and by a smaller number of persons, in the whole, than are requisite in the ordinary mode of spinning. And it is an advantage of great moment that the operations of this mill continue with convenience, during the night, as well as through the day. The prodigious affect of such a Machine is easily conceived. To this invention is to be attributed essentially the immense progress, which has been so suddenly made in Great Britain in the various fabrics of Cotton.

III. As to the additional employment of classes of the community, not ordinarily engaged in the particular business.

This is not among the least valuable of the means, by which manufacturing institutions contribute to augment the general stock of industry and production. In places where those institutions prevail, besides the persons regularly engaged in them, they afford occasional and extra employment to industrious individuals and families, who are willing to devote the leisure resulting from the intermissions of their ordinary pursuits to collateral labours, as a resource of multiplying their acquisitions or their enjoyments. The husbandman himself experiences a new source of profit and support from the encreased industry of his wife and daughters; invited and stimulated by the demands of the neighboring manufactories.

Besides this advantage of occasional employment to classes having different occupations, there is another of a nature allied to it and of a similar tendency. This is—the employment of persons who would otherwise be idle (and in many cases a burthen on the community), either from the byass of temper, habit, infirmity of body, or some other cause, indisposing, or disqualifying them for the toils of the Country. It is worthy of particular remark, that, in general, women and Children are rendered more useful and the latter more early useful by manufacturing establishments, than they would otherwise be. Of the number of persons employed in the Cotton Manufactories of Great Britain, it is computed that 4/7 nearly are women and children; of whom the greatest proportion are children and many of them of a very tender age.

And thus it appears to be one of the attributes of manufactures, and one of no small consequence, to give occasion to the exertion of a greater quantity of Industry, even by the *same number* of persons, where they happen to prevail, than would exist, if there were no such establishments.

IV. As to the promoting of emigration from foreign Countries.

Men reluctandy quit one course of occupation and livelihood for another, unless invited to it by very apparent and proximate advantages. Many, who would go from one country to another, if they had a prospect of continuing with more benefit the callings, to which they have been educated, will often not be tempted to change their situation, by the hope of doing better, in some other way. Manufacturers, who listening to the powerful invitations of a better price for their fabrics, or their labour, of greater cheapness of provisions and raw materials, of an exemption from the chief part of the taxes burthens and restraints, which they endure in the old world; of greater personal independence and consequence, under the operation of a more equal government, and of what is far more precious than mere religious toleration—a perfect equality of religious privileges; would probably flock from Europe to the United States to pursue their own trades or professions, if they were once made sensible of the advantages they would enjoy, and were inspired with an assurance of encouragement and employment, will, with difficulty, be induced to transplant themselves, with a view to becoming Cultivators of Land.

If it be true then, that it is the interest of the United States to open every possible avenue to emigration from abroad, it affords a weighty argument for the encouragement of manufactures; which for the reasons just assigned, will have the strongest tendency to multiply the inducements to it.

Here is perceived an important resource, not only for extending the population, and with it the useful and productive labour of the country, but likewise for the prosecution of manufactures, without deducting from the number of hands, which might otherwise be drawn to tillage; and even for the indemnification of Agriculture for such as might happen to be diverted from it. Many, whom Manufacturing views would induce to emigrate, would afterwards yield to the temptations, which the particular situation of this Country holds out to Agricultural pursuits. And while Agriculture would in other respects derive many signal and unmingled advantages, from the growth of manufactures, it is a problem whether it would gain or lose, as to the article of the number of persons employed in carrying it on.

V. As to the furnishing greater scope for the diversity of talents and dispositions, which discriminate men from each other.

This is a much more powerful means of augmenting the fund of national Industry than may at first sight appear. It is a just observation, that minds of the strongest and most active powers for their proper objects fall below mediocrity and labour without effect, if confined to uncongenial pursuits. And it is thence to be inferred, that the results of human exertion may be immensely increased by diversifying its objects. When all the different kinds of industry obtain in a community, each individual can find his proper element, and can call into activity the whole vigour of his nature. And the community is benefitted by the services of its respective members, in the manner, in which each can serve it with most effect.

If there be anything in a remark often to be met with—namely that there is, in the genius of the people of this country, a peculiar aptitude for mechanic improvements, it would operate as a forcible reason for giving opportunities to the exercise of that species of talent, by the propagation of manufactures.

VI. As to the affording a more ample and various field for enterprise.

This also is of greater consequence in the general scale of national exertion, than might perhaps on a superficial view be supposed, and has effects not altogether dissimilar from those of the circumstance last noticed. To cherish and stimulate the activity of the human mind, by multiplying the objects of enterprise, is not among the least considerable of the expedients, by which the wealth of a nation may be promoted. Even things in themselves not positively advantageous, sometimes become so, by their tendency to provoke exertion. Every new scene, which is opened to the busy nature of man to rouse and exert itself, is the addition of a new energy to the general stock of effort.

The spirit of enterprise, useful and prolific as it is, must necessarily be contracted or expanded in proportion to the simplicity or variety of the occupations and productions, which are to be found in a Society. It must be less in a nation of mere cultivators, than in a nation of cultivators and merchants; less in a nation of cultivators and merchants, than in a nation of cultivators, artificers and merchants.

VII. As to the creating, in some instances, a new, and securing in all a more certain and steady demand, for the surplus produce of the soil.

This is among the most important of the circumstances which have been indicated. It is a principal means, by which the establishment of manufactures contributes to an augmentation of the produce or revenue of a country, and has an immediate and direct relation to the prosperity of Agriculture.

It is evident, that the exertions of the husbandman will be steady or fluctuating, vigorous or feeble, in proportion to the steadiness or fluctuation, adequateness, or inadequateness of the markets on which he must depend, for the vent of the surplus, which may be produced by his labour; and that such surplus in the ordinary course of things will be greater or less in the same proportion.

For the purpose of this vent, a domestic market is greatly to be preferred to a foreign one; because it is in the nature of things, far more to be relied upon.

It is a primary object of the policy of nations, to be able to supply themselves with subsistence from their own soils; and manufacturing nations, as far as circumstances permit, endeavor to procure, from the same source, the raw materials necessary for their own fabrics. This disposition, urged by the spirit of monopoly, is sometimes even carried to an injudicious extreme. It seems not always to be recollected, that nations, who have neither mines nor manufactures, can only obtain the manufactured articles, of which they stand in need, by an exchange of the products of their soils; and that, if those who can best furnish them with such articles are unwilling to give a due course to this exchange, they must of necessity make every possible effort to manufacture for themselves, the effect of which is that the manufacturing nations abrige the natural advantages of their situation, through an unwillingness to permit the Agricultural countries to enjoy the advantages of theirs, and sacrifice the interests of a mutually beneficial intercourse to the vain project of *selling everything* and *buying nothing*.

But it is also a consequence of the policy, which has been noted, that the foreign demand for the products of Agricultural Countries, is, in a great degree, rather casual and occasional, than certain or constant. To what extent injurious interruptions of the demand for some of the staple commodities of the United States, may have been experienced, from that cause, must be referred to the judgment of those who are engaged in carrying on the commerce of the country; but it may be safely assumed, that such interruptions are at times very inconveniently felt, and that cases not unfrequently occur, in which markets are so confined and restricted, as to render the demand very unequal to the supply.

Independently likewise of the artificial impediments, which are created by the policy in question, there are natural causes tending to render the external demand for the surplus of Agricultural nations a precarious reliance. The differences of seasons, in the countries, which are the consumers make immense differences in the produce of their own soils, in different years; and consequently in the degrees of their necessity for foreign supply. Plentiful harvests with them, especially if similar ones occur at the same time in the countries, which are the furnishers, occasion of course a glut in the markets of the latter.

Considering how fast and how much the progress of new settlements in the United States must increase the surplus produce of the soil, and weighing seriously the tendency of the system, which prevails among most of the commercial nations of Europe; whatever dependence may be placed on the force of natural circumstances to counteract the effects of an artificial policy; there appear strong reasons to regard the foreign demand for that surplus as too uncertain a reliance and to desire a substitute for it, in an extensive domestic market.

To secure such a market, there is no other expedient, than to promote manufacturing establishments. Manufacturers who constitute the most numerous class, after the Cultivators of land, are for that reason the principal consumers of the surplus of their labour.

This idea of an extensive domestic market for the surplus produce of the soil is of the first consequence. It is of all things, that which most effectually conduces to a flourishing state of Agriculture. If the effect of manufactories should be to detatch a portion of the hands, which would otherwise be engaged in Tillage, it might possibly cause a smaller quantity of lands to be under cultivation but by their tendency to procure a more certain demand for the surplus produce of the soil, they would, at the same time, cause the lands which were in cultivation to be better improved and more productive. And while, by their influence, the condition of each individual farmer would be meliorated, the total mass of Agricultural production would probably be increased. For this must evidently depend as much, if not more, upon the degree of improvement; than upon the number of acres under culture.

It merits particular observation, that the multiplication manufactories not only furnishes a Market for those articles, which have been accustomed to be produced in abundance, in a country; but it likewise creates a demand for such as were either unknown or produced in inconsiderable quantities. The bowels as well as the surface of the earth are ransacked for articles which were before neglected. Animals, Plants and Minerals acquire an utility and value, which were before unexplored.

The foregoing considerations seem sufficient to establish, as general propositions, That it is the interest of nations to diversify the industrious pursuits of the individuals, who compose them—That the establishment of manufactures is calculated not only to increase the general stock of useful and productive labour; but even to improve the state of Agriculture in particular; certainly to advance the interests of those who are engaged in it. There are other views, that will be hereafter taken of the subject, which, it is conceived, will serve to confirm these inferences.

The objections which are commonly made to the expediency of encouraging, and to the probability of succeeding in manufacturing pursuits, in the United States, having now been discussed; the Considerations which have appeared in the Course of the discussion, recommending that species of industry to the patronage of the Government, will be materially strengthened by a few general and some particular topics, which have been naturally reserved for subsequent Notice.

[. . .] There seems to be a moral certainty, that the trade of a country which is both manufacturing and Agricultural will be more lucrative and prosperous, than that of a Country, which is, merely Agricultural.

One reason for this is found in that general effort of nations (which has been already mentioned) to procure from their own soils, the articles of prime necessity requisite to their own consumption and use; and which serves to render their demand for a foreign supply of such articles in a great degree occasional and contingent. Hence, while the necessities of nations exclusively devoted to Agriculture, for the fabrics of manufacturing states are constant and regular, the wants of the latter for the products of the former, are liable to very considerable fluctuations and interruptions. The great inequalities resulting from difference of seasons, have been elsewhere remarked: This uniformity of demand on one side, and unsteadiness of it, on the other, must necessarily have a tendency to cause the general course of the exchange of commodities between the parties to turn to the disadvantage of the merely agricultural States. Peculiarity of situation, a climate and soil adapted to the production of peculiar commodities, may, sometimes, contradict the rule; but there is every reason to believe that it will be found in the Main, a just one.

Another circumstance which gives a superiority of commercial advantages to states, that manufacture as well as cultivate, consists in the more numerous attractions, which a more diversified market offers to foreign Customers, and greater scope, which it affords to mercantile enterprise. It is a position of indisputable truth in Commerce, depending too on very obvious reasons, that the greatest resort will ever be to those marts where commodities, while equally abundant, are most various. Each difference of kind holds out an additional inducement. And it is a position not less clear, that the field of enterprise must be enlarged to the Merchants of a Country, in proportion to the variety as well as the abundance of commodities which they find at home for exportation to foreign Markets.

A third circumstance, perhaps not inferior to either of the other two, conferring the superiority which has been stated has relation to the stagnations of demand for certain commodities which at some time or other interfere more or less with the sale of all. The Nation which can bring to Market, but few articles is likely to be more quickly and sensibly affected by such stagnations, than one, which is always possessed of a great variety of commodities. The former frequently finds too great a proportion of its stock of materials, for sale or exchange, lying on hand—or is obliged to make injurious sacrifices to supply its wants of foreign articles which are *Numerous* and *urgent*, in proportion to the smallness of the number of its own. The latter commonly finds itself indemnified, by the high prices of some articles, for the low prices of others—and the Prompt and advantageous sale of those articles which are in demand enables its merchant the better to wait for a favorable change, in respect to those which are not. There is ground to believe, that a difference of situation, in this particular, has immensely different effects upon the wealth and prosperity of Nations.

From these circumstances collectively, two important inferences are to be drawn, one, that there is always a higher probability of a favorable balance of Trade, in regard to countries in which manufactures founded on the basis of a thriving Agriculture flourish, than in regard to those, which are confined wholly or almost wholly to Agriculture; the other (which is also a consequence of the first) that countries of the former description are likely to possess more pecuniary wealth, or money, than those of the latter.

Not only the wealth; but the independence and security of a Country, appear to be materially connected with the prosperity of manufactures. Every nation, with a view to those great objects, ought to endeavour to possess within itself all the essentials of national supply. These comprise the means of *Subsistence habitation clothing* and *defence*.

The possession of these is necessary to the perfection of they body politic, to the safety as well as to the welfare of the society; the want of either, is the want of an important organ of political life and Motion; and in the various crises which await a state, it must severely feel the effects of any such deficiency. The extreme embarrassments of the United States during the late War, frorn an incapacity of supplying themselves, are still matter of keen recollection: A future war might be expected again to exemplify the mischiefs and dangers of a situation, to which that incapacity is still in too great a degree applicable, unless changed by timely and vigorous exertion. To effect this change as fast as shall be prudent, merits all the attention and all the Zeal of our Public Councils; 'tis the next great work to be accomplished.

The want of a Navy to protect our external commerce, as long as it shall Continue, must render it a peculiarly precarious reliance, for the supply of essential articles, and must serve to strengthen prodigiously the arguments in favour of manufactures.

To these general Considerations are added some of a more particular nature.

Our distance from Europe, the great fountain of manufactured supply, subjects us in the existing state of things, to inconvenience and loss in two Ways.

The bulkiness of those commodities which are the chief productions of the soil, necessarily imposes very heavy charges on their transportation, to distant markets. These charges, in the Cases, in which the nations, to whom our products are sent, maintain a Competition in the supply of their own markets, principally fall upon us, and form material deductions from the primitive value of the articles furnished. The charges on manufactured supplies, brought from Europe are greatly enhanced by the same circumstance of distance. These charges, again, in the cases in which our own industry maintains no competition, in our own markets, also principally fall upon us; and are an additional cause of extraordinary deduction from the primitive value of our own products; these being the materials of exchange for the foreign fabrics, which we consume.

The equality and moderation of individual property and the growing settlements of new districts, occasion in this country an unusual demand for coarse manufactures; The charges of which being greater in proportion to their greater bulk augment the disadvantage, which has been just described.

As in most countries domestic supplies maintain a very considerable competition with such foreign productions of the soil, as are imported for sale; if the extensive establishment of Manufactories in the United States does not create a similar competition in respect to manufactured articles, it appears to be clearly deducible, from the Considerations which have been mentioned, that they must sustain a double loss in their exchanges with foreign Nations; strongly conducive to an unfavorable balance of Trade, and very prejudicial to their Interests.

Letter to George Washington (August 18, 1792)

Philadelphia

Sir

I am happy to be able, at length, to send you, answers to the objections, which were communicated in your letter of the 29th of July.

They have unavoidably been drawn in haste, too much so, to do perfect justice to the subject, and have been copied just as they flowed from my heart and pen, without revision or correction. You will observe, that here and there some severity appears. I have not fortitude enough always to hear with calmness, calumnies, which necessarily include me, as a principal Agent in the measures censured, of the falsehood of which, I have the most unqualified consciousness. I trust that: I shall always be able to bear, as I ought, imputations of error of Judgment; but I acknowledge that I cannot be entirely patient under charges, which impeach the integrity of my public motives or conduct. I feel, that I merit them *in no degree*; and expressions of indignation sometimes escape me, in spite of every effort to suppress them. I rely on your goodness for the proper allowances.

With high respect and the most affectionate attachment, I have the honor to be, Sir Your most Obedient & humble servant

Alexander Hamilton

Objections and Answers respecting the Administration of the Government

1 Object The public Debt is greater than we can possibly pay before other causes of adding to it will occur; and this has been artificially created by adding together the *whole amount* of the Debtor and Creditor sides of the Account.

Answer The public Debt was produced by the late war. It is not the fault of the present government that it exists; unless it can be proved, that public morality and policy do not require of a Government an honest provision for its debts. Whether it is greater than can be paid before new causes of adding to it will occur is a problem incapable of being solved, but by experience; and this would be the case if it were not one fourth as much as it is. If the policy of the Country be prudent, cautious and *neutral* towards foreign nations, there is a rational probability, that war may be avoided long enough to wipe off the debt. The Dutch in a situation, not near so favorable for it as that of the UStates have enjoyed intervals of peace, longer than with proper exertions would suffice for the purpose. The Debt of the UStates compared with its present and growing abilities is really a very light one. It is little more than 15.000000 of pounds Sterling, about the annual expenditure of Great Britain.

But whether the public Debt shall be extinguished or not within a moderate period depends on the temper of the people. If they are rendered dissatisfied by repressions of the measures of the government, the Government will be deprived of an efficient command of the resources of the community towards extinguishing the Debt. And thus, those who clamour are likely to be the principal causes of protracting the existence of the debt. [. . .]

The general inducements to a provision for the public Debt are—I. To preserve the public faith and integrity by fulfilling as far as was practicable the public engagements. II. To manifest a due respect for property by satisfying the public obligations in the hands of the public Creditors and which were as much their property as their houses or their lands their hats or their coats. III. To revive and establish public Credit; the palladium of public safety. IV. To preserve the Government itself by shewing it worthy of the confidence which was placed in it, to procure to the community the blessings which in innumerable ways attend confidence in the Government and to avoid the evils which in as many ways attend the want of confidence in it.

The particular inducements to an assumption of the state Debts were. I. To consolidate the finances of the country and give an assurance of permanent order in them; avoiding the collisions of thirteen different and independent systems of finance under concurrent and coequal authorities and the scramblings for revenue which would have been incident to so many different systems. II. To secure to the Government of the Union, by avoiding those entanglements, an effectual command of the resources of the Union for present and future exigencies. III. To *equalize the condition* of the *citizens* of the several states in the important article of taxation; rescuing a part of them from being oppressed with burthens, beyond their strength, on account of extraordinary exertions in the war and through the want of certain adventitious resources, which it was the good fortune of others to possess.

A mind naturally attached to order and system and capable of appreciating their immense value, unless misled by particular feelings, is struck at once with the prodigious advantages which in the course of time must attend such a simplification of the financial affairs of the Country as results from placing all the parts of the public debt upon one footing—under one direction—regulated by one provision. The want of this sound policy has been a continual source of disorder and embarrassment in the affairs of the United Netherlands.

The true justice of the case of the public Debt consists in that equalization of the condition of the Citizens of all the states which must arise from a consolidation of the debt and common contributions towards its extinguishment. Little inequalities, as to the past, can bear no comparison with the more lasting inequalities, which, without the assumption, would have characterised the future condition of the people of the UStates; leaving upon those who had done most or suffered most a great additional weight of burthen.

If the foregoing inducements to a provision for the public Debt (including an assumption of the state debts) were sufficiently cogent—then the justification of the Excise law lies within a narrow compass. Some further source of revenue, besides the duties on imports, was indispensable, and none equally productive, would have been so little exceptionable to the Mass of the People.

Other reasons cooperated in the minds of some able men to render an excise at an early period desireable. They thought it well to lay hold of so valuable a resource of revenue before it was generally preoccupied by the State Governments. They supposed it not amiss that the authority of the National Government should be visible in some branch of internal Revenue; lest a total non-exercise of it should beget an impression that it was never to be exercised & next that it ought not to be exercised. It was supposed too that a thing of the kind could not be introduced with a greater prospect of easy success than at a period when the Government enjoyed the advantage of first impressions—when state-factions to resist its authority were not yet matured—when so much aid was to be derived from the popularity and firmness of the actual chief Magistrate.

Facts hitherto do not indicate the measure to have been rash or ill advised. The law is in operation with perfect acquiescence in all the states North of New York, though they contribute most largely. In New York and New Jersey it is in full operation with some very partial complainings fast wearing away. In the greatest part of Pennsylvania it is in operation and with increasing good humour towards it. The four Western Counties continue exceptions. In Delaware it has had some struggle, which by the last accounts was surmounted. In Maryland and Virginia, it is in operation and without material conflict. In South Carolina it is now in pretty full operation, though in the interior parts it has had some serious opposition to overcome. In Georgia no material difficulty has been experienced. North Carolina Kentucke & the four Western Counties of Pensylvania present the only remaining impediments of any consequence to the full execution of the law. The latest advices from NC & Kentuke were more favourable than the former.

It may be added as a well established fact that the effect of the law has been to encourage new enterprises in most of the states in the business of domestic distillation. A proof that it is perceived to operate favorably to the manufacture and that the measure cannot long remain unpopular any where. [. . .]

Objection 11 Paper Speculation nourishes in our Citizens &c.

Answer This proposition within certain limits is true. Jobbing in the funds has some bad effects among those engaged in it. It fosters a spirit of gambling, and diverts a certain number of individuals from other pursuits. But if the proposition be true, that Stock operates as Capital, the effect upon the Citizens at large is different. It promotes among them industry by furnishing a larger field of employment. Though this effect of a funded debt has been called in question in England by some theorists yet most theorists & all practical men allow its existence. And there is no doubt, as already intimated, that if we look into those scenes among ourselves where the largest portions of the Debt are accumulated we shall perceive that a new spring has been given to Industry in various branches.

But be all this as it may, the observation made under the last head applies here. The Debt was the creature of the Revolution. It was to be provided for. Being so, in whatever form, it must have become an object of speculation and jobbing.

Objection 12 The funding of the Debt has furnished effectual means of corrupting &c.

Answer This is one of those assertions which can only be denied and pronounced to be malignant and false. No facts exist to support it, and being a mere matter of fact, no *argument* can be brought to repel it.

The Assertors beg the question. They assume to themselves and to those who think with them infallibility. Take their words for it, they are the only honest men in the community. But compare the tenor of men's lives and *at least* as large a proportion of virtuous and independent characters will be found among those whom they malign as among themselves.

A member of a majority of the Legislature would say to these Defamers—

"In your vocabulary, Gentlemen, *creditor* and *enemy* appear to be synonymous terms—the *support of public credit* and *corruption* of similar import—an *enlarged* and *liberal* construction of the constitution for the public good and for the maintenance of the due energy of the national authority of the same meaning with usurpation and a conspiracy to overturn the republican government of the Country—every man of a different opinion from your own an ambitious despot or a corrupt knave. You bring every thing to the standard of your narrow and depraved ideas, and you condemn without mercy or even decency whatever does not accord with it. Every man who is either too long or too short for your political couch must be stretched or lopped to suit it. But your pretensions must be rejected. Your insinuations despised. Your Politics originate in immorality, in a disregard of the maxims of good faith and the rights of property, and if they could prevail must end in national disgrace and confusion. Your rules of construction for the authorities vested in the Government of the Union would arrest all its essential movements and bring it back in practice to the same state of imbecility which rendered the old confederation contemptible. Your principles of liberty are principles of licentiousness incompatible with all government. You sacrifice every thing that is venerable and substantial in society to the vain reveries of a false and new fangled philosophy. As to the motives by which I have been influenced, I leave my general conduct in private and public life to speak for them. Go and learn among my *fellow citizens* whether I have not uniformly maintained the character of an honest man. As to the love of liberty and Country you have given no stronger proofs of being actuated by it than I have done. Cease then to arrogate to yourself and to your party all the patriotism, and virtue of the Country. Renounce if you can the intolerant spirit by which you are governed—and begin to reform yourself instead of reprobating others, by beginning to doubt of your own infallibility."

Such is the answer which would naturally be given by a member of the Majority in the Legislature to such an Objector. And it is the only one that could be given; until some evidence of the supposed corruption should be produced.

As far as I know, there is not a member of the Legislature who can properly be called a Stock-jobber or a paper Dealer. There are several of them who were proprietors of public debt in various ways. Some for money lent & property furnished for the use of the public during the War others for sums received in payment of Debts—and it is supposable enough that some of them had been purchasers of the public Debt, with intention to hold it, as a valuable & convenient property; considering an honorable provision for it as matter of course.

It is a strange perversion of ideas, and as novel as it is extraordinary, that men should be deemed corrupt & criminal for becoming proprietors in the funds of their Country. Yet I believe the number of members of Congress is very small who have ever been considerably proprietors in the funds.

And as to improper speculations on measures depending before Congress, I believe never was any *body* of men freer from them.

There are indeed several members of Congress; who have become proprietors in the Bank of the United States, and a *few* of them to a pretty large amount say 50 or 60 shares; but all operations of this kind were necessarily subsequent to the determination upon the measure. The subscriptions were of course subsequent and purchases still more so. Can there be any thing really blameable in this? Can it be culpable to invest property in an institution which has been established for the most important national purposes? Can that property be supposed to corrupt the holder? It would indeed tend to render him friendly to the preservation of the Bank; but in this there would be no collision between duty and interest and it could give him no improper byass in other questions.

To uphold public credit and to be friendly to the Bank must be presupposed to be *corrupt things* before the being a proprieter in the funds or of bank Stock can be supposed to have a *corrupting influence.* The being a proprietor in either case is a very different thing from being, in a proper sense of the term, a Stock jobber. On this point of the corruption of the Legislature one more observation of great weight remains. Those who oppose a *funded* debt and mean any provision for it contemplate an *annual* one. Now, it is impossible to conceive a more fruitful source of legislative corruption than this. All the members of it who should incline to speculate would have an annual opportunity of speculating upon their influence in the legislature to promote or retard or put off a provision. Every session the question whether the annual provision should be continued would be an occasion of pernicious caballing and corrupt bargaining. In this very view when the subject was in deliberation, it was impossible not to wish it declared upon once for all & out of the way.

Objection the 13 The Corrupt Squadron &c.

Here again the objectors beg the question. They take it for granted that their constructions of the constitution are right and that the opposite ones are wrong, and with great good nature and candor ascribe the effect of a difference of opinion to a disposition to get rid of the limitations on the Government.

Those who have advocated the constructions which have obtained have met their opponents on the ground of fair argument and they think have refuted them. How shall it be determined which side is right?

There are some things which the General Government has clearly a right to do—there are others which it has clearly no right to meddle with, and there is a good deal of middle ground, about which honest & well disposed men may differ. The most that can be said is that some of this middle ground may have been occupied by the National Legislature; and this surely is no evidence of a disposition to get rid of the limitations in the constitution; nor can it be viewed in that light by men of candor.

The truth is one description of men is disposed to do the essential business of the Nation by a liberal construction of the powers of the Government; another from disaffection would fritter away those powers—a third from an overweening jealousy would do the same thing—a fourth from party & personal opposition are torturing the constitution into objections to every thing they do not like.

The Bank is one of the measures which is deemed by some the greatest stretch of power; and yet its constitutionality has been established in the most satisfactory manner.

And the most incorrigible theorist among its opponents would in one months experience as head of the Department of the Treasury be compelled to acknowledge that it is an absolutely indispensable engine in the management of the Finances, and would quickly become a convert to its perfect constitutionality.

Objection 14 The ultimate object of all.

To this there is no other answer than a flat denial—except this that the project from its absurdity refutes itself.

The idea of introducing a monarchy or aristocracy into this Country, by employing the influence and force of a Government continually changing hands, towards it, is one of those visionary things, that none but madmen could meditate and that no wise men will believe.

If it could be done at all, which is utterly incredible, it would require a long series of time, certainly beyond the life of any individual to effect it. Who then would enter into such plot? For what purpose of interest or ambition?

To hope that the people may be cajoled into giving their sanctions to such institutions is still more chimerical. A people so enlightened and so diversified as the people of this Country can surely never be brought to it, but from convulsions and disorders, in consequence of the acts of popular demagogues.

The truth unquestionably is, that the only path to a subversion of the republican system of the Country is, by flattering the prejudices of the people, and exciting their jealousies and apprehensions, to throw affairs into confusion, and bring on civil commotion. Tired at length of anarchy, or want of government, they may take shelter in the arms of monarchy for repose and security.

Those then, who resist a confirmation of public order, are the true Artificers of monarchy—not that this is the intention of the generality of them. Yet it would not be difficult to lay the finger upon some of their party who may justly be suspected. When a man unprincipled in private life desperate in his fortune, bold in his temper, possessed of considerable talents, having the advantage of military habits—despotic in his ordinary demeanour—known to have scoffed in private at the principles of liberty—when such a man is seen to mount the hobby horse of popularity—to join in the cry of danger to liberty—to take every opportunity of embarrassing the General Government & bringing it under suspicion—to flatter and fall in with all the nonsense of the zealots of the day—It may justly be suspected that his object is to throw things into confusion that he may "ride the storm and direct the whirlwind."

It has aptly been observed that *Cato* was the Tory—*Cæsar* the Whig of his day. The former frequently resisted—the latter always flattered the follies of the people. Yet the former perished with the Republic the latter destroyed it.

No popular Government was ever without its Catalines & its Cæsars. These are its true enemies.

As far as I am informed the anxiety of those who are calumniated is to keep the Government in the state in which it is, which they fear will be no easy task, from a natural tendency in the state of things to exalt the local on the ruins of the National Government. Some of them appear to wish, in a constitutional way, a change in the judiciary department of the Government, from an apprehension that an orderly and effectual administration of Justice cannot be obtained without a more intimate connection between the state and national Tribunals. But even this is not an object of any set of men as a party. There is a difference of opinion about it on various grounds among those who have generally acted together. As to any other change of consequence, I believe nobody dreams of it.

Tis curious to observe the anticipations of the different parties. One side appears to believe that there is a serious plot to overturn the state Governments and substitute monarchy to the present republican system. The other side firmly believes that there is a serious plot to overturn the General Government & elevate the separate power of the states upon its ruins. Both sides may be equally wrong & their mutual jealousies may be materially causes of the appearances which mutually disturb them, and sharpen them against each other.

Objection the 15 This change was contemplated &c.

This is a palpable misrepresentation. No man, that I know of, contemplated the introducing into this country of a monarchy. A very small number (not more than three or four) manifested theoretical opinions favourable in the abstract to a constitution like that of Great Britain, but every one agreed that such a constitution except as to the general distribution of departments and powers was out of the Question in reference to this Country. The Member who was most explicit on this point (a Member from New York) declared in strong terms that the republican theory ought to be adhered to in this Country as long as there was any chance of its success—that the idea of a perfect equality of political rights among the citizens, exclusive of all permanent or hereditary distinctions, was of a nature to engage the good wishes of every good man, whatever might be his theoretic doubts—that it merited his best efforts to give success to it in practice—that hitherto from an incompetent structure of the Government it had not had a fair trial, and that the endeavour ought then to be to secure to it a better chance of success by a government more capable of energy and order.

There is not a man at present in either branch of the Legislature who, that I recollect, had held language in the Convention favourable to Monarchy.

The basis therefore of this suggestion fails. [. . .]

James Madison

A Candid State of Parties (September 26, 1792)

As it is the business of the contemplative statesman to trace the history of parties in a free country, so it is the duty of the citizen at all times to understand the actual state of them. Whenever this duty is omitted, an opportunity is given to designing men, by the use of artificial or nominal distinctions, to oppose and balance against each other those who never differed as to the end to be pursued, and may no longer differ as to the means of attaining it. The most interesting state of parties in the United States may be referred to three periods: Those who espoused the cause of independence and those who adhered to the British claims, formed the parties of the first period; if, indeed, the disaffected class were considerable enough to deserve the name of a party. This state of things was superseded by the treaty of peace in 1783. From 1783 to 1787 there were parties in abundance, but being rather local than general, they are not within the present review.

The Federal Constitution, proposed in the latter year, gave birth to a second and most interesting division of the people. Every one remembers it, because every one was involved in it.

Among those who embraced the constitution, the great body were unquestionably friends to republican liberty; tho' there were, no doubt, some who were openly or secretly attached to monarchy and aristocracy; and hoped to make the constitution a cradle for these hereditary establishments.

Among those who opposed the constitution, the great body were certainly well affected to the union and to good government, tho' there might be a few who had a leaning unfavourable to both. This state of parties was terminated by the regular and effectual establishment of the federal government in 1788; out of the administration of which, however, has arisen a third division, which being natural to most political societies, is likely to be of some duration in ours.

One of the divisions consists of those, who from particular interest, from natural temper, or from the habits of life, are more partial to the opulent than to the other classes of society; and having debauched themselves into a persuasion that mankind are incapable of governing themselves, it follows with them, of course, that government can be carried on only by the pageantry of rank, the influence of money and emoluments, and the terror of military force. Men of those sentiments must naturally wish to point the measures of government less to the interest of the many than of a few, and less to the reason of the many than to their weaknesses; hoping perhaps in proportion to the ardor of their zeal, that by giving such a turn to the administration, the government itself may by degrees be narrowed into fewer hands, and approximated to an hereditary form.

The other division consists of those who believing in the doctrine that mankind are capable of governing themselves, and hating hereditary power as an insult to the reason and an outrage to the rights of man, are naturally offended at every public measure that does not appeal to the understanding and to the general interest of the community, or that is not strictly conformable to the principles, and conducive to the preservation of republican government.

This being the real state of parties among us, an experienced and dispassionate observer will be at no loss to decide on the probable conduct of each.

The antirepublican party, as it may be called, being the weaker in point of numbers, will be induced by the most obvious motives to strengthen themselves with the men of influence, particularly of moneyed, which is the most active and insinuating influence. It will be equally their true policy to weaken their opponents by reviving exploded parties, and taking advantage of all prejudices, local, political, and occupational, that may prevent or disturb a general coalition of sentiments.

The Republican party, as it may be termed, conscious that the mass of people in every part of the union, in every state, and of every occupation must at bottom be with them, both in interest and sentiment, will naturally find their account in burying all antecedent questions, in banishing every other distinction than that between enemies and friends to republican government, and in promoting a general harmony among the latter, wherever residing, or however employed.

Whether the republican or the rival party will ultimately establish its ascendance, is a problem which may be contemplated now; but which time alone can solve. On one hand experience shows that in politics as in war, stratagem is often an overmatch for numbers: and among more happy characteristics of our political situation, it is now well understood that there are peculiarities, some temporary, others more durable, which may favour that side in the contest. On the republican side, again, the superiority of numbers is so great, their sentiments are so decided, and the practice of making a common cause, where there is a common sentiment and common interest, in sight of circumstantial and artificial distinctions, is so well understood, that no temperate observer of human affairs will be surprised if the issue in the present instance should be reversed, and the government be administered in the spirit and form approved by the great body of the people.

ALEXANDER HAMILTON

Pacificus, No. 1 (June 29, 1793)

As attempts are making very dangerous to the peace, and it is to be feared not very friendly to the constitution of the UStates—it becomes the duty of those who wish well to both to endeavour to prevent their success.

The objections which have been raised against the Proclamation of Neutrality lately issued by the President have been urged in a spirit of acrimony and invective, which demonstrates, that more was in view than merely a free discussion of an important public measure; that the discussion covers a design of weakening the confidence of the People in the author of the measure; in order to remove or lessen a powerful obstacle to the success of an opposition to the Government, which however it may change its form, according to circumstances, seems still to be adhered to and pursued with persevering Industry.

This Reflection adds to the motives connected with the measure itself to recommend endeavours by proper explanations to place it in a just light. Such explanations at least cannot but be satisfactory to those who may not have leisure or opportunity for pursuing themselves an investigation of the subject, and who may wish to perceive that the policy of the Government is not inconsistent with its obligations or its honor.

The objections in question fall under three heads—

1. That the Proclamation was without authority
2. That it was contrary to our treaties with France
3. That it was contrary to the gratitude, which is due from this to that country; for the succours rendered us in our own Revolution.
4. That it was out of time & unnecessary.

In order to judge of the solidity of the first of these objection[s], it is necessary to examine what is the nature and design of a proclamation of neutrality.

The true nature & design of such an act is—to *make known* to the powers at War and to the Citizens of the Country, whose Government does the Act that such country is in the condition of a Nation at Peace with the belligerent parties, and under no obligations of Treaty, to become an *associate in the war* with either of them; that this being its situation its intention is to observe a conduct conformable with it and to perform towards each the duties of neutrality; and as a consequence of this state of things, to give warning to all within its jurisdiction to abstain from acts that shall contravene those duties, under the penalties which the laws of the land (of which the law of Nations is a part) annexes to acts of contravention.

This, and no more, is conceived to be the true import of a Proclamation of Neutrality.

It does not imply, that the Nation which makes the declaration will forbear to perform to any of the warring Powers any stipulations in Treaties which can be performed without rendering it an *associate* or *party* in the War. It therefore does not imply in our case, that the UStates will not make those distinctions, between the present belligerent powers, which are stipulated in the 17th and 22d articles of our Treaty with France; because these distinctions are not incompatible with a state of neutrality; they will in no shape render the UStates an *associate* or *party* in the War. This must be evident, when it is considered, that even to furnish *determinate* succours, of a certain number of Ships or troops, to a Power at War, in consequence of *antecedent treaties having no particular reference to the existing war*, is not inconsistent with neutrality; a position well established by the doctrines of Writers and the practice of Nations.

But no special aids, succours or favors having relation to war, not positively and precisely stipulated by some Treaty of the above description, can be afforded to either party, without a breach of neutrality.

In stating that the Proclamation of Neutrality does not imply the non performance of any stipulations of Treaties which are not of a nature to make the Nation an associate or party in the war, it is conceded that an execution of the clause of Guarantee contained in the 11th article of our Treaty of Alliance with France would be contrary to the sense and spirit of the Proclamation; because it would engage us with our whole force as an *associate* or *auxiliary* in the War; it would be much more than the case of a definite limited succour, previously ascertained.

It follows that the Proclamation is virtually a manifestation of the sense of the Government that the UStates are, *under the circumstances of the case, not bound* to execute the clause of Guarantee.

If this be a just view of the true force and import of the Proclamation, it will remain to see whether the President in issuing it acted within his proper sphere, or stepped beyond the bounds of his constitutional authority and duty.

It will not be disputed that the management of the affairs of this country with foreign nations is confided to the Government of the UStates.

It can as little be disputed, that a Proclamation of Neutrality, where a Nation is at liberty to keep out of a War in which other Nations are engaged and means so to do, is a *usual* and a *proper* measure. *Its main object and effect are to prevent the Nation being immediately responsible for acts done by its citizens, without the privity or connivance of the Government, in contravention of the principles of neutrality.*

An object this of the greatest importance to a Country whose true interest lies in the preservation of peace.

The inquiry then is—what department of the Government of the UStates is the proper one to make a declaration of Neutrality in the cases in which the engagements of the Nation permit and its interests require such a declaration.

A correct and well informed mind will discern at once that it can belong neither to the Legislative nor Judicial Department and of course must belong to the Executive.

The Legislative Department is not the *organ* of intercourse between the UStates and foreign Nations. It is charged neither with *making* nor *interpreting* Treaties. It is therefore not naturally that Organ of the Government which is to pronounce the existing condition of the Nation, with regard to foreign Powers, or to admonish the Citizens of their obligations and duties as founded upon that condition of things. Still less is it charged with enforcing the execution and observance of these obligations and those duties.

It is equally obvious that the act in question is foreign to the Judiciary Department of the Government. The province of that Department is to decide litigations in particular cases. It is indeed charged with the interpretation of treaties; but it exercises this function only in the litigated cases; that is where contending parties bring before it a specific controversy. It has no concern with pronouncing upon the external political relations of Treaties between Government and

Government. This position is too plain to need being insisted upon.

It must then of necessity belong to the Executive Department to exercise the function in Question—when a proper case for the exercise of it occurs.

It appears to be connected with that department in various capacities, as the *organ* of intercourse between the Nation and foreign Nations—as the interpreter of the National Treaties in those cases in which the Judiciary is not competent, that is in the cases between Government and Government—as that Power, which is charged with the Execution of the Laws, of which Treaties form a part—as that Power which is charged with the command and application of the Public Force.

This view of the subject is so natural and obvious—so analogous to general theory and practice—that no doubt can be entertained of its justness, unless such doubt can be deduced from particular provisions of the Constitution of the UStates.

Let us see then if cause for such doubt is to be found in that constitution.

The second Article of the Constitution of the UStates, section 1st, establishes this general Proposition, That "The Executive Power shall be vested in a President of the United States of America."

The same article in a succeeding Section proceeds to designate particular cases of Executive Power. It declares among other things that the President shall be Commander in Chief of the army and navy of the UStates and of the Militia of the several states when called into the actual service of the UStates, that he shall have power by and with the advice of the senate to make treaties; that it shall be his duty to receive ambassadors and other public Ministers and to take care that the laws be faithfully executed.

It would not consist with the rules of sound construction to consider this enumeration of particular authorities as derogating from the more comprehensive grant contained in the general clause, further than as it may be coupled with express restrictions or qualifications; as in regard to the cooperation of the Senate in the appointment of Officers and the making of treaties; which are qualifications of the general executive powers of appointing officers and making treaties: Because the difficulty of a complete and perfect specification of all the cases of Executive authority would naturally dictate the use of general terms—and would render it improbable that a specification of certain particulars was design[e]d as a substitute for those terms, when antecedently used. The different mode of expression employed in the constitution in regard to the two powers the Legislative and the Executive serves to confirm this inference. In the article which grants the legislative powers of the Governt the expressions are—"*All Legislative powers herein granted shall be vested in a Congress of the UStates;*" in that which grants the Executive Power the expressions are, as already quoted "The Executive Power shall be vested in a President of the UStates of America."

The enumeration ought rather therefore to be considered as intended by way of greater caution, to specify and regulate the principal articles implied in the definition of Executive Power; leaving the rest to flow from the general grant of that power, interpreted in conformity to other parts of the constitution and to the principles of free government.

The general doctrine then of our constitution is, that the Executive Power of the Nation is vested in the President; subject only to the *exceptions* and *qu[a]lifications* which are expressed in the instrument.

Two of these have been already noticed—the participation of the Senate in the appointment of Officers and the making of Treaties. A third remains to be mentioned the right of the Legislature "to declare war and grant letters of marque and reprisal."

With these exceptions the Executive Power of the Union is completely lodged in the President. This mode of construing the Constitution has indeed been recognized by Congress in formal acts, upon full consideration and debate. The power of removal from office is an important instance.

And since upon general principles for reasons already given, the issuing of a proclamation of neutrality is merely an Executive Act; since also the general Executive Power of the Union is vested in the President, the conclusion is, that the step, which has been taken by him, is liable to no just exception on the score of authority.

It may be observed that this Inference would be just if the power of declaring war had not been vested in the Legislature, but that this power naturally includes the right of judging whether the Nation is under obligations to make war or not.

The answer to this is, that however true it may be, that the right of the Legislature to declare war includes the right of judging whether the Nation be under obligations to make War or not—it will not follow that the Executive is in any case excluded from a similar right of Judgment, in the execution of its own functions.

If the Legislature have a right to make war on the one hand—it is on the other the duty of the Executive to preserve Peace till war is declared; and in fulfilling that duty, it must necessarily possess a right of judging what is the nature of the obligations which the treaties of the Country impose on the Government; and when in pursuance of this right it has concluded that there is nothing in them inconsistent with a *state* of neutrality, it becomes both its province and its duty to enforce the laws incident to that state of the Nation. The Executive is charged with the execution of all laws, the laws of Nations as well as the Municipal law, which recognises and adopts those laws. It is consequently bound, by faithfully executing the laws of neutrality, when that is the state of the Nation, to avoid giving a cause of war to foreign Powers.

This is the direct and proper end of the proclamation of neutrality. It declares to the UStates their situation with regard to the Powers at war and makes known to the Community that the laws incident to that situation will be enforced. In doing this, it conforms to an established usage of Nations, the operation of which as before remarked is to obviate a responsibility on the part of the whole Society, for secret and unknown violations of the rights of any of the warring parties by its citizens.

Those who object to the proclamation will readily admit that it is the right and duty of the Executive to judge of, or to interpret, those articles of our treaties which give to France particular privileges, in order to the enforcement of those privileges: But the necessary consequence of this is, that the Executive must judge what are the proper bounds of those privileges—what rights are given to other nations by our treaties with them—what rights the law of Nature and Nations gives and our treaties permit, in respect to those Nations with whom we have no treaties; in fine what are the reciprocal rights and obligations of the United States & of all & each of the powers at War.

The right of the Executive to receive ambassadors and other public Ministers may serve to illustrate the relative duties of the Executive and Legislative Departments. This right includes that of judging, in the case of a Revolution of Government in a foreign Country, whether the new rulers are competent organs of the National Will and ought to be recognised or not: And where a treaty antecedently exists between the UStates and such nation that right involves the power of giving operation or not to such treaty. For until the new Government is *acknowleged*, the treaties between the nations, as far at least as regards *public* rights, are of course suspended.

This power of determining virtually in the case supposed upon the operation of national Treaties as a consequence, of the power to receive ambassadors and other public Ministers, is an important instance of the right of the Executive to decide the obligations of the Nation with regard to foreign Nations. To apply it to the case of France, if there had been a Treaty of alliance *offensive* and defensive between the UStates and that Country, the unqualified acknowlegement of the new Government would have put the UStates in a condition to become an associate in the War in which France was engaged—and would have laid the Legislature under an obligation, if required, and there was otherwise no valid excuse, of exercising its power of declaring war.

This serves as an example of the right of the Executive, in certain cases, to determine the condition of the Nation, though it may consequentially affect the proper or improper exercise of the Power of the Legislature to declare war. The Executive indeed cannot control the exercise of that power—further than by the exer[c]ise of its general right of objecting to all acts of the Legislature; liable to being overruled by two thirds of both houses of Congress. The Legislature is free to perform its own duties according to its own sense of them—though the Executive in the exercise of its constitutional powers, may establish an antecedent state of things which ought to weigh in the legislative decisions. From the division of the Executive Power there results, in referrence to it, a *concurrent* authority, in the distributed cases.

Hence in the case stated, though treaties can only be made by the President and Senate, their activity may be continued or suspended by the President alone.

No objection has been made to the Presidents having acknowledged the Republic of France, by the

Reception of its Minister, without having consulted the Senate; though that body is connected with him in the making of Treaties, and though the consequence of his act of reception is to give operation to the Treaties heretofore made with that Country: But he is censured for having declared the UStates to be in a state of peace & neutrality, with regard to the Powers at War; because the right of *changing* that state & *declaring war* belongs to the Legislature.

It deserves to be remarked, that as the participation of the senate in the making of Treaties and the power of the Legislature to declare war are exceptions out of the general "Executive Power" vested in the President, they are to be construed strictly—and ought to be extended no further than is essential to their execution.

While therefore the Legislature can alone declare war, can alone actually transfer the nation from a state of Peace to a state of War—it belongs to the "Executive Power," to do whatever else the laws of Nations cooperating with the Treaties of the Country enjoin, in the intercourse of the UStates with foreign Powers.

In this distribution of powers the wisdom of our constitution is manifested. It is the province and duty of the Executive to preserve to the Nation the blessings of peace. The Legislature alone can interrupt those blessings, by placing the Nation in a state of War.

But though it has been thought adviseable to vindicate the authority of the Executive on this broad and comprehensive ground—it was not absolutely necessary to do so. That clause of the constitution which makes it his duty to "take care that the laws be faithfully executed" might alone have been relied upon, and this simple process of argument pursued.

The President is the constitutional Executor of the laws. Our Treaties and the laws of Nations form a part of the law of the land. He who is to execute the laws must first judge for himself of their meaning. In order to the observance of that conduct, which the laws of nations combined with our treaties prescribed to this country, in reference to the present War in Europe, it was necessary for the President to judge for himself whether there was any thing in our treaties incompatible with an adherence to neutrality. Having judged that there was not, he had a right, and if in his opinion the interests of the Nation required it, it was his duty, as Executor of the laws, to proclaim the neutrality of the Nation, to exhort all persons to observe it, and to warn them of the penalties which would attend its non observance.

The Proclamation has been represented as enacting some new law. This is a view of it entirely erroneous. It only proclaims a *fact* with regard to the *existing state* of the Nation, informs the citizens of what the laws previously established require of them in that state, & warns them that these laws will be put in execution against the Infractors of them.

JAMES MADISON

Helvidius, No. 1 (August 24, 1793)

Several pieces with the signature of PACIFICUS were lately published, which have been read with singular pleasure and applause, by the foreigners and degenerate citizens among us, who hate our republican government, and the French revolution; whilst the publication seems to have been too little regarded, or too much despised by the steady friends to both.

Had the doctrines inculcated by the writer, with the natural consequences from them, been nakedly presented to the public, this treatment might have been proper. Their true character would then have struck every eye, and been rejected by the feelings of every heart. But they offer themselves to the reader in the dress of an elaborate dissertation; they are mingled with a few truths that may serve them as a passport to credulity; and they are introduced with professions of anxiety for the preservation of peace, for the welfare of the government, and for the respect due to the present head of the executive, that may prove a snare to patriotism.

In these disguises they have appeared to claim the attention I propose to bestow on them; with a view to shew, from the publication itself, that under colour of vindicating an important public act, of a chief magistrate, who enjoys the confidence and love of his country, principles are advanced which strike at the vitals of its constitution, as well as at its honor and true interest.

As it is not improbable that attempts may be made to apply insinuations which are seldom spared when particular purposes are to be answered, to the author of the ensuing observations, it may not be improper to premise, that he is a friend to the constitution, that he wishes for the preservation of peace, and that the present chief magistrate has not a fellow-citizen, who is penetrated with deeper respect for his merits, or feels a purer solicitude for his glory.

This declaration is made with no view of courting a more favorable ear to what may be said than it deserves. The sole purpose of it is, to obviate imputations which might weaken the impressions of truth; and which are the more likely to be resorted to, in proportion as solid and fair arguments may be wanting.

The substance of the first piece, sifted from its inconsistencies and its vague expressions, may be thrown into the following propositions:

That the powers of declaring war and making treaties are, in their nature, executive powers:

That being particularly vested by the constitution in other departments, they are to be considered as exceptions out of the general grant to the executive department:

That being, as exceptions, to be construed strictly, the powers not strictly within them, remain with the executive:

That the executive consequently, as the organ of intercourse with foreign nations, and the interpreter and executor of treaties, and the law of nations, is authorised, to expound all articles of treaties, those involving questions of war and peace, as well as others; to judge of the obligations of the United States to make war or not, under any casus federis or eventual operation of the contract, relating to war; and, to pronounce the state of things resulting from the obligations of the United States, as understood by the executive:

That in particular the executive had authority to judge whether in the case of the mutual guaranty between the United States and France, the former were bound by it to engage in the war:

That the executive has, in pursuance of that authority, decided that the United States are not bound: And,

That its proclamation of the 22d of April last, is to be taken as the effect and expression of that decision.

The basis of the reasoning is, we perceive, the extraordinary doctrine, that the powers of making war and treaties, are in their nature executive; and therefore comprehended in the general grant of executive power, where not specially and strictly excepted out of the grant.

Let us examine this doctrine; and that we may avoid the possibility of mistating the writer, it shall be laid down in his own words: a precaution the more necessary, as scarce any thing else could outweigh the improbability, that so extravagant a tenet should be hazarded, at so early a day, in the face of the public.

His words are—"Two of these (exceptions and qualifications to the executive powers) have been already noticed—the participation of the Senate in the *appointment of officers*, and the *making of treaties*. A *third* remains to be mentioned—the right of the legislature to *declare war, and grant letters of marque and reprisal*."

Again—"It deserves to be remarked, that as the participation of the Senate in the *making treaties*, and the power of the legislature to *declare war*, are *exceptions* out of the general *executive power*, vested in the President, they are to be construed *strictly*, and ought to be extended no farther than is essential to their execution."

If there be any countenance to these positions, it must be found either 1st, in the writers, of authority, on public law; or 2d, in the quality and operation of the powers to make war and treaties; or 3d, in the constitution of the United States.

[1.] It would be of little use, to enter far into the first source of information, not only because our own reason and our own constitution, are the best guides;

but because a just analysis and discrimination of the powers of government, according to their executive, legislative and judiciary qualities are not to be expected in the works of the most received jurists, who wrote before a critical attention was paid to those objects, and with their eyes too much on monarchical governments, where all powers are confounded in the sovereignty of the prince. It will be found however, I believe, that all of them, particularly Wolfius, Burlamaqui and Vattel, speak of the powers to declare war, to conclude peace, and to form alliances, as among the highest acts of the sovereignty; of which the legislative power must at least be an integral and preeminent part.

Writers, such as Locke and Montesquieu, who have discussed more particularly the principles of liberty and the structure of government, lie under the same disadvantage, of having written before these subjects were illuminated by the events and discussions which distinguish a very recent period. Both of them too are evidently warped by a regard to the particular government of England, to which one of them owed allegiance;[1] and the other professed an admiration bordering on idolatry. Montesquieu, however, has rather distinguished himself by enforcing the reasons and the importance of avoiding a confusion of the several powers of government, than by enumerating and defining the powers which belong to each particular class. And Locke, notwithstanding the early date of his work on civil government, and the example of his own government before his eyes, admits that the particular powers in question, which, after some of the writers on public law he calls *federative*, are really *distinct* from the *executive*, though almost always united with it, and *hardly to be separated into distinct hands*. Had he not lived under a monarchy, in which these powers were united; or had he written by the lamp which truth now presents to lawgivers, the last observation would probably never have dropt from his pen. But let us quit a field of research which is more likely to perplex than to decide, and bring the question to other tests of which it will be more easy to judge.

2. If we consult for a moment, the nature and operation of the two powers to declare war and make treaties, it will be impossible not to see that they can never fall within a proper definition of executive powers. The natural province of the executive magistrate is to execute laws, as that of the legislature is to make laws. All his acts therefore, properly executive, must pre-suppose the existence of the laws to be executed. A treaty is not an execution of laws: it does not pre-suppose the existence of laws. It is, on the contrary, to have itself the force of a *law*, and to be carried into *execution*, like all *other laws*, by the *executive magistrate*. To say then that the power of making treaties which are confessedly laws, belongs naturally to the department which is to execute laws, is to say, that the executive department naturally includes a legislative power. In theory, this is an absurdity—in practice a tyranny.

The power to declare war is subject to similar reasoning. A declaration that there shall be war, is not an execution of laws: it does not suppose pre-existing laws to be executed: it is not in any respect, an act merely executive. It is, on the contrary, one of the most deliberative acts that can be performed; and when performed, has the effect of *repealing* all the *laws* operating in a state of peace, so far as they are inconsistent with a state of war: and of *enacting* as *a rule for the executive*, a *new code* adapted to the relation between the society and its foreign enemy. In like manner a conclusion of peace *annuls* all the *laws* peculiar to a state of war, and *revives* the general *laws* incident to a state of peace.

These remarks will be strengthened by adding that treaties, particularly treaties of peace, have sometimes the effect of changing not only the external laws of the society, but operate also on the internal code, which is purely municipal, and to which the legislative authority of the country is of itself competent and compleat.

From this view of the subject it must be evident, that although the executive may be a convenient organ of preliminary communications with foreign governments, on the subjects of treaty or war; and the proper agent for carrying into execution the final determinations of the competent authority; yet it can

---

1. The chapter on prerogative, shews how much the reason of the philosopher was clouded by the royalism of the Englishman.

have no pretensions from the nature of the powers in question compared with the nature of the executive trust, to that essential agency which gives validity to such determinations.

It must be further evident that, if these powers be not in their nature purely legislative, they partake so much more of that, than of any other quality, that under a constitution leaving them to result to their most natural department, the legislature would be without a rival in its claim.

Another important inference to be noted is, that the powers of making war and treaty being substantially of a legislative, not an executive nature, the rule of interpreting exceptions strictly, must narrow instead of enlarging executive pretensions on those subjects.

3. It remains to be enquired whether there be any thing in the constitution itself which shows that the powers of making war and peace are considered as of an executive nature, and as comprehended within a general grant of executive power.

It will not be pretended that this appears from any *direct* position to be found in the instrument.

If it were *deducible* from any particular expressions it may be presumed that the publication would have saved us the trouble of the research.

Does the doctrine then result from the actual distribution of powers among the several branches of the government? Or from any fair analogy between the powers of war and treaty and the enumerated powers vested in the executive alone?

Let us examine.

In the general distribution of powers, we find that of declaring war expressly vested in the Congress, where every other legislative power is declared to be vested, and without any other qualification than what is common to every other legislative act. The constitutional idea of this power would seem then clearly to be, that it is of a legislative and not an executive nature.

This conclusion becomes irresistible, when it is recollected, that the constitution cannot be supposed to have placed either any power legislative in its nature, entirely among executive powers, or any power executive in its nature, entirely among legislative powers, without changing the constitution, with that kind of intermixture and consolidation of different powers, which would violate a fundamental principle in the organization of free governments. If it were not unnecessary to enlarge on this topic here, it could be shewn, that the constitution was originally vindicated, and has been constantly expounded, with a disavowal of any such intermixture.

The power of treaties is vested jointly in the President and in the Senate, which is a branch of the legislature. From this arrangement merely, there can be no inference that would necessarily exclude the power from the executive class: since the senate is joined with the President in another power, that of appointing to offices, which as far as relate to executive offices at least, is considered as of an executive nature. Yet on the other hand, there are sufficient indications that the power of treaties is regarded by the constitution as materially different from mere executive power, and as having more affinity to the legislative than to the executive character.

One circumstance indicating this, is the constitutional regulation under which the senate give their consent in the case of treaties. In all other cases the consent of the body is expressed by a majority of voices. In this particular case, a concurrence of two thirds at least is made necessary, as a substitute or compensation for the other branch of the legislature, which on certain occasions, could not be conveniently a party to the transaction.

But the conclusive circumstance is, that treaties when formed according to the constitutional mode, are confessedly to have the force and operation of *laws*, and are to be a rule for the courts in controversies between man and man, as much as any *other laws*. They are even emphatically declared by the constitution to be "the supreme law of the land."

So far the argument from the constitution is precisely in opposition to the doctrine. As little will be gained in its favour from a comparison of the two powers, with those particularly vested in the President alone.

As there are but few it will be most satisfactory to review them one by one.

"The President shall be commander in chief of the army and navy of the United States, and of the militia when called into the actual service of the United States."

There can be no relation worth examining between this power and the general power of making treaties. And instead of being analogous to the power of declaring war, it affords a striking illustration of the incompatibility of the two powers in the same hands. Those who are to *conduct a war* cannot in the nature of things, be proper or safe judges, whether *a war ought* to be *commenced, continued,* or *concluded.* They are barred from the latter functions by a great principle in free government, analogous to that which separates the sword from the purse, or the power of executing from the power of enacting laws.

"He may require the opinion in writing of the principal officers in each of the executive departments upon any subject relating to the duties of their respective offices; and he shall have power to grant reprieves and pardons for offences against the United States, except in case of impeachment." These powers can have nothing to do with the subject.

"The President shall have power to fill up vacancies that may happen during the recess of the senate, by granting commissions which shall expire at the end of the next session." The same remark is applicable to this power, as also to that of "receiving ambassadors, other public ministers and consuls." The particular use attempted to be made of this last power will be considered in another place.

"He shall take care that the laws shall be faithfully executed and shall commission all officers of the United States." To see the laws faithfully executed constitutes the essence of the executive authority. But what relation has it to the power of making treaties and war, that is, of determining what the *laws shall be* with regard to other nations? No other certainly than what subsists between the powers of executing and enacting laws; no other consequently, than what forbids a coalition of the powers in the same department.

I pass over the few other specified functions assigned to the President, such as that of convening of the legislature, &c. &c. which cannot be drawn into the present question.

It may be proper however to take notice of the power of removal from office, which appears to have been adjudged to the President by the laws establishing the executive departments; and which the writer has endeavored to press into his service. To justify any favorable inference from this case, it must be shewn, that the powers of war and treaties are of a kindred nature to the power of removal, or at least are equally within a grant of executive power. Nothing of this sort has been attempted, nor probably will be attempted. Nothing can in truth be clearer, than that no analogy, or shade of analogy, can be traced between a power in the supreme officer responsible for the faithful execution of the laws, to displace a subaltern officer employed in the execution of the laws; and a power to make treaties, and to declare war, such as these have been found to be in their nature, their operation, and their consequences.

Thus it appears that by whatever standard we try this doctrine, it must be condemned as no less vicious in theory than it would be dangerous in practice. It is countenanced neither by the writers on law; nor by the nature of the powers themselves; nor by any general arrangements or particular expressions, or plausible analogies, to be found in the constitution.

Whence then can the writer have borrowed it?

There is but one answer to this question.

The power of making treaties and the power of declaring war, are *royal prerogatives* in the *British government,* and are accordingly treated as Executive prerogatives by *British commentators.*

We shall be the more confirmed in the necessity of this solution of the problem, by looking back to the aera of the constitution, and satisfying ourselves that the writer could not have been misled by the doctrines maintained by our own commentators on our own government. That I may not ramble beyond prescribed limits, I shall content myself with an extract from a work which entered into a systematic explanation and defense of the constitution, and to which there has frequently been ascribed some influence in conciliating the public assent to the government in the form proposed. Three circumstances conspire in giving weight to this contemporary exposition. It was made at a time when no application to *persons* or *measures* could bias: The opinion given was not transiently mentioned, but formally and critically elucidated: It related to a point in the constitution which must consequently have been viewed as of importance in the public mind. The passage relates to the power of making treaties; that of declaring war, being arranged with such obvious propriety among the legislative powers, as to be passed over without particular discussion.

"Tho' several writers on the subject of government place that power (*of making treaties*) in the class of *Executive authorities*, yet this is *evidently* an *arbitrary disposition*. For if we attend *carefully*, to its operation, it will be found to partake *more* of the *legislative* than of the *executive* character, though it does not seem strictly to fall within the definition of either of them. The essence of the legislative authority, is to enact laws; or in other words, to prescribe rules for the regulation of the society. While the execution of the laws and the employment of the common strength, either for this purpose, or for the common defense, seem to comprise *all* the functions of the *Executive magistrate*. The power of making treaties is *plainly* neither the one nor the other. It relates neither to the execution of the subsisting laws, nor to the enaction of new ones, and still less to an exertion of the common strength. Its objects are contracts with foreign nations, which have the *force of law*, but derive it from the obligations of good faith. They are not rules prescribed by the sovereign to the subject, but agreements between sovereign and sovereign. The power in question seems therefore to form a distinct department, and to belong properly neither to the legislative nor to the executive. The qualities elsewhere detailed as indispensable in the management of foreign *negotiations*, point out the executive as the most fit agent in those transactions: whilst the vast importance of the trust, and the operation of treaties *as Laws*, plead strongly for the participation of the whole or a part of the *legislative body* in the office of making them." Federalist vol. 2. p. 273.

It will not fail to be remarked on this commentary, that whatever doubts may be started as to the correctness of its reasoning against the legislative nature of the power to make treaties: it is *clear*, *consistent* and *confident*, in deciding that the power is *plainly* and *evidently* not an *executive power*.

Alexander Hamilton

Letter to George Washington (August 2, 1794)

Treasury Department

Sir

In compliance with your requisition I have the honor to submit my Opinion as to the course which it will be advisable for the President to pursue in regard to the armed Opposition recently given in the four Western Counties of Pennsylvania to the execution of the laws of the U. States laying duties upon Spirits distilled within the United States and upon Stills.

The case upon which an Opinion is required is summarily as follows. The four most Western Counties of Pennsylvania since the Commencement of those laws a period of more than three Years, have been in steady and Violent Opposition to them. By formal public meetings of influential individuals, whose resolutions and proceedings had for undisguised objects, to render the laws odious, to discountenance a compliance with them, and to intimidate individuals from accepting and executing Offices under them—by a general Spirit of Opposition (thus fomented) among the Inhabitants—by repeated instances of armed parties going in disguise to the houses of the Officers of the Revenue and inflicting upon them personal violence and outrage—by general combinations to forbear a compliance with the requisitions of the laws by examples of injury to the Property and insult to the persons of individuals who have shewn by their conduct a disposition to comply and by an almost universal noncompliance with the laws—their execution within the Counties in question has been completely frustrated.

Various Alterations have been made in the laws by the Legislature to obviate as far as possible the objections of the Inhabitants of those Counties.

The executive, on its part has been far from deficient in forbearance lenity or a Spirit of Accommodation.

But neither the Legislative nor the Executive accommodations have had any effect in producing compliance with the laws.

The Opposition has continued and matured, till it has at length broke out in Acts which are presumed to amount to Treason.

Armed Collections of men, with the avowed design of Opposing the execution of the laws, have attacked the house of the Inspector of the Revenue, burnt and destroyed his Property and Shed the blood of Persons engaged in its defence—have made Prisoner of the Marshall of the District and did not release him till for the Safety of his life he stipulated to execute no more processes within the disaffected counties—have compelled both him and the Inspector of the Revenue to fly the Country by a circuitous route to avoid personal injury perhaps Assassination—have proposed the Assembling of a Convention of delegates from these Counties and the Neighbouring ones of Virginia probably with a view to systematize measures of more effectual Opposition—have forcibly seized Opened & Spoliated a Mail of the United States.

What in this State of things is proper to be done?

The President has with the advice of the heads of the Departments and the Attorney General, caused to be submitted all the evidence of the foregoing facts to the Consideration of an Associate Judge under the Act intitled "An Act to provide for calling forth the Militia to execute the laws of the Union Suppress Insurrection and repel Invasion."

If the Judge shall pronounce that the case described in the second section of the Act exists—it will follow that a competent force of Militia should be called forth and employed to suppress the insurrection and support the Civil Authority in effectuating Obedience to the laws and the punishment of Offenders.

It appears to me that the very existence of Government demands this course and that a duty of the highest nature urges the Chief Magistrate to pursue it. The Constitution and laws of the United States, contemplate and provide for it.

What force of Militia shall be called out, and from What State or States?

The force ought if attainable to be an imposing one, such if practicable, as will deter from opposition, save the effusion of the blood of Citizens and secure the object to be accomplished.

The quantum must of course be regulated by the resistance to expected. Tis computed, that the four opposing Counties contain upwards of sixteen thousand males of 16 years and more, that of these about seven thousand may be expected to be armed. Tis possible that the union of the neighbouring Counties of Virginia may augment this force. Tis not impossible, that it may receive an accession from some adjacent Counties of this state on this side of the Alleghany Mountain.

To be prepared for the worst, I am of opinion, that twelve thousand Militia ought to be ordered to assemble; 9000 foot and 3000 horse. I should not propose so many horse, but for the probability, that this description of Militia, will be more easily procured for the service.

From what State or States shall these come?

The Law contemplates that the Militia of a State, in which an insurrection happens, if willing & sufficient shall first be employed, but gives power to employ the Milita of other States in the case either of refusal or insufficiency.

The Governor of Pennsylvania in an Official conference this day, gave it explicitly as his opinion to the President, that the Militia of Pennsylvania alone would be found incompetent to the suppression of the insurrection.

This Opinion of the Chief Magistrate of the State is presumed to be a sufficient foundation for calling in, in the first instance, the aid of the Militia of the Neighbouring States.

I would submit then, that Pennsylvania be required to furnish 6000 men of whom 1000 to be horse, New Jersey 2000 of whom 800 to be horse, Maryland 2000 of whom 600 to be horse, Virginia 2000, of whom 600 to be horse.

Or perhaps it may be as elligible to call upon each State for such a number of Troops, leaving to itself the proportion of horse and foot according to convenience. The Militia called for to rendevous at Carlisle in Pennsylvania & Cumberland Fort in Virginia on the 10th of September next.

The law requires that previous to the using of force a Proclamation shall issue, commanding the Insurgents to disperse and return peacably to their respective abodes within a limited time. This step must of course be taken.

The application of the force to be called out and other ulterior measures must depend on circumstances as they shall arise.

With the most perfect respect I have the Honor to be Sir

Your Most Obedient Servant

Alexander Hamilton

Tully, No. 1 (August 23, 1794)

It has from the first establishment of your present constitution been predicted, that every occasion of serious embarrassment which should occur in the affairs of the government—every misfortune which it should experience, whether produced from its own faults or mistakes, or from other causes, would be the signal of an attempt to overthrow it, or to lay the foundation of its overthrow, by defeating the exercise of constitutional and necessary authorities. The disturbances which have recently broken out in the western counties of Pennsylvania furnish an occasion of this sort. It remains to see whether the prediction which has been quoted, proceeded from an unfounded jealousy excited by partial differences of opinion, or was a just inference from causes inherent in the structure of our political institutions. Every virtuous man, every good citizen, and especially EVERY TRUE REPUBLICAN must fervently pray, that the issue may confound and not confirm so ill omened a prediction.

Your firm attachment to the government you have established cannot be doubted.

If a proof of this were wanting to animate the confidence of your public agents, it would be sufficient to remark, that as often as any attempt to counteract its measures appear, it is carefully prepared by strong professions of friendship to the government, and disavowals of any intention to injure it. This can only result from a conviction, that the government carries with it YOUR affections; and that an attack upon it to be successful, must veil the stroke under appearances of good will.

It is therefore very important that YOU should clearly discern in the present instance, the shape in which a design of turning the existing insurrection to the prejudice of the government would naturally assume. Thus guarded, you will more readily discover and more easily shun the artful snare which may be laid to entangle your feelings and your judgment, and will be the less apt to be misled from the path by which alone you can give security and permanency to the blessings you enjoy, and can avoid the incalculable mischiefs incident to a subversion of the just and necessary authority of the laws.

The design alluded to, if it shall be entertained, would not appear in an open justification of the principles or conduct of the insurgents, or in a direct dissuasion from the support of the government. These methods would produce general indignation and defeat the object. It is too absurd and shocking a position to be directly maintained, that forcible resistance by a sixtieth part of the community to the representative will of the whole, and its constitutional laws expressed by that will, and acquiesced in by the people at large, is justifiable or even excusable. It is a position too untenable and disgustful to be directly advocated—that the government ought not be supported in exertions to establish the authority of the laws against a resistance so incapable of justification or excuse.

The adversaries of good order in every country have too great a share of cunning, too exact a knowledge of the human heart, to pursue so unpromising a cause. Those among us would take upon the present occasion one far more artful, and consequently far more dangerous.

They would unite with good citizens, and perhaps be among the loudest in condemning the disorderly conduct of the insurgents. They would agree that it is utterly unjustifiable, contrary to the vital principle of republican government, and of the most dangerous tendency—But they would, at the same time, slily add, that excise laws are pernicious things, very hostile to liberty, (or perhaps they might more smoothly lament that the government had been imprudent enough to pass laws so contrary to the genius of a free people) and they would still more cautiously hint that it is enough for those who disapprove of such laws to submit to them—too much to expect their aid in enforcing them upon others. They would be apt to intimate further, that there is reason to believe that the Executive has been to blame, sometimes by too much forbearance, encouraging the hope that laws would not be enforced, at other times in provoking violence by severe and irritating measures; and they would generally remark, with an affectation of moderation and prudence, that the case is to be lamented, but difficult to be remedied; that a trial of force would be delicate and dangerous; that there is no forseeing how or where it would end; that it is perhaps better to temporize, and by mild means to allay the ferment and afterwards to remove the cause by repealing the exceptionable laws. They would probably also propose, by anticipation of and in concert with the views of the insurgents, plans of procrastination. They would say, if force must finally be resorted to let it not be till after Congress have been consulted, who, if they think fit to persist in continuing the laws, can make additional provisions for enforcing their execution. This too, they would argue, will afford an opportunity for the public sense to be better known, which (if ascertained to be in favor of the laws) will give the government a greater assurance of success in measures of coercion.

By these means, artfully calculated to divert YOUR attention from the true question to be decided, to combat by prejudices against a particular system, a just sense of the criminality and danger of violent resistance to the laws; to oppose the suggestion of misconduct on the part of government to the fact of misconduct on the part of the insurgents; to foster the spirit of indolence and procrastination natural to the human mind, as an obstacle to the vigor and exertion which so alarming an attack upon the fundamental principles of public and private security demands; to distract YOUR opinion on the course proper to be pursued, and consequently on the propriety of the measures which may be pursued. They would expect (I say) by these and similar means, equally insidious and pernicious, to abate YOUR just indignation at the daring affront which has been offered to YOUR authority and YOUR zeal for the maintenance and support of the laws to prevent a competent force, if force is finally called forth, from complying with the call—and thus to leave the government of the Union in the prostrate condition of seeing the laws trampled under foot by an unprincipled combination of a small portion of the community, habitually disobedient to laws, and itself destitute of the necessary aid for vindicating their authority.

Virtuous and enlightened citizens of a now happy country! ye could not be the dupes of artifices so detestable, of a scheme so fatal; ye cannot be insensible to the destructive consequences with which it would be pregnant; ye cannot but remember that the government is YOUR OWN work—that those who administer it are but your temporary agents; that YOU are called upon not to support their power, BUT YOUR OWN POWER. And you will not fail to do what your rights, your best interests, your character as a people, your security as members of society conspire to demand of you.

Tully, No. 3 (August 28, 1794)

If it were to be asked, What is the most sacred duty and the greatest source of security in a Republic? the answer would be, An inviolable respect for the Constitution and Laws—the first growing out of the last. It is by this, in a great degree, that the rich and powerful are to be restrained from enterprises against the common liberty—operated upon by the influence of a general sentiment, by their interest in the principle, and by the obstacles which the habit it produces erects against innovation and encroachment.

It is by this, in a still greater degree, that caballers, intriguers, and demagogues are prevented from climbing on the shoulders of faction to the tempting seats of usurpation and tyranny.

Were it not that it might require too lengthy a discussion, it would not be difficult to demonstrate, that a large and well organized Republic can scarcely lose its liberty from any other cause than that of anarchy, to which a contempt of the laws is the high road.

But, without entering into so wide a field, it is sufficient to present to your view a more simple and a more obvious truth, which is this—that a sacred respect for the constitutional law is the vital principle, the sustaining energy of a free government.

Government is frequently and aptly classed under two descriptions, a government of FORCE and a government of LAWS; the first is the definition of despotism—the last, of liberty. But how can a government of laws exist where the laws are disrespected and disobeyed? Government supposes controul. It is the POWER by which individuals in society are kept from doing injury to each other and are bro't to co-operate to a common end. The instruments by which it must act are either the AUTHORITY of the Laws or FORCE. If the first be destroyed, the last must be substituted; and where this becomes the ordinary instrument of government there is an end to liberty.

Those, therefore, who preach doctrines, or set examples, which undermine or subvert the authority of the laws, lead us from freedom to slavery; they incapacitate us for a GOVERNMENT OF LAWS, and consequently prepare the way for one of FORCE, for mankind MUST HAVE GOVERNMENT OF ONE SORT OR ANOTHER.

There are indeed great and urgent cases where the bounds of the constitution are manifestly transgressed, or its constitutional authorities so exercised as to produce unequivocal oppression on the community, and to render resistance justifiable. But such cases can give no colour to the resistance by a comparatively inconsiderable part of a community, of constitutional laws distinguished by no extraordinary features of rigour or oppression, and acquiesced in by the BODY OF THE COMMUNITY.

Such a resistance is treason against society, against liberty, against every thing that ought to be dear to a free, enlightened, and prudent people. To tolerate [it] were to abandon your most precious interests. Not to subdue it, were to tolerate it. Those who openly or covertly dissuade you from exertions adequate to the occasion are your worst enemies. They treat you either as fools or cowards, too weak to perceive your interest and your duty, or too dastardly to pursue them. They therefore merit, and will no doubt meet your contempt.

To the plausible but hollow harangues of such conspirators, ye cannot fail to reply, How long, ye Catilines, will you abuse our patience.

George Washington

Letter to Henry Lee (August 26, 1794)

German Town

Dear Sir: Your favor of the 17th. came duly to hand, and I thank you for its communications. As the Insurgents in the western counties of this State are resolved (as far as we have yet been able to learn from the Commissioners, who have been sent among them) to persevere in their rebellious conduct until what they call the excise Law is repealed, and acts of oblivion and amnesty are passed; it gives me sincere consolation amidst the regret with which I am filled, by such lawless and outrageous conduct, to find by your letter above mentioned, that it is held in general detestation by the good people of Virginia; and that you are disposed to lend your *personal* aid to subdue this spirit, and to bring those people to a proper sense of their duty.

On this latter point I shall refer you to letters from the War office; and to a private one from Colo. Hamilton (who in the absence of the Secretary of War, superintends the *military* duties of that department) for my sentiments on this occasion.

It is with equal pride and satisfaction I add, that as far as my information extends, this insurrection is viewed with universal indignation and abhorrence; except by those who have never missed an opportunity by side blows, or otherwise, to aim their shafts at the general government; and even among these there is not a Spirit hardy enough, yet, *openly* to justify the daring infractions of Law and order; but by palliatives are attempting to suspend all proceedings against the insurgents until Congress shall have decided on the case, thereby intending to gain time, and if possible to make the evil more extensive, more formidable, and of course more difficult to counteract and subdue.

I consider this insurrection as the first *formidable* fruit of the Democratic Societies; brought forth I believe too prematurely for their own views, which may contribute to the annihilation of them.

That these societies were instituted by the *artful* and *signing* members (many of their body I have no doubt mean well, but know little of the real plan,) primarily to sow the seeds of jealousy and distrust among the people, of the government, by destroying all confidence in the Administration of it; and that these doctrines have been budding and blowing ever since, is not new to any one, who is acquainted with the characters of their leaders, and has been attentive to their manoeuvres. I early gave it as my opinion to the confidential characters around me, that, if these Societies were not counteracted (not by prosecutions, the ready way to make them grow stronger) or did not fall into disesteem from the knowledge of their origin, and the views with which they had been instituted by their father, Genet, for purposes well known to the Government; that they would shake the government to its foundation. Time and circumstances have confirmed me in this opinion, and I deeply regret the probable consequences, not as they will affect me personally, (for I have not long to act on this theatre, and sure I am that not a man amongst them can be more anxious to put me aside, than I am to sink into the profoundest retirement) but because I see, under a display of popular and fascinating guises, the most diabolical attempts to destroy the best fabric of human government and happiness, that has ever been presented for the acceptance of mankind. [. . .]

THOMAS JEFFERSON

Letter to James Madison (1794)

[. . .] The denunciation of the democratic societies is one of the extraordinary acts of boldness of which we have seen so many from the fraction of monocrats. It is wonderful indeed, that the President should have permitted himself to be the organ of such an attack on the freedom of discussion, the freedom of writing, printing & publishing. It must be a matter of rare curiosity to get at the modifications of these rights proposed by them, and to see what line their ingenuity would draw between democratical societies, whose avowed object is the nourishment of the republican principles of our constitution, and the society of the Cincinnati, *a self-created* one, carving out for itself hereditary distinctions, lowering over our Constitution eternally, meeting together in all parts of the Union, periodically, with closed doors, accumulating a capital in their separate treasury, corresponding secretly & regularly, & of which society the very persons denouncing the democrats are themselves the fathers, founders, & high officers. Their sight must be perfectly dazzled by the glittering of crowns & coronets, not to see the extravagance of the proposition to suppress the friends of general freedom, while those who wish to confine that freedom to the few, are permitted to go on in their principles & practices. I here put out of sight the persons whose misbehavior has been taken advantage of to slander the friends of popular rights; and I am happy to observe, that as far as the circle of my observation & information extends, everybody has lost sight of them, and views the abstract attempt on their natural & constitutional rights in all its nakedness. I have never heard, or heard of, a single expression or opinion which did not condemn it as an inexcusable aggression. And with respect to the transactions against the excise law, it appears to me that you are all swept away in the torrent of governmental opinions, or that we do not know what these transactions have been. We know of none which, according to the definitions of the law, have been anything more than riotous. There was indeed a meeting to consult about a separation. But to consult on a question does not amount to a determination of that question in the affirmative, still less to the acting on such a determination; but we shall see, I suppose, what the court lawyers, & courtly judges, & would-be ambassadors will make of it. The excise law is an infernal one. The first error was to admit it by the Constitution; the 2d., to act on that admission; the 3d & last will be, to make it the instrument of dismembering the Union, & setting us all afloat to chuse which part of it we will adhere to. The information of our militia, returned from the Westward, is uniform, that tho the people there let them pass quietly, they were objects of their laughter, not of their fear; that 1000 men could have cut off their whole force in a thousand places of the Alleganey; that their detestation of the excise law is universal, and has now associated to it a detestation of the government; & that separation which perhaps was a very distant & problematical event, is now near, & certain & determined in the mind of every man. I expected to have seen some justification of arming one part of the society against another; of declaring a civil war the moment before the meeting of that body which has the sole right of declaring war; of being so patient of the kicks & scoffs of our enemies, & rising at a feather against our friends; of adding a million to the public debt & deriding us with recommendations to pay it if we can &c., &c. But the part of the speech which was to be taken as a justification of the armament, reminded me of parson Saunders' demonstration why minus into minus make plus. After a parcel of shreds of stuff from Æsop's fables, and Tom Thumb, he jumps all at once into his Ergo, minus multiplied into minus make plus. Just so the 15,000 men enter after the fables, in the speech.—However, the time is coming when we shall fetch up the leeway of our vessel. [. . .]

Alexander Hamilton

Memorandum on the French Revolution (1794)

In the early periods of the French Revolution, a warm zeal for its success was in this Country *a sentiment truly universal.* The love of Liberty is here the ruling passion *of the Citizens of the UStates* pervading every class animating every bosom. As long therefore as the Revolution of France bore the marks of being the cause of liberty it united all hearts, concentered all opinions. But this unanimity of approbation has been for a considerable time decreasing. The excesses which have constantly multiplied, with greater and greater aggravations have successively though slowly detached reflecting men from their partiality for an object which has appeared less and less to merit their regard. Their reluctance to abandon it has however been proportioned to the ardor and fondness with which they embraced it. They were willing to overlook many faults—to apologise for some enormities—to hope that better justifications existed than were seen—to look forward to more calm and greater moderation, after the first shocks of the political earthquake had subsided. But instead of this, they have been witnesses to one volcano succeeding another, the last still more dreadful than the former, spreading ruin and devastation far and wide—subverting the foundations of right security and property, of order, morality and religion—sparing neither sex nor age, confounding innocence with guilt, involving the old and the young, the sage and the madman, the long tried friend of virtue and his country and the upstart pretender to purity and patriotism—the bold projector of new treasons with the obscure in indiscriminate and profuse destruction. They have found themselves driven to the painful alternative of renouncing an object dear to their wishes or of becoming by the continuance of their affection for it accomplices with Vice Anarchy Depotism and Impiety.

But though an afflicting experience has materially lessened the number of the admirers of the French Revolution among us and has served to chill the ardor of many more, who profess still to retain their attachment to it, from what they suppose to be its ultimate tendency; yet the effect of Experience has been thus far much less than could reasonably have been expected. The predilection for it still continues extensive and ardent. And what is extraordinary it continues to comprehend men who are able to form a just estimate of the information which destroys its tide to their favour.

It is not among the least perplexing phœnomina of the present times, that a people like that of the UStates—exemplary for humanity and moderation surpassed by no other in the love of order and a knowledge of the true principles of liberty, distinguished for purity of morals and a just reverence for Religion should so long perservere in partiality for a state of things the most cruel sanguinary and violent that ever stained the annuals of mankind, a state of things which annihilates the foundations of social order and true liberty, confounds all moral distinctions and *substitutes to* the mild & beneficent religion of the Gospel a gloomy persecuting and desolating atheism. To the eye of a wise man, this partiality is the most inauspicious, circumstance, that has appeared in the affairs of this country. It leads involuntarily and irresistibly to apprehensions concerning the soundness of our principles and the stability of our welfare. It is natural to fear that the transition may not be difficult from the approbation of bad things to the imitation of them; a fear which can only be mitigated by a careful estimate of the extraneous causes that have served to mislead the public judgment.

But though we may find in these causes a solution of the fact calculated to abate our solicitude for the consequences; yet we can not consider the public happiness as out of the reach of danger so long as our principles continue to be exposed to the debauching influence of admiration for an example which, it will not be too strong to say, presents the caricature of human depravity. And the pride of national character at least can find no alleviation for the wound which must be inflicted by so ill-judged so unfortunate a partiality.

If there be any thing solid in virtue—the time must come when it will have been a disgrace to have advocated the Revolution of France in its late stages.

This is a language to which the ears of the people of this country have not been accustommed. Every thing has hitherto conspired to confirm the pernicious fascination by which they are enchained. There has been a positive and a negative conspiracy against the truth which has served to shut out its enlightening ray. Those who always float with the popular gale perceiving the prepossession of the people have administered to it by all the acts in their power—endeavouring to recommend themselves by an exaggerated zeal for a favourite object. Others through timidity caution or an ill-judged policy unwilling to expose themselves to the odium of resisting the general current of feeling have betrayed by silence that Truth which they were unable not to perceive. [. . .] Hence the voice of reason has been stifled and the Nation has been left unadmonished to travel on in one of the most degrading delusions that ever disparaged the understandings of an enlightened people.

To recal them from this dangerous error—to engage them to dismiss, their prejudices & consult dispassionately their own good sense—to lead them to an appeal from their own enthusiasm to their reason and humanity would be the most important service that could be rendered to the UStates at the present juncture. The error entertained is not on a mere speculative question. The French Revolution is a political convulsion that in a great or less degree shakes the whole civilized world and it is of real consequence to the principles and of course to the happiness of a Nation to estimate it rightly.

George Washington

Farewell Address (September 19, 1796)

Friends, and Fellow-Citizens: The period for a new election of a Citizen, to Administer the Executive government of the United States, being not far distant, and the time actually arrived, when your thoughts must be employed in designating the person, who is to be cloathed with that important trust, it appears to me proper, especially as it may conduce to a more distinct expression of the public voice, that I should now apprise you of the resolution I have formed, to decline being considered among the number of those, out of whom a choice is to be made.

I beg you, at the same time, to do me the justice to be assured, that this resolution has not been taken, without a strict regard to all the considerations appertaining to the relation, which binds a dutiful citizen to his country, and that, in with drawing the tender of service which silence in my situation might imply, I am influenced by no diminution of zeal for your future interest, no deficiency of grateful respect for your past kindness; but am supported by a full conviction that the step is compatible with both.

The acceptance of, and continuance hitherto in, the office to which your Suffrages have twice called me, have been a uniform sacrifice of inclination to the opinion of duty, and to a deference for what appeared to be your desire. I constantly hoped, that it would have been much earlier in my power, consistently with motives, which I was not at liberty to disregard, to return to that retirement, from which I had been reluctantly drawn. The strength of my inclination to do this, previous to the last Election, had even led to the preparation of an address to declare it to you; but mature reflection on the then perplexed and critical posture of our Affairs with foreign Nations, and the unanimous advice of persons entitled to my confidence, impelled me to abandon the idea.

I rejoice, that the state of your concerns, external as well as internal, no longer renders the pursuit of inclination incompatible with the sentiment of duty, or propriety; and am persuaded whatever partiality may be retained for my services, that in the present circumstances of our country, you will not disapprove my determination to retire.

The impressions, with which I first undertook the arduous trust, were explained on the proper occasion. In the discharge of this trust, I will only say, that I have with good intentions, contributed towards the Organization and Administration of the government, the best exertions of which a very fallible judgment was capable. Not unconscious, in the outset, of the inferiority of my qualifications, experience in my own eyes, perhaps still more in the eyes of others, has strengthened the motives to diffidence of myself; and every day the encreasing weight of years admonishes me more and more, that the shade of retirement is as necessary to me as it will be welcome. Satisfied that if any circumstances have given peculiar value to my services, they were temporary, I have the consolation to believe, that while choice and prudence invite me to quit the political scene, patriotism does not forbid it.

In looking forward to the moment, which is intended to terminate the career of my public life, my feelings do not permit me to suspend the deep acknowledgment of that debt of gratitude wch. I owe to my beloved country, for the many honors it has conferred upon me; still more for the stedfast confidence with which it has supported me; and for the opportunities I have thence enjoyed of manifesting my inviolable attachment, by services faithful and persevering, though in usefulness unequal to my zeal. If benefits have resulted to our country from these services, let it always be remembered to your praise, and as an instructive example in our annals, that, under circumstances in which the Passions agitated in every direction were, liable to mislead, amidst appearances sometimes dubious, viscissitudes of fortune often discouraging, in situations in which not unfrequentiy want of Success has countenanced the spirit of criticism, the constancy of your support was the essential prop of the efforts, and a guarantee of the plans by which they were effected. Profoundly penetrated with this idea, I shall carry it with me to my grave, as a strong incitement to unceasing vows that Heaven may continue to you the choicest tokens of its beneficence; that your Union and brotherly affection may be perpetual; that the free constitution, which is the work of your hands, may be sacredly maintained; that its Administration in every department may be stamped with wisdom and Virtue; that, in fine, the happiness of the people of these States, under the auspices of liberty, may be made complete, by so careful a preservation and so prudent a use of this blessing as will acquire to them the glory of recommending it to the applause, the affection, and adoption of every nation which is yet a stranger to it.

Here, perhaps, I ought to stop. But a solicitude for your welfare, which cannot end but with my life, and the apprehension of danger natural to that solicitude, urge me on an occasion like the present, to offer to your solemn contemplation, and to recommend to your frequent review, some sentiments; which are the result of much reflection, of no inconsiderable observation, and which appear to me all important to the permanency of your felicity as a People. These will be offered to you with the more freedom, as you can only see in them the disinterested warnings of a parting friend, who can possibly have no personal motive to biass his counsel. Nor can I forget, as an encouragement to it, your endulgent reception of my sentiments on a former and not dissimilar occasion.

Interwoven as is the love of liberty with every ligament of your hearts, no recommendation of mine is necessary to fortify or confirm the attachment.

The Unity of Government which constitutes you one people is also now dear to you. It is justly so; for it is a main Pillar in the Edifice of your real independence, the support of your tranquility at home; your peace abroad; of your safety; of your prosperity; of that very Liberty which you so highly prize. But as it is easy to foresee, that from different causes and from different quarters, much pains will be taken, many artifices employed, to weaken in your minds the conviction of this truth; as this is the point in your political fortress against which the batteries of internal and external enemies will be most constantly and actively (though often covertly and insidiously) directed, it is of infinite moment, that you should properly estimate the immense value of your national Union to your collective and individual happiness; that you should cherish a cordial, habitual and immoveable attachment to it; accustoming yourselves to think and speak of it as of the Palladium of your political safety and prosperity; watching for its preservation with jealous anxiety; discountenancing whatever may suggest even a suspicion that it can in any event be abandoned, and indignantly frowning upon the first dawning of every attempt to alienate any portion of our Country from the rest, or to enfeeble the sacred ties which now link together the various parts.

For this you have every inducement of sympathy and interest. Citizens by birth or choice, of a common country, that country has a right to concentrate your affections. The name of American, which belongs to you, in your national capacity, must always exalt the just pride of Patriotism, more than any appellation derived from local discriminations. With slight shades of difference, you have the same Religion, Manners, Habits and political Principles. You have in a common cause fought and triumphed together. The independence and liberty you possess are the work of joint councils, and joint efforts; of common dangers, sufferings and successes.

But these considerations, however powerfully they address themselves to your sensibility are greatly outweighed by those which apply more immediately to your Interest. Here every portion of our country finds the most commanding motives for carefully guarding and preserving the Union of the whole.

The *North*, in an unrestrained intercourse with the *South*, protected by the equal Laws of a common government, finds in the productions of the latter, great additional resources of Maritime and commercial enterprise and precious materials of manufacturing industry. The *South* in the same Intercourse, benefitting by the Agency of the *North*, sees its agriculture grow and its commerce expand. Turning partly into its own channels the seamen of the *North*, it finds its particular navigation envigorated; and while it contributes, in different ways, to nourish and increase the general mass of the National navigation, it looks forward to the protection of a Maritime strength, to which itself is unequally adapted. The *East*, in a like intercourse with the *West*, already finds, and in the progressive improvement of interior communications, by land and water, will more and more find a valuable vent for the commodities which it brings from abroad, or manufactures at home. The *West* derives from the *East* supplies requisite to its growth and comfort, and what is perhaps of still greater consequence, it must of necessity owe the *secure* enjoyment of indispensable *outlets* for its own productions to the weight, influence, and the future Maritime strength of the Atlantic side of the Union, directed by an indissoluble community of Interest as *one Nation*. Any other tenure by which the *West* can hold this essential advantage, whether derived from its own seperate strength, or from an apostate and unnatural connection with any foreign Power, must be intrinsically precarious.

While then every part of our country thus feels an immediate and particular Interest in Union, all the parts combined cannot fail to find in the united mass of means and efforts greater strength, greater resource, proportionably greater security from external danger, a less frequent interruption of their Peace by foreign Nations; and, what is of inestimable value! they must derive from Union an exemption from those broils and Wars between themselves, which so frequently afflict neighbouring countries, not tied together by the same government; which their own rivalships alone would be sufficient to produce, but which opposite foreign alliances, attachments and intriegues would stimulate and imbitter. Hence likewise they will avoid the necessity of those overgrown Military establishments, which under any form of Government are inauspicious to liberty and which are to be regarded as particularly hostile to Republican Liberty: In this sense it is, that your Union ought to be considered as a main prop of your liberty, and that the love of the one ought to endear to you the preservation of the other.

These considerations speak a persuasive language to every reflecting and virtuous mind, and exhibit the continuance of the Union as a primary object of Patriotic desire. Is there a doubt, whether a common government can embrace so large a sphere? Let experience solve it. To listen to mere speculation in such a case were criminal. We are authorized to hope that a proper organization of the whole, with the auxiliary agency of governments for the respective Sub divisions, will afford a happy issue to the experiment. 'Tis well worth a fair and full experiment with such powerful and obvious motives to Union, affecting all parts of our country, while experience shall not have demonstrated its impracticability, there will always be reason, to distrust the patriotism of those, who in any quarter may endeavor to weaken its bands.

In contemplating the causes wch. may disturb our Union, it occurs as matter of serious concern, that any ground should have been furnished for characterizing parties by *Geographical* discriminations: *Northern* and *Southern*; *Atlantic and Western*; whence designing men may endeavour to excite a belief that there is a real difference of local interests and views. One of the expedients of Party to acquire influence, within particular districts, is to misrepresent the opinions and aims of other Districts. You cannot shield yourselves too much against the jealousies and heart burnings which spring from these misrepresentations. They tend to render Alien to each other those who ought to be bound together by fraternal affection. The Inhabitants of our Western country have lately had a useful lesson on this head. They have seen, in the Negociation by the Executive, and in the unanimous ratification by the Senate, of the Treaty with Spain, and in the universal satisfaction at that event, throughout the United States, a decisive proof how unfounded were the suspicions propagated among them of a policy in the General Government and in the Atlantic States unfriendly to their Interests in regard to the Mississippi. They have been witnesses to the formation of two Treaties, that with G: Britain and that with Spain, which secure to them every thing they could desire, in respect to our

Foreign relations, towards confirming their prosperity. Will it not be their wisdom to rely for the preservation of these advantages on the Union by wch. they were procured? Will they not henceforth be deaf to those advisers, if such there are, who would sever them from their Brethren and connect them with Aliens?

To the efficacy and permanency of Your Union, a Government for the whole is indispensable. No Alliances however strict between the parts can be an adequate substitute. They must inevitably experience the infractions and interruptions which all Alliances in all times have experienced. Sensible of this momentous truth, you have improved upon your first essay, by the adoption of a Constitution of Government, better calculated than your former for an intimate Union, and for the efficacious management of your common concerns. This government, the offspring of our own choice uninfluenced and unawed, adopted upon full investigation and mature deliberation, completely free in its principles, in the distribution of its powers, uniting security with energy, and containing within itself a provision for its own amendment, has a just claim to your confidence and your support. Respect for its authority, compliance with its Laws, acquiescence in its measures, are duties enjoined by the fundamental maxims of true Liberty. The basis of our political systems is the right of the people to make and to alter their Constitutions of Government. But the Constitution which at any time exists, 'till changed by an explicit and authentic act of the whole People, is sacredly obligatory upon all. The very idea of the power and the right of the People to establish Government presupposes the duty of every Individual to obey the established Government.

All obstructions to the execution of the Laws, all combinations and Associations, under whatever plausible character, with the real design to direct, controul counteract, or awe the regular deliberation and action of the Constituted authorities are distinctive of this fundamental principle and of fatal tendency; They serve to organize faction, to give it an artificial and extraordinary force; to put in the place of the delegated will of the Nation, the will of a party; often a small but artful and enterprizing minority of the Community; and, according to the alternate triumphs of different parties, to make the public administration the Mirror, of the ill concerted and incongruous projects of faction, rather than the organ of consistent and wholesome plans digested by common councils and modefied by mutual interests. However combinations or Associations of the above description may now and then answer popular ends, they are likely, in the course of time and things, to become potent engines, by which cunning, ambitious and unprincipled men will be enabled to subvert the Power of the People, and to usurp for themselves the reins of Government; destroying afterwards the very engines which have lifted them to unjust dominion.

Towards the preservation of your Government and the permanency of your present happy state, it is requisite, not only that you steadily discountenance irregular oppositions to its acknowledged authority, but also that you resist with care the spirit of innovation upon its principles however specious the pretexts; one method of assault may be to effect, in the forms of the Constitution, alterations which will impair the energy of the system, and thus to undermine what cannot be directly overthrown. In all the changes to which you may be invited, remember that time and habit are at least as necessary to fix the true character of Governments, as of other human institutions; that experience is the surest standard, by which to test the real tendency of the existing Constitution of a country; that facility in changes upon the credit of mere hypotheses and opinion exposes to perpetual change, from the endless variety of hypotheses and opinion: and remember, especially, that for the efficient management of your common interests, in a country so extensive as ours, a Government of as much vigour as is consistent with the perfect security of Liberty is indispensable. Liberty itself will find in such a Government, with powers properly distributed and adjusted, its surest Guardian. It is indeed little else than a name, where the Government is too feeble to withstand the enterprises of faction, to confine each member of the Society within the limits prescribed by the laws and to maintain all in the secure and tranquil enjoyment of the rights of person and property.

I have already intimated to you the danger of Parties in the State, with particular reference to the founding of them on Geographical discriminations. Let me now take a more comprehensive view, and warn you in the most solemn manner against the baneful effects of the Spirit of Party, generally.

This spirit, unfortunately, is inseperable from our nature, having its root in the strongest passions of the human Mind. It exists under different shapes in all Governments, more or less stifled, controuled, or repressed; but, in those of the popular form it is seen in its greatest rankness and is truly their worst enemy.

The alternate domination of one faction over another, sharpened by the spirit of revenge natural to party dissention, which in different ages and countries has perpetrated the most horrid enormities, is itself a frightful despotism. But this leads at length to a more formal and permanent despotism. The disorders and miseries, which result, gradually incline minds of men to seek security and repose in the absolute power of an Individual: and sooner or later the chief of some prevailing faction more able or more fortunate than his competitors, turns this disposition to the purposes of his own elevation, on the ruins of Public Liberty.

Without looking forward to an extremity of this kind (which nevertheless ought not to be entirely out of sight) the common and continual mischiefs of the spirit of Party are sufficient to make it the interest and the duty of a wise People to discourage and restrain it.

It serves always to distract the Public Councils and enfeeble the Public administration. It agitates the Community with ill founded jealousies and false alarms, kindles the animosity of one part against another, foments occasionally riot and insurrection. It opens the door to foreign influence and corruption, which find a facilitated access to the government itself through the channels of party passions. Thus the policy and the will of one country, are subjected to the policy and will of another.

There is an opinion that parties in free countries are useful checks upon the Administration of the Government and serve to keep alive the spirit of Liberty. This within certain limits is probably true, and in Governments of a Monarchical cast Patriotism may look with endulgence, if not with favour, upon the spirit of party; But in those of the popular character, in Governments purely elective, it is a spirit not to be encouraged. From their natural tendency, it is certain there will always be enough of that spirit for every salutary purpose. And there being constant danger of excess, the effort ought to be, by force of public opinion, to mitigate and assuage it. A fire not to be quenched; it demands a uniform vigilance to prevent its bursting into a flame, lest instead of warming it should consume.

It is important, likewise, that the habits of thinking in a free Country should inspire caution in those entrusted with its administration, to confine themselves within their respective Constitutional spheres; avoiding in the exercise of the Powers of one department to encroach upon another. The spirit of encroachment tends to consolidate the powers of all the departments in one, and thus to create whatever the form of government, a real despotism. A just estimate of that love of power, and proneness to abuse it, which predominates in the human heart is sufficient to satisfy us of the truth of this position. The necessity of reciprocal checks in the exercise of political power; by dividing and distributing it into different depositories, and constituting each the Guardian of the Public Weal against invasions by the others, has been evinced by experiments ancient and modern; some of them in our country and under our own eyes. To preserve them must be as necessary as to institute them. If in the opinion of the People, the distribution or modification of the Constitutional powers be in any particular wrong, let it be corrected by an amendment in the way which the Constitution designates. But let there be no change by usurpation; for though this, in one instance, may be the instrument of good, it is the customary weapon by which free governments are destroyed. The precedent must always greatly overbalance in permanent evil any partial or transient benefit which the use can at any time yield.

Of all the dispositions and habits which lead to political prosperity, Religion and morality are indispensable supports. In vain would that man claim the tribute of Patriotism, who should labour to subvert these great Pillars of human happiness, these firmest props of the duties of Men and citizens. The mere Politician, equally with the pious man ought to respect and to cherish them. A volume could not trace all their connections with private and public felicity. Let it simply be asked where is the security for property, for reputation, for life, if the sense of religious obligation *desert* the oaths, which are the instruments of investigation in Courts of Justice? And let us with caution indulge the supposition, that morality can be maintained without religion. Whatever may be conceded to the influence of refined education on minds of peculiar structure, reason and experience both forbid us to expect that National morality can prevail in exclusion of religious principle.

'Tis substantially true, that virtue or morality is a necessary spring of popular government. The rule indeed extends with more or less force to every species of free Government. Who that is a sincere friend to it, can look with indifference upon attempts to shake the foundation of the fabric.

Promote then as an object of primary importance, Institutions for the general diffusion of knowledge. In proportion as the structure of a government gives force to public opinion, it is essential that public opinion should be enlightened.

As a very important source of strength and security, cherish public credit. One method of preserving it is to use it as sparingly as possible: avoiding occasions of expence by cultivating peace, but remembering also that timely disbursements to prepare for danger frequently prevent much greater disbursements to repel it; avoiding likewise the accumulation of debt, not only by shunning occasions of expence, but by vigorous exertions in time of Peace to discharge the Debts which unavoidable wars may have occasioned, not ungenerously throwing upon posterity the burthen which we ourselves ought to bear. The execution of these maxims belongs to your Representatives, but it is necessary that public opinion should cooperate. To facilitate to them the performance of their duty, it is essential that you should practically bear in mind, that towards the payment of debts there must be Revenue; that to have Revenue there must be taxes; that no taxes can be devised which are not more or less inconvenient and unpleasant; that the intrinsic embarrassment inseperable from the selection of the proper objects (which is always a choice of difficulties) ought to be a decisive motive for a candid construction of the Conduct of the Government in making it, and for a spirit of acquiescence in the measures for obtaining Revenue which the public exigencies may at any time dictate.

Observe good faith and justice towds. all Nations. Cultivate peace and harmony with all. Religion and morality enjoin this conduct; and can it be that good policy does not equally enjoin it? It will be worthy of a free, enlightened, and, at no distant period, a great Nation, to give to mankind the magnanimous and too novel example of a People always guided by an exalted justice and benevolence. Who can doubt that in the course of time and things the fruits of such a plan would richly repay any temporary advantages wch. might be lost by a steady adherence to it? Can it be, that Providence has not connected the permanent felicity of a Nation with its virtue? The experiment, at least, is recommended by every sentiment which ennobles human Nature. Alas! is it rendered impossible by its vices?

In the execution of such a plan nothing is more essential than that permanent, inveterate antipathies against particular Nations and passionate attachments for others should be excluded; and that in place of them just and amicable feelings towards all should be cultivated. The Nation, which indulges towards another an habitual hatred, or an habitual fondness, is in some degree a slave. It is a slave to its animosity or to its affection, either of which is sufficient to lead it astray from its duty and its interest. Antipathy in one Nation against another, disposes each more readily to offer insult and injury, to lay hold of slight causes of umbrage, and to be haughty and intractable, when accidental or trifling occasions of dispute occur. Hence frequent collisions, obstinate envenomed and bloody contests. The Nation, prompted by ill will and resentment sometimes impels to War the Government, contrary to the best calculations of policy. The Government sometimes participates in the national propensity, and adopts through passion what reason would reject; at other times, it makes the animosity of the Nation subservient to projects of hostility instigated by pride, ambition and other sinister and pernicious motives. The peace often, sometimes perhaps the Liberty, of Nations has been the victim.

So likewise, a passionate attachment of one Nation for another produces a variety of evils. Sympathy for the favourite nation, facilitating the illusion of an imaginary common interest, in cases where no real common interest exists, and infusing into one the enmities of the other, betrays the former into a participation in the quarrels and Wars of the latter, without adequate inducement or justification: It leads also to concessions to the favourite Nation of privileges denied to others, which is apt doubly to injure the Nation making the concessions; by unnecessarily parting with what ought to have been retained; and by exciting jealousy, ill will, and a disposition to retaliate, in the parties from whom eql. priviledges are withheld: And it gives to ambitious, corrupted, or deluded citizens (who devote themselves to the favourite Nation) facility to betray, or sacrifice the interests of their own country, without odium, sometimes even with popularity; gilding with the appearances of a virtuous sense of obligation a commendable deference for public opinion, or a laudable zeal for public good, the base or foolish compliances of ambition corruption or infatuation.

As avenues to foreign influence in innumerable ways, such attachments are particularly alarming to the truly enlightened and independent Patriot. How many opportunities do they afford to tamper with domestic factions, to practice the arts of seduction, to mislead public opinion, to influence or awe the public Councils! Such an attachment of a small or weak, towards a great and powerful Nation, dooms the former to be the satellite of the latter.

Against the insidious wiles of foreign influence, (I conjure you to believe me fellow citizens) the jealousy of a free people ought to be *constantly* awake; since history and experience prove that foreign influence is one of the most baneful foes of Republican Government. But that jealousy to be useful must be impartial; else it becomes the instrument of the very influence to be avoided, instead of a defence against it. Excessive partiality for one foreign nation and excessive dislike of another, cause those whom they actuate to see danger only on one side, and serve to veil and even second the arts of influence on the other. Real Patriots, who may resist the intriegues of the favourite, are liable to become suspected and odious; while its tools and dupes usurp the applause and confidence of the people, to surrender their interests.

The Great rule of conduct for us, in regard to foreign Nations is in extending our commercial relations to have with them as little *political* connection as possible. So far as we have already formed engagements let them be fulfilled, with perfect good faith. Here let us stop.

Europe has a set of primary interests, which to us have none, or a very remote relation. Hence she must be engaged in frequent controversies, the causes of which are essentially foreign to our concerns. Hence therefore it must be unwise in us to implicate ourselves, by artificial ties, in the ordinary vicissitudes of her politics, or the ordinary combinations and collisions of her friendships, or enmities:

Our detached and distant situation invites and enables us to pursue a different course. If we remain one People, under an efficient government, the period is not far off, when we may defy material injury from external annoyance; when we may take such an attitude as will cause the neutrality we may at any time resolve upon to be scrupulously respected; when belligerent nations, under the impossibility of making acquisitions upon us, will not lightly hazard the giving us provocation; when we may choose peace or war, as our interest guided by our justice shall Counsel.

Why forego the advantages of so peculiar a situation? Why quit our own to stand upon foreign ground? Why, by interweaving our destiny with that of any part of Europe, entangle our peace and prosperity in the toils of European Ambition, Rivalship, Interest, Humour or Caprice?

'Tis our true policy to steer clear of permanent Alliances, with any portion of the foreign world. So far, I mean, as we are now at liberty to do it, for let me not be understood as capable of patronising infidility to existing engagements (I hold the maxim no less applicable to public than to private affairs, that honesty is always the best policy). I repeat it therefore, let those engagements be observed in their genuine sense. But in my opinion, it is unnecessary and would be unwise to extend them.

Taking care always to keep ourselves, by suitable establishments, on a respectably defensive posture, we may safely trust to temporary alliances for extraordinary emergencies.

Harmony, liberal intercourse with all Nations, are recommended by policy, humanity and interest. But even our Commercial policy should hold an equal and impartial hand: neither seeking nor granting exclusive favours or preferences; consulting the natural course of things; diffusing and deversifying by gentle means the streams of Commerce, but forcing nothing; establishing with Powers so disposed; in order to give to trade a stable course, to define the rights of our Merchants, and to enable the Government to support them; conventional rules of intercourse, the best that present circumstances and mutual opinion will permit, but temporary, and liable to be from time to time abandoned or varied, as experience and circumstances shall dictate; constantly keeping in view, that 'tis folly in one Nation to look for disinterested favors frorn another; that it must pay with a portion of its Independence for whatever it may accept under that character; that by such acceptance, it may place itself in the condition of having given equivalents for nominal favours and yet of being reproached with ingratitude for not giving more. There can be no greater error than to expect, or calculate upon real favours from Nation to Nation. 'Tis an illusion which experience must cure, which a just pride ought to discard.

In offering to you, my Countrymen these counsels of an old and affectionate friend, I dare not hope they will make the strong and lasting impression, I could wish; that they will controul the usual current of the passions, or prevent our Nation from running the course which has hitherto marked the Destiny of Nations: But if I may even flatter myself, that they may be productive of some partial benefit, some occasional good; that they may now and then recur to moderate the fury of party spirit, to warn against the mischiefs of foreign Intriegue, to guard against the Impostures of pretended patriotism; this hope will be a full recompence for the solicitude for your welfare, by which they have been dictated.

How far in the discharge of my Official duties, I have been guided by the principles which have been delineated, the public Records and other evidences of my conduct must Witness to You and to the world. To myself, the assurance of my own conscience is, that I have at least believed myself to be guided by them.

In relation to the still subsisting War in Europe, my Proclamation of the 22d. of April 1793 is the index to my Plan. Sanctioned by your approving voice and by that of Your Representatives in both Houses of Congress, the spirit of that measure has continually governed me; uninfluenced by any attempts to deter or divert me from it.

After deliberate examination with the aid of the best lights I could obtain I was well satisfied that our Country, under all the circumstances of the case, had a right to take, and was bound in duty and interest, to take a Neutral position. Having taken it, I determined, as far as should depend upon me, to maintain it, with moderation, perseverence and firmness.

The considerations, which respect the right to hold this conduct, it is not necessary on this occasion to detail. I will only observe, that according to my understanding of the matter, that right, so far from being denied by any of the Belligerent Powers has been virtually admitted by all.

The duty of holding a Neutral conduct may be inferred, without any thing more, from the obligation which justice and humanity impose on every Nation, in cases in which it is free to act, to maintain inviolate the relations of Peace and amity towards other Nations.

The inducements of interest for observing that conduct will best be referred to your own reflections and experience. With me, a predominant motive has been to endeavour to gain time to our country to settle and mature its yet recent institutions, and to progress without interruption, to that degree of strength and consistency, which is necessary to give it, humanly speaking, the command of its own fortunes.

Though in reviewing the incidents of my Administration, I am unconscious of intentional error, I am nevertheless too sensible of my defects not to think it probable that I may have committed many errors. Whatever they may be I fervently beseech the Almighty to avert or mitigate the evils to which they may tend. I shall also carry with me the hope that my Country will never cease to view them with indulgence; and that after forty five years of my life dedicated to its Service, with an upright zeal, the faults of incompetent abilities will be consigned to oblivion, as myself must soon be to the Mansions of rest.

Relying on its kindness in this as in other things, and actuated by that fervent love towards it, which is so natural to a Man, who views in it the native soil of himself and his progenitors for several Generations; I anticipate with pleasing expectation that retreat, in which I promise myself to realize, without alloy, the sweet enjoyment of partaking, in the midst of my fellow Citizens, the benign influence of good Laws under a free Government, the ever favourite object of my heart, and the happy reward, as I trust, of our mutual cares, labours and dangers.

Alexander Addison

On Liberty of Speech and of the Press (1797)

It is of the utmost importance to a free people, that, the just limits of their rights be well ascertained and preserved; for liberty without limit is licentiousness; and licentiousness is the worst kind of tyranny, a tyranny of all. To preserve ourselves against this, and maintain true liberty, a line must be drawn between the rights of each; so well marked, as that it be known by all, and so well guarded, as that it cannot be passed by any with impunity. Thus every man will be free; for every man may exercise his rights to the extent of their just limits, and cannot go beyond those limits and encroach on the rights of others. My right to enjoy implies that no man shall disturb my enjoyment—And it is no restraint on my liberty, that in the exercise of my rights, I am restrained from infringing the rights of others. The rule is *So use your own rights as not to injure those of others.* Invasion of the rights of others is tyranny of the worst kind, for in proportion to the number of oppressors will be the desire and opportunity of oppression. The true friend of liberty, therefore, is he who will set such strong limits round the right of every man, that, in the exercise of them, no man can interrupt the rights of any other. And they are not friends of liberty, but promoters of licentiousness, tyranny, and oppression, who contend, that every man ought to have an unlimited exercise of his own rights, without any regard to the rights of others. I can have no right to injure the rights of another; and if I claim this, I am a tyrant and oppressor.

Reputation, character, good name or opinion is a kind of property or possession, which every man, who has honestly acquired it, has a right to enjoy.[1] Like any other possession or property, it cannot be taken away from us, but by our own acts. The man who invades the reputation invades the right of another. And not only individuals, but more especially men in public station, branches or departments of the government, the whole administration, and the principles, constitution, or system of government, and the principles or system of public religion and morals, have a right, for the sake of the benefits we receive from them, to reputation, good name and opinion; and the invasion of the reputation of either of those is an invasion of right, a lessening of our comfort, and motives to duty.

But Man is indeed with faculties of communicating sentiments, of investigating principles, and of forming opinions and judgments. The exercise of those faculties is a source of pleasure and instruction. A knowledge, and a judgment of principles, of facts, and of characters, may be useful for the improvement of our minds, and the regulation of our conduct. The exercise of those faculties of opinion, reasoning, judgment and communication is part of our natural rights.[2] But the principles of liberty require, that this right, like all our other rights, be limited, for that it never infringe the right of reputation. It must not represent a soleman truth or exercise of religion, as false or ridiculous, an established and useful principle or form of our government, as odious and detestable; a regular and salutary act or motive of the administration as unlawful, pernicious or dishonest; or an upright man as corrupt. For this would be exercising our right of opinion or communication, so as to infringe the right of reputation, and be violating the principles of liberty and natural right.

The principles of liberty, therefore, the rights of Man, require, that our right of communicating information, as to facts and opinions, be so restrained, as not to infringe the right of reputation. Unless it be so restrained, there is no liberty; for there is no just enjoyment of our rights. And if every man's right of communication be unrestrained, every man's right

1. Penn. Constitution, Article i.e. Sec. II.

2. Ib. Sec. 7.

of reputation is unguarded; and there is, in this respect, universal licentiousness, and each man is at the mercy of every man; the most precarious and oppressive of all states. Therefore the freest governments, which have the most regarded and cultivated principles of liberty, as they have so described and limited other rights, that none should infringe any other, have been careful so to define and limit the rights of reputation, and of communication of sentiments, that the right of either should not infringe that of the other.

We communicate our sentiments by words spoken, written, or printed, or by pictures or other signs. The restraints laid on the exercise of this right so as it may not infringe the right of reputation, differ, according to the way in which the right of communication is exercised. If the right of reputation of a private citizen be infringed by words spoken, no indictment will lie for this injury, which is only a ground for a civil action to recover damages. "In fore enscientie," says a learned Author, before the tribunal of conscience, "it is no excuse, that the slanderous words are true; for if a man has been guilty of any thing, which the law prohibits, he is liable to answer for it, in a legal way; but it can answer no good purpose for a private person to accuse him thereof; there is a degree of cruelty in so doing, and it must create ill blood. Yet the law does, in compassion to man's infirmities, allow it to be a justification in an action for words spoken, that they are true." But when words are spoken of the constitution, or administration, or any of its acts or officers, they are ground for an indictment; as a misdemeanor, or breach of the duty of a citizen. The reason of this is evidence for, as for an injury affecting an individual, the remedy is by action, so for an injury affecting the public, the remedy is by indictment.

With respect to Libels, or slander, expressed by words written or printed, or by pictures or other signs, and infringing the right of reputation; "they have," says the same Author, "at all times, and with good reason, been punished in a more exemplary manner than slanderous words; for having a greater tendency to provoke men to breaches of the peace, quarrels, and murders, they are of much more dangerous consequence to society. Words which are frequently the effect of a sudden gust of passion may soon be buried in oblivion. But Libels, besides that the Author is actuated by more deliberate malice, are for the most part so lasting, as to be scarce ever forgiven." For this reason, a libel affecting the reputation of even a private citizen, is restrained by being considered as a public offence, and subject to an indictment. But whether, on the trial of such indictment, the truth of the libel may be given in evidence, will depend on all the nature of the libel [. . .] all truths are not useful or proper for publication, therefore all truths are not to be written, printed, and so uttered or published. And therefore, except in the case of papers investigating the official conduct of officers, or men in a public capacity, or where the matter published is proper for public information, if any man write, print, utter or publish a libel, he may be indicted, convicted and punished, whether the libelous matter be true or not.

Congress, in its last session, has passed a law,[3] enacting, that if any persons shall unlawfully combine together, with intent to oppose any measure of the government of the United States, or impede the operation of any law of the United States, or to prevent any person holding any office under the government of the United States from performing his duty; or shall, with such intent, advise or attempt to procure any insurrection, riot, unlawful assembly or combination; they shall be deemed guilty of a high misdemeanor, and be punished by a fine, not exceeding five thousand dollars, and by imprisonment, for not less than six months, not more than five years; and may further be holden to sureties for good behavior. And it further enacts, that if any person shall write, print, utter or publish, or shall cause or procure to be written, printed, uttered or published, or shall knowingly and willingly aid in writing, printing, uttering or publishing, any false, scandalous, and malicious writing against the government of the United States, or either House of Congress, or the President of the United States, with intent to defame the said government, or either House of Congress, or the President, or to bring them, or either of them, into contempt or disrepute; or to excite against them or either of them, the hatred of the people of the United States; or to excite unlawful combinations therein, for opposing or resisting any law of the United States, or any act of the President of the United States done in pursuance of

3. 14 July, 1798.

any such law, or of the powers vested in him by the constitution of the United States; or to oppose or defeat any such law or acts; or to aid, encourage, or abet any hostile designs of any foreign nation against the United States, their people or government; such person shall be punished by a fine, not exceeding two thousand dollars, and imprisonment, not exceeding two years.

This act, which seems to be best known by the name of the *Sedition Bill*, provides "That if any person shall be prosecuted under it, for writing or publishing any libel, it shall be lawful for him, on the trial of the cause, to give in evidence, in his defense, the truth of the matter contained in the publication charged as a libel. And the jury who shall try the cause shall have a right to determine the law and the fact, under the direction of the court, as in other cases." [. . .]

No law seems to have been resisted in Congress with more vehemence and passion, by those who opposed all the measures adopted as measures of defense against the hostile spirit of France. And, out of doors, it has been attacked with sullen rancor, as a death would to the progress of that detestable system of slander, which has been pursued, with such malignant industry, and calamitous success, against every measure of the administration. And yet, strange as it may seem, this law does not create any new offence; for every thing forbidden by it appears to me to have been, before, an offence at common law. The combinations and attempts therein forbidden are misdemeanors. Any writings of an immoral or illegal tendency is a libel.[4] And slanderous words spoken of the government, or its acts or authority, are punishable by indictment.[5]

It may be said then, why was this law made? Several reasons may be given for it.

1. It is no uncommon thing for a legislature to make an act declaratory of the common law. At this time, it was peculiarly proper to make such an act, as a solemn admonition to wicked or unthinking men to abstain from practices, which spread slanders and falsehood, foment divisions and seditions among the citizens, weaken the energy of the government, and, thus rendering the nation defenseless, encourage France, by a prospect of impunity and success, to measures of aggression and hostility.
2. A doubt had been suggested whether the courts of the United States had cognizance of any offences not expressly declared by the constitution, or some law, or treaty of the United States—I do not think this doubt well founded. The judicial power of the United States extends to all cases arising under the constitution, the laws, and treaties of the United States.[6] Hence results a jurisdiction to try and punish, as misdemeanors, all acts tending to violate or weaken the authority of the constitution, or of any act or measure of the government of the United States. For it cannot be supposed, that such misdemeanors should pass unpunished or that the government of the United States should be obliged to beg protection from the individual States. The doubt however existing, it might be thought proper to remove it.
3. It might be thought proper to pass this law, in order to limit the extent of punishment which might be inflicted on the offender; and to give him the advantage of proving the truth of the libel in his defense. Whatever may have been the motive for making this law, it was opposed on two grounds; 1, as unconstitutional, and, 2, as inexpedient.

1. It was said to be unconstitutional, because the constitution declares that "the powers not delegated to the United States by the constitution, nor prohibited by it to the states, are reserved to the states respectively, or to the people;"[7] and more expressly, that "Congress shall make no law abridging the freedom of speech or of the press."

4. 4 Comm. 150.
5. 4 Bac. 480.
6. Const. Art. Iii. Sec. 2.
7. U.S. Const. Add. Art. xii.

The constitution like every other instrument, must be construed by asking the whole together. Among the powers which the constitution delegates to Congress, is a power "to make all laws, which shall be necessary and proper for carrying into execution all powers vested by this constitution in the government of the United States, or any department or office thereof." It is evident, that the attempts and writings declared punishable by this law, have a direct tendency, differing only in degree from force, to prevent or obstruct the execution of the powers vested by the constitution in the government of the United States. Therefore a law, declaring that such attempts and writings are punishable, is constitutional as necessary and proper for the execution of the powers of government.

If the clause of the constitution which prohibits Congress from making any law abridging the freedom of speech or of the press, is to be construed as prohibiting Congress from making any law declaring libels against the government, acts, or measures of the United States, to be punishable; then by the same construction of the constitution of Pennsylvania, which declares, that no law shall ever be made to restrain this right, the most false and malicious libels might be published, against the government, acts, or measures would have no power to make any law, declaring such libels punishable; and thus absolute impurity for them would be established. This is a construction too absurd to be received as true. Nor will is justify such construction of the constitution of the United States today, that it was intending by that constitution, that the authority of passing laws against libels should be left to the individual fates: for this would be supposing that the government of the United States must, unless the individual chooses to afford it, be without defense against the most dangerous enemy that can attack it, slander; against which, if unrestrained, no government can support itself. This, therefore, would only remove one absurdity by another, and some other construction of this clause of the constitution must be fought for.

To restrain the abuse of my right, or such an exercise of it as shall encroach on a right of another, is no restraint or abridgement of my right: for I can have no right to lessen the right of another. And to claim such an unlimited use of my right, as to encroach on the right of another is to claim, no liberty, but tyranny; no right, but oppression. "I may freely speak, write and print, on any subject;" but "I am responsible for the abuse of liberty." Unless I may speak, write and print, my right will not be sufficiently secured; and unless I be responsible for the abuse of this liberty, the rights of others would not be sufficiently secured. Therefore to secure all, and establish true liberty, I must be free to speak, write and print, but be also responsible for the abuse of that liberty. This is a sound principle, and applies to all rights whatever—It applies to our right of action, as well as to our right of expressing our sentiments in every way. I may ride a horse, but I must not ride over a man. I may walk where I please, but not on my neighbors garden. I may use my cane, but not to strike any man I meet. Such is the liberty of speech or of the press. A law that any printing press should be locked up, and the key kept by a certain officer, or that no book should be printed without permission from a certain officer, would be a law abridging the liberty of press. A law, that a man should not speak without permission, should speak only on certain subjects, or should have a gag put in his mouth, not to be taken out but by a certain officer, would be an abridgement of the freedom of speech, would be indeed a gagging-law. But because the constitution denies the legislature any power to make a law like this, or to make any law laying a previous restraint on speech or the press, to claim therefore a right, from the constitution, to speak, write, or print sedition, impiety, blasphemy, or any falsehood, however gross, indecent, and dangerous, is claiming not liberty but licentiousness. Will any one say, that my right of freedom of speech entitles me to propagate with impunity any slander I please upon all my neighbors? What character would be safe, and what life would be free from misery, were this liberty of speech to be indulged? There is no such liberty. A liberty to destroy reputation would be as unjust, as a liberty to destroy life. Every man is free to speak, but he speaks at his peril, and is answerable for all he says, if it tend to the injury of another. It is not his opinion of its being proper or true, that will justify him.—When he utters it, he is answerable for its truth and propriety; and the opinion of a court and jury, not his opinion must decide on its truth and propriety. Every repeater of the tale is, in like manner answerable as the author. So of libels or written or printed slander, with this difference, that, as the provocation by them is more dangerous, they are less indulged; and, except in the case of matters proper for public information, the proceedings of government, and the official conduct of officers, or men in a public capacity, truth is no justification. Even in cases where truth is a justification, the truth must be made out to the satisfaction of a jury.—That the libeler may have thought it true, though it may extenuate, will not justify the offense: for no man is to be judge in his own cause, and my opinion will not justify me in doing an injury to my neighbor, in his reputation, writes and prints, as he speaks, at his peril: and the publisher of a libel in answerable, in like manner as the author. And both are answerable, as in any other offence, to the judgment of a court and jury, by whole opinion, and not of the offender, must the guilt or innocence of the action be determined. And such restriction, if I may so call it, or correction of the abuse, of freedom, of speech and of the press, is not only perfectly consistent with the principles of civil liberty in general, and with the rules of our constitution: but is necessary for maintaining the genuine liberty of speech and the press. For, of all enemies to liberty, licentiousness is the greatest.

2. I think, the expediency of this law can be as clearly shown, as its constitutionality: and, if so, there will be not only duty, but pleasure in the obedience we yield to it.

Speech, writing and printing, are the great directors of public opinion, and public opinion is the great director of human action. Of such force is public opinion, that, with it on its side, the worst government will support itself; and, with it against it, the best government will fall.—All governments are supported by it; and without it, can no government be supported. What is the force in the power of any government compared to that of the people governed by it, if the people choose to resist? And will they not choose to resist, if their opinions be set against the government, their passions roused to enthusiasm, and an opportunity offered for success. And all this may be done by means of clubs, societies, and the press.—Give to any set of men the command of the press, and you give them the command of the country: for you give them the command of public opinion, which commands every thing. Let therefore, clubs, societies, and the printing presses attack any government, however free, and however strong, they will infallibly destroy it.

It appears evident to me, that this law is not only expedient, but necessary. And it may be laid down as a general rule, that it will be impossible to prevent the corruption of public opinion, or to preserve any government against it; unless there be laws to correct the licentiousness of speech and of the press. True liberty of speech and of the press conflicts in being free to speak, write, and print, but being, as in the exercise of all our liberties, responsible for the abuse of this liberty. And whether we have abused this liberty or not, must, like all other questions of right, be left to the decision of a court and a jury. This is the universal test, by which the exercise of all our rights must be tried. Nor is the subjection of our rights of freedom of speech and of the press to this test, any more a restraint on that right; than the subjection of our rights of life and of property to the same test, is a restraint on those rights. By this test must the exercise of all our rights be tried, or no man could enjoy any right whatever. If while our right to life and to property is submitted to this restriction, we yet believe we are free, shall we think our liberty infringed, by subjecting to the same restrictor, our right to speak and print?

This law takes from no man any liberty but a liberty of doing mischief. And so far is it from being true, that this law is any violation of liberty, that, it may be safely averred, without such laws, for punishing the abuse of the freedom of speech and of the press, liberty cannot be preserved; every man will be a slave to the malignant passions of every other, truth and justice will be banished, the authority of government destroyed, and malice, anarchy, confusion, and every evil work established. No administration or government can stand against the corruption of public opinion; and let me therefore solemnly admonish you, as you value the peace and liberty of yourselves and your posterity, seriously to reflect on the truth of this. We have seen an insurrection promoted by the corruption of public opinion. An invasion is invited by it.—How many shocks of this kind our government is doomed to stand, only the Ruler of the world knows. Let us take warnings from our own experience, and the fate of other nations. Let all friends to liberty and order unite in suppressing slander: for, where it prevails, there will be no happiness, no government. Of all slanders those of the press are most dangerous. Presses established to run down the government are the most destructive of all treasons.—This ought to be well considered; for every one who encourages such presses, or contributes to their support, is a partner in their guilt. Every one who reads their productions with approbation, sucks in disease upon his mind; and every one who repeats them to others, spreads the infection. What would we think of a set of men, who should agree to hire a number of persons to run through the country, and report falsehoods and slanders? Precisely such, and more dangerous, is the guilt of those who contribute to the support of a slanderous Press. They are wounding their own and their country's peace, and undermining the government. [. . .]

THOMAS JEFFERSON

Draft of the Kentucky Resolutions (before October 4, 1798)

1. Resolved that the several states composing the US of America are not united on the principle of unlimited submission to their general government; but that by a compact under the style and title of a Constitution for the US and of amendments thereto, they constituted a general government for special purposes, delegated to that government certain definite powers, reserving, each state to itself, the residuary mass of right to their own self-government; & that whensoever the General government assumes undelegated powers, its acts are unauthoritative, void, & of no force: that to this compact each state acceded as a state, and is an integral party, its co-states forming, as to itself, the other party: that the government created by this compact was not made the exclusive or final judge of the extent of the powers delegated to itself; since that would have made its discretion, & not the constitution, the measure of its powers; but that, as in all other cases of compact among powers having no common judge, each party has an equal right to judge for itself, as well of infractions, as of the mode & measure of redress.

2. Resolved that the constitution of the US having delegated to Congress a power to punish treason, counterfeiting the securities & current coin of the US piracies & felonies committed on the high seas, & offences against the law of Nations, & no other crimes whatsoever, and it being true as a general principle, and one of the Amendments to the constitution having also declared, that "the powers not delegated to the US by the constitution, nor prohibited by it to the states, are reserved to the states respectively, or to the people" therefore the act of Congress passed on the 14th day of July 1798 and intituled "an Act in addition to the act intituled an Act for the punishment of certain crimes against the US" as also the act passed by them on the _____ day of June 1798 intituled "an Act to punish frauds committed on the bank of the US" [and all other their acts which assume to create, define or punish crimes, other than those so enumerated in the Constitution] are altogether void & of no force, & that the power to create, define & punish such other crimes is reserved, & of right appurtains solely & exclusively to the respective states, each within its own territory.

3. Resolved that it is true as a general principle, and is also expressly declared by one of the Amendments to the Constitution that "the powers not delegated to the US by the constitution, nor prohibited by it to the states, are reserved to the states respectively or to the people"; and that no power over the freedom of religion, freedom of speech, or freedom of the press being delegated to the US by the constitution, nor prohibited by it to the states, all lawful powers respecting the same did of right remain, & were reserved, to the states or the people: that thus was manifested their determination to retain to themselves the right of judging how far the licentiousness of speech & of the press may be abridged without lessening their useful freedom, and how far those

abuses which cannot be separated from their use should be tolerated rather than the use be destroyed; and thus also they guarded against all abridgment by the US of the freedom of religious opinions and exercises, & retained to themselves the right of protecting the same, as this state, by a law passed on the general demand of its citizens, had already protected them from all human restraint or interference: And that in addition to this general principle and express declaration, another & more special provision has been made by one of the amendments to the constitution which expressly declares that "Congress shall make no law respecting an establishment of religion, or prohibiting the free exercise thereof or abridging the freedom of speech or of the press," thereby guarding in the same sentence, & under the same words, the freedom of religion of speech & of the press: insomuch that whatever violates either throws down the sanctuary which covers the others, and that libels, falsehood & defamation, equally with heresy & false religion, are witheld from the cognisance of federal tribunals: that therefore the act of Congress of the US passed on the 14th day of July 1798 intituled "an Act in addition to the act intituled an act for the punishment of certain crimes against the US," which does abridge the freedom of the press, is not law, but is altogether void & of no force.

4. Resolved that alien friends are under the jurisdiction and protection of the laws of the state wherein they are; that no power over them has been delegated to the US nor prohibited to the individual states distinct from their power over citizens: and it being true as a general principle, & one of the amendments to the constitution having also declared that "the powers not delegated to the US by the constitution, nor prohibited by it to the States, are reserved to the states respectively, or to the people," the act of the Congress of the US passed on the day ____ of July 1798 intituled "an Act concerning Aliens," which assumes powers over Alien-friends not delegated by the constitution, is not law, but is altogether void & of no force.

5. Resolved that in addition to the general principle, as well as the express declaration, that powers not delegated are reserved, another and more special provision, inserted in the constitution from abundant caution, has declared that "the migration or importation of such persons as any of the states now existing shall think proper to admit, shall not be prohibited by the Congress prior to the year 1808"; that this commonwealth does admit the migration of Alien-friends, described as the subject of the said act concerning aliens; that a provision against prohibiting their migration, is a provision against all acts equivalent thereto, or it would be nugatory; that to remove them when migrated is equivalent to a prohibition of their migration, and is therefore contrary to the said provision of the constitution, and void.

6. Resolved that the imprisonment of a person under the protection of the laws of this commonwealth on his failure to obey the simple *order* of the President to depart out of the US as is undertaken by the said act intituled "an Act concerning Aliens," is contrary to the constitution, one Amendment to which has provided that "no person shall be deprived of liberty without due process of law" and that another having provided that "in all criminal prosecutions the accused shall enjoy the right to a public trial, by an impartial jury, to be informed of the nature and cause of the accusation, to be confronted with the witnesses against him, to have compulsory process for obtaining witnesses in his favor, & to have the assistance of counsel for his defence," the same act, undertaking to authorize the President to remove a person out of the US who is under the protection of the law, on his own suspicion, without accusation, without jury, without public trial, without confrontation of the witnesses against him, without hearing witnesses in his favor, without defence, without counsel, is contrary to these provisions also of the constitution, is therefore not law, but utterly void & of no force; that transferring the power of judging any person, who is under the protection of the laws, from the courts to the President of the US as is undertaken by the same act concerning Aliens, is against the article of the constitution which provides that "the judicial power of the US shall be vested in courts the judges of which shall hold their offices during good behavior" and that the said act is void for that reason also; and it is further to be noted that this transfer of judiciary power is to that magistrate of the general government who already possesses all the Executive, and a negative on all the Legislative powers.

7. Resolved that the construction applied by the General government (as is evidenced by sundry of

their proceedings) to those parts of the constitution of the US which delegate to Congress a power "to lay & collect taxes, duties, imposts & excises, to pay the debts & provide for the common defence & general welfare of the US" and "to make all laws which shall be necessary & proper for carrying into execution the powers vested by the constitution in the government of the US or in any department or officer thereof" goes to the destruction of all the limits prescribed to their power by the constitution; that words meant by that instrument to be subsidiary only to the execution of limited powers, ought not to be so construed as themselves to give unlimited powers, nor a part to be so taken as to destroy the whole residue of that instrument: that the proceedings of the General government under colour of these articles, will be a fit & necessary subject of revisal and correction, at a time of greater tranquility, while those specified in the preceding resolutions, call for immediate redress.

8. Resolved that a committee of conference & correspondence be appointed, who shall have in charge to communicate the preceding resolutions to the legislatures of the several states, to assure them that this commonwealth continues in the same esteem for their friendship and union which it has manifested from that moment at which a common danger first suggested a common union: that it considers union, for specified national purposes, & particularly for those specified in their late federal compact, to be friendly to the peace, happiness & prosperity of all the states; that faithful to that compact, according to the plain intent & meaning in which it was understood & acceded to by the several parties, it is sincerely anxious for its preservation: that it does also believe that to take from the states all the powers of self government, & transfer them to a general & consolidated government, without regard to the special delegations & reservations solemnly agreed to in that compact, is not for the peace, happiness or prosperity of these states: & that therefore this commonwealth is determined, as it doubts not its co-states are, to submit to undelegated, & consequently unlimited powers in no man, or body of men, on earth: that in cases of an abuse of the delegated powers the members of the general government, being chosen by the people, a change by the people would be the constitutional remedy; but, where powers are assumed which have not been delegated, a nullification of the act is the rightful remedy: that every state has a natural right, in cases not within the compact [*casus non foederis*] to nullify of their own authority all assumptions of power by others within their limits: that without this right, they would be under the dominion, absolute and unlimited, of whosoever might exercise this right of judgment for them: that nevertheless this commonwealth, from motives of regard & respect for its co-states, has wished to communicate with them on the subject; that with them alone it is proper to communicate, they alone being parties to the compact, & solely authorized to judge in the last resort of the powers exercised under it, Congress being not a party, but merely the creature of the compact, & subject, as to its assumptions of power, to the final judgment of those by whom, & for whose use, itself, & its powers, were all created & modified: that if the acts before specified should stand, these conclusions would flow from them; that the General government may place any act they think proper on the list of crimes, & punish it themselves, whether enumerated or not enumerated by the constitution as cognisable by them; that they may transfer its cognisance to the President, or any other person, who may himself be the accuser, counsel, judge & jury, whose *suspicions* may be the evidence, his *order* the sentence, his officer the executioner, & his breast the sole record of the transaction: that a very numerous & valuable description of the inhabitants of these states being, by this precedent, reduced, as Outlaws, to the absolute dominion of one man, & the barrier of the constitution thus swept away for us all, no rampart now remains against the passions & the power of a majority in Congress, to protect from a like exportation, or other more grievous punishment, the minority of the same body, the legislatures, judges, governors & counsellors of the states, nor their other peaceable inhabitants, who may venture to reclaim the constitutional rights & liberties of the states & people, or who for other causes, good or bad, may be obnoxious to the views, or marked by the suspicions of the President, or be thought dangerous to his or their elections, or other interests public or personal: that the friendless alien has indeed been selected as the safest subject of a first experiment; but the citizen will soon follow, or rather has already followed; for already has a Sedition act marked him as its prey: that these & successive acts of the same character, unless arrested

at the threshold, necessarily drive these states into revolution & blood, & will furnish new calumnies against republican government, & new pretexts for those who wish it to be believed that man cannot be governed but by a rod of iron: that it would be a dangerous delusion, were a confidence in the men of our choice to silence our fears for the safety of our rights; that confidence is every where the parent of despotism; free government is founded in jealousy, and not in confidence; it is jealousy & not confidence which prescribes limited constitutions, to bind down those whom we are obliged to trust with power: that our constitution has accordingly fixed the limits to which, & no further, our confidence may go: and let the honest advocate of confidence read the Alien and Sedition acts, and say if the constitution has not been wise in fixing limits to the government it created, & whether we should be wise in destroying those limits? Let him say What the government is, if it be not a tyranny, which the men of our choice have conferred on our President, and the President of our choice has assented to, & accepted over the friendly strangers, to whom the mild spirit of our country, & its laws had pledged hospitality & protection: that the men of our choice have more respected the bare *suspicions* of the President, than the solid rights of innocence, the claims of justification, the sacred force of truth, & the forms and substance of law & justice: in questions of power then, let no more be heard of confidence in man, but bind him down from mischief by the chains of the constitution: that this commonwealth does therefore call on its co-states for an expression of their sentiments on the acts concerning aliens, and for the punishment of certain crimes, herein before specified, plainly declaring whether these acts are, or are not authorised by the federal compact? And it doubts not that their sense will be so enounced as to prove their attachment unaltered to limited government, whether general or particular; and that the rights and liberties of their co-states will be exposed to no dangers by remaining embarked in a common bottom with their own: that they will concur with this commonwealth in considering the said acts as so palpably against the constitution as to amount to an undisguised declaration that that compact is not meant to be the measure of the powers of the General government, but that it will proceed in the exercise, over these states, of all powers whatsoever; that they will view this as seizing the rights of the states, and consolidating them in the hands of the General government with a power assumed to bind the states (not merely in the cases made federal [*casus foederis*] but) in all cases whatsoever, by laws made, not with their consent, but by others against their consent; that this would be to surrender the form of government we have chosen, & to live under one deriving its powers from its own will & not from our authority, and that the co-states, recurring to their natural right in cases not made federal, will concur in declaring these acts void and of no force, & will each take measures of its own for providing that neither these acts, nor any others of the general government, not plainly & intentionally authorised by the constitution, shall be exercised within their respective territories.

9. Resolved that the said committee be authorised to communicate, by writing or personal conferences, at any times or places whatever, with any person or persons who may be appointed by any one or more of the co-states to correspond or confer with them; & that they lay their proceedings before the next session of assembly.

James Madison

Virginia Resolutions against the Alien and Sedition Acts (December 21, 1798)

Resolved, that the General Assembly of Virginia doth unequivocally express a firm resolution to maintain and defend the constitution of the United States, and the Constitution of this state, against every aggression, either foreign or domestic, and that they will support the government of the United States in all measures, warranted by the former.

That this Assembly most solemnly declares a warm attachment to the Union of the States, to maintain which, it pledges all its powers; and that for this end, it is their duty, to watch over and oppose every infraction of those principles, which constitute the only basis of that union, because a faithful observance of them, can alone secure its existence, and the public happiness.

That this Assembly doth explicitly and peremptorily declare, that it views the powers of the federal government, as resulting from the compact to which the states are parties; as limited by the plain sense and intention of the instrument constituting that compact; as no farther valid than they are authorised by the grants enumerated in that compact, and that in case of a deliberate, palpable and dangerous exercise of other powers not granted by the said compact, the states who are parties thereto have the right, and are in duty bound, to interpose for arresting the progress of the evil, and for maintaining within their respective limits, the authorities, rights and liberties appertaining to them.

That the General Assembly doth also express its deep regret that a spirit has in sundry instances, been manifested by the federal government, to enlarge its powers by forced constructions of the constitutional charter which defines them; and that indications have appeared of a design to expound certain general phrases (which having been copied from the very limited grant of powers in the former articles of confederation were the less liable to be misconstrued) so as to destroy the meaning and effect of the particular enumeration, which necessarily explains and limits the general phrases; and so as to consolidate the states by degrees into one sovereignty, the obvious tendency and inevitable consequence of which would be, to transform the present republican system of the United States, into an absolute, or at best a mixed monarchy.

That the General Assembly doth particularly protest against the palpable and alarming infractions of the constitution, in the two late cases of the "alien and sedition acts," passed at the last session of Congress; the first of which exercises a power no where delegated to the federal government; and which by uniting legislative and judicial powers, to those of executive, subverts the general principles of free government, as well as the particular organization and positive provisions of the federal constitution: and the other of which acts, exercises in like manner a power not delegated by the constitution, but on the contrary expressly and positively forbidden by one of the amendments thereto; a power which more than any other ought to produce universal alarm, because it is levelled against that right of freely examining public characters and measures, and of free communication among the people thereon, which has ever been justly deemed, the only effectual guardian of every other right.

That this State having by its convention which ratified the federal constitution, expressly declared, "that among other essential rights, the liberty of conscience and of the press cannot be cancelled, abridged, restrained or modified by any authority of the United States" and from its extreme anxiety to guard these rights from every possible attack of sophistry or ambition, having with other states recommended an amendment for that purpose, which amendment was in due time annexed to the Constitution, it would mark a reproachful inconsistency and criminal degeneracy, if an indifference were now shewn to the most palpable violation of one of the rights thus declared and secured, and to the establishment of a precedent which may be fatal to the other.

That the good people of this Commonwealth having ever felt and continuing to feel the most sincere affection for their bretheren of the other states, the truest anxiety for establishing and perpetuating the union of all, and the most scrupulous fidelity to that Constitution which is the pledge of mutual friendship, and the instrument of mutual happiness, the General Assembly doth solemnly appeal to the like dispositions of the other States, in confidence that they will concur with this Commonwealth in declaring, as it does hereby declare, that the acts aforesaid are unconstitutional, and that the necessary and proper measures will be taken by each, for cooperating with this State in maintaining unimpaired the authorities, rights, and liberties, reserved to the States respectively, or to the people.

That the Governor be desired to transmit a copy of the foregoing resolutions to the Executive authority of each of the other States, with a request, that the same may be communicated to the Legislature thereof.

And that a copy be furnished to each of the Senators and Representatives, representing this State in the Congress of the United States.

John Marshall

Report of the Minority on the Virginia Resolutions

(January 22, 1799)

The act intitled "An act in addition to the act instituted as an act for the punishment of certain crimes against the United States," and which is commonly called the sedition law, subjects to a fine not exceeding two thousand dollars, and to imprisonment not exceeding two years, any person who shall write, print, utter, or publish, or cause or procure to be written, printed, uttered or published, any false, scandalous, malicious writing or writings against the government of the United States, with intent to defame the said government of the United States, or either house of Congress of the United States, or the President of the United States, with intent to defame the said government, or either house of Congress, or the said President, or to bring them, or either of them, into contempt or disrepute, or to excite against them, or either or any of them, the hatred of the good people of the United States, or to stir up any sedition within the United States, or to excite any unlawful combination therein for opposing or resisting any law of the United States, or any act of the President of the United States, done in pursuance of such law, or of the powers in him vested by the constitution of the United States, or to resist, oppress, or defeat any such law or act, or to aid, encourage, or abet hostile designs of any foreign nation, against the United States, their people, or government; the person accused is to be tried by jury, and may give in evidence the truth of the matter contained in the libel.

To constitute the crime, the writing must be false, scandalous, and malicious, and the intent must be to effect some of the ill purposes described in the act.

To contend that there does not exist a power to punish writings coming within the description of this law, would be to assert the inability of our nation to preserve its own peace, and to protect themselves from the attempts of wicked citizens, who, incapable of quiet themselves, are incessantly employed in devising means to disturb the public repose.

Government is instituted and preserved for the general happiness and safety—the people therefore are interested in its preservation, and have a right to adopt measures for its security, as well against secret plots as open hostility. But government cannot be thus secured, if by falsehood and malicious slander, it is to be deprived of the confidence and affection of the people. It is vain to urge that truth will prevail, and that slander, when detected, recoils on the calumniator. The experience of the world, and our own experience, prove that a continued course of defamation will at length sully the fairest reputation, and will throw suspicion on the purest conduct. Although the calumnies of the factious and discontented may not poison the minds of the majority of the citizens, yet they will infect a very considerable number, and prompt them to deeds destructive of the public peace and dangerous to the general safety.

This, the people have a right to prevent: and therefore, in all the nations of the earth, where presses are known, some corrective of their licentiousness has been deemed indispensable. But it is contended that though this may be theoretically true, such is the peculiar structure of our government, that this power has either never been confided to, or has been withdrawn from the legislature of this union.—We will examine these positions. The power of making all laws which shall be necessary and proper for carrying into execution all powers vested by the constitution in the government of the United States, or in any department or officer thereof, is by the concluding clause of the eighth section of the first article, expressly delegated to congress. This clause is admitted to authorize congress to pass any act for the punishment of those who would resist the execution of the laws, because such an act would be incontestably necessary and proper for carrying into execution the powers vested in the government. If it authorizes the punishment of actual resistance, does it not also authorize the punishment of those acts, which are criminal in themselves, and which obviously lead to and prepare resistance? Would it not be strange, if, for the purpose of executing the legitimate powers of the government, a clause like that which has been cited should be so construed as to permit the passage of laws punishing open resistance, and yet to forbid the passage of laws punishing acts which constitute the germ from which resistance springs? That the government must look on, and see preparations for resistance which it shall be unable to control, until they shall break out in open force? This would be an unreasonable and improvident construction of the article under consideration. That continued calumnies against the government have this tendency, is demonstrated by uninterrupted experience. They will, if unrestrained, produce in any society convulsions, which if not totally destructive of, will yet be very injurious to, its prosperity and welfare. It is not to be believed that the people of the western parts of Pennsylvania could have been deluded into that unprovoked and wanton insurrection, which called forth the militia of the neighbouring states, if they had not been at the same time irritated and seduced by calumnies with which certain presses incessantly teemed into the opinion that the people of America, instead of supporting their government and their laws, would join in their subversion. Those calumnies men, tended to prevent the execution of the laws of the union, and such seems to be their obvious and necessary tendency.

To punish all malicious calumnies against an individual with an intent to defame him, is a wrong on the part of the calumniator, and an injury to the individual, for which the laws afford redress. To write or print these calumnies is such an aggravation of the crime, as to constitute an offence against the government, and the author of the libel is subject to the additional punishment which may be inflicted under an indictment. To publish malicious calumnies against government itself, is a wrong on the part of the calumniator, and an injury to all those who have an interest in the government. Those who have this interest and have sustained the injury, have the natural right to an adequate remedy. The people of the United States have a common interest in their govenment, and sustain in common the injury which affects that government. The people of the United States therefore have a right to the remedy for that injury, and are substantially the party seeking redress. By the 2d section of the 3d article of the constitution, the judicial power of the United States is extended to controversies to which the United States shall be a party; and by the same article it is extended to all cases in law and equity arising under the constitution, the laws of the United States, and treaties made or which shall be made under their authority. What are cases arising under the constitution, as contradistinguished from those which arise under the laws made in pursuance thereof? They must be cases triable by a rule which exists independent of any act of the legislature of the union. That rule is the common or unwritten law which pervades all America, and which declaring libels against government to be a punishable offence, applies itself to and protects any government which the will of the people may establish. The judicial power of the United States, then, being extended to the punishment of libels against the government, as a common law offence, arising under the constitution which create the government, the general clause gives to the legislature of the union the right to make such laws as shall give that power effect.

That such was the contemporaneous construction of the constitution, is obvious from one of the amendments which have been made to it. The 3d amendment which declares, that Congress shall make no law abridging the liberty of the press, is a general construction made by all America on the original instrument admitting its application to the subject. It would have been certainly unnecessary thus to have modified the legislative powers of Congress concerning the press, if the power itself does not exist.

But altho' the original constitution may be supposed to have enabled the government to defend itself against false and malicious libels, endangering the peace, and threatening the tranquility of the American people, yet it is contended that the 3d amendment to that instrument, has deprived it of this power.

The amendment is in these words,—"Congress shall make no law respecting an establishment of religion, or prohibiting the free exercise thereof, or ABRIDGING the freedom of speech or of the press."

In a solemn instrument, as is a constitution, words are well weighed and considered before they are adopted. A remarkable diversity of expression is not used, unless it be designed to manifest a difference of intention. Congress is prohibited from making any law RESPECTING a religious establishment, but not from making any law RESPECTING the press. When the power of Congress relative to the press is to be limited, the word RESPECTING is dropt, and Congress is only restrained from the passing any law ABRIDGING its liberty. This difference of expression with respect to religion and the press, manifests a difference of intention with respect to the power of the national legislature over those subjects, both in the person who drew, and in those who adopted this amendment.

All ABRIDGMENT of the freedom of the press is forbidden, but it is only an ABRIDGMENT of that freedom which is forbidden. It becomes then necessary in order to determine whether the act in question be unconstitutional or not, to inquire whether it does in fact ABRIDGE the freedom of the press.

The act is believed not to have that operation, for two reasons.

1st. A punishment of the licentiousness is not considered as a restriction of the freedom of the press,

2d. The act complained of does not punish any writing not before punishable, nor does it inflict a more severe penalty than that to which the same writing was before liable.

1st. If by freedom of the press is meant a perfect exemption from all punishment for whatever may be published, that freedom never has, and most probably never will exist. It is known to all, that the person who writes or publishes a libel, may be both sued and indicted, and must bear the penalty which the judgment of his country inflicts upon him. It is also known to all that the person who shall libel the government of the state, is for that offence, punishable in the like manner. Yet this liability to punishment for slanderous and malicious publications has never been considered as detracting from the liberty of the press. In fact the liberty of the press is a term which has a definite and appropriate signification, completely understood. It signifies a liberty to publish, free from previous restraint, any thing and every thing at the discretion of the printer only, but not the liberty of spreading with impunity false and scandalous slanders which may destroy the peace and mangle the reputation of an individual or of a community.

If this definition of the term be correct, and it is presumed that its correctness is not to be questioned, then a law punishing the authors and publishers of false, malicious and scandalous libels can be no attack on the liberty of the press.

But the act complained of is no abridgment of the liberty of the press, for another reason.

2d. It does not punish any writing not before punishable, nor does it inflict a heavier penalty than the same writing was before liable to.No man will deny, that at common law, the author and publisher of a false, scandalous and malicious libel against the government or an individual, were subject to fine and imprisonment, at the discretion of the judge. Nor will it be denied, that previous to our revolution, the common law was the law of the land throughout the now United States.

We believe it to be a principle incontestibly true, that a change of government does not dissolve obligations previously created, does not annihilate existing laws, and dissolve the bonds of society; but that a People passing from one form of government to another, retain in full force all their municipal institutions not necessarily changed by the change of government. If this be true, then the common law continued to be the law of the land after the revolution, and was of complete obligation even before the act of our Assembly for its adoption. Whether similar acts have been passed by the legislature of other states or not, it is certain that in every state the common law is admitted to be in full force, except as it may have been altered by the statute law. The only question is, whether the doctrines of the common law are applicable to libels against the government of the United States, as well as to libels against the governments of particular states. For such a distinction there seems to be no sufficient reason. It is not to a magistrate of this or that description that the rules of the common law apply. That he is a magistrate, that he is cloathed with the authority of the laws, that he is invested with power by the people, is a sufficient title to the protection of the common law. The government of the United States is for certain purposes as entirely the government of each state, chosen by the people thereof, and cloathed with their authority, as the government of each particular state is the government of every subdivision of that state; and no satisfactory reason has been heretofore assigned why a general rule common to all, and punishing generally the malicious calumniators of magistrates, should not be as applicable to magistrates chosen for the whole, as to those chosen for its different parts.

If then it were even true that the punishment of the printer of malicious falsehoods affected the liberty of the press, yet the act does not abridge that liberty, since it does not substitute a harsher or severer rule of punishment than that which before existed.

On points so extremely interesting, a difference of opinion will be entertained. On such occasions all parties must be expected to maintain their real opinions, but to maintain them with moderation and with decency. The will of the majority must prevail, or the republican principle is abandoned and the nation is destroyed. If upon every constitutional question which presents itself, or on every question we choose to term constitutional, the construction of the majority shall be forcibly opposed, and hostility to the government excited throughout the nation, there is an end of our domestic peace, and we may ever bid adieu to our representative government.

The legislature of Virginia has itself passed more than one unconstitutional law, but they have not been passed with an intention to violate the constitution. On being decided to be unconstitutional by the legitimate authority, they have been permitted to fall. Had the judges deemed them constitutional, they should have been maintained. The same check, nor is it a less efficient one, exists in the government of the union. The judges of the United States are as independent as the judges of the state of Virginia, nor is there any reason to believe them less wise and less virtuous. It is their province, and their duty to construe the constitution and the laws, and it cannot be doubted, but that they will perform this duty faithfully and truly. They will perform it unwarmed by political debate, uninfluenced by party zeal. Let us in the mean time seek a repeal of any acts we may disapprove, by means authorized by our happy constitution, but let us not endeavor to disseminate among our fellow citizens the most deadly hate against the government of their own creation, against the government, on the preservation of which we firmly believe the peace and liberty of America to depend, because in some respects its judgment has differed from our own.

Thomas Jefferson

Letter to Elbridge Gerry (January 26, 1799)

Philadelphia

[. . .] In confutation of these and all future calumnies, by way of anticipation, I shall make to you a profession of my political faith; in confidence that you will consider every future imputation on me of a contrary complexion, as bearing on its front the mark of falsehood & calumny.

I do then, with sincere zeal, wish an inviolable preservation of our present federal constitution, according to the true sense in which it was adopted by the States, that in which it was advocated by its friends, & not that which its enemies apprehended, who therefore became its enemies; and I am opposed to the monarchising its features by the forms of its administration, with a view to conciliate a first transition to a President & Senate for life, & from that to a hereditary tenure of these offices, & thus to worm out the elective principle. I am for preserving to the States the powers not yielded by them to the Union, & to the legislature of the Union its constitutional share in the division of powers; and I am not for transferring all the powers of the States to the general government, & all those of that government to the Executive branch. I am for a government rigorously frugal & simple, applying all the possible savings of the public revenue to the discharge of the national debt; and not for a multiplication of officers & salaries merely to make partisans, & for increasing, by every device, the public debt, on the principle of its being a public blessing. I am for relying, for internal defence, on our militia solely, till actual invasion, and for such a naval force only as may protect our coasts and harbors from such depredations as we have experienced; and not for a standing army in time of peace, which may overawe the public sentiment; nor for a navy, which, by its own expenses and the eternal wars in which it will implicate us, will grind us with public burthens, & sink us under them. I am for free commerce with all nations; political connection with none; & little or no diplomatic establishment. And I am not for linking ourselves by new treaties with the quarrels of Europe; entering that field of slaughter to preserve their balance, or joining in the confederacy of kings to war against the principles of liberty. I am for freedom of religion, & against all maneuvres to bring about a legal ascendancy of one sect over another: for freedom of the press, & against all violations of the constitution to silence by force & not by reason the complaints or criticisms, just or unjust, of our citizens against the conduct of their agents. And I am for encouraging the progress of science in all its branches; and not for raising a hue and cry against the sacred name of philosophy; for awing the human mind by stories of raw-head & bloody bones to a distrust of its own vision, & to repose implicitly on that of others; to go backwards instead of forwards to look for improvement; to believe that government, religion, morality, & every other science were in the highest perfection in ages of the darkest ignorance, and that nothing can ever be devised more perfect than what was established by our forefathers. To these I will add, that I was a sincere well-wisher to the success of the French revolution, and still wish it may end in the establishment of a free & well-ordered republic; but I have not been insensible under the atrocious depredations they have committed on our commerce. The first object of my heart is my own country. In that is embarked my family, my fortune, & my own existence. I have not one farthing of interest, nor one fibre of attachment out of it, nor a single motive of preference of any one nation to another, but in proportion as they are more or less friendly to us. But though deeply feeling the injuries of France, I did not think war the surest means of redressing them. I did believe, that a mission sincerely disposed to preserve peace, would obtain for us a peaceable & honorable settlement & retribution; and I appeal to you to say, whether this might not have been obtained, if either of your colleagues had been of the same sentiment with yourself.

These, my friend, are my principles; they are unquestionably the principles of the great body of our fellow citizens, and I know there is not one of them which is not yours also. In truth, we never differed but on one ground, the funding system; and as, from the moment of its being adopted by the constituted authorities, I became religiously principled in the sacred discharge of it to the uttermost farthing, we are united now even on that single ground of difference.

I turn now to your inquiries. The enclosed paper will answer one of them. But you also ask for such political information as may be possessed by me, & interesting to yourself in regard to your embassy. As a proof of my entire confidence in you, I shall give it fully & candidly. When Pinckney, Marshall, and Dana, were nominated to settle our differences with France, it was suspected by many, from what was understood of their dispositions, that their mission would not result in a settlement of differences, but would produce circumstances tending to widen the breach, and to provoke our citizens to consent to a war with that nation, & union with England. Dana's resignation & your appointment gave the first gleam of hope of a peaceable issue to the mission. For it was believed that you were sincerely disposed to accommodation; & it was not long after your arrival there, before symptoms were observed of that difference of views which had been suspected to exist. In the meantime, however, the aspect of our government towards the French republic had become so ardent, that the people of America generally took the alarm. To the southward, their apprehensions were early excited. In the Eastern States also, they at length began to break out. Meetings were held in many of your towns, & addresses to the government agreed on in opposition to war. The example was spreading like a wildfire. Other meetings were called in other places, & a general concurrence of sentiment against the apparent inclinations of the government was imminent; when, most critically for the government, the despatches of Octr 22, prepared by your colleague Marshall, with a view to their being made public, dropped into their laps. It was truly a God-send to them, & they made the most of it. Many thousands of copies were printed & dispersed gratis, at the public expence; & the zealots for war co-operated so heartily, that there were instances of single individuals who printed & dispersed 10 or 12,000 copies at their own expence. The odiousness of the corruption supposed in those papers excited a general & high indignation among the people. Unexperienced in such maneuvres, they did not permit themselves even to suspect that the turpitude of private swindlers might mingle itself unobserved, & give its own hue to the communications of the French government, of whose participation there was neither proof nor probability. It served, however, for a time, the purpose intended. The people, in many places, gave a loose to the expressions of their warm indignation, & of their honest preference of war to dishonor. The fever was long & successfully kept up, and in the meantime, war measures as ardently crowded. Still, however, as it was known that your colleagues were coming away, and yourself to stay, though disclaiming a separate power to conclude a treaty, it was hoped by the lovers of peace, that a project of treaty would have been prepared, ad referendum, on principles which would have satisfied our citizens, & overawed any bias of the government towards a different policy. But the expedition of the Sophia, and as was supposed, the suggestions of the person charged with your despatches, & his probable misrepresentations of the real wishes of the American people, prevented these hopes. They had then only to look forward to your return for such information, either through the Executive, or from yourself, as might present to our view the other side of the medal. The despatches of Oct 22, 97, had presented one face. That information, to a certain degree, is now received, & the public will see from your correspondence with Taleyrand, that France, as you testify, "was sincere and anxious to obtain a reconciliation, not wishing us to break the British treaty, but only to give her equivalent stipulations; and in general was disposed to a liberal treaty." And they will judge whether mr. Pickering's report shews an inflexible determination to believe no declarations the French government can make, nor any opinion which you, judging on the spot & from actual view, can give of their sincerity, and to meet their designs of peace with operations of war. The alien & sedition acts have already operated in the South as powerful sedatives of the X. Y. Z. inflammation. In your quarter, where violations of principle are either less regarded or more concealed, the direct tax is likely to have the same effect, & to excite inquiries into the object of the enormous expences & taxes we are bringing on. And your information supervening, that we might have a liberal accommodation if we would, there can be little doubt of the reproduction of that general movement, by the despatches of Oct. 22. And tho' small checks & stops, like Logan's pretended embassy, may be thrown in the way from time to time, & may a little retard its motion, yet the tide is already turned, and will sweep before it all the feeble obstacles of art. The unquestionable republicanism of the American mind will break through the mist under which it has been clouded, and will oblige its agents to reform the principles & practices of their administration.

You suppose that you have been abused by both parties. As far as has come to my knowledge, you are misinformed. I have never seen or heard a sentence of blame uttered against you by the republicans; unless we were so to construe their wishes that you had more boldly co-operated in a project of a treaty, and would more explicitly state, whether there was in your colleages that flexibility, which persons earnest after peace would have practised? Whether, on the contrary, their demeanor was not cold, reserved, and distant, at least, if not backward? And whether, if they had yielded to those informal conferences which Taleyrand seems to have courted, the liberal accommodation you suppose might not have been effected, even with their agency? Your fellow-citizens think they have a right to full information, in a case of such great concern to them. It is their sweat which is to earn all the expences of the war, and their blood which is to flow in expiation of the causes of it. It may be in your power to save them from these miseries by full communications and unrestrained details, postponing motives of delicacy to those of duty. It rests for you to come forward independently; to take your stand on the high ground of your own character; to disregard calumny, and to be borne above it on the shoulders of your grateful fellow citizens; or to sink into the humble oblivion, to which the Federalists (self-called) have secretly condemned you; and even to be happy if they will indulge you with oblivion, while they have beamed on your colleagues meridian splendor. Pardon me, my dear Sir, if my expressions are strong. My feelings are so much more so, that it is with difficulty I reduce them even to the tone I use. If you doubt the dispositions towards you, look into the papers, on both sides, for the toasts which were given throughout the States on the 4th of July. You will there see whose hearts were with you, and whose were ulcerated against you. Indeed, as soon as it was known that you had consented to stay in Paris, there was no measure observed in the execrations of the war party. They openly wished you might be guillotined, or sent to Cayenne, or anything else. And these expressions were finally stifled from a principle of policy only, & to prevent you from being urged to a justification of yourself. From this principle alone proceed the silence and cold respect they observe towards you. Still, they cannot prevent at times the flames bursting from under the embers, as mr. Pickering's letters, report, & conversations testify, as well as the indecent expressions respecting you, indulged by some of them in the debate on these despatches. These sufficiently show that you are never more to be honored or trusted by them, and that they await to crush you for ever, only till they can do it without danger to themselves.

When I sat down to answer your letter, but two courses presented themselves, either to say nothing or everything; for half confidences are not in my character. I could not hesitate which was due to you. I have unbosomed myself fully; & it will certainly be highly gratifying if I receive like confidence from you. For even if we differ in principle more than I believe we do, you & I know too well the texture of the human mind, & the slipperiness of human reason, to consider differences of opinion otherwise than differences of form or feature. Integrity of views more than their soundness, is the basis of esteem. I shall follow your direction in conveying this by a private hand; tho' I know not as yet when one worthy of confidence will occur. And my trust in you leaves me without a fear that this letter, meant as a confidential communication of my impressions, will ever go out of your hand, or be suffered in anywise to commit my name. Indeed, besides the accidents which might happen to it even under your care, considering the accident of death to which you are liable, I think it safest to pray you, after reading it as often as you please, to destroy at least the 2d & 3d leaves. The 1st contains principles only, which I fear not to avow; but the 2d & 3d contain facts stated for your information, and which, though sacredly conformable to my firm belief, yet would be galling to some, & expose me to illiberal attacks. I therefore repeat my prayer to burn the 2d & 3d leaves. And did we ever expect to see the day, when, breathing nothing but sentiments of love to our country & its freedom & happiness, our correspondence must be as secret as if we were hatching its destruction! Adieu, my friend, and accept my sincere & affectionate salutations. I need not add my signature.

Letter to William Green Munford (June 18, 1799)

Monticello

[. . .] I am among those who think well of the human character generally. I consider man as formed for society, and endowed by nature with those dispositions which fit him for society. I believe also, with Condorcet, as mentioned in your letter, that his mind is perfectible to a degree of which we cannot as yet form any conception. It is impossible for a man who takes a survey of what is already known, not to see what an immensity in every branch of science yet remains to be discovered, & that too of articles to which our faculties seem adequate. In geometry & calculation we know a great deal. Yet there are some desiderata. In anatomy great progress has been made; but much is still to be acquired. In natural history we possess knowlege; but we want a great deal. In chemistry we are not yet sure of the first elements. Our natural philosophy is in a very infantine state; perhaps for great advances in it, a further progress in chemistry is necessary. Surgery is well advanced; but prodigiously short of what may be. The state of medecine is worse than that of total ignorance. Could we divest ourselves of every thing we suppose we know in it, we should start from a higher ground & with fairer prospects. From Hippocrates to Brown we have had nothing but a succession of hypothetical systems each having its day of vogue, like the fashions & fancies of caps & gowns, & yielding in turn to the next caprice. Yet the human frame, which is to be the subject of suffering & torture under these learned modes, does not change. We have a few medecines, as the bark, opium, mercury, which in a few well defined diseases are of unquestionable virtue: but the residuary list of the materia medica, long as it is, contains but the charlataneries of the art; and of the diseases of doubtful form, physicians have ever had a false knowlege, worse than ignorance. Yet surely the list of unequivocal diseases & remedies is capable of enlargement; and it is still more certain that in the other branches of science, great fields are yet to be explored to which our faculties are equal, & that to an extent of which we cannot fix the limits. I join you therefore in branding as cowardly the idea that the human mind is incapable of further advances. This is precisely the doctrine which the present despots of the earth are inculcating, & their friends here re-echoing; & applying especially to religion & politics; 'that it is not probable that any thing better will be discovered than what was known to our fathers.' We are to look backwards then & not forwards for the improvement of science, & to find it amidst feudal barbarisms and the fires of Spitalfields. But thank heaven the American mind is already too much opened, to listen to these impostures; and while the art of printing is left to us, science can never be retrograde; what is once acquired of real knowlege can never be lost. To preserve the freedom of the human mind then & freedom of the press, every spirit should be ready to devote itself to martyrdom; for as long as we may think as we will, & speak as we think, the condition of man will proceed in improvement. The generation which is going off the stage has deserved well of mankind for the struggles it has made, & for having arrested that course of despotism which had overwhelmed the world for thousands & thousands of years. If there seems to be danger that the ground they have gained will be lost again, that danger comes from the generation your cotemporary. But that the enthusiasm which characterises youth should lift its parricide hands against freedom & science, would be such a monstrous phænomenon as I cannot place among possible things in this age & this country. Your college at least has shewn itself incapable of it; and if the youth of any other place have seemed to rally under other banners it has been from delusions which they will soon dissipate. I shall be happy to hear from you from time to time, & of your progress in study, and to be useful to you in whatever is in my power; being with sincere esteem Dear Sir your friend & servt

James Madison

Report on the Virginia Resolutions (January 7, 1800)

Whatever room might be found in the proceedings of some of the states, who have disapproved of the resolutions of the General Assembly of this commonwealth, passed on the 21st day of December, 1798, for painful remarks on the spirit and manner of those proceedings, it appears to the committee most consistent with the duty, as well as dignity, of the General Assembly, to hasten an oblivion of every circumstance which might be construed into a diminution of mutual respect, confidence, and affection, among the members of the union. [. . .]

Clear as the position must seem, that the federal powers are derived from the Constitution, and from that alone, the committee are not unapprized of a late doctrine which opens another source of federal powers, not less extensive and important than it is new and unexpected. The examination of this doctrine will be most conveniently connected with a review of a succeeding resolution. The committee satisfy themselves here with briefly remarking that, in all the contemporary discussions and comments which the Constitution underwent, it was constantly justified and recommended on the ground that the powers not given to the government were withheld from it; and that, if any doubt could have existed on this subject, under the original text of the Constitution, it is removed, as far as words could remove it, by the 12th amendment, now a part of the Constitution, which expressly declares, "that the powers not delegated to the United States by the Constitution, nor prohibited by it to the states, are reserved to the states respectively, or to the people."

The other position involved in this branch of the resolution, namely, "that the states are parties to the Constitution or compact," is in the judgment of the committee, equally free from objection. It is indeed true that the term "States," is sometimes used in a vague sense, and sometimes in different senses, according to the subject to which it is applied. Thus it sometimes means the separate sections of territory occupied by the political societies within each; sometimes the particular governments established by those societies; sometimes those societies as organized into those particular governments; and lastly, it means the people composing those political societies, in their highest sovereign capacity. Although it might be wished that the perfection of language admitted less diversity in the signification of the same words, yet little inconvenience is produced by it, where the true sense can be collected with certainty from the different applications. In the present instance, whatever different construction of the term "States," in the resolution may have been entertained, all will at least concur in that last mentioned; because in that sense, the Constitution was submitted to the "States": In that sense the "States" ratified it; and in that sense of the term "States," they are consequently parties to the compact from which the powers of the Federal Government result.

The next position is, that the General Assembly views the powers of the Federal Government, "as limited by the plain sense and intention of the instrument constituting that compact," and "as no further valid than they are authorized by the grants therein enumerated." It does not seem possible that any just objection can lie against either of these clauses. The first amounts merely to a declaration that the compact ought to have the interpretation, plainly intended by the parties to it; the other, to a declaration, that it ought to have the execution and effect intended by them. If the powers granted be valid, it is solely because they are granted; and if the granted powers are valid, because granted, all other powers not granted, must not be valid.

The resolution having taken this view of the federal compact, proceeds to infer, "that in case of a deliberate, palpable, and dangerous exercise of other powers, not granted by the said compact, the states who are parties thereto, have the right, and are in duty bound, to interpose for arresting the progress of the evil, and for maintaining, within their respective limits, the authorities, rights and liberties appertaining to them."

It appears to your committee to be a plain principle, founded in common sense, illustrated by common practice, and essential to the nature of compacts; that where resort can be had to no tribunal superior to the authority of the parties, the parties themselves must be the rightful judges in the last resort, whether the bargain made, has been pursued or violated. The constitution of the United States was formed by the sanction of the states, given by each in its sovereign capacity. It adds to the stability and dignity, as well as to the authority, of the constitution, that it rests on this legitimate and solid foundation. The states then being the parties to the constitutional compact, and in their sovereign capacity, it follows of necessity, that there can be no tribunal above their authority, to decide in the last resort, whether the compact made by them be violated; and consequently that as the parties to it, they must themselves decide in the last resort, such questions as may be of sufficient magnitude to require their interposition.

It does not follow, however, because the states as sovereign parties to their constitutional compact, must ultimately decide whether it has been violated, that such a decision ought to be interposed either in a hasty manner, or on doubtful and inferior occasions. Even in the case of ordinary conventions between different nations, where, by the strict rule of interpretation, a breach of a part may be deemed a breach of the whole; every part being deemed a condition of every other part, and of the whole, it is always laid down that the breach must be both wilful and material to justify an application of the rule. But in the case of an intimate and constitutional union, like that of the United States, it is evident that the interposition of the parties, in their sovereign capacity, can be called for by occasions only, deeply and essentially affecting the vital principles of their political system.

The resolution has accordingly guarded against any misapprehension of its object, by expressly requiring for such an interposition "the case of a *deliberate, palpable,* and *dangerous* breach of the constitution, by the exercise of *powers not granted* by it." It must be a case, not of a light and transient nature, but of a nature *dangerous* to the great purposes for which the constitution was established. It must be a case moreover not obscure or doubtful in its construction, but plain and *palpable*. Lastly, it must be a case not resulting from a partial consideration, or hasty determination; but a case stampt with a final consideration and *deliberate* adherence. It is not necessary because the resolution does not require, that the question should be discussed, how far the exercise of any particular power, ungranted by the constitution, would justify the interposition of the parties to it. As cases might easily be stated, which none would contend, ought to fall within that description: Cases, on the other hand, might, with equal ease, be stated, so flagrant and so fatal as to unite every opinion in placing them within the description.

But the resolution has done more than guard against misconstruction, by expressly referring to cases of a *deliberate, palpable,* and *dangerous* nature. It specifies the object of the interposition, which it contemplates to be solely that of arresting the progress of the *evil* of usurpation, and of maintaining the authorities, rights and liberties appertaining to the states, as parties to the constitution.

From this view of the resolution, it would seem inconceivable that it can incur any just disapprobation from those, who laying aside all momentary impressions, and recollecting the genuine source and object of the federal constitution, shall candidly and accurately interpret the meaning of the General Assembly. If the deliberate exercise, of dangerous powers, palpably withheld by the constitution, could not justify the parties to it, in interposing even so far as to arrest the progress of the evil, and thereby to preserve the constitution itself as well as to provide for the safety of the parties to it; there would be an end to all relief from usurped power, and a direct subversion of the rights specified or recognized under all the state constitutions, as well as a plain denial of the fundamental principle on which our independence itself was declared.

But it is objected that the judicial authority is to be regarded as the sole expositor of the constitution, in the last resort; and it may be asked for what reason, the declaration by the General Assembly, supposing it to be theoretically true, could be required at the present day and in so solemn a manner.

On this objection it might be observed *first*, that there may be instances of usurped power, which the forms of the constitution would never draw within the controul of the judicial department: secondly, that if the decision of the judiciary be raised above the authority of the sovereign parties to the constitution, the decisions of the other departments, not carried by the forms of the constitution before the judiciary, must be equally authoritative and final with the decisions of that department. But the proper answer to the objection is, that the resolution of the General Assembly relates to those great and extraordinary cases, in which all the forms of the constitution may prove ineffectual against infractions dangerous to the essential rights of the parties to it. The resolution supposes that dangerous powers not delegated, may not only be usurped and executed by the other departments, but that the Judicial Department also may exercise or sanction dangerous powers beyond the grant of the constitution; and consequently that the ultimate right of the parties to the constitution, to judge whether the compact has been dangerously violated, must extend to violations by one delegated authority, as well as by another; by the judiciary, as well as by the executive, or the legislature.

However true therefore it may be that the Judicial Department, is, in all questions submitted to it by the forms of the constitution, to decide in the last resort, this resort must necessarily be deemed the last in relation to the authorities of the other departments of the government; not in relation to the rights of the parties to the constitutional compact, from which the judicial as well as the other departments hold their delegated trusts. On any other hypothesis, the delegation of judicial power, would annul the authority delegating it; and the concurrence of this department with the others in usurped powers, might subvert forever, and beyond the possible reach of any rightful remedy, the very constitution, which all were instituted to preserve.

The truth declared in the resolution being established, the expediency of making the declaration at the present day, may safely be left to the temperate consideration and candid judgment of the American public. It will be remembered that a frequent recurrence to fundamental principles is solemnly enjoined by most of the state constitutions, and particularly by our own, as a necessary safeguard against the danger of degeneracy to which republics are liable, as well as other governments, though in a less degree than others. And a fair comparison of the political doctrines not unfrequent at the present day, with those which characterized the epoch of our revolution, and which form the basis of our republican constitutions, will best determine whether the declaratory recurrence here made to those principles ought to be viewed as unseasonable and improper, or as a vigilant discharge of an important duty. The authority of constitutions over governments, and of the sovereignty of the people over constitutions, are truths which are at all times necessary to be kept in mind; and at no time perhaps more necessary than at present. [. . .]

Samuel Chase

Calder v. Bull (1798)

The decision of one question determines (in my opinion) the present dispute. I shall, therefore, state from the record no more of the case, than I think necessary for the consideration of that question only.

The Legislature of Connecticut, on the 2d Thursday of May 1795, passed a resolution or law, which, for the reasons assigned, set aside a decree of the court of Probate for Harford, on the 21st of March 1793, which decreed disapproved of the will of Normand Morrison (the grandson) made the 21st of August 1779, and refused to record the said will; and granted a new hearing by the said Court of Probate, with liberty of appeal therefrom, in six months. A new hearing was had, in virtue of this resolution, or law, before the said Court of Probate, who, on the 27th of July 1795, approved the said will, and ordered it to be recorded. At August 1795, appeal was then had to the superior court at Harford, who at February term 1796, adjudged, that there were no errors. More than 18 months elapsed from the decree of the Court of Probate (on the 1st of March 1793) and thereby Caleb Bull and wife were barred of all right of appeal, by a statute of Connecticut. There was no law of that State whereby a new hearing, or trial, before the said Court of Probate might be obtained. Calder and wife claim the premises in question, in right of his wife, as heiress of N. Morrison, physician; Bull and wife claim under the will of N. Morrison, the grandson.

The Council for the Plaintiffs in error, content, that the said resolution or law of the Legislature of Connecticut, granting a new hearing, in the above case, is an ex post facto law, prohibited by the Constitution of the United States; that any law of the Federal government, or of any of the State governments, contrary to the Constitution of the United States, is void; and that this court possesses the power to declare such law void.

It appears to me a self-evident proposition, that the several State Legislatures retain all the powers of legislation, delegated to them by the State Constitutions; which are not EXPRESSLY taken away by the Constitution of the United States. The establishing courts of justice, the appointment of Judges, and the making regulations for the administration of justice, within each State, according to its laws, on all subjects not entrusted to the Federal Government, appears to me to be the peculiar and exclusive province, and duty of the State Legislatures: All the powers delegated by the people of the United States to the Federal Government are defined, and NO CONSTRUCTIVE powers can be exercised by it, and all the powers that remain in the State Governments are indefinite; except only in the Constitutions of Massachusetts.

The effect of the resolution or law of Connecticut, above stated, is to revise a decision of one of its Inferior Courts, called the Court of Probate for Harford, and to direct a new hearing of the case by the James Court of Probate, that passed the decree against the will of Normand Morrison. By the existing law of Connecticut a right to recover certain property had vested in Calder and wife (the appellants) in consequence of a decision of a court of justice, but, in virtue of a subsequent resolution or law, and the new hearing thereof, and the decision in consequence, this right to recover certain property was divested, and the right to the property declared to be in Bull and wife, the appellees. The sole enquiry is, whether this resolution or law of Connecticut, having such operation, is an ex post facto law, within the prohibition of the Federal Constitution?

Whether the Legislature of any of the States can revise and correct by law, a decision of any of its Courts of Justice, although not prohibited by the Constitution of the State, is a question of very great importance, and not necessary NOW to be determined; because the resolution or law in question does not go so far. I cannot subscribe to the omnipotence of a State Legislature, or that it is absolute and without controul; although its authority should not be expressly restrained by the Constitution, or fundamental law, of the State. The people of the United States erected their Constitutions, or forms of government, to establish justice, to promote the general welfare, to secure the blessings of liberty; and to protect their persons and property from violence. The purposes for which men enter into society will determine the nature and terms of the social compact; and as they are the foundation of the legislative power, they will decide what are the proper objects of it: The nature, and ends of legislative power will limit the exercise of it. This fundamental principle flows from the very nature of our free Republican governments, that no man should be compelled to do what the laws do not require; nor to refrain from acts which the laws permit. There are acts which the Federal, or State, Legislature cannot do, without exceeding their authority. There are certain vital principles in our free Republicans governments, which will determine and overrule an apparant and flagrant abuse of legislative power; as to authorize manifest injustice by positive law; or to take away that security for personal liberty, or private property, for the protection whereof the government was established. An ACT of the Legislature (for I cannot call it a law) contrary to the great first principles of the social compact, cannot be considered a rightful exercise of legislative authority. The obligation of a law in governments established on express compact, and on republican principles, must be determined by the nature of the power, on which it is founded. A few instances will suffice to explain what I mean. A law that punished a citizen for an innocent action, or, in other words, for an act, which, when done, was in violation of no existing law; a law that destroys, or impairs, the lawful private contracts of citizens; a law that makes a man a Judge in his own cause; or a law that takes property from A. and gives it to B: It is against all reason and justice, for a people to entrust a Legislature with SUCH powers; and, therefore, it cannot be presumed that they have done it. The genius, the nature, and the spirit, of our State Governments, amount to a prohibition of such acts of legislation; and the general principles of law and reason forbid them. The Legislature may enjoin, permit, forbid, and punish; they may declare new crimes; and establish rules of conduct for all its citizens in future cases; they may command what is right, and prohibit what is wrong; but they cannot change innocence into guilt; or punish innocence as a crime; or violate the right of an antecedent lawful private contract; or the right of private property. To maintain that our Federal, or State, Legislature possesses such powers, if they had not been expressly restrained; would, in my opinion, be a political heresy, altogether inadmissible in our free republican governments.

ALL the restrictions contained in the Constitution of the United States on the power of the State Legislatures, were provided in favour of the authority of the Federal Government. The prohibition against their making any ex post facto laws was introduced for greater caution, and very probably arose from the knowledge, that the Parliament of Great Britain claimed and exercised a power to pass such laws, under the denomination of bills of attainder, or bills of pains and penalties; the first inflicting capital, and the other less, punishment. These acts were legislative judgments; and an exercise of judicial power. Sometimes they respected the crime, by declaring acts to be treason, which were not treason, when committed; at other times, they violated the rules of evidence (to supply a deficiency of legal proof) by admitting one witness, when the existing law required two; by receiving evidence without oath; or the oath of the wife against the husband; or other testimony, which the courts of justice would not admit; at other times they inflicted punishments, where the party was not, by law, liable to any punishment; and in other cases, they inflicted greater punishment, than the law annexed to the offence.—The ground for the exercise of such legislative power was this, that the safety of the kingdom depended on the death, or other punishment, of the offender: as if traitors, when discovered, could be so formidable, or the government so insecure! With very few exceptions, the advocates of such laws were stimulated by ambition, or personal resentment, and vindictive malice. To prevent such, and similar, acts of violence and injustice, I believe, the Federal and State Legislatures, were prohibited from passing any bill of attainder; or any ex post facto law. [. . .]

I shall endeavor to shew what law is to be considered an ex post facto law, within the words and meaning of the prohibition in the Federal Constitution. The prohibition, "that no state shall pass any ex post facto law," necessarily requires some explanation; for, naked and without explanation, it is unintelligible, and means nothing. Literally, it is only, that a law shall not be passed concerning, and after the fact, or thing done, or action committed. I would ask, what fact; of what nature, or kind; and by whom done? [. . .] The prohibition, in the letter, is not to pass any law concerning, and after the fact; but the plain and obvious meaning and intention of the prohibition is this; that the Legislatures of the several states, shall not pass laws, after a fact done by a subject, or citizen, which shall have relation to such fact, and shall punish him for having done it. The prohibition considered in this light, is an additional bulwark in favour of the personal security of the subject, to protect his person from punishment by legislative acts, having a retrospective operation. I do not think it was inserted to secure the citizen in his private rights, of either property, or contracts. The prohibitions not to make any thing but gold and silver coin a tender in payment of debts, and not to pass any law impairing the obligation of contracts, were inserted to secure private rights; but the restriction not to pass any ex post facto law, was to secure the person of the subject from injury, or punishment, in consequence of such law. If the prohibition against making ex post facto laws was intended to secure personal rights from being affected, or injured, by such laws, and the prohibition is sufficiently extensive for that object, the other restraints, I have enumerated, were unnecessary, and therefore improper; for both of them are retrospective.

I will state what laws I consider ex post facto laws, within the words and the intent of the prohibition. 1st. Every law that makes an action done before the passing of the law, and which was innocent when done, criminal; and punishes such action. 2d. Every law that aggravates a crime, or makes it greater than it was, when committed. 3d. Every law that changes the punishment, and inflicts a greater punishment, than the law annexed to the crime, when committed. 4th. Every law that alters the legal rules of evidence, and receives less, or different, testimony, than the law required at the time of the commission of the offence, in order to convict the offender. All these, and similar laws, are manifestly unjust and oppressive. In my opinion, the true distinction is between ex post facto laws, and retrospective laws. Every ex post facto law must necessarily be retrospective; but every retrospective law is not an ex post facto law: The former, only, are prohibited. Every law that takes away, or impairs, rights vested, agreeably to existing laws, is retrospective, and is generally unjust, and may be oppressive; and it is a good general rule, that a law should have no retrospect: but there are cases in which laws may justly, and for the benefit of the community, and also of individuals, relate to a time antecedent to their commencement; as statutes of oblivion, or of pardon. They are certainly retrospective, and literally both concerning, and after, the facts committed. But I do not consider any law ex post facto, within the prohibition, that mollifies the rigor of the criminal law; but only those that create, or aggravate, the crime; or encrease the punishment, or change the rules of evidence, for the purpose of conviction. Every law that is to have an operation before the making thereof, as to commence at an antecedent time; or to save time from the statute of limitations; or to excuse acts which were unlawful, and before committed, and the like; is retrospective. But such laws may be proper or necessary, as the case may be. There is a great and apparent difference between making an UNLAWFUL act LAWFUL; and the making an innocent action criminal, and punishing it as a CRIME. The expressions "ex post facto laws," are technical, they had been in use long before the Revolution, and had acquired an appropriate meaning, by Legislators, Lawyers, and Authors. The celebrated and judicious Sir William Blackstone, in his commentaries, considers an ex post facto law precisely in the same light I have done. His opinion is confirmed by his successor, Mr. Wooddeson; and by the author of the Federalist, who I esteem superior to both, for his extensive and accurate knowledge of the true principles of Government. [. . .]

In the present case, there is no fact done by Bull and wife Plaintiffs in Error, that is in any manner affected by the law or resolution of Connecticut: It does not concern, or relate to, any act done by them. The decree of the Court of Probate of Harford (on the 21st, March) in consequence of which Calder and wife claim a right to the property in question, was given before the said law or resolution, and in that sense, was affected and set aside by it; and in consequence of the law allowing a hearing and the decision in favor of the will, they have lost, what they would have been entitled to, if the Law or resolution, and the decision in consequence thereof, had not been made. The decree of the Court of probate is the only fact, on which the law or resolution operates. In my judgment the case of the Plaintiffs in Error, is not within the letter of the prohibition; and, for the reasons assigned, I am clearly of opinion, that it is not within the intention of the prohibition; and if within the intention, but out of the letter, I should not, therefore, consider myself justified to continue it within the prohibition, and therefore that the whole was void.

It was argued by the Counsel for the plaintiffs in error, that the Legislature of Connecticut had no constitutional power to make the resolution (or law) in question, granting a new hearing, &c.

Without giving an opinion, at this time, whether this Court has jurisdiction to decide that any law made by Congress, contrary to the Constitution of the United States, is void; I am fully satisfied that this court has no jurisdiction to determine that any law of any state Legislature, contrary to the Constitution of such state, is void. Further, if this court had such jurisdiction, yet it does not appear to me, that the resolution (or law) in question, is contrary to the charter of Connecticut, or its constitution, which is said by counsel to be composed of its acts of assembly, and usages, and customs. I should think, that the courts of Connecticut are the proper tribunals to decide, whether laws, contrary to the constitution thereof, are void In the present case they have, both in the inferior and superior courts, determined that the Resolution (or law) in question was not contrary to either their state, or the federal, constitution.

To shew that the resolution was contrary to the constitution of the United States, it was contended that the words, ex post facto law, have a precise and accurate meaning, and convey but one idea to professional men which is, "by matter of after fact; by something after the fact." [. . .]

I believe that but one instance can be found in which a British judge called a statute, that affected contracts made before the statute, an ex post facto law; but the judges of Great Britain always considered penal statutes, that created crimes, or encreased the punishment of them, as ex post facto laws.

If the term ex post facto law is to be construed to include and to prohibit the enacting any law after a fact, it will greatly restrict the power of the federal and state legislatures; and the consequences of such a construction may not be foreseen.

If the prohibition to make no ex post facto law extends to all laws made after the fact; the two prohibitions, not to make any thing but gold and silver coin a tender in payment of debts; and not to pass any law impairing the obligation of contracts, were improper and unnecessary.

It was further urged, that if the provision does not extend to prohibit the making any law after a fact, then all choses in action; all lands by Devise; all personal property by bequest, or distribution; by Elegit; by execution, by judgments, particularly on torts; will be unprotected from the legislative power of the states; rights vested may be divested at the will and pleasure of the state legislatures; and, therefore, that the true construction and meaning of the prohibition is, that the states pass no law to deprive a citizen of any right vested in him by existing laws.

It is not to be presumed, that the federal or state legislatures will pass laws to deprive citizens of rights vested in them by existing laws; unless for the benefit of the whole community; and on making full satisfaction. The restraint against making any ex post facto laws was not considered, by the framers of the constitution, as extending to prohibit the depriving a citizen even of a vested right to property; or the provision, "that private property should not be taken for PUBLIC use, without just compensation," was unnecessary.

It seems to me, that the right of property, in its origin, could only arise from compact express, or implied, and I think it the better opinion, that the right, as well as the mode, or manner, of acquiring property, and of alienating or transferring, inheriting, or transmitting it, is conferred by society; is regulated by civil institutions, and is always subject to the rules prescribed by positive law. When I say that a right is vested in a citizen, I mean, that he has the power to do certain actions; or to possess certain things, according to the law of the land.

If any one has a right to property such right is a perfect and exlusive right; but no one can have such right before he has acquired a better right to the property, than any other person in the world: a right, therefore, only to recover property cannot be called a perfect and exclusive right. I cannot agree, that a right to property vested in Calder and wife, in consequence of the decree (of the 21st of March 1783) disapproving of the will of Morrison, the Grandson. If the will was valid, Mrs. Calder could have no rights, as heiress of Morrison, the physician; but if the will was set aside, she had an undoubted title.

The resolution (or law) alone had no manner of effect on any right whatever vested in Calder and wife. The Resolution (or law) combined with the new hearing, and the decision, in virtue of it, took away their right to recover the property in question. But when combined they took away no right of property vested in Calder and wife; because the decree against the will (21st March 1783) did not vest or transfer any property to them.

I am under a necessity to give a construction, or explanation of the words, "ex post facto law," because they have not any certain meaning attached to them. But I will not go farther than I feel myself bound to do; and if I ever exercise the jurisdiction I will not decide any law to be void, but in a very clear case.

I am of opinion, that the decree of the Supreme Court of Errors of Connecticut be affirmed, with costs.

JUDGMENT affirmed.

WILLIAM PATTERSON

Calder v. Bull, Concurrence (1798)

The Constitution of Connecticut is made up of usages, and it appears that its Legislature have, from the beginning, exercised the power of granting new trials. This has been uniformly the case till the year 1762, when this power was, by a legislative act, imparted to the superior and county courts. But the act does not remove or annihilate the pre-existing power of the Legislature, in this particular; it only communicates to other authorities a concurrence of jurisdiction, as to the awarding of new trials. And the fact is, that the Legislature have, in two instances, exercised this power since the passing of the law in 1762. They acted in a double capacity, as a house of legislation, with undefined authority, and also as a court of judicature in certain exigencies. Whether the latter arose from the indefinite nature of their legislative powers, or in some other way, it is not necessary to discuss. From the best information, however, which I have been able to collect on this subject, it appears, that the Legislature, or general court of Connecticut, originally possessed, and exercised all legislative, executive, and judicial authority; and that, from time to time, they distributed the two latter in such manner as they thought proper; but without parting with the general superintending power, or the right of exercising the same, whenever they should judge it expedient. But be this as it may, it is sufficient for the present to observe, that they have on certain occasions, exercised judicial authority from the commencement of their civil policy. This usage makes up part of the Constitution of Connecticut, and we are bound to consider it as such, unless it be inconsistent with the Constitution of the United States. True it is, that the awarding of new trials falls properly within the province of the judiciary; but if the Legislature of Connecticut have been in the uninterrupted exercise of this authority, in certain cases, we must, in such cases, respect their decisions as flowing from a competent jurisdiction, or constitutional organ. And therefore we may, in the present instance, consider the Legislature of the state, as having acted in their customary judicial capacity. If so, there is an end of the question. For if the power, thus exercised, comes more properly within the description of a judicial than of a legislative power; and if by usage or the Constitution, which, in Connecticut, are synonimous terms, the Legislature of that state acted in both capacities; then in the case now before us, it would be fair to consider the awarding of a new trial, as an act emanating from the judiciary side of the department. But as this view of the subject militates against the Plaintiffs in error, their counsel has contended for a reversal of the judgment, on the ground, that the awarding of a new trial, was the effect of a legislative act, and that it is unconstitutional, because an ex post facto law. For the sake of ascertaining the meaning of these terms, I will consider the resolution of the General court of Connecticut, as the exercise of a legislative and not a judicial authority. The question, then, which arises on the pleadings in this cause, is, whether the resolution of the Legislatures of Connecticut, be an ex post facto law, within the meaning of the Constitution of the United States? I am of opinion, that it is not. The words, ex post facto, when applied to a law, have a technical meaning, and, in legal phraseology, refer to crimes, pains, and penalties. Judge Blackstone's description of the terms is clear and accurate. "There is, says he, a still more unreasonable method than this, which is called making of laws, ex post facto, when after an action, indifferent in itself, is committed, the Legislator, then, for the first time, declares it to have been a crime, and inflicts a punishment upon the person who has committed it. Here it is impossible, that the party could foresee that an action, indifferent in itself, is committed, the Legislator, then, for the first time, declares it to have been a crime, and inflicts a punishment upon the person who has committed it. Here it is impossible, that the party could foresee that an action, innocent when it was done, should be afterwards converted to guilt by a subsequent law; he had, therefore, no cause to abstain from it; and all punishment for not abstaining, must, of consequence, be cruel and unjust." 1 Bl. Com. 46. Here the meanings, annexed to the terms ex post facto laws, unquestionably refer to crimes, and nothing else. The historic page abundantly evinces, that the power of passing such laws should be withheld from legislators; as it is a dangerous instrument in the hands of bold, unprincipled, aspiring, and party men, and has been too often used to effect the most detestable purposes.

On inspecting such of our state Constitutions, as take notice of laws made ex post facto, we shall find, that they are understood in the same sense.

The Constitution of Massachusetts, article 24th of the Declaration of Rights: "Laws made to punish for actions done before the existence of such laws, and which have not been declared crimes by preceding laws, are unjust, oppressive, and inconsistent with the fundamental principles of a free government."

The Constitution of Delaware, article 11th of the Declaration of Rights: "That retrospective laws punishing offences committed before the existence of such laws, are oppressive and unjust, and ought not to be made."

The Constitution of Maryland, article 15th of the Declaration of Rights: "That retrospective laws, punishing facts committed before the existence of such laws, and by them only declared criminal, are oppressive, unjust, and incompatible with liberty; wherefore no ex post facto law ought to be made."

The Constitution of North Carolina, article 24th of the Declaration of Rights: "That retrospective laws, punishing facts committed before the existence of such laws, and by them only declared criminal, are oppressive, unjust, and incompatible with liberty; wherefore no ex post facto law ought to be made."

From the above passages it appears, that ex post facto laws have an appropriate signification; they extend to penal statutes, and no further; they are restricted in legal estimation to the creation, and, perhaps, enhancement of crimes, pains and penalties. The enhancement of a crime, or penalty, seems to come within the same mischief as the creation of a crime of penalty; and therefore they may be classed together.

Again, the words of the Constitution of the United States are, "That no State shall pass any bill of attainder, ex post facto law, or law impairing the obligation of contracts." Article 1st. section 10.

Where is the necessity or use of the latter words, if a law impairing the obligation of contracts, be comprehended within the terms ex post facto law? It is obvious from the specification of contracts in the last member of the clause, that the framers of the Constitution, did not understand or use the words in the sense contended for on the part of the Plaintiffs in Error. They understood and used the words in their known and appropriate signification, as referring to crimes, pains, and penalties, and no further. The arrangement of the distinct members of this section, necessarily points to this meaning.

I had an ardent desire to have extended the provision in the Constitution to retrospective laws in general. There is neither policy nor safety in such laws;

and, therefore, I have always had a strong aversion against them. It may, in general, be truly observed of retrospective laws of every description, that they neither accord with found legislation, nor the fundamental principles of the social compact. But on full consideration, I am convinced, that ex post facto laws must be limited in the manner already expressed; they must be taken in their technical, which is also their common and general, acceptation, and are not to be understood in their literal sense.

JAMES IREDELL

Calder v. Bull, Dissent (1798)

Though I concur in the general result of the opinions, which have been delivered, I cannot entirely adopt the reasons that are assigned upon the occasion.

From the best information to be collected, relative to the Constitution of Connecticut, it appears, that the Legislature of that State has been in the uniform, uninterrupted, habit of exercising a general superintending power over its courts of law, by granting new trials. It may, indeed, appear strange to some of us, that in any form, there should exist a power to grant, with respect to suits depending or adjudged, new rights of trial, new privileges of proceeding, not previously recognized and regulated by positive institutions; but such is the established usage of Connecticut, and it is obviously consistent with the general superintending authority of her Legislature Nor is it altogether without some sanction for a Legislature to act as a court of justice. In England, we know, that one branch of the Parliament, the house of Lords, not only exercises a judicial power in cases of impeachment, and for the trial of its own members, but as the court of dernier resort, takes cognizance of many suits at law, and in equity: And that in construction of law, the jurisdiction there exercised is by the King in full Parliament; which shews that, in its origin, the causes were probably heard before the whole Parliament. When Connecticut was settled, the right of empowering her Legislature to superintend the Courts of Justice, was, I presume, early assumed; and its expedience, as applied to the local circumstances and municipal policy of the State, is sanctioned by a long and uniform practice. The power, however, is judicial in its nature; and whenever it is exercised, as in the present instance, it is an exercise of judicial, not of legislative, authority.

But, let us, for a moment, suppose, that the resolution, granting a new trial, was a legislative act, it will by no means follow, that it is an act affected by the constitutional prohibition, that "no State shall pass any ex post facto law." I will endeavour to state the general principles, which influence me on this point, succinctly and clearly, though I have not had an opportunity to reduce my opinion to writing.

If, then, a government, composed of Legislative, Executive and Judicial departments, were established, by a Constitution, which imposed no limits on the legislative power, the consequence would inevitably be, that whatever the legislative power chose to enact, would be lawfully enacted, the judicial power could never interpose to pronounce it void. It is true, that some speculative jurists have held, that a legislative act against natural justice must, in itself, be void; but I cannot think that, under such a government, any Court of Justice would possess a power to declare it so. Sir William Blackstone, having put the strong case of an act of Parliament, which authorise a man to try his own cause, explicitly adds, that even in that case, "there is no court that has power to defeat the intent of the Legislature, when couched in such evident and express words, as leave no doubt whether it was the intent of the Legislature, or no." 1 Bl. Com. 91.

In order, therefore, to guard against so great an evil, it has been the policy of all the American states, which have, individually, framed their state constitutions since the revolution, and of the people of the United States, when they framed the Federal Constitution, to define with precision the objects of the legislative power, and to restrain its exercise within marked and settled boundaries. If any act of Congress, or of the Legislature of a state, violates those constitutional provisions, it is unquestionably void; though, I admit, that as the authority to declare it void is of a delicate and awful nature, the Court will never resort to that authority, but in a clear and urgent case. If, on the other hand, the Legislature of the Union, or the Legislature of any member of the Union, shall pass a law, within the general scope of their constitutional power, the Court cannot pronounce it to be void, merely because it is, in their judgment, contrary to the principles of natural justice. The ideas of natural justice are regulated by no fixed standard: the ablest and the purest men have differed upon the subject; and all that the Court could properly say, in such an event, would be, that the Legislature (possessed of an equal right of opinion) had passed an act which, in the opinion of the judges, was inconsistent with the abstract principles of natural justice. There are then but two lights, in which the subject can be viewed: 1st. If the Legislature pursue the authority delegated to them, their acts are valid. 2d. If they transgress the boundaries of that authority, their acts are invalid. In the former case, they exercise the discretion vested in them by the people, to whom alone they are responsible for the faithful discharge of their trust: but in the latter case, they violate a fundamental law, which must be our guide, whenever we are called upon as judges to determine the validity of a legislative act.

Still, however, in the present instance, the act or resolution of the Legislature of Connecticut, cannot be regarded as an ex post facto law; for, the true construction of the prohibition extends to criminal, not to civil, cases. It is only in criminal cases, indeed, in which the danger to be guarded against, is greatly to be apprehended. The history of every country in Europe will furnish flagrant instances of tyranny exercised under the pretext of penal dispensations. Rival factions, in their efforts to crush each other, have superseded all the forms, and suppressed all the sentiments, of justice; while attainders, on the principle of retaliation and proscription, have marked all the vicissitudes of party triumph. The temptation to such abuses of power is unfortunately too alluring for human virtue; and, therefore, the framers of the American Constitutions have wisely denied to the respective Legislatures, Federal as well as State, the possession of the power itself: They shall not pass any ex post facto law; or, in other words, they shall not inflict a punishment for any act, which was innocent at the time it was committed; nor increase the degree of punishment previously denounced for any specific offence.

The policy, the reason and humanity, of the prohibition, do not, I repeat, extend to civil cases, to cases that merely affect the private property of citizens. Some of the most necessary and important acts of Legislation are, on the contrary, founded upon the principle, that private rights must yield to public exigences. Highways are run through private grounds. Fortifications, Light-houses, and other public edifices, are necessarily sometimes built upon the soil owned by individuals. In such, and similar cases, if the owners should refuse voluntarily to accommodate the public, they must be constrained, as far as the public necessities require; the justice is done, by allowing them a reasonable equivalent. Without the possession of this power the operations of Government would often be obstructed, and society itself would be endangered. It is not sufficient to urge, that the power may be abused, for, such is the nature of all power,—such is the tendency of every human institution: and, it might as fairly be said, that the power of taxation, which is only circumscribed by the discretion of the Body, in which it is vested, ought not to be grounded, because the Legislature, disregarding its true objects, might, for visionary and useless projects, impose a tax to the amount of nineteen shillings in the pound. We must be content to limit power where we can, and where we cannot, consistently with its use, we must be content to repose a salutary confidence. It is our consolation that there never existed a Government, in ancient or modern times, more free from danger in this respect, than the Governments of America.

Upon the whole, though there cannot be a case, in which an ex post facto law in criminal matters is requisite, or justifiable (for Providence never can intend to promote the prosperity of any country by bad means) yet, in the present instance the objection does not arise: Because, 1st. if the act of the Legislature of Connecticut was a judicial act, it is not within the words of the Constitution; and 2d. even if it was a legislative act, it is not within the meaning of the prohibition.

THOMAS JEFFERSON

First Inaugural Address (March 4, 1801)

Friends and Fellow-Citizens,—Called upon to undertake the duties of the first executive office of our country, I avail myself of the presence of that portion of my fellow-citizens which is here assembled to express my grateful thanks for the favor with which they have been pleased to look toward me, to declare a sincere consciousness that the task is above my talents, and that I approach it with those anxious and awful presentiments which the greatness of the charge and the weakness of my powers so justly inspire. A rising nation, spread over a wide and fruitful land, traversing all the seas with the rich productions of their industry, engaged in commerce with nations who feel power and forget right, advancing rapidly to destinies beyond the reach of mortal eye—when I contemplate these transcendent objects, and see the honor, the happiness, and the hopes of this beloved country committed to the issue and the auspices of this day, I shrink from the contemplation, and humble myself before the magnitude of the undertaking. Utterly, indeed, should I despair did not the presence of many whom I here see remind me that in the other high authorities provided by our Constitution I shall find resources of wisdom, of virtue, and of zeal on which to rely under all difficulties. To you, then, gentlemen, who are charged with the sovereign functions of legislation, and to those associated with you, I look with encouragement for that guidance and support which may enable us to steer with safety the vessel in which we are all embarked amidst the conflicting elements of a troubled world.

During the contest of opinion through which we have passed the animation of discussions and of exertions has sometimes worn an aspect which might impose on strangers unused to think freely and to speak and to write what they think; but this being now decided by the voice of the nation, announced according to the rules of the Constitution, all will, of course, arrange themselves under the will of the law, and unite in common efforts for the common good. All, too, will bear in mind this sacred principle, that though the will of the majority is in all cases to prevail, that will to be rightful must be reasonable; that the minority possess their equal rights, which equal law must protect, and to violate would be oppression. Let us, then, fellow-citizens, unite with one heart and one mind. Let us restore to social intercourse that harmony and affection without which liberty and even life itself are but dreary things. And let us reflect that, having banished from our land that religious intolerance under which mankind so long bled and suffered, we have yet gained little if we countenance a political intolerance as despotic, as wicked, and capable of as bitter and bloody persecutions. During the throes and convulsions of the ancient world, during the agonizing spasms of infuriated man, seeking through blood and slaughter his long-lost liberty, it was not wonderful that the agitation of the billows should reach even this distant and peaceful shore; that this should be more felt and feared by some and less by others, and should divide opinions as to measures of safety. But every difference of opinion is not a difference of principle. We have called by different names brethren of the same principle. We are all Republicans, we are all Federalists. If there be any among us who would wish to dissolve this Union or to change its republican form, let them stand undisturbed as monuments of the safety with which error of opinion may be tolerated where reason is left free to combat it. I know, indeed, that some honest men fear that a republican government can not be strong, that this Government is not strong enough; but would the honest patriot, in the full tide of successful experiment, abandon a government which has so far kept us free and firm on the theoretic and visionary fear that this Government, the world's best hope, may by possibility want energy to preserve itself? I trust not. I believe this, on the contrary, the strongest Government on earth. I believe it the only one where every man, at the call of the law, would fly to the standard of the law, and would meet invasions of the public order as his own personal concern. Sometimes it is said that man can not be trusted with the government of himself. Can he, then, be trusted with the government of others? Or have we found angels in the forms of kings to govern him? Let history answer this question.

Let us, then, with courage and confidence pursue our own Federal and Republican principles, our attachment to union and representative government. Kindly separated by nature and a wide ocean from the exterminating havoc of one quarter of the globe; too high-minded to endure the degradations of the others; possessing a chosen country, with room enough for our descendants to the thousandth and thousandth generation; entertaining a due sense of our equal right to the use of our own faculties, to the acquisitions of our own industry, to honor and confidence from our fellow-citizens, resulting not from birth, but from our actions and their sense of them; enlightened by a benign religion, professed, indeed, and practiced in various forms, yet all of them inculcating honesty, truth, temperance, gratitude, and the love of man; acknowledging and adoring an overruling Providence, which by all its dispensations proves that it delights in the happiness of man here and his greater happiness hereafter—with all these blessings, what more is necessary to make us a happy and a prosperous people? Still one thing more, fellow-citizens—a wise and frugal Government, which shall restrain men from injuring one another, shall leave them otherwise free to regulate their own pursuits of industry and improvement, and shall not take from the mouth of labor the bread it has earned. This is the sum of good government, and this is necessary to close the circle of our felicities.

About to enter, fellow-citizens, on the exercise of duties which comprehend everything dear and valuable to you, it is proper you should understand what I deem the essential principles of our Government, and consequently those which ought to shape its Administration. I will compress them within the narrowest compass they will bear, stating the general principle, but not all its limitations. Equal and exact justice to all men, of whatever state or persuasion, religious or political; peace, commerce, and honest friendship with all nations, entangling alliances with none; the support of the State governments in all their rights, as the most competent administrations for our domestic concerns and the surest bulwarks against antirepublican tendencies; the preservation of the General Government in its whole constitutional vigor, as the sheet anchor of our peace at home and safety abroad; a jealous care of the right of election by the people—a mild and safe corrective of abuses which are lopped by the sword of revolution where peaceable remedies are unprovided; absolute acquiescence in the decisions of the majority, the vital principle of republics, from which is no appeal but to force, the vital principle and immediate parent of despotism; a well-disciplined militia, our best reliance in peace and for the first moments of war till regulars may relieve them; the supremacy of the civil over the military authority; economy in the public expense, that labor may be lightly burthened; the honest payment of our debts and sacred preservation of the public faith; encouragement of agriculture, and of commerce as its handmaid; the diffusion of information and arraignment of all abuses at the bar of the public reason; freedom of religion; freedom of the press, and freedom of person under the protection of the habeas corpus, and trial by juries impartially selected. These principles form the bright constellation which has gone before us and guided our steps through an age of revolution and reformation. The wisdom of our sages and blood of our heroes have been devoted to their attainment. They should be the creed of our political faith, the text of civic instruction, the touchstone by which to try the services of those we trust; and should we wander from them in moments of error or of alarm, let us hasten to retrace our steps and to regain the road which alone leads to peace, liberty, and safety.

I repair, then, fellow-citizens, to the post you have assigned me. With experience enough in subordinate offices to have seen the difficulties of this the greatest of all, I have learnt to expect that it will rarely fall to the lot of imperfect man to retire from this station with the reputation and the favor which bring him into it. Without pretensions to that high confidence you reposed in our first and greatest revolutionary character, whose preeminent services had entitled him to the first place in his country's love and destined for him the fairest page in the volume of faithful history, I ask so much confidence only as may give firmness and effect to the legal administration of your affairs. I shall often go wrong through defect of judgment. When right, shall often be thought wrong by those whose positions will not command a view of the whole ground. I ask your indulgence for my own errors, which will never be intentional, and your support against the errors of others, who may condemn what they would not if seen in all its parts. The approbation implied by your suffrage is a great consolation to me for the past, and my future solicitude will be to retain the good opinion of those who have bestowed it in advance, to conciliate that of others by doing them all the good in my power, and to be instrumental to the happiness and freedom of all.

Relying, then, on the patronage of your good will, advance with obedience to the work, ready to retire from it whenever you become sensible how much better choice it is in your power to make. And may that Infinite Power which rules the destinies of the universe lead our councils to what is best, and give them a favorable issue for your peace and prosperity.

7

Liberty, Morality, and Nationalism

Throughout the first half of the nineteenth century the United States experienced vast and multiple expansions. Between 1791 and 1850, eighteen new states entered the Union. The nation doubled its territory with the 1803 purchase of the Louisiana Territory, and it acquired thousands more square miles of land through the annexation of Texas in 1845, the subsequent war with Mexico in 1846 and 1847, and the Oregon Treaty with Great Britain concluded in 1846. Its population increased from 5 million in 1800 to 23 million in 1850. The population explosion brought demands for expanded political participation. New states entered the Union without property restrictions on the adult white male franchise; meanwhile, existing states, particularly in the state constitutional conventions of the 1820s and 1830s, removed such restrictions. In 1850 Virginia became the last state to adopt universal adult white male suffrage. Economically the nation was rapidly transforming as well. Technological changes, the growing importance of banks and corporations, and the emergence of factories produced a market revolution that brought with it profound cultural challenges. The United States in these decades was a vital place, messily expanding and busily striving to define what kind of public society it would be. American politicians, statesmen, and thinkers grappled with the problem of a national identity, even as economic development and demographic expansion wrought profound changes in the nation's social and cultural manners. The selections in this chapter explore the ensuing conversation.

It is these "manners" or mores that Alexis de Tocqueville so brilliantly described in *Democracy in America*. Writing of the "great democratic revolution" he saw "occurring among us," Tocqueville observed that the idea of equality—along with the "equality of conditions"—most indelibly shaped America's cultural and political life. In describing this burgeoning democratic political culture, one that he anticipated would spread worldwide, Tocqueville addressed a question central to American political life in this period: what does it mean to be an American, and more generally, a democratic citizen?

This question, of course, was not new. The Revolutionary period spurred the colonists to contemplate this idea of a distinctly American culture, of which Hector St. John de Crèvecoeur's third *Letter from an American Farmer* (presented in Chapter 4) is a fine example. Further, this question was reflected in public policy debates. The policy battles of the 1790s are significant not only as expressions of differing interpretations of the Constitution but also as expressions of competing political faiths. For Thomas Jefferson and his Republican followers, the policies of Alexander Hamilton and the Federalist Party bespoke of an illiberal concentration of power: political power in the central government—particularly in the executive, as evidenced by George Washington's Neutrality Proclamation—and economic power in the hands of an elite. Indeed, Jefferson and his followers perceived Hamilton's plan for a national bank to be a scheme to reinforce the accumulation of political and economic power in the hands of a small number of men.

After their sweeping electoral victory in 1800, Jefferson and the Republican Congress set out to reverse Federalist policy. According to Jeffersonian Republicans, liberty, along with the virtue or manners necessary to sustain it, was incompatible with a large, commercial empire, which was precisely what Hamilton and the Federalists had been attempting to establish. Jefferson reduced the federal budget, cut taxes, and shifted domestic policy-making power to the state governments. Localized policy making, along with a continued abundance of land, would perpetuate what Jefferson called "the Empire of Liberty" well into the future. He went ahead with the Louisiana Purchase, despite constitutional reservations, because it would guarantee "room enough for our descendants to the thousandth and thousandth generation," thereby delaying the transformation of the American republic into a commercial empire. Similarly, Jefferson sought to reassert a democratic ethos over the perceived elitism and alleged "monarchism" of the Federalist regime, declining, for example, to deliver in person his report on the state of the Union (the practice of delivering the speech before Congress was renewed by Woodrow Wilson over a century later).

William Manning's *The Key of Liberty* is a good representation of the Jeffersonian persuasion. A Massachusetts farmer who lacked formal education, Manning was profoundly distrustful of government. For Manning, good government was limited, frugal government. Standing armies and "needless wars" were the means by which the "Few" sought to destroy free government. More generally, he argued that to hold power the "Few" relied on "A people or nation being . . . trained up from their youths to habits, customs, and manners directly contrary to those necessary in a free government"—habits and manners "not easily changed." Thus, the "Many" of the nation—its farmers, mechanics, and laborers—had to be educated to liberty. They had to be habituated to democracy. One way to do this, he offered, was through a society of laborers, an idea that is interestingly reminiscent of Tocqueville's more famous and developed argument regarding the link between participation in associations and political liberty in America.

Noah Webster and Benjamin Franklin, too, took up the challenge of habituating the nation to republican norms. For Webster, a sense of national identity was inextricably bound up with language. As an independent nation, the United States needed its own language—one that departed from its British roots. A "national language is a band of national union," he wrote, while bemoaning the "astonishing respect for the arts and literature of their parent country, and a blind imitation of its manners" that were "still prevalent among the Americans." Promoting a common tongue—one whose simplicity reflects the habits of a democratic people—would facilitate the respect and friendship that are the social bases of a national identity.

Franklin also perceived that Americans were ripe for "great reformations" in their habits, and that such reformation was essential to the American republican experiment. Franklin's *Autobiography* ranks as an American classic. His analysis extended beyond the mere pursuit of material prosperity to embrace other values, such as friendship and benevolence, as necessary for public as well as private happiness.

Americans also continued to break from their British religious roots. In a series of evangelical revivals that spread across the country in the first years of the nineteenth century, they worked out a distinctive republican emphasis in religion. A new focus on voluntarism led to a host of interdenominational Protestant societies, unions, and associations, committed to Christianizing America's rapidly growing and diverse population. The convictions that sustained the revivals fit well with the Jeffersonian confidence in the capacity of common people to govern themselves. As revivalists like Richard McNemar stressed, "the will of God was made manifest to each individual who honestly sought after it, by an inward light, which shone into the heart." "Heart Religion" underscored the capacity of each individual who chose to strive for it to attain redemption and salvation. The evangelical faith of people like McNemar certainly parted ways with the religious rationalism that had appealed so powerfully to an earlier generation of American statesmen. Nonetheless, the theology of the nineteenth-century revivals represented real continuity with those eighteenth-century Protestant traditions that rejected Calvinist predestination and instead stressed the free capacity of the human will to make moral choices and gain salvation.

In the nineteenth century, then, the latent tendency toward democracy inherent in the reformed tradition's "priesthood of all believers" blossomed into an evangelical faith fully compatible with individual autonomy, liberty, and republican manners. More generally, the essential link between republican government and a citizenry educated in republican norms was a prevailing idea in this period. And, optimism abounded about the ability of common men for self-government. Still, a note of caution about mass democracy could be heard. Luminaries like Jefferson and James Madison extolled the republican principle of majority rule, but they also spoke of the threat that majorities posed to minorities. As he had previously, Madison, writing in 1829, worried that a growing propertyless class "necessarily reduced by a competition for employment to wages which afford them [only] the bare necessities of life," could not be expected to sympathize with or respect property rights. In short, for the republican experiment to succeed, enlightened citizens were needed; but according to satirist Hugh Brackenridge, the idea of an enlightened citizenry was in danger of giving way to the vagaries of an ignorant, unenlightened populace.

Benjamin Franklin

Autobiography (1791)

[Part One]

Twyford, at the Bishop of St. Asaph's 1771

Dear Son,

I have ever had a Pleasure in obtaining any little Anecdotes of my Ancestors. You may remember the Enquiries I made among the Remains of my Relations when you were with me in England; and the journey I took for that purpose. Now imagining it may be equally agreeable to you to know the Circumstances of *my* Life, many of which you are yet unacquainted with; and expecting a Week's Uninterrupted Leisure in my present Country Retirement, I sit down to write them for you. To which I have besides some other Inducements. Having emerg'd from the Poverty and Obscurity in which I was born and bred, to a State of Affluence and some Degree of Reputation in the World, and having gone so far thro' Life with a considerable Share of Felicity, the conducting Means I made use of, which, with the Blessing of God, so well succeeded, my Posterity may like to know, as they may find some of them suitable to their own Situations, and therefore fit to be imitated. That Felicity, when I reflected on it, has induc'd me sometimes to say, that were it offer'd to my Choice, I should have no Objection to a Repetition of the same Life from its Beginning, only asking the Advantage Authors have in a second Edition to correct some Faults of the first. So would I if I might, besides correcting the Faults, change some sinister Accidents and Events of it for others more favorable, but tho' this were denied, I should still accept the Offer. However, since such a Repetition is not to be expected, the Thing most like living one's Life over again, seems to be a *Recollection* of that Life; and to make that Recollection as durable as possible, the putting it down in Writing. Hereby, too, I shall indulge the Inclination so natural in old Men, to be talking of themselves and their own past Actions, and I shall indulge it, without being troublesome to others who thro' respect to Age might think themselves oblig'd to give me a Hearing, since this may be read or not as any one pleases. And lastly, (I may as well confess it, since my Denial of it will be believ'd by no body) perhaps I shall a good deal gratify my own *Vanity*. Indeed I scarce ever heard or saw the introductory Words, *Without Vanity I may say*, etc. but some vain thing immediately follow'd. Most People dislike Vanity in others whatever Share they have of it themselves, but I give it fair Quarter wherever I meet with it, being persuaded that it is often productive of Good to the Possessor and to others that are within his Sphere of Action: And therefore in many Cases it would not be quite absurd if a Man were to thank God for his Vanity among the other Comforts of Life.

And now I speak of thanking God, I desire with all Humility to acknowledge, that I owe the mention'd Happiness of my past Life to his kind Providence, which led me to the Means I us'd and gave them Success. My Belief of This, induces me to *hope*, tho' I must not *presume*, that the same Goodness will still be exercis'd towards me in continuing that happiness, or in enabling me to bear a fatal Reverse, which I may experience as others have done, the Complexion of my future Fortune being known to him only: and in whose Power it is to bless to us even our Afflictions.

The Notes one of my Uncles (who had the same kind of Curiosity in collecting Family Anecdotes) once put into my Hands, furnish'd me with several Particulars, relating to our Ancestors. From those Notes I learned that the Family had liv'd in the same Village, Ecton in Northamptonshire, for 300 Years, and how much longer he knew not, (perhaps from the Time when the Name *Franklin* that before was the Name of an Order of People, was assum'd by them for a Surname, when others took Surnames all over the Kingdom) on a Freehold of about 30 Acres, aided by the Smith's Business which had continued in the Family till his Time, the eldest Son being always bred to that Business. A Custom which he and my Father both followed as to their eldest Sons. When I search'd the Register at Ecton, I found an Account of their Births, Marriages and Burials, from the Year 1555 only, there being no Register kept in that Parish at any time preceding. By that Register I perceiv'd that I was the youngest Son of the youngest Son for 5 Generations back. My Grandfather Thomas, who was born in 1598, lived at Ecton till he grew too old to follow Business longer, when he went to live with his Son John, a Dyer at Banbury in Oxfordshire, with whom my Father serv'd an Apprenticeship. There my Grandfather died and lies buried. We saw his Gravestone in 1758. His eldest Son Thomas liv'd in the House at Ecton, and left it with the Land to his only Child, a Daughter, who with her Husband, one Fisher of Wellingborough, sold it to Mr. Isted, now Lord of the Manor there.

My Grandfather had 4 Sons that grew up, viz. Thomas, John, Benjamin and Josiah. I will give you what Account I can of them at this distance from my Papers, and if those are not lost in my Absence, you will among them find many more Particulars. Thomas was bred a Smith under his Father, but being ingenious, and encourag'd in Learning (as all his Brothers likewise were,) by an Esquire Palmer then the principal Gentleman in that Parish, he qualified himself for the Business of Scrivener, became a considerable Man in the County Affairs, was a chief Mover of all public Spirited Undertakings for the County or Town of Northampton and his own Village, of which many Instances were told us at Ecton, and he was much taken Notice of and patroniz'd by the then Lord Halifax. He died in 1702, Jan. 6, old Stile, just 4 Years to a Day before I was born. The Account we receiv'd of his Life and Character from some old People at Ecton, I remember struck you as something extraordinary from its Similarity to what you knew of mine. Had he died on the same Day, you said one might have suppos'd a Transmigration.

John was bred a Dyer, I believe of Woollens. Benjamin was bred a Silk Dyer, serving an Apprenticeship at London. He was an ingenious Man. I remember him well, for when I was a Boy he came over to my Father in Boston, and lived in the House with us some Years. He lived to a great Age. His Grandson Samuel Franklin now lives in Boston. He left behind him two Quarto Volumes, Manuscript of his own Poetry, consisting of little occasional Pieces address'd to his Friends and Relations, of which the following sent to me, is a Specimen.[1] He had form'd a Shorthand of his own, which he taught me, but never practicing it I have now forgot it. I was nam'd after this Uncle, there being a particular Affection between him and my Father. He was very pious, a great Attender of Sermons of the best Preachers, which he took down in his Shorthand and had with him many Volumes of them. He was also much of a Politician, too much perhaps for his Station. There fell lately into my Hands in London a Collection he had made of all the principal Pamphlets relating to

---

1.

Sent to My Name upon a
Report of his Inclination
to Martial affaires
7 July 1710

Beleeve me Ben. It is a Dangerous Trade
The Sword has Many Marr'd as well as Made
By it doe many fall Not Many Rise
Makes Many poor few Rich and fewer Wise
Fills Towns with Ruin, fields with blood beside
Tis Sloths Maintainer, And the Shield of pride
Fair Citties Rich to Day, in plenty flow
War fills with want, Tomorrow, & with woe
Ruin'd Estates, The Nurse of Vice, broke limbs & scarss
Are the Effects Of Desolating Warrs

Sent to B. F. in N. E.
15 July 1710

B e to thy parents an Obedient Son
E ach Day let Duty constantly be Done
N ever give Way to sloth or lust or pride
I f free you'd be from Thousand Ills beside
A bove all Ills be sure Avoide the shelfe,
M ans Danger lyes in Satan sin and selfe
I n vertue Learning Wisdome progress Make
N ere shrink at Suffering for thy saviours sake

F raud and all Falshood in thy Dealings Flee
R eligious Always in thy station be
A dore the Maker of thy Inward part
N ow's the Accepted time, Give him thy Heart
K eep a Good Consceince 'tis a constant Frind
L ike judge and Witness This Thy Acts Attend
I n Heart with bended knee Alone Adore
N one but the Three in One Forevermore.

Public Affairs from 1641 to 1717. Many of the Volumes are wanting, as appears by the Numbering, but there still remains 8 Volumes Folio, and 24 in Quarto and Octavo. A Dealer in old Books met with them, and knowing me by my sometimes buying of him, he brought them to me. It seems my Uncle must have left them here when he went to America, which was above 50 Years since. There are many of his Notes in the Margins.

This obscure Family of ours was early in the Reformation, and continu'd Protestants thro' the Reign of Queen Mary, when they were sometimes in Danger of Trouble on Account of their Zeal against Popery. They had got an English Bible, and to conceal and secure it, it was fastened open with Tapes under and within the Frame of a Joint Stool. When my Great Great Grandfather read in it to his Family, he turn'd up the Joint Stool upon his Knees, turning over the Leaves then under the Tapes. One of the Children stood at the Door to give Notice if he saw the Apparitor coming, who was an Officer of the Spiritual Court. In that Case the Stool was turn'd down again upon its feet, when the Bible remain'd conceal'd under it as before. This Anecdote I had from my Uncle Benjamin. The Family continu'd all of the Church of England till about the End of Charles the Second's Reign, when some of the Ministers that had been outed for Nonconformity, holding Conventicles in Northamptonshire, Benjamin and Josiah adher'd to them, and so continu'd all their Lives. The rest of the Family remain'd with the Episcopal Church.

Josiah, my Father, married young, and carried his Wife with three Children unto New England, about 1682. The Conventicles having been forbidden by Law, and frequently disturbed, induced some considerable Men of his Acquaintance to remove to that Country, and he was prevail'd with to accompany them thither, where they expected to enjoy their Mode of Religion with Freedom. By the same Wife he had 4 Children more born there, and by a second Wife ten more, in all 17, of which I remember 13 sitting at one time at his Table, who all grew up to be Men and Women, and married. I was the youngest Son and the youngest Child but two, and was born in Boston, New England.

My Mother, the second Wife, was Abiah Folger, a Daughter of Peter Folger, one of the first Settlers of New England, of whom honorable mention is made by Cotton Mather, in his Church History of that Country, (entitled Magnalia Christi Americana) as a *godly learned Englishman,* if I remember the Words rightly. I have heard that he wrote sundry small occasional Pieces, but only one of them was printed which I saw now many Years since. It was written in 1675, in the homespun Verse of that Time and People, and address'd to those then concern'd in the Government there. It was in favor of Liberty of Conscience, and in behalf of the Baptists, Quakers, and other Sectaries, that had been under Persecution; ascribing the Indian Wars and other Distresses that had befallen the Country to that Persecution, as so many judgments of God, to punish so heinous an Offence; and exhorting a Repeal of those uncharitable Laws. The whole appear'd to me as written with a good deal of Decent Plainness and manly Freedom. The six last concluding Lines I remember, tho' I have forgotten the two first of the Stanza, but the Purport of them was that his Censures proceeded from *Goodwill,* and therefore he would be known as the Author,

> because to be a Libeller, (says he)
> I hate it with my Heart.
> From Sherburne Town where now I dwell,
> My Name I do put here,
> Without Offence, your real Friend,
> It is Peter Folgier.

My elder Brothers were all put Apprentices to different Trades. I was put to the Grammar School at Eight Years of Age, my Father intending to devote me as the Tithe of his Sons to the Service of the Church. My early Readiness in learning to read (which must have been very early, as I do not remember when I could not read) and the Opinion of all his Friends that I should certainly make a good Scholar, encourag'd him in this Purpose of his. My Uncle Benjamin too approv'd of it, and propos'd to give me all his Shorthand Volumes of Sermons, I suppose as a Stock to set up with, if I would learn his Character. I continu'd however at the Grammar School not quite one Year, tho' in that time I had risen gradually from the Middle of the Class of that Year to be the Head of it, and farther was remov'd into the next Class above it, in order to go with that into the third at the End of the Year. But my Father in the meantime, from a View of the Expense of a College Education which, having so large a Family, he could not well afford, and the mean Living many so educated were afterwards able to obtain, Reasons that he gave to his Friends in my Hearing, altered his first Intention, took me from the Grammar School, and sent me to a School for Writing and Arithmetic kept by a then famous Man, Mr. George Brownell, very successful in his Profession generally, and that by mild encouraging Methods. Under him I acquired fair Writing pretty soon, but I fail'd in the Arithmetic, and made no Progress in it.

At Ten Years old, I was taken home to assist my Father in his Business, which was that of a Tallow Chandler and Soap-Boiler. A Business he was not bred to, but had assumed on his Arrival in New England and on finding his Dying Trade would not maintain his Family, being in little Request. Accordingly I was employed in cutting Wick for the Candles, filling the Dipping Mold, and the Molds for cast Candles, attending the Shop, going of Errands, etc. I dislik'd the Trade and had a strong Inclination for the Sea; but my Father declar'd against it; however, living near the Water, I was much in and about it, learned early to swim well, and to manage Boats, and when in a Boat or Canoe with other Boys I was commonly allow'd to govern, especially in any case of Difficulty; and upon other Occasions I was generally a Leader among the Boys, and sometimes led them into Scrapes, of which I will mention one Instance, as it shows an early projecting public Spirit, tho' not then justly conducted. There was a Salt Marsh that bounded part of the Mill Pond, on the Edge of which at Highwater, we us'd to stand to fish for Minnows. By much Trampling, we had made it a mere Quagmire. My Proposal was to build a Wharf there fit for us to stand upon, and I show'd my Comrades a large Heap of Stones which were intended for a new House near the Marsh, and which would very well suit our Purpose. Accordingly in the Evening when the Workmen were gone, I assembled a Number of my Playfellows, and working with them diligently like so many Emmets, sometimes two or three to a Stone, we brought them all away and built our little Wharf. The next Morning the Workmen were surpris'd at Missing the Stones; which were found in our Wharf; Enquiry was made after the Removers; we were discovered and complain'd of; several of us were corrected by our Fathers; and tho' I pleaded the Usefulness of the Work, mine convinc'd me that nothing was useful which was not honest.

I think you may like to know something of his Person and Character. He had an excellent Constitution of Body, was of middle Stature, but well set and very strong. He was ingenious, could draw prettily, was skill'd a little in Music and had a clear pleasing Voice, so that when he play'd Psalm Tunes on his Violin and sung withal as he some times did in an Evening after the Business of the Day was over, it was extremely agreeable to hear. He had a mechanical Genius too, and on occasion was very handy in the Use of other Tradesmen's Tools. But his great Excellence lay in a sound Understanding, and solid judgment in prudential Matters, both in private and public Affairs. In the latter indeed he was never employed, the numerous Family he had to educate and the Straitness of his Circumstances, keeping him close to his Trade, but I remember well his being frequently visited by leading People, who consulted him for his Opinion on Affairs of the Town or of the Church he belong'd to and show'd a good deal of Respect for his judgment and Advice. He was also much consulted by private Persons about their Affairs when any Difficulty occur'd, and frequently chosen an Arbitrator between contending Parties. At his Table he lik'd to have as often as he could, some sensible Friend or Neighbor, to converse with, and always took care to start some ingenious or useful Topic for Discourse, which might tend to improve the Minds of his Children. By this means he turn'd our Attention to what was good, just, and prudent in the Conduct of Life; and little or no Notice was ever taken of what related to the Victuals on the Table, whether it was well or ill drest, in or out of season, of good or bad flavor, preferable or inferior to this or that other thing of the kind; so that I was brought up in such a perfect Inattention to those Matters as to be quite Indifferent what kind of Food was set before me; and so unobservant of it, that to this Day, if I am ask'd I can scarce tell, a few Hours after Dinner, what I din'd upon. This has been a Convenience to me in travelling, where my Companions have been sometimes very unhappy for want of a suitable Gratification of their more delicate because better instructed Tastes and Appetites.

My Mother had likewise an excellent Constitution. She suckled all her 10 Children. I never knew either my Father or Mother to have any Sickness but that of which they died, he at 89 and she at 85 Years of age. They lie buried together at Boston, where I some Years since plac'd a Marble stone over their Grave with this Inscription:

Josiah Franklin
And Abiah his Wife
Lie here interred.
They lived lovingly together in Wedlock
Fifty-five Years.
Without an Estate or any gainful Employment,
By constant Labour and Industry,
With God's Blessing,
They maintained a large Family
Comfortably;
And brought up thirteen Children,
And seven Grandchildren
Reputably.
From this Instance, Reader,
Be encouraged to Diligence in thy Calling,
And distrust not Providence.
He was a pious and prudent Man,
She a discreet and virtuous Woman.
Their youngest Son,
In filial Regard to their Memory,
Places this Stone.
J.F. born 1655—Died 1744. Ætat 89
A.F. born 1667—died 1752——85.

By my rambling Digressions I perceive myself to be grown old. I us'd to write more methodically. But one does not dress for private Company as for a public Ball. 'Tis perhaps only Negligence.

To return. I continu'd thus employ'd in my Father's Business for two Years, that is till I was 12 Years old; and my Brother John, who was bred to that Business having left my Father, married and set up for himself at Rhode Island, there was all Appearance that I was destin'd to Supply his Place and be a Tallow Chandler. But my Dislike to the Trade continuing, my Father was under Apprehensions that if he did not find one for me more agreeable, I should break away and go to Sea, as his Son Josiah had done to his great Vexation. He therefore sometimes took me to walk with him, and see Joiners, Bricklayers, Turners, Braziers, etc. at their Work, that he might observe my inclination, and endeavour to fix it on some Trade or other on Land. It has ever since been a Pleasure to me to see good Workmen handle their Tools; and it has been useful to me, having learned so much by it, as to be able to do little jobs myself in my House, when a Workman could not readily be got; and to construct little Machines for my Experiments while the Intention of making the Experiment was fresh and warm in my Mind. My Father at last fix'd upon the Cutler's Trade, and my Uncle Benjamin's Son Samuel who was bred to that Business in London being about that time establish'd in Boston, I was sent to be with him some time on liking. But his Expectations of a Fee with me displeasing my Father, I was taken home again.

From a Child I was fond of Reading, and all the little Money that came into my Hands was ever laid out in Books. Pleas'd with the Pilgrim's Progress, my first Collection was of John Bunyan's Works, in separate little Volumes. I afterwards sold them to enable me to buy R. Burton's Historical Collections; they were small Chapmen's Books and cheap, 40 or 50 in all. My Father's little Library consisted chiefly of Books in polemic Divinity, most of which I read, and have since often regretted, that at a time when I had such a Thirst for Knowledge, more proper Books had not fallen in my Way, since it was now resolv'd I should not be a Clergyman. Plutarch's Lives there was, in which I read abundantly, and I still think that time spent to great Advantage. There was also a Book of Defoe's called an Essay on Projects and another of Dr. Mather's call'd Essays to do Good, which perhaps gave me a Turn of Thinking that had an Influence on some of the principal future Events of my Life.

This Bookish Inclination at length determin'd my Father to make me a Printer, tho' he had already one Son, (James) of that Profession. In 1717 my Brother James return'd from England with a Press and Letters to set up his Business in Boston. I lik'd it much better than that of my Father, but still had a Hankering for the Sea. To prevent the apprehended Effect of such an Inclination, my Father was impatient to have me bound to my Brother. I stood out some time, but at last was persuaded and signed the Indentures, when I was yet but 12 Years old. I was to serve as an Apprentice till I was 21 Years of Age, only I was to be allow'd Journeyman's Wages during the last Year. In a little time I made great Proficiency in the Business, and became a useful Hand to my Brother. I now had

Access to better Books. An Acquaintance with the Apprentices of Booksellers enabled me sometimes to borrow a small one, which I was careful to return soon and clean. Often I sat up in my Room reading the greatest Part of the Night, when the Book was borrow'd in the Evening and to be return'd early in the Morning lest it should be miss'd or wanted. And after some time an ingenious Tradesman who had a pretty Collection of Books, and who frequented our Printing-House, took Notice of me, invited me to his Library, and very kindly lent me such Books as I chose to read. I now took a Fancy to Poetry, and made some little Pieces, My Brother, thinking it might turn to account encourag'd me, and put me on composing two occasional Ballads. One was called the *Light House Tragedy*, and contain'd an Account of the drowning of Capt. Worthilake with his Two Daughters; the other was a Sailor Song on the Taking of *Teach* or Blackbeard the Pirate. They were wretched Stuff; in the Grubstreet Ballad Style, and when they were printed he sent me about the Town to sell them. The first sold wonderfully, the Event being recent, having made a great Noise. This flatter'd my Vanity. But my Father discourag'd me, by ridiculing my Performances, and telling me Verse-makers were generally Beggars; so I escap'd being a Poet, most probably a very bad one. But as Prose Writing has been of great Use to me in the Course of my Life, and was a principal Means of my Advancement, I shall tell you how in such a Situation I acquir'd what little Ability I have in that Way.

There was another Bookish Lad in the Town, John Collins by Name, with whom I was intimately acquainted. We sometimes disputed, and very fond we were of Argument, and very desirous of confuting one another. Which disputatious Turn, by the way, is apt to become a very bad Habit, making People often extremely disagreeable in Company, by the Contradiction that is necessary to bring it into Practice, and thence, besides souring and spoiling the Conversation, is productive of Disgusts and perhaps Enmities where you may have occasion for Friendship. I had caught it by reading my Father's Books of Dispute about Religion. Persons of good Sense, I have since observ'd, seldom fall into it, except Lawyers, University Men, and Men of all Sorts that have been bred at Edinburgh. A Question was once some how or other started between Collins and me, of the Propriety of educating the Female Sex in Learning, and their Abilities for Study. He was of Opinion that it was improper; and that they were naturally unequal to it. I took the contrary Side, perhaps a little for Dispute sake. He was naturally more eloquent, had a ready Plenty of Words, and sometimes as I thought bore me down more by his Fluency than by the Strength of his Reasons. As we parted without settling the Point, and were not to see one another again for some time, I sat down to put my Arguments in Writing, which I copied fair and sent to him. He answer'd and I replied. Three or four Letters of a Side had pass'd, when my Father happen'd to find my Papers, and read them. Without entering into the Discussion, he took occasion to talk to me about the Manner of my Writing, observ'd that tho' I had the Advantage of my Antagonist in correct Spelling and pointing (which I ow'd to the Printing House) I fell far short in elegance of Expression, in Method and in Perspicuity, of which he convinc'd me by several Instances. I saw the Justice of his Remarks, and thence grew more attentive to the *Manner* in Writing, and determin'd to endeavour at Improvement.

About this time I met with an odd Volume of the Spectator. I had never before seen any of them. I bought it, read it over and over, and was much delighted with it. I thought the Writing excellent, and wish'd if possible to imitate it. With that View, I took some of the Papers, and making short Hints of the Sentiment in each Sentence, laid them by a few Days, and then without looking at the Book, tried to complete the Papers again, by expressing each hinted Sentiment at length and as fully as it had been express'd before, in any suitable Words that should come to hand.

Then I compar'd my Spectator with the Original, discover'd some of my Faults and corrected them. But I found I wanted a Stock of Words or a Readiness in recollecting and using them, which I thought I should have acquir'd before that time, if I had gone on making Verses, since the continual Occasion for Words of the same Import but of different Length, to suit the Measure, or of different Sound for the Rhyme, would have laid me under a constant Necessity of searching for Variety, and also have tended to fix that Variety in my Mind, and make me Master of it. Therefore I took some of the Tales and turn'd them into Verse. And after a time, when I had pretty well forgotten the Prose, turn'd them back again. I also sometimes jumbled my Collections of Hints into Confusion, and after some Weeks, endeavour'd to reduce them into the best Order, before I began to form the full Sentences, and complete the Paper. This was to teach me Method in the Arrangement of Thoughts. By comparing my Work afterwards with the original, I discover'd many faults and amended them; but I sometimes had the Pleasure of Fancying that in certain Particulars of small Import, I had been lucky enough to improve the Method or the Language and this encourag'd me to think I might possibly in time come to be a tolerable English Writer, of which I was extremely ambitious.

My Time for these Exercises and for Reading, was at Night after Work, or before Work began in the Morning; or on Sundays, when I contrived to be in the Printing-House alone, evading as much as I could the common Attendance on public Worship, which my Father used to exact of me when I was under his Care: And which indeed I still thought a Duty; tho' I could not, as it seemed to me, afford the Time to practice it.

When about 16 Years of Age, I happen'd to meet with a Book written by one Tryon, recommending a Vegetable Diet. I determined to go into it. My Brother being yet unmarried, did not keep House, but boarded himself and his Apprentices in another Family. My refusing to eat Flesh occasioned an Inconveniency, and I was frequently chid for my singularity. I made myself acquainted with Tryon's Manner of preparing some of his Dishes, such as Boiling Potatoes or Rice, making Hasty Pudding, and a few others, and then propos'd to my Brother, that if he would give me Weekly half the Money he paid for my Board, I would board myself. He instantly agreed to it, and I presently found that I could save half what he paid me. This was an additional Fund for buying Books: But I had another Advantage in it. My Brother and the rest going from the Printing-House to their Meals, I remain'd there alone, and dispatching presently my light Repast, (which often was no more than a Biscuit or a Slice of Bread, a Handful of Raisins or a Tart from the Pastry Cook's, and a Glass of Water) had the rest of the Time till their Return, for Study, in which I made the greater Progress from that greater Clearness of Head and quicker Apprehension which usually attend Temperance in Eating and Drinking. And now it was that being on some Occasion made asham'd of my Ignorance in Figures, which I had twice fail'd in learning when at School, I took Cocker's Book of Arithmetic, and went thro' the whole by myself with great Ease. I also read Seller's and Sturmy's Books of Navigation, and became acquainted with the little Geometry they contain, but never proceeded far in that Science. And I read about this Time Locke on Human Understanding and the Art of Thinking by Messrs. du Port Royal.

While I was intent on improving my Language, I met with an English Grammar (I think it was Greenwood's) at the End of which there were two little Sketches of the Arts of Rhetoric and Logic, the latter finishing with a Specimen of a Dispute in the Socratic Method. And soon after I procur'd Xenophon's Memorable Things of Socrates, wherein there are many Instances of the same Method. I was charm'd with it, adopted it, dropped my abrupt Contradiction and positive Argumentation, and put on the humble Enquirer and Doubter. And being then, from reading Shaftesbury and Collins, become a real Doubter in many Points of our Religious Doctrine, I found this Method safest for myself and very embarassing to those against whom I used it, therefore I took a Delight in it, practic'd it continually and grew very artful and expert in drawing People even of superior Knowledge into Concessions the Consequences of which they did not foresee, entangling them in Difficulties out of which they could not extricate themselves, and so obtaining Victories that neither myself nor my Cause always deserved. I continu'd this Method some few Years, but gradually left it, retaining only the Habit of expressing myself in Terms of modest Diffidence, never using when I advance any thing that may possibly be disputed, the Words, *Certainly, undoubtedly*, or any others that give the Air of Positiveness to an Opinion; but rather say, *I conceive*, or *I apprehend* a Thing to be so or so, *it appears to me*, or *I should think it so or so for such and such reasons*; or I *imagine* it to be so; or *it is so if I am not mistaken*. This Habit I believe has been of great Advantage to me, when I have had occasion to inculcate my Opinions and persuade Men into Measures that I have been from time to time engag'd in promoting. And as the chief Ends of Conversation are to *inform* or to be *informed*, to *please* or to *persuade*, I wish well-meaning sensible Men would not lessen their Power of doing Good by a Positive assuming Manner, that seldom fails to disgust, tends to create Opposition, and to defeat every one of those Purposes for which Speech was given to us, to wit, giving or receiving Information, or Pleasure: For If you would *inform*, a positive and dogmatical Manner in advancing your Sentiments, may provoke Contradiction and prevent a candid Attention. If you wish Information and Improvement from the Knowledge of others, and yet at the same time express yourself as firmly fix'd in your present Opinions, modest, sensible Men, who do not love Disputation, will probably leave you undisturb'd in the Possession of your Error; and by such a Manner you can seldom hope to recommend yourself in *pleasing* your Hearers, or to persuade those whose Concurrence you desire. Pope says, judiciously:

> *Men should be taught as if you taught them not,*
> *And things unknown propos'd as things forgot,*

farther recommending to us,

> *To speak, tho' sure, with seeming Diffidence.*

And he might have coupl'd with this Line that which he has coupled with another, I think, less properly,

> *For want of Modesty is want of Sense.*

If you ask why *less properly*, I must repeat the Lines;

> "Immodest words admit of *no* Defence;
> *For* Want of Modesty is Want of Sense."

Now is not *Want of Sense* (where a Man is so unfortunate as to want it) some Apology for his *Want of Modesty*? and would not the Lines stand more justly thus?

> Immodest words admit *but* this Defence,
> That Want of Modesty is Want of Sense.

This, however, I should submit to better Judgments.

My Brother had, in 1720 or 21, begun to print a Newspaper. It was the second that appear'd in America, and was called *The New England Courant*. The only one before it, was *the Boston News Letter*. I remember his being dissuaded by some of his Friends from the Undertaking, as not likely to succeed, one Newspaper being in their Judgment enough for America. At this time 1771 there are not less than five and twenty. He went on however with the Undertaking, and after having work'd in composing the Types and printing off the Sheets I was employ'd to carry the Papers thro' the Streets to the Customers. He had some ingenious Men among his Friends who amus'd themselves by writing little Pieces for this Paper, which gain'd it Credit and made it more in Demand; and these Gentlemen often visited us. Hearing their Conversations, and their Accounts of the Approbation their Papers were receiv'd with, I was excited to try my Hand among them. But being still a Boy, and suspecting that my Brother would object to printing any Thing of mine in his Paper if he knew it to be mine, I contriv'd to disguise my Hand, and writing an anonymous Paper I put it in at Night under the Door of the Printing-House.

It was found in the Morning and communicated to his Writing Friends when they call'd in as Usual. They read it, commented on it in my Hearing, and I had the exquisite Pleasure, of finding it met with their Approbation, and that in their different Guesses at the Author none were named but Men of some Character among us for Learning and Ingenuity. I suppose now that I was rather lucky in my Judges: And that perhaps they were not really so very good ones as I then esteem'd them. Encourag'd, however, by this, I wrote and convey'd in the same Way to the Press several more Papers, which were equally approv'd; and I kept my Secret till my small Fund of Sense for such Performances was pretty well exhausted, and then I discovered it; when I began to be considered a little more by my Brother's Acquaintance, and in a manner that did not quite please him, as he thought, probably with reason, that it tended to make me too vain. And perhaps this might be one Occasion of the Differences that we began to have about this Time. Tho' a Brother, he considered himself as my Master, and me as his Apprentice; and accordingly expected the same Services from me as he would from another; while I thought he demean'd me too much in some he requir'd of me, who from a Brother expected more Indulgence. Our Disputes were often brought before our Father, and I fancy I was either generally in the right, or else a better Pleader, because the judgment was generally in my favor: But my Brother was passionate and had often beaten me, which I took extremely amiss;[2] and thinking my Apprenticeship very tedious, I was continually wishing for some Opportunity of shortening it, which at length offered in a manner unexpected.

One of the Pieces in our Newspaper, on some political Point which I have now forgotten, gave Offence to the Assembly. He was taken up, censur'd and imprison'd for a Month by the Speaker's Warrant, I suppose because he would not discover his Author. I too was taken up and examin'd before the Council; but tho' I did not give them any Satisfaction, they contented themselves with admonishing me, and dismiss'd me; considering me perhaps as an Apprentice who was bound to keep his Master's Secrets. During my Brother's Confinement, which I resented a good deal, notwithstanding our private Differences, I had the Management of the Paper, and I made bold to give our Rulers some Rubs in it, which my Brother took very kindly, while others began to consider me in an unfavorable Light, as a young Genius that had a Turn for Libelling and Satire. My Brother's Discharge was accompanied with an Order of the House, (a very odd one) *that James Franklin should no longer print the Paper called the New England Courant.* There was a Consultation held in our Printing House among his Friends what he should do in this Case. Some propos'd to evade the Order by changing the Name of the Paper; but my Brother seeing Inconveniences in that, it was finally concluded on as a better Way, to let it be printed for the future under the Name of *Benjamin Franklin.* And to avoid the Censure of the Assembly that might fall on him, as still printing it by his Apprentice, the Contrivance was, that my old Indenture should be return'd to me with a full Discharge on the Back of it, to be shown on Occasion; but to secure to him the Benefit of my Service I was to sign new Indentures for the Remainder of the Term, which were to be kept private. A very flimsy Scheme it was, but however it was immediately executed, and the Paper went on accordingly under my Name for several Months. At length a fresh Difference arising between my Brother and me, I took upon me to assert my Freedom, presuming that he would not venture to produce the new Indentures. It was not fair in me to take this Advantage, and this I therefore reckon one of the first Errata of my Life: But the Unfairness of it weigh'd little with me, when under the Impressions of Resentment, for the Blows his Passion too often urg'd him to bestow upon me, Tho' he was otherwise not an ill-natur'd Man: Perhaps I was too saucy and provoking.

When he found I would leave him, he took care to prevent my getting Employment in any other Printing-House of the Town, by going round and speaking to every Master, who accordingly refus'd to give me Work. I then thought of going to New York as the nearest Place where there was a Printer: and I was the rather inclin'd to leave Boston, when I reflected that I had already made myself a little obnoxious to the governing Party; and from the arbitrary Proceedings of the Assembly in my Brother's Case it was likely I might if I stay'd soon bring myself into Scrapes; and farther that my indiscreet Disputations about Religion began to make me pointed at with Horror by good People, as an Infidel or Atheist; I determin'd on the Point: but my Father now siding with my Brother, I was sensible that if I attempted to go openly, Means would be used to prevent me. My Friend Collins therefore undertook to manage a little for me. He agreed with the Captain of a New York Sloop for my Passage, under the Notion of my being a young Acquaintance of his that had got a naughty Girl with Child, whose Friends would compel me to marry her, and therefore I could not appear or come away publicly. So I sold some of my Books to raise a little Money, was taken on board privately, and as we had a fair Wind, in three Days I found myself in New York near 300 Miles from home, a Boy of but 17, without the least Recommendation to or Knowledge of any Person in the Place, and with very little Money in my Pocket.

My Inclinations for the Sea, were by this time worn out, or I might now have gratified them. But having a Trade, and supposing myself a pretty good Workman, I offer'd my Service to the Printer of the Place, old Mr. William Bradford. He could give me no Employment, having little to do, and Help enough already: But, says he, my Son at Philadelphia has lately lost his principal Hand, Aquila Rose, by Death. If you go thither I believe he may employ

2. I fancy his harsh and tyrannical Treatment of me, might be a means of impressing me with that Aversion to arbitrary Power that has stuck to me thro' my whole life.

you. Philadelphia was 100 Miles farther. I set out, however, in a Boat for Amboy; leaving my Chest and Things to follow me round by Sea. In crossing the Bay we met with a Squall that tore our rotten Sails to pieces, prevented our getting into the Kill, and drove us upon Long Island. In our Way a drunken Dutchman, who was a Passenger too, fell overboard; when he was sinking I reach'd thro' the Water to his shock Pate and drew him up so that we got him in again. His Ducking sober'd him a little, and he went to sleep, taking first out of his Pocket a Book which he desir'd I would dry for him. It prov'd to be my old favorite Author Bunyan's Pilgrim's Progress in Dutch, finely printed on good Paper with copper Cuts, a Dress better than I had ever seen it wear in its own Language. I have since found that it has been translated into most of the Languages of Europe, and suppose it has been more generally read than any other Book except perhaps the Bible. Honest John was the first that I know of who mix'd Narration and Dialogue, a Method of Writing very engaging to the Reader, who in the most interesting Parts finds himself as it were brought into the Company, and present at the Discourse. Defoe in his Cruse, his Moll Flanders, Religious Courtship, Family Instructor, and other Pieces, has imitated it with Success. And Richardson has done the same in his Pamela, etc.

When we drew near the Island we found it was at a Place where there could be no Landing, there being a great Surf on the stony Beach. So we dropped Anchor and swung round towards the Shore. Some People came down to the Water Edge and hallow'd to us, as we did to them. But the Wind was so high and the Surf so loud, that we could not bear so as to understand each other. There were Canoes on the Shore, and we made Signs and hallow'd that they should fetch us, but they either did not understand us, or thought it impracticable. So they went away, and Night coming on, we had no Remedy but to wait till the Wind should abate, and in the mean time the Boatman and I concluded to sleep if we could, and so crowded into the Scuttle with the Dutchman who was still wet, and the Spray beating over the Head of our Boat, leak'd thro' to us, so that we were soon almost as wet as he. In this Manner we lay all Night with very little Rest. But the Wind abating the next Day, we made a Shift to reach Amboy before Night, having been 30 Hours on the Water without Victuals, or any Drink but a Bottle of filthy Rum: The Water we sail'd on being salt.

In the Evening I found myself very feverish, and went ill to Bed. But having read somewhere that cold Water drank plentifully was good for a Fever, I follow'd the Prescription, sweat plentifully most of the Night, my Fever left me, and in the Morning crossing the Ferry, proceeded on my Journey, on foot, having 50 Miles to Burlington, where I was told I should find Boats that would carry me the rest of the Way to Philadelphia.

It rain'd very hard all the Day, I was thoroughly soak'd, and by Noon a good deal tir'd, so I stopped at a poor Inn, where I stayed all Night, beginning now to wish I had never left home. I cut so miserable a Figure too, that I found by the Questions ask'd me I was suspected to be some runaway Servant, and in danger of being taken up on that Suspicion. However I proceeded the next Day, and got in the Evening to an Inn within 8 or 10 Miles of Burlington, kept by one Dr. Browne.

He entered into Conversation with me while I took some Refreshment, and finding I had read a little, became very sociable and friendly. Our Acquaintance continu'd as long as he liv'd. He had been, I imagine, an itinerant Doctor, for there was no Town in England, or Country in Europe, of which he could not give a very particular Account. He had some Letters, and was ingenious, but much of an Unbeliever, and wickedly undertook some Years after to travesty the Bible in doggerel Verse as Cotton had done Virgil. By this means he set many of the Facts in a very ridiculous Light, and might have hurt weak minds if his Work had been publish'd: but it never was. At his House I lay that Night, and the next Morning reach'd Burlington.—But had the Mortification to find that the regular Boats were gone a little before my coming, and no other expected to go till Tuesday, this being Saturday. Wherefore I return'd to an old Woman in the Town of whom I had bought Gingerbread to eat on the Water, and ask'd her Advice; she invited me to lodge at her House till a Passage by Water should offer; and being tired with my foot Travelling, I accepted the Invitation, She understanding I was a Printer, would have had me stay at that Town and follow my Business, being ignorant of the Stock necessary to begin with. She was very hospitable, gave me a Dinner of Ox

Cheek with great Goodwill, accepting only of a Pot of Ale in return. And I thought myself fix'd till Tuesday should come. However walking in the Evening by the Side of the River a Boat came by, which I found was going towards Philadelphia, with several People in her. They took me in, and as there was no Wind, we row'd all the Way; and about Midnight not having yet seen the City, some of the Company were confident we must have pass'd it, and would row no farther, the others knew not where we were, so we put towards the Shore, got into a Creek, landed near an old Fence with the Rails of which we made a Fire, the Night being cold, in October, and there we remain'd till Daylight. Then one of the Company knew the Place to be Cooper's Creek a little above Philadelphia, which we saw as soon as we got out of the Creek, and arriv'd there about 8 or 9 o'Clock, on the Sunday morning, and landed at the Market Street Wharf.

I have been the more particular in this Description of my Journey, and shall be so of my first Entry into that City, that you may in your Mind compare such unlikely Beginning with the Figure I have since made there. I was in my working Dress, my best Clothes being to come round by Sea. I was dirty from my Journey; my Pockets were stuff'd out with Shirts and Stockings; I knew no Soul, nor where to look for Lodging. I was fatigu'd with Travelling, Rowing and Want of Rest. I was very hungry, and my whole Stock of Cash consisted of a Dutch Dollar and about a Shilling in Copper. The latter I gave the People of the Boat for my Passage, who at first refus'd it on Account of my Rowing; but I insisted on their taking it, a Man being sometimes more generous when he has but a little Money than when he has plenty, perhaps thro' Fear of being thought to have but little. Then I walk'd up the Street, gazing about, till near the Market House I met a Boy with Bread. I had made many a Meal on Bread, and inquiring where he got it, I went immediately to the Baker's he directed me to in Second Street, and ask'd for Biscuit, intending such as we had in Boston, but they it seems were not made in Philadelphia, then I ask'd for a three-penny Loaf, and was told they had none such; so not considering or knowing the Difference of Money and the greater Cheapness nor the Names of his Bread, I [bade] him give me three pennyworth of any sort. He gave me accordingly three great Puffy Rolls. I was surpriz'd at the Quantity, but took it, and having no Room in my Pockets, walk'd off, with a Roll under each Arm, and eating the other. Thus I went up Market Street as far as Fourth Street, passing by the Door of Mr. Read, my future Wife's Father, when she standing at the Door saw me, and thought I made as I certainly did a most awkward ridiculous Appearance. Then I turn'd and went down Chestnut Street and part of Walnut Street, eating my Roll all the Way, and coming round found myself again at Market Street Wharf, near the Boat I came in, to which I went for a Draught of the River Water, and being fill'd with one of my Rolls, gave the other two to a Woman and her Child that came down the River in the Boat with us, and were waiting to go farther. Thus refresh'd I walk'd again up the Street, which by this time had many clean dress'd People in it who were all walking the same Way; I join'd them, and thereby was led into the great Meeting House of the Quakers near the Market. I sat down among them, and after looking round awhile and hearing nothing said, being very drowsy thro' Labor and want of Rest the preceding Night, I fell fast asleep, and continu'd so till the Meeting broke up, when one was kind enough to rouse me. This was therefore the first House I was in or slept in, in Philadelphia.

Walking down again toward the River, and looking in the Faces of People, I met a young Quaker Man whose countenance I lik'd, and accosting him requested he would tell me where a Stranger could get Lodging. We were then near the Sign of the Three Mariners. Here, says he, is one Place that entertains Strangers, but it is not a reputable House; if thee wilt walk with me, I'll show thee a better. He brought me to the Crooked Billet in Water Street. Here I got a dinner. And while I was eating it, several sly Questions were ask'd me, as it seem'd to be suspected from my youth and Appearance, that I might be some Runaway. After Dinner my Sleepiness return'd: and being shown to a Bed, I lay down without undressing, and slept till Six in the Evening; was call'd to Supper; went to Bed again very early and slept soundly till next Morning. Then I made myself as tidy as I could, and went to Andrew Bradford the Printer's. I found in the Shop the old Man his Father, whom I had seen at New York, and who travelling on horse back had got to Philadelphia before me. He introduc'd me to his Son, who receiv'd me civilly, gave me a Breakfast, but told me he did not at present want a Hand, being lately supplied with one. But there was another Printer in town lately set up, one Keimer, who perhaps, might employ me; if not, I should be welcome to lodge at his House, and he would give me a little Work to do now and then till fuller Business should offer.

The old Gentleman said, he would go with me to the new Printer: And when we found him, Neighbor, says Bradford, I have brought to see you a young Man of your Business, perhaps you may want such a One. He ask'd me a few Questions, put a Composing Stick in my Hand to see how I work'd, and then said he would employ me soon tho' he had just then nothing for me to do. And taking old Bradford whom he had never seen before to be one of the Townspeople that had a Goodwill for him, enter'd into a Conversation on his present Undertaking and Projects; while Bradford not discovering that he was the other Printer's Father; on Keimer's Saying he expected soon to get the greatest Part of the Business into his own Hands, drew him on by artful Questions and starting little Doubts, to explain all his Views, what Interest he relied on, and in what manner he intended to proceed. I who stood by and heard all, saw immediately that one of them was a crafty old Sophister, and the other a mere Novice. Bradford left me with Keimer, who was greatly surpris'd when I told him who the old Man was.

Keimer's Printing-House I found, consisted of an old shatter'd Press and one small worn-out Fount of English, which he was then using himself, compising in it an Elegy on Aquila Rose before-mentioned, an ingenious young Man of excellent Character much respected in the Town, Clerk of the Assembly, and a pretty Poet. Keimer made Verses, too, but very indifferently. He could not be said to write them, for his Manner was to compose them in the Types directly out of his Head; so there being no Copy, but one Pair of Cases, and the Elegy likely to require all the Letter, no one could help him. I endeavour'd to put his Press (which he had not yet us'd, and of which he understood nothing) into Order fit to be work'd with; and promising to come and print off his Elegy as soon as he should have got it ready, I return'd to Bradford's who gave me a little job to do for the present, and there I lodged and dieted. A few Days after Keimer sent for me to print off the Elegy. And now he had got another Pair of Cases, and a Pamphlet to reprint, on which he set me to work.

These two Printers I found poorly qualified for their Business. Bradford had not been bred to it, and was very illiterate; and Keimer tho' something of a Scholar, was a mere Compositor, knowing nothing of Presswork. He had been one of the French Prophets and could act their enthusiastic Agitations. At this time he did not profess any particular Religion, but something of all on occasion; was very ignorant of the World, and had, as I afterwards found, a good deal of the Knave in his Composition. He did not like my Lodging at Bradford's while I work'd with him. He had a House indeed, but without Furniture, so he could not lodge me: But he got me a Lodging at Mr. Read's before-mentioned, who was the Owner of his House. And my Chest and Clothes being come by this time, I made rather a more respectable Appearance in the Eyes of Miss Read, than I had done when she first happen'd to see me eating my Roll in the Street.

I began now to have some Acquaintance among the young People of the Town, that were Lovers of Reading with whom I spent my Evenings very pleasantly and gaining Money by my Industry and Frugality, I lived very agreeably, forgetting Boston as much as I could, and not desiring that any there should know where I resided except my Friend Collins who was in my Secret, and kept it when I wrote to him. At length an Incident happened that sent me back again much sooner than I had intended.

I had a Brother-in-law, Robert Holmes, Master of a Sloop that traded between Boston and Delaware. He being at New Castle 40 Miles below Philadelphia, heard there of me, and wrote me a Letter, mentioning the Concern of my Friends in Boston at my abrupt Departure, assuring me of their Goodwill to me, and that everything would be accommodated to my Mind if I would return, to which he exhorted me very earnestly. I wrote an Answer to his Letter, thank'd him for his Advice, but stated my Reasons for quitting Boston fully, and in such a Light as to convince him I was not so wrong as he had apprehended. Sir William Keith Governor of the Province, was then at New Castle, and Captain Homes happening to be in Company with him when my Letter came to hand, spoke to him of me, and show'd him the Letter. The Governor read it, and seem'd surpris'd when he was told my Age. He said I appear'd a young Man of promising Parts, and therefore should be encouraged. The Printers at Philadelphia were wretched ones, and if I would set up there, he made no doubt I should succeed; for his Part, he would procure me the public Business, and do me every other Service in his Power. This my Brother-in-Law afterwards told me in Boston. But I knew as yet nothing of it; when one Day Keimer and I being at Work together near the Window, we saw the Governor and another Gentleman (which prov'd to be Colonel French, of New Castle) finely dress'd, come directly across the Street to our House, and heard them at the Door.

Keimer ran down immediately, thinking it a Visit to him. But the Governor enquir'd for me, came up, and with a Condescension and Politeness I had been quite unus'd to, made me many Compliments, desired to be acquainted with me, blam'd me kindly for not having made myself known to him when I first came to the Place, and would have me away with him to the Tavern where he was going with Colonel French to taste as he said some excellent Madeira. I was not a little surpris'd, and Keimer star'd like a Pig poison'd. I went however with the Governor and Colonel French, to a Tavern the Corner of Third Street, and over the Madeira he propos'd my Setting up my Business, laid before me the Probabilities of Success, and both he and Colonel French assur'd me I should have their Interest and Influence in procuring the Public-Business of both Governments, On my doubting whether my Father would assist me in it, Sir William said he would give me a Letter to him, in which he would state the Advantages, and he did not doubt of prevailing with him. So it was concluded I should return to Boston in the first Vessel with the Governor's Letter recommending me to my Father.

In the meantime the Intention was to be kept secret, and I went on working with Keimer as usual, the Governor sending for me now and then to dine with him, a very great Honor I thought it, and conversing with me in the most affable, familiar, and friendly manner imaginable. About the End of April 1724, a little Vessel offer'd for Boston. I took Leave of Keimer as going to see my Friends. The Governor gave me an ample Letter, saying many flattering things of me to my Father, and strongly recommending the Project of my setting up at Philadelphia, as a Thing that must make my Fortune. We struck on a Shoal in going down the Bay and sprung a Leak, we had a blustring time at Sea, and were oblig'd to pump almost continually, at which I took my Turn. We arriv'd safe however at Boston in about a Fortnight. I had been absent Seven Months and my Friends had heard nothing of me, for my Brother Homes was not yet return'd; and had not written about me. My unexpected Appearance surpris'd the Family; all were however very glad to see me and made me Welcome, except my Brother.

I went to see him at his Printing-House: I was better dress'd than ever while in his Service, having a genteel new Suit from Head to foot, a Watch, and my Pockets lin'd with near Five Pounds Sterling in Silver. He receiv'd me not very frankly, look'd me all over, and turn'd to his Work again. The Journeymen were inquisitive where I had been, what sort of a Country it was, and how I lik'd it? I prais'd it much, and the happy Life I led in it; expressing strongly my Intention of returning to it; and one of them asking what kind of Money we had there, I produc'd a handful of Silver and spread it before them, which was a kind of Raree-Show they had not been us'd to, Paper being the Money of Boston. Then I took an Opportunity of letting them see my Watch: and lastly, (my Brother still grum and sullen) I gave them a Piece of Eight to drink and took my Leave. This Visit of mine offended him extremely. For when my Mother some time after spoke to him of a Reconciliation, and of her Wishes to see us on good Terms together, and that we might live for the future as Brothers, he said, I had insulted him in such a Manner before his People that he could never forget or forgive it. In this however he was mistaken.

My Father receiv'd the Governor's Letter with some apparent Surprise; but said little of it to me for some Days; when Captain Homes returning, he show'd it to him, ask'd if he knew Keith, and what kind of a Man he was: Adding his Opinion that he must be of small Discretion, to think of setting a Boy up in Business who wanted yet 3 years of being at Man's Estate. Homes said what he could in favor of the Project; but my Father was clear in the Impropriety of it; and at last gave a flat Denial to it. Then he wrote a civil Letter to Sir William thanking him for the Patronage he had so kindly offered me, but declining to assist me as yet in Setting up, I being in his Opinion too young to be trusted with the Management of a Business so important; and for which the Preparation must be so expensive.

My Friend and Companion Collins, who was a Clerk at the Post-Office, pleas'd with the Account I gave him of my new Country, determin'd to go thither also: And while I waited for my Father's Determination, he set out before me by Land to Rhode Island, leaving his Books which were a pretty Collection of Mathematics and Natural Philosophy, to come with mine and me to New York where he propos'd to wait for me. My Father, tho' he did not approve Sir William's Proposition, was yet pleas'd that I had been able to obtain so advantageous a Character from a Person of such Note where I had resided, and that I had been so industrious and careful as to equip myself so handsomely in so short a time: therefore seeing no Prospect of an Accommodation between my Brother and me, he gave his Consent to my Returning again to Philadelphia, advis'd me to behave respectfully to the People there, endeavour to obtain the general Esteem, and avoid lampooning and libelling to which he thought I had too much Inclination; telling me, that by steady Industry and a prudent Parsimony, I might save enough by the time I was One and Twenty to set me up, and that if I came near the Matter he would help me out with the Rest. This was all I could obtain, except some small Gifts as Tokens of his and my Mother's Love, when I embark'd again for New York, now with their Approbation and their Blessing.

The Sloop putting in at Newport, Rhode Island, I visited my Brother John, who had been married and settled there some Years. He received me very affectionately, for he always lov'd me. A Friend of his, one Vernon, having some Money due to him in Pennsylvania, about 35 Pounds Currency, desired I would receive it for him, and keep it till I had his Directions what to remit it in. Accordingly he gave me an Order. This afterwards occasion'd me a good deal of Uneasiness. At Newport we took in a Number of Passengers for New York: Among which were two young Women, Companions, and a grave, sensible Matronlike Quaker-Woman with her Attendants. I had shown an obliging Readiness to do her some little Services which impress'd her I suppose with a degree of Goodwill towards me. Therefore when she saw a daily growing Familiarity between me and the two Young Women, which they appear'd to encourage, she took me aside and said, Young Man, I am concern'd for thee, as thou has no Friend with thee, and seems not to know much of the World, or of the Snares Youth is expos'd to; depend upon it those are very bad Women, I can see it in all their Actions, and if thee art not upon thy Guard, they will draw thee into some Danger: they are Strangers to thee, and I advise thee in a friendly Concern for thy Welfare, to have no Acquaintance with them. As I seem'd at first not to think so ill of them as she did, she mention'd some Things she had observ'd and heard that had escap'd my Notice; but now convinc'd me she was right. I thank'd her for her kind Advice, and promis'd to follow it. When we arriv'd at New York, they told me where they liv'd, and invited me to come and see them: but I avoided it. And it was well I did: For the next Day, the Captain miss'd a Silver Spoon and some other Things that had been taken out of his Cabin, and knowing that these were a Couple of Strumpets, he got a Warrant to search their Lodgings, found the stolen Goods, and had the Thieves punish'd. So tho' we had escap'd a sunken Rock which we scrap'd upon in the Passage, I thought this Escape of rather more Importance to me.

At New York I found my Friend Collins, who had arriv'd there some Time before me. We had been intimate from Children, and had read the same Books together. But he had the Advantage of more time for Reading, and Studying and a wonderful Genius for Mathematical Learning: in which he far outstripped me. While I liv'd in Boston most of my Hours of Leisure for Conversation were spent with him, and he continu'd a sobered as well as an industrious Lad; was much respected for his Learning by several of the Clergy and other Gentlemen, and seem'd to promise making a good Figure in Life: but during my Absence he had acquir'd a Habit of Setting with Brandy; and I found by his own Account and what I heard from others, that he had been drunk every day since his Arrival at New York, and behav'd very oddly. He had gam'd too and lost his Money, so that I was oblig'd to discharge his Lodgings, and defray his Expences to and at Philadelphia: Which prov'd extremely inconvenient to me. The then Governor of New York, Burnet, Son of Bishop Burnet, hearing from the Captain that a young Man, one of his Passengers, had a great many Books, desired he would bring me to see him. I waited upon him accordingly, and should have taken Collins with me but that he was not sober. The Governor treated me with great Civility, show'd me his Library, which was a very large one, and we had a good deal of Conversation about Books and Authors. This was the second Governor who had done me the Honor to take Notice of me, which to a poor Boy like me was very pleasing,

We proceeded to Philadelphia. I received on the Way Vernon's Money, without which we could hardly have finish'd our journey. Collins wish'd to be employ'd in some Counting House; but whether they discover'd his Dramming by his Breath, or by his Behaviour, tho' he had some Recommendations, he met with no Success in any Application, and continu'd Lodging and Boarding at the same House with me and at my Expense. Knowing I had that Money of Vernon's he was continually borrowing of me, still promising Repayment as soon as he should be in Business. At length he had got so much of it, that I was distress'd to think what I should do, in case of being call'd on to remit it. His Drinking continu'd, about which we sometimes quarrel'd, for when a little intoxicated he was very fractious. Once in a Boat on the Delaware with some other young Men, he refused to row in his Turn: I will be row'd home, says he. We will not row you, says I. You must, says he, or stay all Night on the Water, just as you please. The others said, Let us row; What signifies it? But my Mind being soured with his other Conduct, I continu'd to refuse. So he swore he would make me row, or throw me overboard; and coming along stepping on the Thwarts towards me, when he came up and struck at me, I clapped my Hand under his Crotch, and rising, pitch'd him head-foremost into the River. I knew he was a good Swimmer, and so was under little Concern about him; but before he could get round to lay hold of the Boat, we had with a few Strokes pull'd her out of his Reach. And ever when he drew near the Boat, we ask'd if he would row, striking a few Strokes to slide her away from him. He was ready to die with Vexation, and obstinately would not promise to row; however seeing him at last beginning to tire, we lifted him in; and brought him home dripping wet in the Evening. We hardly exchang'd a civil Word afterwards; and a West India Captain who had a Commission to procure a Tutor for the Sons of a Gentleman at Barbados, happening to meet with him, agreed to carry him thither. He left me then, promising to remit me the first Money he should receive in order to discharge the Debt. But I never heard of him after.

The Breaking into this Money of Vernon's was one of the first great Errata of my Life. And this Affair show'd that my Father was not much out in his Judgment when he suppos'd me too Young to manage Business of Importance. But Sir William, on reading his Letter, said he was too prudent. There was great Difference in Persons, and Discretion did not always accompany Years, nor was Youth always without it. And since he will not set you up, says he, I will do it myself. Give me an Inventory of the Things necessary to be had from England, and I will send for them. You shall repay me when you are able; I am resolv'd to have a good Printer here, and I am sure you must succeed. This was spoken with such an Appearance of Cordiality, that I had not the least doubt of his meaning what he said. I had hitherto kept the Proposition of my Setting up a Secret in Philadelphia, and I still kept it. Had it been known that I depended on the Governor, probably some Friend that knew him better would have advis'd me not to rely on him, as I afterwards heard it as his known Character to be liberal of Promises which he never meant to keep. Yet unsolicited as he was by me, how could I think his generous Offers insincere? I believ'd him one of the best Men in the World.

I presented him an Inventory of a little Printing House, amounting by my Computation to about 100 Pounds Sterling. He lik'd it, but ask'd me if my being on the Spot in England to choose the Types and see that everything was good of the kind, might not be of some Advantage. Then, says he, when there, you may make Acquaintances and establish Correspondences in the Bookselling, and Stationery Way. I agreed that this might be advantageous. Then says he, get yourself ready to go with Annis; which was the annual Ship, and the only one at that Time usually passing between London and Philadelphia. But it would be some Months before Annis sail'd, so I continu'd working with Keimer, fretting about the Money Collins had got from me, and in daily Apprehensions of being call'd upon by Vernon, which however did not happen for some Years after.

I believe I have omitted mentioning that in my first Voyage from Boston, being becalm'd off Block

Island, our People set about catching Cod and haul'd up a great many. Hitherto I had stuck to my Resolution of not eating animal Food; and on this Occasion, I consider'd with my Master Tryon, the taking every Fish as a kind of unprovok'd Murder, since none of them had or ever could do us any Injury that might justify the Slaughter. All this seem'd very reasonable. But I had formerly been a great Lover of Fish, and when this came hot out of the Frying Pan, it smelt admirably well. I balanc'd some time between Principle and Inclination: till I recollected, that when the Fish were opened, I saw smaller Fish taken out of their Stomachs: Then, thought I, if you eat one another, I don't see why we mayn't eat you. So I din'd upon Cod very heartily and continu'd to eat with other People, returning only now and then occasionally to a vegetable Diet. So convenient a thing it is to be a *reasonable Creature*, since it enables one to find or make a Reason for everything one has a mind to do.

Keimer and I liv'd on a pretty good familiar Footing and agreed tolerably well: for he suspected nothing of my Setting up. He retain'd a great deal of his old Enthusiasms, and lov'd an Argumentation. We therefore had many Disputations. I us'd to work him so with my Socratic Method, and had trepann'd him so often by Questions apparently so distant from any Point we had in hand, and yet by degrees led to the Point, and brought him into Difficulties and Contradictions, that at last he grew ridiculously cautious, and would hardly answer me the most common Question, without asking first, *What do you intend to infer from that?* However it gave him so high an Opinion of my Abilities in the Confuting Way, that he seriously propos'd my being his Colleague in a Project he had of setting up a new Sect. He was to preach the Doctrines, and I was to confound all Opponents. When he came to explain with me upon the Doctrines, I found several Conundrums which I objected to, unless I might have my Way a little too, and introduce some of mine. Keimer wore his Beard at full Length, because somewhere in the Mosaic Law it is said, *thou shalt not mar the Comers of thy Beard.* He likewise kept the seventh-day Sabbath; and these two Points were Essentials with him. I dislik'd both, but agreed to admit them upon Condition of his adopting the Doctrine of using no animal Food. I doubt, says he, my Constitution will not bear that. I assur'd him it would, and that he would be the better for it. He was usually a great Glutton, and I promis'd myself some Diversion in half-starving him. He agreed to try the Practice if I would keep him Company. I did so and we held it for three Months. We had our Victuals dress'd and brought to us regularly by a Woman in the Neighborhood, who had from me a List of 40 Dishes to be prepar'd for us at different times, in all which there was neither Fish, Flesh, nor Fowl, and the Whim suited me the better at this time from the Cheapness of it, not costing us above 18 Pence Sterling each, per Week. I have since kept several Lents most strictly, leaving the common Diet for that, and that for the common, abruptly, without the least Inconvenience: So that I think there is little in the Advice of making those Changes by easy Gradations. I went on pleasantly, but Poor Keimer suffer'd grievously, tir'd of the Project, long'd for the Flesh Pots of Egypt, and order'd a roast Pig; He invited me and two Women Friends to dine with him, but it being brought too soon upon table, he could not resist the Temptation, and ate it all up before we came.

I had made some Courtship during this time to Miss Read. I had a great Respect and Affection for her, and had some Reason to believe she had the same for me: but as I was about to take a long Voyage, and we were both very young, only a little above 18, it was thought most prudent by her Mother to prevent our going too far at present, as a Marriage if it was to take place would be more convenient after my Return, when I should be as I expected set up in my Business. Perhaps too she thought my Expectations not so well founded as I imagined them to be.

My chief Acquaintances at this time were, Charles Osborne, Joseph Watson, and James Ralph; All Lovers of Reading. The two first were Clerks to an eminent Scrivener or Conveyancer in the Town, Charles Brockden; the other was Clerk to a Merchant. Watson was a pious sensible young Man, of great Integrity. The others rather more lax in their Principles of Religion, particularly Ralph, who as well as Collins had been unsettled by me, for which they both made me suffer. Obsorne was sensible, candid, frank, sincere, and affectionate to his Friends; but in literary Matters too fond of Criticizing. Ralph, was ingenious, genteel in his Manners, and extremely eloquent; I think I never knew a prettier Talker. Both of them great Admirers of Poetry, and began to try their Hands in little Pieces. Many pleasant Walks we four had together, on Sundays into the Woods near Skuylkill, where we read to one another and conferr'd on what we read. Ralph was inclin'd to pursue the Study of Poetry, not doubting but he might become eminent in it and make his Fortune by it, alledging that the best Poets must when they first began to write, make as many Faults as he did. Osborne dissuaded him, assur'd him he had no Genius for Poetry, and advis'd him to think of nothing beyond the Business he was bred to; that in the mercantile way tho' he had no Stock, he might by his Diligence and Punctuality recommend himself to Employment as a Factor, and in time acquire wherewith to trade on his own Account. I approv'd the amusing oneself with Poetry now and then, so far as to improve one's Language, but no farther. On this it was propos'd that we should each of us at our next Meeting produce a Piece of our own Composing, in order to improve by our mutual Observations, Criticisms and Corrections. As Language and Expression was what we had in View, we excluded all Considerations of Invention, by agreeing that the Task should be a Version of the 18th Psalm, which describes the Descent of a Deity. When the Time of our Meeting drew nigh, Ralph call'd on me first, and let me know his Piece was ready. I told him I had been busy, and having little Inclination had done nothing. He then show'd me his Piece for my Opinion; and I much approv'd it, as it appear'd to me to have great Merit. Now, says he, Osborne never will allow the least Merit in any thing of mine, but makes 1000 Criticisms out of mere Envy. He is not so jealous of you. I wish therefore you would take this Piece, and produce it as yours. I will pretend not to have had time, and so produce nothing: We shall then see what he will say to it. It was agreed, and I immediately transcrib'd it that it might appear in my own hand. We met.

Watson's Performance was read: there were some Beauties in it: but many Defects. Osborne's was read: It was much better. Ralph did it Justice, remark'd some Faults, but applauded the Beauties. He himself had nothing to produce. I was backward, seem'd desirous of being excus'd, had not had sufficient Time to correct; etc. but no Excuse could be admitted, produce I must. It was read and repeated; Watson and Osborne gave up the Contest; and join'd in applauding it immoderately. Ralph only made some Criticisms and propos'd some Amendments, but I defended my Text. Osborne was against Ralph, and told him he was no better a Critic than Poet; so he dropped the Argument. As they two went home together, Osborne express'd himself still more strongly in favor of what he thought my Production, having restrain'd himself before as he said, lest I should think it Flattery. But who would have imagin'd, says he, that Franklin had been capable of such a Performance; such Painting, such Force! such Fire! He has even improv'd the Original! In his common Conversation, he seems to have no Choice of Words; he hesitates and blunders; and yet, good God, how he writes!

When we next met, Ralph discover'd the Trick we had played him, and Osborne was a little laughed at. This Transaction fix'd Ralph in his Resolution of becoming a Poet. I did all I could to dissuade him from it, but he continu'd scribbling Verses, till *Pope* cur'd him. He became however a pretty good Prose Writer. More of him hereafter. But as I may not have occasion again to mention the other two, I shall just remark here, that Watson died in my Arms a few Years after, much lamented, being the best of our Set. Osborne went to the West Indies, where he became an eminent Lawyer and made Money, but died young. He and I had made a serious Agreement, that the one who happen'd first to die, should if possible make a friendly Visit to the other, and acquaint him how he found things in that separate State. But he never fulfill'd his Promise.

The Governor, seeming to like my Company, had me frequently to his House; and his Setting me up was always mention'd as a fix'd thing. I was to take with me Letters recommendatory to a Number of his Friends, besides the Letter of Credit to furnish me with the necessary Money for purchasing the Press and Types, Paper, etc. For these Letters I was appointed to call at different times, when they were to be ready, but a future time was still named. Thus we went on till the Ship whose Departure too had been several times postponed was on the Point of sailing. Then when I call'd to take my Leave and receive the Letters, his Secretary, Dr. Bard, came out to me and said the Governor was extremely busy, in writing, but would be down at New Castle before the Ship, and there the Letters would be delivered to me.

Ralph, tho' married and having one Child, had determined to accompany me in this Voyage. It was thought he intended to establish a Correspondence, and obtain Goods to sell on Commission. But I found afterwards, that thro' some Discontent with his Wife's Relations, he purposed to leave her on their Hands, and never return again. Having taken leave of my Friends, and interchang'd some Promises with Miss Read, I left Philadelphia in the Ship, which anchor'd at New Castle. The Governor was there. But when I went to his Lodging, the Secretary came to me from him with the civillest Message in the World, that he could not then see me being engag'd in Business of the utmost Importance, but should send the Letters to me on board, wish'd me heartily a good Voyage and a speedy Return, etc. I return'd on board, a little puzzled, but still not doubting.

Mr. Andrew Hamilton, a famous Lawyer of Philadelphia, had taken Passage in the same Ship for himself and Son: and with Mr. Denham a Quaker Merchant, and Messrs. Onion and Russel Masters of an Iron Work in Maryland, had engag'd the Great Cabin; so that Ralph and I were forc'd to take up with a Berth in the Steerage: And none on board knowing us, were considered as ordinary Persons. But Mr. Hamilton and his Son (it was James, since Governor) return'd from New Castle to Philadelphia, the Father being recall'd by a great Fee to plead for a seized Ship. And just before we sail'd Colonel French coming on board, and showing me great Respect, I was more taken Notice of, and with my Friend Ralph invited by the other Gentlemen to come into the Cabin, there being now Room. Accordingly we remov'd thither.

Understanding that Colonel French had brought on board the Governor's Dispatches, I ask'd the Captain for those Letters that were to be under my Care. He said all were put into the Bag together; and he could not then come at them; but before we landed in England, I should have an Opportunity of picking them out. So I was satisfied for the present, and we proceeded on our Voyage. We had a sociable Company in the Cabin, and lived uncommonly well, having the Addition of all Mr. Hamilton's Stores, who had laid in plentifully. In this Passage Mr. Denham contracted a Friendship for me that continued during his Life. The Voyage was otherwise not a pleasant one, as we had a great deal of bad Weather.

When we came into the Channel, the Captain kept his Word with me, and gave me an Opportunity of examining the Bag for the Governor's Letters. I found none upon which my Name was put, as under my Care; I pick'd out 6 or 7 that by the Handwriting I thought might be the promis'd Letters, especially as one of them was directed to Basket the King's Printer, and another to some Stationer. We arriv'd in London the 24th of December, 1724. I waited upon the Stationer who came first in my Way, delivering the Letter as from Governor Keith. I don't know such a Person, says he: but opening the Letter, O, this is from Riddlesden; I have lately found him to be a complete Rascal, and I will have nothing to do with him, nor receive any Letters from him. So putting the Letter into my Hand, he turn'd on his Heel and left me to serve some Customer. I was surprised to find these were not the Governor's Letters. And after recollecting and comparing Circumstances, I began to doubt his Sincerity. I found my Friend Denham, and opened the whole Affair to him. He let me into Keith's Character, told me there was not the least Probability that he had written any Letters for me, that no one who knew him had the smallest Dependence on him, and he laughed at the Notion of the Governor's giving me a Letter of Credit, having as he said no Credit to give. On my expressing some Concern about what I should do: He advis'd me to endeavour getting some Employment in the Way of my Business. Among the Printers here, says he, you will improve yourself, and when you return to America, you will set up to greater Advantage.

We both of us happen'd to know, as well as the Stationer, that Riddlesden the Attorney, was a very Knave. He had half ruin'd Miss Read's Father by drawing him in to be bound for him. By his Letter it appear'd, there was a secret Scheme on foot to the Prejudice of Hamilton, (Suppos'd to be then coming over with us,) and that Keith was concern'd in it with Riddlesden. Denham, who was a Friend of Hamilton's, thought he ought to be acquainted with it. So when he arriv'd in England, which was soon after, partly from Resentment and Ill-Will to Keith and Riddlesden, and partly from Goodwill to him: I waited on him, and gave him the Letter. He thank'd me cordially, the Information being of Importance to him. And from that time he became my Friend, greatly to my Advantage afterwards on many Occasions.

But what shall we think of a Governor's playing such pitiful Tricks, and imposing so grossly on a poor ignorant Boy! It was a Habit he had acquired. He wish'd to please everybody; and having little to give, he gave Expectations. He was otherwise an ingenious sensible Man, a pretty good Writer, and a good Governor for the People, tho' not for his Constituents the Proprietaries, whose Instructions he sometimes disregarded. Several of our best Laws were of his Planning, and pass'd during his Administration.

Ralph and I were inseparable Companions. We took Lodgings together in Little Britain at 3 shillings 6 pence per Week, as much as we could then afford. He found some Relations, but they were poor and unable to assist him. He now let me know his Intentions of remaining in London, and that he never meant to return to Philadelphia. He had brought no Money with him, the whole he could muster having been expended in paying his Passage. I had 15 Pistoles. So he borrowed occasionally of me, to subsist while he was looking out for Business, He first endeavoured to get into the Playhouse, believing himself qualified for an Actor; but Wilkes, to whom he applied, advis'd him candidly not to think of that Employment, as it was impossible he should succeed in it. Then he propos'd to Roberts, a Publisher in Paternoster Row, to write for him a Weekly Paper like the Spectator, on certain Conditions, which Roberts did not approve. Then he endeavour'd to get Employment as a Hackney Writer to copy for the Stationers and Lawyers about the Temple: but could find no Vacancy.

I immediately got into Work at Palmer's, then a famous Printing-House in Bartholomew Close; and here I continu'd near a Year. I was pretty diligent; but spent with Ralph a good deal of my Earnings in going to Plays and other Places of Amusement. We had together consum'd all my Pistoles, and now just rubb'd on from hand to mouth. He seem'd quite to forget his Wife and Child, and I by degrees my Engagements with Miss Read, to whom I never wrote more than one Letter, and that was to let her know I was not likely soon to return. This was another of the great Errata of my Life, which I should wish to correct if I were to live it over again. In fact, by our Expenses, I was constantly kept unable to pay my Passage.

At Palmer's I was employ'd in Composing for the second Edition of Wollaston's Religion of Nature. Some of his Reasonings not appearing to me well-founded, I wrote a little metaphysical Piece, in which I made Remarks on them. It was entitled, *A Dissertation on Liberty and Necessity, Pleasure and Pain.* I inscrib'd it to my Friend Ralph. I printed a small Number. It occasion'd my being more consider'd by Mr. Palmer, as a young Man of some Ingenuity, tho' he seriously expostulated with me upon the Principles of my Pamphlet which to him appear'd abominable. My printing this Pamphlet was another Erratum.

While I lodg'd in Little Britain I made an Acquaintance with one Wilcox a Bookseller, whose Shop was at the next Door. He had an immense Collection of second-hand Books. Circulating Libraries were not then in Use; but we agreed that on certain reasonable Terms which I have now forgotten, I might take, read, and return any of his Books. This I esteem'd a great Advantage, and I made as much use of it as I could.

My Pamphlet by some means falling into the Hands of one Lyons, a Surgeon, Author of a Book entitled *The Infallibility of Human Judgment*, it occasioned an Acquaintance between us; he took great Notice of me, call'd on me often, to converse on those subjects, carried me to the Horns, a pale Ale-House in [blank] Lane, Cheapside, and introduc'd me to Dr. Mandeville, Author of the Fable of the Bees who had a Club there, of which he was the soul, being a most facetious entertaining Companion. Lyons too introduc'd me to Dr. Pemberton, at Batson's Coffee House, who promis'd to give me an Opportunity some time or other of seeing Sir Isaac Newton, of which I was extremely desirous; but this never happened.

I had brought over a few Curiosities among which the principal was a Purse made of the Asbestos, which purifies by Fire. Sir Hans Sloane heard of it, came to see me, and invited me to his House in Bloomsbury Square; where he show'd me all his Curiosities, and persuaded me to let him add that to the number, for which he paid me handsomely.

In our House there lodg'd a young Woman, a Milliner, who I think had a Shop in the Cloisters. She had been genteelly bred, was sensible and lively, and of most pleasing Conversation. Ralph read Plays to her in the Evenings, they grew intimate, she took another Lodging, and he follow'd her. They liv'd together some time, but he being still out of Business, and her Income not sufficient to maintain them with her Child, he took a Resolution of going from London, to try for a Country School, which he thought himself well qualified to undertake, as he wrote an excellent Hand, and was a Master of Arithmetic and Accounts. This however he deem'd a Business below him, and confident of future better Fortune when he should be unwilling to have it known that he once was so meanly employ'd, he chang'd his Name, and did me the Honor to assume mine. For I soon after had a Letter from him, acquainting me, that he was settled in a small Village in Berkshire, I think it was, where he taught reading and writing to 10 or a dozen Boys at 6 pence each per Week, recommending Mrs. T. to my Care, and desiring me to write to him directing for Mr. Franklin Schoolmaster, at such a Place. He continu'd to write frequently, sending me large Specimens of an Epic Poem which he was then composing, and desiring my Remarks and Corrections. These I gave him from time to time, but endeavor'd rather to discourage his Proceeding. One of Young's Satires was then just publish'd. I copy'd and sent him a great Part of it, which set in a strong Light the Folly of pursuing the Muses with any Hope of Advancement by them. All was in vain. Sheets of the Poem continu'd to come by every Post. In the mean time Mrs. T. having on his Account lost her Friends and Business, was often in Distresses, and us'd to send for me, and borrow what I could spare to help her out of them. I grew fond of her Company, and being at this time under no Religious Restraints, and presuming on my Importance to her, I attempted Familiarities, (another Erratum) which she repuls'd with a proper Resentment, and acquainted him with my Behaviour. This made a Breach between us, and when he return'd again to London, he let me know he thought I had cancel'd all the Obligations he had been under to me. So I found I was never to expect his Repaying me what I lent to him or advanc'd for him. This was however not then of much Consequence, as he was totally unable. And in the Loss of his Friendship I found myself reliev'd from a Burden. I now began to think of getting a little Money beforehand; and expecting better Work, I left Palmer's to work at Watts's near Lincoln's Inn Fields, a still greater Printing-House. Here I continu'd all the rest of my Stay in London.

At my first Admission into this Printing-House, I took to working at Press, imagining I felt a Want of the Bodily Exercise I had been us'd to in America, where Presswork is mix'd with Composing. I drank only Water, the other Workmen, near 50 in Number, were great Guzzlers of Beer. On occasion I carried up and down Stairs a large Form of Types in each hand, when others carried but one in both Hands. They wonder'd to see from this and several Instances that the Water American as they call'd me was *stronger* than themselves who drunk *strong* Beer. We had an Alehouse Boy who attended always in the House to supply the Workmen. My Companion at the Press drank every day a Pint before Breakfast, a Pint at Breakfast with his Bread and Cheese; a Pint between Breakfast and Dinner; a Pint at Dinner; a Pint in the Afternoon about Six o'clock, and another when he had done his Day's Work. I thought it a detestable Custom. But it was necessary, he suppos'd, to drink *strong* Beer that he might be *strong* to labour. I endeavour'd to convince him that the Bodily Strength afforded by Beer could only be in proportion to the Grain or Flour of the Barley dissolved in the Water of which it was made; that there was more Flour in a Penny-worth of Bread, and therefore if he would eat that with a Pint of Water, it would give him more Strength than a Quart of Beer. He drank on however, and had 4 or 5 Shillings to pay out of his Wages every Saturday Night for that muddling Liquor; an Expense I was free from. And thus these poor Devils keep themselves always under.

Watts after some Weeks desiring to have me in the Composing Room, I left the Pressmen. A new *Bienvenu* or Sum for Drink, being 5 Shillings, was demanded of me by the Compositors. I thought it an Imposition, as I had paid below. The Master thought so too, and forbad my Paying it. I stood out two or three Weeks, was accordingly considered as an Excommunicate, and had so many little Pieces of private Mischief done me, by mixing my Sorts, transposing my Pages, breaking my Matter, etc. etc. if I were ever so little out of the Room, and all ascrib'd to the Chapel Ghost, which they said ever haunted those not regularly admitted, that notwithstanding the Master's Protection, I found myself oblig'd to comply and pay the Money; convinc'd of the Folly of being on ill Terms with those one is to live with continually. I was now on a fair Footing with them, and soon acquir'd considerable Influence. I propos'd some reasonable Alterations in their Chapel Laws, and carried them against all Opposition. From my Example a great Part of them, left their muddling Breakfast of Beer and Bread and Cheese, finding they could with me be supplied from a neighboring House with a large Porringer of hot Water-gruel, sprinkled with Pepper, crumb'd with Bread, and a Bit of Butter in it, for the price of a Pint of Beer, viz, three halfpence. This was a more comfortable as well as cheaper Breakfast, and kept their Heads clearer. Those who continu'd sotting with Beer all day, were often, by not paying, out of Credit at the Alehouse, and us'd to make Interest with me to get Beer, *their Light*, as they phras'd it, *being out.* I watch'd the Pay table on Saturday Night, and collected what I stood engag'd for them, having to pay some times near Thirty Shillings a Week on their Accounts. This, and my being esteem'd a pretty good Riggite, that is a jocular verbal Satirist, supported my Consequence in the Society. My constant Attendance, (I never making a St. Monday), recommended me to the Master; and my uncommon Quickness at Composing, occasion'd my being put upon all Work of Dispatch, which was generally better paid. So I went on now very agreeably. [. . .]

Thus I spent about 18 Months in London. Most Part of the Time, I work'd hard at my Business, and spent but little upon myself except in seeing Plays, and in Books. My Friend Ralph had kept me poor. He owed me about 27 Pounds; which I was now never likely to receive; a great Sum out of my small Earnings. I lov'd him notwithstanding, for he had many amiable Qualities. Tho' I had by no means improv'd my Fortune, I had pick'd up some very ingenious Acquaintance whose Conversation was of great Advantage to me, and I had read considerably.

We sail'd from Gravesend on the 23d of July 1726. For The Incidents of the Voyage, I refer you to my Journal, where you will find them all minutely related. Perhaps the most important Part of that Journal is the *Plan* to be found in it which I formed at Sea for regulating my future Conduct in Life. It is the more remarkable, as being form'd when I was so young, and yet being pretty faithfully adhered to quite thro' to old Age. We landed in Philadelphia the 11th Of October, where I found sundry Alterations. Keith was no longer Governor, being superseded by Major Gordon: I met him walking the Streets as a common Citizen. He seem'd a little asham'd at seeing me, but pass'd without saying anything. I should have been as much asham'd at seeing Miss Read, had not her Friends despairing with Reason of my Return, after the Receipt of my Letter, persuaded her to marry another, one Rogers, a Potter, which was done in my Absence. With him however she was never happy, and soon parted from him, refusing to cohabit with him, or bear his Name, It being now said that he had another Wife. He was a worthless Fellow tho' an excellent Workman which was the Temptation to her Friends. He got into Debt, and ran away in 1727 or 28, went to the West Indies, and died there. Keimer had got a better House, a Shop well supplied with Stationery, plenty of new Types, a number of Hands tho' none good, and seem'd to have a great deal of Business.

Mr. Denham took a Store in Water Street, where we open'd our Goods. I attended the Business diligently, studied Accounts, and grew in a little Time expert at selling. We lodg'd and boarded together, he counsell'd me as a Father, having a sincere Regard for me: I respected and lov'd him: and we might have gone on together very happily: But in the Beginning of February 1726/7 when I had just pass'd my 21st Year, we both were taken ill. My Distemper was a Pleurisy, which very nearly carried me off: I suffered a good deal, gave up the Point in my own mind, and was rather disappointed when I found myself recovering; regretting in some degree that I must now sometime or other have all that disagreeable Work to do over again. I forget what his Distemper was. It held him a long time, and at length carried him off. He left me a small Legacy in a nuncupative Will, as a Token of his Kindness for me, and he left me once more to the wide World. For the Store was taken into the Care of his Executors, and my Employment under him ended: My Brother-in-law Homes, being now at Philadelphia, advis'd my Return to my Business. And Keimer tempted me with an Offer of large Wages by the Year to come and take the Management of his Printing-House that he might better attend his Stationer's Shop. I had heard a bad Character of him in London, from his Wife and her Friends, and was not fond of having any more to do with him. I try'd for farther Employment as a Merchant's Clerk; but not readily meeting with any, I clos'd again with Keimer.

I found in *his* House these Hands: Hugh Meredith, a Welsh- Pensilvanian, 30 Years of Age, bred to Country Work: honest, sensible, had a great deal of solid Observation, was something of a Reader, but given to drink: Stephen Potts, a young Country Man of full Age, bred to the Same, of uncommon natural Parts, and great Wit and Humor, but a little idle. These he had agreed with at extreme low Wages, per week, to be rais'd a Shilling every 3 Months, as they would deserve by improving in their Business, and the Expectation of these high Wages to come on hereafter was what he had drawn them in with. Meredith was to work at Press, Potts at Bookbinding, which he by Agreement, was to teach them, tho' he knew neither one nor t'other. John —— a wild Irishman brought up to no Business, whose Service for 4 Years Keimer had purchas'd from the Captain of a Ship. He too was to be made a Pressman. George Webb, an Oxford Scholar, whose Time for 4 Years he had likewise bought, intending him for a Compositor: of whom more presently. And David Harry, a Country Boy, whom he had taken Apprentice. I soon perceiv'd that the Intention of engaging me at Wages so much higher than he had been us'd to give, was, to have these raw cheap Hands form'd thro' me, and as soon as I had instructed them, then, they being all articled to him, he should be able to do without me. I went on however, very cheerfully; put his Printing-House in Order, which had been in great Confusion, and brought his Hands by degrees to mind their Business and to do it better.

It was an odd Thing to find an Oxford Scholar in the Situation of a bought Servant. He was not more than 18 Years of Age, and gave me this Account of himself; that he was born in Gloucester, educated at a Grammar School there, had been distinguish'd among the Scholars for some apparent Superiority in performing his Part when they exhibited Plays; belong'd to the Witty Club there, and had written some Pieces in Prose and Verse which were printed in the Gloucester Newspapers. Thence he was sent to Oxford; there he continu'd about a Year, but not well-satisfy'd, wishing of all things to see London and become a Player. At length receiving his Quarterly Allowance of 15 Guineas, instead of discharging his Debts, he walk'd out of Town, hid his Gown in a Furz Bush, and footed it to London, where having no Friend to advise him, he fell into bad Company, soon spent his Guineas, found no means of being introduc'd among the Players, grew necessitous, pawn'd his Cloaths and wanted Bread. Walking the Street very hungry, and not knowing what to do with himself, a Crimp's Bill was put into his Hand, offering immediate Entertainment and Encouragement to such as would bind themselves to serve in America. He went directly, sign'd the Indentures, was put into the Ship and came over; never writing a Line to acquaint his Friends what was become of him. He was lively, witty, good-natur'd and a pleasant Companion, but idle, thoughtless, and imprudent to the last Degree.

John the Irishman soon ran away. With the rest I began to live very agreeably; for they all respected me, the more as they found Keimer incapable of instructing them, and that from me they learned something daily. We never work'd on Saturday, that being Keimer's Sabbath. So I had two Days for Reading. My Acquaintance with ingenious People in the Town increased. Keimer himself treated me with great Civility and apparent Regard; and nothing now made me uneasy but my Debt to Vernon, which I was yet unable to pay, being hitherto but a poor Economist. He however kindly made no Demand of it.

Our Printing-House often wanted Sorts, and there was no Letter Founder in America. I had seen Types cast at James's in London, but without much Attention to the Manner: However I now contriv'd a Mold, made use of the Letters we had as Puncheons, struck the Matrices in Lead, and thus supply'd in a pretty tolerable way all Deficiencies. I also engrav'd several Things on occasion. I made the Ink, I was Warehouse-man and everything, in short quite a Factotum.

But, however serviceable I might be, I found that my Services became every Day of less Importance, as the other Hands improv'd in the Business. And when Keimer paid my second Quarter's Wages, he let me know that he felt them too heavy, and thought I should make an Abatement. He grew by degrees less civil, put on more of the Master, frequently found Fault, was captious and seem'd ready for an Outbreaking. I went on nevertheless with a good deal of Patience, thinking that his encumber'd Circumstances were partly the Cause. At length a Trifle snapt our Connections. For a great Noise happening near the Courthouse, I put my Head out of the Window to see what was the Matter. Keimer, being in the Street, look'd up and saw me, call'd out to me in a loud Voice and angry Tone to mind my Business, adding some reproachful Words, that nettled me the more for their Publicity, all the Neighbors who were looking out on the same Occasion being Witnesses how I was treated. He came up immediately into the Printing-House, continu'd the Quarrel, high Words pass'd on both Sides, he gave me the Quarter's Warning we had stipulated, expressing a Wish that he had not been oblig'd to so long a Warning. I told him his Wish was unnecessary for I would leave him that Instant; and so taking my Hat walk'd out of doors, desiring Meredith, whom I saw below to take care of some Things I left, and bring them to my Lodging.

Meredith came accordingly in the Evening, when we talk'd my Affair over. He had conceiv'd a great Regard for me, and was very unwilling that I should leave the House while he remain'd in it. He dissuaded me from returning to my native Country, which I began to think of. He reminded me that Keimer was in debt for all he possess'd, that his Creditors began to be uneasy, that he kept his Shop miserably, sold often without Profit for ready Money, and often trusted without keeping Accounts. That he must therefore fail; which would make a Vacancy I might profit of. I objected my Want of Money. He then let me know, that his Father had a high Opinion of me, and from some Discourse that had pass'd between them, he was sure would advance Money to set us up, if I would enter into Partnership with him. My time, says he, will be out with Keimer in the Spring. By that time we may have our Press and Types in from London: I am sensible I am no Workman. If you like it, Your Skill in the Business shall be set against the Stock I furnish; and we will share the Profits equally. The Proposal was agreeable, and I consented. His Father was in Town, and approv'd of it, the more as he saw I had great Influence with his Son, had prevail'd on him to abstain long from Dramdrinking, and he hop'd might break him off that wretched Habit entirely, when we came to be so closely connected. I gave an Inventory to the Father, who carry'd it to a Merchant; the Things were sent for; the Secret was to be kept till they should arrive, and in the mean time I was to get Work if I could at the other Printing-House. But I found no Vacancy there, and so remain'd idle a few Days, when Keimer, on a prospect of being employ'd to print some Paper-money, in New Jersey, which would require Cuts and various Types that I only could supply, and apprehending Bradford might engage me and get the Job from him, sent me a very civil Message, that old Friends should not part for a few Words, the Effect of sudden Passion, and wishing me to return. Meredith persuaded me to comply, as it would give more Opportunity for his Improvement under my daily Instructions. So I return'd, and we went on more smoothly than for some time before. The New Jersey Job was obtain'd. I contriv'd a Copper-Plate Press for it, the first that had been seen in the Country. I cut several Ornaments and Checks for the Bills. We went together to Burlington, where I executed the Whole to Satisfaction, and he received so large a Sum for the Work, as to be enabled thereby to keep his Head much longer above Water.

At Burlington I made an Acquaintance with many principal People of the Province. Several of them had been appointed by the Assembly a Committee to attend the Press, and take care that no more Bills were printed than the Law directed. They were therefore by Turns constantly with us, and generally he who attended brought with him a Friend or two for Company. My Mind having been much more improv'd by Reading than Keimer's, I suppose it was for that Reason my Conversation seem'd to be more valu'd. They had me to their houses, introduc'd me to their Friends and show'd me much Civility, while he, tho' the Master, was a little neglected. In truth he was an odd Fish, ignorant of common Life, fond of rudely opposing receiv'd Opinions, slovenly to extreme dirtiness, enthusiastic in some Points of Religion, and a little Knavish withal. We continu'd there near 3 Months, and by that time I could reckon among my acquired Friends, Judge Allen, Samuel Bustill, the Secretary of the Province, Isaac Pearson, Joseph Cooper, and several of the Smiths, Members of Assembly, and Isaac Decow the Surveyor General. The latter was a shrewd sagacious old Man, who told me that he began for himself when young by wheeling Clay for the Brickmakers, learned to write after be was of Age, carry'd the Chain for Surveyors, who taught him Surveying, and he had now by his Industry acquir'd a good Estate; and says he, I foresee, that you will soon work this Man out of Business and make a Fortune in it at Philadelphia. He had not then the least Intimation of my Intention to set up there or anywhere. These Friends were afterwards of great Use to me, as I occasionally was to some of them. They all continued their Regard for me as long as they lived.

Before I enter upon my public Appearance in Business, it may be well to let you know the then State of my Mind with regard to my Principles and Morals, that you may see how far those influenc'd the future Events of my Life. My Parents had early given me religious Impressions, and brought me through my Childhood piously in the Dissenting Way. But I was scarce 15 when, after doubting by turns of several Points as I found them disputed in the different Books I read, I began to doubt of Revelation itself. Some Books against Deism fell into my hands; they were said to be the Substance of Sermons preached at Boyle's Lectures. It happened that they wrought an Effect on me quite contrary to what was intended by them: For the Arguments of the Deists which were quoted to be refuted, appeared to me much Stronger than the Refutations. In short I soon became a thorough Deist. My Arguments perverted some others, particularly Collins and Ralph: but each of them having afterwards wrong'd me greatly without the least Compunction, and recollecting Keith's Conduct towards me, (who was another Freethinker) and my own towards Vernon and Miss Read which at Times gave me great Trouble, I began to suspect that this Doctrine tho' it might be true was not very useful. My London Pamphlet, which had for its Motto those Lines of Dryden

——Whatever is, is right
Tho' purblind Man Sees but a Part of
The Chain, the nearest Link,
His Eyes not carrying to the equal Beam,
That poizes all, above.

And from the Attributes of God, his infinite Wisdom, Goodness and Power concluded that nothing could possibly be wrong in the World, and that Vice and Virtue were empty Distinctions, no such Things existing appear'd now not so clever a Performance as I once thought it; and I doubted whether some Error had not insinuated itself unperceiv'd into my Argument, so as to infect all that follow'd, as is common in metaphysical Reasonings. I grew convinc'd that *Truth*, *Sincerity* and *Integrity* in Dealings between Man and Man, were of the utmost Importance to the Felicity of Life, and I form'd written Resolutions, (which still remain in my Journal Book) to practice them ever while I lived. Revelation had indeed no weight with me as such; but I entertain'd an Opinion, that tho' certain Actions might not be bad *because* they were forbidden by it, or good *because* it commanded them; yet probably those Actions might be forbidden *because* they were bad for us, or commanded *because* they were beneficial to us, in their own Natures, all the Circumstances of things considered. And this Persuasion, with the kind hand of Providence, or some guardian Angel, or accidental favorable Circumstances and Situations, or all together, preserved me (thro' this dangerous Time of Youth and the hazardous Situations I was sometimes in among Strangers, remote from the Eye and Advice of my Father) without any *willful* gross Immorality or Injustice that might have been expected from my Want of Religion. I say *willful*, because the Instances I have mentioned, had something of *Necessity* in them, from my Youth, Inexperience, and the Knavery of others. I had therefore a tolerable Character to begin the World with, I valued it properly, and determin'd to preserve it.

We had not been long return'd to Philadelphia, before the New Types arriv'd from London. We settled with Keimer, and left him by his Consent before he heard of it. We found a House to hire near the Market, and took it. To lessen the Rent, (which was then but 24 pounds a Year tho' I have since known it let for 70) We took in Thomas Godfrey a Glazier, and his Family, who were to pay a considerable Part of it to us, and we to board with them. We had scarce opened our Letters and put our Press in Order, before George House, an Acquaintance of mine, brought a Countryman to us; whom he had met in the Street enquiring for a Printer. All our Cash was now expended in the Variety of Particulars we had been obliged to procure, and this Countryman's Five Shillings, being our First Fruits and coming so seasonably, gave me more Pleasure than any Crown I have since earn'd; and from the Gratitude I felt towards House, has made me often more ready than perhaps I should otherwise have been to assist young Beginners. [. . .]

I should have mention'd before, that in the Autumn of the preceding Year, I had formed most of my ingenious Acquaintance into a Club, for mutual Improvement, which we call'd the Junto. We met on Friday Evenings. The Rules I drew up, requir'd that every Member in his Turn should produce one or more Queries on any Point of Morals, Politics or Natural Philosophy, to be discuss'd by the Company, and once in three Months produce and read an Essay of his own Writing on any Subject he pleased. Our Debates were to be under the Direction of a President, and to be conducted in the sincere Spirit of Enquiry after Truth, without fondness for Dispute, or Desire of Victory; and to prevent Warmth, all expressions of Positiveness in Opinion, or of direct Contradiction, were after some time made contraband and prohibited under small pecuniary Penalties. The first Members were, Joseph Breintnall, a Copier of Deeds for the Scriveners; a goodnatur'd friendly middle-ag'd Man, a great Lover of Poetry, reading all he could meet with, and writing some that was tolerable; very ingenious in many little Nicknackeries, and of sensible Conversation. Thomas Godfrey, a self-taught Mathematician, great in his Way, and afterwards Inventor of what is now call'd Hadley's Quadrant. But he knew little out of his way, and was not a pleasing Companion, as like most Great Mathematicians I have met with, he expected unusual Precision in everything said, or was forever denying or distinguishing upon Trifles, to the Disturbance of all Conversation. He soon left us. Nicholas Scull, a Surveyor, afterwards Surveyor General, Who lov'd Books, and sometimes made a few Verses. William Parsons, bred a Shoemaker, but loving Reading, had acquir'd a considerable Share of Mathematics, which he first studied with a View to Astrology that he afterwards laughed at. He also became Surveyor General. William Maugridge, a joiner, and a most exquisite Mechanic, and a solid sensible Man. Hugh Meredith, Stephen Potts, and George Webb, I have Character-is'd before. Robert Grace, a young Gentleman of some Fortune, generous, lively and witty, a Lover of Punning and of his Friends. And William Coleman, then a Merchant's Clerk, about my Age, who had the coolest clearest Head, the best Heart, and the exactest Morals, of almost any Man I ever met with. He became afterwards a Merchant of great Note, and one of our Provincial Judges: Our Friendship continued without Interruption to his Death, upwards of 40 Years. And the Club continu'd almost as long and was the best School of Philosophy, Morals and Politics that then existed in the Province; for our Queries which were read the Week preceding their Discussion, put us on reading with Attention upon the several Subjects, that we might speak more to the purpose: and here too we acquired better Habits of Conversation, everything being studied in our Rules which might prevent our disgusting each other. From hence the long Continuance of the Club, which I shall have frequent Occasion to speak farther of hereafter; But my giving this Account of it here, is to show something of the Interest I had, everyone of these exerting themselves in recommending Business to us.

Breintnall particularly procur'd us from the Quakers, the Printing 40 Sheets of their History, the rest being to be done by Keimer: and upon this we work'd exceeding hard, for the Price was low. It was a Folio, Pro Patria Size, in Pica with Long Primer Notes. I compos'd of it a Sheet a Day, and Meredith work'd it off at Press. It was often 11 at Night and sometimes later, before I had finish'd my Distribution for the next day's Work: For the little Jobs sent in by our other Friends now and then put us back. But so determin'd I was to continue doing a Sheet a Day of the Folio, that one Night when having impos'd my Forms, I thought my Day's Work over, one of them by accident was broken and two Pages reduc'd to Pie, I immediately distributed and compos'd it over again before I went to bed. And this Industry visible to our Neighbors began to give us Character and Credit; particularly I was told, that mention being made of the new Printing Office at the Merchants' Every-night-Club, the general Opinion was that it must fail, there being already two Printers in the Place, Keimer and Bradford; but Doctor Baird (whom you and I saw many Years after at his native Place, St. Andrews in Scotland) gave a contrary Opinion; for the Industry of that Franklin, says he, is superior to anything I ever saw of the kind: I see him still at work when I go home from Club; and he is at Work again before his Neighbors are out of bed. This struck the rest, and we soon after had Offers from one of them to supply us with Stationery. But as yet we did not choose to engage in Shop Business.

I mention this Industry the more particularly and the more freely, tho' it seems to be talking in my own

Praise, that those of my Posterity who shall read it, may know the Use of that Virtue, when they see its Effects in my Favor throughout this Relation.

George Webb, who had found a Friend that lent him wherewith to purchase his Time of Keimer, now came to offer himself as a Journeyman to us. We could not then employ him, but I foolishly let him know, as a Secret, that I soon intended to begin a Newspaper, and might then have Work for him. My Hopes of Success as I told him were founded on this, that the then only Newspaper, printed by Bradford was a paltry thing, wretchedly manag'd, no way entertaining; and yet was profitable to him. I therefore thought a good Paper could scarcely fail of good Encouragement. I requested Webb not to mention it, but he told it to Keimer, who immediately, to be beforehand with me, published Proposals for Printing one himself, on which Webb was to be employ'd. I resented this, and to counteract them, as I could not yet begin our Paper, I wrote several Pieces of Entertainment for Bradford's Paper, under the Title of the Busy Body which Breintnall continu'd some Months. By this means the Attention of the Public was fix'd on that Paper, and Keimer's Proposals which we burlesqu'd and ridicul'd, were disregarded. He began his Paper however, and after carrying it on three Quarters of a Year, with at most only 90 Subscribers, he offer'd it to me for a Trifle, and I having been ready some time to go on with it, took it in hand directly, and it prov'd in a few Years extremely profitable to me.

I perceive that I am apt to speak in the singular Number, though Our Partnership still continu'd. The Reason may be, that in fact the whole Management of the Business lay upon me. Meredith was no Compositor, a poor Pressman, and seldom sober. My Friends lamented my Connection with him, but I was to make the best of it.

Our first Papers made a quite different Appearance from any before in the Province, a better Type and better printed: but some spirited Remarks of my Writing on the Dispute then going on between Governor Burnet and the Massachusetts Assembly, struck the principal People, occasion'd the Paper and the Manager of it to be much talk'd of, and in a few Weeks brought them all to be our Subscribers. Their Example was follow'd by many, and our Number went on growing continually. This was one of the first good Effects of my having learned a little to scribble. Another was, that the leading Men, seeing a Newspaper now in the hands of one who could also handle a Pen, thought it convenient to oblige and encourage me. Bradford still printed the Votes and Laws and other Public Business. He had printed an Address of the House to the Governor in a coarse blundering manner; We reprinted it elegantly and correctly, and sent one to every Member. They were sensible of the Difference, it strengthen'd the Hands of our Friends in the House, and they voted us their Printers for the Year ensuing.

[. . .] Mr. Vernon about this time put me in mind of the Debt I ow'd him: but did not press me. I wrote him an ingenuous Letter of Acknowledgments, crav'd his Forbearance a little longer which he allow'd me, and as soon as I was able I paid the Principal with Interest and many Thanks. So that *Erratum* was in some degree corrected.

But now another Difficulty came upon me, which I had never the least Reason to expect. Mr. Meredith's Father, who was to have paid for our Printing-House according to the Expectations given me, was able to advance only one Hundred Pounds, Currency, which had been paid, and a Hundred more was due to the Merchant; who grew impatient, and su'd us all. We gave Bail, but saw that if the Money could not be rais'd in time, the Suit must soon come to a Judgment and Execution, and our hopeful Prospects must with us be ruined, as the Press and Letters must be sold for Payment, perhaps at half price. In this Distress two true Friends whose Kindness I have never forgotten nor ever shall forget while I can remember anything, came to me separately unknown to each other, and, without any Application from me, offering each of them to advance me all the Money that should be necessary to enable me to take the whole Business upon myself if that should be practicable, but they did not like my continuing the Partnership with Meredith, who as they said was often seen drunk in the Streets, and playing at low Games in Alehouses, much to our Discredit. These two friends were *William Coleman* and *Robert Grace*.

I told them I could not propose a Separation while any Prospect remain'd of the Merediths fulfilling their Part of our Agreement. Because I thought myself under great Obligations to them for what they had done and would do if they could. But if they finally fail'd in their Performance, and our Partnership must be dissolv'd, I should then think myself at Liberty to accept the Assistance of my Friends. Thus the matter rested for some time. When I said to my Partner, perhaps your Father is dissatisfied at the Part you have undertaken in this Affair of ours, and is unwilling to advance for you and me what he would for you alone: If that is the Case, tell me, and I will resign the whole to you and go about my business. No says he, my Father has really been disappointed and is really unable; and I am unwilling to distress him farther. I see this is a Business I am not fit for. I was bred a Farmer, and it was a Folly in me to come to Town and put myself at 30 Years of Age an Apprentice to learn a new Trade. Many of our Welsh People are going to settle in North Carolina where Land is cheap: I am inclin'd to go with them, and follow my old Employment. You may find Friends to assist you. If you will take the Debts of the Company upon you, return to my Father the hundred Pound he has advanc'd, pay my little personal Debts, and give me Thirty Pounds and a new Saddle, I will relinquish the Partnership and leave the whole in your Hands. I agreed to this Proposal. It was drawn up in Writing, sign'd and seal'd immediately. I gave him what he demanded and he went soon after to Carolina; from whence he sent me next Year two long Letters, containing the best Account that had been given of that Country, the Climate, Soil, Husbandry, etc. for in those Matters he was very judicious. I printed them in the Papers, and they gave great Satisfaction to the Public.

As soon as he was gone, I recurr'd to my two Friends; and because I would not give an unkind Preference to either, I took half of what each had offered and I wanted of one, and half of the other; paid off the Company Debts, and went on with the Business in my own Name, advertising that the Partnership was dissolved. I think this was in or about the year 1729.

About this Time there was a Cry among the People for more Paper-Money, only 15,000 Pounds being extant in the Province and that soon to be sunk. The wealthy Inhabitants oppos'd any Addition, being against all Paper Currency, from an Apprehension that it would depreciate as it had done in New England to the Prejudice of all Creditors. We had discuss'd this point in our Junto, where I was on the Side of an Addition, being persuaded that the first small Sum struck in 1723 had done much good, by increasing the Trade, Employment, and Number of Inhabitants in the Province, since I now saw all the old Houses inhabited, and many new ones building, where as I remember'd well, that when I first walk'd about the Streets of Philadelphia, eating my Roll, I saw most of the Houses in Walnut Street between Second and Front Streets with Bills on their Doors, to be let; and many likewise in Chestnut Street, and other Streets; which made me then think the Inhabitants of the City were one after another deserting it. Our Debates possess'd me so fully of the Subject, that I wrote and printed an anonymous Pamphlet on it, entitled *The Nature and Necessity of a Paper Currency.* It was well receiv'd by the common People in general; but the Rich Men dislik'd it; for it increas'd and strengthen'd the Clamor for more Money; and they happening to have no Writers among them that were able to answer it, their Opposition slacken'd, and the Point was carried by a Majority in the House. My Friends there, who conceiv'd I had been of some Service, thought fit to reward me, by employing me in printing the Money, a very profitable Job, and a great Help to me. This was another Advantage gain'd by my being able to write. The Utility of this Currency became by Time and Experience so evident, as never afterwards to be much disputed, so that it grew soon to 55,000 Pounds, and in 1739 to 80,000 Pounds, since which it arose during War to upwards of 350,000 Pounds— Trade, Building and Inhabitants all the while increasing. Tho' I now think there are Limits beyond which the Quantity may be hurtful.

I soon after obtain'd thro' my Friend Hamilton, the Printing of the New Castle Paper Money, another profitable Job, as I then thought it; small Things appearing great to those in small Circumstances. And these to me were really great Advantages, as they were great Encouragements. He procured me also the Printing of the Laws and Votes of that Government which continu'd in my Hands as long as I follow'd that Business.

I now open'd a little Stationer's Shop. I had in it Blanks of all Sorts the correctest that ever appear'd among us, being assisted in that by my Friend

Breintnall; I had also Paper, Parchment, Chapmen's Books, etc. One Whitmarsh, a Compositor I had known in London, an excellent Workman now came to me and work'd with me constantly and diligently, and I took an Apprentice the Son of Aquila Rose. I began now gradually to pay off the Debt I was under for the Printing-House. In order to secure my Credit and Character as a Tradesman, I took care not only to be in *Reality* Industrious and frugal, but to avoid all *Appearances* of the Contrary. I dressed plainly; I was seen at no Places of idle Diversions; I never went out a-fishing or shooting; a Book, indeed, sometimes debauch'd me from my Work; but that was seldom, snug, and gave no Scandal: and to show that I was not above my Business, I sometimes brought home the Paper I purchas'd at the Stores, Thro' the Streets on a Wheelbarrow. Thus being esteeme'd an industrious thriving young Man, and paying duly for what I bought, the Merchants who imported Stationary solicited my Custom, others propos'd supplying me with Books, and I went on swimmingly. In the mean time Keimer's Credit and Business declining daily, he was at last forc'd to sell his Printing-House to satisfy his Creditors. He went to Barbados, and there lived some Years, in very poor Circumstances.

His Apprentice David Harry, whom I instructed while I work'd with him, set up in his Place at Philadelphia, having brought his Materials. I was at first apprehensive of a powerful Rival in Harry, as his Friends were very able, and had a good deal of Interest. I therefore propos'd a Partnership with him; which he, fortunately for me, rejected with Scorn. He was very proud, dress'd like a Gentleman, liv'd expensively, took much Diversion and Pleasure abroad, ran in debt, and neglected his Business, upon which all Business left him; and finding nothing to do, he follow'd Keimer to Barbados; taking the Printing-House with him. There this Apprentice employ'd his former Master as a Journeyman. They quarrel'd often. Harry went continually behind-hand and at length was forc'd to sell his Types and return to his Country Work in Pennsylvania. The Person that bought them employ'd Keimer to use them, but in a few years he died. There remain'd now no Competitor with me at Philadelphia, but the old one, Bradford, who was rich and easy, did a little Printing now and then by straggling Hands, but was not very anxious about the Business. However, as he kept the Post Office, it was imagined he had better Opportunities of obtaining News, his Paper was thought a better Distributer of Advertisements than mine, and therefore had many more, which was a profitable thing to him and a Disadvantage to me. For tho' I did indeed receive and send Papers by the Post, yet the public Opinion was otherwise; for what I did send was by Bribing the Riders who took them privately: Bradford being unkind enough to forbid it: which occasion'd some Resentment on my Part; and I thought so meanly of him for it, that when I afterwards came into his Situation, I took care never to imitate it.

I had hitherto continue'd to board with Godfrey who lived in Part of my House with his Wife and Children, and had one Side of the Shop for his Glazier's Business, tho' he work'd little, being always absorb'd in his Mathematics. Mrs. Godfrey projected a Match for me with a Relation's Daughter, took Opportunities of bringing us often together, till a serious Courtship on my Part ensu'd, the Girl being in herself very deserving. The old Folks encourag'd me by continual Invitations to Supper, and by leaving us together, till at length it was time to explain. Mrs. Godfrey manag'd our little Treaty. I let her know that I expected as much Money with their Daughter as would pay off my Remaining Debt for the Printing-House, which I believe was not then above a Hundred Pounds. She brought me Word they had no such Sum to spare. I said they might mortgage their House in the Loan Office. The Answer to this after some Days was, that they did not approve the Match; that on Enquiry of Bradford they had been inform'd the Printing Business was not a profitable one, the Types would soon be worn out and more wanted, that S. Keimer and D. Harry had fail'd one after the other, and I should probably soon follow them; and therefore I was forbidden the House, and the Daughter shut up.

Whether this was a real Change of Sentiment, or only Artifice, on a Supposition of our being too far engag'd in Affection to retract, and therefore that we should steal a Marriage, which would leave them it Liberty to give or withhold what they pleas'd, I know not: But I suspected the latter, resented it, and went no more. Mrs. Godfrey brought me afterwards some more favorable Accounts of their Disposition, and would have drawn me on again: But I declared absolutely my Resolution to have nothing more to do with that Family. This was resented by the Godfreys, we differ'd, and they removed, leaving me the whole House, and I resolved to take no more Inmates. But this Affair having turn'd my Thoughts to Marriage, I look'd round me, and made Overtures of Acquaintance in other Places; but soon found that the Business of a Printer being generally thought a poor one, I was not to expect Money with a Wife unless with such a one, as I should not otherwise think agreeable. In the mean time, that hard-to-be-govern'd Passion of Youth, had hurried me frequently into Intrigues with low Women that fell in my Way, which were attended with some Expense and great Inconvenience, besides a continual Risk to my Health by a Distemper which of all Things I dreaded, tho' by great good Luck I escaped it.

A friendly Correspondence as Neighbors and old Acquaintances, had continued between me and Mrs. Read's Family who all had a Regard for me from the time of my first Lodging in their House. I was often invited there and consulted in their Affairs, wherein I sometimes was of Service. I pitied poor Miss Read's unfortunate Situation, who was generally dejected, seldom cheerful, and avoided Company. I consider'd my Giddiness and Inconstancy when in London as in a great degree the Cause of her Unhappiness; tho' the Mother was good enough to think the Fault more her own than mine, as she had prevented our Marrying before I went thither, and persuaded the other Match in my Absence. Our mutual Affection was revived, but there were now great Objections to our Union. That Match was indeed look'd upon as invalid, a preceding Wife being said to be living in England; but this could not easily be prov'd, because of the Distance, etc. And tho' there was a Report of his Death, it was not certain. Then, tho' it should be true, he had left many Debts which his Successor might be call'd upon to pay. We ventured however, over all these Difficulties, and I took her to Wife Sept. 1, 1730. None of the Inconveniencies happened that we had apprehended, she prov'd a good and faithful Helpmate, assisted me much by attending the Shop, we throve together, and have ever mutually endeavour'd to make each other happy. Thus I corrected that great *Erratum* as well as I could.

About this Time our Club meeting, not at a Tavern, but in a little Room of Mr. Grace's set apart for that Purpose; a Proposition was made by me, that since our Books were often referr'd to in our Disquisitions upon the Queries, it might be convenient to us to have them all together where we met, that upon Occasion they might be consulted; and by thus clubbing our Books to a common Library, we should, while we lik'd to keep them together, have each of us the Advantage of using the Books of all the other Members, which would be nearly as beneficial as if each owned the whole. It was lik'd and agreed to, and we fill'd one End of the Room with such Books as we could best spare. The Number was not so great as we expected; and tho' they had been of great Use, yet some Inconveniencies occurring for want of due Care of them, the Collection after about a Year was separated, and each took his Books home again.

And now I set on foot my first Project of a public Nature, that for a Subscription Library. I drew up the Proposals, got them put into Form by our great Scrivener Brockden, and by the help of my Friends in the junto, procur'd Fifty Subscribers of 40 Shillings each to begin with and 10 Shillings a Year for 50 Years, the Term our Company was to continue. We afterwards obtain'd a Charter, the Company being increas'd to 100. This was the Mother of all the North American Subscription Libraries now so numerous. It is become a great thing itself, and continually increasing. These Libraries have improv'd the general Conversation of the Americans, made the common Tradesmen and Farmers as intelligent as most Gentlemen from other Countries, and perhaps have contributed in some degree to the Stand so generally made throughout the Colonies in Defense of their Privileges.

Memo.

Thus far was written with the Intention express'd in the Beginning and therefore contains several little family Anecdotes of no Importance to others. What follows was written many Years after in compliance with the Advice contain'd in these Letters, and accordingly intended for the Public. The Affairs of the Revolution occasion'd the Interruption.

[Part Two]

Continuation of the Account of my Life. Begun at Passy, 1784.

[. . .] Not having any Copy here of what is already written, I know not whether an Account is given of the means I used to establish the Philadelphia public Library, which from a small Beginning is now become so considerable, though I remember to have come down to near the Time of that Transaction, 1730. I will therefore begin here, with an Account of it, which may be struck out if found to have been already given.

At the time I establish'd myself in Pennsylvania, there was not a good Bookseller's Shop in any of the Colonies to the Southward of Boston. In New York and Philadelphia the Printers were indeed Stationers, they sold only Paper, etc., Almanacs, Ballads, and a few common School Books. Those who lov'd Reading were oblig'd to send for their Books from England. The Members of the Junto had each a few. We had left the Alehouse where we first met, and hired a Room to hold our Club in. I propos'd that we should all of us bring our Books to that Room, where they would not only be ready to consult in our Conferences, but become a common Benefit, each of us being at Liberty to borrow such as he wish'd to read at home. This was accordingly done, and for some time contented us. Finding the Advantage of this little Collection, I propos'd to render the Benefit from Books more common by commencing a Public Subscription Library. I drew a Sketch of the Plan and Rules that would be necessary, and got a skillful Conveyancer Mr. Charles Brockden to put the whole in Form of Articles of Agreement to be subscribed, by which each Subscriber engag'd to pay a certain Sum down for the first Purchase of Books and an annual Contribution for increasing them. So few were the Readers at that time in Philadelphia, and the Majority of us so poor, that I was not able with great Industry to find more than Fifty Persons, mostly young Tradesmen, willing to pay down for this purpose Forty shillings each, and Ten Shillings per Annum. On this little Fund we began. The Books were imported. The Library was open one Day in the Week for lending them to the Subscribers, on their Promissory Notes to pay Double the Value if not duly returned. The Institution soon manifested its Utility, was imitated by other Towns and in other Provinces, the Libraries were augmented by Donations, Reading became fashionable, and our People having no public Amusements to divert their Attention from Study became better acquainted with Books, and in a few Years were observ'd by Strangers to be better instructed and more intelligent than People of the same Rank generally are in other Countries.

When we were about to sign the above-mentioned Articles, which were to be binding on us, our Heirs, etc. for fifty Years, Mr. Brockden, the Scrivener, said to us, "You are young Men, but it is scarce probable that any of you will live to see the Expiration of the Term fix'd in this Instrument." A Number of us, however, are yet living: But the Instrument was after a few Years rendered null by a Charter that incorporated and gave Perpetuity to the Company.

The Objections, and Reluctances I met with in Soliciting the Subscriptions, made me soon feel the Impropriety of presenting oneself as the Proposer of any useful Project that might be suppos'd to raise one's Reputation in the smallest degree above that of one's Neighbors, when one has need of their Assistance to accomplish that Project. I therefore put myself as much as I could out of sight, and stated it as a Scheme of *a Number of Friends,* who had requested me to go about and propose it to such as they thought Lovers of Reading. In this way my Affair went on more smoothly, and I ever after practic'd it on such Occasions; and from my frequent Successes, can heartily recommend it. The present little Sacrifice of your Vanity will afterwards be amply repaid. If it remains a while uncertain to whom the Merit belongs, someone more vain than yourself will be encourag'd to claim it, and then even Envy will be dispos'd to do you Justice, by plucking those assum'd Feathers, and restoring them to their right Owner.

This Library afforded me the Means of Improvement by constant Study, for which I set apart an Hour or two each Day; and thus repair'd in some Degree the Loss of the Learned Education my Father once intended for me. Reading was the only Amusement I allow'd myself. I spent no time in Taverns, Games, or Frolics of any kind. And my Industry in my Business continu'd as indefatigable as it was necessary. I was in debt for my Printing-House, I had a young Family coming on to be educated, and I had to contend with for Business two Printers who were establish'd in the Place before me. My Circumstances however grew daily easier: my original Habits of Frugality continuing. And My Father having among his Instructions to me when a Boy, frequently repeated a Proverb of Solomon, *"Seest thou a Man diligent in his Calling, he shall stand before Kings, he shall not stand before mean Men."* I from thence consider'd Industry as a Means of obtaining Wealth and Distinction, which encourag'd me: tho' I did not think that I should ever literally stand before Kings, which however has since happened; for I have stood before five, and even had the honor of sitting down with one, the King of Denmark, to Dinner.

We have an English Proverb that says,

He that would thrive
Must ask his Wife,

it was lucky for me that I had one as much dispos'd to Industry and Frugality as myself. She assisted me cheerfully in my Business, folding and stitching Pamphlets, tending Shop, purchasing old Linen Rags for the Paper-makers, etc., etc. We kept no idle Servants, our Table was plain and simple, our Furniture of the cheapest. For instance my Breakfast was a long time Bread and Milk, (no Tea,) and I ate it out of a twopenny earthen Porringer with a Pewter Spoon. But mark how Luxury will enter Families, and make a Progress, in Spite of Principle. Being Call'd one Morning to Breakfast, I found it in a China Bowl with a Spoon of Silver. They had been bought for me without my Knowledge by my Wife, and had cost her the enormous Sum of three and twenty Shillings, for which she had no other Excuse or Apology to make, but that she thought her Husband deserv'd a Silver Spoon and China Bowl as well as any of his Neighbors. This was the first Appearance of Plate and China in our House, which afterwards in a Course of Years as our Wealth increas'd, augmented gradually to several Hundred Pounds in Value.

I had been religiously educated as a Presbyterian; and tho' some of the Dogmas of that Persuasion, such as the Eternal Decrees of God, Election, Reprobation, etc. appear'd to me unintelligible, others doubtful, and I early absented myself from the Public Assemblies of the Sect, Sunday being my Studying-Day, I never was without some religious Principles; I never doubted, for instance, the Existence of the Deity, that he made the World, and govern'd it by his Providence; that the most acceptable Service of God was the doing Good to Man; that our Souls are immortal; and that all Crime will be punished and Virtue rewarded either here or hereafter; these I esteem'd the Essentials of every Religion, and being to be found in all the Religions we had in our Country I respected them all, tho' with different degrees of Respect as I found them more or less mix'd with other Articles which without any Tendency to inspire, promote or confirm Morality, serv'd principally to divide us and make us unfriendly to one another. This Respect to all, with an Opinion that the worst had some good Effects, induc'd me to avoid all Discourse that might tend to lessen the good Opinion another might have of his own Religion; and as our Province increas'd in People and new Places of worship were continually wanted, and generally erected by voluntary Contribution, my Mite for such purpose, whatever might be the Sect, was never refused.

Tho' I seldom attended any Public Worship, I had still an Opinion of its Propriety, and of its Utility when rightly conducted, and I regularly paid my annual Subscription for the Support of the only Presbyterian Minister or Meeting we had in Philadelphia. He us'd to visit me sometimes as a Friend, and admonish me to attend his Administrations, and I was now and then prevail'd on to do so, once for five Sundays successively. Had he been, *in my Opinion*, a good Preacher perhaps I might have continued, notwithstanding the occasion I had for the Sunday's Leisure in my Course of Study: But his Discourses were chiefly either polemic Arguments, or Explications of the peculiar Doctrines of our Sect, and were all to me very dry, uninteresting and unedifying, since not a single moral Principle was inculcated or enforc'd, their Aim seeming to be rather to make us Presbyterians than good Citizens. At length he took for his Text that Verse of the 4th Chapter of Philippians, *Finally, Brethren, Whatsoever Things are true, honest, just, pure, lovely, or of good report, if there be any virtue, or any praise, think on these Things;* and I imagin'd in a Sermon on such a Text, we could not miss of having some Morality: But he confin'd himself to five Points only as meant by the Apostle, viz. 1. Keeping holy the Sabbath Day. 2. Being diligent in Reading the Holy Scriptures. 3. Attending duly the Public Worship. 4. Partaking of the Sacrament. 5. Paying a due Respect to God's Ministers.—These might be all good Things, but as they were not the kind of good Things that I expected from that Text, I despaired of ever meeting with them from any other, was disgusted, and attended his Preaching no more. I had some Years before compos'd a little Liturgy or Form of Prayer for my own private Use, viz, in 1728, entitled, *Articles of Belief and Acts of Religion.* I return'd to the Use of this, and went no more to the public Assemblies. My Conduct might be blameable, but I leave it without attempting farther to excuse it, my present purpose being to relate Facts, and not to make Apologies for them.

It was about this time that I conceiv'd the bold and arduous Project of arriving at moral Perfection. I wish'd to live without committing any Fault at anytime; I would conquer all that either Natural Inclination, Custom, or Company might lead me into. As I knew, or thought I knew, what was right and wrong, I did not see why I might not *always* do the one and avoid the other. But I soon found I had undertaken a Task of more Difficulty than I had imagined: While my Care was employ'd in guarding against one Fault, I was often surpris'd by another. Habit took the Advantage of Inattention. Inclination was sometimes too strong for Reason. I concluded at length, that the mere speculative Conviction that it was our Interest to be completely virtuous, was not sufficient to prevent our Slipping, and that the contrary Habits must be broken and good Ones acquired and established, before we can have any Dependence on a steady uniform Rectitude of Conduct. For this purpose I therefore contriv'd the following Method.

In the various Enumerations of the moral Virtues I had met with in my Reading, I found the Catalogue more or less numerous, as different Writers included more or fewer Ideas under the same Name. Temperance, for Example, was by some confin'd to Eating and Drinking, while by others it was extended to mean the moderating every other Pleasure, Appetite, Inclination or Passion, bodily or mental, even to our Avarice and Ambition. I propos'd to myself, for the sake of Clearness, to use rather more Names with fewer Ideas annex'd to each, than a few Names with more Ideas; and I included after Thirteen Names of Virtues all that at that time occurr'd to me as necessary or desirable, and annex'd to each a short Precept, which fully express'd the Extent I gave to its Meaning.

These Names of Virtues with their Precepts were

1. TEMPERANCE.

Eat not to Dulness. Drink not to Elevation.

2. SILENCE.

Speak not but what may benefit others or yourself. Avoiding trifling Conversation.

3. ORDER.

Let all your Things have their Places. Let each Part of your Business have its Time.

4. RESOLUTION.

Resolve to perform what you ought. Perform without fail what you resolve.

5. FRUGALITY.

Make no Expense but to do good to others or yourself: i.e. Waste nothing.

6. INDUSTRY.

Lose no Time, Be always employ'd in someting useful. Cut off all unnecessary Actions.

7. SINCERITY.

Use no hurtful Deceit. Think innocently and justly; and, if you speak; speak accordingly.

8. JUSTICE.

Wrong none, by doing Injuries or omitting the Benefits that are your Duty.

9. MODERATION.

Avoid Extremes. Forbear resenting Injuries so much as you think they deserve.

10. CLEANLINESS.

Tolerate no Uncleanness in Body, Clothes or Habitation.

11. TRANQUILITY.

Be not disturbed at Trifles, or at Accidents common or unavoidable.

12. CHASTITY.

Rarely use Venery but for Health or Offspring; never to Dulness, Weakness, or the Injury of your own or another's Peace or Reputation.

13. HUMILITY.

Imitate Jesus and Socrates.

My intention being to acquire the *Habitude* of all these Virtues, I judg'd it would be well not to distract my Attention by attempting the whole at once, but to fix it on one of them at a time, and when I should be Master of that, then to proceed to another, and so on till I should have gone thro' the thirteen. And as the previous Acquisition of some might facilitate the Acquisition of certain others, I arrang'd them with that View as they stand above. *Temperance* first, as it tends to procure that Coolness and Clearness of Head, which is so necessary where constant Vigilance was to be kept up, and Guard maintained, against the unremitting Attraction of ancient Habits, and the Force of perpetual Temptations. This being acquir'd and establish'd, *Silence* would be more easy, and my Desire being to gain Knowledge at the same time that I improv'd in Virtue, and considering that in Conversation it was obtain'd rather by the Use of the Ears than of the Tongue, and therefore wishing to break a Habit I was getting into of Prattling, Punning and Joking, which only made me acceptable to trifling Company, I gave *Silence* the second Place. This, and the next, *Order*, I expected would allow me more Time for attending to my Project and my Studies; RESOLUTION once become habitual, would keep me firm in my Endeavors to obtain all the subsequent Virtues; *Frugality* and *Industry*, by freeing me from my remaining Debt, and producing Affluence and Independence would make more easy the Practice of *Sincerity* and *Justice*, etc., etc. Conceiving then that agreeable to the Advice of Pythagoras in his Golden Verses, daily Examination would be necessary, I contriv'd the following Method for conducting that Examination. [. . .]

I made a little Book in which I allotted a Page for each of the Virtues. I rul'd each Page with red Ink so as to have seven Columns, one for each Day of the Week, marking each Column with a Letter for the Day. I cross'd these Columns with thirteen red Lines, marking the Beginning of each Line with the first Letter of one of the Virtues, on which Line and in its proper Column I might mark by a little black Spot every Fault I found upon Examination, to have been committed respecting that Virtue upon that Day.

I determined to give a Week's strict Attention to each of the Virtues successively. Thus in the first Week my great Guard was to avoid every the least Offence against Temperance, leaving the other Virtues to their ordinary Chance, only marking every Evening the Faults of the Day. Thus if in the first Week I could keep my first Line marked T clear of Spots, I suppos'd the Habit of that Virtue so much strengthen'd and its opposite weaken'd, that I might venture extending my Attention to include the next, and for the following Week keep both Lines clear of Spots. Proceeding thus to the last, I could go thro' a Course complete in Thirteen Weeks, and four Courses in a Year. And like him who having a Garden to weed, does not attempt to eradicate all the bad Herbs at once, which would exceed his Reach and his Strength, but works on one of the Beds at a time, and having accomplish'd the first proceeds to a second; so I should have, (I hoped) the encouraging Pleasure of seeing on my Pages the Progress I made in Virtue, by clearing successively my Lines of their Spots, till in the End by a Number of Courses, I should be happy in viewing a clean Book after a thirteen Weeks' daily Examination.

This my little Book had for its Motto these Lines from *Addison's Cato*,

Here will I hold: If there is a Pow'r above us,
(And that there is, all Nature cries aloud
Thro' all her Works) he must delight in Virtue,
And that which he delights in must be happy.

Another from Cicero.

O Vitæ Philosophia Dux! O Virtutum indagatrix, expultrixque vitiorum! Unus dies bene, et ex preceptis tuis actus, peccanti immortalitati est anteponendus.[3]

---

3. ["Philosophy, life's guide! She who seeks virtue, she who drives vice away. Better one day, driven by virtue, than an eternity set before our sin." In *Benjamin Franklin's Autobiography* (Norton Critical Editions), edited by J. A. Leo Lemay and P. M. Zall (New York: W. W. Norton, 1985), it is translated as "O Philosophy, guide of life! O teacher of virtue and corrector of vice. One day of virtue is better than an eternity of vice."]

Another from the Proverbs of Solomon speaking of Wisdom or Virtue;

> Length of Days is in her right hand, and in her Left Hand Riches and Honors; Her Ways are Ways of Pleasantness, and all her Paths are Peace.
>
> III, 16, 17

And conceiving God to be the Fountain of Wisdom, I thought it right and necessary to solicit his Assistance for obtaining it; to this End I form'd the following little Prayer, which was prefix'd to my Tables of Examination, for daily Use.

> *O Powerful Goodness! bountiful Father! merciful Guide! Increase in me that Wisdom which discovers my truest Interests; Strengthen my Resolutions to perform what that Wisdom dictates. Accept my kind Offices to thy other Children, as the only Return in my Power for thy continual Favors to me.*

I us'd also sometimes a little Prayer which I took from Thomson's Poems, viz.

> *Father of Light and Life, thou Good supreme,*
> *O teach me what is good, teach me thy self!*
> *Save me from Folly, Vanity and Vice,*
> *From every low Pursuit, and fill my Soul*
> *With Knowledge, conscious Peace, and Virtue pure,*
> *Sacred, substantial, never fading Bliss!*

The Precept of *Order* requiring *that every Part of my Business should have its allotted Time,* one Page in my little Book contain'd the following Scheme of Employment for the Twenty-four Hours of a natural Day.

I enter'd upon the Execution of this Plan for Self-examination, and continu'd it with occasional Intermissions for some time. I was surpris'd to find myself so much fuller of Faults than I had imagined, but I had the Satisfaction of seeing them diminish. To avoid the Trouble of renewing now and then my little Book, which by scraping out the Marks on the Paper of old Faults to make room for new Ones in a new Course, became full of Holes: I transferr'd my Tables and Precepts to the Ivory Leaves of a Memorandum Book, on which the Lines were drawn with red Ink that made a durable Stain, and on those Lines I mark'd my Faults with a black Lead Pencil, which Marks I could easily wipe out with a wet Sponge. After a while I went thro' one Course only in a Year, and afterwards only one in several Years; till at length I omitted them entirely, being employ'd in Voyages and Business abroad with a Multiplicity of Affairs, that interfered. But I always carried my little Book with me.

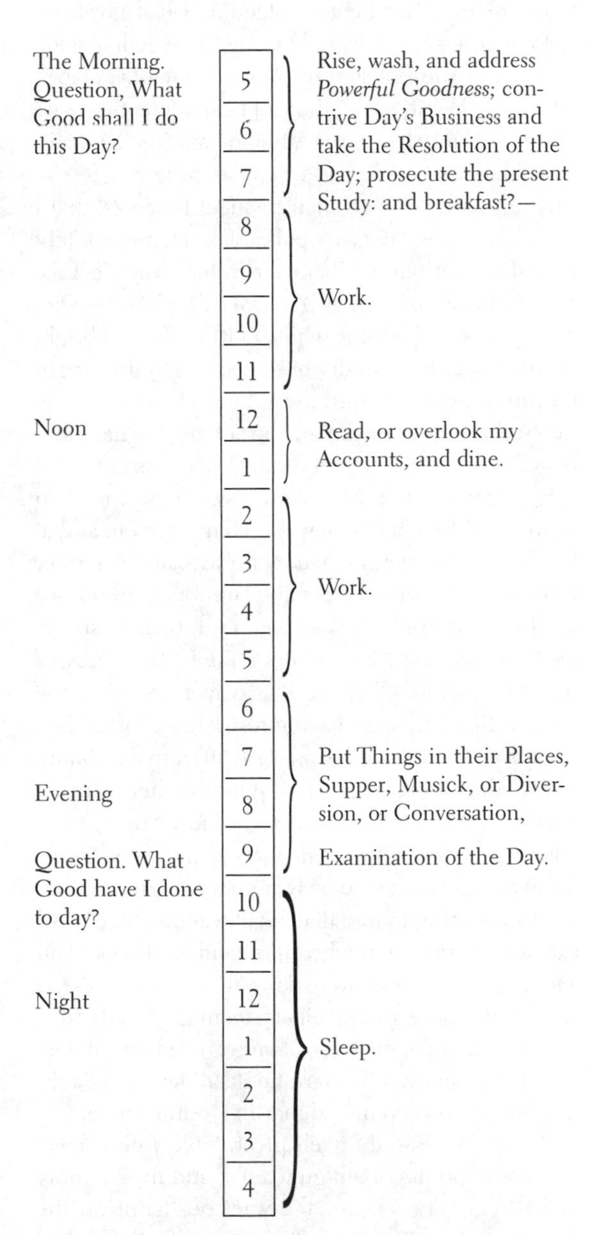

The Morning. Question, What Good shall I do this Day?	5 6 7	Rise, wash, and address *Powerful Goodness;* contrive Day's Business and take the Resolution of the Day; prosecute the present Study: and breakfast?—
	8 9 10 11	Work.
Noon	12 1	Read, or overlook my Accounts, and dine.
	2 3 4 5	Work.
Evening	6 7 8 9	Put Things in their Places, Supper, Musick, or Diversion, or Conversation, Examination of the Day.
Question. What Good have I done to day? Night	10 11 12 1 2 3 4	Sleep.

My Scheme of Order, gave me the most Trouble, and I found, that tho' it might be practicable where a Man's Business was such as to leave him the Disposition of his Time, that of a Journeyman Printer for instance, it was not possible to be exactly observ'd by a Master, who must mix with the World, and often receive People of Business at their own Hours. *Order* too, with regard to Places for Things, Papers, etc. I found extremely difficult to acquire. I had not been early accustomed to it, and having an exceeding good Memory; I was not so sensible of the Inconvenience attending Want of Method. This Article therefore cost me so much painful Attention and my Faults in it vex'd me so much, and I made so little Progress in Amendment, and had such frequent Relapses, that I was almost ready to give up the Attempt, and content myself with a faulty Character in that respect. Like the Man who in buying an Axe of a Smith my Neighbor, desired to have the whole of its Surface as bright as the Edge; the Smith consented to grind it bright for him if he would turn the Wheel. He turn'd while the Smith press'd the broad Face of the Axe hard and heavily on the Stone, which made the Turning of it very fatiguing. The Man came every now and then from the Wheel to see how the Work went on; and at length would take his Axe as it was without farther Grinding. No, says the Smith, Turn on, turn on; we shall have it bright by and by; as yet 'tis only speckled. Yes, says the Man; but—*I think I like a speckled Axe best.*—And I believe this may have been the Case with many who having for want of some such Means as I employ'd found the Difficulty of obtaining good, and breaking bad Habits, in other Points of Vice and Virtue, have given up the Struggle, and concluded that *a speckled Axe was best.* For something that pretended to be Reason was every now and then suggesting to me, that such extreme Nicety as I exacted of myself might be a kind of Foppery in Morals, which if it were known would make me ridiculous; that a perfect Character might be attended with the Inconvenience of being envied and hated; and that a benevolent Man should allow a few Faults in himself, to keep his Friends in Countenance.

In Truth I found myself incorrigible with respect to *Order*; and now I am grown old, and my Memory bad, I feel very sensibly the want of it. But on the whole, tho' I never arrived at the Perfection I had been so ambitious of obtaining, but fell far short of it, yet I was by the Endeavour made a better and a happier Man than I otherwise should have been, if I had not attempted it; As those who aim at perfect Writing by imitating the engraved Copies, tho' they never reach the wish'd for Excellence of those Copies, their Hand is mended by the Endeavour, and is tolerable while it continues fair and legible.

And it may be well my Posterity should be informed, that to this little Artifice, with the Blessing of God, their Ancestor ow'd the constant Felicity of his Life down to his 79th Year in which this is written. What Reverses may attend the Remainder is in the Hand of Providence: But if they arrive, the Reflection on past Happiness enjoy'd ought to help his Bearing them with more Resignation. To *Temperance* he ascribes his long-continu'd Health, and what is still left to him of a good Constitution. To *Industry* and *Frugality* the early Easiness of his Circumstances, and Acquisition of his Fortune, with all that Knowledge which enabled him to be an useful Citizen, and obtain'd for him some Degree of Reputation among the Learned. To *Sincerity* and *Justice* the Confidence of his Country, and the honorable Employs it conferr'd upon him. And to the joint Influence of the whole Mass of the Virtues, even in their imperfect State he was able to acquire them, all that Evenness of Temper, and that Cheerfulness in Conversation which makes his Company still sought for, and agreeable even to his younger Acquaintance. I hope therefore that some of my Descendants may follow the Example and reap the Benefit.

It will be remark'd that, tho' my Scheme was not wholly without Religion there was in it no Mark of any of the distinguishing Tenets of any particular Sect. I had purposely avoided them; for being fully persuaded of the Utility and Excellency of my Method, and that it might be serviceable to People in all Religions, and intending some time or other to publish it, I would not have anything in it that should prejudice anyone of any Sect against it. I purposed writing a little Comment on each Virtue, in which I would have shown the Advantages of possessing it,[4] and the Mischiefs attending its opposite Vice; and I

4. "Nothing so likely to make a Man's Fortune as Virtue."

should have called my Book the ART *of Virtue,* because it would have shown the *Means and Manner* of obtaining Virtue; which would have distinguish'd it from the mere Exhortation to be good, that does not instruct and indicate the Means; but is like the Apostle's Man of verbal Charity, who only, without showing to the Naked and the Hungry how or where they might get Clothes or Victuals, exhorted them to be fed and clothed. *James* 11, 15, 16.

But it so happened that my Intention of writing and publishing this Comment was never fulfilled. I did indeed, from time to time put down short Hints of the Sentiments, Reasonings, etc. to be made use of in it, some of which I have still by me: But the necessary close Attention to private Business in the earlier part of Life, and public Business since, have occasioned my postponing it. For it being connected in my Mind with a *great and extensive Project* that required the whole Man to execute, and which an unforeseen Succession of Employs prevented my attending to, it has hitherto remain'd unfinish'd.

In this Piece it was my Design to explain and enforce this Doctrine, that vicious Actions are not hurtful because they are forbidden, but forbidden because they are hurtful, the Nature of Man alone consider'd: That it was therefore every one's Interest to be virtuous, who wish'd to be happy even in this World. And I should from this Circumstance (there being always in the World a Number of rich Merchants, Nobility, States and Princes, who have need of honest Instruments for the Management of their Affairs, and such being so rare) have endeavoured to convince young Persons, that no Qualities were so likely to make a poor Man's Fortune as those of Probity and Integrity.

My List of Virtues contain'd at first but twelve: But a Quaker Friend having kindly inform'd me that I was generally thought proud; that my Pride show'd itself frequently in Conversation; that I was not content with being in the right when discussing any Point, but was overbearing and rather insolent; of which he convinc'd me by mentioning several Instances; I determined endeavouring to cure myself if I could of this Vice or Folly among the rest, and I added *Humility* to my List, giving an extensive Meaning to the Word. I cannot boast of much Success in acquiring the *Reality* of this Virtue; but I had a good deal with regard to the *Appearance* of it. I made it a Rule to forbear all direct Contradiction to the Sentiments of others, and all positive Assertion of my own. I even forbid myself, agreeable to the old Laws of our Junto, the Use of every Word or Expression in the Language that imported a fix'd Opinion; such as *certainly, undoubtedly,* etc. and I adopted instead of them, I *conceive,* I *apprehend,* or *I imagine* a thing to be so or so, or it so appears to me at present. When another asserted something that I thought an Error, I denied myself the Pleasure of contradicting him abruptly, and of showing immediately some Absurdity in his Proposition; and in answering I began by observing that in certain Cases or Circumstances his Opinion would be right, but that in the present case there *appear'd* or *seem'd* to me some Difference, etc. I soon found the Advantage of this Change in my Manners. The Conversations I engag'd in went on more pleasantly. The modest way in which I propos'd my Opinions, procur'd them a readier Reception and less Contradiction; I had less Mortification when I was found to be in the wrong, and I more easily prevail'd with others to give up their Mistakes and join with me when I happen'd to be in the right. And this Mode, which I at first put on, with some violence to natural Inclination, became at length so easy and so habitual to me, that perhaps for these Fifty Years past no one has ever heard a dogmatical Expression escape me. And to this Habit (after my Character of Integrity) I think it principally owing, that I had early so much Weight with my Fellow Citizens, when I proposed new Institutions, or Alterations in the old; and so much Influence in public Councils when I became a Member. For I was but a bad Speaker, never eloquent, subject to much Hesitation in my choice of Words, hardly correct in Language, and yet I generally carried my Points.

In reality there is perhaps no one of our natural Passions so hard to subdue as *Pride.* Disguise it, struggle with it, beat it down, stifle it, mortify it as much as one pleases, it is still alive, and will every now and then peep out and show itself. You will see it perhaps often in this History. For even if I could conceive that I had completely overcome it, I should probably be proud of my Humility.

Thus far written at Passy, 1784.

[Part Three]

I am now about to write at home, August 1788, but cannot have the help expected from my Papers, many of them being lost in the War. I have however found the following.

Having mentioned *a great and extensive Project* which I had conceiv'd, it seems proper that some Account should be here given of that Project and its Object. Its first Rise in my Mind appears in the following little Paper, accidentally preserv'd, viz.

OBSERVATIONS on my Reading
History in Library, May 9, 1731

"That the great Affairs of the World, the Wars, Revolutions, etc. are carried on and effected by Parties.

"That the View of these Parties is their present general Interest, or what they take to be such.

"That the different Views of these different Parties, occasion all Confusion.

"That while a Party is carrying on a general Design, each Man has his particular private Interest in View.

"That as soon as a Party has gain'd its general Point, each Member becomes intent upon his particular Interest, which thwarting others, breaks that Party into Divisions, and occasions more Confusion.

"That few in Public Affairs act from a mere View of the Good of their Country, whatever they may pretend; and tho' their Actings bring real Good to their Country, yet Men primarily consider'd that their own and their Country's Interest was united, and did not act from a Principle of Benevolence.

"That fewer still in public Affairs act with a View to the Good of Mankind.

"There seems to me at present to be great Occasion for raising an united Party for Virtue, by forming the Virtuous and good Men of all Nations into a regular Body, to be govern'd by suitable good and wise Rules, which good and wise Men may probably be more unanimous in their Obedience to, than common People are to common Laws.

"I at present think, that whoever attempts this aright, and is well qualified, cannot fail of pleasing God, and of meeting with Success.

B.F."

Revolving this Project in my Mind, as to be undertaken hereafter when my Circumstances should afford me the necessary Leisure, I put down from time to time on Pieces of Paper such Thoughts as occur'd to me respecting it. Most of these are lost; but I find one purporting to be the Substance of an intended Creed, containing as I thought the Essentials of every known Religion, and being free of everything that might shock the Professors of any Religion. It is express'd in these Words, viz.

"That there is one God who made all things.

"That he governs the World by his Providence.

"That he ought to be worshipped by Adoration, Prayer and Thanksgiving.

"But that the most acceptable Service of God is doing Good to Man.

"That the Soul is immortal.

"And that God will certainly reward Virtue and punish Vice either here or hereafter."

My Ideas at that time were, that the Sect should be begun and spread at first among young and single Men only; that each Person to be initiated should not only declare his Assent to such Creed, but should have exercis'd himself with the Thirteen Weeks' Examination and Practice of the Virtues as in the before-mention'd Model; that the Existence of such a Society should be kept a Secret till it was become considerable, to prevent Solicitations for the Admission of improper Persons; but that the Members should each of them search among his Acquaintance for ingenuous well-disposed Youths, to whom with prudent Caution the Scheme should be gradually communicated: That the Members should engage to afford their Advice, Assistance and Support to each other in promoting one another's Interest, Business and Advancement in Life: That for Distinction we should be call'd the Society of the *Free and Easy;* Free, as being by the general Practice and Habit of the Virtues, free from the Dominion of Vice, and particularly by the Practice of Industry and Frugality, free from Debt, which exposes a Man to Confinement and a Species of Slavery to his Creditors. This is as much as I can now recollect of the Project, except that I communicated it in part to two young Men, who adopted it with some Enthusiasm. But my then narrow Circumstances, and the Necessity I was under of sticking close to my Business, occasion'd my Postponing the farther Prosecution of it at that time, and my multifarious Occupations public and private induc'd me to continue Postponing, so that it has been omitted till I have no longer Strength or Activity left sufficient for such an Enterprise: Tho I am still of Opinion that it was a practicable Scheme, and might have been very useful, by forming a great Number of good Citizens: And I was not discourag'd by the seeming Magnitude of the Undertaking, as I have always thought that one Man of tolerable Abilities may work great Changes, and accomplish great Affairs among Mankind, if he first forms a good plan, and, cutting off all Amusements or other Employments that would divert his Attention, makes the Execution of that same Plan his sole Study and Business.

In 1732 I first published my Almanac, under the Name of *Richard Saunders*; it was continu'd by me about 25 Years, commonly call'd *Poor Richard's Almanac.* I endeavour'd to make it both entertaining and useful, and it accordingly came to be in such Demand that I reap'd considerable Profit from it, vending annually near ten Thousand. And observing that it was generally read, scarce any Neighborhood in the Province being without it, I consider'd it as a proper Vehicle for conveying Instruction among the common People, who bought scarce any other Books. I therefore filled all the little Spaces that occur'd between the Remarkable Days in the Calendar, with Proverbial Sentences, chiefly such as inculcated Industry and Frugality, as the Means of procuring Wealth and thereby securing Virtue, it being more difficult for a Man in Want to act always honestly, as (to use here one of those Proverbs) *it is hard for an empty Sack to stand upright.* These Proverbs, which contained the Wisdom of many Ages and Nations, I assembled and form'd into a connected Discourse prefix'd to the Almanac of 1757, as the Harangue of a wise old Man to the People attending an Auction. The bringing all these scatter'd Counsels thus into a Focus, enabled them to make greater Impression. The Piece being universally approved was copied in all the Newspapers of the Continent, reprinted in Britain on a Broadside to be stuck up in Houses, two Translations were made of it in French, and great Numbers bought by the Clergy and Gentry to distribute gratis among their poor Parishioners and Tenants. In Pennsylvania, as it discouraged useless Expense in foreign Superfluities, some thought it had its share of Influence in producing that growing Plenty of Money which was observable for several Years after its Publication.

I consider'd my Newspaper also as another Means of communicating Instruction, and in that View frequently reprinted in it Extracts from the Spectator and other moral Writers, and sometimes publish'd little Pieces of my own which had been first compos'd for Reading in our Junto. Of these are a Socratic Dialogue tending to prove, that, whatever might be his Parts and Abilities, a vicious Man could not property be called a Man of Sense. And a Discourse on Self-denial, showing that Virtue was not Secure, till its Practice became a Habitude, and was free from the Opposition of contrary Inclinations. These may be found in the Papers about the beginning of 1735. In the Conduct of my Newspaper I carefully excluded all Libelling and Personal Abuse, which is of late Years become so disgraceful to our Country. Whenever I was solicited to insert anything of that kind, and the Writers pleaded as they generally did, the Liberty of the Press, and that a Newspaper was like a Stage Coach in which any one who would pay had a Right to a Place, my Answer was, that I would print the Piece separately if desired, and the Author might have as many Copies as he pleased to distribute himself, but that I would not take upon me to spread his Detraction, and that having contracted with my Subscribers to furnish them with what might be either useful or entertaining, I could not fill their Papers with private Altercation in which they had no Concern without doing them manifest Injustice. Now many of our Printers make no scruple of gratifying the Malice of Individuals by false Accusations of the fairest Characters among ourselves, augmenting Animosity even to the producing of Duels, and are moreover so indiscrete as to print scurrilous Reflections on the Government of neighboring States, and even on the Conduct of our best national Allies, which may be attended with the most pernicious Consequences. These Things I mention as a Caution to young Printers, and that they may be encouraged not to pollute their Presses and disgrace their Profession by such infamous Practices, but refuse steadily; as they may see by my Example, that such a Course of Conduct will not on the whole be injurious to their Interests.

In 1733, I sent one of my Journeymen to Charleston South Carolina where a Printer was wanting. I furnish'd him with a Press and Letters, of an Agreement of Partnership, by which I was to receive One Third of the Profits of the Business, paying One Third of the Expense. He was a Man of Learning and honest, but ignorant in Matters of Account; and tho' he sometimes made me Remittances, I could get no Account from him, nor any satisfactory State of our Partnership while he lived. On his Decease, the Business was continued by his Widow, who being born and bred in Holland, where as I have been inform'd the Knowledge of Accounts makes a Part of Female Education, she not only sent me as clear a State as she could find of the Transactions past, but continu'd to account with the greatest Regularity and Exactitude every Quarter afterwards; and manag'd the Business with such Success that she not only brought up reputably a Family of Children, but at the Expiration of the Term was able to purchase of me the Printing-House and establish her Son in it. I mention this Affair chiefly for the Sake of recommending that Branch of Education for our young Females, as likely to be of more Use to them and their Children in Case of Widowhood than either Music or Dancing, by preserving them from Losses by Imposition of crafty Men, and enabling them to continue perhaps a profitable mercantile house with establish'd Correspondence till a Son is grown up fit to undertake and go on with it, to the lasting Advantage and enriching of the Family.

About the Year 1734, there arrived among us from Ireland, a young Presbyterian Preacher named Hemphill, who delivered with a good Voice, and apparently extempore, most excellent Discourses, which drew together considerable Numbers of different Persuasions, who join'd in admiring them. Among the rest I became one of his constant Hearers, his Sermons pleasing me as they had little of the dogmatical kind, but inculcated strongly the Practice of Virtue, or what in the religious Style are called Good Works. Those however, of our Congregation, who considered themselves as orthodox Presbyterians, disapprov'd his Doctrine, and were join'd by most of the old Clergy, who arraign'd him of Heterodoxy before the Synod, in order to have him silenc'd. I became his zealous Partisan, and contributed all I could to raise a Party in his Favor; and we combated for him a while with some Hopes of Success. There was much Scribbling pro and con upon the Occasion; and finding that tho' an elegant Preacher he was but a poor Writer, I lent him my Pen and wrote for him two or three Pamphlets, and one Piece in the Gazette of April 1735. Those Pamphlets, as is generally the Case with controversial Writings, tho' eagerly read at the time, were soon out of vogue, and I question whether a single copy of them now exists.

During the Contest an unlucky Occurrence hurt his Cause exceedingly. One of our Adversaries having heard him preach a Sermon that was much admired, thought he had somewhere read that Sermon before, or at least a part of it. On Search he found that Part quoted at length, in one of the British Reviews, from a Discourse of Dr. Forster's. This Detection gave many of our Party Disgust, who accordingly abandoned his Cause, and occasion'd our more speedy Discomfiture in the Synod. I stuck by him, however, as I rather approv'd his giving us good Sermons compos'd by others, than bad ones of his own Manufacture; tho' the latter was the Practice of our common Teachers. He afterwards acknowledg'd to me that none of those he preach'd were his own; adding that his Memory was such as enabled him to retain and repeat any Sermon after one Reading only. On our Defeat he left us, in search elsewhere of better Fortune, and I quitted the Congregation, never joining it after, tho' I continu'd many Years my Subscription for the Support of its Ministers. [. . .]

I began now to turn my thoughts a little to public Affairs, beginning however with small Matters. The City Watch was one of the first Things that I conceiv'd to want Regulation. It was managed by the Constables of the respective Wards in Turn. The Constable warn'd a Number of Housekeepers to attend him for the Night. Those who chose never to attend paid him Six Shillings a Year to be excus'd, which was suppos'd to be for hiring Substitutes; but was in Reality much more than was necessary for that purpose, and made the Constableship a Place of Profit. And the Constable for a little Drink often got such Ragamuffins about him as a Watch, that reputable Housekeepers did not choose to mix with. Walking the Rounds too was often neglected, and most of the Night spent in Tippling. I thereupon wrote a Paper to be read in Junto, representing these Irregularities, but insisting more particularly on the

Inequality of this Six Shilling Tax of the Constables, respecting the Circumstances of those who paid it, since a poor Widow Housekeeper, all whose Property to be guarded by the Watch did not perhaps exceed the Value of Fifty Pounds, paid as much as the wealthiest Merchant who had Thousands of Pounds worth of Goods in his Stores. On the whole I proposed as a more effectual Watch, the Hiring of proper Men to serve constantly in that Business; and as a more equitable Way of supporting the Charge, the levying a Tax that should be proportion'd to Property. This Idea being approv'd by the Junto, was communicated to the other Clubs, but as arising in each of them. And tho' the plan was not immediately carried into Execution, yet by preparing the Minds of People for the Change, it paved the Way for the Law obtained a few Years after, when the Members of our Clubs were grown into more Influence.

About this time I wrote a Paper (first to be read in Junto, but it was afterward publish'd) on the different Accidents and Carelessnesses by which houses were set on fire, with Cautions against them, and Means proposed of avoiding them. This was much spoken of as a useful Piece, and gave rise to a Project, which soon followed it, of forming a Company for the more ready Extinguishing of Fires, and mutual Assistance in Removing and Securing the Goods when in danger. Associates in this Scheme were presently found, amounting to Thirty. Our Articles of Agreement oblig'd every Member to keep always in good Order and fit for Use, a certain Number of Leather Buckets, with strong Bags and Baskets (for packing and transporting of Goods), which were to be brought to every Fire; and we agreed to meet once a Month and spend a social Evening together, in discoursing, and communicating such Ideas as occurred to us upon the Subject of Fires as might be useful in our Conduct on such Occasions. The Utility of this Institution soon appeared, and many more desiring to be admitted than we thought convenient for one Company, they were advised to form another; which was accordingly done. And this went on, one new Company being formed after another, till they became so numerous as to include most of the Inhabitants who were Men of Property; and now at the time of my Writing this, tho' upward of Fifty Years since its Establishment, that which I first formed, called the Union Fire Company, still subsists and flourishes, tho' the first Members are all deceas'd but myself and one who is older by a Year than I am. The small Fines that have been paid by Members for Absence at the Monthly Meetings have been apply'd to the Purchase of Fire Engines, Ladders, Firehooks, and other useful Implements for each Company, so that I question whether there is a City in the World better provided with the Means of putting a Stop to beginning Conflagrations; and in fact since these Institutions, the City has never lost by Fire more than one or two Houses at a time, and the Flames have often been extinguish'd before the House in which they began has been half-consumed.

In 1739 arriv'd among us from England the Rev. Mr. Whitefield, who had made himself remarkable there as an itinerant Preacher. He was at first permitted to preach in some of our Churches; but the Clergy taking a Dislike to him, soon refus'd him their Pulpits, and he was oblig'd to preach in the Fields. The Multitudes of all Sects and Denominations that attended his Sermons were enormous and it was matter of Speculation to me who was one of the Number, to observe the extraordinary Influence of his Oratory on his Hearers, and how much they admir'd and respected him, notwithstanding his common Abuse of them, by assuring them that they were naturally *half Beasts and half Devils.* It was wonderful to see the Change soon made in the Manners of our Inhabitants; from being thoughtless or indifferent about Religion, it seem'd as if all the World were growing Religious; so that one could not walk thro' the Town in an Evening without Hearing Psalms sung in different Families of every Street. And it being found inconvenient to assemble in the open Air, subject to its Inclemencies, the Building of a House to meet in was no sooner propos'd and Persons appointed to receive Contributions, but sufficient Sums were soon receiv'd to procure the Ground and erect the Building which was 100 feet long and 70 broad, about the Size of Westminster Hall; and the Work was carried on with such Spirit as to be finished in a much shorter time than could have been expected. Both House and Ground were vested in Trustees, expressly for the Use of any Preacher of any religious Persuasion who might desire to say something to the People of Philadelphia, the Design in building not being to accommodate any particular Sect, but the Inhabitants in general, so that even if the Mufti of Constantinople were to send a Missionary to preach Mahometanism to us, he would find a Pulpit at his Service.

Mr. Whitefield, in leaving us, went preaching all the Way thro' the Colonies to Georgia. The Settlement of that Province had lately been begun; but instead of being made with hardy industrious Husbandmen accustomed to Labor, the only People fit for such an Enterprise, it was with Families of broken Shopkeepers and other insolvent Debtors, many of indolent and idle habits, taken out of the Jails, who, being set down in the Woods, unqualified for clearing Land, and unable to endure the Hardships of a new Settlement, perished in Numbers, leaving many helpless Children unprovided for. The Sight of their miserable Situation inspir'd the benevolent Heart of Mr. Whitefield with the Idea of building an Orphan House there, in which they might be supported and educated. Returning northward he preach'd up this Charity, and made large Collections;—for his Eloquence had a wonderful Power over the Hearts and Purses of his Hearers, of which I myself was an Instance. I did not disapprove of the Design, but as Georgia was then destitute of Materials and Workmen, and it was proposed to send them from Philadelphia at a great Expense, I thought it would have been better to have built the House here and brought the Children to it. This I advis'd, but he was resolute in his first Project, rejected my Counsel, and I therefore refus'd to contribute.

I happened soon after to attend one of his Sermons, in the Course of which I perceived he intended to finish with a Collection, and I silently resolved he should get nothing from me. I had in my Pocket a Handful of Copper Money, three or four silver Dollars, and five Pistoles in Gold. As he proceeded I began to soften, and concluded to give the Coppers. Another Stroke of his Oratory made me asham'd of that, and determin'd me to give the Silver; and he finish'd so admirably, that I emptied my Pocket wholly into the Collector's Dish, Gold and all. At this Sermon there was also one of our Club, who being of my Sentiments respecting the Building in Georgia, and suspecting a Collection might be intended, had by Precaution emptied his Pockets before he came from home; towards the Conclusion of the Discourse however, he felt a strong Desire to give, and apply'd to a Neighbour who stood near him to borrow some Money for the Purpose. The Application was unfortunately to perhaps the only Man in the Company who had the firmness not to be affected by the Preacher. His Answer was, *At any other time, Friend Hopkinson, I would lend to thee freely; but not now; for thee seems to be out of thy right Senses.*

Some of Mr. Whitefield's Enemies affected to suppose that he would apply these Collections to his own private Emolument; but I, who was intimately acquainted with him, (being employ'd in printing his Sermons and Journals, etc.) never had the least Suspicion of his Integrity, but am to this day decidedly of Opinion that he was in all his Conduct, a perfectly *honest Man.* And methinks my Testimony in his Favour ought to have the more Weight, as we had no religious Connection. He us'd indeed sometimes to pray for my Conversion, but never had the Satisfaction of believing that his Prayers were heard. Ours was a mere civil Friendship, sincere on both Sides, and lasted to his Death.

The following Instance will show something of the Terms on which we stood. Upon one of his Arrivals from England at Boston, he wrote to me that he should come soon to Philadelphia, but knew not where he could lodge when there, as he understood his old friend and Host Mr. Benezet was remov'd to Germantown. My Answer was; You know my house, if you can make shift with its scanty Accommodations, you will be most heartily welcome. He replied, that if I made that kind Offer for Christ's sake, I should not miss of a Reward.—And I return'd, *Don't let me be mistaken; it was not for Christ's sake, but for your sake.* One of our common Acquaintance jocosely remark'd that knowing it to be the custom of the Saints, when they received any favour, to shift the Burden of the Obligation from off their own Shoulders, and place it in Heaven, I had contriv'd to fix it on Earth.

The last time I saw Mr. Whitefield was in London, when he consulted me about his Orphan House Concern, and his Purpose of appropriating it to the Establishment of a College.

He had a loud and clear Voice, and articulated his Words and Sentences so perfectly that he might be heard and understood at a great Distance, especially as his Auditors, however numerous, observ'd the most exact Silence. He preach'd one Evening from the

Top of the Court House Steps, which are in the Middle of Market Street, and on the West Side of Second Street which crosses it at right angles. Both Streets were fill'd with his Hearers to a considerable Distance. Being among the hindmost in Market Street, I had the Curiosity to learn how far he could be heard, by retiring backwards down the Street towards the River, and I found his Voice distinct till I came near Front Street, when some Noise in that Street, obscur'd it. Imagining then a Semicircle, of which my Distance should be the Radius, and that it were fill'd with Auditors, to each of whom I allow'd two square feet, I computed that he might well be heard by more than Thirty Thousand. This reconcil'd me to the Newspaper Accounts of his having preach'd to 25,000 People in the Fields, and to the ancient Histories of Generals haranguing whole Armies, of which I had sometimes doubted.

By hearing him often I came to distinguish easily between Sermons newly compos'd, and those which he had often preach'd in the Course of his Travels. His Delivery of the latter was so improv'd by frequent Repetitions, that every Accent, every Emphasis, every Modulation of Voice, was so perfectly well turn'd and well plac'd, that without being interested in the Subject, one could not help being pleas'd with the Discourse, a Pleasure of much the same kind with that receiv'd from an excellent Piece of Music. This is an Advantage itinerant Preachers have over those who are stationary: as the latter cannot well improve their Delivery of a Sermon by so many Rehearsals.

His Writing and Printing from time to time gave great Advantage to his Enemies. Unguarded Expressions and even erroneous Opinions delivered in Preaching might have been afterwards explain'd, or qualified by supposing others that might have accompanied them; or they might have been denied; but *litera scripta manet.* Critics attack'd his Writings violently, and with so much Appearance of Reason as to diminish the Number of his Votaries, and prevent their Increase: So that I am of Opinion, if he had never written anything he would have left behind him a much more numerous and important Sect. And his Reputation might in that Case have been still growing, even after his Death; as there being nothing of his Writing on which to found a Censure; and give him a lower Character, his Proselytes would be left at Liberty to feign for him as great a Variety of Excellencies, as their enthusiastic Admiration might wish him to have possessed. [. . .]

I had on the whole abundant reason to be satisfied with my being established in Pennsylvania. There were however two things that I regretted: There being no Provision for Defense, nor for a complete Education of Youth. No Militia nor any College. I therefore in 1743, drew up a Proposal for establishing an Academy. [. . .]

Indeed I had some Cause to believe, that the Defense of the Country was not disagreeable to any of them, provided they were not requir'd to assist in it. And I found that a much greater Number of them than I could have imagined, tho' against offensive War, were clearly for the defensive, Many Pamphlets *pro and con* were publish'd on the Subject, and some by good Quakers in favor of Defense, which I believe convinc'd most of their younger People. [. . .]

The honorable and learned Mr. Logan, who had always been of that Sect, was one who wrote an Address to them, declaring his Approbation of defensive War, and supporting his Opinion by many strong Arguments: He put into my Hands Sixty Pounds, to be laid out in Lottery Tickets for the Battery, with Directions to apply what Prizes might be drawn wholly to that Service. He told me the following Anecdote of his old Master William Penn respecting Defense. He came over from England, when a young Man, with that Proprietary, and as his Secretary. It was War Time, and their Ship was chas'd by an armed Vessel suppos'd to be an Enemy. Their Captain prepar'd for Defense, but told William Penn and his Company of Quakers, that he did not expect their Assistance, and they might retire into the Cabin; which they did, except James Logan, who chose to stay upon Deck, and was quarter'd to a Gun. The suppos'd Enemy prov'd a Friend; so there was no Fighting. But when the Secretary went down to communicate the Intelligence, William Penn rebuk'd him severely for staying upon Deck and undertaking to assist in defending the Vessel, contrary to the Principles of *Friends,* especially as it had not been required by the Captain. This Reproof being before all the Company, piqu'd the Secretary, who answer'd, *I being thy Servant, why did thee not order me to come down: but thee was willing enough that I should stay and help to fight the Ship when thee thought there was Danger.*

My being many Years in the Assembly, the Majority of which were constantly Quakers, gave me frequent Opportunties of seeing the Embarrassment given them by their Principle against War, whenever Application was made to them by Order of the Crown to grant Aids for military Purposes. They were unwilling to offend Government on the one hand, by a direct Refusal, and their Friends the Body of Quakers on the other, by a Compliance contrary to their Principles. Hence a Variety of Evasions to avoid Complying, and Modes of disguising the Compliance when it became unavoidable. The common Mode at last was to grant Money under the Phrase of its being *for the King's Use*, and never to enquire how it was applied. But if the Demand was not directly from the Crown, that Phrase was found not so proper, and some other was to be invented. As when Powder was wanting, (I think it was for the Garrison at Louisburg,) and the Government of New England solicited a Grant of some from Pennsylvania, which was much urg'd on the House by Governor Thomas, they could not grant Money to buy Powder, because that was an Ingredient of War, but they voted an Aid to New England, of Three Thousand Pounds, to be put into the hands of the Governor, and appropriated it for the Purchasing of Bread, Flour, Wheat, *or other Grain*. Some of the Council desirous of giving the House still farther Embarrassment, advis'd the Governor not to accept Provision, as not being the Thing he had demanded. But he replied, "I shall take the Money, for I understand very well their Meaning; *Other Grain*, is Gunpowder," which he accordingly bought; and they never objected to it.

It was in Allusion to this Fact, that when in our Fire Company we feared the Success of our Proposal in favor of the Lottery, and I had said to my friend Mr. Syng, one of our Members, if we fail, let us move the Purchase of a Fire Engine with the Money; the Quakers can have no Objection to that: and then if you nominate me, and I you, as a Committee for that purpose, we will buy a great Gun, which is certainly a *Fire-Engine:* I see, says he, you have improv'd by being so long in the Assembly; your equivocal Project would be just a Match for their Wheat *or other grain.*

These Embarrassments that the Quakers suffer'd from having establish'd and publish'd it as one of their Principles, that no kind of War was lawful, and which being once published, they could not afterwards, however they might change their minds, easily get rid of, reminds me of what I think a more prudent Conduct in another Sect among us; that of the Dunkers. I was acquainted with one of its Founders, Michael Welfare, soon after it appear'd. He complain'd to me that they were grievously calumniated by the Zealots of other Persuasions, and charg'd with abominable Principles and Practices to which they were utter Strangers. I told him this had always been the case with new Sects; and that to put a Stop to such Abuse, I imagin'd it might be well to publish the Articles of their Belief and the Rules of their Discipline. He said that it had been propos'd among them, but not agreed to, for this Reason; "When we were first drawn together as a Society, says he, it had pleased God to enlighten our Minds so far, as to see that some Doctrines which we once esteemed Truths were Errors, and that others which we had esteemed Errors were real Truths. From time to time he has been pleased to afford us farther Light, and our Principles have been improving, and our Errors diminishing. Now we are not sure that we are arriv'd at the End of this Progression, and at the Perfection of Spiritual or Theological Knowledge; and we fear that if we should once print our Confession of Faith, we should feel ourselves as if bound and confin'd by it, and perhaps be unwilling to receive farther Improvement; and our Successors still more so, as conceiving what we their Elders and Founders had done, to be something sacred, never to be departed from."

This Modesty in a Sect is perhaps a singular Instance in the History of Mankind, every other Sect supposing itself in Possession of all Truth, and that those who differ are so far in the Wrong: Like a Man travelling in foggy Weather: Those at some Distance before him on the Road he sees wrapped up in the Fog, as well as those behind him, and also the People in the Fields on each side; but near him all appears clear.—Tho' in truth he is as much in the Fog as any of them. To avoid this kind of Embarrassment the Quakers have of late Years been gradually declining the public Service in the Assembly and in the Magistracy. Choosing rather to quit their Power than their Principle. [. . .]

PHILLIS WHEATLEY

Selected Poems (1770–1776)

On Being Brought from Africa to America

'Twas mercy brought me from my pagan land,
Taught my benighted soul to understand
That there's a God, that there's a Saviour too:
Once I redemption neither sought nor knew.
Some view our sable race with scornful eye,
"Their colour is a diabolic die."
Remember, Christians, Negros, black as Cain,
May be refined, and join th' angelic train.

On the Death of the Rev. Mr. George Whitefield

HAIL, happy saint, on thine immortal throne,
Possest of glory, life, and bliss unknown;
We hear no more the music of thy tongue,
Thy wonted auditories cease to throng.
Thy sermons in unequall'd accents flow'd,
And ev'ry bosom with devotion glow'd;
Thou didst in strains of eloquence refin'd
Inflame the heart, and captivate the mind.
Unhappy we the setting sun deplore,
So glorious once, but ah! it shines no more.

Behold the prophet in his tow'ring flight!
He leaves the earth for heav'n's unmeasur'd height,
And worlds unknown receive him from our sight.
There *Whitefield* wings with rapid course his way,
And sails to *Zion* through vast seas of day.
Thy pray'rs, great saint, and thine incessant cries
Have pierc'd the bosom of thy native skies.
Thou moon hast seen, and all the stars of light,
How he has wrestled with his God by night.
He pray'd that grace in ev'ry heart might dwell,
He long'd to see *America* excell;
He charg'd its youth that ev'ry grace divine
Should with full lustre in their conduct shine;
That Saviour, which his soul did first receive,
The greatest gift that ev'n a God can give,
He freely offer'd to the num'rous throng,
That on his lips with list'ning pleasure hung.

"Take him, ye wretched, for your only good,
"Take him ye starving sinners, for your food;
"Ye thirsty, come to this life-giving stream,
"Ye preachers, take him for your joyful theme;
"Take him my dear *Americans*, he said,
"Be your complaints on his kind bosom laid:
"Take him, ye *Africans*, he longs for you,
"*Impartial Saviour* is his title due:
"Wash'd in the fountain of redeeming blood,
"You shall be sons, and kings, and priests to God."

Great *Countess*,[1] we *Americans* revere
Thy name, and mingle in thy grief sincere;
New England deeply feels, the *Orphans* mourn,
Their more than father will no more return.

But, though arrested by the hand of death,
Whitefield no more exerts his lab'ring breath,
Yet let us view him in th' eternal skies,
Let ev'ry heart to this bright vision rise;
While the tomb safe retains its sacred trust,
Till life divine re-animates his dust.

To S. M., a Young African Painter, on Seeing His Works

To show the lab'ring bosom's deep intent,
And thought in living characters to paint,
When first thy pencil did those beauties give,
And breathing figures learnt from thee to live,
How did those prospects give my soul delight,

1. [The Countess of Huntington, an ardent follower of Whitefield.]

A new creation rushing on my sight?
Still, wond'rous youth! each noble path pursue,
On deathless glories fix thine ardent view:
Still may the painter's and the poet's fire
To aid thy pencil, and thy verse conspire!
And may the charms of each seraphic theme
Conduct thy footsteps to immortal fame!
High to the blissful wonders of the skies
Elate thy soul, and raise thy wishful eyes.
Thrice happy, when exalted to survey
That splendid city, crown'd with endless day,
Whose twice six gates on radiant hinges ring:
Celestial Salem blooms in endless spring.

Calm and serene thy moments glide along,
nd may the muse inspire each future song!
Still, with the sweets of contemplation bless'd,
May peace with balmy wings your soul invest!
But when these shades of time are chas'd away,
And darkness ends in everlasting day,
On what seraphic pinions shall we move,
And view the landscapes in the realms above?
There shall thy tongue in heav'nly murmurs flow,
And there my muse with heav'nly transport glow:
No more to tell of *Damon*'s tender sighs,
Or rising radiance of *Aurora*'s eyes,
For nobler themes demand a nobler strain,
And purer language on th' ethereal plain.
Cease, gentle muse! the solemn gloom of night
Now seals the fair creation from my sight.

To His Excellency General Washington

Celestial choir! enthron'd in realms of light;
Columbia's scenes of glorious toils I write.
While freedom's cause her anxious breast alarms,
She flashes dreadful in refulgent arms.
See mother earth her offspring's fate bemoan,
And nations gaze at scenes before unknown!
See the bright beams of heaven's revolving light
Involved in sorrows and the veil of night!

The goddess comes, she moves divinely fair,
Olive and laurel binds her golden hair:
Wherever shines this native of the skies,
Unnumber'd charms and recent graces rise.

Muse! bow propitious while my pen relates
How pour her armies through a thousand gates,
As when Eolus heaven's fair face deforms,
Enwrapp'd in tempest and a night of storms;
Astonish'd ocean feels the wild uproar,
The refluent surges beat the sounding shore;
Or thick as leaves in Autumn's golden reign,
Such, and so many, moves the warrior's train.

In bright array they seek the work of war,
Where high unfurl'd the ensign waves in air.
Shall I to Washington their praise recite?
Enough thou know'st them in the fields of fight.
Thee, first in peace and honor—we demand
The grace and glory of thy martial band.
Fam'd for thy valor, for thy virtues more,
Hear every tongue thy guardian aid implore!

One century scarce perform'd its destined round,
When Gallic powers Columbia's fury found;
And so may you, whoever dares disgrace
The land of freedom's heaven-defended race!
Fix'd are the eyes of nations on the scales,
For in their hopes Columbia's arm prevails.
Anon Britannia droops the pensive head,
While round increase the rising hills of dead.
Ah! cruel blindness to Columbia's state!
Lament thy thirst of boundless power too late.

Proceed, great chief, with virtue on thy side,
Thy ev'ry action let the goddess guide.
A crown, a mansion, and a throne that shine,
With gold unfading, WASHINGTON! be thine.

JOHN MARSHALL

Marbury v. Madison (1803)

Mr. Chief Justice MARSHALL delivered the opinion of the Court.

[. . .] In the order in which the Court has viewed this subject, the following questions have been considered and decided.

1. Has the applicant a right to the commission he demands?
2. If he has a right, and that right has been violated, do the laws of his country afford him a remedy?
3. If they do afford him a remedy, is it a mandamus issuing from this court? [. . .]

It is [. . .] the opinion of the Court,

1. That, by signing the commission of Mr. Marbury, the President of the United States appointed him a justice of peace, for the county of Washington in the District of Columbia; and that the seal of the United States, affixed thereto by the Secretary of State, is conclusive testimony of the verity of the signature, and of the completion of the appointment; and that the appointment conferred on him a legal right to the office for the space of five years.

2. That, having this legal title to the office, he has a consequent right to the commission; a refusal to deliver which, is a plain violation of that right, for which the laws of this country afford him a remedy.

It remains to be enquired whether,

3. He is entitled to the remedy for which applies. This depends on,

1. The nature of the writ applied for and
2. The power of this court.

[. . .] This, then, is a plain case for mandamus, either to deliver the commission, or a copy of it from the record; and it only remains to be enquired, whether it can issue from this court.

The act to establish the judicial courts of the United States authorizes the Supreme Court "to issue writs of mandamus in cases warranted by the principles and usages of law, to any courts appointed, or persons holding office, under the authority of the United States."

The Secretary of State, being a person holding an office under the authority of the United States, is precisely within the letter of the description and if this court is not authorized to issue a writ of mandamus to such an officer, it must be because the law is unconstitutional, and therefore absolutely incapable of conferring the authority, and assigning the duties which its words purport to confer and assign.

The Constitution vests the whole judicial power of the United States in one supreme court, and such inferior courts as Congress shall, from time to time, ordain and establish. This power is expressly extended to all cases arising under the laws of the United States; and, consequently, in some form, may be exercised over the present case; because the right claimed is given by a law of the United States.

In the distribution of this power it is declared that "the Supreme Court shall have original jurisdiction in all cases affecting ambassadors, other public ministers and consuls, and those in which a state shall be a party. In all other cases, the Supreme Court shall have appellate jurisdiction."

It has been insisted at the bar, that, as the original grant of jurisdiction to the Supreme and inferior courts, is general, and the clause assigning original jurisdiction to the Supreme Court contains no negative or restrictive words, the power remains to the legislature to assign original jurisdiction to that court in other cases than those specified in the article which has been recited; provided those cases belong to the judicial power of the United States.

If it had been intended to leave it in the discretion of the legislature to apportion the judicial power between the Supreme and inferior courts according to the will of that body, it would certainly have been useless to have proceeded further than to have defined the judicial power, and the tribunals in which it should be vested. The subsequent part of the section is mere surplusage, is entirely without meaning. If Congress remains at liberty to give this court appellate jurisdiction, where the Constitution has declared their jurisdiction shall be original; and original jurisdiction where the Constitution has declared it shall be appellate, the distribution of jurisdiction made in the Constitution is form without substance.

Affirmative words are often, in their operation, negative of other objects than those affirmed; and in this case, a negative or exclusive sense must be given to them, or they have no operation at all.

It cannot he presumed that any clause in the Constitution is intended to be without effect; and, therefore, such a construction is inadmissible unless the words require it. [. . .]

To enable this court then to issue a mandamus, it must be shown to be an exercise of appellate jurisdiction, or to be necessary to enable them to exercise appellate jurisdiction.

It has been stated at the bar that the appellate jurisdiction may be exercised in a variety of forms, and that, if it be the will of the legislature that a mandamus should be used for that purpose, that will must be obeyed. This is true, yet the jurisdiction must be appellate, not original.

It is the essential criterion of appellate jurisdiction that it revises and corrects the proceedings in a cause already instituted, and does not create that cause. Although, therefore, a mandamus may be directed to courts, yet to issue such a writ to an officer for the delivery of a paper is in effect the same as to sustain an original action for that paper, and, therefore, seems not to belong to appellate, but to original jurisdiction. Neither is it necessary, in such a case as this, to enable the court to exercise its appellate jurisdiction.

The authority, therefore, given to the Supreme Court by the act establishing the judicial courts of the United States, to issue writs of mandamus to public officers, appears not to be warranted by the Constitution; and it becomes necessary to inquire whether a jurisdiction so conferred can be exercised.

The question, whether an act repugnant to the Constitution can become the law of the land, is a question deeply interesting to the United States; but, happily, not of an intricacy proportioned to its interest. It seems only necessary to recognize certain principles, supposed to have been long and well established, to decide it.

That the people have an original right to establish, for their future government, such principles as, in their opinion, shall most conduce to their own happiness is the basis on which the whole American fabric had been erected. The exercise of this original right is a very great exertion; nor can it, nor ought it, to be frequently repeated. The principles, therefore, so established, are deemed fundamental. And as the authority from which they proceed is supreme, and can seldom act, they are designed to be permanent.

This original and supreme will organizes the government, and assigns to different departments their respective powers. It may either stop here, or establish certain limits not to be transcended by those departments.

The government of the United States is of the latter description. The powers of the legislature are defined and limited; and that those limits may not be mistaken, or forgotten, the Constitution is written. To what purpose are powers limited, and to what purpose is that limitation committed to writing, if these limits may, at any time, be passed by those intended to be restrained? The distinction between a government with limited and unlimited powers is abolished if those limits do not confine the persons on whom they are imposed, and if acts prohibited and acts allowed are of equal obligation. It is a proposition too plain to be contested, that the Constitution controls any legislative act repugnant to it; or, that the legislature may alter the Constitution by an ordinary act.

Between these alternatives there is no middle ground. The Constitution is either a superior paramount law, unchangeable by ordinary means, or it is on a level with ordinary legislative acts, and, like other acts, is alterable when the legislature shall please to alter it.

If the former part of the alternative be true, then a legislative act contrary to the Constitution is not law: if the latter part be true, then written constitutions are absurd attempts on the part of the people to limit a power in its own nature illimitable.

Certainly all those who have framed written constitutions contemplate them as forming the fundamental and paramount law of the nation, and consequently, the theory of every such government must be, that an act of the legislature, repugnant to the constitution, is void.

This theory is essentially attached to a written constitution, and is, consequently, to be considered by this court as one of the fundamental principles of our society. It is not therefore to be lost sight of in the further consideration of this subject.

If an act of the legislature, repugnant to the Constitution, is void, does it, notwithstanding its invalidity, bind the courts, and oblige them to give it effect? Or, in other words, though it be not law, does it constitute a rule as operative as if it was a law? This would be to overthrow in fact what was established in theory; and would seem at first view, an absurdity too gross to be insisted on. It shall, however, receive a more attentive consideration.

It is emphatically the province and duty of the judicial department to say what the law is. Those who apply the rule to particular cases must, of necessity, expound and interpret that rule. If two laws conflict with each other, the courts must decide on the operation of each.

So if a law be in opposition to the Constitution; if both the law and the constitution apply to a particular case, so that the court must either decide that case conformably to the law, disregarding the Constitution; or conformably to the Constitution, disregarding the law; the court must determine which of these conflicting rules governs the case. This is of the very essence of judicial duty.

If, then, the courts are to regard the Constitution, and the Constitution is superior to any ordinary act of the legislature, the Constitution, and not such ordinary act, must govern the case to which they both apply.

Those, then, who controvert the principle that the Constitution is to be considered, in court, as a paramount law, are reduced to the necessity of maintaining that courts must close their eyes on the Constitution, and see only the law.

This doctrine would subvert the very foundation of all written constitutions. It would declare that an act which, according to the principles and theory of our government, is entirely void, is yet, in practice, completely obligatory. It would declare that if the legislature shall do what is expressly forbidden, such act, notwithstanding the express prohibition, is in reality effectual. It would be giving to the legislature a practical and real omnipotence, with the same breath which professes to restrict their powers within narrow limits. It is prescribing limits and declaring that those limits may be passed at pleasure.

That it thus reduces to nothing what we have deemed the greatest improvement on political institutions—a written constitution—would of itself be sufficient, in America, where written constitutions have been viewed with so much reverence, for rejecting the construction. But the peculiar expressions of the Constitution of the United States furnish additional arguments in favor of its rejection.

The judicial power of the United States is extended to all cases arising under the Constitution.

Could it be the intention of those who gave this power to say that, in using it, the Constitution should not be looked into? That a case arising under the Constitution should be decided without examining the instrument under which it rises?

This is too extravagant to be maintained.

In some cases then, the Constitution must be looked into by the judges. And if they can open it at all, what part of it are they forbidden to read or to obey?

There are many other parts of the Constitution which serve to illustrate this subject.

It is declared that "no tax or duty shall be laid on articles exported from any state." Suppose a duty on the export of cotton, of tobacco, or of flour; and a suit instituted to recover it. Ought judgment to be rendered in such a case? Ought the judges to close their eyes on the Constitution, and see only the law?

The Constitution declares that "no bill of attainder or ex post facto law shall be passed."

If, however, such a bill should be passed and a person should be prosecuted under it; must the court condemn to death those victims who the Constitution endeavours to preserve?

"No person," says the Constitution, "shall be convicted of treason unless on the testimony of two witnesses to the same overt act, or on confession in open court."

Here the language of the Constitution is addressed especially to the courts. It prescribes, directly for them, a rule of evidence not to be departed from. If the legislature should change that rule, and declare one witness, or a confession out of court, sufficient for conviction, must the constitutional principle yield to the legislative act?

From these, and many other selections which might be made, it is apparent that the framers of the Constitution contemplated that instrument as a rule for the government of courts, as well as of the legislature.

Why otherwise does it direct the judges to take an oath to support it? This oath certainly applies in an especial manner to their conduct in their official character. How immoral to impose it on them, if they were to be used as the instruments, and the knowing instruments, for violating what they swear to support?

The oath of office, too, imposed by the legislature, is completely demonstrative of the legislative opinion on this subject. It is in these words: "I do solemnly swear that I will administer justice without respect to persons, and do equal right to the poor and to the rich; and that I will faithfully and impartially discharge all the duties incumbent on me as according to the best of my abilities and understanding agreeably to the Constitution and laws of the United States."

Why does a judge swear to discharge his duties agreeably to the Constitution of the United States, if that Constitution forms no rule for his government? If it is closed upon him, and cannot be inspected by him?

If such be the real state of things, this is worse than solemn mockery. To prescribe, or take this oath, becomes equally a crime.

It is also not entirely unworthy of observation that, in declaring what shall be the supreme law of the land, the Constitution itself is first mentioned; and not the laws of the United States generally, but those only which shall he made in pursuance of the Constitution, have that rank.

Thus, the particular phraseology of the Constitution of the United States confirms and strengthens the principle, supposed to be essential to all written constitutions, that a law repugnant to the Constitution is void; and that courts, as well as other departments, are bound by that instrument.

The rule must be discharged.

THOMAS JEFFERSON*

Letter to John Adams (October 28, 1813)

Monticello

Dear Sir—According to the reservation between us, of taking up one of the subjects of our correspondence at a time, turn to your letters of Aug. 16. and Sep. 2. [. . .]

For I agree with you that there is a natural aristocracy among men. The grounds of this are virtue and talents. Formerly bodily powers gave place among the *aristoi*. But since the invention of gunpowder has armed the weak as well as the strong with missile death, bodily strength, like beauty, good humor, politeness and other accomplishments, has become but an auxiliary ground of distinction. There is also an artificial aristocracy founded on wealth and birth, without either virtue or talents; for with these it would belong to the first class. The natural aristocracy I consider as the most precious gift of nature for the instruction, the trusts, and government of society. And indeed it would have been inconsistent in creation to have formed man for the social state, and not to have provided virtue and wisdom enough to manage the concerns of the society. May we not even say that that form of government is the best which provides the most effectually for a pure selection of these natural *aristoi* into the offices of government? The artificial aristocracy is a mischievous ingredient in government, and provision should be made to prevent its ascendancy. On the question, What is the best provision, you and I differ; but we differ as rational friends, using the free exercise of our own reason, and mutually indulging its errors. *You* think it best to put the Pseudo-*aristoi* into a separate chamber of legislation where they may be hindered from doing mischief by their coordinate branches, and where also they may be a protection to wealth against the Agrarian and plundering enterprises of the Majority of the people. I think that to give them power in order to prevent them from doing mischief, is arming them for it, and increasing instead of remedying the evil. For if the coordinate branches can arrest their action, so may they that of the coordinates. Mischief may be done negatively as well as positively. Of this a cabal in the Senate of the U.S. has furnished many proofs. Nor do I believe them necessary to protect the wealthy; because enough of these will find their way into every branch of the legislation to protect themselves. From 15 to 20 legislatures of our own, in action for 30 years past, have proved that no fears of an equalisation of property are to be apprehended from them.

I think the best remedy is exactly that provided by all our constitutions, to leave to the citizens the free election and separation of the *aristoi* from the pseudo-*aristoi*, of the wheat from the chaff. In general they will elect the real good and wise. In some instances, wealth may corrupt, and birth blind them; but not in sufficient degree to endanger the society. [. . .]

With respect to Aristocracy, we should further consider that, before the establishment of the American states, nothing was known to History but the Man of the old world, crouded within limits either small or overcharged, and steeped in the vices which that situation generates. A government adapted to such men would be one thing; but a very different one that for the Man of these states. Here every one may have land to labor for himself if he chuses; or, preferring the exercise of any other industry, may exact for it such compensation as not only to afford a comfortable subsistence, but where-with to provide for a cessation from labor in old age. Every one, by his property, or by his satisfactory situation, is interested in the support of law and order. And such men may safely and advantageously reserve to themselves a wholsome controul over their public affairs, and a degree of freedom, which in the hands of the *canaille* of the cities of Europe, would be instantly perverted to the demolition and destruction of every thing public and private. The history of the last 25 years of France, and of the last 40 years in America, nay of its last 200 years, proves the truth of both parts of this observation.

But even in Europe a change has sensibly taken place in the mind of Man. Science had liberated the ideas of those who read and reflect, and the American example had kindled feelings of right in the people. An insurrection has consequently begun, of science, talents and courage against rank and birth, which have fallen into contempt. It has failed in its first effort, because the mobs of the cities, the instrument used for its accomplishment, debased by ignorance, poverty and vice, could not be restrained to rational action. But the world will recover from the panic of this first catastrophe. Science is progressive, and talents and enterprize on the alert. Resort may be had to the people of the country, a more governable power from their principles and subordination; and rank, and birth, and tinsel-aristocracy will finally shrink into insignificance, even there. This however we have no right to meddle with. It suffices for us, if the moral and physical condition of our own citizens qualifies them to select the able and good for the direction of their government, with a recurrence of elections at such short periods as will enable them to displace an unfaithful servant before the mischief he meditates may be irremediable.

I have thus stated my opinion on a point on which we differ, not with a view to controversy, for we are both too old to change opinions which are the result of a long life of inquiry and reflection; but on the suggestion of a former letter of yours, that we ought not to die before we have explained ourselves to each other. We acted in perfect harmony thro' a long and perilous contest for our liberty and independance. A constitution has been acquired which, tho neither of us think perfect, yet both consider as competent to render our fellow-citizens the happiest and the securest on whom the sun has ever shone. If we do not think exactly alike as to its imperfections, it matters little to our country which, after devoting to it long lives of disinterested labor, we have delivered over to our successors in life, who will be able to take care of it, and of themselves. [. . .]

Letter to Samuel Kercheval (July 12, 1816)

Monticello

Sir,—I duly received your favor of June the 13th, with the copy of the letters on the calling a convention, on which you are pleased to ask my opinion. I have not been in the habit of mysterious reserve on any subject, nor of buttoning up my opinions within my own doublet. On the contrary, while in public service especially, I thought the public entitled to frankness, and intimately to know whom they employed. But I am now retired: I resign myself, as a passenger, with confidence to those at present at the helm, and ask but for rest, peace and good will. The question you propose, on equal representation, has become a party one, in which I wish to take no public share. Yet, if it be asked for your own satisfaction only, and not to be quoted before the public, I have no motive to withhold it, and the less from you, as it coincides with your own. At the birth of our republic, I committed that opinion to the world, in the draught of a constitution annexed to the "Notes on Virginia," in which a provision was inserted for a representation permanently equal. The infancy of the subject at that moment, and our inexperience of self-government, occasioned gross departures in that draught from genuine republican canons. In truth, the abuses of monarchy had so much filled all the space of political contemplation, that we imagined everything republican which was not monarchy. We had not yet penetrated to the mother principle, that "governments are republican only in proportion as they embody the will of their people, and execute it." Hence, our first constitutions had really no leading principles in them. But experience and reflection have but more and more confirmed me in the particular importance of the equal representation then proposed. On that point, then, I am entirely in sentiment with your letters; and only lament that a copyright of your pamphlet prevents their appearance in the newspapers, where alone they would be generally read, and produce general effect. The present vacancy too, of other matter, would give them place in every paper, and bring the question home to every man's conscience.

But inequality of representation in both Houses of our legislature, is not the only republican heresy in this first essay of our revolutionary patriots at forming a constitution. For let it be agreed that a government is republican in proportion as every member composing it has his equal voice in the direction of its concerns (not indeed in person, which would be impracticable beyond the limits of a city, or small township, but) by representatives chosen by himself, and responsible to him at short periods, and let us bring to the test of this canon every branch of our constitution.

In the legislature, the House of Representatives is chosen by less than half the people, and not at all in proportion to those who do choose. The Senate are still more disproportionate, and for long terms of irresponsibility. In the Executive, the Governor is entirely independent of the choice of the people, and of their control; his Council equally so, and at best but a fifth wheel to a wagon. In the Judiciary, the judges of the highest courts are dependent on none but themselves. In England, where judges were named and removable at the will of an hereditary executive, from which branch most misrule was feared, and has flowed, it was a great point gained, by fixing them for life, to make them independent of that executive. But in a government founded on the public will, this principle operates in an opposite direction, and against that will. There, too, they were still removable on a concurrence of the executive and legislative branches. But we have made them independent of the nation itself. They are irremovable, but by their own body, for any depravities of conduct, and even by their own body for the imbecilities of dotage. The justices of the inferior courts are self-chosen, are for life, and perpetuate their own body in succession forever, so that a faction once possessing themselves of the bench of a county, can never be broken up, but hold their county in chains, forever indissoluble. Yet these justices are the real executive as well as judiciary, in all our minor and most ordinary concerns. They tax us at will; fill the office of sheriff, the most important of all the executive officers of the county; name nearly all our military leaders, which leaders, once named, are removable but by themselves. The juries, our judges of all fact, and of law when they choose it, are not selected by the people, nor amenable to them. They are chosen by an officer named by the court and executive. Chosen, did I say? Picked up by the sheriff from the loungings of the court yard, after everything respectable has retired from it. Where then is our republicanism to be found? Not in our constitution certainly, but merely in the spirit of our people. That would oblige even a despot to govern us republicanly. Owing to this spirit, and to nothing in the form of our constitution, all things have gone well. But this fact, so triumphantly misquoted by the enemies of reformation, is not the fruit of our constitution, but has prevailed in spite of it. Our functionaries have done well, because generally honest men. If any were not so, they feared to show it.

But it will be said, it is easier to find faults than to amend them. I do not think their amendment so difficult as is pretended. Only lay down true principles, and adhere to them inflexibly. Do not be frightened into their surrender by the alarms of the timid, or the croakings of wealth against the ascendency of the people. If experience be called for, appeal to that of our fifteen or twenty governments for forty years, and show me where the people have done half the mischief in these forty years, that a single despot would have done in a single year; or show half the riots and rebellions, the crimes and the punishments, which have taken place in any single nation, under kingly government, during the same period. The true foundation of republican government is the equal right of every citizen, in his person and property, and in their management. Try by this, as a tally, every provision of our constitution, and see if it hangs directly on the will of the people. Reduce your legislature to a convenient number for full, but orderly discussion. Let every man who fights or pays, exercise his just and equal right in their election. Submit them to approbation or rejection at short intervals. Let the executive be chosen in the same way, and for the same term, by those whose agent he is to be; and leave no screen of a council behind which to skulk from responsibility. It has been thought that the people are not competent electors of judges *learned in the law*. But I do not know that this is true, and, if doubtful, we should follow principle. In this, as in many other elections, they would be guided by reputation, which would not err oftener, perhaps, than the present mode of appointment. In one State of the Union, at least, it has long been tried, and with the most satisfactory success. The judges of Connecticut have been chosen by the people every six months, for nearly two centuries, and believe there has hardly ever been an instance of change; so powerful is the curb of incessant responsibility. If prejudice, however, derived from a monarchical institution, is still to prevail against the vital elective principle of our own, and if the existing example among ourselves of periodical election of judges by the people be still mistrusted, let us at least not adopt the evil, and reject the good, of the English precedent; let us retain amovability on the concurrence of the executive and legislative branches, and nomination by the executive alone. Nomination to office is an executive function. To give it to the legislature, as we do, is a violation of the principle of the separation of powers. It swerves the members from correctness, by temptations to intrigue for office themselves, and to a corrupt barter of votes; and destroys responsibility by dividing it among a multitude. By leaving nomination in its proper place, among executive functions, the principle of the distribution of power is preserved, and responsibility weighs with its heaviest force on a single head.

The organization of our county administrations may be thought more difficult. But follow principle, and the knot unties itself. Divide the counties into wards of such size as that every citizen can attend, when called on, and act in person. Ascribe to them the government of their wards in all things relating to themselves exclusively. A justice, chosen by themselves, in each, a constable, a military company, a patrol, a school, the care of their own poor, their own portion of the public roads, the choice of one or more jurors to serve in some court, and the delivery, within their own wards, of their own votes for all elective officers of higher sphere, will relieve the county administration of nearly all its business, will have it better done, and by making every citizen an acting member of the government, and in the offices nearest and most interesting to him, will attach him by his strongest feelings to the independence of his country, and its republican constitution. The justices thus chosen by every ward, would constitute the county court, would do its judiciary business, direct roads and bridges, levy county and poor rates, and administer all the matters of common interest to the whole country. These wards, called townships in New England, are the vital principle of their governments, and have proved themselves the wisest invention ever devised by the wit of man for the perfect exercise of self-government, and for its preservation. We should thus marshal our government into, 1, the general federal republic, for all concerns foreign and federal; 2, that of the State, for what relates to our own citizens exclusively; 3, the county republics, for the duties and concerns of the county; and 4, the ward republics, for the small, and yet numerous and interesting concerns of the neighborhood; and in government, as well as in every other business of life, it is by division and subdivision of duties alone, that all matters, great and small, can be managed to perfection. And the whole is cemented by giving to every citizen, personally, a part in the administration of the public affairs.

The sum of these amendments is, 1. General Suffrage. 2. Equal representation in the legislature. 3. An executive chosen by the people. 4. Judges elective or amovable. 5. Justices, jurors, and sheriffs elective. 6. Ward divisions. And 7. Periodical amendments of the constitution.

I have thrown out these as loose heads of amendment, for consideration and correction; and their object is to secure self-government by the republicanism of our constitution, as well as by the spirit of the people; and to nourish and perpetuate that spirit. I am not among those who fear the people. They, and not the rich, are our dependence for continued freedom. And to preserve their independence, we must not let our rulers load us with perpetual debt. We must make our election between *economy and liberty*, or *profusion and servitude*. If we run into such debts, as that we must be taxed in our meat and in our drink, in our necessaries and our comforts, in our labors and our amusements, for our callings and our creeds, as the people of England are, our people, like them, must come to labor sixteen hours in the twenty-four, give the earnings of fifteen of these to the government for their debts and daily expenses; and the sixteenth being insufficient to afford us bread, we must live, as they now do, on oatmeal and potatoes; have no time to think, no means of calling the mismanagers to account; but be glad to obtain subsistence by hiring ourselves to rivet their chains on the necks of our fellow-sufferers. Our landholders, too, like theirs, retaining indeed the title and stewardship of estates called theirs, but held really in trust for the treasury, must wander, like theirs, in foreign countries, and be contented with penury, obscurity, exile, and the glory of the nation. This example reads to us the salutary lesson, that private fortunes are destroyed by public as well as by private extravagance. And this is the tendency of all human governments. A departure from principle in one instance becomes a precedent for a second; that second for a third; and so on, till the bulk of the society is reduced to be mere automatons of misery, and to have no sensibilities left but for sinning and suffering. Then begins, indeed, the *bellum omnium in omnia*, which some philosophers observing to be so general in this world, have mistaken it for the natural, instead of the abusive state of man. And the fore horse of this frightful team is public debt. Taxation follows that, and in its train wretchedness and oppression.

Some men look at constitutions with sanctimonious reverence, and deem them like the arc of the covenant, too sacred to be touched. They ascribe to the men of the preceding age a wisdom more than human, and suppose what they did to be beyond amendment. I knew that age well; I belonged to it, and labored with it. It deserved well of its country. It was very like the present, but without the experience of the present; and forty years of experience in government is worth a century of book-reading; and this they would say themselves, were they to rise from the dead. I am certainly not an advocate for frequent and untried changes in laws and constitutions. I think moderate imperfections had better be borne with; because, when once known, we accommodate ourselves to them, and find practical means of correcting their ill effects. But I know also, that laws and institutions must go hand in hand with the progress of the human mind. As that becomes more developed, more enlightened, as new discoveries are made, new truths disclosed, and manners and opinions change with the change of circumstances, institutions must advance also, and keep pace with the times. We might as well require a man to wear still the coat which fitted him when a boy, as civilized society to remain ever under the regimen of their barbarous ancestors. It is this preposterous idea which has lately deluged Europe in blood. Their monarchs, instead of wisely yielding to the gradual change of circumstances, of favoring progressive accommodation to progressive improvement, have clung to old abuses, entrenched themselves behind steady habits, and obliged their subjects to seek through blood and violence rash and ruinous innovations, which, had they been referred to the peaceful deliberations and collected wisdom of the nation, would have been put into acceptable and salutary forms. Let us follow no such examples, nor weakly believe that one generation is not as capable as another of taking care of itself, and of ordering its own affairs. Let us, as our sister States have done, avail ourselves of our reason and experience, to correct the crude essays of our first and unexperienced, although wise, virtuous, and well-meaning councils. And lastly, let us provide in our constitution for its revision at stated periods. What these periods should be, nature herself indicates. By the European tables of mortality, of the adults living at any one moment of time, a majority will be dead in about nineteen years. At the end of that period, then, a new majority is come into place; or, in other words, a new generation. Each generation is as independent as the one preceding, as that was of all which had gone before. It has then, like them, a right to choose for itself the form of government it believes most promotive of its own happiness; consequently, to accommodate to the circumstances in which it finds itself, that received from its predecessors; and it is for the peace and good of mankind, that a solemn opportunity of doing this every nineteen or twenty years, should be provided by the constitution; so that it may be handed on, with periodical repairs, from generation to generation, to the end of time, if anything human can so long endure. It is now forty years since the constitution of Virginia was formed. The same tables inform us, that, within that period, two-thirds of the adults then living are now dead. Have then the remaining third, even if they had the wish, the right to hold in obedience to their will, and to laws heretofore made by them, the other two-thirds, who, with themselves, compose the present mass of adults? If they have not, who has? The dead? But the dead have no rights. They are nothing; and nothing cannot own something. Where there is no substance, there can be no accident. This corporeal globe, and everything upon it, belong to its present corporeal inhabitants, during their generation. They alone have a right to direct what is the concern of themselves alone, and to declare the law of that direction; and this declaration can only be made by their majority. That majority, then, has a right to depute representatives to a convention, and to make the constitution what they think will be the best for themselves. But how collect their voice? This is the real difficulty. If invited by private authority, or county or district meetings, these divisions are so large that few will attend; and their voice will be imperfectly, or falsely pronounced. Here, then, would be one of the advantages of the ward divisions I have proposed. The mayor of every ward, on a question like the present, would call his ward together, take the simple yea or nay of its members, convey these to the county court, who would hand on those of all its wards to the proper general authority; and the voice of the whole people would be thus fairly, fully, and peaceably expressed, discussed, and decided by the common reason of the society. If this avenue be shut to the call of sufferance, it will make itself heard through that of force, and we shall go on, as other nations are doing, in the endless circle of oppression, rebellion, reformation; and oppression, rebellion, reformation, again; and so on forever. [. . .]

John Adams

Letters to Thomas Jefferson (1813)

July 9, 1813

[. . .] Whenever I sit down to write to you, I am precisely in the situation of the wood-cutter on Mount Ida. I cannot see wood for trees. So many subjects crowd upon me, that I know not which to begin. But I will begin at random with Belsham, who is, I have no doubt, a man of merit. He had no malice against you, nor any thought of doing mischief; nor has he done any, though he has been imprudent. The truth is, the dissenters of all denominations in England, and, especially, the Unitarians, are cowed, as we used to say at college. They are ridiculed, insulted, persecuted. They can scarcely hold their heads above water. They catch at straws and shadows to avoid drowning. Priestley sent your letter to Lindsey, and Belsham printed it from the same motive, i.e. to derive some countenance from the name of Jefferson. Nor has it done harm here. Priestley says to Lindsey, "You see he is almost one of us, and he hopes will soon be altogether such as we are." Even in our New England I have heard a high federal divine say, your letters had increased his respect for you.

"The same political parties, which now agitate the United States, have existed through all time." Precisely; and this is precisely the complaint in the preface to the first volume of my Defence. While all other sciences have advanced, that of government is at a stand; little better understood, little better practised now than three or four thousand years ago. What is the reason? I say, parties and factions will not suffer improvements to be made. As soon as one man hints at an improvement, his rival opposes it. No sooner has one party discovered or invented any amelioration of the condition of man, or the order of society than the opposite party belies it, misconstrues it, misrepresents it, ridicules it, insults it, and persecutes it. Records are destroyed. Histories are annihilated or interpolated or prohibited; sometimes by Popes, sometimes by Emperors, sometimes by aristocratical, and sometimes by democratical assemblies, and sometimes by mobs.

Aristotle wrote the history and description of eighteen hundred republics which existed before his time. Cicero wrote two volumes of discourses on government, which, perhaps, were worth all the rest of his works. The works of Livy and Tacitus, &c., that are lost, would be more interesting than all that remain. Fifty gospels have been destroyed. Where are St. Luke's world of books that were written?

If you ask my opinion, who has committed all the havoc? I will answer you candidly. Ecclesiastical and imperial despotisms have done it to conceal their frauds.

Why are the histories of all nations, more ancient than the Christian era, lost? Who destroyed the Alexandrian library? I believe that Christian priests, Jewish rabbis, Grecian sages, and Roman emperors, had as great a hand in it as Turks and Mahometans. Democrats, rebels, and Jacobins, when they possess a momentary power, have shown a disposition both to destroy and to forge records, as Vandatical as priests and despots. Such has been and such is the world we live in.

I recollect, near thirty years ago, to have said carelessly to you, that I wished I could find time and means to write something upon aristocracy. You seized upon the idea, and encouraged me to do it with all that friendly warmth that is natural and habitual to you. I soon began, and have been writing upon that subject ever since. I have been so unfortunate as never to be able to make myself understood. Your *aristoi* are the most difficult animals to manage of any thing in the whole theory and practice of government. They will not suffer themselves to be governed. They not only exert all their own subtilty, industry, and courage, but they employ the commonalty to knock to pieces every plan and model that the most honest architects in legislation can invent to keep them within bounds. Both patricians and plebeians are as furious as the workmen in England to demolish labor-saving machinery. [. . .]

But who are these *aristoi?* Who shall judge? Who shall select these choice spirits from the rest of the congregation? Themselves? We must find out and determine who themselves are. Shall the congregation choose? Ask Xenophon. Perhaps, hereafter I may quote you Greek; too much in a hurry at present; English must suffice. Xenophon says, that the ecclesia always choose the worst men they can find, because none others will do their dirty work. This wicked motive is worse than birth or wealth. Here I want to quote Greek again, but the day before I received your letter of June 27th; I gave the book to George Washington Adams, going to the academy at Hingham. The title is *Ethike Poiesis* a collection of moral sentences from all the most ancient Greek poets. In one of the oldest of them I read, in Greek that I cannot repeat, a couplet, the sense of which was: "Nobility in men is worth as much as it is in horses, asses, or rams; but the meanest-blooded puppy in the world, if he gets a little money, is as good a man as the best of them." Yet birth and wealth together have prevailed over virtue and talents in all ages. The many will acknowledge no other *aristoi.* Your experience of this truth will not much differ from that of your old friend.

July 13, 1813

Let me allude to one circumstance more, in one of your letters to me, before I touch upon the subject of religion in your letter to Priestley. The first time that you and I differed in opinion on any material question was after your arrival from Europe; and that point was the French revolution. You was well persuaded in your own mind that the nation would succeed in establishing a free republican government. I was well persuaded in mine, that a project of such a government, over five-and-twenty millions of people, when four-and-twenty millions and five hundred thousand of them could neither read nor write, was as unnatural, irrational, and impracticable as it would be over the elephants, lions, tigers, panthers, wolves, and bears, in the royal menagerie at Versailles. Napoleon has lately invented a word, which perfectly expressed my opinion at that time and ever since. He calls the project *ideology;* and John Randolph, though he was, fourteen years ago, as wild an enthusiast for equality and fraternity as any of them, appears to be now a regenerated proselyte to Napoleon's opinion and mine, that it was all madness. [. . .]

Inequalities of mind and body are so established by God Almighty in his constitution of human nature, that no art or policy can ever plane them down to a level. I have never read reasoning more absurd, sophistry more gross, in proof of the Athanasian creed, or transubstantiation, than the subtle labors of Helvetius and Rousseau to demonstrate the natural equality of mankind. *Jus cuique,* the golden rule, do as you would be done by, is all the equality that can be supported or defended by reason or common sense.

It is very true, as you justly observe, I can say nothing new on this or any other subject of government. But when Lafayette harangued you, and me, and John Quincy Adams, through a whole evening, in your hotel in the *Cul de Sac,* at Paris, and developed the plans now in operation to reform France, though I was silent as you was, I then thought I could say something new to him. In plain truth, I was astonished at the grossness of his ignorance of government and history, as I had been for years before, at that of Turgot, Rochefoucauld, Condorcet, and Franklin. This gross ideology of them all first suggested to me the thought and the inclination, which I afterwards executed in London, of writing something upon aristocracy. I was restrained for years by many fearful considerations. Who and what was I? Why, a man of no name or consideration in Europe. The manual exercise of writing was painful and distressing to me, almost like a blow on the elbow or the knee; my style was habitually negligent, unstudied, unpolished; I should make enemies of all the French patriots, the Dutch patriots, the English republicans, dissenters, reformers, call them what you will; and, what came nearer home to my bosom than all the rest, I knew I should give offence to many, if not all, of my best friends in America, and, very probably, destroy all the little popularity I ever had in a country where popularity had more omnipotence than the British parliament assumed. Where should I get the necessary books? What printer or bookseller would undertake to print such hazardous writings? But, when the French assembly of notables met, and I saw that

Turgot's "government in one centre, and that centre the nation," a sentence as mysterious or as contradictory as the Athanasian creed, was about to take place; and when I saw that Shays's rebellion was breaking out in Massachusetts; and when I saw that benevolent, the most eloquent and sublime character that has ever been exhibited to man. This is the outline!"

"*Sancte Socrate! Ora pro nobis!*" Erasmus. Priestley, in his letter to Lindsey, inclosing a copy of your letter to him, says, "he is generally considered as an unbeliever. If so, however, he cannot be far from us, and I hope in the way to be not only almost, but altogether what we are. He now attends public worship very regularly, and his moral conduct was never impeached."

Now, I see not but you are as good a Christian as Priestley and Lindsey. Piety and morality were the end and object of the Christian system, according to them and according to you. They believed in the resurrection of Jesus, in his miracles and inspirations. But what inspirations? Not all that is recorded in the New Testament or the Old. They have not yet told us how much they believe or disbelieve. They have not told us how much allegory, how much parable they find, nor how they explained them all in the New Testament or Old.

John Quincy Adams has written, for years, to his sons, boys of ten and twelve, a series of letters, in which he pursues a plan more extensive than yours, but agreeing in most of the essential points. I wish these letters could be preserved in the bosoms of his boys. But women and priests will get them; and I expect, if he makes a peace, he will have to retire, like Jay, to study prophecies to the end of his life.

I have more to say upon this subject of religion.

September 2, 1813

Οὐδὲ γυνὴ κακοῦ ἀνδρὸς ἀναίνεται εἶναι ἄκοιτις
Πλουσίου, ἀλλ' ἀφνεὸν βούλεται ἀντ' ἀγαθοῦ.
Χρήματα γὰρ τιμῶσι· καὶ ἐκ κακοῦ ἐσθλὸς ἔγημε
Καὶ κακὸς ἐξ ἀγαθοῦ· πλοῦτος ἔμιξε γένος.

Grotius renders this into Latin thus:

Nec dedignetur ditemque malumque maritum
Femina: divitiæ præ probitate placent.
In pretio pretium est: genus et prænobile vili,
Obscuruin claro, miscet avaritia.

I should render the Greek into English thus:

"Nor does a woman disdain to be the wife of a bad rich man. But she prefers a man of property before a good man; for riches are honored, and a good man marries from a bad family, and a bad man from a good one. Wealth mingles races."

Now, please to tell me, whether my translation has not hit the sense of Theognis as exactly as that of Grotius?

Tell me, also, whether poet, orator, historian, or philosopher, can paint the picture of every city, county, or State, in our pure, uncorrupted, unadulterated, uncontaminated federal republic, or, in France, England, Holland, and all the rest of Christendom or Mahometanism, in more precise lines or colors? Another translation of the whole passage of Theognis is this:

Arietes quidem et asinos quærimus, Cyrne, et equos,
Generosos, et quisque vult ex bonis admittere; ducere autem malam (filiam)
Mali, non renuit generosus vir, si ei pecunias multas dederit.
Nulla (femina) mali viri recusat esse uxor divitis; sed divitem vult
Pro bono. Opes quidem æstimat, et ex malo (natam) bonus ducet
Et malus ex bono ortam. Divitiæ miscent genus.

Now, my friend, who are the *aristoi?* Philosophers may answer, "the wise and good." But the world, mankind, have, by their practice, always answered, "the rich, the beautiful, and well-born." And philosophers themselves, in marrying their children, prefer the rich, the handsome, and the well-descended, to the wise and good.

What chance have talents and virtues, in competition with wealth and birth and beauty?

Haud facile emergunt quorum virtutibus obstant
Res angustæ domi.

One truth is clear, by all the world confessed,
Slow rises worth, by poverty depressed.

The five pillars of aristocracy are beauty, wealth, birth, genius, and virtue. Any one of the three first can, at any time, overbear any one or both of the two last.

Let me ask again, what a wave of public opinion, in favor of birth, has been spread over the globe by Abraham, by Hercules, by Mahomet, by Guelphs, Ghibellines, Bourbons, and a miserable Scottish chief, Stuart, by Zengis, by——, by——, by a million of others. And what a wave will be spread by Napoleon and by Washington! Their remotest cousins will be sought, and will be proud, and will avail themselves of their descent. Call this principle, prejudice, folly, ignorance, baseness, slavery, stupidity, adulation, superstition, or what you will, I will not contradict you. But the fact in natural, moral, political, and domestic history, I will not deny, or dispute, or question.

And is this great fact in the natural history of man, this unalterable principle of morals, philosophy, policy, domestic felicity, and daily experience from the creation, to be overlooked, forgotten, neglected, or hypocritically waved out of sight, by a legislator, by a professed writer upon civil government, and upon constitutions of civil government?

Thus far had I written, when your favor of August 22d was laid on my table from the post-office. I can only say at present that I can pursue this idle speculation no further, at least till I have replied to this fresh proof of friendship and confidence. Mrs. A. joins in cordial thanks with

J. A.

You may laugh at the introduction of beauty among the pillars of aristocracy. But Madame du Barry says, "*la véritable royauté c'est la beauté*," and there is not a more certain truth. Beauty, grace, figure, attitude, movement, have, in innumerable instances, prevailed over wealth, birth, talents, virtues, and every thing else, in men of the highest rank, greatest power, and, sometimes, the most exalted genius, greatest fame, and highest merit.

Fisher Ames

A Sketch of the Character of Alexander Hamilton (1804)

It is with really great men as with great literary works, the excellence of both is best tested by the extent and durableness of their impression. The public has not suddenly, but after an experience of five-and-twenty years, taken that impression of the just celebrity of Alexander Hamilton, that nothing but his extraordinary intrinsic merit could have made, and still less could have made so deep and maintained so long. In this case, it is safe and correct to judge by effects; we sometimes calculate the height of a mountain, by measuring the length of its shadow.

It is not a party, for party distinctions, to the honor of our citizens be it said, are confounded by the event; it is a nation that weeps for its bereavement. We weep, as the Romans did over the ashes of Germanicus. It is a thoughtful, foreboding sorrow, that takes possession of the heart, and sinks it with no counterfeited heaviness.

It is here proper and not invidious to remark, that as the emulation excited by conducting great affairs commonly trains and exhibits great talents, it is seldom the case that the fairest and soundest judgment of a great man's merit is to be gained, exclusively, from his associates in counsel or in action. Persons of conspicuous merit themselves are, not unfrequently, bad judges and still worse witnesses on this point; often rivals, sometimes enemies; almost always unjust, and still oftener envious or cold. The opinions they give to the public, as well as those they privately formed for themselves, are of course discolored with the hue of their prejudices and resentments.

But the body of the people, who cannot feel a spirit of rivalship towards those whom they see elevated by nature and education so far above their heads, are more equitable, and, supposing a competent time and opportunity for information on the subject, more intelligent judges. Even party rancor, eager to maim the living, scorns to strip the slain. The most hostile passions are soothed or baffled by the fall of their antagonist. Then, if not sooner, the very multitude will fairly decide on character, according to their experience of its impression; and as long as virtue, not unfrequently for a time obscured, is ever respectable when distinctly seen, they cannot withhold, and they will not stint their admiration.

If, then, the popular estimation is ever to be taken for the true one, the uncommonly profound public sorrow for the death of Alexander Hamilton sufficiently explains and vindicates itself. He had not made himself dear to the passions of the multitude by condescending, in defiance of his honor and conscience, to become their instrument; he is not lamented, because a skilful flatterer is now mute for ever. It was by the practice of no art, by wearing no disguise; it was not by accident, or by the levity or profligacy of party, but in despite of its malignant misrepresentation; it was by bold and inflexible adherence to truth, by loving his country better than himself, preferring its interest to its favor, and serving it when it was unwilling and unthankful, in a manner that no other person could, that he rose; and the true popularity, the homage that is paid to virtue, followed him. It was not in the power of party or envy to pull him down; but he rose with the refulgence of a star, till the very prejudice that could not reach, was at length almost ready to adore him.

It is indeed no imagined wound that inflicts so keen an anguish. Since the news of his death, the novel and strange events of Europe have succeeded each other unregarded; the nation has been enchained to its subject, and broods over its grief, which is more deep than eloquent, which though dumb, can make itself felt without utterance, and which does not merely pass, but like an electrical shock, at the same instant smites and astonishes, as it passes from Georgia to New Hampshire.

There is a kind of force put upon our thoughts by this disaster, which detains and rivets them to a closer contemplation of those resplendent virtues, that are now lost, except to memory, and there they will dwell for ever.

That writer would deserve the fame of a public benefactor who could exhibit the character of Hamilton, with the truth and force that all who intimately knew him conceived it; his example would then take the same ascendant as his talents. The portrait alone, however, exquisitely finished, could not inspire genius where it is not; but if the world should again have possession of so rare a gift, it might awaken it where it sleeps, as by a spark from heaven's own altar; for surely if there is any thing like divinity in man, it is in his admiration of virtue.

But who alive can exhibit this portrait? If our age, on that supposition more fruitful than any other, had produced two Hamiltons, one of them might then have depicted the other. To delineate genius one must feel its power; Hamilton, and he alone, with all its inspirations, could have transfused its whole fervid soul into the picture, and swelled its lineaments into life. The writer's mind, expanding with his own peculiar enthusiasm, and glowing with kindred fires, would then have stretched to the dimensions of his subject.

Such is the infirmity of human nature, it is very difficult for a man who is greatly the superior of his associates, to preserve their friendship without abatement; yet, though he could not possibly conceal his superiority, he was so little inclined to display it, he was so much at ease in its possession, that no jealousy or envy chilled his bosom, when his friends obtained praise. He was indeed so entirely the friend of his friends, so magnanimous, so superior, or more properly so insensible to all exclusive selfishness of spirit, so frank, so ardent, yet so little overbearing, so much trusted, admired, beloved, almost adored, that his power over their affections was entire, and lasted through his life. We do not believe that he left any worthy man his foe who had ever been his friend.

Men of the most elevated minds have not always the readiest discernment of character. Perhaps he was sometimes too sudden and too lavish in bestowing his confidence; his manly spirit, disdaining artifice, suspected none. But while the power of his friends over him seemed to have no limits, and really had none, in respect to those things which were of a nature to be yielded, no man, not the Roman Cato himself, was more inflexible on every point that touched, or only seemed to touch, integrity and honor. With him, it was not enough to be unsuspected; his bosom would have glowed, like a furnace, at its own whispers of reproach. Mere purity would have seemed to him below praise; and such were his habits, and such his nature, that the pecuniary temptations, which many others can only with great exertion and self-denial resist, had no attractions for him. He was very far from obstinate; yet, as his friends assailed his opinions with less profound thought than he had devoted to them, they were seldom shaken by discussion. He defended them, however, with as much mildness as force, and evinced, that if he did not yield, it was not for want of gentleness or modesty.

The tears that flow on this fond recital will never dry up. My heart, penetrated with the remembrance of the man, grows liquid as I write, and I could pour it out like water. I could weep too for my country, which, mournful as it is, does not know the half of its loss. It deeply laments, when it turns its eyes back, and sees what Hamilton was; but my soul stiffens with despair when I think what Hamilton would have been.

His social affections and his private virtues are not, however, so properly the object of public attention, as the conspicuous and commanding qualities that gave him his fame and influence in the world. It is not as Apollo, enchanting the shepherds with his lyre, that we deplore him; it is as Hercules, treacherously slain in the midst of his unfinished labors, leaving the world overrun with monsters.

His early life we pass over; though his heroic spirit in the army has furnished a theme that is dear to patriotism and will be sacred to glory.

In all the different stations in which a life of active usefulness has placed him, we find him not more remarkably distinguished by the extent, than by the variety and versatility of his talents. In every place he made it apparent, that no other man could have filled it so well; and in times of critical importance, in which alone he desired employment, his services were justly deemed absolutely indispensable. As secretary of the treasury, his was the powerful spirit that presided over the chaos:

> Confusion heard his voice, and wild uproar
> Stood ruled. . . .

Indeed, in organizing the federal government in 1789, every man of either sense or candor will allow, the difficulty seemed greater than the first-rate abilities could surmount. The event has shown that his abilities were greater than those difficulties. He surmounted them—and Washington's administration was the most wise and beneficent, the most prosperous, and ought to be the most popular, that ever was intrusted with the affairs of a nation. Great as was Washington's merit, much of it in plan, much in execution, will of course devolve upon his minister.

As a lawyer, his comprehensive genius reached the principles of his profession; he compassed its extent, he fathomed its profound, perhaps even more familiarly and easily, than the ordinary rules of its practice. With most men law is a trade; with him it was a science.

As a statesman, he was not more distinguished by the great extent of his views, than by the caution with which he provided against impediments, and the watchfulness of his care over right and the liberty of the subject. In none of the many revenue bills which he framed, though committees reported them, is there to be found a single clause that savors of despotic power; not one that the sagest champions of law and liberty would, on that ground, hesitate to approve and adopt.

It is rare that a man, who owes so much to nature, descends to seek more from industry; but he seemed to depend on industry, as if nature had done nothing for him. His habits of investigation were very remarkable; his mind seemed to cling to his subject till he had exhausted it. Hence the uncommon superiority of his reasoning powers, a superiority that seemed to be augmented from every source, and to be fortified by every auxiliary, learning, taste, wit, imagination, and eloquence. These were embellished and enforced by his temper and manners, by his fame and his virtues. It is difficult, in the midst of such various excellence, to say in what particular the effect of his greatness was most manifest. No man more promptly discerned truth; no man more clearly displayed it; it was not merely made visible, it seemed to come bright with illumination from his lips. But prompt and clear as he was, fervid as Demosthenes, like Cicero full of resource, he was not less remarkable for the copiousness and completeness of his argument, that left little for cavil, and nothing for doubt. Some men take their strongest argument as a weapon, and use no other; but he left nothing to be inquired for more, nothing to be answered. He not only disarmed his adversaries of their pretexts and objections, but he stripped them of all excuse for having urged them; he confounded and subdued as well as convinced. He indemnified them, however, by making his discussion a complete map of his subject, so that his opponents might, indeed, feel ashamed of their mistakes, but they could not repeat them. In fact, it was no common effort that could preserve a really able antagonist from becoming his convert; for the truth, which his researches so distinctly presented to the understanding of others, was rendered almost irresistibly commanding and impressive by the love and reverence which, it was ever apparent, he profoundly cherished for it in his own. While patriotism glowed in his heart, wisdom blended in his speech her authority with her charms.

Such, also, is the character of his writings. Judiciously collected, they will be a public treasure.

No man ever more disdained duplicity or carried frankness further than he. This gave to his political opponents some temporary advantages, and currency to some popular prejudices, which he would have lived down if his death had not prematurely dispelled them. He knew that factions have ever in the end prevailed in free states; and, as he saw no security (and who living can see any adequate?) against the destruction of that liberty which he loved, and for which he was ever ready to devote his life, he spoke at all times according to his anxious forebodings; and his enemies interpreted all that he said according to the supposed interest of their party.

But he ever extorted confidence, even when he most provoked opposition. It was impossible to deny that he was a patriot, and such a patriot as, seeking neither popularity nor office, without artifice, without meanness, the best Romans in their best days would have admitted to citizenship and to the consulate. Virtue so rare, so pure, so bold, by its very purity and excellence inspired suspicion as a prodigy. His enemies judged of him by themselves; so splendid and arduous were his services, they could not find it in their hearts to believe that they were disinterested.

Unparalleled as they were, they were nevertheless no otherwise requited than by the applause of all good men, and by his own enjoyment of the spectacle of that national prosperity and honor which was the effect of them. After facing calumny, and triumphantly surmounting an unrelenting persecution, he retired from office with clean, though empty hands, as rich as reputation and an unblemished integrity could make him.

Some have plausibly, though erroneously inferred, from the great extent of his abilities, that his ambition was inordinate. This is a mistake. Such men as have a painful consciousness that their stations happen to be far more exalted than their talents, are generally the most ambitious. Hamilton, on the contrary, though he had many competitors, had no rivals; for he did not thirst for power, nor would he, as it was well known, descend to office. Of course he suffered no pain from envy when bad men rose, though he felt anxiety for the public. He was perfectly content and at ease in private life. Of what was he ambitious? Not of wealth; no man held it cheaper. Was it of popularity? That weed of the dunghill he knew, when rankest, was nearest to withering. There is no doubt that he desired glory, which to most men is too inaccessible to be an object of desire; but feeling his own force, and that he was tall enough to reach the top of Pindus or of Helicon, he longed to deck his brow with the wreath of immortality. A vulgar ambition could as little comprehend as satisfy his views; he thirsted only for that fame, which virtue would not blush to confer, nor time to convey to the end of his course.

The only ordinary distinction, to which we confess he did aspire, was military; and for that, in the event of a foreign war, he would have been solicitous. He undoubtedly discovered the predominance of a soldier's feelings; and all that is honor in the character of a soldier was at home in his heart. His early education was in the camp; there the first fervors of his genius were poured forth, and his earliest and most cordial friendships formed; there he became enamored of glory, and was admitted to her embrace.

Those who knew him best, and especially in the army, will believe, that if occasions had called him forth, he was qualified, beyond any man of the age, to display the talents of a great general.

It may be very long before our country will want such military talents; it will probably be much longer before it will again possess them.

Alas! the great man who was at all times so much the ornament of our country, and so exclusively fitted in its extremity to be its champion, is withdrawn to a purer and more tranquil region. We are left to endless labors and unavailing regrets.

Such honors Ilion to her hero paid,
And peaceful slept the mighty Hector's shade.

The most substantial glory of a country is in its virtuous great men; its prosperity will depend on its docility to learn from their example. That nation is fated to ignominy and servitude, for which such men have lived in vain. Power may be seized by a nation that is yet barbarous; and wealth may be enjoyed by one that it finds or renders sordid; the one is the gift and the sport of accident, and the other is the sport of power. Both are mutable, and have passed away without leaving behind them any other memorial than ruins that offend taste, and traditions that battle conjecture. But the glory of Greece is imperishable, or will last as long as learning itself, which is its monument; it strikes an everlasting root, and bears perennial blossoms on its grave. The name of Hamilton would have honored Greece in the age of Aristides. May heaven, the guardian of our liberty, grant that our country may be fruitful of Hamiltons, and faithful to their glory!

The Mire of Democracy (1805)

It has been said that every man may be flattered. A fine understanding may make its possessor shrewd to detect the flatterer's art, and great experience in the world may place suspicion as a sentinel at one's door. All this may increase the difficulty of finding access to a man's vanity, but still it is not inaccessible. There are opinions, which every man wishes every other man to entertain of his merit, temper, or capacity, and he is sure to be pleased when he discovers, or thinks he discovers, that his skilful flatterer really entertains them. He indulges a complacency and kindness towards him, who puts him at peace and in good humour with himself. But to flatter the ignorant and inexperienced requires no skill, it scarcely requires any thing more than a disposition to flatter; for with that class of people the very disposition is accepted as an evidence of kindness. It is still easier to make flattery grateful to a multitude, and especially an assembled multitude of such men. No arts are too gross, no topicks of praise disgusting. Popular vanity comes hungry to an election ground, and claims flattery as its proper food. In democracies the people are the depositaries of political power. It is impossible they should exercise it themselves. In such states therefore it is a thing inevitable, that the people should be beset by unworthy flatterers and intoxicated with their philtres. Sudden, blind, and violent in all their impulses, they cannot heap power enough on their favourites, nor make their vengeance as prompt and terrible as their wrath against those, whom genius and virtue have qualified to be their friends and unfitted to be their flatterers. The most skilful sort of flattery is that, which exalts a man in his own estimation by ascribing to his character those qualities, which he is most solicitous to be thought to possess. He mellows into complacency when he finds that his pretensions are rightly understood and cheerfully admitted. As nothing so conspicuously lifts one man above every other man in society as power, of course it is of all topicks of praise the most fascinating and irresistible. When therefore a demagogue invites the ignorant multitude to dwell on the contemplation of their sovereignty, to consider princes as their equals, their own magistrates as their servants and their flatterers, however otherwise distinguished in the world as their slaves, is it to be supposed that aristocratic good sense will be permitted to disturb their feast or to dishonour their triumph? Accordingly we know from history, and we might know if we would from a scrutiny into the human heart, that every democracy, in the very infancy of its vicious and troubled life, is delivered bound hand and foot into the keeping of ambitious demagogues. Their ambition will soon make them rivals, and their bloody discords will surely make one of them a tyrant.

But the fate of democracies, which every man of sense will deem irreversibly fixed, is not so much the object of these remarks as the complexion of popular opinions while they last.

They will all be such as the multitude have an interest, or which is the same thing a pleasure, in believing. Of these, one of the dearest and most delusive is, that the power of the people is their liberty. Yet they can have no liberty without many strong and obnoxious restraints upon their power.

To break down these restraints, to remove these courts and judges, these senates and constitutions, which are insolently as well as artfully raised above the people's heads to keep them out of their reach, will always be the interested counsel of demagogues and the welcome labour of the multitude. The actual state of popular opinion will be ever hostile to the real and efficient securities of the publick liberty. The spirit of '76 is yet invoked by the democrats, because they, erroneously enough, understand it as a spirit to subvert an old government, and not to preserve old rights. Of all flattery, the grossest (gross indeed to blasphemy) is, that the voice of the people is the voice of God; that the opinion of a majority like that of the Pope, is infallible. Hence it is, that the public tranquillity has, and the democrats say ought to have, no more stable basis than popular caprice; hence compacts and constitutions are deemed binding only so long as they are liked by a majority. The temple of the public liberty has no better foundation, than the shifting sands of the desert. It is apparent then that pleasing delusions must become popular creeds. After habit has made praise one of the wants of vanity, it cannot be expected that reproof will be sought or endured, a stomach spoiled by sweets will loathe its medicines. Prudence and duty will be silent.

An individual rarely passes unpunished, who forms and prosecutes his plan of life under a great mistake of his own qualifications and character. And shall a democracy, which is sure to overstretch its rights, to despise its duties, to entrust its traitors and persecute its patriots, to demolish its own bulwarks and invite the host of its assailants to come in, shall such a system last long, or enjoy any degree of tranquillity while it lasts? It is impossible.

Nevertheless, it is assumed as a position of uncontested authority, that the discontents of the people never ripen into resistance and revolution, unless from the oppression and vices of their government. The people are alleged to be always innocent when they refuse evidence, the government is almost always culpable when it exacts it. It may be admitted that no ordinary pressure of grievances would impel a people to rise against government, when that government is possessed of great strength, and is administered with vigour. It cannot be supposed that men conscious of their weakness will attack a superiour power. Yet oppression may at length make a whole nation mad, and when it is perceived that the physical strength is all on one side the political authority will inspire no terror.

But surely there is no analogy between such a government and a democracy. As the force of this latter depends on opinion, and that opinion shifts with every current of caprice, it will not be pretended that the propensity to change is produced only by the vices of the magistrates or the rigour of the laws, that the people can do no wrong when they respect no right, and that the authority of their doings, whether they act for good cause or no cause at all but their own arbitrary pleasure, is a new foundation of right, the more sacred for being new.

To guard against this experienced and always fatal propensity of republics to change and destroy, our sages in the great Convention devised the best distribution of power into separate departments, that circumstances permitted them to select. They intended our government should be a *republic*, which differs more widely from a democracy than a democracy from a despotism. The rigours of a despotism often, perhaps most frequently, oppress only a few, but it is of the very essence and nature of a democracy, for a faction claiming to be a majority to oppress a minority, and that minority the chief owners of the property and the truest lovers of their country. Already the views of the framers of the Constitution are disappointed. The Judiciary is prostrate. Amendments are familiarly resorted to for the purpose of an election, or to wreak the vengeance of an angry demagogue upon the senate. We are sliding down into the mire of a democracy, which pollutes the morals of the citizens before it swallows up their liberties. Our vanity is the parent of our errors, and these, now grown vices, will be the artificers of our fate.

James Madison

Speech to the Virginia Constitutional Convention (1829)

[Mr. Madison now rose and addressed the Chair: the members rushed from their seats, and crowded around him.]

Although the actual posture of the subject before the Committee might admit a full survey of it, it is not my purpose, in rising, to enter into the wide field of discussion, which has called forth a display of intellectual resources and varied powers of eloquence, that any country might be proud of, and which I have witnessed with the highest gratification. Having been, for a very long period, withdrawn from any participation in proceedings of deliberative bodies, and under other disqualifications now of which I am deeply sensible, though perhaps less sensible than others may perceive that I ought to be, I shall not attempt more than a few observations, which may suggest the views I have taken of the subject, and which will consume but little of the time of the Committee, become precious. It is sufficiently obvious, that persons now and property are the two great subjects on which Governments are to act; and that the rights of persons, and the rights of property, are the objects, for the protection of which Government was instituted. These rights cannot well be separated. The personal right to acquire property, which is a natural right, gives to property, when acquired, a right to protection, as a social right. The essence of Government is power; and power, lodged as it must be in human hands, will ever be liable to abuse. In monarchies, the interests and happiness of all may be sacrificed to the caprice and passions of a despot. In aristocracies, the rights and welfare of the many may be sacrificed to the pride and cupidity of the few. In republics, the great danger is, that the majority may not sufficiently respect the rights of the minority. Some gentlemen, consulting the purity and generosity of their own minds, without adverting to the lessons of experience, would find a security against that danger, in our social feelings; in a respect for character; in the dictates of the monitor within; in the interests of individuals; in the aggregate interests of the community. But man is known to be a selfish, as well as a social being. Respect for character, though often a salutary restraint, is but too often overruled by other motives. When numbers of men act in a body, respect for character is often lost, just in proportion as it is necessary to control what is not right. We all know that conscience is not a sufficient safe-guard; and besides, that conscience itself may be deluded; may be misled, by an unconscious bias, into acts which an enlightened conscience would forbid. As to the permanent interest of individuals in the aggregate interests of the community, and in the proverbial maxim, that honesty is the best policy, present temptation is often found to be an overmatch for those considerations. These favourable attributes of the human character are all valuable, as auxiliaries; but they will not serve as a substitute for the coercive provision belonging to Government and Law. They will always, in proportion as they prevail, be favourable to a mild administration of both: but they can never be relied on as a guaranty of the rights of the minority against a majority disposed to take unjust advantage of its power. The only effectual safeguard to the rights of the minority, must be laid in such a basis and structure of the Government itself, as may afford, in a certain degree, directly or indirectly, a defensive authority in behalf of a minority having right on its side.

To come more nearly to the subject before the Committee, viz.: that peculiar feature in our community, which calls for a peculiar division in the basis of our government, I mean the coloured part of our population. It is apprehended, if the power of the Commonwealth shall be in the hands of a majority, who have no interest in this species of property, that, from the facility with which it may be oppressed by excessive taxation, injustice may be done to its owners. It would seem, therefore, if we can incorporate that interest into the basis of our system, it will be the most apposite and effectual security that can be devised. Such an arrangement is recommended to me by many very important considerations. It is due to justice; due to humanity; due to truth; to the sympathies of our nature; in fine, to our character as a people, both abroad and at home, that they should be considered, as much as possible, in the light of human beings, and not as mere property. As such, they are acted upon by our laws, and have an interest in our laws. They may be considered as making a part, though a degraded part, of the families to which they belong.

If they had the complexion of the Serfs in the North of Europe, or of the Villeins formerly in England; in other terms, if they were of our own complexion, much of the difficulty would be removed. But the mere circumstance of complexion cannot deprive them of the character of men. The Federal number, as it is called, is particularly recommended to attention in forming a basis of Representation, by its simplicity, its certainty, its stability, and its permanency. Other expedients for securing justice in the case of taxation, while they amount in pecuniary effect, to the same thing, have been found liable to great objections: and I do not believe that a majority of this Convention is disposed to adopt them, if they can find a substitute they can approve. Nor is it a small recommendation of the Federal number, in my view, that it is in conformity to the ratio recognized in the Federal Constitution. The cases, it is true, are not precisely the same, but there is more of analogy than might at first be supposed. If the coloured population were equally diffused through the State, the analogy would fail; but existing as it does, in large masses, in particular parts of it, the distinction between the different parts of the State, resembles that between the slave-holding and non-slave-holding States: and, if we reject a doctrine in our own State, whilst we claim the benefit of it in our relations to other States, other disagreeable consequences may be added to the charge of inconsistency, which will be brought against us. If the example of our sister States is to have weight, we find that in Georgia, the Federal number is made the basis of Representation in both branches of their Legislature; and I do not learn, that any dissatisfaction or inconvenience has flowed from its adoption. I wish we could know more of the manner in which particular organizations of Government operate in other parts of the United States. There would be less danger of being misled into error, and we should have the advantage of their experience, as well as our own. In the case I mention, there can, I believe, be no error.

Whether, therefore, we be fixing a basis of Representation, for the one branch or the other of our Legislature, or for both, in a combination with other principles, the Federal ratio is a favourite resource with me. It entered into my earliest views of the subject, before this Convention was assembled: and though I have kept my mind open, have listened to every proposition which has been advanced, and given to them all a candid consideration, I must say, that in my judgment, we shall act wisely in preferring it to others, which have been brought before us. Should the Federal number be made to enter into the basis in one branch of the Legislature, and not into the other, such an arrangement might prove favourable to the slaves themselves. It may be, and I think it has been suggested, that those who have themselves no interest in this species of property, are apt to sympathise with the slaves, more than may be the case with their masters; and would, therefore, be disposed, when they had the ascendancy, to protect them from laws of an oppressive character, whilst the masters, who have a common interest with the slaves, against undue taxation, which must be paid out of their labour, will be their protectors when they have the ascendancy.

The Convention is now arrived at a point, where we must agree on some common ground, all sides relaxing in their opinions, not changing, but mutually surrendering a part of them. In framing a Constitution, great difficulties are necessarily to be overcome; and nothing can ever overcome them, but a spirit of compromise. Other nations are surprised at nothing so much as our having been able to form Constitutions in the manner which has been exemplified in this country. Even the union of so many States, is, in the eyes of the world, a wonder; the harmonious establishment of a common Government over them all, a miracle. I cannot but flatter myself, that without a miracle, we shall be able to arrange all difficulties. I never have despaired, notwithstanding all the threatening appearances we have passed through. I have now more than a hope—a consoling confidence, that we shall at last find, that our labours have not been in vain.

Note During the Convention for Amending the Constitution of Virginia

The right of suffrage being of vital importance, and approving an extension of it to House keepers & heads of families, I will suggest a few considerations which govern my judgment on the subject.

Were the Constitution on hand to be adapted to the present circumstances of our Country, without taking into view the changes which time is rapidly producing, an unlimited extension of the right would probably vary little the character of our public councils or measures. But as we are to prepare a system of Government for a period which it is hoped will be a long one, we must look to the prospective changes in the condition and composition of the society on which it is to act.

It is a law of nature, now well understood, that the earth under a civilized cultivation is capable of yielding subsistence for a large surplus of consumers, beyond those having an immediate interest in the soil; a surplus which must increase with the increasing improvements in agriculture, and the labor-saving arts applied to it. And it is a lot of humanity that of this surplus a large proportion is necessarily reduced by a competition for employment to wages which afford them the bare necessaries of life. That proportion being without property, or the hope of acquiring it, can not be expected to sympathize sufficiently with its rights, to be safe depositories of power over them.

What is to be done with this unfavored class of the community? If it be, on one hand, unsafe to admit them to a full share of political power, it must be recollected, on the other, that it cannot be expedient to rest a Republican Government on a portion of the society having a numerical & physical force excluded from, and liable to be turned against it; and which would lead to a standing military force, dangerous to all parties & to liberty itself.

This view of the subject makes it proper to embrace in the partnership of power, every description of citizens having a sufficient stake in the public order, and the stable administration of the laws; and particularly the House keepers & Heads of families; most of whom "having given hostages to fortune," will have given them to their Country also.

This portion of the community, added to those, who although not possessed of a share of the soil, are deeply interested in other species of property, and both of them added to the territorial proprietors, who in a certain sense may be regarded as the owners of the Country itself, form the safest basis of free Government. To the security for such a Government afforded by these combined numbers, may be further added, the political & moral influence emanating from the actual possession of authority and a just & beneficial exercise of it.

It would be happy if a State of Society could be found or framed, in which an equal voice in making the laws might be allowed to every individual bound to obey them. But this is a Theory, which like most Theories, confessedly requires limitations & modifications, and the only question to be decided in this as in other cases, turns on the particular degree of departure, in practice, required by the essence & object of the Theory itself.

It must not be supposed that a crowded state of population, of which we have no example here, and which we know only by the image reflected from examples elsewhere, is too remote to claim attention.

The ratio of increase in the U. S. shows that the present

12 Millions will in	25 years be	24 Mils.
24 " " "	50 " "	48 "
48 " " "	75 " "	96 "
96 " " "	100 " "	192 "

There may be a gradual decrease of the rate of increase: but it will be small as long as agriculture shall yield its abundance. Great Britain has doubled her population in the last 50 years; notwithstanding its amount in proportion to its territory at the commencement of that period, and Ireland is a much stronger proof of the effect of an increasing product of food, in multiplying the consumers.

How far this view of the subject will be affected by the Republican laws of descent and distribution, in equalizing the property of the citizens and in reducing to the minimum mutual surplusses for mutual supplies, cannot be inferred from any direct and adequate experiment. One result would seem to be a deficiency of the capital for the expensive establishments which facilitate labour and cheapen its products on one hand, and, on the other, of the capacity to purchase the costly and ornamental articles consumed by the wealthy alone, who must cease to be idlers and become labourers. Another the increased mass of labourers added to the production of necessaries by the withdrawal for this object, of a part of those now employed in producing luxuries, and the addition to the labourers from the class of present consumers of luxuries. To the effect of the changes, intellectual, moral, and social, the institutions and laws of the Country must be adapted, and it will require for the task all the wisdom of the wisest patriots.

Supposing the estimate of the growing population of the U.S. to be nearly correct, and the extent of their territory to be 8 or 9 hundred Millions of acres, and one fourth of it to consist of inarable surface, there will in a century or a little more, be nearly as crowded a population in the U.S. as in Great Britain or France, and if the present Constitution (of Virginia) with all its flaws, lasted more than half a century, it is not an unreasonable hope that an amended one will last more than a century.

If these observations be just, every mind will be able to develop & apply them.

William Emerson

Fourth of July Oration (July 5, 1802)

Delivered at Faneuil Hall, Boston

It is the glory of nations, as it is of individuals, to increase in wisdom as they advance in age, and to guide their concerns not so much by the result of abstract reasoning as by the dictates of experience. But this glory is no more the uniform felicity of ancient states than of their ancient citizens. In the eighteenth century, the British nation had existed thirteen hundred years; seen ages roll away with wrecks of empires; marked thousands of experiments in the science and the art of civil government; and had risen to a lofty height of improvement, of freedom, and of happiness. It was yet the misfortune and the disgrace of this kingdom, so famous in the annals of modern Europe, to war with the principles of her own constitution, and to tread with presumptuous step the dangerous path of innovation and unrighteousness.

This sentiment will be vindicated by considering, as on this occasion we are bound "to consider, the feelings, manners, and principles which led to the declaration of American Independence, as well as the important and happy effects, whether general or domestic, which have already flowed, or will forever flow, from the auspicious epoch of its date." In assisting your performance of this annual duty, my fellow-citizens, I claim the privilege granted to your former orators, of holding forth the language of truth; and I humbly solicit a favor, of which they had no need, the most liberal exercise of your ingenuousness and benevolence.

The feelings of Americans were always the feelings of freemen. Those venerable men from whom you boast your descent brought with them to these shores an unconquerable sense of liberty. They felt that mankind were universally entitled to be free; that this freedom, though modified by the restrictions of social compact, could yet never be annulled; and that slavery in any of its forms is an execrable monster, whose breath is poison and whose grasp is death. Concerning this liberty, however, they entertained no romantic notions. They neither sought nor wished the freedom of an irrational, but that of a rational being; not the freedom of savages, not the freedom of anchorites, but that of civilized and social man. Their doctrine of equality was admitted by sober understandings. It was an equality not of wisdom, but of right; not a parity of power, but of obligation. They felt and advocated a right to personal security, to the fruits of their ingenuity and toil, to reputation, to choice of mode in the worship of God, and to such a liberty of action as consists with the safety of others and the integrity of the laws.

Of rights like these your ancestors cherished a love bordering on reverence. They had inhaled it with their natal air; it formed the bias and the boast of their minds and indelibly stamped the features of their character. In their eyes honor had no allurement, wealth no value, and existence itself no charms, unless liberty crowned the possession of these blessings. It was for the enjoyment of this ecclesiastic and political liberty that they encountered the greatest dangers and suffered the sharpest calamities. For this they had rived the enchanting bonds which unite the heart to its native country, braved the terror of unknown seas, exchanged the sympathies and intercourse of fondest friendships for the hatred and wiles of the barbarian, and all the elegancies and joys of polished life for a miserable sustenance in an horrible desert.

It was impossible for descendants of such men not to inherit an abhorrence of arbitrary power. Numerous circumstances strengthened the emotion. They had never been taught that property acquires title by labor; and they were conscious of having expended much of the one for little of the other. They were thence naturally tenacious of what they possessed, and conceived that no human power might legally diminish it without their consent. They had also sprung from a commercial people, and they inhabited a country which opened to commerce the most luxuriant prospects. Of course, property with them was an object of unusual importance. Inhabitants of other regions might place their liberty in the election of their governors; but Americans placed it in the control of their wealth, and to them it was a matter of even less consequence who wore the robes of office or held the sword of justice than who had the power of filling the treasury and appropriating its contents. The resolves and attempts, therefore, of the British government to raise an American revenue they viewed as a thrust at their liberties. By these measures they felt themselves wronged, vilified, and insulted. If they acknowledged the pretended right of parliament to bind them in all cases whatever, it cleft, like a ball of lightning, the tree of colonial liberty, giving its foliage to the winds and its fruit to the dust. There was no joy which it did not wither, no hope which it did not blight. An angry cloud of adversity hung over every department of social life. Demands of business, offices of love, and rites of religion were in some sort suspended, and the earliest apprehensions of the American infant were those of servitude and wretchedness. Such were the feelings which impelled resistance of Great Britain and the rejection of her authority. They were the feelings of men who were vigilant of the rights of human nature, of freemen whose liberties had been outraged, of patriots determined never to survive the honor of their country.

American independence was also induced by American manners. The planters of this western world, especially of New England, were eminent for the purity and lustre of their morals. They were industrious from choice, necessity, and habit. Their mode of living rendered them abstinent from enervating pleasures and patient of toil. The difficulties of subduing a rough wilderness, the severities of their climate, and the rigor of paternal discipline were almost alone sufficient to preserve in their offspring this simplicity of life. It had, however, a yet stronger guard in their military and civil, literary and religious institutions. Exposed continually to the incursion of hostile and insidious neighbors, they trained their youth to the exercise of arms, to courage in danger, and to constancy in suffering. The forms of their government were popular. They exercised the right of choosing their rulers, and they chose them from the wisest and best of the people. Virtue and talents were indispensable qualifications for office, and bribery and corruption were unknown and unsuspected. A deep foresight and an expanded generosity directed their plans of education. Colleges were founded in the midst of deserts, and the means of knowledge and goodness were within the reach of all ranks of the community. Every householder was the chaplain of his family, every village had its instructor of children, every parish its minister of the gospel, every town its magistrate, and every county its court of justice. The study of the law, which is ever conservative of liberty, had a due proportion of followers, among whom it numbered as eminent civilians as any age or country has produced. The colonists, in short, enjoyed all those advantages which conduce to intelligence, sobriety, hardihood, and freedom in a people.

Such were the manners which distinguished Americans for a century and a half. They were the manners of men who, though poor, were too rich to be venal, though humble in pretension, too proud for servility, and though overlooked in the mass of mankind, as possessing no national character, yet convinced the proudest monarchy in the world that an attempt to oppress them was dangerous, and to conquer them impossible.

The impossibility of subjugating America consisted not in the feelings and manners only, but likewise in the political principles of her sons. They honestly believed what they boldly avowed, that the assumption of parliament was a violation of law, equity, and ancient usage. These colonies originally were composed of men who were rather ejected from Britain as nuisances of the State than fostered as her duteous children. If, when their increasing population and riches became an object of attention, they owed anything to the parent country, it was to the king who gave them their charters, and not to the parliament which had expended neither cost nor concern in their settlement, and taken no part in the management of their internal affairs. Whilst the governor represented the royal authority, the provincial assembly was to each province what parliament was to Britain. It framed laws, levied taxes, and made every provision for the public exigence. In regard to the single article of commerce, parliament did, indeed, exercise an unquestioned power of monopoly. In all respects else, it was unknown to the colonies. When, therefore, this body in which the colonies were not represented asserted the right of colonial taxation, its claim was unjust; and with the same right in reality, if not in appearance, might the colonial assemblies have gravely maintained the identical supremacy over the people of Britain which parliament assumed over the people of America.

Was it, then, right in the colonies to resist the parliament and wrong to resist the king? No. For the king had joined the latter to oppress the former, and thus became, instead of the righteous ruler, the tyrant of this country, to whom allegiance was no longer due. Americans called themselves free, because they were governed by laws originating in fixed principles, and not in the caprice of arbitrary will. They held that the ruler was equally obliged to construct his laws in consonance with the spirit of the constitution, as were the people to obey them when enacted; and that a departure from duty on his part virtually absolved them from allegiance.

Let not this be deemed a licentious doctrine. Who is the rebel against law and order, the legislator ordaining, or the citizen resisting, unconstitutional measures? It is the unprincipled minister who artfully innovates on the custom of governing; the ambitious senator whose self is his god; the faithless magistrate who tramples on rights which he has sworn to protect,—these are the men who, by perverting the purposes of government, destroy its foundations, bring back society into a state of war, and are answerable for its mischievous effects. Not those who defend, but those who attack the liberties of mankind, are disturbers of the public peace; and not on you, my countrymen, but on thee, O Britain, who killedst thy people with the rod of oppression, be the guilt of all that blood which was spilt in the Revolutionary War!

Here, then, you find the principles which produced the event we this day commemorate. They were the principles of common law and of eternal justice. They were the principles of men who fought not to subvert the government under which they lived, but to save it from degeneracy; not to create new rights, but to preserve inviolate such as they had ever possessed, rights of the same sort by which George III then sat, and still sits, on the throne of England, the rights of prescription. Hence through the progress of our Revolution these principles continued their operation. Armed in the uprightness of your cause, you disdained an appeal to those ferocious passions which commonly desolate society in times of commotion. No man lost his life for resisting the general opinion. Instruction maintained its influence, law its terrors, and religion its divine and powerful authority. Property was secure, and character sacred; and the condition of the country was as remote from a savage democracy as from a sullen despotism.

Such was the American Revolution. It arose not on a sudden, but from the successless petitions and remonstrance of ten long years. It was a revolution not of choice, but of necessity. It grew out of the sorrows and unacknowledged importance of the country, and, having to obtain a definite object by definite means, that object being obtained, was gloriously terminated. [. . .]

Although, then, the American Revolution must be considered, in regard to this country, the most honorable and felicitous and, in the view of the historian, the most splendid, event the world ever saw, yet to legislators in all climes and periods it conveys this solemn instruction; it teaches them in a voice louder than the thunders of heaven to be just and wise: just in not abridging the freedom and invading the properties of their fellow-men, and wise in not abandoning the measures of a temperate policy for the garish projects of innovation.

If, however, this revolution contain a monition to rulers against political speculations, a revolution of later date affords similar warning to every description of men. The vicissitudes of France during the twelve past years defy the pen of description and deter the writer who values his credit with posterity from essaying the record of truth. See there, ye vaunting innovators, your wild and dreadful desolations! Whatever was visionary in metaphysic, or violent in practice, you greedily adopted, and as hastily destroyed whatever bore the semblance of order, rectitude, and antiquity. You fixed no bounds to either your ambition or cupidity. Not content with banishing faith and law and decency from the Gallic dominion, your ever changeful and unhinging policy assumed the forms of hostility to other governments, and threatened to bring upon the whole civilized world the decades of disorder and rapine. Yet what have Frenchmen gained by all this revolutionary error and frenzy? After warring with science, they now encourage it: after abolishing Christianity, they have restored it; and after murdering the mildest of despots, their present republic is a mere mixture of military despotism and of popular slavery. [. . .] For how shall the liberty of individuals be preserved in a state of universal licentiousness? And after the prostration of religious principle how can you hope for purity of manners? What shall support the superstructure when the foundation is removed? Who ever put faith in the national convention of France after it had denied the existence of God? Or what was ever more farcical than a report on morals from the mouth of Robespierre, whilst that monster of faction was wading to empire in the blood of his country? It is, finally, necessary because this unholy spirit of atheism has already deteriorated the political and moral condition of this country, and still menaces our hopes, privileges, and possessions.

Should it be the fate of America to drink still deeper of the inebriating bowl, its government, whose existence depends on the public sentiment, must fall a victim to the draught. Should the rulers of our country especially ever become intoxicated with the poison; should they deviate from the course prescribed by their wise predecessors, incautiously pulling down what had been carefully built; should they mutilate the form or impair the strength of our most excellent constitution; should they amuse themselves with ephemeral experiments instead of adhering to principles of certain utility; and should they despise the religion and customs of our progenitors, setting an example of impiety and dissipation, deplorable will be the consequences. From an head so sick and an heart so faint, disease will extend to the utmost extremities of the political body. As well may you arrest the flight of time or entice the moon from her orbit as preserve your freedom under atheistical rulers and amidst general profligacy of habit. Libertinism and lethargy, anarchy and misrule, will deform our once happy republic, and its liberties will receive an incurable wound. The soil of America will remain; but the name and glory of the United States will have perished forever. This lovely peninsula will continue inhabited; but "the feelings, manners, and principles" of those Bostonians who nobly resisted the various acts of British aggression will be utterly changed. The streams of Concord will flow as formerly, and the hills of Charlestown grow verdant with each return of spring; but the character of the men who mingled their blood with those waters and who eternized those heights will be sought for, but shall not be found.

What execrations shall we merit from posterity if, with the instruction and example of preceding ages and our present advantages, we shall tamely suffer this havoc from the besom of innovation! Compared with ours, the memory of those Goths who overwhelmed in their conquest the arts and literature of Greece and Rome will be glorious and amiable. They destroyed the improvements of their enemies, but we shall have abolished the customs of our forefathers and the worthiest labor of our own hands; they pleaded the necessity of wasting the refinements of civilization to prevent luxury and vice, but the annihilation of our institution will annihilate all our virtue and all our liberty.

Are we willing, then, to bid farewell to our independence and freedom? Shall we relinquish the bright visions of republican bliss which twenty-six years have feasted our imagination? Upon the trial of only half that period will we decry a constitution which is the wonder of the universe? Or, on account of supposed or real injuries which it may have sustained, will we desert the noble fabric? Be such national perverseness and instability far from Americans! The dust of Zion was precious to the exiled Jew, and in her very stones and ruins he contemplated the resurrection of her walls and the augmented magnificence of her towers. A new glory, too, shall yet overspread our beloved constitution. The guardian God of America, he who heard the groans of her oppression and led her hosts to victory and peace, has still an ear for her complaints and an arm for her salvation. That confidence in his care which consists in steadfastness to his eternal statutes will dispel the clouds which darken her hemisphere. [. . .]

With daily and obstinate perseverance, perform this momentous duty. Preserve unchanged the same correct feelings of liberty, the same purity of manners, the same principles of wisdom and piety, of experience and prescription, the same seminaries of learning, temples of worship and castles of defence, which immortalize the memory of your ancestors. You will thus render yourselves worthy of their names and fortunes, of the soil which they watered with the sweat of their brows, and of the freedom for which their blood was the sacrifice. You will thus give consistence, vigor, beauty, and duration to the government of your country; and, rich reward of your fidelity! you will witness a reign of such enlightened policy, firmness of administration and unvaried justice, as shall recall and prolong to your enraptured eyes the age of Washington and of Adams.

WILLIAM MANNING

The Key of Liberty (1798)

To all the Republicans, Farmers, Mechanics, and Laborers in America. Your candid attention is requested to the sentiments of a Laborer.

Learning and knowledge is essential to the preservation of liberty; and unless we have more of it among us, we cannot support our liberties long.

Millions and millions of lives have been lost and oceans of blood have been spilled in revolutions to establish free governments. But melancholy to relate, the history of all ages proves that they have been but of short duration in comparison with arbitrary ones. It is but about twenty years since our revolution in America, when we established governments so free and rational that they commanded not only the wonder and admiration of America but almost all over Europe. Yet we now see a majority of our leading men not only sickening at republican principles but also using their strongest influence to bring us under an arbitrary government. And this too at a time when they are under the greatest struggles to establish free government similar to our own almost all over Europe. At such an important crisis as this, I conceive it to be not only the right but the duty of everyone to search diligently for the causes of this change, and, if possible, to find out a remedy for so great an evil. Under this conviction, I undertake to give you my sentiments on them.

I am not a man of learning, for I never had the advantage of six months schooling in my life. I am no traveler, for I never was fifty miles from where I was born. I am no great reader, for though I have a small landed interest, I always followed labor for a living.

But I always thought it my duty to search into and see for myself in all matters that concerned me as a member of society. And when the revolution began in America I was in the prime of life, and highly taken up with the ideas of liberty and a free government. I was in the Concord fight and saw almost the first blood shed in the cause. I thought then and still think that it is a good cause, which we ought to fight for and maintain. I have also been a constant reader of public newspapers and have closely attended to men and measures ever since—through the war, through the operation of paper money, framing constitutions, and making and construing laws. Seeing what little selfish and contracted ideas of interest would twist and turn the best picked men and bodies of men, I have often almost despaired of ever supporting a free government. But firmly believing it to be the best sort, and the only one approved of by heaven, it has been my unwearied study to find out the real cause of the ruin of republics and a remedy.

I have for many years been satisfied in my own mind what the causes are and what would prove a remedy, provided it was carried into effect. But I had no thoughts of publishing my sentiments until the adoption of the British treaty in the manner it was done. Then, seeing the unwearied pains and the unjustifiable measures taken by a large number of all orders of men who get a living without labor in the adoption of said treaty, and in elections, contrary to the interests of the laborer, I came to a resolution to improve on my constitutional right and state to you my sentiments. [. . .]

The causes that I shall endeavor to make appear are a conceived difference of interest between those that labor for a living and those that get a living without bodily labor. [. . .]

To search into and know ourselves is of the greatest importance, and the want of self-knowledge is the cause of the greatest evils suffered in society. If we knew what alterations might be made in our minds and conduct by alterations in our education, circumstances, and conditions in this life, we should be vastly less censorious of others for their conduct, and more cautious of trusting them when there is no need of it.

Men are born and grow up in this world with a vast variety of capacities, strengths, and abilities both of body and mind, and have strongly implanted in them numerous passions and lusts continually urging them to acts of fraud, violence, and injustice towards each other. Although they have implanted in them a sense of right and wrong (so that if they would always follow the dictates of their consciences and do as they would be done by, they would need no other law or government), yet as they are sentenced by the just decrees of heaven to hard labor for a living in this world, and have so strongly implanted in them a desire of self-support, self-defense, self-love, self-conceit, and self-aggrandizement that it engrosses all their care and attention—so that they can see nothing beyond self. For self (as once described by a divine) is like an object placed before the eye that hinders the sight of every thing beyond.

This selfishness may be discerned in every person, let their conditions in life be what they will; and it operates so powerfully as to disqualify them from judging right in their own cause. There is no station in this life that a man can be raised to that clears him from this selfishness. On the contrary, it is a solemn truth that the higher a person is raised in stations of honor, power, and trust the greater are his temptations to do wrong and gratify those selfish principles. Give a man honor and he wants more. Give him power and he wants more. Give him money and he wants more. In short, he is never easy: but the more he has the more he wants.

The most comprehensive description of man I ever saw was by a writer in the following words, viz.: Man is a being made up of self-love, seeking his own happiness to the misery of all around him, who would damn a world to save himself from temporal or other punishment. And he who denies this to be his real character is either ignorant of himself, or more than a man. [. . .]

From these natural dispositions of mankind arise not only the advantages but the absolute necessity of civil government. Without it, mankind would be continually at war on their own species, stealing and robbing, fighting with, and killing one another. This all nations on earth have been convinced of and have established it in some form or other; and their sole aim in doing it is their safety and happiness. But for want of wisdom or some plan to curb the ambition and govern those to whom they gave power, they have often been brought to suffer as much under their government as they would without any; and it still remains uncertain whether such a plan can be found out or not. [. . .]

The sole business of government is to keep the peace and secure the protection, safety, and happiness of individuals in this life. No government can be free where the rights and liberties of conscience are abridged. Every person has a right to worship and serve his maker in the way his own conscience dictates, and to Him only is accountable for his religious sentiments and conduct in this life. However anxious and concerned a true Christian may be for the future happiness of others, and however confident he may be that his own opinion is right, he cannot enforce it on others in any better way than by timely and friendly arguments, counsels, and admonitions—graced by a Christian life and conduct agreeable to his own profession of faith. And as there can be no religion without morality, so no Christian can refuse obedience to good and wholesome laws made for his protection and happiness in this world.

That government is the most free that causes the greatest sum or degree of individual happiness in this world with the least national expense. The happiness of a person consisteth in eating and drinking and enjoying the good of his own labors, and feeling that his life and liberties (both civil and religious) and his property are all safe and secure; and not in the abundance he possesseth, nor in expensive and national grandeur, which have a tendency to make other men miserable.

Economy in expenditures ought to be the first principle of a free government. The people ought to support just so many without labor as is necessary for the public good and no more, and ought to pay them so much salary and fees as would command sufficient abilities and no more. All taxes for the support of government ought to be laid equally according to the property each one has and the advantage he receives from government, and collected in the easiest and least expensive manner. The sole end of government is the protection of the life, liberty, and property of individuals. The poor man's shilling ought to be as much the care of government as the rich man's pound and no more. Every person ought to have justice done to him freely and promptly, without delay.

These are the principles and objects for which all governments are or ought to be supported. But plain, simple, and just as they appear to be, yet from pride and selfishness of man such have been the contentions and wars about them as has laid a great part of the world in blood and ashes, and near seven-eighths of the people now existing receive little or no advantages from them. [. . .]

In order to support a free government, there are many duties incumbent on every member of the community, especially on those that labor for a living. They must inform themselves about the nature of mankind, the necessity of government, and about their own rights and liberties as established in their constitutions; that all laws made by their representatives must be obeyed, let them be ever so wrong or bad in their opinion; and that there is no remedy for grievances but by petitioning and using their rights in elections.

The same reverence and respect (in a great measure) ought to be paid to the laws and constitution in a free government as is paid to monarchs and great men in arbitrary ones. But at the same time it is not only the right but the duty of everyone to speak their minds freely on all laws and measures of government, and all men in office; and to point out the disadvantages they feel or fear from them. There is also a duty to listen to what others say, as well as what they feel or think themselves (for a majority must govern), and to attend closely and constantly on all elections, using their privileges in them and taking the greatest pains to find out the true characters and abilities of those for whom they vote. Let no private interest, connection, or relation induce them to vote for those that are not true friends to a free government. Also, it is the duty of all to see that their children are well taught to read and write, and that all the above principles are initiated into them in their youths. It is from a neglect of these duties that free governments are destroyed.

I would not be understood as thinking that these political duties are all that are necessary in this life. For there are many religious and social duties which, if neglected, ensure that we cannot be happy here or hereafter, such as:

The duties and worship we owe to our maker, and reverence and respect for the Sabbath and all holy ordinances and institutions.

To cultivate a respect and love for all mankind, and never refuse friendship and good neighborhood to any on account of their sentiments about futurity, let them be ever so contrary to our own, provided they obey the laws and regulations of society in this world.

To cultivate habits of industry, prudence, neatness, and moderation in living and dress.

To be faithful and punctual in our dealings.

To have respect for the aged and for strangers.

To be a kind husband and wife, a kind parent, a kind master, a kind brother and sister, a dutiful child and servant.

To be kind to the poor, to the sick, and those that are unfortunate.

To be always willing to forgive injuries and settle difference in the shortest and cheapest manner.

In short, to obey the injunction of our Savior: "In all cases, whatsoever ye would that men should do to you, do ye even so to them."

All these religious and social duties are an immediate and heartfelt reward to the doer, and if people would only consult their own happiness in putting them into practice they would greatly lessen the expense if not entirely do away with the necessity of government.

Having thus described a free government, I shall proceed.

[. . .] "In the sweat of thy face shalt thou get thy bread until thou return to the ground" is the irreversible sentence of heaven on man for his rebellion. And there is scarcely anything more terrible to human nature than to be sentenced to hard labor during life—especially if one is not brought up to it in youth. Yet it is absolutely necessary that a large majority of the world should labor or we could not subsist. For labor is the sole parent of all property. The land yieldeth nothing without it, and there is no food, clothing, shelter, vessel, or any necessary of life but what costs labor and is generally estimated valuable according to what labor it costs. Therefore no person can possess property without laboring, unless he gets it by force or craft, fraud or fortune, out of the earnings of others.

But from the great varieties of capacities, strength, and abilities of men, there always was and always will be a very unequal distribution of property in the world. Many are so rich that they can live without labor. So, also, can the merchant, physician, lawyer, and divine, the philosopher and schoolmaster, the judicial and executive officers, and many others who can get a living honestly and for the benefit of the community without bodily labors. And as all these professions require a considerable time and expense of property to qualify themselves for them; and as no person after thus qualifying himself and making a pick on a profession by which he means to live can desire to have it dishonorable or unproductive—so they all naturally unite to make these professions as honorable and lucrative as possible.

Also, as ease and rest from labor are reckoned among the greatest pleasures of life, pursued by all with greatest avidity and, when once attained, create a sense of superiority; and as pride and ostentation are natural to the human heart: these orders of men generally associate together and look down with too much contempt on those that labor. On the other hand, the laborer is conscious that it is labor that supports the whole, and that the more there are that live without labor—and the higher they live or the greater their salaries and fees are—so much the harder must he work, or the shorter must he live. This makes both parties look on each other with a jealous and envious eye.

Before I proceed to show how the Few and Many differ in money matters, I will give a short description of what money is. Money is not property of itself, but only the representative of property. Silver and gold are not so valuable as iron and steel for real use, but receive all of their value from the use that is made of them as a medium of trade. Money is simply this: a thing of lighter carriage than property that has an established value set upon it either by law or general consent. For instance, if a dollar, or a piece of paper, or a chip would pass through a nation or the world for a bushel of corn or any other property to the value of said corn, then it would be the representative of so much property. Also, money is a thing that will go where it will fetch the most as naturally as water runs downhill. For the possessor will give it where it will fetch the most. When there is an addition to the quantity of money, or an extraordinary use of barter and credit in commerce, the prices of property will rise. On the other hand, if credit is ruined and the medium of exchange made scarcer, the prices of all kinds of property will fall in proportion.

Here lies the great scuffle between the Few and the Many. [. . .] The sole foundation on which the Few build all their schemes to destroy free government is the ignorance and superstition of, or the want of knowledge among, the Many. Solomon said, "Train up a child in the way he should go, and when he is old he will not depart from it." And it is as true that if a child is trained up in the way he should not go, when he is old, he will keep to it. It is the universal custom and practice of monarchical and arbitrary governments to train up their subjects as much in ignorance as they can as to matters of government and policy, and to teach them to reverence and worship great men in office and to take for truth whatever they say without examining or trying to see for themselves. And they often make an engine of religion, mixing it with their politics to drive their subjects by the terrors of the other world to submit to their tyrannical measures in this one.

A people or nation being thus trained up from their youths to habits, customs, and manners directly contrary to those necessary in a free government, they are not easily changed. Consequently, whenever revolutions are brought about and free governments established, it is done by the influence of a few leading men, who after they have obtained their object can never receive compensation and honors enough from the people for their services. And the people—being brought up from their youths to reverence and respect such men—go on in the old way, neglecting to see for themselves. Being very fond of being flattered, they readily hear those whom they know have done them great services.

These are the principal grounds on which the Few work to destroy free governments. But there always are many among the orders of the Few who are true friends of liberty; and many of the laborers who understand their true interests, who warmly oppose the measures of the Few—so that it requires the utmost precautions and cunning of them to attain their ends. Finding their schemes and views of interest borne down by the Many, to gain the power they cannot constitutionally obtain, the Few endeavor to get it by cunning and corruption.

Conscious at the same time that with usurpation, when once begun, the safety of the usurper consists only in grasping the whole. To effect this, no cost nor pain must be spared. The Few first unite all their orders in societies and conventions, and establish secret correspondences so that they may act in concert with each other. In all measures they then seek to deceive the people and promote their own schemes, aiming principally at the enlargement of their numbers, fees, and salaries, which oppresses and destroys the rights and liberties of the Many. [. . .]

As a knowledge of the laws, of the characters, abilities, and doings of all men in office, and a knowledge of each other's sentiments and circumstances, so that they might unite in elections, is absolutely necessary to the support of liberty; and as this knowledge cannot be obtained but by the liberty of speech, and of the press, and of associations, and by correspondence with each other: so no pains nor arts are spared by the Few to frighten and drive or flatter and deceive the people out of the use and improvement of these all-important rights and privileges. Whenever they can obtain this, the day is theirs. When a people become so negligent and careless as not to improve these privileges, or so cowardly as to give them up, they are just fit for slaves.

Another very important object to the support of liberty is the formation and construction of laws (as I have said before). No care, pains, or precautions ought to be spared to make them as few, plain, comprehensive, and easy to be understood as possible. But instead of this the Few spare no pains nor arts to have them as numerous, intricate, and hard to be understood as possible—so that no person can understand what is law or what not but by applying to a lawyer, or some judicial or executive officer. In this way, also, they add vastly to their numbers and employments.

It also adds vastly to the power and influence of the judicial and executive officers. Here I would observe my opinion that free governments are commonly destroyed by the combinations of the judicial and executive powers in favor of the interests of the Few. They do it by explaining and constructing away the true sense and meaning of the constitutions and laws, and so raise themselves above the legislative power and take the whole administration into their own hands and manage it according to their own wills and the interests of the Few.

The Free Republican in No. 9 saith that in many of the ancient republics, the judicial power became the mere instrument of tyranny and oppression, and he proposes lawyers as a necessary order in a free government to curb the arbitrary will of the judges. But I thought that would be like setting the cat to watch the cream pot. For though they are neither judicial nor executive officers but a kind of mule order engendered by and many times overawing both, yet from their professions and interest lawyers are the most dangerous to liberty and the least to be trusted of any profession whatever.

The greatest curb to the arbitrary will of judges that ever was invented is the trial by juries. But numerous ways have been invented to pick and pack, overawe and mislead them—so that unless the people get knowledge enough to keep the three powers entirely separate from each other, there will always remain great danger of losing our liberties from this quarter. [. . .]

Another great means by which the Few destroy free governments is by raising standing armies and making needless wars. Although it is absolutely necessary for every nation to be in constant readiness to defend itself against foreign invasion or domestic insurrections, yet the best and only safe defense of a free government is by a well-regulated and disciplined militia. Every able-bodied male ought to be trained up to the use of arms and arts of war from his youth, and be constantly equipped for the defense of his liberties and his country—as well as to have a knowledge of what his rights and liberties are—and to have it all done in the cheapest and easiest manner possible.

But this mode of defense doth not suit the views and schemes of the Few. They wish for a standing army of slaves to execute their arbitrary measures. For this end they use all the means in their power to prejudice the people against supporting a militia. By making it as costly as possible, by introducing costly uniforms and large and pompous musters and shows, and by raising all the disputes between officers and soldiers they can, they try to pave the way for a standing army. Also, they will catch hold of every little misunderstanding or uneasiness, either in their own nation or with foreign nations, to raise an insurrection or foreign war only for a pretext to raise and keep a standing army.

So apt is mankind to be wrought up into a passion by false reports and slight offenses that it is an easy matter for artful and cunning men to set peaceable neighbors and families at variance with each other where there are no grounds for it on either side. In the same manner, towns, states, and nations may be (and often have been) set at war against each other, and thousands and millions have been slain on both sides equally thinking that they were fighting in a good cause when the whole matter in dispute would have made little or no uneasiness between honest neighbors.

Nor do I dispute but that it has been often agreed upon by rulers of nations to make war on each other only that they might have a pretext to raise and keep up a standing army to deprive their own subjects of their own rights and liberties. This is a great object with the Few. When attained, it adds so much to their numbers and strength that they have but little more to fear, and the Many have but little reason to expect that they can maintain their liberties long.

There is one more object of the last importance for the Few to carry their points in without which they cannot obtain the foregoing points. That is elections. Here lies the grand scuffle between the two parties. If the Many know their own strength, rights, and minds equal to the Few, they never need to fear any danger from them. For the numbers interested with the Many are near twelve to one of the Few, and every man elected into office remains a man still and is moved by the same principles and passions as other men are—so that the fear of offending his constituents, the honor of the office, the love of the reward, and to be worshipped into the bargain, carries ten thousand charms with it, and he will ever be faithful to that side that was the cause of his election.

Consequently, the Few have to muster all their craft and force in elections. They will all unite in extolling the greatness, goodness, and abilities of their candidate and in running down and blackening the characters and abilities of the candidates on the other side.

Also, they will appear to the electors in a variety of ways. Some they will flatter by promising favors—such as being customers to them; or helping them out of debt or other difficulties; or helping them to a good bargain; or treating them; or trusting them; or lending them money; or even giving them a little if they will vote for such and such a man. Others they will threaten: If you don't vote for such and such a man—or if you do, etc.—you shall pay me what you owe me or I will sue you; or I will turn you out of my house, or off of my farm. I won't be your customer any longer. I will wager a guinea that you dare not vote for such a man, and if you do you shall have a bloody nose for it.

Or they will hire somebody to communicate these things to them.

Also, they will hinder votes from being counted or returned right. And often they will themselves—or hire others to—put in two or three votes apiece.

All these things have been practiced, and may be again. [. . .]

ALEXIS DE TOCQUEVILLE

Democracy in America (1835, 1840)

Volume One (1835)

Introduction

Among the new objects that attracted my attention during my stay in the United States, none struck me with greater force than the equality of conditions. I easily perceived the enormous influence that this primary fact exercises on the workings of the society. It gives a particular direction to the public mind, a particular turn to the laws, new maxims to those who govern, and particular habits to the governed.

I soon recognized that this same fact extends its influence far beyond political mores and laws, and that its empire extends over civil society as well as government: it creates opinions, gives rise to sentiments, inspires customs, and modifies everything that it does not produce.

In this way, then, as I studied American society, I saw more and more, in the equality of conditions, the generative fact from which each particular fact seemed to flow, and I kept finding that fact before me again and again as a central point to which all of my observations were leading.

Then I cast my thoughts back toward our hemisphere, and it seemed to me that I could make out there something analogous to the spectacle that the New World was offering me. I saw the equality of conditions which, without having attained its extreme limits, as it has in the United States, was approaching those limits more each day; and this same democracy, which was reigning over the American societies, appeared to me to be advancing rapidly toward power in Europe.

From that moment, I conceived the idea for this book.

A great democratic revolution is occurring among us; everyone sees it, but everyone does not judge it in the same way. Some think of it as something new, and taking it to be an accident, they hope to be able still to arrest it; whereas others judge it to be irresistible, because it seems to them to be the most unremitting, the most ancient, and the most permanent fact that we know of in history.

Let me turn for a moment to France as it was seven hundred years ago: I find it divided up among a small number of families who possess the earth and govern the inhabitants; the right of command thus descends from generation to generation with their patrimonies; men have only a single means of acting upon one another, force; one finds only a single origin of power, property in land.

But then the political power of the clergy succeeds in establishing a base for itself and soon extends its reach. The clergy opens its ranks to all, to the poor and to the rich, to the commoner and to the lord. Equality begins to penetrate to the heart of the government by way of the Church, and he who had vegetated as a serf in an eternal servitude places himself as a priest in the midst of the nobles, and will often take a seat above the kings.

As the society becomes over time more civilized and more stable, the different relations between men become more complicated and more numerous. The need for civil laws makes itself strongly felt. Then the jurists make their appearance; they leave the obscure precincts of the courts and the dusty nooks of the clerks' offices, and they will sit in the court of the prince, alongside the feudal barons covered in ermine and armor.

The kings ruin themselves in great enterprises; the nobles exhaust themselves in private wars; the commoners enrich themselves in commerce. The influence of money begins to make itself felt on the affairs of State. Trade is a new source that opens the way to power, and the financiers become a political power that is despised and flattered.

Little by little, enlightenment spreads; the taste for literature and the arts is awakened; the mind then becomes an element of success; knowledge is a means of government, intelligence a social force; the learned come to take part in public affairs.

To the extent, however, that new routes for arriving at power are discovered, the value of birth is lowered. In the 11th century, nobility had an inestimable value; by the 13th century, it is purchased. The first act of ennoblement takes place in 1270, and in the end equality is introduced into the government by the aristocracy itself.

During the seven hundred years that have just passed, it sometimes happened that in order to struggle against the royal authority or in order to take power away from their rivals, the nobles gave political power to the people.

Still more often, the kings caused the inferior classes of the State to participate in the government in order to pull down the aristocracy.

In France, the kings showed themselves to be the most active and the most unremitting of levelers. When they were ambitious and strong, they worked to raise the people to the level of the nobles; and when they were modest and weak, they allowed the people to place itself above themselves. The former helped democracy by their talents, the latter by their vices. Louis XI and Louis XIV took care to make everyone equal below the throne, and finally Louis XV himself descended with his court into the dust.

As soon as the citizenry began to possess the earth in ways that did not follow feudal tenure, and personal property, having become widespread, was able in its turn to create influence and give power, discoveries were no longer made in the arts, improvements were no longer introduced into commerce and industry, without creating just so many new elements of equality among men. From this moment, all the techniques that are discovered, all the needs that come into being, all the desires that demand to be satisfied, are advances toward universal leveling. The taste for luxury, the love of war, the empire of fashion, the most superficial passions of the human heart as well as the most profound, seem to work in concert to impoverish the rich and enrich the poor.

From the time that the works of the intellect became sources of power and of riches, each development of science, each new piece of knowledge, each new idea, had to be considered as a source of power placed within the reach of the people. Poetry, eloquence, memory, the charms of the intellect, the fires of the imagination, depth of thought, all these gifts that the heavens distribute haphazardly, were to the benefit of democracy, and even when they were in the possession of its adversaries, they still served its cause by highlighting the natural greatness of man. These conquests therefore spread with those of civilization and enlightenment, and literature was an arsenal open to all, where the weak and the poor came each day to look for arms.

When one searches through the pages of our history, one comes across almost no great events during the last seven hundred years that did not turn to the profit of equality. [. . .] In whatever direction we cast our glance, we perceive the same revolution to be continuing throughout the entire Christian world.

Everywhere, one saw the various incidents in the life of peoples turn to the profit of democracy. All men helped it by their efforts: those who were looking to contribute to its successes and those who had no thought to serve it; those who fought for it and those who declared themselves its enemy; all were pushed pell-mell in the same direction, and all worked in concert, some in spite of themselves and the others unwittingly, blind instruments in the hands of God.

The gradual development of the equality of conditions is thus a providential fact, which has the following principal characteristics: it is universal, it is durable, and each day it escapes human power. All events, as all men, serve its development.

Would it be wise to believe that a social movement that comes from such a distance can be suspended by the efforts of a generation? Do you think that after having destroyed feudalism and vanquished the kings, democracy will retreat before the bourgeois and the rich? Will it stop now that it has become so strong and its adversaries have become so weak?

Where, then, are we heading? None can say, for to begin with we lack the terms of comparison: among Christians in our time, conditions are more equal than they have ever been at any time or in any country in the world; thus the magnitude of what has already occurred prevents us from envisaging what more may occur.

The entire book you are going to read was written under the impression of a sort of religious terror produced in the soul of the author by the sight of this irresistible revolution that has advanced for so many centuries through all obstacles and that one still sees advancing today in the midst of the ruins it has made.

It is not necessary for God himself to speak in order for us to perceive the certain signs of His will; it suffices to examine the ordinary course of nature and the constant tendency of events. I know, without the Creator raising His voice, that the heavenly bodies follow in space the arcs that His finger has traced.

If long observation and sincere meditation work to lead the men of our time to recognize that the gradual and progressive development of equality is at the same time the past and the future of their history, this single discovery would give to this development the sacred character of the will of the sovereign master. To want to stop democracy would then appear to be to struggle against God himself, and it would only remain for the nations to accommodate themselves to the social state that Providence is imposing on them.

The Christian peoples appear to me to offer in our day a fearsome sight. The movement that is sweeping them onward is already so strong that one cannot suspend it, and it is not yet so strong that one despairs of directing it: their fate is in their hands, but soon it will escape them.

To instruct democracy, to reinvigorate if possible its beliefs, to purify its morals, to regulate its movements, to substitute little by little the science of public affairs for its inexperience, the knowledge of its true interests for its blind instincts; to adapt its government to times and places; to modify it according to circumstances and men: such is the first of the duties imposed in our time upon those who direct society.

A new political science is necessary for a wholly new world.

But this is hardly what we are thinking of: placed in the middle of a rapidly flowing current, we fix our eyes obstinately on some remnants that are still visible on the bank, while the current drags and pushes us backward toward the abysses.

There are no peoples in Europe among whom the great social revolution that I have just described has made as rapid progress as among us, but it has always moved forward haphazardly here.

Never have the chiefs of State given any thought to preparing for it in advance; it occurred in spite of them or without their being aware of it. The most powerful, the most intelligent, and the most moral classes of the nation did not seek to seize hold of it in order to direct it. Democracy was thus abandoned to its untamed instincts; it grew like those children, deprived of paternal care, who raise themselves in the streets of our cities and whose only knowledge of society is of its vices and its miseries. We seemed still to be unaware of its existence when it seized power without warning. Then each individual yielded servilely to its slightest desires; it was worshipped as the image of strength. Later, when it was weakened by its own excesses, the legislators conceived the imprudent project of destroying it instead of seeking to instruct and correct it, and without wanting to teach it to govern, they thought only of driving it out of government.

The result of this has been that the democratic revolution has occurred in the matter of the society without the change that was necessary to make this revolution useful occurring in the laws, the ideas, the habits, and the mores. Thus we have democracy, minus that which ought to moderate its vices and emphasize its natural advantages; and seeing already the ills that it causes, we are still unaware of the good it can yield.

When royal power, leaning for support upon the aristocracy, peacefully governed the peoples of Europe, society, in the midst of its miseries, enjoyed several kinds of happiness that are difficult to comprehend and appreciate in our time.

The power of a few subjects raised insurmountable barriers to the tyranny of the prince; and the kings, feeling themselves in any case clothed, in the eyes of the crowd, in an almost divine character, drew, from the very respect that they had fostered, the will to not abuse their power.

Placed at an immense distance from the people, the nobles nevertheless took the kind of benevolent and calm interest in the fate of the people that the pastor accords to his flock; and, without viewing the poor man as their equal, they watched over his destiny as over a trust placed in their hands by Providence.

Not having conceived of the idea of any social state other than its own, nor imagining that it could ever be equal to its leaders, the people received their favors and did not debate their rights. The people loved its leaders when they were mild and just and submitted ungrudgingly and without servility to their rigors, as to unavoidable ills sent to it by the arm of God. Custom and mores had in any case erected boundaries to tyranny and set up a kind of right in the very midst of force.

The noble not having any thought that anyone wanted to take from him the privileges that he believed to be legitimate, and, the serf regarding his inferiority as an effect of the immutable order of nature, it is understandable that a kind of reciprocal benevolence could be set up between these two classes whose lots were divided so differently. One saw, then, inequality and misery in society, but men's souls were not degraded by it.

It is not the exercise of power or the habit of obedience that depraves men, it is the exercise of a power that they regard as illegitimate and the obedience to a power that they regard as usurped and oppressive.

On the one side was property, force, leisure, and with them the pursuit of luxury, the refinements of taste, the pleasures of the intellect, the cultivation of the arts; on the other, work, coarseness, and ignorance.

But in the heart of this ignorant and coarse mass, one came across energetic passions, generous sentiments, profound beliefs, and savage virtues.

The social body organized in this way was able to have stability, strength, and above all, glory.

But here the ranks of society are mixed up with one another; the barriers erected between men are lowered; the great domains are divided, power is split up and shared out, enlightenment is spread, intelligence is equalized; the social state becomes democratic, and the empire of democracy in the end establishes itself peacefully in institutions and in mores.

I conceive, in consequence, a society where all, regarding the law as their own work, would love it and would submit to it without difficulty; where, the authority of the government being respected as necessary and not as divine, the love that one would bear toward the head of the State would be not a passion but a reasoned and calm sentiment. Each one having rights and being assured of conserving these rights, there would be established between all the classes a virile confidence and a sort of reciprocal condescension, as far removed from pride as from servility.

Taught its true interests, the people would understand that in order to profit from society's goods, one must submit to the costs it imposes. The free association of the citizens would be able then to replace the individual power of the nobles, and the State would be protected from tyranny and from licentiousness.

I understand that in a democratic State constituted in this manner, the society will not be immobile; but the movements of the social body will be able to be regulated and progressive. If one encounters less brilliance there than in the bosom of an aristocracy, one also finds less misery; pleasures will be less extreme and well-being more general; the sciences less grand and ignorance rarer; feelings less energetic and habits milder; one will notice there more vices and fewer crimes.

Lacking the enthusiasm and ardor of belief, enlightenment and experience will sometimes obtain great sacrifices from the citizenry. Each man, being equally weak, will feel an equal need of his fellows; and knowing that he cannot obtain their support except on the condition that he lend them his help, he will perceive without difficulty that for him particular interest is mixed up with the general interest.

The nation, taken as a whole, will be less brilliant, less glorious, perhaps less powerful, but the majority of the citizens in it will enjoy a more prosperous lot, and the people in it will prove to be peaceful, not because it despairs of doing better, but because it knows it is doing well.

If all in such an order of things were not good and useful, society at least would have appropriated to itself all that it could of the useful and good, and men, abandoning forever the social advantages that aristocracy can provide, would have taken from democracy all the good things that the latter is able to offer them.

But we, by quitting the social state of our forebears, by throwing pell-mell behind us their institutions, their ideas, and their mores, what have we taken up in their stead?

The prestige of the royal power has vanished without being replaced by the majesty of the laws; in our day, the people has contempt for authority, but it fears it, and this fear extracts from the people more than was formerly given by respect and love.

I perceive that we have destroyed the individual existences that were separately able to fight against tyranny. But I see the government which inherits alone all the prerogatives wrested from some families, corporate bodies, or men: the sometimes oppressive but often conserving power of a small number of citizens has been succeeded by the weakness of all.

The division of fortunes has diminished the distance that separated the poor from the rich; but in coming closer, they seem to have found new reasons to hate each other, and casting glances full of terror and envy at each other, they push each other mutually away from power. For the one as for the other, the idea of rights does not exist, and force appears to both of them to be the only reason in the present, and the only guarantee of the future.

The poor man has kept most of the prejudices of his fathers without their beliefs, their ignorance without their virtues; he has accepted the doctrine of interest in order to regulate his actions, without knowing the science of it, and his egoism is as deprived of enlightenment as was his devotion in former times.

Society is calm, not because it is conscious of its strength and its well-being, but on the contrary because it believes itself to be weak and infirm. It fears that if it makes an effort it will die: each one senses the malady, but no one has the courage and the energy necessary to seek something better; one has desires, regrets, sorrows, and joys that produce nothing visible or durable, much like the passions of old men that end only in impotence.

Thus we have abandoned the good things that the old state of affairs could offer without acquiring the useful things the current state of affairs could offer; we have destroyed an aristocratic society and, stopping complacently in the midst of the ruins of the old structure, we seem to wish to stay there forever.

What has occurred in the intellectual world is no less deplorable.

Hindered in its march or abandoned without support to its disordered passions, democracy in France has upset everything that it came across during its passage, shaking whatever it did not destroy. It has not taken hold of the society little by little, in order to peacefully establish its empire there; it has not ceased to march forward in the midst of the disorders and agitation of battle. Driven by the heat of battle, pushed beyond the natural limits of his opinion by the opinions and excesses of his adversaries, each man loses sight of the very object of his pursuits and uses a language that corresponds badly to his true sentiments and his secret instincts.

From this arises the strange confusion we are constrained to witness.

I search my memory in vain, and I find nothing that merits greater sadness or pity than that which passes beneath our eyes. It seems that in our day the natural connection that unites opinions with tastes and actions with beliefs has been broken; the sympathy that has always been visible between the sentiments and ideas of men appears to be destroyed, and it is as if all the laws of moral analogy were abolished.

Christians full of zeal are still found among us, whose religious souls love to nourish themselves with the truths of the other life; these will be animated without doubt in favor of human liberty, the source of all moral grandeur. Christianity, which made all men equal before God, will not begrudge seeing all men equal before the law. But through a confluence of strange events, religion finds itself momentarily bound to the powers that democracy is toppling, and it often happens that it rejects the equality that democracy loves and curses liberty as an adversary, whereas by taking it by the hand, it would be able to sanctify its efforts.

Besides these religious men, I find others whose gaze is turned toward earth rather than toward heaven. Partisans of liberty, not only because they see in it the origin of the most noble virtues, but above all because they consider it as the source of the greatest goods, they desire sincerely to secure its empire and to give men a taste of its benefits: I know that they will hasten to call religion to their aid because they must know that the reign of liberty cannot be established without that of morals, nor can a foundation be given to morals without beliefs. But they have noticed religion in the ranks of their adversaries, and that is enough for them: some of them attack it, and the others do not dare to defend it.

The past centuries have seen base and venal souls advocate servitude, while independent spirits and generous hearts struggled without hope to save human liberty. But in our day one often comes across naturally noble and proud men whose opinions are in direct opposition to their tastes and who extol the servility and baseness that they have never accepted for themselves. There are others, to the contrary, who speak about liberty as if they were able to sense what is sacred and grand in it and who noisily demand on behalf of humanity the rights that they have always depreciated.

I see virtuous and peaceable men whose pure morals, calm habits, affluence, and enlightenment place them naturally at the head of the populations that surround them. Full of a sincere love for the fatherland, they are ready to make great sacrifices for it: however, civilization often finds them to be its adversaries; they confuse its abuses with its benefits, and in their minds the idea of evil is indissolubly joined to the idea of what is new.

Nearby I see others who, in the name of progress and endeavoring to treat man as having only a material nature, want to discover what is useful without being concerned with what is just, science far removed from beliefs, and well-being separated from virtue: these call themselves the champions of modern civilization, and they place themselves insolently at its head, usurping a position that is abandoned to them and for which they are unworthy.

Where are we then?

Religious men fight against liberty, and friends of liberty attack religions; noble and generous spirits praise servitude, and base and servile souls extol independence; honest and enlightened citizens are enemies of all progress, while men without patriotism and without morals make themselves apostles of civilization and enlightenment!

Have all the centuries thus resembled our own? Has man always had before his eyes, as in our day, a world where nothing is connected, where virtue is without genius, and genius without honor; where the love of order is mixed up with the taste of tyrants, and the sacred cult of liberty with contempt for the laws; where conscience throws only a dubious clarity on human actions; where nothing anymore seems either forbidden, or permitted, or decent, or shameful, or true, or false?

Will I think that the Creator made man in order to leave him to wrestle with himself endlessly in the midst of the intellectual miseries that surround us? I cannot believe it: God is preparing for European societies a more stable and calmer future; I am ignorant of His designs, but I will not cease to believe in them because I cannot penetrate them, and I will prefer to doubt my own lights rather than his justice.

There is a country in the world where the great social revolution I am speaking of seems to have almost reached its natural limits; there, it has taken place in a simple and easy manner, or rather one may say that this country is witness to the results of the democratic revolution that is taking place among us, without having had the revolution itself.

The emigrants who came to settle in America at the beginning of the 17th century disengaged in a certain fashion the principle of democracy from all those against which it struggled in the bosom of the old societies of Europe, and they transplanted it alone on the shores of the New World. There, it was able to grow in liberty and, marching forward with the mores, to develop peacefully within the laws.

It appears to me beyond doubt that sooner or later we will arrive, like the Americans, at the nearly complete equality of conditions. I do not conclude from this that we might be called upon one day to necessarily draw, from a similar social state, the political consequences that the Americans have drawn from it. I am very far from believing that they have found the only form of government that democracy can give to itself; but it suffices that in the two countries the generative cause of the laws and the mores be the same in order for us to have an immense interest in knowing what it has produced in each of them.

It is therefore not only in order to satisfy a curiosity, in any case legitimate, that I have examined America; I wanted to find lessons there from which we might profit. It would be a strange mistake to think that I wanted to write a panegyric; whoever reads this book will be quite well convinced that such was not my design. Nor was my goal to extol such a form of government in general, because I am among those who believe that there is almost never absolute goodness in the laws. I have never even claimed to judge whether the social revolution, whose course seems to me irresistible, was advantageous or disastrous for humanity. I accepted this revolution as an accomplished or nearly accomplished fact, and among the peoples who have seen it occur in their midst, I have sought out the one in which it attained the most complete and peaceful development, in order to discern clearly its natural consequences and to perceive, if possible, the means of making it profitable to men. I admit that in America I saw more than America: I looked there for an image of democracy itself, its inclinations, its character, its prejudices, and its passions. I wanted to get to know it, if only to know at least what we must hope or fear from it. [. . .]

Volume One, Part One, Chapter Two

[. . .] I have already said enough to place the character of Anglo-American civilization in its true light. It is the product (and this point of departure must always be present in our thought) of two elements which are perfectly distinct, which are in addition often at war with one other, but which, in America, have been in some way successfully incorporated in one another, and wonderfully combined. I mean to speak of *the spirit of religion* and *the spirit of liberty*.

The founders of New England were at one and the same time fierce sectarians and passionate innovators. Held within the narrowest bonds of certain religious beliefs, they were free of all political prejudices.

From this came two different but not contrary tendencies whose traces are easy to find everywhere, in mores as well as in laws.

Some men sacrifice their friends, their family, and their country to a religious opinion; one might think them absorbed in the pursuit of this intellectual good that they have come to purchase at so high a price. However, one sees them seek material wealth and moral pleasure with almost equal fervor; heaven in the other world, and material well-being and liberty in this one.

In their hands, political principles, laws, and human institutions seem malleable things which can be bent and combined at will.

Before them the barriers fall which imprisoned the society in the bosom of which they were born; the old opinions which for centuries governed the world vanish. A course almost without limits, a field without a horizon, open up before them: the human mind rushes forward into them; it searches through them in all directions; but, arriving at the limits of the political world, it stops of itself; trembling, it puts away the use of its most formidable faculties; it abjures doubt; it renounces the need to innovate; it abstains even from lifting the veil from the sanctuary; it bows with respect before truths which it accepts without discussion.

Thus, in the moral world, everything is classified, coordinated, anticipated, decided in advance. In the political world, everything is agitated, contested, uncertain; in the one, passive obedience, although voluntary; in the other, independence, contempt for experience, and jealousy of all authority.

Far from damaging each other, these two tendencies, so opposite in appearance, work together in harmony and seem to lend mutual support to one another.

Religion sees in civil liberty a noble exercise of the faculties of man; it sees in the political world a field freed up by the Creator for the efforts of the intellect. Free and powerful in its sphere, satisfied with the place that is reserved for it, it knows that its empire is established all the better because it reigns only by its own strength and dominates the hearts of men without help.

Liberty sees in religion the companion of its struggles and its triumphs, the cradle of its infancy, the divine source of its rights. It considers religion as the safeguard of mores, and mores as the guarantee of the laws and of its own durability [. . .]

Volume One, Part One, Chapter Four

When one wishes to speak of the political laws of the United States, one must always start with the dogma of the sovereignty of the people.

The principle of the sovereignty of the people, which always exists more or less at the bottom of almost all human institutions, ordinarily remains, so to speak, buried there. One obeys it without recognizing it, or if sometimes it happens to appear for a moment in broad daylight, one soon hastens to plunge it back into the shadows of the sanctuary.

The national will is one of those terms that has been the most widely abused by intriguers of all times and demagogues of all ages. Some saw its expression in the votes bought by a few agents of power; others, in the votes of an interested or fearful minority; there are even some who have discovered it fully expressed in the silence of peoples, and who have thought that from the *fact* of obedience issued, for them, the *right* of command.

In America, the principle of the sovereignty of the people is not hidden or sterile as it is among certain nations: it is recognized by the mores, proclaimed by the laws; it expands with liberty and attains its ultimate consequences without obstacles.

If there is a single country in the world where one may hope to appreciate on its just merits the dogma of the sovereignty of the people, to study it in its application to the affairs of society, and to judge its advantages and dangers, that country is assuredly America. [. . .]

The American Revolution broke out. The dogma of the sovereignty of the people emerged from the township and took possession of the government; all classes put themselves at risk for its cause; one fought and triumphed in its name; it became the law of laws.

A change almost as rapid occurred in the interior of the society. The law of inheritance completed the breaking up of local influences.

At the moment when this effect of the laws and of the Revolution began to reveal itself to everyone's eyes, victory had already been irrevocably pronounced in favor of democracy. Power was, by this fact, in democracy's hands. It was no longer even permissible to struggle against it. The upper classes therefore submitted without a murmur and without struggle to an evil that was henceforth inevitable. What ordinarily happens to fallen powers happened to them: individual egoism took hold of their members; since they could no longer tear power from the hands of the people, and because they did not detest the multitude enough to take pleasure in defying it, they no longer thought of anything except winning its goodwill at any price. The most democratic laws were therefore passed in a mutual rivalry by the men whose interests they hurt the most. In this manner, the upper classes did not arouse popular passions against themselves, but they themselves hastened the triumph of the new order. Thus—singular phenomenon!—the democratic impulse was all the more irresistible in the States where aristocracy had the deepest roots.

The state of Maryland, which had been founded by great lords, proclaimed the first universal suffrage and introduced into the whole of its government the most democratic forms.

When a people begins to tamper with the property qualification for voting, one can predict that it will end up, after a more or less long period of time, making it disappear completely. That is one of the most invariable rules governing societies. As the limitation on electoral rights is reduced, the need to reduce it still more is felt; because, after each new concession, the forces of democracy increase and its demands grow with its new power. The ambition of those who are left below the property qualification is inflamed in proportion to the great number of those who are above it. The exception finally becomes the rule; concessions follow upon one another without respite, and one no longer stops until one has arrived at universal suffrage.

In our day, the principle of the sovereignty of the people has attained in the United States all of the practical developments that the imagination can conceive. It has freed itself from all the fictions with which one took care to surround it elsewhere; one sees it assume every form, according to the necessity of the case. Sometimes the people in a body make the laws as in Athens; sometimes deputies, which universal suffrage has created, represent it and act in its name under its almost immediate surveillance.

There are countries where a power, in a way external to the social body, acts on it and forces it to march in a certain path.

There are others where force is divided, being placed at one and the same time in the society and outside of it. Nothing like this is seen in the United States; there, society acts by itself and on itself. Power exists only within it; one comes across almost nobody who dares to conceive and above all express the idea of seeking it elsewhere. The people take part in composing the laws by choosing the legislators and in their application by electing the agents of the executive power. One can say that the people governs itself, so much is the share left to the administration weak and restricted, so much does the latter feel the influence of its popular origin and obey the power from which it emanates. The people reign over the American political world like God over the universe. It is the cause and the end of all things; everything emerges from it and everything is absorbed into it.

Volume One, Part One, Chapter Five

I have said previously that the principle of the sovereignty of the people hangs over the whole political system of the Anglo-Americans. Each page of this book will make known some new applications of this doctrine.

In nations where the doctrine of the sovereignty of the people prevails, each individual forms an equal portion of the sovereign and participates equally in the government of the State.

Each individual is thus assumed to be as enlightened, as virtuous, as strong as any other of his fellow men.

Why then does he obey the society, and what are the natural limits of this obedience?

He obeys the society, not because he is inferior to those who direct it or less capable of governing himself than another man; he obeys society because union with his fellow men seems useful to him and because he knows that this union cannot exist without a controlling power.

In all that concerns the obligations of citizens to one another, he has thus become a subject. In all that regards only himself, he has remained master: he is free and must account for his actions only to God. From which comes this maxim, that the individual is the best as well as the sole judge of his particular interest and that society only has the right to direct his actions when it feels wronged by his act or when it has need to demand his help.

This doctrine is universally accepted in the United States. Elsewhere I will examine what general influence it exercises on the ordinary actions of life, but right now I am speaking about the townships.

The township, taken as a body and in relation to the central government, is only an individual like any other, to whom the theory which I have just pointed out applies.

In the United States, municipal liberty thus flows from the very dogma of the sovereignty of the people. All the American republics have more or less recognized this independence, but among the peoples of New England, circumstances have particularly favored its development. [. . .]

See with what art, in the American township, care has been taken, if I can thus express myself, to *disperse* power, in order to interest more people in public things. Independently of the electors called from time to time to act as the government, how many different offices there are, how many different magistrates, all of whom, within the limits of their jurisdictions, represent the powerful corporate body in whose name they act! How many men in this way make use of municipal power to their own benefit and interest themselves in it for their own sakes!

The American system, at the same time that it breaks up municipal power among a great number of citizens, also does not fear to multiply municipal obligations. In the United States it is thought with reason that love of the fatherland is a species of religion to which men attach themselves through practice.

In this manner, municipal life in a way makes itself felt at each moment; it manifests itself each day by the accomplishment of a duty or the exercise of a right. This political life imparts a movement to the society that is continual but at the same time peaceful, that stirs it up without disrupting it.

The Americans are attached to the town for a reason analogous to that which makes the inhabitants of the mountains love their country. Among them the fatherland has marked and characteristic traits; it has more physiognomy than elsewhere.

The New England townships have in general a happy existence. Their government is to their taste as well as of their choice. In the bosom of the profound peace and material prosperity that prevails in America, the storms of municipal life are few in number. The management of municipal interests is easy. Moreover, the political education of the people was accomplished long ago, or rather they arrived completely educated on the soil that they occupy. In New England, the division of ranks does not even exist in memory; there is therefore no part of the township that is tempted to oppress the other, and injustices, which strike only isolated individuals, are lost in the general contentment. If the government reveals defects, and it is certainly easy to point some out, they do not attract attention, because the government really emanates from the governed and because it is enough that it work more or less well in order for a sort of paternal pride to protect it. Besides, they have nothing else with which to compare it. England formerly reigned over all the colonies, but the people always directed municipal affairs. The sovereignty of the people in the township is therefore not only an ancient state, but a primordial state.

The inhabitant of New England is attached to his township because it is strong and independent; he takes an interest in it because he actively participates in running it; he loves it because he has no reason to complain about his lot in it; he invests in it his ambition and his future; he participates in each of the events of municipal life: in this limited sphere that is within his reach, he tries his hand at governing the society; he habituates himself to the forms without which liberty only progresses by revolutions, is penetrated by their spirit, acquires a taste for order, understands the harmony of the different powers, and, finally, gathers together clear and practical ideas on the nature of his obligations as well as on the extent of his rights. [. . .]

Volume One, Part Two, Chapter One

In America, the people designate the one who makes the law and the one who executes it. The people itself composes the jury that punishes infractions of the law. The institutions are democratic not only in their principle but also in all their elaborations. Thus, the people *directly* designates its representatives and chooses them in general *each year* in order to keep them more fully dependent upon itself. It is therefore really the people that governs, and although the form of government is representative, it is obvious that there are no lasting obstacles that can prevent the opinions, prejudices, interests, and even the passions of the people from manifesting themselves in the daily direction of the society.

In the United States, as in all countries where the people reigns, it is the majority that governs in the name of the people.

This majority is composed principally of peaceful citizens who, either by taste or by interest, sincerely desire the good of the country. About them, in constant agitation, are the parties, who seek to attract them into their midst and to acquire their support. [. . .]

Volume One, Part Two, Chapter Three

Liberty of the press makes its power felt not only on political opinions, but also on all the opinions of men. It modifies not only laws, but mores. In another part of this work, I will try to determine the degree of influence that liberty of the press has exercised on civil society in the United States; I will try to discern the direction that it has given to ideas, and the habits it has caused the minds and sentiments of the Americans to pick up. At this time, I want to examine only the effects produced by liberty of the press in the political world.

I admit that I do not bear toward liberty of the press that complete and immediate love that is given to things supremely good in their nature. I love it out of consideration for the evils it prevents much more than for the goods it provides.

If someone were to show me, between the complete independence and the complete enslavement of thought, an intermediate position where I might hope to hold fast, I would perhaps settle myself there; but who will discover this intermediate position? You start with the licentiousness of the press, and you become a partisan of order: what do you do? First you send the writers before juries; but the juries acquit, and what was only the opinion of an isolated man becomes the opinion of the country. You have thus done too much and too little; it is necessary to go further. You hand over the authors to permanent judges; but the judges are obliged to hear before condemning; what one was afraid to avow in the book, one openly proclaims with impunity in the defense's pleading; what was obscurely said in a single account is thereby repeated in a thousand others. Expression is the external form and, if I can speak in this way, the body of thought, but it is not thought itself. Your tribunals arrest the body, but the soul escapes them and subtly slips between their hands. You have thus done too much and too little; it is necessary to continue to go further. You finally deliver the writers over to the censors. Very fine! We're getting closer. But isn't the political forum free? You have thus again accomplished nothing; I am wrong, you have increased the harm. Do you by chance take thought to be one of those material powers that increases by means of the number of its agents? Do you count writers like the soldiers of an army? Contrary to all material powers, the power of thought is often increased precisely by the small number of those who express it. The speech of one forceful man, which penetrates alone into the depths of the passions of a silent assemblage, has more power than the confused shouting of a thousand orators; and if one may speak freely in a single public place, it's as if one were speaking publicly in every village. You must therefore destroy liberty of speech as well as that of writing. This time, you have arrived in port: everyone is silent. But where have you arrived? You had started with the abuses of liberty, and I find you now under the heel of a despot.

You have been from the utmost independence to the utmost servitude, without finding, over such a long distance, a single place where you could stop.

There are peoples who, independently of the general reasons I have just enunciated, have particular reasons which ought to attach them to the liberty of the press.

Among some nations who claim to be free, each of the agents of power can violate the law with impunity without the constitution of the country giving to the oppressed person the right to bring a complaint before a court. Among these peoples, one must no longer consider the independence of the press as one of the guarantees, but as the sole remaining guarantee of the liberty and security of the citizens.

If therefore the men who govern these nations were to talk about taking away the independence of the press, the whole people might respond to them: "Allow us to prosecute your crimes in the ordinary courts, and perhaps we will then consent to not appeal to the court of opinion."

In a country where the dogma of the sovereignty of the people openly reigns, censorship is not only a danger, but also a great absurdity.

When each person is granted a right to govern the society, it is necessary to grant him the capacity to choose between the different opinions that agitate his contemporaries, and to evaluate the different facts the knowledge of which can guide him.

The sovereignty of the people and the liberty of the press are thus two things that are entirely correlative: censorship and universal suffrage are on the contrary two things that are in contradiction with each other and cannot be joined together for long in the political institutions of a single people. Among the twelve million men who live on the territory of the United States, there is not *a single one* who has yet dared to suggest limiting the liberty of the press. [. . .]

Volume One, Part Two, Chapter Five

[. . .] Many men in Europe believe without saying, or say without believing, that one of the great advantages of universal suffrage is to call to the direction of affairs men worthy of public confidence. The people cannot itself govern, it is said, but it always sincerely wills the good of the State, and its instinct does not fail to point out to it those who are animated by the same desire and who are the most capable of taking power well in hand.

For me, I must say, what I have seen in America does not justify my thinking that this is the case. Upon my arrival in the United States, I was struck with surprise upon discovering to what extent merit was common among the governed, and how little this was the case among the governors. It is invariably the case that, in our day, in the United States, the most remarkable men are rarely called to public office, and one is obliged to recognize that this has been the case to the degree that democracy has gone beyond all its former limits. It is obvious that the race of American statesmen has gotten much smaller over the last half century.

Several causes of this phenomenon may be pointed out.

It is impossible, no matter what one does, to raise the enlightenment of the people above a certain level. However much access to human knowledge is facilitated, methods of instruction improved and learning made a bargain, men will never be made to learn and develop their intelligence without their devoting time to it.

The greater or less ease with which the people can live without working therefore sets the necessary limit of its intellectual progress. This limit is situated further out in certain countries, less far out in others, but in order for it not to exist at all, it would be necessary for the people not to have to be occupied with the material cares of life, that is to say that it would no longer be the people. It is therefore as difficult to conceive of a society in which all men are very enlightened, as it is to conceive of a State in which all the citizens are rich; these are two correlative difficulties. I will readily admit that the mass of citizens very sincerely wills the good of the country; I will go even further and say that the inferior classes of the society seem to me, in general, to mix with this desire fewer schemes of personal interest than the higher classes; but what they always lack, more or less, is the art of judging the means while sincerely willing the end. What long study, what diverse ideas are necessary in order to acquire an exact idea of the character of a single man! As if the multitude might succeed where the greatest geniuses lose their way! The people never finds the time and the means to engage in this work. It must always judge hastily and attach itself to the objects which stand out the most. This is why charlatans of all kinds know so well the secret of pleasing it, whereas, most often, its true friends fail to do so.

Moreover, it is not always the ability to choose men of merit which democracy lacks, but the desire and the taste.

We must not conceal from ourselves the fact that democratic institutions make the sentiment of envy grow in the human heart to a very high degree. It is not so much because they give to each the means of equaling the others, but because these means continually fail those who employ them. Democratic institutions awaken and flatter the passion for equality without ever being able to satisfy it completely. This complete equality always eludes the grasp of the people at the moment they believe they have gotten hold of it, and recedes, as Pascal says, in an eternal flight; the people is excited by the pursuit of this good which is all the more precious for being close enough to be known, and far enough away that it has not been tasted. The chance of succeeding excites it, the uncertainty of success irritates it; it agitates itself, it tires itself out, it becomes embittered. Everything which at some point surpasses it then appears to it as an obstacle to its desires, and there is no superiority so legitimate that the sight of it is not an annoyance to its eyes.

Many men imagine that this secret instinct which causes the inferior classes among us to cut the superior classes off as much as they can from the direction of public affairs is only found in France. This is an error: the instinct I am speaking about is not French, it is democratic; political circumstances may have given it a particular quality of bitterness, but they did not give rise to it.

In the United States, the people has no hatred for the higher classes of the society, but it feels little goodwill for them and is careful to keep them out of power; it does not fear great talents, but it has little taste for them. In general, one notices that everything which raises itself up without its help has difficulty obtaining its favor.

Whereas the natural instincts of democracy cause the people to keep distinguished men out of power, an instinct not less strong causes the latter to eschew the career of politics, in which it is so difficult for them to remain completely themselves and to engage in it without demeaning themselves. It is this thought which is very simply expressed by Chancellor Kent. The celebrated author of whom I speak, after having given great praise to that part of the Constitution which gives the nomination of judges to the executive power, adds: "It is probable, in fact, that the men who are the most fit to fill these places, would have manners too reserved, and principles too severe, to ever be able to attract the majority of votes in an election based on universal suffrage." (Kent's *Commentaries,* v. I, p. 272.) That was printed without contradiction in America in the year 1830.

I take it as proven that those who regard universal suffrage as a guarantee of the goodness of the choices are deluding themselves completely. Universal suffrage has other advantages, but not that one. [. . .] When great dangers threaten the State, the people are often seen to choose felicitously the citizens who are most fit to save it. [. . .] Great characters then appear in relief like those monuments that were obscured by the darkness of night and that one sees suddenly stand out in the glow of a fire. Genius no longer disdains to show itself in its own image, and the people, stupefied by their own peril, temporarily forget their envious passions. Then it is not unusual to see famous names emerge from the ballot box. I said above that in America the statesmen today seem very inferior to those who appeared, fifty years ago, at the head of public affairs. This does not result only from the laws, but from circumstances. When America fought for the most just of causes, that of a people escaping the yoke of another people, when it was a question of bringing forth a new nation into the world, all the people lifted themselves up to reach the height of the goal of their efforts. In this general enthusiasm, the superior men rushed forward to meet the people, and the people, taking them in its arms, placed them at its head. But such events are rare; one must judge on the basis of the normal aspect of things. [. . .]

Volume One, Part Two, Chapter Six

After the general idea of virtue, I know of none more beautiful than that of rights, or rather, these two ideas merge with one another. The idea of rights is nothing other than the idea of virtue introduced into the political world.

It is by means of the idea of rights that men have defined license and tyranny. Enlightened by it, each could be independent without arrogance and submissive without baseness. The man who submits to violence stoops and abases himself, but when he submits to the right to command which he recognizes in his fellow man, he raises himself in a way above the very one who commands him. There are no great men without virtue; there is no great people without respect for rights: one may almost say that there is no society; for what is a union of rational and intelligent human beings whose only linkage is force?

I ask myself what is, in our day, the means of inculcating in men the idea of rights and of making it, so to speak, self-evident to them; and I see only one, to give to all of them the peaceful exercise of certain rights: this is very evident in children, who are men, but without the strength and experience of men. When the child begins to move amid exterior objects, instinct makes him put to use everything that he finds to hand; he does not have the idea of the property of others, not even that of their existence, but as he is made aware of the value of things and discovers that one may, in turn, strip him of them, he becomes more circumspect and ends up respecting in his fellows what he wants one to respect in him.

What happens to the child with regard to his toys, happens later on to the man with regard to all the objects which belong to him. Why is it that in America, the democratic country par excellence, no one hears those complaints against property in general which often resound in Europe? Is there any need to say it? It is that in America there are no proletarians. Since everyone has private property to protect, they recognize in principle the right of property.

It is the same in the political world. In America, the man of the people has conceived a lofty idea of political rights because he has political rights; he refrains from attacking those of others so that his own will not be violated. And whereas in Europe this same man refuses to recognize even the sovereign authority, the American submits without a murmur to the power of the lowest magistrate.

This truth is visible even in the smallest details of the life of peoples. In France, there are few pleasures reserved exclusively for the higher classes of the society; the poor man is admitted almost everywhere where the rich man may enter; therefore one sees him conduct himself with decency and respect everything that serves the rights which he shares. In England, where riches possess the privilege of enjoyment as well as the monopoly of power, one complains that when the poor man succeeds in entering surreptitiously the place reserved for the pleasures of the rich, he takes pleasure in causing pointless damage there: why be surprised by this? One has seen to it that he has nothing to lose.

Democratic government brings the idea of political rights down to the lowest citizen, just as the division of property places the idea of the right of property in general within the reach of all men. In my eyes, that is one of its greatest merits.

I am not saying that it is an easy thing to teach all men to make use of political rights; I am only saying that, when that is possible, the effects which result from it are great.

And I add that if there is any time in which such an undertaking must be attempted, that time is our own.

Do you not see that the religions are becoming weaker and that the divine notion of rights is disappearing? Do you not see that morals are being corrupted and that with them the moral notion of rights is fading?

Do you not see that on all sides belief is giving way to argument, and sentiments to calculations? If, in the midst of this universal tremor, you do not succeed in linking the idea of rights to personal interest, which presents itself as the sole fixed point in the human heart, what then will you be left with for governing the world, except fear?

When, therefore, I am told that the laws are weak and the governed turbulent, that passions are keen and virtue without power, and that in this situation one must not contemplate increasing democratic rights, I respond that it is because of these very things that I believe one must contemplate it; and, in truth, I think that governments have an even greater interest in this than society, because governments perish, and society can never die. Besides, I do not want to overuse the example of America.

In America, the people were invested with political rights at a time when it was difficult to use them badly because the citizens were few in number and simple in their mores. In growing, the Americans have not increased, as it were, the powers of democracy; rather they have increased its fields of activity.

No doubt the moment when political rights are granted to a people who up to then has been deprived of them is a moment of crisis, an often necessary but always dangerous crisis.

The child inflicts death when he is ignorant of the value of life; he takes away the property of others before he knows that one may rob him of his own. The man of the people, at the moment when he is granted political rights, is, in relation to these rights, in the same position as the child *vis-à-vis* all of nature, and in this case the famous saying is applicable to him: *Homo puer robustus.*

This truth is visible even in America. The States where the citizens have enjoyed their rights the longest are those where they still know best how to make use of them.

One cannot say it too often: there is nothing more productive of wonders than the art of being free; but there is nothing harder than the apprenticeship of liberty. This is not the case with despotism. Despotism often appears as the cure for all evils suffered; it is the supporter of just rights, helper of the oppressed, and founder of order. Peoples go to sleep in the bosom of the temporary prosperity to which it gives rise; and when they awaken, they are miserable. Liberty, on the contrary, is usually born in the midst of storms, it establishes itself with difficulty amid civil discord, and it is only when it is already old that one can appreciate its benefits. [. . .]

It is hard to say what place political concerns occupy in the life of a man in the United States. To take part in the government of the society and to talk about it is the greatest business and as it were the only pleasure that an American knows. This is seen even in the smallest habits of his life: women themselves often go to public meetings and divert themselves from the troubles of housework by listening to political speeches. For them, the clubs to a certain extent take the place of theatrical entertainments. An American does not know how to converse, but he debates; he does not talk, he speechifies. He speaks to you always as if to a meeting, and if by chance he happens to become excited, he will say: "Sirs," in addressing his interlocutor.

In certain countries, the inhabitant only accepts with a sort of repugnance the political rights which the law grants him; it seems that occupying him with common interests takes his time away from him, and he likes to shut himself up in a narrow egoism whose exact limit is formed by four ditches topped off by a hedgerow.

From the moment, on the contrary, that the American was reduced to being occupied only with his own affairs, half of his life would be taken from him; he would feel as if there were an immense emptiness in his life, and he would become incredibly unhappy.

I am persuaded that if despotism ever succeeds in being established in America, it will find it still more difficult to conquer the habits which liberty has brought into being than to overcome the love of liberty itself.

This continually recurring agitation, which democratic government introduced into the political world, passes afterward into the civil society. I do not know if, all things considered, this is not the greatest advantage of democratic government, and I praise it much more because of what it causes to be done than because of what it does.

It is incontestable that the people often manage public affairs very badly, but the people cannot participate in public affairs without extending the circle of its ideas and without its mind going outside its ordinary routine. The man of the people who is called to the government of society conceives a certain regard for himself. As he is then one of the authorities, very enlightened intellects are placed in the service of his own. He is constantly asked for his help, and in seeking to deceive him in a thousand different ways, one enlightens him. In politics, he takes part in enterprises which he did not conceive but which give him the general taste for enterprises. Every day new improvements to be made to the common property are pointed out to him, and he feels the desire awaken to improve that which is personal to him. He is neither more virtuous nor happier perhaps, but more enlightened and more active than his predecessors. I do not doubt that democratic institutions, joined to the physical nature of the country, are the cause, not direct, as many men say, but the indirect cause of the prodigious development of industry that one notices in the United States. It is not the laws which give rise to it, but the people learns to produce it by making the law.

When the enemies of democracy claim that a single man accomplishes whatever he takes on better than the government of all, it seems to me that they are right. The government of a single man, assuming an equality of enlightenment on both sides, puts more follow-through into his undertakings than the multitude; he demonstrates more perseverance, a better grasp of the whole, more perfection of detail, and more accurate discernment in his choice of men. Those who deny these things have never seen a democratic republic or have made their judgment only on the basis of a small number of examples. Democracy, even when the local circumstances and the dispositions of the people allow it to survive, does not present the appearance of administrative regularity and methodical order in the government; that is true. Democratic liberty does not execute each of its undertakings with the same perfection as intelligent despotism; often it abandons them before having gotten results from them or takes a risk on dangerous ones. But in the long term it produces more than despotism; it does each thing less well, but it does more things. Under its empire, it is not so much what the public administration executes that is great, it is what is executed without it and outside of it. Democracy does not give the people the most skillful government, but it accomplishes what the most skillful government is often powerless to create; it spreads throughout the whole social body a restless activity, an overabundant force, an energy which never exists without it, and which, if the circumstances are favorable, can bring forth wonders. There are its true advantages.

In this century, when the fate of the Christian world appears in suspense, some hasten to attack democracy as an enemy power while it is still growing; others are already worshipping it like a new god who arises out of nothing; but both of them understand only imperfectly the object of their hate or their desire; they are fighting in the dark and only achieve a hit by chance.

What are you asking of society and of its government? It is necessary to be clear about this.

Do you want to give to the human mind a certain elevation, a generous way of envisioning the things of this world? Do you want to inspire in men a sort of contempt for material goods? Do you desire to bring into being profound convictions and lay the ground for great acts of devotion?

Are you concerned with refining morals, elevating manners, making the arts shine? Do you want poetry, éclat,[1] glory?

Do you intend to organize a people so that they act strongly on all the others? Do you mean it to attempt great enterprises and, whatever the result of these efforts, to leave an immense mark in history?

If such is, according to you, the principal aim which a society must set for itself, do not choose democratic government; it would not lead you with certainty to the goal.

But if it seems to you useful to turn the intellectual and moral activity of man toward the necessities of material life and to use it to produce well-being; if reason appears to you more profitable to men than genius; if your object is not to create heroic virtues but peaceful habits; if you prefer vices to crimes and prefer that there be fewer great deeds on condition

1. [Public fame, brilliance in the public sphere, to surpass others in public achievement.]

that there be fewer crimes; if, instead of acting in the midst of a brilliant society, it is enough for you to live in the midst of a prosperous society; if, finally, the principal object of government is not, according to you, to give to the entire body of the nation the greatest strength or the greatest glory possible, but to obtain the greatest well-being for all of the individuals who compose it and to spare them the greatest misery; then equalize conditions and constitute democratic government.

But if there is no longer time to make a choice, and a force superior to man is already carrying you, without consulting your desires, toward one of the two governments, at least seek to draw from it all the good that it can do, and, knowing its good instincts as well as its bad tendencies, strive to restrain the effect of the second and to develop the first.

Volume One, Part Two, Chapter Seven

The moral empire of the majority is based in part on this idea, that there is more enlightenment and wisdom in many men who are brought together than in one alone, more enlightenment and wisdom in the number than in the choice of legislators. This is the theory of equality applied to the intellect. This doctrine attacks the pride of man in its last refuge: therefore the minority has a hard time accepting it; it becomes accustomed to it only in the long run. Like all the powers, and more perhaps than any of them, the power of the majority therefore needs to last for a long time in order to appear legitimate. When it starts to establish itself, it makes itself obeyed by force; it is only after having lived for a long time under its laws that one begins to respect it.

The idea that the majority possesses the right, by its enlightenment, to govern the society was brought to the soil of the United States by its first inhabitants. This idea, which was alone sufficient for creating a free people, has today passed into the mores, and it is visible even in the smallest habits of daily life.

The French, under the former monarchy, took it as given that the king was infallible; and when he happened to act badly, they thought that the fault lay with his advisors. This facilitated obedience wonderfully. One could grumble against the law without ceasing to love and respect the legislator. The Americans have the same opinion of the majority.

The moral empire of the majority is based on this principle, that the interests of the greatest number must be preferred to those of the minority. Now, it is easy to see that the respect which is professed for this right of the greatest number naturally increases or diminishes according to the state of the parties. When a nation is divided between several great irreconcilable interests, the right of the majority is often refused acceptance because it becomes too difficult to submit to it.

If there existed in America a class of citizens which the legislature was trying to strip of certain exclusive advantages, possessed for centuries, and wished to bring down from an elevated position in order to bring it back into the ranks of the multitude, it is probable that the minority would not easily submit to its laws.

But since the United States was settled by men equal among themselves, there is not yet enough natural and permanent divergence among the interests of its different inhabitants.

There are some social states in which the members of the minority cannot hope to attract to themselves the majority because it would be necessary to abandon the very object of the struggle that they are sustaining against it. An aristocracy, for example, cannot become a majority while conserving its exclusive privileges, and it cannot let go of those privileges without ceasing to be an aristocracy.

In the United States, political questions cannot arise in such a general and absolute manner, and all the parties are ready to recognize the rights of the majority because they all hope to be able one day to exercise them for their own advantage.

The majority thus has in the United States an immense power in fact and a power of opinion almost as great; and once a majority has formed on a question, there are virtually no obstacles which can, never mind stop, but even slow down its march and allow it the time to listen to the complaints of those it crushes in passing.

The consequences of this state of things are disastrous and dangerous for the future. [. . .] I regard as impious and detestable the maxim that in matters of government the majority of a people has the right to do everything, and nevertheless I place the origin of all powers in the wishes of the majority. Am I in contradiction with myself?

There exists a general law which has been made, or at least adopted, not only by the majority of this or that people but by the majority of all men. This law is justice.

Justice thus forms the limit to the right of each people.

A nation is like a jury charged with representing universal society and applying justice, which is its law. Must the jury, which represents society, have more power than the society itself whose laws it applies?

When, therefore, I refuse to obey an unjust law, I do not deny to the majority the right to command; I am only appealing from the sovereignty of the people to the sovereignty of mankind.

There are men who do not fear to say that a people, with respect to the matters that interest only itself, cannot entirely go beyond the limits of justice and reason and that therefore one should not fear giving all power to the majority which represents it. But that is the language of slaves.

What therefore is a majority, taken collectively, except an individual who has opinions and most often interests contrary to another individual whom one calls the minority? Now, if you admit that a man invested with absolute power may abuse it against his adversaries, why do you not admit the same thing for a majority? Have men, by being brought together, changed character? Have they become more patient before obstacles in becoming stronger? For myself, I cannot believe it, and the power to do everything, which I refuse to a single one of my fellow men, I will never grant to several.

It is not that, in order to conserve liberty, I believe that one can mix several principles in the same government in such a manner that they are really opposed to one another.

What is called mixed government has always seemed to me a chimera. In truth, mixed government (in the sense that is given to this word) does not exist, because in each society one ends up finding a principle of action which dominates all the others.

England in the last century, which has been particularly cited as an example of this sort of government, was essentially an aristocratic state, although large elements of democracy existed within it, because the laws and mores were ordered in such a way that, in the long run, aristocracy would always prevail and manage public affairs as it wished.

The error is due to the fact that, constantly seeing the interests of the great in battle with those of the people, one only thought about the struggle instead of paying attention to the result of this struggle, which was the important point. When a society comes to really have a mixed government, that is to say equally divided between contrary principles, it has a revolution, or it breaks up.

I think, therefore, that a social power superior to all the others must always be placed somewhere, but I think liberty in danger when this power finds no obstacle before it which can check its march and give it the time to moderate itself on its own.

Absolute power seems to me in itself a bad and dangerous thing. Its exercise appears to me to be beyond the powers of man, no matter who he is, and I see only God who can be all-powerful without danger, because his wisdom and justice are always equal to His power. There is therefore no authority on earth so respectable in itself, or invested with a right so sacred, that I wish to let it act without control and to dominate without obstacles. Therefore, the moment I see the right and the capability to do everything granted to any power whatsoever, whether one calls it people or king, democracy or aristocracy, whether it is exercised in a monarchy or in a democracy, I say: there is the germ of tyranny, and I try to go live under other laws.

What I reproach the most in democratic government, as it has been organized in the United States, is not, as many men claim in Europe, its weakness, but on the contrary its irresistible force. And what I find most repugnant in America is not the extreme liberty which prevails there; it is the little guarantee against tyranny which one finds there. [. . .]

I am not saying that in the present time in America tyranny occurs frequently; I am saying that there is no guarantee there against it and that the causes of the mildness of government there must be sought in the circumstances and in the mores rather than in the laws. [. . .] It is necessary to distinguish well between arbitrary power and tyranny. Tyranny may be exercised by means of the law itself, and then it is not arbitrary; arbitrary power may be exercised in the interest of the governed, and then it is not tyrannical.

Tyranny usually makes use of arbitrary power, but if necessary it knows how to do without it.

In the United States, the omnipotence of the majority, at the same time that it facilitates the legal despotism of the legislature, also facilitates the arbitrary power of the magistrate. The majority, being absolute master of the making of law and of the supervision of its execution, having an equal control over the governors and the governed, regards public officials as its passive agents and willingly relies on them for the task of carrying out its intentions. It therefore does not go into the detail of their duties in advance and barely takes the trouble to define their rights. It treats them as a master might treat his servants if, seeing them act at all times under his eyes, he could direct or correct their conduct at each moment.

In general, the law leaves American officials much freer than ours within the limits it has marked out for them. Sometimes it even happens that the majority allows them to go beyond those limits. Backed by the opinion of the majority and confident of its support, they then dare things that astonish even a European accustomed to the sight of arbitrary power. Habits are thus formed in the bosom of liberty that may become disastrous for it. [. . .] When one comes to examine the exercise of thought in the United States, it is then that one sees very clearly to what extent the power of the majority surpasses all the powers that we know in Europe.

Thought is an invisible power, and one almost impossible to seize hold of, which mocks all tyrannies. In our day, the most absolute sovereigns of Europe cannot prevent certain thoughts hostile to their authority from circulating silently in their States and even in the heart of their courts. It is not the same in America: to the extent that the majority is in doubt, one speaks; but as soon as it has irrevocably decided, each one falls silent, and friends as well as enemies seem then to attach themselves together to its chariot. The reason for this is simple: there is no monarch so absolute that he can unite in his hands all the forces of society and vanquish resistance, as a majority can when it is invested with the right to make the laws and to execute them.

In addition, a king has only a material power which acts upon behavior and cannot reach wills, but the majority is invested with a force at once material and moral which acts upon the will as much as upon actions and which prevents at one and the same time the act and the desire to act.

I know of no country where there prevails, in general, less independence of mind and less true freedom of discussion than in America.

There is no religious or political theory which cannot be preached freely in the constitutional States of Europe and which does not penetrate the others; for there is no country in Europe so subject to a single power that he who wishes to speak the truth there cannot find some support in it capable of securing him against the consequences of his independence. If he has the misfortune to live under an absolute government, he often has the people on his side; if he lives in a free country, he can take refuge if necessary behind the royal power. The aristocratic fraction of the society supports him in democratic countries, and the democratic fraction does so in the others. But in an organized democracy like that of the United States, there is only a single power, a single element of strength and success, and nothing outside of it.

In America, the majority draws a formidable ring around thought. Within these limits, the writer is free; but woe to him if he dares to go outside of it. It is not that he has to fear being burnt at the stake, but he is exposed to all kinds of execrations and daily persecutions. A political career is closed to him: he has offended the only power which has the capability of opening it up to him. Everything is refused to him, even glory. Before publishing his opinions, he believed that he had partisans; it seems to him that he no longer has any now that he has opened himself up to everyone, because those who condemn him express themselves loudly, and those who think like him, without having his courage, fall silent and withdraw. He gives in, he bows in the end beneath the effort of each day, and he becomes silent again, as if he felt remorse at having told the truth.

Chains and executioners; those are the crude instruments which tyranny formerly employed, but in our day civilization has perfected even despotism itself, which seemed to have nothing more to learn.

The princes had, so to speak, materialized violence; the democratic republics of our day have made it as intellectual as the human will that it wishes to constrain. Under the absolute government of a single man, despotism, in order to reach the soul, crudely strikes the body, and the soul, escaping these blows, rises gloriously above it, but in the democratic republics, tyranny does not proceed in this way; it leaves the body alone and goes straight to the soul. The master no longer says to it: "You will think like me, or you will die;" he says: "You are free to not think like me; your life, your property, all stays with you; but from this day you are a stranger among us. You will keep your political rights, but they will be useless to you; because if you seek the vote of your fellow citizens, they will not give it to you, and if you demand only their esteem, they will still feign refusing it to you. You will remain among men, but you will lose your rights to humanity. When you approach your fellow men, they will avoid you like an impure being; and those who believe in your innocence, those very same ones will abandon you, because they would be avoided in their turn. Go in peace, I leave you your life, but I leave it to you in a condition worse than death."

The absolute monarchies brought despotism into disrepute; let us take care that the democratic republics do not rehabilitate it and that in making it more oppressive for some, they do not take away from it, in the eyes of the majority, its odious appearance and degrading character. [. . .]

Volume Two (1840)

Volume Two, Part One, Chapter Two

[. . .] To the extent that the citizens become more equal and more alike, the inclination of each to believe blindly a certain man or a certain class diminishes. The tendency to believe the mass increases, and it is opinion which increasingly leads the world.

Not only is common opinion the sole guide which remains for individual reason among democratic peoples, but it has, among these peoples, a power infinitely greater than among any other people. In times of equality, men have no faith in one another, due to their similarity, but this same similarity gives them an almost unlimited confidence in the judgment of the public; for it does not appear to them likely that, all of them having a similar level of enlightenment, the truth will not be found on the side of the greatest number.

When the man who lives in a democratic country compares himself individually to all those who surround him, he feels with pride that he is equal to each of them, but when he comes to envisage the whole body of his fellows and place himself alongside this great body, he is immediately overwhelmed by his own insignificance and weakness.

This same equality which renders him independent of each of his fellow citizens individually, abandons him, isolated and without defense, to the influence of the greatest number.

The public thus has, among democratic peoples, a remarkable power of which aristocratic nations could not even conceive the idea. It does not persuade men of its beliefs, it imposes them and makes them penetrate the souls of men by a sort of immense pressure of the mind of all on the intellect of each.

In the United States, the majority takes care of supplying individuals with a host of ready-made opinions and thus relieves them of the obligation of forming their own. There are a great number of theories of philosophy, morality, or politics which everyone there adopts in this way without examination, on the word of the public, and if one looks closely, one will see that religion itself prevails there much less as revealed doctrine than as common opinion.

I know that among the Americans the political laws are such that the majority there governs the society with sovereign power, which greatly increases the influence that it naturally exercises there over the intellect. For there is nothing more usual for man than to acknowledge a superior wisdom in what oppresses him.

This absolute political power of the majority in the United States in fact increases the influence over the mind of each citizen that public opinion would obtain there without it. But it is not the foundation of that influence. It is in equality itself that one must seek the sources of this influence, and not in the more or less popular institutions that equal men may give themselves. It is plausible that the intellectual influence of the greatest number would be less complete among a democratic people subject to a king than in the midst of a pure democracy, but it will always be very complete, and no matter what laws govern men during times of equality, we can foresee that the faith in common opinion will there become a sort of religion whose prophet is the majority.

Thus intellectual authority will be different, but it will not be less; and, far from believing that it must disappear, I foresee that it may easily become too great and that it may happen that it finally confines the action of individual reason within limits that are narrower than befits the grandeur and happiness of mankind. I see clearly two tendencies in equality: one that carries the mind of each man to new thoughts and the other that readily reduces it to no longer thinking at all. And I see how, under the influence of certain laws, democracy may extinguish the intellectual liberty that the democratic social state favors, so that after having broken all the shackles once imposed upon it by classes or by individual men, the human mind would shackle itself tightly to the general will of the majority.

If, in place of all the different powers that encumbered or hampered excessively the activity of individual reason, democratic peoples substituted the absolute power of a majority, the evil would only have changed character. Men would not have found the means to live independently; they would only have discovered—something not easy to do—a new physiognomy of servitude. This, I cannot repeat too often, is matter for profound reflection on the part of those who see in liberty of mind something sacred and who hate not only the despot but despotism. For myself, when I feel the hand of power weighing heavily upon my head, it is of little importance for me to know who oppresses me, and I am not more disposed to place my head in the yoke because a million arms present it to me. [. . .]

Volume Two, Part One, Chapter Five

[. . .] When religion is destroyed among a people, doubt takes over the highest regions of the intellect, and it halfway paralyzes all the others. Everyone becomes used to having only confused and unstable notions about the matters that most interest his fellow men and himself; men defend their opinions badly or abandon them, and since they despair of being able, by themselves alone, to resolve the greatest problems that human fate presents, they are reduced in cowardly fashion to not giving them any thought.

Such a state cannot fail to weaken souls; it relaxes the springs of the will, and it prepares citizens for servitude.

Not only does it then happen that these men allow their liberty to be taken, but often they give it away.

Just as in matters of politics, when authority in matters of religion no longer exists men are soon frightened by the sight of this independence without limits. This perpetual agitation of all things worries and exhausts them. Since everything is in motion in the intellectual world, they wish at least that everything be firm and stable in the material order, and since they are no longer able to recover their former beliefs, they give themselves a master.

For myself, I doubt that man can ever support at the same time complete religious independence and complete political liberty, and I am led to think that if he has no faith, he must serve, and if he is free, he must believe.

I do not know, however, if this great utility of religions is not still more visible among peoples whose conditions are equal than among all the others.

It must be acknowledged that equality, which introduces great goods into the world, nevertheless suggests to men, as will be shown hereafter, some very dangerous instincts; it tends to isolate them from one another, leading each of them to be concerned only with himself alone.

It opens their soul excessively to the love of material pleasures.

The greatest advantage of religions is to inspire completely opposite instincts. There is no religion which does not place the object of man's desires beyond and above earthly goods and which does not raise his soul naturally toward regions far superior to his own. Nor are there any which do not impose upon each man some duties toward mankind, or to be performed in common with it, and which do not in this way draw him away, from time to time, from the contemplation of himself. This is true of the most false and most dangerous religions.

Religious peoples are thus naturally strong precisely where democratic peoples are weak, which shows well how important it is that men keep their religion while becoming equal.

I have neither the right nor the wish to examine the divine means God uses to make a religious belief achieve a place in the heart of man. At this time I am considering religions only from a purely human point of view; I am looking for the manner in which they can most easily conserve their influence during the democratic times that we are entering.

I have shown how, in times of enlightenment and equality, the human mind consents only with difficulty to accept dogmatic beliefs and only feels the need of them strongly with respect to religion. This indicates first that during those times, religions must keep themselves more discreetly than in all others within the limits that are proper to them and not seek to go outside those limits; for, in wanting to extend their power beyond religious matters, they risk no longer being believed in any matter. They must thus mark out with care the sphere within which they claim to decide the human mind, and beyond this leave it entirely free to be entrusted to itself. [. . .]

Volume Two, Part Two, Chapter One

The first and the strongest of the passions that equality of conditions causes to be born, it is not necessary for me to say, is the love of this very equality. It will thus not be surprising if I talk about it before all the others.

Everyone has noticed that in our time, and especially in France, this passion for equality occupies every day a larger place in the human heart. It has been said a hundred times that our contemporaries have a much more ardent and much more tenacious love for equality than for liberty, but I do not think that we have gone far enough back to the causes of this fact. I am going to try to do it.

One can imagine an extreme point where liberty and equality touch one another and merge together.

I assume that all the citizens participate in the government and that everyone has an equal right to participate in it.

Since no one then differs from his fellow men, no one will be able to exercise a tyrannical power; men will be perfectly free because they will all be entirely equal; and they will all be perfectly equal because they will be entirely free. It is toward this ideal that democratic peoples tend.

This is the most complete form that equality can take on earth, but there are a thousand others, which, without being as perfect, are scarcely less dear to these peoples.

Equality may be established in the civil society and not reign in the political world. One may have the right to indulge in the same pleasures, to enter the same professions, and to get together in the same places; in a word, to live in the same manner and pursue wealth by the same means, without everyone taking the same part in government.

A sort of equality may even be established in the political world, although there is no political liberty there. One is the equal of all one's fellow men, save one, who is, without exception, the master of all and who picks the agents of his power from among all men equally.

It would be easy to make several other hypotheses according to which a very great equality might easily be combined with more or less free institutions or even with institutions that are not at all free.

Although men cannot become absolutely equal without being completely free, and consequently equality, in its most extreme degree, merges with liberty, we are therefore justified in distinguishing the one from the other.

The taste that men have for liberty and that which they feel for equality are, in fact, two distinct things, and I am not afraid to add that, among democratic peoples, they are two unequal things.

If one wishes to pay attention, one will find in each age a particular and dominant fact to which the others are attached; this fact almost always gives birth to a mother thought, or to a principal passion that then ends up attracting to itself and sweeping along in its course all sentiments and all ideas. It is like a great river toward which each of the surrounding streams seems to flow.

Liberty manifests itself to men in different times and under different forms; it is not attached exclusively to one social state, and it is found in other places besides democracies. It cannot thus form the distinctive characteristic of democratic times.

The particular and dominant fact that makes these times stand out is the equality of conditions; the principal passion that agitates men in these times is the love of that equality.

Do not ask what singular charm the men of democratic ages find in living as equals nor the particular reasons they may have for being so obstinately attached to equality rather than to the other goods that society offers them: equality forms the distinctive characteristic of the epoch in which they live;

that alone suffices to explain why they prefer it to all the rest.

But, independently of this reason, there are several others that, in all times, normally lead men to prefer equality to liberty.

If a people were ever able itself to destroy or even diminish within itself the equality that prevails there, it would succeed in doing so only by means of long and difficult effort. It would have to modify its social state, abolish its laws, make over its ideas, change its habits, and alter its mores. But, in order to lose political liberty, it suffices to not hold onto it, and it slips away.

Men are therefore attached to equality not only because it is dear to them; they are also attached to it because they believe it is bound to last forever.

There are no men so limited and so thoughtless that they do not see that political liberty may, in its excesses, endanger the tranquility, the patrimony, and the life of private individuals. On the contrary, only attentive and farsighted men perceive the perils with which equality threatens us, and ordinarily they avoid pointing them out. They know that the calamities they fear are a long way off, and they flatter themselves that they will touch only the generations to come, about which the present generation scarcely troubles itself. The evils to which liberty sometimes leads are immediate; they are visible to all, and all, more or less, feel them. The evils that extreme equality can produce only manifest themselves little by little; they insinuate themselves into the social body gradually; they are only seen from time to time, and, at the moment when they become most violent, habit has already made it so that they are no longer felt.

The goods that liberty procures are only visible in the long term, and it is always easy to misconstrue the cause that produces them.

The advantages of equality make themselves felt from the beginning, and every day we see them flow from their source.

Political liberty gives, from time to time, to a certain number of citizens, sublime pleasures.

Equality furnishes every day a multitude of small pleasures to every man. The charms of equality are felt at every moment, and they are within the reach of everyone; the most noble hearts are not insensible to them, and the most ordinary souls delight in them. The passion that equality causes to be born is therefore bound to be at once powerful and general.

Men cannot enjoy political liberty without purchasing it by means of some sacrifices, and they never take full possession of it except by much effort. But the pleasures that equality procures offer themselves of their own accord. Each of the small incidents of private life seems to give rise to them, and in order to savor them, it is necessary only to live.

Democratic peoples love equality in all times, but it is in certain epochs that they push the passion that they feel for it to the point of delirium. This occurs at the moment that the old social hierarchy, under threat for a long time, is completely destroyed after a final internal struggle, and the barriers that separate the citizens are finally overturned. Men then throw themselves upon equality as upon a conquest, and they become attached to it as to a precious good that one wants to take from them. The passion for equality penetrates into every part of the human heart, it spreads there, and it fills it completely. Do not tell men that by so blindly giving way to an exclusive passion, they endanger their most precious interests; they are deaf. Do not point out to them the liberty that is slipping from their hands while they are looking elsewhere; they are blind, or rather they perceive in the entire universe only a single good worthy of desire.

The foregoing applies to all democratic nations. What follows only relates to us.

In the majority of modern nations, and in particular among the peoples of the European continent, the taste for and the idea of liberty only began to appear and grow at the moment when conditions began to become more equal and as a consequence of this very equality. It was the absolute monarchs who did the most work to level ranks among their subjects. Among these peoples, equality preceded liberty; equality was thus an old reality when liberty was still a new thing; the one had already created opinions, customs, and laws that were suited to itself, when the other appeared alone and, for the first time, in the light of day. Thus, the second still only existed in ideas and tastes, while the first had already penetrated into habits, taken possession of mores, and given a particular turn to the slightest actions of life. Why be surprised if the men of our day prefer the one to the other?

I think that democratic peoples have a natural taste for liberty; left to themselves, they seek it, they love it, and they feel pain if it is taken away from them. But they have an ardent, insatiable, eternal, invincible passion for equality; they want equality in liberty, and, if they cannot obtain it, they still want it in slavery. They will put up with poverty, servitude, barbarism, but they will not put up with aristocracy.

This is true in all times, and above all in ours. All the men and all the powers that try to struggle against this irresistible power will be overthrown and destroyed by it. In our day, liberty cannot be established without its support, and despotism itself cannot prevail without it.

Volume Two, Part Two, Chapter Two

I have shown how, in times of equality, each man looks within himself for his beliefs; I wish to show how, in these same times, he turns all his sentiments toward himself alone.

Individualism is a recent expression that a new idea has brought into being. Our fathers only knew about egoism.

Egoism is a passionate and exaggerated love of oneself, which leads man to relate everything only to himself alone and to prefer himself over all things.

Individualism is a reflective and peaceful sentiment that disposes each citizen to isolate himself from the mass of his fellow men and to draw himself off to the side with his family and his friends in such a way that, after having thus created for himself a small society for his own use, he willingly abandons the larger society to itself.

Egoism is born from a blind instinct; individualism proceeds from an erroneous judgment rather than a depraved sentiment. It has its source in the defects of the mind as much as in the vices of the heart.

Egoism dries up the germ of all the virtues; individualism at first only dries up the source of the public virtues, but over the long term it attacks and destroys all the others and eventually becomes absorbed in egoism.

Egoism is a vice as old as the world. It scarcely belongs more to one form of society than to another.

Individualism is in origin democratic, and it risks growing as conditions become more equal.

Among aristocratic peoples, families remain in the same state for centuries and often in the same place. That makes all generations, so to speak, contemporaries. A man almost always knows his ancestors and honors them; he believes he already sees his great-grandchildren, and he loves them. He willingly sets himself duties toward both of them, and he frequently comes to sacrifice his personal pleasures to these beings who no longer exist or do not yet exist.

Aristocratic institutions have, in addition, the effect of tightly connecting each man to several of his fellow citizens.

Since the classes within an aristocratic people are very distinct and immobile, each of them becomes for its members a sort of small fatherland, more visible and more precious than the larger one.

Since in aristocratic societies all citizens are placed in a fixed post, some above the others, it again results that each of them always sees above him a man whose protection he needs, and below he sees another whose aid he may invoke.

The men who live in aristocratic times are therefore almost always connected in a close way to something that is placed outside of themselves, and they are often disposed to forget themselves. It is true that, in these same times, the general notion of *one's fellow man* is obscure and that one scarcely thinks of sacrificing oneself for the cause of humanity, but one often sacrifices oneself for certain men.

In democratic times, on the contrary, when the duties of each individual toward the species are much clearer, devotion to one man becomes rarer: the tie of human affections is stretched and loosened.

Among democratic peoples, new families are constantly emerging from nowhere, other ones fall back into obscurity all the time, and all those that remain change their aspect; the thread of the past is broken at every moment, and the vestige of prior generations is effaced. You easily forget those who have preceded you, and you have no idea of those who will follow you. One takes an interest only in those who are closest to you.

Since each class comes to be similar to the others and is mingled with them, its members become indifferent and like strangers to each other. Aristocracy had made of all its citizens a long chain that went up from the peasant to the king; democracy breaks the chain and separates each link from the others.

As conditions become more equal, there are a larger number of individuals who, while no longer being rich enough or powerful enough to exercise a large influence on the fate of their fellow men, have nonetheless acquired or conserved enough enlightenment and property to be able to be self-sufficient. These men owe nothing to anyone; they expect almost nothing from anyone; they are accustomed to always consider themselves in isolation, and they readily imagine that their whole destiny is in their hands.

In this way, democracy not only makes each man forget his forefathers, but it conceals his descendents from him and separates him from his contemporaries; it leads him back constantly toward himself alone and threatens finally to confine him entirely within the solitude of his own heart. [. . .]

Volume Two, Part Two, Chapter Four

Despotism, which by its nature is fearful, sees in the isolation of men the surest guarantee of its own duration, and it ordinarily devotes all of its attention to isolating them. There is no vice of the human heart that suits it as much as egoism: a despot easily pardons his subjects for not loving him, provided that they do not love one another. He does not demand that they help him to govern the State; it is enough that they do not aspire to govern it themselves. He calls turbulent and restless spirits those who claim to unite their efforts in order to create mutual prosperity, and, changing the natural sense of the words, he calls good citizens those who confine themselves narrowly within themselves.

Thus, the vices that despotism brings into being are precisely those that equality promotes. These two things complement one another and help one another in a way that is lethal.

Equality places men beside each other, without a common link to hold them. Despotism raises barriers between them and separates them. It disposes them to not think about their fellow men and makes indifference into a kind of public virtue.

Despotism, which is dangerous at all times, is thus especially to be feared in democratic times.

It is easy to see that in these same times men have a particular need for liberty.

When citizens are forced to assume responsibility for public affairs, they are necessarily removed from the milieu of their individual interests and drawn away, from time to time, from looking at themselves.

From the moment that one treats common affairs in common, every man sees that he is not as independent of his fellow men as he imagined himself to be at first and that, in order to obtain their help, he must often lend them his active support.

When the public governs, there is no one who does not sense the value of public goodwill and who does not seek to capture it by attracting to himself the esteem and the affection of those in whose midst he must live.

Several of the passions that turn hearts cold and divide them are then obliged to withdraw to the bottom of the soul and conceal themselves there. Pride conceals itself, contempt dares not show itself. Egoism is afraid of itself.

Under a free government, since most public offices are elective, the men for whom the largeness of their soul or the restlessness of their desires leaves them too little space in private life, are aware every day that they cannot do without the population that surrounds them.

It then occurs that one thinks of one's fellow men out of ambition and that often one finds, in a sense, one's interest in forgetting oneself. I know that one can confront me here with all the intrigues that an election occasions, the shameful methods that candidates often make use of, and the calumnies that their enemies spread. These occasion hatreds, and they recur all the more often as elections become more frequent.

These evils are great, without doubt, but they are passing, while the goods that come into being with them remain.

The desire to be elected may momentarily lead certain men to make war on each other, but this same desire leads all men in the long term to lend one another mutual support; and if it happens that an election accidentally divides two friends, the electoral system brings together in a permanent manner a multitude of citizens who would have remained forever strangers to one another. Liberty creates some individual hatreds, but despotism creates general indifference.

The Americans have combated by means of liberty the individualism that equality brought into being, and they have vanquished it.

The lawmakers of America did not believe that in order to cure a malady so natural to the social body in democratic times, and so lethal, it was sufficient to accord the nation as a whole a representation of itself; they thought that, in addition, it was necessary to give a political life to each portion of the territory in order to infinitely multiply the chances for the citizens to act together and to make them feel every day that they depend on one another.

In so doing they conducted themselves wisely.

The general affairs of a country occupy only the leading citizens. Those men are only periodically brought together in the same places, and since it often happens that afterward they lose sight of one another, lasting ties are not established between them. But when it is a matter of having the particular affairs of a county settled by the men who live in it, the same individuals are always in contact, and they are in a way forced to get to know one another and to accommodate one another.

It is difficult to draw a man out of himself in order to interest him in the fate of the whole State because he understands poorly the influence that the fate of the State may exercise on his own lot. But if it is necessary to make a road pass the end of his property, he will see with a glance that there is a relation between this small public affair and his most important private affairs, and he will see, without being shown, the tight link that unites at this point the particular interest and the general interest.

It is therefore by charging the citizens with the administration of small public matters, much more than by handing over to them the government of great ones, that one interests them in the public good and makes them see the continual need that they have of one another in order to produce it.

One may, by an act of brilliance, gain at one stroke the favor of a people; but in order to win the love and respect of the population that surrounds you, a long succession of small services rendered, obscure good offices, a constant habit of kindness, and a well-established reputation for disinterestedness are necessary.

Local liberties, which cause a great number of citizens to value the affection of their neighbors and their close relations, thus continually lead men back toward each other, despite the instincts that draw them apart, and force them to help one another.

In the United States, the wealthiest citizens take great care not to isolate themselves from the people; on the contrary, they approach them constantly, they listen to them willingly and talk to them every day. They know that rich men in democracies always need the poor and that, in democratic times, one attaches the poor to oneself by one's manners more than by largesse. The very magnitude of the largesse, which illuminates the difference of conditions, causes a secret irritation in those who derive advantage from it. But simplicity of manners has almost irresistible charms: their familiarity is captivating and their very lack of refinement does not always displease.

This truth does not penetrate the mind of the rich at first. They ordinarily put up a resistance to it as long as the democratic revolution lasts, and they even refuse to accept it immediately after this revolution is accomplished. They willingly consent to do good to the people, but they want to continue carefully to keep it at a distance. They believe that that is sufficient; they are mistaken. This way, they would bankrupt themselves without warming the heart of the population that surrounds them. It is not the sacrifice of their money that is required of them; it is the sacrifice of their pride.

One has the impression that in the United States there is no imagination that does not exhaust itself in inventing means of increasing the wealth and satisfying the needs of the public. The most enlightened inhabitants of each county constantly make use of their learning in order to discover new secrets suited for increasing the common prosperity, and when they have found some, they hasten to hand them over to the crowd.

When we examine closely the vices and weaknesses that are often exhibited in America by those who govern, we are surprised by the growing prosperity of its people, but we are wrong to be surprised. It is not the elected magistrate who makes American democracy prosper; rather, it prospers because the magistrate is elective.

It would be unfair to think that the patriotism of the Americans and the zeal each of them shows for the well-being of his fellow citizens is not real. Although private interest governs most human actions, in the United States as well as elsewhere, it does not decide all of them.

I must say that I have often seen Americans make great and true sacrifices for the republic, and I have noticed a hundred times that when necessary they almost never fail to give reliable support to one another.

The free institutions that the inhabitants of the United States possess, and the political rights of which they make so much use, remind each citizen, and in a thousand ways, that he lives in society. At every moment they lead his mind back toward this idea, that it is the duty as well as the interest of men to make themselves useful to their fellow men; and, as he sees no particular reason to hate them, since he is never either their slave or their master, his heart easily inclines in the direction of altruism. At first one assumes responsibility for the general interest by necessity, and then by choice; what was a calculation becomes an instinct; and, by dint of working for the good of one's fellow citizens, one finally acquires the habit and the taste for helping them.

Many men in France consider equality of conditions as a pre-eminent evil, and political liberty as a second. When they are obliged to suffer the one, they try hard at least to escape the other. And myself, I say that in order to combat the evils that equality may produce, there is only one effective remedy: that is political liberty.

Volume Two, Part Four, Chapter Six

I had noticed during my stay in the United States that a democratic social state similar to that of the Americans could offer unusual opportunities for the establishment of despotism, and I had seen upon my return to Europe how much the majority of our princes had already made use of the ideas, sentiments, and needs that this same social state gave rise to, in order to extend the sphere of their power.

That led me to believe that the Christian nations would perhaps end up by suffering some oppression similar to that which once weighed heavily upon several of the peoples of antiquity.

A more detailed examination of the subject and five years of further meditations have not diminished my fears, but they have changed their object.

In past times one never saw a sovereign so absolute and so powerful that it undertook to administer by itself, and without the aid of secondary powers, all parts of a great empire. None of them were tempted to subject all their subjects without distinction to the details of a uniform rule, or descended to the side of each of them in order to direct and to lead them. The idea of such an enterprise never presented itself to the human mind, and, if any man had happened to conceive of it, insufficient enlightenment, the imperfection of administrative procedures, and above all the natural obstacles produced by the inequality of conditions would have soon halted such a vast plan in the midst of its execution.

One sees that during the period of the Caesars' greatest power, the different peoples that inhabited the Roman world had still preserved different customs and mores: although subject to a single monarch, the majority of the provinces were administered separately; they were filled with powerful and active municipalities, and although the whole government of the empire was concentrated in the hands of the emperor alone, and although he remained always, when necessary, the arbiter of all things, the details of social life and of individual life normally escaped his control.

The emperors possessed, it is true, a power that was immense and without counterweight, which allowed them to abandon themselves freely to the capriciousness of their inclinations and to employ the entire force of the State to satisfy them. They often abused this power to arbitrarily deprive a citizen of his property or his life: their tyranny weighed very heavily upon some; but it did not extend over a great number; it was attached to a few great principal objects and ignored the rest; it was violent and limited.

It seems that, if despotism were to establish itself among the democratic nations of our time, it would have different characteristics: it would be more far-reaching and milder, and it would degrade men without ill-treating them.

I do not doubt that, in times of enlightenment and equality like ours, sovereigns will succeed more easily in gathering all public powers into their hands alone and in penetrating more normally and more deeply into the sphere of private interests than those of antiquity were ever able to do. But this same equality, which facilitates despotism, tempers it; we have seen how, to the extent that men are more alike and more equal, public mores become more humane and milder; when no citizen has great power or great wealth, tyranny lacks, as it were, opportunity and a theater for action. Since all fortunes are modest, passions are naturally contained, imagination limited, pleasures simple. This universal moderation moderates the sovereign himself and arrests within certain limits the disordered impetus of his desires. [. . .]

Democratic governments may become violent and cruel in certain moments of great turmoil and great danger; but these crises will be rare and temporary.

When I think about the small passions of the men of our day, the softness of their mores, the extent of their enlightenment, the purity of their religion, the mildness of their morality, their industrious and ordered habits, the restraint that they almost all retain in vice as well as in virtue, I do not fear that they will have tyrants for leaders, but rather guardians.

I think therefore that the kind of oppression with which democratic peoples are threatened will not resemble anything that has preceded it in the world. Our contemporaries will not be able to find its image in their memories. I myself search in vain for an expression that reproduces exactly the idea that I form of it and that comprehends it; the ancient words despotism and tyranny are not appropriate. The thing is new; one must therefore try to define it, since I cannot name it.

I want to imagine under what new traits despotism could occur in the world: I see an innumerable mass of similar and equal men who go round and round without respite in order to procure for themselves small and vulgar pleasures, with which they fill their souls. Each of them, withdrawn to the side, has virtually nothing to do with the fate of all the others: his children and his particular friends form for him all of mankind; as for the rest of his fellow citizens, he is next to them, but he does not see them; he touches them and does not sense them; he exists only in himself and for himself alone, and if a family still remains to him, one can at least say that he no longer has a fatherland.

Above them rises an immense and tutelary power, which alone is responsible for securing their pleasure and watching over their fate. It is absolute, detailed, regular, provident, and mild. It would resemble paternal authority if, like it, its object was to prepare men for adulthood; but it seeks only, on the contrary, to keep them irrevocably in childhood; it likes the citizens to enjoy themselves, provided that they think only about enjoying themselves. It works willingly for their happiness, but it wants to be the only agent and the sole judge of that happiness; it provides for their security, anticipates and assures their needs, facilitates their pleasures, conducts their principal affairs, directs their industry, settles their successions, and divides their inheritances. Why may it not entirely spare them the trouble of thinking and the effort of living?

It is in this way that every day it makes the use of free will less necessary and rarer; that it confines the action of the will to a smaller space and gradually robs each citizen even of the use of himself. Equality has prepared men for all these things: it has disposed them to tolerate them and often even to regard them as a benefit.

After having thus taken each individual by turns into his powerful hands and having molded him as he pleases, the sovereign extends his arms over the whole society; he covers its surface with a web of small, complicated, detailed, and uniform rules, through which the most original minds and most vigorous souls are unable to emerge in order to rise above the crowd; it does not break wills, but it softens them, bends them, and directs them; it rarely forces men to act, but it constantly opposes itself to men's acting; it does not destroy, it prevents things from coming into being; it does not tyrannize, it hinders, it presses down upon men, it enervates, it extinguishes, it stupefies, and it finally reduces each nation to no longer being anything but a herd of timid and industrious animals, whose shepherd is the government.

I have always believed that this sort of regulated, mild, and peaceful servitude, whose picture I have just painted, could be combined better than one imagines with some of the exterior forms of liberty and that it would not be impossible for it to establish itself under the very protection of the sovereignty of the people.

Our contemporaries are continually beset by two opposite passions: they feel the need to be led and the desire to remain free. Unable to destroy either the one or the other of these contrary instincts, they try hard to satisfy both of them at the same time. They imagine a power that is unitary, tutelary, all-powerful, but elected by the citizens. They combine centralization and the sovereignty of the people. That gives them some respite. They console themselves for being under tutelage by thinking that they have themselves chosen their guardians. Each individual tolerates being enchained because he sees that it is neither one man nor one class but the people itself that holds the end of the chain.

In this system, the citizens come out of their dependence for a moment in order to indicate their master, and go back into it.

There are, in our day, many men who accommodate themselves very easily to this kind of compromise between administrative despotism and the sovereignty of the people and who think they have sufficiently guaranteed the liberty of individuals, when it is the national power to which they hand them over. That does not suffice for me. The nature of the master is much less important to me than the submission to it.

Nevertheless, I will not deny that such a constitution is infinitely preferable to one which, after having concentrated all powers, places them in the hands of one man or an unaccountable body of men. Of all the different forms that democratic despotism could take, that would assuredly be the worst.

When the sovereign is elective or watched over closely by a really elective and independent legislature, the oppression to which it subjects individuals is sometimes greater; but it is always less degrading because each citizen, although he is hindered and reduced to impotence, can still imagine that by obeying he is only submitting to himself and that it is to one of his wills that he is sacrificing all the others.

I understand as well that when the sovereign represents the nation and depends on it, the powers and the rights that are taken away from each citizen not only serve the head of the State, but benefit the State itself, and that the individuals draw some benefit from the sacrifice of their independence that they have made to the public.

To create a national representation in a very centralized country is thus to diminish the evil that extreme centralization can produce, but not to destroy it.

I see well that, in this way, individual intervention in the most important affairs is retained; but it is not any less suppressed in small and private ones. One forgets that it is especially in the details that it is dangerous to enslave men. For my part, I would be inclined to think liberty less necessary in great things than in smaller ones, if I thought that one could ever be assured of the one without possessing the other.

Subjection in small affairs manifests itself every day and makes itself felt by all citizens without distinction. It does not drive them to despair, but it impedes them constantly and leads them to give up the exercise of their will. It gradually extinguishes their spirit and enervates their soul, whereas the obedience which is owing only in a small number of very grave, but very rare, circumstances, exhibits servitude only from time to time and makes it weigh heavily only upon some men. It will be futile for you to oblige these same citizens, whom you have made so dependent upon the central power, to choose from time to time the representatives of this power; this exercise of their free will, which is so important but so brief and so rare, will not prevent them from gradually losing the ability to think, to feel, and to act on their own, and from thus gradually falling below the level of humanity.

I will add that they will soon become incapable of exercising the great and sole privilege that is left to them. The democratic peoples who have introduced liberty into the political sphere, at the same time that they were increasing despotism in the administrative sphere, have been led into some very strange anomalies. If it is a question of managing small matters where simple good sense may suffice, they judge that the citizens are incompetent; if it is a question of the government of the whole State, they entrust its citizens with immense prerogatives; they make them alternately the playthings of the sovereign and its masters, more than kings and less than men. After having exhausted all the different systems of election without finding one that suits them, they are surprised and recommence their search, as if the ill that they notice were not due to the constitution of the country much more than to that of the electoral body.

It is, in fact, difficult to see how men who have entirely given up the habit of finding their way on their own could succeed in choosing well those who are supposed to lead them; and it is not plausible that a liberal, energetic, and wise government could ever emerge from the votes of a population of servants.

A constitution republican in its head and ultramonarchic in all the other parts has always seemed to me to be an ephemeral monster. The vices of the governors and the stupidity of the governed would not be long in leading it into ruin; and the people, tired of its representatives and of itself, would create freer institutions or soon go back to lying down at the feet of a single master.

Volume Two, Part Four, Chapter Seven

I believe that is is easier to establish an absolute and despotic government among a people where the conditions are equal than among any other, and I think that if such a government were once established among such a people, not only would it oppress men, but in the long run it would deprive each of them of several of the principal attributes of humanity.

Despotism thus appears to me especially to be feared in democratic times.

I would, I think, have loved liberty in any age; but I feel inclined to worship it in the age in which we find ourselves.

I am convinced, on the other hand, that all those who, in the age we are entering, try to base authority on privilege and aristocracy will fail. All those who want to capture and keep authority within the bosom of a single class will fail. In our time, there is no sovereign skillful enough and strong enough to found despotism by reestablishing permanent distinctions between his subjects; nor is there any legislator so wise and so powerful that he can maintain free institutions if he does not take equality for his first principle and credo. It is therefore necessary that all those of our contemporaries who want to create or secure the independence and dignity of their fellow men show themselves to be friends of equality; and the only means worthy of showing oneself to be such is in fact to be one: the success of their holy enterprise depends on it.

Thus, it is not a question of reconstructing an aristocratic society, but of making liberty emerge from the depths of the democratic society where God obliges us to live.

These two primary truths seem to me simple, clear, and fecund, and they lead me naturally to consider what kind of free government can be established among a people where the conditions are equal.

It follows from the very constitution of democratic nations and from their needs that, in them, the power of the sovereign must be more uniform, more centralized, more far-reaching, more penetrating, and more powerful than elsewhere. Society there is naturally more active and stronger, the individual more dependent and weaker: the one does more, the other less; that is inevitable.

It must therefore not be expected that, in democratic countries, the sphere of individual independence will ever be as large as in aristocratic countries. But that is not desirable, for in aristocratic nations, society is often sacrificed to the individual, and the prosperity of the greatest number to the grandeur of a few.

It is at once necessary and desirable that the central power that governs a democratic people be active and powerful. It is not a matter of making it weak or lethargic but only of preventing it from abusing its agility and its strength.

What contributed most to securing the independence of private individuals in aristocratic times was that the sovereign did not take care of governing and administering the citizens alone; he was obliged to leave a portion of this task to the members of the aristocracy, so that the social power, being always divided, never weighed entirely and in the same way upon each man.

Not only did the sovereign not do everything by himself, but the majority of the officials who acted in his stead, drawing their power from the fact of their birth and not from him, were not continually in his control. He could not create or destroy them at any moment, according to his whims, and bend them all equally to his slightest wishes. That again guaranteed the independence of private individuals. [. . .]

Aristocratic countries are replete with rich and influential private individuals who know how to take care of themselves and who cannot be oppressed easily or in secret; and these men keep power within general habits of moderation and restraint.

I know well that democratic countries do not naturally possess such individuals; but one can artificially create something analogous in those countries.

I firmly believe that one cannot once again found an aristocracy in the world; but I think that simple citizens, by uniting together, can constitute very rich, very influential, very strong beings; in a word, aristocratic persons.

In this way one would obtain several of the greatest political advantages of aristocracy without its injustices or its dangers. A political, industrial, commercial or even scientific and literary association is an enlightened and powerful citizen that one cannot bend at will or secretly oppress and which, by defending its particular rights against the demands of power, saves the common liberties.

In aristocratic times, each man is always linked in a very close way to his fellow citizens, so that one cannot attack him without the others coming to his aid. In times of equality, each individual is naturally isolated; he has no hereditary friends whose aid he can lay claim to nor any class whose sympathies are assured to him; he is easily isolated, and he is crushed underfoot with impunity. In our day, an oppressed citizen thus has only one means of defending himself; that is to appeal to the entire nation and, if it is deaf, to mankind. There is only one means of doing that: the press. Liberty of the press is thus infinitely more precious in democratic nations than in all the others; it alone cures the majority of the ills that equality may produce. Equality isolates and weakens men; but the press places beside each of them a very powerful weapon, which the weakest and most isolated can use. Equality deprives each individual of the support of those close to him; but the press allows him to call all his fellow citizens and all his fellow men to his aid. The printing press has hastened the progress of equality, and it is one of its best correctives.

I think that the men who live in aristocracies can, if need be, do without the liberty of the press; but those who live in democratic countries cannot. In order to guarantee the personal independence of the latter, I do not place my trust in great political assemblies, in parliamentary prerogatives, or in the proclamation of the sovereignty of the people.

All those things are reconcilable, up to a certain point, with individual servitude; but this servitude cannot be complete if the press is free. The press is the democratic instrument of liberty par excellence. [. . .]

Another very natural and very dangerous instinct in democratic peoples is that which leads them to have contempt for individual rights and to take little account of them.

Men are in general attached to a right and show respect for it due to its importance or to the long use that they have made of it. The individual rights that one finds among democratic peoples are normally of little importance, very recent, and very unstable; this causes them to be sacrificed easily and violated almost always without remorse.

Now, it happens that at the same time and in the same nations that men conceive a natural disdain for the rights of individuals, the rights of the society spread naturally and strengthen; that is to say that men become less attached to individual rights at the moment when it is most necessary to retain and protect the few of them that remain.

It is therefore especially in the democratic times in which we find ourselves that the true friends of liberty and of human grandeur must constantly be standing and ready to prevent the social power from lightly sacrificing the private rights of a few individuals to the general execution of its designs. In these times there is no citizen so obscure that it is not dangerous to allow him to be oppressed nor individual rights so unimportant that they can be abandoned to arbitrary power without risk. The reason for this is simple: when the private right of an individual is violated during a time when the human mind is steeped in the importance and sacredness of rights of this kind, one does harm only to the one who is despoiled; but to violate such a right, in our day, is to corrupt profoundly the national mores and place the entire society at risk, because among us the very idea of these kinds of rights constantly tends to be degraded and lost. [. . .]

Some see in equality only the anarchic tendencies to which it gives rise. They dread their own free will; they are afraid of themselves.

Others, fewer in number but better enlightened, have another point of view. Alongside the path that, beginning with equality, leads to anarchy, they have in the end discovered another path that seems to lead men irresistibly toward servitude. They bend their souls in advance to this inevitable servitude, and, despairing of remaining free, they are already worshipping at the bottom of their heart the master who must soon arrive.

The first desert liberty because they consider it dangerous; the second because they consider it impossible. [. . .]

Volume Two, Part Four, Chapter Eight

This new society that I have sought to depict and that I wish to judge is only just being born. Time has not yet fixed its form; the great revolution that has created it still persists, and, in what is happening in our time, it is almost impossible to discern what must disappear with the revolution itself and what must remain after it.

The world that is arising is still half-lodged beneath the debris of the world that is falling, and in the midst of the immense confusion that human affairs present, no one can say which of the old institutions and the old mores will remain standing and which of them will completely disappear.

Although the revolution that is occurring in the social state, the laws, the ideas, and the sentiments of men is still very far from being finished, already one cannot compare its works with anything that has previously been seen in the world. I go back from century to century up to the remotest antiquity; I perceive nothing that resembles what is before my eyes. Since the past no longer sheds light on the future, the mind walks in darkness.

Nevertheless, in the midst of a spectacle so vast, so new, so confused, I already have a glimmer of some principal traits that are beginning to emerge, and I will point them out:

I see that goods and evils are apportioned rather equally in the world. Great riches are disappearing; the number of small fortunes is increasing; desires and pleasures are multiplying; there is no longer extraordinary wealth or irremediable poverty. Ambition is a universal sentiment, but there are few vast ambitions. Each individual is isolated and weak; society is agile, provident, and strong; individuals accomplish small things, the State immense ones.

Souls are not energetic, but mores are mild and laws humane. If there are few great acts of self-sacrifice or very elevated, very brilliant, and very pure virtues, habits are well-ordered, violence is rare, cruelty almost unknown. Men's lives become longer and their property more secure. Life does not have much adornment, but it is very comfortable and very peaceful. There are few pleasures that are very refined and few that are very crude, little courteousness in manners and little brutality in tastes. There are scarcely any very learned men nor any very ignorant groups of them. Genius becomes rarer and enlightenment more common. The human mind progresses through the combined small efforts of all men and not by means of the powerful impetus given by a few of them. There is less perfection in men's works, but they bear more fruit. All the ties of race, of class, of fatherland are relaxed; the great tie of humanity tightens.

If among all these different traits, I look for the one that appears to me the most general and the most striking, I come to see that what is noticeable with respect to men's fortunes shows up again in a thousand other forms. Almost all the extremes are becoming attenuated and losing their edge; almost all the points of prominence are being effaced in order to make room for something average, which is at once less high and less low, less brilliant and less obscure than what has been seen in the world.

I scan my eyes over this numberless mass composed of similar beings, where nothing rises to a higher level or sinks to a lower one. The spectacle of this universal uniformity saddens and chills me, and I am tempted to long for the society that no longer exists.

When the world was filled with the very great and the very small, the very rich and the very poor, the very learned and the very ignorant, I used to turn my eyes away from the second ones in order to fix them upon the first, and these delighted my eyes. But I know that this pleasure arose out of my weakness: it is because I cannot take in everything around me at the same time that I was enabled to choose in this way and separate out, among so many objects, those it pleased me to contemplate. It is not the same for the omnipotent and eternal Being, whose eye necessarily takes in all things as a whole and who sees distinctly, even though all at once, all mankind and each individual man.

It is natural to believe that what is most satisfying to the eyes of this creator and preserver of men is not the exceptional prosperity of some of them, but the greatest well-being of all: what seems to me to be decadence is thus in His eyes progress; what offends me pleases Him. Equality is perhaps less elevated, but it is more just, and its justice makes its grandeur and its beauty.

I am making every effort to enter into this point of view of God, and it is from there that I am seeking to consider and judge human things.

No one on earth can yet say in an absolute and general way that the new state of societies is superior to the old; but it is already easy to see that it is different. [. . .]

It is no longer a question of retaining the particular advantages that the inequality of conditions furnishes to men, but of securing the new goods that equality can offer them. We must not try to make ourselves like our ancestors, but must make every effort to attain the kind of grandeur and happiness that is proper to us.

For myself, having arrived at the final conclusion of my journey and viewing from afar, but together, all the different objects that I have contemplated separately in its course, I feel full of fears and full of hopes. I see great dangers that it is possible to avert, great evils that can be avoided or limited, and I am more and more firmly of the belief that in order to be decent and prosperous, it suffices only that democratic nations wish to be so.

I am not unaware that some of my contemporaries have thought that peoples are never masters of themselves here below and that they necessarily obey who knows what insurmountable and unintelligent force that arises from prior circumstances, of race, of soil, or of climate.

These are false and cowardly doctrines, which can never produce anything other than weak men and spineless nations: Providence has not created mankind either completely independent or entirely enslaved. It traces around each man, it is true, a fateful circle from which he cannot escape, but within these vast limits man is powerful and free; so likewise are peoples.

The nations of our day cannot cause conditions within themselves to not be equal. But it depends upon them whether equality leads them to servitude or to liberty, to enlightenment or to barbarism, to prosperity or to wretchedness.

Richard McNemar

The Kentucky Revival (1808)

To the Reader

You have been probably waiting for something to be published from this quarter, and may be a little surprised to find the *Kentucky Revival* our theme; as it is generally known that we profess to have advanced forward into a much greater work.

Admitting this to be the case (which we do not deny) it would nevertheless be improper to forget, or set light by any operation or work of the true spirit, however small it may seem. But far from esteeming the Kentucky Revival a day of small things, we believe it was nothing less that an *introduction* to that work of *final redemption*, which God had promised in the latter days. And to preserve the memory of it among those who have wisely improved it as such, the following particulars have been collected for the press, by one, whose spirit was in it from the beginning, and who is a living witness of the most important particulars which occurred in every stage of it, until the present day.

For the better understanding of the following history, it will be proper to make a few preliminary observations.

I. It will be granted, that God has a particular order and manner of working, in which one thing goes before another. Thus: *the law and the prophets were until John*, after that *the kingdom of heaven is preached*. It then follows that *all men press into it*. The first thing is the *law*, which convinces of sin. 2. The *Prophets*, who minister the promise and hope of salvation. 3. The *kingdom of heaven is preached;* the way and method of salvation made manifest in word and doctrine: and last of all we must *press into it*. This is the order of God, and there is no other. Nothing short of pressing into the kingdom can save the soul. Conviction may die away; hope and comfort desert the breast; and the most lively views of the kingdom be forgotten. Hence the necessity of so often reviving these things among professors. But whatever can die away, is short of the kingdom of God; those who are in the kingdom have everlasting life. Therefore it is plain that the constituent parts of a revival (which are conviction of sin, a hope for deliverance from it, and a manifestation of the *heavenly state*) can only be preparative to entering into it. How many revivals have taken place in these latter days, which for a season would raise the people, as it were, to heaven's gate; and after all, leave them to fall back into their former lifeless state. And why so? Because they did not take the last step, and press into that state which in word and doctrine was opened.

II. It will be granted, that whoever preaches the kingdom of heaven, must preach deliverance from all sin: For where sin is, there can be no heaven. Now when the kingdom has been preached, and honest souls have fixed their eye of faith upon it—longed with intense desire to be in it, and solicitously enquired for the footsteps of those who have already entered: then has been the time for the grand deceiver to come in with his doctrine of procrastination, and preach up sin for term of life;—appeal to the doleful experience of past generation, and confirm the fatal error by the doctrines and decrees of a corrupt church. Thus the most promising revivals have been blasted, and all that near sense of heaven's pure enjoyments (common under the preaching of the kingdom) extinguished by men of corrupt minds.

But the *Kentucky Revival*, from the beginning, spoke better things. Those who were the genuine subjects of it, ever expressed the fullest confidence that it would not terminate as revivals had generally done. It was not a common portion of law conviction; nor that faith in the promise which puts heaven at a distance; nor merely preaching about the kingdom, that drew out the multitudes to encamp for days and nights in the wilderness, &c. It was a near prospect of the true kingdom of God, into which many were determined to press at the expense of all that they held dear upon earth. The late revival was not sent to re-form the churches. It did not come with a piece of new cloth to patch the old garment, to mend up the old hope with some new experience; but to prepare the way for that kingdom of God, in which all things are new: and whether it be in many or few, the purposes whereunto it was sent, shall undoubtedly be answered.

III. That this extraordinary work sprung from some supernatural cause has been universally granted; but whether the cause was good or evil, has been a matter of much debate, even among those who profess to take the scripture for their only guide. Christians so called, of all others have been the most divided in their judgment concerning it; and while some without hesitation have pronounced it a glorious work of God; others who professed to be children of the same father, followers of the same Saviour, and instructed by the same word of God, have with equal confidence pronounced it *witchcraft, enthusiasm, fanaticism*, and *the very energy of delusion*. Hence the various predictions concerning it: Some affirming that it would shortly terminate and leave the unhappy subjects of it, in a worse condition than ever; others that it should *cover the earth, as the waters cover the sea*, and gather the nations into one united body.

IV. As the continuance of the revival was so strongly predicted and asserted by its subjects, it will be proper to consider how far and upon what footing, those predictions and assertions are tenable. That it should always continue in the same measure and appearance without any increase, was never intended; therefore if that same power continues to work, though it should be in a greater degree and more extraordinary manner, and tho' it should be among a different people, this will not prove the above predictions false, provided it be the same power working to the same end.

While the extraordinary power of the revival was exterraneous; while irresistible beams of light presented objects to the view which persons could not avoid seeing, and they were rushed into exercises of body by a force of operation which they could not withstand, the continuance of the work in this fashion, was precarious, knowing that God will not always work upon man like a machine. Therefore in order to allow the continuance of the work, a number of its subjects have found it necessary to receive this extraordinary power as an in-dwelling treasure, to unite with this supernatural agent, to dwell in him and he in them, and become workers together with him, and without force or violence, believe and practise whatever he teaches. And on this pivot the revival turns with each individual. The power or light of God, continues with those who continue in it, his spirit abides only with those who abide in him, and do continually the things that please him; of course such as are willing that Christ and Belial should have day about, light and darkness alternately prevail, must fall off and wither; for no man can serve two masters.

V. Since the spirit and power of the revival has been established upon the above principles, and the divine agent has found a habitation with men, less attention has been paid to former appearances. This new and strange doctrine of receiving Christ, and walking in him, has engrossed the general concern: and while the singular manner of worship, strange bodily exercises, &c. of those the world around, their distinguishing faith has been a matter of serious enquiry with many; especially those who have begun to open their eyes on the hidden glories of the kingdom of Christ, and are beginning to move Zion-ward. But before the *temple of God* can be opened in heaven and the ark of his testament be seen, it will be proper to recognise the various operations by which the materials of the tabernacle were prepared: According as it is written—*"Behold I send my messenger, and he shall prepare the way before me: and the Lord whom ye seek, shall suddenly come to his temple."*

Turtle-Creek, June 20, 1807. R. M.

Of the First Appearances of the Extraordinary Work, in Different Parts of Kentucky, in 1800 and 1801.

The first extraordinary appearances of the power of God in the late revival, began about the close of the last century, in Logan and Christian counties; on the waters of Gasper and Red Rivers. And in the spring of 1801, the same extraordinary work broke out in Mason county, upper part of Kentucky; of which I was an eye witness, and can therefore, with greater confidence, testify what I have heard, seen and felt.

It first began in individuals who had been under deep convictions of sin, and great trouble about their souls, and had fasted and prayed, and diligently searched the scriptures, and had undergone distresses of mind inexpressibly sore, until they had obtained a comfortable hope of salvation. And from seeing and feeling the love of Christ, and his willingness to save all that would forsakc thcir sins and turn to God through him; and feeling how freely his love and goodness flowed to them, it kindled their love to other souls, that were lost in their sins; and an ardent desire that they might come and partake of that spiritual light, life, and comfort, which appeared infinite in its nature, and free to all. And under such an overpowering weight of the divine goodness, as tongue could not express, they were constrained to cry out, with tears and trembling, and testify a full and free salvation in Christ, for all that would come; and to warn their fellow-creatures of the danger of continuing in sin; and entreating them in the most tender and affectionate manner, to turn from it; and seek the Lord, in sure and certain hope that he would be found.

Under such exhortations, the people began to be affected in a very strange manner. At first they were taken with an inward throbbing of heart; then with weeping and trembling: from that to crying out, in apparent agony of soul; falling down and swooning away till every appearance of animal life was suspended, and the person appeared to be in a trance. From this state they would recover under different sensations. [. . .]

And here a new scene was opened, while some trembled like one in a fit of the ague; wept or cried out, lamenting their distance from God, and exposedness to his wrath; others were employed in praying with them, encouraging them to believe on the Son of God—to venture upon his promise—give up their wicked rebellious heart, just as it was; for God to take it away, and give them a heart of flesh;—singing hymns, and giving thanks to God, for the display of his power, without any regard to former rules of order. At this, some were offended and withdrew from the assembly, determined to oppose it, as a work of the wicked one. But all their objections, only tended to open the way for the true nature and spirit of the work to shine out; and encourage the subjects of it, to set out with warmer zeal to promote it. Accordingly a meeting was appointed a few evenings after; to which a crowd of awakened souls flocked, and spent the whole night in singing hymns, praying, and exhorting one another, &c. At this meeting, one man was struck down and lay for about an hour, in the situation above mentioned. This put the matter beyond dispute, that the work was supernatural; and the outcry which it raised against sin, confirmed a number in the belief that it was from above.

From small beginnings, it gradually spread. The news of these strange operations flew about, and attracted many to come and see; who were convinced, not only from seeing and hearing, but feeling; and carried home the testimony, that it was the living work of God. This stirred up others, and brought out still greater multitudes. And these strange exercises still increasing, and having no respect to any stated hours of worship, it was found expedient to encamp on the ground, and continue the meeting day and night. To these encampments the people flocked in hundreds and thousands, on foot, on horseback, and in wagons and other carriages.

At first appearance, those meetings exhibited nothing to the spectator, but a scene of confusion that could scarce be put into human language. They were generally opened with a sermon; near the close of which, there would be an unusual out-cry; some bursting forth into loud ejaculations of prayer, or thanksgiving for the truth. Others breaking out in emphatical sentences of exhortation. Others flying to their careless friends, with tears of compassion, beseeching them to turn to the Lord. Some struck with terror, and hastening through the croud to make their escape, or pulling away their relations.—Others, trembling, weeping and crying out for the Lord Jesus to have mercy upon them: fainting and swooning away, till every appearance of life was gone, and the extremities of the body assumed the coldness of a dead corpse.—Others surrounding them with melodious songs, or fervent prayers for their happy resurrection, in the love of Christ.—Others collecting into circles around this variegated scene, contending with arguments for and against. And under such appearances, the work would continue for several days and nights together. [. . .]

The next general camp-meeting was held at Concord, in the county of Bourbon, about the last of May, or beginning of June. The number of people was supposed to be about 4,000, who attended on this occasion. There were present seven Presbyterian ministers, four of whom were opposed to the work and spoke against it until the fourth day about noon, the evidence then became so powerful, that they all professed to be convinced that it was the work of God; and one of them addressed the assembly with tears, acknowledging that notwithstanding they had long been praying to the Lord to pour out his spirit, yet when it came they did not know it, but wickedly opposed the answer of their own prayers. On this occasion, no sex nor color, class nor description, were exempted from the pervading influence of the spirit; even from the age of eight months to sixty years, there were evident subjects of this marvellous operation.

The meeting continued five days and four nights; and after the people generally scattered from the ground, numbers convened in different places and continued the exercise much longer. And even where they were not collected together, these wonderful operations continued among every class of people and in every situation; in their houses and fields, and in their daily employments, falling down and crying out under conviction, or singing and shouting with unspeakable joy, were so common, that the whole country round about, seemed to be leavened with the spirit of the work. [. . .]

The people among whom the revival began, were generally Calvinists, and altho' they had been long praying in words for the out-pouring of the spirit, and believed that God had *"foreordained whatsoever comes in to pass;"* yet, when it *came to pass* and their prayer was answered, and the spirit began to flow like many waters, from a cloud of witnesses, and souls were convicted of sin and cried for mercy, and found hope and comfort in the news of a Saviour; they rose up and quarreled with the work, because it did not *come to pass* that the subjects of it were willing to adopt their soul stupefying creed. Those who had laboured and travailed to gain some solid hope of salvation, and had ventured their souls upon the covenant of promise, and felt the living zeal of eternal love; could not, dare not preach that salvation was restricted to a certain *definite number*; nor insinuate that any being which God had made, was, by the Creator, laid under the dire necessity of being damned forever. The love of a Saviour constrained them to testify, that one had died for all. This truth, so essential to the first ray of hope in the human breast, was like a dead fly in the ointment of the apothecary, to the Calvinist; hence all this trembling, weeping and groaning under sin, rejoicing in the hope of deliverance and turning from the former practice of it, sent forth a disagreeable savor. Yet these exercises would no doubt, have passed for a good work of God, had they appeared as seals to their doctrine of election, imperfection, and final perseverance. But every thing appeared new, and to claim no relation to the old bed of sand upon which they had been building; and rather than quit the old foundation, they chose to reject, oppose and persecute the truth, accompanied with all that evidence which many of them were obliged to acknowledge was divine. [. . .]

Of the Distinguishing Doctrines and Manner of Worship, among the First Subjects of the Revival.

The first point of doctrine which distinguished the subjects of the revival, was that which respected divine revelation.

The established opinion in the churches had been, that the *Scriptures*, explained according to sound reason and philosophy, was light sufficient; and simply to believe, what we were thus taught, was the highest evidence we could have of the truth of spiritual things. But *these* adopted a very different faith, and taught, as an important truth, that the will of God was made manifest to each individual who honestly sought after it, by an inward light, which shone into the heart.—Hence they received the name of *New-Lights*. Those who were the subjects of this inward light, did not call it *new light*, but a renewed manifestation of *that*, which at sundry times and in divers manners, had been opened to those who were willing and desirous to know the truth for themselves.

This inward light, they denominated *the Lord*, because by it they were instructed, influenced and governed. Hence they spake of seeing *the Lord*, finding *the Lord*, loving *the Lord*, following *the Lord*, offending *the Lord*, &c. by all which expressions was meant, that *inward light* and revelation of truth, by which they could see things in their true colors, and find a measure of peace and consolation, and a comfortable hope of eternal life.

This *new light* first broke out in the Presbyterian church, among those who held the doctrines of Calvin, and therefore it is considered as more immediately contrasted with that system. Those who first embraced it, had also been reputed Calvinists, and belonged to the Presbyterian church, among whom were several persons of distinction in the ministry; of course, the existence of sentiments so very different in the same church, rendered a division unavoidable. This division was gradual, and had its foundation in the above principle of a direct manifestation of spiritual light from God to the soul, which was superior to all the comments that natural men had ever made upon the scriptures. This division in sentiment, with its concomitant effects, drew together a vast multitude out of different churches, who formed a general communion, and for a time, acceded to the doctrines, manner of worship, &c. first opened and practiced among the *New-Lights;* a brief sketch of which is as follows, viz: that all creeds, confessions, forms of worship, and rules of government invented by men, ought to be laid aside; especially the distinguishing doctrines of Calvin.—That all who received the true light of the spirit in the inner man, and faithfully followed it, would naturally see eye to eye, and understand the things of the spirit alike, without any written tenet or learned expositor. That all who received this true light, would plainly see the purity of God—the depravity of man—the necessity of a new birth, and of a sinless life and conversation to evidence it.—That God was no respector of persons—willeth the salvation of all souls—has opened a door of salvation, through Christ, for all—will have all invited to enter, and such as refuse to come in, must blame themselves for their own perdition.

As to worship, they allowed each one to worship God agreeably to their own feelings, whatever impression or consciousness of duty they were under; believing the true wisdom, which "lives through all life," to be a safer guide than human forms, which can only affect the outer man: and hence, so wide a door was opened, and such a variety of exercises were exhibited at their public meetings. All distinction of names was laid aside, and it was no matter what any one had been called before, if now he stood in the present light, and felt his heart glow with love to the souls of men; he was welcome to sing, pray, or call sinners to repentance. Neither was there any distinction as to age, sex, color, or any thing of a temporary nature: old and young, male and female, black and white, had equal privilege to minister the light which they received, in whatever way the spirit directed. And it was moreover generally considered, that such as professed to stand in the light and were not actively engaged some way or other, in time of public meeting, were only dead weights upon the cause.

No one, who has not been an eye witness, can possibly paint in their imagination the striking solemnity of those occasions, on which the thousands of Kentuckians were convened in one vast assembly, under the auspicious influence of the above faith. How striking to see hundreds who never saw each other in the face before, moving uniformly into action, without any preconcerted plan, and each, without intruding upon another, taking that part assigned him by a conscious feeling, and in this manner, dividing into bands over a large extent of ground, interspersed with tents and waggons: some uniting their voices in the most melodious songs; others in solemn and affecting accents of prayer: some lamenting with streaming eyes their lost situation, or that of a wicked world; others lying apparently in the cold embraces of death: some instructing the ignorant, directing the doubtful, and urging them in the day of God's visitation, to make sure work for eternity: others, from some eminence, sounding the general trump of a free salvation, and warning sinners to fly from the wrath to come:—the surrounding forest at the same time, vocal with the cries of the distressed, sometimes to the distance of half a mile or a mile in circumference.

How persons, so different in their education, manners and natural dispositions, without any visible commander, could enter upon such a scene, and continue in it for days and nights in perfect harmony, has been one of the greatest wonders that ever the world beheld.

JOSEPH STORY

Martin v. Hunter's Lessee (1816)

STORY, J., delivered the opinion of the Court.

This is a writ of error from the Court of Appeals of Virginia founded upon the refusal of that Court to obey the mandate of this Court. [. . .]

The Constitution of the United States was ordained and established not by the States in their sovereign capacities, but emphatically, as the preamble of the Constitution declares, by "the people of the United States." There can be no doubt that it was competent to the people to invest the general government with all the powers which they might deem proper and necessary, to extend or restrain these powers according to their own good pleasure, and to give them a paramount and supreme authority. As little doubt can there be that the people had a right to prohibit to the States the exercise of any powers which were, in their judgment, incompatible with the objects of the general compact, to make the powers of the State governments, in given cases, subordinate to those of the nation, or to reserve to themselves those sovereign authorities which they might not choose to delegate to either. The Constitution was not, therefore, necessarily carved out of existing State sovereignties, nor a surrender of powers already existing in State institutions, for the powers of the States depend upon their own Constitutions, and the people of every State had the right to modify and restrain them according to their own views of the policy or principle. On the other hand, it is perfectly clear that the sovereign powers vested in the State governments by their respective Constitutions remained unaltered and unimpaired except so far as they were granted to the Government of the United States.

These deductions do not rest upon general reasoning, plain and obvious as they seem to be. They have been positively recognised by one of the articles in amendment of the Constitution, which declares that "The powers not delegated to the United States by the Constitution, nor prohibited by it to the States, are reserved to the States respectively, or to the people."

The government, then, of the United States can claim no powers which are not granted to it by the Constitution, and the powers actually granted, must be such as are expressly given, or given by necessary implication. On the other hand, this instrument, like every other grant, is to have a reasonable construction, according to the import of its terms, and where a power is expressly given in general terms, it is not to be restrained to particular cases unless that construction grow out of the context expressly or by necessary implication. The words are to be taken in their natural and obvious sense, and not in a sense unreasonably restricted or enlarged.

The Constitution unavoidably deals in general language. It did not suit the purposes of the people, in framing this great charter of our liberties, to provide for minute specifications of its powers or to declare the means by which those powers should be carried into execution. It was foreseen that this would be a perilous and difficult, if not an impracticable, task. The instrument was not intended to provide merely for the exigencies of a few years, but was to endure through a long lapse of ages, the events of which were locked up in the inscrutable purposes of Providence. It could not be foreseen what new changes and modifications of power might be indispensable to effectuate the general objects of the charter, and restrictions and specifications which at the present might seem salutary might in the end prove the overthrow of the system itself. Hence its powers are expressed in general terms, leaving to the legislature from time to time to adopt its own means to effectuate legitimate objects and to mould and model the exercise of its powers as its own wisdom and the public interests, should require.

With these principles in view, principles in respect to which no difference of opinion ought to be indulged, let us now proceed to the interpretation of the Constitution so far as regards the great points in controversy.

The third article of the Constitution is that which must principally attract our attention. [. . .]

Let this article be carefully weighed and considered. The language of the article throughout is manifestly designed to be mandatory upon the Legislature. Its obligatory force is so imperative, that Congress could not, without a violation of its duty, have refused to carry it into operation. The judicial power of the United States shall be vested (not may be vested) in one Supreme Court, and in such inferior Courts as Congress may, from time to time, ordain and establish. [. . .]

If, then, it is a duty of Congress to vest the judicial power of the United States, it is a duty to vest the whole judicial power. The language, if imperative as to one part, is imperative as to all. If it were otherwise, this anomaly would exist, that Congress might successively refuse to vest the jurisdiction in any one class of cases enumerated in the Constitution, and thereby defeat the jurisdiction as to all, for the Constitution has not singled out any class on which Congress are bound to act in preference to others.

The next consideration is as to the Courts in which the judicial power shall be vested. It is manifest that a Supreme Court must be established; but whether it be equally obligatory to establish inferior Courts is a question of some difficulty. If Congress may lawfully omit to establish inferior Courts, it might follow that, in some of the enumerated cases, the judicial power could nowhere exist. The Supreme Court can have original jurisdiction in two classes of cases only, *viz.*, in cases affecting ambassadors, other public ministers and consuls, and in cases in which a State is a party. Congress cannot vest any portion of the judicial power of the United States except in Courts ordained and established by itself, and if, in any of the cases enumerated in the Constitution, the State courts did not then possess jurisdiction, the appellate jurisdiction of the Supreme Court (admitting that it could act on State courts) could not reach those cases, and, consequently, the injunction of the Constitution that the judicial power "shall be vested," would be disobeyed. It would seem therefore to follow that Congress are bound to create some inferior Courts in which to vest all that jurisdiction which, under the Constitution, is exclusively vested in the United States, and of which the Supreme Court cannot take original cognizance. They might establish one or more inferior Courts; they might parcel out the jurisdiction among such Courts, from time to time, at their own pleasure. But the whole judicial power of the United States should be at all times vested, either in an original or appellate form, in some Courts created under its authority. [. . .]

This leads us to the consideration of the great question as to the nature and extent of the appellate jurisdiction of the United States. We have already seen that appellate jurisdiction is given by the Constitution to the Supreme Court in all cases where it has not original jurisdiction, subject, however, to such exceptions and regulations as Congress may prescribe. It is therefore capable of embracing every case enumerated in the Constitution which is not exclusively to be decided by way of original jurisdiction. But the exercise of appellate jurisdiction is far from being limited by the terms of the Constitution to the Supreme Court. There can be no doubt that Congress may create a succession of inferior tribunals, in each of which it may vest appellate as well as original jurisdiction. The judicial power is delegated by the Constitution in the most general terms, and may therefore be exercised by Congress under every variety of form of appellate or original jurisdiction. And as there is nothing in the Constitution which restrains or limits this power, it must therefore, in all other cases, subsist in the utmost latitude of which, in its own nature, it is susceptible.

As, then, by the terms of the Constitution, the appellate jurisdiction is not limited as to the Supreme Court, and as to this Court it may be exercised in all other cases than those of which it has original cognizance, what is there to restrain its exercise over State tribunals in the enumerated cases? The appellate power is not limited by the terms of the third article to any particular Courts. The words are, "the judicial power (which includes appellate power) shall extend to all cases," etc., and "in all other cases before mentioned, the Supreme Court shall have appellate jurisdiction." It is the case, then, and not the court, that gives the jurisdiction. If the judicial power extends to the case, it will be in vain to search in the letter of the Constitution for any qualification as to the tribunal where it depends. It is incumbent, then, upon those who assert such a qualification to show its existence by necessary implication. If the text be clear and distinct, no restriction upon its plain and obvious import ought to be admitted, unless the inference be irresistible.

If the Constitution meant to limit the appellate jurisdiction to cases pending in the Courts of the United States, it would necessarily follow that the jurisdiction of these Courts would, in all the cases enumerated in the Constitution, be exclusive of State tribunals. How otherwise could the jurisdiction extend to all cases arising under the Constitution, laws, and treaties of the United States, or to all cases of admiralty and maritime jurisdiction? If some of these cases might be entertained by State tribunals, and no appellate jurisdiction as to them should exist, then the appellate power would not extend to all, but to some, cases. If State tribunals might exercise concurrent jurisdiction over all or some of the other classes of cases in the Constitution without control, then the appellate jurisdiction of the United States might, as to such cases, have no real existence, contrary to the manifest intent of the Constitution. Under such circumstances, to give effect to the judicial power, it must be construed to be exclusive, and this not only when the *casus foederis* should arise directly, but when it should arise incidentally in cases pending in State courts. This construction would abridge the jurisdiction of such Court far more than has been ever contemplated in any act of Congress.

On the other hand, if, as has been contended, a discretion be vested in Congress to establish or not to establish inferior Courts, at their own pleasure, and Congress should not establish such Courts, the appellate jurisdiction of the Supreme Court would have nothing to act upon unless it could act upon cases pending in the State courts. Under such circumstances it must be held that the appellate power would extend to State courts, for the Constitution is peremptory that it shall extend to certain enumerated cases, which cases could exist in no other Courts. Any other construction, upon this supposition, would involve this strange contradiction that a discretionary power vested in Congress, and which they might rightfully omit to exercise, would defeat the absolute injunctions of the Constitution in relation to the whole appellate power.

But it is plain that the framers of the Constitution did contemplate that cases within the judicial cognizance of the United States not only might, but would, arise in the State courts in the exercise of their ordinary jurisdiction. With this view, the sixth article declares, that "This Constitution, and the laws of the United States which shall be made in pursuance thereof, and all treaties made, or which shall be made, under the authority of the United States, shall be the supreme law of the land, and the judges in every State shall be bound thereby, anything in the Constitution or laws of any State to the contrary notwithstanding."

It is obvious that this obligation is imperative upon the State judges in their official, and not merely in their private, capacities. From the very nature of their judicial duties, they would be called upon to pronounce the law applicable to the case in judgment. They were not to decide merely according to the laws or Constitution of the State, but according to the Constitution, laws and treaties of the United States—"the supreme law of the land."

A moment's consideration will show us the necessity and propriety of this provision in cases where the jurisdiction of the State courts is unquestionable. Suppose a contract for the payment of money is made between citizens of the same State, and performance thereof is sought in the courts of that State; no person can doubt that the jurisdiction completely and exclusively attaches, in the first instance, to such courts. Suppose at the trial the defendant sets up in his defence a tender under a State law making paper money a good tender, or a State law impairing the obligation of such contract, which law, if binding, would defeat the suit. The Constitution of the United States has declared that no State shall make any thing but gold or silver coin a tender in payment of debts, or pass a law impairing the obligation of contracts. If Congress shall not have passed a law providing for the removal of such a suit to the courts of the United States, must not the State court proceed to hear and determine it? Can a mere plea in defence be, of itself, a bar to further proceedings, so as to prohibit an inquiry into its truth or legal propriety when no other tribunal exists to whom judicial cognizance of such cases is confided? Suppose an indictment for a crime in a State court, and the defendant should allege in his defence that the crime was created by an *ex post facto* act of the State, must not the State court, in the exercise of a jurisdiction which has already rightfully attached, have a right to pronounce on the validity and sufficiency of the defence? It would be extremely difficult, upon any legal principles, to give a negative answer to these inquiries. Innumerable instances of the same sort might be stated in illustration of the position, and unless the State courts could sustain jurisdiction in such cases, this clause of the sixth article would be without meaning or effect, and public mischiefs of a most enormous magnitude would inevitably ensue.

It must therefore be conceded that the Constitution not only contemplated, but meant to provide for, cases within the scope of the judicial power of the United States which might yet depend before State tribunals. It was foreseen that, in the exercise of their ordinary jurisdiction, State courts would incidentally take cognizance of cases arising under the Constitution, the laws, and treaties of the United States. Yet to all these cases the judicial power, by the very terms of the Constitution, is to extend. It cannot extend by original jurisdiction if that was already rightfully and exclusively attached in the State courts, which (as has been already shown) may occur; it must therefore extend by appellate jurisdiction, or not at all. It would seem to follow that the appellate power of the United States must, in such cases, extend to State tribunals; and if in such cases, there is no reason why it should not equally attach upon all others within the purview of the Constitution.

It has been argued that such an appellate jurisdiction over State courts is inconsistent with the genius of our Governments, and the spirit of the Constitution. That the latter was never designed to act upon State sovereignties, but only upon the people, and that, if the power exists, it will materially impair the sovereignty of the States, and the independence of their courts. We cannot yield to the force of this reasoning; it assumes principles which we cannot admit, and draws conclusions to which we do not yield our assent.

It is a mistake that the Constitution was not designed to operate upon States in their corporate capacities. It is crowded with provisions which restrain or annul the sovereignty of the States in some of the highest branches of their prerogatives. The tenth section of the first article contains a long list of disabilities and prohibitions imposed upon the States. Surely, when such essential portions of State sovereignty are taken away or prohibited to be exercised, it cannot be correctly asserted that the Constitution does not act upon the States. The language of the Constitution is also imperative upon the States as to the performance of many duties. It is imperative upon the State legislatures to make laws prescribing the time, places, and manner of holding elections for senators and representatives, and for electors of President and Vice-President. And in these as well as some other cases, Congress have a right to revise, amend, or supersede the laws which may be passed by State legislatures. When therefore the States are stripped of some of the highest attributes of sovereignty, and the same are given to the United States; when the legislatures of the States are, in some respects, under the control of Congress, and in every case are, under the Constitution, bound by the paramount authority of the United States, it is certainly difficult to support the argument that the appellate power over the decisions of State courts is contrary to the genius of our institutions. The courts of the United States can, without question, revise the proceedings of the executive and legislative authorities of the States, and if they are found to be contrary to the Constitution, may declare them to be of no legal validity. Surely the exercise of the same right over judicial tribunals is not a higher or more dangerous act of sovereign power.

Nor can such a right be deemed to impair the independence of State judges. It is assuming the very ground in controversy to assert that they possess an absolute independence of the United States. In respect to the powers granted to the United States, they are not independent; they are expressly bound to obedience by the letter of the Constitution, and if they should unintentionally transcend their authority or misconstrue the Constitution, there is no more reason for giving their judgments an absolute and irresistible force than for giving it to the acts of the other coordinate departments of State sovereignty. [. . .]

It has been further argued against the existence of this appellate power that it would form a novelty in our judicial institutions. This is certainly a mistake. In the Articles of Confederation, an instrument framed with infinitely more deference to State rights and State jealousies, a power was given to Congress to establish "courts for revising and determining, finally, appeals in all cases of captures." It is remarkable that no power was given to entertain original jurisdiction in such cases, and consequently the appellate power (although not so expressed in terms) was altogether to be exercised in revising the decisions of State tribunals. This was, undoubtedly, so far a surrender of State sovereignty, but it never was supposed to be a power fraught with public danger or destructive of the independence of State judges. On the contrary, it was supposed to be a power indispensable to the public safety, inasmuch as our national rights might otherwise be compromitted and our national peace been dangered. Under the present Constitution, the prize jurisdiction is confined to the courts of the United States, and a power to revise the decisions of State courts, if they should assert jurisdiction over prize causes, cannot be less important or less useful than it was under the Confederation. [. . .]

It is further argued that no great public mischief can result from a construction which shall limit the appellate power of the United States to cases in their own Courts, first because State judges are bound by an oath to support the Constitution of the United States, and must be presumed to be men of learning and integrity, and secondly because Congress must have an unquestionable right to remove all cases within the scope of the judicial power from the State courts to the courts of the United States at any time before final judgment, though not after final judgment. As to the first reason—admitting that the judges of the State courts are, and always will be, of as much learning, integrity, and wisdom as those of the courts of the United States (which we very cheerfully admit), it does not aid the argument. It is manifest that the Constitution has proceeded upon a theory of its own, and given or withheld powers according to the judgment of the American people, by whom it was adopted. We can only construe its powers, and cannot inquire into the policy or principles which induced the grant of them. The Constitution has presumed (whether rightly or wrongly we do not inquire) that State attachments, State prejudices, State jealousies, and State interests might sometimes obstruct or control, or be supposed to obstruct or control, the regular administration of justice. Hence, in controversies between States, between citizens of different States, between citizens claiming grants under different States, between a State and its citizens, or foreigners, and between citizens and foreigners, it enables the parties, under the authority of Congress, to have the controversies heard, tried, and determined before the national tribunals. [. . .]

This is not all. A motive of another kind, perfectly compatible with the most sincere respect for State tribunals, might induce the grant of appellate power over their decisions. That motive is the importance, and even necessity, of uniformity of decisions throughout the whole United States upon all subjects within the purview of the Constitution. Judges of equal learning and integrity in different States might differently interpret a statute or a treaty of the United States, or even the Constitution itself; if there were no revising authority to control these jarring and discordant judgments and harmonize them into uniformity, the laws, the treaties, and the Constitution of the United States would be different in different States, and might perhaps never have precisely the same construction, obligation, or efficacy in any two States. The public mischiefs that would attend such a State of things would be truly deplorable, and it cannot be believed that they could have escaped the enlightened convention which formed the Constitution. What, indeed, might then have been only prophecy has now become fact, and the appellate jurisdiction must continue to be the only adequate remedy for such evils.

There is an additional consideration, which is entitled to great weight. The Constitution of the United States was designed for the common and equal benefit of all the people of the United States. The judicial power was granted for the same benign and salutary purposes. It was not to be exercised exclusively for the benefit of parties who might be plaintiffs, and would elect the national forum, but also for the protection of defendants who might be entitled to try their rights, or assert their privileges, before the same forum. Yet, if the construction contended for be correct, it will follow that, as the plaintiff may always elect the State court, the defendant may be deprived of all the security which the Constitution intended in aid of his rights. Such a State of things can in no respect be considered as giving equal rights. To obviate this difficulty, we are referred to the power which it is admitted Congress possess to remove suits from State courts to the national Courts, and this forms the second ground upon which the argument we are considering has been attempted to be sustained.

This power of removal is not to be found in express terms in any part of the Constitution; if it be given, it is only given by implication, as a power necessary and proper to carry into effect some express power. The power of removal is certainly not, in strictness of language; it presupposes an exercise of original jurisdiction to have attached elsewhere. The existence of this power of removal is familiar in courts acting according to the course of the common law in criminal as well as civil cases, and it is exercised before as well as after judgment. But this is always deemed in both cases an exercise of appellate, and not of original, jurisdiction. If, then, the right of removal be included in the appellate jurisdiction, it is only because it is one mode of exercising that power, and as Congress is not limited by the Constitution to any particular mode or time of exercising it, it may authorize a removal either before or after judgment. The time, the process, and the manner must be subject to its absolute legislative control. A writ of error is indeed but a process which removes the record of one court to the possession of another court, and enables the latter to inspect the proceedings, and give such judgment as its own opinion of the law and justice of the case may warrant. There is nothing in the nature of the process which forbids it from being applied by the legislature to interlocutory as well as final judgments. And if the right of removal from State courts exist before judgment, because it is included in the appellate power, it must for the same reason exist after judgment. And if the appellate power by the Constitution does not include cases pending in State courts, the right of removal, which is but a mode of exercising that power, cannot be applied to them. Precisely the same objections therefore exist as to the right of removal before judgment as after, and both must stand or fall together. [. . .]

The remedy, too, of removal of suits would be utterly inadequate to the purposes of the Constitution if it could act only on the parties, and not upon the State courts. In respect to criminal prosecutions, the difficulty seems admitted to be insurmountable; and in respect to civil suits, there would, in many cases, be rights without corresponding remedies. If State courts should deny the constitutionality of the authority to remove suits from their cognizance, in what manner could they be compelled to relinquish the jurisdiction? In respect to criminal cases, there would at once be an end of all control, and the state decisions would be paramount to the Constitution; and though, in civil suits, the courts of the United States might act upon the parties, yet the State courts might act in the same way, and this conflict of jurisdictions would not only jeopardise private rights, but bring into imminent peril the public interests.

On the whole, the Court are of opinion that the appellate power of the United States does extend to cases pending in the State courts, and that the 25th section of the judiciary act, which authorizes the exercise of this jurisdiction in the specified cases by a writ of error, is supported by the letter and spirit of the Constitution. We find no clause in that instrument which limits this power, and we dare not interpose a limitation where the people have not been disposed to create one. [. . .]

It is the opinion of the whole Court that the judgment of the Court of Appeals of Virginia, rendered on the mandate in this cause, be reversed, and the judgment of the District Court, held at Winchester, be, and the same is hereby, affirmed.

JOHN MARSHALL

Barron v. Baltimore (1833)

Mr. Chief Justice MARSHALL delivered the opinion of the Court.

The judgment brought up by this writ of error having been rendered by the court of a state, this tribunal can exercise no jurisdiction over it, unless it be shown to come within the provisions of the twenty-fifth section of the judicial act.

The plaintiff in error contends that it comes within that clause in the Fifth Amendment to the Constitution, which inhibits the taking of private property for public use, without just compensation. He insists that this amendment, being in favour of the liberty of the citizen, ought to be so construed as to restrain the legislative power of a state, as well as that of the United States. If this proposition be untrue, the Court can take no jurisdiction of the cause.

The question thus presented is, we think, of great importance, but not of much difficulty.

The Constitution was ordained and established by the people of the United States for themselves, for their own government, and not for the government of the individual states. Each state established a constitution for itself, and, in that constitution, provided such limitations and restrictions on the powers of its particular government as its judgment dictated. The people of the United States framed such a government for the United States as they supposed best adapted to their situation and best calculated to promote their interests. The powers they conferred on this government were to be exercised by itself; and the limitations on power, if expressed in general terms, are naturally, and, we think, necessarily applicable to the government created by the instrument. They are limitations of power granted in the instrument itself; not of distinct governments, framed by different persons and for different purposes.

If these propositions be correct, the Fifth Amendment must be understood as restraining the power of the general government, not as applicable to the states. In their several constitutions they have imposed such restrictions on their respective governments as their own wisdom suggested; such as they deemed most proper for themselves. It is a subject on which they judge exclusively, and with which others interfere no farther than they are supposed to have a common interest.

The counsel for the plaintiff in error insists that the Constitution was intended to secure the people of the several states against the undue exercise of power by their respective state governments; as well as against that which might be attempted by their general government. In support of this argument he relies on the inhibitions contained in the tenth section of the first article.

We think that section affords a strong if not a conclusive argument in support of the opinion already indicated by the Court.

The preceding section contains restrictions which are obviously intended for the exclusive purpose of restraining the exercise of power by the departments of the general government. Some of them use language applicable only to Congress: others are expressed in general terms. The third clause, for example, declares that "no bill of attainder or ex post facto law shall be passed." No language can be more general; yet the demonstration is complete that it applies solely to the government of the United States. In addition to the general arguments furnished by the instrument itself, some of which have been already suggested, the succeeding section, the avowed purpose of which is to restrain state legislation, contains in terms the very prohibition. It declares that "no state shall pass any bill of attainder or ex post facto law." This provision, then, of the ninth section, however comprehensive its language, contains no restriction on state legislation.

The ninth section having enumerated, in the nature of a bill of rights, the limitations intended to be imposed on the powers of the general government, the tenth proceeds to enumerate those which were to operate on the state legislatures. These restrictions are brought together in the same section, and are by express words applied to the states. "No state shall enter into any treaty," etc. Perceiving that in a constitution framed by the people of the United States for the government of all, no limitation of the action of government on the people would apply to the state government, unless expressed in terms; the restrictions contained in the tenth section are in direct words so applied to the states.

It is worthy of remark, too, that these inhibitions generally restrain state legislation on subjects entrusted to the general government, or in which the people of all the states feel an interest. A state is forbidden to enter into any treaty, alliance or confederation. If these compacts are with foreign nations, they interfere with the treaty making power which is conferred entirely on the general government; if with each other, for political purposes, they can scarcely fail to interfere with the general purpose and intent of the Constitution. To grant letters of marque and reprisal, would lead directly to war; the power of declaring which is expressly given to Congress. To coin money is also the exercise of a power conferred on Congress. It would be tedious to recapitulate the several limitations on the powers of the states which are contained in this section. They will be found, generally, to restrain state legislation on subjects entrusted to the government of the union, in which the citizens of all the states are interested. In these alone were the whole people concerned. The question of their application to states is not left to construction. It is averred in positive words.

If the original Constitution, in the ninth and tenth sections of the first article, draws this plain and marked line of discrimination between the limitations it imposes on the powers of the general government, and on those of the state; if in every inhibition intended to act on state power, words are employed which directly express that intent; some strong reason must be assigned for departing from this safe and judicious course in framing the amendments, before that departure can be assumed.

We search in vain for that reason.

Had the people of the several states, or any of them, required changes in their constitutions; had they required additional safeguards to liberty from the apprehended encroachments of their particular governments: the remedy was in their own hands, and would have been applied by themselves. A convention would have been assembled by the discontented state, and the required improvements would have been made by itself. The unwieldy and cumbrous machinery of procuring a recommendation from two-thirds of Congress, and the assent of three-fourths of their sister states, could never have occurred to any human being as a mode of doing that which might be effected by the state itself. Had the framers of these amendments intended them to be limitations on the powers of the state governments, they would have imitated the framers of the original Constitution, and have expressed that intention. Had Congress engaged in the extraordinary occupation of improving the constitutions of the several states by affording the people additional protection from the exercise of power by their own governments in matters which concerned themselves alone, they would have declared this purpose in plain and intelligible language.

But it is universally understood, it is a part of the history of the day, that the great revolution which established the Constitution of the United States, was not effected without immense opposition. Serious fears were extensively entertained that those powers which the patriot statesmen, who then watched over the interests of our country, deemed essential to union, and to the attainment of those invaluable objects for which union was sought, might be exercised in a manner dangerous to liberty. In almost every convention by which the Constitution was adopted, amendments to guard against the abuse of power were recommended. These amendments demanded security against the apprehended encroachments of the general government—not against those of the local governments.

In compliance with a sentiment thus generally expressed, to quiet fears thus extensively entertained, amendments were proposed by the required majority in Congress, and adopted by the states. These amendments contain no expression indicating an intention to apply them to the state governments. This Court cannot so apply them.

We are of opinion that the provision in the Fifth Amendment to the Constitution, declaring that private property shall not be taken for public use without just compensation, is intended solely as a limitation on the exercise of power by the government of the United States, and is not applicable to the legislation of the states. We are therefore of opinion that there is no repugnancy between the several acts of the general assembly of Maryland, given in evidence by the defendants at the trial of this cause, in the court of that state, and the Constitution of the United States. This Court, therefore, has no jurisdiction of the cause; and it is dismissed.

RALPH WALDO EMERSON

Politics (1844)

In dealing with the State, we ought to remember that its institutions are not aboriginal, though they existed before we were born: that they are not superior to the citizen: that every one of them was once the act of a single man: every law and usage was a man's expedient to meet a particular case: that they all are imitable, all alterable; we may make as good; we may make better. Society is an illusion to the young citizen. It lies before him in rigid repose, with certain names, men, and institutions, rooted like oak-trees to the centre, round which all arrange themselves the best they can. But the old statesman knows that society is fluid; there are no such roots and centres; but any particle may suddenly become the centre of the movement, and compel the system to gyrate round it, as every man of strong will, like Pisistratus, or Cromwell, does for a time, and every man of truth, like Plato, or Paul, does forever. But politics rest on necessary foundations, and cannot be treated with levity. Republics abound in young civilians, who believe that the laws make the city, that grave modifications of the policy and modes of living, and employments of the population, that commerce, education, and religion, may be voted in or out; and that any measure, though it were absurd, may be imposed on a people, if only you can get sufficient voices to make it a law. But the wise know that foolish legislation is a rope of sand, which perishes in the twisting; that the State must follow, and not lead the character and progress of the citizen; the strongest usurper is quickly got rid of; and they only who build on Ideas, build for eternity; and that the form of government which prevails, is the expression of what cultivation exists in the population which permits it. The law is only a memorandum. We are superstitious, and esteem the statute somewhat: so much life as it has in the character of living men, is its force. The statute stands there to say, yesterday we agreed so and so, but how feel ye this article today? Our statute is a currency, which we stamp with our own portrait: it soon becomes unrecognizable, and in process of time will return to the mint. Nature is not democratic, nor limited-monarchical, but despotic, and will not be fooled or abated of any jot of her authority, by the pertest of her sons: and as fast as the public mind is opened to more intelligence, the code is seen to be brute and stammering. It speaks not articulately, and must be made to. Meantime the education of the general mind never stops. The reveries of the true and simple are prophetic. What the tender poetic youth dreams, and prays, and paints today, but shuns the ridicule of saying aloud, shall presently be the resolutions of public bodies, then shall be carried as grievance and bill of rights through conflict and war, and then shall be triumphant law and establishment for a hundred years, until it gives place, in turn, to new prayers and pictures. The history of the State sketches in coarse outline the progress of thought, and follows at a distance the delicacy of culture and of aspiration.

The theory of politics, which has possessed the mind of men, and which they have expressed the best they could in their laws and in their revolutions, considers persons and property as the two objects for whose protection government exists. Of persons, all have equal rights, in virtue of being identical in nature. This interest, of course, with its whole power demands a democracy. Whilst the rights of all as persons are equal, in virtue of their access to reason, their rights in property are very unequal. One man owns his clothes, and another owns a county. This accident, depending, primarily, on the skill and virtue of the parties, of which there is every degree, and, secondarily, on patrimony, falls unequally, and its rights, of course, are unequal. Personal rights, universally the same, demand a government framed on the ratio of the census: property demands a government framed on the ratio of owners and of owning. Laban, who has flocks and herds, wishes them looked after by an officer on the frontiers, lest the Midianites shall drive them off, and pays a tax to that end. Jacob has no flocks or herds, and no fear of the Midianites, and pays no tax to the officer. It seemed fit that Laban and Jacob should have equal rights to elect the officer, who is to defend their persons, but that Laban, and not Jacob, should elect the officer who is to guard the sheep and cattle. And, if question arise whether additional officers or watch-towers should be provided, must not Laban and Isaac, and those who must sell part of their herds to buy protection for the rest, judge better of this, and with more right, than Jacob, who, because he is a youth and a traveller, eats their bread and not his own?

In the earliest society the proprietors made their own wealth, and so long as it comes to the owners in the direct way, no other opinion would arise in any equitable community, than that property should make the law for property, and persons the law for persons.

But property passes through donation or inheritance to those who do not create it. Gift, in one case, makes it as really the new owner's, as labor made it the first owner's: in the other case, of patrimony, the law makes an ownership, which will be valid in each man's view according to the estimate which he sets on the public tranquillity.

It was not, however, found easy to embody the readily admitted principle, that property should make law for property, and persons for persons: since persons and property mixed themselves in every transaction. At last it seemed settled, that the rightful distinction was, that the proprietors should have more elective franchise than non-proprietors, on the Spartan principle of "calling that which is just, equal; not that which is equal, just."

That principle no longer looks so self-evident as it appeared in former times, partly, because doubts have arisen whether too much weight had not been allowed in the laws, to property, and such a structure given to our usages, as allowed the rich to encroach on the poor, and to keep them poor; but mainly, because there is an instinctive sense, however obscure and yet inarticulate, that the whole constitution of property, on its present tenures, is injurious, and its influence on persons deteriorating and degrading; that truly, the only interest for the consideration of the State, is persons: that property will always follow persons; that the highest end of government is the culture of men: and if men can be educated, the institutions will share their improvement, and the moral sentiment will write the law of the land.

If it be not easy to settle the equity of this question, the peril is less when we take note of our natural defences. We are kept by better guards than the vigilance of such magistrates as we commonly elect. Society always consists, in greatest part, of young and foolish persons. The old, who have seen through the hypocrisy of courts and statesmen, die, and leave no wisdom to their sons. These believe their own newspaper, as their fathers did at their age. With such an ignorant and deceivable majority, States would soon run to ruin, but that there are limitations, beyond which the folly and ambition of governors cannot go. Things have their laws, as well as men; and things refuse to be trifled with. Property will be protected. Corn will not grow, unless it is planted and manured; but the farmer will not plant or hoe it, unless the chances are a hundred to one, that he will cut and harvest it. Under any forms, persons and property must and will have their just sway. They exert their power, as steadily as matter its attraction. Cover up a pound of earth never so cunningly, divide and subdivide it; melt it to liquid, convert it to gas; it will always weigh a pound: it will always attract and resist other matter, by the full virtue of one pound weight;—and the attributes of a person, his wit and his moral energy, will exercise, under any law or extinguishing tyranny, their proper force,—if not overtly, then covertly; if not for the law, then against it; if not wholesomely, then poisonously; with right, or by might.

The boundaries of personal influence it is impossible to fix, as persons are organs of moral or supernatural force. Under the dominion of an idea, which possesses the minds of multitudes, as civil freedom, or the religious sentiment, the powers of persons are no longer subjects of calculation. A nation of men unanimously bent on freedom, or conquest, can easily confound the arithmetic of statists, and achieve extravagant actions, out of all proportion to their means; as, the Greeks, the Saracens, the Swiss, the Americans, and the French have done.

In like manner, to every particle of property belongs its own attraction. A cent is the representative of a certain quantity of corn or other commodity. Its value is in the necessities of the animal man. It is so much warmth, so much bread, so much water, so much land. The law may do what it will with the owner of property, its just power will still attach to the cent. The law may in a mad freak say, that all shall have power except the owners of property: they shall have no vote. Nevertheless, by a higher law, the property will, year after year, write every statute that respects property. The non-proprietor will be the scribe of the proprietor. What the owners wish to do, the whole power of property will do, either through the law, or else in defiance of it. Of course, I speak of all the property, not merely of the great estates. When the rich are outvoted, as frequently happens, it is the joint treasury of the poor which exceeds their accumulations. Every man owns something, if it is only a cow, or a wheelbarrow, or his arms, and so has that property to dispose of.

The same necessity which secures the rights of person and property against the malignity or folly of the magistrate, determines the form and methods of governing, which are proper to each nation, and to its habit of thought, and nowise transferable to other states of society. In this country, we are very vain of our political institutions, which are singular in this, that they sprung, within the memory of living men, from the character and condition of the people, which they still express with sufficient fidelity,—and we ostentatiously prefer them to any other in history. They are not better, but only fitter for us. We may be wise in asserting the advantage in modern times of the democratic form, but to other states of society, in which religion consecrated the monarchical, that and not this was expedient. Democracy is better for us, because the religious sentiment of the present time accords better with it. Born democrats, we are nowise qualified to judge of monarchy, which, to our fathers living in the monarchical idea, was also relatively right. But our institutions, though in coincidence with the spirit of the age, have not any exemption from the practical defects which have discredited other forms. Every actual State is corrupt. Good men must not obey the laws too well. What satire on government can equal the severity of censure conveyed in the word *politic*, which now for ages has signified *cunning*, intimating that the State is a trick?

The same benign necessity and the same practical abuse appear in the parties into which each State divides itself, of opponents and defenders of the administration of the government. Parties are also founded on instincts, and have better guides to their own humble aims than the sagacity of their leaders. They have nothing perverse in their origin, but rudely mark some real and lasting relation. We might as wisely reprove the east wind, or the frost, as a political party, whose members, for the most part, could give no account of their position, but stand for the defence of those interests in which they find themselves. Our quarrel with them begins, when they quit this deep natural ground at the bidding of some leader, and, obeying personal considerations, throw themselves into the maintenance and defence of points, nowise belonging to their system. A party is perpetually corrupted by personality. Whilst we absolve the association from dishonesty, we cannot extend the same charity to their leaders. They reap the rewards of the docility and zeal of the masses which they direct. Ordinarily, our parties are parties of circumstance, and not of principle; as, the planting interest in conflict with the commercial; the party of capitalists, and that of operatives; parties which are identical in their moral character, and which can easily change ground with each other, in the support of many of their measures. Parties of principle, as, religious sects, or the party of free-trade, of universal suffrage, of abolition of slavery, of abolition of capital punishment, degenerate into personalities, or would inspire enthusiasm. The vice of our leading parties in this country (which may be cited as a fair specimen of these societies of opinion) is, that they do not plant themselves on the deep and necessary grounds to which they are respectively entitled, but lash themselves to fury in the carrying of some local and momentary measure, nowise useful to the commonwealth. Of the two great parties, which, at this hour, almost share the nation between them, I should say, that, one has the best cause, and the other contains the best men. The philosopher, the poet, or the religious man, will, of course, wish to cast his vote with the democrat, for free-trade, for wide suffrage, for the abolition of legal cruelties in the penal code, and for facilitating in every manner the access of the young and the poor to the sources of wealth and power. But he can rarely accept the persons whom the so-called popular party propose to him as representatives of these liberalities. They have not at heart the ends which give to the name of democracy what hope and virtue are in it. The spirit of our American radicalism is destructive and aimless: it is not loving; it has no ulterior and divine ends; but is destructive only out of hatred and selfishness. On the other side, the conservative party, composed of the most moderate, able, and cultivated part of the population, is timid, and merely defensive of property. It vindicates no right, it aspires to no real good, it brands no crime, it proposes no generous policy, it does not build, nor write, nor cherish the arts, nor foster religion, nor establish schools, nor encourage science, nor emancipate the slave, nor befriend the poor, or the Indian, or the immigrant. From neither party, when in power, has the world any benefit to expect in science, art, or humanity, at all commensurate with the resources of the nation.

I do not for these defects despair of our republic. We are not at the mercy of any waves of chance. In the strife of ferocious parties, human nature always finds itself cherished, as the children of the convicts at Botany Bay are found to have as healthy a moral sentiment as other children. Citizens of feudal states are alarmed at our democratic institutions lapsing into anarchy; and the older and more cautious among ourselves are learning from Europeans to look with some terror at our turbulent freedom. It is said that in our license of construing the Constitution, and in the despotism of public opinion, we have no anchor; and one foreign observer thinks he has found the safeguard in the sanctity of Marriage among us; and another thinks he has found it in our Calvinism. Fisher Ames expressed the popular security more wisely, when he compared a monarchy and a republic, saying, "that a monarchy is a merchantman, which sails well, but will sometimes strike on a rock, and go to the bottom; whilst a republic is a raft, which would never sink, but then your feet are always in water." No forms can have any dangerous importance, whilst we are befriended by the laws of things. It makes no difference how many tons weight of atmosphere presses on our heads, so long as the same pressure resists it within the lungs. Augment the mass a thousand fold, it cannot begin to crush us, as long as reaction is equal to action. The fact of two poles, of two forces, centripetal and centrifugal, is universal, and each force by its own activity develops the other. Wild liberty develops iron conscience. Want of liberty, by strengthening law and decorum, stupefies conscience. 'Lynch-law' prevails only where there is greater hardihood and self-subsistency in the leaders. A mob cannot be a permanency: everybody's interest requires that it should not exist, and only justice satisfies all.

We must trust infinitely to the beneficent necessity which shines through all laws. Human nature expresses itself in them as characteristically as in statues, or songs, or railroads, and an abstract of the codes of nations would be a transcript of the common conscience. Governments have their origin in the moral identity of men. Reason for one is seen to be reason for another, and for every other. There is a middle measure which satisfies all parties, be they never so many, or so resolute for their own. Every man finds a sanction for his simplest claims and deeds in decisions of his own mind, which he calls Truth and Holiness. In these decisions all the citizens find a perfect agreement, and only in these; not in what is good to eat, good to wear, good use of time, or what amount of land, or of public aid, each is entitled to claim. This truth and justice men presently endeavor to make application of, to the measuring of land, the apportionment of service, the protection of life and property. Their first endeavors, no doubt, are very awkward. Yet absolute right is the first governor; or, every government is an impure theocracy. The idea, after which each community is aiming to make and mend its law, is, the will of the wise man. The wise man, it cannot find in nature, and it makes awkward but earnest efforts to secure his government by contrivance; as, by causing the entire people to give their voices on every measure; or, by a double choice to get the representation of the whole; or, by a selection of the best citizens; or, to secure the advantages of efficiency and internal peace, by confiding the government to one, who may himself select his agents. All forms of government symbolize an immortal government, common to all dynasties and independent of numbers, perfect where two men exist, perfect where there is only one man.

Every man's nature is a sufficient advertisement to him of the character of his fellows. My right and my wrong, is their right and their wrong. Whilst I do what is fit for me, and abstain from what is unfit, my neighbor and I shall often agree in our means, and work together for a time to one end. But whenever I find my dominion over myself not sufficient for me, and undertake the direction of him also, I overstep the truth, and come into false relations to him. I may have so much more skill or strength than he, that he cannot express adequately his sense of wrong, but it is a lie, and hurts like a lie both him and me. Love and nature cannot maintain the assumption: it must be executed by a practical lie, namely, by force. This undertaking for another, is the blunder which stands in colossal ugliness in the governments of the world. It is the same thing in numbers, as in a pair, only not quite so intelligible. I can see well enough a great difference between my setting myself down to a self-control, and my going to make somebody else act after my views: but when a quarter of the human race assume to tell me what I must do, I may be too much disturbed by the circumstances to see so clearly the absurdity of their command. Therefore, all public ends look vague and quixotic beside private ones. For, any laws but those which men make for themselves, are laughable. If I put myself in the place of my child, and we stand in one thought, and see that things are thus or thus, that perception is law for him and me. We are both there, both act. But if, without carrying him into the thought, I look over into his plot, and, guessing how it is with him, ordain this or that, he will never obey me. This is the history of governments,—one man does something which is to bind another. A man who cannot be acquainted with me, taxes me; looking from afar at me, ordains that a part of my labor shall go to this or that whimsical end, not as I, but as he happens to fancy. Behold the consequence. Of all debts, men are least willing to pay the taxes. What a satire is this on government! Everywhere they think they get their money's worth, except for these.

Hence, the less government we have, the better,—the fewer laws, and the less confided power. The antidote to this abuse of formal Government, is, the influence of private character, the growth of the Individual; the appearance of the principal to supersede the proxy; the appearance of the wise man, of whom the existing government, is, it must be owned, but a shabby imitation. That which all things tend to educe, which freedom, cultivation, intercourse, revolutions, go to form and deliver, is character; that is the end of nature, to reach unto this coronation of her king. To educate the wise man, the State exists; and with the appearance of the wise man, the State expires. The appearance of character makes the State unnecessary. The wise man is the State. He needs no army, fort, or navy,—he loves men too well; no bribe, or feast, or palace, to draw friends to him; no vantage ground, no favorable circumstance. He needs no library, for he has not done thinking; no church, for he is a prophet; no statute book, for he has the lawgiver; no money, for he is value; no road, for he is at home where he is; no experience, for the life of the creator shoots through him, and looks from his eyes.

He has no personal friends, for he who has the spell to draw the prayer and piety of all men unto him, needs not husband and educate a few, to share with him a select and poetic life. His relation to men is angelic; his memory is myrrh to them; his presence, frankincense and flowers.

We think our civilization near its meridian, but we are yet only at the cock-crowing and the morning star. In our barbarous society the influence of character is in its infancy. As a political power, as the rightful lord who is to tumble all rulers from their chairs, its presence is hardly yet suspected. Malthus and Ricardo quite omit it; the Annual Register is silent; in the Conversations' Lexicon, it is not set down; the President's Message, the Queen's Speech, have not mentioned it; and yet it is never nothing. Every thought which genius and piety throw into the world, alters the world. The gladiators in the lists of power feel, through all their frocks of force and simulation, the presence of worth. I think the very strife of trade and ambition are confession of this divinity; and successes in those fields are the poor amends, the fig-leaf with which the shamed soul attempts to hide its nakedness. I find the like unwilling homage in all quarters. It is because we know how much is due from us, that we are impatient to show some petty talent as a substitute for worth. We are haunted by a conscience of this right to grandeur of character, and are false to it. But each of us has some talent, can do somewhat useful, or graceful, or formidable, or amusing, or lucrative. That we do, as an apology to others and to ourselves, for not reaching the mark of a good and equal life. But it does not satisfy *us*, whilst we thrust it on the notice of our companions. It may throw dust in their eyes, but does not smooth our own brow, or give us the tranquillity of the strong when we walk abroad. We do penance as we go. Our talent is a sort of expiation, and we are constrained to reflect on our splendid moment, with a certain humiliation, as somewhat too fine, and not as one act of many acts, a fair expression of our permanent energy. Most persons of ability meet in society with a kind of tacit appeal. Each seems to say, "I am not all here." Senators and presidents have climbed so high with pain enough, not because they think the place specially agreeable, but as an apology for real worth, and to vindicate their manhood in our eyes. This conspicuous chair is their compensation to themselves for being of a poor, cold, hard nature. They must do what they can. Like one class of forest animals, they have nothing but a prehensile tail: climb they must, or crawl. If a man found himself so rich-natured that he could enter into strict relations with the best persons, and make life serene around him by the dignity and sweetness of his behavior, could he afford to circumvent the favor of the caucus and the press, and covet relations so hollow and pompous, as those of a politician? Surely nobody would be a charlatan, who could afford to be sincere.

The tendencies of the times favor the idea of self-government, and leave the individual, for all code, to the rewards and penalties of his own constitution, which work with more energy than we believe, whilst we depend on artificial restraints. The movement in this direction has been very marked in modern history. Much has been blind and discreditable, but the nature of the revolution is not affected by the vices of the revolters; for this is a purely moral force. It was never adopted by any party in history, neither can be. It separates the individual from all party, and unites him, at the same time, to the race. It promises a recognition of higher rights than those of personal freedom, or the security of property. A man has a right to be employed, to be trusted, to be loved, to be revered. The power of love, as the basis of a State, has never been tried. We must not imagine that all things are lapsing into confusion, if every tender protestant be not compelled to bear his part in certain social conventions: nor doubt that roads can be built, letters carried, and the fruit of labor secured, when the government of force is at an end. Are our methods now so excellent that all competitition is hopeless? Could not a nation of friends even devise better ways? On the other hand, let not the most conservative and timid fear anything from a premature surrender of the bayonet, and the system of force. For, according to the order of nature, which is quite superior to our will, it stands thus; there will always be a government of force, where men are selfish; and when they are pure enough to abjure the code of force, they will be wise enough to see how these public ends of the post-office, of the highway, of commerce, and the exchange of property, of museums and libraries, of institutions of art and science, can be answered.

We live in a very low state of the world, and pay unwilling tribute to governments founded on force. There is not, among the most religious and instructed men of the most religious and civil nations, a reliance on the moral sentiment, and a sufficient belief in the unity of things to persuade them that society can be maintained without artificial restraints, as well as the solar system; or that the private citizen might be reasonable, and a good neighbor, without the hint of a jail or a confiscation. What is strange too, there never was in any man sufficient faith in the power of rectitude, to inspire him with the broad design of renovating the State on the principle of right and love. All those who have pretended this design, have been partial reformers, and have admitted in some manner the supremacy of the bad State. I do not call to mind a single human being who has steadily denied the authority of the laws, on the simple ground of his own moral nature. Such designs, full of genius and full of fate as they are, are not entertained except avowedly as air-pictures. If the individual who exhibits them, dare to think them practicable, he disgusts scholars and churchmen; and men of talent, and women of superior sentiments, cannot hide their contempt. Not the less does nature continue to fill the heart of youth with suggestions of this enthusiasm, and there are now men,—if indeed I can speak in the plural number,—more exactly, I will say, I have just been conversing with one man, to whom no weight of adverse experience will make it for a moment appear impossible, that thousands of human beings might share and obey each with the other the grandest and truest sentiments, as well as a knot of friends, or a pair of lovers.

8

Liberty, Order, and the Market

The management of economic and territorial expansion in the United States produced bitter political disputes in early to mid-nineteenth century America. The documents in this chapter in many ways reflect a strong continuity with those of the previous chapter, and there is considerable overlap between them. But whereas the documents of Chapter 7 illuminate a broad moral discussion about national identity and its ends, those that follow here tend to focus on questions of political economy.

The eight years of James Monroe's presidency mark a period of relative quiescence in American political history. Dubbed by the Boston *Columbian Centinel* as the "Era of Good Feelings," Americans in these years asserted a strong sense of national identity, which helped keep sectional differences at bay. Opposition to the War of 1812 gravely weakened the Federalist Party, and by 1820 it had almost entirely withered away. Thus, these years were scarcely roiled by formal, interparty competition. In 1816 the Republican Monroe easily defeated the Federalist presidential candidate, Rufus King. In 1820 the Federalists failed to endorse a presidential candidate at all, and Monroe ran (more or less) unopposed.

Although Republicans dominated the executive and legislative branches, the Federalists still enjoyed the leadership of Supreme Court Chief Justice John Marshall, who in a series of Court opinions promoted and defended a Hamiltonian vision of the Constitution. Under Marshall's guidance, the Court put teeth into the Constitution's contract clause and permitted Congress wide latitude in its exercise of implied power. In *Gibbons v. Ogden* (1824), Marshall provided a broad interpretation of the commerce clause, laying forth a precedent that in the late 1930s the Court and Congress would embrace with profound political consequences. Similarly, under his guidance the Court ruled that the national government, not the states, had authority in Native American affairs.

Moreover, by the mid-1820s fundamental differences over public policy reemerged, sparking renewed party competition. Americans were experiencing a market revolution. Inventions like the steamboat, technological feats like the building of the Erie Canal, and the emergence of factories began to radically transform the American economy. Technological innovations and the specialization of labor made for greater productivity, increased access to domestic and international markets, and rapid economic growth. Henry Clay, the leader of the new Whig Party, embraced this market revolution. Clay believed that economic opportunity would make America wealthier while fostering virtues, such as hard work and frugality, essential to a republic. Further, he sought to engage the help of the national government in spurring that growth, pushing for congressional funding for "internal improvements," like canals and roads, and a protective tariff on imported manufactures. Clay also believed that his "American system" would be "beneficial to all parts of the Union," would be perceived as such, and thus would promote greater national unity.

Although Clay and the Whigs enjoyed the support of numerous Americans, they also faced resistance from many others who were skeptical of their program of strong government and economic development. Though the market revolution spelled opportunity and progress for those farmers and merchants oriented to its possibilities, for many others it was profoundly unsettling. Once-independent artisans now found themselves part of a wage labor force and subject to the vicissitudes of the business cycle. Critics of the market revolution increasingly perceived corporations and banks as threats to

American democracy. Examples of nascent class consciousness found voice in the writings of Theophilus Fisk. Observers hostile to the changes entailed by the vibrant extension of commerce to American society and culture argued for containing corporations under legislative control, and the Supreme Court, now led by Roger Taney, seemed to take them seriously. The Whigs found themselves accused, as the Federalists had been, of "favoring the growth of aristocracy."

The political leader of this attack on corporations, banks, and the Whig Party was Andrew Jackson. "Old Hickory" profoundly changed American politics. He argued convincingly that the president was the most authentic representative of the American people. Further, he promoted a post-Madisonian understanding of democracy, touting respect for popular opinion and the principle that the majority should govern. Jackson identified with the common folk and encouraged them to campaign for him, arguing that the people must choose the president. With all but two states allowing their popular vote to determine their electoral votes, and with Martin Van Buren orchestrating strong party organization, Jackson won the 1828 election for the Democratic Party.

Combining this notion of democracy and the president as voice-of-the-people, Jackson defended an aggressive exercise of presidential authority. He vetoed renewal of the bank, which he perceived to be a threat to the democratic majority. He vetoed the Maysville Road bill, finding it constitutionally suspect and dangerous, and contending that the debt the project would incur would further strengthen the power of the nation's creditors. Like Thomas Jefferson, Jackson saw himself as the defender of a virtuous people, and he echoed the Virginian's call for simple, frugal government and the strict limitation of national political power. At the same time, he would not suffer the states to run roughshod over the national government's constitutional authority. Arguing that the Constitution expressed the will of the people and that the United States "forms a *government*, not a league," he rejected the nullification doctrine and left no doubt that South Carolina's defiance of a federal tariff would be met with armed force.

Jackson's defense of the tariff and the supremacy of federal law should not be mistaken for opposition to slavery. He owned slaves (as did Clay), buying and selling human beings with regularity. Jackson's simultaneous support for slavery and more democracy made him very much a man of his times. While conservatives like James Kent argued that a property requirement for suffrage would help keep democratic excesses in check (the New York state constitution had allowed black men to vote, provided they met the property requirement), so-called democrats sought to abolish the property requirement for white males while disenfranchising blacks altogether. Thus, race became firmly rooted in the ideology and laws of the nation. To be a citizen, one had to be white. Blacks were something else: perpetually childlike, constitutionally incapable of manly independence or virtuous self-government. So, too, were women and Native Americans.

There were critics who saw in the policies of both the Whigs and the Democrats—and in American culture more generally—a coarsening of America's soul. From this critical disillusionment sprang forth myriad new religious communities, like the Shakers, and experimental utopian societies like Hopedale, Brook Farm, and New Harmony. More conventional evangelical denominations like the Methodists and Baptists experienced an explosion of membership. By 1840, more than a million Americans were members of Methodist churches, making that denomination the nation's largest. At the camp meetings of the ongoing Protestant revivals, as in the pulpits of their churches, ministers emphasized the Arminian doctrine of free will as an alternative to Calvinism's more deterministic orientation. These men preached against the narcissism of commercial society and condemned greed and indifference as sin. And yet their message ultimately was ambiguous. They praised the self-controlled, self-ordered autonomous individual, responsible for his or her own salvation. But the character traits they valued—self-reliance, industry, sobriety, and so on—were precisely those rewarded by the expansion of commercial society.

The most important critics were the Transcendentalists. Advocates of democracy, fiercely individualistic, the Transcendentalists found America's religious, economic, and political institutions oppressive.

"I wish to break all prisons," Ralph Waldo Emerson wrote, and no prisons were tougher to break than those fortified by tradition. He rejected evangelical Protestant theology because it presumed the authority of inspired scripture; but for Emerson, the Bible was no more inspired than other great books. Truth had to be sought in one's own experience. Life could not be artificially constricted by tradition or popular prejudice without snuffing out the spirit of the free individual. As Henry David Thoreau explained, it is one's duty to live a life in accordance with principle, even if—particularly if—it leads one to challenge ideas that by convention shape the world around us.

Charles Jared Ingersoll

Inchiquin's Letters (1810)

The lien of this "mighty continental nation" is commercial liberty: not mere political liberty, but positive freedom; geographical absolution from all but the slightest restraints; the inherent and inalienable birthright of this adolescent people, upon the enjoyment of which they entered by a lineal title, the moment they felt strength enough to cast off the trammels of infancy: a heritage as natural as the air they breathe, which, whether it sweeten the toil of New England, where the same farmer who sows and reaps his own field, is also the mariner, who attends his produce on distant ventures, or inflate the pride of the south, where the poor black sows the ground and the rich white reaps the harvest, is still and every where the same "brave spirit," pervading the whole republic, and binding it together by an influence, not the less powerful, because its current is propelled by an animating contrariety. The American people, dispersed over an immense territory, abounding in all the means of commercial greatness, to whom an opportunity was presented at an early period of adapting their government to their circumstances, followed the manifest order of nature, when they adopted a free, republican, commercial federation.

The course and catastrophe of the French revolution have cast a gloom over republicanism, which perhaps it may never shake off; and which, at least for the present, renders it in Europe repulsive and discreditable. But the American republic is the natural fruit of the American soil: the spirit of its freedom is impassioned, perhaps factious, but not furious or bloody. It is in vain to attempt, and absurd to desire, the introduction of the republican polity as a general melioration of the lot of nations. Many causes, that are beyond the reach of man, must concur to its establishment; and there have been few countries predisposed, as they should be, for its reception. The English loathed the adulteration they endured during the area of their commonwealth, when hypocritical lowliness, ferocious fanaticism, and overstained economy, were substituted for the generous and munificent patriotism which ennobled and perpetuated the ancient republics. Yet short as was its duration, and perverted as were its principles, such is the natural vigor of a free commonwealth, that the English received from theirs an impulse, which while it darkened their character, greatly increased their power, and gave it the direction it has ever since followed. The French had none of the ideas or propensities suited to freedom: and whatever may have been the effects of their revolution in deracinating abuses, and regenerating their national energies, it was not to be supposed that a republican government would endure in France. The French had not the raw material. But the American federation is the natural offspring of commerce and liberty, whose correlative interests will bind it together in principle, even after its formal dissolution. What are the merits of those institutions which have been framed by the people of this country it is not necessary here to inquire, or whether the government be calculated for strength and durability. The states, as now organized, may be consolidated or dismembered, may fall asunder by the weight and weakness of the union, or may separate in a convulsion. But it is the perfection of polity, when it rests on natural bases; and disunion of the American states, whatever might be its political consequences, could not destroy or materially change their mutual commercial dependence, and would not probably diminish the almost universal attachment of the people to republican institutions. The empire, in point of extent, is unwieldy. The east and the south are already jealous of each other, and the west regards them both with suspicion. But a community of language, of laws, of political attachments, and a reciprocity of interests are strong bonds of union. So many theories have been projected on the excellence of a federal republic, and so much disgrace has of late been cast upon republicanism by both its advocates and enemies, that the American experiment must be regarded with no small anxiety: for certain it is that an enlightened and predominant republic, such as those of Greece, Carthage and Rome, is the most rational and glorious object the mind can contemplate.

The prevailing character of these national elements is the natural result from their geographical and political combination. It is natural that a people descended so lately from pilgrims and sectaries should be enthusiasts—that a commercial people should be enterprising and ingenious—that a republican people, whose press is free, and whose government is a government of laws and opinion, should be intelligent and licentious—that an adolescent and prosperous people should be aspiring, warlike and vainglorious. This is not the character the Americans bear in Europe. The question there is whether they have any national character at all; and the common impression is that they have not.

There is a great proneness to misrepresent national character, which is a consideration extremely obscured by gross prejudices. That verisimilitude of habits, manners and propensities, indicative of the inhabitants of ancient countries, is not an infallible index to the national character: there are vulgar features, striking, but deceptive. Heroes, poets and historians will adapt national greatness to a poor and enslaved people. Peace, plenty and a certain degree of obscurity render a people happy; and if they are happy, they will commonly be virtuous. But virtue and happiness are not so imposing as greatness, in the national, or in the individual estimate. The same principle that induces a preference of the great to the good, bears admiration from the wise and peaceable commonwealth to the belligerent empire. [. . .] Reflecting men in Europe regard the American revolution as a period when the American character shone forth with considerable distinction. Yet the same nation, in part the same men, after thirty years of peace and prosperity, are supposed to have lost the energy of patriotism they then displayed. An expansion of population, of resources, of territory, of power, of information, of freedom, of every thing that tends to magnify man, is supposed to have degenerated the Americans. Is this the course of nature? All things are said to tend from their origin to a certain degree of perfection, and thence to decline and dissolution. But can the time be so soon arrived for the tide of American declension? According to the common course of events, the genius of the American people should be enhanced, not deteriorated, by the peace and prosperity they have enjoyed since the period of their birth as a nation. By sketches of the present state of their religion, legislation, literature, arts and society, with an aspect never turned from their national characteristics, and embracing no further details that are necessary for their exposition, I propose to endeavour to refute the false opinions inferred from their tranquillity, and at the same time to exhibit their national character.

In this age of infidelity and indifference, to call any people a religious people, is a license, which nothing but a comparative view of the state of religion in this and in other christian countries, can uphold. It is, however, true, that the number of persons devoted to pious exercises, from reflection, independent of education and habit, is greater in the United States, than in any other part of the world, in proportion to the population; and religious morality is more general and purer here than elsewhere. The political ordinance of religious toleration is one of those improvements in the science of politics, for which mankind will acknowledge their obligations to America and the divorce of church and state is an inestimable pledge for the purity and stability of republican government. Religious toleration, says the Prince of Benevento, is one of the most powerful guaranties of social tranquillity; for where liberty of conscience is respected, every other right cannot fail to be so. As Christianity and civilization have hitherto been inseparable companions, it is probable that where the practice of the former is most acceptable, the influence of the latter will be the most pervading. One of the first acts of Fen and Baltimore in their respective provinces, was the absolute separation of ecclesiastical from secular concerns: a catholic and a quaker, the extremes of the christian creed, thus signalizing their administrations by a liberality equally wise and magnanimous, the beneficial effects of which will be felt to the latest generation. In New England, where Presbyterianism is the predominant faith, fanaticism expired slowly, and proscription blazed up more than once, after it was believed and ought to have been extinguished. But at this time persecution is impracticable. Laws, and opinions stronger than laws, prevent it. The churches of

Rome, of England, of Luther, of Wesley and of Fox, in all their various subdivisions and modifications, subsist in peace and harmony, worshipping without molestation, according to their different tenets. Universal toleration has produced numberless particular sects, each maintained by enthusiastic proselytes. Thus the Americans are a nation of freethinkers; and having moreover not only no established church, but being perfectly unrestrained in their belief, those persuasions are most followed, which involve the utmost refinements of enthusiasm, and rejection of ceremonial. After shaking off entirely the shackles of superstition, it is not easy to avoid the phrensy of fanaticism; for one begins where the other ends. But it is the advantage of the latter, that whereas superstition binds the soul in sloth and fear, fanaticism sets it free from their mortification; and though for a time it may float in an unsettled medium, it will settle at last on the right base.

The civil institutions of this country conduce equally with religious toleration to habits of intelligence and independence. Natural equality perhaps does not exist. Birth, affluence and talents create distinctions, notwithstanding political regulations to the contrary. The pride of family, the vanity of wealth, and other adventitious advantages, are not without their sensation in society, even in this young republic. But patrician and plebeian orders are unknown, and that third or middle class, upon which so many theories have been founded, is a section that has no existence here. Luxury has not yet corrupted the rich, nor is there any of that want, which classifies the poor. There is no populace. All are people. What in other countries is called the populace, a compost heap, whence germinate mobs, beggars, and tyrants, is not to be found in the towns; and there is no peasantry in the country. Were it not for the slaves of the south, there would be but one rank. By the facility of subsistence and high price of labour, by the universal education and universal suffrage, almost every man is a yeoman or a citizen, sensible of his individual importance. [. . .]

[. . .] They are most attached to the soil, who own a part of it; from which attachment spring love of country, glory, and that fine union of public with private feelings, which constitutes the strength and ornament of republics. In monarchies, these sentiments are confined to the great. The mass of the people to be sure instinctively love the spot of their nativity, but are seldom animated with that noble, personal, and selfish and obstinate zeal, which citizens feel for what they call their own. Hard labour and low wages stupefy and vitiate the lower classes of most countries. But in the United States wages are very high, and hard labour is altogether optional. Three days work out of seven yields a support. The lassitude and dissipation, which might be expected from so much leisure, are provided against by natural circumstances. On one side the sea, and on the other rich waste lands, present inexhaustible fields of adventure and opulence. The inducement to labour, the recompense, is so great, that the Americans, with the utmost facilities of subsistence, are a most industrious people. As in higher life, learning and assiduity are certain passports to perferment and celebrity, so in the occupations of trade, agriculture, and the sea, persevering industry, almost without a risk of disappointment, leads to comfort and consequence. The proportion of persons of large fortune is small; that of paupers next to nothing. Every one is a man of business; every thing in the progress of emulation and improvement. Universality of successful employment diffuses alacrity and happiness throughout the community. No taxes, no military, no ranks, remove every sensation of restraint. Each individual feels himself rising in his fortunes; and the nation, rising with the concentration of all this elasticity, rejoices in its growing greatness. It is the perfection of civilized society, as far as respects the happiness of its members, when its ends are accomplished with the least pressure from government; and if the principle of internal corruption, and the dangers of foreign aggression, did not render necessary a sacrifice of some of this felicity, to preserve and perpetuate the rest, the Americans might continue to float in undisturbed buoyancy. The happiness, the virtue, and the most desirable character of a people at such a time, and under such circumstances, are most perfect, and should be most distinguished. But a dash of licentiousness already disturbs this happy equilibrium, and it must be overthrown by foreign or domestic violence, unless it be retrenched and protected.

From ignorance and bigotry, the common features of common people, the Americans have less to fear than from the opposite evils of faction and fanaticism. Propensities to the bottle, to conventicles, and to popular assemblies, are founded in enthusiasm, and fomented by freedom. A free and prosperous people will be infected with the lust for novelty; a passion more easily diverted than subdued. It would be practicable for the American government to give such encouragement to public festivals and recreations, as might tend to allay popular restlessness, and to give the popular feeling an innocent and even a patriotic direction. But at present, with all their fondness for public meetings, which is indulged in a numberless variety of associations, religious, political, convivial and social, greatly exceeding that of any other country, the Americans have few national festivals, and they are falling into disuse. [. . .]

In those efforts which are the production of genius rather than erudition, particularly in the accomplishment of public speaking, the Americans have attained to greater excellence than other modern nations, their superiors in age and refinement. In the prevalence of oratory, as a common talent, in the number of good public speakers, in the fire and captivation of their public harangues, parliamentary, popular, forensic and of the pulpit, the English are the only modern people comparable with the Americans, and the English are far from being their equals. Popular representation and freedom of speech, several sovereignties, each one represented in a debating assembly, always rivals and sometimes directly opposed to each other, cultivate and call forth the most striking powers of oratory; whose conceptions are facilitated by the grandeur of surrounding scenery, and sublimity of the images of nature. Not only oratory, but all the arts and sciences are said to flourish in a fresh soil: and Greece will ever remain an illustrious instance, that a cluster of commercial republics is eminently adapted to their propagation and perfection. [. . .]

There is no subject on which a liberal judgment should proceed so cautiously to condemnation, as that of the literary character of a contemporaneous nation. The most distinguished scholars have been the most prejudiced, when they came to weigh the comparative merits of their own and other nations in this respect. Voltaire, notwithstanding all his learning and impartiality in the abstract, and Johnson, take their stations at the head of the prejudices of their respective countries. It is not, therefore, to be wondered at, that the English deny the charms of French poetry, or that the French cannot relish Shakespeare or blank verse.

When a young people, not yet half a century advanced, have already exhibited a genius for oratory and legislation, and their general intelligence is so unrivalled as that of the Americans, we should be slow to conclude, from the paucity of their original writers, that they want an aptitude for composition, or a taste for literature and the arts. Since the invention of printing, and the improvements in commerce, the antiquated principles of gradual amelioration are no longer applicable to any people, especially not to the Americans. Rudiments are obsolete. As the discovery and first settlement of America were the results of, and simultaneous with, the reappearance of the arts and sciences during the 15th and 16th centuries, and as the inhabitants of this country have ever since, by the means of commerce and free presses, been intimately connected with all the most polished nations of the older world, their imitation of successive improvements has been close and constant, sometimes enlivened with distinguished discoveries and useful inventions of their own. While the shackles of a mother country laid upon their genius, it was necessarily somewhat restricted and mortified. The revolution called it forth to action, with all the ardour incident to such occasions. During the short period that has elapsed since their independence, freedom, prosperity and ambition have stimulated its powers; and setting aside two, or perhaps three, of the most enlightened empires of Europe, the literature, arts and sciences of the people of the United States of America, are equal, and their general information and intelligence superior, to those of any other nation. [. . .]

As civilized society rests on reciprocal concessions, its structure is most harmonious when they are best regulated; for, perhaps, the most we can say of human nature is, that it is capable of being rendered amiable by a reciprocity of good offices. The arts of hospitality and politeness, the alternation of business and pleasure, social assemblies, innocent recreations and good breeding, while they give zest to existence, undoubtedly tend to refine and cement society, and to render mankind more virtuous as well as more elegant. Up to the period of enervation, refinements mend the affections as well as the manners: but it is the misfortune of society, that civilization, after a certain point, begins to lose its seemliness; morals give way to manners, and character has no weight against rank, appearance or behaviour.

Though there are few men of very large fortunes in the United States, a great proportion are in easy circumstances, and hospitality and politeness are common virtues. Commercial people are said to be inhospitable. The English and the Dutch are the least hospitable people of modern Europe. But, in the United States, abundance overcomes the calculating spirit of trade, and the east and the south vie with each other in unbounded hospitality. Even this, by some of those Europeans who are prepossessed against this country, may be accounted a remnant of simplicity at least, if not of barbarity. Savages are always hospitable. The Romans found it necessary to prohibit the lavish dispensation of this duty among the Germans. But in the exercise of such a virtue, we admire the vanquished more than their conquerors in its extinction. [. . .]

Commerce, which equalizes fortunes, levels ranks; and parade and stateliness can be kept up only where there is great disproportion of possessions. Expensive establishments, splendid equipages, and magnificent entertainment, are sometimes copied after European models. But they are neither common nor popular. It is difficult and invidious to be magnificent in a republican country, where there is no populace, and so many members of society have wherewithal to be generous and hospitable. [. . .]

Having thus sketched the situation of this country, religious, political and social, let me hasten to such results as have not appeared in the course of the retrospect, and to some brief reflections on that commercial spirit, whose infusion is supposed to debilitate and debase the whole. It must always be borne in mind, that estimates of national character are to be formed from that class of the community, whatever it may be in different nations, which is the largest, and constitutes the most important portion of the population; especially when the Americans are the subject; inasmuch as they have, in fact, but one class of society. But in any nation a few individuals, of either the higher or lowest class, are not to be adopted as national types, nor the impressions they communicate, received as the national character. Our opinions of the French or English would be greatly erroneous, if our inquires were circumscribed to Paris or London.

A republican federation, a free press, general education, abundant subsistence, high price of labour, a warm climate, habits of intemperance, a variety of religious creeds, and the universal sensation of improvement and increase, naturally concur to the constitution of a well informed, ardent, enthusiastic, enterprising and licentious people. Where every man is a citizen, every citizen a freeholder, able and allowed to think, speak, and act for himself, the empire of opinion must be omnipotent: and it is impossible that a free and thinking people can be without a character. Enterprise, public spirit, intelligence, faction and love of country are natural to such a people. No series of ages is requisite to form or consolidate their character. At the earliest date the legend is most decided; and though it may be aggravated, is seldom improved by years or refinements.

Wherever we find foreign commerce, there also we find polished manners. It is commerce that harmonizes the intercourse and dissipates the prejudices of nations; softens their native peculiarities, and approximates their national characters to one common standard. Commerce, and trade, and manufactures, grew under the same shade in which learning flourished.

Such opinions, from such authority, are unanswerable. It is to North America only that their justice is denied. In Europe at least it is a prevailing notion to associate the commercial habits of the United States, with sordid fraud, a distaste for noble pursuits, and a dread of war: and the Americans have incurred the odium and contempt, which will be the lot of any nation that is considered by others to be tame, mercenary and base-spirited. But the policy of the government has been mistaken for the genius of the people. Alert, impetuous, alive to news and public discussions, the vibrations of popular sympathies are in no country so rapid and pervading. As individuals, and as a community, they have exhibited and continue to exhibit every day, the most decided proofs of courage and impetuosity.

The appeal to duels for the decision of private disputes is more frequent in the United States than in any other country whatever: and these private combats are conducted with a scientific ferociousness, and terminate in general with a fatality unknown elsewhere. The severest statutes have in vain pointed their artillery against this chivalric custom, which seems to be inveterate among impassioned and opinioned freeman. It is certain that men have become less free, less courageous, less disposed for great enterprises, than they were in the days of Rome and of suicide, when, as Montesquieu expresses it, they appear to have been born with a greater aptitude for heroism, and by exerting this inconceivable power over themselves, could bid defiance to all other human power. The modern duel is an offspring of this heathen sacrifice, in which similar causes lead to nearly the same effect. [. . .]

As a community, the Americans have always shown themselves no less forward, than as individuals, to face their enemies and aggressors. In most countries it is the government that provokes, declares and maintains wars. But the United States have exhibited continual struggles between the government and the people, in which the latter have been clamorous for hostilities, at one time with one foreign power, at another time with another, while all the influence and forbearance of their rulers has been exercised to restrain this martial intoxication. The revolution was lighted up by a national instinct for independence, called early into action by the allurements of liberty and republicanism; when certainly no incapacity for war was evinced. How illustrious indeed should the conduct and termination of that contest render the Americans, when contrasted with the pusillanimous facility with which the most compact and warlike nations of Europe have lately fallen under the arms of their invaders! The American colonies would not have ventured a war single-handed with the first maritime power of the world, about a trifling tax on tea, had not that military impulse, which inflamed alike the sturdy east, and the impatient south, prompted them to unite for assertion of their independence. It was not oppression that goaded them upon emancipation. But their instinct for liberty: as the author of their epic, with his peculiar propriety of expression, describes their feelings at the time,

> Fame fir'd their courage, freedom edg'd their swords.

A long interval of profound tranquillity and multiplied commerce may have tarnished the fame, perhaps relaxed somewhat the tone of this people. But it was the government, not the nation, who compromised with endurance for emolument; and the same spirit which was once displayed, is still ready to show itself when summoned into action. The same valour, good faith, clemency and patriotism still animate the bosoms of America, as the first burst of their hostilities, whenever it takes place, will convince their calumniators.

Legitimate commerce, instead of demoralizing or debasing a community, refines its sentiments, multiplies its intelligence, and sharpens its ingenuity. Where are the evidences to the contrary in this country?—The Americans, far from being a sordid or venal, are not even a thrifty people. Subsistence is so easy, and competency so common, that those nice calculations of domestic economy which are a branch almost of education in Europe, are scarcely attended to in America; and that long, disgusting catalogue of pretty offences, through which the lower classes of other nations are driven by indigence and wretchedness, has hardly an existence here, though death is almost proscribed from the penal code. Native Americans are very seldom to be met with in menial or the laborious occupations, which are filled by blacks and foreigners, mostly *Europeans*, who are also the common perpetrators of the smaller crimes alluded to. Though the government is supported by the customs, and the punishments for their contravention are merely pecuniary, yet such delinquencies are infinitely less frequent than in Europe or even Asia. The salaries of the public officers are very inconsiderable yet malversation is a crime of rare occurrence; and that essential venality, which pervades almost every department of government in other countries, is altogether unpracticed in this.

In their foreign traffic the Americans have been exposed to all the contumelious indignities which superior power and rapacity could inflict. But have the accusations charged upon them been substantiated? When a young and unarmed people have no other reliance for their advancement than their industry and acuteness, and nevertheless, owing to these and their territorial advantages, succeed against the jealous restrictions and overwhelming maritime strength of older states, it is as natural for the latter to stigmatize them with dishonesty and encroachment, as it was for Rome, when Carthage was half subdued, to proclaim the instability of Punic faith. But the charge contradicts itself: for how could the Americans pursue a successful and augmenting commerce, if their frauds were as numerous as they are declared to be, after the whole world are put on their guard, and in arms, to suppress them? The American merchant can have no other convoy than his neutrality and fairness: and if he have common sense, must perceive that honesty is his only policy. [. . .]

Peter Porter

Speech on Internal Improvements (February 8, 1810)

[. . .] The subject to which I allude, is the internal improvement of the United States by roads and canals; and I intend, before I sit down, to offer a resolution, the object of which will be to ascertain the sense of the house in relation to the expediency of appropriating a part of the public lands to such improvements.

[. . .] I have the honour to represent a portion of the country which is perhaps as little affected by our exterior commercial relations as any part of the United States; and yet I listen, with great attention and interest, to the various plans and propositions which are daily submitted and discussed in this house, and with which, indeed, its time is almost exclusively occupied, for the protection and security of commerce; and I trust that I shall show by my vote, on every proper occasion, that I consider my constituents as bound to support with their persons and their property, and to the last extremity, the just rights of the merchants of this country. On the other hand, I have a right to expect that the gentlemen who represent the mercantile interest will not only hear with patience the proposition I am about to submit, but that they will thank me for the fair opportunity I intend to afford them of proving the sincerity of those professions which we hear so often and so loudly made on this floor, in favour of the agricultural interest. The gentlemen tell us that commerce is only the handmaid of agriculture; and that their zeal to protect commerce arises merely from a desire to promote, through its instrumentality, the great interests of agriculture. I shall not question the sincerity of these declarations, nor the correctness of the principle they assert; but it is to be presumed that the gentlemen will be as willing to give a direct encouragement to agriculture, as to do it indirectly through the medium of commerce.

It will be recollected that a bill was some days ago laid on your table, from the senate, embracing the subject of roads and canals. [. . .] And permit me, in the first place, to say, sir, that some great system of internal navigation, such as is contemplated in the bill introduced into the Senate, is not only an object of the first consequence to the future prosperity of this country, considered as a measure of political economy, but as a measure of state policy, it is indispensable to the preservation of the integrity of this government.

The United States have for twenty years past been favoured in their external commerce, in a manner unequalled perhaps in the history of the world. Our citizens have not only grown rich, but they have gone almost mad in pursuit of this commerce. Such have been its temptations, as to engage in it almost the whole of the floating capital of the country, and a great part of its enterprise; and every other occupation has been considered as secondary and subordinate. This extraordinary success of commerce has been owing partly to our local situation, partly to the native enterprise of our citizens, but primarily to the unparalleled succession of events in Europe. The course of these events, before so propitious to our interests, has of late very materially changed, and with it has changed the tide of our commercial prosperity. I am far, however, from believing that this sudden reverse may not eventually prove fortunate for the true interests of the United States. The embarrassments which the belligerents have thrown in the way of our external commerce, have turned the attention of the people of this country to their own internal resources. And in viewing these resources, we perceive with pride, that there is no country on earth, which in the fertility of its soil, the extent and variety of its climate and productions, affords the means of national wealth and greatness in the measure they are enjoyed by the people of the United States. If these means are properly fostered and encouraged by a liberal and enlightened policy, we shall soon be able not only to defend our independence at home, (which, however, I confidently trust, we have now both the ability and disposition to do, notwithstanding the fears that are attempted to be excited on this subject,) but we shall be able to protect our foreign commerce against the united power of the world. One great object of the system I am about to propose, is to unlock these internal resources, to enable the citizen of one part of the United States to exchange his products for those of another, and to open a great internal commerce, which is acknowledged by all who profess any skill in the science of political economy, to be much more profitable and advantageous than the most favoured external commerce which we could enjoy. The system, however, has another object in view not less important.

The people of the United States are divided by a geographical line into two great and distinct sections—the people who live along the Atlantic on the east side of the Alleghany mountains, and who compose the three great classes of merchants, manufacturers, and agriculturists; and those who occupy the west side of these mountains, who are exclusively agriculturists. This diversity and supposed contrariety of interest and pursuit between the people of these two great divisions of country, and the difference of character to which these occupations give rise, it has been confidently asserted, and is still believed by many, will lead to the separation of the United States at no very distant day. In my humble opinion, sir, this very diversity of interest will, if skilfully managed, be the means of producing a closer and more intimate union of the states. It will be obviously for the interests of the interior states, to exchange the great surplus products of their lands, and the raw materials of manufactures, for the merchandize and manufactured articles of the eastern states; and on the other hand, the interests of the merchants and manufacturers of the Atlantic will be equally promoted by this internal commerce; and it is by promoting this commerce, by encouraging and facilitating this intercourse—it is by producing a mutual dependence of interests between these two great sections, and by these means only, that the United States can ever be kept together.

The great evil, and it is a serious one indeed, sir, under which the inhabitants of the western country labour, arises from the want of a market. There is no place where the great staple articles for the use of civilized life can be produced in greater abundance or with greater ease; and yet as respects most of the luxuries and many of the conveniences of life, the people are poor. They have no vent for their produce at home; because, being all agriculturists, they produce alike the same articles with the same facility; and such is the present difficulty and expense of transporting their produce to an Atlantic port, that little benefits are realized from that quarter. The single circumstance, of the want of a market, is already beginning to produce the most disastrous effects, not only on the industry, but upon the morals of the inhabitants. Such is the fertility of their lands, that one half of their time spent in labour, is sufficient to produce every article which their farms are capable of yielding, in sufficient quantities for their own consumption, and there is nothing to incite them to produce more. They are, therefore, naturally led to spend the other part of their time in idleness and dissipation. Their increase in numbers, and the ease with which children are brought up and fed, far from encouraging them to become manufacturers for themselves, puts a great distance the time, when, quitting the freedom and independence of masters of the soil, they will submit to the labour and confinement of manufacturers. This, sir, is the true situation of the western agriculturist. It becomes then an object of national importance, far outweighing almost every other that can occupy the attention of this house, to inquire whether the evils incident to this state of things, may not be removed by opening a great navigable canal from the Atlantic to the western states; and thus promoting the natural connexion and intercourse between the farmer and the merchant, so highly conducive to the interests of both.

This brings me more immediately to the object of the resolution which I shall have the honour to submit. And I must beg the indulgence of the house while I attempt to show, by a geographical detail, not only the importance but the practicability of such a navigation.

The great ranges of mountains continued from the circular mountain in Georgia, on the south, to the Mohawk River in the state of New York, on the north, intercept and destroy the navigation of all the rivers which discharge into the Atlantic and approach the western country. But when you have passed these mountains from the Atlantic, that country opens a scene of natural internal navigation unequalled in the world. The face of the country is so uniformly level, as to make almost every small stream, by which it is intersected, navigable for boats of considerable size. The chain of western lakes, extending from the north-eastern extremity of Lake Ontario to the south-western termination of Lake Michigan, affords now an excellent navigation for vessels drawing ten feet of water, of fourteen hundred miles in extent; uninterrupted, except by the falls and rapids of Niagara, a distance of only eight miles. To the south and west of these lakes, the waters of the Ohio and Mississippi approach within short distances of, and are interlocked by the waters of the lakes. The lands along these dividing waters are generally level; and the rivers are navigable and might be connected by short canals at little expense. I will mention some of the principal points at which these connexions might be formed. [. . .]

From this view of the western country and the great extent of its natural and internal navigation, we perceive the advantages to be derived by opening it to the Atlantic by a great canal; and we discover also, at the same time, that it is not very important to the inhabitants, by what line this canal approaches them, as their interests would be almost equally promoted by any route that might be adopted. I presume, however, there can be no doubt on this point.

[. . .] The only practicable route for an ascending navigation to the lakes, is by way of the Hudson and Mohawk, in the state of New-York; the Hudson being the only river whose tide waters flow above the Blue Ridge, or eastern chain of mountains. [. . .]

From the place where this canal would connect with Lake Ontario, there is a ship navigation of two hundred miles to the falls of Niagara. A canal with locks sufficiently large for the vessels that navigate the lakes, might be opened around these falls, at an expense, estimated by the secretary of the treasury at one million of dollars. From the Niagara River there is again a ship navigation to every part of Lake Erie. It is presumed that a canal might be opened from Lake Erie to the Ohio, for the sum of five hundred thousand dollars, and another canal cut around the falls of the Ohio, for the like sum of five hundred thousand dollars. And from the falls of the Ohio, there is a good navigation of near two thousand miles to the Gulf of Mexico. And thus, sir, for the sum of 4,200,000 dollars, a great circumnavigation might be formed, embracing the principal part of the United States and their territories, and connecting in its course, by navigable waters, the whole of the western and Atlantic countries. This canal would open to the navigation of the Atlantic on the lakes alone, inclusive of Lake Superior, the navigation to which is now obstructed by a short rapid the River St. Mary's, which connects it with Lake Huron; but which obstruction might be removed by an expense of thrity or forty thousand dollars. I say, sir, it would open to the navigation of the Atlantic, on the lakes alone, a coast of between five and six thousand miles, of as fine and fertile country as any in the world. And it would open on the Mississippi, and its various waters, a country not less fertile and still more extensive. How many hundred millions of dollars such an operation would add to the solid wealth of the western country, I will not venture to conjecture. But, sir, I may well say, that there is no work in the power of man, which would give such life, such vigour, such enterprise, and such riches to the citizens of that country, as the execution of this canal. The inhabitants near the lakes would have a direct communication to and from New York, by means of the canal, and the effect of it would be to double the price of their produce, and to add three or four hundred per cent. to the value of their lands. The people of the Ohio and the Mississippi would descend with their produce to New Orleans, and to any port on the Atlantic, from whence they might return with the articles received in exchange by way of the Hudson and the lakes, to their own homes. The idea of benefitting the people of the Ohio and Mississippi to any great extent by this northern navigation, may perhaps, at first, appear visionary; but I can state it as a fact, that even at this time, under all the disadvantages of that route, goods may be transported from the city of New York, by the way of the Hudson and the lakes, to any part of the Ohio, and to all those parts of the Mississippi above its confluence with the Ohio, at as cheap a rate as they can be transported from any port on the Atlantic, by any other route. The effect of opening this navigation, would then be to reduce the price of transportation to those parts of the country, at least fifty, and probably seventy-five per cent. [. . .] But, sir, aside from all the pecuniary benefits I have mentioned, the great political effect of this work would be, by opening extensive communications, encouraging intercourse, and promoting connexions between the various ports of the Atlantic and western states, to subdue local jealousies, and to bind the union together by the indissoluble ties of interest and friendship.

There may be some, sir, whose fears to do any thing which shall diminish the national resources, may incline them to reject this system of internal improvement at the first view, on account of the magnitude of its expense. Let me ask these gentlemen to give themselves the trouble to trace the consequences of this system on the public wealth, and they will soon be satisfied that there are no possible means by which the aggregate value of the landed property of the United States could be so certainly increased, as by the application of part of these lands to the purposes of opening the great inland navigation which I have before described. The immediate and necessary effect of which would be, to enhance the value of the remaining part to and almost inconceivable extent. [. . .]

Let us now see what will be the probable amount of the sales of land, within a given period, to forward the execution of these improvements.

The present population of the United States is estimated at seven and a half millions.—It is well ascertained that our population doubles once in twenty-three years; and it certainly is increasing, at this time, in as high a ratio as in any former period. According to a calculation of Mr. Blodget (in his statistical tables) something more than one-third of the increasing population of the United States is constantly migrating to the western country.—One-third of the increased population, (or that portion which will migrate) for the next twenty-three years, will amount to two and a half millions. But suppose that only two millions should emigrate, and that only one million of these should settle on the public lands. This population would require fifty millions of acres, or fifty acres to each person, which is about the average quantity taken by new settlers; and it would bring into the treasury, in the space of twenty-three years, the enormous sum of one hundred millions of dollars, upon the supposition that the whole of the land should be purchased at the minimum price of two dollars an acre. It is probable, however, that it will sell much higher, and, if so, the aggregate amount of the sum will be increased in proportion to the increase of the price.

Such a demand for new lands may appear extravagant to those who have not attended to the progressive population and settlement of the United States for the last twenty years. A moment's recurrence to a few well known facts on this subject, will show that such a demand is not only probable, but that, unless some great national calamity befalls us, it is certain. The population of New York has considerably more than doubled within the last twenty years. Upwards of fifteen millions of acres in the western part of that state, which twenty years ago formed a dreary and uninhabited wilderness, are now covered by settlements, and compose one of the most flourishing parts of the United States. Population and settlement have progressed nearly or quite to the same extent in the northern and western parts of the state of Pennsylvania. That tract of country which now forms the state of Ohio, did not contain, twenty years ago, one thousand inhabitants; and now it has a population of more than 200,000. The great states of Kentucky and Tennessee have been almost wholly peopled within the same period; and it is not extravagant to say, that more than one hundred millions of acres have actually been purchased and occupied within the last twenty years in the western country.

It is true, sir, that the rate at which the public lands are now, and have been for some time past selling, is not such as to warrant the calculation I have made as to future sales; but the causes of these sales being so contracted are obvious. One principal cause, which, however, will immediately cease to operate, because it is ceasing to be a fact, has been that the public lands were remote from the inhabited parts of the country. Settlements will always be regular and progressive. People accustomed to the pleasures and advantages of society, do not choose to remove far into the wilderness, when they can purchase lands in the vicinity of old settlements. [. . .]

Another impediment to the sales of public lands arises from the circumstance that you will receive nothing but specie in payment for them. The people who migrate to new countries are, with few exceptions, of the poorer class. They rarely have more than property sufficient to transport their families to their new places of residence, to construct a few temporary accommodations, and to subsist themselves and families until their farms become productive. Then they calculate to pay for their farms by the produce of them. But the products of the public lands in their present occluded situation, will not command money, and settlers are therefore deterred from purchasing. If, instead of confining the payments to money, you were to undertake this system of internal improvement, and issue paper to enable you to execute it, and make this paper receivable at the land offices, the additional facilities which this would afford to payments would not only bring back this paper into the treasury, but large sums of money with it. [. . .]

But, sir, the grand, and all-important operation by which only you can make extensive and effectual sales of the public lands, is to open the produce of them to market, and in this way to make them pay for themselves. Do this, and not only settlers, but monied men will become purchasers. There are now thousands, and I may venture to say millions of dollars in the northern states, ready to be invested in the lands on the lakes, the moment a value shall be stamped on them, by the certainty that they will be speedily opened to the navigation of the Atlantic. Let the United States and the state of New York undertake a canal from the Hudson to the lakes; and so far from draining your treasury by the operation, it will give you in five years, I pledge my reputation on it, an overflowing treasury. There can be no mistake about this business, sir, it is a matter of plain calculation. [. . .]

But, Mr. Speaker, there is one other point of view, in which, although an unpleasant one, I feel it my duty to present this subject to the house: and this regards not only the means of improving that great source of national wealth, the public lands, to the best advantage; but it involves the practicability of enjoying it at all. The people who have purchased and settled on your new lands, are already your debtors to the amount of some millions of dollars; and in as far as they are your debtors, they are (to use a phrase perhaps somewhat too harsh) a species of enemy—and we have already seen to what a formidable extent their powers and numbers are increasing. It is far from my intention, sir, to cast any injurious imputations on the character of these settlers. On the contrary, I know that they are not to be distinguished from the great mass of yeomanry of this country; among whom is to be found most of the real patriotism, as well as the real strength of the nation. It is on them that we are to depend for the security and permanence of our republican institutions. It is to them that this government must resort for protection and support, in every great and dangerous crisis. I say, sir, that I am not about to impeach either the honesty or the patriotism of these settlers; it is their interest and their wish to pay their debts, and to discharge all their duties to government as good and faithful citizens. But let me ask you, sir, let me ask any man of common observation, who has attended in the least, to the situation of the western country, how it is possible for these settlers to pay you fifty or an hundred millions of dollars in specie, when they have no other resources than in their agriculture, and when the produce of this agriculture will not bring them money enough to buy their whiskey. It is impossible, sir, and if you intend to hold those lands, much more if you intend to make them a source of public revenue, you must furnish the means of making them productive, by opening them to market. Every motive of interest and policy unites in urging the government to undertake this system of internal improvement. It is a subject too vast to be accomplished by individual enterprise. The means of the citizens of the western country are peculiarly inadequate to such an undertaking. They cannot construct canals for the very obvious reason that they are already deeply in debt for their lands, and they must continue so until this great work is executed for them. They will then not only be able to pay you for their lands, but they will remunerate you for the expense of opening canals by the tolls which they will be able to pay. In the advantages which these outlets for their produce will give them, and on which their prosperity must so essentially depend, you will have a pledge for their future attachment and fidelity to your government, and which they will never forfeit. But, sir, if you neglect to avail yourselves of the opportunity which this system affords, of securing the affections of the western people if you refuse to extend to them those benefits which their situation so imperiously demands, and which your resources enable you, and your duty enjoins it on you, to extend to them—if, while you are expending millions yearly for the encouragement of commerce, you affect constitutional doubts as to your right to expend any thing for the advancement of agriculture—if you can constitutionally create banks for the accommodation of the merchant, but cannot construct canals for the benefit of the farmer,—if this be the crooked, partial policy which is to be pursued, there is great reason to fear that our western brethren may soon accost us in a tone higher than that of the constitution itself. They may remind us (as the people of this country once did another power, equally regardless of their interests) of the rights with which the God of nature has invested them, by placing them in the possession of a country which they have the physical power to defend; and which it is to be feared, they would defend against all the tax-gatherers we could send among them, supported by all the force of the Atlantic states.

It is unpleasant, sir, to be obliged to press considerations of this sort on the attention of the house. Disagreeable, however, as they are, they are not on that account the less important, and ought not to be disregarded. If you would attach the affections of the western people to your government, you must attach them by their interests. You must appear among them, not in the light of their creditors merely, but as their guardians, their protectors, as the promoters of their welfare. If you avoid all communication with them, except what arises out of your relations as creditors, and go among them only to collect their money, be assured that this is an intercourse which they will soon break off. You have seen how effectual an opposition a few settlers in the north part of Pennsylvania have been able to make to the authority of that great state; and you have seen in a more recent instance, the difficulties which a handful of squatters have opposed to the power of another great state, the state of Massachusetts—and from these examples you may well calculate the effect of an opposition from the host of settlers who are covering your new lands. But I have said enough on this subject.

I am under great obligation to the house, for the attention which have received during this long discussion, and I will not trespass any further. In the various aspects in which I have presented this system of internal improvement, I have considered it principally in reference to the effects which it is calculated to produce on the western country; because, in that point of view I consider it not only most important, but least understood. I have not gone into a particular examination of the benefits to be derived from the proposed canals and roads along the Atlantic, not because I do not think them important, but because this part of the subject is as well and perhaps better understood by the members generally than by myself. For the same reason I have not gone into any minute calculations to show the superior cheapness and safety of canal transportation, over transportation by land. That point is fully illustrated in the report of the secretary of the treasury to which I have before alluded. I believe, however, I have said enough, and more than enough, to satisfy the house of the importance of the subject, and of the propriety of referring it to a committee. This great system, so necessary, in my opinion, to the welfare of this country, is not a measure of speculative or doubtful utility. Its advantages are great and palpable; and the accomplishment of it perfectly within the reach of the resources of the nation. I have not been induced to bring forward this resolution by any personal considerations, but I have done it in obedience to a great duty which I owe my constituents. So far from being a project confined to myself, or even to a few individuals, the proposition, which I now submit, carries with it the anxious wishes, and the best hopes of a large and respectable portion of the population of this country—and permit me to hope, sir, that their expectations may not be disappointed.

Tenkswatawa (The Prophet)

Address at Fort Vincennes (1808)

Father, it is three years since I first began with that system of religion which I now practice. The white people and some of the Indians were against me; but I had no other intention but to introduce among the Indians those good principles of religion which the white people profess. I was spoken badly of by the white people, who reproached me with misleading the Indians; but I defy them to say I did anything amiss.

Father, I was told that you intended to hang me. When I heard this, I intended to remember it, and tell my father, when I went to see him, and relate the truth.

I heard, when I settled on the Wabash, that my father, the Governor, had declared that all the land between Vincennes and Fort Wayne was the property of the Seventeen Fires. I also heard that you wanted to know, my father, whether I was God or man; and that you said if I was the former, I should not steal horses. I heard this from Mr. Wells, but I believed it originated with himself.

The Great Spirit told me to tell the Indians that he had made them, and made the world—that he had placed them on it to do good and not evil.

I told all the red-skins that the way they were in was not good, and that they ought to abandon it.

That we ought to consider ourselves as one man; but we ought to live agreeably to our several customs, the red people after their mode, and the white people after theirs; particularly, that they should not drink whiskey; that it was not made for them, but the white people, who alone knew how to use it; and that it is the cause of all the mischiefs which the Indians suffer; and that they must always follow the directions of the Great Spirit, and we must listen to him, as it was He that made us; determine to listen to nothing that is bad; do not take up the tomahawk, should it be offered by the British, or by the Long-Knives; do not meddle with any thing that does not belong to you, but mind your own business, and cultivate the ground, that your women and your children may have enough to live on.

I now inform you that it is our intention to live in peace with our father and his people forever.

My father, I have informed you what we mean to do, and I call the Great Spirit to witness the truth of my declaration. The religion which I have established for the last three years has been attended to by the different tribes of Indians in this part of the world. These Indians were once different people; they are now but one; they are all determined to practice what I have communicated to them that has come immediately from the Great Spirit through me.

Brother, I speak to you as a warrior. You are one. But let us lay aside this character, and attend to the care of our children, that they may live in comfort and peace. We desire that you will join us for the preservation of both red and white people. Formerly, when we lived in ignorance, we were foolish; but now, since we listen to the voice of the Great Spirit, we are happy.

I have listened to what you have said to us. You have promised to assist us. I now request you, in behalf of all the red people, to use your exertions to prevent the sale of liquor to us. We are all well pleased to hear you say that you will endeavor to promote our happiness. We give you every assurance that we will follow the dictates of the Great Spirit.

We are all well pleased with the attention you have showed us; also with the good intentions of our father, the President. If you give us a few articles, such as needles, flints, hoes, powder, etc., we will take the animals that afford us meat, with powder and ball.

Tecumseh

Three Speeches (1811–1812)

First Speech, September 1811

In view of questions of vast importance, have we met together in solemn council tonight. Nor should we here debate whether we have been wronged and injured, but by what measures we should avenge ourselves; for our merciless oppressors, having long since planned out their proceedings, are not about to make, but have and are still making attacks upon those of our race who have as yet come to no resolution. Nor are we ignorant by what steps, and by what gradual advances, the whites break in upon our neighbors. Imagining themselves to be still undiscovered, they show themselves the less audacious because you are insensible. The whites are already nearly a match for us all united, and too strong for any one tribe alone to resist; so that unless we support one another with our collective and united forces; unless every tribe unanimously combines to give a check to the ambition and avarice of the whites, they will soon conquer us apart and disunited, and we will be driven away from our native country and scattered as autumnal leaves before the wind.

But have we not courage enough remaining to defend our country and maintain our ancient independence? Will we calmly suffer the white intruders and tyrants to enslave us? Shall it be said of our race that we knew not how to extricate ourselves from the three most to be dreaded calamities—folly, inactivity and cowardice? But what need is there to speak of the past? It speaks for itself and asks, "Where today is the Pequot? Where the Narragansetts, the Mohawks, Pocanokets, and many other once powerful tribes of our race?" They have vanished before the avarice and oppression of the white men, as snow before a summer sun. In the vain hope of alone defending their ancient possessions, they have fallen in the wars with the white men. Look abroad over their once beautiful country, and what see you now? Naught but the ravages of the pale-face destroyers meet your eyes. So it will be with you Choctaws and Chickasaws! Soon your mighty forest trees, under the shade of whose wide spreading branches you have played in infancy, sported in boyhood, and now rest your wearied limbs after the fatigue of the chase, will be cut down to fence in the land which the white intruders dare to call their own. Soon their broad roads will pass over the graves of your fathers, and the place of their rest will be blotted out forever. The annihilation of our race is at hand unless we unite in one common cause against the common foe. Think not, brave Choctaws and Chickasaws, that you can remain passive and indifferent to the common danger, and thus escape the common fate. Your people too will soon be as falling leaves and scattering clouds before their blighting breath. You too will be driven away from your native land and ancient domains as leaves are driven before the wintry storms.

Sleep not longer, O Choctaws and Chickasaws, in false security and delusive hopes. Our broad domains are fast escaping from our grasp. Every year our white intruders become more greedy, exacting, oppressive and overbearing. Every year contentions spring up between them and our people and when blood is shed we have to make atonement whether right or wrong, at the cost of the lives of our greatest chiefs, and the yielding up of large tracts of our lands. Before the pale-faces came among us, we enjoyed the happiness of unbounded freedom, and were acquainted with neither riches, wants, nor oppression. How is it now? Wants and oppressions are our lot; for are we not controlled in everything, and dare we move without asking, by your leave? Are we not being stripped day by day of the little that remains of our ancient liberty? Do they not even now kick and strike us as they do their black-faces? How long will it be before they will tie us to a post and whip us, and make us work for them in their corn fields as they do them? Shall we wait for that moment or shall we die fighting before submitting to such ignominy?

Have we not for years had before our eyes a sample of their designs, and are they not sufficient harbingers of their future determinations? Will we not soon be driven from our respective countries and the graves of our ancestors? Will not the bones of our dead be plowed up, and their graves be turned into fields? Shall we calmly wait until they become so numerous that we will no longer be able to resist oppression? Will we wait to be destroyed in our turn, without making an effort worthy our race? Shall we give up our homes, our country, bequeathed to us by the Great Spirit, the graves of our dead, and everything that is dear and sacred to us, without a struggle? I know you will cry with me. Never! Never! Then let us by unity of action destroy them all, which we now can do, or drive them back whence they came. War or extermination is now our only choice. Which do you choose? I know your answer. Therefore, I now call on you, brave Choctaws and Chickasaws, to assist in the just cause of liberating our race from the grasp of our faithless invaders and heartless oppressors. The white usurpation in our common country must be stopped, or we, its rightful owners, be forever destroyed and wiped out as a race of people. I am now at the head of many warriors backed by the strong arm of English soldiers. Choctaws and Chickasaws, you have too long borne with grievous usurpation inflicted by the arrogant Americans. Be no longer their dupes. If there be one here tonight who believes that his rights will not sooner or later be taken from him by the avaricious American pale-faces, his ignorance ought to excite pity, for he knows little of the character of our common foe. And if there be one among you mad enough to undervalue the growing power of the white race among us, let him tremble in considering the fearful woes he will bring down upon our entire race, if by his criminal indifference he assists the designs of our common enemy against our common country. Then listen to the voice of duty, of honor, of nature and of your endangered country. Let us form one body, one heart, and defend to the last warrior our country, our homes, our liberty, and the graves of our fathers.

Choctaws and Chickasaws, you are among the few of our race who sit indolently at ease. You have indeed enjoyed the reputation of being brave, but will you be indebted for it more from report than fact? Will you let the whites encroach upon your domains even to your very door before you will assert your rights in resistance? Let no one in this council imagine that I speak more from malice against the pale-face Americans than just grounds of complaint. Complaint is just toward friends who have failed in their duty; accusation is against enemies guilty of injustice. And surely, if any people ever had, we have good and just reasons to believe we have ample grounds to accuse the Americans of injustice; especially when such great acts of injustice have been committed by them upon our race, of which they seem to have no manner of regard, or even to reflect. They are a people fond of innovations, quick to contrive and quick to put their schemes into effectual execution, no matter how great the wrong and injury to us; while we are content to preserve what we already have. Their design [is] to enlarge their possessions by taking yours in turn; and will you, can you longer dally, O Choctaws and Chickasaws? Do you imagine that that people will not continue longest in the enjoyment of peace who timely prepare to vindicate themselves, and manifest a determined resolution to do themselves right whenever they are wronged? Far otherwise. Then haste to the relief of our common cause, as by consanguinity of blood you are bound; lest the day be not far distant when you will be left single-handed and alone to the cruel mercy of our most inveterate foe.

Second Speech, October 1811

In defiance of the white men of Ohio and Kentucky, I have traveled through their settlements—once our favorite hunting-grounds. No war-whoop was sounded, but there is blood upon our knives. The pale-faces felt the blow, but knew not from whence it came. Accursed be the race that has seized on our country, and made women of our warriors. Our fathers, from their tombs, reproach us as slaves and cowards. I hear them now in the wailing winds. The Muscogee were once a mighty people. The Georgians trembled at our war-whoop; and the maidens of my tribe, in the distant lakes, sung the prowess of your warriors, and sighed for their embraces. Now, your very blood is white, your tomahawks have no edges, your bows and arrows were buried with your fathers. O Muscogees, brethren of my mother! brush from your eyelids the sleep of slavery; once more strike for vengeance—once more for your country. The spirits of the mighty dead complain. The tears drop from the skies. Let the white race perish! They seize your land, they corrupt your women, they trample on your dead! Back! whence they came, upon a trail of blood, they must be driven! Back! back—ay, into the great water whose accursed waves brought them to our shores! Burn their dwellings! Destroy their stock! Slay their wives and children! The red man owns the country, and the pale-face must never enjoy it! War now! War forever! War upon the living! War upon the dead! Dig their very corpses from the graves! Our country must give no rest to a white man's bones. All the tribes of the North are dancing the war-dance. Two mighty warriors across the seas will send us arms.

Tecumseh will soon return to his country. My prophets shall tarry with you. They will stand between you and your enemies. When the white man approaches you the earth shall swallow him up. Soon shall you see my arm of fire stretched athwart the sky. I will stamp my foot at Tippecanoe, and the very earth shall shake.

Third Speech, Winter 1811–1812

Brothers.—We all belong to one family; we are all children of the Great Spirit; we walk in the same path; slake our thirst at the same spring; and now affairs of the greatest concern lead us to smoke the pipe around the same council fire!

Brothers.—We are friends; we must assist each other to bear our burdens. The blood of many of our fathers and brothers has run like water on the ground to satisfy the avarice of the white men. We, ourselves, are threatened with a great evil; nothing will pacify them but the destruction of all the red men.

Brothers.—When the white men first set foot on our grounds, they were hungry; they had no place on which to spread their blankets, or to kindle their fires. They were feeble; they could do nothing for themselves. Our fathers commiserated their distress, and shared freely with them whatever the Great Spirit had given his red children. They gave them food when hungry, medicine when sick, spread skins for them to sleep on, and gave them grounds, that they might hunt and raise corn.—Brothers, the white people are like poisonous serpents: when chilled, they are feeble and harmless; but invigorate them with warmth, and they sting their benefactors to death.

The white people came among us feeble; and now we have made them strong, they wish to kill us, or drive us back, as they would wolves and panthers.

Brothers.—The white men are not friends to the Indians: at first, they only asked for land sufficient for a wigwam; now, nothing will satisfy them but the whole of our hunting grounds, from the rising to the setting sun.

Brothers.—The white men want more than our hunting grounds; they wish to kill our warriors; they would even kill our old men, women, and little ones.

Brothers.—Many winters ago, there was no land; the sun did not rise and set: all was darkness. The Great Spirit made all things. He gave the white people a home beyond the great waters. He supplied these grounds with game, and gave them to his red children; and he gave them strength and courage to defend them.

Brothers.—My people wish for peace; the red men all wish for peace: but where the white people are, there is no peace for them, except it be on the bosom of our mother.

Brothers.—The white men despise and cheat the Indians; they abuse and insult them; they do not think the red men sufficiently good to live. The red men have borne many and great injuries; they ought to suffer them no longer. My people will not; they are determined on vengeance; they have taken up the tomahawk; they will make it fat with blood; they will drink the blood of the white people.

Brothers.—My people are brave and numerous; but the white people are too strong for them alone. I wish you to take up the tomahawk with them. If we all unite, we will cause the rivers to stain the great waters with their blood.

Brothers.—If you do not unite with us, they will first destroy us, and then you will fall an easy prey to them. They have destroyed many nations of red men because they were not united, because they were not friends to each other.

Brothers.—The white people send runners amongst us; they wish to make us enemies, that they may sweep over and desolate our hunting grounds, like devastating winds, or rushing waters.

Brothers.—Our Great Father, over the great waters, is angry with the white people, our enemies. He will send his brave warriors against them; he will send us rifles, and whatever else we want—he is our friend, and we are his children.

Brothers.—Who are the white people that we should fear them? They cannot run fast, and are good marks to shoot at: they are only men; our fathers have killed many of them: we are not squaws, and we will stain the earth red with their blood.

Brothers.—The Great Spirit is angry with our enemies; he speaks in thunder, and the earth swallows up villages, and drinks up the Mississippi. The great waters will cover their lowlands; their corn cannot grow; and the Great Spirit will sweep those who escape to the hills from the earth with his terrible breath.

Brothers.—We must be united; we must smoke the same pipe; we must fight each other's battles; and more than all, we must love the Great Spirit: he is for us; he will destroy our enemies, and make all his red children happy.

PUSHMATAHA

Speech Opposing Tecumseh (1811)

It was not my design in coming here to enter into a disputation with any one. But I appear before you, my warriors and my people, not to throw in my plea against the accusations of Tecumseh; but to prevent your forming rash and dangerous resolutions upon things of highest importance, through the instigations of others. I have myself learned by experience, and I also see many of you, O Choctaws and Chickasaws, who have the same experience of years that I have, the injudicious steps of engaging in an enterprise because it is new. Nor do I stand up before you tonight to contradict the many facts alleged against the American people, or to raise my voice against them in useless accusations. The question before us now is not what wrongs they have inflicted upon our race, but what measures are best for us to adopt in regard to them; and though our race may have been unjustly treated and shamefully wronged by them, yet I shall not for that reason alone advise you to destroy them, unless it was just and expedient for you so to do; nor, would I advise you to forgive them, though worthy of your commiseration, unless I believe it would be to the interest of our common good. We should consult more in regard to our future welfare than our present. What people, my friends and countrymen, were so unwise and inconsiderate as to engage in a war of their own accord, when their own strength, and even with the aid of others, was judged unequal to the task? I well know causes often arise which force men to confront extremities, but, my countrymen, those causes do not now exist. Reflect, therefore, I earnestly beseech you, before you act hastily in this great matter, and consider with yourselves how greatly you will err if you injudiciously approve of and inconsiderately act upon Tecumseh's advice. Remember the American people are now friendly disposed toward us. Surely you are convinced that the greatest good will result to us by the adoption of and adhering to those measures I have before recommended to you; and, without giving too great a scope to mercy or forbearance, by which I could never permit myself to be seduced, I earnestly pray you to follow my advice in this weighty matter, and in following it resolve to adopt those expedients for our future welfare. My friends and fellow countrymen! You now have no just cause to declare war against the American people, or wreak your vengeance upon them as enemies, since they have ever manifested feelings of friendship towards you. It is besides inconsistent with your national glory and with your honor, as a people, to violate your solemn treaty; and a disgrace to the memory of your forefathers, to wage war against the American people merely to gratify the malice of the English.

The war, which you are now contemplating against the Americans, is a flagrant breach of justice; yea, a fearful blemish on your honor and also that of your fathers, and which you will find if you will examine it carefully and judiciously forbodes nothing but destruction to our entire race. It is a war against a people whose territories are now far greater than our own, and who are far better provided with all necessary implements of war, with men, guns, horses, wealth, far beyond that of all our race combined, and where is the necessity or wisdom to make war upon such a people? Where is our hope of success, if thus weak and unprepared we should declare it against them? Let us not be deluded with the foolish hope that this war, if begun, will soon be over, even if we destroy all the whites within our territories, and lay waste their homes and fields. Far from it. It will be but the beginning of the end that terminates in the total destruction of our race. And though we will not permit ourselves to be made slaves, or, like inexperienced warriors, shudder at the thought of war, yet I am not so insensible and inconsistent as to advise you to cowardly yield to the outrages of the whites, or wilfully to connive at their unjust encroachments; but only not yet to have recourse to war, but to send ambassadors to our Great Father at Washington, and lay before him our grievances, without betraying too great eagerness for war, or manifesting any tokens of pusillanimity. Let us, therefore, my fellow countrymen, form our resolutions with great caution and prudence upon a subject of such vast importance, and in which such fearful consequences may be involved.

Heed not, O my countrymen, the opinions of others to that extent as to involve your country in a war that destroys its peace and endangers its future safety, prosperity and happiness. Reflect, ere it be too late, on the great uncertainty of war with the American people, and consider well, ere you engage in it, what the consequences will be if you should be disappointed in your calculations and expectations. Be not deceived with illusive hopes. Hear me, O my countrymen, if you begin this war it will end in calamities to us from which we are now free and at a distance; and upon whom of us they will fall, will only be determined by the uncertain and hazardous event. Be not, I pray you, guilty of rashness, which I never as yet have known you to be; therefore, I implore you, while healing measures are in the election of us all, not to break the treaty, nor violate your pledge of honor, but to submit our grievances, whatever they may be, to the Congress of the United States, according to the articles of the treaty existing between us and the American people. If not, I here invoke the Great Spirit, who takes cognizance of oaths, to bear me witness, that I shall endeavor to avenge myself upon the authors of this war, by whatever methods you shall set me an example. Remember we are a people who have never grown insolent with success, or become abject in adversity; but let those who invite us to hazardous attempts by uttering our praise, also know that the pleasure of hearing has never elevated our spirits above our judgment, nor an endeavor to exasperate us by a flow of invectives to be provoked the sooner to compliance. From tempers equally balanced let it be known that we are warm in the field of battle, and cool in the hours of debate; the former, because a sense of duty has the greater influence over a sedate disposition, and magnanimity the keenest sense of shame; and though good we are at debate, still our education is not polite enough to teach us a contempt of laws, yet by its severity gives us so much good sense as never to disregard them.

We are not a people so impertinently wise as to invalidate the preparations of our enemies by a plausible harangue, and then absolutely proceed to a contest; but we reckon the thoughts of the pale-faces to be of a similar cast with our own, and that hazardous contingencies are not to be determined by a speech. We always presume that the projects of our enemies are judiciously planned, and then we seriously prepare to defeat them. Nor do we found our success upon the hope that they will certainly blunder in their conduct, but upon the hope that we have omitted no proper steps for our own security. Such is the discipline which our fathers have handed down to us; and by adhering to it, we have reaped many advantages. Let us, my countrymen, not forget it now, nor in short space of time precipitately determine a question in which so much is involved. It is indeed the duty of the prudent, so long as they are not injured, to delight in peace. But it is the duty of the brave, when injured, to lay peace aside, and to have recourse to arms; and when successful in these, to then lay them down again in peaceful quiet; thus never to be elevated above measure by success in war, nor delighted with the sweets of peace to suffer insults. For he who, apprehensive of losing the delight, sits indolently at ease, will soon be deprived of the enjoyment of that delight which interested his fears; and he whose passions are inflamed by military success, elevated too high by a treacherous confidence, hears no longer the dictates of judgment.

Many are the schemes, though unadvisedly planned, through the more unreasonable conduct of an enemy, which turn out successfully; but more numerous are those which, though seemingly founded on mature counsel, draw after them a disgraceful and opposite result. This proceeds from that great inequality of spirit with which an exploit is projected, and with which it is put into actual execution. For in council we resolve, surrounded with security; in execution we faint, through the prevalence of fear. Listen to the voice of prudence, oh, my countrymen, ere you rashly act. But do as you may, know this truth, enough for you to know, I shall join our friends, the Americans, in this war.

JOHN MARSHALL

Trustees of Dartmouth College v. Woodward (1819)

Chief Justice John MARSHALL delivered the opinion of the Court.

[. . .] It can require no argument to prove that the circumstances of this case constitute a contract. An application is made to the crown for a charter to incorporate a religious and literary institution. In the application, it is stated, that large contributions have been made for the object, which will be conferred on the corporation, as soon as it shall be created. The charter is granted, and on its faith the property is conveyed. Surely, in this transaction every ingredient of a complete and legitimate contract is to be found.

The points for consideration are, 1. Is this contract protected by the Constitution of the United States? 2. Is it impaired by the acts under which the defendant holds?

1. On the first point, is has been argued, that the word "contract," in its broadest sense, would comprehend the political relations between the government and its citizens, would extend to offices held within a state, for state purposes, and to many of those laws concerning civil institutions, which must change with circumstances, and be modified by ordinary legislation; which deeply concern the public, and which, to preserve good government, the public judgment must control. That even marriage is a contract, and its obligations are affected by the laws respecting divorces. That the clause in the Constitution, if construed in its greatest latitude, would prohibit these laws. Taken in its broad, unlimited sense, the clause would be an unprofitable and vexatious interference with the internal concerns of a state, would unnecessarily and unwisely embarrass its legislation, and render immutable those civil institutions, which are established for purposes of internal government, and which, to subserve those purposes, ought to vary with varying circumstances. That as the framers of the Constitution could never have intended to insert in that instrument, a provision so unnecessary, so mischievous, and so repugnant to its general spirit, the term "contract" must be understood in a more limited sense. That it must be understood as intended to guard against a power, of at least doubtful utility, the abuse of which had been extensively felt; and to restrain the legislature in future from violating the right to property. That, anterior to the formation of the Constitution, a course of legislation had prevailed in many, if not in all, of the states, which weakened the confidence of man in man, and embarrassed all transactions

between individuals, by dispensing with a faithful performance of engagements. To correct this mischief, by restraining the power which produced it, the state legislatures were forbidden "to pass any law impairing the obligation of contracts," that is, of contracts respecting property, under which some individual could claim a right to something beneficial to himself; and that, since the clause in the Constitution must in construction receive some limitation, it may be confined, and ought to be confined, to cases of this description; to cases within the mischief it was intended to remedy.

The general correctness of these observations cannot be controverted. That the framers of the Constitution did not intend to restrain the states in the regulation of their civil institutions, adopted for internal government, and that the instrument they have given us, is not to be so construed, may be admitted. The provision of the Constitution never has been understood to embrace other contracts, than those which respect property, or some object of value, and confer rights which may be asserted in a court of justice.[. . .]

The parties in this case differ less on general principles, less on the true construction of the Constitution in the abstract, than on the application of those principles to this case, and on the true construction of the charter of 1769. This is the point on which the cause essentially depends. If the act of incorporation be a grant of political power, if it create a civil institution, to be employed in the administration of the government, or if the funds of the college be public property, or if the state of New Hampshire, as a government, be alone interested in its transactions, the subject is one in which the legislature of the state may act according to its own judgment, unrestrained by any limitation of its power imposed by the Constitution of the United States.

But if this be a private eleemosynary institution, endowed with a capacity to take property, for objects unconnected with government, whose funds are bestowed by individuals, on the faith of the charter; if the donors have stipulated for the future disposition and management of those funds, in the manner prescribed by themselves; there may be more difficulty in the case, although neither the persons who have made these stipulations, nor those for whose benefit they were made, should be parties to the cause. Those who are no longer interested in the property, may yet retain such an interest in the preservation of their own arrangements, as to have a right to insist, that those arrangements shall be held sacred. Or, if they have themselves disappeared, it becomes a subject of serious and anxious inquiry, whether those whom they have legally empowered to represent them for ever, may not assert all the rights which they possessed, while in being; whether, if they be without personal representatives, who may feel injured by a violation of the compact, the trustees be not so completely their representatives, in the eye of the law, as to stand in their place, not only as respects the government of the college, but also as respects the maintenance of the college charter.

It becomes then the duty of the Court, most seriously to examine this charter, and to ascertain its true character. [. . .]

From this brief review of the most essential parts of the charter, it is apparent, that the funds of the college consisted entirely of private donations. [. . .] It is then an eleemosynary (1 Bl. Com. 471), and so far as respects its funds, a private corporation.

Do its objects stamp on it a different character? Are the trustees and professors public officers, invested with any portion of political power, partaking in any degree in the administration of civil government, and performing duties which flow from the sovereign authority? That education is an object of national concern, and a proper subject of legislation, all admit. That there may be an institution, founded by government, and placed entirely under its immediate control, the officers of which would be public officers, amenable exclusively to government, none will deny. But is Dartmouth College such an institution? Is education altogether in the hands of government? Does every teacher of youth become a public officer, and do donations for the purpose of education necessarily become public property, so far that the will of the legislature, not the will of the donor, becomes the law of the donation? These questions are of serious moment to society, and deserve to be well considered.

Doctor Wheelock, as the keeper of his charity school, instructing the Indians in the art of reading, and in our holy religion; sustaining them at his own expense, and on the voluntary contributions of the charitable, could scarcely be considered as a public officer, exercising any portion of those duties which belong to government; nor could the legislature have supposed, that his private funds, or those given by others, were subject to legislative management, because they were applied to the purposes of education. When, afterwards, his school was enlarged, and the liberal contributions made in England, and in America, enabled him to extend his care to the education of the youth of his own country, no change was wrought in his own character, or in the nature of his duties. Had he employed assistant tutors with the funds contributed by others, or had the trustees in England established a school, with Dr. Wheelock at its head, and paid salaries to him and his assistants, they would still have been private tutors; and the fact, that they were employed in the education of youth, could not have converted them into public officers, concerned in the administration of public duties, or have given the legislature a right to interfere in the management of the fund. The trustees, in whose care that fund was placed by the contributors, would have been permitted to execute their trust, uncontrolled by legislative authority.

Whence, then, can be derived the idea, that Dartmouth College has become a public institution, and its trustees public officers, exercising powers conferred by the public for public objects? Not from the source whence its funds were drawn; for its foundation is purely private and eleemosynary—not from the application of those funds; for money may be given for education, and the persons receiving it do not, by being employed in the education of youth, become members of the civil government. Is it from the act of incorporation? Let this subject be considered.

A corporation is an artificial being, invisible, intangible, and existing only in contemplation of law. Being the mere creature of law, it possesses only those properties which the charter of its creation confers upon it, either expressly, or as incidental to its very existence. These are such as are supposed best calculated to effect the object for which it was created. Among the most important are immortality, and, if the expression may be allowed, individuality; properties, by which a perpetual succession of many persons are considered as the same, and may act as a single individual. They enable a corporation to manage its own affairs, and to hold property, without the perplexing intricacies, the hazardous and endless necessity, of perpetual conveyances for the purpose of transmitting it from hand to hand. It is chiefly for the purpose of clothing bodies of men, in succession, with these qualities and capacities, that corporations were invented, and are in use. By these means, a perpetual succession of individuals are capable of acting for the promotion of the particular object, like one immortal being. But this being does not share in the civil government of the country, unless that be the purpose for which it was created. Its immortality no more confers on it political power, or a political character, than immortality would confer such power or character on a natural person. It is no more a state instrument than a natural person exercising the same powers would be. If, then, a natural person, employed by individuals in the education of youth, or for the government of a seminary in which youth is educated, would not become a public officer, or be considered as a member of the civil government, how is it that this artificial being, created by law, for the purpose of being employed by the same individuals for the same purposes, should become a part of the civil government of the country? Is it because its existence, its capacities, its powers, are given by law? Because the government has given it the power to take and to hold property in a particular form, and for particular purposes, has the government a consequent right substantially to change that form, or to vary the purposes to which the property is to be applied? This principle has never been asserted or recognized, and is supported by no authority. Can it derive aid from reason [. . .] ?

From this review of the charter, it appears, that Dartmouth College is an eleemosynary institution, incorporated for the purpose of perpetuating the application of the bounty of the donors, to the specified objects of that bounty; that its trustees or governors were originally named by the founder, and invested with the power of perpetuating themselves; that they are not public officers, nor is it a civil institution, participating in the administration of government; but a charity-school, or a seminary of education, incorporated for the preservation of its property, and the perpetual application of that property to the objects of its creation.

Yet a question remains to be considered, of more real difficulty, on which more doubt has been entertained, than on all that have been discussed. The founders of the college, at least, those whose contributions were in money, have parted with the property bestowed upon it, and their representatives have no interest in that property. The donors of land are equally without interest, so long as the corporation shall exist. Could they be found, they are unaffected by any alteration in its Constitution, and probably regardless of its form, or even of its existence. The students are fluctuating, and no individual among our youth has a vested interest in the institution, which can be asserted in a court of justice. Neither the founders of the college, nor the youth for whose benefit it was founded, complain of the alteration made in its charter, or think themselves injured by it. The trustees alone complain, and the trustees have no beneficial interest to be protected. Can this be such a contract, as the Constitution intended to withdraw from the power of state legislation? Contracts, the parties to which have a vested beneficial interest, and those only, it has been said, are the objects about which the Constitution is solicitous, and to which its protection is extended.

The Court has bestowed on this argument the most deliberate consideration, and the result will be stated. Dr. Wheelock, acting for himself, and for those who, at his solicitation, had made contributions to his school, applied for this charter, as the instrument which should enable him, and them, to perpetuate their beneficent intention. It was granted. An artificial, immortal being, was created by the crown, capable of receiving and distributing for ever, according to the will of the donors, the donations which should be made to it. On this being, the contributions which had been collected were immediately bestowed. These gifts were made, not indeed to make a profit for the donors, or their posterity, but for something, in their opinion, of inestimable value; for something which they deemed a full equivalent for the money with which it was purchased. The consideration for which they stipulated, is the perpetual application of the fund to its object, in the mode prescribed by themselves. Their descendants may take no interest in the preservation of this consideration. But in this respect their descendants are not their representatives; they are represented by the corporation. The corporation is the assignee of their rights, stands in their place, and distributes their bounty, as they would themselves have distributed it, had they been immortal. So, with respect to the students who are to derive learning from this source; the corporation is a trustee for them also. Their potential rights, which, taken distributively, are imperceptible, amount collectively to a most important interest. These are, in the aggregate, to be exercised, asserted and protected, by the corporation. They were as completely out of the donors, at the instant of their being vested in the corporation, and as incapable of being asserted by the students, as at present.

According to the theory of the British Constitution, their Parliament is omnipotent. To annul corporate rights might give a shock to public opinion, which that government has chosen to avoid; but its power is not questioned. Had Parliament, immediately after the emanation of this charter, and the execution of those conveyances which followed it, annulled the instrument, so that the living donors would have witnessed the disappointment of their hopes, the perfidy of the transaction would have been universally acknowledged. Yet, then, as now, the donors would have no interest in the property; then, as now, those who might be students would have had no rights to be violated; then, as now, it might be said, that the trustees, in whom the rights of all were combined, possessed no private, individual, beneficial interests in the property confided to their protection. Yet the contract would, at that time, have been deemed sacred by all. What has since occurred, to strip it of its inviolability? Circumstances have not changed it. In reason, in justice, and in law, it is now, what is was in 1769.

This is plainly a contract to which the donors, the trustees and the crown (to whose rights and obligations New Hampshire succeeds) were the original parties. It is a contract made on a valuable consideration. It is a contract for the security and disposition of property. It is a contract, on the faith of which, real and personal estate has been conveyed to the corporation. It is, then, a contract within the letter of the Constitution, and within its spirit also, unless the fact, that the property is invested by the donors in trustees, for the promotion of religion and education, for the benefit of persons who are perpetually changing, though the objects remain the same, shall create a particular exception, taking this case out of the prohibition contained in the Constitution.

It is more than possible, that the preservation of rights of this description was not particularly in the view of the framers of the Constitution, when the clause under consideration was introduced into that instrument. It is probable, that interferences of more frequent occurrence, to which the temptation was stronger, and of which the mischief was more extensive, constituted the great motive for imposing this restriction on the state legislatures. But although a particular and a rare case may not, in itself, be of sufficient magnitude to induce a rule, yet it must be governed by the rule, when established, unless some plain and strong reason for excluding it can be given. It is not enough to say, that this particular case was not in the mind of the convention, when the article was framed, nor of the American people, when it was adopted. It is necessary to go further, and to say that, had this particular case been suggested, the language would have been so varied, as to exclude it, or it would have been made a special exception. The case being within the words of the rule, must be within its operation likewise, unless there be something in the literal construction, so obviously absurd or mischievous, or repugnant to the general spirit of the instrument, as to justify those who expound the Constitution in making it an exception.

On what safe and intelligible ground, can this exception stand? There is no expression in the Constitution, no sentiment delivered by its contemporaneous expounders, which would justify us in making it. In the absence of all authority of this kind, is there, in the nature and reason of the case itself, that which would sustain a construction of the Constitution, not warranted by its words? Are contracts of this description of a character to excite so little interest, that we must exclude them from the provisions of the Constitution, as being unworthy of the attention of those who framed the instrument? Or does public policy so imperiously demand their remaining exposed to legislative alteration, as to compel us, or rather permit us, to say, that these words, which were introduced to give stability to contracts, and which in their plain import comprehend this contract, must yet be so construed as to exclude it?

Almost all eleemosynary corporations, those which are created for the promotion of religion, of charity or of education, are of the same character. The law of this case is the law of all. [. . .]

The opinion of the Court, after mature deliberation, is, that this is a contract, the obligation of which cannot be impaired, without violating the Constitution of the United States. This opinion appears to us to be equally supported by reason, and by the former decisions of this Court.

2. We next proceed to the inquiry, whether its obligation has been impaired by those acts of the legislature of New Hampshire, to which the special verdict refers?

From the review of this charter, which has been taken, it appears that the whole power of governing the college, of appointing and removing tutors, of fixing their salaries, of directing the course of study to be pursued by the students, and of filling up vacancies created in their own body, was vested in the trustees. On the part of the crown, it was expressly stipulated, that this corporation, thus constituted, should continue for ever; and that the number of trustees should for ever consist of twelve, and no more. By this contract, the crown was bound, and could have made no violent alteration in its essential terms, without impairing its obligation.

By the revolution, the duties, as well as the powers, of government devolved on the people of New Hampshire. It is admitted, that among the latter was comprehended the transcendent power of Parliament, as well as that of the executive department. It is too clear, to require the support of argument, that all contracts and rights respecting property, remained unchanged by the revolution. The obligations, then, which were created by the charter to Dartmouth College, were the same in the new, that they had been in the old government. The power of the government was also the same. A repeal of this charter, at any time prior to the adoption of the present Constitution of the United States, would have been an extraordinary and unprecedented act of power, but one which could have been contested only by the restrictions upon the legislature, to be found in the constitution of the state. But the Constitution of the United States has imposed this additional limitation, that the legislature of a state shall pass no act "impairing the obligation of contracts."

It has been already stated, that the act "to amend the charter, and enlarge and improve the corporation of Dartmouth College," increases the number of trustees to twenty-one, gives the appointment of the additional members to the executive of the state, and creates a board of overseers, to consist of twenty-five persons, of whom twenty-one are also appointed by the executive of New Hampshire, who have power to inspect and control the most important acts of the trustees.

On the effect of this law, two opinions cannot be entertained. Between acting directly, and acting through the agency of trustees and overseers, no essential difference is perceived. The whole power of governing the college is transferred from trustees, appointed according to the will of the founder, expressed in the charter, to the executive of New Hampshire. The management and application of the funds of this eleemosynary institution, which are placed by the donors in the hands of trustees named in the charter, and empowered to perpetuate themselves, are placed by this act under the control of the government of the state. The will of the state is substituted for the will of the donors, in every essential operation of the college. This is not an immaterial change. The founders of the college contracted, not merely for the perpetual application of the funds which they gave, to the objects for which those funds were given; they contracted also, to secure that application by the constitution of the corporation. They contracted for a system, which should, so far as human foresight can provide, retain for ever the government of the literary institution they had formed, in the hands of persons approved by themselves. This system is totally changed. The charter of 1769 exists no longer. It is reorganized, and reorganized in such a manner as to convert a literary institution, moulded according to the will of its founders, and placed under the control of private literary men, into a machine entirely subservient to the will of government. This may be for the advantage of this college in particular, and may be for the advantage of literature in general; but it is not according to the will of the donors, and is subversive of that contract, on the faith of which their property was given. [. . .]

It results from this opinion, that the acts of the legislature of New Hampshire, which are stated in the special verdict found in this cause, are repugnant to the Constitution of the United States; and that the judgment on this special verdict ought to have been for the plaintiffs. The judgment of the state court must, therefore, be reversed.

McCulloch v. Maryland (1819)

MARSHALL, Chief Justice, delivered the opinion of the Court.

In the case now to be determined, the defendant, a sovereign State, denies the obligation of a law enacted by the legislature of the Union, and the plaintiff, on his part, contests the validity of an act which has been passed by the legislature of that State. The Constitution of our country, in its most interesting and vital parts, is to be considered, the conflicting powers of the Government of the Union and of its members, as marked in that Constitution, are to be discussed, and an opinion given which may essentially influence the great operations of the Government. No tribunal can approach such a question without a deep sense of its importance, and of the awful responsibility involved in its decision. But it must be decided peacefully, or remain a source of hostile legislation, perhaps, of hostility of a still more serious nature; and if it is to be so decided, by this tribunal alone can the decision be made. On the Supreme Court of the United States has the Constitution of our country devolved this important duty.

[1.] The first question made in the cause is—has Congress power to incorporate a bank?

It has been truly said that this can scarcely be considered as an open question entirely unprejudiced by the former proceedings of the Nation respecting it. The principle now contested was introduced at a very early period of our history, has been recognised by many successive legislatures, and has been acted upon by the Judicial Department, in cases of peculiar delicacy, as a law of undoubted obligation. [. . .]

The power now contested was exercised by the first Congress elected under the present Constitution. The bill for incorporating the Bank of the United States did not steal upon an unsuspecting legislature and pass unobserved. Its principle was completely understood, and was opposed with equal zeal and ability. After being resisted first in the fair and open field of debate, and afterwards in the executive cabinet, with as much persevering talent as any measure has ever experienced, and being supported by arguments which convinced minds as pure and as intelligent as this country can boast, it became a law. The original act was permitted to expire, but a short experience of the embarrassments to which the refusal to revive it exposed the Government convinced those who were most prejudiced against the measure of its necessity, and induced the passage of the present law. It would require no ordinary share of intrepidity to assert that a measure adopted under these circumstances was a bold and plain usurpation to which the Constitution gave no countenance.

These observations belong to the cause; but they are not made under the impression that, were the question entirely new, the law would be found irreconcilable with the Constitution.

In discussing this question, the counsel for the State of Maryland have deemed it of some importance, in the construction of the Constitution, to consider that instrument not as emanating from the people, but as the act of sovereign and independent States. The powers of the General Government, it has been said, are delegated by the States, who alone are truly sovereign, and must be exercised in subordination to the States, who alone possess supreme dominion.

It would be difficult to sustain this proposition. The convention which framed the Constitution was indeed elected by the State legislatures. But the instrument, when it came from their hands, was a mere proposal, without obligation or pretensions to it. It was reported to the then existing Congress of the United States with a request that it might be submitted to a convention of delegates, chosen in each State by the people thereof, under the recommendation of its legislature, for their assent and ratification. This mode of proceeding was adopted, and by the convention, by Congress, and by the State legislatures, the instrument was submitted to the people. They acted upon it in the only manner in which they can act safely, effectively and wisely, on such a subject—by assembling in convention. It is true, they assembled in their several States—and where else should they have assembled? No political dreamer was ever wild enough to think of breaking down the lines which separate the States, and of compounding the American people into one common mass. Of consequence, when they act, they act in their States. But the measures they adopt do not, on that account, cease to be the measures of the people themselves, or become the measures of the State governments.

From these conventions the Constitution derives its whole authority. The government proceeds directly from the people; is "ordained and established" in the name of the people, and is declared to be ordained, in order to form a more perfect union, establish justice, insure domestic tranquillity, and secure the blessings of liberty to themselves and to their posterity. The assent of the States in their sovereign capacity is implied in calling a convention, and thus submitting that instrument to the people. But the people were at perfect liberty to accept or reject it, and their act was final. It required not the affirmance, and could not be negatived, by the State Governments. The Constitution, when thus adopted, was of complete obligation, and bound the State sovereignties. [. . .]

It has been said that the people had already surrendered all their powers to the State sovereignties, and had nothing more to give. But surely the question whether they may resume and modify the powers granted to Government does not remain to be settled in this country. Much more might the legitimacy of the General Government be doubted had it been created by the States. The powers delegated to the State sovereignties were to be exercised by themselves, not by a distinct and independent sovereignty created by themselves. To the formation of a league such as was the Confederation, the State sovereignties were certainly competent. But when, "in order to form a more perfect union," it was deemed necessary to change this alliance into an effective Government, possessing great and sovereign powers and acting directly on the people, the necessity of referring it to the people, and of deriving its powers directly from them, was felt and acknowledged by all. The Government of the Union then (whatever may be the influence of this fact on the case) is, emphatically and truly, a Government of the people. In form and in substance, it emanates from them. Its powers are granted by them, and are to be exercised directly on them, and for their benefit.

This Government is acknowledged by all to be one of enumerated powers. The principle that it can exercise only the powers granted to it [. . .] is now universally admitted. But the question respecting the extent of the powers actually granted is perpetually arising, and will probably continue to arise so long as our system shall exist. In discussing these questions, the conflicting powers of the General and State Governments must be brought into view, and the supremacy of their respective laws, when they are in opposition, must be settled.

Among the enumerated powers, we do not find that of establishing a bank or creating a corporation. But there is no phrase in the instrument which, like the Articles of Confederation, excludes incidental or implied powers and which requires that everything granted shall be expressly and minutely described. Even the 10th Amendment, which was framed for the purpose of quieting the excessive jealousies which had been excited, omits the word "expressly," and declares only that the powers "not delegated to the United States, nor prohibited to the States, are reserved to the States or to the people," thus leaving the question whether the particular power which may become the subject of contest has been delegated to the one Government, or prohibited to the other, to depend on a fair construction of the whole instrument. The men who drew and adopted this amendment had experienced the embarrassments resulting from the insertion of this word in the Articles of Confederation, and probably omitted it to avoid those embarrassments. A Constitution, to contain an accurate detail of all the subdivisions of which its great powers will admit, and of all the means by which they may be carried into execution, would partake of the prolixity of a legal code, and could scarcely be embraced by the human mind. It would probably never be understood by the public. Its nature, therefore, requires that only its great outlines should be marked, its important objects designated, and the minor ingredients which compose those objects be deduced from the nature of the objects themselves. That this idea was entertained by the framers of the American Constitution is not only to be inferred from the nature of the instrument, but from the language. Why else were some of the limitations found in the 9th section of the 1st article introduced? It is also in some degree warranted by their having omitted to use any restrictive term which might prevent its receiving a fair and just interpretation. In considering this question, then, we must never forget that it is a Constitution we are expounding.

Although, among the enumerated powers of Government, we do not find the word "bank" or "incorporation," we find the great powers, to lay and collect taxes; to borrow money; to regulate commerce; to declare and conduct a war; and to raise and support armies and navies. The sword and the purse, all the external relations, and no inconsiderable portion of the industry of the nation are intrusted to its Government. It can never be pretended that these vast powers draw after them others of inferior importance merely because they are inferior. Such an idea can never be advanced. But it may with great reason be contended that a Government intrusted with such ample powers, on the due execution of which the happiness and prosperity of the Nation so vitally depends, must also be intrusted with ample means for their execution. The power being given, it is the interest of the Nation to facilitate its execution. It can never be their interest, and cannot be presumed to have been their intention, to clog and embarrass its execution by withholding the most appropriate means. [. . .] Throughout this vast republic, from the St. Croix to the Gulf of Mexico, from the Atlantic to the Pacific, revenue is to be collected and expended, armies are to be marched and supported. The exigencies of the Nation may require that the treasure raised in the north should be transported to the south, that raised in the east, conveyed to the west, or that this order should be reversed. Is that construction of the Constitution to be preferred which would render these operations difficult, hazardous and expensive? Can we adopt that construction (unless the words imperiously require it) which would impute to the framers of that instrument, when granting these powers for the public good, the intention of impeding their exercise, by withholding a choice of means? If, indeed, such be the mandate of the Constitution, we have only to obey; but that instrument does not profess to enumerate the means by which the powers it confers may be executed; nor does it prohibit the creation of a corporation, if the existence of such a being be essential, to the beneficial exercise of those powers. It is, then, the subject of fair inquiry how far such means may be employed.

It is not denied that the powers given to the Government imply the ordinary means of execution. That, for example, of raising revenue and applying it to national purposes is admitted to imply the power of conveying money from place to place as the exigencies of the Nation may require, and of employing the usual means of conveyance. But it is denied that the Government has its choice of means, or that it may employ the most convenient means if, to employ them, it be necessary to erect a corporation. On what foundation does this argument rest? On this alone: the power of creating a corporation is one appertaining to sovereignty, and is not expressly conferred on Congress. This is true. But all legislative powers appertain to sovereignty. The original power of giving the law on any subject whatever is a sovereign power, and if the Government of the Union is restrained from creating a corporation as a means for performing its functions, on the single reason that the creation of a corporation is an act of sovereignty, if the sufficiency of this reason be acknowledged, there would be some difficulty in sustaining the authority of Congress to pass other laws for the accomplishment of the same objects. The Government which has a right to do an act and has imposed on it the duty of performing that act must, according to the dictates of reason, be allowed to select the means, and those who contend that it may not select any appropriate means that one particular mode of effecting the object is excepted take upon themselves the burden of establishing that exception.

The creation of a corporation, it is said, appertains to sovereignty. This is admitted. But to what portion of sovereignty does it appertain? Does it belong to one more than to another? In America, the powers of sovereignty are divided between the Government of the Union and those of the States. They are each sovereign with respect to the objects committed to it, and neither sovereign with respect to the objects committed to the other. We cannot comprehend that train of reasoning, which would maintain that the extent of power granted by the people is to be ascertained not by the nature and terms of the grant, but by its date. Some State Constitutions were formed before, some since, that of the United States. We cannot believe that their relation to each other is in any degree dependent upon this circumstance. Their respective powers must, we think, be precisely the same as if they had been formed at the same time. Had they been formed at the same time, and had the people conferred on the General Government the power contained in the Constitution, and on the States the whole residuum of power, would it have been asserted that the Government of the Union was not sovereign, with respect to those objects which were intrusted to it, in relation to which its laws were declared to be supreme? If this could not have been asserted, we cannot well comprehend the process of reasoning which maintains that a power appertaining to sovereignty cannot be connected with that vast portion of it which is granted to the General Government, so far as it is calculated to subserve the legitimate objects of that Government. The power of creating a corporation, though appertaining to sovereignty, is not, like the power of making war or levying taxes or of regulating commerce, a great substantive and independent power which cannot be implied as incidental to other powers or used as a means of executing them. It is never the end for which other powers are exercised, but a means by which other objects are accomplished. No contributions are made to charity for the sake of an incorporation, but a corporation is created to administer the charity; no seminary of learning is instituted in order to be incorporated, but the corporate character is conferred to subserve the purposes of education. No city was ever built with the sole object of being incorporated, but is incorporated as affording the best means of being well governed. The power of creating a corporation is never used for its own sake, but for the purpose of effecting something else. No sufficient reason is therefore perceived why it may not pass as incidental to those powers which are expressly given if it be a direct mode of executing them.

But the Constitution of the United States has not left the right of Congress to employ the necessary means for the execution of the powers conferred on the Government to general reasoning. To its enumeration of powers is added that of making all laws which shall be necessary and proper for carrying into execution the foregoing powers, and all other powers vested by this Constitution in the Government of the United States or in any department thereof.

The counsel for the State of Maryland have urged various arguments to prove that this clause, though in terms a grant of power, is not so in effect, but is really restrictive of the general right which might otherwise be implied of selecting means for executing the enumerated powers. [. . .] [T]he argument on which most reliance is placed is drawn from that peculiar language of this clause. Congress is not empowered by it to make all laws which may have relation to the powers conferred on the Government, but such only as may be "necessary and proper" for carrying them into execution. The word "necessary" is considered as controlling the whole sentence, and as limiting the right to pass laws for the execution of the granted powers to such as are indispensable, and without which the power would be nugatory. That it excludes the choice of means, and leaves to Congress in each case that only which is most direct and simple.

Is it true that this is the sense in which the word "necessary" is always used? Does it always import an absolute physical necessity so strong that one thing to which another may be termed necessary cannot exist without that other? We think it does not. If reference be had to its use in the common affairs of the world or in approved authors, we find that it frequently imports no more than that one thing is convenient, or useful, or essential to another. To employ the means necessary to an end is generally understood as employing any means calculated to produce the end, and not as being confined to those single means without which the end would be entirely unattainable. Such is the character of human language that no word conveys to the mind in all situations one single definite idea, and nothing is more common than to use words in a figurative sense. Almost all compositions contain words which, taken in a their rigorous sense, would convey a meaning different from that which is obviously intended. It is essential to just construction that many words which import something excessive should be understood in a more mitigated sense—in that sense which common usage justifies. The word "necessary" is of this description. It has not a fixed character peculiar to itself. It admits of all degrees of comparison, and is often connected with other words which increase or diminish the impression the mind receives of the urgency it imports. A thing may be necessary, very necessary, absolutely or indispensably necessary. To no mind would the same idea be conveyed by these several phrases. The comment on the word is well illustrated by the passage cited at the bar from the 10th section of the 1st article of the Constitution. It is, we think, impossible to compare the sentence which prohibits a State from laying "imposts, or duties on imports or exports, except what may be absolutely necessary for executing its inspection laws," with that which authorizes Congress "to make all laws which shall be necessary and proper for carrying into execution" the powers of the General Government without feeling a conviction that the convention understood itself to change materially the meaning of the word "necessary," by prefixing the word "absolutely." This word, then, like others, is used in various senses, and, in its construction, the subject, the context, the intention of the person using them are all to be taken into view.

Let this be done in the case under consideration. The subject is the execution of those great powers on which the welfare of a Nation essentially depends. It must have been the intention of those who gave these powers to insure, so far as human prudence could insure, their beneficial execution. This could not be done by confiding the choice of means to such narrow limits as not to leave it in the power of Congress to adopt any which might be appropriate, and which were conducive to the end. This provision is made in a Constitution intended to endure for ages to come, and consequently to be adapted to the various crises of human affairs. To have prescribed the means by which Government should, in all future time, execute its powers would have been to change entirely the character of the instrument and give it the properties of a legal code. It would have been an unwise attempt to provide by immutable rules for exigencies which, if foreseen at all, must have been seen dimly, and which can be best provided for as they occur. To have declared that the best means shall not be used, but those alone without which the power given would be nugatory, would have been to deprive the legislature of the capacity to avail itself of experience, to exercise its reason, and to accommodate its legislation to circumstances. If we apply this principle of construction to any of the powers of the Government, we shall find it so pernicious in its operation that we shall be compelled to discard it. [. . .]

Take, for example, the power "to establish post-offices and post-roads." This power is executed by the single act of making the establishment. But from this has been inferred the power and duty of carrying the mail along the post road from one post office to another. And from this implied power has again been inferred the right to punish those who steal letters from the post office, or rob the mail. It may be said with some plausibility that the right to carry the mail, and to punish those who rob it, is not indispensably necessary to the establishment of a post office and post road. This right is indeed essential to the beneficial exercise of the power, but not indispensably necessary to its existence. So, of the punishment of the crimes of stealing or falsifying a record or process of a Court of the United States, or of perjury in such Court. To punish these offences is certainly conducive to the due administration of justice. But Courts may exist, and may decide the causes brought before them, though such crimes escape punishment.

The baneful influence of this narrow construction on all the operations of the Government, and the absolute impracticability of maintaining it without rendering the Government incompetent to its great objects, might be illustrated by numerous examples drawn from the Constitution and from our laws. The good sense of the public has pronounced without hesitation that the power of punishment appertains to sovereignty, and may be exercised, whenever the sovereign has a right to act, as incidental to his Constitutional powers. It is a means for carrying into execution all sovereign powers, and may be used although not indispensably necessary. It is a right incidental to the power, and conducive to its beneficial exercise.

[Even] in the absence of this clause, Congress would have some choice of means. That it might employ those which, in its judgment, would most advantageously effect the object to be accomplished. That any means adapted to the end, any means which tended directly to the execution of the Constitutional powers of the Government, were in themselves Constitutional. This clause, as construed by the State of Maryland, would abridge, and almost annihilate, this useful and necessary right of the legislature to select its means. That this could not be intended is, we should think, had it not been already controverted, too apparent for controversy.

We think so for the following reasons:

1st. The clause is placed among the powers of Congress, not among the limitations on those powers.

2d. Its terms purport to enlarge, not to diminish, the powers vested in the Government. It purports to be an additional power, not a restriction on those already granted. No reason has been or can be assigned for thus concealing an intention to narrow the discretion of the National Legislature under words which purport to enlarge it. The framers of the Constitution wished its adoption, and well knew that it would be endangered by its strength, not by its weakness. Had they been capable of using language which would convey to the eye one idea and, after deep reflection, impress on the mind another, they would rather have disguised the grant of power than its limitation. If, then, their intention had been, by this clause, to restrain the free use of means which might otherwise have been implied, that intention would have been inserted in another place, and would have been expressed in terms resembling these. "In carrying into execution the foregoing powers, and all others," etc., "no laws shall be passed but such as are necessary and proper." Had the intention been to make this clause restrictive, it would unquestionably have been so in form, as well as in effect.

The result of the most careful and attentive consideration bestowed upon this clause is that, if it does not enlarge, it cannot be construed to restrain, the powers of Congress, or to impair the right of the legislature to exercise its best judgment in the selection of measures to carry into execution the Constitutional powers of the Government. If no other motive for its insertion can be suggested, a sufficient one is found in the desire to remove all doubts respecting the right to legislate on that vast mass of incidental powers which must be involved in the Constitution if that instrument be not a splendid bauble.

We admit, as all must admit, that the powers of the Government are limited, and that its limits are not to be transcended. But we think the sound construction of the Constitution must allow to the national legislature that discretion with respect to the means by which the powers it confers are to be carried into execution which will enable that body to perform the high duties assigned to it in the manner most beneficial to the people. Let the end be legitimate, let it be within the scope of the Constitution, and all means which are appropriate, which are plainly adapted to that end, which are not prohibited, but consist with the letter and spirit of the Constitution, are Constitutional. [. . .]

That a corporation must be considered as a means not less usual, not of higher dignity, not more requiring a particular specification than other means has been sufficiently proved. [. . .] If a corporation may be employed, indiscriminately with other means, to carry into execution the powers of the Government, no particular reason can be assigned for excluding the use of a bank, if required for its fiscal operations. To use one must be within the discretion of Congress if it be an appropriate mode of executing the powers of Government. That it is a convenient, a useful, and essential instrument in the prosecution of its fiscal operations is not now a subject of controversy. All those who have been concerned in the administration of our finances have concurred in representing its importance and necessity. [. . .] Under the Confederation, Congress, justifying the measure by its necessity, transcended, perhaps, its powers to obtain the advantage of a bank; and our own legislation attests the universal conviction of the utility of this measure. The time has passed away when it can be necessary to enter into any discussion in order to prove the importance of this instrument as a means to effect the legitimate objects of the Government.

But were its necessity less apparent, none can deny its being an appropriate measure; and if it is, the decree of its necessity, as has been very justly observed, is to be discussed in another place. Should Congress, in the execution of its powers, adopt measures which are prohibited by the Constitution, or should Congress, under the pretext of executing its powers, pass laws for the accomplishment of objects not intrusted to the Government, it would become the painful duty of this tribunal, should a case requiring such a decision come before it, to say that such an act was not the law of the land. But where the law is not prohibited, and is really calculated to effect any of the objects intrusted to the Government, to undertake here to inquire into the decree of its necessity would be to pass the line which circumscribes the judicial department and to tread on legislative ground. This Court disclaims all pretensions to such a power.

After this declaration, it can scarcely be necessary to say that the existence of State banks can have no possible influence on the question. No trace is to be found in the Constitution of an intention to create a dependence of the Government of the Union on those of the States, for the execution of the great powers assigned to it. Its means are adequate to its ends, and on those means alone was it expected to rely for the accomplishment of its ends. To impose on it the necessity of resorting to means which it cannot control, which another Government may furnish or withhold, would render its course precarious, the result of its measures uncertain, and create a dependence on other Governments which might disappoint its most important designs, and is incompatible with the language of the Constitution. But were it otherwise, the choice of means implies a right to choose a national bank in preference to State banks, and Congress alone can make the election.

After the most deliberate consideration, it is the unanimous and decided opinion of this Court that the act to incorporate the Bank of the United States is a law made in pursuance of the Constitution, and is a part of the supreme law of the land. [. . .]

It being the opinion of the Court that the act incorporating the bank is constitutional, and that the power of establishing a branch in the State of Maryland might be properly exercised by the bank itself, we proceed to inquire:

2. Whether the State of Maryland may, without violating the Constitution, tax that branch?

That the power of taxation is one of vital importance; that it is retained by the States; that it is not abridged by the grant of a similar power to the Government of the Union; that it is to be concurrently exercised by the two Governments—are truths which have never been denied. But such is the paramount character of the Constitution that its capacity to withdraw any subject from the action of even this power is admitted. The States are expressly forbidden to lay any duties on imports or exports except what may be absolutely necessary for executing their inspection laws. If the obligation of this prohibition must be conceded—if it may restrain a State from the exercise of its taxing power on imports and exports—the same paramount character would seem to restrain, as it certainly may restrain, a State from such other exercise of this power as is in its nature incompatible with, and repugnant to, the constitutional laws of the Union. A law absolutely repugnant to another as entirely repeals that other as if express terms of repeal were used.

On this ground, the counsel for the bank place its claim to be exempted from the power of a State to tax its operations. There is no express provision for the case, but the claim has been sustained on a principle which so entirely pervades the Constitution, is so intermixed with the materials which compose it, so interwoven with its web, so blended with its texture, as to be incapable of being separated from it without rending it into shreds.

This great principle is that the Constitution and the laws made in pursuance thereof are supreme; that they control the Constitution and laws of the respective States, and cannot be controlled by them. From this, which may be almost termed an axiom, other propositions are deduced as corollaries, on the truth or error of which, and on their application to this case, the cause has been supposed to depend. These are, 1st. That a power to create implies a power to preserve; 2d. That a power to destroy, if wielded by a different hand, is hostile to, and incompatible with these powers to create and to preserve; 3d. That, where this repugnancy exists, that authority which is supreme must control, not yield to that over which it is supreme. [. . .]

That the power of taxing it by the States may be exercised so as to destroy it is too obvious to be denied. But taxation is said to be an absolute power which acknowledges no other limits than those expressly prescribed in the Constitution, and, like sovereign power of every other description, is intrusted to the discretion of those who use it. But the very terms of this argument admit that the sovereignty of the State, in the article of taxation itself, is subordinate to, and may be controlled by, the Constitution of the United States. How far it has been controlled by that instrument must be a question of construction. In making this construction, no principle, not declared, can be admissible which would defeat the legitimate operations of a supreme Government. It is of the very essence of supremacy to remove all obstacles to its action within its own sphere, and so to modify every power vested in subordinate governments as to exempt its own operations from their own influence. This effect need not be stated in terms. It is so involved in the declaration of supremacy, so necessarily implied in it, that the expression of it could not make it more certain. We must, therefore, keep it in view while construing the Constitution.

The argument on the part of the State of Maryland is not that the States may directly resist a law of Congress, but that they may exercise their acknowledged powers upon it, and that the Constitution leaves them this right, in the confidence that they will not abuse it.

Before we proceed to examine this argument and to subject it to test of the Constitution, we must be permitted to bestow a few considerations on the nature and extent of this original right of taxation, which is acknowledged to remain with the States. It is admitted that the power of taxing the people and their property is essential to the very existence of Government, and may be legitimately exercised on the objects to which it is applicable, to the utmost extent to which the Government may choose to carry it. The only security against the abuse of this power is found in the structure of the Government itself. In imposing a tax, the legislature acts upon its constituents. This is, in general, a sufficient security against erroneous and oppressive taxation.

The people of a State, therefore, give to their Government a right of taxing themselves and their property, and as the exigencies of Government cannot be limited, they prescribe no limits to the exercise of this right, resting confidently on the interest of the legislator and on the influence of the constituent over their representative to guard them against its abuse. [. . .]

The sovereignty of a State extends to everything which exists by its own authority or is introduced by its permission, but does it extend to those means which are employed by Congress to carry into execution powers conferred on that body by the people of the United States? We think it demonstrable that it does not. Those powers are not given by the people of a single State. They are given by the people of the United States, to a Government whose laws, made in pursuance of the Constitution, are declared to be supreme. Consequently, the people of a single State cannot confer a sovereignty which will extend over them.

If we measure the power of taxation residing in a State by the extent of sovereignty which the people of a single State possess and can confer on its Government, we have an intelligible standard, applicable to every case to which the power may be applied. We have a principle which leaves the power of taxing the people and property of a State unimpaired; which leaves to a State the command of all its resources, and which places beyond its reach all those powers which are conferred by the people of the United States on the Government of the Union, and all those means which are given for the purpose of carrying those powers into execution. We have a principle which is safe for the States and safe for the Union. We are relieved, as we ought to be, from clashing sovereignty; from interfering powers; from a repugnancy between a right in one Government to pull down what there is an acknowledged right in another to build up; from the incompatibility of a right in one Government to destroy what there is a right in another to preserve. We are not driven to the perplexing inquiry, so unfit for the judicial department, what degree of taxation is the legitimate use and what degree may amount to the abuse of the power. The attempt to use it on the means employed by the Government of the Union, in pursuance of the Constitution, is itself an abuse because it is the usurpation of a power which the people of a single State cannot give.

We find, then, on just theory, a total failure of this original right to tax the means employed by the Government of the Union, for the execution of its powers. The right never existed, and the question whether it has been surrendered cannot arise.

But, waiving this theory for the present, let us resume the inquiry, whether this power can be exercised by the respective States, consistently with a fair construction of the Constitution?

That the power to tax involves the power to destroy; that the power to destroy may defeat and render useless the power to create; that there is a plain repugnance in conferring on one Government a power to control the constitutional measures of another, which other, with respect to those very measures, is declared to be supreme over that which exerts the control, are propositions not to be denied. But all inconsistencies are to be reconciled by the magic of the word confidence. Taxation, it is said, does not necessarily and unavoidably destroy. To carry it to the excess of destruction would be an abuse, to presume which would banish that confidence which is essential to all Government.

But is this a case of confidence? Would the people of any one State trust those of another with a power to control the most insignificant operations of their State Government? We know they would not. Why, then, should we suppose that the people of any one State should be willing to trust those of another with a power to control the operations of a Government to which they have confided their most important and most valuable interests? In the Legislature of the Union alone are all represented. The Legislature of the Union alone, therefore, can be trusted by the people with the power of controlling measures which concern all, in the confidence that it will not be abused. This, then, is not a case of confidence, and we must consider it is as it really is.

If we apply the principle for which the State of Maryland contends, to the Constitution generally, we shall find it capable of changing totally the character of that instrument. We shall find it capable of arresting all the measures of the Government, and of prostrating it at the foot of the States. The American people have declared their Constitution and the laws made in pursuance thereof to be supreme, but this principle would transfer the supremacy, in fact, to the States.

If the States may tax one instrument, employed by the Government in the execution of its powers, they may tax any and every other instrument. They may tax the mail; they may tax the mint; they may tax patent rights; they may tax the papers of the custom house; they may tax judicial process; they may tax all the means employed by the Government to an excess which would defeat all the ends of Government. This was not intended by the American people. They did not design to make their Government dependent on the States.

The Court has bestowed on this subject its most deliberate consideration. The result is a conviction that the States have no power, by taxation or otherwise, to retard, impede, burden, or in any manner control the operations of the constitutional laws enacted by Congress to carry into execution the powers vested in the General Government. This is, we think, the unavoidable consequence of that supremacy which the Constitution has declared.

We are unanimously of opinion that the law passed by the Legislature of Maryland, imposing a tax on the Bank of the United States is unconstitutional and void.

This opinion does not deprive the States of any resources which they originally possessed. It does not extend to a tax paid by the real property of the bank, in common with the other real property within the

State, nor to a tax imposed on the interest which the citizens of Maryland may hold in this institution, in common with other property of the same description throughout the State. But this is a tax on the operations of the bank, and is, consequently, a tax on the operation of an instrument employed by the Government of the Union to carry its powers into execution. Such a tax must be unconstitutional.

JAMES KENT

Addresses before the New York State Constitutional Convention (1821)

[. . .] What have we to fear in future? We have no reason to apprehend subjugation by foreign arms, nor conflicts between the states. We have no standing armies to menace our liberties. We have no hereditary aristocracy, nor privileged orders, nor established church to press upon our rights or our income: our liberties are to be assailed from other quarters and by other means. It is not to be disguised that our governments are becoming downright democracies, with all their good, and all their evil. The principle of universal suffrage, which is now running a triumphant career from Maine to Louisiana, is an awful power, which, like gunpowder, or the steam engine, or the press itself, may be rendered mighty in mischief as well as in blessings. We have to fear the corrupting influence of constant struggles for office and power. We have to fear inflammatory appeals to the worst passions of the worst men in society; and we have greatly to dread the disciplined force of fierce and vindictive majorities, headed by leaders flattering their weaknesses and passions, and turning their vengeance upon the heads and fortunes of minorities, under the forms of law. It requires all our wisdom, and all our patriotism, to surround our institutions with a rampart against the corruption and violence of party spirit. We must ingraft something like quarantine laws into our constitution, to prevent the introduction and rage of this great moral pestilence. If we do not, then, take my word for it, we may expect to encounter the same disasters which have corrupted and shaken to the foundation so many popular states. What we have already done, will, as I greatly fear, give a freer operation and an increased impetus to the power of the evil genius of democracy. I need not surely inform this wise assembly, that all unchecked democracies are better calculated for man as he ought to be, than for man as he is, and as he has always appeared to be in the faithful page of history, and as he is declared to be in the volume of divine inspiration.

I hope, sir, I do not press this subject too far. I believe in my conscience, that unless we remove the means of concentrating, at the seat of government, or at any other given place, the elements of faction and the struggles for office, and unless we scatter them in fragments among the counties, our future career will be exceedingly tempestuous and corrupt. [. . .]

[. . .] I have reflected upon the report of the select committee with attention and with anxiety. We appear to be disregarding the principles of the constitution, under which we have so long and so happily lived, and to be changing some of its essential institutions. I cannot but think that the considerate men who have studied the history of republics, or are read in lessons of experience, must look with concern upon our apparent disposition to vibrate from a well balanced government, to the extremes of the democratic doctrines. Such a broad proposition as that contained in the report, at the distance of ten years past, would have struck the public mind with astonishment and terror. So rapid has been the career of our vibration.

Let us recall our attention, for a moment, to our past history.

This state has existed for forty-four years under our present constitution, which was formed by those illustrious sages and patriots who adorned the revolution. It has wonderfully fulfilled all the great ends of civil government. During that long period, we have enjoyed in an eminent degree, the blessings of civil and religious liberty. We have had our lives, our privileges, and our property, protected. We have had a succession of wise and temperate legislatures. The code of our statute law has been again and again revised and corrected, and it may proudly bear a comparison with that of any other people. We have had, during that period, (though I am, perhaps, not the fittest person to say it) a regular, stable, honest, and enlightened administration of justice. All the peaceable pursuits of industry, and all the important interests of education and science, have been fostered and encouraged. We have trebled our numbers within the last twenty-five years, have displayed mighty resources, and have made unexampled progress in the career of prosperity and greatness.

Our financial credit stands at an enviable height; and we are now successfully engaged in connecting the great lakes with the ocean by stupendous canals, which excite the admiration of our neighbours, and will make a conspicuous figure even upon the map of the United States.

These are some of the fruits of our present government; and yet we seem to be dissatisfied with our condition, and we are engaged in the bold and hazardous experiment of remodeling the constitution. Is it not fit and discreet: I speak as to wise men; is it not fit and proper that we should pause in our career, and reflect well on the immensity of the innovation in contemplation? Discontent in the midst of so much prosperity, and with such abundant means of happiness, looks like ingratitude, and as if we were disposed to arraign the goodness of Providence. Do we not expose ourselves to the danger of being deprived of the blessings we have enjoyed?—When the husbandman has gathered in his harvest, and has filled his barns and his granaries with the fruits of his industry, if he should then become discontented and unthankful, would he not have reason to apprehend, that the Lord of the harvest might come in his wrath, and with his lightning destroy them?

The senate has hitherto been elected by the farmers of the state—by the free and independent lords of the soil, worth at least $250 in freehold estate, over and above all debts charged thereon. The governor has been chosen by the same electors, and we have hitherto elected citizens of elevated rank and character. Our assembly has been chosen by freeholders, possessing a freehold of the value of $50, or by persons renting a tenement of the yearly value of $5, and who have been rated and actually paid taxes to the state. By the report before us, we propose to annihilate, at one stroke, all those property distinctions and to bow before the idol of universal suffrage. That extreme democratic principle, when applied to the legislative and executive departments of government, has been regarded with terror, by the wise men of every age, because in every European republic, ancient and modern, in which it has been tried, it has terminated disastrously, and been productive of corruption, injustice, violence, and tyranny. And dare we flatter ourselves that we are a peculiar people, who can run the career of history, exempted from the passions which have disturbed and corrupted the rest of mankind? If we are like other races of men, with similar follies and vices, then I greatly fear that our posterity will have reason to deplore in sackcloth and ashes, the delusion of the day.

It is not my purpose at present to interfere with the report of the committee, so far as respects the qualifications of electors for governor and members of assembly. I shall feel grateful if we may be permitted to retain the stability and security of a senate, bottomed upon the freehold property of the state. Such a body, so constituted, may prove a sheet anchor amidst the future factions and storms of the republic. The great leading and governing interest of this state, is, at present, the agricultural; and what madness would it be to commit that interest to the winds. The great body of the people, are now the owners and actual cultivators of the soil. With that wholesome population we always expect to find moderation, frugality, order, honesty, and a due sense of independence, liberty, and justice. It is impossible that any people can lose their liberties by internal fraud or violence, so long as the country is parceled out among freeholders of moderate possessions, and those freeholders have a sure and efficient control in the affairs of the government. Their habits, sympathies, and employments, necessarily inspire them with a correct spirit of freedom and justice; they are the safest guardians of property and the laws: We certainly cannot too highly appreciate the value of the agricultural interest: It is the foundation of national wealth and power. According to the opinion of her ablest political economists, it is the surplus produce of the agriculture of England, that enables her to support her vast body of manufacturers, her formidable fleets and armies, and the crowds of persons engaged in the liberal professions, and the cultivation of the various arts.

Now, sir, I wish to preserve our senate as the representative of the landed interest. I wish those who have an interest in the soil, to retain the exclusive possession of a branch in the legislature, as a strong hold in which they may find safety through all the vicissitudes which the state may be destined, in the course of Providence, to experience. I wish them to be always enabled to say that their freeholds cannot be taxed without their consent. The men of no property, together with the crowds of dependants connected with great manufacturing and commercial establishments, and the motley and undefinable population of crowded ports, may, perhaps, at some future day, under skilful management, predominate in the assembly, and yet we should be perfectly safe if no laws could pass without the free consent of the owners of the soil. That security we at present enjoy; and it is that security which I wish to retain.

The apprehended danger from the experiment of universal suffrage applied to the whole legislative department, is no dream of the imagination. It is too mighty an excitement for the moral constitution of men to endure. The tendency of universal suffrage, is to jeopardize the rights of property, and the principles of liberty. There is a constant tendency in human society, and the history of every age proves it; there is a tendency in the poor to covet and to share the plunder of the rich; in the debtor to relax or avoid the obligation of contracts; in the majority to tyrannize over the minority, and trample down their rights; in the indolent and the profligate, to cast the whole burthens of society upon the industrious and the virtuous; and *there is a tendency in ambitious and wicked men, to inflame these combustible materials*. It requires a vigilant government, and a firm administration of justice, to counteract that tendency. Thou shalt not covet; thou shalt not steal; are divine injunctions induced by this miserable depravity of our nature. Who can undertake to calculate with any precision, how many millions of people, this great state will contain in the course of this and the next century, and who can estimate the future extent and magnitude of our commercial ports? The disproportion between the men of property, and the men of no property, will be in every society in a ratio to its commerce, wealth, and population. We are no longer to remain plain and simple republics of farmers, like the New-England colonists, or the Dutch settlements on the Hudson. We are fast becoming a great nation, with great commerce, manufactures, population, wealth, luxuries, and with the vices and miseries that they engender. One seventh of the population of the city of Paris at this day subsists on charity, and one third of the inhabitants of that city die in the hospitals; what would become of such a city with universal suffrage? France has upwards of four, and England upwards of five millions of manufacturing and commercial laborers without property. Could these kingdoms sustain the weight of universal suffrage? The radicals in England, with the force of that mighty engine, would at once sweep away the property, the laws, and the liberties of that island like a deluge.

The growth of the city of New-York is enough to startle and awaken those who are pursuing the *ignis fatuus* of universal suffrage.

In 1773	it had	21, 000	souls.
1801	"	60, 000	do.
1806	"	76, 000	do.
1820	"	123, 000	do.

It is rapidly swelling into the unwieldly population, and with the burdensome pauperism, of an European metropolis. New-York is destined to become the future London of America; and in less than a century, that city, with the operation of universal suffrage, and under skilful direction, will govern this state.

The notion that every man that works a day on the road, or serves an idle hour in the militia, is entitled as of right to an equal participation in the whole power of the government, is most unreasonable, and has no foundation in justice. We had better at once discard from the report such a nominal test of merit.

If such persons have an equal share in one branch of the legislature, it is surely as much as they can in justice or policy demand. Society is an association for the protection of property as well as of life, and the individual who contributes only one cent to the common stock, ought not to have the same power and influence in directing the property concerns of the partnership, as he who contributes his thousands. He will not have the same inducements to care, and diligence, and fidelity. His inducements and his temptation would be to divide the whole capital upon the principles of an agrarian law.

Liberty, rightly understood, is an inestimable blessing, but liberty without wisdom, and without justice, is no better than wild and savage licentiousness. The danger which we have hereafter to apprehend, is not the want, but the abuse, of liberty. We have to apprehend the oppression of minorities, and a disposition to encroach on private right—to disturb chartered privileges—and to weaken, degrade, and overawe the administration of justice; we have to apprehend the establishment of unequal, and consequently, unjust systems of taxation, and all the mischiefs of a crude and mutable legislation. A stable senate, exempted from the influence of universal suffrage, will powerfully check these dangerous propensities, and such a check becomes the more necessary, since this Convention has already determined to withdraw the watchful eye of the judicial department from the passage of laws.

We are destined to become a great manufacturing as well as commercial state. We have already numerous and prosperous factories of one kind or another, and one master capitalist with his one hundred apprentices, and journeymen, and agents, and dependents, will bear down at the polls, an equal number of farmers of small estates in his vicinity, who cannot safely unite for their common defence. Large manufacturing and mechanical establishments, can act in an instant with the unity and efficacy of disciplined troops. It is against such combinations, among others, that I think we ought to give to the freeholders, or those who have interest in land, one branch of the legislature for their asylum and their comfort. Universal suffrage once granted, is granted forever, and never can be recalled. There is no retrograde step in the rear of democracy. However mischievous the precedent may be in its consequences, or however fatal in its effects, universal suffrage never can be recalled or checked, but by the strength of the bayonet. We stand, therefore, this moment, on the brink of fate, on the very edge of the precipice. If we let go our present hold on the senate, we commit our proudest hopes and our most precious interests to the waves.

It ought further to be observed, that the senate is a court of justice in the last resort. It is the last depository of public and private rights; of civil and criminal justice. This gives the subject an awful consideration, and wonderfully increases the importance of securing that house from the inroads of universal suffrage. Our country freeholders are exclusively our jurors in the administration of justice, and there is equal reason that none but those who have an interest in the soil, should have any concern in the composition of that court. As long as the senate is safe, justice is safe, property is safe, and our liberties are safe. But when the wisdom, the integrity, and the independence of that court is lost, we may be certain that the freedom and happiness of this state, are fled forever. [. . .]

John Marshall

Gibbons v. Ogden (1824)

Mr. Chief Justice Marshall delivered the opinion of the Court. [. . .]

The appellant contends that this decree is erroneous because the laws which purport to give the exclusive privilege it sustains are repugnant to the Constitution and laws of the United States.

They are said to be repugnant:

1st. To that clause in the Constitution which authorizes Congress to regulate commerce. [. . .]

As preliminary to the very able discussions of the Constitution which we have heard from the bar, and as having some influence on its construction, reference has been made to the political situation of these States anterior to its formation. It has been said that they were sovereign, were completely independent, and were connected with each other only by a league. This is true. But, when these allied sovereigns converted their league into a government, when they converted their Congress of Ambassadors, deputed to deliberate on their common concerns and to recommend measures of general utility, into a Legislature, empowered to enact laws on the most interesting subjects, the whole character in which the States appear underwent a change, the extent of which must be determined by a fair consideration of the instrument by which that change was effected.

This instrument contains an enumeration of powers expressly granted by the people to their government. It has been said that these powers ought to be construed strictly. But why ought they to be so construed? Is there one sentence in the Constitution which gives countenance to this rule? In the last of the enumerated powers, that which grants expressly the means for carrying all others into execution, Congress is authorized "to make all laws which shall be necessary and proper" for the purpose. But this limitation on the means which may be used is not extended to the powers which are conferred, nor is there one sentence in the Constitution which has been pointed out by the gentlemen of the bar or which we have been able to discern that prescribes this rule. We do not, therefore, think ourselves justified in adopting it. What do gentlemen mean by a "strict construction"? If they contend only against that enlarged construction, which would extend words beyond their natural and obvious import, we might question the application of the term, but should not controvert the principle. If they contend for that narrow construction which, in support of some theory not to be found in the Constitution, would deny to the government those powers which the words of the grant, as usually understood, import, and which are consistent with the general views and objects of the instrument; for that narrow construction which would cripple the government and render it unequal to the object for which it is declared to be instituted, and to which the powers given, as fairly understood, render it competent; then we cannot perceive the propriety of this strict construction, nor adopt it as the rule by which the Constitution is to be expounded. As men whose intentions require no concealment generally employ the words which most directly and aptly express the ideas they intend to convey, the enlightened patriots who framed our Constitution, and the people who adopted it, must be understood to have employed words in their natural sense, and to have intended what they have said. If, from the imperfection of human language, there should be serious doubts respecting the extent of any given power, it is a well settled rule that the objects for which it was given, especially when those objects are expressed in the instrument itself, should have great influence in the construction. We know of no reason for excluding this rule from the present case. The grant does not convey power which might be beneficial to the grantor if retained by himself, or which can enure solely to the benefit of the grantee, but is an investment of power for the general advantage, in the hands of agents selected for that purpose, which power can never be exercised by the people themselves, but must be placed in the hands of agents or lie dormant. We know of no rule for construing the extent of such powers other than is given by the language of the instrument which confers them, taken in connexion with the purposes for which they were conferred.

The words are, "Congress shall have power to regulate commerce with foreign nations, and among the several States, and with the Indian tribes."

The subject to be regulated is commerce, and our Constitution being, as was aptly said at the bar, one of enumeration, and not of definition, to ascertain the extent of the power, it becomes necessary to settle the meaning of the word. The counsel for the appellee would limit it to traffic, to buying and selling, or the interchange of commodities, and do not admit that it comprehends navigation. This would restrict a general term, applicable to many objects, to one of its significations. Commerce, undoubtedly, is traffic, but it is something more: it is intercourse. It describes the commercial intercourse between nations, and parts of nations, in all its branches, and is regulated by prescribing rules for carrying on that intercourse. The mind can scarcely conceive a system for regulating commerce between nations which shall exclude all laws concerning navigation, which shall be silent on the admission of the vessels of the one nation into the ports of the other, and be confined to prescribing rules for the conduct of individuals in the actual employment of buying and selling or of barter.

If commerce does not include navigation, the government of the Union has no direct power over that subject, and can make no law prescribing what shall constitute American vessels or requiring that they shall be navigated by American seamen. Yet this power has been exercised from the commencement of the government, has been exercised with the consent of all, and has been understood by all to be a commercial regulation. All America understands, and has uniformly understood, the word "commerce" to comprehend navigation. It was so understood, and must have been so understood, when the Constitution was framed. The power over commerce, including navigation, was one of the primary objects for which the people of America adopted their government, and must have been contemplated in forming it. The convention must have used the word in that sense, because all have understood it in that sense, and the attempt to restrict it comes too late. [. . .]

The word used in the Constitution, then, comprehends, and has been always understood to comprehend, navigation within its meaning, and a power to regulate navigation is as expressly granted as if that term had been added to the word "commerce."

To what commerce does this power extend? The Constitution informs us, to commerce "with foreign nations, and among the several States, and with the Indian tribes."

It has, we believe, been universally admitted that these words comprehend every species of commercial intercourse between the United States and foreign nations. No sort of trade can be carried on between this country and any other to which this power does not extend. It has been truly said that "commerce," as the word is used in the Constitution, is a unit every part of which is indicated by the term.

If this be the admitted meaning of the word in its application to foreign nations, it must carry the same meaning throughout the sentence, and remain a unit, unless there be some plain intelligible cause which alters it.

The subject to which the power is next applied is to commerce "among the several States." The word "among" means intermingled with. A thing which is among others is intermingled with them. Commerce among the States cannot stop at the external boundary line of each State, but may be introduced into the interior.

It is not intended to say that these words comprehend that commerce which is completely internal, which is carried on between man and man in a State, or between different parts of the same State, and which does not extend to or affect other States. Such a power would be inconvenient, and is certainly unnecessary.

Comprehensive as the word "among" is, it may very properly be restricted to that commerce which concerns more States than one. The phrase is not one which would probably have been selected to indicate the completely interior traffic of a State, because it is not an apt phrase for that purpose, and the enumeration of the particular classes of commerce to which the power was to be extended would not have been made had the intention been to extend the power to every description. The enumeration presupposes something not enumerated, and that something, if we regard the language or the subject of the sentence, must be the exclusively internal commerce of a State. The genius and character of the whole government seem to be that its action is to be applied to all the external concerns of the nation, and to those internal concerns which affect the States generally, but not to those which are completely within a particular State, which do not affect other States, and with which it is not necessary to interfere for the purpose of executing some of the general powers of the government. The completely internal commerce of a State, then, may be considered as reserved for the State itself.

But, in regulating commerce with foreign nations, the power of Congress does not stop at the jurisdictional lines of the several States. It would be a very useless power if it could not pass those lines. The commerce of the United States with foreign nations is that of the whole United States. Every district has a right to participate in it. The deep streams which penetrate our country in every direction pass through the interior of almost every State in the Union, and furnish the means of exercising this right. If Congress has the power to regulate it, that power must be exercised whenever the subject exists. If it exists within the States, if a foreign voyage may commence or terminate at a port within a State, then the power of Congress may be exercised within a State.

This principle is, if possible, still more clear, when applied to commerce "among the several States." They either join each other, in which case they are separated by a mathematical line, or they are remote from each other, in which case other States lie between them. What is commerce "among" them, and how is it to be conducted? Can a trading expedition between two adjoining States, commence and terminate outside of each? And if the trading intercourse be between two States remote from each other, must it not commence in one, terminate in the other, and probably pass through a third? Commerce among the States must, of necessity, be commerce with the States. In the regulation of trade with the Indian tribes, the action of the law, especially when the Constitution was made, was chiefly within a State. The power of Congress, then, whatever it may be, must be exercised within the territorial jurisdiction of the several States. The sense of the nation on this subject is unequivocally manifested by the provisions made in the laws for transporting goods by land between Baltimore and Providence, between New York and Philadelphia, and between Philadelphia and Baltimore.

We are now arrived at the inquiry—What is this power?

It is the power to regulate, that is, to prescribe the rule by which commerce is to be governed. This power, like all others vested in Congress, is complete in itself, may be exercised to its utmost extent, and acknowledges no limitations other than are prescribed in the Constitution. These are expressed in plain terms, and do not affect the questions which arise in this case, or which have been discussed at the bar. If, as has always been understood, the sovereignty of Congress, though limited to specified objects, is plenary as to those objects, the power over commerce with foreign nations, and among the several States, is vested in Congress as absolutely as it would be in a single government, having in its Constitution the same restrictions on the exercise of the power as are found in the Constitution of the United States. The wisdom and the discretion of Congress, their identity with the people, and the influence which their constituents possess at elections are, in this, as in many other instances, as that, for example, of declaring war, the sole restraints on which they have relied, to secure them from its abuse. They are the restraints on which the people must often rely solely, in all representative governments.

The power of Congress, then, comprehends navigation, within the limits of every State in the Union, so far as that navigation may be in any manner connected with "commerce with foreign nations, or among the several States, or with the Indian tribes." It may, of consequence, pass the jurisdictional line of New York and act upon the very waters to which the prohibition now under consideration applies.

But it has been urged with great earnestness that, although the power of Congress to regulate commerce with foreign nations and among the several States be coextensive with the subject itself, and have no other limits than are prescribed in the Constitution, yet the States may severally exercise the same power, within their respective jurisdictions. In support of this argument, it is said that they possessed it as an inseparable attribute of sovereignty, before the formation of the Constitution, and still retain it except so far as they have surrendered it by that instrument; that this principle results from the nature of the government, and is secured by the Tenth Amendment; that an affirmative grant of power is not exclusive unless in its own nature it be such that the continued exercise of it by the former possessor is inconsistent with the grant, and that this is not of that description.

The appellant, conceding these postulates except the last, contends that full power to regulate a particular subject implies the whole power, and leaves no residuum; that a grant of the whole is incompatible with the existence of a right in another to any part of it. [. . .]

The grant of the power to lay and collect taxes is, like the power to regulate commerce, made in general terms, and has never been understood to interfere with the exercise of the same power by the State, and hence has been drawn an argument which has been applied to the question under consideration. But the two grants are not, it is conceived, similar in their terms or their nature. Although many of the powers formerly exercised by the States are transferred to the government of the Union, yet the State governments remain, and constitute a most important part of our system. The power of taxation is indispensable to their existence, and is a power which, in its own nature, is capable of residing in, and being exercised by, different authorities at the same time. We are accustomed to see it placed, for different purposes, in different hands. Taxation is the simple operation of taking small portions from a perpetually accumulating mass, susceptible of almost infinite division, and a power in one to take what is necessary for certain purposes is not, in its nature, incompatible with a power in another to take what is necessary for other purposes. Congress is authorized to lay and collect taxes, etc. to pay the debts and provide for the common defence and general welfare of the United States. This does not interfere with the power of the States to tax for the support of their own governments, nor is the exercise of that power by the States an exercise of any portion of the power that is granted to the United States. In imposing taxes for State purposes, they are not doing what Congress is empowered to do. Congress is not empowered to tax for those purposes which are within the exclusive province of the States. When, then, each government exercises the power of taxation, neither is exercising the power of the other. But, when a State proceeds to regulate commerce with foreign nations, or among the several States, it is exercising the very power that is granted to Congress, and is doing the very thing which Congress is authorized to do. There is no analogy, then, between the power of taxation and the power of regulating commerce. [. . .]

The sole question is can a State regulate commerce with foreign nations and among the States while Congress is regulating it?

The counsel for the respondent answer this question in the affirmative, and rely very much on the restrictions in the 10th section as supporting their opinion. They say very truly that limitations of a power furnish a strong argument in favour of the existence of that power, and that the section which prohibits the States from laying duties on imports or exports proves that this power might have been exercised had it not been expressly forbidden, and consequently that any other commercial regulation, not expressly forbidden, to which the original power of the State was competent may still be made.

That this restriction shows the opinion of the Convention that a State might impose duties on exports and imports, if not expressly forbidden, will be conceded, but that it follows as a consequence from this concession that a State may regulate commerce with foreign nations and among the States cannot be admitted.

We must first determine whether the act of laying "duties or imposts on imports or exports" is considered in the Constitution as a branch of the taxing power, or of the power to regulate commerce. We think it very clear that it is considered as a branch of the taxing power. [. . .]

But the inspection laws are said to be regulations of commerce, and are certainly recognised in the Constitution as being passed in the exercise of a power remaining with the States.

That inspection laws may have a remote and considerable influence on commerce will not be denied, but that a power to regulate commerce is the source from which the right to pass them is derived cannot be admitted. The object of inspection laws is to improve the quality of articles produced by the labour of a country, to fit them for exportation, or, it may be, for domestic use. They act upon the subject before it becomes an article of foreign commerce or of commerce among the States, and prepare it for that purpose. They form a portion of that immense mass of legislation which embraces everything within the territory of a State not surrendered to the General Government; all which can be most advantageously exercised by the States themselves. Inspection laws, quarantine laws, health laws of every description, as well as laws for regulating the internal commerce of a State, and those which respect turnpike roads, ferries, etc., are component parts of this mass.

No direct general power over these objects is granted to Congress, and, consequently, they remain subject to State legislation. If the legislative power of the Union can reach them, it must be for national purposes, it must be where the power is expressly given for a special purpose or is clearly incidental to some power which is expressly given. It is obvious that the government of the Union, in the exercise of its express powers—that, for example, of regulating commerce with foreign nations and among the States—may use means that may also be employed by a State in the exercise of its acknowledged powers—that, for example, of regulating commerce within the State. If Congress license vessels to sail from one port to another in the same State, the act is supposed to be necessarily incidental to the power expressly granted to Congress, and implies no claim of a direct power to regulate the purely internal commerce of a State or to act directly on its system of police. So, if a State, in passing laws on subjects acknowledged to be within its control, and with a view to those subjects, shall adopt a measure of the same character with one which Congress may adopt, it does not derive its authority from the particular power which has been granted, but from some other, which remains with the State and may be executed by the same means. All experience shows that the same measures, or measures scarcely distinguishable from each other, may flow from distinct powers, but this does not prove that the powers themselves are identical. Although the means used in their execution may sometimes approach each other so nearly as to be confounded, there are other situations in which they are sufficiently distinct to establish their individuality.

In our complex system, presenting the rare and difficult scheme of one General Government whose action extends over the whole but which possesses only certain enumerated powers, and of numerous State governments which retain and exercise all powers not delegated to the Union, contests respecting power must arise. Were it even otherwise, the measures taken by the respective governments to execute their acknowledged powers would often be of the same description, and might sometimes interfere. This, however, does not prove that the one is exercising, or has a right to exercise, the powers of the other. [. . .]

But if the license be a permit to carry on the coasting trade, the respondent denies that these boats were engaged in that trade, or that the decree under consideration has restrained them from prosecuting it. The boats of the appellant were, we are told, employed in the transportation of passengers, and this is no part of that commerce which Congress may regulate.

If, as our whole course of legislation on this subject shows, the power of Congress has been universally understood in America to comprehend navigation, it is a very persuasive, if not a conclusive, argument to prove that the construction is correct, and if it be correct, no clear distinction is perceived between the power to regulate vessels employed in transporting men for hire and property for hire. The subject is transferred to Congress, and no exception to the grant can be admitted which is not proved by the words or the nature of the thing. A coasting vessel employed in the transportation of passengers is as much a portion of the American marine as one employed in the transportation of a cargo, and no reason is perceived why such vessel should be withdrawn from the regulating power of that government which has been thought best fitted for the purpose generally. The provisions of the law respecting native seamen and respecting ownership are as applicable to vessels carrying men as to vessels carrying manufactures, and no reason is perceived why the power over the subject should not be placed in the same hands. The argument urged at the bar rests on the foundation that the power of Congress does not extend to navigation as a branch of commerce, and can only be applied to that subject incidentally and occasionally. But if that foundation be removed, we must show some plain, intelligible distinction, supported by the Constitution or by reason, for discriminating between the power of Congress over vessels employed in navigating the same seas. We can perceive no such distinction.

If we refer to the Constitution, the inference to be drawn from it is rather against the distinction. The section which restrains Congress from prohibiting the migration or importation of such persons as any of the States may think proper to admit until the year 1808 has always been considered as an exception from the power to regulate commerce, and certainly seems to class migration with importation. Migration applies as appropriately to voluntary as importation does to involuntary arrivals, and, so far as an exception from a power proves its existence, this section proves that the power to regulate commerce applies equally to the regulation of vessels employed in transporting men, who pass from place to place voluntarily, and to those who pass involuntarily.

If the power reside in Congress, as a portion of the general grant to regulate commerce, then acts applying that power to vessels generally must be construed as comprehending all vessels. If none appear to be excluded by the language of the act, none can be excluded by construction. Vessels have always been employed to a greater or less extent in the transportation of passengers, and have never been supposed to be, on that account, withdrawn from the control or protection of Congress. Packets which ply along the coast, as well as those which make voyages between Europe and America, consider the transportation of passengers as an important part of their business. Yet it has never been suspected that the general laws of navigation did not apply to them. [. . .]

If, then, it were even true that the *Bellona* and the *Stoudinger* were employed exclusively in the conveyance of passengers between New York and New Jersey, it would not follow that this occupation did not constitute a part of the coasting trade of the United States, and was not protected by the license annexed to the answer. But we cannot perceive how the occupation of these vessels can be drawn into question in the case before the Court. The laws of New York, which grant the exclusive privilege set up by the respondent, take no notice of the employment of vessels, and relate only to the principle by which they are propelled. Those laws do not inquire whether vessels are engaged in transporting men or merchandise, but whether they are moved by steam or wind. If by the former, the waters of New York are closed against them, though their cargoes be dutiable goods, which the laws of the United States permit them to enter and deliver in New York. If by the latter, those waters are free to them though they should carry passengers only. In conformity with the law is the bill of the plaintiff in the State Court. The bill does not complain that the *Bellona* and the *Stoudinger* carry passengers, but that they are moved by steam. [. . .]

The questions, then, whether the conveyance of passengers be a part of the coasting trade and whether a vessel can be protected in that occupation by a coasting license are not, and cannot be, raised in this case. The real and sole question seems to be whether a steam machine in actual use deprives a vessel of the privileges conferred by a license.

In considering this question, the first idea which presents itself is that the laws of Congress for the regulation of commerce do not look to the principle by which vessels are moved. That subject is left entirely to individual discretion, and, in that vast and complex system of legislative enactment concerning it, which embraces everything that the Legislature thought it necessary to notice, there is not, we believe, one word respecting the peculiar principle by which vessels are propelled through the water, except what may be found in a single act granting a particular privilege to steamboats. With this exception, every act, either prescribing duties or granting privileges, applies to every vessel, whether navigated by the instrumentality of wind or fire, of sails or machinery. The whole weight of proof, then, is thrown upon him who would introduce a distinction to which the words of the law give no countenance. [. . .]

But all inquiry into this subject seems to the Court to be put completely at rest by the act already mentioned, entitled, "An act for the enrolling and licensing of steamboats."

This [1793] act authorizes a steamboat employed, or intended to be employed, only in a river or bay of the United States, owned wholly or in part by an alien, resident within the United States, to be enrolled and licensed as if the same belonged to a citizen of the United States.

This act demonstrates the opinion of Congress that steamboats may be enrolled and licensed, in common with vessels using sails. They are, of course, entitled to the same privileges, and can no more be restrained from navigating waters and entering ports which are free to such vessels than if they were wafted on their voyage by the winds, instead of being propelled by the agency of fire. The one element may be as legitimately used as the other for every commercial purpose authorized by the laws of the Union, and the act of a State inhibiting the use of either to any vessel having a license under the act of Congress comes, we think, in direct collision with that act. [. . .]

Powerful and ingenious minds, taking as postulates that the powers expressly granted to the government of the Union are to be contracted by construction into the narrowest possible compass and that the original powers of the States are retained if any possible construction will retain them may, by a course of well digested but refined and metaphysical reasoning founded on these premises, explain away the Constitution of our country and leave it a magnificent structure indeed to look at, but totally unfit for use. They may so entangle and perplex the understanding as to obscure principles which were before thought quite plain, and induce doubts where, if the mind were to pursue its own course, none would be perceived. In such a case, it is peculiarly necessary to recur to safe and fundamental principles to sustain those principles, and when sustained, to make them the tests of the arguments to be examined.

HENRY CLAY

Speeches on the American System (February 1832)

[. . .] Eight years ago, it was my painful duty to present to the other House of Congress an unexaggerated picture of the general distress pervading the whole land. We must all yet remember some of its frightful features. We all know that the people were then oppressed, and borne down by an enormous load of debt; that the value of property was at the lowest point of depression; that ruinous sales and sacrifices were everywhere made of real estate; that stop laws, and relief laws, and paper money were adopted, to save the people from impending destruction; that a deficit in the public revenue existed, which compelled government to seize upon, and divert from its legitimate object, the appropriations to the sinking fund, to redeem the national debt; and that our commerce and navigation were threatened with a complete paralysis. *In short, sir, if I were to select any term of seven years since the adoption of the present Constitution which exhibited a scene of the most widespread dismay and desolation, it would be exactly that term of seven years which immediately preceded the establishment of the tariff of* 1824.

I have now to perform the more pleasing task of exhibiting an imperfect sketch of the existing state of the unparalleled prosperity of the country. On a general survey, we behold cultivation extended, the arts flourishing, the face of the country improved, our people fully and profitably employed, and the public countenance exhibiting tranquillity, contentment, and happiness. And if we descend into particulars, we have the agreeable contemplation of a people out of debt; land rising slowly in value, but in a secure and salutary degree; a ready though not extravagant market for all the surplus productions of our industry; innumerable flocks and herds browsing and gamboling on ten thousand hills and plains, covered with rich and verdant grasses; our cities expanded, and whole villages springing up, as it were, by enchantment; our exports and imports increased and increasing; our tonnage, foreign and coastwise, swelling and fully occupied; the rivers of our interior animated by the perpetual thunder and lightning of countless steamboats; the currency sound and abundant; the public debt of two wars nearly redeemed; and, to crown all, the public treasury overflowing, embarrassing Congress, not to find subjects of taxation, but to select the objects which shall be liberated from the impost. *If the term of seven years were to be selected, of the greatest prosperity which this people have enjoyed since the establishment of their present Constitution, it would be exactly that period of seven years which immediately followed the passage of the tariff of* 1824.

This transformation of the condition of the country from gloom and distress to brightness and prosperity, has been mainly the work of American legislation, fostering American industry, instead of allowing it to be controlled by foreign legislation, cherishing foreign industry. [. . .]

It is now proposed to abolish the system, to which we owe so much of the public prosperity, and it is urged that the arrival of the period of the redemption of the public debt has been confidently looked to as presenting a suitable occasion to rid the country of the evils with which the system is alleged to be fraught. [. . .]

If the system of protection be founded on principles erroneous in theory, pernicious in practice, above all, if it be unconstitutional, as is alleged, it ought to be forthwith abolished, and not a vestige of it suffered to remain. But before we sanction this sweeping denunciation, let us look a little at this system, its magnitude, its ramifications, its duration, and the high authorities which have sustained it. [. . .] There is scarcely an interest, scarcely a vocation in society, which is not embraced by the beneficence of this system.

It comprehends our coasting tonnage and trade, from which all foreign tonnage is absolutely excluded.

It includes all our foreign tonnage, with the inconsiderable exception made by treaties of reciprocity with a few foreign powers.

It embraces our fisheries, and all our hardy and enterprising fishermen.

It extends to almost every mechanic art. [. . .] The mechanics [. . .] enjoy a measure of protection adapted to their several conditions, varying from twenty to fifty per cent. The extent and importance of some of these artisans may be estimated by a few particulars. The tanners, curries, boot and shoemakers, and other workers in hides, skins, and leather, produce an ultimate value per annum of forty millions of dollars; the manufacturers of hats and caps produce an annual value of fifteen millions; the cabinet-makers, twelve millions; the manufacturers of bonnets and hats for the female sex, lace, artificial flowers, combs, and so forth, seven millions; and the manufacturers of glass, five millions. [. . .]

It affects the cotton planter himself, and the tobacco planter, both of whom enjoy protection.

The total amount of the capital vested in sheep, the land to sustain them, wool, woolen manufactures, and woolen fabrics, and the subsistence of the various persons directly or indirectly employed in the growth and manufacture of the article of wool, is estimated at one hundred and sixty-seven millions of dollars, and the number of persons at one hundred and fifty thousand.

The value of iron, considered as a raw material, and of its manufacturers, is estimated at twenty-six millions of dollars per annum. Cotton goods, exclusive of the capital vested in the manufacture, and of the cost of the raw material, are believed to amount, annually, to about twenty millions of dollars. [. . .]

When gentlemen have succeeded in their design of an immediate or gradual destruction of the American system, what is their substitute? Free trade! Free trade! The call for free trade is as unavailing, as the cry of a spoiled child in its nurse's arms, for the moon, or the stars that glitter in the firmament of heaven. It never has existed, it never will exist. Trade implies at least two parties. To be free, it should be fair, equal, and reciprocal. [. . .] We may break down all barriers to free trade on our part, but the work will not be complete, until foreign powers shall have removed theirs. There would be freedom on one side, and restriction, prohibitions, and exclusions, on the other. [. . .]

Gentlemen deceive themselves. It is not free trade that they are recommending to our acceptance. It is, in effect, the British colonial system that we are invited to adopt; and, if their policy prevail, it will lead substantially to the re-colonization of these States under the commercial dominion of Great Britain. [. . .]

I will now [. . .] proceed to a more particular consideration of the arguments urged against the protective system, and an inquiry into its practical operation, especially on the cotton-growing country. . . . It is alleged that the system operates prejudicially to the cotton planter, by diminishing the foreign demand for his staple; that we can not sell to Great Britain unless we buy from her; that the import duty is equivalent to an export duty, and falls upon the cotton grower; that South Carolina pays a disproportionate quota of the public revenue; that an abandonment of the protective policy would lead to an augmentation of our exports, of an amount not less than one hundred and fifty millions of dollars; and, finally, that the South can not partake of the advantages of manufacturing, if there be any.

The argument comprehends two errors, one of fact and the other of principle. It assumes that we do not in fact purchase of Great Britain. What is the true state of the case? There are certain, but very few articles which it is thought sound policy requires that we should manufacture at home, and on these the tariff operates. But with respect to all the rest, and much the larger number of articles of taste, fashion, and utility, they are subject to no other than revenue duties, and are freely introduced. I have before me from the Treasury a statement of our imports from England, Scotland, and Ireland, [. . .] from which it will appear that [. . .] the last year's importation [. . .] will probably be the greatest in the whole term of eleven years.

Now, if it be admitted that there is a less amount of the protected articles imported from Great Britain, she may be, and probably is, compensated for the deficiency, by the increased consumption in America of the articles of her industry not falling within the scope of the policy of our protection. The establishment of manufactures among us excites the creation of wealth, and this gives new powers of consumption, which are gratified by the purchase of foreign objects. A poor nation can never be a great consuming nation. Its poverty will limit its consumption to bare subsistence.

The erroneous principle which the argument includes, is, that it devolves on us the duty of taking care that Great Britain shall be enabled to purchase from us without exacting from Great Britain the corresponding duty. If it be true on one side that nations are bound to shape their policy in reference to the ability of foreign powers, it must be true on both sides of the Atlantic. [. . .]

But, does Great Britain practice toward us upon the principles which we are now required to observe in regard to her? The exports to the United Kingdom [. . .] fall short of the amount of imports by upward of forty-six millions of dollars. [. . .] It is surprising how we have been able to sustain, for so long a time, a trade so very unequal. [. . .] Great Britain constantly acts on the maxim of buying only what she wants and cannot produce, and selling to foreign nations the utmost amount she can. In conformity with this maxim, she excludes articles of prime necessity, produced by us, equally if not more necessary than any of her industry which we tax, although the admission of those articles would increase our ability to purchase from her, according to the argument of gentlemen. [. . .]

But if there were a diminution of the British demand for cotton equal to the loss of a market for the few British fabrics which are within the scope of our protective policy, the question would still remain, whether the cotton-planter is not amply indemnified by the creation of additional demand elsewhere? With respect to the cotton-grower, it is the totality of the demand, and not its distribution, which affects his interests. If any system of policy will augment the aggregate of the demand, that system is favorable to his interests, although its tendency may be to vary the theater of the demand. It could not, for example, be injurious to him, if, instead of Great Britain continuing to receive the entire quantity of cotton which she now does, two or three hundred thousand bales of it were taken to the other side of the channel, and increased to that extent the French demand. It would be better for him, because it is always better to have several markets than one. Now if, instead of a transfer to the opposite side of the channel, of those two or three hundred thousand bales, they are transported to the northern States, can that be injurious to the cotton-grower? Is it not better for him? Is it not better to have a market at home, unaffected by war, or other foreign causes, for that amount of his staple? [. . .]

[. . .] By its existence at home, the circle of those exchanges is created, which reciprocally diffuses among all who are embraced within it the productions of their respective industry. The cotton-grower sells the raw material to the manufacturer; he buys the iron, the bread, the meal, the coal, and the countless number of objects of his consumption from his fellow-citizens, and they in turn purchase his fabrics. [. . .] The main argument of gentlemen is founded upon the idea of mutual ability resulting from mutual exchanges. They would furnish an ability to foreign nations by purchasing from them, and to our own people, by exchanges at home. If the American manufacture were discontinued, and that of England were to take its place, how would she sell the additional quantity of twenty-four millions of cotton goods, which we now make? To us? That has been shown to be impracticable. To other foreign nations? She has already pushed her supplies to them to the utmost extent. The ultimate consequence would then be to diminish the total consumption of cotton, to say nothing now of the reduction of price that would take place by throwing into the ports of Great Britain the two hundred thousand bales, which, no longer being manufactured in the United States, would go thither. [. . .]

[. . .] It is contended, in the last place, that the South can not, from physical and other causes, engage in the manufacturing arts. I deny the premises, and I deny the conclusion. I deny the fact of inability; and, if it existed, I deny the conclusion, that we must, therefore, break down our manufactures, and nourish those of foreign countries. The South possesses, in an extraordinary degree, two of the most important elements of manufacturing industry—water-power and labor. The former gives to our whole country a most decided advantage over Great Britain. But a single experiment, stated by the gentleman from South Carolina, in which a faithless slave put the torch to a manufacturing establishment, has discouraged similar enterprises. We have in Kentucky the same description of population, and we employ them, almost exclusively, in many of our hemp manufactories. [. . .]

Let it be supposed, however, that the South can not manufacture; must those parts of the Union which can, be therefore prevented? Must we support those of foreign countries? [. . .]

I regret, Mr. President, that one topic has, I think, unnecessarily been introduced into this debate. I allude to the charge brought against the manufacturing system, as favoring the growth of aristocracy. [. . .] The joint-stock companies of the North, as I understand them, are nothing more than associations, sometimes of hundreds, by means of which the small earnings of many are brought into a common stock, and the associates, obtaining corporate privileges, are enabled to prosecute, under one superintending head, their business to better advantage. Nothing can be more essentially democratic or better devised to counterpoise the influence of individual wealth. In Kentucky, almost every manufactory known to me, is in the hands of enterprising and self-made men, who have acquired whatever wealth they possess by patient and diligent labor. Comparisons are odious, and but in defense would not be made by me. But is there more tendency to aristocracy in a manufactory, supporting hundreds of freemen, or in a cotton plantation, with its not less numerous slaves, sustaining perhaps only two white families—that of the master and the overseer? [. . .]

I could extend and dwell on the long list of articles—the hemp, iron, lead, coal, and other items—for which a demand is created in the home market by the operation of the American system; but I should exhaust the patience of the Senate. Where, where should we find a market for all these articles, if it did not exist at home? What would be the condition of the largest portion of our people, and of the territory, if this home market were annihilated? How could they be supplied with objects of prime necessity? What would not be the certain and inevitable decline in the price of all these articles, but for the home market? [. . .]

But if all this reasoning were totally fallacious; if the price of manufactured articles were really higher, under the American system, than without it, I should still argue that high or low prices were themselves relative—relative to the ability to pay them. It is in vain to tempt, to tantalize us with the lower prices of European fabrics than our own, if we have nothing wherewith to purchase them. If, by the home exchanges, we can be supplied with necessary, even if they are dearer and worse, articles of American production than the foreign, it is better than not to be supplied at all. And how would the large portion of our country, which I have described, be supplied, but for the home exchanges? A poor people, destitute of wealth or of exchangeable commodities, has nothing to purchase foreign fabrics with. To them they are equally beyond their reach, whether their cost be a dollar or a guinea. It is in this view of the matter that Great Britain, by her vast wealth, her excited and protected industry, is enabled to bear a burden of taxation, which, when compared to that of other nations, appears enormous, but which, when her immense riches are compared to theirs, is light and trivial. The gentleman from South Carolina has drawn a lively and flattering picture of our coasts, bays, rivers, and harbors; and he argues that these proclaimed the design of Providence, that we should be a commercial people. I agree with him. We differ only as to the means. He would cherish the foreign, and neglect the internal trade. I would foster both. [. . .] By penetrating the bosoms of our mountains, and extracting from them their precious treasures; by cultivating the earth, and securing a home market for its rich and abundant products; by employing the water with which we are blessed; by stimulating and protecting our native industry, in all its forms; we shall but nourish and promote the prosperity of commerce, foreign and domestic.

I have hitherto considered the question in reference only to a state of peace; but a season of war ought not to be entirely overlooked. We have enjoyed nearly twenty years of peace; but who can tell when the storm of war shall again break forth? Have we forgotten, so soon, the privations to which not merely our brave soldiers and our gallant tars were subjected, but the whole community, during the last war, for the want of absolute necessaries? To what an enormous price they rose! And how inadequate the supply was at any price! [. . .] It would be easy to show that the higher prices of peace [. . .] were more than compensated by the lower prices of war, during which, supplies of all essential articles are indispensable to its vigorous, effectual, and glorious prosecution. I conclude this part of the argument with the hope that my humble exertions have not been altogether unsuccessful in showing,

First, that the policy which we have been considering ought to continue to be regarded as the genuine American system.

Secondly, that the free trade system, which is proposed as its substitute, ought really to be considered as the British colonial system.

Thirdly, that the American system is beneficial to all parts of the Union, and absolutely necessary to much the larger portion.

Fourthly, that the price of the great staple of cotton, and of all our chief productions of agriculture, has been sustained and upheld, and a decline averted, by the protective system.

Fifthly, that if the foreign demand for cotton has been at all diminished by the operation of that system, the diminution has been more than compensated in the additional demand created at home.

Sixthly, that the constant tendency of the system, by creating competition among ourselves, and between American and European industry, reciprocally acting upon each other, is to reduce prices of manufactured objects.

Seventhly, that in point of fact, objects within the scope of the policy of protection have greatly fallen in price.

Eighthly, that if, in a season of peace, these benefits are experienced, in a season of war, when the foreign supply might be cut off, they would be much more extensively felt.

Ninthly, and finally, that the substitution of the British colonial system for the American system, without benefiting any section of the Union, by subjecting us to a foreign legislation, regulated by foreign interests, would lead to the prostration of our manufactories, general impoverishment, and ultimate ruin. [. . .]

John C. Calhoun

Fort Hill Address (July 26, 1831)

Fort Hill

I must request you to permit me to use your columns, as the medium to make known my sentiments on the deeply important question, of the relation, which the States and General Government bear to each other, and which is, at this time, a subject of so much agitation.

It is one of the peculiarities of the station I occupy, that while it necessarily connects its incumbent, with the politics of the day, it affords him no opportunity officially to express his sentiments, except accidentally on an equal division of the body, over which he presides. He is thus exposed, as I have often experienced, to have his opinions erroneously and variously represented. In ordinary cases, I conceive, the correct course to be to remain silent, leaving to time and circumstances, the correction of misrepresentations; but there are occasions so vitally important, that a regard both to duty and character would seem to forbid such a course; and such, I conceive, to be the present. The frequent allusions to my sentiments, will not permit me to doubt, that such also is the public conception, and that it claims the right to know, in relation to the question referred to, the opinions of those, who hold important official stations; while on my part, desiring to receive neither unmerited praise, nor blame, I feel, I trust, the solicitude, which every honest and independent man ought, that my sentiments should be truly known, whether they be such, as may be calculated to recommend them to public favour, or not. Entertaining these impressions, I have concluded, that it is my duty to make known my sentiments; and I have adopted the mode, which on reflection seemed to be the most simple, and best calculated to effect the object in view.

The question of the relation, which the States and General Government bear to each other, is not one of recent origin. From the commencement of our system, it has divided public sentiment. Even in the Convention, while the Constitution was struggling into existence, there were two parties, as to what this relation should be, whose different sentiments, constituted no small impediment in forming that instrument. After the General Government went into operation, experience soon proved, that the question had not terminated with the labors of the Convention. The great struggle, that preceded the political revolution of 1801, which brought Mr. Jefferson into power, turned essentially on it; and the doctrines and arguments on both sides were embodied and ably sustained; on the one, in the Virginia and Kentucky resolutions, and the report to the Virginia Legislature; and on the other, in the replies of the Legislature of Massachusetts and some of the other States. These resolutions and this report, with the decision of the Supreme Court of Pennsylvania about the same time, (particularly in the case of Cobbett, delivered by Chief Justice M'Kean and concurred in by the whole bench,) contain, what I believe to be, the true doctrine on this important subject. I refer to them, in order to avoid the necessity of presenting my views, with the reasons in support of them, in detail.

As my object is simply to state my opinions, I might pause with this reference to documents, that so fully and ably state all the points immediately connected with this deeply important subject, but as there are many, who may not have the opportunity, or leisure to refer to them, and, as it is possible, however clear they may be, that different persons may place different interpretations on their meaning, I will, in order that my sentiments may be fully known, and to avoid all ambiguity, proceed to state summarily the doctrines, which I conceive they embrace.

Their great and leading principle is, that the General Government emanated from the people of the several States, forming distinct political communities, and acting in their separate and sovereign capacity, and not from all of the people forming one aggregate political community; that the Constitution of the United States is in fact a compact, to which each State is a party, in the character already described; and that the several States or parties, have a right to judge of its infractions, and in cases of a deliberate, palpable, and dangerous exercise of power not delegated, they have the right, in the last resort, to use the language of the Virginia resolutions, "*to interpose for arresting the progress of the evil, and for maintaining within their respective limits, the authorities, rights and liberties appertaining to them.*" This right of interposition, thus solemnly asserted by the State of Virginia, be it called what it may, State right, veto, nullification, or by any other name, I conceive to be the fundamental principle of our system, resting on facts historically as certain, as our Revolution itself, and deductions, as simple and demonstrative, as that of any political, or moral truth whatever; and I firmly believe that on its recognition depends, the stability and safety of our political institutions.

I am not ignorant, that those opposed to the doctrine have always, now and formerly, regarded it in a very different light, as anarchical and revolutionary. Could I believe such in fact to be its tendency, to me it would be no recommendation. I yield to none, I trust, in a deep and sincere attachment to our political institutions, and the union of these States. I never breathed an opposite sentiment; but on the contrary, I have ever considered them the great instruments of preserving our liberty, & promoting the happiness of ourselves and our posterity; and next to these, I have ever held them most dear. Nearly half my life has passed in the service of the Union, & whatever public reputation I have acquired, is indissolubly identified with it. To be too national has, indeed, been considered by many, even of my friends, to be my greatest political fault. With these strong feelings of attachment, I have examined with the utmost care, the bearing of the doctrine in question; and so far from anarchical, or revolutionary, I solemnly believe it to be, the only solid foundation of our system, and of the Union itself, and that the opposite doctrine, which denies to the States the right of protecting their reserved powers, and which would vest in the General Government, (it matters not through what Department,) the right of determining exclusively and finally the powers delegated to it, is incompatible with the sovereignty of the States, and of the Constitution itself, considered as the basis of a federal Union. As strong as this language is, it is not stronger, than that used by the illustrious Jefferson, who said, to give to the General Government the final and exclusive right to judge of its powers, is to make "*its discretion* and *not the Constitution the measure of its powers*"; and that, "*in all cases of compact between parties having no common Judge, each party has an equal right to judge for itself, as well of the operation as of the mode and measure of redress.*" Language cannot be more explicit; nor can higher authority be adduced.

That different opinions are entertained on this subject, I consider, but as an additional evidence of the great diversity of the human intellect. Had not able, experienced and patriotic individuals, for whom I have the highest respect, taken different views, I would have thought the right too clear to admit of doubt; but I am taught by this, as well as by many similar instances, to treat with deference opinions differing from my own. The error may possibly be with me; but if so, I can only say, that after the most mature and conscientious examination, I have not been able to detect it. But with all proper deference, I must think, that theirs is the error, who deny, what seems to be an essential attribute of the conceded sovereignty of the States; and who attribute to the General Government a right utterly incompatible with what all acknowledge to be its limited and restricted character; an error originating principally, as I must think, in not duly reflecting on the nature of our institutions, and on what constitutes the only rational object of all political constitutions.

It has been well said by one of the most sagacious men of antiquity, that the object of a constitution is to *restrain the government, as that of laws* is to restrain *individuals.* The remark is correct, nor is it less true, where the Government is vested in a majority, than where it is in a single or a few individuals; in a republic, than a monarchy or aristocracy. No one can have a higher respect for the maxim, that the majority ought to govern, than I have, taken in its proper sense, subject to the restrictions imposed by the Constitution, and confined to subjects, in which every portion of the community have similar interests; but it is a great error to suppose, as many do, that the right of a majority to govern is a natural and not a conventional right; and, therefore, absolute and unlimited. By nature every individual has the right to govern himself; and Governments, whether founded on majorities, or minorities, must derive their right from the assent, expressed or implied, of the governed, and be subject to such limitations, as they may impose. Where the interests are the same, that is where the laws that may benefit one, will benefit all, or the reverse, it is just and proper to place them under the control of the majority; but where they are dissimilar, so that the law, that may benefit one portion, may be ruinous to another, it would be on the contrary unjust and absurd to subject them to its will; and such, I conceive to be the theory on which our Constitution rests.

That such dissimilarity of interests may exist, it is impossible to doubt. They are to be found in every community, in a greater, or less degree, however small, or homogeneous; and they constitute, every where, the great difficulty of forming, and preserving free institutions. To guard against the unequal action of the laws, when applied to dissimilar and opposing interests, is, in fact, what mainly renders a constitution indispensable; to overlook which, in reasoning on our Constitution, would be to omit the principal element, by which to determine its character. Were there no contrariety of interests, nothing would be more simple and easy than to form and preserve free institutions. The right of suffrage alone would be a sufficient guaranty. It is the conflict of opposing interests which renders it the most difficult work of man.

Where the diversity of interests exists in separate and distinct classes of the community, as is the case in England, and was formerly the case in Sparta, Rome and most of the free states of antiquity, the rational constitutional provision is, that each should be represented in the Government, as a separate estate, with a distinct voice, and a negative on the acts of its co-estates, in order to check their encroachments. In England, the constitution has assumed expressly this form; while in the governments of Sparta and Rome the same thing was effected under different but not much less efficacious forms. The perfection of their organization, in this particular, was that, which gave to the constitutions of these renowned states all their celebrity, which secured their liberty for so many centuries, and raised them to so great a height of power and prosperity. Indeed, a constitutional provision giving to the great and separate interests of the community the right of self protection, must appear to those who will duly reflect on the subject, not less essential to the preservation of liberty, than the right of suffrage itself. They in fact have a common object, to effect which, the one is as necessary, as the other; to secure *responsibility*, that is, *that those who make and execute the laws should be accountable to those, on whom the laws in reality operate; the only solid and durable foundation of liberty*. If without the right of suffrage, our rulers would oppress us, so, without the right of self-protection, the major, would equally oppress the minor interests of the community. The absence of the former would make the governed the slaves of the rulers, and of the latter the feebler interests the victim of the stronger.

Happily for us, we have no artificial and separate classes of society. We have wisely exploded all such distinctions; but we are not, on that account, exempt from all contrariety of interests, as the present distracted and dangerous condition of our country unfortunately, but too clearly, proves. With us they are almost exclusively geographical, resulting mainly from difference of climate, soil, situation, industry and production, but are not, therefore less necessary to be protected by an adequate constitutional provision, than where the distinct interests exist in separate classes. The necessity is, in truth, greater, as such separate and dissimilar geographical interests, are more liable to come into conflict, and more dangerous when in that state, than those of any other description; so much so, that *ours is the first instance on record, where they have not formed in an extensive territory, separate and independent communities, or subjected the whole to despotic sway*. That such may not be our unhappy fate also, must be the sincere prayer of every lover of his country.

So numerous and diversified are the interests of our country, that they could not be fairly represented in a single government, organized so, as to give to each great and leading interest, a separate and distinct voice, as in governments, to which I have referred. A plan was adopted better suited to our situation, but perfectly novel in its character. The powers of the government were divided, not as heretofore, in reference to classes, but geographically. One General Government was formed for the whole, to which was delegated all of the powers supposed to be necessary to regulate the interests common to all the States, leaving others subject to the separate control of the States, being, from their local and peculiar character, such, that they could not be subject to the will of a majority of the whole Union, without the certain hazard of injustice and oppression. It was thus, that the interests of the whole were subjected, as they ought to be, to the will of the whole, while the peculiar and local interests were left under the control of the States separately, to whose custody only, they could be safely confided. This distribution of power, settled solemnly by a constitutional compact, to which all the States are parties, constitutes the peculiar character and excellence of our political system. It is truly and emphatically *American, without example, or parallel.*

To realize its perfection, we must view the General Government and the States as a whole, each in its proper sphere sovereign and independent, each perfectly adapted to their respective objects; the States acting separately, representing and protecting the local and peculiar interests; acting jointly, through one General Government, with the weight respectively assigned to each by the Constitution, representing and protecting the interest of the whole; and thus perfecting by an admirable, but simple arrangement the great principle of representation and responsibility, without which no government can be free, or just. To preserve this sacred distribution, as originally settled, by coercing each to move in its prescribed orb[it], is the great and difficult problem, on the solution of which, the duration of our Constitution, of our Union, and, in all probability, our liberty depends. How is this to be effected?

The question is new, when applied to our peculiar political organization, where the separate and conflicting interests of society are represented by distinct, but connected Governments; but is in reality an old question under a new form, long since perfectly solved. Whenever separate and dissimilar interests have been separately represented in any Government; whenever the sovereign power has been divided in its exercise, the experience and wisdom of ages have devised but one mode, by which such political organization can be preserved; the mode adopted in England, and by all Governments ancient and modern, blessed with Constitutions deserving to be called free; to give to each co-estate the right to judge of its powers, with a negative, or veto on the acts of the others, in order to protect against encroachments, the interests it particularly represents; a principle which all of our Constitutions recognize in the distribution of power among their respective Departments, as essential to maintain the independence of each, but which to all, who will duly reflect on the subject, must appear, far more essential, for the same object, in that great and fundamental distribution of powers between the States and General Government. So essential is the principle that to withhold the right from either, where the sovereign power is divided, is in fact *to annul the division* itself, and to *consolidate* in the one, left in the exclusive possession of the right, *all* of the powers of the government; for it is not possible to distinguish, practically, between a government having all power, and one having the right to take what powers it pleases. Nor does it in the least vary the principle, whether the distribution of power be between co-estates, as in England, or between distinctly organized, but connected governments, as with us. The reason is the same in both cases, while the necessity is greater in our case, as the danger of conflict is greater, where the interests of a society are divided geographically, than in any other, as has already been shewn.

These truths do seem to me to be incontrovertible; and I am at a loss to understand how any one, who has maturely reflected on the nature of our institutions, or who has read history, or studied the principles of free governments to any purpose, can call them in question. The explanation must, it appears to me, be sought in the fact, that in every free state, there are those, who look more to the necessity of maintaining power, than guarding against its abuses. I do not intend reproach, but simply to state a fact apparently necessary to explain the contrariety of opinions, among the intelligent, where the abstract consideration of the subject, would seem scarcely to admit of doubt. If such be the true cause, I must think the fear of weakening the government too much in this case to be in a great measure unfounded, or, at least that the danger is much less from that, than the opposite side. I do not deny that a power, of so high a nature may be abused by a State; but, when I reflect, that the States unanimously called the general government into existence with all of its powers, which they freely surrendered on their part, under the conviction that their common peace, safety and prosperity required it; that they are bound together by a common origin, and the recollection of common suffering and a common triumph in the great and splendid achievement of their independence; and that the strongest feelings of our nature, and among them, the love of national power and distinction, are on the side of the Union; it does seem to me, that the fear, which would strip the States of their sovereignty, and degrade them, in fact, to mere dependent corporations, lest they should abuse a right indispensable to the peaceable protection of those interests, which they reserved under their own peculiar guardianship, when they created the General Government, is unnatural and unreasonable. If those who voluntarily created the system, cannot be trusted to preserve it, what power can?

So far from extreme danger, I hold, that there never was a free state in which this great conservative principle, indispensable to all, was ever so safely lodged. In others, when the co-estates, representing the dissimilar and conflicting interests of the community came into contact, the only alternative was compromise, submission, or force. Not so in ours. Should the General Government, and a State come into conflict, we have a higher remedy; the power which called the General Government into existence, which gave it all of its authority, and can enlarge, contract, or abolish its powers at its pleasure, may be invoked. The States themselves may be appealed to, three fourths of which, in fact, form a power, whose decrees are the Constitution itself, and whose voice can silence all discontent. The utmost extent then of the power is, that a State acting in its sovereign capacity, as one of the parties to the Constitutional compact, may compel the Government, created by that compact, to submit a question touching its infraction, to the parties, who created it; to avoid the supposed dangers of which, it is proposed to resort to the novel, the hazardous, and, I must add, fatal project of giving to the General Government the sole and final right of interpreting the Constitution, thereby reversing the whole system, making that instrument the creature of its will, instead of a rule of action impressed on it at its creation, and annihilating in fact the authority which imposed it, and from which the government itself derives its existence.

That such would be the result, were the right in question vested in the Legislative, or Executive branch of the Government is conceded by all. No one has been so hardy as to assert, that Congress, or the President ought to have the right, or to deny, that if vested finally and exclusively in either, the consequences, which I have stated would necessarily follow; but its advocates have been reconciled to the doctrine, on the supposition, that there is one Department of the General Government, which, from its peculiar organization, affords an independent tribunal through which the Government may exercise the high authority, which is the subject of consideration, with perfect safety to all.

I yield, I trust, to few in my attachment to the Judiciary Department. I am fully sensible of its importance and would maintain it to the fullest extent in its Constitutional powers and independence; but it is impossible for me, to believe, that it was ever intended by the Constitution, that it should exercise the power in question, or, that it is competent to do so, and, if it were that it would be a safe depository of the power.

Its powers are judicial, and not political, and are expressly confined by the Constitution "to all *cases* in law and equity arising under this Constitution, the laws of the United States and the treaties made, or which shall be made, under its authority";[1] and which I have high authority in asserting, excludes political questions, and comprehends those only, where there are parties amenable to the process of the Court. Nor is its incompetency less clear, than its want of Constitutional authority. There may be many and the most dangerous infractions on the part of Congress, of which, it is conceded by all, the court, as a Judicial tribunal, cannot from its nature take cognizance. The Tariff itself is a strong case in point; and the reason applies equally *to all others where Congress perverts a power, from an object intended, to one not intended, the most insidious and dangerous of all infractions; and which may be extended to all of its powers, more especially to the taxing and appropriating*. But, supposing it competent to take cognizance of all infractions of every description, the insuperable objection still remains, that it would not be a safe tribunal to exercise the power in question.

1. I refer to the authority of Chief Justice Marshall in the case of Jonathan Robbins. I have not been able to refer to the speech and speak from memory.

It is an universal and fundamental political principle, that the power to protect, can safely be confided only to those interested in protecting, or their responsible agents, a maxim not less true in private than in public affairs. The danger in our system is, that the General Government, which represents the interests of the whole, may encroach on the States, which represent the peculiar and local interests, or that the latter may encroach on the former. In examining this point, we ought not to forget, that the Government through all of its Departments, Judicial as well as others, is administered by delegated and responsible agents; and that *the power which really controls ultimately all the movements is not in the agents, but those who elect or appoint them.* To understand then its real character, and what would be the action of the system in any supposable case, we must raise our view from the mere agents, to this high controlling power which finally impels every movement of the machine. By doing so, we shall find all under the control of the will of a majority, compounded of the majority of the States, taken as corporate bodies, and the majority of the people of the States estimated in federal numbers. These united constitute the real and final power, which impels and directs the movements of the General Government. The majority of the States elect the majority of the Senate; of the people of the States, that of the House of Representatives; the two united, the President; and the President and a majority of the Senate appoint the Judges; a majority of whom, and a majority of the Senate and the House with the President, really exercise all of the powers of the Government, with the exception of the cases where the Constitution requires a greater number than a majority. The Judges are, in fact, as truly the Judicial Representatives of this united majority, as the majority of Congress itself, or the President, is its legislative, or executive representative; and to confide the power to the Judiciary to determine finally and conclusively, what powers are delegated, and what reserved, would be in reality to confide it to the majority, whose agents they are, and by whom they can be controlled in various ways; and, of course, to subject, (against the fundamental principle of our system, and all sound political reasoning,) the reserved powers of the States, with all of the local and peculiar interests, they were intended to protect, to the will of the very majority, against which, the protection was intended. Nor will the tenure by which the Judges hold their office, however valuable the provision in many other respects, materially vary the case. Its highest possible effect would be to *retard* and not *finally* to *resist,* the will of a dominant majority.

But it is useless to multiply arguments. Were it possible, that reason could settle a question where the passions and interests of men are concerned, this point would have been long since settled for ever, by the State of Virginia. The report of her Legislature, to which I have already referred, has really, in my opinion, placed it beyond controversy. Speaking in reference to this subject it says, "It has been objected" (to the right of a State to interpose for the protection of her reserved rights) "that the Judicial authority is to be regarded, as the sole expositor of the Constitution; on this objection it might be observed, first, that there may be instances of usurped powers, which the forms of the Constitution could never draw within the control of the Judicial Department; secondly, that if the decision of the Judiciary be raised above the sovereign parties to the Constitution, the decisions of the other departments, not carried by the forms of the Constitution before the Judiciary, must be equally authoritative and final with the decision of that Department. But the proper answer to the objection is, that the resolution of the General Assembly relates to those great and extraordinary cases, in which all the forms of the Constitution may prove ineffectual against infractions dangerous to the essential rights of the parties to it. The resolution supposes, that dangerous powers not delegated, may not only be usurped and executed by the other departments, but that the Judicial Department may also exercise, or sanction dangerous powers beyond the grant of the Constitution, and consequently that the ultimate right of the parties to the Constitution to judge, whether the Compact has been dangerously violated, must extend to violations by one delegated authority, as well as by another—by the Judiciary, as well as by the Executive or Legislative."

Against these conclusive arguments, as they seem to me, it is objected, that if one party has the right to judge of infractions of the Constitution, so has the other, and that consequently in cases of contested powers between a State and the General Government, each would have a right to maintain its opinion, as is the case when sovereign powers differ in the construction of treaties or compacts, and that of course, it would come to be a mere question of force. The error is in the assumption, that the General Government is a party to the Constitutional Compact. The States, as has been shown, formed the compact, acting as sovereign and independent Communities. The General Government is but its creature; and though in reality a government with all the rights and authority which belong to any other government, within the orb of its powers, it is, nevertheless, a government emanating from a compact between sovereigns, and partaking in its nature and object, of the character of a joint commission, appointed to superintend and administer the interests in which all are jointly concerned, but having, beyond its proper sphere, no more power, than if it did not exist. To deny this would be to deny the most incontestible facts, and the clearest conclusions; while to acknowledge its truth is to destroy utterly the objection, that the appeal would be to force, in the case supposed. For if each party has a right to judge, then under our system of government, the final cognizance of a question of contested power would be in the States, and not in the general government. It would be the duty of the latter, as in all similar cases of a contest between one or more of the principals and a joint commission or agency, to refer the contest to the principals themselves. Such are the plain dictates of reason and analogy both. On no sound principle can the agents have a right to final cognizance, as against the principals, much less to use force against them, to maintain their construction of their powers. Such a right would be monstrous; and has never, heretofore, been claimed in similar cases.

That the doctrine is applicable to the case of a contested power between the States and the General Government, we have the authority not only of reason and analogy, but of the distinguished statesman already referred to. Mr. Jefferson, at a late period of his life, after long experience and mature reflection, says, "With respect to our state and federal governments, I do not think their relations are correctly understood by foreigners. They suppose the former are subordinate to the latter. This is not the case. They are co-ordinate departments of one simple and integral whole. But you may ask if the two departments should claim each the same subject of power, where is the umpire to decide between them? In cases of little urgency or importance, the prudence of both parties will keep them aloof from the questionable ground; but if it can neither be avoided nor compromised, a convention of the States must be called, to ascribe the doubtful power to that department which they may think best." It is thus that our Constitution by authorizing amendments, and by prescribing the authority and mode of making them, has by a simple contrivance, with its characteristic wisdom, provided a power which in the last resort, supercedes effectually the necessity, and even the pretext for force; a power to which none can fairly object; with which the interests of all are safe; which can definitively close all controversies in the only effectual mode, by freeing the compact of every defect and uncertainty, by an amendment of the instrument itself. It is impossible for human wisdom, in a system like ours, to devise another mode which shall be safe and effectual, and at the same time consistent with what are the relations and acknowledged powers of the two great departments of our government. It gives a beauty and security peculiar to our system, which, if duly appreciated, will transmit its blessings to the remotest generations; but if not, our splendid anticipation of the future will prove but an empty dream. Stripped of all its covering, the naked question is, whether ours is a federal or a consolidated government; a constitutional or absolute one; a government resting ultimately on the solid basis of the sovereignty of the States, or on the unrestrained will of a majority; a form of government, as in all other unlimited ones, in which injustice, and violence, and force must finally prevail. *Let it never be forgotten that where the majority rules the minority is the subject;* and that if we should absurdly attribute to the former, the exclusive right of construing the Constitution, there would be in fact between the sovereign and subject, under such a government, no Constitution; or at least nothing deserving the name, or serving the legitimate object of so sacred an instrument.

How the States are to exercise this high power of interposition which constitutes so essential a portion of their reserved rights that it *cannot be delegated without an entire surrender of their sovereignty,* and converting our system from a *federal* into a *consolidated* government is a question, that the States only, are competent to determine. The arguments which prove that they possess the power, equally prove, that they are in the language of Jefferson; *"the rightful judges of the mode and measure of redress."* But the spirit of forbearance, as well as the nature of the right itself, forbids a recourse to it, except in cases of dangerous infractions of the Constitution; & then only in the last resort, when all reasonable hope of relief, from the ordinary action of the government, has failed; when if the right to interpose did not exist, the alternative would be submission and oppression on one side, or resistance by force on the other. That our system should afford, in such extreme cases, an intermediate point between these dire alternatives, by which the government may be brought to a pause, and thereby an interval obtained to compromise differences, or, if impracticable, be compelled to submit the question to a constitutional adjustment, through an appeal to the States themselves, is an evidence of its high wisdom; an element not, as is supposed by some, of weakness, but of strength; not of anarchy or revolution, but of peace and safety. *Its general recognition would of itself in a great measure, if not altogether, supercede the necessity of its exercise, by impressing on the movements of the government, that moderation and justice so essential to harmony and peace, in a country of such vast extent, and diversity of interests as ours;* and would, if controversy should come, turn the resentment of the aggrieved, from the system to those who had abused its powers, (a point all important,) and cause them to seek redress, *not in revolution or overthrow, but in reformation.* It is, in fact, properly understood, *a substitute where the alternative would be force, tending to prevent, and if that fails, to correct peaceably, the aberrations to which all political systems are liable, and which, if permitted to accumulate, without correction, must finally end in a general catastrophe.*

I have now said what I intended in reference to the abstract question of the relation of the States to the general government, and would here conclude, did I not believe that a mere general statement on an abstract question, without including that which may have caused its agitation, would be considered by many imperfect, and unsatisfactory. Feeling that such would be justly the case, I am compelled, reluctantly, to touch on the Tariff, so far, at least, as may be necessary to illustrate the opinions which I have already advanced. Anxious, however, to intrude as little as possible, on the public attention, I will be as brief as possible; and with that view, will, as far as may be consistent with my object, avoid all debatable topics.

Whatever diversity of opinion may exist, in relation to the principle, or the effect on the productive industry of the country, of the present, or any other Tariff of protection, there are certain political consequences flowing from the present, which none can doubt, and all must deplore. It would be in vain to attempt to conceal, that it has divided the country into two great geographical divisions, and arrayed them against each other, in opinion at least, if not interests also, on some of the most vital of political subjects; on its finance, its commerce, and its industry; subjects calculated above all others, in time of peace, to produce excitement, and in relation to which, the Tariff has placed the sections in question in deep and dangerous conflict. If there be any point on which the (I was going to say, Southern section, but to avoid, as far as possible, the painful feelings such discussions are calculated to excite, I shall say) weaker of the two sections is unanimous, it is that its prosperity depends, in a great measure, on free trade, light taxes, economical, and, as far as possible, equal disbursements of the public revenue, and unshackled industry, leaving them to pursue whatever may appear most advantageous to their interests. From the Potomac to the Mississippi, there are few indeed, however divided on other points, who would not, if dependent on their volition and if they regarded the interest of their particular section only, remove from commerce and industry every shackle, reduce the revenue to the lowest point that the wants of the government fairly required, and restrict the appropriations to the most moderate scale, consistent with the peace, the security, and the engagements of the public; and who do not believe that the opposite system is calculated to throw on them an unequal burthen, to repress their prosperity, and to encroach on their enjoyment.

On all these deeply important measures, the opposite opinion prevails, if not with equal unanimity, with at least a greatly preponderating majority, in the other and stronger section; so much so, that no two distinct nations ever entertained more opposite views of policy than these two sections do, on all the important points to which I have referred. Nor is it less certain that this unhappy conflict, flowing directly from the Tariff, has extended itself to the halls of legislation, and has converted the deliberations of Congress into an annual struggle between the two sections; the stronger to maintain and increase the superiority it has already acquired, and the other to throw off, or diminish its burdens; a struggle in which all the noble and generous feelings of patriotism are gradually subsiding into sectional and selfish attachments.[2] Nor has the effect of this dangerous conflict ended here. It has not only divided the two sections on the important point already stated, but on the deeper and more dangerous questions, the constitutionality of a protective Tariff, and the general principles and theory of the Constitution itself; the stronger, in order to maintain their superiority, giving a construction to the instrument, which the other believes would convert the General Government into a consolidated, irresponsible government, with the total destruction of liberty; and the weaker seeing no hope of relief with such assumption of powers, turning its eye to the reserved sovereignty of the States, as the only refuge from oppression. I shall not extend these remarks, as I might, by shewing that while the effect of the system of protection was rapidly alienating one section, it was not less rapidly, by its necessary operation, distracting and corrupting the other; and between the two, subjecting the administration to violent and sudden changes, totally inconsistent with all stability and wisdom in the management of the affairs of the nation, of which we already see fearful symptoms. Nor do I deem it necessary to inquire whether this unhappy conflict grows out of true, or mistaken views of interest on either or both sides. Regarded in either light, it ought to admonish us of the extreme danger to which our system is exposed, and the great moderation and wisdom necessary to preserve it. If it comes from mistaken views, if the interests of the two sections as affected by the Tariff, be really the same, and the system instead of acting unequally, in reality diffuses equal blessings, and imposes equal burdens on every part, it ought to teach us how liable those, who are differently situated, and who view their interests under different aspects, are to come to different conclusions; even when their interests are strictly the same; and consequently, with what extreme caution any system of policy ought to be adopted, and with what a spirit of moderation pursued, in a country of such great extent and diversity as ours. But if on the contrary, the conflict springs really from contrariety of interests, if the burden be on one side, and the benefit on the other, then are we taught a lesson not less important, how little regard we have for the interests of others, while in pursuit of our own, or at least, how apt we are to consider our own interest, the interest of all others; and of course how great the danger in a country of such acknowledged diversity of interests, of the oppression of the feebler by the stronger interest, and in consequence of it, of the most fatal sectional conflicts. But whichever may be the cause, the real, or supposed diversity of interest, it cannot be doubted, that the political consequences of the prohibitory system, be its effects in other respects, beneficial, or otherwise, are really such, as I have stated; nor can it be doubted, that a conflict between the great sections on questions so vitally important, indicates a condition of the country, so distempered and dangerous, as to demand the most serious and prompt attention. It is only, when we come to consider of the remedy, that, under the aspect, I am viewing the subject, there can be, among the informed and considerate, any diversity of opinion.

Those, who have not duly reflected on its dangerous and inveterate character, suppose that the disease will cure itself; that events ought to be left to take their own course; and that experience, in a short time, will prove, that the interest of the whole community, is the same, in reference to the Tariff, or, at least, whatever diversity there may now be, time will assimilate. Such has been their language from the beginning, but unfortunately the progress of events has been the reverse. The country is now more divided than in 1824, and then, more than in 1816. The majority may have increased, but the opposite sides are beyond dispute more determined and excited, than at any preceding period. Formerly the system was resisted mainly, as inexpedient; but now, as unconstitutional, unequal, unjust and oppressive.

2. The system if continued, must end, not only in subjecting the industry and property of the weaker section to the control of the stronger, but in proscription and political disfranchisement. It must fully control elections and appointments to offices, as well as acts of legislation, to the great increase of the feelings of animosity, and of the fatal tendency to a complete alienation between the sections.

Then relief was sought exclusively from the General Government; but now, many driven to despair, are raising their eyes to the reserved sovereignty of the States, as the only refuge. If we turn from the past, and present to the future, we shall find nothing to lessen, but much to aggravate the danger. The increasing embarrassment, and distress of the staple States, the growing conviction, from experience, that they are caused by the prohibitory system principally, and that, under its continued operation, their present pursuits must become profitless, and with a conviction, that their great and peculiar agricultural capital, cannot be diverted from its ancient and hereditary channels, without ruinous losses, all concur to increase, instead of dispelling the gloom, that hangs over the future. In fact, to those who will duly reflect on the subject, the hope, that the disease will cure itself, must appear perfectly illusory. The question is in reality one between the exporting and non-exporting interests of the country. *Were there no exports, there would be no Tariff.* It would be perfectly useless. On the contrary, so long as there are States, which raise the great agricultural staples, with the view of obtaining their supplies, and which must depend, on the general market of the world, for their sales, the conflict must remain, if the system should continue, and the disease become more and more inveterate. Their interest, and that of those, who by high duties would confine the purchase of their supplies to the home market, must from the nature of things in reference to the Tariff, be in conflict. Till, then, we cease to raise the great staples cotton, rice and tobacco, for the general market, and till we can find some other profitable investment for the immense amount of capital and labour now employed in their production, the present unhappy and dangerous conflict cannot terminate unless with the prohibitory system itself.

In the meantime, while idly waiting for its termination through its own action, the progress of events, in another quarter, is rapidly bringing the contest, to an immediate and decisive issue. We are fast approaching a period, very novel in the history of nations, and bearing directly and powerfully on the point under consideration, the final payment of a long standing funded debt; a period that cannot be sensibly retarded, or the natural consequences of it eluded, without proving disastrous to those, who may attempt either, if not to the country itself. When it arrives, the Government would find itself in possession of a surplus revenue of $10,000, 000 or $12,000, 000, if not previously disposed of, which presents the important question what previous disposition ought to be made; a question which must press urgently for decision, at the very next session of Congress. It cannot be delayed longer, without the most distracting and dangerous consequences.

The honest and obvious course is, to prevent the accumulation of the surplus in the treasury, by a timely and judicious reduction of the imposts; and thereby to leave the money in the pockets of those who made it, and from whom, it cannot be honestly, nor constitutionally taken, unless required by the fair and legitimate wants of the Government. If, neglecting a disposition so obvious and just, the Government should attempt to keep up the present high duties, when the money was no longer wanted, or to dispose of this immense surplus by enlarging the old, or devising new schemes of appropriations, or, finding that to be impossible, it should adopt the most dangerous, unconstitutional and absurd project ever devised by any government, of dividing the surplus among the States: (a project, which, if carried into execution, could not fail to create an antagonist interest between the States and General Government on all questions of appropriations, which would certainly end in reducing the latter to a mere office of collection and distribution,) either of these modes would be considered by the section suffering under the present high duties as a fixed determination, to perpetuate forever what it considers the present unequal, unconstitutional, and oppressive burden; and from that moment, it would cease to look to the General Government for relief. This deeply interesting period, which must prove so disastrous, should a wrong direction be given, but so fortunate and glorious, should a right one, is just at hand. The work must commence at the next session, as I have stated, or be left undone, or, at least, be badly done. The succeeding session would be too short and too much agitated by the Presidential contest to afford the requisite leisure and calmness, and the one succeeding would find the country in the midst of the crisis, when it would be too late to prevent an accumulation of the surplus; which I hazard nothing in saying, judging from the nature of men and government, if once permitted to accumulate, would create an interest strong enough to perpetuate itself, supported as it would be by others, so numerous and powerful; and thus would pass away a moment, never to be quietly recalled, so precious, if properly used, to lighten the public burden; to equalize the action of the Government; to restore harmony and peace; and to present to the world the illustrious example which could not fail to prove most favourable to the great cause of liberty every where, of a nation the freest, and, at the same time, the best and most cheaply governed; of the highest earthly blessing, at the least possible sacrifice.

As the disease will not, then, heal itself, we are brought to the question, can a remedy be applied, and, if so, what ought it to be?

To answer in the negative, would be to assert, that our union has utterly failed; and that the opinion, so common before the adoption of our Constitution, that a free Government could not be practically extended over a large country, was correct—and that ours had been destroyed by giving it limits so great as to comprehend, not only dissimilar, but irreconcilable interests. I am not prepared to admit a conclusion, that would cast so deep a shade on the future, and that would falsify all the glorious anticipations of our ancestors while it would so greatly lessen their high reputation for wisdom. Nothing but the clearest demonstration, founded on actual experience will ever force me to a conclusion so abhorrent to all of my feelings. As strongly as I am impressed with the great dissimilarity, and, I must add, as truth compels me to do, contrariety of interests in our country, resulting from the causes already indicated, and which are so great, that they cannot be subjected to the unchecked will of a majority of the whole, without defeating the great end of government, and without which it is a curse, justice; yet I see in the union, as ordained by the Constitution, the means, if wisely used, not only of reconciling all diversities, but also the means and the only effectual one, of securing to us justice, peace and security, at home and abroad, and with them, that national power and renown the love of which Providence has implanted for wise purposes so deeply in the human heart; in all of which great objects every portion of our country widely extended and diversified as it is has a common and identical interest. If we have the wisdom to place a proper relative estimate on these more elevated, and durable blessings, the present and every other conflict of like character, may be readily terminated; but if, reversing the scale, each section should put a higher estimate on its immediate and peculiar gains; and acting in that spirit, should push favourite measures of mere policy, without some regard to peace, harmony or justice, our sectional conflicts would then indeed, without some constitutional check, become interminable, except by the dissolution of the Union itself. That we have, in fact so reversed the estimate, is too certain to be doubted, and the result is our present distempered and dangerous condition. The cure must commence in the correction of the error, and not to admit we have erred, would be the worst possible symptom. It would prove the disease to be incurable through the regular and ordinary process of legislation; and would compel finally, a resort to extraordinary, but I still trust, not only constitutional, but safe remedies.

No one would more sincerely rejoice than myself, to see the remedy applied from the quarter, where it could be most easily and regularly done. It is the only way by which those who think that it is the only quarter from which it can constitutionally come, can possibly sustain their opinion. To omit the application by the General Government, would compel even them to admit the truth of the opposite opinion; or force them to abandon our political system in despair; while on the other hand, all their enlightened and patriotic opponents would rejoice at such evidence of moderation and wisdom on the part of the General Government, as would supersede a resort to what they believe to be the higher powers of our political system, as indicating a sounder state of public sentiment than has ever heretofore existed in any country, and thus affording the highest possible assurance of the perpetuation of our glorious institutions to the latest generation. For as a people advance in knowledge, in the same degree they may dispense with mere artificial restrictions in their government: and we may imagine, (but dare not expect to see) a state of intelligence so universal and high, that all the guards of liberty may be dispensed with, except an enlightened public opinion acting through the right of suffrage; but it presupposes a state where every class and every section of the community are capable of estimating the effects of every measure, not only as it may affect itself, but every other class and section; and of fully realizing the sublime truth, that the highest and wisest policy consists in maintaining justice and promoting peace and harmony; and that compared to these, schemes of mere gain are but trash and dross. I fear experience has already proved that we are far removed from such a state, and that we must consequently rely on the old and clumsy, but approved mode of checking power in order to prevent or correct abuses; but I do trust that though far from perfect, we are at least so much so as to be capable of remedying the present disorder in the ordinary way; and thus to prove that with us public opinion is so enlightened, and our political machine so perfect, as rarely to require for its preservation, the intervention of the power that created it. How is this to be effected?

The application may be painful, but the remedy, I conceive, is certain and simple. There is but one effectual cure, an honest reduction of the duties to a fair system of revenue, adapted to the just and constitutional wants of the government. Nothing short of this will restore the country to peace, harmony, and mutual affection. There is already a deep and growing conviction in a large section of the country, that the impost, even as a revenue system, is extremely unequal, and that it is mainly paid by those who furnish the means of paying the foreign exchanges of the country, on which it is laid; and that the case is not varied, taking into the estimate the entire action of the system, whether the producer, or consumer pays in the first instance.

I do not propose to enter formally into the discursion of a point so complex and contested; but as it has necessarily a strong practical bearing on the subject under consideration, in all its relations, I cannot pass it without a few general and brief remarks.

If the producer in reality pays, none will doubt but the burden would mainly fall on the section it is supposed to do. The theory that the consumer pays in the first instance, renders the proposition more complex, and will require, in order to understand where the burden in reality ultimately falls, on that supposition, to consider the protective, or as its friends call it, the American System, under its threefold aspect, of taxation, of protection, and of distribution; or as performing at the same time the several functions of giving a revenue to the government, of affording protection to certain branches of domestic industry, and furnishing the means to Congress of distributing large sums through its appropriations; all of which are so blended in their effects, that it is impossible to understand its true operation, without taking the whole into the estimate.

Admitting then, as supposed, that he who consumes the article pays the tax in the increased price, and that the burden falls wholly on the consumers, without affecting the producers as a class, (which, by the by, is far from being true, except in the single case, if there be such a one, where the producers have a monopoly of an article, so indispensable to life, that the quantity consumed cannot be affected by any increase of price,) and that considered in the light of a tax, merely, the impost duties fall equally on every section, in proportion to its population, still when combined with its other effects, the burden it imposes, as a tax, may be so transferred from one section to the other, as to take it from one, and place it wholly on the other. Let us apply the remark first to its operation as a system of protection.

The tendency of the tax, or duty, on the imported article is, not only to raise its price, but also, in the same proportion, that of the domestic article of the same kind, for which purpose, when intended for protection, it is in fact laid; and of course, in determining where the system ultimately places the burden in reality, this effect also, must be taken into the estimate. If one of the sections exclusively produces such domestic articles, and the other purchases them from it, then it is clear that to the amount of such increased prices, the tax or duty, on the consumption of foreign articles, would be transferred from the section producing the domestic articles to the one that purchased and consumed them, unless the latter in turn, be indemnified by the increased price of the objects of its industry, which none will venture to assert to be the case with the great staples of the country, which form the basis of our exports, the price of which is regulated by the foreign and not the domestic market. To those who grow them, the increased price of the foreign and domestic articles both, in consequence of the duty on the former, is in reality, and in the strictest sense, a tax, while it is clear that the increased price of the latter acts as a bounty to the section producing them, and that as the amount of such increased prices, on what it sells to the other section, is greater or less, than the duty it pays on the imported articles, the system will in fact operate as a bounty or tax; if greater the difference would be a bounty; if less a tax.

Again, the operation may be equal in every other respect, and yet the pressure of the system, relatively, on the two sections, be rendered very unequal by the appropriations, or distribution. If each section receives back what it paid into the treasury, the equality if it previously existed will continue; but if one receives back less, and the other proportionably more than is paid, then the difference in relation to the sections will be to the former a loss, and to the latter a gain; and the system in this aspect would operate to the amount of the difference, as a contribution from the one receiving less than it paid, to the other that receives more. Such would be incontestably its general effects, taken in all its different aspects, even on the theory supposed to be most favourable to prove the equal action of the system, that the consumer pays in the first instance the whole amount of the tax.

To show how, on this supposition, the burden and advantages of the system would actually distribute themselves between the sections, would carry me too far into details; but I feel assured, after full and careful examination, that they are such as to explain, what otherwise would seem inexplicable, that one section should consider its repeal a calamity and the other a blessing; and that such opposite views should be taken by them, as to place them in a state of determined conflict, in relation to the great fiscal and commercial interest of the country. Indeed were there no satisfactory explanation, the opposite views that prevail, in the two sections, as to the effects of the system, ought to satisfy all of its unequal action. There can be no safer, or more certain rule, than to suppose each portion of the country equally capable of understanding their respective interests; and that each is a much better judge of the effects of any system or measures on its peculiar interest, than the other can possibly be.

But whether the opinion, of its unequal action, be correct, or erroneous, nothing can be more certain than that the impression is widely extending itself, that the system, under all its modifications, is essentially unequal; and if to this be added, a conviction still deeper and more universal, that every duty imposed *for the purpose of protection is not only unequal, but also unconstitutional*, it would be a fatal error to suppose, that any remedy, short of that which I have stated, can heal our political disorders.

In order to understand, more fully, the difficulty of adjusting this unhappy contest, on any other ground, it may not be improper to present a general view of the constitutional objection, that it may be clearly seen, how hopeless it is to expect that it can be yielded, by those who have embraced it.

They believe that all the powers, vested by the Constitution in Congress are not only restricted by the limitations expressly imposed, but also by the nature and object of the powers themselves. Thus though the power to impose duties on imports be granted in general terms without any other express limitations, but that they shall be equal, and no preference shall be given to the ports of one State over those of another, yet as being a portion of the taxing power, given with the view of raising revenue, it is from its nature restricted to that object, as much so as if the Convention had expressly so limited it; and that to use it to effect any other purpose, not specified in the Constitution, is an infraction of the instrument, in its most dangerous form; an infraction by perversion, more easily made, and more difficult to resist, than any other. The same view is believed to be applicable to the power of regulating commerce, as well as all the other powers. To surrender this important principle, it is conceived, would be to surrender all power, and to render the government unlimited and despotic; and to yield it up, in relation to the particular power in question, would be in fact to surrender the control of the whole industry and capital of the country to the General Government; and would end in placing the weaker section, in a colonial relation with the stronger. For nothing are more dissimilar in their nature, or may be more unequally affected by the same laws, than different descriptions of labour and property; and if taxes, by increasing the amount and changing the intent only, may be perverted, in fact, into a system of penalties and rewards, it would give all the power that could be desired, to subject the labour and property of the minority to the will of the majority, to be regulated without regarding the interest of the former, in subserviency to the will of the latter. Thus thinking, it would seem unreasonable to expect, that any adjustment, based on the recognition of the correctness of a construction of the Constitution, which would admit the exercise of such a power, would satisfy the weaker of the two sections, particularly with its peculiar industry and property, which experience has shown may be so injuriously effected by its exercise. Thus much for one side.

The just claim of the other ought to be equally respected. Whatever excitement, the system has justly caused, in certain portions of our country, I hope, and believe, all will conceive that the change, should be made with the least possible detriment to the interests of those, who may be liable to be affected by it, consistently with what is justly due to others and the principles of the Constitution. To effect this, will require the kindest spirit of conciliation, and the utmost skill; but, even with these, it will be impossible to make the transition, without a shock greater or less, though I trust, if judiciously effected, it will not be without many compensating advantages. That there will be some such, cannot be doubted. It will, at least, be followed by greater stability, and will tend to harmonize the manufacturing with all of the other great interests of the country, and bind the whole in mutual affection. But these are not all. Another advantage, of essential importance to the ultimate prosperity of our manufacturing industry will follow. *It will cheapen production;* and, in that view, the loss of any one branch, will be nothing like in proportion to the reduction of duty on that particular branch. Every reduction will, in fact, operate as a bounty to every other branch, except the one reduced; and thus the effect of a general reduction will be to cheapen, universally, the price of production, by cheapening living, wages and materials; so as to give, if not equal profits after the reduction, profits by no means reduced proportionally to the duties; an effect, which, as it regards the foreign market, is of the utmost importance. It must be apparent on reflection, that the means adopted to secure the home market, for our manufactures are precisely the opposite of those necessary to obtain the foreign. In the former, the increased expense of production in consequence of a system of protection may be more than compensated by the increased price at home of the article protected; but, in the latter this advantage is lost, and as there is no other corresponding compensation, the increased cost of production must be a dead loss in the foreign market. But whether these advantages and many others, that might be mentioned, will ultimately compensate to the full extent, or not, the loss to the manufacturers on the reduction of the duties, certain it is, that we have approached a point at which a great change cannot be much longer delayed; and that the more promptly it may be met, the less excitement there will be, and the greater leisure and calmness for a cautious and skilful operation in making the transition; and which it becomes those more immediately interested duly to consider. Nor ought they to overlook, in considering the question, the different character of the claims of the two sides. The one asks from the Government no advantage, but simply to be let alone in the undisturbed possession of their natural advantages, and to secure which, as far as was consistent with the other objects of the Constitution, was one of their leading motives in entering into the Union; while the other side claims, for the advancement of their prosperity, the positive interference of the Government. In such cases, on every principle of fairness and justice, such interference ought to be restrained within limits strictly compatible with the natural advantages of the other. He who, looking to all of the causes in operation; the near approach of the final payment of the public debt, the growing disaffection and resistance to the system, in so large a section of the country, the deeper principles on which opposition to it is gradually turning, must be, indeed, infatuated not to see a great change is unavoidable; and that the attempt to elude or much longer delay it must finally, but increase the shock, and disastrous consequences which may follow.

In forming the opinions, I have expressed, I have not been actuated by any unkind feeling towards our manufacturing interest. I now am, and ever have been decidedly friendly to them, though I cannot concur in all of the measures which have been adopted to advance them. I believe, considerations higher than any question of mere pecuniary interest, forbids their use. But subordinate to these higher views of policy, I regard the advancement of mechanical and chemical improvements in the arts with feelings little short of enthusiasm; not only, as the prolific source of national & individual wealth, but, as the great means of enlarging the domain of man over the material world; and, thereby, of laying the solid foundation of a highly improved condition of society, morally and politically. I fear not, that we shall extend our power too far over the great agents of nature; but, on the contrary, I consider such enlargement of our power, as tending, more certainly and powerfully, to better the condition of our race, than any one of the many powerful causes, now operating to that result. With these impressions, I not only rejoice at the general progress of the arts in the world, but in their advancement in our own country; and, as far as protection can be incidentally afforded, in the fair and honest exercise of our constitutional powers, I think now, as I have always done, that sound policy, connected with the security, independence and peace of the country, requires them to be protected, but, that we cannot go a single step beyond, without jeopardizing our peace, our harmony and our liberty; considerations of infinitely more importance to us than any measure of mere policy, can possibly be.

In thus placing my opinions before the public, I have not been actuated by the expectation of changing the public sentiment. Such a motive, on a question so long agitated, and so beset with feelings of prejudice and interest, would argue, on my part, an insufferable vanity, and a profound ignorance of the human heart. To avoid, as far as possible, the imputation of either, I have confined my statement on the many and important points, on which I have been compelled to touch, to a simple declaration of my opinion, without advancing any other reasons to sustain them, than what, appeared to me, to be indispensable to the full understanding of my views; and, if they should, on any point, be thought to be not clearly and explicitly developed, it will, I trust, be attributed to my solicitude to avoid the imputations to which I have alluded; and not from any desire to disguise my sentiments; nor the want of arguments and illustrations to maintain positions, which so abound in both, that it would require a volume to do them any thing like justice. I can only hope, that truths, which I feel assured, are essentially connected with all that we ought to hold most dear, may not be weakened in the public estimation by the imperfect manner, in which I have been by the object in view compelled to present them.

With every caution on my part, I dare not hope, in taking the step I have, to escape the imputation of improper motives; though I have without reserve, freely expressed my opinions, not regarding whether they might, or might not, be popular. I have no reason to believe, that they are such, as will conciliate public favour, but the opposite; which I greatly regret, as I have ever placed a high estimate on the good opinion of my fellow citizens. But be that as it may, I shall, at least, be sustained by feelings of conscious rectitude. I have formed my opinions after the most careful and deliberate examination, with all the aids, which, my reason and experience could furnish; I have expressed them honestly and fearlessly, regardless of their effects personally; which, however interesting to me individually, are of too little importance, to be taken into the estimate, where the liberty and happiness of our country are so vitally involved.

John Marshall

Cherokee Nation v. State of Georgia (1831)

Mr. Chief Justice Marshall delivered the opinion of the Court.

This bill is brought by the Cherokee nation, praying an injunction to restrain the state of Georgia from the execution of certain laws of that state, which, as is alleged, go directly to annihilate the Cherokees as a political society, and to seize, for the use of Georgia, the lands of the nation which have been assured to them by the United States in solemn treaties repeatedly made and still in force.

If Courts were permitted to indulge their sympathies, a case better calculated to excite them can scarcely be imagined. A people once numerous, powerful, and truly independent, found by our ancestors in the quiet and uncontrolled possession of an ample domain, gradually sinking beneath our superior policy, our arts and our arms, have yielded their lands by successive treaties, each of which contains a solemn guarantee of the residue, until they retain no more of their formerly extensive territory than is deemed necessary to their comfortable subsistence. To preserve this remnant, the present application is made.

Before we can look into the merits of the case, a preliminary inquiry presents itself. Has this Court jurisdiction of the cause?

The third article of the Constitution describes the extent of the judicial power. The second section closes an enumeration of the cases to which it is extended, with "controversies" "between a state or the citizens thereof, and foreign states, citizens, or subjects." A subsequent clause of the same section gives the Supreme Court original jurisdiction in all cases in which a state shall be a party. The party defendant may then unquestionably be sued in this Court. May the plaintiff sue in it? Is the Cherokee nation a foreign state in the sense in which that term is used in the Constitution?

The counsel for the plaintiffs have maintained the affirmative of this proposition with great earnestness and ability. So much of the argument as was intended to prove the character of the Cherokees as a state, as a distinct political society, separated from others, capable of managing its own affairs and governing itself, has, in the opinion of a majority of the judges, been completely successful. They have been uniformly treated as a state from the settlement of our country. The numerous treaties made with them by the United States recognize them as a people capable of maintaining the relations of peace and war, of being responsible in their political character for any violation of their engagements, or for any aggression committed on the citizens of the United States by any individual of their community. Laws have been enacted in the spirit of these treaties. The acts of our government plainly recognize the Cherokee nation as a state, and the courts are bound by those acts.

A question of much more difficulty remains. Do the Cherokees constitute a foreign state in the sense of the Constitution?

The counsel have shown conclusively that they are not a state of the union, and have insisted that individually they are aliens, not owing allegiance to the United States. An aggregate of aliens composing a state must, they say, be a foreign state. Each individual being foreign, the whole must be foreign.

This argument is imposing, but we must examine it more closely before we yield to it. The condition of the Indians in relation to the United States is perhaps unlike that of any other two people in existence. In the general, nations not owing a common allegiance are foreign to each other. The term foreign nation is, with strict propriety, applicable by either to the other. But the relation of the Indians to the United States is marked by peculiar and cardinal distinctions which exist no where else. The Indian territory is admitted to compose a part of the United States. In all our maps, geographical treatises, histories, and laws, it is so considered. In all our intercourse with foreign nations, in our commercial regulations, in any attempt at intercourse between Indians and foreign nations, they are considered as within the jurisdictional limits of the United States, subject to many of those restraints which are imposed upon our own citizens. They acknowledge themselves in their treaties to be under the protection of the United States; they admit that the United States shall have the sole and exclusive right of regulating the trade with them, and managing all their affairs as they think proper; and the Cherokees in particular were allowed by the treaty of Hopewell, which preceded the Constitution, "to send a deputy of their choice, whenever they think fit, to Congress." Treaties were made with some tribes by the state of New York, under a then unsettled construction of the confederation, by which they ceded all their lands to that state, taking back a limited grant to themselves, in which they admit their dependence.

Though the Indians are acknowledged to have an unquestionable, and, heretofore, unquestioned right to the lands they occupy, until that right shall be extinguished by a voluntary cession to our government; yet it may well be doubted whether those tribes which reside within the acknowledged boundaries of the United States can, with strict accuracy, be denominated foreign nations. They may, more correctly, perhaps, be denominated domestic dependent nations. They occupy a territory to which we assert a title independent of their will, which must take effect in point of possession when their right of possession ceases. Meanwhile they are in a state of pupilage.

Their relation to the United States resembles that of a ward to his guardian.

They look to our government for protection; rely upon its kindness and its power; appeal to it for relief to their wants; and address the president as their great father. They and their country are considered by foreign nations, as well as by ourselves, as being so completely under the sovereignty and dominion of the United States, that any attempt to acquire their lands, or to form a political connexion with them, would be considered by all as an invasion of our territory, and an act of hostility.

These considerations go far to support the opinion, that the framers of our Constitution had not the Indian tribes in view, when they opened the courts of the union to controversies between a state or the citizens thereof, and foreign states.

In considering this subject, the habits and usages of the Indians, in their intercourse with their white neighbours, ought not to be entirely disregarded. At the time the Constitution was framed, the idea of appealing to an American court of justice for an assertion of right or a redress of wrong, had perhaps never entered the mind of an Indian or of his tribe. Their appeal was to the tomahawk, or to the government. This was well understood by the statesmen who framed the Constitution of the United States, and might furnish some reason for omitting to enumerate them among the parties who might sue in the courts of the union. Be this as it may, the peculiar relations between the United States and the Indians occupying our territory are such, that we should feel much difficulty in considering them as designated by the term foreign state, were there no other part of the Constitution which might shed light on the meaning of these words. But we think that in construing them, considerable aid is furnished by that clause in the eighth section of the third article; which empowers Congress to "regulate commerce with foreign nations, and among the several states, and with the Indian tribes."

In this clause they are as clearly contradistinguished by a name appropriate to themselves, from foreign nations, as from the several states composing the union. They are designated by a distinct appellation; and as this appellation can be applied to neither of the others, neither can the appellation distinguishing either of the others be in fair construction applied to them. The objects, to which the power of regulating commerce might be directed, are divided into three distinct classes—foreign nations, the several states, and Indian tribes. When forming this article, the convention considered them as entirely distinct. We cannot assume that the distinction was lost in framing a subsequent article, unless there be something in its language to authorize the assumption.

The counsel for the plaintiffs contend that the words—"Indian tribes" were introduced into the article, empowering Congress to regulate commerce, for the purpose of removing those doubts in which the management of Indian affairs was involved by the language of the ninth article of the confederation. Intending to give the whole power of managing those affairs to the government about to be instituted, the convention conferred it explicitly; and omitted those qualifications which embarrassed the exercise of it as granted in the confederation. This may be admitted without weakening the construction which has been intimated. Had the Indian tribes been foreign nations, in the view of the convention; this exclusive power of regulating intercourse with them might have been, and most probably would have been, specifically given, in language indicating that idea, not in language contradistinguishing them from foreign nations. Congress might have been empowered "to regulate commerce with foreign nations, including the Indian tribes, and among the several states." This language would have suggested itself to statesmen who considered the Indian tribes as foreign nations, and were yet desirous of mentioning them particularly.

It has been also said, that the same words have not necessarily the same meaning attached to them when found in different parts of the same instrument: their meaning is controlled by the context. This is undoubtedly true. In common language the same word has various meanings, and the peculiar sense in which it is used in any sentence is to be determined by the context. This may not be equally true with respect to proper names. Foreign nations is a general term, the application of which to Indian tribes, when used in the American Constitution, is at best extremely questionable. In one article in which a power is given to be exercised in regard to foreign nations generally, and to the Indian tribes particularly, they are mentioned as separate in terms clearly contradistinguishing them from each other. We perceive plainly that the Constitution in this article does not comprehend Indian tribes in the general term "foreign nations," not we presume because a tribe may not be a nation, but because it is not foreign to the United States. When, afterwards, the term "foreign state" is introduced, we cannot impute to the convention the intention to desert its former meaning, and to comprehend Indian tribes within it, unless the context force that construction on us. We find nothing in the context, and nothing in the subject of the article, which leads to it.

The Court has bestowed its best attention on this question, and, after mature deliberation, the majority is of opinion that an Indian tribe or nation within the United States is not a foreign state in the sense of the Constitution, and cannot maintain an action in the Courts of the United States.

A serious additional objection exists to the jurisdiction of the Court. Is the matter of the bill the proper subject for judicial inquiry and decision? It seeks to restrain a state from the forcible exercise of legislative power over a neighbouring people, asserting their independence; their right to which the state denies. On several of the matters alleged in the bill, for example on the laws making it criminal to exercise the usual powers of self government in their own country by the Cherokee nation, this Court cannot interpose; at least in the form in which those matters are presented.

That part of the bill which respects the land occupied by the Indians, and prays the aid of the Court to protect their possession, may be more doubtful. The mere question of right might perhaps be decided by this Court in a proper case with proper parties. But the Court is asked to do more than decide on the title. The bill requires us to control the legislature of Georgia, and to restrain the exertion of its physical force. The propriety of such an interposition by the Court may be well questioned. It savours too much of the exercise of political power to be within the proper province of the judicial department. But the opinion on the point respecting parties makes it unnecessary to decide this question.

If it be true that the Cherokee nation have rights, this is not the tribunal in which those rights are to be asserted. If it be true that wrongs have been inflicted, and that still greater are to be apprehended, this is not the tribunal which can redress the past or prevent the future.

The motion for an injunction is denied.

Worcester v. Georgia (1832)

Mr. Chief Justice MARSHALL delivered the opinion of the Court.

This cause, in every point of view in which it can be placed, is of the deepest interest.

The defendant is a state, a member of the union, which has exercised the powers of government over a people who deny its jurisdiction, and are under the protection of the United States.

The plaintiff is a citizen of the state of Vermont, condemned to hard labour for four years in the penitentiary of Georgia; under colour of an act which he alleges to be repugnant to the Constitution, laws, and treaties of the United States. [. . .]

The indictment charges the plaintiff in error, and others, being white persons, with the offence of "residing within the limits of the Cherokee nation without a license," and "without having taken the oath to support and defend the Constitution and laws of the state of Georgia."

The defendant in the state court appeared in proper person, and filed the following plea:

> And the said Samuel A. Worcester, in his own proper person, comes and says, that this Court ought not to take further cognizance of the action and prosecution aforesaid, because, he says, that, on the 15th day of July in the year 1831, he was, and still is, a resident in the Cherokee nation; and that the said supposed crime or crimes, and each of them, were committed, if committed at all, at the town of New Echota, in the said Cherokee nation, out of the jurisdiction of this Court, and not in the county Gwinnett, or elsewhere,

within the jurisdiction of this Court: and this defendant saith, that he is a citizen of the state of Vermont, one of the United States of America, and that he entered the aforesaid Cherokee nation in the capacity of a duly authorised missionary of the American Board of Commissioners for Foreign Missions, under the authority of the president of the United States, and has not since been required by him to leave it: that he was, at the time of his arrest, engaged in preaching the gospel to the Cherokee Indians, and in translating the sacred scriptures into their language, with the permission and approval of the said Cherokee nation, and in accordance with the humane policy of the government of the United States for the civilization and improvement of the Indians; and that his residence there, for this purpose, is the residence charged in the aforesaid indictment; and this defendant further saith, that this prosecution the state of Georgia ought not to have or maintain, because, he saith, that several treaties have, from time to time, been entered into between the United States and the Cherokee nation of Indians . . . all which treaties have been duly ratified by the senate of the United States of America; and, by which treaties, the United States of America acknowledge the said Cherokee nation to be a sovereign nation, authorised to govern themselves, and all persons who have settled within their territory, free from any right of legislative interference by the several states composing the United States of America, in reference to acts done within their own territory. . . .

This plea was overruled by the Court. And the prisoner, being arraigned, plead not guilty. The jury found a verdict against him, and the Court sentenced him to hard labour, in the penitentiary, for the term of four years. [. . .]

The plea avers, that the residence, charged in the indictment, was under the authority of the president of the United States, and with the permission and approval of the Cherokee nation. That the treaties, subsisting between the United States, and the Cherokees, acknowledge their right as a sovereign nation to govern themselves and all persons who have settled within their territory, free from any right of legislative interference by the several states composing the United States of America. That the act under which the prosecution was instituted is repugnant to the said treaties, and is, therefore, unconstitutional and void. That the said act is, also, unconstitutional; because it interferes with, and attempts to regulate and control, the intercourse with the Cherokee nation, which belongs, exclusively, to Congress; and, because, also, it is repugnant to the statute of the United States, entitled "an act to regulate trade and intercourse with the Indian tribes, and to preserve peace on the frontiers," [. . .]

The first step, then, in the inquiry, which the Constitution and laws impose on this Court, is an examination of the rightfulness of this claim.

America, separated from Europe by a wide ocean, was inhabited by a distinct people, divided into separate nations, independent of each other and of the rest of the world, having institutions of their own, and governing themselves by their own laws. It is difficult to comprehend the proposition, that the inhabitants of either quarter of the globe could have rightful original claims of dominion over the inhabitants of the other, or over the lands they occupied; or that the discovery of either by the other should give the discoverer rights in the country discovered, which annulled the pre-existing rights of its ancient possessors. [. . .]

But power, war, conquest, give rights, which, after possession, are conceded by the world; and which can never be controverted by those on whom they descend. We proceed, then, to the actual state of things, having glanced at their origin; because holding it in our recollection might shed some light on existing pretensions.

The great maritime powers of Europe discovered and visited different parts of this continent at nearly the same time. [. . .] To avoid bloody conflicts, which might terminate disastrously to all, it was necessary for the nations of Europe to establish some principle which all would acknowledge, and which should decide their respective rights as between themselves. This principle, suggested by the actual state of things, was, "that discovery gave title to the government by whose subjects or by whose authority it was made, against all other European governments, which title might be consummated by possession."

This principle, acknowledged by all Europeans [. . .] gave to the nation making the discovery [. . .] the sole right of acquiring the soil and of making settlements on it. It was an exclusive principle which shut out the right of competition among those who had agreed to it; not one which could annul the previous rights of those who had not agreed to it. It regulated the right given by discovery among the European discoverers; but could not affect the rights of those already in possession, either as aboriginal occupants, or as occupants by virtue of a discovery made before the memory of man. It gave the exclusive right to purchase, but did not found that right on a denial of the right of the possessor to sell. [. . .]

Soon after Great Britain determined on planting colonies in America, the king granted charters to companies of his subjects who associated for the purpose of carrying the views of the crown into effect, and of enriching themselves. [. . .] They purport, generally, to convey the soil, from the Atlantic to the South Sea. [. . .] They were well understood to convey the title which, according to the common law of European sovereigns respecting America, they might rightfully convey, and no more. This was the exclusive right of purchasing such lands as the natives were willing to sell. The crown could not be understood to grant what the crown did not affect to claim; nor was it so understood. [. . .]

[O]ur history furnishes no example, from the first settlement of our country, of any attempt on the part of the crown to interfere with the internal affairs of the Indians, farther than to keep out the agents of foreign powers, who, as traders or otherwise, might seduce them into foreign alliances. [. . .] He [. . .] purchased their alliance and dependence by subsidies; but never intruded into the interior of their affairs, or interfered with their self-government, so far as respected themselves only. [. . .]

Such was the policy of Great Britain towards the Indian nations inhabiting the territory from which she excluded all other Europeans; such her claims, and such her practical exposition of the charters she had granted: she considered them as nations capable of maintaining the relations of peace and war; of governing themselves, under her protection; and she made treaties with them, the obligation of which she acknowledged.

This was the settled state of things when the war of our revolution commenced. The influence of our enemy was established; her resources enabled her to keep up that influence; and the colonists had much cause for the apprehension that the Indian nations would, as the allies of Great Britain, add their arms to hers. This, as was to be expected, became an object of great solicitude to Congress. Far from advancing a claim to their lands, or asserting any right of dominion over them, Congress resolved "that the securing and preserving the friendship of the Indian nations appears to be a subject of the utmost moment to these colonies."

The early journals of Congress exhibit the most anxious desire to conciliate the Indian nations. Three Indian departments were established; and commissioners appointed in each, "to treat with the Indians in their respective departments, in the name and on the behalf of the United Colonies, in order to preserve peace and friendship with the said Indians, and to prevent their taking any part in the present commotions."

The most strenuous exertions were made to procure those supplies on which Indian friendships were supposed to depend; and every thing which might excite hostility was avoided. [. . .]

The treaty of Hopewell seems not to have established a solid peace. To accommodate the differences still existing between the state of Georgia and the Cherokee nation, the treaty of Holston was negotiated in July 1791. [. . .] The mutual desire of establishing permanent peace and friendship, and of removing all causes of war, is honestly avowed, and, in pursuance of this desire, the first article declares, that there shall be perpetual peace and friendship between all the citizens of the United States of America and all the individuals composing the Cherokee nation.

The second article repeats the important acknowledgement, that the Cherokee nation is under the protection of the United States of America, and of no other sovereign whosoever.

The meaning of this has been already explained. The Indian nations were, from their situation, necessarily dependent on some foreign potentate for the supply of their essential wants, and for their protection from lawless and injurious intrusions into their country. That power was naturally termed their protector. They had been arranged under the protection of Great Britain: but the extinguishment of the British power in their neighbourhood, and the establishment of that of the United States in its place, led naturally to the declaration, on the part of the Cherokees, that they were under the protection of the United States, and of no other power. They assumed the relation with the United States, which had before subsisted with Great Britain.

This relation was that of a nation claiming and receiving the protection of one more powerful: not that of individuals abandoning their national character, and submitting as subjects to the laws of a master. [. . .]

To the general pledge of protection have been added several specific pledges, deemed valuable by the Indians. Some of these restrain the citizens of the United States from encroachments on the Cherokee country, and provide for the punishment of intruders.

From the commencement of our government, Congress has passed acts to regulate trade and intercourse with the Indians; which treat them as nations, respect their rights, and manifest a firm purpose to afford that protection which treaties stipulate. All these acts, and especially that of 1802, which is still in force, manifestly consider the several Indian nations as distinct political communities, having territorial boundaries, within which their authority is exclusive, and having a right to all the lands within those boundaries, which is not only acknowledged, but guarantied by the United States.

In 1819, Congress passed an act for promoting those humane designs of civilizing the neighbouring Indians. [. . .]

This act avowedly contemplates the preservation of the Indian nations as an object sought by the United States, and proposes to effect this object by civilizing and converting them from hunters into agriculturists. Though the Cherokees had already made considerable progress in this improvement, it cannot be doubted that the general words of the act comprehend them. [. . .] This act furnishes strong additional evidence of a settled purpose to fix the Indians in their country by giving them security at home.

The treaties and laws of the United States contemplate the Indian territory as completely separated from that of the states; and provide that all intercourse with them shall be carried on exclusively by the government of the union. Is this the rightful exercise of power, or is it usurpation?

While these states were colonies, this power, in its utmost extent, was admitted to reside in the crown. When our revolutionary struggle commenced [. . .], Congress was considered as invested with all the powers of war and peace, and Congress dissolved our connexion with the mother country, and declared these United Colonies to be independent states. Without any written definition of powers, they employed diplomatic agents to represent the United States at the several courts of Europe; offered to negotiate treaties with them, and did actually negotiate treaties with France. From the same necessity, and on the same principles, Congress assumed the management of Indian affairs; first in the name of these United Colonies; and, afterwards, in the name of the United States. Early attempts were made at negotiation, and to regulate trade with them. These not proving successful, war was carried on under the direction, and with the forces of the United States, and the efforts to make peace, by treaty, were earnest and incessant. The confederation found Congress in the exercise of the same powers of peace and war, in our relations with Indian nations, as will those of Europe. [. . .]

The Indian nations had always been considered as distinct, independent political communities, retaining their original natural rights, as the undisputed possessors of the soil, from time immemorial, with the single exception of that imposed by irresistible power, which excluded them from intercourse with any other European potentate than the first discoverer of the coast of the particular region claimed: and this was a restriction which those European potentates imposed on themselves, as well as on the Indians. The very term "nation," so generally applied to them, means "a people distinct from others." The Constitution, by declaring treaties already made, as well as those to be made, to be the supreme law of the land, has adopted and sanctioned the previous treaties with the Indian nations, and consequently admits their rank among those powers who are capable of making treaties. The words "treaty" and "nation" are words of our own language, selected in our diplomatic and legislative proceedings, by ourselves, having each a definite and well understood meaning. We have applied them to Indians, as we have applied them to the other nations of the earth. They are applied to all in the same sense.

Georgia, herself, has furnished conclusive evidence that her former opinions on this subject concurred with those entertained by her sister states, and by the government of the United States. Various acts of her legislature have been cited in the argument, including the contract of cession made in the year 1802, all tending to prove her acquiescence in the universal conviction that the Indian nations possessed a full right to the lands they occupied, until that right should be extinguished by the United States, with their consent: that their territory was separated from that of any state within whose chartered limits they might reside, by a boundary line, established by treaties: that, within their boundary, they possessed rights with which no state could interfere: and that the whole power of regulating the intercourse with them, was vested in the United States. [. . .]

The Cherokee nation, then, is a distinct community occupying its own territory, with boundaries accurately described, in which the laws of Georgia can have no force, and which the citizens of Georgia have no right to enter, but with the assent of the Cherokees themselves, or in conformity with treaties, and with the acts of Congress. The whole intercourse between the United States and this nation, is, by our Constitution and laws, vested in the government of the United States.

The act of the state of Georgia, under which the plaintiff in error was prosecuted, is consequently void, and the judgment a nullity. [. . .]

T. Hartley Crawford

Annual Report of the Commissioner of Indian Affairs (1838)

[. . .] The principal lever by which the Indians are to be lifted out of the mire of folly and vice in which they are sunk is education. The learning of the already civilized and cultivated man is not what they want now. It could not be advantageously ingrafted on so rude a stock. In the present state of their social existence, all they could be taught, or would learn, is to read and write, with a very limited knowledge of figures. There are exceptions, but in the general the remark is true, and perhaps more is not desirable or would be useful. As they advance, a more liberal culture of their minds may be effected, if happily they should yield to the influences that, if not roughly thrust back, will certainly follow in the wake of properly directed efforts to improve their understandings. To attempt too much at once is to insure failure. You must lay the foundations broadly and deeply, but gradually, if you would succeed. To teach a savage man to read, while he continues a savage in all else, is to throw seed on a rock. In this particular there has been a general error. If you would win an Indian from the waywardness and idleness and vice of his life, you must improve his morals, as well as his mind, and that not merely by precept, but by teaching him how to farm, now to work in the mechanic arts, and how to labor profitably; so that, by enabling him to find his comfort in changed pursuits, he will fall into those habits which are in keeping with the useful application of such education as may be given him. Thus too, only, it is conceived, are men to be christianized; the beginning is some education, social and moral lives, the end may be the brightest hope: but this allusion ought not, perhaps, to have been made; upon it I certainly will not enlarge; it is in better hands. Manual-labor schools are what the Indian condition calls for. The Missionary Society of the Methodist Episcopal Church has laid before the department a plan, based upon the idea suggested, for establishing a large central school for the education of the Western Indians. Into their scheme enter a farm, and shops for teaching the different mechanic arts. Experience, they say, has shown them, after much opportunity for judging correctly, that separate schools for the respective tribes, though productive of much good, are not so useful as one common school for the benefit of all would be. They assert truly that a knowledge of the English language is necessary, and they think that it can be best acquired in an establishment of the latter description. I would not hazard a different opinion; and yet it may not be improper to state that the funds which have been set apart for education purposes belong to the several tribes, without whose consent the Government could not devote them to a general school; and this the society admits. There is no disposition to discourage the efforts of those who choose to labor in this work of benevolence. On the contrary, there is, as there should be, an eagerness to meet any advance which promises greater facilities for improving the mind and morals of the Indian. Upon success in this department hangs every hope. All that can be done to encourage and cheer on those who have devised this scheme of goodness and charity, I think, should be done. But, whatever reform may be deemed advisable in the direction and economy of the separate schools, it appears to me that if the proposed central school shall be established, they should be kept up too. [. . .]

There is one measure that, in my judgment, is of great importance; it has heretofore attracted the attention of Congress, and I hope will meet with favor. As any plan for the government of the western tribes of Indians contemplates an interior police of their own, in each community, and that their own laws shall prevail, as between themselves, for which some of their treaties provide, this, as it seems to me, indispensable step to their advancement in civilization cannot be taken without their own consent. Unless some system is marked out by which there shall be a separate allotment of land to each individual whom the scheme shall entitle to it, you will look in vain for any general casting off of savagism. Common property and civilization cannot co-exist. The few instances to be found in the United States and other countries of small abstracted communities, who draw their subsistence and whatever comforts they have from a common store, do not militate against this position. Under a show of equality, the mass work for two or three rulers or directors, who enjoy what they will, and distribute what they please. The members never rise beyond a certain point, (to which they had reached, generally, before they joined the society,) and never will while they remain where they are. But if they should, these associations are so small and confined as to place their possessions in the class of individual estates. At the foundation of the whole social system lies individuality of property. It is, perhaps, nine times in ten the stimulus that manhood first feels. It has produced the energy, industry, and enterprise that distinguish the civilized world, and contributes more largely to the good morals of men than those are willing to acknowledge who have not looked somewhat closely at their fellow-beings. With it come all the delights that the word home expresses; the comforts that follow fixed settlements are in its train, and to them belongs not only an anxiety to do right that those gratification may not be forfeited, but industry that they may be increased. Social intercourse and a just appreciation of its pleasures result, when you have civilized, and, for the most part, moral men. This process, it strikes me, the Indians must go through, before their habits can be materially changed, and they may, after what many of them have seen and know, do it very rapidly. If, on the other hand, the large tracts of land set apart for them shall continue to be joint property, the ordinary motive to industry (and the most powerful one) will be wanting. A bare subsistence is as much as they can promise themselves. A few acres of badly cultivated corn about their cabins will be seen, instead of extensive fields, rich pastures, and valuable stock. The latter belong to him who is conscious that what he ploughs is his own, and will descend to those he loves; never to the man who does not know by what tenure he holds his miserable dwelling. Laziness and unthrift will be so general as not to be disgraceful; and if the produce of their labors should be thrown into common stock, the indolent and dishonest will subsist at the expense of the meritorious. Besides, there is a strong motive in reference to ourselves for encouraging individual ownership. The history of the world proves that distinct and separate possessions make those who hold them averse to change. The risk of losing the advantages they have, men do not readily encounter. By adopting and acting on the view suggested, a large body will be created whose interest would dispose them to keep things steady. They would be the ballast of the ship.

Plans have at various times been proposed for a confederation of the Indian tribes west of the Mississippi, embracing those who shall hereafter remove. I incline much to doubt the expedience of such a measure. It could only be executed with the consent of the tribes that might become members of it. The Choctaws have twice signified their disinclination to it. The treaty with the Cherokees of December, 1835, discourages it. The idea of such a bond between dependant communities is new. The league could only be for regulation among themselves, and not for mutual protection, which is the usual object of such combinations. They have no common property to secure, or common interest to advance. Any plan I have seen is based upon the power of the President to reject their articles of association, which exhibits strikingly their true position. They may be likened to colonies, among whom a confederation does not exist. They are governed, and their legislation, by each community for itself, is supervised and controlled, by the parent country. When they contemplate a different attitude, they confederate. A general council of the Indians might pass resolutions of a pacific character, or to arrest actual hostilities, and to regulate their intercourse with each other, but this could be done better by Congress, leaving to each tribe the management of its own internal concerns, not interfering with treaties or laws. There are inherent difficulties in the dissimilar conditions of the tribes. Some of them are semi civilized, others as wild as the game they hunt. Some are rich, others poor. Some number but a few hundred souls, others more thousands. We cannot frame for them, much less could they do it, articles of confederation which would bring into council a just representation of the different tribes. If you allot so many representatives to a tribe, looking to its population, the smaller would be swallowed up in the larger. If you limit to a certain number, or within or between two numbers, you are unjust to the larger tribes, which a combination of the smaller, with fewer motives to rectitude, might control. A small proportion of all might come into the confederation, and these separated from each other by bands who would not join in the arrangement, and would not on any principle be bound by the resolves of the general council. We owe duties to ourselves. Cogent reasons for not giving to these neighboring communities more concentration than they have must be seen. While they are treated with all kindness, tenderness even, and liberality, prudential considerations would seem to require that they should be kept distinct from each other. Let them manage their internal police after their own views. One or more superintendents, and as many agencies as may be deemed proper, with such regulation of their intercourse with each other, and such guards for their protection, as Congress shall think fit to prescribe, would, it appears to me, meet the emergence. Through the officers thus stationed among them, they could make their complaints known, and ask redress for grievances, which would be afforded when it was proper. It is not understood that the deliberations of the council could result in any act that would be valid, until approved by the chief magistrate, which does not lessen the force of what has been said.

It would perhaps be judicious not to pay a compliment at some hazard, especially where it would not be appreciated, but to assert directly for general purposes the authority which actually exists, and which must, upon any suggestion that may be adopted, be really felt and acknowledged. At some future period, if circumstances should be so changed as to call for a territorial government, or for any other alteration in the system, the United States can, in the guardian position they occupy, make such modification as sound judgment and an anxious desire to benefit the Indians shall dictate.

ANDREW JACKSON

Veto of the Maysville Road Bill (1830)

[. . .] The constitutional power of the Federal Government to construct or promote works of internal improvement presents itself in two points of view—the first as bearing upon the sovereignty of the States within whose limits their execution is contemplated, if jurisdiction of the territory which they may occupy be claimed as necessary to their preservation and use; the second as asserting the simple right to appropriate money from the National Treasury in aid of such works when undertaken by State authority, surrendering the claim of jurisdiction. In the first view the question of power is an open one, and can be decided without the embarrassments attending the other, arising from the practice of the Government. Although frequently and strenuously attempted, the power to this extent has never been exercised by the Government in a single instance. It does not, in my opinion, possess it; and no bill, therefore, which admits it can receive my official sanction.

But in the other view of the power the question is differently situated. The ground taken at an early period of the Government was "that whenever money has been raised by the general authority and is to be applied to a particular measure, a question arises whether the particular measure be within the enumerated authorities vested in Congress. If it be, the money requisite for it may be applied to it; if not, no such application can be made." The document in which this principle was first advanced is of deservedly high authority, and should be held in grateful remembrance for its immediate agency in rescuing the country from much existing abuse and for its conservative effect upon some of the most valuable principles of the Constitution. The symmetry and purity of the Government would doubtless have been better preserved if this restriction of the power of appropriation could have been maintained without weakening its ability to fulfill the general objects of its institution, an effect so likely to attend its admission, notwithstanding its apparent fitness, that every subsequent Administration of the Government, embracing a period of thirty out of the forty-two years of its existence, has adopted a more enlarged construction of the power. [. . .]

The bill before me does not call for a more definite opinion upon the particular circumstances which will warrant appropriations of money by Congress to aid works of internal improvement, for although the extension of the power to apply money beyond that of carrying into effect the object for which it is appropriated has, as we have seen, been long claimed and exercised by the Federal Government, yet such grants have always been professedly under the control of the general principle that the works which might be thus aided should be "of a general, not local, national, nor State," character. A disregard of this distinction would of necessity lead to the subversion of the federal system. That even this is an unsafe one, arbitrary in its nature, and liable, consequently, to great abuses, is too obvious to require the confirmation of experience. It is, however, sufficiently definite and imperative to my mind to forbid my approbation of any bill having the character of the one under consideration. I have given to its provisions all the reflection demanded by a just regard for the interests of those of our fellow-citizens who have desired its passage, and by the respect which is due to a coordinate branch of the Government, but I am not able to view it in any other light than as a measure of purely local character; or, if it can be considered national, that no further distinction between the appropriate duties of the General and State Governments need be attempted, for there can be no local interest that may not with equal propriety be denominated national. [. . .]

In the other view of the subject, and the only remaining one which it is my intention to present at this time, is involved the expediency of embarking in a system of internal improvement without a previous amendment of the Constitution explaining and defining the precise powers of the Federal Government over it. Assuming the right to appropriate money to aid in the construction of national works to be warranted by the contemporaneous and continued exposition of the Constitution, its insufficiency for the successful prosecution of them must be admitted by all candid minds. If we look to usage to define the extent of the right, that will be found so variant and embracing so much that has been overruled as to involve the whole subject in great uncertainty and to render the execution of our respective duties in relation to it replete with difficulty and embarrassment. It is in regard to such works and the acquisition of additional territory that the practice obtained its first footing. In most, if not all, other disputed questions of appropriation the construction of the Constitution may be regarded as unsettled if the right to apply money in the enumerated cases is placed on the ground of usage. [. . .]

If it be the wish of the people that the construction of roads and canals should be conducted by the Federal Government, it is not only highly expedient, but indispensably necessary, that a previous amendment of the Constitution, delegating the necessary power and defining and restricting its exercise with reference to the sovereignty of the States, should be made. Without it nothing extensively useful can be effected.

Message on Removal of Southern Indians (1835)

[. . .] All preceding experiments for the improvement of the Indians have failed. It seems now to be an established fact that they can not live in contact with a civilized community and prosper. Ages of fruitless endeavors have at length brought us to a knowledge of this principle of intercommunication with them. The past we can not recall, but the future we can provide for. Independently of the treaty stipulations into which we have entered with the various tribes for the usufructuary rights they have ceded to us, no one can doubt the moral duty of the Government of the United States to protect and if possible to preserve and perpetuate the scattered remnants of this race which are left within our borders. In the discharge of this duty an extensive region in the West has been assigned for their permanent residence. It has been divided into districts and allotted among them. Many have already removed and others are preparing to go, and with the exception of two small bands living in Ohio and Indiana, not exceeding 1,500 persons, and of the Cherokees, all the tribes on the east side of the Mississippi, and extending from Lake Michigan to Florida, have entered into engagements which will lead to their transplantation.

The plan for their removal and reestablishment is founded upon the knowledge we have gained of their character and habits, and has been dictated by a spirit of enlarged liberality. A territory exceeding in extent that relinquished has been granted to each tribe. Of its climate, fertility, and capacity to support an Indian population the representations are highly favorable. To these districts the Indians are removed at the expense of the United States, and with certain supplies of clothing, arms, ammunition, and other indispensable articles; they are also furnished gratuitously with provisions for the period of a year after their arrival at their new homes. In that time, from the nature of the country and of the products raised by them, they can subsist themselves by agricultural labor, if they choose to resort to that mode of life; if they do not they are upon the skirts of the great prairies, where countless herds of buffalo roam, and a short time suffices to adapt their own habits to the changes which a change of the animals destined for their food may require. Ample arrangements have also been made for the support of schools; in some instances council houses and churches are to be erected, dwellings constructed for the chiefs, and mills for common use. Funds have been set apart for the maintenance of the poor; the most necessary mechanical arts have been introduced, and blacksmiths, gunsmiths, wheelwrights, millwrights, etc., are supported among them. Steel and iron, and sometimes salt, are purchased for them, and plows and other farming utensils, domestic animals, looms, spinning wheels, cards, etc., are presented to them. And besides these beneficial arrangements, annuities are in all cases paid, amounting in some instances to more than $30 for each individual of the tribe, and in all cases sufficiently great, if justly divided and prudently expended, to enable them, in addition to their own exertions, to live comfortably. And as a stimulus for exertion, it is now provided by law that "in all cases of the appointment of interpreters or other persons employed for the benefit of the Indians a preference shall be given to persons of Indian descent, if such can be found who are properly qualified for the discharge of the duties."

Such are the arrangements for the physical comfort and for the moral improvement of the Indians. The necessary measures for their political advancement and for their separation from our citizens have not been neglected. The pledge of the United States has been given by Congress that the country destined for the residence of this people shall be forever "secured and guaranteed to them. A country west of Missouri and Arkansas has been assigned to them, into which the white settlements are not to be pushed. No political communities can be formed in that extensive region, except those which are established by the Indians themselves or by the United States for them and with their concurrence. A barrier has thus been raised for their protection against the encroachment of our citizens, and guarding the Indians as far as possible from those evils which have brought them to their present condition. Summary authority has been given by law to destroy all ardent spirits found in their country, without waiting the doubtful result and slow process of a legal seizure. I consider the absolute and unconditional interdiction of this article among these people as the first and great step in their melioration. Halfway measures will answer no purpose. [. . .]

Memorial and Protest of the Cherokee Nation (1836)

The undersigned representatives of the Cherokee nation, east of the river Mississippi, impelled by duty, would respectfully submit, for the consideration of your honorable body, the following statement of facts: It will be seen, from the numerous subsisting treaties between the Cherokee nation and the United States, that from the earliest existence of this government, the United States, in Congress assembled, received the Cherokees and their nation into favor and protection; and that the chiefs and warriors, for themselves and all parts of the Cherokee nation, acknowledged themselves and the said Cherokee nation to be under the protection of the United States of America, and of no other sovereign whatsoever: they also stipulated, that the said Cherokee nation will not hold any treaty with any foreign power, individual State, or with individuals of any State; that for, and in consideration of, valuable concessions made by the Cherokee nation, the United States solemnly guaranteed to said nations all their lands not ceded, and pledged the faith of the government, that "all white people who have intruded, or may hereafter intrude, on the lands reserved for the Cherokees, shall be removed by the United States, and proceeded against, according to the provisions of the act, passed 30th March, 1802," entitled "An act to regulate trade and intercourse with the Indian tribes, and to preserve peace on the frontiers." It would be useless to recapitulate the numerous provisions for the security and protection of the rights of the Cherokees, to be found in the various treaties between their nation and the United States. The Cherokees were happy and prosperous under a scrupulous observance of treaty stipulations by the government of the United States, and from the fostering hand extended over them, they made rapid advances in civilization, morals, and in the arts and sciences. Little did they anticipate, that when taught to think and feel as the American citizen, and to have with him a common interest, they were to be despoiled by their guardian, to become strangers and wanderers in the land of their fathers, forced to return to the savage life, and to seek a new home in the wilds of the far west, and that without their consent. An instrument purporting to be a treaty with the Cherokee people, has recently been made public by the President of the United States, that will have such an operation, if carried into effect. This instrument, the delegation aver before the civilized world, and in the presence of Almighty God, is fraudulent, false upon its face, made by unauthorized individuals, without the sanction, and against the wishes, of the great body of the Cherokee people. [. . .]

Roger Taney

Charles River Bridge Co. v. Warren Bridge Co. (1837)

Taney, Ch. J., delivered the opinion of the Court. [. . .]

It appears, from the record, that in the year 1650, the legislature of Massachusetts granted to the president of Harvard College "the liberty and power" to dispose of the ferry from Charlestown to Boston, by lease or otherwise, in the behalf, and for the behoof, of the college; and that under that grant, the college continued to hold and keep the ferry, by its lessees or agents, and to receive the profits of it, until 1785. In the last-mentioned year, a petition was presented to the legislature, by Thomas Russell and others, stating the inconvenience of the transportation by ferries, over Charles River, and the public advantages that would result from a bridge; and praying to be incorporated, for the purpose of erecting a bridge in the place where the ferry between Boston and Charlestown was then kept. Pursuant to this petition, the legislature, on the 9th of March 1785, passed an act incorporating a company, by the name of "The Proprietors of the Charles River Bridge," for the purposes mentioned in the petition. Under this charter, the company were empowered to erect a bridge, in "the place where the ferry was then kept," certain tolls were granted, and the charter was limited to forty years from the first opening of the bridge for passengers; and from the time the toll commenced, until the expiration of this term, the company were to pay £200 annually, to Harvard College; and at the expiration of the forty years, the bridge was to be the property of the commonwealth; "saving (as the law expresses it) to the said college or university, a reasonable annual compensation, for the annual income of the ferry, which they might have received, had not the said bridge been erected."

The bridge was accordingly built, and was opened for passengers on the 17th of June 1786. In 1792, the charter was extended to seventy years from the opening of the bridge; and at the expiration of that time, it was to belong to the commonwealth. The corporation have regularly paid to the college the annual sum of £200 and have performed all of the duties imposed on them by the terms of their charter.

In 1828, the legislature of Massachusetts incorporated a company by the name of "The Proprietors of the Warren Bridge" for the purpose of erecting another bridge over Charles River. This bridge is only sixteen rods, at its commencement, on the Charlestown side, from the commencement of the bridge of the plaintiffs; and they are about fifty rods apart, at their termination on the Boston side. The travelers who pass over either bridge, proceed from Charlestown square, which receives the travel of many great public roads leading from the country; and the passengers and travelers who go to and from Boston, used to pass over the Charles River Bridge, from and through this square, before the erection of the Warren Bridge.

The Warren Bridge, by the terms of its charter, was to be surrendered to the state, as soon as the expenses of the proprietors in building and supporting it should be reimbursed; but this period was not, in any event, to exceed six years from the time the company commenced receiving toll.

When the original bill in this case was filed, the Warren Bridge had not been built; and the bill was filed, after the passage of the law, in order to obtain an injunction to prevent its erection, and for general relief. The bill, among other things, charged as a ground for relief, that the act for the erection of the Warren Bridge impaired the obligation of the contract between the commonwealth and the proprietors of the Charles River Bridge; and was, therefore, repugnant to the Constitution of the United States. [. . .]

[S]ince the filing of the [. . .] bill, a sufficient amount of toll had been reserved by the proprietors of the Warren Bridge to reimburse all their expenses, and that the bridge is now the property of the state, and has been made a free bridge; and that the value of the franchise granted to the proprietors of the

Charles River Bridge, has by this means been entirely destroyed. [. . .]

It is very clear that [. . .] the plaintiffs, in claiming under either of these rights, must place themselves on the ground of contract. [. . .] [T]hey must show that the title which they claim, was acquired by contract, and that the terms of that contract have been violated by the charter to the Warren Bridge. In other words, they must show that the state had entered into a contract with them, or those under whom they claim, not to establish a free bridge at the place where the Warren Bridge is erected. Such, and such only, are the principles upon which the plaintiffs in error can claim relief in this case.

The nature and extent of the ferry right granted to Harvard College, in 1650, must depend upon the laws of Massachusetts. [. . .] But in the view which the Court take[s] of the case before them, it is not necessary to express any opinion on these questions. For, assuming that the grant to Harvard College, and the charter to the bridge company, were both contracts, and that the ferry right was as extensive and exclusive as the plaintiffs contend for; still they cannot enlarge privileges granted to the bridge, unless it can be shown that the rights of Harvard College in this ferry have, by assignment, or in some other way, been transferred to the proprietors of the Charles River Bridge, and still remain in existence, vested in them, to the same extent with that in which they were held and enjoyed by the college, before the bridge was built. [. . .]

But upon what ground can the plaintiffs in error contend, that the ferry rights of the college have been transferred to the proprietors of the bridge? If they have been thus transferred, it must be by some mode of transfer known to the law; and the evidence relied on to prove it, can be pointed out in the record. How was it transferred? It is not suggested, that there ever was, in point of fact, a deed of conveyance executed by the college to the bridge company. Is there any evidence in the record, from which such a conveyance may, upon legal principle, be presumed? The testimony before the Court, so far from laying the foundation for such a presumption, repels it, in the most positive terms. The petition to the legislature, in 1785, on which the charter was granted, does not suggest an assignment, nor any agreement or consent on the part of the college; and the petitioners do not appear to have regarded the wishes of that institution, as by any means necessary to insure their success. They place their application entirely on considerations of public interest and public convenience, and the superior advantages of a communication across Charles River, by a bridge, instead of a ferry. The legislature, in granting the charter, show, by the language of the law, that they acted on the principles assumed by the petitioners. The preamble recites, that the bridge "will be of great public utility," and that is the only reason they assign, for passing the law which incorporates this company. The validity of the character is not made to depend on the consent of the college, nor of any assignment or surrender on their part; and the legislature deal with the subject, as if it were one exclusively within their own power, and as if the ferry right were not to be transferred to the bridge company, but to be extinguished, and they appear to have acted on the principle, that the state, by virtue of its sovereign powers and eminent domain, had a right to take away the franchise of the ferry; because, in their judgment, the public interest and convenience would be better promoted by a bridge in the same place; and upon that principle, they proceed to make a pecuniary compensation to the college, for the franchise thus taken away. [. . .]

It does not, by any means, follow that, because the legislative power of Massachusetts in 1650 may have granted to a justly favored seminary of learning, the exclusive right of ferry between Boston and Charlestown, they would, in 1785, give the same extensive privilege to another corporation, who were about to erect a bridge in the same place.

The fact that such a right was granted to the college, cannot, by any sound rule of construction, be used to extend the privileges of the bridge company, beyond what the words of the charter naturally and legally import. Increased population, longer experience in legislation, the different character of the corporations which owned the ferry from that which owned the bridge, might well have induced a change in the policy of the state in this respect; and as the franchise of the ferry, and that of the bridge, are different in their nature, and were each established by separate grants, which have no words to connect the privileges of the one with the privileges of the other, there is no rule of legal interpretation, which would authorize the Court to associate these grants together, and to infer that any privilege was intended to be given to the bridge company, merely because it had been conferred on the ferry. The charter to the bridge is a written instrument which must speak for itself, and be interpreted by its own terms.

This brings us to the act of the legislature of Massachusetts, of 1785, by which the plaintiffs were incorporated by the name of "The Proprietors of the Charles River Bridge," and it is here, and in the law of 1792, prolonging their charter, that we must look for the extent and nature of the franchise conferred upon the plaintiffs. Much has been said in the argument of the principles of construction by which this law is to be expounded, and what undertakings, on the part of the state, may be implied. The Court think there can be no serious difficulty on that head. It is the grant of certain franchises, by the public, to a private corporation, and in a matter where the public interest is concerned. The rule of construction in such cases is well settled, both in England, and by the decisions of our own tribunals. [. . .]

Borrowing, as we have done, our system of jurisprudence from the English law; and having adopted, in every other case, civil and criminal, its rules for the construction of statutes; is there anything in our local situation, or in the nature of our political institutions, which should lead us to depart from the principle, where corporations are concerned? Are we to apply to acts of incorporation, a rule of construction differing from that of the English law, and, by implication, make the terms of a charter, in one of the states, more unfavorable to the public, than upon an act of parliament, framed in the same words, would be sanctioned in an English court? Can any good reason be assigned, for excepting this particular class of cases from the operation of the general principle; and for introducing a new and adverse rule of construction, in favor of corporations, while we adopt and adhere to the rules of construction known to the English common law, in every other case, without exception? We think not; and it would present a singular spectacle, if, while the courts in England are restraining, within the strictest limits, the spirit of monopoly, and exclusive privileges in nature of monopolies, and confining corporations to the privileges plainly given to them in their charter; the courts of this country should be found enlarging these privileges by implication; and construing a statute more unfavorably to the public, and to the rights of community, than would be done in a like case in an English court of justice.

But we are not now left to determine, for the first time, the rules by which public grants are to be construed in this country. The subject has already been considered in this Court; and the rule of construction, above stated, fully established. [. . .]

[T]he case most analogous to this, and in which the question came more directly before the Court, is the case of the *Providence Bank v. Billings*, 4 Pet. 514, which was decided in 1830. In that case, it appeared, that the legislature of Rhode Island had chartered the bank, in the usual form of such acts of incorporation. The charter contained no stipulation on the part of the state, that it would not impose a tax on the bank, nor any reservation of the right to do so. It was silent on this point. Afterwards, a law was passed, imposing a tax on all banks in the state; and the right to impose this tax was resisted by the Providence Bank, upon the ground, that if the state could impose a tax, it might tax so heavily as to render the franchise of no value, and destroy the institution; that the charter was a contract, and that a power which may in effect destroy the charter is inconsistent with it, and is impliedly renounced by granting it. But the Court said that the taxing power was of vital importance, and essential to the existence of government; and that the relinquishment of such a power is never to be assumed. And in delivering the opinion of the Court, the late chief justice states the principle, in the following clear and emphatic language. Speaking of the taxing power, he says, "as the whole community is interested in retaining it undiminished, that community has a right to insist that its abandonment ought not to be presumed, in a case in which the deliberate purpose of the state to abandon it does not appear." The case now before the Court is, in principle, precisely the same. It is a charter from a state; the act of incorporation is silent in relation to the contested power. The argument in favor of the proprietors of the Charles River Bridge, is the same, almost in words, with that used by the Providence Bank; that is, that the power claimed by the state, if it exists, may be so used as to destroy the value of the franchise they have granted to the corporation. The argument must receive the same answer; and the fact that the power has been already exercised, so as to destroy the value of the franchise, cannot in any degree affect the principle. The existence of the power does not, and cannot, depend upon the circumstance of its having been exercised or not.

It may, perhaps, be said, that in the case of the Providence Bank, this Court were speaking of the taxing power; which is of vital importance to the very existence of every government. But the object and end of all government is to promote the happiness and prosperity of the community by which it is established; and it can never be assumed, that the government intended to diminish its power of accomplishing the end for which it was created. And in a country like ours, free, active and enterprising, continually advancing in numbers and wealth, new channels of communication are daily found necessary, both for travel and trade, and are essential to the comfort, convenience and prosperity of the people. A state ought never to be presumed to surrender this power, because, like the taxing power, the whole community have an interest in preserving it undiminished. And when a corporation alleges, that a state has surrendered, for seventy years, its power of improvement and public accommodation, in a great and important line of travel, along which a vast number of its citizens must daily pass, the community have a right to insist, in the language of this Court, above quoted, "that its abandonment ought not to be presumed, in a case, in which the deliberate purpose of the state to abandon it does not appear." The continued existence of a government would be of no great value, if, by implications and presumptions, it was disarmed of the powers necessary to accomplish the ends of its creation, and the functions it was designed to perform, transferred to the hands of privileged corporations. The rule of construction announced by the Court, was not confined to the taxing power, nor is it so limited, in the opinion delivered. On the contrary, it was distinctly placed on the ground, that the interests of the community were concerned in preserving, undiminished, the power then in question; and whenever any power of the state is said to be surrendered or diminished, whether it be the taxing power, or any other affecting the public interest, the same principle applies, and the rule of construction must be the same. No one will question, that the interests of the great body of the people of the state, would, in this instance, be affected by the surrender of this great line of travel to a single corporation, with the right to exact toll, and exclude competition, for seventy years. While the rights of private property are sacredly guarded, we must not forget, that the community also have rights, and that the happiness and well-being of every citizen depends on their faithful preservation.

Adopting the rule of construction above stated as the settled one, we proceed to apply it to the charter of 1785, to the proprietors of the Charles River Bridge. This act of incorporation is in the usual form, and the privileges such as are commonly given to corporations of that kind. It confers on them the ordinary faculties of a corporation, for the purpose of building the bridge; and establishes certain rates of toll, which the company are authorized to take: this is the whole grant. There is no exclusive privilege given to them over the waters of Charles River, above or below their bridge; no right to erect another bridge themselves, nor to prevent other persons from erecting one, no engagement from the state, that another shall not be erected; and no undertaking not to sanction competition, nor to make improvements that may diminish the amount of its income. Upon all these subjects, the charter is silent; and nothing is said in it about a line of travel, so much insisted on in the argument, in which they are to have exclusive privileges. No words are used, from which an intention to grant any of these rights can be inferred; if the plaintiff is entitled to them, it must be implied, simply, from the nature of the grant; and cannot be inferred, from the words by which the grant is made.

The relative position of the Warren Bridge has already been described. It does not interrupt the passage over the Charles River Bridge, nor make the way to it, or from it, less convenient. None of the faculties or franchises granted to that corporation, have been revoked by the legislature; and its right to take the tolls granted by the charter remains unaltered. In short, all the franchises and rights of property, enumerated in the charter, and there mentioned to have been granted to it, remain unimpaired. But its income is destroyed by the Warren Bridge; which, being free, draws off the passengers and property which would have gone over it, and renders their franchise of no value. This is the gist of the complainant; for it is not pretended, that the erection of the Warren Bridge would have done them any injury, or in any degree affected their right of property, if it had not diminished the amount of their tolls. In order, then, to entitle themselves to relief, it is necessary to show, that the legislature contracted not to do the act of which they complain; and that they impaired, or in other words, violated, that contract, by the erection of the Warren Bridge.

The inquiry, then, is, does the charter contain such a contract on the part of the state? Is there any such stipulation to be found in that instrument? It must be admitted on all hands, that there is none; no words that even relate to another bridge, or to the diminution of their tolls, or to the line of travel. If a contract on that subject can be gathered from the charter, it must be by implication; and cannot be found in the words used. Can such an agreement be implied? The rule of construction before stated is an answer to the question: in charters of this description, no rights are taken from the public, or given to the corporation, beyond those which the words of the charter, by their natural and proper construction, purport to convey. There are no words which import such a contract as the plaintiffs in error contend for, and none can be implied; and the same answer must be given to them that was given by this Court to Providence Bank. The whole community are interested in this inquiry, and they have a right to require that the power of promoting their comfort and convenience, and of advancing the public prosperity, by providing safe, convenient and cheap ways for the transportation of produce, and the purposes of travel, shall not be construed to have been surrendered or diminished by the state; unless it shall appear by plain words, that it was intended to be done. [. . .]

Indeed, the practice and usage of almost every state in the Union, old enough to have commenced the work of internal improvement, is opposed to the doctrine contended for on the part of the plaintiffs in error. Turnpike roads have been made in succession, on the same line of travel; the later ones interfering materially with the profits of the first. These corporations have, in some instances, been utterly ruined by the introduction of newer and better modes of transportation and traveling. In some cases, railroads have rendered the turnpike roads on the same line of travel so entirely useless, that the franchise of the turnpike corporation is not worth preserving. Yet in none of these cases have the corporation supposed that their privileges were invaded, or any contract violated on the part of the state. [. . .]

And what would be the fruits of this doctrine of implied contracts, on the part of the states, and of property in a line of travel, by a corporation, if it would now be sanctioned by this Court? To what results would it lead us? If it is to be found in the charter to this bridge, the same process of reasoning must discover it, in the various acts which have been passed, within the last forty years, for turnpike companies. [. . .] If this Court should establish the principles now contended for, what is to become of the numerous railroads established on the same line of travel with turnpike companies; and which have rendered the franchises of the turnpike corporations of no value? Let it once be understood, that such charters carry with them these implied contracts, and give this unknown and undefined property in a line of traveling; and you will soon find the old turnpike corporations awakening from their sleep, and calling upon this Court to put down the improvements which have taken their place. The millions of property which have been invested in railroads and canals, upon lines of travel which had been before occupied by turnpike corporations, will be put in jeopardy. We shall be thrown back to the improvements of the last century, and obliged to stand still, until the claims of the old turnpike corporations shall be satisfied; and they shall consent to permit these states to avail themselves of the lights of modern science, and to partake of the benefit of those improvements which are now adding to the wealth and prosperity, and the convenience and comfort, of every other part of the civilized world. Nor is this all. This Court will find itself compelled to fix, by some arbitrary rule, the width of this new kind of property in a line of travel; for if such a right of property exists, we have no lights to guide us in marking out its extent, unless, indeed, we resort to the old feudal grants, and to the exclusive rights of ferries, by prescription, between towns; and are prepared to decide that when a turnpike road from one town to another, had been made, no railroad or canal, between these two points, could afterwards be established. This Court are not prepared to sanction principles which must lead to such results. [. . .]

The judgment of the Supreme Judicial Court of the commonwealth of Massachusetts, dismissing the plaintiffs' bill, must, therefore, be affirmed, with costs.

Joseph Story

Charles River Bridge Co. v. Warren Bridge Co., Dissent (1837)

Story, Justice, dissenting. [. . .]

The only question, over which this Court possesses jurisdiction in this case (it being an appeal from a state court and not from the circuit court) is, as has been stated at the bar, whether the obligation of any contract, within the true intent and meaning of the Constitution of the United States, has been violated. [. . .]

But, before we can properly enter upon the consideration of this subject, a preliminary inquiry is presented, as to the proper rules of interpretation applicable to the charter. Is the charter to receive a strict or a liberal construction? Are any implications to be made, beyond the express terms? And if so, to what extent are they justifiable, by the principles of law [. . .] ?

I admit that, where the terms of a grant are to impose burdens upon the public, or to create a restraint injurious to the public interest, there is sound reason for interpreting the terms, if ambiguous, in favor of the public. But at the same time, I insist that there is not the slightest reason for saying, even in such a case, that the grant is not to be construed favorably to the grantee, so as to secure him in the enjoyment of what is actually granted. [. . .]

[W]ith a view to induce the Court to withdraw from all the common rules of reasonable and liberal interpretation in favor of grants, we have been told at the argument, that this very charter is a restriction upon the legislative power; that it is in derogation of the rights and interests of the state, and the people; that it tends to promote monopolies and exclusive privileges; and that it will interpose an insuperable barrier to the progress of improvement. Now, upon every one of these propositions, which are assumed, and not proved, I entertain a directly opposite opinion; and if I did not, I am not prepared to admit the conclusion for which they are adduced. If the legislature has made a grant, which involves any or all of these consequences, it is not for courts of justice to overturn the plain sense of the grant, because it has been improvidently or injuriously made.

But I deny the very groundwork of the argument. This charter is not [. . .] any restriction upon the legislative power; unless it be true, that because the legislature cannot grant again, what it has already granted, the legislative power is restricted. If so, then every grant of the public land is a restriction upon that power; a doctrine, that has never yet been established, nor (so far as I know) ever contended for. Every grant of a franchise is, so far as that grant extends, necessarily exclusive; and cannot be resumed or interfered with. All the learned judges in the state court admitted, that the franchise of Charles River Bridge, whatever it be, could not be resumed or interfered with. The legislature could not recall its grant, or destroy it. It is a contract, whose obligation cannot be constitutionally impaired. In this respect, it does not differ from a grant of lands. In each case, the particular land, or the particular franchise, is withdrawn from the legislative operation. The identical land, or the identical franchise, cannot be regranted, or avoided by a new grant. But the legislative power remains unrestricted. The subject-matter only (I repeat it) has passed from the hands of the government. [. . .]

Then, again, how is it established, that this is a grant in derogation of the rights and interests of the people? No individual citizen has any right to build a bridge over navigable waters; and consequently, he is deprived of no right, when a grant is made to any other persons for that purpose. Whether it promotes or injures the particular interest of an individual citizen, constitutes no ground for judicial or legislative interference, beyond what his own rights justify. When, then, it is said, that such a grant is in derogation of the rights and interests of the people, we must understand, that reference is had to the rights and interests common to the whole people, as such (such as the right of navigation), or belonging to them as a political body; or, in other words, the rights and interests of the state. Now, I cannot understand, how any grant of a franchise is a derogation from the rights of the people of the state, any more than a grant of public land. The right, in each case, is gone, to the extent of the thing granted, and so far may be said to derogate from, that is to say, to lessen the rights of the people, or of the state. But that is not the sense in which the argument is pressed; for, by derogation, is here meant an injurious or mischievous detraction from the sovereign rights of the state. On the other hand, there can be no derogation from the rights of the people, as such, except it applies to rights common there before; which the building of a bridge over navigable waters certainly is not. If it had been said, that the grant of this bridge was in derogation of the common right of navigating the Charles River, by reason of its obstructing, pro tanto, a free and open passage, the ground would have been intelligible. So, if it had been an exclusive grant of the navigation of that stream. But, if at the same time, equivalent public rights of a different nature, but of greater public accommodation and use, had been obtained; it could hardly have been said, in a correct sense, that there was any derogation from the rights of the people, or the rights of the state. It would be a mere exchange of one public right for another.

Then, again, as to the grant being against the interests of the people. I know not how that is established; and certainly, it is not to be assumed. It will hardly be contended, that every grant of the government is injurious to the interests of the people; or that every grant of a franchise, must necessarily be so. The erection of a bridge may be of the highest utility to the people. It may essentially promote the public convenience, and aid the public interests, and protect the public property. And if no persons can be found willing to undertake such a work, unless they receive in return the exclusive privilege of erecting it, and taking toll; surely, it cannot be said, as of course, that such a grant, under such circumstances, is, per se, against the interests of the people. Whether the grant of a franchise is, or is not, on the whole, promotive of the public interests, is a question of fact and judgment, upon which different minds may entertain different opinions. It is not to be judicially assumed to be injurious, and then the grant to be reasoned down. It is a matter exclusively confided to the sober consideration of the legislature; which is invested with full discretion, and possesses ample means to decide it. For myself, meaning to speak with all due deference for others, I know of no power or authority confided to the judicial department, to rejudge the decisions of the legislature upon such a subject. It has an exclusive right to make the grant, and to decide whether it be, or be not, for the public interests. It is to be presumed, if the grant is made, that it is made from a high sense of public duty, to promote the public welfare, and to establish the public prosperity. [. . .]

No sound lawyer will, I presume, assert that the grant of a right to erect a bridge over a navigable stream is a grant of a common right. Before such grant, had all the citizens of the state a right to erect bridges over navigable streams? Certainly, they had not; and therefore, the grant was no restriction of any common right. It was neither a monopoly; nor, in a legal sense, had it any tendency to a monopoly. It took from no citizen what he possessed before; and had no tendency to take it from him. It took, indeed, from the legislature the power of granting the same identical privilege or franchise to any other persons. But this made it no more a monopoly, than the grant of the public stock or funds of a state for a valuable consideration. Even in cases of monopolies, strictly so called, if the nature of the grant be such that it is for the public good, as in cases of patents for inventions, the rule has always been, to give them a favorable construction, in support of the patent. [. . .]

But it has been argued, and the argument has been pressed in every form which ingenuity could suggest, that if grants of this nature are to be construed liberally, as conferring any exclusive rights on the grantees, it will interpose an effectual barrier against all general improvements of the country. [. . .] For my own part, I can conceive of no surer plan to arrest all public improvements, founded on private capital and enterprise, than to make the outlay of that capital uncertain and questionable, both as to security and as to productiveness. No man will hazard his capital in any enterprise, in which, if there be a loss, it must be borne exclusively by himself; and if there be success, he has not the slightest security of enjoying the rewards of that success, for a single moment. If the government means to invite its citizens to enlarge the public comforts and conveniences, to establish bridges, or turnpikes, or canals, or railroads, there must be some pledge, that the property will be safe; that the enjoyment will be co-extensive with the grant; and that success will not be the signal of a general combination to overthrow its rights and to take away its profits. [. . .]

I have thus endeavored to answer, and I think I have successfully answered all the arguments (which indeed run into each other) adduced to justify a strict construction of the present charter. I go further, and maintain, not only that it is not a case for strict construction; but that the charter, upon its very face, by its terms, and for its professed objects, demands from the Court, upon undeniable principles of law, a favorable construction for the grantees. In the first place, the legislature has declared, that the erecting of the bridge will be of great public utility; and this exposition of its own motives for the grant, requires the Court to give a liberal interpretation, in order to promote, and not to destroy, an enterprise of great public utility. In the next place, the grant is a contract for a valuable consideration, and a full and adequate consideration. The proprietors are to lay out a large sum of money (and in those times it was a very large outlay of capital) in erecting a bridge; they are to keep it in repair, during the whole period of forty years; they are to surrender it in good repair, at the end of that period, to the state, as its own property; they are to pay, during the whole period, an annuity of £200 to Harvard College; and they are to incur other heavy expenses and burdens, for the public accommodation. In return for all these charges, they are entitled to no more than the receipt of the tolls, during the forty years, for their reimbursement of capital, interest and expenses. With all this, they are to take upon themselves the chances of success; and if the enterprise fails, the loss is exclusively their own. Nor let any man imagine, that there was not, at the time when this charter was granted, much solid ground for doubting success. In order to entertain a just view of this subject, we must go back to that period of general bankruptcy, and distress and difficulty. The Constitution of the United States was not only not then in existence, but it was not then even dreamed of. The union of the states was crumbling into ruins, under the old confederation. Agriculture, manufactures and commerce were at their lowest ebb. There was infinite danger to all the states, from local interests and jealousies, and from the apparent impossibility of a much longer adherence to that shadow of a government, the Continental Congress. And even four years afterwards, when every evil had been greatly aggravated, and civil war was added to other calamities, the Constitution of the United States was all but shipwrecked, in passing through the state conventions; it was adopted by very slender majorities. These are historical facts, which required no coloring to give them effect, and admitted of no concealment, to seduce men into schemes of future aggrandizement. I would even now put it to the common sense of every man, whether, if the Constitution of the United States had not been adopted, the charter would have been worth a forty years' purchase of the tolls.

This is not all. It is well known historically that this was the very first bridge ever constructed in New England over navigable tidewaters so near the sea. The rigors of our climate, the dangers from sudden thaws and freezing, and the obstructions from ice in a rapid current were deemed by many persons to be insuperable obstacles to the success of such a project. It was believed, that the bridge would scarcely stand a single severe winter. And I myself am old enough to know, that in regard to other arms of the sea, at much later periods, the same doubts have had a strong and depressing influence upon public enterprises. If Charles River Bridge had been carried away, during the first or second season after its erection, it is far from being certain, that up to this moment, another bridge, upon such an arm of the sea, would ever have been erected in Massachusetts. I state these things, which are of public notoriety, to repel the notion that the legislature was surprised into an incautions grant, or that the reward was more than adequate to the perils. There was a full and adequate consideration, in a pecuniary sense, for the charter. But, in a more general sense, the erection of the bridge, as a matter of accommodation, has been incalculably beneficial to the public. Unless, therefore, we are wholly to disregard the declarations of the legislature, and the objects of the charter, and the historical facts of the times; and indulge in mere private speculations of profit and loss, by our present lights and experience; it seems to me, that the Court is bound to come to the interpretation of this charter, with a persuasion that it was granted in furtherance, and not in derogation, of the public good. [. . .]

But I do not insist upon any extraordinary liberality in interpreting this charter. All I contend for is, that it shall receive a fair and reasonable interpretation; so as to carry into effect the legislative intention, and secure to the grantees a just security for their privileges. [. . .]

Now, I put it to the common sense of every man, whether if, at the moment of granting the charter, the legislature had said to the proprietors; you shall build the bridge; you shall bear the burdens; you shall be bound by the charges; and your sole reimbursement shall be from the tolls of forty years: and yet we will not even guaranty you any certainty of receiving any tolls; on the contrary; we reserve to ourselves the full power and authority to erect other bridges, toll or free bridges, according to our own free will and pleasure, contiguous to yours, and having the same termini with yours; and if you are successful, we may thus supplant you, divide, destroy your profits, and annihilate your tolls, without annihilating your burdens: if, I say, such had been the language of the legislature, is there a man living, of ordinary discretion or prudence, who would have accepted such a charter, upon such terms? I fearlessly answer, no. There would have been such a gross inadequacy of consideration, and such a total insecurity of all the rights of property, under such circumstances, that the project would have dropped still-born. And I put the question further, whether any legislature, meaning to promote a project of permanent, public utility (such as this confessedly was), would ever have dreamed of such a qualification of its own grant, when it sought to enlist private capital and private patronage to insure the accomplishment of it?

Yet, this is the very form and pressure of the present case. It is not an imaginary and extravagant case. Warren Bridge has been erected, under such a supposed reserved authority, in the immediate neighborhood of Charles River Bridge; and with the same termini, to accommodate the same line of travel. For a half-dozen years, it was to be a toll bridge, for the benefit of the proprietors, to reimburse them for their expenditures; at the end of that period, the bridge is to become the property of the state, and free of toll; unless the legislature should thereafter impose one. In point of fact, it has since become, and now is, under the sanction of the act of incorporation, and other subsequent acts, a free bridge, without the payment of any tolls, for all persons. So that, in truth, here now is a free bridge, owned by and erected under the authority of the commonwealth, which necessarily takes away all the tolls from Charles River Bridge; while its prolonged charter has twenty years to run. And yet the act of the legislature establishing Warren Bridge, is said to be no violation of the franchise granted to the Charles River Bridge. The legislature may annihilate, nay, has annihilated, by its own acts, all chance of receiving tolls, by withdrawing the whole travel; though it is admitted, that it cannot take away the barren right to gather tolls, if any should occur, when there is no travel to bring a dollar. According to the same course of argument, the legislature would have a perfect right to block up every avenue to the bridge, and to obstruct every highway which should lead to it, without any violation of the chartered rights of Charles River Bridge; and at the same time, it might require every burden to be punctiliously discharged by the proprietors, during the prolonged period of seventy years. I confess, that the very statement of such propositions is so startling to my mind, and so irreconcilable with all my notions of good faith, and of any fair interpretation of the legislative intentions, that I should always doubt the soundness of any reasoning which should conduct me to such results.

But it is said that there is no prohibitory covenant in the charter, and no implications are to be made of any such prohibition. The proprietors are to stand upon the letter of their contract, and the maxim applies. [. . .] And yet it is conceded, that the legislature cannot revoke or resume this grant. Why not, I pray to know? There is no negative covenant in the charter; there is no express prohibition to be found there. The reason is plain. The prohibition arises by natural, if not by necessary, implication. It would be against the first principles of justice, to presume that the legislature reserved a right to destroy its own grant. That was the doctrine in *Fletcher v. Peck* (1810), in this Court; and in other cases turning upon the same great principle of political and constitutional duty and right. Can the legislature have power to do that indirectly, which it cannot do directly? If it cannot take away, or resume, the franchise itself, can it take away its whole substance and value? If the law will create an implication, that the legislature shall not resume its own grant, is it not equally as natural and as necessary an implication, that the legislature shall not do any act directly to prejudice its own grant, or to destroy its value [. . .]?

But it is urged that some local limits must be assigned to such grants, and the Court must assign them, for otherwise they would involve the absurdity of being co-extensive with the range of the river; for every other bridge or ferry must involve some diminution of toll; and how much (it is asked) is necessary to constitute an infringement of the right? I have already given an answer, in part, to this suggestion. The rule of law is clear. The application of it must depend upon the particular circumstances of each case. Wherever any other bridge or ferry is so near, that it injures the franchise, or diminishes the toll, in a positive and essential decree, there it is a nuisance, and is actionable. It invades the franchise, and ought to be abated. But whether there be such an injury or not, is a matter, not of law, but of fact. Distance is no otherwise important than as it bears on the question of fact. All that is required, is, that there should be a sensible, positive injury. In the present case, there is no room to doubt upon this point, for the bridges are contiguous; and Warren Bridge, after it was opened, took away three-fourths of the profits of the travel from Charles River Bridge; and when it became free (as it now is), it necessarily took away all the tolls, or all except an unimportant and trivial amount. [. . .]

What I have said, however, is to be understood with this qualification, that the franchise of the bridge has no assigned local limits; but it is a simple grant of the right to erect a bridge across a river, from one point to another, without being limited between any particular villes or towns, or by other local limits. In the case now before the Court, I have already stated, that my judgment is, that the franchise is merely to erect a bridge between Charlestown and Boston; and therefore, it does not, necessarily, exclude the legislature from making any other grant, for the erecting of a bridge between Boston and any other town. The exclusive right being between those towns, it only precludes another legislative grant between those towns, which is injurious to Charles River Bridge. [. . .] And there is the greatest reason for supporting such rights, because the owners of ferries are bound, at their peril, to supply them to the public use; and are, therefore, fairly entitled to the public advantage arising from them. [. . .]

To sum up, then, the whole argument on this head: I maintain, that, upon the principles of common reason and legal interpretation, the present grant carries with it a necessary implication, that the legislature shall do no act to destroy or essentially to impair the franchise; that (as one of the learned judges of the state court expressed it) there is an implied agreement that the state will not grant another bridge between Boston and Charlestown, so near as to draw away the custom from the old one; and (as another learned judge expressed it) that there is an implied agreement of the state to grant the undisturbed use of the bridge and its tolls, so far as respects any acts of its own, or of any persons acting under its authority. In other words, the state impliedly contracts not to resume its grant, or to do any act to the prejudice or destruction of its grant. I maintain, that there is no authority or principle established in relation to the construction of crown grants, or legislative grants, which does not concede and justify this doctrine. Where the thing is given, the incidents, without which it cannot be enjoyed, are also given; [. . .] I maintain, that a different doctrine is utterly repugnant to all the principles of the common law, applicable to all franchises of a like nature; and that we must overturn some of the best securities of the rights of property, before it can be established. I maintain, that the common law is the birthright of every citizen of Massachusetts, and that he holds the title deeds of his property, corporeal and incorporeal, under it. I maintain, that under the principles of the common law, there exists no more right in the legislature of Massachusetts, to erect the Warren Bridge, to the ruin of the franchise of the Charles River Bridge, than exists to transfer the latter to the former, or to authorize the former to demolish the latter. If the legislature does not mean in its grant to give any exclusive rights, let it say so, expressly, directly, and in terms admitting of no misconstruction. The grantees will then take at their peril, and must abide the results of their overweening confidence, indiscretion and zeal. [. . .]

Upon the whole, my judgment is that the act of the legislature of Massachusetts granting the charter of Warren Bridge is an act impairing the obligation of the prior contract and grant to the proprietors of Charles River Bridge; and, by the Constitution of the United States, it is, therefore, utterly void. I am for reversing the decree to the state court (dismissing the bill); and for remanding the cause to the state court for further proceedings, as to law and justice shall appertain.

Daniel Webster

Speech on the Presidential Veto of the Bank Bill (July 1832)

Mr. President, no one will deny the high importance of the subject now before us. Congress, after full deliberation and discussion, has passed a bill, by decisive majorities, in both houses, for extending the duration of the Bank of the United States. It has not adopted this measure until its attention had been called to the subject, in three successive annual messages of the President. The bill having been thus passed by both houses, and having been duly presented to the President, instead of signing and approving it, he has returned it with objections. These objections go against the whole substance of the law originally creating the bank. They deny, in effect, that the bank is constitutional; they deny that it is expedient; they deny that it is necessary for the public service.

It is not to be doubted, that the Constitution gives the President the power which he has now exercised; but while the power is admitted, the grounds upon which it has been exerted become fit subjects of examination. The Constitution makes it the duty of Congress, in cases like this, to reconsider the measure which they have passed, to weigh the force of the President's objections to that measure, and to take a new vote upon the question.

Before the Senate proceeds to this second vote, I propose to make some remarks upon those objections. And, in the first place, it is to be observed, that they are such as to extinguish all hope that the present bank, or any bank at all resembling it, or resembling any known similar institution, can ever receive his approbation. He states no terms, no qualifications, no conditions, no modifications, which can reconcile him to the essential provisions of the existing charter. He is against the bank, and against any bank constituted in a manner known either to this or any other country. One advantage, therefore, is certainly obtained by presenting him the bill. It has caused the President's sentiments to be made known. There is no longer any mystery, no longer a contest between hope and fear, or between those prophets who predicted a *veto* and those who foretold an approval. The bill is negatived; the President has assumed the responsibility of putting an end to the bank; and the country must prepare itself to meet that change in its concerns which the expiration of the charter will produce. Mr. President, I will not conceal my opinion that the affairs of the country are approaching an important and dangerous crisis. At the very moment of almost unparalleled general prosperity, there appears an unaccountable disposition to destroy the most useful and most approved institutions of the government. Indeed, it seems to be in the midst of all this national happiness that some are found openly to question the advantages of the Constitution itself; and many more ready to embarrass the exercise of its just power, weaken its authority, and undermine its foundations. How far these notions may be carried, it is impossible yet to say. We have before us the practical result of one of them. The bank has fallen, or is to fall. [. . .]

[. . .] [I]f the President thinks lightly of the authority of Congress in construing the Constitution, he thinks still more lightly of the authority of the Supreme Court. He asserts a right of individual judgment on constitutional questions, which is totally inconsistent with any proper administration of the government, or any regular execution of the laws. Social disorder, entire uncertainty in regard to individual rights and individual duties, the cessation of legal authority, confusion, the dissolution of free government,—all these are the inevitable consequences of the principles adopted by the message, whenever they shall be carried to their full extent. Hitherto it has been thought that the final decision of constitutional questions belonged to the supreme judicial tribunal. The very nature of free government, it has been supposed, enjoins this; and our Constitution, moreover, has been understood so to provide, clearly and expressly. It is true, that each branch of the legislature has an undoubted right, in the exercise of its functions, to consider the constitutionality of a law proposed to be passed. This is naturally a part of its duty; and neither branch can be compelled to pass any law, or do any other act, which it deems to be beyond the reach of its constitutional power. The President has the same right, when a bill is presented for his approval, for he is, doubtless, bound to consider, in all cases, whether such bill be compatible with the Constitution, and whether he can approve it consistently with his oath of office. But when a law has been passed by Congress, and approved by the President, it is now no longer in the power, either of the same President, or his successors, to say whether the law is constitutional or not. He is not at liberty to disregard it; he is not at liberty to feel or to affect "constitutional scruples," and to sit in judgment himself on the validity of a statute of the government, and to nullify it, if he so chooses. After a law has passed through all the requisite forms; after it has received the requisite legislative sanction and the executive approval, the question of its constitutionality then becomes a judicial question, and a judicial question alone. In the courts that question may be raised, argued, and adjudged; it can be adjudged nowhere else.

The President is as much bound by the law as any private citizen, and can no more contest its validity than any private citizen. He may refuse to obey the law, and so may a private citizen; but both do it at their own peril, and neither of them can settle the question of its validity. The President may *say* a law is unconstitutional, but he is not the judge. Who is to decide that question? The judiciary alone possesses this unquestionable and hitherto unquestioned right. The judiciary is the constitutional tribunal of appeal for the citizens, against both Congress and the executive, in regard to the constitutionality of laws. It has this jurisdiction expressly conferred upon it, and when it has decided the question, its judgment must, from the very nature of all judgments that are final, and from which there is no appeal, be conclusive. Hitherto, this opinion, and a correspondent practice, have prevailed, in America, with all wise and considerate men. If it were otherwise, there would be no government of laws; but we should all live under the government, the rule, the caprices, of individuals. If we depart from the observance of these salutary principles, the executive power becomes at once purely despotic; for the president, if the principle and the reasoning of the message be sound, may either execute or not execute the laws of the land, according to his sovereign pleasure. He may refuse to put into execution one law, pronounced valid by all branches of the government, and yet execute another, which may have been by constitutional authority pronounced void.

On the argument of the message, the President of the United States holds, under a new pretence and a new name, a *dispensing power* over the laws as absolute as was claimed by James the Second of England, a month before he was compelled to fly the kingdom. That which is now claimed by the President is in truth nothing less, and nothing else, than the old dispensing power asserted by the kings of England in the worst of times; the very climax, indeed, of all the preposterous pretensions of the Tudor and the Stuart races. According to the doctrines put forth by the President, although Congress may have passed a law, and although the Supreme Court may have pronounced it constitutional, yet it is, nevertheless, no law at all, if he, in his good pleasure, sees fit to deny it effect; in other words, to repeal and annul it. Sir, no President and no public man ever before advanced such doctrines in the face of the nation. There never before was a moment in which any President would have been tolerated in asserting such a claim to despotic power. After Congress has passed the law, and after the Supreme Court has pronounced its judgment on the very point in controversy, the President has set up his own private judgment against its constitutional interpretation. It is to be remembered, Sir, that it is the present law, it is the act of 1816, it is the present charter of the bank, which the President pronounces to be unconstitutional. It is no bank *to be created*, it is no law proposed to be passed, which he denounces; it is the *law now existing*, passed by Congress, approved by President Madison, and sanctioned by a solemn judgment of the Supreme Court, which he now declares unconstitutional, and which, of course, so far as it may depend on him, cannot be executed. If these opinions of the President be maintained, there is an end of all law and all judicial authority. Statutes are but recommendations, judgments no more than opinions. Both are equally destitute of binding force. Such a universal power as is now claimed for him, a power of judging over the laws and over the decisions of the judiciary, is nothing else but pure despotism. If conceded to him, it makes him at once what Louis the Fourteenth proclaimed himself to be when he said, "I am the State." [. . .]

According to that mode of construing the Constitution which was adopted by Congress in 1791, and approved by Washington, and which has been sanctioned by the judgment of the Supreme Court, and affirmed by the practice of nearly forty years, the question upon the constitutionality of the bank involves two inquiries. First, whether a bank, in its general character, and with regard to the general objects with which banks are usually connected, be, in itself, a fit means, a suitable instrument, to carry into effect the powers granted to the government. If it be so, then the second, and the only other question is, whether the powers given in a particular charter are appropriate for a bank. If they are powers which are appropriate for a bank, powers which Congress may fairly consider to be useful to the bank or the country, then Congress may confer these powers; because the discretion to be exercised in framing the constitution of the bank belongs to Congress. One man may think the granted powers not indispensable to the particular bank; another may suppose them injudicious, or injurious; a third may imagine that other powers, if granted in their stead, would be more beneficial; but all these are matters of expediency, about which men may differ; and the power of deciding upon them belongs to Congress.

I again repeat, Sir, that if, for reasons of this kind, the President sees fit to negative a bill, on the ground of its being inexpedient or impolitic, he has a right to do so. But remember, Sir, that we are now on the constitutional question; remember, that the argument of the President is, that, because powers were given to the bank by the charter of 1816 which he thinks unnecessary, that charter is unconstitutional. Now, Sir, it will hardly be denied, or rather it was not denied or doubted before this message came to us, that, if there was to be a bank, the powers and duties of that bank must be prescribed in the law creating it. Nobody but Congress, it has been thought, could grant these powers and privileges, or prescribe their limitations. It is true, indeed, that the message pretty plainly intimates, that the President should have been *first* consulted, and that he should have had the framing of the bill; but we are not yet accustomed to that order of things in enacting laws, nor do I know a parallel to this claim, thus now brought forward, except that, in some peculiar cases in England, highly affecting the royal prerogative, the assent of the monarch is necessary, before either the House of Peers, or his Majesty's faithful Commons, are permitted to act upon the subject, or to entertain its consideration. But supposing, Sir, that our accustomed forms and our republican principles are still to be followed, and that a law creating a bank is, like all other laws, to originate with Congress, and that the President has nothing to do with it till it is presented for his approval, then it is clear that the powers and duties of a proposed bank, and all the terms and conditions annexed to it, must, in the first place, be settled by Congress.

This power, if constitutional at all, is only constitutional in the hands of Congress. Anywhere else, its exercise would be plain usurpation. If, then, the authority to decide what powers ought to be granted to a bank belong to Congress, and Congress shall have exercised that power, it would seem little better than absurd to say, that its act, nevertheless, would be unconstitutional and invalid, if, in the opinion of a third party, it had misjudged, on a question of expediency, in the arrangement of details. According to such a mode of reasoning, a mistake in the exercise of jurisdiction takes away the jurisdiction. If Congress decide right, its decision may stand; if it decide wrong, its decision is nugatory; and whether its decision be right or wrong another is to judge, although the original power of making the decision must be allowed to be exclusively in Congress. This is the end to which the argument of the message will conduct its followers. [. . .]

The truth is, Mr. President, that if the general object, the subject-matter, properly belong to Congress, all its incidents belong to Congress also. If Congress is to establish post-offices and post-roads, it may, for that end, adopt one set of regulations or another; and either would be constitutional. So the details of one bank are as constitutional as those of another, if they are confined fairly and honestly to the purpose of organizing the institution, and rendering it useful. One *bank* is as constitutional as another *bank*. If Congress possesses the power to make a bank, it possesses the power to make it efficient, and competent to produce the good expected from it. It may clothe it with all such power and privileges, not otherwise inconsistent with the Constitution, as may be necessary, in its own judgment, to make it what government deems it should be. It may confer on it such immunities as may induce individuals to become stockholders, and to furnish the capital; and since the extent of these immunities and privileges is matter of discretion, and matter of opinion, Congress only can decide it, because Congress alone can frame or grant the charter. A charter, thus granted to individuals, becomes a contract with them, upon their compliance with its terms. The bank becomes an agent, bound to perform certain duties, and entitled to certain stipulated rights and privileges, in compensation for the proper discharge of these duties; and all these stipulations, so long as they are appropriate to the object professed, and not repugnant to any other constitutional injunction, are entirely within the competency of Congress. And yet, Sir, the message of the President toils through all the commonplace topics of monopoly, the right of taxation, the suffering of the poor, and the arrogance of the rich, with as much painful effort, as if one, or another, or all of them, had something to do with the constitutional question.

What is called the "monopoly" is made the subject of repeated rehearsal, in terms of special complaint. By this "monopoly," I suppose, is understood the restriction contained in the charter, that Congress shall not, during the twenty years, create another bank. Now, Sir, let me ask, Who would think of creating a bank, inviting stockholders into it, with large investments, imposing upon it heavy duties, as connected with the government, receiving some millions of dollars as a *bonus* or premium, and yet retaining the power of granting, the next day, another charter, which would destroy the whole value of the first? If this be an unconstitutional restraint on Congress, the Constitution must be strangely at variance with the dictates both of good sense and sound morals. Did not the first Bank of the United States contain a similar restriction? And have not the States granted bank charters with a condition, that, if the charter should be accepted, they would not grant others? States have certainly done so; and, in some instances, where no *bonus* or premium was paid at all; but from the mere desire to give effect to the charter, by inducing individuals to accept it and organize the institution. The President declares that this restriction is not necessary to the efficiency of the bank; but that is the very thing which Congress and his predecessor in office were called on to decide, and which they did decide, when the one passed and the other approved the act. And he has now no more authority to pronounce his judgment on that act than any other individual in society. It is not his province to decide on the constitutionality of statutes which Congress has passed, and his predecessors approved. [. . .]

As to the taxing power of the States, about which the message says so much, the proper answer to all it says is, that the States possess no power to tax any instrument of the government of the United States. It was no part of their power before the Constitution, and they derive no such power from any of its provisions. It is nowhere given to them. Could a State tax the *coin* of the United States at the mint? Could a State lay a stamp tax on the process of the courts of the United States, and on custom-house papers? Could it tax the transportation of the mail, or the ships of war, or the ordnance, or the muniments of war, of the United States? The reason that these cannot be taxed by a State is, that they are means and instruments of the government of the United States. The establishment of a bank exempt from State taxation takes away no existing right in a State. It leaves it all it ever possessed. But the complaint is, that the bank charter does not *confer* the power of taxation. This, certainly, though not a new (for the same argument was urged here), appears to me to be a strange mode of asserting and maintaining State rights. The power of taxation is a sovereign power; and the President and those who think with him are of opinion, in a given case, that this sovereign power should be conferred on the States by an act of Congress. There is, if I mistake not, Sir, as little compliment to State sovereignty in this idea, as there is of sound constitutional doctrine. Sovereign rights held under the grant of an act of Congress present a proposition quite new in constitutional law.

The President himself even admits that an instrument of the government of the United States ought not, as such, to be taxed by the States; yet he contends for such a power of taxing property connected with this instrument, and essential to its very being, as places its whole existence in the pleasure of the

States. It is not enough that the States may tax all the property of all their own citizens, wherever invested or however employed. The complaint is, that the power of State taxation does not reach so far as to take cognizance over persons out of the State, and to tax them for a franchise lawfully exercised under the authority of the United States. Sir, when did the power of the States, or indeed of any government, go to such an extent as that? Clearly never. The taxing power of all communities is necessarily and justly limited to the property of its own citizens, and to the property of others, having a distinct local existence as property, within its jurisdiction; it does not extend to rights and franchises, rightly exercised, under the authority of other governments, nor to persons beyond its jurisdiction. As the Constitution has left the taxing power of the States, so the bank charter leaves it. Congress has not undertaken either to take away, or to confer, a taxing power; nor to enlarge, or to restrain it; if it were to do either, I hardly know which of the two would be the least excusable.

I beg leave to repeat, Mr. President, that what I have now been considering are the President's objections, not to the policy or expediency, but to the constitutionality of the bank; and not to the constitutionality of any new or proposed bank, but of the bank as it now is, and as it has long existed. If the President had declined to approve this bill because he thought the original charter unwisely granted, and the bank, in point of policy and expediency, objectionable or mischievous, and in that view only had suggested the reasons now urged by him, his argument, however inconclusive, would have been intelligible, and not, in its whole frame and scope, inconsistent with all well-established first principles. His rejection of the bill, in that case, would have been, no doubt, an extraordinary exercise of power; but it would have been, nevertheless, the exercise of a power belonging to his office, and trusted by the Constitution to his discretion. But when he puts forth an array of arguments such as the message employs, not against the expediency of the bank, but against its constitutional existence, he confounds all distinctions, mixes questions of policy and questions of right together, and turns all constitutional restraints into mere matters of opinion. As far as its power extends, either in its direct effects or as a precedent, the message not only unsettles every thing which has been settled under the Constitution, but would show, also, that the Constitution itself is utterly incapable of any fixed construction or definite interpretation, and that there is no possibility of establishing, by its authority, any practical limitations on the powers of the respective branches of the government. [. . .]

Mr. President, we have arrived at a new epoch. We are entering on experiments, with the government and the Constitution of the country, hitherto untried, and of fearful and appalling aspect. This message calls us to the contemplation of a future which little resembles the past. Its principles are at war with all that public opinion has sustained, and all which the experience of the government has sanctioned. It denies first principles; it contradicts truths, heretofore received as indisputable. It denies to the judiciary the interpretation of law, and claims to divide with Congress the power of originating statutes. It extends the grasp of executive pretension over every power of the government. But this is not all. It presents the chief magistrate of the Union in the attitude of arguing away the powers of that government over which he has been chosen to preside; and adopting for this purpose modes of reasoning which, even under the influence of all proper feeling towards high official station, it is difficult to regard as respectable. It appeals to every prejudice which may betray men into a mistaken view of their own interests, and to every passion which may lead them to disobey the impulses of their understanding. It urges all the specious topics of State rights and national encroachment against that which a great majority of the States have affirmed to be rightful, and in which all of them have acquiesced. It sows, in an unsparing manner, the seeds of jealousy and ill-will against that government of which its author is the official head. It raises a cry, that liberty is in danger, at the very moment when it puts forth claims to powers heretofore unknown and unheard of. It affects alarm for the public freedom, when nothing endangers that freedom so much as its own unparalleled pretences. This, even, is not all. It manifestly seeks to inflame the poor against the rich; it wantonly attacks whole classes of the people, for the purpose of turning against them the prejudices and the resentments of other classes. It is a state paper which finds no topic too exciting for its use, no passion too inflammable for its address and its solicitation.

Such is this message. It remains now for the people of the United States to choose between the principles here avowed and their government. These cannot subsist together. The one or the other must be rejected. If the sentiments of the message shall receive general approbation, the Constitution will have perished even earlier than the moment which its enemies originally allowed for the termination of its existence. It will not have survived to its fiftieth year.

Theophilus Fisk

Capital against Labor (1835)

The history of the producers of wealth, of the industrious classes, is that of a continued warfare of *honesty* against *fraud, weakness* against *power, justice* against *oppression.* The purchasers of labor have in all ages had the advantage of the sellers and they have rarely failed to use their power to the furtherance of their own interest. Until within a comparatively short period of time, the laboring classes even in England and Scotland were slaves, serfs, bondmen. Colliers in the latter country even down to as late a period as 1776 were slaves in fact as well as in name. Gradually, however, the rust of time weakened their chains of bondage; the period at length arrived when the grievous burdens upon their shoulders were too galling longer to be borne; the collar was slipped from the galled neck, and their aristocratic masters, finding it impossible longer to *ride* in safety, consented with an ill grace to forego a privilege they were no longer able to preserve. But in losing the *name* of slaves, we are not to suppose that the sellers of labor were allowed to assume the place in society that God and nature designed for them. That the laborer had natural, inalienable rights, that they were free and independent members of society and possessed the right, if they sold their labor, to fix their own price upon it would have been scouted at as of all things the most levelling, disorganizing and dangerous. Hence the government, those who purchased labor, were continually passing partial, unequal, unjust laws and paying for it according to the ideas of its value by those who wanted to use it. Then commenced the struggle between the two great dealers in the market of the world, viz., Capital and Labor; and as Capital had always the government with its legion of bayonets to support its claims, the result may easily be imagined.

During the existence of the ancient monopolies, called "guilds or fraternities," capital and labor were identified. These fraternities were composed both of masters and workmen whose interests were one and the same; at length, however, the privileges of these bodies which had originally been conferred upon them for their protection against the violence of the feudal nobility became so odious and oppressive that it became indispensable that they should be abridged. The parties then became opponents; the one endeavoring to raise, the other to depress the prices of labor. Combinations were then formed. As early as 1548, we find a notice in a preamble of an act of Parliament, in these words: "artificers, handicrafts men and laborers have made confederacies and promises and have sworn mutual oaths, not only that they should not meddle with one another's work and perform and finish that another hath begun, but also to constitute and appoint *how much work they shall do in a day and what hours and times* they shall work, contrary to the laws and statutes of this realm, to the great injury and impoverishment of his majesty's subjects." Parliament also passed sundry acts expressly prohibiting combinations for the purpose of raising the prices of labor. In 1824, after long experience had tested the folly and inutility of laws of that nature, that they were partial and unjust, that they raised one class and depressed another, that they were impolitic, unwise, and inexpedient, the system was abandoned and the laws repealed.

By this brief and imperfect outline, it may be seen that those who live without labor are and have been the enemies of the producing classes. Their interests, although naturally, where justice prevails, one and the same, have almost always clashed with each other. We find by glancing at the past that the laboring classes have been struggling for centuries under the iron yoke of despotism, against fraud, tyranny, and injustice. "Upward and onward" has been their watchword until now they are enabled from the proud eminence to which they have attained to look forward and behold the promised land. If they are true to themselves they must inevitably enter in and possess it. Although the Jebusites and Gershashites and [Perizzites], all the various classes, castes, and tribes of the Canaanites who live by prey and plunder may look fierce and "talk big," the inheritance is ours.

The history of the amelioration, improvement, and elevation of the working classes is but the history of the progress of wealth, civilization, and all that ennobles, dignifies, and exalts humanity. It is the history of all the wonderful improvements in the arts and sciences, in manufactures and commerce.

The record of the past affords the highest encouragement for the present and the future. If the laboring classes have been able with all the stupendous obstacles that have been thrown in their way to fight an uphill battle against the omnipotent power of Capital and to possess themselves of many of the privileges that belong to free citizenship, we can easily determine the question of their ultimate emancipation and triumph. The controversy will never cease, the warfare will never end, until all are placed upon the broad tableland of perfect political equality. The sellers of labor will yet wrest from the unholy grasp of the apostles of Mammon the right to govern themselves, to make their own laws, and to select their own agents to execute them.

Though the power of wealth in the hands of the *few* may for a time keep down the industrious *many*, yet the hazard of experimenting too far with those who have suffered so much and so long had better be taken into the calculation before a system of continued, permanent robbery be determined upon; before they determined to treat the unmanacled workingman as they would a convict in the state prison, they would do well to pause. Beneath their feet an earthquake slumbers. There is a period in the affairs of men when forbearance ceases to be a virtue, when patient endurance becomes criminal. Let the interested beware how they accelerate the sands in Time's hourglass and thereby hasten a season when resistance and not resignation and passive obedience will be the rallying watchword.

The laws by which we are governed were not made by us although said to be—had they been, they would have been equal, equitable, and impartial—for the benefit and protection of the masses, the great whole of which society is composed. It is quite impossible for the laboring classes to make laws to rob one another; they cannot steal from themselves by partial legislation. What is for the interest of one is for the interest of all. But let the privileged few make the laws and what is the result? What has been the natural consequence in all past time? Why, that the many have been ground up to feed the nabobs. What has been, will be. Like causes produce like effects under similar circumstances. Pore over the musty folios of the past and the startling truth meets you at every page that all laws made by rich men have been in favor of Capital, never in favor of Labor. And yet our blood-proud and purse-proud nobility talk of *protecting the laborer!* "Such protection as the vulture gives to Iambs, covering and devouring them!" Their misnamed laws of *protection* always have made them rich at our expense, have ever added to their already overflowing coffers by filching the products of industry from the pockets of the poor. The laborer asks no protection, their offers therefore are entirely gratuitous; the laborer can and does both protect himself and the non-producer into the bargain. In case of invasion or insurrection, who talks of protecting them? When the appalling cry of "fire!" falls upon the ear, who protects the scanty property of the laborer, the "palaces of the poor?" Not the men who make the laws. They do not even protect their own gorgeous mansions from the devouring element. No. We ask no protection; we simply desire *to be let alone.*

A great deal of affectionate regard is, and has been, manifested by the aristocracy for the interests of the "dear people." They have clung to them like the poisonous ivy to the monarch of the wood, palsying the faculties, throwing fetters of bondage upon the intellect until at last they perish in the entwining folds of hollow-hearted dissimulation. All the friendly embraces of those who fatten upon the toil of others are, like the hug of the bear, certain death. Let our motto be, "Take your delicate fingers from our throats; 'white paws,' if you please, gentlemen."

But the monopolists, the professional men, the men of wealth, *they* labor, it is said, as well as the farmer and the mechanic. They do labor to be sure, but *it is laboring to collect that which others have earned*. The lawyer's "may it please your honor" never made the pot boil. The presidents' and cashiers' printed paper rags, covered with false promises to pay, never crowned the hill with ripening sheaf, nor made the valley smile. The lazy drone by sucking a quill behind his ear never yet felled the boundless forest and reared the castle's dome, breaking the repose of ages with the busy tones of hardy enterprise. If our houses could spring up spontaneously like mushrooms, if we could sit in our seats like dried mummies and by single scratch of a pen could construct canals, bridges, and railroads, we might then talk about equality of rights and privileges with some degree of propriety. But no. If houses are to be erected, it is to be done by the hard hand of labor, in sweat, and toil, and fatigue. The legislature grants no charters for the *workingmen* to build houses without labor and to grow rich without being industrious.

We hear at almost every corner of the streets the stereotyped Billingsgate about the "lower classes." "Lower classes" indeed! The time has been when they were as low as the sordid spirit of avarice and the iron heel of bloodsucking ambition could tread them down; thousands living and dying mere cogs in the social machine; dragging out a miserable existence in the squalor of toil, want, and degradation. They have stood still as stocks, quiet as the charnel house, while "lisping infancy" has been foredoomed by the unholy lust of gold to labor 12, 14, 16 hours per day, withering and blasting the bud of youth ere its petals were unfolded to the sun. If they dared to remonstrate, to utter a word of expostulation, the dry, hard, cold lip of unfeeling selfishness would contract with scorn and malignity, and the stony eye of unpitying brutality would "look daggers," while the hand used them. This has been borne; their taskmasters were rich, and could talk Latin.

The natural consequences of laziness, the penalty of idleness, has fallen upon the industrious classes instead of the rich capitalist who lives without labor, those who earn and save have been compelled to toil early and late for a pittance barely sufficient to keep their families from starving that the indolent drones might be clothed in purple and fine linen and fare sumptuously every day. The natural reward of honest industry has been wrested from the laborer by unjust laws and given to those who were never guilty of earning a dollar in their lives, who are too lazy to work, and too proud to beg; but the days of oppression are numbered; God grant they may soon be finished.

The subject which has called us from our homes this evening is vitally important inasmuch as it seems the dawning light of a coming day. It will have this good effect if nothing more: it will teach those who live by plunder that a part of mankind were never born to be hewers of wood and drawers of water to those no better than themselves. It will call upon the public for their strong reasons why the producers of wealth should be kept in ignorance, servility, and bondage; why they must longer be debarred the blessings they have purchased with tears and blood, and lazy men riot upon the miseries of the poor! It calls upon the philanthropist and Christian to advocate and demand the immediate emancipation of the "white slaves of the North," and to declare to the world that the workers "are, and of right ought to be, free and independent citizens of these United States."

The recent movements among our industrious fellow citizens speak a language that can neither be perverted nor misunderstood. The world is told by acts that speak more plainly than volumes of words, that he who will shun the exertions and sacrifices necessary to qualify him to know his rights, and also to maintain them, deserves to be duped, to groan in perpetual slavery, to wear the inextricable chains the *few* are forging for the *many*."

Knowledge and virtue being the only sure foundation of American Liberty, you have taken the proper steps towards a resumption of your sacred rights. By reducing the number of hours of labor, you give yourselves opportunity to obtain that knowledge which is power. They whose god is gain have long feared that if the laborer should be allowed to take his nose from the grindstone five minutes at a time, he would be learning how to govern and provide for himself, so he must be compelled to toil on like a galley slave at the oar. "Is there not," exclaims an eloquent gentleman in the British Parliament, "something inexpressibly cruel, most disgustingly selfish in thus attempting to ascertain the utmost limits to which labor and fatigue may be carried without their certainly occasioning misery and destruction, the full extent of profitable torture that may be safely inflicted and in appealing to learned and experienced doctors to fix the precise point beyond which it would be murder to proceed?" Eight hours for work, eight hours for sleep, and eight hours for amusement and instruction is the equitable allotment of the twenty-four. But to a great majority of the buyers of labor even the granting of your present just demand that ten hours shall constitute a day's work seems preposterous in the extreme. They think that mankind were not only born to trouble as the sparks fly upward, but according to their creed we were born to labor as the sweat drops downwards. Says *Blackwood's Magazine*, "Are not the poor the 'working classes'? Then let them work—work—work. If they are to have resting hours on weekdays, pray, what is the use of the Sabbath? Work is the chief end and whole duty of man." Nobody thinks of asking what rest does the law of nature require? We are governed by the laws of avarice which, like bigotry, "has no head, and cannot think, no heart and cannot feel." We even seem to forget there ever were laws of nature, we are groping in such an unnatural state of society. We might almost as well talk of the empire of Chaos as of the empire of mind while it is fettered with chains of midnight.

The proverb "All work, and no play, makes Jack a dull boy" is truth, but not the whole truth. Sir Anthony Carlisle, an English physician of great eminence, says that after 40 years observation and practice, he is satisfied that vigorous health and the ordinary duration of life cannot be generally maintained under the circumstances of twelve hours labor, day by day. Dr. Farre says "Man can do more than he is allowed or permitted to do by nature, and in attempting to transgress the bounds Providence has pointed out to him, he abridges his life in the exact proportion in which he transgresses the laws of nature and the divine command." When will the mass learn that the life is more than meat, the body more than raiment?

Dr. Green, surgeon of St. Thomas' Hospital, draws a most frightful picture of the maladies that are engendered by long continued, unremitting toil. The medical profession in England raise their united voices against a system that demands uniform, unceasing labor. They declare that the average labor of full grown, strong, healthy men ought not to exceed twelve hours, meals included. The vigor of life is well known to depend upon the perfection of the blood. "If the arterial circulation be too much exhausted, an accumulation takes place on the venous side, the blood is deteriorated, and organic diseases are produced which abridge life." So far they regard man as an animal!—over-exertion having the same baneful influence upon both. But man is to be considered as vastly superior to an animal; over-labor has a most debasing influence upon his mind, that faculty alone which renders him more exalted in the scale of being than the animal creation. "The bonds of domestic love become relaxed; and as a consequence, the filial and paternal duties are uncultivated. The overworked artisan has not time to cherish these feelings by the familiar and grateful arts which are their constant food, and without which nourishment they perish." An apathy benumbs his better sympathies, chills his spirit, and turns the heart to stone. Such is the natural, aye, almost inevitable result of the barbarous system against which you have so nobly taken up arms; should you succeed, of which I do not entertain a shade of doubt, if you are true to yourselves, the blessings of posterity will be showered upon your memories. The cruel system of slavery must be robbed of its sting; the venom must be destroyed. We demand not mere justice to the animal body, but time to do justice to the heart and mind, time to grow in knowledge, and the practice of equity and virtue. We wish to see the beacon of knowledge lighted up in every hilltop and shedding its hallowed rays across the path of ignorance, shining with a saving light, brighter and brighter even unto the perfect day. [. . .]

A mighty spirit is abroad in the earth overthrowing the pillars of despotism and the fetters of bondage. With the friends of freedom throughout the world let us be co-workers. Let the present effort be but the glimmering twilight of a day of unclouded glory. Remember that this is but the lopping off of but one single head of the political monster that feeds on human gore; the other ninety-nine are hissing and sputtering fiercely as ever. So long as you allow capital to make laws for labor, standing out for higher wages or reducing the hours of toil will only be doing the work by halves. There must be a radical reform and this can only be accomplished at the ballot boxes. Allow the capitalists to make a compromise with you, allow them to play the lawgiver, and they will not care a brass farthing how few hours you work or what prices you receive. They will take good care how to strike the balance when they come to pay you for your labor. For every hour you abstract from toil, they will levy an indirect tax upon you that shall treble its value. No. There is not a nabob in Boston that would raise a finger to prevent the "ten hour system," if he thought the great work of reform would stop there; for all that could be remedied in a hundred ways by partial legislation next winter. But the great fear of those who grow rich upon your industry is that if you get time to improve your minds, you will get your eyes open to the monstrous frauds that have been perpetrated upon you by the heathen idolaters, the worshippers of Mammon. Let their worst fears be realized. Shoulder to shoulder, man to man, our fathers fought and triumphed; let their sons profit by their illustrious example. Shrink not, disband not, and fear nothing.

Teach the lawgivers a salutary lesson at the polls; vote for no man who is not pledged to maintain your cause at all risks and at every hazard. If you are united, your strength is well nigh omnipotent. Throw away all party names; *all parties* are, and ever have been, opposed to your interests. Form a party of your own that shall be all-controlling and uncontrollable. Take any name you please, I care not. Call yourselves Whigs, Tories, Democrats, Federalists—it is all one to me, so that you are united. Your opposers will seek to divide you by some party jealousy because they know that divide and ruin is the only policy that will overthrow you. Bind yourselves together by the strongest of all bonds: that of self-interest. You have all one common cause, one common name, one common interest: the interest of Labor, the interest of honest industry. Keep this one single object in view, no longer at elections throw the rope over the roof of the house and pull at each end, but all one way; give one steady "yo yeave yoo" the long, strong and the pull altogether, and the mass of human wrong, inequality, and oppression will be scattered to the four winds of heaven.

David Henshaw

Remarks upon the Rights and Powers of Corporations, and the Rights, Powers and Duties of the Legislature toward Them (1837)

Business corporations, excluding banks and all large corporations for trading in money, when judiciously granted and suitably regulated, seem to me generally beneficial and the natural offspring of our social condition. But if they are to be placed beyond legislative control and are thus to become monopolies and perpetuities, they assume an aspect the reverse of this and become alarming excrescences upon the body politic. We may assume this axiom as perfectly sound: that *Corporations can hold their rights upon no firmer basis nor different tenure than individuals hold theirs.* The legislature exercises the undisputed right to regulate the business of individuals and to define their rights to property. It has first prohibited, then licensed, and then made penal, the selling of lottery tickets. It prohibits the selling of certain articles without a license therefor from designated officers. It forbids the selling of goods at auction without a license and the payment of a tax. It forbids the selling of other articles, except in certain quantities, and with certain brands put upon them by public officers—unwise and vexatious regulations, I grant, but still who disputes the legality of the inspection laws? It requires, in other cases, that the name of the vender or packer be branded on the article sold. It prohibits people from doing business on certain days and on particular hours, as in the case of the laws respecting the observance of the Lord's day, and selling goods by auction after sunset. It prohibits certain amusements, and has even affixed a fine to a particular exercise of the liberty of speech, as may be seen in the laws against gaming and profane swearing. It regulates the rights of inheritance, prescribes the rules for the transfer of property from individuals to individuals, and their rights and remedies in matters of private contract; and all these rules are changed at the will of the legislature. What particular quality, then, is there, in a law, in the form of a charter, or limited copartnership to a number of individuals, that places it beyond the power that created it, the legislative power, and gives to it the character of a contract in perpetuity? From the very nature of the case, the legislature must have the same right to repeal as to grant a charter. It has the same right, inherently, to repeal a special law or charter creating a bank, insurance company, manufactory, or any other business corporation that it has to repeal the general law of limited copartnerships. But this right to repeal the charters gives it no right to the private property of the corporation, any more than the right to repeal the general law of limited copartnerships gives it the right to the property of the partners.

In this state, the legislature transcends its constitutional power if it attempt to farm out the rights of the community and of succeeding generations by means of corporate perpetuities to individual or associated grantees. Our institutions abhor private perpetuities and monopolies as much as nature abhors a vacuum. The constitution of Massachusetts says: "No man, nor corporation, or association of men, have any other title to obtain advantages or *particular* or exclusive privileges, distinct from those of the community, than what arises from considerations of services rendered to the public." It also says, "that government is instituted for the *common good;* for the protection, safety, prosperity and happiness of the *people,* and *not* for the profit, honor, or private interest of any one man, family or class of men: Therefore, the people alone have an incontestable, unalienable, and indefeasible right to institute government, to reform, alter or totally change the same, when their protection, safety, prosperity and happiness require it." Again it says, "that the legislature ought frequently to assemble for the redress of grievances, for *correcting,* strengthening and confirming the laws, and for making new laws, as the *common good* requires."

The constitution of this state, though it allows and supposes that "particular and exclusive privileges, distinct from those of the community" may be granted by the legislature "to individuals, corporations and associations of men," allows them to be granted only for services rendered. They must be considered by the legislature to be generally beneficial; they must conduce to the common good, or it has no constitutional power to grant them. The framers of the constitution well knew that corporations and associations of men possessing "particular" privileges adapted to the nature and purposes of their pursuits were necessary in this community; that the charter for a college would not answer for the business of a church; that a charter to a glass manufactory would not answer for a bank; and they hence clothed the legislature with power to make these grants, limited, however, by the consideration that they are in consequence of the benefit they will confer on the public, that they will conduce to the *common good.* They were, from their constitutional origin, to be considered public laws, for public purposes; and whenever they should cease to minister to the purposes of their creation, the *common good,* the legislature, for the time being, not only has a right, but is in duty bound by the same constitution, to "correct" them, either by making new laws respecting them, or amending the old ones. There is no more propriety in saying that these institutions can only be controlled by general laws than in assuming that they can only be created by general laws; or than there would be in saying that the legislature cannot regulate the affairs of a single town or city by a particular or special law. Indeed, if these acts of incorporation or charters are not to be considered laws of the land, great wrong has been committed under them in so considering them for some purposes. The legislature has no constitutional right, by a special act, to permit my neighbor to take my land for his own use against my consent. But it has a right to take my land or other property for public purposes, paying me therefor a just equivalent. If railroad, turnpike, canal, and the like corporations are mere private associations, existing for the benefit of the corporations and not for the *common good*, I would ask, What right have they to occupy my land against my consent? All these corporations then exist by the law of the land and, like all other laws, are liable to modification at the legislative will. Such, in effect, has been the decision of the Supreme Court of the United States in regard to the Bank of the United States, in the cases of Maryland and Ohio, which states taxed that bank. The court decided that the Bank of the United States was a *public institution*. Such, too, was the opinion of the legislature of Massachusetts in revising the laws of the state. In the third section of the second chapter of the revised code, it is declared that "all acts of incorporation shall be deemed public acts." There is more sound than substance in the term "vested rights," as applied to acts of incorporation. Every right any citizen holds is a vested right until he is divested of it; and the remark applies with equal truth to corporations as to individuals. But it by no means follows that, because they have a "vested right," they may not be legally divested of it. Last year our farmers had a vested right to screw their hay into bundles and sell it as they pleased; this year the legislature has divested them of that right, unless they put the name of the packer on the bundle. This year a bank has a vested right, vested for the common good, to loan its credit; next year the legislature may, if it choose, divest it of that right, if it will more conduce to the common good to divest it. And this, too, inherently, and without any special reservation in the charter to that effect. Numerous instances, in this and other States, might be cited, where this power has been exercised upon banks, and other charters of incorporation; but I omit them, preferring the question should be decided in the mind of the reader upon its own merits to relying upon precedents. Mere precedents have little binding force upon my mind.

The safety of the public and of corporations themselves depends on the establishing of these principles. Corporate charters would not be repealed, admitting this right to exist, as all experience teaches us, unless they had become a public grievance in the opinion of the legislature; in which case their "particular" privileges ought to be taken from them. They were originally granted to promote the common good; and whenever they cease to accomplish the purposes of their creation, an end should be put to their existence. [. . .]

With respect to the rights of wives, a married woman, now, has a right, and of course a vested right, to the use of certain portions of her husband's real estate, if she survive him, of which her husband cannot divest her without her consent; but the legislature can change the law, and divest her of this right, and this, too, though she has no voice in choosing the representatives.

Under existing laws the personal property of the wife becomes the property of the husband on marriage, but not her real estate. The legislature could change the law, and vest in the husband the real as well as the personal estate. Can corporations, then, *the mere creatures of the law, created not for themselves, but for the common good*, claim rights superior to those of individuals, and above the reach of the legislative power? In maintaining the legislative authority to alter, amend, or totally to abolish all charters, I am far from advocating any general, indiscriminate, or wanton exercise of that power. The legislature, composed as it is of the representatives of the whole people, chosen annually, could have no motive to legislate upon this subject, unless necessity and the common good required it, nor unless the people sanctioned it. When any institution of this kind, in any of its branches, from age or other causes, has ceased to answer the design of its creation, the common good, there should be a power in the legislature, and it ought to be exercised, to put an end to such institution. Who shall judge of the wants of the existing generation, the living or the dead? Who shall control the property of this world and prescribe its application, the dead, who once owned it in part, or the living, who own it entire? The conservatives cling to the dead; I am for the living. This right is inherent and exists in all communities, from the very nature of civil society; and, in this country, the principle is recognized in our written and fundamental law. The constitution gives to the legislature, for the time being, authority to pass laws creating and regulating these institutions for the *common good*; but one legislature has no constitutional competency to bind its successor, who is coequal in power, both holding their authority from the same constitution, and not the one from the other. Hence, happily, one legislature cannot bind another, and thus farm out, irrevocably, the rights of succeeding generations.

Where lies the difficulty in applying these principles to practice by amending or repealing all such acts of incorporation as may be found objectionable? The difficulty arises from the assumption of authority on the part of the Supreme Court of the United States, which, if submitted to, prostrates the power of the states to the footstool of that bench, that acts of incorporation are contracts between the state granting them and the corporators; and cannot be annulled except with the consent of the corporators, because the Constitution of the United States, the paramount law of the land, says that no state shall pass any laws impairing the obligation of contracts. This principle was maintained, if not established, in the case of the Dartmouth College, tried before the Supreme Court at Washington, in 1819. It may be necessary therefore to a right understanding of this subject and to a just appreciation of the principles laid down by the court and of their effect upon the rights and interests of the states, to take a view of the facts in this case and of the course of reasoning which brought the court to such an extraordinary result.

In the year 1769, a charter was granted in the name of the King of Great Britain, George the 3d, through his governor of the then province of New Hampshire, John Wentworth, by and with the advice of the council of the province, to Eleazer Wheelock and others for a college, authorizing them by voluntary endowments to support suitable teachers and other officers therein named. The object of the charter is recited in the preamble, and is to further the exertions of Dr. Wheelock in spreading the truths of the Gospel and the lights of civilization among the Indians and in giving the best means of education to the people of New Hampshire, for their own benefit. [. . .] It was an institution, not for private emolument, but to promote the public good, the civilization and Christianizing the Indians, and for the education of the people of New Hampshire. By the Revolution the people of New Hampshire succeeded to all the rights of sovereignty held before by the crown, the parliament of Great Britain, and by the colony of New Hampshire. Every kind of civil and political power, before held, jointly or severally, by the different or collective branches of the government of the mother country and of the province of New Hampshire, devolved upon the state of New Hampshire at the time of the revolution. The powers thus acquired still remain to be exercised by the legislature, except so far as they may have been restricted by their own state constitution or that of the United States. In the year 1816, the legislature of New Hampshire, for the purpose of making the college more useful to the people of New Hampshire, the Indians, for whose benefit it was originally, in part, founded, having become extinct, and the funds being no longer applied or applicable to their use, passed an act enlarging and changing the government of the college. The trustees, disliking to lose their power and the profits of office, as they were likely to do by this act, resisted, on the ground that the charter vested in them rights of which the legislature had no authority to divest them; that the charter was a "contract" within the meaning of the Constitution of the United States; and that the act aforesaid impaired its obligation, contrary to the Constitution. They brought a suit in the state courts, contesting the validity of the law, which was decided against them. The trustees then carried it by appeal to the Supreme Court of the United States; and that tribunal decided in their favor. Chief Justice Marshall, who presided at the trial, *assumed* the whole question, as settled, as follows: "It can require *no argument* to prove that the circumstances of this case constitute a contract. An application is made to the *crown* for a charter to incorporate a religious and literary institution. In the application, it is stated, that large contributions have been made in England for the object, which will be conferred on the corporation as soon as it shall be created.

"The charter is granted, and on its faith the property is conveyed. Surely, in this transaction, every ingredient of a complete contract is to be found." That may be true, but is it such a contract as was intended by the framers of the Federal Constitution and the people who adopted it should come within the reach of the inhibitory clause in that instrument? The institution of government is a contract between the whole body of citizens and each citizen; but does it hence follow that we cannot impair that contract, that we cannot change the constitution without the unanimous assent of the citizens? Every civil institution is in some sense a contract; but does it follow that, hence, we cannot change those institutions? This charter was a contract of this kind, given by the provincial executive, containing express and implied conditions, the former limited, qualified, and controlled by the latter. The trustees were declared to be a corporation, with power to hold forever certain gifts, grants, and other property for certain purposes, subject, however, to the fundamental laws of the colony, liable to taxation, and to such laws as subsequent legislatures might deem proper to enact, within their legislative competency; and their powers, at the time, over local grants, were plenary. If the grant had emanated directly from the king, which it did not, it must have been limited by these well-known, though implied conditions. The king himself was legally incompetent to make any grant other than thus limited. The Chief Justice, apparently conscious of the sophistical position he had assumed, comes, subsequently, more to the point, and asks:

First, "Is this a contract protected by the Constitution of the United States?"

Second, "Is it impaired by the acts under which the defendant holds?"

The last question it is unnecessary to consider, for, notwithstanding the finely-spun arguments of the state counsel to show that the law did not impair the charter, even if it were a contract, that to change and enlarge the charter was not to impair the contract, I am free to admit that there is more ingenuity than candor in it, and that the law of New Hampshire did abridge and impair the rights of the trustees under the charter. Judge Marshall says the general correctness of these observations cannot be controverted, viz., "That the framers of the Constitution did not intend to restrain the states in the regulation of their civil institutions adopted for internal government, and that the instrument they have given us is not to be so construed, may be admitted. This provision of the Constitution never has been understood to embrace other contracts than those which respect some object of value, and confer rights which may be asserted in a court of justice." Does not this embrace every possible case or transaction in society, particularly if it come before a judge avowing the vicious principle on which most English and some Anglo-American judges act, that "the first duty of a good judge is to extend his jurisdiction?"

It has extended to officers appointed by the executive who have demanded a compulsory process to procure a commission made out for an officer, but subsequently withheld by order of the President. The office was an object of value, though not a "freehold," and the appointment and commission conferred rights which were asserted in a court of justice; and hence the case comes within that clause of the Federal Constitution respecting contracts, as expounded and defined above by Judge Marshall. If the appointment of men to office be a contract, charters of incorporation contracts, and marriage be a contract, as Judge Marshall pretty plainly, and Judge Story unequivocally, intimates, coming within the scope of the before-cited inhibitory clause of the Federal Constitution, it would seem to follow that every other transaction of civil society may be engulfed in this vortex and whirled under the jurisdiction of the Supreme Court; and that the people of the states, instead of having governments adapted to their wants, liable to be modified, altered, repealed, or totally changed, as was supposed to be their inherent and unalienable right, have, in fact, myriads of little perpetuities beyond the control of state and national legislation, and subject only to the will of their directors or of the lord patrons.

Judge Marshall says, respecting the contract of marriage, "When any state legislature shall pass an act annulling all marriage contracts (and if they can annul one they can many), or allowing either party to annul it without the consent of the other, it will be time enough to inquire whether such an act be constitutional."

Judge Story, in the same case, was much more explicit, and develops the doctrine of the court on the subject of contracts more boldly than Judge Marshall. He says, "As to the case of the contract of marriage, which the argument supposes not to be within the reach of the prohibitory clause, because it is a matter of civil institution, *I profess I do not feel the weight of the reason assigned for the exception.* In a legal sense, *all contracts* recognized as valid in any country, may be properly said to be *matters* of *civil institution,* since they obtain their obligation and construction *jure loci contractus.*" [. . .]

"But," continues the judge, "if the argument means to assert that the legislature has power to dissolve such contracts without any breach on either side, against the wishes of the parties, and without *judicial* inquiry to ascertain the breach, I certainly am not prepared to admit such a power. [. . .] "A man has just as good a right to his *wife*, as he has to the *property* acquired under a marriage contract. He has a legal right to her *society*, and her *fortune;* and to divest such right without his default, and against *his will*, would be as flagrant a violation of the principles of justice as the confiscation of his own estate."

Judge Marshall says, "According to the theory of the British constitution, their parliament is omnipotent. To annul corporate rights, might give a shock to public opinion which that government has chosen to avoid; but the power is not questioned." (Here the judge mistakes, for Great Britain has exercised this power in many cases in that of church funds, as I have before shown.) "By the Revolution," continues Judge Marshall, "the duties as well as the powers of government devolved on the people of New Hampshire. It is admitted, that among the latter was comprehended the transcendent power of parliament, as well as of the executive. . . . Religion, charity, and education, are, in the law of England, legatees or donees, capable of receiving bequests or donations in this form." (But they are not under our laws, and the fact of their capability in England, to say the least, is irrelevant.) [. . .]

"This," continues the judge, "is plainly a contract, to which the donors, the trustees, and the crown, to whose rights and obligations New Hampshire succeeds, were the original parties. It is a contract made for a valuable consideration. It is a contract for the security and disposition of property. It is a contract, on the faith of which real and personal estate has been conveyed to the corporation. It is then a contract within the letter of the Constitution; and within its spirit also, unless the fact that property is invested by the donors in trustees for the promotion of religion and education, for the benefit of persons who are perpetually changing, though the objects remain the same, shall create a particular exception, taking this case out of the prohibition contained in the Constitution.

"It is *more than possible*, that the preservation of rights of this description was *not* particularly in view of the framers of the Constitution, when the clause under consideration was introduced into that instrument.

[. . .] "It is not enough to say that this particular case (or class of cases) was not in the mind of the convention when the article was framed, nor of the American people when it was adopted. It is necessary to go further, and to say that, had this particular case been suggested, the language would have been so varied as to exclude it, or it would have been made a special exception"!! Can there be anywhere found upon record a more unsound and dangerous stretch of judicial law? What can more directly shake the public confidence in the judgment of the court than these admissions? Judge Marshall admits, what everybody knows, that the prohibitory clause in the Constitution was *not* intended by the convention who framed, nor the people who adopted that instrument, to extend to cases of this kind. It had reference only to money contracts, and was intended to restrict the states from cancelling those obligations by bankrupt laws, stop laws, and tender laws.

This construction, too, violates well-settled principles of law and of common sense, long and often recognized by the Supreme Court itself. Every man knows that the *intention* of the parties in making laws is to be the rule of construction. Their intentions are to be gathered from the words of the law, and if they be ambiguous, from any other credible source. [. . .]

Whatever was granted in the Constitution was meant to be a well-defined grant. It was never intended by those who framed, and the people who adopted the Constitution, that its powers should be enlarged by construction. So jealous and careful were the people upon this point, that they adopted an amendment to guard against the apprehended evil. It is the 10th article of amendment in the Constitution, as follows: "The powers not delegated to the United States by the Constitution, nor prohibited by it to the states, are reserved to the states respectively, or to the people." The framers intended a specific thing in the clause, inhibiting the states from passing laws impairing the obligations of contracts; they made use of the word *contracts* in its ordinary meaning, as it was then well understood. It was to remedy the then well-known evil of tender laws, stop laws, and absolving laws. It was never designed to apply to the civil institutions of the states, but was confined in its application to contracts for the buying and selling of things. If there were any doubt as to this fact—but there appears to be none even on the mind of the Chief Justice—the testimony of Luther Martin, a member of the convention from Maryland, in his letter or report to the legislature of his state, would remove it. It was meant, he says, only to secure the rights of debtor and creditor from the operations of state tender laws, stop laws, and bankrupt laws. Mr. Madison, another member of the convention, in the *Federalist,* written about the period the Constitution was adopted, bears his testimony corroborative of the same fact.

The principle assumed by Judge Marshall and sanctioned by all the court except Judge Duval in effect annihilates the Federal Constitution, or makes it a plastic mass in the hands of the Supreme Court to mean anything or nothing. It can mold the state institutions to suit the will of the court.

The Chief Justice admits that this kind of contract was not in view when the convention adopted and the people approved the inhibitory clause. But that, he says, is not enough; you must go further; you must show that if this case had been presented to them at the time, they would have rejected it; *and of this probability the court assume the sole right to judge.* The counsel for the state show that the convention had not this class of contracts in view when they framed the clause; their object and design were confined to property contracts and private rights; and all history bears testimony that the states never would have surrendered the very object for which they had contended before the Revolution and encountered its miseries and perils to attain, the right to regulate their own internal civil institutions. "Very true," say the court, "but this particular class of cases did not occur to them at the time, and if it had, would they have excluded it? We decide that they would not; and consequently it is embraced within the meaning of the clause."

Thus the authority to regulate some of the most important civil institutions, and particularly that of education in the higher branches of literature and the sciences, the control over those seminaries where the citizens are educated who are destined to fill what are termed the liberal professions and, as ministers, lawyers, physicians, and men of letters, are to enter every city, town, hamlet, and family in the state and directly to influence the condition of society, is wrested from the states and confided to irresponsible perpetuities, thus made independent within the limits of the state. With such latitudinous and farfetched constructions, the Federal Constitution is whatever the Federal judiciary may please to make it; and the states are in fact in possession of little more power than the bailiffs who officiate in the Federal courts.

The case, from beginning to end, was tried and decided, in all its cardinal points, upon an assumption of facts and principles that have no real existence here. It is an English, not an American decision; made by a court who are English in all their legal learning and principles. The rights, powers, privileges, and duties of the corporation are gathered, not from the *laws* of New Hampshire, where alone we should look for them, but from British "authorities," that is, from the opinions of English judges, in what the court assume to be analogous cases, and English law writers, who have figured on the British bench, in British "reports," and British law books, for the last five hundred or a thousand years. The industrious research into the musty precedents of English judges and the misty opinions of English jurists so quaintly displayed by some members of the court in deciding this cause might have been very praiseworthy and perhaps useful if they had been sitting on the king's bench in Westminster; but they appear sadly grotesque from the supreme bench at Washington. [. . .]

We repeat, if the charter were originally such a contract as to make it a perpetuity, the constitution of New Hampshire, made before the Constitution of the United States, destroyed that quality and placed the institution on the footing of all other public institutions, controllable by the legislative will. The Constitution of the United States could not confer any new rights upon the college. It could at most only preserve what it then possessed; and as the charter, by the state constitution, if it ever possessed the character of a contract, had been deprived of that character, the inhibition of the United States Constitution, subsequently made, was inoperative upon it. But, waiving all these considerations, and take the admission of Judge Marshall before quoted, and it is conclusive that the case was brought within the reach of that clause only by the boldest and most licentious construction, viz., "That it is more than possible the preservation of rights of this description was not particularly in the view of the framers of the Constitution when the clause under consideration was introduced into that instrument, [. . .] nor of the American people when they adopted it;" but as Judge Marshall did not know that this view would have been rejected if it had been presented, the court *assume* that the clause does therefore embrace this class of civil institutions and give judgment accordingly. I repeat that admitting, for argument sake, the English definitions of corporations, as laid down by the court, to apply to Dartmouth College charter, and that it held its rights originally from the king in England, and not from the provincial authority, then, from the foregoing admission of the Chief Justice, the case did not come within the inhibitory clause of the Constitution. The conclusions drawn by the court are at war with their own premises. [. . .]

RALPH WALDO EMERSON

Divinity School Address (1838)

In this refulgent summer, it has been a luxury to draw the breath of life. The grass grows, the buds burst, the meadow is spotted with fire and gold in the tint of flowers. The air is full of birds, and sweet with the breath of the pine, the balm-of-Gilead, and the new hay. Night brings no gloom to the heart with its welcome shade. Through the transparent darkness the stars pour their almost spiritual rays. Man under them seems a young child, and his huge globe a toy. The cool night bathes the world as with a river, and prepares his eyes again for the crimson dawn. The mystery of nature was never displayed more happily. The corn and the wine have been freely dealt to all creatures, and the never-broken silence with which the old bounty goes forward has not yielded yet one word of explanation. One is constrained to respect the perfection of this world in which our senses converse. How wide; how rich; what invitation from every property it gives to every faculty of man! In its fruitful soils; in its navigable sea; in its mountains of metal and stone; in its forests of all woods; in its animals; in its chemical ingredients; in the powers and path of light, heat, attraction and life, it is well worth the pith and heart of great men to subdue and enjoy it. The planters, the mechanics, the inventors, the astronomers, the builders of cities, and the captains, history delights to honor.

But when the mind opens and reveals the laws which traverse the universe and make things what they are, then shrinks the great world at once into a mere illustration and fable of this mind. What am I? and What is? asks the human spirit with a curiosity new-kindled, but never to be quenched. Behold these out-running laws, which our imperfect apprehension can see tend this way and that, but not come full circle. Behold these infinite relations, so like, so unlike; many, yet one. I would study, I would know, I would admire forever. These works of thought have been the entertainments of the human spirit in all ages.

A more secret, sweet, and overpowering beauty appears to man when his heart and mind open to the sentiment of virtue. Then he is instructed in what is above him. He learns that his being is without bound; that to the good, to the perfect, he is born, low as he now lies in evil and weakness. That which he venerates is still his own, though he has not realized it yet. *He ought.* He knows the sense of that grand word, though his analysis fails to render account of it. When in innocency or when by intellectual perception he attains to say,—"I love the Right; Truth is beautiful within and without for evermore. Virtue, I am thine; save me; use me; thee will I serve, day and night, in great, in small, that I may not be virtuous, but virtue;"—then is the end of the creation answered, and God is well pleased.

The sentiment of virtue is a reverence and delight in the presence of certain divine laws. It perceives that this homely game of life we play, covers, under what seem foolish details, principles that astonish. The child amidst his baubles is learning the action of light, motion, gravity, muscular force; and in the game of human life, love, fear, justice, appetite, man, and God, interact. These laws refuse to be adequately stated. They will not be written out on paper, or spoken by the tongue. They elude our persevering thought; yet we read them hourly in each other's faces, in each other's actions, in our own remorse. The moral traits which are all globed into every virtuous act and thought,—in speech we must sever, and describe or suggest by painful enumeration of many particulars. Yet, as this sentiment is the essence of all religion, let me guide your eye to the precise objects of the sentiment, by an enumeration of some of those classes of facts in which this element is conspicuous.

The intuition of the moral sentiment is an insight of the perfection of the laws of the soul. These laws execute themselves. They are out of time, out of space, and not subject to circumstance. Thus in the soul of man there is a justice whose retributions are instant and entire. He who does a good deed is instantly ennobled. He who does a mean deed is by the action itself contracted. He who puts off impurity, thereby puts on purity. If a man is at heart just, then in so far is he God; the safety of God, the immortality of God, the majesty of God do enter into that man with justice. If a man dissemble, deceive, he deceives, himself, and goes out of acquaintance with his own being. A man in the view of absolute goodness, adores, with total humility. Every step so downward, is a step upward. The man who renounces himself, comes to himself.

See how this rapid intrinsic energy worketh everywhere, righting wrongs, correcting appearances, and bringing up facts to a harmony with thoughts. Its operation in life, though slow to the senses, is at last as sure as in the soul. By it a man is made the Providence to himself, dispensing good to his goodness, and evil to his sin. Character is always known. Thefts never enrich; alms never impoverish; murder will speak out of stone walls. The least admixture of a lie,—for example, the taint of vanity, any attempt to make a good impression, a favorable appearance,—will instantly vitiate the effect. But speak the truth, and all nature and all spirits help you with unexpected furtherance. Speak the truth, and all things alive or brute are vouchers, and the very roots of the grass underground there do seem to stir and move to bear you witness. See again the perfection of the Law as it applies itself to the affections, and becomes the law of society. As we are, so we associate. The good, by affinity, seek the good; the vile, by affinity, the vile. Thus of their own volition, souls proceed into heaven, into hell.

These facts have always suggested to man the sublime creed that the world is not the product of manifold power, but of one will, of one mind; and that one mind is everywhere active, in each ray of the star, in each wavelet of the pool; and whatever opposes that will is everywhere balked and baffled, because things are made so, and not otherwise. Good is positive. Evil is merely privative, not absolute: it is like cold, which is the privation of heat. All evil is so much death or nonentity. Benevolence is absolute and real. So much benevolence as a man hath, so much life hath he. For all things proceed out of this same spirit, which is differently named love, justice, temperance, in its different applications, just as the ocean receives different names on the several shores which it washes. All things proceed out of the same spirit, and all things conspire with it. Whilst a man seeks good ends, he is strong by the whole strength of nature. In so far as he roves from these ends, he bereaves himself of power, or auxiliaries; his being shrinks out of all remote channels, he becomes less and less, a mote, a point, until absolute badness is absolute death.

The perception of this law of laws awakens in the mind a sentiment which we call the religious sentiment, and which makes our highest happiness. Wonderful is its power to charm and to command. It is a mountain air. It is the embalmer of the world. It is myrrh and storax, and chlorine and rosemary. It makes the sky and the hills sublime, and the silent song of the stars is it. By it is the universe made safe and habitable, not by science or power. Thought may work cold and intransitive in things, and find no end or unity; but the dawn of the sentiment of virtue on the heart, gives and is the assurance that Law is sovereign over all natures; and the worlds, time, space, eternity, do seem to break out into joy.

This sentiment is divine and deifying. It is the beatitude of man. It makes him illimitable. Through it, the soul first knows itself. It corrects the capital mistake of the infant man, who seeks to be great by following the great, and hopes to derive advantages *from another*,—by showing the fountain of all good to be in himself, and that he, equally with every man, is an inlet into the deeps of Reason. When he says, "I ought;" when love warms him; when he chooses, warned from on high, the good and great deed; then, deep melodies wander through his soul from Supreme Wisdom.—Then he can worship, and be enlarged by his worship; for he can never go behind this sentiment. In the sublimest flights of the soul, rectitude is never surmounted, love is never outgrown.

This sentiment lies at the foundation of society, and successively creates all forms of worship. The principle of veneration never dies out. Man fallen into superstition, into sensuality, is never quite without the visions of the moral sentiment. In like manner, all the expressions of this sentiment are sacred and permanent in proportion to their purity. The expressions of this sentiment affect us more than all other compositions. The sentences of the oldest time, which ejaculate this piety, are still fresh and fragrant. This thought dwelled always deepest in the minds of men in the devout and contemplative East; not alone in Palestine, where it reached its purest expression, but in Egypt, in Persia, in India, in China. Europe has always owed to oriental genius its divine impulses. What these holy bards said, all sane men found agreeable and true. And the unique impression of Jesus upon mankind, whose name is not so much written as ploughed into the history of this world, is proof of the subtle virtue of this infusion.

Meantime, whilst the doors of the temple stand open, night and day, before every man, and the oracles of this truth cease never, it is guarded by one stern condition; this, namely; it is an intuition. It cannot be received at second hand. Truly speaking, it is not instruction, but provocation, that I can receive from another soul. What he announces, I must find true in me, or reject; and on his word, or as his second, be he who he may, I can accept nothing. On the contrary, the absence of this primary faith is the presence of degradation. As is the flood, so is the ebb. Let this faith depart, and the very words it spake and the things it made become false and hurtful. Then falls the church, the state, art, letters, life. The doctrine of the divine nature being forgotten, a sickness infects and dwarfs the constitution. Once man was all; now he is an appendage, a nuisance. And because the indwelling Supreme Spirit cannot wholly be got rid of, the doctrine of it suffers this perversion, that the divine nature is attributed to one or two persons, and denied to all the rest, and denied with fury. The doctrine of inspiration is lost; the base doctrine of the majority of voices usurps the place of the doctrine of the soul. Miracles, prophecy, poetry, the ideal life, the holy life, exist as ancient history merely; they are not in the belief, nor in the aspiration of society; but, when suggested, seem ridiculous. Life is comic or pitiful as soon as the high ends of being fade out of sight, and man becomes nearsighted, and can only attend to what addresses the senses.

These general views, which, whilst they are general, none will contest, find abundant illustration in the history of religion, and especially in the history of the Christian church. In that, all of us have had our birth and nurture. The truth contained in that, you, my young friends, are now setting forth to teach. As the Cultus, or established worship of the civilized world, it has great historical interest for us. Of its blessed words, which have been the consolation of humanity, you need not that I should speak. I shall endeavor to discharge my duty to you, on this occasion, by pointing out two errors in its administration, which daily appear more gross from the point of view we have just now taken.

Jesus Christ belonged to the true race of prophets. He saw with open eye the mystery of the soul. Drawn by its severe harmony, ravished with its beauty, he lived in it, and had his being there. Alone in all history, he estimated the greatness of man. One man was true to what is in you and me. He saw that God incarnates himself in man, and evermore goes forth anew to take possession of his world. He said, in this jubilee of sublime emotion, "I am divine. Through me, God acts; through me, speaks. Would you see God, see me; or, see thee, when thou also thinkest as I now think." But what a distortion did his doctrine and memory suffer in the same, in the next, and the following ages! There is no doctrine of the Reason which will bear to be taught by the Understanding. The understanding caught this high chant from the poet's lips, and said, in the next age, "This was Jehovah come down out of heaven. I will kill you, if you say he was a man." The idioms of his language, and the figures of his rhetoric, have usurped the place of his truth; and churches are not built on his principles, but on his tropes. Christianity became a Mythus, as the poetic teaching of Greece and of Egypt, before. He spoke of miracles; for he felt that man's life was a miracle, and all that man doth, and he knew that this daily miracle shines, as the character ascends. But the word Miracle, as pronounced by Christian churches, gives a false impression; it is Monster. It is not one with the blowing clover and the falling rain.

He felt respect for Moses and the prophets; but no unfit tenderness at postponing their initial revelations, to the hour and the man that now is; to the eternal revelation in the heart. Thus was he a true man. Having seen that the law in us is commanding, he would not suffer it to be commanded. Boldly, with hand, and heart, and life, he declared it was God. Thus is he, as I think, the only soul in history who has appreciated the worth of a man.

1. In this point of view we become very sensible of the first defect of historical Christianity. Historical Christianity has fallen into the error that corrupts all attempts to communicate religion. As it appears to us, and as it has appeared for ages, it is not the doctrine of the soul, but an exaggeration of the personal, the positive, the ritual. It has dwelt, it dwells, with noxious exaggeration about the *person* of Jesus. The soul knows no persons. It invites every man to expand to the full circle of the universe, and will have no preferences but those of spontaneous love. But by this eastern monarchy of a Christianity, which indolence and fear have built, the friend of man is made the injurer of man. The manner in which his name is surrounded with expressions, which were once sallies of admiration and love, but are now petrified into official titles, kills all generous sympathy and liking. All who hear me, feel, that the language that describes Christ to Europe and America, is not the style of friendship and enthusiasm to a good and noble heart, but is appropriated and formal,—paints a demigod, as the Orientals or the Greeks would describe Osiris or Apollo. Accept the injurious impositions of our early catachetical instruction, and even honesty and self-denial were but splendid sins, if they did not wear the Christian name. One would rather be

> A pagan, suckled in a creed outworn,

than to be defrauded of his manly right in coming into nature, and finding not names and places, not land and professions, but even virtue and truth foreclosed and monopolized. You shall not be a man even. You shall not own the world; you shall not dare, and live after the infinite Law that is in you, and in company with the infinite Beauty which heaven and earth reflect to you in all lovely forms; but you must subordinate your nature to Christ's nature; you must accept our interpretations; and take his portrait as the vulgar draw it.

That is always best which gives me to myself. The sublime is excited in me by the great stoical doctrine, Obey thyself. That which shows God in me, fortifies me. That which shows God out of me, makes me a wart and a wen. There is no longer a necessary reason for my being. Already the long shadows of untimely oblivion creep over me, and I shall decease forever.

The divine bards are the friends of my virtue, of my intellect of my strength. They admonish me, that the gleams which flash across my mind, are not mine, but God's; that they had the like, and were not disobedient to the heavenly vision. So I love them. Noble provocations go out from them, inviting me to resist evil; to subdue the world; and to Be. And thus by his holy thoughts, Jesus serves us, and thus only. To aim to convert a man by miracles, is a profanation of the soul. A true conversion, a true Christ, is now, as always, to be made, by the reception of beautiful sentiments. It is true that a great and rich soul, like his, falling among the simple, does so preponderate, that, as his did, it names the world. The world seems to them to exist for him, and they have not yet drunk so deeply of his sense, as to see that only by coming again to themselves, or to God in themselves, can they grow forevermore. It is a low benefit to give me something; it is a high benefit to enable me to do somewhat of myself. The time is coming when all men will see, that the gift of God to the soul is not a vaunting, overpowering, excluding sanctity, but a sweet, natural goodness, a goodness like thine and mine, and that so invites thine and mine to be and to grow.

The injustice of the vulgar tone of preaching is not less flagrant to Jesus, than to the souls which it profanes. The preachers do not see that they make his gospel not glad, and shear him of the locks of beauty and the attributes of heaven. When I see a majestic Epaminondas, or Washington; when I see among my contemporaries, a true orator, an upright judge, a dear friend; when I vibrate to the melody and fancy of a poem; I see beauty that is to be desired.

And so lovely, and with yet more entire consent of my human being, sounds in my ear the severe music of the bards that have sung of the true God in all ages. Now do not degrade the life and dialogues of Christ out of the circle of this charm, by insulation and peculiarity. Let them lie as they befell, alive and warm, part of human life, and of the landscape, and of the cheerful day.

2. The second defect of the traditionary and limited way of using the mind of Christ is a consequence of the first; this, namely; that the Moral Nature, that Law of laws, whose revelations introduce greatness,—yea, God himself, into the open soul, is not explored as the fountain of the established teaching in society. Men have come to speak of the revelation as somewhat long ago given and done, as if God were dead. The injury to faith throttles the preacher; and the goodliest of institutions becomes an uncertain and inarticulate voice.

It is very certain that it is the effect of conversation with the beauty of the soul, to beget a desire and need to impart to others the same knowledge and love. If utterance is denied, the thought lies like a burden on the man. Always the seer is a sayer. Somehow his dream is told: somehow he publishes it with solemn joy: sometimes with pencil on canvas; sometimes with chisel on stone; sometimes in towers and aisles of granite, his soul's worship is builded; sometimes in anthems of indefinite music; but clearest and most permanent, in words.

The man enamored of this excellency, becomes its priest or poet. The office is coeval with the world. But observe the condition, the spiritual limitation of the office. The spirit only can teach. Not any profane man, not any sensual, not any liar, not any slave can teach, but only he can give, who has; he only can create, who is. The man on whom the soul descends, through whom the soul speaks, alone can teach. Courage, piety, love, wisdom, can teach; and every man can open his door to these angels, and they shall bring him the gift of tongues. But the man who aims to speak as books enable, as synods use, as the fashion guides, and as interest commands, babbles. Let him hush.

To this holy office, you propose to devote yourselves. I wish you may feel your call in throbs of desire and hope. The office is the first in the world. It is of that reality, that it cannot suffer the deduction of any falsehood. And it is my duty to say to you, that the need was never greater of new revelation than now. From the views I have already expressed, you will infer the sad conviction, which I share, I believe, with numbers, of the universal decay and now almost death of faith in society. The soul is not preached. The Church seems to totter to its fall, almost all life extinct. On this occasion, any complaisance would be criminal which told you, whose hope and commission it is to preach the faith of Christ, that the faith of Christ is preached.

It is time that this ill-suppressed murmur of all thoughtful men against the famine of our churches;—this moaning of the heart because it is bereaved of the consolation, the hope, the grandeur that come alone out of the culture of the moral nature,—should be heard through the sleep of indolence, and over the din of routine. This great and perpetual office of the preacher is not discharged. Preaching is the expression of the moral sentiment in application to the duties of life. In how many churches, by how many prophets, tell me, is man made sensible that he is an infinite Soul; that the earth and heavens are passing into his mind; that he is drinking forever the soul of God? Where now sounds the persuasion, that by its very melody imparadises my heart, and so affirms its own origin in heaven? Where shall I hear words such as in elder ages drew men to leave all and follow,—father and mother, house and land, wife and child? Where shall I hear these august laws of moral being so pronounced as to fill my ear, and I feel ennobled by the offer of my uttermost action and passion? The test of the true faith, certainly, should be its power to charm and command the soul, as the laws of nature control the activity of the hands,—so commanding that we find pleasure and honor in obeying. The faith should blend with the light of rising and of setting suns, with the flying cloud, the singing bird, and the breath of flowers. But now the priest's Sabbath has lost the splendor of nature; it is unlovely; we are glad when it is done; we can make, we do make, even sitting in our pews, a far better, holier, sweeter, for ourselves.

Whenever the pulpit is usurped by a formalist, then is the worshipper defrauded and disconsolate. We shrink as soon as the prayers begin, which do not uplift, but smite and offend us. We are fain to wrap our cloaks about us, and secure, as best we can, a solitude that hears not. I once heard a preacher who sorely tempted me to say I would go to church no more. Men go, thought I, where they are wont to go, else had no soul entered the temple in the afternoon. A snow-storm was falling around us. The snow-storm was real, the preacher merely spectral, and the eye felt the sad contrast in looking at him, and then out of the window behind him into the beautiful meteor of the snow. He had lived in vain. He had no one word intimating that he had laughed or wept, was married or in love, had been commended, or cheated, or chagrined. If he had ever lived and acted, we were none the wiser for it. The capital secret of his profession, namely, to convert life into truth, he had not learned. Not one fact in all his experience had he yet imported into his doctrine. This man had ploughed and planted and talked and bought and sold; he had read books; he had eaten and drunken; his head aches, his heart throbs; he smiles and suffers; yet was there not a surmise, a hint, in all the discourse, that he had ever lived at all. Not a line did he draw out of real history. The true preacher can be known by this, that he deals out to the people his life,—life passed through the fire of thought. But of the bad preacher, it could not be told from his sermon what age of the world he fell in; whether he had a father or a child; whether he was a freeholder or a pauper; whether he was a citizen or a countryman; or any other fact of his biography. It seemed strange that the people should come to church. It seemed as if their houses were very un-entertaining, that they should prefer this thoughtless clamor. It shows that there is a commanding attraction in the moral sentiment, that can lend a faint tint of light to dulness and ignorance coming in its name and place. The good hearer is sure he has been touched sometimes; is sure there is somewhat to be reached, and some word that can reach it. When he listens to these vain words, he comforts himself by their relation to his remembrance of better hours, and so they clatter and echo unchallenged.

I am not ignorant that when we preach unworthily, it is not always quite in vain. There is a good ear, in some men, that draws supplies to virtue out of very indifferent nutriment. There is poetic truth concealed in all the common-places of prayer and of sermons, and though foolishly spoken, they may be wisely heard; for each is some select expression that broke out in a moment of piety from some stricken or jubilant soul, and its excellency made it remembered. The prayers and even the dogmas of our church are like the zodiac of Denderah and the astronomical monuments of the Hindoos, wholly insulated from anything now extant in the life and business of the people. They mark the height to which the waters once rose. But this docility is a check upon the mischief from the good and devout. In a large portion of the community, the religious service gives rise to quite other thoughts and emotions. We need not chide the negligent servant. We are struck with pity, rather, at the swift retribution of his sloth. Alas for the unhappy man that is called to stand in the pulpit, and *not* give bread of life. Everything that befalls, accuses him. Would he ask contributions for the missions, foreign or domestic? Instantly his face is suffused with shame, to propose to his parish that they should send money a hundred or a thousand miles, to furnish such poor fare as they have at home and would do well to go the hundred or the thousand miles to escape. Would he urge people to a godly way of living;—and can he ask a fellow-creature to come to Sabbath meetings, when he and they all know what is the poor uttermost they can hope for therein? Will he invite them privately to the Lord's Supper? He dares not. If no heart warm this rite, the hollow, dry, creaking formality is too plain, than that he can face a man of wit and energy, and put the invitation without terror. In the street, what has he to say to the bold, village blasphemer? The village blasphemer sees fear in the face, form, and gait of the minister.

Let me not taint the sincerity of this plea by any oversight of the claims of good men. I know and honor the purity and strict conscience of numbers of the clergy. What life the public worship retains, it owes to the scattered company of pious men, who minister here and there in the churches, and who, sometimes accepting with too great tenderness the tenet of the elders, have not accepted from others, but from their own heart, the genuine impulses of virtue, and so still command our love and awe, to the sanctity of character. Moreover, the exceptions are not so much to be found in a few eminent preachers, as in the better hours, the truer inspirations of all,—nay, in the sincere moments of every man. But, with whatever exception, it is still true that tradition characterizes the preaching of this country; that it comes out of the memory, and not out of the soul; that it aims at what is usual, and not at what is necessary and eternal; that thus historical Christianity destroys the power of preaching, by withdrawing it from the exploration of the moral nature of man; where the sublime is, where are the resources of astonishment and power. What a cruel injustice it is to that Law, the joy of the whole earth, which alone can make thought dear and rich; that Law whose fatal sureness the astronomical orbits poorly emulate;—that it is travestied and depreciated, that it is behooted and behowled, and not a trait, not a word of it articulated. The pulpit in losing sight of this Law, loses its reason, and gropes after it knows not what. And for want of this culture the soul of the community is sick and faithless. It wants nothing so much as a stern, high, stoical, Christian discipline, to make it know itself and the divinity that speaks through it. Now man is ashamed of himself; he skulks and sneaks through the world, to be tolerated, to be pitied, and scarcely in a thousand years does any man dare to be wise and good, and so draw after him the tears and blessings of his kind.

Certainly there have been periods when, from the inactivity of the intellect on certain truths, a greater faith was possible in names and persons. The Puritans in England and America found in the Christ of the Catholic Church and in the dogmas inherited from Rome, scope for their austere piety and their longings for civil freedom. But their creed is passing away, and none arises in its room. I think no man can go with his thoughts about him into one of our churches, without feeling that what hold the public worship had on men is gone, or going. It has lost its grasp on the affection of the good and the fear of the bad. In the country, neighborhoods, half parishes are *signing off*, to use the local term. It is already beginning to indicate character and religion to withdraw from the religious meetings. I have heard a devout person, who prized the Sabbath, say in bitterness of heart, "On Sundays, it seems wicked to go to church." And the motive that holds the best there is now only a hope and a waiting. What was once a mere circumstance, that the best and the worst men in the parish, the poor and the rich, the learned and the ignorant, young and old, should meet one day as fellows in one house, in sign of an equal right in the soul, has come to be a paramount motive for going thither.

My friends, in these two errors, I think, I find the causes of a decaying church and a wasting unbelief. And what greater calamity can fall upon a nation than the loss of worship? Then all things go to decay. Genius leaves the temple to haunt the senate or the market. Literature becomes frivolous. Science is cold. The eye of youth is not lighted by the hope of other worlds, and age is without honor. Society lives to trifles, and when men die we do not mention them.

And now, my brothers, you will ask, What in these desponding days can be done by us? The remedy is already declared in the ground of our complaint of the Church. We have contrasted the Church with the Soul. In the soul then let the redemption be sought. Wherever a man comes, there comes revolution. The old is for slaves. When a man comes, all books are legible, all things transparent, all religions are forms. He is religious. Man is the wonder-worker. He is seen amid miracles. All men bless and curse. He saith yea and nay, only. The stationariness of religion; the assumption that the age of inspiration is past, that the Bible is closed; the fear of degrading the character of Jesus by representing him as a man;—indicate with sufficient clearness the falsehood of our theology. It is the office of a true teacher to show us that God is, not was; that He speaketh, not spake. The true Christianity,—a faith like Christ's in the infinitude of man,—is lost. None believeth in the soul of man, but only in some man or person old and departed. Ah me! no man goeth alone. All men go in flocks to this saint or that poet, avoiding the God who seeth in secret. They cannot see in secret; they love to be blind in public. They think society wiser than their soul, and know not that one soul, and their soul, is wiser than the whole world. See how nations and races flit by on the sea of time and leave no ripple to tell where they floated or sunk, and one good soul shall make the name of Moses, or of Zeno, or of Zoroaster, reverend forever. None assayeth the stern ambition to be the Self of the nation and of nature, but each would be an easy secondary to some Christian scheme, or sectarian connection, or some eminent man. Once leave your own knowledge of God, your own sentiment, and take secondary knowledge, as St. Paul's, or George Fox's, or Swedenborg's, and you get wide from God with every year this secondary form lasts, and if, as now, for centuries,—the chasm yawns to that breadth, that men can scarcely be convinced there is in them anything divine.

Let me admonish you, first of all, to go alone; to refuse the good models, even those which are sacred in the imagination of men, and dare to love God without mediator or veil. Friends enough you shall find who will hold up to your emulation Wesleys and Oberlins, Saints and Prophets. Thank God for these good men, but say, "I also am a man." Imitation cannot go above its model. The imitator dooms himself to hopeless mediocrity. The inventor did it because it was natural to him, and so in him it has a charm. In the imitator something else is natural, and he bereaves himself of his own beauty, to come short of another man's.

Yourself a newborn bard of the Holy Ghost, cast behind you all conformity, and acquaint men at first hand with Deity. Look to it first and only, that fashion, custom, authority, pleasure, and money, are nothing to you,—are not bandages over your eyes, that you cannot see,—but live with the privilege of the immeasurable mind. Not too anxious to visit periodically all families and each family in your parish connection,—when you meet one of these men or women, be to them a divine man; be to them thought and virtue; let their timid aspirations find in you a friend; let their trampled instincts be genially tempted out in your atmosphere; let their doubts know that you have doubted, and their wonder feel that you have wondered. By trusting your own heart, you shall gain more confidence in other men. For all our penny-wisdom, for all our soul-destroying slavery to habit, it is not to be doubted that all men have sublime thoughts; that all men value the few real hours of life; they love to be heard; they love to be caught up into the vision of principles. We mark with light in the memory the few interviews we have had, in the dreary years of routine and of sin, with souls that made our souls wiser; that spoke what we thought; that told us what we knew; that gave us leave to be what we inly were. Discharge to men the priestly office, and, present or absent, you shall be followed with their love as by an angel.

And, to this end, let us not aim at common degrees of merit. Can we not leave, to such as love it, the virtue that glitters for the commendation of society, and ourselves pierce the deep solitudes of absolute ability and worth? We easily come up to the standard of goodness in society. Society's praise can be cheaply secured, and almost all men are content with those easy merits; but the instant effect of conversing with God will be to put them away. There are persons who are not actors, not speakers, but influences; persons too great for fame, for display; who disdain eloquence; to whom all we call art and artist, seems too nearly allied to show and by-ends, to the exaggeration of the finite and selfish, and loss of the universal. The orators, the poets, the commanders encroach on us only as fair women do, by our allowance and homage. Slight them by preoccupation of mind, slight them, as you can well afford to do, by high and universal aims, and they instantly feel that you have right, and that it is in lower places that they must shine. They also feel your right: for they with you are open to the influx of the all-knowing Spirit, which annihilates before its broad noon the little shades and gradations of intelligence in the compositions we call wiser and wisest.

In such high communion let us study the grand strokes of rectitude: a bold benevolence, an independence of friends, so that not the unjust wishes of those who love us shall impair our freedom, but we shall resist for truth's sake the freest flow of kindness, and appeal to sympathies far in advance; and,—what is the highest form in which we know this beautiful element,—a certain solidity of merit, that has nothing to do with opinion, and which is so essentially and manifestly virtue, that it is taken for granted that the right, the brave, the generous step will be taken by it, and nobody thinks of commending it. You would compliment a coxcomb doing a good act, but you would not praise an angel. The silence that accepts merit as the most natural thing in the world, is the highest applause. Such souls, when they appear, are the Imperial Guard of Virtue, the perpetual reserve, the dictators of fortune. One needs not praise their courage,—they are the heart and soul of nature. O my friends, there are resources in us on which we have not drawn. There are men who rise refreshed on hearing a threat; men to whom a crisis which intimidates and paralyzes the majority,—demanding not the faculties of prudence and thrift, but comprehension, immovableness, the readiness of sacrifice,—comes graceful and beloved as a bride. Napoleon said of Massena, that he was not himself until the battle began to go against him; then, when the dead began to fall in ranks around him, awoke his powers of combination, and he put on terror and victory as a robe. So it is in rugged crises, in unweariable endurance, and in aims which put sympathy out of question, that the angel is shown. But these are heights that we can scarce remember and look up to without contrition and shame. Let us thank God that such things exist.

And now let us do what we can to rekindle the smouldering, nigh quenched fire on the altar. The evils of the church that now is are manifest. The question returns, What shall we do? I confess, all attempts to project and establish a Cultus with new rites and forms, seem to me vain. Faith makes us, and not we it, and faith makes its own forms. All attempts to contrive a system are as cold as the new worship introduced by the French to the Goddess of reason,—today, pasteboard and filigree, and ending tomorrow in madness and murder. Rather let the breath of new life be breathed by you through the forms already existing. For if once you are alive, you shall find they shall become plastic and new. The remedy to their deformity is first, soul, and second, soul, and evermore, soul. A whole popedom of forms one pulsation of virtue can uplift and vivify. Two inestimable advantages Christianity has given us; first the Sabbath, the jubilee of the whole world, whose light dawns welcome alike into the closet of the philosopher, into the garret of toil, and into prison-cells, and everywhere suggests, even to the vile, the dignity of spiritual being. Let it stand forevermore, a temple, which new love, new faith, new sight shall restore to more than its first splendor to mankind. And secondly, the institution of preaching,—the speech of man to men,—essentially the most flexible of all organs, of all forms. What hinders that now, everywhere, in pulpits, in lecture-rooms, in houses, in fields, wherever the invitation of men or your own occasions lead you, you speak the very truth, as your life and conscience teach it, and cheer the waiting, fainting hearts of men with new hope and new revelation?

I look for the hour when that supreme Beauty which ravished the souls of those Eastern men, and chiefly of those Hebrews, and through their lips spoke oracles to all time, shall speak in the West also. The Hebrew and Greek Scriptures contain immortal sentences, that have been bread of life to millions. But they have no epical integrity; are fragmentary; are not shown, in their order to the intellect. I look for the new Teacher that shall follow so far those shining laws that he shall see them come full circle; shall see their rounding complete grace; shall see the world to be the mirror of the soul; shall see the identity of the law of gravitation with purity of heart; and shall show that the Ought, that Duty, is one thing with Science, with Beauty, and with Joy.

HENRY DAVID THOREAU

Civil Disobedience (1849)

I heartilly accept the motto,—"That government is best which governs least;" and I should like to see it acted up to more rapidly and systematically. Carried out, it finally amounts to this, which also I believe,—"That government is best which governs not at all;" and when men are prepared for it, that will be the kind of govenment which they will have. Government is at best but an expedient; but most governments are usually, and all govenments are sometimes, inexpedient. The objections which have been brought against a standing army, and they are many and weighty, and deserve to prevail, may also at last be brought against a standing government. The standing army is only an arm of the standing government. The government itself, which is only the mode which the people have chosen to execute their will, is equally liable to be abused and perverted before the people can act through it. Witness the present Mexican war, the work of comparatively a few individuals using the standing government as their tool; for, in the outset, the people would not have consented to this measure.

This American government,—what is it but a tradition, though a recent one, endeavoring to transmit itself unimpaired to posterity, but each instant losing some of its integrity? It has not the vitality and force of a single living man; for a single living man can bend it to his will. It is a sort of wooden gun to the people themselves. But it is not the less necessary for this; for the people must have some complicated machinery or other, and hear its din, to satisfy that idea of government which they have. Governments show thus how successfully men can be imposed on, even impose on themselves, for their own advantage. It is excellent, we must all allow. Yet this government never of itself furthered any enterprise, but by the alacrity with which it got out of its way. *It* does not keep the country free. *It* does not settle the West. *It* does not educate. The character inherent in the American people has done all that has been accomplished; and it would have done somewhat more, if the govenment had not sometimes got in its way. For government is an expedient by which men would fain succeed in letting one another alone; and, as has been said, when it is most expedient, the governed are most let alone by it. Trade and commerce, if they were not made of India-rubber would never manage to bounce over the obstacles which legislators are continually putting in their way; and, if one were to judge these men wholly by their effects of their actions and not partly by their intentions, they would deserve to be classed and punished with those mischievous persons who put obstructions on the railroads.

But, to speak practically and as a citizen, unlike those who call themselves no-government men, I ask for, not at once no government, but *at once* a better government. Let every man make known what kind of government would command his respect, and that will be one step toward obtaining it.

After all, the practical reason why, when the power is once in the hands of the people, a majority are permitted, and for a long period continue, to rule is not because they are most likely to be in the right, nor because this seems fairest to the minority, but because they are physically the strongest. But a government in which the majority rule in all cases cannot be based on justice, even as far as men understand it. Can there not be a government in which majorities do not virtually decide right and wrong, but conscience?—in which majorities decide only those questions to which the rule of expediency is applicable? Must the citizen ever for a moment, or in the least degree, resign his conscience to the legislator? Why has every man a conscience, then? I think that we should be men first, and subjects afterward. It is not desirable to cultivate a respect for the law, so much as for the right. The only obligation which I have a right to assume is to do at any time what I think right. It is truly enough said, that a corporation has no conscience; but a corporation of conscientious men is a corporation *with* a conscience. Law never made men a whit more just; and, by means of their respect for it, even the well-disposed are daily made the agents of injustice. A common and natural result of an undue respect for law is, that you may see a file of soldiers, colonel, captain, corporal, privates, powder-monkeys, and all, marching in admirable order over hill and dale to the wars, against their wills, ay, against their common sense and consciences, which makes it very steep marching indeed, and produces a palpitation of the heart. They have no doubt that it is a damnable business in which they are concerned; they are all peaceably inclined. Now, what are they? Men at all? or small movable forts and magazines, at the service of some unscrupulous man in power? Visit the Navy-Yard, and behold a marine, such a man as an American government can make, or such as it can make a man with its black arts,—a mere shadow and reminiscence of humanity, a man laid out alive and standing, and already, as one may say, buried under arms with funeral accompaniments, though it may be,—

> Not a drum was heard, not a funeral note,
> As his corse to the rampart we hurried;
> Not a soldier discharged his farewell shot
> O'er the grave where our hero we buried.

The mass of men serve the state thus, not as men mainly, but as machines, with their bodies. They are the standing army, and the militia, jailors, constables, posse comitatus, etc. In most cases there is no free exercise whatever of the judgment or of the moral sense; but they put themselves on a level with wood and earth and stones; and wooden men can perhaps be manufactured that will serve the purpose as well. Such command no more respect than men of straw or a lump of dirt. They have the same sort of worth only as horses and dogs. Yet such as these even are commonly esteemed good citizens. Others—as most legislators, politicians, lawyers, ministers, and office-holders—serve the state chiefly with their heads; and, as they rarely make any moral distinctions, they are as likely to serve the Devil, without *intending* it, as God. A very few, as heroes, patriots, martyrs, reformers in the great sense, and *men*, serve the state with their consciences also, and so necessarily resist it for the most part; and they are commonly treated as enemies by it. A wise man will only be useful as a man, and will not submit to be "clay," and "stop a hole to keep the wind away," but leave that office to his dust at least:—

> I am too high-born to be propertied,
> To be a secondary at control,
> Or useful serving-man and instrument
> To any sovereign state throughout the world.

He who gives himself entirely to his fellow-men appears to them useless and selfish; but he who gives himself partially to them is pronounced a benefactor and philanthropist.

How does it become a man to behave toward this American government to-day? I answer, that he cannot without disgrace be associated with it. I cannot for an instant recognize that political organization as *my* government which is the *slave's* government also.

All men recognize the right of revolution; that is, the right to refuse allegiance to, and to resist, the government, when its tyranny or its inefficiency are great and unendurable. But almost all say that such is not the case now. But such was the case, they think, in the Revolution of '75. If one were to tell me that this was a bad government because it taxed certain foreign commodities brought to its ports, it is most probable that I should not make an ado about it, for I can do without them. All machines have their friction; and possibly this does enough good to counterbalance the evil. At any rate, it is a great evil to make a stir about it. But when the friction comes to have its machine, and oppression and robbery are organized, I say, let us not have such a machine any longer. In other words, when a sixth of the population of a nation which has undertaken to be the refuge of liberty are slaves, and a whole country is unjustly overrun and conquered by a foreign army, and subjected to military law, I think that it is not too soon for honest men to rebel and revolutionize. What makes this duty the more urgent is the fact that the country so overrun is not our own, but ours is the invading army. [. . .]

Practically speaking, the opponents to a reform in Massachusetts are not a hundred thousand politicians at the South, but a hundred thousand merchants and farmers here, who are more interested in commerce and agriculture than they are in humanity, and are not prepared to do justice to the slave and to Mexico, *cost what it may*. I quarrel not with far-off foes, but with those who, near at home, cooperate with, and do the bidding of, those far away, and without whom the latter would be harmless. We are accustomed to say, that the mass of men are unprepared; but improvement is slow, because the few are not materially wiser or better than the many. It is not so important that many should be as good as you, as that there be some absolute goodness somewhere; for that will leaven the whole lump. There are thousands who are *in opinion* opposed to slavery and to the war, who yet in effect do nothing to put an end to them; who, esteeming themselves children of Washington and Franklin, sit down with their hands in their pockets, and say that they know not what to do, and do nothing; who even postpone the question of freedom to the question of free-trade, and quietly read the prices-current along with the latest advices from Mexico, after dinner, and, it may be, fall asleep over them both. What is the price-current of an honest man and patriot today? They hesitate, and they regret, and sometimes they petition; but they do nothing in earnest and with effect. They will wait, well disposed, for others to remedy the evil, that they may no longer have it to regret. At most, they give only a cheap vote, and a feeble countenance and God-speed, to the right, as it goes by them. There are nine hundred and ninety-nine patrons of virtue to one virtuous man. But it is easier to deal with the real possessor of a thing than with the temporary guardian of it.

All voting is a sort of gaming, like checkers or backgammon, with a slight moral tinge to it, a playing with right and wrong, with moral questions; and betting naturally accompanies it. The character of the voters is not staked. I cast my vote, perchance, as I think right; but I am not vitally concerned that that right should prevail. I am willing to leave it to the majority. Its obligation, therefore, never exceeds that of expediency. Even voting *for the right* is *doing* nothing for it. It is only expressing to men feebly your desire that it should prevail. A wise man will not leave the right to the mercy of chance, nor wish it to prevail through the power of the majority. There is but little virtue in the action of masses of men. When the majority shall at length vote for the abolition of slavery, it will be because they are indifferent to slavery or because there is but little slavery left to be abolished by their vote. *They* will then be the only slaves. Only *his* vote can hasten the abolition of slavery who asserts his own freedom by his vote.

I hear of a convention to be held at Baltimore, or elsewhere, for the selection of a candidate for the Presidency, made up chiefly of editors, and men who are politicians by profession; but I think, what is it to any independent, intelligent, and respectable man what decision they may come to? Shall we not have the advantage of his wisdom and honesty, nevertheless? Can we not count upon some independent votes? Are there not many individuals in the country who do not attend conventions? But no: I find that the respectable man, so called, has immediately drifted from his position, and despairs of his country, when his country has more reason to despair of him. He forthwith adopts one of the candidates thus selected as the only *available* one, thus proving that he is himself *available* for any purposes of the demagogue. His vote is of no more worth than that of any unprincipled foreigner or hireling native, who may have been bought. O for a man who is a *man*, and, as my neighbor says, has a bone in his back which you cannot pass your hand through! Our statistics are at fault: the population has been returned too large. How many *men* are there to a square thousand miles in this country? Hardly one. [. . .]

It is not a man's duty, as a matter of course, to devote himself to the eradication of any, even the most enormous wrong; he may still properly have other concerns to engage him; but it is his duty, at least, to wash his hands of it, and, if he gives it no thought longer, not to give it practically his support. If I devote myself to other pursuits and contemplations, I must first see, at least, that I do not pursue them sitting upon another man's shoulders. I must get off him first, that he may pursue his contemplations too. See what gross inconsistency is tolerated. I have heard some of my townsmen say, "I should like to have them order me out to help put down an insurrection of the slaves, or to march to Mexico;—see if I would go;" and yet these very men have each, directly by their allegiance, and so indirectly, at least, by their money, furnished a substitute. The soldier is applauded who refuses to serve in an unjust war by those who do not refuse to sustain the unjust government which makes the war; is applauded by those whose own act and authority he disregards and sets at naught; as if the state were penitent to that degree that it hired one to scourge it while it sinned, but not to that degree that it left off sinning for a moment. Thus, under the name of Order and Civil Government, we are all made at last to pay homage to and support our own meanness. After the first blush of sin comes its indifference; and from immoral it becomes, as it were, *un*moral, and not quite unnecessary to that life which we have made.

The broadest and most prevalent error requires the most disinterested virtue to sustain it. The slight reproach to which the virtue of patriotism is commonly liable, the noble are most likely to incur. Those who, while they disapprove of the character and measures of a government, yield to it their allegiance and support are undoubtedly its most conscientious supporters, and so frequently the most serious obstacles to reform. [. . .]

Unjust laws exist: shall we be content to obey them, or shall we endeavor to amend them, and obey them until we have succeeded or shall we transgress them at once? Men generally, under such a government as this, think that they ought to wait until they have persuaded the majority to alter them. They think that, if they should resist, the remedy would be worse than the evil. But it is the fault of the government itself that the remedy *is* worse than the evil. *It* makes it worse. Why is it not more apt to anticipate and provide for reform? Why does it not cherish its wise minority? Why does it cry and resist before it is hurt? [. . .]

If the injustice is part of the necessary friction of the machine of government let it go, let it go: perchance it will wear smooth,—certainly the machine will wear out. If the injustice has a spring, or a pulley, or a rope, or a crank, exclusively for itself, then perhaps you may consider whether the remedy will not be worse than the evil; but if it is of such a nature that it requires you to be the agent of injustice to another, then, I say, break the law. Let your life be a counter friction to stop the machine. What I have to do is to see, at any rate, that I do not lend myself to the wrong which I condemn.

As for adopting the ways which the state has provided for remedying the evil, I know not of such ways. They take too much time, and a man's life will be gone. I have other affairs to attend to. I came into this world, not chiefly to make this a good place to live in, but to live in it, be it good or bad. A man has not everything to do, but something; and because he cannot do *everything,* it is not necessary that he should do *something* wrong. It is not my business to be petitioning the Governor or the Legislature any more than it is theirs to petition me; and if they should not hear my petition, what should I do then? But in this case the state has provided no way: its very Constitution is the evil. This may seem to be harsh and stubborn and unconciliatory; but it is to treat with the utmost kindness and consideration the only spirit that can appreciate or deserves it. So is all change for the better, like birth and death, which convulse the body.

I do not hesitate to say, that those who call themselves Abolitionists should at once effectually withdraw their support, both in person and property, from the government of Massachusetts and not wait till they constitute a majority of one, before they suffer the right to prevail through them. I think that it is enough if they have God on their side, without waiting for that other one. Moreover, any man more right than his neighbors constitutes a majority of one already.

I meet this American government, or its representative, the state government, directly, and face to face, once a year—no more—in the person of its tax-gatherer; this is the only mode in which a man situated as I am necessarily meets it; and it then says distinctly, Recognize me; and the simplest, most effectual, and, in the present posture of affairs, the indispensablest mode of treating with it on this head, of expressing your little satisfaction with and love for it, is to deny it then. My civil neighbor, the tax-gatherer, is the very man I have to deal with,—for it is, after all, with men and not with parchment that I quarrel,—and he has voluntarily chosen to be an agent of the government. How shall he ever know well what he is and does as an officer of the government, or as a man, until he is obliged to consider whether he shall treat me, his neighbor, for whom he has respect, as a neighbor and well-disposed man, or as a maniac and disturber of the peace, and see if he can get over this obstruction to his neighborliness without a ruder and more impetuous thought or speech corresponding with his action. I know this well, that if one thousand, if one hundred, if ten men whom I could name,—if ten *honest* men only,—ay, if *one* HONEST man, in this State of Massachusetts, *ceasing to hold slaves,* were actually to withdraw from this copartnership, and be locked up in the county jail therefor, it would be the abolition of slavery in America. [. . .]

Under a government which imprisons any unjustly, the true place for a just man is also a prison. The proper place to-day, the only place which Massachusetts has provided for her freer and less desponding spirits, is in her prisons, to be put out and locked out of the State by her own act, as they have already put themselves out by their principles. It is there that the fugitive slave, and the Mexican prisoner on parole, and the Indian come to plead the wrongs of his race should find them; on that separate, but more free and honorable ground, where the State places those who are not *with* her, but *against* her,—the only house in a slave State in which a free man can abide with honor. If any think that their influence would be lost there, and their voices no longer afflict the ear of the State, that they would not be as an enemy within its walls, they do not know by how much truth is stronger than error, nor how much more eloquently and effectively he can combat injustice who has experienced a little in his own person. Cast your whole vote, not a strip of paper merely, but your whole influence. A minority is powerless while it conforms to the majority; it is not even a minority then; but it is irresistible when it clogs by its whole weight. If the alternative is to keep all just men in prison, or give up war and slavery, the State will not hesitate which to choose. If a thousand men were not to pay their tax-bills this year, that would not be a violent and bloody measure, as it would be to pay them, and enable the State to commit violence and shed innocent blood. This is, in fact, the definition of a peaceable revolution, if any such is possible. If the tax-gatherer, or any other public officer, asks me, as one has done, "But what shall I do?" my answer is, "If you really wish to do anything, resign your office." When the subject has refused allegiance, and the officer has resigned his office, then the revolution is accomplished. But even suppose blood should flow. Is there not a sort of blood shed when the conscience is wounded? Through this wound a man's real manhood and immortality flow out, and he bleeds to an everlasting death. I see this blood flowing now.

I have contemplated the imprisonment of the offender, rather than the seizure of his goods,—though both will serve the same purpose,—because they who assert the purest right, and consequently are most dangerous to a corrupt State, commonly have not spent much time in accumulating property. To such the State renders comparatively small service, and a slight tax is wont to appear exorbitant, particularly if they are obliged to earn it by special labor with their hands. If there were one who lived wholly without the use of money, the State itself would hesitate to demand it of him. But the rich man—not to make any invidious comparison—is always sold to the institution which makes him rich. Absolutely speaking, the more money, the less virtue; for money comes between a man and his objects, and obtains them for him; and it was certainly no great virtue to obtain it. It puts to rest many questions which he would otherwise be taxed to answer; while the only new question which it puts is the hard but superfluous one, how to spend it. Thus his moral ground is taken from under his feet. The opportunities of living are diminished in proportion as what are called the "means" are increased. [. . .]

I have paid no poll-tax for six years. I was put into a jail once on this account, for one night; and, as I stood considering the walls of solid stone, two or three feet thick, the door of wood and iron, a foot thick, and the iron grating which strained the light, I could not help being struck with the foolishness of that institution which treated me as if I were mere flesh and blood and bones, to be locked up. I wondered that it should have concluded at length that this was the best use it could put me to, and had never thought to avail itself of my services in some way. I saw that, if there was a wall of stone between me and my townsmen, there was a still more difficult one to climb or break through before they could get to be as free as I was. I did not for a moment feel confined, and the walls seemed a great waste of stone and mortar. I felt as if I alone of all my townsmen had paid my tax. They plainly did not know how to treat me, but behaved like persons who are underbred. In every threat and in every compliment there was a blunder; for they thought that my chief desire was to stand the other side of that stone wall. I could not but smile to see how industriously they locked the door on my meditations, which followed them out again without let or hindrance, and *they* were really all that was dangerous. As they could not reach me, they had resolved to punish my body; just as boys, if they cannot come at some person against whom they have a spite, will abuse his dog. I saw that the State was half-witted, that it was timid as a lone woman with her silver spoons, and that it did not know its friends from its foes, and I lost all my remaining respect for it, and pitied it.

Thus the State never intentionally confronts a man's sense, intellectual or moral, but only his body, his senses. It is not armed with superior wit or honesty, but with superior physical strength. I was not born to be forced: I will breathe after my own fashion. Let us see who is the strongest. What force has a multitude? They only can force me who obey a higher law than I. They force me to become like themselves. I do not hear of *men* being *forced* to live this way or that by masses of men. What sort of life were that to live? When I meet a government which says to me, "Your money or your life," why should I be in haste to give it my money? It may be in a great strait, and not know what to do: I cannot help that. It must help itself; do as I do. It is not worth the while to snivel about it. I am not responsible for the successful working of the machinery of society. I am not the son of the engineer. I perceive that, when an acorn and a chestnut fall side by side, the one does not remain inert to make way for the other, but both obey their own laws, and spring and grow and flourish as best they can, till one, perchance, overshadows and destroys the other. If a plant cannot live according to its nature, it dies; and so a man. [. . .]

I have never declined paying the highway tax, because I am as desirous of being a good neighbor as I am of being a bad subject; and as for supporting schools, I am doing my part to educate my fellow-countrymen now. It is for no particular item in the tax-bill that I refuse to pay it. I simply wish to refuse allegiance to the State, to withdraw and stand aloof from it effectually. I do not care to trace the course of my dollar, if I could, till it buys a man or a musket to shoot with,—the dollar is innocent,—but I am concerned to trace the effects of my allegiance. In fact, I quietly declare war with the State, after my fashion, though I will still make what use and get what advantage of her I can, as is usual in such cases.

If others pay the tax which is demanded of me, from a sympathy with the State, they do but what they have already done in their own case, or rather they abet injustice to a greater extent than the State requires. If they pay the tax from a mistaken interest in the individual taxed, to save his property, or prevent his going to jail, it is because they have not considered wisely how far they let their private feelings interfere with the public good.

This, then, is my position at present. But one cannot be too much on his guard in such a case, lest his action be biased by obstinacy or an undue regard for the opinions of men. Let him see that he does only what belongs to himself and to the hour.

I think sometimes, Why, this people mean well, they are only ignorant; they would do better if they knew how: why give your neighbors this pain to treat you as they are not inclined to? But I think again, This is no reason why I should do as they do, or permit others to suffer much greater pain of a different kind. Again, I sometimes say to myself, When many millions of men, without heat, without ill will, without personal feeling of any kind, demand of you a few shillings only, without the possibility, such is their constitution, of retracting or altering their present demand, and without the possibility, on your side, of appeal to any other millions, why expose yourself to this overwhelming brute force? You do not resist cold and hunger, the winds and the waves, thus obstinately; you quietly submit to a thousand similar necessities. You do not put your head into the fire. [. . .]

I do not wish to quarrel with any man or nation. I do not wish to split hairs, to make fine distinctions, or set myself up as better than my neighbors. I seek rather, I may say, even an excuse for conforming to the laws of the land. I am but too ready to conform to them. Indeed, I have reason to suspect myself on this head; and each year, as the tax-gatherer comes round, I find myself disposed to review the acts and position of the general and State governments, and the spirit of the people, to discover a pretext for conformity.

> We must affect our country as our parents,
> And if at any time we alienate
> Our love or industry from doing it honor,
> We must respect effects and teach the soul
> Matter of conscience and religion,
> And not desire of rule or benefit.

I believe that the State will soon be able to take all my work of this sort out of my hands, and then I shall be no better a patriot than my fellow-countrymen. Seen from a lower point of view, the Constitution, with all its faults, is very good; the law and the courts are very respectable; even this State and this American government are, in many respects, very admirable, and rare things, to be thankful for, such as a great many have described them; but seen from a point of view a little higher, they are what I have described them; seen from a higher still, and the highest, who shall say what they are, or that they are worth looking at or thinking of at all?

However, the government does not concern me much, and I shall bestow the fewest possible thoughts on it. It is not many moments that I live under a government, even in this world. If a man is thought-free, fancy-free, imagination-free, that which *is not* never for a long time appearing *to be* to him, unwise rulers or reformers cannot fatally interrupt him.

I know that most men think differently from myself; but those whose lives are by profession devoted to the study of these or kindred subjects content me as little as any. Statesmen and legislators, standing so completely within the institution, never distinctly and nakedly behold it. They speak of moving society, but have no resting-place without it. They may be men of a certain experience and discrimination, and have no doubt invented ingenious and even useful systems, for which we sincerely thank them; but all their wit and usefulness lie within certain not very wide limits. They are wont to forget that the world is not governed by policy and expediency. Webster never goes behind government, and so cannot speak with authority about it. His words are wisdom to those legislators who contemplate no essential reform in the existing government; but for thinkers, and those who legislate for all time, he never once glances at the subject. I know of those whose serene and wise speculations on this theme would soon reveal the limits of his mind's range and hospitality. Yet, compared with the cheap professions of most reformers, and the still cheaper wisdom and eloquence of politicians in general, his are almost the only sensible and valuable words, and we thank Heaven for him. Comparatively, he is always strong, original, and, above all, practical. Still, his quality is not wisdom, but prudence. The lawyer's truth is not Truth, but consistency or a consistent expediency. Truth is always in harmony with herself, and is not concerned chiefly to reveal the justice that may consist with wrong-doing. He well deserves to be called, as he has been called, the Defender of the Constitution. There are really no blows to be given by him but defensive ones. He is not a leader, but a follower. His leaders are the men of '87. [. . .]

They who know of no purer sources of truth, who have traced up its stream no higher, stand, and wisely stand, by the Bible and the Constitution, and drink at it there with reverence and humility; but they who behold where it comes trickling into this lake or that pool, gird up their loins once more, and continue their pilgrimage toward its fountainhead.

No man with a genius for legislation has appeared in America. They are rare in the history of the world. There are orators, politicians, and eloquent men, by the thousand; but the speaker has not yet opened his mouth to speak who is capable of settling the much-vexed questions of the day. We love eloquence for its own sake, and not for any truth which it may utter, or any heroism it may inspire. Our legislators have not yet learned the comparative value of free-trade and of freedom, of union, and of rectitude, to a nation. They have no genius or talent for comparatively humble questions of taxation and finance, commerce and manufactures and agriculture. If we were left solely to the wordy wit of legislators in Congress for our guidance, uncorrected by the seasonable experience and the effectual complaints of the people, America would not long retain her rank among the nations. For eighteen hundred years, though perchance I have no right to say it, the New Testament has been written; yet where is the legislator who has wisdom and practical talent enough to avail himself of the light which it sheds on the science of legislation?

The authority of government, even such as I am willing to submit to,—for I will cheerfully obey those who know and can do better than I, and in many things even those who neither know nor can do so well,—is still an impure one: to be strictly just, it must have the sanction and consent of the governed. It can have no pure right over my person and property but what I concede to it. The progress from an absolute to a limited monarchy, from a limited monarchy to a democracy, is a progress toward a true respect for the individual. Even the Chinese philosopher was wise enough to regard the individual as the basis of the empire. Is a democracy, such as we know it, the last improvement possible in government? Is it not possible to take a step further towards recognizing and organizing the rights of man? There will never be a really free and enlightened State until the State comes to recognize the individual as a higher and independent power, from which all its own power and authority are derived, and treats him accordingly. I please myself with imagining a State at last which can afford to be just to all men, and to treat the individual with respect as a neighbor; which even would not think it inconsistent with its own repose if a few were to live aloof from it, not meddling with it, nor embraced by it, who fulfilled all the duties of neighbors and fellow-men. A State which bore this kind of fruit, and suffered it to drop off as fast as it ripened, would prepare the way for a still more perfect and glorious State, which also I have imagined, but not yet anywhere seen.

Walden (1854)

Where I Lived, and What I Lived For

At a certain season of our life we are accustomed to consider every spot as the possible site of a house. I have thus surveyed the country on every side within a dozen miles of where I live. In imagination I have bought all the farms in succession, for all were to be bought, and I knew their price. I walked over each fanner's premises, tasted his wild apples, discoursed on husbandry with him, took his farm at his price, at any price, mortgaging it to him in my mind; even put a higher price on it—took everything but a deed of it—took his word for his deed, for I dearly love to talk—cultivated it, and him too to some extent, I trust, and withdrew when I had enjoyed it long enough, leaving him to carry it on. This experience entitled me to be regarded as a sort of real-estate broker by my friends. Wherever I sat, there I might live, and the landscape radiated from me accordingly. What is a house but a *sedes*, a seat?—better if a country seat. I discovered many a site for a house not likely to be soon improved, which some might have thought too far from the village, but to my eyes the village was too far from it. Well, there I might live, I said; and there I did live, for an hour, a summer and a winter life; saw how I could let the years run off, buffet the winter through, and see the spring come in. The future inhabitants of this region, wherever they may place their houses, may be sure that they have been anticipated. An afternoon sufficed to lay out the land into orchard, wood-lot, and pasture, and to decide what fine oaks or pines should be left to stand before the door, and whence each blasted tree could be seen to the best advantage; and then I let it lie, fallow, perchance, for a man is rich in proportion to the number of things which he can afford to let alone.

My imagination carried me so far that I even had the refusal of several farms—the refusal was all I wanted—but I never got my fingers burned by actual possession. The nearest that I came to actual possession was when I bought the Hollowell place, and had begun to sort my seeds, and collected materials with which to make a wheelbarrow to carry it on or off with; but before the owner gave me a deed of it, his wife—every man has such a wife—changed her mind and wished to keep it, and he offered me ten dollars to release him. Now, to speak the truth, I had but ten cents in the world, and it surpassed my arithmetic to tell, if I was that man who had ten cents, or who had a farm, or ten dollars, or all together. However, I let him keep the ten dollars and the farm too, for I had carried it far enough; or rather, to be generous, I sold him the farm for just what I gave for it, and, as he was not a rich man, made him a present of ten dollars, and still had my ten cents, and seeds, and materials for a wheelbarrow left. I found thus that I had been a rich man without any damage to my poverty. But I retained the landscape, and I have since annually carried off what it yielded without a wheelbarrow. With respect to landscapes,

I am monarch of all I *survey*,
My right there is none to dispute.[1]

I have frequently seen a poet withdraw, having enjoyed the most valuable part of a farm, while the crusty farmer supposed that he had got a few wild apples only. Why, the owner does not know it for many years when a poet has put his farm in rhyme, the most admirable kind of invisible fence, has fairly impounded it, milked it, skimmed it, and got all the cream, and left the farmer only the skimmed milk.

The real attractions of the Hollowell farm, to me, were: its complete retirement, being, about two miles from the village, half a mile from the nearest neighbor, and separated from the highway by a broad field; its bounding on the river, which the owner said protected it by its fogs from frosts in the spring, though that was nothing to me; the gray color and ruinous state of the house and barn, and the dilapidated fences, which put such an interval between me and

---

1. William Cowper (1731–1800) English poet, hymnist, *The Solitude of Alexander Selkirk*—a surveyor.

the last occupant; the hollow and lichen-covered apple trees, gnawed by rabbits, showing what kind of neighbors I should have; but above all, the recollection I had of it from my earliest voyages up the river, when the house was concealed behind a dense grove of red maples, through which I heard the house-dog bark. I was in haste to buy it, before the proprietor finished getting out some rocks, cutting down the hollow apple trees, and grubbing up some young birches which had sprung up in the pasture, or, in short, had made any more of his improvements. To enjoy these advantages I was ready to carry it on; like Atlas,[2] to take the world on my shoulders—I never heard what compensation he received for that—and do all those things which had no other motive or excuse but that I might pay for it and be unmolested in my possession of it; for I knew all the while that it would yield the most abundant crop of the kind I wanted, if I could only afford to let it alone. But it turned out as I have said.

All that I could say, then, with respect to farming on a large scale—I have always cultivated a garden—was, that I had had my seeds ready. Many think that seeds improve with age. I have no doubt that time discriminates between the good and the bad; and when at last I shall plant, I shall be less likely to be disappointed. But I would say to my fellows, once for all, As long as possible live free and uncommitted. It makes but little difference whether you are committed to a farm or the county jail.

Old Cato,[3] whose "De Re Rustica" is my "Cultivator," says—and the only translation I have seen makes sheer nonsense of the passage—"When you think of getting a farm turn it thus in your mind, not to buy greedily; nor spare your pains to look at it, and do not think it enough to go round it once. The oftener you go there the more it will please you, if it is good." I think I shall not buy greedily, but go round and round it as long as I live, and be buried in it first, that it may please me the more at last.

The present was my next experiment of this kind, which I purpose to describe more at length, for convenience putting the experience of two years into one. As I have said, I do not propose to write an ode to dejection, but to brag as lustily as chanticleer in the morning, standing on his roost, if only to wake my neighbors up.

When first I took up my abode in the woods, that is, began to spend my nights as well as days there, which, by accident, was on Independence Day, or the Fourth of July, 1845, my house was not finished for winter, but was merely a defence against the rain, without plastering or chimney, the walls being of rough, weather-stained boards, with wide chinks, which made it cool at night. The upright white hewn studs and freshly planed door and window casings gave it a clean and airy look, especially in the morning, when its timbers were saturated with dew, so that I fancied that by noon some sweet gum would exude from them. To my imagination it retained throughout the day more or less of this auroral character, reminding me of a certain house on a mountain which I had visited a year before. This was an airy and unplastered cabin, fit to entertain a travelling god, and where a goddess might trail her garments. The winds which passed over my dwelling were such as sweep over the ridges of mountains, bearing the broken strains, or celestial parts only, of terrestrial music. The morning wind forever blows, the poem of creation is uninterrupted; but few are the ears that hear it. Olympus[4] is but the outside of the earth everywhere.

The only house I had been the owner of before, if I except a boat, was a tent, which I used occasionally when making excursions in the summer, and this is still rolled up in my garret; but the boat, after passing from hand to hand, has gone down the stream of time. With this more substantial shelter about me, I had made some progress toward settling in the world. This frame, so slightly clad, was a sort of crystallization around me, and reacted on the builder. It was suggestive somewhat as a picture in outlines. I did not need to go outdoors to take the air, for the atmosphere within had lost none of its freshness. It was not so much within doors as behind a door where I sat, even in the rainiest weather. The Harivansa[5] says,

2. In Greek mythology Atlas supported the heavens on his shoulders.

3. Marcus Porcius Cato (234–149 B.C.), Roman agricultural author.

4. In Greek mythology, home of the gods.

5. 5th century Hindu epic poem.

"An abode without birds is like a meat without seasoning." Such was not my abode, for I found myself suddenly neighbor to the birds; not by having imprisoned one, but having caged myself near them. I was not only nearer to some of those which commonly frequent the garden and the orchard, but to those smaller and more thrilling songsters of the forest which never, or rarely, serenade a villager—the wood thrush, the veery, the scarlet tanager, the field sparrow, the whip-poor-will, and many others.

I was seated by the shore of a small pond, about a mile and a half south of the village of Concord and somewhat higher than it, in the midst of an extensive wood between that town and Lincoln, and about two miles south of that our only field known to fame, Concord Battle Ground; but I was so low in the woods that the opposite shore, half a mile off, like the rest, covered with wood, was my most distant horizon. For the first week, whenever I looked out on the pond it impressed me like a tarn high up on the side of a mountain, its bottom far above the surface of other lakes, and, as the sun arose, I saw it throwing off its nightly clothing of mist, and here and there, by degrees, its soft ripples or its smooth reflecting surface was revealed, while the mists, like ghosts, were stealthily withdrawing in every direction into the woods, as at the breaking up of some nocturnal conventicle. The very dew seemed to hang upon the trees later into the day than usual, as on the sides of mountains.

This small lake was of most value as a neighbor in the intervals of a gentle rain-storm in August, when, both air and water being perfectly still, but the sky overcast, mid-afternoon had all the serenity of evening, and the wood thrush sang around, and was heard from shore to shore. A lake like this is never smoother than at such a time; and the clear portion of the air above it being, shallow and darkened by clouds, the water, full of light and reflections, becomes a lower heaven itself so much the more important. From a hill-top near by, where the wood had been recently cut off, there was a pleasing vista southward across the pond, through a wide indentation in the hills which form the shore there, where their opposite sides sloping toward each other suggested a stream flowing out in that direction through a wooded valley, but stream there was none. That way I looked between and over the near green hills to some distant and higher ones in the horizon, tinged with blue. Indeed, by standing on tiptoe I could catch a glimpse of some of the peaks of the still bluer and more distant mountain ranges in the northwest, those true-blue coins from heaven's own mint, and also of some portion of the village. But in other directions, even from this point, I could not see over or beyond the woods which surrounded me. It is well to have some water in your neighborhood, to give buoyancy to and float the earth. One value even of the smallest well is, that when you look into it you see that earth is not continent but insular. This is as important as that it keeps butter cool. When I looked across the pond from this peak toward the Sudbury meadows, which in time of flood I distinguished elevated perhaps by a mirage in their seething valley, like a coin in a basin, all the earth beyond the pond appeared like a thin crust insulated and floated even by this small sheet of intervening water, and I was reminded that this on which I dwelt was but *dry land.*

Though the view from my door was still more contracted, I did not feel crowded or confined in the least. There was pasture enough for my imagination. The low shrub oak plateau to which the opposite shore arose stretched away toward the prairies of the West and the steppes of Tartary, affording ample room for all the roving families of men. "There are none happy in the world but beings who enjoy freely a vast horizon"—said Damodara,[6] when his herds required new and larger pastures.

Both place and time were changed, and I dwelt nearer to those parts of the universe and to those eras in history which had most attracted me. Where I lived was as far off as many a region viewed nightly by astronomers. We are wont to imagine rare and delectable places in some remote and more celestial corner of the system, behind the constellation of Cassiopeia's Chair, far from noise and disturbance. I discovered that my house actually had its site in such a withdrawn, but forever new and unprofaned, part of the universe. If it were worth the while to settle in those parts near to the Pleiades or the Hyades, to Aldebaran[7] or Altair, then I was really there, or at an

---

6. Another name for the Hindu god Krishna.

7. Cassiopeia's Chair, Pleiades, and Hyades are constellations.

equal remoteness from the life which I had left behind, dwindled and twinkling with as fine a ray to my nearest neighbor, and to be seen only in moonless nights by him. Such was that part of creation where I had squatted,—

> There was a shepherd that did live,
> And held his thoughts as high
> As were the mounts whereon his flocks
> Did hourly feed him by.[8]

What should we think of the shepherd's life if his flocks always wandered to higher pastures than his thoughts?

Every morning was a cheerful invitation to make my life of equal simplicity, and I may say innocence, with Nature herself. I have been as sincere a worshipper of Aurora[9] as the Greeks. I got up early and bathed in the pond; that was a religious exercise, and one of the best things which I did. They say that characters were engraven on the bathing tub of King Tchingthang[10] to this effect: "Renew thyself completely each day; do it again, and again, and forever again." I can understand that. Morning brings back the heroic ages. I was as much affected by the faint hum of a mosquito making its invisible and unimaginable tour through my apartment at earliest dawn, when I was sitting with door and windows open, as I could be by any trumpet that ever sang of fame. It was Homer's requiem; itself an Iliad and Odyssey[11] in the air, singing its own wrath and wanderings. There was something cosmical about it; a standing advertisement, till forbidden, of the everlasting vigor and fertility of the world. The morning, which is the most memorable season of the day, is the awakening hour. Then there is least somnolence in us; and for an hour, at least, some part of us awakes which slumbers all the rest of the day and night. Little is to be expected of that day, if it can be called a day, to which we are not awakened by our Genius, but by the mechanical nudgings of some servitor, are not awakened by our own newly acquired force and aspirations from within, accompanied by the undulations of celestial music, instead of factory bells, and a fragrance filling the air—to a higher life than we fell asleep from; and thus the darkness bear its fruit, and prove itself to be good, no less than the light. That man who does not believe that each day contains an earlier, more sacred, and auroral hour than he has yet profaned, has despaired of life, and is pursuing a descending and darkening way. After a partial cessation of his sensuous life, the soul of man, or its organs rather, are reinvigorated each day, and his Genius tries again what noble life it can make. All memorable events, I should say, transpire in morning time and in a morning atmosphere. The Vedas[12] say, "All intelligences awake with the morning." Poetry and art, and the fairest and most memorable of the actions of men, date from such an hour. All poets and heroes, like Memnon,[13] are the children of Aurora, and emit their music at sunrise. To him whose elastic and vigorous thought keeps pace with the sun, the day is a perpetual morning. It matters not what the clocks say or the attitudes and labors of men. Morning is when I am awake and there is a dawn in me. Moral reform is the effort to throw off sleep. Why is it that men give so poor an account of their day if they have not been slumbering? They are not such poor calculators. If they had not been overcome with drowsiness, they would have performed something. The millions are awake enough for physical labor; but only one in a million is awake enough for effective intellectual exertion, only one in a hundred millions to a poetic or divine life. To be awake is to be alive. I have never yet met a man who was quite awake. How could I have looked him in the face?

We must learn to reawaken and keep ourselves awake, not by mechanical aids, but by an infinite expectation of the dawn, which does not forsake us in our soundest sleep. I know of no more encouraging fact than the unquestionable ability of man to elevate his life by a conscious endeavor. It is something to be able to paint a particular picture, or to carve a statue, and so to make a few objects beautiful; but it is far

---

8. Anonymous, published 1610.

9. In Roman mythology, the goddess of dawn.

10. Another name for Confucius.

11. *Iliad* and *Odyssey*, attributed to Homer, 8th cent. B.C. Greek epic poet.

12. Brahmin religious books.

13. Statue in ancient Egypt said to produce music at dawn.

more glorious to carve and paint the very atmosphere and medium through which we look, which morally we can do. To affect the quality of the day, that is the highest of arts. Every man is tasked to make his life, even in its details, worthy of the contemplation of his most elevated and critical hour. If we refused, or rather used up, such paltry information as we get, the oracles would distinctly inform us how this might be done.

I went to the woods because I wished to live deliberately, to front only the essential facts of life, and see if I could not learn what it had to teach, and not, when I came to die, discover that I had not lived. I did not wish to live what was not life, living is so dear; nor did I wish to practise resignation, unless it was quite necessary. I wanted to live deep and suck out all the marrow of life, to live so sturdily and Spartan-like as to put to rout all that was not life, to cut a broad swath and shave close, to drive life into a corner, and reduce it to its lowest terms, and, if it proved to be mean, why then to get the whole and genuine meanness of it, and publish its meanness to the world; or if it were sublime, to know it by experience, and be able to give a true account of it in my next excursion. For most men, it appears to me, are in a strange uncertainty about it, whether it is of the devil or of God, and have *somewhat hastily* concluded that it is the chief end of man here to "glorify God and enjoy him forever."[14]

Still we live meanly, like ants; though the fable tells us that we were long ago changed into men; like pygmies we fight with cranes; it is error upon error, and clout upon clout, and our best virtue has for its occasion a superfluous and evitable wretchedness. Our life is frittered away by detail. An honest man has hardly need to count more than his ten fingers, or in extreme cases he may add his ten toes, and lump the rest. Simplicity, simplicity, simplicity! I say, let your affairs be as two or three, and not a hundred or a thousand; instead of a million count half a dozen, and keep your accounts on your thumb-nail. In the midst of this chopping sea of civilized life, such are the clouds and storms and quicksands and thousand-and-one items to be allowed for, that a man has to live, if he would not founder and go to the bottom and not make his port at all, by dead reckoning, and he must be a great calculator indeed who succeeds. Simplify, simplify. Instead of three meals a day, if it be necessary eat but one; instead of a hundred dishes, five; and reduce other things in proportion. Our life is like a German Confederacy,[15] made up of petty states, with its boundary forever fluctuating, so that even a German cannot tell you how it is bounded at any moment. The nation itself, with all its so-called internal improvements, which, by the way are all external and superficial, is just such an unwieldy and overgrown establishment, cluttered with furniture and tripped up by its own traps, ruined by luxury and heedless expense, by want of calculation and a worthy aim, as the million households in the land; and the only cure for it, as for them, is in a rigid economy, a stern and more than Spartan[16] simplicity of life and elevation of purpose. It lives too fast. Men think that it is essential that the *Nation* have commerce, and export ice, and talk through a telegraph, and ride thirty miles an hour, without a doubt, whether *they* do or not; but whether we should live like baboons or like men, is a little uncertain. If we do not get out sleepers,[17] and forge rails, and devote days and nights to the work, but go to tinkering upon our *lives* to improve *them*, who will build railroads? And if railroads are not built, how shall we get to heaven in season? But if we stay at home and mind our business, who will want railroads? We do not ride on the railroad; it rides upon us. Did you ever think what those sleepers are that underlie the railroad? Each one is a man, an Irishman, or a Yankee man. The rails are laid on them, and they are covered with sand, and the cars run smoothly over them. They are sound sleepers, I assure you. And every few years a new lot is laid down and run over; so that, if some have the pleasure of riding on a rail, others have the misfortune to be ridden upon. And when they run over a man that is walking in his sleep, a supernumerary sleeper in the wrong position, and wake him up, they suddenly stop the

14. Westminster Catechism.

15. Group of European states, 1815–1866.

16. Like the Spartans of ancient Greece, disciplined, austere.

17. Wooden railroad ties that support the rails.

cars, and make a hue and cry about it, as if this were an exception. I am glad to know that it takes a gang of men for every five miles to keep the sleepers down and level in their beds as it is, for this is a sign that they may sometime get up again.

Why should we live with such hurry and waste of life? We are determined to be starved before we are hungry. Men say that a stitch in time saves nine, and so they take a thousand stitches today to save nine tomorrow. As for *work*, we haven't any of any consequence. We have the Saint Vitus' dance,[18] and cannot possibly keep our heads still. If I should only give a few pulls at the parish bell-rope, as for a fire, that is, without setting the bell, there is hardly a man on his farm in the outskirts of Concord, notwithstanding that press of engagements which was his excuse so many times this morning, nor a boy, nor a woman, I might almost say, but would forsake all and follow that sound, not mainly to save property from the flames, but, if we will confess the truth, much more to see it burn, since burn it must, and we, be it known, did not set it on fire—or to see it put out, and have a hand in it, if that is done as handsomely; yes, even if it were the parish church itself. Hardly a man takes a half-hour's nap after dinner, but when he wakes he holds up his head and asks, "What's the news?" as if the rest of mankind had stood his sentinels. Some give directions to be waked every half-hour, doubtless for no other purpose; and then, to pay for it, they tell what they have dreamed. After a night's sleep the news is as indispensable as the breakfast. "Pray tell me anything new that has happened to a man anywhere on this globe"—and he reads it over his coffee and rolls, that a man has had his eyes gouged out this morning on the Wachito River;[19] never dreaming the while that he lives in the dark unfathomed mammoth cave of this world, and has but the rudiment of an eye himself.

For my part, I could easily do without the post-office. I think that there are very few important communications made through it. To speak critically, I never received more than one or two letters in my life—I wrote this some years ago—that were worth the postage. The penny-post is, commonly, an institution through which you seriously offer a man that penny for his thoughts which is so often safely offered in jest. And I am sure that I never read any memorable news in a newspaper. If we read of one man robbed, or murdered, or killed by accident, or one house burned, or one vessel wrecked, or one steam-boat blown up, or one cow run over on the Western Railroad, or one mad dog killed, or one lot of grasshoppers in the winter—we never need read of another. One is enough. If you are acquainted with the principle, what do you care for a myriad instances and applications? To a philosopher all news, as it is called, is gossip, and they who edit and read it are old women over their tea. Yet not a few are greedy after this gossip. There was such a rush, as I hear, the other day at one of the offices to learn the foreign news by the last arrival, that several large squares of plate glass belonging to the establishment were broken by the pressure—news which I seriously think a ready wit might write a twelve-month, or twelve years, beforehand with sufficient accuracy. As for Spain, for instance, if you know how to throw in Don Carlos and the Infanta, and Don Pedro and Seville and Granada,[20] from time to time in the right proportions—they may have changed the names a little since I saw the papers—and serve up a bull-fight when other entertainments fail, it will be true to the letter, and give us as good an idea of the exact state or ruin of things in Spain as the most succinct and lucid reports under this head in the newspapers: and as for England, almost the last significant scrap of news from that quarter was the revolution of 1649; and if you have learned the history of her crops for an average year, you never need attend to that thing again, unless your speculations are of a merely pecuniary character. If one may judge who rarely looks into the newspapers, nothing new does ever happen in foreign parts, a French revolution not excepted.

What news! how much more important to know what that is which was never old! "Kieou-he-yu[21]

---

18. Chorea, a nervous disorder characterized by involuntary movements.

19. River in Arkansas and Louisiana.

20. Relating to Spanish & Portuguese politics, 1830s & 1840s.

21. Character in a book by Confucius.

(great dignitary of the state of Wei) sent a man to Khoung-tseu to know his news. Khoung-tseu caused the messenger to be seated near him, and questioned him in these terms: What is your master doing? The messenger answered with respect: My master desires to diminish the number of his faults, but he cannot accomplish it. The messenger being gone, the philosopher remarked: What a worthy messenger! What a worthy messenger!" The preacher, instead of vexing the ears of drowsy farmers on their day of rest at the end of the week—for Sunday is the fit conclusion of an ill-spent week, and not the fresh and brave beginning of a new one—with this one other draggle-tail of a sermon, should shout with thundering voice, "Pause! Avast! Why so seeming fast, but deadly slow?"

Shams and delusions are esteemed for soundest truths, while reality is fabulous. If men would steadily observe realities only, and not allow themselves to be deluded, life, to compare it with such things as we know, would be like a fairy tale and the Arabian Nights' Entertainments. If we respected only what is inevitable and has a right to be, music and poetry would resound along the streets. When we are unhurried and wise, we perceive that only great and worthy things have any permanent and absolute existence, that petty fears and petty pleasures are but the shadow of the reality. This is always exhilarating and sublime. By closing the eyes and slumbering, and consenting to be deceived by shows, men establish and confirm their daily life of routine and habit everywhere, which still is built on purely illusory foundations. Children, who play life, discern its true law and relations more clearly than men, who fail to live it worthily, but who think that they are wiser by experience, that is, by failure. I have read in a Hindoo book, that "there was a king's son, who, being expelled in infancy from his native city, was brought up by a forester, and, growing up to maturity in that state, imagined himself to belong to the barbarous race with which he lived. One of his father's ministers having discovered him, revealed to him what he was, and the misconception of his character was removed, and he knew himself to be a prince. So soul," continues the Hindoo philosopher, "from the circumstances in which it is placed, mistakes its own character, until the truth is revealed to it by some holy teacher, and then it knows itself to be *Brahme*."[22] I perceive that we inhabitants of New England live this mean life that we do because our vision does not penetrate the surface of things. We think that that is which *appears* to be. If a man should walk through this town and see only the reality, where, think you, would the "Mill-dam" go to? If he should give us an account of the realities he beheld there, we should not recognize the place in his description. Look at a meeting-house, or a court-house, or a jail, or a shop, or a dwelling-house, and say what that thing really is before a true gaze, and they would all go to pieces in your account of them. Men esteem truth remote, in the outskirts of the system, behind the farthest star, before Adam and after the last man. In eternity there is indeed something true and sublime. But all these times and places and occasions are now and here. God himself culminates in the present moment, and will never be more divine in the lapse of all the ages. And we are enabled to apprehend at all what is sublime and noble only by the perpetual instilling and drenching of the reality that surrounds us. The universe constantly and obediently answers to our conceptions; whether we travel fast or slow, the track is laid for us. Let us spend our lives in conceiving then. The poet or the artist never yet had so fair and noble a design but some of his posterity at least could accomplish it.

Let us spend one day as deliberately as Nature, and not be thrown off the track by every nutshell and mosquito's wing that falls on the rails. Let us rise early and fast, or break fast, gently and without perturbation; let company come and let company go, let the bells ring and the children cry—determined to make a day of it. Why should we knock under and go with the stream? Let us not be upset and overwhelmed in that terrible rapid and whirlpool called a dinner, situated in the meridian shallows. Weather this danger and you are safe, for the rest of the way is down hill. With unrelaxed nerves, with morning vigor, sail by it, looking another way, tied to the mast like Ulysses.[23] If the engine whistles, let it whistle till

---

22. Brahma, Hindu god of creation.

23. Roman name for Odysseus, character in Homer's *Iliad* and *Odyssey*.

it is hoarse for its pains. If the bell rings, why should we run? We will consider what kind of music they are like. Let us settle ourselves, and work and wedge our feet downward through the mud and slush of opinion, and prejudice, and tradition, and delusion, and appearance, that alluvion which covers the globe, through Paris and London, through New York and Boston and Concord, through Church and State, through poetry and philosophy and religion, till we come to a hard bottom and rocks in place, which we can call *reality*, and say, This is, and no mistake; and then begin, having a *point d'appui*,[24] below freshet and frost and fire, a place where you might found a wall or a state, or set a lamp-post safely, or perhaps a gauge, not a Nilometer,[25] but a Realometer, that future ages might know how deep a freshet of shams and appearances had gathered from time to time. If you stand right fronting and face to face to a fact, you will see the sun glimmer on both its surfaces, as if it were a cimeter, and feel its sweet edge dividing you through the heart and marrow, and so you will happily conclude your mortal career. Be it life or death, we crave only reality. If we are really dying, let us hear the rattle in our throats and feel cold in the extremities; if we are alive, let us go about our business.

Time is but the stream I go a-fishing in. I drink at it; but while I drink I see the sandy bottom and detect how shallow it is. Its thin current slides away, but eternity remains. I would drink deeper; fish in the sky, whose bottom is pebbly with stars. I cannot count one. I know not the first letter of the alphabet. I have always been regretting that I was not as wise as the day I was born. The intellect is a cleaver; it discerns and rifts its way into the secret of things. I do not wish to be any more busy with my hands than is necessary. My head is hands and feet. I feel all my best faculties concentrated in it. My instinct tells me that my head is an organ for burrowing, as some creatures use their snout and fore paws, and with it I would mine and burrow my way through these hills. I think that the richest vein is somewhere hereabouts; so by the divining rod and thin rising vapors I judge; and here I will begin to mine.

24. A point of support; a solid footing.

25. A device used to measure the rise and fall of the Nile River in Ancient Egypt.

9

Slavery and Secession

Since the earliest days of the colonies, slavery militated against the full development of an American democratic polity. As Walt Whitman noted, it allowed cynics to ridicule "your vaunted America" for its "infidelism, even to itself and its own program." The incongruity between slavery and the Revolutionists' cry for liberty had not gone unnoticed during the decade prior to independence. "How is it that we hear the loudest yelps for liberty from the drivers of Negros?" Samuel Johnson had caustically asked. James Otis, in his influential pamphlet, *The Rights of the British Colonies Asserted and Proved* (1764), had declared, "That the colonists, black and white, born here, are free born British subjects, and entitled to all the essential civil rights of such. . . ." On the eve of the American Revolution, Thomas Paine had sternly denounced the existence of slavery and the moral folly of slave owners who pretended to be Christians. In short, the essential ideals of individual liberty and political equality—ideals at the core of the Revolution—were hobbled by the chains of African slavery. "Our republican robe is soiled," Abraham Lincoln lamented in 1854, "and trailed in the dust."

The glaring hypocrisy between the colonists' words and actions reverberated politically throughout the thirteen colonies. In 1774 Rhode Island became the first colony to abolish the slave trade. Other colonies, as well as the Continental Congress, passed similar laws. In most of the Northern states these legislative restrictions on the slave trade were soon followed by laws abolishing slavery altogether, although in some cases the abolition was gradual. In Massachusetts, a jury ruling in the Mum Bett case, followed shortly by the ruling of Judge William Cushing in the Quock Walker case that slavery was "incompatible and repugnant" to the state's constitution, facilitated a rapid end to slavery. Even Southern legislatures recognized the injustice and illiberality of slavery, and while they stopped short of abolishing the institution, many enacted laws permitting manumission. Virginia did so in 1782, and by 1790 ten thousand slaves had been set free by their owners. To many, slavery appeared to be dying a natural death. Thus a political solution to the problem of slavery seemed unnecessary.

The reality, of course, was more complicated and tragic. Slavery had never gained a strong foothold in the North, but in the Revolutionary-era South, slaves counted for (roughly) one-third of the population in North Carolina and Georgia, two-fifths of the population of Virginia, and half the population in South Carolina. Philosophical arguments about liberty and equality ran up against economic interests. Further, a century-and-a-half of slavery and legislation aimed at preserving it had indelibly shaped public attitudes and mores. Even the most liberal democratic thinkers harbored notions of African inferiority. Thomas Jefferson might "tremble for my country" when contemplating the injustice of slavery and the fact that "God is just." But he also suggested that Africans were less capable of reason and more prone to passion—a mix that was incompatible with democratic self-government. He feared, too, as did many Southerners, that if slaves were freed, they would be incapable of caring for themselves, or worse, would erupt in vengeful violence against their former masters.

In sum, when the Constitution's Framers met in Philadelphia in the spring of 1787, conditions were not favorable to a political solution to the problem of slavery. Many recognized it for the moral and political evil it was. And yet, preserving the Union while abolishing slavery seemed to most of them an unachievable goal. As one South Carolina delegate warned, "if the Committee should fail to insert some security to the Southern States [against] an emancipation of slaves, and taxes on exports, he [should] be bound by duty to his State to vote [against] their Report." Driven by the overriding fear of disunion—the potential consequences of which Alexander Hamilton brilliantly mapped in *The Federalist* (particularly in #7, 8, and 11; see Chapter 5)—the delegates compromised.

Criticisms of the Framers on this score are common and not without merit. As William Lloyd Garrison argued, the Constitution does appear to be an "infamous bargain" that "dethroned the Most High God" and trampled the "solemn and heaven-attested Declaration." Various constitutional provisions—in particular, the three-fifths clause and the protection of the slave trade against *congressional* prohibition until 1808—are evidence of political compromise that today we have trouble comprehending. At the same time, the Framers took special care to avoid language that might be construed as providing slavery moral or legal sanction. It is not by chance that the words *slave, slavery, slave trade,* and so on do not appear in the Constitution until the Thirteenth Amendment abolished slavery.

It was the Framers' express refusal to recognize slavery's legitimacy that allowed Frederick Douglass to declare the Constitution a "Glorious Liberty Document." The Framers, he argued, understood slavery to be inconsistent with republican government and had left it to his generation finally to abolish the institution, an obligation his generation had failed to fulfill. In his newspaper (*The North Star*) and in speeches, like his great Fourth of July oration in 1852, Douglass called on his compatriots to finish the Framers' work. But slave rebellions—notably, the Haitian slave rebellion in 1791, along with domestic slave rebellions, such as Gabriel Prosser's rebellion in 1800 and Nat Turner's bloody insurrection of August 1831—exacerbated Southerners' paranoia about postemancipation reprisal killings of whites by blacks. Further, by the turn of the nineteenth century, technological advances like the cotton gin helped strengthen and broaden the Southern investment in slavery. Industrialization of textile manufacture in England and New England led to a voracious appetite for cotton and generated huge profits for the cotton plantations that produced it. In the 1790s, the commodities produced by slave plantations in the United States had faced uncertain markets. But the surge in demand for cotton starting in the early years of the nineteenth century stimulated the Southern economy and renewed Southern confidence in and commitment to the "peculiar institution." Slavery accrued powerful advocates—including religious clergy (though some religious sects, like the Quakers, had long argued against the institution)—who defended the practice scripturally. Proponents of slavery by the 1820s rejected the vision of slavery as a lamentable evil, whose existence must be tolerated but whose eventual end was anticipated. For some apologists, slavery could serve as a civilizing institution, necessary for a race incapable of exercising the virtues essential to self-government.

If slavery was a positive good and if, as many began to claim, it was a right positively asserted in the Constitution, there was no reason for it not to grow along with the nation. If, on the other hand, slavery was a moral and political abomination, albeit one that must be tolerated where it had long existed, it was critical that it be prevented from spreading to new territories. Thus were sown the seeds of the continual crises and resulting political compromises regarding federal territories in the first half of the nineteenth century. Slavery had been prohibited in the old northwest under the 1787 Northwest Ordinance, but substantial acquisitions of land, especially as a result of the Louisiana Purchase (1803) and the Mexican-American War (1846–48), continually brought the problem of slavery's future to the fore of American politics. According to many Northerners, passage of the 1820 Missouri Compromise committed the nation to a policy of containment while anticipating the eventual abolition of slavery. In their eyes, its broad prohibition against the spread of slavery made it a sacred compact, one that they saw betrayed by the Compromise of 1850, the Kansas-Nebraska Act (1854), and finally by the Supreme Court's ruling in *Dred Scott v. Sandford* (1857).

This legislation and the *Dred Scott* ruling shared a common impetus, namely, the search to find a peaceful resolution to the problem of slavery. But, perhaps, the problem had grown intractable. Slavery's apologists, including those on the U.S. Supreme Court, asserted slavery to be a constitutionally recognized right and even beneficial to the slave. Its spread westward through the territories could and should not be checked. Abolitionists like Douglass denied—correctly—the Court's claim that the "right of property in a slave is distinctly and expressly affirmed in the Constitution." Moreover, like Lincoln, many believed that a "new *Dred Scott* decision" would soon be forthcoming, one that would require existing free states to open their borders to slavery. Given what clearly seemed to be slavery's advancement throughout the Union, what strategy was best suited to check its advance?

On this question the antislavery forces offered competing answers. Abolitionist leaders like William Lloyd Garrison and David Walker were militant in their language, attacking the integrity of and arguments offered by slavery's defenders, demanding the immediate and uncompensated liberation of all slaves, and emphasizing full equality for African Americans. Other, comparatively more politically moderate voices downplayed Garrison's vision of a national, moral metamorphosis, seeking instead a political solution to the slavery crisis—including emancipation with compensation for slave owners and the colonization abroad of newly freed slaves. The advocates of such plans rejected calls for the social and political equality for African Americans. By 1840, the Garrisonians broke from this more moderate wing of the movement, declaring the Constitution to be a "compact with Satan" and calling for "no union with slaveholders." Garrison now argued for political disengagement, asserting the Constitution to be a pro-slavery document and participation in its political process a tacit endorsement of slavery.

In the wake of the Mexican-American War, debate over the status of slavery in the territories seemed poised to rip the Union asunder. Alarmed, politicians sought to defuse the issue. For the new Republican Party, led by Abraham Lincoln, this meant reinstating the ban on slavery in the territories while tolerating it in those states where it already existed. Stephen Douglas, as architect of the 1854 Kansas-Nebraska Act, promoted a policy of popular sovereignty, in which "the people of each Territory, when coming into the Union, [would] . . . decide . . . for themselves, to have slavery or not." The idea was to denationalize the slavery issue; that is, to make it merely a local policy issue, of no particular moral import to the nation.

Lincoln persuasively attacked this doctrine as morally bankrupt while successfully manipulating it to divide the Democratic Party, a political tactic instrumental to Republican electoral success in 1860. Moreover, the policy of popular sovereignty only further inflamed the nation over the slavery issue, for it encouraged local groups to seek control of the political process. It took little time for such efforts to turn violent, as the armed clashes in Kansas between abolitionists (including John Brown) and Missouri's "border ruffians" demonstrated. With the powder keg of slavery about to explode, the Supreme Court weighed in, issuing in *Dred Scott v. Sandford* an opinion that it hoped would finally settle and hence defuse the issue. It was simultaneously a politically hubristic and futile act. Within three years Chief Justice Roger Taney would retire, John Brown would lead a raid on the federal arsenal at Harper's Ferry, Southern troops would attack Fort Sumter, and Civil War would begin.

James Forten et al.

A Voice from Philadelphia (1817)

Philadelphia, January, 1817

At a numerous meeting of the people of color, convened at Bethel church, to take into consideration the propriety of remonstrating against the contemplated measure, that is to exile us from the land of our nativity; James Forten was called to the chair, and Russell Parrott appointed secretary. The intent of the meeting having been stated by the chairman, the following resolutions were adopted, without one dissenting voice.

Whereas our ancestors (not of choice) were the first successful cultivators of the wilds of America, we their descendants feel ourselves entitled to participate in the blessings of her luxuriant soil, which their blood and sweat manured; and that any measure or system of measures, having a tendency to banish us from her bosom, would not only be cruel, but in direct violation of those principles, which have been the boast of this republic.

Resolved, That we view with deep abhorrence the unmerited stigma attempted to be cast upon the reputation of the free people of color, by the promoters of this measure, "that they are a dangerous and useless part of the community," when in the state of disfranchisement in which they live, in the hour of danger they ceased to remember their wrongs, and rallied around the standard of their country.

Resolved, That we never will separate ourselves voluntarily from the slave population in this country; they are our brethren by the ties of consanguinity, of suffering, and of wrong; and we feel that there is more virtue in suffering privations with them, than fancied advantages for a season.

Resolved, That without arts, without science, without a proper knowledge of government, to cast into the savage wilds of Africa the free people of color, seems to us the circuitous route through which they must return to perpetual bondage.

Resolved, That having the strongest confidence in the justice of God, and philanthropy of the free states, we cheerfully submit our destinies to the guidance of Him who suffers not a sparrow to fall, without his special providence.

Resolved, That a committee of eleven persons be appointed to open a correspondence with the honorable Joseph Hopkinson, member of Congress from this city, and likewise to inform him of the sentiments of this meeting, and that the following named persons constitute the committee, and that they have power to call a general meeting, when they in their judgment may deem it proper.

Rev. Absalom Jones, Rev. Richard Allen, James Forten, Robert Douglass, Francis Perkins, Rev. John Gloucester, Robert Gorden, James Johnson, Quamoney Clarkson, John Summersett, Randall Shepherd.

James Forten, Chairman.
Russell Parrott, Secretary.

Resolved unanimously, That the following address, signed on behalf of the meeting, by the Chairman and Secretary, be published and circulated.

To the humane and benevolent Inhabitants of the city and county of Philadelphia.

The free people of color, assembled together, under circumstances of deep interest to their happiness and welfare, humbly and respectfully lay before you this expression of their feelings and apprehensions.

Relieved from the miseries of slavery, many of us by your aid, possessing the benefits which industry and integrity in this prosperous country assure to all its inhabitants, enjoying the rich blessings of religion, by opportunities of worshipping the only true God, under the light of Christianity, each of us according to his understanding; and having afforded to us and to our children the means of education and improvement; we have no wish to separate from our present homes, for any purpose whatever. Contented with our present situation and condition, we are not desirous of increasing their prosperity but by honest efforts, and by the use of those opportunities for their improvement, which the constitution and laws allow to all. It is therefore with painful solicitude, and sorrowing regret, we have seen a plan for colonizing the free people of color of the United States on the coast of Africa, brought forward under the auspices and sanction of gentlemen whose names give value to all they recommend, and who certainly are among the wisest, the best, and the most benevolent of men, in this great nation.

If the plan of colonizing is intended for our benefit; and those who now promote it, will never seek our injury; we humbly and respectfully urge, that it is not asked for by us; nor will it be required by any circumstances, in our present or future condition; as long as we shall be permitted to share the protection of the excellent laws and just government which we now enjoy, in common with every individual of the community.

We, therefore, a portion of those who are the objects of this plan, and among those whose happiness, with that of others of our color, it is intended to promote; with humble and grateful acknowledgments to those who have devised it, renounce and disclaim every connexion with it; and respectfully but firmly declare our determination not to participate in any part of it.

If this plan of colonization now proposed, is intended to provide a refuge and a dwelling for a portion of our brethren, who are now held in slavery in the south, we have other and stronger objections to it, and we entreat your consideration of them.

The ultimate and final abolition of slavery in the United States, by the operation of various causes, is, under the guidance and protection of a just God, progressing. Every year witnesses the release of numbers of the victims of oppression, and affords new and safe assurances that the freedom of all will be in the end accomplished. As they are thus by degrees relieved from bondage, our brothers have opportunities for instruction and improvement; and thus they become in some measure fitted for their liberty. Every year, many of us have restored to us by the gradual, but certain march of the cause of abolition—parents, from whom we have been long separated—wives and children whom we had left in servitude—and brothers, in blood as well as in early sufferings, from whom we had been long parted.

But if the emancipation of our kindred shall, when the plan of colonization shall go into effect, be attended with transportation to a distant land, and shall be granted on no other condition; the consolation for our past sufferings and of those of our color who are in slavery, which have hitherto been, and under the present situation of things would continue to be, afforded to us and to them, will cease for ever. The cords, which now connect them with us, will be stretched by the distance to which their ends will be carried, until they break; and all the sources of happiness, which affection and connexion and blood bestow, will be ours and theirs no more.

Nor do we view the colonization of those who may become emancipated by its operation among our southern brethren, as capable of producing their happiness. Unprepared by education, and a knowledge of the truths of our blessed religion, for their new situation, those who will thus become colonists will themselves be surrounded by every suffering which can afflict the members of the human family.

Without arts, without habits of industry, and unaccustomed to provide by their own exertions and foresight for their wants, the colony will soon become the abode of every vice, and the home of every misery. Soon will the light of Christianity, which now dawns among that portion of our species, be shut out by the clouds of ignorance, and their day of life be closed, without the illuminations of the gospel.

To those of our brothers, who shall be left behind, there will be assured perpetual slavery and augmented sufferings. Diminished in numbers, the slave population of the southern states, which by its magnitude alarms its proprietors, will be easily secured. Those among their bondmen, who feel that they should be free, by rights which all mankind have from God and from nature, and who thus may become dangerous to the quiet of their masters, will be sent to the colony; and the tame and submissive will be retained, and subjected to increased rigor. Year after year will witness these means to assure safety and submission among their slaves, and the southern masters will colonize only those whom it may be dangerous to keep among them. The bondage of a large portion of our brothers will thus be rendered perpetual.

Should the anticipations of misery and want among the colonists, which with great deference we have submitted to your better judgment, be realized; to emancipate and transport to Africa will be held forth by slaveholders as the worst and heaviest of punishments; and they will be threatened and successfully used to enforce increased submission to their wishes, and subjection to their commands.

Nor ought the sufferings and sorrows, which must be produced by an exercise of the right to transport and colonize such only of their slaves as may be selected by the slaveholders, escape the attention and consideration of those whom with all humility we now address. Parents will be torn from their children—husbands from their wives—brothers from brothers—and all the heart-rending agonies which were endured by our forefathers when they were dragged into bondage from Africa, will be again renewed, and with increased anguish. The shores of America will, like the sands of Africa, be watered by the tears of those who will be left behind. Those who shall be carried away will roam childless, widowed, and alone, over the burning plains of Guinea.

Disclaiming, as we emphatically do, a wish or desire to interpose our opinions and feelings between all plans of colonization, and the judgment of those whose wisdom as far exceeds ours as their situations are exalted above ours; *we humbly*, respectfully, and fervently entreat and beseech your disapprobation of the plan of colonization now offered by 'the American Society for colonizing the free people of color of the United States.'—Here, in the city of Philadelphia, where the voice of the suffering sons of Africa was first heard; where was first commenced the work of abolition, on which heaven has smiled, for it could have had success only from the Great Maker; let not a purpose be assisted which will stay the cause of the entire abolition of slavery in the United States, and which may defeat it altogether; which proffers to those who do not ask for them what it calls benefits, but which they consider injuries; and which must insure to the multitudes whose prayers can only reach you through us, MISERY, *sufferings, and perpetual slavery.*

JAMES FORTEN, Chairman.
RUSSELL PARROTT, Secretary.

RICHARD FURMAN

Exposition of the Views of Baptists, Relative to the Coloured Population in the United States, in a Communication to the Governor of South Carolina (1822)

Charleston, 24th December, 1822

SIR,

When I had, lately, the honour of delivering to your Excellency an Address, from the Baptist Convention in this State, requesting that a Day of Public Humiliation and Thanksgiving might be appointed by you, as our Chief Magistrate, to be observed by the Citizens of the State at large, in reference to two important recent events, in which the interposition of Divine Providence has been conspicuous, and in which the interests and feelings of our Citizens have been greatly concerned,—viz: The protection afforded them from the horrors of an intended Insurrection; and the affliction they have suffered from the ravages of a dreadful Hurricane—I took the liberty to suggest, that I had a further communication to make on behalf of the Convention, in which their sentiments would be disclosed respecting the policy of the measure proposed; and on the lawfulness of holding slaves—the subject being considered in a moral and religious point of view.

The Political propriety of bringing the intended Insurrection into view by publicly acknowledging its prevention to be an instance of the Divine Goodness, manifested by a providential, gracious interposition, is a subject, which has employed the serious attention of the Convention; and, if they have erred in the judgment they have formed upon it, the error is, at least, not owing to a want of consideration, or of serious concern. They cannot view the subject but as one of great magnitude, and intimately connected with the interests of the whole State. The Divine Interposition has been conspicuous; and our obligations to be thankful are unspeakably great. And, as principles of the wisest and best policy leads nations, as well as individuals, to consider and acknowledge the government of the Deity, to feel their dependency on him and trust in him, to be thankful for his mercies, and to be humbled under his chastening rod; so, not only moral and religious duty, but also a regard to the best interests of the community appear to require of us, on the present occasion, that humiliation and thanksgiving, which are proposed by the Convention in their request. For a sense of the Divine Government has a meliorating influence on the minds of men, restraining them from crime, and disposing them to virtuous action. To those also, who are humbled before the Heavenly Majesty for their sins, and learn to be thankful for his mercies, the Divine Favour is manifested. From them judgments are averted, and on them blessings are bestowed.

The Convention are aware that very respectable Citizens have been averse to the proposal under consideration; the proposal for appointing a Day of Public Thanksgiving for our preservation from the intended Insurrection, on account of the influence it might be supposed to have on the Black Population—by giving publicity to the subject in *their view*, and by affording them excitements to attempt something further of the same nature. These objections, however, the Convention view as either not substantial, or overbalanced by higher considerations. As to publicity, perhaps no fact is more generally known by the persons referred to; for the knowledge of it has been communicated by almost every channel of information, public and private, even by documents under the stamp of Public Authority; and has extended to every part of the State. But with the knowledge of the conspiracy is united the knowledge of its frustration; and of that, which Devotion and Gratitude should set in a strong light, *the merciful interposition of Providence,* which produced that frustration. The more rational among that class of men, as well as others, know also, that our preservation from the evil intended by the conspirators, is a subject, which should induce us to render thanksgivings to the Almighty; and it is hoped and believed, that the truly enlightened and religiously disposed among them, of which there appear to be many, are ready to unite in those thanksgivings, from a regard to their own true interests: if therefore it is apprehended, that an undue importance would be given to the subject in their view, by making it the matter of public thanksgiving; that this would induce the designing and wicked to infer our fear and sense of weakness from the fact, and thus induce them to form some other scheme of mischief: Would not our silence, and the omission of an important religious duty, under these circumstances, undergo, at least, as unfavorable a construction, and with more reason?

But the Convention are persuaded, that publicity, rather than secrecy is the true policy to be pursued on this occasion; especially, when the subject is taken into view, in connexion with other truths, of high importance and certainty, which relate to it, and is placed in a just light; the evidence and force of which truths, thousands of this people, when informed, can clearly discern and estimate. It is proper, the Convention conceives, that the Negroes should know, that however numerous they are in some parts of these Southern States, they, yet, are not, even including all descriptions, bond and free, in the United States, but little more than one sixth part of the whole number of inhabitants, estimating that number which it probably now is, at Ten Millions; and the Black and Coloured Population, according to returns made at 1,786,000: That their destitution in respect to arms, and the knowledge of using them, with other disabilities, would render their physical force, were they all united in a common effort, less than a tenth part of that, with which they would have to contend. That there are multitudes of the best informed and truly religious among them, who, from principle, as well as from prudence, would not unite with them, nor fail to disclose their machinations, when it should be in their power to do it: That, however in some parts of our Union there are Citizens, who favour the idea of general emancipation; yet, were they to see slaves in our Country, in arms, wading through blood and carnage to effect their purpose, they would do what both their duty and interest would require; unite under the government with their fellow citizens at large to suppress the rebellion, and bring the authors of it to condign punishment: That it may be expected, in every attempt to raise an insurrection (should other attempts be made) as well as it was in that defeated here, that the prime movers in such a nefarious scheme, will so form their plan, that in case of exigency, they may flee with their plunder and leave their deluded followers to suffer the punishment, which law and justice may inflict: And that therefore, there is reason to conclude, on the most rational and just principles, that whatever partial success might at any time attend such a measure at the onset, yet, in this country, it must finally result in the discomfiture and ruin of the perpetrators; and in many instances pull down on the heads of the innocent as well as the guilty, an undistinguishing ruin.

On the lawfulness of holding slaves, considering it in a moral and religious view, the Convention think it their duty to exhibit their sentiments, on the present occasion, before your Excellency, because they consider their duty to God, the peace of the State, the satisfaction of scrupulous consciences, and the welfare of the slaves themselves, as intimately connected with a right view of the subject. The rather, because certain writers on politics, morals and religion, and some of them highly respectable, have advanced positions, and inculcated sentiments, very unfriendly to the principle and practice of holding slaves; and by some these sentiments have been advanced among us, tending in their nature, *directly* to disturb the domestic peace of the State, to produce insubordination and rebellion among the slaves, and to infringe the rights of our citizens; and *indirectly*, to deprive the slaves of religious privileges, by awakening in the minds of their masters a fear, that acquaintance with the Scriptures, and the enjoyment of these privileges would naturally produce the aforementioned effects; because the sentiments in opposition to the holding of slaves have been attributed, by their advocates, to the Holy Scriptures, and to the genius of Christianity. These sentiments, the Convention, on whose behalf I address your Excellency, cannot think just, or well-founded: for the right of holding slaves is clearly established by the Holy Scriptures, both by precept and example. In the Old Testament, the Israelites were directed to purchase their bond-men and bond-maids of the Heathen nations; except they were of the Canaanites, for these were to be destroyed. And it is declared, that the persons purchased were to be their "bond-men forever;" and an "inheritance for them and their children." They were not to go out free in the year of jubilee, as the Hebrews, who had been purchased, were: the line being clearly drawn between them. [See Leviticus XXV. 44, 45, 46, &c.] In example, they are presented to our view as existing in the families of the Hebrews as servants, or slaves, born in the house, or bought with money: so that the children born of slaves are here considered slaves as well as their parents. And to this well known state of things, as to its reason and order, as well as to special privileges, St. Paul appears to refer, when he says, "But I was free born." [. . .]

Had the holding of slaves been a moral evil, it cannot be supposed, that the inspired Apostles, who feared not the faces of men, and were ready to lay down their lives in the cause of their God, would have tolerated it, for a moment, in the Christian Church. If they had done so on a principle of accommodation, in cases where the masters remained heathen, to avoid offences and civil commotion; yet, surely, where both master and servant were Christian, as in the case before us, they would have enforced the law of Christ, and required, that the master should liberate his slave in the first instance. But, instead of this, they let the relationship remain untouched, as being lawful and right, and insist on the relative duties. [. . .] If the holding of slaves is lawful, or according to the Scriptures; then this Scriptural rule can be considered as requiring no more of the master, in respect of justice (whatever it may do in point of generosity) than what he, if a slave, could consistently, wish to be done to himself, while the relationship between master and servant should still be continued.

In this argument, the advocates for emancipation blend the ideas of injustice and cruelty with those which respect the existence of slavery, and consider them as inseparable. But, surely, they may be separated. A bond-servant may be treated with justice and humanity as a servant; and a master may, in an important sense, be the guardian and even father of his slaves.

They become a part of his family, (the whole, forming under him a little community) and the care of ordering it and providing for its welfare, devolves on him. The children, the aged, the sick, the disabled, and the unruly, as well as those, who are capable of service and orderly, are the objects of his care: The labour of these, is applied to the benefit of those, and to their own support, as well as that of the master. Thus, what is effected, and often at a great public expense, in a free community, by taxes, benevolent institutions, bettering houses, and penitentiaries, lies here on the master, to be performed by him whatever contingencies may happen; and often occasions much expense, care and trouble, from which the servants are free. Cruelty, is, certainly, inadmissible; but servitude may be consistent with such degrees of happiness as men usually attain in this imperfect state of things.

Some difficulties arise with respect to bringing a man, or class of men, into a state of bondage. For crime, it is generally agreed, a man may be deprived of his liberty. But, may he not be divested of it by his own consent, directly, or indirectly given: And, especially, when this assent, though indirect, is connected with an attempt to take away the liberty, if not the lives of others? The Jewish law favours the former idea: And if the inquiry on the latter be taken in the affirmative, which appears to be reasonable, it will establish a principle, by which it will appear, that the Africans brought to America were slaves by their own consent, before they came from their own country, or fell into the hands of white men.

Their law of nations, or general usage, having, by common consent the force of law, justified them while carrying on their petty wars, in killing their prisoners or reducing them to slavery; consequently, in selling them, and these ends they appear to have proposed to themselves; the nation, therefore, or individual which was overcome, reduced to slavery, and sold would have done the same by the enemy, had victory declared on their, or his side. Consequently, the man made slave in this manner, might be said to be made so by his own consent, and by the indulgence of barbarous principles.

That Christian nations have not done all they might, or should have done, on a principle of Christian benevolence, for the civilization and conversion of the Africans: that much cruelty has been practised in the slave trade, as the benevolent Wilberforce, and others have shown; that much tyranny has been exercised by individuals, as masters over their slaves, and that the religious interests of the latter have been too much neglected by many cannot, will not be denied. But the fullest proof of these facts, will not also prove, that the holding men in subjection, as slaves, is a moral evil, and inconsistent with Christianity. Magistrates, husbands, and fathers, have proved tyrants. This does not prove, that magistracy, the husband's right to govern, and parental authority, are unlawful and wicked. The individual who abuses his authority, and acts with cruelty, must answer for it at the Divine tribunal; and civil authority should interpose to prevent or punish it; but neither civil nor ecclesiastical authority can consistently interfere with the possession and legitimate exercise of a right given by the Divine Law.

If the above representation of the Scriptural doctrine, and the manner of obtaining slaves from Africa is just; and if also purchasing them has been the means of saving human life, which there is great reason to believe it has; then, however the slave trade, in present circumstances, is justly censurable, yet might motives of humanity and even piety have been originally brought into operation in the purchase of slaves, when sold in the circumstances we have described. If, also, by their own confession, which has been made in manifold instances, their condition, when they have come into the hands of humane masters here, has been greatly bettered by the change; if it is, ordinarily, really better, as many assert, than that of thousands of the poorer classes in countries reputed civilized and free; and, if, in addition to all other considerations, the translation from their native country to this has been the means of their mental and religious improvement, and so of obtaining salvation, as many of themselves have joyfully and thankfully confessed—then may the just and humane master, who rules his slaves and provides for them, according to Christian principles, rest satisfied, that he is not, in holding them, chargeable with moral evil, nor with acting, in this respect, contrary to the genius of Christianity.—It appears to be equally clear, that those, who by reasoning on abstract principles, are induced to favour the scheme of general emancipation, and who ascribe their sentiments to Christianity, should be particularly careful however benevolent their intentions may be, that they do not by a perversion of the Scriptural doctrine through their wrong views of it, not only invade the domestic and religious peace and rights of our Citizens, on this subject; but, also by an intemperate zeal, prevent indirectly, the religious improvement of the people they design, professedly, to benefit; and, perhaps, become, evidently, the means of producing in our country, scenes of anarchy and blood; and all this in a vain attempt to bring about a state of things, which, if arrived at, would not probably better the state of that people; which is thought by men of observation, to be generally true of the Negroes in the Northern states, who have been liberated. [. . .]

The Convention, Sir, are far from thinking that Christianity fails to inspire the minds of its subjects with benevolent and generous sentiments; or that liberty rightly understood, or enjoyed, is a blessing of little moment. The contrary of these positions they maintain. But they also consider benevolence as consulting the truest and best interests of its objects; and view the happiness of liberty as well as of religion, as consisting not in the name or form, but in the reality. While men remain in the chains of ignorance and error, and under the domination of tyrant lusts and passions, they cannot be free. And the more freedom of action they have in this state, they are but the more qualified by it to do injury, both to themselves and others. It is, therefore, firmly believed, that general emancipation to the Negroes in this country, would not, in present circumstances, be for their own happiness, as a body; while it would be extremely injurious to the community at large in various ways: And, if so, then it is not required even by benevolence. But acts of benevolence and generosity must be free and voluntary; no man has a right to compel another to the performance of them. This is a concern, which lies between a man and his God. If a man has obtained slaves by purchase, or inheritance, and the holding of them as such is justifiable by the law of God; why should he be required to liberate them, because it would be a generous action, rather than another on the same principle, to release his debtors, or sell his lands and houses, and distribute the proceeds among the poor? These also would be generous actions: Are they, therefore, obligatory? Or, if obligatory, in certain circumstances, as personal, voluntary acts of piety and benevolence, has any man or body of men, civil or ecclesiastic, a right to require them? Surely those, who are advocates for compulsory, or strenous measures to bring about emancipation, should duly weigh this consideration.

Should, however, a time arrive, when the Africans in our country might be found qualified to enjoy freedom; and, when they might obtain it in a manner consistent with the interest and peace of the community at large, the Convention would be happy in seeing them free: And so they would, in seeing the state of the poor, the ignorant and the oppressed of every description, and of every country meliorated; so that the reputed free might be free indeed, and happy. But there seems to be just reason to conclude that a considerable part of the human race, whether they bear openly the character of slaves or are reputed freemen, will continue in such circumstances, with mere shades of variation, while the world continues. It is evident, that men are sinful creatures, subject to affliction and to death, as the consequences of their nature's pollution and guilt: That they are now in a state of probation; and that God as a Righteous, All-wise Sovereign, not only disposes of them as he pleases, and bestows upon them many unmerited blessings and comforts, but subjects them also to privations, afflictions and trials, with the merciful intention of making all their afflictions, as well as their blessings, work finally for their good; if they embrace his salvation, humble themselves before him, learn righteousness, and submit to his holy will. To have them brought to this happy state is the great object of Christian benevolence, and of Christian piety; for this state is not only connected with the truest happiness, which can be enjoyed at any time, but is introductory to eternal life and blessedness in the future world: And the salvation of men is intimately connected with the glory of their God and Redeemer.

And here I am brought to a part of the general subject, which, I confess to your Excellency, the Convention, from a sense of their duty, as a body of men, to whom important concerns of Religion are confided, have particularly at heart, and wish it may be seriously considered by all our Citizens: This is the religious interests of the Negroes. For though they are slaves, they are also men; and are with ourselves accountable creatures; having immortal souls, and being destined to future eternal reward. Their religious interests claim a regard from their masters of the most serious nature; and it is indispensable. Nor can the community at large, in a right estimate of their duty and happiness, be indifferent on this subject. To the truly benevolent it must be pleasing to know, that a number of masters, as well as ministers and pious individuals, of various Christian denominations among us, do conscientiously regard this duty; but there is a great reason to believe, that it is neglected and disregarded by many. [. . .]

The result of this inquiry and reasoning, on the subject of slavery, brings us, sir, if I mistake not, very regularly to the following conclusions:—That the holding of slaves is justifiable by the doctrine and example contained in Holy writ; and is; therefore consistent with Christian uprightness, both in sentiment and conduct. That all things considered, the Citizens of America have in general obtained the African slaves, which they possess, on principles, which can be justified; though much cruelty has indeed been exercised towards them by many, who have been concerned in the slave-trade, and by others who have held them here, as slaves in their service; for which the authors of this cruelty are accountable. That slavery, when tempered with humanity and justice, is a state of tolerable happiness; equal, if not superior, to that which many poor enjoy in countries reputed free. That a master has a scriptural right to govern his slaves so as to keep it in subjection; to demand and receive from them a reasonable service; and to correct them for the neglect of duty, for their vices and transgressions; but that to impose on them unreasonable, rigorous services, or to inflict on them cruel punishment, he has neither a scriptural nor a moral right. At the same time it must be remembered, that, while he is receiving from them their uniform and best services, he is required by the Divine Law, to afford them protection, and such necessaries and conveniences of life as are proper to their condition as servants; so far as he is enabled by their services to afford them these comforts, on just and rational principles. That it is the positive duty of servants to reverence their master, to be obedient, industrious, faithful to him, and careful of his interests; and without being so, they can neither be the faithful servants of God, nor be held as regular members of the Christian Church. That as claims to freedom as a *right*, when that right is forfeited, or has been lost, in such a manner as has been represented, would be unjust; and as all attempts to obtain it by violence and fraud would be wicked; so all representations made to them by others, on such censurable principles, or in a manner tending to make them discontented; and finally, to produce such unhappy effects and consequences, as been before noticed, cannot be friendly to them (as they certainly are not to the community at large,) nor consistent with righteousness: Nor can the conduct be justified, however in some it may be palliated by pleading benevolence in intention, as the motive. That masters having the disposal of the persons, time and labour of their servants, and being the heads of families, are bound, on principles of moral and religious duty, to give these servants religious instruction; or at least, to afford them opportunities, under proper regulations to obtain it: And to grant religious privileges to those, who desire them, and furnish proper evidence of their sincerity and uprightness: Due care being at the same time taken, that they receive their instructions from right sources, and from their connexions, where they will not be in danger of having their minds corrupted by sentiments unfriendly to the domestic and civil peace of the community. That, where life, comfort, safety and religious interest of so large a number of human beings, as this class of persons is among us, are concerned; and, where they must necessarily, as slaves, be so much at the disposal of their masters; it appears to be a just and necessary concern of the Government, not only to provide laws to prevent or punish insurrections, and other violent and villanous conduct among them (which are indeed necessary) but, on the other hand, laws, also, to prevent their being oppressed and injured by unreasonable, cruel masters, and others; and to afford them, in respect of morality and religion, such privileges as may comport with the peace and safety of the State, and with those relative duties existing between masters and servants, which the word of God enjoins. It is, also, believed to be a just conclusion, that the interest and security of the State would be promoted, by allowing, under proper regulations, considerable religious privileges, to such of this class, as know how to estimate them aright, and have given suitable evidence of their own good principles, uprightness and fidelity; by attaching them, from principles of gratitude and love, to the interests of their masters and the State; and thus rendering their fidelity firm and constant. While on the other hand, to lay them under an interdict, as some have supposed necessary, in a case where reason, conscience, the genius of Christianity and salvation are concerned, on account of the bad conduct of others, would be felt as oppressive, tend to sour and alienate their minds from their masters and the public, and to make them vulnerable to temptation. All which is, with deference, submitted to the consideration of your Excellency.

With high respect, I remain, personally, and on behalf of the Convention,

Sir, your very obedient and humble servant,

RICHARD FURMAN
President of the Baptist State Convention

JAMES MADISON

Letter to Edward Everett (August 28, 1830)

I have duly recd. your letter in wch. you refer to the "nullifying doctrine," advocated as a constitutional right by some of our distinguished fellow citizens; and to the proceedings of the Virga. Legislature in 98 & 99, as appealed to in behalf of that doctrine; and you express a wish for my ideas on those subjects.

I am aware of the delicacy of the task in some respects; and the difficulty in every respect of doing full justice to it. But having in more than one instance complied with a like request from other friendly quarters, I do not decline a sketch of the views which I have been led to take of the doctrine in question, as well as some others connected with them; and of the grounds from which it appears that the proceedings of Virginia have been misconceived by those who have appealed to them. In order to understand the true character of the Constitution of the U.S. the error, not uncommon, must be avoided of viewing it through the medium either of a consolidated Government or of a confederated Govt. whilst it is neither the one nor the other, but a mixture of both. And having in no model the similitudes & analogies applicable to other systems of Govt. it must more than any other be its own interpreter, according to its text & *the facts of the case.*

From these it will be seen that the characteristic peculiarities of the Constitution are 1. The mode of its formation, 2. The division of the supreme powers of Govt. between the States in their united capacity and the States in their individual capacities.

1. It was formed, not by the Governments of the component States, as the Federal Govt. for which it was substituted was formed; nor was it formed by a majority of the people of the U.S. as a single community in the manner of a consolidated Government.

It was formed by the States—that is by the people in each of the States, acting in their highest sovereign capacity; and formed, consequently by the same authority which formed the State Constitutions.

Being thus derived from the same source as the Constitutions of the States, it has within each State, the same authority as the Constitution of the State; and is as much a Constitution, in the strict sense of the term, within its prescribed sphere, as the Constitutions of the States are within their respective spheres; but with this obvious & essential difference, that being a compact among the States in their highest sovereign capacity, and constituting the people thereof one people for certain purposes, it cannot be altered or annulled at the will of the

States individually, as the Constitution of a State may be at its individual will.

2. And that it divides the supreme powers of Govt. between the Govt. of the United States, & the Govts. of the individual States, is stamped on the face of the instrument; the powers of war and of taxation, of commerce & of treaties, and other enumerated powers vested in the Govt. of the U.S. being of as high & sovereign a character as any of the powers reserved to the State Govts.

Nor is the Govt. of the U.S. created by the Constitution, less a Govt. in the strict sense of the term, within the sphere of its powers, than the Govts. created by the constitutions of the States are within their several spheres. It is like them organized into Legislative, Executive, & Judiciary Departments. It operates like them, directly on persons & things. And, like them, it has at command a physical force for executing the powers committed to it. The concurrent operation in certain cases is one of the features marking the peculiarity of the system.

Between these different constitutional Govts.—the one operating in all the States, the others operating separately in each, with the aggregate powers of Govt. divided between them, it could not escape attention that controversies would arise concerning the boundaries of jurisdiction; and that some provision ought to be made for such occurrences. A political system that does not provide for a peaceable & authoritative termination of occurring controversies, would not be more than the shadow of a Govt.; the object & end of a real Govt. being the substitution of law & order for uncertainty confusion, and violence.

That to have left a final decision in such cases to each of the States, then 13 & already 24, could not fail to make the Constn. & laws of the U.S. different in different States was obvious; and not less obvious, that this diversity of independent decisions, must altogether distract the Govt. of the Union & speedily put an end to the Union itself. A uniform authority of the laws, is in itself a vital principle. Some of the most important laws could not be partially executed. They must be executed in all the States or they could be duly executed in none. An impost or an excise, for example, if not in force in some States, would be defeated in others. It is well known that this was among the lessons of experience wch. had a primary influence in bringing about the existing Constitution. A loss of its general authy. would moreover revive the exasperating questions between the States holding ports for foreign commerce and the adjoining States without them, to which are now added all the inland States necessarily carrying on their foreign commerce through other States.

To have made the decisions under the authority of the individual States, co-ordinate in all cases with decisions under the authority of the U.S. would unavoidably produce collisions incompatible with the peace of society, & with that regular & efficient administration which is the essence of free Govts. Scenes could not be avoided in which a ministerial officer of the U.S. and the correspondent officer of an individual State, would have rencounters in executing conflicting decrees, the result of which would depend on the comparative force of the local posse attending them, and that a casualty depending on the political opinions and party feelings in different States.

To have referred every clashing decision under the two authorities for a final decision to the States as parties to the Constitution, would be attended with delays, with inconveniences, and with expenses amounting to a prohibition of the expedient, not to mention its tendency to impair the salutary veneration for a system requiring such frequent interpositions, nor the delicate questions which might present themselves as to the form of stating the appeal, and as to the Quorum for deciding it.

To have trusted to negotiation, for adjusting disputes between the Govt. of the U.S. and the State Govts. as between independent & separate sovereignties, would have lost sight altogether of a Constitution & Govt. for the Union; and opened a direct road from a failure of that resort, to the ultima ratio between nations wholly independent of and alien to each other. If the idea had its origin in the process of adjustment between separate branches of the same Govt. the analogy entirely fails. In the case of disputes between independent parts of the same Govt. neither part being able to consummate its will, nor the Gov. to proceed without a concurrence of the parts, necessity brings about an accommodation. In disputes between a State Govt. and the Govt. of the U. States the case is practically as well as theoretically different; each party possessing all the Departments of an organized Govt. Legisl, Ex. & Judiciary; and having each a physical force to support its pretensions.

Although the issue of negotiation might sometimes avoid this extremity, how often would it happen among so many States, that an unaccommodating spirit in some would render that resource unavailing? A contrary supposition would not accord with a knowledge of human nature or the evidence of our own political history.

The Constitution, not relying on any of the preceding modifications for its safe & successful operation, has expressly declared on the one hand; 1. "That the Constitution, and the laws made in pursuance thereof, and all Treaties made under the authority of the U.S. shall be the supreme law of the land; 2. That the judges of every State shall be bound thereby, anything in the Constn. or laws of any State to the contrary notwithstanding; 3. That the judicial power of the U.S. shall extend to all cases in law & equity arising under the Constitution, the laws of the U.S. and Treaties made under their authority &c."

On the other hand, as a security of the rights & powers of the States in their individual capacities, agst. an undue preponderance of the powers granted to the Government over them in their united capacity, the Constitution has relied on, 1. The responsibility of the Senators and Representatives in the Legislature of the U.S. to the Legislatures & people of the States. 2. The responsibility of the President to the people of the U. States; & 3. The liability of the Ex. and Judiciary functionaries of the U.S. to impeachment by the Representatives of the people of the States, in one branch of the Legislature of the U.S. and trial by the Representatives of the States, in the other branch; the State functionaries, Legislative, Executive, & judiciary, being at the same time in their appointment & responsibility, altogether independent of the agency or authority of the U. States.

How far this structure of the Govt. of the U.S. be adequate & safe for its objects, time alone can absolutely determine. Experience seems to have shown that whatever may grow out of future stages of our national career, there is as yet a sufficient controul in the popular will over the Executive & Legislative Departments of the Govt. When the Alien & Sedition laws were passed in contravention to the opinions and feelings of the community, the first elections that ensued put an end to them. And whatever may have been the character of other acts in the judgment of many of us, it is but true that they have generally accorded with the views of a majority of the States and of the people. At the present day it seems well understood that the laws which have created most dissatisfaction have had a like sanction without doors; and that whether continued varied or repealed, a like proof will be given of the sympathy & responsibility of the Representative Body to the Constituent Body. Indeed, the great complaint now is, not against the want of this sympathy and responsibility, but against the results of them in the legislative policy of the nation.

With respect to the Judicial power of the U.S. and the authority of the Supreme Court in relation to the boundary of jurisdiction between the Federal & the State Govts. I may be permitted to refer to the [39] number of the "Federalist" for the light in which the subject was regarded by its writer, at the period when the Constitution was depending; and it is believed that the same was the prevailing view then taken of it, that the same view has continued to prevail, and that it does so at this time notwithstanding the eminent exceptions to it.

But it is perfectly consistent with the concession of this power to the Supreme Court, in cases falling within the course of its functions, to maintain that the power has not always been rightly exercised. To say nothing of the period, happily a short one, when judges in their seats did not abstain from intemperate & party harangues, equally at variance with their duty and their dignity, there have been occasional decisions from the Bench which have incurred serious & extensive disapprobation. Still it would seem that, with but few exceptions, the course of the judiciary has been hitherto sustained by the predominant sense of the nation.

Those who have denied or doubted the supremacy of the judicial power of the U.S. & denounce at the same time nullifying power in a State, seem not to have sufficiently adverted to the utter inefficiency of a supremacy in a law of the land, without a supremacy in the exposition & execution of the law; nor to the destruction of all equipoise between the Federal Govt. and the State governments, if, whilst the functionaries of the Fedl. Govt. are directly or indirectly elected by and responsible to the States & the functionaries of the States are in their appointments & responsibility wholly independent of the U.S. no constitutional control of any sort belonged to the U.S. over the States. Under such an organization it is evident that it would be in the power of the States individually, to pass unauthorized laws, and to carry them into complete effect, anything in the Constn. and laws of the U.S. to the contrary notwithstanding. This would be a nullifying power in its plenary character; and whether it had its final effect, through the Legislative Ex. or Judiciary organ of the State, would be equally fatal to the constitutional relation between the two Govts.

Should the provisions of the Constitution as here reviewed be found not to secure the Govt. & rights of the States agst. usurpations & abuses on part of the U.S. the final resort within the purview of the Constn. lies in an amendment of the Constn. according to a process applicable by the States.

And in the event of a failure of every constitutional resort, and an accumulation of usurpations & abuses, rendering passive obedience & non-resistence a greater evil, than resistence & revolution, there can remain but one resort, the last of all, an appeal from the cancelled obligations of the constitutional compact, to original rights & the law of self-preservation. This is the ultima ratio under all Govt. whether consolidated, confederated, or a compound of both; and it cannot be doubted that a single member of the Union, in the extremity supposed, but in that only would have a right, as an extra & ultra constitutional right, to make the appeal.

This brings us to the expedient lately advanced, which claims for a single State a right to appeal agst. an exercise of power by the Govt. of the U.S. decided by the State to be unconstitutional, to the parties of the Const. compact; the decision of the State to have the effect of nullifying the act of the Govt. of the U.S. unless the decision of the State be reversed by three-fourths of the parties.

The distinguished names & high authorities which appear to have asserted and given a practical scope to this doctrine, entitle it to a respect which it might be difficult otherwise to feel for it.

If the doctrine were to be understood as requiring the three-fourths of the States to sustain, instead of that proportion to reverse, the decision of the appealing State, the decision to be without effect during the appeal, it wd. be sufficient to remark, that this extra constl. course might well give way to that marked out by the Const. which authorizes ⅔ of the States to institute and ¾ to effectuate, an amendment of the Constn. establishing a permanent rule of the highest authy. in place of an irregular precedent of construction only.

But it is understood that the nullifying doctrine imports that the decision of the State is to be presumed valid, and that it overrules the law of the U.S. unless overuled by ¾ of the States.

Can more be necessary to demonstrate the inadmissibility of such a doctrine than that it puts it in the power of the smallest fraction over ¼ of the U.S.—that is, of 7 States out of 24—to give the law and even the Constn. to 17 States, each of the 17 having as parties to the Constn. an equal right with each of the 7 to expound it & to insist on the exposition. That the 7 might, in particular instances be right and the 17 wrong, is more than possible. But to establish a positive & permanent rule giving such a power to such a minority over such a majority, would overturn the first principle of free Govt. and in practice necessarily overturn the Govt. itself.

It is to be recollected that the Constitution was proposed to the people of the States as a *whole,* and unanimously adopted by the States as a *whole,* it being a part of the Constitution that not less than ¾ of the States should be competent to make any alteration in what had been unanimously agreed to. So great is the caution on this point, that in two cases when peculiar interests were at stake, a proportion even of ¾ is distrusted, and unanimity required to make an alteration.

When the Constitution was adopted as a whole, it is certain that there were many parts which if separately proposed, would have been promptly rejected. It is far from impossible, that every part of the Constitution might be rejected by a majority, and yet, taken together as a whole be unanimously accepted. Free constitutions will rarely if ever be formed without reciprocal concessions; without articles conditioned on & balancing each other. Is there a constitution of a single State out of the 24 that wd. bear the experiment of having its component parts submitted to the people & separately decided on?

What the fate of the Constitution of the U.S. would be if a small proportion of States could expunge parts of it particularly valued by a large majority, can have but one answer.

The difficulty is not removed by limiting the doctrine to cases of construction. How many cases of that sort, involving cardinal provisions of the Constitution, have occurred? How many now exist? How many may hereafter spring up? How many might be ingeniously created, if entitled to the privilege of a decision in the mode proposed?

Is it certain that the principle of that mode wd. not reach farther than is contemplated. If a single State can of right require ¾ of its co-States to overrule its exposition of the Constitution, because that proportion is authorized to amend it, would the plea be less plausible that, as the Constitution was unanimously established, it ought to be unanimously expounded?

The reply to all such suggestions seems to be unavoidable and irresistible, that the Constitution is a compact; that its text is to be expounded according to the provision for expounding it, making a part of the compact; and that none of the parties can rightfully renounce the expounding provision more than any other part. When such a right accrues, as it may accrue, it must grow out of abuses of the compact releasing the sufferers from their fealty to it.

In favour of the nullifying claim for the States individually, it appears, as you observe, that the proceedings of the Legislature of Virga. in 98 & 99 agst. the Alien and Sedition Acts are much dwelt upon.

It may often happen, as experience proves, that erroneous constructions, not anticipated, may not be sufficiently guarded against in the language used; and it is due to the distinguished individuals who have misconceived the intention of those proceedings to suppose that the meaning of the Legislature, though well comprehended at the time, may not now be obvious to those unacquainted with the contemporary indications and impressions.

But it is believed that by keeping in view the distinction between the Govt. of the States & the States in the sense in which they were parties to the Constn.; between the rights of the parties, in their concurrent and in their individual capacities; between the several modes and objects of interposition agst. the abuses of power, and especially between interpositions within the purview of the Constn. & interpositions appealing from the Constn. to the rights of nature paramount to all Constitutions; with these distinctions kept in view, and an attention, always of explanatory use, to the views & arguments which were combated, a confidence is felt, that the Resolutions of Virginia, as vindicated in the Report on them, will be found entitled to an exposition, showing a consistency in their parts and an inconsistency of the whole with the doctrine under consideration.

That the Legislature cd. not have intended to sanction such a doctrine is to be inferred from the debates in the House of Delegates, and from the address of the two Houses to their constituents on the subject of the resolutions. The tenor of the debates wch. were ably conducted and are understood to have been revised for the press by most, if not all, of the speakers, discloses no reference whatever to a constitutional right in an individual State to arrest by force the operation of a law of the U.S. Concert among the States for redress against the alien & sedition laws, as acts of usurped power, was a leading sentiment, and the attainment of a concert the immediate object of the course adopted by the Legislature, which was that of inviting the other States "to *concur* in declaring the acts to be unconstitutional, and to *co-operate* by the necessary & proper measures in maintaining unimpaired the authorities rights & liberties reserved to the States respectively & to the people." That by the necessary and proper measures to be *concurrently* and co-operatively taken, were meant measures known to the Constitution, particularly the ordinary controul of the people and Legislatures of the States over the Govt. of the U.S. cannot be doubted; and the interposition of this controul as the event showed was equal to the occasion.

It is worthy of remark, and explanatory of the intentions of the Legislature, that the words "not law, but utterly null, void, and of no force or effect," which had followed, in one of the Resolutions, the word "unconstitutional," were struck out by common consent. Though the words were in fact but synonymous with "unconstitutional," yet to guard against a misunderstanding of this phrase as more than declaratory of opinion, the word unconstitutional alone was retained, as not liable to that danger.

The published address of the Legislature to the people their constituents affords another conclusive evidence of its views. The address warns them against the encroaching spirit of the Genl. Govt., argues the unconstitutionality of the alien & sedition acts, points to other instances in which the constl. limits had been overleaped; dwells upon the dangerous mode of deriving power by implications; and in general presses the necessity of watching over the consolidating tendency of the Fedl. policy. But nothing is sd. that can be understood to look to means of maintaining the rights of the States beyond the regular ones within the forms of the Constn.

If any farther lights on the subject cd. be needed, a very strong one is reflected in the answers to the Resolutions by the States which protested agst. them. The main objection to these, beyond a few general complaints agst. the inflammatory tendency of the resolutions was directed agst. the assumed authy. of a State Legisle. to declare a law of the U.S. unconstitutional, which they pronounced an unwarrantable interference with the exclusive jurisdiction of the Supreme Ct. of the U.S. Had the resolns. been regarded as avowing & maintaining a right in an indivl. State, to arrest by force the execution of a law of the U.S. it must be presumed that it wd. have been a conspicuous object of their denunciation.

DAVID WALKER

Appeal in Four Articles to the Colored Citizens of the World (1830)

My dearly beloved Brethren and Fellow Citizens.

Having travelled over a considerable portion of these United States, and having, in the course of my travels, taken the most accurate observations of things as they exist—the result of my observations has warranted the full and unshaken conviction, that we, (coloured people of these United States,) are the most degraded, wretched, and abject set of beings that ever lived since the world began; and I pray God that none like us ever may live again until time shall be no more. They tell us of the Israelites in Egypt, the Helots in Sparta, and of the Roman Slaves, which last were made up from almost every nation under heaven, whose sufferings under those ancient and heathen nations, were, in comparison with ours, under this enlightened and Christian nation, no more than a cypher—or, in other words, those nations of antiquity, had but little more among them than the name and form of slavery; while wretchedness and endless miseries were reserved, apparently in a phial, to be poured out upon our fathers, ourselves and our children, by *Christian* Americans!

These positions I shall endeavour, by the help of the Lord, to demonstrate in the course of this APPEAL, to the satisfaction of the most incredulous mind—and may God Almighty, who is the Father of our Lord Jesus Christ, open your hearts to understand and believe the truth. [. . .]

I am fully aware, in making this appeal to my much afflicted and suffering brethren, that I shall not only be assailed by those whose greatest earthly desires are, to keep us in abject ignorance and wretchedness, and who are of the firm conviction that Heaven has designed us and our children to be slaves and *beasts of burden* to them and their children. I say, I do not only expect to be held up to the public as an ignorant, impudent and restless disturber of the public peace, by such avaricious creatures, as well as a mover of insubordination—and perhaps put in prison or to death, for giving a superficial exposition of our miseries, and exposing tyrants. But I am persuaded, that many of my brethren, particularly those who are ignorantly in league with slave-holders or tyrants, who acquire their daily bread by the blood and sweat of their more ignorant brethren—and not a few of those too, who are too ignorant to see an inch beyond their noses, will rise up and call me cursed—Yea, the jealous ones among us will perhaps use more abject subtlety, by affirming that this work is not worth perusing, that we are well situated, and there is no use in trying to better our condition, for we cannot. I will ask one question here.—Can our condition be any worse? [. . .] The fact is, the labour of slaves comes too cheap to the avaricious usurpers, and is (as they think) of such great utility to the country where it exists, that those who are actuated by sordid avarice only, overlook the evils, which will as sure as the Lord lives, follow after the good. In fact, they are so happy to keep in ignorance and degradation, and to receive the homage and the labour of the slaves, they forget that God rules in the armies of heaven and among the inhabitants of the earth, having his ears continually open to the cries, tears and groans of his oppressed people; and being a just and holy Being will at one day appear fully in behalf of the oppressed, and arrest the progress of the avaricious oppressors; for although the destruction of the oppressors God may not effect by the oppressed, yet the Lord our God will bring other destructions upon them—for not unfrequently will he cause them to rise up one against another, to be split and divided, and to oppress each other, and sometimes to open hostilities with sword in hand.

Some may ask, what is the matter with this united and happy people?—Some say it is the cause of political usurpers, tyrants, oppressors, &c. But has not the Lord an oppressed and suffering people among them? Does the Lord condescend to hear their cries and see their tears in consequence of oppression? Will he let the oppressors rest comfortably and happy always? Will he not cause the very children of the oppressors to rise up against them, and ofttimes put them to death? "God works in many ways his wonders to perform." [. . .]

All persons who are acquainted with history, and particularly the Bible, who are not blinded by the God of this world, and are not actuated solely by avarice—who are able to lay aside prejudice long enough to view candidly and impartially, things as they were, are, and probably will be—who are willing to admit that God made man to serve Him *alone*, and that man should have no other Lord or Lords but Himself—that God Almighty is the *sole proprietor* or *master* of the WHOLE human family, and will not on any consideration admit of a colleague, being unwilling to divide his glory with another—and who can dispense with prejudice long enough to admit that we are *men*, notwithstanding our *improminent noses* and *woolly heads*, and believe that we feel for our fathers, mothers, wives and children, as well as the whites do for theirs.—I say, all who are permitted to see and believe these things, can easily recognize the judgments of God among the Spaniards. Though others may lay the cause of the fierceness with which they cut each other's throats, to some other circumstances, yet they who believe that God is a God of justice, will believe that SLAVERY *is the principal cause*. [. . .] I would only mention that the Egyptians, were Africans or coloured people, such as we are—some of them yellow and others dark—a mixture of Ethiopians and the natives of Egypt—about the same as you see the coloured people of the United States at the present day.—I say, I call your attention then, to the children of Jacob, while I point out particularly to you his son Joseph, among the rest, in Egypt. [. . .]

Now I appeal to heaven and to earth, and particularly to the American people themselves, who cease not to declare that our condition is not *hard*, and that we are comparatively satisfied to rest in wretchedness and misery, under them and their children. Not, indeed, to show me a coloured President, a Governor, a Legislator, a Senator, a Mayor, or an Attorney at the Bar.—But to show me a man of colour, who holds the low office of a Constable, or one who sits in a Juror Box, even on a case of one of his wretched brethren, throughout this great Republic!!—But let us pass Joseph the son of Israel a little farther in review, as he existed with that heathen nation. [. . .]

Compare the above, with the American institutions. Do they not institute laws to prohibit us from marrying among the whites? I would wish, candidly, however, before the Lord, to be understood, that I would not give a *pinch of snuff* to be married to any white person I ever saw in all the days of my life. And I do say it, that the black man, or man of colour, who will leave his own colour (provided he can get one, who is good for any thing) and marry a white woman, to be a double slave to her, just because she is *white*, ought to be treated by her as he surely will be, viz: as a NIGER!!!! It is not, indeed, what I care about intermarriages with the whites, which induced me to pass this subject in review; for the Lord knows, that there is a day coming when they will be glad enough to get into the company of the blacks, notwithstanding, we are, in this generation, levelled by them, almost on a level with the brute creation: and some of us they treat even worse than they do the brutes that perish. I only made this extract to show how much lower we are held, and how much more cruel we are treated by the Americans, than were the children of Jacob, by the Egyptians.—We will notice the sufferings of Israel some further, under *heathen Pharaoh,* compared with ours under the *enlightened Christians of America.* [. . .]

But to prove farther that the condition of the Israelites was better under the Egyptians than ours is under the whites. I call upon the professing Christians, I call upon the philanthropist, I call upon the very tyrant himself, to show me a page of history, either sacred or profane, on which a verse can be found, which maintains, that the Egyptians heaped the *insupportable insult* upon the children of Israel, by telling them that they were not of the *human family.* Can the whites deny this charge? Have they not, after having reduced us to the deplorable condition of slaves under their feet, held us up as descending originally from the tribes of *Monkeys* or *Orang-Outangs?* O! my God! I appeal to every man of feeling—is not this insupportable? Is it not heaping the most gross insult upon our miseries, because they have got us under their feet and we cannot help ourselves? Oh! pity us we pray thee, Lord Jesus, Master.—Has Mr. Jefferson declared to the world, that we are inferior to the whites, both in the endowments of our bodies and of minds? It is indeed surprising, that a man of such great learning, combined with such excellent natural parts, should speak so of a set of men in chains. [. . .]

Are we MEN!!—I ask you, O my brethren! are we *MEN?* Did our Creator make us to be slaves to dust and ashes like ourselves? Are they not dying worms as well as we? Have they not to make their appearance before the tribunal of Heaven, to answer for the deeds done in the body, as well as we? Have we any other Master but Jesus Christ alone? Is he not their Master as well as ours?—What right then, have we to obey and call any other Master, but Himself? How we could be so *submissive* to a gang of men, whom we cannot tell whether they are *as good* as ourselves or not, I never could conceive. However, this is shut up with the Lord, and we cannot precisely tell—but I declare, we judge men by their works.

The whites have always been an unjust, jealous, unmerciful, avaricious and blood-thirsty set of beings, always seeking after power and authority.—We view them all over the confederacy of Greece, where they were first known to be any thing, (in consequence of education) we see them there, cutting each other's throats—trying to subject each other to wretchedness and misery—to effect which, they used all kinds of deceitful, unfair, and unmerciful means. We view them next in Rome, where the spirit of tyranny and deceit raged still higher. We view them in Gaul, Spain, and in Britain.—In fine, we view them all over Europe, together with what were scattered about in Asia and Africa, as heathens, and we see them acting more like devils than accountable men. But some may ask, did not the blacks of Africa, and the mulattoes of Asia, go on in the same way as did the whites of Europe. I answer, no—they never were half so avaricious, deceitful and unmerciful as the whites, according to their knowledge.

But we will leave the whites or Europeans as heathens, and take a view of them as Christians, in which capacity we see them as cruel, if not more so than ever. In fact, take them as a body, they are ten times more cruel, avaricious and unmerciful than ever they were; for while they were heathens, they were bad enough it is true, but it is positively a fact that they were not quite so audacious as to go and take vessel loads of men, women and children, and in cold blood, and through devilishness, throw them into the sea, and murder them in all kind of ways. While they were heathens, they were too ignorant for such barbarity. But being Christians, enlightened and sensible, they are completely prepared for such hellish cruelties.

Now suppose God were to give them more sense, what would they do? If it were possible, would they not *dethrone* Jehovah and seat themselves upon his throne? I therefore, in the name and fear of the Lord God of Heaven and of earth, divested of prejudice either on the side of my colour or that of the whites, advance my suspicion of them, whether they are *as good by nature* as we are or not. Their actions, since they were known as a people, have been the reverse, I do indeed suspect them, but this, as I before observed, is shut up with the Lord, we cannot exactly tell, it will be proved in succeeding generations. [. . .] Oh! coloured people of these United States, I ask you, in the name of that God who made us, have we, in consequence of oppression, nearly lost the spirit of man, and, in no very trifling degree, adopted that of brutes? Do you answer, no?—I ask you, then, what set of men can you point me to, in all the world, who are so abjectly employed by their oppressors, as we are by our *natural enemies?*

How can, Oh! how can those enemies but say that we and our children are not of the HUMAN FAMILY, but were made by our Creator to be an inheritance to them and theirs for ever? How can the slave-holders but say that they can bribe the best coloured person in the country, to sell his brethren for a trifling sum of money, and take that atrocity to confirm them in their avaricious opinion, that we were made to be slaves to them and their children? How could Mr. Jefferson but say,[1] "I advance it therefore as a suspicion only, that the blacks, whether originally a distinct race, or made distinct by time and circumstances, are *inferior* to the whites in the endowments both of body and mind?" "It," says he, "is not against experience to suppose, that different species of the same genus, or varieties of the same species, may possess different qualifications." [Here, my brethren, listen to him.] "Will not a lover of natural history, then, one who views the gradations in all the races of *animals* with the eye of philosophy, excuse an effort to keep those in the department of MAN as *distinct* as nature has formed them?"—I hope you will try to find out the meaning of this verse—its widest sense and all its bearings: whether you do or not, remember the whites do. This very verse, brethren, having emanated from Mr. Jefferson, a much greater philosopher the world never afforded, has in truth injured us more, and has been as great a barrier to our emancipation as any thing that has ever been advanced against us. I hope you will not let it pass unnoticed. He goes on further, and says: "This *unfortunate* difference of colour, and *perhaps of faculty*, is a powerful obstacle to the emancipation of these people. Many of their advocates, while they wish to vindicate the liberty of human nature are anxious also to preserve its *dignity* and *beauty*. Some of these, embarrassed by the question, 'What further is to be done with them?' join themselves in opposition with those who are actuated by sordid avarice only."

Now I ask you candidly, my suffering brethren in time, who are candidates for the eternal worlds, how could Mr. Jefferson but have given the world these remarks respecting us, when we are so submissive to them, and so much servile deceit prevail among ourselves—when we so *meanly* submit to their murderous lashes, to which neither the Indians nor any other people under Heaven would submit? No, they would die to a man, before they would suffer such things from men who are no better than themselves, and *perhaps not so good*. Yes, how can our friends but be embarrassed, as Mr. Jefferson says, by the question, "What further is to be done with these people?" For while they are working for our emancipation, we are, by our treachery, wickedness and deceit, working against ourselves and our children—helping ours, and the enemies of God, to keep us and our dear little children in their infernal chains of slavery!!! Indeed, our friends cannot but relapse and join themselves "with those who are actuated by *sordid avarice* only!!!"

For my own part, I am glad Mr. Jefferson has advanced his positions for your sake; for you will either have to contradict or confirm him by your own actions, and not by what our friends have said or done for us; for those things are other men's labours, and do not satisfy the Americans, who are waiting for us to prove to them ourselves, that we are MEN, before they will be willing to admit the fact; for I pledge you my sacred word of honour, that Mr. Jefferson's remarks respecting us, have sunk deep into the hearts of millions of the whites, and never will be removed this side of eternity.—For how can they, when we are confirming him every day, by our *groveling submissions* and *treachery?* I aver, that when I look over these United States of America, and the world, and see the ignorant deceptions and consequent wretchedness of my brethren, I am brought ofttimes solemnly to a stand, and in the midst of my reflections I exclaim to my God, "Lord didst thou make us to be slaves to our brethren, the whites?" But when I reflect that God is just, and that millions of my wretched brethren would meet death with glory—yea, more, would plunge into the very mouths of cannons and be torn into particles as minute as the atoms which compose the elements of the earth, in preference to a mean submission to the lash of tyrants, I am with streaming eyes, compelled to shrink back into

1. See his Notes on Virginia, page 213.

nothingness before my Maker, and exclaim again, thy will be done, O Lord God Almighty. [. . .]

God will show the whites what we are, yet. I say, from the beginning, I do not think that we were natural enemies to each other. But the whites having made us so wretched, by subjecting us to slavery, and having murdered so many millions of us, in order to make us work for them, and out of devilishness—and they taking our wives, whom we love as we do ourselves—our mothers, who bore the pains of death to give us birth—our fathers and dear little children, and ourselves, and strip and beat us one before the other—chain, hand-cuff, and drag us about like rattle-snakes—shoot us down like wild bears, before each other's faces, to make us submissive to, and work to support them and their families. They (the whites) know well, if we are *men*—and there is a secret monitor in their hearts which tells them we are—they know, I say, if we *are* men, and see them treating us in the manner they do, that there can be nothing in our hearts but death alone, for them, notwithstanding we may appear cheerful, when we see them murdering our dear mothers and wives, because we cannot help ourselves.

Man, in all ages and all nations of the earth, is the same. Man is a peculiar creature—he is the image of his God, though he may be subjected to the most wretched condition upon earth, yet the spirit and feeling which constitute the creature, man, can never be entirely erased from his breast, because God who made him after his own image, planted it in his heart; he cannot get rid of it. The whites knowing this, they do not know what to do; they know that they have done us so much injury, they are afraid that we, being men, and not brutes, will retaliate, and woe will be to them; therefore, that dreadful fear, together with an avaricious spirit, and the natural love in them, to be called masters, (which term will yet honour them with to their sorrow) bring them to the resolve that they will keep us in ignorance and wretchedness, as long as they possibly can,[2] and make the best of their time, while it lasts. Consequently they, themselves, (and not us) render themselves our natural enemies, by treating us so cruel. [. . .]

Americans! notwithstanding you have and do continue to treat us more cruel than any heathen nation ever did a people it had subjected to the same condition that you have us. Now let us reason—I mean you of the United States, whom I believe God designs to save from destruction, if you will hear. For I declare to you, whether you believe it or not, that there are some on the continent of America, who will never be able to repent. God will surely destroy them, to show you his disapprobation of the murders they and you have inflicted on us. I say, let us reason; had you not better take our body, while you have it in your power, and while we are yet ignorant and wretched, not knowing but a little, give us education, and teach us the pure religion of our Lord and Master, which is calculated to make the lion lay down in peace with the lamb, and which millions of you have beaten us nearly to death for trying to obtain since we have been among you, and thus at once, gain our affection while we are ignorant? Remember Americans, that we must and shall be free and enlightened as you are, will you wait until we shall, under God, obtain our liberty by the crushing arm of power? Will it not be dreadful for you? I speak Americans for your good. We must and shall be free I say, in spite of you. You may do your best to keep us in wretchedness and misery, to enrich you and your children, but God will deliver us from under you. And woe, woe, will be to you if we have to obtain our freedom by fighting. Throw away your fears and prejudices then, and enlighten us and treat us like men, and we will like you more than we do now hate you,[3]

2. And still hold us up with indignity as being incapable of acquiring knowledge!!! See the inconsistency of the assertions of those wretches—they beat us inhumanely, sometimes almost to death, for attempting to inform ourselves, by reading the *Word* of our Maker, and at the same time tell us, that we are beings *void of intellect!!!* How admirably their practices agree with their professions in this case. Let me cry shame upon you Americans, for such outrages upon human nature!!! If it were possible for the whites always to keep us ignorant and miserable, and make us work to enrich them and their children, and insult our feelings by representing us as *talking Apes*, what would they do? But glory, honour and praise to Heaven's King, that the sons and daughters of Africa, will, in spite of all the opposition of their enemies, stand forth in all the dignity and glory that is granted by the Lord to his creature man.

3. You are not astonished at my saying we hate you, for if we are men, we cannot but hate you, while you are treating us like dogs.

and tell us now no more about colonization, for America is as much our country, as it is yours.—

Treat us like men, and there is no danger but we will all live in peace and happiness together. For we are not like you, hard hearted, unmerciful, and unforgiving. What a happy country this will be, if the whites will listen. What nation under heaven, will be able to do any thing with us, unless God gives us up into its hand? But Americans, I declare to you, while you keep us and our children in bondage, and treat us like brutes, to make us support you and your families, we cannot be your friends. You do not look for it, do you? Treat us then like men, and we will be your friends. And there is not a doubt in my mind, but that the whole of the past will be sunk into oblivion, and we yet, under God, will become a united and happy people. The whites may say it is impossible, but remember that nothing is impossible with God.

Abraham Lincoln

Address before the Young Men's Lyceum of Springfield, Illinois (1838)

As a subject for the remarks of the evening, "The perpetuation of our political institutions" is selected.

In the great journal of things happening under the sun, we, the American people, find our account running under date of the nineteenth century of the Christian era. We find ourselves in the peaceful possession of the fairest portion of the earth as regards extent of territory, fertility of soil, and salubrity of climate. We find ourselves under the government of a system of political institutions conducing more essentially to the ends of civil and religious liberty than any of which the history of former times tells us. We, when mounting the stage of existence, found ourselves the legal inheritors of these fundamental blessings. We toiled not in the acquirement or establishment of them; they are a legacy bequeathed us by a once hardy, brave, and patriotic, but now lamented and departed, race of ancestors. Theirs was the task (and nobly they performed it) to possess themselves, and through themselves us, of this goodly land, and to uprear upon its hills and its valleys a political edifice of liberty and equal rights; 'tis ours only to transmit these—the former unprofaned by the foot of an invader, the latter undecayed by the lapse of time and unborn by usurpation—to the latest generation that fate shall permit the world to know. This task of gratitude to our fathers, justice to ourselves, duty to posterity, and love for our species in general, all imperatively require us faithfully to perform.

How then shall we perform it? At what point shall we expect the approach of danger? By what means shall we fortify against it? Shall we expect some transatlantic military giant to step the ocean and crush us at a blow? Never! All the armies of Europe, Asia, and Africa combined, with all the treasure of the earth (our own excepted) in their military chest, with a Bonaparte for a commander, could not by force take a drink from the Ohio or make a track on the Blue Ridge in a trial of a thousand years.

At what point then is the approach of danger to be expected? I answer, If it ever reach us it must spring up amongst us; it cannot come from abroad. If destruction be our lot we must ourselves be its author and finisher. As a nation of freemen we must live through all time, or die by suicide.

I hope I am over wary; but if I am not, there is even now something of ill omen amongst us. I mean the increasing disregard for law which pervades the country—the growing disposition to substitute the wild and furious passions in lieu of the sober judgment of courts, and the worse than savage mobs for the executive ministers of justice. This disposition is awfully fearful in any community; and that it now exists in ours, though grating to our feelings to admit, it would be a violation of truth and an insult to our intelligence to deny. Accounts of outrages committed by mobs form the every-day news of the times. They have pervaded the country from New England to Louisiana; they are neither peculiar to the eternal snows of the former nor the burning suns of the latter; they are not the creature of climate, neither are they confined to the slaveholding or the non-slaveholding States. Alike they spring up among the pleasure-hunting masters of Southern slaves, and the order-loving citizens of the land of steady habits. Whatever then their cause may be, it is common to the whole country.

It would be tedious as well as useless to recount the horrors of all of them. Those happening in the State of Mississippi and at St. Louis are perhaps the most dangerous in example and revolting to humanity. In the Mississippi case they first commenced by hanging the regular gamblers—a set of men certainly not following for a livelihood a very useful or very honest occupation, but one which, so far from being forbidden by the laws, was actually licensed by an act of the legislature passed but a single year before. Next, negroes suspected of conspiring to raise an insurrection were caught up and hanged in all parts of the State; then, white men supposed to be leagued with the negroes; and finally, strangers from neighboring States, going thither on business, were in many instances subjected to the same fate. Thus went on this process of hanging, from gamblers to negroes, from negroes to white citizens, and from these to strangers, till dead men were seen literally dangling from the boughs of trees upon every roadside, and in numbers almost sufficient to rival the native Spanish moss of the country as a drapery of the forest.

Turn then to that horror-striking scene at St. Louis. A single victim only was sacrificed there. This story is very short, and is perhaps the most highly tragic of anything of its length that has ever been witnessed in real life. A mulatto man by the name of McIntosh was seized in the street, dragged to the suburbs of the city, chained to a tree, and actually burned to death; and all within a single hour from the time he had been a freeman attending to his own business and at peace with the world.

Such are the effects of mob law, and such are the scenes becoming more and more frequent in this land so lately famed for love of law and order, and the stories of which have even now grown too familiar to attract anything more than an idle remark.

But you are perhaps ready to ask, "What has this to do with the perpetuation of our political institutions?" I answer, "It has much to do with it." Its direct consequences are, comparatively speaking, but a small evil, and much of its danger consists in the proneness of our minds to regard its direct as its only consequences. Abstractly considered, the hanging of the gamblers at Vicksburg was of but little consequence. They constitute a portion of population that is worse than useless in any community; and their death, if no pernicious example be set by it, is never matter of reasonable regret with any one. If they were annually swept from the stage of existence by the plague or smallpox, honest men would perhaps be much profited by the operation. Similar too is the correct reasoning in regard to the "burning of the negro at St. Louis. He had forfeited his life by the perpetration of an outrageous murder upon one of the most worthy and respectable citizens of the city, and had he not died as he did, he must have died by the sentence of the law in a very short time afterward. As to him alone, it was as well the way it was as it could otherwise have been. But the example in either case was fearful. When men take it in their heads to-day to hang gamblers or burn murderers, they should recollect that in the confusion usually attending such transactions they will be as likely to hang or burn some one who is neither a gambler nor a murderer as one who is, and that, acting upon the example they set, the mob of to-morrow may, and probably will, hang or burn some of them by the very same mistake. And not only so; the innocent, those who have ever set their faces against violations of law in every shape, alike with the guilty fall victims to the ravages of mob law; and thus it goes on, step by step, till all the walls erected for the defense of the persons and property of individuals are trodden down and disregarded. But all this, even, is not the full extent of the evil. By such examples, by instances of the perpetrators of such acts going unpunished, the lawless in spirit are encouraged to become lawless in practice; and having been used to no restraint but dread of punishment, they thus become absolutely unrestrained. Having ever regarded government as their deadliest bane, they make a jubilee of the suspension of its operations, and pray for nothing so much as its total annihilation. While, on the other hand, good men, men who love tranquillity, who desire to abide by the laws and enjoy their benefits, who would gladly spill their blood in the defense of their country, seeing their property destroyed, their families insulted, and their lives endangered, their persons injured, and seeing nothing in prospect that forebodes a change for the better, become tired of and disgusted with a government that offers them no protection, and are not much averse to a change in which they imagine they have nothing to lose. Thus, then, by the operation of this mobocratic spirit which all must admit is now abroad in the land, the strongest bulwark of any government, and particularly of those constituted like ours, may effectually be broken down and destroyed—I mean the attachment of the people. Whenever this effect shall be produced among us; whenever the vicious portion of population shall be permitted to gather in bands of hundreds and thousands, and burn churches, ravage and rob provision-stores, throw printing-presses into rivers, shoot editors, and hang and burn obnoxious persons at pleasure and with impunity, depend on it, this government cannot last. By such things the feelings of the best citizens will become more or less alienated from it, and thus it will be left without friends, or with too few, and those few too weak to make their friendship effectual. At such a time, and under such circumstances, men of sufficient talent and ambition will not be wanting to seize the opportunity, strike the blow, and overturn that fair fabric which for the last half century has been the fondest hope of the lovers of freedom throughout the world.

I know the American people are much attached to their government: I know they would suffer much for its sake; I know they would endure evils long and patiently before they would ever think of exchanging it for another,—yet, notwithstanding all this, if the laws be continually despised and disregarded, if their rights to be secure in their persons and property are held by no better tenure than the caprice of a mob, the alienation of their affections from the government is the natural consequence; and to that, sooner or later, it must come.

Here, then, is one point at which danger may be expected.

The question recurs, "How shall we fortify against it?" The answer is simple. Let every American, every lover of liberty, every well-wisher to his posterity swear by the blood of the Revolution never to violate in the least particular the laws of the country, and never to tolerate their violation by others. As the patriots of seventy-six did to the support of the Declaration of Independence, so to the support of the Constitution and laws let every American pledge his life, his property, and his sacred honor—let every man remember that to violate the law is to trample on the blood of his father, and to tear the charter of his own and his children's liberty. Let reverence for the laws be breathed by every American mother to the lisping babe that prattles on her lap; let it be taught in schools, in seminaries, and in colleges; let it be written in primers, spelling-books, and in almanacs; let it be preached from the pulpit, proclaimed in legislative halls, and enforced in courts of justice. And, in short, let it become the political religion of the nation; and let the old and the young, the rich and the poor, the grave and the gay of all sexes and tongues and colors and conditions, sacrifice unceasingly upon its altars.

While ever a state of feeling such as this shall universally or even very generally prevail throughout the nation, vain will be every effort, and fruitless every attempt, to subvert our national freedom.

When I so pressingly urge a strict observance of all the laws, let me not be understood as saying there are no bad laws, or that grievances may not arise for the redress of which no legal provisions have been made. I mean to say no such thing. But I do mean to say that although bad laws, if they exist, should be repealed as soon as possible, still, while they continue in force, for the sake of example they should be religiously observed. So also in unprovided cases. If such arise, let proper legal provisions be made for them with the least possible delay, but till then let them, if not too intolerable, be borne with.

There is no grievance that is a fit object of redress by mob law. In any case that may arise, as, for instance, the promulgation of abolitionism, one of two positions is necessarily true—that is, the thing is right within itself, and therefore deserves the protection of all law and all good citizens, or it is wrong, and therefore proper to be prohibited by legal enactments; and in neither case is the interposition of mob law either necessary, justifiable, or excusable.

But it may be asked, "Why suppose danger to our political institutions? Have we not preserved them for more than fifty years? And why may we not for fifty times as long?"

We hope there is no sufficient reason. We hope all danger may be overcome; but to conclude that no danger may ever arise would itself be extremely dangerous. There are now, and will hereafter be, many causes, dangerous in their tendency, which have not existed heretofore, and which are not too insignificant to merit attention. That our government should have been maintained in its original form, from its establishment until now, is not much to be wondered at. It had many props to support it through that period, which now are decayed and crumbled away. Through that period it was felt by all to be an undecided experiment; now it is understood to be a successful one. Then, all that sought celebrity and fame and distinction expected to find them in the success of that experiment. Their all was staked upon it; their destiny was inseparably linked with it. Their ambition aspired to display before an admiring world a practical demonstration of the truth of a proposition which had hitherto been considered at best no better than problematical—namely, the capability of a people to govern themselves. If they succeeded they were to be immortalized; their names were to be transferred to counties, and cities, and rivers, and mountains; and to be revered and sung, toasted through all time. If they failed, they were to be called knaves, and fools, and fanatics for a fleeting hour; then to sink and be forgotten. They succeeded. The experiment is successful, and thousands have won their deathless names in making it so. But the game is caught; and I believe it is true that with the catching end the pleasures of the chase. This field of glory is harvested, and the crop is already appropriated. But new reapers will arise, and they too will seek a field. It is to deny what the history of the world tells us is true, to suppose that men of ambition and talents will not continue to spring up amongst us. And when they do, they will as naturally seek the gratification of their ruling passion as others have done before them. The question then is, Can that gratification be found in supporting and maintaining an edifice that has been erected by others? Most certainly it cannot. Many great and good men, sufficiently qualified for any task they should undertake, may ever be found whose ambition would aspire to nothing beyond a seat in Congress, a gubernatorial or a presidential chair; but such belong not to the family of the lion, or the tribe of the eagle. What! think you these places would satisfy an Alexander, a Cassar, or a Napoleon? Never! Towering genius disdains a beaten path. It seeks regions hitherto unexplored. It sees no distinction in adding story to story upon the monuments of fame erected to the memory of others. It denies that it is glory enough to serve under any chief. It scorns to tread in the footsteps of any predecessor, however illustrious. It thirsts and burns for distinction; and if possible, it will have it, whether at the expense of emancipating slaves or enslaving freemen. Is it unreasonable, then, to expect that some man possessed of the loftiest genius, coupled with ambition sufficient to push it to its utmost stretch, will at some time spring up among us? And when such an one does, it will require the people to be united with each other, attached to the government and laws, and generally intelligent, to successfully frustrate his designs.

Distinction will be his paramount object, and although he would as willingly, perhaps more so, acquire it by doing good as harm, yet, that opportunity being past, and nothing left to be done in the way of building up, he would set boldly to the task of pulling down.

Here then is a probable case, highly dangerous, and such an one as could not have well existed heretofore.

Another reason which once was, but which, to the same extent, is now no more, has done much in maintaining our institutions thus far. I mean the powerful influence which the interesting scenes of the Revolution had upon the passions of the people as distinguished from their judgment. By this influence, the jealousy, envy, and avarice incident to our nature, and so common to a state of peace, prosperity, and conscious strength, were for the time in a great measure smothered and rendered inactive, while the deep-rooted principles of hate, and the powerful motive of revenge, instead of being turned against each other, were directed exclusively against the British nation. And thus, from the force of circumstances, the basest principles of our nature were either made to lie dormant, or to become the active agents in the advancement of the noblest of causes—that of establishing and maintaining civil and religious liberty.

But this state of feeling must fade, is fading, has faded, with the circumstances that produced it.

I do not mean to say that the scenes of the Revolution are now or ever will be entirely forgotten, but that, like everything else, they must fade upon the memory of the world, and grow more and more dim by the lapse of time. In history, we hope, they will be read of, and recounted, so long as the Bible shall be read; but even granting that they will, their influence cannot be what it heretofore has been. Even then they cannot be so universally known nor so vividly felt as they were by the generation just gone to rest. At the close of that struggle, nearly every adult male had been a participator in some of its scenes. The consequence was that of those scenes, in the form of a husband, a father, a son, or a brother, a living history was to be found in every family—a history bearing the indubitable testimonies of its own authenticity, in the limbs mangled, in the scars of wounds received, in the midst of the very scenes related—a history, too, that could be read and understood alike by all, the wise and the ignorant, the learned and the unlearned. But those histories are gone. They can be read no more forever. They were a fortress of strength; but what invading foeman could never do, the silent artillery of time has done—the leveling of its walls. They are gone. They were a forest of giant oaks; but the all-restless hurricane has swept over them, and left only here and there a lonely trunk, despoiled of its verdure, shorn of its foliage, unshading and unshaded, to murmur in a few more gentle breezes, and to combat with its mutilated limbs a few more ruder storms, then to sink and be no more.

They were pillars of the temple of liberty; and now that they have crumbled away that temple must fall unless we, their descendants, supply their places with other pillars, hewn from the solid quarry of sober reason. Passion has helped us, but can do so no more. It will in future be our enemy. Reason—cold, calculating, unimpassioned reason—must furnish all the materials for our future support and defense. Let those materials be molded into general intelligence, sound morality, and, in particular, a reverence for the Constitution and laws; and that we improved to the last, that we remained free to the last, that we revered his name to the last, that during his long sleep we permitted no hostile foot to pass over or desecrate his resting place, shall be that which to learn the last trump shall awaken our Washington.

Upon these let the proud fabric of freedom rest, as the rock of its basis; and as truly as has been said of the only greater institution, "the gates of hell shall not prevail against it."

William Lloyd Garrison

The Liberator (1831–1844)

January 1, 1831 (Inaugural Issue)

To the Public

In the month of August, I issued proposals for publishing "The Liberator" in Washington City; but the enterprise, though hailed in different sections of the country, was palsied by public indifference. Since that time, the removal of the *Genius of Universal Emancipation* to the Seat of Government has rendered less imperious the establishment of a similar periodical in that quarter.

During my recent tour for the purpose of exciting the minds of the people by a series of discourses on the subject of slavery, every place that I visited gave fresh evidence of the fact, that a greater revolution in public sentiment was to be effected in the free States—and particularly in New-England—than at the South. I found contempt more bitter, opposition more active, detraction more relentless, prejudice more stubborn, and apathy more frozen, than among slave-owners themselves. Of course, there were individual exceptions to the contrary. This state of things afflicted, but did not dishearten me. I determined, at every hazard, to lift up the standard of emancipation in the eyes of the nation, within sight of Bunker Hill and in the birthplace of liberty. That standard is now unfurled; and long may it float, unhurt by the spoliations of time or the missiles of a desperate foe—yea, till every chain be broken, and every bondman set free! Let Southern oppressors tremble—let their secret abettors tremble—let their Northern apologists tremble—let all the enemies of the persecuted blacks tremble.

I deem the publication of my original Prospectus unnecessary, as it has obtained a wide circulation. The principles therein inculcated will be steadily pursued in this paper, excepting that I shall not array myself as the political partisan of any man. In defending the great cause of human rights, I wish to derive the assistance of all religions and of all parties.

Assenting to the "self-evident truth" maintained in the American Declaration of Independence, "that all men are created equal, and endowed by their Creator with certain inalienable rights—among which are life, liberty and the pursuit of happiness," I shall strenuously contend for the immediate enfranchisement of our slave population. In Park-Street Church, on the Fourth of July, 1829, I unreflectingly assented to the popular but pernicious doctrine of gradual abolition. I seize this moment to make a full and unequivocal recantation, and thus publicly to ask pardon of my God, of my country, and of my brethren the poor slaves, for having uttered a sentiment so full of timidity, injustice, and absurdity. A similar recantation, from my pen, was published in the *Genius of Universal Emancipation* at Baltimore, in September, 1829. My conscience is now satisfied.

I am aware that many object to the severity of my language; but is there not cause for severity? I will be as harsh as truth, and as uncompromising as justice. On this subject, I do not wish to think, or to speak, or write, with moderation. No! no! Tell a man whose house is on fire to give a moderate alarm; tell him to moderately rescue his wife from the hands of the ravisher; tell the mother to gradually extricate her babe from the fire into which it has fallen;—but urge me not to use moderation in a cause like the present. I am in earnest—I will not equivocate—I will not excuse—I will not retreat a single inch—AND I WILL BE HEARD. The apathy of the people is enough to make every statue leap from its pedestal, and to hasten the resurrection of the dead.

It is pretended, that I am retarding the cause of emancipation by the coarseness of my invective and the precipitancy of my measures. The charge is not true. On this question of my influence,—humble as it is,—is felt at this moment to a considerable extent, and shall be felt in coming years—not perniciously, but beneficially—not as a curse, but as a blessing; and posterity will bear testimony that I was right. I desire to thank God, that he enables me to disregard "the fear of man which bringeth a snare," and to speak his truth in its simplicity and power. And here I close with this fresh dedication:

Oppression! I have seen thee, face to face,
And met thy cruel eye and cloudy brow,
But thy soul-withering glance I fear not now—
For dread to prouder feelings doth give place
Of deep abhorrence! Scorning the disgrace
Of slavish knees that at thy footstool bow,
I also kneel—but with far other vow
Do hail thee and thy herd of hirelings base:—
I swear, while life-blood warms my throbbing veins,
Still to oppose and thwart, with heart and hand,
Thy brutalizing sway—till Africa's chains
Are burst, and Freedom rules the rescued land,—
Trampling Oppression and his iron rod:
Such is the vow I take—SO HELP ME GOD!
[by the Scottish poet Thomas Pringle]

July 30, 1831

The solemn inquiries are often anxiously made, what shall be done for the abolition of slavery, and wherein can the people of the free States act efficiently? A full and satisfactory reply to these inquiries demands a series of numbers. In the present essay, I shall sketch out only the outlines of a few feasible schemes.

First of all, I want every man and every woman to discard their criminal prejudices, their timorous fears, and their paralyzing doubts. I want them to feel that two millions of their brothers and sisters are groaning under the thraldom of slavery; that they are bound, by every conceivable motive, to assist in breaking their fetters; and that they are capable of effecting their desires, through divine assistance.—The work of reform must commence with *ourselves*. Until *we* are purified, it will be fruitless and intrusive for *us* to cleanse *others*. I say, then, that the *entire abstinence* from the products of slavery is the duty of every individual. [. . .]

"For this thing which it cannot bear, the earth is disquieted." The Gospel of Peace and Mercy preached by him who steals, buys and sells the purchase of the Messiah's blood! [. . .]

3dly. The formation of an American Anti-Slavery Society is of the utmost importance; and it is now, I am happy to say, in embryo. The objects of this Society will be, to consolidate the moral power of the nation, so that Congress and the State Legislatures may be inundated with petitions;—to scatter tracts, like rain-drops, over the land, on the subject of slavery;—to employ active and eloquent agents to plead the cause constantly, and to form auxiliaries;—to encourage planters to cultivate their lands by freemen, by offering large premiums;—to promote education and the mechanical arts among the free people of color, and to recover their lost rights. The people, at large, are astonishingly ignorant of the horrors of slavery. Let information be circulated among them as prodigally as the light of heaven, and they cannot long act and reason as they now do.

4thly. Slavery in the District of Columbia is sustained in our national capacity: it ought, therefore, to be prostrated at a blow.

5thly. The clause in the Constitution should be erased, which tolerates, greatly to the detriment and injustice of the free states, a slave representation in Congress. Why should property be represented from the impoverished south, and not from the opulent north?

6thly. We want, at this moment, at least one hundred periodicals over the land, expressly devoted to the cause of emancipation. [. . .]

January 7, 1832

The past has been a year more than ordinarily eventful to this country and the world. Henceforth there is to be no peace on the earth—no cessation of revolutionary movements—no exhausted imbecility—until unjust rule be at an end; until personal thraldom be broken; until thrones be scattered in ashes to the winds; until hereditary titles and distinctions be effaced; until knowledge be diffused as freely as sunlight, and be as readily inhaled by all classes of the people as the vital atmosphere; until landed monopolies be distributed in equitable shares; until all labor be voluntary, receive its just remuneration, be protected in its own earnings, be a crown of honor and not a mark of servitude; until every government be elective and republican; until the right to worship God, according to the dictates of every man's conscience, be secured; until, in short, freedom of thought and speech and writing—freedom of choice—freedom of action—be not only the inalienable right but the positive exercise of every rational creature. The Spirit of Liberty is no longer young and feeble—it is no longer to make an abortive struggle, and then be passive for years: it is abroad with power—thundering at castle-gates and prison-doors: from revolutionizing neighborhoods, it is going on to revolutionize nations: instead of agitating a kingdom, as formerly, it is now shaking the world. When it once fairly gets the mastery over its enemy Oppression, will not its retaliation be terrible? Wo to those who dress in purple and fine linen, and fare sumptuously every day, having defrauded the laborer of his hire and oppressed the poor! Wo to those who entrench themselves behind hereditary privileges and conduct, and declare that for the crimes which they commit, their ancestors must be responsible! Wo to that policy or system which has no other foundation than injustice, tyranny and wrong! which consults expediency and not right! which expects to satisfy the hungry with a crumb of knowledge—to content the benighted wanderer with a few scattered rays of light—to comfort the naked with half a blanket, or a whole suit of rags! which mocks the remonstrances of prudence, repels the suggestions of wisdom, forgets all the lessons of history, discredits the uniform results of experience, defies the moral and physical power of its victims! Wo, wo, for all that is oppressive—for all that lives by usurpation—for those who hearken not to the voice of nature—for the persecutors of their fellow men, wherever they may be found! There will be no discrimination with God or man, in favor of any class of despots: they who tread, with iron heels, upon the necks of their slaves in this country, will not be thought less blameworthy than the tyrants of Europe. Despotism in a republic is as sure of punishment, as in a monarchy.

Happy will it be for us, as a people, if, treasuring up these truths in our memories, we check the retributive thunders of justice "in mid volley," by a timely repentance. We are a nation of blind, unrelenting, haughty, cruel, heaven-daring oppressors. The chains which we rivet upon the bodies of two millions of our fellow-countrymen, are as galling and heavy as were ever forged for human limbs. Shall those chains be broken by physical or moral power? Infatuated as we may be, we are conscious that, at some period or other, in some way or other, our slaves must be free. Gigantic as may be our strength, we are too intelligent to believe that it will enable us always to oppress with impunity. Secure as we may feel, we tremble for posterity—for our children, and our children's children. [. . .]

[. . .] So long as we continue one body—a union—a nation—the compact involves us in the guilt and danger of slavery. If the slaves, goaded to desperation by their cruel masters, should rise *en masse* to obtain redress, do the citizens of New-England reflect, that they are constitutionally bound to assist the southern taskmasters in subduing or exterminating the blacks and are liable to be drafted at a moment's warning? Perhaps we imagine, that there is little danger of a general insurrection among the slaves—(the recent events at the south to the contrary, notwithstanding)—but does this circumstance remove the responsibility from our shoulders? No matter what is the *probability* in this case. The question is, whether we are not solemnly pledged to put down a black rebellion in the south? At the present moment, indeed, appearances seem to indicate a double rebellion in that section of the Union; a rebellion against the Government by the whites, and a rebellion against the whites by the blacks; so that the "tug of war" may be nearer than the people of the free states imagine. What protects the south from instant destruction? Our physical force. Break the chain which binds her to the Union, and the scenes of St. Domingo would be witnessed throughout her borders. She may affect to laugh at this prophecy; but she knows that her security lies in northern bayonets. Nay, she has repeatedly taunted the free states with being pledged to protect her: tyrannise long and cruelly as she may, they are bound to give her life, and, if necessary, to slaughter her slaves. How, then, do we make the inquiry, with affected astonishment, "what have we to do with the guilt of slavery?" Is this a novel view of the subject? Must we now begin to inquire, for the first time, what are our duties and responsibilities as American citizens?

Perhaps we internally resolve never to march against the blacks—never to bear arms south of the Potomac. But such a decision would be full of treachery to the people of the south. Let us give them fair warning when we intend to leave them to their fate; and let us not practice studied cruelty and deceit. Hear the language of a Representative from Massachusetts [Mr. Dwight] in the Congressional session of 1827:

> In an internal commotion in Georgia, where should its white population seek a shelter? Not, certainly, in the little fort of Savannah. In such an event, [and he hoped the day was far distant,] they would not look to the forts erected for maritime defence, but to the *stout hearts* and *sympathetic feelings* of their *northern brethren*; and he did not hazard too much in saying, that in such a case the north will *pour out its blood like water* to assist the south!

Are these indeed our sentiments? Can we cover ourselves with laurels in a war of oppression? What! ready to pour out our blood like water, in order that a large portion of our fellow countrymen may be kept in servile bondage!

It is awful to reflect, that it is solely by the authority of the free states that slavery is tolerated in our land. The south is only our agent. We form a powerful combination which cannot be resisted, and give her a broad license to kidnap, plunder and oppress; promising our united aid, in case she is in personal danger! Yet we complacently wipe our mouths, and say, "We commit no evil—the south is the victim to be sacrificed." This is certainly an improvement upon the Holy Alliance. We are guilty—all guilty—horribly guilty. [. . .]

July 14, 1832

Two capital errors have extensively prevailed, greatly to the detriment of the cause of abolition. The first is, a proneness on the part of the advocates of immediate and universal emancipation to overlook or depreciate the influence of women in the promotion of this cause; and the other is, a similar disposition on the part of the females in our land to undervalue their own power, or through a misconception of duty, to excuse themselves from engaging in the enterprise. These errors, we repeat, are capital, and should no longer be suffered to prevail. The cause of bleeding humanity is always, legitimately, the cause of woman. Without her powerful assistance, its progress must be slow, difficult, imperfect.

A million females in this country, are recognized and held as property—liable to be sold or used for the gratification of the lust or avarice or convenience of unprincipled speculators—without the least protection for their chastity—cruelly scourged for the most trifling offences—and subjected to unseemly and merciless tasks, to severe privations, and to brutish ignorance! Have these no claims upon the sympathies—prayers—charities—exertions of our white countrywomen? [. . .]

December 29, 1832

[. . .] There is much declamation about the sacredness of the compact which was formed between the free and slave states, on the adoption of the Constitution. A sacred compact, forsooth! We pronounce it the most bloody and heaven-daring arrangement ever made by men for the continuance and protection of a system of the most atrocious villany ever exhibited on earth. Yes—we recognize the compact, but with feelings of shame and indignation; and it will be held in everlasting infamy by the friends of justice and humanity throughout the world. It was a compact formed at the sacrifice of the bodies and souls of millions of our race, for the sake of achieving a political object—an unblushing and monstrous coalition to do evil that good might come. Such a compact was, in the nature of things and according to the law of God, null and void from the beginning. No body of men ever had the right to guarantee the holding of human beings in bondage. Who or what were the framers of our government, that they should dare confirm and authorize such high-handed villany—such a flagrant robbery of the inalienable rights of man—such a glaring violation of all the precepts and injunctions of the gospel—such a savage war upon a sixth part of our whole population?—They were men like ourselves—as fallible, as sinful, as weak, as ourselves. By the infamous bargain which they made between themselves, they virtually dethroned the Most High God, and trampled beneath their feet their own solemn and heaven-attested Declaration, that all men are created equal, and endowed by their Creator with certain inalienable rights—among which are life, liberty, and the pursuit of happiness. They had no lawful power to bind themselves, or their posterity, for one hour—for one moment—by such an unholy alliance. It was not valid then—it is not valid now. Still they persisted in maintaining it. A sacred compact! a sacred compact! What, then, is wicked and ignominious?

This, then, is the relation in which we of New-England stand to the holders of the slaves at the south, and this is virtually our language toward them—"Go on, most worthy associates, from day to day, from month to month, from year to year, from generation to generation, plundering two millions of human beings of their liberty and the fruits of their toil . . . we do not wish nor mean to interfere, for the rescue of your victims, even by expostulation or warning—we like your company too well to offend you by denouncing your conduct—although we know that by every principle of law which does not utterly disgrace us by assimilating us to pirates, that they have as good and as true a right to the equal protection of the law as we have; and although we ourselves stand prepared to die, rather than submit even to a fragment of the intolerable load of oppression to which we are subjecting them—yet, never mind—let that be—they have grown old in suffering and we iniquity—and we have nothing to do now but to speak *peace, peace,* to one another in our sins. [. . .] Go on, from bad to worse—add link to link to the chains upon the bodies of your victims—add constantly to the intolerable burdens under which they groan—and if, goaded to desperation by your cruelties, they should rise to assert their rights and redress their wrongs, fear nothing—we are pledged, by a sacred compact, to shoot them like dogs and rescue you from their vengeance. [. . .] We pledge you our physical strength, by the sacredness of the national compact—a compact by which we have enabled you already to plunder, persecute and destroy two millions of slaves, who now lie beneath the sod; and by which we now give you the same piratical license to prey upon a much larger number of victims and all their posterity. Go on—and by this sacred instrument, the Constitution of the United States, *dripping as it is with human blood,* we solemnly pledge you our lives, our fortunes, and our sacred honor, that we will stand by you to the last."

People of New-England, and of the free States! is it true that slavery is no concern of yours? Have you no right even to protest against it, or to seek its removal? Are you not the main pillars of its support? How long do you mean to be answerable to God and the world, for spilling the blood of the poor innocents? Be not afraid to look the monster Slavery boldly in the face. He is your implacable foe—the vampyre who is sucking your life-blood—the ravager of a large portion of your country, and the enemy of God and man. Never hope to be a united, or happy, or prosperous people while he exists. He has an appetite like the grave—a spirit as malignant as that of the bottomless pit—and an influence as dreadful as the corruption of death. Awake to your danger! the struggle is a mighty one—it cannot be avoided—it should not be, if it could.

It is said if you agitate this question, you will divide the Union. Believe it not; but should disunion follow, the fault will not be yours. You must perform your duty, faithfully, fearlessly and promptly, and leave the consequences to God: that duty clearly is, to cease from giving countenance and protection to southern kidnappers. Let them separate, if they can muster courage enough—and the liberation of their slaves is certain. Be assured that slavery will very speedily destroy this Union *if it be let alone*; but even if the Union can be preserved by treading upon the necks, spilling the blood, and destroying the souls of millions of your race, we say it is not worth a price like this, and that it is in the highest degree criminal for you to continue the present compact. Let the pillars thereof fall—let the superstructure crumble into dust—if it must be upheld by robbery and oppression.

November 17, 1837

A Short Catechism Adapted to All Parts of the United States

1. Why is American slaveholding in all cases not sinful?

Because its victims are *black*.

2. Why is gradual emancipation right?

Because the slaves are *black*.

3. Why is immediate emancipation wrong and dangerous?

Because the slaves are *black*.

4. Why ought one-sixth portion of the American population to be exiled from their native soil?

Because they are *black*.

5. Why would the slaves if emancipated, cut the throats of their masters?

Because they are *black*.

6. Why are our slaves not fit for freedom?

Because they are *black*.

7. Why are American slaveholders not thieves, tyrants and men-stealers?

Because their victims are *black*.

8. Why does the Bible justify American slavery?

Because its victims are *black*.

9. Why ought not the Priest and the Levite, "passing by on the other side," to be sternly rebuked?

Because the man who has fallen among thieves, and lies weltering in his blood, is *black*.

10. Why are abolitionists fanatics, madmen and incendiaries?

Because those for whom they plead are *black*.

11. Why are they wrong in their principles and measures?

Because the slaves are *black*.

12. Why is all the prudence, moderation, judiciousness, philanthropy and piety on the side of their opponents?

Because the slaves are *black*.

13. Why ought not the free discussion of slavery to be tolerated?

Because its victims are *black*.

14. Why is Lynch law, as applied to abolitionists, better than common law?

Because the slaves, whom they seek to emancipate, are *black*.

15. Why are the slaves contented and happy?

Because they are *black!*

16. Why don't they want to be free?

Because they are *black!*

17. Why are they not created in the image of God?

Because their skin is *black.*

18. Why are they not cruelly treated, but enjoy unusual comforts and privileges?

Because they are *black!*

19. Why are they not our brethren and countrymen?

Because they are *black.*

20. Why is it unconstitutional to pity and defend them?

Because they are *black.*

21. Why is it a violation of the national compact to rebuke their masters?

Because they are *black.*

22. Why will they be lazy, improvident, and worthless, if set free?

Because their skin is *black.*

23. Why will the whites wish to amalgamate with them in a state of freedom?

Because they are *black!!*

24. Why must the Union be dissolved, should Congress abolish slavery in the District of Columbia?

Because the slaves in that District are *black.*

25. Why are abolitionists justly treated as outlaws in one half of the Union?

Because those whose cause they espouse are *black.*

26. Why is slavery "the corner-stone of our republican edifice?"

Because its victims are *black.*

We have thus given twenty-six replies to those who assail our principles and measures—that is, one reply, unanswerable and all-comprehensive, to all the cavils, complaints, criticisms, objections and difficulties which swarm in each State in the Union, against our holy enterprize. The victims are BLACK! "That alters the case!" There is not an individual in all this country, who is not conscious before God, that if the slaves at the South should be to-day miraculously transformed into men of white complexions, to-morrow the abolitionists would be recognized and cheered as the best friends of their race; their principles would be eulogized as sound and incontrovertible, and their measures as rational and indispensable! Then, indeed, immediate emancipation would be the right of the slaves, and the duty of the masters! [. . .]

December 8, 1837

It required a sanguinary conflict of seven years, on the part of the American colonies with the mother country, to maintain the "self-evident truths," that all men are created equal, and endowed by their Creator with an inalienable right to liberty. That a people who had made such sacrifices, and suffered their blood to be so lavishly shed in the cause of HUMAN RIGHTS, might degenerate even to servility, within half a century, was deemed a possible, though not a very probable occurrence:—That, on achieving their independence, they would immediately begin to doubt or deny the soundness of the doctrines for which they had contended, as applied to all mankind, who would have ventured to predict?—That, instead of emancipating the four hundred thousand slaves whom they held in bondage, while they themselves were struggling for freedom, they would multiply them to MILLIONS within three-score years, and make their yokes heavier and their fetters more galling, was a supposition too absurd, too atrocious for human conception or utterance.

All these dreadful inconsistencies, however, are cherished realities. Nearly one-fifth part of the American people are at this moment held in chains and slavery! by their own countrymen!—and it is far more perilous to plead for their deliverance, than it was for the colonists to denounce the oppression of England. We have been engaged in a moral campaign to redeem them from bondage, for a period equal in duration to the revolutionary war; yet they clank their chains, and their cries continue to enter into the ear of the Lord of Sabaoth!

When we first unfurled the banner of the Liberator, we anticipated a severe struggle with the foul Spirit of Slavery, whose name is BLASPHEMY. [. . .] We knew it would prove no childish controversy, and that the whole land would rock with the excitement. We were sure, that if a huge system of licentiousness, robbery and oppression could thrive on the American soil, it must be because there were deep corruption and almost total insensibility on the part of the people. But, we confess, of the awful state of this nation, which subsequent developements have made manifest, we had no adequate conception. Whatever scenes of violence might transpire in the slaveholding States, we did not anticipate that, in order to uphold southern slavery, the free States would voluntary trample under foot all order, law and government, or brand the advocates of universal liberty as incendiaries and outlaws. It did not occur to us, that nearly every religious sect, and every political party, would rally on the side of the oppressor; that Doctors of Divinity, Professors of Theology, Presidents of Colleges, and those who claim to be ministers of the gospel would have the impiety to justify the enslavement of men by the Bible; that public halls and meeting-houses would be closed against those who might wish to "plead for justice, in the name of humanity, and according to the law of the living God"—and opened to those who were the deadliest enemies of freedom and Christianity; or that the right of petition would be denied to the people by Congress, respecting the existence of slavery in those portions of territory over which it holds entire jurisdiction. We did not dream that the free discussion of any system or institution, in the republic, would be regarded as dangerous or unconstitutional;—least of all that it would be necessary for any man to lay down his life, in a free State, in defence of the liberty of the press.

The whole land has been thoroughly proved, by a series of tests, to be diseased beyond the power of recovery. "There is no healing of its bruise—its wound is grievous." In the solemn language of another—"The violence of mobs—the fury of oppressors—the violence and madness of their protectors and apologists in Church and State, are but the tremendous convulsions, the fearful delirium, the dying throes of an expiring nation." The American people are waging war, not against England or France, or the combined powers of Europe; but against the Rights of Mankind, against the image of God, against Divine Revelation, against Life and Immortality, against the Throne of the Eternal.

December 15, 1837

The motto upon our banner has been from the commencement of our moral warfare, "Our country is the world—our countrymen are all mankind." We trust that it will be our only epitaph. Another motto we have chosen is, "Universal Emancipation." Up to this time, we have limited its application to those who are held in this country, by southern taskmasters, as marketable commodities, goods and chattels, and implements of husbandry. Henceforth, we shall use it in its widest latitude: the emancipation of our whole race from the dominion of man, from the thraldom of self, from the government of brute force, from the bondage of sin—and bringing them under the dominion of God, the control of an inward spirit, the government of the law of love, and into the obedience and liberty of Christ, who is "*the same*, yesterday, to-day, and forever." [. . .]

Next to the overthrow of slavery, the cause of peace will command our attention. The doctrine of non-resistance, as commonly received and practised by Friends, and certain members of other religious denominations, we conceive to be utterly indefensible in its application to national wars;—not that it "goes too far," but that it does not go far enough. If a nation may not redress its wrongs by physical force—if it may not repel or punish a foreign enemy who comes to plunder, enslave or murder its inhabitants—then it may not resort to arms to quell an insurrection, or send to prison or suspend upon a gibbet any transgressors upon its soil. If the slaves of the South have not an undoubted right to resist their masters in the last resort, then no man, or body of men, may appeal to the law of violence in self-defence—for none have suffered, or can suffer, more than they.

[. . .] If, when men are robbed of their earnings, their liberties, their personal ownership, their wives and children, they may not resist, in no case can physical resistance be allowable, either in an individual or collective capacity. Now, the doctrine we shall endeavor to inculcate is, that the kingdoms of this world are to become the kingdoms of our Lord and of his Christ; consequently, that they are all to be supplanted, whether they are called despotic, monarchical or republican, and he only who is King of kings, and Lord of lords, is to rule in righteousness. The kingdom of God is to be established in all the earth, and it shall never be destroyed, but it shall "break in pieces and consume all others:" its elements are righteousness and peace, and joy in the Holy Ghost: without are dogs, and sorcerers, and whoremongers and murderers, and idolators, and whatsoever loveth and maketh a lie. Its government is one of love, not of military coercion or physical restraint: its laws are not written upon parchment, but upon the hearts of its subjects—they are not conceived in the wisdom of man, but framed by the Spirit of God: its weapons are not carnal, but spiritual: its soldiers are clad in the whole armor of God. . . . Hence, when smitten on the one cheek, they turn the other also; being defamed, they entreat; being reviled, they bless; being persecuted, they suffer it; they take joyfully the spoiling of their goods; they rejoice, inasmuch as they are partakers of Christ's sufferings; they are sheep in the midst of wolves; in no extremity whatever, even if their enemies are determined to nail them to the cross with Jesus, and if they like him could summon legions of angels to their rescue, will they resort to the law of violence.

As to the governments of this world, whatever their titles or forms, we shall endeavor to prove, that, in their essential elements, and as at present administered, they are all Anti-Christ; that they can never, by human wisdom, be brought into conformity to the will of God; that they cannot be maintained, except by naval and military power; that all their penal enactments being a dead letter without an army to carry them into effect, are virtually written in human blood; and that the followers of Jesus should instinctively shun their stations of honor, power and emolument—at the same time "submitting to every ordinance of man for the Lord's sake," and offering no *physical* resistance to any of their mandates, however unjust or tyrannical. [. . .]

So long as men contemn the perfect government of the Most High, and will not fill up the measure of Christ's sufferings in their own persons, just so long will they desire to usurp authority over each other—just so long will they pertinaciously cling to human governments, *fashioned in the likeness and administered in the spirit of their own disobedience.* Now, if the prayer of our Lord be not a mockery; if the kingdom of God is to come universally, and his will be done ON EARTH as it is IN HEAVEN; and if, in that kingdom, no carnal weapon can be wielded, and swords are beaten into ploughshares, and spears into pruning hooks, and there is none to molest or make afraid, and no statute-book but the bible, and no judge but Christ; then why are not Christians obligated to come out NOW, and be separate from "the kingdoms of this world," which are all based upon the principle of violence, and which require their officers and servants to govern and be governed by that principle? How, then, is the wickedness of men to be overcome? Not by lacerating their bodies, or incarcerating them in dungeons, or putting them upon tread-mills, or exiling them from their native country, or suspending them upon gibbets—O no!—but simply by returning good for evil, and blessing for cursing; by using those spiritual weapons which are "mighty, through God, to the pulling down of strongholds"; by the power of that faith which overcomes the world; by ceasing to look to man for a redress of injuries, however grievous, but committing the soul in well-doing, as unto a faithful Creator, and leaving it with God to bestow recompense—"for it is written, Vengeance is mine; I will repay, saith the Lord." [. . .]

Robert Hayne and Daniel Webster

Speeches in Debate over Foot's Resolution (1830)

Hayne's First Speech, January 19

[. . .] I have not risen, [. . .] Mr. President, for the purpose of discussing the propriety of instituting the inquiry recommended by the resolution, but to offer a few remarks on another and much more important question, to which gentlemen have alluded in the course of this debate—I mean the policy which ought to be pursued in relation to the public lands. Every gentleman who has had a seat in Congress for the last two or three years, or even for the last two or three weeks, must be convinced of the great and growing importance of this question. More than half of our time has been taken up with the discussion of propositions connected with the public lands; more than half of our acts embrace provisions growing out of this fruitful source. Day after day the changes are rung on this topic, from the grave inquiry into the right of the new States to the absolute sovereignty and property in the soil, down to the grant of a preemption of a few quarter sections to actual settlers. In the language of a great orator in relation to another "vexed question," we may truly say, "that year after year we have been lashed round the miserable circle of occasional arguments and temporary expedients." No gentleman can fail to perceive that this is a question no longer to be evaded; it must be met—fairly and fearlessly met. A question that is pressed upon us in so many ways; that intrudes in such a variety of shapes; involving so deeply the feelings and interests of a large portion of the Union; insinuating itself into almost every question of public policy, and tinging the whole course of our legislation, cannot be put aside, or laid asleep. We cannot long avoid it; we must meet and overcome it, or it will overcome us. Let us, then, be prepared to encounter it in a spirit of wisdom and of justice, and endeavor to prepare our own minds and the minds of the people, for a just and enlightened decision. The object of the remarks I am about to offer is merely to call public attention to the question, to throw out a few crude and undigested thoughts, as food for reflection, in order to prepare the public mind for the adoption, at no distant day, of some fixed and settled policy in relation to the public lands. I believe that, out of the Western country, there is no subject in the whole range of our legislation less understood, and in relation to which there exists so many errors, and such unhappy prejudices and misconceptions.

There may be said to be two great parties in this country, who entertain very opposite opinions in relation to the character of the policy which the Government has heretofore pursued, in relation to the public lands, as well as to that which ought, hereafter, to be pursued. I propose, very briefly, to examine these opinions, and to throw out for consideration a few ideas in connexion with them. Adverting first, to the past policy of the Government, we find that one party, embracing a very large portion, perhaps at this time a majority of the people of the United States, in all quarters of the Union, entertain the opinion, that, in the settlement of the new States and the disposition of the public lands, Congress has pursued not only a highly just and liberal course, but one of extraordinary kindness and indulgence. We are regarded as having acted towards the new States in the spirit of parental weakness, granting to froward children, not only every thing that was reasonable and proper, but actually robbing ourselves of our property to gratify their insatiable desires. While the other party, embracing the entire West, insist that we have treated them, from the beginning, not like heirs of the estate, but in the spirit of a hard taskmaster, resolved to promote our selfish interests from the fruit of their labor. Now, sir, it is not my present purpose to investigate all the grounds on which these opposite opinions rest; I shall content myself with noticing one or two particulars, in relation to which it has long appeared to me, that the West have had some cause for complaint. I notice them now, not for the purpose of aggravating the spirit of discontent in relation to this subject, which is known to exist in that quarter—for I do not know that my voice will ever reach them—but to assist in bringing others to what I believe to be a just sense of the past policy of the Government in relation to this matter. In the creation and settlement of the new States, the plan has been invariably pursued, of selling out, from time to time, certain portions of the public lands, for the highest price that could possibly be obtained for them in open market, and, until a few years past, on long credits. In this respect, a marked difference is observable between our policy and that of every other nation that has ever attempted to establish colonies or create new States. [. . .]

Let us now consider for a moment, [. . .] the effect of these two opposite systems on the condition of a new State. I will take the State of Missouri, by way of example. Here is a large and fertile territory, coming into the possession of the United States without any inhabitants but Indians and wild beasts—a territory which is to be converted into a sovereign and independent State. You commence your operations by surveying and selling out a portion of the lands, on long credits, to actual settlers; and, as the population progresses, you go on, year after year, making additional sales on the same terms; and this operation is to be continued, as gentlemen tell us, for fifty or a hundred years at least, if not for all time to come. The inhabitants of this new State, under such a system, it is most obvious, must have commenced their operations under a load of debt, the annual payment of which must necessarily drain their country of the whole profits of their labor, just so long as this system shall last. This debt is due, not from some citizens of the State to others of the same State, (in which case the money would remain in the country) but it is due from the whole population of the State to the United States, by whom it is regularly drawn out, to be expended abroad. Sir, the amount of this debt has, in every one of the new States, actually constantly exceeded the ability of the people to pay, as is proved by the fact that you have been compelled, from time to time, in your great liberality, to extend the credits, and in some instances even to remit portions of the debt, in order to protect some land debtors from bankruptcy and total ruin. Now, I will submit the question to any candid man, whether, under this system, the people of a new State, so situated, could, by any industry or exertion, ever become rich and prosperous. What has been the consequence, sir? Almost universal poverty; no money; hardly a sufficient circulating medium for the ordinary exchanges of society; paper banks, relief laws, and the other innumerable evils, social, political, and moral, on which it is unnecessary for me to dwell. Sir, under a system by which a drain like this is constantly operating upon the wealth of the whole community, the country may be truly said to be afflicted with a curse which it has been well observed is more grievous to be borne "than the barrenness of the soil, and the inclemency of the seasons." It is said, sir, that we learn from our own misfortunes how to feel for the sufferings of others; and perhaps the present condition of the Southern States has served to impress more deeply on my own mind, the grievous oppression of a system by which the wealth of a country is drained off to be expended elsewhere. In that devoted region, sir, in which my lot has been cast, it is our misfortune to stand in that relation to the Federal Government, which subjects us to a taxation which it requires the utmost efforts of our industry to meet. Nearly the whole amount of our contributions is expended abroad: we stand towards the United States in the relation of Ireland to England. The fruits of our labor are drawn from us to enrich other and more favored sections of the Union; while, with one of the finest climates and the richest products in the world, furnishing, with one-third of the population, two-thirds of the whole exports of the country, we exhibit the extraordinary, the wonderful, and painful spectacle of a country enriched by the bounty of God, but blasted by the cruel policy of man. The rank grass grows in our streets; our very fields are scathed by the hand of injustice and oppression. Such, sir, though probably in a less degree, must have been the effects of a kindred policy on the fortunes of the West. It is not in the nature of things that it should have been otherwise.

Let gentlemen now pause and consider for a moment what would have been the probable effects of an opposite policy. Suppose, sir, a certain portion of the State of Missouri had been originally laid off and sold to actual settlers for the quit rent of a "peppercorn" or even for a small price to be paid down in cash. Then, sir, all the money that was made in the country would have remained in the country, and, passing from hand to hand, would, like rich and abundant streams flowing through the land, have adorned and fertilized the whole. Suppose, sir, that all the sales that have been effected had been made by the State, and that the proceeds had gone into the State treasury, to be returned back to the people in some of the various shapes in which a beneficent local government exerts its powers for the improvement of the condition of its citizens. Who can say how much of wealth and prosperity, how much of improvement in science and the arts, how much of individual and social happiness, would have been diffused throughout the land! But I have done with this topic. [. . .]

I distrust, [. . .] sir, the policy of creating a great permanent national treasury, whether to be derived from public lands or from any other source. If I had, sir, the powers of a magician, and could, by a wave of my hand, convert this capital into gold for such a purpose, I would not do it. If I could, by a mere act of my will, put at the disposal of the Federal Government any amount of treasure which I might think proper to name, I should limit the amount to the means necessary for the legitimate purposes of the Government. Sir, an immense national treasury would be a fund for corruption. It would enable Congress and the Executive to exercise a control over

States, as well as over great interests in the country, nay, even over corporations and individuals—utterly destructive of the purity, and fatal to the duration of our institutions. It would be equally fatal to the sovereignty and independence of the States. Sir, I am one of those who believe that the very life of our system is the independence of the States, and that there is no evil more to be deprecated than the consolidation of this Government. It is only by a strict adherence to the limitations imposed by the constitution on the Federal Government, that this system works well, and can answer the great ends for which it was instituted. I am opposed, therefore, in any shape, to all unnecessary extension of the powers, or the influence of the Legislature or Executive of the Union over the States, or the people of the States; and, most of all, I am opposed to those partial distributions of favors, whether by legislation or appropriation, which has a direct and powerful tendency to spread corruption through the land; to create an abject spirit of dependence; to sow the seeds of dissolution; to produce jealousy among the different portions of the Union, and finally to sap the very foundations of the Government itself.

But, sir, there is another purpose to which it has been supposed the public lands can be applied, still more objectionable. I mean that suggested in a report from the Treasury Department, under the late administration, of so regulating the disposition of the public lands as to create and preserve, in certain quarters of the Union, a population suitable for conducting great manufacturing establishments. It is supposed, sir, by the advocates of the American System, that the great obstacle to the progress of manufactures in this country is the want of that low and degraded population which infest the cities and towns of Europe, who, having no other means of subsistence, will work for the lowest wages, and be satisfied with the smallest possible share of human enjoyment. And this difficulty it is proposed to overcome, by so regulating and limiting the sales of the public lands, as to prevent the drawing off this portion of the population from the manufacturing States. Sir, it is bad enough that Government should presume to regulate the industry of man; it is sufficiently monstrous that they should attempt, by arbitrary legislation, artificially to adjust and balance the various pursuits of society, and to "organize the whole labor and capital of the country." But what shall we say of the resort to such means for these purposes! What! create a manufactory of paupers, in order to enable the rich proprietors of woollen and cotton factories to amass wealth? From the bottom of my soul do I abhor and detest the idea, that the powers of the Federal Government should ever be prostituted for such purpose. Sir, I hope we shall act on a more just and liberal system of policy. The people of America are, and ought to be for a century to come, essentially an agricultural people; and I can conceive of no policy that can possibly be pursued in relation to the public lands, none that would be more "for the common benefit of all the States," than to use them as the means of furnishing a secure asylum to that class of our fellow-citizens, who in any portion of the country may find themselves unable to procure a comfortable subsistence by the means immediately within their reach. I would by a just and liberal system convert into great and flourishing communities, that entire class of persons, who would otherwise be paupers in your streets, and outcasts in society, and by so doing you will but fulfil the great trust which has been confided to your care. [. . .]

Webster's First Speech, January 20

I now proceed, sir, to some of the opinions expressed by the gentleman from South Carolina. Two or three topics were touched by him, in regard to which he expressed sentiments in which I do not at all concur.

In the first place, sir, the honorable gentleman spoke of the whole course and policy of the Government towards those who have purchased and settled the public lands and seemed to think this policy wrong. He held it to have been, from the first, hard and rigorous; he was of opinion that the United States had acted towards those who had subdued the Western wilderness, in the spirit of a step-mother; that the public domain had been improperly regarded as a source of revenue; and that we had rigidly compelled payment for that which ought to have been given away. He said we ought to have followed the analogy of other Governments, which had acted on a much more liberal system than ours, in planting colonies. He dwelt particularly upon the settlement of America by colonists from Europe; and reminded us that their governments had not exacted from those colonists payment for the soil; with them, he said, it had been thought that the conquest of the wilderness was, itself, an equivalent for the soil; and he lamented that we had not followed the example, and pursued the same liberal course towards our own emigrants to the West.

Now, sir, I deny altogether, that there has been any thing harsh or severe in the policy of the Government towards the new States of the West. On the contrary, I maintain that it has uniformly pursued towards those States, a liberal and enlightened system, such as its own duty allowed and required, and such as their interests and welfare demanded. The Government has been no step-mother to the new States; she has not been careless of their interests, nor deaf to their requests; but from the first moment, when the Territories which now form those States, were ceded to the Union, down to the time in which I am now speaking, it has been the invariable object of the Government to dispose of the soil, according to the true spirit of the obligation under which it received it; to hasten its settlement and cultivation, as far and as fast as practicable; and to rear the new communities into equal and independent States, at the earliest moment of their being able, by their numbers, to form a regular government.

I do not admit sir, that the analogy to which the gentleman refers is just, or that the cases are at all similar. There is no resemblance between the cases upon which a statesman can found an argument. The original North American colonists either fled from Europe, like our New England ancestors, to avoid persecution, or came hither at their own charges, and often at the ruin of their fortunes, as private adventurers. Generally speaking, they derived neither succor nor protection from their governments at home. Wide, indeed, is the difference between those cases and ours. From the very origin of the Government, these Western lands, and the just protection of those who had settled or should settle on them, have been the leading objects in our policy, and have led to expenditures, both of blood and treasure, not inconsiderable; not indeed exceeding the importance of the object, and not yielded grudgingly or reluctantly certainly; but yet not inconsiderable, though necessary sacrifices, made for high proper ends. The Indian title has been extinguished at the expense of many millions. Is that nothing? There is still a much more material consideration. These colonists, if we are to call them so, in passing the Alleghany, did not pass beyond the care and protection of their own Government. Wherever they went, the public arm was still stretched over them. A parental Government at home was still ever mindful of their condition, and their wants; and nothing was spared which a just sense of their necessities required. Is it forgotten that it was one of the most arduous duties of the Government, in its earliest years, to defend the frontiers against the Northwestern Indians? Are the sufferings and misfortunes under Harmar and St. Clair not worthy to be remembered? Do the occurrences connected with these military efforts show an unfeeling neglect of Western interests? And here, sir, what becomes of the gentleman's analogy? What English armies accompanied our ancestors to clear the forests of a barbarous foe? What treasures of the exchequer were expended in buying up the original title to the soil? What governmental arm held its aegis over our fathers heads, as they pioneered their way in the wilderness? Sir, it was not till General Wayne's victory, in 1794, that it could be said we had conquered the savages. It was not till that period that the Government could have considered itself as having established an entire ability to protect those who should undertake the conquest of the wilderness. And here, sir, at the epoch of 1794, let us pause, and survey the scene. It is now thirty-five years since that scene actually existed. Let us, sir, look back, and behold it. Over all that is now Ohio, there then stretched one vast wilderness, unbroken, except by two small spots of civilized culture, the one at Marietta, and the other at Cincinnati. At these little openings, hardly each a pin's point upon the map, the arm of the frontiersman had leveled the forest, and let in the sun. These little patches of earth, and themselves almost shadowed by the over hanging boughs of that wilderness, which had stood and perpetuated itself, from century to century, ever since the creation, were all that had then been rendered verdant by the hand of man. In an extent of hundreds and thousands of square miles, no other surface of smiling green attested the presence of civilization. The hunters path crossed mighty rivers, flowing in solitary grandeur, whose sources lay in remote and unknown regions of the wilderness. It struck, upon the North, on a vast inland sea, over which the wintry tempests raged as on the ocean; all around was bare creation. It was a fresh, untouched, unbounded, magnificent wilderness! And, sir, what is it now? Is it imagination only, or can it possibly be fact, that presents such a change, as surprises and astonishes us, when we turn our eyes to what Ohio now is? Is it reality, or a dream, that, in so short a period even as thirty-five years, there has sprung up, on the same surface, an independent State, with a million of people? A million of inhabitants! an amount of population greater than that of all the cantons of Switzerland; equal to one third of all the people of the United States, when they undertook to accomplish their independence. This new member of the republic has already left far behind her a majority of the old States. She is now by the side of Virginia and Pennsylvania; and in point of numbers, will shortly admit no equal but New York herself. If, sir, we may judge of measures by their results, what lessons do these facts read us upon the policy of the Government? [. . .]

But there was another observation of the honorable member, which, I confess, did not a little surprise me. As a reason for wishing to get rid of the public lands as soon as we could, and as we might, the honorable gentleman said, he wanted no permanent sources of income. He wished to see the time when the Government should not possess a shilling of permanent revenue. If he could speak a magical word, and by that word convert the whole capital into gold, the word should not be spoken. The administration of a fixed revenue, [he said] only consolidates the Government, and corrupts the people! Sir, I confess I heard these sentiments uttered on this floor not without deep regret and pain.

I am aware that these, and similar opinions, are espoused by certain persons out of the capitol, and out of this Government; but I did not expect so soon to find them here. Consolidation!—that perpetual cry, both of terror and delusion—consolidation! Sir, when gentlemen speak of the effects of a common fund, belonging to all the States, as having a tendency to consolidation, what do they mean? Do they mean, or can they mean, any thing more than that the Union of the States will be strengthened, by whatever continues or furnishes inducements to the people of the States to hold together? If they mean merely this, then, no doubt, the public lands as well as every thing else in which we have a common interest, tends to consolidation; and to this species of consolidation every true American ought to be attached; it is neither more nor less than strengthening the Union itself. This is the sense in which the framers of the constitution use the word consolidation; and in which sense I adopt and cherish it. They tell us, in the letter submitting the constitution to the consideration of the country, that, "in all our deliberations on this subject, we kept steadily in our view that which appears to us the greatest interest of every true American—the consolidation of our Union—in which is involved our prosperity, felicity, safety; perhaps our national existence. This important consideration, seriously and deeply impressed on our minds, led each State in the Convention to be less rigid, on points of inferior magnitude, than might have been otherwise expected."

This, sir, is General Washington's consolidation. This is the true constitutional consolidation. I wish to see no new powers drawn to the General Government; but I confess I rejoice in whatever tends to strengthen the bond that unites us, and encourages the hope that our Union may be perpetual. And, therefore, I cannot but feel regret at the expression of such opinions as the gentleman has avowed; because I think their obvious tendency is to weaken the bond of our connexion. I know that there are some persons in the part of the country from which the honorable member comes, who habitually speak of the Union in terms of indifference, or even of disparagement. The honorable member himself is not, I trust, and can never be, one of these. They significantly declare, that it is time to calculate the value of the Union; and their aim seems to be to enumerate, and to magnify all the evils, real and imaginary, which the Government under the Union produces.

The tendency of all these ideas and sentiments is obviously to bring the Union into discussion, as a mere question of present and temporary expediency; nothing more than a mere matter of profit and loss. The Union to be preserved, while it suits local and temporary purposes to preserve it; and to be sundered whenever it shall be found to thwart such purposes. Union, of itself, is considered by the disciples of this school as hardly a good. It is only regarded as a possible means of good; or on the other hand, as a possible means of evil. They cherish no deep and fixed regard for it, flowing from a thorough conviction of its absolute and vital necessity to our welfare. Sir, I deprecate and deplore this tone of thinking and acting. I deem far otherwise of the Union of the States; and so did the framers of the constitution themselves. What they said I believe; fully and sincerely believe, that the Union of the States is essential to the prosperity and safety of the States. I am a Unionist, and in this sense a National Republican. I would strengthen the ties that hold us together. Far, indeed, in my wishes, very far distant be the day, when our associated and fraternal stripes shall be severed asunder, and when that happy constellation under which we have risen to so much renown, shall be broken up, and be seen sinking, star after star, into obscurity and night! [. . .]

I come now to that part of the gentleman's speech which has been the main occasion of my addressing the Senate. The East! the obnoxious, the rebuked, the always reproached East! We have come in, sir, on this debate, for even more than a common share of accusation and attack. If the honorable member from South Carolina was not our original accuser, he has yet recited the indictment against us, with the air and tone of a public prosecutor. He has summoned us to plead on our arraignment; and he tells us we are charged with the crime of a narrow and selfish policy; of endeavoring to restrain emigration to the West, and, having that object in view, of maintaining a steady opposition to Western measures and Western interests. And the cause of all this narrow and selfish policy, the gentleman finds in the tariff. I think he called it the accursed policy of the tariff. This policy, the gentleman tells us, requires multitudes of dependent laborers, a population of paupers, and that it is to secure these at home that the East opposes whatever may induce to Western emigration. Sir, I rise to defend the East. I rise to repel, both the charge itself, and the cause assigned for it. I deny that the East has, at any time, shown an illiberal policy towards the West. I pronounce the whole accusation to be without the least foundation in any facts, existing either now, or at any previous time. I deny it in the general, and I deny each and all its particulars. I deny the sum total, and I deny the detail. I deny that the East has ever manifested hostility to the West, and I deny that she has adopted any policy that would naturally have led her in such a course. But the tariff! the tariff!! Sir, I beg to say, in regard to the East, that the original policy of the tariff is not hers, whether it be wise or unwise. New England is not its author. If gentlemen will recur to the tariff of 1816, they will find that that was not carried by New England votes. It was truly more a Southern than an Eastern measure. And what votes carried the tariff of 1824? Certainly, not those of New England. It is known to have been made matter of reproach, especially against Massachusetts, that she would not aid the tariff of 1824; and a selfish motive was imputed to her for that also. In point of fact, it is true that she did, indeed, oppose the tariff of 1824. There were more votes in favor of that law in the House of Representatives, not only in each of a majority of the Western States, but even in Virginia herself also, than in Massachusetts. It was literally forced upon New England; and this shows how groundless, how void of all probability any charge must be, which imputes to her hostility to the growth of the Western States, as naturally flowing from a cherished policy of her own. But leaving all conjectures about causes and motives, I go at once to the fact, and I meet it with one broad, comprehensive, and emphatic negative. I deny that, in any part of her history, at any period of the Government, or in relation to any leading subject, New England has manifested such hostility as is charged upon her. On the contrary, I maintain that, from the day of the cession of the territories by the States to Congress, no portion of the country has acted, either with more liberality or more intelligence, on the subject of the Western lands in the new States, than New England. [. . .]

Those immense regions, large enough almost for an empire, were to be appropriated to private ownership. How was this best to be done? What system for sale and disposition should be adopted? Two modes for conducting the sales presented themselves; the one a Southern, and the other a Northern mode. It would be tedious, sir, here, to run out these different systems into all their distinctions, and to contrast their opposite results. That which was adopted was the Northern system, and is that which we now see in successful operation in all the new States. That which was rejected, was the system of warrants, surveys, entry, and location; such as prevails South of the Ohio. It is not necessary to extend these remarks into invidious comparisons. This last system is that which, as has been emphatically said, has shingled over the country to which it was applied with so many conflicting titles and claims. Every body acquainted with the subject knows how easily it leads to speculation and litigation—two great calamities in a new country. From the system actually established, these evils are banished. Now, sir, in effecting this great measure, the first important measure on the whole subject, New England acted with vigor and effect, and the latest posterity of those who settled Northwest of the Ohio, will have reason to remember, with gratitude, her patriotism and her wisdom. The system adopted was her own system. She knew, for she had tried and proved its value. It was the old fashioned way of surveying lands, before the issuing of any title papers, and then of inserting accurate and precise descriptions in the patents or grants, and proceeding with regular reference to metes and bounds. This gives to original titles, derived from Government, a certain and fixed character; it cuts up litigation by the roots, and the settler commences his labors with the assurance that he has a clear title. It is easy to perceive, but not easy to measure, the importance of this in a new country. New England gave this system to the West; and while it remains, there will be spread over all the West one monument of her intelligence in matters of government, and her practical good sense.

At the foundation of the constitution of these new Northwestern States, we are accustomed, sir, to praise the lawgivers of antiquity; we help to perpetuate the fame of Solon and Lycurgus; but I doubt whether one single law of any lawgiver, ancient or modern, has produced effects of more distinct, marked, and lasting character, than the ordinance of '87. That instrument was drawn by Nathan Dane, then, and now, a citizen of Massachusetts. It was adopted, as I think I have understood, without the slightest alteration; and certainly it has happened to few men, to be the authors of a political measure of more large and enduring consequence. It fixed, forever, the character of the population in the vast regions Northwest of the Ohio, by excluding from them involuntary servitude. It impressed on the soil itself, while it was yet a wilderness, an incapacity to bear up any other than free men. It laid the interdict against personal servitude, in original compact, not only deeper than all local law, but deeper, also, than all local constitutions. Under the circumstances then existing, I look upon this original and seasonable provision, as a real good attained. We see its consequences at this moment, and we shall never cease to see them, perhaps, while the Ohio shall flow. It was a great and salutary measure of prevention. Sir, I should fear the rebuke of no intelligent gentleman of Kentucky, were I to ask whether, if such an ordinance could have been applied to his own State, while it yet was a wilderness, and before Boone had passed the gap of the Alleghany, he does not suppose it would have contributed to the ultimate greatness of that Commonwealth? It is, at any rate, not to be doubted, that, where it did apply, it has produced an effect not easily to be described, or measured in the growth of the States, and the extent and increase of their population. Now, sir, this great measure again was carried by the North, and by the North alone. There were, indeed, individuals elsewhere favorable to it; but it was supported, as a measure, entirely by the votes of the Northern States. If New England had been governed by the narrow and selfish views now ascribed to her, this very measure was, of all others, the best calculated to thwart her purposes. It was, of all things, the very means of rendering certain a vast emigration from her own population to the West. She looked to that consequence only to disregard it. She deemed the regulation a most useful one to the States that would spring up on the territory, and advantageous to the country at large. She adhered to the principle of it perseveringly, year after year, until it was finally accomplished.

Leaving, then, sir, these two great and leading measures, and coming down to our own times, what is there in the history of recent measures of Government that exposes New England to this accusation of hostility to Western interests? I assert, boldly, that in all measures conducive to the welfare of the West, since my acquaintance here, no part of the country has manifested a more liberal policy. I beg to say, sir, that I do not state this with a view of claiming for her any special regard on that account. Not at all. She does not place her support of measures on the ground of favor conferred; far otherwise. What she has done has been consonant to her view of the general good, and, therefore, she has done it. She has sought to make no gain of it; on the contrary, individuals may have felt, undoubtedly, some natural regret at finding the relative importance of their own states diminished by the growth of the West. [. . .] But every inducement has been held out to them to settle in the West, until our population has become sparse; and then the effects of this sparseness are now to be counteracted by another artificial system. Sir, I say if there is any object worthy the attention of this Government, it is a plan which shall limit the sale of the public lands. If those lands were sold according to their real value, be it so. But while the Government continues, as it now does, to give them away, they will draw the population of the older States, and still farther increase the effect which is already distressingly felt, and which must go to diminish the value of all those States possess. And this, sir, is held out to us as a motive for granting the present appropriation. I would not, indeed, prevent the formation of roads on these considerations, but I certainly would not encourage it. Sir, there is an additional item in the account of the benefits which this Government has conferred on the Western States. It is the sale of the public lands at the minimum price. At this moment we are selling to the people of the West, lands at one dollar and twenty-five cents an acre, which are fairly worth fifteen, and which would sell at that price if the markets were not glutted.

"[. . .] The gentleman from South Carolina supposes that, if our population had been confined to the old thirteen States, the aggregate wealth of the country would have been greater than it now is. But, sir, it is an error that the increase of the aggregate of the national wealth is the object chiefly to be pursued by Government. The distribution of the national wealth is an object quite as important as its increase. He was not surprised that the old States were not increasing in population so fast as was expected (for he believed nothing like a decrease was pretended) should be an idea by no means agreeable to gentlemen from those States; we are all reluctant in submitting to the loss of relative importance: but this was nothing more than the natural condition of a country densely populated in one part, and possessing, in another, a vast tract of unsettled lands. The plan of the gentleman went to reverse the order of nature, vainly expecting to retain men within a small and comparatively unproductive territory, 'who have all the world before them where to choose.' For his own part, he was in favor of letting population take its own course; he should experience no feeling of mortification if any of his constituents liked better to settle on the Kansas, or the Arkansas, or the Lord knows where, within our territory; let them go, and be happier, if they could. The gentleman says our aggregate of wealth would have been greater, if our population had been restrained within the limits of the old States; but does he not consider population to be wealth? And has not this been increased by the settlement of a new and fertile country? Such a country presents the most alluring of all prospects to a young and laboring man; it gives him a freehold; it offers to him weight and respectability in society; and, above all, it presents to him a prospect of a permanent provision for his children. Sir, these are inducements which never were resisted, and never will be; and, were the whole extent of country filled with population up to the Rocky Mountains, these inducements would carry that population forward to the shores of the Pacific Ocean. Sir, it is in vain to talk; individuals will seek their own good, and not any artificial aggregate of the national wealth. A young, enterprising, and hardy agriculturist can conceive of nothing better to him than plenty of good, cheap land."

Sir, with the reading of these extracts, I leave the subject. The Senate will bear me witness that I am not accustomed to allude to local opinions, nor to compare nor contrast different portions of the country. I have often suffered things to pass which I might, properly enough, have considered as deserving a remark, without any observation. But I have felt it my duty, on this occasion, to vindicate the State I represent from charges and imputations on her public character and conduct, which I know to be undeserved and unfounded. If advanced elsewhere, they might be passed, perhaps, without notice. But whatever is said here, is supposed to be entitled to public regard, and to deserve public attention; it derives importance and dignity from the place where it is uttered. As a true Representative of the State which has sent me here, it is my duty, and a duty which I shall fulfil, to place her history and her conduct, her honor and her character, in their just and proper light, so often as I think an attack is made upon her so respectable as to deserve to be repelled.

Hayne's Second Speech, January 25

[. . .] Little did I expect [. . .] to be called upon to meet such as was yesterday urged by the gentleman from Massachusetts [Mr. WEBSTER.] Sir, I questioned no man's opinions; I impeached no man's motives; I charged no party, or State, or section of country, with hostility to any other; but ventured, I thought in a becoming spirit, to put forth my own sentiments in relation to a great national question of public policy. Such was my course. [. . .] The honorable gentleman from Massachusetts, after deliberating a whole night upon his course, comes into this chamber to vindicate New England, and; instead of making up his issue with the gentleman from Missouri,[1] on the charges which he had preferred, chooses to consider me as the author of those charges; and, losing sight entirely of that gentleman, selects me as his adversary, and pours out all the vials of his mighty wrath upon my devoted head. Nor is he willing to stop there. He goes on to assail the institutions and policy of the South, and calls in question the principles and conduct of the State which I have the honor to represent. When I find a gentleman of mature age and experience, of acknowledged talents and profound sagacity, pursuing a course like this, declining the contest offered from the West, and making war upon the unoffending South, I must believe, I am bound to believe, he has some object in view that he has not ventured to disclose. [. . .]

The gentleman from Massachusetts, in reply to my remarks on the injurious operation of our land system on the prosperity of the West, pronounced an extravagant eulogium on the paternal care which the Government had extended towards the West, to which he attributed all that was great and excellent in the present condition of the new States. The language of the gentleman on this topic fell upon my ears like the almost forgotten tones of the tory leaders of the British Parliament, at the commencement of the American Revolution. They, too, discovered, that the colonies had grown great under the fostering care of the mother country; and I must confess, while listening to the gentleman, I thought the appropriate reply to his argument was to be found in the remark of a celebrated orator, made on that occasion: "They have grown great in spite of your protection."

The gentleman, in commenting on the policy of the Government, in relation to the new States, has introduced to our notice a certain Nathan Dane, of Massachusetts, to whom he attributes the celebrated ordinance of '87, by which he tells us, "slavery was forever excluded from the new States north of the Ohio." After eulogizing the wisdom of this provision, in terms of the most extravagant praise, he breaks forth in admiration of the greatness of Nathan Dane—and great, indeed, he must be, if it be true, as stated by the Senator from Massachusetts, that "he was greater than Solon and Lycurgus, Minos, Numa Pompilius, and all the legislators and philosophers of the world," ancient and modern. Sir, to such high authority it is certainly my duty, in a becoming spirit of humility, to submit. And yet, the gentleman will pardon me when I say, that it is a little unfortunate for the fame of this great legislator, that the gentleman from Missouri should have proved that he was not the author of the ordinance of '87, on which the Senator from Massachusetts has reared so glorious a monument to his name. Sir, I doubt not the Senator will feel some compassion for our ignorance, when I tell him, that so little are we acquainted with the modern great men of New England, that, until he informed us yesterday, that we possessed a Solon and a Lycurgus in the person of Nathan Dane, he was only known to the South as a member of a celebrated assembly called and known by the name of "the Hartford Convention." In the proceedings of that assembly, which I hold in my hand, [. . .] will be found, in a few lines, the history of Nathan Dane; and a little further on, there is conclusive evidence of that ardent devotion to the interests of the new States, which it seems, has given him a just claim to the title of "Father of the West." By the 2d resolution of the "Hartford Convention," it is declared, "that it is expedient to attempt to make provision for restraining Congress in the exercise of an unlimited power to make new States, and admitting them into the Union." So much for Nathan Dane, of Beverly, Massachusetts.

In commenting upon my views in relation to the public lands, the gentleman insists that it being one of the conditions of the grants, that these lands should be applied to "the common benefit of all the

1. [Sen. Thomas Hart Benton]

States, they must always remain a fund for revenue," and adds, "they must be treated as so much treasure." Sir, the gentleman could hardly find language strong enough to convey his disapprobation of the policy which I had ventured to recommend to the favorable consideration of the country. And what, sir, was that policy, and what is the difference between that gentleman and myself, on this subject? I threw out the idea, that the public lands ought not to be reserved forever as "a great fund for revenue;" that they ought not to be "treated as a great treasure;" but that the course of our policy should rather be directed towards the creation of new States, and building up great and flourishing communities. [. . .]

The gentleman may boast as much as he pleases of the friendship of New England for the West, as displayed in their support of Internal Improvement; but, when he next introduces that topic, I trust that he will tell us when that friendship commenced, how it was brought about, and why it was established. Before I leave this topic, I must be permitted to say that the true character of the policy now pursued by the gentleman from Massachusetts and his friends, in relation to appropriations of land and money, for the benefit of the West, is, in my estimation, very similar to that pursued by Jacob of old towards his brother Esau; "it robs them of their birthright for a mess of pottage."

The gentleman from Massachusetts, in alluding to a remark of mine, that, before any disposition could be made of the public lands, the national debt (for which they stand pledged) must be first paid, took occasion to intimate "that the extraordinary fervor which seems to exist in a certain quarter [meaning the South, sir] for the payment of the debt, arises from a disposition to weaken the ties which bind the people to the Union." While the gentleman deals us this blow, he professes an ardent desire to see the debt speedily extinguished. He must excuse me, however, for feeling some distrust on that subject until I find this disposition manifested by something stronger than professions. I shall look for acts, decided and unequivocal acts: for the performance of which an opportunity will very soon (if I am not greatly mistaken) be afforded. Sir, if I were at liberty to judge of the course which that gentleman would pursue, from the principles which he has laid down in relation to this matter, I should be bound to conclude that he will be found acting with those with whom it is a darling object to prevent the payment of the public debt. He tells us he is desirous of paying the debt, "because we are under an obligation to discharge it." Now, sir, suppose it should happen that the public creditors, with whom we have contracted the obligation, should release us from it, so far as to declare their willingness to wait for payment for fifty years to come, provided only the interest shall be punctually discharged. The gentleman from Massachusetts will then be released from the obligation which now makes him desirous of paying the debt; and, let me tell the gentleman, the holders of the stock will not only release us from this obligation, but they will implore, nay, they will even pay us not to pay them. But, adds the gentleman, "so far as the debt may have an effect in binding the debtors to the country, and thereby serving as a link to hold the States together, he would be glad that it should exist forever." Surely then, sir, on the gentleman's own principles, he must be opposed to the payment of the debt.

Sir, let me tell that gentleman that the South repudiates the idea that a pecuniary dependence on the Federal Government is one of the legitimate means of holding the States together. A moneyed interest in the Government is essentially a base interest; and just so far as it operates to bind the feelings of those who are subjected to it to the Government; just so far as it operates in creating sympathies and interests that would not otherwise exist; is it opposed to all the principles of free government, and at war with virtue and patriotism. Sir, the link which binds the public creditors, as such, to their country, binds them equally to all governments, whether arbitrary or free. In a free government, this principle of abject dependence, if extended through all the ramifications of society, must be fatal to liberty. Already have we made alarming strides in that direction. The entire class of manufacturers, the holders of stocks, with their hundreds of millions of capital, are held to the Government by the strong link of pecuniary interests; millions of people, entire sections of country, interested, or believing themselves to be so, in the public lands, and the public treasure, are bound to the Government by the expectation of pecuniary favors. If this system is carried much further, no man can fail to see that every generous motive of attachment to the country will be destroyed, and in its place will spring up those low, grovelling, base, and selfish feelings which bind men to the footstool of a despot by bonds as strong and as enduring as those which attach them to free institutions. Sir, I would lay the foundation of this Government in the affections of the People; I would teach them to cling to it by dispensing equal justice, and, above all, by securing the "blessings of liberty to themselves and to their posterity."

The honorable gentleman from Massachusetts has gone out of his way to pass a high eulogium on the State of Ohio. In the most impassioned tones of eloquence, he described her majestic march to greatness. He told us that, having already left all the other States far behind, she was now passing by Virginia, and Pennsylvania, and about to take her station by the side of New York. To all this, sir, I was disposed most cordially to respond. When, however, the gentleman proceeded to contrast the State of Ohio with Kentucky, to the disadvantage of the latter, I listened to him with regret; and when he proceeded further to attribute the great, and, as he supposed, acknowledged superiority of the former in population, wealth, and general prosperity, to the policy of Nathan Dane, of Massachusetts, which had secured to the people of Ohio (by the ordinance of '87) a population of freemen, I will confess that my feelings suffered a revulsion, which I am now unable to describe in any language sufficiently respectful towards the gentleman from Massachusetts. In contrasting the State of Ohio with Kentucky, for the purpose of pointing out the superiority of the former, and of attributing that superiority to the existence of slavery, in the one State, and its absence in the other, I thought I could discern the very spirit of the Missouri question intruded into this debate, for objects best known to the gentleman himself. Did that gentleman, sir, when he formed the determination to cross the southern border, in order to invade the State of South Carolina, deem it prudent, or necessary, to enlist under his banners the prejudices of the world, which like Swiss troops, may be engaged in any cause, and are prepared to serve under any leader? Did he desire to avail himself of those remorseless allies, the passions of mankind, of which it may be more truly said, than of the savage tribes of the wilderness, "that their known rule of warfare is an indiscriminate slaughter of all ages, sexes, and conditions?" Or was it supposed, sir, that, in a premeditated and unprovoked attack upon the South, it was advisable to begin by a gentle admonition of our supposed weakness, in order to prevent us from making that firm and manly resistance, due to our own character, and our dearest interest? Was the significant hint of the weakness of slave-holding States, when contrasted with the superior strength of free States—like the glare of the weapon half drawn from its scabbard—intended to enforce the lessons of prudence and of patriotism, which the gentleman had resolved, out of his abundant generosity, gratuitously to bestow upon us. The impression which has gone abroad, of the weakness of the South, as connected with the slave question, exposes us to such constant attacks, has done us so much injury, and is calculated to produce such infinite mischiefs, that I embrace the occasion presented by the remarks of the gentleman from Massachusetts, to declare that we are ready to meet the question promptly and fearlessly. It is one from which we are not disposed to shrink, in whatever form or under whatever circumstances it may be pressed upon us. We are ready to make up the issue with the gentleman, as to the influence of slavery on individual and national character—on the prosperity and greatness, either of the United States, or of particular States. Sir, when arraigned before the bar of public opinion, on this charge of slavery, we can stand up with conscious rectitude, plead not guilty, and put ourselves upon God and our country. Sir, we will not stop to inquire whether the black man, as some philosophers have contended, is of an inferior race, nor whether his color and condition are the effects of a curse inflicted for the offences of his ancestors. We deal in no abstractions. We will not look back to inquire whether our fathers were guiltless in introducing slaves into this country. If an inquiry should ever be instituted in these matters, however, it will be found that the profits of the slave trade were not confined to the South. Southern ships and Southern sailors were not the instruments of bringing slaves to the shores of America, nor did our merchants reap the profits of that "accursed traffic." But, sir, we will pass over all this. If slavery, as it now exists in this country, be an evil, we of the present day found it ready made to our hands. Finding our lot cast among a people, whom God had manifestly committed to our care, we did not sit down to speculate on abstract questions of theoretical liberty. We met it as a practical question of obligation and duty. We resolved to make the best of the situation in which Providence had placed us, and to fulfil the high trust which had developed upon us as the owners of slaves, in the only way in which such a trust could be fulfilled, without spreading misery and ruin throughout the land. We found that we had to deal with a people whose physical, moral, and intellectual habits and character, totally disqualified them from the enjoyment and blessings of freedom. We could not send them back to the shores from whence their fathers had been taken; their numbers forbade the thought, even if we did not know that their condition here is infinitely preferable to what it possibly could be among the barren sands and savage tribes of Africa; and it was wholly irreconcileable with all our notions of humanity to tear asunder the tender ties which they had formed among us, to gratify the feelings of false philanthropy. What a commentary on the wisdom, justice, and humanity, of the Southern slave owner is presented by the example of certain benevolent associations and charitable individuals elsewhere. Shedding weak tears over sufferings which had existence only in their own sickly imaginations, these "friends of humanity" set themselves systematically to work to seduce the slaves of the South from their masters. By means of missionaries and political tracts, the scheme was in a great measure successful. Thousands of these deluded victims of fanaticism were seduced into the enjoyment of freedom in our Nothern cities. And what has been the consequence? Go to these cities now, and ask the question. Visit the dark and narrow lanes, and obscure recesses, which have been assigned by common consent as the abodes of those outcasts of the world—the free people of color. Sir, there does not exist, on the face of the whole earth, a population so poor, so wretched, so vile, so loathsome, so utterly destitute of all the comforts, conveniences, and decencies of life, as the unfortunate blacks of Philadelphia, and New York, and Boston. Liberty has been to them the greatest of calamities, the heaviest of curses. Sir, I have had some opportunities of making comparisons between the condition of the free negroes of the North and the slaves of the South, and the comparision has left not only an indelible impression of the superior advantages of the latter, but has gone far to reconcile me to slavery itself. Never have I felt so forcibly that touching description, "the foxes have holes, and the birds of the air have nests, but the son of man hath not where to lay his head," as when I have seen this unhappy race, naked and houseless, almost starving in the streets, and abandoned by all the world. Sir, I have seen in the neighborhood of one of the most moral, religious, and refined cities of the North, a family of free blacks, driven to the caves of the rock, and there obtaining a precarious subsistence from charity and plunder.

When the gentleman from Massachusetts adopts and reiterates the old charge of weakness as resulting from slavery, I must be permitted to call for the proof of those blighting effects which he ascribes to its influence. I suspect that when the subject is closely examined, it will be found that there is not much force even in the plausible objection of the want of physical power in slave holding States. The power of a country is compounded of its population and its wealth; and, in modern times, where, from the very form and structure of society, by far the greater portion of the people must, even during the continuance of the most desolating wars, be employed in the cultivation of the soil, and other peaceful pursuits, it may be well doubted whether slave holding States, by reason of the superior value of their productions, are not able to maintain a number of troops in the field, fully equal to what could be supported by States with a larger white population, but not possessed of equal resources.

It is a popular error to suppose, that in any possible state of things, the people of a country could ever be called out *en masse*, or that a half, or a third, or even a fifth part of the physical force of any country could ever be brought into the field. The difficulty is not to procure men, but to provide the means of maintaining them; and in this view of the subject, it may be asked whether the Southern States are not a source of strength and power, and not to weakness, to the country? whether they have not contributed, and are not now contributing, largely, to the wealth and prosperity of every State in the Union? From a statement which I hold in my hand, it appears that, in ten years (from 1818 to 1827 inclusive) the whole amount of the domestic exports of the United States was five hundred and twenty-one millions eight hundred and eleven thousand and forty-five dollars. Of which, three articles, the product of slave labor, namely, cotton, rice, and tobacco, amounted to three hundred and thirty-nine millions two hundred and three thousand two hundred and thirty-two dollars; equal to about two-thirds of the whole. It is not true, as has been supposed, that the advantages of this labor is confined almost exclusively to the Southern States. Sir, I am thoroughly convinced that, at this time, the States North of the Potomac actually derive greater profits from the labor of our slaves, than we do ourselves. It appears, from our public documents, that, in seven years, (from 1821 to 1827 inclusive) the six Southern States exported to the amount of one hundred and ninety millions three hundred and thirty-seven thousand two hundred and eighty-one dollars; and imported to the value of fifty-five millions six hundred and forty-six thousand three hundred and one dollars. Now, the difference between these two sums, near one hundred and forty millions of dollars, passed through the hands of the Northern merchants, and enabled them to carry on their commercial operations with all the world. Such part of these goods as found its way back to our hands, came charged with the duties, as well as the profits of the merchant, the ship owner, and a host of others, who found employment in carrying on these immense exchanges; and, for such part as was consumed at the North, we received in exchange Northern manufactures, charged with an increased price, to cover all the taxes which the Northern consumer had been compelled to pay on the imported article. It will be seen, therefore, at a glance, how much slave labor has contributed to the wealth and prosperity of the United States; and how largely our Northern brethren have participated in the profits of that labor. Sir, on this subject I will quote an authority which will, I doubt not, be considered by the Senator from Massachusetts as entitled to high respect. It is from the great father of the American System—honest Mathew Carey; no great friend, it is true, at this time, to Southern rights and Southern interests, but not the worst authority, on that account, on the point in question.

Speaking of the relative importance to the Union of the Southern and the Eastern States, Mathew Carey, in the sixth edition of his "Olive Branch," [. . .] after exhibiting a number of statistical tables, to show the decided superiority, of the former, thus proceeds:

"But I am tired of this investigation. I sicken for the honor of the human species. What idea must the world form of the arrogance of the pretensions on the one side, [the East] and of the folly and weakness of the rest of the Union, to have so long suffered them to pass without exposure and detection? The naked fact is, that the demagogues in the Eastern States, not satisfied with deriving all the benefit from the Southern section of the Union that they would from so many wealthy colonies; with making princely fortunes by the carriage and exportation of its bulky and valuable productions, and supplying it with their own manufactures, and the productions of Europe, and the East and West Indies, to an enormous amount, and at an immense profit, have uniformly treated it with outrage, insult, and injury. And, regardless of their vital interests, the Eastern States were lately courting their own destruction, by allowing a few restless, turbulent men, to lead them blindfold to a separation, which was pregnant with their certain ruin. Whenever that event takes place they sink into insignificance. If a separation were desirable to any part of the Union, it would be to the Middle and Southern States, particularly the latter, who have been so long harassed with the complaints, the restlessness, the turbulence, and the ingratitude, of the Eastern States, that their patience has been tried almost beyond endurance. "Jeshurun waxed fat and kicked;" and he will be severely punished for his kicking, in the event of a dissolution of the Union."

Sir, I wish it to be distinctly understood that I do not adopt these sentiments as my own. I quote them to show that very different sentiments have prevailed in former times, as to the weakness of the slave holding States, from those which now seem to have become fashionable in certain quarters. I know it has been supposed, by certain ill informed persons, that the South exists only by the countenance and protection of the North. Sir, this is the idlest of all idle and ridiculous fancies that ever entered into the mind of man. In every State of this Union, except one, the free white population actually preponderates; while in the British West India Islands, where the average white population is less than ten per cent of the whole, the slaves are kept in entire subjection. It is preposterous to suppose that the Southern States could even find the smallest difficulty in this respect. On this subject, as in all others, we ask nothing of our Northern brethren but to "let us alone;" leave us to the undisturbed management of our domestic concerns, and the direction of our own industry, and we will ask no more. Sir, all our difficulties on this subject have arisen from interference from abroad, which has disturbed, and may again disturb, our domestic tranquillity, just so far as to bring down punishment upon the heads of the unfortunate victims of a fanatical and mistaken humanity.

There is a spirit, which, like the father of evil, is constantly "walking to and fro about the earth, seeking whom it may devour." It is the spirit of false philanthropy. The persons whom it possesses do not indeed throw themselves into the flames, but they are employed in lighting up the torches of discord throughout the community. Their first principle of action is to leave their own affairs, and neglect their own duties, to regulate the affairs and the duties of others. Theirs is the task to feed the hungry and clothe the naked, of other lands, whilst they thrust the naked, famished, and shivering beggar from their own doors; to instruct the heathen, while their own children want the bread of life. When this spirit infuses itself into the bosom of a statesman, (if one so possessed can be called a statesman) it converts him at once into a visionary enthusiast. Then it is that he indulges in golden dreams of national greatness and prosperity. He discovers that "liberty is power;" and not content with vast schemes of improvement at home, which it would bankrupt the treasury of the world to execute, he flies to foreign lands, to fulfil obligations to "the human race," by inculcating the principles of "political and religious liberty," and promoting the "general welfare" of the whole human race. It is a spirit which has long been busy with the slaves of the South, and is even now displaying itself in vain efforts to drive the Government from its wise policy in relation to the Indians. It is this spirit which has filled the land with thousands of wild and visionary projects, which can have no effect but to waste the energies and dissipate the resources of the country. It is the spirit, of which the aspiring politician dexterously avails himself, when, by inscribing on his banner the magical words "liberty and philanthropy," he draws to his support that entire class of persons who are ready to bow down at the very names of their idols.

But, sir, whatever difference of opinion may exist as to the effect of slavery on national wealth and prosperity, if we may trust to experience, there can be no doubt that it has never yet produced any injurious effects on individual or national character. Look through the whole history of the country, from the commencement of the Revolution down to the present hour; where are there to be found brighter examples of intellectual and moral greatness, than have been exhibited by the sons of the South? From the Father of his Country, down to the distinguished chieftain who has been elevated, by a grateful people, to the highest office in their gift, the interval is filled up by a long line of orators, of statesmen, and of heroes, justly entitled to rank among the ornaments of their country, and the benefactors of mankind. Look at "the Old Dominion," great and magnanimous Virginia, "whose jewels are her sons." Is there any State in this Union which has contributed so much to the honor and welfare of the country? Sir, I will yield the whole question; I will acknowledge the fatal effects of slavery upon character; if any one can say that, for noble disinterestedness, ardent love of country, exalted virtue, and a pure and holy devotion to liberty, the people of the Southern States have ever been surpassed by any in the world. I know, sir, that this devotion to liberty has sometimes been supposed to be at war with our institutions; but it is in some degree the result of those very institutions. Burke, the most philosophical of statesmen, as he was the most accomplished of orators, well understood the operation of this principle, in elevating the sentiments and exalting the principles of the people in slaveholding States. I will conclude my remarks on this branch of the subject, by reading a few passages from his speech "on moving his resolutions for conciliation with the colonies, the 22d of March, 1775."

"There is a circumstance attending the Southern colonies, which makes the spirit of liberty still more high and haughty than those to the Northward. It is, that in Virginia and the Carolinas they have a vast multitude of slaves. Where this is the case, in any part of the world, those who are free are by far the most proud and jealous of their freedom. Freedom is to them not only an enjoyment, but a kind of rank and privilege. Not seeing there, as in countries where it is a common blessing, and as broad and general as the air, that it may be united with much abject toil, with great misery, with all the exterior of servitude, liberty looks among them like something more noble and liberal. I do not mean, sir, to commend the superior morality of this sentiment, which has, at least, as much of pride as virtue in it; but I cannot alter the nature of man. The fact is so, and these people of the Southern colonies are much more strongly, and with a higher and more stubborn spirit, attached to liberty, than those to the Northward. Such were all the ancient commonwealths; such were our Gothic ancestors; such, in our days, were the Poles; and such will be all masters of slaves who are not slaves themselves. In such a people, the haughtiness of domination, combined with the spirit of freedom, fortifies it, and renders it invincible."

In the course of my former remarks, I took occasion to deprecate, as one of the greatest of evils, the consolidation of this Government. The gentleman takes alarm at the sound. "Consolidation," like the "tariff," grates upon his ear. He tells us, "we have heard much, of late, about consolidation; that it is the rallying word for all who are endeavoring to weaken the Union by adding to the power of the States." But consolidation, says the gentleman, was the very object for which the Union was formed; and in support of that opinion, he read a passage from the address of the President of the Convention to Congress (which he assumes to be authority on his side of the question.) But, sir, the gentleman is mistaken. The object of the framers of the constitution, as disclosed in that address, was not the consolidation of the Government, but "the consolidation of the Union." It was not to draw power from the States, in order to transfer it to a great National Government, but, in the language of the constitution itself, "to form a more perfect union;" and by what means? By "establishing justice," "promoting domestic tranquillity," and "securing the blessings of liberty to ourselves and our posterity." This is the true reading of the constitution. But, according to the gentleman's reading, the object of the constitution was to consolidate the Government, and the means would seem to be, the promotion of injustice, causing domestic discord, and depriving the States and the people "of the blessings of liberty" forever. The gentleman boasts of belonging to the party of national republicans. National republicans! a new name, sir, for a very old thing. The national republicans of the present day were the federalists of '98, who became federal republicans during the war of 1812, and were manufactured into national republicans somewhere about the year 1825. As a party, (by whatever name distinguished) they have always been animated by the same principles, and have kept steadily in view a common object—the consolidation of the Government.

Sir, the party to which I am proud of having belonged from the very commencement of my political life to the present day, were the democrats of '98. Anarchists, antifederalists, revolutionists, I think they were sometimes called. They assumed the name of democratic republicans in 1812, and have retained their name and their principles up to the present hour. True to their political faith, they have always, as a party, been in favor of limitations of power; they have insisted that all powers not delegated to the Federal Government are reserved, and have been constantly struggling, as they are now struggling, to preserve the rights of the States, and prevent them from being drawn into the vortex, and swallowed up by one great consolidated Government. Sir, any one acquainted with the history of parties in this country will recognize in the points now in dispute between the Senator from Massachusetts and myself, the very grounds which have, from the beginning, divided the two great parties in this country, and which [. . .] will divide them forever. [. . .] [T]wo distinct orders of men—the lovers of freedom, and the devoted advocates of power. [. . .]

Sir, nothing has been further from my thoughts than to impeach the character or conduct of the people of New England. For their steady habits and hardy virtues, I trust I entertain a becoming respect. I fully subscribe to the truth of the description given before the Revolution, by one whose praise is the highest eulogy, "that the perseverance of Holland, the activity of France, and the dexterous and firm sagacity of English enterprise, have been more than equalled by this 'recent people.'" Hardy, enterprising, sagacious, industrious, and moral, the people of New England of the present day, are worthy of their ancestors. Still less has it been my intention to say any thing that could be construed into a want of respect for that party, who, trampling on all narrow, sectional feelings, have been true to their principles in the worst of times—I mean the democracy of New England.

Sir, I will declare that, highly as I appreciate the democracy of the South, I consider even higher praise to be due to the democracy of New England—who have maintained their principles "through good and through evil report," who at every period of our national history have stood up manfully for "their country, their whole country, and nothing but their country." In the great political revolution of '98, they were found united with the democracy of the South, marching under the banner of the constitution, led on by the patriarch of liberty, in search of the land of political promise, which they lived not only to behold, but to possess and to enjoy. Again, sir, in the darkest and most gloomy period of the war, when our country stood single handed, against "the conqueror of the conquerors of the world," when all about and around them was dark, and dreary, disastrous and discouraging, they stood a Spartan band in that narrow pass, where the honor of their country was to be defended, or to find its grave. And in the last great struggle, when, as we believe, the very existence of the principle of popular sovereignty was at stake, where were the democracy of New England? Where they always have been found, Sir, struggling side by side with their brethren of the South and the West, for popular rights, and assisting in that glorious triumph by which the man of the People was elevated to the highest office in their gift.

Who, then, Mr. President, are the true friends of the Union? Those who would confine the federal government strictly within the limits prescribed by the constitution—who would preserve to the States and the people all powers not expressly delegated—who would make this a federal and not a national Union—and who, administering the government in a spirit of equal justice, would make it a blessing and not a curse. And who are its enemies? Those who are in favor of consolidation; who are constantly stealing power from the States and adding strength to the federal government; who, assuming an unwarrantable jurisdiction over the States and the people, undertake to regulate the whole industry and capital of the country. But, Sir, of all descriptions of men, I consider those as the worst enemies of the Union, who sacrifice the equal rights which belong to every member of the confederacy, to combinations of interested majorities for personal or political objects. But the gentleman apprehends no evil from the dependence of the States on the Federal Government; he can see no danger of corruption from the influence of money or of patronage. Sir, I know that it is supposed to be a wise saying, "that patronage is a source of weakness," and in support of that maxim it has been said, that "every ten appointments make a hundred enemies." But I am rather inclined to think, with the eloquent and sagacious orator now reposing on his laurels on the banks of the Roanoke, that "the power of conferring favors creates a crowd of dependants." He gave a forcible illustration of the truth of the remark when he told us of the effect of holding up the savory morsel to the eager eyes of the hungry hounds gathered around his door. It mattered not whether the gift was bestowed on Towser or Sweetlips, "Tray, Blanch, or Sweetheart," while held in suspense they were all governed by a nod; and when the morsel was bestowed, the expectation of the *favors of to-morrow* kept up the *subjection of to-day*.

The Senator from Massachusetts, in denouncing what he is pleased to call the *Carolina doctrine*, has attempted to throw ridicule upon the idea that a State has any constitutional remedy by the exercise of its sovereign authority against "a gross, palpable, and deliberate violation of the Constitution." He called it "an idle" or "a ridiculous notion," or something to that effect; and added, that it would make the Union "a mere rope of sand." Now, Sir, as the gentleman has not condescended to enter into an examination of the question, and has been satisfied with throwing the weight of his authority into the scale, I do not deem it necessary to do more than to throw into the opposite scale, the authority on which South Carolina relies; and there, for the present, I am perfectly willing to leave the controversy. The South Carolina doctrine, that is to say, the doctrine contained in an exposition reported by a committee of the Legislature in December, 1828, and published by their authority, is the good old Republican doctrine of '98, the doctrine of the celebrated "Virginia Resolutions," of that year, and of "Madison's Report," of '99. It will be recollected that the Legislature of Virginia, in December, '98, took into consideration the Alien and Sedition Laws, then considered by all Republicans as a gross violation of the Constitution of the United States, and on that day passed, among others, the following resolution:

"The General Assembly doth explicitly and peremptorily declare, that it views the powers of the Federal Government as resulting from the compact to which the States are parties, as limited by the plain sense and intention of the instrument constituting that compact, as no further valid than they are authorized by the grants enumerated in that compact; and that, in case of *a deliberate, palpable, and dangerous exercise of other powers not granted by the said compact*, the States who are parties thereto, *have the right, and are in duty bound, to interpose, for arresting the progress of the evil*, and for maintaining within their respective limits, the authorities, rights and liberties appertaining to them."

In addition to the above resolutions, the General Assembly of Virginia "appealed to the other States, in the confidence that they would concur with that Commonwealth, that the acts aforesaid [the Alien and Sedition Laws] are unconstitutional, and that the necessary and proper measures would be taken by each for co-operating with Virginia *in maintaining unimpaired the authorities, rights, and liberties*, reserved to the States respectively, or to the people."

The Legislatures of several of the New England States having, (contrary to the expectation of the Legislature of Virginia) expressed their dissent from these doctrines, the subject came up again for consideration during the session of '99–1800, when it was referred to a Select Committee, by whom was made that celebrated report, which is familiarly known as "Madison's Report," and which deserves to last as long as the Constitution itself. In that report, which was subsequently adopted by the Legislature, the whole subject was deliberately examined, and the objections urged against the Virginia doctrines carefully considered; the result was, that the Legislature of Virginia re-affirmed all the principles laid down in the resolutions of '98, and issued to the world that admirable report which has stamped the character of Mr. Madison as the preserver of that Constitution, which he had contributed so largely to create and establish. I will here quote from Mr. Madison's report one or two passages which bear more immediately on the point in controversy. "The resolution having taken this view of the federal compact, proceeds to infer, that, in case of a deliberate, palpable, and dangerous exercise of powers, not granted by the said compact, the States who are parties thereto have the right, and are in duty bound, to interpose for arresting the progress of the evil, and for maintaining, within their respective limits, the authorities, rights, and liberties appertaining to them.

"It appears to your committee to be a plain principle, founded in common sense, illustrated by common practice, and essential to the nature of compacts, that, where resort can be had to no tribunal, superior to the authority of the parties, *the parties themselves must be the rightful judges* in the last resort, whether the bargain made has been pursued or violated. The constitution of the United States was formed by the sanction of *the States*, given by each in its sovereign capacity. It adds to the stability and dignity, as well as to the authority of the Constitution, that it rests upon this legitimate and solid foundation. The States, then, being the parties to the Constitutional compact, and in their sovereign capacity, it follows of necessity, that there can *be no tribunal above their authority*, to decide, in the last resort, whether the compact made by them be violated; and, consequently, that, as the parties to it, they must themselves decide, in the last resort, such questions as may be of sufficient magnitude to require their interposition.

"The resolution has guarded against any misapprehension of its object, by expressly requiring for such an interposition 'the case of a *deliberate, palpable, and dangerous* breach of the Constitution, by the exercise of *powers not granted by* it.' It must be a case, not of a light and transient nature, but of a nature dangerous to the great purposes for which the Constitution was established." [. . .]

[. . .] Resting on authority like this, I will ask gentlemen whether South Carolina has not manifested a high regard for the Union, when, under a tyranny ten times more grievous than the alien and sedition laws, she has hitherto gone no further than to *petition, remonstrate*, and solemnly *protest* against a series of measures which she believes to be wholly unconstitutional, and utterly destructive of her interests. Sir, South Carolina has not gone one step further than Mr. Jefferson himself was disposed to go, in relation to the very subject of our present complaints,—not a step further than the statesmen from New England were disposed to go, under similar circumstances,—no further than the Senator from Massachusetts himself once considered as within "the limits of a constitutional opposition." The doctrine that it is the right of a State to judge of the violations of the Constitution on the part of the Federal Government, and to protect her citizens from the operations of unconstitutional laws, was held by the enlightened citizens of Boston, who assembled in Faneuil Hall on the 25th January, 1809. They state in that celebrated memorial, that "they looked only to the State Legislature, who were *competent to devise relief* against the unconstitutional acts of the General Government. That your power (say they) is adequate to that object, is evident *from the organization of the Confederacy.*"

A distinguished Senator, from one of the New England States, (Mr. HILLHOUSE) in a speech delivered *here,* on a bill for enforcing the embargo, declared I feel myself bound in conscience to declare, (lest the blood of those who shall fall in the execution of this measure, shall be on my head) that I consider this to be an act which directs a mortal blow at the liberties of my country—an act containing *unconstitutional provisions,* to which the PEOPLE ARE NOT BOUND TO SUBMIT, and to which, in my opinion, they will not submit.

And the Senator from Massachusetts himself, in a speech delivered on the same subject, in the other House, said,—"This opposition is constitutional and legal; it is also conscientious. It rests on settled and sober conviction, that such policy is destructive to the interests of the people, and *dangerous to the being of the government.* The experience of every day confirms these sentiments. Men who act from such motives, are not to be discouraged by trifling obstacles, nor *awed by any dangers.* [. . .]

Thus it will be seen, Mr. PRESIDENT, that the South Carolina doctrine is the republican doctrine of '98; that it was first promulgated by the Fathers of the Faith—that it was maintained by Virginia and Kentucky, in the worst of times—that it constituted the very pivot on which the political revolution of that day turned—that it embraced the very principles the triumph of which at that time "saved the Constitution at its last gasp;" and which New England Statesmen were not unwilling to adopt, when they believed themselves to be the victims of unconstitutional legislation! Sir, as to the doctrine that the Federal Government is the exclusive judge of the extent as well as the limitations of its powers, it seems to be utterly subversive of the sovereignty and independence of the States. It makes but little difference, in my estimation, whether Congress or the Supreme Court, are invested with this power. If the Federal Government, in all or any of its departments, are to prescribe the limits of its own authority; and the States are bound to submit to the decision, and are not to be allowed to examine and decide for themselves, when the barriers of the Constitution shall be overleaped, this is practically "a Government without limitation of powers;" the States are at once reduced to mere petty corporations, and the people are entirely at your mercy. I have but one word more to add. In all the efforts that have been made by South Carolina to resist the unconstitutional laws which Congress has extended over them, she has kept steadily in view the preservation of the Union, by the only means by which she believes it can be long preserved—a firm, manly, and steady resistance against usurpation. The measures of the Federal Government have, it is true, prostrated her interests, and will soon involve the whole South in irretrievable ruin. But this evil, great as it is, is not the chief ground of our complaints. It is the principle involved in the contest, a principle which, substituting the discretion of Congress for the limitations of the Constitution, brings the States and the people to the feet of the Federal Government, and leaves them nothing they can call their own. Sir, if the measures of the Federal Government were less oppressive, we should still strive against this usurpation. The South is acting on a principle she has always held sound—resistance to *unauthorized taxation.* These, Sir, are the principles which induced the immortal Hampden to resist the payment of a tax of twenty shillings—"Would twenty shillings have ruined his fortune? No—but the payment of half twenty shillings, on the principle on which it was demanded, would have made him a slave." Sir, if, in acting on these high motives—if, animated by that ardent love of liberty which has always been the most prominent trait in the Southern character, we should be hurried beyond the bounds of a cold and calculating prudence, who is there with one noble and generous sentiment in his bosom, who would not be disposed in the language of Burke, to exclaim, "YOU MUST PARDON SOMETHING TO THE SPIRIT OF LIBERTY."

Webster's Second Speech, January 26–27

Mr. President:

When the mariner has been tossed, for many days, in thick weather, and on an unknown sea, he naturally avails himself of the first pause in the storm, the earliest glance of the sun, to take his latitude, and ascertain how far the elements have driven him from his true course. Let us imitate this prudence, and, before we float farther, refer to the point from which we departed, that we may at least be able to conjecture where we now are. I ask for the reading of the resolution.

[The Secretary read the resolution, as follows:

> *Resolved,* That the Committee on Public Lands be instructed to inquire and report the quantity of the public lands remaining unsold within each State and Territory, and whether it be expedient to limit, for a certain period, the sales of the public lands to such lands only as have heretofore been offered for sale, and are now subject to entry at the minimum price. And, also, whether the office of Surveyor General, and some of the Land Offices, may not be abolished without detriment to the public interest; or whether it be expedient to adopt measures to hasten the sales, and extend more rapidly the surveys of the public lands.]

We have thus heard, sir, what the resolution is, which is actually before us for consideration; and it will readily occur to every one that it is almost the only subject about which something has not been said in the speech, running through two days, by which the Senate has been now entertained by the gentleman from South Carolina. Every topic in the wide range of our public affairs, whether past or present—every thing, general or local, whether belonging to national politics, or party politics, seems to have attracted more or less of the honorable member's attention, save only the resolution before us. He has spoken of every thing but the public lands. They, have escaped his notice. To that subject, in all his excursions, he has not paid even the cold respect of a passing glance. [. . .]

We approach, at length, sir, to a more important part of the honorable gentleman's observations. Since it does not accord with my views of justice and policy to give away the public lands altogether, as mere matter of gratuity, I am asked by the honorable gentleman on what ground it is, that I consent to vote them away, in particular instances? How, he inquires, do I reconcile with these professed sentiments, my support of measures appropriating portions of the lands to particular roads, particular canals, particular rivers, and particular institutions of education in the West? This leads, sir, to the real and wide difference, in political opinion, between the honorable gentleman and myself. On my part, I look upon all these objects, as connected with the common good, fairly embraced in its object and its terms; he, on the contrary, deems them all, if good at all, only local good. This is our difference. The interrogatory which he proceeded to put, at once explains this difference. "What interest," asks he, "has South Carolina in a canal in Ohio?" Sir, this very question is full of significance. It develops the gentleman's whole political system; and its answer expounds mine. Here we differ, *toto coelo.* I look upon a road over the Allegany, a canal round the Falls of the Ohio, or a canal or railway from the Atlantic to the western waters, as being objects large and extensive enough to be fairly said to be for the common benefit. The gentleman thinks otherwise, and this is the key to open his construction of the powers of the Government. He may well ask, upon his system, what interest has South Carolina in a canal in Ohio? On that system, it is true, she has no interest. On that system, Ohio and Carolina are different Governments, and different countries, connected here, it is true, by some slight and ill-defined bond of union, but, in all main respects, separate and diverse. On that system, Carolina has no more interest in a canal in Ohio than in Mexico. The gentleman, therefore, only follows out his own principles; he does no more than arrive at the natural conclusions of his own doctrines; he only announces the true results of that creed, which he has adopted himself, and would persuade others to adopt, when he thus declares that South Carolina has no interest in a public work in Ohio. Sir, we narrow-minded people of New England do not reason thus. Our *notion* of things is entirely different. We look upon the States, not as separated, but as united. We love to dwell on that union, and on the mutual happiness which it has so much promoted, and the common renown which it has so greatly contributed to acquire. In our contemplation, Carolina and Ohio are parts of the same country; States, united under the same General Government, having interests, common, associated, intermingled. In whatever is within the proper sphere of the constitutional power of this Government, we look upon the States as one. We do not impose geographical limits to our patriotic feeling or regard; we do not follow rivers and mountains, and lines of latitude, to find boundaries, beyond which public improvements do not benefit us. We who come here, as agents and representatives of these narrow-minded and selfish men of New England, consider ourselves as bound to regard, with equal eye, the good of the whole, in whatever is within our power of legislation. Sir, if a rail road or a canal, beginning in South Carolina, and ending in South Carolina, appeared to me to be of national importance and national magnitude, believing, as I do, that the power of Government extends to the encouragement of works of that description, if I were to stand up here, and ask, what interest has Massachusetts in a rail road in South Carolina, I should not be willing to face my constituents. These same narrow-minded men would tell me, that they had sent me to act for the whole country, and that one who possessed too little comprehension, either of intellect or feeling; one who was not large enough, in mind and heart, to embrace the whole, was not fit to be entrusted with the interest of any part. Sir, I do not desire to enlarge the powers of the Government, by unjustifiable construction; nor to exercise any not within a fair interpretation. But when it is believed that a power does exist, then it is, in my judgment, to be exercised for the general benefit of the whole. So far as respects the exercise of such a power, the States are one. It was the very object of the constitution to create unity of interests, to the extent of the powers of the General Government. In war and peace, we are one; in commerce, one; because the authority of the General Government reaches to war and peace, and to the regulation of commerce. I have never seen any more difficulty, in erecting light houses on the lakes, than on the ocean; in improving the harbors of inland seas, than if they were within the ebb and flow of the tide; or of removing obstructions in the vast streams of the West, more than in any work to facilitate commerce on the Atlantic coast. If there be power for one, there is power also for the other; and they are all and equally for the country.

There are other objects, apparently more local, or the benefit of which is less general, towards which, nevertheless, I have concurred, with others, to give aid, by donations of land. It is proposed to construct a road, in or through one of the new States, in which this Government possesses large quantities of land. Have the United States no right, as a great and untaxed proprietor, are they under no obligation, to contribute to an object thus calculated to promote the common good of all the proprietors, themselves included? And even with respect to education, which is the extreme case, let the question be considered. In the first place, as we have seen, it was made matter of compact with these States, that they should do their part to promote education. In the next place, our whole system of land laws proceeds on the idea that education is for the common good; because, in every division, a certain portion is uniformly reserved and appropriated for the use of schools. And, finally, have not these new States singularly strong claims, founded on the ground already stated, that the Government is a great untaxed proprietor, in the ownership of the soil? It is a consideration of great importance, that, probably, there is in no part of the country, or of the world, so great a call for the means of education, as in those new States; owing to the vast numbers of persons within those ages in which education and instruction are usually received, if received at all. This is the natural consequence of recency of settlement and rapid increase. The census of these States shows how great a proportion of the whole population occupies the classes between infancy and manhood. These are the wide fields, and here is the deep and quick soil, for the seeds of knowledge and virtue; and this is the favored season, the very spring-time for sowing them. Let them be disseminated without stint. Let them be scattered with a bountiful, broad cast. Whatever the Government can fairly do towards these objects, in my opinion, ought to be done.

These, sir, are the grounds, succinctly stated, on which my votes for grants of lands for particular objects rest; while I maintain, at the same time, that it is all a common fund, for the common benefit. And reasons like these, I presume, have influenced the votes of other gentlemen from New England. Those who have a different view of the powers of the Government, of course, come to different conclusions, on these, as on other questions. I observed, when speaking on this subject before, that, if we looked to any measure, whether for a road, a canal, or any thing else, intended for the improvement of the West, it would be found, that, if the New England *ayes* were struck out; of the lists of votes, the Southern *noes* would always have rejected the measure. The truth of this has not been denied, and cannot be denied. [. . .]

[. . .] [L]et me observe that the eulogium pronounced on the character of the State of South Carolina, by the honorable gentleman, for her Revolutionary and other merits, meets my hearty concurrence. I shall not acknowledge that the honorable member goes before me in regard for whatever of distinguished talent, or distinguished character, South Carolina has produced. I claim part of the honor, I partake in the pride, of her great names. I claim them for countrymen, one and all. The Laurenses, the Rutledges, the Pinckneys, the Sumpters, the Marions—Americans, all—whose fame is no more to be hemmed in by State lines, than their talents and patriotism were capable of being circumscribed within the same narrow limits. In their day and generation, they served and honored the country, and the whole country; and their renown is of the treasures of the whole country. [. . .]

[L]et me remind you that in early times no States cherished greater harmony, both of principle and of feeling, than Massachusetts and South Carolina. Would to God, that harmony might again return! Shoulder to shoulder they went through the Revolution—hand in hand they stood round the Administration of Washington, and felt his own great arm lean on them for support. Unkind feeling, if it exist, alienation and distrust, are the growth, unnatural to such soils, of false principles since sown. They are weeds, the seeds of which that same great arm never scattered.

Mr. President, I shall enter on no encomium upon Massachusetts—she needs none. There she is—behold her, and judge for yourselves. There is her history—the world knows it by heart. The past, at least, is secure. There is Boston, and Concord, and Lexington, and Bunker Hill—and there they will remain forever. The bones of her sons, falling in the great struggle for Independence, now lie mingled with the soil of every State, from New England to Georgia; and there they will lie forever. And, sir, where American liberty raised its first voice; and where its youth was nurtured and sustained, there it still lives, in the strength of its manhood, and full of its original spirit. If discord and disunion shall wound it—if party strife and blind ambition shall hawk at and tear it—if folly and madness—if uneasiness, under salutary and necessary restraint—shall succeed to separate it from that Union, by which alone its existence is made sure, it will stand, in the end, by the side of that cradle in which its infancy was rocked; it will stretch forth its arm, with whatever of vigor it may still retain, over the friends who gather round it; and it will fall at last, if fall it must, amidst the proudest monuments of its own glory, and on the very spot of its origin.

There yet remains to be performed, Mr. President, by far the most grave and important duty, which I feel to be devolved on me, by this occasion. It is to state, and to defend, what I conceive to be the true principles of the Constitution under which we are here assembled. I might well have desired that so weighty a task should have fallen into other and abler hands. I could have wished that it should have been executed by those, whose character and experience give weight and influence to their opinions, such as cannot possibly belong to mine. But, sir, I have met the occasion, not sought it; and I shall proceed to state my own sentiments, without challenging for them any particular regard, with studied plainness, and as much precision as possible.

I understand the honorable gentleman from South Carolina to maintain, that it is a right of the State Legislatures to interfere, whenever, in their judgment, this Government transcends its constitutional limits, and to arrest the operation of its laws.

I understand him to maintain this right, as a right existing *under* the Constitution; not as a right to overthrow it, on the ground of extreme necessity, such as would justify violent revolution.

I understand him to maintain an authority, on the part of the States, thus to interfere, for the purpose of correcting the exercise of power by the General Government, of checking it, and of compelling it to conform to their opinion of the extent of its powers.

I understand him to maintain, that the ultimate power of judging of the constitutional extent of its own authority, is not lodged exclusively in the General Government, or any branch of it; but that, on the contrary, the States may lawfully decide for themselves, and each State for itself, whether, in a given case, the act of the General Government transcends its power.

I understand him to insist, that if the exigency of the case, in the opinion of any State Government, require it, such State Government may, by its own sovereign authority, annul an act of the General Government, which it deems plainly and palpably unconstitutional.

This is the sum of what I understand from him, to be the South Carolina doctrine; and the doctrine which he maintains. I propose to consider it, and to compare it with the Constitution. Allow me to say, as a preliminary remark, that I call this the South Carolina doctrine, only because the gentleman himself has so denominated it. I do not feel at liberty to say that South Carolina, as a State, has ever advanced these sentiments. I hope she has not, and never may. That a great majority of her people are opposed to the Tariff laws, is doubtless true. That a majority, somewhat less than that just mentioned, conscientiously believe these laws unconstitutional, may probably also be true. But, that any majority holds to the right of direct State interference, at State discretion, the right of nullifying acts of Congress, by acts of State legislation, is more than I know, and what I shall be slow to believe. [. . .]

I need not say that I have much respect, for the constitutional opinions of Mr. Madison; they would weigh greatly with me, always. But, before the authority of his opinion be vouched for the gentleman's proposition, it will be proper to consider what is the fair interpretation of that resolution,[1] to which Mr. Madison is understood to have given his sanction. As the gentleman construes it, it is an authority for him. Possibly, he may not have adopted the right construction. That resolution declares, that, *in the case of the dangerous exercise of powers not granted, by the General Government, the States may interpose to arrest the progress of the evil.* But how interpose, and what does this declaration purport? Does it mean no more, than that there may be extreme cases, in which the People, in any mode of assembly, may resist usurpation, and relieve themselves from a tyrannical government? No one will deny this. Such resistance is not only acknowledged to be just in America, but in England also. Blackstone admits as much, in the theory, and practice, too, of the English Constitution. We, sir, who oppose the Carolina doctrine, do not deny that the People may, if they choose, throw off any government, when it become oppressive and intolerable, and erect a better in its stead. We all know that civil institutions are established for the public benefit, and that when they cease to answer the ends of their existence, they may be changed. But I do not understand the doctrine now contended for to be that which, for the sake of distinctness, we may call the right of revolution. I understand the gentleman to maintain, that, without revolution, without civil commotion, without rebellion, a remedy for supposed abuse and transgression of the powers of the General Government lies in a direct appeal to the interference of the State Governments. [Mr. HAYNE here rose: He did not contend, he said, for the mere right of revolution, but for the right of constitutional resistance. What he maintained, was, that, in case of a plain, palpable violation of the Constitution, by the General Government, a State may interpose; and that this interposition is constitutional.] Mr. WEBSTER resumed: So, Sir, I understood the gentleman, and am happy to find that I did not misunderstand him. What he contends for, is, that it is constitutional to interrupt the administration of the Constitution itself, in the hands of those who are chosen and sworn to administer it, by the direct interference, in form of law, of the States, in virtue of their sovereign capacity. The inherent right in the People to reform their government, I do not deny; and they have another right, and that is, to resist unconstitutional laws, without overturning the Government. It is no doctrine of mine, that unconstitutional laws bind the People. The great question is, *whose prerogative is it to decide on the constitutionality or unconstitutionality of the laws?* On that, the main debate hinges. The proposition, that, in case of a supposed violation of the Constitution by Congress, the States have a constitutional right to interfere, and annul the law of Congress, is the proposition of the gentleman: I do not admit it. If the gentleman had intended no more than to assert the right of revolution, for justifiable cause, he would have said only what all agree to.

1. [Virginia Resolution, 1798.]

But I cannot conceive that there can be a middle course, between submission to the laws, when regularly pronounced constitutional, on the one hand, and open resistance, which is revolution, or rebellion, on the other. I say, the right of a State to annul a law of Congress, cannot be maintained, but on the ground of the unalienable right of man to resist oppression; that is to say, upon the ground of revolution. I admit that there is an ultimate violent remedy, above the Constitution, and in defiance of the Constitution, which may be resorted to, when a revolution is to be justified. But I do not admit that, under the Constitution, and in conformity with it, there is any mode in which a State Government, as a member of the Union, can interfere and stop the progress of the General Government, by force of her own laws, under any circumstances whatever.

This leads us to inquire into the origin of this Government, and the source of its power. Whose agent is it? Is it the creature of the State Legislatures, or the creature of the People? If the Government of the United States be the agent of the State Governments, then they may control it, provided they can agree in the manner of controlling it; if it be the agent of the People, then the People alone can control it, restrain it, modify, or reform it. It is observable enough, that the doctrine for which the honorable gentleman contends, leads him to the necessity of maintaining, not only that this General Government is the creature of the States, but that it is the creature of each of the States severally; so that each may assert the power, for itself, of determining whether it acts within the limits of its authority. It is the servant of four-and-twenty masters, of different wills and different purposes, and yet bound to obey all. This absurdity (for it seems no less) arises from a misconception as to the origin of this Government and its true character. It is, sir, the People's Constitution, the People's Government; made for the People; made by the People; and answerable to the People. The People of the United States have declared that this Constitution shall be the Supreme Law. We must either admit the proposition, or dispute their authority. The States are, unquestionably, sovereign, so far as their sovereignty is not affected by this supreme law. But the State Legislatures, as political bodies, however sovereign, are yet not sovereign over the People. So far as the People have given power to the General Government, so far the grant is unquestionably good, and the Government holds of the People, and not of the State Governments. We are all agents of the same supreme power, the People. The General Government and the State Governments derive their authority from the same source. Neither can, in relation to the other, be called primary, though one is definite and restricted, and the other general and residuary. The National Government possesses those powers which it can be shown the People have conferred on it, and no more. All the rest belongs to the State Governments or to the People themselves. So far as the People have restrained State sovereignty, by the expression of their will, in the Constitution of the United States, so far, it must be admitted, State sovereignty is effectually controlled. I do not contend that it is, or ought to be, controlled farther. The sentiment to which I have referred, propounds that State sovereignty is only to be controlled by its own "feeling of justice;" that is to say, it is not to be controlled at all: for one who is to follow his own feelings is under no legal control. Now, however men may think this ought to be, the fact is, that the People of the United States have chosen to impose control on State sovereignties. There are those, doubtless, who wish they had been left without restraint, but the Constitution has ordered the matter differently. To make war, for instance, is an exercise of sovereignty; but the Constitution declares that no State shall make war. To coin money is another exercise of sovereign power; but no State is at liberty to coin money. Again, the Constitution says that no sovereign State shall be so sovereign as to make a treaty. These prohibitions, it must be confessed, are a control on the State sovereignty of South Carolina, as well as of the other States, which does not arise "from her own feelings of honorable justice." Such an opinion, therefore, is in defiance of the plainest provisions of the Constitution.

There are other proceedings of public bodies which have already been alluded to, and to which I refer again for the purpose of ascertaining, more fully, what is the length and breadth of that doctrine, denominated the Carolina doctrine, which the honorable member has now stood up on this floor to maintain. In one of them I find it resolved, that "the Tariff of 1828, and every other Tariff designed to promote one branch of industry at the expense of others, is contrary to the meaning and intention of the

Federal compact; and, as such, a dangerous, palpable, and deliberate usurpation of power, by a determined majority, wielding the General Government beyond the limits of its delegated powers, as calls upon the States which compose the suffering minority, in their sovereign capacity, to exercise the powers which, as sovereigns, necessarily devolve upon them, when their compact is violated."

Observe, sir, that this resolution holds the Tariff of 1828, and every other Tariff, designed to promote one branch of industry at the expense of another, to be such a dangerous, palpable, and deliberate usurpation of power, as calls upon the States, in their sovereign capacity, to interfere by their own authority. This denunciation, Mr. President, you will please to observe, includes our old Tariff of 1816, as well as all others; because that was established to promote the interest of the manufactures of cotton, to the manifest and admitted injury of the Calcutta cotton trade. Observe, again, that all the qualifications are here rehearsed and charged upon the Tariff, which are necessary to bring the case within the gentleman's proposition. The Tariff is a usurpation; it is a dangerous usurpation; it is a palpable usurpation; it is a deliberate usurpation. It is such a usurpation, therefore, as calls upon the States to exercise their right of interference. Here is a case, then, within the gentleman's principles, and all his qualifications of his principles. It is a case for action. The Constitution is plainly, dangerously, palpably, and deliberately violated; and the States must interpose their own authority to arrest the law. Let us suppose the State of South Carolina to express this same opinion, by the voice of her Legislature. That would be very imposing; but what then? Is the voice of one State conclusive? It so happens that at the very moment when South Carolina resolves that the Tariff laws are unconstitutional, Pennsylvania and Kentucky, resolve exactly the reverse. *They* hold those laws to be both highly proper and strictly constitutional. And now, sir, how does the honorable member propose to deal with this case? How does he relieve us from this difficulty, upon any principle of his? His construction gets us into it; how does he propose to get us out?

In Carolina, the Tariff is a palpable, deliberate usurpation; Carolina, therefore, may *nullify* it, and refuse to pay the duties. In Pennsylvania, it is both clearly constitutional, and highly expedient; and there, the duties are to be paid. And yet, we live under a Government of uniform laws, and under a Constitution, too, which contains an express provision, as it happens, that all duties shall be equal in all the States! Does not this approach absurdity?

If there be no power to settle such questions, independent of either of the States, is not the whole Union a rope of sand? Are we not thrown back again, precisely, upon the old Confederation?

It is too plain to be argued. Four-and-twenty interpreters of constitutional law, each with a power to decide for itself, and none with authority to bind any body else, and this constitutional law the only bond of their Union! What is such a state of things, but a mere connexion during pleasure, or, to use the phraseology of the times, *during feeling*? And that feeling, too, not the feeling of the People, who established the Constitution, but the feeling of the State Governments.

In another of the South Carolina Addresses, having premised that the crisis requires "all the concentrated energy of passion," an attitude of open resistance to the laws of the Union is advised. Open resistance to the laws, then, is the constitutional remedy, the conservative power of the State, which the South Carolina doctrines teach for the redress of political evils, real or imaginary. And its authors further say, that, appealing with confidence to the Constitution itself, to justify their opinions, they cannot consent to try their accuracy by the Courts of Justice. In one sense, indeed, sir, this is assuming an attitude of open resistance in favor of liberty. But what sort of liberty? The liberty of establishing their own opinions, in defiance of the opinions of all others; the liberty of judging and of deciding exclusively themselves, in a matter in which others have as much right to judge and decide as they; the liberty of placing their own opinions above the judgment of all others, above the laws, and above the Constitution. This is their liberty, and this is the fair result of the proposition contended for by the honorable gentleman. Or it may be more properly said, it is identical with it, rather than a result from it. [. . .]

I was forcibly struck, sir, with one reflection, as the gentleman went on in his speech. He quoted Mr. Madison's resolutions to prove that a State may interfere, in a case of deliberate, palpable, and dangerous exercise of a power not granted. The honorable member supposes the Tariff law to be such an exercise of power; and that, consequently, a case has arisen in which the State may, if it see fit, interfere by its own law. Now it so happens, nevertheless, that Mr. Madison himself deems this same Tariff law quite constitutional. Instead of a clear and palpable violation, it is, in his judgment, no violation at all. So that, while they use his authority for a hypothetical case, they reject it in the very case before them. All this, sir, shows the inherent—futility—I had almost used a stronger word—of conceding this power of interference to the States, and then attempting to secure it from abuse by imposing qualifications, of which the States themselves are to judge. One of two things is true; either the laws of the Union are beyond the discretion, and beyond the control of the States; or else we have no Constitution of General Government, and are thrust back again to the days of the Confederacy.

Let me here say, sir, that if the gentleman's doctrine had been received and acted upon in New England, in the times of the embargo and non-intercourse, we should probably not now have been here. The Government would, very likely, have gone to pieces, and crumbled into dust. No stronger case can ever arise than existed under those laws; no States can ever entertain a clearer conviction than the New England States then entertained; and if they had been under the influence of that heresy of opinion, as I must call it, which the honorable member espouses, this Union would, in all probability, have been scattered to the four winds. I ask the gentleman, therefore, to apply his principles to that case; I ask him to come forth and declare, whether, in his opinion, the New England States would have been justified in interfering to break up the embargo system, under the conscientious opinions which they held upon it? Had they a right to annul that law? Does he admit or deny? If that which is thought palpably unconstitutional in South Carolina, justifies that State in arresting the progress of the law, tell me, whether that which was thought palpably unconstitutional also in Massachusetts, would have justified her in doing the same thing? Sir, I deny the whole doctrine. It has not a foot of ground in the Constitution to stand on. No public man of reputation ever advanced it in Massachusetts, in the warmest times, or could maintain himself upon it there at any time. [. . .]

I must now beg to ask, sir, whence is this supposed right of the States derived?—where do they find the power to interfere with the laws of the Union? Sir, the opinion which the honorable gentleman maintains, is a notion, founded in a total misapprehension, in my judgment, of the origin of this Government, and of the foundation on which it stands. I hold it to be a popular Government, erected by the People; those who administer it responsible to the People; and itself capable of being amended and modified, just as the People may choose it should be. It is as popular, just as truly emanating from the People, as the State Governments. It is created for one purpose; the State Governments for another. It has its own powers; they have theirs. There is no more authority with them to arrest the operation of a law of Congress, than with Congress to arrest the operation of their laws. We are here to administer a Constitution emanating immediately from the People, and trusted, by them, to our administration. It is not the creature of the State Governments. It is of no moment to the argument, that certain acts of the State Legislatures are necessary to fill our seats in this body. That is not one of their original State powers, a part of the sovereignty of the State. It is a duty which the People, by the Constitution itself, have imposed on the State Legislatures; and which they might have left to be performed elsewhere, if they had seen fit. So they have left the choice of President with electors; but all this does not affect the proposition, that this whole Government, President, Senate, and House of Representatives, is a popular Government. It leaves it still all its popular character. The Governor of a State, (in some of the States) is chosen, not directly by the People, but by those who are chosen by the People, for the purpose of performing, among other duties, that of electing a Governor. Is the Government of the State, on that account, not a popular Government? This Government, sir, is the independent offspring of the popular will. It is not the creature of State Legislatures; nay, more, if the whole truth must be told, the People brought it into existence, established it, and have hitherto supported it, for the very purpose, amongst others, of imposing certain salutary restraints on State sovereignties. The States cannot now make war; they cannot contract alliances; they cannot make, each for itself, separate regulations of commerce; they cannot lay imposts; they cannot coin money. If this Constitution, sir, be the creature of State Legislatures, it must be admitted that it has obtained a strange control over the volitions of its creators.

The People, then, sir, erected this Government. They gave it a Constitution, and in that Constitution they have enumerated the powers which they bestow on it. They have made it a limited Government. They have defined its authority. They have restrained it to the exercise of such powers as are granted; and all others, they declare, are reserved to the States or the People. But, sir, they have not stopped here. If they had, they would have accomplished but half their work. No definition can be so clear, as to avoid possibility of doubt; no limitation so precise, as to exclude all uncertainty.

[. . .] [T]he People have wisely provided, in the Constitution itself, a proper, suitable mode and tribunal for settling questions of constitutional law. There are, in the Constitution, grants of powers to Congress; and restrictions on these powers. There are, also, prohibitions on the States. Some authority must, therefore, necessarily exist, having the ultimate jurisdiction to fix and ascertain the interpretation of these grants, restrictions, and prohibitions. The Constitution has itself pointed out, ordained, and established that authority. How has it accomplished this great and essential end? By declaring, sir, that *"the Constitution and the laws of the United States, made in pursuance thereof, shall be the supreme law of the land, any thing in the Constitution or laws of any State to the contrary notwithstanding."*

This, sir, was the first great step. By this, the supremacy of the Constitution and laws of the United States is declared. The People so will it. No State law is to be valid, which comes in conflict with the Constitution, or any law of the United States. But who shall decide this question of interference? To whom lies the last appeal? This, sir, the Constitution itself decides, also by declaring, *"that the Judicial power shall extend to all cases arising under the Constitution and Laws of the United States."* These two provisions, sir, cover the whole ground. They are, in truth, the key-stone of the arch. With these, it is a Constitution; without them, it is a Confederacy. In pursuance of these clear and express provisions, Congress established, at its very first session, in the Judicial act, a mode for carrying them into full effect, and for bringing all questions of constitutional power to the final decision of the Supreme Court. It then, sir, became a Government. It then has the means of self-protection; and, but for this, it would, in all probability, have been now among things which are past. Having constituted the Government, and declared its powers, the People have further said, that since somebody must decide on the extent of these powers, the Government shall itself decide; subject, always, like other popular governments, to its responsibility to the People. And now, sir, I repeat, how is it that a State Legislature acquires any power to interfere? Who, or what, gives them the right to say to the People, "We, who are your agents and servants for one purpose, will undertake to decide, that your other agents and servants, appointed by you for another purpose, have transcended the authority you gave them!"? The reply would be, I think, not impertinent—"Who made you a judge over another's servants? To their own masters they stand or fall."

Sir, I deny this power of State Legislatures altogether. It cannot stand the test of examination. Gentlemen may say, that, in an extreme case, a State Government might protect the People from intolerable oppression. Sir, in such a case, the People might protect themselves, without the aid of the State Governments. Such a case warrants revolution. It must make, when it comes, a law for itself. A nullifying act of a State Legislature cannot alter the case, nor make resistance any more lawful. In maintaining these sentiments, sir, I am but asserting the rights of the People. I state what they have declared, and insist on their right to declare it. They have chosen to repose this power in the General Government, and I think it my duty to support it, like other constitutional powers. [. . .]

And now, Mr. President, let me run the honorable gentleman's doctrine a little into its practical application. Let us look at his probable *modus operandi*. If a thing can be done, an ingenious man can tell *how* it is to be done. Now, I wish to be informed *how* this State interference is to be put in practice, without violence, bloodshed, and rebellion. We will take the existing case of the Tariff law. South Carolina is said to have made up her opinion upon it. If we do not repeal it, (as we probably shall not,) she will then apply to the case the remedy of her doctrine. She will, we must suppose, pass a law of her Legislature, declaring the several acts of Congress, usually called the Tariff Laws, null and void, so far as they respect

South Carolina, or the citizens thereof. So far, all is a paper transaction, and easy enough. But the collector at Charleston is collecting the duties imposed by these Tariff Laws—he, therefore, must be stopped. The Collector will seize the goods if the Tariff duties are not paid. The State authorities will undertake their rescue: the Marshal, with his posse, will come to the Collector's aid, and here the contest begins. The militia of the State will be called out to sustain the nullifying act. They will march, sir, under a very gallant leader: for I believe the honorable member himself commands the militia of that part of the State. He will raise the NULLIFYING ACT on his standard, and spread it out as his banner! It will have a preamble, bearing, that the Tariff Laws are palpable, deliberate, and dangerous violations of the Constitution! He will proceed, with this banner flying, to the Customhouse in Charleston:

> All the while,
> Sonorous metal blowing martial sounds.

Arrived at the custom-house, he will tell the Collector that he must collect no more duties under any of the Tariff laws. This, he will be somewhat puzzled to say, by the way, with a grave countenance, considering what hand South Carolina herself had in that of 1816. But, sir, the Collector would, probably, not desist at his bidding—here would ensue a pause: for they say, that a certain stillness precedes the tempest. Before this military array should fall on the custom-house, collector, clerks, and all, it is very probable some of those composing it, would request of their gallant commander-in-chief, to be informed a little upon the point of law; for they have, doubtless, a just respect for his opinions as a lawyer, as well as for his bravery as a soldier. They know he has read Blackstone and the Constitution, as well as Turrene and Vauban. They would ask him, therefore, something concerning their rights in this matter. They would inquire, whether it was not somewhat dangerous to resist a law of the United States. What would be the nature of their offence, they would wish to learn, if they, by military force and array, resisted the execution in Carolina of a law of the United States, and it should turn out, after all, that the law *was constitutional?* He would answer, of course, treason. [. . .] We are not afraid of bullets, but treason has a way of taking people off, that we do not much relish. How do you propose to defend us? "Look at my floating banner," he would reply; "see there the *nullifying law!*" Is it your opinion, gallant commander, they would then say, that if we should be indicted for treason, that same floating banner of yours would make a good plea in bar? "South Carolina is a sovereign State," he would reply. That is true—but would the Judge admit our plea? "These tariff laws," he would repeat, "are unconstitutional, palpably, deliberately, dangerously." That all may be so; but if the tribunals should not happen to be of that opinion, shall we swing for it? We are ready to die for our country, but it is rather an awkward business, this dying without touching the ground! After all, that is a sort of *hemp*-tax, worse than any part of the Tariff.

Mr. President, the honorable gentleman would be in a dilemma, like that of another great General. He would have a knot before him, which he could not untie. He must cut it with his sword. He must say to his followers, defend yourselves with your bayonets; and this is war—civil war.

Direct collision, therefore, between force and force, is the unavoidable result of that remedy for the revision of unconstitutional laws which the gentleman contends for. [. . .]

[. . .] If any thing be found in the National Constitution, either by original provision, or subsequent interpretation, which ought not to be in it, the People know how to get rid of it. If any construction be established, unacceptable to them, so as to become, practically, a part of the Constitution, they will amend it, at their own sovereign pleasure. But while the people choose to maintain it, as it is; while they are satisfied with it, and refuse to change it; who has given, or who can give, to the State Legislatures a right to alter it, either by interference, construction, or otherwise? Gentlemen do not seem to recollect that the People have any power to do any thing for themselves; they imagine there is no safety for them, any longer than they are under the close guardianship of the State Legislatures. Sir, the People have not trusted their safety, in regard to the general Constitution, to these hands. They have required other security, and taken other bonds. They have chosen to trust themselves, first, to the plain words of the instrument, and to such construction as the Government itself, in doubtful cases, should put on its own powers, under their oaths of office, and subject to their responsibility to them; just as the People of a State trust their own State Governments with a similar power. Secondly, they have reposed their trust in the efficacy of frequent elections, and in their own power to remove their own servants and agents, whenever they see cause. Thirdly, they have reposed trust in the Judicial power, which, in order that it might be trust-worthy, they have made as respectable, as disinterested, and as independent as was practicable. Fourthly, they have seen fit to rely, in case of necessity, or high expediency, on their known and admitted power, to alter or amend the Constitution, peaceably and quietly, whenever experience shall point out defects or imperfections. And, finally, the People of the United States have, at no time, in no way, directly or indirectly, authorized any State Legislature to construe or interpret *their* high instrument of Government; much less to interfere, by their own power, to arrest its course and operation.

If, sir, the People, in these respects, had done otherwise than they have done, their Constitution could neither have been preserved, nor would it have been worth preserving. And, if its plain provisions shall now be disregarded, and these new doctrines interpolated in it, it will become as feeble and helpless a being as its enemies, whether early or more recent, could possibly desire. It will exist in every State, but as a poor dependent on State permission. It must borrow leave to be; and will be, no longer than State pleasure, or State discretion, sees fit to grant the indulgence, and to prolong its poor existence.

But, sir, although there are fears, there are hopes also. The People have preserved this, their own chosen Constitution, for forty years, and have seen their happiness, prosperity, and renown, grow with its growth, and strengthen with its strength. They are now, generally, strongly attached to it. Overthrown by direct assault, it cannot be; evaded, undermined, NULLIFIED, it will not be, if we, and those who shall succeed us here, as agents and representatives of the People, shall conscientiously and vigilantiy discharge the two great branches of our public trust—faithfully to preserve, and wisely to administer it.

Mr. President, I have thus stated the reasons of my dissent to the doctrines which have been advanced and maintained. I am conscious of having detained you and the Senate much too long. I was drawn into the debate, with no previous deliberation such as is suited to the discussion of so grave and important a subject. But it is a subject of which my heart is full, and I have not been willing to suppress the utterance of its spontaneous sentiments. I cannot, even now, persuade myself to relinquish it without expressing, once more, my deep conviction, that, since it respects nothing less than the Union of the States, it is of most vital and essential importance to the public happiness. I profess, sir, in my career, hitherto, to have kept steadily in view the prosperity and honor of the whole country, and the preservation of our Federal Union. It is to that Union we owe our safety at home, and our consideration and dignity abroad. It is to that Union that we are chiefly indebted for whatever makes us most proud of our country. That Union we reached only by the discipline of our virtues in the severe school of adversity. It had its origin in the necessities of disordered finance, prostrate commerce, and ruined credit. Under its benign influences, these great interests immediately awoke, as from the dead, and sprang forth with newness of life. Every year of its duration has teemed with fresh proofs of its utility and its blessings; and, although our territory has stretched out wider and wider, and our population spread farther and farther, they have not outrun its protection or its benefits. It has been to us all a copious fountain of national, social, and personal happiness. I have not allowed myself, sir, to look beyond the Union, to see what might lie hidden in the dark recess behind. I have not coolly weighed the chances of preserving liberty, when the bonds that unite us together shall be broken asunder. I have not accustomed myself to hang over the precipice of disunion, to see whether, with my short sight, I can fathom the depth of the abyss below; nor could I regard him as a safe counsellor in the affairs of this Government, whose thoughts should be mainly bent on considering, not how the Union should be best preserved, but how tolerable might be the condition of the People when it shall be broken up and destroyed. While the Union lasts, we have high, exciting, gratifying prospects spread out before us, for us and our children. Beyond that I seek not to penetrate the veil. God grant that, in my day, at least, that curtain may not rise. God grant that on my vision never may be opened what lies behind. When my eyes shall be turned to behold, for the last time, the sun in Heaven, may I not see him shining on the broken and dishonored fragments of a once glorious Union; on States dissevered, discordant, belligerent; on a land rent with civil feuds, or drenched, it may be, in fraternal blood! Let their last feeble and lingering glance, rather behold the gorgeous Ensign of the Republic, now known and honored throughout the earth, still full high advanced, its arms and trophies streaming in their original lustre, not a stripe erased or polluted, nor a single star obscured—bearing for its motto, no such miserable interrogatory as, *What is all this worth?* Nor those other words of delusion and folly, *Liberty first, and Union afterwards*—but every where, spread all over in characters of living light, blazing on all its ample folds, as they float over the sea and over the land, and in every wind under the whole Heavens, that other sentiment, dear to every true American heart—Liberty *and* Union, now and forever, one and inseparable!

HENRY HIGHLAND GARNET

An Address to the Slaves of the United States of America (1843)

Your brethren of the North, East, and West have been accustomed to meet together in National Conventions, to sympathize with each other, and to weep over your unhappy condition. In these meetings we have addressed all classes of the free, but we have never, until this time, sent a word of consolation and advice to you. We have been contented in sitting still and mourning over your sorrows, earnestly hoping that before this day your sacred liberties would have been restored. But, we have hoped in vain. Years have rolled on, and tens of thousands have been borne on streams of blood and tears to the shores of eternity. While you have been oppressed, we have also been partakers with you; nor can we be free while you are enslaved. We, therefore, write to you as being bound with you.

Many of you are bound to us, not only by the ties of a common humanity, but we are connected by the more tender relations of parents, wives, husbands, and sisters, and friends. As such we most affectionately address you.

Slavery has fixed a deep gulf between you and us, and while it shuts out from you the relief and consolation which your friends would willingly render, it afflicts and persecutes you with a fierceness which we might not expect to see in fiends of hell. But still the Almighty Father of mercies has left to us a glimmering ray of hope, which shines out like a lone star in a cloudy sky. Mankind are becoming wiser, and better—the oppressor's power is fading, and you, every day, are becoming better informed, and more numerous. Your grievances, brethren, are many. We shall not attempt, in this short address, to present to the world all the dark catalogue of the nation's sins, which have been committed upon an innocent people. Nor is it indeed necessary, for you feel them from day to day, and all the civilized world looks upon them with amazement.

Two hundred and twenty-seven years ago the first of our injured race were brought to the shores of America. They came not with glad spirits to select their homes in the New World. They came not with their own consent, to find an unmolested enjoyment of the blessings of this fruitful soil. The first dealings they had with men calling themselves Christians exhibited to them the worst features of corrupt and sordid hearts: and convinced them that no cruelty is too great, no villainy and no robbery too abhorrent for even enlightened men to perform, when influenced by avarice and lust. Neither did they come flying upon the wings of Liberty to a land of freedom. But they came with broken hearts, from their beloved native land, and were doomed to unrequited toil and deep degradation. Nor did the evil of their bondage end at their emancipation by death. Succeeding generations inherited their chains, and millions have come from eternity into time, and have returned again to the world of spirits, cursed and ruined by American slavery.

The propagators of the system, or their immediate successors, very soon discovered its growing evil, and its tremendous wickedness, and secret promises were made to destroy it. The gross inconsistency of a people holding slaves, who had themselves "ferried o'er the wave" for freedom's sake, was too apparent to be entirely overlooked. The voice of Freedom cried, "Emancipate your slaves." Humanity supplicated with tears for the deliverance of the children of Africa. Wisdom urged her solemn plea. The bleeding captive plead his innocence, and pointed to Christianity who stood weeping at the cross. Jehovah frowned upon the nefarious institution, and thunderbolts, red with vengeance, struggled to leap forth to blast the guilty wretches who maintained it. But all was vain. Slavery had stretched its dark wings of death over the land, the Church stood silently by—the priests prophesied falsely, and the people loved to have it so. Its throne is established, and now it reigns triumphant.

Nearly three millions of your fellow-citizens are prohibited by law and public opinion (which in this country is stronger than law) from reading the Book of Life. Your intellect has been destroyed as much as possible, and every ray of light they have attempted to shut out from your minds. The oppressors themselves have become involved in the ruin. They have become weak, sensual, and rapacious—they have cursed you—they have cursed themselves—they have cursed the earth which they have trod. [. . .]

SLAVERY! How much misery is comprehended in that single word. What mind is there that does not shrink from its direful effects? Unless the image of God be obliterated from the soul, all men cherish the love of liberty. The nice discerning political economist does not regard the sacred right more than the untutored African who roams in the wilds of Congo. Nor has the one more right to the full enjoyment of his freedom than the other. In every man's mind the good seeds of liberty are planted, and he who brings his fellow down so low, as to make him contented with a condition of slavery, commits the highest crime against God and man. [. . .]

Brethren, the time has come when you must act for yourselves. It is an old and true saying that, "if hereditary bondmen would be free, they must themselves strike the blow." You can plead your own cause, and do the work of emancipation better than any others. [. . .] Think of the undying glory that hangs around the ancient name of Africa—and forget not that you are native-born American citizens, and as such you are justly entitled to all the rights that are granted to the freest. Think how many tears you have poured out upon the soil which you have cultivated with unrequited toil and enriched with your blood; and then go to your lordly enslavers and tell them plainly, that you *are determined to be free*. Appeal to their sense of justice, and tell them that they have no more right to oppress you than you have to enslave them. Entreat them to remove the grievous burdens which they have imposed upon you, and to remunerate you for your labor. Promise them renewed diligence in the cultivation of the soil, if they will render to you an equivalent for your services. Point them to the increase of happiness and prosperity in the British West Indies since the Act of Emancipation. Tell them in language which they cannot misunderstand of the exceeding sinfulness of slavery, and of a future judgment, and of the righteous retributions of an indignant God. Inform them that all you desire is FREEDOM, and that nothing else will suffice. Do this, and forever after cease to toil for the heartless tyrants, who give you no other reward but stripes and abuse. If they then commence work of death, they, and not you, will be responsible for the consequences. You had far better all die—*die immediately*, than live slaves, and entail your wretchedness upon your posterity. [. . .]

Fellowmen! patient sufferers! behold your dearest rights crushed to the earth! See your sons murdered, and your wives, mothers and sisters doomed to prostitution. In the name of the merciful God, and by all that life is worth, let it no longer be a debatable question, whether it is better to choose *liberty* or *death*.

In 1822, Denmark Veazie, of South Carolina, formed a plan for the liberation of his fellowmen. In the whole history of human efforts to overthrow slavery, a more complicated and tremendous plan was never formed. He was betrayed by the treachery of his own people, and died a martyr to freedom. Many a brave hero fell, but history, faithful to her high trust, will transcribe his name on the same monument with Moses, Hampden, Tell, Bruce, and Wallace, Toussaint L'Ouverture, Lafayette, and Washington. [. . .]

The patriotic Nathaniel Turner followed Denmark Veazie. He was goaded to desperation by wrong and injustice. By despotism, his name has been recorded on the list of infamy, and future generations will remember him among the noble and brave.

Next arose the immortal Joseph Cinque, the hero of the Amistad. He was a native African, and by the help of God he emancipated a whole ship-load of his fellowmen on the high seas. And he now sings of liberty on the sunny hills of Africa and beneath his native palm-trees, where he hears the lion roar and feels himself as free as the king of the forest.

Next arose Madison Washington, that bright star of freedom, and took his station in the constellation of true heroism. He was a slave on board the brig *Creole*, of Richmond, bound to New Orleans, that great slave mart, with a hundred and four others. Nineteen struck for liberty or death. But one life was taken, and the whole were emancipated, and the vessel was carried into Nassau, New Providence.

Noble men! Those who have fallen in freedom's conflict, their memories will be cherished by the true-hearted and the God-fearing in all future generations; those who are living, their names are surrounded by a halo of glory.

Brethren, arise, arise! Strike for your lives and liberties. Now is the day and the hour. Let every slave throughout the land do this, and the days of slavery are numbered. You cannot be more oppressed than you have been—you cannot suffer greater cruelties than you have already. *Rather die freemen than live to be slaves.* Remember that you are FOUR MILLIONS! [. . .]

Let your motto be resistance! *resistance!* RESISTANCE! No oppressed people have ever secured their liberty without resistance. What kind of resistance you had better make you must decide by the circumstances that surround you, and according to the suggestion of expediency. Brethren, adieu! Trust in the living God. Labor for the peace of the human race, and remember that you are FOUR MILLIONS!

FREDERICK DOUGLASS

What to the Slave Is the Fourth of July? (1852)

Mr. President, Friends and Fellow Citizens: He who could address this audience without a quailing sensation, has stronger nerves than I have. I do not remember ever to have appeared as a speaker before any assembly more shrinkingly, nor with greater distrust of my ability, than I do this day. A feeling has crept over me, quite unfavorable to the exercise of my limited powers of speech. The task before me is one which requires much previous thought and study for its proper performance. I know that apologies of this sort are generally considered flat and unmeaning. I trust, however, that mine will not be so considered. Should I seem at ease, my appearance would much misrepresent me. The little experience I have had in addressing public meetings, in country school houses, avails me nothing on the present occasion.

The papers and placards say, that I am to deliver a 4th [of] July oration. This certainly, sounds large, and out of the common way, for me. It is true that I have often had the privilege to speak in this beautiful Hall, and to address many who now honor me with their presence. But neither their familiar faces, nor the perfect gage I think I have of Corinthian Hall, seems to free me from embarrassment.

The fact is, ladies and gentlemen, the distance between this platform and the slave plantation, from which I escaped, is considerable—and the difficulties to be overcome in getting from the latter to the former, are by no means slight. That I am here to-day, is, to me, a matter of astonishment as well as of gratitude. You will not, therefore, be surprised, if in what I have to say, I evince no elaborate preparation, nor grace my speech with any high sounding exordium. With little experience and with less learning, I have been able to throw my thoughts hastily and imperfectly together; and trusting to your patient and generous indulgence, I will proceed to lay them before you.

This, for the purpose of this celebration, is the 4th of July. It is the birthday of your National Independence, and of your political freedom. This, to you, is what the Passover was to the emancipated people of God. It carries your minds back to the day, and to the act of your great deliverance; and to the signs, and to the wonders, associated with that act, and that day. This celebration also marks the beginning of another year of your national life; and reminds you that the Republic of America is now 76 years old. I am glad, fellow-citizens, that your nation is so young. Seventy-six years, though a good old age for a man, is but a mere speck in the life of a nation. Three score years and ten is the allotted time for individual men; but nations number their years by thousands. According to this fact, you are, even now only in the beginning of your national career, still lingering in the period of childhood. I repeat, I am glad this is so. There is hope in the thought, and hope is much needed, under the dark clouds which lower above the horizon. The eye of the reformer is met with angry flashes, portending disastrous times; but his heart may well beat lighter at the thought that America is young, and that she is still in the impressible stage of her existence. May he not hope that high lessons of wisdom, of justice and of truth, will yet give direction to her destiny? Were the nation older, the patriot's heart might be sadder, and the reformer's brow heavier. Its future might be shrouded in gloom, and the hope of its prophets go out in sorrow. There is consolation in the thought, that America is young.—Great streams are not easily turned from channels, worn deep in the course of ages. They may sometimes rise in quiet and stately majesty, and inundate the land, refreshing and fertilizing the earth with their mysterious properties. They may also rise in wrath and fury, and bear away, on their angry waves, the accumulated wealth of years of toil and hardship. They, however, gradually flow back to the same old channel, and flow on as serenely as ever. But, while the river may not be turned aside, it may dry up, and leave nothing behind but the withered branch, and the unsightly rock, to howl in the abyss-sweeping wind, the sad tale of departed glory. As with rivers so with nations.

Fellow-citizens, I shall not presume to dwell at length on the associations that cluster about this day. The simple story of it is, that, 76 years ago, the people of this country were British subjects. The style and title of your "sovereign people" (in which you now glory) was not then born. You were under the British Crown. Your fathers esteemed the English Government as the home government; and England as the fatherland. This home government, you know, although a considerable distance from your home, did, in the exercise of its parental prerogatives, impose upon its colonial children, such restraints, burdens and limitations, as, in its mature judgment, it deemed wise, right and proper.

But, your fathers, who had not adopted the fashionable idea of this day, of the infallibility of government, and the absolute character of its acts, presumed to differ from the home government in respect to the wisdom and the justice of some of those burdens and restraints. They went so far in their excitement as to pronounce the measures of government unjust, unreasonable, and oppressive, and altogether such as ought not to be quietly submitted to. I scarcely need say, fellow-citizens, that my opinion of those measures fully accords with that of your fathers. Such a declaration of agreement on my part, would not be worth much to anybody. It would, certainly, prove nothing, as to what part I might have taken, had I lived during the great controversy of 1776. To say *now* that America was right, and England wrong, is exceedingly easy. Everybody can say it; the dastard, not less than the noble brave, can flippantly discant on the tyranny of England towards the American Colonies. It is fashionable to do so; but there was a time when, to pronounce against England, and in favor of the cause of the colonies, tried men's souls. They who did so were accounted in their day, plotters of mischief, agitators and rebels, dangerous men. To side with the right, against the wrong, with the weak against the strong, and with the oppressed against the oppressor! *here* lies the merit, and the one which, of all others, seems unfashionable in our day. The cause of liberty may be stabbed by the men who glory in the deeds of your fathers. But, to proceed.

Feeling themselves harshly and unjustly treated, by the home government, your fathers, like men of honesty, and men of spirit, earnestly sought redress. They petitioned and remonstrated; they did so in a decorous, respectful, and loyal manner. Their conduct was wholly unexceptionable. This, however, did not answer the purpose. They saw themselves treated with sovereign indifference, coldness and scorn. Yet they persevered. They were not the men to look back.

As the sheet anchor takes a firmer hold, when the ship is tossed by the storm, so did the cause of your fathers grow stronger, as it breasted the chilling blasts of kingly displeasure. The greatest and best of British statesmen admitted its justice, and the loftiest eloquence of the British Senate came to its support. But, with that blindness which seems to be the unvarying characteristic of tyrants, since Pharoah and his hosts were drowned in the Red sea, the British Government persisted in the exactions complained of.

The madness of this course, we believe, is admitted now, even by England; but we fear the lesson is wholly lost on our present rulers.

Oppression makes a wise man mad. Your fathers were wise men, and if they did not go mad, they became restive under this treatment. They felt themselves the victims of grievous wrongs, wholly incurable in their colonial capacity. With brave men there is always a remedy for oppression. Just here, the idea of a total separation of the colonies from the crown was born! It was a startling idea, much more so, than we, at this distance of time, regard it. The timid and the prudent (as has been intimated) of that day, were, of course, shocked and alarmed by it. [. . .]

On the 2d of July, 1776, the old Continental Congress, to the dismay of the lovers of ease, and the worshippers of property, clothed that dreadful idea with all the authority of national sanction. They did so in the form of a resolution; and as we seldom hit upon resolutions, drawn up in our day, whose transparency is at all equal to this, it may refresh your minds and help my story if I read it.

> Resolved, That these united colonies *are*, and of right, ought to be free and Independent States; that they are absolved from all allegiance to the British Crown; and that all political connection between them and the State of Great Britain is, and ought to be, dissolved.

Citizens, your fathers made good that resolution. They succeeded; and to-day you reap the fruits of their success. The freedom gained is yours; and you, therefore, may properly celebrate this anniversary. The 4th of July is the first great fact in your nation's history—the very ring-bolt in the chain of your yet undeveloped destiny.

Pride and patriotism, not less than gratitude, prompt you to celebrate and to hold it in perpetual remembrance. I have said that the Declaration of Independence is the ring-bolt to the chain of your nation's destiny; so, indeed, I regard it. The principles contained in that instrument are saving principles. Stand by those principles, be true to them on all occasions, in all places, against all foes, and at whatever cost. [. . .]

Fellow Citizens, I am not wanting in respect for the fathers of this republic. The signers of the Declaration of Independence were brave men. They were great men too—great enough to give fame to a great age. It does not often happen to a nation to raise, at one time, such a number of truly great men. The point from which I am compelled to view them is not, certainly, the most favorable; and yet I cannot contemplate their great deeds with less than admiration. They were statesmen, patriots and heroes, and for the good they did, and the principles they contended for, I will unite with you to honor their memory.

They loved their country better than their own private interests; and, though this is not the highest form of human excellence, all will concede that it is a rare virtue, and that when it is exhibited, it ought to command respect. He who will, intelligently, lay down his life for his country, is a man whom it is not in human nature to despise. Your fathers staked their lives, their fortunes, and their sacred honor, on the cause of their country. In their admiration of liberty, they lost sight of all other interests.

They were peace men; but they preferred revolution to peaceful submission to bondage. They were quiet men; but they did not shrink from agitating against oppression. They showed forbearance; but that they knew its limits. They believed in order; but not in the order of tyranny. With them, nothing was *"settled"* that was not right. With them, justice, liberty and humanity were *"final;"* not slavery and oppression. You may well cherish the memory of such men. They were great in their day and generation. Their solid manhood stands out the more as we contrast it with these degenerate times.

How circumspect, exact and proportionate were all their movements! How unlike the politicians of an hour! Their statesmanship looked beyond the passing moment, and stretched away in strength into the distant future. They seized upon eternal principles, and set a glorious example in their defence. Mark them! [. . .]

We have to do with the past only as we can make it useful to the present and to the future. To all inspiring motives, to noble deeds which can be gained from the past, we are welcome. But now is the time, the important time. Your fathers have lived, died, and have done their work, and have done much of it well. You live and must die, and you must do your work. You have no right to enjoy a child's share in the labor of your fathers, unless your children are to be blest by your labors. You have no right to wear out and waste the hard-earned fame of your fathers to cover your indolence. Sydney Smith tells us that men seldom eulogize the wisdom and virtues of their fathers, but to excuse some folly or wickedness of their own. This truth is not a doubtful one. There are illustrations of it near and remote, ancient and modern. It was fashionable, hundreds of years ago, for the children of Jacob to boast, we have "Abraham to our father," when they had long lost Abraham's faith and spirit. That people contented themselves under the shadow of Abraham's great name, while they repudiated the deeds which made his name great. Need I remind you that a similar thing is being done all over this country to-day? Need I tell you that the Jews are not the only people who built the tombs of the prophets, and garnished the sepulchres of the righteous? Washington could not die till he had broken the chains of his slaves. Yet his monument is built up by the price of human blood, and the traders in the bodies and souls of men, shout—"We have Washington to *our father.*" Alas! that it should be so; yet so it is.

The evil that men do, lives after them,
The good is oft' interred with their bones.

Fellow-citizens, pardon me, allow me to ask, why am I called upon to speak here to-day? What have I, or those I represent, to do with your national independence? Are the great principles of political freedom and of natural justice, embodied in that Declaration of Independence, extended to us? and am I, therefore, called upon to bring our humble offering to the national altar, and to confess the benefits and express devout gratitude for the blessings resulting from your independence to us?

Would to God, both for your sakes and ours, that an affirmative answer could be truthfully returned to these questions! Then would my task be light, and my burden easy and delightful. For *who* is there so cold, that a nation's sympathy could not warm him? Who so obdurate and dead to the claims of gratitude, that would not thankfully acknowledge such priceless benefits? Who so stolid and selfish, that would not give his voice to swell the hallelujahs of a nation's jubilee, when the chains of servitude had been torn from his limbs? I am not that man. In a case like that, the dumb might eloquently speak, and the "lame man leap as an hart."

But, such is not the state of the case. I say it with a sad sense of the disparity between us. I am not included within the pale of this glorious anniversary! Your high independence only reveals the immeasurable distance between us. The blessings in which you, this day, rejoice, are not enjoyed in common.—The rich inheritance of justice, liberty, prosperity and independence, bequeathed by your fathers, is shared by you, not by me. The sunlight that brought life and healing to you, has brought stripes and death to me. This Fourth [of] July is *yours*, not *mine*. *You* may rejoice, I must mourn. To drag a man in fetters into the grand illuminated temple of liberty, and call upon him to join you in joyous anthems, were inhuman mockery and sacrilegious irony. Do you mean, citizens, to mock me, by asking me to speak to-day? If so, there is a parallel to your conduct. And let me warn you that it is dangerous to copy the example of a nation whose crimes, towering up to heaven, were thrown down by the breath of the Almighty, burying that nation in irrecoverable ruin! I can to-day take up the plaintive lament of a peeled and woe-smitten people!

"By the rivers of Babylon, there we sat down. Yea! we wept when we remembered Zion. We hanged our harps upon the willows in the midst thereof. For there, they that carried us away captive, required of us a song; and they who wasted us required of us mirth, saying, Sing us one of the songs of Zion. How can we sing the Lord's song in a strange land? If I forget thee, O Jerusalem, let my right hand forget her cunning. If I do not remember thee, let my tongue cleave to the roof of my mouth."

Fellow-citizens; above your national, tumultous joy, I hear the mournful wail of millions! whose chains, heavy and grievous yesterday, are, to-day, rendered more intolerable by the jubilee shouts that reach them. If I do forget, if I do not faithfully remember those bleeding children of sorrow this day, "may my right hand forget her cunning, and may my tongue cleave to the roof of my mouth!" To forget them, to pass lightly over their wrongs, and to chime in with the popular theme, would be treason most scandalous and shocking, and would make me a reproach before God and the world. My subject, then, fellow-citizens, is AMERICAN SLAVERY. I shall see, this day, and its popular characteristics, from the slave's point of view. Standing, there, identified with the American bondman, making his wrongs mine, I do not hesitate to declare, with all my soul, that the character and conduct of this nation never looked blacker to me than on this 4th of July! Whether we turn to the declarations of the past, or to the professions of the present, the conduct of the nation seems equally hideous and revolting. America is false to the past, false to the present, and solemnly binds herself to be false to the future. Standing with God and the crushed and bleeding slave on this occasion, I will, in the name of humanity which is outraged, in the name of liberty which is fettered, in the name of the constitution and the Bible, which are disregarded and trampled upon, dare to call in question and to denounce, with all the emphasis I can command, everything that serves to perpetuate slavery—the great sin and shame of America! "I will not equivocate; I will not excuse;" I will use the severest language I can command; and yet not one word shall escape me that any man, whose judgment is not blinded by prejudice, or who is not at heart a slaveholder, shall not confess to be right and just.

But I fancy I hear some one of my audience say, it is just in this circumstance that you and your brother abolitionists fail to make a favorable impression on the public mind. Would you argue more, and denounce less, would you persuade more, and rebuke less, your cause would be much more likely to succeed. But, I submit, where all is plain there is nothing to be argued. What point in the anti-slavery creed would you have me argue? On what branch of the subject do the people of this country need light? Must I undertake to prove that the slave is a man? That point is conceded already. Nobody doubts it. The slaveholders themselves acknowledge it in the enactment of laws for their government. They acknowledge it when they punish disobedience on the part of the slave. There are seventy-two crimes in the State of Virginia, which, if committed by a black man, (no matter how ignorant he be,) subject him to the punishment of death; while only two of the same crimes will subject a white man to the like punishment.—What is this but the acknowledgement that the slave is a moral, intellectual and responsible being? The manhood of the slave is conceded. It is admitted in the fact that Southern statute books are covered with enactments forbidding, under severe fines and penalties, the teaching of the slave to read or to write.—When you can point to any such laws, in reference to the beasts of the field, then I may consent to argue the manhood of the slave. When the dogs in your streets, when the fowls of the air, when the cattle on your hills, when the fish of the sea, and the reptiles that crawl, shall be unable to distinguish the slave from a brute, *then* will I argue with you that the slave is a man!

For the present, it is enough to affirm the equal manhood of the negro race. Is it not astonishing that, while we are ploughing, planting and reaping, using all kinds of mechanical tools, erecting houses, constructing bridges, building ships, working in metals of brass, iron, copper, silver and gold; that, while we are reading, writing and cyphering, acting as clerks, merchants and secretaries, having among us lawyers, doctors, ministers, poets, authors, editors, orators and teachers; that, while we are engaged in all manner of enterprises common to other men, digging gold in California, capturing the whale in the Pacific, feeding sheep and cattle on the hill-side, living, moving, acting, thinking, planning, living in families as husbands, wives and children, and, above all, confessing and worshipping the Christian's God, and looking hopefully for life and immortality beyond the grave, we are called upon to prove that we are men!

Would you have me argue that man is entitled to liberty? that he is the rightful owner of his own body? You have already declared it. Must I argue the wrongfulness of slavery? Is that a question for Republicans? Is it to be settled by the rules of logic and argumentation, as a matter beset with great difficulty, involving a doubtful application of the principle of justice, hard to be understood? How should I look today, in the presence of Americans, dividing, and subdividing a discourse, to show that men have a natural right to freedom? speaking of it relatively, and positively, negatively, and affirmatively. To do so, would be to make myself ridiculous, and to offer an insult to your understanding.—There is not a man beneath the canopy of heaven, that does not know that slavery is wrong *for him.*

What, am I to argue that it is wrong to make men brutes, to rob them of their liberty, to work them without wages, to keep them ignorant of their relations to their fellow men, to beat them with sticks, to flay their flesh with the lash, to load their limbs with irons, to hunt them with dogs, to sell them at auction, to sunder their families, to knock out their teeth, to burn their flesh, to starve them into obedience and submission to their masters? Must I argue that a system thus marked with blood, and stained with pollution, is *wrong?* No! I will not. I have better employments for my time and strength, than such arguments would imply.

What, then, remains to be argued? Is it that slavery is not divine; that God did not establish it; that our doctors of divinity are mistaken? There is blasphemy in the thought. That which is inhuman, cannot be divine! *Who* can reason on such a proposition? They that can, may; I cannot. The time for such argument is past.

At a time like this, scorching irony, not convincing argument, is needed. O! had I the ability, and could I reach the nation's ear, I would, to-day, pour out a fiery stream of biting ridicule, blasting reproach, withering sarcasm, and stern rebuke. For it is not light that is needed, but fire; it is not the gentle shower, but thunder. We need the storm, the whirlwind, and the earthquake. The feeling of the nation must be quickened; the conscience of the nation must be roused; the propriety of the nation must be startled; the hypocrisy of the nation must be exposed; and its crimes against God and man must be proclaimed and denounced.

What, to the American slave, is your 4th of July? I answer; a day that reveals to him, more than all other days in the year, the gross injustice and cruelty to which he is the constant victim. To him, your celebration is a sham; your boasted liberty, an unholy license; your national greatness, swelling vanity; your sounds of rejoicing are empty and heartless; your denunciations of tyrants, brass fronted impudence; your shouts of liberty and equality, hollow mockery; your prayers and hymns, your sermons and thanksgivings, with all your religious parade, and solemnity, are, to him, mere bombast, fraud, deception, impiety, and hypocrisy—a thin veil to cover up crimes which would disgrace a nation of savages. There is not a nation on the earth guilty of practices, more shocking and bloody, than are the people of these United States, at this very hour.

Go where you may, search where you will, roam through all the monarchies and despotisms of the old world, travel through South America, search out every abuse, and when you have found the last, lay your facts by the side of the every day practices of this nation, and you will say with me, that, for revolting barbarity and shameless hypocrisy, America reigns without a rival. [. . .]

By an act of the American Congress, not yet two years old, slavery has been nationalized in its most horrible and revolting form. By that act, Mason & Dixon's line has been obliterated; New York has become as Virginia; and the power to hold, hunt, and sell men, women, and children, as slaves remains no longer a mere state institution, but is now an institution of the whole United States. The power is coextensive with the star-spangled banner, and American Christianity. Where these go, may also go the merciless slave-hunter. Where these are, man is not sacred. He is a bird for the sportsman's gun. By that most foul and fiendish of all human decrees, the liberty and person of every man are put in peril. Your broad republican domain is hunting ground for *men. Not* for thieves and robbers, enemies of society, merely, but for men guilty of no crime. Your law-makers have commanded all good citizens to engage in this hellish sport. Your President, your Secretary of State, your *lords, nobles*, and ecclesiastics, enforce, as a duty you owe to your free and glorious country, and to your God, that you do this accursed thing. Not fewer than forty Americans have, within the past two years, been hunted down, and, without a moment's warning, hurried away in chains, and consigned to slavery, and excruciating torture. Some of these have had wives and children, dependent on them for bread; but of this, no account was made. The right of the hunter to his prey stands superior to the right of marriage, and to *all* rights in this republic, the rights of God included! For black men there are neither law, justice, humanity, nor religion. The Fugitive Slave *Law* makes MERCY TO THEM, A CRIME; and bribes the judge who tries them. An American JUDGE GETS TEN DOLLARS FOR EVERY VICTIM HE CONSIGNS to slavery, and five, when he fails to do so. The oath of any two villains is sufficient, under this hell-black enactment, to send the most pious and exemplary black man into the remorseless jaws of slavery! His own testimony is nothing. He can bring no witnesses for himself. The minister of American justice is bound by the law to hear but *one* side; and *that* side, is the side of the oppressor. Let this damning fact be perpetually told. Let it be thundered around the world, that, in tyrant-killing, king-hating, people-loving, democratic, Christian America, the seats of justice are filled with judges, who hold their offices under an open and palpable *bribe*, and are bound, in deciding in the case of a man's liberty, *to hear only his accusers!*

In glaring violation of justice, in shameless disregard of the forms of administering law, in cunning arrangement to entrap the defenceless, and in diabolical intent, this Fugitive Slave Law stands alone in the annals of tyrannical legislation. I doubt if there be another nation on the globe, having the brass and the baseness to put such a law on the statute-book. If any man in this assembly thinks differently from me in this matter, and feels able to disprove my statements, I will gladly confront him at any suitable time and place he may select.

I take this law to be one of the grossest infringements of Christian Liberty, and, if the churches and ministers of our country were not stupidly blind, or most wickedly indifferent, they, too, would so regard it.

At the very moment that they are thanking God for the enjoymen of civil and religious liberty, and for the right to worship God acording to the dictates of their own consciences, they are utterly silent in respect to a law which robs religion of its chief significance, and makes it utterly worthless to a world lying in wickedness. Did this law concern the "*mint, anise* and *cummin*"—abridge the right to sing psalms, to partake of the sacrament, or to engage in any of the ceremonies of religion, it would be smitten by the thunder of a thousand pulpits. A general shout would go up from the church, demanding *repeal, repeal, instant repeal!*—And it would go hard with that politcian who presumed to solicit the votes of the people without inscribing this motto on his banner. [. . .] The fact that the church of our country, (with fractional exceptions,) does not esteem "the Fugitive Slave Law" as a declaration of war against religious liberty, implies that that church regards religion simply as a form of worship, an empty ceremony, and *not* a vital principle, requiring active benevolence, justice, love and good will towards man. It esteems sacrifice above mercy; psalm-singing above right doing; solemn meetings above practical righteousness. A worship that can be conducted by persons who refuse to give shelter to the houseless, to give bread to the hungry, clothing to the naked, and who enjoin obedience to a law forbidding these acts of mercy, is a curse, not a blessing to mankind. The Bible addresses all such persons as "scribes, pharisees, hypocrites, who pay tithe of *mint, anise*, and *cummin*, and have omitted the weightier matters of the law, judgment, mercy and faith." [. . .]

Americans! your republican politics, not less than your republican religion, are flagrantly inconsistent. You boast of your love of liberty, your superior civilization, and your pure Christianity, while the whole political power of the nation, as embodied in the two great political parties, is solemnly pledged to support and perpetuate the enslavement of three millions of your countrymen. You hurl your anathemas at the crowned headed tyrants of Russia and Austria, and pride yourselves on your Democratic institutions, while you yourselves consent to be the mere *tools* and *body-guards* of the tyrants of Virginia and Carolina. You invite to your shores fugitives of oppression from abroad, honor them with banquets, greet them with ovations, cheer them, toast them, salute them, protect them, and pour out your money to them like water; but the fugitives from your own land, you advertise, hunt, arrest, shoot and kill. You glory in your refinement and your universal education; yet you maintain a system as barbarous and dreadful, as ever stained the character of a nation—a system begun in avarice, supported in pride, and perpetuated in cruelty. You shed tears over fallen Hungary, and make the sad story of her wrongs the theme of your poets, statesmen and orators, till your gallant sons are ready to fly to arms to vindicate her cause against her oppressors; but, in regard to the ten thousand wrongs of the American slave, you would enforce the strictest silence, and would hail him as an enemy of the nation who dares to make those wrongs the subject of public discourse! You are all on fire at the mention of liberty for France or for Ireland; but are as cold as an iceberg at the thought of liberty for the enslaved of America.—You discourse eloquently on the dignity of labor; yet, you sustain a system which, in its very essence, casts a stigma upon labor. You can bare your bosom to the storm of British artillery, to throw off a threepenny tax on tea; and yet wring the last hard-earned farthing from the grasp of the black laborers of your country. You profess to believe "that, of one blood, God made all nations of men to dwell on the face of all the earth." and hath commanded all men, everywhere to love one another; yet you notoriously hate, (and glory in your hatred,) all men whose skins are not colored like your own. You declare, before the world, and are understood by the world to declare, that you "*hold these truths to be self evident, that all men are created equal; and are endowed by their Creator with certain inalienable rights; and that, among these are, life, liberty, and the pursuit of happiness;*" and yet, you hold securely, in a bondage, which according to your own Thomas Jefferson, "*is worse than ages of that which your fathers rose in rebellion to oppose,*" *a seventh part* of the inhabitants of your country.

Fellow-citizens! I will not enlarge further on your national inconsistencies. The existence of slavery in this country brands your republicanism as a sham, your humanity as a base pretence, and your Christianity as a lie. It destroys your moral power abroad; it corrupts your politicians at home. It saps the foundation of religion; it makes your name a hissing, and a by-word to a mocking earth. It is the antagonistic force in your government, the only thing that seriously disturbs and endangers your *Union*. It fetters your progress; it is the enemy of improvement, the deadly foe of education; it fosters pride; it breeds insolence; it promotes vice; it shelters crime; it is a curse to the earth that supports it; and yet, you cling to it, as if it were the sheet anchor of all your hopes. Oh! be warned! be warned! a horrible reptile is coiled up in your nation's bosom; the venomous creature is nursing at the tender breast of your youthful republic; *for the love of God, tear away,* and fling from you the hideous monster, and *let the weight of twenty millions, crush and destroy it forever!*

But it is answered in reply to all this, that precisely what I have now denounced is, in fact, guaranteed and sanctioned by the Constitution of the United States; that the right to hold, and to hunt slaves is a part of that Constitution framed by the illustrious Fathers of this Republic.

Then, I dare to affirm, notwithstanding all I have said before, your fathers stooped, basely stooped

> To palter with us in a double sense:
> And keep the word of promise to the ear,
> But break it to the heart.

And instead of being the honest men I have before declared them to be, they were the veriest imposters that ever practised on mankind. *This* is the inevitable conclusion, and from it there is no escape; but I differ from those who charge this baseness on the framers of the Constitution of the United States. *It is a slander upon their memory*, at least, so I believe. There is not time now to argue the constitutional question at length; nor have I the ability to discuss it as it ought to be discussed. The subject has been handled with masterly power by Lysander Spooner, Esq., by William Goodell, by Samuel E. Sewall, Esq., and last, though not least, by Gerritt Smith, Esq. These gentlemen have, as I think, fully and clearly vindicated the Constitution from any design to support slavery for an hour.

Fellow-citizens! there is no matter in respect to which, the people of the North have allowed themselves to be so ruinously imposed upon, as that of the pro-slavery character of the Constitution. In *that* instrument I hold there is neither warrant, license, nor sanction of the hateful thing; but, interpreted, as it *ought* to be interpreted, the Constitution is a GLORIOUS LIBERTY DOCUMENT. Read its preamble, consider its purposes. Is slavery among them? Is it at the gateway? or is it in the temple? it is neither. While I do not intend to argue this question on the present occasion, let me ask, if it be not somewhat singular that, if the Constitution were intended to be, by its framers and adopters, a slave-holding instrument, why neither *slavery*, *slaveholding*, nor *slave* can anywhere be found in it. What would be thought of an instrument, drawn up, *legally* drawn up, for the purpose of entitling the city of Rochester to a track of land, in which no mention of land was made? Now, there are certain rules of interpretation, for the proper understanding of all legal instruments. These rules are well established. They are plain, common-sense rules, such as you and I, and all of us, can understand and apply, without having passed years in the study of law. I scout the idea that the question of the constitutionality, or unconstitutionality of slavery is not a question for the people. I hold that every American citizen has a right to form an opinion of the Constitution, and to propagate that opinion, and to use all honorable means to make his opinion the prevailing one. Without this right, the liberty of an American citizen would be as insecure as that of a Frenchman. Ex-Vice-President Dallas tells us that the Constitution is an object to which no American mind can be too attentive, and no American heart too devoted. He further says, the Constitution, in its words, is plain and intelligible, and is meant for the home-bred, unsophisticated understandings of our fellow-citizens. Senator Berrien tells us that the Constitution is the fundamental law, that which controls all others. The charter of our liberties, which every citizen has a personal interest in understanding thoroughly. The testimony of Senator Breese, Lewis Cass, and many others that might be named, who are everywhere esteemed as sound lawyers, so regard the Constitution. I take it, therefore, that it is not presumption in a private citizen to form an opinion of that instrument.

Now, take the Constitution according to its plain reading, and I defy the presentation of a single pro-slavery clause in it. On the other hand it will be found to contain principles and purposes, entirely hostile to the existence of slavery.

I have detained my audience entirely too long already. At some future period I will gladly avail myself of an opportunity to give this subject a full and fair discussion.

Allow me to say, in conclusion, notwithstanding the dark picture I have this day presented, of the state of the nation, I do not despair of this country. There are forces in operation, which must inevitably, work the downfall of slavery. *"The arm of the Lord is not shortened,"* and the doom of slavery is certain. I, therefore, leave off where I began, with *hope*. While drawing encouragement from the Declaration of Independence, the great principles it contains, and the genius of American Institutions, my spirit is also cheered by the obvious tendencies of the age. Nations do not now stand in the same relation to each other that they did ages ago. No nation can now shut itself up, from the surrounding world, and trot round in the same old path of its fathers without interference. The time *was* when such could be done. Long established customs of hurtful character could formerly fence themselves in, and do their evil work with social impunity. Knowledge was then confined and enjoyed by the privileged few, and the multitude walked on in mental darkness. But a change has now come over the affairs of mankind. Walled cities and empires have become unfashionable. The arm of commerce has borne away the gates of the strong city. Intelligence is penetrating the darkest corners of the globe. It makes its pathway over and under the sea, as well as on the earth. Wind, steam, and lightning are its chartered agents. Oceans no longer divide, but link nations together. From Boston to London is now a holiday excursion. Space is comparatively annihilated.—Thoughts expressed on one side of the Atlantic are distinctly heard on the other.

The far off and almost fabulous Pacific rolls in grandeur at our feet. The Celestial Empire, the mystery of ages, is being solved. The fiat of the Almighty, "*Let there be Light*," has not yet spent its force. No abuse, no outrage whether in taste, sport or avarice, can now hide itself from the all-pervading light. The iron shoe, and crippled foot of China must be seen, in contrast with nature. *Africa must rise and put on her yet unwoven garment. "Ethiopia shall stretch out her hand unto God."* In the fervent aspirations of William Lloyd Garrison, I say, and let every heart join in saying it:

God speed the year of jubilee
  The wide world o'er!
When from their galling chains set free,
Th' oppress'd shall vilely bend the knee,
And wear the yoke of tyranny
  Like brutes no more.
That year will come, and freedom's reign,
To man his plundered rights again
  Restore.

God speed the day when human blood
  Shall cease to flow!
In every clime be understood,
The claims of human brotherhood,
And each return for evil, good,
  Not blow for blow;
That day will come all feuds to end,
And change into a faithful friend
  Each foe.

God speed the hour, the glorious hour,
  When none on earth
Shall exercise a lordly power,
Nor in a tyrant's presence cower;
But all to manhood's stature tower,
  By equal birth!
THAT HOUR WILL COME, to each, to all,
And from his prison-house, the thrall
  Go forth.

Until that year, day, hour, arrive,
With head, and heart, and hand I'll strive,
To break the rod, and rend the gyve,
The spoiler of his prey deprive—
  So witness Heaven!
And never from my chosen post,
Whate'er the peril or the cost,
  Be driven.

George Fitzhugh

Sociology for the South (1854)

[. . .] Now it has been the practice in all countries and in all ages, in some degree, to accommodate the amount and character of government control to the wants, intelligence, and moral capacities of the nations or individuals to be governed. A highly moral and intellectual people, like the free citizens of ancient Athens, are best governed by a democracy. For a less moral and intellectual one, a limited and constitutional monarchy will answer. For a people either very ignorant or very wicked, nothing short of military despotism will suffice. So among individuals, the most moral and well-informed members of society require no other government than law. They are capable of reading and understanding the law, and have sufficient self-control and virtuous disposition to obey it. Children cannot be governed by mere law; first, because they do not understand it, and secondly, because they are so much under the influence of impulse, passion and appetite, that they want sufficient self-control to be deterred or governed by the distant and doubtful penalties of the law. They must be constantly controlled by parents or guardians, whose will and orders shall stand in the place of law for them. Very wicked men must be put into penitentiaries; lunatics into asylums, and the most wild of them into straight jackets, just as the most wicked of the sane are manacled with irons; and idiots must have committees to govern and take care of them. Now, it is clear the Athenian democracy would not suit a negro nation, nor will the government of mere law suffice for the individual negro. He is but a grown up child, and must be governed as a child, not as a lunatic or criminal. The master occupies towards him the place of parent or guardian. We shall not dwell on this view, for no one will differ with us who thinks as we do of the negro's capacity, and we might argue till dooms-day, in vain, with those who have a high opinion of the negro's moral and intellectual capacity.

Secondly. The negro is improvident; will not lay up in summer for the wants of winter; will not accumulate in youth for the exigencies of age. He would become an insufferable burden to society. Society has the right to prevent this, and can only do so by subjecting him to domestic slavery.

In the last place, the negro race is inferior to the white race, and living in their midst, they would be far outstripped or outwitted in the chase of free competition. Gradual but certain extermination would be their fate. We presume the maddest abolitionist does not think the negro's providence of habits and money-making capacity at all to compare to those of the whites. This defect of character would alone justify enslaving him, if he is to remain here. In Africa or the West Indies, he would become idolatrous, savage and cannibal, or be devoured by savages and cannibals. At the North he would freeze or starve.

We would remind those who deprecate and sympathize with negro slavery, that his slavery here relieves him from a far more cruel slavery in Africa, or from idolatry and cannibalism, and every brutal vice and crime that can disgrace humanity; and that it christianizes, protects, supports and civilizes him; that it governs him far better than free laborers at the North are governed. There, wife murder has become a mere holiday pastime; and where so many wives are murdered, almost all must be brutally treated. Nay, more: men who kill their wives or treat them brutally, must be ready for all kinds of crime, and the calendar of crime at the North proves the inference to be correct. Negroes never kill their wives. If it be objected that legally they have no wives, then we reply, that in an experience of more than forty years, we never yet heard of a negro man killing a negro woman. Our negroes are not only better off as to physical comfort than free laborers, but their moral condition is better. [. . .]

Negro slavery would be changed immediately to some form of peonage, serfdom or villienage, if the negroes were sufficiently intelligent and provident to manage a farm. No one would have the labor and trouble of management, if his negroes would pay in hires and rents one-half what free tenants pay in rent in Europe. Every negro in the South should be soon liberated, if he would take liberty on the terms that white tenants hold it. The fact that he cannot enjoy liberty on such terms, seems conclusive that he is only fit to be a slave. [. . .]

It is a common remark, that the grand and lasting architectural structures of antiquity were the results of slavery. The mighty and continued association of labor requisite to their construction, when mechanic art was so little advanced, and labor-saving processes unknown, could only have been brought about by a despotic authority, like that of the master over his slaves. It is, however, very remarkable, that whilst in taste and artistic skill the world seems to have been retrograding ever since the decay and abolition of feudalism, in mechanical invention and in great utilitarian operations requiring the wielding of immense capital and much labor, its progress has been unexampled. Is it because capital is more despotic in its authority over free laborers than Roman masters and feudal lords were over their slaves and vassals?

Free society has continued long enough to justify the attempt to generalize its phenomena, and calculate its moral and intellectual influences. It is obvious that, in whatever is purely utilitarian and material, it incites invention and stimulates industry. Benjamin Franklin, as a man and a philosopher, is the best exponent of the working of the system. His sentiments and his philosophy are low, selfish, atheistic and material. They tend directly to make man a mere "featherless biped," well-fed, well-clothed and comfortable, but regardless of his soul as "the beasts that perish." [. . .]

But far the worst feature of modern civilization, which is the civilization of free society, remains to be exposed. Whilst labor-saving processes have probably lessened by one half, in the last century, the amount of work needed for comfortable support, the free laborer is compelled by capital and competition to work more than he ever did before, and is less comfortable. The organization of society cheats him of his earnings, and those earnings go to swell the vulgar pomp and pageantry of the ignorant millionaires, who are the only great of the present day. These reflections might seem, at first view, to have little connexion with negro slavery, but it is well for us of the South not to be deceived by the tinsel glare and glitter of free society, and to employ ourselves in doing our duty at home, and studying the past, rather than in insidious rivalry of the expensive pleasures and pursuits of men whose sentiments and whose aims are low, sensual and grovelling.

We need never have white slaves in the South, because we have black ones. Our citizens, like those of Rome and Athens, are a privileged class. We should train and educate them to deserve the privileges and to perform the duties which society confers on them. Instead, by a low demagoguism depressing their self-respect by discourses on the equality of man, we had better excite their pride by reminding them that they do not fulfil the menial which white men do in other countries. Society does not feel the burden of providing for the few helpless paupers in the South. And we should recollect that here we have but half the people to educate, for half are negroes; whilst at the North they profess to educate all. It is in our power to spike this last gun of the abolitionists. We should educate all the poor. The abolitionists say that it is one of the necessary consequences of slavery that the poor are neglected. It was not so in Athens, and in Rome, and should not be so in the South. If we had less trade with and less dependence on the North, all our poor might be profitably and honorably employed in trades, professions and manufactures. Then we should have a rich and denser population. Yet we but marshal her in the way that she was going. The South is already aware of the necessity of a new policy, and has begun to act on it. Every day more and more is done for education, the mechanic arts, manufactures and internal improvements. We will soon be independent of the North.

We deem this peculiar question of negro slavery of very little importance. The issue is made throughout the world on the general subject of slavery in the abstract. The argument has commenced. One set of ideas will govern and control after awhile the civilized world. Slavery will everywhere be abolished, or every where be re-instituted. We think the opponents of practical, existing slavery, are estopped by their own admission; nay, that unconsciously, as socialists, they are the defenders and propagandists of slavery, and have furnished the only sound arguments on which its defence and justification can be rested. We have introduced the subject of negro slavery to afford us a better opportunity to disclaim the purpose of reducing the white man any where to the condition of negro slaves here. It would be very unwise and unscientific to govern white men as you would negroes. Every shade and variety of slavery has existed in the world. In some cases there has been much of legal regulation, much restraint of the master's authority; in others, none at all. The character of slavery necessary to protect the whites in Europe should be much milder than negro slavery, for slavery is only needed to protect the white man, whilst it is more necessary for the government of the negro even than for his protection. But even negro slavery should not be outlawed. We might and should have laws in Virginia, as in Louisiana, to make the master subject to presentment by the grand jury and to punishment, for any inhuman or improper treatment or neglect of his slave.

We abhor the doctrine of the "Types of Mankind;" first, because it is at war with scripture, which teaches us that the whole human race is descended from a common parentage; and, second, because it encourages and incites brutal masters to treat negroes, not as weak, ignorant and dependent brethren, but as wicked beasts, without the pale of humanity. The Southerner is the negro's friend, his only friend. Let no intermeddling abolitionist, no refined philosophy, dissolve this friendship.

Henry David Thoreau

Slavery in Massachusetts (1854)

I lately attended a meeting of the citizens of Concord, expecting, as one among many, to speak on the subject of slavery in Massachusetts; but I was surprised and disappointed to find that what had called my townsmen together was the destiny of Nebraska, and not of Massachusetts, and that what I had to say would be entirely out of order. I had thought that the house was on fire, and not the prairie; but though several of the citizens of Massachusetts are now in prison for attempting to rescue a slave from her own clutches, not one of the speakers at that meeting expressed regret for it, not one even referred to it. It was only the disposition of some wild lands a thousand miles off which appeared to concern them. The inhabitants of Concord are not prepared to stand by one of their own bridges, but talk only of taking up a position on the highlands beyond the Yellowstone River. Our Buttricks and Davises and Hosmers are retreating thither, and I fear that they will leave no Lexington Common between them and the enemy. There is not one slave in Nebraska; there are perhaps a million slaves in Massachusetts.

They who have been bred in the school of politics fail now and always to face the facts. Their measures are half measures and makeshifts merely. They put off the day of settlement indefinitely, and meanwhile the debt accumulates. Though the Fugitive Slave Law had not been the subject of discussion on that occasion, it was at length faintly resolved by my townsmen, at an adjourned meeting, as I learn, that the compromise compact of 1820 having been repudiated by one of the parties, "Therefore, the Fugitive Slave Law of 1850 must be repealed." But this is not the reason why an iniquitous law should be repealed. The fact which the politician faces is merely that there is less honor among thieves than was supposed, and not the fact that they are thieves.

As I had no opportunity to express my thoughts at that meeting, will you allow me to do so here?

Again it happens that the Boston Court-House is full of armed men, holding prisoner and trying a MAN, to find out if he is not really a SLAVE. Does any one think that justice or God awaits Mr. Loring's decision? For him to sit there deciding still, when this question is already decided from eternity to eternity, and the unlettered slave himself and the multitude around have long since heard and assented to the decision, is simply to make himself ridiculous. We may be tempted to ask from whom he received his commission, and who he is that received it; what novel statutes he obeys, and what precedents are to him of authority. Such an arbiter's very existence is an impertinence. We do not ask him to make up his mind, but to make up his pack.

I listen to hear the voice of a Governor, Commander-in-Chief of the forces of Massachusetts. I hear only the creaking of crickets and the hum of insects which now fill the summer air. The Governor's exploit is to review the troops on muster days. I have seen him on horseback, with his hat off, listening to a chaplain's prayer. It chances that that is all I have ever seen of a Governor. I think that I could manage to get along without one. If he is not of the least use to prevent my being kidnapped, pray of what important use is he likely to be to me? When freedom is most endangered, he dwells in the deepest obscurity. A distinguished clergyman told me that he chose the profession of a clergyman because it afforded the most leisure for literary pursuits. I would recommend to him the profession of a Governor. [. . .]

I had thought that the Governor was, in some sense, the executive officer of the State; that it was his business, as a Governor, to see that the laws of the State were executed; while, as a man, he took care that he did not, by so doing, break the laws of humanity; but when there is any special important use for him, he is useless, or worse than useless, and permits the laws of the State to go unexecuted. Perhaps I do not know what are the duties of a Governor; but if to be a Governor requires to subject one's self to so much ignominy without remedy, if it is to put a restraint upon my manhood, I shall take care never to be Governor of Massachusetts. I have not read far in the statutes of this Commonwealth. It is not profitable reading. They do not always say what is true; and they do not always mean what they say. What I am concerned to know is, that that man's influence and authority were on the side of the slaveholder, and not of the slave,—of the guilty, and not of the innocent,—of injustice, and not of justice. [. . .]

The whole military force of the State is at the service of a Mr. Suttle, a slaveholder from Virginia, to enable him to catch a man whom he calls his property; but not a soldier is offered to save a citizen of Massachusetts from being kidnapped! Is this what all these soldiers, all this *training*, have been for these seventy-nine years past? Have they been trained merely to rob Mexico and carry back fugitive slaves to their masters?

These very nights I heard the sound of a drum in our streets. There were men *training* still; and for what? I could with an effort pardon the cockerels of Concord for crowing still, for they, perchance, had not been beaten that morning; but I could not excuse this rub-a-dub of the "trainers." The slave was carried back by exactly such as these; *i.e.*, by the soldier, of whom the best you can say in this connection is that he is a fool made conspicuous by a painted coat.

Three years ago, also, just a week after the authorities of Boston assembled to carry back a perfectly innocent man, and one whom they knew to be innocent, into slavery, the inhabitants of Concord caused the bells to be rung and the cannons to be fired, to celebrate their liberty,—and the courage and love of liberty of their ancestors who fought at the bridge. As if *those* three millions had fought for the right to be free themselves, but to hold in slavery three million others. Nowadays, men wear a fool's cap, and call it a liberty-cap. I do not know but there are some who, if they were tied to a whipping-post, and could but get one hand free, would use it to ring the bells and fire the cannons to celebrate *their* liberty. So some of my townsmen took the liberty to ring and fire. That was the extent of their freedom; and when the sound of the bells died away, their liberty died away also; when the powder was all expended, their liberty went off with the smoke.

The joke could be no broader if the inmates of the prisons were to subscribe for all the powder to be used in such salutes, and hire the jailers to do the firing and ringing for them, while they enjoyed it through the grating.

This is what I thought about my neighbors.

Every humane and intelligent inhabitant of Concord, when he or she heard those bells and those cannons, thought not with pride of the events of the 19th of April, 1775, but with shame of the events of the 12th of April, 1851. But now we have half buried that old shame under a new one. [. . .]

I wish my countrymen to consider, that whatever the human law may be, neither an individual nor a nation can ever commit the least act of injustice against the obscurest individual, without having to pay the penalty for it. A government which deliberately enacts injustice, and persists in it, will at length even become the laughing-stock of the world.

Much has been said about American slavery, but I think that we do not even yet realize what slavery is. If I were seriously to propose to Congress to make mankind into sausages, I have no doubt that most of the members would smile at my proposition, and if any believed me to be in earnest, they would think that I proposed something much worse than Congress had ever done. But if any of them will tell me that to make a man into a sausage would be much worse,—would be any worse,—than to make him into a slave,—than it was to enact the Fugitive Slave Law,—I will accuse him of foolishness, of intellectual incapacity, of making a distinction without a difference. The one is just as sensible a proposition as the other.

I hear a good deal said about trampling this law under foot. Why, one need not go out of his way to do that. This law rises not to the level of the head or the reason; its natural habitat is in the dirt. It was born and bred, and has its life, only in the dust and mire, on a level with the feet; and he who walks with freedom, and does not with Hindoo mercy avoid treading on every venomous reptile, will inevitably tread on it, and so trample it under foot,—and Webster, its maker, with it, like the dirt-bug and its ball.

Recent events will be valuable as a criticism on the administration of justice in our midst, or, rather, as showing what are the true resources of justice in any community. It has come to this, that the friends of liberty, the friends of the slave, have shuddered when they have understood that his fate was left to the legal tribunals of the country to be decided. Free men have no faith that justice will be awarded in such a case. The judge may decide this way or that; it is a kind of accident, at best. It is evident that he is not a competent authority in so important a case. It is no time, then, to be judging according to his precedents, but to establish a precedent for the future. I would much rather trust to the sentiment of the people. In their vote you would get something of some value, at least, however small; but in the other case, only the trammeled judgment of an individual, of no significance, be it which way it might.

It is to some extent fatal to the courts, when the people are compelled to go behind them. I do not wish to believe that the courts were made for fair weather, and for very civil cases merely; but think of leaving it to any court in the land to decide whether more than three millions of people, in this case a sixth part of a nation, have a right to be freemen or not! But it has been left to the courts of *justice*, so called,—to the Supreme Court of the land,—and, as you all know, recognizing no authority but the Constitution, it has decided that the three millions are and shall continue to be slaves. Such judges as these are merely the inspectors of a pick-lock and murderer's tools, to tell him whether they are in working order or not, and there they think that their responsibility ends. There was a prior case on the docket, which they, as judges appointed by God, had no right to skip; which having been justly settled, they would have been saved from this humiliation. It was the case of the murderer himself.

The law will never make men free; it is men who have got to make the law free. They are the lovers of law and order who observe the law when the government breaks it.

Among human beings, the judge whose words seal the fate of a man furthest into eternity is not he who merely pronounces the verdict of the law, but he, whoever he may be, who, from a love of truth, and unprejudiced by any custom or enactment of men, utters a true opinion or *sentence* concerning him. He it is that *sentences* him. Whoever can discern truth has received his commission from a higher source than the chiefest justice in the world who can discern only law. He finds himself constituted judge of the judge. Strange that it should be necessary to state such simple truths!

I am more and more convinced that, with reference to any public question, it is more important to know what the country thinks of it than what the city thinks. The city does not *think* much. On any moral question, I would rather have the opinion of Boxboro' than of Boston and New York put together. When the former speaks, I feel as if somebody *had* spoken, as if *humanity* was yet, and a reasonable being had asserted its rights,—as if some unprejudiced men among the country's hills had at length turned their attention to the subject, and by a few sensible words redeemed the reputation of the race. When, in some obscure country town, the farmers come together to a special town-meeting, to express their opinion on some subject which is vexing the land, that, I think, is the true Congress, and the most respectable one that is ever assembled in the United States.

It is evident that there are, in this Commonwealth at least, two parties, becoming more and more distinct,—the party of the city, and the party of the country. I know that the country is mean enough, but I am glad to believe that there is a slight difference in her favor. But as yet she has few, if any organs, through which to express herself. The editorials which she reads, like the news, come from the seaboard. Let us, the inhabitants of the country, cultivate self respect. Let us not send to the city for aught more essential than our broadcloths and groceries; or, if we read the opinions of the city, let us entertain opinions of our own.

Among measures to be adopted, I would suggest to make as earnest and vigorous an assault on the press as has already been made, and with effect, on the church. The church has much improved within a few years; but the press is, almost without exception, corrupt. I believe that in this country the press exerts a greater and a more pernicious influence than the church did in its worst period. We are not a religious people, but we are a nation of politicians. We do not care for the Bible, but we do care for the newspaper. At any meeting of politicians,—like that at Concord the other evening, for instance,—how impertinent it would be to quote from the Bible! how pertinent to quote from a newspaper or from the Constitution! The newspaper is a Bible which we read every morning and every afternoon, standing and sitting, riding and walking. It is a Bible which every man carries in his pocket, which lies on every table and counter, and which the mail, and thousands of missionaries, are continually dispersing. It is, in short, the only book which America has printed, and which America reads. So wide is its influence. The editor is a preacher whom you voluntarily support. Your tax is commonly one cent daily, and it costs nothing for pew hire. But how many of these preachers preach the truth? I repeat the testimony of many an intelligent foreigner, as well as my own convictions, when I say, that probably no country was ever ruled by so mean a class of tyrants as, with a few noble exceptions, are the editors of the periodical press in this country. And as they live and rule only by their servility, and appealing to the worse, and not the better, nature of man, the people who read them are in the condition of the dog that returns to his vomit. [. . .]

The majority of the men of the North, and of the South and East and West, are not men of principle. If they vote, they do not send men to Congress on errands of humanity; but while their brothers and sisters are being scourged and hung for loving liberty, while—I might here insert all that slavery implies and is—it is the mismanagement of wood and iron and stone and gold which concerns them. Do what you will, O Government, with my wife and children, by mother and brother, my father and sister, I will obey your commands to the letter. It will indeed grieve me if you hurt them, if you deliver them to overseers to be hunted by hounds or to be whipped to death; but, nevertheless, I will peacably pursue my chosen calling on this fair earth, until perchance, one day, when I have put on mourning for them dead, I shall have persuaded you to relent. Such is the attitude, such are the words of Massachusetts.

Rather than do thus, I need not say what match I would touch, what system endeavor to blow up; but as I love my life, I would side with the light, and let the dark earth roll from under me, calling my mother and brother to follow.

I would remind my countrymen that they are to be men first, and Americans only at a late and convenient hour. No matter how valuable law may be to protect your property, even to keep soul and body together, if it do not keep you and humanity together.

I am sorry to say that I doubt if there is a judge in Massachusetts who is prepared to resign his office, and get his living innocently, whenever it is required of him to pass sentence under a law which is merely contrary to the law of God. I am compelled to see that they put themselves, or rather are by character, in this respect, exactly on a level with the marine who discharges his musket in any direction he is ordered to. They are just as much tools, and as little men. Certainly, they are not the more to be respected, because their master enslaves their understandings and consciences, instead of their bodies.

The judges and lawyers,—simply as such, I mean,—and all men of expediency, try this case by a very low and incompetent standard. They consider, not whether the Fugitive Slave Law is right, but whether it is what they call *constitutional.* Is virtue constitutional, or vice? Is equity constitutional, or iniquity? In important moral and vital questions, like this, it is just as impertinent to ask whether a law is constitutional or not, as to ask whether it is profitable or not. They persist in being the servants of the worst of men, and not the servants of humanity. The question is, not whether you or your grandfather, seventy years ago, did not enter into an agreement to serve the Devil, and that service is not accordingly now due; but whether you will not now, for once and at last, serve God,—in spite of your own past recreancy, or that of your ancestor,—by obeying that eternal and only just CONSTITUTION, which He, and not any Jefferson or Adams, has written in your being.

The amount of it is, if the majority vote the Devil to be God, the minority will live and behave accordingly,—and obey the successful candidate, trusting that, some time or other, by some Speaker's casting-vote, perhaps, they may reinstate God. This is the highest principle I can get out or invent for my neighbors. These men act as if they believed that they could safely slide down a hill a little way,—or a good way,—and would surely come to a place, by and by, where they could begin to slide up again. This is expediency, or choosing that course which offers the slightest obstacles to the feet, that is, a downhill one. But there is no such thing as accomplishing a righteous reform by the use of "expediency." There is no such thing as sliding up hill. In morals the only sliders are backsliders.

Thus we steadily worship Mammon, both school and state and church, and on the seventh day curse God with a tintamar from one end of the Union to the other.

Will mankind never learn that policy is not morality,—that it never secures any moral right, but considers merely what is expedient? chooses the available candidate,—who is invariably the Devil,—and what right have his constituents to be surprised, because the Devil does not behave like an angel of light? What is wanted is men, not of policy, but of probity,—who recognize a higher law than the Constitution, or the decision of the majority. The fate of the country does not depend on how you vote at the polls,—the worst man is as strong as the best at that game; it does not depend on what kind of paper you drop into the ballot-box once a year, but on what kind of man you drop from your chamber into the street every morning.

What should concern Massachusetts is not the Nebraska Bill, nor the Fugitive Slave Bill, but her own slaveholding and servility. Let the State dissolve her union with the slave-holder. She may wriggle and hesitate, and ask leave to read the Constitution once more; but she can find no respectable law or precedent which sanctions the continuance of such a union for an instant.

Let each inhabitant of the State dissolve his union with her, as long as she delays to do her duty. [. . .]

Covered with disgrace, the State has sat down coolly to try for their lives and liberties the men who attempted to do its duty for it. And this is called *justice!* They who have shown that they can behave particularly well may perchance be put under bonds for *their good behavior.* They whom truth requires at present to plead guilty are, of all the inhabitants of the State, preeminently innocent. While the Governor, and the Mayor, and countless officers of the Commonwealth are at large, the champions of liberty are imprisoned.

Only they are guiltless who commit the crime of contempt of such a court. It behooves every man to see that his influence is on the side of justice, and let the courts make their own characters. My sympathies in this case are wholly with the accused, and wholly against their accusers and judges. Justice is sweet and musical; but injustice is harsh and discordant. The judge still sits grinding at his organ, but it yields no music, and we hear only the sound of the handle. He believes that all the music resides in the handle, and the crowd toss him their coppers the same as before.

Do you suppose that that Massachusetts which is now doing these things,—which hesitates to crown these men, some of whose lawyers, and even judges, perchance, may be driven to take refuge in some poor quibble, that they may not wholly outrage their instinctive sense of justice,—do you suppose that she is anything but base and servile? that she is the champion of liberty?

Show me a free state, and a court truly of justice, and I will fight for them, if need be; but show me Massachusetts, and I refuse her my allegiance, and express contempt for her courts.

The effect of a good government is to make life more valuable,—of a bad one, to make it less valuable. We can afford that railroad and all merely material stock should lose some of its value, for that only compels us to live more simply and economically; but suppose that the value of life itself should be diminished! How can we make a less demand on man and nature, how live more economically in respect to virtue and all noble qualities, than we do? I have lived for the last month—and I think that every man in Massachusetts capable of the sentiment of patriotism must have had a similar experience—with the sense of having suffered a vast and indefinite loss. I did not know at first what ailed me. At last it occurred to me that what I had lost was a country. I had never respected the government near to which I lived, but I had foolishly thought that I might manage to live here, minding my private affairs, and forget it. For my part, my old and worthiest pursuits have lost I cannot say how much of their attraction, and I feel that my investment in life here is worth many per cent, less since Massachusetts last deliberately sent back an innocent man, Anthony Burns, to slavery. I dwelt before, perhaps, in the illusion that my life passed somewhere only *between* heaven and hell, but now I cannot persuade myself that I do not dwell *wholly within* hell. The site of that political organization called Massachusetts is to me morally covered with volcanic scoriae and cinders, such as Milton describes in the infernal regions. If there is any hell more unprincipled than our rulers, and we, the ruled, I feel curious to see it. Life itself being worth less, all things with it, which minister to it, are worth less. Suppose you have a small library, with pictures to adorn the walls,—a garden laid out around,—and contemplate scientific and literary pursuits and discover all at once that your villa, with all its contents, is located in hell, and that the justice of the peace has a cloven foot and a forked tail,—do not these things suddenly lose their value in your eyes?

I feel that, to some extent, the State has fatally interfered with my lawful business. It has not only interrupted me in my passage through Court Street on errands of trade, but it has interrupted me and every man on his onward and upward path, on which he had trusted soon to leave Court Street far behind. What right had it to remind me of Court Street? I have found that hollow which even I had relied on for solid.

I am surprised to see men going about their business as if nothing had happened. I say to myself, "Unfortunates! they have not heard the news." I am surprised that the man whom I just met on horseback should be so earnest to overtake his newly bought cows running away,—since all property is insecure, and if they do not run away again, they may be taken away from him when he gets them. Fool! does he not know that his seed-corn is worth less this year,—that all beneficent harvests fail as you approach the empire of hell? No prudent man will build a stone house under these circumstances, or engage in any peaceful enterprise which it requires a long time to accomplish. Art is as long as ever, but life is more interrupted and less available for a man's proper pursuits. It is not an era of repose. We have used up all our inherited freedom. If we would save our lives, we must fight for them.

I walk toward one of our ponds; but what signifies the beauty of nature when men are base? We walk to lakes to see our serenity reflected in them; when we are not serene, we go not to them. Who can be serene in a country where both the rulers and the ruled are without principle? The remembrance of my country spoils my walk. My thoughts are murder to the State, and involuntarily go plotting against her.

But it chanced the other day that I scented a white water-lily, and a season I had waited for had arrived. It is the emblem of purity. It bursts up so pure and fair to the eye, and so sweet to the scent, as if to show us what purity and sweetness reside in, and can be extracted from, the slime and muck of earth. I think I have plucked the first one that has opened for a mile. What confirmation of our hopes is in the fragrance of this flower! I shall not so soon despair of the world for it, notwithstanding slavery, and the cowardice and want of principle of Northern men. It suggests what kind of laws have prevailed longest and widest, and still prevail, and that the time may come when man's deeds will smell as sweet. Such is the odor which the plant emits. If Nature can compound this fragrance still annually, I shall believe her still young and full of vigor, her integrity and genius unimpaired, and that there is virtue even in man, too, who is fitted to perceive and love it. It reminds me that Nature has been partner to no Missouri Compromise. I scent no compromise in the fragrance of the water-lily. It is not a *Nymphœa* DOUGLASII. In it, the sweet, and pure, and innocent are wholly sundered from the obscene and baleful. I do not scent in this the time-serving irresolution of a Massachusetts Governor, nor of a Boston Mayor. So behave that the odor of your actions may enhance the general sweetness of the atmosphere, that when we behold or scent a flower, we may not be reminded how inconsistent your deeds are with it; for all odor is but one form of advertisement of a moral quality, and if fair actions had not been performed, the lily would not smell sweet. The foul slime stands for the sloth and vice of man, the decay of humanity; the fragrant flower that springs from it, for the purity and courage which are immortal.

Slavery and servility have produced no sweet-scented flower annually, to charm the senses of men, for they have real life: they are merely a decaying and a death, offensive to all healthy nostrils. We do not complain that they *live,* but that they do not *get buried.* Let the living bury them; even they are good for manure.

Roger Taney

Dred Scott v. Sandford (1857)

Mr. Chief Justice Taney delivered the opinion of the Court.

The question is simply this: can a negro whose ancestors were imported into this country and sold as slaves become a member of the political community formed and brought into existence by the Constitution of the United States, and as such become entitled to all the rights, and privileges, and immunities, guarantied by that instrument to the citizen [. . .] ?

It will be observed that the plea applies to that class of persons only whose ancestors were negroes of the African race, and imported into this country and sold and held as slaves. The only matter in issue before the court, therefore, is, whether the descendants of such slaves, when they shall be emancipated, or who are born of parents who had become free before their birth, are citizens of a State in the sense in which the word "citizen" is used in the Constitution of the United States. And this being the only matter in dispute on the pleadings, the court must be understood as speaking in this opinion of that class only, that is, of those persons who are the descendants of Africans who were imported into this country and sold as slaves. [. . .]

The words "people of the United States" and "citizens" are synonymous terms, and mean the same thing. They both describe the political body who, according to our republican institutions, form the sovereignty and who hold the power and conduct the Government through their representatives. They are what we familiarly call the "sovereign people," and every citizen is one of this people, and a constituent member of this sovereignty. The question before us is whether the class of persons described in the plea in abatement compose a portion of this people, and are constituent members of this sovereignty? We think they are not, and that they are not included, and were not intended to be included, under the word "citizens" in the Constitution, and can therefore claim none of the rights and privileges which that instrument provides for and secures to citizens of the United States. On the contrary, they were at that time considered as a subordinate and inferior class of beings who had been subjugated by the dominant race, and, whether emancipated or not, yet remained subject to their authority, and had no rights or privileges but such as those who held the power and the Government might choose to grant them.

It is not the province of the court to decide upon the justice or injustice, the policy or impolicy, of these laws. The decision of that question belonged to the political or lawmaking power, to those who formed the sovereignty and framed the Constitution. The duty of the court is to interpret the instrument they have framed with the best lights we can obtain on the subject, and to administer it as we find it, according to its true intent and meaning when it was adopted.

In discussing this question, we must not confound the rights of citizenship which a State may confer within its own limits and the rights of citizenship as a member of the Union. It does not by any means follow, because he has all the rights and privileges of a citizen of a State, that he must be a citizen of the United States. He may have all of the rights and privileges of the citizen of a State and yet not be entitled to the rights and privileges of a citizen in any other State. For, previous to the adoption of the Constitution of the United States, every State had the undoubted right to confer on whomsoever it pleased the character of citizen, and to endow him with all its rights. But this character, of course, was confined to the boundaries of the State, and gave him no rights or privileges in other States beyond those secured to him by the laws of nations and the comity of States. Nor have the several States surrendered the power of conferring these rights and privileges by adopting the Constitution of the United States. Each State may still confer them upon an alien, or anyone it thinks proper, or upon any class or description of persons, yet he would not be a citizen in the sense in which that word is used in the Constitution of the United States, nor entitled to sue as such in one of its courts, nor to the privileges and immunities of a citizen in the other States. The rights which he would acquire would be restricted to the State which gave them. The Constitution has conferred on Congress the right to establish an uniform rule of naturalization, and this right is evidently exclusive, and has always been held by this court to be so. Consequently, no State, since the adoption of the Constitution, can, by naturalizing an alien, invest him with the rights and privileges secured to a citizen of a State under the Federal Government, although, so far as the State alone was concerned, he would undoubtedly be entitled to the rights of a citizen and clothed with all the rights and immunities which the Constitution and laws of the State attached to that character.

It is very clear, therefore, that no State can, by any act or law of its own, passed since the adoption of the Constitution, introduce a new member into the political community created by the Constitution of the United States. It cannot make him a member of this community by making him a member of its own. And, for the same reason, it cannot introduce any person or description of persons who were not intended to be embraced in this new political family which the Constitution brought into existence, but were intended to be excluded from it.

The question then arises, whether the provisions of the Constitution, in relation to the personal rights and privileges to which the citizen of a State should be entitled, embraced the negro African race, at that time in this country or who might afterwards be imported, who had then or should afterwards be made free in any State, and to put it in the power of a single State to make him a citizen of the United States and endue him with the full rights of citizenship in every other State without their consent? Does the Constitution of the United States act upon him whenever he shall be made free under the laws of a State, and raised there to the rank of a citizen, and immediately clothe him with all the privileges of a citizen in every other State, and in its own courts?

The court think the affirmative of these propositions cannot be maintained. And if it cannot, the plaintiff in error could not be a citizen of the State of Missouri within the meaning of the Constitution of the United States, and, consequently, was not entitled to sue in its courts.

It is true, every person, and every class and description of persons who were, at the time of the adoption of the Constitution, recognised as citizens in the several States became also citizens of this new political body, but none other; it was formed by them, and for them and their posterity, but for no one else. And the personal rights and privileges guarantied to citizens of this new sovereignty were intended to embrace those only who were then members of the several State communities, or who should afterwards by birthright or otherwise become members according to the provisions of the Constitution and the principles on which it was founded. It was the union of those who were at that time members of distinct and separate political communities into one political family, whose power, for certain specified purposes, was to extend over the whole territory of the United States. And it gave to each citizen rights and privileges outside of his State which he did not before possess, and placed him in every other State upon a perfect equality with its own citizens as to rights of person and rights of property; it made him a citizen of the United States.

It becomes necessary, therefore, to determine who were citizens of the several States when the Constitution was adopted. And in order to do this, we must recur to the Governments and institutions of the thirteen colonies when they separated from Great Britain and formed new sovereignties, and took their places in the family of independent nations. [. . .]

In the opinion of the court, the legislation and histories of the times, and the language used in the Declaration of Independence, show that neither the class of persons who had been imported as slaves nor their descendants, whether they had become free or not, were then acknowledged as a part of the people, nor intended to be included in the general words used in that memorable instrument.

It is difficult at this day to realize the state of public opinion in relation to that unfortunate race which prevailed in the civilized and enlightened portions of the world at the time of the Declaration of Independence and when the Constitution of the United States was framed and adopted. But the public history of every European nation displays it in a manner too plain to be mistaken.

They had for more than a century before been regarded as beings of an inferior order, and altogether unfit to associate with the white race either in social or political relations, and so far inferior that they had no rights which the white man was bound to respect, and that the negro might justly and lawfully be reduced to slavery for his benefit. He was bought and sold, and treated as an ordinary article of merchandise and traffic whenever a profit could be made by it. This opinion was at that time fixed and universal in the civilized portion of the white race. It was regarded as an axiom in morals as well as in politics which no one thought of disputing or supposed to be open to dispute, and men in every grade and position in society daily and habitually acted upon it in their private pursuits, as well as in matters of public concern, without doubting for a moment the correctness of this opinion.

And in no nation was this opinion more firmly fixed or more uniformly acted upon than by the English Government and English people. They not only seized them on the coast of Africa and sold them or held them in slavery for their own use, but they took them as ordinary articles of merchandise to every country where they could make a profit on them, and were far more extensively engaged in this commerce than any other nation in the world.

The opinion thus entertained and acted upon in England was naturally impressed upon the colonies they founded on this side of the Atlantic. And, accordingly, a negro of the African race was regarded by them as an article of property, and held, and bought and sold as such, in every one of the thirteen colonies which united in the Declaration of Independence and afterwards formed the Constitution of the United States. The slaves were more or less numerous in the different colonies as slave labor was found more or less profitable. But no one seems to have doubted the correctness of the prevailing opinion of the time.

The legislation of the different colonies furnishes positive and indisputable proof of this fact. [. . .]

The province of Maryland, in 1717, ch. 13, s. 5, passed a law declaring

> that if any free negro or mulatto intermarry with any white woman, or if any white man shall intermarry with any negro or mulatto woman, such negro or mulatto shall become a slave during life, excepting mulattoes born of white women, who, for such intermarriage, shall only become servants for seven years, to be disposed of as the justices of the county court where such marriage so happens shall think fit, to be applied by them towards the support of a public school within the said county. And any white man or white woman who shall intermarry as aforesaid with any negro or mulatto, such white man or white woman shall become servants during the term of seven years, and shall be disposed of by the justices as aforesaid, and be applied to the uses aforesaid.

The other colonial law to which we refer was passed by Massachusetts in 1705. It is entitled "An act for the better preventing of a spurious and mixed issue," etc., and it provides, that

> if any negro or mulatto shall presume to smite or strike any person of the English or other Christian nation, such negro or mulatto shall be severely whipped, at the discretion of the justices before whom the offender shall be convicted.

And

> that none of her Majesty's English or Scottish subjects, nor of any other Christian nation, within this province, shall contract matrimony with any negro or mulatto; nor shall any person, duly authorized to solemnize marriage, presume to join any such in marriage, on pain of forfeiting the sum of fifty pounds; one moiety thereof to her Majesty, for and towards the support of the Government within this province, and the other moiety to him or them that shall inform and sue for the same, in any of her Majesty's courts of record within the province, by bill, plaint, or information.

We give both of these laws in the words used by the respective legislative bodies because the language in which they are framed, as well as the provisions contained in them, show, too plainly to be misunderstood the degraded condition of this unhappy race. They were still in force when the Revolution began, and are a faithful index to the state of feeling towards the class of persons of whom they speak, and of the position they occupied throughout the thirteen colonies, in the eyes and thoughts of the men who framed the Declaration of Independence and established the

State Constitutions and Governments. They show that a perpetual and impassable barrier was intended to be erected between the white race and the one which they had reduced to slavery, and governed as subjects with absolute and despotic power, and which they then looked upon as so far below them in the scale of created beings, that intermarriages between white persons and negroes or mulattoes were regarded as unnatural and immoral, and punished as crimes, not only in the parties, but in the person who joined them in marriage. And no distinction in this respect was made between the free negro or mulatto and the slave, but this stigma of the deepest degradation was fixed upon the whole race.

We refer to these historical facts for the purpose of showing the fixed opinions concerning that race upon which the statesmen of that day spoke and acted. It is necessary to do this in order to determine whether the general terms used in the Constitution of the United States as to the rights of man and the rights of the people was intended to include them, or to give to them or their posterity the benefit of any of its provisions.

The language of the Declaration of Independence is equally conclusive:

[. . .] It [declares],

> We hold these truths to be self-evident: that all men are created equal; that they are endowed by their Creator with certain unalienable rights; that among them is life, liberty, and the pursuit of happiness; that to secure these rights, Governments are instituted, deriving their just powers from the consent of the governed.

The general words above quoted would seem to embrace the whole human family, and if they were used in a similar instrument at this day would be so understood. But it is too clear for dispute that the enslaved African race were not intended to be included, and formed no part of the people who framed and adopted this declaration, for if the language, as understood in that day, would embrace them, the conduct of the distinguished men who framed the Declaration of Independence would have been utterly and flagrantly inconsistent with the principles they asserted, and instead of the sympathy of mankind to which they so confidently appealed, they would have deserved and received universal rebuke and reprobation.

Yet the men who framed this declaration were great men—high in literary acquirements—high in their sense of honor, and incapable of asserting principles inconsistent with those on which they were acting. They perfectly understood the meaning of the language they used, and how it would be understood by others, and they knew that it would not in any part of the civilized world be supposed to embrace the negro race, which, by common consent, had been excluded from civilized Governments and the family of nations, and doomed to slavery. [. . .]

This state of public opinion had undergone no change when the Constitution was adopted, as is equally evident from its provisions and language. [. . .]

[T]here are two clauses in the Constitution which point directly and specifically to the negro race as a separate class of persons, and show clearly that they were not regarded as a portion of the people or citizens of the Government then formed.

One of these clauses reserves to each of the thirteen States the right to import slaves until the year 1808 if it thinks proper. And the importation which it thus sanctions was unquestionably of persons of the race of which we are speaking, as the traffic in slaves in the United States had always been confined to them. And by the other provision the States pledge themselves to each other to maintain the right of property of the master by delivering up to him any slave who may have escaped from his service, and be found within their respective territories. By the first above-mentioned clause, therefore, the right to purchase and hold this property is directly sanctioned and authorized for twenty years by the people who framed the Constitution. And by the second, they pledge themselves to maintain and uphold the right of the master in the manner specified, as long as the Government they then formed should endure. And these two provisions show conclusively that neither the description of persons therein referred to nor their descendants were embraced in any of the other provisions of the Constitution, for certainly these two clauses were not intended to confer on them or their posterity the blessings of liberty, or any of the personal rights so carefully provided for the citizen. [. . .]

Indeed, when we look to the condition of this race in the several States at the time, it is impossible to believe that these rights and privileges were intended to be extended to them. [. . .]

The legislation of the States [. . .] shows in a manner not to be mistaken the inferior and subject condition of that race at the time the Constitution was adopted and long afterwards, throughout the thirteen States by which that instrument was framed, and it is hardly consistent with the respect due to these States to suppose that they regarded at that time as fellow citizens and members of the sovereignty, a class of beings whom they had thus stigmatized, whom, as we are bound out of respect to the State sovereignties to assume they had deemed it just and necessary thus to stigmatize, and upon whom they had impressed such deep and enduring marks of inferiority and degradation, or, that, when they met in convention to form the Constitution, they looked upon them as a portion of their constituents or designed to include them in the provisions so carefully inserted for the security and protection of the liberties and rights of their citizens. It cannot be supposed that they intended to secure to them rights and privileges and rank, in the new political body throughout the Union which every one of them denied within the limits of its own dominion. More especially, it cannot be believed that the large slaveholding States regarded them as included in the word citizens, or would have consented to a Constitution which might compel them to receive them in that character from another State. For if they were so received, and entitled to the privileges and immunities of citizens, it would exempt them from the operation of the special laws and from the police regulations which they considered to be necessary for their own safety. It would give to persons of the negro race, who were recognised as citizens in any one State of the Union, the right to enter every other State whenever they pleased, singly or in companies, without pass or passport, and without obstruction, to sojourn there as long as they pleased, to go where they pleased at every hour of the day or night without molestation, unless they committed some violation of law for which a white man would be punished; and it would give them the full liberty of speech in public and in private upon all subjects upon which its own citizens might speak; to hold public meetings upon political affairs, and to keep and carry arms wherever they went. And all of this would be done in the face of the subject race of the same color, both free and slaves, and inevitably producing discontent and insubordination among them, and endangering the peace and safety of the State. [. . .]

But it is said that a person may be a citizen, and entitled to that character, although he does not possess all the rights which may belong to other citizens—as, for example, the right to vote, or to hold particular offices—and that yet, when he goes into another State, he is entitled to be recognised there as a citizen, although the State may measure his rights by the rights which it allows to persons of a like character or class resident in the State, and refuse to him the full rights of citizenship.

This argument overlooks the language of the provision in the Constitution of which we are speaking.

Undoubtedly a person may be a citizen, that is, a member of the community who form the sovereignty, although he exercises no share of the political power and is incapacitated from holding particular offices. Women and minors, who form a part of the political family, cannot vote, and when a property qualification is required to vote or hold a particular office, those who have not the necessary qualification cannot vote or hold the office, yet they are citizens.

So, too, a person may be entitled to vote by the law of the State, who is not a citizen even of the State itself. And in some of the States of the Union, foreigners not naturalized are allowed to vote. And the State may give the right to free negroes and mulattoes, but that does not make them citizens of the State, and still less of the United States. And the provision in the Constitution giving privileges and immunities in other States does not apply to them.

Neither does it apply to a person who, being the citizen of a State, migrates to another State. For then he becomes subject to the laws of the State in which he lives, and he is no longer a citizen of the State from which he removed. And the State in which he resides may then, unquestionably, determine his status or condition, and place him among the class of persons who are not recognised as citizens, but belong to an inferior and subject race, and may deny him the privileges and immunities enjoyed by its citizens. [. . .]

But so far as mere rights of person are concerned, the provision in question is confined to citizens of a State who are temporarily in another State without taking up their residence there. It gives them no political rights in the State as to voting or holding office, or in any other respect. For a citizen of one State has no right to participate in the government of another. But if he ranks as a citizen in the State to which he belongs, within the meaning of the Constitution of the United States, then, whenever he goes into another State, the Constitution clothes him, as to the rights of person, will all the privileges and immunities which belong to citizens of the State. And if persons of the African race are citizens of a State, and of the United States, they would be entitled to all of these privileges and immunities in every State, and the State could not restrict them, for they would hold these privileges and immunities under the paramount authority of the Federal Government, and its courts would be bound to maintain and enforce them, the Constitution and laws of the State to the contrary notwithstanding. And if the States could limit or restrict them, or place the party in an inferior grade, this clause of the Constitution would be unmeaning, and could have no operation, and would give no rights to the citizen when in another State. He would have none but what the State itself chose to allow him. This is evidently not the construction or meaning of the clause in question. It guaranties rights to the citizen, and the State cannot withhold them. And these rights are of a character and would lead to consequences which make it absolutely certain that the African race were not included under the name of citizens of a State, and were not in the contemplation of the framers of the Constitution when these privileges and immunities were provided for the protection of the citizen in other States. [. . .]

[U]pon a full and careful consideration of the subject, the court is of opinion, that, upon the facts stated in the plea in abatement, Dred Scott was not a citizen of Missouri within the meaning of the Constitution of the United States, and not entitled as such to sue in its courts, and consequently that the Circuit Court had no jurisdiction of the case, and that the judgment on the plea in abatement is erroneous. [. . .]

[T]he plaintiff [. . .] admits that he and his wife were born slaves, but endeavors to make out his title to freedom and citizenship by showing that they were taken by their owner to certain places, hereinafter mentioned, where slavery could not by law exist, and that they thereby became free, and, upon their return to Missouri, became citizens of that State.

Now if the removal of which he speaks did not give them their freedom, then, by his own admission, he is still a slave, and whatever opinions may be entertained in favor of the citizenship of a free person of the African race, no one supposes that a slave is a citizen of the State or of the United States. If, therefore, the acts done by his owner did not make them free persons, he is still a slave, and certainly incapable of suing in the character of a citizen. [. . .]

We proceed, therefore, to inquire whether the facts relied on by the plaintiff entitled him to his freedom.

The case, as he himself states it, on the record brought here by his writ of error, is this:

The plaintiff was a negro slave, belonging to Dr. Emerson, who was a surgeon in the army of the United States. In the year 1834, he took the plaintiff from the State of Missouri to the military post at Rock Island, in the State of Illinois, and held him there as a slave until the month of April or May, 1836. At the time last mentioned, said Dr. Emerson removed the plaintiff from said military post at Rock Island to the military post at Fort Snelling, situate on the west bank of the Mississippi river, in the Territory known as Upper Louisiana, acquired by the United States of France, and situate north of the latitude of thirty-six degrees thirty minutes north, and north of the State of Missouri. Said Dr. Emerson held the plaintiff in slavery at said Fort Snelling from said last-mentioned date until the year 1838.

In the year 1835, Harriet, who is named in the second count of the plaintiff's declaration, was the negro slave of Major Taliaferro, who belonged to the army of the United States. In that year, 1835, said Major Taliaferro took said Harriet to said Fort Snelling, a military post, situated as herein before stated, and kept her there as a slave until the year 1836, and then sold and delivered her as a slave, at said Fort Snelling, unto the said Dr. Emerson herein before named. Said Dr. Emerson held said Harriet in slavery at said Fort Snelling until the year 1838.

In the year 1836, the plaintiff and Harriet intermarried, at Fort Snelling, with the consent of Dr. Emerson, who then claimed to be their master and owner. Eliza and Lizzie, named in the third count of the plaintiff's declaration, are the fruit of that marriage. Eliza is about fourteen years old, and was born on board the steamboat *Gipsey*, north of the north line of the State of Missouri, and upon the river Mississippi. Lizzie is about seven years old, and was born in the State of Missouri, at the military post called Jefferson Barracks.

In the year 1838, said Dr. Emerson removed the plaintiff and said Harriet and their said daughter Eliza from said Fort Snelling to the State of Missouri, where they have ever since resided.

Before the commencement of this suit, said Dr. Emerson sold and conveyed the plaintiff, and Harriet, Eliza, and Lizzie, to the defendant, as slaves, and the defendant has ever since claimed to hold them, and each of them, as slaves.

In considering this part of the controversy, two questions arise: 1. Was he, together with his family, free in Missouri by reason of the stay in the territory of the United States herein before mentioned? And 2. If they were not, is Scott himself free by reason of his removal to Rock Island, in the State of Illinois, as stated in the above admissions?

We proceed to examine the first question.

The act of Congress upon which the plaintiff relies declares that slavery and involuntary servitude, except as a punishment for crime, shall be forever prohibited in all that part of the territory ceded by France, under the name of Louisiana, which lies north of thirty-six degrees thirty minutes north latitude, and not included within the limits of Missouri. And the difficulty which meets us at the threshold of this part of the inquiry is whether Congress was authorized to pass this law under any of the powers granted to it by the Constitution; for if the authority is not given by that instrument, it is the duty of this court to declare it void and inoperative, and incapable of conferring freedom upon anyone who is held as a slave under the laws of anyone of the States.

The counsel for the plaintiff has laid much stress upon that article in the Constitution which confers on Congress the power "to dispose of and make all needful rules and regulations respecting the territory or other property belonging to the United States," but, in the judgment of the court, that provision has no bearing on the present controversy, and the power there given, whatever it may be, is confined, and was intended to be confined, to the territory which at that time belonged to, or was claimed by, the United States, and was within their boundaries as settled by the treaty with Great Britain, and can have no influence upon a territory afterwards acquired from a foreign Government. It was a special provision for a known and particular territory, and to meet a present emergency, and nothing more. [. . .]

[T]he power of Congress over the person or property of a citizen can never be a mere discretionary power under our Constitution and form of Government. The powers of the Government and the rights and privileges of the citizen are regulated and plainly defined by the Constitution itself. And when the Territory becomes a part of the United States, the Federal Government enters into possession in the character impressed upon it by those who created it. It enters upon it with its powers over the citizen strictly defined, and limited by the Constitution, from which it derives its own existence and by virtue of which alone it continues to exist and act as a Government and sovereignty. It has no power of any kind beyond it, and it cannot, when it enters a Territory of the United States, put off its character and assume discretionary or despotic powers which the Constitution has denied to it. It cannot create for itself a new character separated from the citizens of the United States and the duties it owes them under the provisions of the Constitution. The Territory being a part of the United States, the Government and the citizen both enter it under the authority of the Constitution, with their respective rights defined and marked out, and the Federal Government can exercise no power over his person or property beyond what that instrument confers, nor lawfully deny any right which it has reserved. [. . .]

For example, no one, we presume, will contend that Congress can make any law in a Territory respecting the establishment of religion, or the free exercise thereof, or abridging the freedom of speech or of the press, or the right of the people of the Territory peaceably to assemble and to petition the Government for the redress of grievances. [. . .]

These powers, and others in relation to rights of person which it is not necessary here to enumerate, are, in express and positive terms, denied to the General Government, and the rights of private property have been guarded with equal care. Thus, the rights of property are united with the rights of person, and placed on the same ground by the Fifth Amendment to the Constitution, which provides that no person shall be deprived of life, liberty, and property, without due process of law. And an act of Congress which deprives a citizen of the United States of his liberty or property merely because he came himself or brought his property into a particular Territory of the United States, and who had committed no offence against the laws, could hardly be dignified with the name of due process of law. [. . .]

The powers over person and property of which we speak are not only not granted to Congress, but are in express terms denied, and they are forbidden to exercise them. And this prohibition is not confined to the States, but the words are general, and extend to the whole territory over which the Constitution gives it power to legislate, including those portions of it remaining under Territorial Government, as well as that covered by States. It is a total absence of power everywhere within the dominion of the United States, and places the citizens of a Territory, so far as these rights are concerned, on the same footing with citizens of the States, and guards them as firmly and plainly against any inroads which the General Government might attempt under the plea of implied or incidental powers. And if Congress itself cannot do this—if it is beyond the powers conferred on the Federal Government—it will be admitted, we presume, that it could not authorize a Territorial Government to exercise them. It could confer no power on any local Government established by its authority to violate the provisions of the Constitution. [. . .]

Now, as we have already said in an earlier part of this opinion upon a different point, the right of property in a slave is distinctly and expressly affirmed in the Constitution. The right to traffic in it, like an ordinary article of merchandise and property, was guarantied to the citizens of the United States in every State that might desire it for twenty years. And the Government in express terms is pledged to protect it in all future time if the slave escapes from his owner. This is done in plain words—too plain to be misunderstood. And no word can be found in the Constitution which gives Congress a greater power over slave property or which entitles property of that kind to less protection that property of any other description. The only power conferred is the power coupled with the duty of guarding and protecting the owner in his rights.

Upon these considerations, it is the opinion of the court that the act of Congress which prohibited a citizen from holding and owning property of this kind in the territory of the United States north of the line therein mentioned is not warranted by the Constitution, and is therefore void, and that neither Dred Scott himself nor any of his family were made free by being carried into this territory, even if they had been carried there by the owner with the intention of becoming a permanent resident. [. . .]

Benjamin Curtis

Dred Scott v. Sandford, Dissent (1857)

Mr. Justice Curtis dissenting.

I dissent from the opinion pronounced by the Chief Justice, and from the judgment which the majority of the court think it proper to render in this case. [. . .]

[U]nder the allegations contained in this plea and admitted by the demurrer, the question is whether any person of African descent, whose ancestors were sold as slaves in the United States, can be a citizen of the United States. If any such person can be a citizen, this plaintiff has the right to the judgment of the court that he is so, for no cause is shown by the plea why he is not so, except his descent and the slavery of his ancestors.

The first section of the second article of the Constitution uses the language, "a citizen of the United States at the time of the adoption of the Constitution." One mode of approaching this question is to inquire who were citizens of the United States at the time of the adoption of the Constitution.

Citizens of the United States at the time of the adoption of the Constitution can have been no other than citizens of the United States under the Confederation. By the Articles of Confederation, a Government was organized, the style whereof was "The United States of America." This Government was in existence when the Constitution was framed and proposed for adoption, and was to be superseded by the new Government of the United States of America, organized under the Constitution. When, therefore, the Constitution speaks of citizenship of the United States existing at the time of the adoption of the Constitution, it must necessarily refer to citizenship under the Government which existed prior to and at the time of such adoption. [. . .]

To determine whether any free persons, descended from Africans held in slavery, were citizens of the United States under the Confederation, and consequently at the time of the adoption of the Constitution of the United States, it is only necessary to know whether any such persons were citizens of either of the States under the Confederation at the time of the adoption of the Constitution.

Of this there can be no doubt. At the time of the ratification of the Articles of Confederation, all free native-born inhabitants of the States of New Hampshire, Massachusetts, New York, New Jersey, and North Carolina, though descended from African slaves, were not only citizens of those States, but such of them as had the other necessary qualifications possessed the franchise of electors, on equal terms with other citizens. [. . .]

An argument from speculative premises, however well chosen, that the then state of opinion in the Commonwealth of Massachusetts was not consistent with the natural rights of people of color who were born on that soil, and that they were not, by the Constitution of 1780 of that State, admitted to the condition of citizens, would be received with surprise by the people of that State who know their own political history. It is true, beyond all controversy that persons of color, descended from African slaves, were by that Constitution made citizens of the State, and such of them as have had the necessary qualifications have held and exercised the elective franchise, as citizens, from that time to the present.

The Constitution of New Hampshire conferred the elective franchise upon "every inhabitant of the State having the necessary qualifications," of which color or descent was not one.

The Constitution of New York gave the right to vote to "every male inhabitant, who shall have resided," etc., making no discrimination between free colored persons and others.

That of New Jersey, to "all inhabitants of this colony, of full age, who are worth £50 proclamation money, clear estate." [. . .]

I shall not enter into an examination of the existing opinions of that period respecting the African race, nor into any discussion concerning the meaning of those who asserted, in the Declaration of Independence, that all men are created equal; that they are endowed by their Creator with certain inalienable rights; that among these are life, liberty, and the pursuit of happiness. My own opinion is that a calm comparison of these assertions of universal abstract truths and of their own individual opinions and acts would not leave these men under any reproach of inconsistency; that the great truths they asserted on that solemn occasion, they were ready and anxious to make effectual, wherever a necessary regard to circumstances, which no statesman can disregard without producing more evil than good, would allow; and that it would not be just to them nor true in itself to allege that they intended to say that the Creator of all men had endowed the white race, exclusively, with the great natural rights which the Declaration of Independence asserts. But this is not the place [to] vindicate their memory. As I conceive, we should deal here not with such disputes, if there can be a dispute concerning this subject, but with those substantial facts evinced by the written Constitutions of States and by the notorious practice under them. And they show, in a manner which no argument can obscure, that, in some of the original thirteen States, free colored persons, before and at the time of the formation of the Constitution, were citizens of those States.

The fourth of the fundamental articles of the Confederation was as follows:

> The free inhabitants of each of these States, paupers, vagabonds, and fugitives from justice, excepted, shall be entitled to all the privileges and immunities of free citizens in the several States.

The fact that free persons of color were citizens of some of the several States, and the consequence that this fourth article of the Confederation would have the effect to confer on such persons the privileges and immunities of general citizenship, were not only known to those who framed and adopted those articles, but the evidence is decisive that the fourth article was intended to have that effect, and that more restricted language, which would have excluded such persons, was deliberately and purposely rejected.

On the 25th of June, 1778, the Articles of Confederation being under consideration by the Congress, the delegates from South Carolina moved to amend this fourth article by inserting after the word "free," and before the word "inhabitants," the word "white," so that the privileges and immunities of general citizenship would be secured only to white persons. Two States voted for the amendment, eight States against it, and the vote of one State was divided. The language of the article stood unchanged, and both by its terms of inclusion, "free inhabitants," and the strong implication from its terms of exclusion, "paupers, vagabonds, and fugitives from justice," who alone were excepted, it is clear that under the Confederation, and at the time of the adoption of the Constitution, free colored persons of African descent might be, and, by reason of their citizenship in certain States, were, entitled to the privileges and immunities of general citizenship of the United States.

Did the Constitution of the United States deprive them or their descendants of citizenship?

That Constitution was ordained and established by the people of the United States, through the action, in each State, or those persons who were qualified by its laws to act thereon in behalf of themselves and all other citizens of that State. In some of the States, as we have seen, colored persons were among those qualified by law to act on this subject. These colored persons were not only included in the body of "the people of the United States" by whom the Constitution was ordained and established, but, in at least five of the States, they had the power to act, and doubtless did act, by their suffrages, upon the question of its adoption. It would be strange if we were to find in that instrument anything which deprived of their citizenship any part of the people of the United States who were among those by whom it was established.

I can find nothing in the Constitution which, *proprio vigore*, deprives of their citizenship any class of persons who were citizens of the United States at the time of its adoption, or who should be native-born citizens of any State after its adoption, nor any power enabling Congress to disfranchise persons born on the soil of any State, and entitled to citizenship of such State by its Constitution and laws. And my opinion is that, under the Constitution of the United States, every free person born on the soil of a State, who is a citizen of that State by force of its Constitution or laws, is also a citizen of the United States. [. . .]

It has been often asserted that the Constitution was made exclusively by and for the white race. It has already been shown that, in five of the thirteen original States, colored persons then possessed the elective franchise, and were among those by whom the Constitution was ordained and established. If so, it is not true, in point of fact, that the Constitution was made exclusively by the white race. And that it was made exclusively for the white race is, in my opinion, not only an assumption not warranted by anything in the Constitution, but contradicted by its opening declaration that it was ordained and established by the people of the United States, for themselves and their posterity. And as free colored persons were then citizens of at least five States, and so in every sense part of the people of the United States, they were among those for whom and whose posterity the Constitution was ordained and established. [. . .]

The conclusions at which I have arrived on this part of the case are:

First. That the free native-born citizens of each State are citizens of the United States.

Second. That, as free colored persons born within some of the States are citizens of those States, such persons are also citizens of the United States.

Third. That every such citizen, residing in any State, has the right to sue and is liable to be sued in the Federal courts, as a citizen of that State in which he resides.

Fourth. That, as the plea to the jurisdiction in this case shows no facts, except that the plaintiff was of African descent, and his ancestors were sold as slaves, and as these facts are not inconsistent with his citizenship of the United States and his residence in the State of Missouri, the plea to the jurisdiction was bad, and the judgment of the Circuit Court overruling it was correct.

I dissent, therefore, from that part of the opinion of the majority of the court in which it is held that a person of African descent cannot be a citizen of the United States, and I regret I must go further and dissent both from what I deem their assumption of authority to examine the constitutionality of the act of Congress commonly called the Missouri Compromise Act and the grounds and conclusions announced in their opinion. [. . .]

The material facts agreed bearing on this part of the case are that Dr. Emerson, the plaintiff's master, resided about two years at the military post of Fort Snelling, [. . .] in the Territory of Wisconsin. This may or may not have been with such intent as to make it his technical domicile. The presumption is that it was. [. . .]

On what ground can it be denied that all valid laws of the United States, constitutionally enacted by Congress for the government of the Territory, rightfully extended over an officer of the United States and his servant who went into the Territory to remain there for an indefinite length of time, to take part in its civil or military affairs? They were not foreigners, coming from abroad. Dr. Emerson was a citizen of the country which had exclusive jurisdiction over the Territory, and not only a citizen, but he went there in a public capacity, in the service of the same sovereignty which made the laws. Whatever those laws might be, whether of the kind denominated personal statutes or not, so far as they were intended by the legislative will, constitutionally expressed, to operate on him and his servant, and on the relations between them, they had a rightful operation, and no other State or country can refuse to allow that those laws might rightfully operate on the plaintiff and his servant, because such a refusal would be a denial that the United States could, by laws constitutionally enacted, govern their own servants, residing on their own Territory, over which the United States had the exclusive control, and in respect to which they are an independent sovereign power. Whether the laws now in question were constitutionally enacted, I repeat once more, is a separate question. But, assuming that they were, and that they operated directly on the status of the plaintiff, I consider that no other State or country could question the rightful power of the United States so to legislate, or, consistently with the settled rules of international law, could refuse to recognise the effects of such legislation upon the status of their officers and servants, as valid everywhere. [. . .]

What, then, shall we say of the consent of the master that the slave may contract a lawful marriage, attended with all the civil rights and duties which belong to that relation; that he may enter into a relation which none but a free man can assume—a relation which involves not only the rights and duties of the slave, but those of the other party to the contract, and of their descendants to the remotest generation? In my judgment, there can be no more effectual abandonment of the legal rights of a master over his slave than by the consent of the master that the slave should enter into a contract of marriage in a free State, attended by all the civil rights and obligations which belong to that condition. [. . .]

I have thus far assumed, merely for the purpose of the argument that the laws of the United States respecting slavery in this Territory were constitutionally enacted by Congress. It remains to inquire whether they are constitutional and binding laws. [. . .]

Under the Confederation, the unsettled territory within the limits of the United States had been a subject of deep interest. Some of the States insisted that these lands were within their chartered boundaries, and that they had succeeded to the title of the Crown to the soil. On the other hand, it was argued that the vacant lands had been acquired by the United States by the war carried on by them under a common Government and for the common interest.

This dispute was further complicated by unsettled questions of boundary among several States. It not only delayed the accession of Maryland to the Confederation, but at one time seriously threatened its existence. Under the pressure of these circumstances, Congress earnestly recommended to the several States a cession of their claims and rights to the United States. And before the Constitution was framed, it had been begun. That by New York had been made on the 1st day of March, 1781; that of Virginia on the 1st day of March, 1784; that of Massachusetts on the 19th day of April, 1785; that of Connecticut on the 14th day of September, 1786; that of South Carolina on the 8th day of August, 1787, while the Convention for framing the Constitution was in session.

It is very material to observe in this connection that each of these acts cedes, in terms, to the United States as well the jurisdiction as the soil.

It is also equally important to note that, when the Constitution was framed and adopted, this plan of vesting in the United States, for the common good, the great tracts of ungranted lands claimed by the several States, in which so deep an interest was felt, was yet incomplete. It remained for North Carolina and Georgia to cede their extensive and valuable claims. These were made by North Carolina on the 25th day of February, 1790, and by Georgia on the 24th day of April, 1802. The terms of these last-mentioned cessions will hereafter be noticed in another connection, but I observe here that each of them distinctly shows upon its face that they were not only in execution of the general plan proposed by the Congress of the Confederation, but of a formed purpose of each of these States existing when the assent of their respective people was given to the Constitution of the United States. [. . .]

The Ordinance of 1787 had made provision for the temporary government of so much of the territory actually ceded as lay northwest of the river Ohio.

But it must have been apparent both to the framers of the Constitution and the people of the several States who were to act upon it that the Government thus provided for could not continue unless the Constitution should confer on the United States the necessary powers to continue it. That temporary Government, under the ordinance, was to consist of certain officers, to be appointed by and responsible to the Congress of the Confederation, their powers had been conferred and defined by the ordinance. So far as it provided for the temporary government of the Territory, it was an ordinary act of legislation, deriving its force from the legislative power of Congress and depending for its vitality upon the continuance of that legislative power. But the officers to be appointed for the Northwestern Territory, after the adoption of the Constitution, must necessarily be officers of the United States, and not of the Congress of the Confederation, appointed and commissioned by the President and exercising powers derived from the United States under the Constitution.

Such was the relation between the United States and the Northwestern Territory which all reflecting men must have foreseen would exist when the Government created by the Constitution should supersede that of the Confederation. That if the new Government should be without power to govern this Territory, it could not appoint and commission officers, and send them into the Territory to exercise there legislative, judicial, and executive power, and that this Territory, which was even then foreseen to be so important, both politically and financially, to all the existing States, must be left not only without the control of the General Government in respect to its future political relations to the rest of the States, but absolutely without any Government, save what its inhabitants, acting in their primary capacity, might from time to time create for themselves. [. . .]

There is another consideration applicable to this part of the subject, and entitled, in my judgment, to great weight.

The Congress of the Confederation had assumed the power not only to dispose of the lands ceded, but to institute Governments and make laws for their inhabitants. In other words, they had proceeded to act under the cession, which, as we have seen, was as well of the jurisdiction as of the soil. This ordinance was passed on the 13th of July, 1787. The Convention for framing the Constitution was then in session at Philadelphia. The proof is direct and decisive that it was known to the Convention. It is equally clear that it was admitted and understood not to be within the legitimate powers of the Confederation to pass this ordinance.

The importance of conferring on the new Government regular powers commensurate with the objects to be attained, and thus avoiding the alternative of a failure to execute the trust assumed by the acceptance of the cessions made and expected, or its execution by usurpation, could scarcely fail to be perceived. That it was in fact perceived is clearly shown by the *Federalist*, No. 38, where this very argument is made use of in commendation of the Constitution.

Keeping these facts in view, it may confidently be asserted that there is very strong reason to believe, before we examine the Constitution itself, that the necessity for a competent grant of power to hold, dispose of, and govern territory ceded and expected to be ceded could not have escaped the attention of those who framed or adopted the Constitution, and that, if it did not escape their attention, it could not fail to be adequately provided for. [. . .]

The admission of new States, to be framed out of the ceded territory, early attracted the attention of the Convention. Among the resolutions introduced by Mr. Randolph, on the 29th of May, was one on this subject, which, having been affirmed in Committee of the Whole, on the 5th of June, and reported to the Convention on the 13th of June, was referred to the Committee of Detail, to prepare the Constitution, on the 26th of July. This committee reported an article for the admission of new States "lawfully constituted or established." Nothing was said concerning the power of Congress to prepare or form such States. This omission struck Mr. Madison, who, on the 18th of August, moved for the insertion of power to dispose of the unappropriated lands of the United States, and to institute temporary Governments for new States arising therein.

On the 29th of August, the report of the committee was taken up, and after debate, which exhibited great diversity of views concerning the proper mode of providing for the subject, arising out of the supposed diversity of interests of the large and small States, and between those which had and those which had not unsettled territory, but no difference of opinion respecting the propriety and necessity of some adequate provision for the subject, Gouverneur Morris moved the clause as it stands in the Constitution. This met with general approbation, and was at once adopted. The whole section is as follows:

> New States may be admitted by the Congress into this Union, but no new State shall be formed or erected within the jurisdiction of any other State, nor any State be formed by the junction of two or more States, or parts of States, without the consent of the Legislatures of the States concerned, as well as of Congress.
>
> The Congress shall have power to dispose of and make all needful rules and regulations respecting the territory or other property belonging to the United States, and nothing in this Constitution shall be so construed as to prejudice any claims of the United States or any particular State.

That Congress has some power to institute temporary Governments over the territory, I believe all agree, and if it be admitted that the necessity of some power to govern the territory of the United States could not and did not escape the attention of the Convention and the people, and that the necessity is so great that, in the absence of any express grant, it is strong enough to raise an implication of the existence of that power, it would seem to follow that it is also strong enough to afford material aid in construing an express grant of power respecting that territory, and that they who maintain the existence of the power, without finding any words at all in which it is conveyed, should be willing to receive a reasonable interpretation of language of the Constitution, manifestly intended to relate to the territory, and to convey to Congress some authority concerning it.

It would seem, also that when we find the subject matter of the growth and formation and admission of new States, and the disposal of the territory for these ends, were under consideration, and that some provision therefor was expressly made, it is improbable that it would be, in its terms, a grossly inadequate provision, and that an indispensably necessary power to institute temporary Governments, and to legislate for the inhabitants of the territory, was passed silently by, and left to be deduced from the necessity of the case. [. . .]

At the time of the adoption of the Constitution, the United States held a great tract of country northwest of the Ohio, another tract, then of unknown extent, ceded by South Carolina, and a confident expectation was then entertained, and afterwards realized, that they then were or would become the owners of other great tracts claimed by North Carolina and Georgia. These ceded tracts lay within the limits of the United States and out of the limits of any particular State, and the cessions embraced the civil and political jurisdiction and so much of the soil as had not previously been granted to individuals.

These words, "territory belonging to the United States" were not used in the Constitution to describe an abstraction, but to identify and apply to these actual subjects matter then existing and belonging to the United States and other similar subjects which might afterwards be acquired, and, this being so, all the essential qualities and incidents attending such actual subjects are embraced within the words "territory belonging to the United States" as fully as if each of those essential qualities and incidents had been specifically described.

I say, the essential qualities and incidents. But in determining what were the essential qualities and incidents of the subject with which they were dealing, we must take into consideration not only all the particular facts which were immediately before them, but the great consideration, ever present to the minds of those who framed and adopted the Constitution, that they were making a frame of government for the people of the United States and their posterity under which they hoped the United States might be what they have now become—a great and powerful nation, possessing the power to make war and to conclude treaties, and thus to acquire territory. With these in view, I turn to examine the clause of the article now in question.

It is said this provision has no application to any territory save that then belonging to the United States. I have already shown that, when the Constitution was framed, a confident expectation was entertained, which was speedily realized, that North Carolina and Georgia would cede their claims to that great territory which lay west of those States. No doubt has been suggested that the first clause of this same article which enabled Congress to admit new States refers to and includes new States to be formed out of this territory expected to be thereafter ceded by North Carolina and Georgia, as well as new States to be formed out of territory northwest of the Ohio, which then had been ceded by Virginia. It must have been seen, therefore, that the same necessity would exist for an authority to dispose of and make all needful regulations respecting this territory, when ceded, as existed for a like authority respecting territory which had been ceded.

No reason has been suggested why any reluctance should have been felt by the framers of the Constitution to apply this provision to all the territory which might belong to the United States, or why any distinction should have been made, founded on the accidental circumstance of the dates of the cessions—a circumstance in no way material as respects the necessity for rules and regulations or the propriety of conferring on the Congress power to make them. And if we look at the course of the debates in the Convention on this article, we shall find that the then unceded lands, so far from having been left out of view in adopting this article, constituted, in the minds of members, a subject of even paramount importance.

Again, in what an extraordinary position would the limitation of this clause to territory then belonging to the United States, place the territory which lay within the chartered limits of North Carolina and Georgia. The title to that territory was then claimed by those States, and by the United States; their respective claims are purposely left unsettled by the express words of this clause, and when cessions were made by those States, they were merely of their claims to this territory, the United States neither admitting nor denying the validity of those claims, so that it was impossible then, and has ever since remained impossible, to know whether this territory did or did not then belong to the United States, and consequently to know whether it was within or without the authority conferred by this clause to dispose of and make rules and regulations respecting the territory of the United States. This attributes to the eminent men who acted on this subject a want of ability and forecast, or a want of attention to the known facts upon which they were acting, in which I cannot concur.

There is not, in my judgment, anything in the language, the history, or the subject matter of this article which restricts its operation to territory owned by the United States when the Constitution was adopted. [. . .]

There was to be established by the Constitution a frame of government under which the people of the United States and their posterity were to continue indefinitely. To take one of its provisions, the language of which is broad enough to extend throughout the existence of the Government and embrace all territory belonging to the United States throughout all time, and the purposes and objects of which apply to all territory of the United States, and narrow it down to territory belonging to the United States when the Constitution was framed, while at the same time it is admitted that the Constitution contemplated and authorized the acquisition, from time to time, of other and foreign territory, seems to me to be an interpretation as inconsistent with the nature and purposes of the instrument as it is with its language, and I can have no hesitation in rejecting it.

I construe this clause, therefore, as if it had read

> Congress shall have power to make all needful rules and regulations respecting those tracts of country, out of the limits of the several States, which the United States have acquired, or may

> hereafter acquire, by cessions, as well of the jurisdiction as of the soil, so far as the soil may be the property of the party making the cession, at the time of making it.

It has been urged that the words "rules and regulations" are not appropriate terms in which to convey authority to make laws for the government of the territory.

But it must be remembered that this is a grant of power to the Congress—that it is therefore necessarily a grant of power to legislate—and, certainly, rules and regulations respecting a particular subject, made by the legislative power of a country, can be nothing but laws. Nor do the particular terms employed, in my judgment, tend in any degree to restrict this legislative power. Power granted to a Legislature to make all needful rules and regulations respecting the territory is a power to pass all needful laws respecting it. [. . .]

If, then, this clause does contain a power to legislate respecting the territory, what are the limits of that power?

To this I answer that, in common with all the other legislative powers of Congress, it finds limits in the express prohibitions on Congress not to do certain things; that, in the exercise of the legislative power, Congress cannot pass an *ex post facto* law or bill of attainder; and so in respect to each of the other prohibitions contained in the Constitution.

Besides this, the rules and regulations must be needful. But undoubtedly the question whether a particular rule or regulation be needful must be finally determined by Congress itself. Whether a law be needful is a legislative or political, not a judicial, question. Whatever Congress deems needful is so, under the grant of power. [. . .]

But it is insisted that, whatever other powers Congress may have respecting the territory of the United States, the subject of negro slavery forms an exception.

The Constitution declares that Congress shall have power to make "*all* needful rules and regulations" respecting the territory belonging to the United States.

The assertion is, though the Constitution says "all," it does not mean all—though it says "all" without qualification, it means all except such as allow or prohibit slavery. It cannot be doubted that it is incumbent on those who would thus introduce an exception not found in the language of the instrument to exhibit some solid and satisfactory reason, drawn from the subject matter or the purposes and objects of the clause, the context, or from other provisions of the Constitution, showing that the words employed in this clause are not to be understood according to their clear, plain, and natural signification. [. . .]

There is nothing in the context which qualifies the grant of power. The regulations must be "respecting the territory." An enactment that slavery may or may not exist there is a regulation respecting the territory. Regulations must be needful, but it is necessarily left to the legislative discretion to determine whether a law be needful. No other clause of the Constitution has been referred to at the bar, or has been seen by me, which imposes any restriction or makes any exception concerning the power of Congress to allow or prohibit slavery in the territory belonging to the United States. [. . .]

The only one suggested is that clause in the fifth article of the amendments of the Constitution which declares that no person shall be deprived of his life, liberty, or property, without due process of law. I will now proceed to examine the question whether this clause is entitled to the effect thus attributed to it. It is necessary, first, to have a clear view of the nature and incidents of that particular species of property which is now in question.

Slavery, being contrary to natural right, is created only by municipal law. This is not only plain in itself, and agreed by all writers on the subject, but is inferable from the Constitution and has been explicitly declared by this court. The Constitution refers to slaves as "persons held to service in one State, under the laws thereof." Nothing can more clearly describe a status created by municipal law. In *Prigg v. Pennsylvania* [1842], this court said: "The state of slavery is deemed to be a mere municipal regulation, founded on and limited to the range of territorial laws." [. . .]

Is it conceivable that the Constitution has conferred the right on every citizen to become a resident on the territory of the United States with his slaves, and there to hold them as such, but has neither made nor provided for any municipal regulations which are essential to the existence of slavery?

Is it not more rational to conclude that they who framed and adopted the Constitution were aware that persons held to service under the laws of a State are property only to the extent and under the conditions fixed by those laws that they must cease to be available as property, when their owners voluntarily place them permanently within another jurisdiction, where no municipal laws on the subject of slavery exist, and that, being aware of these principles, and having said nothing to interfere with or displace them, or to compel Congress to legislate in any particular manner on the subject, and having empowered Congress to make all needful rules and regulations respecting the territory of the United States, it was their intention to leave to the discretion of Congress what regulations, if any, should be made concerning slavery therein? Moreover, if the right exists, what are its limits, and what are its conditions? If citizens of the United States have the right to take their slaves to a Territory, and hold them there as slaves, without regard to the laws of the Territory, I suppose this right is not to be restricted to the citizens of slaveholding States. A citizen of a State which does not tolerate slavery can hardly be denied the power of doing the same thing. And what law of slavery does either take with him to the Territory? If it be said to be those laws respecting slavery which existed in the particular State from which each slave last came, what an anomaly is this? Where else can we find, under the law of any civilized country, the power to introduce and permanently continue diverse systems of foreign municipal law, for holding persons in slavery? I say not merely to introduce, but permanently to continue, these anomalies. For the offspring of the female must be governed by the foreign municipal laws to which the mother was subject, and when any slave is sold or passes by succession on the death of the owner, there must pass with him, by a species of subrogation, and as a kind of unknown *jus in re,* the foreign municipal laws which constituted, regulated, and preserved, the status of the slave before his exportation. Whatever theoretical importance may be now supposed to belong to the maintenance of such a right, I feel a perfect conviction that it would, if ever tried, prove to be as impracticable in fact as it is, in my judgment, monstrous in theory. [. . .]

If the Constitution prescribe one rule, and the law another and different rule, it is the duty of courts to declare that the Constitution, and not the law, governs the case before them for judgment. If the law include no case save those for which the Constitution has furnished a different rule, or no case which the Legislature has the power to govern, then the law can have no operation. If it includes cases which the Legislature has power to govern, and concerning which the Constitution does not prescribe a different rule, the law governs those cases, though it may, in its terms, attempt to include others on which it cannot operate. In other words, this court cannot declare void an act of Congress which constitutionally embraces some cases, though other cases within its terms are beyond the control of Congress or beyond the reach of that particular law. If, therefore, Congress had power to make a law excluding slavery from this territory while under the exclusive power of the United States, the use of the word "forever" does not invalidate the law so long as Congress has the exclusive legislative power in the territory. [. . .]

For these reasons, I am of opinion that so much of the several acts of Congress as prohibited slavery and involuntary servitude within that part of the Territory of Wisconsin lying north of thirty-six degrees thirty minutes north latitude and west of the river Mississippi, were constitutional and valid laws.

I have expressed my opinion, and the reasons therefor, at far greater length than I could have wished, upon the different questions on which I have found it necessary to pass to arrive at a judgment on the case at bar. These questions are numerous, and the grave importance of some of them required me to exhibit fully the grounds of my opinion. I have touched no question which, in the view I have taken, it was not absolutely necessary for me to pass upon to ascertain whether the judgment of the Circuit Court should stand or be reversed. I have avoided no question on which the validity of that judgment depends. To have done either more or less, would have been inconsistent with my views of my duty.

Abraham Lincoln

Fragments on Government (1854?)

I

Government is a combination of the people of a country to effect certain objects by joint effort. The best framed and best administered governments are necessarily expensive; while by errors in frame and maladministration most of them are more onerous than they need be, and some of them very oppressive. Why, then, should we have government? Why not each individual take to himself the whole fruit of his labor, without having any of it taxed away, in services, corn, or money? Why not take just so much land as he can cultivate with his own hands, without buying it of any one?

The legitimate object of government is "to do for the people what needs to be done, but which they can not, by individual effort, do at all, or do so well, for themselves." There are many such things—some of them exist independently of the injustice in the world. Making and maintaining roads, bridges, and the like; providing for the helpless young and afflicted; common schools; and disposing of deceased men's property, are instances.

But a far larger class of objects springs from the injustice of men. If one people will make war upon another, it is a necessity with that other to unite and cooperate for defense. Hence the military department. If some men will kill, or beat, or constrain others, or despoil them of property, by force, fraud, or noncompliance with contracts, it is a common object with peaceful and just men to prevent it. Hence the criminal and civil departments.

II

The legitimate object of government is to do for a community of people whatever they need to have done, but cannot do at all, or cannot so well do, for themselves, in their separate and individual capacities. In all that the people can individually do as well for themselves, government ought not to interfere. The desirable things which the individuals of a people cannot do, or cannot well do, for themselves, fall into two classes: those which have relation to wrongs, and those which have not. Each of these branch off into an infinite variety of subdivisions.

The first—that in relation to wrongs—embraces all crimes, misdemeanors, and non-performance of contracts. The other embraces all which, in its nature, and without wrong, requires combined action as public roads and highways, public schools, charities, pauperism, orphanage, estates of the deceased, and the machinery of government itself.

From this it appears that if all men were just, there still would be some, though not so much, need of government.

Fragments on Slavery (1854?)

I

The ant who has toiled and dragged a crumb to his nest will furiously defend the fruit of his labor against whatever robber assails him. So plain that the most dumb and stupid slave that ever toiled for a master does constantly know that he is wronged. So plain that no one, high or low, ever does mistake it, except in a plainly selfish way; for although volume upon volume is written to prove slavery a very good thing, we never hear of the man who wishes to take the good of it by being a slave himself.

Most governments have been based, practically, on the denial of the equal rights of men, as I have, in part, stated them; ours began by affirming those rights. They said, some men are too ignorant and vicious to share in government. Possibly so, said we; and, by your system, you would always keep them ignorant and vicious. We proposed to give all a chance; and we expected the weak to grow stronger, the ignorant wiser, and all better and happier together.

We made the experiment, and the fruit is before us. Look at it, think of it. Look at it in its aggregate grandeur, of extent of country, and numbers of population—of ship, and steamboat, and railroad.

II

Equality in society alike beats inequality, whether the latter be of the British aristocratic sort or of the domestic slavery sort. We know Southern men declare that their slaves are better off than hired laborers amongst us. How little they know whereof they speak! There is no permanent class of hired laborers amongst us. Twenty-five years ago I was a hired laborer. The hired laborer of yesterday labors on his own account to-day, and will hire others to labor for him to-morrow. Advancement—improvement in condition—is the order of things in a society of equals. As labor is the common burden of our race, so the effort of some to shift their share of the burden onto the shoulders of others is the great durable curse of the race. Originally a curse for transgression upon the whole race, when, as by slavery, it is concentrated on a part only, it becomes the double-refined curse of God upon his creatures.

Free labor has the inspiration of hope; pure slavery has no hope. The power of hope upon human exertion and happiness is wonderful. The slave-master himself has a conception of it, and hence the system of tasks among slaves. The slave whom you cannot drive with the lash to break seventy-five pounds of hemp in a day, if you will task him to break a hundred, and promise him pay for all he does over, he will break you a hundred and fifty. You have substituted hope for the rod. And yet perhaps it does not occur to you that to the extent of your gain in the case, you have given up the slave system and adopted the free system of labor.

III

If A can prove, however conclusively, that he may of right enslave B, why may not B snatch the same argument and prove equally that he may enslave A? You say A is white and B is black. It is color, then; the lighter having the right to enslave the darker? Take care. By this rule you are to be slave to the first man you meet with a fairer skin than your own. You do not mean color exactly? You mean the whites are intellectually the superiors of the blacks, and therefore have the right to enslave them? Take care again. By this rule you are to be slave to the first man you meet with an intellect superior to your own. But, say you, it is a question of interest, and if you make it your interest you have the right to enslave another. Very well. And if he can make it his interest he has the right to enslave you.

IV. Letter to Joshua Speed, 1855

You know I dislike slavery; and you fully admit the abstract wrong of it. So far there is no cause of difference. But you say that sooner than yield your legal right to the slave—especially at the bidding of those who are not themselves interested, you would see the Union dissolved. I am not aware that any one is bidding you to yield that right; very certainly I am not. I leave that matter entirely to yourself. I also acknowledge your rights and my obligations, under the constitution, in regard to your slaves. I confess I hate to see the poor creatures hunted down, and caught, and carried back to their stripes, and unrewarded toils; but I bite my lip and keep quiet. In 1841 you and I had together a tedious low-water trip, on a Steam Boat from Louisville to St. Louis. You may remember, as I well do, that from Louisville to the mouth of the Ohio there were, on board, ten or a dozen slaves, shackled together with irons. That sight was a continual torment to me; and I see something like it every time I touch the Ohio, or any other slave-border. It is hardly fair to you to assume, that I have no interest in a thing which has, and continually exercises, the power of making me miserable. You ought rather to appreciate how much the great body of the Northern people do crucify their feelings, in order to maintain their loyalty to the constitution and the Union.

I do oppose the extension of slavery, because my judgment and feelings so prompt me; and I am under no obligation to the contrary.

"House Divided" Speech (1858)

If we could first know where we are, and whither we are tending, we could better judge what to do, and how to do it. We are now far into the fifth year since a policy was initiated with the avowed object, and confident promise, of putting an end to slavery agitation. Under the operation of that policy, that agitation has not only not ceased, but has constantly augmented. In my opinion, it will not cease, until a crisis shall have been reached and passed. "A house divided against itself cannot stand." I believe this government cannot endure permanently half slave and half free. I do not expect the Union to be dissolved—I do not expect the house to fall—but I do expect it will cease to be divided. It will become all one thing, or all the other. Either the opponents of slavery will arrest the further spread of it, and place it where the public mind shall rest in the belief that it is in the course of ultimate extinction; or its advocates will push it forward, till it shall become alike lawful in all the States, old as well as new—North as well as South.

Have we no tendency to the latter condition?

Let any one who doubts, carefully contemplate that now almost complete legal combination—piece of machinery, so to speak—compounded of the Nebraska doctrine, and the Dred Scott decision. Let him consider not only what work the machinery is adapted to do, and how well adapted; but also, let him study the history of its construction, and trace, if he can, or rather fail, if he can, to trace the evidences of design, and concert of action, among its chief architects, from the beginning.

The new year of 1854 found slavery excluded from more than half the States by State Constitutions, and from most of the national territory by Congressional prohibition. Four days later, commenced the struggle which ended in repealing that Congressional prohibition. This opened all the national territory to slavery, and was the first point gained.

But, so far, Congress only had acted; and an indorsement by the people, real or apparent, was indispensable, to save the point already gained, and give chance for more.

This necessity had not been overlooked; but had been provided for, as well as might be, in the notable argument of "squatter sovereignty," otherwise called "sacred right of self-government," which latter phrase, though expressive of the only rightful basis of any government, was so perverted in this attempted use of it as to amount to just this: That if any one man choose to enslave another, no third man shall be allowed to object. That argument was incorporated into the Nebraska bill itself, in the language which follows: "It being the true intent and meaning of this act not to legislate slavery into any Territory or State, nor to exclude it therefrom; but to leave the people thereof perfectly free to form and regulate their domestic institutions in their own way, subject only to the Constitution of the United States." Then opened the roar of loose declamation in favor of "Squatter Sovereignty," and "sacred right of self-government." "But," said opposition members, "let us amend the bill so as to expressly declare that the people of the Territory may exclude slavery." "Not we," said the friends of the measure; and down they voted the amendment.

While the Nebraska bill was passing through Congress, a law case involving the question of a negro's freedom, by reason of his owner having voluntarily taken him first into a free State and then into a Territory covered by the Congressional prohibition, and held him as a slave for a long time in each, was passing through the U. S. Circuit Court for the District of Missouri; and both Nebraska bill and law suit were brought to a decision in the same month of May, 1854. The negro's name was "Dred Scott," which name now designates the decision finally made in the case. Before the then next Presidential election, the law case came to, and was argued in, the Supreme Court of the United States; but the decision of it was deferred until after the election. Still, before the election, Senator Trumbull, on the floor of the Senate, requested the leading advocate of the Nebraska bill to state his opinion whether the people of a Territory can constitutionally exclude slavery from their limits; and the latter answers: "That is a question for the Supreme Court."

The election came. Mr. Buchanan was elected, and the indorsement, such as it was, secured. That was the second point gained. The indorsement, however, fell short of a clear popular majority by nearly four hundred thousand votes, and so, perhaps, was not overwhelmingly reliable and satisfactory. The outgoing President, in his last annual message, as impressively as possible echoed back upon the people the weight and authority of the endorsement. The Supreme Court met again; did not announce their decision, but ordered a re-argument. The Presidential inauguration came, and still no decision of the court; but the incoming President in his inaugural address, fervently exhorted the people to abide by the forthcoming decision, whatever it might be. Then, in a few days, came the decision.

The reputed author of the Nebraska bill finds an early occasion to make a speech at this capital indorsing the Dred Scott decision, and vehemently denouncing all opposition to it. The new President, too, seizes the early occasion of the Silliman letter to indorse and strongly construe that decision, and to express his astonishment that any different view had ever been entertained!

At length a squabble springs up between the President and the author of the Nebraska bill, on the mere question of fact, whether the Lecompton Constitution was or was not, in any just sense, made by the people of Kansas; and in that quarrel the latter declares that all he wants is a fair vote for the people, and that he cares not whether slavery be voted down or voted up. I do not understand his declaration that he cares not whether slavery be voted down or voted up, to be intended by him other than as an apt definition of the policy he would impress upon the public mind—the principle for which he declares he has suffered so much, and is ready to suffer to the end. And well may he cling to that principle. If he has any parental feeling, well may he cling to it. That principle is the only shred left of his original Nebraska doctrine. Under the Dred Scott decision "squatter sovereignty" squatted out of existence, tumbled down like temporary scaffolding—like the mould at the foundry served through one blast and fell back into loose sand—helped to carry an election, and then was kicked to the winds. His late joint struggle with the Republicans, against the Lecompton Constitution, involves nothing of the original Nebraska doctrine. That struggle was made on a point—the right of a people to make their own constitution—upon which he and the Republicans have never differed.

The several points of the Dred Scott decision, in connection, with Senator Douglas's "care not" policy, constitute the piece of machinery, in its present state of advancement. This was the third point gained. The working points of that machinery are:

First, That no negro slave, imported as such from Africa, and no descendant of such slave, can ever be a citizen of any State, in the sense of that term as used in the Constitution of the United States. This point is made in order to deprive the negro, in every possible event, of the benefit of that provision of the United States Constitution, which declares that "The citizens of each State, shall be entitled to all privileges and immunities of citizens in the several States."

Secondly, That "subject to the Constitution of the United States," neither Congress nor a Territorial Legislature can exclude slavery from any United States territory. This point is made in order that individual men may fill up the Territories with slaves, without danger of losing them as property, and thus to enhance the chances of permanency to the institution through all the future.

Thirdly, That whether the holding a negro in actual slavery in a free State, makes him free, as against the holder, the United States courts will not decide, but will leave to be decided by the courts of any slave State the negro may be forced into by the master. This point is made, not to be pressed immediately; but, if acquiesced in for awhile, and apparently indorsed by the people at an election, then to sustain the logical conclusion that what Dred Scott's master might lawfully do with Dred Scott, in the free State of Illinois, every other master may lawfully do with any other one, or one thousand slaves, in Illinois, or in any other free State.

Auxiliary to all this, and working hand in hand with it, the Nebraska doctrine, or what is left of it, is to educate and mould public opinion, at least Northern public opinion, not to care whether slavery is voted down or voted up. This shows exactly where we now are; and partially, also, whither we are tending.

It will throw additional light on the latter, to go back, and run the mind over the string of historical facts already stated. Several things will now appear less dark and mysterious than they did when they were transpiring. The people were to be left "perfectly free," "subject only to the Constitution." What the Constitution had to do with it, outsiders could not then see. Plainly enough now, it was an exactly fitted niche, for the Dred Scott decision to afterward come in, and declare the perfect freedom of the people to be just no freedom at all. Why was the amendment, expressly declaring the right of the people, voted down? Plainly enough now: the adoption of it would have spoiled the niche for the Dred Scott decision. Why was the court decision held up? Why even a Senator's individual opinion withheld, till after the Presidential election? Plainly enough now: the speaking out then would have damaged the perfectly free argument upon which the election was to be carried. Why the outgoing President's felicitation on the indorsement? Why the delay of a reargument? Why the incoming President's advance exhortation in favor of the decision? These things look like the cautious patting and petting of a spirited horse preparatory to mounting him, when it is dreaded that he may give the rider a fall. And why the hasty after-indorsement of the decision by the President and others?

We cannot absolutely know that all these exact adaptations are the result of preconcert. But when we see a lot of framed timbers, different portions of which we know have been gotten out at different times and places and by different workmen—Stephen, Franklin, Roger and James, for instance—and when we see these timbers joined together, and see they exactly make the frame of a house or a mill, all the tenons and mortices exactly fitting, and all the lengths and proportions of the different pieces exactly adapted to their respective places, and not a piece too many or too few—not omitting even scaffolding—or, if a single piece be lacking, we see the place in the frame exactly fitted and prepared yet to bring such a piece in—in such a case, we find it impossible not to believe that Stephen and Franklin and Roger and James all understood one another from the beginning, and all worked upon a common plan or draft drawn up before the first blow was struck.

It should not be overlooked that, by the Nebraska bill, the people of a State as well as Territory, were to be left "perfectly free," "subject only to the Constitution." Why mention a State? They were legislating for Territories, and not for or about States. Certainly the people of a State are and ought to be subject to the Constitution of the United States; but why is mention of this lugged into this merely Territorial law? Why are the people of a Territory and the people of a State therein lumped together, and their relation to the Constitution therein treated as being precisely the same? While the opinion of the court, by Chief Justice Taney, in the Dred Scott case, and the separate opinions of all the concurring Judges, expressly declare that the Constitution of the United States neither permits Congress nor a Territorial Legislature to exclude slavery from any United States Territory, they all omit to declare whether or not the same Constitution permits a State, or the people of a State, to exclude it. Possibly, this is a mere omission; but who can be quite sure, if McLean or Curtis had sought to get into the opinion a declaration of unlimited power in the people of a State to exclude slavery from their limits, just as Chase and Mace sought to get such declaration, in behalf of the people of a Territory, into the Nebraska bill;—I ask, who can be quite sure that it would not have been voted down in the one case as it had been in the other? The nearest approach to the point of declaring the power of a State over slavery, is made by Judge Nelson. He approaches it more than once, using the precise idea, and almost the language, too, of the Nebraska act. On one occasion, his exact language is, "except in cases where the power is restrained by the Constitution of the United States, the law of the State is supreme over the subject of slavery within its jurisdiction." In what cases the power of the States is so restrained by the United States Constitution, is left an open question, precisely as the same question, as to the restraint on the power of the Territories, was left open in the Nebraska act. Put this and that together, and we have another nice little niche, which we may, ere long, see filled with another Supreme Court decision, declaring that the Constitution of the United States does not permit a State to exclude slavery from its limits. And this may especially be expected if the doctrine of "care not whether slavery be voted down or voted up," shall gain upon the public mind sufficiently to give promise that such a decision can be maintained when made.

Such a decision is all that slavery now lacks of being alike lawful in all the States. Welcome, or unwelcome, such decision is probably coming, and will soon be upon us, unless the power of the present political dynasty shall be met and overthrown. We shall lie down pleasantly dreaming that the people of Missouri are on the verge of making their State free, and we shall awake to the reality instead, that the Supreme Court has made Illinois a slave State. To meet and overthrow the power of that dynasty, is the work now before all those who would prevent that consummation. That is what we have to do. How can we best do it?

There are those who denounce us openly to their own friends, and yet whisper us softly, that Senator Douglas is the aptest instrument there is with which to effect that object. They wish us to infer all, from the fact that he now has a little quarrel with the present head of the dynasty; and that he has regularly voted with us on a single point, upon which he and we have never differed. They remind us that he is a great man, and that the largest of us are very small ones. Let this be granted. But "a living dog is better than a dead lion." Judge Douglas, if not a dead lion, for this work, is at least a caged and toothless one. How can he oppose the advances of slavery? He don't care anything about it. His avowed mission is impressing the "public heart" to care nothing about it. A leading Douglas democratic newspaper thinks Douglas's superior talent will be needed to resist the revival of the African slave trade. Does Douglas believe an effort to revive that trade is approaching? He has not said so. Does he really think so? But if it is, how can he resist it? For years he has labored to prove it a sacred right of white men to take negro slaves into the new Territories. Can he possibly show that it is less a sacred right to buy them where they can be bought cheapest? And unquestionably they can be bought cheaper in Africa than in Virginia. He has done all in his power to reduce the whole question of slavery to one of a mere right of property; and as such, how can he oppose the foreign slave trade—how can he refuse that trade in that "property" shall be "perfectly free"—unless he does it as a protection to the home production? And as the home producers will probably not ask the protection, he will be wholly without a ground of opposition.

Senator Douglas holds, we know, that a man may rightfully be wiser today than he was yesterday—that he may rightfully change when he finds himself wrong. But can we, for that reason, run ahead, and infer that he will make any particular change, of which he, himself, has given no intimation? Can we safely base our action upon any such vague inference? Now, as ever, I wish not to misrepresent Judge Douglas's position, question his motives, or do aught that can be personally offensive to him. Whenever, if ever, he and we can come together on principle so that our cause may have assistance from his great ability, I hope to have interposed no adventitious obstacle. But clearly, he is not now with us—he does not pretend to be—he does not promise ever to be.

Our cause, then, must be intrusted to, and conducted by, its own undoubted friends—those whose hands are free, whose hearts are in the work—who do care for the result. Two years ago the Republicans of the nation mustered over thirteen hundred thousand strong. We did this under the single impulse of resistance to a common danger, with every external circumstance against us. Of strange, discordant, and even hostile elements, we gathered from the four winds, and formed and fought the battle through, under the constant hot fire of a disciplined, proud and pampered enemy. Did we brave all then, to falter now?—now, when that same enemy is wavering, dissevered and belligerent? The result is not doubtful. We shall not fail—if we stand firm, we shall not fail. Wise counsels may accelerate, or mistakes delay it, but, sooner or later, the victory is sure to come.

Abraham Lincoln and Stephen Douglas

Selected Debates (1858)

At Ottawa, August 21

Lincoln

My Fellow-Citizens: When a man hears himself somewhat misrepresented, it provokes him—at least, I find it so with myself; but when misrepresentation becomes very gross and palpable, it is more apt to amuse him. [. . .]

Now, gentlemen, I hate to waste my time on such things, but in regard to that general Abolition tilt that Judge Douglas makes, when he says that I was engaged at that time in selling out and Abolitionizing the Old Whig party, I hope you will permit me to read a part of a printed speech that I made then at Peoria, which will show altogether a different view of the position I took in that contest of 1854. [Voice: "Put on your specs."] Yes, sir, I am obliged to do so. I am no longer a young man.

> This is the repeal of the Missouri Compromise. The foregoing history may not be precisely accurate in every particular; but I am sure it is sufficiently so for all the uses I shall attempt to make of it, and in it we have before us the chief materials enabling us to correctly judge whether the repeal of the Missouri Compromise is right or wrong.
>
> I think, and shall try to show, that it is wrong; wrong in its direct effect, letting slavery into Kansas and Nebraska and wrong in its prospective principle, allowing it to spread to every other part of the wide world where men can be found inclined to take it.
>
> This declared indifference, but, as I must think, covert real zeal for the spread of slavery, I cannot but hate. I hate it because of the monstrous injustice of slavery itself. I hate it because it deprives our republican example of its just influence in the world; enables the enemies of free institutions, with plausibility, to taunt us as hypocrites; causes the real friends of freedom to doubt our sincerity, and especially because it forces so many really good men amongst ourselves into an open war with the very fundamental principles of civil liberty-criticizing the Declaration of Independence, and insisting that there is no right principle of action but self-interest.
>
> Before proceeding, let me say I think I have no prejudice against the Southern people. They are just what we would be in their situation. If slavery did not now exist among them, they would not introduce it. If it did now exist among us, we should not instantly give it up. This I believe of the masses North and South. Doubtless there are individuals on both sides who would not hold slaves under any circumstances; and others who would gladly introduce slavery anew, if it were out of existence. We know that some Southern men do free their slaves, go North, and become tip-top Abolitionists; while some Northern ones go South, and become most cruel slavemasters.
>
> When Southern people tell us they are no more responsible for the origin of slavery than we, I acknowledge the fact. When it is said that the institution exists, and that it is very difficult to get rid of it in any satisfactory way, I can understand and appreciate the saying. I surely will not blame them for not doing what I should not know how to do myself. If all earthly power were given me, I should not know what to do as to the existing institution. My first impulse would be to free all the slaves, and send them to Liberia—to their own native land. But a moment's reflection would convince me that whatever of high hope (as I think there is) there may be in this in the long run, its sudden execution is impossible. If they were all landed there in a day, they would all perish in the next ten days; and there are not surplus shipping and surplus money enough in the world to carry them there in many times ten days. What then? Free them all, and keep them among us as underlings? Is it quite certain that this betters their condition? I think I would not hold one in slavery at any rate; yet the point is

not clear enough to me to denounce people upon. What next? Free them, and make them politically and socially our equals? My own feelings will not admit of this; and if mine would, we well know that those of the great mass of white people will not. Whether this feeling accords with justice and sound judgment is not the sole question, if indeed, it is any part of it. A universal feeling, whether well or ill-founded, cannot be safely disregarded. We cannot make them equals. It does seem to me that systems of gradual emancipation might be adopted; but for their tardiness in this, I will not undertake to judge our brethren of the South.

When they remind us of their constitutional rights, I acknowledge them, not grudgingly, but fully and fairly; and I would give them any legislation for the reclaiming of their fugitives, which should not, in its stringency, be more likely to carry a free man into slavery, than our ordinary criminal laws are to hang an innocent one.

But all this, to my judgment, furnishes no more excuse for permitting slavery to go into our own free territory, than it would for reviving the African slave trade by law. The law which forbids the bringing of slaves from Africa, and that which has so long forbidden the taking of them to Nebraska, can hardly be distinguished on any moral principle; and the repeal of the former could find quite as plausible excuses as that of the latter.

I have reason to know that Judge Douglas knows that I said this. I think he has the answer here to one of the questions he put to me. I do not mean to allow him to catechize me unless he pays back for it in kind. I will not answer questions one after another, unless he reciprocates; but as he has made this inquiry, and I have answered it before, he has got it without my getting anything in return. He has got my answer on the fugitive-slave law.

Now, gentlemen, I don't want to read at any great length, but this is the true complexion of all I have ever said in regard to the institution of slavery and the black race. This is the whole of it, and anything that argues me into his idea of perfect social and political equality with the negro is but a specious and fantastic arrangement of words, by which a man can prove a horse-chestnut to be a chestnut horse. I will say here, while upon this subject, that I have no purpose, either directly or indirectly, to interfere with the institution of slavery in the States where it exists. I believe I have no lawful right to do so, and I have no inclination to do so. I have no purpose to introduce political and social equality between the white and the black races. There is a physical difference between the two, which, in my judgment, will probably forever forbid their living together upon the footing of perfect equality; and inasmuch as it becomes a necessity that there must be a difference, I, as well as Judge Douglas, am in favor of the race to which I belong having the superior position. I have never said anything to the contrary, but I hold that, notwithstanding all this, there is no reason in the world why the negro is not entitled to all the natural rights enumerated in the Declaration of Independence—the right to life, liberty, and the pursuit of happiness. I hold that he is as much entitled to these as the white man. I agree with Judge Douglas he is not my equal in many respects—certainly not in color, perhaps not in moral or intellectual endowment. But in the right to eat the bread, without the leave of anybody else, which his own hand earns, he is my equal and the equal of Judge Douglas, and the equal of every living man. [. . .]

As I have not used up so much of my time as I had supposed, I will dwell a little longer upon one or two of these minor topics upon which the judge has spoken. He has read from my speech in Springfield in which I say that "a house divided against itself cannot stand." Does the judge say it can stand? I don't know whether he does or not. The judge does not seem to be attending to me just now, but I would like to know if it is his opinion that a house divided against itself can stand. If he does, then there is a question of veracity, not between him and me, but between the judge and an authority of a somewhat higher character.

Now, my friends, I ask your attention to this matter for the purpose of saying something seriously. I know that the judge may readily enough agree with me that the maxim which was put forth by the Saviour is true, but he may allege that I misapply it; and the judge has a right to urge that in my application I do misapply it, and then I have a right to show that I do not misapply it. When he undertakes to say that because I think this nation, so far as the question of slavery is concerned, will all become one thing or all the other, I am in favor of bringing about a dead uniformity in the various States in all their institutions, he argues erroneously. The great variety of the local institutions in the States, springing from differences in the soil, differences in the face of the country, and in the climate, are bonds of union. They do not make "a house divided against itself," but they make a house united. If they produce in one section of the country what is called for by the wants of another section, and this other section can supply the wants of the first, they are not matters of discord but bonds of union, true bonds of union. But can this question of slavery be considered as among these varieties in the institutions of the country? I leave it to you to say whether, in the history of our government, this institution of slavery has not always failed to be a bond of union, and, on the contrary, been an apple of discord and an element of division in the house.

I ask you to consider whether, so long as the moral constitution of men's minds shall continue to be the same, after this generation and assemblage shall sink into the grave, and another race shall arise with the same moral and intellectual development we have—whether, if that institution is standing in the same irritating position in which it now is, it will not continue an element of division? If so, then I have a right to say that, in regard to this question, the Union is a house divided against itself; and when the judge reminds me that I have often said to him that the institution of slavery has existed for eighty years in some States, and yet it does not exist in some others, I agree to the fact, and I account for it by looking at the position in which our fathers originally placed it—restricting it from the new Territories where it had not gone, and legislating to cut off its source by the abrogation of the slave-trade, thus putting the seal of legislation against its spread. The public mind did rest in the belief that it was in the course of ultimate extinction. But lately, I think—and in this I charge nothing on the judge's motives—lately, I think, that he, and those acting with him, have placed that institution on a new basis, which looks to the perpetuity and nationalization of slavery. And while it is placed upon this new basis, I say, and I have, that I believe we shall not have peace upon the question until the opponents of slavery arrest the further spread of it, and place it where the public mind shall rest in the belief that it is in the course of ultimate extinction; or, on the other hand, that its advocates will push it forward until it shall become alike lawful in all the States, old as well as new, North as well as South. Now I believe if we could arrest the spread, and place it where Washington and Jefferson and Madison placed it, it would be in the course of ultimate extinction, and the public mind would, as for eighty years past, believe that it was in the course of ultimate extinction. The crisis would be past, and the institution might be let alone for a hundred years—if it should live so long—in the States where it exists, yet it would be going out of existence in the way best for both the black and the white races. [A voice: "Then do you repudiate popular sovereignty?"] Well, then, let us talk about popular sovereignty! What is popular sovereignty? Is it the right of the people to have slavery or not have it, as they see fit, in the Territories? I will state—and I have an able man to watch me—my understanding is that popular sovereignty, as now applied to the question of slavery, does allow the people of a Territory to have slavery if they want to, but does not allow them not to have it if they do not want it. I do not mean that if this vast concourse of people were in a Territory of the United States, any one of them would be obliged to have a slave if he did not want one; but I do say that, as I understand the Dred Scott decision if any one man wants slaves, all the rest have no way of keeping that one man from holding them. [. . .]

When I made my speech at Springfield, of which the judge complains, and from which he quotes, I really was not thinking of the things which he ascribes to me at all. I had no thought in the world that I was doing anything to bring about a war between the free and slave States. I had no thought in the world that I was doing anything to bring about a political and social equality of the black and white races. It never occurred to me that I was doing anything or favoring anything to reduce to a dead uniformity all the local institutions of the various States. But I must say, in all fairness to him, if he thinks I am doing something which leads to these bad results, it is none the better that I did not mean it. It is just as fatal to the country, if I have any influence in producing it, whether I intend it or not. But can it be true, that placing this institution upon the original basis—the basis upon which our fathers placed it—can have any tendency to set the Northern and the Southern States at war with one another, or that it can have any tendency to make the people of Vermont raise sugar-cane because they raise it in Louisiana, or that it can compel the people of Illinois to cut pine logs on the Grand Prairie, where they will not grow, because they cut pine logs in Maine, where they do grow? The judge says this is a new principle started in regard to this question. Does the judge claim that he is working on the plan of the founders of the government? I think he says in some of his speeches—indeed, I have one here now—that he saw evidence of a policy to allow slavery to be south of a certain line, while north of it should be excluded, and he saw an indisposition on the part of the country to stand upon that policy, and therefore he set about studying the subject upon original principles, and upon original principles he got up the Nebraska bill! I am fighting it upon these "original principles"—fighting it in the Jeffersonian, Washingtonian, and Madisonian fashion. [. . .]

[. . .] I want to ask your attention to a portion of the Nebraska bill which Judge Douglas has quoted: "It being the true intent and meaning of this act, not to legislate slavery into any Territory or State, nor to exclude it therefrom, but to leave the people thereof perfectly free to form and regulate their domestic institutions in their own way, subject only to the Constitution of the United States." Thereupon Judge Douglas and others began to argue in favor of "popular sovereignty"—the right of the people to have slaves if they wanted them, and to exclude slavery if they did not want them. "But," said, in substance, a senator from Ohio (Mr. Chase, I believe), "we more than suspect that you do not mean to allow the people to exclude slavery if they wish to; and if you do mean it, accept an amendment which I propose expressly authorizing the people to exclude slavery." I believe I have the amendment here before me, which was offered, and under which the people of the Territory, through their proper representatives, might, if they saw fit, prohibit the existence of slavery therein. And now I state it as a fact, to be taken back if there is any mistake about it, that Judge Douglas and those acting with him voted that amendment down. I now think that those men who voted it down had a real reason for doing so. They know what that reason was. It looks to us, since we have seen the Dred Scott decision pronounced, holding that, under the Constitution the people cannot exclude slavery—I say it looks to outsiders, poor, simple, "amiable, intelligent gentlemen," as though the niche was left as a place to put that Dred Scott decision in, a niche which would have been spoiled by adopting the amendment. And now I say again, if this was not the reason, it will avail the Judge much more to calmly and good-humoredly point out to these people what that other reason was for voting the amendment down, than swelling himself up to vociferate that he may be provoked to call somebody a liar.

Again: there is in that same quotation from the Nebraska bill this clause: "It being the true intent and meaning of this bill not to legislate slavery into any Territory or State." I have always been puzzled to know what business the word "State" had in that connection. Judge Douglas knows. He put it there. He knows what he put it there for. We outsiders cannot say what he put it there for. The law they were passing was not about States, and was not making provision for States. What was it placed there for? After seeing the Dred Scott decision which holds that the people cannot exclude slavery from a Territory, if another Dred Scott decision shall come, holding that they cannot exclude it from a State, we shall discover that when the word was originally put there, it was in view of something which was to come in due time, we shall see that it was the other half of something. I now say again, if there is any different reason for putting it there, Judge Douglas, in a good-humored way, without calling anybody a liar, can tell what the reason was. [. . .]

At Freeport, August 27

Douglas

[. . .] In reference to Kansas, it is my opinion, that as she has population enough to constitute a slave State, she has people enough for a free State. [Cheers.] I will not make Kansas an exceptional case to the other States of the Union. [Sound, and "Hear, hear."] I hold it to be a sound rule of universal application to require a Territory to contain the requisite population for a member of Congress, before it is admitted as a State into the Union. I made that proposition in the Senate in 1856, and I renewed it during the last session, in a bill providing that no Territory of the United States should form a Constitution and apply for admission until it had the requisite population. On another occasion I proposed that neither Kansas, or any other Territory, should be admitted until it had the requisite population. Congress did not adopt any of my propositions containing this general rule, but did make an exception of Kansas. I will stand by that exception. [Cheers.] Either Kansas must come in as a free State, with whatever population she may have, or the rule must be applied to all the other Territories alike. [Cheers.] I therefore answer at once, that it having been decided that Kansas has people enough for a slave State, I hold that she has enough for a free State. ["Good," and applause.] I hope Mr. Lincoln is satisfied with my answer; ["He ought to be," and cheers,] and now I would like to get his answer to his own interrogatory—whether or not he will vote to admit Kansas before she has the requisite population. ["Hit him again."] I want to know whether he will vote to admit Oregon before that Territory has the requisite population. Mr. Trumbull will not, and the same reason that commits Mr. Trumbull against the admission of Oregon, commits him against Kansas, even if she should apply for admission as a free State. ["You've got him," and cheers.] [. . .]

The next question propounded to me by Mr. Lincoln is, can the people of a Territory in any lawful way, against the wishes of any citizen of the United States, exclude slavery from their limits prior to the formation of a State Constitution? I answer emphatically, as Mr. Lincoln has heard me answer a hundred times from every stump in Illinois, that in my opinion the people of a Territory can, by lawful means, exclude slavery from their limits prior to the formation of a State Constitution. Mr. Lincoln knew that I had answered that question over and over again. He heard me argue the Nebraska bill on that principle all over the State in 1854, in 1855, and in 1856, and he has no excuse for pretending to be in doubt as to my position on that question. It matters not what way the Supreme Court may hereafter decide as to the abstract question whether slavery may or may not go into a Territory under the Constitution, the people have the lawful means to introduce it or exclude it as they please, for the reason that slavery cannot exist a day or an hour anywhere, unless it is supported by local police regulations. ["Right, right."] Those police regulations can only be established by the local legislature, and if the people are opposed to slavery they will elect representatives to that body who will by unfriendly legislation effectually prevent the introduction of it into their midst. If, on the contrary, they are for it, their legislation will favor its extension. Hence, no matter what the decision of the Supreme Court may be on that abstract question, still the right of the people to make a slave Territory or a free Territory is perfect and complete under the Nebraska bill. I hope Mr. Lincoln deems my answer satisfactory on that point.

In this connection, I will notice the charge which he has introduced in relation to Mr. Chase's amendment. I thought that I had chased that amendment out of Mr. Lincoln's brain at Ottawa; [laughter] but it seems that still haunts his imagination, and he is not yet satisfied. I had supposed that he would be ashamed to press that question further. He is a lawyer, and has been a member of Congress, and has occupied his time and amused you by telling you about parliamentary proceedings. He ought to have known better than to try to palm off his miserable impositions upon this intelligent audience. ["Good," and cheers.] The Nebraska bill provided that the legislative power, and authority of the said Territory, should extend to all rightful subjects of legislation consistent with the organic act and the Constitution of the United States. It did not make any exception as to slavery, but gave all the power that it was possible for Congress to give, without violating the Constitution to the Territorial Legislature, with no exception or limitation on the subject of slavery at all. The language of that bill which I have quoted, gave the full power and the full authority over the subject of slavery, affirmatively and negatively, to introduce it or exclude it, so far as the Constitution of the United States would permit. What more could Mr. Chase give by his amendment? Nothing. He offered his amendment for the identical purpose for which Mr. Lincoln is using it, to enable demagogues in the country to try and deceive the people. ["Good, hit him again," and cheers.]

His amendment was to this effect. It provided that the Legislature should have the power to exclude slavery: and General Cass suggested, "why not give the power to introduce as well as exclude?" The answer was, they have the power already in the bill to do both. Chase was afraid his amendment would be adopted if he put the alternative proposition and so make it fair both ways, but would not yield. He offered it for the purpose of having it rejected. He offered it, as he has himself avowed over and over again, simply to make capital out of it for the stump. He expected that it would be capital for small politicians in the country, and that they would make an effort to deceive the people with it, and he was not mistaken, for Lincoln is carrying out the plan admirably. ["Good, good."] Lincoln knows that the Nebraska bill, without Chase's amendment, gave all the power which the Constitution would permit. Could Congress confer any more? ["No, no."] Could Congress go beyond the Constitution of the country? We gave all a full grant, with no exception in regard to slavery one way or the other. We left that question as we left all others, to be decided by the people for themselves, just as they pleased. I will not occupy my time on this question. I have argued it before all over Illinois. I have argued it in this beautiful city of Freeport; I have argued it in the North, the South, the East, and the West, avowing the same sentiments and the same principles. I have not been afraid to avow my sentiments up here for fear I would be trotted down into Egypt. [Cheers and laughter.]

The third question which Mr. Lincoln presented is, if the Supreme Court of the United States shall decide that a State of this Union cannot exclude slavery from its own limits, will I submit to it? I am amazed that Lincoln should ask such a question. ["A schoolboy knows better."] Yes, a schoolboy does know better. Mr. Lincoln's object is to cast an imputation upon the Supreme Court. He knows that there never was but one man in America, claiming any degree of intelligence or decency, who ever for a moment pretended such a thing. It is true that the Washington *Union,* in an article published on the 17th of last December, did put forth that doctrine, and I denounced the article on the floor of the Senate, in a speech which Mr. Lincoln now pretends was against the President. The *Union* had claimed that slavery had a right to go into the free States, and that any provision in the Constitution or laws of the free States to the contrary were null and void. I denounced it in the Senate, as I said before, and I was the first man who did. Lincoln's friends, Trumbull, and Seward, and Hale, and Wilson, land the whole Black Republican side of the Senate, were silent. They left it to me to denounce it. [Cheers.] And what was the reply made to me on that occasion? Mr. Toombs, of Georgia, got up and undertook to lecture me on the ground that I ought not to have deemed the article worthy of notice, and ought not to have replied to it; that there was not one man, woman or child south of the Potomac, in any slave State, who did not repudiate any such pretension. Mr. Lincoln knows that that reply was made on the spot, and yet now he asks this question. He might as well ask me, suppose Mr. Lincoln should steal a horse, would I sanction it; [laughter] and it would be as genteel in me to ask him, in the event he stole a horse, what ought to be done with him. He casts an imputation upon the Supreme Court of the United States, by supposing that they would violate the Constitution of the United States. I tell him that such a thing is not possible. [Cheers.] It would be an act of moral treason that no man on the bench could ever descend to. Mr. Lincoln himself would never in his partisan feelings so far forget what was right as to be guilty of such an act. ["Good, good."]

The fourth question of Mr. Lincoln is, are you in favor of acquiring additional territory, in disregard as to how such acquisition may affect the Union on the slavery questions? This question is very ingeniously and cunningly put.

The Black Republican creed lays it down expressly, that under no circumstances shall we acquire any more territory unless slavery is first prohibited in the country. I ask Mr. Lincoln whether he is in favor of that proposition. Are you [addressing Mr. Lincoln] opposed to the acquisition of any more territory, under any circumstances, unless slavery is prohibited in it? That he does not like to answer. When I ask him whether he stands up to that article in the platform of his party, he turns, Yankee-fashion, and without answering it, asks me whether I am in favor of acquiring territory without regard to how it may affect the Union on the slavery question. ["Good."] I answer that whenever it becomes necessary, in our growth and progress, to acquire more territory, that I am in favor of it, without reference to the question of slavery, and when we have acquired it, I will leave the people free to do as they please, either to make it slave or free territory, as they prefer. [Here Deacon Bross spoke; the reporter believes that he said, "That's bold." It was said solemnly.] It is idle to tell me or you that we have territory enough. Our fathers supposed that we had enough when our territory extended to the Mississippi river, but a few years' growth and expansion satisfied them that we needed more, and the Louisiana territory, from the West branch of the Mississippi to the British possessions, was acquired. Then we acquired Oregon, then California and New Mexico. We have enough now for the present, but this is a young and a growing nation. It swarms as often as a hive of bees, and as new swarms are turned out each year, there must be hives in which they can gather and make their honey. ["Good."] In less than fifteen years, if the same progress that has distinguished this country for the last fifteen years continues, every foot of vacant land between this and the Pacific Ocean, owned by the United States, will be occupied. Will you not continue to increase at the end of fifteen years as well as now? I tell you, increase, and multiply, and expand, is the law of this nation's existence. ["Good."] You cannot limit this great Republic by mere boundary lines, saying, "thus far shalt thou go, and no further." Any one of you gentlemen might as well say to a son twelve years old that he is big enough, and must not grow any larger, and in order to prevent his growth put a hoop around him to keep him to his present size. What would be the result? Either the hoop must burst and be rent asunder, or the child must die. So it would be with this great nation. With our natural increase, growing with a rapidity unknown in any other part of the globe, with the tide of emigration that is fleeing from despotism in the old world to seek refuge in our own, there is a constant torrent pouring into this country that requires more land, more territory upon which to settle, and just as fast as our interests and our destiny require additional territory in the North, in the South, or on the Islands of the ocean, I am for it, and when we acquire it, will leave the people, according to the Nebraska bill, free to do as they please on the subject of slavery and every other question. ["Good, good, hurrah for Douglas."]

I trust now that Mr. Lincoln will deem himself answered on his four points. He racked his brain so much in devising these four questions that he exhausted himself, and had not strength enough to invent the others. [Laughter.] As soon as he is able to hold a council with his advisers, Lovejoy, Farnsworth, and Fred Douglass, he will frame and propound others. ["Good, good," etc. Renewed laughter, in which Mr. Lincoln feebly joined, saying that he hoped with their aid to get seven questions, the number asked him by Judge Douglas, and so make *conclusions* even.] You Black Republicans who say good, I have no doubt think that they are all good men. ["White, white."] I have reason to recollect that some people in this country think that Fred Douglass is a very good man. The last time I came here to make a speech, while talking from the stand to you, people of Freeport, as I am doing today, I saw a carriage, and a magnificent one it was, drive up and take a position on the outside of the crowd; a beautiful young lady was sitting on the box-seat, whilst Fred Douglass and her mother reclined inside, and the owner of the carriage acted as driver. [Laughter, cheers, cries of "Right," "What have you to say against it," etc.] I saw this in your own town. ["What of it."] All I have to say of it is this, that if you, Black Republicans, think that the negro ought to be on a social equality with your wives and daughters, and ride in a carriage with your wife, whilst you drive the team, you have perfect right to do so. I am told that one of Fred Douglass' kinsmen, another rich black negro, is now traveling in this part of the State making speeches for his friend Lincoln as the champion of black men. ["White men, white men," and "What have you to say against it?" "That's right," etc.] All I have to say on that subject is, that those of you who believe that the negro is your equal and ought to be on an equality with you socially, politically, and legally, have a right to entertain those opinions, and of course will vote for Mr. Lincoln. ["Down with the negro," no, no, etc.] [. . .]

[. . .] [Y]ou see every member from your Congressional District voted for Mr. Lincoln, and they were pledged not to vote for him unless he was committed to the doctrine of no more slave States, the prohibition of slavery in the Territories, and the repeal of the Fugitive Slave law. Mr. Lincoln tells you today that he is not pledged to any such doctrine. Either Mr. Lincoln was then committed to those propositions, or Mr. Turner violated his pledges to you when he voted for him. Either Lincoln was pledged to each one of those propositions, or else every Black Republican Representative from this Congressional District violated his pledge of honor to his constituents by voting for him. I ask you which horn of the dilemma will you take? Will you hold Lincoln up to the platform of his party, or will you accuse every Representative you had in the Legislature of violating his pledge of honor to his constituents? There is no escape for you. Either Mr. Lincoln was committed to those propositions, or your members violated their faith. Take either horn of the dilemma you choose. There is no dodging the question; I want Lincoln's answer. He says he was not pledged to repeal the Fugitive Slave law, that he does not quite like to do it; he will not introduce a law to repeal it, but thinks there ought to be some law; he does not tell what it ought to be; upon the whole, he is altogether undecided, and don't know what to think or do. That is the substance of his answer upon the repeal of the Fugitive Slave law. I put the question to him distinctly, whether he indorsed that part of the Black Republican platform which calls for the entire abrogation and repeal of the Fugitive Slave law. He answers no! that he does not indorse that, but he does not tell what he is for, or what he will vote for. His answer is, in fact, no answer at all. Why cannot he speak out and say what he is for and what he will do?

In regard to there being no more slave States, he is not pledged to that. He would not like, he says, to be put in a position where he would have to vote one way or another upon that question. I pray you, do not put him in a position that would embarrass him so much. Gentlemen, if he goes to the Senate, he may be put in that position, and then which way will he vote?

[A Voice—"How will you vote?"]

Douglas—I will vote for the admission of just such a State as by the form of their Constitution the people show they want; if they want slavery, they shall have it; if they prohibit slavery it shall be prohibited. They can form their institutions to please themselves, subject only to the Constitution; and I for one stand ready to receive them into the Union. Why cannot your Black Republican candidates talk out as plain as that when they are questioned?

I do not want to cheat any man out of his vote. No man is deceived in regard to my principles if I have the power to express myself in terms explicit enough to convey my ideas.

Mr. Lincoln made a speech when he was nominated for the United States Senate which covers all these Abolition platforms. He there lays down a proposition so broad in its abolitionism as to cover the whole ground.

> In my opinion it [the slavery agitation] will not cease until a crisis shall have been reached and passed. "A house divided against itself cannot stand." I believe this Government cannot endure permanently half slave and half free. I do not expect the house to fall—but I do expect it will cease to be divided. It will become all one thing or all the other. Either the opponents of Slavery will arrest the further spread of it, and place it where the public mind shall rest in the belief that it is in the course of ultimate extinction, or its advocates will push it forward till it shall become alike lawful in all the States—old as well as new, North as well as South.

There you find that Mr. Lincoln lays down the doctrine that this Union cannot endure divided as our fathers made it, with free and slave States. He says they must all become one thing, or all the other; that they must all be free or all slave, or else the Union cannot continue to exist. It being his opinion that to admit any more slave States, to continue to divide the Union into free and slave States, will dissolve it. I want to know of Mr. Lincoln whether he will vote for the admission of another slave State.

He tells you the Union cannot exist unless the States are all free or all slave; he tells you that he is opposed to making them all slave, and hence he is for making them all free, in order that the Union may exist; and yet he will not say that he will not vote against another slave State, knowing that the Union must be dissolved if he votes for it. I ask you if that is fair dealing? The true intent and inevitable conclusion to be drawn from his first Springfield speech is, that he is opposed to the admission of any more slave States under any circumstance. If he is so opposed, why not say so? If he believes this Union cannot endure divided into free and slave States, that they must all become free in order to save the Union, he is bound as an honest man, to vote against any more slave States. If he believes it he is bound to do it. Show me that it is my duty in order to save the Union to do a particular act, and I will do it if the Constitution does not prohibit it. [Applause.] I am not for the dissolution of the Union under any circumstances. [Renewed applause.] I will pursue no course of conduct that will give just cause for the dissolution of the Union. The hope of the friends of freedom throughout the world rests upon the perpetuity of this Union.

The down-trodden and oppressed people who are suffering under European despotism all look with hope and anxiety to the American Union as the only resting place and permanent home of freedom and self-government.

Mr. Lincoln says that he believes that this Union cannot continue to endure with slave States in it, and yet he will not tell you distinctly whether he will vote for or against the admission of any more slave States, but says he would not like to be put to the test. [Laughter.] I do not think he will be put to the test. [Renewed laughter.] I do not think that the people of Illinois desire a man to represent them who would not like to be put to the test on the performance of a high constitutional duty. [Cries of "Good."] I will retire in shame from the Senate of the United States when I am not willing to be put to the test in the performance of my duty. I have been put to severe tests. ["That is so."] I have stood by my principles in fair weather and in foul, in the sunshine and in the rain. I have defended the great principles of self-government here among you when Northern sentiment ran in a torrent against me, [a voice—"That is so,"] and I have defended that same great principle when Southern sentiment came down like an avalanche upon me. I was not afraid of any test they put to me. I knew I was right—I knew my principles were sound—I knew that the people would see in the end that I had done right, and I knew that the God of Heaven would smile upon me if I was faithful in the performance of my duty. [Cries of "Good," cheers, and laughter.]

At Jonesboro, September 15

Lincoln

LADIES AND GENTLEMEN: There is very much in the principles that Judge Douglas has here enunciated that I most cordially approve, and over which I shall have no controversy with him. In so far as he has insisted that all the States have the right to do exactly as they please about all their domestic relations, including that of slavery, I agree entirely with him. He places me wrong in spite of all I can tell him, though I repeat it again and again, insisting that I have made no difference with him upon this subject. I have made a great many speeches, some of which have been printed, and it will be utterly impossible for him to find anything that I have ever put in print contrary to what I now say upon this subject. I hold myself under constitutional obligations to allow the people in all the States, without interference, direct or indirect, to do exactly as they please, and I deny that I have any inclination to interfere with them, even if there were no such constitutional obligation. I can only say again that I am placed improperly—altogether improperly, in spite of all I can say—when it is insisted that I entertain any other view or purpose in regard to that matter.

While I am upon this subject, I will make some answers briefly to certain propositions that Judge Douglas has put. He says, "Why can't this Union endure permanently, half slave and half free?" I have said that I supposed it could not, and I will try, before this new audience, to give briefly some of the reasons for entertaining that opinion. Another form of his question is, "Why can't we let it stand as our fathers placed it?" That is the exact difficulty between us. I say that Judge Douglas and his friends have changed it from the position in which our fathers originally placed it. I say, in the way our fathers originally left the slavery question, the institution was in the course of ultimate extinction, and the public mind rested in the belief that it was in the course of ultimate extinction. I say when this government was first established, it was the policy of its founders to prohibit the spread of slavery into the new Territories of the United States, where it had not existed. But Judge Douglas and his friends have broken up that policy, and placed it upon a new basis by which it is to become national and perpetual. All I have asked or desired anywhere is that it should be placed back again upon the basis that the fathers of our government originally placed it upon. I have no doubt that it would become extinct, for all time to come, if we but readopted the policy of the fathers by restricting it to the limits it has already covered—restricting it from the new Territories.

I do not wish to dwell at great length on this branch of the subject at this time, but allow me to repeat one thing that I have stated before. Brooks, the man who assaulted Senator Sumner on the floor of the Senate, and who was complimented with dinners, and silver pitchers, and gold-headed canes, and a good many other things for that feat, in one of his speeches declared that when this government was originally established, nobody expected that the institution of slavery would last until this day. That was but the opinion of one man, but it was such an opinion as we can never get from Judge Douglas, or anybody in favor of slavery in the North at all. You can sometimes get it from a Southern man. He said at the same time that the framers of our government did not have the knowledge that experience has taught us—that experience and the invention of the cotton-gin have taught us that the perpetuation of slavery is a necessity. He insisted, therefore, upon its being changed from the basis upon which the fathers of the government left it to the basis of its perpetuation and nationalization.

I insist that this is the difference between Judge Douglas and myself—that Judge Douglas is helping that change along. I insist upon this government being placed where our fathers originally placed it. [. . .]

[. . .] At Freeport I answered several interrogatories that had been propounded to me by Judge Douglas at the Ottawa meeting. The judge has yet not seen fit to find any fault with the position that I took in regard to those seven interrogatories, which were certainly broad enough, in all conscience, to cover the entire ground. In my answers, which have been printed, and all have had the opportunity of seeing, I take the ground that those who elect me must expect that I will do nothing which will not be in accordance with those answers. I have some right to assert that Judge Douglas has no fault to find with them. But he chooses to still try to thrust me upon different ground without paying any attention to my answers, the obtaining of which from me cost him so much trouble and concern. At the same time, I propounded four interrogatories to him, claiming it as a right that he should answer as many interrogatories for me as I did for him, and I would reserve myself for a future installment when I got them ready. The judge, in answering me upon this occasion, put in what I suppose he intends as answers to all four of my interrogatories. The first one of these interrogatories I have before me, and it is in these words:

Question 1. If the people of Kansas shall, by means entirely unobjectionable in all other respects, adopt a State constitution, and ask admission into the Union under it, before they have the requisite number of inhabitants according to the English bill—some ninety-three thousand—will you vote to admit them?

As I read the judge's answer in the newspaper, and as I remember it as propounded at the time, he does not give any answer which is equivalent to yes or no—I will or I won't. He answers at very considerable length, rather quarreling with me for asking the question, and insisting that Judge Trumbull had done something that I ought to say something about; and finally getting out such statements as induce me to infer that he means to be understood he will, in that supposed case, vote for the admission of Kansas. I only bring this forward now for the purpose of saying that, if he chooses to put a different construction upon his answer, he may do it But if he does not, I shall from this time forward assume that he will vote for the admission of Kansas in disregard of the English bill. He has the right to remove any misunderstanding I may have. I only mention it now that I may hereafter assume this to be the true construction of his answer, if he does not now choose to correct me.

The second interrogatory that I propounded to him was this:

Question 2. Can the people of a United States Territory, in any lawful way, against the wish of any citizen of the United States, exclude slavery from its limits prior to the formation of a State constitution?

To this Judge Douglas answered that they can lawfully exclude slavery from the Territory prior to the formation of a constitution. He goes on to tell us how it can be done. As I understand him, he holds that it can be done by the territorial legislature refusing to make any enactments for the protection of slavery in the Territory, and especially by adopting unfriendly legislation to it. For the sake of clearness, I state it again: that they can exclude slavery from the Territory—first, by withholding what he assumes to be an indispensable assistance to it in the way of legislation; and, second, by unfriendly legislation. If I rightly understand him, I wish to ask your attention for a while to his position.

In the first place, the Supreme Court of the United States has decided that any congressional prohibition of slavery in the Territories is unconstitutional—they have reached this proposition as a conclusion from their former proposition, that the Constitution of the United States expressly recognizes property in slaves; and from that other constitutional provision, that no person shall be deprived of property without due process of law. Hence they reach the conclusion that as the Constitution of the United States expressly recognizes property in slaves, and prohibits any person from being deprived of property without due process of law, to pass an act of Congress by which a man who owned a slave on one side of a line would be deprived of him if he took him on the other side is depriving him of that property without due process of law. That I understand to be the decision of the Supreme Court. I understand also that Judge Douglas adheres most firmly to that decision; and the difficulty is, how is it possible for any power to exclude slavery from the Territory unless in violation of that decision? That is the difficulty.

In the Senate of the United States, in 1856, Judge Trumbull, in a speech, substantially, if not directly, put the same interrogatory to Judge Douglas, as to whether the people of a Territory had the lawful power to exclude slavery prior to the formation of a constitution? Judge Douglas then answered at considerable length, and his answer will be found in the "Congressional Globe," under the date of June 9, 1856. The judge said that whether the people could exclude slavery prior to the formation of a constitution or not was a question to be decided by the Supreme Court. He put that proposition, as will be seen by the "Congressional Globe," in a variety of forms, all running to the same thing in substance—that it was a question for the Supreme Court. I maintain that when he says, after the Supreme Court has decided the question, that the people may yet exclude slavery by any means whatever, he does virtually say that it is not a question for the Supreme Court. He shifts his ground. I appeal to you whether he did not say it was a question for the Supreme Court? Has not the Supreme Court decided that question? When he now says that the people may exclude slavery, does he not make it a question for the people? Does he not virtually shift his ground and say that it is not a question for the court, but for the people? This is a very simple proposition—a very plain and naked one. It seems to me that there is no difficulty in deciding it. In a variety of ways he said that it was a question for the Supreme Court. He did not stop then to tell us that, whatever the Supreme Court decides, the people can by withholding necessary "police regulations" keep slavery out. He did not make any such answer. I submit to you now, whether the new state of the case has not induced the judge to sheer away from his original ground. Would not this be the impression of every fair-minded man?

I hold that the proposition that slavery cannot enter a new country without police regulations is historically false. It is not true at all. I hold that the history of this country shows that the institution of slavery was originally planted upon this continent without these "police regulations" which the judge now thinks necessary for the actual establishment of it. Not only so, but is there not another fact—how came this Dred Scott decision to be made? It was made upon the case of a negro being taken and actually held in slavery in Minnesota Territory, claiming his freedom because the act of Congress prohibited his being so held there. Will the judge pretend that Dred Scott was not held there without police regulations? There is at least one matter of record as to his having been held in slavery in the Territory, not only without police regulations, but in the teeth of congressional legislation supposed to be valid at the time. This shows that there is vigor enough in slavery to plant itself in a new country even against unfriendly legislation. It takes not only law but the enforcement of law to keep it out. That is the history of this country upon the subject.

I wish to ask one other question. It being understood that the Constitution of the United States guarantees property in slaves in the Territories, if there is any infringement of the right of that property, would not the United States courts, organized for the government of the Territory, apply such remedy as might be necessary in that case? It is a maxim held by the courts, that there is no wrong without its remedy; and the courts have a remedy for whatever is acknowledged and treated as a wrong.

Again: I will ask you, my friends, if you were elected members of the legislature, what would be the first thing you would have to do before entering upon your duties? Swear to support the Constitution of the United States. Suppose you believe, as Judge Douglas does, that the Constitution of the United States guarantees to your neighbor the right to hold slaves in that Territory—that they are his property—how can you clear your oaths unless you give him such legislation as is necessary to enable him to enjoy that property? What do you understand by supporting the Constitution of a State, or of the United States? Is it not to give such constitutional helps to the rights established by that Constitution as may be practically needed? Can you, if you swear to support the Constitution, and believe that the Constitution establishes a right, clear your oath, without giving it support? Do you support the Constitution if, knowing or believing there is a right established under it which needs specific legislation, you withhold that legislation? Do you not violate and disregard your oath. I can conceive of nothing plainer in the world. There can be nothing in the words "support the Constitution," if you may run counter to it by refusing support to any right established under the Constitution. And what I say here will hold with still more force against the judge's doctrine of "unfriendly legislation." How could you, having sworn to support the Constitution, and believing that it guaranteed the right to hold slaves in the Territories, assist in legislation intended to defeat that right? That would be violating your own view of the Constitution. Not only so, but if you were to do so, how long would it take the courts to hold your votes unconstitutional and void? Not a moment.

Lastly I would ask—Is not Congress itself under obligation to give legislative support to any right that is established under the United States Constitution? I repeat the question—Is not Congress itself bound to give legislative support to any right that is established in the United States Constitution? A member of Congress swears to support the Constitution of the United States, and if he sees a right established by that Constitution which needs specific legislative protection, can he clear his oath without giving that protection? Let me ask you why many of us who are opposed to slavery upon principle give our acquiescence to a fugitive-slave law? Why do we hold ourselves under obligations to pass such a law, and abide by it when it is passed? Because the Constitution makes provision that the owners of slaves shall have the right to reclaim them. It gives the right to reclaim slaves, and that right is, as Judge Douglas says, a barren right, unless there is legislation that will enforce it.

The mere declaration, "No person held to service or labor in one State under the laws thereof, escaping into another, shall in consequence of any law or regulation therein be discharged from such service or labor, but shall be delivered up on claim of the party to whom such service or labor may be due," is powerless without specific legislation to enforce it. Now, on what ground would a member of Congress who is opposed to slavery in the abstract vote for a fugitive-slave law, as I would deem it my duty to do? Because there is a constitutional right which needs legislation to enforce it. And although it is distasteful to me, I have sworn to support the Constitution, and having so sworn, I cannot conceive that I do support it if I withhold from that right any necessary legislation to make it practical. And if that is true in regard to a fugitive-slave law, is the right to have fugitive slaves reclaimed any better fixed in the Constitution than the right to hold slaves in the Territories? For this decision is a just exposition of the Constitution, as Judge Douglas thinks. Is the one right any better than the other? Is there any man who, while a member of Congress, would give support to the one any more than the other? If I wished to refuse to give legislative support to slave property in the Territories, if a member of Congress, I could not do it, holding the view that the Constitution establishes that right. If I did it at all, it would be because I deny that this decision properly construes the Constitution. But if I acknowledge, with Judge Douglas, that this decision properly construes the Constitution, I cannot conceive that I would be less than a perjured man if I should refuse in Congress to give such protection to that property as in its nature it needed. [. . .]

At Galesburg, October 7

Douglas

[. . .] You find that Mr. Lincoln there proposed that if the doctrine of the Declaration of Independence, declaring all men to be born equal, did not include the negro and put him on an equality with the white man, that we should take the statute-book and tear it out. He there took the ground that the negro race is included in the Declaration of Independence as the equal of the white race, and that there could be no such thing as a distinction in the races, making one superior and the other inferior. I read now from the same speech:

"My friends" [he says], "I have detained you about as long as I desire to do, and I have only to say let us discard all this quibbling about this man and the other man—this race and that race and the other race being inferior, and therefore they must be placed in an inferior position, discarding our standard that we have left us. Let us discard all these things, and unite as one people throughout this land, until we shall once more stand up declaring that all men are created equal." ["That's right," etc.]

Yes, I have no doubt that you think it is right, but the Lincoln men down in Coles, Tazewell, and Sangamon counties do not think it is right. In the conclusion of the same speech, talking to the Chicago Abolitionists, he said: "I leave you, hoping that the lamp of liberty will burn in your bosoms until there shall no longer be a doubt that all men are created free and equal." ["Good, good!"] Well, you say good to that, and you are going to vote for Lincoln because he holds that doctrine. I will not blame you for supporting him on that ground, but I will show you, in immediate contrast with that doctrine, what Mr. Lincoln said down in Egypt in order to get votes in that locality where they do not hold to such a doctrine. In a joint discussion between Mr. Lincoln and myself, at Charleston, I think, on the 18th of last month, Mr. Lincoln, referring to this subject, used the following language:

"I will say, then, that I am not nor ever have been in favor of bringing about in any way the social and political equality of the white and black races; that I am not nor ever have been in favor of making voters of the free negroes, or jurors, or qualifying them to hold office, or having them to marry with white people. I will say in addition, that there is a physical difference between the white and black races, which, I suppose, will forever forbid the two races living together upon terms of social and political equality, and inasmuch as they cannot so live, that while they do remain together, there must be the position of superior and inferior, that I as much as any other man am in favor of the superior position being assigned to the white man." ["Good for Lincoln!"]

Fellow-citizens, here you find men hurrahing for Lincoln, and saying that he did right when in one part of the State he stood up for negro equality, and in another part, for political effect, discarded the doctrine, and declared that there always must be a superior and inferior race. Abolitionists up north are expected and required to vote for Lincoln because he goes for the equality of the races, holding that by the Declaration of Independence the white man and the negro were created equal, and endowed by the divine law with that equality, and down south he tells the Old Whigs, the Kentuckians, Virginians, and Tennesseeans that there is a physical difference in the races, making one superior and the other inferior, and that he is in favor of maintaining the superiority of the white race over the negro.

Now, how can you reconcile those two positions of Mr. Lincoln? He is to be voted for in the south as a pro-slavery man, and he is to be voted for in the north as an Abolitionist. Up here he thinks it is all nonsense to talk about a difference between the races, and says that we must "discard all quibbling about this race and that race and the other race being inferior, and therefore they must be placed in an inferior position." Down south he makes this "quibble" about this race and that race and the other race being inferior as the creed of his party, and declares that the negro can never be elevated to the position of the white man. You find that his political meetings are called by different names in different counties in the State. Here they are called Republican meetings, but in old Tazewell, where Lincoln made a speech last Tuesday, he did not address a Republican meeting, but "a grand rally of the Lincoln men." There are very few Republicans there, because Tazewell County is filled with old Virginians and Kentuckians, all of whom are Whigs or Democrats, and if Mr. Lincoln had called an Abolition or Republican meeting there, he would not get many votes. Go down into Egypt, and you will find that he and his party are operating under an alias there, which his friend Trumbull has given them, in order that they may cheat the people. When I was down in Monroe County a few weeks ago addressing the people, I saw handbills posted announcing that Mr. Trumbull was going to speak in behalf of Lincoln, and what do you think the name of his party was there? Why, the "Free Democracy." Mr. Trumbull and Mr. Jehu Baker were announced to address the Free Democracy of Monroe County, and the bill was signed "Many Free Democrats." The reason that Mr. Lincoln and his party adopted the name of "Free Democracy" down there was because Monroe County has always been an old-fashioned Democratic county, and hence it was necessary to make the people believe that they were Democrats, sympathized with them, and were fighting for Lincoln as Democrats. Come up to Springfield, where Lincoln now lives and always has lived, and you find that the convention of his party which assembled to nominate candidates for the legislature, who are expected to vote for him if elected, dare not adopt the name of Republican, but assembled under the title of "All opposed to the Democracy." Thus you find that Mr. Lincoln's creed cannot travel through even one half of the counties of this State, but that it changes its hues and becomes lighter and lighter as it travels from the extreme north, until it is nearly white when it reaches the extreme south end of the State. I ask you, my friends, why cannot Republicans avow their principles alike everywhere? I would despise myself if I thought that I was procuring your votes by concealing my opinions, and by avowing one set of principles in one part of the State, and a different set in another part.

If I do not truly and honorably represent your feelings and principles, then I ought not to be your senator; and I will never conceal my opinions, or modify or change them a hair's-breadth, in order to get votes. I tell you that this Chicago doctrine of Lincoln's—declaring that the negro and the white man are made equal by the Declaration of Independence and by Divine Providence—is a monstrous heresy. The signers of the Declaration of Independence never dreamed of the negro when they were writing that document. They referred to white men, to men of European birth and European descent, when they declared the equality of all men. I see a gentleman there in the crowd shaking his head. Let me remind him that when Thomas Jefferson wrote that document he was the owner, and so continued until his death, of a large number of slaves. Did he intend to say in that Declaration that his negro slaves, which he held and treated as property, were created his equals by divine law, and that he was violating the law of God every day of his life by holding them as slaves? It must be borne in mind that when that Declaration was put forth, every one of the thirteen colonies were slave-holding colonies, and every man who signed that instrument represented a slaveholding constituency. Recollect, also, that no one of them emancipated his slaves, much less put them on an equality with himself, after he signed the Declaration. On the contrary, they all continued to hold their negroes as slaves during the Revolutionary War. Now, do you believe—are you willing to have it said—that every man who signed the Declaration of Independence declared the negro his equal, and then was hypocrite enough to hold him as a slave, in violation of what he believed to be the divine law? And yet when you say that the Declaration of Independence includes the negro, you charge the signers of it with hypocrisy.

I say to you frankly, that in my opinion this government was made by our fathers on the white basis. It was made by white men for the benefit of white men and their posterity forever, and was intended to be administered by white men in all time to come. But while I hold that under our Constitution and political system the negro is not a citizen, cannot be a citizen, and ought not to be a citizen, it does not follow by any means that he should be a slave. On the contrary, it does follow that the negro as an inferior race ought to possess every right, every privilege, every immunity which he can safely exercise consistent with the safety of the society in which he lives. Humanity requires, and Christianity commands, that you shall extend to every inferior being, and every dependent being, all the privileges, immunities, and advantages which can be granted to them consistent with the safety of society. If you ask me the nature and extent of these privileges, I answer that that is a question which the people of each State must decide for themselves. Illinois has decided that question for herself. We have said that in this State the negro shall not be a slave, nor shall he be a citizen. Kentucky holds a different doctrine. New York holds one different from either, and Maine one different from all. Virginia, in her policy on this question, differs in many respects from the other, and so on, until there are hardly two States whose policy is exactly alike in regard to the relation of the white man and the negro. Nor can you reconcile them and make them alike. Each State must do as it pleases. Illinois had as much right to adopt the policy which we have on that subject as Kentucky had to adopt a different policy. The great principle of this government is that each State has the right to do as it pleases on all these questions, and no other State or power on earth has the right to interfere with us, or complain of us merely because our system differs from theirs. In the compromise measures of 1850, Mr. Clay declared that this great principle ought to exist in the Territories as well as in the States, and I reasserted his doctrine in the Kansas and Nebraska bill in 1854. [. . .]

[. . .] I hold that in this country there is no power on the face of the globe that can force any institution on an unwilling people. The great fundamental principle of our government is that the people of each State and each Territory shall be left perfectly free to decide for themselves what shall be the nature and character of their institutions. When this government was made, it was based on that principle. At the time of its formation there were twelve slaveholding States, and one free State, in this Union. Suppose this doctrine of Mr. Lincoln and the Republicans, of uniformity of laws of all the States on the subject of slavery, had prevailed; suppose Mr. Lincoln himself had been a member of the convention which framed the Constitution, and that he had risen in that august body, and, addressing the Father of his Country, had said as he did at Springfield:

> A house divided against itself cannot stand. I believe this government cannot endure permanently half slave and half free. I do not expect the Union to be dissolved—I do not expect the house to fall, but I do expect it will cease to be divided. It will become all one thing, or all the other.

What do you think would have been the result? Suppose he had made that convention believe that doctrine, and they had acted upon it, what do you think would have been the result? Do you believe that one free State would have outvoted the twelve slaveholding States, and thus abolished slavery? On the contrary, would not the twelve slaveholding States have outvoted the one free State, and under his doctrine have fastened slavery by an irrevocable constitutional provision upon every inch of the American republic? Thus you see that the doctrine he now advocates, if proclaimed at the beginning of the government, would have established slavery everywhere throughout the American continent; and are you willing, now that we have the majority section, to exercise a power which we never would have submitted to when we were in the minority? If the Southern States had attempted to control our institutions, and make the States all slave when they had the power, I ask would you have submitted to it? If you would not, are you willing, now that we have become the strongest under that great principle of self-government that allows each State to do as it pleases, to attempt to control the Southern institutions? Then, my friends, I say to you that there is but one path of peace in this republic, and that is to administer this government as our fathers made it, divided into free and slave States, allowing each State to decide for itself whether it wants slavery or not. If Illinois will settle the slavery question for herself, and mind her own business and let her neighbors alone, we will be at peace with Kentucky, and every other Southern State. If every other State in the Union will do the same, there will be peace between the North and South, and in the whole Union. [. . .]

Lincoln

[. . .] The Judge has alluded to the Declaration of Independence, and insisted that negroes are not included in that Declaration; and that it is, a slander upon the framers of that instrument to suppose that negroes were meant therein; and he asks you: Is it possible to believe that Mr. Jefferson, who penned the immortal paper, could have supposed himself applying the language of that instrument to the negro race, and yet held a portion of that race in slavery? Would he not at once have freed them? I only have to remark upon this part of the Judge's speech (and that, too, very briefly, for I shall not detain myself, or you, upon that point for any great length of time), that I believe the entire records of the world, from the date of the Declaration of Independence up to within three years ago, may be searched in vain for one single affirmation, from one single man, that the negro was not included in the Declaration of Independence; I think I may defy Judge Douglas to show that he ever said so, that Washington ever said so, that any president ever said so, that any member of Congress ever said so, or that any living man upon the whole earth ever said so, until the necessities of the present policy of the Democratic party, in regard to slavery, had to invent that affirmation. And I will remind Judge Douglas and this audience that while Mr. Jefferson was the owner of slaves, as undoubtedly he was, in speaking upon this very subject, he used the strong language that "he trembled for his country when he remembered that God was just"; and I will offer the highest premium in my power to Judge Douglas if he will show that he, in all his life, ever uttered a sentiment at all akin to that of Jefferson. [. . .]

Now a few words in regard to these extracts from speeches of mine which Judge Douglas has read to you, and which he supposes are in very great contrast to each other. Those speeches have been before the public for a considerable time, and if they have any inconsistency in them, if there is any conflict in them, the public have been able to detect it. When the judge says, in speaking on this subject, that I make speeches of one sort for the people of the northern end of the State, and of a different sort for the southern people, he assumes that I do not understand that my speeches will be put in print and read north and south. I knew all the while that the speech that I made at Chicago and the one I made at Jonesboro and the one at Charleston would all be put in print, and all the reading and intelligent men in the community would see them and know all about my opinions; and I have not supposed, and do not now suppose, that there is any conflict whatever between them. But the judge will have it that if we do not confess that there is a sort of inequality between the white and black races which justifies us in making them slaves, we must, then, insist that there is a degree of equality that requires us to make them our wives. Now, I have all the while taken a broad distinction in regard to that matter; and that is all there is in these different speeches which he arrays here, and the entire reading of either of the speeches will show that that distinction was made. Perhaps by taking two parts of the same speech he could have got up as much of a conflict as the one he has found. I have all the while maintained that in so far as it should be insisted that there was an equality between the white and black races that should produce a perfect social and political equality, it was an impossibility. This you have seen in my printed speeches, and with it I have said that in their right to "life, liberty, and the pursuit of happiness," as proclaimed in that old Declaration, the inferior races are our equals. And these declarations I have constantly made in reference to the abstract moral question, to contemplate and consider when we are legislating about any new country which is not already cursed with the actual presence of the evil—slavery. I have never manifested any impatience with the necessities that spring from the actual presence of black people amongst us, and the actual existence of slavery amongst us where it does already exist; but I have insisted that, in legislating for new countries where it does not exist, there is no just rule other than that of moral and abstract right. With reference to those new countries, those maxims as to the right of a people to "life, liberty, and the pursuit of happiness" were the just rules to be constantly referred to. There is no misunderstanding this, except by men interested to misunderstand it. I take it that I have to address an intelligent and reading community who will peruse what I say, weigh it, and then judge whether I advance improper or unsound views, or whether I advance hypocritical and deceptive and contrary views in different portions of the country. I believe myself to be guilty of no such thing as the latter, though, of course, I cannot claim that I am entirely free from all error in the opinions I advance.

The judge has also detained us awhile in regard to the distinction between his party and our party. His he assumes to be a national party—ours a sectional one. He does this in asking the question whether this country has any interest in the maintenance of the Republican party? He assumes that our party is altogether sectional—that the party to which he adheres is national; and the argument is that no party can be a rightful party—can be based upon rightful principles—unless it can announce its principles everywhere. I presume that Judge Douglas could not go into Russia and announce the doctrine of our national Democracy; he could not denounce the doctrine of kings and emperors and monarchies in Russia; and it may be true of this country, that in some places we may not be able to proclaim a doctrine as clearly true as the truth of Democracy, because there is a section so directly opposed to it that they will not tolerate us in doing so. Is it the true test of the soundness of a doctrine, that in some places people won't let you proclaim it? Is that the way to test the truth of any doctrine? Why, I understand that at one time the people of Chicago would not let Judge Douglas preach a certain favorite doctrine of his. I commend to his consideration the question, whether he takes that as a test of the unsoundness of what he wanted to preach.

There is another thing to which I wish to ask attention for a little while on this occasion. What has always been the evidence brought forward to prove that the Republican party is a sectional party? The main one was that in the Southern portion of the Union the people did not let the Republicans proclaim their doctrines amongst them. That has been the main evidence brought forward—that they had no supporters, or substantially none, in the slave States. The South have not taken hold of our principles as we announce them; nor does Judge Douglas now grapple with those principles. We have a Republican State platform, laid down in Springfield in June last, stating our position all the way through the questions before the country. We are now far advanced in this canvass. Judge Douglas and I have made perhaps forty speeches apiece, and we have now for the fifth time met face to face in debate, and up to this day I have not found either Judge Douglas or any friend of his taking hold of the Republican platform or laying his finger upon anything in it that is wrong. I ask you all to recollect that. Judge Douglas turns away from the platform of principles to the fact that he can find people somewhere who will not allow us to announce those principles. If he had great confidence that our principles were wrong, he would take hold of them and demonstrate them to be wrong. But he does not do so. The only evidence he has of their being wrong is in the fact that there are people who won't allow us to preach them. I ask again is that the way to test the soundness of a doctrine? I ask his attention also to the fact that by the rule of nationality he is himself fast becoming sectional. I ask his attention to the fact that his speeches would not go as current now south of the Ohio River as they have formerly gone there. I ask his attention to the fact that he felicitates himself today that all the Democrats of the free States are agreeing with him, while he omits to tell us that the Democrats of any slave State agree with him. If he has not thought of this, I commend to his consideration the evidence in his own declaration, on this day, of his becoming sectional too. I see it rapidly approaching. Whatever may be the result of this ephemeral contest between Judge Douglas and myself, I see the day rapidly approaching when his pill of sectionalism, which he has been thrusting down the throats of Republicans for years past, will be crowded down his own throat.

Now in regard to what Judge Douglas said (in the beginning of his speech) about the compromise of 1850 containing the principle of the Nebraska bill; although I have often presented my views upon that subject, yet as I have not done so in this canvass, I will, if you please, detain you a little with them. I have always maintained so far as I was able that there was nothing of the principle of the Nebraska bill in the compromise of 1850 at all—nothing whatever.

Where can you find the principle of the Nebraska bill in that compromise? If anywhere, in the two pieces of the compromise organizing the Territories of New Mexico and Utah. It was expressly provided in these two acts that, when they came to be admitted into the Union, they should be admitted with or without slavery, as they should choose, by their own constitutions. Nothing was said in either of those acts as to what was to be done in relation to slavery during the territorial existence of those Territories, while Henry Clay constantly made the declaration (Judge Douglas recognizing him as a leader) that, in his opinion, the old Mexican laws would control that question during the territorial existence, and that these old Mexican laws excluded slavery. How can that be used as a principle for declaring that during the territorial existence, as well as at the time of framing the constitution, the people, if you please, might have slaves if they wanted them? I am not discussing the question whether it is right or wrong; but how are the New Mexican and Utah laws patterns for the Nebraska bill? I maintain that the organization of Utah and New Mexico did not establish a general principle at all. It had no feature establishing a general principle. The acts to which I have referred were a part of a general system of compromises. They did not lay down what was proposed as a regular policy for the Territories; only an agreement in this particular case to do in that way, because other things were done that were to be a compensation for it. They were allowed to come in that shape, because in another way it was paid for—considering that as a part of that system of measures called the compromise of 1850, which finally included half a dozen acts. It included the admission of California as a free State, which was kept out of the Union for half a year because it had formed a free constitution. It included the settlement of the boundary of Texas, which had been undefined before, which was in itself a slavery question; for if you pushed the line further west, you made Texas larger, and made more slave Territory; while if you drew the line toward the east, you narrowed the boundary and diminished the domain of slavery, and by so much increased free Territory. It included the abolition of the slave-trade in the District of Columbia. It included the passage of a new fugitive-slave law. All these things were put together, and though passed in separate acts, were nevertheless in legislation (as the speeches at the time will show) made to depend upon each other. Each got votes, with the understanding that the other measures were to pass, and by this system of compromise, in that series of measures, those two bills—the New Mexico and Utah bills—were passed; and I say for that reason they could not be taken as models, framed upon their own intrinsic principle, for all future Territories. And I have the evidence of this in the fact that Judge Douglas, a year afterward, or more than a year afterward perhaps, when he first introduced bills for the purpose of framing new Territories, did not attempt to follow these bills of New Mexico and Utah; and even when he introduced this Nebraska bill, I think you will discover that he did not exactly follow them. But I do not wish to dwell at great length upon this branch of the discussion. My own opinion is that a thorough investigation will show most plainly that the New Mexico and Utah bills were part of a system of compromise, and not designed as patterns for future territorial legislation, and that this Nebraska bill did not follow them as a pattern at all.

The judge tells us, in proceeding, that he is opposed to making any odious distinctions between free and slave States. I am altogether unaware that the Republicans are in favor of making any odious distinctions between the free and slave States. But there still is a difference, I think, between Judge Douglas and the Republicans in this. I suppose that the real reference between Judge Douglas and his friends and the Republicans, on the contrary, is that the judge is not in favor of making any difference between slavery and liberty—that he is in favor of eradicating, of pressing out of view, the questions of preference in this country for free or slave institutions; and consequently every sentiment he utters discards the idea that there is any wrong in slavery. Everything that emanates from him or his coadjutors in their course of policy carefully excludes the thought that there is anything wrong in slavery. All their arguments, if you will consider them, will be seen to exclude the thought that there is anything whatever wrong in slavery. If you will take the judge's speeches, and select the short and pointed sentences expressed by him,—as his declaration that he "don't care whether slavery is voted up or down,"—you will see at once that this is perfectly logical, if you do not admit that slavery is wrong. If you do admit that it is wrong, Judge Douglas cannot logically say he don't care whether a wrong is voted up or voted down. Judge Douglas declares that if any community wants slavery they have a right to have it. He can say that logically, if he says that there is no wrong in slavery; but if you admit that there is a wrong in it, he cannot logically say that anybody has a right to do wrong.

He insists that, upon the score of equality, the owners of slaves and owners of property—of horses and every other sort of property—should be alike, and hold them alike in a new Territory. That is perfectly logical, if the two species of property are alike, and are equally founded in right. But if you admit that one of them is wrong, you cannot institute any equality between right and wrong. And from this difference of sentiment—the belief on the part of one that the institution is wrong, and a policy springing from that belief which looks to the arrest of the enlargement of that wrong; and this other sentiment, that it is no wrong, and a policy sprung from that sentiment which will tolerate no idea of preventing that wrong from growing larger, and looks to there never being an end of it through all the existence of things—arises the real difference between Judge Douglas and his friends on the one hand, and the Republicans on the other. Now, I confess myself as belonging to that class in the country who contemplate slavery as a moral, social, and political evil, having due regard for its actual existence amongst us, and the difficulties of getting rid of it in any satisfactory way, and to all the constitutional obligations which have been thrown about it; but who, nevertheless, desire a policy that looks to the prevention of it as a wrong, and looks hopefully to the time when as a wrong it may come to an end. [. . .]

While we were at Freeport, in one of these joint discussions, I answered certain interrogatories which Judge Douglas had propounded to me, and there in turn propounded some to him, which he in a sort of way answered. The third one of these interrogatories I have with me, and wish now to make some comments upon it. It was in these words: "If the Supreme

Court of the United States shall decide that States cannot exclude slavery from their limits, are you in favor of acquiescing in, adopting, and following such decision as a rule of political action?"

To this interrogatory Judge Douglas made no answer in any just sense of the word. He contented himself with sneering at the thought that it was possible for the Supreme Court ever to make such a decision. He sneered at me for propounding the interrogatory. I had not propounded it without some reflection, and I wish now to address to this audience some remarks upon it.

In the second clause of the sixth article, I believe it is, of the Constitution of the United States, we find the following language: "This Constitution and the laws of the United States which shall be made in pursuance thereof, and all treaties made, or which shall be made, under the authority of the United States, shall be the supreme law of the land; and the judges in every State shall be bound thereby, anything in the constitution or laws of any State to the contrary notwithstanding."

The essence of the Dred Scott case is compressed into the sentence which I will now read: "Now, as we have already said in an earlier part of this opinion, upon a different point, the right of property in a slave is distinctly and expressly affirmed in the Constitution." I repeat it, "The right of property in a slave is distinctly and expressly affirmed in the Constitution"! What is to be "affirmed" in the Constitution? Made firm in the Constitution—so made that it cannot be separated from the Constitution without breaking the Constitution—durable as the Constitution, and part of the Constitution? Now, remembering the provision of the Constitution which I have read, affirming that that instrument is the supreme law of the land; that the judges of every State shall be bound by it, any law or constitution of any State to the contrary notwithstanding; that the right of property in a slave is affirmed in that Constitution, is made formed into, and cannot be separated from it without breaking it; durable as the instrument, part of the instrument—what follows as a short and even syllogistic argument from it? I think it follows, and I submit to the consideration of men capable of arguing, whether as I state it, in syllogistic form, the argument has any fault in it?

Nothing in the constitution or laws of any State can destroy a right distinctly and expressly affirmed in the Constitution of the United States.

The right of property in a slave is distinctly and expressly affirmed in the Constitution of the United States.

Therefore, nothing in the constitution or laws of any State can destroy the right of property in a slave.

I believe that no fault can be pointed out in that argument; assuming the truth of the premises, the conclusion, so far as I have capacity at all to understand it, follows inevitably. There is a fault in it, as I think, but the fault is not in the reasoning; the falsehood, in fact, is a fault in the premises. I believe that the right of property in a slave is not distinctly and expressly affirmed in the Constitution, and Judge Douglas thinks it is. I believe that the Supreme Court and the advocates of that decision may search in vain for the place in the Constitution where the right of property in a slave is distinctly and expressly affirmed. I say, therefore, that I think one of the premises is not true in fact. But it is true with Judge Douglas. It is true with the Supreme Court who pronounced it. They are stopped from denying it, and being stopped from denying it, the conclusion follows that the Constitution of the United States, being the supreme law, no constitution or law can interfere with it. It being affirmed in the decision that the right of property in a slave is distinctly and expressly affirmed in the Constitution, the conclusion inevitably follows that no State law or constitution can destroy that right. I then say to Judge Douglas, and to all others, that I think it will take a better answer than a sneer to show that those who have said that the right of property in a slave is distinctly and expressly affirmed in the Constitution are not prepared to show that no constitution or law can destroy that right. I say I believe it will take a far better argument than a mere sneer to show to the minds of intelligent men that whoever has so said is not prepared, whenever public sentiment is so far advanced as to justify it, to say the other.

This is but an opinion, and the opinion of one very humble man; but it is my opinion that the Dred Scott decision, as it is, never would have been made in its present form if the party that made it had not been sustained previously by the elections. My own opinion is that the new Dred Scott decision, deciding against the right of the people of the States to exclude slavery, will never be made if that party is not sustained by the elections. I believe, further, that it is just as sure to be made as tomorrow is to come, if that party shall be sustained. I have said upon a former occasion, and I repeat it now, that the course of argument that Judge Douglas makes use of upon this subject (I charge not his motives in this) is preparing the public mind for that new Dred Scott decision. I have asked him again to point out to me the reasons for his first adherence to the Dred Scott decision as it is. I have turned his attention to the fact that General Jackson differed with him in regard to the political obligation of a Supreme Court decision. Jefferson said that "judges are as honest as other men, and not more so." And he said, substantially, that whenever a free people should give up in absolute submission to any department of government, retaining for themselves no appeal from it, their liberties were gone. I have asked his attention to the fact that the Cincinnati platform, upon which he says he stands, disregards a time-honored decision of the Supreme Court, in defying the power of Congress to establish a national bank. I have asked his attention to the fact that he himself was one of the most active instruments at one time in breaking down the Supreme Court of the State of Illinois, because it had made a decision distasteful to him—a struggle ending in the remarkable circumstance of his sitting down as one of the new judges who were to overslaugh that decision, getting his title of judge in that very way.

So far in this controversy I can get no answer at all from Judge Douglas upon these subjects. Not one can I get from him, except that he swells himself up and says: "All of us who stand by the decision of the Supreme Court are the friends of the Constitution; all you fellows that dare question it in any way are the enemies of the Constitution." Now in this very devoted adherence to this decision, in opposition to all the great political leaders whom he has recognized as leaders—in opposition to his former self and history, there is something very marked. And the manner in which he adheres to it—not as being right upon the merits, as he conceives, because he did not discuss that at all), but as being absolutely obligatory upon every one simply because of the source from whence it comes—as that which no man can gainsay, whatever it may be—this is another marked feature of his adherence to that decision. It marks it in this respect, that it commits him to the next decision, whenever it comes, as being as obligatory as this one, since he does not investigate it, and won't inquire whether this opinion is right or wrong. So he takes the next one without inquiring whether it is right or wrong. He teaches men this doctrine, and in so doing prepares the public mind to take the next decision when it comes without any inquiry. In this I think I argue fairly (without questioning motives at all) that Judge Douglas is most ingeniously and powerfully preparing the public mind to take that decision when it comes; and not only so, but he is doing it in various other ways. In these general maxims about liberty—in his assertions that he "don't care whether slavery is voted up or voted down"; that "whoever wants slavery has a right to have it"; that "upon principles of equality it should be allowed to go everywhere"; that "there is no inconsistency between free and slave institutions"—in this he is also preparing (whether purposely or not) the way for making the institution of slavery national. I repeat again, for I wish no misunderstanding, that I do not charge that he means it so; but I call upon your minds to inquire, if you were going to get the best instrument you could, and then set it to work in the most ingenious way, to prepare the public mind for this movement, operating in the free States, where there is now an abhorrence of the institution of slavery, could you find an instrument so capable of doing it as Judge Douglas, or one employed in so apt a way to do it?

I have said once before, and I will repeat it now, that Mr. Clay, when he was once answering an objection to the Colonization Society, that it had a tendency to the ultimate emancipation of the slaves, said that "those who would repress all tendencies to liberty and ultimate emancipation must do more than put down the benevolent efforts of the Colonization Society—they must go back to the era of our liberty and independence, and muzzle the cannon that thunders its annual joyous return—they must blot out the moral lights around us—they must penetrate the human soul, and eradicate the light of reason and the love of liberty"! And I do think—I repeat, though I said it on a former occasion—that Judge Douglas, and whoever, like him, teaches that the negro has no share, humble though it may be, in the Declaration of Independence, is going back to the era of our liberty and independence, and, so far as in him lies muzzling the cannon that thunders its annual joyous return; that he is blowing out the moral lights around us, when he contends that whoever wants slaves has a right to hold them; that he is penetrating, so far as lies in his power the human soul, and eradicating the light of reason and the love of liberty, when he is in every possible way preparing the public mind, by his vast influence, for making the institution of slavery perpetual and national. [. . .]

And now it only remains for me to say that I think it is a very grave question for the people of this Union to consider whether, in view of the fact that this slavery question has been the only one that has ever endangered our republican institutions—the only one that has ever threatened or menaced a dissolution of the Union—that has ever disturbed us in such a way as to make us fear for the perpetuity of our liberty—in view of these facts, I think it is an exceedingly interesting and important question for this people to consider whether we shall engage in the policy of acquiring additional territory, discarding altogether from our consideration, while obtaining new territory, the question how it may affect us in regard to this the only endangering element to our liberties and national greatness. The judge's view has been expressed. I, in my answer to his question, have expressed mine. I think it will become an important and practical question. Our views are before the public. I am willing and anxious that they should consider them fully—that they should turn it about and consider the importance of the question, and arrive at a just conclusion as to whether it is or is not wise in the people of this Union, in the acquisition of new territory, to consider whether it will add to the disturbance that is existing among us—whether it will add to the one only danger that has ever threatened the perpetuity of the Union or our own liberties. I think it is extremely important that they shall decide, and rightly decide, that question before entering upon that policy.

And now, my friends, having said the little I wish to say upon this head, whether I have occupied the whole of the remnant of my time or not, I believe I could not enter upon any new topic so as to treat it fully without transcending my time, which I would not for a moment think of doing. I give way to Judge Douglas.

At Quincy, October 13

Lincoln

[. . .] We have in this nation the element of domestic slavery. It is a matter of absolute certainty that it is a disturbing element. It is the opinion of all the great men who have expressed an opinion upon it, that it is a dangerous element. We keep up a controversy in regard to it. That controversy necessarily springs from difference of opinion, and if we can learn exactly—can reduce to the lowest elements—what that difference of opinion is, we perhaps shall be better prepared for discussing the different systems of policy that we would propose in regard to that disturbing element. I suggest that the difference of opinion, reduced to its lowest terms, is no other than the difference between the men who think slavery a wrong and those who do not think it wrong. The Republican party think it wrong—we think it is a moral, a social, and a political wrong. We think it is a wrong not confining itself merely to the persons or the States where it exists, but that it is a wrong which in its tendency, to say the least, affects the existence of the whole nation. Because we think it wrong, we propose a course of policy that shall deal with it as a wrong. We deal with it as with any other wrong, in so far as we can prevent its growing any larger, and so deal with it that in the run of time there may be some promise of an end to it. We have a due regard to the actual presence of it amongst us, and the difficulties of getting rid of it in any satisfactory way, and all the constitutional obligations thrown about it. I suppose that in reference both to its actual existence in the nation, and to our constitutional obligations, we have no right at all to disturb, it in the States where it exists, and we profess that we have no more inclination to disturb it than we have the right to do it. We go further than that: we don't propose to disturb it where, in one instance, we think the Constitution would permit us. We think the Constitution would permit us to disturb it in the District of Columbia. Still we do not propose to do that, unless it should be in terms which I don't suppose the nation is very likely soon to agree to—the terms of making the emancipation gradual and compensating the unwilling owners. Where we suppose we have the constitutional right, we restrain ourselves in reference to the actual existence of the institution and the difficulties thrown about it. We also oppose it as an evil so far as it seeks to spread itself. We insist on the policy that shall restrict it to its present limits. We don't suppose that in doing this we violate anything due to the actual presence of the institution, or anything due to the constitutional guaranties thrown around it.

We oppose the Dred Scott decision in a certain way, upon which I ought perhaps to address you a few words. We do not propose that when Dred Scott has been decided to be a slave by the court, we, as a mob, will decide him to be free. We do not propose that, when any other one, or one thousand, shall be decided by that court to be slaves, we will in any violent way disturb the rights of property thus settled, but we nevertheless do oppose that decision as a political rule, which shall be binding on the voter to vote for nobody who thinks it wrong, which shall be binding on the members of Congress or the President to favor no measure that does not actually concur with the principles of that decision. We do not propose to be bound by it as a political rule in that way, because we think it lays the foundation not merely of enlarging and spreading out what we consider an evil, but it lays the foundation for spreading that evil into the States themselves. We propose so resisting it as to have it reversed if we can, and a new judicial rule established upon this subject.

I will add this, that if there be any man who does not believe that slavery is wrong in the three aspects which I have mentioned, or in any one of them, that man is misplaced and ought to leave us. While, on the other hand, if there be any man in the Republican party who is impatient over the necessity springing from its actual presence, and is impatient of the constitutional guaranties thrown around it, and would act in disregard of these, he too is misplaced, standing with us. He will find his place somewhere else; for we have a due regard, so far as we are capable of understanding them, for all these things. This, gentlemen, as well as I can give it, is a plain statement of our principles in all their enormity.

I will say now that there is a sentiment in the country contrary to me—a sentiment which holds that slavery is not wrong, and therefore it goes for the policy that does not propose dealing with it as a wrong. That policy is the Democratic policy, and that sentiment is the Democratic sentiment. If there be a doubt in the mind of any one of this vast audience that this is really the central idea of the Democratic party, in relation to this subject, I ask him to bear with me while I state a few things tending, as I think, to prove that proposition. In the first place, the leading man—I think I may do my friend Judge Douglas the honor of calling him such—advocating the present Democratic policy never himself says it is wrong. He has the high distinction, so far as I know, of never having said slavery is either right or wrong. Almost everybody else says one or the other but the judge never does. If there be a man in the Democratic party who thinks it is wrong, and yet clings to that party, I suggest to him in the first place that his leader don't talk as he does, for he never says that it is wrong. In the second place, I suggest to him that if he will examine the policy proposed to be carried forward, he will find that he carefully excludes the idea that there is anything wrong in it. If you will examine the arguments that are made on it, you will find that every one carefully excludes the idea that there is anything wrong in slavery. Perhaps that Democrat who says he is as much opposed to slavery as I am, will tell me that I am wrong about this. I wish him to examine his own course in regard to this matter a moment, and then see if his opinion will not be changed a little. You say it is wrong; but don't you constantly object to anybody else saying so? Do you not constantly argue that this is not the right place to oppose it? You say it must not be opposed in the free States, because slavery is not there; it must not be opposed in the slave States, because it is there; it must not be opposed in politics, because that will make a fuss; it must not be opposed in the pulpit, because it is not religion. Then where is the place to oppose it? There is no suitable place to oppose it. There is no plan in the country to oppose this evil overspreading the continent, which you say yourself is coming. Frank Blair and Gratz Brown tried to get up a system of gradual emancipation in Missouri, had an election in August, and got beat; and you, Mr. Democrat, threw up your hat and hallooed, "Hurrah for Democracy!"

So I say again, that in regard to the arguments that are made, when Judge Douglas says he "don't care whether slavery is voted up or down," whether he means that as an individual expression of sentiment, or only as a sort of statement of his views on national policy, it is alike true to say that he can thus argue logically if he don't see anything wrong in it; but he cannot say so logically if he admits that slavery is wrong. He cannot say that he would as soon see a wrong voted up as voted down. When Judge Douglas says that whoever or whatever community wants slaves, they have a right to have them, he is perfectly logical if there is nothing wrong in the institution; but if you admit that it is wrong, he cannot logically say that anybody has a right to do wrong. When he says that slave property and horse and hog property are alike to be allowed to go into the Territories, upon the principles of equality, he is reasoning truly if there is no difference between them as property; but if the one is property, held rightfully, and the other is wrong, then there is no equality between the right and wrong; so that, turn it in any way you can, in all the arguments sustaining the Democratic policy, and in that policy itself, there is a careful studied exclusion of the idea that there is anything wrong in slavery. Let us understand this. I am not, just here, trying to prove that we are right and they are wrong. I have been stating where we and they stand, and trying to show what is the real difference between us; and I now can say that whenever we can get the question distinctly stated—can get all these men who believe that slavery is in some of these respects wrong to stand and act with us in treating it as a wrong—then, and not till then, I think, will we in some way come to an end of this slavery agitation. [. . .]

Judge Douglas also makes the declaration that I say the Democrats are bound by the Dred Scott decision, while the Republicans are not. In the sense in which he argues, I never said it; but I will tell you what I have said and what I do not hesitate to repeat today. I have said that, as the Democrats believe that decision to be correct, and that the extension of slavery is affirmed in the National Constitution, they are bound to support it as such; and I will tell you here that General Jackson once said each man was bound to support the Constitution, "as he understood it." Now, Judge Douglas understands the Constitution according to the Dred Scott decision, and he is bound to support it as he understands it. I understand it another way, and therefore I am bound to support it in the way in which I understand it. And as Judge Douglas believes that decision to be correct, I will remake that argument if I have time to do so. Let me talk to some gentleman down there among you who looks me in the face. We will say you are a member of the territorial legislature, and, like Judge Douglas, you believe that the right to take and hold slaves there is a constitutional right. The first thing you do is to swear you will support the Constitution and all rights guaranteed therein; that you will, whenever your neighbor needs your legislation to support his constitutional rights, not withhold that legislation. If you withhold that necessary legislation for the support of the Constitution and constitutional rights, do you not commit perjury? I ask every sensible man if that is not so? That is undoubtedly just so, say what you please. Now, that is precisely what Judge Douglas says—that this is a constitutional right. Does the judge mean to say that the territorial legislature in legislating may, by withholding necessary laws or by passing unfriendly laws, nullify that constitutional right? Does he mean to say that? Does he mean to ignore the proposition, so long and well established in law, that what you cannot do directly, you cannot do indirectly? Does he mean that? The truth about the matter is this: Judge Douglas has sung paeans to his "popular sovereignty" doctrine until his Supreme Court, cooperating with him, has squatted his squatter sovereignty out. But he will keep up this species of humbuggery about squatter sovereignty. He has at last invented this sort of do-nothing sovereignty—that the people may exclude slavery by a sort of "sovereignty" that is exercised by doing nothing at all. Is not that running his popular sovereignty down awfully? Has it not got down as thin as the homeopathic soup that was made by boiling the shadow of a pigeon that had starved to death? But at last, when it is brought to the test of close reasoning, there is not even that thin decoction of it left. It is a presumption impossible in the domain of thought. It is precisely no other than the putting of that most unphilosophical proposition, that two bodies can occupy the same space at the same time.

The Dred Scott decision covers the whole ground, and while it occupies it, there is no room even for the shadow of a starved pigeon to occupy the same ground. [. . .]

[. . .] The judge has taken great exception to my adopting the heretical statement in the Declaration of Independence, that "all men are created equal," and he has a great deal to say about negro equality. I want to say that in sometimes alluding to the Declaration of

Independence, I have only uttered the sentiments that Henry Clay used to hold. Allow me to occupy your time a moment with what he said. Mr. Clay was at one time called upon in Indiana, and in a way that I suppose was very insulting, to liberate his slaves, and he made a written reply to that application, and one portion of it is in these words: "What is the foundation of this appeal to me in Indiana to liberate the slaves under my care in Kentucky? It is a general declaration in the act announcing to the world the independence of the thirteen American colonies, that 'men are created equal.' Now, as an abstract principle, there is no doubt of the truth of that declaration, and it is desirable in the original construction of society, and in organized societies, to keep it in view as a great fundamental principle. [. . .]"

Abraham Lincoln

Cooper Union Address (1860)

Mr. President and fellow citizens of New York:

The facts with which I shall deal this evening are mainly old and familiar; nor is there anything new in the general use I shall make of them. If there shall be any novelty, it will be in the mode of presenting the facts, and the inferences and observations following that presentation.

In his speech last autumn, at Columbus, Ohio, as reported in "The New-York Times," Senator Douglas said:

"Our fathers, when they framed the Government under which we live, understood this question just as well, and even better, than we do now."

I fully indorse this, and I adopt it as a text for this discourse. I so adopt it because it furnishes a precise and an agreed starting point for a discussion between Republicans and that wing of the Democracy headed by Senator Douglas. It simply leaves the inquiry: "What was the understanding those fathers had of the question mentioned?"

What is the frame of government under which we live?

The answer must be: "The Constitution of the United States." That Constitution consists of the original, framed in 1787, (and under which the present government first went into operation,) and twelve subsequently framed amendments, the first ten of which were framed in 1789.

Who were our fathers that framed the Constitution? I suppose the "thirty-nine" who signed the original instrument may be fairly called our fathers who framed that part of the present Government. It is almost exactly true to say they framed it, and it is altogether true to say they fairly represented the opinion and sentiment of the whole nation at that time. Their names, being familiar to nearly all, and accessible to quite all, need not now be repeated.

I take these "thirty-nine," for the present, as being "our fathers who framed the Government under which we live."

What is the question which, according to the text, those fathers understood "just as well, and even better than we do now?"

It is this: Does the proper division of local from federal authority, or anything in the Constitution, forbid our *Federal Government* to control as to slavery in *our Federal Territories?*

Upon this, Senator Douglas holds the affirmative, and Republicans the negative. This affirmation and denial form an issue; and this issue—this question—is precisely what the text declares our fathers understood "better than we."

Let us now inquire whether the "thirty-nine," or any of them, ever acted upon this question; and if they did, how they acted upon it—how they expressed that better understanding?

In 1784, three years before the Constitution—the United States then owning the Northwestern Territory, and no other, the Congress of the Confederation had before them the question of prohibiting slavery in that Territory; and four of the "thirty-nine" who afterward framed the Constitution, were in that Congress, and voted on that question. Of these, Roger Sherman, Thomas Mifflin, and Hugh Williamson voted for the prohibition, thus showing that, in their understanding, no line dividing local from federal authority, nor anything else, properly forbade the Federal Government to control as to slavery in federal territory. The other of the four—James M'Henry—voted against the prohibition, showing that, for some cause, he thought it improper to vote for it.

In 1787, still before the Constitution, but while the Convention was in session framing it, and while the Northwestern Territory still was the only territory owned by the United States, the same question of prohibiting slavery in the territory again came before the Congress of the Confederation; and two more of the "thirty-nine" who afterward signed the Constitution, were in that Congress, and voted on the question. They were William Blount and William Few; and they both voted for the prohibition—thus showing that, in their understanding, no line dividing local from federal authority, nor anything else, properly forbids the Federal Government to control as to slavery in Federal territory. This time the prohibition became a law, being part of what is now well known as the Ordinance of '87.

The question of federal control of slavery in the territories, seems not to have been directly before the Convention which framed the original Constitution; and hence it is not recorded that the "thirty-nine," or any of them, while engaged on that instrument, expressed any opinion on that precise question.

In 1789, by the first Congress which sat under the Constitution, an act was passed to enforce the Ordinance of '87, including the prohibition of slavery in the Northwestern Territory. The bill for this act was reported by one of the "thirty-nine," Thomas Fitzsimmons, then a member of the House of Representatives from Pennsylvania. It went through all its stages without a word of opposition, and finally passed both branches without yeas and nays, which is equivalent to a unanimous passage. In this Congress there were sixteen of the thirty-nine fathers who framed the original Constitution. They were John Langdon, Nicholas Gilman, Wm. S. Johnson, Roger Sherman, Robert Morris, Thos. Fitzsimmons, William Few, Abraham Baldwin, Rufus King, William Paterson, George Clymer, Richard Bassett, George Read, Pierce Butler, Daniel Carroll, James Madison.

This shows that, in their understanding, no line dividing local from federal authority, nor anything in the Constitution, properly forbade Congress to prohibit slavery in the federal territory; else both their fidelity to correct principle, and their oath to support the Constitution, would have constrained them to oppose the prohibition.

Again, George Washington, another of the "thirty-nine," was then President of the United States, and, as such approved and signed the bill; thus completing its validity as a law, and thus showing that, in his understanding, no line dividing local from federal authority, nor anything in the Constitution, forbade the Federal Government, to control as to slavery in federal territory.

No great while after the adoption of the original Constitution, North Carolina ceded to the Federal Government the country now constituting the State of Tennessee; and a few years later Georgia ceded that which now constitutes the States of Mississippi and Alabama. In both deeds of cession it was made a condition by the ceding States that the Federal Government should not prohibit slavery in the ceded territory. Besides this, slavery was then actually in the ceded country. Under these circumstances, Congress, on taking charge of these countries, did not absolutely prohibit slavery within them. But they did interfere with it—take control of it—even there, to a certain extent. In 1798, Congress organized the Territory of Mississippi. In the act of organization, they prohibited the bringing of slaves into the Territory, from any place without the United States, by fine, and giving freedom to slaves so bought. This act passed both branches of Congress without yeas and nays. In that Congress were three of the "thirty-nine" who framed the original Constitution. They were John Langdon, George Read and Abraham Baldwin. They all, probably, voted for it. Certainly they would have placed their opposition to it upon record, if, in their understanding, any line dividing local from federal authority, or anything in the Constitution, properly forbade the Federal Government to control as to slavery in federal territory.

In 1803, the Federal Government purchased the Louisiana country. Our former territorial acquisitions came from certain of our own States; but this Louisiana country was acquired from a foreign nation. In 1804, Congress gave a territorial organization to that part of it which now constitutes the State of Louisiana. New Orleans, lying within that part, was an old and comparatively large city. There were other considerable towns and settlements, and slavery was extensively and thoroughly intermingled with the people. Congress did not, in the Territorial Act, prohibit slavery; but they did interfere with it—take control of it—in a more marked and extensive way than they did in the case of Mississippi. The substance of the provision therein made, in relation to slaves, was:

First. That no slave should be imported into the territory from foreign parts.

Second. That no slave should be carried into it who had been imported into the United States since the first day of May, 1798.

Third. That no slave should be carried into it, except by the owner, and for his own use as a settler; the penalty in all the cases being a fine upon the violator of the law, and freedom to the slave.

This act also was passed without yeas and nays. In the Congress which passed it, there were two of the "thirty-nine." They were Abraham Baldwin and Jonathan Dayton. As stated in the case of Mississippi, it is probable they both voted for it. They would not have allowed it to pass without recording their opposition to it, if, in their understanding, it violated either the line properly dividing local from federal authority, or any provision of the Constitution.

In 1819–20, came and passed the Missouri question. Many votes were taken, by yeas and nays, in both branches of Congress, upon the various phases of the general question. Two of the "thirty-nine"—Rufus King and Charles Pinckney—were members of that Congress. Mr. King steadily voted for slavery prohibition and against all compromises, while Mr. Pinckney as steadily voted against slavery prohibition and against all compromises. By this, Mr. King showed that, in his understanding, no line dividing local from federal authority, nor anything in the Constitution, was violated by Congress prohibiting slavery in federal territory; while Mr. Pinckney, by his votes, showed that, in his understanding, there was some sufficient reason for opposing such prohibition in that case.

The cases I have mentioned are the only acts of the "thirty-nine," or of any of them, upon the direct issue, which I have been able to discover.

To enumerate the persons who thus acted, as being four in 1784, two in 1787, seventeen in 1789, three in 1798, two in 1804, and two in 1819–20—there would be thirty of them. But this would be counting John Langdon, Roger Sherman, William Few, Rufus King, and George Read each twice, and Abraham Baldwin, three times. The true number of those of the "thirty-nine" whom I have shown to have acted upon the question, which, by the text, they understood better than we, is twenty-three, leaving sixteen not shown to have acted upon it in any way.

Here, then, we have twenty-three out of our thirty-nine fathers "who framed the government under which we live," who have, upon their official responsibility and their corporal oaths, acted upon the very question which the text affirms they "understood just as well, and even better than we do now;" and twenty-one of them—a clear majority of the whole "thirty-nine"—so acting upon it as to make them guilty of gross political impropriety and willful perjury, if, in their understanding, any proper division between local and federal authority, or anything in the Constitution they had made themselves, and sworn to support, forbade the Federal Government to control as to slavery in the federal territories. Thus the twenty-one acted; and, as actions speak louder than words, so actions, under such responsibility, speak still louder.

Two of the twenty-three voted against Congressional prohibition of slavery in the federal territories, in the instances in which they acted upon the question. But for what reasons they so voted is not known. They may have done so because they thought a proper division of local from federal authority, or some provision or principle of the Constitution, stood in the way; or they may, without any such question, have voted against the prohibition, on what appeared to them to be sufficient grounds of expediency. No one who has sworn to support the Constitution can conscientiously vote for what he understands to be an unconstitutional measure, however expedient he may think it; but one may and ought to vote against a measure which he deems constitutional, if, at the same time, he deems it inexpedient. It, therefore, would be unsafe to set down even the two who voted against the prohibition, as having done so because, in their understanding, any proper division of local from federal authority, or anything in the Constitution, forbade the Federal Government to control as to slavery in federal territory.

The remaining sixteen of the "thirty-nine," so far as I have discovered, have left no record of their understanding upon the direct question of federal control of slavery in the federal territories. But there is much reason to believe that their understanding upon that question would not have appeared different from that of their twenty-three compeers, had it been manifested at all.

For the purpose of adhering rigidly to the text, I have purposely omitted whatever understanding may have been manifested by any person, however distinguished, other than the thirty-nine fathers who framed the original Constitution; and, for the same reason, I have also omitted whatever understanding may have been manifested by any of the "thirty-nine" even, on any other phase of the general question of slavery. If we should look into their acts and declarations on those other phases, as the foreign slave trade, and the morality and policy of slavery generally, it would appear to us that on the direct question of federal control of slavery in federal territories, the sixteen, if they had acted at all, would probably have acted just as the twenty-three did. Among that sixteen were several of the most noted anti-slavery men of those times—as Dr. Franklin, Alexander Hamilton and Gouverneur Morris—while there was not one now known to have been otherwise, unless it may be John Rutledge, of South Carolina.

The sum of the whole is, that of our thirty-nine fathers who framed the original Constitution, twenty-one—a clear majority of the whole—certainly understood that no proper division of local from federal authority, nor any part of the Constitution, forbade the Federal Government to control slavery in the federal territories; while all the rest probably had the same understanding. Such, unquestionably, was the understanding of our fathers who framed the original Constitution; and the text affirms that they understood the question "better than we."

But, so far, I have been considering the understanding of the question manifested by the framers of the original Constitution. In and by the original instrument, a mode was provided for amending it; and, as I have already stated, the present frame of "the Government under which we live" consists of that original, and twelve amendatory articles framed and adopted since. Those who now insist that federal control of slavery in federal territories violates the Constitution, point us to the provisions which they suppose it thus violates; and, as I understand, that all fix upon provisions in these amendatory articles, and not in the original instrument. The Supreme Court, in the Dred Scott case, plant themselves upon the Fifth Amendment, which provides that no person shall be deprived of "life, liberty or property without due process of law;" while Senator Douglas and his peculiar adherents plant themselves upon the Tenth Amendment, providing that "the powers not delegated to the United States by the Constitution" "are reserved to the States respectively, or to the people."

Now, it so happens that these amendments were framed by the first Congress which sat under the Constitution—the identical Congress which passed the act already mentioned, enforcing the prohibition of slavery in the Northwestern Territory. Not only was it the same Congress, but they were the identical, same individual men who, at the same session, and at the same time within the session, had under consideration, and in progress toward maturity, these Constitutional amendments, and this act prohibiting slavery in all the territory the nation then owned. The Constitutional amendments were introduced before, and passed after the act enforcing the Ordinance of '87; so that, during the whole pendency of the act to enforce the Ordinance, the Constitutional amendments were also pending.

The seventy-six members of that Congress, including sixteen of the framers of the original Constitution, as before stated, were pre-eminently our fathers who framed that part of "the Government under which we live," which is now claimed as forbidding the Federal Government to control slavery in the federal territories.

Is it not a little presumptuous in any one at this day to affirm that the two things which that Congress deliberately framed, and carried to maturity at the same time, are absolutely inconsistent with each other? And does not such affirmation become impudently absurd when coupled with the other affirmation from the same mouth, that those who did the two things, alleged to be inconsistent, understood whether they really were inconsistent better than we—better than he who affirms that they are inconsistent?

It is surely safe to assume that the thirty-nine framers of the original Constitution, and the seventy-six members of the Congress which framed the amendments thereto, taken together, do certainly include those who may be fairly called "our fathers who framed the Government under which we live." And so assuming, I defy any man to show that any one of them ever, in his whole life, declared that, in his understanding, any proper division of local from federal authority, or any part of the Constitution, forbade the Federal Government to control as to slavery in the federal territories. I go a step further. I defy any one to show that any living man in the whole world ever did, prior to the beginning of the present century, (and I might almost say prior to the beginning of the last half of the present century,) declare that, in his understanding, any proper division of local from federal authority, or any part of the Constitution, forbade the Federal Government to control as to slavery in the federal territories. To those who now so declare, I give, not only "our fathers who framed the Government under which we live," but with them all other living men within the century in which it was framed, among whom to search, and they shall not be able to find the evidence of a single man agreeing with them.

Now, and here, let me guard a little against being misunderstood. I do not mean to say we are bound to follow implicitly in whatever our fathers did. To do so, would be to discard all the lights of current experience—to reject all progress—all improvement. What I do say is, that if we would supplant the opinions and policy of our fathers in any case, we should do so upon evidence so conclusive, and argument so clear, that even their great authority, fairly considered and weighed, cannot stand; and most surely not in a case whereof we ourselves declare they understood the question better than we.

If any man at this day sincerely believes that a proper division of local from federal authority, or any part of the Constitution, forbids the Federal Government to control as to slavery in the federal territories, he is right to say so, and to enforce his position by all truthful evidence and fair argument which he can. But he has no right to mislead others, who have less access to history, and less leisure to study it, into the false belief that "our fathers who framed the Government under which we live" were of the same opinion—thus substituting falsehood and deception for truthful evidence and fair argument. If any man at this day sincerely believes "our fathers who framed the Government under which we live," used and applied principles, in other cases, which ought to have led them to understand that a proper division of local from federal authority or some part of the Constitution, forbids the Federal Government to control as to slavery in the federal territories, he is right to say so. But he should, at the same time, brave the responsibility of declaring that, in his opinion, he understands their principles better than they did themselves; and especially should he not shirk that responsibility by asserting that they "understood the question just as well, and even better, than we do now."

But enough! *Let all who believe that "our fathers, who framed the Government under which we live, understood this question just as well, and even better, than we do now," speak as they spoke, and act as they acted upon it. This is all Republicans ask—all Republicans desire—in relation to slavery. As those fathers marked it, so let it be again marked, as an evil not to be extended, but to be tolerated and protected only because of and so far as its actual presence among us makes that toleration and protection a necessity. Let all the guarantees those fathers gave it, be, not grudgingly, but fully and fairly, maintained.* For this Republicans contend, and with this, so far as I know or believe, they will be content.

And now, if they would listen—as I suppose they will not—I would address a few words to the Southern people.

I would say to them:—You consider yourselves a reasonable and a just people; and I consider that in the general qualities of reason and justice you are not inferior to any other people. Still, when you speak of us Republicans, you do so only to denounce us a reptiles, or, at the best, as no better than outlaws. You will grant a hearing to pirates or murderers, but nothing like it to "Black Republicans." In all your contentions with one another, each of you deems an unconditional condemnation of "Black Republicanism" as the first thing to be attended to. Indeed, such condemnation of us seems to be an indispensable prerequisite—license, so to speak—among you to be admitted or permitted to speak at all. Now, can you, or not, be prevailed upon to pause and to consider whether this is quite just to us, or even to yourselves? Bring forward your charges and specifications, and then be patient long enough to hear us deny or justify.

You say we are sectional. We deny it. That makes an issue; and the burden of proof is upon you. You produce your proof; and what is it? Why, that our party has no existence in your section—gets no votes in your section. The fact is substantially true; but does it prove the issue? If it does, then in case we should, without change of principle, begin to get votes in your section, we should thereby cease to be sectional. You cannot escape this conclusion; and yet, are you willing to abide by it? If you are, you will probably soon find that we have ceased to be sectional, for we shall get votes in your section this very year. You will then begin to discover, as the truth plainly is, that your proof does not touch the issue. The fact that we get no votes in your section, is a fact of your making, and not of ours. And if there be fault in that fact, that fault is primarily yours, and remains until you show that we repel you by some wrong principle or practice. If we do repel you by any wrong principle or practice, the fault is ours; but this brings you to where you ought to have started—to a discussion of the right or wrong of our principle. If our principle, put in practice, would wrong your section for the benefit of ours, or for any other object, then our principle, and we with it, are sectional, and are justly opposed and denounced as such. Meet us, then, on the question of whether our principle, put in practice, would wrong your section; and so meet it as if it were possible that something may be said on our side. Do you accept the challenge? No! Then you really believe that the principle which "our fathers who framed the Government under which we live" thought so clearly right as to adopt it, and indorse it again and again, upon their official oaths, is in fact so clearly wrong as to demand your condemnation without a moment's consideration.

Some of you delight to flaunt in our faces the warning against sectional parties given by Washington in his Farewell Address. Less than eight years before Washington gave that warning, he had, as President of the United States, approved and signed an act of Congress, enforcing the prohibition of slavery in the Northwestern Territory, which act embodied the policy of the Government upon that subject up to and at the very moment he penned that warning; and about one year after he penned it, he wrote LaFayette that he considered that prohibition a wise measure, expressing in the same connection his hope that we should at some time have a confederacy of free States.

Bearing this in mind, and seeing that sectionalism has since arisen upon this same subject, is that warning a weapon in your hands against us, or in our hands against you? Could Washington himself speak, would he cast the blame of that sectionalism upon us, who sustain his policy, or upon you who repudiate it? We respect that warning of Washington, and we commend it to you, together with his example pointing to the right application of it.

But you say you are conservative—eminently conservative—while we are revolutionary, destructive, or something of the sort. What is conservatism? Is it not adherence to the old and tried, against the new and untried? We stick to, contend for, the identical old policy on the point in controversy which was adopted by "our fathers who framed the Government under which we live;" while you with one accord reject, and scout, and spit upon that old policy, and insist upon substituting something new. True, you disagree among yourselves as to what that substitute shall be. You are divided on new propositions and plans, but you are unanimous in rejecting and denouncing the old policy of the fathers. Some of you are for reviving the foreign slave trade; some for a Congressional Slave-Code for the Territories; some for Congress forbidding the Territories to prohibit Slavery within their limits; some for maintaining Slavery in the Territories through the judiciary; some for the "gur-reat pur-rinciple" that "if one man would enslave another, no third man should object," fantastically called "Popular Sovereignty;" but never a man among you is in favor of federal prohibition of slavery in federal territories, according to the practice of "our fathers who framed the Government under which we live." Not one of all your various plans can show a precedent or an advocate in the century within which our Government originated. Consider, then, whether your claim of conservatism for yourselves, and your charge or destructiveness against us, are based on the most clear and stable foundations.

Again, you say we have made the slavery question more prominent than it formerly was. We deny it. We admit that it is more prominent, but we deny that we made it so. It was not we, but you, who discarded the old policy of the fathers. We resisted, and still resist, your innovation; and thence comes the greater prominence of the question. Would you have that question reduced to its former proportions? Go back to that old policy. What has been will be again, under the same conditions. If you would have the peace of the old times, readopt the precepts and policy of the old times.

You charge that we stir up insurrections among your slaves. We deny it; and what is your proof? Harper's Ferry! John Brown!! John Brown was no Republican; and you have failed to implicate a single Republican in his Harper's Ferry enterprise. If any member of our party is guilty in that matter, you know it or you do not know it. If you do know it, you are inexcusable for not designating the man and proving the fact. If you do not know it, you are inexcusable for asserting it, and especially for persisting in the assertion after you have tried and failed to make the proof. You need to be told that persisting in a charge which one does not know to be true, is simply malicious slander.

Some of you admit that no Republican designedly aided or encouraged the Harper's Ferry affair, but still insist that our doctrines and declarations necessarily lead to such results. We do not believe it. We know we hold to no doctrine, and make no declaration, which were not held to and made by "our fathers who framed the Government under which we live." You never dealt fairly by us in relation to this affair. When it occurred, some important State elections were near at hand, and you were in evident glee with the belief that, by charging the blame upon us, you could get an advantage of us in those elections. The elections came, and your expectations were not quite fulfilled. Every Republican man knew that, as to himself at least, your charge was a slander, and he was not much inclined by it to cast his vote in your favor. Republican doctrines and declarations are accompanied with a continual protest against any interference whatever with your slaves, or with you about your slaves. Surely, this does not encourage them to revolt. True, we do, in common with "our fathers, who framed the Government under which we live," declare our belief that slavery is wrong; but the slaves do not hear us declare even this. For anything we say or do, the slaves would scarcely know there is a Republican party. I believe they would not, in fact, generally know it but for your misrepresentations of us, in their hearing. In your political contests among yourselves, each faction charges the other with sympathy with Black Republicanism; and then, to give point to the charge, defines Black Republicanism to simply be insurrection, blood and thunder among the slaves.

Slave insurrections are no more common now than they were before the Republican party was organized. What induced the Southampton insurrection, twenty-eight years ago, in which, at least three times as many lives were lost as at Harper's Ferry? You can scarcely stretch your very elastic fancy to the conclusion that Southampton was "got up by Black Republicanism." In the present state of things in the United States, I do not think a general, or even a very extensive slave insurrection is possible. The indispensable concert of action cannot be attained. The slaves have no means of rapid communication; nor can incendiary freemen, black or white, supply it. The explosive materials are everywhere in parcels; but there neither are, nor can be supplied, the indispensable connecting trains.

Much is said by Southern people about the affection of slaves for their masters and mistresses; and a part of it, at least, is true. A plot for an uprising could scarcely be devised and communicated to twenty individuals before some one of them, to save the life of a favorite master or mistress, would divulge it. This is the rule; and the slave revolution in Hayti was not an exception to it, but a case occurring under peculiar circumstances. The gunpowder plot of British history, though not connected with slaves, was more in point. In that case, only about twenty were admitted to the secret; and yet one of them, in his anxiety to save a friend, betrayed the plot to that friend, and, by consequence, averted the calamity. Occasional poisonings from the kitchen, and open or stealthy assassinations in the field, and local revolts extending to a score or so, will continue to occur as the natural results of slavery; but no general insurrection of slaves, as I think, can happen in this country for a long time. Whoever much fears, or much hopes for such an event, will be alike disappointed.

In the language of Mr. Jefferson, uttered many years ago, "It is still in our power to direct the process of emancipation, and deportation, peaceably, and in such slow degrees, as that the evil will wear off insensibly; and their places be, *pari passu*, filled up by free white laborers. If, on the contrary, it is left to force itself on, human nature must shudder at the prospect held up."

Mr. Jefferson did not mean to say, nor do I, that the power of emancipation is in the Federal Government. He spoke of Virginia; and, as to the power of emancipation, I speak of the slaveholding States only. The Federal Government, however, as we insist, has the power of restraining the extension of the institution—the power to insure that a slave insurrection shall never occur on any American soil which is now free from slavery.

John Brown's effort was peculiar. It was not a slave insurrection. It was an attempt by white men to get up a revolt among slaves, in which the slaves refused to participate. In fact, it was so absurd that the slaves, with all their ignorance, saw plainly enough it could not succeed. That affair, in its philosophy, corresponds with the many attempts, related in history, at the assassination of kings and emperors. An enthusiast broods over the oppression of a people till he fancies himself commissioned by Heaven to liberate them. He ventures the attempt, which ends in little else than his own execution. Orsini's attempt on Louis Napoleon, and John Brown's attempt at Harper's Ferry were, in their philosophy, precisely the same. The eagerness to cast blame on old England in the one case, and on New England in the other, does not disprove the sameness of the two things.

And how much would it avail you, if you could, by the use of John Brown, Helper's Book, and the like, break up the Republican organization? Human action can be modified to some extent, but human nature cannot be changed. There is a judgment and a feeling against slavery in this nation, which cast at least a million and a half of votes. You cannot destroy that judgment and feeling—that sentiment—by breaking up the political organization which rallies around it. You can scarcely scatter and disperse an army which has been formed into order in the face of your heaviest fire; but if you could, how much would you gain by forcing the sentiment which created it out of the peaceful channel of the ballot-box, into some other channel? What would that other channel probably be? Would the number of John Browns be lessened or enlarged by the operation?

But you will break up the Union rather than submit to a denial of your Constitutional rights.

That has a somewhat reckless sound; but it would be palliated, if not fully justified, were we proposing, by the mere force of numbers, to deprive you of some right, plainly written down in the Constitution. But we are proposing no such thing.

When you make these declarations, you have a specific and well-understood allusion to an assumed Constitutional right of yours, to take slaves into the federal territories, and to hold them there as property. But no such right is specifically written in the Constitution. That instrument is literally silent about any such right. We, on the contrary, deny that such a right has any existence in the Constitution, even by implication.

Your purpose, then, plainly stated, is that you will destroy the Government, unless you be allowed to construe and enforce the Constitution as you please, on all points in dispute between you and us. You will rule or ruin in all events.

This, plainly stated, is your language. Perhaps you will say the Supreme Court has decided the disputed Constitutional question in your favor. Not quite so. But waiving the lawyer's distinction between dictum and decision, the Court have decided the question for you in a sort of way. The Court have substantially said, it is your Constitutional right to take slaves into the federal territories, and to hold them there as property. When I say the decision was made in a sort of way, I mean it was made in a divided Court, by a bare majority of the Judges, and they not quite agreeing with one another in the reasons for making it; that it is so made as that its avowed supporters disagree with one another about its meaning, and that it was mainly based upon a mistaken statement of fact—the statement in the opinion that "the right of property in a slave is distinctly and expressly affirmed in the Constitution."

An inspection of the Constitution will show that the right of property in a slave is not "*distinctly* and *expressly* affirmed" in it. Bear in mind, the Judges do not pledge their judicial opinion that such right is *impliedly* affirmed in the Constitution; but they pledge their veracity that it is "*distinctly* and *expressly*" affirmed there—"distinctly," that is, not mingled with anything else—"expressly," that is, in words meaning just that, without the aid of any inference, and susceptible of no other meaning.

If they had only pledged their judicial opinion that such right is affirmed in the instrument by implication, it would be open to others to show that neither the word "slave" nor "slavery" is to be found in the Constitution, nor the word "property" even, in any connection with language alluding to the things slave, or slavery; and that wherever in that instrument the slave is alluded to, he is called a "person;"—and wherever his master's legal right in relation to him is alluded to, it is spoken of as "service or labor which may be due,"—as a debt payable in service or labor. Also, it would be open to show, by contemporaneous history, that this mode of alluding to slaves and slavery, instead of speaking of them, was employed on purpose to exclude from the Constitution the idea that there could be property in man.

To show all this, is easy and certain.

When this obvious mistake of the Judges shall be brought to their notice, is it not reasonable to expect that they will withdraw the mistaken statement, and reconsider the conclusion based upon it?

And then it is to be remembered that "our fathers, who framed the Government under which we live"—the men who made the Constitution—decided this same Constitutional question in our favor, long ago—decided it without division among themselves, when making the decision; without division among themselves about the meaning of it after it was made, and, so far as any evidence is left, without basing it upon any mistaken statement of facts.

Under all these circumstances, do you really feel yourselves justified to break up this Government unless such a court decision as yours is, shall be at once submitted to as a conclusive and final rule of political action? But you will not abide the election of a Republican president! In that supposed event, you say, you will destroy the Union; and then, you say, the great crime of having destroyed it will be upon us! That is cool. A highwayman holds a pistol to my ear, and mutters through his teeth, "Stand and deliver, or I shall kill you, and then you will be a murderer!"

To be sure, what the robber demanded of me—my money—was my own; and I had a clear right to keep it; but it was no more my own than my vote is my own; and the threat of death to me, to extort my money, and the threat of destruction to the Union, to extort my vote, can scarcely be distinguished in principle.

A few words now to Republicans. *It is exceedingly desirable that all parts of this great Confederacy shall be at peace, and in harmony, one with another. Let us Republicans do our part to have it so. Even though much provoked, let us do nothing through passion and ill temper. Even though the southern people will not so much as listen to us, let us calmly consider their demands, and yield to them if, in our deliberate view of our duty, we possibly can.* Judging by all they say and do, and by the subject and nature of their controversy with us, let us determine, if we can, what will satisfy them.

Will they be satisfied if the Territories be unconditionally surrendered to them? We know they will not. In all their present complaints against us, the Territories are scarcely mentioned. Invasions and insurrections are the rage now. Will it satisfy them, if, in the future, we have nothing to do with invasions and insurrections? We know it will not. We so know, because we know we never had anything to do with invasions and insurrections; and yet this total abstaining does not exempt us from the charge and the denunciation.

The question recurs, what will satisfy them? Simply this: We must not only let them alone, but we must somehow, convince them that we do let them alone. This, we know by experience, is no easy task. We have been so trying to convince them from the very beginning of our organization, but with no success. In all our platforms and speeches we have constantly protested our purpose to let them alone; but this has had no tendency to convince them. Alike unavailing to convince them, is the fact that they have never detected a man of us in any attempt to disturb them.

These natural, and apparently adequate means all failing, what will convince them? This, and this only: cease to call slavery *wrong*, and join them in calling it *right*. And this must be done thoroughly—done in *acts* as well as in *words*. Silence will not be tolerated—we must place ourselves avowedly with them. Senator Douglas' new sedition law must be enacted and enforced, suppressing all declarations that slavery is wrong, whether made in politics, in presses, in pulpits, or in private. We must arrest and return their fugitive slaves with greedy pleasure. We must pull down our Free State constitutions. The whole atmosphere must be disinfected from all taint of opposition to slavery, before they will cease to believe that all their troubles proceed from us.

I am quite aware they do not state their case precisely in this way. Most of them would probably say to us, "Let us alone, do nothing to us, and say what you please about slavery." But we do let them alone—have never disturbed them—so that, after all, it is what we say, which dissatisfies them. They will continue to accuse us of doing, until we cease saying.

I am also aware they have not, as yet, in terms, demanded the overthrow of our Free-State Constitutions. Yet those Constitutions declare the wrong of slavery, with more solemn emphasis, than do all other sayings against it; and when all these other sayings shall have been silenced, the overthrow of these Constitutions will be demanded, and nothing be left to resist the demand. It is nothing to the contrary, that they do not demand the whole of this just now. Demanding what they do, and for the reason they do, they can voluntarily stop nowhere short of this consummation. Holding, as they do, that slavery is morally right, and socially elevating, they cannot cease to demand a full national recognition of it, as a legal right, and a social blessing.

Nor can we justifiably withhold this, on any ground save our conviction that slavery is wrong. If slavery is right, all words, acts, laws, and constitutions against it, are themselves wrong, and should be silenced, and swept away. If it is right, we cannot justly object to its nationality—its universality; if it is wrong, they cannot justly insist upon its extension—its enlargement. All they ask, we could readily grant, if we thought slavery right; all we ask, they could as readily grant, if they thought it wrong. Their thinking it right, and our thinking it wrong, is the precise fact upon which depends the whole controversy. Thinking it right, as they do, they are not to blame for desiring its full recognition, as being right; but, thinking it wrong, as we do, can we yield to them? Can we cast our votes with their view, and against our own? In view of our moral, social, and political responsibilities, can we do this?

Wrong as we think slavery is, we can yet afford to let it alone where it is, because that much is due to the necessity arising from its actual presence in the nation; but can we, while our votes will prevent it, allow it to spread into the National Territories, and to overrun us here in these Free States? If our sense of duty forbids this, then let us stand by our duty, fearlessly and effectively. Let us be diverted by none of those sophistical contrivances wherewith we are so industriously plied and belabored—contrivances such as groping for some middle ground between the right and the wrong, vain as the search for a man who should be neither a living man nor a dead man—such as a policy of "don't care" on a question about which all true men do care—such as Union appeals beseeching true Union men to yield to Disunionists, reversing the divine rule, and calling, not the sinners, but the righteous to repentance—such as invocations to Washington, imploring men to unsay what Washington said, and undo what Washington did.

Neither let us be slandered from our duty by false accusations against us, nor frightened from it by menaces of destruction to the Government nor of dungeons to ourselves. Let us have faith that right makes might, and in that faith, let us, to the end, dare to do our duty as we understand it.

Address in Independence Hall, Philadelphia (1861)

Mr. Cuyler: I am filled with deep emotion at finding myself standing in this place, where were collected together the wisdom, the patriotism, the devotion to principle, from which sprang the institutions under which we live. You have kindly suggested to me that in my hands is the task of restoring peace to our distracted country. I can say in return, sir, that all the political sentiments I entertain have been drawn, so far as I have been able to draw them, from the sentiments which originated in and were given to the world from this hall. I have never had a feeling, politically, that did not spring from the sentiments embodied in the Declaration of Independence. I have often pondered over the dangers which were incurred by the men who assembled here and framed and adopted that Declaration. I have pondered over the toils that were endured by the officers and soldiers of the army who achieved that independence. I have often inquired of myself what great principle or idea it was that kept this Confederacy so long together. It was not the mere matter of separation of the colonies from the motherland, but that sentiment in the Declaration of Independence which gave liberty not alone to the people of this country, but hope to all the world, for all future time. It was that which gave promise that in due time the weights would be lifted from the shoulders of all men, and that all should have an equal chance. This is the sentiment embodied in the Declaration of Independence. Now, my friends, can this country be saved on that basis? If it can, I will consider myself one of the happiest men in the world if I can help to save it. If it cannot be saved upon that principle, it will be truly awful. But if this country cannot be saved without giving up that principle, I was about to say I would rather be assassinated on this spot than surrender it. Now, in my view of the present aspect of affairs, there is no need of bloodshed and war. There is no necessity for it. I am not in favor of such a course; and I may say in advance that there will be no bloodshed unless it is forced upon the government. The government will not use force, unless force is used against it.

My friends, this is wholly an unprepared speech. I did not expect to be called on to say a word when I came here. I supposed I was merely to do something toward raising a flag. I may, therefore, have said something indiscreet. [Cries of "No, no."] But I have said nothing but what I am willing to live by, and, if it be the pleasure of Almighty God, to die by.

First Inaugural Address (1861)

Fellow-Citizens of the United States:

In compliance with a custom as old as the Government itself, I appear before you to address you briefly and to take in your presence the oath prescribed by the Constitution of the United States to be taken by the President before he enters on the execution of this office.

I do not consider it necessary at present for me to discuss those matters of administration about which there is no special anxiety or excitement.

Apprehension seems to exist among the people of the Southern States that by the accession of a Republican Administration their property and their peace and personal security are to be endangered. There has never been any reasonable cause for such apprehension. Indeed, the most ample evidence to the contrary has all the while existed and been open to their inspection. It is found in nearly all the published speeches of him who now addresses you. I do but quote from one of those speeches when I declare that—

I have no purpose, directly or indirectly, to interfere with the institution of slavery in the States where it exists. I believe I have no lawful right to do so, and I have no inclination to do so.

Those who nominated and elected me did so with full knowledge that I had made this and many similar declarations and had never recanted them; and more than this, they placed in the platform for my acceptance, and as a law to themselves and to me, the clear and emphatic resolution which I now read:

> Resolved, That the maintenance inviolate of the rights of the States, and especially the right of each State to order and control its own domestic institutions according to its own judgment exclusively, is essential to that balance of power on which the perfection and endurance of our political fabric depend; and we denounce the lawless

> invasion by armed force of the soil of any State or Territory, no matter what pretext, as among the gravest of crimes.

I now reiterate these sentiments, and in doing so I only press upon the public attention the most conclusive evidence of which the case is susceptible that the property, peace, and security of no section are to be in any wise endangered by the now incoming Administration. I add, too, that all the protection which, consistently with the Constitution and the laws, can be given will be cheerfully given to all the States when lawfully demanded, for whatever cause—as cheerfully to one section as to another.

There is much controversy about the delivering up of fugitives from service or labor. The clause I now read is as plainly written in the Constitution as any other of its provisions:

> No person held to service or labor in one State, under the laws thereof, escaping into another, shall in consequence of any law or regulation therein be discharged from such service or labor, but shall be delivered up on claim of the party to whom such service or labor may be due.

It is scarcely questioned that this provision was intended by those who made it for the reclaiming of what we call fugitive slaves; and the intention of the lawgiver is the law. All members of Congress swear their support to the whole Constitution—to this provision as much as to any other. To the proposition, then, that slaves whose cases come within the terms of this clause "shall be delivered up" their oaths are unanimous. Now, if they would make the effort in good temper, could they not with nearly equal unanimity frame and pass a law by means of which to keep good that unanimous oath?

There is some difference of opinion whether this clause should be enforced by national or by State authority, but surely that difference is not a very material one. If the slave is to be surrendered, it can be of but little consequence to him or to others by which authority it is done. And should anyone in any case be content that his oath shall go unkept on a merely unsubstantial controversy as to how it shall be kept?

Again: In any law upon this subject ought not all the safeguards of liberty known in civilized and humane jurisprudence to be introduced, so that a free man be not in any case surrendered as a slave? And might it not be well at the same time to provide by law for the enforcement of that clause in the Constitution which guarantees that "the citizens of each State shall be entitled to all privileges and immunities of citizens in the several States"?

I take the official oath today with no mental reservations and with no purpose to construe the Constitution or laws by any hypercritical rules; and while I do not choose now to specify particular acts of Congress as proper to be enforced, I do suggest that it will be much safer for all, both in official and private stations, to conform to and abide by all those acts which stand unrepealed than to violate any of them trusting to find impunity in having them held to be unconstitutional.

It is seventy-two years since the first inauguration of a President under our National Constitution. During that period fifteen different and greatly distinguished citizens have in succession administered the executive branch of the Government. They have conducted it through many perils, and generally with great success. Yet, with all this scope of precedent, I now enter upon the same task for the brief constitutional term of four years under great and peculiar difficulty. A disruption of the Federal Union, heretofore only menaced, is now formidably attempted.

I hold that in contemplation of universal law and of the Constitution the Union of these States is perpetual. Perpetuity is implied, if not expressed, in the fundamental law of all national governments. It is safe to assert that no government proper ever had a provision in its organic law for its own termination. Continue to execute all the express provisions of our National Constitution, and the Union will endure forever, it being impossible to destroy it except by some action not provided for in the instrument itself.

Again: If the United States be not a government proper, but an association of States in the nature of contract merely, can it, as a contract, be peaceably unmade by less than all the parties who made it? One party to a contract may violate it—break it, so to speak—but does it not require all to lawfully rescind it?

Descending from these general principles, we find the proposition that in legal contemplation the Union is perpetual confirmed by the history of the Union itself. The Union is much older than the Constitution. It was formed, in fact, by the Articles of

Association in 1774. It was matured and continued by the Declaration of Independence in 1776. It was further matured, and the faith of all the then thirteen States expressly plighted and engaged that it should be perpetual, by the Articles of Confederation in 1778. And finally, in 1787, one of the declared objects for ordaining and establishing the Constitution was "to form a more perfect Union."

But if destruction of the Union by one or by a part only of the States be lawfully possible, the Union is less perfect than before the Constitution, having lost the vital element of perpetuity.

It follows from these views that no State upon its own mere motion can lawfully get out of the Union; that resolves and ordinances to that effect are legally void, and that acts of violence within any State or States against the authority of the United States are insurrectionary or revolutionary, according to circumstances.

I therefore consider that in view of the Constitution and the laws the Union is unbroken, and to the extent of my ability, I shall take care, as the Constitution itself expressly enjoins upon me, that the laws of the Union be faithfully executed in all the States. Doing this I deem to be only a simple duty on my part, and I shall perform it so far as practicable unless my rightful masters, the American people, shall withhold the requisite means or in some authoritative manner direct the contrary. I trust this will not be regarded as a menace, but only as the declared purpose of the Union that it will constitutionally defend and maintain itself.

In doing this there needs to be no bloodshed or violence, and there shall be none unless it be forced upon the national authority. The power confided to me will be used to hold, occupy, and possess the property and places belonging to the Government and to collect the duties and imposts; but beyond what may be necessary for these objects, there will be no invasion, no using of force against or among the people anywhere. Where hostility to the United States in any interior locality shall be so great and universal as to prevent competent resident citizens from holding the Federal offices, there will be no attempt to force obnoxious strangers among the people for that object. While the strict legal right may exist in the Government to enforce the exercise of these offices, the attempt to do so would be so irritating and so nearly impracticable withal that I deem it better to forego for the time the uses of such offices.

The mails, unless repelled, will continue to be furnished in all parts of the Union. So far as possible the people everywhere shall have that sense of perfect security which is most favorable to calm thought and reflection. The course here indicated will be followed unless current events and experience shall show a modification or change to be proper, and in every case and exigency my best discretion will be exercised, according to circumstances actually existing and with a view and a hope of a peaceful solution of the national troubles and the restoration of fraternal sympathies and affections.

That there are persons in one section or another who seek to destroy the Union at all events and are glad of any pretext to do it I will neither affirm nor deny; but if there be such, I need address no word to them. To those, however, who really love the Union may I not speak?

Before entering upon so grave a matter as the destruction of our national fabric, with all its benefits, its memories, and its hopes, would it not be wise to ascertain precisely why we do it? Will you hazard so desperate a step while there is any possibility that any portion of the ills you fly from have no real existence? Will you, while the certain ills you fly to are greater than all the real ones you fly from, will you risk the commission of so fearful a mistake?

All profess to be content in the Union if all constitutional rights can be maintained. Is it true, then, that any right plainly written in the Constitution has been denied? I think not. Happily, the human mind is so constituted that no party can reach to the audacity of doing this. Think, if you can, of a single instance in which a plainly written provision of the Constitution has ever been denied. If by the mere force of numbers a majority should deprive a minority of any clearly written constitutional right, it might in a moral point of view justify revolution; certainly would if such right were a vital one. But such is not our case. All the vital rights of minorities and of individuals are so plainly assured to them by affirmations and negations, guaranties and prohibitions, in the Constitution that controversies never arise concerning them. But no organic law can ever be framed with a provision specifically applicable to every question which may occur in practical administration. No foresight can anticipate nor any document of reasonable length contain express provisions for all possible questions. Shall fugitives from labor be surrendered by national or by State authority? The Constitution does not expressly say. May Congress prohibit slavery in the Territories? The Constitution does not expressly say. Must Congress protect slavery in the Territories? The Constitution does not expressly say.

From questions of this class spring all our constitutional controversies, and we divide upon them into majorities and minorities. If the minority will not acquiesce, the majority must, or the Government must cease. There is no other alternative, for continuing the Government is acquiescence on one side or the other. If a minority in such case will secede rather than acquiesce, they make a precedent which in turn will divide and ruin them, for a minority of their own will secede from them whenever a majority refuses to be controlled by such minority. For instance, why may not any portion of a new confederacy a year or two hence arbitrarily secede again, precisely as portions of the present Union now claim to secede from it? All who cherish disunion sentiments are now being educated to the exact temper of doing this.

Is there such perfect identity of interests among the States to compose a new union as to produce harmony only and prevent renewed secession?

Plainly the central idea of secession is the essence of anarchy. A majority held in restraint by constitutional checks and limitations, and always changing easily with deliberate changes of popular opinions and sentiments, is the only true sovereign of a free people. Whoever rejects it does of necessity fly to anarchy or to despotism. Unanimity is impossible. The rule of a minority, as a permanent arrangement, is wholly inadmissible; so that, rejecting the majority principle, anarchy or despotism in some form is all that is left.

I do not forget the position assumed by some that constitutional questions are to be decided by the Supreme Court, nor do I deny that such decisions must be binding in any case upon the parties to a suit as to the object of that suit, while they are also entitled to very high respect and consideration in all parallel cases by all other departments of the Government. And while it is obviously possible that such decision may be erroneous in any given case, still the evil effect following it, being limited to that particular case, with the chance that it may be overruled and never become a precedent for other cases, can better be borne than could the evils of a different practice. At the same time, the candid citizen must confess that if the policy of the Government upon vital questions affecting the whole people is to be irrevocably fixed by decisions of the Supreme Court, the instant they are made in ordinary litigation between parties in personal actions the people will have ceased to be their own rulers, having to that extent practically resigned their Government into the hands of that eminent tribunal. Nor is there in this view any assault upon the court or the judges. It is a duty from which they may not shrink to decide cases properly brought before them, and it is no fault of theirs if others seek to turn their decisions to political purposes.

One section of our country believes slavery is right and ought to be extended, while the other believes it is wrong and ought not to be extended. This is the only substantial dispute. The fugitive-slave clause of the Constitution and the law for the suppression of the foreign slave trade are each as well enforced, perhaps, as any law can ever be in a community where the moral sense of the people imperfectly supports the law itself. The great body of the people abide by the dry legal obligation in both cases, and a few break over in each. This, I think, can not be perfectly cured, and it would be worse in both cases after the separation of the sections than before. The foreign slave trade, now imperfectly suppressed, would be ultimately revived without restriction in one section, while fugitive slaves, now only partially surrendered, would not be surrendered at all by the other.

Physically speaking, we can not separate. We can not remove our respective sections from each other nor build an impassable wall between them. A husband and wife may be divorced and go out of the presence and beyond the reach of each other, but the different parts of our country can not do this. They can not but remain face to face, and intercourse, either amicable or hostile, must continue between them. Is it possible, then, to make that intercourse more advantageous or more satisfactory after separation than before? Can aliens make treaties easier than friends can make laws? Can treaties be more faithfully enforced between aliens than laws can among friends? Suppose you go to war, you can not fight always; and when, after much loss on both sides and no gain on either, you cease fighting, the identical old questions, as to terms of intercourse, are again upon you.

This country, with its institutions, belongs to the people who inhabit it. Whenever they shall grow weary of the existing Government, they can exercise their constitutional right of amending it or their revolutionary right to dismember or overthrow it. I can not be ignorant of the fact that many worthy and patriotic citizens are desirous of having the National Constitution amended. While I make no recommendation of amendments, I fully recognize the rightful authority of the people over the whole subject, to be exercised in either of the modes prescribed in the instrument itself; and I should, under existing circumstances, favor rather than oppose a fair opportunity being afforded the people to act upon it. I will venture to add that to me the convention mode seems preferable, in that it allows amendments to originate with the people themselves, instead of only permitting them to take or reject propositions originated by others, not especially chosen for the purpose, and which might not be precisely such as they would wish to either accept or refuse. I understand a proposed amendment to the Constitution—which amendment, however, I have not seen—has passed Congress, to the effect that the Federal Government shall never interfere with the domestic institutions of the States, including that of persons held to service. To avoid misconstruction of what I have said, I depart from my purpose not to speak of particular amendments so far as to say that, holding such a provision to now be implied constitutional law, I have no objection to its being made express and irrevocable.

The Chief Magistrate derives all his authority from the people, and they have referred none upon him to fix terms for the separation of the States. The people themselves can do this if also they choose, but the Executive as such has nothing to do with it. His duty is to administer the present Government as it came to his hands and to transmit it unimpaired by him to his successor.

Why should there not be a patient confidence in the ultimate justice of the people? Is there any better or equal hope in the world? In our present differences, is either party without faith of being in the right? If the Almighty Ruler of Nations, with His eternal truth and justice, be on your side of the North, or on yours of the South, that truth and that justice will surely prevail by the judgment of this great tribunal of the American people.

By the frame of the Government under which we live this same people have wisely given their public servants but little power for mischief, and have with equal wisdom provided for the return of that little to their own hands at very short intervals. While the people retain their virtue and vigilance no Administration by any extreme of wickedness or folly can very seriously injure the Government in the short space of four years.

My countrymen, one and all, think calmly and well upon this whole subject. Nothing valuable can be lost by taking time. If there be an object to hurry any of you in hot haste to a step which you would never take deliberately, that object will be frustrated by taking time; but no good object can be frustrated by it. Such of you as are now dissatisfied still have the old Constitution unimpaired, and, on the sensitive point, the laws of your own framing under it; while the new Administration will have no immediate power, if it would, to change either. If it were admitted that you who are dissatisfied hold the right side in the dispute, there still is no single good reason for precipitate action. Intelligence, patriotism, Christianity, and a firm reliance on Him who has never yet forsaken this favored land are still competent to adjust in the best way all our present difficulty.

In your hands, my dissatisfied fellow-countrymen, and not in mine, is the momentous issue of civil war. The Government will not assail you. You can have no conflict without being yourselves the aggressors. You have no oath registered in heaven to destroy the Government, while I shall have the most solemn one to "preserve, protect, and defend it."

I am loath to close. We are not enemies, but friends. We must not be enemies. Though passion may have strained it must not break our bonds of affection. The mystic chords of memory, stretching from every battlefield and patriot grave to every living heart and hearthstone all over this broad land, will yet swell the chorus of the Union, when again touched, as surely they will be, by the better angels of our nature.

Alexander Stephens

Cornerstone Speech[1] (March 21, 1861)

Savannah, Georgia

Mr. Mayor, and Gentlemen of the Committee, and Fellow-Citizens: For this reception you will please accept my most profound and sincere thanks. The compliment is doubtless intended as much, or more, perhaps, in honor of the occasion, and my public position, in connection with the great events now crowding upon us, than to me personally and individually. It is however none the less appreciated by me on that account. We are in the midst of one of the greatest epochs in our history. The last ninety days will mark one of the most memorable eras in the history of modern civilization. [. . .] I very much regret that every one who desires cannot hear what I have to say. Not that I have any display to make, or any thing very entertaining to present, but such views as I have to give, I wish *all*, not only in this city, but in this State, and throughout our Confederate Republic, could hear, who have a desire to hear them.

I was remarking, that we are passing through one of the greatest revolutions in the annals of the world. Seven States have within the last three months thrown off an old government and formed a new. This revolution has been signally marked, up to this time, by the fact of its having been accomplished without the loss of a single drop of blood. [Applause.]

This new constitution, or form of government, constitutes the subject to which your attention will be partly invited. In reference to it, I make this first general remark. It amply secures all our ancient rights, franchises, and liberties. All the great principles of Magna Charta are retained in it. No citizen is deprived of life, liberty, or property, but by the judgment of his peers under the laws of the land. The great principle of religious liberty, which was the honor and pride of the old constitution, is still maintained and secured. All the essentials of the old constitution, which have endeared it to the hearts of the American people, have been preserved and perpetuated. [Applause.] Some changes have been made. Of these I shall speak presently. Some of these I should have preferred not to have seen made; but these, perhaps, meet the cordial approbation of a majority of this audience, if not an overwhelming majority of the people of the Confederacy. Of them, therefore, I will not speak. But other important changes do meet my cordial approbation. They form great improvements upon the old constitution. So, taking the whole new constitution, I have no hesitancy in giving it as my judgment that it is decidedly better than the old. [Applause.]

Allow me briefly to allude to some of these improvements. The question of building up class interests, or fostering one branch of industry to the prejudice of another under the exercise of the revenue power, which gave us so much trouble under the old constitution, is put at rest forever under the new. We allow the imposition of no duty with a view of giving advantage to one class of persons, in any trade or business, over those of another. All, under our system, stand upon the same broad principles of perfect equality. Honest labor and enterprise are left free and unrestricted in whatever pursuit they may be engaged. This subject came well nigh causing a rupture of the old Union, under the lead of the gallant Palmetto State, which lies on our border, in 1833. This old thorn of the tariff, which was the cause of so much irritation in the old body politic, is removed forever from the new. [Applause.]

Again, the subject of internal improvements, under the power of Congress to regulate commerce, is put at rest under our system. The power claimed by construction under the old constitution, was at least

1. [Delivered extemporaneously by Stephens. There is no known original draft for this speech available to us. The excerpt was taken from an article in the *Savannah Republican* and included in a collection of Stephens' work edited by Henry Cleveland, *Alexander Stephens in Public and Private* . . . (Philadelphia, 1886), 717–29.]

a doubtful one—it rested solely upon construction. We of the South, generally apart from considerations of constitutional principles, opposed its exercise upon grounds of its inexpediency and injustice. Notwithstanding this opposition, millions of money, from the common treasury had been drawn for such purposes. Our opposition sprang from no hostility to commerce, or all necessary aids for facilitating it. With us it was simply a question, upon whom the burden should fall. In Georgia, for instance, we have done as much for the cause of internal improvements as any other portion of the country according to population and means. We have stretched out lines of railroads from the seaboard to the mountains; dug down the hills, and filled up the valleys at a cost of not less than twenty-five millions of dollars. All this was done to open an outlet for our products of the interior, and those to the west of us, to reach the marts of the world. No State was in greater need of such facilities than Georgia, but we did not ask that these works should be made by appropriations out of the common treasury. The cost of the grading, the superstructure and equipments of our roads, was borne by those who entered on the enterprise. Nay, more—not only the cost of the iron, no small item in the aggregate cost, was borne in the same way—but we were compelled to pay into the common treasury several millions of dollars for the privilege of importing the iron, after the price was paid for it abroad. What justice was there in taking this money, which our people paid into the common treasury on the importation of our iron, and applying it to the improvement of rivers and harbors elsewhere?

The true principle is to subject the commerce of every locality, to whatever burdens may be necessary to facilitate it. If Charleston harbor needs improvement, let the commerce of Charleston bear the burden. If the mouth of the Savannah river has to be cleared out, let the sea-going navigation which is benefited by it bear the burden. So with the mouths of the Alabama and Mississippi river. Just as the products of the interior, our cotton, wheat, corn, and other articles, have to bear the necessary rates of freight over our railroads to reach the seas. This is again the broad principle of perfect equality and justice. [Applause.] And it is especially set forth and established in our new constitution. [. . .] The new constitution has put at rest, *forever*, all the agitating questions relating to our peculiar institution—African slavery as it exists amongst us—the proper *status* of the negro in our form of civilization. This was the immediate cause of the late rupture and present revolution. Jefferson in his forecast, had anticipated this, as the "rock upon which the old Union would split." He was right. What was conjecture with him, is now a realized fact. But whether he fully comprehended the great truth upon which that rock *stood* and *stands*, may be doubted. The prevailing ideas entertained by him and most of the leading statesmen at the time of the formation of the old constitution, were that the enslavement of the African was in violation of the laws of nature; that it was wrong in *principle*, socially, morally, and politically. It was an evil they knew not well how to deal with, but the general opinion of the men of that day was that, somehow or other in the order of Providence, the institution would be evanescent and pass away. This idea, though not incorporated in the constitution, was the prevailing idea at that time. The constitution, it is true, secured every essential guarantee to the institution while it should last, and hence no argument can be justly urged against the constitutional guarantees thus secured, because of the common sentiment of the day. Those ideas, however, were fundamentally wrong. They rested upon the assumption of the equality of races. This was an error. It was a sandy foundation, and the government built upon it fell when the "storm came and the wind blew."

Our new government is founded upon exactly the opposite idea; its foundations are laid, its cornerstone rests upon the great truth, that the negro is not equal to the white man; that slavery—subordination to the superior race—is his natural and normal condition. [Applause.] This, our new government, is the first, in the history of the world, based upon this great physical, philosophical, and moral truth. This truth has been slow in the process of its development, like all other truths in the various departments of science. It has been so even amongst us. Many who hear me, perhaps, can recollect well, that this truth was not generally admitted, even within their day. The errors of the past generation still clung to many as late as twenty years ago. Those at the North, who still cling to these errors, with a zeal above knowledge, we justly denominate fanatics. All fanaticism springs from an aberration of the mind—from a defect in reasoning. It is a species of insanity. One of the most striking characteristics of insanity, in many instances, is forming correct conclusions from fancied or erroneous premises; so with the anti-slavery fanatics; their conclusions are right if their premises were. They assume that the negro is equal, and hence conclude that he is entitled to equal privileges and rights with the white man. If their premises were correct, their conclusions would be logical and just—but their premise being wrong, their whole argument fails. I recollect once of having heard a gentleman from one of the northern States, of great power and ability, announce in the House of Representatives, with imposing effect, that we of the South would be compelled, ultimately, to yield upon this subject of slavery, that it was as impossible to war successfully against a principle in politics, as it was in physics or mechanics. That the principle would ultimately prevail. That we, in maintaining slavery as it exists with us, were warring against a principle, a principle founded in nature, the principle of the equality of men. The reply I made to him was, that upon his own grounds, we should, ultimately, succeed, and that he and his associates, in this crusade against our institutions, would ultimately fail. The truth announced, that it was as impossible to war successfully against a principle in politics as it was in physics and mechanics, I admitted; but told him that it was he, and those acting with him, who were warring against a principle. They were attempting to make things equal which the Creator had made unequal.

In the conflict thus far, success has been on our side, complete throughout the length and breadth of the Confederate States. It is upon this, as I have stated, our social fabric is firmly planted; and I cannot permit myself to doubt the ultimate success of a full recognition of this principle throughout the civilized and enlightened world.

As I have stated, the truth of this principle may be slow in development, as all truths are and ever have been, in the various branches of science. It was so with the principles announced by Galileo—it was so with Adam Smith and his principles of political economy. It was so with Harvey, and his theory of the circulation of the blood. It is stated that not a single one of the medical profession, living at the time of the announcement of the truths made by him, admitted them. Now, they are universally acknowledged. May we not, therefore, look with confidence to the ultimate universal acknowledgment of the truths upon which our system rests? It is the first government ever instituted upon the principles in strict conformity to nature, and the ordination of Providence, in furnishing the materials of human society. Many governments have been founded upon the principle of the subordination and serfdom of certain classes of the same race; such were and are in violation of the laws of nature. Our system commits no such violation of nature's laws. With us, all of the white race, however high or low, rich or poor, are equal in the eye of the law. Not so with the negro. Subordination is his place. He, by nature, or by the curse against Canaan, is fitted for that condition which he occupies in our system. The architect, in the construction of buildings, lays the foundation with the proper material—the granite; then comes the brick or the marble. The substratum of our society is made of the material fitted by nature for it, and by experience we know that it is best, not only for the superior, but for the inferior race, that it should be so. It is, indeed, in conformity with the ordinance of the Creator. It is not for us to inquire into the wisdom of his ordinances, or to question them. For his own purposes, he has made one race to differ from another, as he has made "one star to differ from another star in glory."

The great objects of humanity are best attained when there is conformity to his laws and decrees, in the formation of governments as well as in all things else. Our confederacy is founded upon principles in strict conformity with these laws. This stone which was rejected by the first builders "is become the chief of the corner"—the real "corner-stone"—in our new edifice. [Applause.]

I have been asked, what of the future? It has been apprehended by some that we would have arrayed against us the civilized world. I care not who or how many they may be against us, when we stand upon the eternal principles of truth, *if we are true to ourselves and the principles for which we contend,* we are obliged to, and must triumph. [Immense applause.]

Thousands of people who begin to understand these truths are not yet completely out of the shell; they do not see them in their length and breadth. We hear much of the civilization and christianization of the barbarous tribes of Africa. In my judgment, those ends will never be attained, but by first teaching them the lesson taught to Adam, that "in the sweat of his brow he should eat his bread," [applause,] and teaching them to work, and feed, and clothe themselves. [. . .]

But to return to the question of the future. What is to be the result of this revolution?

Will every thing, commenced so well, continue as it has begun? In reply to this anxious inquiry, I can only say it all depends upon ourselves. A young man starting out in life on his majority, with health, talent, and ability, under a favoring Providence, may be said to be the architect of his own fortunes. His destinies are in his own hands. He may make for himself a name, of honor or dishonor, according to his own acts. If he plants himself upon truth, integrity, honor and uprightness, with industry, patience and energy, he cannot fail of success. So it is with us. We are a young republic, just entering upon the arena of nations; we will be the architects of our own fortunes. Our destiny, under Providence, is in our own hands. With wisdom, prudence, and statesmanship on the part of our public men, and intelligence, virtue and patriotism on the part of the people, success, to the full measures of our most sanguine hopes, may be looked for. But if unwise counsels prevail—if we become divided—if schisms arise—if dissensions spring up—if factions are engendered—if party spirit, nourished by unholy personal ambition shall rear its hydra head, I have no good to prophesy for you. Without intelligence, virtue, integrity, and patriotism on the part of the people, no republic or representative government can be durable or stable.

We have intelligence, and virtue, and patriotism. All that is required is to cultivate and perpetuate these. Intelligence will not do without virtue. France was a nation of philosophers. These philosophers become Jacobins. They lacked that virtue, that devotion to moral principle, and that patriotism which is essential to good government. Organized upon principles of perfect justice and right—seeking amity and friendship with all other powers—I see no obstacle in the way of our upward and onward progress. Our growth, by accessions from other States, will depend greatly upon whether we present to the world, as I trust we shall, a better government than that to which neighboring States belong. If we do this, North Carolina, Tennessee, and Arkansas cannot hesitate long; neither can Virginia, Kentucky, and Missouri. They will necessarily gravitate to us by an imperious law. We made ample provision in our constitution for the admission of other States; it is more guarded, and wisely so, I think, than the old constitution on the same subject, but not too guarded to receive them as fast as it may be proper. Looking to the distant future, and, perhaps, not very far distant either, it is not beyond the range of possibility, and even probability, that all the great States of the north-west will gravitate this way, as well as Tennessee, Kentucky, Missouri, Arkansas, etc. Should they do so, our doors are wide enough to receive them, but not until they are ready to assimilate with us in principle.

The process of disintegration in the old Union may be expected to go on with almost absolute certainty if we pursue the right course. We are now the nucleus of a growing power which, if we are true to ourselves, our destiny, and high mission, will become the controlling power on this continent. To what extent accessions will go on in the process of time, or where it will end, the future will determine. So far as it concerns States of the old Union, this process will be upon no such principles of *reconstruction* as now spoken of, but upon *reorganization* and new assimilation. [Loud applause.] Such are some of the glimpses of the future as I catch them. [. . .]

Our object is *peace*, not only with the North, but with the world. All matters relating to the public property, public liabilities of the Union when we were members of it, we are ready and willing to adjust and settle upon the principles of right, equity, and good faith. War can be of no more benefit to the North than to us. Whether the intention of evacuating Fort Sumter is to be received as an evidence of a desire for a peaceful solution of our difficulties with the United States, or the result of necessity, I will not undertake to say. I would fain hope the former. Rumors are afloat, however, that it is the result of necessity. All I can say to you, therefore, on that point is, keep your armor bright and your powder dry. [. . .] [Enthusiastic cheering.]

10

THE CIVIL WAR AND RECONSTRUCTION

Five events reverberated ominously throughout America in the antebellum decade of the 1850s: the publication of Harriet Beecher Stowe's *Uncle Tom's Cabin* in 1852; the outbreak of armed conflict in the Kansas Territory over the future of slavery in 1855; the decision and reasoning of the Taney Court in *Dred Scott v. Sandford* in 1857; the Lincoln-Douglas debates in 1858; and the raid on Harper's Ferry in 1859 by abolitionist and warrior-prophet John Brown. Each event served as a signpost to the coming war. Stowe's novel gave the issue of slavery a flesh-and-bones reality to the majority of Americans who had never seen a slave and had thus remained distant from its practice. The *Dred Scott* case appeared to empower slaveholding, rather than liberty, with the weight of the rule of law. The bloodshed in Kansas, where Brown first emerged on the national scene, and the episode at Harper's Ferry, where he met his end, presaged the violence that would soon characterize an America divided against itself. In what might be seen as a further omen, it was at Harper's Ferry that Robert E. Lee led federal forces against Brown's insurrection. Thus, even before the Southern attack on Fort Sumter, Lee joined the battle over the one great issue that menaced the republic's survival.

The debates between senatorial candidates Abraham Lincoln (Republican) and Stephen Douglas (Democrat) demonstrated just how divisive and intractable the issue of slavery had become. With violence already erupting on the Great Plains, Lincoln challenged Douglas' assumption that the nation could survive half free and half slave. Further, he denounced chattel slavery as a moral and political evil, an institution at odds with the Declaration of Independence and the Constitution. At the same time, however, Lincoln maintained as his highest obligation the preservation of the Union. His task, then, was to denounce slavery and to work toward its eventual demise, while retaining the Union. As a result, his political solution to the crisis of slavery was more conservative, more gradualist, than that demanded by abolitionists like John Brown or William Lloyd Garrison: contain slavery where it already existed, tolerate it as far as it goes, but deny its constitutional legitimacy and encourage its gradual, natural death.

But by 1858 Lincoln was operating in political waters with contrary currents. Douglas' policy of "popular sovereignty" and the Court's ruling in *Dred Scott* opened the territories—and perhaps even the free states—to slavery. Further, the Court affirmed what slavery's apologists already insisted: namely, that the Constitution recognized the right to own slaves. In this political environment, even Douglas' profession of indifference toward the future of slavery in the territories was unacceptable to almost every prominent Southern politician. Lincoln's insistence, in turn, that the growth of slavery in the federal territories must and legislatively could be stopped, along with his denial that the Constitution recognized a right to own slaves, were perceived as threats to the very institution itself.

That the South seceded in order to preserve the institution of slavery is undeniable. The states' secession declarations bear out this thesis convincingly. Moreover, it wasn't simply the economy of the South that Lincoln appeared to threaten,—it was an entire way of life, a way of looking at and ordering the world. For if slavery was abolished, would that not imply that blacks were equal to whites? And if blacks were equal, were they not entitled to *full* equality—social, political, and economic? These questions necessarily followed any discussion of abolition, and the answers were potentially troubling to white Americans everywhere. For while many people, black and white, objected to slavery on moral and political grounds, many whites nonetheless stopped well short of demanding true equality for the former slave. Douglas knew this well, and he exploited it in his debates with Lincoln, claiming that the future president was at heart a radical abolitionist who favored full equality for blacks. That charge evidently had bite, for Lincoln felt the need to deny it during their fourth debate.

> While I was at the hotel today, an elderly gentleman called upon me to know whether I was really in favor of producing a perfect equality between the negroes and white people. [Great Laughter. . . .] I will say . . . that I am not, nor ever have been, in favor of bringing about in any way the social and political equality of the white and black races, [applause]—that I am not nor ever have been in favor of making voters or jurors of negroes, nor of qualifying them to hold office, nor to intermarry with white people; and I will say in addition to this that there is a physical difference between the white and black races which I believe will forever forbid the two races living together on terms of social and political equality.

The point here is not to denigrate Lincoln's great and well-deserved name, nor to charge that Lincoln failed to envision in fact what equality necessarily entails in principle. Reputable scholars disagree here, and we leave it to the reader to decide whether Lincoln was progressive for his times but not for ours, or whether the cagey debater and politician was ahead of his times and acted in order to influence them. Rather, the point is that the Lincoln-Douglas debates reveal the depth of the racial prejudice that dominated American culture; for that racial prejudice and indeed animus that shaped antebellum politics would in turn indelibly shape the politics of Reconstruction.

Reconstruction is the term that denotes the government's policies toward rebuilding and reuniting the nation in the wake of the Civil War. Even before it ended, debate arose over the goals that drove the Civil War. Was the war fought in the name of abolition alone, or was a concerted public effort toward greater, more meaningful equality for blacks morally and politically mandated? Lincoln implemented the first Reconstruction measures in 1864, putting forth a policy of readmission to the Union for Louisiana that members of his party in Congress believed too lenient. The "Radical Republicans" in Congress proposed their own policy in the Wade-Davis bill. The measure failed, but it signaled that debate over Reconstruction was going to be divisive.

The differences between Presidential Reconstruction and Congressional (or Radical) Reconstruction would grow after Lincoln's death. In January 1865 General William Tecumseh Sherman issued Field Order 15, which set aside portions of coastal Florida, Georgia, and South Carolina for former slaves, who were to be given title to forty acres and a mule. In March the Freedman's Bureau was established to help former slaves with immediate needs, such as medical care, housing, and negotiating labor contracts. In his last speech, President Lincoln talked of extending the suffrage to black war veterans—roughly 180,000 men in all. But after Lincoln's assassination, President Andrew Johnson showed little disposition to punish white Confederates or to lend significant assistance to the millions of newly freed blacks in the South. In late summer he ordered that confiscated land, including land seized by General Sherman, be returned to its former owners. "White men alone must manage the South," President Johnson asserted. In the fall the Thirteenth Amendment was ratified, but at the same time Southern legislatures began to enact "black codes," statutory restrictions aimed at reimposing a form of servitude on blacks. Under these laws, blacks could work only as field hands; unemployed blacks could be prosecuted for vagrancy and then "loaned" to landowners as a way to pay off their fine; blacks were prohibited from voting, sitting on juries, and testifying against whites in court. When in December President Johnson declared Reconstruction over, a political battle ensued over the nature of Reconstruction in America.

Congress responded to Johnson's leniency by refusing to seat scores of former Confederates elected to Congress. Then, in April 1866, Congress passed—over Johnson's veto—a civil rights bill that granted citizenship to African Americans and, significantly, established specific legal rights that the states were obligated to respect and which federal officials were empowered to enforce. The act was a response to the black codes and to the violence and denial of rights that African Americans were experiencing throughout the South. In June Congress sent the Fourteenth Amendment to the states with the intent of giving constitutional status to the provisions of the 1866 Civil Rights Act. (Its passage two years later radically redefined citizenship in the United States and gave the federal government powers over the states when enforcing constitutional rights.) Later that year Congress again overrode a presidential veto, this of another Freedman's Bureau bill. In 1867 it once more overcame presidential opposition in passing a bill enfranchising black voters in Washington, D.C. And it enacted a law that divided the South into military zones, gave police powers to federal troops patrolling in those zones, and required the former Confederate states to write new constitutions providing for African American male suffrage before being readmitted to the Union (this right was inscribed in the national Constitution three years later, in the Fifteenth Amendment).

By many measures Reconstruction was a success, particularly for African Americans. More than 700,000 African Americans were registered to vote. They participated in Southern state constitutional conventions and were elected to Southern legislatures. In fact, in every legislature except Virginia, freedmen, working with "carpetbaggers" from the North and native Southern Republican sympathizers ("scalawags"), briefly constituted the majority in power. In South Carolina, African American delegates comprised a majority in the legislature's lower chamber, and Joseph Rainey and Hiram Revels became the first African Americans to serve in the U.S. House and Senate, respectively. Socially and economically, African Americans made advances, too. The Freedmen's Bureau built more than 100 hospitals and 4,000 public schools. The first African American colleges were constructed, including Fisk (1866) and Howard (1867) Universities.

Still, the problems of Reconstruction in the South were enormous. The Civil War freed 4 million slaves into an economy devastated by the conflict. Inevitably, many lived in poverty, and black crime—much of it motivated by need—fed preexisting fears about the social costs of abolition. Moreover, racial animus toward the new freedmen brought forth a reign of terror against African Americans. Racial violence broke out quickly in response to Radical Reconstruction, with white mobs killing scores of African Americans in Memphis and New Orleans (1866), and in Opelousas (St. Landry Parish), Louisiana (1868). It's important to bear in mind that the violence (and threat of violence) against African Americans and white Republicans was constant throughout the South. In this period white supremacist groups, like the Knights of the White Camellia, systematically disenfranchised African Americans across the South by threats and violence. Perhaps the most appalling example of racial violence occurred on Easter Sunday, 1873, at the Colfax Courthouse, in Grant Parish, Louisiana, when a dispute over the outcome of an election led to a race riot in which more than 100 African Americans were killed, many of them after they had been taken as prisoners. Remarkably, three men were convicted of civil rights violations under the 1870 Enforcement Act, but the U.S. Supreme Court overturned those convictions in 1875, in the case of *United States v. Cruikshank*.

The Court ruling was a clear indication that resistance to Radical Reconstruction could be expected from many quarters. Moreover, by 1876 even Northerners, perhaps war weary and disillusioned by growing charges of corruption in Republican-led governments, had lost the intense commitment to the plight of the freedmen necessary to sustain an aggressive Reconstruction policy. A bitterly fought and disputed presidential election that year eventually led to a back-room deal in which congressional Republicans agreed to end Reconstruction; in return, Republican Rutherford B. Hayes was declared president. Soon after taking office Hayes ordered the removal of remaining federal troops in the South. By April 1877, a federal police presence in the South was no more, and the veil of segregation and political disempowerment began to descend on African Americans.

Abraham Lincoln

Letter to Orville H. Browning (September 22, 1861)

(Private and Confidential.)

Executive Mansion, Washington

Hon. O. H. Browning.

My dear Sir: Yours of the 17th is just received; and coming from you, I confess it astonishes me. That you should object to my adhering to a law which you had assisted in making and presenting to me less than a month before is odd enough. But this is a very small part. General Frémont's proclamation as to confiscation of property and the liberation of slaves is purely political and not within the range of military law or necessity. If a commanding general finds a necessity to seize the farm of a private owner for a pasture, an encampment, or a fortification, he has the right to do so, and to so hold it as long as the necessity lasts; and this is within military law, because within military necessity. But to say the farm shall no longer belong to the owner, or his heirs forever, and this as well when the farm is not needed for military purposes as when it is, is purely political, without the savor of military law about it. And the same is true of slaves. If the general needs them, he can seize them and use them; but when the need is past, it is not for him to fix their permanent future condition. That must be settled according to laws made by law-makers, and not by military proclamations. The proclamation in the point in question is simply "dictatorship." It assumes that the general may do anything he pleases—confiscate the lands and free the slaves of loyal people, as well as of disloyal ones. And going the whole figure, I have no doubt, would be more popular with some thoughtless people than that which has been done! But I cannot assume this reckless position, nor allow others to assume it on my responsibility.

You speak of it as being the only means of saving the government. On the contrary, it is itself the surrender of the government. Can it be pretended that it is any longer the Government of the United States—any government of constitution and laws—wherein a general or a president may make permanent rules of property by proclamation? I do not say Congress might not with propriety pass a law on the point, just such as General Fremont proclaimed. I do not say I might not, as a member of Congress, vote for it. What I object to is, that I, as President, shall expressly or impliedly seize and exercise the permanent legislative functions of the government.

So much as to principle. Now as to policy. No doubt the thing was popular in some quarters, and would have been more so if it had been a general declaration of emancipation. The Kentucky legislature would not budge till that proclamation was modified; and General Anderson telegraphed me that on the news of General Fremont having actually issued deeds of manumission, a whole company of our volunteers threw down their arms and disbanded. I was so assured as to think it probable that the very arms we had furnished Kentucky would be turned against us. I think to lose Kentucky is nearly the same as to lose the whole game. Kentucky gone, we cannot hold Missouri, nor, as I think, Maryland. These all against us, and the job on our hands is too large for us. We would as well consent to separation at once, including the surrender of this capital. On the contrary, if you will give up your restlessness for new positions, and back me manfully on the grounds upon which you and other kind friends gave me the election and have approved in my public documents, we shall go through triumphantly. You must not understand I took my course on the proclamation because of Kentucky. I took the same ground in a private letter to General Fremont before I heard from Kentucky.

You think I am inconsistent because I did not also forbid General Frémont to shoot men under the proclamation. I understand that part to be within military law, but I also think, and so privately wrote General Frémont, that it is impolitic in this, that our adversaries have the power, and will certainly exercise it, to shoot as many of our men as we shoot of theirs. I did not say this in the public letter, because it is a subject I prefer not to discuss in the hearing of our enemies.

There has been no thought of removing General Frémont on any ground connected with his proclamation, and if there has been any wish for his removal on any ground, our mutual friend Sam. Glover can probably tell you what it was. I hope no real necessity for it exists on any ground. Your friend, as ever,

A. Lincoln

Message to Congress Recommending Compensated Emancipation (March 6, 1862)

Fellow-citizens of the Senate and House of Representatives: I recommend the adoption of a joint resolution by your honorable bodies, which shall be substantially as follows:

> *Resolved,* That the United States ought to cooperate with any State which may adopt gradual abolishment of slavery, giving to such State pecuniary aid, to be used by such State, in its discretion, to compensate for the inconveniences, public and private, produced by such change of system.

If the proposition contained in the resolution does not meet the approval of Congress and the country, there is the end; but if it does command such approval, I deem it of importance that the States and people immediately interested should be at once distinctly notified of the fact, so that they may begin to consider whether to accept or reject it. The Federal Government would find its highest interest in such a measure, as one of the most efficient means of self-preservation. The leaders of the existing insurrection entertain the hope that this government will ultimately be forced to acknowledge the independence of some part of the disaffected region, and that all the slave States north of such part will then say, "The Union for which we have struggled being already gone, we now choose to go with the Southern section." To deprive them of this hope substantially ends the rebellion; and the initiation of emancipation completely deprives them of it as to all the States initiating it. The point is not that all the States tolerating slavery would very soon, if at all, initiate emancipation; but that while the offer is equally made to all, the more Northern shall, by such initiation, make it certain to the more Southern that in no event will the former ever join the latter in their proposed confederacy. I say "initiation" because, in my judgment, gradual and not sudden emancipation is better for all. In the mere financial or pecuniary view, any member of Congress, with the census tables and treasury reports before him, can readily see for himself how very soon the current expenditures of this war would purchase, at fair valuation, all the slaves in any named State. Such a proposition on the part of the General Government sets up no claim of a right by Federal authority to interfere with slavery within State limits, referring, as it does, the absolute control of the subject in each case to the State and its people immediately interested. It is proposed as a matter of perfectly free choice with them.

In the annual message, last December, I thought fit to say, "The Union must be preserved, and hence all indispensable means must be employed." I said this not hastily, but deliberately. War has been made, and continues to be, an indispensable means to this end. A practical reacknowledgment of the national authority would render the war unnecessary, and it would at once cease. If, however, resistance continues, the war must also continue; and it is impossible to foresee all the incidents which may attend and all the ruin which may follow it. Such as may seem indispensable, or may obviously promise great efficiency, toward ending the struggle, must and will come.

The proposition now made, though an offer only, I hope it may be esteemed no offense to ask whether the pecuniary consideration tendered would not be of more value to the States and private persons concerned than are the institution and property in it, in the present aspect of affairs?

While it is true that the adoption of the proposed resolution would be merely initiatory, and not within itself a practical measure, it is recommended in the hope that it would soon lead to important practical results. In full view of my great responsibility to my God and to my country, I earnestly beg the attention of Congress and the people to the subject.

Abraham Lincoln

Washington, March 6, 1862.

Proclamation Revoking General Hunter's Martial Order of Emancipation (May 9, 1862)

Whereas there appears in the public prints what purports to be a proclamation of Major-General Hunter, in the words and figures following, to wit:

(General Orders No. 11.)

HEADQUARTERS DEPARTMENT OF THE SOUTH,
HILTON HEAD, PORT ROYAL, S.C., May 9, 1862.

The three States of Georgia, Florida, and South Carolina, comprising the military department of the South, having deliberately declared themselves no longer under the protection of the United States of America, and having taken up arms against the said United States, it became a military necessity to declare martial law. This was accordingly done on the 25th day of April, 1862. Slavery and martial law in a free country are altogether incompatible; the persons in these three States—Georgia, Florida, and South Carolina—heretofore held as slaves, are therefore declared forever free.

By command of Major-General D. Hunter:
(Official.) ED. W. SMITH,
Acting Assistant Adjutant-General.

And whereas the same is producing some excitement and misunderstanding: therefore,

I, Abraham Lincoln, President of the United States, proclaim and declare that the Government of the United States had no knowledge, information, or belief of an intention on the part of General Hunter to issue such a proclamation; nor has it yet any authentic information that the document is genuine. And further, that neither General Hunter, nor any other commander or person, has been authorized by the Government of the United States to make a proclamation declaring the slaves of any State free; and that the supposed proclamation now in question, whether genuine or false, is altogether void so far as respects such a declaration.

I further make known that, whether it be competent for me, as commander-in-chief of the army and navy, to declare the slaves of any State or States free, and whether, at any time, in any case, it shall have become a necessity indispensable to the maintenance of the government to exercise such supposed power, are questions which, under my responsibility, I reserve to myself, and which I cannot feel justified in leaving to the decision of commanders in the field. These are totally different questions from those of police regulations in armies and camps.

On the sixth day of March last, by special message, I recommended to Congress the adoption of a joint resolution, to be substantially as follows:

> Resolved, That the United States ought to cooperate with any State which may adopt gradual abolishment of slavery, giving to such State pecuniary aid, to be used by such State, in its discretion, to compensate for the inconvenience, public and private, produced by such change of system.

The resolution, in the language above quoted, was adopted by large majorities in both branches of Congress, and now stands an authentic, definite, and solemn proposal of the nation to the States and people most immediately interested in the subject-matter. To the people of those States I now earnestly appeal. I do not argue—I beseech you to make arguments for yourselves. You cannot, if you would, be blind to the signs of the times. I beg of you a calm and enlarged consideration of them, ranging, if it may be, far above personal and partizan politics. This proposal makes common cause for a common object, casting no reproaches upon any. It acts not the Pharisee. The change it contemplates would come gently as the dews of heaven, not rending or wrecking anything. Will you not embrace it? So much good has not been done, by one effort, in all past time, as in the providence of God it is now your high privilege to do. May the vast future not have to lament that you have neglected it.

In witness whereof, I have hereunto set my hand and caused the seal of the United States to be affixed.

[L. S.] Done at the city of Washington, this nineteenth day of May, in the year of our Lord one thousand eight hundred and sixty-two, and of the independence of the United States the eighty-sixth.

ABRAHAM LINCOLN

By the President: WILLIAM H. SEWARD,
Secretary of State

Address on Colonization to a Committee of Colored Men (August 14, 1862)

Washington

This afternoon the President of the United States gave an audience to a committee of colored men at the White House. They were introduced by Rev. J. Mitchell, Commissioner of Emigration. E.M. Thomas, the chairman, remarked that they were there by invitation to hear what the Executive had to say to them.

Having all been seated, the President, after a few preliminary observations, informed them that a sum of money had been appropriated by Congress, and placed at his disposition, for the purpose of aiding the colonization in some country of the people, or a portion of them, of African descent, thereby making it his duty, as it had for a long time been his inclination, to favor that cause. And why, he asked, should the people of your race be colonized, and where? Why should they leave this country? This is, perhaps, the first question for proper consideration. You and we are different races. We have between us a broader difference than exists between almost any other two races. Whether it is right or wrong I need not discuss; but this physical difference is a great disadvantage to us both, as I think. Your race suffer very greatly, many of them, by living among us, while ours suffer from your presence. In a word, we suffer on each side. If this is admitted, it affords a reason, at least, why we should be separated. You here are freemen, I suppose?

A voice: Yes, sir.

The President: Perhaps you have long been free, or all your lives. Your race is suffering, in my judgment, the greatest wrong inflicted on any people. But even when you cease to be slaves, you are yet far removed from being placed on an equality with the white race. You are cut off from many of the advantages which the other race enjoys. The aspiration of men is to enjoy equality with the best when free, but on this broad continent not a single man of your race is made the equal of a single man of ours. Go where you are treated the best, and the ban is still upon you. I do not propose to discuss this, but to present it as a fact with which we have to deal. I cannot alter it if I would. It is a fact about which we all think and feel alike, I and you. We look to our condition. Owing to the existence of the two races on this continent, I need not recount to you the effects upon white men, growing out of the institution of slavery.

I believe in its general evil effects on the white race. See our present condition—the country engaged in war—our white men cutting one another's throats—none knowing how far it will extend—and then consider what we know to be the truth. But for your race among us there could not be war, although many men engaged on either side do not care for you one way or the other. Nevertheless, I repeat, without the institution of slavery, and the colored race as a basis, the war could not have an existence. It is better for us both, therefore, to be separated. I know that there are free men among you who, even if they could better their condition, are not as much inclined to go out of the country as those who, being slaves, could obtain their freedom on this condition. I suppose one of the principal difficulties in the way of colonization is that the free colored man cannot see that his comfort would be advanced by it. You may believe that you can live in Washington, or elsewhere in the United States, the remainder of your life as easily, perhaps more so, than you can in any foreign country; and hence you may come to the conclusion that you have nothing to do with the idea of going to a foreign country.

This is (I speak in no unkind sense) an extremely selfish view of the case. You ought to do something to help those who are not so fortunate as yourselves. There is an unwillingness on the part of our people, harsh as it may be, for you free colored people to remain with us. Now, if you could give a start to the white people, you would open a wide door for many to be made free: If we deal with those who are not free at the beginning, and whose intellects are clouded by slavery, we have very poor material to start with. If intelligent colored men, such as are before me, would move in this matter, much might be accomplished. It is exceedingly important that we have men at the beginning capable of thinking as white men, and not those who have been systematically oppressed. There is much to encourage you. For the sake of your race you should sacrifice something of your present comfort for the purpose of being as grand in that respect as the white people. It is a cheering thought throughout life, that something can be done to ameliorate the condition of those who have been subject to the hard usages of the world. It is difficult to make a man miserable while he feels he is worthy of himself and claims kindred to the great God who made him. In the American Revolutionary war sacrifices were made by men engaged in it, but they were cheered by the future. General Washington himself endured greater physical hardships than if he had remained a British subject, yet he was a happy man because he was engaged in benefiting his race, in doing something for the children of his neighbors, having none of his own.

The colony of Liberia has been in existence a long time. In a certain sense it is a success. The old President of Liberia, Roberts, has just been with me—the first time I ever saw him. He says they have within the bounds of that colony between three and four hundred thousand people, or more than in some of our old States, such as Rhode Island or Delaware, or in some of our newer States, and less than in some of our larger ones. They are not all American colonists or their descendants. Something less than 12,000 have been sent thither from this country. Many of the original settlers have died; yet, like people elsewhere, their offspring outnumber those deceased. The question is, if the colored people are persuaded to go anywhere, why not there?

One reason for unwillingness to do so is that some of you would rather remain within reach of the country of your nativity. I do not know how much attachment you may have toward our race. It does not strike me that you have the greatest reason to love them. But still you are attached to them, at all events.

The place I am thinking about for a colony is in Central America. It is nearer to us than Liberia—not much more than one fourth as far as Liberia, and within seven days' run by steamers. Unlike Liberia, it is a great line of travel—it is a highway. The country is a very excellent one for any people, and with great natural resources and advantages, and especially because of the similarity of climate with your native soil, thus being suited to your physical condition. The particular place I have in view is to be a great highway from the Atlantic or Caribbean Sea to the Pacific Ocean, and this particular place has all the advantages for a colony. On both sides there are harbors—among the finest in the world. Again, there is evidence of very rich coal-mines. A certain amount of coal is valuable in any country. Why I attach so much importance to coal is, it will afford an opportunity to the inhabitants for immediate employment till they get ready to settle permanently in their homes. If you take colonists where there is no good landing, there is a bad show; and so where there is nothing to cultivate and of which to make a farm.

But if something is started so that you can get your daily bread as soon as you reach there, it is a great advantage. Coal land is the best thing I know of with which to commence an enterprise.

To return—you have been talked to upon this subject, and told that a speculation is intended by gentlemen who have an interest in the country, including the coal-mines. We have been mistaken all our lives if we do not know whites, as well as blacks, look to their self-interest. Unless among those deficient of intellect, everybody you trade with makes something. You meet with these things here and everywhere. If such persons have what will be an advantage to them, the question is, whether it cannot be made of advantage to you! You are intelligent, and know that success does not so much depend on external help as on self-reliance. Much, therefore, depends upon yourselves. As to the coal-mines, I think I see the means available for your self-reliance. I shall, if I get a sufficient number of you engaged, have provision made that you shall not be wronged. If you will engage in the enterprise, I will spend some of the money intrusted to me. I am not sure you will succeed. The government may lose the money; but we cannot succeed unless we try; and we think, with care, we can succeed. The political affairs in Central America are not in quite as satisfactory a condition as I wish. There are contending factions in that quarter; but, it is true, all the factions are agreed alike on the subject of colonization, and want it, and are more generous than we are here.

To your colored race they have no objection. I would endeavor to have you made equals, and have the best assurance that you should be, the equals of the best.

The practical thing I want to ascertain is, whether I can get a number of able-bodied men, with their wives and children, who are willing to go when I present evidence of encouragement and protection. Could I get a hundred tolerably intelligent men, with their wives and children, and able to "cut their own fodder," so to speak? Can I have fifty? If I could find twenty-five able-bodied men, with a mixture of women and children,—good things in the family relation, I think,—I could make a successful commencement. I want you to let me know whether this can be done or not. This is the practical part of my wish to see you. These are subjects of very great importance—worthy of a month's study, instead of a speech delivered in an hour. I ask you, then, to consider seriously, not pertaining to yourselves merely, nor for your race and ours for the present time, but as one of the things, if successfully managed, for the good of mankind—not confined to the present generation, but as

From age to age descends the lay
  To millions yet to be,
Till far its echoes roll away
  Into eternity.

The above is merely given as the substance of the President's remarks.

The chairman of the delegation briefly replied that they would hold a consultation, and in a short time give an answer.

The President said: Take your full time—no hurry at all.

The delegation then withdrew.

Letter to Horace Greeley (August 22, 1862)

Executive Mansion, Washington

Hon. Horace Greeley.

Dear Sir: I have just read yours of the 19th, addressed to myself through the New York "Tribune." If there be in it any statements or assumptions of fact which I may know to be erroneous, I do not, now and here, controvert them. If there be in it any inferences which I may believe to be falsely drawn, I do not, now and here, argue against them. If there be perceptible in it an impatient and dictatorial tone, I waive it in deference to an old friend whose heart I have always supposed to be right.

As to the policy I "seem to be pursuing," as you say, I have not meant to leave any one in doubt.

I would save the Union. I would save it the shortest way under the Constitution. The sooner the national authority can be restored, the nearer the Union will be "the Union as it was." If there be those who would not save the Union unless they could at the same time save slavery, I do not agree with them. If there be those who would not save the Union unless they could at the same time destroy slavery, I do not agree with them. My paramount object in this struggle is to save the Union, and is not either to save or to destroy slavery. If I could save the Union without freeing any slave, I would do it; and if I could save it by freeing all the slaves, I would do it; and if I could save it by freeing some and leaving others alone, I would also do that. What I do about slavery and the colored race, I do because I believe it helps to save the Union; and what I forbear, I forbear because I do not believe it would help to save the Union. I shall do less whenever I shall believe what I am doing hurts the cause, and I shall do more whenever I shall believe doing more will help the cause. I shall try to correct errors when shown to be errors, and I shall adopt new views so fast as they shall appear to be true views.

I have here stated my purpose according to my view of official duty; and I intend no modification of my oft-expressed personal wish that all men everywhere could be free.

Yours,

A. Lincoln

Reply to a Committee from the Churches of Chicago Requesting the Issuance of an Emancipation Proclamation (1862)

The subject presented in the memorial is one upon which I have thought much for weeks past, and I may even say for months. I am approached with the most opposite opinions and advice, and that by religious men who are equally certain that they represent the divine will. I am sure that either the one or the other class is mistaken in that belief, and perhaps in some respects both. I hope it will not be irreverent for me to say that if it is probable that God would reveal his will to others on a point so connected with my duty, it might be supposed he would reveal it directly to me; for, unless I am more deceived in myself than I often am, it is my earnest desire to know the will of Providence in this matter. And if I can learn what it is, I will do it. These are not, however, the days of miracles, and I suppose it will be granted that I am not to expect a direct revelation. I must study the plain physical facts of the case, ascertain what is possible, and learn what appears to be wise and right.

The subject is difficult, and good men do not agree. For instance, the other day four gentlemen of standing and intelligence from New York called as a delegation on business connected with the war; but, before leaving, two of them earnestly beset me to proclaim general emancipation, upon which the other two at once attacked them. You know also that the last session of Congress had a decided majority of antislavery men, yet they could not unite on this policy. And the same is true of the religious people. Why, the rebel soldiers are praying with a great deal more earnestness, I fear, than our own troops, and expecting God to favor their side; for one of our soldiers who had been taken prisoner told Senator Wilson a few days since that he met with nothing so discouraging as the evident sincerity of those he was among in their prayers. But we will talk over the merits of the case.

What good would a proclamation of emancipation from me do, especially as we are now situated? I do not want to issue a document that the whole world will see must necessarily be inoperative, like the Pope's bull against the comet. Would my word free the slaves, when I cannot even enforce the Constitution in the rebel States? Is there a single court, or magistrate, or individual that would be influenced by it there? And what reason is there to think it would have any greater effect upon the slaves than the late law of Congress, which I approved, and which offers protection and freedom to the slaves of rebel masters who come within our lines? Yet I cannot learn that that law has caused a single slave to come over to us. And suppose they could be induced by a proclamation of freedom from me to throw themselves upon us, what should we do with them? How can we feed and care for such a multitude? General Butler wrote me a few days since that he was issuing more rations to the slaves who have rushed to him than to all the white troops under his command. They eat, and that is all; though it is true General Butler is feeding the whites also by the thousand, for it nearly amounts to a famine there. If, now, the pressure of the war should call off our forces from New Orleans to defend some other point, what is to prevent the masters from reducing the blacks to slavery again? For I am told that whenever the rebels take any black prisoners, free or slave, they immediately auction them off. They did so with those they took from a boat that was aground in the Tennessee River a few days ago. And then I am very ungenerously attacked for it! For instance, when, after the late battles at and near Bull Run, an expedition went out from Washington under a flag of truce to bury the dead and bring in the wounded, and the rebels seized the blacks who went along to help, and sent them into slavery, Horace Greeley said in his paper that the government would probably do nothing about it. What could I do?

Now, then, tell me, if you please, what possible result of good would follow the issuing of such a proclamation as you desire? Understand, I raise no objections against it on legal or constitutional grounds; for, as commander-in-chief of the army and navy, in time of war I suppose I have a right to take any measure which may best subdue the enemy; nor do I urge objections of a moral nature, in view of possible consequences of insurrection and massacre at the South. I view this matter as a practical war measure, to be decided on according to the advantages or disadvantages it may offer to the suppression of the rebellion.

I admit that slavery is the root of the rebellion, or at least its *sine qua non*. The ambition of politicians may have instigated them to act, but they would have been impotent without slavery as their instrument. I will also concede that emancipation would help us in Europe, and convince them that we are incited by something more than ambition. I grant, further, that it would help somewhat at the North, though not so much, I fear, as you and those you represent imagine. Still, some additional strength would be added in that way to the war, and then, unquestionably, it would weaken the rebels by drawing off their laborers, which is of great importance; but I am not so sure we could do much with the blacks. If we were to arm them, I fear that in a few weeks the arms would be in the hands of the rebels; and, indeed, thus far we have not had arms enough to equip our white troops. I will mention another thing, though it meet only your scorn and contempt. There are fifty thousand bayonets in the Union armies from the border slave States. It would be a serious matter if, in consequence of a proclamation such as you desire, they should go over to the rebels. I do not think they all would—not so many, indeed, as a year ago, or as six months ago—not so many to-day as yesterday. Every day increases their Union feeling. They are also getting their pride enlisted, and want to beat the rebels. Let me say one thing more: I think you should admit that we already have an important principle to rally and unite the people, in the fact that constitutional government is at stake. This is a fundamental idea going down about as deep as anything. Do not misunderstand me because I have mentioned these objections. They indicate the difficulties that have thus far prevented my action in some such way as you desire. I have not decided against a proclamation of liberty to the slaves, but hold the matter under advisement; and I can assure you that the subject is on my mind, by day and night, more than any other. Whatever shall appear to be God's will, I will do. I trust that in the freedom with which I have canvassed your views I have not in any respect injured your feelings.

Proclamation Suspending Writ of Habeas Corpus (September 24, 1862)

Whereas it has become necessary to call into service not only volunteers, but also portions of the militia of the States by draft, in order to suppress the insurrection existing in the United States, and disloyal persons are not adequately restrained by the ordinary processes of law from hindering this measure, and from giving aid and comfort in various ways to the insurrection:

Now, therefore, be it ordered—

First. That during the existing insurrection, and as a necessary measure for suppressing the same, all rebels and insurgents, their aiders and abettors within the United States, and all persons discouraging volunteer enlistments, resisting militia drafts, or guilty of any disloyal practice affording aid and comfort to rebels against the authority of the United States, shall be subject to martial law, and liable to trial and punishment by courts martial or military commissions.

Second. That the writ of *habeas corpus* is suspended in respect to all persons arrested, or who are now, or hereafter during the rebellion shall be, imprisoned in any fort, camp, arsenal, military prison, or other place of confinement, by any military authority, or by the sentence of any court martial or military commission.

In witness whereof, I have hereunto set my hand and caused the seal of the United States to be affixed.

[L. S.] Done at the city of Washington, this twenty-fourth day of September, in the year of our Lord one thousand eight hundred and sixty-two, and of the independence of the United States the eighty-seventh.

Abraham Lincoln

By the President: William H. Seward,
Secretary of State

Meditation on Divine Will (1862)

The will of God prevails. In great contests each party claims to act in accordance with the will of God. Both may be, and one must be, wrong. God cannot be for and against the same thing at the same time. In the present civil war it is quite possible that God's purpose is something different from the purpose of either party; and yet the human instrumentalities, working just as they do, are of the best adaptation to effect his purpose. I am almost ready to say that this is probably true; that God wills this contest, and wills that it shall not end yet. By his mere great power on the minds of the now contestants, he could have either saved or destroyed the Union without a human contest. Yet the contest began. And, having begun, he could give the final victory to either side any day. Yet the contest proceeds.

Emancipation Proclamation (January 1, 1863)

Whereas, on the twenty-second day of September, in the year of our Lord one thousand eight hundred and sixty-two, a proclamation was issued by the President of the United States, containing, among other things, the following, to wit:

"That on the first day of January, in the year of our Lord one thousand eight hundred and sixty-three, all persons held as slaves within any State, or designated part of a State, the people whereof shall then be in rebellion against the United States, shall be then, thenceforward, and forever free; and the Executive Government of the United States, including the military and naval authority thereof, will recognize and maintain the freedom of such persons, and will do no act or acts to repress such persons, or any of them, in any efforts they may make for their actual freedom.

"That the Executive will, on the first day of January aforesaid, by proclamation, designate the States and parts of States, if any, in which the people thereof respectively shall then be in rebellion against the United States; and the fact that any State, or the people thereof, shall on that day be in good faith represented in the Congress of the United States by members chosen thereto at elections wherein a majority of the qualified voters of such State shall have participated, shall in the absence of strong countervailing testimony be deemed conclusive evidence that such State and the people thereof are not then in rebellion against the United States."

Now, therefore, I, Abraham Lincoln, President of the United States, by virtue of the power in me vested as commander-in-chief of the army and navy of the United States, in time of actual armed rebellion against the authority and government of the United States, and as a fit and necessary war measure for suppressing said rebellion, do, on this first day of January, in the year of our Lord one thousand eight hundred and sixty-three, and in accordance with my purpose so to do, publicly proclaimed for the full period of 100 days from the day first above mentioned, order and designate as the States and parts of States wherein the people thereof, respectively, are this day in rebellion against the United States, the following, to wit:

Arkansas, Texas, Louisiana (except the parishes of St. Bernard, Plaquemines, Jefferson, St. John, St. Charles, St. James, Ascension, Assumption, Terre Bonne, Lafourche, St. Mary, St. Martin, and Orleans, including the city of New Orleans), Mississippi, Alabama, Florida, Georgia, South Carolina, North Carolina, and Virginia (except the forty-eight counties designated as West Virginia, and also the counties of Berkeley, Accomac, Northampton, Elizabeth City, York, Princess Ann, and Norfolk, including the cities of Norfolk and Portsmouth), and which excepted parts are for the present left precisely as if this proclamation were not issued.

And by virtue of the power and for the purpose aforesaid, I do order and declare that all persons held as slaves within said designated States and parts of States are, and henceforward shall be, free; and that the Executive Government of the United States, including the military and naval authorities thereof, will recognize and maintain the freedom of said persons.

And I hereby enjoin upon the people so declared to be free to abstain from all violence, unless in necessary self-defense; and I recommend to them that, in all cases when allowed, they labor faithfully for reasonable wages.

And I further declare and make known that such persons of suitable condition will be received into the armed service of the United States to garrison forts, positions, stations, and other places, and to man vessels of all sorts in said service.

And upon this act, sincerely believed to be an act of justice, warranted by the Constitution upon military necessity, I invoke the considerate judgment of mankind and the gracious favor of Almighty God.

In witness whereof, I have hereunto set my hand, and caused the seal of the United States to be affixed.

[L. S.] Done at the city of Washington, this first day of January, in the year of our Lord one thousand eight hundred and sixty-three, and of the independence of the United States of America the eighty-seventh.

ABRAHAM LINCOLN

By the President: WILLIAM H. SEWARD,
Secretary of State

Letter to Erastus Corning et al. (June 12, 1863)

Gentlemen: Your letter of May 19, inclosing the resolutions of a public meeting held at Albany, New York, on the 16th of the same month, was received several days ago.

The resolutions, as I understand them, are resolvable into two propositions—first, the expression of a purpose to sustain the cause of the Union, to secure peace through victory, and to support the administration in every constitutional and lawful measure to suppress the rebellion; and, secondly, a declaration of censure upon the administration for supposed unconstitutional action, such as the making of military arrests. And from the two propositions a third is deduced, which is that the gentlemen composing the meeting are resolved on doing their part to maintain our common government and country, despite the folly or wickedness, as they may conceive, of any administration. This position is eminently patriotic, and as such I thank the meeting, and congratulate the nation for it. My own purpose is the same; so that the meeting and myself have a common object, and can have no difference, except in the choice of means or measures for effecting that object.

And here I ought to close this paper, and would close it, if there were no apprehension that more injurious consequences than any merely personal to myself might follow the censures systematically cast upon me for doing what, in my view of duty, I could not forbear. The resolutions promise to support me in every constitutional and lawful measure to suppress the rebellion; and I have not knowingly employed, nor shall knowingly employ, any other. But the meeting, by their resolutions, assert and argue that certain military arrests, and proceedings following them, for which I am ultimately responsible, are unconstitutional. I think they are not. The resolutions quote from the Constitution the definition of treason, and also the limiting safeguards and guarantees therein provided for the citizen on trials for treason, and on his being held to answer for capital or otherwise infamous crimes, and in criminal prosecutions his right to a speedy and public trial by an impartial jury. They proceed to resolve "that these safeguards of the rights of the citizen against the pretensions of arbitrary power were intended more especially for his protection in times of civil commotion." And, apparently to demonstrate the proposition, the resolutions proceed: "They were secured substantially to the English people after years of protracted civil war, and were adopted into our Constitution at the close of the revolution." Would not the demonstration have been better if it could have been truly said that these safeguards had been adopted and applied during the civil wars and during our revolution, instead of after the one and at the close of the other? I, too, am devotedly for them after civil war, and before civil war, and at all times, "except when, in cases of rebellion or invasion, the public safety may require" their suspension. The resolutions proceed to tell us that these safeguards "have stood the test of seventy-six years of trial under our republican system, under circumstances which show that while they constitute the foundation of all free government, they are the elements of the enduring stability of the republic." No one denies that they have so stood the test up to the beginning of the present rebellion, if we except a certain occurrence at New Orleans hereafter to be mentioned; nor does any one question that they will stand the same test much longer after the rebellion closes. But these provisions of the Constitution have no application to the ease we have in hand, because the arrests complained of were not made for treason—that is, not for the treason defined in the Constitution, and upon the conviction of which the punishment is death—nor yet were they made to hold persons to answer for any capital or otherwise infamous crimes; nor were the proceedings following, in any constitutional or legal sense, "criminal prosecutions." The arrests were made on totally different grounds, and the proceedings following accorded with the grounds of the arrests. Let us consider the real case with which we are dealing, and apply to it the parts of the Constitution plainly made for such cases.

Prior to my installation here it had been inculcated that any State had a lawful right to secede from the national Union, and that it would be expedient to exercise the right whenever the devotees of the doctrine should fail to elect a president to their own liking. I was elected contrary to their liking; and, accordingly, so far as it was legally possible, they had taken seven States out of the Union, had seized many of the United States forts, and had fired upon the United States flag, all before I was inaugurated, and, of course, before I had done any official act whatever. The rebellion thus begun soon ran into the present civil war; and, in certain respects, it began on very unequal terms between the parties. The insurgents had been preparing for it more than thirty years, while the government had taken no steps to resist them. The former had carefully considered all the means which could be turned to their account. It undoubtedly was a well-pondered reliance with them that in their own unrestricted effort to destroy Union, Constitution and law, all together, the government would, in great degree, be restrained by the same Constitution and law from arresting their progress. Their sympathizers pervaded all departments of the government and nearly all communities of the people. From this material, under cover of "liberty of speech," "liberty of the press," and "*habeas corpus*" they hoped to keep on foot amongst us a most efficient corps of spies, informers, suppliers, and aiders and abettors of their cause in a thousand ways. They knew that in times such as they were inaugurating, by the Constitution itself the "*habeas corpus*" might be suspended; but they also knew they had friends who would make a question as to who was to suspend it; meanwhile their spies and others might remain at large to help on their cause. Or if, as has happened, the Executive should suspend the writ without ruinous waste of time, instances of arresting innocent persons might occur, as are always likely to occur in such cases; and then a clamor could be raised in regard to this, which might be at least of some service to the insurgent cause. It needed no very keen perception to discover this part of the enemy's program, so soon as by open hostilities their machinery was fairly put in motion. Yet, thoroughly imbued with a reverence for the guaranteed rights of individuals, I was slow to adopt the strong measures which by degrees I have been forced to regard as being within the exceptions of the Constitution, and as indispensable to the public safety. Nothing is better known to history than that courts of justice are utterly incompetent to such cases. Civil courts are organized chiefly for trials of individuals, or, at most, a few individuals acting in concert—and this in quiet times, and on charges of crimes well defined in the law. Even in times of peace bands of horse-thieves and robbers frequently grow too numerous and powerful for the ordinary courts of justice. But what comparison, in numbers, have such bands ever borne to the insurgent sympathizers even in many of the loyal States? Again, a jury too frequently has at least one member more ready to hang the panel than to hang the traitor. And yet again, he who dissuades one man from volunteering, or induces one soldier to desert, weakens the Union cause as much as he who kills a Union soldier in battle. Yet this dissuasion or inducement may be so conducted as to be no defined crime of which any civil court would take cognizance.

Ours is a case of rebellion—so called by the resolutions before me—in fact, a clear, flagrant, and gigantic case of rebellion; and the provision of the Constitution that "the privilege of the writ of *habeas corpus* shall not be suspended unless when, in cases of rebellion or invasion, the public safety may require it," is the provision which specially applies to our present case. This provision plainly attests the understanding of those who made the Constitution that ordinary courts of justice are inadequate to "cases of rebellion"—attests their purpose that, in such cases, men may be held in custody whom the courts, acting on ordinary rules would discharge. *Habeas corpus* does not discharge men who are proved to be guilty of defined crime; and its suspension is allowed by the Constitution on purpose that men may be arrested and held who cannot be proved to be guilty of defined crime, "when, in cases of rebellion or invasion, the public safety may require it."

This is precisely our present case—a case of rebellion wherein the public safety does require the suspension. Indeed, arrests by process of courts and arrests in cases of rebellion do not proceed altogether upon the same basis. The former is directed at the small percentage of ordinary and continuous perpetration of crime while the latter is directed at sudden and extensive uprisings against the government, which, at most, will succeed or fail in no great length of time. In the latter case arrests are made not so much for what has been done, as for what probably would be done. The latter is more for the preventive and less for the vindictive than the former. In such cases the purposes of men are much more easily understood than in cases of ordinary crime. The man who stands by and says nothing when the peril of his government is discussed, cannot be misunderstood. If not hindered, he is sure to help the enemy; much more if he talks ambiguously—talks for his country with "buts," and "ifs" and "ands." Of how little value the constitutional provision I have quoted will be rendered if arrests shall never be made until defined crimes shall have been committed, may be illustrated by a few notable examples: General John C. Breckinridge, General Robert E. Lee, General Joseph E. Johnston, General John B. Magruder, General William B. Preston, General Simon B. Buckner, and Commodore Franklin Buchanan, now occupying the very highest places in the rebel war service, were all within the power of the government since the rebellion began, and were nearly as well known to be traitors then as now. Unquestionably if we had seized and held them, the insurgent cause would be much weaker. But no one of them had then committed any crime defined in the law. Every one of them, if arrested, would have been discharged on *habeas corpus* were the writ allowed to operate. In view of these and similar cases, I think the time not unlikely to come when I shall be blamed for having made too few arrests rather than too many.

By the third resolution the meeting indicate their opinion that military arrests may be constitutional in localities where rebellion actually exists, but that such arrests are unconstitutional in localities where rebellion or insurrection does not actually exist. They insist that such arrests shall not be made "outside of the lines of necessary military occupation and the scenes of insurrection." Inasmuch, however, as the Constitution itself makes no such distinction, I am unable to believe that there is any such constitutional distinction. I concede that the class of arrests complained of can be constitutional only when, in cases of rebellion or invasion, the public safety may require them; and I insist that in such cases they are constitutional wherever the public safety does require them, as well in places to which they may prevent the rebellion extending, as in those where it may be already prevailing; as well where they may restrain mischievous interference with the raising and supplying of armies to suppress the rebellion, as where the rebellion may actually be; as well where they may restrain the enticing men out of the army, as where they would prevent mutiny in the army; equally constitutional at all places where they will conduce to the public safety, as against the dangers of rebellion or invasion. Take the particular case mentioned by the meeting. It is asserted in substance, that Mr. Vallandigham was, by a military commander, seized and tried "for no other reason than words addressed to a public meeting in criticism of the course of the administration, and in condemnation of the military orders of the general." Now, if there be no mistake about this, if this assertion is the truth and the whole truth, if there was no other reason for the arrest, then I concede that the arrest was wrong. But the arrest, as I understand, was made for a very different reason. Mr. Vallandigham avows his hostility to the war on the part of the Union; and his arrest was made because he was laboring, with some effect, to prevent the raising of troops, to encourage desertions from the army, and to leave the rebellion without an adequate military force to suppress it. He was not arrested because he was damaging the political prospects of the administration or the personal interests of the commanding general, but because he was damaging the army, upon the existence and vigor of which the life of the nation depends. He was warring upon the military, and this gave the military constitutional jurisdiction to lay hands upon him. If Mr. Vallandigham was not damaging the military power of the country, then his arrest was made on mistake of fact, which I would be glad to correct on reasonably satisfactory evidence.

I understand the meeting whose resolutions I am considering to be in favor of suppressing the rebellion by military force—by armies. Long experience has shown that armies cannot be maintained unless desertion shall be punished by the severe penalty of death. The case requires, and the law and the Constitution sanction, this punishment. Must I shoot a simple-minded soldier boy who deserts, while I must not touch a hair of a wily agitator who induces him to desert? This is none the less injurious when effected by getting a father, or brother, or friend into a public meeting, and there working upon his feelings till he is persuaded to write the soldier boy that he is fighting in a bad cause, for a wicked administration of a contemptible government, too weak to arrest and punish him if he shall desert. I think that, in such a case, to silence the agitator and save the boy is not only constitutional, but withal a great mercy.

If I be wrong on this question of constitutional power, my error lies in believing that certain proceedings are constitutional when, in cases of rebellion or invasion, the public safety requires them, which would not be constitutional when, in absence of rebellion or invasion, the public safety does not require them: in other words, that the Constitution is not in its application in all respects the same in cases of rebellion or invasion involving the public safety as it is in times of profound peace and public security. The Constitution itself makes the distinction, and I can no more be persuaded that the government can constitutionally take no strong measures in time of rebellion, because it can be shown that the same could not be lawfully taken in time of peace, than I can be persuaded that a particular drug is not good medicine for a sick man because it can be shown to not be good food for a well one. Nor am I able to appreciate the danger apprehended by the meeting, that the American people will by means of military arrests during the rebellion lose the right of public discussion, the liberty of speech and the press, the law of evidence, trial by jury, and *habeas corpus* throughout the indefinite peaceful future which I trust lies before them any more than I am able to believe that a man could contract so strong an appetite for emetics during temporary illness as to persist in feeding upon them during the remainder of his healthful life.

In giving the resolutions that earnest consideration which you request of me, I cannot overlook the fact that the meeting speak as "Democrats." Nor can I, with full respect for their known intelligence, and the fairly presumed deliberation with which they prepared their resolutions, be permitted to suppose that this occurred by accident, or in any way other than that they preferred to designate themselves "Democrats" rather than "American citizens." In this time of national peril I would have preferred to meet you upon a level one step higher than any party platform, because I am sure that from such more elevated position we could do better battle for the country we all love than we possibly can from those lower ones where, from the force of habit, the prejudices of the past, and selfish hopes of the future, we are sure to expend much of our ingenuity and strength in finding fault with and aiming blows at each other. But since you have denied me this, I will yet be thankful for the country's sake that not all Democrats have done so. He on whose discretionary judgment Mr. Vallandigham was arrested and tried is a Democrat, having no old party affinity with me, and the judge who rejected the constitutional view expressed in these resolutions, by refusing to discharge Mr. Vallandigham on *habeas corpus*, is a Democrat of better days than these, having received his judicial mantle at the hands of President Jackson. And still more, of all those Democrats who are nobly exposing their lives and shedding their blood on the battle-field, I have learned that many approve the course taken with Mr. Vallandigham, while I have not heard of a single one condemning it. I cannot assert that there are none such. And the name of President Jackson recalls an instance of pertinent history. After the battle of New Orleans, and while the fact that the treaty of peace had been concluded was well known in the city, but before official knowledge of it had arrived, General Jackson still maintained martial or military law. Now that it could be said the war was over, the clamor against martial law, which had existed from the first, grew more furious. Among other things, a Mr. Louaillier published a denunciatory newspaper article. General Jackson arrested him. A lawyer by the name of Morel procured the United States Judge Hall to order a writ of *habeas corpus* to release Mr. Louaillier. General Jackson arrested both the lawyer and the judge. A Mr. Hollander ventured to say of some part of the matter that "it was a dirty trick." General Jackson arrested him. When the officer undertook to serve the writ of *habeas corpus*, General Jackson took it from him, and sent him away with a copy. Holding the judge in custody a few days, the general sent him beyond the limits of his encampment, and set him at liberty with an order to remain till the ratification of peace should be regularly announced, or until the British should have left the southern coast. A day or two more elapsed, the ratification of the treaty of peace was regularly announced, and the judge and others were fully liberated. A few days more, and the judge called General Jackson into court and fined him $1000 for having arrested him and the others named. The general paid the fine, and then the matter rested for nearly thirty years, when Congress refunded principal and interest. The late Senator Douglas, then in the House of Representatives, took a leading part in the debates in which the constitutional question was much discussed. I am not prepared to say whom the journals would show to have voted for the measure.

It may be remarked—first, that we had the same Constitution then as now; secondly, that we then had a case of invasion, and now we have a case of rebellion; and, thirdly, that the permanent right of the people to public discussion, the liberty of speech and of the press, the trial by jury, the law of evidence, and the *habeas corpus*, suffered no detriment whatever by that conduct of General Jackson, or its subsequent approval by the American Congress.

And yet, let me say that, in my own discretion, I do not know whether I would have ordered the arrest of Mr. Vallandigham. While I cannot shift the responsibility from myself, I hold that, as a general rule, the commander in the field is the better judge of the necessity in any particular case. Of course I must practice a general directory and revisory power in the matter.

One of the resolutions expresses the opinion of the meeting that arbitrary arrests will have the effect to divide and distract those who should be united in suppressing the rebellion, and I am specifically called on to discharge Mr. Vallandigham. I regard this as, at least, a fair appeal to me on the expediency of exercising a constitutional power which I think exists. In response to such appeal I have to say, it gave me pain when I learned that Mr. Vallandigham had been arrested (that is, I was pained that there should have seemed to be a necessity for arresting him), and that it will afford me great pleasure to discharge him so soon as I can by any means believe the public safety will not suffer by it.

I further say that, as the war progresses, it appears to me, opinion and action, which were in great confusion at first, take shape and fall into more regular channels, so that the necessity for strong dealing with them gradually decreases. I have every reason to desire that it should cease altogether, and far from the least is my regard for the opinions and wishes of those who, like the meeting at Albany, declare their purpose to sustain the government in every constitutional and lawful measure to suppress the rebellion. Still, I must continue to do so much as may seem to be required by the public safety.

A. Lincoln

Letter to Governor Johnson (September 11, 1863)

Executive Mansion, Washington

Hon. Andrew Johnson.

My dear Sir: All Tennessee is now clear of armed insurrectionists. You need not to be reminded that it is the nick of time for reinaugurating a loyal State government. Not a moment should be lost. You and the cooperating friends there can better judge of the ways and means than can be judged by any here. I only offer a few suggestions. The reinauguration must not be such as to give control of the State and its representation in Congress to the enemies of the Union, driving its friends there into political exile. The whole struggle for Tennessee will have been profitless to both State and nation if it so ends that Governor Johnson is put down and Governor Harris is put up. It must not be so. You must have it otherwise. Let the reconstruction be the work of such men only as can be trusted for the Union. Exclude all others, and trust that your government so organized will be recognized here as being the one of republican form to be guaranteed to the State, and to be protected against invasion and domestic violence. It is something on the question of time to remember that it cannot be known who is next to occupy the position I now hold, nor what he will do. I see that you have declared in favor of emancipation in Tennessee, for which may God bless you. Get emancipation into your new State government—constitution—and there will be no such word as fail for your case. The raising of colored troops, I think, will greatly help every way.

Yours very truly,

A. Lincoln

Proclamation Suspending Writ of Habeus Corpus (September 15, 1863)

Whereas, the Constitution of the United States has ordained that the privilege of the writ of *habeas corpus* shall not be suspended unless when, in cases of rebellion or invasion, the public safety may require it; and whereas, a rebellion was existing on the third day of March, 1863, which rebellion is still existing; and whereas, by a statute which was approved on that day, it was enacted by the Senate and House of Representatives of the United States, in Congress assembled, that during the present insurrection the President of the United States, whenever in his judgment the public safety may require it, is authorized to suspend the privilege of the writ of *habeas corpus* in any case throughout the United States, or any part thereof; and whereas, in the judgment of the President, the public safety does require the privilege of the said writ shall now be suspended, throughout the United States, in the cases where, by the authority of the President of the United States, military, naval, and civil officers of the United States, or any of them, hold persons under their command, or in their custody, either as prisoners of war, spies, or aiders or abettors of the enemy, or officers, soldiers, or seamen enrolled or drafted or mustered or enlisted in, or belonging to, the land or naval forces of the United States, or as deserters therefrom, or otherwise amenable to military law, or the rules and articles of war, or the rules or regulations prescribed for the military or naval service by authority of the President of the United States; or for resisting a draft, or for any other offense against the military or naval service:

Now, therefore, I, Abraham Lincoln, President of the United States, do hereby proclaim and make known to all whom it may concern, that the privilege of the writ of *habeas corpus* is suspended throughout the United States in the several cases before mentioned, and that this suspension will continue throughout the duration of the said rebellion, or until this proclamation shall, by a subsequent one to be issued by the President of the United States, be modified or revoked. And I do hereby require all magistrates, attorneys, and other civil officers within the United States, and all officers and others in the military and naval service of the United States, to take distinct notice of this suspension, and to give it full effect, and all citizens of the United States to conduct and govern themselves accordingly, and in conformity with the Constitution of the United States and the laws of Congress in such cases made and provided.

[L. S.] In testimony whereof, I have hereunto set my hand, and caused the seal of the United States to be affixed, this fifteenth day of September, in the year of our Lord one thousand eight hundred and sixty-three, and of the independence of the United States of America the eighty-eighth.

ABRAHAM LINCOLN

By the President: WILLIAM H. SEWARD, Secretary of State

Gettysburg Address (1863)

Fourscore and seven years ago our fathers brought forth on this continent a new nation, conceived in liberty, and dedicated to the proposition that all men are created equal.

Now we are engaged in a great civil war, testing whether that nation, or any nation so conceived and so dedicated, can long endure. We are met on a great battle-field of that war. We have come to dedicate a portion of that field as a final resting-place for those who here gave their lives that that nation might live. It is altogether fitting and proper that we should do this.

But, in a larger sense, we cannot dedicate—we cannot consecrate—we cannot hallow—this ground. The brave men, living and dead, who struggled here, have consecrated it far above our poor power to add or detract. The world will little note nor long remember what we say here, but it can never forget what they did here. It is for us, the living, rather, to be dedicated here to the unfinished work which they who fought here have thus far so nobly advanced. It is rather for us to be here dedicated to the great task remaining before us—that from these honored dead we take increased devotion to that cause for which they gave the last full measure of devotion; that we here highly resolve that these dead shall not have died in vain; that this nation, under God, shall have a new birth of freedom; and that government of the people, by the people, for the people, shall not perish from the earth.

Proclamation of Amnesty and Reconstruction (December 8, 1863)

Whereas, in and by the Constitution of the United States, it is provided that the President "shall have power to grant reprieves and the pardons for offenses against the United States, except in cases of impeachment"; and

Whereas a rebellion now exists whereby the loyal State governments of several States have for a long time been subverted, and many persons have committed, and are now guilty of, treason against the United States; and

Whereas, with reference to said rebellion and treason, laws have been enacted by Congress, declaring forfeitures and confiscation of property and liberation of slaves, all upon terms and conditions therein stated, and also declaring that the President was thereby authorized at any time thereafter, by proclamation, to extend to persons who may have participated in the existing rebellion, in any State or part thereof, pardon and amnesty, with such exceptions and at such times and on such conditions as he may deem expedient for the public welfare; and

Whereas the congressional declaration for limited and conditional pardon accords with well-established judicial exposition of the pardoning power; and

Whereas, with reference to said rebellion, the President of the United States has issued several proclamations, with provisions in regard to the liberation of slaves; and

Whereas it is now desired by some persons heretofore engaged in said rebellion to resume their allegiance to the United States, and to reinaugurate loyal State governments within and for their respective States; therefore

I, Abraham Lincoln, President of the United States, do proclaim, declare, and make known to all persons who have, directly or by implication, participated in the existing rebellion, except as hereinafter excepted, that a full pardon is hereby granted to them and each of them, with restoration of all rights of property, except as to slaves, and in property cases where rights of third parties shall have intervened, and upon the condition that every such person shall take and subscribe an oath, and thenceforward keep and maintain said oath inviolate; and which oath shall be registered for permanent preservation, and shall be of the tenor and effect following, to wit:

> I, ——, do solemnly swear, in presence of almighty God, that I will henceforth faithfully support, protect, and defend the Constitution of the United States, and the union of the States thereunder; and that I will, in like manner, abide by and faithfully support all acts of Congress passed during the existing rebellion with reference to slaves, so long and so far as not repealed, modified, or held void by Congress, or by decision of the Supreme Court; and that I will, in like manner, abide by and faithfully support all proclamations of the President made during the existing rebellion having reference to slaves, so long and so far as not modified or declared void by decision of the Supreme Court. So help me God.

The persons exempted from the benefits of the foregoing provisions are all who are, or shall have been, civil or diplomatic officers or agents of the so-called Confederate Government; all who have left judicial stations under the United States to aid the rebellion; all who are or shall have been military or naval officers of said so-called Confederate Government above the rank of colonel in the army or of lieutenant in the navy; all who left seats in the United States Congress to aid the rebellion; all who resigned commissions in the army or navy of the United States and afterward aided the rebellion; and all who have engaged in any way in treating colored persons, or white persons in charge of such, otherwise than lawfully as prisoners of war, and which persons may have been found in the United States service as soldiers, seamen, or in any other capacity.

And I do further proclaim, declare, and make known that whenever, in any of the States of Arkansas, Texas, Louisiana, Mississippi, Tennessee, Alabama, Georgia, Florida, South Carolina, and North Carolina, a number of persons, not less than one tenth in number of the votes cast in such State at the presidential election of the year of our Lord one thousand eight hundred and sixty, each having taken the oath aforesaid and not having since violated it and being a qualified voter by the election law of the State existing immediately before the so-called act of secession, and excluding all others, shall reestablish a State government which shall be republican, and in no wise contravening said oath, such shall be recognized as the true government of the State, and the State shall receive thereunder the benefits of the constitutional provision which declares that "the United States shall guaranty to every State in this Union a republican form of government, and shall protect each of them against invasion; and, on application of the legislature, or the executive (when the legislature cannot be convened), against domestic violence."

And I do further proclaim, declare, and make known, that any provision which may be adopted by such State government in relation to the freed people of such State, which shall recognize and declare their permanent freedom, provide for their education, and which may yet be consistent as a temporary arrangement with their present condition as a laboring, landless, and homeless class, will not be objected to by the national executive.

And it is suggested as not improper that, in constructing a loyal State government in any State, the name of the State, the boundary, the subdivisions, the constitution, and the general code of laws, as before the rebellion, be maintained, subject only to the modifications made necessary by the conditions herein before stated, and such others, if any, not contravening said conditions, and which may be deemed expedient by those framing the new State government.

To avoid misunderstanding, it may be proper to say that this proclamation, so far as it relates to State governments, has no reference to States wherein loyal State governments have all the while been maintained.

And, for the same reason, it may be proper to further say, that whether members sent to Congress from any State shall be admitted to seats, constitutionally rests exclusively with the respective houses, and not to any extent with the executive. And still further, that this proclamation is intended to present the people of the States wherein the national authority has been suspended, and loyal State governments have been subverted, a mode in and by which the national authority and loyal State governments may be reestablished within said States, or in any of them; and while the mode presented is the best the executive can suggest, with his present impressions, it must not be understood that no other possible mode would be acceptable.

[L. S.] Given under my hand at the city of Washington, the eighth day of December, in the year of our Lord one thousand eight hundred and sixty-three, and of the independence of the United States of America the eighty-eighth.

ABRAHAM LINCOLN

By the President: WILLIAM H. SEWARD, Secretary of State

Letter to Albert G. Hodges (April 4, 1864)

Executive Mansion, Washington

A. G. Hodges, Esq., Frankfort, Kentucky.

My dear Sir: You ask me to put in writing the substance of what I verbally said the other day in your presence, to Governor Bramlette and Senator Dixon. It was about as follows:

"I am naturally antislavery. If slavery is not wrong, nothing is wrong. I cannot remember when I did not so think and feel, and yet I have never understood that the presidency conferred upon me an unrestricted right to act officially upon this judgment and feeling. It was in the oath I took that I would, to the best of my ability, preserve, protect, and defend the Constitution of the United States. I could not take the office without taking the oath. Nor was it my view that I might take an oath to get power, and break the oath in using the power. I understood, too, that in ordinary civil administration this oath even forbade me to practically indulge my primary abstract judgment on the moral question of slavery. I had publicly declared this many times, and in many ways. And I aver that, to this day, I have done no official act in mere deference to my abstract judgment and feeling on slavery. I did understand, however, that my oath to preserve the Constitution to the best of my ability imposed upon me the duty of preserving, by every indispensable means, that government—that nation, of which that Constitution was the organic law. Was it possible to lose the nation and yet preserve the Constitution? By general law, life and limb must be protected, yet often a limb must be amputated to save a life; but a life is never wisely given to save a limb. I felt that measures otherwise unconstitutional might become lawful by becoming indispensable to the preservation of the Constitution through the preservation of the nation. Right or wrong, I assumed this ground, and now avow it. I could not feel that, to the best of my ability, I had even tried to preserve the Constitution, if, to save slavery or any minor matter, I should permit the wreck of government, country, and Constitution all together. When, early in the war, General Frémont attempted military emancipation, I forbade it, because I did not then think it an indispensable necessity. When, a little later, General Cameron, then Secretary of War, suggested the arming of the blacks, I objected because I did not yet think it an indispensable necessity. When, still later, General Hunter attempted military emancipation, I again forbade it, because I did not yet think the indispensable necessity had come. When in March and May and July, 1862, I made earnest and successive appeals to the border States to favor compensated emancipation, I believed the indispensable necessity for military emancipation and arming the blacks would come unless averted by that measure. They declined the proposition, and I was, in my best judgment, driven to the alternative of either surrendering the Union, and with it the Constitution, or of laying strong hand upon the colored element. I chose the latter. In choosing it, I hoped for greater gain than loss; but of this, I was not entirely confident. More than a year of trial now shows no loss by it in our foreign relations, none in our home popular sentiment, none in our white military force—no loss by it anyhow or anywhere. On the contrary it shows a gain of quite a hundred and thirty thousand soldiers, seamen, and laborers. These are palpable facts, about which, as facts, there can be no caviling. We have the men; and we could not have had them without the measure.

"And now let any Union man who complains of the measure test himself by writing down in one line that he is for subduing the rebellion by force of arms; and in the next, that he is for taking these hundred and thirty thousand men from the Union side, and placing them where they would be but for the measure he condemns. If he cannot face his case so stated, it is only because he cannot face the truth."

I add a word which was not in the verbal conversation. In telling this tale I attempt no compliment to my own sagacity. I claim not to have controlled events, but confess plainly that events have controlled me. Now, at the end of three years' struggle, the nation's condition is not what either party, or any man, devised or expected. God alone can claim it. Whither it is tending seems plain. If God now wills the removal of a great wrong, and wills also that we of the North, as well as you of the South, shall pay fairly for our complicity in that wrong, impartial history will find therein new cause to attest and revere the justice and goodness of God.

Yours truly,

A. Lincoln

Proclamation Concerning Reconstruction (July 8, 1864)

Whereas, at the late session, Congress passed a bill to "guarantee to certain States, whose governments have been usurped or overthrown, a republican form of government," a copy of which is hereunto annexed;

And whereas the said bill was presented to the President of the United States for his approval less than one hour before the *sine die* adjournment of said session, and was not signed by him;

And whereas the said bill contains, among other things, a plan for restoring the States in rebellion to their proper practical relation in the Union, which plan expresses the sense of Congress upon that subject, and which plan it is now thought fit to lay before the people for their consideration:

Now, therefore, I, Abraham Lincoln, President of the United States, do proclaim, declare, and make known, that, while I am (as I was in December last, when by proclamation I propounded a plan for restoration) unprepared, by a formal approval of this bill, to be inflexibly committed to any single plan of restoration; and, while I am also unprepared to declare that the free-State constitutions and governments already adopted and installed in Arkansas and Louisiana shall be set aside and held for nought, thereby repelling and discouraging the loyal citizens who have set up the same as to further effort, or to declare a constitutional competency in Congress to abolish slavery in States, but am at the same time sincerely hoping and expecting that a constitutional amendment abolishing slavery throughout the nation may be adopted, nevertheless I am fully satisfied with the system for restoration contained in the bill as one very proper plan for the loyal people of any State choosing to adopt it, and that I am, and at all times shall be, prepared to give the executive aid and assistance to any such people, so soon as the military resistance to the United States shall have been suppressed in any such State, and the people thereof shall have sufficiently returned to their obedience to the Constitution and the laws of the United States, in which cases military governors will be appointed, with directions to proceed according to the bill.

In testimony whereof, I have hereunto set my hand, and caused the seal of the United States to be affixed.

[L. S.] Done at the city of Washington, this eighth day of July, in the year of our Lord one thousand eight hundred and sixty-four, and of the independence of the United States the eighty-ninth.

ABRAHAM LINCOLN

By the President: WILLIAM H. SEWARD,
Secretary of State

Second Inaugural Address (1865)

Fellow-countrymen: At this second appearing to take the oath of the presidential office, there is less occasion for an extended address than there was at the first. Then a statement, somewhat in detail, of a course to be pursued, seemed fitting and proper. Now, at the expiration of four years, during which public declarations have been constantly called forth on every point and phase of the great contest which still absorbs the attention and engrosses the energies of the nation, little that is new could be presented. The progress of our arms, upon which all else chiefly depends, is as well known to the public as to myself; and it is, I trust, reasonably satisfactory and encouraging to all. With high hope for the future, no prediction in regard to it is ventured.

On the occasion corresponding to this four years ago, all thoughts were anxiously directed to an impending civil war. All dreaded it—all sought to avert it. While the inaugural address was being delivered from this place, devoted altogether to saving the Union without war, insurgent agents were in the city seeking to destroy it without war—seeking to dissolve the Union, and divide effects, by negotiation. Both parties deprecated war; but one of them would make war rather than let the nation survive; and the other would accept war rather than let it perish. And the war came.

One-eighth of the whole population were colored slaves, not distributed generally over the Union, but localized in the Southern part of it. These slaves constituted a peculiar and powerful interest. All knew that this interest was, somehow, the cause of the war. To strengthen, perpetuate, and extend this interest was the object for which the insurgents would rend the Union, even by war; while the government claimed no right to do more than to restrict the territorial enlargement of it.

Neither party expected for the war the magnitude or the duration which it has already attained. Neither anticipated that the cause of the conflict might cease with, or even before, the conflict itself should cease. Each looked for an easier triumph, and a result less fundamental and astounding. Both read the same Bible, and pray to the same God; and each invokes his aid against the other. It may seem strange that any men should dare to ask a just God's assistance in wringing their bread from the sweat of other men's faces; but let us judge not, that we be not judged. The prayers of both could not be answered—that of neither has been answered fully.

The Almighty has his own purposes. "Woe unto the world because of offenses! for it must needs be that offenses come; but woe to that man by whom the offense cometh." If we shall suppose that American slavery is one of those offenses which, in the providence of God, must needs come, but which, having continued through his appointed time, he now wills to remove, and that he gives to both North and South this terrible war, as the woe due to those by whom the offense came, shall we discern therein any departure from those divine attributes which the believers in a living God always ascribe to him? Fondly do we hope—fervently do we pray—that this mighty scourge of war may speedily pass away. Yet, if God wills that it continue until all the wealth piled by the bondman's two hundred and fifty years of unrequited toil shall be sunk, and until every drop of blood drawn with the lash shall be paid by another drawn with the sword, as was said three thousand years ago, so still it must be said, "The judgments of the Lord are true and righteous altogether."

With malice toward none; with charity for all; with firmness in the right, as God gives us to see the right, let us strive on to finish the work we are in; to bind up the nation's wounds; to care for him who shall have borne the battle, and for his widow, and his orphan—to do all which may achieve and cherish a just and lasting peace among ourselves, and with all nations.

WADE-DAVIS MANIFESTO (1864)

We have read without surprise, but not without indignation, the Proclamation of the President of the 8th of July.

The President, by preventing this bill from becoming a law, holds the electoral votes of the Rebel States at the dictation of his personal ambition.

If those votes turn the balance in his favor, is it to be supposed that his competitor, defeated by such means will acquiesce?

If the Rebel majority assert their supremacy in those States, and send votes which elect an enemy of the Government, will we not repel his claims?

And is not that civil war for the Presidency, inaugurated by the votes of Rebel States? Seriously impressed with these dangers, Congress, "*the proper constitutional authority*," formally declared that there are no State Governments in the Rebel States, and provided for their erection at a proper time; and both the Senate and the House of Representatives rejected the Senators and Representatives chosen under the authority of what the President calls the Free Constitution and Government of Arkansas.

The President's proclamation "*holds for naught*" this judgment, and discards the authority of the Supreme Court, and strides headlong toward the anarchy his Proclamation of the 8th of December inaugurated.

If electors for President be allowed to be chosen in either of those States, a sinister light will be cast on the motives which induced the President to "*hold for naught*" the will of Congress rather than his Government in Louisiana and Arkansas.

That judgment of Congress which the President defies was the exercise of an authority exclusively vested in Congress by the Constitution to determine what is the established Government in a State, and in its own nature and by the highest judicial authority binding on all other departments of the Government.

A more studied outrage on the legislative authority of the people has never been perpetrated.

Congress passed a bill; the President refused to approve it, and then by proclamation puts as much of it in force as he sees fit, and proposes to execute those parts by officers unknown to the laws of the United States and not subject to the confirmation of the Senate!

The bill directed the appointment of Provisional Governors by and with the advice and consent of the Senate.

The President, after defeating the law, proposes to appoint without law, and without the advice and consent of the Senate, *Military* Governors for the Rebel States!

He has already exercised this dictatorial usurpation in Louisiana, and he defeated the bill to prevent its limitation.

The President has greatly presumed on the forbearance which the supporters of his Administration have so long practiced, in view of the arduous conflict in which we are engaged, and the reckless ferocity of our political opponents.

But he must understand that our support is of a cause and not of a man; that the authority of Congress is paramount and must be respected; that the whole body of the Union men of Congress will not submit to be impeached by him of rash and unconstitutional legislation; and if he wishes our support, he must confine himself to his executive duties—to obey and execute, not make the laws—to suppress by arms armed Rebellion, and leave political reorganization to Congress.

If the supporters of the Government fail to insist on this, they become responsible for the usurpations which they fail to rebuke, and are justly liable to the indignation of the people whose rights and security, committed to their keeping, they sacrifice.

Let them consider the remedy for these usurpations, and, having found it, fearlessly execute it.

James McKaye

The Mastership and Its Fruits (1864)

The mastership and its fruits: the emancipated slave face to face with his old master. A supplemental report to Hon. Edwin M. Stanton, secretary of war, by James McKaye, special commissioner.

The Emancipated Slave, Face to Face with His Old Master.

(Valley of the Lower Mississippi.)

To the Hon. Edwin M. Stanton, Secretary of War:

Of all portions of the slave region to which the Commission have had access, the valley of the lower Mississippi affords the most interesting field for the observation and study of the slave system, as well as of the great changes which, at the present moment, slave society is everywhere undergoing. Unlike most other sections visited by the Commission, here are found all the elements of that society still in existence; but in a state of revolution and transformation. Here, facing the board river on either side, still stands the great white mansion of the planter; by its side, just without its shadow, the long rows of cabins called the negro quarters, and, a little in the rear, the great quadrangular structure, usually of brick, known as the sugarhouse. In many instances the old master still occupies the mansion, and the negroes their old quarters; but under circumstances and in relations quite new, strange, and full of anxiety to both.

During a recent visit to the neighborhood of these mansions and negro quarters, many important facts came to light, and many important suggestions occurred, not elsewhere presented. [. . .]

As I have before said, here, upon the banks of the great river, these results and products are still to be seen, side by side, the colored man, as slavery has left him, and the white man, as slavery has made him.

Allow me briefly to present them, not in the light of my own personal observation alone, but rather in that of the experience of those whose duty it has been to mingle with them, and to deal practically with many of the troublesome and disturbing questions arising out of the great transformation going on in their midst.

And, first, as to the colored man. Gen. Banks, in command of the Department of the Gulf, whose experience and earnest study of the subject matter under consideration, gives weight to his testimony, declared to me that he had learned far more of the colored men than of the white; that they understood much better the requirements of their own peculiar position in the present exigency than the white men did of theirs, and accepted them much more readily and wisely; and that, in his judgment, "whoever else might fail in the great revolution, it would not be the black man."

And, in a letter from Alexandria, Louisiana, in answer to certain inquiries addressed to him, previous to my departure from New Orleans, under date of March 28th, 1864, Gen. Banks writes: "I entertain no doubt whatever of the capabilities of the emancipated colored people to meet and discharge the duties incident to the great change in their condition. I have seen them in all situations, within the last year and a half, and it is with much pleasure I say, as I stated to you in person, that they seem to me to have a clearer comprehension of their position, and the duties which rest upon them, than any other class of our people, accepting the necessity of labour which rests upon them as as upon others. The conditions they uniformly impose show the good sense with which they approach in their condition.

"They demand, in the first instance, that to whatever punishment they may be subjected, they shall not be flogged.

"2d. That they shall labor only when they are well treated.

"3d. That families should not be separated.

"4th. That their children shall be educated.

"With these stipulations I have never found any person of that race who did not readily accept the necessity of continuous and faithful labor at just rates of compensation, which they seem willing to leave to the Government. As far as the experiment goes in this department, they have justified in the fullest degree this conclusion, and, subject to the conditions which they impose, they are willing to and have rendered faithful labor.

"There were in this department, when I assumed command, many thousands of colored persons without employment or home, who were decimated by disease and death of the most frightful character. To these, natives of the plantations in the department, have been added many thousand fugitives from the surrounding States, of every age and condition. There are not, at this time, 500 persons that are not self-supporting, and there has not been in the last year, any day when we would not have gladly accepted ten or twenty thousand, irrespective of their condition, in addition to those we have of our own. Except that the negro understood the necessities of his position, and was able, in the language of your letter, 'to meet and discharge the duties incident to the great change in his condition,' this result would have been physically impossible.

"Wherever, in the department, they have been well treated, and reasonably compensated, they have invariably rendered faithful service to their employers.

"From many persons who manage plantations, I have received the information that there is no difficulty whatever in keeping them at work, if the conditions to which I have above referred are complied with."

And George U. Hanks, Colonel of the 15th Regiment, Corps d'Afrique, member of the Board of Enrollment, and Superintendent of negro labor in the Department of the Gulf, under date of February 6th, 1864, deposes: "that he went to Louisiana as a Lieutenant in the 12th Connecticut Regiment, under Gen. Butler; that he was appointed superintendent of contrabands under Brig. Gen. T.W. Sherman. The negroes, he says, came in scarred, wounded, and some with iron collars round their necks. I set them at work on abandoned plantations, and on the fortifications. At one time we had 6,500 of them; there was not the slightest difficulty with them. They are more willing to work, and more patient than any set of human beings I ever saw. It is true there is a general dislike to return to their old masters; and those who have remained at home are suspicious of foul play, and feel it to be necessary to run away to test their freedom. This year the dislike has very much lessened; they begin to feel themselves more secure, and do not hesitate to return for wages. The negroes *willingly accept the condition of labor for their own maintenance, and the musket for their freedom.* [. . .]"

Next to the right to work for his own maintenance and that of his family, the colored man here, as elsewhere, asks for the privilege of sending his children to school. "The colored people," says Col. Hanks, "manifest the greatest anxiety to educate their children, and they thoroughly appreciate the benefits of education. I have known a family to go with two meals a day, in order to save fifty cents a week to pay an indifferent teacher for their children."

The universal and urgent desire of the colored people for education was most strikingly illustrated by a fact that came to my knowledge during a recent visit to Port Hudson. In each of the camps of the colored regiments, the best built cabin was a school-house. These regiments had obtained the authorization of Gen. Andrews for the establishment of regimental schools. They proceeded with their own hands to erect school-houses, and, at their own cost, to procure teachers (in some of the regiments the chaplains undertook that duty); and, according to the testimony of their officers, all their leisure time was most assiduously and perseveringly devoted to their studies. Ought not the Government to encourage this most praiseworthy desire of the colored regiments, by providing for each, at least one permanent teacher? A disabled veteran white soldier, might be thus employed.

A desire for education, a love of knowledge in any community or people have been always considered the surest proofs of their intrinsic worth, the most hopeful signs of their capacity for civilization and future advancement. The extraordinary manifestation of this love and desire among the emancipated colored people, when taken in connection with their previous condition of degradation, is one of the most amazing facts with respect to them. And when contrasted with the almost universal indifference, even contempt, with which the poor Southern whites regard that matter, is well calculated to stagger the white man's boast of the great superiority of his race. The colored man came out of Africa without a single element of civilization. Not even a tradition of any trace of education belongs to his ancestry. On the other hand, what are called *"the poor white trash"* of the Slave States, are for the most part, the descendants of the same race as the men who have carried our civilization from the hills of New England through the great wilderness, to the shores of the Pacific Ocean. They set out upon their career with many advantages of climate and soil, and with equal opportunities for education and enlightenment. But there stood in their way the formidable barriers of the *mastership*. Its all devouring darkness swallowed them up, and to-day it can only be said of them, that no more ignorant, demoralized, and pitiable community of human beings ever lived in any civilized country, in any age. [. . .]

It is hardly necessary for me to speak of the character of the colored man as a soldier, as presented here in the Valley of the Mississippi. The universal official attestation to his soldierly bearing and true valor under the severest trials, has put that beyond question. Nor are his sobriety, orderliness, and willing submission to discipline, less conspicuous. Gen. Andrews, in command at Port Hudson, recently assured me that his colored troops were his best troops, that they performed all their duties, and especially fatigue duties, with greater cheerfulness and more faithfully than the white regiments; and that, with competent officers, he believed no troops would be more reliable. [. . .]

On the other hand, what is to be said of the white man, his old master, and of his capacity, disposition, and attitude relative to the part which he is called upon to perform in the new industrial and social system?

Col. Hanks, a large portion of whose daily life, for two years past, has been spent in daily intercourse with the planters in the Department of the Gulf, declares that "although they begin to see that slavery is dead, yet the spirit of Slavery still lives among them. Many of them are even more rampant to enslave the negro than ever before. They make great endeavors to recover *what they call their own negroes*. One planter offered me $5,000 to return his negroes. They have even hired men to steal them from my own camp. (The old spirit still prompting to the old crime, which, long ago, was declared felony by the law of nations if perpetrated in Africa.)" "They yield," he continues, "to the idea of freedom only under compulsion. They submit to the terms dictated by the Government, because obliged so to do. Mr. V.B. Marmillon, one of the richest and most extensive sugar planters in the whole valley of the Mississippi, took the oath of allegiance, but refused to work his plantation unless he could have *his own negroes* returned to him. He had 1,450 acres of cane under cultivation; his whole family of plantation hands left him and came to New Orleans, reporting themselves to me. Among them could be found every species of mechanic and artisan. I called them up and informed them that the Government had taken possession of old master's crop, and that they were needed to take it off, and would be paid for their labor. All consented to return; but next morning when the time came for their departure, not one would go. One of them said: 'I will go anywhere else to work, but you may shoot me before I will returned to the old plantation.' I afterwards ascertained that Marmillon, whom they called 'Old Cotton Beard,' had boasted in the presence of two colored girls, house servants, how he would serve them when he once more had them in his power. These girls had walked more than thirty miles in the night to bring the information to their friends." These people were set to work elsewhere.

"It is undoubtedly true," says Col. Hanks, "that this year a change for the better seems to be taking place. In some parishes the letting of plantations to

Northern men has a powerful effect. The disposition of the planters, however, towards their old slaves, when they consent to hire them, is by no means friendly. I told a planter recently, that it was the express order of Gen. Banks that the negroes should be educated. He replied that, 'no one should teach *his negro*.'"

Col. Hanks further declares it as his deliberate judgment that "if civil government be established here, and military rule withdrawn, there is the greatest danger that the negro would become subject to some form of serfdom." [. . .]

The simple truth is, that the virus of slavery, the lust of ownership, in the hearts of these old masters, is as virulent and active to-day as it ever was. Many of them admit that the old form of slavery is for the present, broken up. They do not hesitate even to express the opinion that the experiment of secession is a failure; but they scoff at the idea of freedom for the negro, and repeat the old argument of his incapacity to take care of himself, or to entertain any higher motive for exertion than that of the whip. They await with impatience the withdrawal of the military authorities, and the re-establishment of the civil power of the State to be controlled and used as hitherto for the maintenance of what, to them doubtless, appears the paramount object of all civil authority, of the State itself, some form of the slave system.

With slight modifications, the language recently used by Judge Humphrey in a speech delivered at a Union meeting at Huntsville, Alabama, seems most aptly to express the hopes and purposes of a large proportion of the old masters in the Valley of the Mississippi, who have consented to qualify their loyalty to the Union by taking the oath prescribed by the President's Proclamation of Amnesty. After advising that Alabama *should at once return to the Union by simply rescinding the ordinance of secession*, and after expressing the opinion that the old institution if slavery was gone, Judge Humphery says; "I believe, in case of a return to the Union, we would receive *political co-operation*, so as to secure the management of that labor by those who were slaves. *There is really no difference, in my opinion, whether we hold them as absolute slaves, or obtain their labor by some other method.* Of course we prefer the old method. But that question is not before us." [. . .]

For the sake of greater perspicuity, I have hitherto refrained from any reference to the treatment and actual condition of the emancipated population, or to the labor system recently introduced in the Department of the Gulf. In what I deem it my duty to say of the former, I refer for the most part to a period antecedent to the date of the proclamation of Gen. Banks prescribing the latter; that proclamation having been issued but a few days previous to my arrival at New Orleans. [. . .]

I do not deem it necessary here to enter further into the details of these several systems. The proclamation and the orders under which they are established, are undoubtedly of record in the War and Treasury departments. Nor do I desire to criticise too closely plans adopted, doubtless with the best intentions, to meet the urgent necessities which presented themselves in the confusion and chaos consequent upon the breaking up of the old systems, in the midst of a great war. Neither, however, seems to me sufficiently to recognize the freedman's right to intervene in his own affairs, or to contemplate sufficiently the great end of educating him to self control, self reliance, and to the exercise of the rights and duties of civilized life.

This must, be a work of time. But unless a system be speedily adopted which shall embrace these as its fundamental and primary objects, the practical freedom and future well-being of the emancipated population, no less than the great industrial interests dependent upon their voluntary, enlightened, and justly compensated labor, will be seriously, if not fatally jeopardied.

But, in the judgment of the Commission, the most serious error in connection with the present arrangements for the care and protection of these people arises out of the assignment to a different agency of the care and disposal of the abandoned plantations. To enter into the detail of all the evils and abuses that have arisen out of this error, and which are unavoidable, so long as it continues to exist, would occupy too great a space in this report. Suffice it to say that it is the source of the greatest confusion and a perpetual collision between the different local authorities, in which not only the emancipated population but the Government itself, suffers the most serious injuries and losses. Gen. Banks, in the letter hereinbefore so often quoted, says: "The assignment of the abandoned or forfeited plantations to one department of the Government, and the protection and support of the emancipated people to another, is a fundamental error productive of incalculable evils, and cannot be too soon or too thoroughly corrected." And this is the purport of all the testimony which the Commission has been able to obtain, not in the Department of the Gulf only, but everywhere, in relation to this matter. The unhesitating judgment of every person, official or other, not interested in the opportunities it affords for peculation, with whom we have consulted, coincides with that of Gen. Banks. All, without exception, declare that no system can avail to effect the great objects contemplated, that does not assign to one and the same authority, the care and disposal of the abandoned plantations, and the care and protection of the emancipated laborers who are to cultivate them.

And, after the most thorough investigations, I am authorized in saying that this is the deliberate judgment of the Commission.

If, in the preceding cursory survey of the present state of things in the valley of the Mississippi, I have succeeded in presenting the two constituent elements of the old slave society in their true light, it cannot fail to suggest the intrinsic nature of the antagonisms that stand in the way of the successful introduction of the free labor system there, and of the political reconstruction based upon it. Every analysis of slave society everywhere brings us to a like conclusion. The difficulty is not with the emancipated slave; but with the old master, still enthralled by his old infatuation.

[. . .] [W]hat is certain is that these masters, isolating themselves, in their fierce pride, from the great movements of the free, democratic society and civilization of their country and age, had come to entertain some very strange and erroneous beliefs, as well with regard to themselves as with regard to the world around them. With their hearts filled with the indisputable ownership of broad domains and toiling slaves, is it strange that the fumes of unrestrained and illicit power and dominion, should have mounted into their heads and perverted, not their own self consciousness only, but their whole sense of truth and of the quality of actions and of things, even to the extent of believing their monstrous system of organized barbarism, the supermost and most excellent product of the ages, and its maintenance the one paramount concern of the world? What to them was the value of constitution, government, or country, compared with the interests of their God-ordained slave commonwealth and mastership?

Seldom has the ethical providence of the world had to deal with so profound a blindness and degeneration. It is only to be paralleled by that of an order of men whose *regime* was extinguished in its own blood at the end of the last century in France. Apparently that ancient "noblesse" was as besotted with pride and disdain as even this new order of the slave-whip. They seem to have entertained as supreme a contempt for the poor, white-skinned drudges, upon whose spoilated labor they had lived and prospered and revelled for a thousand years, as any master for his black-skinned chattels. [. . .]

The culmination of the masters' infatuation in their present atrocious war would seem to indicate a somewhat similar kind of Providential survey, to have been necessary for them.

However this may be, had not their infatuation and blindness infected and demoralized the mind and heart of the whole people of the United States and of their public servants, the intrinsic nature of their mastership, and the utter incompatibility of its existence, with that of our free democratic institutions and civilization, would long ago have been recognized and acted upon frankly, and without equivocations or reservations. Every diagnosis of the malady under which the body politic is writing and staggering in the present hour, discloses its nucleus in the old mastership. That in this mastership is the seat of the disease, containing the pestiferous virus by which the whole nation has been infected. That this seed of national dishonor, dissolution, and death, was brought from Africa, and landed upon the banks of the James River, Virginia, in the autumn of that same year (1620) in which the Pilgrims, with the germs of our national life, civilization, and glory, landed upon Plymouth Rock. That this fatal virus has spread and increased in virulence for more than two hundred years, until the glow of the fever had come to be mistaken for the bloom of health; until the summits of the mountainous social carbuncle generated by it, had come to be regarded as the heights of national culture, wealth, and glory. Let us thank God that it has burst at last, and opened up to the eyes of all men its loathsome depths, so that the merest tyro in the science of social and political health and statesmanship, need no longer be mistaken as to its nature, or as to the treatment proper for its cure.

Let us indeed thank God, that under the operation of his own infinitely just and inexorable laws, the white man's great enterprise of nearly four hundred years' duration, to rob the negro race of its labor and enrich himself with it, approaches its final termination.

A more stupendous scheme of human selfishness and wrong was never projected or prosecuted on earth. Taking it from its beginnings, in the slave-hunts in Africa, in which it is said two human beings, on an average, were destroyed for every one taken—through the nameless atrocities of the middle passage, in the course of which it is estimated that more than two millions of human bodies, dead and alive, were cast into the sea, to its final consummation on this continent, in a gigantic system of organized inhumanity and barbarism, it involved the commission of every crime known to civilized nations.

It could not be otherwise; the very nature of the enterprise made the commission of all crimes a necessary incident, to its successful prosecution. Viewed then, simply, in the light of its own legitimate operations, the slave system may well be defined "the sum of all villainies." Viewed in the light of its own essential idea, of its own intrinsic nature, it involves a still profounder guilt; for it not only contemplated the overthrow in morals and legislation, of the distinction fundamental to all human civilization, between person and property, but the extinction in the whole race of men, of that divine spark which constitutes the manhood, and gives to distinction its validity. Thus, in import and intention it outreached all secular crime, to sap the innermost foundations of the immortal life.

Only in the terrible glare cast upon it by the present war did the true nature of the mastership, and the order of slavery founded upon it, begin to reveal itself to the popular understanding. We may well believe that when the great revolution now transpiring shall have swept out of existence all its interests and passions, all the blindness and infatuation engendered by it, it will be difficult for the future historian to realize or recall that state of the public conscience in which its enormities were not only deemed innocent, but here in the United States, were accepted as an essential, component part of a great System of Democratic Liberty and Christian civilization.

We still stand in the midst of that revolution. Its great work, the regeneration of the reason and conscience of the nation and of its public servants, has yet by no means been fully accomplished. By a great law of the ethical Providence, the struggle must continue until both are cleansed of the moral and political pollutions and lies, that slavery has engendered there, and the people and their rulers, accept with all their hearts and in their true and broadest meaning "the self evident truths" of the great declaration: "that all men are created equal, that they are endowed by their Creator with certain inalienable rights; that among these are life, liberty, and the pursuit of happiness." For, let us rest assured, that in these truths are contained the germs, the vital forces of whatever national prosperity, civilization, and history is possible to us as a people.

In all manner of official proclamations and manifestoes, it has been repeatedly declared that the war on our part was waged alone for the preservation of the constitution and the re-establishment of the Union. But what would be the value of the letter of the constitution unless quickened by the spirit of these "self-evident truths." And what would the Union be, without the inherent principle of cohesion, the living unity founded in these truths?

Reunion then, and the preservation of the essential life of the constitution, demand, not only the release of the slave population from their bonds and the degradation thereby imposed upon them; but the deliverance of the master population also, wholly and forever, from their mastership, and from their fatal delusions and depravations that are inherent in it. This is the primary necessity of any rational attempt to establish free labor and a better social order in the Slave States, the very first step towards any wise, or well-founded reconstruction; for in no other way can the rebel States ever be rehabilitated with a truly loyal, democratic, concurrent citizenship.

And this brings me to speak of the means which, in the judgment of the Commission are deemed necessary to give practical effect to the acts of Congress and the President's Proclamation of January, 1863, "to the end that the colored population thereby emancipated may defend and support themselves." Their recommendations embrace three principal measures, which with more or less completeness have been heretofore, in their several preliminary reports and are herewith, in their final report, submitted to the War Department.

The object of the first of these measures is to secure beyond any possible peradventure or doubt, the civil right of the colored man to personal freedom, by placing that right, in the new order of thing, on the same broad basis as that of the white man. In the Declaration of Independence, and in the Bills of Right, contained in nearly all of the Constitutions of the States, even in those of the Slave States, this right of Personal Liberty, with others, considered as personal endowments of the Creator, attributes of the human nature—are expressly reserved as above all governmental interference, as too sacred to be meddled with by human legislatures. And this doctrine is the keystone of our whole system of Free Democratic Institutions. These rights are as sacred in the person of the colored man as of the white man; and upon every consideration of justice to him, as of safety to the commonweal and honor of the nation, ought to be as securely guarantied, as sacredly guarded. This is to be effected most surely by an amendment of the Constitution of the United States. That measure is already before Congress, and although not exactly in the form recommended by the Commission, yet it is believed sufficient, especially if accompanied with other legislation in the same spirit and with a like intent, to accomplish the great object proposed, and every true lover of his country's permanent peace, prosperity, and honor, cannot but await with the greatest anxiety its final consummation.

The second is a measure of scarcely less importance, and considering the exigencies of the approaching crisis and the present temper and disposition of the master class, even more immediately urgent than the first.

Whenever civil authority shall be re-established in the rebel States, and they shall be re-admitted to the Federal Union, the greater portion of the civil and political rights of their inhabitants, necessarily fall under the jurisdiction and control of State authority. In all these States the colored people, even such of them as have been always free, have been uniformly debarred the enjoyment of all political and many civil rights. Unless, therefore, the emancipated population have secured to them their civil and political rights by national authority, antecedent to such re-admission, they will stand in imminent danger of being defrauded of any practical freedom, notwithstanding "the acts of Congress and the President's Proclamation."

In the language of a witness whose intimate acquaintance with the spirit of the master-class, gives great weight to his words: "They had much better be slaves with the present feelings of the Southern whites against them, than to be left without national guarantees for the maintenance of their rights as freemen."

It is the producing class—that class whose whole life is devoted to toil—that under every form of civil government is most in danger of being made the victim of the leisure, capital, and opportunities of the non-producing class. Under the most favorable circumstances, therefore, it is this class that most needs and deserves to be fenced about with civil and political guarantees. But the circumstances and position of the emancipated population are most unfavorable and critical. Without their own volition, without previous preparation, and as a measure of national self-preservation, they have been suddenly precipitated into new and wholly untried relations with an antagonistic, far more able and adroit class. To leave them in this position, defenceless and at the mercy of their old masters, would in its cruelest meaning be to keep with them "the word of promise to the ear and break it to the hope."

Nay, not only the national honor, but future national peace and well-being demand that the National Government should secure to these people now, while they are still under the sole jurisdiction and control of that government, the permanent possession of such civil and political rights as will enable them "to defend and support themselves," against the machinations and schemes of any class or power to subject them again to any form of slavery of serfdom.

To this end, I cannot too earnestly urge that Congress be invoked to fix and establish by law antecedent to, and as a condition precedent to reconstruction, the civil rights of the emancipated population; and, at the same time, to provide for the future enjoyment by all free persons of color of the fundamental right of citizenship in a free government, the right to the elective franchise, based upon the acquisition on their part, of such qualifications only, as are deemed essential in their white fellow-citizens.

Another matter intimately connected with the foregoing, and as I believe profoundly involving the existence and future prosperity of free society in the Southern States, is the disposition to be made of the confiscated estates, or other forfeited lands in these States. No such thing as free, democratic society can exist in any country where all the lands are owned by one class of men and are cultivated by another. Such ownership of the lands of a country constitutes the basis of the most permanent and oppressive aristocracies. Upon this foundation stood, for a thousand years, the feudal aristocracy of France. And, to-day, the aristocracy of England maintain their supremacy upon the basis of the partition and tenure of the soil of England, robbed by William the Conqueror from the original owners, the people of England, and granted in large estates to his captains.

So incompatible has that tenure become with modern civilization and the well-being of society in that country, that the wisest statesmen there are beginning to apprehend the most fearful consequences from its continued existence.

In the sugar and cotton producing portions of the South, almost all the cultivated soil has been hitherto held in large tracts by the master-class.

I need not stop to argue the utter incompatibility of such a state of things with the existence of a free, independent, democratic yeomanry, or with the development of free democratic institutions. The poor whites of the South are a sufficient illustration of its pernicious influence and effect upon a whole community, of the same race with the landholders.

If not for the sake of the emancipated colored people, then for the the sake of these poor whites, these most pitiable men of our own race, the whole scheme and tenure of the mastership would be overthrown. The great necessity, as I have before intimated from another point of view, which at the present hour lies upon the people and Government of the United States, is not so much a political as a social reconstruction of the Southern States. Any well founded plan for the former, to be effectual and permanent must include the latter; and for the latter, the initiation of a policy on the part of the National Government, which shall have for its aim the ultimate division of the great plantations, into moderate sized farms, to be held and cultivated by the labor of their owners, is of the utmost importance.

I am aware that an opinion has been hitherto generally entertained that sugar and cotton cultivation, could only be profitably carried on upon large estates, and by the employment of large gangs of laborers, principally because a large capital is necessary to the erection of the sugar mills, cotton gins, and other machinery connected with the production of these commodities. All the investigations of the Commission go to show, that this opinion is but a part of the system of slavery, and has no foundation in the necessities of the case. There is, in reality, no more reason why the sugar cane should be raised and converted into sugar by the planter alone, than there is that wheat should be converted into flour, only by the farmer who raises it. And so with the raising, ginning, and baling of cotton. On the contrary, a proper division of labor in the raising and manufacture of sugar and cotton, would almost inevitably lead to a great development in their production; while, at the same time, it would tend not only to mitigate the labor, but to secure the industrial prosperity and independence of all those employed in that production, and thus constitute an entirely different order of social relation and condition in these States. I consider this a matter next in importance to the permanent security of the civil and political rights of the emancipated population, and beg leave to recommend it to the earnest attention of the national authorities.

And, finally, permit me once more to call the attention of Government to the third of the measures proposed by the Commission—the establishment of some uniform system of supervision and guardianship for the emancipated population in the interim of their transition from slavery to freedom. No one acquainted with the facts could hesitate a moment as to the necessity and propriety of such a system; not only for the sake of the emancipated, but for the general interest of Government and country.

In the letter so frequently hereinbefore mentioned, General Banks most forceibly says: "It is undoubtedly true, as you say, that for some time to come, and until the new order of things shall be better understood by the employer and the employed, and the free-labor system be more completely established, there will be a necessity for some kind of Government supervision and protectorate for the benefit of both parties.

"But this is not specially incident to the new system of negro labor. It is only by Governmental supervision and assistance that the labor of any race has been fostered and established. It is of course as necessary for the blacks as for the whites, and if you look at the stipulations which in this department have themselves suggested, as the condition of their service, you will find that their ideas embody in substance and in character, the spirit of all statute legislation for the protection of white labor.

"It is no more incident to the condition of the blacks than of any other class of people, except that they enter the arena of civilization at a later period and the difficulties of their position are presented at a glance and a remedy instantly demanded."

All of which is respectfully submitted.

J. McKaye, *Special Commissioner.*

Charles Soule

Letter to General Oliver Otis Howard, Commissioner of the Freedmen's Bureau (June 12, 1865)

Orangeburg, S.C.

General. [. . .] Upon the occupation of this District by the U.S. troops, affairs were found to be in a very unsettled state. The "scouts" who had latterly enforced local order and preserved discipline upon the plantations, were disbanded; no civil magistrates had power to act; the planters, uncertain as to the wishes of the United States authorities, were afraid even to defend themselves against aggression and robbery;—while the negro laborers, who in this neighborhood outnumber the whites five to one, already excited by the prospect of freedom, were urged to lawlessness and acts of violence by the advice of many of the colored soldiers. Not only was there every prospect that the crops would be neglected, but it also seemed probable that the negroes would revenge themselves by theft, insults, and violence, upon their former owners. To avert disorder and starvation, officers detailed for the purpose were sent into the country to explain to white and black alike their condition under the new state of affairs, and to induce the laborers, if possible, to resume work upon the crops, which are now in the most critical stage. It was soon found, however, that uniformity was needed in these operations; and during the last week in May, Brevet Brigadier General Hartwell, commanding the Brigade, appointed a Special Commission to have charge over all the relations between proprietor and laborer; to supervise contracts, made under Brig. General Hatch's orders, and to act also as Provost Judges in cases of disorder or crime upon the plantations. The commission originally consisted of four members; afterwards of five; and this number is at present reduced to two by the establishment of an auxiliary board in Columbia, S.C.

In the two weeks which have passed since the Commission was appointed, several hundred contracts have been approved, as many plantations visited, and probably two thousand whites and ten thousand blacks have been addressed. The officers engaged in this work have frequently ridden alone and unarmed twenty-five miles, or further, from the Post, and have almost invariably met with courteous and hospitable treatment at the hands of the planters,—most of whom seem desirous to comply in good faith with the wishes and orders of the Government and to make the best of a system of labor in which, notwithstanding, they thoroughly disbelieve.

It is found very difficult to disabuse the negroes of the false and exaggerated ideas of freedom they have received, in a great measure, from our own colored troops. They have been led to expect that all the property of their former masters was to be divided out to them; and the most reasonable fancy which prevails is that besides receiving their food, clothes, free rent of houses and gardens, and the privilege of keeping their hogs and poultry, they are to take for themselves all day Saturday and Sunday, and to receive half the crops. Their long experience of slavery has made them so distrustful of all whites, that on many plantations they persist still in giving credit only to the rumors set afloat by people of their own color, and believe that the officers who have addressed them are rebels in disguise. Even where they are satisfied that the idea of freedom comprehends law, order, and hard labor, there are many whom the absence of the usual restraint and fear of punishment renders idle, insolent, vagrant and thievish. Owing to the entire want of cavalry in this Department it has been found possible to investigate a few only of the cases brought before the board in its judicial capacity; and the members view with solicitude the alarming increase of vagrancy throughout the country, and the idleness, half-way-work, and turbulence of a large portion of the negro population, which they are powerless to check, except in the immediate vicinity of a military force.

In the opinion of a majority of the Commission, little danger to the welfare of society, or of the country, need be apprehended from the former slave-owners, who appear generally desirous to become good citizens. It is the ignorance, the prejudice, the brutality, and the educated idleness,—if so it can be termed—of the freedmen,—all attributable, not so much to their race, as to the system of slavery under which they have lived,—that's mainly to be watched and placed under restraint. To supply the place of the rigid plantation discipline now suddenly done away with Some well digested code of laws and punishments, adapted to the peculiar position of affairs, should be applied throughout the entire South. The impossibility of attaching, in future, money value to the former slaves, will breakup, in practice, as the Emancipation proclamation has done in theory, the system of slavery; and the interests of the capitalists and landowners of the South will lead them to make the best possible use of freed labor: but it will be more difficult to convince the freedmen themselves of their true position and prospects. Only actual suffering, starvation, and punishment will drive many of them to work. It is a general complaint on the part of the planters that although the laborers have had fair offers made to them of compensation, including a share of the crops, they nearly all have shortened their day's work several hours, and persist in taking to themselves every Saturday.

In districts remote from our posts of occupation the plantation discipline still prevails, and cases of flogging and shooting are continually brought to the notice of the Commission from places sixty or eighty miles from Orangeburg. Nor are the planters always to be blamed for such measures of self-defence. There must be some restraint in every community, and where there are but two classes, the one educated and intelligent; the other ignorant and degraded, it is preferable, if one class must govern, that it be the former. It is to be hoped, however, that civil or military authority will soon supplant such an exercise of irresponsible power which is liable to great abuse.

A form for making contracts, adapted after consultation with a number of planters, is enclosed herewith. It was found, at the outset of our operations, that half the crop,—which General Hatch had recommended as fair compensation, was too much to give, if the laborers were also to be fed and clothed until the end of the year. At the wish of General Hartwell, therefore, the planters have been left to make their own proposals, the Commission reserving the right to disapprove such contracts as seemed unjust to the workmen. It has been found, however, that in almost every instance, the offers have been very liberal. It is usual to promise food, and as far as possible, clothing, to all the people on the plantations, both workers and dependents; and in addition, either a certain share of the crop, varying according to circumstances from one-tenth to one-half (the latter in very rare instances), to he divided among the laborers only;—or, so many bushels of corn to every hand,—usually a year's supply. In consideration of the fact that only one third of the people supported, on the average, are laborers, and that General Sherman's armies have destroyed the fences, taken the stock, and devastated the whole region hereabouts, the Commission are of opinion that these contracts are very favorable to the workmen. It would appear that so low, uneducated and inefficient a class of laborers as these now suddenly freed, should not receive more pay than Northern farm laborers,—allowance being made for difference of circumstances. A day laborer at the North, with a large family, usually has to pay all his wages for food, clothing, and house-rent. If he can have his own little garden, and a stock of poultry and pigs—as most of the freedmen have, he is fortunate; and if in addition to all this be gets a share of the crops—say a year's supply of food, over and above expenditures, he is prospering beyond most of his fellows. Were the freedmen to receive more, the relation between capital and labor would be disturbed, and an undue value placed upon the latter, to the prejudice and disadvantage, in the end, of the laborers themselves.

For the present year, a better condition of affairs than that now prevailing can hardly be looked for. An influx of immigrants from Europe and from the Northern States, increasing the proportion of the white inhabitants to the blacks, dividing into smaller farms the arable lands of the South, and introducing a system of money payments for labor, together with the gradual education of the negroes themselves, will, it is to be hoped, bring order out of this chaos. The plan adopted by the Commission is only meant to compose matters, as far as possible, in order that the crops may be tilled and reaped. [. . .]

In addition to the form for contracts, is enclosed an address to the colored people of the District, which embodies all that the visiting officers include in their speeches. All the points upon which any doubt or question has arisen are touched upon and explained in the simplest and most familiar terms which can be used.

Awaiting instructions for the future, I have the honor, General, to remain Your obedient servant,

Charles C. Soule

To the Freed People of Orangeburg District.

You have heard many stories about your condition as freemen. You do not know what to believe: you are talking too much; waiting too much; asking for too much. If you can find out the truth about this matter, you will settle down quietly to your work. Listen, then, and try to understand just how you are situated.

You are now free, but you must know that the only difference you can feel yet, between slavery and freedom, is that neither you nor your children can be bought or sold. You may have a harder time this year than you have ever had before; it will be the price you pay for your freedom. You will have to work hard, and get very little to eat, and very few clothes to wear. If you get through this year alive and well, you should be thankful. Do not expect to save up anything, or to have much corn or provisions ahead at the end of the year. You must not ask for more pay than free people get at the North. There, a field hand is paid in money, but has to spend all his pay every week, in buying food and clothes for his family and in paying rent for his house. You cannot be paid in money,—for there is no good money in the District,—nothing but Confederate paper. Then, what can you be paid with? Why, with food, with clothes, with the free use of your little houses and lots. You do not own a cent's worth except yourselves. The plantation you live on is not yours, nor the houses, nor the cattle, mules and horses; the seed you planted with was not yours, and the ploughs and hoes do not belong to you. Now you must get something to eat and something to wear, and houses to live in. How can you get these things? By hard work—and nothing else, and it will be a good thing for you if you get them until next year, for yourselves and for your families. You must remember that your children, your old people, and the cripples belong to you to support now, and all that is given to them is so much pay to you for your work. If you ask for anything more; if you ask for a half of the crop, or even a third, you ask too much; you wish to get more than you could get if you had been free all your lives. Do not ask for Saturday either: free people everywhere else work Saturday, and you have no more right to the day than they have. If your employer is willing to give you part of the day, or to set a task that you can finish early, be thankful for the kindness, but do not think it is something you must have. When you work, work hard. Begin early at sunrise, and do not take more than two hours at noon. Do not think, because you are free you can choose your own kind of work. Every man must work under orders. The soldiers, who are free, work under officers, the officers under the general, and the general under the president. There must be a head man everywhere, and on a plantation the head man, who gives all the orders, is the owner of the place. Whatever he tells you to do you must do at once, and cheerfully. Never give him a cross word or an impudent answer. If the work is hard, do not stop to talk about it, but do it first and rest afterwards. If you are told to go into the field and hoe, see who can go first and lead the row. If you are told to build a fence, build it better than any fence you know of. If you are told to drive the carriage Sunday, or to mind the cattle, do it, for necessary work must be done even on the Sabbath. Whatever the order is, try and obey it without a word.

There are different kinds of work. One man is a doctor, another is a minister, another a soldier. One black man may be a field hand, one a blacksmith, one a carpenter, and still another a house-servant. Everyman has his own place, his own trade that he was brought up to, and be must stick to it. The house-servants must not want to go into the field, nor the field hands into the house. If a man works, no matter in what business, he is doing well. The only shame is to be idle and lazy.

You do not understand why some of the white people who used to own you, do not have to work in the field. It is because they are rich. If every man were poor, and worked in his own field, there would be no big farms, and very little cotton or corn raised to sell; there would be no money, and nothing to buy. Some people must be rich, to pay the others, and they have the right to do no work except to look out after their property. It is so everywhere, and perhaps by hard work some of you may by-and-by become rich yourselves.

Remember that all your working time belongs to the man who hires you: therefore you must not leave work without his leave not even to nurse a child, or to go and visit a wife or husband. When you wish to go off the place, get a pass as you used to, and then you will run no danger of being taken up by our soldiers. If you leave work for a day, or if you are sick, you cannot expect to be paid for what you do not do; and the man who hires you must pay less at the end of the year.

Do not think of leaving the plantation where you belong. If you try to go to Charleston, or any other city, you will find no work to do, and nothing to eat. You will starve, or fall sick and die. Stay where you are, in your own homes, even if you are suffering. There is no better place for you anywhere else.

You will want to know what to do when a husband and wife live on different places. Of course they ought to be together, but this year, they have their crops planted on their own places, and they must stay to work them. At the end of the year they can live together. Until then they must see each other only once in a while.

In every set of men there are some bad men and some fools; who have to be looked after and punished when they go wrong. The Government will punish grown people now, and punish them severely, if they steal, lie idle, or hang around a man's place when he does not want them there, or if they are impudent. You ought to be civil to one another, and to the man you work for. Watch folks who have always been free, and you will see that the best people are the most civil.

The children have to be punished more than those who are grown up, for they are full of mischief. Fathers and mothers should punish their own children, but if they happen to be off, or if a child is caught stealing or behaving badly about the big house, the owner of the plantation must switch him, just as he should his own children.

Do not grumble if you cannot get as much pay on your place as some one else, for on one place they have more children than others, on one place the land is poor, an another it is rich; on one place Sherman took everything, on another perhaps, almost everything was left safe. One man can afford to pay more than another. Do not grumble, either, because the meat is gone or the salt hard to get. Make the best of everything, and if there is anything which you think is wrong, or hard to bear, try to reason it out: if you cannot, ask leave to send one man to town to see an officer. Never stop work on any account, for the whole crop must be raised and got in, or we shall starve. The old men, and the men who mean to do right, must agree to keep order on every plantation. When they see a hand getting lazy or shiftless, they must talk to him, and if talk will do no good, must take him to the owner of the plantation.

In short, do just about as the good men among you have always done. Remember that even if you are badly off, no one can buy or sell you: remember that if you help yourselves, *God* will help you, and trust hopefully that next year and the year after will bring some new blessing to you.

Joseph Daniel Pope

Report and Remarks on Post-War Conditions in South Carolina (June 29, 1865)

Charleston So Car

Sir. At the suggestion and by the invitation of Gen Hartwell and through the courtesy of Gen Hatch and yourself I have been enabled to visit Port Royal and the adjacent Islands which have been in the military occupancy of the United States since the autumn of 1861; and at your request I have the honor of submitting to you my views and observations. I am sure after so long an absence that any one will be agreeably surprised and impressed with the fact that so little damage has been done to the physical aspect of country. [. . .]

[. . .] [V]isiting the plantations on the Islands of Hilton Head St Helena and Port Royall I was very far from being agreeably impressed. Neglect and decay overgrown roads and badly cultivated fields were visible everywhere. [. . .] Can the freed Negroes be made a useful and efficient peasantry? I propose to give you my views with great frankness and candor for in the present agony of the country this is no time for flattery self delusion or varnished statements. In the middle and upper parts of the State which I had but recently left there was a universal complaint that the negro labor upon the plantations could not be controlled. While the planters appeared to be willing to make contracts with their own slaves and others and to engage in the present crop with zeal they assured me that the "freedmen" would not stand to any engagement whatever and the planters had no means of compelling a performance on their part. This is a grave difficulty; important to the whole country North and South. In visiting the Islands above named I was very anxious to see how matters had worked there in the last four years. The opportunity was good for in the same community were white contractors trying to cultivate their crops with hired negro labor and "freedmen" trying to cultivate them for themselves. I visited several plantations in the first class and the crops were miserable beyond description. [. . .] I invariably asked "Why is this"? and the invariable answer was "the negroes will not work regularly or systematically." [. . .] The negroes employed work when they please and do just as much as they please, they visit the neighbouring cities or plantations as they please, do not work on Saturdays at all, get paid for just what they do and rely largely upon hunting and fishing to make up for what they lose in the field; and in this way a crop that is planted for thirty hands is attended by the aggregate labor of ten or twelve hands and the result is certain failure—ruin to the master of the plantation and to the prospects of the country. Labor must be commanded completely or the production of the cotton crop must be abandoned. [. . .]

So much for the experience and testimony of the contractor. I will now call your attention to the *independent* negro farmer. His condition is even much worse than the contractor's for as a general thing the latter has secured the best lands. Many of the negroes that I saw and whose crops I visited had a small patch here and there of cotton corn and potatoes. Almost universally these crops will not support those who are now cultivating them. Upon inquiry I found that scarcely one of them had applied any manures; and as an illustration of the thrift of this class I will give you an example. One of my own negroes came to see me as soon as he heard I had arrived. I felt gratified at the warmth of friendship he expressed for me. After some conversation I remarked to him that he would for the future have to take care of himself; he would no longer have me to think for him & I would therefore try to help him to think a little for himself. I had during the day seen his crop and asked him how much he had planted. He said he had three acres of cotton and four acres of corn and some potatoes. I then said to him "How much do you think your cotton will make?" "I dont know Sir" "Do you think it will make over 25 lbs to the acre?" "I dont think it Sir" "Very well I do not think it will make so much but I will allow that much and your three acres will make you 75 lbs (or what we call one quarter of a bag of cotton). "Now" I continued "how much do you expect to get for it?" "I cant tell Sir" "Well I will tell you: before the war the kind of cotton you are planting would have sold for about 25 cts per lb but I will allow you 50 cts per lb and thus estimated your whole crop will yield you $37.50." So much for the cotton: "Now" I inquired of him "how much corn do you expect to make?" He gave me the same answer "Can't tell Sir." "Well I will tell you: you *may* make eight bushels to the acre and your four will yield you 32 bushels of corn." He had in addition one hog and potatoes. I then asked him how many he had in family to feed. He answered "I have my wife and three children and myself and a horse" "How long do you expect $37.50 and 32 bushels of corn and one hog to support your family giving them food clothing shoes and paying medical bills besides this feeding your horse? Can it last you a year?" "No Sir" "Can it last you six months?" "No Sir" "What then do you propose to do? How do you expect to live?" I said to him "Can't you get some day labor?" "No Sir there are so many people and the work is slacking off now and I cant get any." "But you must get something to do or you can't get along." He finally said his son was in the army and would help him out with his pay. This was sensible and a very good calculation. Just as long as the Government can employ in one way or another the very large number of negroes on these Islands just so long will they live. Money has heretofore been freely expended at Port Royal by the Government for war purposes but the war is now over and these expenditures must sensibly diminish. The *immorality* of both males and females has caused a large circulation of money from hand to hand but when large numbers of soldiers and sailors are no longer paid off at Port Royal this supply will fail. What then must be result? The Government is not going to support them; that is certain. What will become of the thousands over and above the capacity of the soil support? What will become of the crowd of non-producers at Mitchellville and Beaufort who have no trade no arts no invention? The Community will not be self-supporting much less will there be a surplus. The example I have furnished you above will be the general rule. Those do better will be the exceptions. Some will support themselves, some will do even better than that, but I do mean to say that as an agricultural experiment, the present Crop in and around Port Royal is going to be a failure. [. . .] The negro when placed under a contractor will not labor more than one third of his time—he does not care about violating his engagements—his labor cannot be calculated upon with certainty from one day to another; and when left to himself he succeeds even much worse for with his natural disposition to self-indulgence he has of all human beings the least administrative capacity or the ability by a present combination to secure a future result. In other words he exists and lives from day to day without plans for the future. The result of all this, I very much fear will be, that as soon as these negroes in the lower part of the State have wasted or consumed or been cheated out of what they shall make in the present crop they will depredate in bands upon the interior and middle District of the State and we shall have precipitated upon us a state of things *fearful to contemplate*. The negroes are armed, the whites are unarmed. May God protect the people in this extremity. [. . .]

[. . .] Any system of Labor whether slave or hireling must take many years to accommodate itself to any new order of things. Careful and judicious legislation from time to time will be necessary. The whole question at the north as well as at the South must be treated as a practical question and not a fanciful one. For the present I would make a few practical suggestions:

1. Let the whole white population of the South be at once let in to the cultivation of their lands and the quiet enjoyment of their homes. Those who understand the cultivation of the soil and of the Sea Island cotton crop particularly must be restored to its cultivation or we shall witness nothing but failure. These valuable cotton and provision lands are now entirely occupied by freed negroes and are groaning under mismanagement and an idle, superfluous colored population, and results have been already noticed. Were it even the policy of the Government to punish for the past we would respectfully suggest that the abolition of slavery has worked the most gigantic practical confiscation of property that has ever been enforced in the history of the world. It is too a confiscation not for life but for all time. It is so much

property that can never be restored again to one or to one's posterity. If we are to expect any kind of prosperity the lands at least must be restored.

2. The great number of negroes now accumulated and accumulating on the coast should be sent back to the places from whence they came. In and around Port Royal are negroes from every State in the South are there collected far beyond the capacity of the soil to support them. They are generally the worst characters of communities from which they have come. Let them all be sent back to the States or communities where they belong: Why should the community at Port Royal white or black be saddled with the pauperism, the vice, the disease, the idleness, the filth of so many negroes who are not identified with the soil in any way and whose homes are hundreds of miles removed.

3. The immediate establishment of some system of "permits" or passports by which the freed negro will be prevented from running over the country vagabondizing from city to city and idling from one place in the country to another as is now the case. This will tend in a great degree to hold him to his engagements to labor, prevent vagrancy and remove many of the evils now experienced. It has been found necessary to have a system of "permits" in the army and in the navy and in every service where *obedience* is necessary to *success*. The soldier or the sailor is compelled to obey; and the free negro laborer must be subjected to some Similar system. In the one organization obedience is compelled by punishment both certain and secure; and in the industrial organization rewards and punishments must also be established upon some system or there can be no success.

4. The quartering of negro soldiers in a community of negro laborers must always be attended with evil consequences. The negro soldiers are not uncivil to the white citizens but the influence is bad upon the colored population because the negro soldier sets the example (upon a peace establishment) of idleness that is injurious. He encourages habits of immorality and dissipation which must destroy the usefulness of the laborer; and the contact while it cannot improve the discipline of the negro soldier will detract very much *from* the character of the negro laborer. [. . .]

I designed to touch at some length upon the political aspect of affairs in South Carolina and furnish some hint at what I believe to be the temper of our people, but I have already trespassed too long. The war which has just closed was probably inevitable. Men do not usually go to war for the mere pleasure of slaying each other. A war presupposes a previous conflict of long cherished opinions that could be settled by no other arbitrament. In the present contest the South submitted in my judgment two grave questions: 1 The doctrine of state rights. 2 The question of African slavery. For forty years the statesmen and divines of the South discussed these questions without any satisfactory practical result. Who was to decide them? These two questions, however we may have differed about them and discussed them heretofore, are decided by the war. To go back after an appeal to the sword to argumentation again would be simply childish. Our high duty is to meet the responsibility *as* we find it today. The stern logic of events is more potent than the most refined legal speculations. I believe that the people of the South are prepared to accept the conclusion. *Tempora mutanta et nos mutamal in illis*. With a liberal spirit on the one hand and good faith on the other let the North and the South wake up to a sense of mutual obligation to the instincts of justice and mercy, and to the fearful crisis that lies before both, If the overwhelming difficulties that surround us can be overcome let them be overcome. If *free black labor* can not be made industrious tractable and profitable let us know the fact at once in order that it may be made to yield its position *to free white labor*. No one can look upon the future without fearful misgivings but now that the war is over we should look forward with a hopeful trust in the providence of God and an assurance of returning prosperity to the Country if we discharge our duty. [. . .]

Jos. Dan'l Pope

Thaddeus Stevens

Speech at Lancaster, Pennsylvania (1865)

Fellow Citizens:

In compliance with your request, I have come to give my views of the present condition of the rebel States—of the proper mode of reorganizing the Government, and the future prospects of the Republic. During the whole progress of the war, I never for a moment felt doubt or despondency. I knew that the loyal North would conquer the rebel despots who sought to destroy freedom. But since that traitorous confederation has been subdued, and we have entered upon the work of "reconstruction" or "restoration," I cannot deny that my heart has become sad at the gloomy prospects before us.

Four years of bloody and expensive war, waged against the United States by eleven States, under a government called the "Confederate States of America," to which they acknowledged allegiance, have overthrown all governments within those States which could be acknowledged as legitimate by the Union. The armies of the Confederate States having been conquered and subdued, and their territory possessed by the United States, it becomes necessary to establish governments therein which shall be republican in form and principles and form a more "perfect Union" with the parent government. It is desirable that such a course should be pursued as to exclude from those governments every vestige of human bondage, and render the same forever impossible in this nation; and to take care that no principles of self-destruction shall be incorporated therein. In effecting this, it is to be hoped that no provision of the Constitution will be infringed, and no principle of the law of nations disregarded. Especially must we take care that in rebuking this unjust and treasonable war, the authorities of the Union shall indulge in no acts of usurpation which may tend to impair the stability and permanency of the nation. Within these limitations, we hold it to be the duty of government to inflict condign punishment on the rebel belligerents, and so weaken their hands that they can never again endanger the Union; and so reform their municipal institutions as to make them republican in spirit as well as in name.

We especially insist that the property of the chief rebels should be seized and appropriated to the payment of the National debt, caused by the unjust and wicked war which they instigated.

How can such punishments be inflicted and such forfeiture produced without doing violence to established principles?

Two positions have been suggested.

First—To treat those States as never having been out of the Union, because the Constitution forbids secession, and therefore a fact forbidden by law could not exist.

Second—To accept the position to which they placed themselves as severed from the Union; an independent government *de facto,* and an alien enemy to be dealt with according to the laws of war.

It seems to me that while we do not aver that the United States are bound to treat them as an alien enemy, yet they have the right to elect so to do it if be for the interest of the Nation; and that the "Confederate States" are estopped from denying that position. South Carolina, the leader and embodiment of the rebellion, in the month of January, 1861, passed the following resolution by the unanimous vote of her Legislature.

"*Resolved,* That the separation of South Carolina from the Federal Union *is final,* and she has no further interests in the Constitution of the United States; and that the only appropriate negotiations between her and the Federal Government are as to their mutual relations as *foreign* States."

The convention that formed the Government of the Confederate States, and all the eleven States that composed it, adopted the same declaration, and pledged their lives and fortunes to support it. That Government raised large armies and by its formidable power compelled the nations of the civilized world as well as our own Government to acknowledge them as an independent belligerent, entitled by the law of nations to be considered as engaged in a public war, and not merely in an insurrection. It is idle to deny that we treated them as a belligerent, entitled to all the rights, and subject to all the liabilities of an alien enemy. We blockaded their ports, which is an undoubted belligerent right; the extent of coast blockaded marked the acknowledged extent of their territory—a territory criminally acquired but *de facto* theirs. We acknowledged their sea-rovers as privateers, and not as pirates, by ordering their captive crews to be treated as prisoners of war. We acknowledged that a commission from the Confederate Government was sufficient to screen Semmes and his associates from the fate of lawless buccaneers. Who but an acknowledged government *de jure* or *de facto*, could have power to issue such a commission? The invaders of the loyal States were not treated as outlaws, but as soldiers of war, because they were commanded by officers holding commissions from that government. The Confederate States were for four years what they claimed to be, an alien enemy, in all their rights and liabilities. To say that they were States under the protection of that constitution which they were rendering, and within the Union which they were assaulting with bloody defeats, simply because they became belligerents through crime, is making theory overrule fact to an absurd degree. It will, I suppose, at least be conceded that the United States, if not obliged so to do, have a right to treat them as an alien enemy, now conquered, and subject to all the liabilities of a vanquished foe.

If we are also at liberty to treat them as never having been out of the Union, and that their declarations and acts were all void because they contravened the constitution, and therefore they were never engaged in a public war, but were merely insurgents, let us inquire which position is best for the United States. If they have never been otherwise than States in the Union, and we desire to try certain of the leaders for treason, the constitution requires that they should be indicted and tried "by an impartial jury of the State and district wherein the crime shall have been committed, which district shall have been previously ascertained by law."

The crime of treason can be committed only where the person is actually or potentially present. Jefferson Davis, sitting in Richmond, counseling, or advising, or commanding an inroad into Pennsylvania, has committed no overt act in this State, and can be tried, if anywhere, only in the Richmond District. The doctrine of constructive presence, and constructive treason, will never, I hope, pollute our statutes, or judicial decisions. Select an impartial jury from Virginia, and it is obvious that no conviction could ever be had. Possibly a jury might be packed to convict, but that would not be an "impartial" jury. It would be judicial murder, and would rank in infamy with the trial of Lord RUSSEL, except only that the one was the murder of an innocent man, the other of a traitor. The same difficulties would exist in attempting forfeitures, which can only follow conviction in States protected by the Constitution; and then it is said only for the life of the malefactor. Congress can pass no "bill of attainder."

Nor, under that theory, has Congress, much less the Executive, any power to interfere in remodeling those States upon reconstruction. What reconstruction is needed? Here are States which they say have never been out of the Union, and which are, consequently, now in it without asking leave of anyone. They are competent to send Senators and members to Congress. The state of war has broken no constitutional ligaments, for it was only an insurrection of individuals, not a public war waged by States. Such is the reasoning, notwithstanding every State acted in its municipal capacity; and the court in the prize cases (2 Black, 673) say "Hence in organizing this rebellion they have acted as States." It is no loose, unorganized rebellion, having no defined boundary or possessions. It has a boundary, marked by lines of bayonets, and which can be crossed only by force—south of this line is enemy's territories, because it is claimed and held in possession by an ["]organized, hostile and belligerent power." What right has any one to direct a convention to be held in a sovereign State of this Union, to amend its constitution and prescribe the qualifications of voters? The sovereign power of the nation is lodged in Congress. Yet where is the warrant in the constitution for such sovereign power, much less in the Executive, to intemeddle with the domestic institutions of a State, mold its laws, and regulate the elective franchise? It would be rank, dangerous and deplorable usurpation. In reconstruction, therefore, no reform can be effected in the Southern States if they have never left the Union. But reformation must be effected; the foundation of their institutions, both political, municipal and social, must be broken up and re-laid, or all our blood and treasure have been spent in vain. This can only be done by treating and holding them as a conquered people. Then all things which we can desire to do, follow with logical and legitimate authority. As conquered territory, Congress would have full power to legislate for them; for the territories are not under the constitution, except so far as the express power to govern them is given to Congress. They would be held in a territorial condition until they are fit to form State Constitutions, republican in fact, not in form only, and ask admission into the Union as new States. If Congress approve of their constitutions, and think they have done works meet for repentance, they would be admitted as new States. If their constitutions are not approved of, they would be sent back, until they have become wise enough so to purge their old laws as to eradicate every despotic and revolutionary principle—until they shall have learned to venerate the Declaration of Independence. I do not touch on the question of negro suffrage. If in the Union, the States have long ago regulated that, and for the Central Government to interfere with it would be mischievous impertinence. If they are to be admitted as new States they must form their own constitutions; and no enabling act could dictate its terms. Congress could prescribe the qualifications of voters while a Territory, or when proceeding to call a convention to form a State government. That is the extent of the power of Congress over the elective franchise, whether in a Territorial or State condition. The President has not even this or any other power to meddle in the subject, except by advice to Congress—and they on Territories. Congress, to be sure, has some sort of compulsory power by refusing the States admission until they shall have complied with its wishes over this subject. Whether those who have fought our battles should all be allowed to vote, or only those of a paler hue, I leave to be discussed in the future when Congress can take legitimate cognizance of it.

If capital punishments of the most guilty are deemed essential as examples, we have seen that, on the one theory, none of them can be convicted on fair trials—the complicity if the triers would defeat it. But, as a conquered enemy, they could not escape. Their trials would take place by court-martial. I do not think they could thus be tried for treason; but they could be tried as belligerents, who had forfeited their lives, according to the laws of war. By the strict rights of war, as anciently practiced, the victor held the lives, the liberty and the property of the vanquished at his disposal. The taking of life, or reduction to bondage of the captives, have long ceased to be practiced in case of ordinary wars, but the abstract right—the *summum jus*—is still recognized in exceptional cases where the cause of the war, or the character of the belligerent, or the safety of the victors justify its exercise. The same thing may be said of the seizure of property on land. Halleck says some modern writers—Hautefeuille, for example—contends for the ancient rule, that private property on land may be subject to seizure. They are undoubtedly correct, with regard to the general abstract right, as deduced from ["]the law of nature and ancient practice." Vattel says: "When, therefore, he has subdued a hostile nation, he undeniably may, in the first place, do himself justice respecting the object which has given rise to the war, and indemnify himself for the expenses and damages which he has sustained by it." And at page 369: "A conqueror, who has taken up arms not only against the sovereign but against the nation herself, and whose intention it was to subdue a fierce and savage people, and once for all to reduce an obstinate enemy, such a conqueror may, with justice, lay burdens on the conquered nation, both as a compensation for the expenses of war, and as a punishment."

I am happy to believe that the government has come to this conclusion. I cannot otherwise see how Capt. Wirz can be tried by a court-martial at Washington for acts done by him at Andersonville. He was in no way connected with our military organization, nor did he as a citizen connect himself with our army as to bring his case within any of the acts of Congress. If he committed murder in Georgia, and Georgia was a state in the Union, the he should be tried according to her laws. The General Government has no jurisdiction over such crime, and the trial and execution of this wretch by a United States military court would be illegal. But if he was an officer of a belligerent enemy, making war as an independent people, now being conquered, it is competent, holding them as a conquered foe, to try him for doing acts contrary to the laws of war, and if found guilty to execute or otherwise punish him. As I am sure the loyal men at the head of the government will not involve the nation in illegal acts and thus set a precedence injurious to our national character, I am glad to believe that hereafter we shall treat the enemy as conquered, and remit the condition and reconstruction to the sovereign power of the nation.

In short, all writers agree that the victor may inflict punishment upon the vanquished enemy, even to taking of life, liberty, or the confiscation of all his property; but that this extreme right is never exercised except upon a cruel, barbarous, obstinate, or dangerous foe who has waged an unjust war.

Upon the character of the belligerent, and the justice of the war, and the manner of conducting it, depends our right to take the lives, liberty and property of the belligerent. This war had its origin in treason without one spark of justice. It was prosecuted before notice of it, by robbing our forts and armories, and our navy-yards; by stealing our money from the mints and depositories, and by surrendering our forts and navies by perjuries who had sworn to support the constitution. In its progress our prisoners, by the authority of their government, were slaughtered in cold blood. Ask Fort Pillow and Fort Wagner. Sixty thousand of our prisoners have been deliberately starved to death because they would not enlist in the rebel armies. The graves at Andersonville have each an accusing tongue. The purpose and avowed object of the enemy "to found an empire whose cornerstone should be slavery," rendered its perpetuity or revival dangerous to human liberty.

Surely, these things are sufficient to justify the exercise of the extreme rights of war—"to execute, to imprison, to confiscate." How many captive enemies it would be proper to execute, as an example to nations, I leave others to judge. I am not fond of sanguinary punishments, but surely some victims must propitiate the manes of our starved, murdered, slaughtered martyrs. A court-martial could do justice according to law. But we propose to confiscate all the estates of every rebel belligerent whose estate was worth $10,000, or whose land exceeded two hundred acres in quantity. Policy if not justice would require that the poor, the ignorant, and the coerced should be forgiven. They followed the example and teachings of their wealthy and intelligent neighbors. The rebellion would never have originated with them. Fortunately those who would thus escape, form a lax majority of the people, though possessing but a small portion the wealth. The proportion of those exempt compared with punished would be I believe about nine-tenths.

There are about six millions of freedmen in the South. The number of acres of land is 465,000,000. Of this, those who own above two hundred acres each number about 70,000 persons, holding in the aggregate, (together with the states,) about 394,000,000 acres, leaving for all the others below 200 each about 71,000,000 of acres. By thus forfeiting the estates of the leading rebels, the government would have 394,000,000 of acres, beside their property, and yet nine-tenths of the people would remain untouched. Divide this land into convenient farms. Give, if you please, forty acres to each adult male freedman. Suppose there are one million of them. That would require 40,000,000 acres, which, deducted from 394,000,000, leaves 354,000,000 of acres for sale. Divided into suitable farms, and sell it to the highest bidders. I take it, including town pro[p]erty, would average at least $10 per acre. That would produce $3,540,000,000—three billions five hundred forty millions of dollars.

Let that be applied as follows to wit:

1. Invest $300,000,000 in six per cent government bonds and add the interest semiannually to the pensions of those who have bec[o]me entitled by this vill[ai]nous war.

2. Appropriate $200,000,000 to pay the damages done to loyal men, North and South, by the rebellion.

3. Pay the residue, being 3,040,000,000 towards payment of the National debt.

What loyal man can object to this? Look around you, and even where behold your neighbors, some with an arm, some with a leg, some with an eye, carried away by rebel bullets. Others horribly mutilated in every form. And yet numerous others wearing the weed which mark the death of those on whom they leaned for support. Contemplate these monuments of rebel perfidy, and of patriotic suffering, and then say if too much is asked for our valiant soldiers.

Look again, and see loyal men reduced to poverty by the confiscations by the Confederate States, and by the rebel States, see Union men robbed of their property, and their dwellings laid to ashes by rebel raiders, and say if too much is asked for them. But, above all, let us inquire whether imperative duty to the present generation and to posterity, does not command us to comply the wicked enemy to pay the expenses of this unjust war. By ordinary transactions, he who raise a false clamor, and prosecutes an unfounded suit, is adjudged to pay the costs on his defeat. We have seen that, by the law of nations, the vanquished in an unjust war must pay the expense.

Our war debt is estimated at from three to four billions of dollars. In my judgment, when all is funded, and the pensions capitalized, it will reach more than four billions.

The interest at 6 per cent, only (now much more)	$240,000,000
The ordinary expenses of our government are	$120,000,000
For some years the ordinary expense our army and Navy will be	$110,000,000
Total	$470,000,000

Four hundred and seventy millions to be raised by taxation—our present heavy taxes will not, in ordinary years, produce but little more than half that sum. Can our people bear double their present taxation? He who unnecessarily causes it will be accursed from generation to generation. It is fashionable to belittle our public debt, lest the people should become alarmed, and political parties should suffer. I have never found it wise to deceive the people. They can always be trusted with the truth. Capitalists will not be affected, for they can not be deceived. Confide in the people, and you will avoid repudiation. Deceive them, and lead them into false measures, and you may produce it.

We pity the poor Englishmen whose national debt and burdensome taxation we have heard deplored from our childhood. The debt of Great Britain is just about as much as ours, ($4,000,000,000) four billions. But in effect it is but half as large—it bears but three per cent, interest. The current year, the Chancellor of the Exchequer tells us, the interest was $131,806,990. Ours, when all shall be funded, will be nearly double.

The plan we have proposed would pay at least three-fourths of our debt. The balance could be managed with our present taxation. And yet to think that even that is to be perpetual is sickening. If it is to be doubled, as it must be, if "restoration" instead of "reconstruction" is to prevail, would to God the authors of it could see themselves as an excreting public and posterity will see them.

Our new Doctors of National law, who hold that the "Confederate States" were never out of the Union, but only insurgents and traitors, have become wiser than Grotius, and Puffendorf, and Rutherford, and Vattel, and all modern publicists down to Halleck and Phillimore. They all agree that such a state of things as has existed here for four years is public war, and constitutes the parties independent belligerents, subject to the same rules of war as foreign nations engaged in open warfare.

The learned and able professor at law in the Cambridge University, Theophilus Parsons, lately said in a public speech:

> As we are victorious in war we have a right to impose upon the defeated party any terms necessary for our security. This right is perfect. It is not only in itself obvious, but it is asserted in every book on this subject, and is illustrated by all the wars of history. The rebels forced a war upon us; it was a long and costly and bloody war; and now that we have conquered them, we have all the rights which victory confers.

The only argument of the Restorationists is, that the States could not and did not go out of the Union because the Constitution forbids it. By the same reasoning you could prove that no crime ever existed. No man ever committed murder for the law forbids it! He is a shallow reasoner who could make theory overrule fact!

I prefer to believe the ancient and modern publicists, and the learned professors of legal science, to the extemporized doctrines of modem sciolists.

If "Restoration," as it is now properly christened, is to prevail over "Reconstruction," will some learned pundit of that school inform me in what condition slavery and the slave laws are? I assert that upon that theory not a slave has been liberated, not a slave law has been abrogated, but on the "Restoration" the whole slave code is in legal force. Slavery was protected by our constitution in every state in the Union where it existed. While they remained under that protection no power in the Federal Government could abolish slavery. If, however, the Confederate States were admitted to be what they claimed, an independent belligerent *de facto*, then the war broke all treaties, compacts and ties between the parties, and slavery was left to its rights under the law of nations. These rights were none; for the law declares that "Man can hold no property in man." (Phillimore, page 316.) Then the laws of war enabled us to declare every bondsman free, so long as we held them in military possession. And the conqueror, through Congress, may declare them forever emancipated. But if the States are "States in the Union," then when war ceases they resume their positions with all their privileges untouched. There can be no "mutilated" restoration. That would be the work of Congress alone, and would be "Reconstruction."

While I hear it said everywhere that slavery is dead, I cannot learn who killed it. No thoughtful man has pretended that Lincoln's proclamation, so noble in sentiment, liberated a single slave. It expressly excluded from its operation all those within our lines. No slave within any part of the rebel States in our possession, or in Tennessee, but only those beyond our limits and beyond our power were declared free. So Gen. Smith conquered Canada by a proclamation! The President did not pretend to abrogate the slave laws of any of the States. "Restoration," therefore, will leave the "Union as it was,["]—a hideous idea. I am aware that a very able and patriotic gentleman, and learned historian, Mr. Bancroft, has attempted to place their freedom on different grounds. He says, what is undoubtedly true, that the proclamation of freedom did not free a slave. But he liberates them on feudal principles. Under the feudal system, when a king conquered his enemy, he parceled out his lands and conquered *subjects* among his chief retainers; the lands and serfs were held on condition of fealty and rendering military service when required. If the subordinate chief rebelled, he broke the condition on which he held them, and the lands and serfs became forfeited to the Lord paramount. But it did not free the serfs. They, with the manors, were bestowed on other favorites. But the analogy fails in another important respect. The American slave-holder does not hold, by virtue of any grant from any Lord paramount—least of all by a grant from the General Government. Slavery exists by no law of the Union, but simply by local laws, by the laws of the States. Rebellion against the National authority is a breach of no condition of their tenure. It were more analogous to say that rebellion against a State under whose laws they held, might work a forfeiture. But rebellion against neither government would *per se* have any such effect. On whom would the Lord paramount again bestow the slaves? The theory is plausible, but has no solid foundation.

The president says to the rebel states: "Before you can participate in the government you must abolish slavery and reform your election laws." That is the command of a conqueror. That is reconstruction, not restoration—reconstruction too by assuming the powers of Congress. This theory will lead to melancholy results. Nor can the constitutional amendment abolishing slavery ever be ratified by three-fourths of the States, if they are States to be counted. Bogus conventions of those States may vote for it. But no convention honestly and fairly elected will ever do it. The frauds will not permanently avail. The cause of liberty must rest on a firmer basis. Counterfeit governments, like the Virginia, Louisiana, Tennessee, Mississippi and Arkansas pretend, will be disregarded by the sober sense of the people, by future law, and by the courts. "[R]estoration" is replanting the seeds of rebellion which, within the next quarter of a century will germinate and produce the same bloody strife which has just ended.

But, it is said, by those who have more sympathy with rebel wives and children than for the widows and orphans of loyal men, that this stripping the rebels of their estates and driving them to exile or to honest labor, would be harsh and severe upon innocent women and children. It may be so; but that is the result of the necessary laws of war. But it is revolutionary, say they. This plan would, no doubt, work a radical reorganization in Southern institutions, habits and manners. It is intended to revolutionize their principles and feelings. This may startle feeble minds and shake weak nerves. So do all great improvements in the political and moral world. It requires a heavy impetus to drive forward a sluggish people. When it was first proposed to free the slaves and arm the blacks, did not the nation tremble? The prim conservatives, the snobs, and the male waiting-maids in Congress, were in hysterics.

The whole fabric of southern society must be changed, and never can it be done if this opportunity is lost. Without this, this Government can never be, as it never has been, a true republic. Heretofore, it had more the features of aristocracy than of democracy. The Southern States have been despotisms, not governments of the people. It is impossible that any practical equality of rights can exist where a few thousand men monopolize the whole landed property. The larger the number of small proprietors the more safe and stable the government. As the landed interest must govern, the more it is subdivided and held by independent owners, the better. What would be the condition of the State of New York if it were not for her independent yeomanry? She would be overwhelmed and demoralized by the Jews, Milesians and vagabonds of licentious cities. How can republican institutions, free schools, free churches, free social intercourse exist in a mingled community of nabobs and serfs; of the owners of twenty thousand acre manors with lordly palaces, and the occupants of narrow huts inhabited by "low white trash?" If the South is ever to be made a safe republic, let her lands be cultivated by the toil of the owners or the free labor of intelligent citizens. This must be done even though it drive her nobility into exile. If they go, all the better. It will be hard to persuade the owner of a thousand acres of land, who drives a coach and four, that he is not degraded by sitting at the same table, or in the same pew, with the embrowned and hard-handed farmer who has himself cultivated his own thriving homestead of 150 acres. This subdivision of the lands will yield ten bales of cotton to one that is made now, and he who produced it will own it and *feel himself a man.*

It is far easier and more beneficial to exile 70,000 proud, bloated and defiant rebels, than to expatriate four millions of laborers, native to the soil and loyal to the Government. This latter scheme was a favorite plan of the BLAIRS, with which they had for awhile inoculated our late sainted President. But a single experiment made him discard it and its advisers. Since I have mentioned the BLAIRS, I may say a word more of these persistent apologists of the South. For, when the virus of Slavery has once entered the veins of the slave holder, no subsequent effort seems capable of wholly eradicating it. They are a family of considerable power, some merit, of admirable audacity and execrable selfishness. With impetuous alacrity they seize the White House, and hold possession of it, as in the late administration, until shaken off by the overpowering force of public indignation. Their pernicious counsel had well nigh defeated the reelection of ABRAHAM LINCOLN; and if it should prevail with the present administration, pure and patriotic as President JOHNSON is admitted to be, it will render him the most unpopular Executive—save one—that ever occupied the Presidential chair. But there is no fear of that. He will soon say, as MR. LINCOLN did: "Your time has come!"

This remodeling the institutions, and reforming the rooted habits of a proud aristocracy, is undoubtedly a formidable task, requiring the broad mind of enlarged statesmanship, and the firm nerve of the hero. But will not this mighty occasion produce—will not the God of Liberty and order give us—such men? Will not a Romulus, a Lycurgus, a Charlemagne, a Washington arise, whose expansive views will found a free empire, to endure till time shall be no more?

This doctrine of Restoration shocks me. We have a duty to perform which our fathers were incapable of, which will be required at our hands by God and our country. When our ancestors found a "more perfect Union" necessary, they found it impossible to agree upon a constitution without tolerating, nay, guaranteeing, slavery. They were obliged to acquiesce, trusting to time to work a speedy cure, in which they were disappointed. They had some excuse, some justification. But we can have none if we do not thoroughly eradicate slavery and render it forever impossible in this republic. The slave power made war upon the nation. They declared the "more perfect Union" dissolved—solemnly declared themselves a foreign nation, alien to this republic; for four years were in fact what they claimed to be. We accepted the war which they tendered and treated them as a government capable of making war. We have conquered them, and as a conquered enemy we can give them laws; can abolish all their municipal institutions and form new ones. If we do not make those institutions fit to last through generations of free men, a heavy curse will be on us. Our glorious, but tainted republic has been born to new life through bloody, agonizing pains. But this frightful "Restoration" has thrown it into "cold obstruction, and to death." If the rebel States have never been out of the Union, any attempt to reform their State institutions, either by Congress or the President, is rank usurpation.

Is then all lost? Is this great conquest to be in vain? That will depend upon the virtue and intelligence of the next Congress. To Congress alone belongs the power of reconstruction—of giving law to the vanquished. This is expressly declared by the Supreme Court of the United States in the Dorr case, 7th Howard, 42. The court says, "Under this article of the constitution (the 4th) it rests with Congress to decide what government is the established one in a State, for the United States guarantees to each a republican form of government," etc. But we know how difficult it will be for a majority of Congress to overcome preconceived opinions. Besides, before Congress meets, things will be so inaugurated—precipitated—it will be still more difficult to correct. If a majority of Congress can be found wise and firm enough to declare the Confederate States a conquered enemy, reconstruction will be easy and legitimate; and the friends of freedom will long rule in the councils of the nation. If restoration prevails the prospect is gloomy, and new "lords will make new laws." The Union party will be overwhelmed. The Copperhead party has become extinct with succession. But with succession it will revive. Under "restoration" every rebel State will send rebels to Congress, and they, with their allies in the North, will control Congress, and occupy the White House. Then restoration of laws and ancient constitutions will be sure to follow, our public debt will be repudiated, or the rebel national debt will be added to ours, and the people be crushed beneath heavy burdens.

Let us forget all parties, and build on the broad platform of "reconstructing" the government out of the conquered territory converted into new and free States, and admitted into the Union by the sovereign power of Congress, with another plank—"THE PROPERTY OF REBELS SHALL PAY OUR NATIONAL DEBT, *and indemnify freedmen and loyal suffers*—and that under no circumstances will we suffer the national debt to be repudiated, or the interest scaled below the contract rates; nor permit any part of the rebel debt to be assumed by the nation."

Let all who approve of these principles rally with us. Let all others go with Copperheads and rebels. Those will be the opposing parties. Young men, this duty devolves on you. Would to God, if only for that, that I were still in the prime of life, that I might aid you to fight through this last and greatest battle of freedom.

Petitions of the Freedmen of Edisto Island, South Carolina, to General O. O. Howard, Freedmen's Bureau Commissioner, and to the President of the United States (October 1865)

[Edisto Island, S.C. October 28?, 1865]

General, It Is with painfull Hearts that we the Committe address you, we Have thoroughly considerd the order which you wished us to Sign, we wish we could *do* so but cannot feel our rights Safe If we do so,

General we want Homesteads; we were promised Homesteads by the government; if it does not carry out the promises its agents made to us, if the government Having concluded to befriend its late enemies and to neglect to observe the principles of common faith between its self and us its allies in the war you said was over, now takes away from them all right to the soil they stand upon save such as they can get by again working for *your* late and their *all time enemies.*—If the government does so we are left in a more unpleasant condition than our former

[W]e are at the mercy of those who are combined to prevent us from getting land enough to lay our Father's bones upon. We have property in horses, cattle, carriages, & articles of furniture, but we are landless and homeless, from the homes we have lived in in the past we can only do one of three things Step Into the public *road or the sea* or remain on them working as in former time and subject to their will as then. We can not resist it in any way without being driven out homeless upon the road.

You will see this Is not the condition of really freemen

You ask us to forgive the land owners of our island, *you* only lost your right arm. In war and might forgive them. The man who tied me to a tree & gave me 39 lashes & who stripped and flogged my mother & sister & who will not let me stay in his empty hut except I will do his planting & be satisfied with his price & who combines with others to keep away land from me well knowing I would not Have any thing to do with him if I had land of my own.—that man, I cannot well forgive. Does it look as if he has forgiven me, seeing how he tries to keep me in a condition of helplessness

General, we cannot remain here in such condition and if the government permits them to come back we ask it to help us to reach land where we shall not be slaves nor compelled to work for those who would treat us as such

[W]e Have not been treacherous, we have not for selfish motives allied to us those who suffered like us from a common enemy & then haveing gained *our* purpose left our allies in their hands There is no rights secured to us there is no law likely to be made which our hands can reach. The state will make laws that we shall not be able to hold land even if we pay for it landless, homeless, voteless, we can only pray to god & hope for *his help, your infuence & assistance* with consideration of esteem Your Obt Servts

In behalf of the people

Committee — Henry Bram, Ishmael Moultrie, yates Sampson

Edisto Island S.C. Oct 28th, 1865

To the President of these United States. We the freedmen of Edisto Island South Carolina have learned From you through Major General O. O. Howard commissioner of the Freedmans Bureau, with deep sorrow and painful hearts of the possibility of government restoring These lands to the former owners. We are well aware Of the many perplexing and trying questions that burden your mind, and do therefore pray to god (the preserver of all and who has through our Late and beloved President (Lincoln) proclamation and the war made us A free people) that he may guide you in making your decisions, and give you that wisdom that cometh from above to settle these great and Important questions for the best interests of the country and the colored race: Here is where secession was born and nurtured here is were we have toiled nearly all our lives as slaves and were treated like dumb driven cattle, This is our home, we have made these lands what they are. [W]e were the only true and loyal people that were found in posession of these lands. [W]e have been always ready to strike for liberty and humanity yea to fight if needs be to preserve this glorious union. Shall not we who are freedman and have been always true to this Union have the same rights as are enjoyed by others? Have we broken any Law of these United States? Have we forfeited our rights of property in land?—If not then are not our rights as a free people and good citizens of these United States to be considered before the rights of those who were found in rebellion against this good and just Government (and now being conquered) come (as they seem) with penitent hearts and beg forgiveness for past offences and also ask if their lands cannot be restored to them are these rebellious spirits to be reinstated in thier *possessions* and we who have been abused and oppressed for many long years not to be allowed the privilige of purchasing land but be subject to the will of these large land owners? God forbid, land monopoly is injurious to the advancement of the course of freedom, and if Government does not make some provision by which we as freedmen can obtain a homestead, we have not bettered our condition.

We have been encouraged by Government to take up these lands in small tracts, receiving certificates of the same—we have thus far taken sixteen thousand (16000) acres of land here on this Island. We are ready to pay for this land when government calls for it, and now after what has been done will the good and just government take from us all this right and make us subject to the will of those who have cheated and oppressed us for many years God forbid!

We the freedmen of this island and of the State of South Carolina—do therefore petition to you as the President of these United States, that some provisions be made by which every colored man can purchase land and hold it as his own. We wish to have a home if it be but a few acres. [W]ithout some provision is made our future is sad to look upon. [Yes] our Situation is dangerous. [W]e therefore look to you in this trying hour as A true friend of the poor and neglected race, for protection and equal rights, with the privilege of purchasing a homestead—a homestead right here in the heart of South Carolina.

We pray that God will direct your heart in making such provision for us as freedmen which will tend to unite these states together stronger than ever before—May God bless you in the administration of your duties as the President of these United States is the humble prayer of us all.—

In Behalf of the Freedmen

Committee — Henry Bram, Ishmael Moultrie., yates Sampson

South Carolina Black Code (1865)

[. . .] VIII. One who is a pauper, or a charge to the public, shall not be competent to contract marriage. Marriage between a white person and a person of color, shall be illegal and void.

IX. The marriage of an apprentice shall not, without the consent of the master, be lawful.

XLVIII. Visitors or other persons shall not be invited, or allowed by the servant, to come or remain upon the premises of the master, without his express permission.

XLIX. Servants shall not be absent from the premises without the permission of the master.

Mechanics, Artisans and Shop-keepers

LXXI. No person of color shall pursue or practice the art, trade or business of an artisan, mechanic or shop-keeper, or any other trade, employment or business (besides that of husbandry, or that of a servant under a contract for services or labor) on his own account and for his own benefit, or in partnership with a white person, or as agent or servant of any person, until he shall have obtained a license therefor from the Judge of the District Court, which license shall be good for one year only. This license the Judge may grant upon petition of the applicant, and upon being satisfied of his skill and fitness, and of his good moral character, and upon payment, by the applicant, to the Clerk of the District Court of one-hundred dollars, if a shop-keeper or pedlar, to be paid annually, and ten dollars if a mechanic artisan, or to engage in any other trade, also to be paid annually: *Provided, however*, That upon complaint being made and proved to the District Judge of an abuse of such license, he shall revoke the same, and: *Provided, also*, That no person of color shall practice any mechanical art or trade, unless he shows that he has served an apprenticeship in such trade or art, or is now practicing such trade or art. [. . .]

Andrew Johnson

Veto of Freedman's Bureau Bill (1866)

To the Senate of the United States:

I have examined with care the bill, which originated in the Senate and has been passed by the two houses of Congress, to amend an act entitled "An act to establish a bureau for the relief of freedmen and refugees," and for other purposes. Having with much regret come to the conclusion that it would not be consistent with the public welfare to give my approval to the measure, I return the bill to the Senate with my objections to its becoming a law.

I might call to mind in advance of these objections that there is no immediate necessity for the proposed measure. The act to establish a bureau for the relief of freedmen and refugees, which was approved in the month of March last, has not yet expired. It was thought stringent and extensive enough for the purpose in view in time of war. Before it ceases to have effect, further experience may assist to guide us to a wise conclusion as to the policy to be adopted in time of peace.

I share with Congress the strongest desire to secure to the freedmen the full enjoyment of their freedom and property and their entire independence and equality in making contracts for their labor, but the bill before me contains provisions which in my opinion are not warranted by the Constitution and are not well suited to accomplish the end in view.

The bill proposes to establish, by authority of Congress, military jurisdiction over all parts of the United States containing refugees and freedmen. It would by its very nature apply with most force to those parts of the United States in which the freedmen most abound, and it expressly extends the existing temporary jurisdiction of the Freedmen's Bureau, with greatly enlarged powers, over those states "in which the ordinary course of judicial proceedings has been interrupted by the rebellion."

The source from which this military jurisdiction is to emanate is none other than the President of the United States, acting through the War Department and the commissioner of the Freedmen's Bureau. The agents to carry out this military jurisdiction are to be selected either from the Army or from civil life; the country is to be divided into districts and subdistricts, and the number of salaried agents to be employed may be equal to the number of counties or parishes in all the United States where freedmen and refugees are to be found.

The subjects over which this military jurisdiction is to extend in every part of the United States include protection to "all employees, agents, and officers of this bureau in the exercise of the duties imposed" upon them by the bill. In eleven states it is further to extend over all cases affecting freedmen and refugees discriminated against "by local law, custom, or prejudice." In those eleven states the bill subjects any white person who may be charged with depriving a freedman of "any civil rights or immunities belonging to white persons" to imprisonment or fine, or both, without, however, defining the "civil rights and immunities" which are thus to be secured to the freedmen by military law. This military jurisdiction also extends to all questions that may arise respecting contracts.

The agent who is thus to exercise the office of a military judge may be a stranger, entirely ignorant of the laws of the place and exposed to the errors of judgment to which all men are liable. The exercise of power over which there is no legal supervision by so vast a number of agents as is contemplated by the bill must, by the very nature of man, be attended by acts of caprice, injustice, and passion.

The trials having their origin under this bill are to take place without the intervention of a jury and without any fixed rules of law or evidence. The rules on which offenses are to be "heard and determined" by the numerous agents are such rules and regulations as the President, through the War Department, shall prescribe. No previous presentment is required nor any indictment charging the commission of a crime against the laws; but the trial must proceed on charges and specifications. The punishment will be, not what the law declares, but such as a court-martial may think proper; and from these arbitrary tribunals there lies no appeal, no writ of error to any of the courts in which the Constitution of the United States vests exclusively the judicial power of the country.

While the territory and the classes of actions and offenses that are made subject to this measure are so extensive, the bill itself, should it become a law, will have no limitation in point of time, but will form a part of the permanent legislation of the country. I cannot reconcile a system of military jurisdiction of this kind with the words of the Constitution which declare that "no person shall be held to answer for a capital or otherwise infamous crime unless on a presentment or indictment of a grand jury, except in cases arising in the land or naval forces, or in the militia, when in actual service in time of war or public danger," and that "in all criminal prosecutions the accused shall enjoy the right to a speedy and public trial, by an impartial jury of the state and district wherein the crime shall have been committed."

The safeguards which the experience and wisdom of ages taught our fathers to establish as securities for the protection of the innocent, the punishment of the guilty, and the equal administration of justice are to be set aside; and for the sake of a more vigorous interposition in behalf of justice, we are to take the risks of the many acts of injustice that would necessarily follow from an almost countless number of agents established in every parish or county in nearly a third of the states of the Union, over whose decisions there is to be no supervision or control by the federal courts. The power that would be thus placed in the hands of the President is such as in time of peace certainly ought never to be entrusted to any one man.

If it be asked whether the creation of such a tribunal within a state is warranted as a measure of war, the question immediately presents itself whether we are still engaged in war. Let us not unnecessarily disturb the commerce and credit and industry of the country by declaring to the American people and to the world that the United States are still in a condition of civil war. At present there is no part of our country in which the authority of the United States is disputed. Offenses that may be committed by individuals should not work a forfeiture of the rights of whole communities. The country has returned, or is returning, to a state of peace and industry, and the rebellion is in fact at an end. The measure, therefore, seems to be as inconsistent with the actual condition of the country as it is at variance with the Constitution of the United States. [. . .]

Undoubtedly the freedman should be protected, but he should be protected by the civil authorities, especially by the exercise of all the constitutional powers of the courts of the United States and of the states. His condition is not so exposed as may at first be imagined. He is in a portion of the country where his labor cannot well be spared. Competition for his services from planters, from those who are constructing or repairing railroads, and from capitalists in his vicinage or from other states will enable him to command almost his own terms. He also possesses a perfect right to change his place of abode, and if, therefore, he does not find in one community or state a mode of life suited to his desires or proper remuneration for his labor, he can move to another where that labor is more esteemed and better rewarded.

In truth, however, each state, induced by its own wants and interests, will do what is necessary and proper to retain within its borders all the labor that is needed for the development of its resources. The laws that regulate supply and demand will maintain their force, and the wages of the laborer will be regulated thereby. There is no danger that the exceedingly great demand for labor will not operate in favor of the laborer.

Neither is sufficient consideration given to the ability of the freedmen to protect and take care of themselves. It is no more than justice to them to believe that as they have received their freedom with moderation and forbearance, so they will distinguish themselves by their industry and thrift, and soon show the world that in a condition of freedom they are self-sustaining, capable of selecting their own employment and their own places of abode, of insisting for themselves on a proper remuneration, and of establishing and maintaining their own asylums and schools. It is earnestly hoped that instead of wasting away they will by their own efforts establish for themselves a condition of respectability and prosperity. It is certain that they can attain to that condition only through their own merits and exertions.

In this connection the query presents itself whether the system proposed by the bill will not, when put into complete operation, practically transfer the entire care, support, and control of 4 million emancipated slaves to agents, overseers, or taskmasters, who, appointed at Washington, are to be located in every county and parish throughout the United States containing freedmen and refugees. Such a system would inevitably tend to a concentration of power in the executive which would enable him, if so disposed, to control the action of this numerous class and use them for the attainment of his own political ends.

I cannot but add another very grave objection to this bill. The Constitution imperatively declares, in connection with taxation, that each state *shall* have at least one representative, and fixes the rule for the number to which, in future times, each state shall be entitled. It also provides that the Senate of the United States *shall* be composed of two senators from each state, and adds with peculiar force "that no state, without its consent, shall be deprived of its equal suffrage in the Senate." The original act was necessarily passed in the absence of the states chiefly to be affected, because their people were then contumaciously engaged in the rebellion. Now the case is changed, and some, at least, of those states are attending Congress by loyal representatives, soliciting the allowance of the constitutional right for representation.

At the time, however, of the consideration and the passing of this bill, there was no senator or representative in Congress from the eleven states which are to be mainly affected by its provisions. The very fact that reports were and are made against the good disposition of the people of that portion of the country is an additional reason why they need and should have representatives of their own in Congress to explain their condition, reply to accusations, and assist by their local knowledge in the perfecting of measures immediately affecting themselves. While the liberty of deliberation would then be free and Congress would have full power to decide according to its judgment, there could be no objection urged that the states most interested had not been permitted to be heard.

The principle is firmly fixed in the minds of the American people that there should be no taxation without representation. Great burdens have now to be borne by all the country, and we may best demand that they shall be borne without murmur when they are voted by a majority of the representatives of all the people. I would not interfere with the unquestionable right of Congress to judge, each house for itself, "of the elections, returns, and qualifications of its own members"; but that authority cannot be construed as including the right to shut out in time of peace any state from the representation to which it is entitled by the Constitution. At present all the people of eleven states are excluded—those who were most faithful during the war not less than others.

The state of Tennessee, for instance, whose authorities engaged in rebellion, was restored to all her constitutional relations to the Union by the patriotism and energy of her injured and betrayed people. Before the war was brought to a termination, they had placed themselves in relations with the general government, had established a state government of their own, and, as they were not included in the Emancipation Proclamation, they by their own act had amended their constitution so as to abolish slavery within the limits of their state. I know no reason why the state of Tennessee, for example, should not fully enjoy "all her constitutional relations to the United States."

The President of the United States stands toward the country in a somewhat different attitude from that of any member of Congress. Each member of Congress is chosen from a single district or state; the President is chosen by the people of all the states. As eleven states are not at this time represented in either branch of Congress, it would seem to be his duty on all proper occasions to present their just claims to Congress. There always will be differences of opinion in the community and individuals may be guilty of transgressions of the law, but these do not constitute valid objections against the right of a state to representation. I would in no way interfere with the discretion of Congress with regard to the qualifications of members; but I hold it my duty to recommend to you, in the interests of peace and the interests of union, the admission of every state to its share in public legislation when, however insubordinate, insurgent, or rebellious its people may have been, it presents itself, not only in an attitude of loyalty and harmony but in the persons of representatives whose loyalty cannot be questioned under any existing constitutional or legal test.

It is plain that an indefinite or permanent exclusion of any part of the country from representation must be attended by a spirit of disquiet and complaint. It is unwise and dangerous to pursue a course of measures which will unite a very large section of the country against another section of the country, however much the latter may preponderate. The course of emigration, the development of industry and business, and natural causes will raise up at the South men as devoted to the Union as those of any other part of the land; but if they are all excluded from Congress, if in a permanent statute they are declared not to be in full constitutional relations to the country, they may think they have cause to become a unit in feeling and sentiment against the government. Under the political education of the American people the idea is inherent and ineradicable that the consent of the majority of the whole people is necessary to secure a willing acquiescence in legislation.

The bill under consideration refers to certain of the states as though they had not "been fully restored in all their constitutional relations to the United States." If they have not, let us at once act together to secure that desirable end at the earliest possible moment. It is hardly necessary for me to inform Congress that in my own judgment most of those states, so far, at least, as depends upon their own action, have already been fully restored and are to be deemed as entitled to enjoy their constitutional rights as members of the Union. Reasoning from the Constitution itself and from the actual situation of the country, I feel not only entitled but bound to assume that with the federal courts restored and those of the several states in the full exercise of their functions the rights and interests of all classes of people will, with the aid of the military in cases of resistance to the laws, be essentially protected against unconstitutional infringement or violation.

Should this expectation unhappily fail, which I do not anticipate, then the executive is already fully armed with the powers conferred by the act of March 1865 establishing the Freedmen's Bureau, and hereafter, as heretofore, he can employ the land and naval forces of the country to suppress insurrection or to overcome obstructions to the laws.

In accordance with the Constitution, I return the bill to the Senate in the earnest hope that a measure involving questions and interests so important to the country will not become a law, unless upon deliberate consideration by the people it shall receive the sanction of an enlightened public judgment.

Veto of Civil Rights Act of 1866 (1866)

To the Senate of the United States:

I regret that the bill, which has passed both houses of Congress, entitled "An act to protect all persons in the United States in their civil rights and furnish the means of their vindication" contains provisions which I cannot approve consistently with my sense of duty to the whole people and my obligations to the Constitution of the United States. I am therefore constrained to return it to the Senate, the house in which it originated, with my objections to its becoming a law.

By the 1st Section of the bill, all persons born in the United States and not subject to any foreign power, excluding Indians not taxed, are declared to be citizens of the United States. This provision comprehends the Chinese of the Pacific states, Indians subject to taxation, the people called gypsies, as well as the entire race designated as blacks, people of color, Negroes, mulattoes, and persons of African blood. Every individual of these races born in the United States is by the bill made a citizen of the United States.

It does not purport to declare or confer any other right of citizenship than federal citizenship. It does not purport to give these classes of persons any status as citizens of states except that which may result from their status as citizens of the United States. The power to confer the right of state citizenship is just as exclusively with the several states as the power to confer the right of federal citizenship is with Congress.

The right of federal citizenship thus to be conferred on the several excepted races before mentioned is now for the first time proposed to be given by law. If, as is claimed by many, all persons who are native-born already are, by virtue of the Constitution, citizens of the United States, the passage of the pending bill cannot be necessary to make them such. If, on the other hand, such persons are not citizens, as may be assumed from the proposed legislation to make them such, the grave question presents itself whether, when eleven of the thirty-six states are unrepresented in Congress at the present time, it is sound policy to make our entire colored population and all other excepted classes citizens of the United States.

Four million of them have just emerged from slavery into freedom. Can it be reasonably supposed that they possess the requisite qualifications to entitle them to all the privileges and immunities of citizens of the United States? Have the people of the several states expressed such a conviction? It may also be asked whether it is necessary that they should be declared citizens in order that they may be secured in the enjoyment of the civil rights proposed to be conferred by the bill.

Those rights are, by federal as well as state laws, secured to all domiciled aliens and foreigners, even before the completion of the process of naturalization; and it may safely be assumed that the same enactments are sufficient to give like protection and benefits to those for whom this bill provides special legislation. Besides, the policy of the government, from its origin to the present time, seems to have been that persons who are strangers to and unfamiliar with our institutions and our laws should pass through a certain probation, at the end of which, before attaining the coveted prize, they must give evidence of their fitness to receive and to exercise the rights of citizens as contemplated by the Constitution of the United States.

The bill in effect proposes a discrimination against large numbers of intelligent, worthy, and patriotic foreigners, and in favor of the Negro, to whom, after long years of bondage, the avenues to freedom and intelligence have just now been suddenly opened. He must, of necessity, from his previous unfortunate condition of servitude, be less informed as to the nature and character of our institutions than he who, coming from abroad, has to some extent at least, familiarized himself with the principles of a government to which he voluntarily entrusts "life, liberty, and the pursuit of happiness."

Yet it is now proposed, by a single legislative enactment, to confer the rights of citizens upon all persons of African descent, born within the extended limits of the United States, while persons of foreign birth who make our land their home must undergo a probation of five years and can only then become citizens upon proof that they are "of good moral character, attached to the principles of the Constitution of the United States, and well-disposed to the good order and happiness of the same."

The 1st Section of the bill also contains an enumeration of the rights to be enjoyed by these classes so made citizens "in every state and territory in the United States." These rights are "to make and enforce contracts; to sue, be parties, and give evidence; to inherit, purchase, lease, sell, hold, and convey real and personal property," and to have "full and equal benefit of all laws and proceedings for the security of person and property as is enjoyed by white citizens." So, too, they are made subject to the same punishment, pains, and penalties, in common with white citizens and to none other.

Thus a perfect equality of the white and colored races is attempted to be fixed by federal law in every state of the Union over the vast field of state jurisdiction covered by these enumerated rights. In no one of these can any state ever exercise any power of discrimination between the different races. In the exercise of state policy over matters exclusively affecting the people of each state, it has frequently been thought expedient to discriminate between the two races.

By the statutes of some of the states, Northern as well as Southern, it is enacted, for instance, that no white person shall intermarry with a Negro or mulatto. Chancellor Kent says, speaking of the blacks, that:

> Marriages between them and the whites are forbidden in some of the states where slavery does not exist, and they are prohibited in all the slaveholding states; and when not absolutely contrary to law, they are revolting and regarded as an offense against public decorum.

I do not say that this bill repeals state laws on the subject of marriage between the two races, for as the whites are forbidden to intermarry with the blacks, the blacks can only make such contracts as the whites themselves are allowed to make, and therefore cannot under this bill enter into the marriage contract with the whites. I cite this discrimination, however, as an instance of the state policy as to discrimination and to inquire whether if Congress can abrogate all state laws of discrimination between the two races in the matter of real estate, of suits, and of contracts generally, Congress may not also repeal the state laws as to the contract of marriage between the two races.

Hitherto every subject embraced in the enumeration of rights contained in this bill has been considered as exclusively belonging to the states. They all relate to the internal policy and economy of the respective states. They are matters which, in each state, concern the domestic condition of its people, varying in each according to its own peculiar circumstances and the safety and well-being of its own citizens. I do not mean to say that upon all these subjects there are not federal restraints—as, for instance, in the state power of legislation over contracts there is a federal limitation that no state shall pass a law impairing the obligations of contracts; and, as to crimes, that no state shall pass an *ex post facto* law; and, as to money, that no state shall make anything but gold and silver a legal tender.

But where can we find a federal prohibition against the power of any state to discriminate, as do most of them, between aliens and citizens, between artificial persons, called corporations, and natural persons, in the right to hold real estate? If it be granted that Congress can repeal all state laws discriminating between whites and blacks in the subjects covered by this bill, why, it may be asked, may not Congress repeal in the same way all state laws discriminating between the two races on the subjects of suffrage and office? If Congress can declare by law who shall hold lands, who shall testify, who shall have capacity to make a contract in a state, then Congress can by law also declare who, without regard to color or race, shall have the right to sit as a juror or as a judge, to hold any office, and, finally, to vote "in every state and territory of the United States."

As respects the territories, they come within the power of Congress, for as to them the lawmaking power is the federal power; but as to the states, no similar provision exists vesting in Congress the power "to make rules and regulations" for them.

The object of the 2nd Section of the bill is to afford discriminating protection to colored persons in the full enjoyment of all the rights secured to them by the preceding section. It declares:

> That any person who, under color of any law, statute, ordinance, regulation, or custom, shall subject, or cause to be subjected, any inhabitant of any state or territory to the deprivation of any right secured or protected by this act, or to different punishment, pains, or penalties on account of such person having at any time been held in a condition of slavery or involuntary servitude, except as a punishment for crime whereof the party shall have been duly convicted, or by reason of his color or race, than is prescribed for the punishment of white persons, shall be deemed guilty of a misdemeanor, and on conviction shall be punished by fine not exceeding $1,000, or imprisonment not exceeding one year, or both, in the discretion of the court.

This section seems to be designed to apply to some existing or future law of a state or territory which may conflict with the provisions of the bill now under consideration. It provides for counteracting such forbidden legislation by imposing fine and imprisonment upon the legislators who may pass such conflicting laws or upon the officers or agents who shall put or attempt to put them into execution. It means an official offense, not a common crime committed against law upon the persons or property of the black race. Such an act may deprive the black man of his property but not of the *right* to hold property. It means a deprivation of the right itself, either by the state judiciary or the state legislature.

It is therefore assumed that under this section members of state legislatures who should vote for laws conflicting with the provisions of the bill, that judges of the state courts who should render judgments in antagonism with its terms, and that marshals and sheriffs who should, as ministerial officers, execute processes sanctioned by state laws and issued by state judges in execution of their judgments, could be brought before other tribunals and there subjected to fine and imprisonment for the performance of the duties which such state laws might impose.

The legislation thus proposed invades the judicial power of the state. It says to every state court or judge: If you decide that this act is unconstitutional; if you refuse, under the prohibition of a state law, to allow a Negro to testify; if you hold that over such a subject matter the state law is paramount, and "under color" of a state law refuse the exercise of the right to the Negro, your error of judgment, however conscientious, shall subject you to fine and imprisonment. I do not apprehend that the conflicting legislation which the bill seems to contemplate is so likely to occur as to render it necessary at this time to adopt a measure of such doubtful constitutionality.

In the next place, this provision of the bill seems to be unnecessary as adequate judicial remedies could be adopted to secure the desired end without invading the immunities of legislators, always important to be preserved in the interest of public liberty; without assailing the independence of the judiciary, always essential to the preservation, of individual rights; and without impairing the efficiency of ministerial officers, always necessary for the maintenance of public peace and order. The remedy proposed by this section seems to be in this respect not only anomalous but unconstitutional; for the Constitution guarantees nothing with certainty if it does not insure to the several states the right of making and executing laws in regard to all matters arising within their jurisdiction, subject only to the restriction that in cases of conflict with the Constitution and constitutional laws of the United States the latter should be held to be the supreme law of the land.

The 3rd Section gives the district courts of the United States exclusive "cognizance of all crimes and offenses committed against the provisions of this act," and concurrent jurisdiction with the circuit courts of the United States or all civil and criminal cases "affecting persons who are denied or cannot enforce in the courts or judicial tribunals of the state or locality where they may be any of the rights secured to them by the first section." The construction which I have given to the second section is strengthened by this third section, for it makes clear what kind of denial or deprivation of the rights secured by the first section was in contemplation. It is a denial or deprivation of such rights "in the courts or judicial tribunals of the state."

It stands, therefore, clear of doubt, that the offense and the penalties provided in the second section are intended for the state judge who, in the clear exercise of his functions as a judge, not acting ministerially but judicially, shall decide contrary to this federal law. In other words, when a state judge, acting upon a question involving a conflict between a state law and a federal law and bound, according to his own judgment and responsibility, to give an impartial decision between the two, comes to the conclusion that the state law is valid and the federal law is invalid, he must not follow the dictates of his own judgment, at the peril of fine and imprisonment. The Legislative Department of the government of the United States thus takes from the Judicial Department of the states the sacred and exclusive duty of judicial decision and converts the state judge into a mere ministerial officer, bound to decide according to the will of Congress.

It is clear that in states which deny to persons whose rights are secured by the first section of the bill any one of those rights, all criminal and civil cases affecting them will, by the provisions of the third section, come under the exclusive cognizance of the federal tribunals. It follows that if, in any state which denies to a colored person any one of all those rights, that person should commit a crime against the laws of a state—murder, arson, rape, or any other crime—all protection and punishment through the courts of the state are taken away, and he can only be tried and punished in the federal courts.

How is the criminal to be tried? If the offense is provided for and punished by federal law, that law, and not the state law, is to govern. It is only when the offense does not happen to be within the purview of federal law that the federal courts are to try and punish him under any other law. Then resort is to be had to "the common law, as modified and changed" by state legislation, "so far as the same is not inconsistent with the Constitution and laws of the United States." So that over this vast domain of criminal jurisprudence provided by each state for the protection of its own citizens and for the punishment of all persons who violate its criminal laws, federal law, whenever it can be made to apply, displaces state law.

The question here naturally arises, from what source Congress derives the power to transfer to federal tribunals certain classes of cases embraced in this section. The Constitution expressly declares that the judicial power of the United States "shall extend to all cases, in law and equity, arising under this Constitution, the laws of the United States, and treaties made or which shall be made under their authority; to all cases affecting ambassadors, other public ministers, and consuls; to all cases of admiralty and maritime jurisdiction; to controversies to which the United States shall be a party; to controversies between two or more states, between a state and citizens of another state, between citizens of different states, between citizens of the same state claiming lands under grants of different states, and between a state, or the citizens thereof, and foreign states, citizens, or subjects."

Here the judicial power of the United States is expressly set forth and defined; and the act of September 24, 1789, establishing the judicial courts of the United States, in conferring upon the federal courts jurisdiction over cases originating in state tribunals, is careful to confine them to the classes enumerated in the above-recited clause of the Constitution. This section of the bill undoubtedly comprehends cases and authorizes the exercise of powers that are not, by the Constitution, within the jurisdiction of the courts of the United States. To transfer them to those courts would be an exercise of authority well calculated to excite distrust and alarm on the part of all the states, for the bill applies alike to all of them, as well to those that have as to those that have not been engaged in rebellion.

It may be assumed that this authority is incident to the power granted to Congress by the Constitution, as recently amended, to enforce, by appropriate legislation, the article declaring that:

> Neither slavery nor involuntary servitude, except as a punishment for crime whereof the party shall have been duly convicted, shall exist within the United States or any place subject to their jurisdiction.

It cannot, however, be justly claimed that, with a view to the enforcement of this article of the Constitution, there is at present any necessity for the exercise of all the powers which this bill confers. Slavery has been abolished, and at present nowhere exists within the jurisdiction of the United States; nor has there been, nor is it likely there will be, any attempt to revive it by the people or the states. If, however, any such attempt shall be made, it will then become the duty of the general government to exercise any and all incidental powers necessary and proper to maintain inviolate this great constitutional law of freedom.

The 4th Section of the bill provides that officers and agents of the Freedmen's Bureau shall be empowered to make arrests and also that other officers may be specially commissioned for that purpose by the President of the United States. It also authorizes circuit courts of the United States and the superior courts of the territories to appoint, without limitation, commissioners, who are to be charged with the performance of quasi-judicial duties.

The 5th Section empowers the commissioners so to be selected by the courts to appoint in writing, under their hands, one or more suitable persons from time to time to execute warrants and other processes described by the bill. These numerous official agents are made to constitute a sort of police, in addition to the military, and are authorized to summon a *posse comitatus*, and even to call to their aid such portion of the land and naval forces of the United States, or of the militia, "as may be necessary to the performance of the duty with which they are charged." This extraordinary power is to be conferred upon agents irresponsible to the government and to the people, to whose number the discretion of the commissioners is the only limit and in whose hands such authority might be made a terrible engine of wrong, oppression, and fraud.

The general statutes regulating the land and naval forces of the United States, the militia, and the execution of the laws are believed to be adequate for every emergency which can occur in time of peace. If it should prove otherwise, Congress can at any time amend those laws in such manner as, while subserving the public welfare, not to jeopard the rights, interests, and liberties of the people.

The 7th Section provides that a fee of $10 shall be paid to each commissioner in every case brought before him, and a fee of $5 to his deputy or deputies "for each person he or they may arrest and take before any such commissioner," "with such other fees as may be deemed reasonable by such commissioner," "in general for performing such other duties as may be required in the premises." All these fees are to be "paid out of the Treasury of the United States," whether there is a conviction or not; but in case of conviction they are to be recoverable from the defendant. It seems to me that under the influence of such temptations bad men might convert any law, however beneficent, into an instrument of persecution and fraud.

By the 8th Section of the bill, the United States courts, which sit only in one place for white citizens, must migrate with the marshal and district attorney (and necessarily with the clerk, although he is not mentioned) to any part of the district upon the order of the President, and there hold a court, "for the purpose of the more speedy arrest and trial of persons charged with a violation of this act;" and there the judge and officers of the court must remain, upon the order of the President, "for the time therein designated."

The 9th Section authorizes the President, or such person as he may empower for that purpose, "to employ such part of the land or naval forces of the United States, or of the militia, as shall be necessary to prevent the violation and enforce the due execution of this act." This language seems to imply a permanent military force that is to be always at hand and whose only business is to be the enforcement of this measure over the vast region where it is intended to operate.

I do not propose to consider the policy of this bill. To me the details of the bill seem fraught with evil. The white race and the black race of the South have hitherto lived together under the relation of master and slave—capital owning labor. Now, suddenly, that relation is changed, and, as to ownership, capital and labor are divorced. They stand now each master of itself. In this new relation, one being necessary to the other, there will be a new adjustment, which both are deeply interested in making harmonious. Each has equal power in settling the terms, and, if left to the laws that regulate capital and labor, it is confidently believed that they will satisfactorily work out the problem. Capital, it is true, has more intelligence, but labor is never so ignorant as not to understand its own interests, not to know its own value, and not to see that capital must pay that value.

This bill frustrates this adjustment. It intervenes between capital and labor and attempts to settle questions of political economy through the agency of numerous officials whose interest it will be to foment discord between the two races; for, as the breach widens, their employment will continue, and when it is closed their occupation will terminate.

In all our history, in all our experience as a people living under federal and state law, no such system as that contemplated by the details of this bill has ever before been proposed or adopted. They establish for the security of the colored race safeguards which go infinitely beyond any that the general government has ever provided for the white race. In fact, the distinction of race and color is by the bill made to operate in favor of the colored and against the white race. They interfere with the municipal legislation of the states, with the relations existing exclusively between a state and its citizens, or between inhabitants of the same state—an absorption and assumption of power by the general government which, if acquiesced in, must sap and destroy our federative system of limited powers and break down the barriers which preserve the rights of the states.

It is another step, or rather stride, toward centralization and the concentration of all legislative powers in the national government. The tendency of the bill must be to resuscitate the spirit of rebellion and to arrest the progress of those influences which are more closely drawing around the states the bonds of union and peace.

My lamented predecessor, in his proclamation of the 1st of January, 1863, ordered and declared that all persons held as slaves within certain states and parts of states therein designated were and thenceforward should be free; and further, that the executive government of the United States, including the military and naval authorities thereof, would recognize and maintain the freedom of such persons. This guarantee has been rendered especially obligatory and sacred by the amendment of the Constitution abolishing slavery throughout the United States. I, therefore, fully recognize the obligation to protect and defend that class of our people whenever and wherever it shall become necessary, and to the full extent compatible with the Constitution of the United States.

Entertaining these sentiments, it only remains for me to say that I will cheerfully cooperate with

Congress in any measure that may be necessary for the protection of the civil rights of the freedmen, as well as those of all other classes of persons throughout the United States, by judicial process, under equal and impartial laws, in conformity with the provisions of the federal Constitution.

I now return the bill to the Senate, and regret that in considering the bills and joint resolutions—forty-two in number—which have been thus far submitted for my approval, I am compelled to withhold my assent from a second measure that has received the sanction of both houses of Congress.

Lyman Trumbull

Speech to the United States Senate (1866)

Mr. President, I fully share with the President of the United States the regret expressed that he was unable to sign the bill "to protect all persons in the United States in their civil rights and secure the means of their vindication." I regret it on my own account because the just expectations raised when this bill was presented to the President before its introduction into the Senate have been disappointed. I regret it on the President's account because it is calculated to alienate him from those who elevated him to power and would gladly have rallied around his administration to sustain him in the principles upon which he was elected. But above all, sir, I regret it for liberty's sake, to secure which to ourselves and our posterity this government was founded. Yet, if the bill is unconstitutional or unjust to the whole people, I would not have had the President approve it. [. . .]

Gladly would I refrain from speaking of the spirit of this message, of the dangerous doctrines it promulgates, of the inconsistencies and contradictions of its author, of his encroachments upon the constitutional rights of Congress, of his assumption of unwarranted powers, which, if persevered in and not checked by the people, must eventually lead to a subversion of the government and the destruction of liberty.

Congress, in the passage of the bill under consideration, sought no controversy with the President. So far from it, the bill was proposed with a view to carry out what were supposed to be the views of the President and was submitted to him before its introduction into the Senate. I am not about to relate private declarations of the President; but it is right that the American people should know that the controversy which exists between him and Congress in reference to this measure is of his own seeking. Soon after Congress met it became apparent that there was a difference of opinion between the President and some members of Congress in regard to the condition of the rebellious states and the rights to be secured to freedmen.

The President in his annual message had denied the constitutional power of the general government to extend the elective franchise to Negroes, but he was equally decided in the assertion of the right of every man to life, liberty, and the pursuit of happiness.

This was his language:

> But while I have no doubt that now, after the close of the war, it is not competent for the general government to extend the elective franchise in the several states, it is equally clear that good faith requires the security of the freedmen in their liberty and their property.

There were some members of Congress who expressed the opinion that in the reorganization of the rebellious states the right of suffrage should be extended to the colored man, though this was not the prevailing sentiment of Congress. All were anxious for reorganization of the rebellious states and their admission to full participation in the federal government as soon as these relations could be restored with safety to all concerned. Feeling the importance of harmonious action between the different departments of the government and an anxious desire to sustain the President, for whom I had always entertained the highest respect, I had frequent interviews with him during the early part of the session.

Without mentioning anything said by him, I may with propriety state that, acting from the considerations I have stated and believing that the passage of a law by Congress, securing equality in civil rights when denied by state authorities to freedmen and all other inhabitants of the United States, would do much to relieve anxiety in the North, to induce the Southern states to secure these rights by their own action, and thereby remove many of the obstacles to an early reconstruction, I prepared the bill substantially as it is now returned with the President's objections. After the bill was introduced and printed, a copy was furnished him; and, at a subsequent period, when it was reported that he was hesitating about signing the Freedmen's Bureau Bill, he was informed of the condition of the Civil Rights Bill then pending in the House, and a hope expressed that if he had objections to any of its provisions he would make them known to its friends that they might be remedied, if not destructive of the measure; that there was believed to be no disposition on the part of Congress, and certainly none on my part, to have bills presented to him which he could not approve.

He never indicated to me, nor, so far as I know, to any of its friends, the least objection to any of the provisions of the bill till after its passage. And how could he, consistently with himself? The bill was framed, as was supposed, in entire harmony with his views, and certainly in harmony with what he was then and has since been doing in protecting freedmen in their civil rights all through the rebellious states. It was strictly limited to the protection of the civil rights belonging to every freeman, the birthright of every American citizen, and carefully avoided conferring or interfering with political rights or privileges of any kind.

The bill neither confers nor abridges the rights of anyone but simply declares that in civil rights there shall be an equality among all classes of citizens and that all alike shall be subject to the same punishment. Each state, so that it does not abridge the great fundamental rights belonging, under the Constitution, to all citizens, may grant or withhold such civil rights as it pleases; all that is required is that, in this respect, its laws shall be impartial.

And yet this is the bill now returned with the President's objections; and such objections! What are they? That:

> In all our history, in all our experience as a people, living under federal and state laws, no such system as that contemplated by the details of this bill has ever before been proposed or adopted. . . .

He says "the tendency of this bill must be to resuscitate the spirit of the rebellion." What assumption in one who denies the authority to punish those who violate United States laws under color of sure authority—a doctrine from which the rebellion sprung and in entire harmony with the declaration of Mr. Buchanan, that there was no power to coerce a state. But, sir, out of the mouth of Senator Andrew Johnson I will prove that President Andrew Johnson has violated the spirit of the Constitution, if not its letter, in vetoing this bill. It will be remembered that the bill passed both houses of Congress by more than a two thirds majority—the vote in the Senate being, yeas 33 to nays 12, and, in the House, yeas 111, nays 38. I will read from the remarks of Senator Andrew Johnson on the veto of the Homestead Bill by Mr. Buchanan:

> The President of the United States *presumes*—yes, sir, I say *presumes*—to dictate to the American people and to the two houses of Congress, in violation of the spirit, if not the letter, of the Constitution, that this measure shall not become a law. Why do I say this? I ask, is there any difference in the spirit of the Constitution whether a measure is sanctioned by a two-thirds vote before its passage or afterward? When a measure has been vetoed by the President, the Constitution requires that it shall be reconsidered and passed by a two-thirds vote in order to become a law. But here, in the teeth of the Executive, there was a two-thirds vote in favor of this bill. The vote was 36 to 2 in this body. The two houses have said that this bill is constitutional and right. In the other house, reflecting the popular sentiment of the nation, the vote was 112 to 51—ten more than the

> two-thirds majority which the Constitution requires; and when there is a two-thirds vote for a measure, I say it is against the spirit of the Constitution for the Executive to say, "No, you shall not have this measure; I will take all the chances of vetoing it."

Apply this language to the facts connected with this bill and then say who has violated the spirit of the Constitution.

This bill in no manner interferes with the municipal regulations of any state which protects all alike in their rights of person and property. It could have no operation, in Massachusetts, New York, Illinois, or most of the states of the union. How preposterous, then, to charge that unless some state, can have and exercise the right to punish somebody or to deny somebody a civil right on account of his color, its rights as a state as I am sure will be destroyed. It is manifest that, unless this bill can be passed, nothing can be done to protect the freedmen in their liberty and their rights.

Whatever may have been the opinion of the President at one time as to "good faith, requiring the security of the freedmen, their liberty and their property," it is now manifest from the character of his objections to this bill that he will approve no measure that will accomplish the object. That the second clause of the constitutional amendment gives this power, there can be no question. Some have contended that it gives the power even to confer the right of suffrage. I have not thought so, because I have never thought suffrage any more necessary to the liberty of a freedman than of a non-voting white, whether child or female. But his liberty under the Constitution he is entitled to, and whatever is necessary to secure it to him he is entitled to have, be it the ballot or the bayonet. If the bill now before us, and which goes no further than to secure civil rights to the freedman, cannot be passed, then the constitutional amendment proclaiming freedom to all the inhabitants of the land is a cheat and a delusion.

Civil Rights Act of 1866 (April 6, 1866)

An Act to protect all Persons in the United States in their Civil Rights, and furnish the Means of their Vindication.

Be it enacted by the Senate and House of Representatives of the United States of America in Congress assembled, That all persons born in the United States and not subject to any foreign power, excluding Indians not taxed, are hereby declared to be citizens of the United States; and such citizens, of every race and color, without regard to any previous condition of slavery or involuntary servitude, except as a punishment for crime whereof the party shall have been duly convicted, shall have the same right, in every State and Territory in the United States, to make and enforce contracts, to sue, be parties, and give evidence, to inherit, purchase, lease, sell, hold, and convey real and personal property, and to full and equal benefit of all laws and proceedings for the security of person and property, as is enjoyed by white citizens, and shall be subject to like punishment, pains, and penalties, and to none other, any law, statute, ordinance, regulation, or custom, to the contrary notwithstanding.

Sec. 2. And be it further enacted, That any person who, under color of any law, statute, ordinance, regulation, or custom, shall subject, or cause to be subjected, any inhabitant of any State or Territory to the deprivation of any right secured or protected by this act, or to different punishment, pains, or penalties on account of such person having at any time been held in a condition of slavery or involuntary servitude, except as a punishment for crime whereof the party shall have been duly convicted, or by reason of his color or race, than is prescribed for the punishment of white persons, shall be deemed guilty of a misdemeanor, and, on conviction, shall be punished by fine not exceeding one thousand dollars, or imprisonment not exceeding one year, or both, in the discretion of the court.

Sec. 3. And be it further enacted, That the district courts of the United States, within their respective districts, shall have, exclusively of the courts of the several States, cognizance of all crimes and offences committed against the provisions of this act, and also, concurrently with the circuit courts of the United States, of all causes, civil and criminal, affecting persons who are denied or cannot enforce in the courts or judicial tribunals of the State or locality where they may be any of the rights secured to them by the first section of this act; and if any suit or prosecution, civil or criminal, has been or shall be commenced in any State court, against any such person, for any cause whatsoever, or against any officer, civil or military, or other person, for any arrest or imprisonment, trespasses, or wrongs done or committed by virtue or under color of authority derived from this act or the act establishing a Bureau for the relief of Freedmen and Refugees, and all acts amendatory thereof, or for refusing to do any act upon the ground that it would be inconsistent with this act, such defendant shall have the right to remove such cause for trial to the proper district or circuit court in the manner prescribed by the "Act relating to habeas corpus and regulating judicial proceedings in certain cases," approved March three, eighteen hundred and sixty-three, and all act amendatory thereof. The jurisdiction in civil and criminal matters hereby conferred on the district and circuit courts of the United States shall be exercised and enforced in conformity with the laws of the United States, so far as such laws are suitable to carry the same into effect; but in all cases where such laws are not adapted to the object, or are deficient in the provisions necessary to furnish suitable remedies and punish offences against law, the common law, as modified and changed by the constitution and statutes of the State wherein the court having jurisdiction of the cause, civil or criminal, is held, so far as the same is not inconsistent with the Constitution and laws of the United States, shall be extended to and govern said courts in the trial and disposition of such cause, and, if of a criminal nature, in the infliction of punishment on the party found guilty.

Sec. 4. And be it further enacted, That the district attorneys, marshals, and deputy marshals of the United States, the commissioners appointed by the circuit and territorial courts of the United States, with powers of arresting, imprisoning, or bailing offenders against the laws of the United States, the officers and agents of the Freedmen's Bureau, and every other officer who may be specially empowered by the President of the United States, shall be, and they are hereby, specially authorized and required, at the expense of the United States, to institute proceedings against all and every person who shall violate the provisions of this act, and cause him or them to be arrested and imprisoned, or bailed, as the case may be, for trial before such court of the United States or territorial court as by this act has cognizance of the offence. And with a view to affording reasonable protection to all persons in their constitutional rights of equality before the law, without distinction of race or color, or previous condition of slavery or involuntary servitude, except as a punishment for crime, whereof the party shall have been duly convicted, and to the prompt discharge of the duties of this act, it shall be the duty of the circuit courts of the United States and the superior courts of the Territories of the United States, from time to time, to increase the number of commissioners, so as to afford a speedy and convenient means for the arrest and examination of persons charged with a violation of this act; and such commissioners are hereby authorized and required to exercise and discharge all the powers and duties conferred on them by this act, and the same duties with regard to offences created by this act, as they are authorized by law to exercise with regard to other offences against the laws of the United States.

Sec. 5. And be it further enacted, That it shall be the duty of all marshals and deputy marshals to obey and execute all warrants and precepts issued under the provisions of this act, when to them directed; and should any marshal or deputy marshal refuse to receive such warrant or other process when tendered, or to sue all proper means diligently to execute the same, he shall, on conviction thereof, be fined in the sum of one thousand dollars, to the use of the person upon whom the accused is alleged to have committed the offence. And the better to enable the said commissioners to execute their duties faithfully and efficiently, in conformity with the Constitution of the United States and the requirements of this act, they are hereby authorized and empowered, within their counties respectively, to appoint, in writing, under their hands, any one or more suitable persons, from time to time, to execute all such warrants and other process as may be issued by them in the lawful performance of their respective duties; and the persons so appointed to execute any warrant or process as aforesaid shall have authority to summon and call to their aid the bystanders or posse comitatus of the proper county, or such portion of the land or naval forces of the United States, or of the militia, as may be necessary to the performance of the duty with which they are charged, and to insure a faithful observance of the clause of the Constitution which prohibits slavery, in conformity with the provisions of this act; and said warrants shall run and be executed by said officers anywhere in the State or Territory within which they are issued.

Sec. 6. And be it further enacted, That any person who shall knowingly and wilfully obstruct, hinder, or prevent any officer, or other person charged with the execution of any warrant or process issued under the provisions of this act, or any person or persons lawfully assisting him or them, from arresting any person for whose apprehension such warrant or process may have been issued, or shall rescue or attempt to rescue such person from the custody of the officer, other person or persons, or those lawfully assisting as aforesaid, when so arrested pursuant to the authority herein given and declared, or shall aid, abet, or assist any person so arrested as aforesaid, directly or indirectly, to escape from the custody of the officer or other person legally authorized as aforesaid, or shall harbor or conceal any person for whose arrest a warrant or process shall have been issued as aforesaid, so as to prevent his discovery and arrest after notice or knowledge of the fact that a warrant has been issued for the apprehension of such personel, shall, for either of said offences, be subject to a fine not exceeding one thousand dollars, and imprisonment not exceeding six months, by indictment and conviction before the district court of the United States for the district in which said offence may have been committed, or before the proper court of criminal jurisdiction, if committed within any one of the organized Territories of the United States.

Sec. 7. And be it further enacted, That the district attorneys, the marshals, their deputies, and the clerks of the said district and territorial courts shall be paid for their services the like fees as may be allowed to them for similar services in other cases; and in all cases where the proceedings are before a commissioner, he shall be entitled to a fee of ten dollars in full for his services in each case, inclusive of all services incident to such arrest and examination. The person or persons authorized to execute the process to be issued by such commissioners for the arrest of offenders against the provisions of this act shall be entitled to a fee of five dollars for each person he or they may arrest and take before any such commissioner as aforesaid, with such other fees as may be deemed reasonable by such commissioner for such other additional services as may be necessarily performed by him or them, such as attending at the examination, keeping the prisoner in custody, and providing him with food and lodging during his detention, and until the final determination of such commissioner, and in general for performing such other duties as may be required in the premises; such fees to be made up in conformity with the fees usually charged by the officers of the courts of justice within the proper district or county, as near as may be practicable, and paid out of the Treasury of the United States on the certificate of the judge of the district within which the arrest is made, and to be recoverable from the defendant as part of the judgment in case of conviction.

Sec. 8. And be it further enacted, That whenever the President of the United States shall have reason to believe that offences have been or are likely to be committed against the provisions of this act within any judicial district, it shall be lawful for him, in his discretion, to direct the judge, marshal, and district attorney of such district to attend at such place within the district, and for such time as he may designate, for the purpose of the more speedy arrest and trial of persons charged with a violation of this act; and it shall be the duty of every judge or other officer, when any such requisition shall be received by him, to attend at the place and for the time therein designated.

Sec. 9. And be it further enacted, That it shall be lawful for the President of the United States, or such person as he may empower for that purpose, to employ such part of the land or naval forces of the United States, or of the militia, as shall be necessary to prevent the violation and enforce the due execution of this act.

Sec. 10. And be it further enacted, That upon all questions of law arising in any cause under the provisions of this act a final appeal may be taken to the Supreme Court of the United States.

SCHUYLER COLFAX,
Speaker of the House of Representatives.

LAFAYETTE S. FOSTER,
President of the Senate, pro tempore.

In the Senate of the United States, April 6, 1866.

The President of the United States having returned to the Senate, in which it originated, the bill entitled "An act to protect all persons in the United States in their civil rights, and furnish the means of their vindication," with his objections thereto, the Senate proceeded, in pursuance of the Constitution, to reconsider the same; and,

Resolved, That the said bill do pass, two-thirds of the Senate agreeing to pass the same.

Attest: J. W. Forney, Secretary of the Senate

In the House of Representatives U.S. April 9th, 1866.

The House of Representatives having proceeded, in pursuance of the Constitution, to reconsider the bill entitled "An act to protect all persons in the United States in their civil rights, and furnish the means of their vindication," returned to the Senate by the President of the United States, with his objections, and sent by the Senate to the House of Representatives, with the message of the President returning the bill:

Resolved, That the bill do pass, two-thirds of the House of Representatives agreeing to pass the same.

Attest: Edward McPherson, Clerk,
by, Clinton Lloyd, Chief Clerk.

ALEXANDER STEPHENS

Testimony before the Joint Congressional Committee on Reconstruction (1866)

Question: If the proposition were to extend [the] right of suffrage to those who could read and to those who had served in the Union armies, would that modification affect the action of the state?

Answer: I think the people of the state would be unwilling to do more than they have done for restoration. Restricted or limited suffrage would not be so objectionable as general or universal. But it is a matter that belongs to the state to regulate. The question of suffrage, whether universal or restricted, is one of state policy exclusively, as they believe. Individually, I should not be opposed to a proper system of restricted or limited suffrage to this class of our population. But, in my judgment, it is a matter that belongs of constitutional right to the states to regulate respectively each for itself. [. . .]

The only view in their opinion that could possibly justify the war which was carried on by the federal government against them was the idea of the indissolubleness of the Union; that those who held the administration for the time were bound to enforce the execution of the laws and the maintenance of the integrity of the country under the Constitution. And since that was accomplished, since those who had assumed the contrary principle—the right of secession and the reserved sovereignty of the states—had abandoned their cause, and the administration here was successful in maintaining the idea upon which war was proclaimed and waged, and the only view in which they supposed it could be justified at all—when that was accomplished, I say, the people of Georgia supposed their state was immediately entitled to all her rights under the Constitution. That is my opinion of the sentiment of the people of Georgia, and I do not think they would be willing to do anything further as a condition precedent to their being permitted to enjoy the full measure of their constitutional rights.

I only give my opinion of the sentiment of the people at this time. They expected as soon as the Confederate cause was abandoned that immediately the states would be brought back into their practical relations with the government as previously constituted. That is what they looked to. They expected that the states would immediately have their representatives in the Senate and in the House; and they expected, in good faith, as loyal men, as the term is frequently used—loyal to law, order, and the Constitution—to support the government under the Constitution. That was their feeling. They did what they did believing it was best for the protection of constitutional liberty.

Toward the Constitution of the United States the great mass of our people were always as much devoted in their feelings as any people ever were toward any laws or people. This is my opinion. As I remarked before, they resorted to secession with a view of more securely maintaining these principles. And when they found they were not successful in their object in perfect good faith, as far as I can judge from meeting with them and conversing with them, looking to the future development of their country in its material resources as well as its moral and intellectual progress, their earnest desire and expectation was to allow the past struggle, lamentable as it was in its results, to pass by and to cooperate with the true friends of the Constitution, with those of all sections who earnestly desire the preservation of constitutional liberty and the perpetuation of the government in its purity.

They have been a little disappointed in this, and are so now. They are patiently waiting, however, and believing that when the passions of the hour have passed away, this delay in representation will cease. They think they have done everything that was essential and proper, and my judgment is that they would not be willing to do anything further as a condition precedent. They would simply remain quiet and passive.

Question: Does your own judgment approve the view you have given as the opinion of the people of the state?

Answer: My own judgment is very decided that the question of suffrage is one that belongs, under the Constitution, and wisely so too, to the states, respectively and exclusively.

Question: Is it your opinion that neither of the alternatives suggested in the question ought to be accepted by the people of Georgia?

Answer: My own opinion is that these terms ought not to be offered as conditions precedent. In other words, my opinion is that it would be best for the peace, harmony, and prosperity of the whole country that there should be an immediate restoration, an immediate bringing back of the states into their original practical relations; and let all these questions then be discussed in common council. Then the representatives from the South could be heard, and you and all could judge much better of the tone and temper of the people than you could from the opinions given by any individuals.

You may take my opinion, or the opinions of any individual, but they will not enable you to judge of the condition of the state of Georgia so well as for her own representatives to be heard in your public councils on her own behalf. My judgment, therefore, is very decided that it would have been better, as soon as the lamentable conflict was over, when the people of the South abandoned their cause and agreed to accept the issue, desiring as they do to resume their places for the future of the Union, and to look to the arena of reason and justice for the protection of their rights of the Union—it would have been better to have allowed that result to take place, to follow under the policy adopted by the administration, than to delay it or hinder it by propositions to amend the Constitution in respect to suffrage or any other new matter.

I think the people of all the Southern states would in the halls of Congress discuss these questions calmly and deliberately, and if they did not show that the views they entertained were just and proper, such as to control the judgement of the people of the other sections and states, they would quietly, philosophically, and patriotically yield to whatever should be constitutionally determined in common council. But I think they feel very sensitively the offer to them of propositions to accept while they are denied all voice in the common council of the Union, under the Constitution, in the discussion of these propositions. I think they feel very sensitively that they are denied the right to be heard. And while, as I have said, they might differ among themselves in many points in regard to suffrage, they would not differ upon the question of doing anything further as a condition precedent to restoration. And in respect to the alternate conditions to be so presented, I do not think they would accept the one or the other.

My individual general views as to the proper course to be pursued in respect to the colored people are expressed in a speech made before the Georgia legislature, referred to in my letter to Senator Stewart. This was the proper forum, as I conceive, to address them, and my utmost exertions shall be, if I live, to carry out those views. But I think a great deal depends in the advancement of civilization and progress, that these questions should be considered and kept before the proper forum.

Question: Suppose the states that are represented in Congress, and Congress itself, should be of the opinion that Georgia should not be permitted to take its place in the government of the country except upon its assent to one or the other of the two propositions suggested. Is it, then your opinion that, under such circumstances, Georgia ought to decline?

Witness: You mean the states now represented, and those only?

Mr. Boutwell: Yes.

Witness: You mean by Congress, Congress as it is now constituted, with the other eleven states excluded?

Mr. Boutwell: I do.

Witness: And you mean the same alternative propositions to be applied to all the eleven states as conditions precedent to their restoration?

Mr. Boutwell: I do.

Answer: I think she ought to decline under the circumstances and for the reasons stated, and so ought the whole eleven. Should such an offer be made and declined, and those states, should they be kept out, a singular spectacle would be presented—a complete reversal of positions would be presented. In 1861 these states thought they could not remain safely in the Union without new guarantees; and now, when they agree to resume their former practical relations in the Union, under the Constitution, the other states turn upon them and say they cannot permit them to do so safely to their interests without new constitutional guarantees. The Southen states would thus present themselves as willing for immediate union, under the Constitution, while it would be the Northern states opposed to it. The former disunionists would thereby become the unionists, and the former unionists the practical disunionists.

REPORT OF THE JOINT COMMITTEE ON RECONSTRUCTION (1866)

When Congress assembled in December last, the people of most of the states lately in rebellion had, under the advice of the President, organized local governments, and some of them had acceded to the terms proposed by him. In his annual message he stated, in general terms, what had been done, but he did not see fit to communicate the details for the information of Congress. While in this and in a subsequent message the President urged the speedy restoration of these states, and expressed the opinion that their condition was such as to justify their restoration, yet it is quite obvious that Congress must either have acted blindly on that opinion of the President, or proceeded to obtain the information requisite for intelligent action on the subject. The impropriety of proceeding wholly on the judgment of any one man, however exalted his station, in a matter involving the welfare of the republic in all future time, or of adopting any plan, coming from any source, without fully understanding all its bearings and comprehending its full effect, was apparent.

The first step, therefore, was to obtain the required information. A call was accordingly made on the President for the information in his possession as to what had been done, in order that Congress might judge for itself as to the grounds of the belief expressed by him in the fitness of states recently in rebellion to participate fully in the conduct of national affairs. This information was not immediately communicated. When the response was finally made, some six weeks after your committee had been in actual session, it was found that the evidence upon which the President seemed to have based his suggestions was incomplete and unsatisfactory. Authenticated copies of the new constitutions and ordinances adopted by the conventions in three of the states had been submitted, extracts from newspapers furnished scanty information as to the action of one other state, and nothing appears to have been communicated as to the remainder. There was no evidence of the loyalty of those who had participated in these conventions, and in one state alone was any proposition made to submit the action of the conventions to the final judgment of the people. [. . .]

The evidence of an intense hostility to the federal Union, and an equally intense love of the late Confederacy, nurtured by the war, is decisive. While it appears that nearly all are willing to submit, at least for the time being, to the federal authority, it is equally clear that the ruling motive is a desire to obtain the advantages which will be derived from a representation in Congress. Officers of the Union Army, on duty, and Northern men who go South to engage in business, are generally detested and proscribed. Southern men who adhered to the Union are bitterly hated and relentlessly persecuted. In some localities prosecutions have been instituted in state courts against Union officers for acts done in the line of official duty, and similar prosecutions are threatened elsewhere as soon as the United States troops are removed. All such demonstrations show a state of feeling against which it is unmistakably necessary to guard.

The testimony is conclusive that after the collapse of the Confederacy the feeling of the people of the rebellious states was that of abject submission. Having appealed to the tribunal of arms, they had no hope except that, by the magnanimity of their conquerors, their lives, and possibly their property, might be preserved. Unfortunately, the general issue of pardons to persons who had been prominent in the Rebellion, and the feeling of kindliness and conciliation manifested by the executive, and very generally indicated through the Northern press, had the effect to render whole communities forgetful of the crime they had committed, defiant toward the federal government, and regardless of their duties as citizens.

The conciliatory measures of the government do not seem to have been met even halfway. The bitterness and defiance exhibited toward the United States under such circumstances is without a parallel in the history of the world. In return for our leniency we receive only an insulting denial of our authority. In return for our kind desire for the resumption of fraternal relations we receive only an insolent assumption of rights and privileges long since forfeited. The crime we have punished is paraded as a virtue, and the principles of republican government which we have vindicated at so terrible a cost are denounced as unjust and oppressive.

If we add to this evidence the fact that, although peace has been declared by the President, he has not, to this day, deemed it safe to restore the writ of habeas corpus, to relieve the insurrectionary states of martial law, nor to withdraw the troops from many localities, and that the commanding general deems an increase of the army indispensable to the preservation of order and the protection of loyal and well-disposed people in the South, the proof of a condition of feeling hostile to the Union and dangerous to the government throughout the insurrectionary states would seem to be overwhelming.

With such evidence before them, it is the opinion of your committee:

1. That the states lately in rebellion were, at the close of the war, disorganized communities, without civil government, and without constitutions or other forms, by virtue of which political relations could legally exist between them and the federal government.

2. That Congress cannot be expected to recognize as valid the election of representatives from disorganized communities, which, from the very nature of the

case, were unable to present their claim to representation under those established and recognized rules, the observance of which has been hitherto required.

3. That Congress would not be justified in admitting such communities to a participation in the government of the country without first providing such constitutional or other guarantees as will tend to secure the civil rights of all citizens of the republic; a just equality of representation; protection against claims founded in rebellion and crime; a temporary restoration of the right of suffrage to those who have not actively participated in the efforts to destroy the Union and overthrow the government, and the exclusion from positions of public trust of, at least, a portion of those whose crimes have proved them to be enemies to the Union and unworthy of public confidence.

Your committee will, perhaps, hardly be deemed excusable for extending this report further; but inasmuch as immediate and unconditional representation of the states lately in rebellion is demanded as a matter of right, and delay and even hesitation is denounced as grossly oppressive and unjust, as well as unwise and impolitic, it may not be amiss again to call attention to a few undisputed and notorious facts, and the principles of public law applicable thereto, in order that the propriety of that claim may be fully considered and well understood.

The state of Tennessee occupies a position distinct from all the other insurrectionary states, and has been the subject of a separate report, which your committee have not thought it expedient to disturb. Whether Congress shall see fit to make that state the subject of separate action, or to include it in the same category with all others so far as concerns the imposition of preliminary conditions, it is not within the province of this committee either to determine or advise.

To ascertain whether any of the so-called Confederate States "are entitled to be represented in either house of Congress," the essential inquiry is, whether there is, in any one of them, a constituency qualified to be represented in Congress. The question how far persons claiming seats in either house possess the credentials necessary to enable them to represent a duly qualified constituency is one for the consideration of each house separately, after the preliminary question shall have been finally determined.

We now propose to restate, as briefly as possible, the general facts and principles applicable to all the states recently in rebellion:

First. The seats of the senators and representatives from the so-called Confederate States became vacant in the year 1861, during the second session of the Thirty-sixth Congress, by the voluntary withdrawal of their incumbents, with the sanction and by direction of the legislatures or conventions of their respective states. This was done as a hostile act against the Constitution and government of the United States, with a declared intent to overthrow the same by forming a Southern confederation. This act of declared hostility was speedily followed by an organization of the same states into a Confederacy, which levied and waged war, by sea and land, against the United States.

This war continued more than four years, within which period the Rebel armies besieged the national capital, invaded the loyal states, burned their towns and cities, robbed their citizens, destroyed more than 250,000 loyal soldiers, and imposed an increased national burden of not less than $3,500 million, of which $700 million or $800 million have already been met and paid. From the time these confederated states thus withdrew their representation in Congress and levied war against the United States, the great mass of their people became and were insurgents, rebels, traitors, and all of them assumed and occupied the political, legal, and practical relation of enemies of the United States. This position is established by acts of Congress and judicial decisions, and is recognized repeatedly by the President in public proclamations, documents, and speeches.

Second. The states thus confederated prosecuted their war against the United States to final arbitrament, and did not cease until all their armies were captured, their military power destroyed, their civil officers, state and confederate, taken prisoners or put to flight, every vestige of state and confederate government obliterated, their territory overrun and occupied by the federal armies, and their people reduced to the condition of enemies conquered in war, entitled only by public law to such rights, privileges, and conditions as might be vouchsafed by the conqueror. This position is also established by judicial decisions, and is recognized by the President in public proclamations, documents, and speeches.

Third. Having voluntarily deprived themselves of representation in Congress for the show that they are qualified to resume federal relations. In order to do this, they must prove that they have established, with the consent of the people, republican forms of government in harmony with the Constitution and laws of the United States, that all hostile purposes have ceased, and should give adequate guarantees against future treason and rebellion—guarantees which shall prove satisfactory to the government against which they rebelled, and by whose arms they were subdued.

Fourth. Having, by this treasonable withdrawal from Congress, and by flagrant rebellion and war, forfeited all civil and political rights and privileges under the Federal Constitution, they can only be restored thereto by the permission and authority of that constitutional power against which they rebelled and by which they were subdued.

Fifth. These rebellious enemies were conquered by the people of the United States, acting through all the coordinate branches of the government, and not by the Executive Department alone. The powers of conqueror are not so vested in the President that he can fix and regulate the terms of settlement and confer congressional representation on conquered rebels and traitors. Nor can he, in any way, qualify enemies of the government to exercise its lawmaking power. The authority to restore rebels to political power in the federal government can be exercised only with the concurrence of all the departments in which political power is vested; and hence the several proclamations of the President to the people of the Confederate States cannot be considered as extending beyond the purposes declared, and can only be regarded as provisional permission by the commander in chief of the army to do certain acts, the effect and validity whereof is to be determined by the constitutional government, and not solely by the executive power.

Sixth. The question before Congress is, then, whether conquered enemies have the right, and shall be permitted at their own pleasure and on their own terms, to participate in making laws for their conquerors; whether conquered Rebels may change their theater of operations from the battlefield, where they were defeated and overthrown, to the halls of Congress, and, through their representatives, seize upon the government which they fought to destroy; whether the national Treasury, the Army of the nation, its Navy, its forts and arsenals, its whole civil administration, its credit, its pensioners, the widows and orphans of those who perished in the war, the public honor, peace and safety, shall all be turned over to the keeping of its recent enemies without delay, and without imposing such conditions as, in the opinion of Congress, the security of the country and its institutions may demand.

Seventh. The history of mankind exhibits no example of such madness and folly. The instinct of self-preservation protests against it. The surrender by Grant to Lee, and by Sherman to Johnston, would have been disasters of less magnitude, for new armies could have been raised, new battles fought, and the government saved. The anticoercive policy, which, under pretext of avoiding bloodshed, allowed the rebellion to take form and gather force, would be surpassed in infamy by the matchless wickedness that would now surrender the halls of Congress to those so recently in rebellion until proper precautions shall have been taken to secure the national faith and the national safety.

Eigth. As has been shown in this report, and in the evidence submitted, no proof has been afforded to Congress of a constituency in any one of the so-called Confederate states; unless we except the state of Tennessee, qualified to elect senators and representatives in Congress. No state constitution, or amendment to a state constitution, has had the sanction of the people. All the so-called legislation of state conventions and legislatures has been had under military dictation. If the President may, at his will, and under his own authority, whether as military commander or chief executive, qualify persons to appoint senators and elect representatives, and empower others to appoint and elect them, he thereby practically controls the organization of the Legislative Department. The constitutional form of government is thereby practically destroyed, and its powers absorbed in the executive. And while your committee do not for a moment impute to the President any such design, but cheerfully concede to him the most patriotic motives, they cannot but look with alarm upon a precedent so fraught with danger to the republic.

Ninth. The necessity of providing adequate safeguards for the future, before restoring the insurrectionary states to a participation in the direction of public affairs, in apparent form the bitter hostility to the govenment and people of the United States yet existing throughout the conquered territory, as proved incontestably by the testimony of many witnesses and by undisputed facts.

Tenth. The conclusion of your committee, therefore, is that the so-called Confederate States are not, at present, entitled to representation in the Congress of the United States; that, before allowing such representation, adequate security for future peace and safety should be required; that this can only be found in such changes of the organic law as shall determine the civil rights and privleges of all citizens in all parts of the republic, shall place representation on an equitable basis, shall fix a stigma upon treason, and protect the loyal people against future claims for the expenses incurred in support of rebellion and for manumitted slaves, together with an express grant of power in Congress to enforce those provisions. To this end they offer a joint resolution for amending the Constitution of the United States, and the two several bills designed to carry the same into effect, before reffered to.

Before closing this report, your committee beg leave to state that the specific recommendations submitted by them are the results of mutual concession, after a long and careful comparison of conflicting opinions. Upon a question of such magnitude, infinitely important as it is to the future of the republic, it was not to be expected that all should think alike. Sensible of the imperfections of the scheme, your committee submit it to Congress as the best they could agree upon, in the hope that its imperfections may be cured, and its deficiencies supplied, by legislative wisdom; and that, when finally adopted, it may tend to restore peace and harmony to the whole country, and to place our republican institutions on a more stable foundation.

DAVID DAVIS

Ex Parte Milligan (1866)

Mr. Justice DAVIS delivered the opinion of the Court.

On the 10th day of May, 1865, Lambdin P. Milligan presented a petition to the Circuit Court of the United States for the District of Indiana to be discharged from an alleged unlawful imprisonment. The case made by the petition is this: Milligan is a citizen of the United States; has lived for twenty years in Indiana, and, at the time of the grievances complained of, was not, and never had been, in the military or naval service of the United States. On the 5th day of October, 1864, while at home, he was arrested by order of General Alvin P. Hovey, commanding the military district of Indiana, and has ever since been kept in close confinement.

On the 21st day of October, 1864, he was brought before a military commission, convened at Indianapolis by order of General Hovey, tried on certain charges and specifications, found guilty, and sentenced to be hanged, and the sentence ordered to be executed on Friday, the 19th day of May, 1865.

On the 2d day of January, 1865, after the proceedings of the military commission were at an end, the Circuit Court of the United States for Indiana met at Indianapolis and empaneled a grand jury, who were charged to inquire whether the laws of the United States had been violated. and, if so, to make presentments. The court adjourned on the 27th day of January, having, prior thereto, discharged from further service the grand jury, who did not find any bill of indictment or make any presentment against Milligan for any offence whatever, and, in fact, since his imprisonment, no bill of indictment has been found or presentment made against him by any grand jury of the United States.

Milligan insists that said military commission had no jurisdiction to try him upon the charges preferred, or upon any charges whatever, because he was a citizen of the United States and the State of Indiana, and had not been, since the commencement of the late Rebellion, a resident of any of the States whose citizens were arrayed against the government, and that the right of trial by jury was guaranteed to him by the Constitution of the United States. [. . .]

The importance of the main question presented by this record cannot be overstated, for it involves the very framework of the government and the fundamental principles of American liberty. [. . .]

The controlling question in the case is this: upon *the facts* stated in Milligan's petition and the exhibits filed, had the military commission mentioned in it jurisdiction legally to try and sentence him? Milligan, not a resident of one of the rebellious states or a prisoner of war, but a citizen of Indiana for twenty years past and never in the military or naval service, is, while at his home, arrested by the military power of the United States, imprisoned, and, on certain criminal charges preferred against him, tried, convicted, and sentenced to be hanged by a military commission, organized under the direction of the military commander of the military district of Indiana. Had this tribunal the *legal* power and authority to try and punish this man?

No graver question was ever considered by this court, nor one which more nearly concerns the rights of the whole people, for it is the birthright of every American citizen when charged with crime to be tried and punished according to law. The power of punishment is alone through the means which the laws have provided for that purpose, and, if they are ineffectual, there is an immunity from punishment, no matter how great an offender the individual may be or how much his crimes may have shocked the sense of justice of the country or endangered its safety. By the protection of the law, human rights are secured; withdraw that protection and they are at the mercy of wicked rulers or the clamor of an excited people. If there was law to justify this military trial, it is not our province to interfere; if there was not, it is our duty to declare the nullity of the whole proceedings. The decision of this question does not depend on argument or judicial precedents, numerous and highly illustrative as they are. These precedents inform us of the extent of the struggle to preserve liberty and to relieve those in civil life from military trials. The founders of our government were familiar with the history of that struggle, and secured in a written constitution every right which the people had wrested from power during a contest of ages. By that Constitution and the laws authorized by it, this question must be determined. The provisions of that instrument on the administration of criminal justice are too plain and direct to leave room for misconstruction or doubt of their true meaning. Those applicable to this case are found in that clause of the original Constitution which says "That the trial of all crimes, except in case of impeachment, shall be by jury," and in the fourth, fifth, and sixth articles of the amendments. [. . .]

These securities for personal liberty thus embodied were such as wisdom and experience had demonstrated to be necessary for the protection of those accused of crime. And so strong was the sense of the country of their importance, and so jealous were the people that these rights, highly prized, might be denied them by implication, that, when the original Constitution was proposed for adoption, it encountered severe opposition, and, but for the belief that it would be so amended as to embrace them, it would never have been ratified.

Time has proven the discernment of our ancestors, for even these provisions, expressed in such plain English words that it would seem the ingenuity of man could not evade them, are now, after the lapse of more than seventy years, sought to be avoided. Those great and good men foresaw that troublous times would arise when rulers and people would become restive under restraint, and seek by sharp and decisive measures to accomplish ends deemed just and proper, and that the principles of constitutional liberty would be in peril unless established by irrepealable law. The history of the world had taught them that what was done in the past might be attempted in the future. The Constitution of the United States is a law for rulers and people, equally in war and in peace, and covers with the shield of its protection all classes of men, at all times and under all circumstances. No doctrine involving more pernicious consequences was ever invented by the wit of man than that any of its provisions can be suspended during any of the great exigencies of government. Such a doctrine leads directly to anarchy or despotism, but the theory of necessity on which it is based is false, for the government, within the Constitution, has all the powers granted to it which are necessary to preserve its existence, as has been happily proved by the result of the great effort to throw off its just authority.

Have any of the rights guaranteed by the Constitution been violated in the case of Milligan?, and, if so, what are they?

Every trial involves the exercise of judicial power, and from what source did the military commission that tried him derive their authority? Certainly no part of judicial power of the country was conferred on them, because the Constitution expressly vests it "in one supreme court and such inferior courts as the Congress may from time to time ordain and establish," and it is not pretended that the commission was a court ordained and established by Congress. They cannot justify on the mandate of the President, because he is controlled by law, and has his appropriate sphere of duty, which is to execute, not to make, the laws, and there is "no unwritten criminal code to which resort can be had as a source of jurisdiction."

But it is said that the jurisdiction is complete under the "laws and usages of war."

It can serve no useful purpose to inquire what those laws and usages are, whence they originated, where found, and on whom they operate; they can never be applied to citizens in states which have upheld the authority of the government, and where the courts are open and their process unobstructed. This court has judicial knowledge that, in Indiana, the Federal authority was always unopposed, and its courts always open to hear criminal accusations and redress grievances, and no usage of war could sanction a military trial there for any offence whatever of a citizen in civil life in nowise connected with the military service. Congress could grant no such power, and, to the honor of our national legislature be it said, it has never been provoked by the state of the country even to attempt its exercise. One of the plainest constitutional provisions was therefore infringed when Milligan was tried by a court not ordained and established by Congress and not composed of judges appointed during good behavior.

Why was he not delivered to the Circuit Court of Indiana to be proceeded against according to law? No reason of necessity could be urged against it, because Congress had declared penalties against the offences charged, provided for their punishment, and directed that court to hear and determine them. And soon after this military tribunal was ended, the Circuit Court met, peacefully transacted its business, and adjourned. It needed no bayonets to protect it, and required no military aid to execute its judgments. It was held in a state, eminently distinguished for patriotism, by judges commissioned during the Rebellion, who were provided with juries, upright, intelligent, and selected by a marshal appointed by the President. The government had no right to conclude that Milligan, if guilty, would not receive in that court merited punishment, for its records disclose that it was constantly engaged in the trial of similar offences, and was never interrupted in its administration of criminal justice. If it was dangerous, in the distracted condition of affairs, to leave Milligan unrestrained of his liberty because he "conspired against the government, afforded aid and comfort to rebels, and incited the people to insurrection," the law said arrest him, confine him closely, render him powerless to do further mischief, and then present his case to the grand jury of the district, with proofs of his guilt, and, if indicted, try him according to the course of the common law. If this had been done, the Constitution would have been vindicated, the law of 1863 enforced, and the securities for personal liberty preserved and defended.

Another guarantee of freedom was broken when Milligan was denied a trial by jury. The great minds of the country have differed on the correct interpretation to be given to various provisions of the Federal Constitution, and judicial decision has been often invoked to settle their true meaning; but, until recently, no one ever doubted that the right of trial by jury was fortified in the organic law against the power of attack. It is *now* assailed, but if ideas can be expressed in words and language has any meaning, *this right*—one of the most valuable in a free country—is preserved to everyone accused of crime who is not attached to the army or navy or militia in actual service. The Sixth Amendment affirms that, "in all criminal prosecutions, the accused shall enjoy the right to a speedy and public trial by an impartial jury," language broad enough to embrace all persons and cases; but the fifth, recognizing the necessity of an indictment or presentment before anyone can be held to answer for high crimes, "*except* cases arising in the land or naval forces, or in the militia, when in actual service, in time of war or public danger," and the framers of the Constitution doubtless meant to limit the right of trial by jury in the Sixth Amendment to those persons who were subject to indictment or presentment in the fifth.

The discipline necessary to the efficiency of the army and navy required other and swifter modes of trial than are furnished by the common law courts, and, in pursuance of the power conferred by the Constitution, Congress has declared the kinds of trial, and the manner in which they shall be conducted, for offences committed while the party is in the military or naval service. Everyone connected with these branches of the public service is amenable to the jurisdiction which Congress has created for their government, and, while thus serving, surrenders his right to be tried by the civil courts. *All other persons*, citizens of states where the courts are open, if charged with crime, are guaranteed the inestimable privilege of trial by jury. This privilege is a vital principle, underlying the whole administration of criminal justice; it is not held by sufferance, and cannot be frittered away on any plea of state or political necessity. When peace prevails, and the authority of the government is undisputed, there is no difficulty of preserving the safeguards of liberty, for the ordinary modes of trial are never neglected, and no one wishes it otherwise; but if society is disturbed by civil commotion—if the passions of men are aroused and the restraints of law weakened, if not disregarded—these safeguards need, and should receive, the watchful care of those intrusted with the guardianship of the Constitution and laws. In no other way can we transmit to posterity unimpaired the blessings of liberty, consecrated by the sacrifices of the Revolution.

It is claimed that martial law covers with its broad mantle the proceedings of this military commission. The proposition is this: that, in a time of war, the commander of an armed force (if, in his opinion, the exigencies of the country demand it, and of which he is to judge) has the power, within the lines of his military district, to suspend all civil rights and their remedies and subject citizens, as well as soldiers to the rule of *his will*, and, in the exercise of his lawful authority, cannot be restrained except by his superior officer or the President of the United States.

If this position is sound to the extent claimed, then, when war exists, foreign or domestic, and the country is subdivided into military departments for mere convenience, the commander of one of them can, if he chooses, within his limits, on the plea of necessity, with the approval of the Executive, substitute military force for and to the exclusion of the laws, and punish all persons as he thinks right and proper, without fixed or certain rules.

The statement of this proposition shows its importance, for, if true, republican government is a failure, and there is an end of liberty regulated by law. Martial law established on such a basis destroys every guarantee of the Constitution, and effectually renders the "military independent of and superior to the civil power"—the attempt to do which by the King of Great Britain was deemed by our fathers such an offence that they assigned it to the world as one of the causes which impelled them to declare their independence. Civil liberty and this kind of martial law cannot endure together; the antagonism is irreconcilable, and, in the conflict, one or the other must perish.

This nation, as experience has proved, cannot always remain at peace, and has no right to expect that it will always have wise and humane rulers sincerely attached to the principles of the Constitution. Wicked men, ambitious of power, with hatred of liberty and contempt of law, may fill the place once occupied by Washington and Lincoln, and if this right is conceded, and the calamities of war again befall us, the dangers to human liberty are frightful to contemplate. If our fathers had failed to provide for just such a contingency, they would have been false to the trust reposed in them. They knew—the history of the world told them—the nation they were founding, be its existence short or long, would be involved in war; how often or how long continued human foresight could not tell, and that unlimited power, wherever lodged at such a time, was especially hazardous to freemen. For this and other equally weighty reasons, they secured the inheritance they had fought to maintain by incorporating in a written constitution the safeguards which time had proved were essential to its preservation. Not one of these safeguards can the President or Congress or the Judiciary disturb, except the one concerning the writ of *habeas corpus*.

It is essential to the safety of every government that, in a great crisis like the one we have just passed through, there should be a power somewhere of suspending the writ of *habeas corpus*. In every war, there are men of previously good character wicked enough to counsel their fellow-citizens to resist the measures deemed necessary by a good government to sustain its just authority and overthrow its enemies, and their influence may lead to dangerous combinations. In the emergency of the times, an immediate public investigation according to law may not be possible, and yet the period to the country may be too imminent to suffer such persons to go at large. Unquestionably, there is then an exigency which demands that the government, if it should see fit in the exercise of a proper discretion to make arrests, should not be required to produce the persons arrested in answer to a writ of *habeas corpus*. The Constitution goes no further. It does not say, after a writ of *habeas corpus* is denied a citizen, that he shall be tried otherwise than by the course of the common law; if it had intended this result, it was easy, by the use of direct words, to have accomplished it. The illustrious men who framed that instrument were guarding the foundations of civil liberty against the abuses of unlimited power; they were full of wisdom, and the lessons of history informed them that a trial by an established court, assisted by an impartial jury, was the only sure way of protecting the citizen against oppression and wrong. Knowing this, they limited the suspension to one great right, and left the rest to remain forever inviolable. But it is insisted that the safety of the country in time of war demands that this broad claim for martial law shall be sustained. If this were true, it could be well said that a country, preserved at the sacrifice of all the cardinal principles of liberty, is not worth the cost of preservation. Happily, it is not so.

It will be borne in mind that this is not a question of the power to proclaim martial law when war exists in a community and the courts and civil authorities are overthrown. Nor is it a question what rule a military commander, at the head of his army, can impose on states in rebellion to cripple their resources and quell the insurrection. The jurisdiction claimed is much more extensive. The necessities of the service during the late Rebellion required that the loyal states should be placed within the limits of certain military districts and commanders appointed in them, and it is urged that this, in a military sense, constituted them the theater of military operations, and as, in this case, Indiana had been and was again threatened with invasion by the enemy, the occasion was furnished to establish martial law. The conclusion does not follow from the premises. If armies were collected in Indiana, they were to be employed in another locality, where the laws were obstructed and the national authority disputed. On her soil there was no hostile foot; if once invaded, that invasion was at an end, and, with it, all pretext for martial law. Martial law cannot arise from a *threatened* invasion. The necessity must be actual and present, the invasion real, such as effectually closes the courts and deposes the civil administration.

It is difficult to see how the *safety* for the country required martial law in Indiana. If any of her citizens were plotting treason, the power of arrest could secure them until the government was prepared for their trial, when the courts were open and ready to try them. It was as easy to protect witnesses before a civil as a military tribunal, and as there could be no wish to convict except on sufficient legal evidence, surely an ordained and establish court was better able to judge of this than a military tribunal composed of gentlemen not trained to the profession of the law.

It follows from what has been said on this subject that there are occasions when martial rule can be properly applied. If, in foreign invasion or civil war, the courts are actually closed, and it is impossible to administer criminal justice according to law, *then*, on the theatre of active military operations, where war really prevails, there is a necessity to furnish a substitute for the civil authority, thus overthrown, to preserve the safety of the army and society, and as no power is left but the military, it is allowed to govern by martial rule until the laws can have their free course. As necessity creates the rule, so it limits its duration, for, if this government is continued *after* the courts are reinstated, it is a gross usurpation of power. Martial rule can never exist where the courts are open and in the proper and unobstructed exercise of their jurisdiction. It is also confined to the locality of actual war. Because, during the late Rebellion, it could have been enforced in Virginia, where the national authority was overturned and the courts driven out, it does not follow that it should obtain in Indiana, where that authority was never disputed and justice was always administered. And so, in the case of a foreign invasion, martial rule may become a necessity in one state when, in another, it would be "mere lawless violence." [. . .]

If the military trial of Milligan was contrary to law, then he was entitled, on the facts stated in his petition, to be discharged from custody by the terms of the act of Congress of March 3d, 1863. [. . .]

First Reconstruction Act (1867)

An act to provide for the more efficient government of the Rebel states.

Whereas no legal state governments or adequate protection for life or property now exists in the Rebel states of Virginia, North Carolina, South Carolina, Georgia, Mississippi, Alabama, Louisiana, Florida, Texas, and Arkansas; and *whereas* it is necessary that peace and good order should be enforced in said states until loyal and republican state governments can be legally established; therefore,

Be it enacted by the Senate and House of Representatives of the United States of America in Congress assembled, that said Rebel states shall be divided into military districts and made subject to the military authority of the United States as hereinafter prescribed, and for that purpose Virginia shall constitute the first district; North Carolina and South Carolina the second district; Georgia, Alabama, and Florida the third district; Mississippi and Arkansas the fourth district; and Louisiana and Texas the fifth district.

Section 2. *And be it further enacted,* that it shall be the duty of the President to assign to the command of each of said districts an officer of the Army, not below the rank of brigadier general, and to detail a sufficient military force to enable such officer to perform his duties and enforce his authority within the district to which he is assigned.

Section 3. *And be it further enacted,* that it shall be the duty of each officer assigned as aforesaid to protect all persons in their rights of person and property, to suppress insurrection, disorder, and violence, and to punish or cause to be punished all disturbers of the public peace and criminals; and to this end he may allow local civil tribunals to take jurisdiction of and to try offenders, or, when in his judgment it may be necessary for the trial of offenders, he shall have power to organize military commissions or tribunals for that purpose, and all interference under color of state authority with the exercise of military authority under this act shall be null and void.

Section 4. *And be it further enacted,* that all persons put under military arrest by virtue of this act shall be tried without unnecessary delay, and no cruel or unusual punishment shall be inflicted, and no sentence of any military commission or tribunal hereby authorized affecting the life or liberty of any person shall be executed until it is approved by the officer in command of the district, and the laws and regulations for the government of the Army shall not be affected by this act, except insofar as they conflict with its provisions: *Provided,* that no sentence of death under the provisions of this act shall be carried into effect without the approval of the President.

Section 5. *And be it further enacted,* that when the people of any one of said Rebel states shall have formed a constitution of government in conformity with the Constitution of the United States in all respects, framed by a convention of delegates elected by the male citizens of said state, twenty-one years old and upward, of whatever race, color, or previous condition, who have been resident in said state for one year previous to the day of such election, except such as may be disfranchised for participation in the rebellion or for felony at common law, and when such constitution shall provide that the elective franchise shall be enjoyed by all such persons as have the qualifications herein stated for electors of delegates, and when such constitution shall be ratified by a majority of the persons voting on the question of ratification who are qualified as electors for delegates, and when such constitution shall have been submitted to Congress for examination and approval, and Congress shall have approved the same; and when said state, by a vote of its legislature elected under said constitution, shall have adopted the amendment to the Constitution of the United States, proposed by the Thirty-ninth Congress and known as Article Fourteen, and when said article shall have become a part of the Constitution of the United States, said state shall be declared entitled to representation in Congress, and senators and representatives shall be admitted therefrom on their taking the oath prescribed by law, and then and thereafter the preceding sections of this act shall be inoperative in said state: *Provided*, that no person excluded from the privilege of holding office by said proposed amendment to the Constitution of the United States shall be eligible to election as a member of the convention to frame a constitution for any of said Rebel states, nor shall any such person vote for members of such convention.

Section 6. *And be it further enacted*, that, until the people of said Rebel states shall be by law admitted to representation in the Congress of the United States, any civil governments which may exist therein shall be deemed provisional only, and in all respects subject to the paramount authority of the United States at any time to abolish, modify, control, or supersede the same; and in all elections to any office under such provisional governments all persons shall be entitled to vote, and none others, who are entitled to vote under the provisions of the 5th Section of this act; and no person shall be eligible to any office under any such provisional governments who would be disqualified from holding office under the provisions of the 3rd Article of said constitutional amendment.

Andrew Johnson

Veto of the First Reconstruction Act (1867)

To the House of Representatives:

I have examined the bill "to provide for the more efficient government of the Rebel states" with the care and anxiety which its transcendent importance is calculated to awaken. I am unable to give it my assent for reasons so grave that I hope a statement of them may have some influence on the minds of the patriotic and enlightened men with whom the decision must ultimately rest. [. . .]

All the information I have on the subject convinces me that the masses of the Southern people and those who control their public acts, while they entertain diverse opinions on questions of federal policy, are completely united in the effort to reorganize their society on the basis of peace and to restore their mutual prosperity as rapidly and as completely as their circumstances will permit.

The bill, however, would seem to show upon its face that the establishment of peace and good order is not its real object. The 5th Section declares that the preceding sections shall cease to operate in any state where certain events shall have happened. These events are, first, the selection of delegates to a state convention by an election at which Negroes shall be allowed to vote; second, the formation of a state constitution by the convention so chosen; third, the insertion into the state constitution of a provision which will secure the right of voting at all elections to Negroes and to such white men as may not be disfranchised for rebellion or felony; fourth, the submission of the constitution for ratification to Negroes and white men not disfranchised, and its actual ratification by their vote; fifth, the submission of the state constitution to Congress for examination and approval, and the actual approval of it by that body; sixth, the adoption of a certain amendment to the federal Constitution by a vote of the legislature elected under the new constitution; seventh, the adoption of said amendment by a sufficient number of other states to make it a part of the Constitution of the United States.

All these conditions must be fulfilled before the people of any of these states can be relieved from the bondage of military domination; but when they are fulfilled, then immediately the pains and penalties of the bill are to cease, no matter whether there be peace and order or not, and without any reference to the security of life or property. The excuse given for the bill in the preamble is admitted by the bill itself not to be real. The military rule which it establishes is plainly to be used, not for any purpose of order or for the prevention of crime but solely as a means of coercing the people into the adoption of principles and measures—to which it is known that they are opposed and upon which they have an undeniable right to exercise their own judgment.

I submit to Congress whether this measure is not in its whole character, scope, and object without precedent and without authority, in palpable conflict with the plainest provisions of the Constitution, and utterly destructive to those great principles of liberty and humanity for which our ancestors on both sides of the Atlantic have shed so much blood and expended so much treasure. [. . .]

It is plain that the authority here given to the military officer amounts to absolute despotism. But to make it still more unendurable, the bill provides that it may be delegated to as many subordinates as he chooses to appoint, for it declares that he shall "punish or cause to be punished." Such a power has not been wielded by any monarch in England for more than 500 years. In all that time no people who speak the English language have borne such servitude. It reduces the whole population of the ten states—all persons, of every color, sex, and condition, and every stranger within their limits—to the most abject and degrading slavery. No master ever had a control so absolute over the slaves as this bill gives to the military officers over both white and colored persons.

It may be answered to this that the officers of the Army are too magnanimous, just, and humane to oppress and trample upon a subjugated people. I do not doubt that Army officers are as well entitled to this kind of confidence as any other class of men. But the history of the world has been written in vain if it does not teach us that unrestrained authority can never be safely trusted in human hands. [. . .]

I come now to a question which is, if possible, still more important. Have we the power to establish and carry into execution a measure like this? I answer, certainly not, if we derive our authority from the Constitution and if we are bound by the limitations which it imposes.

This proposition is perfectly clear, that no branch of the federal government—executive, legislative, or judicial—can have any just powers except those which it derives through and exercises under the organic law of the Union. Outside of the Constitution we have no legal authority more than private citizens, and within it we have only so much as that instrument gives us. This broad principle limits all our functions and applies to all subjects. It protects not only the citizens of states which are within the Union but it shields every human being who comes or is brought under our jurisdiction. We have no right to do in one place more than in another that which the Constitution says we shall not do at all. If, therefore, the Southern states were in truth out of the Union, we could not treat their people in a way which the fundamental law forbids.

Some persons assume that the success of our arms in crushing the opposition, which was made in some of the states to the execution of the federal laws, reduced those states and all their people—the innocent as well as the guilty—to the condition of vassalage and gave us a power over them which the Constitution does not bestow or define or limit. No fallacy can be more transparent than this. Our victories subjected the insurgents to legal obedience, not to the yoke of an arbitrary despotism. When an absolute sovereign reduces his rebellious subjects, he may deal with them according to his pleasure, because he had that power before. But when a limited monarch puts down an insurrection, he must still govern according to law.

If an insurrection should take place in one of our states against the authority of the state government and end in the overthrow of those who planned it, would that take away the rights of all the people of the counties where it was favored by a part or a majority of the population? Could they for such a reason be wholly outlawed and deprived of their representation in the legislature? I have always contended that the government of the United States was sovereign within its constitutional sphere; that it executed its laws, like the states themselves, by applying its coercive power directly to individuals, and that it could put down insurrection with the same effect as a state and no other. The opposite doctrine is the worst heresy of those who advocated secession and cannot be agreed to without admitting that heresy to be right.

Invasion, insurrection, rebellion, and domestic violence were anticipated when the government was framed, and the means of repelling and suppressing them were wisely provided for in the Constitution; but it was not thought necessary to declare that the states in which they might occur should be expelled from the Union. Rebellions, which were invariably suppressed, occurred prior to that out of which these questions grow; but the states continued to exist and the Union remained unbroken. In Massachusetts, in Pennsylvania, in Rhode Island, and in New York, at different periods in our history, violent and armed opposition to the United States was carried on; but the relations of those states with the federal government were not supposed to be interrupted or changed thereby after the rebellious portions of their population were defeated and put down.

It is true that in these earlier cases there was no formal expression of a determination to withdraw from the Union, but it is also true that in the Southern states the ordinances of secession were treated by all the friends of the Union as mere nullities and are now acknowledged to be so by the states themselves. If we admit that they had any force or validity or that they did in fact take the states in which they were passed out of the Union, we sweep from under our feet all the grounds upon which we stand in justifying the use of federal force to maintain the integrity of the government. [. . .]

It will be observed that of the three kinds of military jurisdiction which can be exercised or created under our Constitution there is but one that can prevail in time of peace, and that is the code of laws enacted by Congress for the government of the national forces. That body of military law has no application to the citizen, nor even to the citizen soldier enrolled in the militia in time of peace. But this bill is not a part of that sort of military law, for that applies only to the soldier and not to the citizen, while, contrariwise, the military law provided by this bill applies only to the citizen and not to the soldier. [. . .]

This bill holds every person not a soldier answerable for all crimes and all charges without any presentment. The Constitution declares that "no person shall be deprived of life, liberty, or property without due process of law." This bill sets aside all process of law and makes the citizen answerable in his person and property to the will of one man, and as to his life, to the will of two. Finally, the Constitution declares that "the privilege of the writ of habeas corpus shall not be suspended unless when, in case of rebellion or invasion, the public safety may require it"; whereas this bill declares martial law (which of itself suspends this great writ) in time of peace, and authorizes the military to make the arrest, and gives to the prisoner only one privilege and that is a trial "without unnecessary delay." He has no hope of release from custody, except the hope, such as it is, of release by acquittal before a military commission.

The United States are bound to guarantee to each state a republican form of government. Can it be pretended that this obligation is not palpably broken if we carry out a measure like this, which wipes away every vestige of republican government in ten states and puts the life, property, liberty, and honor of all the people in each of them under the domination of a single person clothed with unlimited authority? [. . .]

The purpose and object of the bill—the general intent which pervades it from beginning to end—is to change the entire structure and character of the state governments and to compel them by force to the adoption of organic laws and regulations which they are unwilling to accept if left to themselves. The Negroes have not asked for the privilege of voting; the vast majority of them have no idea what it means. This bill not only thrusts it into their hands but compels them, as well as the whites, to use it in a particular way. If they do not form a constitution with prescribed articles in it and afterward elect a legislature which will act upon certain measures in a prescribed way, neither blacks nor whites can be relieved from the slavery which the bill imposes upon them.

Without pausing here to consider the policy or impolicy of Africanizing the southern part of our territory, I would simply ask the attention of Congress to that manifest, well-known, and universally acknowledged rule of constitutional law which declares that the federal government has no jurisdiction, authority, or power to regulate such subjects for any state. To force the right of suffrage out of the hands of the white people and into the hands of the Negroes is an arbitrary violation of this principle. [. . .]

The bill also denies the legality of the governments of ten of the states which participated in the ratification of the amendment to the federal Constitution abolishing slavery forever within the jurisdiction of the United States and practically excludes them from the Union. If this assumption of the bill be correct, their concurrence cannot be considered as having been legally given, and the important fact is made to appear that the consent of three fourths of the states—the requisite number—has not been constitutionally obtained to the ratification of that amendment, thus leaving the question of slavery where it stood before the amendment was officially declared to have become a part of the Constitution.

That the measure proposed by this bill does violate the Constitution in the particulars mentioned and in many other ways which I forbear to enumerate is too clear to admit of the least doubt. [. . .]

While we are legislating upon subjects which are of great importance to the whole people, and which must affect all parts of the country, not only during the life of the present generation but for ages to come, we should remember that all men are entitled at least to a hearing in the councils which decide upon the destiny of themselves and their children. At present, ten states are denied representation, and when the Fortieth Congress assembles on the 4th day of the present month, sixteen states will be without a voice in the House of Representatives. This grave fact, with the important questions before us, should induce us to pause in a course of legislation which, looking solely to the attainment of political ends, fails to consider the rights it transgresses, the law which it violates, or the institutions which it imperils.

Samuel J. Tilden

Speech on Reconstruction (1868)

A complete and harmonious restoration of the revolted states would have been effected if the Republican Party had not proved to be totally incapable of acting in the case with any large, wise, or firm statesmanship.

A magnanimous policy would not only have completed the pacification of the country but would have effected a reconciliation between the Republican Party and the white race in the South. Every circumstance favored such a result. The Republican Party possessed all the powers of the government, and held sway over every motive of gratitude, fear, or interest. The Southern people had become thoroughly weary of the contest; more than half of them had been originally opposed to entering into it, and had done so only when nothing was left to them but to choose on which side they would fight.

Few would ever have favored the measures which led to the conflict of arms if they had anticipated such a conflict; many had all the while felt a lingering regret in ceasing to belong to a great country which they had been accustomed to regard with proud ambition; and all remembered that they had been prosperous, contented, and happy as American citizens. The mass yearned to come back to what was left of their birthright. On the surrender of General Lee, every hostile sword fell, and the abolition of slavery was yielded as a peace offering with universal alacrity.

All that was necessary to heal the bleeding wounds of the country and to allow its languishing industries to revive, was that the Republican Party—which boasts its great moral ideas and its philanthropy—should rise to the moral elevation of an ordinary pugilist, and cease to strike its adversary after it was down.

This crisis was the trial of the Republican Party. The question was whether it could become a permanent party in the country, continuing to govern for the present, capable of being, from time to time, called to govern; or whether it must admit itself to be but a revolutionary faction, accepted by the people during the war, accepted for the venom, if not the vigor, with which it could strike, acting often "outside the Constitution," often converting the regular and lawful organs of the government into a French committee of public safety or a Jacobin club, and now incapable of adapting itself to the work of pacification when that has become the commanding public necessity; and therefore, its mission being fulfilled, having nothing left to it but to die and be forever dismissed from our national history.

In this trial the Republican Party completely failed. [. . .]

The Republican Party recoiled for a while on the fatal brink of the policy on which it at last embarked. It had not the courage to conciliate by magnanimity, and to found its alliances and its hopes of success upon the better qualities of human nature. It totally abandoned all relations to the white race of the ten states. It resolved to make the black race the governing power in those states, and by means of them to bring into Congress twenty senators and fifty representatives—practically appointed by itself in Washington.

It is evident that the internal government of those states was not the main object of this desperate expedient. The state organizations had been comparatively neglected. It was only through new state organizations and new electoral bodies that the twenty senators and fifty representatives could be secured to the Republican Party after it refused to trust to pacification.

The effect of a gain to the Republican Party of twenty senators and fifty representatives is to strengthen its hold on the federal government against the people of the North. Nor is there the slightest doubt that the paramount object and motive of the Republican Party is by these means to secure itself against a reaction of opinion adverse to it in our great populous Northern commonwealths. The effect of its system and its own real purpose is to establish a domination over us of the Northern states.

When the Republican Party resolved to establish Negro supremacy in the ten states in order to gain to itself the representation of those states in Congress, it had to begin by governing the people of those states by the sword. The 4,500,000 whites composed the electoral bodies. If they were to be put under the supremacy of the 3 million Negroes, and twenty senators and fifty representatives were to be obtained through these 3 million Negroes, it was necessary to obliterate every vestige of local authority, whether it had existed before the Rebellion, or been instituted since by Mr. Lincoln or by the people. A bayonet had to be set to supervise and control every local organization. The military dictatorship had to be extended to the remotest ramifications of human society. That was the first necessity.

The next was the creation of new electoral bodies for those ten states, in which, by exclusions, by disfranchisements and proscriptions, by control over registration, by applying test oaths operating respectively and prospectively, by intimidation, and by every form of influence, 3 million Negroes are made to predominate over 4,500,000 whites. These 3 million Negroes—three-fourths of the adult male portion of whom are field hands who have been worked in gangs on the plantations, and are immeasurably inferior to the free blacks whom we know in the North, who have never had even the education which might be acquired in the support of themselves or in the conduct of any business, and who, of all their race, have made the least advance from the original barbarism of their ancestors—have been organized in compact masses to form the ruling power in these ten states. They have been disassociated from their natural relations to the intelligence, humanity, virtue, and piety of the white race, set up in complete antagonism to the whole white race, for the purpose of being put over the white race, and of being fitted to act with unity and become completely impervious to the influence of superior intellect and superior moral and social power in the communities of which they form a part.

Of course such a process has repelled, with inconsiderable exceptions, the entire white race in the ten states. It has repelled the moderate portion who had reluctantly yielded to secession. It has repelled those who had remained Unionists. The first fruit of the Republican policy is the complete separation of the two races, and to some extent their antagonism. [. . .]

If those 3 million Negroes elect twenty senators and fifty representatives, they will have ten times as much power in the Senate of the United States as the 4 million whites in the state of New York. On every question which concerns the commercial metropolis—every question of trade, of finance, of currency, of revenue, and of taxation—these 3 million liberated African slaves will count ten times as much in the Senate as 4 million New Yorkers. One freedman will counterbalance thirteen white citizens of the Empire State. These 3 million blacks will count ten times as much as 3 million white people in Pennsylvania; ten times as much as 2,500,000 in Ohio; ten times as much as 2,225,000 or 2,500,000 in Illinois; ten times as much as 1,500,000 in Indiana. These 3 million blacks will have twice the representation in the Senate which will be possessed by the five great commonwealths—New York, Pennsylvania, Ohio, Indiana, and Illinois—embracing 13,500,000 of our people.

Let me not be told that this enormous wrong is nothing more than an original defect of the Constitution. I answer that it derives most of its evil and its danger from the usurpations of the Republican Party.

We have now reached a period when everything valuable in the Constitution and in the government as formed by our fathers is brought into peril. Men's minds are unsettled by the civil strifes through which we have passed. The body of traditionary ideas which limited the struggles of parties within narrow and fixed boundaries is broken up. A temporary party majority, having complete sway over the legislative bodies, discards all standards, whether embodied in laws, constitutions, or in elementary and organic principles of free government; acts its own pleasure as absolutely as if it were a revolutionary convention; and deems everything legitimate which can serve its party aims.

Changes are dared and attempted by it with a success which, I trust, is but temporary—changes which revolutionize the whole nature of our government.

1. If there be anything fundamental in government or in human society, it is the question, what elements shall compose the electoral bodies from which emanate all the governing powers. The Constitution left the states with exclusive power over the suffrage, and the states have always defined and protected the suffrage from change by their fundamental laws. Congress now usurps control over the whole subject in the ten states and creates Negro constituencies, and vests them with nearly a third of the whole representation in the Senate, and nearly a quarter of the whole representation in the House. The leaders of the Republican Party also claim the power by congressional act to regulate the suffrage in the loyal states, and, without the consent of the people of those states, to alter their constitutions and involve them in a political partnership with inferior races.

2. Congress, by the methods and means I have traced, usurps control over the representation in the two branches of the national legislature and packs those bodies with delegates, admitting or rejecting for party ends, and at length attempting to create a permanent majority by deputies from Negro constituencies formed for that purpose.

3. Congress has not only fettered the trade and industries of the country for the benefit of special interests and classes but it has absorbed many powers and functions of the state governments which are, in the words of Mr. Jefferson's celebrated inaugural, "the most competent administrations for our domestic concerns, the surest bulwark against anti-republican tendencies"; and it is rapidly centralizing all our political institutions.

4. Congress is systematically breaking down all the divisions of power between the coordinate departments of the federal government which the Constitution established, and which have always been considered as essential to the very existence of constitutional representative government.

The conviction of all our revered statesmen and patriots is, in the language of Mr. Jefferson, that "the concentration of legislative, executive, and judicial powers in the same hands is precisely the definition of despotic government." "An elective despotism," said he, "was not the government we fought for, but one which should not only be founded on free principles but in which the powers of government should be so divided among several bodies of magistracy as that no one could transcend their legal limits without being effectually checked and restrained by the others."

In violation of these principles, Congress has stripped the President of his constitutional powers over his subordinates in the executive function, and even over his own confidential advisers, and vested these powers in the Senate. It is now exercising the power of removing from office the President elected by the people and appointing another in his place, under the form of a trial, but without the pretense of actual crime, or anything more than a mere difference of opinion.

It has menaced the judiciary, at one time proposing to create by law an incapacity in the Supreme Court to act by a majority in any case where it should disagree with Congress; at another time proposing to divest that tribunal of jurisdiction, exercised by it from the foundation of the government, to decide between an ordinary law and the Constitution, which is the fundamental and supreme law. There is reason to believe also that a plan has been matured to overthrow the court by the creation of new judges, to make a majority more subservient to Congress than the judges appointed by Mr. Lincoln are found to be.

These changes are organic. They would revolutionize the very nature of the government. They would alter every important part of its structure on which its authors relied to secure good laws and good administration, and to preserve civil liberty. They would convert it into an elective despotism. The change could not by possibility stop at that stage.

I avow the conviction, founded on all history and on the concurring judgment of all our great statesmen and patriots, that such a system, if continued, would pass into imperialism. I feel not less certain that the destruction of all local self-government in a country so extensive as ours, and embracing such elements of diversity in habits, manners, opinions, and interests, and the exercise by a single, centralized authority of all the powers of society over so vast a region and over such populations, would entail upon us an indefinite series of civil commotions and repeat here the worst crimes and worst calamities of history.

It is time for the people to stay these destructive tendencies, and to declare that the reaction from secession toward centralism shall not effect the ruin which secession could not directly accomplish. [. . .]

The masses of the Republicans do not understand the real nature of the system they are contributing to establish. They are misled by party association and party antagonism, by the animosities created by the war, and the unsettled ideas which grow out of the novelty of the situation. The leaders are full of party passion and party ambition, and will not easily surrender the power of a centralized government, or the patronage and profits which are incident to an official expenditure of $500 million a year. The grim Puritan of New England—whose only child, whose solitary daughter is already listening to the soft music of a Celtic wooer—stretches his hand down along the Atlantic coast to the receding and decaying African, and says: "Come, let us rule this continent together!" The twelve senators from New England, with twenty from the ten states, would require only a few from Missouri, Tennessee, West Virginia, and from new states to make a majority.

I do not forbid the banns; I simply point to the region which stretches from the Hudson to the Missouri. It is there that the democracy must display their standards in another, and I trust final, battle for constitutional government and civil liberty. I invited you to that theater last year; I come now to bid you Godspeed!

Every business, every industrial interest is paralyzed under excessive taxation, false systems of finance, extravagant cost of production, diminished ability to consume. You cannot obtain relief until you change your governmental policy. You cannot change that until you change the men who administer your government. The causes of the dangers in respect to our political institutions and civil liberty and the causes of your suffering in business are identical. For the safety of the one and for the relief of the other you must demand of the people a change of administration as now carried on by Congress.

Constitution and Ritual of the Knights of the White Camellia (1868)

Preamble

Whereas, Radical legislation is subversive of the principles of the government of the United States as originally adopted by our fathers:

And whereas, our safety and our prosperity depend on the preservation of those grand principles and believing that they can be peacefully maintained; therefore, we adopt the following:

Constitution

Title I. Division of the Order

Article 1. This Order shall consist of a Supreme Council of the United States, and of Grand, Central, and Subordinate Councils.

Title II. Supreme Council

Article 2. The Supreme Council shall be organized as soon as five states shall have established each a Grand Council.

Article 3. This Council shall be composed of delegates from each state in which a Grand Council shall be established.

Article 4. Each state shall send to the Supreme Council five delegates, whose appointment shall continue for one year and who shall be elected, from their own bodies, by the several Grand Councils of the Order.

Article 5. All past grand commanders in good standing shall be ex-officio members of the Grand Council and shall be entitled to all the rights and privileges of the members of that body.

Article 6. The Supreme Council shall hold its sessions in the city of New Orleans, state of Louisiana, but may, by a vote of two-thirds of its members, change its place of meeting to any other city in the United States.

Article 7. The Supreme Council shall be the head of the Order and the court of last appeal in all matters of disagreement, except in cases hereinafter specified. It shall make all laws for the general government of the Order; shall take cognizance of all acts; and shall be the arbiter of all disputes which may arise between the Grand and Central Councils of any state and Grand Councils and their grand commanders.

Article 8. The officers of the Supreme Council shall be as follows: (1) supreme commander; (2) supreme lieutenant commander; (3) supreme sentinel; (4) supreme corresponding secretary; (5) supreme treasurer.

Questions

1. Do you belong to the white race? *Answer.*—I do.

2. Did you ever marry any woman who did not, or does not, belong to the white race? *Ans.*—No.

3. Do you promise never to marry any woman but one who belongs to the white race? *Ans.*—I do.

4. Do you believe in the superiority of your race? *Ans.*—I do.

5. Will you promise never to vote for anyone for any office of honor, profit, or trust who does not belong to your race? *Ans.*—I do.

6. Will you take a solemn oath never to abstain from casting your vote at any election in which a candidate of the Negro race shall be opposed to a white man attached to your principles, unless or prevented by severe illness or any other physical disability? *Ans.*—I will.

7. Are you opposed to allowing the control of the political affairs of this country to go in whole or in part into the hands of the African race, and will you do everything in your power to prevent it? *Ans.*—Yes.

8. Will you devote your intelligence, energy, and influence to the furtherance and propagation of the principles of our Order? *Ans.*—I will.

9. Will you, under all circumstances, defend and protect persons of the white race in their lives, rights, and property against all encroachments or invasions from any inferior race, and especially the African? *Ans.*—Yes.

10. Are you willing to take an oath forever to cherish these grand principles and to unite yourself with others who, like you, believing in their truth, have firmly bound themselves to stand by and defend them against all? *Ans.*—I am.

The commander shall then say: If you consent to join our Association, raise your right hand and I will administer to you the oath which we have all taken:

Oath

I do solemnly swear, in the presence of these witnesses, never to reveal, without authority, the existence of this Order, its objects, its acts, and signs of recognition; never to reveal or publish, in any manner whatsoever, what I shall see or hear in this Council; never to divulge the names of the members of the Order or their acts done in connection therewith. I swear to maintain and defend the social and political superiority of the white race on this continent; always and in all places to observe a marked distinction between the white and African races; to vote for none but white men for any office of honor, profit, or trust; to devote my intelligence, energy, and influence to instill these principles in the minds and hearts of others; and to protect and defend persons of the white race in their lives, rights, and property against the encroachments and aggressions of an inferior race.

I swear, moreover, to unite myself in heart, soul, and body with those who compose this Order; to aid, protect, and defend them in all places; to obey the orders of those who, by our statutes, will have the right of giving those orders; to respond at the peril of my life to a call, sign, or cry coming from a fellow member whose rights are violated; and to do everything in my power to assist him through life. And to the faithful performance of this oath, I pledge my life and sacred honor. [. . .]

Charge

Brothers:

You have been initiated into one of the most important Orders which have ever been established on this continent; an Order, which, if its principles are faithfully observed and its objects diligently carried out, is destined to regenerate our unfortunate country and to relieve the white race from the humiliating condition to which it has lately been reduced in this republic. It is necessary, therefore, that before taking part in the labors of this Association, you should understand fully its principles and objects and the duties which devolve upon you as one of its members.

As you may have already gathered from the questions which were propounded to you, and which you have answered so satisfactorily, and from the clauses of the oath which you have taken, our main and fundamental object is the *maintenance of the supremacy of the white race* in this republic. History and physiology teach us that we belong to a race which nature has endowed with an evident superiority over all other races, and that the Maker, in thus elevating us above the common standard of human creation, has intended to give us over inferior races a dominion from which no human laws can permanently derogate. The experience of ages demonstrates that, from the origin of the world, this dominion has always remained in the hands of the Caucasian race, while all the other races have constantly occupied a subordinate and secondary position; a fact which triumphantly confirms this great law of nature.

Powerful nations have succeeded each other on the face of the world and have marked their passage by glorious and memorable deeds; and among those who have thus left on this globe indelible traces of their splendor and greatness, we find none but descended from the Caucasian stock. We see, on the contrary, that most of the countries inhabited by the other races have remained in a state of complete barbarity; while the small number of those who have advanced beyond this savage existence have, for centuries, stagnated in a semi-barbarous condition, of which there can be no progress or improvement. And it is a remarkable fact that as a race of men is more remote from the Caucasian and approaches nearer to the black African, the more fatally that stamp of inferiority is affixed to its sons and irrevocably dooms them to eternal imperfectibility and degradation.

Convinced that we are of these elements of natural ethics, we know, besides, that the government of our republic was established by white men, for white men alone, and that it never was in the contemplation of its founders that it should fall into the hands of an inferior and degraded race. We hold, therefore, that any attempt to wrest from the white race the management of its affairs in order to transfer it to control of the black population is an invasion of the sacred prerogatives vouchsafed to us by the Constitution, and a violation of the laws established by God Himself; that such encroachments are subversive of the established institutions of our republic; and that no individual of the white race can submit to them without humiliation and shame.

It, then, becomes our solemn duty, as white men, to resist strenuously and persistently those attempts against our natural and constitutional rights, and to do everything in our power in order to maintain, in this republic, the supremacy of the Caucasian race and restrain the black or African race to that condition of social and political inferiority for which God has destined it. This is the object for which our Order was instituted; and, in carrying it out, we intend to infringe no laws, to violate no rights, and to resort to no forcible means, except for purposes of legitimate and necessary defense.

As an essential condition of success, this Order proscribes absolutely all social equality between the races. If we were to admit persons of African race on the same level with ourselves, a state of personal relations would follow which would unavoidably lead to political equality; for it would be a virtual recognition of *status*, after which we could not consistently deny them an equal share in the administration of our public affairs. The man who is good enough to be our familiar companion is good enough also to participate in our political government; and if we were to grant the one, there could be no good reason for us not to concede the other of these two privileges.

There is another reason, brothers, for which, we condemn this social equality. Its toleration would soon be a fruitful source of intermarriages between individuals of the two races; and the result of this miscegenation would be gradual amalgamation and the production of a degenerate and bastard offspring, which would soon populate these states with a degraded and ignoble population, incapable of moral and intellectual development, and unfitted to support a great and powerful country. We must maintain the purity of the white blood if we would preserve it for that natural superiority with which God has ennobled it.

To avoid these evils, therefore, we take the obligation *to observe a marked distinction between the two races,* not only in the relations of public affairs but also in the more intimate dealings and intercourse of private life which, by the frequency of their occurrence, are more apt to have an influence on the attainment of the purposes of the Order.

Now that I have laid before you the objects of this Association, let me charge you specially in relation to one of your most important duties as one of its members. Our statutes make us bound to respect sedulously the rights of the colored inhabitants of this republic and, in every instance, to give to them whatever lawfully belongs to them. It is an act of simple justice not to deny them any of the privileges to which they are legitimately entitled; and we cannot better show the inherent superiority of our race than by dealing with them in that spirit of firmness, liberality, and impartiality which characterizes all superior organizations. Besides, it would be ungenerous for us to undertake to restrict them to the narrowest limits as to the exercise of certain rights, without conceding to them, at the same time, the fullest measure of those which we recognize as theirs; and a fair construction of a white man's duty toward them would be not only to respect and observe their acknowledged rights but also to see that these are respected and observed by others.

From the brief explanation which I have just given you, you must have satisfied yourselves that our Association is not a political party and has no connection with any of the organized parties of the day. Nor will it lend itself to the personal advancement of individuals or listen to the cravings of any partisan spirit. It was organized in order to carry out certain great principles from which it must never swerve by favoring private ambitions and political aspirations. These, as well as all sentiments of private enmity, animosity, and other personal feelings, we must leave at the door before we enter this Council. You may meet here, congregated together, men who belong to all the political organizations which now divide, or may divide, this country; you see some whom embittered feuds and irreconcilable hatred have long and widely separated; they have all cast away these rankling feelings to unite cordially and zealously in the labors of our great undertaking. Let their example be to you a useful lesson of the disinterestedness and devotedness which should characterize our efforts for the success of our cause!

Brothers, I now consign you to the lieutenant commander of this Council, who will instruct you as to the signs and other means of recognition of this Association and other details of its organization and order.

The lieutenant commander will now instruct the new brothers as to the sign, grip, cry, dialogue, rap, password, etc., taking care to charge them particularly as to the circumstances and occasion of their use. He will also inform them of the mode of initiation and other details of order which they are required to know.

Raleigh Daily Sentinel

Editorial (1869)

That the State has been cursed and almost mined by a class of "carpet bag" vultures from the North, aided by degenerate and too often corrupt natives, is patent to anybody who opens his eyes. We have not been slow to tell the people of the villainies that have been perpetrated and are yet being perpetrated, day and night, by the present State government, at the expense and injury of the people, black and white. We intend to continue to do so regardless of cost or consequences.

Our firm conviction is that the people will not tolerate these villainies a great while longer; the day of reckoning cometh, and it will be terrible. The "carpet bagger" race will then hurry off to some other field of spoils and laugh at the calamity of their dupes and co-workers in iniquity; but the *native* culprit must answer at the bar of public opinion, and in many cases at the bar of the Court for high crimes. We tell the native scalawags that the day is not far distant, when the thin veil that now hides their crimes from public gaze will be withdrawn, and they will be exposed to the scorn and indignation of an outraged people. Yes, and that small class of our people who claim to be good and true men, who, for the sake of a little gain, have *secretly* colluded with the bad wretches who have plundered and impoverished the people without mercy, they, too, will be exposed. Yes, we repeat, the day will be mercilessly exposed. And such perpetration or crime will thenceforth be a *stench* in the nostrils of all decent men, white and black. Everybody will bate them, mock and hiss at them as they pass by. The Penitentiary fraud will be exposed, the Railroad frauds will be exposed; it will yet be known how much money was used to corrupt the members of the Legislature, who used it, who paid it, and where it came from; it will yet be known how many warrants have been made on the Treasury not authorized by law. We have the best of reasons for saying that the passage of the Railroad acts cost the State tens and hundreds of thousands of dollars. The people will yet ferret out those who so recklessly and criminally spent the treasure of the people. Yes, gentlemen, the day of reckoning will come. Mark what we say! Let every man watch how he connects himself even innocently with those who have so outraged the State and the people.

Petition to Congress of the Committee of Grievances of the Colored Citizens of Frankfort, Kentucky (1871)

To the Senate and House of Representatives
in Congress assembled:

We the colored citizens of Frankfort and vicinity do this day memorialize your honorable bodies upon the condition of affairs now existing in this state of Kentucky.

We would respectfully state that life, liberty, and property are unprotected among the colored race of this state. Organized bands of desperate and lawless men, mainly composed of soldiers of the late Rebel armies, armed, disciplined, and disguised, and bound by oath and secret obligations, have by force, terror, and violence subverted all civil society among colored people, thus utterly rendering insecure the safety of persons and property, overthrowing all those rights which are the primary basis and objects of the government which are expressly guaranteed to us by the Constitution of the United States as amended.

We believe you are not familiar with the description of the Ku Klux Klan's riding nightly over the country, going from county to county, and in the county towns spreading terror wherever they go by robbing, whipping, ravishing, and killing our people without provocation, compelling colored people to break the ice and bathe in the chilly waters of the Kentucky River.

The legislature has adjourned; they refused to enact any laws to suppress Ku Klux disorder. We regard them as now being licensed to continue their dark and bloody deeds under cover of the dark night. They refuse to allow us to testify in the state courts where a white man is concerned. We find their deeds are perpetrated only upon colored men and white Republicans. We also find that for our services to the government and our race we have become the special object of hatred and persecution at the hands of the Democratic Party.

Our people are driven from their homes in great numbers, having no redress, only the U.S. courts, which is in many cases unable to reach them. We would state that we have been law-abiding citizens, pay our tax, and, in many parts of the state, our people have been driven from the polls—refused the right to vote. Many have been slaughtered while attempting to vote; we ask how long is this state of things to last.

We appeal to you as law-abiding citizens to enact some laws that will protect us and that will enable us to exercise the rights of citizens. We see that the senator from this state denies there being organized bands of desperadoes in the state; for information we lay before you a number of violent acts [that] occurred during his administration. Although he, Stevenson, says half-dozen instances of violence did occur, these are not more than one-half the acts that have occurred.

The Democratic Party has here a political organization composed only of Democrats; not a single Republican can join them. Where many of these acts have been committed, it has been proven that they were the men, done with arms from the state arsenal. We pray you will take some steps to remedy these evils.

Done by a committee of grievances appointed at a meeting of all the colored citizens of Frankfort and vicinity.

REPORT OF A FEDERAL GRAND JURY ON THE KU KLUX KLAN (1871)

In closing the labors of the present term, the grand jury beg leave to submit the following presentment.

During the whole session we have been engaged in investigations of the most grave and extraordinary character—investigations of the crimes committed by the organization known as the Ku Klux Klan. The evidence elicited has been voluminous, gathered from the victims themselves and their families, as well as those who belong to the Klan and participated in its crimes. The jury has been shocked beyond measure at the developments which have been made in their presence of the number and character of the atrocities committed, producing a state of terror and a sense of utter insecurity among a large portion of the people, especially the colored population. The evidence produced before us has established the following facts:

1. That there has existed since 1868, in many counties of the state, an organization known as the "Ku Klux Klan," or "Invisible Empire of the South," which embraces in its membership a large proportion of the white population of every profession and class.

2. That this Klan [is] bound together by an oath, administered to its members at the time of their initiation into the order, of which the following is a copy:

Obligation

> I [name], before the immaculate Judge of Heaven and earth, and upon the Holy Evangelists of Almighty God, do, of my own free will and accord, subscribe to the following sacredly binding obligation:
>
> 1. We are on the side of justice, humanity, and constitutional liberty, as bequeathed to us in its purity by our forefathers.
>
> 2. We oppose and reject the principles of the Radical Party.
>
> 3. We pledge mutual aid to each other in sickness, distress, and pecuniary embarrassment.
>
> 4. Female friends, widows, and their households shall ever be special objects of our regard and protection.
>
> Any member divulging, or causing to be divulged, any of the foregoing obligations, shall meet the fearful penalty and traitor's doom, which is Death! Death! Death!

That, in addition to this oath, the Klan has a constitution and bylaws, which provides, among other things, that each member shall furnish himself with a pistol, a Ku Klux gown, and a signal instrument. That the operations of the Klan were executed in the night, and were invariably directed against members of the Republican Party by warnings to leave the country, by whippings, and by murder.

3. That in large portions of the counties of York, Union, and Spartanburgh, to which our attention has been more particularly called in our investigations during part of the time for the last eighteen months, the civil law has been set at defiance and ceased to afford any protection to the citizens.

4. That the Klan, in carrying out the purposes for which it was organized and armed, inflicted summary vengeance on the colored citizens of these counties by breaking into their houses at the dead of night, dragging them from their beds, torturing them in the most inhuman manner, and in many instances murdering them; and this, mainly, on account of their political affiliations. Occasionally, additional reasons operated, but in no instance was the political feature wanting.

5. That for this condition of things, for all these violations of law and order and the sacred rights of citizens, many of the leading men of those counties were responsible. It was proven that large numbers of the most prominent citizens were members of the order. Many of this class attended meetings of the Grand Klan. At a meeting of the Grand Klan held in Spartanburgh County, at which there were representatives from the various dens of Spartanburgh, York, Union, and Chester counties, in this state, besides a number from North Carolina, a resolution was adopted that no raids should be undertaken or

anyone whipped or injured by members of the Klan without orders from the Grand Klan. The penalty for violating this resolution was 100 lashes on the bare back for the first offense; and for the second, death.

This testimony establishes the nature of the discipline enforced in the order, and also the fact that many of the men who were openly and publicly speaking against the Klan, and pretending to deplore the work of this murderous conspiracy, were influential members of the order and directing its operations, even in detail.

The jury has been appalled as much at the number of outrages as at their character, it appearing that 11 murders and over 600 whippings have been committed in York County alone. Our investigation in regard to the other counties named has been less full; but it is believed, from the testimony, that an equal or greater number has been committed in Union, and that the number is not greatly less in Spartanburgh and Laurens.

We are of the opinion that the most vigorous prosecution of the parties implicated in these crimes is imperatively demanded; that without this there is great danger that these outrages will be continued, and that there will be no security to our fellow citizens of African descent.

We would say further that unless the strong arm of the government is interposed to punish these crimes committed upon this class of citizens, there is every reason to believe that an organized and determined attempt at retaliation will be made, which can only result in a state of anarchy and bloodshed too horrible to contemplate.

Ulysses S. Grant

Memoirs (1885)

Morale of the Two Armies—Relative Conditions of the North and South—President Lincoln Visits Richmond—Arrival at Washington—President Lincoln's Assassination—President Johnson's Policy

After the fall of Petersburg, and when the armies of the Potomac and the James were in motion to head off Lee's army, the *morale* of the National troops had greatly improved. There was no more straggling, no more rear guards. The men who in former times had been falling back, were now, as I have already stated, striving to get to the front. For the first time in four weary years they felt that they were now nearing the time when they could return to their homes with their country saved. On the other hand, the Confederates were more than correspondingly depressed. Their despondency increased with each returning day, and especially after the battle of Sailor's Creek. They threw away their arms in constantly increasing numbers, dropping out of the ranks and betaking themselves to the woods in the hope of reaching their homes. I have already instanced the case of the entire disintegration of a regiment whose colonel I met at Farmville. As a result of these and other influences, when Lee finally surrendered at Appomattox, there were only 28,356 officers and men left to be paroled, and many of these were without arms. It was probably this latter fact which gave rise to the statement sometimes made, North and South, that Lee surrendered a smaller number of men than what the official figures show. As a matter of official record, and in addition to the number paroled as given above, we captured between March 29th and the date of surrender 19,132 Confederates, to say nothing of Lee's other losses, killed, wounded and missing, during the series of desperate conflicts which marked his headlong and determined flight. The same record shows the number of cannon, including those at Appomattox, to have been 689 between the dates named.

There has always been a great conflict of opinion as to the number of troops engaged in every battle, or all important battles, fought between the sections, the South magnifying the number of Union troops engaged and belittling their own. Northern writers have fallen, in many instances, into the same error. I have often heard gentlemen, who were thoroughly loyal to the Union, speak of what a splendid fight the South had made and successfully continued for four years before yielding, with their twelve million of people against our twenty, and of the twelve four being colored slaves, non-combatants. I will add to their argument. We had many regiments of brave and loyal men who volunteered under great difficulty from the twelve million belonging to the South.

But the South had rebelled against the National government. It was not bound by any constitutional restrictions. The whole South was a military camp. The occupation of the colored people was to furnish supplies for the army. Conscription was resorted to early, and embraced every male from the age of eighteen to forty-five, excluding only those physically unfit to serve in the field,—and the necessary number of civil officers of State and intended National government. The old and physically disabled furnished a good portion of these. The slaves, the non-combatants, one-third of the whole, were required to work in the field without regard to sex, and almost without regard to age. Children from the age of eight years could and did handle the hoe; they were not much older when they began to hold the plough. The four million of colored non-combatants were equal to more than three times their number in the North, age for age and sex for sex, in supplying food from the soil to support armies. Women did not work in the fields in the North, and children attended school.

The arts of peace were carried on in the North. Towns and cities grew during the war. Inventions were made in all kinds of machinery to increase the products of a day's labor in the shop, and in the field. In the South no opposition was allowed to the government which had been set up and which would have become real and respected if the rebellion had been successful. No rear had to be protected. All the troops in service could be brought to the front to contest every inch of ground threatened with invasion. The press of the South, like the people who remained at home, were loyal to the Southern cause.

In the North, the country, the towns and the cities presented about the same appearance they do in time of peace. The furnace was in blast, the shops were filled with workmen, the fields were cultivated, not only to supply the population of the North and the troops invading the South, but to ship abroad to pay a part of the expense of the war. In the North the press was free up to the point of open treason. The citizen could entertain his views and express them. Troops were necessary in the Northern States to prevent prisoners from the Southern army being released by outside force, armed and set at large to destroy by fire our Northern cities. Plans were formed by Northern and Southern citizens to burn our cities, to poison the water supplying them, to spread infection by importing clothing from infected regions, to blow up our river and lake steamers—regardless of the destruction of innocent lives. The copperhead disreputable portion of the press magnified rebel successes, and belittled those of the Union army. It was, with a large following, an auxiliary to the Confederate army. The North would have been much stronger with a hundred thousand of these men in the Confederate ranks and the rest of their kind thoroughly subdued, as the Union sentiment was in the South, than we were as the battle was fought.

As I have said, the whole South was a military camp. The colored people, four million in number, were submissive, and worked in the field and took care of the families while the able-bodied white men were at the front fighting for a cause destined to defeat. The cause was popular, and was enthusiastically supported by the young men. The conscription took all of them. Before the war was over, further conscriptions took those between fourteen and eighteen years of age as junior reserves, and those between forty-five and sixty as senior reserves. It would have been an offence, directly after the war, and perhaps it would be now, to ask any able-bodied man in the South, who was between the ages of fourteen and sixty at any time during the war, whether he had been in the Confederate army. He would assert that he had, or account for his absence from the ranks.

Under such circumstances it is hard to conceive how the North showed such a superiority of force in every battle fought. I know they did not.

During 1862 and '3, John H. Morgan, a partisan officer, of no military education, but possessed of courage and endurance, operated in the rear of the Army of the Ohio in Kentucky and Tennessee. He had no base of supplies to protect, but was at home wherever he went. The army operating against the South, on the contrary, had to protect its lines of communication with the North, from which all supplies had to come to the front. Every foot of road had to be guarded by troops stationed at convenient distances apart. These guards could not render assistance beyond the points where stationed. Morgan was footloose and could operate where his information—always correct—led him to believe he could do the greatest damage. During the time he was operating in this way he killed, wounded and captured several times the number he ever had under his command at any one time. He destroyed many millions of property in addition. Places he did not attack had to be guarded as if threatened by him. Forrest, an abler soldier, operated farther west, and held from the National front quite as many men as could be spared for offensive operations. It is safe to say that more than half the National army was engaged in guarding lines of supplies, or were on leave, sick in hospital or on detail which prevented their bearing arms. Then, again, large forces were employed where no Confederate army confronted them. I deem it safe to say that there were no large engagements where the National numbers compensated for the advantage of position and intrenchment occupied by the enemy.

While I was in pursuit of General Lee, the President went to Richmond in company with Admiral Porter, and on board his flagship. He found the people of that city in great consternation. The leading citizens among the people who had remained at home surrounded him, anxious that something should be done to relieve them from suspense. General Weitzel was not then in the city, having taken offices in one of the neighboring villages after his troops had succeeded in subduing the conflagration which they had found in progress on entering the Confederate capital. The President sent for him, and, on his arrival, a short interview was had on board the vessel, Admiral Porter and a leading citizen of Virginia being also present. After this interview the President wrote an order in about these words, which I quote from memory: "General Weitzel is authorized to permit the body calling itself the Legislature of Virginia to meet for the purpose of recalling the Virginia troops from the Confederate armies."

Immediately some of the gentlemen composing that body wrote out a call for a meeting and had it published in their papers. This call, however, went very much further than Mr. Lincoln had contemplated, as he did not say the "Legislature of Virginia" but "the body which called itself the Legislature of Virginia." Mr. Stanton saw the call as published in the Northern papers the very next issue and took the liberty of countermanding the order authorizing any meeting of the Legislature, or any other body, and this notwithstanding the fact that the President was nearer the spot than he was.

This was characteristic of Mr. Stanton. He was a man who never questioned his own authority, and who always did in war time what he wanted to do. He was an able constitutional lawyer and jurist; but the Constitution was not an impediment to him while the war lasted. In this latter particular I entirely agree with the view he evidently held. The Constitution was not framed with a view to any such rebellion as that of 1861–5. While it did not authorize rebellion it made no provision against it. Yet the right to resist or suppress rebellion is as inherent as the right of self-defence, and as natural as the right of an individual to preserve his life when in jeopardy. The Constitution was therefore in abeyance for the time being, so far as it in any way affected the progress and termination of the war.

Those in rebellion against the government of the United States were not restricted by constitutional provisions, or any other, except the acts of their Congress, which was loyal and devoted to the cause for which the South was then fighting. It would be a hard case when one-third of a nation, united in rebellion against the national authority, is entirely untrammelled, that the other two-thirds, in their efforts to maintain the Union intact, should be restrained by a Constitution prepared by our ancestors for the express purpose of insuring the permanency of the confederation of the States.

After I left General Lee at Appomattox Station, I went with my staff and a few others directly to

Burkesville Station on my way to Washington. The road from Burkesville back having been newly repaired and the ground being soft, the train got off the track frequently, and, as a result, it was after midnight of the second day when I reached City Point. As soon as possible I took a dispatch-boat thence to Washington City.

While in Washington I was very busy for a time in preparing the necessary orders for the new state of affairs; communicating with my different commanders of separate departments, bodies of troops, etc. But by the 14th I was pretty well through with this work, so as to be able to visit my children, who were then in Burlington, New Jersey, attending school. Mrs. Grant was with me in Washington at the time, and we were invited by President and Mrs. Lincoln to accompany them to the theatre on the evening of that day. I replied to the President's verbal invitation to the effect, that if we were in the city we would take great pleasure in accompanying them; but that I was very anxious to get away and visit my children, and if I could get through my work during the day I should do so. I did get through and started by the evening train on the 14th, sending Mr. Lincoln word, of course, that I would not be at the theatre.

At that time the railroad to New York entered Philadelphia on Broad Street; passengers were conveyed in ambulances to the Delaware River, and then ferried to Camden, at which point they took the cars again. When I reached the ferry, on the east side of the City of Philadelphia, I found people awaiting my arrival there; and also dispatches informing me of the assassination of the President and Mr. Seward, and of the probable assassination of the Vice-President, Mr. Johnson, and requesting my immediate return.

It would be impossible for me to describe the feeling that overcame me at the news of these assassinations, more especially the assassination of the President. I knew his goodness of heart, his generosity, his yielding disposition, his desire to have everybody happy, and above all his desire to see all the people of the United States enter again upon the full privileges of citizenship with equality among all. I knew also the feeling that Mr. Johnson had expressed in speeches and conversation against the Southern people, and I feared that his course towards them would be such as to repel, and make them unwilling citizens; and if they became such they would remain so for a long while. I felt that reconstruction had been set back, no telling how far.

I immediately arranged for getting a train to take me back to Washington City; but Mrs. Grant was with me; it was after midnight and Burlington was but an hour away. Finding that I could accompany her to our house and return about as soon as they would be ready to take me from the Philadelphia station, I went up with her and returned immediately by the same special train. The joy that I had witnessed among the people in the street and in public places in Washington when I left there, had been turned to grief; the city was in reality a city of mourning. I have stated what I believed then the effect of this would be, and my judgment now is that I was right. I believe the South would have been saved from very much of the hardness of feeling that was engendered by Mr. Johnson's course towards them during the first few months of his administration. Be this as it may, Mr. Lincoln's assassination was particularly unfortunate for the entire nation.

Mr. Johnson's course towards the South did engender bitterness of feeling. His denunciations of treason and his ever-ready remark, "Treason is a crime and must be made odious," was repeated to all those men of the South who came to him to get some assurances of safety so that they might go to work at something with the feeling that what they obtained would be secure to them. He uttered his denunciations with great vehemence, and as they were accompanied with no assurances of safety, many Southerners were driven to a point almost beyond endurance.

The President of the United States is, in a large degree, or ought to be, a representative of the feeling, wishes and judgment of those over whom he presides; and the Southerners who read the denunciations of themselves and their people must have come to the conclusion that he uttered the sentiments of the Northern people; whereas, as a matter of fact, but for the assassination of Mr. Lincoln, I believe the great majority of the Northern people, and the soldiers unanimously, would have been in favor of a speedy reconstruction on terms that would be the least humiliating to the people who had rebelled against their government. They believed, I have no doubt, as I did, that besides being the mildest, it was also the wisest, policy.

The people who had been in rebellion must necessarily come back into the Union, and be incorporated as an integral part of the nation. Naturally the nearer they were placed to an equality with the people who had not rebelled, the more reconciled they would feel with their old antagonists, and the better citizens they would be from the beginning. They surely would not make good citizens if they felt that they had a yoke around their necks.

I do not believe that the majority of the Northern people at that time were in favor of Negro suffrage. They supposed that it would naturally follow the freedom of the Negro, but that there would be a time of probation, in which the ex-slaves could prepare themselves for the privileges of citizenship before the full right would be conferred; but Mr. Johnson, after a complete revolution of sentiment, seemed to regard the South not only as an oppressed people, but as the people best entitled to consideration of any of our citizens. This was more than the people who had secured to us the perpetuation of the Union were prepared for, and they became more radical in their views. The Southerners had the most power in the executive branch, Mr. Johnson having gone to their side; and with a compact South, and such sympathy and support as they could get from the North, they felt that they would be able to control the nation at once, and already many of them acted as if they thought they were entitled to do so.

Thus Mr. Johnson, fighting Congress on the one hand, and receiving the support of the South on the other, drove Congress, which was overwhelmingly republican, to the passing of first one measure and then another to restrict his power. There being a solid South on one side that was in accord with the political party in the North which had sympathized with the rebellion, it finally, in the judgment of Congress and of the majority of the legislatures of the States, became necessary to enfranchise the Negro, in all his ignorance. In this work, I shall not discuss the question of how far the policy of Congress in this particular proved a wise one. It became an absolute necessity, however, because of the foolhardiness of the President and the blindness of the Southern people to their own interest. As to myself, while strongly favoring the course that would be the least humiliating to the people who had been in rebellion, I had gradually worked up to the point where, with the majority of the people, I favored immediate enfranchisement.

Conclusion

The cause of the great War of the Rebellion against the United States will have to be attributed to slavery. For some years before the war began it was a trite saying among some politicians that "A state half slave and half free cannot exist." All must become slave or all free, or the state will go down. I took no part myself in any such view of the case at the time, but since the war is over, reviewing the whole question, I have come to the conclusion that the saying is quite true.

Slavery was an institution that required unusual guarantees for its security wherever it existed; and in a country like ours where the larger portion of it was free territory inhabited by an intelligent and well-to-do population, the people would naturally have but little sympathy with demands upon them for its protection. Hence the people of the South were dependent upon keeping control of the general government to secure the perpetuation of their favorite institution. They were enabled to maintain this control long after the States where slavery existed had ceased to have the controlling power, through the assistance they received from odd men here and there throughout the Northern States. They saw their power waning, and this led them to encroach upon the prerogatives and independence of the Northern States by enacting such laws as the Fugitive Slave Law. By this law every Northern man was obliged, when properly summoned, to turn out and help apprehend the runaway slave of a Southern man. Northern marshals became slave-catchers, and Northern courts had to contribute to the support and protection of the institution.

This was a degradation which the North would not permit any longer than until they could get the power to expunge such laws from the statute books. Prior to the time of these encroachments the great majority of the people of the North had no particular quarrel with slavery, so long as they were not forced to have it themselves. But they were not willing to play the role of police for the South in the protection of this particular institution.

In the early days of the country, before we had railroads, telegraphs and steamboats—in a word, rapid transit of any sort—the States were each almost a separate nationality. At that time the subject of slavery caused but little or no disturbance to the public mind. But the country grew, rapid transit was established, and trade and commerce between the States got to be so much greater than before, that the power of the National government became more felt and recognized and, therefore, had to be enlisted in the cause of this institution.

It is probably well that we had the war when we did. We are better off now than we would have been without it, and have made more rapid progress than we otherwise should have made. The civilized nations of Europe have been stimulated into unusual activity, so that commerce, trade, travel, and thorough acquaintance among people of different nationalities, has become common; whereas, before, it was but the few who had ever had the privilege of going beyond the limits of their own country or who knew anything about other people. Then, too, our republican institutions were regarded as experiments up to the breaking out of the rebellion, and monarchical Europe generally believed that our republic was a rope of sand that would part the moment the slightest strain was brought upon it. Now it has shown itself capable of dealing with one of the greatest wars that was ever made, and our people have proven themselves to be the most formidable in war of any nationality.

But this war was a fearful lesson, and should teach us the necessity of avoiding wars in the future.

The conduct of some of the European states during our troubles shows the lack of conscience of communities where the responsibility does not come upon a single individual. Seeing a nation that extended from ocean to ocean, embracing the better part of a continent, growing as we were growing in population, wealth and intelligence, the European nations thought it would be well to give us a check. We might, possibly, after a while threaten their peace, or, at least, the perpetuity of their institutions. Hence, England was constantly finding fault with the administration at Washington because we were not able to keep up an effective blockade. She also joined, at first, with France and Spain in setting up an Austrian prince [Maximilian] upon the throne in Mexico, totally disregarding any rights or claims that Mexico had of being treated as an independent power. It is true they trumped up grievances as a pretext, but they were only pretexts which can always be found when wanted.

Mexico, in her various revolutions, had been unable to give that protection to the subjects of foreign nations which she would have liked to give, and some of her revolutionary leaders had forced loans from them. Under pretence of protecting their citizens, these nations seized upon Mexico as a foothold for establishing a European monarchy upon our continent, thus threatening our peace at home. I, myself, regarded this as a direct act of war against the United States by the powers engaged, and supposed as a matter of course that the United States would treat it as such when their hands were free to strike. I often spoke of the matter to Mr. Lincoln and the Secretary of War, but never heard any special views from them to enable me to judge what they thought or felt about it. I inferred that they felt a good deal as I did, but were unwilling to commit themselves while we had our own troubles upon our hands.

All of the powers except France very soon withdrew from the armed intervention for the establishment of an Austrian prince upon the throne of Mexico; but the governing people of these countries continued to the close of the war to throw obstacles in our way. After the surrender of Lee, therefore, entertaining the opinion here expressed, I sent Sheridan with a corps to the Rio Grande to have him where he might aid Juarez in expelling the French from Mexico. These troops got off before they could be stopped; and went to the Rio Grande, where Sheridan distributed them up and down the river, much to the consternation of the troops in the quarter of Mexico bordering on that stream. This soon led to a request from France that we should withdraw our troops from the Rio Grande and to negotiations for the withdrawal of theirs. Finally [A. F.] Bazaine was withdrawn from Mexico by order of the French Government. From that day the empire began to totter. Mexico was then able to maintain her independence without aid from us.

France is the traditional ally and friend of the United States. I did not blame France for her part in the scheme to erect a monarchy upon the ruins of the Mexican Republic. That was the scheme of one man [Napoleon III], an imitator without genius or merit. He had succeeded in stealing the government of his country, and made a change in its form against the wishes and instincts of his people. He tried to play the part of the first Napoleon, without the ability to sustain that role. He sought by new conquests to add to his empire and his glory; but the signal failure of his scheme of conquest was the precursor of his own overthrow.

Like our own war between the States, the Franco-Prussian war was an expensive one; but it was worth to France all it cost her people. It was the completion of the downfall of Napoleon III. The beginning was when he landed troops on this continent. Failing here, the prestige of his name—all the prestige he ever had—was gone. He must achieve a success or fall. He tried to strike down his neighbor, Prussia—and fell.

I never admired the character of the first Napoleon; but I recognize his great genius. His work, too, has left its impress for good on the face of Europe. The third Napoleon could have no claim to having done a good or just act.

To maintain peace in the future it is necessary to be prepared for war. There can scarcely be a possible chance of a conflict, such as the last one, occurring among our own people again; but, growing as we are, in population, wealth and military power, we may become the envy of nations which led us in all these particulars only a few years ago; and unless we are prepared for it we may be in danger of a combined movement being some day made to crush us out. Now, scarcely twenty years after the war, we seem to have forgotten the lessons it taught, and are going on as if in the greatest security, without the power to resist an invasion by the fleets of fourth-rate European powers for a time until we could prepare for them.

We should have a good navy, and our sea-coast defenses should be put in the finest possible condition. Neither of these cost much when it is considered where the money goes, and what we get in return. Money expended in a fine navy, not only adds to our security and tends to prevent war in the future, but is very material aid to our commerce with foreign nations in the meantime. Money spent upon sea-coast defenses is spend among our own people, and all goes back again among the people. The work accomplished, too, like that of the navy, gives us a feeling of security.

England's course towards the United States during the rebellion exasperated the people of this country very much against the mother country. I regretted it. England and the United States are natural allies, and should be the best of friends. They speak one language, and are related by blood and other ties. We together, or even either separately, are better qualified than any other people to establish commerce between all the nationalities of the world.

England governs her own colonies, and particularly those embracing the people of different races from her own, better than any other nation. She is just to the conquered, but rigid. She makes them self-supporting, but gives the benefit of labor to the laborer. She does not seem to look upon the colonies as outside possessions which she is at liberty to work for the support and aggrandizement of the home government.

The hostility of England to the United States during our rebellion was not so much real as it was apparent. It was the hostility of the leaders of one political party [Whig]. I am told that there was no time during the civil war when they were able to get up in England a demonstration in favor of secession, while these were constantly being gotten up in favor of the Union, or, as they called it, in favor of the North. Even in Manchester, which suffered so fearfully by having the cotton cut off from her mills, they had a monster demonstration in favor of the North at the very time when their workmen were almost famishing.

It is possible that the question of a conflict between races may come up in the future, as did that between freedom and slavery before. The condition of the colored man within our borders may become a source of anxiety, to say the least. But he was brought to our shores by compulsion, and, he now should be considered as having as good a right to remain here as any other class of our citizens. It was looking to a settlement of this question that led me to urge the annexation of Santo Domingo during the time I was President of the United States.

Santo Domingo was freely offered to us, not only by the administration, but by all the people, almost without price. The island is upon our shores, is very fertile, and is capable of supporting fifteen millions of people. The products of the soil are so valuable that labor in her fields would be so compensated as to enable those who wished to go there to quickly repay the cost of their passage. I took it that the colored people would go there in great numbers, so as to have independent states governed by their own race. They would still be States of the Union, and under the protection of the General Government; but the citizens would be almost wholly colored.

By the war with Mexico, we had acquired, as we have seen, territory almost equal in extent to that we already possessed. It was seen that the volunteers of the Mexican war largely composed the pioneers to settle up the Pacific coast country. Their numbers, however, were scarcely sufficient to be a nucleus for the population of the important points of the territory acquired by that war. After our rebellion, when so many young men were at liberty to return to their homes, they found they were not satisfied with the farm, the store, or the work-shop of the villages, but wanted larger fields. The mines of the mountains first attracted them; but afterwards they found that rich valleys and productive grazing and farming lands were there. This territory, the geography of which was not known to us at the close of the rebellion, is now as well mapped as any portion of our country. Railroads traverse it in every direction, north, south, east, and west. The mines are worked. The high lands are used for grazing purposes, and rich agricultural lands are found in many of the valleys. This is the work of the volunteer. It is probable that the Indians would have had control of these lands for a century yet but for the war. We must conclude, therefore, that wars are not always evils unmixed with some good.

Prior to the rebellion the great mass of the people were satisfied to remain near the scenes of their birth. In fact an immense majority of the whole people did not feel secure against coming to want should they move among entire strangers. So much was the country divided into small communities that localized idioms had grown up, so that you could almost tell what section a person was from by hearing him speak. Before, new territories were settled by a "class"; people who shunned contact with others; people who, when the country began to settle up around them, would push out farther from civilization. Their guns furnished meat, and the cultivation of a very limited amount of the soil, their bread and vegetables. All the streams abounded with fish. Trapping would furnish pelts to be brought into the States once a year, to pay for necessary articles which they could not raise—powder, lead, whiskey, tobacco and some store goods. Occasionally some little articles of luxury would enter into these purchases—a quarter of a pound of tea, two or three pounds of coffee, more of sugar, some playing cards, and if anything was left over of the proceeds of the sale, more whiskey.

Little was known of the topography of the country beyond the settlements of these frontiersmen. This is all changed now. The war begot a spirit of independence and enterprise. The feeling now is, that a youth must cut loose from his old surroundings to enable him to get up in the world. There is now such a commingling of the people that particular idioms and pronunciation are no longer localized to any great extent; the country has filled up "from the centre all around to the sea"; railroads connect the two oceans and all parts of the interior; maps, nearly perfect, of every part of the country are now furnished the student of geography.

The war has made us a nation of great power and intelligence. We have but little to do to preserve peace, happiness and prosperity at home, and the respect of other nations. Our experience ought to teach us the necessity of the first; our power secures the latter.

I feel that we are on the eve of a new era, when there is to be great harmony between the Federal and Confederate. I cannot stay to be a living witness to the correctness of this prophecy; but I feel it within me that it is to be so. The universally kind feeling expressed for me at a time when it was supposed that each day would prove my last, seemed to me the beginning of the answer to "Let us have peace."

The expressions of these kindly feelings were not restricted to a section of the country, nor to a division of the people. They came from individual citizens of all nationalities; from all denominations—the Protestant, the Catholic, and the Jew; and from the various societies of the land—scientific, educational, religious, or otherwise. Politics did not enter into the matter at all.

I am not egotist enough to suppose all this significance should be given because I was the object of it. But the war between the States was a very bloody and a very costly war. One side or the other had to yield principles they deemed dearer than life before it could be brought to an end. I commanded the whole of the mighty host engaged on the victorious side. I was, no matter whether deservedly so or not, a representative of that side of the controversy. It is a significant and gratifying fact that Confederates should have joined heartily in this spontaneous move. I hope the good feeling inaugurated may continue to the end.

Jourdan Anderson

Letter to My Old Master (1865)

Big Spring, Tennessee

Sir: I got your letter, and was glad to find that you had not forgotten Jourdan, and that you wanted me to come back and live with you again promising to do better for me than anybody else can. I have often felt uneasy about you. I thought the Yankees would have hung you long before this, for harboring Rebs they found at your house. I suppose they never heard about your going to Colonel Martin's to kill the Union soldier that was left by his company in their stable. Although you shot at me twice before I left you, I did not want to hear of your being hurt, and am glad you are still living. It would do me good to go back to the dear old home again, and see Miss Mary and Miss Martha and Allen, Esther, Green, and Lee. Give my love to them all, and tell them I hope we will meet in the better world, if not in this. I would have gone back to see you all when I was working in the Nashville Hospital, but one of the neighbors told me that Henry intended to shoot me if he ever got a chance.

I want to know particularly what the good chance is you propose to give me. I am doing tolerably well here. I get twenty-five dollars a month, with victuals and clothing; have a comfortable home for Mandy—the folks call her Mrs. Anderson—and the children—Milly, Jane, and Grundy—go to school and are learning well. The teacher says Grundy has a head for a preacher. They go to Sunday school, and Mandy and me attend church regularly. We are kindly treated. Sometimes we overhear others saying, "Them colored people were slaves" down in Tennessee. The children feel hurt when they hear such remarks; but I tell them it was no disgrace in Tennessee to belong to Colonel Anderson. Many darkeys would have been proud, as I used to be, to call you master. Now if you will write and say what wages you will give me, I will be better able to decide whether it would be to my advantage to move back again.

As to my freedom, which you say I can have, there is nothing to be gained on that score, as I got my free papers in 1864 from the Provost-Marshal-General of the Department of Nashville. Mandy says she would be afraid to go back without some proof that you were disposed to treat us justly and kindly; and we have concluded to test your sincerity by asking you to send us our wages for the time we served you. This will make us forget and forgive old scores, and rely on your justice and friendship in the future. I served you faithfully for thirty-two years, and Mandy twenty years. At twenty-five dollars a month for me, and two dollars a week for Mandy, our earnings would amount to eleven thousand six hundred and eighty dollars. Add to this the interest for the time our wages have been kept back, and deduct what you paid for our clothing, and three doctor's visits to me, and pulling a tooth for Mandy, and the balance will show what we are in justice entitled to. Please send the money by Adam's Express, in care of V. Winters, Esq., Dayton, Ohio. If you fail to pay us for for faithful labors in the past, we can have little faith in your promises in the future. We trust the good Maker has opened your eyes to the wrongs which you and your fathers have done to me and my fathers, in making us toil for you for generations without recompense. Here I draw my wages every Saturday night; but in Tennessee there was never any pay-day for the Negroes any more than for the horses and cows. Surely there will be a day of reckoning for those who defraud the laborer of his hire.

In answering this letter, please state if there would be any safety for my Milly and Jane, who are now grown up, and both good-looking girls. You know how it was with poor Matilda and Catherine. I would rather stay here and starve—and die, if it come to that—than have my girls brought to shame by the violence and wickedness of their young masters. You will also please state if there has been any schools opened for the colored children in your neighborhood. The great desire of my life now is to give my children an education, and have them form virtuous habits.

Say howdy to George Carter, and thank him for taking the pistol from you when you were shooting at me.

From Your Old Servant,

Jourdan Anderson

Credits

William Byrd, "Letter to John Perceval, Earl of Egmont" (1736) from Marion Tinling, ed., *The Correspondence of the Three William Byrds of Westover, Virginia, Volume II*. Reprinted with the permission of the University of Virginia Press.

Thomas Hutchinson, "A Dialogue between an American and a European Englishman" (1768), edited by Bernard Bailyn, from *Perspectives in American History* 9 (1975): 390–394. Reprinted with permission.

Henry Laurens, excerpt from letter to John Laurens (1776) from *The Papers of Henry Laurens, Volume XI*. Reprinted with the permission of the University of South Carolina Press.

Charles-Louis de Secondat, Baron de la Brede et de Montesquieu, excerpts from *The Spirit of the Laws*, translated and edited by Anne Cohler, Basia Miller, and Harold Stone. Copyright © 1989 by Cambridge University Press. Reprinted with the permission of Cambridge University Press.

Samuel Pufendorf, excerpts from "On the Law of Nature and Nations" (1672) from *The Political Writings of Samuel Pufendorf*, edited by Craig L. Carr, translated by Michael J. Seidler. Copyright © 1994 by Oxford University Press. Reprinted with the permission of Oxford University Press, Inc.

Benjamin Rush, letter to Ebenezer Hazard (October 22, 1768), from *Letters of Benjamin Rush, Volume I*, edited by L. H. Butterfield. Originally in Rush Mss., Vol. 39, page 24. Reprinted with the permission of The Library Company of Philadelphia.